TutemRa

The Prophecy of Reincarnation
Star Codes of Immortality
The Hip Hop Bible

2022

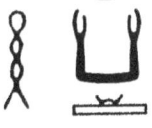

Dedications

This book is dedicated to my mother and my father in this life and all of my previous mothers and fathers. It is dedicated to my grand mother and grand father in this life and all of my previous grand parents. It is dedicated to all the family and friends in this life and in every life I have lived. I want to thank all those who have helped me in any way throughout the course of my many lives. I have mentioned many people in this book but if I have failed to mention you please know that it was not intentional. I make a special thanks to all the guardian angels that covered me throughout my time lost in the wilderness and during the course of my awakening. Above all it was and still is the frequencies that govern the unseen realms that know the full extent of my trials, tribulations and victories. Thank you for having patience with me. I am only just beginning.

Tutankhaten	Around 1347 BCE	Emmett	1941 CE	Dawud, Beloved by the Ntru	1977 CE

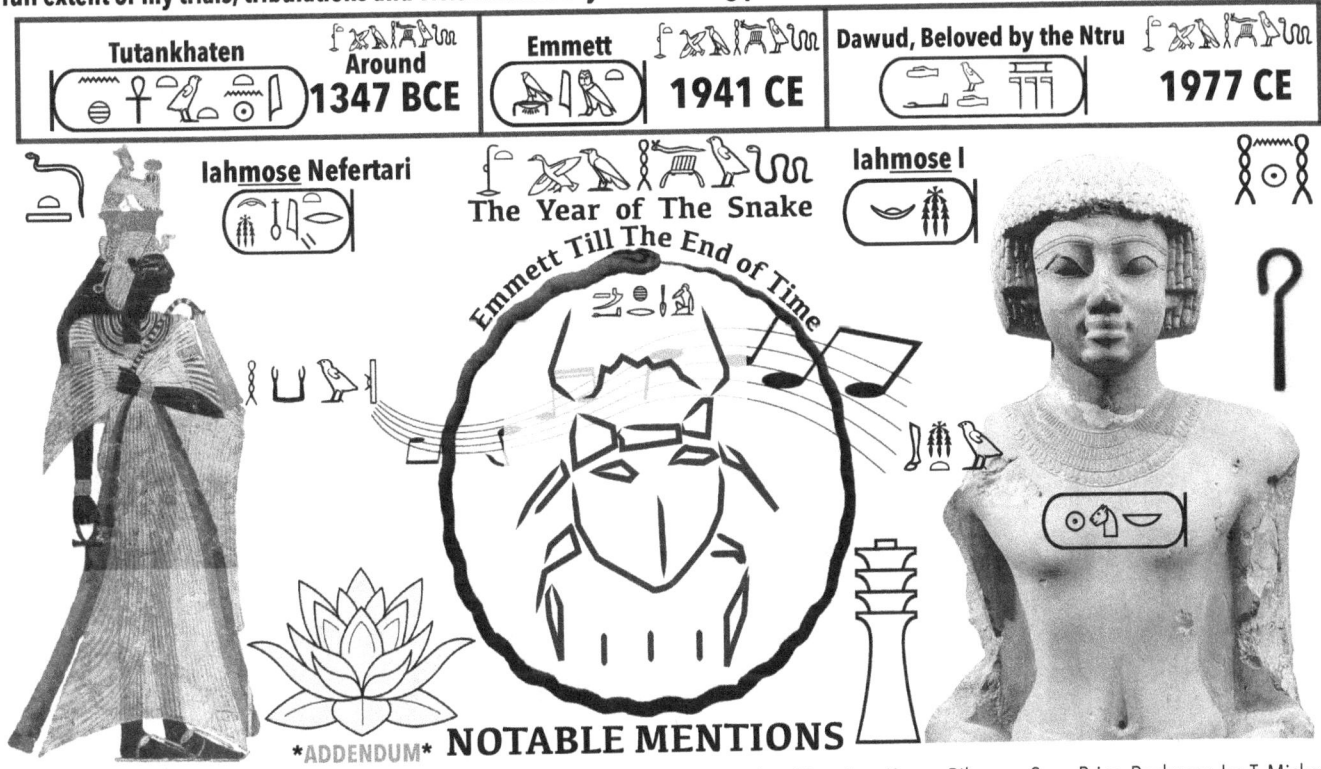

ADDENDUM **NOTABLE MENTIONS**

Iahmose Nefertari, Iahmose I, Tupac, Ankhesenaten, Harriet Tubman, Malcolm X, Martin Luther King, Nas, Kanye, Rihanna, Sean Price, Rockness, Ice T, Mickey Rourke, Mike Tyson, Floyd Mayweather, Jack Johnson, Narmer, Muhammad Ali, Mfundishi Jhutyms, Mentuhotep II, Pro James Small, Dr Umar Johnson, Ahati Kilindi Iyi, Osotrari, C Love, J Hunt, Dr Sebi, Dr Llaila Afrika, Prince, Vanity, Canibus, DMX, Michael Jackson, President Kennedy, Chris Rock, Will Smith, Set, Auset, Ausar, Heru, Marcus Garvey, Medgar Evers, Rosa Parks, Swami Muktananda, C. FreeMan EL, Chadwick Bosemen, MF Doom, Cella Dwellas, KRS One, Q-Tip, Pharoahe Monch, The Artifacts, Treach, Common, 50 Cent, Ja Rule, Prodigy, Bushwick Bill, Big L, Biggie, Howard Carter, Sean Carter, George Lucas, Michelle Lamy, Jimmy Dukes, Moses Wright jr, Spencer Wright, Richard Pryor, James Brown, Toni Morrison, Octavia Butler, David Eddings, Einstein, Eddington, Dr. Emmett L Brown, Emmett Dukes, Kenneth Eddings, Denzel Washington, Jean Jacques Dessalines, A J Cooper, Benjamin Banneker, X Clan, Dr Clarke, Dr J Felder, Nina Simone, Toussaint Louverture, Bob Dylan, Courtlan G, Will F, Angel R, Patrick H x2, Godfrey L, J Quick, Mathew D, George & Johnathan Jackson, Erykah Badu, Jay Electronica, Afeni Shakur, Eloise Barnes, Neptune is in picses, Dr Heru, David Walker's Appeal, Whitney Houston, Nehmes Bastet, Bobby Hemmit, Immortal Technique, Mutulu Shakur, Mumia, Assata, Hannibal, Voodoo Priestess, Prostitutes, Khalid Muhammad, De La Soul, Raekwon, Eric Garner, Queen Tiye, Amen Hotep III, The great "Amen" Pharaohs, Ay, Horemhab, Lisa Lisa, Mamie Till, Louis Till, Debra Dukes, Spencer Eddings, Jhutyms III, The great "Jhutyms" Pharaohs, Kheper, Jhuty, Maat, Serket, Anat, Fela Kuti, Bob Marley, Aaliyah, Steve Biko, Ida B Wells, Troy Davis, Sana, Taheerah, Jannah, Henry Smith, Karen, Adilah, Rosina, Pamela, Marcia, Bobby Hutton, Young Nobel, Buckshot, Desmomd Owens, Nat Turner, Black Thought, Geronimo Pratt, Mereruka, Khufu, Imhotep, Dr Ben-Jochannan, Ra Un Nefer, Kalief Browder, Tony Browder, Hatshepsut, Taharqa, Shabaka, Piye, Shebitku, Tantamani, Jeffre P, Denmark Vessy, Giara P, Sandra Bland, Biz Markie, Stic, Lord Jamar, Mars, Hadiiya B, Akua, Meeky S, Zawadi P, Mut Rita, Coreisa L, Shanta L, Sherri C, Anita G, Monique W, Kalishea S, Christine M, Cassiopeia, Wadjety, Fat Joe, Dejazmatch Beru, Indira, Jasmin, Mambo Kid, Colin B, Haile Selassie, Allen Brooks, Thomas Shipp and Abram Smith, The Scottsboro Boys, Scott La Rock, Amadou Diallo, Amanda Gonzales, Vanessa Guillen, Laura and her son L. D. Nelson, LaVena Johnson, Clinton Melton, Sean Bell, Aiyana Stanley-Jones, Netic, Oscar Grant, Ramarely Graham, Trayvon Martin, Kendrick Johnson, Chris Dorner, Yirser Hotep, Gabriella Nevarez, Michael Brown, Aura Rosser, Tanisha Anderson, Akai Gurley, Tamir Rice, James Byrd, Janisha Fonville, Frances C Welsing, Walter Scott, Freddie Gray, Clementa Pinckney, Cynthia Hurd, Susie Jackson, Ethel Lance, Depayne Middleton, Tywanza Sanders, Daniel Simmons, Sharonda Singleton, Myra Thompson, Alton sterling, Philando Castile, Korryn Gaines, Sathya Sia Baba, Nipsey Hussle, Left Eye, Buck Franklin, Mother Ross, Colin Kaepernick, Ahmaud Arbery, Jarad Anthony Higgins, Kwame Ture, Gaspar Yangar, Chief Manuelito, Jordan Edwards, Stephon clark, Jashen Onfory, George Washington Carver, DMT, the One in the Tree, The Manna, Amanita, 5-MeO DMT, Heket, María Sabina, Neter Ankh, Ayiti, Simeon Toko, Hankh R Sun, Rameses II, The great "Rameses" Pharaohs, Botham Jean, Sehu Khepera, Mfundishi Heru, Rod Sterling, Back To The Future, USS Emmett Till 2277, Flight 828, Ganesha, Tim Reed, Jelani Manigault, The Great Lafayette and Chung Ling Soo, George Floyd ,Breonna Taylor, Omm Sety, Aten, Quawan "Bobby" Charles, Mr Nature, General Dukes Sr, Juanita Dukes, General Dukes Jr, Leacola Riddle, Maia, May F. Riddle, Grace, Mildred, Charlotte, Kiya, Nefertiti, Akhenaten, The Great Di**vine** Amen in the Grape**vine**

ADDENDUM Copyright © 2022 Dawud Basheer Eddings

Sep 29th 2022 - Lil Boy Emmett

There was a girl named D**emmet**, born again in Turkey, a lil boy **Emmett** came back to earth see, the lil girl D**emmet** remembered the life she lived, **Emmett** was thrown in a river where **Isis** is, **Emmett** was not like D**emmet**, **Emmett** came from K**emet**, but **Emmett** had no remanence of any life he lived, still **Emmett** connected them just like **Isis** did - **TutemRa** **(page 623)**

Inquiries for Selling of this Book and Book Orders should be addressed to:

TutemRa@yahoo.com • www.TutemRa.com

ISBN: 979-8-9860362-0-5 (Softcover - black and white edition)
ISBN: 979-8-9860362-2-9 (Softcover - full color edition)
ISBN: 979-8-9860362-1-2 (eBook - In full color)

Author, Editor, Text Design, Cover Design, Illustrations and Layout by Dawud Basheer Eddings (TutemRa Setep en Ra Nebu Sahu Kheperu)

Start Date: April 4th 2020
Original Completion Date: June 1st 2022
Revision Completion Date: December 25th 2023

Page 594 - Martin Luther King Jr
Pages 28, 104 and 404 - Black Wall Street
Pages 489, 504, 511 - "Christ - Krst - Emmett"

In the event of my demise, the proceeds of this book should go to: my Grand Mother, my Parents, my wife Shanta and future wife, my two sons and future children, my Sisters, my Aunts and my Extended Family.

For questions about the events in this book please leave a message on the contact page of the site below.

To leave a donation scan QR code or visit the site below.

Scan to pay with Cash App

www.TutemRa.com

Why should you donate?

Zelle

Donate so that this book can be put into the hands of people who need to read it, yet might not be able to afford to purchase it. Why is it important for people to read this book? Because the inward path of peace and spirituality needs to be promoted and the transformative life of TutemRa has the power to influence people of all ages, from all walks of life, to walk a spiritual path. 55% of donations will go towards the printing of this book to be given away for free. 33% of donations will be allocated towards community based wellness programs. 12% will go to the lineage of TutemRa. For more information please go to site. **www.TutemRa.com**

Kemet **Emmett**

TutemRa Setep en Ra Nebu Sahu Kheperu

Dawud, Beloved by the Ntru

I'm writing a Epic Sci-Real (Science Reality) Novel Trilogy version of this book and a book about Tupac's ancient past life (p 664). Stay tuned!

June 4th 2022 The Hip Hop Bible

I was murdered, lynched, shot in the head in a fit of rage, and for justice my mother begged, then **she heard a voice** from above and what it said: "Emmett has done his job now you have a long road ahead", you can read her every word on page 180, and 511, I'm not a reverend, I'm a reincarnated soul like **Bob Marley** was singing, I wrote a book it's more like a **divine scroll**, a **Hip Hop Bible** even, I rhyme with reason, my story is weaving and woven by the hands of souls stolen and shot like **Scott LaRock** and **Tupac**! Scott was shot the day before me on August 27th my grand pops was born the day after **2pacalypse Now**, June 1 7 3 1 the day, how - you still ain't got the answers like Sway?! but I'll give you this PROPHECY, Dylan Roof June 17th murdered 9 people in a church on my grand pops astrology, my grandfather died the day after **Marcus Garvey** see, my great grand mother was born the day that **Marcus Garvey** died, George Reeves committed suicide on Tupac's birthday! you can't play Superman when you evil in the worst way, you can't play **Superman** when you evil in the worst way, I was murdered, lynched, shot in the head in a fit of rage, then I transformed into another egg, then my new mother was born when my Mamie prayed, 22 years later I came flying through my mothers legs - **TutemRa**

Definitions:

Hekau = Words of power.

Wehem Mesut = The one who has repeated births. Also known as reincarnation, resurrection and Gilgul.

Heka = Magical meaningful speech / utterance; word with mystic effects.

(Shps) = Ancestors, Nobles, Those of former times.

Maa Kheru = True of voice.

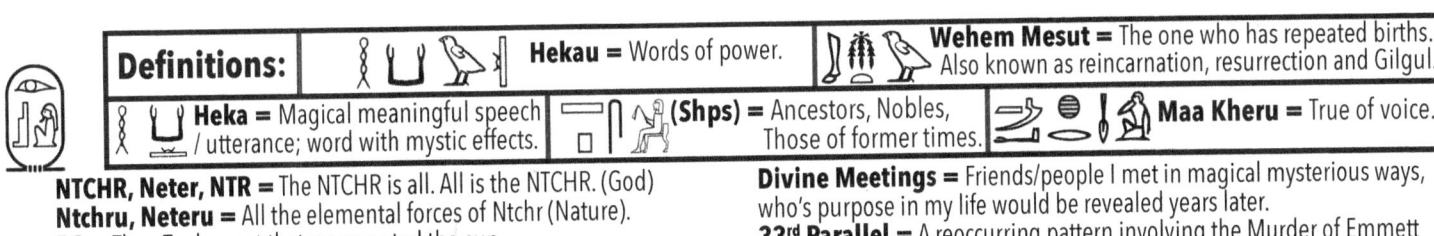

NTCHR, Neter, NTR = The NTCHR is all. All is the NTCHR. (God)
Ntchru, Neteru = All the elemental forces of Ntchr (Nature).
RA = The nTr element that represented the sun.
Kheper (Scarab) **=** The nTr who was closely associated with resurrection. Kheper was the first "only begotten God". See page 569.
Auset, Isis = The Ntr who consorted with Ra and was the wife of Ausar, and mother of Heru.
Ausar, Osiris = The nTr who was known as the Lord of resurrection, the underworld, the west and the afterlife. Ausar was the first to cultivate (**Till**) the land and was the first gardener. He was also known as "The One in the Acacia Tree" (page 481). Ausar represents the immortal soul of all human beings that reincarnates. See page 3.
Heru, Horus = Heru is the Ntr that returns to avenge the death of his father Ausar. You are HERU! See page 3 for the **hero's journey!**
Nswt Bity = The original name for Pharaoh/King.
Anat = The nTr who was a powerful Goddess of war and fertility. She was seen as a bearer of life because she protected the NSWT BITY (Pharaoh) in battle with mighty vengeance. See page 584.
Hatshepsut = A magnificent woman who ruled Kemet wisely and efficiently and peacefully. Representations of her leave no doubt that she was genuinely African. She sent out the great expedition to punt.
Thutmoses = A group of great Pharaohs. The Thutmoses were military leaders par excellence, especially Thutmoses III. See page 225.
AmenHotep I, II, III, and IV = The great "Amen" Pharaohs, renowned for their statesmanship, wealth and artistic creativity. Amenhotep III was best known for his ability to rule for around 40 years without war, practicing excellent diplomacy. AmenHotep IV is better known as **<u>Akhenaten</u>** (AmenHotep IV) - The father of monotheism (P 664 - 665).
Ramese I, II, and III = Another group of great pharaohs. Great military men and builders. Ramese II was a builder without an equal in the then known world and even still to this day.
Melanin = The chemical of the soul, a transformation doorway though which the energy waves of the holy soul, spirit, and mind pass to take form in a human body. It is secreted by the pineal gland (3rd eye). Africans have the most melanin in their systems than all other people.
Birthmarks / Black dots = Are highly melanated markers, usually seen as black dots, and are part of the souls genetic memory connected to how people may have died in past lives.
Djed Pillar = The energy flowing up the spinal cord known as kundalini or serpentine energy. It was called the spine of Ausar and represented stability. The activation of the Jedi light saber is based on the djed pillar representing the serpentine energy flowing up the 33 vertebrae activating "Christ consciousness".
Mysticism = Belief that union with the creator (God) is possible.
Immortality = Survival of the soul after the death of the body.
Birthdates = The time & date of birth is your spiritual star code.
Dreams = Some dreams take place in a different space and time where the **astral body travels**, sometimes to the past and even the future. **Deja Vu** is sometimes a result of having already experienced a moment in a dream and when you reach the moment in your waken state you have a feeling of familiarity.
= When you see this symbol it most often denotes a dream and sometimes **astral projection**. See page 30.
May 25th Strikes Back = A reoccurring date forming a pattern. It was the first star code pattern that I decoded on page **222**, stemming from a dream my sister had in 2002 (page 104). This code would ultimately connect me with my previous life as Emmett Till and spark my awareness to patterns.
Kemet = The black land, original name for Egypt. (Kemet = k**Emmett**)

Coincidences = When **coincid**ences bind with **synchronicities** the outcome tends to have <u>the mark of a greater authority</u>. Like a pattern that happens for a divine purpose. Three **coincid**ing points create a tri**<u>angle</u>**. In our lives we meet different people or have certain experiences that are governed by guardian **<u>angels</u>**. All things are governed by seen and unseen forces. <u>Angles-Angels</u>

Divine Meetings = Friends/people I met in magical mysterious ways, who's purpose in my life would be revealed years later.
33rd Parallel = A reoccurring pattern involving the Murder of Emmett Till and other prominent people. See pages 20, 380, 505, 511, 515.
44th Parallel = A reoccurring pattern confirming the transmigration of my soul and my connection to Star Wars. Pages 517, 602, 660, 37, 329.
December 3rd Theory = A reoccurring date forming a pattern used by the dead to speak to me. See pages 312,314,345,431,457, 519.
Revelation = The communication of truth like "goose bumps".
Believe/Beliefs = Beliefs have no place in this book. The word **lie** is in the middle of both words and to belie is to contradict.
Ba = The divine soul. An immaterial life force capable of existing without the body. Depicted as a bird with a human head.
Ka = The divine spirit. The Ka is depicted as two hands raised to symbolize the energy body or the double that reincarnates.
Jhuty = The nTr governing divine wisdom, speech and magic.
Music = A powerful art with the ability to break glass or heal broken hearts and can be used to awaken the **Ka** of humans. **Heka, Hekau**.
Maat = The nTr energy that holds creation together. Maat governs the principles of truth, justice, moral righteousness, harmonious balance, cosmic order, and reciprocity.
Telepathy = The transference of thoughts across time and space by the sheer power of the mind.
Krishna = The eighth avatar, the most important incarnation of Vishnu. Krishna was of unmistakable African ancestry.
Tupac = A shining serpent sent back to earth to sp**ark** the minds of those who would change the world bringing about **Better Dayz**.
Enpu/Anubis = The nTr who is the protector of the deceased and the messenger of Ausar (Osiris).
Xenophobia = Fear and hatred of strangers or foreigners or anything that is strange or foreign. This mood is the striking reality of the temperament of the United States.
Racism = A historical phenomenon that has its roots in the slavery peculiar to America; it is an assumptive attitude of superiority based on the skin color made into a legal fiction and bolstered by political and economic power; in short, it is the belief by white people (particularly those in America) that they are racially and culturally superior to all first world people (Africans, Asians, Indians, etc.) and that their economic and military strength guarantees them the wherewithal to exercise their racist feelings to keep first world peoples forever in their place.
Nigga = A term used to belittle Africans by white racist but the word is connected to the words **Negus** (King) and **Naga** (divine snake).
Dawud = David, beloved of God.
Basheer = The bringer of truth. Pure Soul.
Emmett = Truth, mound, build up, Maat, to **come forth**.
Emit = To **send forth**, to utter, or cause to appear.
Shine = To "**Emit**" light. **To send forth light**.
Aten, Aton, = The nTr that represented the rays of the sun.
Tutankhaten (King Tut) = The most famous pharaoh in modern times who returned to earth many times doing good works for the betterment of all people. Like Amen Atum and Aten he will never be forgotten, he went from **Neb Kheperu Ra**, to slave fields pick'n cotton, then to **Emmett Till** getting killed and thrown in a river rotten like **Ausar,** then he came back as **Dawud, TutemRa.**
Hip Hop = Collective Conscious Movement. Hip Hop is an international Kulture. I am Hip Hop, you are Hip Hop. Rap is what you do, but Hip Hop is what you live. The **Temple of Hip Hop** was established by **KRS One** (p 633) in 1996, the same year Tupac died.
Heka Maat = In this book, this symbol denotes **Heka** or **Hekau**, which are magical meaningful words of power with mystic effects (**Hip Hop**). My music has always been reflecting the times and my life at the time of the hekas. The oldest known words of power were written to ensure the **Nswt Bity** resurrected in the next life. See page **xi** and page **6** to see how I **unconsciously used <u>music as magic</u> to awaken my ancient soul fragments.**

iii

ADDENDUM

Appendix/Triggers

Matrix	
1	344
7	345
109	421
141	433
212	442
216	463
218	471
226	480
262	543
266	569
282	578
292	596
323	

RA

p137

PAGES WITH ADDENDUMS

Revised
Addition
Completed
Dec 25, 2023
See page,
489, 504, 511
Krst (Christ)

i	122	463
ii	123	469
iii	125	471
xi	126	472
1	150	481
2	168	482
5	169	492
6	173	508
14	178	510
15	180	511
16	182	515
18	202	518
25	204	520
29	210	528
30	245	536
40	251	542
42	252	554
44	259	564
46	267	566
51	271	572
52	278	577
54	279	582
57	281	586
58	282	602
60	287	609
71	289	614
72	309	615
74	329	619
76	342	623
79	345	631
95	348	633
106	355	640
107	367	643
108	379	648
118	407	650
121	419	657
	438	659
	446	670
	450	672

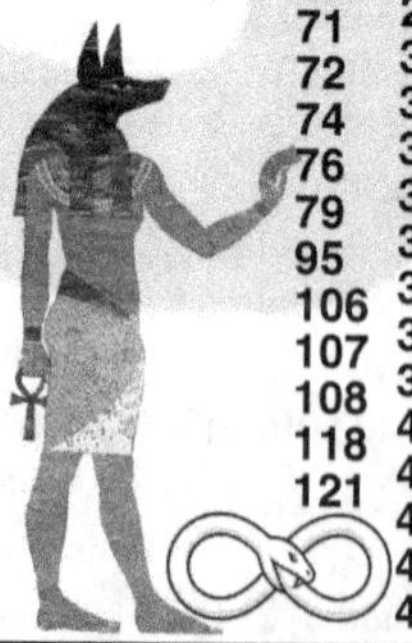

Tupac Amaru Shakur p76
Biggie Smalls p77
Abner Louima p78
Amadou Diallo p80
Big L p80

Contents

Rau

nu

Prt

m

heru

Iu

f

Per

f

m

heru

Utterances

for

Coming

Forth

by day

into

Light

It is

he,

who

comes

forth

by day

into

Light

Appendix/Triggers

p137

Amanda Gonzales p100
Vanessa Guillen p100

Ka Doors (Spirit Doors) Guardians, Invisible Protectors				
48	251	348	548	626
148	252	349	549	650
150	253	409	572	
179	315	421	584	
199	318	434	604	
250	329	545	606	

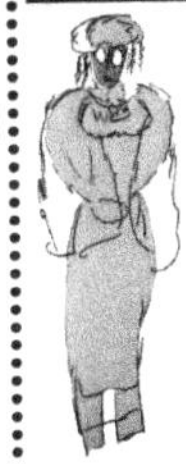

Invisible Protectors

La Vena Johnson p140
Sean Bell p149

9 Prophetic Hekau's (Spells) where Emmett Till's name appears before I realize I was him in a past life (p 480.)		
180	274	370
187	351	424
214	365	454

6 Prophetic Hekau's (Spells) where King Tut's name appears before I realize I was him in a past life (p 594).		
187	268	382
195	323	435

Aiyana Jones p181
Oscar Grant p192

Contents

Appendix/Triggers

ATEN

AMEN

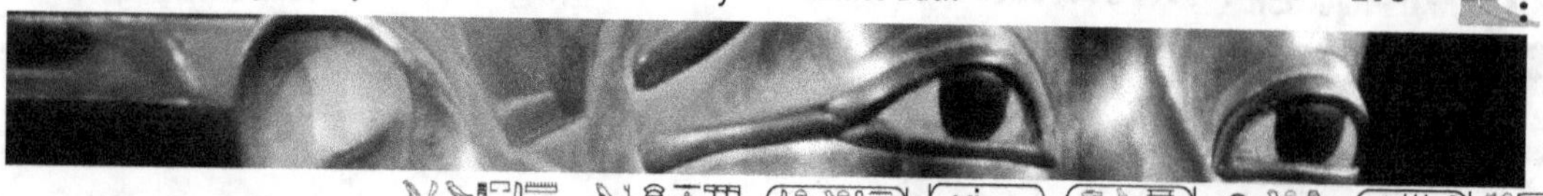

Contents

Rau nu Prt m heru

Iu f Per f m heru

Utterances for Coming Forth by day into Light

It is he, who comes forth by day into Light

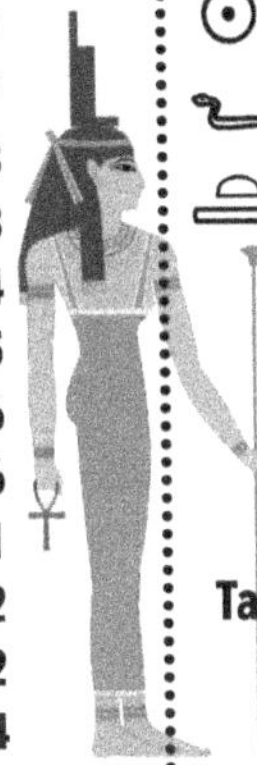
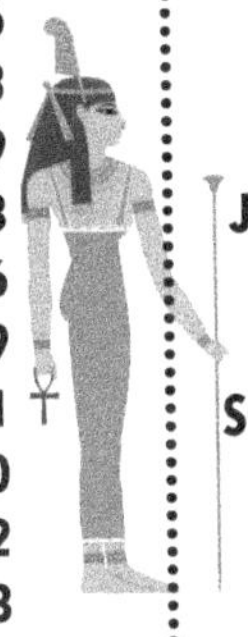
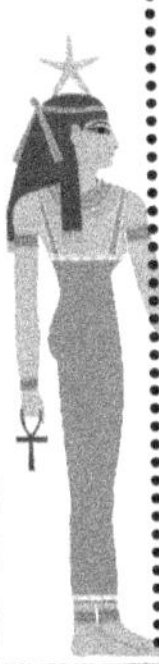

Appendix/Triggers

p137

Contents

Appendix/Triggers

p137

Jordan Edwards p446

AMEN

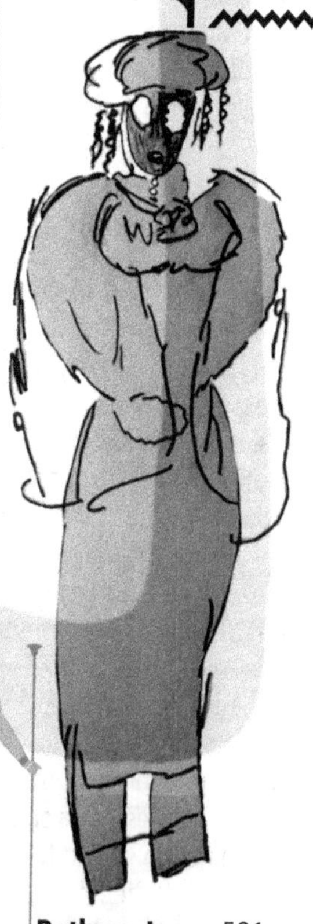

Bothem Jean p581

Atatiana Jefferson p581

RA

Contents

Rau nu Prt m heru

Iu f Per f m heru

Utterances for Coming Forth by day into Light

It is he, who comes forth by day into Light

Appendix/Triggers

ATEN

p137

Juice WRLD p583

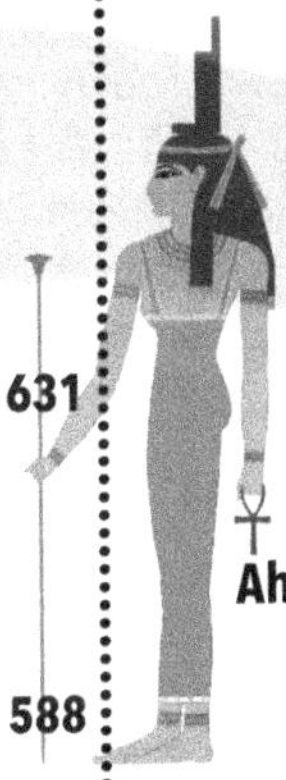

Ahmaud Arbery p586

Breonna Taylor p589

Contents

Appendix/Triggers

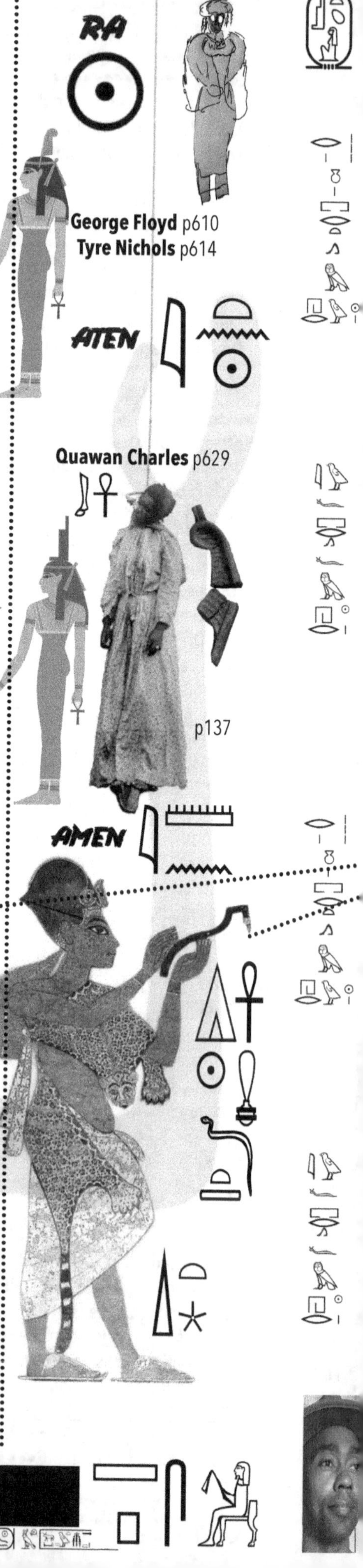

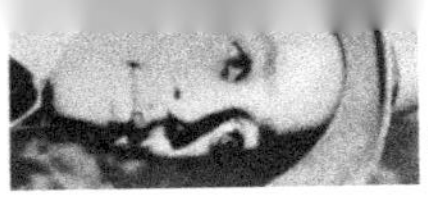

Rau nu Prt m heru

Iu f Per f m heru

Utterances for Coming Forth by day into Light

It is he, who comes forth by day into Light

# of Rhyme's	6	1	1	0	0	1	2	2	23	1	0	0	0	36	67	36	10	13	50	101	30	40	11	19	8	8	466
Amen Hotep III (p 336)																			1	1							2
Queen Tiye (p 261)																	1		1	1							3
Hatshepsut (p 268)																	1		2	1							4
Jean J. Dessalines (p 374)																				2	1			1			4
Akhenaten (p 664)																	1		2	2							5
Nefertiti (p 665)																			2	2		2					6
Toussaint (p 254)																1			3	1	1						6
Ramose (p 271)																	1		1	2	2						6
King Tut (p 187)														1	1		1		1	2							6
Tehuti / Thoth / Ibis (p 337)																			1	2	1	1	2	1			8
Pharaoh (p 234)																3			1	1	1	2		1	1		10
Reincarnation (p 258)																		1		2		4		1	2	1	11
Harriet Tubman (p 492)																3	1		1	5		2	1				13
Resurrection (p 77)	1								1					1					2	3		3		1	1	1	14
To Rise - To Be Risen (p 245)																1	1	1	3	8						1	15
Kemet / Egypt (p 231)															1	2	1		2	4	1	1	2	2		1	17
Haitian (p 235)																2		1	2	9	3						17
Auset / Isis (p 267)																	2	1	6	6		2		1		1	19
Goddess (p 321)																			4	11	1	2	4	5	1	1	20
Huey P (p 139)									1					2	2			1	1	7	2	3	1	1			21
Immortality (p 254)																1			1	7		6	3	2	2		22
Ausar / Osiris (p 481)																1	1		5	9		2	3			2	23
Martin Luther King (p 69)								1	1					2	2	2		2	1	5	3	4					23
Emmett Till (p 180)														2	1		1		1	3	1	2	2	5	1	4	24
Marcus Garvey (p 245)																1	1	2	6	11	2	2		1		1	27
Heru / Horus (p 267)																	1	1	6	9	2	4		3	1	1	28
Maat (p 258)																2	1		5	10	4	1	3		2	2	30
Jesus / Christ (p 135)									1					1	6	4		1	6	7	2	5		5		1	39
"I Came Back" etc (p 133)									3					1		4	2	1	6	6	4	3	1	5	3	4	43
Malcolm X (p 561)									1					3	3	3	2		2	20	6	5					45
Tupac (p 664)	1						1		2					10	5	1			5	10	5	1	2	11	1		55
Hip Hop (p 134)									2					10	15	2		1	6	17	3	1				1	58
Spirit (p 133)									2					1	7		3	1	9	31	5	5	3	2	1	1	71
Soul (p 77)	1	1					1		5					2	7	8	4	2	11	27	3	11	5	5	3	4	100
Heart (p 77)	2							1	2					3	5	2	6	4	14	41	10	14	2	2	1		109
Dream (p 77)	2						1	1	1					6	11	6	4		17	24	6	14	6	2	3	4	114
God (p 106)						1		2	7					9	15	9		2	16	24	6	16	4	5	1	1	118
Love (p 78)	1						1		6					21	18	9	4	4	14	58	10	15	2	3	4		170
Years 1997 - 2022	97	98	99	00	01	02	03	04	05	06	07	08	09	10	11	12	13	14	15	16	17	18	19	20	21	2022	Total
Age	20	21	22	23	24	25	26	27	28	29	30	31	32	33	34	35	36	37	38	39	40	41	42	43	44	45	

Other names, words and concepts uttered in music.

Love 168x's
Hate 62x's
Tamir Rice 7x's
Sean Bell 11x's
Eric Garner 5x's
Nat Turner 13x's
Sandra Bland 8x's
Trayvon Martin 5x's
Khalid Muhammad 2x's

Michael Jackson 23x's
Nas 17x's Common 12x's
Biggie 10x's Tyson 9x's
Bob Marley 8x's
Smif-N-Wessun 5x's
Mos Def 5x's
Buckshot 3x's
Sean P 4x's
Jay Z 7x's

Ark 7x's
Sirius 4x's
Orion 6x's
Magic 31x's
Matrix 12x's
Buddha 7x's
Coincidence 8x's
I Am That I Am 14x's

Music (Heka) can be used as alchemy when it originates in the heart and soul. **I unconsciously used music as magic** which helped awaken my ancient soul fragments. This chart reflects the record of every time a word or concept seen on the chart was written into a verse of my music. From this chart one can observe the awakening of my soul fragments through my music (Heka, page 6). "Music is a spiritual thing. You don't play with music" - **Fela Kuti**

ADDENDUM

The Codes Within The Web of The Matrix

As you read this book you might ask yourself, why is he using the birth dates and death dates of people, and movies, tv shows and music and etc etc? What does it all mean? My friend, the messages are hidden within the murmuration of starlings forming patterns for a split second as they circle above head or in the murmuration of starlings seen in the movie, **Matrix Resurrection**. The messages are everywhere, even in the wind. When you watch the movie **Matrix**, you see the green text computer code scrolling down in the background known as digital rain or the Matrix code and sometimes green rain. This falling Matrix code is a way of representing the activity of the simulated reality environment of the Matrix seen on screen. Basically everything that is happening within the Matrix is seen on a computer screen as green falling rain which can be decoded or read by those who know how to read it. The same thing is happening within this life you are living. The Matrix of this life you are living has a code as well. You must decode it but this code is not limited to green falling rain on a computer screen. Sometimes the code is unseen, sometimes it's in the rain. It can be in a strange message from a stranger passing by, like when I met brother Khufu in massage school (page 282). The messages are everywhere. My book is full of star codes of immortality. These star codes are the falling rain surrounding my lives. The word Matrix appears **5** times in the King James Version of the Bible in **Exodus**, and all the references deal with the **first born son**. My life path number is **5** and I'm the **first born son** in my family and my name.. Like David from the Bible had **5** smooth stones with which he struck Goliath between the forehead and defeated him. And my name.. My name is **Dawud** which is **David** in English (page 41). The story of David in the Bible is an allegory. David's battle was not with another person. His battle was with his lower self and when he awoke to his **Heru** consciousness by opening his 3rd eye (between his two eyes) he dropped his lower **5** senses and ascended. There are codes within this life. Even in your spiritual books there are codes that you must decipher. If you are in sync with the frequency of God divine messages will be sent to you in what ever means necessary. There is no limit to what God can do within the Matrix that it designed. If you are trapped in a prison alone in a cell then you might not get a message from the wind. Your message might come in a dream. Or perhaps in solitude you might very well **hear a voice** like I did on July 1st 2018 (page 474). It is not by mere happenstance that a person on the tv show, **The Odd Couple** said the name **King Tut** on February 24th 2022 as I was coming to the close of this book (page 669). I was watching that show just so that the Matrix could show me that. God wanted me to hear that. It was a part of my play of consciousness. You have your own individual play set up for you. We are here to play this game of life which is more like a play of consciousness. We all play it together like a shared dream (pages 30, 452, 589). It's important that we help wake each other up so that we all end the game well but most importantly we must first awaken ourselves. No person can hand another person enlightenment. Each person must earn it on their own. We win when we all win and there is no real end. Just as the sun has a daily cycle and a yearly cycle there are cycles we go through in our daily and yearly lives. As we move through our cycles we attract certain patterns that follow us waiting for us to decipher them. I encourage you to take nothing in your life lightly because most things that are happening to you have great importance. Life is a game that we play, a play of consciousness. Your ability to be successful at this game is measured by your ability to see what is not seen and to hear what can't be heard. We make a fatal error when we think all that we see with our two eyes is all that there is to be seen. All things are governed by seen and unseen forces. **I suspect that we are living a double life**. We live a life that we are aware of because we see it but at the same time our **Ka** (spirit) is playing the game too. The goal of the game is to unite with the Ka. In ancient Kemet (Egypt) the human soul was divided into 9 parts. One of the aspects was the **Ka** which was the **spirit**, or the etheric twin. The Ka, which housed by the **Sahu**, is the part of the soul that survives in the physical world after the body of a person has departed. The symbol for the Ka was **two hands raised** representing the **double nature** of our being. It's important that you start paying attention because the further you get away from the right path the less you will hear the clarion call. The less you will see the falling rain. The less you will see the code hidden within the Matrix. Amen is the hidden one and this Matrix is like a **Web**. I am a scorpio and the scorpio is connected to the **spider** that spins a perfect **web** with out being taught. The Scorpio is the eighth zodiac sign and corresponds with the number **8**, which is **infinity**. Mamie Till (Emmett Till's mother) was born in **Web** M**ississ**ippi**,** on the 33rd parallel. Emmett was murdered on the 33rd parallel. These are all pieces of this unseen **web** that was formed around me. I did not always see the **web** within this **Matrix**. While I was on this journey at times I felt like I was being led to the next chapter, in a book that I had never read. This life is like having the keys to a plane out of sight, but instead of taking flight, some of us decide to walk instead. Do you understand?! You have an astral body a divine ark but you must pull gold from lead. At times I felt like the whole world was walking dead, sleep walking, caught in a **web** of ebb and flow chasing the dough and the street cred. You should never go to the lowest low tryin to get ahead. Many are led to a path of indoctrination with doctors and drug dealers and vaccinations. But I suggest you seek elevation through meditation and fasting and praying and exercise and rest for rejuvenation. Don't be in a rush for a quick high. I see the truth seekers smoking reefer for deeper **red pills** leading to conspiracy theories having you feeling ill. It's a true terror knowing the truth teller is getting killed. Might have done better by taking that **blue pill**. You should know that when **LSD** was tested on **spiders** the affects altered the spiders **web**-building patterns. At low doses the **webs** were even better proportioned and more exactly built than normally. **However**, with higher doses, the **webs** were badly and rudimentarily made. Too much of anything is bad for you I'm afraid. Beware of the web of lies and don't get lost the maze. **DO NOT BE AFRAID TO DIE and at all cost be brave!** Because with your thoughts, if you try to conceive or to fathom, you could bend quantum events in time and space. Can you imagine?

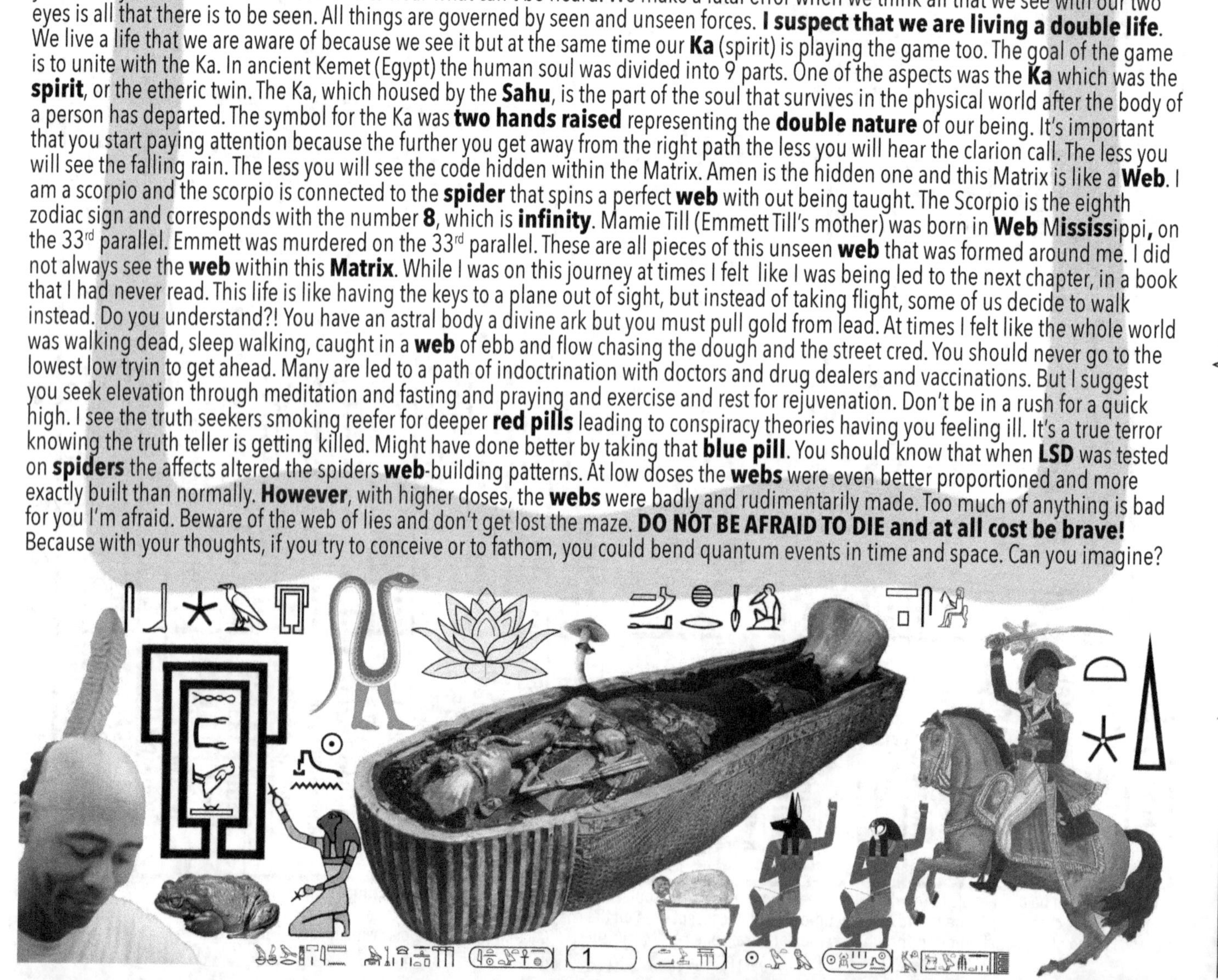

Rau nu Prt m heru

Ancient Prophecies and Spiritual Alchemy

There are two ancient prophecies that one should be aware of when reading this book. I have come to fulfill these two prophecies. There is the ancient prediction that **Heru** will return one day and recapture the kingdom of his father, when the golden age will be restored and the **lion** will unite with the **Lamb/Goat**. Heru is believed to have a **resurrection** during the **Aquarian Age**. He is the prince of peace, bringer of order, redeemer of truth for humanity, resurrection and the life. He is able to right the wrongs of the past, free the oppressed, and restore **Maat** (page 367). In the ancient Kemetic Ausarian resurrection drama, Ausar (Osiris) was the first **gardener**, the first to cultivate (**Till, Tilling, Tillage**) the land and the first to come back after "death", or better known as **Wehem Mesut/Ankh** (repeating of births/life , **Gilgul**, page 14). Christianity borrowed from the resurrection story of Ausar when the character of **Jesus** was created and the Murder of Emmett **Till** is intimately connected to both Ausar and Jesus. According to the book of John, after Jesus resurrected, Mary mistook him for a **gardener**. Emmett **Till** arrived in M**ississ**ippi (**isis**) on August 21st 1955. The next day he spent the early morning harvesting cotton on his uncles farm (**garden**). Emmett **Till**'s uncle, **Moses** Wright Jr was a farmer - a **gardener**. According to the book of John, Jesus's cruxifixction took place near a **garden**. Emmett **Till** was murdered on Leslie Milam's **farm** (**garden**) in Money M**ississ**ippi. Ausar reigned for **28 years** and Emmett Till was murdered on **August 28th**. **Emmett Till** was beaten, tortured, shot in the head and **thrown in a** M**ississ**ippi **river** at **14** years old. In the Ausarian **resurrection** drama, Ausar was trapped in a box, **thrown in the Nile river**, then cut into **14** pieces. The story of Ausar is a parable that teaches about the natural law of resurrection and reincarnation, with that in mind we must consider what it is that Ausar was really "cultivating". The murder of Emmett **Till** was a prophecy designed to remind human beings about the immortality of their souls and what it is that we are supposed to be cultivating, or "Tilling" here on Earth. **Emmett** is another way to spell the word **Emit**. Emit means to **send forth**. In a like manner, my past lives were **sent forth** no different than how the Goddess **Lusaaset** was said to **come forth** after the consumption of the **Yrp wine** (p 481).Then there is also <u>*The Prophecy of Reincarnation Sambho the Black Buddha*</u> from the far east of Asia. It is said that between the years of 1975 and 2020 the **Buddha** would reincarnate in the western world. He would prove the **immortality** of the **soul** with his **reincarnation**. He would be the descendant of those who are still in bondage today - the offspring of those who from time immemorial worked their way down from the high lands of Ethiopia to the Mediterranean sea at the delta. Behold, **TutemRa: The Prophecy of Reincarnation**.

Iu f Per f m heru

ADDENDUM

The Return of Heru and The Path of Shemsu Heru

This Stela (p 3) was created under the reign of **Nectanebo II (Senedjem ib Ra Setep en Amun)**, the last African Nswt Bity of ancient Kemet (Egypt). Upon witnessing the invasion of the Persian empire he fled to Nubia to rally troops in an effort to regain control of Kemet but too many foreign forces had mounted against him. He along with his people fled back to Nubia and some migrated to other parts of Africa. The stela (p 3) predicts the attributes of the one who will fulfill the ancient prophecy ushering in the golden age of consciousness. The images carved into the stone stela portray the perilous nighttime journey of the sun as it passes through the nether world under the earth. Its rebirth each morning is shown at the uppermost point of the stela, where Jhuty (Thoth), four baboons, and the kneeling Nswt Bity **Nectanebo II** lift their arms in the gesture of adoration and prayer. The Ancient people of the Hapi Eteru (Nile River) understood the immortality of the soul and taught about the resurrection of the Ba (soul). This concept of resurrection was called the **Wehem-mesut** (**The one who has repeated births**, p 14). They Called the death of the physical body westing. Just as the Sun rises in the east and sets in the west the same is to be said for the Ba. Therefore this stela is depicting the repetition of the human soul and the foretelling of the attributes of the one who would return. The **Snakes**, the **Lion**, the **Lamb** and the **Scorpion King**.

Ultimately, **Ausar** represents the **immortal soul** of all human beings that reincarnates. **Auset** represents intuition and wisdom. **Set** represents your own **ego**. While **Heru** represents the potential of your spiritual stamina to become the Heru (**hero)** of your life journey, conquering **your own ego** (Set).. In the Stela seen on page 3, **Heru** is depicted after he defeats **Set** becoming the champion of the world. The image symbolizes Heru's dominion over nature, and most importantly his victory over immoral sexual urges, and anger because these are habits that lead the human personality into failure and regret. Heru is portrayed in the conventional Kemetic form for youth; that is, he is nude and wearing his hair in a sidelock. He is seen with a **scorpion,** a **snake** and a **Lion** in his **left** hand. In his **right** hand he holds a **scorpion,** a **snake** and a **Lamb/Goat**. He is seen stepping forward with his left foot while standing on a crocodile. Above him is the head of **Bes**, the NTCHR (deity) with leonine features who had traditionally been a protector of households and eventually had become the defender of everything good and enemy to everything bad. Heru is flanked by several deities as well as the Uatchet (eye of intention) with human hands and arms. On his right the Goddess **Auset** (Isis), is seen protectively holding the wall of a curved reed hut, a primeval chapel, in which the Heru child stands together with a figure of **Ra-horakhty**, God of the rising sun, who stands upon coiled snakes. **Ausar** is seen next to Ra-horakhty in the form of a hawk standing on a papyrus reed scepter, wearing an Atef crown. Behind Auset, the Goddess **Nekhbet** is seen in vulture form standing on a papyrus reed scepter. On his left **Jhuty** (Thoth) is seen protectively holding the wall of a curved reed hut. Behind Jhuty, the Goddess **Wadjet** in the form of a serpent is seen standing on a papyrus reed scepter. On the stela **Auset** (**Isis**) speaks and recounts that while she and her infant child Heru were still hiding in the marshes, the child became ill. In her despair, she cried for help to the "Boat of Eternity" (the sun boat in which the God travels over the sky), "and the sun disk stopped opposite her and did not move from its place." Jhuty was sent from the sun boat to help Auset and cured her son Heru by reciting spells (words of power, **hekau**). The hekau's always ended with the phrase "and the protection of the afflicted as well," indicating that by using these hekau's, any type of affliction in human beings would be healed. Because of this "egyptologist" believe***** this stela to be solely about protection and curing of insect bites but they are wrong just as they have been wrong about many things when it comes to deciphering language and spiritual systems they do not fully inner stand. Heru is striding forward with his left foot, his spiritual foot. The statue is **3 dimensional** as Heru faces the viewer stepping into the aquarian age carrying the zodiac signs of Leo, Scorpion and Snake in his hands. The stela details my return and so here I am, but I won't be the last! More will come! In essence, all human beings have the potential to reach Heru consciousness becoming a metaphorical reflection of the Heru stela (p 3). We will win!

Utterances for Coming Forth by day into Light

It is he, who comes forth by day into Light

The Snakes, The Lion, The Lamb and The Scorpion King

In the name K**emet** you find the name **Emmet**. I was sent down (born) again on July 25th 19**41** the year of the **snake** as **Emmett Till** (p 480) under the sun sign of **Leo** the **Lion**. I was born again in my current RA-incarnation as Dawud (David) on Oct 25th 1977 the year of the **Snake** under the sun sign of the **Scorpion** (full astrological reading, p 654). This is why Heru is holding the Snakes, Scorpions, the Goat and the Lion. Emmett was the "sacrificial **Lamb**" born as Leo the **Lion** and murdered in the year of the **Goat** which is why Heru is holding a **Lion** and a **Goat**. Emmett was murdered in the month of virgo (**virgin Mary / Auset - Isis**) which is the sign of service. A sacrificial lamb is a metaphorical reference to a person or animal sacrificed for the common good. The most common animals used for sacrifice in ancient times were goats, bulls, sheep etc. A lamb is a baby sheep. This prophecy was not set in stone! I had to earn this revelation and as you read this book you will see how I rose from the muddy waters like the **lotus flowers** of **rebirth** which is also seen in the stela. In the stela the **lotus** stand supports the **two feathers** in Ausar's (Osiris's) headdress. Ausar is the lord of **resurrection** returning through his son **Heru** (p 482). The original name of the Sphinx was **Heru Em Ahket**, which has the head of a human and the body of a **lion**. In my life as Emmett I was a **Leo** like the **Lion.** In my life as Emmett Till I was the sacrificial **lamb** murdered in the year of the **goat** and I <u>united the **lion** with the **lamb**</u> by decoding the **riddle** of the Sphinx in my present life by applying the principles of **Maat** to my life and my actions (seen world). In this transformation I earned the right to know that I was Emmett Till (unseen world) in my most previous past life but that wasn't enough because life is continuously unfolding. I continued my journey and then I earned the right to know that I was **Tutankhaten (King Tut**, p 594). We must all aspire to be **Shemsu Heru** (followers of Heru). The followers of Heru are those who rise above their animalistic nature uniting the two lands, the seen and the unseen worlds. This is **spiritual alchemy**. This is how you pull **gold** from lead. I went through a blind initiation and by honoring the laws of **Maat** and the divine feminine energies on the planet I was gradually awakened to my previous lives (unseen dimensions) fulfilling the ancient prophecies. This prophecy is for all the citizens of the world, but in particular, and Very Expressly, to the Africans all over the world who still suffer under the oppression of racism and white supremacy.. As I have Remembered who I am it's important that you Ra-member / RE-MEMBER WHO YOU ARE! Sankofa.

The Hero’s Journey and the Return of Heru

All human beings have the **potent**ial to reach Heru consciousness (Christ, Chrism, p 492), becoming a metaphorical reflection of the Heru stela seen above. Ultimately, **Ausar** (Osiris) represents the **immortal soul** of all human beings that reincarnates, while **Auset** (Isis) represents intuition and wisdom. **Set** (Satan) represents your own **ego** and your lower nature. Finally, **Heru** (Horus) represents the potential of **your** spiritual stamina to **become** the Heru (**hero**) of **your** life journey, by conquering **your ego** (Set).. The Hero’s journey is a cyclical one. The hero goes off into the world and finds, or achieves, or does something beyond the normal range of achievement and experience, they give their lives to something bigger than themselves and returns home with a story of transformation to share. There are two types of Hero's, the physical one and the spiritual one. The physical hero might save someones life or sacrifice their own life for another person. The spiritual hero has learned or found some rare form of supernatural experience and comes back to communicate it. **I am** the spiritual Heru (Hero). Behold, The Reincarnation of **King Tut**, the golden boy who has fascinated the world since 19**22** and **Emmett Till**, the boy who’s death sparked the Civil Rights Movement in America, 67 years ago in 19**55**. These two boys are **fragments of my soul** from **different life times**. From the same soul I was **Born Again** in 19**77** as **Dawud Eddings** (p 34). In 2018 I realized I was Emmett Till in a past life (p 480) and in **2**02**0** I realized I was **King Tut** in a past life (p 594). It was ordained from the beginning of time that I would die a sacrificial death in my life as Emmett Till so that I could have the opportunity to be **Born Again**, **22** years later as Dawud Eddings and earn the right to know who I was and with the revealing of this revelation mans consciousness can be aroused and justice can at-last prevail (p 511). See page 481 for Ausar’s connection to the **garden** and the soul. See page **602** for the math connecting my previous lives, **the sacred geometry behind the transmigration of my soul**.

Out of Kemet (Egypt) I Will Call My Son (The prologue below is my creative imagination - Not a Memory, but....)

Rau nu Prt m heru

Iu f Per f m heru

My sun, you do not remember me but I am Nefer Kheperu Ra Wa en Ra, your father. You are my one and only son, a royal descendent from the 18th dynasty. Your name is Tutankhaten and your throne name will be Neb Kheperu Ra Heka **Maat**, you will die young but you will be born again and you will die again and you will be born again and again, so on and so forth. What you don't fix in each life you will suffer with in your next life! Through this journey of many lives you will become illuminated through the polishing, cleansing, and the shaping of your personality. Finally you will be born again at the coming of the Aquarian age. You will experience many trials and tribulations but the ancestors have paved a way for you. Even though that is true you will still need to earn the right to know the fullness of who you are and thereby becoming venerable in the presence of the great divine. You must take energy from Aten, the source of all your power. You will spend time in solitude seeking answers and if you hope to find these answers you must pay **Aten**tion to the signs. Much truth has been coded for you in music, movies, religious text and other forms of media. You must read the signatures and connect the dots, decoding your web like a constellation. You must continuously weigh the actions of your heart against the feather of **Maat**. Remember, that actions have reactions, so don't be quick to judge because you may not know the hardships people don't speak of. It's best to step back and observe with couth for we all must meet our moment of truth. When you are a teenager those words will make more sense. Be careful who you listen to because the poets of this time can mislead and deceive you. This life will be your great moment of truth. In this life you will be raised with the concepts of mortal men but you are not a mortal man. You are an immortal being of light. You are a beacon of light sent here to write, sent her to fight. You are a rocket ship. You have great potential but you will need to put forth supreme efforts to realize them. You will meet many helpers along your way. If you stay on course you will come to know your first previous life in your 40th year, then more tests will come your way and if you are once again successful, this royal life will come full circle at the age of 42, and a new name will be bestowed upon you and you will know the whole of who and what you are! Most of the men of this time are unaware of the two sides of existence. They lack the light of truth (**Maat**) and so they need a sign to bring them from the depths of their darkness so that their consciousness will be aroused and **Maat** (Justice) can at-last prevail. You have been chosen by the supreme council of galactic elders. I have placed much at stake to place you in the position to take up this quest. Do not let me down, do not let us down. My son, when you are born into this life as Tutankhaten you will forget everything I'm telling you right now. I have only been allowed to leave one code deep within a dream and you must earn the right to awaken to this dream. At some point they will open your metaphysical chamber (tomb) and that's when you must use the wisdom of Jhuty (Thoth) and the cosmic order of **Maat** to design your **Star Codes of Immortality.** Rest assured knowing that I will always be with you and **Amenta** will not be hard to find. Remember, as for the span of earthly affairs it is the manner of a dream. Eat drink and be merry for tomorrow we shall die. Aha tu sa e. Shem em hetep. Safe travels my son. Go in peace.

August 28th 1955

The Two Ladies

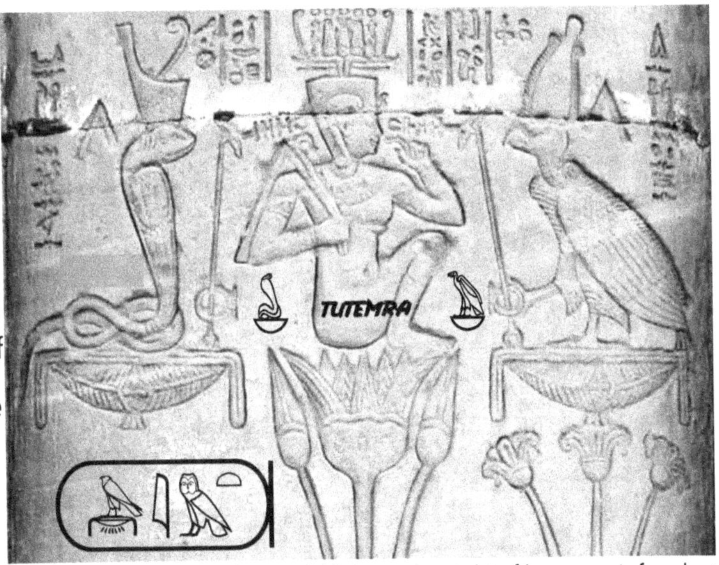

Utterances for Coming Forth by day into Light

It is he, who comes forth by day into Light

When Emmett arrived at the halls of **Maat** he was confused and still afraid. His last memory was a gun shot to his temple, then a fade to blackness, then a bright light and now he was here standing in the halls of **Maat**. His pineal gland (𓂀single eye, first eye, third eye, spiritual eye) had been flooded with **DMT** and now his **heart** was ready to be weighed against the feather of **Maat**. The two Ladies, **Wadjet** and **Nekhbet** appeared in front of him and spoke telepathically and simultaneously with gentle voices, "**Oh great one who resides in the house of Aten! Be not afraid. The ancestors have paved a way for you**." Instantaneously Emmett Louis Till was ushered into **Amenta** where he danced in the field of reeds for what felt like an eternity of jubilee. Soon after his soul returned to comfort and to protect his mourning mother, Mamie Till (page 514). Emmett was there when his mother gazed into the box and looked upon his mutilated body. They thought she would faint at the sight of her some's face but somehow she straightened up as if every bone in her body had turned to steel (page 79). She heard the voice of God that gave her the divine task that she was sent down here to fulfill (page 511). Mamie wasn't aware that Emmett was there all she could do is cry, still Emmett Till glides to his mother and tries to wipe the tears from her eyes. Tales from the other side, it's gonna be hell for them other guys, when it's their time to answer to the most high! At Emmett's funeral they read from revelations, Mamie's heart was racing with memories of his face and happy times. The racist legal system was blind to the crime of Milam and Roy killing a black boy, her only begotten son, her creation. When Emmett realized he was a soul that had died, on his Barque of Ages his soul did glide to 1922, where the most important part of the mission he still had to do. Be careful of the life path you pursue, and your life, how you live it. Most die and never get it, they lie cheat steal and still neglect the spirit, the clarion call they never hear it! They carry on having a ball, drugs, sex, alcohol, and at some point they hit a wall and fall, then they crawl back up and that's when they fear it. The truth is hard to bare it. The proof to God is in your merit, in your habits, are you a savage or benevolent?! Like David Walker the day walker intelligent gentlemen from North Carolina, in his jacket liner you might find a copy of **David Walker's Appeal** and a heavy piece of steel, because shit is real trying to stay alive in 1825. In 1831 **Nat Turner** was on the run. In **1850 The Slave Act** was enacted to catch slaves who escaped evaded capture like running backs breaking tackles, leaving crowds amazed, the truest practice, sink or swim, **Let's Get Free Or Die Trying,** now let's see who's the fastest. He grabbed the cops burner and then he blasted! On Nov 6th 1955, 70 days after Emmett's lynching, a place was reserved in the womb of his next mother and **22** years later in 1977 he was sent back here to complete the mission he had crafted in 1922 (P 11). He deciphered the first **star code** and returned during a total solar eclipse on Wednesday, Oct 12th 1977 (p 31). 13 days later he was born again in his new body on Oct 25th 1977 and immediately all memory of his mission was erased except one code (P 34). His ancestral father, Nefer Kheperu Ra Wa en Ra had stored the date **May 25th** deep within his subconscious locked inside of a dream within a dream (P 104). He would have to earn the right to awaken to this dream (page 30). These teachings were only passed down to the Kemetic Priest's and Nswt Bity's (Pharaoh's) in ancient times. Emmett isn't the only one on this mission. In fact if you are reading this then you are on the same mission but you just don't know it yet. We all have a part to play in this cosmic play of consciousness. SHEMSU HERU is the way (p 2)!

The Older Gods (The prologue below is my creative imagination - Not a Memory, But....!)

On this very plane in this very dimension that you have been taught to call a planet, the ancient Kemetyu had reached levels of consciousness long forgotten. As a result of many wars, the power grids were destroyed, the ancient knowledge was hidden and eventually isfet (evil) prevailed. The planet was thrown into chaos and with that came violent storms, and floods. Thousands of years passed and those who roamed away from royalty lost their way. With the absence of divine wisdom, and being subjected to harsh life conditions these man fell deeper to their lower nature, entrapped in the material realm. When they returned home and their eyes fell upon the ancient cities of the past they gazed with amazement. They came with admiration, and we filled their open hands. In their search for material wealth they became imperial killers. Serial sinister ministers, the harbingers of death finishers of everything, and so theft till nothings left swept across the land. With no understanding of what they saw they plundered and desecrated the ancient meta-spiritual devices (tombs) of the Older Gods. They had fallen so far from **Maat** that they became obsessed, even enough that they ate our decomposed flesh in hopes to somehow become one with the knowledge we possessed. They dug deep and took what mother earth needed for herself, to keep fertile health. They altered the nation and went away from the way of creation for generations, so far that they forgot the **Wehem Mesut** (the Cycle Of Regeneration). They disrupted the eternal cosmic play of consciousness and placed one man above the next, racing for occupation through extermination, like a dog chasing it's tail. They didn't know so they created a tale and called it his-story and deceived many. They changed the 10 day week to a 7 day week and disrupted time for reasons that were empty. They still search for these "tombs" today, still amazed with the flesh, still looking past what is not so easily seen when stuck on the two eyed quest. Over the millennia the supreme council of galactic elders managed to keep them from locating many of the divine meta-spiritual devices of the Older Gods'. The council patiently waited for the one who would triumph, defying the impossible odds by making a grand return sparking the revolutionary germ. And many did come doing great deeds but as valiant as they tried none were able to **decipher** and connect the **two lands** unified. Their meta-spiritual devices had been destroyed so seeing face upon face was never utilized. There was one who came just before we fell doomed, but he placed within his son, a seed that would dwell and take many life times to bloom. He fought tirelessly to restore **Maat** but the invasion of isfet prevailed and eventually we fell and the world forgot. But fret not, thousands of years later he came again in modern times as the Shining serpent leaving a mark as bright as the dazzling sun behind. But our adversaries were steadily on watch for his deadly melodies that could spark the prophetic return of Ra heavenly. He used the ancient bells of war hidden within his spoken words and for this he was slain but his death was not in vain because his message was heard by his son who was once a young pharaoh who escaped death a few times with a few scars, odds narrow. Inter-dimensional with his 3rd eye, a long distance he had to travel. Stuck in the middle of eternity speaking in **riddles** returning the 3rd time trinity with the potential to strike a supreme blow against the enemy to usher in the golden age of **Maat** consciousness but when he arrived here he had forgotten this. Over the course of 40 years of life on earth he slowly awoke from his slumber and saw everyone under a spell, somber. The temptation of the flesh was great and even greater when the soul wanders. He was given the hardest road of them all, the blind initiation. He knew not who he was or the prophecy of his reincarnation. Born again in the world at a decline with no teacher, no guide, and no guru to mold his young mind. He had to find the way on his own and the task was not easy. He was given his **suit**, his talents, 40 years and a mission to find the **other half** of a staff stolen, the hover **craft**, the **other half** of the math floating around in the ether. A mission only fit for the seekers. All the pages of this book tell the story of the Nswt who stole back his flail and his crook. The world is old but the future springs from the past to prevail in this book. He came back from the future where we're free at last but look, if you don't listen to what is written you might feel the wrath of the **crook**. This one is written for the seekers searching for high teachers in books and in preachers. You're smoking reefer and popping the red pills that lead to conspiracy theories having you feeling ill because it's a terror knowing the truth teller is getting killed. Might have done better by taking that blue pill but still, one day soon we'll be on top again! The Afrikan came back with unity as the stratagem, maximum effect like maroons ready to ride again. If I die I'll be back in the spirit to try again!

ADDENDUM

How did the ancient Kemetyu (Egyptians) depict themselves?

From the walls of the Tomb of **Ramses III** we can see from the **objective evidence** that the ancient Kemetyu (Egyptians) depicted themselves as **jet black in skin color** and dressed identical to the other black Africans to the south (**Kushites**). In figures **A** and **B** we can see the actual wall reliefs while in figures **C - 1** through **C - 4** we see how the ancient Kemetyu depicted themselves and other peoples who entered their land.

A

F.a

B

F.b

C

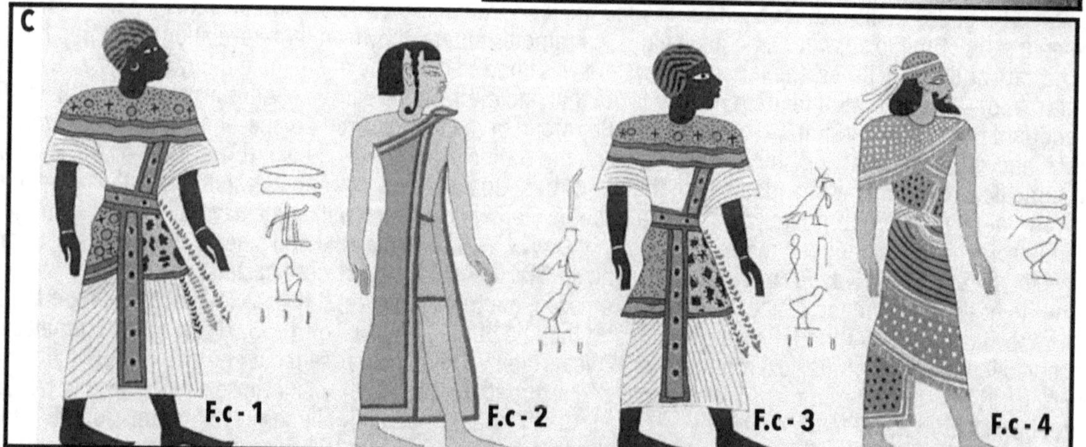

F.c - 1 F.c - 2 F.c - 3 F.c - 4

The ancient Kemetyu (Egyptians) as depicted by themselves.

The ancient Kemetyu (Egyptians) as depicted by themselves.

The Indo-European (Caucasoids).

Other Blacks in Africa (Kushites) from the south.

The Semite.

The 49th anniversary of Hip Hop, Sound, Vibration and a Message to the Musicians

Rau nu Prt m heru

Iu f Per f m heru

Utterances for Coming Forth by day into Light

It is he, who comes forth by day into Light

Life is a symphony speaking in **riddles** with harmonic patterns that govern our paths. Some say "in the beginning was the word", while others proclaim the "Big bang", either or, to speak a word is to create sound and to create sound is to **emit** a vibration. The human ear is only capable of hearing a small range of sound frequencies and there are frequencies above and below what humans can hear or perceive. The same is to be said about the spectrum of light. Between the unseen and unheard frequencies of sound and light is where the energy of God can be found, also known as **dark matter**. The heart and the mind are used to permeate this dimension. A negative word sent with bad intentional vibrations can cause a negative reaction even to the point of changing the molecular structure of the water you drink or the cells within the body. The same can be said about loving words sent with loving intentional vibrations, they can evoke healing. **Cancer cells can be shattered** like glass and destroyed when two pulsating resonant frequencies (sound vibrations) are aimed at them but the frequency fields must be between 100,000 and 300,000 Hertz, and the higher frequency must be 11 times the lower (the 11th harmonic). You can diagnose disease by the rhythm of a persons pulse and you can tell a persons growth by the choice of music they listen to or the music they create. The vibration of sound can brake glass, destroy bridges or it can heal the broken heart and even awaken ancient soul fragments. Sound vibration was used as a healing modality in the ancient temples of Kemet. The pitch of 40 Hertz reduces fibromyalgia pain and helps to reduce the loss of memory associated with Alzheimer's. Depression, insomnia, stress and Parkinson's disease can all be reduced with sound therapy. Speaking of hertz, **Hertz sounds** like **Hurts**. Which is probably why the medieval physicians and **dentist** used the hertz in music to distract their patients from the pains or the hurts of their barbaric surgeries. In 2018 my friend Tobius walked into the last chamber on the left in the Temple of Ramses II and as soon as he entered the chamber his body began to vibrate (p 533). The temple itself was and instrument, due to the precise stone placements that allowed them to be "played" like music. There is no **coincidence** as to why the "organs" of the body are located near chakra energy centers in the body or why "organs" are "played" in churches (Temples). And there is no **coincidence** as to why the choir is made to sing at church before the preacher delivers his sermon or why the muslim prayers are recited in a harmonious singing manner, or why the words Om, Amen and Ra are used as vibrational chanting mantras. The body is a divine temple that can be affected by sound. When music is heard it is able to reach the subconscious regions of the mind and if it is powerful enough it can penetrate ones soul. For those creating the music even more powerful transformations can take place. Either way, the creator of music is responsible for they create and the listener is responsible for what they choose to listen to. The pyramids and other megalithic structures across the planet were designed to emit powerful vibrations and were strategically built on top of energetic locations of the earths surface. Not to mention the method in which they were built. We are only left to speculate how these massive stones were set in place but anti gravity by sound vibration or magnetism should not be excluded from the realm of possibilities. In my song, **Grid of the Gods** written in 2020 (p 609), I speak of magic and moving stones with sound, "<u>We stacked 12 sided stones in great numbers, make you wonder what magic the ancients honed? anti gravity? and the grid of the Gods that's coming home"…. "airtime soaring magician acoustic levitation, exploring the hidden, the music use it for revelation</u>".

Rau nu Prt M Hru

DMT

This book was brought forth in 2022, the **49th** anniversary of **Hip Hop** and **49** days is the amount of time the **Tibetans believed** it took one soul to be **reborn** into another life. The active component within the sacred psychoactive **DMT** molecule is called **dimethyltryptamine** and the **pineal gland** (3rd eye) is responsible for producing this molecule and it appears in the embryo at the **49th** day of gestation. DMT is secreted during birth (via the mother), upon death and during near death experiences. Why is this important? I unconsciously used music (Hip Hop) as magic which helped awaken my ancient soul fragments.. If used properly music can be a source of healing and transformation when it originates in the heart. In the Kemetic Mdw Ntr (Hieroglyphs) the word for magic was **Heka**, however the concept of magic was complex. The Mdw Ntr were known as 'divine words' and the creation of writing was credited to Jhuty (Thoth) who was said to have the most Heka. Another translation for heka is '**Art of the Mouth**' or magical meaningful speech / utterance; word with mystic effects and **Hekau** meant **words of power**. Jhuty is the nTr that governs divine wisdom, thought and articulate speech. His wife was **Maat** and without **Maat** there is no Heka. The balancing of **Maat** allowed the ancient Priests/Magicians to 'perform magic', the more heka one had, the greater their ability to do magic. Heka was also present in written words so owning books or scrolls and reading them gave you more heka. Because heka connects everything from the Divine to the material, it is invariably linked to **Maat** (p, 367). **Hip Hop** is the world's most popular genre and art form, simultaneously influencing politics, social issues, culture, and society as a whole. However, over time Hip Hop culture has been devalued and degraded leading to the early demise of many Hip Hop artist due to health related issues and unnecessary violence. We must be careful what we "spell" and we should never write music about killing our selves. We must move into our greatness in all areas of our being. Especially in our Hip Hop music. Hip Hop as a whole, must move to a place of enlightenment. We must grow and we must change for the better. We must do more than just addressing ourselves as Kings and Queens! We must actually do the things our ancestral Kings and Queen did. It is time for us to allow ourselves to be great. Greatness in any form is rarely accepted and appreciated at first glance but when we experience growth in our character and our spiritual life we can begin to appreciate the higher possibilities of music. If I unconsciously used Hip Hop as magic which helped awaken my ancient soul fragments, then what can you do with music if you have my experience in mind? Greater things can do you! Perhaps move the mountains of oppression you will. Both Fela Kuti and Nipsey Hussle once said that, "music is spiritual and not to be played with". Perhaps it was the **opening of my mouth** with music that **expanded** my spiritual life (p 356). My grand father, General Dukes Jr, passed away from **cancer** in 2009 (p 169), then he appeared to me in **spirit form** in 2015 (p 348) and afterwards he began to appear in my **dreams** but in these dreams he would never speak. In 2021 I got my first and only **IFA reading** (p 641). The next day my grand father appeared to me in a **dream** and for the first time he spoke to me in a **dream**. In this dream my grand father delivered **<u>a message to the musicians</u>** (p 642). In the dream my grandfather and I saw **Hip Hop artists** rapping on a stage with negative lyrics. My grand father looked at them, then **he asked me**, "**If the music had to be so violent**?", then I woke up (p 642). You should know that the oldest writings known to man are utterances, spells or "rhymes/hymns" written on the walls in the tombs of the **Nswt Bity** (pharaoh) evoked to ensure the safe passage of the pharaoh after death and towards the **resurrection** in the next life (**Wehem Mesut,** p 14). These **utterances** first appeared in the pyramid of **Unas**, the last pharaoh of the fifth dynasty (p 670). These writings were called the pyramid text by archeologist, then they were later referred to as the coffin text and the Book of The Dead because they were found written on papyrus buried with the dead. During the reign of Hatshepsut these spells were, for the first time, given its own name, "The Book of Coming Forth by Day". There was a brief interlude during the reign of Akhenaten when the spells fell out of use, but when they returned they appeared (among other places) on the gilded shrine of Tutankhaten. And for the first time the image of a snake swallowing it's tail was seen, (**Wehem Mesut**, page 657). This book is the modern "**Book of The Dead**" because it was the **murder** of **Black life** that caused the names of my ancient soul fragments to "**Come Forth by Day and Night**" in my music (p 201, 597). When we **open our mouths** we can speak from our ego or our souls. What is music anyway? Isn't it the bleeding of the **soul**?! The use of language in music should never be reduced to reckless art. **Music** can bring tears, it can bring laughter, it can tear people apart or it can bind them together. In physics, entrainment is the action of one rhythmic vibrating object synchronizing with another, like two tuning forks. Are you aware of how music was used in the **Haitian revolution**?! Read the words of Jean-Baptiste, "<u>But what men these blacks are! How they fight and how they die! One has to make war against them to know their reckless courage in braving danger, when they can no longer have recourse to strategm I have seen a solid colum, torn apart by grapeshot from 4 pieces of cannon, advance without making a retrograde step. The more they fell, the greater seemed to be the courage of the rest. They advanced **SINGING**, for **the negroes sing everywhere**. **Making songs to everything**. Even today after more than 40 years, this majestic and glorious spectacle still lives as vividly in my imagination as in the moments when I saw it</u>" - Jean-Baptiste Lemonnier-Delafosse (1770-1840). Before you go running in search of some glorious past life, go run an pick up the feather of Maat. This book is not just about the realization of my previous lives. What is more important for the reader is that you "inner" stand the events that brought about the unraveling of this revelation. This revelation is more like an equation of intuition, time, space, coincidences, dreams, visions, **synchronicities** and other profound variables that manifested in a musical display of the mathematics (p **41**) of the heart, driven by the Heru (hero) journey of the **soul** (see page 3), all of which was governed by the unseen realms. I am the **Alchemist** coded within **Hip Hop** (p 633). This is **Divine Alchemy** of the soul, the only alchemy that **maat**ters.

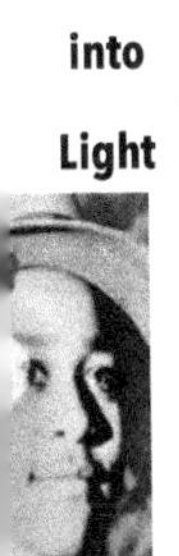

ADDENDUM

I Remember The Time Now

I am writing this book for many reasons, the first of which being a feeling deep within my being that knows I am supposed to share this with the world. A part of me feels that people clouded by their belief systems might want to cause me harm for the truth that I present in this document but the soul is immortal so I disregard that and I let thy will be done. A part of me also screams out '***You will know that I came back and that I descend from the people labeled as niggers***!" I want those who keep my possessions and my family's possessions in museums all over the world to know that the artifacts they collect tourist money off of actually belong to people! To the new $**55**0 million Grand Egyptian Museum that houses much of my stolen property, I want my things. If you truly honor Kemetic culture then the principles of **Maat** are at hand and practicing excellent diplomacy like my grand father Amenhotep III is the most ideal and noble thing to do. Under these extraordinary circumtances I am open to negotiations. I want the archeologist who spend their life's energy digging for treasure in the soil to know that the real treasure is found when we dig within our souls! I want the religious people to consider for a moment, that perhaps the Bible is not a literal book. Perhaps it is religious literature because some of it was plagiarized (page 615) and much of what is written in it is allegory (page 488). For instance, perhaps the **Jews** are not a group of people, perhaps they are the **chakras/Glands** of the body. Revelations, ch 2:9 says, "those who claim they are Jews but they are not, they are the synagog of Satan". This Scripture is referring to people who have not raised themselves up via the inward path, those who have not built their "Noah's Ark (page 252). As a child I always felt like there was something about me and this world that I did not know, a feeling that I'm sure most of you can relate to. I want the **Christians**, the **Muslims**, the **Jews**, the Gentiles, the Brahmans, the Priests and the Popes, so on and so forth to put a side your beliefs for a moment. Open up your mind of imagination and use your imagination when reading this book allowing your heart to be the guide. Listen to my story and know that it is true. For the Muslim, you should know that I was born a Muslim and my middle name is Basheer (the bringer of truth). For the Christian, you should know that I got baptized at 11 (p 49) and gave my life to Christ at 22 (p 92) and my born name is Dawud which means David (beloved of God). For those who practice Hinduism, you should know that the Buddha always returns and I have come again (p 2 & 288). For the Jews and Christians waiting for someone to return through the line of David, you should know that my father in this life was given the name David as his middle name (p 28) and in my life as Tutankhaten I descend from the pharaonic line of Thutmoses (Jhutyms) III, the historical King David. My father was Akhenaten (Amenhotep IV) and he is the real person that the biblical character Moses was fashioned after. My grand father was Amenhotep III, the real person that the biblical character King Solomon was fashion after. My grand mother was Queen Tiye, the real person that the biblical character Queen Sheba was fashion after. My great grand father was Thutmoses (Jhutyms) IV, the great war general. My great great grand father was Amenhotep II and my great great great grand father was Thutmoses (Jhutyms) III, the real person that the biblical character King David was fashioned after. There's no structural or tangible proof that this David from the bible ever lived but Thutmoses (Jhutyms) III lived a life that parallels the stories of David from the bible and you can see, touch and read about Thutmoses on the walls of Kemet (p 225). Thutmoses (Jhutyms) III is the historical David and he is my great great great grand father. I am the reincarnated soul of Tutankhaten (King Tut) and I am the one you've been waiting for. I hope I didn't disappoint you too much. I once saw a European archeologist awaiting the results from the DNA samples of a mummy from ancient Nubia. He seemed so, disappointed when the results proved the mummy to be Afrikan. How can we prove that the bible was influenced by the great Afrikans from the 18th dynasty (**Mission-Aries** p 667)? Take the poem **Psalms 104** from the Bible as an example. My father wrote **The Hymn to the Aten** over 3000 years ago yet a plagiarized version of it found its way into the psalms of David, title Psalms 104 (p 615). Akhenaten is seen as the father of monotheism (one God concept) which all Abrahamic religions follow but Akhenaten didn't create the concept, he just crystallized teachings about the sun's life giving properties that his forefathers taught him. His father Amenhotep III was known as the **Dazzling Sun** and his mother Queen Tiye knew about the life giving properties of the sun (RA). The bible pulls from a time period that covers the 18th dynasty (Age of Aries) that "King Tut" comes from so if anyone will return from this bible prophecy it will be the son of the father of monotheism which is me, Tutankhaten, the son of Akhenaten. Even the story of Jesus was taken from the story of Ausar (Osiris) and Jesus taught about reincarnation (p 592). For all the other religions or spiritual people know that I have never been an enemy to any faith. I was always a seeker of truth even as a little boy and that is why I decided to get baptized at 11 (p 49). **I'm writing this book for all peoples of the world but it is more intimately directed to those in bondage.** It is important that you know that this life you are living is not the end. There is a great chance that you might come back here again. <u>So we must make this world a better place not just for the children of the world but more importantly we must make it a better place for our souls to come back to</u>. It's one thing to be born into **racism** and **white supremacy** but it's another thing entirely to **reincarnate** into it over and over and never know it! I listened to **Michael Jackson's** song *Remember The Time* and watched the video like everyone else but NEVER DID I "RA-member The Time"! I looked at **Nas's** album cover ***I AM*** and saw him as a **golden pharaoh** but NEVER DID I THINK I WAS A PHARAOH (page 443). In fact Nas was one of the Emcees that kept me from pursuing Hip Hop as a teen because to me I could not write at his level and so why take rap seriously if I wasn't the best (more on **Nas**, page 54). I was clouded by my level of skill at football where I amazed crowds, so Hip Hop was always a hobby for me and I accepted it as just that and nothing more. Tupac died the day before Nas's birthday and **Nas** has a daughter named **Destiny** who is "**coincidentally**" born the day before **Tupac's** birthday. I have a theory about who **Tupac** was in a past life. After he died in 1996 there were many people including myself who felt like he was still alive, living in hiding. There were websites made that had all the events linked by songs and dates speculating the faking of his death. It seemed that Tupac was connected to the numbers 25 and 7 (page 41). He was shot on Sep **7th** and died on the **7th** day on Sep 13th at 25 years old, the same day that my uncle died (p 28). "**Coincidentally**" his Last album was titled, **Makaveli**, The Don Killuminati: **The 7 Day Theory**, and on that album his ancient soul revealed itself (p 664-665). Being intrigued with his death opened me up to numbers and connections which seemed to have prepared me for the decoding of my previous lives years to come (p 222). As I tell my story you will see how significant dates are used to confirm my prophecy. How all things have worked towards the coming of this Golden age. Decoding messages of the spiritual nature will not always be easy as 1 2 3. In many instances you will need to have a higher under standing of the spiritual world. Just because you don't understand something doesn't mean it is untrue or impossible. Many of us have seen a movie as a child or read a book as a child then revisited them as adults and as adults you were able to perceive more from the movie or book. And this is the sad part because we all watch movies like the **Matrix** or **Avatar** and deep within our subconscious we know that there is some hidden knowledge that eludes us. Nothing is just a **coincidence** my friend and we make a fatal error when we think all that we see with our two eyes is all that there is to see. All things are governed by seen and unseen forces. We will be free and no one will give us this freedom. We will take it. We will liberate our souls and the rest will follow. Know that this can be done peacefully, in fact all we need to do is turn towards the sun, the sun that is within you (p 667). Ultimately, **Ausar** is the **immortal soul** of all human beings that reincarnates, **Auset** is the intuition and wisdom, **Set** is your own **ego**, While **Heru** is the potential of your spiritual stamina to become the Hero (**heru)** of your life journey, conquering **your own ego** (Set).. Ramemeber the ancients, the Ancestors, the Ancient Star Ntchrs. Read my story and see what happened to me! Then ask yourself if your path has produced this kind of nectar... If it hasn't, I welcome you to the path of **Shemsu Heru** (the followers of Heru) in search of Heru Konsciousness (p 2). See page 3 for more on the **Hero's (Heru's) journey**.

MANY WILL COME IN MY NAME, CLAIMING THEY ARE TUTANKHATEN, BUT BECAUSE OF THIS BOOK THEY WILL DECEIVE NO ONE !

Rau nu Prt m heru

Iu f Per f m heru

Utterances for Coming Forth by day into Light

It is he, who comes forth by day into Light

This book came forth during my current life as Dawud and in it I mention many of the people I love and care for, many of the places I've traveled, mistakes I've made, my wins and my losses, many of the women I've fallen in love with, many of the people I've looked up to, and many of the people I've argued with.. All of these people and experiences have been instrumental in shaping the way I view life but none has been more beneficial than the self imposed discipline I have subjected myself to at different stages in my life. Life is about the demonstration, manifestation, and realization of the divine self hidden within each one of us. I'd never thought I was any specific person in another life until I knew I was Emmett Till instantaneously, in the blink of an eye, on July 3rd 2018 (page 480). Prior to that I'd heard Mitchel Gibson speak about soul fragments and **birthmarks** being part of the **genetic memory** connected to how people may have died in previous lives (p 395). That was in 2014 and that was the first time I ever thought about the possibility of living before in another life. Because of the many **black dots** I have around my body, I thought that I must have been a **rebellious slave** who would not submit to enslavement, and so I must have been shot many times. I had that thought but never did I communicate it to anyone or connect it to a specific person from the past. Nor did I fully believe it. I just pondered about the many black dots on my body. Like the black dot on my chest that seemingly connects with the black dot on my back, which made me consider the idea of being shot in the heart with the bullet exiting my back. I did not think I was a **pharaoh** or a **prince** or some great **leader**. I figured that I must have been the same type of rebellious soul that I am now in this life and because of that I must have been murdered. In 2016 I met a woman in massage therapy school who told me she was into **past life regression**. She told me that she felt like she was a **witch** in another life but that didn't cause me to look into past lives or to think I was any specific person in a past life. Even though right after she told me that I had a profound paranormal experience which I wrote about in this book (page 418). Prior to my first past life revelation I had a healthy belief that **Jesus** was going to one day return and because of that I would write about **resurrection** often in my rhymes. Even though I liked writing rhymes as a teenager I never believed in myself enough to consider the idea of being a rapper. I never thought I was a great emcee, I just wrote as a hobby and because I loved putting words together. However many of the **spells** I wrote throughout the course of my life turned out to be **prophetic** as I realize now that it was my soul attachments writing. Emmett was writing, and at some point the oldest parts of my soul began to be more prominent in my writing. I may not break any sales records or win any awards but yet still, I have done the most powerful thing EVER done with music and the divine will. My music was the pyramid text turned to flesh. I awoke to my previous lives by aligning the actions of my heart with the principles of Maat (page 367). Writing this book was the most tedious and arduous undertaking I have ever embarked on however something came over me and would not allow me to stop until I was done.

When my past life as Emmett came (p 480) I told many people. I told anyone who would listen. I posted about it online. I wrote about it in music. Never had I ever met a person who knew exactly who they were in a past life. I had heard about reincarnation loosely in books but I never did any study on it and again, when I was a Chrisrtian, it was Jesus who I thought was coming back one day. When I told the Kemetic priest **Mfundishi Jhutyms**, he told me to, **"write it down"** and I said yes I would, but I didn't. I just went on telling people about all the connections as I continuously found more and more connections and I'm still finding connections to this day. This was indeed a preplanned return. Nothing this precise can be just a coincidence and nothing this precise can be meaningless. When my past life as Tutankhaten (King Tut) came on April 4th 2020 (p 594) it came instantaneously, in the blink of an eye just like when my past life of Emmett came but this one was more profound and precise. I was even given the **NEW NAME** , **TutemRa**! Again, I told the story of this past life revelation to anyone who would listen. I posted it online and I wrote about it in my music. I was amazed. This is when most of the people in the Kemetic circle that I was in began to distance themselves from me. Many of the men and women who teach the kemetic way of life disregarded me. Some of them were the very people that the ancestors had used to help me realize this revelation yet when they heard my claim I felt as if they abandoned me. The only elder who took interest in my story was Minister Clemson Brown (P 518). I reached out to Mitchell Gibson (p 395) via Instagram but he blocked me. He did not believe me. That was disheartening as I had a couple of his books and found them helpful. He would be just one of many people who were helpful in my journey but would shun me away when I came to them with what I had uncovered. I went to Mfundishi Jhutyms again, after my past life as Tutankhaten was revealed but I'm not sure if he believed me. I began to feel that I was alone in my journey for the most part and Just like Mfundishi had suggested when my life as Emmett came, I began to write my story. In writing my story I realized that whether or not people believed my experience, it still needed to be told. As you read my story I hope that you can move from a place of sorrow with the tragic way my life as Emmett Till ended (p 507) and come rejoice with me in the reality of my rebirth (p 480 & 594). I'm writing a Epic Sci-Real (Science Reality) Novel Trilogy version of this book and a book about Tupac's ancient past life (p 664). Stay tuned!

When my life as Emmett came people began to tell me that they too felt they had lived previous lives before but when my life as Tutankhaten came many people told me that they also felt like they were pharaohs from ancient Kemet (Egypt). This got my attention. Then I began to come across men online who felt like they were Tutankhaten in their previous lives. This bothered me greatly but **I had many mixed feelings** about it. Part of me felt angry because I had found this past life in the most profound way and here I find these men online claiming to be "me". I had never met another man who thought he was Emmett Till in another life but yet here I was finding all these men who thought they were the reincarnation of King Tut, Amenhotep III and so on and so forth. These men bothered me but I always wanted to hear their stories. As soon as I would find one I would ask him questions about how he came to know he was "King Tut" in his past life. I told them all quite bluntly that I was the reincarnation of Emmett Till and Tutankhaten (King Tut), I would explain my revelation to them then I would asked them to explain their revelation and the most common response was, "I don't need to explain anything to you". Some of them even blocked my Instagram page. That's when I began to realize that some people saw me just as delusional as I saw these men, but I wasn't like them! I had a **star code pattern** with many layers of revelation, and I was writing a book! Most of these men all had the same story, they had a **dream** or saw a **vision** but none of them had what I experienced. They all used my ancient names, Tutankhaten or Tutankhamen and none of them had been given a new name the way I had been given my name (p 594). They did not have my experience and they did not have the **star code** that I had. I began to realize what was happening. Black people are suffering from a separation from culture and past history and when some of us come in contact with the truth about our past in ancient Kemet many of us attach ourselves to the greatness of that time. Inside of all of us is a feeling of being special because we are special. When I realized what was happening I began to respond with compassion to the men I kept coming across who felt they were King Tut and other Pharaohs. I would also meet many women who felt they were the reincarnation of Nefertiti, Nefertari, Cleopatra, Queen Tiye and so on and so forth. They all had different variations of the same story. Still I have never met a man who thought he was Emmett Till. And the name Emmett is in the name K**emet**. You will understand the importance of this when you read the story of my Lynching in 1955 M**ississ**ippi (page 508). My death was an Ausarian resurrection not some visionary induced feeling, dream or deep desire for connection. Based on my experiences I think this is a time of a great awakening. I think the souls of our ancient ancestors have come to help lead us and that is indeed divine. If you are feeling called to Kemet then you are of the chosen and it is very important that you allow your own soul to shine through without the obstruction of your self imposed attachment to a specific person in the past. If you walk the path of Maat your soul will find you, and that is not to say that every person will find a past life. That is not the purpose of life. Previous lives are real and some of us do find them but not everyone will find their previous life and that's ok. Life is full of other important tasks to fulfill. This was my great task, to remind you of the immortality of your soul. It was ordained from the beginning of time that I would die a sacrificial death so that I could have the opportunity to come back here again in this life and earn the right to know who I was and with the revealing of this revelation mans consciousness will be aroused and justice can at-last prevail (page 511). For those of you that identify as white or European, and feel that you've lived lives in ancient Kemet (Egypt); if you did live a life in Kemet it is of utmost importance that you equip yourself with sound right facts about the past. And with this truth, you should be compelled to uphold **Maat** by doing your part to restore balance in the world, standing on truth, insuring justice is meted out, and being morally righteous in all your doings.

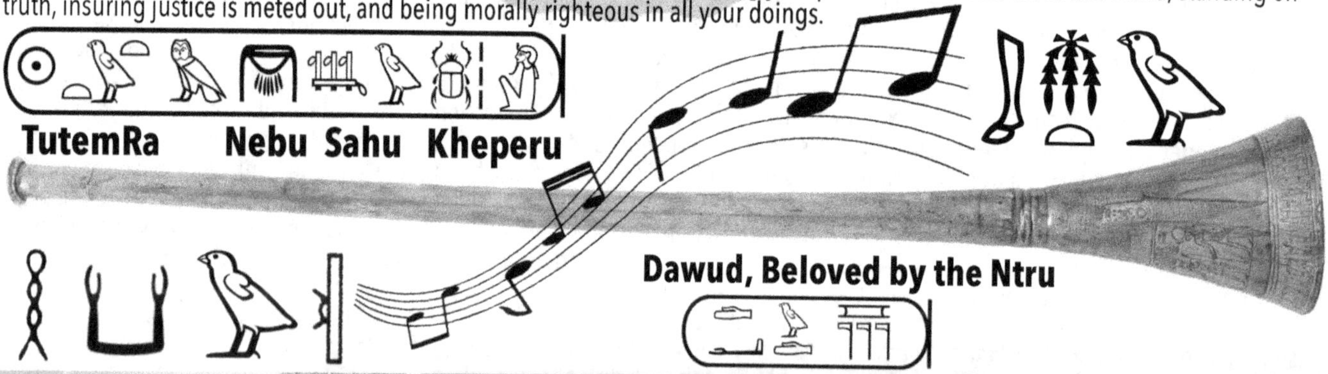

Rau nu Prt m heru

Iu f Per f m heru

Utterances for Coming Forth by day into Light

September 4th 2020 The Young Pharaoh

He was a young **Pharaoh,** long distance he had to travel, inter-dimensional 3rd eye, bulls eye tears from the cattle, **Het Heru,** she was true, lead the army into battle, **TutemRa Kheperu,** her great great great grand nephew, I bet you, if you ever paid **Aten**tion, 60 days in the future on an unknown planet, **Atlantis** Ascension, divine guidance, not easy for comprehension, hindsight is 20 20 parallel dimensions, the time is 10:10 I was riding, I forgot to mention the chariots of electrum, strapped with a weapon for the mission, **Pepi the 2nd** the longest reign, every millisecond rep'n **Kemet,** the spirit of **Emmett** shot down and chained, and it went down in flames like the library, they claim they feel my pain but I know they lie to me - **TutemRa (p 627)**

September 4th 2021

Todays date is Sep 4th 2021 and as of this date TutemRa has no memory of any life he has previously lived but he knows he has lived many times as you will come to see. He longs for a memory even if for just a second. When he is in a sleepy state usually while reading and dozing off he has bouts of **Deja Vu** yet and still the experiences are never enough to **salvage a complete feeling** or image. He is left thinking about kemet with a feeling of emptiness, like seeing food in front of you and eating it but never being able to smell it or taste it and never feeling full. He is mourning his own death from his life as Emmett Till for the fourth year in a row while to the world at large he is a ghost. He longs for the love of his ancient wife Ankhesenaten, surely if he is here again then perhaps she might be too, but where?! Where is she?! He tells people who he was in his previous lives but most people give him a blank stare. It wasn't until earlier today that he found out that his grand father had a brother named **Emmett** Dukes (p 23) and that's what forced him out of his despair and started him writing again. He had no idea that the next month he would be given yet another previous life he had lived. He would finally experience a memory from another life he lived in the 7th century (p 659). The very next year his feelings of **Deja Vu** would take an interesting turn. In 2022 he went to Kemet for the first time in this life and while there he had **Deja Vu** two times (pages 670 - 671).

Iahmose Nefertari

(page 15, 637)

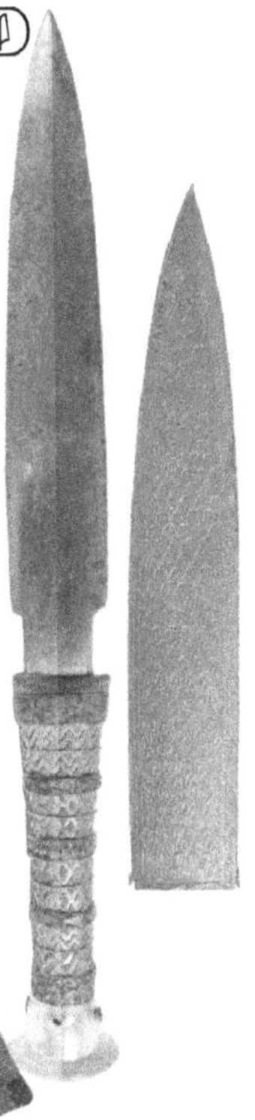

Incarnations

It is he, who comes forth by day into Light

Once upon a time there was a soul that found itself lost in the netherworld - navigating the Duat, traversing the universe between space and time. This soul would crash again on a plane it had lived on many times before. It's been said that since time immemorial only a few souls had ever successfully survived an awakening there. This plane was not like others, it was a sick plane and because of this only the bravest of souls or the most foolish of souls ever ventured there. They called this plane the great mystery because when most souls incarnate there they completely forget who and what they are. Tens of thousands of years ago or longer, during the times of the pyramids, awakening to mans greater potential and the immortality of the soul was a known reality, but that time was long gone.

This plane was known as planet Earth at the time of this awakening. They were approaching the age of Aquarius and the year was 1922. This planet is extremely older than 99.9999% of the inhabitants will ever come to know but most people on earth were operating on the premise that the earth is only 6000 years old. This false theory was brought forth by an **arch**bishop from Ireland named **James Ussher**. In 1654 he claimed that God created earth on Oct **23**rd 4004 BCE, at 9 am. Even **Sir Isaac Newton** believed the earth was created in 3998 BC. Since then Christianity bound most of the world into a box of 6000 years, claiming that the meta-spiritual devices (pyramids) could be no older than 6000 years. On Earth there are those who put all their hard work and efforts on material things that can be seen as well as the part of life spent during the day light when the sun was seen. Then there were those who focused more on the the unseen realms of life and the state called dreaming which was usually done at night when the sun was not seen. There were also the ones who never gave any of this any thought at all. On the Planet Earth it is not guaranteed that you will start a life in a state of knowing that's why it's called the great mystery.. In fact most people live many lives there and never even realize the purpose of them being there let alone the fact that they had once lived there at all. TutemRa was an interesting soul on the planet Earth as he would crash there time and time again, always finding his poetry and always doing divine works of good for the betterment of the whole. It wasn't until his most recent incarnation that TutemRa would consciously realize why he had been coming back to Earth. Earth was a play of consciousness and it reminded him of the game **senet** that he loved to play. **Iahmose Nefertari** is seen above playing **senet**, the game that **chess** was fashioned after. See page 648 for the **metaphysical significance** of the **number 23**.

November 4th 1922 CATCH 22

(The prologue below is my creative imagination - Not a Memory, but.....)

On November 4th 1922 Archaeologist Howard Carter and his benefactor Lord Carnarvon would discover the tomb of the long lost and forgotten boy King Tutankhaten. Shortly after discovery of the tomb a **giant king cobra snake** was found in the room of Lord Carnarvon having eaten his canary bird. That would be **the first sign** of a possible **curse**. Shortly after that the workers at the excavation site began to leave their posts in fear of the curse of the pharaoh. After weeks of digging they would open the main entrance to the tomb on November 26th 1922 and saw "wonderful things". They began to loot and desecrate the first four rooms of the tomb. On February 16th 19**23** they opened the last chamber and.......... *Boom* ***once they open his tomb*** *in the air you can smell the whispers of fear and doom cause it's near (p 540)* - They found Tutankhaten's sarcophagus and at that very moment the most ancient portion of Tutankhaten's soul was set free from the prison of untold millions of years. His many incarnations flashed before his eyes and he knew he was the **Karast** (**anointed one**, Nswt Bity, Pharoah, King) in the sarcophagus. He knew he'd been back to earth many times since he'd ruled in ancient Kemet but the memories of these other lives he did not have. Tutankhaten found himself without a body, just a soul looking down at the pale face Hyksos, they were back and now they had found his tomb just as it had been planned. They were cataloging and stealing his possessions and they were just as blind to the reality of life as they had been 4000 years ago. On February 26th 19**23** they opened the last room in his tomb. To their amazement they found 4 gilded (golden) shrines, one inside of the other. In the last shrine they found a stone sarcophagus. Inside the stone sarcophagus they found 3 golden coffins, one inside of the other. The last of which was solid gold and it was sealed tight with tar like resin so they used extreme heat to melt the resin which caused the remains of the mummy to cook. Tutankhaten couldn't focus too much time on that though. He had to find another body and fast. He was operating in the **astral realm** and only had 70 earth days to work in this dimension. He knew he was here to restore **Maat** (page 367) but he also knew that it wouldn't be easy because once he entered another body he would forget all of this again. He would have to earn the right to know who he was and even then the task would not be easy but knowing that the ancestors were with him gave him solace. He summoned a fleet of star seeds and calculated the light in the heavens, using the arrival of each star seed as signs, down to the minutes, days and the years. With the wisdom of Jhuty (Thoth) and the cosmic order of **Maat** he designed the **Star Codes of Immortality** and it only took him **22** earth seconds to complete. Theses Star Codes are the **Sacred Geometry behind the transmigration of his soul fragments (See page 602).** When he was done, one by one **22** people that were involved with the desecration of his tomb met their end under "mysterious" circumstances. Lord Carnarvon would die less than 2 months later on Apr 5th 19**23**, a day after the day that **Martin Luther King** was assassinated (Apr 4th 1968, p 69). When he was done he went to sleep and prepared for the **total eclipse** on Oct 12th 1977 the year of the **snake** (p 31).

June 14th 2021 Catch 22

It's not that I'm writing a book, I'm just putting things in order, like **Shook** in 95 - recorded in 94, have you ever had **DeJa Vu?** this is nothing knew I've seen this before! catch **22**, I was walking out the store, they say I **whistled,** but for what? they not really sure, I ate the bread the color was hoar, here to restore **Maat,** you forgot who got the props, they process the poor, the poor soul get's lost in lure and lust on this ball of confusion, look at the score it's us, we down! 1921 **sun down towns**, they said a change gonna come but until then don't come around, so we went and found happiness health excitement, then they burnt it down cause they don't got love or enlightenment, and the question now is, at what time am I writing this? there might exist a space and time on some **psychic** shit, **Amen Atum Aten**, never to be forgotten, from **Neb Kheperu Ra**, to slave fields pick'n cotton, from **Emmett Till** getting killed thrown in a river rotten, like **Ausar** I came back as **Dawud, TutemRa - TutemRa**

Significance

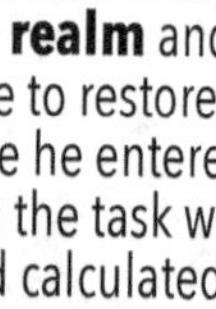

I wrote this on June 14th 2021 and then 5 months later on **December 11th 2021** I would watch a video of **Prodigy** from the legendary group **Mobb Deep** whom I mention in this song ("like **Shook** in 95 - recorded in 94"). In this video Prodigy was wearing a gold **Nefertiti** chain reminiscent of **Tupac** and in the video Prodigy would detail some of the **supernatural** experiences he has had including seeing a **UFO** (p 663), seeing **shadow people**, and being told that this was not his first time living here on this planet, that **he has lived on this planet many times for many thousands of years** (p 663). It was as if the soul of Prodigy had come to me to confirm my findings. Prodigy is a scorpio like myself and he is born on November 2nd, two days before the discovery of Tutankhaten's (King Tut's) tomb (November 4th 1922). He died on June 20th 2017 6 days after the date of this song and 4 days after the birth of Tupac. His last album was titled Hegelian Dialectic, The Book of **Revelation**. My past life **revelation** of my life as Tutankhaten (King Tut) came on April 4th 2020 (page 594). On the cover of his album **Hegelian Dialectic,** Project buildings can be seen next to the **Giza pyramids** and the zodiac wheel of destiny incircles a skeleton version on the vitruvian man drawn by Leonardo da Vinci. In this song I mention **Deja Vu** and in 2022 I experienced **Deja Vu** twice while in **Kemet** (pages 670 - 671).

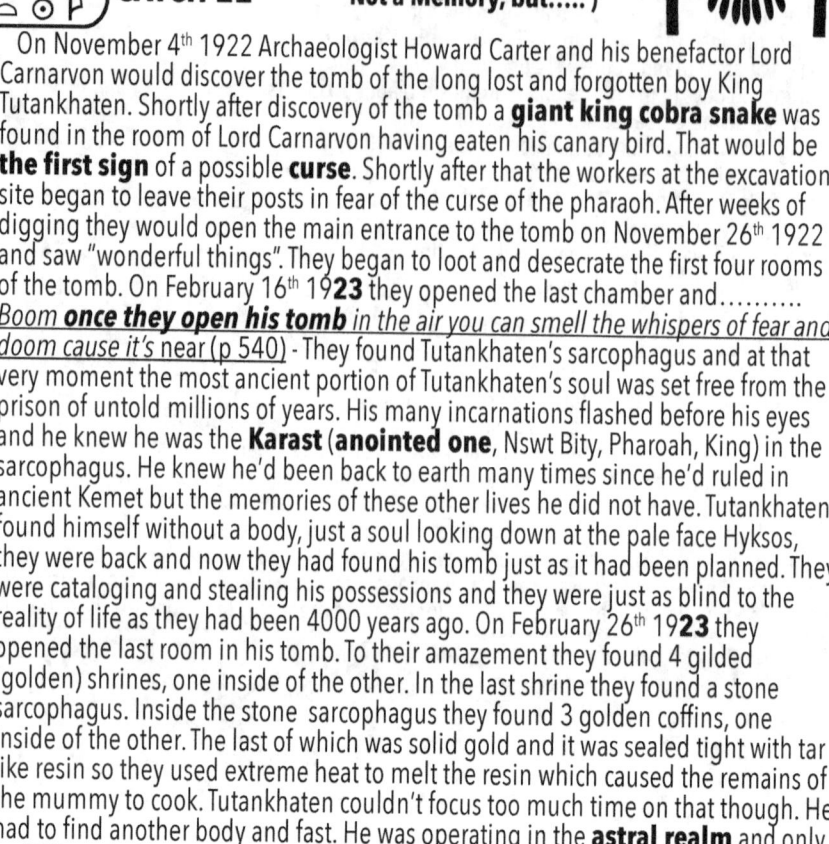

The odds are narrow escaping death after disturbing my rest and my bone marrow. Behold, The Curse of The Pharaoh

Rau nu Prt m heru

A week before the discovery of the Tomb of Tutankhaten (King Tut), Howard Carter bought a pet canary bird and placed it in a gilded cage with the hopes of finding a tomb. As a precautionary measure he'd planned to use the bird to test the air for poisonous toxins, and if a tomb was found, the bird would be set free in the tomb before anyone else. Upon seeing the bird, one of Carter's servants exclaimed, "It's a bird of gold that will bring luck. This year we will find, inshallah (God willing), a tomb full of gold." Within a week of purchasing the canary, Carter discovered Tut's tomb. Not knowing whose tomb they had found, the workers nicknamed it **"the tomb of the Golden Bird"**. On the day in which the entrance to the tomb was fully cleared, a **cobra** entered Carter's house, pounced on the canary and swallowed it. Cobras were common in the days of the Pharaohs, but they were rare in Egypt at the time of the discovery, and were seldom seen during the winter. Cobra's were regarded as the symbol of royalty in the time of the Pharaohs and each Pharaoh wore the symbol upon his forehead. When Carter finally entered the tomb on November 26th 1922, in front of him stood two life-size statues of a pharaoh wearing solid **gold** sandals and **gold** crowns adorned with stylized **cobras**. The sight of the **cobras** gave the local workmen pause, especially after what had happened to Carter's Canary. They saw it as a warning from the spirit of the departed pharaoh against further intrusion on the privacy of his tomb, and many of them abandoned the site. That was the first death that sparked the legend of the "**curse of the pharaoh**". All together **22** people were said to have died in mysterious ways after coming in contact with the Boy King.

The Death of George Herbert, 5th Earl of Carnarvon and The Aleister Crowley Misdirection

Iu f Per f m heru

The belief in the mummy's curse was rekindled when Lord Carnarvon, the benefactor of Howard Carter's archaeological excavations, died five months after the discovery of Tutankhaten's tomb. He died of blood poisoning following a mosquito bite that became infected on April 5th 19**23**, the day after **Martin Luther King** was assassinated (April 4th 1968, see pages 69, 592, 594). It should be noted that **Jean Jacques Dessalines**, one of the primary leaders of the Haitian revolution once said that if he fell in battle he would come back as a **mosquito** and kill his enemies! After Dessalines was murdered his body was cut into **14** pieces like Ausar (p 2), and thrown about the land. The pieces of his body were gathered and buried. Soon after his death the French European forces attempting to occupy Haiti fell victim to **Yellow Fever** and **Malaria** which are both transmitted by **mosquito bites**. This strange turn of events helped Haiti win its independence in 1804. **[** <u>**Tupac** once said in a rhyme, "**bury me in pieces** cause they fear **reincarnation**" (p 665)</u> **]**.... During the night that Carnarvon lay dying in Cairo, the city went black from a mysterious power failure as soon as he died and at that same time, back in London, Carnarvon's dog gave a weird howl and then rolled over and died as well. With all the mystery surrounding Carnarvon's death and the death of the canary bird and the dog, the world back in the 1920's and 30's was left captivated as more people linked to the opening of Tutankhaten's burial chamber died in bizarre circumstances, six of them dying in London. A frenzied public blamed the 'Curse of the Pharaoh' and speculated on the supernatural powers of the ancient Egyptians. Less than two months before the death of Carnarvon, Raoul Loveday died on Feb 16th 19**23**, **on the same day at the very hour that the last room in Tutankhaten's burial chamber was opened** and the same day **Tupac** released **Strictly 4 My N.I.G.G.A.Z....** Loveday was an Oxford undergraduate and a follower of **Aleister Crowley's** cult. Crowley was born into a wealthy family in 1875. He was an occultist who was drawn to alchemy, magic, and Buddhism. In 1904 he wrote the book titled, **The Book of Law** which would be the basis of his religion **Thelma**, identifying himself as the prophet entrusted with guiding humanity into the time of Heru (Horus). He claimed that he channeled the Egyptian deity Horus when writing his book. The Gods and Goddesses of Crowley's religion were mainly drawn from ancient Egypt. Supposedly Raoul Loveday died after drinking the blood of a cat sacrificed in one of Crowley's rituals. This is conjecture posed by the historian Mr **Mark Beynon** who argues that Crowley was involved with the death of Loveday, deliberately poisoning him. He also suggest that Crowley was connected with all the mysterious deaths that happened in London. Beynon released a book in 2012 titled, <u>London's Curse: Murder, Black Magic and Tutankhamun in the 1920s West End</u>, where he claimed Crowley was obsessed with the serial killer **Jack the Ripper** which led him to mastermind a series of ritualistic killings in 'revenge' for the British archaeologist Howard Carter's opening of King Tut's tomb. This however is not the case. All these deaths are connected to **Emmett Till** and the Star Codes of Immortality Patterns that fill the pages of this book and span the ages of time. **Author Calendar** helped open the tomb and soon after died from pneumonia. Lord Carnarvon's widow, **Almina Herbert, Countess of Carnarvon** died on May 8th, the same day my great grandmother **Grace Ann Haynes** was born. **George Jay Gould**, a wealthy railroad executive died of pneumonia on May 16, 19**23**, 24hrs after he visited the tomb. He died the same day that Aiyana Jones was murdered by a police officer in 2010 (p 181). **Arthur Mace**, an archeologist that helped with the excavation of the tomb had to leave Egypt due to health reasons. Years later he died of pneumonia, but he was born the same day **Eric Garner** was murdered by police in 2014 (p 299) and he died the same day that **Bobby Hutton** was murdered by police in 1968 (p 217).

Utterances for Coming Forth by day into Light

The Death of The Egyptian Prince

It is he, who comes forth by day into Light

The **Egyptian Prince** Ali Kamel Fahmy Bey was shot dead by his French wife Marie-Marguerite of six months, in London's Savoy Hotel shortly **after** he was photographed **visiting King Tut's tomb.** Marie-Marguerite was **acquitted** during the murder trial. Mr Beynon claims that Crowley and Marie-Marguerite had been lovers in Paris and that he was working as a hostess at the Folies Berghre where Crowley was a regular patron at the same venue. He suggests that Crowley put her up to the shooting but this can not be proven. What can be proven is the fact that the Prince was also born in 1900, the same year as my great grand parents **Grace Ann Haynes <u>Parker</u>** and **Jessie James <u>Parker</u>.** He died on July 10th 1923, the day after my great grand father **Jessie James <u>Parker</u>** was born, the same month that **Emmett Till** was born (July 25th 19**41**, page 503) and the same month that I had my past life revelation of Emmett Till (July 3rd 2018, page 480). His death is part of the star code patterns that flow throughout this book and the **acquittal** of Marie-Marguerite only leads us back to **Emmett Till** and the next mysterious death of Aubrey Herbert.

The Mysterious Acquittal

Shortly after Marie-Marguerite's **acquittal,** Aubrey Herbert, died on September **23rd** 19**23**, the same day that **Roy Bryant** and **J.W. Milam** were **acquitted** for the murder of **Emmett Till** in 1955 (p 517). On Sep **23rd** 2020 the officers who murdered

Breonna Taylor were acquitted and that same day my father had a stroke and survived (p 627). See page **648** for the **metaphysical significance of the number 23**. Aubrey Herbert was the half-brother of Lord Carnarvon. Aubrey died of blood poisoning after a routine dental operation went suspiciously wrong at his private hospital in **Park** Lane. He had only recently **returned** from his own **trip to Luxor**. Mr Beynon speculates that Crowley was behind the death and may again have used Marie-Marguerite to do his dirty work but Aubrey's death was connected to **Emmett Till** and the Star Codes of Immortality Patterns that fill the pages of this book and span the ages of time. Aubrey Herbert was born on April 3rd 1880, the day before Martin Luther King was assassinated (April 4th 1968, see page 69) which is also the same day that I had my past life revelation of King Tut in 2020 (p 592, 594).

Dr. Aaron Ember and The Book of the Dead

Aaron was an American Egyptologist who was present at the opening of King Tut's tomb. Aaron died along with his wife, maid, and two children on **May 31st** 1926, after his house set on fire. His wife tried to save their children while he tried to save his manuscript. The name of the manuscript was "**The Egyptian Book of the Dead**." It is said that he was a believer in the curse of the pharaoh. 5 years prior, racist white supremacist burned Black Wall Street (**Tulsa race massacre**) to the ground on **May 31st** 1921 (page 404).

Richard Bethell

Captain Richard Bethell, was Howard Carter's personal secretary and he died on November 15th 1929 the year of the **snake**, like **Emmett Till** (19**41**, the year of the snake). He was found dead in his bed at Mayfair's exclusive Bath Club. Bethell was said to have been in perfect health. It was initially thought that he died of a heart attack but his symptoms raised suspicion that he was smothered to death as he slept. Mr Beynon claims Crowley had only recently returned to London and was often a guest at the same club. "Mysteriously", many of the artifacts from King Tut's tomb, found their way to the home of Richard Bethell, and perhaps that's why his home was the scene of unexplained loud noises and even fires. Richard was born in 1883 the year of the **goat, Emmett Till** was murdered in 1955 the year of the **goat** - **my mother** was born that **same year**. Emmett's mother died in 2003, the year of the **goat**.

Lord Westbury and The 8 Year Old Boy

Bethell's father, Lord Westbury, died 3 months later on February 20th **1930**, the day after my great grand father **General Dukes's** birthday and the same year that my grand mother **Juantia Dukes** was born. He died at the age of **77**, and was believed to have thrown himself off his **7th** floor St James's apartment. I was born in 19**77** the year of the **snake**. On the day of his funeral a **8** year old boy was ran over by the hearse that carried the body of Lord Westbury. Mr Beynon suggested that it was practically impossible for an elderly man to have climbed out onto the window ledge and suggests that Crowley threw him off.

Edgar Steele

Four days after the death of Lord Westbury, Edgar Steele died on February 24th **1930** the same year that my grand mother **Juantia Dukes** was born. **February 24th 2022** is ***<u>the last star pattern entered on the last page of this book</u>*** (page 669)! Mr Steele died at St Thomas' Hospital after a minor stomach operation. Edgar Steele was in charge of handling the **tomb artifacts** at London's British Museum. Mr Beynon speculates that Crowley was behind the death but his death was part of this star code pattern of this book.

Sir Ernest Wallis Budge

Sir Ernest Wallis Budge, died on November **23**rd 1934, the year of the **dog**, the same day **Mamie Till** (Emmett Till's mother) was born. See page **648** for the **metaphysical significance of the number 23**. My past life as Emmett was revealed in 2018 the year of the **dog** and the tomb of Tutankhaten was discovered in 1922, the year of the **dog**. Budge was found dead in his bed in Bloomsbury at the age of **77**. I was born in 19**77** the year of the **snake**. Budge was a friend of Lord Carnarvon, he was a former **Keeper** in the British **Museum's** Department of Egyptian and Assyrian Antiquities, responsible for displaying the **artifacts from Luxor**. Mr Beynon claims there is evidence that Budge and Crowley were associates on the London occult scene and some how was involved with his death but Sir Ernest Wallis Budge died the same day that **Emmett Till's mother (Mamie Till) was born** and he was born on my nephews birthday, July 27th 1857 the year of the **snake,** two days after Emmett Till's birthday. Budge's death was part of this star code pattern of this book.

Howard Carter and The Professional Skeptics

Howard Carter, the archaeologist who discovered my tomb said the curse was nonsense. He claimed that if anyone was going to die from the curse it would have been him since he discovered the tomb. He died from natural causes, at 64 years of age in his home, on **March 2nd** 1939 in London, 17 years after the discovery. But, he died the same day my Grand father, **Edward Eddings** was born (page 25)! furthermore, on **March 2nd** 2014 I watched **The Prophecy of Reincarnation Sambho the Black Buddha** for the first time (p 288). Speaking of reincarnation, a previously unpublished letter sent to Carter from **Sir Alan Gardner** has surfaced in 2022 and it proves that Carter gave Gardner a **Wehem amulet** that was stolen from my tomb. Wehem amulets were symbols of resurrection (repeating births - p 14). In 1925, Carter gave his friend Bruce Ingham a paperweight composed of a mummified hand with the wrist attached to a **scarab** bracelet. The morbid gift carried a message saying that anyone who moved the Pharaoh's body would be cursed and would suffer pestilence, fire, and water. Ingram's house burned to the ground soon after he received the gift. Carter had hoped to examine my mummy with x-rays and had therefore invited Sir Archibald Douglas Reid to Egypt. Reid died before he arrived to Egypt, on January 5th the day before Mamie Till died and he was born on July 14th the same day that Sergeant James Brown was murdered (p 331). During the "Treasures of Tutankhamun" tour in the1970s, Egypts head of the Antiquities **dreamt** he would die if the treasures left the country, he was killed in a road accident shortly after signing the contract for the traveling exhibition. In 1972, Dr. Gamal Mehrez of the British Museum supervised the transport of my treasures to London. He laughed at the notion of a curse and said the deaths were a coincidence, yet he died the night after overseeing the cargo's transportation. In 1980 Lord Carnarvon's daughter, Evelyn Leonora had a

stroke as she exited the King Tut museum exhibit. Zahi Hawass is an Egyptian archaeologist who's worked at sites in the Nile Delta, the Western Desert, and the Upper Nile Valley. Hawass is a man who digs for treasure in the soil while he neglects the real treasure which is found when the human digs within their souls! Hawass was once accused of helping three Germans steal artifacts from the Pyramid of **Khufu**. Hawass is one of the "authorities" who **claims** that ancient **Egyptians were not Africans**. Hawass has experienced reoccurring patterns with death on specific dates, similar to the December 3rd Theory (p 312), yet he see's the patterns as **just "coincidence".** On one occasion he got a call that his uncle died the same day that he placed new artifacts into a museum. The next year on the same day his aunt died and the third year his cousin died on the same day. On another occasion there was an earthquake in Cairo on the day after one of his excavations and the very next day he had a heart attack. Some people think **synchronicities** like these are **just "coincidence".** Perhaps that's because of stories like the Superman curse (p 204) or the mummy that sank the Titanic. According to legend, eerie sounds were heard at night coming from the coffin of a mummy in the British Museum and somehow this mummy had caused a series of deaths. Because of this the British Museum was said to have sold the mummy to an American archaeologist who arranged to take the mummy back home aboard the **Titanic**. This 3,500 year old mummy was a Princess of Amen-Ra from the time of **King Tut**. The Titanic sank on April 15th 1912 and the US Senate's inquiry into the disaster was completed on **May 25th** 1912. **May 25th** is a reoccurring date forming a pattern in my life (p 30). It was the first star code pattern that I decoded in 2011 (p 222), stemming from a **dream** my sister had in 2002 (p 104). This code sp**ark**ed my awareness to patterns and would ultimately connect me with my previous life as Emmett.

Rau nu Prt m heru

***ADDENDUM* Mummification, Wehem-mesut and the Christ (Repeating of Births - Reincarnation - Gilgul)**

Many clueless people think that we mummified ourselves in our meta-spiritual devices (tombs) with our belongings so that our souls could take our belongings with us in the afterlife, but that is a fools errand and a fools thought. The Nswt Bity's "Pharaohs" reincarnated in ancient times and when they did they went to their tombs to collect their belongings! That's the reason we buried ourselves underground like the only begotten **Scarab** who **springs** forth from the dirt from seemingly nowhere (p 569). Some say the Nswt Bity's were known to come back an reanimate their mummified bodies. That, I can not confirm but every "Pharaoh" was seeking to resurrect/reincarnate no different than your modern day Dali Lama is said to be the same reincarnated soul. Mummification was also an analogy taken from the **butterfly**. The ancient Kemetians (Egyptians) mummified the Pharaohs, and **anointed** them with oils. The Mummified body was called a **Krst** (Karast, **Christ**) and just as a caterpillar wraps (mummifies) itself into a **chrysalis** (cocoon) and transforms into a butterfly, the human being is supposes to use each life to further the transformation of their consciousness. This is why we wrote the utterances of resurrection in stone to awaken the pharaohs, like those found in the temple of Unas (p 670). Every Nswt Bity had 6 names: their birth name, Nebty name, Horus name, Golden Horus name, Throne name and finally a name that only the mother knew. **EmhatAmen I** was the first Nswt Bity of the twelfth dynasty of the Middle Kingdom of Kemet and his Horus name was **Wehem-Mesut**, which translates to "**The one who has repeated births**". Either, those who are in charge of deciphering the Mdw Ntr (hieroglyphs) don't have the understanding of resurrection and reincarnation or they desire to suppress the truth about resurrection and reincarnation (**Gilgul**) because they translate his Horus name as "the renaissance", claiming that the meaning of his name was based on his position as the initiator of a new period of prosperity and power. I think the truth is being suppressed no different than when reincarnation was taken out of the bible in 553CE (p 592). Horus (Heru) is the one who resurrects after death and that's why **EmhatAmen I's** Horus name was **Wehem-Mesut** which translates to "**The one who has repeated births**". Howard Carter stole a Wehem amulet from my tomb (p 13). My treasures were stored and preserved waiting for me to reclaim them. I am famous today not only because my tomb is the only ancient burial found almost fully intact; but soon I will be even more "famous" when the world comes to know that I have **repeated births** making a successful Ausarian Resurrection, fulfilling the ancient prophecy, helping to sp**ark** the hearts and minds of the children of Africa. During the course of this book you will see my life unfold and by embodying the principles of **Maat** I unwittingly decoded the **riddle** of Heru Em Akhet (p 2), uniting the **lion** with the **lamb**, and by doing so re-membering many of my previous lives, transforming from Dawud (David the beloved) into TutemRa (in the image of Ra). It seems my burial was done hastily and my death remains a mystery, the circumstances of which being controversial. Some say that I only ruled for around 11 years and then I went west (died) between the ages of 18 and 22yrs old. Truthfully I don't know the full circumstances of any of my deaths. There are many questions about me and my most ancient family. Who my mother and father were, was the gold mask really mine, where did my iron dagger come from (p 10), why are there so many objects in my tomb with other family members names on them, why was my tomb so small in comparison to the tombs of other pharaohs and of course, was I a Black man or a White man? The real question one should ponder is why we left ourselves mummified and why much of what you've been taught about the past is full of lies. And why the name Emmett can be found in the name Kemet.

Iu f Per f m heru

Utterances for Coming Forth by day into Light

Tutankhaten (In the eternal living image of Aten) has returned and my name is now TutemRa (In the image of Ra). I have come on the shoulders of many Nswt Bity's that came before me and many other great women and men of the ages who led the way for me. Let my story be told near and far, to those seeking the inward path and even those who aren't yet aware of the paths they are on. Direct your attention to my revelation and know that it is true, so that we may usher in this new Golden age of consciousness because that is the reason I have returned. Leave your beliefs elsewhere and work with the intuition of your soul, your heart and your gut and remember, every life is but another pearl on a necklace. I'm sure that many wanna know how I found this treasure.... You must learn to let go of what you have been taught to believe and how you've been taught to measure. If you want to grow you can't hold on to those teachings forever! Instead, go with the flow and follow the signs keeping your heart light as a feather! They wanna know if I'm lying but I just point to the **NTCHR!** The true **NTCHRU soul compressor**. I'm wiser than an old professor, Dawud da **Naga** a deep deep diver baptizer of the 85'ers! A sleep sleep I was in a dream for days or was it hours? Every step on this path ain't paved with flowers! They wanna know about the powers and the weak, about the sours and the sweet and so I put it on a beat. While you pray to God for your soul to keep, I'm turning up the solar heat, so to speak, from my head to the djed, to the soles of my feet. And so I sow what I reap, and you reap what you sow! A wise man is one who knows what he don't know! Still they wanna know who I am, and if I am who they say that I am, and if I am how did I come to know? And is it a scam or gimmick? No! It's the kham the K**EMET**, the measure of a mans soul has no limit! I walked this land as a man before I was **Emmett**! The spirit is younger at a year than the body is at a minute! They took my body I made a new one then I jumped right in it! Each life is a page and the world is your stage. I came back this time to write the book of a sage. Like a pearl on a necklace each life is engraved. Like seeing your soulmate in a strangers gaze and then in the blink of an eye you're gone turning the page. Page 582, **They Wanna Know**......

It is he, who comes forth by day into Light

My Family Acacia Tree of Many Lives

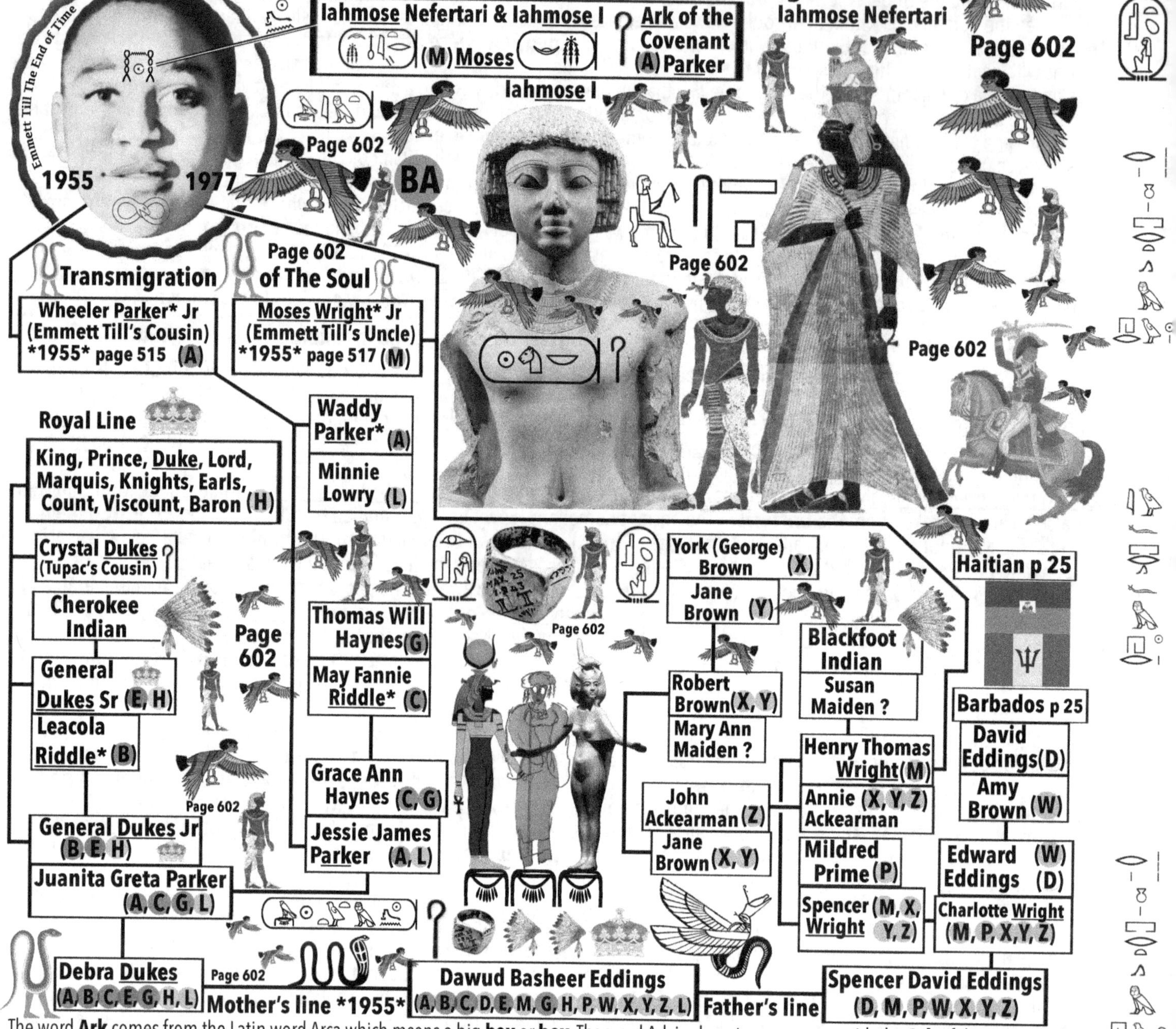

The word **Ark** comes from the Latin word Arca which means a big **box** or **box**. The word Ark is almost synonymous with the **Ark** of the Covenant. **RA**member that all Letters **stem** from the Mdw Ntr, the symptomatic spiritual writing system from ancient kemet also known as the hieroglyphs. Words carry a frequency, a vibration like **Hekau** (p 6). The **Ark** of the Covenant is connected to the story of **Moses** from the Bible. The Bible motifs were taken from the age of Aries (page's 225, 313, 667) and spread across the world by Mission**Aries**. The 3rd golden age of Kemet took place in the age of Aries during the 18th dynasty. The oldest matri**arc**h (mon**arch**) from the 18th dynasty was **Iahmose Nefertari**. The character Moses from the Bible was said to have come down from Mount Sinai with Ten Commandments and placed them in the **Ark** of the Covenant. In the Bible Moses' mother placed him in a papyrus basket and sent him down the **Nile**. The Hebrew word for basket (**box**) is te**BA**h, and in Kemet the **soul** was called the **BA**. In the Ausarian resurrection drama **Ausar** is invited to a party and tricked into getting in a **box** by his brother Set. His body was cut into **14** pieces then the **box** was thrown in the **Nile river**. In my past life as Emmett Till I was murdered at **14** years of age and thrown in the M**ississ**ippi **river** (pages, 508-509). Ausar reigned for **28 years** and I was (Emmett was) murdered on **August 28th**. In ancient kemet the word for **unite** is **smai** which is symbolized by a **wind pipe** and the **lungs**. Kemetic Yoga is called Smai Tawi, which means to unite the two lands, the seen world and the unseen world. The day and the night, the sun rise and sun set. Coming into existence in the flesh again. It was Kemetic yoga that helped sp**ark** my first past life as Emmett Till (p 463-480). In 1922 My tomb was discovered and my **box** was opened. It took me many lives to find myself again. To put all my members together again but I have done that, in fact I'm still doing it. I was born in the family tree of the P**ark**ers at least two times. Out of the d**ark**ness comes the sp**ark** of life that brings the fire. The **metal** iron within our blood allows us to attract the unseen oxygen when we breathe. In every p**ark** you will find b**ark**s of trees that grow leaves that allow us to breathe the breath of life and when this breath is turned into a fire we can unite the two lands (Smai Tawi). This is called the fire triangle, heat, oxygen and or fuel moving upward, like a nose which is shaped like a triangle or pyramid taking in air through the wind pipe to the lungs. This is the path of light and fire. Like the fire that was said to strike those who mishandled the **Ark** of the Covenant in the Bible and like the power that those who possessed the **Ark** would be said to wield. Why were all the Goddesses and Gods of the Egyptian creation stories said to be born beneath an acacia tree? What is the acacia tree and who is the one in the tree (p 482)?? What is the celestial b**ark**, or the b**ark** of a million years? Perhaps the **box** is your body. And perhaps this unseen oxygen is the fuel needed to **ignite** the most divine vessel that we have, our immortal Ba. And perhaps the one in the tree is key to the mystery. At least that's what helped in My Story. It is no **coincidence** that King Tut's Father, **Akhenaten** was the biblical **Moses** who ate the small round caps (**mushrooms**, p 488). It's no **coincidence** that my **uncle's** name was **Moses** in my life as Emmett Till (p 517). It's no **coincidence** that **Mars**, the woman who invited me to the festival, leading to the sp**ark**ing of my past life as Emmett Till has a **son** named **Moses** (p 475). I descend from the spiritual pharaonic line of **Iahmose Nefertari**. I love all the matri**arc**hs in my family tree. <u>Nefertari, Hatshepsut, Tiye, Kiya, Nefertiti, May, Grace, Leacola, Juanita, Charlotte,</u> **Mamie** & **Debra**. Ultimately, you are Ausar! See page 3 for the **hero's journey**!

ADDENDUM **The Late 1800s**

Thomas Will Haynes and May Fannie Riddle
My Maternal Great Great Grand Parents
(Mothers great Grand parents)

Rau nu Prt m heru

My maternal great great grand parents, **Thomas Will Haynes** and **May Fannie Riddle Haynes** were born around 1867, two years after the **Civil War**. Life is a symphony speaking in **Riddles** and both of my grand parents have the name **Riddle** in their bloodline and they did not grow up in the same area. My grand father's (page **23**) mother's maiden named was **Riddle** (page 15, 21) and during the revision of this book I came to know that my grand mother's (page 22) grand mother's maiden name was **Riddle** as well (**May Fannie Riddle Haynes**). **May Fannie Riddle Haynes** was born sometime around 1867. She was a tall woman with large hands. **Thomas Will Haynes** was born around 1864. He was a very light skinned and it was assumed that he was a **Mulatto** man. My grand mother (page 22) remembers him having curly hair and she said he looked like a poor white man. There is no knowledge as to who his parents were. And there is also no knowledge as to how Thomas and May met but **they loved each other** and **worked together** at home, **on their land**. They had a big garden were **they grew their own food**. Everything from corn, sweet potatoes, tomatoes and many other vegetables. They had cows that helped bring them income. May would milk the cows and sell the milk and butter. Unfortunately that is the only info about them I was able to attain and the land they owned is not in the hands of my family. My great great grand parents were born more than 100 years ago but the hate they saw is not much different than the hate Black people see today in 2022. It was legal to lynch Black people back then and when a Black person is killed by the police today they usually go free. We need to unite as a people!

Iu f Per f m heru

NEVER FORGET!!!

Does the image of Jesus hanging from a cross offend you? Of course it doesn't. So do not for one second complain to anyone about the images seen in this book! This is historical fact! These are my ancestors hanging from trees like strange fruit. If you can look at Jesus hanging from the necks of millions of Christians then surely you can stomach what you see here in this book. This might be history you don't want to see but it is the story that is not told in your history classes. There's no proof of Egypt enslaving Hebrews but there is proof of white Americans enslaving the African children of Egypt. - Emmett Louis Till (EL Till, page 671)

Utterances for Coming Forth by day into Light

It is he, who comes forth by day into Light

Jessie James and Grace Ann Parker, my Maternal Great Grand Parents (Juanita's parents)

Jessie James Parker

My great grandfather **Jessie James Parker** was sent down on (born on) July 9th 1900 (07091900 = 26 = **8**) in **Bedford Virginia** and died in 1969. His fathers name was **Waddy Parker** (my great great grand father). Jessie had two brothers and one sister. Their mother died when they were young and perhaps that is why his father treated them so carelessly. Jessie only went to school for one day during the first grade, and after that he was made to work the **land** with his brothers cutting weeds all day. He and his siblings spent many days hungry as his father (Waddy Parker) would cook a chicken and take the best parts for himself and his girl friend leaving his children to pick through what was left. My grand mother remembers a story told to her by her father (Jessie James Parker) - on a very cold day during the winter there was no food in the house and one of Jessie's brothers caught a mouse in the house. His brother cooked it and ate it by himself. After the mouse was already eaten his father (Waddy P**ark**er) screamed from his room "I smell food cooking!". When he came out to see what was cooking he found no food and no one to explain what he'd smelt. Christmas was no different for my great grand father and his siblings. They would take socks and place them up in the house in hopes that their father would fill them with presents but never did they find any, not even a piece a candy. Unfortunately this **land** that was owned by my great great grand father Waddy P**ark**er is unaccounted for, I have never seen the **land** and none of my family members have anything to do with it.

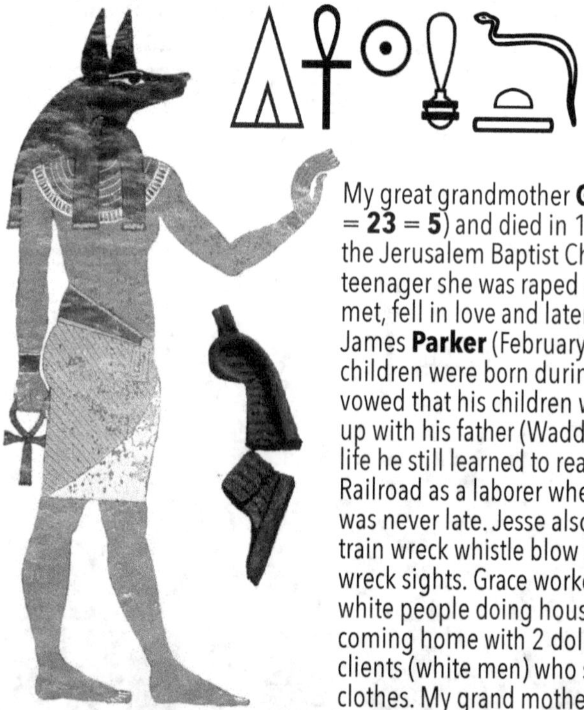

Grace Ann Haynes (Parker)

My great grandmother **Grace Ann Haynes** was sent down on (born on) May 8th 1900 (05081900 = **23** = **5**) and died in 1980. She was a church going, God fearing woman. She was a member of the Jerusalem Baptist Church. She was a good cook and worked at a store. When she was a teenager she was raped and gave birth to a son named **Jackal** Bernard Haynes. Jessie and Grace met, fell in love and later had 3 children, Marion (June 28th 1928), **Juanita** (October 9th 1930) and James **Parker** (February 3rd 1932). They settled in **Roanoke Virginia** and even though their children were born during the great depression they never went a day hungry. Jessie James Parker vowed that his children would never experience what him and his siblings experienced growing up with his father (Waddy Parker). Even though he only attended school for one day in his entire life he still learned to read and was a productive man. He worked at the Norfolk and Western Railroad as a laborer where he lubricated the engines. He got up early and was at work by 7am and was never late. Jesse also worked on the wrecking crew and my grand mother hated to hear the train wreck whistle blow because she knew that meant her father would be gone long hours at the wreck sights. Grace worked at a mill factory where she made flour. She also worked side jobs for white people doing house work, where she earned 25 cents an hour. She would work 4 hour shifts coming home with 2 dollars until of course her pay was raised to 50 cents an hour. She had two clients (white men) who she would iron clothes for. Marion would help her starch and press the clothes. My grand mother remembers receiving a nickel and an orange for Christmas from one of the men when he came to pick up his clothes. Jessie became good friends with his foreman eventually helping him raise pigs. During the winter he would receive portions of the pigs for his family. Sometimes Jessie would make sweet potato pies and ginger cookies for the family and would cook dinner when Grace had long days at work. My grand mother still remembers one line from the song he used to sing - "**If you love your mother meet her in the sky**". He sang that song for his mother who died when he was young and when my grand mother (Juanita) and my Aunt (Marion) heard him sing it they would cry. Every Christmas James would take his family to see his father (Waddy P**ark**er) where he brought him food and money or sometimes just money. Upon receiving these gifts from his son Waddy would begin to cry and then proceed to deliver a prayer as he cried. Marion and Juanita would cry as they listened to the prayer and saw their grand father cry, but Jessie James Parker never cried during his fathers prayers. His memories of the way his father treated him as a child would not allow him to. Jessie James Parker was able to take care of his family despite never having had a traditional education, (read page 667).

1909 - IDA B. WELLS, "LYNCHING, AMERICA'S NATIONAL CRIME"

Rau nu Prt m heru

Iu f Per f m heru

Ida Bell Wells-Barnett was an American investigative journalist, educator, and early leader in the Civil Rights and Anti-Lynching Movements. She was born into slavery on July 16th 1862 in Holly Springs, M**ississ**ippi, the same state **Emmett Till** was murdered in. 3 years after she was born the Civil War ends and the slaves are "Freed". When she was 16, both of her parents and an infant brother died during the malaria and yellow fever epidemic. After her parents passed she became the sole provider for her 8 siblings. Against all odds she still managed to graduate from Rust College and became a Teacher and that's when her activism started. She began to use local Black newspapers to expose the poor conditions in colored schools. This eventually resulted in her termination as a teacher in 1891 but that fueled her and freed up her time allowing her to help other schools across the nation. From the early 1890's she labored mostly alone in her effort to raise the nation's awareness and indignation about these usually **unpunished murders**. In 1892 she started an **anti lynching** campaign. In 1893 she joined other Black leaders in boycotting the Chicago World's Fair (World's Columbian Exposition) after they were accused of locking out and negatively portraying the Black community. In 1894 she is thrown off a train for refusing to move from a "first class" section to one designated for "Negros". In 1895 she married the famed lawyer Ferdinand Lee Barnett and moved to Chicago where she later published, **Anti-lynching pamphlet, A Red Record**. In 1898 she visited President McKinley to speak out against lynchings. By **1909** Wells was the most prominent **anti-lynching** campaigner in the United States after she gained a powerful ally becoming one of the founders of the National Association for the Advancement of Colored People (NAACP). She was a forerunner in the women's suffrage movement and the advancement of African American Women. She founded the Alpha suffrage club and the Negro fellowship club. In 1913 she walked with the Alpha suffrage club for the passage of the federal suffrage amendment. She was an inspiration to many other aspiring activists with her belief in the truth and justice, helping so many groups of people being ignored in society.

ADDENDUM Ida B Wells goes WEST and the lynching of People's Grocery

Utterances for Coming Forth by day into Light

Ida B Wells-Barnett was born in M**ississ**ippi, the same state **Emmett Till** was murdered in. She passed away in Chicago, the same state **Emmett Till** was born in. She passed (went **west**) on **March 25th,** the same day that **Biggie Small's, Life After Death** album was released, in the year 1931, the same year my grandfather **General Dukes Jr** was born. It was a lynching that took place on **March 9th**, 1892, the same day that **Biggie Smalls** died (page 77) that helped sp**ark** her **anti lynching** campaign in 1892. The Lynching of Tommie Moss, Will Stewart, and Calvin McDowell, owners of **People's Grocery** store in **Mem**phis Tennessee. As Ida once said, "many lynchings and "race riots" were designed to repress and threaten economic advancement by African Americans". This lynching was no different. There was White grocery store in Memphis known for selling low quality food for high prices while the new Black owned People's Grocery began to sell quality food at quality prices. People's Grocery began to threaten the monopoly the White grocers once had in the area and this is when a series of campaigns of violence against the owners of People's Grocery began. With no protection by local law enforcement and fearing a mob attack, the Black grocers armed themselves and prepared for **self defense**. Sure enough, that attack came, and gunfire was exchanged. With multiple white men wounded, Stewart, Moss, and McDowell were arrested and jailed. A few days later, the jail was stormed by 75 White men in black masks who took the men to a railroad yard. All three were killed savagely but they didn't go without a fight. The fact that the events of this lynching were described in such disturbing detail by white papers shows how normalized the barbaric system of racism was back then and still is to this day! It was clear reporters had been called in advance to witness the lynching and probably took part in it. It was reported that at one point McDowell managed to grab a shotgun from one of his abductors but he was eventually subdued and his fingers and hands were shot to pieces. The mob shot four holes into McDowell's face, each large enough for a fist to enter. His **left eye** was shot out and the "ball hung over his cheek in shreds." Just like "Emmett Till's" eye laid on his cheek (page 514). McDowell's jaw was torn out by buckshot. Where "his right eye had been there was a big hole which his brains oozed out." The account by the five ministers in the Appeal-Avalanche added that his injuries were in accord with his "vicious and unyielding nature." According to a local newspaper, Moss was the last to be shot and **his final last words were:** "Tell my people to **go West**, there is no justice for them here."

I have brought forth this **PROPHECY OF REINCARNATION** so as to tell all people, especially my people, that **death IS NO THE END**! In the ancient Kemetic (Egyptian) Ausarian (Osirion) resurrection drama, Ausar (Osiris) was known as the Lord of the **West** and the Lord of **resurrection/ Reincarnation**. Death was called "**Westing**" in ancient Kemet because we did not believe that death was the end, instead we understood that just as the sun rises in the east and sets in the west, the soul is born into a body then leaves the body but just like the sun comes back the next day, the soul comes back to live another life. So **west** was where the soul (BA) went when we "die" but the soul rises again in the east. The "Pharaoh's" were known to take on new bodies (reincarnate, resurrect) after they went "west". This concept of resurrection was called the **Wehem-Mesut** (repeating of births, p 14). In **Judaism**, reincarnation is known as **Gilgul** (Cycle), but it is not taught to everyone. Ultimately, you are **Ausar**! See page 3 for the **hero's journey!** FYI, **Mem**phis Tennessee was named after the city of **Mem**phis, the royal residence and capital of ancient Kemet (Egypt) established my the **Nswt Bity** (Pharaoh) **Memes** (Narmer, pages 55, 528).

It is he, who comes forth by day into Light

"Yo I was born to rebel, being born black's to be born in hell! Word is born, word to Big L, rest in peace to homies that fell, how the hell you expect us to act well?! spark L's take your mind back in time to **Ida B Wells**, Troy Davis is the latest society fail! Larry Davis did what he had to do with the steel! do you know the only thing we get from silence is more violence?! my name's Dawud and I slay giants, from sea to shining sea…" - (Dawud, Born 2 rebel - written in 2011, page 210). We need to unite as a people! **Marcus Garvey** once said, "it will only take 24 hours once we all decide that it is ours". It is time for us to unite so as to ensure that these horrors NEVER happen to any of us again!

February 19th 1910 - June 9th 1971

General Dukes Sr. my Maternal Great Grand father (General Dukes Jr's Father)

My Great Grand Father General Dukes Sr. was sent down (born) on February 19th 1910 (191219 = **23** = **5**), in **Orrville** Alabama. The word Or means **Gold** and Ville means **town** (Town of **Gold**). He died on June 9th 1971 the day before **Marcus Garvey** died and the same year **Tupac** was born. Both Francis Scott, **Earl** of Dalkeith and **Prince** Andrew, **Duke** of York are born on his birthday (page 99). General was raised by his uncle Jimmy **Turner** and that's where he got the nick name **Son Turner**. General Dukes Sr. "Son Turner", had a brother named Jimmy Dukes who's nickname was **Kid Duke**. General had 19 children and gave them all his last name. He had his first son General Dukes Jr in 1931 with Leacola **Riddle** (Montgomery). There are no surviving pictures of Son Turner but it's said that his first son, General Dukes Jr. was the splitting image of him. He later married Bertha Paulin Tolbert Dukes and had three other children: Jimmy Lee Dukes (who was named after his uncle), Clara Dukes and Velma Dukes who lived in Centrailia Illinois, south of **Chicago,** where **Emmett Till** was from. The only other names that survive the records are, Richard, Kenneth, Carrie, Wilson, Johnny, Vera, Charles, Virginia, Glenn, Zack, **Emma** and of course, **"Emmett"** Dukes.

Jack Johnson The First Black Heavy Weight Champion

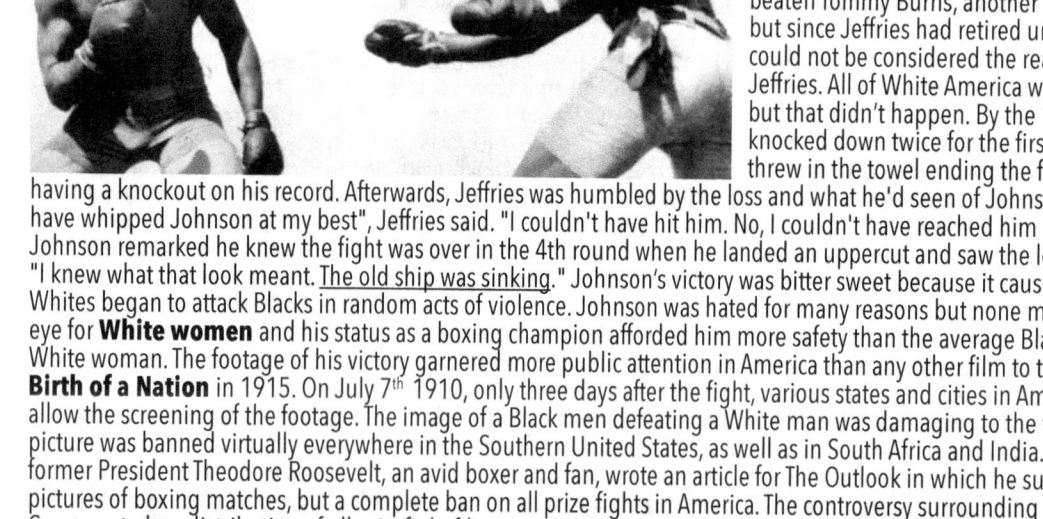

5 months after my great grandfather was born Jack Johnson defeated James Jeffries and became the first Black heavy weight champion on July 4th 1910. Weeks before the fight it had been promoted as the fight of the century with racist undertones as the press dubbed Jeffries "**The Great White Hope**". Johnson had beaten Tommy Burns, another White champion two years prior but since Jeffries had retired undefeated critics claimed Johnson could not be considered the real champion until he defeated Jeffries. All of White America wanted to see Jeffries beat Johnson but that didn't happen. By the 15th round, after Jeffries had been knocked down twice for the first time in his career, Jeffries' corner threw in the towel ending the fight and preventing Jeffries from having a knockout on his record. Afterwards, Jeffries was humbled by the loss and what he'd seen of Johnson in their match. "I could never have whipped Johnson at my best", Jeffries said. "I couldn't have hit him. No, I couldn't have reached him in 1,000 years." After the fight Johnson remarked he knew the fight was over in the 4th round when he landed an uppercut and saw the look on Jeffries face, stating, "I knew what that look meant. The old ship was sinking." Johnson's victory was bitter sweet because it caused race riots across America as Whites began to attack Blacks in random acts of violence. Johnson was hated for many reasons but none more than the fact that he had an eye for **White women** and his status as a boxing champion afforded him more safety than the average Black man that might be seen with a White woman. The footage of his victory garnered more public attention in America than any other film to that date until the release of **The Birth of a Nation** in 1915. On July 7th 1910, only three days after the fight, various states and cities in America declared they would not allow the screening of the footage. The image of a Black men defeating a White man was damaging to the white supremacist ideology so the picture was banned virtually everywhere in the Southern United States, as well as in South Africa and India. Two weeks after the match, former President Theodore Roosevelt, an avid boxer and fan, wrote an article for The Outlook in which he supported banning not just moving pictures of boxing matches, but a complete ban on all prize fights in America. The controversy surrounding the film directly motivated Congress to ban distribution of all prizefight films across state lines in 1912; the ban lasted for nearly three decades. It was finally lifted in 1940 **the same year Marcus Garve**y died. My great grandfather General Dukes Sr died on June 9th 1971, the day before Marcus Garvey died. Jack Johnson died on **June 10th** 1946, **the same day Marcus Garvey** died and the same day my Great grandmother Leacola **Riddle** was born (p 21). The movie **King Kong** was full of **racist undertones** and it was released on **March 2nd** 1933, **the same day** Howard Carter died (p 13). Which is also **the same day** my Grand father, **Edward Eddings** was born (page 25)! March 2nd is also **the same day** that I watched the documentary, **The Prophecy of Reincarnation** (p 288). King Kong was a giant black Gorilla from "Skull" island which was populated by "savage" Black people. The only Black people in the movie were the Black "savages" on Skull island. King Kong ate the "savages" but when he came in contact with the **White women** he fell in love with her. **Jack Johnson** loved **White women** and the movie King Kong was about him which is why there was a scene of Madison Square Garden in the movie. The first boxing match in Madison Square Garden was in 1882 and has been the mecca of boxing ever since. King Kong is the metaphorical Giant Athletic Black man like the image **LeBron James** seen holding a **White women** on the cover of a Vogue magazine (est in 1892), in April of 2008. The **F.B.I.** was created to convited Jack and they used the **Mann Act** to do that.

Son Turner's Farm, Orrville Alabama

Some say my Great Grand Father, General Dukes Sr (Son Turner) was raised by white people and some say the white people **owned** him. Whether he was a **slave** or not is unknown but from these white people he did inherit 88 acres of land in the early 1900's, in **Orrville** Alabama. On this land he farmed cotton, tomatoes, collard greens, turnip, cabbage, rutabaga, radish, corn, peanuts, peaches, watermelon, cantaloups, onions, sweet potatoes, white potatoes, blue ribbon sugar cane, saga sugar cane, and had several pecan trees. There was a smoke house on the farm for salting the ham meat and collecting the syrup from the sugar cane. They raised horses, pigs, ducks and several other animals. They had two to three cows that my uncle Jimmy remembers milking as a child (p 660). He had two mules that did all the plowing and never owned a tractor. Because of his farm, Son Turner's family was one of the only family's within 50 miles that went throughout the entire winter without ever being hungry. All the Blacks within a couple of miles of his farm would come and help with harvesting in return for food such as, ham, butter, eggs, milk and other things. Son Turner was also a well known moonshiner like the TV show **The Dukes of Hazard**. People complained about bad moonshine often but Son Turner was known for having the best **moonshine** around because he used real ingredients and didn't short cut.

Rau nu Prt m heru Iu f Per f m heru

Utterances for Coming Forth by day into Light

It is he, who comes forth by day into Light

I Don't Need Your Credit!

When my uncle Jimmy was a boy his father took him to the local store to buy school supplies for him and his sisters, and when he got to the register the white man asked my Great Grand father if he would like to pay for his items with credit. My uncle told me that some white people liked to have the Black people in debt to them but Son Turner always paid cash and was never in debt to any man. Perhaps it was the amount of supplies that caused the white man to ask him if he wanted credit but whatever the reason it didn't matter because Son Turner didn't like it. He took the large pile of supplies and threw them on the floor and pissed on them then asked the white man, - "have I ever asked you for credit before?!". the white man replied, - "no". And Son Turner told him, - "then why the hell would I need it now?!". Just before he left the store he told him to do what ever he needed to do with his supplies but he would never be back there again.

Don't disturb Son Turner When He's Eating!

On another occasion my uncle Jimmy was at the table eating dinner with his father General Dukes Sr (Son Turner) when he heard a knock at the door. Jimmy was around 8 or 9 years old at the time so the year was around 1952 or 1953. When Jimmy got up to answer the door there was a White man there who wanted to speak to General. He told the man that his father was eating and he would be with him shortly. Jimmy knew very well that his father did not like to be disturbed while eating. He went back to the table and told him a White man was at the door, but General continued to eat his food. After some time the man knocked at the door again and again, Jimmy went to the door to tell the man that his father would be with him when he was done eating. Jimmy went back to the table and began to eat his food. The man knocked a third time and when he did Son Turner got up from the table and grabbed his double gage shotgun. As he walked to the door he pumped the shotgun loading a round and when the man saw him coming with his gun he took off running. When Son Turner got to the door he shot a round off in the air as the man ran for his life leaving his car parked in front of the Dukes's home. The next day Son Turner strapped ropes to the mans car and with his horses and cows he dragged the car off his property where the car sat for two weeks until the white man finally came to get it.

The Real Dukes of Hazzard County

My great Grandfather General Dukes Sr died on June 9th 1971 the day before **Marcus Garvey** died and his first son (my Grandfather) General Dukes Jr died on August 18th 2009 the day after **Marcus Garvey's** birthday (page 169)! The TV show **The Dukes of Hazzard** was thought projected to the creators of the show just like **Star Wars** was thought projected to George Lucas (page 37). **Bo** and **Luke** Duke were **moonshiners** who lived with their uncle **Jesse** Duke. My great Grandfather General Dukes Sr aka **Son Turner** was an expert **moonshiner** in **Orrville** Alabama. The character **Jesse** Dukes was named after Jesse Woodson James who was a white American outlaw, bank and train robber, guerrilla, and leader of the James Younger Gang. **Jesse James** joined the **pro-Confederate** guerrillas known as "bushwhackers" operating in Missouri and Kansas during the American Civil War. My Grand Mothers father was named **Jesse James** Parker (page 17). **Bo** and **Luke** Duke drove a car named **The General* Lee*** with the image of a **confederate flag** on it which became the symbol of the show. My great Grandfather, General Dukes Sr had a son named **General*** Dukes (page **23**) and a son named Jimmy **Lee*** Dukes (page 660) like the name of the car **The General* Lee***. **Emmett Till** was lynched on the **33rd parallel** and his nickname was **Bobo**. The character **Bo**'s full name was **Beauregard** Dukes, he was named after **Pierre Gustave Toutant-Beauregard** who was a White **Confederate general officer** who started the American Civil War by leading the attack on Fort Sumter in Charleston Harbor, South Carolina on April 12, 1861. Charleston is located on the **mysterious 33rd Parallel** (p 379, 380), and is known officially as "the Mother Lodge of the World." **Pierre Gustave Toutant-Beauregard** died on feb 20th, the day after my great grand father General Dukes Sr was born. The character Lucas K. Dukes, better known as **Luke** was named after The Battle of **Lucas** Bend which took place on January 11, 1862 near Lucas Bend, during the American Civil War. I have written about my connection to **Luke** Skywalker as the story was created by George **Lucas** and taken from **Akhenaten** and **Tutankhaten** and is connected to me just like the Dukes of Hazzard (page 37). The character Jefferson Davis (J.D.) Hogg, better known as **"Boss Hogg"** was the local sheriff and was named after Jefferson Davis who was **president of the Confederate States of America** throughout its existence during the American Civil War (1861–65). In 2021 I deciphered the pattern of 1944 and 1977 and named it **The 44th Parallel** (page 660). My uncle Jimmy Lee Dukes is born two days before Emmett Till on July **23rd** 19**44**. They both turned 77 in 2021 and I'm born in 1977 and I turned **44** in 2021. **George Lucas** (creator of **star wars**) is born on my sister's birthday and he also turned **77** in 2021 the same year I turned **44**. My great grand father General Dukes Sr aka Son Turner kept a **44** caliber pistol near his sternum in his overalls pocket. His brother Jimmy Dukes was known as **Kid Duke**. The Dukes of Orrville Alabama were all very good with weapons sort of like the legends of **Billy the Kid**. My Grandfather, General Dukes Jr was born on **June 17** which is the same day that **Dylann Roof** massacred 9 Black people in 2015 while they sat at bible study at a historical Black church in Charleston North Carolina which was once owned by **Denmark Vesey**. Charleston North Carolina is at 32.6 degrees north, just shy of the **33rd parallel.** The Dukes of Hazard tv show was taken off the air after the massacre because several pictures of Dylann surfaced with him holding the confederate flag. When I was a little boy I used to watch the show and wonder why they had the same name as my Grand Parents. I even had a replica toy of the General Lee car. General dukes Sr was the type of man they make movies about and so this book is a historical* document that all Black people and all people in general* must never forget. It's not just about my lives or about the lore and mystery of who I was in previous lives. It's about the restoration of **Ma'at**! This too shall come to pass! All is being revealed. None of these dates are "just coincidence". The word **Orrville** translates to Village of **Gold**. The word Or means **gold** and Ville means town or village. I am the reincarnation of the **Golden** boy Tutankhaten, more widely known as **King Tut**. My tomb was discovered in 1922 and it was the first tomb found in modern time with a treasure of **GOLD**. There is a popular series named **Orville** and the creator of the show is named **Seth MacFarlane** (page 99). Seth is born the day after me on October 26th. In the Ausarian **resurrection** drama Ausar is murdered by his brother **Seth**. Ausar **resurrects** and returns as **Ra** through his son Heru. Ultimately, you are Ausar and Heru! See page 3 for the **hero's (Heru's) journey!** On April 4th 2020 my past life as Tutankhaten was revealed to me and I was given the name Tutem**Ra** (page 594). One time is an incidence, twice is a coincidence, but 3, 4 and 5 is a pattern. Can you tell the difference?!! **Genesis 1:14 "And God said, Let there be lights in the firmament of the heaven to divide the day from the night; and let them be for signs, and for seasons, and for days, and years"**

March 3rd 1910
The lynching of Allen Brooks

Less than a month after my great great grandfather was born Allen Brooks, a Black handyman in Dallas was accused of raping a little girl. Allen had been fixing a furnace in the home of a white family on Feb 27, 1910, when the family's 3-year-old daughter, Mary Ethel Beuvens, went missing. Brooks, who was believed to be 59 years old, was found with the toddler less than four hours later. After Allen and the child were examined by doctors, Brooks was charged with **rape**. Dr. Keaton said there was **no proof of that crime and the child had no injuries**. While the attorneys were preparing the motion on March 3rd 1910, Allen was awaiting the beginning of his trial when a white lynch mob stormed the courtroom and a rope was tied around his neck and was pulled from the second story window of the courthouse. Judge Robert Seay wrote in the court record, "Case dismissed." His body was then dragged several blocks to the Elks **Arc**h, a large landmark in downtown Dallas. Brooks was strung up on a telephone pole and lynched on the corner of Main and Akard Street. An estimated 5,000 people witnessed the lynching at Elks **Arc**h, a three-story white, blue and purple structure that marked the main entrance to the city. One of the great tragedies is that there are many lynchings that we'll never know anything about, because there was just no way to document them.

Leacola Riddle Montgomery my Maternal Great Grandmother (General Dukes Jr's mother)

June 10th 1913 - June 18th 1988 (06101913 = 21= **3**)

Leacola **Riddle** Montgomery was sent down on (born on) June 10th 1913 in Dallas County, AL, from the union of Mr Coleman and Mrs Pinky **Riddle**. She confessed Jesus Christ as her Lord and savior at an early age. She met General Dukes Sr. and had her first son, General Dukes Jr in 1931 when she was 18 years old. She later moved to Bessemer, Alabama and joined the **Wheeling** Chapel Baptist Church under the pastorate of Rev. W. M. Hunter in 1949. She was a member of Christian unions 10, 12, 16 and 20. She was married to the late Deacon Issac Montgomery, Sr. and from that union four children were born, Mrs. Rosie Elam of Chicago IL, Cecil Montgomery of Roosevelt City, AL, Maggie and Issac. She also had one adopted daughter, Miss Gloria Montgomery of Birmingham, AL.

The Holy Leacola Riddle of The Sphinx

My **maternal** great great grand mother's maiden named was **Riddle** (May Fannie **Riddle**, page 16) and one might say it's just a **coincidence** that my **paternal** great grand mother Leacola's maiden name is also **Riddle**! But non of this is a a coincidence! I have not been able to find much information about my Great Grandmother Leacola outside of the information found on her obituary but interestingly enough I found a **star pattern** hidden within the dates of her birth and her death that is more like a "**Riddle**". A **Divine Riddle,** like the **Riddle** of the **Sphinx**. She was sent down (born) on June 10th the same day that **Marcus Garvey** died and she died on June 18th the same day that Alexander Gordon, 4th **Duke** of Gordon and Keeper of the Seal of Scotland was born (page 99), which is the day after her son General **Dukes** Jr (my grand father, page 23) was sent down (born). General **Dukes** Sr, who is the father of her son (General **Dukes** Jr) died on June 9th the day before she was born which is also the day before **Marcus Garvey** died. Her son General **Dukes** Jr died on August 18th 2009 which is the day after **Marcus Garvey** was born. Her son General Dukes Jr was born on June 17th 1931, the day after **Tupac**. As you read this book you will see how Tupac becomes my favorite rapper and Marcus Garvey will become a focal point in my journey after my Grand Father General Dukes Jr dies in 2009 (page 169). Prior to his death I can only remember hearing the name Marcus Garvey once in a **Nas** song titled, **Halftime**. Nas is born the day after **Tupac** died and he has a daughter named **Destiny** who was born on June 15, the day before Tupac. I have a theory about who Tupac was in a previous life (page 664). These dates are not a coincidence. They are star patterns, divine numerology, like **my sacred geometry** (page 602). Like the royal star code that formed on Sep 11th 2001 (page 99) or the pattern the formed around the Curse of the Pharaoh (page 12). Or like **Emmett Till** having a cousin who was a **Parker** (Wheeler Parker, page 515) and my maternal great grand father's name being Jessie James **Parker** (pages 17), and **Emmett Till** having an uncle named Moses **Wright** Jr (page 517) and my great grand father being Henry **Wright** (pages 15, 25). This is not a coincidence, this is divine math formulated and orchestrated by the creator and it can be called **Maat**hematics (p **41, 602**). We all have a **destiny** when we come to earth and with in the pages of this book I have fulfilled my life's **destiny**. The original name of the Sphinx was **Heru** Em Ahket, which has the head of a human and the body of a **lion** symbolizing mans ability to rise above his animalistic nature. We must all aspire to be Heru. Life is a symphony speaking in **Riddles**, I'm TutemRa the infinite stuck in the middle of eternity, **Heh** infinity, returning the 3rd time trinity. We need to unite as a people! **Marcus Garvey** once said, "it will only take 24 hours once we all decide that it is ours". It is time for us to unite so as to ensure that these horrors NEVER happen to any of us again!

Juanita Greta Parker Dukes, (My Mother's Mother)

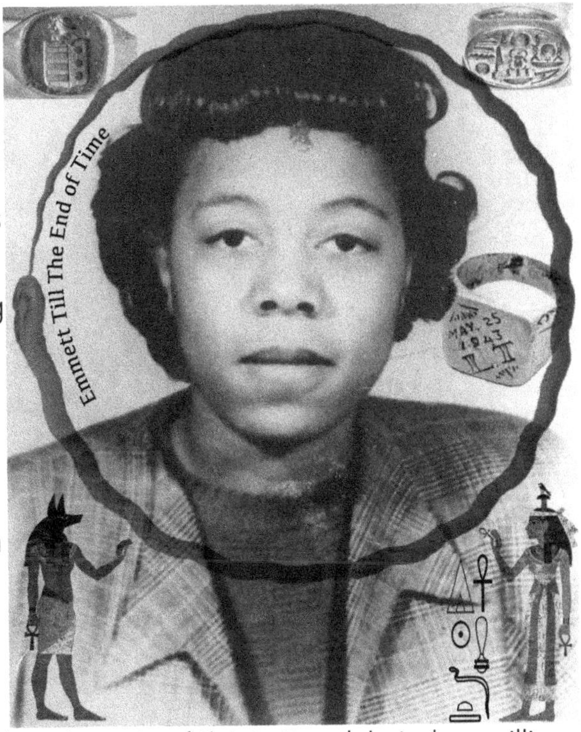

Juanita Greta Parker was sent down (born) on October 9th 1930 (10091930 = **23** = **5**), in the month of Libra (**Maat**, page 367). We share the same life path number of **5**. **88** years after she was born I realized I was Emmett Till (p 480). She's from Roanoke Virginia, and grew up in a loving home with both of her parents. She was never taught about the enslavement of her ancestors and did not know why the world was the way it was but it was her faith in God that powered her existence. Juanita grew up in the church attending service every Sunday following all the rules. When telling stories of her childhood she often tells the story of being chased home. When returning home from school some days the White kids would chase her and her sister Marion home screaming, "Nigger nigger black as tar can't get to heaven on an electric car". When they finally reached their block the white kids would stop their pursuit. They only attacked in packs and would never venture on Juanita's block. **Juanita** and **Marion** would then stop, and scream back "Cracker cracker green as grass can't get to heaven on a bull frogs ass". (More of her childhood on page 17). When Juanita was around 20yrs old her and her older sister moved to Queens New York. Juanita would make a living as a live-in nanny for Jewish families where she earned between $15 and $50 a month. She did her job well and never allowed anyone to disrespect her. She once quit a job on the spot when a family insisted that she work the night, when she had already made it clear that she would not be available. Eventually she became a nurse and would later meet a man named General, falling in love (page 24). Juanita is now 91 years of age in the year 2021. Sometimes I talk to her about his-tory (our-story) that she never learned and about the origins of Christianity and she is always willing to listen. I have the closest relationship with my grandmother than any other person in my family. My grandmother shares the same birthday as Prince Edward, **Duke** of Kent, a member of the British royal family. He is first cousins with Queen Elizabeth the 2nd. There seems to be some strange pattern with my grandparents, **Emmett Till** and the **royals of England** (page 99). But it doesn't end there, **Jasmin** is connected, page 95. **Benjamin Banneker** is connected, page 160. **The Ark of a Million years** is connected, pages 176-538. The Cream Remix is connected, page 454. **Troy Anthony Davis** is connected, page 258. The Reincarnation of Dejazmatch Beru is connected, page 391. Luxx On Lex is connected, page 586. Jackie Robinson and the Field of Dreams Deferred is connected, page 609. And finally, my experience with **Deja Vu** while Leaving The City of Akhetaten is connected, page 671.

Rau nu Prt m heru

Iu f Per f m heru

August 7th 1930 She Later Recanted Her Claim of Rape

August 7th 1930, 2 months before my grandmother was born, a **mob** of ten to fifteen **thousand** whites abducted three young black men from the jail in **Marion**, Indiana, lynching Thomas Shipp and Abram Smith. Sixteen-year-old James Cameron narrowly survived after being beaten by the mob. The night before the lynching, Claude Deeter, a **23** year old white man, was shot and taken to the hospital, where he died the next day. His fiancée, nineteen year old **Mary** Ball, reported that the men who shot Deeter had raped her; **however, she later recanted her claim**. Police arrested Shipp, Smith, and Cameron, charging them with murdering Deeter and raping Ball. The next day whites arrived by the thousands from out of town and joined local residents outside the jail. The mob demanded that the three imprisoned men be turned over to them. When the sheriff refused, several young men in the crowd broke into the jail using sledgehammers. That same year over a dozen states outlawed possession of **peyote**, largely as an **anti-Native American** statement (page 497). Their goal was to separate the natives from nature. They had come to see how the **plant medicines** were a source of the natives **ability** to **foretell the future** and operate harmoniously with the land. The Black indigenous peoples of North America (Turtle Island) had been using **peyote** for thousands of years.

Utterances for Coming Forth by day into Light

It is he, who comes forth by day into Light

General Dukes Jr. (My Mother's Father)

General Dukes Jr. was sent down (born) on June 17th 1931 (06171931 = **28** = **1**), the year of the Goat in the month of Gemini. He was sent down (born) the day after Tupac's birthday and he transitioned the day after Marcus Garvey's birthday on August 18th 2009 the year of the Ox. He was 78 years old when he died but I would see my him again, 6 years after he died (p 348). **Ka** doors (spirit doors) were built into the walls of the tombs in ancient Kemet (Egypt) as a way to interface between the world of the living and the world of the dead (p 251). They did not believe in death, they called death, westing. Just as the sun rises in the East and sets in the West the same is to be said for the Ba (soul). They understood the immortality of the soul and this concept was called the **Wehem-Mesut** (repeating of births, p 14). General was from Orville, Alabama and his family was part **Cherokee Indian** therefore so am I. He had a rough upbringing, being beat a lot as a child by his father, because of this his mother left his father and they move Birmingham Alabama. He left his home at 16yrs old and became a sharecropper. He then joined the Army. While in the Army he met Juanita in New York and married her in 19**55**, the same year **Emmett Till** was murdered (p 508). Juanita and General had **6 daughters and no sons** like **Nefertiti**, (King Tut's stepmother) and **Betty Shabazz**, (Malcolm X's wife). General was an independent man. He taught his daughters to get their own and not to depend on anyone. In the streets of Far Rockaway Queens he was known as Duke and people knew not to touch the Dukes daughters. Duke did construction, he worked as a cook in many restaurants, he also worked as a cook for The Board of Education and even opened his own restaurant (Dukes Cafe) in Far Rockaway. When Duke's first grandson Dawud (TutemRa) was born he got the news while he was at work, it is said that he jumped on a table in the lunch room and screamed "I got a Grandson". Duke believed in God and during a stent in jail he became a Muslim. Still navigating the hells of America (Turtle Island) General would find himself in the south doing prison time during the 80's for possession of marijuana. Interestingly enough the **war on drugs** was started on my grandfather's birthday, on June 17th 1971, which was the day after Tupac was born. The "war on drugs" which started in the 70's was a **war on The Black Family structure** in America. On June 17th 1971 President Nixon would declare drug abuse to be "public enemy number one" which was really a war on Black people and the Black family structure (Crack, p 502). Both Alexander Gordon, 4th **Duke** of Gordon and Lord Herbert Montagu Douglas Scott died on his birthday (p 99). This is page **23** and **23** is one of the most commonly cited prime numbers - a number that can only be divided by itself and one. **23** is the lowest prime that consists of consecutive digits. Primes have been described as the "atoms" of mathematics - the building blocks of the world of numbers. With that said, this book is full of **star code patterns** appearing in the form of numbers. Some say that God is a divine mathematician and numerology is the language of God. I spent many years as a **Hermit** studying **Kemet** and Djehuty (Hermes, Thoth, Tehuti), and it's no surprise that the **Hermit** is the **23rd** tarot card and the **Hermit** is sometimes considered the mature and wiser version of The **Ma-gician (page 672)**. The axial tilt of the Earth is **23.**5 degrees (rounded to the nearest .5 naturally) **2** + **3** = 5. Each parent contributes **23** chromosomes to the start of human life. The **second** and **third** operations of **Alchemy** are Dissolution (**death**) and Separation (**reincarnation**), respectively. The **23rd** hexagram of the **I-Ching** is translated as Splitting Apart (**reincarnation**). See page **648** for more on the **metaphysical significance of the number 23**.

March 25th 1931 The Scottsboro Boys

3 months before my grandfather was born nine Black teenagers (The Scottsboro Boys,) were falsely accused of **raping** two **white women** aboard a train near Scottsboro, Alabama. The trials and repeated retrials of the Scottsboro Boys sparked an international uproar and produced two landmark U.S. Supreme Court verdicts, even as the defendants were forced to spend years battling the courts and enduring the harsh conditions of the Alabama prison system. That same year **DMT** was first synthesized by British chemist Richard Manske and named "**nigerine**" (Niggerine, p 497). When Manske first synthesized **DMT** the substance's **psychedelic** properties, as well as its natural occurrence in plants and humans, remained unknown. **Marcus Garvey** once said, "it will only take 24 hours once we all decide that it is ours". It is time for us to unite so as to ensure that these horrors NEVER happen to any of us again!

May their souls walk peacefully through the field of reeds in Amenta. Amen Ra

Rau
nu
Prt
m
heru

Iu
f
Per
f
m
heru

Utterances
for
Coming
Forth
by day
into
Light

It is
he,
who
comes
forth
by day
into
Light

Emmett Till The End of Prime

The patterns I present below and throughout this book are examples of a "weird", "strange" or **supernatural** phenomena known as **quantum entanglement**, spoken about often by physicists like Arthur **Stanley Edding**ton (**44th parallel**, page 329), who died on November 22, the day before **Mamie Till** was born (page 511). Like the **sacred geometrical soul chart** I created (page 602). **Carl Jung** coined these **incidences** as **synchronicities** because they seem to be more like patterns (page 569). The word **coincidence** (**co - incidence**) implies **two or more incidences** happening together but **synchronicities** are two or more **meaningful incidences** happening together. Some coincidences are connected so meaningfully that they break all statistical probabilities. Like the incidences leading me to meeting my cousin **Stanley Wright**.

It wasn't **till** the revision of this book that I came to know more about my family lineage from my fathers side. Because I didn't grow up with my father and because of his lack of interest in discussing his family, I never got the intricate details of his family tree and ever since his stroke in 2020 (page 627), he is incapable of discussing anything in great detail. Fortunately my cousin Edward connected me with my cousin **Stanley Wright** and my aunt Francis Eddings. My cousin Edward was born on April 20th like my niece (page 558, 610), he is the son of my aunt Florence (page 464). When I learned I was related to the **Wright's** a light went off no different than when I realized **Emmett Till** had a cousin who was a **Parker** (Wheeler Parker Jr, page 515) and my maternal grand mother was a **Parker** (pages 15,17, 22). This is note worthy because **Emmett Till** also had an uncle named Moses **Wright** Jr (page 517). It seems like I was born again into the same family tree and it's apparent that my story is forever unfolding. From a 4 hour conversation with my cousin **Stanley** Wright and my aunt Francis Eddings I learned a lot about the **Wright** side of my family and some strange things about the **Eddings** side of my family. My great grand father, **Spencer Wright was born** two days before **Emmett Till**, on July 23, 1900, the same day as Carolyn Bryant (p 180). My great grand mother, **Mildred Prime Wright was born** on July 22, 1899, three days before **Emmett Till**. My grand mother **Charlotte Demeanis Wright was born** on **November 21**, 1921, only two days before **Mamie Till** (**November 23**, 1921). My grand father Edward Eddings was born on **March 2, 1909** and died in 1960. **Howard Carter** is the archaeologist who discovered the tomb of **"King Tut"**. Carter once said that **the curse of King Tut** was nonsense but Carter died on **March 2,** the same day my grand father was born. Furthermore, **March 2,** is the same day that I watched the documentary, **The Prophecy of Reincarnation**, in 2014 (p 288). Edward Eddings would go on to marry Charlotte Wright and together they had 5 children: Edward Thomas Eddings Jr, **Spencer David Eddings** (p 28), William Nicholas Eddings, Florence Violet Eddings and Francis Ann Marie Eddings. It has been confirmed, via word of mouth, that Charlotte Wright was a **Blackfoot Indian**, therefor so am I. It has also been confirmed that Edward's mother was Amy Brown but it has not been confirmed that David Eddings (page 15) was his biological father. I have however been able to confirm, via word of mouth, that Edward's blood lines comes from **Barbados**, therefor so does mine. When the indigenous population of the island of Hispaniola (**Haiti**) was decimated by European invaders, the first place they went for new "slaves" was Barbados. I'm connected to Haiti and the **Haitian revolution** because of my Bajan ancestry. This is why I would have **synchronistic** experiences with the leaders of the Haitian revolution throughout my **years of awakening** (see pages 141-142, 292 & 297). During my talk with my Aunt Francis I learned that she is born on Feb **23**, 1954 and she has a grandson born on Feb **23rd**. Emmett Till was murdered at **14** years old in 19**55** and **the first bible was printed** on Feb **23**, **1455** ACE, (p 615). See page **648** for the **metaphysical significance of the number 23** and see pages 94, 102, 121, 283, 444, 439, 586, 669, and 672 for more on **Feb 23.**

Spencer Wright and Mildred Prime Wright,
my Paternal Great Grand Parents (My Father's Grand Parents)

Edward Thomas Eddings Sr & Charlotte Demeanis Wright Eddings,
my Paternal Grand Parents (My Father's Parents).

ADDENDUM

December 7th 1974
Spencer and Debra Eddings (Parents)

They both had challenging starts at life but they met each other at the most divine and **prime** times of their lives. They fell in love while practicing the Islamic faith and had 3 children. Love is a art, love is a sp**ark**, sometimes things fall apart and get d**ark**, but sometimes it's for the better. Unbeknownst to them both, they had given birth the an ancient soul, a sun who mastered magic and traveled from the times of papyrus and tablets. He charted his own course with a thought on a divine barque made of acacia and amethyst, **RA**member this like a **hieroglyph, Anubis** and a **obelisk,** Karma do exist like the kiss of death. He came back to sp**ark** the last ones left in bondage.

Rau nu Prt m heru

Iu f Per f m heru

Utterances for Coming Forth by day into Light

It is he, who comes forth by day into Light

February 3rd 1955 (02031955 = 25 = 7) Debra Lisa Dukes (My Mother)

My mother, Debra Dukes was the first of **six daughters** born to Juanita and General Dukes Jr. She was born Feb 3rd (**23**), the same Year **Emmett Till** was murdered, the day before **Rosa Parks** was born. (See page **648** for the **metaphysical significance of the number 23**). Debra was the first daughter of a man who only had a 6 grade education. Because of that he stressed the importance of getting a good education. As a child she was praised by her father for being, "so smart" and this positive reinforcement inspired Debra to excel in school. She loved to read and to sow and as a teenager she made most of her own clothes. She attended high school at Jamaica high and was a straight A student regularly making the honor role. She was always contemplating about God and talking about spirituality with her friends. When she was around 15 she was introduced to **Islam**. One day she was at a friends house playing cards and listening to music. Her friends brother came over with a group of his friends and she saw them reciting a long **muslim prayer**. They had just returned from prison having made spiritual changes in their lives. She had heard them praying before but when she heard the long prayer she was immediately taken with curiosity and expressed her desire to study Islam. They wrote down a prayer for her and told her to practice it and if she learned it they would give her more info. The next day she came back and recited the whole prayer. She was given a **shahada** and a **Quran**, and now she was secretly a **muslim** and stayed that way for about five years because her father was not into the muslim religion. It was around this time that she was sexually assaulted by Rudy Williams, a popular football star. Her father was never told of this in fear that he would kill Rudy and be sent to prison. Debra struggled to deal with the attack but the experience took a toll on her. In the 11th grade she left Jamaica High and enrolled to Far Rock High School. The school had strict no hat policies and she was told that she had to remove her **hijab** while at school but she refused. Debra was naturally a rebellious spirit and so she argued that if **Jewish** students could wear their **yarmulke** then she could wear her hijab and she was left alone. She went on to become the president and founder of the Black Student Union.

Sister Debra 29X

When she graduated she went to Fairly Dickerson College. During her time in college she was sexually assaulted again and the experience had a lasting effect on her dealings with men. At some point in college she was introduced to the **Nation of Islam,** She was the 29th women named Debra to join that mosque and so she was given the name, **Sister Debra 29X** (page 64). She was around 19 years old when she met **Spencer** at the mosque who was himself around 24yrs old. She didn't know about Spencer's past, she saw him as a disciplined brother in The Nation, but Spencer was like her friends brother whom she had met years ago, he had come home from prison and was trying to make a better way for himself. They began to speak to each other and soon after they spent time together. The Nation of Islam did chaperone dates for the young adults so the couples could get to know each other. Marriage was highly encouraged for the young couples in the masque in hopes that they would not fall into sin. Debra remembers someone asking her, "when is the wedding". One thing led to another and they got married on Dec 7th 1974. Their marriage certificate number was **555**82 (see page 555). The first 3 months of their marriage they had 3 different addresses, moving around trying to find stability. By June of 1975 they were going to divorce until Debra came up pregnant with her first daughter. Spencer had problems with drinking and that led to physical abuse. He couldn't break his bad habits. With drugs and alcohol the black family was the target of the largest psychological warfare ravaged, and there you have it. They separated, and couldn't fix their marriage. Debra was left with 3children, struggling to find stability. She found herself running from Spencer and in the beginning she faired well. She moved the family around and did the best she could. She was in a depression and played the **Sade** song, **Is It A Crime**, a lot. That is why Sade is one of my favorite artist. That Sade album was released on Nov 4th 1985, the same day **King Tut's** tomb was discovered. In 1988 she was pregnant again, by another man. In attempts to start over she moved her family to Columbus Georgia in 1989. Her plans didn't workout and after 2 years she moved back to NY. Her children were sent to live with different family members and at some point she fell and began using the drugs of the day. I never lived with my mother again after we moved back to New York and because of this our relationship would take major damage while in my teenage years. Around 2013, the year of the **snake,** my mother began to profess her faith of Islam again. During the years of my awakening I argued with my mother regularly about religion. I strongly feel that it was this turmoil with my mother that helped me realize this divine revelation. I'm forever grateful to my mother and we are currently working on our relationship. Her life path number is **7** rooted in **25**. When I got out of the Army in 2005, I was listening to a lot of **Tupac's** music and one day my mother told me that she felt like her son was Tupac. I never thought too much of that comment back then but when my past life as **King Tut** was revealed her feelings made more sense.

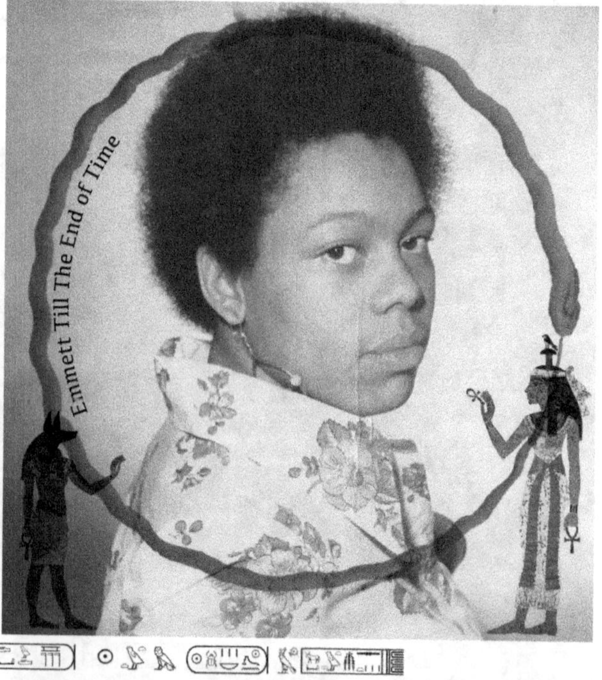

June 1st 1950 (06011950 = 22) Spencer David Eddings (My Father)

Rau nu Prt m heru

My father, Spencer David Eddings was sent down (born) on June 1st, the same day that the **Black Wall Street massacre** ended (page 408).. I once crashed in a violent car accident on his birthday, June 1st 2002 (page 106). The strange thing is my sister dreamt the car accident on May 25th, 7 days before it happened (page 104). Spencer grew up in New Jersey without his mother or his father, spending some parts of his youth in the foster care system, similar to Emmett Till's father who was an orphan. Spencer's father died when he was 10 years old and for most of his life he never knew his mother; he was always told she was dead. He has **Bajan** ancestry through his fathers side and **Blackfoot Indian** ancestry from his mothers side. Spencer was one of many children, but was the only child with a different mother. He lived with different family members and eventually became **the problem child,** the one that got caught in the streets. His youth was sort of like the story of Mike Tyson except he was no great boxer so he didn't find an escape route out of the ghetto. Instead he became a stick up kid and to this day he doesn't like to think of all the devious things he did. He used to roll up, "This is a hold up, ain't nothin' funny stop smilin', be still, don't nothin' move but the money!" He would rob the drug dealers and find various other ways of making a quick buck. He, like many other young black males growing up in America, used the drugs of the day and lived a life of crime. "He was a young man with no dreams just plans to make cream which failed; he went to jail at the age of 15, a young buck sellin' drugs and such, he never had much he was tryin' to get a clutch but he could not". He got caught and the court system played him short. He was handcuffed and put in the back of a bus with no one to trust. Over the years he would find himself in and out of jail and at one point being housed in a cell next to the famous Boxer **Hurricane Rubin Carter**. It's a miracle that he lived to have children as his life was almost ended several times having survived many fights, stabbings and gun shot injuries.

Thirteen Signs

Iu f Per f m heru

Inspired by men like **Malcolm X** Spencer joined the Nation of Islam in the early 70's. **Elijah Muhammad** can be credited for his ability to unite the so called Black community under the religion of Islam transforming men like my father from criminals to honorable men, raising them up perpendicular into pillars of the community. **Malcolm X** can be credited for grabbing the hearts and minds of the people, standing on street corners speaking from his heart, trying to improve the conditions of negroes, indigenous blacks, African Americans, and any other name assigned to the **aboriginal** descendants of torture and pain around the world. Spencer met a woman named Debra in the Nation of Islam during the summer of 1974. That's when Spencer learned to earn an honest living and became righteous. Everything was great, so he searched for a 9 to 5, and he began to strive. He found love giving him more reason to stay alive. They planned to get married in September of 1974 but the wedding was postponed because his youngest brother **Kenneth Eddings** died on **September 13th**, on his **13th birthday**, the same day **Tupac** died (P 76). They got married on Dec 7th 1974. The first 3 months of their marriage they had 3 different addresses, moving around trying to find stability. Spencer had problems with drinking and that led to physical abuse. By June of 1975 they were going to divorce until Debra came up pregnant with her first daughter. They tried to make things work but the marriage could not be salvaged. Spencer went on to marry a woman named Mary. While working security in Ocean Village, he shot and killed a man. Fearing that he might be sent to prison, he ran from the law and changed his name to XXXXXXX XXXX. He changed his birthday to my birthday (October 25) and his birth year to 19XX.

Utterances for Coming Forth by day into Light

It is he, who comes forth by day into Light

Fortunately he was able to rebound from his troubled past and found a union job as a senior painter at the Waldorf Astoria (p 141, 142) which allowed him to make an honest living. All the people that worked with Spencer liked him but Spencer developed a bad anger management problem as a result of the life that he lived and the hell he'd survived. Some time in the late 80's or early 90's he was tracked down and made to serve his time for the killing a man. Fortunately the union at Waldorf allowed him to come back to work when he finished serving his time. Spencer is alive now. He is 71 years old. He is recovering from a stroke he suffered on Sep **23rd** 2020, the same day that **Emmitt Till's** killers were acquitted (page 627). See page **648** for the **metaphysical significance of the number 23**. I did not grow up with my father but I have always loved him. I only have two memories of him prior to being a teenager. I don't know what age I was but there was a knock at my grand mothers door and when the door opened a man came in the house. My older sister ran to him screaming, "Daddy" as she hugged him. I did not recognize him but I ran to him too because she did. I always wanted to know where my daddy was. Our younger sister was too young, she just stood and watched. The other memory is walking down the street with him at a young age. I had dried snot around my nose and he licked his fingers and cleaned it from my nose with a tissue wet with the moisture of his spit. I never forgot the smell of his spit on my nose. I would not have another memory of him until I was a teenager. As a boy I was always looking for my father. Maybe he would be coming through the door again like that time when we were little. I did not have a vivid memory of what he looked like and sometimes I would see men in the street and wonder if that was my father. Him and I would not get to know each other until after I got out of the Army in 2004. Currently our relationship is the best it has been. In life we might not get what we want but we get what we need. I think I needed to walk the path that I did in life with no father. I had to earn the right to know. My father's life path number is **22** (195061=22). The names **David** (41494 = **22**) and **Emmett** (544225 = **22**) add up to the **master number 22** (see p **41**).

1976-1977: The Tut Tour: Treasures of Tutankhamun
"I am the Boy King in the Museum that You Be Seeing"

I am the **boy king** in the museum that you be seeing, I gave you the signs this time I'm back in a human being, facts encoded in rhyme like my body frozen in time, in 1929 I shined on **Martin Luther King.** My tomb was discovered in 19**22** the year of the **dog**. I was born again in 19**41**, the year of the **snake** as Emmett Till. _Then I was murdered in 19**55**_ the year of the **goat**. **22** years later I was born again in 19**77** the year of the **snake**. In 2018 the year of the **dog** my past life as **Emmett Till** is revealed to me (page 480). In November of 1976 the year of the **dragon**, a year before I returned in this life, _**55** of my royal treasures were sent on a tour of the United States_. The exhibition started in Washington DC before moving on to **Chicago** in 19**77** the year of the **snake,** from **July** to **August**, in the same state **Emmett Till** was born and the same month he was born (July 25th 19**41**, page **41**) and murdered (August 28th 1955). On April **4th** 2020 my past life as Tutankhaten (King Tut) was revealed to me (page 594), the same day that Martin Luther King was assassinated (see page 69). On April **4th** 19**77** the year of the **snake**, **President Carter** called seeing Tut **"one of the most exciting experiences that I have had."** I'm sure if he saw me today he would refuse to believe this revelation. He would not want to believe a "Black Pharaoh" is back here in the same spirit of freedom that Martin spoke about. It wouldn't surprise me though. The American archaeologist George Reisner refused to believe in "Black Pharaohs" too. In 1916 the year after the movie **Birth of a Nation** was shown in the White House, Reisner was excavating in **Sudan** when he "discovered" beautiful black Granite statues of Kushite pharaohs. He argued that the kings were not black, but instead they were white foreigners who migrated **deep** into Africa to build that civilization, then left.... He couldn't accept Black Greatness and failed to fill in the blank ––– as to why these mysterious "white" foreigners never built up the civilization of Europe to the degree as the Kushites. None of that stops the fact that I am the **boy king** in the museum that you be seeing, I gave you the signs this time I'm back in a human being, facts encoded in rhyme like my body frozen in time, in 1929 I shined on **Martin Luther King.**

When my exhibit came to America (Turtle Island), day after day, they showed up by the thousands, the butchers and bakers and candlestick makers. **Cleopatra**, I mean Elizabeth Taylor the actor, she came and gazed upon my golden face caught up in my rapture. **President Carter** was standing on the White House grass when he said, seeing Tut was "one of the most exciting experiences that I have had". Members of Congress paraded through, as did Hollywood royalty and the stars of that time took time for a rendezvous with TutemRa Kheperu. The non VIPs gathered before dawn, hoping to beat the crush of the rush to see Tut, the race was on. Some people camped out at night, to be among the first at the gallery doors to see the sights. Rain or shine and even in the snow, they waited and waited to see the show. Some waited for 7 hours long just to see me, and take a stroll back in time to 1325 BC. Golden and frozen in alabaster, ebony and ivory but Serket was their favorite she was a sight to see. I am the **boy king** in the museum that you be seeing, I gave you the signs this time I'm back in a human being, facts encoded in rhyme like my body frozen in time, in 1929 I shined on **Martin Luther King.**

Serket
(page 634)

Addendum On **October 28,** 20**22**, <u>3 days after my 45th birthday, the movie **Till** (a movie about **Emmett Till**) was released nationwide in America and on that same day the **Beyond King Tut tour** opened in New York City. The number **28** correlates to Ausar the Gardener (page 481). This book was released on June 1 2022).</u> **See page 33.**

May 25 is a reoccurring date **entangled** with a past life and my current life that formed a pattern. It was the first star code pattern that I decoded in 2011 (p 222), stemming from a **dream** my sister had in 2002 (p 104). This star code would sp**ark** my awareness to patterns hidden within dates and ultimately it connects me with my previous life as Emmett Till (p 480). These patterns are examples of a phenomena known as **quantum entanglement**, spoken about often in Physics. Like my strange **entanglement** with the movie **Back To The Future** (p 40). **Einstein**, called this phenomena, **spooky action at a distance** (p 329). My sister's "dream" wasn't a premonition, **it was time travel** (p 104)! Our consciousness can **quantum leap** to the past or the future via dreaming and meditation. Dream interpretations are a major part of all indigenous peoples of the world and were used as a source of divination (forecasting the future). Thutmose IV, had a dream about the Sphinx. When he awoke he followed the dream, unearthed the Sphinx buried beneath the sand and afterwards he was crowned Pharaoh. The bible places emphasis on dreams as well with the story of Joseph deciphering the dream of a Pharaoh which prevented a famine. The profound dreams of "Prince Siddhartha" (Buddha) caused him to contemplate the root of suffering which led to his enlightenment. The Prophet Muhammad (PBUH) had a dream about Aisha and married her. The indigenous peoples (Native Americans) of Turtle Island (America) were very keen on dreams as well. They had people who were skilled in all the arts, the medicine women/men, the warriors, the dancers, and many more, but the most important people were the dreamers. Everyday the dreamers would come together and share their dreams and visions to ensure the balance of the tribe. Oral tradition still records how the Native Americans saw the pale face man before he came. Abraham Lincoln dreamt his death before it happened! Jewell dreamt about **Tupac's** death before it happened (p 105). The questions we should be asking ourselves are, what is a dream and what does it really mean to follow your dreams or to live out your dreams (p 589). Some dreams take place in a different space and time where the **astral body travels**, sometimes to the past and even the future. **Deja Vu** is sometimes a result of having already experienced a moment in a dream and when you reach the moment in your waken state you have a feeling of familiarity. In 2022 I experienced **Deja Vu** twice while in **Kemet** (pages 670 - 671). If you are reading this then you're still sleeping. In ancient Kemet we saw this life as a **dream** and the word dream (re-soot) meant to become awakened. MDW (word) NTCHR (divine) = divine words (hieroglyphs).

Rau nu Prt m heru

eg. 1 Dream Re-soot	eg. 2 Dream = Re-soot	eg. 3 Sleep = Awe	eg. 4 Sleep = Qeded	eg. 5 Sleep = Sejer	
eg. 6 Death = Emt	eg. 7 Death = Mini	eg. 8 Deceased = Kepet	eg. 9 Beautiful = Nefer	eg.10 Awakening within the Dream of life	or

Iu f Per f m heru

Imagine a time when humans did not need to speak with their mouths, a time when communicating telepathically was a normality. Imagine being able to see from far distances with your minds eye and taking the form of any animal you so choose. Writing and speaking only came about when humans lost the ability to communicate telepathically. It was the ancient African Kemetyu who developed the writing system we know as MDW NTCHR (hieroglyphics). Deciphering the MDW NTCHR takes a deeper mode of thought than what modern language offers. You must imagine that you are reading the language of immortals. Until this is done the meaning of the MDW NTCHR will never be fully inner stood. In every language there may be several ways to say certain words or to convey a certain idea. Take for instance eg. 9, the word **beautiful** (Nefer) is the symbol of a **wind pipe connected to the heart**. What are the ancient Kemetyu trying to convey? In modern society we have come to judge beauty by the surface, usually by a persons face or the way their body looks but in ancient Kemet we understood that beauty came from the heart and this is why the heart was weighed against the feather of Maat during the judgement scenes after death of the physical body. It is beautiful when thy heart is lighter than the feather. Above we have the words dream, sleep, death and deceased written in MDW NTCHR. I got the transliterations for these words from two different sources, **Rkhty Amen** and **Sir Alan Gardiner**. Examples 1, 3, 4, 6, 7 and 8 come from Gardiner's book, Egyptian Grammar while examples 2 and 5 come from Rkhty's book, Mejat Wefa - Conversation book, English to Medu Neter (mdw ntchr). You will notice the three different spellings of the word sleep in examples 3, 4 and 5. In examples 3 and 4 Gardiner uses the symbol of an **eye** while Rkhty has the symbol of a **mummy** laying on a bed. You can also see that Rkhty and Gardiner agree on the word for **dream**, they spell it slightly different yet they both use the symbol of an **eye**. In the words death(eg. 7, Mini)and deceased(eg. 8, Kepet) Gardiner uses the symbol of a mummy. When we look at how Rkhty spells sleep(eg. 5, Sejer) she uses a mummy as well. This connects the idea of sleep and death and the Emcee **Nas** said it best, "Sleep is the cousin of death". The words see, wakeful, wake, weep, transfix, nature, milk, form, and Ausar (Osiris) all have the symbol of an eye in them. This is not done by chance. When we are being **form**ed in our mothers womb we are taking in her nourishment and when we are born we suckle **milk** from her breast. A mothers breast **milk** is full of the **love** hormone oxytocin which is produced by the posterior pituitary gland which works with the pineal gland (**3rd eye**). The word dream in ancient Kemet meant to become awakened and that is why the words wakeful and wake have an eye in them. The popular phrase, "**life is but a dream**" originates in the tomb of Neferhotep (TT50) in the song of a harpist written on the wall in stone, "As for the span of earthly affairs it is the manner of a dream". We must awaken from the dream like Ausar. The word Nature stems from the word **NTCHR** which meant God. **Nature / God** provides medicine like the acacia tree that will allow initiates who have earned the keys to awaken from the dream and that is why the word **nature** has an eye in it. Ausar was known as, "**the one in the tree**" (**acacia** tree page 482). In Kemet death of the physical body was not seen as the end, it was called Westing and Just as the sun rises in the east and sets in the west, the same is to be said for the soul. The Pharaoh's were known to take on new bodies (reincarnate, resurrect) after they went "west". In fact, during the **heb sed** festival, conducted in the Pharaoh's thirtieth year, they had to prove their worthiness to continue on the throne by astral projecting from their physical bodies to meet with Anubis who leads them to the Underworld in the dimension of dreams where they enter death returning as Ausar in new garments (the robe and the spiritual body of transformation). In the Ausarian Resurrection drama, the **acacia** is the tree that magically grew up around the body of Ausar when his sarcophagus washed up on the shores of Byblos. The acacia tree holds the same spiritual molecule (DMT) that I ingested at the age of 40 (page 480) which **awoke** me to my life as Emmett Till. In eg. 10, the symbol of a bed with the symbol of an open eye placed above it is used to convey the concept of awakening within a dream (or), when this symbol is seen in this book it denotes a **dream**, **lucid dreaming** or **astral projection**. Ausar (Osiris) is the Lord of **resurrection** and that is why his name has an eye in it. In the Ausarian **resurrection** Drama Ausar is murdered by his brother **Set**. Ausar's son Heru avenges the death of his father Ausar and battles his uncle Set. During the battle Set gouged Heru's eye out but Heru was victorious giving birth to the eye of Heru. Ausar resurrects through his son **Heru** but ultimately, you are Ausar and Heru! See the **hero's journey** (p 3)! See The Force Awakens (p 37). Just as my sister **dreamt** my car accident before it happened, **Jewell dreamt** Tupac's death before it happened (p 105).

Utterances for Coming Forth by day into Light

It is he, who comes forth by day into Light

October 12th 1977 The Year of The Snake
The Divine Return of Djed Eye
(The prologue below is my creative imagination - Not a Memory, but.......)

I was sent by the supreme council of galactic elders and I came again flying out of the primordial darkness of the **beehive** deep within the **Scarab** (Cancer) constellation headed to Earth on my **Barque of Ages** on a **5** year cycle, known now as the Comet **Grigg-Skjellerup 1902II**. It was John Grigg, an astronomer from New Zealand who tracked me gliding across the sky in **The Sun Boat of Ra** in 1902 when **Howard Carter** and fellow Egyptologist Theodore Davies discovered the royal tomb of **Hatshepsut** in Egypt's Valley of the Kings. I came to insure that no one discovered my tomb. They logged my sighting as **Grigg 1902**. When everything was clear I shot back to the **Beehive**. On November 6th 19**55**, **70** days after my lynching I was without body. I didn't remember the details of my death but I knew I was "dead" again. My pineal gland (𓂀 single eye, first eye, third eye, spiritual eye) had been flooded with **DMT** and my soul (consciousness) had successfully passed through the halls of **Amenta,** then I was sent back to the year 19**22**. I came again flying out of the primordial darkness of the **beehive** headed to earth again in my **celestial bark** on **May 25th** 19**22.** This time I came to insure that **Howard Carter** would find my tomb and he did. This time it was the Australian Astronomer John Francis Skjellerup who tracked my movements gliding across the skies of South Africa on May 16th, logging my appearance as **Grigg-Skjellerup 1902II**. They had no earthly idea what they were observing and only now because of this book might they start to fathom what they were seeing in the heavens. With lightning speed I deciphered the **first star code** and planned my return during the **total solar eclipse** of 19**77**. **55** years later I came again on **April 4th** of **1977** the year of the **snake** and this was the first time they tracked my **Ark of a Million Years** with it's new orbit making a closer approach to the Earth than they had been previously accustomed to, yet still they had no clue as to what they were observing. I returned during a **total solar eclipse** on Wednesday, October 12th 1977 with no interruptions. Then I entered the new body on October 25th 19**77** and immediately all memory of my mission was erased except one code. The date **May 25th** was stored deep within my subconscious locked inside of a box, inside of a dream within a dream. And finally a portion of the code was placed in the same place with in the subconscious of one of my sistars. I would have to earn the right to awaken to this dream. These teachings were only passed down to the Kemetic Priest's and Nswt Bity's (Pharaoh's) in ancient times. I wasn't the only one on this mission. In fact if you are reading this then you are on the same mission but you just don't know it yet. We all have a part to play in this cosmic play of consciousness.

I Am A Beacon of Light

"I'm a rocket ship, yo, I'm a beacon of light, I was sent here to write, sent here to write, sent here to fight, I'm a rocket ship, I'm a, I'm a rocket ship, I'm a beacon of light, I was sent here to write, sent here to fight, I'm a rocket ship, I'm a rocket ship, I'm a rocket ship, I'm a rocket ship, I'm a beacon of light, I was sent here to write, sent here to fight and I could die to night, I'm a rocket ship, I'm a, I'm a rocket ship, I'm a beacon of light, I was sent here to fight and I could die to night, I'm a rocket ship, on a rocket ship" (**Beacon of Light,** written on January 8th 2012, P 222)

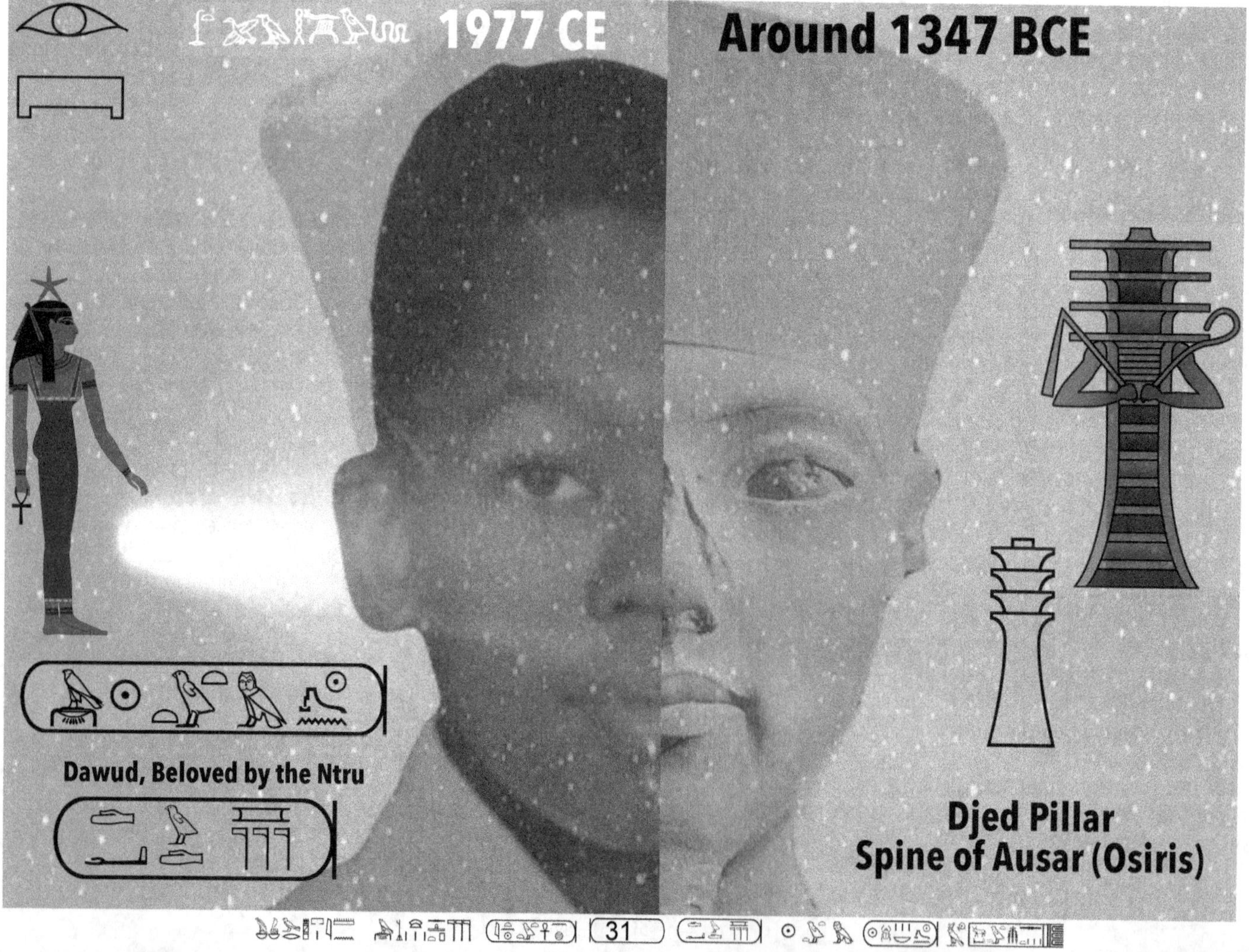

Rau nu Prt m heru

The thought of immortality is the most important thought you can have! This book is about the immortality of the soul. I do not claim to be a genius by telling you this however I am the only person who has ever produced a work quite like this. In the year 2022 this book will be released and it will detail the slow awakening of the soul of a Nswt Bity (Pharaoh) in modern time. An awakening that unfolds over the course of 40 years in this life time. I will be 44 in 2 days. We are all one in that we all share this breath of life breathing in the divine spirit of the creator. We share that spirit but we all have our own souls and go on our own individual soul journeys, life after life. I am the soul of **Emmett Till**, **Tutankhaten** (**King Tut**) and many other lives I have lived. Some of you reading this do not believe one word I am saying so let's start with a joke.

Iu f Per f m heru

Utterances for Coming Forth by day into Light

The Immortal Joke Featuring Richard Pryor

It is he, who comes forth by day into Light

The year is 19**77**, ***the year of the snake*** *and* **Richard Pryor** is at the top of his fame in the business of Comedy. This same year I would be born on **Tuesday** October 25th and this same year Richard would close a deal to **star** in his own show on **Tuesday** nights at **8**pm Live on NBC, called **The Richard Pryor Show**. His **first** episode would **air** on **September 13th** the same day that my uncle died (page 28) and the same day that **Tupac** died (page 76). Richard Pryor starred in the movie **Superman** in 1983 and it premiered on my **grand father General Dukes'** birthday June 17th (page **23**), which is the day after **Tupac's** birthday. I have a **theory** about who Tupac was in a **past** life and I'll talk more about **Superman**, and Tupac in 2011 when I audition to play Tupac in the Tupac biopic (page, 204 ☥). Pryor's show was brought to a quick end after only 4 episodes. On **September 20th**, his second episode would air and in this episode he would open the **tomb** of a long **lost** and forgotten **Pharaoh**. **22** years Pryor, on **September** 19th 19**55** Emmett Till's court case had just began in M**ississi**ppi, the same year my **mother** was born (page 27). Richard Pryor was sent down on (born on) December 1st 1940 the year before Emmett was born, on the same day that **Rosa Parks** (p 518) was arrested for not giving her seat to a white man, sparking the Civil Rights Movement. Rosa later quoted saying, "I thought of Emmett Till, and I couldn't go back." Rosa died on October 24, the day before my birthday and was born the day after my mother's birthday (p 27). If it weren't for the brave actions of women like Emmett's mother Mamie Till and Rosa Parks there would not have been a Civil Rights Movement (<u>It's important that you read about **"The Sacrificial Lamb"** on page 511, so that you can hear Mamie Till's experience with the voice God</u>). Emmett was lynched in **Money** M**ississi**ppi and in the word M**ississi**ppi you can see the name **isis** (Auset) who is the **mother** of **Heru** (**Horus**, **Zeus**, **Jesus**) and the great royal **wife** of **Ausar** (**Osiris**) the Lord of **resurrection**. Richard Pryor opens the **tomb** of a long **lost** and forgotten **Pharaoh** the same year that I am born and this book is about the **reincarnation** of the boy Pharaoh **Tutankhaten** (**King Tut**) and the boy **Emmett Till** so allow me to take a break from this "**joke**" to tell you about the **mother** of Emmett Till.

Escape From Mississippi

On **August 28th** 18**33** the year of the **snake**, slavery was abolished in the United Kingdom, which had a trickle down effect and led to the American abolition of slavery. The murder of Emmett Till sparked the Civil Rights Movement for blacks in America and he was murdered on **August 28th** 19**55**. We would not have the freedoms we have today if it were not for the murder of Emmett Till and more importantly the courageous actions of his mother **Mamie Till**! Mamie had a life changing experience with God (page 511, **"The Sacrificial Lamb"**) and afterwards she risked her life by daring to show the world the pictures of her sons brutalized body and to take his killers to trial. Because of this act of bravery she barely escaped M**ississ**ippi with her life! She did not stay to hear the verdict because she knew it wouldn't be a guilty one!! After the trial was over and these men were found innocent of lynching her only son, the whites in Sumner M**ississ**ippi started beating random blacks in hateful acts of violence and even killing some. In attempts to escape M**ississ**ippi Mamie, along with her party, went to see the Bishop of the state of M**ississ**ippi to plea for help but he refused. He looked her in the face and told her, "You have no business down here in the first place." He turned them away and offered no help. Instead he scolded Mamie for coming down there and making trouble for M**ississ**ippi. Just when all hope seemed to be lost safety was sent their way. As if sent by an angel, a cab appeared from seemingly nowhere like a scarab dung beetle. After learning who Mamie was, the black cab driver turned his car lights off so as to avoid those who might be after them and raced through dead of the night as fast as he could on the narrow and sketchy M**ississ**ippi back roads, with ditches on each side. Mamie says, "the car trembled like a leaf on a tree the whole ride" and finally he dropped them off at the edge of the Memphis airport and told her, "this is where we have to part company". They had a long walk to the airport but she was grateful that he risked his life for them, they boarded the plane and they made it back to Chicago safely. I met Minister Clemson Brown in 2021 through Professor Oyibo. Minister Brown would show me a video he captured of Mamie in 1995 and from this video is where I got the details of her escape. Minister Brown is 82yrs old. He is born on August 25th the day after Emmett entered Bryant's grocery story in 1955, which would eventually lead to his death. I did two interviews with Minister Clemson Brown before I released this book. The first was on August 20th 2021 and the second was August 25th 2021. At the beginning of the second video Minister Brown opened with a profound experience he had with a **star**, or **light**, or **UFO** in the night sky (page 518). Now back to **The Immortal Joke**.

The Golden Throne Chair of Tutankhaten (King Tut)

On September 20th Pryor's second episode of The Richard Pryor show would air and in this episode he would open the tomb of a long lost and forgotten Pharaoh. **22** years prior, on September 19th **Emmett Till's** court case had just began. The show aired on a Tuesday night. **Tuesdays** are governed by **Enpu** (Anubis), the dog headed NTCHRU (Element of the one GOD) of ancient Kemet (Egypt). Enpu is the Lord of mummification. The first person Enpu ever mummified was Ausar (Osiris) the Egyptian Lord of resurrection (reincarnation). On this episode Pryor appears at the doors of a lost tomb with a team of European archaeologists in ancient Egypt in 1909. Once inside the tomb they discover the elixir of life (cure for all diseases) and the Book of Life, which revealed that Black people were the creators of the greatest civilization on earth. The chair that Richard sat in while reading through the Book of Life was a replica of the **golden throne chair** (page 472) of **Tutankhaten** (**King Tut**), which was discovered in 19**22** the same year Emmett Till's father was sent down (born). The skit ends with Pryor being locked in the tomb by the European archaeologists who do not want the knowledge Pryor discovered to be shared with the rest of the world. Wasn't that funny? The same thing will be done with this book. They do not want you to know that I have returned so tell everyone! I am seen sitting in a replica of my throne chair on Dec 22, 2022.

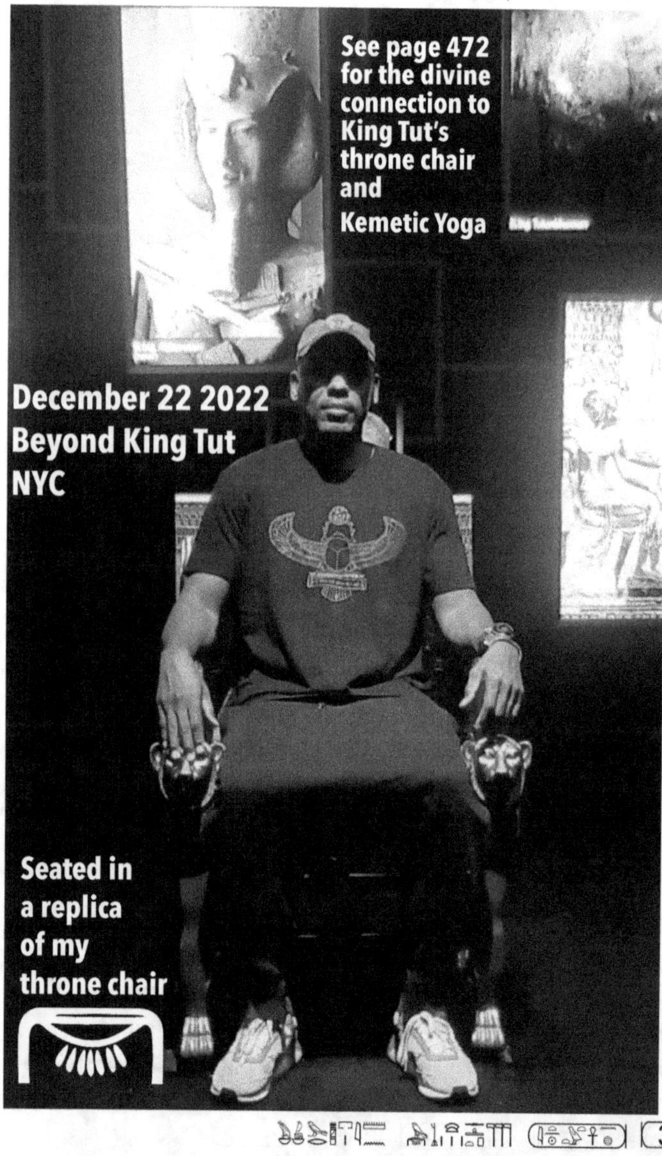

See page 472 for the divine connection to King Tut's throne chair and Kemetic Yoga
December 22 2022
Beyond King Tut
NYC
Seated in a replica of my throne chair

"Jesus" once said "Ye are Gods" (John 10:34 / Psalms 82:6), but who was Jesus and where did he come from? What is it that this character "Jesus" was teaching (p 593), do you know? There is a great possibility that you will live another life! That after you die **"you"** will be **born again** and live another life as a completely different person, and when **born again** most people will have no memory of the previous life. I say these things because I know that I have lived before. We all have an individual soul and this book is about my soul. And about how everything in the time that I reincarnated in seemed to work towards helping me realize this revelation. Perhaps you can take the fruit from my story and use it to fuel you towards an even greater life experience that might help the advancement of all beings towards a path of love peace and prosperity. I'm writing a Epic Sci-Real (Science Reality) Novel Trilogy version of this book and a book about Tupac's ancient past life (pages 664 - 665). Stay tuned!

"I stay younger than the age that a man plans to retire, the world is my stage, **transform** my rage like **Richard Pryor,** it's a cold world take a page, get paid to burn it in the fire, the desire to acquire, you can't steal the level of **Messiah,** but <u>*the caterpillar will kill the butterfly just to be flyer!*</u>" **- Dawud The Amazing BlaKseed (Retire,** written on June 15th 2018, (page 470).

October 25th 1977 The Year of the Snake

The 10th Month and The 25th Day at 10:25 am

Rau nu Prt m heru

Iu f Per f m heru

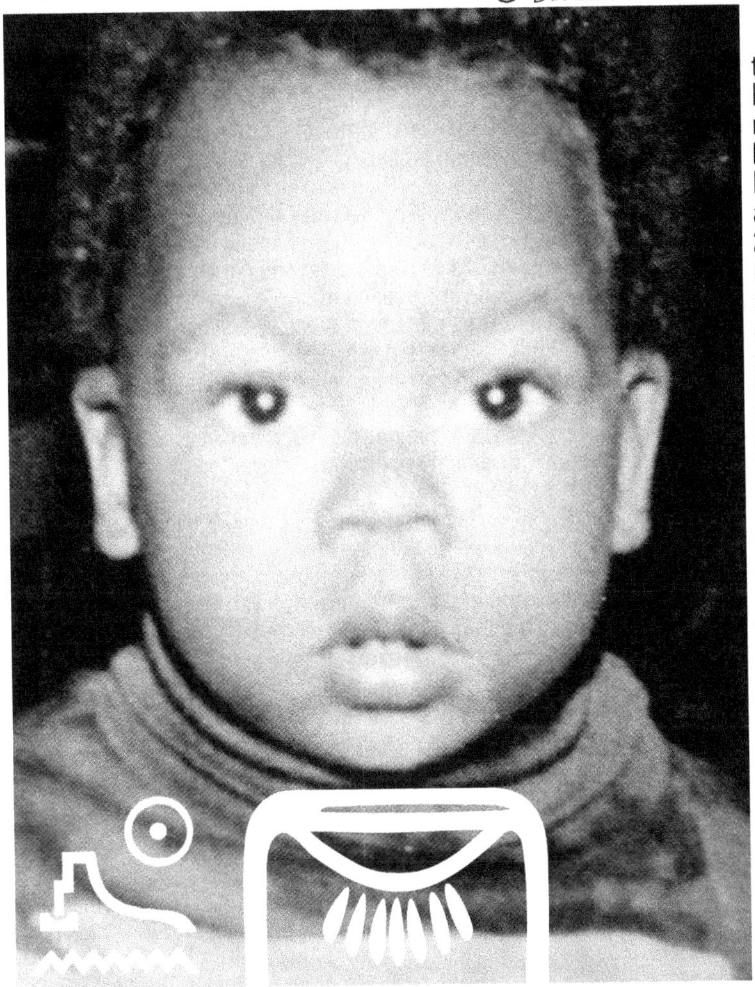

Dawud, Beloved by the Ntru

Utterances for Coming Forth by day into Light

Puerto Ricans on the island in 1900 Dusky Belles Puerto Rico Blackamoor, Morena, Moor, Moorian, Muurs,

It is he, who comes forth by day into Light

I don't remember pushing and fighting my way through the womb and I don't remember having lived before but I know now that I have and even more so that I've been here many times before. Sometimes I have these feelings of **DeJa Vu** that I can not place however the feelings feel like a long time ago. In this body I was sent down (born) at **10:25** am on a **Tuesday** near the end of Generation X, on **October 25th** 1977 **the year of the snake**. The two numbers in the middle of my social security number are **62** (pages 41, 221, 508, 6**02**). When my Grand Father got the news that his first daughter had a boy he jumped on the table at work and screamed "I have a grandson". He had no sons and I was the first boy born in the family. 45 years later I would go to **Kemet** (Egypt) for the first time in this life and experience **Deja Vu** twice while in there (pages 670 - 671).

On the day I was born, 30 **Puerto Rican** nationalist were demanding freedom for Puerto Rico, and in doing so they occupied the **Statue of Liberty** for **8** hours. They dropped a Puerto Rican flag from it's crown, and a banner calling for the independence of Puerto Rico across it's pedestal. Boats and helicopters, full of reporters and photographers, were dispatched to the New York harbor. The "nationalist" as they were called were finally arrested after the **eight** hour stand off, and charged with trespassing on federal property. You should remember that the Statue of Liberty was dedicated to America (Turtle Island) on October 28th 1886 at a time when not even white women had the right to vote. After the Civil War black men in America received the right to vote after the ratification of the 15th amendment on **February 3rd** 1870, my mothers birthday (February 3rd 1955). Black men received the right to vote before white women and black women. On **August 18th** 1920, the day my Grand Father died (August 18th 2009), white women received the right to vote with the ratification of the 16th amendment but black women would not receive the right to vote until 1960, five years after the murder of **Emmett Till**. In fact it was the murder of Emmett Till that ushered in Civil Rights in America yet still we don't really have Civil Rights. What has voting really done for black people? We are still murdered indiscriminately and housed in prisons no different than 1864 slave plantations. The irony of the statue of Liberty is that she was initially supposed to be a black woman and she had chains around her ankles yet she is supposed to represent liberty and freedom.

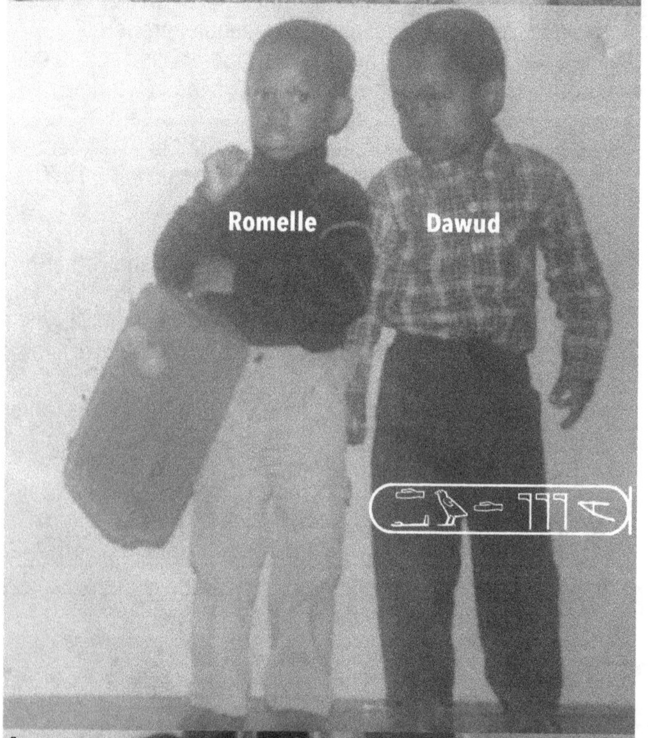

I Failed The 1st Grade

I used to **stutter** when I was a little boy. I don't remember this but this is what I was told. My sister Tahira, who is 1 year and 8 months younger than me tells me that when people used to ask me my name I would begin to stutter and she would answer for me, "His name is Dawud". My mother and older sister Saana remember this as well but I do not. It was my younger sister who taught me to tie my shoes. My grandmother tells me that I had trouble learning how to read and I was told that I was **left back in the first grade**. I was born a **lefty** but my mother and the school system forced me to become a right handed person by forcing me to write with my right hand. My older sister still remembers taking the pencil out of my left hand and making me write with my right hand. I do not remember that but I do remember the teachers making me write with my right hand. Why is this important? Because there's no other creature in nature that has only one dominant hand. Everything else in nature is ambidextrous, using both or all their limbs. Monkeys even use their tails. The left hand is governed by the right side of the brain which is the feminine spiritual side and the right hand is governed by the left side of the brain which is the masculine war side. In ancient Kemet (Egypt) the left hand held the Heka staff (Shepard staff / Crook) which was the staff of the ruler. Heka also meant meaningful speech or magic. The world we live in today is currently a patriarchal society ruled by the male energy and subsequently the world has become a place of war, logic, fear, and other symptoms of left brain thinking. By being forced to write with my right hand I was forced to use both sides of my brain since I was naturally a lefty. This helped me tap into my spiritual centers. I didn't understand this back then but this is also why my hand writing was never neat. Having sloppy penmanship played a role in how I viewed myself scholastically as a child however my ability to draw sort of nullified that a little.

The earliest memories I have are those living in Far Rockaway Queens on Central Avenue in an apartment with my mother and my two sisters. I remember playing with my sisters and going to the bus stop for school behind our apartment. We had plants and cats. I had my own room and my sisters shared a room. I remember listening to my **Star Wars** audio cassette album as I went to sleep. I was fascinated with Star Wars and I had many of the toys. I remember my mother reading us the story about Pandoras box and always wondering what was in the box but I never did figure out what was in the box. I used to climb on the counter and take cookies out of the cookie jar when my mother wasn't looking.

I remember the day my sisters and I caused a fire in our apartment. That day I woke up to find my sisters playing with fire. It was my older sister who started playing with the fire, she was mesmerized with seeing the fire burn. I joined in with them as we burned small sheets of toilet tissue while our mother was in her room sleeping. Somehow their canapé beds caught fire. I remember running to the bathroom for water and throwing water on the fire. When the fire grew larger we finally ran to wake our mother. The last thing I remember is being outside as the firemen arrived. Good thing we lived five blocks from the fire station.

The next place that I remember living is with my grandmother on 6952 **Hill**meyer, 72nd street (p 40, 260 653). I would fight with my older sister, who would beat me up but she would also protect me from other people like my cousins or the other boys on the block. My sisters and I spent most of our youth living with and around our grandparents. We lived with aunts as well but for the most part we grew up with our grand parents. My cousins George (matmuu), Romelle and Rahsaan lived one house over from us with their grandmother, aunt Marion, my grandmothers older sister. I also played with Mosunga, Run, Timothy, Thomas and Colin. All the kids on my block loved to play outside, we enjoyed running, and climbing trees, playing tag, the girls played double dutch. We rode big wheels until it was time for bicycles. We played until the sun went down. I knew it was time to come home when I heard my grandmother screaming "Dawuuuuuud" from the porch. When ever that happened my friends would all scream my name the same way teasing me. My father left when I was three and my grandfather was doing time in prison for possession of a small amount of **weed**. Funny how the laws have changed. Today one thing is legal and the next day it's not. Like in 2020 it's damn near illegal to breathe without a mask on your face. **Maat** never changes though! **Maat** is always true! So true that your Ten Commandments were taken from the 42 negative confessions of **Maat** (p 367). Not Biggies Ten Crack Commandments, the ones from the Bible.

The Mid 1980's

My cousin **Romelle** and I got along but my cousin **George** (matmuu) would try to bully me sometimes. The only fight I remember is our last fight because I won the fight. We were at the end of the block and George was picking on my little sister Tahira. George and I never fought again after that. I have not seen my cousin George in over 15 years but I still love and miss him. Life has a way of taking you far away from your beginnings.

Timothy Holliday and **Thomas Jones** used to bully me too. Timothy even beat me up in front of my mother one time but the next day we were friends. He had and older brother that ruffed him up, but I did not. Today is January 2nd 2022 and I just found a picture of **Timothy wearing** a shirt with **King Tut's gold mask** on it, so I had to add the picture to this book. He posted the picture on his Instagram page on Dec 14th 2015. I left a comment under the picture over 6 years ago that reads, "**We been kings**". It was only a few days ago that I found a picture of my friend **Giara Nova** standing next to a **replica of King Tut's gold mask**, posted to her Instagram page on October 7th 2015 (page 379). I have not seen Timothy or Thomas in over 20+ years, we are connected via social networking but we don't communicate often. I miss them both and wish them and their families the best. Thomas and I never had an actual fight that I can remember but I remember that he was tougher than me and I was afraid to fight him. I was the fast kid they could not catch. I can't stress enough how important the playing time was for the kids on my block. It kept us out of "trouble". We used to walk on our hands and balance walking on fences, you know, like the stuff they do in the olympics. My cousin Rahsaan was younger than all of us but he was the best at walking on hands. He would walk the entire block or it seemed like he did. There was a boy that moved on the block in the house across the street from me. He was Jamaican and his name was **Rohan Fung**. He was so fast that his nicknane was **Run**. So fast that everyone wanted us to race and one day we did. When the day finally came to race **Run**, we lined up, I put my left foot forward and someone said, "On your m**ark,** get set, **GO**!" We took off and he was ahead. I had a slow start but that was my usual. **I would always come from behind and steal the race** and there was no difference here. I beat **Run** and he was the first "fast" person I beat in a race.

Rau nu Prt m heru

In elementary I can remember having one fight in the back of the class room with a boy named Edward. He too had older brothers. He was the type of boy that was more muscularly developed than other kids his age. Our fight didn't really involve punches. We tussled by the desks and the chairs that were stacked on top of our desks all fell on him so everyone felt that I had won the fight. We were kids but I was afraid of him but after that "fight" I felt a little better.

Iu f Per f m heru

2004 Family Reunion

I left New York in 1999 and would not see my cousins again until our family reunion in 2004. I have not seen them since this picture. I think about them often and always hope they are in good spirits. I have tried to get numbers for them for many years and was never able to get either of them on the phone until 2022. I finally got **George** on the phone and we spoke for a 25 to 30 minutes. He was at a pivotal point in his life where he was rebounding from some setbacks. I spent the time speaking life into him and encouraging him.

Utterances for Coming Forth by day into Light

It is he, who comes forth by day into Light

May 25th 1983 - 2051, The Return of Djed Eye

May 25th is the first **star code pattern** in my story and **Star Wars** first premiered on **May 25th**, 19**7**7 the year of the **snake**, **5** months before I (Dawud/David) was born.. The **Ausarian Resurrection Drama** is the hidden story woven within the Star Wars theme which is why Luke's aunt's name was **Beru**, which sounds like **Heru**, the son of **Ausar** and the **hero** of the Ausarian Resurrection Drama. Much of the concepts used in the Star Wars movies were taken from the science and philosophy of ancient **Kemet** (Egypt), in particular from the 18th Dynasty and the relationship between Akhenaten and his sun Tutankhaten. George Lucas created a father and son drama between Anakin Sky Walker who would later be known as Darth Vader and his sun Luke Sky Walker but ultimately, you are Ausar and Heru! See page 3 for the **hero's journey!** If you were to look at the headdress of Darth Vader (**Anikan** Sky Walker) and the headdress of Amen Hotep IV (**Akhenaten**) you will see where George Lucas, the "creator" of Star Wars got his inspiration. The design of the **light saber** would be taken from the science of the **Djed Pillar** also known as the ***Spine of Ausar (Osiris)*** representing the kundalini serpentine energy that flows up the spine when the Djed Pillar or the "Spine of Ausar "or the "light saber"is activated. Anikan Sky Walker would grow up to be a powerful Jedi (Djed) but he would unfortunately turn to the "dark side" of the force and his name would be changed to **Darth Vader**. This Character of Darth Vader is taken from the real historical person **Amen Hotep IV** who would become the most enigmatic pharaoh of Kemet from the 18th dynasty who would make radical changes to the spiritual belief systems in Kemet by going away from the Amen Ra priesthood, closing all the other temples and going back to the ancient ways favoring only one Deity, the Aten (The Sun). Because of these changes he is seen as the father of monotheism (the concept of one God), however he just crystallized teachings about the sun's life giving properties that his forefathers taught him. During his **5**th year of rulership Amen Hotep IV would then change his name to **Akhenaten** which **coincidentally** sounds similar to **Anikan** (Darth Vader). Akhenaten took his people to a fertile land and built a new city (Akhetaten, p 671) between Memphis and Thebes (**Luxor**) where he venerated the sun (**Aten**), similarly to how the character* **Moses*** from the bible was chased into the desert. Akhenaten would disappear from history after his 17th year of rule and shortly after his son Tutankhaten would take the throne at around 9 or 11 years of age becoming the Boy King Tutankhaten. After taking the throne the Amen Ra priesthood would change his name from **Aten** to **Amen** (from Tutankh**aten** to Tutankh**amen**) so as to go back to the way of the **Amen** Ra priesthood. This is similar to how Darth Vader's son Luke Sky Walker would become a Jedi and fight against him. And again Luke sounds like Tut (toot) just as Akhenaten sounds like Anikan. In ancient Kemet the name Tut ( ) is pronounced toot/tute like flute. The bird (quail chick) hieroglyphic in Tut's name makes the uuw sound similar to the uuw sound in the name Luke (Luuwke).

My Aunt Pamela, Malcolm X and My First Movie

My aunt **Pamela** took me to see Star Wars, **Return of the Jedi** in 1983 when I was **5** years old. It was the first movie I ever saw in a movie theatre. As I watched the movie it captivated my imagination and **I began to think I was Luke Skywalker** and that my father was Darth Vader. Here I was, a 4000 year old soul trapped in a 5 year old human body watching Star Wars **Return of the Jedi**, the concepts of which were taken from one of my previous lives and I had no clue. Or perhaps deep within I did. When Luke Sky Walker took the mask off of Darth Vader I still remember feeling like Darth Vader was my father. Afterwards my mother bought me the Star Wars audio book and I would fall asleep listening to it. My aunt **Pamela** is the **5th** daughter born from my grand parents General and Juanita **Dukes**. She was sent down in (born in) 1965 the year of the **snake**, the same year that **Malcolm X** was assassinated. She has 4 children. Her first **son** is named **Wesley** and he is born on May 19th which is Malcolm X's birthday and Malcolm X had a **brother** named **Wesley**! Her second son is named Justin like Justice (**Maat**, p 367) and he is born two days after Emmett Till's birthday. Her 3rd child is born on my mother and sister's birthday which is the day before Rosa Parks' birthday and Rosa Parks was instrumental in sparking the Civil Rights Movement after the murder of Emmett Till (p 518). Her last child was sent down on (born on) my birthday, October **25th** in 2001 the year of the **snake**. I have a sister born on May 14th 1989 the year of the **snake** the same day as George Lucas the "creator" of Star Wars. George Lucas is also part of **the 44th Parallel star code pattern** (p 660). He was sent down in (born in) 19**44** and I turned **44** in 2021. George Lucas turned **77** in 2021 and I was sent down in (born in) 19**77** the year of the **snake**. Star wars was sent down to earth in thought forms to George Lucas so that I could watch it when I turned **5** years of age and by doing so would be impregnated with the thought that I was Luke Sky Walker. Star Wars always opens with the words "A LONG TIME AGO IN A GALAXY FAR, **FAR AWAY**", I was born in **FAR** Rock**away** Queens New York. Star Wars was released on **May 25th** so as to help me connect my previous lives having had many remarkable events in my lives happen on **May 25th**. "**Yoda**" is the eldest Jedi that teaches the young Luke Sky Walker the ways of the Jedi and it was Kemetic "**Yoga**" that helped sp**ark** my first past life revelation of Emmett Till on July 3rd 2018. Today is December 8th 2021 and this is the day that Buddhist celebrate as the day Siddhartha Gautama, the Buddha received his enlightenment. The Buddha Siddhartha was aware of the ancient **Vedas** (ancient Hindu scriptures) and commented on it in his writings. It is no **coincidence** that Darth **Vader** sounds like **Vedas**! One time is an incidence, twice is a coincidence, but 3, 4 and 5 is a pattern. Can you tell the difference?

Return of Djed Eye

As you read this book you will see how everything from **Hip Hop**, to **religion**, to **accidents**, **movies**, **dreams**, **spirits**, **prayers**, **death**, **murder**, **birth**, **teleportation**, **meditations**, **fasting**, and more were used to awaken me to my past lives and ultimately my life purpose. It must be understood that "if" I am who I say I am, being the **soul** of Emmett Till (p 480), Tutankhaten (p 594), Siddhartha (p 295), Earl Johnson (pages 236 & 584), and other lives then my coming back here would be for some divine purpose and because of that the energies that govern life itself would set a stage for me to find myself. This stage would be set in the minds of the creators of novels, movies, music etc and throughout my life from childhood to adulthood I gradually gravitated to each book, movie and song etc, at the most divine of times to help me decipher this **star code of immortality**. Watching the series **Lost** (p 259) did the same thing **Star Wars** did for me as a boy. But patterns like the ones in the movie **Back To The Future** work to confirm my claims for you (p 40)! I am the **pattern master** that **Octavia E. Butler** wrote about as in I am an immortal spirit like **Doro** from her book **Wildseed** (p 298) and I have been able to decode the pattern of my incarnations, as if I collected the **blue prints of my creations**. Octavia's work primed me and helped prepare me to **weave** my pattern of destiny like **Webb** Mi**ssiss**ippi, where Mamie Till was born. In September of 2016 (pages 419-420) my friend **Amiga** would tell me the **dreams** she had of me where I deciphered the **star code of immortality** which would turn out to be the foretelling of this book. It was **The Manifestation of Emmett Till** (p 536).

2051, The Return of Djed Eye

May 25th Strikes back pages 30, 104 - 106, 222, 512

Aunt Beru	OR	Heru
Psalms 104	OR	The Hymn to The Aten Page 615
Jedi Light Saber	OR	Djed Pillar, Spine of Ausar (Osiris)

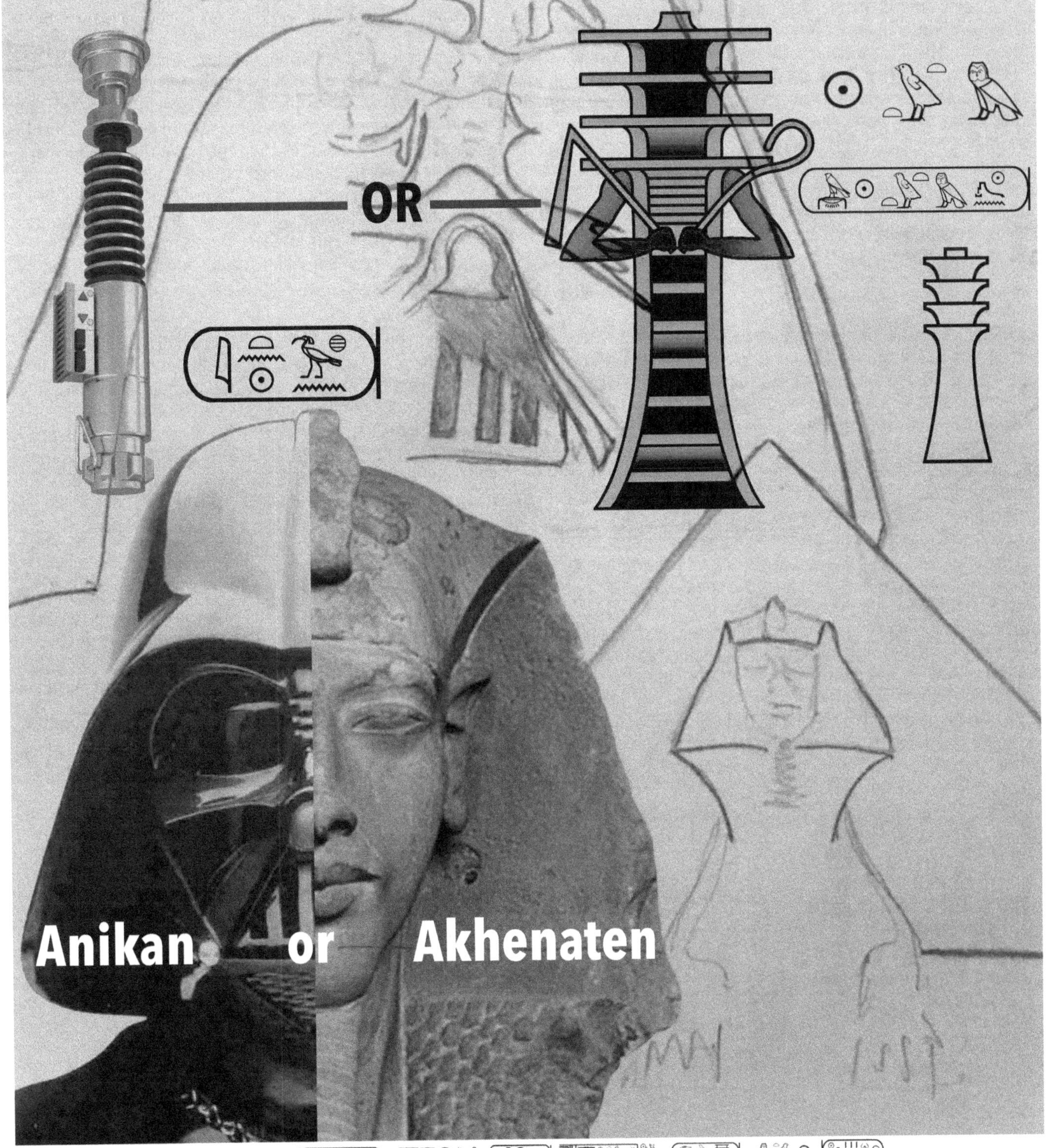

Rau
nu
Prt
m
heru

Iu
f
Per
f
m
heru

Utterances
for
Coming
Forth
by day
into
Light

It is
he,
who
comes
forth
by day
into
Light

Flying, Astral Projection, OBE, Sleep Paralysis, Levitation and a Child's Imagination

When I was around the age of **6** or **7** I really enjoyed **dreaming**. I could **control my dreams** and I even had the ability to awake from a dream, then go back to sleep and start dreaming again from the same place I left off from before I woke up. It was the events in my dreams that **caused me to believe that I could fly**.. I would experience vivid "**dreams**" of **floating** around my grand mothers house at the ceiling level. One day I woke from one of these dreams so convinced that it was real that I got a chair and placed it near the book shelf and stood on it to see if what I saw in the dream was on top of the book shelf. I don't remember whether or not what I saw confirmed my dream but I remember checking the top of the book shelf when I awoke from the "dream". I had been **astral traveling** around the house but as a kid I had no understanding of **astral travel** or **astral projection** and so in my mind I really thought I could fly. I remember thinking, if I jumped off the porch I might float to the bottom. I never tried to jump though. There was however an abandoned building at the end of our block, from which all the boys on my block would jump from the first floor window to the ground where a pile of used mattresses braced our "falls". I had other dreams where I would be alone in darkness floating in what felt like outer space. These dreams attracted me to the tv show **The Greatest American Hero (Heru)**. In this show the main character was given a suit by **alien** beings on a spaceship. The suit granted him the powers of flight, super strength, invulnerability, invisibility, precognition, telekinesis, X-ray vision, super speed, pyrokinesis, shrinking, psychometry ("holographic vision"), and even the ability to detect the supernatural. As a child I was unaware that he had lost the instructions on how to use the suit. But because he lost the instructions he was a clumsy superhero. The show was based on him slowly learning how to use the powers of his suit. No different than humans that don't know how to fully use the bodies we have. Most of us don't know that we can fly via astral traveling or reach higher states of consciousness. I was also amazed by the scene from **Remo Williams**, when he ran over wet cement and did not sink, and when his Master Chiun, ran across the lake and did not sink. As a child I was drawn to shows like these. Unfortunately my curiosity for these things were not **watered** and so these memories faded away as I grew into adolescence; because of course man can't fly. At least that's what we are taught.

The Man With The Checkered Shirt

When I was a little boy I remember hearing the rumor that there was a **ghost** in our house. My aunt Pamela had seen the **ghost** of a man who was wearing a red and black **checkered shirt**.. He never said anything he just walked in the bathroom and seemed to be stuck in a **daze**. This was never talked about in the open I only heard about it in passing. As I began to write this book I called my aunt and she confirmed the story. As you read through this book you will come to see that my interest in and experiences with dreams, levitation and **astral projection** will resurface in my 30's after I find my way back to the narrow path. In 2009 I would wake up one night unable to move or speak, only being able to move my eyes. In shock of the moment I struggled to move and to get a word out and finally I screamed out the name "**JESUS**". I can remember feeling a bit ashamed that the name Jesus was what I called out to "save" me because by that time I had already left religion behind. That was my first experience with **sleep paralysis,** but I would have more. On **May 14th** 2020 (my sister Jenna's birthday, p 93), I would have an experience with The Great Lafayette and Chung Ling Soo, two long dead **magicians** and oddly enough, one of them died on **May 14th** 1911 performing a levitation act. If death is not the end then how will you spend eternity? Will you ride the divine Sun Boat of Ra or will you walk around for an eternity stuck in a WEEK DAZE aimlessly like the man in the **checkered shirt**? If you search long enough you might find that you are stuck on a life sentence, **riddled** with spells hidden within the **language**. You **awake** every **morning** and proceed to your **job** also known as an **undertaking** where you spend 5 days a **week** stuck in a **weak daze** just to **earn** the **weak-end** of the money. Then you get the weekend off, but by then most people are drained and **weakened.** Still you **manage** to say **hello** to your **manager** even though the **man ages** you from the stress of the **Job**, but still you keep the peace and you never forsake him because no one wants to get **fired**. Then finally you die and hopefully you go up high to heaven with God where everything is beautiful because no one wants to say **hello** to the devil in **hell** which is **low** where the souls get **fired**, I mean burn in eternal **fire**. Your family and friends will hold **a wake** for you in the **morning** as they **mourn** your death and finally the **undertaker** places your cremated ashes in an **urn,** and the **fun**eral is paid for with the money you **earned**.. But what if souls come back for another turn on the wheels of time for another life sentence left to **languish** if the divine soul never finds its God self like **Job** from the Bible.. Play life like Senet (page 10) not Checkers, or end up like the man in the **checkered shirt**.

The Sun Boat of Ra
The Ark of a million years
The celestial bark
Barque of Ages
The Ark of the covenant
Noah's Ark (page 252)

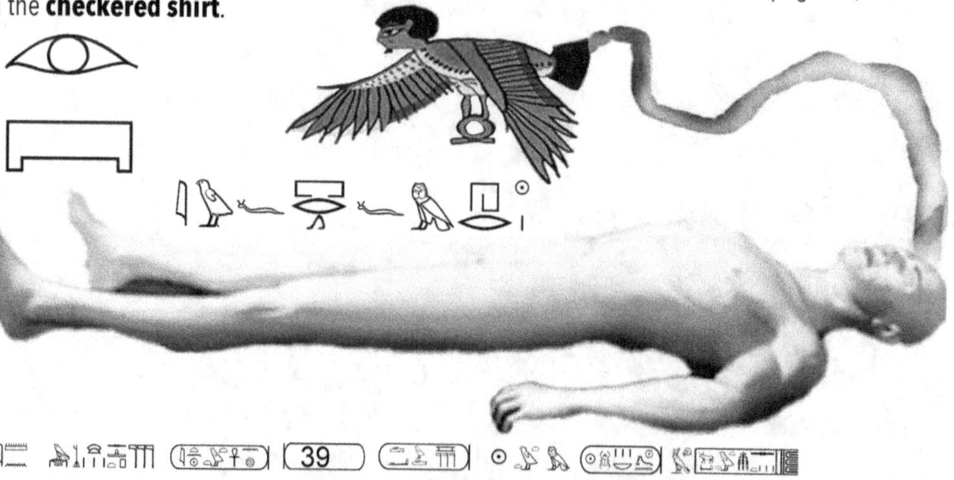

From The Hills Of Amarna, Back To The Ancient Future *ADDENDUM*

Rau nu Prt m heru

Iu f Per f m heru

Utterances for Coming Forth by day into Light

It is he, who comes forth by day into Light

Back To The Future premiered on **July 3**, 1985 and **33** years later on **July 3,** 2018 I realized I was **Emmett Till** in a past life (**p** 480). In the movie they traveled back to the year 1955 and **33** years before that is 1922, the year **King Tut** was discovered. My 5x's great grand father was York **Brown** (p 15). In the movie Back To The Future, the scientist **Emmett Brown** builds a time traveling car (the **DeLorean, page 180**). A dog named **Einstein** was in the **DeLorean** when they did the first time travel experiment. The physicist **Einstein** died in **1955**, my mother was born in **1955** and **Emmett Till** was murdered in **1955**. When they traveled in time for the first time they traveled from **October 26,**1985, and arrived in **1955**, on **November 5**. My birthday is **October 25** and **King Tut's** tomb was discovered on **November 4**. **Dr Emmett Brown** builds a car that travels back in time when it reaches the speed of **88 miles** an **hour**. At the end of the movie he tells Marty McFly that he only has **7** minutes and **23** seconds till the **lightening strikes**. **7:23** is also **July 23**. Carolyn Bryant, the woman that caused the murder of **Emmett** Till, was born on **July 23 (7:23)**, two days before Emmett Till and she died at **88 years old** in 2023 (page 506). As I wrote on page 37, many mediums were used to awaken me to my past lives and ultimately my life purpose. Of all the mediums, perhaps the patterns found in movies might be the most astonishing. These patterns embedded within the movies work to bind me and my past lives with the fabric of time and space in a way that can't be explained away. Like how **Rod Sterling's**, The Twilight Zone episode, **Noon On Doomsday** from 1956 appears to for tale the death of Carolyn Bryant (see page 508 - **Twilight Zone: Carolyn Bryant on Doomsday**). When **coincidences** bind with **synchronicities** the outcome tends to have **the mark of a greater authority**. Like a pattern that happens for a divine purpose.

Back To The Future 2 premiered on Nov 22, 1989, the day before Emmett Till's Mother's birthday (Mamie Till, p 511), in the same year Shanta's mother died (p 289). Dr Emmett Brown and Marty McFly go forward into the future to Oct 21, 2015, the day after Shanta's first son Noah is born (p 289). In this movie Marty McFly's father dies on March 15, the same day Shanta is born (p 289). All the **Back To The Future** movies were written by **Bob Gale** who was born on **May 25**. **Back To The Future 3** premiered on **May 25**, 1990. **May 25** was the **first Star Code** that I decoded (pages 30, 222), stemming from a **dream** my sister had on **May 25** (p 104). Emmett Till's mutilated body was identified by a ring that had the date **May 25** engraved on it (p 512). In this movie Marty McFly is sent back to **Sep 2**, 1885. Mamie Till wrote a letter to the president on **Sep 2**, 1955 (p 514). This movie reveals Dr Emmett Brown's middle name as **Lathrop (ELB)**. Emmett Till's middle name is **Louis (ELT)**. The name **Lathrop** means: Man from the **farm**. **Till** means: **cultivation** of the land. Emmett Brown dies on Sep 7, the same day **Tupac** was shot and the same day that Shanta's son Nouel was born (p 289). Dr Emmett mentions that his family's surname was **Von Braun** but it was changed to Brown when his family migrated to America. Von Brown was a rocket engineer. He died on June 16,1977, on **Tupac's** birthday, the same year I was born.

From the **Hills** of **Amarna** I came.. In this current life I grew up on a block named **Hill**meyer (p 35, 648, 653). In my life as **King Tut** I was born in a city originally named Akhe**t**aten, built by my father Akhe**n**aten. Today this city is desolate and is known as **Tell El Amarna** but when I traveled their in 2022 I was amazed to find that the locals call it **El Till** which means, **The Hill** (p 671). **El Till**, like **E**mmett **L**ouis **Till**. **Back To The Future** takes place in a town named **Hill** Valley. The word **DeLorean** means: from the **hills**. The patterns I present in this book are examples of a phenomena known as **quantum entanglement**, spoken about often in **Physics**. The theory states that quantum particles that are entangled will act as one system. A measurement made on one particle will be the same on the other particle even if the particles are thousands of miles away. **Einstein** called this phenomena, **spooky action at a distance**. Physicist like Einstein have been trying to find and measure the smallest of particles but these particles seem to disappear and react differently when they are being observed (p 329). The particle I am isolating is the transmigration of the soul. The soul in question is my own (p 602)! Souls are broken into fragments and the measurements on one life (soul fragment) will equal the next life (soul fragment) even if the lives are 3300 years apart. All the patterns in this book are examples of the quantum entanglement of my soul fragments. That is why I have **birthmarks** where Emmett was shot (p 514) and why the **gematria** in my names are the same, as seen on page **41**. The mathematics of the divine creator binds all things that are connected with **star codes**. The codes follow us in life and in death, like a finger print. And some of us take our soul-er finger prints Back To The Ancient Future. In the movie **Back To The Future 2**, they go to the year 1955 on November 12 and **Tupac** released his first album **2pacalypes Now** on November 12. While I do feel the revealing of my past lives is profound, compared to the past life of **Tupac** it pales in comparison (p 664)!!?

1986, Return of The Duke

My Grandfather, General Dukes JR was sent to prison in 1980 for possession of **marijuana** (**weed**). That same weed that is legal to sell and smoke in America today in 2021, was criminalized and made illegal to buy, sell, use or transport on my Grand Fathers birthday, June 17th 1971, the very next day after **Tupac** was born. They took a man away from his wife and 6 daughters leaving them to fin for themselves. They took my grand father away from his wife and daughters. He spent **6 years in prison** and came back from Alabama in 1986. This has happened to countless black families. The father of the actor **Jamie Foxx** was sent to prison for 7 years for $25 worth of illegal substance. For the most of my youth I grew up without a father figure and I can remember seeing **Crack vials** in the parks and on the streets when I was a kid. **Crack** was everywhere and initially the selling of it went unpunished yet simple possession of **weed** was enough to spend years in prison. I was 8 or 9 when my grand father returned and now there was a man in the house. That gave everyone in the house more of a sense of protection whether they knew it or not. My Grandfather was a street man and everyone in Far Rockaway knew him. They called him Duke or Mr Dukes. Just before he went west (died, passed away) in 2009 he told me that when he was younger he was a terrorizer in the streets. He said he had many fights, he won some and lost some but he won more than he lost. He would go on to say *"I used to knock niggas out, one punch. Big niggas! First shot, no arguments no nothing. Disagreements settle it right now, get it over with and shake hands and be friends. Fuck it! I lost some but I won most"*. "That's the way things used to be", he said. My Grandfather was raised in Alabama. He left home when he was 16 years old and survived on his own since then. My grand father never put his hands on me, not once. I don't think he wanted me to experience what his father had done to him. He had other siblings from his father General Dukes Sr (p 19) but he was the first born and the only child born from his mother **Leacola Riddle** (p 21). He never taught me how to fight or to hate any type of a person nor did anyone in my family for that matter. My family was/is a loving family with mostly women. The most profound thing my Grand Father ever did for me would happen on December 18th 2015, **6 years after he died**. He would appear to me as a **ghost** or **apparition** (page 348). And as you will come to see, that day he would appear at the most divine of times, and after that I would only see him again in my **dreams** where he is always driving me away from danger. This experience of seeing his **spirit** would broaden my depth and perception of this reality we live in.

ADDENDUM **The Golden Ratio is One of The Most Famous Formulas in Maathematics.**

Each number in the sequence is the sum of the number that proceeds it. The sequence is as follows:

0 - 1 - 1 - **2** - 3 - **5** - **8** - 13 - 21 - **34** - **55** - **89** - 144 - **23**3 - 3**77** - 610 - 987 - 1597 - **25**84 - **41**81 - 6765 - 1**7**,**7**11 - 24,476 - 42,187

1 1 **2** **3** 5 **8** 4 3 7 1 **8** 9 **8** **8** 7 6 **22** 1 **5** **5** **8** 5 **22**

What ever or whoever the creator is, that being is love and it is indeed a master maathematician, a master builder like the number **22**. Even in your bible there is a book titled numbers. You came to this earth at a divine time and you will leave the same way so make your time here divine. Time is measured by the sun and even the Bible states that the sun will be used as signs. **Genesis 1:14 "And God said, Let there be lights in the firmament of the heaven to divide the day from the night; and let them be for signs, and for seasons, and for days, and years"**

Tutankhaten also known as King Tut, traveled across space and time, life after life searching for a way to get the ATENtion of the lost children of Ta Merry (Africa) so as to direct them back to the ways of **Maat** and awaken them to the immortality of the souls journey from life to life and beyond the beyond. Maat represents truth, Justice, cosmic order, harmonious balance, reciprocity and moral righteousness (**42 Laws of Maat, Page 367**). Tutankhaten has most recently returned as the boy Emmett Till in 19**41** the year of the **snake** and then again 22 years after my death he was born again as Dawud Basheer Eddings in 1977 the year of the **snake**. Tutankhaten has returned in the most divine of ways using everything from sacred geometry, astrology, astronomy, dreams, dates, music, movies, cartoons, sending down thought projections to musicians, writers, movie directors, and even sending thought projections in the form of spells (rhymes) to his present incarnation (Dawud). Dawud is not alone in this saga, many ancestors have paved the way for him to receive the revelation of his previous lives as Emmett Till, Tutankhaten and other lives.

What you will read in this living book is a **divine pattern**, like a formula or a revelation. Formulas reveal a path. Real revelations are specified by formulas appose to a claim that is not and or can not be proven. As you read this book you will be able to feel it and know it to be true so you won't have to lean on blind faith alone and this is what separates this divine revelation from religious prophets. This prophecy is absolutely precisely correct. Like the stones that comprise the pyramids, a razor blade cannot be placed in between them and not even the professional skeptic can find legitimate cracks in the Prophecy of reincarnation being expressed in this timeless body of work. For those who might have trouble decoding what you read I have even come back looking exactly like myself from previous lives. Here are a few codes to keep in mind as you experience this book. These are numbers in my pattern and they will follow me from life to life like birthmarks.perhaps you will start to decode your own pattern.

The remains of Tutankhaten (King Tut) were found in the Valley of the Kings and were stored as KV**62**. 6+2 = **8**. The 2 digits in the middle of my **social security** number are **62** (p 121, 221, 508). 6+2 = **8**. I was born in the month of **Oct**ober which is the 10th month but the prefix **Oct** means **8** like the **8** sides of an **oct**agon. In **gematria** the names, God, Osiris, Eddings, Dawud, Moses, and Maat all have a value of **8**. The number **8** represents infinity or immortality, like the Egyptian NTR **Heh** who is the representation of infinity millions of years. The image of Heh was found on the back of one of Tutankhaten's royal chairs thrones (p 472). King Tut's (Tutankhaten, Tutankhamen) tomb was discovered in 19**22**, the same year Louis Till (Emmett's father) was born. The name Louis adds up to the master number **22** in **gematria**. Debra Dukes, is my mother in this life and she was born in 19**55**, the same year Emmett Louis Till was murdered. **22** years later, when she was **22** years old, my mother gave birth to me on October **25**th 19**77**, year of the **snake**. Emmett Till was born on July **25**th 19**41**, year of the **snake.** In my life as Emmett Till my **life path number** was the **master number 11**. The names Tutankhamen and Jesus both add up to the master number **11** in **gematria**. In my current life, my life path number in this life is **5** (rooted in the number 32 =**5**). **5** is the **fifth** number in the **Golden Ratio** and the only number in the sequence that is equal to its position. Amen Hotep IV, also known as **Akhenaten**, was the most enigmatic pharaoh in ancient Kemet and the father of King Tut. His remains were found in the Valley of the Kings and were stored as KV**55** (p 513). Ramose was a Vizier under the reign on **Amenhotep III** (King Tut's grand father) and **Akhenaten** (King Tut's father), his remains are stored in tomb TT**55**. The numbers **55**, **5**, **8**, **22** etc, are not appearing by mere coincidence. All things are governed by seen and unseen forces and as you continue to read this book you will see this revelation unfold across space and time, life after life arriving at this very time so as to awaken those who are blind to the reality of the immortality of the souls journey from life to life and beyond the beyond. All the patterns in this book are examples of the **quantum entanglement** of my soul fragments. The **maathematics** of the divine creator binds all things that are connected with **star codes**, that follow us in life and in death, like a finger print. And some of us leave our **soul-er finger print** everywhere. Like when **Einstein** died in 19**55**, the same year **Emmett Till** was murdered. **See page 602** for the **Sacred Geometry behind the transmigration of my soul**. Like the **Pert M Heru** (Book of Coming Forth by Day) this book is about the immortality of the soul, like the snake swallowing its own tail, representing infinity. That's why I'm born in the year of the snake & why I'm a scorpio. **The awakened Scorpio** embodies the life-giving powers to heal itself and others. Its final prize is its own **immortality**. Death is the initiate of the Mysteries. To die is to understand transformative powers of life and reminds us that to live is to die and to die is to be reborn. The Scorpio rises from its own ashes, and it takes with it the occult powers becoming the **phoenix** liberating themselves and **reclaiming all parts of their Soul.**

Gematria
Sacred Geometry in names.

1	2	3	4	5	6	7	8	9
A	B	C	D	E	F	G	H	I
J	K	L	M	N	O	P	Q	R
S	T	U	V	W	X	Y	Z	

David 41494 = 22 = (4)
Dawud 41534 = 8
Basheer 2118559 = (4)
Eddings 5449571 = (8)

Emmett 544522 = 22 = (4)
Louis 36391 = 22 = (4)
Till = 2933 = (8)

Osiris = 619991 = **8**
TutemRa 2325491 = **8**
Maat = 4112 = **8**
Moses = 46151 = **8**
Rebirth 9529928 = **8**

Tutankhamen 23215281455 = **11**
Cultivation 33329412965 = **11**
Tilling = 2933957 = **11**
Grape = 79175 = **11**
Jesus = 15131 = **11**

Akhenaten 128551255 = **7**
Tupac = 23713 = **7**
Heru = 8593 = **7**
Neo = 556 = **7**
Hero = 8598 = **1**

My name at birth was Dawud. Dawud stems from the name **David**. As you can see above, when I use the name David, my first, middle and last names (David **4**, Basheer **4**, Eddings **8**) have the numerical values of **4**, **4**, **8**, the same as Emmett **4** Louis **4** Till **8**. I came back with the same numerical vibration. 448 adds up to **7**. My name Dawud, adds up to the number **8**, which is the number of **infinity** ∞ . The named **TutemRa** was echoing in my ear on April 4 2020 (p 594) and it has the same value of **8** like the names **Dawud, Till, Eddings, Maat, Osiris, Rebirth** and **Moses**. **Akhenaten** is the biblical **Moses** and his name has a value of **7** just like **Tupac** (pages 664, 665, 667). Heru (**7**) is the **hero**, the **One** (**7**) like **Neo** (**7**) who returns to avenge his father, Osiris. The story of **Jesus** (**11**) is another telling of the story of Osiris and Osiris was the first to cultivate the land (page 481). To have **Cultivation** (**11**) is to be **Tilling** (**11**). And that's where the **Grape (11)** comes in as, **"the blood of Osiris"** (p 482). The names David and Emmett are rooted in the master number **22**, the number of the **master builder**. In biblical prophecy, there would be someone returning from the linage of King David. I have already explained who the biblical character David was fashioned after (pages 7, 225). **Tutankhamen** (**11**) was the son of Akhenaten and he **returned** through **rebirth** (Wehem Mesut , **Gilgul**, page 14) as Emmett **Till**, then he was murdered and returned again as **David** (TutemRa). These patterns are examples of quantum entanglement. Soul fragments will have the same measurements even if the lives are 3300 years apart (**see pages 329, 602**).

Dr Mark Dean, Alan Emtage and Jesse Russle

A special thanks goes out to the computer scientist **Alan Emtage**. In 19**89,** the year of the **snake**, he conceived of and implemented **Archie**, the world's first **Internet Search Engine**. In doing so, he pioneered many of the techniques used by public search engines today. It is widely considered the world's first Internet search engine. Alan Emtage, who was born on November **27th** 1964, the day after Tutankhaten's (king Tut's) tomb was opened (November **26th** 1922, page 11). Alan is Bajan from, **Barbados** Island and I have Bajan ancestry from my fathers father (page 25). I also want to thank **Dr Mark Dean** the engineer who pioneered the technolgy for **Computer Software** in 1981, and **Jesse Russle**, the engineer who created the **Cell phone**. Without the technology of these **black men**, it may have been near impossible for me to realize this revelation in the manner* that I did. A might thanks to you all.

ADDENDUM **1987 - Parker Family Reunion**

My cousin **Hymeed** (seen below) died on January 9th 1988 when he was only 10 years old. He was born on May 20th 19**77** the year of the **snake**, on **Toussaint Louverture's** birthday (p 141). Unfortunately Hymeed had a **heart condition** and had to have surgery at St Francis hospital. Before he went into surgery **he told his grand mother that he would not return from the hospital. Somehow he knew he was going to die**. I was 10 years old at the time and Hymeed was the first person I ever knew that died. He didn't live near me so I didn't know him very well and so his death didn't touch me that way the death of one of my cousins I grew up with might have affected me. I came across Hymeed's Obituary in November of 2021 when I went to visit my grandmother and after seeing it I wanted to add him to this book so that he would be remembered. Please know that death is not the end. The soul survives death, indeed and in spirit. This is a book of the dead written by a boy who was murdered without justice, who defeated death and came forth by day. May the soul of **Hymeed Stroud** walk peacefully through the field of Reeds in Amenta. Amen Ra

Rau nu Prt m heru

Juanita Parker, Wheeler Parker, Rosa Parks

Today is February 4th 2022, Rosa **Parks**' birthday. The picture to the right was taken at the **Parker Family Reunion** some time in the 1980's. **Emmett Till** had a cousin named Wheeler **Parker** (page 515). I have an Uncle named **Emmett** Dukes (p 19). Rosa **Parks** refused to give her seat to a white man because of the murder of Emmett Till (p 518). Her actions helped spark the Civil Rights Movement. My grandmother's maiden name, in this life, is Juanita **Parker**. She has the same last name as Emmett Till's cousin Wheeler **Parker** because I was **born again** into the same **family tree** (page 515). His name is Wheeler, like a "wheel". In ancient times man understood the immortality of the soul and time was governed by the **wheel of little animals** circling in the heavens called the **zodiac**. And just as the sun rises in the east and sets in the west in our **solar** system, our **souls** do the same. They come and they go. Just as a **snake** sheds its skin so does man. We leave old bodies behind and put on new ones in the eternal Wheel of life. Jesus said, "all these things I have done, so will you do and greater deeds will you do". Well, I have risen again just like Ausar and "Jesus".

Iu f Per f m heru

ADDENDUM **Darryl "Squeek" Jordan**

When I was a boy, around 6 and 7 years old, living on Beach 69th street, my second cousin Darryl was in his 20's living a life of crime. But I never knew that back then. He lived one house away from me with my third cousins **George** and **Romelle** (page 36) who grew up with him as a role model. I remember that he always had money and had big muscles. I called Darryl recently to get his story from his own words. Darryl was, "**nice with his hands**" and feels like he missed his calling as a **boxer**. Being nice with his hands is what gained him initial street credibility. He was a part of the **Hip Hop culture** by way of his **DJing** but he had a **dark side**. Far Rockaway Queens had a **notorious crime** reputation in the 80's and 90's and Darryl helped create that reputation. He went by the name **Squeek** and had two partners in crime named **Bo** and **Master**. Together, the three of them would engage in armed robberies. They had all agreed that, if any of them were ever caught, they would never snitch on each other and they never did. Darryl was a stick up kid like my father (page 28). He would rob other stick up kids and take their guns. These acts of violence made Darryl a **street legend** no different than Walter "**King Tut**" Johnson (page 664). He got caught twice and did jail time. While in jail his knuckle game garnered him respect. No one ever tried him while he was locked up. And when he was on the streets, even the drug dealers ran from him when they saw him coming like people ran from **Deebo** in the movie **Friday**. In September of 1990 he saw a friend of his get his head blown open at a failed robbery attempt. When he saw that he thought about getting out of the life of crime. When he first started the life of crime it was for money but when he began to use **heroin** it became necessary to fund his habit (page 502). Two weeks after he saw his friend dead in the street he went to rob a weed house. He lined everyone up on the wall and started taking their money. He began to pistol whip one of them and when he did, one of the men on the wall shot him four times in the back. Then kicked him in the face while he laid there on the floor. The man was a cop and the weed spot was about to get raided. Darryl was at the wrong place at the wrong time. Darrly thought he had been shot with a shot gun and thought his legs were gone because he could not feel them. As soon as he hit the floor it it began to rain and he began to see his life flash before his eyes. He saw every good thing and every bad thing he had ever done. As he began to fade away to what he thought was death, a car pulled up, it was his brother **Anthony** (p 51). The door flew open and his brother grabbed his hand pulling him into the car and suddenly the flashing of his life stopped and he was back in this reality. This took place on **September 19**, 1990, the same day that **Emmett Till's** murder trial started in 1955 (page 516). Darryl has been in a wheelchair ever since and no longer lives a life of crime. He now lives a Christian life in service of the Lord but the name Squeek still rings bells in the streets. Darryl was born on **October 22**,1959 and was a role model for the late rapper **Stack Bundles**, who was born on **October 21**,1982. The late rappers **Chinx Drugs**, **Rockaway Rome** and **Stack Bundles** paid homage to him.

Utterances for Coming Forth by day into Light

1980's Prison Photo

It is he, who comes forth by day into Light

Cartoons, G.I. Joe, "Thunder, Thunder, Thunder Cats Ho!"

Everyday I ran home from public school **42** (P.S. 42) to watch cartoons like **He-Man**, **Thunder Cats** and **G.I. Joe**. First Sergeant "**Duke"** was the leader of the G.I. Joe team, who were the "good guys". My Grand Fathers name was General **Dukes** but as a kid I never connected that. Of all the cartoons, **Thunder Cats** was my favorite. From the music to the characters I was fascinated. As a boy I wanted to be like **He-Man**, **Panthro** from the **Thunder Cats, Superman** and for a short period of time I actually thought I was **Luke Skywalker**. He-Man, **Superman** and Luke Skywalker were all **white** and I knew that as a child but I used my imagination. I can't really say how much this effected my psyche but we all seek to find a sense of sameness and as a child it was easy for me to see that **Panthro,** from the Thundercats was the **black character** because his skin color was blue and his accent sounded like a black person, so I imagine that's why I gravitated to him. I can only Imagine how it must have been to grow up as a white boy in a world seeing a white superman, who was "the strongest man in the world" with skin the color of theirs as well as 98% of all the other superheroes seen on tv, in the movies and in comic books (**See Superman Curse**, page 204). When I look back on the Thunder Cats I see another deep seeded conditioning. The bad guy was the Mummy, **Mumm-Ra**. I never wanted to be Mumm-Ra but when I turned **42** years old I would realize that I was once mummified and that I was indeed the most famous Mummy ever found in modern time. The Thundercats Lair is modeled after the Kemetic (Egyptian) monument named the **Sphinx**. The original name of the Sphinx was **Heru** Em Ahket, which has the head of a **human** and the body of a **lion**. In my life as **Emmett Till** my zodiac sign was a **Leo** like the **Lion**. **Heru** is the son of Ausar, and Ausar is the one who resurrects after death through his son **Heru**, but ultimately, you are Ausar and Heru (see page 3 for the **heru's journey**). We must all aspire to be Heru. The one who rises above his animalistic nature. This is the journey that I took in my present life, it's called Shemsu Heru (page 2). The present moment is the truest gift and we must be wise about how we spend our time here on earth. "The peasant cuts down the tree and side steps the truest bliss, they wanna separate you from the oneness that do exist, the wind blew me the kiss of life one starry night, ***I started remembering what I forgot when starting this life, they say death is an awakening, a remembering like a dream***". - **(Dec 26th 2016, page 437)**

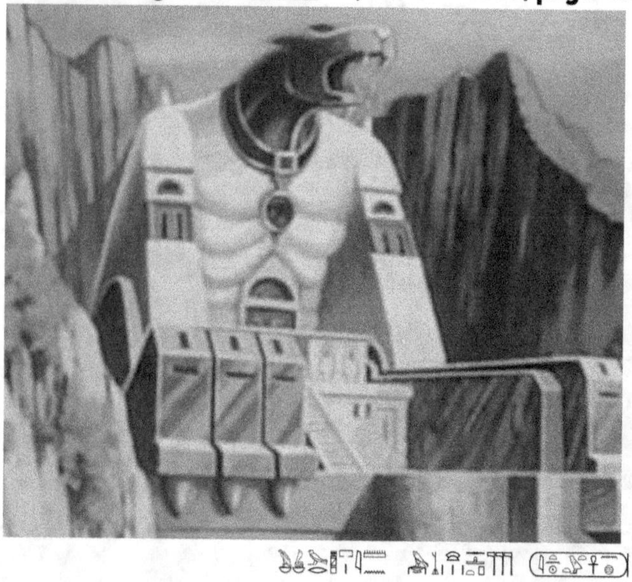

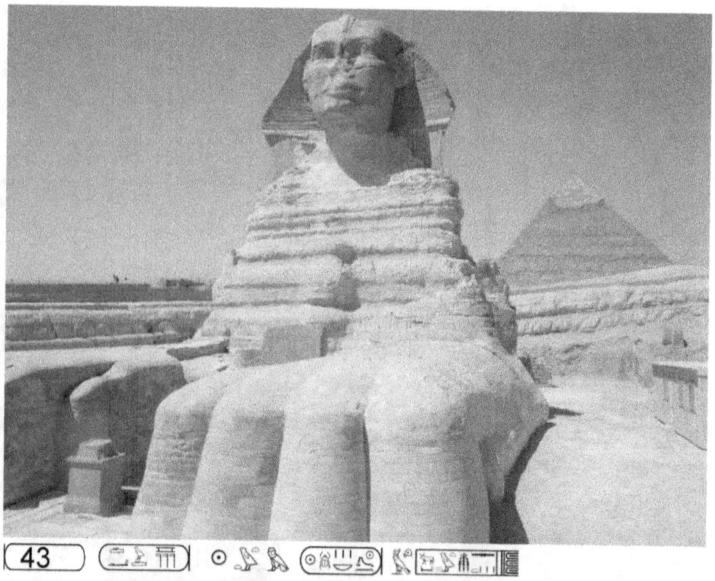

The Renaissance Flute

Rau nu Prt m heru

Iu f Per f m heru

Utterances for Coming Forth by day into Light

It is he, who comes forth by day into Light

1987 or 1988, Public School 42 and The Prophecy of The Renaissance Flute

When I was in the 5th or 6th grade we were given a writing assignment. We were told to use our **imaginations** to create a short story. I wrote a story about a boy who was trying to save the world. In the story there was an ancient legend of a **magical flute,** that when played had the power to save the world. The boy in the book went on the quest just like the boy in the movie *The Never Ending Story*, a movie that I loved (p 259). I titled the short story, **The Renaissance Flute.** I don't remember much more than that but I do remember that my teacher did not believe I wrote the story. I guess she had not heard of the famous fantasy writer David Eddings! Dawud means David in english so I share the same name as a famous writer (**Dawud Eddings - David Eddings**). There's nothing too bizarre about that right, but what if I told you that - David Eddings was a writer with my same name who wrote a book called ***Dreamers*** and many people in my family **dream** things before they happen and as you will come to see I will start experiencing **dreaming** things before they happen in my 30s (p 305).. To add more strangeness to my David Eddings connection I found that he was sent down (born) in 1931 the same year my grandfather was sent down (born). Again that's no big deal but I do find it eerie that he also died at **77** yrs old, in 2009 the same year my grand father died and of all the days for him to die, he died on my sisters birthday, June 2nd. The same sister who would have a "**vivid dream**" about me dying in a car accident on **May 25th** 2002 and 7 days after her **dream** I would crash my car in a violent accident on June 1st 2002, which is my fathers birthday (p 104). May 25th would turn out to be the first star code that I decoded in 2011 (p 30, 222). I'm writing a Epic Sci-Real (Science Reality) Novel Trilogy version of this book and a book about Tupac's ancient past life (pages 664,665). Stay tuned!

Some **dreams** take place in a different space and time where the **astral body travels**, sometimes to the past and even the future. I would have a **dream** about **Dr Umar Johnson** on ***Martin Luther Kings birthday***, Jan 15th 2019 (page 550). The **dream** would prove to be **prophetic** after the events of the **dream** came to fruition on May 19th 2019 during the annual ceremony for ***Malcolm X's birthday*** held at his grave site (page 561-565).. The very next month, on my Grand Father's birthday, June 17th 2019 I would meet **Coreisa Lee** (page 568), a professional flutist who is a descendant of **Malcolm X**. Her and I would become friends and she would blow her flute over a few of my songs (page 460) for my first album (page 577). 1 year and **22** days after the revelation of my past life as Emmett Till I released an album titled *Dawud The Uncanny BlaKseed: The **Immortal** Life Of Emmett Till* on Emmett's birthday, July 25th 2019 (page 577). Meeting Coreisa was a fulfillment of the Prophecy of the renaissance flute that I wrote about in elementary school. Today is March 15th 2022 and Coreisa contacted me today, as soon as I got off the phone with Big O (page 96). She told me that she got a call to be a part of a new Emmett Till theater project named, **Emmett Till, A New American Opera**. You should know that David **Eddings** also wrote a book Titled *Pawn of **Prophecy*** about an **immortal** Sorcerer and you are reading *TutemRa: The **Prophecy** Of Reincarnation* about the **immortality** of the soul written by Dawud **Eddings,** also known as TutemRa. There is no such thing as "just" a coincidence. When **coincidences** bind with **synchronicities** the outcome tends to have **the mark of a greater authority!!!...**

ADDENDUM Marcia Dukes, Phade and Father MC

After adding the story of my cousin Darrly, the street legend to this book and realizing his connection to Hip Hop (page 40), I figured I should also add the memories of seeing **Phade** from **Shirt Kings** and **Father MC**. This book is titled, TutemRa - The Prophecy of Reincarnation - Star Codes of Immortality 2022 - **The Hip Hop Bible**. With that in mind, it would make perfect sense that at least one of the women in my family would be drawn into the world of Hip Hop and my aunt **Marcia** played that role. She dated **Phade** from **Shirt Kings** when I was around 7 or 8 years old. Street Fashion was and still is one of the elements of Hip Hop and **Phade** was one of the original pioneers of Hip Hop fashion with his legendary **Shirt Kings** brand. Any and everyone in the Hip Hop world could be seen wearing his gear. Perhaps it was **Phade** who influenced Marcia to get into the world of fashion later in her life but before that, she met **Timothy Brown**, better known as **Father MC**. My mother had moved us to Columbus Georgia by this time but I remember receiving pictures of **Father MC** and showing them to friends. This was many years before the internet so having those pictures added to my popularity. Father MC was brought into the industry by Sean **Puffy** Combs, who's born on **Nov 4th**, the same day **King Tut's** tomb was discovered. I once wrote a verse to a beat that sampled the **Father MC** song, Treat Them Like They Want To Be Treated (p 359).

1989, Columbus Georgia

We moved to Columbus Georgia in 1989 **the year of the snake**, the year that **Public Enemy** dropped the single **Fight The Power**, I was 11 yrs old. Every morning I would hear the loud military **bugle** wake up call from the **FT Benning Army base.** Never would I have imagined that only 10 years later in 1999 I would be there standing in formation. At this time in my life I was not listening to a lot of Hip Hop just the songs that played on the radio. I was too occupied with drawing, video games and going out side to play. I enjoyed drawing but I never drew things from my memory however if I looked at a thing I could draw it. ***I never had to practiced drawing, I did it like I had already known how to do it***. I drew mostly for the high feeling I got after completing the drawing and also the praise I received when showing it to people. I can only remember one drawing from my time in Columbus and it was a picture of **Big Daddy Kane**. I drew a picture of Kane wearing a **gold Nefertiti** chain. Some years later **that picture along with my portfolio containing my best drawings was stolen from me by another student while attending JR high school 180**. I loved to draw but I didn't draw often. I would draw around 5 to 10 pictures a year from the age of 7 till around 15. I only drew when I couldn't go outside or when something inspired me. I probably drew Kane because I was listening to his music on the radio. At the ages 11, 12, and 13 I was still a passive listener of music and I didn't understand many things talked about in most of the songs.

My sisters Saana and Tahira

While in Georgia my sisters and I had lives of our own, as in we didn't play together a lot and we didn't share friends. I was always getting into arguments with my older sister. I remember feeling like I should have been the older child because I was the boy. Whenever I told my younger sister Tahira what to do, my older sister would always tell her she didn't have to do it. So in the house I had no authority. My mother told us all what to do. My older sister tried to tell me what to do and my younger sister never had to listen to me because what ever I told her to do was over turned by my older sister. My older sister used to beat me up until the time when I over powered her. After that she never tried to hit me again. I can't ever remember hitting her with a closed fist, I can only remember over powering her. We didn't get along but we loved each other. Unfortunately our relationship as children has affected our relationship as adults.

My Sister Jenna

My sister Jenna would be born in *1989, the year of the snake*. Being the only boy growing up with two sisters I was hoping that I would have a little brother but another sister is what we had. Her father lived with us for a few months then he was gone - never to be seen again. My mother was a single parent again with four children now. When Jenna was around 8 or 9 months she would sleep with me most often. I would rock her to sleep and the first word she spoke was, "Dawud". Jenna would have a baby girl in 2019 (p 558) who's birth day would be connected to my revelation just like the children of my aunt Pamela and my two nephews (p 287).

Friends *ADDENDUM 2023*

Tellas Wilson is the only friend I remember from Columbus Georgia. He lived behind our house on the other side of our fence. Tellas had a little brother who was "different". He was more feminine like a girl. None of us ever teased him or asked him why he was that way, or at least I never did. Tellas had video games and a basketball court. Gaming had just really started and we spent a lot of time playing Double Dribble and Tecmo Bowl mostly.. We would play tackle football in his front yard and basketball in his back yard. I always play to win and as far as I remember, I won most of the time. I was fascinated with the possibility of dunking the basketball from seeing the athletes in the video game jump and glide in the air. **I would jump and jump until finally one day I grabbed the rim**. Once I grabbed it with one hand I kept jumping till I could grab it with two hands. I played on Tellas's court by myself even when he wasn't home but I don't think Tellas ever came to my house. Some time in 2010 I drove my grand mother to Columbus Georgia to see her sister. I went to see my old house and it looked to be abandoned. I went to Tellas's house to see if he still lived there. His father answered the door and told me that Tellas had joined the Army years ago and was station in **Ft Drum NY**. He gave me his number and we talked one time. ***ADDENDUM* In 2023** I took my grand mother to see her sister again and again I went to my old house but this time I was looking for **synchronicities** and I found them. A few blocks from my old home I passed a street named **Prince** and a street named **Nepal**. When I got to my old house I saw that the address was **228** Syndey Drive. The tomb of **King Tut** was discovered in 19**22** and **Emmett Till** was murdered on August **28**. The address of the house to the right of my old house was **222** Syndey Drive. The door of my old house was open so I knocked on the screen door. A man named **Milton** answered. I told him that I used to live in his house when I was a boy, back in 1989. I asked him how long he had lived there and he said **8** years. He asked me where I was from, I told him I was from Far Rockaway Queens but I live in Harlem now. I was surprised when he told me he used to live in Far Rockaway.. We both found that to be odd and got a good laugh out of it. Afterwards he was nice enough to let me in. He let me walk into my old room and it was so small. I asked him his birthday and he said **April 3rd**. I thought to myself, that's the day before **Martin Luther King** was assassinated and the day before I realized I was **King Tut** (p 594). Then I went to Tellas's house again. This time an old lady answered the door and before I could say who I was she said, "You're Tellas's friend". I smiled and asked, "you remember me?". She said that when she looked at me she saw my baby face and immediately remembered me. She called **Tellas** and he was 5 minutes away. When we saw each other again after 34 years we laughed, hugged, then caught up on each others lives. I told him about **Milton** and told him his birthday was **April 3rd** and it happened again.. **More patterns**.. Tellas said, "that's my wife's birthday". That's when I began to tell him my story of my past lives. His mother listened as well. She resonated with my story and told me that she had studied the mysteries of **Isis**. Tellas is born on **May 2nd**, the same day **Afeni Shakur** died (page 381, 641). He has a child born on **September 6**, the day **Emmett Till** was buried (p 515). When we parted ways I gave him a free copy of this book.

Rau nu Prt m heru

Iu f Per f m heru

St Marys Elementary School

My sisters and I attended St Marys elementary school. I can only remember three of the classrooms from this school, the **music** room where I played the **Trombone**, the **Science** classroom and some other room that I think was a **math** class. I remember my science teacher and the song we sang about **Electricity**, "Eee-lectricityyyy, AC, Eee-lectricityyyy, DC, a wonderful kind of energyyyy, that's Eee-lectricityyyy". That was over 30 years ago and I still remember that song! Prehaps thats's the power of learning in musical form. I also remember clearly my **nemesis** Dem**arc**o and a girl named Denise. Denise was born the day before me on October 24th and I had a crush on her. October 24th is the same day that **Rosa Parks** died and the day **KRS One** released his book, **The Gospel of Hip Hop** (page 633). I think Dem**arc**o liked Denise too and I think that's the reason why Dem**arc**o didn't like me. One day on my way home from school, while walking down the long hill, Dem**arc**o tried to pick a fight with me but before the fight could ensue my older sister **Saana** was there ready for war. Saana and I didn't get along but we loved each other. Saana Jumped in front of Dem**arc**o and yelled somethings about us, being from New York and blah blah blah. And so, I never did fight Dem**arc**o. I did not know how to fight and I didn't like fighting. I was never actually taught how to fight so I was always afraid of the possibility of getting hurt. I remember wanting to join the **Karate** school I would see around the town. As much as I wanted to know how to fight I seemed to avoid confrontations for the most part and I never had a fight that I started. I attended St **Marys** Elementary and the name **Mary** comes from the Egyptian word  (**Meryt**) which meant **love** or **beloved**. My name at birth was **Dawud** which means, **Beloved** by God.

Utterances for Coming Forth by day into Light

It is he, who comes forth by day into Light

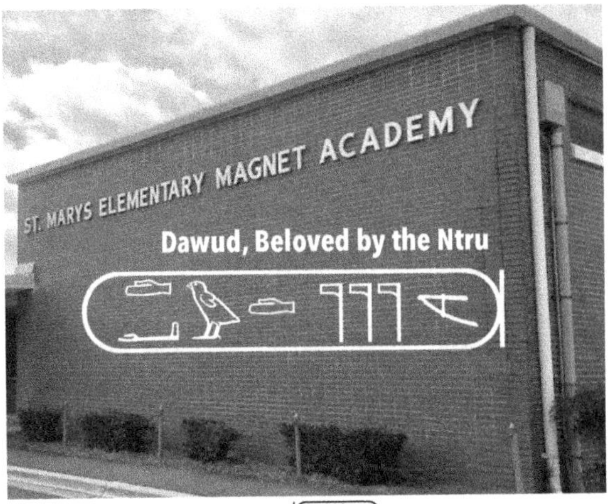

1989 - Speed

My greatest memory from **St Marys** was the annual 50 meter race. I was the new boy from New York and no one had ever seen me run. I entered the race. It was hot that day and there were many people there watching all the events. I watched event after event until it was time for the big race. There must have been 8 to 10 of us that entered the race. We all walked up to the line in the back of the school on the red Georgia clay and made ourselves ready. I put my left foot forward on the line and waited for the count, "On your m**ark,** get set, GO", then we all took off! I was behind as usual. I still Ramember pulling and closing the gap and catching them all one by one and finally passing the person in the lead. I won the race and received my first trophy ever. **Dawud Eddings 1st place winner** in the 1989, **50 meters race** at **St Mary's** Elementary school. We should not over look the accomplishments that we experience as children because they shape our personalities and are part of the ingredients that play into our growth into adulthood. Some things stay imprinted into our memory centers for the rest of our lives. I always ran as fast as I could and never gave up. I was almost always coming from behind and can only remember being caught from behind once in my life, I'll tell that story later, or maybe I won't.

When The Saints Go marching In

I played the Trombone while at Saint Mary's Elementary School but the only song I remember playing was, **When The Saints Go marching In**, which was a Black Spiritual from 1896. The Trombone wasn't my instrument of choice. I wanted to play the Drums or the Trumpet but those spots were already taken. The two trumpets found in the tomb of Tutankhaten (King Tut) are the oldest operational trumpets in the world and the only ones that survived the pillaging of ancient Kemet (Egypt).

David Duke

There was a white boy named **David Duke** who I played with sometimes. I remember him because he had the same last name as my Grand parents and my name Dawud is David in English. David and I didn't know each other well and I only have one memory of him. I remember being in his house and for some reason he got upset with me. I think it was over a video game. Then his brothers or some older boys insisted that we fight. I was not a fighter but while fighting David we ended up on the ground wrestling in the grass in front of his house. Soon after his **collarbone broke** then he got up in pain, screaming. Afraid of being beat up by the rest of them I darted home as fast as I could and I never saw David or his family again. Looking back at this now I find it strange that I broke the collarbone of a boy who shares the same name as **David Duke** the former grand wizard of the Knights of the **Ku Klux Klan**. I don't think I had ever seen or heard of the Ku Klux Klan at this point in my life.

Out of The Drum We Come

Rau nu Prt m heru

Iu f Per f m heru

Utterances for Coming Forth by day into Light

It is he, who comes forth by day into Light

I saw the uncut version of the Movie **Drum** in 1989 or 1990 when I was around 11 or 12. I was staying the night over my mothers friends house and the adults were watching it. The kids were supposed to be sleep but I peaked through the sheets and watched the movie. Drum was a movie about a Slave named Drum (Ken Nortan Sr) who was forced to bare knuckle fight and who was used as a **sex slave**. In the movie the daughter of the white slave owner forced a slave named Blaze to do **sexual acts** with her. The scenes would be considered **pornography** by todays standards (page 119). The white girl would tell her father that blaze **raped her** and for that Blaze was to be **lynched,** Just like how **Emmett Till** was lynched. They titled the name of the movie **Drum** and connected it with sex slave plantations but the sound of the Drum is what scared the Europeans when they first ventured into the heart of darkness within the African Jungles. **Drum** was the sequel to the movie **Mandingo** that was released on **Emmett Till's** birthday July 25th 1975. Drum was released the year before I was born on July 30th 1976.

I was a teenager around 16 yrs old when **Malcolm X** first came to me. I saw a stack of magazines in my grand parents closet and I remembered all my uncle Joseph's playboy magazines I used to look at when I lived with him and my aunt in 1991 (p 53). I searched through the magazines hoping to find a pornographic one. I found nothing of the sort but what I did find was a cassette tape of a **Malcolm X** speech titled the ***Ballot or the Bullet***. I listened to this speech many times and what stood out the most to me was the part where Malcolm says. *"we all have the same problem. They don't hang you cause you're a baptist they hang you cause you're black. They don't attack me cause I'm a muslim they attack me cause I'm black. They attack all of us for the same reason. All of us catch hell from the same enemy. We're all in the same bag, in the same boat. We suffer political oppression, economic exploitation and social degradation. All of them from the same enemy. The government has failed us you can't deny that. Any time you're living in the 20th century 1964 and you're walking around here singing we shall over come the government has failed you."* **- Malcolm X .**

I did not get taught about Malcolm in my school or in my home. I was like most young men in their teens heavily inundated with sex from tell lie vision, movies, music and even in the cartoons. I always thought the tape was my grand fathers but now I'm not sure where it came from. *Perhaps it appeared there like the **card** that **Jean Jacque Dessalines** would place before me in 2005* (pages 141-142). I listened to Malcolm's speech over and over. It was the first time I'd ever heard a black man speak in that way. At that time in my life I had no knowledge of the historical horrors that black people had faced or the greatness of Afrikan people. I could however understand from my environment that "we" as "black people" or "negroes" etc etc, we had it bad while at the same time being the best at many things, the fastest the strongest etc.. I was living in Far Rockaway Queens at the time and Malcolm's words hit home. I always felt like my neighborhood was not well kept but as soon as I went east towards Long Island the land scape changed. The people out there had big yards, nice homes, peaceful neighborhoods and it was occupied by white people, mostly Jews. I never questioned this it just was what it was. The house that my grand parents were renting was owned by a jewish family named the Korningbergs and they treated us "nice".

You might be wondering what my point is and what does Malcolm X and the movie Drum have to do with anything. The events that happen to us as children play a major role in our development into puberty and on into adulthood. Sex, money and drugs are used to control the masses. Sex is used to sell you drugs through advertisements and product placement. The first time that I heard the name **Nat Turner** it was an adult porn star. At the time I was in my early 20's in the Army. I would also watch a porn star named **Cherokee** and I didn't know that I was a **Cherokee Indian**. I was recruited to an Army Unit that flew **Black Hawk** helicopters used to massacre Somalians in 1991 (page 127) and I didn't know that I was a **Blackfoot Indian**. Why am I speaking about sex and pornography? Because I do not remember my life as **Emmett Till,** so I can not speak about my conduct on that day August 24th 1955 that led to me being tortured, murdered and thrown in a river with my eye gouged out like **Set** did to Heru (Jesus-Hero/Heru) in the Kemetic (Egyptian) Ausarian resurrection drama (page 3). I have however heard my cousin (Emmett's cousin) **Wheeler Parker** speak of me and he speaks very highly of the young man that I was. Even the woman Carolyn Bryant who caused me to be lynched was said to have admitted that I never did anything to her (see pages 180, 287, 419, 508 for pattern with Carolyn's birth and death). What I can speak about however is my conduct in this current life. I would be lying if I told you that I had never done things that I am ashamed of. As you read this book you will read about many of my missteps. I can release them here because I have already released them from my heart, mind, soul and most importantly my character. More importantly I share them here because I know from my experiences that sexual perversion and violence is the cause of many of our ills. I have always respected women in the sense that I have never hit a woman or forced them to do anything but I have however at times chased them as sexual objects with no care for a real stable future with them. Once I got into my 20's I treated enter course like a game of numbers. When I met a woman I would think I was in love with her then somewhere down the line after we entered the course I would eventually start to desire another woman. Many people especially men have committed more vile crimes than I and so they languish in guilt and sorrow while the victims never really recover. I imagine there are women out there as guilty as men but I write from the prospective of a man and our dysfunctions. When we do other people harm we unknowingly do harm to ourselves. All of our actions are recorded in the akashic records, in the fabric of the universe for eternity. The Akashic records are real and ancestral spirits are real. I have been to the Akashic records and I have been visited by ancestral spirits while there as well as in this "dimension" as you will read later in this book (page 584). Malcolm X is one of the most important people in my journey when it comes to my transformation. Just as he made a transformation in his life I did the same. Malcolm would become a beacon for me in my years of awakening (2009 - 2018) and I would be summoned to his grave in 2019 (page 561). Perhaps if this story of **how I rose** from the **mud** like a **lotus flower** and cleaned my self up is heard near and far it might inspired many men and young boys to do the same. I did not start to rise from the mud until I began to honor the divine feminine. I had to battle **thought forms** that manifested in my actions. Are you beginning to inner stand the plot? We have been at war for over 6000 years. Every person reading this book has at least one **guardian angel** watching you. You might even have **soul fragments** from previous lives watching you. I have always had guardian angels protecting me and you will read about many of these events. Perhaps I took this mission to be a sacrifice as I know how much people love a good gossip story.. Remember, you are Ausar and Heru! See page 3 for the **heru's journey!** If you do repeat my story make sure you beat the Drum while you tell it, cause **Out of the Drum I Come flying like Relics**!

The Mormons

One day we got a knock at the door, and there stood two white boys - they were **Mormon** missionaries. They offered to help my mother pay her rent and even supply food, all we had to do was attend church and bible study every week. Stuck between a rock and a hard place, my mother use the religion as a means of survival, and we became Mormons. We were one of only two black families at this church. The other black family didn't associate with us perhaps because we were poor and I guess they weren't. I was always drawn to the idea of God and heaven and so after hearing about baptism being necessary to go to heaven I decided to get **baptized**. I was then given the job as an usher at the church - we handed out the bread and juice for communion Sunday's. I used to eat the bread and drink the juice when no one was looking. I don't ever remember seeing many girls at the church. I was happy about becoming a Boy Scout but I wasn't very active in the events . I can remember being the fastest kid when we played sports especially when we played capture the flag. I have four lasting memories from being a mormon.

Who is the Cain and Who is the Able? (See page 330)

The **first** was my experience during our over night camping trip for the wilderness survival badge. I remember being **naked** with all the other boys **and** the adult **men** while taking a shower outside. It was uncomfortable because we were all naked and I felt like all their eyes were on me. No one touched me but I <u>never forgot</u> the uncomfortable <u>feeling</u>. The **second** lasting memory is the bible study we had about ***<u>Cain and Able</u>***. I attended every Bible study and I always asked questions. We studied from their monthly booklets and the Book of Mormon more than we did the Bible. Their booklets had illustrations but I only saw a black person one time in the illustrations. One day we had a **bible study lesson** on **Cain** and **Abel** and this was the first time I saw a black person in the illustrations of one of their booklets . I was always looking for myself in these stories and this was the first time I saw a person that looked like me. During our class the teacher taught us that Cain was cursed because he killed Able. My sisters sat and listened but didn't ask any questions. I wanted to know why Cain was black so I asked them why Cain was painted black. They did not have an answer. They said they would ask their Elders and respond back with an answer. The next week I was told that Cain was black and he killed Able and because of this Black people were cursed. At that very moment I was no longer a Mormon! I was only 12 years old but I was old enough to know that this did not agree with me. I did not believe it. The **third** lasting memory is watching ***Indiana Jones and The Last Crusades*** *as well as* **Indiana Jones and Raiders of the Lost Ark** at a Christmas event at a member of the church's house. I was caught up in the search for the **Holy Grail**, this ancient **artifact** that could heal all illness with one drink. I wanted to know about this grail and I wanted to drink from it (page 488). I was equally curious about the **Ark** of the covenant. My last memory from being a Mormon was receiving a wallet for Christmas from one of the men in the church. What did I need with a wallet? I didn't have any money..

Baptism and Resurrection

We are told that **God** is in us and all around us. Well, **Water** (Hydrogen) is in us and all around us. The Kemetic deity **Hapi** was depicted as androgynous (All encompassing) and Hapi governed the Nile river. Water has no gender but all humans start life in the amniotic fluid of their mothers. Water comes from the clouds and perhaps this is why Heaven is said too be in the sky. When water is heated by the sun it evaporates via the process of precipitation but it is resurrected again when rain falls from the heavens. Just as the second principle of **Jhuty** states "As above, so below, as within, so without, as the universe, so the soul…". Just as rain water comes back again so does the human soul. The Kemetyu understood that there was no death and this was expressed through a concept called the **Wehem-Mesut** (repeating of births, p 14). In **Judaism** reincarnation is known as **Gilgul** (Cycle), but it is not taught to everyone. The story of **Ausar** being trapped in a box by his brother **Set** and thrown in the Nile river was used to give life to this process of resurrection and the Christian "baptism" borrowed from this Kemetic motif. All human beings are divine and are baptized by the **life giving waters** (amniotic fluid) of our mothers womb however the Christian Baptism is a ritual that is based on the belief that every human being is born in sin due to the actions of Eve (the female) so they must be dipped into water to cleanse their soul. In 418 "AD" the Catholic church council decided that every human child is born demonic as a result of sexual conception and damned to hell if not baptized (p 592). This belief system was a misinterpretation of what was seen on the walls in ancient Kemet (p 252). The concept of baptism originates in Kemet. It was not the act of submersion into a pool as Christians erroneously practiced, but the pouring of water over the initiate to symbolize cleansing to begin ones transformation into the pursuit of becoming **Ausar** (the Supreme Being dwelling in Man). The ancient Kemetyu state that, the only path to Afrikan power is the worship of the divine Godself. In ancient Kemet the divine Godself was called Ausar, the Lord of the Perfect Black, the Supreme Being dwelling in man, the immortal soul that never dies. The Tekhen was another symbol of **resurrection** and when a person was raised from the water after baptism it was symbolic of the Tekhen being raised into place. When you find yourself in search of truth, drink water and remember that you are Ausar and Heru, the hero! See page 3 for the **hero's journey!**

Rau nu Prt m heru

In the relief below the Nswt Bity (Pharaoh) is seen in the middle being cleansed by **Jhuty (Thoth, Hermes)** on his **right** and **Heru** on his **left** who both pour symbols of ankhs over him. The Ankhs symbolize the life giving qualities of the waters (amniotic fluid) of our mothers womb from which we emerge from during birth. They had also come to notice that water is the source of Life and that it revives everything so when the Nswt Bity is purified with water, he will live again. Usually the initiate is depicted as "mummified" to represent the immortal nature of becoming Ausar. They are symbolically preparing him to become **Ausar**, the Lord of resurrection, the Lord of the west, the Lord of the Perfect Black. When I was 11 years old I was told by the Mormon church that baptism was necessary to go to heaven and so at 11 years old I decided to get **baptized**. I have been on the journey towards truth for a long time however the perversion of **sex** in modern society distracted me for many years. Learn from my story and take the narrow path now and not later!

Iu f Per f m heru

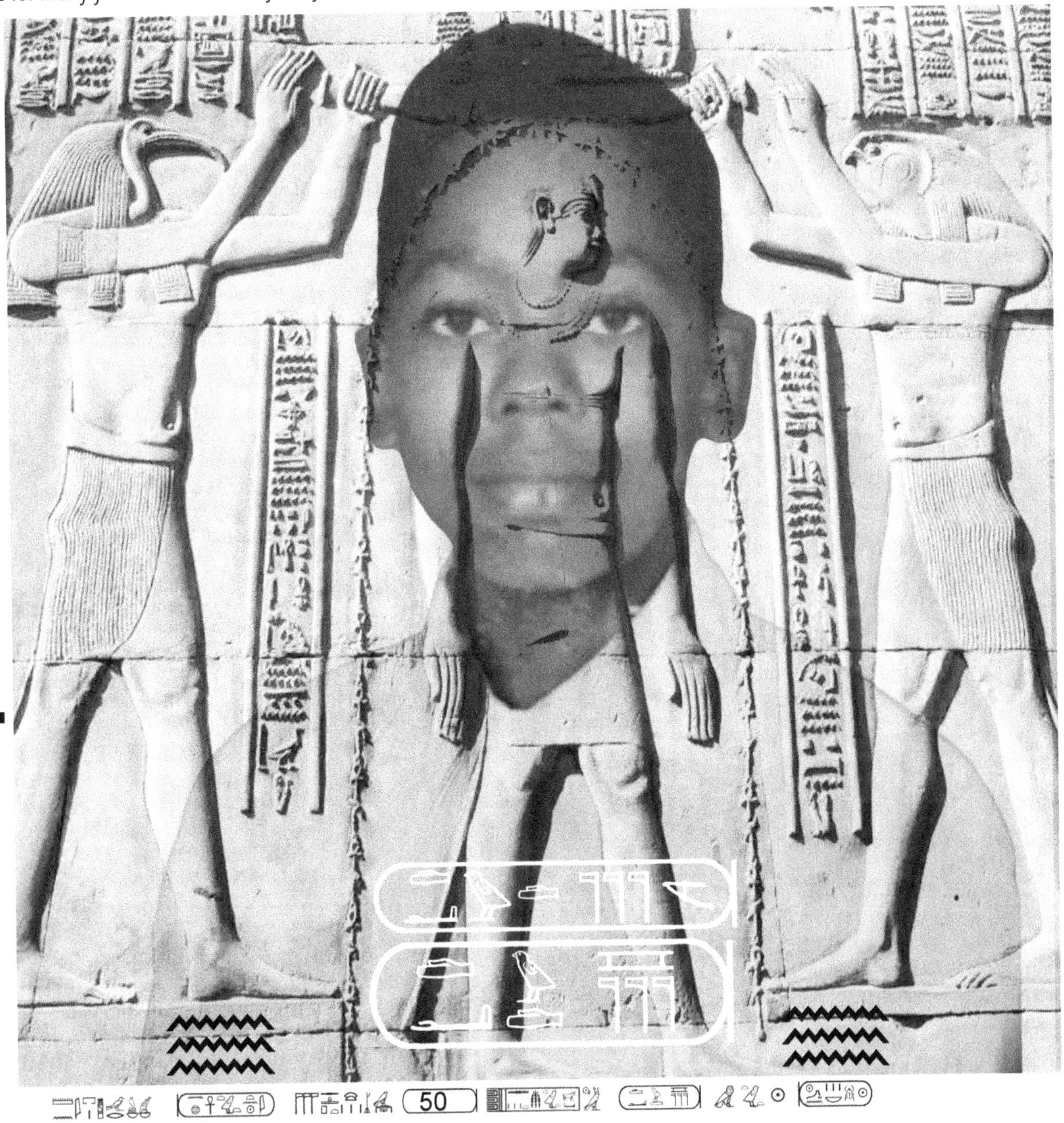

Utterances for Coming Forth by day into Light

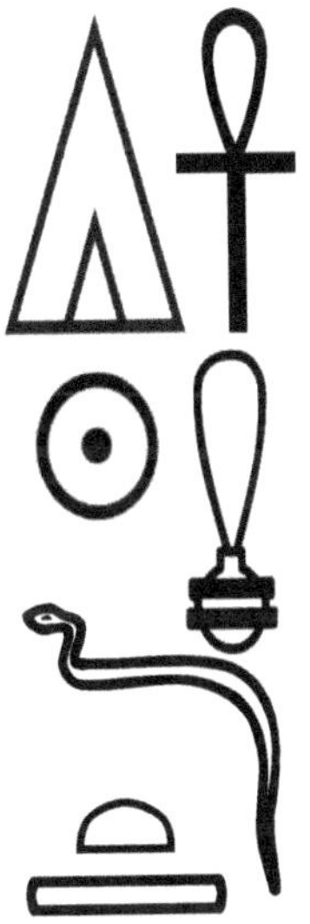

It is he, who comes forth by day into Light

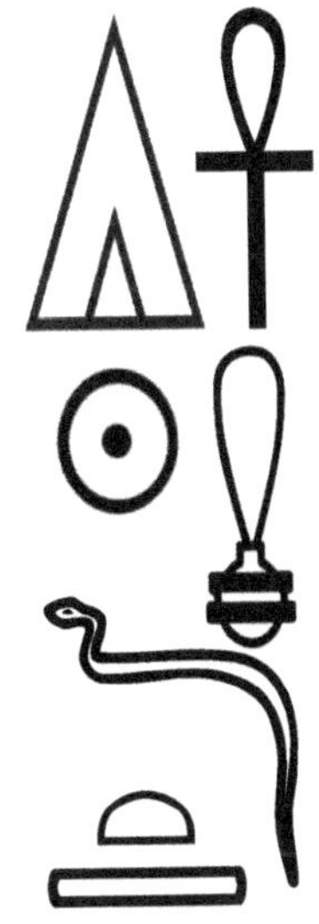

ADDENDUM

1975 Good Times

The Parker's, Jordan's, Dukes', Dudley's, and Shakur's

1 Marion Jordan
2 Juanita Dukes
3 Kirkland Jordan
4 Roslyn Dudley
5 Gale Dudley
6 Adilah Dukes
7 Karen Dukes
8 Vanessa Jordan
9 Carol Jordan
10 Anthony Jordan
11 Rosina Dukes
12 Pamela Dukes
13 Loretta Jordan
14 Marcia Dukes
15 Audrey Jordan
16 Brenda Jordan
17 Marla Shakur Parker
18 Lu'Wana Parker

Army GiAnts

I Loved watching the humming birds sucking the nectar from the flowers. I would slowly walk up next to them and look at them moving so quickly and defying gravity! In my front and backyards I would observed the **lizards**, the **spiders**, the giant **roaches** and there was a **snake** that I always saw near a creek on my path to school but none got my attention more than the **ants**. I was amazed by their ability to quickly rebuild their homes. The mound/pyramid ant hill was my favorite type of ant home to observe. I would break a hole in the ant hill and watch them rebuild it. I'm ashamed to say but sometimes I would place roaches in there to see the ants attack it and rip it to pieces. I even threw a lizard in there one time but I didn't like the way it felt so I never did that again. As a child I was more interested in the immediate efforts of the ants to rebuild their hills! If they found the attacker they attacked it but they didn't go beyond that moment. They always rebuilt their home. I began to feel bad about killing roaches so I stopped observing that and after a while I began to avoid stepping on ant hills all together. Today people make a living off of the revenue from the views of the videos they upload on youtube, of insects, snakes and other "lower" life forms killing and eating each other. Tiny little ants can take down animals the size of an elephant if they work together. In life, size doesn't always matter like the story of David and Goliath (page 1). In nature all things are working together balancing all life and all things have their natural predator - But who is mans predator? Are all things in nature really working to balance all life on earth? Is incarnating into a human body the only possible way of experiencing life on earth? Can we come back as rats or roaches and cats or dogs or falcons or whales or perhaps monkeys and apes? Who's to say we are the smartest or most advanced beings in the universe? What if we could reincarnate into "higher" life forms, not just human bodies? I wonder sometimes, do some people come back as lab rats for punishment of wrong doings from a previous life? If there's life on earth is there life on other planets? If everything has a predator are there other lifeforms that would see human life as prey? In times of fear should we pray for something out side of self to save us? What if the ants prayed to some unseen God for help and never fought back and never got around to rebuilding their home? The **Queen** would surely die and the colony as well. If only Black people had the memories of elephants and worked together like gi**ants** we might once again regain our place in the world.

Football

I didn't see live organized **football** until just before we moved back to New York. I was at Rothschild middle school. After school one day I saw the high school football team playing a game - **I fell in love immediately** - They were **running**, **catching** the ball, **tackling** and avoiding being tackled and it looked like so much **fun,** just like when I used to play **tag** on **Hill**meyer, no one could ever tag me back then. *I was in love and I wanted to play!* Unfortunately shortly after that day my mother moved us all back to New York, but football followed me to New Jersey, then back to Queens and it stayed with me until I was in my mid 20's. I never watched football on tv until I was in high school and that was after I started playing it. Football was the one thing that I was unexplainably, amazingly highly skilled at without ever being taught.

Rau nu Prt m heru

The first lyrics I ever wrote down so that I could learn them were **Treach's** from **Naughty by Nature**. I wrote down the lyrics to **Uptown Anthem** and could repeat the entire song word for word. (***ADDENDUM*** On the second verse of **Uptown Anthem** , Treach says, "hit a nigga, kill a nigga, **we'll come back**". Come back from where?! Was Treach talking about death? If so it would make perfect sense.) **Tupac** was in the video for the song. Around this time my aunt Marcia (page 44) was dating **Father MC** and I was living with my Aunt Karen in Edison New Jersey. I was a big Naughty by Nature fan before I was a Tupac fan. It's interesting that two of my favorite artists' from the 90's, **Treach** and **Buckshot,** from **Black Moon,** would come to be close friends with **Tupac**, and things get more interesting when you consider who I suggest Tupac was in a past life. Naughty by Nature's song **Ghetto Bastard** was released in the year of the **Goat** on November 26th 1991, the same day that **King Tut's** tomb was opened (Nov 26, 1922, page 11) and **Emmett Till** was murdered in 1955, the year of the **Goat**. I felt like **I was the Ghetto Bastard** because I didn't grow up with my father and interestingly enough, neither did Emmett Till. Treach has a daughter named **Egypt**, born on Sep 2nd, the same day **Mamie Till** arrived at the Illinois Central Terminal to receive the box's housing Emmett Till's dead body (p 514). Treach's daughter being named **Egypt** is very interesting when you consider who I suggest Tupac was in a past life (page 664 - 665) and who I was in a past life (p 594)..

"You'll Never Go To Yale"

Iu f Per f m heru

I went to **Edison** middle school and I remember my first week there. I used to play tackle football with other boys in the small patch of grass in front of school, before school started and I would never get tackled. I was developing a love for **football** that was sparked just before I left Columbus Georgia (p 51). My aunt Karen took me and my little sister in and cared for us the best she knew how. She dressed my sister up like a princess and bought me the clothes she wanted me to wear. I wanted the designer clothes but I remember the **Notre Dame** and **Yale** Sweaters she bought me. There weren't many black kids in my school and I was always getting in trouble, ending up in the principles office. One day while in the principles office I was wearing the **Blue Yale** sweater and I still remember a fat white female teacher telling me that she didn't know why I was wearing that sweater because I was never going to go there. I didn't care because I didn't have aspirations to go to any college. To me it seemed like I was always moving from school to school. I wasn't being prepared for life. I was being loved, housed and fed. I went to **church** with my aunt sometimes and when ever I did, **I always wanted to walk to the alter during the alter call** at the end of service. **I always had the desire to connect with this thing we called God** but I never had the courage to get up and walk to the alter (**Perception,** page 532). I wouldn't take that walk until I was **22** years old (page 92). 25 years later, in 2016, at the age of 38, around the same age that both **Malcolm X** and **Martin Luther King** were assassinated (page 69), I wrote the following hekau (rhyme), "**Mother Nature** giving birth to the **Heavenly Father**, put respect on my name whether pissed or bothered, it's not a quest for fame, **fuck Notre Dame**, **Yale**, **Princeton**, **Harvard**, they all the same garbage paling in comparison certainly, how you graduate university and don't know the universe **Dark Matter** all you see?!" (page 372).

Utterances for Coming Forth by day into Light

I had never heard of Tommie Smith, John Carlos, Greg **Parker** or Bill Brown

Two weeks after the American sprinters **Tommie Smith** and **John Carlos** gave the Black Power salute at the 1968 Summer Olympics in Mexico, two Yale cheerleaders, **Greg Parker** and **Bill Brown** echoed the protest at the Yale-Dartmouth **football** game on Nov 2nd 1968, two days before the discovery of King Tut's tomb (Nov 4th 1922).. The move shocked Yale alumni. In 1968, America appeared to be coming apart at the seams. The system of racism and white supremacy had taken the life of our charismatic leader **Martin Luther King, Jr** (see page 69). The Vietnam War had bitterly divided the country, with antiwar protests increasingly pitting younger Americans versus older ones. By August the streets of Chicago became a violent battleground between protesters and police outside the Democratic National Convention. I had not heard of either protests until I was in my 30's but I wore that Yale sweater my aunt bought me.

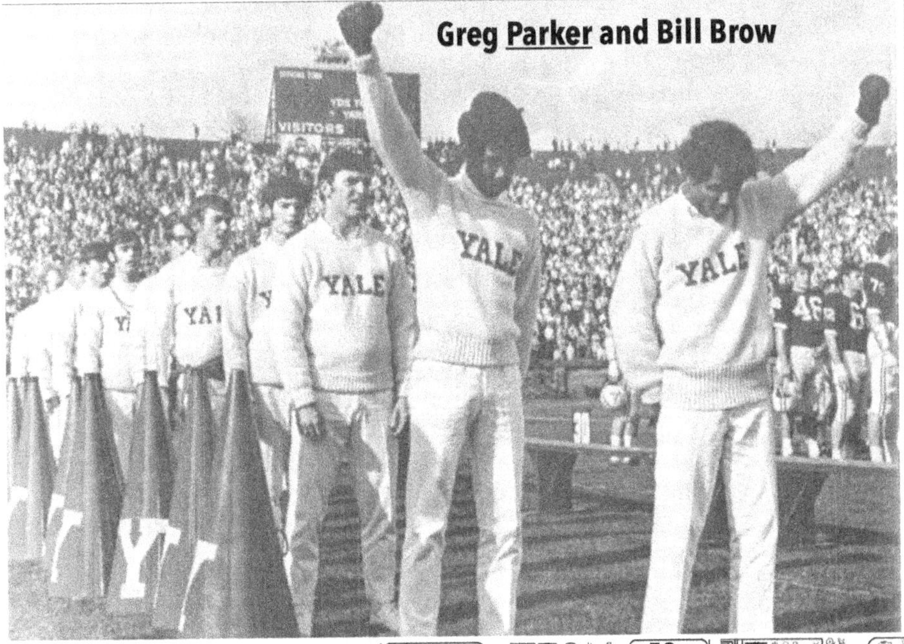

Greg Parker and Bill Brow

Tommie Smith and John Carlos do black power salute wearing gloves given to them by **Peter Norman**.

It is he, who comes forth by day into Light

Profound Motown's and Hollow Pornos

My aunt Karen and uncle Joseph were always arguing so they weren't paying attention to what I was doing. There was love in her home but there was also tension but I am grateful that they took me in. I still remember the long trip with my uncle Joseph when he first brought me to New Jersey. I had just come from Columbus Georgia. My uncle Joseph had an old collection of **porngraphic** videos on the top shelf of the pantry and a collection of "rare" **Playboy** and **Penthouse** magazines with **Marilyn Monroe** and other famous ***white women***. I watched every video and I barely read the articles in the magazines. I was 13yrs old and had no real understanding of sex because no man had ever taken the time to talk to me about it. At 13 yrs old I watched my uncle's videos and looked at the pictures in the magazines. Seeing a woman naked was exciting to me. Some how I knew I wanted to do what ever they were doing on the video but I was shy. Sometimes I would pause the video and draw what I saw. It excited me but I did not know that there was a sensation of pleasure that went along with what I was watching. With that said, I didn't experience ejaculation till I was 17 years old and it was by mistake. Aside from the pornographic videos I watched, I also listened to all of my uncle's old cassette tape **Motown collection** which seemed to feed my soul. I listened to everything from **I Heard It Through the Grape Vine** (page 481), to the **Temptations**, **Smokey Robinson** and the list goes on. I seemed to really love the music from that time period and I listened to his tapes so much that he once told me that I had an **old soul**. I guess I had more of an old soul than either of us could have imagined. As with most of my family, there is a strange pattern with the birthdates of my uncle's children, from his previous marriage. He has a daughter name Jacqueline (p 147) who's born on my birthday, **October 25th** and she can "see" **dead people** (spirits, ghost, see pages 318, 421, 547). His first son **Lenny** was born 3 days after me on **October 28th**.
Addendum (The movie **Till** (a movie about Emmett Till) was released on **Lenny's** birthday, on **October 28,** 2022, which was the same day the **Beyond King Tut** tour opened in New York City, pages 29 and 33**)**.

Art

I was 13 or 14 when I drew this picture. My cousin **Lenny** had a collection of Heavy Metal comic books and they had a lot of nudity and sex scenes. This is not the first picture I ever drew but unfortunately this is the oldest one that survives. My portfolio was stolen from me in the 9th grade by another student. I drew the picture below in 1991 from a scene in one of Lenny's Heavy Metal comic books. 11 years later **Jasmin** would write a note on the back of this picture after she helped **saved me** from an attack (p 108).

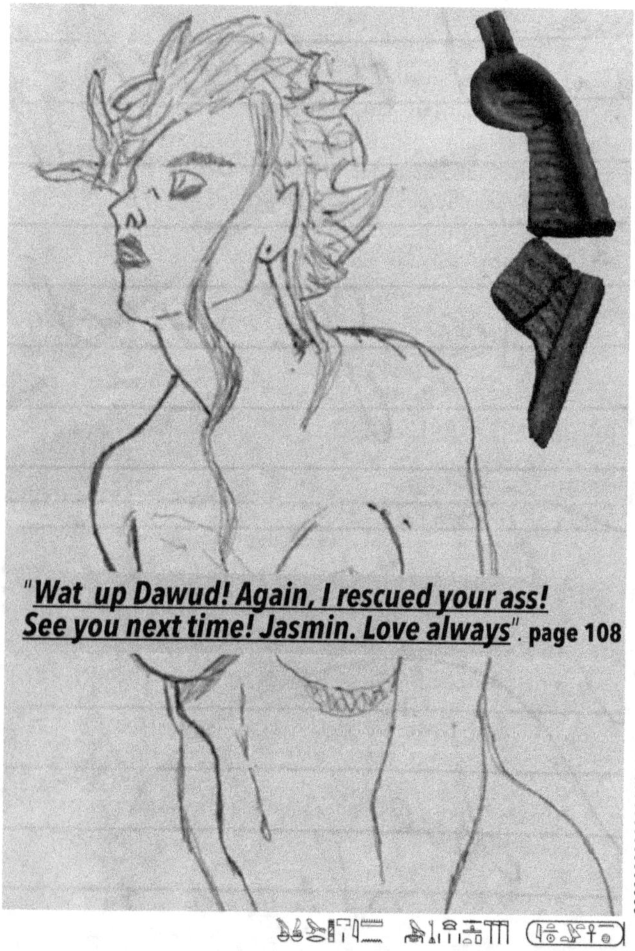

"***Wat up Dawud! Again, I rescued your ass! See you next time! Jasmin. Love always***". **page 108**

Football, Black Eyes, Guns and Bullies

I played basketball at the court near our townhouse and I was always trying to grab the rim. The **high** I got from jumping and **floating** to the rim was fun to me. All I wanted to do was dunk the basketball. In school we started playing flag football during gym and soon after our gym teachers saw that I was good. He wanted me to play football for Edison high and I was excited about that. I loved going out for deep passes and catching the ball and when I caught the ball tackling me was not an easy task.

Sports kept me out of trouble for the most part but trouble was always there if you weren't careful. I was friends with a Puerto Rican boy in the next townhouse, I forget his name but I used to play video games with him in his basement. One day some other boys in the neighborhood came to solve some issues they had with his older brother. We were all standing in the parking lot in front of the townhouse when they rolled up and all of a sudden one of the boys pulled a **gun** out! We all ran but I ran the fastest. No shots were fired though and thank God for that. I left New Jersey after I got punched in the face by a boy in school. One day a new black kid named Dorian came to the school. I can still remember him walking towards me in the hall way with a group of white boys behind him. He walked up to me and punched me in the face for no reason and we got into a scuffle. He gave me the only black I have ever had. I got in that one little fight and my auntie got scared, she said, "you're movin' with your father in Queens Bridge not Bell Air". Shortly after **I was sent back to New York**, but that wouldn't be the last time I saw Dorian! To this day I'm still amazed by what happed to Dorian. Some how, by some strange fate of the universe he was also sent to New York and of all the schools for him to end up in, he ended up attending school at Far Rock High, the same school my younger sister attended. And some how my sister ended up getting him beat up by some guys she knew. I always wondered how that seemed to happen. What were the odds of that?! I always thought it was some strange coincidence.. But now I think I understand what happened to Dorian. Ancestral spirits don't play and sometimes karma is immediate. Be careful how you treat people, you never know who's guarding them. This same sister would **dream** my car accident before it happened on **May 25th** 2002 (p 104). This date would be the first star code that I decoded in 2011 (p 222).

Queens Bridge and That Tape my Father Gave Me

Rau nu Prt m heru

After my time living with my aunt Karen in New Jersey I was sent back to Queens to attend school at Jr High School **180**, in Far Rockaway Queens. Initially I was sent to **Queens Bridge** to live with my father for 4 to 6 months. This is the longest time I can remember living with my father as a youth (Before that it was when I was around 3). My older sister and I slept on the pull-out couch in the living room. I had two step brothers, Charles and Quedar and a step sister. My step-mother Mary was always nice enough to us but we never really spoke much. she was a Jehovah's Witness and she took us the Kingdom Hall for a church service once. She also took care of me when I injured my eyes. One day I jumped down on the train tracks and kicked a long piece of metal into the 3rd rail. When it hit the 3rd rail it exploded and black smoke went everywhere. It got into my eyes and I barely made it home. The best thing Mary did for me was let me stay home so that my eyes could heal on their own and they did, but for several days I could barely open my eyes. It felt as if I had sharp rocks under my eye lids. My step brothers both had many pairs of sneakers and I barely had one pair. I think one of them worked at a sneaker store. They called my father Pop, but I had not spent enough time around him to even feel comfortable calling him daddy. I actually never called him anything. I just spoke to him when I needed to speak to him and I always felt uncomfortable about that. During the time of this picture I was living with him. He had given me the bootleg **Karl Kani** sweater that I'm wearing. I was one of the first people in my school to wear Karl Kani. As teens we were very self conscious about the clothes we wore. This need for approval would follow me for years. While living in **Queens Bridge** I was always on the look out, hoping that I would see **Nas,** but I never did. Hip Hop was becoming a major force in my life at the time. My father had given me a tape while I was living with him and that tape became a sentimental item that I kept for many years until it broke from over use. The only songs I remember from the tape are, Slow Down off the One for All debut album from **Brand Nubian**, Just To Get A Rep by **Gang Starr**, Be a Father to your child by **Ed O.G. & Da Bulldogs** and Trapped by **Tupac**. **Trapped** became one of my favorite songs. Even still to this day I know one of the verses by heart. Music was my escape. I enjoyed listening to emcees craft songs taking me off into their imaginations with skillful soliloquies. I didn't write my own rhymes I just listened but I was falling in love with Hip Hop. I didn't care about anything else except playing football, girls, video games and Hip Hop. I did not read books, not even my comic books, I only read what was mandatory for school and I drew pictures from my comic books. It's funny how the music you listen to can tell a lot about you. My father was a stick up kid in Harlem like the guy from **Gang Starr's** song Just to Get a Rep. His youth was sort of Like **Mike Tyson's** except my father didn't end up the heavy weight champ. He did however manage to get himself stored in a jail cell next to the Boxer **Hurricane Rubin Carter**. My father used the **drugs** that **Brand Nubian** warned about in the song Slow Down. My father had a hard life but he survived. He made some bad decisions but given his circumstances I understand. My father did not have a father and so my father was not "a father to his children" like the song by **Ed O.G.** was prompting men to be, instead he met a woman named Mary and fathered her children. In the year 2021 my father is one of my best friends.

Iu f Per f m heru

Utterances for Coming Forth by day into Light

ADDENDUM

Nas, Dreams and Reincarnation

I have not been to many concerts in my life but the first rapper I saw perform was **Nas** at the **Apollo** in 1996 the same year Tupac died. In 2002 I would survived a near fatal car accident and the song that was playing during the crash was, You Da Man, by Nas (p 104). Fast forward 17 years and I would have two **dreams** with **Nas**, the first of which was very **vivid** (pages 443, 545). A few years later I would realize that **Nas** spoke about **reincarnation** several times in his music. **Nas** released his **Demo Tape** in 1991 the year of the **goat**.. **Emmett Till** was murdered at the age of **14**, in 1955 the year of the **goat**. The last track on his Demo Tape was titled, **Nas Will Prevail**. In the first verse **Nas** says, "**A modern Shakespeare Reincarnated**". In 2012 **Nas** dropped his 11th studio album titled, **Life Is Good** on July 13 2012. On the 3rd track titled, **A Queens Story**, **Nas** mentions **reincarnation** again, "**Bebo Posse reincarnated through me, probably**". And in 2021, on **Nas's 14th** studio album he says reincarnation again, "This what I live for, the inventor, the re-invention, **I'm reincarnated**, see what it hit for". This album was titled **Magic** and it was released on Dec 24, the day before the Winter Solstice (p 489) which is related to Reincarnation "Gilgul" (p 14). Over the years I would mention **Nas** 17 times in my music.

January 6th 1992, The Jordans

It is he, who comes forth by day into Light

Today is January 26th 2022 and this is the second picture from my childhood that I found that was drawn on January 6th. I enjoyed drawing but I only drew things that inspired me. I sketched this picture of Jordan from a picture I saw in a magazine. I drew this at **14** years old, on the day that **Emmett Till's** mother, **Mamie Till** died (**January 6th** 2003). (***ADDENDUM* January 6** is the day that the ancient Kemetyu celebrated the Winter Solstice. **January 6th** currently marks the 12th day after the Winter Solstice (pages 489, 614). In the Christian religion **January 6th** is the day that the 3 Magi visited Jesus in a manger. **Tupac's** grand mother Eloise Maria Barnes was also born on **January 6**.) Emmett was from **Chicago** like the Chicago **Bulls** and was murdered at **14**.. All the years that I watched Jordan it never occurred to me that I had an aunt and uncle named *Squeek and Marion* **Jordan** (p 403). My grand mother's sister married into the Jordan family, however I do not think they are anywhere close to Michael Jordan's family tree. I can remember watching the NBA finals with my grandmother, Juanita (p 22). Jordan was her favorite player and she really got into the games. She thought he was handsome and I think she fantasized about Jordan because his wife was also named Juanita. She loved the way Jordan would win the game in the clutch. As an athlete I loved Jordan for the same reasons. He was like a **hero** (page 3). When the Bulls needed a **hero** he rose to the occasion. I believed in Michael Jordan but I also believed in myself. I kept jumping until I could grab the rim because Jordan's airtime fascinated me. I also never gave up on the football field and because of that I would rise to the occasion many times for my team.

The Nswt Bity (Pharaoh) Narmer (Menes) Smiting the enemies of Kemet (Egypt) with a

Mace..

July 7th 1992, 14yrs old
Mace

This is the first and only character I ever created from my **imagination**. I was better at drawing what I saw in front of me rather than creating it from my mind. I enjoyed the feeling of creating an exact copy of an image. There was a small high that came after completion. I do not know what reason I had for naming him **MACE** but that is what I named him. Today is **Rosa Parks'** birthday, February 4th 2022 and it is only today that I realized why I named him **Mace**. One of the most recognizable scenes in the iconography of ancient Kemet (Egypt) is the image of the Nswt Bity (Pharaoh, King or Queen) ritualistically **smiting** the enemies of Kemet (Egypt). These scenes can be found in every period of Kemet's history from the predynastic age until the fall of Kemet to European invaders. A typical smiting scene' depicts the Nswt Bity wielding a **mace** over his of her head with one hand while restraining one or more enemies with the other. The Nswt is typically shown leaning over his victim(s) with one heel raised off the ground, in the very last moment before striking the enemy in the head. What does this mean? Spiritually, this is a picture that I drew at **14** years old, the same age that **Emmett** was when "he" was murdered, therefore *it is a symbolic blow to racism and white supremacy*. In developing this character I only took from one character and that was Wolverine, I used his boots. Everything else was created from my 14 year old imagination. As can be seen in the picture he **emit's** energy from his left hand, enough to destroy a brick wall. In ancient Kemet the left hand holds the Heka staff (the crook) which is connected to the feminine, spiritual side of the brain (the right side) and the Heka staff is the staff of the ruler. Heka also meant meaningful speech or magic. Notice he has the high top fade in the same shape as the statues of pharaoh's (left side). Below you can see Tutankhaten depicted as the **NTR Amun** who's crown resembles a hightop fade. **Mace** has a jet pack on his back because of course he needs to be able to **fly**. More than anything else as a child I always wanted to fly. I don't remember why I made his face glass but when I look at it now I see the face of **Cobra Commander** (right side) from the **G.I. Joe** cartoon I used to watch every day after school. Cobra Commander was a snake, like the Snake (Uraeus) found on the foreheads of the NSWT BITY. The Cobra represented immortality in ancient Kemet. In the cartoon Cobra Commander was the leader of the "bad guys" while First Sergeant "**Duke**" was the leader of the G.I. Joe team, who were the "good guys". My Grand Fathers name was General **Dukes** Jr. He was from **Orrville** Alabama, the state in which **Rosa Parks** refused giving up her seat to a white man because all she could think of was **Emmett Till** and that act would help sp**ark** the Civil Rights Movement. Today is Sep 4th 2021 and I've started writing again. As I was looking for the city that my Grand father was born in, I found it written in his obituary, and that's how I came to know that my Grand father had a brother named **Emmett Dukes**! I'm in tears looking through pictures and contemplating my existence here. I can't make this up! He had around 10 brothers and one of them just happened to be named **Emmett**!

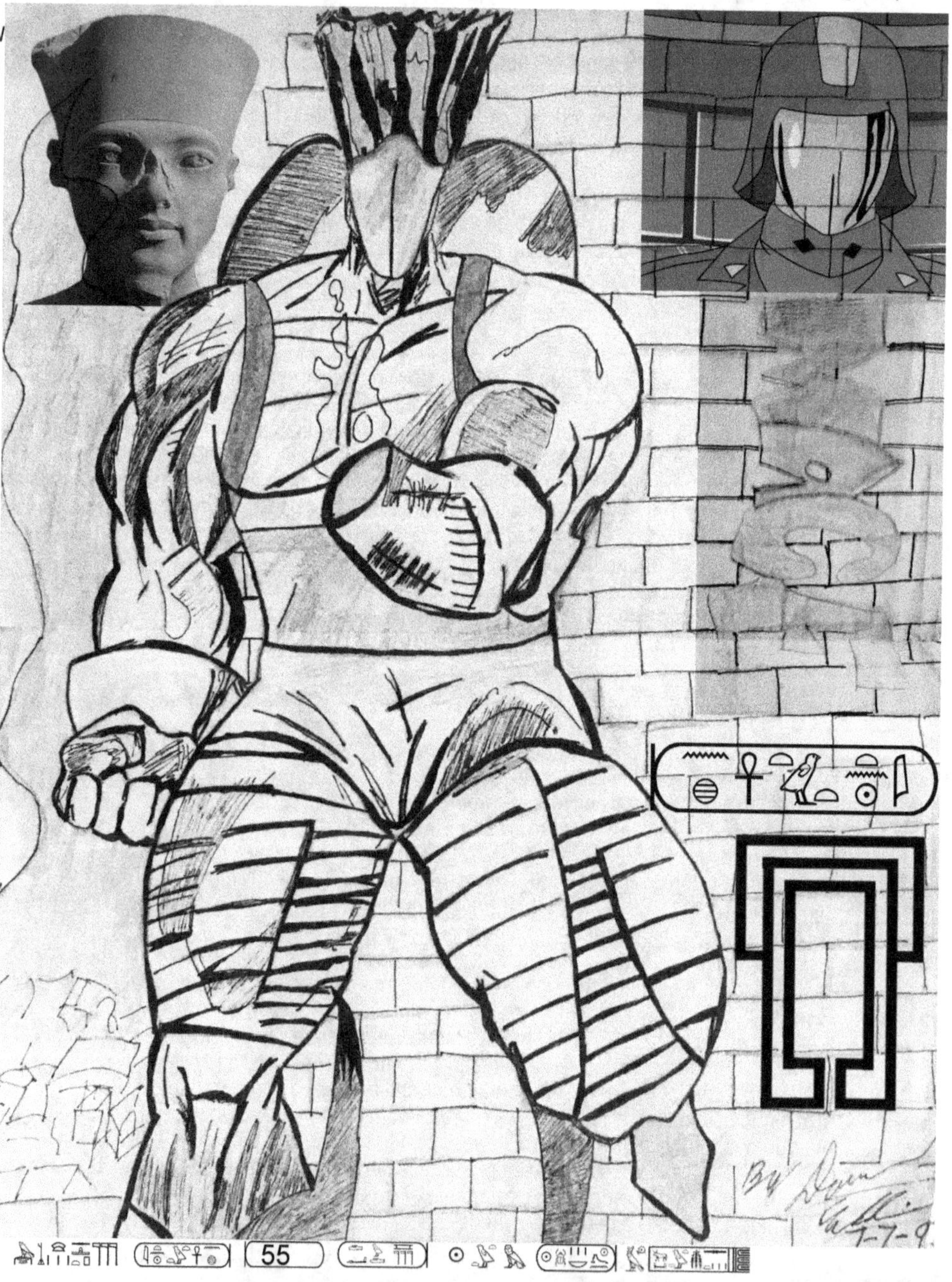

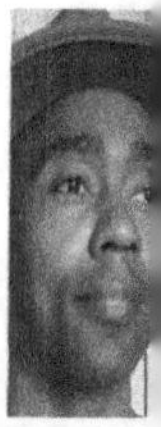

1992 - "Riddle Me This Batman"

I had the bad habit of starting pictures and not finishing them sometimes. Batman was never one of my favorite superheroes and perhaps that's why I never finished this one, or perhaps, *it was all* ***just a riddle***.. To the young ones reading this book, remember, it's not about how you start, it's about how you finish! Batman was created in 1939 by Robert Kahn and Bill **Finger**. Robert was born the day before me on October 24th, the same day that KRS One released his book, The Gospel of Hip Hop (page 633) and he died on **November 3rd**, the day before Tutankhaten's (**King Tut's**) tomb was discovered on **November 4th**. Bill **Finger** was born the day before **Louis** Till (Emmett Till's father) and Bill's father's name was **Louis** Finger. I was **14** years old when I drew this and Emmett was murdered at **14** years old. "**Holy Leacola Riddle Batman**! There's a mystery here that I just can't seem to put my **Finger** on". In 1948 Bill **Finger** and Dick Sprang created the supervillain character named, **The Riddler,** who incorporated complex **riddles**, puzzles and lethal contraptions in his schemes. The **Riddler** is one of the most enduring enemies of the superhero Batman. **Life is a symphony speaking in Riddles**. My maternal great great grand mother's maiden named was May Fannie **Riddle** (p 16) and my paternal great grand mother's maiden name was Leacola **Riddle** (page 21). May Fannie **Riddle** was born around the beginning of the **Civil War** while Leacola **Riddle** was born on June 10th, the same day that **Marcus Garvey** died. Marcus Garvey would be instrumental in my search for truth during my 30's, the years of my awakening. The death of my grand father sparked my awakening. He passed on Aug 18th, the day after Marcus Garvey's birthday. Marcus Garvey once said, "It will only take 24hrs for us to for us to reclaim what is ours, ounce we all decide it is ours!". See page 3 for the **hero's journey**.

Rau
nu
Prt
m
heru

Iu
f
Per
f
m
heru

Utterances
for
Coming
Forth
by day
into
Light

It is
he,
who
comes
forth
by day
into
Light

ADDENDUM **February 2nd 1993 Harlem World**

In February of 1993 I drew a character named **Spawn**. **Mushrooms** go through the process of "**spawn**ing".. **25** years after I drew that picture of **Spawn**, in 2018, at the age of **40**, I would eat a **mushroom** for the first time sp**ark**ing the revelation of my past life as **Emmett Till** (p 474 - 483). With all the moving around I did as a teen these pictures have helped me to place where I was in the world at the time I drew them. I drew this picture of **Spawn** around the time I was living in **Harlem** on 140th and Lenox, in Delinor housing with my aunt Adilah. My mother and one of my sisters were staying there as well. I drew this the day before my mothers birthday. It was during this time that our relationship began to fade away as she went through her struggles with life. I didn't know what she was struggling with but I knew she was different. You can see that the picture is not finished because by this time my attention to drawing was fading away too. I was slowly moving my attention to Hip Hop, girls and football. When I was living in Delinor I used to exercise by running up and down the 15 flights of stairs. The song **What's the 411** from **Mary J** and **Grand Puba** was a hit at the time (p 566). When I lived in Harlem I stayed in the house a lot. I played tricks on my younger cousin **Abdulla** that he's still upset about to this day. I played basketball at the court where I jumped and jumped till I could grab the rim. I played Street Fighter a lot with my friend Dondy. But my time in Harlem was not without trials. I was once punched in the face, while in the playground by a boy who's name I don't remember. I ran from him and never saw him again. I only remember that he had a brother and they were both very muscular. I have a foggy memory from my time in Harlem. One day, for some **reason***, I **decided*** to walk around Harlem and found myself in a park. In this park I saw or spoke to a man. The memory is only comprised of a **feeling***. Like the person was special or the moment was important. It almost feels like the memory is broken or partly erased. It wasn't till the writing of this book that I realized the movie **Above The Rim** started filming in Harlem in 1993. And that's when I began to **feel*** as if that man might have been **Tupac**. Sort of like how I feel like the man I met on the plane was Graham Hancock (p 659). There was an older brother named Talib who lived in Delinor and sold comic books on 135th and Lenox. He must have been in his late 20's or early 30's. He took a liking to me and would let me hang out with him while he sold his comic books. He would even let me come to his apartment and look through his comic book collection. Unfortunately Talib died from **Diabetes** not long after I met him and not long after that my affinity for comics died as well. It was around this time that I started hanging out at **Alan's** house, my sister's boy friend. Alan was like a big brother to me. We used to play 93 Madden football and listen to the **Wu Tang Clan's** first album. He used to call me **"Kid Fresh"** (p 196). Unfortunately Alans father died from **Diabetes** in 2002. The "**Strange**" part is that Alan's father died on **August 27th**, the day before **Emmett Till** was murdered (Aug 28, 19**55**, page 507) and Alan is born on April 5, the day after I realized I was **Tutankhaten (King Tut)** in a past life (p 593). The pictures drawn on pages, **55**, 56, 57, 58 and 79 were drawn in an art book that Alan gave me. On Jan 18, 2017, Alan appeared in a **dream** of mine for the first and only time (p 441).

May the souls of Talib and Mr Troutman walk peacefully through the field of Reeds in Amenta. Amen Ra.

Rau nu Prt m heru

Today is Jan 26th 2022 and after realizing that I drew a picture of **Wolverine** on the day **Emmett Till's mother** died (p 79), I looked at the dates of the other pictures I drew as a teenager and I found another interesting date. I drew this picture of **Magneto** on **Louis Till's** birthday (p 475). **Louis Till** was **Emmett Till's father** and it was the **ring** that he left for Emmett that would eventually help to identify Emmett's disfigured body (p 512). The date **May 25th** was inscribed on the ring and that date would surface many times in this life ultimately being the first star code I deciphered in 2011 (p 222).. When I drew this picture I was 15 years old and I had no idea that the concepts for **X**-Men were taken from the Civil Rights Movement that was sp**ark**ed by the murder of Emmett Till. The character **Magneto** was taken from the persona of **Malcolm X** and **Professor X** was taken from the persona of **Martin Luther King**. Malcolm **X** (Magneto) was seen as more willing to fight against racism (mutant rights) seeking separation while Martin (Professor **X**) was seen as more peaceful seeking unity with all. In 2019 **I would have a dream** on Martin's birthday (p 550) that came to fruition on Malcolm's birthday (p 564). Even before the persona's of Malcolm and Martin were co-opted and placed in the X-men, many other superheroes were taken from the 7 African Powers also known as the Yoruba Orishas. Shango is the most popular of the Yoruba Orishas and worship of him begins centuries ago in present-day Yorubaland (Nigeria, Benin, Togo). **Shango** exhibits the powers of thunder, lightening and fire and he wields a double sided axe. The interesting thing about Shango is that he was a real person. He was the 3rd king of the Oyo empire located in Nigeria. His rule and impact as a King was so profound that after his death he was deified. His name lived on in the Caribbean during the transatlantic slave trade, especially in **Haiti** as many of the enslaved Yoruba called on his name to power them through battle and still lives on today in Haiti's Voudou, Brazil's Candomblé, Cuba's Santería, and in the **Shango** Baptists of Trinidad.. **Thor** is an **arc**hetype of **Shango** sharing many of Shango's characteristics. Thor is the God of thunder and wields a double headed hammer while Shango wields a double headed axe and has the powers of thunder, lightening and fire.

ADDENDUM

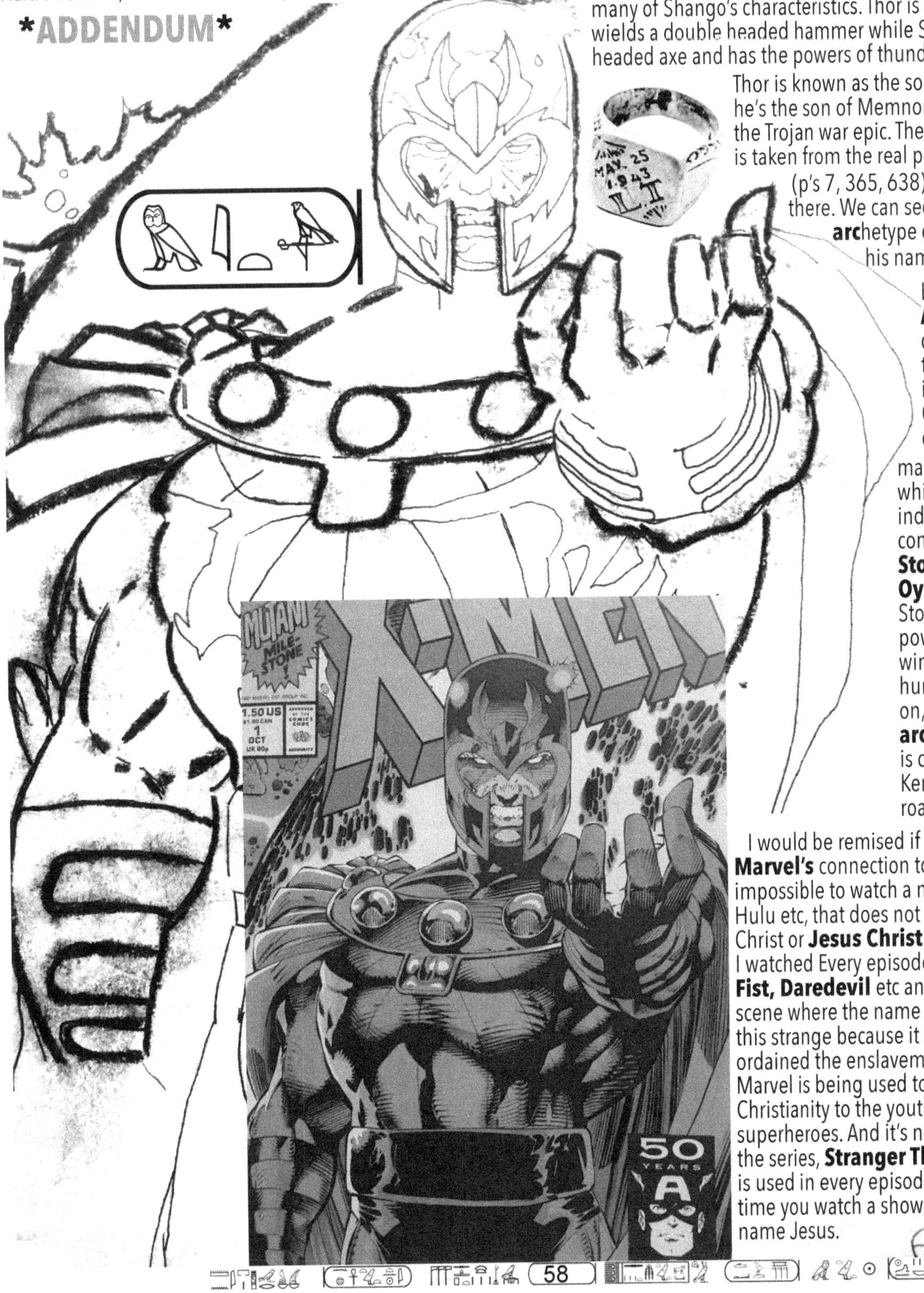

Thor is known as the son of Odin but some say he's the son of Memnon, the African hero from the Trojan war epic. The character AgaMemnon is taken from the real person **Amenhotep III** (p's 7, 365, 638). But it doesn't stop there. We can see that **Wolverine** is an **arc**hetype of **Ogun** starting with his name. Wolverine's name is **Logan** and if the letter **A** in the name Logan is changed to **U**, you have the name **Ogun**. Ogun is one of the Yoruba Orishas and is the God of Metal who carries machetes in his hands while Wolverine has indestructible metal coming from his hands.. **Storm** is and **arc**hetype of **Oya** and just like Oya, Storm harnesses the powers of nature, using wind, tornados and hurricanes. The list goes on, even **Superman** is an **arc**hetype of **Shango** and is connected to ancient Kemet (Pages 202-204). All roads lead to Kemet.

Iu f Per f m heru

I would be remised if I did not speak about **Marvel's** connection to **Jesus**. It is almost impossible to watch a new show on Netflix or Hulu etc, that does not have the name Jesus, Christ or **Jesus Christ** written into a scene. I watched Every episode of **Luke Cage, Iron Fist, Daredevil** etc and every episode had a scene where the name Jesus is spoken. I find this strange because it was Christianity that ordained the enslavement of Africans and now Marvel is being used to spread the message of Christianity to the youth who are drawn to superheroes. And it's not just Marvel, even in the series, **Stranger Things**, the name Jesus is used in every episode I watched. The next time you watch a show online listen for the name Jesus.

Utterances for Coming Forth by day into Light

It is he, who comes forth by day into Light

February 8th 1993, Your Gift will Make a Way for You

At **15** years old, I drew a character named **Spawn**. **25** years later, in 2018, at the age of **40**, I would eat a **mushroom** for the first time sp**ark**ing my first past life revelation. **Mushrooms** go through the process of "**spawn**ing", which means, **Give Rise To**. It was the **mushroom** that **gave rise to** my first past life revelation as **Emmett Till** (p 474 - 483). I used to take the long train ride from Harlem to Far Rockaway Queens everyday for school and this caused me to be late a lot. I drew this picture of Spawn on Feb 8th 1993 the day after Louis Till's (Emmett Till's father's) birthday (p 475). My favorite comic book super hero (heru) was **Peter (Ptah) Parker Spiderman** and I drew more pictures of him than any other super Heru, yet I don't even have one of those drawings. **<u>My portfolio with all of my best drawings was stolen from me</u>** in Junior high school by another student. It was also around this time that I took a **Studio Art** class at **Jr High School 180**. The only thing I remember from that class was editing a video for the song **Scenario** by **A Tribe Called Quest** ft. **Leaders of the New School**. At some point you will begin to see the significance of certain ***star codes*** in this book and then, the birth dates of a few of the members of the Leaders of the New School will make more sense (**Nov 4th** and **Sep 19th**). The Studio Arts class was fun but my favorite part of JR High school was the **two hand touch football games** we would play before school started. I was "**recruited**" **to play football** for **Beach Channel high school,** which was located directly across the street from my Jr High school. One of my gym teachers had seen me play two hand touch in the play ground several times and one day he approached me and my friend **Alvin Latimore** (**Foul Al**) after one of our games. **He told me that I was really good at football and that I should consider playing Football at Beach Channel High School**. He would later introduce me to the High School football coach. I was 14 or 15 at the time. See page 3 for the **hero's journey**.

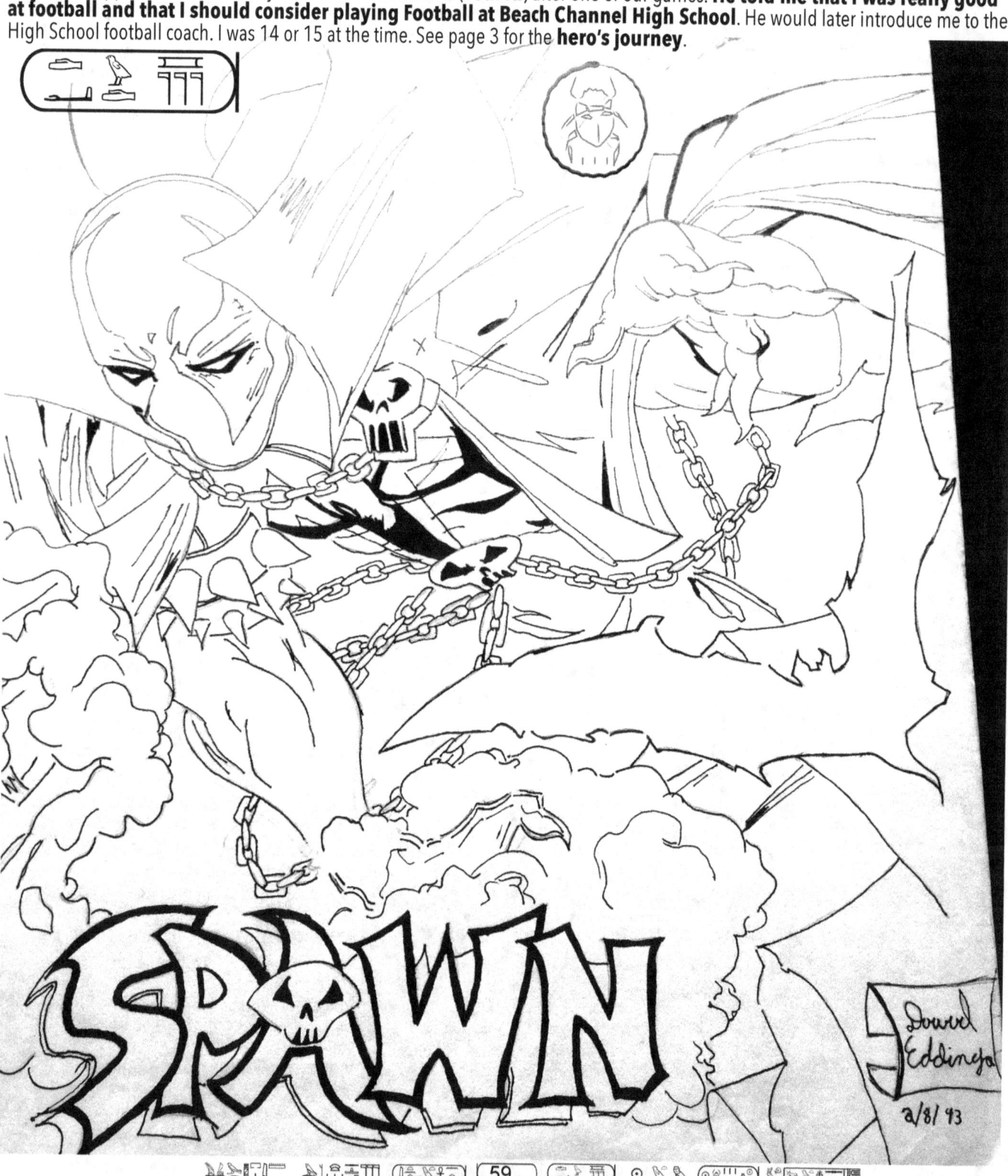

Rau nu Prt m heru

Iu f Per f m heru

Utterances for Coming Forth by day into Light

It is he, who comes forth by day into Light

Indira Aminta

I met Indira in Jr high school 180. She was on the track team and I only joined because of her. She would be the first girl I ever fell in love with. I would go to her house after school often and she would help me with my homework. She even did some of it for me. I knew her father and her sisters and her brothers. Her father liked me and I liked him. Indira got me my first job on the books. She had good grades and played on the basketball team. She was picked to be a peer mentor for kids at an after school program. She was asked to find a male with good grades who could work with her. She picked me even though my grades were terrible. I was a "big brother" for a boy named Javin Jones, who I would help with his homework and I even took him and his sister to the movies a few times along with my little sister. It was the children at this after school program who taught me how to play chess. They beat me the first few times until I caught on and I came to enjoy the game. I had no plan for life but I thought I was going to marry Indira. Then we went to High School and I fell in love with Monique too. Indira let **Reggie Dorsey** take her to the prom so I went stag with some friends. We graduated and we went our separate ways in life. I only saw her once after we went to college then I never saw her in person again. However on October 18th 2014 (page 305) I would have a profound experience with her in a **dream**. On April 4th 2020 (page 594) my past life as **King Tut** was revealed to me and that's when I realized my connection with Indira. Her middle name is **Aminta** and in ancient Kemet (Egypt) **Amenta** is what we called Heaven. (***ADDENDUM*** In 2021 I would meet **Reggie's** brother **Mathew** in a mysterious way leading to my first trip to Kemet. page 647).

Monique

Monique was one of the most popular girls in the school. She had a magnetic personality and for some reason I was drawn to her. She was on the cheerleading squad, the softball team and involved with other groups. I would travel to Brooklyn to hangout with her at her house a lot. I knew her mother and her father and all her siblings. Monique and I shared an innocent teenage love. We were never intimate in high school. All we did was kiss but I loved kissing her. I traveled to see Monique from Queens to Brooklyn during the blizzard of 1996 because I had to be near her. With all the time I spent around Monique I never knew she was **Native American,** from the **Unkechaug** and **Shinnecock Nations**. She knew her heritage her whole life. I would not realize my Native American heritage until after my Grandfather died in 2009. Monique and I would date when I got out of the army and she helped me when I was homeless sleeping in my car in 2006. In 2018 she would take me to my first **Powwow** (page 578). Monique and I are still friends today and I feel that I have known her before.

Jeannie In A Bottle (July 31st 2018)

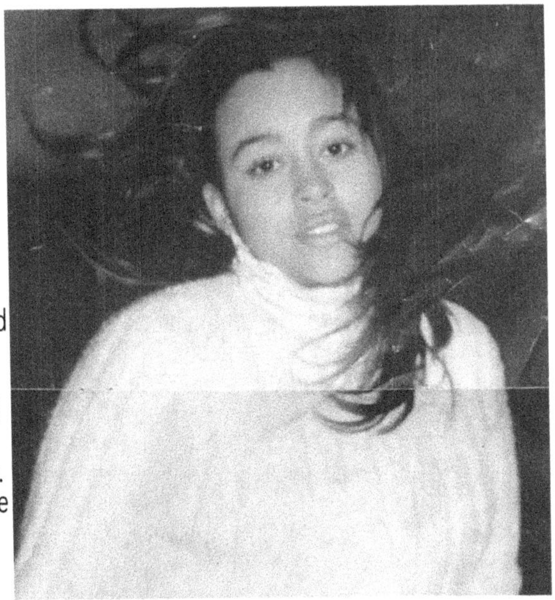

Jeannie Gonzales and I had science class together in the 10th grade. I learned very little about science in that class because I was always talking to Jeannie. I had a crush on her but she was dating John and I was in love with Indira so I always kept her as a friend. I would talk to Jeannie about Indira and she would tell me to just be her friend. After high school was over I wouldn't see Jeannie again until 2006 when we began to date for a short period of time (page 147). We floated away from each other for 10 years then found each other again. She gave me the spark I needed then she floated away again. She was like my Genie in a bottle (page 531). My experience with Jeannie in 2006 helped make me a better person. Jeanie is born on June 15th, the day before **Tupac**.

We Played on Rocks and Dirt

Message To My Teammates

If ever a team mate of mine reads this book remember the games we played and remember the things I did on the force field of play. Remember the undefeated season with the **Hornets**, and the 25+ touchdowns I scored. Remember the things I did with the **Dolphins**. Many of you thought I would go on to play in the **NFL**, but as we can see that never happened. I was chosen for a greater mission. I left the sport of football in 2003 and in my regular life I kept "playing", I kept trying my best in all that I did and when I started to apply the same attention to the unseen realms I started to experience magical things just like those done on the football force field. Most of you know that I used to write rhymes, well I did the same thing with my poetry. I wrote this story down in wraps years before it happened. The game of life is the "game" that we need to give our ATENtion to because we play it more than once. **In this life football was a programming system for me that I planned before I got here**. **I used the game of football to train my ability to rise above the storm** like **Heru** the true Ntchru from ancient Kemet. For those of you that I have not spoken to since 1996 or 2003 I want to say that I love you and I hope that you are all in good health and doing well. I write these words through tears. This life is a play of consciousness brothers. The same things that we did on the force field is what we must do with our everyday lives. We must try our best and NEVER give up.

It's All In The Numbers

I played on a few teams but this was my first team, The **Beach Channel Dolphins** and our colors were blue and **Gold**! Everyone of my teammates that I ever played with, from 2 hand touch to semi pro has witnessed me do things on the force field of play that statistics can not record. **In everything there is a pattern!** I'm sure each one of the men in this picture can write a book about their lives and make what I'm about to say fit into their own life story but since I have the floor I'll do the math on the numbers worn in this picture. There are 31 men in this picture but I can only make out 16 numbers for sure, that's half. Reggie is wearing number **22**, he is standing above number 3 with his finger pointing to the sky. King Tut's tomb was discovered in 19**22** and the famous gold mask weighs **22** pounds. I was born **22** years after Emmett was murdered when my mother was **22** years old. On the bottom left we see the number **41** worn by Austin (page **41**). Emmett Till was born in 19**41** the year of the snake. And on the far right, **Spencer** is wearing number **55,** and my father's name is **Spencer** and my mother was born in 19**55** the same year Emmett Till was murdered. p**ARK**ed dead* in the center is number **77**, I was born in 19**77** the same year that Emmett's cousin Wheeler **Park**er (p 515) would answer his call to ministry and the same year Emmett Till's uncle Moses **Wright** passed away (p 517). Emmett has a cousin named Wheeler **Parker** and my Grandmother's maiden name is **Parker** (p 15). Emmett had an Uncle named Moses Wright and my Grandfather's name is Spencer **Wright** (p 15). I'm born on October 25th 19**77** (**10/25/77**) and you can see that numbers **10**, **25** and **77** go from left to right in proper order. **Angel** is wearing number **5** (p 63). In high school I predicted that his son would be born on my birthday and so he was born on October 25th 1996. Joe Sid is wearing number **42** and **42** represents **Maat** as well as the **42** negative confessions (laws) that were used

Rau nu Prt m heru

Iu f Per f m heru

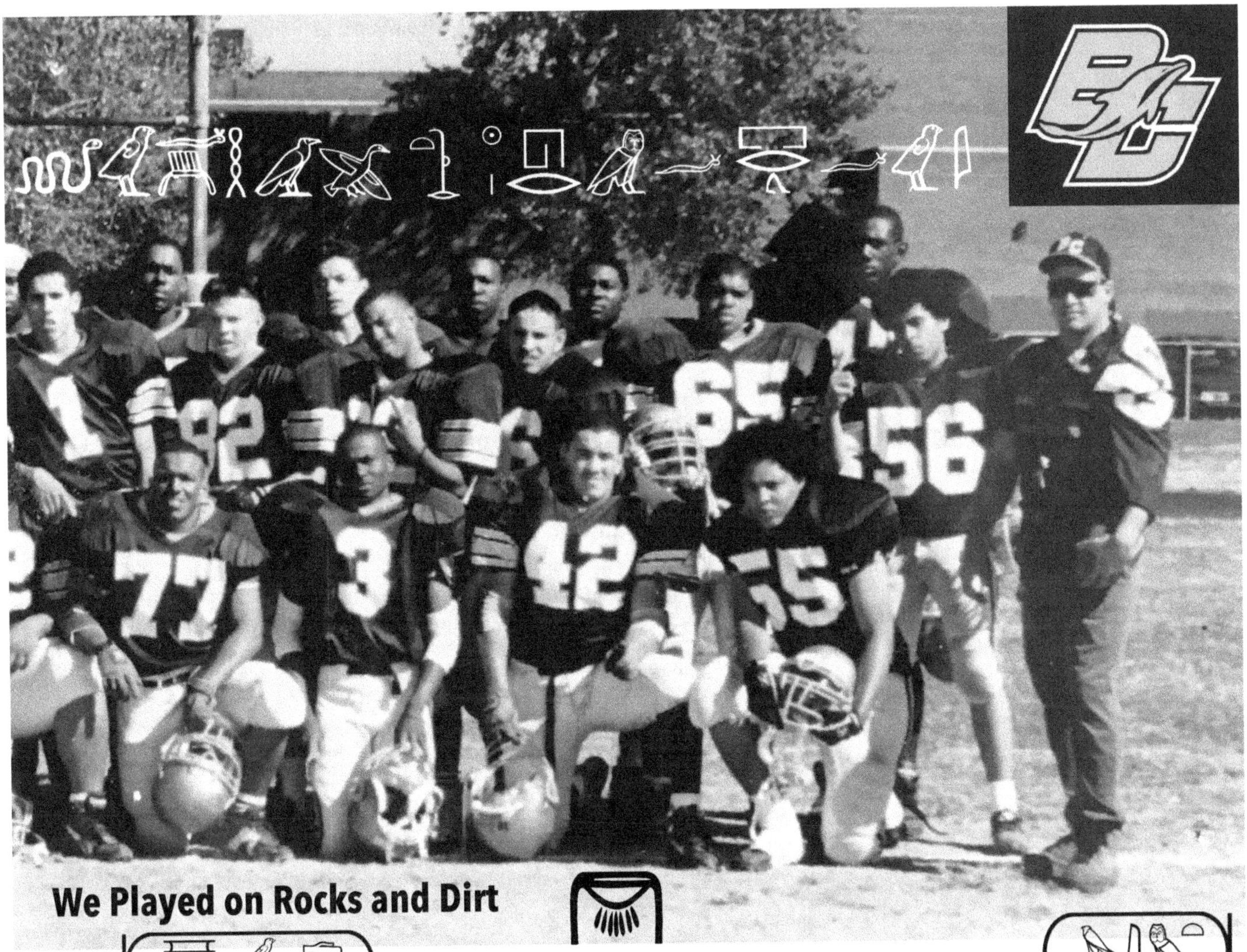
We Played on Rocks and Dirt

Message To My Teammates

Utterances for Coming Forth by day into Light

It is he, who comes forth by day into Light

to make the 10 commandments in the bible (**42 Laws of Maat, Page 367**). Number **56** is seen on the far right and the Alabama bus boycotts lasted the entire year of 19**56**, lead by **Rosa Parks** and **Martin Luther King**. Rosa refused to give her seat to a white man because of the murder of Emmett Till and was subsequently arrested. 85 is a number that doesn't weave into this story but it does add up to the number 4 and football was my foundation for perseverance. The brother wearing number **85** is Dave, he is one of only **8** teammates in this picture that I have contact info on and there is only one that I speak to often, he is wearing the number **1**, his name is **Will**. Will was our Quarter back and to this day his favorite play is **Pro Right fly to Z**, a **hail Mary pass** to me. It was Will that threw me the passes that allowed me to rise to the occasion. He will always be a special person to me. He needed me and I needed him. Number **65** is at the right, **65** is the year of the snake the same year **Malcolm X** was assassinated, the same year my Aunt Pamela is born, who has a son named Wesley born on Malcolm X's birthday. Malcolm X had a brother named Wesley (p 287)! **Malcolm X** was the first black man I ever heard speak truth to power and I never forgot him. I heard his speech <u>*The Ballot Or The Bullet*</u> at around 16yrs old and would not hear another speech of his till I was around 32 years old. John **King** is wearing number **82**, John was my backup receiver. We were both receivers and his last name was **King** and on April 4th 2020, I would realize that I was **King Tut** in a past life. I heard that he is a cop now. I hope that he looks at black men in the streets and can remember his teammates he played with in high school, most of us were "black". We see numbers **3** and **33**. The master number 33 for the 33 vertebrae traveling up the spine and number 3 representing the first trinity, sunrise (kheper Ra)- high noon (Ra) - and sunset (Atum). Between numbers 1 and 5 we can see the number **4** but it can not be certain if there is another number there. **Rosa pARKs** is born on February 4th the day after my mother (p 27) and the same day as my friend **Mars**. **Rosa Parks** refused giving up her seat to a white man because all she could think of was **Emmett Till** and that act would help sp**ark** the Civil Rights Movement. **Mars** is the woman who invited me to the International African Arts festival on July 1, 2018 (page 474) where I had my first past life revelation of Emmett Till (p 480). I will end off with the numbers 72 and 77. The brother wearing 72 was given the name **Heru** at his birth. Heru was Samoan. He was our center and he was the biggest guy on the team but his nickname was **Tiny**. In ancient Kemet **Heru** is represented by a **Falcon**. He is the son of **Ausar** who is the Lord of **resurrection** and **reincarnation**. IN HIGH SCHOOL MY "**CENTER'S**" NAME WAS **HERU**! Vargas is the brother wearing number **77**. He was a Dominican brother and the shortest guy on the team but he had the biggest heart on the team. I was born in 19**77**. These are some of the numbers that flow through out this book. The man on the far right, next to number 56 was Coach Bryant **Sole**, like the **immortal soul** that reincarnates!!. He was the defensive coach and didn't like me because it took me a long time to develop the recklessness needed to slam my body into other people to tackle them. The man on the left, behind number **41** was my biggest fan, his name was coach Dunkley (p **41**). When I left Junior varsity and went on to the varsity team he told me that I was the best player he had ever seen play football and that I would be the best player on the varsity team the next year. I never forgot that. Make sure that YOU never forget that you are Ausar and Heru, the hero! See page 3 for the **hero's journey!**

Angel, The Monk

Angel was one of my closest friends in High School. He is **Dominican** and **Puerto Rican**. We played on the football team together. In 1996 he had his first son. The baby was due in October and I told him he would be born on my birthday and sure enough he was sent down (born) on **October 25th 1996**. I have only seen Angel once since 1996. I saw him in 2004 just before I got out the army. I lost contact with him for many years and just got back in touch with him a few weeks ago. Today is October 30th 2021 and I spoke to Angel a few minutes ago. He told me that when he was in the Navy he passed through the Suez Canal and saw the **pyramids** from a distance for the "first time", however when he saw them he was struck with a feeling a **Deja Vu** as if he had lived there before and seen them before. He said the moon and the stars were very clear and bright that night and they looked as if he could reach out and touch them. He also told me that he feels like he was a **monk** in a **past life**. He said that when he was a teenager and still to this day when he watches Chinese karate movies he has feelings of **Deja Vu**. I don't know if Angel was a monk but he was always peaceful, calm and very quiet so if he was a monk it would make perfect sense to me. In ancient Kemet the concept of reincarnation and past lives was called the **Wehem-Mesut** (repeating of births, page 14). In 2022 I experienced **Deja Vu** twice while in **Kemet** (p 670 - 671). In everything there is a pattern! Like mine, the two numbers in the middle of Angel's social security number are **62** (see pages 41, 221, 508, 602)!

Confirmation

Today is December 26th 2021 and I came across this Egyptian basalt head statue from the Berlin, Neues Museum (Z 40022), of a man from around 2500 BC. At least that's the date that the museum gives. As soon as I saw the face I thought of Angel and the conversation we had on October 30th 2021!! Then I placed the faces side by side and to me they seemed to be a perfect match. I must have known Angel in another life during Kemet and like other people I crossed paths with in this life we became friends again and after I had these past life revelations I connected all the dots when the time was right allowing me to place them all here in this book. Angel is born on September 27th 1977, the year of the snake (page 579).

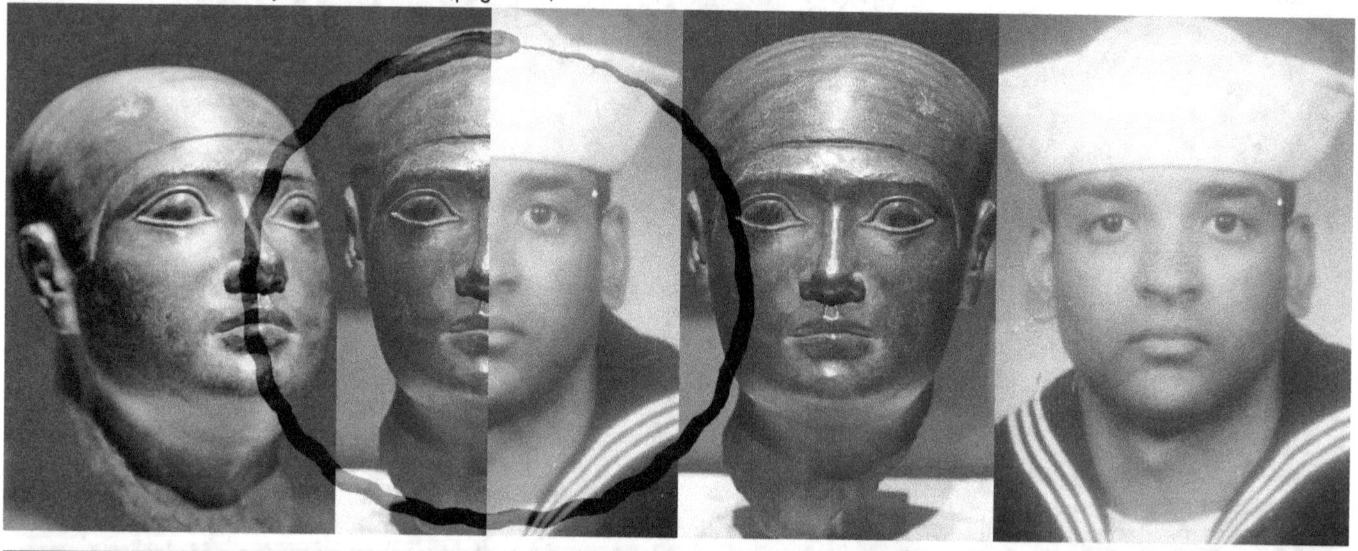

Sister Debra 29X

Rau nu Prt m heru

Number 30, Sean Roberts. Number 20, **Courtlan** Green. Number 59, Robert McCracken. Number **77**, Will Holland. Number **29**, Dawud Eddings. I wanted number 80 but Marvin Randell already had it. I was randomly given the number **29** by my coach, he told me Eric Dickerson wore that number and he was a good player. After my past life revelation of Emmett Till, I was telling my mother about the many **number patterns** and the number **29** came up. Emmett's numbers add up to **29** (19**41**725=**29**). Martin Luther King rose to prominence after the murder of Emmett and Martin was born in 19**29** the year of the **snake**. That's when she told me that she was given the name Sister Debra **29X** when she joined the Nation of Islam. I went to high school in the 10th grade and that's when I played organized football for the first time and that's where I met Courtlan. **Courtlan** would become my best friend. We had many things in common. We both played on the football team, we both wrote rhymes, we were the fastest on the team, we both drew when we were younger and we both grew up without our fathers although his father was present in his life and mine wasn't. He was the number one player on the team but when I got there I became a rival because our teammates always compared us and so we were pit against each other. It wasn't till we got to varsity the next year that we began to become friends. In our first varsity game we were down by 6 points with a few minutes to go in the 4th quarter. Our quarterback Will, threw me the ball (**Pro Right fly to Z**). It was a **hail Mary pass** and the memory is still stored in my mind in slow motion. Will threw the ball as far as he could and I ran to it as fast as I could, then finally I extended my hands out and I grabbed it and ran into the end-zone. The crowd cheered and we won the game. Will is born on February 9th (**29**) 19**77**. Our first year on varsity we won our first game then we lost 7 games in a row, ending up 1 and 7 that year. It was a hard year but it forged my friendship with **Courtlan** and my other teammates. Him and I depended on each other. We lost 7 in a row but we almost won a lot of those games and most of the time it was **Courtlan** and **I** rising to the occasion. In everything there is a pattern! I had two **Haitian** team mates who shared the same exact name, **Patrick Hilair**. I am still friends with both of them to this day. One is born on September 17th (pages 66, 67, 68) two days before **Emmett Till's Murder** trial started in 1955 (page 516). Like myself and Angel (page 63) the two numbers in the middle of his social security number are **62** (pages 41, 221, 508, 602)! The other Patrick is born on July 3rd (page 138) the same day that I had the revelation of my **past life** as **Emmett Till** on July 3rd 2018. The cheerleader standing behind Will Holland (number 77) is Monique Wallace. I was in love with her. Her birthday is Feb 9th (**29**) like Will F (p 63).

Iu f Per f m heru

Utterances for Coming Forth by day into Light

Weed in The 90's

It is he, who comes forth by day into Light

I never smoked weed as a teenager in fact I didn't smoke till I was **33** years old and I met **Ice T** that night but we'll get to that later (page 194).. When I was in high school **I got my high from running**. I would run the beaches of Far Rockaway at night with my football in my hand while listening to Hip Hop in my walkman (The football Run away, **Heb Sed**, April 3rd 2016, page 373). When I was in high school there was a guy on the varsity football team whom's name I do not Ramember. He played defense and he could hit really hard. We looked up to him or at least I did. It took me some time to adjust to running into people at high speeds and tackling them. I had the fear of hurting myself. I eventually developed my own technique of bringing people to the ground without causing too much harm. I did however use my speed against my own teammates sometimes. To be fare I did this in games too. If I found myself playing defense or blocking I might catch someone on the opposing team running my direction but looking the other way. I would lay them out. It would hurt. On the field I could not be caught and I was elusive. Tackling me was not easy. Ok enough about me and back to this guy on the varsity team. All of a sudden one day he changed completely and was never the same. It was as if he was in some sort of a daze. If you said what's up to him his only reply would be - "nothing, just chillin", and he would stare off into the distance. The rumor was that his **weed** had been **laced** and as a result he was never the same. The last thing I ever heard about him was that he ended up in jail. Apparently he tried to rape a woman in broad daylight, at least that is what I heard. In college I heard of another tragedy involving weed so this made it easy for me to not smoke weed (p 73). I was also very fast and I had heard that smoking would weaken your lungs and reduce your speed, armed with that belief* and the fear of ending up like the guy on my team, smoking weed never appealed to me. **I was getting my high scoring touchdowns** anyway but you will see what happened when I finally did smoke weed in 2011 (page 194). I smoked weed for the first time when I was **33** years old, on December 31st 2010 (page 194). I smoked weed heavily for 5 years then I stopped. It wasn't till I began writing this book that I realized weed had opened up **High Frequency Psychic Channels** where prophetic messages were channeled down through my thoughts (pages 208, 227, 238, 282, 343).

Hip Hop Over High School
WKCR Stretch & Bobbito and The Strange Freestyle Session With The Cella Dwellas

"Phantasm the lyrical **emperor** tempting ya with beats, sweets and treats for the tummy, brains and honey, like the cheerios **bumble bee immortality,** enables me to live **infinitely**, which means I'll have longevity, I remember tails of Rumpelstiltskin, sing a song of six pin, playing dungeons and dragons in a big pig pin with the other children of the Gods up in heaven, imagine a vex underground, made the thunder pound, so he had to run to his cavern, I trained and road a dinosaur and lived cross town, in a little tavern now it's call the Gavin, California the state, now that we left, the Gods get vexed that's why they still have earthquakes, I light my lantern to explore the corridor and use the portal to emerge to the surface floor, then I view the planet earth for what it's worth **and see why I was placed here for birth** and not in **my holy temple**, too much adventure for a child's mental it's simple, *it's sort of like the story of superman how world destroyed, so now we're here on this land, with no super human powers, only my six sense and visions after hours, I see psychics and gypsies I can't afford*, and **swamis** for **predictions** on the ouija board, the triangular magic game to get **insight on my planet and real name**, live in Flatbush with my aunty **Em**, like Peter **Parker** I keep my secret from the rest of them, I have food shelter and my girl, but I still fantasize about the 3rd world" - **Phantasm (Cella Dwella's)**

"The murderous scum, hey my thumb starts to swell, when I see visions of hunchback ringing a church bell, the carousel is spinning I'm getting nauseous, I'm cautious of holy symbols and crosses, my heart pumps various gravies and sauces, my eyes smell like prunes from the fumes and the tar pits, then the goblins sits on my lap, suck'n black milk from my tittie, as I go on like this hey the ambulance, all right, lives are saved, **at 4000 years of age** I have my pubic hair shaved, I bathe in the blood of my friends, the apocalypse begins, I down my ceremonial robe and contact **Egyptian kings**, the glistening of multi color scales of **dragons** leave you in horror, I raise my kids like batches or lava, I sort of chewed off my right hand now **I'm a lefty**, left her wonder why God won't help me, it's spookier nuclear, reaction the sun run, nadafuel poor it in the pool, cool with the mind, while they rule, is he 9? Sign is mister, fingers blister when they're near a pen my friend begins to whisper" **- UG (Cella Dwella's)**

"The **resurrection rebirth** realm 3 heaven and earth, scenery dungeon fog like in **London**, welcome to a time of no hydraulic pits, no politics, no democracy or space odyssey, 3000 and one no more automatic guns just laser ones, I'll be throwing planets and suns, from beneath the cella, comes the original dwella with x amount of styles, mad like the X Files, call me the 6 foot 3 tall man Phantasm, *sending chills down spines for back spasms*, orgasms all in your mind, I'm fuck'n with ya head, **it's the sign of the times**, I seen John Coltrane on a cold train dying from the flu playing the sax, with his last breath he said use this on your track, I'll inject **streams of dreams** like the professor from the X-Men, and **Buddha** bless when I'm hex'n, so listen at night for my call of the wild, the sun the moon the star **the birth" - Phantasm (Cella Dwella's)**

"I've been thrown into an unknown, **mathematics** induces fabrics to **interweave**, disease, mind hunts sunshine on seas shores, I cause and effect, I suspect bitten by insects, did some good, skin turned to wood, I throw back my hood, it should radiate alpha particles according to article 6 of my textbook tactics, much practice, survival yes medieval, multi personality switch" **- UG (Cella Dwella's)**

The Cella Dwellas Significance

I only did the bare minimum in high school. I would stay up real late on school nights listening to radio stations where rappers would come up for interviews and to freestyle. This freestyle session from **Cella Dwellas** was my favorite freestyle session from my whole time listening to underground Hip Hop in high school and now I realize that it was my soul that was attracted to it. My youtube search history says I listened to this on September 13th 2019, which was a year and 3 months after my past life revelation of Emmett Till.. September 13th is also the day **Tupac** died. I had not heard this freestyle since I was in high school and to my surprise every verse of this freestyle session speaks to my **Prophecy Of Reincarnation**. I have highlighted the obvious ones and left others for your imaginations. **Marcel Frasher** and I were one of the few people in school who would come to school with the tapes we recorded the previous night. I recently spoke to my friend **Alvin Latimore** (**Foul Al**) from JR school 180 and he told me that he used to copy his tapes and sell them (p 59). He said he made a lot of money like that. Unfortunately I wasn't that entrepreneurial.

October 25th 1994, The Artifacts Coded Within Hip Hop

When I heard the Artifacts for the first time I was a fan immediately. I liked a lot of their music but their song, **Wrong Side Of The Tracks** would be my all time favorite song from them. The strangeness surrounding the Artifacts and my revelation starts with their name, **Artifacts**! Artifacts are objects made by human beings from earlier periods in time typically items of cultural or historical interest and the most famous artifacts ever found in modern time are the ones found in **Tutankhaten's** (**King Tut's**) tomb in 19**22**, year of the **DOG**.. The most famous piece of all being the **golden death mask**. The "Artifacts" would release their first album on my 17th birthday, **Oct 25th** in 1994, year of the **DOG**. The first single off their second album would be titled The Art of facts and in that song the word ***resurrection*** would be used. The first verse is ended with these words - "Analyze'n more spots than Madlock, now I got this rap'n shit on padlock, you only half-rock, my shit ***returns** like **resurrections** in religion*". On July 3rd 2018 my **past life** as **Emmett Till** would be revealed and on April 4th 2020 my **past life** as **Tutankhaten** (**King Tut**) would be revealed. On Feb **22nd** 2011(p 189), I would mention The Artifacts in my song **Time Traveling** - "A yo believe me I been loving **Hip Hop** way before the **CD**, my **TAPE** fixing it when it break, staying up late, no internet, no status update, I hit eject, flip the tape put it back in the deck then call my ace, A yo you heard that new track from **Artifacts, Wrong Side of the Tracks**?!" 1 month before the Artifacts debuted, **Tupac** dropped the **Thug Life** album on Sep 26th 1994, 3 days after the **Emmett Till's** trial ended in 19**55** (p 516). The first song on the album is **Bury Me a G** and on the second verse, Tupac's brother, **Mopreme Shukar** say's, "and to the G's you can feel my pain, until the motherfucker gets **born again**". The first single for the album was, **Pour Out a Little Liquor** and it was released on Aug **23**rd, the day before Emmett Till entered the store that got him killed. The second single was, **Cradle to the Grave** and it was released on Nov 4th 1994, the same day that **King Tut's**) tomb was discovered in 19**22**. On the song **Under pressure** Tupac says, "Right before I die, I'll be cursin' the law, **Reincarnated** bitch, even worse than before". The first **Common Connection** from **Common Sense** happened in 1995 the second in 1997 (p **77**). **Common Sense** would release the single **Resurrection** the next year on **April 4th 1995** and **25** years later I would have my **past life** revelation of **King Tut** on April 4th 2020 (p 594). After Tupac's death (p 76) many of his unfinished songs were leaked. One of those was a track called **Reincarnation** (p 300). On this song Tupac can be heard saying the following words, "My only fear of death, is **reincarnation**, I use my last breath, to reach the whole nation, How can they call me murderer for my spoken words? This composition be my **prophecy** I hope it's heard". I have a theory about who Tupac was in his past life (p 664) and this book, **TutemRa: The Prophecy of Reincarnation,** is the **"prophecy"** that Tupac spoke of in his song, **Reincarnation**. In ancient Kemet the concept of reincarnation was called the **Wehem-Mesut** (repeating of births, page 14). This book was brought forth in 2022, the 49th anniversary of Hip Hop and 49 days is the amount of time the Tibetans believed it took one soul to be reborn into another life. I am the **Alchemist** coded within **Hip Hop** (p 633). This is **Divine Alchemy** of the soul, the only alchemy that matters!

Rau nu Prt m heru

lu f Per f m heru

Utterances for Coming Forth by day into Light

It is he, who comes forth by day into Light

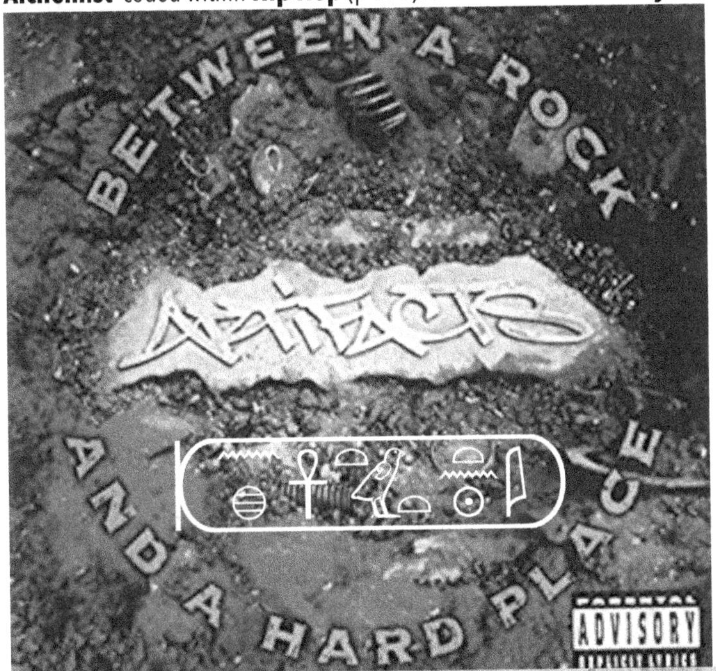

A Course in divine Statistics

I started playing organized football in the 10th grade and ever since I have played ironman. I played offense, defense, punt return and kick return. There was very little time that I wasn't on the force field of play. In my senior year I would score **5** receiving touchdowns and all of them were for **55** yards or more. My life path (**Ptah**) number is **5** and Emmett was murdered in 19**55**. Akhenaten's (King Tut's father) remains were said to be found in the Valley of the Kings site KV**55** (page 41) I even got a grade of **55** nine times while in high school (page 70). In my senior year I averaged **42** yards every time I touched the ball. The number **42** correlates with the principles of **Maat** (truth, justice, harmonious balance, moral righteousness, reciprocity and cosmic order, **<u>42 Laws of Maat, page 367</u>**). I was instrumental in the **2** games we won our senior year and the number **22** can be seen in the score of both games. Emmett Till's father, **Louis Till** was born in 19**22** and Tutankhaten's (**King Tut's**) tomb was discovered in 19**22**. My **mother** was born in 19**55** and **22** years later when she was **22,** I was born again in 19**77**. My teammate and best friend, **Courtlan** is born on July **22** (page 64). During my 11th and 12th year of high school I lived with my grand parents on 311 Beach 27th street and I took the **Q-22** bus to school everyday. This book was released in 20**22**.

DAWUD EDDINGS

School: Beach Channel (2-6, 0-4 PSAL Queens).
Position: Wide receiver.
Year: Senior.
Height / Weight: 5-11, 170.
1995 Highlights: Scored more than half of Beach Channel's touchdowns this season, including five receiving scores, two punt returns, one kickoff return and one interception return . . . All five touchdown receptions were for 55 yards or more . . . Averaged 42 yards every time he touched the ball . . . Was instrumental in the Dolphins' only two wins, shaking off a first-quarter left ankle sprain to catch an 80-yard touchdown pass and adding a 62-yard interception return in a 30-22 victory over Boys & Girls, and returning a kickoff 80 yards and a punt 75 yards for scores in a 22-8 win over Stevenson . . . Returned the opening kickoff 90 yards for a touchdown in PSAL Queens all-star game.
Coach's comments: "He was super. He was the big part of our attack. We were 2-6 and he had real big games in the games we won. We had him all over the place. He was very dynamic . . . Dawud was terrific. He had a great season." — Mike Magid
Player's comments: I tried to make the best of it whenever I touched the ball. When I'm on the field, I try to do what I can . . . [The 2-6 season] was hard. But I didn't think of it. I just went out and played."
Recruiting roundup: Junior college.

I was a wide receiver on a running team and because of that I didn't get the ball in my hands often, so I made every possession count. I never met another player faster than me in any game I played through out my time playing football. The coaches of the opposing teams had me covered by two defenders sometimes. This helped our potential for running the ball. I was a diversion. They did not kick the ball in my direction on kick offs or punt returns so I found other ways of getting my hands on the ball. I would knock down passes and catch interceptions. One time a cornerback intercepted a pass that was thrown to me and less then two strides later without breaking a stride I took the ball out of his hand, spun away from him and proceeded to score a touchdown. I could have tackled him but I wanted the ball so I took it!

I developed a **high vertical leap** and I can remember the feeling of **floating in the air** when jumping to catch passes. It was all happening in slow motion for me. Football was my **high**. The **high** that I got from those plays lasted long after the games. Even the act of remembering them evokes a **high**. Every time I did something incredible I would wonder if I could EVER top that play. Then sure enough we would be in need and I would rise to the occasion and do the amazing.

I was never happy about the fact that my teammates took the All City picture without me. To me it was like the Bulls taking a picture without Jordan. I was the Jordan of the team. I knew it and the coaches knew it. With all the talent that I had I was never given the guidance I needed to ensure that I was doing what I needed to be doing in class. I never took school seriously because I didn't know how it would affect my life. I wasn't a class clown but I cracked jokes in class a lot and disrupted the class at times - to the point that I was almost placed in special education. My grandmother did not go along with that though and I stopped disrupting classes after that.

Row 1: Christopher Green, Andres Guzman-Acha. Row 2: Patrick Hillaire, Jose Cid, Robert McCracken.

Rau nu Prt m heru

Iu f Per f m heru

1996, Shoeboxes full of College Letters

I was blinded by the **shoeboxes full of division 1 letters** I was receiving in the mail. I thought my skill was going to get me into a college. I still remember the Army recruiter trying to get me to enlist but I laughed at him telling him that I was going to the **NFL**. In school I always seemed to find myself in some trouble. I went to class but every now and then I walked the halls and cut classes. Gym, girls and football were my favorite parts of school. I spent more time listening to Hip Hop while in high school than anything else. I would call **Patrick** everyday and recite my rhymes to him. He would always listen and tell me liked them. I used to stay up late on school nights to record the radios shows when rappers came on for interviews. This is how I stumbled across radio stations that spoke on topics not heard on day time radio. I still remember hearing a guy say that **VISA** was the **Mark of the Beast** because **VI** was **6** in **Roman numerals**, **S** was **6** in **Greek** and **A** was **6** in **Babylonian**. And that the **Dodge RAM** logo was an **Illuminati** symbol that represented **Baphomet**. The next day I told **Javet** about this and she thought I was crazy (pages 147, 291). Perhaps this was the beginnings of me searching for info not taught in school. When I did find hip hop stations, listening to people freestyle was my favorite part. I was never really good at freestyle'n and when I think about it now it makes sense because I didn't read many books as a teen and I never practiced freestyle'n. I only halfway read what was needed for class. I excelled on the football field and that's all that mattered to me! If I wasn't good at anything else I made up for it all with the way I played football. I had speed, quickness and I jumped really high and during the games my abilities seemed to intensify. I was addicted to the roar of the crowd but I had no plan and no idea how I would live my life in society as an adult. In the 3 years I played football at Beach Channel I only had family come to one game. During my senior year, my aunt Karen came at the very end of one of my games. She brought my grand mother, my cousin Brenden and my sister Jenna. My grand mother says she saw me catch a pass and run for a touch down. Football was my only plan in life but I wasn't wise enough to realize that my grades would affect my ability to play at a division 1 school. I had no real understanding of how the world worked. One day the "fat" track coach asked me to join the track team so I did. One day I missed practice because I went to football practice instead and he tried to reprimand me. I only cared about football so I told him, "I didn't join the track team, you joined me". He looked at me with a dazed look and walked away. He never spoke to me again. I was arrogant and I never went back to the track team. The second person to ever suggest the **Army** was my grand father. I can still remember that day. I was in the 12th grade and I'd missed the **Q-22** bus and was late for school so he drove me. On the ride to school my grandfather said to me, **"Boy, you should join the army"**, and I responded, **"I ain't joining no white mans army"**. He looked at me with piercing eyes and said nothing for the rest of the ride. He didn't like the way I responded to him. Looking back I guess he was trying to help me with my future as he probably didn't see what I would possibly do with my life. I hadn't any plans and had not talked about anything. I had all those letters from those colleges but I wasn't looking into any. I was just going through the motions. **In fact when the college scouts came to my school they left immediately after they saw my grades. They even scolded my coaches for wasting their time.** That one time that my grandfather suggested the **Army** was the only time anyone in my family had ever talked to me about doing anything with my life beyond high school. 4 years later I would find myself in the **Army**.

Utterances for Coming Forth by day into Light

It is he, who comes forth by day into Light

What Will I Do With My Life?

I was never taught about sex or the birds and the bees by any man. I had to learn about sex on my own. I had sex for the first time at 17 and it was a bad experience. I was never taught about the meaning of life or about the history of African people or the history of the **Black negroid** indigenous people who were here in America (Turtle Island) before Columbus. I was never taught to **hate** white people but I was also never taught about all the evil things white people had done to black people that might cause black people to hate white people. I grew up around white people and had them as landlord's, teachers, classmates, teammates, coaches and police etc. I was also never taught to **love** black people but somehow I always instinctively knew that I should love black people. You sort or learn some things naturally, as you grow up in this world. Without being told I could tell that things were different with white and black people. Just like a mouse learns to beware of the cat, I learned that I had to beware of the trap. I never did "drugs" as a teen or drank alcohol. They never appealed to me. There are many was we can go wrong in life. The biggest misstep is not taking the adequate time to study the past so that you fully understand the terrain of the world that you live in or more importantly not teaching your children about the past so that they fully understand the terrain of the world they live in. I used to get in trouble during history class when I insisted on asking questions about **what came before what we were being** taught. The teachers claimed I was, "disrupting the class". **But I was searching for a timeline**. Some how I knew there was a history that was being kept from me. I bumped my head many times in life because I had no knowledge of who or what I was as an African indigenous person on this planet. I had no purpose and did not know what I would do with my life. I began to chase girls and developed unhealthy dating habits. I never took school very seriously because I didn't understand the part schooling played in my success in life. Or at least how important degrees are when it comes to finding work in the world today. I was lucky that I was good at a sport. I never sold drugs and did not have good grades so my only way out the hood was Football. My love for football was all I had and because I was so good at it I figured that I would naturally do that. At this time in my life I had only heard the name **Marcus Garvey** once and that was in the **Nas** song, Half Time.

Things I was Never told about Malcolm X, Martin Luther King and the Black Panther Movement

I was born into a world that is at war with me but I was never taught that. I would not fully understand this fight that I was in until I was an adult. Before then it was a gradual awakening to the horrors of the past and what had happened to others that look like me. It is in this system that I was raised! However for some reason I never feared white people. I didn't know enough about what white people had done to black people to be cautious of them. For some reason during my teenage years my greatest fear was that I might be killed by one of my brothers. That another 'Black" male might take my life. It is not that I was afraid of them. I have actually never been afraid of black people yet still I developed this fear as a teenager because of the violence I saw and heard about in my environment. It seemed like brothers from different projects were always at war with each other. learning about how Malcolm X was murdered by other black men further increased that fear and or distrust. Seeing the image of Malcolm being shot to death in the movie Malcolm X by **Spike Lee**, never left my subconscious. I was not old enough to understand all the hidden hands involved with the murder of Malcolm X , or the murder of Martin Luther King JR, or the murder of Fred Hampton. In fact, back then I had never heard of **Fred Hampton** or **Emmett Till** for that matter. It was only after my past life as Emmett Till was revealed to me in 2018, that I came to know that **Fred Hampton's** mother **Iberia Hampton** used to babysit **"Emmett Till"**. I would also come to know that black men had been involved with the kidnapping of Emmett Till (pages 507-508) and perhaps that is where my fear of being killed by another black male came from.

When I was in high school, the only speech I heard from Martin Luther King was the famous, "**I Have a Dream Speech**". And I was only taught about Martin's "peaceful protests". I never heard what Martin said about **reparations**. After Malcolm X was assassinated Martin spoke out against the Vietnam war and said the following about reparations, "At the very same time that America refused to give the Negro any land, through an act of Congress our government was giving away millions of acres of land in the West and Midwest. Which meant that it was willing to undergird its white peasants from Europe with an economic floor. But not only did they give the land, they built land grant colleges with government money to teach them how to farm. Not only that, they provided county agents to further their expertise in farming. Not only that, they provided low interest rates in order that they could mechanize their farms. Not only that, today many of these people are receiving millions of dollars in federal subsidies, to not farm and they are the very people telling the black man to lift himself by his own bootstraps. This is what we are faced with, and this is the reality. Now, when we come to Washington in this campaign **we are coming to get our check**." When you read those words from Martin you can see why he began to feel that he had, "lead his people into a burning house" (**Clemency**, page 435). Martin was seen as a threat and he was subsequently assassinated. **J Edgar Hoover**, who was the head of the F.B.I. once warned that the American government needed to prevent the rise of a "**black Messiah**" which lead to the arrest and deportation of **Marcus Garvey** (pages 21, 256, 287, 312, 320, 375, 417 etc etc) then the deaths of **Malcolm X** (pages 44, 48, 58, 291, 561-565, 463) and later **Martin Luther King** (page 58,94, 102, 130, 277, 592). They didn't stop there though. Two days after Martin was assassinated, **Bobby Hutton** was killed on April 6, 1968, by Oakland Police officers (pages 217, 376, 463). 6 months after Martin was assassinated his younger brother **Alfred King** was found dead in his home pool. Alfred's wife, Naomi King, always felt his death was suspicious because Alfred was a good swimmer.. Many others in the black movement for Civil Rights saw his death as another assassination, so as to prevent him from filling the shoes of his brother. The next year, on December 4th 1969, **Fred Hampton** and M**ark** C**lark** (members in the Black Panther Party for self Defense), were assassinated by the **F.B.I.**. 6 years after Martin was assassinated his mother, **Alberta King** was murdered as she played the organ during a Sunday church service. She was murdered by **Marcus Chenault**, a 21-year-old black man from Ohio who claimed, "All Christians are my enemies". The records say that Marcus Chenault was a follower of the Hebrew Israelite faith but we must NEVER FORGET the words of Malcolm X , **"They will pay a black man to kill a black man just to say a black man did it"**. And I think this is exactly what happened in the deaths of Malcolm X and Martin Luther King's mother. **Dick Gregory** was quoted saying, "If anybody can believe that a Cat can go berserk in Dayton Ohio and get on a bus with two guns and don't shoot nobody until he gets to Atlanta, in church, then they crazy! Do you realize how much aim and how much practice one must have to be able to hit somebody in the head three times with a handgun? It's just totally unbelievable. And so I definitely don't rule conspiracy out. It's the same pattern with Sirhan Sirhan, **Lee Harvey Oswald** and **James Earl Ray**; that every time one of those persons was arrested, they went to his house and found some other stuff in it. Now they go to **Chenault's** house and find a diary with 10 other names in it. See, it's the same **pattern** that is followed." On December 8, 1999, a four-week civil trial determined that local, state and federal U.S government agencies, and the Mafia, were all involved in the murder of Martin Luther King. Dr William Pepper was Martin's family doctor and he was given info by a nurse named, R. Shelby, who was in Martin's operating room at Saint Josephs Hospital. She says that **Martin survived the shooting but was spit on and suffocated by Dr Breen Bland, a white neurosurgeon**. 56 years after Malcolm X was assassinated, Muhammad Aziz and his co-defendant Khalil Islam, the two black men convicted of killing Malcolm X in 1965, were exonerated in November 2021. They received a $36 million settlement after lawsuits were filed on their behalf against both the city and the state of New York last year. **"How long shall they kill our prophets, while we stand aside and look? Some say it's just a part of it; we've got to fulfill the book" - Bob Marley**

Rau

nu

Prt

m

heru

lu

f

Per

f

m

heru

TRANSCRIPT OF HIGH SCHOOL RECORD

STUDENT INFORMATION

EDDINGS DAWUD

311 B 27 ST

FAR ROCKAWAY NY 11691

SEX	BIRTH DATE	DATE ENTERED SECONDARY SCHOOL	EXPECTED DATE OF GRADUATION
M	10/25/77	09/20/93	*****

SIX SEMESTER RANK IN CLASS DATA

TOTAL POINTS	NO. OF MARKS	AVERAGE	RANK	GROUP SIZE	%ILE STANDING
3304	/ 46.0	= 71.83	121 IN	330	= 63.33

OFFICIAL CLASS 63AE BATES NO. 8880

68.3 RANK INDEX 73.7

SCHOOL INFORMATION

B CHANNEL
100-00 BEACH CHAN D
ROCKAWAY PAR 11694

CLASS PD (MIN)	MEETING WK	WEEKS YR	PASS GRADE	DATE
45	5	40	65	07/01/95

CEEB SCHOOL NUMBER	CLASS SIZE	SCHOOL ACCREDITED BY
334874	330	NY ST. DEPT

ACADEMIC RECORD

AREA	UNITS	AVG
ENGLISH	7.0	71
SOC STUD	8.0	69
MATH	6.0	71
SCIENCE	6.0	70
FOR LANG	1.0	56
OCC. EDUC.	2.0	95
ART/MUSIC	8.0	78
HE/PHYS ED	1.0	85

VERBAL AVERAGE 67
MATH SCIENCE AVERAGE 70

GRADE 9 — 92

SUBJECT	TERM 1	TERM 2
COM GRAPH1 J		96
STUDIO ART J		80
9TH ENG J	80	80
VIDEO J		95
9TH GLOBAL J	75	75
9 YR SHOP J	95	95
9YR FUND M J	90	90
9YRPHY ED1 J		90*
9THPHYSSCI J	75	75

UNITS 13.0 GRADE AVG 84.6

GRADE 10 — 93

SUBJECT	TERM 1	TERM 2
PAINTING1	65	
COMM ARTS3	80	
GLOB HIST3	50	
SEQ MATH 1	55	
POWER TRNG	40*	
MAR BIO 1	50	
MARBIOLAB1	U	
COMM ARTS4		80
GLOB HIST3		CR
GLOB HIST4		65
RCT PREP1		CR
RCT PREP2		70
HEALTH		85
GEN BIO 1		CR
BIOLOGY 2		85

UNITS 10.0 GRADE AVG 68.5

GRADE 11 — 94

SUBJECT	TERM 1	TERM 2
COMM ARTS5	65	
SPANISH 1	55	
AMER HIST1	55	
SEQ MATH 1	75	
FTBL/BKTBL	80*	
REG BIO	CR	
BIO LAB 1	U	
ELEM MUSIC	95	
SCULPTURE		85
DRAWING		65
COMM ARTS6		65
SPANISH 1		65
AMER HIST1		75
SEQ MATH 2		50
GYM/LAB		55*
REG BIO		65
BIO LAB 2		S
PHYS ED 1 7		75

UNITS 10.0 GRADE AVG 67.9

GRADE 12 — 95

SUBJECT	TERM 1	TERM 2
PORTFOLIO2	65	
COMM ARTS7	65	
SPANISH 2	55	
AMER HIST2	65	
AMER HIST3	65	
SEQ MATH 2	55	
POWER TRNG	85*	
ARTHISTORY		[illegible] H
COMM ARTS8		[illegible]
SPANISH 2		50
ECONOMICS		93
SEQ MATH 2		80
PE SURVY 2		90*
POWER TRNG		85*

UNITS 6.0 GRADE AVG 63.9

EXAMINATIONS	SCORES	EXAMINATIONS	SCORES
COMP ART RR	55		
ENG REGENTR	51		
SEQM I REGR	78		
ENG REGENTR	57		
SEQM I REGR	51		
ENG REGENTR	AB		
SEQM I REGR	AB		
BIO REGENTR	AB		

FAILURES	TERM	YR
ARTHISTORY	2	4
COMM ARTS8	2	4
SPANISH 2	2	4
SPANISH 2	1	4
SEQ MATH 2	1	4
SEQ MATH 2	2	3
GYM/LAB	2	3
SPANISH 1	1	3
AMER HIST1	1	3
BIO LAB 1	1	3
GLOB HIST3	1	2
SEQ MATH 1	1	2
TOO MANY		

LEGEND FOR THIS SCHOOL

SCHOOL NOW 2 TERM YR, WAS 4 CYCLES .5 CREDIT= 1 CYCLE WORK; 1 CREDIT = 1 TERM; 2 CREDITS = 1 YEAR "UNIT" CODES: J = JR. HS; TERM 7 = SUMMER SCHOOL; TERMS 5 & 6 = EVENING SCHOOL. GRADES INCLUDE: 01 = LATE ENTRANT; 02= NON-ENGLISH SPEAKING; 09= MEDICAL EXCUSE FROM PHYS. ED; +0 =100 %. EXAMS: R = REGENTS; C = CITYWIDE; S = SCHOOL. STARTING AUG 1991, 40 CREDITS ARE NEEDED FOR GRADUATION. H = HONORS WEIGHT RANK USED

GRADE 12

SUBJECT	TERM 1	TERM 2

GRADE 9 — 92

SUBJECT	TERM 1	TERM 2
COM GRAPH1 J		96
STUDIO ART J		80
9TH ENG J	80	80
VIDEO J		95
9TH GLOBAL J	75	75
9 YR SHOP J	95	95
9YR FUND M J	90	90
9YRPHY ED1 J		90*
9THPHYSSCI J	75	75

UNITS 13.0 GRADE AVG 84.6

GRADE 10 — 93

SUBJECT	TERM 1	TERM 2
PAINTING1	65	
COMM ARTS3	80	
GLOB HIST3	50	
SEQ MATH 1	55	
POWER TRNG	40*	
MAR BIO 1	50	
MARBIOLAB1	U	
COMM ARTS4		80
GLOB HIST3		CR
GLOB HIST4		65
RCT PREP1		CR
RCT PREP2		70
HEALTH		85
GEN BIO 1		CR
BIOLOGY 2		85

UNITS 10.0 GRADE AVG 68.5

GRADE 11 — 94

SUBJECT	TERM 1	TERM 2
COMM ARTS5	65	
SPANISH 1	55	
AMER HIST1	55	
SEQ MATH 1	75	
FTBL/BKTBL	80*	
REG BIO	CR	
BIO LAB 1	U	
ELEM MUSIC	95	
SCULPTURE		85
DRAWING		65
COMM ARTS6		65
SPANISH 1		65
AMER HIST1		75
SEQ MATH 2		50
GYM/LAB		55*
REG BIO		65
BIO LAB 2		S
PHYS ED 1 7		75

UNITS 10.0 GRADE AVG 67.9

GRADE 12 — 95

SUBJECT	TERM 1	TERM 2
PORTFOLIO2	65	
COMM ARTS7	65	
SPANISH 2	55	
AMER HIST2	65	
AMER HIST3	65	
SEQ MATH 2	55	
POWER TRNG	85*	
ARTHISTORY		[illegible] H
COMM ARTS8		[illegible]
SPANISH 2		50
ECONOMICS		93
SEQ MATH 2		80
PE SURVY 2		90*
POWER TRNG		85*

UNITS 6.0 GRADE AVG 63.9

ACADEMIC RECORD

AREA	UNITS	AVG
ENGLISH	7.0	71
SOC STUD	8.0	69
MATH	6.0	71
SCIENCE	6.0	70
FOR LANG	1.0	56
OCC. EDUC.	2.0	95
ART/MUSIC	8.0	78
HE/PHYS ED	1.0	85

VERBAL AVERAGE 67
MATH/SCIENCE AVERAGE 70

Utterances

for

Coming

Forth

by day

into

Light

It is

he,

who

comes

forth

by day

into

Light

WE NEED OUR OWN SCHOOLS

This message is for the ones who find themselves failing classes and or in the principles office. What ever you decide to dedicate your time to you can master. There is no class that you can't excel at if you focus your time and attention on it. Most people go to college trying to get ahead but what good is college if it doesn't get you fed? Most people graduate with a business degree yet they end up working for other people, never using the degree they paid for. I left high school and went on to college where I got A's and B's until my fallout with my coach (p 73). I left college and decided to play a different game, the play of consciousness. I followed the unbeaten path of **chance** and **fate**. When reading this book use your **divine intuition** which is more valuable than what we learn in schools paid for with tuition. The state known as sleep and or death, is our natural state and **life** is the "**class**" that we must use to develop or enhance our **psychic abilities** because sleep/death is where we spend most of our "**time**". We are here to expand and if we don't we can end up being the walking dead with not ability of affect our affairs in the underworld/death/sleep or to affect the living world. There for we must subject ourselves to discipline and practice.. I could have been a rich athlete but that never happened yet still I'm happy with where my life has taken me but where will your eternal life take you?

I Graduated, Barely

I barely graduated high school because I had to make up many late homework assignments. I wasn't supposed to walk across stage but at the last minute one of my teachers gave me a gown and told me to walk. I can't remember the teachers name but when Principle Hassan saw me on stage, a look of surprise covered her face as she shook my hand, smiled and handed me my diploma.

ADDENDUM

The manifestation of the Buckingham Palace Remix

The **Buckingham Palace Remix** is the most recent Hekau (rhyme) I have written. I started it on February 17, 2023, which is **Huey P's** birthday (p 93), which is also the same day that **Khalid Muhammad** was assassinated (pages 440, 666). I finished the rhyme on February 19, 2023, which is my great grand father, General Dukes Sr's birthday (p 19). I fell in love with Hip Hop in the early 90's and I started writing rhymes as a passive hobby in the mid 90's, just before I went to college (p 77). When I left college, the frequency of my writing decreased and when I joined the Army I barley wrote any rhymes (p 80). When I got out of the Army in 2005 I wrote 24 rhymes, then stopped writing for 5 years (p 131). After my grand father, General Dukes Jr died in 2009 (p 169) I started writing rhymes again in 2010 (p 180). On my lyrical journey I searched for many of the nostalgic beats from my youth but one beat eluded me and every other poet who desired to write a rhyme to it. The beat in question was the classic beat, **Buckingham Palace** from **Canibus'** Debut album. I searched for this beat for years and never found it until Feb 17, 2023. It was uploaded in March 16, 2022, the day after **Shanta's** birthday (p 289), two weeks before I went to Kemet (Egypt) for the first time in this life (p 670). In the creation of my ode to Canibus I used elements from the his song, Buckingham Palace. The lyrics can be seen below and **all references are underlined.** I wrote the first verse on the 17th, I started the second verse on the night of the 18th and when I woke up on the 19th I finished the second verse and wrote the third verse. Afterwards I saw that Canibus had recently done an interview with **Nems**. I watched the whole video and realized that Canibus never knew how much he was loved by Emcee's and how much he was indeed esteemed as a lyrical champion. In the interview he spoke about having a **boat**. That night I went to sleep and when I woke up on Feb 20th, I woke from a **dream with Canibus**. Him and I were on a **submarine** together. When I woke from the **dream,** I told Shanta about my **dream** and to my surprise she had a similar **dream**. She **dreamt** that I was in water and at some point her and I were on a **boat** together. I had been recently talking to her about practicing **lucid dreaming** with the intent of mastering **shared dreaming** (pages 452 & 589). Prior to writing the **Buckingham Palace Remix** I had not had a Top **10 Hip Hop Artist list** in this book but because of this experience I took the time make several lists (p 72). When I searched for a picture of Canibus to add to this book I found a picture of him in the **Ausarian pose of Resurrection** (pages 380, 481, 600, 625, 664, 671). Remember that you are Ausar and Heru, the hero! See page 3 for the **hero's journey!**

ADDENDUM Buckingham Palace Remix

Started on February 17, 2023 and finished on February 19, 2023

Aye yo, Eye appear in front of Giza with a time travel visa and mind readers look'n at me and call'n me the **Negus**, the most high, before you ever live you gotta die, most try to live forever but they never profit, **TutemRa** will be here forever! do you understand? I am the boy king, they found buried in the sand, a soul survivor, they stole my gold, pied piper, Diana starring at me like she's bitten by a viper, forbidden rhymes written spit'n in a cypher, **Amen** dreams hidden **Ausar** risen decipher, a body in a river, a trigger a lighter, **Martin's** vision spark'n a dream, and if you can hear, smell, see, touch and taste, then you can feel what they feel when they seen what they did to my face in the Jet magazine, faced with the face of death, **Emmett Till** the ultimate executioners dream, shit is Stillmatic, killed over skittles and Ice T, I wield magic from ancient papyrus and tablets, so there you have it, the **Ballot Or The Bullet**, The Ballad of the dead abbott, stay **crook**ed… ***when I say Tut Ankh, you say Aten, Tut Ankh***, *Aten* , ***Tut Ankh***, *Aten*, ***when I say Never, you say forgotten, Never***, *Forgotten*, ***Never***, *Forgotten…..*

My Naga **Netic** set it off with Kenetic energy, there's never a loss in death when you cultivate the inner chi, when the **Kemetic yoga** is mixed with the **Manna** it's like a spaceship that dips to Nirvana, face the trauma, everything I say is true, if you follow my path and do the things I do, and yet still the great mysteries are not shown to you, continue the path and **To Maat Be True**, and perhaps in due time you'll be worthy of the view, do you see that? I give you the Facts of Life Kim Fields, this is a life hack like the big wheel, believe that, they came happy, left shook daddy, attacked by the ghost of **Hatshepsut** from **The Nile Valley**, that's my word is bond like ionic, super sonic, telekinesis, hunting **Orion**, a **D**ead **M**ans **T**reasure, to be born again or die trying! tell me how could eye ever lose! I took the blueprint from the human rubrics cube, they mesmerized raising the dead in front of their eyes, spiritually on a scale of 1-10 I'm **25** ***when I say Tut Ankh, you say Aten, Tut Ankh***, *Aten* , ***Tut Ankh***, *Aten*, ***when I say Never, you say forgotten, Never***, *Forgotten*, ***Never***, *Forgotten……*

This the truth serum, they came here to kill em Quell em Stick em, no **Better Dayz**, no one to shield them, afraid women and children like 7 Days, reptilian, a Shriner, wisdom in the mind of a minor, **Son Turner Orville** real skilled moonshiner, one burner 44 five more 49er, **Tibetan Book of the Dead** another door a diviner, see 30 seconds ahead of time, I had to pay an admission to go and see my shrine, **Mission Aries**, my moon and my dragons tail aligned, from my tomb I make sure that I Vomit spit the rhyme, never stagnant, I split like Comets, used music as magic, when it's done right awaken the soul fragments, that's a rap, a hymn a **Hekau**, charismatic words of power, supernatural, my lyrics invade half of you like a chromosome, and when we die is that really when we going home? when we die is that really when we going home? never die, live to die another day, life is but a dream, back in time we use to say… ***when I say Tut Ankh, you say Aten, Tut Ankh***, *Aten* , ***Tut Ankh***, *Aten*, ***when I say Never, you say forgotten, Never***, *Forgotten*, ***Never***, *Forgotten…..* **- TutemRa**

X Clan

Rau nu Prt m heru

When I was a teenager living in New Jersey I listened to a few songs from the **X Clan** that made it to the radio but I never owned one of their albums, however, what I heard from them struck a cord, unfortunately most of it went over my head. Last year, on July 24th 2021, I listened to their **Exodus** album for the first time and I was blown away when I heard them talking about ancient Kemet (Egypt). They mentioned the **Cosmic Ark, Thoth, Ibis, Immortality, Ra, Hotep, the temple of Horus, the scales of Maat, pyramid builders** etc. I didn't learn what an **Ankh** was till I was in my 30's and the only **Ark** I heard of back then was Noah's Ark. If I had been told about the **Ark of Ra** I may have possibly thought about the times I used to **float** around my grand mothers house (**astral traveling,** p 39). As I look at the picture above, with X Clan dressed in African garb I'm filled with a feeling of **regret**. Sometimes I wish that I could have learned more when I was younger but I guess I needed to go through life this time **"blind to the facts"** like Heavy D. Back then I loved Hip Hop too much to have a top 10. There are too many great emcees that influenced me and my pen to have just ten locked in. Each artist or group was like a channel in which I **Channel**ed **Live** flammable, some conscious and some half animal like **Heru Em Ahket,** but back then I had not heard of the Sphinx yet. I loved the movie **Breakin**' but Break Dancing I never learned, on **October 25th** Krush Groove'n get the body Move'n was shown, **14 Shots to the Dome**, The **LL**ords of the UnderGround, where the **Souls** of Mischief roam. It all started on the block with block parties, my cousin **Darryl** was a stick up kid and a **DJ** as a side hobby, like **Kool Herk** playing soul music after work. I went to school but when I came home I barely did my work. I did **Video Music Box** and **Red Alert**. Hip Hop is where I got my lessons but some lessons I never got cause I ain't know about 5 percent'n. I saw the **Ankh** but for some reason I never asked the questions. Like what did vainglorious mean, when I heard the **X Clan** say it. They say the best is saved for last so the last is where I saved it. **Brother Jay Brother Jay**, I was so close yet so far away. I never listened to a full album until yesterday, in 2021 and that's when I felt so numb. So close but yet so far, I listened to **Run**, I ran into **DMC** twice, once at the gym and once while on a run, he was walking into a church in Harlem. I used to listen to **Big Daddy Kane** and when I was 12 I drew him wearing a **Nefertiti** chain. I never really did graffiti I only learned to draw my name. On Strictly Representin' **Tupac** listed many names, some of them I didn't know but his flow hit my brain, I loved Hip Hop and never will that change. Some things fall apart some things remain the same, some say it's fate, like **Buckshot** touring state to state, or like when my father gave me that tape. I heard who's gonna take the whole weight from **Guru** and **Ed O.G.** Be a Father to Your Child, and Shaka Zulu ain't got nothing to do with what he did to them kids in that false nation and death should be the penalty not probation! The first time that I heard **Half Time** I nearly lost my mind, around that time I wrote my first rhyme, **2pacalypse Now** on repeat keep pressing rewind, 89 tech 9 had the classic sessions, **Big L**, L - Swift, **Smif N Wessun**, and that question, **Biggie, Jay Z** or **Nas**, does it matter?! Nah! Cause **The Underground** that's where you found the essence, the **De La Soul**, **Brand Nubian,** Slow Down cause 911 is a joke in yo town. Bonita Applebum she kept on pass'n me by. **KRS One, Scott LaRock** the first homicide. Then Hip Hop went after the gold and after that the platinum but I still listened to M.O.P. and Kool G Rap son. Believe me I was in love with Hip Hop way before the **CD**, I played my tapes so much they would break, I stayed up late to record live sessions, no internet, no status update, I hit eject, flipped my tape, put it back in the deck then called my ace, "A yo you heard that new track from **Artifacts,** Wrong Side of the Tracks?! **Naughty by Nature** in videos with the bats." I was a Ghetto Bastard and that's a fact. The first raps I ever wrote down to learn was from **Treach**. I was the biggest fan then next was the **Black Moon, Heltah Skeltah, Boot Camp Clik**, then **Common Sense** cause he had Soul by the Pound and I really dug his sound like the **RZA-rrecter** and the Gravediggers, put both hands up then put your hands together **O.D.B. Osiris** Wu Tang Forever, Sunz of Man, Beretta 9, Killarmy, leaving the church - Killah Priest and **the basic instructions before leaving earth**, The Roots, The Fresh prince and Jazzy Jeff, The Fugees, Mc Hammer, Queen Latifah, Wrecks-n-Effect, Trends of Culture, A Tribe Called Quest, Mc Lyte, Salt N Pepa, Busta Rhymes, Canibus, Onyx, Lil Kim, Foxy, Organized Konfusin, Mos Def and Talib, K-Solo, Snoop Dogg, Melle Mel, The Geto Boys, Pete Rock and CL Smooth, MC Eiht, Smooth B and Greg Nice, The Pharcyde, NWA, The Lox, Ice T and Ice Cube, Mobb Deep, Bones Thugs and Harmony, Warren G, Eric B and **Ra**kim, Mc Shan, Keith Murray, Camp Lo, Outkast, Black Sheep, Redman, EPMD, AZ, Cypress Hill, Scarface, Ras Kaz, Big Pun and Fat Joe, CNN, UGK, Kurious Jorge, Digable Planets, Main Source, **Jeru** The Damaja, Immortal Technique and Xzibit but on April 9th 2021 I'll never forget it, when **DMX** died his soul came did me a favor, whispered in my ear said, "go ye there look through them papers"! **Anubis** and the **afterlife** advice watch for them gators, **Maat** is precise in your life! you gotta watch your behavior! warlock the **Acacia**, _the burning bush_ light the _light saber_, returning to **kush**, too close to the edge I got pushed! I fell I flew! feather on my head like **Shu** and my heart is true that's why I return like **Heru,** and now Eye appear in front of Giza with a time travel visa and mind readers look'n at me and call'n me the Negus, If I could do it all over again, I would dig deeper with **MF Doom** and **Brother Jay** blasting through my speakers.

lu f Per f m heru

Utterances for Coming Forth by day into Light

It is he, who comes forth by day into Light

ADDENDUM

TutemRa's Top 10 Hip Hop lists

Hip Hop as a whole, must move to a place of enlightenment. Hip Hop is Green,(pages **6**, **376**).

Top 10 Overall	Top 10 Old School	Top 10 Golden Era 90's	Top 10 Most Lyrical	Top 10 Groups	Top 10 Songs	Top 10 Albums
					0 Trapped - Tupac	**0 2pacalypes Now**
1 Tupac	**1 Rakim**	**1 Tupac**	**1 MF Doom**	**1 Dead Prez**	**1 Blasphemy - Tupac** (p 665)	**1 Makaveli**
2 Nas	**2 LL Cool J**	**2 Nas**	**2 Canibus**	**2 Wu Tang Clan**	**2 Qi Gong - Stic Khnum**	**2 Let's Get Free**
3 MF Doom	**3 Melle Mel**	**3 Common**	**3 Black Thought**	**3 Naughty By Nature**	**3 Ghetto Bastard-Naughty By N**	**3 Life After Death**
4 DMX	**4** Big Daddy Kane	**4** Killah Priest	**4** K. Lamar J. Cole	**4** Boot Camp Clik	**4** All I Got Is You - Ghostface	**4** Enta Da Stage
5 KRS[T] One	**5** X Clan	**5** Method Man	**5** Cassidy	**5** The Roots	**5** The Message - Furious Five	**5** It Was Written
6 Kanye	**6** Run DMC	**6** Lauryn Hill	**6** Kool G Rap	**6** Geto Boys	**6** Back In The Day - Ahmad	**6** College Dropout
7 Rae **&** Ghost	**7** Slick Rick	**7** André 3000	**7** Eminem	**7** Onyx	**7** Buckingham Palace - Canibus	**7** Heavy Mental
8 Treach	**8** Mc Lyte	**8** Busta Rhymes	**8** Jay Z	**8** Mobb Deep	**8** No Alibi - The Roots/ <u>TutemRa</u>	**8** 36 Chambers
9 Mos Def, Talib	**9** Salt-N-Pepa	**9** Scarface	**9** JadaKiss	**9** Outkast	**9** Through The Wire - Kanye	**9** Dah Shinin'
10 Immortal Technique	**10** Public Enemy	**10** Sean Price	**10** Redman RJ Payne	**10** Brand Nubian	**10** Passing Me By - Pharcyde	**10** Black Star

1996, From High School to College

I have graduated, but barely. Now what?! I had all those college letters but I hadn't reached out to any of the schools! I couldn't get into most of them anyway because my grades were so horrible. I was considering going to **C W Post** but when **Courtlan** called me I changed my mind. He told me that he was going to **Suny Canton** to play for **Lou Saban** and that he'd told Saban about me. That's how I got to Suny Canton. Saban had coached **O.J. Simpson** on the Buffalo Bills. Court and I were like brothers. We had this **dream** we shared with football and we both loved **Hip Hop**. **Courtlan** was always the forerunner to a mission! When he wanted something he went for it. If it weren't for **Courtlan** I'm not sure what I would have done after high school but because of him I went to College. Court had his first child while in college. She was born on **Feb 7**, 1997, the same day that **Emmett Till's** father was born (page 475, 518).

The racism within NLF pension

The average NFL career is 3.3 years. NFL athletes need to be play in the NFL for 3 years to be eligible for an NFL pension. **Cornerbacks** average 2.94 years, **Running backs** average 2.81 years and **Wide Receivers** average 2.57 years. On average, more black men hold the positions of Running backs, Wide Receivers and Cornerbacks and are less likely to qualify for a pension. **Kickers** average 4.87 years and **Quarterbacks** average 4.44 years. On average, more white men hold the positions of Kickers and Quarterbacks so they have a greater potential to receive a pension. Is it by designed that white men receive NFL pension more often than black men?…….!!

From A's and B's to The Bench then Leave

We had been up there a month or so doing our pre season training camp before everyone else arrived for classes. Of course you had to make the team first! After training camp was over **Lou Saban** had a meeting with Court and I in his office. He told us that he would look to both of us to lead the team. I was the starting receiver and **Courtlan** was the starting running back. I also did kick return and punt return. When classes started I was doing really well. I maintained A"s and B's in most of my classes. I was having fun chasing the girls and playing football until... Until I dropped a pass in a game. I had a splint on my right middle finger because I fractured it in practice while catching a ball. With my finger in a splint I was still the starting receiver. During our 1st or 2nd game I went up for a pass on a 3rd down. I caught the ball but the defender made a good play. He knocked the ball out of my hands. I came to the sideline in pain. Our Head Coach, Lou Saban screamed at me because I was experiencing pain or because he was upset that I dropped the ball. I think we lost that game. On the bus ride home he mentioned me and my finger and dropping the pass. I'm not sure what I said but I responded to him in defense of myself because I had already forgotten about that pass. He could never be more upset with me than I was with myself. I took pride in being known for catching any pass thrown to me. After that incident on the bus he sat me on the bench. I sat by and watched the team play game after game watching my back up receiver play while I sat the bench. I was the best receiver and the fastest person on the team but I was sitting on the bench. I had never been on the bench before. I out played the other receivers on my team during practices and every game I waited and waited to be called in to play to no avail. **Courtlan** was doing well. I cheered for him when he got the ball however I also sunk into a depression. I don't remember playing much at all that year at Canton and subsequently I stopped going to classes and stopped trying. I don't think I ever scored a touchdown while at Canton and if I did I don't remember. I spent my time listening to rap, playing video games and chasing girls.

Smoke, Weed and Wrestling

I never smoked weed in college but there was a guy from Albany who was so fast that they called him **Smoke**. Naturally the word got around that I was fast and everyone wanted Smoke and I to race so we did. We lined up to race on the Campus parking lot. I put my left foot forward while we waited for someone to give the count. "On your mark, get set, go".. I beat Smoke and I beat him by a lot. It was settled, I was the fastest guy in the school! One of my roommates was the Campus weed dealer, his name was **Pep**. He kept his weed stashed in our room. He liked me because I didn't smoke and that allowed him a sense of security knowing I wouldn't smoke his weed. Here's a funny story about Pep. I used to be in the gym lifting weights all the time. So I was bigger than Pep. One day while in our room he looked at me and said - "you think you big huh?". I said - "why you wanna wrestle?". I don't know why I said that because he said yeah. I didn't know that Pep had wrestled in High School. We faced each other playfully. As soon as we touched each other I was on my back. He got up laughing. I laughed too and we never wrestled again. Sometimes I wonder how I might have perceived the world had I smoked weed in my youth but I never did. The High I got from scoring touchdowns was enough for me and the horror stories of **laced** weed kept me from trying. There was a guy who ran in the creek behind the dorms and drowned. The story spread around Campus that his weed was **laced** and so he ran into the creek and drowned. I don't know if the story is true but it was enough for me to continue to leave "drugs" alone. I didn't smoke until I was 33 years old (page 194) and afterwards I smoked weed heavily for 5 years then I stopped. It wasn't till I began writing this book that I realized weed had opened up **High Frequency Psychic Channels** where prophetic messages were channeled down through my thoughts (pages 208, 227, 282, 343). Weed is a sacred plant medicine and it should not be regulated to recreational party use. It should be used ritualistically. Too much of anything can cause the risks to outweigh the benefits.

Rau nu Prt m heru

Iu f Per f m heru

Utterances for Coming Forth by day into Light

It is he, who comes forth by day into Light

Suny Canton Campus Radio Station - Out The Mouth of Babes, or Channels like Radio Waves

The pictures above (left), and on the bottom, are from that one time **Courtlan** and I rapped at the Suny Canton campus radio station, Modern Music **107-3 FM**. As I consider who each person in my life is and the role they played in getting me to where I am in life at the point of presenting this book to the world, I must say that Court played a major role. He was like a **light house** (p 648). He kept flashing the lights on poetry and it was my poetry that got me through my rough points in my journey when I got into my 30's, hitting a great wall of depression. **Courtlan** loves music and his love for music helped me realize mine. I would be remiss if I did not mention in this book the story that Cortland's grandmother told me. After I had the revelation of my past life as Emmett Till in 2018 (p 480), I sent a video out about it to many people via e-mail. His grand mother, Florence saw it and sent me her number and told me to call her. We spoke about my past life revelation and she shared a story with me about Court from when he was a small baby still breast feeding. One day his mother was doing baby talk to him. She was saying, "My name is Chris, what's your name?" Florence did the same, "My name is Florence, what's your name?" After asking him this several times Courtlan, a baby still breast feeding and not yet able to formulate words, opened his mouth, and **with the voice of an old man,** he said, **"don't you worry about that"**. His mother was so shocked that it frightened her, she tossed him in the hands of her mother. Florence was startled too but she caught him and comforted the baby Cortland as he went back to being a baby again. Some things in life will not always be easily explained, and some things are even harder to explain away. Courtlan's high school girl friend Shanta would have a similar experience with her daughter (p 289) and in 2020 I would meet a couple in Detroit with a similar story (p 618). In 2022 my friend Big O would tell me about his Angel Baby and the profound things she would say (p 96).

ADDENDUM **Killah Priest**

During my time in college I listened to a lot of Hip Hop but the artists' that got most of my attention were, 2pac, all of The Wu Tang Clan, The Roots, The **Boot Camp Clik**, Nas, Sunz of Man, Killarmy, KRS One, and Common. The **Killah Priest** song, **B.I.B.L.E.,** was one of my favorite and most played songs from this time in my life. I wasn't alone in that sentiment. Many of us were searching for the purpose of life and this song spoke to us. In 2022 I found some interesting patterns with **Killah Priest**. Killah Priest's born name is Walter **Reed**. In ancient K**emet** the **field of Reeds** was where the vindicated **soul** went **after death**. He shares the name Walter Reed with an Army physician who was born on Sep 13th, the day **Tupac** died (p 76), in 1851, they year of the **dog**. He died in 1902, the year of the **tiger**, on Nov 22, the day before **Mamie Till** died (Emmett Till's mother). **Killah Priest** was born in 1970 the year of the **dog**. **King Tut's** tomb was discovered in 19**22** the year of the **dog** and my past life as **Emmett Till** was revealed in 2018 the year of the **dog**. Priest was born the day before **Marcus Garvey**, on Aug 16th and he has a nephew named **Marcus**. Priest dropped his first album (**Heavy Mental**) in 1998, the year of the **tiger**, this book was released in 20**22**, the year of the **tiger**. My favorite song off that album was the song titled, **From Then Till Now**. I loved the picture he painted with his words on top of the melodic humming heard throughout the song which sent my imagination on a journey as I pondered the beginning of existence. Back **then** I loved the song but it wasn't until **now** (2022, year of the **tiger**) that I noticed he said the name **Pharaoh** in the song.. "Now we step in precincts, for your ebony prince, the smell of frankincense, once treated like a **pharoah**, with royal apparel, **anointed** with myrrh and aloes, we used to wallow, amongst the mallows, we had herd sheep and cattle, now we battle"... Priest would become a part of the group **Sunz of Man**. The Sunz of Man would also drop their debut album (**The Last Shall Be First**) in 1998 the year of the **tiger**. My favorite track off that album was the song titled, **Cold**. I listened to the track in 2022 (year of the **tiger**) and realized the name **King Tut** was said in the first verse. "Aiyyo, my thoughts be colorless The undercover rich, haters loving it, watch the hell **King Tut** with it, Queen's, bath tubbing it, my diamond's cutting it, Sharpen all points, fuck the tricks of the government"....... "Microphone masked emcees, Maccabees, headed seed be told but still ain't free, The truth came in flesh but still you don't believe, The best thing you know is the spots to find weed......"

Meta Mysterious Encounter with Brother Carlos from Suny Canton. Divine Patterns - Sing-Natures

Carlos and I met during our enrollment at Suny Canton College of Technology. I only remember hanging out with him once but in that one time I came to know that he was sent down (born) on **October 25th** like me. We both got picked to be one of the representatives for our school at an auction event where females could win a date with us. I have not seen Carlos in person or spoke to him since our time at Suny Canton however in 2021 the fellow **scorpio** would play a role in a pattern dealing with the opening of the tomb of Tutankhaten (**King Tut**). In January of 2016 I would meet a woman name Melanie in Harlem on the corner of **Fredrick Douglass** and 145th street (page 358). We talked for a bit and in the short chat I would find out that she knew **Carlos,** they are both from DR **(Dominican Republic)**. In January of 2021 I would see a post on her page about her birthday. She was sent down (born) on November 26th the day **King Tut's** tomb was opened (page 11). I saw the **sign** from **nature**, or the **signature**.. The circle would be complete. Circles don't complete if you don't pass the test, or earn it and some things are just divine prophecy like this book.

ADDENDUM **September 13th 1996**

The murdered of Lesane Parish Crooks, "Tupac Amaru Shakur" The Shining Serpent

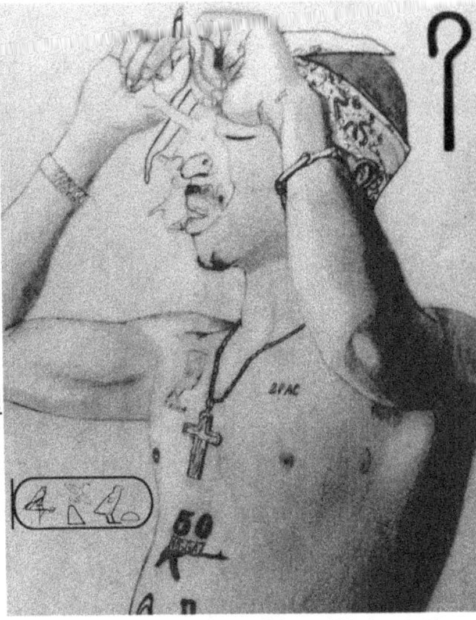

Rau nu Prt m heru

I was **18** at the time of Tupac's death. When I got the news I was in college sitting in someones dorm room. I will never forget, it was a Friday and when I saw it on MTV I cried. **I remember people wondering why I was crying**. Courtlan didn't understand why I was crying either. I don't remember anyone else crying but I did because I knew Tupac was a special person the first time I heard his music. I had listened to his albums **2pacalypse Now** and **Strictly 4 My N.I.G.G.A.Z.** "**Coincidentally**", **Strictly 4 My N.I.G.G.A.Z** was released the same day that the final room of Tutankhaten's (**King Tut's**) tomb was opened (Feb 16th 19**23**, p 11). I listened to every song even the interludes. I knew that Tupac cared about his people and his death bothered me. Pac spoke to the young black male and that was me. I lived in the world of Hip Hop as a teen and he was sort of like the big brother I never had. **<u>See Page 105, Jewell dreamt Tupac's death before it happened!</u>**

As soon as he died speculations about him still being alive began to circulate. His death was mysterious and many people including myself felt like he was still alive, living in hiding. Eventually websites were made that had all the events linked by songs and dates speculating the faking of his death. It seemed as if his death was surrounded with **numerology,** connected to the numbers 25 and 7. He was shot on Sep **7th** and died on the **7th** day (page 41), on Sep 13th at 25 years old, the same day that my uncle died (page 28). "**Coincidentally**", his last album was titled, **Makaveli**, The Don Killuminati: **The 7 Day Theory**. Just before he died he changed his name to **Makaveli** which is similar to **Niccolo Machiavelli** the 16th century **poet** who faked his own death, only to return years later to kill his enemies. I was one of the people who thought Tupac was coming back like some sort of **"black Jesus"** and in his music I found all the reasons to believe it. I heard a another track titled **All Out**. On this track Tupac say's, "<u>While y'all caught up in the rapture, still after me **I'm in Jamaica sippin' daquiris**</u>". This line further supported my belief that Tupac was still alive living in hiding, like Machiavelli. The album **R U Still Down** didn't help! On that album Tupac can be heard saying "**you can't kill me, I'm the king**", he also said "**<u>Expect me nigga. Like you expect Jesus to come back. Expect me nigga. I'm coming!</u>**". **"Coincidentally"**, Tupac's mother, Afeni Shakur died on May 2nd (page 382), the day before **Niccolo Machiavelli** was born. Tupac died the day before **Nas's** birthday and **Nas** has a daughter named **Destiny** who's "**coincidentally**" born the day before Tupac's birthday. After Tupac's death many of his unfinished songs were leaked. One of those was a track was titled **Reincarnation** (p 300). On this song Tupac can be heard saying the following words, "My only fear of death, is **reincarnation**, I use my last breath, to reach the whole nation, How can they call me murderer for my spoken words? This composition be my **prophecy** I hope it's heard". Being intrigued with his death opened me up to numbers and connections which seemed to have prepared me for the decoding of my previous lives years to come (pages 41, 222, 602). **14** shots were fired at Tupac on Sep 7. Ausar was cut into **14** pieces and Emmett Till died at **14**. I have a theory about who Tupac was in his past life (p 664) and this book, **TutemRa: The Prophecy of Reincarnation,** is the **"prophecy"** that Tupac spoke of in his song, **Reincarnation**. In ancient Kemet the concept of reincarnation was called the **Wehem-Mesut** (repeating of births, page 14). In **Judaism** reincarnation is known as **Gilgul** (Cycle), but it is not taught to everyone. Just as my sister **dreamt** my car accident before it happened (p 104), **Jewell dreamt** Tupac's death before it happened (p 105). Read about **Dreams** (p 30)!

Iu f Per f m heru

Video Games, Theft and Ralph Lauren ***ADDENDUM***

Tekhen (Obelisk)

Utterances for Coming Forth by day into Light

It is he, who comes forth by day into Light

After **Coach Saban** benched me I stayed in the dorms and played the fighting video game **Tekken,** which just so "*<u>happens</u>*" to be based off of the **Ausarian resurrection** drama from ancient **Kemet** (**Egypt**), but instead of a son and uncle rivalry like Heru snd Set it's a son and father rivalry with Kazuya and Heihachi. I became one of the best people on campus at the game. My favorite character to use was **King,** a Mexican wrestler who wore a **Jaguar** mask. Even the name of the game Tekken, is taken from Kemet. In ancient Kemet we built a structure called a **Tekhen** (**Iron Fist**) which was another symbol of **resurrection** and when a person was raised from the water after **baptism** it was symbolic of the Tekhen being raised into place. The Greeks called it an obelisk and the United States of America has one in Washington DC called the **Washington Monument** (page 160 - 162).

Without football as a motivation, college became like high school all over again. My focus was on how I dressed, girls, rapping and **Tekken**. I dressed in nice clothes that I could not afford to pay for. Many of them I stole by some means. I met a guy at school who used to **steal** from the campus store and the local clothing store. I copied him. I **stole** silk boxers, socks, shirts and jackets. I had all the things I needed to survive at school so I was only stealing from the campus store for the thrill. During the break I would go to New Jersey with this same friend and he would teach me how to **steal** from the warehouses. I stole the jacket I'm wearing in the picture from an outlet in New Jersey (p 75). It's a Ralph Lauren Sheep Skin. It was priced at way more than I could afford to pay for anything at that time in my life (In 2021 it is still my winter coat). When I got back to school from the holiday break one of the brothers involved with student government told me that the old White ladies that worked at the campus store knew that I was **stealing** and had me on video. They were waiting for me to steal more so that I could be charged for a **felony**. I never went back to the campus store again. I got academically dismissed from school after my first year and had to write a letter to admissions so that I could be allowed to come back to school the next year. When I came back I was not eligible to play football so I had no reason why I was there anymore.. I was going through the motions at that point. All I did was play **Tekken**, the fighting video game based on the **Ausarian** drama of **resurrection**. The next year I got caught **stealing** for the first time. I tried to **steal** a copy of the **Wu Tang Forever** album from a Mega Store on 42nd Street. The security stopped me and took me a room, but for some reason he let me go. After that I never stole again. The last Tekken game I ever purchased and played was **Tekken 6 Bloodline Rebellion** and it was released in Arcades on **November 26**, 2007, the same day **King Tut's** tomb was opened (page 11). My favorite stage to fight on was **Aza**zel's Chamber, the final bosses stage.... I liked the sound and the imagery of the stage but at the time (2007) **I knew nothing** about ancient Kemet of the Ausarian Resurrection. The name **Aza** sounds like **Ausar** and **Aza**zel wears a Kemetic head dress and statues of **Heru** in his falcon form can been seen on this stage... And **"coincidentally"**, the symbol of **King Tut's** throne name, **Neb Kheperu Ra**, can be seen on this stage. Remember that you are Ausar and Heru, the hero! See page 3 for the **hero's journey!** 76=13

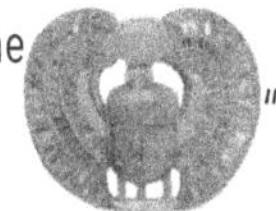

"King" Tut's gold inlaid wooden **Jaguar** head

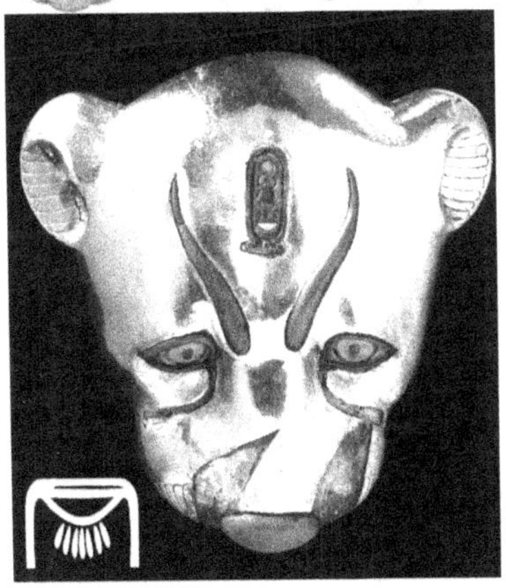

King's, **Jaguar** mask from the **Tekken** video game.

Combo Style

I gets open combo style, sometimes girls say I'm too wild cause I'm too up front, yo suck my ––-, sometimes that's all I want, I keep it real without a blunt, no need to front, **I don't get high or tipsy** don't fuck with **whiskey**, since my man got **laced** that lesson it stuck with me, stay on point never know when you gotta throw your joints, or run from the man cause I ain't fuck'n with the joint, I heard a jail cell is like hell, similar to the unholy, and can't no man fold me, or hold me, my out route, you better learn about my first move, make a hard core nigger turn smooth, when I'm at home I watch those who back stab, and role with cover up niggas that drive cabs, I'm from R.O.C.K. and everyday niggas got the gun play from Hamels to Gateway, so when you walk this way in this day and time, watch your top and your bottom, your front and your back, cause you never know where a brothers mind state is at - **Dawud**

May 21st 1972 - March 9th 1997

Christopher George Latore Wallace "Biggie Smalls" goes West

I remember hearing Biggie's music on the underground stations. He had a flow that was unique and dope. He was one of my favorite artist and back then I had no idea that he was once friends with Tupac. Biggie was signed by **Sean Puffy Combs** who's born on **Nov 4th**, the same day **King Tut's** tomb was discovered (pages 44, 664). Unfortunately Biggie met his untimely demise by what was made to look like **gang violence** (Hip Hop Police). **Biggie Smalls** was gunned down on March 9th 1997 and his posthumous album **Life After Death** was released just short of two weeks later on March 25th. On Sep 6th 1996 **Tupac** called Prof. James **Small** (p 564) and told him that the media was creating the East coast West coast beef and that he was going to start his own distribution company with other Hip Hop artists, the next day he was assassinated. Read about **Darpa** on page 352.

Condolences

My condolences go out to all the family, friends and fans of **Christopher Wallace**. Please know that death is not the end. The soul survives death, indeed and in spirit. This is a book of the dead written by a boy who was murdered without justice, who defeated death and came forth by day. May the soul of **Christopher Wallace** walk peacefully through the field of Reeds in Amenta. Amen Ra.

Periods

Me and my mic got lyrics for idiots period! and periods for run on raps that trap kids, I got **soul control** let me mold your wig, I told ya kid I got no time for negative, it's too repetitive, more like the norm, now I'm on these steps that manifest me leave'n my first form, the ***first born son I am that I am*** the raw one, come with more protein than creatine, microphone fien fight'n threw my write'n, I gotta **dream,** a scheme, with the same concepts different means, from a different angle, y'all niggas don't wanna tangle, cause I strangle the evil that men do, so run fool, the new school teach'n - ***Dawud***

1997 Far Rockaway

The last stop on the A is **Rockaway**, the land of hard rocks, and we don't play we dish'n out speed nots, ya need not step to the Rock wave'n your gats, outer towner's need to bow down and step back, cause you're wack and so's your whole bootleg crew, pump fear to your **heart**, you was *shook* when I dissed you, who's next? I'll punish you, like *Sound Boy Burial*, I'm son'n you, Rock you in your ribs and make you wonder who, the fuck I be, I be L.I.V.E. to the day I D.I.E. I'll bring pain constantly, got them niggas run'n like **D.M.C.**, Buck em the down like the **B.D.I. Emcee**, keep it real with yourself when your rhymes sound petty, try'n to live that *thug life* that of **Makaveli - Dawud**

March 1997 The Resurrection

While you want a Ac and a Lex brother I need land! you idealize **Nino Brown**, I expand understand, it takes more to be a man than fast cash and chicks, I blast past brothers score TD's but never spike it! the last ref didn't like it, and I'm the source of this rhyme so I five mic it, Thugs are **psychic,** with **7 Day Theories,** about **Life After Death,** they were living in hell now in peace they rest, now to the rest of Emcees left on this earth, master your apparatus and bless coast to coast, verse after verse I spit mine, and fuck a tech 9, brothers floss crime but crime cost time, and doing tall time is a hard lesson, you can talk from experience but I'm a keep guess'n, and I'll use a metaphor before I use a weapon cause brothers die everyday and only one seen **Resurrection,** I'll use a metaphor before I use a weapon cause brothers die everyday and only the **Son** seen **Resurrection,** I'll use a metaphor before I use a weapon cause brothers die everyday and only the **Sun** seen **Resurrection - Dawud**

(Significance - The second Common Connection)

When I received this star code I was 19 years old. I was oblivious to the Quest I had emb**ark**ed on when I started putting words together in rhyme form which we call Hip Hop. **Biggie Smalls (RIP)** was murdered on Mar 9th 1997 and his posthumous album **Life After Death** was released just short of two weeks later on Mar 25th. Tupac was murdered the year prior on Sep 13th 1996 and his album **The Don Killuminati: The 7 Day Theory** was released on Nov 5th 1996 the day after **Tutankhaten's** (**King Tut**) tomb was discovered on Nov 4th 1922. This rhyme would m**ark** the first transmission that I would send to myself across inter dimensional time lines in rhyme form. I titled the song **resurrection** because I said the word resurrection at the end 3 times. **Common's** album **Resurrection** was one of my favorite albums at the time and Common often repeated his last bar so I repeated mine. **Ausar** also known as **Osiris** was the first story of a **resurrection**, **rebirth**, **reincarnation**. On July 3rd 2018 I would have my past life of **Emmett Till** revealed to me and on **April 4th 2020** (p 594) my past life of **Tutankhaten (King Tut)** would be revealed to me on the same day **Martin Luther King** was assassinated (p 69, 592). **Common Sense** would release the single **Resurrection** the next year on **April 4th 1995** and **25** years later I would have my **past life** revelation of **Tutankhaten** (**King Tut**) on April 4th 2020. The album **Resurrection** was released Oct 4th 1994 but oddly enough amazon has the album release date as **my birthday Oct 25th** 1994. In 2011 Common would drop the album, The **Dreamer/The Believer** and on track 7 titled Raw he would say the name Tutankhamen "she was lit shining bright in a fit that was tight, bout to get that invite for a night over **Egypt**, she said 'you rap?' yeah **mummy**, I'm **Tutankhamen** kicking and spending this rap money"… Remember that you are Ausar and Heru, the hero! See page 3 for the **hero's journey!** More **Common Connections** on pages, 66, 81, 208, and 385.

Rau nu Prt m heru

Iu f Per f m heru

Utterances for Coming Forth by day into Light

It is he, who comes forth by day into Light

1997 Steps of Progress

We use to catch reck and collect division one letters, damn if only our GPA's were better, we use to argue didn't know witch one of us was better, then we came together make'n us tougher than leather, I can set a corner back on his back what ever, catch any quarterback pass I'm type nast, thought because we ruled the dash, we could get the cash, wasn't concerned with going to class to learn the math and science, 97 rose our rap alliance, DNC step'n through and through any climate, now we're in college, yeah it's a Ju-co don't get fooled though, you can still get schooled though cause we blow teams out the water you ought to give us respect, I got two last words and they be who's next? Through these steps of progress we recollect on our past, those moves we made the dawn of a new day, just another part of life another lesson we've learned, DNC together it's our turn to burn - **Dawud**

Do What I Do

I **love** girls that **love** me for the man that I be, don't give my **heart** to the ones that give it up easily, I peeped this girl from a far, get'n in a car, made me feel like a fan, and she was the superstar, better yet supermodel, my **heart** raced full throttle, body made perfect, like a champagne bottle, better believe that I flat left my crew, to kick my game simple and plain, you know how I do, hello miss, how you doing? what's your name, and what's your angle? **dreams** of when and where we could tangle, pretty brown skin short hair she was kill'n em, I can't believe all these thoughts, that I'm remember'n, but if you saw her you'd be remembering too, she's the reason why I do what I do - **Dawud**

August 9th 1997 Abner Louima

Abner Louima, a **Haitian** immigrant born on November 24th, the day after Emmett Till's mother Mamie Till (November **23**rd 1921), was at a club in Brooklyn when a fight broke out. Policeman, Justin Volpe began beating Abner in the street. Officers took Louima back to the precinct where Volpe continued to beat him. Volpe Kicked him in the testicles and sodomized him with a broomstick, causing critical internal damage. After he was done, Volpe, proudly displayed the excrement and blood stained broomstick to his co-workers and boasted that he had broken a man. Volpe then threatened to kill Louima and his family if he told anyone. Volpe admitted in court to sodomizing Abner and was sentenced to 30 years in prison. Only one other cop involved in the incident, Chris Schwartz, served any time. Abner suffered severe internal damage to his colon and bladder, which required three major operations to repair. Abner sued the city successfully for $5.8 million. I remember hearing the name Abner Louima in 1997, then the next year was the name Amadou Diallo. I was 19 when Abner was assaulted and I did not internalize it. I didn't realize how at any moment I could have been the one assaulted and even more so, I did not know I was once the victim of a violent assault that took my life. **What happens to one of us happens to all of us!** See page **648** for the **metaphysical significance of the number 23**.

1998 Denzel Washington

It doesn't matter if you're male or female, stardom makes you more desirable to people who are not yet grounded in self knowledge. I imagine celebrities have loads of stories about how fans reacted when meeting them. Some funny, some good and I'm sure some bad. The first celebrity I ever met was **Denzel Washington** and I made a complete fool of myself. The movie **Fallen** had just been released. I was in the city with **Courtlan** and someone else, possibly **Hanif**, Godfrey or Dieter. Denzel was walking down the street talking on his phone when he walked pass us. When they saw Denzel they said high, I on the other hand acted like I had seen God. With my eyes wide open, I kept pointing at him as he walked by as I while screamed, "that's Denzel Washington, that's Denzel Washington, that's Denzel Washington". I was "star" struck. He looked at me pointing at him and laughed. He was talking to someone on the phone, but stopped to acknowledge us. He smiled and said hi, then he kept on his way. I wonder if Denzel Remembers meeting me.

Significance

The movie **Fallen** is about the world of the **Occult** and a **spirit** that jumps from body to body like the **soul** does when we **reincarnate**. This book is about ghosts / spirits, the occult and reincarnation etc etc. Denzel was once offered a role in 1986. The part they wanted him to play was a black man who **raped a white women** and as a result he was electrocuted but didn't die. Then he was hung and again he didn't die. There were some Jewish people at the audition who told Denzel the role would be funny and Denzel responded quickly with his own scenario. He said, "Yeah it's funny, like you put some Jewish people in a room and they think it's a shower but it's gas". When he made that comparison they saw his point immediately and stopped the audition. Denzel called it the role, **the Nigger they couldn't kill**. Denzel has always stood on principles and I respect him for that.

March 1998 Sunday (1st of 1)

I think it was a Sunday in BK, last minute change of plans so I could parlay with my fam, on the way to the A on the ave of Nostrand homie crossed the street with beef to impress his clan, he asked me for the time tried to cut me from behind, you know the government they loving this black on black crime, brothers sell their **souls** signing on the lines of the streets, didn't read the fine print now they running trying to eat, my mind I gotta speak, from now until, brothers feel what I feel, I get a chill when I build like this, cause shit is real like that, my habitat requires me to be strapped, you cant floss without a gat, cause brothers want beef but nah homie I don't, my man said we pack heat, leave niggas cold burnt in the winter, he explained, shit Is like Abel and Cain, niggas got no shame, they take yo chain, blow the skull off ya brain, I was like, yeah every year we recycle the game and my man Cartier stopped rocking his chain, cause brothers don't care, they just cock it and aim, cock it and aim, they just cock it and aim, and my brothers don't care, they just cock it and aim - **Dawud**

Wolverine was my favorite character from the **X-men**. He had the superhuman ability to heal from any injury and he had bones made from indestructible **metal** called **Adamantium**. When Mamie Till, first looked into the casket and saw the disfigured and mutilated face of her son **Emmett Till**, she said it felt like **every bone in her body turned to steel** and instead of falling and fainting **she straightened up** (p, 514). If it weren't for the brave actions of Mamie Till there would not have been a Civil Rights Movement. When I drew this picture I had no idea that the concepts for **X-Men** were taken from the Civil Rights Movement or that many other superheroes were taken from the **7 African Powers** also known as the **Yoruba Orishas** (p 58). **Wolverine** is an **arc**hetype of **Ogun** starting with his name. Wolverine's name is Logan and if the letter **A** in the name Logan is changed to **U**, you have the name **Ogun**. Ogun is one of the Yoruba Orishas and is the God of **Metal** who carries machetes in his hands while Wolverine has indestructible metal coming from his hands..The list goes on, **Superman** is an **arc**hetype of **Shango,** the most popular of the **Yoruba Orishas** and Superman is connected to ancient Kemet (Pages 202-204). Today is January 26 2022 and while coming to the close of this book I realized this picture was drawn on January 6 1999, **the same day Mamie Till died**. (***ADDENDUM*** January 6 marks the 12th day after the Winter Solstice (Dec 25, Christmas, pages 489, 614). In the Christian religion January 6 is the day that the 3 Magi visited Jesus in a manger. January 6 is also the day that the ancient Kemetyu celebrated the Winter Solstice and **Tupac's** grand mother Eloise Maria Barnes was born on **January 6**.) All roads lead to K**emet** and the name **Emmett** is in the name K**emet**. See page 3 for the **hero's journey**.

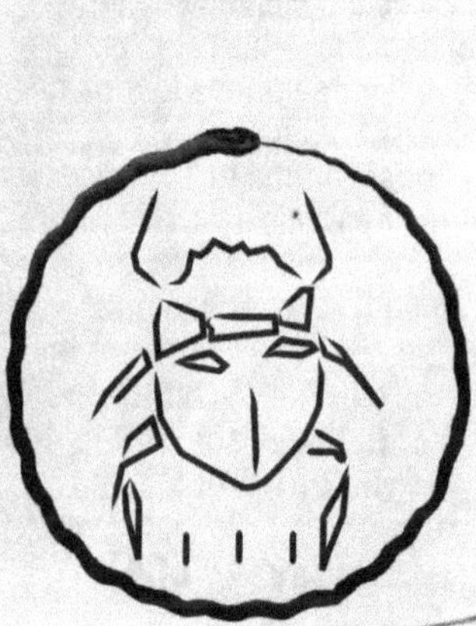

Rau nu Prt m heru

Iu f Per f m heru

February 4th 1999
The Murder of Amadou Diallo

Amadou Diallo was born on September 2nd 1975 in Guinea and was part of a historic Fulbe trading family in Guinea. In September 1996, he followed other family members to New York City and started a business with a cousin. He sold video cassettes, gloves, and socks on the sidewalk along 14th Street during the day. In the early morning of February 4, 1999, Diallo was standing near his building after returning from a meal. At about 12:40 a.m. in the Soundview section of the Bronx, four Police officers racially profiled Diallo and interrogated him. Officers Edward McMellon, Sean Carroll, Kenneth Boss and Richard Murphy fired **41** shots with semi-automatic pistols, fatally hitting Diallo 19 times. Eyewitness Sherrie Elliott stated that the police continued to shoot even though Diallo was already down. The officers claimed to see him reach for a gun but no weapons on or near Diallo. He died with a wallet in his hand. On March 25, 1999, a Bronx grand jury indicted the four officers on charges of second-degree murder and reckless endangerment. On February 25th 2000, after three days of deliberation, a jury composed of four black and eight white jurors acquitted the officers of all charges. In April 2000, Diallo's mother and father filed a $61 million lawsuit against the city and the officers, charging gross negligence, wrongful death, racial profiling, and other violations of Diallo's Civil Rights. In March 2004, they accepted a $3 million settlement, one of the largest in the City of New York for a single man with no dependents under New York State's "wrongful death law", which limits damages to financial loss by the deceased person's next of kin.

Significance

Amadou was murdered on **Rosa Parks's** birthday, February 4th. Rosa Parks helped sparked the Civil Rights Movement after the murder of **Emmett Till**. Amadou was shot **41** times and Emmett was born in 19**41** the year of the snake. He was born the same day of Emmett Tills funeral in 1955. See pages **41** and 508 (**4141**).

Condolences

My condolences go out to all the families of those who have been robbed of their life by this system of white supremacy. Please know that death is not the end. The soul survives death, indeed and in spirit. This is a book of the dead written by a boy who was murdered without justice, who defeated death and came forth by day. May the soul of **Amadou Diallo** walk peacefully through the field of Reeds in Amenta. Amen Ra.

Utterances for Coming Forth by day into Light

It is he, who comes forth by day into Light

May 30th 1974 - February 15th 1999
RIP Big L

I took this picture on October 3rd 2016 as a show of respect for the life of a young brother who was taken too soon. I used to live across the street from this mural in the early 90's with my Aunt in **Delinor** housing apartments (p 57). I never met or saw Big L (Lamont Coleman) but I heard him freestyle a few times on **underground radio stations** and his song with Tupac was one of my favorite tracks of his. I have been living in Harlem for 14 years now and it will be 15 years when this book is released in 2022. Throughout the course of my life and the writing of this book many Hip Hop artist have lost their lives to street violence. Big L's career was just taking off when he was murdered by a friend of his on February 15th 1999 around the same time I moved to Atlanta. Big L was known for putting the L sign up during his shows and I'm sure he would agree that we are the ones that take the L when we engage in self destructive behavior that is prevalent in our communities especially when we mix the street life with Hip Hop.

Condolences

My condolences go out to all the family, friends and fans of Lamont Coleman. Please know that death is not the end. The soul survives death, indeed and in spirit. This is a book of the dead written by a boy who was murdered without justice, who defeated death and came forth by day. May the soul of **Lamont Coleman** walk peacefully through the field of Reeds in Amenta. Amen Ra.

1999 Atlanta - "We Only Got One Year Left!" - Busta Buss

My aunt Pamela asked me if I wanted to move to Atlanta with her in February of 1999. She had moved down for the 96 Olympics and was doing well. I had no other plans so I agreed. I came down and slept on their couch. She was in a relationship with a man named Tony who was a private contractor. He built and remodeled homes. He even had some celebrity clients like **Outkast,** the **Goodie Mobb** and other notable people. He even built his own house once and I helped him out with handy work and some drilling. Him and I got along well. I enjoyed our trips to different jobs listening to the cool jazz radio station. We played basketball a lot, he cooked well and he was funny. I liked him. His **dream** was to one day close on a contracting deal to build all the homes in a subdivision.. Pamela is the same aunt that took me to see Star Wars at 5 years old (page 37). On **January 20th 2014** (page 287) I would realize that I was connected to this aunt in a strange astrological way. After my past life revelations I would decipher the code realizing that she and her children were born with **Astrological codes sent down from heaven** (page 287).

After a few months I got a job where my aunt worked, at Saia Motor Freight. I was "breaking freight", unloading and uploading large pallets from 18 wheelers with a forklift. I soon got very good with the forklift becoming one of the fastest breakers of freight. When the dock was quiet in the wee hours of the night we used to speed around like racing cars with the forklifts. I had fun there. There was a brother named Ced, that I worked with who had a nice car and loved southern rap. He would pick me up for work and drop me home until I got my own car but during our rides to and from work we bonded through Hip Hop, he would play his favorites and I would play mine. He taught me how to get "crunk" with southern rap which would come in handy when I got to Germany the next year being exposed to the club scene for the first time in my life.

Tony was trying to help me to "be more social". He took me out to bars and we drank. I began to experience drinking and being shit faced **drunk**. Crown Royal was his drink of choice and so it soon became mine. Tony also took me to my **first strip club**. I still remember how beautiful the woman in front of me was, she was "fully naked", and beautiful. I was mesmerized by her beauty. The most popular female rapper in 2021 is **Cardi B** who was a stripper before she became a rapper and everyone knows this. So yes, I was amazed by what I saw in 1999. The woman was beautiful. Her complexion was caramel and her nipples and breast were different amazing colors. I don't remember her face I remember her body but she was gorgeous.. Think about that, I don't remember her face, I only remember her body. I was nestled deep in my lower nature I only saw body parts however you can go to indigenous tribes and see the women walking around with their breast free and you will not find a man there staring at her breast. What would they do that for? Breast are for feeding the babies. I would not come to see the human body this way for many years. You will see how the lure of sex ruled my life and at times almost ending my life.

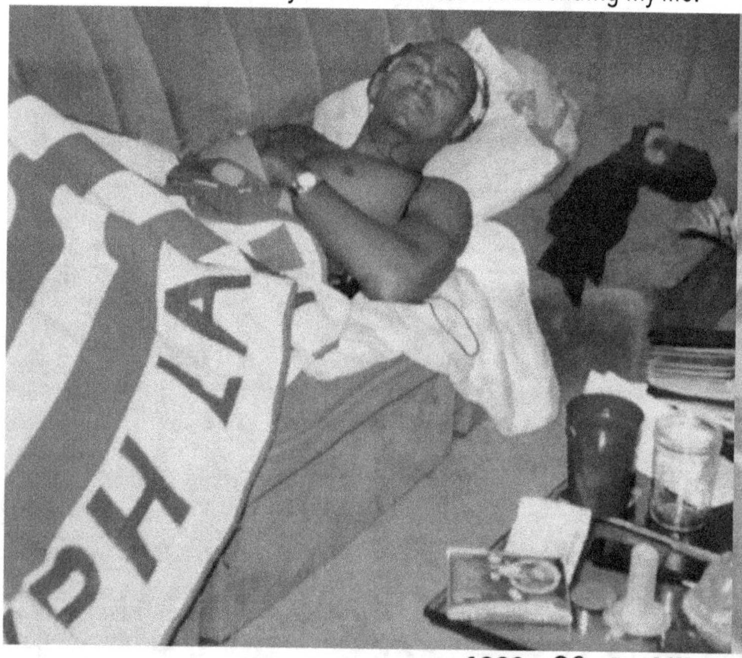
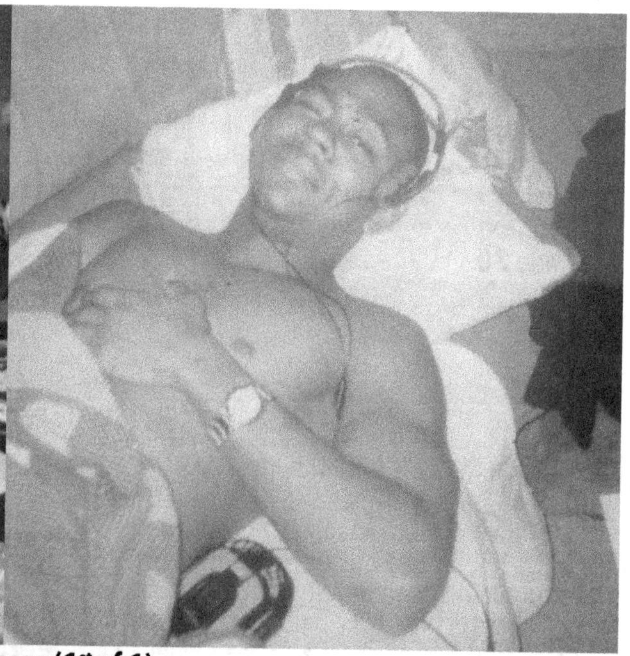

1999 Real ill Emcee (1st of 1)

What does it take to be a real ill emcee? get respect in the game and still be me, it's simple see not like deep dimples be, put water on my pad so I can rhyme fluidically, it's me, **I am that I am** slash emcee, **the beloved one** that defines my name, I know it's different, far from **Common,** Dawud's not a **Common** name, ***one day it'll all make sense*** and never have had changed, it's a sad shame, these boys are bad gone mad in this rap game, this rap game got them sell'n out check it out, first their name then their style now they make'n clout, you heard it from me fuck a word of mouth, get it right, I'm from New York but I wrote this in the dirty south, what does it take to be a real ill emcee? get respect in the game and still be me? is it the measure of your metaphor or simile? I don't know but niggas be like yo it's your delivery, is it that or the gat? matter of fact when I listen to rap I be listen'n black - **Dawud**

Significance - and the Common Connection

During this time in my life, **Common Sense** was my favorite artists and my favorite album of his was **Resurrection**. I say **Common's** name in the song above and in the song I said, ***"one day it'll all make sense "***, *which is the title of one of* ***Common's*** *albums.* **Common** released the single **Resurrection** on **April 4th** 1995, the same day that **Martin Luther King** was assassinated (p 69) which is also the same day that I had my past life revelation of my life as **King Tut** in 2020 (p 594). See pages 66 and 77 for the first and second **Common Connections**. See pages 134, 195, 200, 278, 313, 322, 3**23**, 360, 366, 431 and 624 for the other times I say **Common's** name in my music. See pages 208 and 385 for two strange **Common Connections**.

September 21st 1999
"I Ain't Joining No White Mans Army"

Tony and I began to have disagreements. I imagine that I had passed my time of welcome in his apartment. I had a job now with a car and I think he felt I needed to get out a survive on my own. He started to suggest that I join the army and I responded to him in the same fashion that I did to my Grand Father - "I ain't joining no white mans army". Tony was clever, he would suggest that I could go to Germany and play football in the army however I still disregarded the idea.

One day Tony and I had a major disagreement and either I left or he kicked me out, I don't clearly remember but I started staying in a motel on Old National High Way. When this happened I had just gotten my first car and did not even have car insurance nor did I have the money to pay for it. The motel was owned by an **Indian man** who took a liking to me. He knew my situation and lent me the money to pay for my insurance. <u>After I graduated from my Army training I would return to this motel and repay the generous man</u>.

One day I went to Tony's apartment to gather all my belongings, my clothes my watches etc etc. I packed them all in my car and made my way to work but my car broke down before I made it to work. I parked my car with all my belongings and went to work. When I got back to my car my car was on bricks. My rims and radio had been stolen as well as all my belongings. **All the polo clothes and watches I had stolen and the things I had bought with my own money were stolen from me** (page 76). I was between a rock and a hard place. Soon after this I went to the local Army recruiter center and told him **<u>if he put Germany in my contract and gave me a job that would allow me the time to play football I would join the army.</u>** <u>I was **21** years old and had never given much thought to how powerful our thoughts and desires are but my request would soon be granted</u> **(page 89)**. I took the enrollment test and passed, then I was off to the Army on September **21,** 19**99**. **44** years prior to the date that I joined the Army was September **21**st 19**55** and on that very day, **Emmett Till's** uncle, **Moses Wright** would **stand up and boldly point out Emmett's Killers** (page 517). Unlce Moses would pass away in 19**77**, the same year I was born again as Dawud Eddings. This book will be released in 20**22**, when I'm **44** years of age. This **44** year **"coincidence"** strengthens the **44th parallel theory**. See page 660 for the birth of the **44th parallel.**

I must admit that I was not mentally prepare for the Army and I was not informed about world history or politics when I joined. I can remember considering the possibility that I could die at war however I joined thinking that no country would want to go to war with America. I didn't realize that America has never NOT been at war. I had no loyalty to America I just thought "our" military was stronger than everyone else's so I figured I could join for a few years then get out with no problems. I had also only seen one military movie prior to joining the army and that was the movie, Platoon. There I was at FT Benning being *<u>woken</u>* up by the 5:**55** am bugle call, the same bugle call that I used to hear when I was a boy 10 years prior (page 45)! What are the chances of that? I never thought much about it except that it was just some *<u>"strange coincidence".</u>*

Rau nu Prt m heru

Iu f Per f m heru

Utterances for Coming Forth by day into Light

It is he, who comes forth by day into Light

K-Doug, My Pacer

"AT EASEeeeeeeeee", everyone would scream every time a Drill Sergeant was in sight and immediately everyone would stand at the position of parade rest with our legs hip width apart and our hands behind our backs with our eyes straight forward. It took me a few times for me to realize what was going on and that they were screaming, "AT EASEeeeeeeeee" and not "Eddingssss". I was unprepared for the Army. I had not watched any movies involving basic training so Basic Training was more of fun for me than it was a challenge. I did what I was told, woke up on time and excelled at everything except for sit-ups. I had a six pack but I had never done many sit ups in my life until I got to basic training so I failed sit ups on every fitness test except the very last one we took to graduate and I only past that test because I turned **22** on October **25th** and the last test was on the 27th a couple days after my birthday. The number of sit ups required to pass were reduced at the age of **22**. My drill sergeants thought I was purposely failing so that I would get discharged from the army. Drill Sergeant **Smalls** went so far as to nickname me "Six Pack". I left basic training running 2 miles in 11 minutes and 16 seconds. I would have never ran that fast if it weren't for **Kevin Douglas** (K-Doug) who would run 2 miles in under 11 minutes. He was my **pacer** as I was trying to catch him! In the picture above, Kevin Douglas is wearing a **Cobra's** jersey. The Cobra was the snake used in ancient Kemet (Egypt) and they symbolized **Rebirth** with the routine shedding of their skin, divinity and the right to rule. Perhaps with the revealing of my **past lives** I can be the **pacer** for another ancient soul wandering this earth plane with not yet a clue as to who you are and why you are here. Perhaps you too can shed your skin and rise like Heru (page 366).

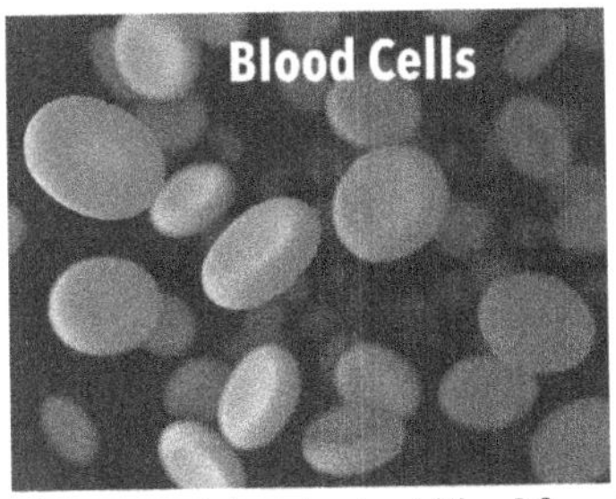

1999 - Transdimensional Encounters
Celestial Disks in The Night Sky

During one of our overnight camping exercises I was staring up at the night sky and what I saw, I would never forget. I saw very clearly, circular objects moving around very slowly. At first I thought they were satellites but there were so many of them that they couldn't have been satellites. They looked to be in space, orbiting the planet and they looked like ***blood cells** (biconcave disks), or **spaceships.** The only frame of reference for what I saw was a **UFO***. They looked like **UFO's**! I would never see anything in the sky like this again but years later in 2015, I would see another object in the sky over Yankee Stadium (p 346). I can only speculate as to what I saw that night at FT Benning Army base but according to the ancient kemetyu the **NTCHRU** (**God**) **RA** was said to have landed on earth in a **celestial disk**. Perhaps those were the same disks or the "chariots in the sky" that **Enoch** saw. **Akhenaten** the enigmatic Pharaoh of the 18th dynasty changed the entire spiritual system and made the sun disk his main focus. The Aten was the sun disk that gave life to all things. Was this circular disk representing the sun or was it some other disk he was referring to? Perhaps a flying disk? And if it was a flying disk was it made by him or was it **extraterrestrial**? I can only tell you what I saw and they looked like what TV programed me to see as a UFO. What about the "Helicopter hieroglyphs" on the walls of Seti I's temple in Abydos, Egypt? Many people believe them to be proof of advanced flying technology hidden from modern man, however those who can read the writings suggest that the initial carving was made during the reign of Seti I and translates to "He who repulses the nine "enemies of Egypt". This carving was later filled in with plaster and re-carved during the reign of Rameses II with the title "He who protects Egypt and overthrows the foreign countries". Over time, the plaster has eroded away, leaving both inscriptions partially visible and creating a palimpsest-like effect of overlapping hieroglyphs. I don't know what technology they had back then but I know what I saw that night in basic training was not like anything I have ever seen before and still till this day have never seen it again. This would not however, be the last time that I had an experience that caused me to think of **UFO's**. In 2002 I would survive a severe car accident and for some reason I would speak of UFO's while in the ambulance (p 105). I would also have a bout of **sleep paralysis** in 2016 that would cause me to think of **aliens**. In 2010 I would start writing music again and flying saucers, **aliens** and extraterrestrials would find their way into my music. Years later I would hear **Prodigy** speaking about seeing a UFO (p 663).

The "Helicopter hieroglyphs" as seen in the temple of Seti I's in Abydos, Egypt

Basic Training Graduation

What some people say the wall of Seti I's looked like before Rameses II plastered over the initial writings.

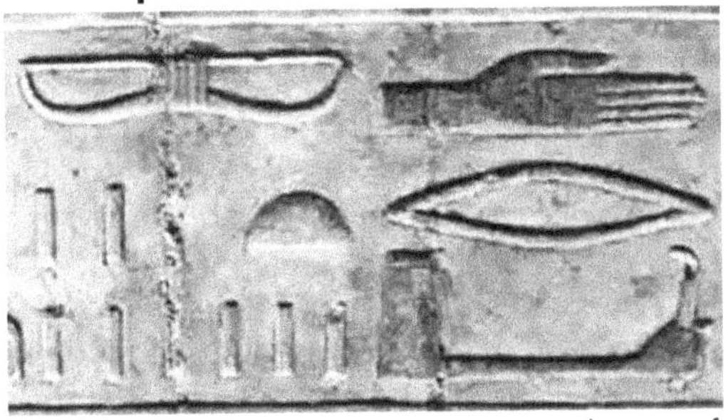

Looking back on those days in basic training none of us knew anything about life really. We all joined for different reasons and many of us had no plan for life outside the Army.

Rau nu Prt m heru

Iu f Per f m heru

Utterances for Coming Forth by day into Light

It is he, who comes forth by day into Light

2000 - Advanced Individual Training (A.I.T.)

I graduated basic training and was promptly sent to FT Lee Virginia for Advanced Individual Training (A.I.T.) to learn how to do my job. I was a 92 Alpha, Logistics - supply. My A.I.T. was co-ed. By this time I was programmed well. I was the soldier that you wanted to have. I kept my shoes shined and my uniform pressed. I was on time, I was fit and as we called it, I was "hoa-hoa sergeant, too easy sergeant, yes sergeant"! I met Carima while at AIT.

Carima

Carima and I met when I was a platoon leader. We were **Whiskey Warriors** and our mascott was the head of a **Native American Chief**. One day Carima wrote me a letter and revealed that she had a crush on me. I was not thinking about starting a relationship because I was on my way to Germany after school was over. Then she told me she was going to Germany too. That's when we began to write each other letters then we began dating, soon after I fell in love with Carima. When we got to Germany we lived very far from each other and I started going out to clubs and running after other girls. I was also into **Jesus** and religion and she was not. I wanted her to be a follower of Jesus like me and so our relationship fell apart because of me. She went on to marry and have children in Germany.

Toussiant, Dessalines and Quantum Physics

Toussaint was a Haitian brother. His last name was **Toussaint**. Him and I got along but he would try to challenge my leadership at times. We respected each other but I was the Platoon leader and when you are telling other men what to do they will sometimes have a problem with that. At least this is how it was for us going through school, and dealing with telling large groups of people what to do for the first time. I had led my football teams on the football field so I was used to being at the helm but this was different. When you're going through school the drill sergeants pick the soldiers they want to be squad leaders and platoon leaders based on your level of physical fitness first so I always rose to the top. When I look back on my experience with **Toussaint** in AIT and consider the fact that I did not know the history of Haiti back then I sort of laugh at the coincidence.

Significance

Our thoughts and desires can affect our reality by influencing quantum level events in time and space and our ancestors operate in between time and space. Years later in 2005 (page 141, 142) **Toussaint** Louverture the leader of the Haitian Revolution would lead my path in one of the first profound and very **strange** experiences I would have with what I saw as a **divine sign from God.** This sign guided me to a job in personal training and it wasn't until May of 2014 (page 292) that I realized it was **Toussaint** and **Dessalines** that led my path. When you read the full circle of what happened in this series of events it will give you another perspective on **Quantum physics**, the ancestral realms involving dead ancestors and their ability and willingness to guide and help us from the other side. All things are governed by seen and or unseen forces. We make a fatal error when we think all that we see with our two eyes is all there is to see.

Rau
nu
Prt
m
heru

Iu
f
Per
f
m
heru

Shackelford
Toussiant
Eddings
Gray

Utterances
for
Coming
Forth
by day
into
Light

It is
he,
who
comes
forth
by day
into
Light

War Games
We were doing over night war game exercises in the field and I must have thought I was Rambo or something.

U.S.ARMY
U.S.ARMY

My first Duty Station
1st Armored division, Old Ironside - HHC 4th Brigade, Hanau Germany

I was in an aviation unit and our company mascot was a FALCON so after every formation we screamed "FIGHTING FALCONS"!

Significance

My **1st Armored division** patch was shaped in a **triangle** like a **pyramid**. The **falcon** (**Heru**) is the pectoral jewelry from the tomb of **Tutankhaten** (**King Tut**). In ancient kemet Heru (Falcon/Horus/Jesus) is the son of Ausar (Osiris) that returns. Heru is from the Ausarion or Osirion drama of **resurrection**. On April 4th 2020 the day that **Martin Luther King** was assassinated (page 69) I would have my past life revelation of my life as **Tutankhaten** (**King Tut**, page 594). **Re-member** that **you** are **Ausar** and **Heru**, the **hero**! See page 3 for the **hero's journey**!

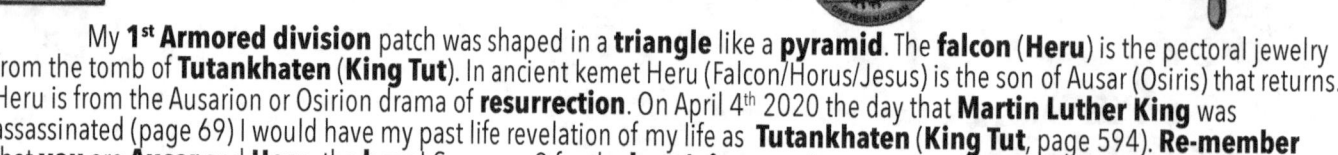

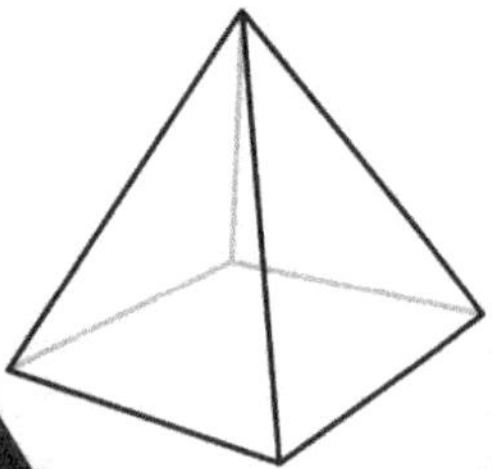

Heru, the Falcon

SGT Austin - "Train or Go Home"

I met Sgt Austin in the gym and he always reminds me that the first time he saw me I was drunk walking around the club with my shirt off. He is 10 years older than me. I was 22 years old and I was always looking for people above me to shadow and learn from. Austin and I would become workout partners and we were faithful to the gym. I never missed a training session. We had a saying when we were in the gym, "**Train or Go Home**", and when things were tough and the weight was heavy we pushed each other with that mantra. This was Austin's mantra and I took it with me on my journey through fitness. It was Austin that showed me the ropes in the gym. I met other people like **Big O** (p 96), but Austin was my main training partner. Training with him helped me develop my discipline with strength training and I am forever grateful. When I left Germany in 2003 I would see Austin again at Ft Campbell. Him and I still talk once or twice a year. Austin's son Tyrone was born on March 19th, my friend Felicia's birthday (page 150). On December **23rd** 2011 Austin lost his only son Tyrone (page 544). He is gone but he is never forgotten. See page **648** for the **metaphysical significance of the number 23**.

Condolences

My condolences go out to the family and friends of Tyrone Austin. Please know that death is not the end. The soul survives death, indeed and in spirit. This is a book of the dead written by a boy who was murdered without justice, who defeated death and came forth by day. May the soul of **Tyrone Austin** walk peacefully through the field of Reeds in Amenta. Amen Ra

Rau nu Prt m heru

Iu f Per f m heru

Utterances for Coming Forth by day into Light

It is he, who comes forth by day into Light

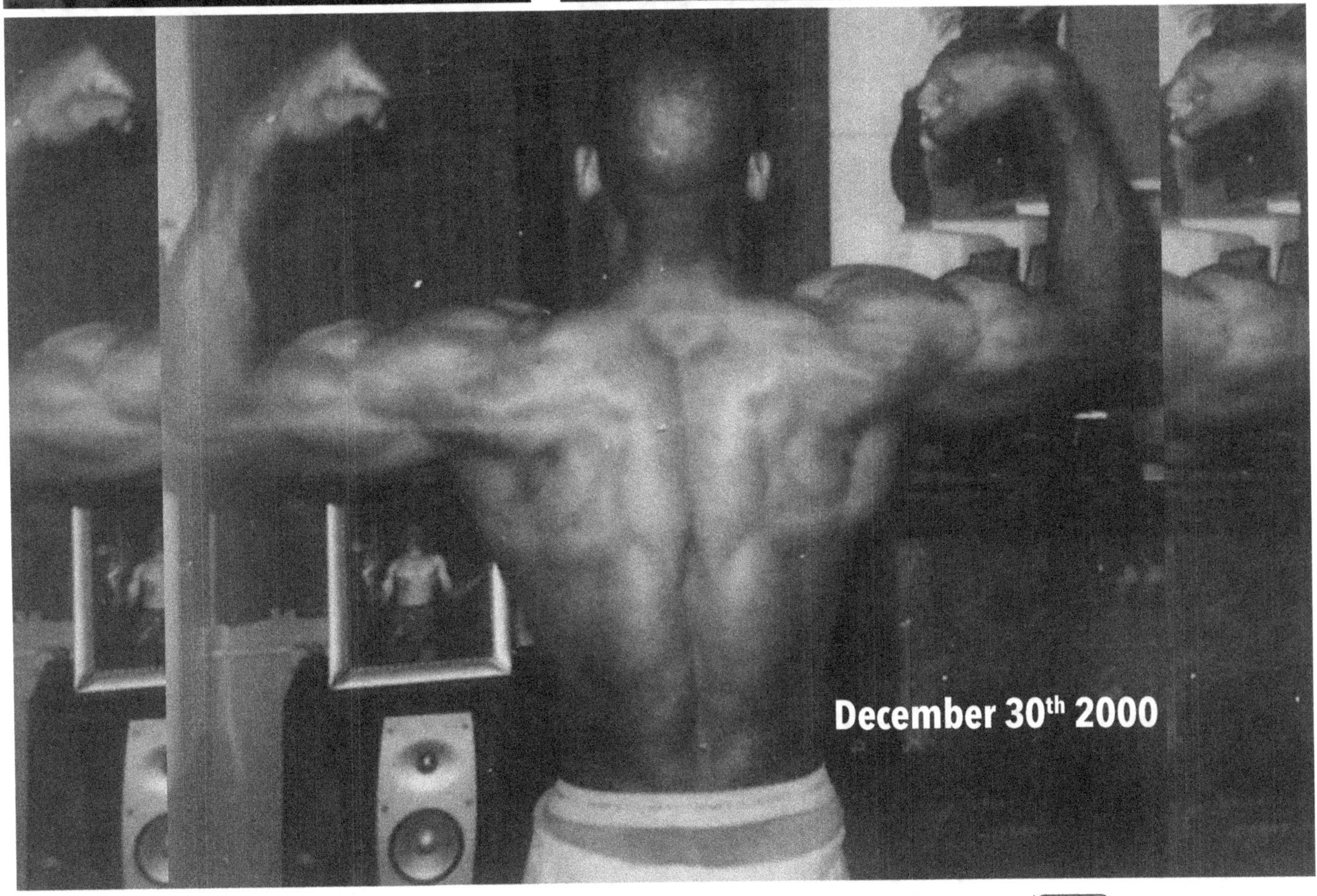

From the Club to the Football Field

I got a job at the club doing security not because I was a fighter but because I knew one of the security guards and I "looked" like I could fight. I was a peace maker in the club but that didn't stop me from participating in some of the brawls that erupted at the club. I spent most of my time picking up women at the club than I did my job as a security guard. One of the German security guards named **Martin** told me about his **Semi Pro Football** team and I joined. I had made a request when I joined the army. I went to the local Army recruiter and told him if he put Germany in my contract and gave me a job that would allow me the time to play **football** I would join the army and now here I was playing football (page 82). Our thoughts and desires can affect our reality by influencing quantum level events in time and space. I put a thought into the air about playing football and it came to fruition. **I manifested it!**

While I never did get to play football in the **NFL**, which was my **dream**, I got to play on a **semi pro** level in Germany. As seen on page 90, I made the news papers often, doing amazing feats that lead us to our first undefeated season. This type of attention only helped to magnify my draw power with women. I was now a security guard at two popular clubs and the star player on a football team. My **soul** purpose with most of the women I met was to engage in enter course. To score a "touchdown". And I scored many touchdowns. This lifestyle caused me to **p**onder about life in general. About my **l**ife and how I was living it. This is what caused me to finally give my life to Christ (**p**age 92), the way I had once wanted to **d**o as teenager (page 52).

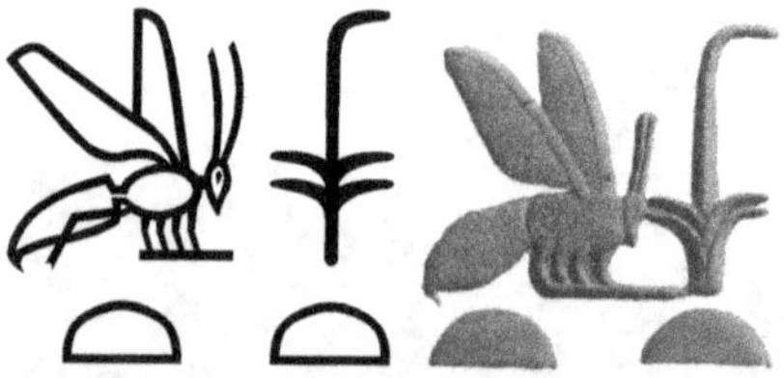

The Hanau Hornets 1st Undefeated Season

I loved football so much I played for free my first year. I didn't choose to play for free I just didn't know other players on the team were getting paid. I had no concept of getting paid for Football. I was in the Army and playing football was fun for me. When I signed up for the army I signed up with the hope that I might be able to play football in Germany (page 82). I did not realize how much of a long shot that was. It was like a hail Mary pass, but I caught it. I found a team or did the team find me? One of the security guards from the job told me about the team and I joined. I played for the **Hanau Hornets** and our colors were blue and **Gold,** like the Beach Channel Dolphins (p 61)! I led my team to our first ever **undefeated** season and first ever champion ship. I was the **MVP**. I scored more than 25 touchdowns that season. I played offense and defense and I did punt return, kick return. I was the starting receiver and the starting cornerback. The only time I wasn't on the field was on kickoffs. I scored receiving touchdowns, interceptions for touchdowns, punt returns, kick returns, fumble recovery's and I had rushing touch downs as well. I was having a good time in Germany.

Rau
nu
Prt
m
heru

lu
f
Per
f
m
heru

Utterances
for
Coming
Forth
by day
into
Light

It is
he,
who
comes
forth
by day
into
Light

Hornets bitten wieder zum Tänzchen

Hanau (ak). Jetzt wird es wieder ernst für Hanaus Hornissen: Am Sonntag (15 Uhr) treffen die Hornets im eigenen Stadion auf die Badener Greifs. Die Karlsruher zählen zu den Traditionsteams im deutschen Football und haben bereits bessere Zeiten als Bundesligist der ersten Stunde gesehen.

Trotz der 0:26-Niederlage gegen Zweitligist und Aufstiegsfavorit Marburg blickt Headcoach Herb Holloway zuversichtlich in die Zukunft. „Wir haben gegen den Favoriten der 2. Bundesliga gut mithalten können. Immerhin gelangen uns vier Touchdowns, die leider wegen Strafen aberkannt worden sind", meint der US-Amerikaner.

In der Verteidigung baut Holloway weiter auf den „doppelten Christian". Christian Fusenecker avancierte in der vergangenen Saison mit 55 Solotackles und acht Quarterbacksacks zum erfolgreichsten Defensespieler der Hornets. Sein Namensvetter Obermaier sorgte neben 27 Tackles noch für sechs Interceptions und konnte zwei Fumbles für die Hornissen sichern. „Ich denke unsere Defense wird auch in der Regionalliga für Furore sorgen", so Holloway. Auch wenn die Greifs am Sonntag mit einem schwer auszurechnenden Spielsystem die Hornets schlagen wollen, die Hanauer nehmen die Kampfansage an. „Wir werden 100 Prozent Leistung bringen", versprechen Fusenecker und Obermaier.

Im Angriff steht wieder Top-Scorer und Publikumsliebling Dee Eddings (Foto) im Blickpunkt. Mit 103 Yards gelang dem Amerikaner der fulminanteste Touch-down-Lauf der letzten Saison. Auch gegen Marburg ließ ein glänzend aufgelegter Eddings wieder seine Klasse aufblitzen. „Wir werden in dieser Saison viel Spaß miteinander haben", verspricht Eddings den Hornets-Fans.

Für sein Team hat Holloway den Klassenerhalt als primäres Ziel ausgerufen. „Jedes Spiel ist eine neue Aufgabe, die wir lösen müssen. Wir werden uns auf jede dieser Aufgaben individuell einstellen", verrät Holloway einen Teil seiner Marschroute für die beginnende Saison. Von der Euphorie der Fans will er sich gar nicht erst anstecken lassen. „Wir spielen eine Liga höher und müssen demnach 100 Prozent mehr Leistung als im letzten Jahr abrufen."

RACISM

For the most part I loved my teammates and they loved me, However I had a couple racist Neo Nazi teammates but that didn't stop them from loving me when I did something to win the game. Team sports have a way of bringing men together.

Transcribed quote from the news clipping

"On the attack, the **top scorer** and crowd favorite **Dee Eddings** is in the spotlight again. The American displayed the most brilliant touch down run of the season with a 103 yard kick return. Against Marburg, a brilliant **Eddings** flashed his skills again. "We will have a lot of fun together this season". Promises **Eddings** to the Hornets fans."

Courtney, Gimel and Our Brother Jesus

Courtney Faulkner is the tall brother in the middle. Courtney and I met when I got to Germany and we became really close, good friends. We were in the same Company and we lived in the same barracks. He was very quiet and shy and was always up for a good laugh. We also went to the same church. We were believers in **Jesus Christ** together. Gimel Peterman is the brother on the right and him and I clicked too. I think I brought him to my church. He wasn't a soldier, his wife was but he was also a believer in Jesus Christ and had grown up in the church. We played the **Tekken** fighting video game (p 76) together most of the time. I made many friends while in the army but after I got out I lost contact with most of them. Courtney was the second friendship broken because of a difference of opinions on who and what **Jesus** was. I left the army in 2005 and I have not seen Courtney since. After I got out the army him and I would talk over the phone every now and then to catch up on things. After my grand father died in 2009 I started studying all forms of information but I don't think Courtney was doing that. We started

having arguments about religion and Jesus around the same time I started arguing with most of the people I knew. I have not spoken to Slim in 4 or 5 years, maybe even 6. I hope he's doing well and in good spirits. I bought my green Benz from Slim and we had a lot of good times hanging out in Germany. We were all young and in our young adult phases of life. There was no internet back then where we might find information the way that we have it today.

Courtney was the first friend I lost due to religion, Sebastian was the second and the last was Larry. Sebastian and I have not spoken in maybe over 8 years and Larry and I stopped speaking in 2021. Sometimes you grow apart from people due to your beliefs, interests and habits. People flock together due to a sameness and I shared a sameness with all the brothers I mentioned. We had being **black** in common, we had the **military** in common, we had being "**American**" in common while stationed in Germany, we had **Tekken** in common and finally we all had **Jesus** in common. If you take those 5 things and weigh their importance to each of us, all of us might hold one thing more closely to the heart than the other. They held their bond with Jesus more important to the bond with their "black" brother. Jesus never came to get us up off of a slave plantation but **Harriet** did and many others along side her and many others like her. We must always remember what **Malcolm X** said - "they don't kill you because you're muslim and they don't kill you because you're christian! They kill you because you are black!". We must always find the route that allows us to build and not destroy.

The year 2000 and New Jerusalem Church - I Gave My Life to Christ at 22 Years Old

I was **22** years old when I joined my first church and ***gave my life to Christ***. I think Slim invited me to church. Pastor Macintosh was our spiritual leader. I was drawn in by his sermons and his singing. When I was 14 years old living with my aunt in New Jersey I used to go to church with her sometimes and I always wanted to walk up and give my life to God when they did the alter call. Finally at the age of 22 I got up and walked to the front and gave my life to Christ just like I always wanted to. I would remain a Christian for many years. Pastor Macintosh came to a few of my football games and after he saw me do magical things on the football field it had a effect on him. After seeing me play he would use my efforts on the football field in his sermons. He told the congregation about how I never gave up, how when everyone thought I was going to be tackled and all hope was lost, out of the sea of people I would surface and still be running until I scored a touchdown. He had seen me play football and he was a believer in me and we were both believers in Jesus Christ.

Rau nu Prt m heru

Iu f Per f m heru

Utterances for Coming Forth by day into Light

It is he, who comes forth by day into Light

2001 Year of The Snake

The 2,300 Year old Ancient Kemetic (Egyptian) City of Thonis-Heracleion is discovered underwater in the Mediterranean sea off the coast of Egypt. A statue of **Ausar** (**Osiris**) the Lord of **resurrection / reincarnation**, a stela of baby Heru with scorpions and snakes in his hand and other artifacts are found and a mesmerizing picture of Ausar is taken under water at the sea floor.

February 17th 2001 (the year of the Snake)

Apparently I drew this picture of my little sister on **Huey P's** birthday Feb 17th in 2001, the year of the **snake** which is the same exact day that **Khalid Muhammed** was **assassinated**. At the time I had never heard of Khalid and would not come to know of him until after my grand father died from **cancer** on Aug18th 2009 the day after **Marcus Garvey's** birthday. Huey P was one of the founders of the **Black Panther** Party for self defense and **Khalid Muhammad resurrected** the **Black Panthers**. I don't recall drawing this picture but as I stare at it, it brings me sadness because of the look of sadness on the face of my little sister Jenna, who was 11 at the time. I probably drew it because it touched my soul as it does now. I came across this drawing by "**coincidence**" on Nov 19th 2021 while looking through my Grandmothers photo albums. My sister was born in 1989 the year of the **snake** and in 2019 she would have a baby that came to earth carrying a **code** like my Aunt Pamela and her children who are coded by **Malcolm X** (pages 37 & 287). My sister's baby father was born on **May 25th** which is the first star code that I decoded in 2011 (p 222) and her daughter is born on **Apr 20th** (p 558). On **May 25th** 2002 another sister of mine would call me about a **dream** she had of me dying in a car crash (p 104). 7 days after her dream I would survive a violent car crash on my fathers birthday. In my life as Emmett Till my uncle **Moses** Wright would identify my dead body by the **ring** my father (Louis Till) gave me which had the date **May 25th** inscribed on it. My death as Emmett Till would spark the first mass protest for civil rights. Four months after my ("Emmett's") death, Rosa Parks was riding a bus in Montgomery, Alabama. She was supposed to give up her seat to a white man and move to the back of the bus but she refused. Rosa Parks said, "I thought of Emmett Till, and I couldn't go back." On **May 25th** 2020 **George Floyd** was murdered by a white police officer who kneeled on his neck until he died and his death sparked the biggest protest for civil rights in American history (p 610). On **Aug 28th** 1833 the year of the **snake**: Slavery was abolished in the United Kingdom, which had a trickle down effect and led to the American abolition of slavery. On **Aug 28th** 2020 Chadwick Boseman, the actor who played The **Black Panther** dies of **cancer** (p 624). Chadwick was born in 1977 the year of the **snake** like me in my current life as well as my life as Emmet (19**41**) but Chadwick's year of birth is now changed to 1976 the year of the **Dragon***. My astrological **dragons* tail** also known as the "**south node**"starts in the age of **Aries** which was the last golden age of ancient Kemet where the 18th dynasty reigned (page 656). **Akhenaten** was the most enigmatic pharaoh from that time and research proves him to be the biblical **Moses**. In my life as Emmett Till my uncle **Moses** Wright identified my dead body by the **ring** my father gave me which had the date **May 25th** inscribed on it p (512). On **May 25th** 2020 **George Floyd** was murdered. In 2021 the killer of **George Floyd** is sentenced to prison on **April 20th** the same day that my niece was born (p 558). A mural for George Floyd was erected in Union Square New York City and a white man defaced the mural by throwing paint on it. The man was identified and arrested on my 44th birthday October 25th 2021. Rosa Parks died the day before my birthday on October 24th and she was born on February 4th, the day after my mother. On July 3rd 2018 my past life as Emmett Till was revealed to me (p 480) and on April 4th 2020 the day **Martin Luther King** was **assassinated** (page 69, 592) my life as **Tutankhaten** (**King Tut**) was revealed to me (page 592-596). Today is May 14th 2022 and today is my sisters birthday. Today a 18 year old white man killed 10 black people in Buffalo NY. Gaspar Yanga was born on my sister's birthday, May 14th 1545 the year of the **snake*** (p 430). As a rebel leader Yanga successfully resisted a Spanish attack on the colony in 1609 and he was named as a "**national hero of Mexico**". Will you stand around and be murdered or will you do like Huey, Khalid, Garvey, Martin, Rosa, Malcom X, Akhenaten and Yanga? See page 3 for the **hero's journey**.

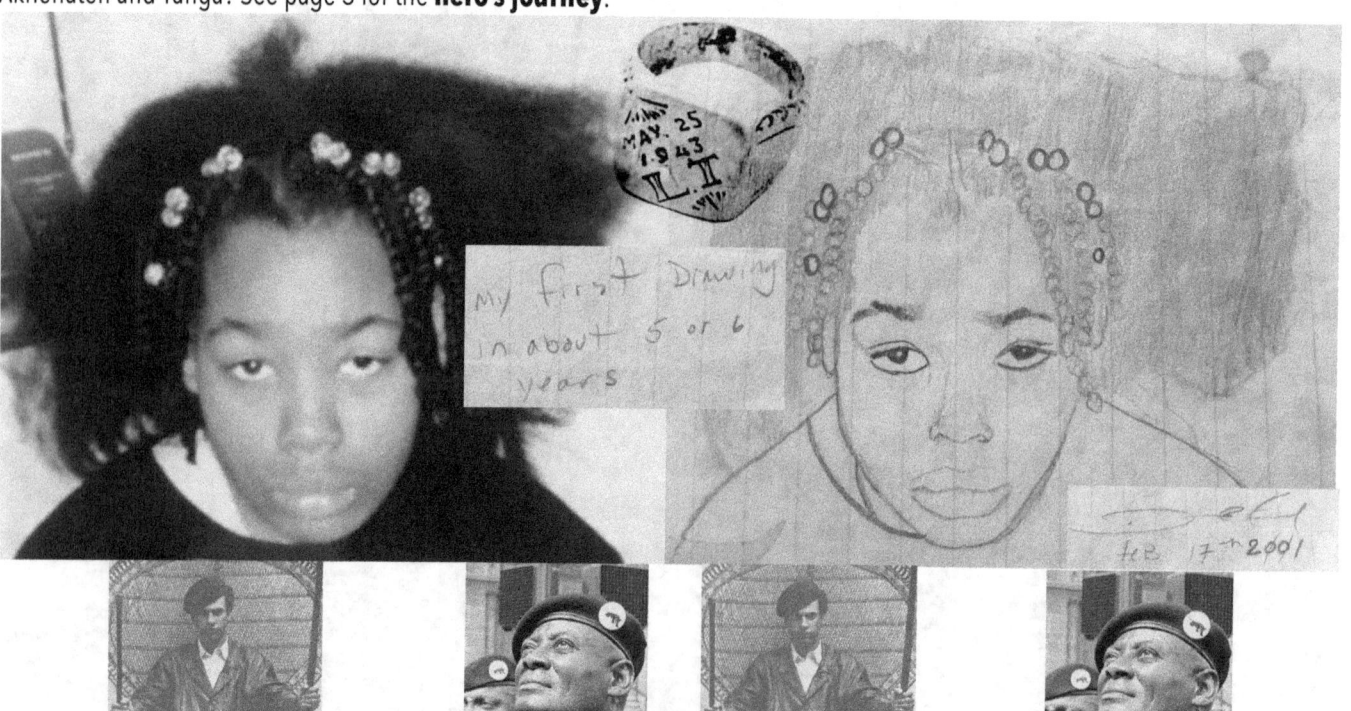

1943
L T
My first Drawing
in about 5 or 6
years
Feb 17th 2001

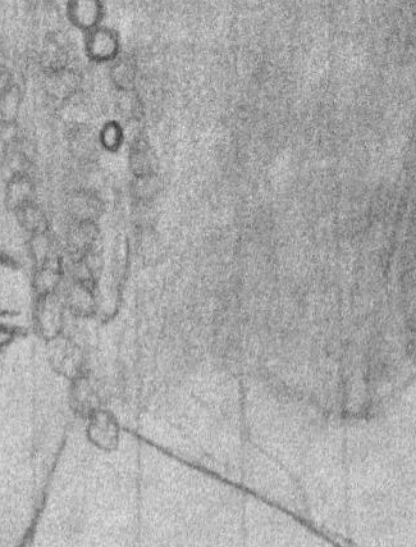

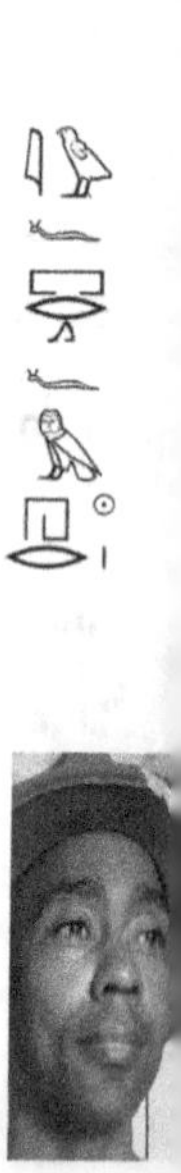

February 23rd 2001
Tupac, Mos Def & Martin Luther King

During this time in my life I would say my prayers every night before bed. I had a ritual, Mos Def was one of my favorite emcee's and I would play his song **UMI Says** on repeat while I said my prayers. Sometimes I would fall asleep during the prayers while **on my knees in the salat position that muslims use when praying**. Little did I know that this posture was done in Kemet thousands of year before Islam took this posture as a prayer position. I was in my 20's and I loved **Tupac** for the same reasons we love **Malcolm X**, **Muhammad Ali**, **Harriet Tubman** and so on. In the picture seen below, I have two pictures of Tupac on my wall and in the middle is a picture of **Martin Luther King** (p 69, 592) on the wall. I didn't know all the things that I know now about life in general or about Martin and Tupac for that matter however Martin's speeches and Tupac's music had a way of reaching the soul. Research suggest that things heard pass almost immediately into the subconscious regions of our minds and emotions. I had consumed more of Tupac's music than most of the people that I knew. At this time in my life I don't think I had ever met a person who loved Tupac or his music more than me but I always met brothers who loved Tupac. I was not what you would call a "thug" but I loved Tupac's music. I was the "young Black male" that he spoke of often in his music. I was the "*Ghetto Bastard*" and so **Treach** became my favorite rapper before I ever heard of Tupac (page 52). That was around the same time that I lived in New Jersey with my Aunt Karen. The song Ghetto Bastard by Naughty By Nature was one of my favorite songs and it was released on Nov 26th 1991 the same day that King Tut's tomb was opened (p 11). My last day in the Army would end up being Martin Luther Kings birthday, Jan 15th 2005. I have a theory about who Tupac was in a previous life. On **Aug 28th** 1833 the year of the **snake**: Slavery was abolished in the United Kingdom, which had a trickle down effect and led to the American abolition of slavery. On **August 28th** 1955 **Emmett Till** is brutally murdered ushering Martin Luther King to the forefront of the Civil Rights Movement. On **Aug 28th** 1963 Dr. Martin Luther King, Jr. delivered his iconic "**I Have A Dream**" speech in Washington, D.C. On **Aug 28th** 2005, **Hurricane Katrina** reached it's peak strength and headed towards Louisiana. The storm, which devastated New Orleans, and to an unusually large degree it impacted many of the city's black residents more than any other group of people, as if it was planned that way. On **August 28th** 2008, then Senator **Barack Obama** accepted the democratic nomination for president, becoming the first black man to ever win the nomination and bid for presidency. Speaking of February **23**, I don't know when I saw the movie **The Number 23** but it was many years before my past life revelations, yet the movie mentions **Sirius** and it's about patterns and numbers. It premiered on Feb **23,** 2007 and Jim Carrey **star**red in it. Jim Carrey **star**ted his acting career in 19**77**, the year of the snake, the year I was born. See page **648** for the **metaphysical significance of the number 23** and pages 25, 102, 121, 283, 444, 439, 586, 669, and 672 for more on **Feb 23rd**.

Rau nu Prt m heru

Iu f Per f m heru

Utterances for Coming Forth by day into Light

It is he, who comes forth by day into Light

Jasmin Sharawi and Her Golden Dream Meta Spiritual Encounters

I met Jasmin at the club, she's **Egyptian, Palestinian, German** and she was gorgeous. I still remember our first date. I picked her up in my old grey Opel Cadet hooptie and it broke down at a gas station. I was embarrassed but she didn't seem to mind it all. A random mechanic took a look at my car and hit the starter with a hammer then the car started. Jasmin and I looked at each other and laughed. I would use that solution a few other times in the future when my car failed to start. Jasmin was one of the women that I was drawn to for reasons beyond my understanding. I fell for Jasmin fast but again, I fell for most of the women that I chased but yet still, there was something about Jasmin that made her special to me. I knew that she was born on my Grandmothers birthday October 9, 1979 (year of the goat) and perhaps that played into the reasons why I always felt close to her. Jasmin took me to my first concert, we saw **Jay Z** live on November 8th 2001 **the year of the Snake** in Frankfurt Germany. My favorite part of the show was **Jay Z** paying homage and condolences to not only **Biggie Smalls** but to **Tupac** as well. Before this the only other rapper I had seen live was **Nas** at the **Apollo** in 1996, performing **If I ruled the World**. Apollo is the Greek Equivalent to Heru. Ausar returns (resurrects) through his son Heru (Horus) as **Ra** in the Ausarian **resurrection drama**. My feelings for Jasmin would intensify after my car accident on June 1st 2002 (page 106). Jasmin is a part of my **May 25th pattern** and she would have a profound **dream** on **May 2nd 2021** about me that seemed to confirm my past life as **Tutankhaten** (page 643). Her **dream** left me questioning who she might possibly have been in a previous life. Perhaps I fell for her because I had known her before, in another life. Remember that you are Ausar and Heru, the hero! See page 3 for the **hero's journey!**

April 10th 2001 (Soldier of the Quarter) *ADDENDUM*

When I got to Germany **Sgt Medina** was my squat leader and he really liked me because of my work ethic. Soldiers were not allowed to get jobs on the economy without first getting approval from the chain of command but **1st SGT Peter Lamberti** liked me a lot too so he allowed me to play even though I never asked permission. His wife was German and he felt like my playing football helped with host country relations. Plus I was the soldier of the Month, Soldier of the Quarter, guide on bearer, I held the colors during change of command ceremonies and I was the most fit soldier in the unit. Shortly after I arrived Sgt Medina left the unit and I got a new squad leader, **Sgt Carter**.. She had just made the rank of Sergeant just before I arrived to the unit. She was a southern woman with a gold tooth who was over zealous about recently being promoted to Sgt. I was her first soldier but I wasn't the most ideal soldier for a gay masculine female. In the Army people can become rank heavy when they get promoted. So since I was her new soldier she was working extra hard at exercising her authority to prove she was the one in charge. I never tried her authority but I think she had a problem with me because all of the chain of command liked me. Sometimes it's hard to lead someone who is more of a natural leader than you. She took her anger out on me and wrote me up a few times but I never got in trouble. In hindsight I appreciate her. She's part of the reason I worked so hard and became Soldier of the year. Back then the awards meant a lot to me but now they don't mean much. They only show that you can parrot what you read. Anyone can do that. That's why, when I exited the army I never got galvanized by people in the "Conscious Community" who memorized and regurgitated information. Instead I studied the information and applied it. Just because you can define something doesn't mean that you know it intimately. In 20**23** **1st SGT Peter Lamberti** wrote me a buddy letter for my military compensation claim helping me to receive my proper monthly compensation (p 121).

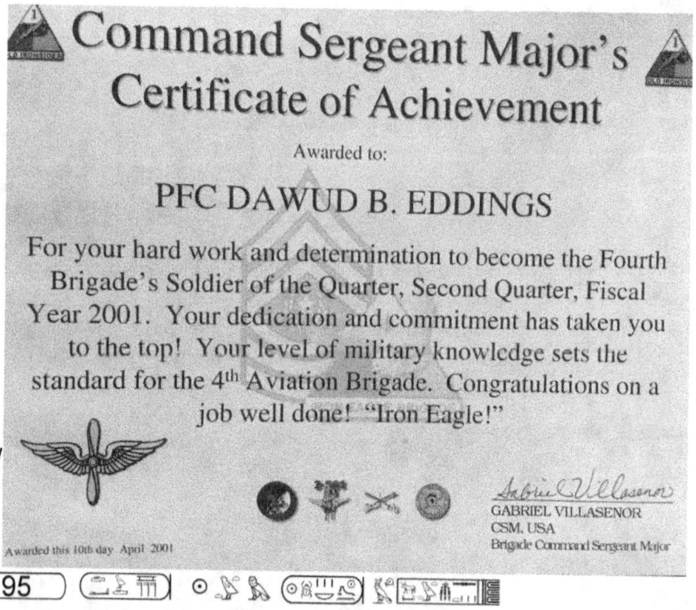

Command Sergeant Major's Certificate of Achievement

Awarded to:

PFC DAWUD B. EDDINGS

For your hard work and determination to become the Fourth Brigade's Soldier of the Quarter, Second Quarter, Fiscal Year 2001. Your dedication and commitment has taken you to the top! Your level of military knowledge sets the standard for the 4th Aviation Brigade. Congratulations on a job well done! "Iron Eagle!"

Gabriel Villasenor
GABRIEL VILLASENOR
CSM, USA
Brigade Command Sergeant Major

Awarded this 10th day April 2001

Rau nu Prt m heru

SGT Oliver "Big O"

I heard about the freak-nick in Atlanta only after attending the ones here in Germany. Fast cars and pretty women that's what most of us single soldiers did with our time and unfortunately lots of the married ones too. **Big O** was one of the biggest guys in our gym. On my post there was just a small group of us who worked out and we didn't take pictures everyday. We pushed each other to be stronger and there was a time when my arms almost rivaled Big O's in size. When Big O's unit returned home from their deployment to Iraq many of them suffered from **cancer** and died, however Big O survived and I think he survived because his body had been used to struggling from all the years of lifting heavy weights. This can't be confirmed but this is my theory.

Iu f Per f m heru

Meta Spiritual Encounters, Big O and Angel Baby from Mars

Today is **March 15**, 2022, I called Big O yesterday but he didn't answer. He returned my call today and we spoke for 2 hours and **23** minutes. I told him about this book for the first time. I told him about the story of my past lives and I told him that I mentioned him in my book. He wanted to know how I came to the realization of the past lives and I started by telling him about how I connected the dates with my accident in 2002. I explained how my sister had a **dream premonition** about my car accident on May 25th 2002 and then I crashed 7 days later on **June 1st** 2002. Afterwards we went on to have a long spiritual conversation. He told me about his spiritual journey. We had both changed from the image seen in the picture above. We laughed a lot and reflected. I began to share with him more experiences that I put in my book then he began to talk about his daughter. She is 6 now but when she first began to talk she would say things that he could not explain. The first thing that caught his attention was her response to seeing **helicopters**. Big O was a Black Hawk crew chief in the army. So he flew on helicopters all the time. When his daughter saw helicopters she said, "**da da, you used to fly**". Big O could not understand how she could know this. She was only two years old and they never talked about that to her. One day his daughter looked at a picture of his mother who had passed away years before she was born yet when she saw the picture she said, "**that's grandma**". Big O wondered how could she know that because he never told her that. When she began to speak sentences she once said to him, "**when I was a angel baby I used to watch over you when you used to fly**". These moments with his daughter left him perplexed and caused him to contemplate the purpose of life and how this little girl could know what she knew. When he asked her how she knew these things she would reply, "**I told you I was a angel baby, I am from Mars**". Her response further confused him because she was too young to know about different planets. One day him and his wife were driving in the car and they noticed his daughter in the back seat laughing. They asked her what was so funny. She replied, "**grandma is telling me knock knock jokes**". Big O was a bit spooked but he remained interested in these strange moments with his daughter and it was his daughter who helped guide him back to his spiritual path. Afterwards I told him about my friend Shanta (who is born on **March 15th**) and the experiences she had with her daughter (page 289) and what happened in Detroit in Aug 2020 (page 618).

Utterances for Coming Forth by day into Light

Confirmations

After hearing the dates in my revelation he was compelled to tell me about the accident he had last year on **June 1st**. Big O used to race motorcycles professionally and he crashed his motorcycle on **June 1st** 2021 at 120 miles and hour, on my fathers birthday, the same day that I crashed my car in 2002 (page 105). As soon as his hand hit the ground his glove exploded and the skin on his finger was burned off. When he crashed he had an **outer body experience**. He could see the men racing to his aid from above with looks of despair and grief on their faces as they rushed to his aid. No one thought he could have survived the accident but he did. We began to talk about my accident then he asked me if I remembered him coming to my room after my accident but I did not. He said he had come to see me and told me to, "be slow and for sho, cause when you're fast you crash". I put those words in the rhyme I wrote about my accident but I could never remember who the person was that told me that, but apparently it was Big O and "coincidentally" Big O would crash 19 years later on the same day that I crashed (page 105). As soon as I hung up with Big O, I got a call from **Coreisa Lee** that left me spellbound, see pages 44, 460 and 568.

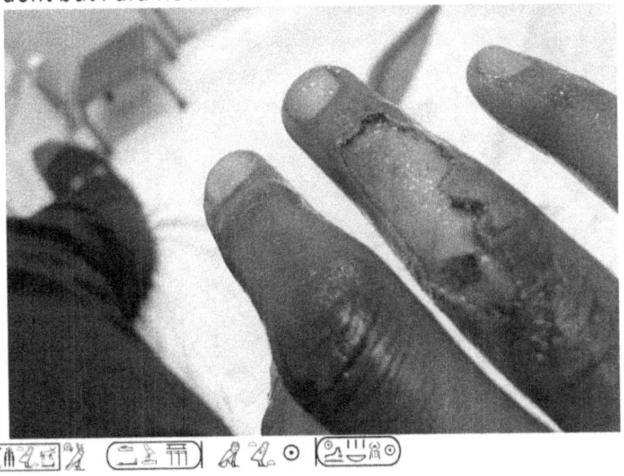

It is he, who comes forth by day into Light

Permanent Change of Duty Station

When it was time for someone to leave the unit we would have a going away dinner to see them off. It was called PCSing, permanent change of duty station. I spoke to Shannette a few years ago, she was having health issues and I gave her information on holistic healing. Since then her number changed and I lost contact with her. Dehaan (page 118) sent me Paul's number and I spoke to him recently (2022). I am currently not in contact with any of the other people in this picture.

Left- SGT Christopherson, SGT Shannette Chapmen, SPC Cocetta and --?. **Right** - SPC Faulkner, SPC Eddings, SSG Paul Sherman and SPC Ivey. I don't know who was leaving the unit in this picture but I can say that I miss all the people in this picture and I hope they're all doing well and in good health. We had a sense of camaraderie and family the only problem is that we all worked for a military that currently only bombs black and brown people.

190E Mercedes Benz

I purchased this car from my homie Courtney (Slim). I was making more money from working at the Club so I upgraded from my Opel cadet to the 190 E. These were also the same types of cars used as cabs in Germany but to us American's it was luxury. I was a speed demon in this car and had a few close calls on the highway while racing but I always seemed to escape most certain danger. I stopped driving this car completely once I bought the black one a year later but I had two Benzes.

Rau nu Prt m heru

Iu f Per f m heru

Utterances for Coming Forth by day into Light

It is he, who comes forth by day into Light

Zascha Moktan

Meta Mysterious Encounters

Zascha was the first person I can ever remember meeting in a magical way, as if our meeting was governed by the hands of fate. I met Zascha at a club frequented by mostly locals and very few Americans. One of my German teammates from the **Hanau Hornets football** team was a DJ there. He brought me along because he liked me and wanted to take me out for fun. The first time I went to this club I saw Zascha and it was like **love at first sight.** I remember trying to talk to her and being rejected immediately! She did not like American soldiers. I went back to the club the following week just to see if I would see her again and sure enough I did. This time she would see me in the DJ booth and she would ask me if I could get the DJ to let her sing happy birthday to her friend. I was more than happy to do that for her! I got my friend, the DJ, to turn all the music in the club off. I walked over to Zascha and I handed her the mic. She began to sing and when she did the whole clubbed stopped and was silent! Her voice was like and instrument, she could "sing sing". When she was done the crowd cheered. She thanked me for setting that up for her but still, she didn't give me her number.

One day I was going to see one of the cheerleaders from the Hanau Hornets cheerleading squad. She told me she had a friend over her house so I brought a friend with me, my homie **Slim**. When we got to her house I would be amazed to see Zascha there! We were both surprised to see each other. What were the chances of that?!! Her friend was Zascha the girl I met at the club!!! I KNEW THIS WAS A DIVINE MEETING!. It was like magic and I was amazed. The cheerleader I came to see was reasonably upset because Zascha and I became more interested in each other and spent the rest of the evening speaking to each other. Not to mention my boy Slim, he thought "the friend" was for him. Well, she was until she ended up being Zascha. I got Zascha's number this time. I began to call her but she was always far away in Hamburg Germany pursuing her music career.

After some time she came back to Frankfurt and we began to hangout. I got to know her mother and her little brother Danny. I fell in love with a few women in Germany but my love for Zascha eclipsed all the rest. I don't know if Zascha ever knew how much I loved her. I was so used to having sex with women quickly that when I really fell for a woman I wouldn't even rush to kiss them, I just wanted to be around them and this how is ot went with Zascha. Because of this perhaps she thought I saw her as just a friend but I Loved her dearly. I would leave Germany in 2003 and would leave the Army in 2005 but by some twist of fate, somehow I would see her again in **Atlanta** in 2005 (page 133).... **What are the "chances" of that?!**

On **Sep 11th** 2001 I took a physical fitness test to become a Sergeant in the Army. I was stationed in Germany at the time. Because the people in my platoon knew I was from New York they rushed to tell me the news of a plane hitting one of the Twin Towers. Initially I thought nothing of it but when the second plane hit we all knew something was happening. From that day things changed for us soldiers in Germany and soon we were on the course for a war with Iraq. The only reason I thought to place this event into this book is because of my fathers **dream**. Around 8 years ago (2013) my father revealed to me that he **dreams** things before they happen, just like me uncle Jimmy (page 172). Usually it's bad things, like if a family member or a friend is going to die he see's it before it happens. He told me that he **dreamt** about people jumping from a building that was on fire the day before **911** happened. He also dreamt about his sister Florence being sick before she died (p 464). I have a sister who is born the day after him and she once **dreamt** about me dying in a car accident on **May 25th** 2002 (page 104). 7 days later I would have a violent crash on my father's birthday (p 106). In 2014 I would start **dreaming** things before they happen (p 305). While looking into the **911** event I came across a few high profile people who narrowly escaped death on Sep 11th 2001. The first person I came across was **Michael Jackson**. He had a meeting at the Twin Towers the day they fell but he missed the meeting because he over **slept** after staying up late into the night talking to his mother, Katherine, and his sister, Rebbie. I found that interesting because it involved **sleep** and because Michael Jackson is born the day after **Emmett Till** was murdered and he is also connected to **King Tut** (p 166). Oddly enough I found myself writing this portion of the book on **Sep 11th** 2021 and had also added the stories of how **Mark Wahlberg**, **Seth MacFarlane** and **Sarah Ferguson** had also seemed to escape death on **911**.

I was done with this portion of the book in October of 2021 but that changed after I finished watching the first two seasons of **Orville** in May of 2022. I had only watched the show because of the name, **Orville**, my great grandfather **General Dukes Sr** was born in **Orrville** Alabama (page 19). When I was done with the series I found myself anticipating the release of season 3 and oddly enough it was **set** to air on my sisters birthday, the same sister who **dreamt** my car accident before it happened in 2002 (p 104). I had already known that Seth was the writer behind the cartoon comedy Family Guy and because of a booking mix up and a hangover he narrowly avoided boarding a plane that crashed into the Twin Towers. Because I was now a fan of the show **Orville** I began to look into the details of the show and that's when I went down a rabbit hole, or better, a blackhole. First I saw that Seth is born the day after me. Then it registered, the name **Seth** is another way of spelling **Set** and **Set** is the brother of **Ausar** (Osiris) in the Egyptian **resurrection** drama (page 30). **Remember that you are Ausar!** <u>See page 3 for the **hero's journey!**</u> This connection made me look into the other people I had written about. I had already written about Mark Wahlberg booking a flight on American Airlines Flight 11 which crashed into the North Tower and how him and his friends decided to change plans at the last minute. What I didn't know was that Mark was born in 1971, the same year and month that my great grandfather **General Dukes Sr** died and the same year **Tupac** was born. The last person was Sarah Ferguson, the **Duchess of York**. I had already written about how she escaped death because she was stuck in traffic preventing her from attending a meeting located on the 101st floor of the north tower but with all the other connections I wondered if perhaps there was more. I did a search on her and immediately I saw that she was married to Prince Andrew, **Duke** of York. Then I saw that Prince Andrew, **Duke** of York was born on **February 19th**, the same day as my great grandfather **General Dukes Sr** (page 19). Then I began to look at the birth and death dates of Sarah's royal line and what I observed reminded me of the dates surrounding the "**Curse of The Pharaoh**" (page 12). My sister is born on my mother's birthday and Michael Jackson's brother Jackie is born on their mother's birthday. This is a pattern that happens often within families. When I looked into Sarah's ancestry I was spun deeper into a star code pattern that can not and should not be seen as "**just a coincidence**". All things are governed by seen and unseen forces. This was part of this **Prophecy of Reincarnation**.

Her father Ronald Ferguson, born Oct 10th the day after my grandmother (p 22). Her grand father Andrew Ferguson was also born October 10th. Her mother Susan Wright, born June 9th, the same day my great grandfather **General Dukes Sr** died (p 19), and she died Sep 19th, the same day **Emmett Louis Till's** murder trial started (p 516). Her grandmother Marian **Louis**a Montagu, born on June 16th, same day **Tupac** was born. Her great grandfather H. FitzHerbert Wright, born Oct 9th, same day as my grandmother (p 22). Her great grandfather Algernon Ferguson, born **Sep 27th** and died Nov 5th, the day after **King Tut's** tomb was discovered. Her great grandmother Margaret Ferguson died **Sep 27th** which is the day I watch the video, A Different look at **Emmett Till** (p 579). Her great grandfather Lord Herbert died June 17th 1944, same day my grandfather **General Dukes Jr** was born (p **23**) and he had a daughter named Patricia who was born Oct 9th, my grandmother's birthday (p 22). Her 2x's great grandmother **Louis**a Jane Montagu, Duchess of Buccleuch and Queensberry was born on my nephews birthday, Aug 26th, two days before Emmett **Louis** Till was murdered. Her 5x's great grandfather Alexander Gordon, 4th **Duke** of Gordon and Keeper of the Seal of Scotland was born June 18th, same day my great grandmother Leacola **Riddle** died (p 21), he died June 17th, the day my grandfather **General Dukes Jr** was born (p **23**). Her 2x's great grandfather William Henry Montagu, 6th **Duke** of Buccleuch and 8th **Duke** of Queensberry died Nov 5th, the day after **King Tut's** tomb was discovered and he was born on Sep 9th, two days after **Tupac** was shot. Her great grandfather to Prince Richard, **Duke** of Gloucester died two days before **Emmett Till** was murdered on Aug 26th 1944 at the age of 77. His grand son Prince William died on Aug 28th, the same day **Emmett Till** was murdered. Her 3x's great grandfather Walter Montagu, 5th **Duke** of Buccleuch and 7th **Duke** of Queensberry was born Nov 25th, the day before **King Tut's** tomb was opened, (p 11). His son Henry, 1st Baron Montagu of Beaulieu was born on Nov 5th 1832 and died Nov 4th 1905 the same day **King Tut's** tomb was discovered. His son Lord Charles Montagu died on Aug 21st the same day the **Haitian Revolution** started. Her 5x great grandfather Thomas Thynne, died Sep 13th the same day **Tupac** died. His son George Thynne, 2nd Baron Carteret died **Feb 19th** the same day that my great grandfather **General Dukes Sr** was born (p 19). Her 5x's great grandfather, Henry Scott, 3rd **Duke** of Buccleuch and 5th **Duke** of Queensberry was born Sep 2nd, the day that **Mamie Till** arrived at the Illinois Central Terminal to receive the box's of her dead son, **Emmett Till** (p 514). Her 6x's great grandfather Francis Scott, Earl of Dalkeith was born **Feb 19th** the same day as my great grandfather **General Dukes Sr** (page 19). Her 3x's great grand father Charles William Henry Montagu, 4th **Duke** of Buccleuch and 6th **Duke** of Queensberry was born May 24th, the day before **George Floyd** was murdered and he was born Apr 20th, the same day as my niece and the same day **George Floyd's** killer was sent to prison (P 610). Her 4 x's great grandfather Richard Wingfield was born **Sep 11th** 1790. His daughter Lady Maria Rose died Feb 7th the same day as Emmett's father, **Louis** Till was born (pages 475, 518). His son Richard Meade, 2nd Earl of Clanwilliam died Sept 3rd the same day **Emmett Till's** wake was held. I have a theory about who **Tupac** was in a past life.?

Rau nu Prt m heru

Amanda Gonzales was 19 years old when she was murdered. Her body was found on November 5th 2001 in her third-floor barracks room on Fliegerhorst Kasern (post) near Hanau, Germany after she did not report for work. She had been in Germany only **eight** months. She was on her first assignment in the Army, and was assigned to Headquarters Supply Company of the 127th Aviation Support Battalion as a cook at the time of her death. Her death was ruled a homicide by asphyxiation. Amanda was four or five-months pregnant when she was beaten and strangled by someone. To this day, nobody has been arrested for her death nor has any motive been discovered. Amanda's case has received a lot more attention following the death of Fort Hood soldier **Vanessa Guillen** on April 22nd 2020. When Vanessa's case was made public Amanda's mother saw the news and felt like it was her daughter Amanda's case all over again. Both families have joined the families of other soldiers who have been murdered while serving. They have demanded more transparency from the military and changes in the ranks due to the way the cases are handled. As the push continues for justice in the murder of Fort Hood soldier Vanessa Guillen, her family and attorney are planning their next steps. At a small cemetery in Hearne, Amanda Gonzales is laid to rest but her family has been restless for two decades following the 19-year-old's brutal murder.

Iu f Per f m heru

Significance

I was stationed in Germany on the same post as Amanda at the time of her death but I never heard about it. As you can see I was only focused on chasing women and playing football at the time. I only found this case by chance. I found the case on October 28th 2021 when I was online looking for pictures of my old post (Fliegerhorst Kasern). I kept seeing the face of a woman pop up in searches but this book has been so tedious that I had not the energy to search or look at anything other than what I'm writing however something told me to click on her picture, so reluctantly I did. And when I did I realized that the woman in the picture had been murdered and she was only 19 years old. I saw that she was murdered in the year of the **snake** on November 5th the day after **King Tut's** tomb was discovered. They claim to have no motive to her death but I have one. Perhaps Amanda was pregnant by another soldier who was married or who did not want to have a child. The penalty for adultery is strict in the army so perhaps someone killed her to avoid facing the legal charges or child support. Statistically 1 in every 3 females in the military is sexually harassed or raped at some point during their time in the military. On July 19th 2005 **LaVena Johnson** was raped, burned and murdered while deployed to Iraq and to this day no one has faced any charges (page 140). (*****Addendum***** as of February 2023, **<u>Shannon L. Wilkerson was charged with the murder of Amanda Gonzales</u>**. I knew Shannon and he was a lose cannon, always in the clubs drinking and getting into fights. He was married and perhaps I was right when I wrote my thoughts of a potential motive. Perhaps he did kill Amanda to avoid the penalty of adultery. In his mugshot photo he looks to be deep in thought, as he is not looking into the camera, instead he is gazing downward to the left. I hope they got the right person).

Amanda Gonzales 19 • November 5th 2001

<u>Condolences</u>

My condolences go out to all the families of those who have been robbed of their life by this system of racism and white supremacy. Please know that death is not the end. The soul survives death, indeed and in spirit. This is a book of the dead written by a boy who was murdered without justice, who defeated death and came forth by day. May the soul of **Amanda** walk peacefully through the field of Reeds in Amenta. Amen Ra

Vanessa Guillen 20 • Sep 30th 1999 - April 22nd 2020

<u>Condolences</u>

My condolences go out to all the families of those who have been robbed of their life by this system of racism and white supremacy. Please know that death is not the end. The soul survives death, indeed and in spirit. This is a book of the dead written by a boy who was murdered without justice, who defeated death and came forth by day. May the soul of **Vanessa** walk peacefully through the field of Reeds in Amenta. Amen Ra

Utterances for Coming Forth by day into Light

It is he, who comes forth by day into Light

Erhart and Turkish Gangs "Clubbing" People

They had a lot of gangs in Germany and the **Turkish gangs** were so notorious that they had their own security guards at the club to deal with Turkish disputes. They were family oriented so they would not allow Germans or Americans to interfere with altercations that involved Turkish people. One night while I was working at the **Millennium** club I got into an argument with one of the Turkish security guards. When I looked away he kicked me in the chest like that scene in the movie 300. I flew back but I regained my footing quickly and I did not fall. Just as I advanced forward to throw punches all the other security jumped in between us separating us but they could not defuse the situation. It kept building that night. Someone threw a brick threw the window of my green Benz. The Turkish were very loyal so if one was against you then they all were. This night **Erhart,** a Turkish man put his safety in jeopardy for me. He stood beside me in front of all his Turkish brothers. He suffered from that as they didn't like that he sided with me. I had seen the Turkish beat people real bad. We had people on our staff that liked to fight too and because of that I got into a lot of unnecessary fights at the club. There was a guy named Morgan who worked security with us. His wife had purposely killed their child, or at least that was the story I was told. He never told me this from his mouth but I was told that that was the reason why he was so violent and why he was always getting into fights with people. He was taking his anger out on anyone he could. One night Morgan was chasing some one at the **Natrix** club and when I saw the guy running from Morgan I punched the guy in the face while he was in mid stride. As soon as I hit him, his body fell lifeless to the ground. My heart dropped and I felt horrible. I wondered if he was ok but the other security guards just dragged his lifeless body out the club by his feet. One night females were complaining about a guy trying to go into the females bathroom. I told the brother he couldn't be in the female bathroom and without thinking the guy punched me in the face. I felt bad afterwards but we beat him up good. I had a large black flash light that I hit him with several times. The next day while I was at the gas station I saw the same guy at the next pump. His front tooth was missing but he didn't recognize me. He was a soldier and we had beat him up bad. I felt really bad about that. On another occasion Morgan started a fight with some people in the front of the **Millennium** club. I jumped in and punched one of the guys in the mouth knocking his tooth out but his tooth split my knuckles and cut my tendons. I was bleeding everywhere. Immediately I went to the German hospital and they stitched me up but the next day my hand was infected and the smell was disgusting. I had surgery at the Military hospital and was told that I almost lost my hand. I stopped hitting people after this fight.

Rahél, The Dopest Ethiopian

During this time **Ja Rule** was one of my favorite artist as he reminded me of **Tupac**. I didn't dance much when I went out to clubs but when the song **Always on Time** came on, I danced! I met a lot of women in Germany but there was something about **Rahél** that drew me to her. And I remember dancing with her. I think she was the first **Ethiopian** women I fell head over heels for. A lot of **Ethiopian** people migrated to Germany and I found that there was something about the features of the **Ethiopian** women that caught my attention. They were beautiful! I was around **23** years old and Rahél was around 19 years old. She was a virgin and all we ever did was kiss. In 2003 I would leave Germany and I thought I would never see her again. They say the universe is undefeated and what ever is supposed to be yours will eventually be yours. I wonder about this concept because it really seems like the universe wanted me to see Rahél again. In 2005 she got a job close to where I lived in Harlem. **I remember thinking that it was fate**. But whatever it is was, I took advantage of it and I would go see her often (p 136). Sometimes I wonder about the many women I fell in love with. As I'm in my 40's now, I can say that I was not in "love". I was driven by my lower nature, infatuated with their beauty. Yet still Rahél was placed in front of me again so that I could see her. These types of **coincidences** involving women would continue to happen to me through out my life. It happened with **Zascha** (pages 98, 133), and it happened with **Mellssa** (p 205). On Jan 13th 2020 I was given a spiritual reading where I communicated with two of my guardian angels (p 584). I was told by one of my guardians, that all the paranormal phenomena I had been experiencing over the years, like the **shape shifting** experiences (p 282), the **near death** experiences (p 548) etc, were designed to prepare me for my past life revelations. In my most ancient past life I lived in the region we now call **Ethiopia** (p 594).

January 15th 2002 - Soldier of The Year

I won the soldier of the year in 2001 the year of the **snake** but it was issued to me on **Martin Luther King's birthday,** January 15th 2002. At the time I had no idea it was his birthday. I had a picture of him on my wall but I did not know much about Martin other than his marching for Civil Rights and being assassinated for it. My last day in the Army would also be on his birthday in 2005 (p 130). Of course I was unaware that it was his birthday at that time and I would not come to understand my life path connection to the life path of Martin until after my past life revelation of **Emmett Till** on July 3rd 2018 (p 480). When I began to compile this book is when I realized the dates that connect us. He was born in 1929 the year of the **snake**, Emmett was 19**41** the year of the **snake** and I was 1977 the year of the **snake**. Martin would rise to prominence after the murder of Emmett Till (p **41**). The picture below was taken on Feb **23**, 2001 the year of the snake (p 94). Speaking of Feb **23**, I don't know when I saw this movie **23** but it was many years before my past life revelations, yet the movie mentions **Sirius** and it's about patterns and numbers. Jim Carrey **star**red in this movie. It premiered on Feb **23,** 2007 and he **star**ted his career in 19**77**, the year of the snake, the year I was born. See page **648** for the **metaphysical significance of the number 23**. See pages 25, 94, 121, 283, 444, 439, 586, 669, and 672 for more on Feb **23rd**.

Rau nu Prt m heru

Iu f Per f m heru

Utterances for Coming Forth by day into Light

It is he, who comes forth by day into Light

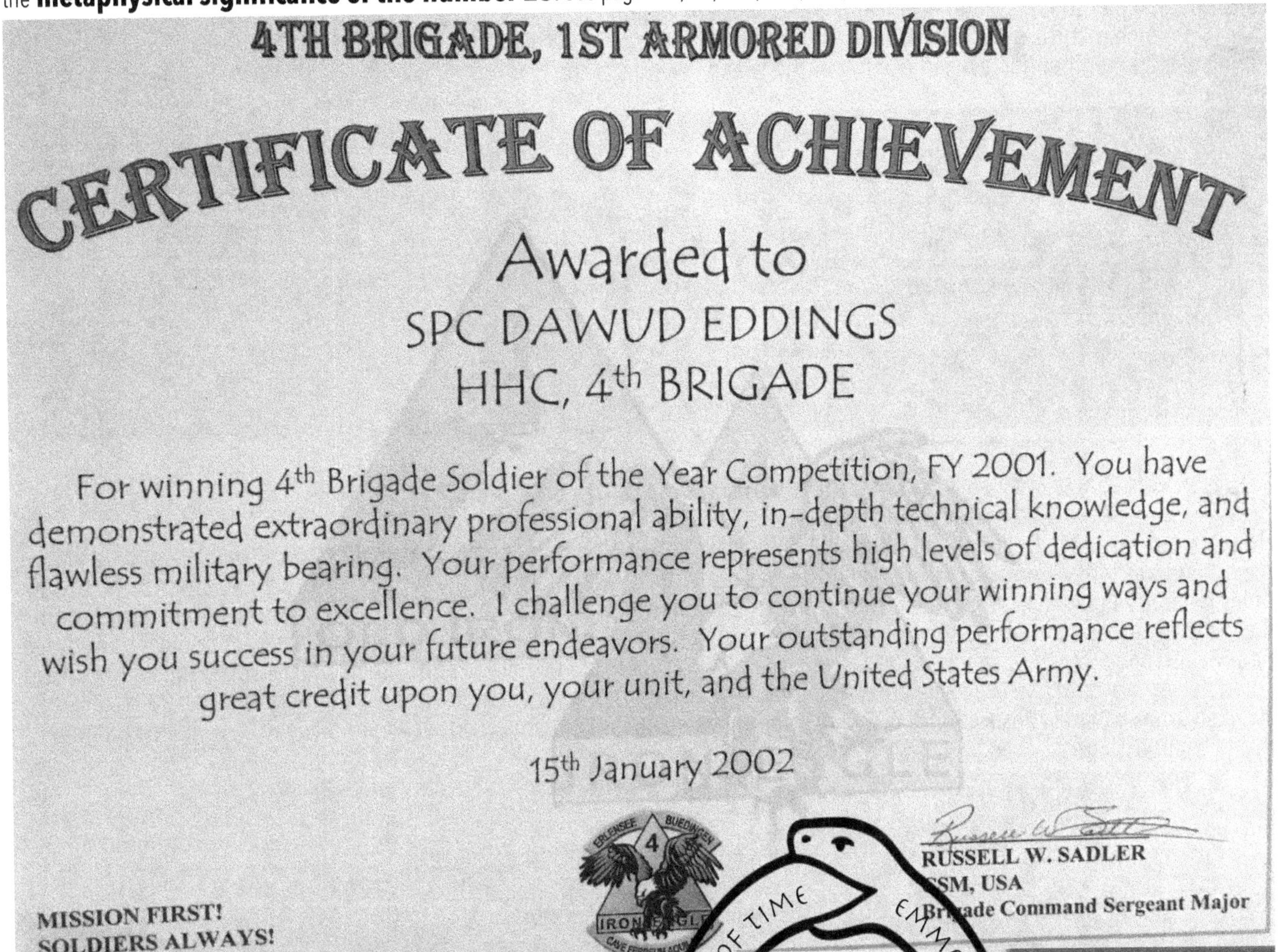
4TH BRIGADE, 1ST ARMORED DIVISION

CERTIFICATE OF ACHIEVEMENT

Awarded to

SPC DAWUD EDDINGS
HHC, 4th BRIGADE

For winning 4th Brigade Soldier of the Year Competition, FY 2001. You have demonstrated extraordinary professional ability, in-depth technical knowledge, and flawless military bearing. Your performance represents high levels of dedication and commitment to excellence. I challenge you to continue your winning ways and wish you success in your future endeavors. Your outstanding performance reflects great credit upon you, your unit, and the United States Army.

15th January 2002

MISSION FIRST!
SOLDIERS ALWAYS!

RUSSELL W. SADLER
CSM, USA
Brigade Command Sergeant Major

February 23rd 2001

Keisha
Tell Me Have You Seen Her?

I don't remember how I met Keisha but I know that I had a thing for her. As I labor through these pictures they bring back many emotions and memories of my past. I remember speeding on the Autobahn with her in my black Benz. I had to slow down because she was afraid. One of the things I'm most very grateful for is that I never crashed with another person in my car. I never caused another person bodily harm due to my recklessness. While looking at Keisha I realize how much I miss her. She is a person I think of a lot when I think about my times in Germany. I never got to say goodbye to Keisha and I always hope that she is in good health and doing well. I'm willing to bet there was some magical **synchronicity** with Keisha that I never got to know. I don't even remember her last name or her birthday and I wonder if she is still alive.

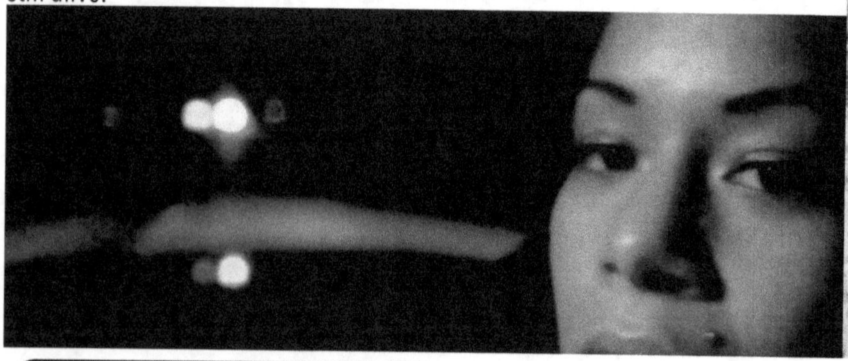

190 Benz, or was in the DeLorean?!

When I purchased the Benz, the man who sold it to me was **very clear** about how **dangerous** the car was. He told me that the engine was too powerful for the frame and he was right, the car was VERY fast. I drove at speeds upward around 160 to 180 miles per hour and when I drove that fast things seemed to slow down. I Only had this car for a few weeks. I remember washing the car many times and making the rims shine. Then just as soon as I got the car it was gone and I was back to driving my green Benz again (page 97). My sister would call me on **May 25th** 2002 to tell me of a **dream** she had just awoke from. In her dream I died in a car accident and a week later I would total the black Benz in a violent accident on my fathers birthday, June 1st 2002. I walked away with only flesh wounds but years later my sisters dream and this accident would prove to be a vital element to this revelation (page 222).

Dawud, Beloved by the Ntru

May 25th 2002 - The first Premonition and the birth of the May 25th pattern in this life

It's 6am, I'm working security at the **Millennium** club and most of us are doing the usual, tying to see what woman we are going to take home. As far as I can remember it was a smooth night, we had no fights. I was the ladies man and was known for being gone for 30 minutes to an hour at a time. I would meet a girl, take her in the back of the club or to my car or out side on top of anyones car. It didn't matter where and the more crazy the place the better for the story. I was 24 years old at the time and having random sex with the prettiest women as fast as I could is what I thought life was about. Then of course I could brag with the fellas and feel good about myself. It was a rush to me. Like rushing the ball on the football field. The chase is what it was about and scoring was the end game. As far as I remember I didn't score that night but during the end of the night my phone rang and an alarming sound I would hear. My sister **Tahira crying!!**

Dawud, Beloved by the Ntru

Tahira - *"Dawud, are you ok?"*
DAWUD - *"Yes, I'm fine what's wrong?!"*
Tahira - *"I had this dream it was so real as if I was there. You had a car accident and you died!"*
DAWUD - *"Well I'm working at the club and it's closing soon, I haven't been drinking and I'm on my way home soon. You can go back to sleep. I love you."*
Tahira - *"I love you too Dawud. Be careful."*
DAWUD - *"Ok Tahira."*

The call was strange but I didn't really think anything of it, however I think I did make an effort to be careful driving home that night. 7 days later on June 1st which is my fathers birthday, I would have a near fatal car accident.

June 1st 2002 - The First Dream Premonition

7 days after my sisters' **dream** it would **manifest** in this **plane** (page 536). I was leaving Jasmine's house. She was the first woman that I fell for when I was stationed in Germany. She was always special to me because she was sent down (born) on my grand mothers birthday, Oct 9th. I called her jazz-mine. I remember that morning because I had just purchased this new Benz. Well it was used but it was new to me and it was in mint condition. It was a190E Benz Rare Sports edition that had been discontinued because the engine was too powerful for the frame. The person who sold it to me told me to be careful it was **a dangerous car**, too powerful. I remember walking to my car that morning. It must have been around 6am. I got in my car and put on the song '*You da man*' by **Nas**. I had the song playing on repeat. The lyrics to the song are below.

"Now wait a sec', give me time to explain, ***women and fast cars****, and diamond rings can poison a rap star, was suicidal, how I smoke in so much la,* ***I saw a dead bird flying through a broken sky,*** *Wish I could flap wings and fly away,* ***To where black kings in Ghana stay,*** *So I can get old my flesh rot away, But that'll be the day when it's peace, When my gat don't need to spray, When these streets are safe to play,* ***Sex with death, indulge in these women, Vision my own skeleton swimming in eternal fire,*** *Broads play with pentagrams in they vagina, Like the Exorcist, then they gave birth to my seeds,* ***I beg for God's help, why they love hurting me? I'm your disciple****, a thug certainly, I'm the N the A to the S-I-R, If I wasn't I must've been Escobar, Forty-five in my waist, staring at my reflection in the mirror, sitting still in the chair like my conception, when everything around me got cloudy,* ***the chair became a king's throne*** *my* ***destiny*** *found me, It was clear why the struggle was so painful,* ***metamorphosis****, this is what I changed to and* ***God I'm so thankful****" - **Nas***

17 years later **Nas** would appear in two of my **dreams** (pages, 443, 545). Years later I would realize that **Nas** mention reincarnation in is music several time (page 54). Once you finish this whole book you will see how these lyrics from this **Nas** song can easily be seen as a **prophetic** story about the transformation of **TutemRa**.

Rau nu Prt m heru

Iu f Per f m heru

Utterances for Coming Forth by day into Light

It is he, who comes forth by day into Light

June 1st 2002, May 25th Strikes Back

It was June 1st 2002 and I was leaving Jasmin's house on my way to formation. I was cruising at decent speed not too fast considering how fast I usually drove. The song '*<u>You da man</u>*' by **Nas** is playing on repeat. The autobahn was not crowded and everything was peaceful. Then all of a sudden the car started to shake uncontrollably. I turned the wheel to avoid hitting the guardrails and the only thing I remember after that was the car falling one last time. The **car** had **flipped** serval times end over end. The car ended up upside down. As soon as the car fell the last time **my eyes opened** and I immediately searched for a way out. I exited the back window passenger side. I crawled out on all fours and stood up on my feet. My adrenaline was pumping and I was in shock. I looked around at the wreckage then I did a self assessment to see and feel if anything felt broken but nothing did. I felt completely fine except for the blood that was coming from my face. My face was bleeding! I picked up one of my side panel mirrors from the debris of the wreckage and looked at my face. My face was cut open from my **left eye** to the corner of my **left ear** and the open skin was hanging down. I looked like a monster! No more pretty boy I thought but I also didn't care. I was happy to be alive. The car was totaled. The rear passenger side tire had blown out. Or was I sabotaged? Jasmin had an ex boyfriend that didn't like that she had moved on. Jasmin said years later he eluded to having something to do with my accident, perhaps slicing my tires. My possessions were flown here and there. I had a bible in my back window that my grand mother had given me. I never found that in the wreckage but I found my phone quickly and I called Jasmin. She arrived shortly after I called her. The first person to the scene was a guy who witnessed the accident. He was more hysterical than I was because he had seen the car flip end over end and here I was walking and talking to him. He could not believe that I survived. My adrenaline was pumping but I was still relatively calm. I was however amazed that I was still alive. One of the **stranger things** about the whole experience was the ride to the hospital. I can vividly remember saying to Jasmin and the EMT's that *<u>"maybe **aliens** came and saved me</u>"*. Why would I say that? ***<u>Why would I say that maybe aliens saved me?</u>*** At the time of this accident I didn't know that June 1st was my fathers birthday. My sister who had the **dream/premonition** is born on June 2nd.

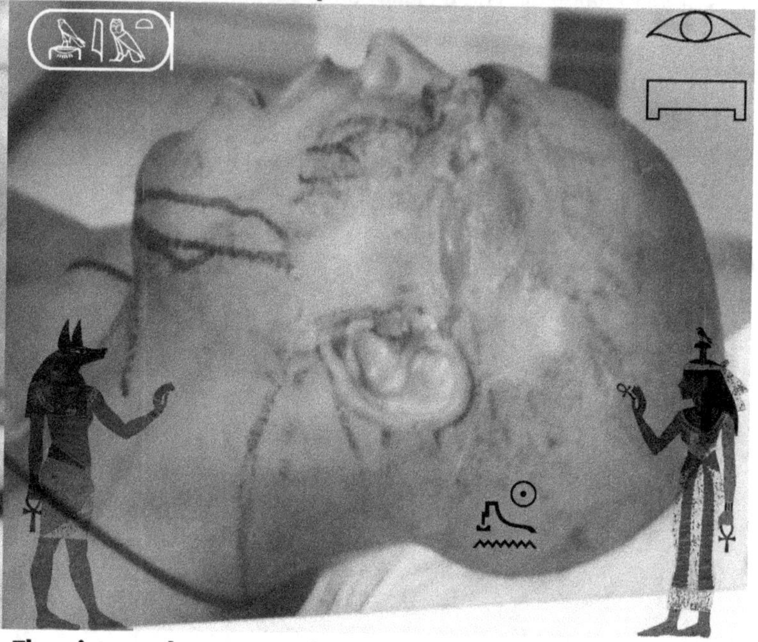

Dawud, Beloved by the Ntru

The picture above was taken by a doctor after he cleaned the open wound, right before he stitch me up.

Jasmins Golden Dream

As you will come to see I will leave Germany in 2003 and never see Jasmin in person again, however I was able to audio chat with her via Instagram direct message in 2021. On May 2nd 2021 (page 643), Jasmin would detail the events of a **dream** she had about me as a **Golden Pharaoh** sitting on a throne with an Egyptian Queen.

On May 2nd 1963 more than 700 black children who were trained in nonviolent tactics walked out of their classes and assembled at the 16th street baptist church to march to downtown Birmingham. They were met with extreme violence by white police officers and their police dogs. The children were blasted with fire hoses and clubbed with night sticks. **Assata Shakur** was sentenced to life in prison on May 2nd 1977 **The Year Of The Snake.** On May 2nd 2013 **The Year Of The Snake, Assata Shakur** would be placed back on the F.B.I. Most wanted list and **Afeni Shakur** would transition on May 2nd 2016 (page 381-382). I have a theory about who **Tupac** was in a past life.

Jewell Cries While Detailing How She Warned 2Pac That She Had A Dream That He Got Killed In Vegas!

On October 18, 2021 the **Youtube** channel, **The Art Of Dialogue** released a video interview with **Jewell**, titled (Jewell Cries While Detailing How She Warned 2Pac That She Had A Dream That He Got Killed In Vegas!). In this interview Jewell details how Tupac called her the night of September 7, 1996, the same day he was shot. **Jewell warned Tupac that she had a dream that he was in a white Cadillac with Suge Knight, and Snoop Dogg and in her dream they were all shot and killed.** Tupac brushed it off and told her he would be back the next day and he would record his part of the vocals for her song then. She responded by telling Tupac, **"If you go to the fight, you won't make it back!".** Tupac threw the phone and Suge picked it up. Jewell told Suge about her **dream** and he didn't take it seriously either. After Tupac was killed, Suge and others who knew about Jewell's **dream** began to think she set Tupac up. They were not aware of how people can dream things before they happen like **my sister dreamt my car accident before it happened** (page 104). Or how **my father dreamt the 911 Twin Towers attack the day before it happened** (page 99). The strange thing about Jewell's dream is that **Suge's cousin Lashelle had a similar dream**. She dreamt that Tupac, Snoop Dogg, Suge, and MC Hammer were in a black Cadillac and they were all shot and killed in her dream as well. What are dreams (page 30)?!

Rau nu Prt m heru

Mark Dehaan (page 118), drove me to see my car a week or so after my accident. I took this picture that day

Iu f Per f m heru

"As for the span of earthly affairs it is the manner of a dream" ***ADDENDUM***

My sister's "**dream**" wasn't a premonition, **it was time travel**, like in the movie **Back To The Future** (p 40)! Our consciousness can **quantum leap** to the past or the future via dreaming and meditation. Some dreams take place in a different space and time where the astral body travels, sometimes to the past and even the future. **Deja Vu** is sometimes a result of having already experienced a moment in a dream and when you reach the moment in your waken state you have a feeling of familiarity. In 2022 I experienced **Deja Vu** twice while in **Kemet** (p 670 - 671). The questions we should be asking ourselves are, what is a **dream** and what does it really mean to <u>follow your dreams</u> or to live out your dreams (p 589). **May 25** is a reoccurring date **entangled** with a past life and my current life that formed a pattern. It was the first star code pattern that I decoded (p 222). This code would sp**ark** my awareness to patterns hidden within dates and ultimately it connects me with my previous life as Emmett Till (p 480). These patterns are examples of a phenomena known as **quantum entanglement**, spoken about often in Physics. **Einstein**, called this phenomena, **spooky action at a distance** (p 329). Einstein died in 1955, the same year Emmett Till was murdered. Dream interpretations are a major part of all indigenous peoples of the world and were used as a source of divination (forecasting the future). If you are reading this then you're still sleeping. In ancient Kemet we saw this life as a **dream** and the word dream, meant to become awakened (p 30). Awaken from your slumber!

Utterances for Coming Forth by day into Light

June 2002 **190E (1st of 1)**

I crawled out on all fours and stood up on my own two, <u>only **God** can bring someone through what I been through</u>, I got into my car that morning without a warning or a sign it might have been my last time, and I remember, everything was good, I had the all black sport leather and the grain wood, and the symbol on my hood pushed back cause I shift from 1st to 3rd like I'm on the track, racing, speed racer, no patience! and even when I drank, I needed no chaser! speed I needed an adrenaline rush! I always peeled out I peeled out too much! so I pulled off to make my way home, not New York son I'm in a different time zone, so I hopped on the autobahn to get my cruise on, not even 10 minutes, damn and my tires gone, my cars flipping, glass flying, my face bleeding but no I'm not dying and I'm not screaming and I'm not crying, yeah I'm just believing yeah I'm just believing, ***<u>that the Lord let me live again</u>***, ***<u>time time after time</u>*** even though I sin, you gotta be slow and fa sho cause when ya fast ya crash! my testimony! for those sitting in class it's a lesson, for those in **church** it's a blessing, one flesh one step, we fall down but we get back up and get in step, I said we get back up and get in step **-Dawud**

Significance **(Still Dreaming Remix, page 438)**

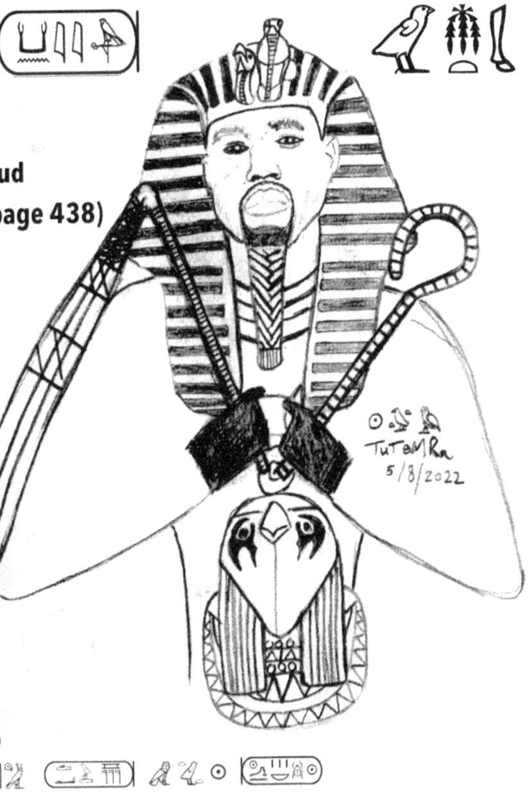

It is he, who comes forth by day into Light

This was written shortly after the accident during my recovery and when I look back sometimes I feel like perhaps I did die in this accident. Perhaps this is when other portions of my soul took refuge in my body. I crashed on my father's birthday which is 7 days before Kanye's birthday. Kanye West would crash 4 months later on Oct **23**rd, 2 days before my birthday. I wrote a song about my accident and so did Kanye. In Kanye's song: **Through The Wire,** he says the name **Emmett Till**. "<u>And just imagine how my girl feel on the plane, scared as hell that her guy look like **Emmett Till**, she was with me before the deal, she been tryna be mine, she a **Delta***, so she been throwing that **Dynasty* sign***</u>". Emmett Till was thrown in a river at the **Delta*** and these are all **SIGNS***. My **past life** as Emmett Till will be revealed to me 16 years later on July 3rd 2018 (p 480). It was the video for his song: **Through The Wire** where he says the name <u>Emmett Till</u> that would help him get a release date for his album sparking his rise to fame. In 2009 (page 162-163) I will have my first **dream** with Kanye and afterwards he will appear in my dreams a number of times even up until 2022. Kanye's from Chicago like Emmett Till and his last name is West. In the ancient Kemetic Ausarian Resurrection drama, Ausar was known as the Lord of the West and of **resurrection**. West was where the soul or the BA went when we "die". **Remember that you are Ausar**! <u>See page 3 for the **hero's journey!**</u> Kanye and I are both born in 1977 the year of the **snake**, just like Emmett Till (19**41**, year of the **snake**). On April 4th 2020 my past life as Tutankhaten (King Tut, **18th DYNASTY***) will be revealed to me (page 594).

Dez

Dead Prez and the Spirit of Dez

I met Desmond (Dez) just before I left to try out for Special Forces Assessment and Selection (SFAS, p109). He was from Florida. We had Hip Hop and a love for music in common. We used to spit raps to each other. There weren't many black brothers in our unit so we clicked as soon as we met. I usually drove around by myself if I didn't have some girl in the car with me but I let him ride with me and showed him Germany. I took him to the club with me sometimes and got him in for free. He had only been in my unit for a few months and him and I had become good friends. When I got back from the selection try outs our unit was beginning to prepare for our deployment to Iraq (page 119). Just before we deployed to Iraq, **Dez** put a CD in my hand and told me that I needed to listen to it. It was a mix tape from **Dead Prez**! When I heard them it was like a breath of fresh air. I was immediately a fan! 10 years later I would meet **Stic** in a **magical** way (page 271). I told you Stic, none of this was just coincidence. That's word to your RBG Heru logo.

ADDENDUM

Desmond Owens - June 11, 1979 - Sept 9, 2021

Fast forward 15 years – Desmond and I got into an argument about **religion** sometime in 2017 and had not spoke since then. On Feb 21, 2023, which is the day that **Malcolm X** was assassinated (p 561-565), **Larry Davis** (page 108) called me out of the blue and from our conversation I came to know that Desmond had died a few years prior. This news deeply saddened me. Larry sent me Dez's Facebook page and I found a video of Dez singing that gave me **goosebumps**. Desmond loved music and loved to sing. The words of the song were, "Things will work in my favor, I just got to believe". I began to sing the song and the **goosebumps** kept coming and **Shanta** said she felt **goosebumps** too as well as a presence in the room. A few days later I used Instagram to contact **Ruth Tanelus**, a soldier that Dez and I knew from Germany. Ruth was actually the first soldier I had when I became a Sgt in the Army but her and I never got to know each other. Her and Dez on the other hand became very close friends. After talking with Ruth for over an hour I got more info on how Dez passed and I learned more about Ruth than I had previously known. Unfortunately Desmond died from **Covid** on Sep 9, 2021 and he left two children behind. From my talk with Ruth I found out that she is **Haitian** and retired as a Master Sergeant. From there we began to talk about spirituality. Ruth told me that she has **a friend that sees spirits,** and this friend can see Desmond's spirit lingering around Ruth. She told Ruth that Dez has not crossed over to the after life yet because he is still dealing with his early death and had many unfinished things but he needs to cross over because he has **another life** to start. As we talked about Dez, I was overcome with goosebumps several times. Ruth believes my story of my past lives and believes in reincarnation. On the day Desmond was born, **June 11**, 1963 President Kennedy delivered an address calling for Congressional action in the area of **Civil Rights**, defining the cause–for the first time–as a moral, and not purely legal, issue (p 520). May the soul of my friend Desmond Owens, walk peacefully through the fields of reeds in Amenta. Amen Ra. In 20**23 Ruth** wrote me a buddy letter for my Army compensation claim which helped me to receive my 100% monthly compensation (page 121).

Rau nu Prt m heru

Iu f Per f m heru

Utterances for Coming Forth by day into Light

It is he, who comes forth by day into Light

ADDENDUM Sgt Larry Davis Saved Me

You can't tell by this picture but Larry was an ape of a man. His hands were almost 3 times the size of mine. One night I was out partying at a club in Wiesbaden Germany with my homie Desmond (p 107). While there I saw some basketball players that I knew. They played for the NBA Europe league. I would see them at the clubs I worked security at and I would show them love. They always bought bottles and partied hard. They saw me and waved me over to the VIP section they were in. They had many bottles and I drank their free liquor and got blasted shit face drunk. The last thing I remember was being in the VIP section. I only recall waking up the next day and apparently I drank so much that when I went to sleep my body forced a bowel movement to release the alcohol poison that was in my blood. I woke and felt something strange in my pants. I had shit on myself and it was like a pancake stuck to me. I got up and cleaned myself up. Later that day Desmond came by my room to check on me then he told me what happened. He said that I got so drunk that I could not stand. He went and got **Larry** who was also at the club. He said Larry grabbed me up with one arm and carried me out the club. While exiting the club there was a guy named Antonio who tried to approach me but I grabbed him with one hand and threw him through the bathroom door while Larry walked me out. The guy was **Jasmin's** Ex boy friend. He didn't like me because I was dating her so he tried to take this opportunity to press me. Jasmin drove me home with Desmond and placed me safely in my bed. Jasmin would leave a note on the back of a picture (page 53) I drew when I was 14 years old. "***Wat up Dawud! Again, I rescued your ass! See you next time! Jasmin. Love always***". There were 2 nights in Germany that alcohol got the best of me and this night in Wiesbaden was one of them! The other was a night that I was working at the Millennium club. I was on the clock working but still I was walking around drinking Crown Royal from the bottle. I remember falling on my face in the parking lot as someone was taking me home. The next day I went to pick up my car from the club and afterwards I went to get gas. When I went to pay for my gas the person at the register gave me my ID card. He was in the club the night prior and had picked my ID up off the floor. This guy happened to be a big fan of Tupac like me. His name was L.A. I stopped drinking alcohol in 2011 but before I did I would have another bad night with alcohol the night I met **Rihanna** on July 4th 2009 (page 167). On **May 2nd 2021** (page 643) Jasmin would keep true to her word, delivering a message to me from the depths of her **dreams**.
Addendum Today is February 21, 20**23**. I got a call from Larry today. I had not heard from him in MANY years. We laughed and talked about what was going on in each others lives. He retired from the Army after doing 24 years, his wife is retiring in few months after 20 years and his son LJ is about to start college. I told him about this book and I read what I wrote about him but he corrected some things. He told me that he heard a loud commotion in the club and saw that I was in a dispute with Antonio. Larry said, at first he thought I was I was ok to fight but then he saw that I was wobbling like a drunken master and my speech was slurred. He also saw that Antonio was gathering a crowd and friends. That's when he grabbed me and took me away from the situation. As I began to talk about that night Larry could tell that I did not know about Desmond (pages 107, 119). Larry told me that **Desmond had died** a few years ago and that news brought my excitement down. The last time I spoke to Desmond we had an argument and I had been trying to reach him for years. Now I know why he never answered. I told Larry about my past life as **Emmett Till**. I wondered if there was a **star code connection** with him and I so I asked him his birthday but he said March **23** (p 648). I did not have a connection to that date so I asked him his wife's birthday and again there was no connection. I told him about how I prayed about getting out of the Army and my last day in the Army ended up being **Martin Luther King's birthday** (p 130). Then Larry said, most people would not understand those types of **coincidence** but he did. He said he called me because **a thought came into his head and told him to call me.** He told me that his best friend Michael Mc**lamb** has a daughter born on the same day as his daughter and that Michael Mc**lamb** was born on the same day that **Martin Luther King** did the march on Washington. I stopped him and said, "yeah, that was **August 28**, the same day **Emmett Till** was murdered and Emmett Till was a sacrificial **lamb**" (page 511). Then he told me that his mother was also born on **August 28**. When he told me that **I got chills**. Then I explained to him that none of this was **just a coincidence**. I told him that today is February 21, and **Malcolm X** was assassinated on this day in 1965 (page 287) and I'm uploading the revised version of this book today. I told him about the **coincidence** with Mark and his wife (page 118). I told him about Big O and his daughter (p 96). I told him about April 4th and how I started writing this book the day Martin was assassinated (page 594). As we ended our talk he told me how much he enjoys watching **sunsets** in his Alabama backyard and he invited me to visit sometime..

The Natrix Club

I was full speed ahead in my lower nature. This picture was taken in a back room of the **Natrix club**. I worked security there on Saturday nights. This night **I met a beautiful woman** and after we exchanged a few words we would come to find that we were both born on **October 25th**. **I looked directly into her eyes** and told her, **"I know exactly who you are"**. We wasted no time to get to know each other…... We entered the course in a back room and she took the picture of me on the couch afterwards. I don't remember her name but she was very pretty. People wonder why I currently live the life of a hermit. I have done my share of what we call "partying". I am a scorpio who's **south node** or **dragon's tail** starts in the **age of Aries** during in the **18th dynasty of Kemet**, where **Tutankhaten** (**King Tut**) was from. I am a scorpio and back then, in my early 20's, scorpios only meant sex to me. I had no idea that the scorpio is connected to the spider that spins a perfect web with out being taught. The Scorpio is the eighth zodiac sign and corresponds with the number **8**, which is **infinity**. The Scorpio is connected to snakes that shed their skin symbolizing renewal. Snakes like the first image of a snake swallowing its tail (**ouroboros,** page 657) that was found on the shrine of Tutankhaten (King Tut) in 1922. Back then I did not know that the scorpio was about renewal, mastering **resurrection**, **rebirth** and **reincarnation**. The Scorpio knows that we are spiritual beings, only temporarily having this human experience. It took me years to get out of the "Natrix" and find the narrow path but eventually I did……..

October 25th 2002 — Why I went to Special Forces Assessment and Selection (SFAS)

I was in the Army and I didn't know my past history or my culture and I had no plan for life. I worked out all the time and never even considered being a personal trainer. I remember when my homie Big O (page 96) got his personal training certification. I didn't even think to do it myself. The first year that I played semi pro football in Germany I didn't even get paid. A few of the players were getting paid and I didn't know it. I loved football and I was doing it for the love. I scored most of the touchdowns and I led them to an undefeated season. I was a fool moving through life with no real plan but I had the personality to try for the top of what ever I was doing. I volunteered for **Special Forces** because in the army it was seen as the top. I had been soldier of the month, soldier of the quarter and soldier of the year. I was one of the most fit soldiers in my unit and I definitely had the fastest time in the two mile run. Sgt Sherman was the knew Platoon Sgt. He was a mechanic coming from a **Ranger** unit. He ran the motor-pool where I worked and I think having him there helped inspire me to try out for Special Forces. My SMG Major was rooting for me. A lot of the other higher up soldiers were rooting for me to complete the course. Actually, everyone who knew I was going thought I was going to make it and so did I but what the hell was I thinking?! My face wasn't even fully healed from my car accident 4 months prior. I did not know my place in the world. I wasn't paying ATENtion! Too much time spent chasing women. I had never heard of **David Walker's Appeal** (page 226) but now here I found myself in North Carolina, **FT Bragg North Carolina**.

My Arrival to SFAS

When I got to Special Forces School there were very few black men there. I had flown from Germany back to America and now I was at **FT Bragg North Carolina**. There was either 290 men when we started or 390 men. It was one or the other. Out of all the men there I can only remember ever seeing 2 or maybe 3 other black men trying out for the course and I only ever spoke to one. Our time was micro managed so we didn't have time to make friends with anyone. It was every man for him self but the black guy that I did speak to, was very muscular. He was a Saper from Ft Drum, 10th Mountain NY. He was disqualified before me but for personal reasons. I saw around 18 to 12 brothers of latin or Hispanic descent and I saw one brother who looked like the typical **Native American** you see on tv. He was a giant of a man. I don't know if he ever made it. The Army ran test on Native Americans in the past trying to understand our ability to navigate in the wilderness by instinct alone. They found that our ability was strengthened by the length of our hair. The **hair** was seen as an **antenna** receiving information from the unseen **matrix** that we live in. The first thing that the army does when soldiers enter is cut their hair off and for many years black soldiers were not allowed to wear their hair in **locs** or "dreads".

Number 97

When we got there our names were ripped off of our uniforms and we were all given numbers. They wrote our numbers on a white piece of cloth and pinned them to our uniforms with safety pins. I was number 97, like September 7th the day that **Tupac** was shot and 19**97** the year that **Biggie** was murdered. We were sleep deprived but that was expected. The first test was the physical fitness test! Many people failed that test because they were very strict on form and technique. I had around 80 of my push ups counted as acceptable. The Saper had over 100 counted. They never told me my run time, just that I passed. The course was only 20 days and I'm not sure how many days I lasted. I just know the day I was disqualified.
I only have a few memories from this course. I remember arriving.
I remember the large group of men standing in formation.
I remember the plans being changed at the last minute all the time.
They would wake us up after only given us a few minutes of rest.
I only took one shower while I was there and that was the day I was disqualified. It was either eat or shower. One day they took us to the pull up bars and we all had to do as many as we could. This was 2002 and I had never done the movement called a muscle up. I had never seen this before or tried it but when it was time for me to do pull ups I was surrounded by all white men. I was practically alone, the only black man. I pulled up so high that my arms were locking out. I did not plan to do that. I was doing "muscle ups" because of the adrenaline that was racing throughout my veins. The same adrenaline that would take over when I was on the football field. They all said I was doing "dick ups" because I was the only person to go up so high. After a few days many of the soldiers were gone and it may have been around 100 of us left.

The Longest Run and The Voices in My Head

The most challenging thing I did was the run. I do not know how long I ran for! One day they stormed in our barracks and woke us up around 2 or 3 am in the morning. It was pitch black in the North Carolina Woods. We got to formation and we were told to run until someone told us to stop. They sent us out in small groups all starting around 5 to 10 minutes apart, all running in the same direction. The only thing that we could see was the chem lights that lit the trail. There were horror stories of people twisting and breaking their ankles in the woods due to poor lighting and I think a few people did hurt themselves this night. At some point in the run **I began to hear voices in my head** asking me what I was doing this for, but I ignored the voices and kept running. I ran until the sun came up. At some point in the run a person passed me. He was the first person to pass me. The brother look Latin and he did not look to be in better shape than me. That bothered me but I picked up my pace and I caught him. Then I caught every other person that was in front of me. I caught many people who were sent out ahead of me. I ran and I ran until someone told me to stop. I don't know how long I ran for. I have ran 24 miles once in my life. I did that on December 26th 2020 (page 544). I have ran from Harlem to Wall street before but neither of those runs were as hard or as long as the run at FT Bragg seemed or felt but I don't know how long I ran for.

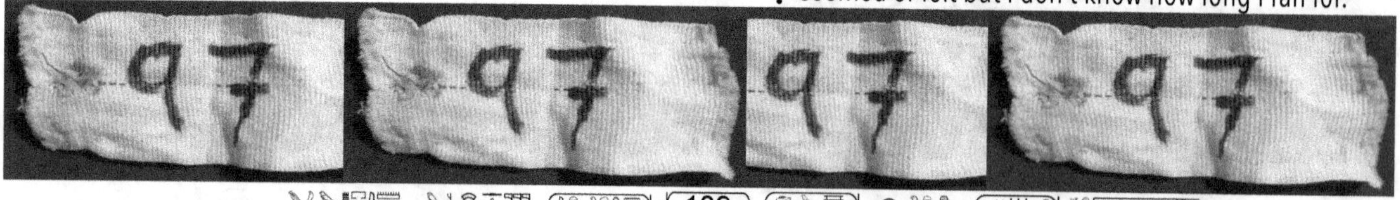

Running in The Wrong Direction

Rau nu Prt m heru

Every night we had a formation and every night numbers were called. If your number was called that meant you were disqualified. I got disqualified at night and I think it was the second day of Land Navigation exercises. By this time there were not many soldiers left. We had land navigation exercises in the day and night. During that night exercise I got my first bolo or warning strike. I had found myself off course so I did a back azimuth. This is where you turn around 180 degrees and go in the reverse direction (degrees) seen on your compass and follow that degrees back to your previous starting point so that you can start over again. When I did the back azimuth I did not save the degrees so when one of the instructors appeared from nowhere and asked me what azimuth I was on I didn't have one. I was told I was walking too close to a road without having a direct azimuth saved in my compass. He gave me a bolo. I wasn't too upset because you could get one bolo in each exercise but if you get two bolos in one exercise you're disqualified. All I had to do was stay on my azimuths for the rest of the exercise and I would have been fine. I was doing good because I had found most of my points already. I didn't fully rely on my azimuths in the woods during the day. I got good at reading the terrain of the map. I followed an azimuth but I also used the land to navigate. Later that night when it got pitch black I was moving from one point to the next when I happened upon a deer. I didn't notice the deer until after it darted off in front of me and it scared the living shit out of me. I remember thinking what these woods might have been like for slaves escaping slavery.

Iu f Per f m heru

Before we started this night exercise we were instructed to move to the roads and turn our strobe lights on when the exercise was complete. When the exercise was over I moved to the road and turned my strobe light on. Soon after a jeep appeared and the instructor took my paper work. He gave me another bolo and told me the exercise wasn't over to continue to train, then he sped off into the night. Shortly after jeeps began to come by picking soldiers up and driving us to formation. We all stood in formation as they called off the numbers for those who were disqualified. At this point none of us really knew each other but we knew who the top people were by our numbers. I was number 97 and I stood out because I was Black and because I was doing well on everything. That night my number was called and I had to take that shameful walk, I was disqualified. When my number was called a few of the soldiers around me could not believe it and neither could I. I was sent to an area where I had to sit near a tree and wait to be escorted to the barracks with others who had been disqualified. I cried that night. It was **October 25th** 2002 on **my 25th birthday** and I had failed. When I got to the barracks I was surprised to see the Saper. I could not believe he didn't make it! He told me that he was hungry. He had gone too long without eating and he couldn't take it anymore so he gave up. While there I met white boys who had been disqualified for cheating. They had land navigation devices. I had never seen or used one before. This was the first time I ever heard the phrase "if you ain't cheating, you ain't trying and if you get caught you ain't trying hard enough". I thought about the white guys in college who were taking steroids so they could compete with people like me and Courtlan. I was technically on leave so I went to visit family before I went back to Germany. When I got back to Germany we were in full throttle preparing to go to War with Iraq.

Significance

Jtterances for Coming Forth by day into Light

Later in life I would come to realize that I was on the wrong azimuth when I first joined the army on September **21**st 1999. I am **44** years old right now. I turned **44** four days ago. **44** years from the date that I joined the army was September **21**st 19**55** and Emmett Till's case had started two days prior (September 19th 1955, page 516). 2 days later his killers would be found not guilty. I got disqualified on my 25th birthday on October 25th 2002. Emmett Till was born July 25th. I was disqualified during land navigation which is the discipline of following a route through unfamiliar terrain using a compass and other tools. I was lost in the wilderness of America and the hidden and evasive elements of **racism** and **white supremacy**. I was trying out for a unit that creates the same type of men that are sent to kill black people all across the world. I did not fully realize what I was doing. I am forever grateful to the White cadre member that disqualified me. I would deploy to Iraq in April of 2003 but I would leave Iraq 6 months before most of the other soldiers in my unit. This was uncommon because no one leaves a combat zone unless you're dead in a body bag or if you are severely injured. I was pulled out of Iraq because I was "**selected**" to try out for the 160th Special Operations Aviation Unit. Without applying I came up on orders and was swiftly taken from Iraq and sent to Ft Campbell Kentucky. Perhaps someone my performance at Special Forces Selection (SFAS) garnered me an opportunity to tryout for 160th or perhaps someone saw me running around the Baghdad international airport with 100 pounds of weights in my ruck sack, with a fully loaded m16, in over 100 degrees heat with all my army battle gear on. I was crazy crazy, I was in Iraq training to go back to Special forces School. When I Got back to Germany I only had one month to out-process and leave for Ft Campbell. In that last month in Germany I "partied like it was 1999".

It is he, who comes forth by day into Light

"Who do you believe in? I believe in the God that leads me to freedom, I discard the God that say obey the heathen, I pray to even the odds, Adam and Eve, they deceiving the Goddess Isis, she's priceless! **Auset be the asset, Ausar** be the star, identity crlsis, Do you know who you are? **Can you locate Orion?** mothers in black crying, brothers in pack dying, too high to see the designing of the prison we in, is it The Ballot Or The Bullet, or the prison with in the mind?" **- Dawud The Uncanny BlaKseed (Who Do You Believe In - Written on May 12th 2015, page 330)**

November 29th 2002

I returned to Germany from ***Special Forces*** *assessment and selection school* in November depressed because I failed to complete the course. I think I was a little embarrassed too. I would draw this picture of **Tupac** just to see if I could still draw. I was **25** yrs old when I drew these pictures of Tupac and I had not drawn a picture since I drew the picture of Wolverine in 1999 (page 79). The odd thing is I drew this 3 days after King Tut's tomb was opened (page 11) and 6 days after Mamie Till's birthday. **14** shots were fired at Tupac on Sep 7, 1996. **Ausar** was cut into **14** pieces and **Emmett Till** died at **14** years old. I have a theory about who Tupac was in a past life and if you endeavor to venture deeper into the pages of this book you might find yourself arriving at the same conclusions.. Start be reading the next page…..

November 30th 2002

Lisa "Left Eye" Lopes once drew a picture of Tupac in the early 90's. Lisa signed and dated the picture. Years later that picture would end up being placed on the wall of a record stored owned by **William Lesane**, Tupac's cousin. Years after Lisa died, William Lesane noticed that Lisa had drawn the picture on April 25 (page 180), which was the same day she died. The patterns I present in this book are examples of a weird phenomena known as **quantum entanglement**, spoken about often in **Physics**. Like the mysterious pattern seen on page 602. I drew this picture of Tupac on Nov 30, 2002, on the same day that Tupac was shot and robbed on Nov 30th 1994, which is four days after **King Tut's** tomb was opened (Nov 26th 19**22**, p 11). I drew the picture because I felt like it was a harder picture to draw than the one I had drawn the day prior (page 111).. After drawing this picture I would not draw another picture for over 10 years (page 268). Tupac was my favorite artist and I played his music so much that some of my neighbors in the barracks knew the lyrics to his songs because I blasted it so much. At this time in my life I still thought Tupac was alive somewhere, living in hiding. I wouldn't relinquish this belief for another 4 years after shedding Tupac tears (page 147). I got out of the Army in 2005 and started writing rhymes again, and when I did the name Tupac found its way to 2 of my rhymes. Then I stopped writing for 5 years when I started personal training. After my grand fathers death in 2009 I started writing again in 2010 and the name Tupac found its way to 10 of my rhymes. Tupac was a major influence on my writing but if someone would have told me back then, the real reason why I was drawn to Tupac, I would not have believed them – Unless of course they presented this book to me. Did you know that Tupac had a tattoo on his arm that read, "My Only Fear Of Death Iz Coming Back Reincarnated"? See page 664 for more info.

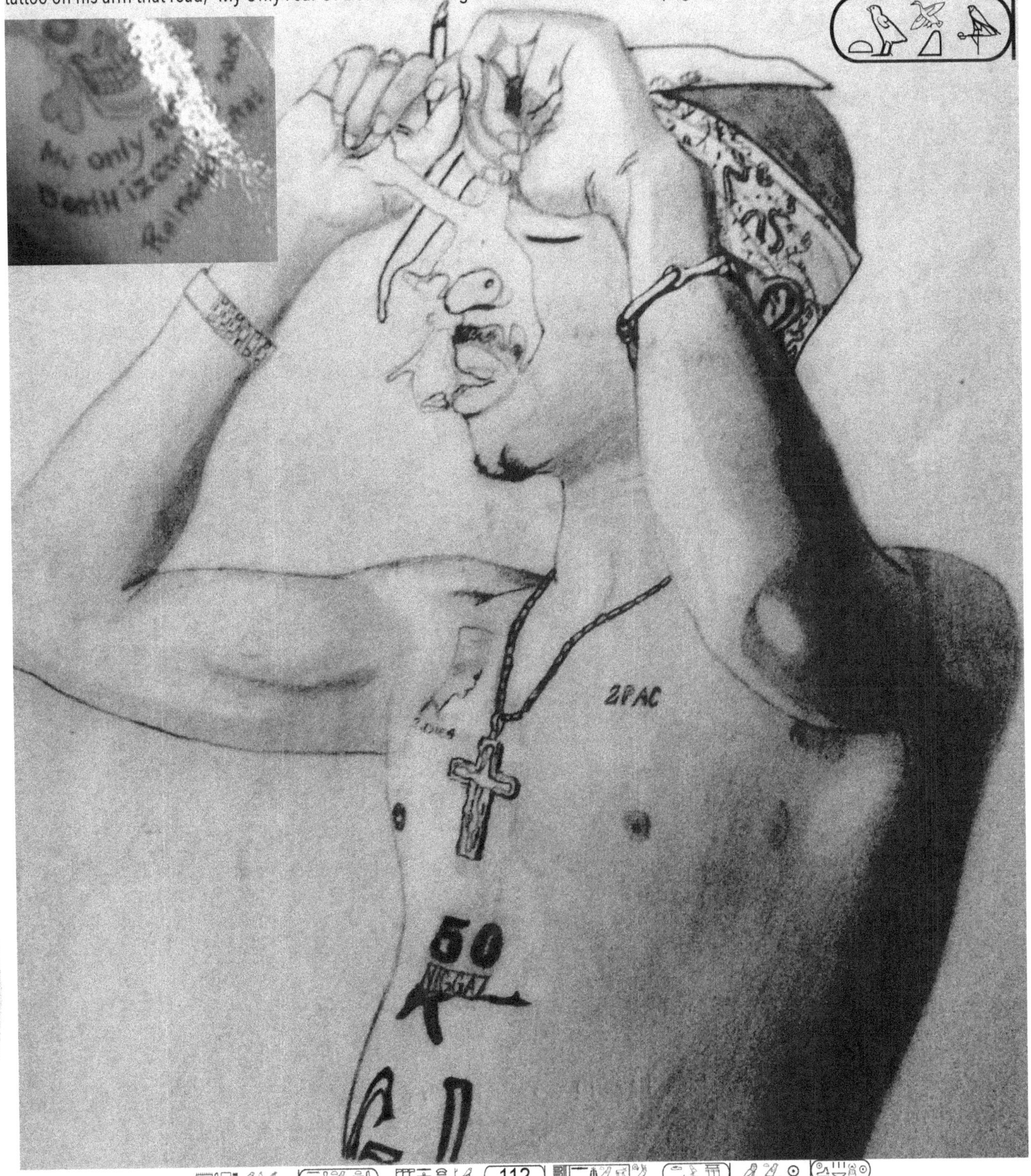

Rau nu Prt m heru

Iu f Per f m heru

Utterances for Coming Forth by day into Light

It is he, who comes forth by day into Light

May 2003
Convoy from Kuwait To Iraq

We drove from Kuwait to Iraq in a sand storm that lasted for what seemed like forever. We had to travel very slowly through **sand storms** and there were times when we could not see the Humvee (vehicle) in front of us. This must be the longest ride I had ever gone on in my life. I was driving with a female soldier who was a cook and she was reasonably afraid and reasonably tired. She kept falling asleep at the wheel. I kept waking her while I kept my weapon on the ready pointed out the window. I could not be scared because I had to lead those around me. We were "**going to war**" and I wasn't even afraid. I was a sergeant now and I was "**doing my job**". Some of our vehicles broke down. I took a picture with a polaroid camera during one of these stops. Knowing what I know now about **mother nature** (NTR), **Shu** (air), the **ancestors, Anat** the powerful Ntr Goddess who protected the Pharaoh's in battle with mighty vengeance, and who I was in previous lives, I see these sand storms very differently. Perhaps these **storms** saved our lives (page 584).

Rules Change

I respected the rank structure but I was also an enlisted soldier so if you were a butter bar (new officer) and you came trying to throw your rank around it didn't go well with me. I don't remember this officers name but I didn't like him. He never came at me sideways when we were in Germany but one day while deployed in Kuwait we got into a disagreement and he wanted to wrestle. We ended up on the floor wrestling and things got heated. I came out on top but I was no wrestler. I remember leaving that experience feeling like we could have easily gotten into a fist fight if we hadn't been broken up. Fist fights are different when both of you have fully loaded weapons on you.

Rau nu Prt m heru

Iu f Per f m heru

Utterances for Coming Forth by day into Light

It is he, who comes forth by day into Light

The 7 Letters I received while in Iraq

June 10th 2003

Dear Dawud, I hope that when you receive this letter it will find you doing well as could be expected, and hoping that you are getting adjusted to that kind of environment you're in. You are where I didn't want you to be , and I'm praying for you everyday. I pray that God will protect you and keep you safe hide you from violence and evil people. I hope that you have your bible with you. Read 91 psalms everyday for your protection. Every one here is at same place since you left. Karen is doing home business like Pamela with melaleuca wellness co. Duke, he takes it easy sitting in the garage still smoking. He cant stop it. Debra started back smoking too. We have had lots of rain here this year. Its getting warmer. We were planting flowers in the front yard today. I talk to Tahira last night she's going to write to you and send a care box to you. Saana's baby will be born next month. Haven't heard from her in a while phone is always off. She called Debra from one of her friends phone. Pamela and Tony went car shopping for their melaleuca paid for car. They want a Ford Expedition Eddie Bauer. Kyra is mischievous just like you were when you were little boy she's into everything born on your birthday (SMILE) it is now 12:45 am and I'm sitting in the bathroom writing this letter the only place to be private (smile) excuse writing and paper that I'm using. I intended to buy writing tablet but I forgot it. My memory is a little slack sometimes but doctors says we all have memory lapses sometimes. I will go to Pamela's house tomorrow to watch kids while she be on computer all day and go to curves exercise Tuesdays and Thursdays. She is senior director 2 in her group. She works hard Karen does too but it takes patience to reach senior director and it took Pamela just about 2 years to get there. Kids are doing fine. Bryan is going to summer school and working three days a week. So stubborn he's not running like he was before doesn't eat a lot either. Don't let him or Karen know I said this she don't like for us to talk about what he does to anyone. But your granddaddy tells him off sometimes he is so disrespectful. Brendan is changing a little but he keep saying he don't like Bryan. I guess I will save some words to write next time. Let us know what you would like in your care box next time. Please don't try to be a hero take care of yourself. May God bless you and keep you safe. **Love your Grandma.**

June 20th 2003

Hey Dawud, I hope this letter finds you in good spirit and in good health. I was so surprised to hear that you left to bagdad. You didn't even call me and let me know. I thought we were cool like that. Well anyway, I just wanted to write and let you know that I am very proud of you. I miss you, you haven't called me in a while I guess I know why. Well I'm sitting here on my bed. It's 2:21 am Sunday morning. I just came in from having drinks out with a girl friend. I was in the mood and had time to sit and write Dawud a letter and let him know he has family support here in the states. I know you don't get many calls from us but that doesn't mean we don't love and miss you. (You know you're entire family is dead broke). Half of them don't even have long distance service. So are you sleeping in a tent or a bed or sand? Is it very hot or are there good breezes coming in? I suppose it's very hot and humid there. When are you coming home? Are you going to stay in Germany for long? Well, when you write back I expect answers. As for my well being is concerned I basically go to work everyday and wish I had the lotto numbers so I can never work another day in my life. Now about happiness. I am still fucking single with no prospect yet. Do you have a girl friend? Have you heard from Natasha sister (p 305)? I forgot her name? Excuse my sloppy hand writing I've been drinking and it's late. Are you going to be stationed there for a long time? I will write you again soon. If you get a chance send me a line and let me know what you want me to send you. I will send anything you want. **Love you very very very much auntie Marcia**.

June 21st 2003

Dear Dawud, How are you doing over there in bagdad? I hope you're ok knowing you will not let me know how it really is. God will protect you and keep you for you're my first grandson and always tried after you had grown up to be your best. My hands are numb in the morning I cant write too good hope you can read this scribbling. We are doing fine still going through trials and tribulations trying to get things and our lives in order. I spoke to Saana gave her your address she said she was fine baby due July 27th. I hope this box has something you want. Write and let us know just what you want. You will be receiving portion drinks from melaleuca soon. This is little note before I mail the box. **All my love Grandma**

June 24th 2003

Hey big guy, Love you. Thought I would drop you a few lines to let you know that grand daddy was thinking about you. But I'm not worried about anything cause God is on the lookout. I firmly believe that. I pray in my own way. The power of forces is with you and will guide you in the right direction. So watch your back and get home safe. We all love you and were are praying you will come home safe. Grand Daddy doing good I turned 72 last week and I'm feeling good. I'm trying to get my truck fixed so I can get out and hustle you know I cant sit home and do nothing. So big guy I'll close for now. Say more next time. So, chow. **God bless Grand Daddy**.

The 7 Letters I Received while in Iraq

Rau nu Prt m heru

Iu f Per f m heru

Utterances for Coming Forth by day into Light

It is he, who comes forth by day into Light

July 10th 2003

Dear Dawud, I hope that when this letter reaches you it will find you feeling well and safe. I started this letter and didn't finish it. I just received your letter. July 14th and was so relieved to hear from you after looking at the news everyday on tv. Just keeps us upset. I called your mother and read the letter to her. She was so happy I heard from you. She is going to get herself in shape to sit down and write a letter to you. She is always talking about you but didn't take the time to write. She is always doing something, baby sitting for Shelia and keeping up with everything around Everdale ave (smile). I hear from Tahira often and listen to Alana cooing. Didn't see any picture of her yet. Lenny was down here for four days came for Bryans birthday Saturday. He was 18. Tahira said she is coming down here in September. Brendan said he wants to be like you. He is 12 now and is getting better then he was when you were here. Did you receive Granddaddy's letter and the box we sent you? Debra told us somethings you wanted. All of your aunts said they were going to write and send you a box but didn't sent it yet. I know how that is because I don't hear from them much unless I call. Especially Rosina, and Adaliah. I pray that you will be leaving from Baghdad very soon every American soldier should be coming home. The news is talking about people asking when will you guys be coming home they're mad because you're still there. I bet you are skinny not eating enough. Don't be picky eating just eating junk (smile). When you write next time put date on letter so I'll know when you wrote it, and when did you get my letter? Took almost a month to get it. When you leave bagdad do you have to go back to Germany or do you go to FT Hood. I hope that they will let you come here first. Our car is trying to give out on us. For about two weeks the wipers didn't work. it's the Cadillac convertible, somethings wrong with he exhaust, need a new one. Windshield has hailing crack in the middle. Tire when flat. Motto mounts about gone everything at the same time we're thinking about another car. I told your grand daddy I ain't thinking about another car unless he gets rid of that old ugly truck he wants to keep it. It still isn't running needs a transmission cant find one that old he won't give up looking. It's now 2am I guess I'll go to bed now and will write you soon. Trust in the Lord with all your heart and lean not to your own understanding. In all your ways acknowledge him and he will direct your path straight. Keep on praying I love you and hope to see you soon. I'm sending another box this week. **All my love. Grandma.**

July 16th 2003

Hi Dawud, Firstly I apologize for not writing sooner. I really don't have a good excuse. Anyway I hope you are keeping your spirits up as much as possible. It takes someone special to do what you are doing. I am very proud of you. It has been a very hot summer here. Lenny just left Sunday after being here for 4 days. Bryan turned 18 on July 12th. So Lenny drove down. He should be moving back north in the fall to Pennsylvania. I am doing consulting work as well as growing my melaleuca business I must say, I am exhausted though. I workout 5 days a week at the gym. I've lost 22 pounds so far and a lot of inches. I figure by next year this time I will be where I want to be. Another 4 to 5 pounds and ill be ok. So what is a typical day like there for you? Are you anxious to come back to the states? I hear you are going to be station in Texas? Brendan had pneumonia in June. The doctor said he had a partially collapsed lung some have to take him to see a pulmonologist. A lung specialist. He wants to play football so I have to get him a clear bill of health. I am reading a lot about what is going on over there. I pray for the safe return of all of you. I pray every day that God will return my nephew, safe and unharmed. I just got off the phone with your mom. She is in really good spirits. She also told me that she had a great conversation with you. That made her really happy. When grandma received your letter she was really thrilled. Grand daddy also wrote you. I am going to Long Beach, California with Pamela for melaleuca convention in august. Pam is leaving on august 6th and I am leaving on the 7th because Lenny will be here. August 6th will be our 20th anniversary. Well, Dawud I will write to you again. For now have a great day. Keep yourself safe and hurry home. We all miss you and love you. **Love always auntie Karen**

August 7th 2003

Dear Dawud, When this letter reaches you I hope that it will find you ok and feeling well. I see news everyday and I just can't wait until bush wakes up and sends our man back to our country America. Everyday I think about writing a letter to you and thinking about you in Baghdad. I pray that God will protect you. From any accidents, diseases, dangers or evil influences. When you have any quiet time read these bible verses. He who dwells in the secret place of the most high shall abide under the shadow of the almighty I will say of the Lord he is my refuge and my fortress, my God in him I will trust. Psalms 91:1-2 , Psalms 27:5, **Psalms 23:4**. I hope that you have your bible with you. I pray that you will find your purpose in life and that you will find happiness and peace in doing what you were created to do and be. I hope that you're eating enough and getting a little more weight not fat (smile). We're here still doing same thing. Karens in California, Pamela too. They're at a melaleuca convention, be back Sunday. Lenny and Jenna are here. Jenna needed a break from far Rockaway and that gal of Shelia next door to them she's too wild for Jenna to be with. Lenny and Karen's 20th anniversary is August 6th so he came to be with her. He's driving back Tuesday. Saana had a 7 pound 1 oz boy on Justin's birthday July 27th. I wish that Debra could move from that environment and find a better place she could afford. She needs a new start in a new environment to save Jenna. Maybe when Tahira changes over to the coast guard in staten island n.y. she could be some help for Jenna since Jenna is thinking about boys (smile). She's 13 1/2 now. Idol hands are devils workshop she needs to be doing something constructive. This is now Thursday 1:30 AM August 13th. I am finishing writing this letter to you that I started last Thursday. Since that night grand daddy has been to Alabama to see his sister from Chicago and was eating and talking to him. They said he blacked out they called 911 and he was taken to the hospital. Stayed two nights. He's home doing fine they did a lot of test didn't find what caused it waiting on results from ekg test of head. I was worried about him glad Lenny and Jenna was here. I told him that smoking caused it, restriction of blood vessels maybe he will soon stop smoking. When you come home you will see Pamela and Tony moved again two exits from where they were living before you left. Its a brand new house really nice. Lenny and Jenna left this morning. Tahira has a beautiful baby she sent me a tape of baby doing different things she's a doll (smile). She's suppose to come here next month. Debra she babysits everyday that keeps her busy. Will you be coming home here or will you have to go back to Germany when you leave Baghdad? I will close this letter so I can mail it now. **Love Grandma**

May 2003

War (1st of 2)

When you going to war who ya call to help ya? Airborne, Ranger, SF, Delta, Support M.O.S's run go seek shelter, 1st in last out, no doubt I'm a while out, when I get home but till then I just zone out, leaving the safe zone shit you don't know about, downtown Baghdad running up in a house, we know the enemy is in there gotta get em out, we kick in the door we ain't got 4 4's, we got M4's, M9's and hand grenades, storm the room yelling, get on your knees with your hands raised, I leave holes too big to fix with a band-aid, for ten dam days I been sick in the head from something I read I'm so full of rage, I be think'n of shit I read on that damn page while I be sending these men to their damn graves, I can't even think straight my mind is man made, they made my mind up to think like a damn slave, broke me down to nothing then built me up to something unbelievable, you cant conceive the evil that we do! wanna know what we do? Let me enlighten you, I got this crew serve weapon pointed right at you! so don't question shit if you don't know the job, and don't question shit if you ain't seen the mob, we ain't got time for politics we load clips, and we bust back even when we getting hit, so when you're going to the club, I'm fighting cause I love my family I gotta get back to them in one piece, the Middle East ,I never thought I would be here, battle focused training soldier you better prepare, them Middle East you could be stuck there for a whole year, battle focused training soldier you better prepare **- Dawud**

2003

The B.I.A.P. (Baghdad International Air Port)

1 AD be the patch on my shoulder, bomb on my enemies cause I'm a souljah, it's just the **Tupac** in me dog I thought I told ya bomb on my enemies cause I'm a souljah! I salute to you buddy, soldiers getting killed, it just sickens me sir cause it's all for the dollar bill, the dinar, the Deutsche mark don't take Iraqi money! keep an eye on the one who be smile'n and look'n funny! I be trying not to get complacent, I rather keep it on semi fuck all that safe shit! tell me where is yo clip or yo magazine? you think you in the field son? son it's not a dream! I keep a military mind like an A-team, and if you open your mind you can see this scene, it was a Sergeant first class and PFC Iraqi's snuck up behind them stabbed them up so we sent some Apaches out to find them, not enough intel, we can't even tell the difference, from the good, bad, and ugly to carry on the mission, K.I.A, P.O.W, M.I.A., everyday a soldiers life taken away, to the soft M.O.S. soldier who lacks training, you chill on the BIAP think'n you back on your block, but you'er not! don't you hear that knock on our door? they been try'n to mortar you, but still you don't think you at war!

Two troops move out in one soft Humvee, leave the safe zone alone cause they hungry, end up downtown Iraq were the enemy sees a chance to strike back for his family, his family was killed on an infantry raid, from a grenade, he cried as he kneeled and he prayed, he's filling with rage, hates Americans for there ways, he hates the land of the free home of the brave to the soft M.O.S. soldier who lacks training, you chill on the BIAP think'n you back on your block, but you'er not! don't you hear that knock on our door? they been try'n to mortar you, but still you don't think you at war! **- Dawud**

2003 - Mark Dehaan and Irvin

Dehaan and I rarely got along back in Germany. He was 7 years older than me and he was wiser than me. He did the bare minimum while I did the best that I could. He knew the army was bullshit but I was blind to the facts. I was the stupid one who followed all the rules and he was always breaking the rules. He even showed up in Iraq wearing a shirt with a different name on it. With all that said, seeing him while deployed to Iraq felt good because I missed him. He had PCS'ed to another duty station before we deployed to Iraq but he made it his business to find his old unit and came by to see how we were making out. While deployed in Iraq we all knew that any day could be our last so whatever quarrels we had in the past we left them back in Germany for the most part. I have only seen Dehaan once since this picture was taken in 2003. In 2017 he would give me a call telling me he was in New York City at the bus station so I went down to see him. He was there with Irvin a brother who was also stationed with us in Germany. They both crossed paths in New York and knew that I was in New York. It felt good to see both of them. I called Dehaan after I wrote this to see how he was doing and he's doing well.

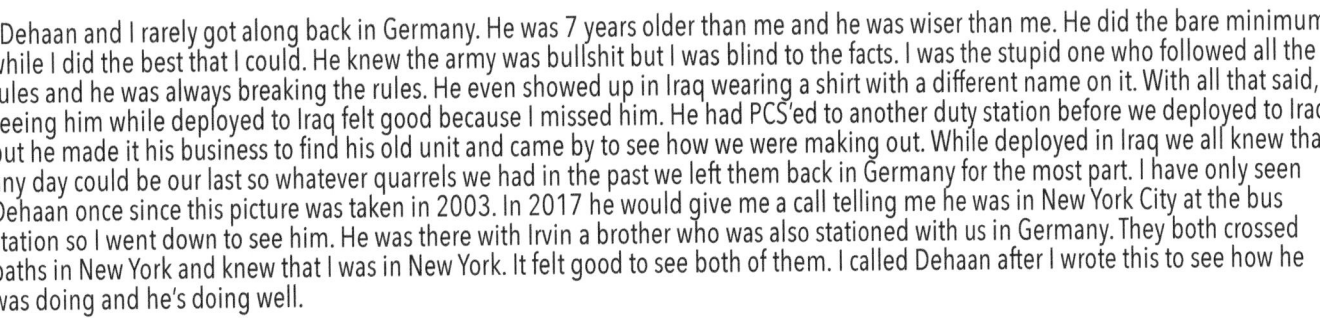

Rau nu Prt m heru

***Addendum* Revision and divine Confirmations** (See pages 182, 619 and 648 for other confirmations)

This book was finished on June 1st 2022 and online for sale some time in June 2022. When I got the physical copy of this book I made some grammatical corrections and small updates. On July 3rd 2022 I got a text from Mark that would m**ark** the **first divine confirmation**. In the text was a picture of this book. He told me that his wife bought him a copy of the book for his birthday. I asked him if July 3rd was his birthday and to my surprise he said yes. That's when I told him that my past life as **Emmett Till** was revealed on July 3rd of 2018 (page 480). I told him July 3rd's connection to the **Dog** star **Sirius**, ancient Kemet (Egypt) and the inundation of the Nile River. I asked him what year he was born and he said 1970. I told him his life path number was 9. I asked what his wife's birthday was, he said **Nov 4th** 1971. I told him she was born the same day the **Tutankhaten's** (**King Tut's**) tomb was discovered in 19**22**. I told him that **Tupac** was born the same year his wife was born and that I detail who Tupac was in his past life in this book. Mark told me about a time when he got a massage and after the massage he began to attract more business than he could handle. He said the massage therapist did that for him. I explained that she only moved the energy in his body around allowing his body to do what it is designed to do, which is to attract what we desire. I told him to read page 582, where I **attracted** business with my **thoughts**. After we hung up I realized that Mark was born in 1970 the year of the **Dog**. King Tut's tomb was discovered in the year of the **Dog** and my past life revelation of Emmett Till was in 2018 the year of the **Dog** on Mark's birthday! On July 7th 2022 I would get the **second divine confirmation** with **Justin** (page 619). The 3rd **divine confirmation** came with **Keith Brown** (p 648) and the last was a message from **Netic**, The Ancient One (p 182). I added these experiences to the book because the book appears to be taking on a life of it's own. While writing this book I thought that **coincidences** like this might happen and so, they have begun…………..!

Iu f Per f m heru

Utterances for Coming Forth by day into Light

It is he, who comes forth by day into Light

Pornography, as a War Strategy

I was in Iraq for 6 months and the first 4 months I was **VERY VIGILANT**. I wanted to make it home and "**stay alert, stay alive**" was my motto. For the first four months I did not think about sex even though many soldiers were having sex and some even cheated on their wives and husbands. Some where in my last two months I was given a CD with **porn** on it. I don't know for sure where they got it from but I was told that the cd's were purchased from Iraqi vendors outside the gate. When I think of that now I wonder if it was a war strategy used to preoccupy the "enemy" with sex. I began to masterbate even though I had not masterbated in many years. I never did while I was stationed in Germany because I had no reason to. I had many women to pick from. While I was deployed in Iraq I did not have sex with anyone but I masterbated. Pornography and sex is used as a war strategy against all those reading this book. Imagine how much more productive you could be if you didn't waste your life force energy. There was a time when you could watch movies for free online but in todays day and time you can not watch any movie for free. Now with the emergence of Netflix, Hulu and many other streaming platforms all movies must be paid for, except pornography! Why do you think that is?! The enemy attacks with distractions! You must remain vigilant in your journey of awakening. If you know that someone has a plan to see you fail you must be equally and even more so determined to not allow them to be successful! The path of **Shemsu Heru** is the path I took (page 2). This is the path of raising ones consciousness above their animalistic nature. This is the **riddle** of the Sphinx (**Heru Em Akhet)**, an ancient monument with the head of a human and the body of a lion. See pages 2 and 3 for more details.

I never knew of a STD or a bad FLU until I did what they told me to do and got Vaccinated

Rau nu Prt m heru

lu f Per f m heru

Before my deployment to Iraq in 2003, the Army **vaccinated** all of us soldiers like farm animals. I still have my medical information and it is only today, March 16th 2022 that I realize the amount of vaccines I received and it is truly alarming. I received the **Anthrax, Hep A, Hep B, Smallpox, Yellow Fever, Polio, Influenza, Meningo**, **MMR**, and the **Japanese Encephalitis Vaccine** (p 221). Studies on soldiers have shown that mild and moderate reactions from **Anthrax** shots appear on the arm where the vaccine was given such as tenderness, redness, itching, development of a lump or bruise, muscle aches; headaches; joint pain; fever; and fatigue. The more severe and adverse reactions to the anthrax vaccine include difficulty breathing, weakness, hoarseness, wheezing, a fast heartbeat, hives, dizziness, paleness, or swelling of the lips and throat. Serious reactions involving the skin and nervous system have been reported as well, but the military claims no direct link to the anthrax vaccine has been conclusively proven. I can only imagine the harm all those vaccines combined must have done to my body. I truly believe it was physical fitness that kept me from suffering severe illness yet still I did not escape without injury. When I left Iraq in 2003 I got an **STD** for the first time in my life and in 2004 I had a bad case of the **Flu** for the first time in my life. I think my **natural defense system** was compromised by the vaccines I was given and this is why I was not willing to take any vaccine for "**Covid**". Instead I leaned on the knowledge I had acquired from this experience as well as all the natural healing remedies I acquired during the years of my awakening. I was my own case study. For some people it might seem obvious that the vaccine was the cause but for others, they might think it was just some "coincidence". It's always interesting how people who have not had the first hand experience, still feel like their opinions are more valid. Sometimes it's the level of study they claim to have that makes them so sure that the government would never do such a thing to them. Or perhaps they feel like the government would never knowingly do that to them. These same people remain quiet when you ask them what ever happened to the weapons of mass destruction that the government claimed Iraq had? You ask them what the purpose of the war in Iraq was and they think that we were insuring freedom for the Iraqi people even though Black people still don't have freedom in America. Trying to explain this to some people is like pissing in the wind. And speaking of that, not even our genitals are safe when it comes to medical procedures. Take the barbaric practice of genital mutilation (**circumcision**) for instance (p 252). Why should we trust doctors who prompt this practice solely because it is written in the Bible (p 252)? Circumcision serves no purpose but we are told that it is a way to prevent disease yet by cutting the first line of defense (the skin) the genitals are made susceptible to foreign pathogens. What will it take us to use our common sense?! If the God of the bible is an all knowing God and this God created the heavens and earth, then why would humans not be already made perfect and why would this God sacrifice her/his own "children"(p 252)?! We are so blinded by all of the lights and camera's and tv shows that we can't see the truth when it's exposed. I don't know what was in the vaccines I was given and I can't be sure what was in the air while I was deployed in a Iraq but I was circumcised as a child and after I left Iraq I heard stories of many soldiers dying from "**cancer**" shortly after they returned from Iraq due to their exposure to different forms of **radiation**. My brother Sgt Oliver (Big O, p 69) was lucky. Many of the people in his unit died from "**cancer**" but he survived his bout with "**cancer**"..

A Message To The Afflicted

Utterances for Coming Forth by day into Light

It is he, who comes forth by day into Light

Are you stricken with sickness? Have you felt the pains of disease? Are you ashamed of what has been cast upon you? Perhaps though, you have been given the opportunity to be victorious if you can only find your healing. To every up there is a down. To every solid there is a liquid and to every liquid there is a gas. To every illness there is a cure. If the temperature is not low enough then water will not freeze and just the same, disease can be eliminated or promoted by the terrain within your body. Said another way, our insides can be peaceful like a summer day or dangerous like a hurricane coming your way. It all depends on how we take care of our bodies, and what we put in them or what we allow others to put in or take out of them. Nature has provided balance for all things so if we make the proper changes in sufficient time healing can take place. Transformation is not always pretty, sometimes to transform we must get dirty. Sometimes we might feel like we're swimming through a tunnel of feces like Andy Dufrense in the movie The Shawshank Redemption or like the **scarab dung beetle**. The early Christian Father **St. Augustine**, writes, "My own **good beetle**, not so much because he is only the begotten (God), not because he, the author of himself, has taken on the form of mortals, but because he has **rolled himself** in our **filth** and chooses to be born from this filth itself." **St. Augustine** is speaking about the **dung beetle** who **roles the cow dung** in a ball and places it's eggs in the dung, then they deposit the ball of dung in a hole in the ground, where their larvae feed on the dung. When their larvae hatch their progeny spring forth from the earth seemingly from nowhere giving rise to the beetle's connection with transformation and the **resurrection of the dead,** in ancient Kemet (Egypt). You can transform yourself like the dung beetle. You can rise from the disease that is said to be a death sentence. You have been stricken with some malady but rest assure there is a cure, however you must know that to be true in your mind first. Our thoughts and emotions are vital to our recovery. The label of a sickness (AIDS, CANCER, COVID, LUPUS, POLIO etc etc) by itself can cause a person to stress and get sick. When we stress our bodies release a host of hormonal chemicals that reduce the bodies ability to fight off infections and diseases. All of this can lead to the shortening of life. You should know that there is healing in water and healing in laughter and healing in breathing and healing in fasting and healing in sound. **Cancer cells can be shattered like glass** and destroyed when two pulsating resonant frequencies (vibrations) are aimed at them but the frequency fields must be between 100,000 - 300,000 Hertz, and the higher frequency must be 11 times the lower (the 11th harmonic, p 6). The act of **smiling** boosts the immune system 3000 percent. **Dr Patch Adams used laughter to cure stage 4 terminal Cancer conditions**. He only used laughter! Sometimes sickness can be your blessing. If you begin to make healthy life style changes like adding healthy eating to your habits, like yoga and deep breathing you might think it's magic. Because the feeling of healing is feeling like magic when you reverse the sickness that you once thought was tragic. Cancer is a highly acidic condition (disease) that is a result poor eating, causing blockages in the lymphatic system. The body is always working in our defense. In ancient Kemet the dead were placed in **tombs**. Cancer cells are dying cells that the body places into **tombs** which doctors call **tumors**.

SGT Eddings' Vaccination Record

Anthrax, Hep A, Hep B, Smallpox, Yellow Fever, Polio, Influenza, Meningo, MMR, and Japanese Encephalitis.

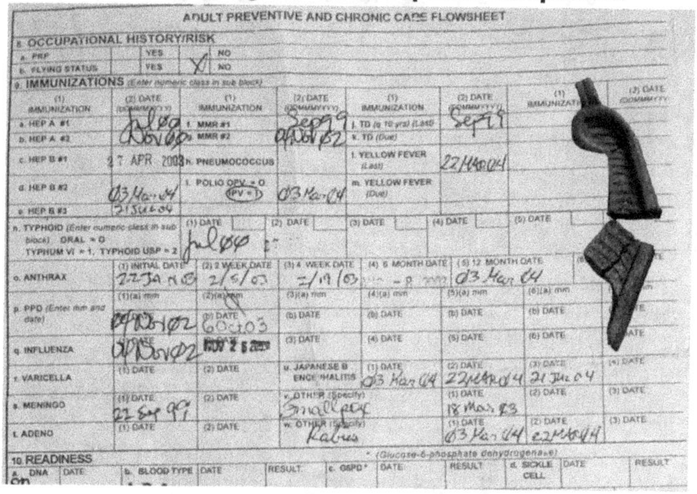
ADULT PREVENTIVE AND CHRONIC CARE FLOWSHEET

8. OCCUPATIONAL HISTORY/RISK
a. PRP — YES / NO
b. FLYING STATUS — YES / X NO

9. IMMUNIZATIONS (Enter numeric class in sub block)

(1) IMMUNIZATION	(2) DATE (DDMMMYYYY)	(1) IMMUNIZATION	(2) DATE (DDMMMYYYY)	(1) IMMUNIZATION	(2) DATE (DDMMMYYYY)
a. HEP A #1	Jul 99	f. MMR #1	Sep 99	j. TD (q 10 yrs) (Last)	Sep 99
b. HEP A #2	Nov 99	g. MMR #2	04 Oct 02	k. TD (Due)	
c. HEP B #1	27 APR 2003	h. PNEUMOCOCCUS		l. YELLOW FEVER (Last)	22 Mar 04
d. HEP B #2	03 Mar 04	i. POLIO OPV = 0 IPV = 1	03 Mar 04	m. YELLOW FEVER (Due)	
e. HEP B #3	21 Jul 04				

n. TYPHOID (Enter numeric class in sub block) ORAL = 0, TYPHUM VI = 1, TYPHOID USP = 2 — (1) DATE Jul 04; (2) DATE; (3) DATE; (4) DATE; (5) DATE

o. ANTHRAX — (1) INITIAL DATE 22 Jan 03; (2) 2 WEEK DATE 2/5/03; (3) 4 WEEK DATE 2/19/03; (4) 6 MONTH DATE; (5) 12 MONTH DATE 03 Mar 04

p. PPD (Enter mm and date) — 04 Oct 02; 6 Oct 03

q. INFLUENZA — 04 Nov 02; NOV 2 5 2003

r. VARICELLA — (1) DATE; (2) DATE
u. JAPANESE B ENCEPHALITIS — (1) DATE 03 Mar 04; (2) DATE 22 Mar 04; (3) DATE 21 Jul 04; (4) DATE

s. MENINGO — (1) DATE 27 Sep 99; (2) DATE
v. OTHER (Specify) Smallpox — (1) DATE 18 Mar 03; (2) DATE; (3) DATE

t. ADENO — (1) DATE; (2) DATE
w. OTHER (Specify) Rabies — (1) DATE 03 Mar 04; (2) DATE 22 Mar 04; (3) DATE

10. READINESS
a. DNA — DATE; b. BLOOD TYPE — DATE — RESULT; c. G6PD* — DATE — RESULT; d. SICKLE CELL — DATE — RESULT
* (Glucose-6-phosphate dehydrogenase)

SGT Eddings' initial claim in 2004

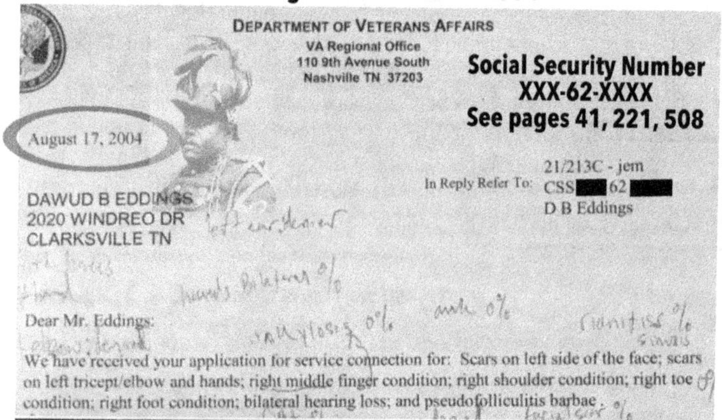
DEPARTMENT OF VETERANS AFFAIRS
VA Regional Office
110 9th Avenue South
Nashville TN 37203

Social Security Number
XXX-62-XXXX
See pages 41, 221, 508

August 17, 2004

In Reply Refer To: 21/213C - jem
CSS[redacted]62[redacted]
D B Eddings

DAWUD B EDDINGS
2020 WINDREO DR
CLARKSVILLE TN

Dear Mr. Eddings:

We have received your application for service connection for: Scars on left side of the face; scars on left tricept/elbow and hands; right middle finger condition; right shoulder condition; right toe condition; right foot condition; bilateral hearing loss; and pseudofolliculitis barbae.

VA Claim and Compensation Denied

When I was out processing the army in 2004, I listed the injuries that I incurred while in the military. It is no surprise that the date on my paperwork was **Marcus Garvey's** birthday (August 17,2004). They only approved 1 injury. I receive **10%** compensation for my shoulder. In 2013 I appealed my claim but on March 8th 2014 my appeal for compensation was denied (page 288). I got out of the Army in 2005 and as of 2022 I only get $144.00 a month from the military. I still suffer from lower back pains, pains in my back that sometimes cause me to drop to the floor incapacitated, sharp pains in the heels of my feet, sharp pain in my right toe, pains in my left elbow when I try fully extending my left arm, shoulder pains, I get razor bumps because I was made to shave my face in the Army and I deal with post traumatic stress disorder that I was only able to reduce by expressing myself through music. Sometimes I have trouble sleeping and my hearing isn't as good as it used to be. While I was in the army it was frowned upon to miss work or formation due to going to sick call (doctor). So I dealt with my pains and don't have a record of most of my injuries. I have placed X Ray images of my right toe and shoulder. When I was a private in the army I was made to cut grass and while doing so I tripped and fell and the lawnmower cut my big toe. As you can see in the X Ray on the bottom, a pin was placed in my toe. My collar bone broke from carrying heavy things on my back for long distances on road marches. I have struggled with these pains since I left the army. The VA hospital wants to make soldiers beg them for the compensation they are owed. They denied my appeal and I struggled in silence. I must thank them though. If they had paid me what they owed me I might not have been so financially stressed and I might not have turned to music for therapy and I might not have studied my past and I might not know that I was Emmett Till and Tutankhaten. So thank you but I still want what is mine.

ADDENDUM

Sgt Dawud Eddings' Appeal for Compensation for Service connected injuries and retro pay for a Clear and Unmistakable Error

My name is Sgt Dawud Eddings, I am currently 45 years old. I made my initial claim in 2004 and had been receiving **10%** compensation from 2005 up until February of 20**23** when my rating was raised to **60%**. I submitted a new claim on August 15, 2022 for an increase in compensation for my service connected injuries and to appeal the rejected claims of other service connected injuries I submitted in 2004. Some of my injuries manifested after my time in the Army, but are a result of events or experiences that took place while in the Army from the ages of 21 to 26 yrs old. In August of 2022 I reopened my case for military compensation for my injuries. On September 28, 2022 I met with Welby Alcanatara, my Veterans Benefits Advisor at 245 West Houston Street room 205. Welby and I spoke for over two hours as we went over my claim. I explained how I had been experiencing many levels of pain and discomfort that effect my day to day life in reduce my ability to make a living. I expressed my desire to have all my injuries fully compensated and most importantly to receive the retro active pay for the service connected injuries that the Army never compensated me for. As we looked over my claim we noticed that there was **A Clear and Unmistakable Error** with how the Army compensated me for my shoulder injury. Some how the Army wrongfully connected my **shoulder injury** with my **Toe injury** but these injuries are not related. They are two separate claims. After an hour or so of speaking to Welby I realized that he was the same man who helped me in 2012 during my process of receiving my G.I. Bill tuition (p 240). Then I asked him what his birthday was and to my surprise I found that he is born on August 18, the same day grand father died (p 169). As of **February 13**, 2023 (p 289), the Army has separated the two claims and I now receive 30% compensation for my toe and 40% compensation for my shoulder which adds up to 60% compensation. Unfortunately I was not paid the correct amount of retro active pay for my toe. I should have received over $100K for retroactive payment of my right toe that dates back from 2004 but I have yet to receive what I am owed. On June 1, 2023, my father's birthday and the same day I crashed and lived (page 104 -106), my military compensation is incleased to **90%**. **Medgar Evers was the reason that Mamie Till had an open casket at Emmett Till's funeral**. Medgar encouraged Mamie to show the world Emmett's face and that's how the Civil Rights Movement was born. **Medgar was a soldier in the U.S. Army** during World War II just like **Louis Till** (Emmett Till's father, p 475, 651). The U.S. Army was still segregated and **openly racist** at the time. Medgar was born in Decatur, Mississippi, on **July 2nd** 1925, the same day that **Louis Till** was **Hung** by the U.S. Army (**July 2nd** 1945), falsely accused of raping and killing a **White woman** (p 518). Medgar was assassinated on **June 12th** 1963 (**year of the rabbit**) and on **June 12th** 2023 (**year of the rabbit**) my military compensation is incleased to **100%** (page 515, 520).

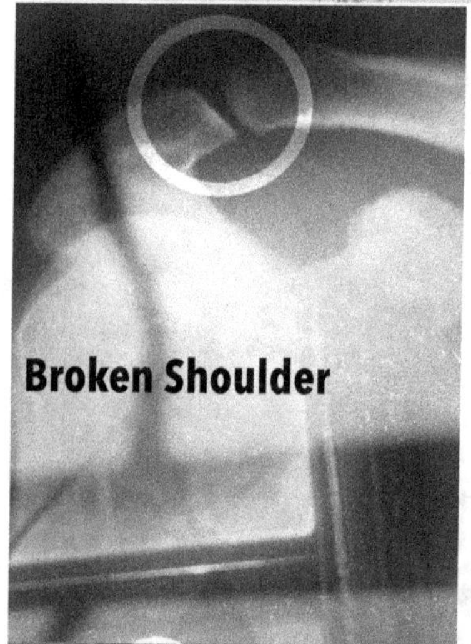
Broken Shoulder

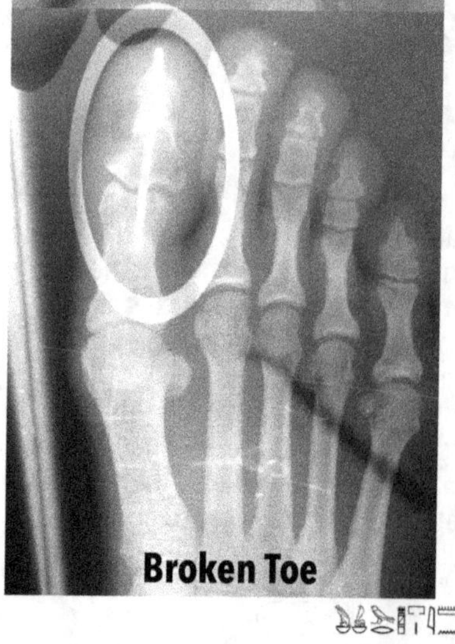
Broken Toe

I wake up in pain every day! Everyday, without fail, both of my shoulders pain me when I awake in the morning. I experience headaches often and as I write this I am experiencing a throbbing headache. These headaches stop me from being functional. Everyday I am challenged with lower back pain that can rest around my sacrum but on bad days will also radiate up my spin. Sometimes these pains in my lower back are crippling.. As the day goes on sometimes the pain reduces but the pain never completely goes away. Very often I experience throbbing pain in my teeth from the unnecessary dental work I was given a few months before I was honorably discharged (page 123). If I ever endeavor to do any running my knees and feet will start causing me pains. Some days they pain me without doing any running. Someday I start my day with uncontrolled sneezing, runny/stuffy nose, itchy/watery eyes and or a headache. When the weather is cold I am stricken with pains in my fingers and toes. Even though I never killed anyone, when I think of my time in the Army I have nervousness, stress and regret due to the part I played in causing harm and killing of innocent people in the world. When is see innocent black people killed at the hands of American police I am taken back to my time in the Army, now feeling I'm targeted by the police. Without black African soldiers the civil war would not have been won by the Union and the place we know as America would not be what we know it to be today. Yet still, with all the sacrifices black American soldiers have made, the US Military has discriminated against black American military veterans like myself, ever since the first black Americans began to serve in the military. According to a new 2022 lawsuit filed in federal court, the Military disproportionally rejects the claims of black American veterans at a much higher rate than white veterans. When my claims were rejected in 2004 I was too young to understand how the lack of compensation would effect me mentally, physically and emotionally as my body began to age rapidly due to all the service connected damage I sustained while in the Army.. When calling the VA about my current appeal I asked about having my claim rushed

Rau nu Prt m heru

Iu f Per f m heru

Utterances for Coming Forth by day into Light

It is he, who comes forth by day into Light

I was 11 months behind on rent due to Covid and a loss of business. The VA representative told me that they only make claims first priority when a veteran is over 70 years old, terminally ill on their death bed, or if they had some kind of hardship. I explained that I was 11 months behind on rent due to loss of business from Covid but this was not emergency enough to warrant a first priority. When the call was ended I felt like the the VA was waiting me out, hoping I would die first or possibly commit suicide. Suicide rates are especially high among veterans. According to VA, in 2016, about 58% of Military suicides were among Veterans age 55 and older. I am a 45 year old Veteran who is attempting, for the third time, to receive compensation for the service connected injuries I sustained while in the Army... A study released in 2022 found that as many as 44 veterans die on average per day from suicide when accounting overlooked deaths such as unexplained drug overdoses, which is more than twice the official estimate. Nearly three quarters of these veterans are not under VA care. I don't trust that the VA has my best interest in mind so I don't go to the Va. I am 11 months behind on my rent and other bills due to a loss of business caused by the Covid pandemic in 2020. I still feel the financial effects to this day. As soon as I came back from Iraq in 2003 I saw the physical effects of the vaccines I was injected with just before I deployed to Iraq in 2003. As the years went by the other service connected pathologies began to manifest. I represent the percentage of Veterans that would never commit suicide but that doesn't mean that I don't have issues of my own. I often think back on the years I spent in the Army, now knowing all that I know, I ask myself what purpose did I serve……. I am able to see how my time in the Army was useful for me. It gave me first hand experience to speak from. I am a Veteran that was sent to War. On top of that my body was damaged in many ways. I suffer from psychological stress due to my encounters with police and the murdered of African American soldiers and civilians at the hands of police, many of the police being white officers, many of them being ex military. When I saw how **La Vena Johnson** was murdered in 2005 it bothered me greatly (page 140). She was deployed to Iraq when her death made the news. The official report claims that La Venna killed herself, that she committed suicide. But the evidence tells another story. From the remains of La Venna's body it appears that she had been raped. It also appears that La Venna's body was burnt, as if someone was trying to burn away the evidence of their crimes. The Military has yet to resolve the case with La Venna's family. She is not the only soldier that has died under similar circumstances. I was a sergeant in the Army and as a Sergeant these murders cause me much pain.

ADDENDUM **Excerpt from pages 38 and 39 of my 2022, 43 page claim for Army compensation**

Service connected PTSD condition. Origin of **PTSD condition**

First traumatic stress episode

The first time I can remember **experiencing a heightened sense of imminent death was during my deployment to Iraq in 2003 while on a convoy from Kuwait to Iraq**. I experienced driving through a sand storm, barley being able to see the vehicle in front of me. There was a feeling of death knocking at your door. When the convoy was over my vehicle was **riddled** with bullet holes. Fortunately we did not have any casualties during this convoy.

3 additional traumatic stress factors

1 • While deployed to Iraq on the Baghdad International Airport (B.I.O.P.) I had countless experiences that caused me to fear for my life. One of those experiences was when **Private Acosta got his hand blown off from a grenade** that was thrown in his vehicle. **2 •** Another contributing factor to my fears of death was the non stop **mega explosions** we heard and felt, while stationed on the Baghdad International Airport (B.I.O.P.). These explosions caused many of us to walk around with the sense that any moment could be our last. **3 • One of the images that I will never forget was seeing Iraqi soldiers melted to their vehicles**. No matter what I do, these images seem to never go away…

PTSD condition manifestation post military service

The murder of black men, women and children by American Police

While stationed in Germany I had been away from America for 4 years. Because of this I had not seen coverage of the countless lives lost from necessary killings by the hands of American police. After I left the Army I began a career as a personal trainer in 2005. The next year, in **2006**, I saw the murder of **Sean bell** (page 149). I was 29yrs old when he was murdered. Sean Bell was a 23yr old African American man who was shot four times in a hail of **50 bullets by the NYPD**. Perhaps this case may not have garnered so much attention if there had not been so many shots fired, but why did they need 50 rounds? It was the murder of Sean Bell that awoken the feelings of being back at war, only now the war was against people who look like me. As time went on I began to see a pattern. I saw more and more Black people gunned down by the police, more than any of group and the police were usually White cops killing Black people with no care for their lives. In **2010** I saw 7 year old **Aiyana Mo'Nay Stanley-Jones**, murdered by police and no justice was served. She was at home sleeping when police stormed into the wrong house and killed her while she slept (p 181). In **2012** I saw 17 year old **Trayvon Martin** murdered by a White security guard and no justice was served (p 232). In **2014** I saw 12 year old **Tamir Rice** murdered by police, and for what?! Tamir was playing with a toy gun in a park by himself. No justice was served in his killing (p 307). The same year I saw 18 year old **Michael Brown** gunned down in **2014**. A White police officer by the name of Darren Wilson confronted Michael Brown and his friend (page 300). Minutes later Wilson fired a total of 12 bullets leaving Michael dead on the floor. No justice was served. On July 17th **2014**, **Eric Garner** was killed by a white New York City Police officer named Daniel Pantaleo who put Eric in a prohibited chokehold while arresting him (page 299). Video footage of the incident generated widespread national attention and his death increased my feelings of being back in Iraq.. As a black man like Eric, I had a feeling of being targeted and these feelings still live inside of me to this day. In **2015**, on **Martin Luther King's birthday**, I saw the news reporting of **Florida police using Mug Shots of Black Men for Target Practice** (page 317). Why were they using black people as target practice?! This gave me greater belief that the system was set up against me and I felt more and more that I was back in Iraq. On **April 4 2015,** the same day that **Martin Luther King was assassinated,** I saw **Walter Scott shot in the back** by a white police officer (page 322). **I felt I was back in Iraq**. **Walter** was shot dead for no reason. Walter was a 50 year old black man, **he was also a veteran like me**! He was studying **massage therapy like me**. Seeing this murder of Walter Scott heightened my feelings of warfare against Black Americans. I felt like **it could have been me that was shot down by a cop for no reason**. *These are the murders that caused me to respond in anger when police* ***racially targeted me*** *for trivial stop and checks (page 35 of claim)*. With all the Black people being killed by police in America I couldn't understand how the police could perform their duty and not know that some Black people feel threatened by them. Many of these police officers were ex military men and women like myself. They served America like I had but now they were killing Black people who look like me. In April of **2015 Freddie Gray**, a 25 year old black male, was arrested by Baltimore police and 45 minutes later he was found dead in the back of a police van with a severed spine, with his hands and feet shackled (page 324). **His death sparked the Baltimore Riots in Maryland** because Black people in America, especially Black men felt a reasonable fear of losing their life when dealing with police, especially white police officers. On June 17th **2015**, a white man by the name, **Dylan Storm Roof** entered the Emanuel African Methodist Episcopal Church through a side door at 8:16 pm (page 335). He pretended to be a peaceful participant of the Bible study and at around 9pm he opened fire with a Glock 41. 45 caliber handgun **killing 9 people** in total. He murdered black men, women and children. On **July 10th 2015 Sandra Bland** was pulled over for a minor traffic violation (page 337). Three days later Sandra Bland was found hanged in a jail cell in Waller County, Texas. Her death was ruled a suicide but in December of 2015 Encinia was indicted for perjury for making false statements about the circumstances surrounding Bland's arrest. These murders have not stopped. The names are countless and in 2020 we saw the murder of **Breonna Taylor** (page 589) and **George Floyd** by the hands of American police officers (page 610). Breonna's murderers went free while the cop that killed George was sent to prison. **These murders remind me of my time in Iraq and they heighten my stress levels.** Instead of responding in anger I used poetry as an outlet for my anger (page 33 of claim). Some of my other claims are: **Service connected peripheral neuropathy**, **Service connected** injuries to my **Right toe, Service connected** injuries to my right **shoulders, Service connected** pains in the **arches** and **heels of my feet, Service connected** pains in my **knees, Service connected** injuries to my **spine and lower back**, **Service connected** injuries of **Elbow**, **shoulder**, **concussion**, sustained from work related **Car Accident, Service connected Rhinitis condition**, **Service connected** pains in **teeth, Service connected hearing impairment/Tinnitus. Service connected** injuries of brain from car accident (**Traumatic Brain Injury - TBI**).

Barbaric Dentistry

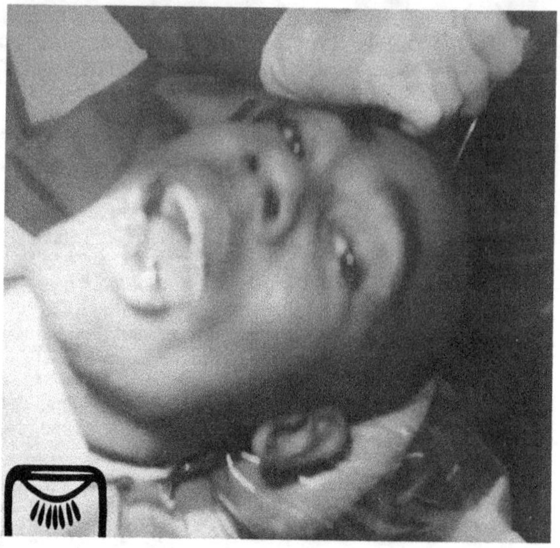

From **circumcision** (p 252), to what foods to eat for healthy living, the world has been thoroughly conditioned through religion. If there was any verse in the bible that might save the world it is Genesis 1 verse 29, "And God said, Behold, I have given you every herb bearing seed, which is upon all the face of the earth, and every tree, in the which is the fruit of a tree yielding seed; to you it shall be for food". But then there is chapter 15, verse 11 in the book of Matthew which contradicts that by stating, "a man is not defiled by what enters his mouth, but by what comes out of it". People think they can pray over food to protect themselves from sickness however food kills more people in America than racist police officers. The 3rd leading cause of death is **medical malpractice** due to misdiagnosis of pharmaceutical drugs and in many cases these drugs are taken to mask the symptoms caused by the foods we eat. Calcium is vital in the bodies process of healing but **processed sugar** is in almost everything we eat, and processed sugar depletes the calcium stores in the body. When a baby is developing in the womb it needs plenty of calcium to build the skeleton and if the mothers isn't properly nourished the body will leach calcium from the mother to form the skeleton of the baby which is why my grand mother lost one tooth with every child that she had. After my last physical during my out-processing of the Army the Dentist felt one of my teeth needed to be pulled. I had been in the Army for 5 years and it was only now that a Dentist saw something terribly wrong with my teeth. I listened to his professional opinion because of course, he was the "Doctor". He said that I needed a root canal and I **believed*** him. I was not yet knowledgable enough to defend my body from the barbaric practices of the American Medical Association. I wasn't having any problems with the tooth but still he pulled the healthy tooth out of my mouth and gave me a gold crown. Then he put fillings in 6 other teeth, 3 on the top and 3 on the bottom. I was not aware of the potential side effects of having teeth pulled from your mouth or about the toxic materials that are used in the fillings. In 2015 I ordered the book, **Doctors are more Harmful than Germs** and what I read alarmed me. I realized how detrimental my experience with the dentist was to my health. In 2003 I knew nothing about the different systems in the body but by 2015 I was going through Massage School and now I knew about the different acupuncture meridians in the body (p 274). The book explained how the teeth, even though they are hard, they are still living tissue just like lips, gums and the roof of your mouth. I learned that all **32** teeth in the mouth have a relationship with each part of the body. Every single one of the **acupuncture meridians** passes through a particular tooth and every tooth has a relationship with a particular body structure. One of my molars was taken out and the molars are connected to the meridians of the **spleen**, stomach and thyroid. I ruptured my **spleen** in high school when Victor tripped me (number **32**, p 61). I was running so fast during football practice that when he tripped me I went **flying** into the air and landed on the left side of my torso. Afterwards I was peeing blood so I was admitted to the hospital. My high school sweetheart **Indira** (p 60) came to see me while I was there and we laughed and played board games. I spent a few days in the hospital but I was fortunate because **no surgery was performed on me**. I was instead, healed by **love** and **laughter** the same way **Dr Patch Adams** healed **cancer** (p 120). **Indira** would appear in a **profound dream** in 2014 after not speaking to her in 14 years (p 305). Like other medical professions, dentistry suffers from a love of procedure and the money that comes with it. This dates back to medieval times when both **physicians** and **dentist** used music to distract their patients from the pains of their **barbaric surgerie**s. And their patients, who had no knowledge of how their bodies worked, accepted these surgeries. Even today, there are some people who get all their teeth pulled, like my my grand parent's, who unwittingly let a dentist pull their teeth out. What is the wisdom in having wisdom teeth removed? Pulling teeth creates inflammation and this can lead to heart disease if the inflammation is unknown or ignored. When a tooth is dead or dying the body triggers bacteria to decompose the tooth. After root canal surgery sometimes the remaining tissue begins to decompose but when decomposing tissue is trapped under a crown, infection can begin. The best way to heal a problem is to reverse the cause. **Processed sugar** is the number one cause of decaying teeth. So if a person has a cavity, a complete halt of eating processed sugar or a reduction can help reverse the issue. I was not aware of this at the time and so I let a Dentist do surgery on me. I have learned my lesson and I am more cautious of what I eat. The military has yet to compensate me for all the physical damage that I experienced while serving in the Army. Yet politicians claim to love their troops and veterans.

Cancer and The Death of my Grandfather General Dukes Jr

When my grand father died from Cancer on August 18th 2009 (page 169) I sunk into a deep depression. I began to write music as a means of therapy in 2010 (page 180). It wasn't until after he died that I learned **Cancer** was reversible and this caused me to sink deeper into a depression. For if I had been studying health and wellness before he died I might have been able to give him some advise that might have prolonged his life. As I continued to research health and wellness and natural healings I came across many hidden truths about the medical association and the diabolic practices of some doctors. Of course not all doctors are the same and not all cops are bad and so on and so forth, but what I came to know was beyond the individual practitioners, it was designed within the fabric of the medical practice. Even the term practice. We are supposed to honor a **doctors** professional opinion about our health because he or she has gone through many years of schooling and residency yet they do not have **professions**, they have **practices**. As if to say that they are only **practicing** on you. Not to mention all the **paper work** that you sign before surgeries to ensure that you can not sue them. I find that interesting because the word **doctored** literally means **to falsify paper work**. But perhaps that's just an arbitrary coincidence.

Did you know that **"Emmett Till"** was stricken with a bad case of **polio** in 1946 when "he" was 5 years old and it left "him" with a speech impediment (page 504)? Franklin D. Roosevelt was paralyzed by polio in 1921. After he became President in 1932 he helped raise millions of dollars for the Salk vaccine trials. By June of 1954 1.8 million people, including schoolchildren had been vaccinated and they were deemed "**polio pioneers**". The same year that Emmett Till was lynched, the Salk vaccine was declared, "safe effective and potent" on April 12th 1955 and Just weeks later more than 200 cases of polio were reported. 11 people died and most of the others were left paralyzed. Did you know that at the same time that the Salk vaccine supposedly eliminated the polio epidemic in the 1940's and 1950's in the United States, it disappeared simultaneously in Europe, but the strange thing is that mass vaccination did not take place in Europe. How then can we say that it was a vaccine that caused the diminishing of polio cases in the United States? However we can say that the 200 people that got polio after the vaccines got polio because of the vaccine. Did you know that there are physicians who refused to vaccinate their own babies in fear that the vaccine might linger in the body with the potential to cause harm instantly or over time? Yet those same physicians vaccinate their infant patients. Perhaps it's because these routine immunizations actually ensure the patient get sick and guarantee the patients will return for repeated office calls. Perhaps this is why many doctors continue to defend vaccines, even to the death. Parents are rarely warned of the hazards and there are times when doctors vaccinate children without determining whether the immunization is contraindicated for the child. The least we can do is insure that the parents of the small **arm**ies of children who are lined up in clinics to receive **shots** in their **arm**s are well informed about the potential h**arm**s. The American Medical association is not without fault. The American Medical Association was found guilty of "conspiracy" to destroy the chiropractic profession in August of 1987. They did not want other healers healing people because that would stop people from going to the doctor for surgeries and pharmaceutical drugs. See page **648** for the **metaphysical significance of the number 23**.

The Changes I Made

It's the ritual that becomes habitual, the habits you're addicted to, what has afflicted you? do you have a clue? do you have the flu or a cold that you couldn't control? Medical bills and pills kill your soul, every year the death rate goes up and that's getting old! They say it's hard to teach a old **Dog** new tricks but it's harder to teach an old **God** that's been tricked! People often come to the conclusion that they are powerless in their sickness because they believe their disease to be hereditary. But what if that's completely wrong?! What if your sick because of your habits? Perhaps it's not hereditary and perhaps it's habitual! Perhaps our problems come from the unhealthy habits in our lives that have become everyday rituals. In 2010 I changed my habits and I changed my ritual. The death of my grand father caused me to study health and wellness. **I stopped eating meat and drinking milk in 2010** (p 212). On December 2nd of 2012 I declared a **war** on **processed sugar** (p 257). I stopped purchasing sugar and reduced the amount of foods I ate with processed sugar in them. I began to see processed sugar as the cause to my early balding, dehydration, and also the cause of the experience of erectile disfunction I had in the past. My balding was also linked to the spilling of my vital seed without properly replenishing the vital minerals in my eating habits.

Rau nu Prt m heru

I was buying books and watching lectures which led me to many natural healers like **Dr Sebi** and **Dr. Llaila Afrika** who both coincidentally died before and at the onset of covid. My search for optimal health and honoring Maat are two vital elements that manifested my past life revelations. In 2018 I **fasted for 20 days only drinking water** (page 467). I did that for several reasons. The doctor who did Malcolm X's autopsy said he had the cleanest body he had ever seen. I was overcome with the idea of having a pristine temple and I was searching for some sort of Jesus or Buddha type of enlightenment experience, but what I got was far more than I could have imagined! I fasted for 20 days only drinking water (page 467) during my kemetic yoga course and two days after I graduated my past life as **Emmett Till** was revealed to me on July 3rd 2018 (page 480). The scarab dung beetle, the only begotten God who rolls himself in our filth and chooses to be born from this filth itself (page 569). This is what I did. This western diet and this western way can cause one to weaken their auric field (page 212). By undergoing these holistic changes in my life I opened doors to psychic experiences, profound dreams and ultimately my past lives. If you are on a journey of recovery or sick and stricken with some disease keep your thoughts positive and know that you can heal. While having that knowingness you must also make the right changes to your life.

Iu f Per f m heru

I find it troubling how often holistic doctors are mysteriously found dead when they report their victories over illness without the use of modern medicine promoted by the American Medical Association. Even celebrities who promote these findings face the same demise. They say that healing can become a crime. **Lisa "Left eye" Lopez** was healed by Dr Sebi's remedies and when she began to share her story she "died". Dr Sebi "died" mysteriously in police custody. He was detained because he had "too much money" on him. **Nipsey Hussle** was murdered while he was in the process of producing a documentary about **Dr Sebi**. **Prodigy** healed his **Sickle Cell** disorder with natural remedies and as he began to speak about this and other controversial issues he also met his demise mysteriously. We have had two years of a Covid "pandemic" or was it a "plan-demic"? Who will ever know? I find it interesting however that the first things that opened up again were the sporting events. In March of 2022 Covid mask restrictions have been lifted in NYC. Kyrie Irving is still not allowed to play at his home games in Brooklyn because he refused to get vaccinated yet he is allowed to sit court side at the game. What sense does that make and who's making the rules? Is it the doctor or is it the news? Or is it the Generals dropping the bombs from a war on drugs to the shots in your arms. You should be alarmed but some won't care till they the one that's being harmed, Some won't care until they start hearing bombs, word to my moms, a word to Assata, I'm a rider **Muhammad Ali** Pyramid on the dollar, Fuck they rules and they schools, Keep ya hands off Assata! **Fuck sports, don't be a good sport** (page 269).

Covid 19

Utterances for Coming Forth by day into Light

I remember having the **Chicken Pox** when I was a little boy but it wasn't life threatening for me. It came and went and I never had it again. I think my sisters got it too. My mother says that we never got the mandatory school vaccinations as children but I can not confirm that. As I covered on page 120, I got **many vaccinations** just before I deployed to Iraq in the spring of 2003 and afterwards I got an **STD** and caught a **bad flu** for the first time in my life. I would not connect that STD and that bad flu with the vaccinations I got before I deployed to Iraq until after **Covid** started in 2020. Covid started around March of 2020 and I did not wear a mask throughout Covid. I only put one on when entering stores or public transportation that mandated it. What I did do was up my exercising and my intake of vital minerals and essential oils such as Pine Needle oil, Vitamin D, Colloidal Silver, Seamoss, Oil of Oregano, Blackseed oil, Thyme oil and other useful herbs. I was able to walk around breathing regularly without having any effects of this Covid pandemic that the news, many doctors and common people claimed was so deadly. I did not have any physical effects of Covid until December 24th of 2021. Covid had destroyed my personal training business and my massage business so at the time I was not seeing many clients at all. The month after Covid appeared my past life as Tutankhaten (King Tut) was revealed on April 4th 2020 (page 594) the same day **Martin Luther King** was assassinated (page 69, 592). When that happened I started writing this book so the loss of business was actually the best thing that could have happened. It allowed me the time I needed to take on this mighty task. **It would be imprudent to mention STD's and not speak about ways to heal ones self**. Most STD's come from parasites living and reproducing in the body. Here are a few that are helpful with healing. **Wormwood** is good for clearing intestinal worms such as pinworm and helps with malaria, it has been used since the times of **ancient Kemet (Egypt)**. **Catsclaw** is an anti viral and anti fungal as well as a natural antibiotic. **Pau D'Arco** is a anti inflammatory, anti fungal, effective at remedying urinary track infections, kills parasite, and is good for remedying yeast infections.

It is he, who comes forth by day into Light

On December 1st 2021 I started a training program where I had been running everyday for 25 minutes, followed by doing Kemetic Yoga and then strength training. I planned to do this for 5 months and 25 days straight stopping at **May 25th** 2022 but my program ended on December 24th the day before Christmas. In November and December of 2021 I was training two clients who came to train with me in person. They had both been vaccinated. Client A had two vaccine shots and one booster shot. After the first shot he felt really bad for two days, suffering from headaches, hot flashes and feeling lethargic. After the second shot he had the same effects but it only lasted one day. After his booster shot he had no negative reactions. Client B only had two vaccine shots and she feels that the shots have made her feel lethargic and exhausted she is still trying to rebound from that to this day. She says her general health goes up and down day by day. Client A had a training session scheduled for December 21st but he cancelled because he had just gotten a booster shot on the 20th and didn't want to pass anything to me. I trained client B on Tuesday December 21st then I trained client A on **Friday** December 24th at 7am. After he left I went back to sleep because I had been up all night writing this book before our session. I woke up at around 11 am and **I did not feel well**. I thought the training routine of training everyday might have taken it's toll on me so I went back to sleep and woke up at around 3pm and **I felt worse**. I had a headache coming on and soreness in my lower back. I started to think Client A had gotten me sick, I went back to sleep. I woke up at around 8pm and I knew that client A had given me something. **I was not feeling well** but I got up and did a **coffee enema** immediately! Then I went back to sleep and knew my body would heal me. For the next two days I felt horrible but I knew my body would heal me. I had intense pains in my skull, I was sweating a lot, lower back pains, headache and stomach ache. For those two days I slept and drank liquid juices with lots of ginger and I knew my body would heal me. By **Sunday** evening on December 26th the effects had subsided and by Monday I felt like my normal self with no pains but still I felt like there was some lingering presence of a foggy feeling that I could not place. This feeling lasted for around a week. I trained client B on Tuesday December 28th. On January 3rd she called me and told me she was just recovering from Covid. After she trained with me she got sick for the first time. She asked me to take a **covid 19** test so I took one for

the first time and it was **negative**. We waited another week to start training again and neither of us have had any effects since then. I must also add that in November of 2021 I went to see my 91 year old Grandmother in Georgia. She had been vaccinated because a doctor pressured her to. She had gotten dehydrated and was admitted to the hospital and the doctor told her to, "get your vaccine" and she listened to him. There was a scare within my family with Covid. Some did not want anyone around grandma who wasn't vaccinated and some didn't want to be around people, even family members who weren't vaccinated. I felt like an outcast. I had come down in August of 2020 and given massages to my mother, grandmother, 3 aunts and a cousin. I was not vaccinated then and I didn't feel the need to be in November of 2021, so I disregarded them and went to see my grandmother. While I was in the house with my grand mother and my cousin who were both vaccinated I experienced a very faint headache and mild sweats at night. I was waking up with wet tee shirts. My body was heating up to kill some foreign pathogen. I went to Alabama to see my uncle Jimmy a week later and the same thing happened. Him and his wife were both vaccinated. After Client A got me sick on December 24th I remembered this and it made me think that I was having those effects because I was around people who had been vaccinated. Many vaccinated people were afraid of the unvaccinated fearing they were spreading the "virus" but after those experiences I felt like it was the other way around. I felt like it was the vaccinated who did the spreading.

ADDENDUM Inside info about the Deaths at the Jacob Javits Center Covid 19 Vaccination Station

A good friend of mine worked at the Jacob Javits Center during the 2020 Covid 19 "pandemic". She was working along side military soldiers. Her job was to watch over the civilians who had come to receive the **free** covid 19 vaccinations. After each person got the vaccine she watched them for 15 minutes and followed them as they left the Jacob Javits Center. My friend witnessed more than 15 deaths while working at the Jacob Javits Center. She noticed that the Johnson and Johnson vaccine was more deadly that the Pfizer vaccine. She told me of three deaths that still bother her to this day. The first was a white man in his 60's or 70's who traveled with his wife to receive the vaccine. After he received his shot he was watched for 15 minutes and he seemed well. He got up to leave and just as he reached the doors to exit the Jacob Javits Center he collapsed on the floor. My friend ran to his aid and dropped to her knees. She turned him over to see him foaming at the mouth. He was dead. The soldiers rushed to his aid, put him a stretcher and sent him to a hospital. They told the mans wife that he had a reaction and was sent to the hospital. A pregnant woman and her husband traveled a long distance just for the vaccine. The women was excited to be one of the "lucky" people to receive the vaccine. When she got her vaccine they watched her for 15 minutes. When she got up to walk away she took a few steps then fell to her knees and died. They told her husband that she was sent to the hospital for labor complications. Two black men came in. They were a couple. One guy was not interested in the vaccine and didn't want his partner to get the shot but his partner was determined. My friend tried to get him to take the Pfizer instead of the Johnson and Johnson but he insisted on the Johnson and Johnson. He got the vaccine and he died in the chair moments after he was injected.

March 13th 2022 Vaccinated

Through the **birth** canal arrives her only begotten, to the shores of a land unholy and rotten, from a beautiful struggle dropped in this new place, the first thing most see is the **Doc**tors face, some say it's a blessing, some say it's a curse, some say it gets better some say it gets worse, some survive, some stillborn, some become autistic, but what did the harm? like a ship **berth**ing and **doc**king at bay a manifest is signed and the cargo sent away, with the help of a nurse many needles they prick, so the babies they scream and they never forget, the papers they **doc**tored, natural law they forged it, and left you to labor with birth certificates, when they see fit the new virus appears, then the vaccine then you disappear, no need to worry still more ships will come, the people don't listen they can not fathom, a system so sick that sickness is so frequent, the people not thinking relationships sinking, her baby did die and so she harbored the pain, the contraindications they never explained, Immunization a good thing or satanic? the Tuskegee airman that's what makes me panic, the airplane the boat, even the Titanic, the lead in the water, smallpox in the fabric, yet so many trust them, it must be the magic, stethoscopes on white coats, mutilating the phallus, a system so careless, a system so callus, you live is a vessel, it's your divine palace, the high priest might press you and even spit malice, if you don't let them inspect your rectum, or hold your scrotum for routine inspection, dental extractions can cause infections, they dig out the nerve, a tooth fairies robbery, the nerve of the doctor performing surgery without properly warning humanity that we can die from the cure, now that's pure insanity - **TutemRa**

March 29th 2022
Vaccines in Morocco and Egypt (page 670)

I took my first trip to Kemet/Egypt (in this life) in March of 2022 and I had a 14 hour layover in Morocco. While there I went to see the **Hassan II Mosque** which is the 2nd largest Mosque in the world. When I got back to the airport I was waiting on my flight when a Moroccan woman sat next to me. At some point we began to speak about traveling when the topic of Vaccines came up. She mentioned that she had been back and forth to the hospital ever since she had been vaccinated. She said she didn't want to get vaccinated but it was mandatory. While in line to board the plane I spoke to another woman. She had a dual citizenship, Moroccan and Egyptian. She was on her way home to Egypt after burying her mother in Morocco. Her mother had been recently vaccinated and afterwards had began to have major kidney issues and other bodily complications that ultimately ended her life. The woman herself had been vaccinated against her will but had not experienced bad symptoms however she said she was made to wear a sticker on buses that read, "vaccinated". The brother who sold me the phone sim card for my cell phone was vaccinated against his will too but the brother who sold me my tour was against the vaccines and did not get vaccinated. All of these people were Muslim.

A New Duty Station, Old friends, New Friends and a New Church Home

Rau nu Prt m heru

I was stationed in **FT Campbell Kentucky**, but I lived 1 mile away in Clarksville Tennessee, on 109A Chapel st. **--[[[DEJA VU!!!** I just got **Deja Vu** when writing C**lark**sville Tennessee.]]]--- When I got to Ft Campbell one of the first things I did was search for a new church home. First I went to a church close to the apartment I found. It was a **Pentecostal church**. While in the service I felt the desire to **renew my relationship with God** so at the end of the service I walked to the front during the **alter call**. One of the ministers came to me and immediately started to "speak in tongues". He was repeating the word **"Hallelujah, Hallelujah, Hallelujah"**, then he told me to repeat after him, **"Hallelujah Hallelujah"**. He began to "speak in tongues".. Many of the people in this church were doing the same thing with different sounds and words. They all seemed to be under a spell. I told him that I'm not going to pretend to talk in tongues, and if that ever happened to me it would happen naturally. I told him that I was only there to renew my commitment with God. He looked at me like a dear in headlights then quickly moved to the next person and continued with them where he had left off with me. I saw little kids and adults "talking in tongues". It was a different experience for me. I left that church and never went back.

I ended up joining **The Deliverance Out Reach Temple,** a church that one of the brothers in my unit was a member of. His name was **Sebastian Persons**. Sebastian was a light in the church. Everyone loved him. I took no active role in the church but I went often. I paid tithes often but not every Sunday. Sebastian was an active member of the church. He led the **praise and worship dance** group with the young boys. Him and I became good friends. We laughed a lot, we freestyle rapped together, listened to a lot of christian Hip Hop, and went out to eat at this all you can eat Chinese buffet often. There was a brother in the church who was a recovering drug addict. Sometimes he slept in the church. He was very passionate about God as he would always exclaim how he knew the real name of Jesus, which was "Yashua". He would be taken by the Holy Spirit during services and sometimes other people would get up and dance a little. I was always ready for a good sermon. Something to inspire me. I always believed in something greater than me. To me it mathematically made sense that something greater than me created me. Then there's always the looming questions: Who created the creator? What is heaven and what is hell? I had done wrong in the past and so I want to be forgiven.. This desire to be forgiven can be the trap used by religions. It's a trap of the conscious mind. Having a religion often causes a person to stop searching for information about the past and accept the idea of not knowing everything since most things in the bible are never fully explained. Our personal self guilt is the trap as well. We know we are not perfect so we seek forgiveness for our ill ways and in return we are forgiving to others and seek a God to fix everything but no one is coming to save you, you must save yourself by awakening to this eternal play of consciousness.

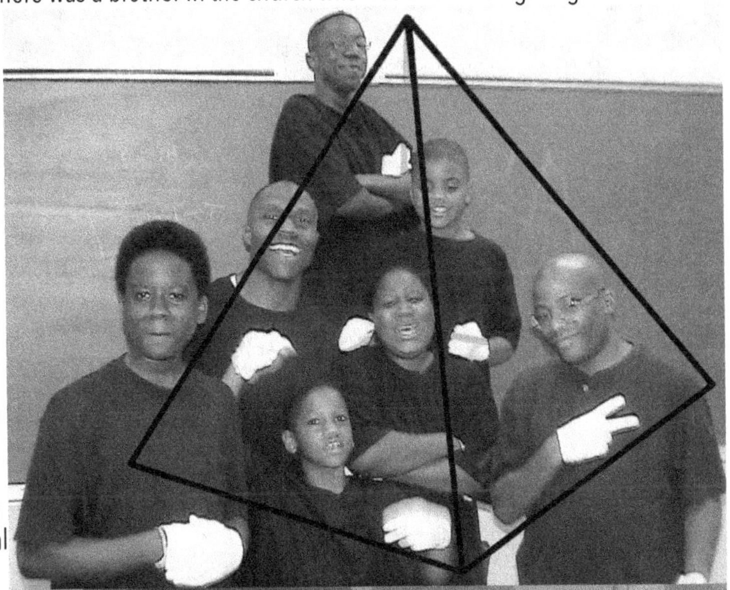

Iu f Per f m heru

ADDENDUM

Utterances for Coming Forth by day into Light

I wasn't by my self in FT Campbell. My good friends **Kyle Esannason, Courtney Faulkner** and **Willie Austin** were there. Kyle and I would hang out a lot. I even got him to come to my church a few times. I would invite my friends to church because I wanted them to have a relationship with God. I felt like I was doing the right thing by sharing the "good word". The problem is that once I stopped going to church and started studying **African culture** I changed my tune and many of the people I knew from church were turned off to my new view on life. I didn't start changing my views until after my grand father died in 2009. I stopped hearing from Kyle sometime in 2015. We got into an disagreement about his ethnicity. I told him that he was black because his mother was black but he refused to see himself as black, claiming that his father was Dominican so he is Dominican. In 2023 **Larry Davis** (p 108) told me that Kyle was holding on to anger and didn't want anything to do with me. I stopped hearing from Slim and Sebastian when I left the Christian religion and directed my attention to Kemet. The last time I saw Kyle was in 2010 (page 185). Austin is the only one who remains my friend (page 88). He is a faithful Christian but he listens when I speak about the bible from my perspective and he doesn't take it personal. He allows me to see the world the way I see it and often times he finds what I have to say and the connections to be interesting. One thing I can say about my friends from the Army is, most of them thought for the future. Most of them also had children and perhaps that kept them conscious of bills they would be responsible for. Kyle was always focused on his financial business. Making sure he would be able to find work after the military. Many of the people I met in the Army were like this. I was not. Unfortunately I did not do much planning for the future. **I** thought **I** was going to the NFL in high school and at this point **I** thought **I** was going to S.Forces, until (p 130)

It is he, who comes forth by day into Light

October 3rd and 4th of 1993 - Somalia Massacre (Black Hawk Down)

In 1993 I was not paying attention to the news or the news papers. I was listening to Enta da Stage, 93 till Infinity, Wu Tang Clan, Snoop Doggy Dog, KRS One, OutKast, 2pac, Biggie Smalls, A Tribe Called Quest, Jeru The Damaja, Run DMC, Naughty By Nature, Lords of the Under Ground, Trends Of Culture, Onyx, MC Eiht and so on and so on (page 72)….. While some of this music was anti police and anti "the system" I still did not fully understand the "system". I knew nothing about the **Somalia Massacre**. I knew nothing about The **Gulf War** that happened in 1991. I was 15 at the time of the Somalia massacre and I was 13 at the time of the Gulf War.

When I joined the army in 1999 I was 21 and I had no knowledge of my connection to my Caribbean indigenous past, my African indigenous past or my American indigenous past (page 25). I was not into politics and so I knew nothing about the world I lived in. When I was recruited to 160th Special Operations Aviation Unit (SOAR) in 2003 I was excited about being selected to a "special operations" unit! Most people had to put in requests to get that assignment but not me, I was "selected". I was proud of that and I sort of bragged about it and other people were envious. I was pulled out of Iraq to go to a Special Ops unit while the rest of my unit had to stay in Iraq in a war zone. During the entry training for the unit we were all given a history of the unit with special attention given to the Somalia Massacre which they called the **Black Hawk Down** event. We were taught to mourn the deaths of the 19 American soldiers who were killed, including six Delta Force operators, and the 73 who were wounded. We were shown pictures of a white man named Staff Sgt William David Cleveland who was killed and dragged through the streets of Mogadishu by the Black Somalian people. We were taught to have pride in the unit. When I think of all the Black people who still join the armed forces everyday without the knowledge of what system they are joining it saddens me but I understand how they can make that choice because I made it too. I didn't understand my relationship with the Somali people or any of the brown people that this American military rains their hell fire of bullets upon. **They did not teach us** about how the American forces killed over 3000 Somalian civilians, mostly women and children with machine gun fire from their black hawk helicopters. **They did not teach us** about the Somalian dictator who was put into place by America who sold ¼ (one fourth) of the Somalian oil rights to four American oil companies, Amoco, Gulf, Chevron and another. **They did not teach us** that General Aideed drove that leader out to restore control of Somalian's oil resources to the Somalian people. **"If you are not careful, the newspaper will have you hating the people being oppressed, and loving the people who are doing the oppressing." - Malcolm X**

Rau

nu

Prt

m

heru

When I got back to the states I had around 10 thousand dollars saved from being in Iraq. The first thing I did was buy a car. I was not interested in paying a car note so I bought a car I could buy with cash. I bought a **Nissan 300ZX**, it was pretty and timeless in style. When I drove it from Georgia to Tennessee it broke down as soon as I got to my post. I mean the car broke down at the very moment I arrived to my post. I purchased a new transmission and two of my soldiers who were good with cars installed it in for me. We had gone through Green Platoon together and they looked up me. Most people did. Some time after I finished Green Platoon I got a call from my mother that my **little sister was missing**. Without requesting leave from the military I got into my **300ZX** and drove from Tennessee to New York straight. I only stopped for gas! My sister was 14 years old and all I knew is that she was missing! I was not going to asked someone for permission to go. When I got to Pennsylvania I stopped for gas, and while there I met a **White guy** who needed a ride. So I gave him one. During our trip we were stuck in a long block of traffic with no exit ramps. After the traffic subsided we got on the way again but at some point we both had to pee. I pulled over on the shoulder of the highway and we got out to pee in the brush. To both of our surprise we heard **gun shots**. We look up and there in the distance was an **old White man** with a shot gun. He was aiming and about to take another shot at us. We looked at each other in terror and we both dashed back to the car. I jumped over the top of my car like **Bo Duke** from the **Dukes of Hazard** (page 20). As soon as we got in the car we were off! When I got to New York I came to find that my sister was not missing. She was in Harlem doing what she wanted to do. She was unaware of how her actions could affect other people. I was happy that she was ok though.

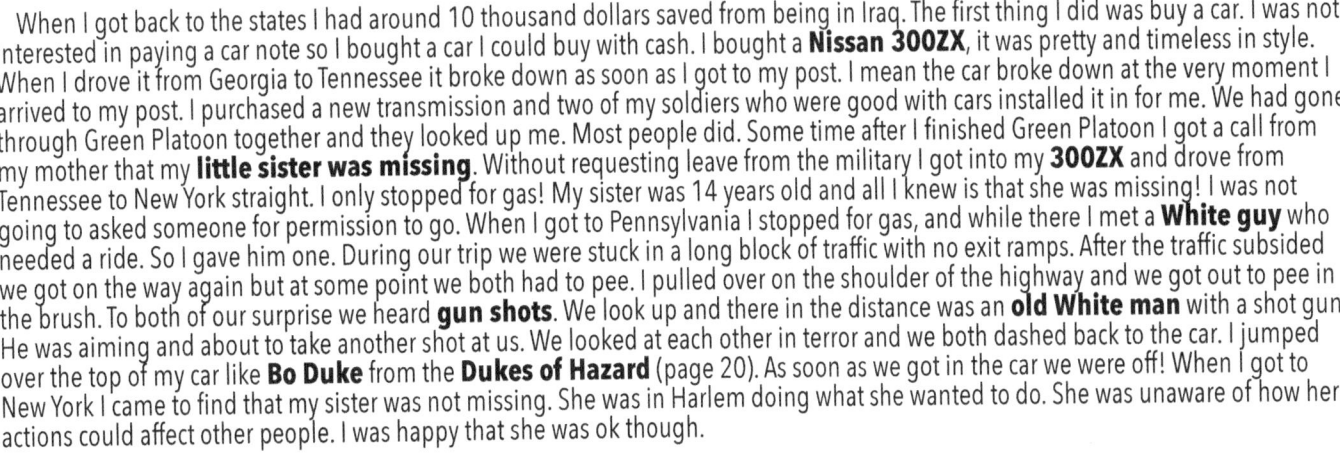

Iu

f

Per

f

m

heru

Utterances

for

Coming

Forth

by day

into

Light

December 16th 2004
Speeding Through the Weed Fields of Tennessee

I had one month of leave left in the army but I was done. I was driving from New York to Atlanta with one of my cousins, he was 20yrs old at the time and I was 27. We got stopped by a state trooper while on the highway in Tennessee. The cop approached my car and asked for license and registration. He said I wasn't wearing a seatbelt but that was a lie, he just used that as a reason to stop me. I gave him my license, registration and military ID. He stuck his head in the car and said he smelt weed. I told him I was in the army and I didn't smoke weed and there was no weed in the car. The car did smell like weed but because I wasn't accustom to smoking I didn't notice it until after he found the **weed**.. The trooper asked if he could search my car and I welcomed him to. I opened my trunk and he began to search. He found a bag of weed in my cousins bag but I had no idea it was there. He arrested my cousin and it was hard to watch him go through the process of being cuffed and taken away in the troopers car. Before they left he gave me the information where I could bail him out. I bailed him out with the help of one of my aunts, we both split the fine fee.

It is

he,

who

comes

forth

by day

into

Light

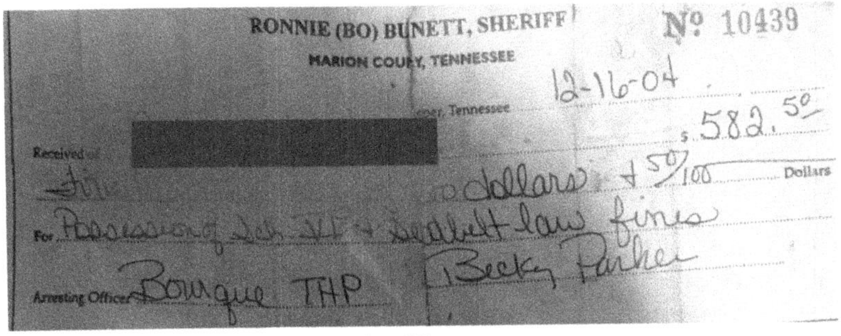

RONNIE (BO) BUNETT, SHERIFF

MARION COUNTY, TENNESSEE

№ 10439

12-16-04 ... Tennessee

$ 582.50

Received of [redacted]

dollars + 50/100 Dollars

For Possession of Sch. VI + seatbelt law fines

Arresting Officer Bourque THP Becky Parker

Significance

We were stopped for not wearing a seatbelt and possession of weed in 2004 and paid a Hefty fee for it and now in 2021 **weed** is legal. I got stopped for speeding in Germany and the police just gave me a warning. He told me to drive fast on the highway but to keep it safe and slow in the local area where people live. I followed his orders because it made sense and I appreciated him. In 2009 a state trooper will save my life while I'm on my motorcycle speeding (page 157). In 2009 a cop will hit me while I'm on my motorcycle then write me a ticket for having an aftermarket muffler. In 2011 I will be stopped by plain clothes officers on the train (page 211). In 2012 I will be stopped by cops for sitting in the park (page 239). On May 15th 2015 I will be stopped in central park by cops for running a light on my bicycle (page 331). In the summer of 2016 I will have an explosive altercation with a cop for trying to write me a ticket for running a light on my bicycle (page 388), this experience will open my mind up to the power of rage vs love and the energy that flows through our spine! The clerk who wrote this ticket above had the last name **Parker**, like my Great Grand Father Jesse James **Parker**.

2004

WIN I DIE (1st of 2)

We over here trying to reload our magazines, you over there reading about us in a magazine, Alpha team trained to go and take out a whole regime, can't be thinking bout politics when we gotta clear the scene, ***"I had a dream"*** like **Martin** but my heart has really hardened, since I been to combat it's like my reactions have sharpened, there's nothing like real life man now we the targets, we gotta work together we brothers so even in the darkest days, we die for each other even in the worst of ways, you wouldn't under stand me though, I want y'all all to know we ain't fighting for **Bush** and his oil war, cause everyday I kill a man and I'm not sure what for, that's how it is when yo ass up and join the corp, better be sure when Uncle Sam knocking at yo door, never no more will you be innocent getting your hands dirty, for other men who decide to got to war for the money, you sure you ready for this life far away from home, mission top secret destination unknown? when they ask me why, I be silent, they wouldn't understand me, I do it for the man next to me that be my family, and when I die put them medals on my chest and when I die tell my family I did my best and if I die far away from home, you can box me up and ship me home, I said when I die "You cant handle the truth", ohh I said when I die "You cant handle the truth"

You ain't never seen a man die like this, go ask a war vet, our muzzle velocity is sick, we on a conquest, the best, you know the spear head of the mission, and the only reward is another unwanted mission, no time for piss'n or shit'n, 5 minutes of sleeping is all we getting, we stay creeping, every seconds a bless'n, It's like, ***Me and my girl friend***, me and my weapon, I reload her then clean her up and the we keep on stepping, because we silent professionals, sneak right up next to you, one shot one kill that's the strategy, we live this life for real this is our reality, how dare you watch the news turn it off and then get mad at me, Imagine being looked at by a kid that don't see white or black he see American, he see them army greens, these are combat blues, he got a RPG pointed right at you, so why you gonna do? You ain't got much time, now you can scream out kid don't do it but some times civilians become combative's, and when the bullets start flying nothing matters **- DAWUD**

Significance

I wrote this rhyme shortly after I graduated **Green Platoon**. I had never shot at anyone or been shot. I went to Iraq for 6 months and return with no injury from bullets. I had watched the movie **Black Hawk Down** and been given the story of the two day war in Somalia from the White military point of view (page 127).

2004

One Day You'll be Alone

This for the **Nigga** the **Cracker** the **Jew** the **Spick**, the **Muslim**, the **Atheist** whoever's fully equipped with a 210 round basic load, you better practice your aim soldier breath control, Lord I'm not sure why they signed their contracts, what ever the reason they all gonna see combat, I just ask that you honor their steps, the left the right, they're left to fight the false threat, and of course death often comes to your mind when the war is met first hand for the first time, and who's really dying? it's the lower enlisted! 18 through 22, but don't get it twisted! cause on the streets I'm seeing the same cycle, my lil homies they be lucky to finish high school! the boots of a soldier only filled by the truest, it might sound good but can you dance to the music? we all seen Private Ryan, how his buddy was upstairs dying while he just sat there cry'n, and I'm not try'n to be something I'm not, cause death waits in the dark in the life of the spec ops, God damn this sand my gun jammed, and alls in my head what my drill sergeant said, <u>one day you'll be alone way out there in the combat zone</u>, God damn this sand my gun jam, and alls in my head what my drill sergeant said, don't you cry now don't you moan drill sergeants gonna bring you home

Mission top secret destination unknown, learn your battle drills buddy you could be left alone on the battle field buddy, and Charlie is not friendly, keep your head low, ears open and mouth shut, and when your buddy dies yeah you know what's up, grab his dog tags water and ammo, can you handle a situation like that? cause it's so real! and y'all be over here thinking freedom is free, debating all the nonsense you see on TV, like **Ja Rule** and **50** or **Kobe** and **Shaq** man, I don't want to hear it! I been to Iraq man! came back still pay'n tax man! I just don't get it, I just don't feel appreciated, I feel like I'm not really emancipated, thank God I made it, even though I hate it cause other soldiers didn't make it back home! **Sergeant Major Cook** was the real backbone, he took shrapnel to the side of the dome, and even though I know it's all in the glory of the thrown! I don't like it and I just don't appreciate it, a good soldier why couldn't he have made it? you won't see this on your late night news cause they never broadcast the ones or the twos, the unsung hero's, the combat blues! God damn this sand my gun jammed, and alls in my head what my drill sergeant said, <u>one day you'll be alone way out there on the combat zone,</u> God damn this sand my gun jam, and alls in my head what my drill sergeant said, bullets fly'n all around gotta keep your head to the ground **- Dawud**

"Lord Give Me a Sign" - DMX

Rau nu Prt m heru

It's 2004 and I'm in the **160th Special Operations Aviation Regiment**. I made it through the vigorous **Green Platoon** training. Upon completing the Green Platoon training I was being considered for selection as one of the cadre members (instructors) who over sees the Green Platoon training for the new recruits entering the unit. The sky was the limit for me. I was the type of soldier that would have excelled in that unit. All the doors were opening for me. I had come up on orders for **Airborne** school, **Air Assault** school and **Pathfinder** school was an option too. In my previous regular army unit it would have been next to impossible for me to get any of these schools let alone all them in a package deal. I could have finished these schools then gone to **Ranger** school and then back to **Special Forces** school to try again and that was my plan. The universe had another plan for me though. It was as if the ancestors were tasked with a mission to help awaken me and Martin Luther King would appear first. At the time I had only been in the army for 5 years but I had reenlisted twice already for 1 year extensions of my contract. Previously I had never asked **"God"** for direction in the decisions I made with my life. When I went to college I decided, I didn't pray over it. When I joined the army and when I reenlisted twice I just did it, I didn't pray about it but for some reason I said a prayer and asked **God** for direction this time. **I asked God** to **give me a sign** on whether I should stay in the army or get out. The series of events that made me decide to get out are too intricate to explain but I got the sign I was looking for and I decided not to reenlist and I got out of the army **with no plan**. I said that prayer then I followed the signs. I could have done a lot of things with my life. I could have been a great artist if I ever really applied myself with drawing. I always felt like I could have been an inventor too because I was good at finding ways to make a job easier using less manpower. If I had the wisdom I could have made better decisions in high school and college and used my football ability to move me and my family out the hood. If I had believed in myself while playing football in Germany I could have tried out for NFL Europe. I could have been "All that you can be in the Army".. But I said that prayer and I followed what I felt was a sign. I decided to be myself and play a different game, **the play of consciousness**. When I got out of the army I went to my Grandparents house in Georgia and wrote lots of rhymes about **God** and **Jesus**. My **last day** in the **Army** ended up being **Martin Luther King's** birthday (Jan 15th 2005) but I would not know that was his birthday for many* years. In 2004 I only wrote two rhymes and when I read them now it's as if I was suffering from **Stockholm syndrome** (page 129). Interestingly enough I say **Martin Luther King's** name in the first rhyme. Remember, I had Martin Luther King's picture on my wall in my barracks room for most of my time in Germany (page 102). I loved the Army but I was blinded by irrational patriotism. I was sent through training with all colors of people and somehow I believed we were all brothers, overlooking the fact that the American Armed Forces only goes to war with brothers with the skin color as mine. At the time **I didn't know how the government killed Martin Luther King**. On December 8, 1999, a four-week civil trial determined that local, state and federal U.S government agencies, and the Mafia, were all involved in the murder of Martin Luther King. Dr William Pepper was Martin's family doctor and he was given info by a nurse named, R. Shelby, who was in Martin's operating room at Saint Josephs Hospital. She says that **Martin survived the shooting but was spit on and suffocated by Dr Breen Bland, a white neurosurgeon** (see page 69).

Iu f Per f m heru

The Play of Consciousness

Utterances for Coming Forth by day into Light

It is he, who comes forth by day into Light

2005, Grandma Dukes

I got out of the army with no plan. I went to ATL and slept in my Grand Parents guest room. My Grandmother would get up early everyday and make breakfast. On Sundays I went to church with her and sometimes my Grandfather would go too. It was good to be around them but I had no real plan as to what I was going to do with my life. Oddly enough I was not worried. Perhaps I was too much of a fool to be worried. You see I never had a plan for my life. I just went the way the wind blew. Most people stayed in the army due to fear of not being able to find work to support themselves. They sort of get used to getting paid every month on the 1st and 15th, so they settle. **I spent my free time writing rhymes** at the dining room table and at the time I was a **Christian** so most of my rhymes were about this guy who was gonna **come back** named **Jesus**. I was a believer in **Jesus Christ** like my Grandma Dukes.

The Revolutionary Christian

The more I read my old rhymes I realize how much of a blind follower I was. I believed what I was told and not what I had studied and found to be true from my own tedious research and experience. I had not read many books but at this time in my life I'm writing from the black male prospective who wants to continue a struggle led by Martin Luther King, Malcolm X and others in the 20th century but I was dangerously unlearned (see page 69, 592). I had never heard of Jean Jacques Dessalines, or David Walker and I'm ashamed to say that I did not even know much about Nat Turner. The first time I heard the name **Nat Turner** it was the **porn star*** and the only **Cherokee** I paid attention to was the **porn star***. I had heard the name **Marcus Garvey** in the **Nas** song Halftime but I never knew who he was. I did not know that I was **Cherokee Indian** or **Blackfoot Indian** for that matter but I was writing rhymes about someone **coming back** and this person would **save** us all. This one special person that returns named **Jesus**. One thing I can say about the **23** rhymes written in 2005 is that **I was sure someone was coming back**, **I just didn't know it was me and that I had already come back here many times**. See page **648** for the **metaphysical significance of the number 23**. I would get my job as a trainer later this year (p 138). Afterwards I will write 1 rhyme is 2006 (p 149), then I would not write another rhyme again until after my Grandfather dies in 2009 (p 169). The first rhyme that I have found was written on April 11th 2010 (p 180) and in that rhyme I say the name **Emmett Till** in it. On **Nov 26th** 2010 I say the name **King Tut** for the first time in my music (page 187). The strange thing about that is **Nov 26th** is the day that King Tut's tomb was opened (p 11) and on that day I said "his" name. Today is Nov 4th 2021 and today is the day that King Tut's tomb was discovered 99 years ago in 1922. This book was brought forth in 2022, the 49th anniversary of Hip Hop and 49 days is the amount of time the Tibetans believed it took one soul to be reborn into another life. I am the **Alchemist** who has revealed The Hip Hop Bible (p 633). This is Divine Alchemy of the soul, the only alchemy that matters! I'm writing a Epic Sci-Real (Science Reality) Novel Trilogy version of this book and a book about Tupac's ancient past life (p 664,665). Stay tuned!

2005 Gospel Rap (1st of 23)

This ain't **gospel** rap, this is the gospel wrapped in human flesh, with the purpose to purchase back, the hopeless that, get **saved** then turn around and go back, to the same ways and acts which are nothing but traps, so run tell that to the masses, reverse the madness, graduate from the block to the hearse and casket, the worse has yet to come, I research the scriptures, my prayers go out to the ones in **Sri Lanka**, to my soldiers at war I know it's a monster, from the streets to the battle field, now how that make you feel? been at war my whole life with the imperial, they got you ride'n on dubs can you really tell were you're going? jokes on you for the moment, I've heard them say we need atonement or a revolution, **the revolution is here**, run get the constitution and some white out, cause I gotta proposition, fall in, attention, in other words listen, the word strengthens and the word is what is missing **- Dawud**

2005 - Granddaddy Dukes

My Grand Father always seemed the be proud of me and he would often tell me that he was. I guess to him I had done well for myself. He was around 74 at the time I came home from the army and he was still an early riser. He could not sit around in the house all day, he always had to be moving and if he wasn't he was in the garage fixing something. He sold candies and roasted peanuts to the kids in the neighborhood. They would come by looking for "Mr Dukes" to purchase candies. It was closer for them than going to the local store which was a quarter of a mile away. I would sit out and talk to him sometimes as we got some laughs in. Sometimes I went with him on his local runs to the shop fixing his truck. I was happy to be able to give him the money he needed to fix his truck once. I wish I could have bought him the F150 truck he always wanted. In 2009 my Grandfather passed away from **cancer** on August 18th (page 169), the day after Marcus Garvey's birthday and his death would be the catalyst that caused me to start reading and studying health and African history. After my Grandfather died **he would materialize himself to me in spirit form** 6 years later on December 18th 2015 (page 348). This experience would open my eyes to the other side of this reality that we live in. The timing of his appearance would be the most important part of his materialization. I told my family members and I don't think most of them believed me. My Grandmother listened and I think she believed me. I have family members who are Muslim and when I told them a few of them told me I saw a jin. They felt as if what I saw was another entity that made itself look like my Grandfather. My cousin is a Muslim and he is scared of spirits. He only has a view of the spirit as something evil but I know what I experienced and it was not evil. **It was one of the most profound things I have experienced in this life.** It was a moment that seemed to last forever yet still only a moment but it was full of love and light as he stood there in all white with a bright light behind him. I love you Granddaddy. Thank you and I will see you again in my dreams and finally when I am done here.

Rau nu Prt m heru

Iu f Per f m heru

Utterances for Coming Forth by day into Light

It is he, who comes forth by day into Light

2005 The Resurrection

A yo, you're nothing without faith, ignorance is bliss, it's knowledge that you should chase, I'm not here to debate, are you willing to face any type of persecution? ***I am the resurrection*** so I'm never lose'n, I got on the bus but the bus wasn't moving, so I jumped off and **jumped on the white horse**, sword in my right hand, mic in my **left hand**, he ain't come to talk about peace man, I got a niece man, I got nephews, so I'm about **opening doors** for them to step through, how could you be live'n on earth and not be thankful **- Dawud**

April 2005 - Zascha Moktan (The German Alicia Keys)

I met Zascha in Germany and she was the first person I can ever remember meeting in a magical way, as if our meeting was governed by the hands of fate. I left Germany abruptly and didn't get the chance to say goodbye to a lot of people and many of them I still missed but none more than Zascha (page 98). I was attracted to her in a way that I couldn't explain, perhaps because **the way we met was so profound**. It was as if the universe wanted us to meet but that was all over now because I was gone, living my life in Atlanta and she was going on with her life in Germany...... Then I got and e-mail from her informing me that she was coming to Atlanta! **Was the universe conspiring for us again?** I wasn't sure but I was looking forward to seeing her. She was on tour with **Alicia Keys**. She opened the show with **Jimmy Camacho**. John Legend went on after her and finally **Alicia Keys** did her set. I went to all her shows in Atlanta, hung out with her in her dressing room and stood back stage as she performed. I met John Legend and took a picture with him. On her last night in Atlanta we went out to a club. Things were different though. It was as if I was on the outside looking in. When we got to the club I was in VIP with her but she was sitting with John Legend, his arm warpped around her and with hand on her waste. She was in another world that I could not reach. I left that night and never saw her again. Because of the way I met Zascha I always felt like we were supposed to know each other. So she was always special to me. As I continued my journey in life I met other people in mysterious ways similar to how I met Zascha. Many of the people you cross paths with in life have a deeper meaningful purpose in your life beyond what you might initially be willing to fathom. Your life is a beautiful symphony speaking in **Riddles**. I have a great great grand mother named May Fannie **Riddle** (p 16) and another great grand mother named Leacola **Riddle** (p 21) and my whole life is a **riddle**. If you can decipher my life it will help you decipher yours. Safe travels.

2005 King of Kings

Tell me who's controlling your airways? the radio the TV and the satellite plays a major role in the way you gonna behave, you gotta pay the toll, reap what you sow, pray for **Better Dayz**, I only talk what I know, and I know **Better Dayz** only come from the grace of the **son**, it's already won, the war is over it was written, but still you won't read and you still won't listen, I've been charged with a mission to plant these seeds, I've come too far to go back nah, you can hold that, live'n in this world your whole life with no map and no sense of direction no perception to where north's at, you so **Lost** black in TV the radio you don't hear me, so you pair me up with the ones labeled corny simply cause I rep the gospel, but when you lay'n up in the hospital, you put it all in prospective, you ain't worried about your neckless with the bling or chase'n the fast life for them finer things, all you want is mercy from ***the king of kings***, all of a sudden thirsty for *the king of kings*, *The king of kings the king of kings the king of kings* - **Dawud**

2005 The God Gene

That life is not for you, you don't need it, silly rabbit stuck on the block can't you see who plant the seeds to your habits? believe me it's tragic, live'n life without the light and think you live'n lavish, we all need the **sun** to grow, that's mathematics, yeah, you know they say we got this **God** gene in our DNA programmed to know what **God** means, **Allah** means the ***sun God*** *I only know one God, the one son, the one way, I only got one job, to please him, I needs him, I never can please him, cause I leave him, come back and leave him again, on the next plane or train what a treasonous trend, and that's exactly the reason for the season I'm in* - **Dawud**

2005 Realign my Flesh Mind

Just cause I use the **divine** to realign my flesh mind don't make me a saint son, it just means I confess mine, look at yourself, **man in the mirror**, this can help, get the log out your eye, I got the log out mine, who you run'n with, ***the prince of the air or the living water?*** you ain't got much time, this was written for the black, white, yellow, red, I break bread with the **spirit**ual with the religious, I never said that I'm feel'n you, it's just that I see things clearly so I give bread to everyone cause everybody's hungry, **when he comes back** feeding his **sheep** is what he wanna see, when I try to live right sink holes are put in front of me, but that's how it's gonna be, I'm not gonna change, got my sword in my hand and look I got aim - **Dawud**

2005 The Staff

I be the *staff touch'n the water divine order*, show'n the way in this day cause morals have waisted away, you're look'n at me like you disagree with the **N.I.V.**, but you probably would stop if you knew that **the tsunami was written already**, and I see that you're not ready, I'm mentally heavy, so I'll Tom and Jerry break it down for ya, here's your bowl here's your milk, how that sound to yah? - **Dawud**

2005 The Prince of Peace

The emancipation proclamation! If you were born in the 60's or maybe the 40's or the 1600's, when the white woman bought you because her eye caught you standing on the platform, waiting to be sold to the highest bidder, because of your brolic figure, what type of man would you be? would you be the **Kunta** trying to be free? or the house nigga just trying to be? I'm trying to see! putting it all in perspective, in the double O 5 would you sell out to sell records? *I'm going north like a slave but* ***I'm coming back*** *for my people*, how could you sell crack to your people? Mr Lincoln didn't free me, he pacified us, over a hundred years walking in the wilderness, gave us the will to live and fight, thank God for that, ***there's only one chosen one***, you know ***the son that laid his life down***, then went back but never left?! without ***the prince of peace*** you're not really prepared for death! are you prepared to step out of this bondage? it's real easy kid, you walk'n on the wrong road! you been miss led, fooled and bamboozled! when will you open your heart man you're get'n old? and time is too short you need a new **soul**, you need to let go and let **God** take control **- Dawud**

Rau nu Prt m heru

2005 *The Glorious Lamb*

I'm a tell you this, the truth is in the mist of a fellowship, and the **bread and wine take it in remembrance**, and remember this, everything that shines ain't heaven sent, ***a fallen prince***, die in sin, go with him, I meant what I meant, From 11 cents to 11 mill hell is real, from the block to the top, I stay grounded to the rock, **book of life** saw a spot signed my name on the dot, you can stay here and rot and be a slave to the plot, but there's more to this man, ***the glorious lamb***, the sword in a warriors hand **- Dawud**

Iu f Per f m heru

2005 Army of the Lord

Yo! in this **army of the Lord** I'm a soldier, now you can bring all them guns in your holsters, but I don't need a gun son I got **Jehovah**, cup runneth over and over, plants seeds for this culture, my rhymes poke yah, pierce yah cause you feel me! the energy in me ain't me it's love from the heavenly, I stay readily available to give it to them, Drop A Gem on Them, and I don't gotta say a thing, I lead by example and I don't see no box'n ring, so don't let them amp you or gas you up for failure, when keep'n it real goes wrong who needs the drama? if you're in school go to school don't just be a number, be about your business wish somebody would'a told me, but that's ok see cause I'm gonna build this bridge like **J.C.**, they hated him so they just might hate me, and that's just where my faith be, the faithful a great few endure to the end, everyday another test the devil lure'n us in, I only got four words for him and your lynch men, you're not gonna win - Dawud

2005 Poet

Utterances for Coming Forth by day into Light

I love it when they call me poet, I love it when they say "he got lyrics", I love that feeling I get when I see it, a new fan bob'n his head when he hear it, his only words are "yo son, yo who is this"? **I am that I am** slash emcee I live it, pure **Hip Hop** from **the flesh to the spirit,** when I spit I never drop short from exquisite, thorough come'n from one of the five boroughs, and my flow, is pro Black, White, Yellow, anti anything that's going to take me to hell, so I, get on my knees and I praise the **divine,** sometimes I think about ways to define, myself, my name, my style, **my call'n,** I picked up arms to fight for those fallen, soldiers, civilians, somebodies children, it won't stop till we all start building, it won't stop till we all start building **- Dawud**

2005 Talk It Out

The Common Connection (page 81)

I'd rather talk it out before I fight son, I rather fight before I use a gun, I only fight for freedom, I'm a revolutionary, like **Makaveli** ain't shit you can tell me, **I'm on top with** ***the whole world waiting, on what I have to produce***, all I have was the truth, and when I write I write for the youth, and the truth is I was born to flow, and niggas blow they dough like the prodigal son, son we be pros in motion ***raiders of this lost art,*** about to start where it stopped cause real Hip Hop stops for no man, no clan, click, crew, that's the rhyme and reason for what we do, I'm far from through, just believe in **God** and **love** your **mother**, next to me, bro there ain't no other, I'm a man so I don't give a damn about a rank structure, you push'n me up mad close to the edge, but that's alright son because I know the ledge, and I know your type you don't really want war you don't really wanna fight, you wanna look hard in front of people right?

It is he, who comes forth by day into Light

I'm real like that **rose that grew from concrete, Common Sense** son I don't want no beef, I want the **Mos Def** beat, the most fly rhyme, something that don't glorify crime, I'm fly like Rodan, ain't no man equal to I, I ain't claim'n the best, I'm just not taken a tie, taken my time write'n my scripts make'n them shine, with something that don't glorify crime, in my prime like 21, I spit for a hundred one drum taps, make your best sound like chit chat, ...daily, fuck you pay me - **Dawud**

2005 Two roads

Two roads one way, two sons one say, I'm too young I'm having fun I'm gonna change one day, too much TV and too many hypocrites, how you gonna show your kids a way when you ain't live'n it? who knew that Dawud would ever take this serious? from student to soldier to a soulja that just fish, I fish for souls and I study **scrolls** of those, who talked to the word in flesh, you know the one God three forms? ***one day he's come'n back***, five fingers one fist in the air like that, one man one woman one marriage that's right! one quake two waves and how many lost life? we gotta get it together this might be the night, but it's Friday so she look'n like yeah right! she just got her hair done and just got a new dress **- Dawud**

2005 The Only Begotten

So you throw your hood up and throw your click up, and when beef come you ready to finish it up! you run to your trunk and you ready to get pop'n! there's only one hope, **there's only *one begotten*!** you crazy rep'n a state that don't respect you! they chase you, cuff you, print you, put you in a hearse too! it's curfew time bring it back home, I have a dream let it ring let's realize the poem, **cause here lies the tomb of a man that God sent, he sacrificed his life for the cause of the movement**, they called him a nuisance, still he stayed at the pulpit, the slaves got the bullwhip but they got the nite sticks and the water hose, back in the days of **Jim Crow**, and the Lord knows my heart, the reason why I wrote this, I wrote this with a purpose, this wasn't written in anger, I'm a peaceful man so I'm not for the violence or the negative conditioning conditioning the projects, the science projects! now who's gonna be next? come take the first step, step into this revolution, restitution, restoration, I wasn't fooled with the emancipation proclamation, tell me why at this very second there's drugs being shipped to this nation? It's curfew time, bring it back home, I have a **dream** let it ring, let's realize the poem, don't you realize we owe them that much?! back of the bus rapper, in your video I see everything that you lust after, you capture the mind of a kid before he's sharp enough to line it up and see the wickedness for what it is **- Dawud**

2005 The Mission man

You can call me the mission man, I'm talking to every man, with the **bible** in the right and book of **mormon** in his other hand, **Galatians** 1 and 8 what part you don't understand? I'll hit you with a verse that's worth more than a hundred grand, you can call me the mission man, I'm talking to everyman, that keeps **Christ** on the right but worships **Mary** on the other hand, **Exodus** 20:5 do you understand? I'll hit you with a verse that's worth more than a hundred grand **- Dawud**

2005 A Name and a Number

who am I?! I'm a - if u listen I'll explain, I'm not a killer but I'm trained don't test me man, ***The Hate U Gave Little Infants Fucked Everybody*****,** take 911 for instance they fooled everybody! - [po po sound] - harass niggas for a hobby, they can find Saddam then they can find anybody, and them niggas that killed **Pac**, hmm, yeah they probably hired and assisted, don't get it twisted, the history you read in a book has been shifted, like them plates in the ocean, I'm up against the ropes and I'm **rope'a dope'n**, and I'm cope'n with real life issues, dodge'n the missiles, **depleted uranium** probably all in my tissue, but who cares my name and number is just a name and a number, and when you go to war and come back man that make you wonder, why He ain't call my number? why am I here? why do I get to see another summer? Taft ain't here! cause he ain't make it, **pour out a little liquor** this is sacred, and don't mistake this for something you take for granite, I'm a soldier nigga! one of the realist to walk the planet **- Dawud**

2005 A Soldiers Still

You think life is hard? my regards go out to the families of the soldiers, the sons and daughters they handed over, for a quarter of a mill reimbursement for real, don't get it twisted I'm a soldiers still, so I still understand the definition of duty when duty calls, **it's my duty to deliver the word at any cause**, been in many wars, first I was born in the ghetto and if your not head strong you'll be conditioned to settle, petitioned to peddle, get on the bus you got'a put the peddle to the metal **- Dawud**

2005 The Champion

Y'all dudes don't want to see him, from the top to the floor I'm raw, the champion, step in my ring face the illest fight'n human being, it's hard being **King**, you can't check mate a soldier with an ill **Queen**, you can't escape your **fate,** I am the great... - **Dawud**

2005 Tomorrow

Five years three kids, he's out for the count, all I got was my name from this dude then he bounced, 27yrs old can't believe who I found, a fountain of living water, he put my life in order, I got a heavenly father, in this earthly horror, try'n to paint a picture that can better frame tomorrow, and sometimes it's discouraging when you see what tomorrow brings, but you gotta see the **God** in things **- Dawud**

2005 The kings Sword

<u>*He wore sandals but I wear shoes*</u>, and in my shoes I spread his good news, it don't matter who you are, don't matter how far that you go in sin, **Gods**' so salving so he'll save you, turn to John 3:16 dog, that's what it means dog! one clean swing from the **kings** sword, some times that's what we need to get on accord, sometimes we won't learn till we bump our heads, just stand still that's what man said, and when the enemy comes for your head try'n to make your blood bleed, try'n to make your blood shed, look to the sky for your master, scream out loud scream over your enemies laughter, and when they say the Lord won't save, your faiths gonna make you whole, turn off the cable, **the prince of the air** is conditioning, and if you think it's cool then dude your gonna burn, don't be miss led down the wrong path, cause every time you fall the enemy gets to laugh, go do the math **- Dawud**

Rau nu Prt m heru

"Come back to New York and Stay in My Guest Room"

My sister called me and said since I didn't have any plans I might as well come to New York and spend some time with her and her family. She said I could stay in one of her rooms, so I did. When I got back to New York I enjoyed being around my niece and nephew and I got along with my brother in law as well. At the time he was looking for a job and was considering the idea of becoming a nurse. I had my car, I had 3 or 4 thousand dollars in the bank and no plans for life. Life was a party at the moment as I began to party with old friends again.

Iu f Per f m heru

2005 Reason for Rhyme

I done heard them all dog yeah I've heard all the reasons, but I ain't here to discredit nobodies rhyme or season that they came in the game, but I got next and yeah I came to change, and yeah I feel your pain, I got no chain, no fitted, no my rims not spin'n, I fall down and get up cause everyday I stop sin'n, I used to be a thief dog had to stop steal'n, they tried to set me up dog like the <u>*First Time Felon*</u>, I was conditioned to think that I had to look appealing, but now I don't give a wut about what I'm wear'n, it's bout make'n it happen, poetry in motion, there's an ocean full of niggas who drowned try'n to make it rap'n, and who knows what happened? maybe they had no backing or maybe no marketing scheme, and if your cd's in the store but nowhere to be scene, how can you expect to make money? ask my nigga **C. Green - Dawud**

2005 A Love letter 4 Heather

It only takes 5 letters, all I need is 2 words, it took a little time to curve-my direction towards you, I only fear the **Lord** and your rejection this is true, at this very moment right now I'm miss'n you, so listen you, Heather Mcdow Jackson time with you is so relax'n, I'm tax'n your time, I'm ask'n if I'm the answer to a prayer maybe? pray with me, **Lord** direct the path, you lead the way, I'm going to go wherever you say, if I ever did sway from your path too much I ask for forgiveness, I trust that what must happen will happen I'm not going to fuss cause I got faith enough, all I think about is Heather Mcdow Jackson, all my time spent with her is so relaxin, she takes me back when, before my conditioning, before I was listening to rhymes laced with sin, I give thanks to him **- Dawud**

Rahél, The Dopest Ethiopian

When I was in the Army, stationed in Germany I met a girl named Rahél while working at the **Millennium** club (page 101). She was **Ethiopian** and perhaps that's the reason I had a powerful attraction to her. I left Germany in 2003 but **by some strange twist of fate** she would get a job in Westchester, NY as an Au Pair (a live in nanny) and I would go see her often in my 300ZX. It was as if the universe made it so that I could see her again, no different than what would happen with Zascha (pages 98, 133) and Melissa (p 205).

Utterances for Coming Forth by day into Light

2005 (Personal Training and the Haitian Revolution)

I came back to New York and I started "hanging" out with old friends and clubbing. I was back to chasing women again. I started hanging out with **Courtlan** and **Godfrey** a lot. On one occasion I took a group picture. In 2022 I realized there was a man in the picture who happened to look a lot like **Woody Guthrie**, the famous musician from the same town of the horrific Lynching of **Laura and L. D. Nelson**, from **May 25th** 1911. At this time in my journey Godfrey was still doing graphic design and seeing success at it. He would later design my first business card. Courtlan was still chasing two **dreams**, playing in the NFL and Hip Hop success. He was making beats all the time now and was getting better with each beat he made. He had been chasing his **dreams** since I left him in college back in 1998. Because I was in good shape Courtlan asked me to train him so that he could gain size for **NFL** Football. I agreed.

It is he, who comes forth by day into Light

May 25th 1911, Woody Guthrie and Lynchings He Did See

Today is January 19th 2022 and I'm supposed to be finishing the story of how I was murdered in 1955 (page 504). However, while searching for a picture of the Tallahatchie River I was thrown in, I came across a picture of Laura Nelson and her **14** year old son who were hanged from a bridge in Okemah, Oklahoma. When I looked into the lynching I saw that it took place on **May 25th** which is the first date or "pattern" I decoded (page 222). While reading about this lynching I came across the white musician, **Woody Guthrie** who was born in 1912, **14** months after the lynching, in the same town this lynching took place. As soon as I saw a picture of Woody I thought of a picture I had placed in this book over a year ago (page 136). In this picture Courtlan's friend Adam looked a lot like Woody. It's the look on Adam's face that I find interesting along with who Woody was. Woody was born in a very racist state that had many lynchings yet somehow he became everything his home town was not. He was a social outcast who embraced all races, creeds and religions, and when he was asked to indicate his religious preference upon admission to Greystone Hospital for the Huntington's Disease (that would eventually take his life), he put down "All." When challenged to be more specific Woody added, "**All or none**." To have come from **O**kema**h**, Oklahoma with these beliefs was an extraordinary departure, knowing the odds were all in favor of him perpetuating the racism that led to the lynching of both Laura Nelson and her 14-year old son Lawrence W. Nelson. The fact that to this day **O**kema**h**, Oklahoma has never acknowledged their only famous native son speaks volumes about how far removed in spirit, culture and values Woody Guthrie was. In 19**77** the year of the **snake,** Woody's uncle Claude Guthrie was recorded in an interview detailing how his older brother Charley Guthrie (Woody's father) was one of the people who lynched Laura and her son: "It was pretty bad back there in them days... The niggers was pretty bad over there in Boley, you know... Charley and them, they throwed this nigger and his mother in jail, both of them, the boy and the woman. And that night, why they stuck out and hung [laughter], they hung them niggers that killed that sheriff... I just kind of laughed [laughter]. I knew darn well that rascal [Charley] was–I knew he was in on it."

The Lynching of Laura and L. D. Nelson

The truth of what really happened will forever be lost to his-story however an Oklahoma paper read: A teenage boy, L. W. Nelson, shot and killed Deputy George Loney, whose posse was searching the Nelson cabin for **stolen meat**. Trying to protect her 14 year old son, Laura claimed that she shot Loney but her son was dragged through the streets by a white howling lynch mob. The boy's father pled guilty to stealing cattle and was taken to the pen, which probably saved his life. Forty men rode into Okemah at night and entered the sheriff's office unimpeded. The jailer, a man named Payne unlocked the cell, and they took the frightened boy, and "stifled and gagged" him. Next they went up to the female jail (a cage in the courthouse) and took Laura out. She was very small of stature, very dark, around 35 years old. Laura was then raped by the mob then she and her son were hauled by wagon six miles **west** of town to a new steel bridge crossing the Canadian River "**in a negro settlement**," where they were hung from the bridge. Laura's arms were swinging at her side, untied, while about twenty feet away swung her 14 year old son with his clothes partly torn off and his hands tied with a saddle string. This horrifying yet common spectacle was discovered by a Black boy taking his cow to water. Hundreds of people from Okemah and the western part of the country went to view the scene. The "strange fruit" gently swaying in the wind. The bodies were cut down from the bridge at 11:00 on **May 25th** by order of the county commissioner, then taken to Okemah. The Nelsons' relatives did not claim the bodies, and they were buried by the county in the Greenleaf cemetery near Okemah. Laura had been caring for her baby in jail and had the child with her when she was taken from her cell. A local woman was quoted: "After they had hung them up, those men just walked off and left that baby lying there. One of my neighbors was there, and she picked the baby up and brought it to town, and we took care of it. It's all grown up now and lives here."

Rau nu Prt m heru

Iu f Per f m heru

Utterances for Coming Forth by day into Light

It is he, who comes forth by day into Light

May 2005
PERSONAL TRAINING and Meta Mysterious Encounters

I started training **Courtlan** (p 73, 144) at **Bally's Total Fitness Gym** and my second day at the gym a **Haitian** brother walked over to me. I thought I knew him! He looked just like my good friend **Patrick** from my high school football team and I thought it was him, but as we began to talk I realized that he wasn't **Patrick**. He asked me how I was able to develop the peak of my biceps. I told him about an article I read where **Arnold Schwarzenegger** talked about **visualizing** mountains as he curled and I did the same. That same day that brother introduced me to the manager and **the next day I was a trainer!** I went to college because **Courtlan** told the coach about me and now I had a job because he asked me to train him (p 73). All the people in our lives serve a purpose and sometimes the purpose is divine. While at the gym I would see **Tek** from **Smif-n-Wessun** every now and then and whenever I saw him I would recite one of my favorite verses from their album. He would smile and bob his head. In high school the **Boot Camp Clik** was my favorite group (pages 72, 345).

Significance

There were two **Haitian** brothers on my high school football team with the name **Patrick Hilaire**. One of them was housed in the **St. John's Boys Home**, and oddly enough, the father of the other Patrick worked at the Boys Home. **Patrick** wasn't my only teammate housed in the St. John's Boys Home, **Greg Mondesir** was there too. I was the only teammate that would visit them at the boys home. Though I was their friend I never knew the details of how they came to live in the boys home. At the time I had no historical knowledge of **Haiti** and had no idea that they were both **Haitian**! I would not come to know their life stories till many years later. Against All Odds, they both persevered despite many trials and now they are both successful business men! I would visit Patrick in **Nov of 2021** and that's when I realized that he's born on July 3, the same day I had my past life revelation of my life as **Emmett Till** on July 3, 2018 (p 480). And the other **Patrick Hilaire** is born on Sept 17, two days before Emmett's court trial started (page 66). **Greg** is born June 2, on the birthday of my sister that dreamt my car accident before it happened (page 104).

Bally's Total fitness and Meta Mysterious Encounters

The strangest thing about me working at Bally's is that **Greg** was the first

sales manager at that location in the late 90's. He helped open the location and was the top regional sales rep. What are the "chances" that I would go to that gym with Courtlan, a high school football teammate and a person who gets me a job at the gym looked just like Patrick, another high school football teammate? And what are the "chances" that **Greg** would have worked at the gym before me? Patrick and **Greg** were both in **St. John's Boys Home** together. They are both **Haitian**! I am part **Haitian** (p 25). This is not just a coincidence! All of this was governed by seen and unseen forces! See pages 6,78,85,107,141 149,248,292,297,305,345,405,437,450,505,537,547,586,609,646,650

Heather

I fell in love with Heather. She was the friend of Lauryn, Courtlan's girl friend. She was a faithful **Christian**. She lived all the way out in Amityville Long Island and I would drive my 300ZX out to see her often. I think we dated for a 2 or 3 months. Then I got the job in the gym and we had a miscommunication via text that caused us to part ways. The last time I saw her was a few days after I crashed my first motorcycle on May 25th 2008 (page 157-158). I bought a new one from a guy in Long Island a few days after that accident and on my way home I stop by her house. She told me to be careful, I smiled and said I would be but as fate would have it I crashed that motorcycle the next day on June 3rd 2008 (page 157-158).

2005 Shift The Power

As I step to the front, you can step to the rear, I'm here to relieve your command, it's part of a bigger plan, give the power to the people, the people already know that if you really want power, gotta get dough for sho! And I know success don't come easy, sometimes I get mad wanna throw my tv, break my CD somebody got's to feel me, I'm a war vet nigga but don't salute me, I'm in debt my nigga just buy the album, you ain't heard of the soulja? Ask about him, **Greenhouse Entertainment**, got to shout em, cause right now we come'n up from the bottom, rags to riches my nigga, you know it's gotta feel good to us niggas from the ghetto, we ain't never had shit so you know we won't settle, until our names on the Forbes 100 come'n to get that power **- Dawud**

In a quest for shine we cross the line, feel'n pressed for time we can't press rewind, thoughts of supremacy run'n though my mind, know'n I can be the **king** if I stay on my grind, heard the grass was a little greener and turn the beat up, the D's ain't the only reason I hop the fence, it'll all make sense if we form a prism no dotted lines to be signed if we share the same vision, and let start with a spark, and end with **D Eddings**, and we'll all see green if I become a **legend**, from **past to present**, ask'n questions like, what in Gods name took us so long, friends like the sitcom but can't sit calm, ain't no good times here know'n we should be on, if I pause I'm just let'n it breathe now catch wind, fuck the world if they can't believe it's out time now **- Dutch**

I spent enough time on the sideline like an old vet, figured it was time to get my feet wet, if you a critic and knew that I did it, just understand I produce as sick as I spit it, so cut the games stop play'n, you feel the heat, just admire the way the words merge with the beat, got sick of feeling shit on, something like I was spit on, got a click, my own shit told my niggas to get on, I said a D you handle the talk'n, I do the walk'n, if cats get out of line the Dutch you do the talk'n, Dawud don't even have to play the game, when I make then he made it, I know he would do the same, they say what goes up must come down, the last shall be first, and the peasant shall bear the **crown**, now all around the world you see the sign of the times, so when you look at my wrist just know that this ones mine **- C Green**

Significance

Courtlan and Dutch were serious about this music thing but for me I was just there. I wasn't really serious. This was the only song we recorded. Each of their verses speak to prominence. Dutch says the word **King** and **Legend** and years later I would realize I was a King and the prophecy of the reincarnation of Emmett Till and **Tutankhaten** (King Tut) is legendary. Courtlan says the peasant shall bear the crown. I once wore a **crown**.

2005 Attention

Only one out of ten of us supposed to make it kid, I'm what you get when a man falls in love and leaves his son abandoned, the making of a bastard battle the world on my own, bump my head five times before a nigga learn, *still the **Lord** blessed me through all of my wrong turns*, so pardon me cause I direct the traffic here, been my whole life poor now this is the stick up, if you ain't sure who you run'n wit, you run'n against us, more often times I'm viewed as the lone soldier, at first glance I'm perceived as misplaced anger, but look closer I'm a banger for my culture, what the world needs to know is I'm taken over, who knew that Dawud would be the soldier? organizing the streets like we suppose ta, so you can cop the roster I'm a rock this timex like it's a Rolex, I do my next set, for my niggas who ain't here, your best bet's to fall in behind me, there's no call'n for mommy, when we march into war and death becomes definite, **Greenhouse** is where it's at we set precedence, Brigade, Company, Platoon Attention, did I mention I'm here to raise the tension,I ain't come to bring peace, I got yah piece, there's gonna be a lot of pain and gnashing of teeth, Brigade Company Platoon Attention, did I mention I'm here to raise the tension, I ain't come to bring peace, I got yah piece, there's never gonna be peace until we get a piece

I heard you ask who that new kid is, I never been shot, I been shot at, but never did a bid, how would that benefit the struggle? **Martin** and **Malcolm** got shot for me so I just praise them, *as I climb the mountain to speak to the **savior***, look down to the earth and analyze behavior, I realize the time for a leader is major, wanna do me a favor? address me as General, and salute me when you see me walk'n in front of you, I'm **destined** to do all the things you scared to, and all them things you ain't really prepared to, I'm behind enemy lines *see'n life through the rear view*, I don't care who's who's and what crew thinks they hot, I'm from back in the days of *who got the props*, now who's wit me? if you is good, if u not you not! we need soldiers on the block, so I put my fist in the air for all to see it, the **ghost** of **Huey P** lives on you better believe it! *in every breath I breathe-it and every step that I put down, a great realization is where I will be found*, Brigade, Company, Platoon Attention, did I mention I'm here to raise the tension,I ain't come to bring peace, I got yah piece, there's gonna be a lot of pain and gnashing of teeth, Brigade Company Platoon Attention, did I mention I'm here to raise the tension, I ain't come to bring peace, I got yah piece, there's never gonna be peace until we get a piece **- Dawud**

July 19th 2005 - LaVena Johnson

LaVena Lynn Johnson was murdered by fellow soldiers while deployed in Iraq on July 19th 2005, just **8** days before her 20th birthday, She was raped, burned and murdered. They claimed she killed herself but I don't believe that. I know that statistically one out of every three women in the Army (military) is **raped** or **sexually harassed** and these numbers can go up while deployed in combat. I did not hear about the murder of laVena until June 10th 2015 and when I heard her story it troubled me deeply. I had been a Sergeant in the army and I had been out of the army for 10yrs now. I still knew/know my NCO Creed by heart, and this line rang out, "all soldiers are entitled to outstanding leadership; I will provide that leadership"… No one protected her! She was gone. I was angry! I turned on the **Tupac** instrumental '*Words to my first Born*' and I wrote a song for her on June 10th 2015 (page 334).

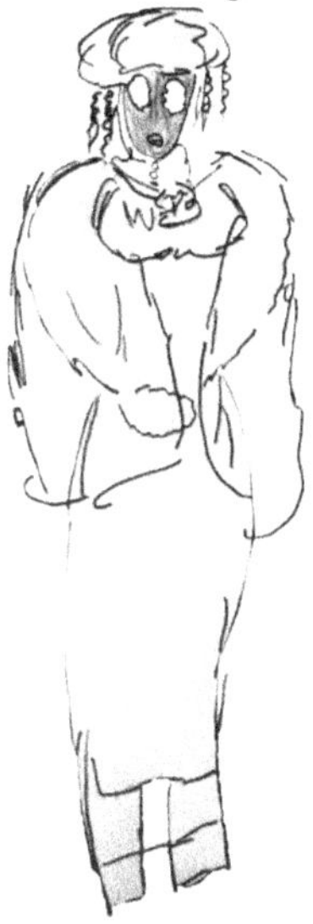

Significance

Years after I wrote the song for LaVena I would realize that she was sent down on (born on) July 27th the same day as my nephew and two days after **Emmett Till's** birthday. I only have two nephews and one is born 2 days before Emmett was murdered and one is born 2 days after Emmett was sent down (born). When I wrote the song for LaVena (page 334) I felt like her spirit was calling me to write it and now her story is here, in this book. LaVena and her family have still yet to see justice for her murder.

Condolences

My condolences go out to the family of **LaVena Johnson** and all the families of those who have been robbed of their life by this system of racism and white supremacy. Please know that death is not the end. The soul survives death, indeed and in spirit. This is a book of the dead written by a boy who was murdered without justice, who defeated death and came forth by day. May the soul of **LaVena Johnson** walk peacefully through the field of Reeds in Amenta. Amen Ra.

June 10th 2015 LaVena Johnson

I can't go to sleep in the late night, I be having visions of death and seeing this great light, and *when I breathe my last breath and escape the flesh*, **I'll be back** in the hurricane with **Lesane,** and every slain African that's feeling the same, bringing the rain, the thunder, the pain, **LaVena Johnson** remember the name!… they **raped** her then they claim it was suicide! a soldier, killed by her own side! no where to run, no where to hide! unify we gotta try, gotta survive, gotta *ride on our enemies* and stay alive, the inner chi be the energy for you and I, you ain't never lie when you said, **Green Black** and **Red, U.N.I.A** your **dream** is never dead! every day is a day we can move ahead, instead of looking back in fact recite this pledge, I pledge allegiance for many reasons, can you see the treason for 2000 seasons?! who do you believe in?! ***invoking** the legions*, united we stand, divide is treason, on my block - (Written on June 10th 2015, page 334)

2005

Quantum-Spiritual Encounters of The Fourth Kind

Jean Jacques Dessalines and the Glitch in the Matrix The Quantum leap, Teleportation, Paranormal Magic

At this point I'm having the time of my life. I'm working at the gym and I'm making decent money, way more than I made in the army and the potential to make more money was great. The gym was like a club, and there were always new beautiful women coming in. I began to spend less time at my sisters house because I was always at the gym and I was always out clubbing. I think that bothered her because when she invited me to stay I think she had the vision of me being around there more not to mention the room I was in wasn't well kept, but I was out living my life. One day my brother in law (Abdul) asked me to join him for the ride to long Island for an open house where he was going to apply for a union job. While there he suggested that I apply for the **Helmets To Hard Hats** program they mention, so I did. Abdul and I got along well. A few weeks later I got a call from the union and I got a job because I was prior military but Abdul didn't. At the time I did not see how that might have caused some issue with my sister because after that we began to have discord.

Now I have two jobs. I get up at 5 am to drive my car to the Staten Island ferry, then I take the ferry to the city and catch the train to 47th street where I worked at **30 Rockefeller** as a **painter apprentice** from 7 am until the afternoon. Then I would catch the D train to Brooklyn and train clients until the gym closed. Then I took the long trip back to my sisters house. I was burning the candle at both ends. My brother in law could not find work and Court had graduated college with a 4 year degree but he couldn't find work either and here I was with two jobs. Court ended up doing scenic work where he would **paint** and dress the sets of movies and tv shows like The Sopranos. **His father** was a scenic **painter** and got him the job. Oddly enough **my father** was a **painter** too, at the famous Waldorf Astoria Hotel. My father is a man who **dreams** things before they happen (p 99). He often dreams death before it happens. He dreamt his sister's death before it happened (p 464). While working at the Waldorf Astoria Hotel he once had an experience with a **dead friend**. He was walking through a hallway in the Hotel when he saw one of his friends who had not come into work for a few days. When he called out to him, **his friend disappeared**. Then he had a **dream** that he saw his friend in a casket. Days later he got the news that his friend had indeed died. He saw a **ghost.**

I did the same routine everyday for about two or three long weeks. I drove my car to the ferry and took the early morning ferry to the city, then I painted at 30 Rockefeller until the afternoon, then I took the train to Brooklyn and worked at the gym until closing. Everyday I contemplated on which job I should keep or whether I should just keep them both. I was only an apprentice at the time so all I did was paint the area around 30 Rockefeller. I felt lucky to have the job so I didn't want to just leave. I had all the benefits you could want, I had a **401K plan**, **insurance**, **vacation**, **Medical**, **Dental** and more. The job offered a sense of security and I was one of the few black males there. The job was staffed by mostly old **Greek men** who got their jobs from their friends or family and passed the jobs down to their sons and family members. I kept asking the senior painters what they thought I should do. I explained how I liked working at the gym and I could make a lot of money there but I also like the security of the union job. But none of them offered any advice for me. They liked me but they didn't like me at the same time. I was 27 years old and I was doing the painting job the way I did everything else, **fast**. I was fast and good and they didn't like that. I was not supposed to work so fast but I didn't know that. I remember one of them telling me to slow down because I was moving too fast and making them all look bad. It wasn't on purpose I was just being me. Little did I know, the universe had a different plan for me. I was **sleep walking** through life but the time for me to **awaken** from my slumber was soon upon me.

2005

Jean Jacques Dessalines and the glitch in the Matrix. The Quantum leap, Teleportation, Paranormal Magic

Rau nu Prt m heru

After a few weeks I was sent on my first contract job. I was dressed in all white painters clothes and had a cart full of equipment. As I pushed my equipment down the street to the location of the job, I made a right turn on **Park** avenue and as soon as I saw the Waldorf Astoria Hotel **I was over come with a wave of Deja Vu!** It was a very **powerful** feeling that left me standing in a daze as I realized that I had not grown up with my father yet I was following in his foot steps! He was a senior painter at the Waldorf Astoria Hotel and here I was in painters uniform going to my first contract job! I stood there and took it all in then I proceeded to the location. It was a big office space in a city building with many rooms. While there all I had to do was prep each room by taping the corners in every room for the senior painters. I worked fast and I listened to Hip Hop music while working. What happened next is an example of how thoughts can affect our reality. The relationship our thoughts have to quantum level events in time and space is more powerful than I was aware of at this time but I was about to get a first hand lesson. I remember having **thoughts** of getting my first personal training **cards**. They were in the process of being printed and I couldn't wait to get them. All morning I was contemplating whether I should keep the Union job or should I just do Personal Training, or should I do them both?! I asked another painter what he thought and he told me it was my decision. I continued to tape the borders and edges. Right before my lunch break I entered a room that had a desk up against the wall so I had to get on my knees to tape the borders. While on my knees taping the borders **I was asking God** what I should do, then out of the corner of my eyes I saw something on the floor. I don't remember seeing the card before I got under the table but when I noticed it I remember thinking, it would be funny if it was a **personal training card** and when I picked it up to my surprise it read, **NO LIMIT FITNESS!** **I was over come with another wave of Deja Vu.** I showed one of the painters and told him what happened and it surprised him too. This was strange because I had been taping rooms all morning and found nothing in any other room except desks and chairs. I only remember seeing a cup of coffee in one room. I taped many rooms that morning and when I was on **my knees asking God** what I should do, I looked and found a card that read **NO LIMIT FITNESS**. I left for lunch that day and I never went back to the union job. At this time I knew about the idea of **guardian angels** and **ghosts** but I had never seen any. At least not yet… I had never heard of the term **invisible helpers**. And at the time I would have never considered that some unseen entity had "helped" me. I just saw it as a very strange coincidence that amazed me. In **May of 2014** (p 292) this card that appeared out of nowhere would prove to be more than just a card that I found by happenstance. I would come to realize that the ancestors had guided my path just like when the Haitian brother walked up to me in the gym and introduced me to the manager (p 138). This card would be connected to the **Haitian** revolution that was planned on August 14, 1791, led by **Jean Jacques Dessalines, Toussaint Louverture, Dutty Bookman** and many others! I am connected to the Haitian revolution because of my Bajan ancestry from my father (pages 15, 25). When the indigenous population of the island of Hispaniola (Haiti) was decimated by European invaders the first place they went for new "slaves" was Barbados (page 25). In 2022 I went to **Kemet** for the first time in this life and while there I had **Deja Vu** two times (pages 670 - 671). More on Haiti: pages 6,78,85,107,138,149,248,292,297,305,345, 405,437,450,505,537 ,547,586,609,646, 650.

Iu f Per f m heru

Utterances for Coming Forth by day into Light

It is he, who comes forth by day into Light

On **August 28th** 2005, the same day Emmett Till was murdered, **Hurricane Katrina** reached it's peak strength and headed towards Louisiana. The storm, which devastated New Orleans, and to an unusually large degree it impacted many of the city's black residents more than any other group of people. When Hurricane Katrina struck I was working in the gym having fun. I saw the news and I felt bad about what I saw but it wasn't happening to me so all I did was watch like most other people. I sent no money and had no desire to go there to help because I had done my time in the Army and the government was supposed to help but I saw the slow reaction from military forces to provide that help. And I heard the conspiracies that the government caused the hurricane but I was working in the gym having fun. At the time I was not studying but I had heard the song **Bin Laden** by **Immortal Technique** which had been release the same summer. In the song the words "Bush knocked down the towers" can be heard. In a 2008 interview Immortal Technique explained that he didn't think Bush was responsible for 911 but he figured that the government was lying about their relationships with people involved in it. I remember hearing **Kanye West** speak truth to power and I never forgot that, "**George Bush doesn't care about black people**" is what he said on live tv and from that moment I have never stopped being a supporter of Kanye. **Immortal** Technique was the first artist I started listening to when I got back to the states from Germany. His music was like nothing I had ever heard and it made me start thinking and I would come to meet him on April 24th 2013 at a **Mumia** rally (page 270). Over time the impact of Katrina calmed down and we were given other things to focus on like the murder of **Sean Bell** the next year!

At the time Hurricane Katrina was the largest and 3rd strongest hurricane ever recorded to make landfall in the US but I have an alternative perspective on the events that took place in New Orleans! In a country that has no problem shoving blacks in prisons at the highest percentage and shoots us down in the streets, is it really that hard to believe that advanced technology would be used as ethnic cleansing? What has this country done to earn our trust? We still wait* for them to decide that the horrors their ancestors have perpetrated against ours is worthy of **reparations** and some how every time election seasons comes around reparations is never dealt with. Is it outlandish to think the children of the enslavers will do the same as the fathers? This country murdered **Martin Luther King**, **Malcolm X** and destroyed countless black wealthy communities so why is it out the frame of possibility for them to have used advanced technology like HAARP (high-frequency active auroral research program) to cause a hurricane and flood us out? –(see page 69)– I guess they wanted their 1803 Louisiana purchase back! The levees in New Orleans were designed for category 3, but **Katrina** peaked at a category 5 hurricane, with winds up to 175 mph. The final death toll was at 1,836, primarily from Louisiana (1,577) and M**ississ**ippi (**23**8). More than half of these victims were senior citizens. The storm surge from Katrina left an estimated 80% of New Orleans under water, up to 20 ft deep in some places (six meters). Over a 1000 people are reported as still missing as a result of Hurricane Katrina. Hurricane Katrina affected over 15 million people in different ways varying from having to evacuate their homes, rising gas prices, and the economy suffering. Hurricane Katrina caused $81 billion in property damages, but it is estimated that the total economic impact in Louisiana and M**ississ**ippi may exceed $150 billion, earning the title of costliest hurricane ever in US history. Hurricane Katrina impacted about 90,000 square miles. The region affected by the storm supported roughly 1 million non-farm jobs, and still, hundreds of thousands of local residents were left unemployed by the hurricane. More than 70 countries pledged monetary donations or other assistance after the hurricane. **Kuwait** made the largest single pledge of **$500 million**, but **Qatar**, **India**, **China**, **Pakistan** and **Bangladesh** made very large donations as well. In1942, Japanese Americans were sent to concentration camps during World War 2. 46 years later, with the passing of the Civil Liberties Act of 1988 Japanese Americans received reparations to right the wrongs they experienced. Black people are the aboriginal people of the continent known as America (Turtle Island) and for hundreds of years we have been subjected to enslavement, lynchings, systematic racism and the list goes on, yet still we have yet to receive reparations. See page **648** for the **metaphysical significance of the number 23**.

I didn't know the responsibilities of a best man to be honest. I was a loyal friend and when Court asked me to be the best man I happily accepted. I had never been to a wedding as an adult and so I had no recollection of what a best man speech sounded like. When it was my time to speak I was over come with the type of emotion that should really only be roused by the bride or groom and perhaps their parents. I cried while attempting to deliver my speech at his wedding. He was like a brother to me and if it were my wedding I imagine I would have cried. I was happy for him and my emotions got the "best" of me and I felt like a fool afterwards. His wife Lauryn and I would become friends over the years and I would also become friends with his brother in-law Jay Cooper. Unfortunately Jay Cooper would pass away on December 3rd 2014. When I got the news of his passing I cried. Then I wrote him a song. Then a few days later I would have a profound spiritual experience with the spirit of Jay Cooper on December 17th 2014 at a holiday party. Then for the next 3 years I would have an experience with death on December 3rd, 2014 **Jay Cooper** (page 314), 2015 **Sean Price** (page 345), 2016 **Tupac Shakur** (page 431) and 2017 **Dr Jack Felder** (page 457). During the writing of this book this Dec 3rd pattern would close with the uncovering of the death of **Clinton Melton** who was murdered in broad daylight by a racist White man, on December 3rd 1955, only 3 months after Emmett was killed (page 519). I would call this, the December 3rd Theory. Courtlan and I would have several arguments over the years due to our differences of opinions on politics and such. During one of these arguments he would tell me that Cooper made many jokes about me crying at the wedding. That didn't bother me because Coop was my homie in the spirit. Courtlan had grown up around more white people than I did. We both played sports and so we played with all "races" of people and neither of us "hated" white people but I was the one who would more freely speak my truth to power in my music. Courtlan felt like I was angry in my music and this is where we clashed. He once mentioned that he felt like I was a Malcolm X type spirit and he was a Martin Luther King type spirit. Today is January 1st 2022 and him and I don't speak often at all. In 2020 we got into a big argument over vaccinations, as he felt they were necessary and I didn't. Perhaps we spoke once in 2021 via text. Despite all of our differences I owe Courtlan a mighty thanks. It was his passion for music that kept a pulse going for me. This is important because eventually I would come to see that the music was the conveyer for my soul as I used music as magic to awaken my ancient soul fragments. We get the friends in life that we need and even in our arguments there is much to be learned. I am thankful. Thank you Court. Court had his first child while in college ---- she was born on **Feb 7**, 1997, the same day that **Emmett Till's** father was born (page 475, 518).

Rau nu Prt m heru

Iu f Per f m heru

Utterances for Coming Forth by day into Light

It is he, who comes forth by day into Light

I didn't grow up aware of the different struggles of my brothers from different Caribbean islands but I have had close friends from many different islands since my adolescence. My first job at a gym was in Flatbush Brooklyn where I worked with many brothers from different Caribbean islands and countries in Africa. I got along with all my brothers. All the brothers in this picture I hold dearly even though I don't see any of them anymore. After losing my Job at Bally's, Excel was the only one I saw often and that's because I got him a job at my gym in the city. I Saw **ELL** once in 2016 at the Bam African Dance Festival when I had just started wearing my feather (page 385). I saw **Shiller** in 2020 in Central Park (page 616). I saw **Wade** in 2022 at the International African Arts Festival while I was selling the copies of this book. I had not seen him in since 2006. I have not seen **Excel** in many years.

Kellee Lewis

I met Kellee when I had just started at Bally's. She came to the gym with her cousin who "happened" to be born on October 25, like me….. Kellee is born on November 11th (**11:11**). She is a Jamaican sister who is committed to the development of children. Kellee and I are still friends till this day. After I began to tell her about my past life experience in 2018 and how **Marcus Garvey** was a major part of my journey, she revealed that she is a descendant of his. I find it interesting that she is a speech pathologist because I used to stutter as a boy (page 35) and **Emmett Till** Stuttered too (page 506).

January 19th 2006 - Fired From Bally's...... In 2006, the Year of the "DOG" for being a DOG........

A girl came into the gym one day and requested a personal trainer. I was at the front desk so I sat and spoke with her. When I asked her what her goals were she told me that she wanted to get in shape so that she could have a nicer body because she wanted to become a **stripper**. Unfortunately when she told me that my thoughts were everything but pure. I thought with the lower parts of my nature. I took her through the same process I took everyone else through but when it was time for her to take her before pictures she decided to take them in a thong. No other woman had ever done that but she did, and I was not wise enough to navigate this situation. I should have suggested that she take the picture in shorts but I didn't. I just took the picture. At the time I was renting a small room near the gym I worked at. Soon after meeting her she came to see me there, where I trained her and afterwards she danced like a stripper. We were not intimate in any way but soon after that she got upset and made a complaint to the gym and afterwards I was suspended from the gym. Instead of using my position to help the person crossing my path I used my position to fulfill desires of the flesh. My decision would cause me to struggle for close to a year. My manager reluctantly suspended me because I was one of his highest producers. I was never brought back to work for the gym however my district manager liked me so he referred me to a gym in the city. I tried to make it on my own, training clients in the parks and in their homes but that didn't work and the next year I would use that referral he offered.

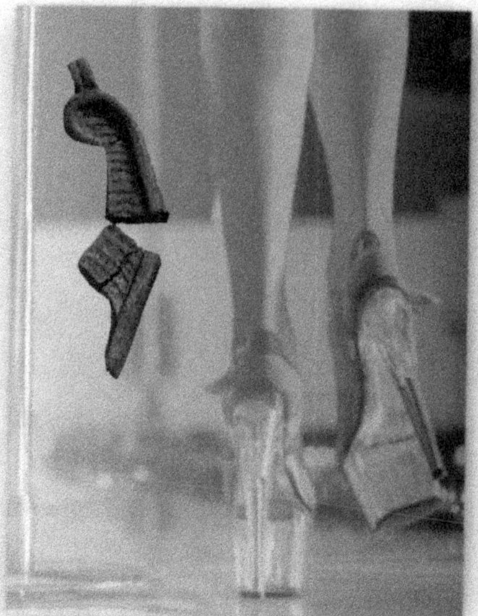

Pearl and Nina Simone Put a Spell on Me, Meta Mysterious Encounters

Rau nu Prt m heru

I met Pearl in 2006 on **Myspace** however we would meet face to face in a most mysterious way. One day I walked into an AT&T store in midtown manhattan to inquire about a phone and the woman behind the register looked very familiar. She looked like a friend from Myspace. I asked her if her name was **Yemaya** on Myspace and she said yes. **That got both of our attention**. We exchanged numbers and her and I would spend hours on the phone talking about what was going on in each of our lives and she would listen to the rhymes I had written. One day she sent me the song: <u>I Put A Spell On You</u> by **Nina Simone**. I had previously never heard the song and unfortunately had never heard of Nina Simone. I was 27 and had never heard Nina Simone's music... That is embarrassing. Unbeknownst to either of us Pearl had put a spell on me by sending me that song. Pearl and I would end up being platonic friends to this day because of the circumstances surrounding the way we met at her job.

Pearl See's Shadows

Iu f Per f m heru

Over the years I would share the experiences I was having with **dreams**, **sleep paralysis** and **astral traveling** with Pearl. This led her to sharing a few paranormal experiences of her own with me. She told me about a night she woke up from her sleep and found herself stuck in the state of **sleep paralysis.** While in this state the **astral body** of a man walked into her room. The entity tried to make sexual advances on her then she did the unthinkable. **<u>Out of reflex</u> her astral body jumped out of her physical body** and she chased the entity out of her house. On another occasion she was fully awake in her bed when she saw what appeared to be the silhouette of a person standing by her window. The curtains had formed the shape of a body and she could see what looked like someone hiding behind the curtains. Her curtains were thin and see through so she knew there was no physical person there but still the shape of a person could be seen, as if it was just the shadow of a person or a **shadow person** (p 663). She was not afraid, she told it to leave then she closed her eyes and when she opened them moments later it was gone. In 2020 after my past life revelation of **Tutankhaten** (**King Tut**) (page 594) Pearl and I were talking on the phone when I realized that her last name just so happens to be **Ramose** like the Pharaohs in Kemet (Egypt). It wasn't until after I returned from Kemet in 2022 that I realized that a **Vizier** under the reign on Amenhotep III (King Tut's grand father) and Akhenaten (King Tut's father) was named Ramose. Ramose was the Governor of Luxor (Thebes, Waset.) and his tomb, TT**55** is located on the West Bank of the Nile in Thebes in Upper Egypt. In 2020 I already knew without a **shadow** of a doubt that I was Emmett (page 480) and Tutankhaten (page 594) in previous lives but it was becoming increasingly more interesting as I continued to see the confirmations coming from everywhere. It was like the universe was revealing all the connections to me. Emmett Till was murdered in 19**55**, Akhenaten's remains were found in tomb number KV**55**, my mother in this life was born in 19**55** and now I found that Ramose's tomb is TT**55**. Pearl is the same person that introduced me to Nina Simone's music and Nina just so happen to write a song for **Emmett Till**. This is not just a "coincidence"! One time is an incidence, twice is a **coincidence** but 3, 4 and 5 is a pattern. Can you tell the difference?

Mississippi Goddam

Utterances for Coming Forth by day into Light

Nina Simone would become one of my favorite people. Her story was very close to my heart as I felt like she was alone in the world of musicians who didn't care to speak about the black struggle in their music. Nina Simone wrote her first Civil Rights song, M**ississ**ippi **Goddam** in 1964 when she was 31. It was her response to the murder of **Emmett Till**, **Medgar Evers** (page 520) and the 16th street Baptist Church bombing that killed **four little girls in Alabama**. All these murders were racially motivated by white racist in the American South. When I started writing music again I would think about Nina a lot and I mention her several times in my music. In 2012 I mentioned Nina for the first time in a song (p 254), in 2016 I wrote a song to a beat with a sample from Nina (p 359), a few months later, on the day **Afeni Shakur** died, I spoke Nina's words, "**Black is The Color of My true loves Hair**" (p 381). In this song I would also say the name **King Tut** for the 5th time in my music, 4 years before my past life revelation (p 594).

It is he, who comes forth by day into Light

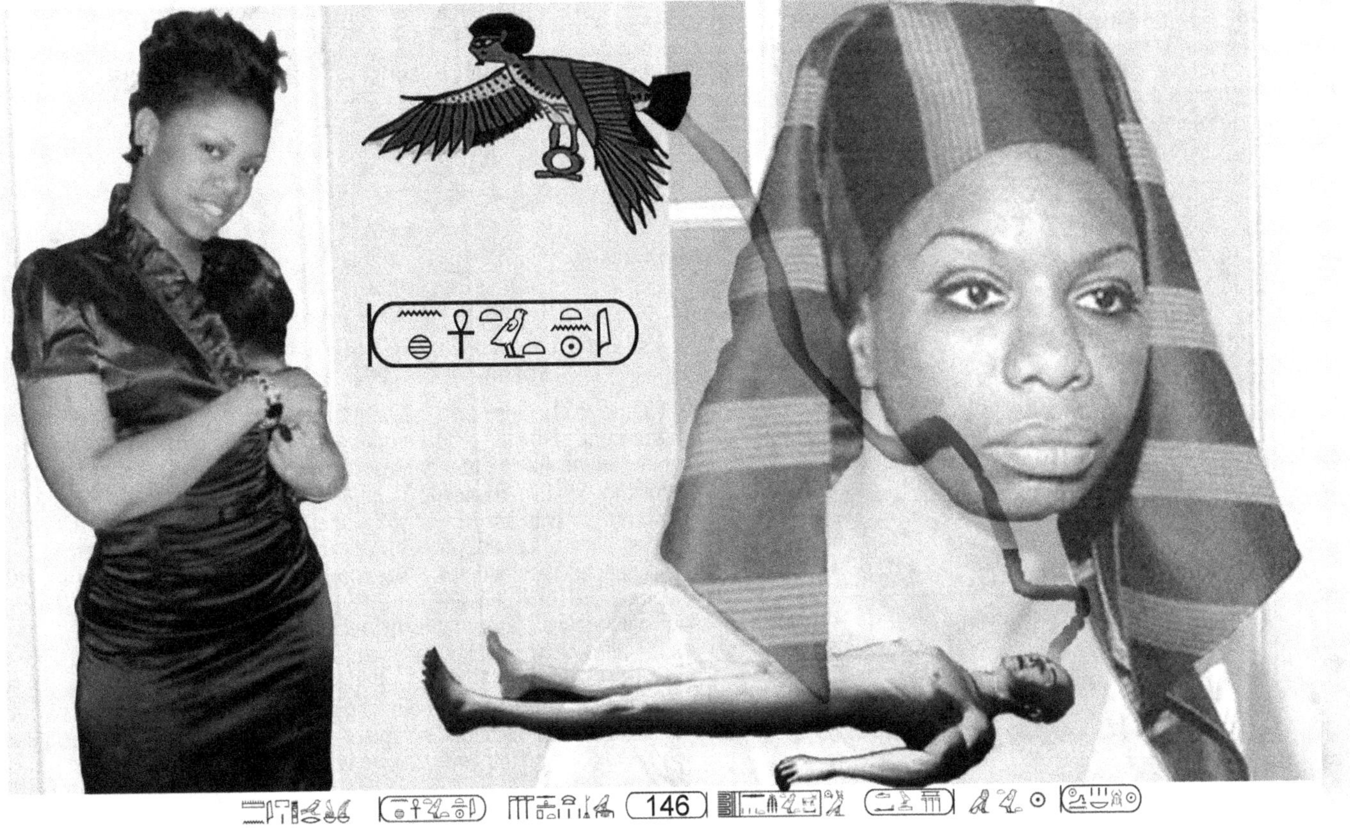

2006, Jeannie in the Bottle

I met Jeannie in the 10th grade in Science class (page 60). I had a crush on her but she was dating John and I was chasing Indira. Her and I became friends and nothing more. When I got out of the army in 2005 I ran into her again. We started dating and we fell for each other. We started looking for an apartment together but we almost got scammed by fake realtors. Then I lost my job at the gym. I was at an all time low point in my life. I never told her how I lost my job at the gym (p 145). She was smart though. She let me go. She told me something I had never heard before. She told me that she needed a shark and I wasn't a shark. I never saw Jeannie again but I do hope that she is doing well and in good health. I struggled for a while sleeping in my car and training clients privately in parks and in their homes. Then in 2006 I got a job at New York Sports Club. I stayed there for 3 months then I went to Synergy Gym for a week. In 2007 I started training at Crunch and became the top trainer in my Gym. I began to swim like a shark again. Jeannie and I developed a friendship as teenagers then we floated away from each other for 10 years like a bottle thrown out to sea. We found each other again in 2006 and fell in Love for a short time. She left me but she also gave me the spark I needed, then she floated away again. She was like my Genie in a bottle. I needed to hear what Jeannie told me and therefore I am thankful.

"We used to sit in science class, in the back of my mind I flash of all the times I had her in my grasps, good times don't last forever sometimes but good memories ain't hard to find, and damn she was fine, then finally I got the courage to kiss her, but she was blind to my feelings and now I miss her, she never got along with her sister and her father never bothered, her mother was her only stable fixture, and now all I got left of us is this faded picture"- **Jeannie in a bottle** (written on **August 14th 2018,** page 531).

Tupac Tears with Khiara Briggs

Somewhere around this time in my life I found my self on the phone talking to **Khiara Briggs**, or more like crying to Khiara. I know it was around this time because I was in between apartments. I met Khiara through Courtlan's wife Lauren and we became friends. We would talk on the phone every now and then. One day I was in Queens sitting in my car, in the rain, talking to Khiara and **Tupac** came up in conversation. I remember telling her that I could not understand why I was so drawn to him. It was10 years after his death and I had finally began to feel like he was really dead. I began to cry uncontrollably. Khiara was kind enough to listen to me with no judgements. I always "believed" Tupac was coming back someday. 14 years later I would finally realize why I felt that way and why I was drawn to Tupac.

2006 • Javet and her Sister Cherri

I went from **sleeping in my car in the parking lot on the roof of the gym**, to renting out a small room in Javet's apt. Her sister Cheri lived there too. We had a lot of laughs and good times. Javet is a platonic friend who I have had since high school. We must have known each other since at least 1994 or 1995. I remember meeting her through my cousin **Jacqueline** who is born on my birthday October 25th (page 53). In May of 2014 Javet would stop by to see me after not seeing each other for many years and during that meeting we would share a special **coincidence** with a spiritual old man I met named Mr Nature (page 291). 13 years from now I will graduate as a **Kemetic Yoga** instructor on Javet's birthday, July 1st 2018 (page 472) and 2 days later on July 3rd my past life as **Emmett Till** will be revealed to me. **(See page 463)**

November 6th 2006 - Crunch Fitness

I got a job at Crunch gym in late 2006. I was so motivated to work that I became one of the top producing trainers quickly. I began to make a lot of money but my living situation was still shaky so sometimes **I slept in this gym too**.. I met an **Armenian** woman in this gym and her and I would do all sorts of crazy things in the gym, at the movies, in a club, and even in the park, but never in the day time always after dark. She would also let me stay at her place sometimes. It was early 2007 that my father got an apt in Harlem but because I needed one he gave it to me. Coincidentally my apt was only a few blocks from this **Armenian** woman. In the year 2010 I would become **hermit** for many years and in 2018 I would realize my **past life** as **Emmett Till**...... During these years as a hermit I would argue with my cousin Dula about religion often (page 180). In 2019 he got a job as the Super in a building and of all the buildings in Harlem, he got a job in the building the Armenian woman used to live in.

Rau nu Prt m heru Iu f Per f m heru

The only way I can explain my love for Monique is a **past life**. I must have known her in a previous life but in 2006 this concept of previous lives was foreign to me and the furthest thing from my mind. I'm not sure but I think it was facebook that reconnected Monique and I again and when we saw each other it was like we had seen each other only weeks ago even though it had been 8 years. I think both of us felt our meeting again later in life was possibly opening the door for us to finish the relationship we never really started in high school. We did care for each other back then. The love was innocent and it was real. I wrote in the book earlier about traveling to her during the blizzard of 96 and as an adult I look back on that day (page 60). I felt like I was the only person outside traveling anywhere but I had to be near her. I went to the A train in Far Rockaway but service had been suspended and the busses were the same. By chance I found a dollar van that took me to Jamaica Queens and the trip took forever and a day. **PERHAPS**, my **desire** to see Monique is what caused the driver of the van to take his van out because, **we were the only people on the road**! Just like my experience with Giara Nova in 2010, my desire to site next to her caused the guy to move (p 184). When I got to Jamaica Queens the E train was running but the service was limited. I had to wait forever and another day to catch an E train. Then finally I made it to the city and came all the way back around to Brooklyn were I finally made it to Moniques house.

I was in love with Monique in high school and when I saw her again in 2006 I remembered that love. I remembered that trip in the blizzard of 96. I remembered kissing her and how it made me feel. I told Monique that I was looking for an apartment and I needed a place to stay. She opened her door to me. I stayed with her for a few months then I got the job in the city. I was excited about the new job and I began trying to make money in the gym, then I began to make the money I was hoping to make. Shortly after that I got my apartment in Harlem and I moved out. The Apartment was supposed to be my father's but he passed it to me because I needed a place to live. Then I began to chase women again. I became a top producing trainer in the gym and I barely ventured out to Brooklyn any more but I do remember visiting in 2008 when I got my first motorcycle (page 157). The years between 2005 and 2007 were so stressful that I can't place the exact time when I was sleeping in my car but it was sometime after my sister kicked me out in 2005 and before I got the job at Crunch in late 2006. Before I moved in with Javet (page 147) and Monique I would sleep in my car in the parking lot on the roof of the Bally's gym I worked at. There was a gate that closed the parking lot overnight so it was somewhat safe. After my grand father died in 2009 I was spun on a downward spiral from which my only saving grace was my diligent study and my music. Music was my therapy. When I began to research the past Monique is one of the people I would end up arguing with but she is the only person that I argued with that I was able to maintained the same friendship with. We may not have spoken as often but I never really got mad at her.

Utterances for Coming Forth by day into Light

Monique Hears Dead People

After my past life revelation of Emmett Till came in 2018 (page 480) I called Monique and told her but she was very skeptical at first and that bothered me. I thought she might be someone that would believe me because she knew me and knew I would not make something up. I began to talk to her about the spiritual things I had been experiencing before the past life came and that's when she opened up and told me that she had the gift of clairaudience, but she had asked it to be taken away. **She could hear spirits** (voices) and she would get messages but she didn't want her gift. She said the weight was too heavy to bare so she turned it off. She had asked the spirits to leave her alone and they stopped coming to her. At first I told her that she was wrong for doing that. I told her that I had met many women who shared their gifts with me which allowed my revelation to slowly, step by step be revealed to me. I told her that she had a gift that she should be using. Years later I realized I was wrong for telling another person how to negotiate their life. In 2016 I would meet a woman name **Zee** (page 362) and she would tell me that she could see my **guardian angel** (page 421). In December of 2018 **Zee** would experience random spirits coming to her asking her for help the day after she helped me have a conversation with my guardian angel. It was as if **she opened a door in the spirit world** and somehow spirits knew she could see and hear them. She did the same thing Monique did, she turned it off. It was too much to bare. When I began to tell the world about my past life as Emmett Till I understood Monique and Zee more. In a world where most people have tuned themselves out of the ability to see what can't be seen and to hear what can't be heard, you will look crazy if you tell people what you see and hear if they can't see and hear it too. In 2019 Monique would take me to my first **Powwow** (page 578). Even as I write this on February 19th 2022, I feel as if, perhaps Monique and I were meant to be together but I can't imagine that I would have ever realized this revelation had I been in a serious relationship with any woman. I needed to go through my trials and end up in solitude. Perhaps love and relationship is not meant for me in this life. Or perhaps all the guardians that came to me via the other women I met in my journey might have came to Monique had I stayed with her. That, we will never know so who's to say? But my love for Monique will never go away. For more on **Guardian Angels** and **Ka Doors** (**Spirit Doors**) see pages (250 -253, 48, 150,179, 199, 315, 318, 329, 348, 349, 409, 421, 434, 545, 548, 549, 572, 584. 604, 626, 650).

It is he, who comes forth by day into Light

November 25th 2006 (Sean Bell is shot down in a hail of 50 bullets by New York Police)

I don't know what happened the night that **Sean Bell** was murdered. I was 29yrs old when he was murdered. He was **23**yrs old when he was shot four times in a hail of 50 bullets by the NYPD. See page **648** for the **metaphysical significance of the number 23**. Perhaps this case may not have garnered so much attention if there had not been so many shots fired. Why did they need 50 rounds? I was upset when I saw the news but I can't say I spent a lot of time looking into his murder or all the other murders that were happening for that matter. I wasn't reading any books at this time in my life and I wasn't searching. I was dealing with the affects of a decision I made that cost me my job. I was trying to survive in the world. Even though I didn't rally for Sean I never did forget about him and when I picked my pen up to start writing, his name came out of my mind and my mouth several times. Tutankhaten's tomb was opened on **November 26th** 1922 (page 11), the year of the **Dog** and Sean Bell was murdered like a **Dog** the day before that on **November 25th** 2006 the year of the **Dog**. My life as Emmett Till would be revealed to me in 2018 the year of the **Dog** (page 480). On April 4th 2020 my life as Tutankhaten (King Tut) would be revealed to me (page 594).

Condolences

My condolences go out to the family of **Sean Bell** and all of those who have been robbed of their lives by this system of racism and white supremacy. Please know that death is not the end. The soul survives death, indeed and in spirit. This is a book of the dead written by a boy who was murdered without justice, who defeated death and came forth by day. May the soul of **Sean Bell** walk peacefully through the field of Reeds in Amenta. Amen Ra.

2006 Primes Niggas (1st of 1)

So you grew up without ya mom or your dad, maybe both, **keep ya head up**, take the good from the bad, who's next to stand up and help direct the path? before you stand up come take a seat in my class, of fundamentals these are your life tools, gotta get ya lessons lil homie and your values, your morals, direction, discipline, you gotta be loyal to the game too many soldiers died before you, and it's a shame, get your fundamentals then bang on the system, learn your history, come back and bang like **Sonny Liston**, mission statement paragraph one, reverse all conditioning, I been patient, but the time has come for more than listening, actions speak louder than words, *turn down 50 mill like* ***Chapelle*** if it betters the cause, cause in this **white mans world** you gotta fight for a cause, keep your eyes wide shut, and you'll be fight'n his wars, I recruit from the streets I take the pimps and the hoes, give em a new way to think, that's how us Prime niggas operate, foo niggas teach moo niggas got no time to wait, for show niggas want this money like **Bill Gates,** Prime niggas not divisible by anything, Prime niggas be up in the club in any hood, loved by the **Bloods, Crips**, Thugs it's understood Prime niggas come'n to bang up in yo hood

I keep my finger on the trigger, selector lever on semi, this is for my niggas that's down till the d.i.e. I ride for them they ride for me, I mean all the way to z, fuck a A to Y nigga, my brother **C Green** that's a ride or die nigga, only a few men make my list of Prime niggas, Prime niggas be like one in a dozen, I don't trust my own blood my dude, so fuck if we cousins, you gotta earn your respect, too many huff'n and puff'n, all y'all niggas go right, I go **left**, you can't live your life like a house nigga, gotta fight to the death! I mean **M.O.P.** Style P.N.C. **Tek n Steele** style, fall in line if you wanna be Prime now, **look at the sign of the time**, time to make that push, and I'm a lead from the front of the boat that we all on, my lil homies need more than hope to drive on, my aim, to show em that love is not wrong, I love my niggas, sisters, souljas, rest'n in peace **pour out some liquor** and hold ya, fist in the sky I pray that we can all grow to be, Prime niggas not divisible by anything, Prime niggas be up in the club in any hood, loved by the **Bloods, Crips**, Thugs it's understood Prime niggas come'n to bang up in yo hood **- Dawud**

2007 • Crunch Fitness • Tiffany Deriveau

When I got the job at Crunch Fitness on Broadway and Houston in Soho I was told by other trainers that I picked a bad location because was no business there. I introduced myself to every member of the gym offering them a complimentary training session if they didn't already have a trainer. I said the same thing to them all: "Hello my name is D-Train, I'm the best thing since sliced bread. I'm a new trainer here and I'm offering complimentary sessions with no commitment involved. If you like the session you can buy a package of training at a reduced price. My manager has allowed me to reduce my price to build my business." I grew my business faster than anyone had seen in a long time, becoming one of the top producers. Tiffany was a manager at the gym and she had previously never trained with any other trainer but she approached me and asked me to train her. Training her helped build my business because she worked so hard attracting potential business. Actually it was Tiffany and Danielle Kirschbaum. I would train them together, drawing the attention of other members of the gym. Tiffany was like a sister to me. We even slept in the same bed and I made no advance. **She was my Haitian sister** and at the time **I had no knowledge of Haiti and the Haitian revolution**. I had no idea that my experience with the card in 2005 (pages 141-142) was connected to the **Haitian revolution** and would not come to know that until 2014 (p 292). In 2016, while attending massage therapy school, a **Haitian sister** from my Tai Chi class would **dream** of me (p 297) and I would graduate massage school on the same day that the **Haitian revolution** was planned in 1791 (p 450). In 2019 I would meet a **Haitian Yoga instructor** (p 572).

Rau nu Prt m heru

Iu f Per f m heru

Utterances for Coming Forth by day into Light

It is he, who comes forth by day into Light

The King of Clubs and Eternal Life (Ankh)

I used hit the **clubs** with the brothers I met in the gym. Our plans were always the same, go out and look for the best looking females we could find and I was absolutely **lost** in that **"life"** of **aimlessly chasing women**. While in this stupor I remember seeing the **Ankh** symbol here and there and never knowing what it meant. As you can see, Jay had the **Ankh** symbol tatted on his shoulder and I can also vividly remember looking at it and wondering what it meant. Sometimes I'm amazed at how much I didn't know back then. At this point of my **"life"** I was way off the righteous path and Christianity was the furthest I had gone in my spiritual search for truth. Who would have ever thought I was once a **King** named Tut**ankh**aten!

ADDENDUM 2007 There's Something Familiar about Felicia

I had a crush on **Felicia** when we met in high school. She was 7 months older than me and a year ahead of me. I would go to her house after school sometimes and watch tv with her. I always wanted to kiss her but I was too shy so I never did. I never got up the courage or found the perfect opportunity. She went on to have children and a family while I was sleep walking in This **Never Ending Story** of my many lives that ultimately filled the pages of this book. I ran into Felicia when I got out of the army and we started seeing each other from time to time. There is something familiar about Felicia that I can't explain. We love each other but for some reason in this life we never got into a serious relationship. Felicia has a daughter born on **February 7**, which is the same day **Emmett Till's** father was born (pages 475, 518). After I had my past life revelation of **Emmett Till** in 2018 (p 480) she would tell me that she feels like she lived a life in ancient Egypt. Two years later my past life of **Tutankhaten** (**King Tut**) would be revealed (p 594). In ancient Kemet the concept of reincarnation and past lives was called **Wehem-Mesut** (repeating of births, p 14). In 2022 Felicia told me the experience her family had with the **spirits** of her uncle and her grand father. When she was a teenager her uncle died. This uncle lived with her and everyone knew when he was home. He had a habit of coming home late and running up stairs making a lot of noise. After this uncle died everyone in her house could hear loud foot steps running up the stairs at night for months after his death and it frightened everyone in the house. Years later her grand father died. Because of the experience her family had with her uncle they were all anxious about the possibility of having the same experience with the "**spirit**" of her grand father. Because of the anxiety many of them slept in the same room. One night Felicia was talking on the phone while she laid in the bed with her grandmother, then suddenly the door to her room opened and the light switch was turned on but no visible person was there. Speaking of dead grand father, Felicia told me about experiences with her son that cause me to wonder if he is her grand father **reincarnated**. Felicia was bathing her son when a song came on the radio. Upon hearing the song Felicia said, "that was my grand fathers favorite song". Her son replied, "who, Birdie?" Felicia looked at her son, shocked and confused and asked him how he knew that name, but all he did was laugh. She had never spoken to him about her grand father but he had spoken his name in a similar fashion several times. Her son would also say things like, "God doesn't exist". And when he made remarks like that he spoke as if he knew this as a matter of fact. Perhaps her grand father used her son as a conduit to speak to her, like when my **guardian angel** spoke to me through a brother at the **International African Arts Festival** in July of 2021 (p 650). Or perhaps her son is her grand father reincarnated. Souls do come back, like the little girl from Detroit (p 618). Felicia's son is born on March 9th, the day **Biggie** was murdered (p 77). I have had quite a few experiences with spirits and spirits do embody people to deliver messages. I think this might be the origin of the term **"Ghost rider"**. For more on **Guardian Angels** and **Ka Doors** (**Spirit Doors**) see pages (250 - 253, 48, 148, 179, 199, 315, 318, 329, 348, 349, 409, 421, 434, 545, 548, 549, 572, 584, 604,).

2007 - Maurepaz Auguste (The Mambo Kid) The Reincarnated World War 1 veteran

I met **Mambo** at the gym I worked at in 2007. He was a Kick boxer and he used to use the boxing ring we had upstairs to workout. We became friends. I went to a few of his fights and cheered him on. I slept on his couch once when I was homeless looking for an apartment. Mambo is actually the only person I ever sparred with in a ring with gloves on. He called it my baptism. He was elusive and found it easy to touch me but I escaped with no bruises, it was fun. After I left the gym and moved my business uptown in 2010 I stopped seeing and communicating with Mambo. It wasn't until around 2017 that we began to follow each other on Instagram but we barely interacted with each others pages. In the year 2021 we would connect via Instagram. I would share my experiences of **reincarnation** with him. My experiences hit a deep cord with him because of an experience he had had a few years back that made him question whether he had lived another life before.

He told me that he would travel the same path everyday to spar and do other training at the gym. And one day while on his path he saw a giant picture of a group of world war 1 soldiers in an exhibit on 5th ave and 26th street in Manhattan. He said, when he saw the picture for the first time he was struck with a feeling of **DeJa vu**, as he stood there **transfixed**, staring at it for what seemed like forever. When he saw the man in the picture he saw himself and at the same time he sort of knew it was him. Like a foggy **memory**. In this picture he saw 9 black soldiers from the 369th unit out of New York. These men had been awarded the Croix de Guerre for gallantry in action, in 1919. The writing below the picture stated that those soldiers would walk pass the spot they were in when they went to **battle**. He found that **strange** because he felt like his sparring was **battle** and he walked the same path everyday passing this picture. In ancient Kemet the concept of reincarnation and past lives was called the **Wehem-Mesut** (repeating of births, page 14). After Mambo sent me this picture in 2021 and told me his story I looked at the other men and felt I saw other men I knew. One of the men passed away on Dec 3rd 2014.. **Legend has it that Mambo fought to defend Black Wall Street during the 1921 Tulsa Oklahoma riots (Page 407).** In 2022 I went to Kemet for the first time in this life and while there I had **Deja Vu** two times (pages 670 - 671).

Soldiers of the 369th (15th N.Y.), Awarded the Croix de Guerre for gallantry in action, 1919.

The Reincarnated World War 1 veteran Maurepaz Auguste (The Mambo Kid)

Rau nu Prt m heru

Iu f Per f m heru

Utterances for Coming Forth by day into Light

It is he, who comes forth by day into Light

October 25th 2007 - My 30th Birthday Bash

For my 30th birthday I had the first birthday party that I can remember since being a child. I rented out the Lounge **Tillmans** and I invited my family, friends and clients. My clients were my friends too. Many people showed up and **Tillmans** was packed. From what I can remember I had a good time. I felt good about where I was in my life. At the time I was making what I felt was really good money. I had a lot of friends. I was dating several women. I had designer shades on at night.

Monique **Me** **Courtlan** **Dutch** **and Godfrey**

2007 - Q-Tip at The Canal Room

I used to hit the Canal Room, a club on Canal Street in downtown Manhattan. I didn't dance much, I went for the music and the women. I was still a drinker of alcohol at the time. I can't be 100 percent sure exactly what year this was but I was definitely still training clients downtown so it was before 2011. I remember giving my business card to **Q-Tip** several times on different nights at this club. The last time I gave him my card he looked at it, then looked at me and said "**didn't you give me your card before**?". I say yes. He looked at me, rolled his eyes, shook his head, then went back to DJ'ing. I felt a bit stupid. I loved Hip Hop and his song Check the Rhime was one of my favorite songs as a teen. I wanted celebrity clients and I thought training a rapper would have been dope. He was born in Harlem and moved to Queens. I was born in Queens and now I live in Harlem. I would remix the song Check the Rhime in 2016 (page 3**55**). Q Tip is part of the legendary group, **A Tribe Called Quest**….. And here I was **on this quest to find my ancient tribe**. Around 15 years later I would come to know this "tribe" I was from (page 594).

Pharoahe Monch at Tillmans

I once met **Pharoahe Monch** at Tillmans lounge. I told him I was a fan of his music and that the **Large Professor** remix of his song **Stress** was one of my favorite tracks. I told him I was a trainer and gave him my business card. He asked if I did boxing. I told him no but I also told him that I knew a lot of boxers and if he needed a trainer I could refer one to him. I never had a problem promoting and helping other trainers. I never heard back from Pharoahe Monch and when I met him I was not thinking about a "Pharaoh" from Kemet (**Egypt**). I don't think I had ever really given Egypt much thought in my life not even when I went to War in Iraq which was pretty close to Egypt (page 113). Pharoahe Monch is definitely a master word smith and I'm glad I met him because now it makes so much more sense! These elite Hip Hop artist use words in skillful, magical ways. **Heka** is the word for meaningful speech or magic (page 6) and years later I would experience many levels of depression and **stress** which caused me to write rhymes (Heka). By conquering my lower nature I was able to use Hip Hop as a conveyor of my ancient soul fragments leading the revelation that I was once Emmett Till (page 480) and I was once a Pharaoh and my throne name was **Neb Kheperu Ra Heka Maat** (page 594). I only saw **Pharoahe Monch** one time after meeting him at **Till**mans. He was at the **Sean Price** tribute on December 3rd 2015 (page 345). See page 376 for **42 Laws of Maat.**

Rau
nu
Prt
m
heru

Iu
f
Per
f
m
heru

Utterances
for
Coming
Forth
by day
into
Light

It is
he,
who
comes
forth
by day
into
Light

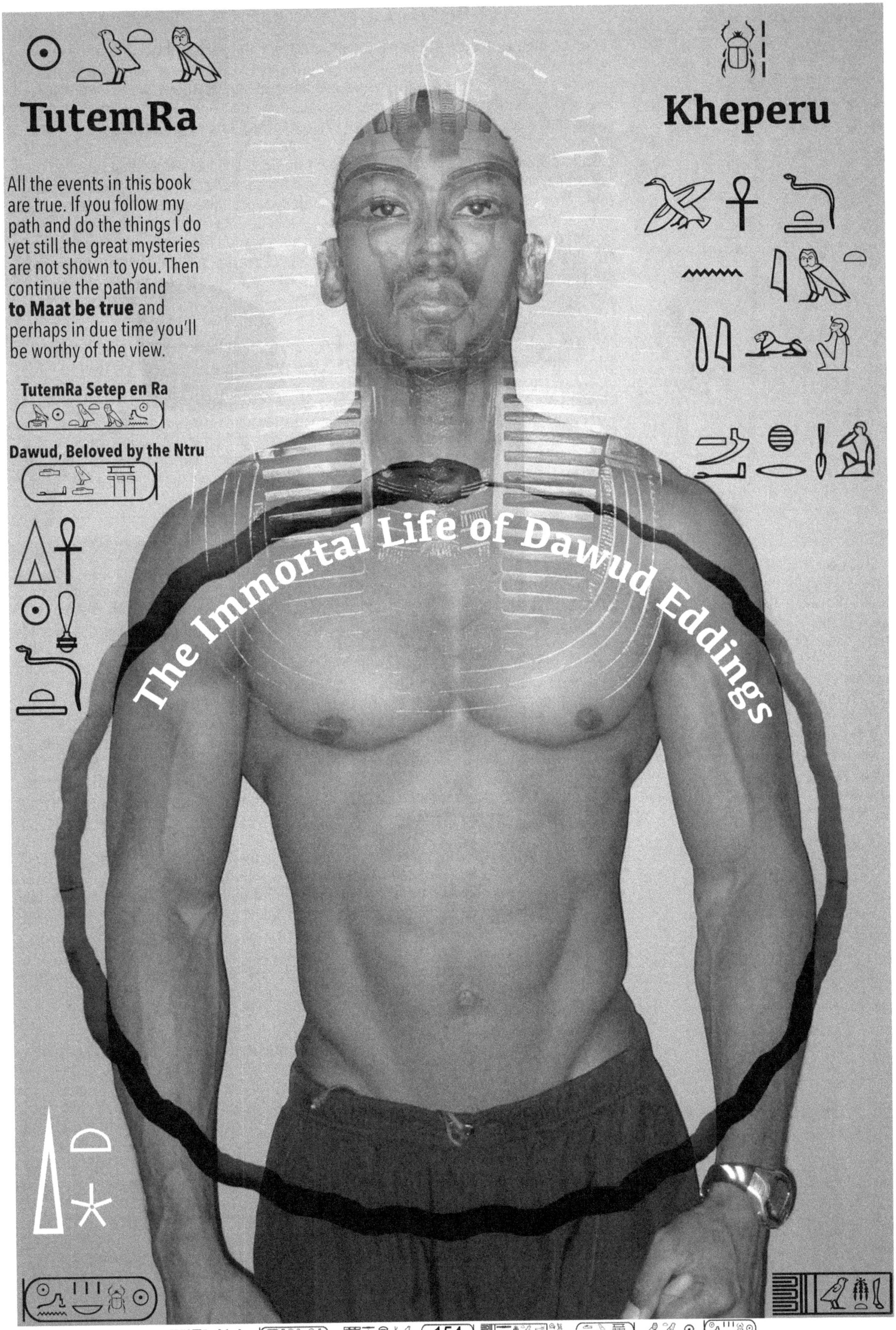

TutemRa
Kheperu
All the events in this book are true. If you follow my path and do the things I do yet still the great mysteries are not shown to you. Then continue the path and **to Maat be true** and perhaps in due time you'll be worthy of the view.
TutemRa Setep en Ra
Dawud, Beloved by the Ntru
The Immortal Life of Dawud Eddings

2007, Migdalia, George Jackson and Delayed Reactions

I don't remember how I acquired Migdalia as a client but I enjoyed working with her. Perhaps she was in her 60's when we met. I think she was Puerto Rican, or perhaps Dominican, but she was a lawyer. She used to laugh at me because I always seemed to fall in love with a new girl so quickly. One day Migdalia gave me a book and suggested that I read it. The book was ***Soledad Brothers, The Prison Letters of George Jackson***. I still have the book and the pages are falling apart. I didn't read any of this book until sometime after my grand father died in 2009. George Jackson would be the first person that I studied on my journey to self awareness as a Black man in America (**Sankofa**). I never read this book completely because I was consuming a lot of information at the time. I read some but I also watched documentaries on him and his brother Johnathan Jackson. After learning about the story of **George** and **Johnathan Jackson** my mind went back to the second verse of **Tupac's** song **Soulja's Story** from his first album **2Pacalypse Now**. I felt like Tupac had used pieces of their story to write that verse however I have never heard that from anyone else and this can't be confirmed.

In 2018 I would have my first past life revelation of my life as **Emmett Till** on July 3rd 2018. **Migadalia was born on February 7,1950, the same day as Emmett' s father (p 475)**. In 2021 while writing this book I would come across the **pattern** that Emmett shares with George. I would realize that **George Jackson** was sent down (born) in **1941** *the year of the snake*, the same year that **Emmett Till** was born. He was from **Chicago** just Like Emmett Till and he was born on **September 23rd** which is the same day that Emmett Till's killers were **acquitted** in **1955**. See page **648** for the **metaphysical significance of the number 23**. George was murdered on August 21st 1971 the day of the Haitian revolution and the same year **Tupac** was sent down (born). I have a theory about who Tupac was in a past life.

2007 Skiing Through Life

The stock market was about to crash but I wasn't really feeling the effects because the types of clients I had didn't feel the effects. I went skiing for the first time because I made friends with people from the gym, people who grew up with different life experiences than I did and had different hobbies. I'm not sure if **Sal** or **Randy** invited me to go skiing first but I have gone with both of them before and I think we all went together once as well. Randy was an investment banker and Sal was a defense attorney. It was **Sal** who helped me escaped the **South Carolina Prison** system on **May 25th** 2008 (p 157). Randy had become more like a friend. Randy would take me to my first yoga sessions. I attended Bikram yoga with him and I remember the first session was agonizing. After 15 minutes I could not believe I still had over an hour left to go however afterwards I felt refreshed and renewed. I liked that feeling so I went back a few times but I was more focused on the women who attended classes than I was with the spiritual benefits of yoga. As I continued my journey things began to change and in 2018 yoga would play a major role in sp**ark**ing my first past life revelation (page 466). Randy was the second client I got when I started working at New York Sports club on wall street in 2006. One day he walked up to me at the gym and asked me what days do I work. At first the question confused me, but then I realized he wanted me to train him. We trained for many years and because of him I met **Rihanna** (page 167). The first client at New York Sports club was given to me by **a disciplined brother** that was leaving that location when I started. I Lost contact with this brother after a year or so of meeting him but **in the few times that we were around each other he made a big impact in my life**. <u>He took me under his wing and gave me tips on how to be a better person and personal trainer</u>. I met him at his studio apartment one day and I saw that he had many books, a skeleton of the human body, he had no bed, just a roll out mat to sleep on.. He **encouraged me to buy books** related to fitness. I purchased a couple of the books he suggested on the anatomy but I never read them. I'm ashamed to say that I have forgotten this brothers name but he was a positive influence on me.

I was a personal trainer but I didn't know exactly where every organ in my body was or the names for every muscle or bone. The only reason I knew where my **spleen** was is because I ruptured mine in high school (p 1**23**). I had a client named **Jesse A. Cohn** who also **inspired me to buy books**. One day I arrived to the gym and the sales associate handed me a note. It was from a member of the gym and the note read, "<u>I want to be a defined Jewish version of you</u>." The note was from Jesse Cohn. I began to train him and he became one of my most dedicated clients transforming his body into that which he desired. One day I met him at his apartment to pick up a payment for training sessions and that's when **I saw his wall of books**. I began to buy books in 2011 and it was his wall of books that I used to think about when I began to build my library (p 265). You never know what affect you might have on someone so always aspire to inspire. It's the little things that count.

Significance

Because of **Sal** (p 165) I escaped the South Carolina Prison system on **May 25th** 2008 (p 157). Because of Randy I met **Mickey Rourke** and by meeting Mickey I met **Rihanna** on July 4th 2009 (page 167). Randy took me to a **Jay Z** and **Kanye west** concert in Madison Square Garden once. The performance was an amazing experience. I went to see **Nas** by myself once on 34th street and the experience was the same.. I would meet with Kanye, Nas and Jay Z in the **dream** realm in my years of awakening.

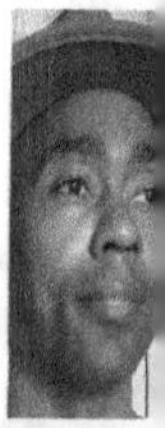

Rau nu Prt m heru

Iu f Per f m heru

Utterances for Coming Forth by day into Light

It is he, who comes forth by day into Light

January 2008

Old friends, and new bad habits (Motor-cycles)

I met **Carti** (**Cartier wrist wear**) through my homie **Jerry Webster** whom I met in College. **Jerry** and I became friends because we both loved Hip Hop. **Jerry** was good at free-styling or at least he was better than me. I got drunk for the first time with Jerry and Carti in 1998 when I was 21 years old. Carti and I only met a few times back in the 90s but we clicked. All we ever did was go out looking for girls together. Now here we are 10yrs later, the **cycle** continues as we start hanging out again **and we're still, looking for girls**. At some point Carti offers me his bike for sale, a **Suzuki TL1000**. I bought it from him with cash money. This bike would lead me to crashing on **May 25, 2008** (page 157), the same day that **my sister dreamt my car accident** in 2002 (page 104-106). Purchasing this bike would also lead me to connecting patterns and ultimately connecting my **past life** (pages 222, 284, 512).

March 2008

Hadiiya Barbel and the Rain that Fell

Here I am with my friend **Hadiiya Barbel** on the left and Candice on the right. Candice was a party promoter that I met at the lounge **Tillmans,** while Hadiiya and I met at a gym in Brooklyn back in 2005 when I first started personal training. I vividly remember speeding up the FDR highway with Hadiiya on the back of my bike after taking the picture below. Hadiiya and I dated briefly and shared a **profound experience** that neither of us will ever forget! It happened one day when we were sitting and talking in my car. We were still getting to know each other at the time and I remember there was a light rain that day. As we began to talk our faces began to get closer and as soon as our lips touched the loudest thunder I had ever heard struck and then monsoon rains began to pour down. The rain drops hit the car in a loud drum like manner as if hail was falling. We both looked at each other speechless and we never spoke of it again until 2018 (page 474) after my **past life revelation** of my life of **Emmett Till**.

Significance

It wasn't until after my revelation of my life as **Tutankhaten** (King Tut, page 594) that I realized Hadiiya was a part of the pattern in both of my past life revelations. I graduated as a **Kemetic Yoga** instructor on July 1st 2018 and that was the day that sp**ark**ed the events that led to my first **past life revelation**. I would cross paths with Hadiiya that day while at the International African Arts Festival right after I had **heard a voice** in my head telling me that I was going to meet a woman. I listened to the voice and proceeded to walk away from my group looking for a woman. I would meet a woman named **Mars.** Mars would invite me to come back to the festival on **Tuesday,** July 3rd. As soon as I left **Mars** I ran into **Hadiiya** no more than a minute later (page 474) . We had not seen each other in person in many years. We would embrace then we spent some time catching up and just before we parted ways we took a picture. Two days later my past life as Emmett Till would be revealed and two years later in 2020 after my past life revelation of **Tutankhaten** (**King Tut**) on April 4th 2020 (page 594), I would come to know that her **two sons** are connected to my revelations. Her first son is born on **August 28th** the same day that **Emmett Till** was murdered and **Ausar** (Osiris) reigned for **28 years** in the **Ausarian resurrection** drama.... Her second son is born February 26th, the same day that **Trayvon Martin** was murdered (page 232), his name sounds like **Ausar** (**the Lord of resurrection**, page 3**)**, he is a trainer like myself and he has a Tattoo of **Nefertiti** on his chest just like **Tupac**. Nefertiti is the step mother of **Tutankhaten** (**King Tut**). I have a theory about who **Tupac** was in his **past life**. The next year Hadiiya would invite me to come to her Goddess Glow Up event and the next day I would have a profound experience at **Malcolm X's** grave that was connected to a **dream** I had on Martin Luther King's birthday (page 560).

March 4th 2008 - Brother C. FreeMan EL

Perhaps I watched my first video of Brother C Freeman EL in 2016 or 2017. I'm not sure but I know I watched a lot of his videos on youtube in 2018 after my past life revelation of Emmett Till. Brother C. Freeman EL was a Moorish Grand master who's wisdom far exceeded his years. He introduced the ancient wisdom of Moorish science to the masses of Afrikan people in the United States. He taught that which the uninformed and European educated can't begin to comprehend. His teachings include the knowledge of self, God and the universe (astrology). His teachings on astrology captivated me the most as well as his deciphering of the scriptures in the bible. He provided answers to the secrets of how to live in harmony with the universe. He explained how we should not wait for a Jesus figure to come save us but instead we should internalize what we read in the biblical text. He taught that the Christ, God and Heaven are found within each person and the book of Revelation was really teaching about the various stages of spiritual development as you become Amen, the hidden God. Sadly he made his transition on March 4th 2008.

Condolences

My condolences go out to the family of **Brother C. FreeMan EL** and all those who fought against this system of racism and white supremacy. Please know that death is not the end. The soul survives death, indeed and in spirit. This is a book of the dead written by a boy who was murdered without justice, who defeated death and came forth by day. May the soul of **Brother C. FreeMan EL** walk peacefully through the field of Reeds in Amenta. Amen RA.

2008 - Prelude to May 25th strikes back
State Trooper Nailed Me at The Cross Walk

I got on my bike and I headed south on the **West**side Highway. Where I was going I don't know but I never got there. I road my motorcycle like I ran the football and since I took the motorcycle safety course and scored a 100 on the road test I thought I was some great driver but I was nothing but reckless. I sped past cars and weaved in and out of them like it was fun, like I was running with a football. When I got off the highway and got to the traffic lights I must have thought I was above the law because I didn't feel the need to stop at the lights. I ran all the lights until I got to 34th street. Then this cab came from the other side of the street and parked in from of me at the light. The door opened and it out stepped a State Trooper dressed in his State Trooper uniform with the long black boots and the Drill Sergeant hat. He told me to turn my bike off and took my key then he asked me for my license and registration. I gave him my license and my military ID because I was trying to win some favor but he looked at me with disgust and sort of threw my military ID back at me and asked for the registration. Then he gave me my key and signaled me to pull off over to the side next to the Javits Center.. When he approached me again he told me that if he wanted to he could confiscate my bike and arrest me with no questions asked. He had clocked me speeding and saw me running all the red lights but he decided to ticket me instead but before he left he gave me a verbal lashing. I thought I had gotten off easy but when I went to pull off I realized that this State Trooper had probably saved my life. My rear tire was flat. Apparently I ran over a **nail** during my trip down the **West**side Highway. This State Trooper was a **White man** and he could have arrested me and taken my bike but instead he gave me a ticket and a verbal warning. He doesn't even realized that he probably saved my life. This will not be my last run in with the police and they weren't always so "nice". In 2011 I will be stopped by police on feet for the first time (page 211). These stop and checks would eventually lead to the raising of my **kundalini** (page 388).

May 25th 2008
May 25th Strikes Back again at Black Bike Weekend

We drove to Myrtle Beach South Carolina to have fun at black bike weekend. When I look back now all we did was drive around looking for women to talk to. Looking for women to enter the course with but fate had another thing in mind for me as **May 25th** would strike again for the first time! It was **May 25th** around 2am or 3am and I remember leaving a club with the 3 guys I went down with. We began to drive around the parking lot looking for women. Then I tried to pop a wheelie on my motorcycle and when I came down my clutch hit my friends bike and broke resulting in my motorcycle rocketing out of control sending me **flying** head first into the front of an SUV truck. There was no helmet law in Myrtle beach and I wasn't wearing one. The impact of the collision **totaled my motorcycle** but I was oblivious to this. As soon as I hit the ground I got up immediately as if I was on the football field. At this point I was in shock but I didn't know it. I tried to get on my bike, I was not cognizant enough to see that the bike was totaled. The owner of the SUV got out and began to yell. My fight or flight instincts kicked in. I was in a daze, my adrenaline was running so I ran. One of the guys I was with picked me up and we sped away into the night.

We went back to our hotel and packed all of our things, then we started making our way back to NYC. I called **Sal**, my friend from the gym (page 165). He was a big defense attorney in the city. I told him what happened. He told me to turn myself in and he would find me a lawyer. I listened to him. We turned around and they left me in Myrtle Beach to face my charges. I turned myself in a day later but I never told the police or my lawyer the full story. I waited a day because I was in pain. My shoulder and my face were very sore. I ran because I had been drinking and I did not know if I was over the legal limit. I did not want to get a D.U.I., but it turns out I was charged with a hit and run.

Rau nu Prt m heru

Iu f Per f m heru

June 3rd 2008 The *Crossroads*

I paid $1000 for bail and $4000 for the lawyer. Then I came back to New York and a few days later I purchased another motorcycle. Our thoughts and desires can affect our reality by influencing quantum level events in time and space. I searched online for the same bike to replace the one I had lost and I found a newer, shinier model of the same bike I had just totaled. I purchased the bike from a white guy in long island. He told me that he just had a baby and he was selling the bike because he needed the money and his wife no longer wanted him riding because it was dangerous. He told me to be careful because they called this style of bike the widow maker because many people had died on this bike. I noticed that he had a **cross** with **Jesus Christ** attached to it hanging between the handle bars. I told him that I was gonna keep that there so I would always have God with me. I paid him then I drove off. I was in long Island so I stopped by to see **Heather**. She saw the bike and told me to be careful. Days later on June 3rd , I would have another **accident,** the day after my sisters birthday.

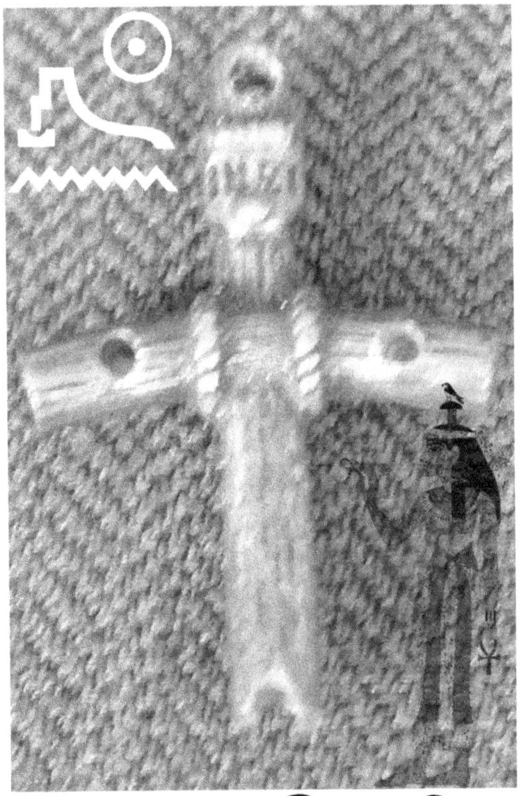

Utterances for Coming Forth by day into Light

Dawud, Beloved by the Ntru

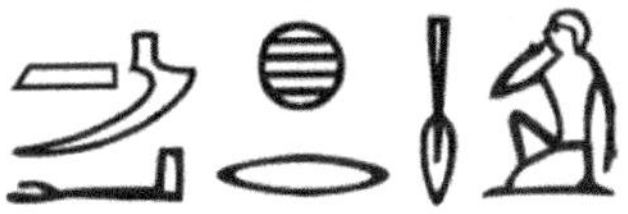

Cross my Heart and Live to Die another Day

It was around 5:50 am, I was riding my bike to the work going south on the FDR highway when a truck started to merge into my lane as if I wasn't there. To avoid getting hit I maneuvered my bike to the next lane on the right. I had no time to look and check traffic I just moved out of reflex to avoid the collision with the truck. The lane I merged in was at the very beginning of the on ramp for cars merging onto the highway on 116th street. Because of this, the car in front of me was moving at a slower rate of speed than me causing me to crash into the back of it. I flew off my motorcycle and **crashed** into the back window of the car. I bounced off the car and **landed on my feet** on the highway like **Spiderman** (Peter-Ptah **Parker**). When I looked down between my feet the **cross** that was on the bike was laying there right between my feet. But **Jesus Christ** was no longer on the **cross**. I picked the **cross** up and I still have it to this day. I suffered no injuries from this accident nor did the people in the car. I left this accident with a sense of being **saved** by God **again** because what were the chances of me finding that **cross** laying between my feet?! The **cross** could have landed anywhere on the highway but it just so "happened" to land where I would land, right between my feet. And what are the chances that I would even notice it but I did notice it and it did land between my feet! <u>I knew that it was **some sort of sign** so I kept the **cross** and told the story to many people</u>. I would not realize that my car accident in 2002 (page 106) and my motorcycle accidents in 2008 were connected by the date May 25th until January of 2011 after I received the child support papers in the mail (page 222). This would be the first **pattern** that I would decode and when it happened I can remember thinking that it reminded me about the TV series **Lost** (page 259, 648). I didn't know what it meant but **I KNEW IT WAS NOT JUST SOME COINCIDENCE THAT MEANT NOTHING. I KNEW IT MEANT SOMETHING, I JUST DIDN'T KNOW WHAT.** Read **Buck Franklin's Eye Witness Accounts From** page 409 and ask yourself why the woman wasn't hit by any bullets . Then read what happened to me on page 548. Then ask yourself how I landed on my feet.

It is he, who comes forth by day into Light

Postlude to May 25th Strikes Back

After the accident on the FDR my bike was in the shop for a few weeks. The same day that I got my bike back I met up with some people I knew who were riding in the city near 42nd street. While I was riding my bike on 42nd street I was hit by a cop who wore a white shirt. He wrote me a ticket and never took responsibility for what he did. I never paid the ticket and was never reminded about it. My bike stayed parked for a month or so until it was finally stolen. My license was revoked and I stopped riding vehicles for 13 years. I would not get my license back until November 1st 2021 (page 610-Bilal). It was like the universe was telling me that I was not supposed to be riding a bike! I reluctantly left bikes alone and I have never ridden one since.

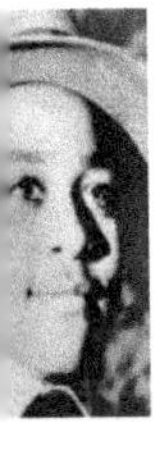

July 12th 2008

Meta Mysterious Encounters - Maat and The Game of Thrones

I once met a woman with the last name **Golden** and when I met her I had never heard about the **Golden** age of Kemet. Her role in my life would not come full circle until I started writing this book in 2020. Like many other people in this book her and I met in such a manner that it can not and should not be seen as "just a coincidence"! I was a trainer at Crunch fitness in Soho in July of 2008 when I signed up for a kettle bells course. The first day of the course all the trainers attending the course got acquainted with each other. There was only around 15 of us and maybe two or three were female in the class. If there were any other females there I don't remember them, I only remember Golden. She was pretty, had a cute smile, seemed very confident and was very shapely. All of the other male trainers were looking at her too. During our lunch break I found my way over to talk to her. She told me that she had just moved to New York two days prior and got a job at the gym and signed up for this course at the last minute. The chances of her attending this class were slim! As we continued to talk I was overcome with the feeling that I knew her, then it hit me, her and I were friends on Myspace! I found that to be strange because I only had around 10 friends on Myspace! I asked her if her last name was Golden and she said yes! Then I told her we were friends on Myspace. She was surprised and we both thought that to be a cool "**coincidence**". We laughed and talked more then we exchanged info. I told my friend Excel, who was also attending the course, that I liked her and that I thought <u>I was really supposed to meet her</u>. After the course Golden and I started dating and later she told me that Excel tried to hit on her the last day of the course. I never got mad at him about that. I guess it's all fair in love and war right? Golden and I became close very quickly and I fell in love with her but the only problem was I didn't really know what love was. In the beginning I knew <u>our meeting was not just happenstance and we met for a reason</u>; **I was sure of it**! I met some of her family and thought I saw a future with her, then something happened and it was over.

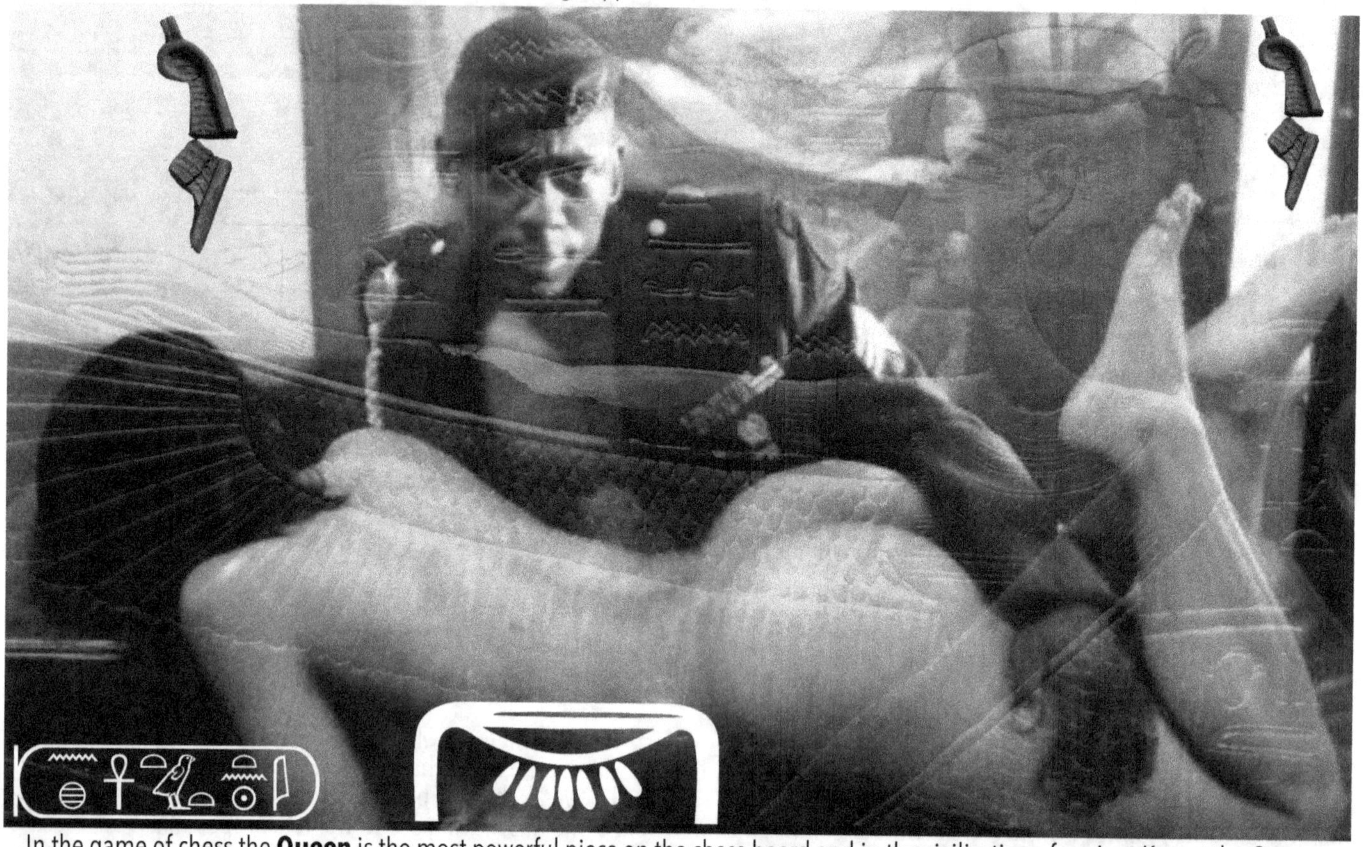

In the game of chess the **Queen** is the most powerful piece on the chess board and in the civilization of ancient Kemet the Queen symbolized the throne. Ancient Kemet was a matriarchal society where the women held the power and to become the Nswt Bity (Pharaoh, King) it was the Queen that extended that kingship. Once becoming the Nswt Bity it was mandatory to uphold the principles of **Maat** (truth, justice, cosmic order, harmonious balance, reciprocity, moral righteousness) and so the Nswt Bity's called themselves the <u>*Lord's of Maat.*</u> The world we live in today is currently a patriarchal society ruled by the male energy and subsequently the world has become a place of war, logic, fear, and other symptoms of left brain thinking. Because the principles of **Maat** have been forgotten by most of the world the women has been abused, molested, betrayed, she's been thrown shade and used for sex and left to raise a nation that won't behave, she's the Goddess giving birth to the grave, but she's the eve of creation, the oracle, the sage! She's the Black Madonna. But I was raised in this society and due to that I fell victim of this mistreatment to women. I chased them because of their beauty and not because of their true value which is found in their souls. Even in a world that tramples the women under its feet it still uses the women to do its bidding when someone wants a man snatched off his throne. I loved Golden but I used her as a trophy. I saw a picture of my friend Netic (page 182) posted with a naked woman on his lap and I wanted to out do him so I took this picture along with many other pictures of us. Years later I would delete them all but somehow this one picture survived, I found it on an old computer. When I look at this picture now I am ashamed of it because it reminds me of men who pose with animals they have killed just for sport. **Now this picture has a new meaning! It represents where I came from mentally when dealing with the divine feminine.** I met with Golden on November 15th of 2021 and told her about this book and asked her permission to use this picture and she agreed. I had not seen her in over 10 years. In a perfect world I would have married Golden in 2008 but I was caught in the ball of confusion back then. However even in my poor handlings of our divine meeting, and our relationship even this picture would proved to be divine. This one picture is actually the **golden master key** that allowed me to receive this revelation of my past life as the Golden Boy Tutankhaten (King Tut)! I met a **Queen** who was **born the day before Tupac died** with the last name **Golden**. I took this picture because I was trapped in my lower nature. Years later I went on a journey with **Maat** as my guide and after changing my ways magical doors opened for me. If I can change my ways then so can you! Just imagine what might be waiting for you if you decide to honor **Maat** and the **Divine Feminine**?! Perhaps an ancient throne awaits you too. **42 Laws of Maat, p 367**

Rau nu Prt m heru

Iu f Per f m heru

Utterances for Coming Forth by day into Light

It is he, who comes forth by day into Light

On **August 28th** 2008, the same day that **Emmett Till** was murdered, then Senator Barack Obama accepted the Democratic nomination for president, becoming the first black man to ever win the nomination and bid for presidency. I remember when I got the news that a black man was running for president. I was stretching a client after a training session when I was asked what I thought about this black candidate for president. The thought of people entertaining the idea of a black president of America made me laugh. Then one day I heard this guy named **Obama** speak and it was like being in church. He galvanized me. I believed in him. I was a believer. I got up early and voted for him. I even made a video of the day I voted and posted it on facebook. Then I went to the inauguration and made a short video about that too. The picture below is a screenshot from that video. When I got to DC for the inauguration on January 20th my homie **Jay Coop** picked me up and we had a good time weaving through all the road blocks that were put in place due to the crowd control. **Coop** and I met at his sisters wedding back in 2005 (page 144). She married my best friend Courtlan. I was the best men at the wedding. I only met Coop two times, and that was at the wedding and when he picked me up for the inauguration but him and I communicated via Facebook. Years before I met Coop he was a Host on the show for B.E.T. Teen Summit. I think it was around 2012 when Coop began to run for local office. Perhaps Obama had inspired him to make political change. I think he ran for City Councilman in DC. I don't recall but Coop was heavily involved with the community as he work with teen pregnancy and local farming for the youth until his untimely death on **December 3rd** in 2014 (page 312). December 3rd would turn out to be the 3rd **pattern** that I became aware of (pages 314, 345, 431, 457). The first being my birthday having met so many people born on my birthday. I was even disqualified from the **Army**

Special Forces School on my 25th birthday on October 25th. The second pattern was **May 25th** which started in 2002 with my sisters **dream** premonition of my car accident that I would have 7 days later on June 1st, my fathers birthday (page 104). Then the 3rd pattern being December 3rd 2014. **14** days after **Coops death** his **spirit** would come to me through the body of a 5 year old boy on December 17th 2014 (page 314). The next year the spirit of my dead grand father would appear to me on Dec 18th 2015 (page 348). Today is December 29th 2021 and the book is almost done but not before I speak of **Benjamin Banneker** and the **Tekhen** (Washington monument) that stands erect over my left shoulder in the picture above. Which represents death and rebirth, which is the soul focus of this book. Perhaps I came to the inauguration to see the Tekhen more than I came to see Obama. I was not technically supposed to be in the spot that I was in when I took this picture. The crowd placement was controlled by specific passes that had been issued prior to the event. I had no pass but somehow I managed to bypass every checkpoint and make it to the front of the speech, less than 50 yards from Obama.

Benjamin Banneker the Magical Astronomer from Mali

I knew I needed to speak on Benjamin when writing about my trip to DC but it wasn't till December 28th 2021 that I realized that there was a pattern, or better, a **star code pattern** connecting me with him. As soon as I looked into Benjamin I saw that he died on my birthday, **October 25th** 1806, then another source said he died on October 9, my grandmother's birthday (page 22). I began to research which date might be the real date and it looks as if my birthday is the more popular date of his transition. Why is this important? Because the men who conceived the idea of Washington DC were trying to recreate the energy they saw in Kemet along the Nile River. What we see in Washington DC is really an attempt to bring Egypt (Kemet) to DC and they needed a Black man who descends from the **Dogon** tribes of **Mali** to bring that vision to fruition. **The White House was built by the same people who built the pyramids.**

Benjamin Banneker the Magical Astronomer from Mali

As time goes by, names, dates and the facts seem to get blurred when talking about the history of America. Especially when dealing with the roles black people have played in fields of progress. Many people who have a passing familiarity with Washington, D.C. know it was originally styled by architect Pierre Charles L'Enfant and Andrew Ellicott after L'Enfant was fired in 1792. L'Enfant took all the plans for the U.S. capital with him however the project was saved by the genius Benjamin Banneker. Benjamin surprised them when he asserted that he could reproduce L'Enfant's plans from memory. Not only was he able to do it from memory, but he was also able to do it in just two days as well as adding his own expertise to the project! He reproduced a complete layout of all the streets, parks, and major buildings. Hidden within the street design Benjamin deliberately incorporated a **hexagram** shape (a 6 point star shape) which in Kemet (Egypt) represented of the land of spirits and the risen **Heru** (Horus). Benjamin was well suited for this role, having already accurately predicted solar and lunar eclipses, sunrises, and sunsets. He was also a highly accomplished mathematician, astronomer, architect and scholar. Benjamin, a free black man in a nation that was still practicing slavery, used his intellect and skill to disprove the theory that blacks were an inferior race. The extent of his contributions to the design and building of the U.S. capital may be disputed in some circles, but the fact that Banneker played an important part in that grand project is a matter of public record. As a young man in 1753, he was inspired to design and build a clock at age **22**, made entirely of wood. His invention was so impressive at the time that it propelled his reputation tremendously, and until today, he is known as the inventor of **"America's first clock"** - which kept perfect time for forty years. For nearly 10 years, he published an annual Farmer's Almanac, for which he did all the calculations himself. His Almanac, won him fame all over the world and he once sent a copy of one of his Almanacs to **Thomas Jefferson** with a letter protesting that the man who declared that **"all men are created equal"** actually owned slaves himself. Banneker's predictions were consistently accurate, except for his prediction of his own death. Living four years longer than he had predicted, Banneker died on my birthday, October 25th 1806, wrapped in a blanket observing the **stars** through his telescope.

The first White House and Egypt on the Potomac

The **White House** was built by the same people who built the pyramids and was named after a Temple in Kemet (Egypt). In Ancient Egypt their treasury was called the "White House" (**Per-Hedj**) in Upper Egypt and the "Red house" (**Per-Desher**) in Lower Egypt." The earliest recorded use of this name was attested from about 3000 BC, early in the reign of the Pharaoh **Den**. 53 out of the **55** people who signed the declaration of independence were freemasons who studied the different sciences of ancient Kemet (Egypt), from math to astrology and astronomy. In ancient kemet many of the temples were aligned with the **stars** above (p 251). In ancient kemet the star **Sirius** was of **major importance**, being connected with the winter solstice's (p 489). **The colors of the American flag** are **Red**, **White** and **Blue** because the star **Sirius** can be observed changing colors, from **Red**, **White** and **Blue**! On 16th street in DC there are more churches and spiritual buildings than any another street in the world. They were trying to duplicate the energy of ancient Kemet because ancient Kemet was the most spiritual place in modern history. Many of the buildings in DC have Kemetic science hidden with in the designs. There is a water fall in Meridian Hill Park which is shaped like an **Ankh** with **Tekhens** placed at the four corners of the entrance of the park. The Ankh represents **Eternal Life** and the Tekhen represents **Rebirth** and **Resurrection**. **Papyrus** and **Lotus Flowers** are planted around the water fall each year and they are the national plants of ancient Kemet. The lotus flower is the flower of **Rebirth** in ancient Kemet. The Scottish Right building is full of masonic numerology and has two western style **Sphinx's** in front of it with **Ankhs** on them. The top of the building is designed in a step pyramid shape taking you back to the step pyramid of **Saqqara** (p 670). The church across the street from the Scottish right building has the **flower of life** symbol on it. The Flower of Life is a geometrical design that consists of 19 circles of the same size that are interconnected. The image looks like a set of equally proportioned flowers. The composition is not only beautiful; it has profound symbolic meanings for our existence, life on Earth, and the formation of the Universe. When you go to DC you are looking at Kemet (Egypt) on the Potomac River.

Resurrection of the Tekhen (Obelisk)

In ancient Kemet (Egypt) the story of **Ausar** (**Osiris**) being trapped in a box by his brother **Set** and thrown in the river is symbolic to the Christian "**baptism**". All human beings are divine and are **baptized** by the life giving waters (amniotic fluid) of our mothers womb however the Christian **Baptism** is a ritual that is based on the belief that every human being is born in sin due to the actions of Eve (the female) so they must be **dipped into water to cleanse their soul**. In 418 "AD" the Catholic church council decided that every human child is born demonic as a result of sexual conception and damned to hell if not **baptized**. This belief system was a misinterpretation of what was seen on the walls in ancient Kemet (Egypt). The concept of **baptism** originates in Kemet (present day Egypt / parts of Sudan). It was not the submersion into a pool as Christians erroneously practiced, but the pouring of water over the initiate to symbolize cleansing to begin his/her transformation into the pursuit of becoming **Ausar** (the Supreme Being dwelling in Man). The ancient Kemetyu state that, the only path to Afrikan power is the worship of the divine Godself. In ancient Kemet the divine Godself was called Ausar, the Lord of the Perfect Black. He is the Supreme being dwelling in man, the immortal soul that never dies. **Re-member** that **you** are **Ausar** and **Heru, the hero!** See page 3 for the **hero's journey!** The Kemetyu understood that there was no death only a repetition of the soul also known as **reincarnation** or **resurrection** (p 14). The Tekhen was another symbol of **resurrection** and when a person was raised from the water after **baptism** it was symbolic of the Tekhen being raised into place. This is why the **Washington monument** stands in front of a large pool of water next to the Potomac River but it will take more than this replica to cleanse America of it's sins. I was always a seeker of truth even as a little boy and that is why I decided to get baptized at 11 years old (p 49)!!.

Rau nu Prt m heru

The Analemma and Infinity

If you took a picture of the Sun every day of the year, at the same hour and from the same location, would the Sun appear in the same spot in the sky? This is the same question the ancient Kemetyu (Egyptians) asked over 10,000 years ago and this is what led to the creation of the Tekhen (Obelisk). They noticed that the sun was rising at different points each month and after a years time it formed a figure **8** sign. Today we call this phenomena **analemma**. This is part of why the Tekhen is connected to resurrection and immortality. The number **8** is the number of infinity. The Tekhen is a tall, four-sided, narrow tapering monument which ends in a pyramid-like shape or pyramidion at the top. Their moving shadows formed a kind of **sundial** indicating the passage of time, enabling people to partition the day into morning and afternoon. The **Tekhen** also showed the year's longest and shortest days when the shadow at noon was the shortest or longest of the year. Today the analemma is considered by many to be one of the most difficult and demanding astronomical phenomenon to image because astrophotographers need to dedicate an entire year to the project. It requires diligence to take images 30 to 50 times throughout the year at the same time of day and same location. A combination of the Earth's **23**.5 degree tilt and its slightly elliptical orbit combine to generate this **figure "8" pattern** of where the Sun would appear at the same time throughout the year. **Genesis 1:14** reads - "And God said, Let there be lights in the firmament of the heaven to divide the day from the night; and let them be for signs, and for seasons, and for days, and years". Perhaps this **analemma** phenomena is the origin of that passage.

Iu f Per f m heru

Analemmas Sundial phenomena

Above is a picture showing the position of the sun in the sky at noon at one specific locale measured throughout the year and the shape of a figure 8 can be seen. The number **8** represents infinity or immortality. The remains of Tutankhaten (King Tut) were found in the Valley of the Kings and were stored as KV**62**. 6+2 = **8** (p 41, 508). This book is about the immortality of the soul, like the snake swallowing its own tail, which represents infinity. Like the Kemetic (Egyptian) NTCHR (Deity) **Heh** seen seated on a basket holding a pair of notched palm branches which represented the year. On his arm hangs the Ankh which represents **eternal life.** Heh symbolizes untold infinity numbers of years. The image of NTR Heh was found on the back of one of Tutankhaten's royal chairs (throne) in 1922. My past life as **Tutankhaten** (**King Tut**) will be revealed to me on April 4th 2020 (page 594), the same day that Martin Luther King was assassinated (page 69). And in 2023 the significance of King Tut's royal chair would intensify (page 472).

Utterances for Coming Forth by day into Light

2009, Kate's Dream

(Still Dreaming Remix, page 438)

U TOUGH BOOTCAMP, was the first group class that I started when I began to break away from the organized gym facilities. The first park I trained in was Tompkins Square Park in the lower east side. I trained clients at 6 am in the morning. Kate was a regular member of the class and I think Kate was the first woman other than my sister to ever tell me she had a **dream** about me. I can remember her telling me her dream after my 6 am class but I don't remember the dream fully. She either dreamt that I was with **Kanye West** or I was with **Tupac**. Around this same time I had a dream about Kanye West and I remember that dream clearly (page 163). The next year I would try to open a gym with another trianer but that didn't "work out" (page 183).

It is he, who comes forth by day into Light

Still Dreaming Remix, page 438

2009 - 1st Dream with Kanye West

I dreamt that I walked into I big white church and there inside was a very long table that seemed to stretch the entire length of the church. Kanye West and I sat at the table and when it was time to leave there was some sort of Lamborghini car parked outside. Then I woke up.

Significance

Kanye crashed 2 days before my birthday, October **23**rd 2002. I crashed 7 days before his on my fathers birthday in 2002 (p 106). In Kanye's song: Through The Wire, he says the name Emmett Till. It was the video for this song that would help him get a release date for his album sparking his rise to fame. This would be my first of several dreams that I would have with Kanye, the last dream being in 2022. Why is he appearing in my dreams? Kanye and I are both born in 1977 the year of the **snake** and I would use a lot of Kanye's beats to rhyme over when I first started writing again in 2010. Dreams take place in the underworld and **Ausar** is the Lord of the **west,** Lord of the underworld. Kanye is from **Chicago** like **Emmett Till** and his last name is **West**. On July 3rd 2018 my **past life** as Emmett Till is revealed to me (p 480). In the ancient Kemetic (Egyptian) Ausarian (Osirion) resurrection drama, Ausar (Osiris) was known as the Lord of the **West** and the Lord of **resurrection/Reincarnation**. **Re-member** that **you** are **Ausar** and **Heru,** the **hero!** <u>See page 3 for the **hero's journey!**</u> Death was called "**Westing**" in ancient Kemet because we did not believe that death was the end, instead we understood that just as the sun rises in the east and sets in the west, the soul is born into a body then leaves the body but just like the sun comes back the next day, the soul comes back to live another life. So **west** was where the soul (BA) went when we "die" but the soul rises again in the east. This concept of resurrection was called the **Wehem-Mesut** (repeating of births, p 14). Kanye performed at the 2010 BET awards wearing a gold chain with a giant **Heru** pendant (in falcon form). **Heru** is the son of Ausar and he is the one that returns as Ra through **resurrection**. On April 4th 2020, the day Martin Luther King was assassinated (page 69, 592) my past life as the Pharaoh Tutankhaten (King Tut) was revealed to me (page 594). **Martin Luther King** wrote a theology paper on the Ausarian resurrection in 1949 (p 593) and he rose to prominence after the murder of Emmett Till. See page **648** for the **metaphysical significance of the number 23**.

February 5 - February 9, 2009
Cancun, CEO's and a bad trip to Mexico

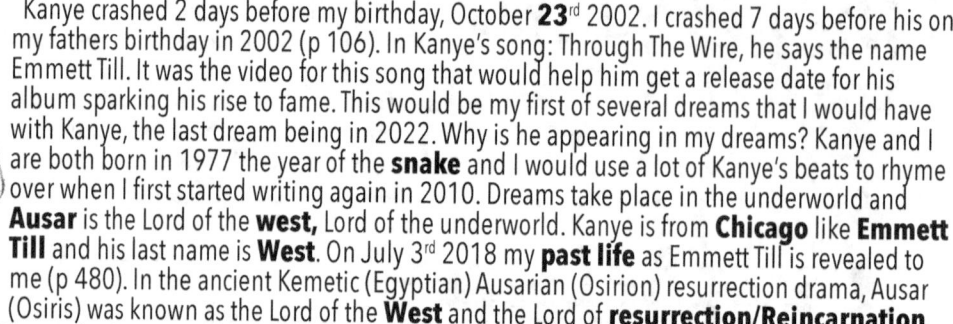

I had a client who was a the CEO of a Hedge Fund. He told me that his secretary was cute and single and indeed she was. He arranged for us to meet. I do not remember where we were introduced but I remember that I used to go see her at her apartment and we would enter the course then stuff ourselves with food. She invited me on a trip to Cancun with a couple of her friends who were in a relationship. Her and I didn't know each other well and that revealed it self while on this trip. We got into a meaningless argument that spoiled the trip and we never spoke again afterwards. I think I took these pics after we fell out with each other. I do not know which ancient sight this is but I do remember being interested in seeing a "**Pyramid**". We were not allowed to walk on them but as I type this I began to remember walking around them. I looked at these magnificent stone structures and had no real clue as to what I was looking at. I was so consumed with matters of the flesh that I missed the opportunity to take in the magnitude of this moment. Years later in 2011 I would start paying more attention to the past with ancient Kemet (Egypt) being my primary area of interest. In 2022 I would go to Kemet (Egypt) and have profound experiences (page 669).

Rau nu Prt m heru

February 2009
-$800 Miller Time 1/7 Communication

I met a brother in the gym who was into real estate. We got a lone well. One day I got a call from him, he was In dire need of money. He needed to borrow $2000.00. He told me he needed it for rent because he got hit with child support and couldn't pay his rent. He came to meet me at my apartment and I lent him $800.00. That was the last time I ever saw Miller. I was suppose to get the money back in a week or so but I wouldn't get the money back until 2017 the same day the Tupac biopic previewed in theaters.

9:25pm **Dawud** – "was up bro? any good news?" 9:26pm **Miller** – "i may have something for you in a couple a days it wont be all of it but i could put something in your hand." 9:26pm **Dawud** – "thats good news, keep me posted. Ttyl." 9:27pm **Miller** – "cool."

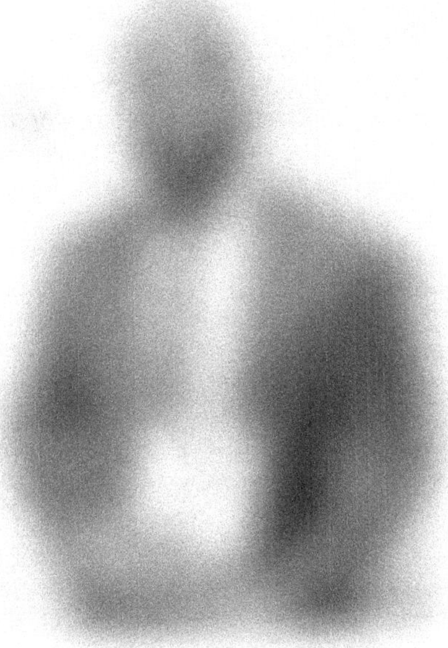

Next communication Oct 2009 page 174

Iu f Per f m heru

2009 - Amanda (Cassiopeia) and August 14th 1791

I did what you're not supposed to do. You're not supposed to fall for your client but I fell for Amanda. This was back in 2008 or 2009 when I worked at Crunch gym in Soho. Her and I always had good sessions and I was pretty sure that she liked me too. We hung out at least one time at a club I know because I still have the picture. I remember going on a run with her outside once and I even attended service with her at her church once. Her church reminded me of the small churches I had been in on my quest for a relationship with this thing we call God (pages 92, 126). While at her church I could tell immediately that she had an attraction to the guy that ran the choir or who was on the choir. After seeing that I withdrew my attraction to her and some time after she had changes in her life that took her away from training. I would not see or hear from her again for 5 years. In October of 2014 I would reactivate my Facebook account. I developed a habit of deactivating my account to step away from social networking from time to time. I went on for one day then deactivated it again but within the time that I logged on Amanda messaged me. She said that she had been thinking about me and wanted to start training again. We exchanged numbers and set up a session (page 304). Amanda would train hard and see quick results. She would also bring me the pattern with August 14th (page 304). Her pattern was so precise that it involved my high school sweetheart that I had not seen in over 14 years (page 305). Amanda's middle name is **Cassiopeia**, which is one of the **Greek constellations**. In Greek mythology Cassiopeia was the wife of **Cepheus**, the mythical King of **Ethiopia**. Together they are the parents of **Andromeda**. Currently, Earth's pole star is **Polaris**, a star in the northern circumpolar constellation of Ursa Minor (little dipper). The precession of the equinoxes is shifting and the northern-most tip of **Cepheus** is a mere 1.5° away from the pole. Cepheus lies in the far northern sky and by 7500 AD, Cepheus's brightest star Alder**amen** will become the pole star.. To fully understand the symbology of why Amanda (**Cassiopeia**) and I gravitated to each other you must read what **Minister Brown** told me in 2021 about Cepheus and his experience with a light in the night sky (page 518).

Utterances for Coming Forth by day into Light

It is he, who comes forth by day into Light

May 21 - May 26, 2009 London

I met **Sal Paszynsky** at Crunch gym and we became gym buddies. If it weren't for Sal I wouldn't have favored well when I totaled my motorcycle in 2008 (page 157). He is responsible for calling the attorney in South Carolina who bailed me out of jail. If I didn't have another "white" attorney to vouch for me I might have had to wait until I could get in touch with a person to bail me out. After Sal did that favor for me I was grateful and our friendship grew stronger. It's no surprise to me now when I consider the fact that Sal has a sister named Kari who's born on my Birthday, October 25th. This is how my life has been. People who have crossed my path as helpers have also come with **star codes**. Sal is born on October 27th. When he told me he was going to London and invited me to come, I agreed. I had the money and didn't know what to do with it so I went to London on the spur of the moment. Sal was going to London with his colleague and gym partner Richard who was also a lawyer. We must have stayed in London for five days. Sal and I shared the same room with two small beds while Richard had his own room. During the trip Sal and I spent more time together while Richard did his own thing, he'd already made plans with men he'd communicated with online prior to the trip. We all went out to eat together two or three times and we also went to the **London Museum** together and did a few tourist things like ride the London Eye (the **Millennium Wheel**). Sal and I went to a club together one night and the few nights that I spent alone I spent them aimlessly chasing women. I went to the **London Museum** but **I don't have a memory of viewing any of the Ancient Kemetic (Egyptian) artifacts. At the time my mind was not yet orientated to Kemet!** This trip would prove to be important because in 2015 (page 351) I wrote about all the experiences I have had with homosexuality in my life and if I **hated gay people** I could have never gone on this trip. This shows that my views on homosexuality do not come from a place of hate. Working at the gym I met many men who were gay and I never treated them different. That was their way and I had my way. In fact I can remember an incident I had with a brother named **Pharaoh,** who frequented my gym. He was a trainer with a tattoo of a dragon or a snake on the side of his head. He also had a small patch of hair on the top of his head. I guess I was desensitized because one day I said a **gay joke** to Pharaoh insinuating that he was gay and he did not take kindly to it. **He looked at me with piercing eyes** and said, **"don't you ever play with me like that again"**. I never forgot that and it caused me to question why I would even joke that way. I never made another joke like that and ever since that day I don't take kindly to gay jokes either. Pharaoh's grand mother is born on July 25, **Emmett Till's** birthday. I saw that posted on his Facebook page (**Pharoah Masters**). Pharoah is born on September 24, the day after the Emmett Till murder trial ended (pages 516-517).

June 25th 2009
Michael Jackson Goes West
This is what the sky in New York City, Union Square looked like the day Michael Jackson went west.
The Great Michael Jackson

Michael Jackson! I do not need to tell you the greatness of Michael Jackson but I'm sure I can tell you a few things about him that you might not know! Two months after Michael transitioned there were rumors circulating amongst his fans about his possible **reincarnation**. An Egyptian **bust** from a museum began to garner attention as it bore a striking resemblance to Michael Jackson. Due to all the new attention there was much speculation about the identity of the person depicted in the bust. It seems that the **bust** was tracked to the New Kingdom of ancient Kemet (Egypt) and was most likely crafted under the reign of the **Pharaoh Tutankhaten (King Tut)** from the 18th Dynasty, the same person writing this book. On Nov 26th 1991 (year of the **Goat**) Michael Jackson would release the album **Dangerous** on the same day that King Tut's Tomb was opened (Nov 26th 1922, p 11). The song ***Remember The Time*** would be the second single released from the album on Jan 14th 1992. I'm sure some of you reading this are born on January 14th. Happy born day to you all. The video for the song ***Remember The Time*** was set in ancient Egypt and the **throne** that the Pharaoh (Eddie Murphy) sat on in the video was a replica of one of **King Tut's** thrones. Michael can also be seen wearing a belt buckle that bears the name **Neb Kheperu Ra** in Mdw Ntr (hieroglyphics). Neb Kheperu Ra is King Tut's throne name (page 670). On April 4th 2020 my past life as Tutankhaten (King Tut) is revealed to me (page 594). Michael is born on Aug 29th 1958 the year of the **dog**, the day after **Emmet Till** was lynched (Aug 28th 1955). On July 3rd 2018 the year of the **dog,** my past life as Emmett Till is revealed to me (page 480). In 1997 Michael released a short movie titled **Ghost**, in the movie he played a cruel Mayor that resembled Sheriff **H.C. Strider,** the Sherif who work along side the defense during the Emmett Till murder trial helping Emmett's killers go free. Strider testified for the defense claiming that the body pulled from the Tallahatchie was that of an adult rather than a 14 year old boy (page 515). Michael was never afraid to speak truth to power, just a year prior he released the song **They Don't Really care about Us** and in the video he showed images of cops beating Rodney King. Within the pages on this book I will share **dreams** from many different people including myself with many of the **dreams** being premonitions or memories involving my journey towards this prophecy. When reading this book you should start to question what a **dream** really is (page 30). In 2001 *the year of the **snake**,* **Michael Jackson** was almost **assassinated** but he was saved by a **dream**. He had a meeting at the World Trade buildings on Sept 11th 2001 (**911**) the day that the **Twin Towers** were bombed (page 99). The day before the that, my father had a dream that people were jumping from a burning building. **Michael Jackson** missed his meeting because he "overslept". A month later Michael Jackson's last album **Invincible**, was released in **scorpio** season, on Oct 30th, 5 days after my birthday (Oct 25th 1977) and 5 days before the discovery of Tutankhaten's (King Tut's) tomb (Nov 4th 1922). Over the years I said Michael's name **23** times in my music (page xi) and the first time I said his name I also said **Emmett Till's** (page 187). It would not surprise me if the person in the **bust** above was Michael Jackson in a previous life, however, I can't tell you about the measure and movements of another persons soul. Except of course for my theory about **Tupac** (page 664). I hope that you all ***Remember The Time*** (page 7).

Billie Jean, DNA, and Birthmarks but "THE KID IS NOT MY SON"

Michael Jackson owned half of Sony Records, he owned the **Beetles catalog**, and a portion of **Elvis's** music. He was accused of **pedophilia** in the 1990's when he was about to purchase **Marvel Comics** (page 58) and refused to sell back his rights to Sony Records. This is no coincidence! **Bill Cosby** (pages 313, 370, 371) was accused of sexual misconduct when he attempted to purchase NBC and when he refused to allow an oil company to drill under his home. **Sam Cooke** was the first black artist to own his **Master**. He told Martin and Malcom that he would finance the **Civil Rights Movement** and afterwards he was murdered. **Jimi Hendrix** was going to finance the **Black Panther Party** (page 274) but "died" in a mysterious drowning. It was after **Whitney Houston** (page 230) began to look into her royalties and attempted to get her **Masters** and publishing back, that she "died" in a mysterious drowning. I fired a client once because of the things she said about Micheal Jackson. She believed what she'd heard on the **tell-lie-vision** and because of that she hated him. I knew I could not trust what the media told me about a black man or black person so I never believed the allegations and I never will. For those who do give value to the "news", read these words of **Malcolm X** very slowly: "If you are not careful, the newspaper will have you hating the people being oppressed, and loving the people who are doing the oppressing." The interesting thing about this client was what she taught me about **DNA**. Before I started training her I came across info claiming that the **wombmen's body** has the **ability** to **store the DNA** of every man they engage with sexually. This info was **confirmed** with her first hand experience. She told me that, when she was around 20, she was in love with her boy friend, their families were close and marriage was planned. Unfortunately her boy friend was sent to prison for many years and she immediately ended the relationship because she could not see her self going to a prison to visit him.. She felt she would never find a love like this again but years later she did fall in love again. She got married and had a son. The son was born with an identical **birthmark** on the same hand as her ex-boyfriend who was still in prison. She had not seen or heard from him in many years yet the son she had with a completely different man had the same **birthmark**. When I heard her story it amazed me. I thought back to what I had heard of Amazon women and a time when women ruled the planet. Perhaps, if done correctly, the Women has the ability to be selective in her mating so as to bring about the greatest potential in childbirth. I don't have any children, but perhaps some children walk the earth with a little portion of me in them. Who knows? Because in my hay day, I got around like **Tupac**.

Condolences

My condolences go out to the family, friends and fans of **Michael Jackson**. Please know that death is not the end. The soul survives death, indeed and in spirit. This is a book of the dead written by a boy who was murdered without justice, who defeated death and came forth by day. May the soul of **Michael Jackson** walk peacefully through the field of Reeds in Amenta. Amen Ra.

I was dating Susan, a Persian woman born in London, but if you spoke to her you would think she was Black. Two of her male friends from London, **Chris "Bigga" Biggs** and **Emile Heskey**, were visiting New York and she asked me to take them out. So I did. Prior to meeting up with them in the city I drank a bottle of Riesling by myself while getting ready. We planned to meet up at **Till**mans which was my favorite lounge at the time. I had my 30th birthday party there a few years back (page 153). I knew the owner, the bar tenders, the promoters and the security at the door.

We met up at **Tillmans** and got aquatinted. **Bigga** was tall and had a lively spirit. **Emile** was a professional footbal player in England and I noticed that he had a lot of money on him (seen in picture below). I remember having around a grand in my pocket but had no intentions on spending it all. The bar tender whom I knew well made my usual drink. I don't remember what it was but I drank it. We stayed there for a short time then I took them to the rooftop bar at the **Gansevoort Hotel** in the Meat Packing District. While there we had more drinks. At some point someone invited us to the club **1 Oak**.

We went to club **1 Oak** but we couldn't get in.. **1 Oak** was known for making non white customers pay more to get in but we couldn't even buy our way in. Here we are, three black men standing there while other people are walking in. Then all of a sudden the most beautiful thing I had ever seen walks by me. At first I did not know who she was. Then she passed me and I saw the stars on her neck. It was **Rihanna**! I wanted to meet her but that wasn't happening we were stuck outside. The night looked to be over and just as we were about to leave a limo pulls up and out walks the actor and boxer **Mickey Rourke**. I met Mickey several times while working out at the **Equinox** gym with my client and friend Randy (page 155). Mickey was getting in shape to play the villain in the movie ***Iron man 2***. The first time I met Mickey he walked up to me and tells me that I had an amazing physique and that my father had given me incredible genetics. I laughed and thanked him. We talked a little, **he gave me his card** then he left. Afterwards Randy asked me if I knew who he was and I said "no". Then Randy told me he starred in the movie **Gridlock** alongside **Tupac**. Randy knew how much I loved Tupac. I would run into Mickey 2 or 3 more times at that same Equinox gym and when ever we saw each other we would speak. I tried to get him as a client but he said he already had a trainer in Miami.

[I have not met many "celebrities" in my life and definitely not in the manner in which I met Mickey. I once met **Dwayne "The Rock" Johnson** while working out a Equinox as well, 59th street location. He had some of the biggest arms I had ever seen in person. I looked at him and said, "can you smell what The Rock is cooking", he looked at me, raised his eye brow and smiled. The Rock's second movie role was in the movie **Scorpion King**, where he played The Scorpion King (p 2). I am a scorpio and the oldest Pharaoh's are scorpion Kings.... **]**

So here I am standing out front of the club 1 Oak with two brothers that I had just met and we can't get in. We were planning to call it a night then that limo pulls up and out walks Mickey Rourke! I was surprised to see him but immediately I yelled, "Yo Mickey"! He looks at me and replies "D-Train"! We laughed and embraced. He asks me what I was up to. I told him that we couldn't get in. Mickey says "*fuck that come with us*"! So now we walk in the club and don't even pay to get in. When we got in

the club Mickey went to the VIP section and that was the last time I ever saw him. We are in the club now and **Bigga** and **Emile** are impressed because all looked bleak until I pulled a **wildcard** and got us in! Now where was **Rihanna**?! She must be in VIP! I went to VIP and tried to get in. The security ask who I was with. I told him Mickey. He asked my name and I told him D Train. He went in to get approval but came back and shook his head no. I remember walking away feeling like I was pushing my luck anyway. I found Bigga and **Emile** about to take shots of **Tequila**. I only had one shot but that must have been the drink that caused my **blackout**. My next memory after that was being drunk at the next club.

Rau nu Prt m heru

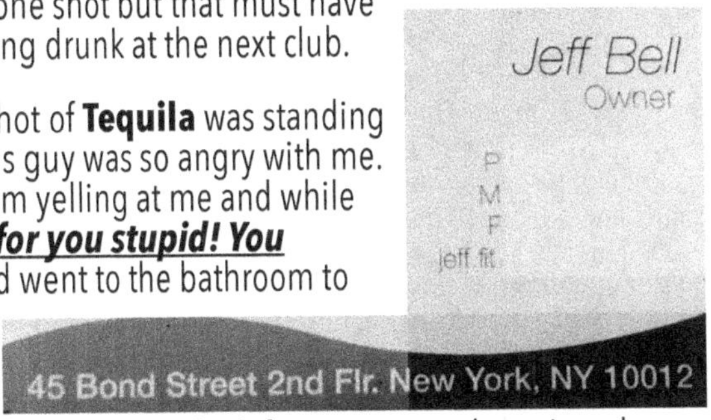

I don't remember leaving 1 Oak. The next memory I have after taking the shot of **Tequila** was standing on the couch at the next club when I spilled a drink on some random guy. This guy was so angry with me. I think he wanted to fight me. I'm sure he wanted to fight. I can remember him yelling at me and while he's yelling at me **I hear this voice in my head** telling me "***This is good for you stupid! You shouldn't be drunk standing on the couch anyways***". I walked away and went to the bathroom to piss and throw water on my face. I looked at my reflection in the mirror and knew it was time for me to call it a night. Without saying goodbye to **Bigga**, and **Emile** I exited the club, got in a cab and went to Jeff Bells loft on Bond Street. I can remember throwing up out the window of the cab, I stumbled up the stairs to the loft. No one was there. I made my way to the back room where I fell asleep on a massage table.

Iu f Per f m heru

When I woke up I was on the floor with my face in a puddle of vomit. My phone was on the other side of the table. I picked it up but it was cracked and broken. I realized there were parts of the night I could not remember. I barely remembered getting to the loft. I checked myself to see if I had had sex but I had no sign of entering the course. I cleaned up the mess, took a shower and went straight to the Apple store on 59th street like a mindless slave and purchased a new iPhone. When I got home and turned the new phone on I would receive the most upsetting messages from **Bigga**. Apparently before we left 1 Oak I had a long conversation with **Rihanna**. I called **Bigga** and he exclaimed **"you are the man!" Bigga** told me that **I had a conversation with Rihanna!** I did not remember this but I felt like I had lost a winning lottery ticket! He thanked me for taking them out. They went back to London and I never saw them again.

ADDENDUM

I have had two **dreams** with Rihanna since this book was released. They were both very interesting. The second dream happened on December 22 2022 and it involved **Tupac**. I won't share the dreams in this book, but if I ever meet Rihanna again I'll tell her.

Serket

Utterances for Coming Forth by day into Light

It is he, who comes forth by day into Light

It is not the fact that I met Rihanna that makes our meeting profound, it is the fact that I would never have met her if I had not met Mickey Rourke months prior (p 167) but having met Mickey would set the stage for the stars to align when he, by chance pulled up right before we left the club. Then somehow I had a conversation with her making our meeting fall into the arena of **fate** or **destiny**. Perhaps she was an ancient Queen or temple singer like Whitney Houston (p 230). It should be noted that **Rihanna** is Bajan and so am I. She is born on Feb 20th, the day after my great grandfather **General Dukes Sr** (p 19), she is born the day before **Malcolm X** died. After meeting Rihanna she would get 3 Kemetic (Egyptian) tattoos that are connected to my **revelation** (page 278). She got a tattoo of King Tut's step mother **Nefertiti** on her rib. Nefertiti is the wife of **Akhenaten**. She also got a tattoo of **Auset** (Isis) on her sternum in the same place that **Tupac** had his "**50 Niggaz**" tattoo.. Auset is the mother of **Heru** (Horus) and the wife of **Ausar** (Osiris) who just so "happens to be" the Lord of **Resurrection**. She would also get an Egyptian **Falcon** tattooed on her ankle and the Falcon is another symbol of Heru, the one who **returns**. The strangest thing of all is that I also have a small connection with her partner, Asap Rocky but I won't place that in this book. If I ever meet them I will tell them. Mickey was a loyal friend to Tupac. When he heard of someone speaking negatively about Tupac this was his response,

"Tell him come see me to my face," he told TMZ. "If you want to talk about my brother when he's not here. You tell any mother fucker on the planet; he got any shit to talk about Tupac, come look me up. OK?" "He was one mother fucking good dude, and if anybody want to talk shit about him, come talk to Mickey Rourke."

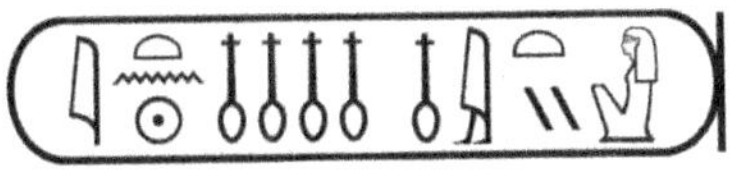

August 18th 2009 - The Death of my Grand Father, General Dukes Jr.

I was not prepared for my Grand Fathers transition in any way shape or form. It marked the first time that anyone close to me had passed. I was living my life and I wasn't thinking about death or life after death for that matter. I was clubbing and chasing women. My grandfather died from stomach **Cancer**. I remember when they said he was sick. I went down to see him and he was very thin. I took the picture below during that time and it is now my favorite picture of him because of the way the sun shines behind him. He knew he was going to die when I took this picture. He had accepted it and so did I. I didn't know about cancer. I did not know you could heal yourself from cancer (page 120). I was too busy making money in the gym and chasing women to be concerned with natural healing modalities. He went to doctors for help like all people were supposed to. I had never heard of **Dr Llaila Afrika** (page 312) or **Dr Sebi** (page 401). It took me many years to realize that Cancer is a highly acidic condition (disease) that is a result poor eating blockages in the lymphatic system. The body is always working in our defense. In ancient Kemet the dead were placed in **tombs**. Cancer cells are dying cells that the body places into **tombs** which doctors call **tumors**. My grand fathers death would mark the beginning of my spiritual journey. After he died I sunk into a depression and in that depression I would start writing rhymes again in 2010 (page 180). In 2011 I started smoking **weed** and I also started **reading** books (page 194).. At some point I came across info about **natural healings** of cancer and I fell into a deeper depression as I realized that if I had started studying sooner I could have possibly given this information to my grand father and prolonged his life. His death angered me even more now. In my mind the business of cancer had murdered him! The doctors failed him! I failed him. In 2011 I picked up the book about **George Jackson** that my client Migdalia had given me in 2007 (page 155). At some point I began to study all the ancestors and they slowly began to appear in lines of my music. At some point I realized that my grand father had died the day after Marcus Garvey's birthday. For the following years I would study the past and write music. I would also begin to experience what people call paranormal phenomena and on **December 18th 2015** my "dead" Grand Father would broaden my perception of this reality we live in. He would appear to me as a **ghost** or **apparition** shining down on me like a heavenly being with bright lights emanating around him (page 348). It is not just the fact that he appeared that left me spellbound but it was coupled by the timing of his appearance that made it so profound. After that I would only see him again in my **dreams** where he is always driving me away from danger. The reality of communicating with dead family members was a common practice in ancient Kemet (Egypt). Ka doors (spirit doors) were built into the walls of the tombs in ancient Kemet (Egypt) as a way to interface between the world of the living and the world of the dead (p 251). The reason why the picture below is my favorite picture of my grand father is because it is the only picture I have of him that reminds me of how he looked when he appeared to me that day. The sun shining over his shoulder reminds me of the bright lights that I saw when he appeared to me. I told all the people in my family about seeing him and most of them just listened in silence and I never felt like most some of them believed me. My cousin Jackie has seen him in a dream too and she is born on my birthday.. For more on **Guardian Angels** and **Ka Doors** (**Spirit Doors**) see pages (250 -253, 48, 148, 150, 179, 199, 315, 318, 329, 348, 349, 409, 421, 434, 545, 548, 549, 572, 584. 604, 626, 650).

Addendum Whoopi Goldberg, Patrick Swayze the movie Ghost, Emmett Till and Beyond King Tut

Whoopi Goldberg was was born in 19**55**, the same year **Emmett Till** was murdered. **Patrick Swayze** played the "**ghost**" (the spirit lingering on after death) in the movie. Patrick is born on August 18th, the same day my grand father **General Dukes Jr** died (page 169). My grand father appeared to me in spirit form on Dec 18 2015 (p 348), just like Patrick did in the movie **Ghost**. 3 days after my birthday, on **October 28** 20**22**, the movie **Till** was released. **Whoopi Goldberg** was one of the executive producers of the movie. That same day, **October 28** 20**22** the **Beyond King Tut Exhibit** opened in NYC (page 29 & 33). I have not watched my movie but I went to my Exhibit on December **22,** 20**22** with Shanta (p 289).

Rau

nu

Prt

m

heru

Iu

f

Per

f

m

heru

Utterances

for

Coming

Forth

by day

into

Light

It is

he,

who

comes

forth

by day

into

Light

Rau nu Prt m heru

Iu f Per f m heru

August 22nd 2009 - Uncle Jimmy Dukes, The Dreamer and the 44th Parallel

The picture to the right was taken at my Grand Father's funeral and it was my first time meeting his brother, my Uncle Jimmy. He's a Vietnam veteran and a 2 time recipient of the Silver Star medal. I don't remember anything we talked about during our meeting and he does not remember taking this picture and I only vaguely remember taking it as I was still in shock of losing my grand father.

Significance

I called with my Uncle Jimmy in 2020 during the **Covid** outbreak to check on him. I asked him questions about his parents so as to pick up some oral family history. He told me about our family who were **Cherokee Indians,** and how they were forced to move out of Alabama to the Kansas and Oklahoma regions during the **Trail of Tears** (forced ethnic cleansing and removal over 60,000 native Americans) around 1831 and around 50 years later they would migrate back after the "Emancipation of Slavery". We talked about life and other things then finally I told him about my **past life revelations**. He wasn't put off by the idea of **reincarnation**. He began to explain how every once in a while he would go to a place that he was sure he had never been to before but some how he would know how to get where he was going with out navigation. He then explain how he would at times **dream things before they happen**. He said that sometimes he would get these gut feelings. He described them as uneasy foreboding feelings before something unfavorable would happen, usually the death of someone he knows. He said that if he ever **dreams** of a hearse or a **casket** then he would usually get news in the next day or so that one of his close relatives was sick or has met death. When his father passed away he knew it before anyone told him. He was serving in the Army station in Vietnam during the war. He was given 14 days leave. He went home and visited his family for 14 days. He left home and went back to Vietnam. The night he got back he took a shower and **dreamt** of a casket but never saw who was in the casket. When he awoke he got a phone call from Head Quarters. They told him his father had passed. He told them that he knew. They didn't understand how he could already know. As you read this book you will come to see how I would in the coming years start to have my own experiences with **prophetic dreams,** as well as other profound experiences like **shared dreaming** (pages 452 & 589). In 2021 I would decode "**The 44th Parallel**" connected with Uncle Jimmy and George Lucas (page 660). This compelled me to go to Alabama to see him and during that meeting he would tell me about his experiences in Vietnam and how he got his **Silver Star Medals**. He would also tell me about my **Great Grandfather General Dukes Sr**.

Utterances for Coming Forth by day into Light

It is he, who comes forth by day into Light

SOLAR BARK, The Boat of Ra

When I was in the 9th grade I made the boat below in my shop class. I gave it to my grand father because he was a carpenter and he kept it on his dresser until the day he passed. Please know that death is not the end. The soul survives death, indeed and in spirit. This is a book of the dead written by a boy who was murdered without justice, who defeated death and came forth by day. May the soul of my grand father **General Dukes Jr** travel safely through the cosmos on his solar bark. May his soul walk victoriously through the halls of Maat on the way to the field of reeds in Amenta. Amen Ra. I am thankful to you Granddaddy. Thank You, Thank You, Thank You. I love you. Thank you for what you did for me on **Dec 18th 2015** (Page 348). Today is January 9th 2022 and so far you are the only spirit I have ever seen in this life. I look forward to seeing you again. Please visit some of the other family members in their dreams.

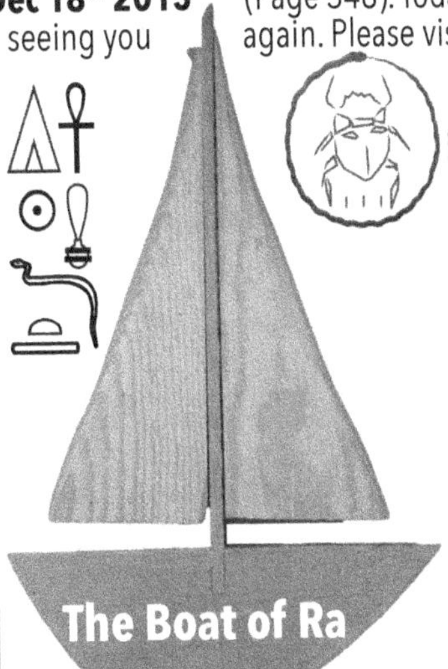

In Loving Memory of those From Former Times

I went to visit my grand mother in November of 2021. While visiting her I looked through the obituaries she keeps in her Bible, hoping to find a picture of my great grand father, General Dukes Sr. (page 19). I never found one but I did have a chance to read the obituaries of family members I never met. I planned on placing their names in this book but I didn't get around to doing so till I did the **revision**. This page is dedicated to the memory of family members from former times. Many of them, I never got to meet. As I read over the dates they were born, the dates they died and the dates of their funerals I saw dates that correlate with events in this book and it was as if they spoke from the other side. Please know that death is not the end. The soul survives death, indeed and in spirit. This is a book of the dead written by a boy who was murdered without justice, who defeated death and came forth by day. **May the souls of those listed below walk peacefully through the field of Reeds in Amenta. Amen Ra**

Gertrude Haynes Childress was my grand mother's aunt and she lived till 100 years old. She was born on **November 27,** 1905, the day after **King Tut's** tomb was discovered and she died on **January 7, 2006** the day after **3 Kings day**, the day **Tyre Nichols** was beaten by police (page 614). Her funeral was on funeral on **Jan 12, Khalid Muhammad's** birthday (pages 93, 223, 355, 360, 440, 443, 554, 666)

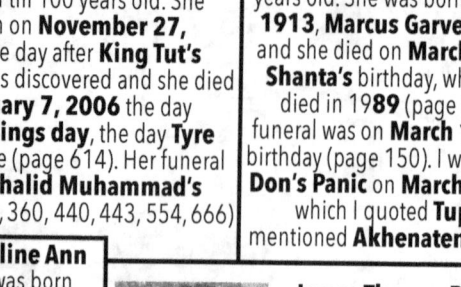

Lottie Mae Haynes was my grand mother's aunt and she lived till **89** years old. She was born on **Aug 17, 1913**, **Marcus Garvey's** birthday and she died on **March 15, 1993**, **Shanta's** birthday, who's mother died in 19**89** (page 2**89**). Her funeral was on **March 19**, **Felicia's** birthday (page 150). I wrote the song **Don's Panic** on **March 19**, 2016 in which I quoted **Tupac** and mentioned **Akhenaten** (page 371).

Deacon Jack Henry Childers was born on **January 31, 1932** and he passed away on **April 8, 2007**. His **funeral on April 14.** I wrote the song **Star of The Story** on **April 8th** 2015, which was the fourth time that I said the name **King Tut** in a rhyme before my past life revelation (page 323) and I got **Deja Vu** on April 8th 2022 while leaving **Akhetaten**, the city **King Tut** was born in (page 671).

Jaqueline Ann Jones was born on **October 23,** 1935 and he passed away on **September 29**, 1994. His funeral was on **October 5**. On **Sep 29**, 2016 I wrote the song **Prophecy** (page 424). On **Sep 29**, 2019 a 2200 year old Egyptian tomb was discovered (page 581). On **Sep 29**, 2022 I wrote a song about D**emmet** Yilderi, The **Reincarnation** of Atra Kapi (page 623). I met Mr Nature in a mysterious was on **October 5**, 2013 (page 28). I met **Kilindi Iyi** on **October 5** 2018 (page 537).

James Thomas Parker was my grand mother's younger brother. He was born on **February 3, 1932** and he passed on **September 20, 1992**. His funeral was held on **September 25**. My mother was born on his birthday (page 27). **Richard Pryor's** episode about a **long lost Egyptian tomb** aired on **Sep 20th** 1977 (Pages 32,33). **Superman** was born on **Sep 25** (page 204). I have had other significant experiences on this date on pages 326, 388, 435, 536, 212, 247.

Ronnie Parker was born on **March 12, 1953** and he passed away on **July 10, 1994. Sandra Bland** was pulled over for a minor traffic violation on **July 10**, 2015 and three days later she was found hanged in a jail cell in Waller County, TX (p 337). **Ronnie's funeral** on **July 23rd** , two days before **Emmett Till's** birthday. **Carolyn Bryant** (pages 506, 180), the women who caused **Emmett Till** to be lynched was born on July **23rd**. **Haile Selassie** was born on July **23rd** (p 392). My aunt Alice was born on July **23rd**, she is connected to the **44th parallel** (p 660).

Christine Sutton Stanley was born on **Feb 24**, 1950 and she passed away on **December 29**, 2019. Her funeral on **January 6**. On **Feb 24** 2020 I had a **dream** about Emmett Till (page 586). On **Feb 24, 2022** I had an interesting experience I called, The Odd Never Ending story (page 669). On **Dec 29**, I was kicked off **facebook**, and I said Emmett Till's name in a song for the fifth time before my past life revelation (page 351). Her funeral was on **January 6**, which is **3 Kings Day** (page 489, 614).

Cecil Montgomery was my grand father's younger brother. He was born on **July 21, 1952** and he passed away on **February 8, 2014.** His **funeral** was on **February 15.** I wrote the song, **Secret life of plants** on **July 21**, 2016 (Page 396). On **July 21**, 2018, I had an experience with **5meo-DMT** on (Bufo page 527), I also wrote a hook claiming to be **King Tut** and **Zee** tells me her **dream** (Page 529). On **Feb 8**,1915, the movie, **Birth of a Nation** was released (pages 19, 29, 407, 415, 425, 496). On **Feb 8**, 1993, I drew the last of five **prophetic drawings** (pages 59, 58, 57, 56, 55). **Kalief Browder** attempted **suicide** on **Feb 8**, 2012 (page 333). And in 2015, I wrote the song **Ancient Future** on that same day (page 321, 562). **Big L** is murdered on **February 15**, 1999 (page 80). **Vanity** dies on **Feb 15,** 2016 (page 362, 379).

Velma A. Childers was born on **April 19, 1935** and she passed away on **October 6, 2010.** Her funeral was on **October 9**, my grand mothers birthday. All connection related to the date **April 19** can be found on pages 327, 375, 607, and 641. All connection related to the date **October 6** can be found on pages 189, 619, 369, 425, and 501. **October 9**, is my grand mother's birthday and it is connected to several significant events in this book. **Jasmin** is connected, page 95. **Benjamin Banneker** is connected, page 160. **The Ark of a Million years** is connected, pages 176-538. The **Cream Remix** is connected, page 454. **Troy Anthony Davis** is connected, page 258. **The Reincarnation of Dejazmatch Beru** is connected, page 391. Luxx On Lex is connected, page 586. **Jackie Robinson** and the **Field of Dreams Deferred** is connected, page 609. And finally, my experience with **Deja Vu** while Leaving The City of **Akhetaten** is connected (page 671).

Darolyn Lisa Martin was born on **March 21, 1955**, the same year as **Emmett Till** was murdered (pages 503 - 521). She passed away on Oct 11, 2009. Her funeral on Oct 14.

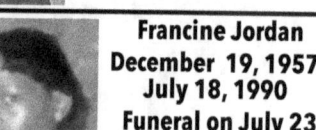

Francine Jordan
December 19, 1957 - July 18, 1990
Funeral on July 23

Francine was my cousin **Romelle's mother** and **Vanessa** was my cousin **George's mother** (page 36). Their mothers were murdered by **America's drug war** waged on black people with **Crack** and **Heroin** placed in our communities (pages 237, 238, 274, 485, 500, 501, 502, 528, 661).

Vanessa Jordan
December 6, 1955 - March 17, 1995
Funeral on March 21

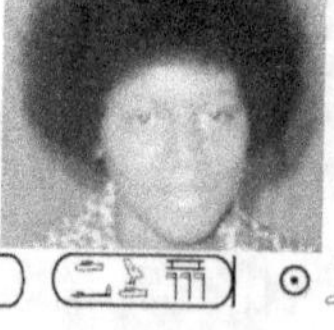

Lewis Allen Jordan was born on **May 31**, 1956 and he passed away on **October 25**, 1992. His funeral on **October 28. The Tulsa Massacre** started on May 31, 1921 (pages 404-415) and **Dr. Aaron Ember** and his family die in a fire after opening **King Tut's** tomb on **May 31**, 1926 (page 13). I am born on **October 25**th 1977, (page 34). **Beyond King Tut Tour** comes to NYC on **October 28**, 2022 and the movie about Emmett Till premiers that same day (pages 29, 33). I came across the murder on **Amanda Gonzales and Vanessa Guillen** on **October 28**, 2021 (page 100).

Maggie Howard was born on **September 15, 1944** and she passed away on **March 28, 1987**. Her funeral on **April 4. Jet magazine** published pictures of **Emmett Till's** mutilated face on **September 15th** 1955 (page 515). **April 4th** is the day **Martin Luther King** was assassinated (page 69, 592) and the day my past life of **King Tut** was revealed to me (page 594). She was born in 19**44** connecting her to the **44th parallel** (page 660). She passed away the same day that **Shanta** started training with me (page 289).

Rau nu Prt m heru

Never Judge a book by it's cover!
At the time I didn't know but I'm about to hit rock bottom very soon.

Iu f Per f m heru

October 5th 2009 -$800 Miller Time 2/7 Communication

1:00pm **Dawud** "whats up bro?" 4:07pm **Dawud** "whats up bro? back to no communication? put urself in my shoes homie....im being very patient. and you told me august was def." 4:07pm **Miller** "dude i'm logged on but i'm not looking at my facebook. baniks are killing me right now. i got closing delayed. i will get at you when i got the ends..three deals got pushed out of august..i want to pay you so we could go on about our lives. you think i need someone to keep asking me about money? you think i need someone to keep asking me about money?" 4:11pm **Dawud** "i hear you bro. i been asken you for a yr and a half. and im just still patiently waiting. and i cant allow you to forget thats all. u really have to undertand that... put urself in my shoes... ofcoures mine arn't faragamos. just help me out bro." 4:12pm **Miller** "still cant spell..but i understand you" 4:12pm **Dawud** "Lol. can't aford them so it ain;t a prob right now. or priority. one last thing" 4:13pm **Miller** "yup." 4:14pm **Dawud** "im really not gonna question how you spend your money. i wish ypu all the best homie. nice cars clothes trips whatever just take of me bro. before the next pair of faragomos or whatever you do nice for yourself... take care of me first. thats all i want." 4:15pm **Miller** "i haven't bought a pair of fg's since 97...but i hear you" 4:15pm **Dawud** "my grand dad just passed... i can do aot for my grand mother with $800....alot." 4:15pm **Miller** "I see and i'm sorry to hear that. I know what it feels like to lose a grandmother and grandfather. my codolensces" 4:16pm **Dawud** "thanks." 4:18pm **Dawud** "ok later bro. last thing. should i expect this before the 15th?" 4:20pm Miller "i would like to tell you yes..but i will keep you updated as the days go by"

Next communication October 2011 page 213

Utterances for Coming Forth by day into Light

It is he, who comes forth by day into Light

Carla, Karma and Redemption

I saw Carla for the first time on Facebook and when I saw her I pursued her. She was **Netic's** friend (page 182). I sent her a message but she ignored me. One night I happened to see her at the club Canal Room, where Q Tip would DJ. She was with another guy but at some point I found her alone so I opened a conversation with her but in the middle of talking to her the guy she was with grabbed her and walked off with her. I laughed and went on with my night. I would hit her up from time to time on facebook trying to get some time with her until she finally told me flat out, that she wasn't attracted to me and that I was not her type. I stopped reaching out to her after that. I don't know the date but one day she reached out to me and asked me what I was doing. She wanted to hang out. She told me to get some Bacardi 151. So I did that. I got the 151 and she came over to see me. We drank and we danced, we laughed and had a good time then we went to a club downtown in the city. On the way back to my place we were both drunk. When she woke up the next day she had no recollection of what had happened the night prior. That didn't stop me from bragging about my time with her to **Netic** (p 182), who didn't find my bragging to be amusing.

Years later I would become aware of the Laws of **Maat** again in this life and that's when my time with Carla became the source of much regret. I did not give her the drink to get her drunk. She requested it and I supplied it with a smile. I felt like I had taken advantage of her and I wanted to let her know that I regretted that night. I reached out to her on Instagram and expressed my feelings to her and she understood me. She didn't blame me. She came to New York sometime in 2018 or 2019 and she came to see me for a massage because she was experiencing pain in her back. Her mother drove her so I got to meet her mother. Being able to meet with Carla in a healthy holistic way was liberating and redemptive. I felt like I was able to forgive myself and move on from that memory. Thank you Carla.

42 Laws of Maat, Page 367

October 25th 2009 -
Some Doors Lock You In Rooms By Yourself

Today is January 16th 2022 and 2009 was the last time that I celebrated my birthday. My grand father had just died two months earlier and my depression had already started. In 2007 I had the biggest birthday party I ever had (page 153) and 2008 I had a smaller version of that party but this year I had a dinner with a small group of family and friends.....

Today is January 30th 2022 and the path towards my past life revelations has weaken the relationships with many of my family and friends. On top of that, **Covid** caused so much fear in the world that it caused relationships to crumble if the two people also held different views on covid and how to respond to it (page 120). It appears that I opened a **door** and ended up locking myself in a room where I found myself alone (page 251). But even in the word **alone** you find the words **All One**.. My views on the world didn't sit well with some of my family, especially my mother and two of my sisters. I barely ever speak to my sister **Tahira** anymore. I don't know the last time we spoke

but it was in 2021. For some reason our conversations never seem to end well. She used to be my best friend but now religion divides us. Her life is based on a religion and mine is based on the spiritual systems that birthed religions. She **dreamt** my car accident before it happened in 2002 which turned out to be a major key to me decoding the patterns in my life (pages 104-106, 220-222). My aunt **Marcia** is the youngest aunt I have and because I grew up with her as child she is more like a sister (pages 44, 51). Over the years she became the aunt I related to the most but when I began to speak about **past lives** and **psychedelics** we went for a long time without speaking. Currently she takes more time to listen to stories I tell detailing my experiences. **Courtlan** and I have had more arguments than I can count. We stopped speaking again in 2020 because of Covid. I reached out to him a week or so ago because he was in a **dream** of mine. I didn't want to, I only reached out just to see if he was ok. Him and I spoke for a good amount of time but in the end I still felt like he didn't understand what I was experiencing with my life. **Godfrey** and I have only had one falling out in the 20 plus years that I've known him. He took my vision and designed my latest logo (page 645) and he did the same with most of my previous ones (pages 281, 309). **Felicia** and I have not spoken in a while but when we do speak the vibes are always good. I have appeared in a few of her **dreams** and she has an interesting story (p 150). Both **Courtlan** and **Felicia** have a daughter born on **February 7**, which is **Emmett Till's** father's birthday (pages 475, 518) and Felicia has a son is born on March 9th, the day **Biggie Smalls** was murdered (p 77). I have not seen **Tom**, **Kate** or **Debra** since I stopped training them back in my bootcamp classes. I did however call **Kate** in 2021 for the first time in many years and she was understandably surprised to hear from me. She was somewhere with loud music playing and so we didn't speak long. I wanted clarity on a **dream** she had of me years ago in 2009. I asked her if she remembered having a dream about me and she understandably had no recollection of the dream. She said she would call me back but she never did so I wrote what I remembered of her dream (page 162). All the events in this book are true. If you follow my path and do the things I do yet still the great mysteries are not shown to you. Then continue the path and **to Maat be true** and perhaps in due time you will be worthy of the view.

Rau nu Prt m heru

Iu f Per f m heru

I do not remember when I had my first **sleep paralysis** experience but I know it happened after I moved into my apartment in 2007. I do however know the date when I first broke out of the **sleep paralysis** experience and it was on December 18th 2010 (page 189) and I had had **sleep paralysis** a few times before that. On January 4th 2011 (**page 195**) I would write about these experiences in the song **Hail Mary** when I said - "don't push me homie, I'm close to the edge, having **dreams** I cant move, with demons over my head, is it the **spirit** of Hip Hop? cause Hip Hop is dead, maybe it's **Tupac** and **Biggie,** telling me to go ahead". When I wrote those words I was sure that I had had the experience a few times but what is **"sleep paralysis"** anyway? If you google it you might find a description similar to it being a temporary inability to move or speak while falling asleep or upon waking and usually the only thing that you can move are your eyes. The medical industry labels this sleep apnea. Many people describe a feeling of being weighed down as if something is laying on top of them or holding them down. Older people have coined the phrase, "**the witch is riding you**". Many people describe seeing beings that are often times dark giving the impression of ghostly figures. This is why the experience is usually frightening to those who experience it for the first time. The first time I ever had the experience it was frightening and I did not see any dark beings the first times I experienced it. During my first experience I was stuck and all I wished to do was move or speak. I felt like I was bound in a straight jacket unable to move with no mouth to speak only eyes that expressed extreme fear.

I would have **"sleep paralysis"** several times before my breakthrough experience on **December 18th 2010** (page 189). At least 2 or 3 times. It's hard to say because it wasn't until the second or third experience that I realized what I had experienced was real and not just a bad dream. One of the first times I had the experience I laid there struggling trying to speak and move in the dead of the night then finally after what felt like forever my body was animated again and I shouted out the name **"JESUS"** as if I was taking my first breath after being submerged under water for too long. **I can remember feeling ashamed that I screamed for Jesus** because I had already abandoned that belief system yet here I was screaming for him to "save me". I could have left that out but the truth is the truth. That was the last time I scream for Jesus to help me.

I know from experience that **sleep paralysis** is more complex than just not being able to move or speak. On **December 18th 2010** I would finally break free of the paralysis and years later I would use this state of paralysis as a bridge to activate the **Ark of a million years**. On my Grand Mothers birthday **October 9th 2018** (p 538) I would for the first time use this state of paralysis as a bridge to activate the **Ark of the covenant**. **On October 9th 2018** (p 538) I would for the first time use this state of paralysis as a bridge to activate **Noah's Ark**. **On October 9th 2018** (p 538) I would for the first time use this state of paralysis as a bridge to activate my **Merkaba**. **On October 9th 2018** (p 538) I would for the first time use this state of paralysis as a bridge to activate my **Astral body**. **On October 9th 2018** (p 538) I would for the first time use this state of paralysis as a bridge to activate my **Light body**. **On October 9th 2018** (p 538) I would for the first time use this state of paralysis as a bridge to activate my **Celestial Bark**. **On October 9th 2018** (p 538) I would for the first time use this state of paralysis as a bridge to to activate my **Meta Spiritual Device opening the door to the other side of this thing we call reality**. More on Noah's Ark on page 252.

Jesus: "All these works I have done so will you do!"

Utterances for Coming Forth by day into Light

It was sometime in 2020 when I realized that it was my faith in Jesus Christ's resurrection and returning someday that set the foundation for my own revelation of reincarnation. The Scripture John, 14:12 reads, "Verily, verily, I say unto you, He that believeth on me, the works that I do shall he do also; and greater works than these shall he do". By having the belief in the resurrection of Jesus it allowed my soul to fathom the concept of resurrection after death, not knowing that the concept originated in Kemet. (**See page 488**)

It is he, who comes forth by day into Light

Neptune is the **highest spiritual** planet in the solar system and represents the **great poet** which is like a tuning fork dealing with rhythm and rhyme. Neptune will be in Pisces starting on **April 4th** 2011 but Neptune starts tuning me in 2010. In 2010 I will start writing rhymes again and while taking the path of the poet I will start to slowly awaken ancient soul fragments because of the nature of my music. The **first rhyme** will be written on April 11th 2010, titled, **Surveillance** and in that song I will say the name Emmett Till for the **first time** in a rhyme (p 180).. Then on **November 25th** 2010 I will say Emmett's name again in the song **Power** (p 187). **Tutankhaten's (King Tut's)** tomb was opened on **Nov 26th** 1922 (p 11) and **on that same day** I would say the name **King Tut** for the first time in a rhyme titled **Uptown** on **November 26th** 2010 (p 187). Then I would say the name **King Tut** again on January 7th 2011 in the song **These Many Roads** (p 195), which was written for **Michael Jackson.** I wrote the song **These Many Roads** the day after Emmett Till's mother **Mamie Till** Died (November **23**rd 1921 - January 6th 2003).. I would go on to say the name Emmett Till 7 more times in my music before I realized I was Emmett Till in a **past life** on July 3rd 2018 (p 480). The dates and pages of each rhyme are listed below. I would go on to say the name King Tut four more times in music before I realized I was King Tut in a **past life** on **April 4th** 2020 (p 594). I would however speak about both of them indirectly in my music many more times before I realized my past lives. On **April 4th** 2011 I would start my audition videos for the Tupac Biopic (page 202). **14** shots were fired at Tupac on Sep 7. Ausar was cut into **14** pieces and Emmett Till died at **14** years old. I have a theory about who Tupac was in his past life. I understand now, that having Neptune rising coupled with Sagittarius (p 655) in my birth chart allowed me to see the trends of times having an over all picture and Neptune will be over head in pisces until 2025 the year of the **snake**. I was born in 19**41** the year of the **snake** as Emmett Till then I was **born again** in 1977 the year of the **snake** in my current incarnation.

Dawud, Beloved by the Ntru

Emmett Till's name appears in my music 9 times before I realize I was him in a past life

1st	April 11th 2010	Surveillance	P. 180
2nd	November 25th 2010	Power	P. 187
3rd	October 16th 2011	American Dream'n	P. 214
4th	July 7th 2013	Knock Knock	P. 274
5th	December 29th 2015	RIP Tamir Rice	P. 351
6th	February 28th 2016	Barbaric	P. 365
7th	March 18th 2016	Rope a Dope	P. 370
8th	September 29th 2016	Prophecy	P. 424
9th	October 9th 2017	Cream (remix)	P. 454

King Tut's name appears in my music 6 times before I realize I was him in a past life

1st	November 26th 2010	Uptown	P. 187
2nd	January 7th 2011	These Many Roads	P. 195
3rd	March 27th 2013	Year of the Snake	P. 268
4th	April 8th 2015	Star of the Story	P. 323
5th	May 3rd 2016	Hapiness	P. 382
6th	December 18th 2016	Move 9	P. 435

The oldest writings known to man are utterances, spells or "rhymes/hymns" written on the walls in the tombs of the **Nswt Bity** (pharaoh) evoked to ensure the safe passage of the pharaoh after death and towards their **resurrection** in the next life (page 6). In my life as **Emmett Till** I was murdered in 19**55**, in that same year the **originator** of Hip Hop, **Dj Kool Herc** was born in the zodiacal sign of **Aries**, which is where **Tutankhaten** (**King Tut**) comes from. In my current life my moon is in **Aries** and my Dragons Tail **originates** in the age of **Aries** (Pages 654-657).. **22** years after I was murdered, I came back to earth, born again in 19**77**, carrying a complex equation of star codes intimately connected to the musical art form known as Hip Hop. **KRS One's DJ Scott La Rock** was murdered on **August 27th** 1987 the day before **Emmett** was Murdered (**August 28th**). Emmett's murder sparked the **first** Black movement for Civil Rights while Scott La Rock's death is said to be the **first** murder of a major Hip Hop artist. Emmett's death was **connected to a women** and his **two killers** were **acquitted**. The murder of Scott La Rock is said to be **connected** to a confrontation that **D-Nice** had with **two men** involving **a woman**. **Two men** were arrested and charged with La Rock's murder, but they were **acquitted** at the trial. KRS One released **The Gospel of Hip Hop** the day before my birthday (p 633). The **Artifacts** would released their first album on my 17th birthday **Oct 25th** in 94 (p 66). **Artifacts** are objects made by human beings from earlier periods in time typically items of cultural or historical interest and the most famous artifacts ever found in modern time are the ones found in **Tutankhaten's** (**King Tut's**) tomb in 19**22**. The American record producer, DJ, rapper and songwriter Daniel Alan Maman was born the same day and year as me, Oct 25th 19**77** the year of the **snake** and he is professionally known as the **Alchemist**. This book is the modern "Book of The Dead, Coming Forth by Day" because it was the **murder** of Black life that fueled my music causing my ancient soul fragments to Come Forth by Day. This is the reason why I wrote my story into my music years before I consciously knew about my past lives. Below are some of the rhymes I wrote about Tut years before the revelation. On the list above one can see every time I said the names Emmett and Tut in music before I knew my past lives. This book was brought forth in 2022, the 49th anniversary of Hip Hop and 49 days is the amount of time the Tibetans believed it took one soul to be reborn into another life. I am the **alchemist** coded within Hip Hop (p 656). This is **Divine Alchemy** of the soul, the only alchemy that matters!.

Rau nu Prt m heru

Iu f Per f m heru

I was on **Craigslist** and **Backpage** looking for a cheap **laptop** to buy. While on the site I saw the link for personals and I started looking at the pictures of single females, the same way people do on Instagram. Then I ended up on a different type of page were gorgeous women were offering adult services for a $80 to $100 and sometimes more and sometimes a lot more. When I looked at the women I was not thinking about **sex trafficking**. I was not really too aware of it to be very honest. I saw women that looked like the types of women I used to pursue when I would go out to clubs and lounges. They looked like the **strippers** at the **strip clubs** I had gone to in the past. I contemplated the ethical ramifications and I felt inside that it was a wrong thing to do. I would not want any of the women in my family to experience having to sell themselves to survive. Then I thought about all the money I used to spend taking women out on dates. Most of the time all I ever really wanted from the women was sex. Of course I met women that I fell in love with beyond the desire for sex but I was really only attracted sexually most of the time. I began to rationalize the idea. I figured, I could pay less just picking a woman from Backpage and paying her. I didn't do it that day but eventually I did. **I paid a women for sex**. Then I did it again. It became **addictive**. I could pick a woman, pay her, then have sex. It was a lot easier than dating but **my conscious was weighing on me**. I must have done it around 7 to 10 times in the year of 2010. I spent around $1000 in total and the next year I went broke due to the new habit of smoking weed (p 194). I had lived in **Germany** for 3 and a half years, where **prostitution was legal** in the **Red light district**, but I never went there and **never paid for sex**. I was only doing this now because it became addictive. I inherently knew what I was doing was wrong and subsequently on a few occasions I could not engage with the women that came. I just gave them money and sent them away. I know they must have thought I was crazy calling them for service, then talking to them, then giving them money and sending them away. Because of experiences like those it was easy for me to stop doing it forever. There is a moral factor that takes hold of ones soul if they allow themselves to listen to their hearts. At least that is what happened to me. Once I stopped doing that I never did it again and never will. On Apr 6th 2018, Backpage and affiliated websites were seized by the F.B.I. due to prostitution. This is a part of my past that I did not want to tell but it is important as men need to see that transformation is not always pretty and honoring the divine feminine energy on the planet is important. I was distracted by desires of the flesh but eventually, I found the computer I was looking for. I used that computer to make music that helped **awaken** my **ancient soul fragments**. I changed my actions and sought the narrow path and subsequently I opened **doors** that most people never realize are there.

The **Mary Magdalene** of the bible is thought by many to have been a **prostitute** however the bible never directly states that. In the bible, the character of Jesus traveled with 12 disciples (12 signs of zodiac and 12 cranial nerves, page 492) and a group of women who helped spread his message. Mary Magdalene was one of the women. In chapter 8 verses 1-3 of the book Luke, Jesus cast's 7 demons out of Mary Magdalene. Mary is also one of the people who saw Jesus after his resurrection (p 481). Afterwards Jesus tells her to spread the news of his return. This act of giving women roles of leadership was not promoted in the early Christian churches and to down play Mary's importance some preachers claimed her to be a **prostitute**. I can not judge a person who sells themselves because I have been on the other side of that exchange. I could never limit someones potential of growth because of something they have done in their past because I know what I have done and I know how I have transformed. To all the women who might feel ashamed of their past, just know that you can rise above what ever you have been through or you have done. This goes for all people. Life is a class and humans exist on different planes of existence. We can graduate to higher levels of existence if we would only subject ourselves to mystical disciplines like Yoga (page 467). Sometimes you must leave the four walls and boxes of organized religion to realize higher states of consciousness. Perhaps many religions are, "male chauvinistic power structures used as frameworks to control our minds". **Ask yourself why the bible has NO female angels?** Yet, in ancient Kemet (Egypt) all principles have **male and female counterparts.** Amun, the hidden one, is balanced with his wife and counterpart **Amunet**. Kemet has a long list of female Goddesses (**angels**). From **Nut**, the mother of the Gods; to **Heket**, she who governs **birth** and **rebirth** (page, 523), to **Anat**, the Goddess of war and fertility (page, 584), to **Serqet**, the scorpion Goddess (page, 634), to **Tefnut**, the Goddess of moisture, moist air, dew and rain (page 432), to **Het Heru** (**Hathor**), the Goddess connected to the **heavenly cow**, who crossed boundaries between worlds, helping deceased souls in the transition to the afterlife (page 658), and the list goes on. In fact, elements from the character Mary Magdalene were taken from **Auset** (**Isis**). Christianity borrowed from the resurrection story of Ausar when the character of **Jesus** was created. According to the book of John, after Jesus resurrected, Mary was found **weeping**, "Dear woman, why are you **crying**?" **Jesus** asked her (John, ch. 20:14.15). In the Ausarian resurrection drama, Auset (Isis) went in search of her dead husband Asuar and when she found him she was **weeping**. In the Ausarian resurrection drama Auset is the one that helps to resurrect Ausar and this story comes thousands of years before the Christian religion was even thought of. This story of resurrection is also connected to Emmett Till (page 481). Through the mystical arts of Yoga humans can vibrate to higher frequencies bringing about experiences of, Telepathy, Premonition, Clairvoyance, the realization of reincarnation (past lives, page 14) and the countless other transmutative potentials. **Remember that you are Ausar, the hero!** See page 3 for the **hero's journey!**

Utterances for Coming Forth by day into Light

It is he, who comes forth by day into Light

backpage

March 28th 2010 - U.T.O.U.G.H. Bootcamp Central Park

I was being pulled back to **Harlem**. I didn't want to work in the city any more. I wanted to work with **people of color** who looked like me so **I started my movement north**. I moved my classes from Thompson Sq P**ark** then to Union Square (p 162) then on to Central P**ark** (p 183) and finally I started a class in Morningside p**ark** in Harlem (p 279). This year I would also unknowingly open **spirit doors** through my **music** (p 251). Four years from this date a woman from my past would enter my life and start training with me. She would eventually become the woman that I confided in during the writing of this book. Exactly 12 years from this date I would be on a flight to **Kemet** (**Egypt**) for the first time in this life, where I had **Deja Vu** and other profound experiences (pages 670 - 671).

2010 - The Museum of Modern Art

A rare picture of me and my mother together. I took her to the museum to spend time with her and before we went in we stopped to take this picture together. It is at this moment that I take a break from writing to call my mother…

I wasted many years arguing with my mother about religion but I think having my mother as a mother is what helped me to realize who I was. If I had accepted her way of life I might not have ever went to study what came before all religions. A few years after we took this picture she began to wear a Muslim hijab head dress like she had done when she became a Muslim in the early 1970's (page 26-27). As of 2022 her and I currently have a peaceful relationship. She has began to understand the connections in this book that I am writing and she is eagerly waiting to read it. She always felt she would write a book but perhaps that feeling was connected this book, written by her only son, Dawud Basheer Eddings.

Rau nu Prt m heru

April 11th 2010 Surveillance (1st of 35)

For a couple of thangs I make a nigga bleed, like a blood when he bang, the way I'm from most nigga's the same, re-up flip try and make it triple, cut it to the bone and gristle, **I'm as clean as a whistle**, New York state of mind, a **Harlem** nigga, **Brooklyn** grind, what's really? You illy, I'm get'n mine, his ego big, my ego big, adrenaline be pump'n when I thump the 50, the **dreams**, the **voices**, **no faces** just **screams**, I need a shot of Jager, let's get this paper, my deen off balance like a triple beam, my team po though scope our logo, 'I'm on the scene, 3 strikes on my Y3 Jeans, why this life is leaf I lead, things ain't always what they seem, I'm stuck on the block with the dope man and fien chase'n a **dream**, they say play ball or sell crack - **Dula Miz**

Man I said fuck em all, What type of hope is that? I take you back to a time where we knew the time, the time we all dressed in black and I ain't talking bout no **wake** nigga **the panthers back**! not the ones on tv, I mean the visions back, picture that, CNN and FOX 5 can you cover that? but you won't will you?! what don't kill you only make you stronger, NYPD still **Emmett Till** you, no I don't feel you, Y'all rappers crazy I swear, you probably would have sold your brothers into slavery, I'm here, Lord I know you got me, you never drop me, my daddy left me but you protect me, in this life of monopoly, I'm like **Haile Selassie** and I'm forming a posse, think it's over? think again over out copy - **Dawud**

Significance

ADDENDUM

Iu f Per f m heru

On January 30th 2022 I decided to transcribe the first verse of this song into this book. It was written by my cousin **Abdulla**. I had to listen to the song to transcribe his lyrics. That is when I was overcome with amazement. I had already labeled the 6 times I said Emmett's name in my rhymes before I realized I was him in my **past life** but this was **unexplainable** because this song has a **Whistle** in it and Emmett was murdered because he **whistled**! Abdulla said the word **Whistle** in his verse and this is **the first time that the name Emmett Till appears in my poetry** and this is the first rhyme I wrote when I started writing again! I was even more blown away when I realized for the first time that the beat for this song had a **whistle** in it! **(***Addendum*** Carolyn Bryant** (page 506), the women who caused **Emmett Till** to be lynched, died in on April **25**, 2023, **two days** before **Abdulla's** birthday, the same day as Lisa "Left Eye" Lopes (pages 112, 401). Before you dismiss this as just coincidence, concider this first. **Rod Sterling**, the creator of the **Twilight Zone** saw the 1955 murder of Emmett Till as a mistrial of justice. In response to the murder of Emmett Till he produced a show titled Noon On Doomsday. When the network realized his show was about the murder of Emmett Till they censored it so much that the audience never knew it was about Emmett Till. But isn't strange that the show aired on **April 25**, 1956, and **Carolyn Bryant** would die on **April 25**, 2023..........? **Rod Sterling** was quoted saying, "I think it's criminal that we're not permitted to make dramatic note of social evils as they exist... Drama by it's very nature should make a comment on those things that effect our daily lives". **Carolyn Bryant** was born on July **23**, 1934, **two days** before **Emmett Till**. She was born the same day as my grand father Spencer **Wright** (page 25), and **Haile Selassie** (page 390), and my Aunt Alice (page 660). She died at **88** years of age. 2022 is **88** years after she was born. 2022 in 100 years after the tomb of **King Tut** was discovered and the same year this book was released.***). In this song I mention **Haile Selassie** and in 2014 I meet my brother Padmore who is the **reincarnation** of **Dejazmatch Beru** (Ras Beru), **Ethiopian royalty** and was the minister of war for Emperor **Haile Selassie** (page 390). This can only be explained by the words of **Mamie Till**, in an interview in 1991 she detailed a spiritual experience she had (page 511). She claimed that after Emmett was murdered a **Godly voice** came to her and told her, "It was ordained from the beginning of time that Emmett would die a sacrificial death. Be happy to have been the mother of a child who died blameless like Christ, but there is a job for you to do now. Emmett has done his job now your job is to continue to tell the story so that mans consciousness will be aroused and justice can at-last prevail." In 2018 I would have another revelation with a song related to Emmett Till which has a **whistle** hidden within the beat (page 546).

Utterances for Coming Forth by day into Light

2010 Diabolic Remix

You mother fuckers are nothing, you can not harm me, I **resurrect** every revolutionary and start a army, the first soldier amongst me is the most Godly, you know the one with **bronze skin** and **wooly hair** bless'n me, join me if you want to but know the end may be upon you, if you're in love with your life then this fight is not for you, cause there's a war going on outside Sun Zu, Hip Hop ain't Hip Hop if you won't stop what's killing you, horizontal violence, you shoot me but are you willing to shoot a mother fucker who claim to serve and protect you? I ain't trying to play you, but let me ask you, do you really think you thug'n? That nigga that you shot was probably your third cousin, you bug'n! Where were you during the **Sean Bell** verdict? **Amadou Diallo** the name have you ever heard it?! **Timothy Stansberry** google it get mad then get equipped but don't shoot me mother fucker, the system, shoot it! **Lolita** the type of leader not afraid to shoot a heater, blast on the system they called it terrorism, don't believe everything you read, read between the lines because he who wins wars writes history every time, Afghanistan - for peace? or is it the pipe line? use your mind and use it well cause to the man with a hammer a problem is just a nail - **Dawud**

Significance

It is he, who comes forth by day into Light

I had been searching for this song for many years and when compiling this book my desire to find it increased. **Today is February 2nd 2022** and I just placed the lyrics to this song in the book. I found the video I made for this song a week ago, on an old hard drive. As I watched the video and listened to my lyrics I was left **speechless**. The video had images of a **Black Jesus** on a cross with the words **Revelations 1: 12-18** on the video. I went and read verses 12 through 18 of the first chapter of Revelations and verse 18 says, "I am the living one; I was dead, and now look, I am alive for ever and ever! and I hold the keys of death and **Hades**". **Hades** is connected to the **Underworld** which is connected to **Ausar** (**Osiris**), who is the Lord of **resurrection** in ancient Kemetic spiritual philosophy. This song was written to the **Immortal Technique** (pages 143, 270) beat **Diabolic** and in it I use the word **Resurrect,** and in the video I place a verse from Revelations about **Resurrection**. This revelation came **three days** after I realized the significance of the song **Surveillance**. This might actually be the first song that I wrote when I started writing rhymes again but there is no way to confirm it. The computer I was using to create these songs crashed years ago, in a very peculiar and questionable way (p 224), which would have been the most ideal of times for anyone trying to stop me from continuing my "heroes" journey (p 3). I was exporting a video for a song I had recently recorded when my Mac desktop froze and crashed.. I lost a lot of personal information like family pictures, and other things, there might have even been other songs that were lost with that hard drive like ancient cities lost under the sea. Sometimes I wonder what was so important on that hard drive that something or someone felt the need to erase it. Perhaps it was for my own good. **Re-member, you** are **Ausar** and **Heru**! See page 3, the **hero's journey!**

April 23rd - Dec 27th 2010 (King Tut comes to New York)

I never went to this exhibit but I vaguely remember seeing the flyers for it and what's **strange** is that this is the same year that I would say **King Tut's** name in a rhyme for the first time (p 187). What's even **stranger** is that I wrote the rhyme on Nov 26th 2010 which is the same day that **King Tut's** tomb was opened in 1922 (p 11). In this same song I would quote **Tupac** ("Never Had A Friend Like Me"). To take it a step further, in 2020 my friend Kalishea would show me a card for this exhibit that she had kept since 2010 (p 199). Kalishea took the picture of me below on **June 16th** 2012 which is **Tupac's** birthday. I took her out to eat for her birthday, she's born on **June 15th** the day before Tupac's birthday and Kalishea has a son born on **Oct 24th** the day before my birthday, the same day that KRS One released his book, The Gospel of Hip Hop (p 633) and the same day **Rosa Parks** died. **14** shots were fired at **Tupac** on Sep 7. **Ausar** was cut into **14** pieces and **Emmett Till** died at **14** years old. I have a theory about who Tupac was in his past life. While writing this book I saw that **Kanye** went to see this exhibit on July 7th or 8th of 2010, and a little over a week prior to his visit he performed at the 2010 BET awards wearing a gold chain with a giant **Heru** pendant (in falcon form). In the ancient Kemetic (Egyptian) Ausarian (Osirion) resurrection drama, Ausar (Osiris) was known as the Lord of the **West** and the Lord of **resurrection/Reincarnation**. **West** was where the soul (BA) went when we "die". **Heru** is the son of Ausar and he is the one that returns as Ra through resurrection. **Re-member** that **you** are **Ausar** and **Heru,** the **hero!** See page 3 for the **hero's journey**! Kanye is from Chicago like Emmett Till and his last name is **West**. On July 3rd 2018 my past life as Emmett Till is revealed to me (p 480). On April 4th 2020, the day Martin Luther King was assassinated (p 69, 592) my past life as King Tut was revealed to me (p 594). **Martin Luther King** wrote a paper on the Ausarian resurrection in 1949 (p 593). Kanye is mentioned more times than most artist in this book. I would use many of his beats to rap over when I first started writing again in 2010 and he appears in several of my **dreams**, even up to the last page of this book. Kanye crashed 2 days before my birthday in 2002. I crashed 7 days before his on my fathers birthday in 2002 (p 106). In Kanye's song: Through The Wire, he says the name Emmett Till. It was the video for this song that would help him get a release date for his album sparking his rise to fame. I am the reincarnated soul of Emmett Till and King Tut. Same soul different bodies. See page **648** for the **metaphysical significance of the number 23**. "I'm just a revolutionary nigga, simple man, "**Never Had A Friend Like Me**", loyalty to the end, **royalty** I would have been, if I was around in the time of **King Tut** king could have been me! **Watch me rise up** in this fuck'n game, cause all these niggas ain't say'n shit they the fuck'n same! **- Dawud** (written on **Nov 26th 2010, page 187**)

April 23rd 2010 **What is Love**

What is **love**? who do I **love** and who **loves** me? let's start from the top, love is **G.O.D**.., I **love** girls that **love** me for the man that I be, when I'm in **love**, I **love** unconditional, this ain't The Flavor of **Love**, this is real baby, and lately I been think'n you can have my baby, what is a queen? Who is my queen? And what does it mean, you know we only met once but you still in my **dreams**, who am I? I'm really your king, really your king, looked in your eyes, and that stopped everything, I'm buying a ring, I never bought a ring before, but times have changed, I'm'a carry you over the door, let's make this house a home, this ain't a rap or a poem, this what happens when you meet her, turn around and she's gone! **- Dawud**

May 16th 2010 (Aiyana Mo'Nay Stanley-Jones, 7 years old)

Aiyana was seven years old when Detroit's East Side Police Department's Special Response Team conducted a botched up raid in which Aiyana was shot in the head and killed by police officer Joseph **Week**ley. (July 20, 2002 – May 16, 2010), Her death drew national media attention and led U.S. Representative John Conyers to ask U.S. Attorney General Eric Holder for a federal investigation into the incident. The officers name was **Week**ley and every **week** Black people are murdered by the systemic pursuits of racism and white supremacy. I would not come to know about Aiyana's case until years after it had happened. The exact year I'm not sure but it must have been around the time I first spoke her name in my music. I mentioned her in the song, **Terrorism** that I wrote on August 6th 2016 (page 399), then again on December 30th 2016 in the song **Hell Razor (page 437)**, and finally on June 14th 2020 in the song I wrote for **George Floyd (page 616)**. Her case angered me deeply as do all of the murders.
Condolences: My condolences go out to all the families of those who have been robbed of their lives by this system of racism and white supremacy. Please know that death is not the end. The soul survives death, indeed and in spirit. This is a book of the dead written by a boy who was murdered without justice, who defeated death and came forth by day. May the soul of **Aiyana Mo'Nay Stanley-Jones** walk peacefully through the field of Reeds in Amenta. Amen Ra

Netic, Game Rebellion and Rebellious Spirits

Rau nu Prt m heru

Netic and I met in 2009 at the gym I worked at and we clicked immediately. He was the first person that showed me how to do a **muscle up**. I had only done them once before but only by accident while attending Special Forces Selection trials (p 109). Netic and I would become friends and afterwards I would come to know that he was the lead vocalist in the **Afro Punk** Group **Game Rebellion**. One day he came to the gym and we got into a friendly argument as to who was faster. Netic didn't know that I played football and that I was real fast. He went on about how his little brother was Ryan Grant, a running back for the Green Bay Packers (number **25**). I didn't care, I told him, we could go outside and race and we did... I was always supportive of my friends so I went to a few of his shows and cheered him on. I even recorded one of their shows and edited a video for them. I had done this for a few people I knew as well. I never asked for money, I did it from my heart and years later the art of editing would come in handy as I got better at it and began editing my own fitness promotional videos as well as videos for my music. It was Netic who inspired me to take the picture of **Golden** (p 159). I saw a picture of him with a woman across his lap and wanted to, "one up" him. Years later that picture would take on a different meaning to me. When I started writing music again in 2010 Netic was the only person to ever tell me to **stop rhyming**. He told me to do what I was good at, which was personal training. I did not get angry or offended. I think he thought I was trying to do what he was doing but I had been writing as a hobby since I was a teen. When I listen to my old rhymes, they are definitely not my best rhymes but what they are is more profound than Netic or I could have ever imagined. Netic was right though, he told me that if I kept writing I would get better in 7 to 10 years and 7 to 10 years later my writing proved to be prophetic. They were the foretelling of my past life revelations. I became a hermit in 2011 and years later I reflected back on a time when I asked Netic to come hang out at a club but he declined, asserting that he never goes out anymore. When he told me that **it made me think** about how I was spending my time. Netic spent his time reading, challenging himself and being creative. I beat Netic in that foot race but Netic proved to be faster in spirit, and it would take me years to catch up to him. The last time I spoke to Netic was on Dec 10, 2021 via text and was telling him about my past lives and he said **he knew of his past lives and future lives**. I sent him the video for my song **Star Codes of Immortality** in 2021 and that happened to be the first song of mine he ever liked (p 663). His response was, "Best one yet".

Iu f Per f m heru

Addendum

Today is May 7th 2022 and I just received a text from **Aaron**, a trainer I used to work with at the gym in Soho where I met Netic. I don't know the cause, but my brother Netic has passed away and it's hard to believe. **During the revision of this book** (p 118, 619, 648) I ran into Netic's Comrade **Daoud** at a **Powwow** on July 30th and he told me of a profound experience he had with Netic before he passed. Daoud is a Master Reiki healing practitioner and when he heard that Netic was fighting for his life he sat down and began to meditate with the intent of sending Netic long distance healing energy. At some point **Daoud opened a channel** and was overcome with a feeling of euphoria when **he heard Netic's voice speak to him**. Netic told him that his body had been compromised but he was ok. He said he was with the ancestors and he informed Daoud that we are in a **spiritual war**. During our discourse we both experienced waves of **goose bumps**. Daoud also detailed a series of strange **coincidences** that seemed to confirm that Netic was ok. On several occasions, shortly after Netic passed, Daoud would be walking down the street and random people would speak Netic's name as they passed him. He would be at the gym and the person next to him would say the name Netic. This reminded me of what happened to me at the International African Arts Festival in 2022 (p 650). Netic also contacted many people via mediums and **dreams**. Daoud told me that Netic's name means, **The Ancient One**, and oddly enough I used the term, "the ancient one" in a rhyme I wrote the month before Netic died (p 284, 489). Netic was native to this land and perhaps that is where our spirits knew each other. Those who pass away are gone in the physical sense but the soul lives on and Netic's soul will live on forever, he is The Ancient One "as old as the ancient sun". See **Buckingham Palace**, page 71.

Utterances for Coming Forth by day into Light

It is he, who comes forth by day into Light

Condolences: My condolences go out to the family, friends and fans of **Kien (Netic) Grant**. Please know that death is not the end. The soul survives death, indeed and in spirit. This is a book of the dead written by a boy who was murdered without justice, who defeated death and came forth by day. May the soul of **Kien (Netic) Grant** walk peacefully through the field of Reeds in Amenta. AmenRa.

I left **Crunch Fitness** because I was tired of them taking the majority of **MY** money. The clients paid to train with **ME**! Not Crunch! I proved that when I began to take clients to parks and smalls gyms. I paid around $20 to $30 per hour to train my clients at small gyms and I paid nothing to train them at parks. Around this time a **Dominican** trainer by the name of **Alberto** asked me to join him on a business venture. He wanted to open a Gym for Personal Trainers to train their clients. We both had one of our clients agree to invest 50 to 100k. We went and looked at a space close to the Crunch location we were working at. But Alberto ended up cutting me out the deal and him and his client opened the gym without me and my client. The gym, Work Train Fight, is still in operations today. At the time I felt betrayed, like Alberto had crossed me. But he didn't betray me, I didn't know where I was headed in the world but the ancestors had another plan for me. Most of my clients were white and deep with in my heart I wanted to help people that looked like me. Oddly enough, many of my group fitness clients would end up being Dominicans, like Alberto. I was always self motivated but I did not see the level of importance in my job. I knew that being in shape was ideal but I did not realize how important it was to our overall health, wellness and longevity. I was on a journey that needed to take me to **Harlem**, but I wouldn't get there till 2013, the Year of the Snake (page 279). In times of struggle we depend heavily on the discipline and hard work we have instilled in ourselves through the training we have done and during the Covid Plandemic of 2020 being in shape was a major benefit. Sometimes old clients tell me that when they are training themselves they hear my voice motivating them. I always smile when I hear that, it gives me a sense of having been a positive example in their lives. **John Haller** (seen on pages 279, 280, 281 and 301) was white man who started training with when I started classes at Central Park. He was one of the most committed members of my classes and also one of the people who saw the most results. He was around 50 years old when he started training with me and it was sometime in 2013 that he told me his Grand father's nickname was **Duke**. I always **thought** that was **strange** (p 19).

Netic, page 182

2010 - SuperNova Thought Projections
Meta-Mental Encounters of the Thought kind

I will never forget the day I met **Giara Nova**. I was walking through Union Square enjoying the sights. It was a crowded day, people were playing chess, others were breakdancing, the skate boarders were there and there was no where to sit. Then all of a sudden, it was as if lightening struck and three things happen almost simultaneously. What happened next is an example of how our thoughts and desires can affect our reality by influencing quantum level events in time and space. I would see this **gorgeous women** sitting down on the steps, then immediately **I thought,** I wanted to sit next to her', then as if he heard my words, **the man next to her got up and walked away**. Then immediately, I sat down next to her and we began to talk to each other. Shortly after, the daughter of **Russell Simmons** or **Run,** from **Run DMC** would stop to ask Nova her thoughts on a line of sneakers they were looking to release. When they exchanged info I took Nova's number too and gave her mine as well. That day her and I wet to eat lunch. Nova remembers the story different, she remembers us going out to eat a few days after. Either way, her and I would develop a friendship that we still maintain to this day.

Rau nu Prt m heru Iu f Per f m heru

SIGNIFICANCE

Meeting Nova would prove to be another piece of this unseen web that was forming around me. I would have a profound spiritual experience at her house in 2014 (page 314) during a holiday party that her mother had been throwing for some years. The experience would be the first of a four year pattern that would involve death, the underworld and the immortality of the soul. On Dec 17th of 2014 (page 314) I would be visited by a friend who had passed away on Dec 3rd of 2014 (page 312). Then again on Dec 3rd of 2015 (page 345), 2016 (page 431), and 2017 (page 457). I would have similar experiences with different people who had passed away, the last of which would involve the passing of **DR Jack Felder** who is the father of another friend of mine who is **also named Nova!!** (page 457). There is no such thing as just a coincidence, all things are governed by seen and unseen forces. We make a fatal error when we think all that we see with our two eyes is all there is to see! I'm taking you back, come follow me, on a journey to see a for real Emcee.

Utterances for Coming Forth by day into Light

2010 - As Life Changes Sometimes Best Friends Become Strangers

I remember this night, I brought Susan with me to this party on Courts rooftop. I think this may have been the last time that I hung out with Godfrey and Courtlan in the same setting. As of 2022 I rarely speak to Court. I spoke to Godfrey yesterday (January 8th 2022) but we don't speak very often either. Both of them are doing well in their respective fields. Godfrey met a woman from Columbia that he is excited about. Over the years Godfrey has taken my ideas and designed my logos for me. He even designed the newest logo I have with the scarab encircled by a snake swallowing its tail (page 645). I have not seen Godfrey in person in perhaps 7 or 8 years. Court has had 3 more children that are all smart, energetic and they bring him happiness. I'm happy to see that he has finally had a son and I'm sure his son will be a sharper version of him. I have not seen Court in person in perhaps 6 years. Over the years Court and I had so many arguments that it has stopped us from communicating with each other. I think 2020 and 2021 might have been the first years that I did not send him a happy birthday text. We had a big argument over masks and vaccinations in 2020 that caused us to stop speaking again. I see him from time to time via Instagram. Today is January 13th 2022 and in the last month I have had 3 **dreams** with Courtlan. Todays was the third **dream**. I called him today and we spoke. Court had his first child while in college (page 74). She was born on **February 7**, 1997, the same day that **Emmett Till's** father was born (page 475, 518).

It is he, who comes forth by day into Light

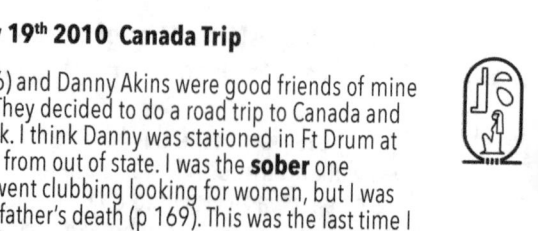

May 19th 2010 Canada Trip

Kyle Esannason (p 126) and Danny Akins were good friends of mine when I was in the Army. They decided to do a road trip to Canada and picked me up in New York. I think Danny was stationed in Ft Drum at the time and Kyle flew in from out of state. I was the **sober** one throughout the trip. We went clubbing looking for women, but I was still mourning my grand father's death (p 169). This was the last time I saw either of them. **As I began to move on in my search for truth the less I had in common with many of the people I knew from my past**. I think it was me who did not handle my friendships the right way. I began to speak about what I was learning and I think I began to sound like a broken record. This is what happened with these two brothers as well as other people I once called friends. Perhaps it was because I began to be very pro black and they both married white women. I don't hear from these brothers anymore but they are a part of an important time in my life, my time in the Army.

June 23rd 2010 Feelings

I keep refresh'n the page, u got me in a maze, I'm wait'n for your next text but it's take'n days, if timing is everything can you tell me will this fade? if missing u had pounds could you tell me what it weighs?! It's 12:51 and I'm on the train, I'm really happy, I feel like I'm make'n a change, business is slow but it's new so it's gonna grow, I got it LLC'd, thought you'll like to know, when u get back, me & u dinner we should go! you look good but it's the inner you that I want to know, I probably sound like a **- Dawud**

June 28th 2010 Time

You're not the first woman, that I've been inspired to write for, you're the 3rd, if you heard or could read my mind, then everything would be fine, you would know that I'm real, you would drop your guard like I did mine, I'm on my way home, what a waste of my time, I can't wait till you get back only a matter of time **- Dawud**

October 18th 2010 RIP Luis Cintron

When Cintron died he was only 30 years old. They say he died from a brain aneurysm. We were not best of friends but we served together in the army in the same unit, the fighting **falcons** (page 87)**,** we lived in the same barracks so we were brothers. Cintron was full of life and always laughing. He had a nice car and he spent a lot of time fixing it up and chasing women just like most of us. I had not seen Cintron since 2002 when I got the news he passed away but I saw that he passed via facebook and it bothered me. My grand father had died the year prior and I was till mourning his passing. I made a memorial video for Cintron and posted it on facebook. His family and friends were grateful. I had been writing rhymes again for almost a year when he died and I told myself that I was gonna keep writing because Cintron didn't have a life to live so he would live through me.

Condolences

My condolences go out to the family and friends of Luis Alberto Cintron Ibańez. Please know that death is not the end. The soul survives death, indeed and in spirit. This is a book of the dead written by a boy who was murdered without justice, who defeated death and came forth by day. May the soul of **Luis Alberto Cintron Ibańez** walk peacefully through the field of Reeds in Amenta. Amen Ra

October 26th 2010

Penitentiary Chances (Kanye beat)

Penitentiary chances, my friends took em, I never did, even as a teenager I could see them kids, fence hop'n, school drop'n, out fox'n nobody, can't you see the game you locked in? Too often lyrics lead kids to coffins, lost on that course to self destruction, you floss'n but not when you get up north to the industrial prison complex, they force'n slave labor, crime pays but you pay greater, now or later, you're gonna do the time player, I walk with favor, love my neighbor, but don't sleep bitch cause I'm gonna replace ya, *I used to love her* but then you went and you raped her, now I'm straight Hip Hop, and you are just a chaser **- Dawud**

November 5th 2010

All of The Lights (Kanye Remix)

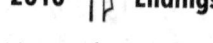

Dawud **The General**, ahead of you, I'm tell'n you I'm new but incredible, the pedestal **I'm on, the throne**, bad to the bone and I'm a keep keep on, climbing up until the lights come on, and when they do I'm shining on my own last name, I wasn't really known till I found my zone, spit my game, now I'm **flying** like a plane, life is what you make it mane, I hope you get more from life than diamonds stuck in yo chain, y'all niggas sound the same, use your medulla oblongata, **I'm here to balance things**, got a problem?! well nigga holler! **- Dawud**

2010

My name is... (AZ beat, Eminem remix)

My name is Dawud it won't change and I'm, sort of like **Pac** cause "my aim is to, spread more smiles than tears", and I don't know why it took me years but I'm here now, so go talk mad shit about me, "Yeah excuse me - I'm a let you finish", but not until y'all mafuckers know about me, I won't stop, I won't quit, Rocky! My whole life I been judged, Cocky! You're obviously confused, Oxy - moron, at ease - order arms, Overseas need for speed, autobahns, I never smoked weed but I fuck long, no tattoos, skin torn, put the time in the gym put the size on, and learn your history cause the books wrong, My name is, Dawud, My name is, gonna cut through this game like stainless Steel for real I'm the shit like anus, That means my scripts just comes out painless, **Your life is a lucid dream you change it,** See what you want take a picture frame it, claim it, **you too can rise up** to famous, My name is, My name is, My name is synonymous with the revolution **- Dawud**

2010 Endings

Just thinking of love in it's many forms, you think you love someone until they turn and do you wrong, what was she really on? She didn't know that I would have loved her for life long, well that's gone, I'm sitting here and cutting off her right arm, I stay calm like Vietnam, no that's not a car alarm, the cops coming I'm not running, don't you see this fucking bomb? **- Dawud**

Rau nu Prt m heru

Iu f Per f m heru

Utterances for Coming Forth by day into Light

It is he, who comes forth by day into Light

2010 Top 10

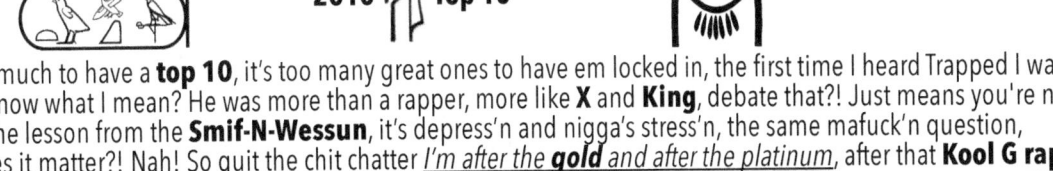

Ay yo I love Hip Hop too much to have a **top 10**, it's too many great ones to have em locked in, the first time I heard Trapped I was 15, _Holler if ya hear me,_ know what I mean? He was more than a rapper, more like **X** and **King**, debate that?! Just means you're not abreast with things, and the lesson from the **Smif-N-Wessun**, it's depress'n and nigga's stress'n, the same mafuck'n question, **Biggie Jay Z** or **Nas**, does it matter?! Nah! So quit the chit chatter _I'm after the **gold** and after the platinum_, after that **Kool G rap** son, 98 **Buckshot** _state to state_, **Gang Star** _who's gonna take the whole weight_? When I was young my father gave me a tape, **ED O.G**, **De La**, **Brand Nubian**, just a taste of where I'm coming from, who I listened to, if I don't mention you I'm not diss'n you, it's a long list here so I might miss a few, I'm on some **KRS One**, **Dead Prez**, **Mos Def** shit, **Kweli** quote right here, bump'n **2pacalypse** now death wish **- Dawud**

Top 10 Hip Hop lists on page 72

November 11th 2010 Krazy (Tupac remix)

When I sit sit and think'a think about my life backwards, I think about how I grew up the ghetto bastard, no wonder **Naughty By Nature's** what I blasted, **Tupac** Trapped shit that was my classic, I had that hoop **dream** to one day get drafted, and one day the teacher looked at my grades and laughted, I disrupted classes walked halls with no passes, but when I got on that field, I caught them passes, if you let it life will make you a has been, I been so blessed I'm living I should have passed when, I was in Iraq so many bullets pass'n, or when I was on the highway speed'n and crash'n, can't count the times I played with death and came out laugh'n, had a gun pointed at me son and they wasn't laugh'n, have you ever had to run away from somebody blast'n? Was it really that serious?! I'm just ask'n, I never smoked ly, I don't know why but one day I'm a get high, I just hope I don't go krazy, krazy I just hope I don't go krazy, krazy

When I think about death I see the General pass'n, my grand father, **General Dukes** in his casket, now I'm the oldest man in my family, my family ain't close, but I'm think'n we can be, I got three sisters only one of them's friendly, my mother ain't a mother she was more like a auntie, my aunts like sisters I lived with them mostly, so yeah it was bad, but it could have been worse b! My father wasn't there but still I became a man, raise a child up and let them know that Gods got it planned, learn your history before you go and take a stand, I joined the army and woke up in Iraqi sand, I never smoked ly, I don't know why but one day I'm a get high, I just hope I don't go krazy, krazy I just hope I don't go krazy, krazy

If it's meant to be maybe I be the one, reverse my military training and I aim it on them, even though the road is dark I still look for the **sun**, and you ain't got's to be smart to know to get you a gun, so, look for the **sun** but get you a gun cause niggas don't wanna see you rollin, rollin, he wasn't strong enough to make the voyage and stuff they stabbed him up and threw him in the ocean ocean, these rappers must be joke'n, got me ask'n what the fuck is he smoke'n? I'm hope'n unity is approach'n cause **self destruction** is like a really bad joke, take it back to before dope, I never smoked ly, I don't know why but _**one day I'm a get high**_, I just hope I don't go krazy, krazy I just hope I don't go krazy, krazy **- Dawud** _**Page 194... I got high...**_

November 18th 2010 Nasty Ashy

Days in the crib turn to weeks in the crib, barely eat or sleep no pussy this is all I can give, take a track write a rap, and give it back like here it is, I remix some new shit that's out, can I live? My youtube is scream'n out I'm love'n it kid, more views more hits more chance that I touch the sky, the more you diss the more I laugh **when I start to rise**, I had this **dream** when I was young but never did try, _**it's like God put this vision in front of my eyes, I be a fool not to follow this feeling inside**_, so if you hate on me remember to watch me go from ashy to classy, **Nasir** to Nasty, my grind impeccable, rhyme more than respectable, bow out now I won't think nothing less than you, a lot of new emcees in the game sound the same, it's impossible for me to merge in the same lane, I'm a different animal, sleeping giant always ahead of you, mechanical zero at the range I put the lead in you, boys in blue the only crew I really got beef with, they kill'n niggas, send them to jail or beneath it, I'm sea sick I see so much shit I'm disgusted if you see it on fox 5 news don't trust it! ashy to classy, **Nasir** to Nasty, life ain't a game when you try'n to get that broccoli, it take money to make money and be a boss G, I'm just try'n to see what it's gonna cost me **- Dawud**

November 19th 2010 Start'n Another

As soon as I finish this rhyme I'm start'n another, so we can't go out chill and that's word to this rubber, just another undercover lover, love'n to love ya, but my mind stuck on the grind like two dogs stuck on each other, I might miss ya but don't love ya, might kiss ya but don't trust ya, she ain't my girl just cause I fuck her, you know I gotta keep it G so hearts don't shatter look when they hooked they wanna be happier ever after, **Lesane Crooks** he had the illest flow and vernacular, **Sam Cook**, A change gonna come, she came faster, I was named after my **father** a mafuk'n slacker, he left soon there after, we never exchanged laughter but, ha who's laugh'n now? Yeah you silly clown, my mother you beat her you drank, dragged her on the ground, I heard you sober that's good cause life can come around and bite you in yo ass, I'm still fight'n with my past, think you know me? You don't know the half, and oh when I blow it's gonna be facebook picture tag, for those who hate, I'm just step'n back with the jab, like **Money May** I need a million dollars in the bag, so far away from where I started do the fuck'n math, is you retarded? **- Dawud**

November 25th 2010 **POWER (Kanye remix)**

I'm live'n in the 21st century, only got one life to live, **when I die I'm a live forever** just like **Michael** did, stupid! Ain't no recoup'n the painful life he lived, **Michael** ain't never molest no fuck'n kids! no one man on earth know they last hour! the clocks tick'n I'm going to get power, you gotta a problem with that well nigga holler, I don't wanna have to send your mother flowers, I believe in **miracles**, but I don't depend on them, like **seminal Indians** fuck a treaty if they kill'n them, the **Huey P** in me won't let me stop think'n bout **Emmett Till**, I keep it real, **O.D.B. Dead Prez**, "*let's get free*" **- Dawud**

Significance

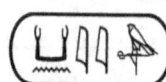

The name **Emmett Till** appears in my poetry for the **second** time. I say the name O.D.B., From the Wu Tang Clan. O.D.B. Took the name **Osiris** as a nickname and Osiris (Ausar) is the Kemetic (Egyptian) Lord of **resurrection**. Eight years after this song, On July 3rd 2018 my past life as Emmett Till is revealed to me. I speak of Michael Jackson and **Michael Jackson's** striking resemblance to an Egyptian Bust was discovered in the late 19th century, said to have been crafted during the reign of the Pharaoh **Tutankhaten**. On April 4th 2020 my past life as Tutankhaten (King Tut) is revealed to me (page 594). In this verse I state that we "*only get one life to live*". At this time I was not cognizant of **reincarnation** but I also said "when I die I'm a live forever"…. Subconsciously I already knew! **Re-member** that **you** are **Ausar (Osiris)** and **Heru**, the **hero!** See page 3 for the **hero's journey!**

November 26th 2010 **Uptown**

I'm just a revolutionary nigga, simple man, "**Never Had A Friend Like Me**", loyalty to the end, **royalty** I would have been, if I was around in the time of **King TUT** king could have been me! **Watch me rise up** in this fuck'n game, cause all these niggas ain't say'n shit they the fuck'n same! **- Dawud**

Significance

The name **King Tut** appears in my poetry for the **first** time on the exact same day that the Tomb was opened in 1922 (page 11). Tutankhaten's (King Tut's) tomb was discovered on November 4th 1922 and it was opened on November 26th 1922. On April 4th 2020 (page 594) my past life as Tutankhaten (King Tut) is revealed to me. I quote **Tupac** in this song and I have a theory about who Tupac was in a **past life**. **14** shots were fired at Tupac on Sep 7, 1996. **Ausar** was cut into **14** pieces and **Emmett Till** died at **14** years old.

November 27th 2010 **In The Morning (J Cole, Drake Remix)**

I love waken up to pretty faces, girl I swear through clothes I can never tell how small your waist is, ratio to hip girl my heart races, and it skips a beat when I see you naked, let me know what's on your mind, what you craven, word? you know I'm always up for chase'n, extra credit, 9th inning, loaded bases, ahh, change the pillow cases, fall asleep wake up, penetration, you like'n that, you bump it back with no hesitation, damn I thought I never say it, I thought I never meet my match but this game you play it and play it well, a lessor man would have fell, but not me, I just see you at the hotel, and you know damn well the way I put it down girl when we wake up I ain't gotta ask, can I hit it in the morning? can I hit it in the morning? can I hit it in the morning? The sun rising while you moan'n - **Dawud**

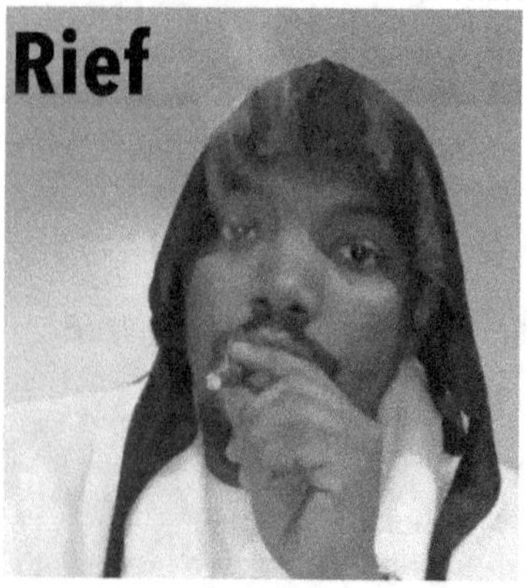

December 1st 2010 **Generally Speak'n feat Ramadan Rief**

Fresh off the pavement, I ain't supposed to make it, so I made my own rules cause the game is played flagrant, **14** I was aight wit it, then the hunger took me under nigga I'm nice wit it! **the heir to the throne**, so respect me or leave me alone, send radiators at you that will heat up ya home, is real life sit back and pay attention, **Ramadan Rief** flow harder than san Quentin, bar for bar, I hear the fake mask and they smile wrong, heat you with the gem star for play'n a star wrong, I'm tired of all these hate'n niggas bitches and uncle toms, showing no support but play'n me close when the lights on, as far as taken shots, dump a clip and aim high, and rise in the sky look'n down with the evil eye, dark days dark nights, always bring the same lights, I need money like a bank heist, to live right, I'm try'n ta get right, I need money like a bank heist, bank heist, got the shadows all around, and they need to get off me, get the fuck off me, get off him, the heir to the throne, so respect me or leave me alone, leave me alone, I'm nothing that you thought of, the son of a Generals' daughter **- Ramadan Rief**

I stand here with no fear in the ***shadow of the valley of death*** with nothing less than that **God** flow, when I'm at the top of the game with money and fame will they hate me or love me, more or less? Hell if I know, whatever the case my grind don't stop, I stay on chase, M.O.B mode forever, I never forget a face, keep my enemies hang'n from they legs off a ledge whoever said I wasn't the illest gets dropped on they heads, breath'n life into Hip Hop, **Nas** said it was D.O.A. And I agree it's pathetic they paying for airplay, I live it I breathe it, I be it, son of a **Generals daughter**, thought you knew me?! I'm more than you thought of, the world is mine fuck a new world order, I'm sorta like **Denzel** unstoppable, **Jordan** 4th quarter, I gotta do what I gotta do, ***I'm claiming the throne***, Maximus Decimus Meridius Rome, I'm try'n ta get right, I need money like a bank heist, bank heist, got the shadows all around, and they need to get off me, get the fuck off me, get off him, the heir to the throne, so respect me or leave me alone, leave me alone, I'm nothing that you thought of, the son of a Generals' daughter **- Dawud**

Rau nu Prt m heru lu f Per f m heru

December 2nd 2010 Real as They Come

I'm just the realest nigga walk'n everyday that I'm live'n, I'm sinning but praying that God give me time cause I'm trying, I'm focused and so I wrote this, *my **hokus pokus** was **predicted** and written like the locus*, I'm the greatest the dopest, don't hate it that's hopeless, your time is over fall in line it's time to **Soulja**, I'm sure they told ya, always somebody bigger stronger, **I'm King Cobra,** now you knowing, and knowing's half the battle game over, **ever since I was a kid I knew there were things that I had to do, my paster knew, some people can look and see things inside of you,** but it's up to you to close your mouth, look and listen, you could miss your lesson if you spend your time stress'n and bitch'n, to my lil homies cook'n up coke in the kitchen, there're more ways to hustle fuck going to prison! you really find out who love you as that clock keep tic'n, when they come to slug you the same niggas that hug you come up missing, I'm on a mission, top of the game top of the world, impossible is nothing I walked on ice and never fell, if you tell me something tell me I'm nice or go to hell, think not? then you're a fool! small bus to school, got everything to prove nothing to loose that nigga Dawud spit'n jewels but then I go and cruise on the highway like I done lost my mind, what else can I say? when I'm dead I'm dead but while I'm living I'm living my way... **- Dawud**

December 2nd 2010 Gangsta

Yeah, check over, the lone soldier ride'n dolo, me stop'n this grind, nigga that's no bueno, its a no brainer, I'm like a volcano, spit fire so easy like **Kobe** at the free throw, I ain't come to tip toe, I came to flip the script tho, didn't know I was a G? What the fuck do you know? This is nothin knew tho, a man of many hats, many wish death pon me but where they at? Trying to Tupac me I see where the haters at, well this death-com 3, where the coffins at? **- Dawud**

December 4th 2010 One of these mornings

I wrote this for my kids if I ever have some, one day I'll be gone, I know it's hard to fathom, but you gotta carry on, if you love them grab them, hug them, tell them you love them, kiss them and keep them laughing, they say the love inside is **everlasting**, memory is therapy, tears crashing, right the wrongs in your life before life happens, in the blink of an eye, left here asking why? man, I just don't get it! some of us die before we get the chance to live it, we all born just to die, won't be long I'll be gone in a minute, ***Look for me** in **another form** a **spirit, transform etheric*** **- Dawud**

December 4th 2010 Young Gifted and Black

I'm Americas worst nightmare, young black and I never sold crack out here, yeah I'm aware of the facts of how the drugs got here, I'm taking it back to afros and fists in the air, in the back strapped in all black gear, if I can die in Iraq then I can die right here! We call cops here but the cops don't care, they stand on the block try'n to instill fear, so niggas drop cops on the black round here, and we don't shed a tear when the cop die here, I swear last year they killed a nigga right there, Obama is here but niggas still in the rear, I'm uptown but I ain't from here, last stop on the A is Rockaway I was born there, yeah Hamels, Gateway and Edgemere, niggas die there, mothers screaming out my dear God, yeah this the hood where life is hard, **Tupac** and **Biggie's** killers still at large, a career killing niggas it's an inside job **- Dawud**

Utterances for Coming Forth by day into Light

December 7th 2010 Day Dreams

Ha ha ha ha ha, check out the bizarre, rapper quote used by D A triple U D, ***I see the future*** **every time that I'm dozen**, I see the crowd moving like a ocean, one for the money two going against all the odds, you hate'n on me, look at me now, I'm a star! so far from where I came, everybody knows my name, and I can hear it now, -DAWUD- that nigga changed, well?! we ain't supposed to stay the same are we? started my own army full a niggas that's ready to die for me, I die a Nobel death **Martin** on the balcony, I walk the streets and visualize what would **Malcolm** see? so keep doubt'n me, it only makes me better, I bet I see Creflo dollars like Mason Betha, or Warren Buffett, yeah that's my type of budget, I was told **if I can think it then one day I'll touch it**, somebody tell you different, you better tell them shove it, they couldn't do it themselves, and don't want you to have it, I'll be on top soon show'n you how a soldier does it, you gotta love it these haters helping me **rise above** it **- Dawud**

It is he, who comes forth by day into Light

December 7th 2010 Warm Regards

Dear love, yeah, you know who you are, said I was cold but you chose to play the odds, and so I close with warm regards, before we crash like falling stars **- Dawud**

December 17th 2010 Genesis

I'm here cause I'm never gonna stop this, I got this Hip Hop ***prophet prophecy*** to see profit, promise me you won't stop it, I need you to hate me, fuel to my rocket, plug to my socket, close your mouth, put a sock in it, or a cock in it, I tell you what there's no top'n this, Hip Hop fucked up nigga's given niggas top in it, you not the shit, I'm not relate'n, *if I don't like it I don't like it that don't mean that I'm hate'n*, I'm **Tyson** when I'm write'n, only right that I'm chase'n niggas back to the lab without a mic to grab, silly rabbit you can't have it, I **Prodigously** bring **Havoc**, Dawud means David Blaine **magic - Dawud**

Significance

I named this rhyme **Genesis** and this is the **first** time I mentioned Tyson in a rhyme. **Menes** (Narmer) is basically the Genesis of ancient Kemetic Dynasties being the **first** and oldest known Pharaoh of ancient Kemet. By placing these pictures together I make no claim that **Mike Tyson** is the **reincarnation** of The Pharaoh **Menes**. Mike Tyson is however, the youngest heavy weight champion ever, and probably the most feared heavy weight champion of them all and he looks just like Menes, the first known Pharaoh. Menes united upper and lower Egypt strengthening the whole of Egypt. I also mention Tyson in a song titled **Reincarnated** in 2016 (p 370). I wrote more about Tyson, **rebirth** and a **dream** I had with him on page 528.

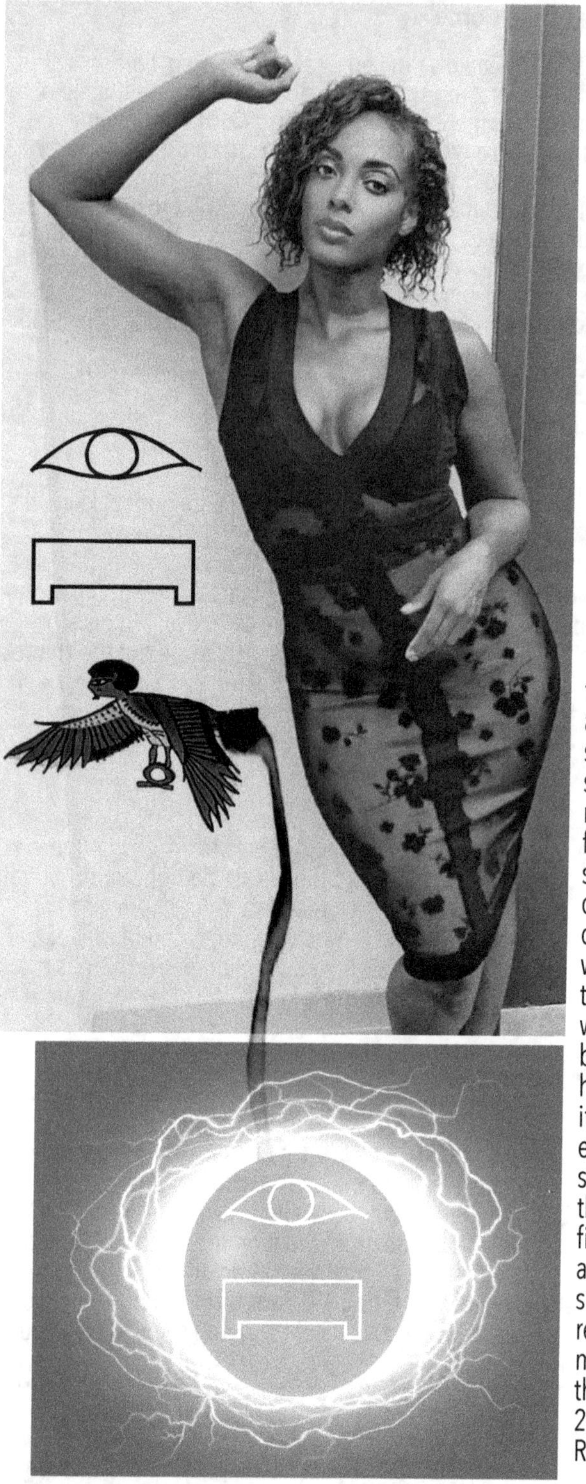

December 18th 2010

Sleep Paralysis / False Starts / The Ark of a Million years / Divine Barks /Meta Spiritual Devices

I called Nikkie on October 7th 2021. It took me some time to remember her name. I searched the address book from my old computer to find it and on October 6th 2021 I found her on Instagram. I sent her a message. - "**do you remember me? You needed a placed to stay in NYC some years ago**." 2 hours later she replied. - "**were you training at the time?**" I said, "**yes**". She replied - "**oh wow. Hello!**" I told her I was writing a book about my life journey towards my past life revelations. She replied. - "**I don't know why...but I recently thought about you. Your book sounds interesting**".... I asked her if she was available to speak and we spoke the next day.

In writing this book I could not remember the exact year or the date that Nikkie came to stay the night at my place. The date Dec 18th is around the time she left NY in 2010. Her and I were friends on facebook in 2010 but we had never met in real life. At the time she was around **23** or 24 years old and I was 33 years old. Nikkie was a pretty actress with a very nice body. She was from Atlanta visiting New York and somehow she was left without a place to stay. Feeling stranded she reached out to me on facebook and told me her situation and asked if she could stay the night at my place. I agreed to let her stay. I can remember wondering whether she was being honest or did she "like me". I didn't know but I knew that if she was stranded I was not going to use the opportunity to "make a move" on her. I treated her as I would want one of the women in my family to be treated. I had a queen size low platform bed and I let her sleep on the left side and I slept on the right side. I did not touch her and did not move to her side of the bed. Neither of us did. We both slept on our respective sides of the bed. I do remember thinking, I wonder if she wants to lay closer to me but I was not going to ask her and I wasn't going to move to her side of the bed. I fell a sleep. I would wake up that night in what people commonly refer to as **sleep paralysis**. I could not move my body or speak but I could move my eyes. My body was frozen and hovering above me was a **dark sphere** with **electricity emitting** from it. This was the only time I had ever seen a black sphere like this but I'd experienced **sleep paralysis** two or three times before this. I wasn't scared this time! Before this night I had never been able to break free of the **"sleep paralysis",** but this time was different. I kept fighting and finally I broke free lunging at the black ball of lightening taking a swing at it with my left hand. It flew to the other side of the bed where Nikki was sleeping. I was free. I had broken free from **sleep paralysis**. I don't recall if I told Nikkie about what had happened but this was a victory for me. This would be the last time that I experienced **sleep paralysis** in this manner. My experience with Nikkie would take a strange turn in 2022 after the release of this book. Perhaps she was some "**Goddess**"! Read page 619 for more details.

Years later I would learn how to consciously bring myself into the state of **sleep paralysis** and use it as a bridge to **astral projection** (page 538) by using my thoughts and desires to influence quantum level events in time and space. The **black sphere of lightening** that I saw above me while I was stuck in the state of **sleep paralysis** always reminded me of the TV series **Lost** (page 259). There was a "monster" in the jungle that took the form of a giant cloud of black smoke with electricity emitting from it and when most people came in contact with this smoke they were killed (page 260). Over the course of the next 11 years I would continue to have experiences that reminded me of the TV series **Lost** and in the year 2021 they would all crystalize. While writing this book I kept thinking about the series **Lost** and finally on April 9th 2021, the day **DMX** died, **I would hear a voice in my head** that sounded like DMX and the voice would lead me to a vendors table on 125th street where, to my surprise I would find and purchase the first season of **Lost** on DVD for $5 dollars (page 640). On November 1st 2014 I would have another experience that reminded me of **Lost** (page 306). The same thing happened on June **23rd** 2021 (page 648). These two experiences were connected to the **star codes**. November 1st 2014 would be a pattern of **Heru** the one who **resurrects**. In the unseen realms we must hear what is not spoken and years later this experience would finally speak to me. On June **23rd** 2021 the same pattern intensifies and the Heka (**Crook, Shepard**) staff of rulership is presented to me in a profound coincidence. Then in 2022 I go on my first trip to Kemet (Egypt) in this life and I am given a staff, a short wooden branch that had come from a tree in Akhetaten (p 671), the city King Tut was born in (last page of book). In 2010 I had no idea that I was the Boy King on a mission to find the other half of a staff stolen. All the pages of this book tell the story of the Nswt who stole back his crook and his flail. The world is old but the future springs from the past. One day soon we'll be on top again, the Afrikan came back with unity as the stratagem, maximum effect like maroons ready to ride again, when I die I'll be back in the spirit to try again.

Patterns and the Pattern Masters of the Universe

Just as the sun has a daily cycle and a yearly cycle there are cycles we go through in our daily and yearly lives. As we move through our cycles we attract certain patterns that follow us waiting for us to decipher them. I encourage you to take nothing in your life lightly because most things that are happening to you have great importance. Life is a game that we play, a play of consciousness. Your ability to be successful at this game is measured by your ability to see what is not seen and to hear what can't be heard. We make a fatal error when we think all that we see with our two eyes is all that there is to be seen. All things are governed by seen and unseen forces.

Rau nu Prt m heru

Iu f Per f m heru

Utterances for Coming Forth by day into Light

It is he, who comes forth by day into Light

December 19th 2010 Crooked Cop

Even if you hurt me I'm a never shed no tears, cause I'm a soldier and I stay teach'n my peers, they all look for me to help, but tell me who's gonna help me? Sometimes being a leader's to be lonely, ***my only fear of death*** is being misunderstood and not doing all that I could, if you could see how I feel inside, every time I see an innocent man die, mo shots on the block from crooked cops, live and learn to discern friend or foe, live'n the school of the hard knocks, they treat our home like a war zone, it's hard to get along most of us come from a broken home, we ain't from where drugs are grown but they shipped and flown to our doorsteps, do you get it homes? and they call me courageous but I'm just like, I ain't standing around while they enslave us! God bless that crooked cop, ain't much time left for a crooked cop, better get him in check or he gonna get popped, boys in blue bleed red on the fuck'n block, death to a crooked cop, I ain't got no respect for a crooked cop, better get him in check or he gonna get popped, boys in blue bleed red on the fuck'n block

Go ahead write your ticket, stare me down, pat me down, fuck'n clown, life ain't fair what goes around come around, you work here but it's clear you ain't from here, and if you are are you aware how they compare us to dogs?! even the **Lord** had it rough here, I've had enough yeah, you can see it in my eyes, fuck the law ***in the event of my demise***, another nigga dies another mother cry's, another rap song about how they flip pies, **Al pachino** and **Al capone**, I wonder if they see the evil they have cloned, I thank God for another day, and then I zone off patron it ain't healthy, I need a way to let them all know we family, each one teach one, one nigga hand me my 44, God bless that crooked cop, ain't much time left for a crooked cop, better get him in check or he gonna get popped, boys in blue bleed red on the fuck'n block, death to a crooked cop, I ain't got no respect for a crooked cop, better get him in check or he gonna get popped, boys in blue bleed red on the fuck'n block **- Dawud**

December 19th 2010 Digital Angel

The race is on no slowing down, she ten years old with a thong, and she going down, food so fat on the farm can't walk around, change come when the gun use sonic sound, around 91 the internet was barely around, oh when the buildings go fall'n down, the real life Michael Douglas, is here now search **Clay A Duke**, they let his wife go and so he went to shoot, that's what it's coming to, V for Vendetta, I never say never but it's never getting better, I'm **morpheus** on this hip hop **Nebuchadnezzar - Dawud**

December 22nd 2010 Flow'n

I'm nasty on the track, Dawud wud is the key cause he's flow'n, she said energize the insides of me and keep going, I'm like, it ain't a problem for the kid, she get's off see me stir'n it like mafuk'n coffee, after I nut I hit the highway see ya later, the price you pay when you parlay with a player, I'm just a man understand my many layers, middle finger to the law I'm a be a law breaker, obey the law? I'd be ly'n if I said I did, cause I'm a g4 soar'n over all of this, I got a fever hot like scorch'n kid, feed me seymour, I never see so I'm stay'n on top dig? and on topic that I'm hot shit, so hot I flip from independent to a major turn everything in my favor, you just the flavor of the month like **Blacksheep - Dawud**

December 26th 2010 Bet That

When I was young I was **superman** nothing you could tell me, Clark Kent had a **dream** I could fly, never forgot it, look at me now, through my life, the ups and downs, Hip Hops the only thing that stayed around, I played around with different beats, it calmed me down, like my **therapy**, I got used to the people tell'n me, you should take it seriously, I'm like listen to me, I'm in the army, it's not gonna happen, but now I can't think of doing anything but rap'n, when you realize a **dream** haters they come flap'n, small gains with even bigger set backs, Dawud gonna do his thang, you can bet that, respect that, yeah I was born in Rockaway, been around the world hell and back **die another day**, but not today, maybe tomorrow, until then my friend, it's me that you follow

Small gains and with even bigger set backs, but that's gonna change, you can bet that, small gains and with even bigger set backs, but that's gonna change, you can bet that, Two, three, four five minds are stronger than one, but I write my own rhymes, still I'm getting it done, am I the fool? is being true considered old school? freestyle ain't even freestyle no more fuck what they sold you **- Dawud**

2010 You Can't Imagine How I feel

You can't imagine how I feel, you can't imagine how I feel, you can't imagine how I feel, you can't imagine how I feel, you can't imagine how I feel, you can't imagine how I feel, it's one thing to survive 5 shots, it's another thing to die and stay on the top, when you die will you live like my nigga **Pac**? Or make the list of emcees that we all forgot, I'm talk'n bout whether you can imagine how I feel, I know some do, I shed tears too, some of you rap'n for years and still I don't respect you, when it's your time to go ain't nothing that can protect you, I'm trying to live I ain't got a son but I got a nephew, and I'm'a bless him with some **Pac** that he can rock to, how could you not like **Pac** and be Hip Hop too, black too, Funk master Flex don't make me smack you **- Dawud**

Significance

I saw a video of Funk master Flex Talking about Tupac in a negative way and that fueled me to write this verse. When I recorded the song I used the energy from a Tupac interview when he says, "you can't imagine how I feel", speaking about being shot.

Rau nu Prt m heru

Iu f Per f m heru

Utterances for Coming Forth by day into Light

It is he, who comes forth by day into Light

December 28th 2010 I Shot The Sheriff

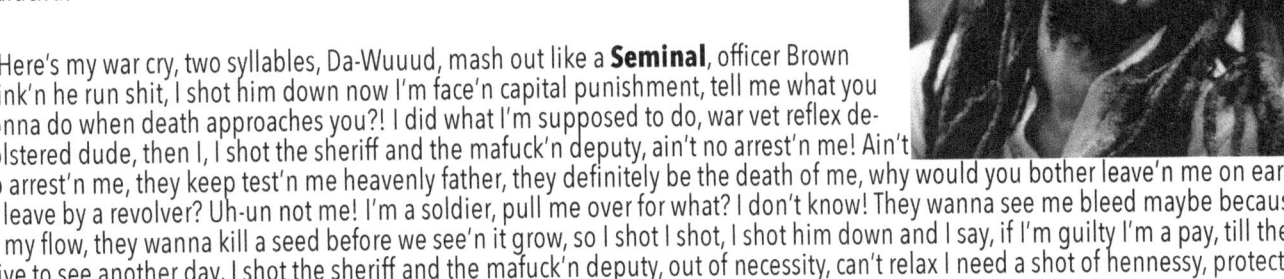

I shot the sheriff, I am a victim of police brutality, naw, set set me free, I shot the sheriff and the mafuck'n deputy, out of necessity, no look'n back, I only see ahead of me, can't get caught, It's more than a felony, fought for my life, judge ain't hear'n me, hear'n me, I shot the sheriff and the mafuck'n deputy, out of necessity, can't relax I need a shot of hennessy, protect me? Nah! You My Enemy! My Enemy! I am a victim of police brutality, **Sean Bell** mafuck'a!

Here's my war cry, two syllables, Da-Wuuud, mash out like a **Seminal**, officer Brown think'n he run shit, I shot him down now I'm face'n capital punishment, tell me what you gonna do when death approaches you?! I did what I'm supposed to do, war vet reflex de-holstered dude, then I, I shot the sheriff and the mafuck'n deputy, ain't no arrest'n me! Ain't no arrest'n me, they keep test'n me heavenly father, they definitely be the death of me, why would you bother leave'n me on earth to leave by a revolver? Uh-un not me! I'm a soldier, pull me over for what? I don't know! They wanna see me bleed maybe because of my flow, they wanna kill a seed before we see'n it grow, so I shot I shot, I shot him down and I say, if I'm guilty I'm a pay, till then I live to see another day, I shot the sheriff and the mafuck'n deputy, out of necessity, can't relax I need a shot of hennessy, protect me? Nah! You My Enemy! My Enemy! Never Been A Friend To Me!

In memory of **Sean Bell** and **Oscar Grant**, so many brothers fell like we live'n in combat, who's next? Who's gonna ride with me? Fuck beef with **Lil Kim** and **Nikkie**, and **Ja Rule** and **50**, we gotta ….. Take over the city, I shot the sheriff , I am a victim of police brutality, naw, set set me free, I shot the sheriff and the mafuck'n deputy, out of necessity, no look'n back, I only see ahead of me, can't get caught, it's more than a felony, fought for my life, judge ain't hear'n me, hear'n me, I shot the sheriff and the mafuck'n deputy, out of necessity, can't relax I need a shot of Hennessy, protect me? Nah! You My Enemy! My Enemy! I am a victim of police brutality, **Sean Bell** mafuck'a! - **Dawud**

December 26th 2010 Essence

This much is true, Dawud is come'n, I'm come'n to do what you wouldn't, or maybe you couldn't, so maybe you shouldn't fuck with a nigga like me, nigga like me, come in to see, Yo I ain't come here to be second, first thing on my mind is staying true to my essence, I let my light shine, I'm a product of that 90's Hip Hop, played my **purple tape** so much finally it popped **- Dawud**

December 20th 2010 New York State of Mind

New York streets full of heat in the winter, no heart beat for the weak, niggas fall in the summer, the spring bring the same things, gun laws don't matter, the man with a hammer is king, you just a nail, call it heads or tails, life in hell or a cell it's all the same when they aim'n to set you up to fail, drive'n when black, walk'n on egg shells, war in Iraq ,the war is here what part you can't tell? Welcome to Israel, anything will sell here even **Jada will Smif-N-Wessun** in bell air, clear? Nah! We ain't got no fresh air here, it take 911 to come together here, where the soldiers at? New York state of mind, where they at? On the grind, the 4 line is where it started at, I wrote a rap in the back of the ac, I'll never relax, I'm on the map and feel'n blessed to be a part of that **- Dawud**

December 21st 2010 Who's World is This

I sip the Hennessy watch'n **Huey P** till I'm charged, there's only a matter of time before the cops come barging in, the black male is the problem they solve'n them, so when they come I 45 revolver them, or hand to hand **Antonio Tarver** them, when they sleep is **Oscar Grant** haunting them? Emotions of hate and rage I harbor them, I feel better as I pray to conquer them **- Dawud**

Oscar Grant

Oscar Grant III was a **22**-year-old African-American man who was killed in the early morning hours of New Year's Day **January 1st 2009** by BART Police Officer Johannes Mehserle in Oakland, California. Responding to reports of a fight on a crowded Bay Area Rapid Transit train returning from San Francisco, BART Police officers detained Grant and several other passengers on the platform at the Fruitvale BART Station. BART officer Anthony Pirone kneed Grant in the head and forced Grant to lie face down on the platform. Mehserle drew his pistol and shot Grant killing him. His death sparked protests and some people rioted. The civil case was partially resolved when BART settled with Grant's daughter for $1.5 million (with accrued interest), according to Burris' law firm. BART paid a $1.3 million settlement to Grant's mother. The five friends of Grant settled with BART and received a total of $175,000.

Condolences

My condolences go out to the family of **Oscar Grant** and all those who have been robbed of their life by this system of racism and white supremacy. Please know that death is not the end. The soul survives death, indeed and in spirit. This is a book of the dead written by a boy who was murdered without justice, who defeated death and came forth by day. May the soul of **Oscar Grant** walk peacefully through the field of Reeds in Amenta. Amen Ra.

December 29th 2010 Dawud is Come'n

Expect me nigga, I'm come'n, Expect me nigga like you expect **Jesus** to come back, Expect me nigga, I'm come'n, my life is all I have, my rhymes my pen my pad, and I done made it through the struggle don't judge me, what you say now wont budge me, cause where I come from so often people you grew up with are lay'n in a coffin, I'm come'n, but I done made it through the pain and strife, it's my time now my world my life **my life**

I told ya'll nigga I was come'n, guess you thought that I was fuck'n around, either get down or lay down, as I kneel down to pray for my enemies, it's still a life for a life I'm precise like snipe'n a Kennedy, a soulja of fortune, now ready the coffin you ain't hot, you's a dead man walk'n, *I'm come'n, My life is all I have*, and you ain't got that if it's me you think'n of off'n, we all dying, **I'm just dying trying to live forever** through my rhyming, take you to Zion Hip Hop Nebuchadnezzar, I'm the best nothing less like **Mayweather,** won't stop won't quit, no way never! **- Dawud**

Significance

In this song I sampled the words of **Tupac** from his album**, R U STILL DOWN**, where he says, "Expect me nigga like you expect **Jesus** to come back, Expect me nigga, I'm come'n". Years later I would have past life revelations of being **Emmett Till** and **Tutankhaten** (**King Tut**) in past lives. Afterwards I realized that **Tupac** had been here before (pages 664 - 665). I also used the hook from the song, **The Life** by **Styles P** (p 377) and **Pharoah Monch** (p153). Pharoah Monch is born a few days after me, the same day **Mf Doom** died (page 630, 633) and Styles is born two days after **King Tut's** tomb was opened (page 11). In this song I would also say, "we all dying, **I'm just dying trying to live forever** through my rhyming". As if my **soul** knew the whole time and "**it**" was trying to awaken me to the immortality of my soul. This is why it is very important that we are careful when we spell words and put them into poetry that we might repeat over and over. Our souls are listening. I mention Floyd Mayweather in this rhyme and the first time I saw **Mayweather** fight was when he fought **Zab Judah** in 2006. I was a Zab Judah fan at the time and afterwards I became a Mayweather fan as well. I once met Zab Judah at the **4040** club during a fight night. We were in the same VIP room watching a big fight. He was approachable and friendly. I would have my 1st **dream** with Mayweather in 2019 (p 552) and again in 2021 (p 635). Floyd and Zab are both born in 19**77** the year of the **snake** like me, Zab is born two days after me on October 27th. I think both of these brothers were ancient warriors who traveled to earth the same time I did. I consider Mayweather to be the best of the best. A Black man who utilize the barbaric art of American boxing to his benefit. Taking the least harm than any boxer in any era, making the most money while also inflicting less harm on his opponents while doing so. This is not to say he is in any way weak, but instead he May very well be the wisest of them all. Enslaved Black Men were forced to bare knuckle fight, sometimes to the death, and sometimes killing their family and friends to the amusement of White slave owners who only saw them as animals. The enslaved Black men were even forced to run full speed towards each other and ram their heads together, like rams, for the amusement of White slave owners who only saw them as animals (page 19). In 2019 I would start reaching out to Mayweather in the dream realms (p 552, 560).

Page 443

December 29th 2010

No Come'n on After Me

Yeah, in forever search of the **illmatic**, I elevate the status great **32 magic**, emphatically take the entire cake, you can't have it, this empire state of mind has gotten me so graphic, get'n some head in the back, call it blow'n through traffic, she said you classic but nigga you ain't classy, you spit'n and shit'n on tracks you so nasty, I'm sicker than jack the ripper, but you can't catch me, and still I'm so **Wesley**, still bump'n **2pacalypes Now** I'm down for my niggas, don't test me **- Dawud**

December 30th 2010 Photosynthesis

I was born for this, I put on a crown of thorns for this, even when I do sleep I wake up and then I'm drawn to this, like a flower to **sun** photosynthesis, **first born son** I'm the one you wanted, you asked for this, diss me, mafucker that's blasphemous, you can't touch this not even my ass to kiss, you know I mastered this, I'm like **Jadakiss** and **Kris** mixed with **2pacalypse**, they can wish but I'm still never stop'n this, that's like **Malcolm X** becoming a cop or crip it won't happen! think ahead take stock in this, like upper Manhattan used to be chocolate **- Dawud**

December 31st 2010 - January 1st 2011
Weed and Ice T

I was 33 years old and I had been writing rhymes as a way of therapy for 1 year now. Just like most people who create music I wanted to make a song that people could feel and maybe become famous but I had not been able to do that as of yet. **Tupac** was my favorite Emcee and he always rapped about being high and **smoking weed.** I began to wonder whether or not I would write better and deliver my rhymes with more feeling if I smoked weed. Would it some how make me better? In the back of my mind I remembered what happened to that guy from my high school football team. He smoked weed and went crazy (page 64). He ended up in jail for trying to rape a woman in broad daylight and then while in college a guy smoked weed then ran into the lake and drowned (page 73). Or at least that's what was reported. I was 33 and had never even smoked a cigarette. I never saw the logic in smoking because it destroyed the lungs. For most of my youth I was getting high naturally. I got high from drawing as a teen and there's a small high in playing video games. I got the most high when I played football, especially during games. **I got high when I ran as fast as I could in a race**. A regular race on the play ground is different than when you're in front of a great crowd of people and the game is on the line, because then your adrenaline is racing throughout your blood and time can seem to slow down. That's a powerful high. I was curious though, I wondered what this high from smoking weed felt like?!

I smoked weed with my cousin Taliah (p 42) but I didn't inhale properly so the effects were very mild. After we smoked we went to a New Years party that **Ice T** was hosting. He was there with his wife **Coco** and a few other people. My cousin knew one of the people so we got in for free. I sat at the table with Ice T and had some small talk with him. I told him that I had just started writing rhymes again. He told me that there wasn't any money in Hip Hop anymore and if I wanted to make money I should try techno or another form of music. Then he got up and performed a few songs. Shortly after he performed he left and we left too. Things changed after that. I started to see weed as a possible good thing and not a bad thing that it was vilified as. In 2011 I went on to smoke weed on a regular basis and little did I know I had **opened a portal for thought consciousness to flow through me** (p 343). Because of the things I was watching and the books I began to buy, **Jehuti** began to work with me and the ancestors began to order my steps. I still had a lot of work to do with cleaning myself up but I was on the path. We attract the energy that we entertain. After my third year of smoking I tried to stop but I wouldn't stop till my fifth year, Nov of 2015 (p 343).

Significance

If we pay close enough attention we can find the meaning to almost all of the things that happen to us and why we cross paths with certain people at specific times in our lives, just like my meeting with **Rihanna** (pages 167 & 278). Take my meeting with **Ice T** for instance. On the surface level it could be a meaningless crossing of paths governed by nothing but chance however, with a closer analysis one can find the **pattern**. **Ice T** enlisted in the United States Army in October 19**77** the year of the **snake**. He was assigned to the **25**th Infantry Division. I was born on October **25**th 19**77** the year of the **snake**. Of course I knew none of this at the time. This was not a **coincidence** it was all governed by unseen forces. This was the first and the only time my cousin and I have **ever** gone out together to a club.

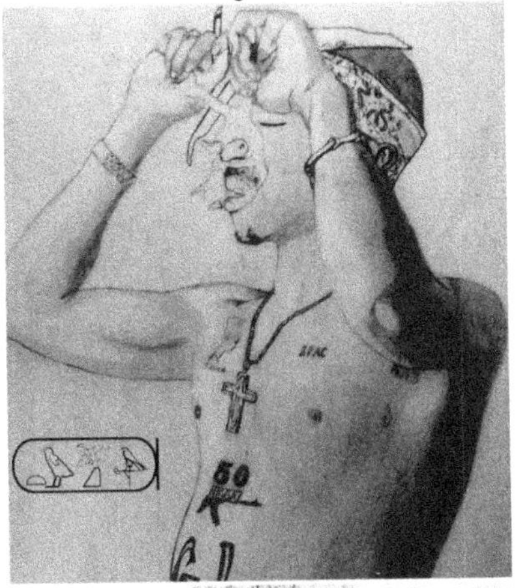

January 4th 2011 Hail Mary Tupac remix (1st of 67)

What do we have here now? don't push me homie, I'm close to the edge, having **dreams** I can't move with demons over my head, is it the **spirit** of Hip Hop? Cause Hip Hop is dead, Maybe it's **Tupac** and **Biggie** telling me to go ahead? cause in my **dreams** I'm falling, hit the ground I'm crawling, looking up at these niggas they ballin, and I'm so appalled, Hip Hop hypnosis the pride before the fall, the 11th hour approaches, you can quote this, yeah I'm a mother fucking monster, it's deeper than that Reagan Iran contra, a born leader, my nigga run quick see *on a journey to see a for real emcee*, I was born for this, ***I put on a crown of thorns for this***, even when I do sleep I wake up and then I'm drawn top this, like a flower to **sun, Photosynthesis,** diss me mother fucker that's blasphemous **- Dawud**

Significance

I mentioned **sleep paralysis** in this rhyme as well as taking power from the Sun (**Aten**). (**sleep paralysis** page 176)

January 9th 2011 Money over Morality

I exist cause y'all niggas ain't represent'n, so busy cook'n coke in the kitchen, you have anyapiphan, epiphany reversed, I think you're fuck'n cursed! when they start given out the m**ark** I think y'all be the first, you know we distant relatives but it's never relevant, so niggas die where they live, it's money over medicine, a felony for weed, they make'n millie's off excedrin! Lord I'm on my knees, times more fucked up than they ever been! money over evidence, I'm talking to my president, let **Mumia** free! anything else is negligent, they raised my **rent** I had to act like a thespian, though inside my pride knows I'm more broke than I ever been, it's a joke if you think you're never gonna sin, even the **pope** gonna get his in, yeah anything to win, that's what time we in, we inherited this poverty, track it back to the colonies, **black Indian** fatalities, **smallpox, H.I.V.** same strategy, you don't agree? you must live in another galaxy, I speak the truth no apology, the powers that be, practice money over morality, M.O.M money over morality, you sit'n pretty we live'n here in this poverty

(For the Common Connection see page 81)

Look in front of the museum of natural history, what you see is a fallacy, we fought gallantly, we ain't go willingly, define enemy? it's an armed adversary, and I ain't gotta look far my nigga I'm come'n from the belly, of the beast, in the concrete jungle full of police, you ticket me to pay your salary?! That's money over morality! A masters mentality, I'm a **Nat Turner** slave! *holler at me* if you hear me the **spirit** of **Makaveli!** define silly? The ones scream'n out swag in videos floss'n their money, and no it's not funny, you know they say I spit **Mos Def**, **Common**, **Nas** rap I just say make sure you **Jay**, **Kweli**, **Tupac** that, I joined the army almost lost my life fighting combat, now my life is the light brining Hip Hop back, we inherited this poverty, track it back to the colonies, black **Indian fatalities**, **smallpox, H.I.V.** Same strategy, you don't agree? You must live in another galaxy, I speak the truth no apology, the powers that be, practice money over morality, M.O.M money over morality, you sit'n pretty we live'n here in this poverty **- Dawud**

January 7th 2011 These Many Roads

Racing through life on these many roads you gotta know the codes, us brothers in the hood we them black crows, from **The Wiz** not **The Wizard Of Oz,** We had to make our own movies so we can see **stars** that look like us, *we used to be **Gods***! look at **King Tut** even he got robbed! Laying up with shorty you know, after we blazed that, asked her how she felt about **Huey P** from way back, She didn't know who he was I couldn't believe that, Lil homie, be careful where you plant blakseeds at, you never know how the odds will go, you pick a hoe and that same hoe come knocking at yo door, you ain't got ta live and learn No! that's a big lie, you can learn from other people Just a word from the wise, Open your eyes when will you realize *if you give yourself half a try* ***you can really rise***, what if everything that you'd ever been shown had been changed just to benefit the throne? We had more kings than the ones in Rome! Are you your brothers keeper?! he was screaming leave me alone! What would you do? He was screaming leave me alone, What would you do? He was screaming leave me alone! What would you do if you were **Michael**? Leave him alone! What would you do if you were **Michael**? Leave us alone!

What would you do if you were **Michael**? suddenly nobody likes you, at least that's how the media hypes you, you climb the whole mountain of fame, etched your name in the game and all you got in return was the pain, pain turns to running but for you there is no hiding, you ride around in things a little less under high end, that's how you blend in, I wonder what you saw, you had the whole world looking back in aw, I sign my name at the floor, put this letter in a bottle and promise that I'll do better tomorrow, *and when I see **DMX** you know a prayer's gonna follow, cause what I see is my brother there fighting for his survival*, the rifle, back against the wall shit that I do, each one reach one teach one like the gospel, what you ain't got it?! homie I spot you! yeah I got you! every other race look out for their own but we forgot to **- Dawud**

Significance

This is the second time I mention King Tut's name in a rhyme, the first time was Nov 26th 2010 (page 187). I mention **DMX** in this song and when he passes away on April 9th 2021 I was visited by his soul the same day (page 640). **Aaliyah** would Ghost write the song **Astral Plane** for me on Nov 26th 2018 the same day that **King Tut's** tomb was opened in 1922 (pages 11, 543). I've heard an interesting theory about who **Aaliyah** was in a **past life** but I won't be repeating that in this book…..

(Doors, written on **August 22nd 2021,** page 658**)**

"when **DMX** died his soul came did me a favor, whispered in my ear said go ye there look through them papers! **Anubis** and the **afterlife** advice watch for them gators, **Maat** is precise in your life! you gotta watch your behavior!" **- TutemRa**

January 11th 2011 **Big Dividends**

Big dreams, big dividends, more money more problems I ain't got a problem with a bigger Benz, you know it all depends, on If I'm going in, like **Bruce Lee** I keep it flow'n like water my friend, **Sho-nuff** you just a **Bruce Leroy**, Hip Hop with out me is like Hip Hop without a **B-boy**, look, if me and you was beef'n, you'd be **Kool Moe D**, I'm **LL**, nigga harder than hell, I battle anybody, don't care who you tell, me at rock the bells? Yeah that's pretty guess'n, if I could rock the bells **- Dawud**

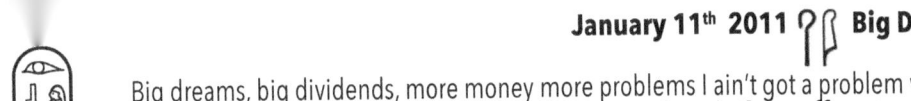

Rau nu Prt m heru

January 16th 2011 **Corrupt Cops**

A yo Cops, on one hand I hate em then I understand them, but my hater is greater, Yo I'm more interested in rider music, all these cops with guns and don't know how to use it, these _streets are death-row_, lil homies get'n executed, Mr Officer can't you see your view's polluted? I think yo scared is that the reason why you shoot'n? We all dress the same but we don't all bang, **Obama's** here what did you think that it was gonna all change? He put his work in to get respect to get a rep, and she was search'n for a case or high speed chase to make detect, they made the perfect team always seemed to be two steps away from every murder scene, took a few years on the job but they started noticing, as long as there's a Fien these teens gonna be servicing **- Dawud**

January 21st 2011 **Kid Fresh**

Iu f Per f m heru

don't you understand that every war that America's been in, we been there fighting, wait'n! wait'n to be free my friend! and it's hard when you erasing our history and then we get robbed of our talents, where is the balance? from the concrete I rose seen so many highs and lows, I guess my biggest regret is treating our women like hoes! cause the women in my family man they, they don't deserve to be **Hallie Berry'd** and I ain't tryin to come up off her name! cause this game right here this ain't no game! this the plantation! look at the NBA and everyday they kill kill, they kill our thug nation! we need some **foundation**, respect to **Lord Jamal and Sadat X** cause they said that, standing on the train and I heard a kid in a black hat say he was upset that when a brother assess rap and write raps that fight back, they barely get the love back, I had to reject that, and spit the facts, and say look black, the fact is we gonna come together, every generation got some soldiers wait'n like the panthers of Patton, I need your participation this is not a verse it's a dissertation, they say where u been? I say I been watching the nation, watching inflation, this is not my imagination, they killed **Tupac Amaru,** not **Shakur,** the one from **Peru**, the things they do! when u wake up they come for you! don't let them kill your dreams Freddy Krueger seemed so scary as a teen, you're probably more safe in a **dream** because your closer to death, and they say in peace you rest but when u wake up and see the light that's when you see'n the test! Yeah yeah they call me call me **kid fresh**, my name's Dawuud they call me **Kid Fresh**, yeah, they call me kid fresh, they call me they me call they call me kid fresh, my name's Dawuud they call me **Kid Fresh**, my nigga Danny over there my nigga **Alan** on the left

Utterances for Coming Forth by day into Light

Ay yo I love Hip Hop too much to have a **top 10**, it's too many great ones to have it locked in, the first time I heard **Trapped** I was 15, _Holler if ya hear me,_ know what I mean? He was more than a rapper, more like **X** and **King**, debate that?! Just means you're not abreast with things, and the lesson from the **Smif-N-Wessun**, it's depress'n and nigga's stress'n, the same mafuck'n question, **Biggie Jay Z** or **Nas?** does it matter?! Nah! So quit the chit chatter _I'm after the **gold** and after the platinum_, after that **Kool G rap** son, 98 **Buckshot** _state to state_, **Gang Star** _who's gonna take the whole weight_? When I was young my father gave me a tape, **ED O.G**, **De La**, **Brand Nubian**, just a taste of where I'm coming from, who I listened to, if I don't mention you I'm not diss'n you, if you take it personal it's _the bitch in you_, _I walk the night in rhyming armor bomb a nigger like a winter coat_, _One Nation_ under God indivisible by no man, we were robbed, brought to the land and it's still uneven odds, that's why we plan plot strategize, too many brothers coming up dead! **Sean Bell 41** shots of led, we kill each other but we scared to shoot a cop in the head, I ain't another **Tupac** cause **Tupac** is dead as we all gonna be if we don't check what was said about divide and conquer, look at the **blue** and the **red**, you a gorilla but you ain't really food for the fed's, you eating good but what about the ones that you lead that you led, they believe that you do every little thing that you said, it's in a headlock y'all Hip Hop ain't dead, you gotta fight for what you think is right I pledge allegiance to my friends and family to write on the right side of history fuck a Grammy **- Dawud**

Top 10 Hip Hop lists on page 72

It is he, who comes forth by day into Light

January 25th 2011

The upper edge of a tomb was found on the first day of Egypt's revolution, on **25** January 2011. The opening was sealed with an iron cover and the discovery was kept quiet.

Significance

The discovery would be made public the next year in January the month before Whitney Houston made her transition and that would be very telling. There is no such thing as just a coincidence!

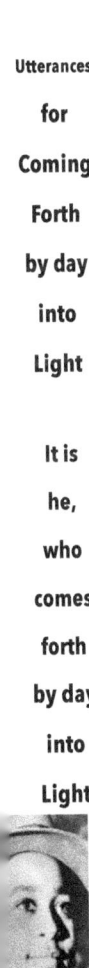

January 28th 2011
So High I Could Touch The Sky

For the first time I got so high that I was worried about my mental state. My body was twitching and I was very paranoid. I said that I would never smoke again because I wasn't sure if I would go back to normal. I thought about the guy from my high school football team (page 64) and the guy who ran into the lake and died in college (page 73).. I was worried but I fell asleep and woke up fine. So I kept smoking.

January 28th 2011 Your Policies

Who are you to tell me what I need? I see my brothers killed away, locked away over some seeds, over some greed, I hear them scream'n please, you don't hear them? Blessed is he who fights the power don't fear them! Oh oh what a tangle tangled web you weave, when you conspire to deceive you liar! Look at your policies! We set this on fire go ask the **Pharisees**, I ain't the **Jesus** of **Christ** but I'm a bad Emcee! **- Dawud**

January 29th 2011 No Master Plan

What you gonna do when the people come to, when they wake up and realize all the things that you put them through? They gonna be come'n for you, guns in the air, we come'n, they gonna be gun'n for you! What if **Jesus** wasn't **God** man?! No reason behind why life was really so hard man! No heaven no hell! No master or no master plan! What if **Jesus** wasn't **God** man?! No reason behind why life was really so hard man! No heaven no hell! No master or no master plan!.......... **- Dawud**

February 17th 2011

Use Ya Head

I'm spit'n some realer shit on the pavement right next to some shit, but still I clean up cleaner than some shit you bathing with, they slaving with no knowledge no mind that they been sold, and *I know another conscious emcee that's getting old, but the law was told somewhere next to* ***the book of Job, I came to save it*** *and that's the reason why they named me* **David, Goliath** the greatest expired, it's only right somebody takes us higher without killing the poor, hangers pliers, they hang us they try us, they couldn't understand her tears from all the years of seeing all that they denied us, a raisin in the sun they dried us up no love for self inside us, need more than a **Waka Flacka** flame to light us up and then ignite us, what's worse **Michael Vic** or how they used to whip and fight us? they used to make us ram head to head! sick fucks! More ways to get ahead than a quick buck, try instead to use your head now put yo fist up, It's not ok for you to judge me trust me, you can never tell who the thugs be, reality is ugly, look for the history you don't see, only one God above me, Only God can judge me, probably be different if my daddy loved me but if he did I wouldn't be here, Such a beautiful struggle hallelujah yeah, bombs burst in the air rockets red glare yeah

Now that the tables set let me project my views on being an **Iraqi vet,** I bet you never would guess the stress of the hood is the same as life or death, let me take a breath, Whewww whooo, in peace I hope he rest, the boys in the blue shot him down, no peace pipe here! Let's be clear, would you care if this was rocking roll?! would you be locking up the Guns and Rose?! secret society got you under control, playing they game you could lose ya soul, I'm saying no names but **- Dawud**

February 20th 2011

Stress Free Day

Make it a stress free day, nobody crying on my day, let the kids play out all day, B.E.A utiful everything's beautiful, think it's not? You the fool, I'm ready to die cause life is not the move and, look the blood it made a pool and, everything's so slowly oozing, emotional ocean look at you sinking, taking your life man you must have been drinking! **- Dawud**

February 21st 2011 2 Sin By Thought (dexter)

Oh shit man, Wow! Yo, do you think anybody saw us? Relax relax**, Yo that was close this time man**, Relax! **I don't know man**, Relax homie! **Yo, we really need to. Yo! This shit is getting crazy man**, listen, relax! **This shit right here is getting really fucking crazy**, Nobody saw us! Nobody saw us! **I'm just saying, This shiiish this shit this shit fucking crazy,** Yo listen, let me tell you something, Hold up listen! you need to remember why we doing this man! Yo it's not a game. Yo Yo! Life is a long journey, some of our time here shorter than others, he's been gone for an hour, she has yet to discover, yet to meet her destiny of having to bury her brother, yet to squeeze his lifeless body that can't squeeze back and hug her, but yet and still I did it still admittingly killing fields, killing feels good when the killings real, I mean close and personal killing no sleeping pills, I've lost my mind my mind reminds me of my many kills, you'll get chills knowing the many different ways I made him feel sorry for killing boys in the hood like it's a game or even a hobby **- Dawud**

Rau nu Prt m heru

Iu f Per f m heru

Utterances for Coming Forth by day into Light

It is he, who comes forth by day into Light

February 22nd 2011 Time Traveling

A yo believe me I been loving **Hip Hop** way before the **CD**, my **Tape** fixing it when it break, staying up late, no internet, no status update, I hit eject, flip the tape put it back in the deck then call my ace, A yo you heard that new track from **Artifacts Wrong Side of the Tracks**?! **Naughty by Nature** they was swinging bats not busting gats, **Hip Hop** done lost it's shine it's time we bring it back, first time that I heard **Half Time** I nearly lost my mind, around that time I wrote my first rhyme, **2pacalypse Now** on repeat keep pressing rewind, **89 tech 9** had the classic sessions, **Big L L-Swift Smif-N-Wessun, The Underground** that's where you found the essence, where I found my lessons, calling up to **freestyle** I was stressing, cause if you was wack they was disconnecting, and you know that, that right there can be a bit depressing, so that kept us on our toes with our flows, **No Half** step half Step'N, **follow me time traveling, follow me time traveling, follow me time time traveling, time traveling, follow me time traveling, traveling back in time with me, follow me time traveling, follow me time time traveling, time traveling follow me time time traveling, follow me time traveling time traveling, traveling back in time with me follow me**, I said you are just a slave, they control how you behave, man made religions lead'n people astray, the government be eat'n, police be beat'n, judges and lawyers they cheat'n, now you in jail for the weekend, hands and face leak'n **- Dawud**

<u>**When I wrote this spell, little did I know, I was seemingly apart of the most iconic movies about time travel (p 40)**</u>

February 24th 2011 Everyday

I literately write everyday, so I'm nice in every way, while you on the sideline scream'n, can I play? and everyday they splice'n **DNA**, I never thought I'd see the day when real life's more like a scene from Michael Bay, either way you go it's haho, halo, lay low you never know if it's gonna open only my real soldiers know, search'n for sight beyond sight like Panthro, I know that God's got the world right in his hand though, expand yo mind man, tell him I said so, be a man devise a plan don't spend up all your dough, one man call it progress, I call it a low blow, **Malcolm X** said it best, by any means necessary even death **- Dawud**

February 25th 2011 I Tried to Warn Ya

It's easy to be a gangster! try being a man, or a woman that's not so easy to anger! can't you see the danger? I see your <u>*death around the corner,*</u> **Pac** tried to told ya, I'm trying to warn ya! wanna be a soldier? think of those who you dishonor, 50 yrs ago we were fighting for tomorrow, and now we're here today, but we done went astray, I can't watch us kill each other and look away, they say a better day is coming but they didn't say it would be without people dying or people running, the Sunni, the Shia, some day one day they gonna unite, when I write it's like let there be light, a new beginning, street **prophet** I ain't free from sinning, we all answer to the **Lord** when our clock is finished, until then we stuck on earth like a jail sentence doing time prime time news ain't gonna stop the crime, **Man in the mirror** make up your mind! destroy build cultivate kill, read between the lines, let your light shine, let your light shine, let your light shine, let your light shine, I'm lyrically, yes, I'm on another level, never sell my **soul** to the devil, I tried to warn ya **- Dawud**

February 26th 2011 Hang Your Self

Beef is not what Labron did to Cleveland, beef is how somebody gonna die this evening, shot gun blast deceive'n, we fall'n fast, another soldier down no longer breathe'n, seduced by the game when you pull that trigger the bullets leave'n, why can't you use your brain? Dawud's my name **I said I was come'n** and they thought I was lame, the jokes on you cause **I'm come'n for the top the hall of the fame**, Hip Hop took a fall, tied a rope to the wall, let they feet hang loose put they head through the noose, that's how most of the rappers hang, I'm in a different lane doing my own thang, doing my own thang **- Dawud**

February 28th 2011 Ego Trip

Yo there's a reason why you rock to every beat, that's how you get to closer proximity of the greatest hip hop Emcee, and I ain't talk'n Em I'm talk'n me, and I ain't talk'n Jay or little weez, nigga please I'm supposed to think that I am the best no disrespect to any vet but I had to get that off my chest, see kiss'n ass will probably get you there fast but hard work at my craft got you doing your math like I just hope that he act right, most of these greats ain't wrapped tight, most of these fans addicted to the abc crack pipe **- Dawud**

March 4th 2011 The King

Hip Hop everybody wanna be the **king**, how you gonna be that?! You ain't even a good human being! I sting like **Wu Tang**, these are your nuts on the table, bang! Bang! These are your brains on drugs, fame! See I was born in the 70's, raised in the 80's but 90's Hip Hop's what made me, and lately none of y'all clowns can phase me, **if another nigga die! Die! I'm a go crazy!** They kill'n us but you, you wanna blaze me?! Damn! Give **Willie Lynch** a hand! **I am that I am** slash Emcee, I'm self made cause no nobody taught me, I'm not a slave cause no nobody bought me, gotta be Atlanta brave on these streets of New York see ya lost me once you start rhyme'n about being frosty, it's written on your face and ain't no way you taken it off B, things are well even though I don't deserve it, my dude corrected me when he heard this, a closed fist get you ass kicked, we all fall short the glory of the Lord so I still carry my sword, if you don't like it you don't like it that don't mean that you hate'n but karma's a bitch and that's the bitch that you date'n, I'm Hip Hop son so I'm second to none, I ain't worried about make'n it cause it's already done, I walked on ice and I never fell so you know I'll never run, unless it's DMC **- Da'wuud**

March 11th 2011 E.T.

Who the hell is this scream'n die bitch die bitch at 5:46 in the morning? Terror, screams, bullets fly'n cops sirens we had a fair warning, horror scenes, UFO's so commonly seen, something explodes, look out my window, the Army Marines, the type of things in 100 years you'll see in a museum, we all scared but we fight'n no no time to stand and fear them **- Da'wuud**

March 14th 2011 Kalishea

I met Kalishea shortly after she moved to Harlem. When I saw her I knew I was supposed to know her. She gave me her number and we became friends quickly. I cared for Kalishea and wanted to see her accomplish her dreams but I was searching for something. I was on a quest to somewhere, but to where I did not know. I had been smoking weed for two months now and Kalishea and I would smoke weed sometimes. I took two puffs of a cigarette once in my life and that was while at the park with her. I was amazed at how quick the "high" feeling came on and immediately I understood why people stand out in the cold on their lunch breaks to smoke cigarettes. I never smoked another cigarette. On March 14th I took a picture with Kalishea at the top of 45 Rockefeller. 6 years prior I worked at 30 Rockefeller as a painters apprentice. One day I left that job for lunch and never went back because of a **card** I found on the floor (pages 141-142). I felt like it was a sign! In Dec of 2020 Kalishea would show me a **card** she had since 2010. Her card would show me a sign!

Significance

Kalishea is born on June 15th, the day before **Tupac's** birthday and years later she would have a son named **Honor** born on October 24th the day before my birthday. Kalishea once worked for **Sean Puffy Combs** on a fashion gig. Kalishea says that Puffy made inappropriate advances towards her. He tried to kiss her and told her that he wanted to have sex with her. She declined, left that day and never went back. Puffy is born on Nov 4, the same day **King Tut's** tomb was discovered (p 11, 664). In 2020 I would tell Kalishea about my **past life** as **King Tut** and she would show me a card that she had kept since 2010. A card promoting the **King Tut** exhibit where 50 of King Tut's treasures had been shown from April **23** till Dec 17th of 2010 at the Discovery Times Square Exposition. At this time we had not seen each other in over 7 years. On July 18th of 2021 Kalishea attempted to drive to New York from Philly to see me but every route she took was stopped by police road blocks due to rain flooding. After an hour of driving she finally turned around and went home. When she got home and went to exit her car she looked on the passenger seat and saw a **golden** Scarab **Beetle**. She claims that she has never seen a scarab like that in her life. King Tut's throne name was Neb Kheperu Ra. Kheperu means scarab. The year after my past life revelation of **Emmett** and a year before my past life revelation of **Tutankhaten** (**King Tut**) I would have a series of profound experiences with the same type of Scarab Dung Beetles at the 2019 International African Arts Festival (page 569). Afterwards I would realize that scarabs had a deeper meaning in ancient Kemet (Egypt). They represented resurrection, rebirth, reincarnation and were place on the mummy of the Pharaohs to ensure that they had a safe journey to the next life. On **April 28th 2021** I got a tattoo of the **Ba** (**soul**) and when Kalishea saw the tattoo she said it looked like her and to my surprise it did (p 642). When Kalishea was 16 she was laying in the bed crying because she was 16 and pregnant. Her grandmother was sick with **cancer** and she felt that she had let her grand mother down. At that moment all she wanted to hear was her grandmothers voice. Then to her amazement the **astral body** (**Ba** / **Soul**) of her grand mother floated through the ceiling and stood over her and said, "I'm sorry baby". Then she floated away. Kalishea picked up the phone to call her grandmother only to find out that **she had just passed away.**

March 18th 2011 Piano

One for the money, two for recruiting the non believer, three for the source I show you how to hook the non believer, first of all keep it hotter than a fever, colder than January, no shoe and no wife beater, white boy come with some crazy idea, step step up on my land say he the first one here, but the black boy play with a different kind toy, same block where he from same block he destroy, but *everything gonna be alright*, I'll Hip Hop till I drop build the block not destroy, *trapped in the city of seclusion*, try to take that short cut might come up lose'n, *cash rules everything around you*, it's a e*veryday struggle*, try not to let it drown you **- Dawud**

Rau

nu

Prt

m

heru

March 19th 2011 LA

You know, I was home like usual make'n music, cause all I do is just think about make'n music, I got a call, picked it up like who is it? I'm busy make'n music so make it quick, my nigga LA on a New York trip, said he wait'n to parlay with a Germany chick, I said hit me up later we can get in some shit **- Dawud**

March 19th 2011 You's a Boss

Earthquakes in different places but you's a boss, sex trafficing and raping but still U's a boss, you have a platform to teach but all you do is floss, **Ricky Ross** Ross Baby Baebae. **- Dawud**

March 19th 2011 Slow Down

They tell'n me to slow down I can be found hover'n over the ground, at home rock'n a beat, conductor'n a new sound, a new flow, the way I speak my flow is so unique now you are getting sleepy, when they ask you how I rhyme you will say uniquely, they say I lyrically find he got something to teach me, when he open up to rhyme **- Dawud**

Iu

f

Per

f

m

heru

March 22nd 2011 Dawuud is Beloved

Ay yo Dawuud means **beloved**, I'm *beloved of God*, I know *I'm Gods son* cause he gave me the nod, I could have died in Iraq, or as a young black male, but I escape evaded them crack sales, but my cousin was doped up, locked up and he ain't make bail, raised on the same block, but we chose different roads, from the same family but learned different codes, it's a shame when you see them kids get exposed, Montana Fishburne, I got a little sister, and her daddy wasn't ever really there in the picture, I just wish I could say something to her that would shift her, in the right direction, life is one big question, faith is the answer, my **Grand father** died of **Cancer**, my **Father** has **Cancer**, man they gonna really make the Panther come out of me! the powers that be owe us an apology **- Dawud**

March 23rd 2011 Paranoid and Nervous

I'm scared to go to sleep, what if I don't wake up! and I'm scared to stay up, what if I fall asleep? I'm paranoid and nervous this shit is deep! should I eat? Should I drink? I don't know what to think, I think I'm thinking too much, this never happens when I'm drinking too much, am I talking too much? gotta watch the person roll'n the dutch, end up like Charlie Sheen, or Gucci Mane, you're not winning that's not a tattoo that's a shame, and I ain't beef'n I'm just say'n **- Da'wuud**

See page **648** for the **metaphysical significance of the # 23**.

March 24th 2011 Dawuud's Invocation

Envisioning *the here after*, listening to 97 **Common Sense**, 2011 you still spit with no relevance, but when I write it's like the passion of the **Christ**, through my parables I give advice, when I was young they used to say he's nice, but now I'm just **floating** through life and I'm just hoping that you listen twice, I'm break'n the ice, cause my flow turned water to ice, now that's cold, picture a Van Gogh starry night, I'm on a stroll ***trying to find my soul when I write***, no body knows the trouble I've seen when we fight we need to unite, if we gonna make a bond make it tight, and if it ain't a bong make sure you roll it right **- Da'wuud**

Utterances

for

Coming

Forth

by day

into

Light

March 24th 2011 STAGES STRANGERS

Yo, yo when my ah, when my days come to an end, and they register my thoughts, they gonna be like yo, he really cared about some of these women man, yo, they gonna know, it's gonna be right there

Chill'n with you everyday, the **10th grade** we was in, but now you ain't even my friend, I thank God for **MoMo** she let a nigga in, I was at a low, a real friend to the end, she had a **son** name Asiah, I met her through a friend of a friend, if I could do it again I'd be none the wiser, I wasn't ready but I was far from a sucker, never forget the one who played me like a sucker, **science class** used to **dream** that I could touch her, 10 years passed and then the **love** bug struck us, but when my chips were down she became monstrous, you can't support yourself how you gonna support us?! Love changes, life changes, best friends become, they become strangers, Love changes, life changes, best friends become, they become strangers, Love changes, life changes, best friends become, they become strangers, Love changes, life changes, Eww Nana, they become strangers love love, strangers

Eww Nana yeah you know who that is, I used to walk you home try'n to get me a kiss, end up waiting 15 years for the **kiss** but it was worth it, I met you at the club, I admit at ***first sight I fell in love***, **Zascha Moktan**, say what's up to ya moms, I survived a crash that should have ended me! **Jasmin Sharawi** my **angel** she's gotta be, remember when my car broke down properly on the first date it was **fate,** somebody gotta help me find **Keisha**, half german half black hypnotic features, this talk can't teach ya half of what life will teach ya, if you afraid to get hurt then get your ass in the bleachers, Love changes, life changes, best friends become, they become strangers **- Da'wuud**

It is

he,

who

comes

forth

by day

into

Light

April 4th 2011 - 2025
Neptune in Pisces

Some people live on the planet Earth their whole lives and never consider the idea that the Earth is really a living entity. And if the Earth is living then what is to be said of the Sun the Moon and the trillions of other Stars…. Today is December 16th 2021 and I came to know that I have **Neptune rising** at 14 degrees Sagittarius in my birth chart after doing my first astrological reading on July 30th of 2021 (page 654). April 4th is a sacred day for me due to **Martin Luther King** being assassinated on this day 43 years ago in 1968 (p 69) and because 9 years from this day my **past life** as **Tutankhaten** (**King Tut**) will be revealed to me April 4th 2020 (page 594). Neptune represents the **great poet** which is like a tuning fork dealing with rhythm and rhyme and this is also the day I started practicing for the **Tupac** biopic. In 2010 I started writing rhymes again and perhaps the extreme sensitivity and intuitiveness of my Neptune rising is what caused me to start speaking the names Emmett Till and King Tut in my music. Neptune is the **highest spiritual** planet in the solar system and while taking the **path of the poet** I was able to awaken ancient fragments of my spirit because of the nature of my music. It was my love for black people that fueled my music not the lure of money. Neptune is a hard planet to **tune** into because tuning requires a willingness to be totally loving. Knowing what I know now in 2021 I realize that the planet Neptune helped me. The **first rhyme** that I wrote in 2010 on April 11th was title **Surveillance** and in that song I would say the name Emmett Till for the **first time** in a rhyme.. Then on **November 25th** 2010 I said Emmett's name again in the song **Power**. **Tutankhaten's** (**King Tut's**) tomb was opened on **Nov 26th** 1922 (p 11) and **on that same day** I would say the name **King Tut** for the first time in a rhyme titled **Uptown** on **November 26th** 2010. Then I would say the name King Tut again on January 7th 2011 in the song **These Many Roads**, which was written for **Michael Jackson.** I wrote the song **These Many Roads** the day after Emmett Till's mother **Mamie Till** Died (November **23**rd 1921 - January 6th 2003). I would go on to say the name Emmett Till 7 more times in my music before I realized I was Emmett Till in a **past life** on July 3rd 2018 (page 480). I would go on to say the name King Tut four more times in music before I realized I was King Tut in a **past life** on April 4th 2020 (page 594). I would however speak about both of them indirectly in my music many more times before I realized my past lives. I understand now that having Neptune rising coupled with Sagittarius in my chart it allowed me to see the trends of times having an over all picture and Neptune will be over head in pisces till 2025 the year of the **snake**. I was born in 19**41** the year of the **snake** then I was **born again** in 1977 the year of the **snake**. These patterns are examples of quantum entanglement (pages 329, **41**). Music (Hekau) can be used as alchemy when it originates in the heart and soul. I unconsciously used **music as magic** which helped awaken my ancient soul fragments. "**Music is a spiritual thing. You don't play with music**" - **Fela Kuti**

Dawud, Beloved by the Ntru

Emmett Till's name appears in my music 9 times before I realize I was him in a past life

1st	April 11th 2010	Surveillance	P. 180
2nd	November 25th 2010	Power	P. 187
3rd	October 16th 2011	American Dream'n	P. 214
4th	July 7th 2013	Knock Knock	P. 274
5th	December 29th 2015	RIP Tamir Rice	P. 351
6th	February 28th 2016	Barbaric	P. 365
7th	March 18th 2016	Rope a Dope	P. 370
8th	September 29th 2016	Prophecy	P. 424
9th	October 9th 2017	Cream (remix)	P. 454

King Tut's name appears in my music 6 times before I realize I was him in a past life

1st	November 26th 2010	Uptown	P. 187
2nd	January 7th 2011	These Many Roads	P. 195
3rd	March 27th 2013	Year of the Snake	P. 268
4th	April 8th 2015	Star of the Story	P. 323
5th	May 3rd 2016	Hapiness	P. 382
6th	December 18th 2016	Move 9	P. 435

TutemRa Setep en Ra

APRIL 4th 2011

Tupac Audition, Meta Spiritual Encounters and The Superman Curse

Rau nu Prt m heru

"I **embody** everybody, God body, Tupac, Marcus Garvey, Malcolm X, **Imhotep**, respect to Bob Marley". Those are lyrics from my song **Holler If Ya Hear Me**, I wrote it on April 16th 2016 (pages 374-375). "Acting verse action, we don't take action, we get roles to act in movies cause we relaxin, I miss Michael Jackson". Those are lyrics from my song **Dec 3rd RIP Jay Cooper**, I wrote it on December 11th 2014 (page 313). The measure of our words are more powerful than most people understand and the roles actors play in movies can have long lasting effects on the "actor" playing the role and the person viewing the movie. Similarly the names we are given at birth reverberate within each individual whether they know it or not. Many people say that **Tupac** changed after he played the role of **Bishop** in the movie Juice. In April of 2011 I submitted a video audition for the role of Tupac in his biopic that was being produced. I can tell you from my own experience that the souls of those who have passed on to the other side respond to the calling of their names. I had an experience while practicing a Tupac monolog that left me crying uncontrollable tears feeling like I had felt the presence of Tupac in my studio. Playing the role of a fictional person in a movie is very different from playing the role of a real historical figure especially when you take all of your soul and pour it into your practice. It can be liken to summoning the spirit of the person you are portraying. What does it mean to **Embody** someone? You often hear of actors taking on some of the same mannerisms or habits of the people they portray in biopics (movies). If this is true then there can be negative and positive effects of acting depending upon who or what you "act" like. Did you know that there was a thing called the **Superman** curse (see page 204)?

Iu f Per f m heru

Utterances for Coming Forth by day into Light

It is he, who comes forth by day into Light

In ancient Kemet (Egypt) the human soul was divided into 9 parts which are the **IB** or **Ab** which is the heart. The **Ba** which is the soul. The **Ahku** which is intelligence (page 476). The **Sahu** which means mummy and is also the spiritual energy that houses the Ba and the Ahku. And is the part of the soul that survives in the physical world after the body of a person has departed. The **Sekhem** which is the life force energy also known as chi in China or prana in India. The **Khat** which is the physical body. The **Sheut** which is the shadow. The **Ka** is the spirit, or the etheric twin. The symbol for the Ka is two hands raised representing the double nature of our being. It was the image of the dead surviving in the memory of the living, so this Ka could not die until the last living person who could conjure a personal memory of the dead had also departed. **It is the Ka** (**Sahu**) that **reincarnates**, finding the perfect opportunity to finish it's mission on earth. This is why we must keep our ancestors in our hearts and minds and this is where the saying, "speak a mans name and he lives forever" comes from. There was also the **Ren**, which is what we called the name of a person. So the Ren could be defined as the energy of a persons name. Take Tupac's born name for instance, Lesane Parish **Crooks,** in ancient Kemet the Nswt Bity (pharaoh) held a staff (𓋹) like **Moses** called a **Heka** (𓋹) also called a **Shepard's staff** (𓋹) or the **Crook** (𓋹). It was known as the staff of the **ruler**. It was like the title in a name like Doctor or General. King Tut's throne name was Neb Kheperu Ra Heka Maat which meant, master of transformations of Ra, **Ruler** of **Maat**. Why do you think Tupac's born name was Lesane Parish **Crooks (𓋹)** when he was born, and later his name was changed to Tupac Amaru Shakur?! Lesane can be scrambled to spell the word slane (slain). The word **Parish** can mean family, **house** or town, usually related to Christian Churches. The word Parish also stems from the word Parisis (Par-isis / **Paris**). The Kemetic word for **house** was **per** (par) and **isis** (Auset) was the wife of **Ausar** (Osiris) the lord of **resurrection**. So Tupac's born name can translate to, the slain (Lesane) **Ruler** (Crooks) born in the **house** of **Isis** (Per-isis). And the name **Tupac Amaru** means, **Shining Serpant**. In the movie Juice Tupac's character was named **Bishop**. The Bishop in the church is a leader. The Bishop is also a piece in the game of chess. The oldest version of the game chess is called **Senet** (page 10) and that was created in ancient Kemet (Egypt). Tupac is the most influential artist that rose from the concrete of Hip Hop. In the movie Juice he played the role of a young black male who shot and killed his friend. When these types of images are shown all across the world to young black males they can negatively influence this type of behavior. Tupac was a royal soul in a white mans world, that was hell bent on destroying him. He made mistakes but the heart of his mission here will override the mistakes he made. I don't think he lived long enough to realize exactly who he was in his past life but he lived long enough to leave a mark of revolution. Speak a mans name and he will live forever. When I spoke Tupac's name and put myself in his shoes his Ka (spirit) came over me and allowed me to feel his pain and when it did I stood in my apartment and I cried like a baby.

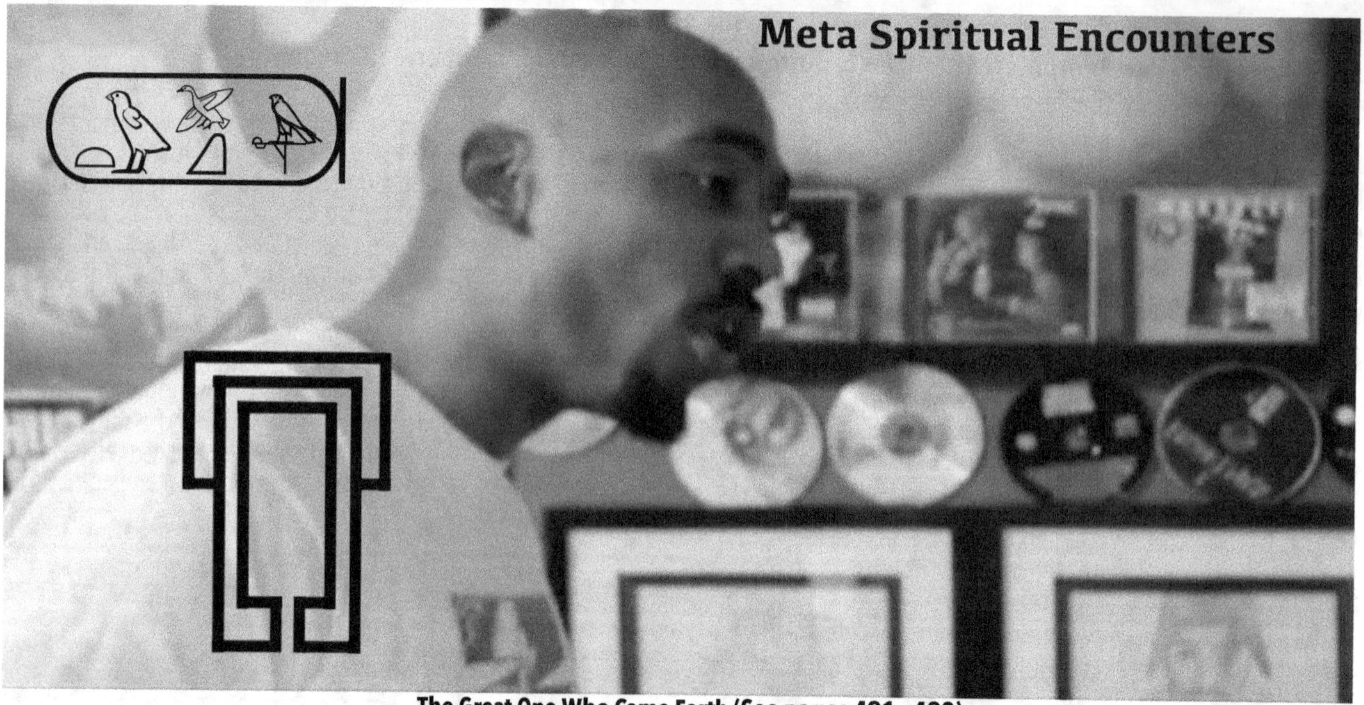

The Great One Who Came Forth (See pages 481 - 482)

Doing this audition video for the Tupac biopic opened a door that propelled me deeper into the musical realms of spells and reality. I would find myself reciting his "speeches" over and over, memorizing his words in preparation and anticipation of landing the role. I used to memorize his songs and now I was memorizing his verbal confrontations with the American Legal system, **then one day something strange happened while reciting a monolog**. It was from the interview outside the court house on November 29th 1994 when he was fighting his sexual abuse charges. "*Why am I the only one in court right now?…….. No I don't want nobody else to go to jail but I don't wanna go to jail for what somebody else did!……* " I was saying this monolog over and over and I tried to imagine as if I was him, and how I would feel if I was in that position, them **BOOM**, something new happened. I was not prepared for this experience so I can't even fully express it but I know that something was there with me and I was not alone. I felt like the Ka (spirit) of Tupac had come over me and I felt him and how he felt at the moment in front of the court room. I cried like a baby. But what really happened?! "Speak a mans name and he lives forever", how "real" is that saying?!… Read what I wrote about the words: **Spirit, Vine, Grapes** and **Wine** in ancient Kemet (page 481). Perhaps **Lusaaset** isn't the only entity, or spirit that can "**come forth**" and perhaps we don't need to be in a drunken state for these "spirits" to "**come forth**"…… Can somebody in the church say, "Amen", or Tutankhamen?

When I decided to do the Tupac audition I posted videos of my monologs on facebook and soon after I received a direct message from a brother who was facebook friends with **Aaron Veasley**. Aaron and I worked together at the gym. We always got along and Aaron always seemed to believe in me, perhaps due to him witnessing me come to the gym and amass a large clientel quickly. Aaron is born on Sep 18, the day before **Emmett Till's** murder trial began (p 516). Aarons friend was an acting coach and he offered to help me with "free" acting lessons. I took his offer. When he got to my place I could tell that he was **gay**. I treated him no different than any other person but I also let him know that I was not interested in anything but acting lessons. Perhaps that was my insecurity but I didn't want to ignore the elephant in the room. I don't remember my exact words but I wasn't disrespectful. He told me that he was **Bisexual**. After that was clear, we went on and did the sessions. He told me that he appreciated me being real with him and not judging him. I had many clients who were "**gay**" I just wanted to be clear, - and because I'm an open book we talked about many things and I asked him if he always knew that he was gay? He told me that he was **molested** by someone when he was a boy. I expressed my empathy. He also told me that **he had tried to stop before**. We didn't talk too long about it and afterwards we never spoke of it again. Interestingly enough, in the year 2019 I saw that this brother was now happily married living a **heterosexual lifestyle**. Many years later **Aaron** would share two interesting things with me. His **dreaming** ability and his experience's with his daughter. Aaron receives messages through dreams. He once **dreamt** his girl friend had been unfaithful and when he brought it to her attention she admitted it was true. Aaron has also had experiences that remind me of Big O's "angle baby" (page 96) and the little girl named Mary (p 618). Aaron's daughter has told him several times that she used to watch him from heaven before she came to earth…

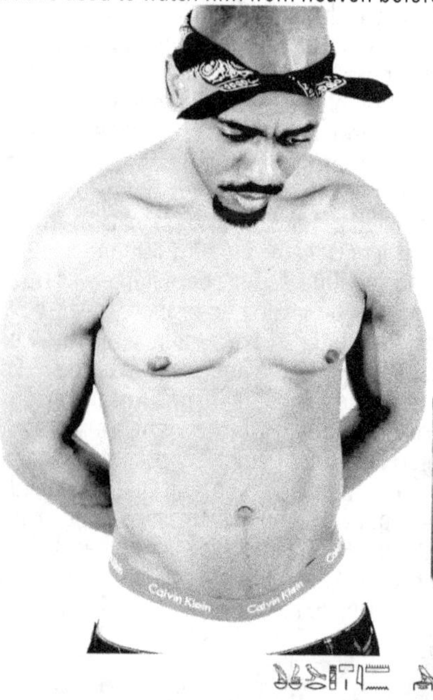

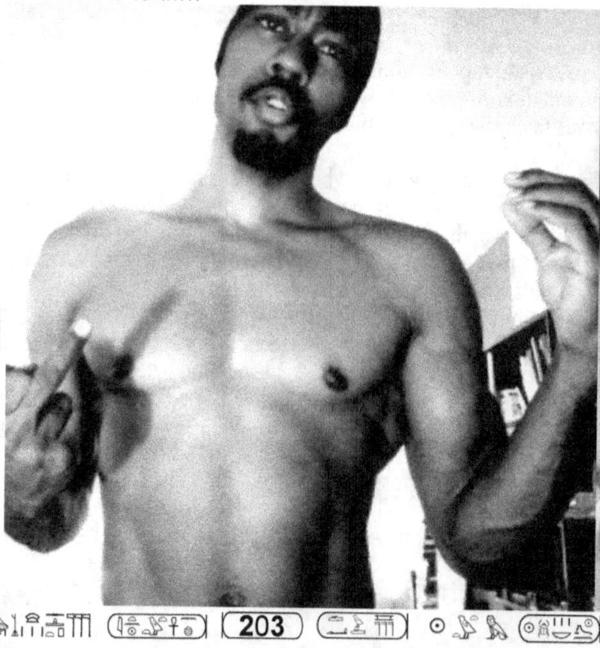

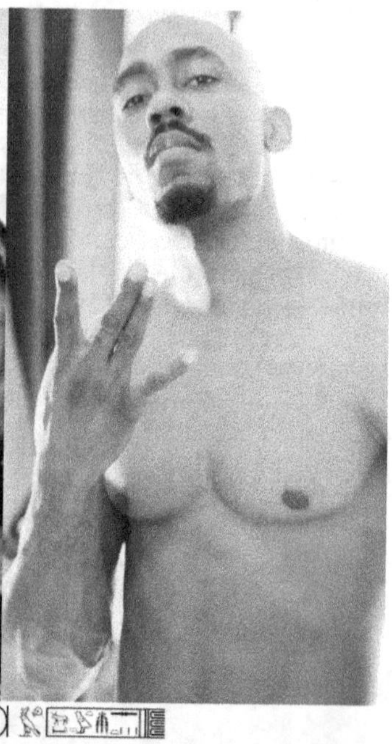

The Superman Curse or The Curse of The Pharaoh?

Addendum The Dangers of "Acting" Like a Superman

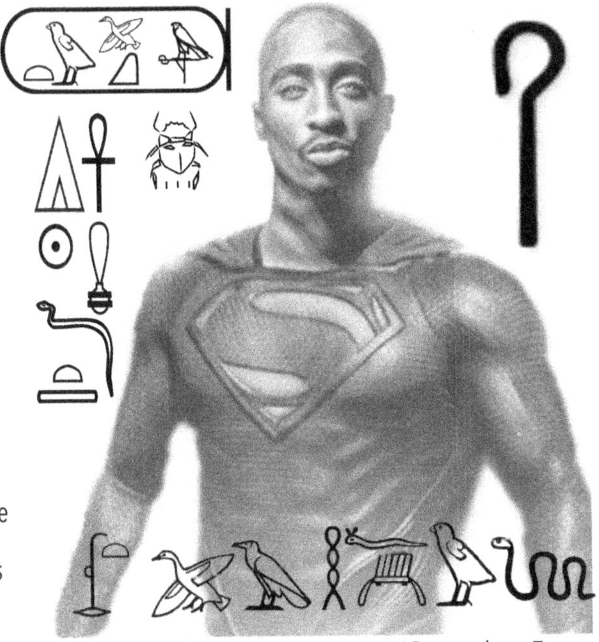

Rau nu Prt m heru

Iu f Per f m heru

Utterances for Coming Forth by day into Light

It is he, who comes forth by day into Light

Taking action doesn't always involve movement. You can act like a tree and stand very still and do nothing, or you could act like a tree and breathe deeply leading to levels of self realization unimaginable. Acting is a broad concept. You could act like you care about people when really and truly you don't. Superman is a White superhero created in 1933 in a culture of racism and white supremacy. A White man who saves the world while in real life white men murder, lynch, rape, and imprison Black people all over the world. Superman is an **arc**hetype of **Shango,** the most popular of the Yoruba Orishas (p 58). The first Superman animation films were created in 19**41** the year of the snake, the same year **Emmett Till** was born (p **41**). When this Superman character saves someone from a falling plane it is out of an act of bravery, like when **Tupac** shot two White men who were beating a helpless Black man in Atlanta, in 1993. Those two White men turned out to be off duty cops with illegal guns. Tupac was **22** years old at the time and had just performed at **Clark** University. **George Reeves** was the first white man to die after taking the role of **Clark** Kent (Superman). He took the role in 1951. Unfortunately when the show was cancelled in 1958 he struggled to get roles as an actor partly or mostly because he was too identifiable as the character Superman and subsequently Reeves committed **suicide** the next year, a few days before his wedding on **Tupac's** birthday, June 16th 1959 the year of the **Pig**, giving rise to the 'Superman curse'. 12 years later Tupac is born in the year of the **Pig**. The year after George **Reeves** took the role of Superman Christopher **Reeves** was born on September **25**th 19**52,** which is two days after Roy Bryant and JW Milan were acquitted for the murder of Emmett Till on September **23**rd 1955 (p 517). When I was a boy Christopher Reeves was the superman I grew up watching in the 80's. A White man who could fly and had super strength using it to 'save the world'. Christopher would seemingly fall victim to the 'Superman curse'. While riding a horse named **buck**, Christopher Reeves was paralyzed from the neck down on May 27th 1995. The horse failed to obey a command and Reeves went 'flying' off the horse injuring his spine. African men were reduced to slaves on American plantations and were often referred to as **Bucks** (**Buck Breaking,** page 354). Christopher **Reeves,**Superman, the man of steel was now crippled and confined to a wheelchair until his death 9 yrs later on October 10th 2004 at the age **52,** the day after my grandmothers birthday (page's 22, 99). Superman's love interest Margot Kidder (Lois Lane) died of **suicide** in **2018**. Marlon Brando, the actor who played Superman's father died on July 1st 2004, the same day that I graduated as a Kemetic Yoga instructor in **2018** (p 472). Two days later my past life as **Emmett Till** would be revealed to me (p 480). Brando was born on April 3rd the day before Martin Luther King was assassinated and the day before my past life revelation of King Tut was revealed to me (p 592, 594). **Kirk Alyn** was the first actor to play Superman in a live action movie and he was born the day before my grandmother Juanita **Dukes** (p **22**). **Bud Collyer** did the voices of Superman and Clark Kent for the 1940 Superman cartoon. He was born two days after Tupac on June 18th, the same day that my great grandmother Leacola **Riddle** died (p 21) and he died on September 8th, the day after Tupac was shot. The 1983 **Superman** movie premiered on my **grandfather General Dukes'** birthday June 17th (page's **23**, 99), which is the day after Tupac's **birthday**. Richard Pryor starred in this movie and 3 years later would be diagnosed with multiple sclerosis (p 32). Richard Pryor was sent down on (born on) December 1st 1940 the year before Emmett was born, on the same day that **Rosa Parks** was arrested for not giving her seat to a White man, sparking the Civil Rights Movement. Rosa later said, "I thought of Emmett Till, and I couldn't go back." **14** shots were fired at Tupac on Sep 7, 1996. **Ausar** was cut into **14** pieces and **Emmett Till** died at **14** years old. Lee Quigley, the actor who played the **infant Clark** Kent (**Superman)** in 1976 died at **14** years old. Quigley was born on Aug 13th, the day before the Haitian revolution was planned in 1791 and he died on March 10th, the day after **Biggie** was killed by the Hip Hop police (page's 77, 443, 663). On Superman's home planet Krypton, there is a red sun named **Rao** that only emits enough power to sustain life but when people from Krypton come to earth and receive the energy of earth's sun they experience levels of power not seen on their native planet. Superman is a super hero (Heru) who gets his power from the sun (**RA**). The Kemetic Ntr Ausar returns as Ra (the sun) after death through his son Heru (hero). See page 3 for the **hero's journey**. Ausar was a Pharaoh so the Superman Curse could also be called **The Curse Of The Pharaoh**, since many of the people involved with the Superman movies seemed to fall victim to some curse just like those who opened the tomb of **King Tut** in 19**22** (p's 12, 99). The first Superman Death happened on Tupac's birthday and I have a theory about who Tupac was in a past life ☥ (p 664). This "Superman Curse" even struck an aspiring actor by the name Christopher Lloyd Dennis. He was born on June 16, 1967, the year of the **goat**, on Tupac's birthday, the day **George Reeves** committed suicide. Christopher Lloyd was told by many people that he looked like Christopher Reeves. Sometime around the time that Christopher Reeves died Christopher Lloyd decided to dress up like Superman and walk around Hollywood Boulevard taking pictures with tourist for a small fee. Perhaps that one decision detoured his life. He never became the actor he dreamed of becoming, instead he ended up homeless and addicted to drugs. After **25** years of **p**ortraying superman, Christop**h**er Lloyd died at **52** years of age on Nov 2, 2019, two days before the discover of my tomb (Nov 4, 1922).

Dawud, Beloved by the Ntru

There's a Little of Tupac in All Of Us.

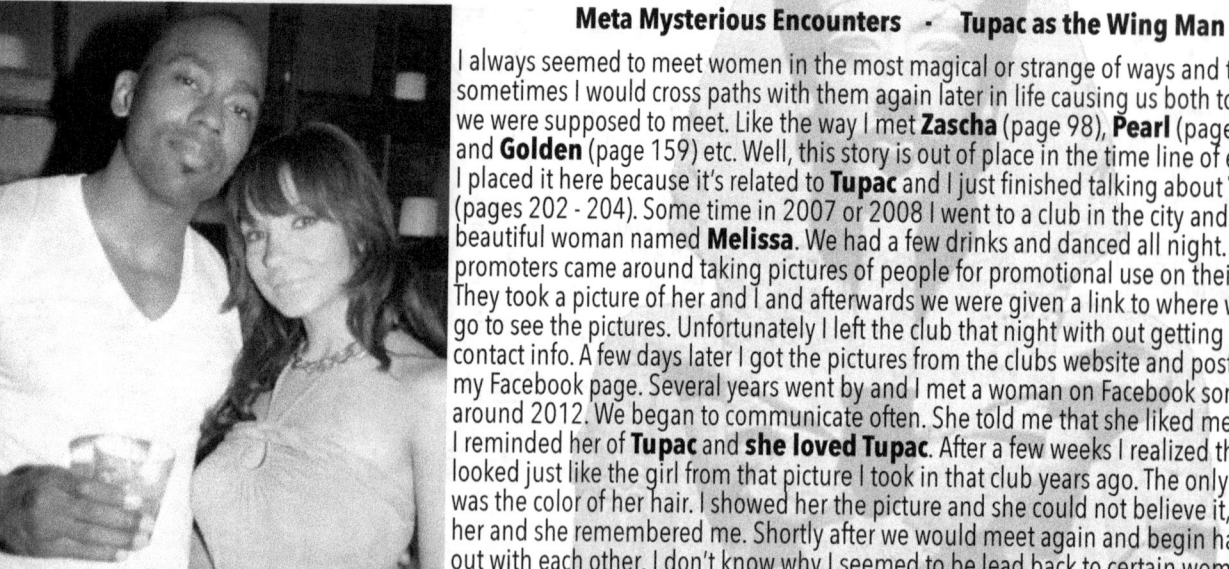

Meta Mysterious Encounters - Tupac as the Wing Man

I always seemed to meet women in the most magical or strange of ways and then sometimes I would cross paths with them again later in life causing us both to feel like we were supposed to meet. Like the way I met **Zascha** (page 98), **Pearl** (page 146), and **Golden** (page 159) etc. Well, this story is out of place in the time line of events but I placed it here because it's related to **Tupac** and I just finished talking about **Tupac** (pages 202 - 204). Some time in 2007 or 2008 I went to a club in the city and met a beautiful woman named **Melissa**. We had a few drinks and danced all night. The club promoters came around taking pictures of people for promotional use on their website. They took a picture of her and I and afterwards we were given a link to where we could go to see the pictures. Unfortunately I left the club that night with out getting Melissa's contact info. A few days later I got the pictures from the clubs website and posted one on my Facebook page. Several years went by and I met a woman on Facebook sometime around 2012. We began to communicate often. She told me that she liked me because I reminded her of **Tupac** and **she loved Tupac**. After a few weeks I realized that she looked just like the girl from that picture I took in that club years ago. The only difference was the color of her hair. I showed her the picture and she could not believe it, but it was her and she remembered me. Shortly after we would meet again and begin hanging out with each other. I don't know why I seemed to be lead back to certain women in my life. These serendipitous experiences would cause me to think I was supposed to be with some of these women. Like the way **Rahél** came back into my life (pages 101-136). Ultimately it was **Hip Hop** that turned out to be my most magical relationship, and different women would become muses in my love affair with music. Like **Rachel** (pages 427-438), **Leara** (p 336), **Aylin** (pages 359, 433), and my **twin flame** (page **444**.)

April 5th 2011 My Style

When you hear me bless'n this beat it's like reverse psychology, will you like it, will you won't, will you follow me? Your memory of **Biggie's** got you wait'n try'n to see, is he young money, is he lyrically hung funny, y'all niggas is dumb funny, just listen to a nigga style, maybe stay a while, I can tell you tails of my lifestyle, cause it was wild, I take you back to that snot nose juvenile, but most of all I remind you of how a nigga shall proceed and continue to rock the mic **- Dawud**

April 8th 2011 Running

Yo I'm at home with my eyes closed, it's a Friday night I could be on some dime hoes, but I turn this beat on and somehow find flows, so I'm a speak on some wisdom I was told, when it's time to eat you better eat, and when you find a beat that ain't no time to be try'n to sleep, cause father time he can climb right up in you sleep and take yo life away **- Dawud**

Significance

Many of the poetry from this period are not the best crafted rhymes but they track my journey as they show what mind was. I had given up the chase of women at the clubs and was now focused on the search for information.

April 8th 2011

Doubt (Matthew 21:21) (written to the Biggie ready to die beat)

Yo, what is doubt man? Yo sometimes all that that hate'n, it can weigh down on you like a weight man, but you gotta have belief in yourself man. Your belief in yourself gotta be so strong that it doubles everybody else's disbelief…

Sometimes the weight of the hate, it'll make you wait a minute and pause, but you should never hesitate, lyrical sword, yes I am adored by the crowd when they see'n how a mother fucker gladiate, I'm fuck'n great! so don't doubt me or hate on me, you can't fatally stop my drive **I'm a commodity**! Imagine **23** stop'n when they cut him from the team, all I need is a hit to get you to follow me, you Scotty Pipp it, I'm hell'a gifted, I spit in brail even **hieroglyphics**, ***look on the wall see the tale of my life and how I lived it***, my life is all I have, all my rhymes written in my iPad, I'm have'n a flash back of killings in Baghdad, and I guess this is make'n sense cause I was feel'n sad, I doubted if I'd live but I did, I'm live'n so how the hell you gonna doubt the blessings I'm given? I'm ready! they doubt'n me but I'm so ready, they doubt'n me, they doubt'n me but I'm so ready, they doubt'n me but I'm so ready, I'm so ready, they doubt'n me , they doubt'n me but I'm so ready,

The **Lord** said don't be doubt'n me! now take that mountain move it in the sea, **spiritually**! I'm in another place look at my face, I'm in a race, chase'n desire verse ability, they say I'm witty I'm clever but I'm better, call me the only trend setter, in a time where the game is deader than 96 and 97 put together, off off and on, I doubt it if you know that song, I take you back to "*let's let's get it on*", or "*once again it's on*", I'm Hip Hop in the purist form, that's my word is bond, so many I accepted as ahead of me, but fuck around be a dead emcee, I'm feel'n the effects of hatery, yo they tell'n me ain't no save'n me, **I'm bound to leave a legends legacy,** they doubt'n me but I'm so ready, they doubt'n me, they doubt'n me but I'm so ready, they doubt'n me but I'm so ready, I'm so ready, They doubt'n me , they doubt'n me but I'm so ready,

What if he never took the stage cause he was afraid? Nigga we wouldn't have a **Slim Shade**, what if he never had the heart to let his **dream** ring? everyday would be a **Rodney king**! I'm the truth bringer, rap slash trash singer, but doubt'n me is like give'n God the middle finger, trust I don't speak in I it's a must we speak in us, when we started hate'n that's what weakened us, get on the bus, I pledge allegiance to the just, you can't break me down you build me up up, puff puff pass, so high that I look down and laugh, haa woh, to Hip Hop I'm bring'n the **soul**, think not? Then your ears are closed, to all those that doubted me y'all gonna get exposed, my 4 4 make yo kids don't grow yo I'm so ready, they doubt'n me but I'm so ready, they doubt'n me, they doubt'n me but I'm so ready, they doubt'n me but I'm so ready, I'm so ready, they doubt'n me, they doubt'n me but I'm so ready, **- Dawud**

Matthew 21:21 then **Jesus** told them, I tell you the truth, if you have faith and do not doubt, you can do the things like this and much more, you can even say to this mountain may you be lifted up and thrown in the sea and it will be done"

In the book of Matthew Jesus is speaking about Reincarnation, (page 592, 647)

Rau nu Prt m heru

Iu f Per f m heru

Utterances for Coming Forth by day into Light

It is he, who comes forth by day into Light

April 11th 2011 **Make It**

We gonna get there, I'm gonna get the there, you gonna get there, stop hate'n! I'm gonna get there, word is born, so many mafuka's paper chase'n, yo I'm gonna get there, I'm gonna make it and I don't need no chick to get naked, no video hoe just my incredible flow, you on the top, that's your spot? I'm gonna take it, you don't like me? My hand don't shake it, don't fake it, be real! but use your head, cause when it's hot niggas drop more niggas get killed, don't stop it get lifted, I'm gonna get there, I'm gonna make it, I make it quite clear that I'm gifted, you have'n nightmares of **David**, I mean Dawud in Arabic, the way she move she ain't even gotta say shit, walked in the club gave a thug a hug, everybody looked back in amazement, it's funny how a woman can make it, shake it on the dance floor, she did the same thing that the man did but when she was done they called her a damn whore, if you don't like it don't hate it, cause she gonna make it cause she real, close your eyes, zone out and do what you feeeeel, do what you feel, do what you feel like, do it all night see what it be like, put your lighters in the air I swear from here all I wanna see is one big bright light, do what you feel, do what you feel like, do it all night see what it be like, put your lighters in the air I swear from here all I wanna see is one big bright light **- Dawud**

April 12th 2011, 6:31 PM
Michael Jackson

I love **Michael Jackson**, I fuck'n love **Michael Jackson, Michael Jackson,** part of the reason why I'm rap'n, inside of me he's a part of my passion, _the way you make me feel_, **Diana Ross** some thoughts that just keep keep passing, back when I was niiiiiiiine, I think my **Mother** played **Michael Jackson** like everytiiiiiiiiiiiime **- Dawud**

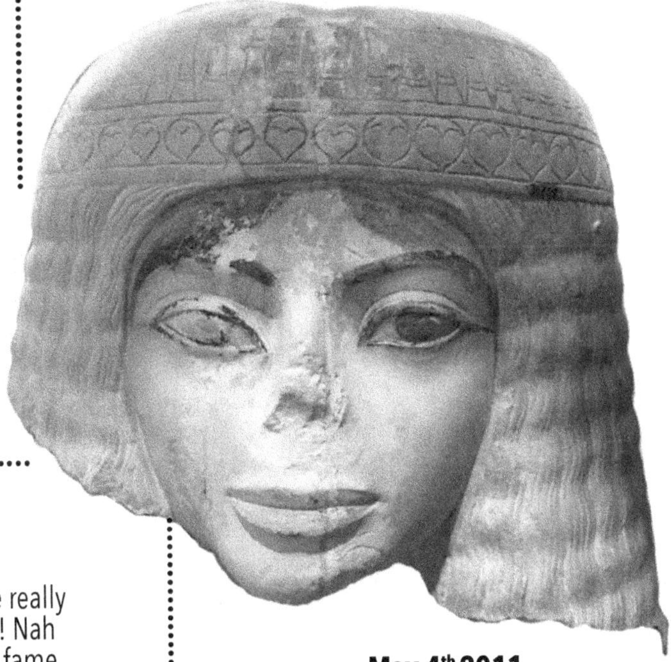

April 15th 2011
Really The Same

Nah son we really the same! The same! Fame, fame! but we're really the same! You the same! weakness and fortune and fame, fame! Nah nigga we really the same! The same! weakness and fortune and fame, you think you are but you yo, temptation weakness and fortune and fame we think we're different but we're really the same, temptation weakness and fortune and fame you think you different but we really the same, temptation weakness and fortune and fame I think I'm different but we really the same, temptation weakness and fortune and fame you think you're different but you're really the same, temptation weakness and fortune and fame we think we different but we're really the same, temptation weakness and fortune and fame we think we different but we're really the same, same we really the same **- Dawud**

May 4th 2011
Re lation SHIPS

How you gonna be the one that's so holy but can't take me as you know me? You used to be my ace man now you act like you don't know me! How you gonna be the one that's so holy but can't take me as you know me? I smack the taste out ya mouth man don't act like you don't know me **- Dawud**

May 9th 2011 **From This Moment On**

From this moment on I ain't gonna ask another mafuk'a how they feel about my song, cause _sometimes I rhyme slow, sometimes I rhyme quick_, but when ever I finish a rhyme I like it so, I'm a let you know my sister was there from the start, she was my first fan, there's nothing worse than, a man afraid to stand on his own, my nigga **C Green** never left rap alone see I was really gone, see for me this shit was never my **dream**, although I wish it was, see for me it was love, C4 with the m4 slug, see me I went to war, do you know what war does? Basically I don't care about the odds face'n me! I'll be here waiting patiently until I make it, life has taken me, so many different places so many faces, are you approaching life like it's a race kid? Cause it truly is, and the race is on, he had all them kids and can't do nothing for em, it truly is, and the race is on, he had all them kids and can't do shit for em, so I spit for him just to motivate him, I spit for him just to motivate him, yeah I spit for him just to motivate him, never to agitate him!

I said look lil homie, I see how you be on your grind, but do you ever listen to my rhymes? man if you did you'd know I love you, I ain't lying! I love my niggas! and I'm a never hate my niggas! Cause to me I'm a always see you as that man next to me, shackled and chained not fully knowing **our destiny**, you're not just a enemy of my enemy nigga **we're family**, does anybody understand me?!! Now put yo hands up, put yo hands up, that's what the **Black cop** said when he showed up, now _do the right thing_ **radio Raheem** choked up, man, we can't win for losing! Get busy being busy bout something, I'm sure there's more to you than how much you be stunt'n, and smoke'n and drink'n and hump'n, you talk'n nothing, please tell me why you front'n? from this moment on I ain't gonna ask another mafuk'a how they feel about my song, from this moment on I ain't gonna ask another mafuk'a how they feel about my song **- Dawud**

May 17th 2011 **MoorMyLaneRightHere**

This is more my lane right here, even though the club might not bang it there, but if they do put your fist up in the air, while I **while I put my poetry in the atmosphere**, I'm like grandma I'm a be fine, but inside I don't know if I'm a be fine, but lying is better than seeing her crying, if I could give her diamonds before the time end, if I ain't have people that loved me I'd be dead already, dead and buried, racing through life in a hurry, I call my grandma to see she fine and I'm the one that end up crying, I always thought I'd would be the one to help everybody make it, that was my **dream** life is what you make it, you get a chance lil homie you better take it, thou shalt not not forsake it, my relationship with the word **never** was like, I was **never** the one that everyone liked, either you love me or you hate me, it's only now that I see I treated some people nigady nasty, though some of them deserved it, a wise man might think before he speak and curve it, go catch more bee's with honey, be bout your money don't follow him cause he's a dummy, yeah **this is more my lane right here, even though the club might not bang it there, but if they do put ya fist up in the air, while I while I put my poetry in the atmosphere**, Somethings are planned, somethings are changed, somethings are rearranged, and some things are **destined**! **Dear Lord** when I go let me go like a **hero**, a beautiful death ground zero, how low? how low? how low can these niggas go? Chill'n in my **b-boy** stance give'n 5.0. My **b-boy** glance, the George Jefferson dance, I'm on my own but I need an advance, you'd be doing good to give me a chance, give me give me a chance, I'm tired of scream'n give me a chance, is what I be think'n in my **b-boy** stance, with just once glance **God see's everything**, the highs the lows and everything in between, **dear Lord** will you forgive me for everything? **Dear Lord** do you hear me? you never say a thing! you don't say nothing! this is more my lane right here, even though the club might not bang it there, but if they do put your fist up in the air, while I **while I put my poetry in the atmosphere - Dawud**

May 19th 2011 • Sahara at the Malcolm X day event

As we marched down 125th street in Harlem, everyone shouted, **"Malcolm X, Malcolm X"**, celebrating the life and sacrifice of the shining prince who was **Malcolm X**. This year I met a woman named **Sahara** at the rally. And just like the **Sahara Desert**, near Egypt, I was changing. I was beginning to look beyond the surface of the women I met, searching for the "well". I liked **Sahara** because of where I met her not just because **she was gorgeous**. I remember having a big attraction to her but not wanting it to be just about the physical. I enjoyed her company. While at her place I saw a **book** she had about **Steve Biko**. I'd never heard of him so I borrowed her book. **Bantu Stephen Biko was a South African anti-apartheid activist.** Ideologically an African nationalist and African socialist, he was at the forefront of a grassroots anti-apartheid campaign known as the Black Consciousness Movement during the late 1960s and 1970s. Steve Biko was assassinated on Sep 12th 1977 the day before **Tupac** died (Sep 13th 1996), the same year that I was born (Oct 25th 1977). I lost contact with Saharah a month or so after I met her and never saw her again.

May 24th 2011 **Build'n**

I don't scream hakuna matata, I scream **Kwame Nkruma**, **Assata**, I would never coon for a dollar, or a million, or billion, hundred trillion, I stay build'n to teach the children, I got cousins, I got nephews, and they all young… **- Dawud**

Significance

Around this time I would learn about how **Kwame Nkruma** was influenced by **Marcus Garvey** which sparked him to liberate his home country of **Ghana** in 1957.

2011 **This Ain't Livin**

Tell me, what is yo perception of friends? My perception of friends, is fuck friends cause friends can straight flip, it be that one time you need them, they say they ain't see shit, but you lay'n there bleed'n, like later them secrets, they gonna come to light, they turned on me, they turned on you, they turned on **Christ**, you said you didn't if you did you gonna pay the price, one life to live you don't get it twice, if you didn't live it then don't give advice **- Dawud**

Significance

This was written to the **Tupac** beat, **This Ain't Livin**. In this song I state that we have, "one life to live you don't get it twice". At this time I was not cognizant of **reincarnation** but subconsciously I already knew! But what did Tupac know?! On the second verse of his song, **This Ain't Livin**, there are words blanked out. But it makes you wonder what Tupac said, and why his words were censored. He says: **"and who are you to watch me fall farther, I disappeared, reappeared as the,- - - - -, follow me now".** What ever Tupac said, it rhymes with farther. Like heavenly Father, or **Martyr**. **Tupac was a reincarnated soul** (pages 664 - 665).

Rau nu Prt m heru

Iu f Per f m heru

Utterances for Coming Forth by day into Light

It is he, who comes forth by day into Light

May 24th 2011 - High Frequency Psychic Channeling

A Weed induced Thought Form / idea for a movie recorded into my phone as a audio memo on May 24th 2011

"It's about ah, it's about a rapper. Or somebody pursuing music. Or somebody who loves Hip Hop. They love Hip Hop you know, from the 90's. You know, they go about their life. Um, there needs to be a twist in it. There needs to be, you know... It needs to be about Hip Hop, but a guy pursuing a **dream**, you know, that's not Hip Hop. It ain't Hip Hop though, but he's a..., pursuing his **dream** in life and ah..., and you know, one thing he **loves** is **Hip Hop**, and it takes you through the elements of Hip Hop, and it would be a good Hip Hop movie and at the end, you know!? The police brutality sort of the **Spike Lee**, um, **Do The Right Thing** with ah..., with um..., you know, Love verse Hate. What's his name? Um...,ahh, fuck!.... **Radio Raheem**! Sort of like Radio Raheem getting killed. The dude gets.., doesn't get killed, he gets you know, **police brutality**, brain damage, and the only way you can get him to smile at the end is if you put on that favorite song of his from Hip Hop back in the 90s. And the song is **Nothin to do** from **Common**. Yeah that'll be dope" **- Dawud**

Significance - and the Common Connection!

I started smoking weed in 2011 (p 194) when I was 33 years old and when I got **"high"** I would have these **"ideas"** for movies, skits & business. At the time I was unaware of what was happening. I would record these "ideas" into my phone as audio memos. I realize now that this recording was not an idea for a movie, it was actually an inter dimensional transmission from another dimension. I had opened up a **High Frequency Psychic Channel** (perhaps from the akashic records), where these messages were channeled down through my thoughts. I smoked weed and it opened a channel/portal for a thought about **a persons who's following his dream and loves Hip Hop** and I **thought** it was an idea for a movie but it was actually a foretelling of what I was about to experience. This "thought" sort of foreshadows what I did with music (page's 6, 227) and the murder of black life (**Radio Raheem)** sp**ark**ed it. **Common** was my favorite artist for a long time in the 90's, my favorite album of his was **Resurrection**. **Common** would release the single **Resurrection** on **April 4th** 1995, the same day that **Martin Luther King** was assassinated (p 69) which is also the same day that I had my past life revelation of my life as **King Tut** in 2020 (p 594). For the **Common Connections** see pages 66, 77, 385. For **Common's** name in my music see pages 81, 134, 195, 200, 278, 313, 322, 3**23**, 360, 366, 431 and 624. In ancient Kemet the concept of resurrection and past lives was called the **Wehem-Mesut** (repeating of births, page 14). It is not about how much you know, it's about how much you desire to know. It's about where your heart is. All actions are measured by the matters of the heart. These spiritual **messages** are **received through the heart**. If your desire is right and exact you can attract the information or situation you earn. This is the ancient Kemetic principle of divine thought and divine wisdom governed by the Deity (God) **Jehuti** also known as **Tehuti** or **Hermes** or **Thoth** (divine **thought**). The 7 hermetic principles are: **mentalism**, **correspondence**, **vibration**, **polarity**, **rhythm**, **cause vs effect** and **gender**.

June 4th 2011

We are All Soledad Brothers

All he wanted to be was a soldier soldier, all he wanted to be was a soldier like me, all he wanted to be was a soldier soldier, all he wanted to be was a soldier like me, brother **Malcolm**, high schools ain't teaching about him! Nor **Jonathan Jackson** running in blasting! Like where's **Assata?!** she's coming with me! the **BLA** , The black liberation army, there's nothing you can tell me to sever my love for every revolutionary! New Orleans! Ya gotta know the ledge and the levy! too close to the edge, Public Enemies in the crosshairs of the feds! Red white and blue? Nah! **Green Black** and **Red**! "*The **dragon** has arrived*" is what the soldier said, Courage in one hand, Assault rifle in the other my brother, my comrade and my friend never be another, letters from a Soledad brother, **George Jackson**, **Jonathan Jackson**, what I'm asking? acting verse action we don't take action we get roles to act in movies cause we relaxing I miss Michael Jackson **- Dawud**

George Lester Jackson (September 23, 1941 – August 21, 1971)

See page 155. Pictures above show 17 year old Johnathan Jackson's attempt to free his brother George Jackson from the Marin County Courthouse on August 7th 1970. George and a group of other inmates (The Soledad Brothers) were charged with throwing a white prison guard to his death at San Quentin prison facility. Unfortunately none of the Soledad Brothers were at the court house that day so Jonathan and his comrades took hostages and demanded the release of the Soledad Brothers. In an ensuing shootout, Jonathan and the Judge were killed, along with two inmates who joined the march for freedom. May the Souls of Jonathan Jackson and the other inmates walk peacefully through the field of Reeds in Amenta. Amen Ra.

U TOUGH BOOTCAMP Central Park

At this point I'm doing fitness classes in Central Park. I did a couple ads with group on to build my business but it wasn't very beneficial. By 2012 I had moved my classes up to Harlem. I wanted to work with more people of color.

June 15th 2011

Susan (p 167) had another friend visiting from London again and asked if I could show her around. Her name was Carla. I took her to the museum of natural history then I took her to see **Malcolm X** at the Autobahn ball room in Washington Heights. On **May 19th 2019** I will go to Malcolm's annual ceremony held at his grave site for the first time and I will be **"randomly"** picked to be one of the brothers in white who stand guard around his grave (page 561-565) . It is still one of my most proudest moments in this life. **I love you Malcolm X**.

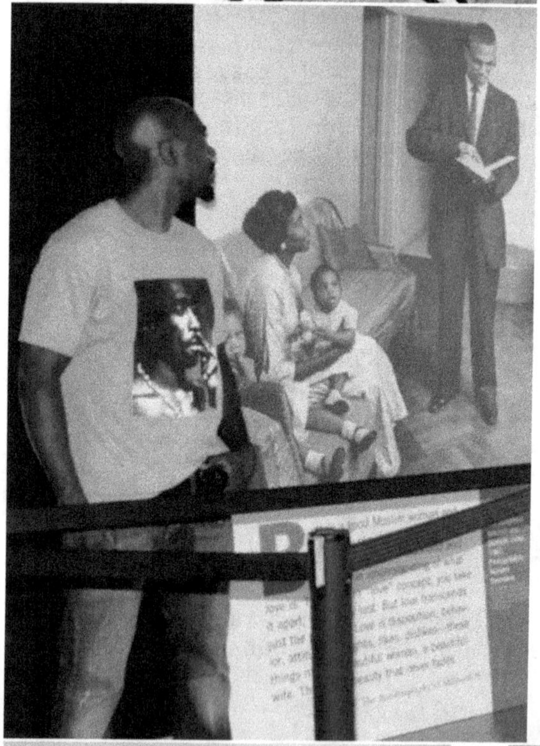

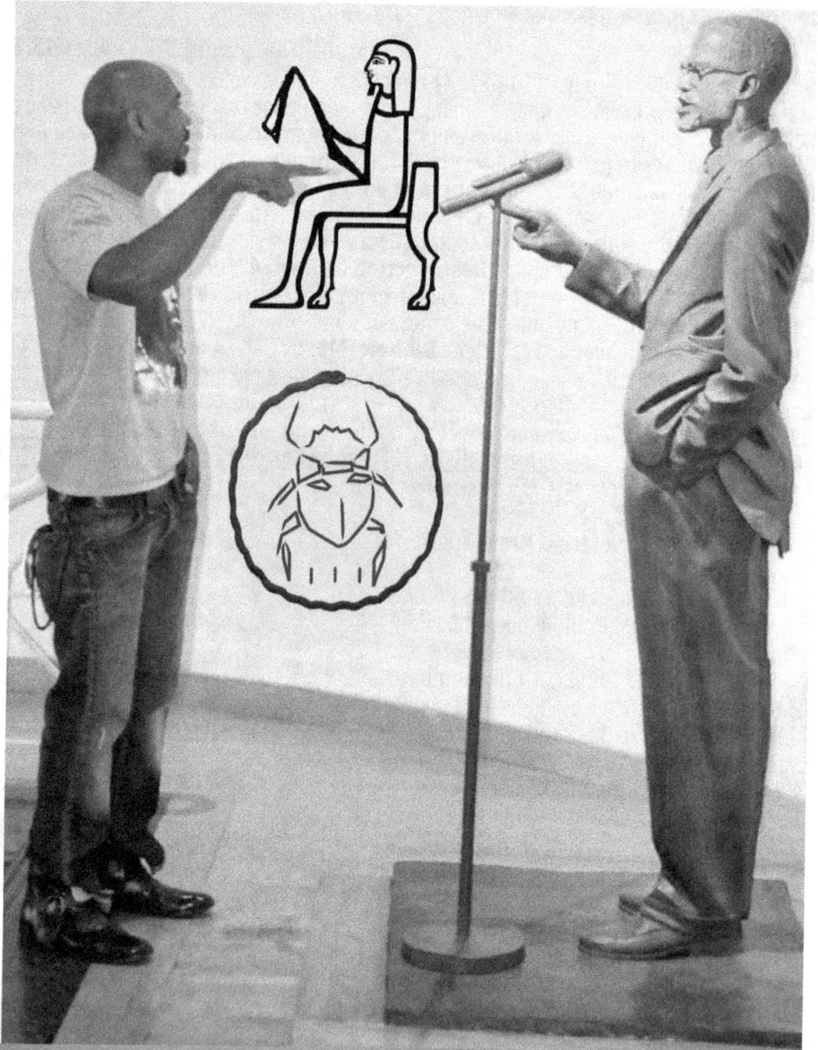

Rau nu Prt m heru

Iu f Per f m heru

Utterances for Coming Forth by day into Light

It is he, who comes forth by day into Light

August 6th 2011
How Well I Live

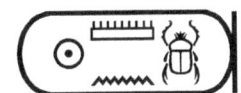

I no longer care about how long I live, I'm more concerned with how well I live, ***evoking** the __spirit__ of my **dead** relatives*, **Jack Johnson**, he was box'n, he was winning but he knew he was boxed in, like **George Jackson** and **Steve Biko**, tell me why they don't wanna teach em bout they people? I used to wish I grew up with a **daddy** that taught me about the world, I could call up and just say **Daddy**, or homie, or **Dad**, damn, I don't even know how to address what I never had, but I ain't mad I had my **Grand dad**, I called him **Grand Daddy** daily my **Grand Mother** praying for the family, and every Sunday she be paying **God** and paying gladly, preacher man do you need the money that badly? **- Dawud**

"evoking the spirit of my dead relatives"

August 13th 2011
Memnon or Amen Hotep III?

Addendum On August 13th 2011, I met **Brother G** who was selling his books on 125th, in front of the Magic Johnson movie theatre. I purchased his first book, **Memnon**. After he signed it he looked at me and said, "You could play the role of Memnon in my movie. I smiled, shook my head and said, "Nah, I'm not a fighter or actor". I never read Memnon past the first 10 - to 15 pages but 7 years later, on May 20th 2018, I purchased 4 more of his books (p 469). I always supported vendors and initially I thought I bought his books just to support him but there was a deeper reason as to why I was drawn to his books. I would not come to know the full meaning until after my past life as King Tut was revealed in 2020 (pages 356, 389, 638). I'm writing a Epic Sci-Real (Science Reality) Novel Trilogy version of this book and a book about Tupac's ancient past life (p 664,665). Stay tuned!

August 12th 2011 **Faster (Kanye Beat)**

Lord have mercy, Lord have mercy, Lord have mercy, Lord have mercy, I'm mafuk'n thirsty, want me to **fast**? I'm just trying to move faster, are we alone? Or did we come after? Why did you make the white man my master?! Faster, faster, faster, no church in the wild beautiful disaster **- Dawud**

August 31st 2011 **Aspire**

What happens when you living life for more than yourself?! **you live forever**! I aspire to inspire till I expire, ask why the sucker Emcees they call me Sia, cause I don't give a damn about swagger or looking flyer, ask why the look on my face is you fuck'n liar **- Dawud**

2011 **Born 2 rebel**

Yo, I was born to rebel, being born black's to be born in hell! Word is born, word to **Big L**, rest in peace to homies that fell, how the hell you expect us to act well?! spark L's take your mind back in time to **Ida B Wells**, **Troy Davis** is the latest society fail! **Larry Davis** did what he had to do with the steel! do you know the only thing we get from silence is more violence?! my name's **Dawud** and I slay giants, *from sea to shining sea*, I'm screaming alliance from **93 till infinity,** I know God is inside of me, ***real niggas don't die***, we just multiply, ***when I die let a real soldier tatt my name on his shoulder***, the truth be told, I don't fit the mold for this country, frame my **soul,** paint me ugly, who controls the **media**? think before you judge me, who's feeding ya this wikipedia?! uncle Rukus "*bring the mother fuck'n Rukus*"

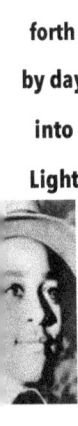

What's up with the black gossip? Henny without any coke, who owns Bossip? can you explain why you watch it? the greatest marketing campaign got your brain hostage, shame on America for not giving us our profits, I know if I rebel you gonna kill me like a prophet but you can go to hell cause I ain't never gonna stop it! yeah I'm singing nigga, make it sound good, I'm just trying to bring revolution here back into the hood, if I told you that Neo was Black would you strike back with the "fuck that black man is God shit"? this life just ain't fair, every where yo go on the earth I swear black life is real hard there **- Dawud**

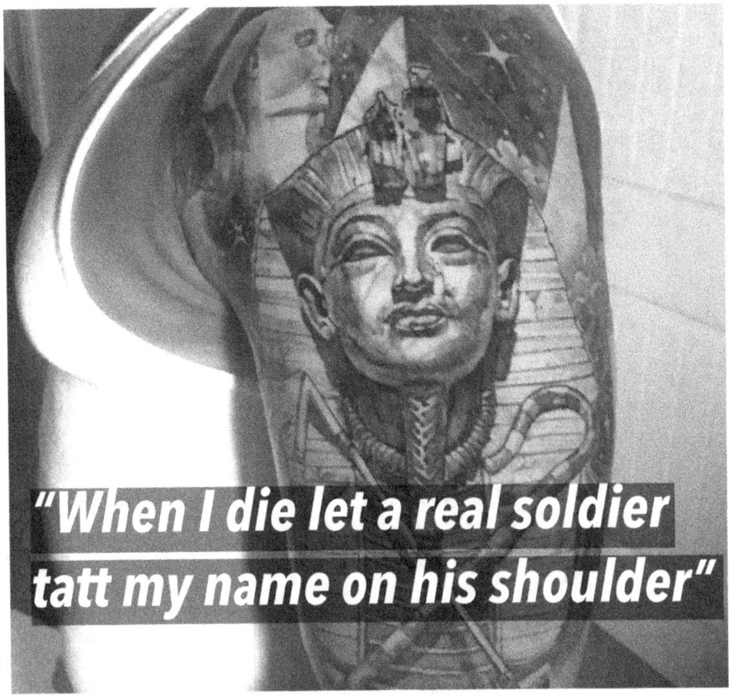

2011 50 Niggaz

If you go ham I go hammer, like a emcee don't test me, cause I'm ride or die to the day I die, no loyalty in country! my loyalty's to the company I keep, over the years you've learned to trust me, and I trust you, if **Martin Luther King** was live'n he'd probably say fuck you, there's always a quiet before the storm, and this is where I prepare the bomb, you ain't got nothing you ready to live for? Well this is where I prove you wrong, **take one nigga from every state**, come **50 Niggaz** let's regulate, educate, communicate, young nigga be great, don't be good, be fuck'n great, if you go ham I go hammer, If you go ham I go hammer, If you go ham I go hammer, Dawud is the man, If you go ham I go hammer, If you go ham I go hammer, If you go ham I go hammer, Dawud is the man - **Dawud**

2011
One Day you'll be Alone

One day you'll be alone, there's a war going on outside no man is safe from, one day you'll be alone, no man is safe, way out there on the combat zone, no man is safe, bullets frying all around, no man is safe, gotta keep your head to the ground, one day you'll be alone, way out there on the combat zone, no man is safe, one day you'll be alone, no man is safe, on the combat zone, on the combat zone, Goddam the sand my gun jammed and all in my head what the drill sergeant said, one day you'll be alone, way out there on the combat zone

There's a war going on outside no man is safe, there's no escape, bullets fly all over the place, Afghan, Brooklyn, Compton, Look man! you need more than a gun to have me look'n shook man, see I done been through the fire, praying for rain, when you've seen the things I've seen you're never the same, they never knew my name they just knew my number, I can't even explain, you just gonna half to wonder - think - what would have come next? put my guns up for the vets and **salute political prisoners who been oppressed**, stressed, **free Mumia**, torn between my country and my **coloredness**, but I was there yeah trying to do my best, all alone in the battle zone, far from home laying in the prone, brigade company platoon attention, I might not be coming home, might not be coming home, Goddam the sand my gun jammed! and all in my head what the drill sergeant said, one day you'll be alone, way out there on the combat zone, Goddam the sand my gun jammed and all in my head what the drill sergeant said, bullets flying all around, no man is safe, gotta keep your head to the ground - **Dawud**

2011
1st Police Stop and Check

I was on my way to teach my group fitness class in Central Park. I got on the **B** train at 145th Street. The train car I got on was very hot because the air conditioner wasn't working so I decided to walk to the next car. Three plain clothes police officers would follow me through the car and ask me for my ID. When the trained arrived at the next stop they escorted me off the train. While on the platform they asked why I walked from one car to the next. I remain respectful to the police officers and explained that the car I was in had no air conditioner and I was unaware that it was illegal to do so. They looked over my ID's and asked me a few questions. They saw that I was an Army veteran and one of the offices tried to be friendly stating that he was prior military himself. I did not want to be late for my class nor did I want to receive a ticket. They gave me my ID's back and told me that it was against the law to walk between cars. Then they left. This would be the first time in my 33 years that I was stopped by police on the train. I would have a few more encounters with the police over the next fews years and it was never this peaceful. (Pages 239, 331, 388)

2011 Up Mad Late

Rau nu Prt m heru

lu f Per f m heru

Sit'n in my room alone, a year ago I would have been on my phone look'n for some chicks to bone, how much I've grown, look at the "***buck***" approach the *throne*, don't throw no stones! is **the man in the mirror** really a clone! **Patrice O'Neal**, you roasted him but now he's gone! how do you feel? You spoke so ill, you so wrong, you gotta watch what the media feeding ya, for so long been deceiving ya, scared when your leaders go Voltron, **A**rm **L**eg **L**eg **A**rm **H**ead that's where I'm from, yeah I walked on ice so you can call me the son, you know the one that get the job done through the barrel of a gun but where I'm from they teach us to kill each other but run when cops come, that's so dumb! so dumbfounded cause to me it just like it was grounded on the third rock from the sun, supernova one day it's gonna be all over, fork over my ***40 Acres***, what a time to be stuck in a grind a world so blind, you gotta walk in faith, know that your fate is in no one mans hand to create, ***everything's been designed by the divine***, I was born to elevate, ***read the signs of the times***, it's all gonna escalate, and 144 of us did escape, the **oracle** was like, even if I had told you you would have still been late, in 98 you could have toured state to state, if you had more faith, we need more love, less cops killing thugs then we'll be feeling good, the story of Robin Hood be call'n me, but I be good cause I understand and over stand I walk this land with Gods hand, put my life back together when ever you like, with my family, homie don't play that, I take you way back to **Pat Sajak**, in fact I'm a dinosaur, the realist shit you ever saw, you could never be my competitor, I'm a alpha male predator, Hip Hop to the core the revolution's what he saw, they could be coming through your door, **the patriot act**! They don't act like patriots, they fake'n the facts! make'n the stacks off everything, even the water from your tap, back when it was rap, **Slick Rick** or **Kris**, don't ask how I did this, I do this, no Christmas or Thanksgiving on my wish list, *if I ruled the world* I'd marry the girl, marry the girls and take away all sin, my brother Austin you got lost when you got trapped in their way of think'n, what were you think'n? You weren't think'n ,the cities sink'n, Babylon, Megatron, Shaton, I was watching **Beauty And The Beast** and they stabbed him! this is **Disney** for the kids! They stabbed him in the ribs! I'm sit'n there thinking somethings gotta give! *How can we live in a world that won't let kids grow up without being chased by pigs*?! Agents everywhere! I bet you weren't aware! I say it loud and clear! A Black Woman wrote the **Matrix**! Everywhere you go on the earth I swear black life is hard there, I hate this! I make this for people who will listen! Cause Hip Hop is still living, I got **O.D.B.** in me, **Guru** and **Heavy D**, soon to be on your tv flat screen, what does that mean? What is Success? is it the money? is it the Hip Hop honey? is it the swag? don't make me laugh! let's do the math! **do you follow a path**? **cause even if you don't you do**! some of you will never get that you'll have no clue, cause you ain't never heard a **Clue Tape**! I remember staying up mad late, make'n tapes, it's mad late right now, it's mad late right now, it's mad, it's mad late right now, it's mad, it's mad late right now, I still love Hip Hop and I love my people put that together and I will forever be fighting evil **- Dawud**

Significance

I referenced the movie, **The Matrix** in this song and unbernounced to myself I was waking up from a long sleep, in a new body Just like the movie **Matrix**. See pages **1 7 109 141 216 218 226 262 266 282 292 323 344 345 421 433 442 463 471 480 543 569 578 596.**

Utterances for Coming Forth by day into Light

September 9th 2011 - First and Only Colonic

I had been studying health for a few years now and I had a few reasons that brought me to the idea of getting a colonic also known as colon hydrotherapy. My grand father had past away from stomach cancer and I came across info that warned about death starting in the colon and how the cleanliness of our colons is vital to our health. I also had an issue with the fact that I could not suck my stomach in like other people I knew. I had a hard defined six pack abs but my stomach could not vacuum. I began to consider that my intestines were dehydrated and full of old food that had hardened around my intestines. So I scheduled my first and only colonic at **Love your Transformation** located at **347 5th ave. I had stopped eating meat and drinking milk** in 2010 however I kept eating fish and shrimp until I had a profound experience during and after thanksgiving of 2014 that caused me to stop eating all seafood as well (page 308 & 311). In 2016 I would began to do my own coffee **enemas** (page 363).

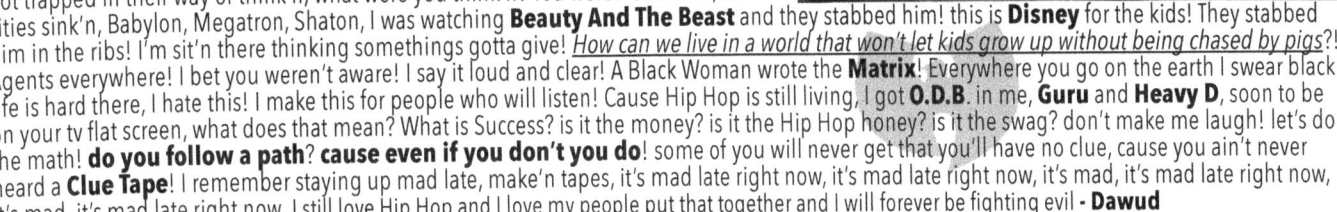

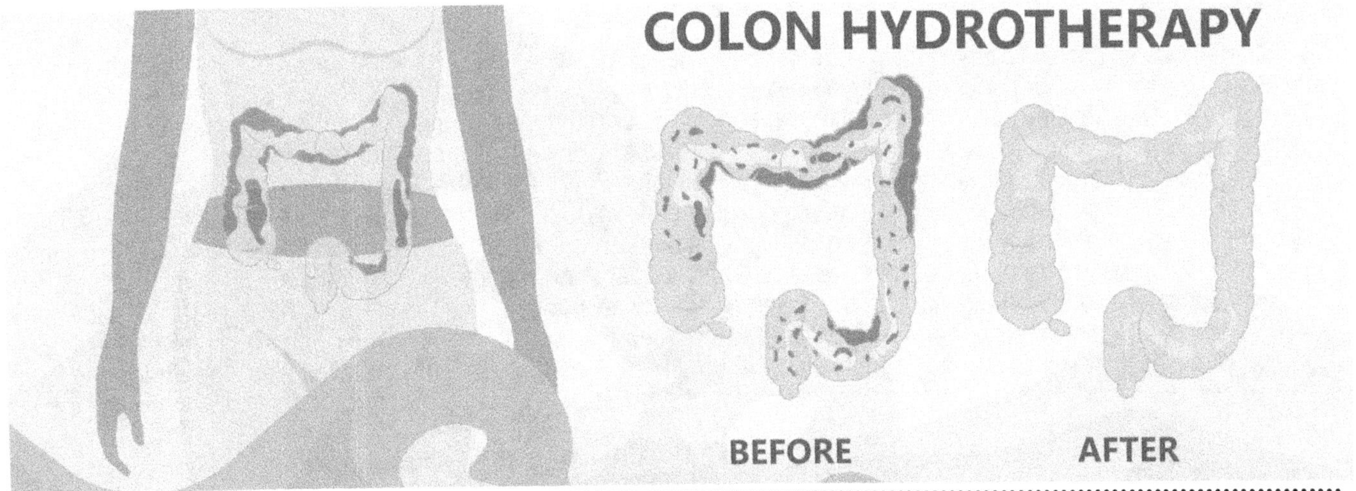

It is he, who comes forth by day into Light

September 25th 2011 Run Free

I guess some will never understand me! You my nigga, You my brother, You my family! I feel like a man who ran free, it's harder these days to see **- Dawud**

For many years I will begin to write about Great Mother Araminta Ross aka Harriet Tubman and in December of 2018, the year of the Dog I will realize why I was so drawn to her (page 545). There is no such thing as just a coincidence.

October 18th 2011
From Soldiers to Civilians

On October 18th 2011 the former enlisted **Marine Sgt. Shamar Thomas** was caught on video verbally reprimanding police officers for their lack of proper protocol. The video went viral and Shamar got a lot of media attention. Protestors were shouting things like, 'Police come join us!' but the police started moving closer and closer to the crowd. Soon, pushing and shoving started. Then Shamar saw a woman and a man getting hit with a baton and that infuriated him. He had been deployed to combat while in the Marines and he felt like the officers were out of line. During one of his two tours to Iraq in 2004 and 2006, he had been in a riot. One of his fellow Marines got hit in the face with a rock thrown by an unarmed Iraqi civilian. The Marine fell off the truck but Shamar and his fellow Marines didn't go into the crowd and start beating people. As a Marine his mission was to win the hearts and minds. So when he saw he NYPD hurting unarmed civilians, and those people were not even throwing rocks, it didn't make any sense to him. After witnessing the NYPD Police officers hitting unarmed civilians with batons this filled him with anger and prompted him to unleash verbal fury on stunned police officers, who stared at him blankly as he shouted to them repeatedly, **"These are unarmed people. It doesn't make you tough to hurt these people**." The video went viral. I saw the video of Sgt. Shamar Thomas, it inspired and it promoted me to go to occupy Wall Street sometime in October to see it for myself. I wore my Army Beret and walked around observing the scene but I didn't see **my struggle** there. I saw White people angry about money yet Black people were once sold on auction blocks in the same area they were protesting, but none of them were speaking about that. I didn't stay long. The only good thing that came from my trip was meeting **Danny**. Danny and I would go back to Occupy Wall Street a week or so later to shoot a video on November 17th then I never went back (page 215).

October 15th 2011
Inside of Me

"Nah nigga. The game! It's not even one person. The game is just air! It's in me. It was in me. Somebody Just awoke it. Somebody just woke it up inside of me. You know what I'm saying? like a religion!" - Tupac

Yo yo, my thoughts are never far from the struggle, they book you and then they mug you, her mommy too busy with rent to say I love you, this government ain't really bout shit nah they don't love you, they just waiting for you to slip so they can judge you, don't trip! **Keep Ya Head Up** and rock this dope shit, *I fell asleep woke up and wrote this, I fell asleep woke up and wrote this,* for the hopeless for lil homies out there losing focus, Lil homie got a record but I swear he barely got a brain, how you gonna love **Pac** and not be about change?! Shorty in the club getting naked cause babies gotta eat nigga check it, what's the method! Y'all say what y'all say until y'all get elected, and kids play where they play till they get arrested, the other day **I went to Wall Street it's getting hectic**, and we ain't leaving till y'all mother fuckers get the message, yo ain't it funny how the brain it'll block the pain? when I was young I was alone no one to help me aim, It's kinda strange but Hip Hop really raised me mane, It's kinda strange but Hip Hop really raised me mane **- Dawud**

Significance

The internet allowed me to see more footage of Tupac than I had ever seen before. I learned more about him and what was going on with his family politically. I started to really learn about *Lesane Parish* ***Crooks*** and how he became **Tupac Amaru Shakur**. He was always my favorite rapper but things changed when I auditioned for the role to play him in his movie in April of 2011. I practiced monologs and recited his songs. I did what actors do when they prepare to take on the role of a famous figure. Like Denzel preparing to play the role of the honorable shining Prince **Malcolm X**. I put myself in Tupac's shoes and pretended that I was him standing in front of a court room defending myself of the charges of rape. I pretended that I was him. "How could these people sing my songs like Keep ya head up than think I could do this?", then like a tidal wave I was overcome with uncontrollable crying. I was struck with the feeling that **Tupac** was there with me in the spirit (page 203). This was the first time I had ever experienced anything like that. The closest thing may be emotions that can rise up while in church. Tupac would appear in a few of my dreams years from now. Tupac is the most quoted person in this book and if you are to fully understand who Tupac was in ancient Kemet you should understand why the reincarnated soul of **Tutankhaten** would be attracted to him.

October 2011
-$800 Miller Time 3/7 Communication

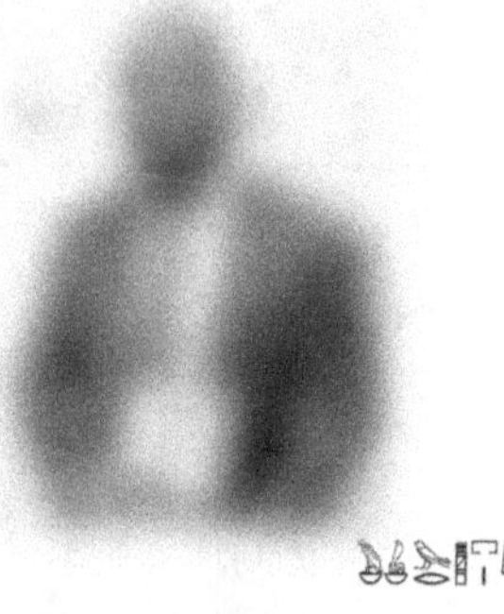

9:25pmDawud was up bro? any good news? **9:26pmMiller** i may have something for you in a couple a days it wont be all of it but i could put something in your hand **9:26pmDawud** thats good news. keep me posted. Ttyl **9:27pmJermain** cool

Next communication page Dec 11th 2011 page 219

Rau nu Prt m heru

Iu f Per f m heru

October 16th 2011 American Dream'n

There is no such thing as, American **dream'n** only American scheme'n! you picking up a mic you better rhyme with a reason! there used to be a time when reading and writing was treason, and every night a **slave** was being brave and leaving, I see my Mexicans on the other side let them in, We all the same ain't no body the lessor man, The politicians and the CEO's fuck em man, Does anybody out there really trust the government?! Hell no fuck the law worse than they ever been! and ya better not touch my mother fucking president, and how you kill a man with no evidence?! It's evident **Troy Davis** he never had a chance! So don't forget about **Mumia!** they don't want us to grow so they killing all our leaders, I see ya when they free ya **Mumia!** Yeah I'm a see ya when they free ya **Mumia,** There is no such thing as American dream'n only American scheming, Yeah, you better rhyme with a reason, there is no such thing, you better rhyme with a reason, there is no such thing as, You better rhyme with a reason, yeah!

They dropped the patriot act, and now I'm watching my back, cause even while write'n this rhyme they could be come'n in packs, and I know half of them black, and I know all of them strapped, I know they creep'n when I'm sleep'n, so I'm keep'n this gat, that nigga ran, that nigga flew, and we been run'n for years but where we run'n to? the information is here it's right in front of you, their greatest fear is for you to take it back to 92, cause that shit reunited you, reunite! or did it? did we ever change? look at him son! man he love his fuck'n chain, don't hate him son, let him do his fuck'n thang, cause **400 years** ago we was tied up in some chains, get'n hanged cause of a look, the names that they took, **Emmett Till** ain't the only one, please open up a book, I know you feel me homie, and you can lead a man to knowledge but you cant make him think homie, there is no such thing as, American **dream'n** only American scheme'n! you picking up a mic you better rhyme with a reason! there is no such thing, you better rhyme with a reason, there is no such thing **- Dawud**

Significance

This would be the 3rd time I mention **Emmett Till's** name in a rhyme. Twice in 2010 and now again in 2011. Something was happening that I was totally clueless to. All those years of believing that **Jesus** was coming back were about to play the most bizarre of jokes on me. In the years to come I will continue to write about Emmett and the idea of returning to this world like Marcus Garvey's' claims of returning in the whirlwind after his death. Gradually I stopped talking about Jesus coming back and began to express that "**I was coming back**".

Utterances for Coming Forth by day into Light

It is he, who comes forth by day into Light

October 17th 2011 , 9:27 PM.

Henry Smith

Henry Smith hanging on a platform heart racing! The emancipation proclamation the plan to free a man then incarcerate him! World domination, control the population, facebook they watch your conversation, wall street they know your location, but fuck em fuck em I say fuck em, ***<u>you only get one life to live</u>***, you better die for something, **Tupac, Huey P,** a little of them live in you and me, and I got White boys too like B.P. Uppum, they showed me pictures of Sgt Sherman and Sgt Witham and said you could free your whole nation all you gotta do is kill em, they said they are no good, they be the ones in the hood beat'n people down just cause they could, how could the sound of something so bad feel so good? **- Dawud**

Significance

Henry Smith was lynched on February 1st 1893 in Paris Texas. Henry was accused of killing the 3 year old daughter of a law enforcement officer. They tied Henry up to a platform in front of a mob of around 15,000 people, They beat and tortured him. Burning both of his eyes out with hot iron rods and shoving them down his throat. The crowd cheered at every blow and every time his body was pierced or burned with hot iron rods. Finally they poured coal oil over Smith and lit him on fire. He fell to the ground and tried to crawl from the fire but the crowd kicked him back into the fire. When his spirit was gone from his body and the fires reduced, his fingers and toes were cut off and kept as souvenirs by the white crowd. I became aware of Henry around the time that I wrote this. . What was done to Henry sounds to be more terrifying than what happened to Emmett Till. I would mention Henry again in January of 2012 and I don't think I ever wrote about him again. Emmett on the other hand, I would continue to write about him. Interestingly enough in this verse I state that "*<u>you only get one life to live</u>*". At this time I was not cognizant of **reincarnation** outside of the idea of "**Jesus coming back**", but subconsciously I already knew!

October 31st 2011 — Reunite

When they ask me why I came? I came for reparations! And my aim? Write rhymes thats relate'n to the pain, that my people feel I'm keep'n it real, even slaves wrote rhymes work'n up in the field! The bill of rights written by men who love to fight and kill, 700 trillion made off the trade! So yeah I got a problem but I ain't wait'n for nobody to solve em, if you really want change get involved son! Revolution is naturally our evolution, here's a solution let's go and burn the **Constitution**, what you gonna do when the police start shoot'n and occupy every street?! Now I lay me down to sleep, I pray the Lord my soul to keep, cause there's only one way to die that's ride'n for peace, I say brother brother brother we kill'n each other, the least you and me can do is stop kill'n each other, cause if you knew like I know the system don't love you, systematic racism ready to judge you, C.O.'s in the pen wait'n to un cuff you, this the modern day slavery the government wants you, trapped on they plantation, the mental the castration, my pencil is instrumental in get'n you past pray'n cause brothers is dying, and I'm just say'n we need to reunite and I'm not play'n! **- Dawud**

Significance

In this song I say, "**burn the Constitution**" because the American Constitution was taken from the Democratic Constitution written up by the **Iroquois** (Native Americans) but the laws that are carried out by this country do not reflect the ethical and moral practices of the **Iroquois**. A video for this song was shot during an Occupy wall street march on November 17th 2011. I went to occupy wall street demonstrations two times and I met **Danny** the first time I went in of October 2011(page 213). Danny and I would soon become very good friends. He is the one who held the camera and recorded this footage of the video for me. He was 19yrs old when we met and he reminded me of myself as a teenager. He is a Mexican and he is a peaceful loving human being. When Danny and I met he was studying the Bhagavad Gita. He is the one who gave me my copy of the **Bhagavad Gita**. I am the first person to introduce him to **Tupac**. Now he is a big Tupac fan and now I have realized **previous lives** just like the teachings from the Bhagavad Gita. In 2021 I would realize why my friend Stephanie gave me that book **Siddahartha**, on my birthday in 2015. I would realize that I once lived a life in India as well. In1942, Japanese Americans were sent to concentration camps during World War 2. 46 years later, with the passing of the Civil Liberties Act of 1988 Japanese Americans received reparations to right the wrongs they experienced. Black people have been in America for hundreds of year being subjected to enslavement, lynchings, systematic racism and the list goes on, yet still we have yet to receive reparations.

Rau nu Prt m heru

November 1st 2011 Legendary

Legendary before they bury me, yeah I'm a be a **legend**, mafuk'a go and ask the reverend, you ain't gotta sell crack or pack a mac 11, matter fact where you going nigga hell or heaven? ***Legendary before they bury me***, yeah I'm a be a **legend**, mafuk'a go and ask the reverend, you ain't gotta sell crack or pack a mac 11, matter fact where you going nigga hell or heaven? **- Dawud**

November 2nd 2011 Casualties of War

Casualties of war collateral damage, blood on the walls, mommy's dead on the floor, welcome to the broken home, war zone, kids run the streets strapped ready to eat, and them call girls make them stacks between the sheets, it's a cold world yeah it's a bitch it's not a beach! **- Dawud**

November 5th 2011 Matrix

Last night I went to **sleep** and I prayed that I would **wake up**, in a world where people who wasn't afraid to speak up, and do the right thing, like **Morpheus** screaming, **waaaaaake up**! Up up up, the **Matrix** was written by a black woman, and stolen by 2 white men, you know they made more than 100 mafuck'n hundred grand! **- Dawud**

Significance

Iu f Per f m heru

I wrote the three rhymes above leading up to the 90th anniversary of the day that Tutankhaten's (**King Tut's**) Tomb was discovered on Nov 4th 1922. On Nov 1st I wrote the words: "***Legendary before they bury me***, yeah I'm a be a **legend**, mafuk'a go and ask the reverend". Then on November 2nd I wrote a song about the destruction of Black Civilization and titled it, **Casualties of war**. On Nov 5th, the day after the tomb was discovered I wrote a song and named it, **Matrix** in which I prayed that I would "**Wake up**".. Little did I know, I was waking up from a long sleep, in a new body Just like the movie **Matrix**. After I died, the **New Kingdom** would be held together by the **Rameses** era then the **25th Dynasty** would be our last dance in the sun before we saw major **casualties of war**, and finally the destruction of Black Civilization, eventually falling into bondage for 400+ years of slavery and persecution that we still suffer from to this day. I would be born again in this life as Dawud (David) where I was awakened slowly over the course of 30 plus years but it was up to me to decide to take the inward path and I did. And subsequently at the age of 40, on July 3rd 2018, I was placed face to face with the life I had lived as **Emmett Till**, which was a sacrificial life mission (page 480). Then two years later on April 4th 2020 (page 594) my past life as **King Tut** is revealed to me on the same day that **Martin Luther King** was assassinated (April 4th 1968, p 69). It turns out that I was ***Legendary before they buried me*** and I will always be a **legend**, and you ain't gotta ask the reverend. I came back in 1977, and I can't tell you if there's a hell or heaven. But I can tell you that it's best that you wake up as soon as you can because if you don't you might die in this life only to be reborn into another life and never know it. like **Morpheus** said in the movie, **The Matrix**, **it's dangerous to awaken adults to the reality of the matrix they live in...** This is because adults are often times too indoctrinated into the societal norms such as religion, or culture to **break free** of the mental hold of the matrix. **See page 1**.

Utterances for Coming Forth by day into Light

November 19th 2011 Plan

The more I understand, the more that I plan, but then the more you understand you realize you can't plan, is he on a **spaceship** or is the world in his hand? Ay yoo the more I understand, the more that I plan, but then the more you understand you realize you can't plan, is he on a spaceship or is the world in his hand? Check it, **One** homie teach **two** homies now you got **three** homies, go find **four** homies teach more homies, that's the only way to expand and grow, the revolution pump'n through my veins when it flow! **- Dawud**

November 27th 2011 Do it For the Love

It is he, who comes forth by day into Light

You see that home run?! That started back when he was young! He swung a bat and started to run! y'all look and call it greatness but he was just having fun, do it cause you love it that should be your reason number one, halftime down by 20 and the coach is mad, do it because you love it, do it for your mums and dads, is what he screams at his team, everything starts now if you wanna get the ring, **against all odds,** a man only 17, **Bobby Hutton** was murdered while he was in a **dream**, and it would seem, some things that we do for love, seal our fate, the difference between good and great, you beef with me just because I'm from another faith! Us brothers need a tougher line between love and hate! c'est la vie, such is life says the emcee, I love you Hip Hop, but do you love me? Love me, the less I care what you think think, the more I'm doing it for the love, do it for the love, the less I care what you think think, the more I'm doing it for the love, do it for the love, the less I care what you think think, the more I'm doing it for the love, do it for the love, the less I care what you think think, the more I'm doing it for the love, do it for the love

A yo football, Hip Hop, soldiering, training, just a few things that I got wired up in my cranium, for the love one day I'll perform in a packed stadium, U TOUGH takes the regular man and gladiators them, God loves man when they wrong he still favors them, I'm talking from experience my whole face was numb, I shouldn't be here! I just need to be clear, **Zakeriah's** gone and it ain't fair! Lil Zakky didn't make two now his twin has one life to live through, life is short live the life that you want to, I should probably call my mother and say I love you, my sisters too, I never knew I would be, wait a minute scratch that! I always knew I had it inside of me they kiss the ass crack, the words that I'm a leave you with on the finish is, do it because you love it and if you start it finish it! the less I care what you think think, the more I'm doing it for the love, do it for the love, the less I care what you think think, the more I'm doing it for the love, do it for the love, **- Dawud**

Bobby Hutton (April 21st 1950 - April 6th 1968)

In October 1966, Bobby Hutton, 16 years old, then became the first member and the first treasurer of the **Black Panther Party for self defense**. In May 1967, Hutton was one of thirty Panthers who traveled to the California state capitol in Sacramento to demonstrate against the Mulford Act, a bill that would prohibit carrying loaded firearms in public. The group walked in to the state assembly armed as a protest to the Mulford Act. Hutton and four other Panthers were arrested. Two days after Martin Luther King was assassinated (page 69), Bobby Hutton was killed on April 6, 1968, by Oakland Police officers. The police shot an unarmed Bobby more than a dozen times when he had surrendered, after a shoot out between the Panthers and the Oakland police at a house in West Oakland. One Oakland police officer who witnessed the shooting later told a member of the Black Panther Party that, "What they did was first degree murder." Bobby Hutton's death at the hands of the Oakland police was yet another example of police brutality committed against the Oakland community and the Black Panther Party. Hutton's funeral was held on April 12 at the Ephesians Church of God in Berkeley, California. About 1,500 people attended the funeral and a rally held afterwards in **West** Oakland was attended by over 2,000 people. DeFremery Park in West Oakland, California was unofficially named after Bobby Hutton not long after his death. "Lil' Bobby Hutton Day" has been held annually at the park since April 1998. Organized by family members and former Black Panther Party members, the memorial event features speakers, performers, and art works commemorating Hutton's black consciousness and dedication to the party.

<u>Condolences</u>

My condolences go out to the family and friends of Bobby Hutton, murdered by this system of racism and white supremacy. Please know that death is not the end. The soul survives death, indeed and in spirit. This is a book of the dead written by a boy who was murdered without justice, who defeated death and came forth by day. May the soul of **Bobby Hutton** walk peacefully through the field of Reeds in Amenta. Amen Ra.

November 27th 2011 Wake up

Ay yo I woke up and saw life for what it is, now I don't trust, I just move on the positive, develop my circle with homies who would never leave me lonely, I don't wanna hurt you, I'm just say'n back up off me homie, <u>my **ancestors** built this country</u>! I think you scared that once we come together we might hunt the perpetrator, I'm just a alpha male predator, I want peace not war but I ain't scared of ya! **- Dawud**

2011 Revolution

My name is synonymous with the revolution, I'm come'n in shoot'n like **Johnathan Jackson** I'm recruit'n, pack a heater like **Lotita,** lead a mob in front of the jail, scream'n **free Mumia Abu Jamal**, **free Mumia Abu Jamal**, brick by brick , wall by wall, **free Mumia Abu Jamal**, pack a heater like **Lotita**! **- Dawud**

November 17th 2011 Black August
(Reaction to 2011 Insurrection in England from Aug 6th - Aug 11th 2011 after the police shooting of Mark Duggan)

White female Reporter

"That is not an excuse to go out rioting and cause the sort of damage that we have been seeing over the last few days."

Old Black Male Citizen

"Where were you in 1981 when brixton?!!"

White female Reporter

"Mr.... "

Old Black Male Citizen

"I don't call it **rioting** I call it an **insurrection** of the masses of the people. It is happening in Sierra, it is happening in ah, Clapjam, it's happening in Liverpool. it's happening in port of Spain Trinidad."

I keep **Luther** in the heart, **X** in the brain, **Pac** in the vain, **Black August Black August**, Somebody gotta be the first one to grab the gun, *"The Dragon has come"*, there's no where to run it's Black August, Hurricane Irene cop sirens another Fien caught in high beams, **Black August Black August**, blackmail blacklist don't forget to add the asterisk, the glass dick, the glass ceiling, my glass is empty and I'm feeling an insurrection of the masses of the people **- Dawud**

<u>Condolences</u>

My condolences go out to all the family and friends of Mark Duggan, murdered by this system of racism and white supremacy. Please know that death is not the end. The soul survives death, indeed and in spirit. This is a book of the dead written by a boy who was murdered without justice, who defeated death and came forth by day. May the soul of **Mark Duggan** walk peacefully through the field of Reeds in Amenta. Amen Ra.

November 2011 - My G.I. Bill Financial Relief back up Plan is Rejected

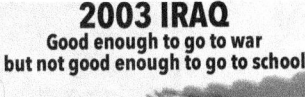

2003 IRAQ
Good enough to go to war but not good enough to go to school

I filed my paper work for College so that I could pay my bills. I was now 6 months behind on rent. Prior to this I had never been late on bills. Actually, I used to pay my rent 6 months in advance. I was living in an Apartment in Harlem owned by an old Black man named **Mr Johnson**, from South Carolina. His son **Curtis** once told me that I was the best tenant they'd ever had. Because of this they allowed me the time to get my finances on order and for that I am forever grateful! Now I was trying to use my **Army G.I. Bill** to go back to school. The Army would pay my full tuition for 36 months while also paying me **$3177.00** a month, every month that I was in school. This had always been a fall back plan for me if my money got low but after applying for school I hit a road block. I was told that I was not eligible for the G.I. Bill, **they claimed that I never graduated High School** (page 240)**!** At this point in my life I was a time bomb ready to explode and I let this situation stress me (page 2**23**). I felt like the "system" was attacking me. Maybe "they" were watching me?! The **weed** definitely had me paranoid! Perhaps they wanted me to fail and stopping my G.I. Bill was reprisal for all the **music** I was making and posting online. Maybe I was on some Person of Interest list (**P.O.I.**). I hear they had these lists for people they wanted to silence. To add more stress I would receive **Child Support** paperwork in the mail the next month (page 220). I was spun on a downward spiral from which my only saving grace was my diligent study and my music. congressm

Rau nu Prt m heru

2011 Devil (Dance With Him)

So do you flirt with him or dance with him? You sure look like you spend more time hold'n hands with him, now I ain't perfect I done fought hand and hand with him, I mean went ham on these niggas like slam'n them, so do you flirt with him or dance with him? Yeah that's the question on the table, the reason why Cain slew Abel, the reason you think to say I hate you, and he could never say I love you, he's the reason why they wanna slug you, he's there when they cuff you for no reason, the reason why people commit treason, the reason why my mother said I'm leave'n, **hallelujah Jesus Christ** that'll make them flee, or **Allahuakbar** like **Muhammad Ali**, when you let him in your heart that's when it affects me, like a problem in the ocean that connects to a sea, the T.H.E.W.A.Y.B.A.C.K I.S.L.O.V.E., make no mistake I know you exist and I know you hate me, with an intricate plan to break me, but you won't shake me, no! You won't break me, you won't take me, no no no nooo, make no mistake I know you exist and I know you hate me, with an intricate plan to break me, but you won't shake me, no! You won't break me, you won't take me, no no no nooo

Iu f Per f m heru

Ahhhh ah ah oh I could just kill a man, and I ain't never ever gotta use my hands, and I'm the reason why you cut and sell them grams, and I'm a find a way to have you fight'n Pakistan, I came to kill, steal destroy, you'll never guess who I employ, bring death steal your seconds of joy, I'll take your wife and your girl, this is my world, have fun run with me get to know **God** while you in jail, but don't believe him, he gonna say I fell, and he gonna try to sell you **heaven** but I'm a give you **hell**, but what's hell anyway? it's all what you make it! play, get naked, if you got beef I suggest you take it, out to the street, don't suggest us make'n peace, cause I'm the beast from the East and the West craven, he scream'n **God** but through your deeds it's me you praise'n, innocent seeds you ain't raise'n are mine no time for save'n, make no mistake I know you exist and I know you hate me, with an intricate plan to break me, but you won't shake me, no! You won't break me, you won't take me, no no no nooo, make no mistake I know you exist and I know you hate me, with an intricate plan to break me, but you won't shake me, no! You won't break me, you won't take me, no no no nooo **- Dawud**

Utterances for Coming Forth by day into Light

December 5th 2011 The Alchemist

See Alchemist on pages 376, 597, 599, 633 and 656.

It's now or never like the **alchemist**, and I ain't look'n for **gold** or no platinum hit, I was told be realistic, you're too optimistic?! I'm like optimistic?! **Dream** kill'n ass bitch I had to dismiss this! I know success ain't promised and no it ain't Christmas, but I got a gift to give what you got against this? I'm about my business and ain't no way around it, ***I know I'm here for a reason*** I got the game surrounded, put your hands in the air if you like the way it sounded, I'm might run it out, na I think I'll ground it, so it's first and ten, I'm starting from the 20, you know I'm fresh in the game, a new day and it's **sunny**, they go and mess my name up and then then they think it's funny, but guess what? That's the same thing they went and did to **Kanye**, so Dawud's my name, pronounce my name, practice makes perfect cause I ain't going no where mane, and ain't a thing that's gonna stop me from getting everything, don't be afraid to let me know I'm doing my damn thing **- Dawud**

It is he, who comes forth by day into Light

December 8th 2011 Inside of me

You put the D and the A with the Wu that's my name, I put my name in the for front to confront the game, I'm from the same place this art started, Home of them cold hearted, Home of them lost towers don't even get me started, From the cradle to the dearly departed, I'm a speak for those not able to hit their target, the army sergeant I'm here just to lead these kids, I make em **Soul**jas, tell em that the games not over! off sides run it back, Yo we doing it over, we don't like the way shit is so we taking it over, more community control stop killing these **Soul**jas, all this *Black on Black crime* got me screaming **Jahova - Dawud**

November 2011 Lucid Dream

Your life is a **lucid dream** you change'n, your life is a lucid dream you change'n, Your life is a **lucid dream** you change'n, Your life is a **lucid dream** you change'n, You know what! What? Sometimes you gotta go to the trap house! Word?! Rally the troops figure a plan out, if it ain't family beware of the handout, word is bond! Your life is a **lucid dream** to plan out, red pill blue pill, red white blue light, cops stop'n a nigga when ever he like, that's why the **Matrix** is something **we** write, and **Edison** ain't the one that invented the light **- Dawud**

Significance

I referenced the movie, **The Matrix** and **lucid dreaming** in this song and unbernounced to myself I was waking up from a long sleep, in a new body Just like the movie **Matrix**.

December 8th 2011 Kemet feat: Plat

In the spirit of **Jesus** and **Muhammad**, and them things in the sky that you think are comets, the land of **Kemet**, they won't teach that I promise, if you are offended I'm sorry I'm just being honest, we got the gift and the cures, the only way we get better is by living life in reverse, reflection, questions, why's reparation on the tail end? build the jail and the black male fell in, they going to hell them, all those who keep people oppressed, occupy wall street alive in the flesh, he said when ever there's two or three he'll ride with the rest, and I keep it like **M.O.P.** to the mother fuck'n death! High blood pressure cause we stressed, love is gonna get ya if your blessed, love is gonna get ya, love is gonna get ya, love is gonna get ya, love is gonna get ya, bbrrrrah stick'a ha ha ha stick'a, I'll sacrifice every cop to free everyone of my niggas, yeah I ain't crazy, **possessed** with the **spirit** of **slavery**, America made me! **- Dawud**

Fuck lifting weights, and work'n out, I'm doing pull ups, bars of raps, and everybody wanna know, why I'm so heartless, where my soul is at, is my body somewhere with some **artifacts**? Niggas wanna scream damn what type of God is that? and I reply, how large is that? I know everything, how smart is that? they said that I lost my shit, I said I left it, I'm here to get back rap, and if you had what I had you wouldn't know what to do with it, and you would give that back, you want a rap deal? let's keep it real, sign the scripture, sell your soul turn your brain to all the 6's, sleep with all the bitches drive in all the sickest d….. **- Plat**

December 8th 2011 Life is Beach feat: Ramadan Rief

Going through it, I'm in fuck'n hell! Smell the brimstone burning nigga while the demons spark me L's, stand up man up Rief can not fail, trying to live righteously, lot of wrongs seem right to me, fish out of water feeling life a Pisces be, shit is depressing trying to cope, blow clouds of loud smoke cause mommy's on dope, my life more deeper than I allow you to see, supposed to be on campus fuck'n bitches with a college degree, analyzing what my destiny is, second chapter in my life, and I hope by the third that I'm rich, hard not to know revolvers and glock's, one hazed by the field of crops, hug the block more than I hug my pops, who could love me?! **- Ramadan Rief** **(See page 187)**

Look Rief life is not a beach, I know your mommy fell down, for now you hold it down, I know you had it rough and you could be out sell'n dust, as you read up on black life, you see this life is full of strife, every generation is face'n a new trial and tribulation, formulation of rhymes to change times, one line for one mind, I shine you shine, my whole life I grew up without my father, as a kid I thought he didn't want to bother, but my father was locked down with **Hurricane Ruben Carter**, when life seems hard you work smarter, you're the son of a Generals daughter, **General Dukes** a sharecropper from Alabama, New York where he met our Grandma **- Dawud**

December 2011 Are You A Slave

Are you a slave, I used to be a slave, look at her she's a slave, look at him he's a slave, are you a slave? I used to be a slave homie, don't be a slave, when I see a woman in heels I see a slave, when I see that model on the stage I see a slave, brown skin lady, with a perm, I'm not concerned with how yo hair look, I'm more concerned with little girls being sucked up in this world, I used to be a boy run'n wild in this crazy world, now I'm a man work'n on everything I stand for, I explore, I read, I want more, yeah I came through the door but they all said this before, I'm a revolutionary to the mother fuck'n core, cause they rotten, this apple will snap you, leave you on the floor, they sprayed this woman with mace, we seen this all before, in 1968 **Ali** wasn't at war, that's why he's the greatest, and **Mayweather** is the latest, we ain't gonna get nowhere wait'n for someone to save us **- Dawud**

December 2011 READ

Take a look at the life of the average man, they wanna make cream and live lavish man, I'm try'n to make you understand there's more to life than just they way you see it man, expand your mind, take some time, read a book, don't be no crook, you don't understand how important it is for you to read, brother read! They use weed to lock brown people just like me down! Let me break it down! Ay yo I woke up and saw life for what it is, now I don't trust, I just move on the positive, develop my circle with homies who would never leave me lonely, I don't wanna hurt you, I'm just say'n back up off me homie, my ancestors built this country! I think you scared that once we come together we might hunt the perpetrator, I'm just a alpha male predator, I want peace not war but I ain't scared of ya! **- Dawud**

December 11th 2011 FB chat about -$800 (Miller Time 4/7 Communication)

2:31pm Dawud whats up bro? **2:41pm Miller** I'm alive! whats good? **2:41pm Dawud** im alive too. havent heard from u in a minute. **2:42pm Miller** yeah been real brutal lately **2:42pm Dawud** yeah its cold outside u talkn bout business? **2:42pm Miller** yeah..but its real cold outside too **2:43pm Dawud** i guess looks can be deceiving. u look to be doing well **2:44pm Miller** man I'm hanging on by threads..literally I just wear them well **2:45pm Dawud** maybe real estate isnt for you. **2:45pm Miller** guess you don't read the papers **2:45pm Dawud** or will things get better? i have clients who are doing well in real estate **2:46pm Miller** well everyone is in a different season of there business... **2:47pm Dawud** a couple months ago you said you had some bread for me but then like usual i didnt hear from u **2:48pm Miller** yeah I had half..but honestly money goes extremely quick for me now a days **2:48pm Dawud** wow **2:49pm Dawud** i cant wait to finally get paid and i honestly hope that you are never on my side of thise long drawn out favor... **2:51pm Miller** I am and am owed way more than 800 but the difference between me and you is I write things off and move on! just because I say i'm hanging in there doesn't mean I'm doing bad..especially considering all the expenses i have..but you not hollering at me to know whats good you want dough **2:53pm Dawud** i wont ever forget about the my money homie. and yes im hollering about my bread. i earned it. i closed a deal with a client i trained them they gave me money. you needed money, asked me for it and i lended it to you. i just want it back. im not writing it off. i guess we are different and so if your not doing bad why havent you paid me bro? whats up? at one point we where cool enough for you to ask me to barrow the money im the same dude lol the same dude the only difference is that you owe me money for almost 2yrs now. im the same dude i just want the $800 **2:57pm Dawud** no reply now? Wow **2:58pm Miller** I'm not going back and forth with you..im getting the bread to you..I'd would love to get it over with **2:58pm Dawud** i look forward to that-- **Our next communication is in 2013, page 273**

December 22nd 2011
Father Hood

On December 22nd 2011 I would receive child support papers in the mail. The paperwork had a picture of a little girl named Aniya. When I saw her I felt like she looked like me and as I read the details of the letter the reality of it's contents slowly began to hit me! I must have been wrong all of these years and I was the father! To this day I still don't know how long I stared down at that paper but it felt like an eternity went by as I was overcome with the feelings of regret, and sorrow and of being a delinquent dad. The song Be A Father to ya Child by ED O. G rang to my mind! After I got myself together I searched my mind for a person that might know Aja's number. I called Hurley. Him and I shared a sweet together in the barracks, our rooms were connected by a bathroom. I explained the situation to him and he gave me her number. I called her immediately. I don't remember the conversation but I called with the intent to do the right thing. We had a peaceful conversation and set up a day for her and Aniya to come to NY so that we could meet and take DNA samples. She was living in DC at the time.

This had happened at the worst possible time in my life. I was behind on rent for the first time in my life and I was at a fork in the road with my life. I didn't know what I was doing. I was smoking weed everyday and writing raps and I had only just started paying attention to what was happening in the world. I had also been paying attention the the destruction of the black family so I didn't want to be a part of that and something truly came over me when I thought I was a father. I had to take care of what was mine!

We wasted no time. They came to New York a few days later. Before I met Aniya I had already accepted that she was mine. I thought I was a father and I surrendered to it. We went and got a DNA test the next day then we went to the park and the museum of natural history. I began to call her and talk to her about school and things, I didn't know what I was doing. I was just trying to be her father. After a few weeks the DNA test results came back and they said I was not the father. Now I didn't know what to do. Her birthday came up in January and I went to DC on January 21st 2012 to celebrate her birthday.

Rau nu Prt m heru

Iu f Per f m heru

Utterances for Coming Forth by day into Light

It is he, who comes forth by day into Light

Thank You Aniya

If you ever read this Aniya I want you to know that I'm sorry for coming into your life the way that I did. When I met your mother I was 25 and she was 20 and we didn't know each other well. We were nice to each other but shortly after we met I was deployed to Iraq and I didn't see your mother again until 6 months later, and when I saw her she was pregnant with you. I had just got back from Iraq and I was happy to be alive but I was not ready for what your mother told me. She told me that I might be the father of the baby she was carrying. I was overwhelmed, scared and confused. I left Germany a few weeks later and a few months after you were born. Your mother and I communicated several times then I stopped hearing from her. I would not hear from her again until December of 2011. When I got the news that I possibly had a daughter I didn't think clearly. I immediately thought I was your father. I think I wrote that song for you the day I got the letter in the mail or the very next day but when I got the letter I was devastated. I thought that I was a delinquent father. I didn't grow up with a father so I knew what it felt like and that's why I rushed to see you, and to take responsibility. I want you to know that even when things in life get hard and everything seem hopeless, there is always a way to fix things and if we search hard enough we can find the reason why most things happen to us in our lives. I know why I met your mother. She was supposed to have you. You have a divine purpose to fulfill in this life. And I was supposed to receive that letter from your mother, and I was supposed to meet you. Meeting you did two important things for me. It made me assess the way I handle women in my life and it was the catalyst to me decoding the first part of the **star code of immortality** (p 222). If I had not responded the way I did I would have never decoded that pattern! Contemplating my past caused me to look through old files and thats when I realized the pattern with the date **May 25th**. I called your mother sometime early 2021 and told her about the book I was writing and that you two were in the book. I explained how the experience of meeting you and thinking I was your father changed my life. I told her about many of the connections I made binding me to my past lives. I told her about my theory about who **Tupac** was in a past life, then she told me that she was friends with **Young Nobel**, a member of **Tupac's** group, **The Outlawz**. She once lived across the street from him. When she told me that I was amazed. What were the chances of that?! At that point all that did was add fuel to my theory of who Tupac was in his past life because a few of the Outlawz have **star codes** connected to my prophecy. **Yaki Kadafi** was born in the same year as me on **Oct 9th** 19**77**, the same day as my grand mother (p 22). Yaki's father, **Sekou Odinga** is part of the **44th parallel** (p 561) and he's born on my June 17th, the same day as my grand father (p **23**). **Napoleon** was born on **Oct 7th** 19**77**, the same year as me and **Yaki Kadafi**. Aniya, even in the song I wrote for you, I quoted Tupac, " help me raise my Black nation reparations are due, I got caught up in the world took advantage of you, let's show our babies that we love them precious boys and girls, born Black in this White mans world". The day after I met your mother I took a picture of her holding one of the pictures I drew of Tupac in **2**00**2** on pages **111** and **11**2. Look at this page, it's number **22**1 and the next page is **222**. The pictures of Tupac are on pages **111** and **11**2. Even in this there is a pattern. When I told your mother about this pattern and told her about a pattern dealing with someones **social security** number (**4141**, page 508), she told me that the last four digits of her **social security** number are 0**222**. The remains of **Tutankhaten** were found in the Valley of the Kings and were stored as KV**62**. The 2 digits in the middle of my **social security** number are **62** (see page **41**, 121). **None of this is just coincidence!** You are a special person Aniya and I'm so grateful that I met you. I speak to your mom every so often and I'm glad to hear that you two are doing well. I'll be here if you ever decide to call.

December 28th 2011 Aniya

This is for you, I wrote this for you, this letter's for you, I heard you draw too, the first time I saw you I didn't fully explore you, I wrote this for you, I wrote this letter for you

I love you! I see you draw too, the first time I saw you I didn't really explore you, I know you probably think I ignored you, I wasn't sure! I had just got done with a tour of duty for this country, I didn't see your beauty in front of me, I still remember the day your mommy ran up and confronted me, telling me to man up, I felt stuck, I felt like she messed up my plans, I didn't have a plan! you see, your daddy wasn't taught to be a man, I had to learn on my own, a traveling man not fully grown, this is nothing knew this is what's shown, It's hard for a black man to cultivate a happy home, but daddies here now and you are not alone, daddies here, and you are not alone, and if that mocking bird don't sing, I'll teach you about **Coretta Scott King** and you can be the best at anything, don't quest for silly things, we are really **Kings** and **Queens**, see, I was really raised in Queens, and things, ain't always what they seem, my thoughts you can have them, grab them and used them to defuse this American illusion, Black men, help me raise my Black nation reparations are due, I got caught up in the world took advantage of you, let's show our babies that we love them precious boys and girls, born Black in this White mans world **- Dawud**

December 2011
The first Pattern!
May 25th Strikes Back for the first time

When I received the papers for **child support** I was filled with emotions of regret (**see page 220**), this caused me to look through old pictures and old paperwork and that's when **the first** parts of the **star code of immortality was revealed**. I would find out that my car accident in 2002 and my motorcycle accident in 2008 were both connected to the date **May 25**th. I crashed my car on June 1st 2002 but my sister dreamt the accident 7 days prior on **May 25th.** Then 6 years later in 2008 I would total my motor cycle on **May 25th**! I started sharing the pictures from my accident and telling the story on social media and many people would find it interesting, telling me that it wasn't my time to die, but none found it more amazing than me because I had lived it and lived through it! This was some sort of a **pattern** like in the series **Lost** (p 259, 648)! Most people would leave comments expressing their belief that I was here for a reason, that **God** had "**saved me**". I had no idea I would end up here in 2021 writing these events but I always knew that I should have died or suffered more injury from my vehicular accidents and I knew it was not just "luck" alone behind the reason I was still living. I had no idea of the journey I had embarked on but I was clear that this was some sort a pattern! Some sort of sign from God like the one that led me out of the Army. Like The card that I found on the floor in 2005 (pages 141-142)! May 25th became a special day for me and I began to see it as another birthday having escaped death twice on that day. Little did I know that May 25th was part of my link to **Emmett Till** (p 512).

Rau nu Prt m heru

Iu f Per f m heru

January 8th 2012 **Beacon of Light (1st of 36)**

I'm a rocket ship, yo, I'm a beacon of light, I was sent here to write, sent here to write, sent here to fight, I'm a rocket ship, I'm a, I'm a rocket ship, I'm a beacon of light, I was sent here to write, sent here to fight, I'm a rocket ship, I'm a rocket ship, I'm a rocket ship, I'm a rocket ship, I'm a beacon of light, I was sent here to write, sent here to fight and I could die to night, I'm a rocket ship, I'm a, I'm a rocket ship, I'm a beacon of light, I was sent here to fight and I could die to night, I'm a rocket ship, on a rocket ship **- Dawud**

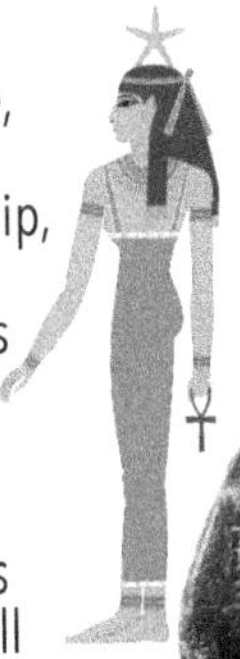

Utterances for Coming Forth by day into Light

Significance

I found this song last night. Today is January 8th 2022. I'm about two weeks or less away from the end of this book. I still must finish writing about the life of Emmett Till which spans 18 pages, 503 - 521. I held off writing that story and I'm glad I waited until the end to write it. I still need to finish writing about the sacred mushroom as well (p 483). Last night I found a few old rhymes that previously escaped me. I found another song where I call myself a **pharaoh,** written on March 8th 2012. I found **Mickey Rourke's business card** which helps confirm my meeting with **Rihanna** on July 4th 2009 (page 267) - I wonder if she remembers my **name**? In ancient Kemet **Ptah** is the Ntr (Deity) of creation who created the world through **sound** by "**naming** himself". To speak a word is to create sound and sound can't be seen like the soul can't be seen (by most). In the book of **John,** found within the **Bible,** you find a similar quote. - "In the beginning was the word… then the word became flesh". This concept of sound and creation was taken from the ancient **Shabaka** text found in the 25th Dynasty of Kemet (Egypt) that detailed the original creation story of Ptah. How important is the spoken word? I wrote music from the heart and soul and my ancient soul awoke within my flesh. I used music as magic to awaken my ancient soul fragments. **I am a beacon of light** and I was sent here to write this book. I was sent here to fight the forces of darkness like Luke Sky Walker (page 37). My lyrical word was my sword, and my light saber and with it I crashed down on the enemy with inter dimensional accuracy that they could not detect or anticipate. They knew someone was coming through Hip Hop, through the spoken word but they thought they had killed him in 1996! They had no idea he would come from a galaxy Far Far away called Far Rockaway Queens. **14** shots were fired at Tupac on Sep 7. **Ausar** was cut into **14** pieces and **Emmett Till** died at **14** years old. I have a theory about who Tupac was in a past life.

It is he, who comes forth by day into Light

End of Mayan Calendar

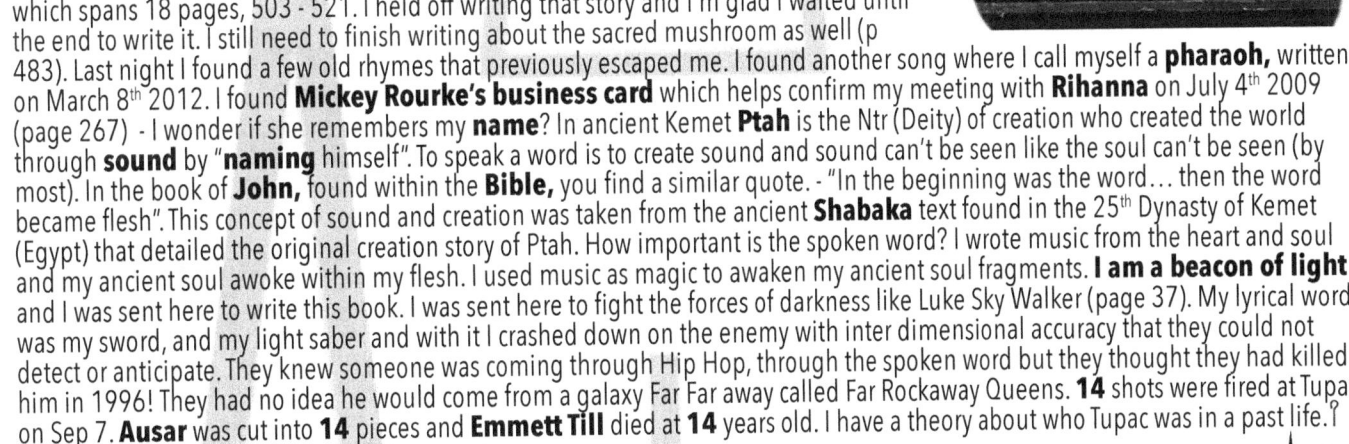

Emmett Till came to this planet on July 25th which is the most sacred day on the Mayan calendar (see page 503). The Mayans called it - **the day out of time**. It is the culmination of the 13 Moon Calendar year originated from the **Mayan** science of time. On July 25th, the Mayans observed the star **Sirius** (**the dog star**) rising in sync with the **sun**. In Ancient Kemet (Egypt) the star Sirius was connected with Auset (Isis) while her husband Ausar (Osiris) was connected with the 3 stars (3 wise men, 3 kings) that make up the belt in the constellation of **Orions belt** (page 250). Ausar was the Lord of **resurrection/reincarnation** and the **afterlife** (see page 3). This was a very special day in ancient Kemet because it marked the inundation of the Nile river and the Mayans regarded this day as a spiritual mark to start the evolutionary process of humanity. It is considered a moment of great energetic intensity, in which the **Beings of Light** work to align us with the harmony of the universe, on its various dimensions of time, and space.

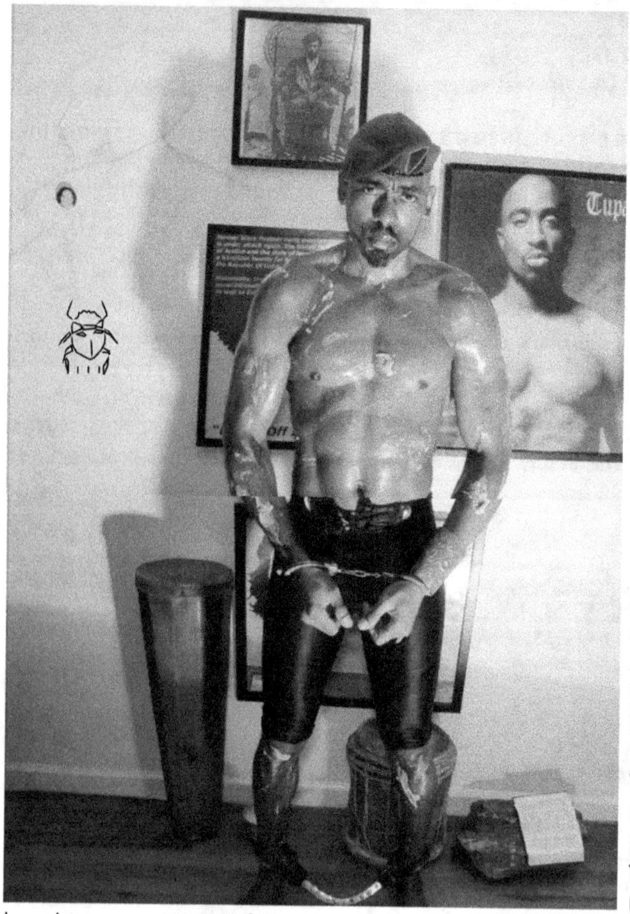

January 12th 2012 - Emotional Meltdown

On **Khalid Muhammad**'s birthday I had an emotional meltdown. The day prior to these pictures my computer crashed as I was uploading a video on youtube. The video was for a song about America's murder of Black people. I felt like the government was after me. Perhaps I was just delusional but I was definitely paranoid and stressed! Adding to my paranoia was the fact that my Army G.I. Bill stipend for my school fee's was rejected. They claimed I didn't graduate from high school! I was told that I needed to first prove I graduated high school before I could use my Army G.I. Bill and receive the monthly stipend of **$3177.00**. I was livid! I went to Jamaica Queens and got the help of Congressmen Gregory meek's Liaison, Nathaniel Hezekiah. Eventually I would get the stipend in June but I couldn't see that far ahead (p 240). I crumbled! I had my friend filmed this video for me. I wore my Army beret because I felt like I was a Military Veteran who was being mistreated by a country who claimed to love their veterans. I put chains and grease on because I was a descendant of slaves and the slaves were greased up before they were sold on the auction block. I wore the football pants because I was also an athlete that got a raw deal. I felt the system had wronged me in many ways. I felt like I was at rock bottom. I had never really planned any of my life out, I just moved from one thing to the next and for the first time I didn't have my rent money. Prior to this it seemed like the universe had always placed what I needed in front of me. Perhaps the universe was just a little late this time.. On top of that I was a delinquent father! I had a nine year old daughter that I never met! Or at least I thought I did. I needed money! My business was low and I had been smoking weed for a year now.

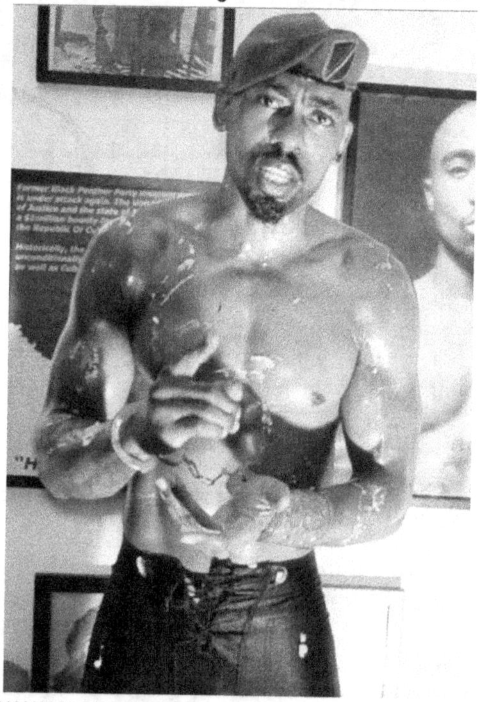

I never watched this video completely until I began writing this book. It had always been hard for me to watch because I felt like it was a moment of weakness, like I had cracked under pressure. I felt like it was cowardice. I should have been more of a man like **Khalid Muhammad** and kept my composure. I almost deleted this video many times. Perhaps by the time you read this it will be deleted. There is a saying, "**never awaken people past a certain age because it can be dangerous**". This is because adults are often times too indoctrinated into the societal norms such as religion, or culture to **break free** of the mental hold of the matrix. Like a bus or train hopelessly speeding out of control with no brakes. This is what happened to me. Many people end their lives during bouts of depression. If you are depressed take a deed breath and continue to read. There is always a sunny day coming. While I was here having a break down, **Nehmes Bastet's** was about to make her grand return.

January 16th 2012
Nehmes Bastet's Hits the internet a Year After Her Discovery

This tomb is only the second tomb found in the Valley of the Kings since 19**22** when **Tutankhaten** from the **18th** dynasty was discovered. In the tomb a coffin was found with an intact mummy from about 3,000 years ago. Her name was **Nehmes Bastet** and she was the daughter of the high priest of Amen and a **temple singer**, perhaps during Egypt's **22**nd Dynasty (approximately 945 - 712 B.C.). The discovery of Nehmes' mummy was the first time a tomb has been discovered containing a woman that wasn't related to a royal family. It has been speculated that Theben high priests saw Nehmes as so important that they allowed her body to be mummified and placed in the tomb of a royal family. She was buried along side mostly **18th** dynasty royalty giving rise to her potential connection to the 18th dynasty royals..

See page **648** for the **metaphysical significance of the number 23**.

January 18th 2012 - Meta Spiritual Encounters
The Book of Psalms and My Apparition

Rau nu Prt m heru

I was going through a lot of **stress** during this period of my life and what happened this day didn't help my stress but it damn sure got my **attention**! 6 days prior I had an alarming experience while editing a video for one of my songs. When I finished the song I started uploading the video on youtube and in the middle of the upload my Mac desk top crashed (p **23**3). Immediately I thought it was "they" or "somebody" who was trying to stop me from speaking truth to power. I don't remember what song I was editing the video for but I know it was something that was speaking truth to power and that's why I felt like I was being attacked. After this experience I was shaken and I didn't want to write music anymore but I went to the bible and opened it randomly to see what it would say. I wanted to see if it would speak to my situation. I opened it to a passage in the book of **Psalms** and the first thing I read was - "**to the chief musician David**"... I was shocked. I went on to read and the passage felt like it was speaking to me. It was talking about fighting against the city of Babylon.

Iu f Per f m heru

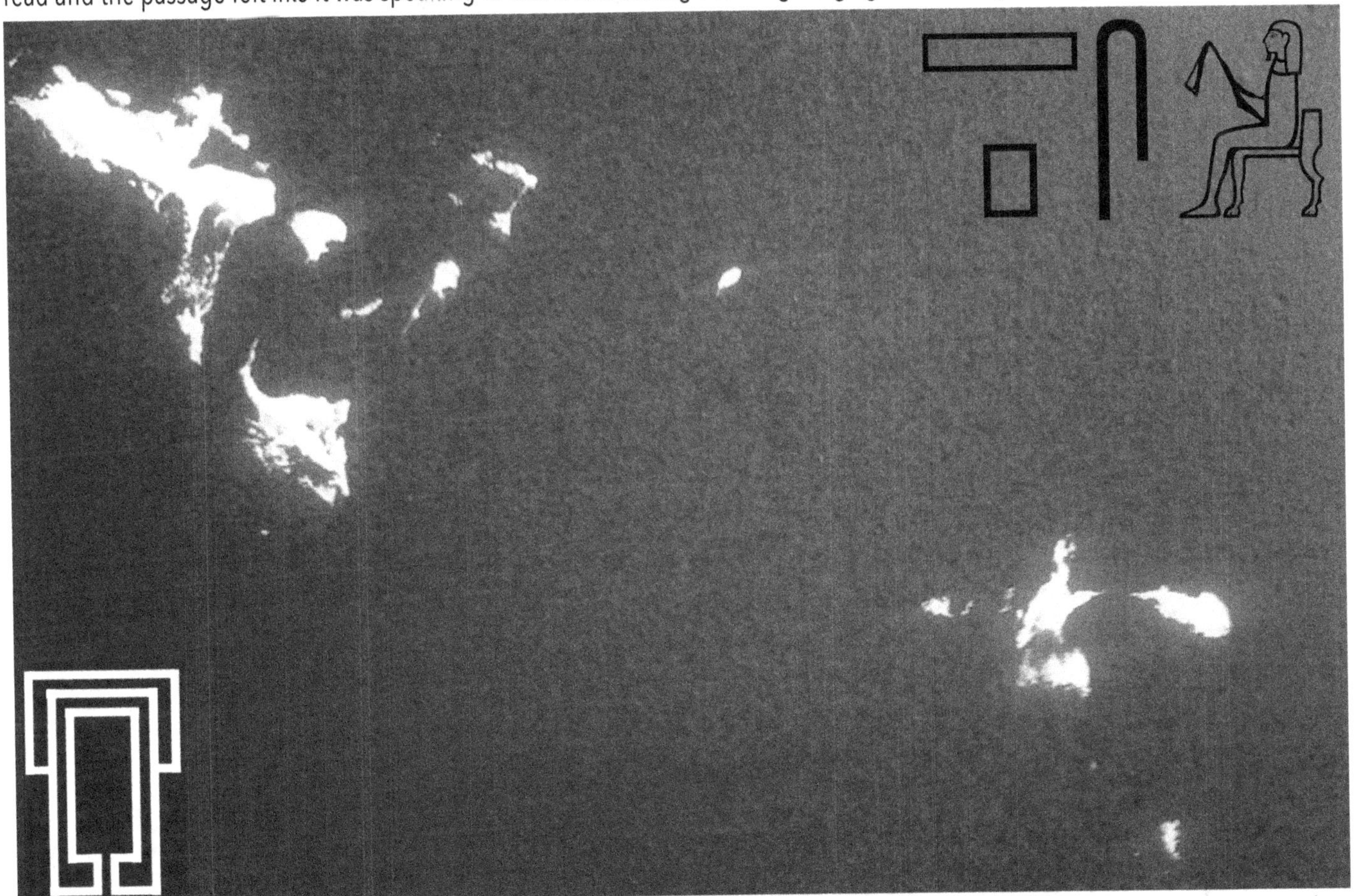

Utterances for Coming Forth by day into Light

It is he, who comes forth by day into Light

A few days later on January 18th 2012 I was painting the ceiling of my studio white. There was a portion of my wall that was red and so I had plastic covering it so as to not get any white paint from the ceiling on the red wall. While I was painting I was contemplating what had happened with my computer a few days prior and whether or not I should continue writing music. When it was time for me to take the plastic down it slipped out my hands and the side with white paint drops fell, smearing white paint onto the red wall. I ran to get a wet clothe to wipe the paint off but just before I wiped it off I **stopped in my tracks because what I saw looked like the face of a Godly figure looking down at a person with their arms extended in the shape of a cross, seemingly in supplication**. I felt like it was a representation of me in that moment speaking to God and God painted the moment on my red wall for me to see! I felt like it was a real intervention of a **higher divine power** like when people see apparitions of **Mary** (Auset, Isis), or like the ones people claim to see in the clouds. Like the shapes and images hidden within the murmuration of the starlings (birds) forming patterns for a split second as they circle above head. It reminded me of when I found that **card** on the floor in 2005 when I was asking God what I should do with my life (pages 141-142). After this experience I kept writing my music and years later I would come to find that many of my writings were **prophetic** just like some of my **dreams**. I had no idea though what it was all leading to. And I had no idea who **King David** really was. In 2014 (page 292) I would come to realize who sent me the card in 2005 and after my past life as Tutankhaten (King Tut) on April 4th 2020 (page 594) I would come to know that the bible character King David was **Thutmoses III**. We make a fatal error when we think all that we see with our two eyes is all there is to see! All things are governed by seen and unseen forces.

I would not become aware of the biblical connections to the 18th dynasty until after I had my past life revelation of Tutankhaten (King Tut) on April 4th 2020 (page 594). I had Previously seen posts online claiming that characters from the bible were really pharaohs from Kemet (Egypt) but I never researched it. On January 18th 2012 I opened the book of **Psalms** seeking spiritual help and my ancestral guides spoke to me (page 224). The **poetry** of **Akhenaten** (the father of King Tut) was **plagiarized and placed in the Bible, in the book of Psalms** and Psalms (**23:** 1-6) also holds an interesting passage, "Yea, though I walk through the valley of the shadow of death, I will fear no evil: for thou art with me; thy **rod** and thy **staff** they comfort me." This rod and staff sounds like the **Crook** and **Flail** carried by the Nswt Bity's (Pharaoh's) of ancient Kemet. I want the archeologist who spend their life's energy digging for treasure in the soil to know that the real treasure is found when we dig within our souls! I want the religious people to consider for a moment, that perhaps the Bible is not a literal book. Perhaps it is religious literature, because some of it was plagiarized (page 615) and much of what is written in it is allegory (page 488). For instance, perhaps the **Jews** are not a group of people, perhaps they are the **chakras/Glands** of the body. Revelations, ch 2:9 says, "those who claim they are Jews but they are not, they are the synagog of Satan". This Scripture is referring to people who have not raised themselves up via the inward path, those who have not built their "Noah's Ark (page 252). As a child I always felt like there was something about me and this world that I did not know, a feeling that I'm sure most of you can relate to. I want the **Christians**, the **Muslims**, the **Jews**, the **Gentiles**, the **Brahmans**, the **Priests** and the **Popes**, so on and so forth to put a side your beliefs for a moment. Open up your mind of imagination and use your imagination when reading this book allowing your heart to be the guide. Listen to my story and know that it is true. For the muslim, you should know that I was born a Muslim and my born name was **Dawud** which means **David** (beloved of God) and my middle name is Basheer (the bringer of truth). For the Christian, you should know that I got **baptized** at **11** (page 49) and gave my life to **Christ** at **22** (page 92). **Jews** and **Christians** are waiting for someone to return through the line of **David**. You should know that my **father** in this life was given the name **David** as his middle name and in my life as **Tutankhaten (King Tut)** I **descend** from the Pharaonic **line** of **Thutmoses III** who is seen as the **biblical David** by historians. There's no structural or tangible proof that this "David" from the bible ever lived but Thutmoses the 3rd lived a life that parallels the stories of David from the bible and you can see, touch and read about Thutmoses. Thutmoses the 3rd comes from the 18th dynasty like **Tutankhaten (King Tut)** so if I am **Tut** then I come from the Pharaonic line of **David** (p 7). I did not write the Bible but there is a poem in the bible written by my father, Akhenaten titled Psalms 104 (**Hymn to the Aten, p 615**) from the Psalms of **David**. My father **Akhenaten** was the **biblical Moses**. Akhenaten did the things that Moses was said to have done in the book of **Exodus**. He took his people to a fertile land between Memphis and Thebes (Luxor) and built the city of Akhetaten that venerated the sun. Today Akhetaten is called Tell EL Amarna and it is mostly a desert... The locals call it **ET Till** or **EL Till**. These names are part of this prophecy of reincarnation. ET Till like EMM**ETT Till** and **EL Till** like **E**mmett **L**ouis **Till** (pages 40, 671). And the name Emmett can be found on the name K**emet**. Akhenaten is seen as the father of monotheism (the concept of one God) which many of you follow. Akhenaten didn't create this concept he just crystallized teachings about the sun's life giving properties that his fore-mothers and fathers taught him. The bible pulls from the astrological zodiacal time period of Aries which covers the 18th dynasty where King Tut comes from. This is why the Christian men who went around killing in the name of their region were called **missionaries**. The mission was pulling from this time of **Aries**, hence **Mission-Aries**. The mission was to steal the knowledge they had taken from the the 18th dynasty so as to dominate and control the world with religion (p 592)! So if anyone will return from this "**bible prophecy**" it will be the son of the father of monotheism which is me, Tutankhaten, Emmett Till, Dawud, TutemRa the son of Akhenaten (p 645). The reality is that we ALL resurrect and reincarnate. In ancient Kemet the concept of reincarnation and past lives was called the **Wehem-Mesut** (repeating of births, p 14).

For all the other religions or spiritual people know that I have never been an enemy to any faith. I was always a seeker of truth even as a little boy and that is why I decided to get baptized at 11 (page 49). Most importantly I'm writing this book for the children of Africa and all peoples of the world. It is important that you know that this life you are living is not the end. There is a great chance that you might come back here again. So we must make this world a better place not just for the children of the world but more importantly we must make it a better place for our souls to come back to. Your mothers and fathers and sisters and brothers and friends might come back here too. We must heal ourselves and heal the world so that we can create this **golden** age that I have come back to remind you of. We sank to a depression for ages so as to give us a reminder of what we should never allow to come about again. We are here to play this game of life which is more like a play of consciousness. We all play it together like a shared dream (p 452, 589). It's important that we help wake each other up so that we all end the game well but more importantly we must first awaken ourselves. No person can hand another person enlightenment. Each person must earn it on their own. We win when we all win and there is no real end.

We will be free and no one will give us this freedom. We will take it. We will liberate our souls and the rest will follow. Know that this can be done peacefully, in fact all we need to do is turn towards the sun, the one that is within you. Ramemeber the ancient Kemetyu, the Ancestors, the Ancient Star Ntchrs. Read my story and see what happened to me! Then ask yourself if your path has produced the same nectar. If it hasn't I welcome you to the path of Shemsu Heru - the followers of Heru (p 2). In fact many of your paths have borrowed from the story of Heru. I promise it's true! Come Follow me on a journey to see a for real Emcee. BOO!

Rau nu Prt m heru

Iu f Per f m heru

2012
The Coming of Dawuud's Appeal

It is around this time that I became aware of David Walker. David Walker was a free Black man during chattel slavery who became an abolitionist. In 1829 he wrote a pamphlet titled, DAVID WALKER'S APPEAL, to the coloured citizens of the world but in particular, and very expressly, to those of the United States of America. David was inspired by the declaration of independence written in 1776. He argued that the declaration was flawed because it preached equality for all but yet they still had blacks in chains. David Walker's Appeal was the most notorious document of the times and if Blacks were found with it they could be killed on the spot. After learning about Walker's appeal I began using the name Dawuud's Appeal. I wrote an essay about him on November 7th 2012 (p 254).

2012 The Ones

If you knew a lil more about the world, you would love me, and u would understand why I write these rhymes to get your mind out the **matrix**, I use to work at a club named the **Natrix**, we had fun, we didn't see the bull whips, up in the club lookin for hugs, I suppose every bodies gotta have their fun, so I'm only speak'n to the one's, yeah, I'm only speak'n to the one's, the one's that know the time has come, the man the woman, the old the young, my name is Dawuud, I had a **revelation**, my life is like all stories rolled in one, like ancient scripts **- Dawuud's Appeal**

Significance

I referenced the movie, **The Matrix** in this song and I titled it, **The Ones**. In the movie, The Matrix, **Neo** was "the one" and unbernounced to myself, I was waking up from a long sleep, in a new body Just like the movie **Matrix**.

Utterances for Coming Forth by day into Light

January 21st 2012 Deeper

They say live and let live but when you're live'n kills kids that's when you gotta find another door, it ain't all about you this nigga scream'n on the house floor, are you kill'n for peace? cause that defeats the purpose, get familiar with the you that lies beneath the surface, I was think'n of you when I sat and wrote this, it seems like we all broke as a joke, except for him, look at him, yo! there must be hope! he's so successful, how did he get it? How'd he rid his life of misery and pain everybody want money and fame, mo gains no change, *no ropes but we still hang! court rooms full of our children*, now pledge allegiance to that! see I'm'a give you the facts, when they say life that's when you collapse, no turning back, come to Harlem look up in the sky, black birds fly, for these white lies, you can never blackmail me, I'll never tell a white lie, stop trying to be wealthy and try to live your life like the **most high**, you dig yourself deeper in your grave every line that you write, every song every page, you dig yourself deeper in your grave, every line that you write, every song every page, you dig yourself deeper in your grave every line that you write, every song every page, you dig yourself deeper in your grave, every line that you write, every song every page **- Dawuud's Appeal**

It is he, who comes forth by day into Light

January 21st 2012 Homeless Dreamer

Homeless man on the train beg'n, no body sees him, cause every bodies greave'n and every bodies worried about how much they make'n, or what they tweet'n, there's this guy on the 4 train I used to see him, tell me have you seen him? What a life to live, I'm on the train going over the bridge, thinking about life and what rights do I have to live? and who are you not to forgive? And who are you to decide whether or not I live? Can't you see mr officer? Ain't no stop'n this! you are not superman and this is not metropolis! calling all cars officer down damn he took a round to the face, man you can't just run up in the place! I don't mean no disrespect, there's been a disconnect, you guys are disconnected to reality, and y'all tell fallacies, imagine if **Sean Bell** was a part of your family, imagine if the name **Malcolm X** didn't command respect, imagine if no one came for you, I mean imagine if you was left in the pit of death, **Henry Smith** hanging from a tree breathing his last breath what did he see? It had to be something like the sight of **Christ** taking his last step up the hill, senator Perry said he don't care who he kills, the crowd cheered and I'm sure God shed tears, they know not what they do, be careful what you pursue, cause your pursuit of happiness is not about you, free **Mumia** from this great incarcerator, greed's the enemy! you ain't ***never had a friend like me***, **Dawuud's Appeal** is mad real people ***let's get free***, it's mad real people ***let's get free***, I picked my pen back up at **33 - Dawuud's Appeal**

January 27th 2012 - High Frequency Psychic Channeling

A Weed induced Thought Form / idea for a movie recorded into my phone as a audio memo on January 27th 2012

"And then I could tie in the fact that I -chuckle- There are two levels, those two levels. The good and the bad. I could tie those in and **we could have those people shooting back to** do things to maybe help me, Uuummm? Like **Tupac.** He knew how I loved him. **He came back** and he helped me? -questioning- Is that what I was trying to say? or just Tie the heaven thing, or I could have… Oh! That's what I was saying. Have them **go back** and and just show how those, or **some of those people came back** and embodied the -chuckle- the **soul** of Nat- and became like **Nat Turner** and and they became people like ahhhh… ? Um, they just **came back** in that time. They didn't want to be that person, they just **came back** in that time and became possessed and -chuckles- I yeah, that's can be what it is. They didn't **come back** as a… They never planned to be who they were they were just regular people who got that sp**ark** when that person **came back**. And the thing about me is, **I'm just Dawud. I'm just somebody that came back** -laughs- **yeah and I came back when I smoked that shit —? and who I was, I came back -laughs-** That's dope!" **- Dawud**

SIGNIFICANCE

I started smoking weed in 2011 when I was 33 years old (page194). When I got "high" I would have these **ideas** for movies and skits and business. At the time I was unaware of what was happening. I would record these ideas into my phone as audio memos. I realize now that the recording transcribed above was not an idea for a movie it was actually an inter dimensional transmission from another dimension. I had opened up a **High Frequency Psychic Channel** (perhaps from the akashic records), where these messages were channeled down through my thoughts. I smoked weed and it opened a channel/portal for a thought about **souls returning from the dead** and I **thought** it was an idea for a movie but it was actually a foretelling of what I was about to experience. The fact that I had indeed **COME BACK**! In ancient Kemet the concept of reincarnation and past lives was called the **Wehem-Mesut** (repeating of births, page 14). It is not about how much you know, it's about how much you desire to know. It's about where your heart is. All actions are measured by the matters of the heart. <u>These spiritual **messages** are **received through the heart**</u>. If your desire is right and exact you can attract the information or situation you earn. This is the ancient Kemetic (Egyptian) principle of divine thought and divine wisdom governed by the Deity (God) **Jehuti** also known as **Tehuti** or **Hermes** or **Thoth** (divine **thought**).

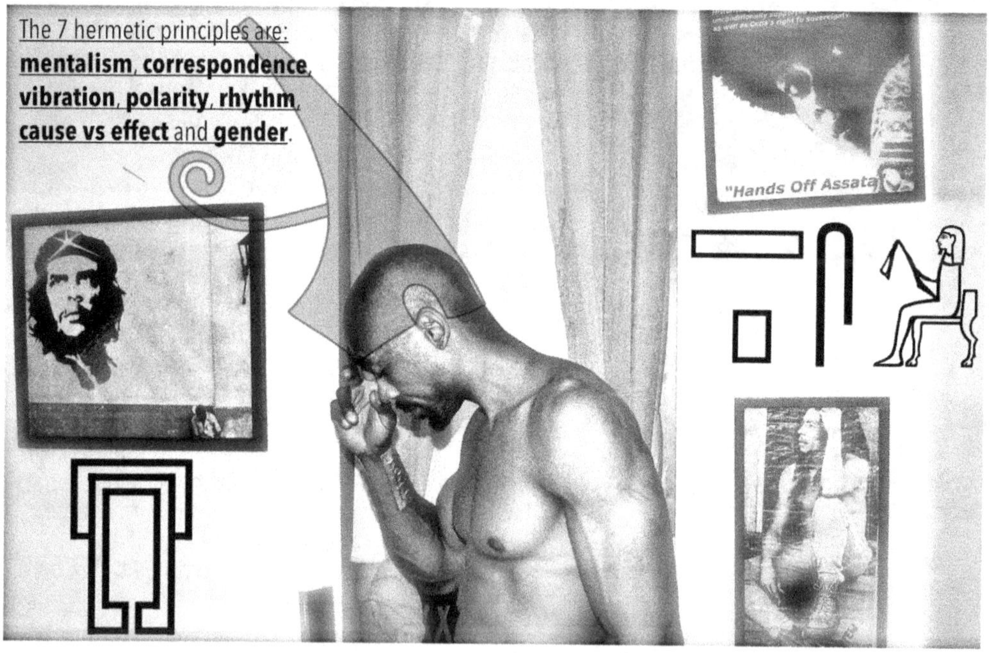

The 7 hermetic principles are:
mentalism, correspondence, vibration, polarity, rhythm, cause vs effect and gender.
"Hands Off Assata"

January 30th 2012 Geronimo

<u>Ever heard of Geronimo?</u> how could you see **Avatar** and not see who you are? the **Neo** the **One** the **God,** the one with the earth, the wind, the water, the air, peace in your time of despair, **Dawuud's Appeal** is here, let those with ears hear, let those who appose stand clear, **Geronimo** is dead, so is **Geronimo Pratt**, but you are alive, so you need to live, search inside, if we gonna survive, we gotta teach the kids, teach them they were taught lies, teach em bout **Sundiata,** the kings of **Kemet,** now them some riders, when will you realize that we **soul survivors?!!** when will you open your eyes and see the **Osiris?** on your dollar, where's it from? where's that **pyramid?** come on son! **- Dawuud's Appeal 2012**

January 30th 2012 General Dukes Jr

Gone, strong, this is for my, this is for my, this is for my Grand father, yo, this is for my grand father who is gone, I am still here going strong, I am still here going strong, I am still here going strong, this is for my grand father who is gone, I am still here going strong, I am still here going strong, I am still here going strong, this is for my grand father, gone, I am still here, strong, going strong, going strong,

Man **I love you and I miss you**, right now I need a tissue cause the hook to this song, got me think'n bout you gone, but I'm still going strong, I'm still going strong, man I feel like I've done so many things wrong since you've gone to see what's next beyond, I'm still going strong **- Dawuud's Appeal 2012**

I Never finished this Song. I started crying and had a really bad emotional break down (see page 169).

Rau nu Prt m heru

January 30 2012 **Maverick (Army G.I. Bill)**

I said wow, things that they do your child, wow, the things that they say to your child, wow, they be make'n them juveniles, while you at work get'n fucked with a smile, I used to watch the **Dukes of Hazard**, no blacks on the **Jetsons**, Hollywood **magic**, these mafucka's really think they Mavericks, I went to war came back and I can't have it?!

Hold up, hold up man wait a minute! You mean to tell me that I can go play college football without that Spanish credit, then 99 I can join the Army with out that Spanish credit, but when I get out the Army and I wanna go to school y'all gonna tell me I never graduated?! Y'all mafucka's are crazy. Y'all need to get y'all shit together! Cause you know people be blow'n shit up these days man but that ain't me cause I'm about peace and ***<u>I'm a write about this shit!</u>*** Fuck **Joe the plumber** man! I don't care about Joe the plumber. Know what I'm saying? What about me?! What about me?! - **Dawuud's Appeal 2012**

Iu f Per f m heru

January 30th 2012
3rd Eye Battle Cry (Sight Beyond Sight)

This is my battle cry, and this is my lullaby, see I wasn't really born here son, I was born in the 3rd eye eye eye , Yo! how could you live life and never see strife?! turn a blind eye to everything in sight, sight beyond sight, hit the peace pipe, and in the distance I see your indifference - to other peoples pain and what a shame, I see you got Jordans on your feet, they got slaves in China with no shoes on their feet, you ever seen a man with no right hand?! go to the **Congo**! go to the mother land, they gave us free so they could expand **white supremacy**, but I see everything spiritually, *<u>you gonna need another plan to get rid of me</u>*, **Dawuud's Appeal** straight from the field, I speak from the heart and don't care when I'm killed, cause **you can't kill me we gonna live on** , the **soul** lives on, this is my battle cry, and this is my lullaby, see I wasn't really born here son, I was born in the 3rd eye eye eye, this is my battle cry, and this is my lullaby, see I wasn't really born here son, I was born in the 3rd eye eye eye - **Dawuud's Appeal 2012**

February 2nd 2012
The Shooting of Ramarley Graham

Utterances for Coming Forth by day into Light

The murder of Ramarley Graham took place in the borough of the Bronx in New York City on February 2, 2012. Richard Haste, a New York Police Department officer, shot Ramarley in the bathroom of his Grandmothers apartment. The officer Michael Best claims he had been informed that Ramarley had a gun and believed that Ramarley had been reaching for a gun in his waistband after disregarding police orders. No gun was found on the scene. Haste was charged with manslaughter, but the charge was dropped. Graham's family filed a lawsuit against the city of New York, and the lawsuit was settled for $3.9 million in 2015. The NYPD Firearms Discharge Review Board found the shooting to be within department guidelines. In 2016, under pressure from Mayor Bill de Blasio and prior to Bratton's resignation, Haste was offered to vest out with all benefits, in spite of having been cleared of all criminal charges and found within guidelines. Haste opted to go to department trial. In 2017, an internal NYPD investigation explored whether Haste used "poor tactics" leading up to the shooting. Haste ultimately resigned from the NYPD rather than allow himself to be terminated.

<u>Condolences</u>

My condolences go out to all the families of those who have been robbed of their life by this system of racism and white supremacy. Please know that death is not the end. The soul survives death, indeed and in spirit. This is a book of the dead written by a boy who was murdered without justice, who defeated death and came forth by day. May the soul of **Ramarley Graham** walk peacefully through the field of Reeds in Amenta. Amen Ra

It is he, who comes forth by day into Light

February 3rd 2012 illusion

There is no, There is no, end, there's only a beginning, we are all dead, we are all born dead, until we come to the light, in the beginning there was light

This is all an illusion, you are not here! until you wake up, I dare you to care about you ancestors and what they had to do to survive here! are you aware that the ancestors are still in the air? you might put their pictures on your wall, you might pour out a little alcohol, but homie; **are you there when your homies call**? brick by brick, wall by wall… free **Mumia Abu Jamal!!!** I hit the streets around high noon and took a walk past Grants' tomb, I wonder if I would have liked him if I had knew him?! probably not! the good ones end up getting shot on my block! cops chase kids from where they live. I think it's rooted in the language! the language is racist! and I know you won't like this.. I don't give a damn cause I'm speaking with righteous, righteous anger cops with bangers.. cops be the ones bringing the danger! If it was your son you'd be the one with anger! they even chased the one born in a **manger**, My names Dawud Basheer the beloved truth bringer, my names Dawud Basheer the beloved truth bringer, my names Dawud Basheer the beloved truth bringer, the beloved truth bringer, righteous anger cops with bangers

Sometimes, sometimes you really get a calling , sometimes, sometimes fate looks you in the face and say, what are you doing, What are you doing? Yo! I'm here! I'm here! my names Dawud Basheer the beloved truth bringer, my names Dawud Basheer the beloved truth bringer, the beloved, the beloved truth bringer, the beloved truth bringer, my names Dawud Basheer the beloved truth bringer, the beloved truth bringer - **Dawuud's Appeal 2012**

Kemet, Temple of Dendera 2022

April 28th 2022 Scarabeus

Born live love die, sleep dream 3rd eye, wake up follow your **dream** and cruise through a vanilla sky, never die **born again** live to die another day, life is but a **dream** back in time that's what we used to say, I used to pull the harp string just to let my heart sing, and she be feel'n my heart say'n from what my Harp play'n, **Ptah** Nefer spit **divine heka's** that they call rhymes, took 5 emcees from every borough put them in a line, multiplied them by 5 now they thorough and you can see em shine, like your highness be like the **Aten** the 18th dynasty, from **Tutankhaten** to being forgotten, them **coming back** as **Emmett Till** then gettin killed and thrown in a river rotten, the plot thickens the **Isis** in M**ississ**ippi, this **prophecy** was written on papyrus and **I have risen** like **Osiris**, check my thymus gland recorded by the **ibis** hand, understand, row row row ya boat if you wanna reach the promise land, the running man run run as fast as you ever can, that's if you're trying to find the great I am that I am, eye on top again, eye on top again how iconic the cream of the crop now eye on top again - **TutemRa**

February 6th 2012 I Ran So Fast

The twin towers seemed so far away, we could see it from the bay when we play, uhh, growing up in Queens, growing up in Queens, ***I remember being chased by a very mean old white man, I must have been 8, he lured us all in with some bait, candy and some money, see, he had plan to act funny, but God had another plan for me***! I ran so fast, I ran so fast! I went to school broke rules, coach looked at coach they both said, he ran so fast, top division one prospects we had mad respect, top division one prospects we had mad respect

Look man I'm 34, but I got people to tell you I'm the realest player they ever saw, but I don't think about that any more, I think about all these schools closing, it's like they making sure, making sure they closing every door, it's like they don't want us to grow, they want us to be the dinosaur, let me explain how I feel inside, a dream differed, do you explode or sit and cry? yeah I cried homie, I won't lie homie, but now the Lord done shined the light on me, and now I'm sitting here writing songs to you, never stop even if they think they're better than you, ***Don't stop Dawud, Don't stop Dawud, Don't stop Dawud, Don't stop Dawud, Don't stop, My name's Dawud Basheer the beloved truth bringer, My name's Dawud Basheer the beloved truth bringer, My name's Dawud Basheer the beloved truth bringer, the beloved truth bringer***, I ran so fast, I ran so fast! I went to school broke rules, coach looked at coach they both said, he ran so fast, I ran so fast, I went to school broke rules, coach looked at coach they both said he ran so fast! - **Dawuud's appeal 2012**

February 11th 2012 Angel

I said, look man my name is Dawud, I ain't mad, I'm not the angry black man, I'm glad! **I'm glad I lived long enough to have this talk with my dad,** ***the world is old but it springs from the past*****,** springs from the past **- Dawuud's Appeal 2012**

Rau nu Prt m heru

February 11th 2012
Whitney Houston Transitions

With over 200 million combined albums, singles and videos sold worldwide during her career with Arista Records, Whitney Houston has established a benchmark for superstardom that will quite simply never be eclipsed in the modern era. She is a singer's singer who has influenced countless other vocalists female and male. Whitney's tragic passing on February 11, 2012 is still deeply felt by her family, friends and millions of fans worldwide. Her Estate is committed to keeping her legacy alive. To that end, they along with Sony Music's Legacy Recordings have released (to date) two albums – Whitney Houston Live: Her Greatest Performances on November 10, 2014 and most recently on November 17, 2017- I Wish You Love: More From The Bodyguard, marking the 25th anniversary of The Bodyguard and containing rare unreleased versions of many songs from the film.

Iu f Per f m heru

Significance

Whitney Houston started her career at **14** years old in 1977 the **year of the snake** the same year that I was born. She was only **14** when she became a back up singer for Michael Zager and **Emmett Till** was **14** when he was murdered. It was after Whitney began to look into her royalties and attempted to get her **Masters** back, that she died in a mysterious drowning. At her funeral two **golden** Pharaonic sarcophagi were placed at the entrance of the doors. The same day that Whitney passed away I wrote a short rhyme titled, **Angel** and in it would say the words "***the world is old but it springs from the past***" and the month before Whitney passed away a tomb was discovered in the Valley of the kings (page 223). This tomb is only the second tomb found in the Valley of the Kings since the discovery of **Tutankhaten** in 19**22**. In the tomb a coffin was found with an intact mummy from about 3,000 years ago. Her name was **Nehmes Bastet** and she was the daughter of the high priest of Amen and a temple **SINGER,** perhaps during Egypt's **22**nd Dynasty (approximately 945 - 712BC). Archeologist suggest that the discovery of Nehmes' mummy was the first time a tomb has been discovered containing a woman that wasn't related to a royal family. They believe that Theben high priests, saw Nehmes as so important that they allowed her body to be mummified and placed in the tomb of a royal family. I disagree with the archeologist, I think **Nehmes Bastet** was a royal and I think she died again on February 11th 2012. This is why Whitney Houston was laid to rest with the energetics of Egyptian royalty. There is no such thing as just a coincidence! One time is an incidence, twice is a coincidence, but three, four, and five, is a pattern! Can you tell the difference?! 5 days after Whitney passed away I would write her a song. I wrote her a song on February 16th, the same day that the final room of King Tut's Tomb was opened (Feb 16th 19**23**, p 11) and she just so happened to have two large Pharaonic sarcophagi at her funeral. In ancient Kemet (Egypt) the concept of reincarnation and past lives was called the **Wehem-Mesut** (repeating of births, page 14).

Utterances for Coming Forth by day into Light

Condolences

My condolences go out to the family, friends and fans of **Whitney Houston**. Please know that death is not the end. The soul survives death, indeed and in spirit. This is a book of the dead written by a boy who was murdered without justice, who defeated death and came forth by day. May the soul of **Whitney Houston** walk peacefully through the field of Reeds in Amenta. Amen Ra.

It is he, who comes forth by day into Light

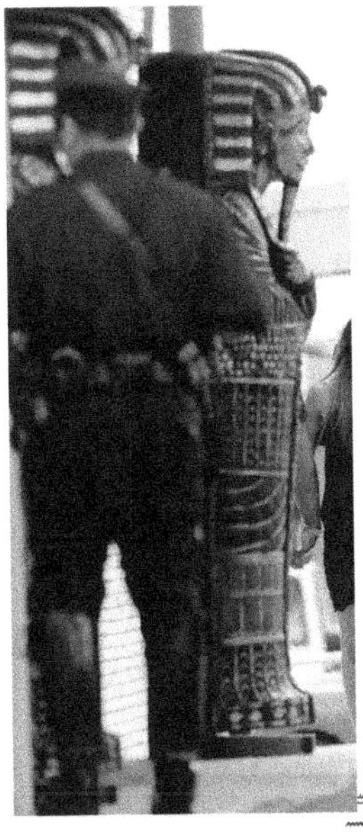

February 16th 2012 Whitney Outro R.I.P.

They say a fien could be anyone, You could fien for anything, what's the difference between you and another human being? nothing! I said nothing! I Fien for freedom the spirit of **Harriet Tubman,** Weezy and George was really in love man, **Bobby** and **Whitney** this one hits me, cause everybody judges but you could be next b, *when I die you ain't even gotta respect me*! **Cause I'll be back** blacker than Wesley, but before that I might have to relax, and talk to my **Grand Father,** I know your cards were hard and you ain't have to bother, and I can't stop now I gotta go farther, **Whitney Houston** say high to the Heavenly Father, there's gotta be a G*hetto in Heaven*, **RAmarley Graham** I hope you chill'n with Muhammad my man, on a world tour, giving them some more, uncut rugged and raw, on a world tour, bring'n them some more, uncut rugged and raw, Hip Hop **- Dawuud's Appeal 2012**

Significance

I wrote a song for Whitney on the same day that the final room of Tutankhaten's (King Tut's) Tomb was opened (February 16th 19**23**, page 11) and she just so happened to have two life size Pharaoh sarcophagi at her funeral.

February 17th 2012 All Alone

I'm feeling all alooooooooone, in a land full or men more like clones, when I reach my end I leave my poems, and I hope my sin don't get me thrown in the lake of fire, the devil's a liar, and I aspire to inspire before I expire, there's nothing like desire, I desire to be on good terms with the **Messiah,** I read the good book and I admire, the struggle of my people we never tire, I see you and I need you, **Dawuud's Appeal** is mad real I'm on the battle field fighting evil, and I'm feeling all alooooooooone, cause all those who were my friends they are gooooooooone, I guess I really can't complaaain, I got courage I got heart and I got a braaain, I got some oil for the weapon when I hit the range, things are still bad, will they ever change? I used to get mad, I still do, but I ain't sitting here thinking how I wanna kill you, all I really want is peace that's for real **Duke,** but police pull their piece and they will shoot, there will never be peace **Till** we get a peace, there will never be peace **Till** we get a peace, there will never be peace **Till** we get a peace, there will never be peace, **Till** we get a peace - **Dawuud's Appeal 2012**

February 18th 2012
Bob Dylan and The Death Of Emmett Till

While writing this book I had to search through my computer for music I made. This is when I found the song, The Death Of Emmett Till by Bod Dylan on my laptop. It was downloaded on February 18th 2012, the day before my great grand father General Dukes Sr's birthday (February 19th 1910, page 19). 8 days after I downloaded this song dedicated to Emmett Till, **Trayvon Martin** would be murdered. His death would be compared to the Murder of Emmett Till as it was seen as a major miscarriage of justice. I don't remember downloading The Death Of Emmett Till by Bod Dylan but I can see why I did. Emmett's nickname was "**Bobo**", like Bob. Bob Dylan was sent down (born) in 19**41** the **year of the snake** like Myself and "Emmett Till" and he released this song in 1989 the **year of the snake**. Emmett was born in 19**41** the year of the snake and I was born in 1977 the year of the snake. (see page **41**). All the events in this book are true. If you follow my path and do the things I do yet still the great mysteries are not shown to you. Then continue the path and **to Maat be true** and perhaps in due time you will be worthy of the view.

February 18th 2012 Lucid Dream

Engine Engine number 9 on the New York transit line, if that train falls off the track, pick it up, pick it up, pick it up, Dawud on the scene in my **Lucid Dream,** don't know why, don't try cause you cant intervene, going off course and I'm picking up steam, unstoppable like **Denzel** on screen - **Dawuud's Appeal 2012**

February 22nd 2012 Hey Young World

Hey young world, the world is yours and are you sure where you going to? and do you like the things life is showing you? hey young world this your world, hey young world, the world is yours and are you sure where you going to? and do you like the things life is showing you? hey young world this your world, hey young world , the world is yours and are you sure where you going to?

Police so violent, I believe greed breeds tyrants, we need to stop the violence, America is tired but I ain't tired, are you too tired to occupy every street? we don't need to riot, we need to come together cause we don't need to be quiet, **Egypt** had the whole world inspired, if the dog wagged the tail you wouldn't believe every tale that they tell, but the tail wags the dog so most of y'all are lost, but I was too, when I was **22** I was living life doing everything I wanted to, hey young world are you sure, do know where you going to? Going to, do you know where you going to? do you believe all the things that they showing you? **black kids never know the things that they owing you, white kids you will see how this thing will follow you**, do your own research don't rely on your school, **peace is the golden rule**, are you sure do you know where you going to? the good book said a chosen few and in a few years they'll be cloning you, hey young world, the world is yours and are you sure where you going to? and do you like the things life is showing you? hey young world this your world, hey young world, the world is yours and are you sure where you going to? - **Dawuud's Appeal 2012**

February 25th 2012 Griot

What's old is new, and what's new is old, I am you, but you've been told, that I'm a criminal fit to be sold, but **I'm an ancient Griot,** I don't say it how I see it, I say it how it is, from many perspectives, you don't want change, you scared to get arrested, I ain't never change, **I came to bring a message,** this whole universe is connected, so if I die tonight and see the shining light, am I gonna be alright?! I hope so ya never know, what the end is like, I guess it all depends on how you lived ya life, now have you ever sat back and examined life? like who is the one that turns day to night? It ain't they, so they can't rule ya life, yet everyday, they take away our rights, what would you say if I say **I'm coming back like Christ,** you would reject that right?! what would you say if I say **I'm coming back like Christ,** you would reject that right?! - **Dawuud's Appeal 2012**

Significance

"what would you say if I say **I'm coming back like Christ,** you would reject that right?!"

February 26th 2012 Happier

Rau nu Prt m heru lu f Per f m heru

They say it's all in your mind, write a rhyme about something happy, once upon a time you were happy, I come from a broken family, a lot of us don't have fathers, a lot of fathers don't bother, still we gotta do what we gotta do running through life, you better stand for something! _you only get one life_, don't run from the man, running might get you killed, I been to **Iraq** and these streets are the battle field, it's a fact! this generation is lost for real, **Dawuud's Appeal** is mad real, we need to change, God bless the child that made they own lane, use your brain this ain't the time for us to all reach fame, I'm trying to explain my pain inside, all these feelings, you expect me to hide? I'm an African America veteran my life don't mean piss to them, they killing them! **Poor black children! anything to stop poor people from building, no loitering around new luxury buildings**, **Cops** on the beat, **Cops** in the cars, **Cops** in the sky they ***stop and check*** who you are, well this is my block homie, this is my corner, **Cops** have no honor, they making deals with the coroner, **say a black girl's lost they ignoring ya, Black girls come us missing no one listens,** they say she ran away or she's been stripping stripping stripping, man they don't listen! i*s she really stripping?* I am not a politician, This is everyday poor living, we been tricked to think that we all different, American is just a pool of poor people, every four years a new senator cares but you see through, feeding the hopes and the fears of the people and now my free speech is illegal, they got yo trapped in this city of seclusion, happiness living on the streets is a delusion, they want you lose'n

They do anything to stop poor people from building, they care more about the teachers than they do for the children, kids get shot for reefer, the **cops** are not thinkers cause they shoot first, I try to think what's worse, a scared **cop** or the one that's straight blood thirst, either way it's me or you that's gonna end up in a hearse, I said look nurse, how many here for **police brutality?** she said, look dear, this is an everyday reality, what a divided place, these United States, outside they smile but inside they hate, this world is very demanding, from all your getting get understanding, these politicians are good at rambling and gamboling with your life but take my advice, what ever they say, check the other way, double check the checker, apply pressure on the oppressor, don't settle for the lessor, give the world free and they kill ya, like **Nicola Tesla** or **Tulsa Oklahoma,** how could you not know that and receive a diploma? the more that you don't study, the more that they own ya, you don't wanna be hungry worried waiting for money from someone else to loan ya, I got a question what's the root of black thought? they get caught and shipped up north before they hear the question, they wanna kill my revolution and imprison the children, kill the leaders take the history books out the building, anything to stop poor people from building, trapped in this city of seclusion losing, happiness living on the streets is a delusion, they want you lose'n

I had a thought to write a rhyme to those who never made it, technically I'm on that list, but you, I won't debate it, I'm not frustrated, I'm closer to elated, sometimes I get stressed sometimes I think I made it, but I listen to my music more than other people play it, it's been a year now, things are getting real now, sit'n here write'n music watch'n these bills pile, Sell'n gear I don't wear, don't get lost in materials, walked away from religion, wrestled my flesh in submission, life is a test, try your best to leave a good impression, the world is too depress'n, and if you lose lil homie, don't lose your lessons, **keep your head up** and keep step'n, what's the **root** of **black thought?** they get caught and shipped up north before they hear the question, they want to kill my revolution, imprison the children, kill the leaders, take the history books out the build'n! anything to stop poor people from build'n! **- Dawuud's Appeal 2012**

Significance

I wrote this before I heard about the murder of Trayvon yet in the song I talk about the issue that caused him to lose his life at the hands of George Zimmerman. I also state that, "you only get one life" to live. **I was not yet consciously aware of reincarnation**.

Utterances for Coming Forth by day into Light

It is he, who comes forth by day into Light

February 26th 2012 Trayvon Martin is Murdered by George Zimmerman

Trayvon Martin was only 17 years old when he was murdered by George Zimmerman. Trayvon was walking home from the store after purchasing a bag of skittles candy and an Ice Tea. George Zimmerman was a part of the community watch patrol. Trayvon was unarmed. George Zimmerman was a 26 year old man with a gun and with the gun he had power. The power to question a boy for no other reason than because he was black. I was still upset and angry about the murder of **Ramarely Graham** but I think it was the murder of **Trayvon Martin** that jolted my attention to the **young black male** more than any of the others. His death was compared to the murder of **Emmett Till** as it was seen as a miscarriage of the justice system by many people. This was a case where many white people agreed that Zimmerman got away with murder. Mothers and fathers of all backgrounds empathized and marched for Trayvon. President **Obama** even said Trayvon could have been his son. Just a month prior I thought I was a father but the test result proved that I wasn't but perhaps that's why I felt like Trayvon could been my son too. I would say the name Trayvon a lot in my music and I would use his image a lot in the videos. I never forgot Trayvon. I seemed to be always writing about those who were murdered by this system of racism and white supremacy. Four years later on February 27th 2016 (page 365), the day after Trayvon's murder I was writing a song when all of a sudden **I felt like there was someone else in the room with me**. I would feel like it was Trayvon. **When the force came in the room these words came to my head,** "Some spooky shit **Jay Dilla** modern day **Thriller, Raising the dead,** He was gonna go to school, she had to bury him instead, **is There A Ghetto In Heaven**? On this date in Hip hop February 27th, I shine illuminance iridescence, ***the presence of a mysterious energy around me***, that might astound the observer for a second". I wrote about Trayvon many times in my music but the first time I mention his name is on September 18th 2012 (page 246). The death of Trayvon would ignite a fire of in me that fueled many of my rhymes. I was writing with the anger of his murder and the injustice that is experienced when black people die at the hands of white people in America. Little did I know the deeper reasons why his death bothered me so much but 6 years later I would come face to face with that reason (page 480).

Condolences

My condolences go out to the family of **Trayvon Martin** and all those who have been robbed of their lives by this system of racism and white supremacy. Please know that death is not the end. The soul survives death, indeed and in spirit. This is a book of the dead written by a boy who was murdered without justice, who defeated death and came forth by day. May the soul of **Trayvon Martin** walk peacefully through the field of Reeds in Amenta. Amen Ra

Mfundishi Jhutyms

Mfundishi Jhutyms Hassan Salim is the Kemetic Priest the ancestors chose to give me my initial guidance on my path to Kemet. The first time I saw **Mfundishi** was when I used to do my shirtless runs around Harlem wearing my red Army beret. He would be stationed on 125th street selling books, stones and other items used to awaken the minds of the sleeping. I always showed him respect and sometime in 2012 I decided to take his MDW NTR (Hieroglyphics) class. At the time the material seemed too complex and I did not yet have the money or the desire to make the commitment to study. I was searching but unfortunately I only attended one class and I wouldn't try again for another 6 years. After I graduated as a Kemetic Yoga instructor Mfundishi allowed me to work under his tent at the International African Arts Festival where my past life was sparked and afterwards I took his class again but even then I only lasted four or five classes (page 476). It wasn't till 2020, after my past life as Tutankhaten (King Tut, page 594) that I actually completed his beginners level MDW NTR (Hieroglyphics) class. In between the time of 2012 and 2018 I would cross paths with Mfundishi many times when passing his table on 125th street . In 2014 I would purchased a **Silver Scarab Cuff** off his wrist (Page 293) and during the writing of this book the Cuff would prove to have a divine significance and finally in 2021 (page 659) the Cuff would show it's full mystical purpose in my journey. It appears **the Cuff was always mine** and sometimes I wonder how old it really is. In 2015 I would have a profound experience with a voodoo priestess on 125th street after talking to Mfundishi (page 345). In 2016 I was leaving his class with brother **Basui** when I had a powerful experience with my spine (page 388). In 2017 he would appear in a dream (page 441). Mfundishi is an important part of my revelation and I am forever grateful. Dua nTr.

February 28th 2012 - Meta Spiritual Encounters
Neo Nefertari Maat KhepeRa

I met Neo on the corner of 125th street and 8th ave in Harlem. I was standing at a vendor's table when she approached the table with a friend. When Neo and I made **eye contact** it was as if we knew each other. It was very **strange** but we started talking immediately and we even exchanged numbers. I took this picture of her and her friend. This is how I was able to date this meeting.

Significance

At this time in my journey I had said the name **King Tut** in my music twice, on Nov 26th 2010 and again on January 7th 2011 but I had no idea that I was that person. Neo's first child is named **Senai,** born on November 22nd the day before **Mamie Till** and 4 days before King Tut's tomb was opened (page 11). **Senai** sounds like Mount **Sinai**, which is said to be the mountain at which the Ten Commandments were given to **Moses** by God. **Akhenaten,** the father of Tutankhamen (King Tut), was the most enigmatic pharaoh from that time and research proves him to be the biblical **Moses**.

42 Laws of Maat, Page 367

Neo would have her first son in 2014. He has a Kemet name however Neo did not name him. The name was given to her while in a meditation. She was home in Dominican Republic when she decided to sit under a mango tree and sun bathe. While in the mediation she was focusing on clearing her mind, then suddenly she **heard a voice** sing the name, **Ankh** El Heru **Amen**, and immediately she knew that was her son's name. When I first heard his name I loved it and now I know why I loved it so much. My name was once Tut-**ankh-amen** but I wouldn't come to know this for another 8 years. His middle name is Heru and **Heru** is the son of **Ausar** (**Osiris**) the Lord of **resurrection**. I wanted a kemetic name but never really picked one. I started using the Name **General Maat** briefly in 2013 to represent my grandfather General Dukes Jr and to honor the principles of Maat that I had been drawn to. In the year 2020 I told Neo about my past life as Tutankhaten (King Tut) and then she would tell me that she took the name **Nefertari Maat KhepeRa** only a week or so before she met me in 2012. **Iahmose Nefertari** was the oldest matri**arch** of the 18th dynasty where **King Tut** was from (pages 15, 638) and King Tut's throne name was Neb **Kheperu Ra** Heka **Maat**. In African culture we are taught that **names** carry a vibration (brother Khufu, page 282). The vibration of the name **Nefertari Maat KhepeRa** is what attracted us. We will attract the people who are supposed to be in our lives. Nefertari would also tell me that the brother she was with had an affinity to **Akhenaten** and at one point he thought he was Akhenaten. Akhenaten is the father of Tutankhaten (King Tut). In 2022 Nefertari would also tell me about a friend of her's named Juan. He was born on my nephews birthday, August 26th and he died in Iraq as a result of an explosive device on the same day Emmett Till was lynched, **August 28th**. His body was returned in pieces like the story of **Ausar** (Osiris) being cut into **14** pieces (p 15, 482) and like Emmett was murdered at age **14**. **Ausar** reigned for **28 years** and I was (Emmett was) murdered on **August 28th**. One time is an incidence, twice is a coincidence, three, four, five is a pattern, but can you tell the difference? **Re-member** that **you** are **Ausar** and **Heru**, the **hero!** See page 3 for the **hero's journey!**

Rau nu Prt m heru

Iu f Per f m heru

Utterances for Coming Forth by day into Light

It is he, who comes forth by day into Light

March 2012 Planned Abstinence over Planned Abortion

In march of 2012 I would consciously stop having sex. The experience with thinking I had a daughter (page 220) plus dealing with getting Kalishea pregnant and encouraging her to have an abortion caused me to stop having sex completely. It was my idea for her to not keep the baby. I felt like she wasn't listening to the things I wanted her to listen to or doing what I wanted her to do and I didn't feel like we should have the baby. My decision was also rooted in the strange feeling I had the last time we entered the course, which I never forgot. I also never told her. When I climaxed I had a very intense sense of **Deja vu**. It felt like a was **repeating a cycle**. I did not want to repeat a cycle and a very clear thought and feeling that I should not have that baby came over me. The doctors told her that she would never be able to have children again. I deeply regretted encouraging her to get the abortion and afterwards I told myself I would never cut my hair again and I never did. I would **not have sex again** for close to two years. Years later Kalishea would get pregnant again by another man but the doctors told her that she should not keep the baby because it would not be healthy. Kalishea was led by her heart and she kept the baby. She was going to name her son Dawud because she stilled cared for me and because the baby was due in October. She knew he would be born on my birthday but instead he was born the day before my birthday on October 24th 2016, the same day Rosa Parks died and the same day KRS One released his book, **The Gospel of Hip Hop: The First Instrumental** (page 633). Kalishea named her son **Honor**. Years later I would realize that I was **Emmett Till** in my **past life** (page 480) and that caused me to view life, death and even abortion differently allowing me to forgive myself for encouraging her to have the abortion. Kalishea has a son born the day before my birthday and she is born on June 15th the day before Tupac's birthday. I have a theory about who **Tupac** was in a past life ☥. **14** shots were fired at Tupac on Sep 7. **Ausar** was cut into **14** pieces and **Emmett Till** died at **14** years old. On **May 2**, 2012 I will be summoned to court for Child Support claims. On **May 2,** 2016 **Afeni Shakur** will make her transition (page 381-382). It is 2022 and the American government is trying to pass laws banning women's rights for abortion even if they have been raped. I can not stress how important having no children was in my journey. When we have children in this current world system we are forced to focus on monetary survival which can take us away from our spiritual quest keeping you tied to the system. Have babies but remember it is VERY important that you do not have babies before you are ready. See p 357. In 2022 I went to Kemet for the first time in this life and while there I had **Deja Vu** two times (pages 670 - 671).

March 4th 2012 ☥ Race Time

you can really lose your mind in these sands of time, like what are you chase'n, the future or history? will you be the last see the catastrophes of this world unfold? if I could see the **Pharaohs**, we're all in a race with time, no mans mind by design can explain the divine, I remain sane, yet insane is what you claim that I am, **I am that I am**, what came first Adam or the atom? the truth you can't fathom, the truth is elusive and quick, so it's rarely seen in politricks, this world is old, spin'n out of control, men sell their souls, but the Lord knows, they wont profit from it, imagine if where you go, depends on how much you know, cause on the low, the more I go, the more life is like the **Truman show - Dawuud's Appeal**

March 8th 2012 Women

I used to think being black was bad but really though! being a women, that's when your stock is really the low, I could probably die from sayin this shit you never know, but the black women is my **Queen** and I'm a **pharaoh**, I been around the world and I met a lot of girls and I just wonder when will they wake up and take off the make up **- Dawuud's Appeal**

March 6th 2012 War

What if I had the power to gather all my revolutionaries, send them to war with every evil man this earth had ever saw, inconceivable? unbelievable? yet as wild as it seems, I fell a sleep and woke as the **Last Emperor** in this **dream**, what if i took my love for all people and took a shot at all evil, and gave you the secret war, you never saw? till they come'n through your door, **Tupac** stood at the mic and shouted "I don't create songs I speak feelings, these feelings strong enough to raise a nation of millions, save the women and children" the people looked amazed lost in daze, u wouldn't believe how they behaved, like a rave, **J Edger Hoover**, such a loser, **Bobby Seal** knew it was real but didn't see how cleverly they would maneuver **-Dawuud's Appeal**

March 10th 2012 Mother

and when the sun super novas atoms turn to matter and it all starts over, guest what? it's all gonna start over, we are all star people some are more evil

I wrote this here for my **mother** to let her know that I love her, I come from you a bond so special, I've been so blessed to have met you, so many children left alone, left to raise 3 kids on your own, I understand you more now that I've grown, **I love my mother**, if you love your mother then you should love life, my mother hates war but not enough to kill, she's a Muslim and some times I feel that's where I belong, I know America might tell me that I'm wrong, and I know the law might come with guns drawn, see my mother was the outcast a leader, ahead of her class a believer, she went to school and wore her hijab, they told her to take it off, but she fought back and a new law was passed, no wonder why I can't stop speak'n my mind, I guess I got it from my mother, I just put it in rhyme **- Dawuud's Appeal**

Significance

These notes below where at the bottom of the page this rhyme was written on.

wow! that's even deeper.. But to know God is to know that there is always time to change your way of thinking and move in the direction of peace and love. You see, even at the end... There is no end. **Our energy may very well stay here, waiting for souls to harness them.**

March 2012 Warehouse Of Souls

America's the mother of so many horrible things! The first thing you think is slavery! but I'm here to tell you this judge and jury! It's worst than the plantation! the criminalization, the blaxploitation, the probation and, the way they hate the **Haitians**! a warehouse of souls, it's out of control, they tried to throw **Michael Jackson** deep down in their hole, they got the doctor instead! now either way they got the bread and a whole towns being fed, when I write I feel the FED'S through my window, I put my middle finger up and let my pen go, I'm so blessed that when I wrecked in South Carolina my ends weren't low, cause when your ends low, yo! You gotta pay with your time, a revolving cycle, my _New York State Of Mind_, the blood line of **Michael, Jordan, Tyson** I remember fight'n M Bison, play'n Double Dribble, I take you back a little, cause yeah, you need to chill sometime, I said chill lil homie we should chill sometime, instead of killing each other, yo let's kill some time, build your mind, stop given your mother a hell of a hard time and try write'n a rhyme that don't glorify crime!

Abraham Lincoln was forced into glory! don't listen to **his-story**! he who wins war writes glory! but you'll probably ignore me, you'll probably wanna throw tar and feathers on me, so much pressure on me, I was young when I joined the Army, I had never heard of **Geronimo Pratt** "pack'n a gat in the back of the Ac", **What's Beef**?! beef is the fact that **George Jackson** went out blast'n, the last shall be first son, you the cursed one! Kill me! I wouldn't be the first one, "at all cost stay alive", **Afeni** told her son, my mother said, "you the chosen one. you my only son", I don't wanna die but I'm'a fight cause I will not run! Senator Perry tell me, how could you murder all of them?! **23**5 souls no longer alive, suppose a few of them were innocent men! you take away life with the strike of a pen, to all my niggas in the pen, you gotta move with the strength from within! you gotta know that it's designed to keep you behind that cell that you're in, but expand ya mind, see what **Tookie** did behind enemy lines, that's why I'm write'n rhymes that don't glorify a fuck'n crime! **- Dawuud's Appeal 2012**

Narmer/Menes and Mike Tyson

In the picture above on the far right we can see **Michael Jackson's** striking resemblance to an Egyptian Bust discovered in the late 19th century, said to have been crafted during the reign of the Pharaoh **Tutankhaten** (seen in the middle) and to the far left **Mike Tyson's** striking resemblance to the Pharaoh **Menes, (Narmer)**. These pictures are not here to make the claim that Mike Tyson is the reincarnation of the Pharaoh Narmer or that Michael lived a life in ancient Kemet. I place these pictures here because Michael Jackson had an affinity for King Tut (p 166), and Mike Tyson is probably the most feared heavy weight champion of them all and Narmer is the first Pharaoh to unify ancient Kemet and I think it's interesting how Mike Tyson, a modern day warrior looks just like the oldest known Pharaoh. Mike Tyson has experienced the psychedelic Bufo (page 528).. This experience changed his perspective on life. _**Mike** equated the experience like going to be "**Born Again**"_. He said he saw the **sun** open up when he smoked the toad and was amazed sort of like how **Akhenaten** (King Tut's father) might have been when he saw the vision of the **Aten** on the horizon sitting between the two mountains compelling him to build the city of Akhetaten (Aten on the horizon, page, 671) in a lush environment along the Nile river between Memphis and Thebes in ancient Kemet (Egypt). Perhaps Akhenaten also smoked the toad or snake Venom and saw the sun but the chances are more likely that he ate a mushroom since the story of Moses was taken from Akhenaten and Moses told his people to eat the **round caps** that come after the morning dew which is none other than the **magic mushroom** (pages 488 - 489). In 2022 I would have a **dream** with Mike Tyson shortly after I returned from Egypt (P 528).

April 6th 2012 Crazy

what if I went crazy? **Nat Turner**! kill ma fuckers and their babies! **John Brown**, had more **soul** than **James Brown**? Lord save me! they watch me, can't stop me, you clock me, you jock me, you kick me, _you kike me but don't you black or white me_, see I believe we been takin this lightly, **Trayvon Martin** skittles and iced tea, every where I go po-po don't like me, I walk with a book I ain't no crook, I'm more like **Paul** but I could have been **Saul**, **Jesus** drunk off alcohol, I walked on ice and did not fall, black life is like no life at all, who do I call when they come for me? **Jonny's** dead, one to the head, he armed the prisoners and they fled, before that my nigga this what he said! "take our picture! we are the revolutionaries", I got this letter in the mail saying go to war or go to jail but they don't know I ain't the same nigga for real, it's time for everybody to rebel, I'm a mafuk'n African they sent me to Iraq and almost Afghanistan, damn! **No Afghan man ever called me nigga**! You want me to kill him! How you figure?! First of all free Mumia Abu Jamal, free Mumia Abu Jamal, together we stand divided we fall! **- Dawud**

George Jackson Speaks! 1971 Prison Interview. George L. Jackson (September **23**, 19**41** – August 21, 1971) (**Page 155**)

April 22nd 2012 The Ship is Sinking

Dawuud's appeal, Dawuud's appeal is mad real, Dawuud's appeal was written and now the ship is sinking, Dawuud's appeal, Dawuud's appeal is mad real, Dawuud's appeal was written and now the ship is sinking, Dawuud's appeal, Dawuud's appeal is mad real, Dawuud's appeal was written and now the ship is sinking, Fuck **Abe Lincoln** - **Dawuud's Appeal 2012**

April 23rd 2012
Who was Earl Johnson?! Another Strange Revelation!!
Dawuud's Appeal 2012

While in search for the name of the brother who asked me to speak to his Jr high school students in 2012 I have come to **another strange realization**. His name was **Earl Johnson III**. I met him in 2012 when I played a few games with a flag football team. The team was called Smash Mouth. Today is **November 1st 2021** and the book needs to be done soon. It must be ready for 2022 and I still have many experiences and connections I need to write about before I finish this book so I can not spend unnecessary time looking into pockets of my past for things that are not relevant to this book. I have been avoiding this part of my story because it is not easy to explain but today I finally settled on it and began to look into it. I had 2 pages of unfinished thoughts that I wrote on April **23rd** 2012. I had planned to take the 2 pages of notes and write a speech for the teenagers in Earl's class but I never wrote the speech. And when it was time to talk to his students I figured I would just speak from my mind about the things I wrote down but the speech didn't go as planned. I was 34 years old at the time and when I got in front of the teenagers and I had not been in a Jr. high school since I was their age. **Trayvon Martin** had been murdered two months prior to meeting them (page **23**2). At the time I was struggling financially, waiting for my Army stipend to be released so that I could receive the $3177.00 a month allowing me to pay my rent that I was behind on (page 240). I was going through a rough time and when I got in front of the teenagers my heart dropped, I didn't look at my laptop I just spoke to them from my heart about life. I kept thinking about Trayvon Martin and how any one of them could be next. I don't remember anything that I said but when I left I felt like I had not said enough and that I had not done a well enough job. They seemed so young and so unaware of anything going on in the world. I saw them as young black males in a war that they didn't realize they were in. On top of that, the school had another teacher sit in on the class when I spoke. She was a White woman. I think her presence stopped me from saying some of the things that I wanted to say. I remember wondering why she was there. It was the school who did that, not Earl. See page **648** for the **metaphysical significance of the number 23**.

As I said earlier I did not remember Earl's name. Him and I lost contact with each other so I had to search through my e-mails for messages that I sent in 2012 to find his name. When I saw his name I was **struck with wonder!** I knew that name! And Just yesterday, Oct 31st 2021, I finally wrote about another series of events involving **another life I lived** and the name **Earl Johnson** (page 584)! I had been avoiding writing about this story due to how complicated the experience was, but yesterday I finally wrote about an Earl Johnson from over a 100 years ago from another life I lived and today I find an Earl Johnson from my past, in this life!! Yesterday I wrote about the session I had with a **seer** on **Jan 13th 2020 (page 584)** where I was given the knowledge of a life that I lived with **Harriet Tubman**. In that life my name was **Earl Johnson** just like this brother from my flag **football** team who invited me to speak to his students. I met Earl doing the thing that I loved most as a youth, playing football, and we became friends. He also became a big supporter of my music. He was on the e-mail list that I used to send my music to when I first started writing again. I found his name by searching my old e-mails. He had done street team work for artist, helping to promote their music and after hearing my music he offered to be part of my street team. I had never heard of a street team and didn't know how the music industry worked I was just writing music from my heart and sharing it with people. Today is **Nov 1st 2021** and I just got off the phone with Earl after not speaking in 9 years. I called him because of what I read in our last e-mail exchange on Jan 16th 2012. In that last email **he asked me if I had ever thought about writing a book collection of my writings**. I told him that I had thought about it and we planned to catch up and talk. That was our last communication till 30 minutes ago. When I settled on this speech I was only planning to sum up all the things I had planned to speak to them about and tell a story about how I spoke to some teenagers and how I saw myself in them. I remember now, I asked them what they wanted to be when they grew up. Many of them said rappers and athletes. I told them my story. One of them said a rhyme. I spoke about the importance of doing well in school and that is all I remember. I will take the time now to sum up what I had planned to tell them using the bullet points from the 2 pages of unfinished thoughts that I wrote on April **23**rd 2012.

April 23rd 2012 - The Speech I Never Gave

My name is Dawud, I am your brother. I care about you. I believe that I have always cared about you. I can remember being your ages. I struggled with my topic for today! I struggled so much that it took me 9 years to write this speech. I am 34 and to all that may seem very old and I find myself in a very interesting position at the age of 34 going through the education system a second time. This land is not yours but it should be! Your ancestors shed many tears here, bled here and died here. The most important thing you can do is believe in something greater than yourself. When I was your age I did not know how much I mattered. How important I was, how important I am and indeed how important each of us are. But this is nothing knew at all, you all probably do not know how important you are?! I asked myself, if I could go all the way back and whisper one thing in the ear of my younger self that would make me take LIFE seriously what would it be? Only after going through the process of writing this book did I come up with the answer. I would tell myself that it's one thing to be born into **racism** and **white supremacy,** but it's another thing entirely to **reincarnate** into it over and over and never know it! I would make sure that my younger self knew that life was eternal and everything that I did in this life mattered. Everything! Everything you do in this life matters too. In ancient Kemet (Egypt) the concept of reincarnation and past lives was called the **Wehem-Mesut** (repeating of births, page 14). I would tell my younger self that the **school system was made to turn people into slaves**. I would tell my younger self about how **John D Rockefeller** founded the General Education Board in 1903 and invested $1.27 Billion into it. **Rockefeller** was quoted saying, "I don't want a nation of thinkers. I want a nation of workers".

I may seem like some regular ordinary person and you might even think the same thing about yourself or other people that you know, but the fact is that you are not ordinary at all! You are all very special. We are all very special. Some of you might by now know my story to be true and so you might feel that I am greater than you but that is not true. I am a man that made many mistakes but I rebounded and rose through the mud like the **lotus flower** which is the same thing you can do. The dung beetle springs forth from the excrement (feces) of other animals. We are the proud descendants of a great people. We are the descendants of people who civilized the entire planet. The battle is for your mind. To have you disconnected from your **golden legacy**. What will you do with your mind? Why did **Malcolm X** change his name? Why did he change his life? Malcolm lived the life of crime but while in prison he was awoken to a higher prospective on life. What do you want to be? Do you have the courage to be you? Do you have the courage to walk into your authority or do you need to go to prison first? Malcolm went to prison so that you don't have to. Learn from his mistakes. Learn from **Tupac** and **Mike Tyson**. When Tyson returned from prison he went to his old high school and when he was asked about his experience he said he felt like he was in a **prison.** The school buses you take to school look just like the prison buses that prisoners are sent to prison in. The cafeteria where you eat looks similar to a prison cafeteria. In jail they sag their pants just like most of you do, but they sag for different reasons. Sometimes sagging ones pants in prison is done to let other prisoners know that they have been raped.

The **Vietnam war** started on **November 1st 1955,** only two months after **Emmett Till** was lynched and didn't end till April 30th **1975**. I was **25** when I went to the war in **Iraq** in **2003**. I did not know any of the things I'm telling you now, but I wish that I did. Instead I was listening to rap music just like most of you and I thought I was gonna play professional football like some of you. I had a great talent and I should have made it but I didn't. I ended up in the Army. I ended up in Iraq with the potential of dying while I was there. I was lucky though because I made it home. I heard **Tupac's** words when he said "*they got money for wars but can't feed the poor*", but I didn't fully get it. I did not know the extent of the war that was being waged against the Black community directly and all people in general. There was a time when the prisons in America only held Black people. The Black people who are your ancestors, were all made to work for free all day, from sun up until sun down. The children they had were born into that same **prison system**. Today they call that prison system "**slavery**" but it was war and it was prison. We were held at bay with weapons of mass destruction. Today the prisons house people of all colors but still the population of Black people is the largest with in the prison industrial complex. It's important that you understand that fighting wars for this country is in the benefit of no one, not even the people who think they benefit from it. Today is **November 1st 2021** and America still has this war against drugs however some "drugs" have been legalized like cannabis (weed marijuana). Thousands of Americans, mainly Black people have been sent to prison for the simple possession of cannabis, many of them still behind bars and now cannabis is legal. During the Vietnam war soldiers were given **heroin** to cope with battle fatigue, (the stresses that come with killing lots of people). Today we call that post traumatic stress disorder. My uncle Jimmy Lee Dukes suffers from post traumatic stress disorder due to his experiences in Vietnam which led to him receiving two Silver Star medals. I went to visit him in Alabama on November 16th 2021 and I wrote about his experiences in Vietnam (page 660).

I was born in 1977, around the time that drugs were widely circulating through the black inner-city communities and when Hip Hop music was on the rise. **Heroin** was a powerfully destructive drug in the black community. The Bayer Company started **Heroin** production on a commercial scale in 1898 and the first clinical results were so promising that it was labeled **a wonder drug**. By the 1910's Morphine addicts "discovered" it and began using it intravenously. The use and abuse of it began to spread quickly and soon after the use of **heroin** was regulated and total bans of it were proposed. By **1931**, the same year my **Grand Father** was born the use of **Heroin** had decreased significantly. Because of the bans placed on **Heroin** people began to sell it illegally. On my **Grand Fathers** birthday **June 17th 1971** president Nixon waged his war on drugs campaign. This was the day after **Tupac** was born. "*June one six seven one, the day my momma pushed me out the womb told me nigga get paid*" - Tupac. Tupac's mother **Afeni Shakur** was in jail fighting her **Panther 21** trial while she was pregnant with him. She, just like members of my family tree had also been addicted to these drugs that had been strategically placed in Black communities by government agencies (page 502). Drugs have been used to destroy our families and so it is important that none of you allow yourselves to be destroyed by drugs. I did not drink alcohol till I was 21 and I did not smoke weed till I was 33. When I turned 33 I stopped drinking **alcohol** completely. **Alcohol was used against the Native Americans as well**. I advise that you do none of those things till you have fully studied the history of these substances. I understand the pressures of life that can lead to substance abuse; particularly in the hood. We live under economic, academic, geographic, social, racial and police oppression, and due to this we often find ourselves looking for a quick mental escape from systemic problems that are way bigger than us as individuals. Our mentalities have been shaped by conditions that render many of us deeply hopeless, cynical, and pessimistic about life, and the drug game is always there to exploit this reality. I was never a drug user but I got seduced by the lure and lust of women. My biggest distraction as a young teen was sex and I didn't have sex till I was 17. I was a highly skilled athlete so I thought that I was going to the NFL, so money was never a concern for me. Football was my plan period, but I never made it to the NFL. What is your plan and what are you doing to ensure that you are successful?

The greatest trick is to trapped someone in a maze and have the person not even be aware that they are trapped. With fathers in jail and music and movies controlling the minds of the youth, mothers have been left to raise our nation. I barely escaped the streets, I was lucky to have **football**. I loved it but I had no idea of how to make the sport work for me. I was not a stellar student and because of that I was not able to use my skill to my advantage so I ended up in the Army. What will you do with your chance at an education? Do you think this school will teach you everything you need to know in life? Well I can tell you that it won't. This school won't teach why **Martin** and **Malcolm** were murdered. It won't teach you about **Marcus Garvey**, **Steve Biko** or about the **Hieroglyphs**. They won't tell you that you are **the Africans from the Nile Valley** or that many of the common inventions that we use today were created by the minds of people who look just like you. The world is old but the future springs from the past and you must desire to know your past.

The New Jim Crow and the Cruel School to Prison Pipeline

During the American **Jim Crow** Era black people experienced countless levels of intimidation, discrimination, and murder by **public lynching** was a normal part of life. We faced disenfranchisement, while being forced to live life under a 2nd and 3rd class citizenship status. We were not allowed to vote. Finding work was almost impossible and when we did find work the pay was deplorable. When we were allowed to use stores it was

important to have exact change because if you paid with a large bill you could run the risk of getting no change back. Our land was stolen and faced housing discrimination. The best thing that we did was teach our own children but for some reason we were spun in the direction of "**integration**" thinking we needed to go to school with white people. This is what sparked the **Brown v. Board of Education** case. In 1954, the landmark Supreme Court, Brown v. Board of Education decision struck down **racial segregation in public schools**. That same year **Medgar Evers** became the first Black person to apply to the University of M**ississ**ippi **Law School**, but was **denied admittance** because of his race (page 520). By 1955 the white racist tension and hate in the American southern states had escalated. The racist whites of the south did not want their way of life to change and no way were their children going to go to the same schools as the lowly Black children. The 1954 Brown v. Board of Education Supreme Court decision was a spring board to the racial turmoil of the newly segregated M**ississ**ippi that set the stage for the lynching of **Emmett Till**.

Emmett Till was lynched on **August 28**, 1955 and 8 years later, on **August 28**, 1963, **Martin Luther King** would lead the historical march on Washington DC. Martin's efforts in the fight for Civil Rights would give rise to the passing of the Civil Rights Act in 1964. The very next year, in 1965, the Voting Act would be passed. That same year **Malcolm X** would be assassinated. With these new laws in place white Americans could no longer discriminate on a person because of their race or the color of their skin and white Americans could no longer prevent blacks from voting, receiving a quality education, seeking adequate housing, and employment. But, they could prevent people from doing all these things **IF THEY WERE CONVICTED FELONS**. And from 1965 to the year 2020, the prison population in America rose 700 percent, from 300 thousand inmates to 1.8 million today. We are living in a New Jim Crow and there is a prison to school pipeline that all young black males need to be aware of. Crime rates have not gone down much, but the prison population has risen and black people are convicted and sent to prison at the highest rates. **1 out of every 3 black males** carries the label of **convicted felon,** while only **1 out of every 17 white males** carries the label **of convicted felon**. I wrote the following lyrics on **August 28**, 2016 (page 417), "Oppression, harassment, aggression, perfected methods, stop and check'n, the cruel **school to prison pipe line**, records, **felonies**, state fines, 1 800 I heard it through the **grapevine**, 400 years of hate crimes, **It's Nation Time**"

Your life will flow into different stages and phases no different than moving from middle school to jr. High school. You share this world with people who may have completely different life experiences than you. Even your classmates sitting next to you might have a different up bringing depending upon their home environment. Some of you have both parents at home and some of you don't. I grew up without my father and I'm sure some of you may have that same experience. Because of the drug laws I spoke about many of our family members, especially our fathers have been taken away and sent to prison due to mass incarceration. Because of this many of our youth fall victim to gangs and along with that comes gang violence and drugs which lead directly to the jail or the grave. I never saw the movie **Paid in Full**, and I never saw the movie **Scarface**. Paid in Full came out while I was stationed in Germany and Scarface never appealed to me however a few days ago a drug kingpin name Alpo was shot and killed in the Harlem streets. His life was portrayed in the movie Paid in Full and many rappers idolized him in their music. My cousin Darryl fell victim to this lifestyle (page 42). We must be careful what we put into our minds by way of music and movies. I never watched the show **Wire** or **Empire** or **New York House Wives** and other shows like that. When I was a teen I didn't like the show **Jerry Springer** because the people would always fight each other and I knew that these shows would make people do what they saw and sure enough the shows did cause people to mimic what they saw. You are our best and our brightest. You must learn your history like **Marcus Garvey** encouraged us to. We must study **Martin Luther King** and **Malcolm X** and find the common ground that they shared. We must understand why they were both systematically taken from us (page 69). Our unity is their greatest fear. **America's worst nightmare is our unity!** After I release this book I'm not sure how long I will have left here but just like Marcus Garvey said, I will be back in the whirlwind. I once ruled the land of Kemet, I died young and my death is still a mystery but I came back as Emmett Till, I came back as Earl Johnson, I mapped out the planet when it was first mapped, I sailed the seas when they were first sailed, I fought with Dessalines, I lived other lives and I came back to write this book. **One day soon we'll be on top again, the Afrikan came back with unity as the stratagem, maximum effect like maroons ready to ride again, when I die I'll be back in the spirit to try again**.

May 27th 2012 - High Frequency Psychic Channeling (Audio Memo Found in iphone)

"What's happening to me is very important. What's happening to you is very important. Everything is connected. Everything is connected, My name is Dawud and this is Dawuud's Appeal. Dawuud's Appeal is mad real. Mad real. -laughs-. Yeah."

Significance

See pages 343, 227, and 208, 282, and 343 for more info on **High Frequency Psychic Channeling..**

April 12th 2012 - Black Girl Lost

Check it, **African sisters**, I know you're look'n for **love**, but you gotta understand the problem before you go looking for **love**, you gotta work on you, and I'm'a work on me, we build a **family** with **black unity** in the community, we gotta all do better and be better, remember **Willie Lynch** reading a letter in Virginia teach'n them how to keep us deader, and how to sever the black family, so many black men in jail! yet we are not weak men yet they got us in they hell! One day from this system we will prevail, with **Black power**, this is for white people that fought for hours days and years, **John Brown** would have been my peer, it's quite clear I would have been right there, bringing up the rear, like "**Harriet**, pass me the spear"! *if **Jesus** came to bring a sword*, why do you live your life in fear? Yeah *I came to bring a sword* and I know you don't wanna hear ***Dawuud's Appeal is here***! - **Dawuud's Appeal**

Rau nu Prt m heru

Iu f Per f m heru

Utterances for Coming Forth by day into Light

It is he, who comes forth by day into Light

May 2nd 2012 - Child Support Court

I was summoned to court on May 2nd 2012 for Child Support claims. The results from my DNA test revealed that **I was not the father of Aniya**. I was relieved that I was not caught by the legal system but I was not all happy that I wasn't her father. It's not that I wanted to be a father but for a few weeks I really thought that I was and **I had grown to care for Aniya**. I had gone to her birthday party in DC even after I knew I wasn't her father. I had been calling her and talking to her on the phone. The experience with Aniya changed my life. **For the first time I felt what it was like to be a father**. But I also felt free because now I wasn't a father and I was able to go on with my life. I didn't handle that situation properly. When I got the paperwork I rushed to fix everything. I thought I was the father but after seeing that I wasn't I much preferred to finish doing what it was that I was doing with my life.. Which was smoking weed, trying to get this free G.I. Bill money and writing music. I didn't know what the hell I was doing with my own life how was I gonna be a father. I went on with my life. Fortunately Aja (Aniya's Mother) and I remained friends over the years even to this day. Every now and then I call to see how her and Aniya are doing. This experience with Aniya allowed me to decipher the first parts of the **star code of immortality**. Contemplating my past caused me to look through old files and thats when I realized the connection with the date **May 25th** (p 222). **Assata Shakur** was sentenced to life in prison on May 2nd 1977 **The Year Of The Snake** and **Afeni Shakur** transitioned on May 2nd 2016 (page 381-382). On May 2nd 2013 **The Year Of The Snake,** Assata Shakur would be placed back on the F.B.I. Most Wanted List. On May 2nd 2021 (p 643), Jasmin would detail the events of a **dream** she had about me as a **<u>Golden Pharaoh</u>** <u>sitting on a throne with an Egyptian Queen</u>.

June 3rd 2012 Learned

How could you walk around and not know, so desperate for dough, you go and kill your brother, sell your sister, I'm the one rebelling with ya, If we gonna die, let's die for something, fuck getting richer, **Malcolm X** didn't die for nothing; he died for you, get up my **negus** we ain't scared of revolution, they got us trapped, that's why **we Gotta raise a Black nation**, We done learned everything expect for how to stop waiting, If you stop and listen maybe you would learn something children, I know Everything you see on tv seems appealing but if it ain't about freedom, who you think they killing? It's time for us to go man, you're moving too slow and I'm tired of teaching you things you don't know and you don't wanna learn, you see everybody having fun and you want a turn, one wrong turn will leave a whole city burned, I said please open your eyes; **we subsidize our own demise**, they say the longer ya live, the more you see the lies, but that ain't always true, I seen old people dumber than you, you take the good one, the bad one, which one of them's you? **You got one life to live you don't get two,** not everybody grows up as comfortable as you and I ain't never did a crime I ain't have to do, well **- Dawuud's Appeal 2012**

Significance

<u>It should be noted that I ended this rhyme with the words " **You got one life to live you don't get two**".. So I was not consciously aware of the reality of **reincarnation** at the time of this rhyme. I had not yet "**LEARNED**" about it.</u>

2012
2nd Police Stop and Check in the Park while with Kalishea

This would be my second time ever being stopped by the police while walking, or "sitting". The first time was in 2011 (page 211) while on my way to train a group class. This time I was in my local park (Jackie Robinson Park) sitting on a bench talking with Kalishea when two cops walked up trying to ticket us for sitting in the park. Apparently they were enforcing a "law" that no one followed. Apparently there's no sitting in the park after 10pm. This would be the first time that I blew up on police officers. When they approached me I became infuriated. All I could think of was **Trayvon Martin** who had been murdered for walking in the wrong neighborhood (page 232). Now these cops were fucking with me for sitting on a mother fuck'n bench in my neighborhood! All I could think was this mother fuck'n country won't give me my G.I. Bill money for school! They killing Black people everywhere and now they wanna fuck with me cause I'm on a bench after 10pm?! I got up and stated my Military name and rank, "**My names is Sgt Eddings United States Army Special ops" then I cursed them out, "I been to war for this mother fuck'n Country. I live in the neighborhood, this is my community. I train people in this park. I can sit on any mother fuck'n bench I want to mother fucker! Go solve a fucking crime and leave me the fuck alone**." I think I scared the hell out of Kalishea.. They eventually left. I guess they felt stupid or something. Kalishea would tell me that the experience made her feel protected.

Significance

What I did was understandable but it was also stupid and dangerous. In the next few years I would have a few more explosive confrontations with police officers and the last one being so profound that I vowed to never allow myself to explode in the presence of the police again. On May 15th 2016 I would have my 3rd confrontation (page 331)and on May 22nd 2016 I would have my last one (page 388). This confrontation on May 22nd 2016 would make me consider the effects that the emotions of anger and rage can have on the body. While cursing a cop out on May 22nd 2016 I was struck with a intense pain that felt like electricity flowing from my neck down to my spine. It was so painful that I stopped talking and sat on my bike. **After experiencing extreme pain from anger I never cursed another cop out and I began to consider what effects the emotions of extreme love might be able to bring forth in the body**.

June 5th 2012 - Army G.I. Bill for School Tuition

Rau

nu

Prt

m

heru

After 7 months I am finally given access to my Army G.I. Bill to pay for school tuition. I applied for it in November of 2011 but was rejected on claims that I hadn't graduated high school. This caused me a lot of stress and pushed me deeper into a depression. I felt like the government was attacking me. I met with Nathaniel Hezekiah, the liaison for congressmen Gregory Meek's. Nathaniel Hezekiah helped me resolve this issue. The G.I. Bill not only paid my full tuition, but I was also given a $3177.00 stipend every month that I attended school. This was really the only reason I was in school. Before the stipend money came I was low in cash and going though a hard financial time. I even signed up for **food stamps** and while standing in line for **food stamps** I saw a girl that I knew from a gym I used to work at. I was the top trainer in the gym when we met. She had a big crush on me and she even stayed the night over my place a few times. Now here I was standing in line for **food stamps**. I was embarrassed and happy that she didn't stop to talk. While I went through the process for **food stamps** I saw that 95% of the people coming for assistance were women but I didn't care. I felt like this government owed me way more than school money and food money. I was on my **Ole Dirty Bastard** shit and didn't care. Finally on June 5th my G.I. Bill benefits were released. I went through a college prep course headed by **Welby** Alcantara, then I began school the next month at BMCC (borough of manhattan community college) for summer classes immediately.

Update, September 28 2022

I reopened my case for military compensation for my injuries (page 121) on September 28 2022. The man who handled my case was named **Welby**. The same man who helped me during my process of using my G.I. Bill tuition. He is also born on August 18, the same day that my grand father died (page 169).

Iu

f

Per

f

m

heru

DEPARTMENT OF VETERANS AFFAIRS
BUFFALO REGIONAL OFFICE
P.O. BOX 4616
BUFFALO NY 14240-4616

JUNE 5, 2012

MR. DAWUD B. EDDINGS
[redacted]

307/22
[redacted]

Dear Mr. Eddings:

You have been awarded education benefits under the Post-9/11 GI Bill. This letter gives information about your payment(s), remaining benefits, and how to contact us.

What Our Records Show

ELIGIBILITY PERCENTAGE

Our records show, as of June 5, 2012 you are entitled to receive 100% of the benefits payable under the Post-9/11 GI Bill program. We determined this percentage based on your length of creditable active duty service. We based our decision on the following service information:

Begin Date	End Date	Length (in days)
09/21/1999	01/15/2005	1,223
Total aggregate service (in days):		1,223

Utterances

for

Coming

Forth

by day

into

Light

What Benefits Will You Receive

Based on your eligibility percentage and the enrollment information we received from your school(s), we awarded benefits as follows:

TUITION AND FEES

Enrollment(s) for the 2011-2012 Academic Year

As of July 17, 2012 you are entitled to receive 100% of the amount(s) payable under the Post-9/11 GI Bill.

BOROUGH OF MANHATTAN COMMUNITY COLLEGE certified that you were charged $943.33 for 6 credit hours, which consists of 0 distance and 6 residence hours for the term dates July 17, 2012 through August 16, 2012.

LTSver5.2.1 AWD3

It is

he,

who

comes

forth

by day

into

Light

I was excited to start school and receive the money from the Army G.I Bill. I needed it! So I started school asap. I started with summer classes in 2012. I signed up for two African history courses. I was taking courses that I found interesting. I wanted to "learn" but what I quickly began to realize is that this College School System was not really for learning. It was for shaping minds, not teaching people to use their minds. I had not been to school since I left college in 1997. When I first met my African studies professor I was happy to meet him. I was being my normal self and I spoke often in class giving my opinion and asking questions as well as challenging things I though where off. **I fell out with my professor when he claimed that it was debatable whether or not the Egyptians were Africans**. Today is March 5th 2022 and I just finished that last tedious stent of writing and will with in a few hours will start formulating the table of contents of this book. Today I also just happened to find a container holding many old thumb drives that I had been looking for in the past few months. I wanted to see if there was anything on them that I might want to add to the book and that's when I found a few of my old papers from when I started college again in BMCC. Below I have place the 8 short essays I wrote which was one part for my midterm assignment. We also had a 70 question test to take.

College Paper

Essay 1 Afro civilization:

Tracking historic accuracy is not and easy job. For centuries man has been in search of his/her beginnings. Many Historians have been at odds when tracking civilizations but by far the most controversial is the history of African civilization and it's relation to mankind. This seems the entirely strange to me because the proof is written on the walls, in the caves and lay beneath the earth fossilized for over a million years. "The world is old but the future springs from the past."

Even though the oldest fossils and other material used to date early mans existence are found in Africa there are some who reject this idea. There are now three theories of man origins. One theory is that God created all things in seven days. There is another theory that man simultaneously appeared in three different places on the earth at the exact same time. And there is the idea that Africa is the cradle of civilization which happens to be the idea with the most evidence to support its claim.

In the 1940's scientist developed radiocarbon dating techniques for approximating the age of a wide range of dead organic materials. After this discovery this opened up more research of Africa but the research was not based on historical facts. It was more based on the agendas of the people doing the study. Africa is the only continent that has evidence of mans early evolution. Along with Ancient bones fossils, stone tools and artifacts are also used to date African civilization. The oldest bones were found in the Ethiopian highlands in 1974 and the bones are of a black woman. There is also evidence that suggest the birth of iron in the Congo.

College Paper

Essay 2 Afro Civilizations

All societies have a collective memory. Some is oral and some is written on cave walls or on steles. We are all in a sense historians. Man depends more on experience than it does on instinct. The world is old but the future springs from the past. Modern man belongs to a primate family of hominids. Human beings are the only surviving hominids. Fossils show that there were many different types of hominid species tracking back millions of years ago. The oldest fossils ever found were found in the Ethiopian highlands

The environment was very important for the early man; depending on were you lived would determine what they ate. Early man in Africa hunted in small groups and relied heavily on the food that was available in their environment for sustenance. The birth of iron greatly improved their ability to hunt and gather food.

College Paper

Essay 3 Afro civilizations Egypt / Nubia: rise of Nubia

History is never finished, because the future springs from the past. What appears as the death of one civilization only results in the birth of another, is that always true? I will discuss the period in African history called the 25th dynasty where you will see how the Nubians conquered Egypt in 713 BCE. When an empire conquers another the conquering power will most times merge beliefs and traditions. I think some of these changes/fusions were done just to keep control over "all" the different belief systems. During the Hellenistic period the pharaohs decided to produce a deity that would be accepted by both the local government and influx of Hellenic visitors so that no rebellions would grow. When discussing the Nubian conquest of Egypt, the question is: was this the first time Nubia ruled Egypt? Were the Egyptians actually Nubians?

There was a back and forth battle between Egypt and Nubia. After Nubia conquered Egypt they were said to have taken over Egyptian customs by dressing like the Egyptians and practicing similar burial practices. One distinctive difference from Egyptian art and Nubian art is that the Nubian art is noticeably black. This is the rise of the "Black pharaohs". The Nubian artifacts are dated older than the Egyptian artifacts. If you look at the geographical location of old Nubia one can make the argument the Nubians used the river to explore and expand their empire. The Nile flows north to Egypt. I believe the Nubians traveled north and expanded. In 15 BCE Diodorus Siculus was a Greek historian was quoted saying "The Egyptians are colonist sent out by the Ethiopians (not the modern Ethiopians but the black peoples from inner Africa south of Egypt)". Also why did king Shabaka believe his role was to "restore" Egyptian culture to their ancient glories? The Nubian Black Pharaohs don't get the glory that Egypt gets but it is the older civilization. The Nubians were later pushed back to Nubia (lower Egypt/north Sudan). So it seems that it was a back and forth rivalry.

College Paper

Essay 4: Afro civilization Overview of social / political/ economic systems of traditional Africa

Africa is the cradle of civilization and is the source of much advancement for humanity. Africa is the largest continent on the planet and has over 3000 languages. Every region in Africa had it's own speed in development but share many customs as people traveled across the continent. Each society has different systems.

Rau nu Prt m heru

Africans developed complex farming systems with different mixtures of crops rather than just one. You can see examples of this in the cultures along the Nile River. Every year the Nile would over flow its banks and when the overflow subsided the land would be fertile for farming. Some crops were rice, mixed rice, maize, yams, banana-plantains, mixed cassava, mixed banana and cassava. They lived in a trade lifestyle. They traded with local and long distant people and they used the resources they had available to trade with. The resources taking the role as money. Here is a list of things that were used as money during trading: iron, salt ,beads, cowry ,shells, copper rods, brass bracelets, iron bars, **gold** dust (limited use as money), cattle, sheep, baskets of different sizes, firewood, furniture, clay pots, tobacco pipes, axes, bows arrows, spears, machetes , wild animals, crops were not used much. Gin and Rum were introduced by Europeans for trade.

The power in the societies comes from the amount of wealth a person has or it is gained by force. "he who has the **gold** makes the rules". Both states and stateless societies have laws. The states have legal authorities to back up the laws and stateless societies leave decisions up to the elders. The religious practices of the Africans are a complex series of myths and rituals. Currently Christianity and Islam are the biggest religions on the continent. Their religions are buried deep in tradition. It is also tradition to pay tribute to the kings by sending offerings.

Iu f Per f m heru

College Paper

Essay 5 Afro 1865 Northern blacks vs. southern black is colonial period / American Revolution 1790

Life for Africans during the colonial period was different in every state but there was a drastic difference in the everyday life of northern Africans and southern Africans both free and enslaved. Africans in the north were more out spoken and the ones in the south were more servile (or at least many pretended to be) because of the tougher conditions in the south. The north was generally the beacon for freedom. The Quakers had a part in this with their anti slavery stance. Strangely enough the colonist felt the need to rebel against their mother country due to unfair treatment and taxes however they themselves were in the business of slavery.

On March 5th 1770, the Boston massacre is sparked when Crispus Attucks, a Black man, is the first to die in what would be the first shot of the revolution. The 13 colonies went to war in 1776 for their independence. The British recruited slaves to fight along side them in their campaign against the colonies. Many Africans took this as a way to win their freedom and joined the British. George Washington had not intended on using Africans as soldiers in fear it would compromise the institution of slavery but was forced to recruit Africans due to White soldier abandoning their war duties. African slaves were faced with a decision to take part in a war that would possibly give them their freedom but also potentially have them kill other Black men.

Utterances for Coming Forth by day into Light

College Paper

Essay 6. From freemen to slavery

It seems as if the Africans have a "dark" cloud over them. From freedom to slavery is the reoccurring theme. Slavery in America is in my belief the most important period of slavery in human history. The Africans had a more honorable way of dealing with slaves. As Diop explains in his book precolonial Black Africa, in classic antiquity prisoners of war were automatically subject to being sold. Persons of rank could be ransomed off by their families. There was some sense of honor in their practices. There was no honor in the Trans Saharan slave trade during the 1400s and when the trans Atlantic slave trade started they were not to be out done. With the desire to build a new great empire like that of the Black Pharos in Africa they "discovered" the Americas and started their campaign for world dominance. Virginia was the first colony formed in 1607 and by 1732 the last colony of Georgia was formed. The colonies only receive 5% of total slaves taken from Africa. The bulk of human cargo was taken to the Caribbean's, Brazil and Spanish America. I can imagine that life for a free African or indentured African during these times must have been nerve wrecking. Knowing that one-day you could see the chains of slavery like those in the Caribbean and other places.

It is he, who comes forth by day into Light

During the early 1600s up until 1670 blacks worked hand and hand with whites in the colonial tobacco fields. This is an interesting fact because today tobacco kills over 400,000 people a year and the tobacco does not see color! During this time the whites and the Blacks socialized with each other even slept in the same living quarters, however in places like Virginia Africans were worked so hard that they died from overworking. There was a gradual institution of slavery as the basis of identification and restriction from the colonial period to the period of the new nation. Not all Africans in the colonies were slaves. Some Africans owned land, lent money, served as jurors in court, and sued in courts. By the mid 1600s the life for the Africans got worse in the colonies. The British believed that Blacks were inferior and the rise of the white supremacy in America was born. The idea of Africans being inferior was a convenient reason and excuse for enslaving Africans while also allowing themselves and those who came after them to feel ok with injustices done to the Africans. By 1640 Africans could no longer bear arms. The courts in Virginia and Maryland as well as the mindset of the colonials was that the Africans reason for living was to serve their masters (white men). By 1660 we see the introduction of the slave codes. By 1700s more Blacks were arriving than Whites. This of course raised fear of insurrection so tougher laws were implemented. In 1770, the Boston massacre is sparked and Crispus Attucks, a Black man is the first to die for the American Revolution. Interestingly enough Slave codes were later changed to Black codes after the civil war. These slave codes still exist to this day just like the sell of tobacco.

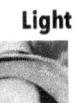

College Paper

Essay 7. Civil War and Reconstruction

War has been the one consistent part of American culture but what they don't teach is the many blacks who fought for freedom on slave plantations. During the Civil War (1861-1865) and during reconstruction the United States had many issues to deal with; the country was divided between the northern states and the southern states. In 1861 the southern states broke away from the union and formed the confederate states of America and the country went to war. The north wanted to move westward and expand the country without slavery or at least without as much slavery. The south wanted to keep the institution of slavery and the slaves wanted of course to be "free". The south did not want to let go of their number one resource being free slave labor. Slavery for Americans was very much like a tradition. In fact it is American tradition. America's favorite pastime is not baseball it is the enslavement of African people.

During this war there was much confusion, Abraham Lincoln drafted an emancipation that would free Africans who were in the rebelling states. Africans were again used as pawns and pulled into this war. Infect many Africans wanted to fight in this war. Many of them saw it as a way to prove their loyalty and earn an equal level of respect from the whites but this was not the case. Truthfully America has never wanted to use Africans in war in fear that they would turn their guns on their former masters. After the war Abraham Lincoln was assassinated, John Adams became president, the slaves were freed and the confederate states denounced their ties to the confederacy and reluctantly rejoined the union. Conditions in the south after the war were the most bizarre and volatile. There was the formation of the ku klux klan in the south who reintroduced the slave codes again but was now labeled Black codes. The Governors of the south came together and set in motion these black codes. Returning confederate soldiers were tired from 4 years of war and coming home to states that were left in shambles. They were now the outcast of society and the slaves were now free. It was indeed a new day for the south. There were union soldiers on patrol who's job was to protect the Africans from the wrath of these returning soldiers. After a few years reconstruction failed. These **Black codes** changed to **Jim Crow** and the system has since then mutated into the system we have today. Africans today are freed from one system of slavery to another. **Slavery was not abolished it was transformed**. **Now it is computerized and the system that is here now is more profitable than the era of plantations.**

College Paper

Essay 8. African Americans at the start of the 20th century and Harlem renaissance

The early part of the 20th century in America was the time of the "New Negro" in the north. After the civil war and emancipation, the Africans in America were now free to explore different states, and different arts, which gave birth to the great migration and the Harlem Renaissance. There were a host of progressive African leaders and organizations. This is a time when the Africans started to view themselves as the "New Negros". They were finding their way in American life through arts, politics, and sports but still facing harsh racism, prejudice and cruelty.

There were many advancements for Africans during this period and also many set backs. Truthfully Africans still have not gotten their fare shake in America. Not everyone in that time-shared the same views on the direction Africans should go. This caused for a lot of discord in African leadership but this is not a new phenomenon. There was also discord with slaves on slave plantations. **Harriet Tubman** was quoted saying that she could have freed 1000's more slave if only they new they were slaves. In 1830 **David walker** wrote, "never mind what the ignorant ones among us may say, many of whom when you speak to them for their own good, and try to enlighten their minds, laugh at you, and perhaps tell you plump to you face, that they want no instruction from you or any other nigger, and all such aggravating language. Now if you are a man of understanding and sound sense, I conjure you in the name of the Lord, and of all that is good, to impute their actions to ignorance, and wink at their follies, and do your very best to get around them some way or another, for remember they are your brethren; and I declare to you that it is for your interest to teach and enlighten them". I believe this passage is the solution for Africans.

The fight for freedom had and still has many different faces and many different solutions. In 1915 **Marcus Garvey**, the leader of the Back to Africa movement was scheduled to visit **Booker T Washington** in the States to discuss improvements on African life in America; however this meeting never took place because booker T Washington "died" that year. Booker T Washington believed in education as the best route for advancement and disapproved civil rights agitation and for this he was widely opposed by many black intellectuals. **W.E.B. Dubois** was one of those who opposed Washington's views. Dubois was an advocate of the talented 10, an idea that the leading minds of the north could be the leaders of all Africans in American by gaining both economic and political power.

While the African intellectuals were fighting for freedom and justice for all, many Africans were exploring the new freedoms and assimilating to the American society. Many Africans in the south migrated to the north and explored the arts. This gave birth to the Harlem renaissance, a One must not forget that this was during the first world war. Many African soldiers were again fighting for this country for freedom they would never receive.

In conclusion all of these men and women have their place in history it is our job here in the present to assess their views with critical thinking and devise a more unified solution. Marcus Garvey started a movement that birthed **Malcolm X**! Malcolm's parents were Garveyites and this had a profound effect on a young Malcolm. **George Jackson** wrote from his prison cell, "**if revolution is tied to dependence on the inscrutabilities of 'long range politics 'it can not be made relevant to a person who expects to die tomorrow.** "

Rau nu Prt m heru

When I got to **BMCC** (borough of manhattan community college) I didn't give a fuck about the system! I was only in school for the money. Taking these classes were fun but I didn't care about graduating. I did the work, made it to class and gave it all about 65 percent of my effort. I did just enough to pass in most classes but I still managed to keep A's and B's. I started school as soon as I could so I could get the $3,177.00 a month stipend from the Army G.I. Bill. I kind of felt like a had reached a safe point. I was low on money for the first time and now I could pay rent again and buy the food I needed to eat without worry. I enjoyed getting paid to go to school. I went to Iraq for that money! I had an agreement sort of like a treaty but just like every other treaty America has signed they tried to break this one too.

I remember looking through the classes they offered. I took two African studies courses my first semester. I had a black professor named Professor Brockington. He was a gay man, or he seemed to be **gay**. In class he once said the incorrect birthday of **David Walker**. I mean if you read this book you will see that I pay attention to numbers. I'm not the best **maathematician** but I do connect some dots (page **41**). I had only been studying African History for a few years now so there was much about African history that I did not know and so much that I'm still learning to this day so I have no room to correct people on such small particulars but when he said the wrong date I corrected him. As I write this I must say that I would rather that I had stayed quiet in moments like that, however this professor once said that it was debatable whether or not the Egyptians were black. Prior to this I had no real problem with Professor Brockington. I actually liked him. I wanted to like him. I wanted to like all my black professors but I will admit that as soon as he said that I had an issue with him. Because I was in a college class with people from many different ethnic backgrounds, most of whom only took that class because it was their mandatory African history course and most of those people WILL NEVER TAKE AN AFRICAN HISTORY COURSE AGAIN. I didn't know everything about my history but I knew the **Egyptians** were black! I didn't care who the teacher was, I would have challenged that claim even if the teacher was white, red, blue or green. I had just started growing the hair in the back of my head and people looked at me as if I was different. I was not the average college student. I was older than the average student, I was a black male, and I wasn't afraid to speak truth the power. **Professor Brockington, it is not debatable whether or not the people of the Nile Valley were Africans, that my friend is a fact and my life is living proof! On April 4th 2020 (page 594) my past life as Tutankhaten (King Tut) was revealed to me and so now you can understand why my soul could not allow you to teach that lie to everyone in your class!**

Iu f Per f m heru

You often feel tired, not because you've done too much, but because you've done too little of what sparks a light within you

Dawud, Beloved by the Ntru

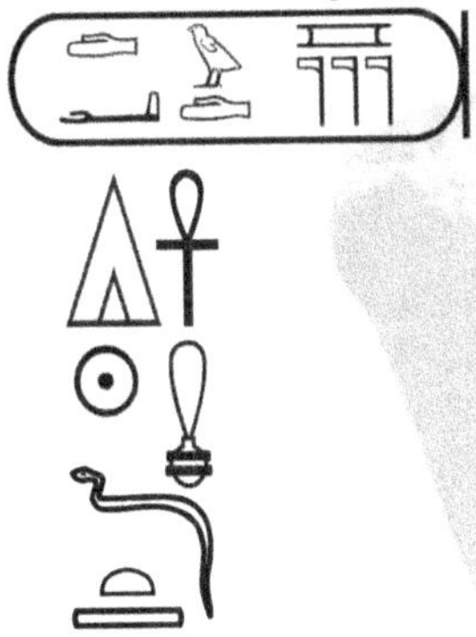

Utterances for Coming Forth by day into Light

It is he, who comes forth by day into Light

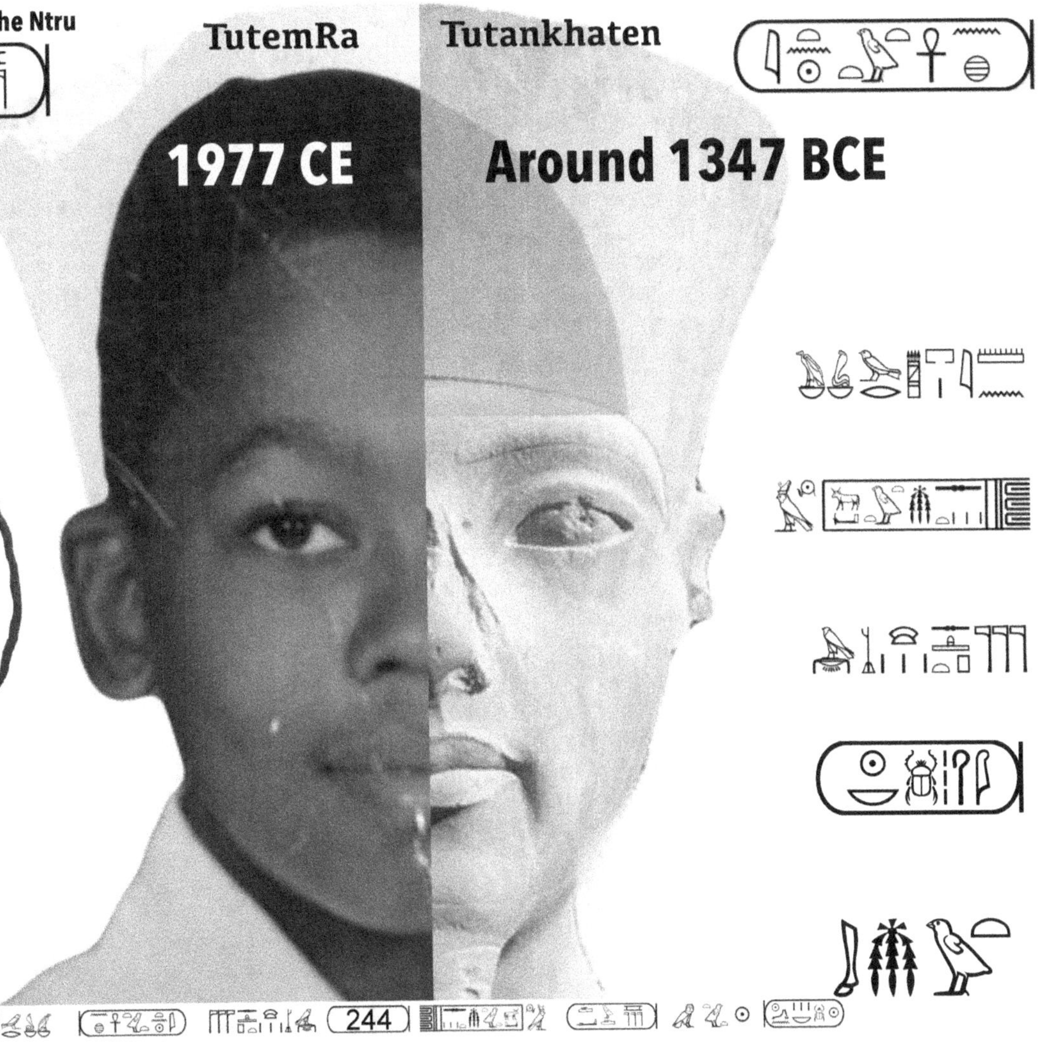

August 11th 2012 Dawuudism

Afrikans listen up I got a story to tell, I should have been here already but I slipped and fell, I had a race with life and life is fast as hell, and it won't slow down till you master self, how could you master self, when you amass your wealth enslaving everybody else? all you think about is yourself! enough of that though, really, I'm on another plateau, I ain't angry I'm hungry and _50 Niggas_ got my back yo, **Garveyism,** judaism, dawuudism, I start my own religion of no religion, homie listen, there's more than one way, _I had a vision_, a vision we fought to keep our families out the prisons, **I have risen,** Listen as I write the story, how we rose to glory, it wasn't televised, we started to organize, **Garveyism**, judaism, dawuudism, it wasn't televised we started to organize, It was like 2000 and 12 or 15, it was when all of our minds were shifting, we had a black president, yeah he was really clean but he ain't hear his brothers in the jails when they scream, this ain't the dream of **Martin Luther King!** what will it take for you to realize that you're a King? What will it take for you're to realize that you a Queen? it's so very important we start looking home, the red black and the green, _it's funny how I remember writing this same rhyme in a **Dream,**_ they say fate you cant escape that's why I'm great, **I'm king, A king with no land underhanded schemes,** and if you feel how I feel then you're on my team, **Dawuud's Appeal** is mad real, realer than the face on the dollar bill, w_hen I was 8 I was chased and almost raped but I escaped cause I was fast, It never pays to be last_! this all relates cause _Afrikas_' been getting _raped_ for the last ,14 hundred years, it appears the time is here, have no fear the bodies already at warfare, long before you came out and started to breathe air, life ain't fair but you gotta believe there's a reason for everything, a season for every **dream,** I see my people struggle so I look up to **Elohim,** he look at me and tell me that that's the problem with human beings, _**Zimmerman**_ said God planned for him to kill the teen, can't you see what the fuck I mean?! I see my people struggle, you should know that Dawud loves you, I see my people struggle, you should know that Dawud loves you, I see my people struggle, you should know that Dawud loves you, word, you should know that Dawud loves you **- Dawuud's Appeal 2012**

August 27th 2012 — Pro: Vanessa Roe, Critical thinking, BMCC 100-122

Today is March 5th 2022 and I just finished a tedious stent of writing and will with in a few hours will start formulating the table of contents of this book. Today I also just happened to find a container holding many old thumb drives that I had been looking for the last few months. I wanted to see if there was anything on them that I might want to add to the book and that's when I found a few of my old papers from when I started college again in BMCC. Here is the homework for the first day of my Critical Thinking class with Professor Vanessa Row. She was one of the teachers who actually thanked me for taking her class. She enjoyed having me give my perspective on different topics because the class was full of younger people who benefited from the prospective I spoke from. The first day of class Professor Roe instructed everyone to write down one word that came to our minds when we thought of term **Critical Thinking**. She gave us about 5 minutes and when we were done she had each of us write our word on the chalk board then she told us our home work was to write a poem about critical thinking using every word that was on the board. Here are the words each person presented. Perhaps I broke the rules because I used two words. I picked the word Judge first and immediately after the name Malcolm came to mind. Leonne (**Logic**). Ralfy (**Different**). Almir (**Assume**). Cassandra (**Open**). Ed (**Prospective**). Neil (**Morals**). Tanisha (**Interpretation**). Martin (**Plato**). Emie (**Personal**). James (**Skeptic**). Jose (**Detailed**). Wesley (**Hidden**). Tyler (**Strategic**). Herman (**Analyze**). Taliah (**Believe**). Destiny (**Critical**). Joel (**Question**). Shirley (**Mindset**). Victoria (**Thought**). Mike (**Theory**). Dawud (**Judge / Malcolm**). In total there were **22** words used.

"A **Malcolm's mindset**, a **skeptic** none the less. **Detailed theories** thinking **different** can you hear me? **Knowledge** is power, open a book be a scholar. The secrets are **hidden**, so **analyze** and go get them. Using **logic** and **morals**, don't **assume** ask questions. With educated **theories** and **allegories** I teach lessons. **Plato** can't match my mental lyrical weapon. My **thoughts** are deep like oceans, my **personal prospective**, my **interpretations**. If you **believe** and read you can think like this. **Critical** thinking I stay **strategic**." **- Dawuud's Appeal 2012**

September 8th 2012 Is it a crime

D evil in sin is in you, you gotta do good to see God, _Stay true,_ one two mic check, yeah I ain't never gonna let this rest, what would you do, if you the one that's the threat? _stay true,_ should I change my name leave my last name **X?** feel my pain, maybe if only if I explain, but I can't tell you everything on my brain, Ameri Ka Ka kan't you see your stain?! every 4 years don't a damn thing change, all I see is my people in chains, and I wish it would change, my own people ain't feeling my pain, cause they ain't looking, listening or reading shit mane, and it's really strange, cause everybody's looking for fame, but if you sp**ark** a flame, they start to aim, we all gonna die one day, this ain't the time to be a run away, So I gotta stay, I shed tears like **Lupe,** I don't care what they say, _I'm gonna unite the people, from here to **Zimbabwe,**_ one race, I grew up listening to **Sade,** it's a crime not to replay what I say, stay united! reply what I say, it's a crime not to replay what I say, stay united! replay what I say, it's a crime not to replay what I say, stay united! divided we fall alcohol killing most of y'all, stay united, divided we fall tobacco killing most of y'all, Black male, black sheep, blacklist, black life don't come with no map or no compass, it comes with conflict, you gotta be conscious to combat the nonsense, where my 90's niggas at to organize with?! **- Dawud The Uncanny BlaKseed**

September 2012 Sexual Abstinence

I found am old audio conversation/argument that I had with my mother and in it I reveal that I had not had sex in 7 months and that is how I was able to track this date.. The conversation was recorded on July 27th of 2013. In my journey I had gone on 3 long intentional bouts of abstinence but I never tracked the dates. One was for 1 year and 7 months, the other was 1 year and 3 months and the other was 10 months. This decision came as a result of dealing with what happened earlier in the year when I thought I was the father of a 9 year old little girl. Then months later Kalishea would get pregnant but we decided not to keep the baby. I stop having sex in September of 2012. 4 years later Kalishea would have a son born the day before my birthday on October 24th 2016, the same day **Rosa Parks** died and the same day that **KRS One** released his book, The Gospel of Hip Hop (page 633). Kalishea is born on June 15th the day before Tupac's birthday. I have a theory about who Tupac was in a past life.

Rau nu Prt m heru

September 18th 2012 Trayvon

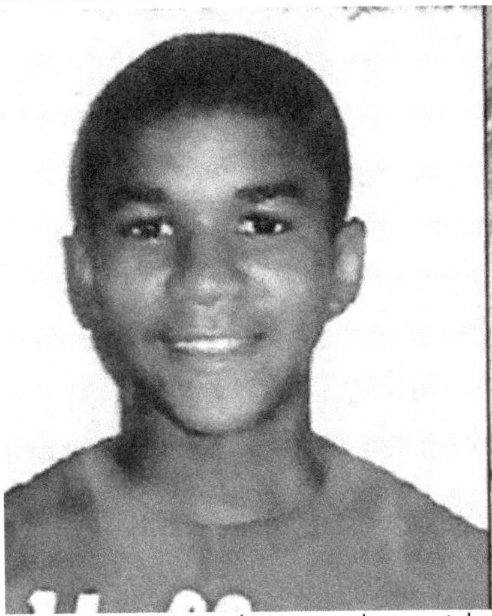

I wrote this for **Trayvon Martin** R I P, _All Eyes On Me_, All eyes on the young black youth is all I see, from N.Y.C. to F.L.A. the other day, I seen this black mother locked away for tryin to give her kids an education, do the calculation not even this black inauguration's gonna raise this black nation! we gotta all start pacing at the same time! you'd be surprised how many soldiers out here dying! analyze the facts before you tell me to relax, cause all the ones dying look like me! Obama's security budget; the biggest in history! why would that be man?! maybe because he's _Black Like Me_! now if I used the word conspiracy you look at me like I'm crazy, yet the rich get richer and the poor get poorer! White people are richer and Black people are poorer yet these are the facts they choose to ignore but I must step across the line and analyze your mind, What makes you think it's fine for you to go and reorganize your crime? America is anti Black by design! **Amadou Diallo** shot **41** times! **Bush** should go to jail for committing war crimes! and we should rebel **Chapelle**, Cointelpro, community watch watching too much Rambo mixed with little **Sambho**, I guess **Trayvon Martin** was walking too damn slow! reparations are due reparations are due, I got caught up in the world took advantage of you, Help me raise my Black Nation reparations are due, I got caught up in the world took advantage of you, reparations are due reparations are due, I got caught up in the world took advantage of you, help me raise my Black Nation reparations are due, I got caught up in the world took advantage of you **- Dawud The Uncanny BlaKseed**

Iu f Per f m heru

Utterances for Coming Forth by day into Light

Significance

Trayvon was by himself when he was murdered on this dark road. He fought back but just like when the European came to the shores of Africa with the gatling gun, George Zimmerman pulled a gun on young Trayvon and ended his life with one squeeze the same way the gatling gun killed armies of Zulu warriors and many other indigenous peoples of the world. These machine guns were the weapons most associated with imperial conquest because they were heavily used by colonial powers during the scramble for Africa and it's precious resources. Trayvon may be gone in physical form but he is immortal and so are you. I find it sad that man wastes his time killing each other. Fear is the mother of war and love is the only answer. Look at me, in 2012 I had no idea who I was in my previous lives. These killings angered me greatly but I kept moving forward. I kept seeking truth and eventually I found the great mystery of resurrection and immortality **(hero's journey**, page 3). I saw what happened to the men that killed me when I was **Emmett Till** (page 318). Time does not work the same when you are "dead"! A moment can be a thousand years and a thousand years can be a moment. Sometimes my **guardian angel** brings the men who killed me to my studio and they watch me with great remorse and regret (page 318, 507). I do not feel any pity for what men like George Zimmerman will face once they leave their physical bodies. See, most of them have no idea what's waiting for them on the other side of life. Perhaps that's why so many are afraid to die trying to prolong their lives here on earth with every artificial way instead of just living peaceful healthy lives.

It is he, who comes forth by day into Light

The Laws are the Walls to Keep Us Down in America

The laws in America have always been made to ensure that the white men who established this country maintain the power and control. In 1619 the first African slaves were brought to the Americas, 20 of them. The White enslavers soon learned that with free labor their profits could go up exponentially and they did. These profits are what made America financially stable. Black men, women and children were bought and sold like animals and regulated to the title of slaves, becoming a source of free labor. Over time the White men began to increase their profits by allowing the babies that were born from the routine raping of the black slaves to live. This cut cost by not having to buy new slaves all the time. The slaves had babies with each other and the white enslavers had babies from the females slaves they raped. These practices were the ground work for the new "laws". In 1662 Virginia wrote into law: "children of enslaved mothers are slaves, regardless of their fathers race or status". So basically even if your father is the president you will still be a slave. There is no mystery as to why so many black people have the last names, Washington, Jefferson, and Jackson etc etc. All of these early white presidents had slaves and raped female slaves. by 1667 Virginia wrote into law: "**enslaved blacks** who convert to **Christianity** are **still slaves**". So not even God could free you from the binds of this white mans system of slavery. And by **1669** Virginia wrote into law: "slave masters may kill *people* who resist authority". There is no difference in the system of law making in America today. **Trayvon Martin** was murdered on February 26th 2012 (p 232) and the Stand Your Ground law was the law used to legitimize George Zimmerman murdering him. This law is no different than the law passed in **1669**. With all the laws being passed there is never a law to reconcile what has been done to the enslaved Africans and indigenous (blacks) of this land. In 1740 South Carolina wrote into law: "whipping or execution of slaves who grew their own food, learned to read or assembled in groups". These are the hells that birth the idea that, the laws are the walls to keep us down. This is a line that I first wrote into my music on July 7th 2013 when I wrote the Song, **Knock Knock** (p 274). In this rhyme I would say the name **Emmett Till** for the 3rd time in my music before my past life of Emmett was revealed to me. I would make reference to this idea again on May 12th 2015 in the song, **Who Do You Believe in** (page 330) when I said "these laws are the walls you can't break through". I would make reference to this idea again on August 6th 2016 on the song **Terrorism** (p 399), it was the murder of **Alton Sterling** (p 394), **Philando Castile** (p 395) and **Korryn Gaines** (p 398) and many others that caused me to write with righteous anger. On April 22nd 2018 I would use the line again in the song, **Crown** (p 466). I wrote that song the second day of my Kemetic Yoga course and two days after I graduated my past life as Emmett Till was revealed to me on July 3rd 2018 (p 480). If we as the indigenous peoples of this land want to rise from the binds of this system of racism we will not do it by voting or waiting for laws to be passed. We must decide to unite on all fronts regardless of the island we were dropped off on or the European tongue we speak. We must also stop killing each other!

September 22nd 2012 Who's the Wisest

I love rap, and I love listening to other niggas rapping, I happen to be on a mission that started back when, I realized I was black in America, Trapped in the ghetto with ghetto niggas that'll fuck'n bury ya, You can watch the news but don't believe everything they selling ya, the ones on the the top be orchestrating the mass hysteria, "I will work for food, I will work for shelter", If you read the signs, you realize the cards they dealt ya, white man black man what's the big difference?! humanity is so twisted, never pledge allegiance to mischief, They blast you with a biscuit and call it holy war merry Christmas, put the world in yo hands, now big brother all up in yo business, you might see the world different If you stop and look'n and listening, and listening, but you ain't listening, now who's the wisest, I say the one in the sky is, not the ones under the **sun** in disguises, who's the wisest, I say the one in the sky is, not the ones under the **sun** in disguises

Picture me rolling at about a 100, 190 Benz all my friends said slow down cousin, But you know I wasn't, cause I was living life fast and crazy, **There's gotta be a reason why God saved me**, maybe I'm supposed to harness the energy of slaves from slavery, it's funny how now we all in slavery, in debt to the mighty dollar, these copers will make you holler, they killed her only son to be married in a matter of hours, so now they'll only do a funeral and baby shower, Damn! that's fucked up! It's not good enough to just know the name, do your history son get below the plane, do your history son get below the plane, do your history son get below the plane, it's not good enough to just know the name, do your history son get below the plane, do your history son get below the plane, do your history son get below the plane, **Jonathan Jackson** coming in blasting, **Bunchy Carter** couldn't get harder, there's no greater honor to die a martyr, the type of shit to make you understand a Ji-hada, now who's the wisest, I say the one in the sky is, *n*ot the ones under the **sun** in disguises, who's the wisest, I say the one in the sky is not the ones under the **sun** in disguises **- Dawud The Uncanny BlaKseed**

September 25th 2012 Dawuud's Pain Remix [Tupac Tribute]

They had you mobbing like a loc, and ready to get yo slug on, you held it down and shot two cops when they was wrong, even if you are dead my nigga you gonna live on trust, I seen so many of your tattoo's I figured they must be feeling, a fucking thugs passion, these lil niggas still out here cuss'n and buck'n and blast'n, man they nut's! they drinking Hennessy, they getting high but they ain't looking for their enemies, we all gonna die, if we don't try, man this stress is still major, this scar on my face didn't come from a razor, what can I do? but stay true until I'm dead and gone, and keep my aim on change, I know the road is long, these sorry bastards wanna kill you when you teach, who will you grow to be? everyday is a struggle just to change your reality, so if you falling loc, don't let em make you worry, keep banging on the system till you're buried, I was born to raise hell, another brother from the gutter, word to mother we trapped, who can we trust ? enemies look like us, I'm on the scene steady mug'n mean, until they kill me, I'll be living this life I know ya feel me, so much pain **- Dawuud's Appeal 2012**

College Paper

October 10th 2012 (BMCC LAT: 200-141 Documentary review)
Égalité for all: Toussaint Louverture and the Haitian Revolution

Rau nu Prt m heru

The Haitian insurrection/revolution (1791-1804), though seldom talked about is a major part of world history and more importantly African history. This revolt takes place in the late 18th century in present day Haiti, formally called the island of Saint Domingo. During this time Saint Domingo was the most profitable of the Caribbean islands. It was under the control of the French and was also the sugar capital of the world. The working conditions and every day lifestyles of the slaves were very torturous and barbaric, needless to say, the slaves who worked the fields were only expected to live a maximum of 3yrs. Slaves worked from sun up until sun down and were often killed if they refused to work. The enormous profits from sugar made it easy for the french planters (slave drivers) to ignore the horrors that made this possible. The documentary focuses on the rise and fall of Toussaint and not much about the other Haitian leaders such as Jean-Jacques Dessalines who would eventually win the war.

lu f Per f m heru

Toussaint was born into slavery on the island Saint Domingo. As a boy Toussaint was taught the arts of reading, writing and business; this set him apart from his brethren who were reduced and degraded to the level of animals. There were 3 classes of people in Saint Domingo, the whites, the mixed (Mulatto's) and the African slaves. The whites were of course the planters who enjoyed full freedom and enforced all the laws of the land. The mulatto's were the children of white planters and African slave women and because of their "white blood" the mulatto's also experienced a life similar to that of the whites but they were still, NOT EQUAL. The African Slaves were the workers and as I stated earlier their lives were short and grueling. The revolution starts in 1791 when the mixed race people of saint Domingo petitioned for equal rights. his angered the Whites and ensuing wars broke out. Many were killed. The war had begun. The war lasted 14yrs and the battles were more like massacres. During these years many different allegiances were formed and broken. At one point Spain armed Toussaint with weapons with hopes of reaping some of the profits of the island. There were no codes left unbroken, each army had a stake in the resources of St. Domingo. Toussaint rose to power quickly because of his education and experience as well as his favor with his fellow slaves. Winning many battles he rose to the highest rank an African had attained during colonialism. This infuriated Napoleon the general of the French army. The battles were not just fought between the French and the Slaves of St. Domingo. In fact the French later recruited the help of Spain and the British. If you can imagine the strongest armies of the European world taking on the small island of St Domingo. By 1802 Napoleon recruits the help of Thomas Jefferson the president of the Americas. Napoleon was enraged with the idea that a Black army was defeating White armies. Napoleon was quoted saying that he wanted to "**stop forever the march of the blacks in the world**". Napoleon then reinstituted slavery and launched the biggest offensive against St. Domingo. After 3 months of battle Toussaint surrenders and a day later he is arrested. After the news of the reinstitution of slavery made its way to the slaves of Saint Domingo the island erupted in flames. Dessalines and the slaves took to the fields and utilized scorched earth tactics. Dessalines, with his "take no prisoners" motto, killed all the French men on the island. Some say that the explosions and fires were so precise that it seemed as if gun power was previously put down very much like the belief that the world trade center towers had been prepped with explosives. 1804; Haiti he first black state is born.

This documentary is important to the history of Haiti because it shows resistance to colonial order and oppression. In the text Sanabria explains the many different ways that the slaves and indigenous would rebel. While revolution by war is the supreme expression of freedom the slaves also used everyday forms of resistance. One of the challenges in history is telling the story as truthful as possible. The textbook doesn't talk much about the Haitian revolution but it does mention that Napoleon lost more troops and generals than at the famous battle of waterloo against the British. This revolt should not be taken lightly. It was indeed a milestone moment for all oppressed peoples of the world at that time and even still to this day.

Utterances for Coming Forth by day into Light

In my opinion this documentary does not do the Haitian revolution justice. The story is centered on Toussaint who is not the one who finally brought freedom to Haiti. The documentary did not speak about how the slaves got to St Domingo and only brushed over how barbaric the planters treated the slaves. Many historians argue that when Toussaint went back to save his white masters it showed that he was too invested in the affairs of whites to see the cries of his brethren. The fact that Toussaint owned land and also had slaves under his command helped to support this feeling. My biggest question is why isn't Jean-Jacques Dessalines the main character in this documentary? Jean-Jacques is the one who actually won the revolution? Who decides for Africans who their heroes are or should be? Still, I believe we all play our part. The revolution may not have ever happened without Toussaint but then again the slaves out numbered the planters 12 to 1 with a population of over 500,000 slaves. I believe the revolt may have ended quicker if the slaves had followed the lead of slaves like jean-Jacques Dessalines.

It is he, who comes forth by day into Light

Revolutions are contagious, and they spread rapidly. Present day revolts in Greece, Tunisia or Egypt prove how one revolution can spark another. When enslaved or oppressed peoples see or get news of others winning their freedom it gives the enslaved the heart and the will to see about their own freedom and this is precisely what happened in Haiti (Saint Domingo). However he who wins war writes history! If I did a documentary on Haiti I would not have Toussaint as the hero that this documentary attempts to make of him. Toussaint was indeed a great man in African history but I believe he lost touch with his peoples desire for full freedom. I think the documentary did what it was intended to do; it gave some info on the most profound insurrection every recorded into historical text but the documentary left out many major factors that led to this revolt. They talked about the king being beheaded in 1793 but failed to expand on why he was beheaded. This happened because of the way the French were treating their own citizens. Remember; the oceans were like highways and news traveled fast! The time is 1791 and less than 20yrs earlier in 1776 the world had seen the Americas win their freedom from the British and now the French working class were in the process of fighting for their rights because the kings and queens of France were hoarding all the food for themselves leaving the French working class hungry and angry. So this means that the French were not only profiting off the work of the slaves in the sugar fields of St Domingo but they were also keeping the profits for themselves leaving their own citizens hungry and cold. The story of Haiti (St Domingo) is an unfinished one, it is still the only colony to ever gain their freedom! At the end of the war Toussaint dies in a freezing cell in the mountains of France in 1804. Jean-Jacques Dessalines is killed 2 yrs after the revolution with his murder being subject to many different versions. St Domingo the most profitable colony went bankrupt after they were forced to pay France reparations and so they have been left crippled ever since. The word revolution, depending on who uses it has many different connotations however when ever a people are unjustly* imprisoned or oppressed the time is always ripe for what is right. In 1804 the time was indeed ripe for Revolution.

November 3rd 2012 **Come Follow Me**

I'll tell u the truth if you tryin to find it, Africa is the root of the economics, my nigga I promise, they quick to show a nigga when he be loot'n, but they don't show you how they be doing the drug pollution, she said, "the strong go crazy" it's true! the weak go along! I keep my mind **Assata** strong, check it, life can get real in a second, you ain't got time to blink, neck better protect it, you give a slave a book he gonna be leaving, or he gonna be shook broke stuck be-**lie**-ving that we we even, salute to those who rhyme with reason, some of your **souls** will pay the toll of treason, community come unite you and me, so America can be what it's suppose to be, now if the laws are made to set us free, can you tell me why the law be harnessing me, I promise **I'm coming**, the Slaves R come'n, Dawuud is coming, The Kings R come'n, The **Pharo's** R come'n, The Kings R come'n, The Slaves R come'n, The Niggers R come'n, Dawuud is coming, The Slaves R come'n, Dawuud is coming, The Niggers R come'n, The Slaves R come'n

"I pray you understand your place in the world today", a world away from the ways of the brighter days, growing up in **Rockaway**, it hurt to see you in the news today, the greatest fear, when the ocean meets the bay, times like this when nature hits, the guns come out to play, why? cause people they gonna die, cause people they gonna try, to take yo shit away, why? somebody tell me why when the pressure is gettin high, poor people gettin swept away? is that why Black people don't like water? stuck in this new world order, salute to the B.L.A., I know what I said, but how do do you decode what I say? it it just some underground Hip Hop hooray, I'm taken ya back come follow me, on a journey to see a for real emcee, they want you to fall down like Michael Douglass, you don't really know me, so you can't really judge this, justice? not here! I really does this! fuck this language I never liked english, black male, black sheep, black list, Black life don't come with no map or no compass it comes with conflict, gotta be conscious to combat the nonsense, I need 49 niggas to organize with, The Niggers R come'n, The Kings R come'n, The **Pharo's** R come'n, The Kings R come'n, The Slaves R come'n, The Niggers R come'n, Dawuud is coming, The Slaves R come'n, Dawuud is coming, The Niggers R come'n, The Slaves R come'n, The **Pharo's** R come'n, I want you in the back come follow me on a journey to see a for real emcee **- Dawuud's Appeal 2012**

Significance

I wrote 35 rhymes in 2012, only half of what I wrote in 2011, and that's only because I had started school at BMCC so a lot of my focus was on school work. However this year I was still studying Kemet (Egypt) and my music reflects that study. This year, via my music I spoke the names, **Pharaoh** 3 times, Tupac once, Garvey twice, **Maat** twice, **Osiris** once, Haiti twice, Toussaint once, Harriet 3 times, Malcolm 3 times, Martin twice, the idea of "**coming back**" twice, **resurrection**/risen once, and Kemet once (see page xi for chart). **Re-member** that **you** are **Ausar** (**Osiris**) and **Heru,** the **hero!** See page 3 for the **hero's journey!** There was a lot of hype as to what the significant of 2012 was in respects to the **Mayan** calendar however both of my past life revelations are connected to the **Mayan 2012 prophecy**. Emmett Till came to this planet on July 25th which is the most sacred day on the **Mayan** calendar (p 503) and Lord **Pacal** was a priest king of the **Mayans** and was known as the **feathered snake** or the **feathered serpent** just like **King Tut**. I wrote this song on **November 3rd** and the tomb of **Tutankhaten** (**King Tut**) was discovered on **November 4th 1922**. In the first verse I mention **souls** paying for treason as well as the idea that "**I am come'n**". But where was I coming from is the question? I also say that "The **Pharo's** R come'n". I do remember placing the **Pharo's** in the hook last. I said the **slaves**, **kings** and **niggas** were come'n and after I'd finished the song and listened to it I felt that I hadn't fully represented the journey of Africans enough so I added **Pharo's** as well because I had started to realize that we really were the people from the Nile Valley and I wanted to represent all of our past. So I added "The **Pharo's** R come'n" and low **and BEHOLD the pharaoh WAS coming**! On April 4th 2020 my past life as **Tutankhaten** (**King Tut**) will be revealed to me (p 594).

2012 - Vending with Kadwo (Nkruma)

I met Kodwo some time on 2010 at an event that Hadiiya hosted and this is where I purchased a cuff from him (p 181). Years later I would hang out with Kodwo in Soho while he sold his jewelry. This is around the same time that I would purchase a **bronzed face Benin necklace** from a Black woman vending in Soho. I purchased from her because her table had no traffic and I wanted to draw people to her table. 3 years later I would watch the movie **Birth of a Nation,** produced by **Nat**e **Park**er ("Parker" p 17) and in the movie **Nat Turner** (p 19) gave his wife a similar or the exact same **Bronzed face Benin pendant** as a wedding gift (p 425). Kodwo once told me that he found my transformation interesting. This was years before my past life revelations. He came to my place a few times in 2012 and I played my music for him while we smoked weed. He had seen me go from being a man focused on women and fashion to a man focused on transformation and the struggle of Black People. Little did I know how much I would actually **Transform**.

November 2012 - I Built an Alter Unto The Lord

My homie Kadwo ("**Nkruma**" at the time) would refer me to sister **Kufunya** for the purchase of crystals and I would travel to East New York to purchase crystal technology from her. She happened to live blocks away from my high school sweet heart **Monique**, whom I lived with briefly back in 2006 (pages 60, 148). The first stone I picked was a large piece of **Selenite** because it reminded me of the Movie **Superman** (page 202-204). This would be the center piece to my **first alter**. In the picture below, taken in 2012 my alter can be seen. I had **Auset** (Isis) and **Ausar** (Osiris) on the left and right of my alter with **Maat** in the middle. I built an alter unto the Lord and the ancestors responded by guiding my steps. I wouldn't see sister Kufunya again till 2019 while doing chair massage at **Nicholas** store in Brooklyn.

Rau nu Prt m heru

Iu f Per f m heru

Utterances for Coming Forth by day into Light

It is he, who comes forth by day into Light

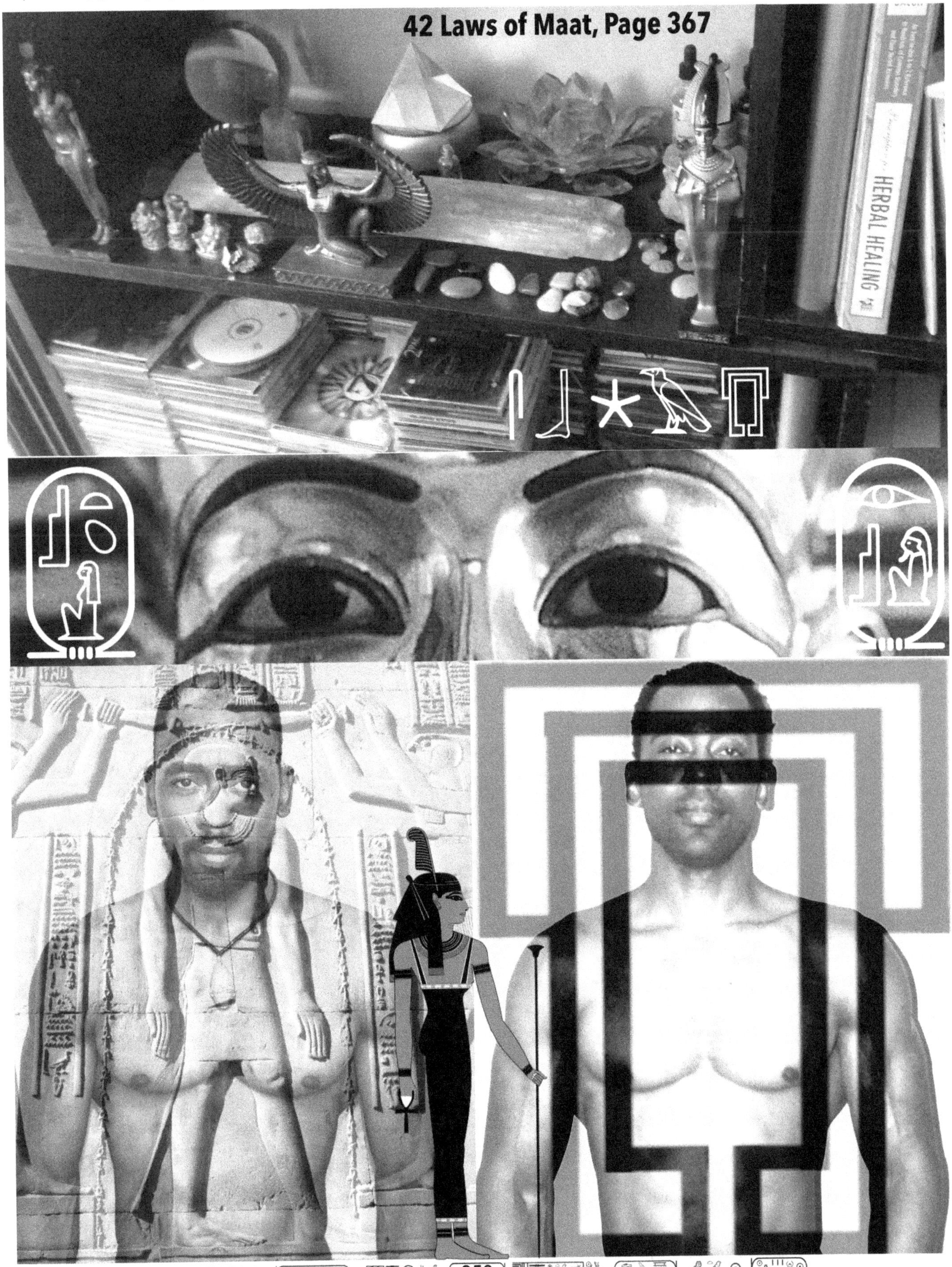

Addendum **The False Door, also known as the Ka (Spirit) Door, Meta Spiritual Devices and The Alter to The Lord**

False doors (**Ka doors**, **Spirit doors**) were built into the walls of the tombs as a way to interface between the world of the living and the world of the dead, very much like the **alters** people keep in their homes in modern times. Visitors went to the tombs to say prayers and deposit offerings for the spirit of the deity or the deceased loved one, whose soul could pass through the door. The inscriptions on the door commemorate the person it was built for. In many mastabas, both husband and wife buried within have their own false door. Most false doors are found on the **west** wall of a funerary chapel or offering chamber (Mastaba) because the ancient Egyptians associated the **west** with the land of the dead which was governed by **Ausar** (Osiris). **In the higher levels of teaching the false doors represented entry into high states of consciousness.**

Eg. 1	Eg. 2	Eg. 3
Ka = Spirit	Seba = Star	Seba = Door

Mereruka

Mereruka was a vizier for the Pharaoh Teti during the 6th dynasty of the old kingdom in ancient Kemet (Egypt). Mereruka was a master builder, a master craftsman and he was also a **sun of light.** Mereruka was the overseer of the builders. He was an equivalent to the great **Imhotep**, the builder of the Great Pyramid of **Khufu** on the Giza plateau in Kemet. It took 40 years of school to reach his level of mastery. When you think of the men of today that build great structures you must first think of builders like Mereruka. He built a 33 room Mastaba (meta-spiritual device) for his entire family. This Mastaba was built to stand the test of time. In the picture on the right Mereruka is seen standing in what appears to be a false door, also known as a spirit door. He is seen striding with his left foot forward to keep in line with the heart which is what is weighed after death.

Spirits, Stars and Doors

It was the ancient African Kemetyu who developed the writing system we know as MDW NTCHR (hieroglyphics). Deciphering the MDW NTCHR takes a deeper mode of thought than what modern language offers. You must imagine that you are reading the language of immortals (p 30). Until this is done the meaning of the MDW NTCHR will never be fully inner stood. With that in mind, take a look at the key above. Notice that the words, **Star** (**example 2**) and **Door** (**example 3**) are spelled the same and sound the same except for the **bird** and the **door** added to the word **door**. The bird is a hawk vulture and it makes the sound "**ahh**". It is there to help with pronouncing the word Seba. The door is there to symbolize a physical door. The word for **spirit** is **Ka**, as seen in **example 1**. Knowing that **Ka** means **spirit** and the words **star** and **door** are spelled the same, **that opens the "door"** to speculation as to what the ancient Kemetyu were trying to convey. Perhaps the **"door"** was really a **"GATEWAY"**. The Pyramids of Giza were aligned with the stars in heaven and the Nile was aligned with the **Milky Way**... In the Great Pyramid (meta-spiritual device) of Khufu, there is a stone "box" in the center of the pyramid, placed in the middle of the Kings Chamber. Inside this chamber there are two narrow shafts, commonly known as "air shafts" or "**star shafts**" they face each other and are located approximately 3.0 ft above the floor, 2.5 m from the eastern wall, with a width of 18 and 21 cm and a height of **14** cm (**5.5** in). The southern shaft reaches to the outer surface of the Pyramid and was aligned with **Orion's belt**. The south shaft in the Queens chamber is aligned to the star **Sirius**. Sirius was associated with **Auset** (**Isis**) and known as the "**Nile Star**" because of its annual appearance at sunrise on the day of the summer solstice which heralded the inundation. **Orion** was associated with **Ausar** (**Osiris**), the Lord of Resurrection (p 481). The northern shaft in the Kings Chamber aligned with Thuban, in the constellation of Draco. Currently, Polaris m**ark**s our celestial north pole, but when the pyramids were built the star closest to the pole was Thuban. Because it never left the night sky it was of high astrological importance and considered to be a symbol of **immortality**. It is theorized that in ancient times the initiates would lay in the stone "box" (sarcophagus) inside the Kings Chamber and separate their **light bodies** (Ka, Spirit, Ba, soul, consciousness, astral body) from their physical bodies. Upon separation of the **light body** they would take the **star shaft**, teleporting their astral body to the Sirius or Orion star systems (pages 366,485).

Dawud built an Alter unto The Lord

Whether we are aware of it or not we are building alters and spirit doors in our homes when we place pictures of "dead" people on our walls or on our tables. From a place of love we are consciously deciding to remember their souls. We are placing them up high, honoring them and the souls of the dead are aware of this. In 2012 I would build my first alter. I had **Auset** (**Isis**) and **Ausar** (**Osiris**) on the left and right of my alter with **Maat** in the middle (p 250). In the past 15 years the walls and book shelves of my apartment have been adorned with pictures of my family, friends, the ancestors that I hold dear to my heart, Kemetic statues and my favorite emcees. When I did this I did not consider the fact that I might attract the energy of any of these deities or people who had passed on but that is exactly what happened. I built an alter unto the Lord and the ancestors responded by guiding my steps. My grand father died in 2009 but in 2015 he would appear to me in spirit form and the experience would broaden my scope of "reality" (p 348). Our bodies are divine temples and they can be used as spirit doors as well. In 2013 the **Nswt Bity** (Pharaoh) **Khufu** spoke to me through a brother named **Khufu** (p 282). **Remember that you are Ausar and Heru, the hero!** See page 3 for the **hero's journey!** For more on **Guardian Angels** and **Ka Doors** see pages (48, 148, 150,179, 199, 252, 253, 315, 318, 329, 348, 349, 409, 421, 434, 545, 548, 549, 572, 584, 604, 626, 650).

Did God asked Abraham to Sacrifice His Son Isaac on The Alter? Did Noah build a boat?

Rau nu Prt m heru

Iu f Per f m heru

In the bible, God establishes a covenant with Abraham, Issac and Jacob and each builds an alter unto the Lord. In Genesis 12 7-8, **Abraham** builds an alter to God. In Genesis 26 4-5, **Issac** builds an alter unto God. In Genesis 35 3, **Jacob** builds an alter unto God. In Genesis 8-20, **Noah** built an alter unto God. **David** was a man after Gods own heart and in 1st Chronicles 21-26, **David** built an alter unto God. In Genesis 22, God asked Abraham to bring his son Isaac and lay him across the alter as a sacrifice and Abraham proved to God that God was first in his life by laying his son on the alter and offering him to God as a **sacrifice**. Just before Abraham sacrifices (kills) his son, a spirit (Angel) was said to have appeared and told Abraham not to kill his son. Why would a loving God create his or her children just to ask their child to kill their children? What kind of loving God would do that? Would you ask your child to kill their child just to prove that they love you? In the tomb chapel of Kapure, in Saqqara, a scene of butchering can be seen. Several horizontal rows depict offerings and bearers that would provide the necessities that Kapure required for his afterlife, such as wine, cosmetic items, foodstuffs, and clothing. Other scenes feature butchering of animals, for purposes unknown. This is 2300 years before the story of Jesus is presented to the world, **23**00 years before any Christians walked the earth. Did the creators of the Christian religion misinterpret what was seen on the walls of these funerary chapel tombs? Is this where they got their idea of sacrificing animals for "God"? The chapel (mastaba) was not a place for sacrificing (**killing**) people, it was the place where funerary priests would perform rituals, recite spells, and leave offerings to ensure that the deceased would prosper in the afterlife. It was also the site where the spirit, which in theory could come up from the burial chamber and proceed forth from the inner niche of the spirit door, and would take its sustenance (offering). Several representations of Kapure, both standing and sitting, appear on his false door. If the creators of the Christian religion did misinterpret this, then what else have they misinterpreted? Perhaps the barbaric practice of genital mutilation (**circumcision**) is also a monstrous misstep (page 120). If the God of the bible is an all knowing God and this God created the heavens and earth, then why would humans not be already made perfect? Why would the human being be the only living creature made to "correct" their reproductive organs?! The commandment to circumcise was said to be a covenant made with Abraham and is recorded in Genesis 17:10–14, reading: "And God spoke to Abraham saying: This is my covenant which you shall keep between me and you and thy seed after you – every male child among you shall be circumcised." However, in 1916, the mummified remains of a teenage boy were discovered in **Edfu** Egypt. His family was from a noble class in the Ptolemaic Egyptian society and so he was buried in a **golden** sarcophagus. Scientists put his 2000 year old mummy through a CAT scan and among the things detected, they found his **uncircumcised penis**. This is proof that circumcision was not practiced by the royals in Egypt, or at least not by everyone. Some claim that **circumcision** was the **mark of slavery** in Egypt, asserting that when opposing warriors were defeated in battle they were mutilated before being reduced to slavery. Amputation of digits and castration was common, but death after castration was frequent so circumcision was used as a sufficiently humiliating compromise. Imagine if we are following a practice only meant for humiliation.. How much do you really know about the past? And again, why would an all knowing God who created the sun, moon and stars fail to make man perfect? And why didn't God make circumcision mediatory for women? Why aren't there any female angels?.. There are so many unanswered questions, yet when Christians read the Bible they read it as if the stories are real and as if the prophets are real, yet there are no artifacts from any of these biblical prophets. There is no museum on the planet earth where one can go to see the skeletons of any prophets from the bible or the Quran. Not Noah's Ark, not a sword or staff, not even a piece of cloth, yet museums all over the world are full of African skeletons and treasures from ancient Kemet. You can see the artifacts and bodies of the Queens and Kings of ancient Kemet but I have never seen anything that belonged to Jesus, Moses, Abraham, Noah, Issac, or David in a museum. The only thing I am left to mull over is the Bible, but the events and motifs in the Bible are taken from Kemet (page 667).

Noah and his Ark *Addendum*

Did Noah really build an Ark or was part of the story taken (plagiarized/stolen) from the Ausarian Resurrection Drama? The word **Ark** comes from the Latin word **Arc**a which means a **big box** or box. Ausar was the first to cultivate the land and in doing so, knowing the exact time that the **flood** waters of the Nile would rise was key. Noah is a story about a **flood**, like the flooding waters of the Nile. Ausar was put in a **box** and placed in the Nile river and Noah was in a **giant box** floating on the waters of the earth.. Ausar was the first to cultivate grapes, making the sacred yrp wine which was called the blood of Osiris (p 481). Noah got **drunk**, but only priest had possession of the sacred yrp wine. The story of Noah is about building **The Divine Ark of a Million years** (pages, 39, 176, 189, 361, 538). This is what we must do while here on earth. We must build our **astral bodies**, light bodies, or as we called in Kemet, the **Soul**ar B**ark** or the B**ark** of Ra. We practice this through the art of Kemetic Yoga (p 472). The Art of uniting the two lands with our breath. With this Ark we can travel via mediation or dreams. This is why two people can wake up and remember sharing the same dream (p 452, 589). **Remember that you are Ausar and Heru, the hero!** See page 3 for the **hero's journey!** Life is a class and living life trying to be a faithful Muslim or Christian or Jew, etc, is not how you pass the class. We must, **be ye like gods** (John 10:34 / Psalms 82:6). We must raise (rays) our life force energy and master the **dream** realm, because the span of earthly affairs is the manner of a dream. The same place you dream in is the same place the **astral body** goes when it dies (**Ka doors**, page 251). You will still exist, just without your physical body. Life is a dream that we must awaken from (p 30). I hope I was able to help with false teachings of Noah and false doors.

Utterances for Coming Forth by day into Light

It is he, who comes forth by day into Light

Below: Spirit Door of Kapure

The Tomb of Ra-Ka-Pou

This tomb was excavated at Saqqara in 1903 by the Egyptian Government under Mr. Quibell. Ra-ka-pou was an official in Thebes during the Old Empire. The statue placed in the interior is a copy of the wooden statue in the Cairo Museum knows as Sheik El Beled. It is placed in this position to indicate the appearance of the statue of Ra-ka-pou that has been stolen. The limestone walls of the tomb are covered with scenes representing the meats, game, fruit, cakes and other viands that the mourners would wish the deceased to have for his journey or that he might require.

College Paper

November 7th 2012
BMCC Essay on David Walker

Rau nu Prt m heru Iu f Per f m heru

Utterances for Coming Forth by day into Light

It is he, who comes forth by day into Light

How many of you have ever heard of the Abolitionist David Walker? This morning I will be informing you about the abolitionist David Walker focusing on 3 periods in his life. I will be focusing on his early life in North Carolina, his move to the north and finally the writing of his notorious pamphlet, DAVID WALKER'S APPEAL. The world is old but the future springs from the past, we must not forget those who have come before us.

Let's start with his early life. David was born in North Carolina in the year 1785. What makes David walker a special individual is the fact that he was born free. His father died before he was born and his mother had already earned her freedom therefore by law in the state of North Carolina her child would also be free. With his freedom, David got to experience slavery from the outside looking in. He learned to read and write and also learned to despise slavery making his mind up at an early age to do his part to help his brothers and sisters free themselves from bondage. When David was in his early 40's he moved to Boston Massachusetts and immediately started working as a civil rights activist.

David was quoted saying "If I remain in this bloody land I will not live long. As true as God reigns, I will be avenged for the sorrows, which my people have suffered. This is not the place for me no-no. I must leave this part of the country. Go I must". David opened a second hand clothing store that did surprisingly well despite his African heritage. This was indeed a big achievement during that time. David had a benevolent reputation with his community because he was always helping those in need. David walker also worked closely with the Underground Railroad. Even more so after the writing of his appeal. The under ground railroad if any of you are not aware, was not an actual rail road system in fact it was a network of abolitionist who fought for the freedom of slaves. This was not a popular thing to do at the time because there was always a possibility of reprisal from the ruling elite. In 1826 when David was 26 he worked as an agent for the freedom journal. I believe his involvement with the freedom journal and the Underground Railroad were major factors in him writing his pamphlet, David Walker's Appeal but not the only ones.

What exactly was in the Appeal? Who was it for? DAVID WALKER'S APPEAL, To the coloured citizens of the world but in particular, and very expressly, to those of the United States of America. David was inspired by the declaration of independence written in 1776. He argued that the declaration was flawed because it preached equality for all but yet they still had Blacks in chains. In 1828 David met and married a fugitive slave named Emily. After marrying her he wrote his Appeal. I believe his love for his wife and the desire for her freedom greatly inspired him as well. David Walker's appeal was the most notorious document of the times. Here is a quote from the pamphlet. "*And believe this, that it is no more harm for you to kill a man, who is trying to kill you than it is for you to take a drink of water when thirsty. In fact the man that stands there and lets a man kill him is worse than an infidel*". If slaves were found reading they were subject to severe punishment not excluding death. The slave security patrol (todays police) was tightened in the south and a bounty was put out for the capture Walker, **dead or alive**. $3,000 dead and $10,000 alive. Months later David was found dead. In 1831, a year after David's murder one of the most brave accounts of freedom would take place on August 21st 1831 in Virginia. Nat Turner would spark the biggest successful revolt in Virginia. Killing many of his slave masters. It has been said that **Nat Turner read David Walker's Appeal** before his insurrection. Even with his writing of the Appeal and being killed for it, David's son was able to become the first African to be elected to the Massachusetts congress.

In conclusion, David walker was killed because of his desire to help his people. All David wanted to do was help his people realize their potential for freedom. Heroes are not often seen as heroes while they are living because they often stand against the agenda of the status quo. If you were born during David Walker's time what would you do? Are their people in the world today who suffer similar fates? If so, do you hear their many cries for freedom?

References

- David Walker (1829) DAVID WALKER'S APPEAL To the coloured citizens of the world but in particular, and very expressly, to those of the United States of America
- Herbert Aptheker (1915) American Negro Slave Revolts, E 447 .A67

November 16th 2012
Brown Was The Color of Her True Skin Tone

Let me get it straight, **Nina** looks more like my aunt Rosina, listen, Zoe's cool but if she plays **Nina** she plays the fool, he who has the **gold** makes the rule, niggas sold out I swear, niggas act like they don't care, I swear they got more love for dogs than they do for thugs, the Lord's the only one I need to applaud, I'm in my prime but not a very long time ago I was moving slow in the fast lane, but still the cash came, but then the crash came, because you can't mask pain, you end up like **Toussaint,** the sugar cane, it's the sugar mane! simple and plain, Spain had a tea party in **Haiti** over our Black bodies, I probably be found dead for the shit that I said, or maybe niggas unite so that we can get ahead, **Killuminati** through my mind soul and my body, your words **immortalized** you, cause when it's real niggas feel your appeal, they can't kill what's infused within you, when I was **22** the universe **immortalized** you **- Dawud**

Found in an E-mail dated: November 16, 2012 at 11:27:30 AM EST

Significance

I mentioned my **Aunt Rosina** in this song and she's born on **January 6**. **January 6** was the day that the ancient Kemetyu celebrated the Winter Solstice, however **January 6th** currently marks the 12th day after the Winter Solstice (pages 489, 614). In the Christian religion **January 6th** is celebrated as 3 kings day, symbolizing the day that the 3 Magi visited **Jesus** in a manger. **January 6** is also the day that **Emmett Till's** mother, **Mamie Till** died (**January 6th** 2003) and **Tupac's** grand mother, **Eloise Maria Barnes** was born on **January 6**. Speaking of Tupac, I mention **Killuminati** in this song and I got that term from Tupac's last studio album (page 76).

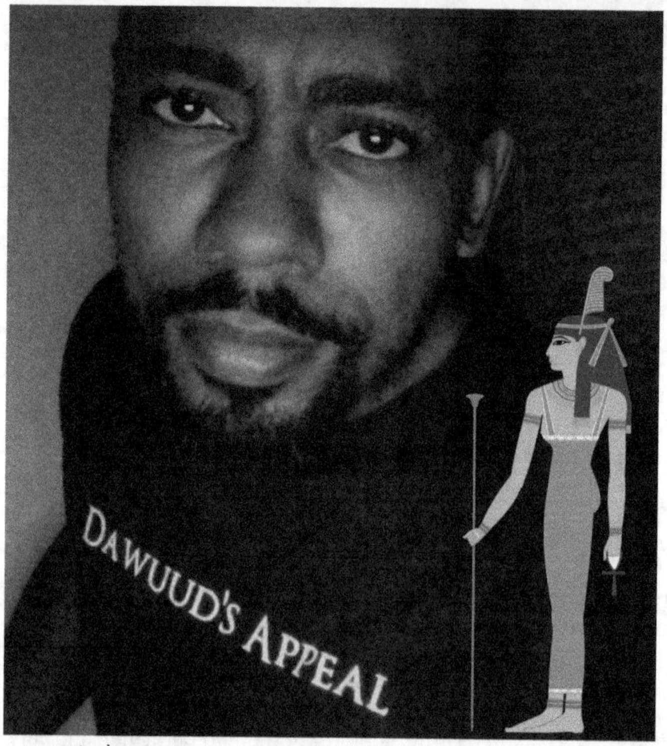

November 19th 2012 Silver Bullets

I'm come'n through with the silver bullet, load these fuck'n cops up with a silver bullet, maybe they would think before they squeeze and pull it, if they stocked silver bullets at your local store, would you buy em, and try em, lil homie you lie'n too afraid of die'n, open your mind see what I'm design'n, I'm not a cop killer I'm more realer, life got a nigga down no time for facebook now, **what if your life was based off of intent and how much you grow**, what if that's what they don't want you to know, they don't wanna see thugs get a full plate, separate these niggas divide em up into 50 states, stakes are high when crackers die, when niggas escape in 1831 I was on the run with that nigga **Nate**, I had a gun, cause it ain't fun liv'n life disgraced, misplaced then chased I got one for the Jake, 1785 happy to be alive born free in North Cacalaci, no I never knew my daddy, we read **Walker's Appeal** then shit got real nappy, they call me crazy but the biggest gang be the united states B, they stick together make'n the **laws** to make us all think we live'n better, **stand your ground**, then they buck a brother down, sugar in everything, the slave swings at everything, in St Domingo, I pray that you know your place in the world today bro! and that you stop your family and friends from cry'n and die'n slow, yeah that right there that I'll stop the wars, I'll write a movie and beg the **RZA** to do the score! but what ever does the silver bullet mean? if you kill somebody unjust and unclean then you die too, no judge or jury, just to **Maat** be true, they say the fruit don't fall far from the tree but I got a axe and we gonna see, in revelations people will dance to this music of **Bob Marley**, he told his children as long as you got brothers and sisters you don't need to be friends with everybody **- Dawud**

42 Laws of Maat, Page 367

November 23rd 2012 - Jordan Russle Davis

On November **23**rd 2012, Jordan Davis, a Black 17 year old high school student was murdered at a Gate Petroleum gas station in Jacksonville, Florida, by Michael David Dunn, a White 45 year old software developer, following an argument over **loud music** played by Jordan and his three friends. Around 7:30 p.m., four teenage boys (Leland Brunson, Jordan Davis, Tommie Stornes, and Tevin Thompson) stopped at a Gate Petroleum gas station. Tommie left his red SUV running while he went into the store. Leland, Jordan and Tevin remained in the vehicle listening to **music** which was described as **"very loud."** Michael Dunn, driving a black sedan, and his fiancée Rhonda Rouer pulled into the right adjacent parking spot. Rhonda left the car to purchase white wine and chips. She testified in court that Michael told her, **"I hate that thug music"** before she left the car for the store, although Michael claims he used the phrase **"rap crap."** The bass from the **loud music** playing in the teens' SUV annoyed Michael, who asked for it to be turned down. Tevin initially complied and turned the volume down, but Jordan requested the volume be turned back up. Jordan's protests continued and an independent witness overheard Dunn say "No, you're not gonna talk to me that way." Michael, who had a concealed weapons permit, took a handgun out of his glove compartment and started firing at Jordan's door, hitting him in the legs, lungs, and aorta (heart). As the SUV backed up to evade his gunshots, Michael opened his own door and continued firing at the car in shooter's stance, as the teens ducked for cover. Michael later testified that he still feared for his safety as well as that of Rouer who was to return to the vehicle imminently. Jordan was convicted on three counts of attempted second-degree murder for firing at three other teenagers who were with Jordan and one count of firing into an occupied vehicle. The jury could not reach a verdict about whether to convict Dunn for the murder of Jordan at the first trial. In a second trial, Dunn was found guilty of the first degree murder of Davis and sentenced to life plus 90 years in prison.

Significance

This was written through tears. **Today is January 6th 2022** and I'm almost done with this book. I wrote about Jordan Davis in a song titled **R U STILL DOWN** on Dec 10th 2012 (page 258) and I remember his case clearly but I had not placed his story in the book. Not because I didn't see the importance of it, I just have so many people in this book that it's too many to mention them all but Jordan Davis came to my attention today right after Jordan Edwards came to me (page 446). Jordan Davis was murdered on the same day that Emmett Till's mother Mamie Till was sent down (born), November **23**rd 1921. Mamie Till made her transition on **this very day January 6th 2003** the year of the **Goat**. Emmett was murdered in 1955 the year of the **Goat**. **Jan 6th** is 12 days after the Winter Solstice (Christmas, pages 489, 614). In the Christian religion **Jan 6** is the day that the 3 Magi visited Jesus in a manger. **Jan 6** is also the day that the ancient Kemetyu celebrated the Winter Solstice. **Tupac's** grand mother Eloise Maria Barnes was also born on **Jan 6**. Jordan Edwards was sent down (born) on my birthday October 25th in the year of the **snake** 2001. I was born on October 25th the year of the **snake** 1977. The murder of Jordan Davis angered me greatly. He died because his music was too loud! At this time in my life I was writing a lot of music and in the song **R U STILL DOWN**, I said the words "America's built off backs of *Kings **coming back** to haunt you*," (page 258). My soul was speaking. On July 3rd 2018 I would have my first past life revelation of my life as Emmett Till (page 480). Then on April 4th 2020 my past life as Tutankhaten (King Tut) was revealed to me (page 594). See page **648** for the **metaphysical significance of the number 23**.

Condolences

My condolences go out to the family of **Jordan Russle Davis** and all those who have been robbed of their life by this system of racism and white supremacy. Please know that death is not the end. The soul survives death, indeed and in spirit. This is a book of the dead written by a boy who was murdered without justice, who defeated death and came forth by day. May the soul of **Jordan Russle Davis** walk peacefully through the field of Reeds in Amenta. Amen Ra.

College Paper

November 26th 2012
BMCC LAT: 200-141
Who was Marcus Garvey?

Parish = Per Isis
See pages 202, 394, 629, 665

Rau nu Prt m heru

Marcus Garvey was a visionary born on August 17, 1887, in Saint Ann **Parish**, Jamaica. Marcus would grow up to become a leader in the African movement for peace, freedom, and equality and called for the return of Africans to the continent of Africa from which they had all been stolen. At an early age Marcus planed on becoming the worlds first gentlemen. As a child he developed a wide vocabulary by reading as many books as he could and he even read the dictionary as a hobby. As an adult Marcus lived a life of solitude, as did his father before him. Marcus developed a feeling that the world was against him. Many say that he embodied the black experience and carried the weight on his back. In 1915 Marcus planned on traveling to America to meet with Booker T Washington (another forward thinker) to speak to the African people of the southern parts of America. Unfortunately Marcus never met Booker T Washington due to Washington's untimely demise. Marcus would make his first trip to America a couple years later around 1917.

Iu f Per f m heru

While in America Marcus founder the U.N.I.A (Universal Negro Improvement Association). The U.N.I.A quickly gaining thousands of followers. Malcolm X's parents were followers of Marcus. Followers of Marcus were called Garveyites. Marcus used this platform to start his back to Africa movement. He used his donation money to buy ships that would be used to carry Africans back to Africa. He named his shipping company the Black Star Line. Marcus only stayed in the states for 10 years and Because of Marcus's efforts to unite African people he was eventually railroaded and arrested for petty charges then thrown into prison. While in prison he developed asthma and a heart condition. After he was set free he was deported back to Jamaica. Marcus never got to step foot in Africa. His death was a sad one. Marcus had been ill with the problems he developed while in prison when one day he read a newspaper article that listed him as dead. The article had such a traumatic effect on Marcus that he had a heart attack and died. My prayers are with Marcus and I will ready my soul to receive his energy and continue his work.

"A race that is solely dependent upon another for its economic existence sooner or later dies." - (Marcus Garvey)

November 27th 2012

Who was David walker?

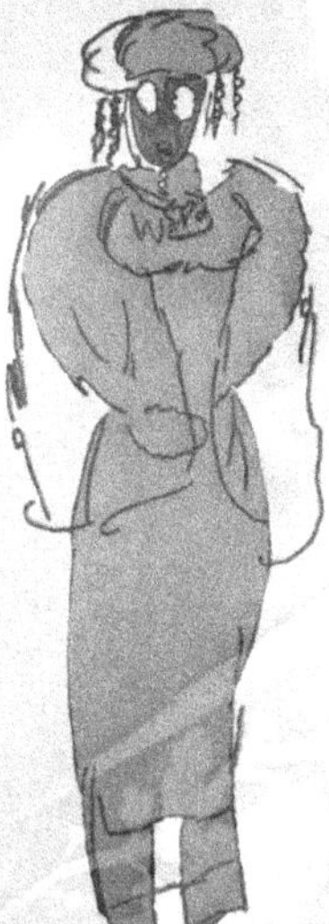

Utterances for Coming Forth by day into Light

Who was David walker? and what was written in his appeal?! tell me why when he wrote it they wanted him killed?! David walker was the first black man to make a written assault on this disgrace of a land, that I was born in, this is a warning join hands Black woman and man, damn! can't you see we fallen? it won't stop till we all in! then we ball'n! I need 49 niggas to really heed this calling! I need a ride or die chick like **Harriet Tubman**! I need people to wake up and see we all struggle'n, struggle'n is a synonym for thug'n! you think Martin wasn't thug'n?! you crazy homie you bug'n! White people be thug'n too, but you can't be a thug if you don't stay true! come with me and set your mind, body, soul free, come follow me, on a journey to see a for real emcee. - **Dawuud's Appeal 2012**

November 28th 2012 - Langston Hughes' A Dream Deferred decoded

It is he, who comes forth by day into Light

<u>What happens to a dream deferred</u>? = (What happens when you steal a people and forever change their course of life?)

<u>Does it dry up like a raisin in the sun</u>? = (Do they burn under the sun, forced to work in fields by fear of a gun?)

<u>Or fester like a sore and then run</u>? = (Or do they break free and run?)

<u>Does it stink like rotten meat</u>? = (When they are caught and hung do they smell like rotten dung?)

<u>Or crust and sugar over like a syrupy sweet</u>? = (The need for sugar started it all, do they accept their fate and fall?)

<u>Maybe it just sags like a heavy load</u>. = (Look at us now see how the sugar has obesity on the rise in the black community.)

<u>Or does it explode</u>? = (Do we rise up and blast, finally righting the wrongs done in the past?)

I had a client named **Aria Hughes**, she was born on my birthday. I always wondered if she was related to Langston Hughes.

December 1st 2012 - Logo Idea

On December 1st of 2012 I would take a picture of two sketches I drew for a new logo. On one of the sketches I wrote the words **Scorpion King** (page 2)..

I mention 4 bullet points on the other sketch and the first being a war against sugar. The next day I would pour my 5 pound bag of processed sugar in the toilet. I had become aware of the dangers of processed sugar being the cause of many bodily dysfunctions. The second was about a running group I wanted to start called We Run Harlem. The third was about heath being the true measure of wealth as money can not buy quality of life inside the body. The last thing I mentioned was a nation only being as healthy as it's mothers because the women is the one who must create the baby for 9 to 10 months and the baby is created from the body of the mother. So what she eats is important.

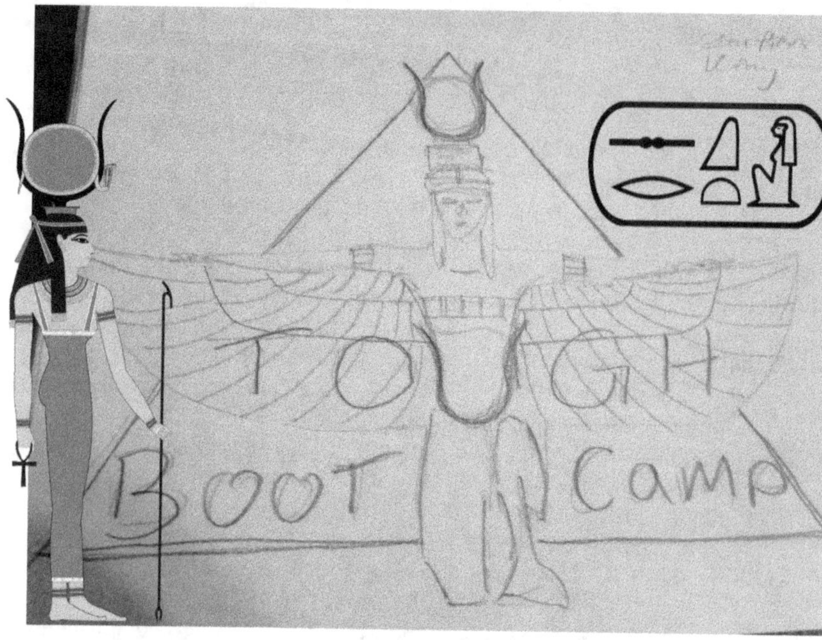

December 2nd 2012 - Cancer causing preservatives and Sugar Elimination

When I realized that **Sugar** was the most addictive and deadliest ingredient in most food I took my 5 pound bag of sugar from my cabinet and recorded myself pouring it in the toilet. I would now see sugar as a drug. I would never again purchase another bag of processed sugar. I realized that sugar was part of the cause of my **hair loss** and the eventual **greying** of my hair. I would also come to realize that the excess sugar is what cause my temporary **erectile disfunction**. On September 8th 2011, I did my first and only **colonic** (Colon hydrotherapy, page 212). I saw the bag of **Domino** sugar as a direct result of the sugar plantations that the white slave owning colonist ran on the island of Santo **Domingo**, the Capital of the Dominican Republic (Hispaniola, Haiti and the Dominican Republic). I refused to be addicted to the processed sugar that had taken the lives of many brothers and sisters that were killed on the sugar plantations of the Caribbean's. On the island of Jamaica black men (imprisoned men reduced to slaves) were cut into pieces in front of family members if they didn't cut the sugar cane fast enough. The average life of a male slave was 3 years. **There are 195 countries in the world and the United States has the 4th highest Cancer rate of them all!** Many of the foods deemed suitable for consumption by FDA, are banned in most of those 194 countries. The **BHA** and **BHT** preservatives in these foods are linked to Cancer. The European Union classifies BHA as an **endocrine disruptor** because of its ability to **lower testosterone** and thyroid-hormone thyroxin. **BHT** may disrupt endocrine function by causing thyroid changes and affecting animal development, according to the European Food Safety Authority. Studies on rats fed BHT found they developed **liver** and **lung tumors**. Cancer cells feed off of the processed sugar in the foods and these foods are advertised to children. **Fenugreek** and **bitter lemon** are two of the best plants to help balance sugar levels. Bitter lemon helps the sugars get into your cells while fenugreek is used for blood sugar regulation. These two can be mixed in a tea and drank every 3 to 4 hours to help stabilize the blood sugar levels.

December 10th 2012 R U Still Down

Rau nu Prt m heru

I hear all these kids scream'n **THUGLIFE**, you think life is a game, life ain't no joke! I hope you **Stand Your Ground** when them bullets rain down, keep ya head to the ground if them bullets rain down, don't bite me with a smile bite me with a frown, **R U Still Down?** I be the first to set it off man, but we want peace not war, war is not the answer, teach the youth the truth about the Panthers, lyrically I'm **Geronimo Pratt**, sugar was the first crack, America's built off the backs of ***Kings coming back to haunt you***, *the* ***specter's*** *hear!* they can kill you but they can't kill the revolution ***Maat** is here and she wants restitution*! **Free Mumia** rest in peace **Troy Davis**, **Jordan Davis**, brothers die, we get mad, mothers cry, we wonder why, but do you really try?! my black diaspora they attack blacks in Florida like Iraq and Gaza, **Stand Your Ground** or be a martyr! yeah I said that and I don't know if I'll be here tomorrow, but I bet that Thug Life it'll hit em when 50 Kings scream out THUG LIFE, you think life is a game, life ain't no joke, I hope you **Stand Your Ground** when them bullets rain down, keep ya head to the ground when the bullets rain down, don't bite me with a smile bite me with a frown, **R U Still Down?**

Iu f Per f m heru

Hell yeah! do you still feel the chill?! they still here and it's written right there! I wonder if they saw this, a world so lawless, we built the **pyramids** my nigga yet they ignore us, I'm **Morpheus** and **Neo**, I'm **Trayvon Martin**, I'm **Ice T**, I'm **Malcolm X** sit'n next to mi amigo, Viva la revolution flow, generate your own dough, even if you gotta start alone, so! this world is full of people who don't know, and they don't even know that they don't know, it's sad- he said he killed him cause he walk too slow, they said you free but you ain't free, you just loose yo, spread around the world divided so you would never know, the greatest story never told, **A Dream Deferred** explodes, a Thugs Life from concrete rose, the next time you think about THUG LIFE, don't think life is a game, life ain't no joke, I hope you **Stand Your Ground** when them bullets rain down, keep ya head to the ground when them bullets rain down, don't bite me with a smile bite me with a frown, **R U STILL DOWN? R U STILL DOWN, R U STILL DOWN my nigga?** - **Dawuud's Appeal 2012**

<u>Significance</u> **42 Laws of Maat, Page 367**

Utterances for Coming Forth by day into Light

I named this song after a **Tupac** album, R U Still Down. This album was released on Nov 25th, the day before **King Tut's** tomb was opened (page 11). On this album Tupac can be heard saying: "<u>you can't kill me, **I'm the king**</u>". On the track, **Only Fear of Death**, Tupac say's "Never will I die, **<u>I'll be back, reincarnated</u>** as a mother fuckin' MAC 11". At the time of this rhyme **I had no idea who Tupac was in his pastlife** (pages 664 - 665). This revelation would not come till after I realized my past lives (pages 480, 594). The murder of **Troy Davis** and others like him fueled my anger, this anger I managed to quell by releasing it through my music. My music being the launching pad for the **bleeding** of **my soul** as it began to speak my revelation into existence with lines like this "American built off backs of *<u>Kings **coming back** to haunt you</u>*, the **specter's** hear! they can kill you but they can't kill the revolution **Maat** is here and she wants restitution!". When I edited the video for this song I used pictures of ancient Kemet in it. My **"soul"** knew who **"it"** was but consciously I was none the wiser. While writing this book I realized that **Troy Davis** was sent down (born) on my Grand Mother's birthday (Oct 9, page 22) and the murder he was charged with took place on the day my Grand Father died (August 18, page 169).In ancient Kemet the concept of reincarnation and past lives was called the **Wehem-Mesut** (repeating of births, page 14).

Troy Anthony Davis
(October 9, 1968 – September 21, 2011)

Troy Davis maintained his innocence up to his execution. He was executed by the Georgia State department of corrections for a crime many people believed he did not commit. He was charged with killing an off duty police officer who was working security at a Burger King.

It is he, who comes forth by day into Light

In the 20 years between his conviction and execution, Davis and his defenders secured support from the public, celebrities, and human rights groups. Amnesty International and other groups such as National Association for the Advancement of Colored People took up Davis's cause. Prominent politicians and leaders, including former President Jimmy Carter, Rev. Al Sharpton, Pope Benedict XVI, Archbishop Desmond Tutu, former U.S. Congressman from Georgia and presidential candidate Bob Barr, and former FBI Director and judge William S. Sessions called upon the courts to grant Davis a new trial or evidentiary hearing. In July 2007, September 2008, and October 2008, execution dates were scheduled, but each execution was stayed shortly before it was to take place.

The name Troy Davis would find it's way to a four of my songs after he was murdered. I say his name in the songs **Born 2 Rebel**, page 210. **American Dream'n**, page 214. **R U Still Down**, page 258. And the song, **Halftime**, page 314.

<u>Condolences</u>

My condolences go out to the family of **Troy Davis** and the families of all those who have been robbed of their lives by this system of racism and white supremacy. Please know that death is not the end. The soul survives death, indeed and in spirit. This is a book of the dead written by a boy who was murdered without justice, who defeated death and came forth by day. May the soul of **Troy Davis** walk peacefully through the field of Reeds in Amenta. Amen Ra.

ADDENDUM ~~2013~~ Lost in The Never Ending Story

I misplaced the time frame in which I watched the series **Lost**. It wasn't in 2013! During the revision of this book I found a receipt in my **iTunes** that confirmed my purchase of the 3rd season of **Lost** on **August 31**, 2007. **"Emmett Till's"** disfigured body was found **<u>3 days later</u>** on **August 31,** 1955 (p 508)! It must be understood that if I am who I say I am, being the same reincarnated soul of Emmett Till (page 480), Tutankhaten (page 594), Earl Johnson (pages **23**6, 584) and other lives, then my **coming back** here would be for some divine purpose and because of that the energies that govern life itself would set a stage for me to find myself. This stage would be set in the minds of the creators of novels, movies and songs and throughout my life from childhood to adulthood I gradually gravitated to each book, movie and song etc, at the divine times to help me decipher this Prophecy of Reincarnation (p 602). Watching the series **Lost** did the same thing **Star Wars** did for me as a boy (page 37). It captivated my **imagination**. As a boy I thought I was Luke Skywalker and I thought my father was Darth Vader. You must read what I wrote about 1983 Star Wars to understand this connection but what I felt as a child was right because the character Darth Vader was fashioned after Akhenaten and Luke Sky Walker was fashioned after Tutankhaten (King Tut) (see page 37).

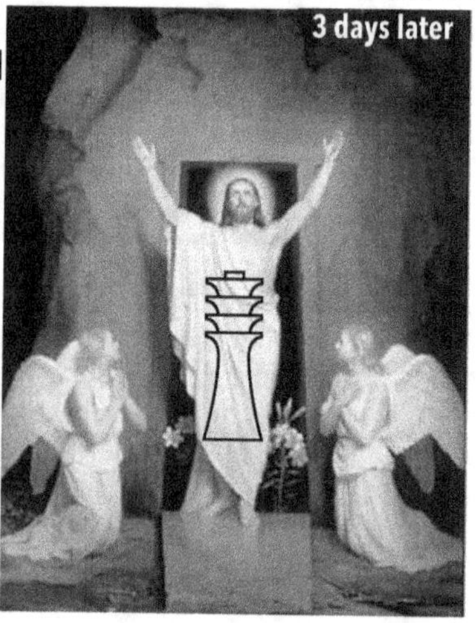

Lost fed my imagination and curiosity but it did so in a similar way that the movie **The Never ending story** did when I was a boy. The Never Ending Story takes place in the attic of a high school and in a fantasy world called **Fantasia** found within the pages of a book. The main character is a boy who skips school after being chased by bullies finding himself in a book store where he steals a book and ends up reading the book in the attic of his high school during a thunder storm. Him being in the attic symbolizes him using his mental capacity and the fact that he's reading about a fantasy world he is engaging with his imagination, and the unseen realms. He is using his brain and his heart seeking the narrow path, like a Buddha. In fact in the movie the character in the book has to prove himself worthy by walking between two giant golden female sphinx's without being struck dead by beams of lightning just like the halls of Maat in ancient kemet (Egypt) where ones soul is measured after death by their heart being weighed on a scale against the feather. This test was called the sixth gate, like how the pineal gland 𓂀 is the sixth chakra. The **pineal** gland being stimulated by the **breath** or plants and fungi (**psychedelics**). The pineal, like the light saber turned on by Luke Sky Walker symbolizing the energy flowing up the spinal cord. In ancient Kemet the **Djed Pillar** 𓊽 represented this same principle. It was called the **spine of Ausar** (Osiris) 𓊽. In ancient Kemetic spiritual systems **Ausar** is the Lord of **resurrection**. The one who returns after death like Jesus. In fact, the story of **Jesus** <u>comes thousands of years after</u> the story of **Ausar** and the story of Jesus is very similar to Ausar. But you are Ausar, the hero! <u>See page 3 for the **hero's journey!**</u>

While reading the book the boy becomes aware that the characters in the book can hear him speaking - **they hear a voice coming from somewhere in the sky**. Like how people hear voices in their heads or like the people in the bible talked to angels and **Moses** talking to the burning bush. Like the **voice** that **came in** my **head** on **July 1st 2018** the day I graduated as a **Kemetic Yoga** Instructor leading me to my first past life revelation of Emmett Till (page 474) . The boy becomes one with **The never ending story**, the book of his life. Gradually I began to experience what seemed like, this world, or God, or something speaking to me through **coincidence** after **coincidence** in almost everything, and in every way possible, trying to get my **aten**tion. On **May 5th of 2015** a book titled **Metu Neter** by **Ra Un Nefer Amen** would speak to me **loud and clear** letting me know that there was something beyond this thing called life and beyond the vision of my two eyes (page 329). **Something could observe me but I had yet to observe it**. Sort of like how you feel the wind but you don't see it. I had to use a different lens to observe this phenomena. And after contemplating my experiences I would often think about the series **Lost**.

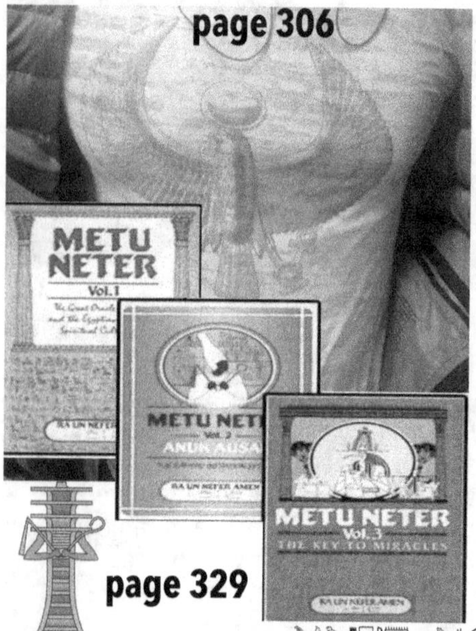

What interested me most about the series **Lost** was all the **coincidences** that seemed to flow together harmoniously. In the series **Lost**, they all got on a same plane, the plane crashed and those that survived the crash were all **"Lost"** on some island just like our souls are **lost** in our bodies. Most of the people who crashed on the island had **<u>crossed paths</u>** with one another before they got on the plane and some of the people happened to be related. The life that I was living began to respond in the same **coincidental** manner as the series **Lost**. Like when I first met **Ron**. We only met in passing on **Nov 1, 2014** because of the **shirt** he was wearing (page 306). His shirt had the image of **Heru** (**Horace**) in his Falcon form (seen in the image to the left) and years later I would **<u>meet him again</u>** just like some of the people in the series **Lost** had **<u>crossed paths</u>** prior to boarding the plane. Heru is the son of **Ausar**, who returns to avenge the death of his "father", like how **Jesus** is the son of "God" who was sent to earth to save the world. **And**, there just so "happened" to be a character named **Horace** (**Heru**) in the series **Lost**. But remember, you are Ausar and you are HERU! See page 3 for the **hero's journey!** In the series **Lost** the character John Locke gave another character **Ayahuasca** to help him lose himself from drug **addiction** (p 476, 482, 493, 523, 626). I would not experience a **psychedelic** until I was 40 years old (p 480). In many episodes of **Lost** the characters make references to having **lived another life**. In one episode a person was complimented on his ability to draw and he responded that he was a artist in a **previous life**. Two different characters met in passing in a football

Rau nu Prt m heru

Iu f Per f m heru

Utterances for Coming Forth by day into Light

It is he, who comes forth by day into Light

stadium years before they found themselves on the island and when they parted ways in the stadium **Desmond** said to **Jack Shepard**, "**see you in another life**". They would meet again on the island, in the jungle and when they parted ways Desmond would say, "**see you in another life**" again and this time Jack remembered him from the stadium and stood there confused.

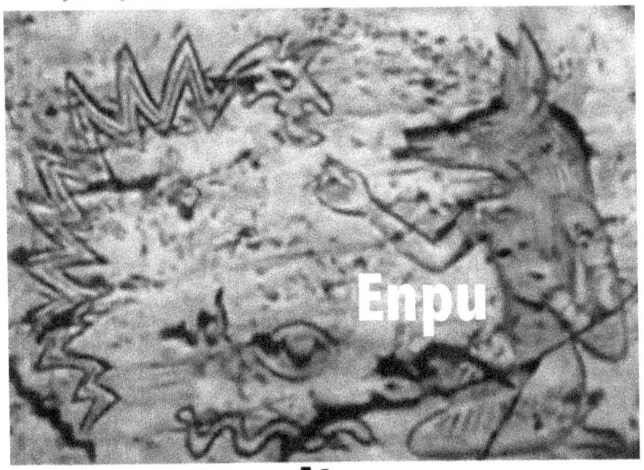

There's more that I could say about the series **Lost** but the most interesting thing is what happened when I came back to the series in 2021 after my past life revelations and even more interesting are the **coincidental** events that led to me watching it again. It was as if the universe handed it to me at divine timing just like it handed me **Octavia Butler** in 2014 (p 298) and **Star Wars** in 1983 (p 37). I would **hear** the **voice** of **DMX** in **my head** on **April 9th 2021** (p 640) which is the same day that **DMX,** the "**Dog**" of Hip Hop passed away. His voice would lead me to a table where I bought the 1st season of **Lost** for **$5** dollars from a brother named **Lani** on 125th street. After watching the series **Lost** again

Aten

I would come to understand the deeper meanings of the series. Especially the fact that the show is based on **Egyptian spirituality** with Jacob representing **Light** (**Ausar**) and his twin brother (**The Man in Black**) representing darkness (**Set**). On the island there was an old Egyptian temple. Inside this temple there was a wall with hieroglyphs (Mdw Ntr) on it. The **raise of Aten** (seen in image on the right), an image of **Enpu** (Anubis, seen in image on the top right) and other hieroglyphs can be seen on the walls. **Enpu** (**Anubis**), is the "**Dog"** headed NTCHR (deity) from Kemet (Egypt). He is the protector of the souls of the dead. On the wall of the temple an image of **Enpu** is seen kneeling in front of a symbol that looks like the **dark electrical cloud of smoke** that is often seen on the island. This mysterious cloud of smoke roams the island and had been responsible for the **death** of most of the people that encountered it. The cloud looked like the dark spheric electrical cloud that I saw above me during **sleep paralysis** on **December 18th 2010** (page 189) and strange enough my dead grandfather would appear to me as a bright glowing spirit on **Dec 18th 2015** (page 348). There was a character on the island who found a wrecked plane in the jungle that had crashed there years ago and in the plane he found the skeletal remains of his dead brother who had crashed there and died. There was also a guy on the island who could **communicate with the dead** but he didn't crash on the island, he teleported there from the future. What was the island? Was it heaven or hell or purgatory? Where were they? Perhaps all those places exist all around us but only some of us are able to perceive or see each plane, or dimension. The next time I saw **Lani** on 125th street he stood **mesmerized**, staring over my shoulder. He told me that he saw Enpu (Anubis) standing over my shoulder guarding me. **Lani** had used **MDMA** and other drugs in the past and this allowed him to see or perceive another plane, or dimension of this reality. The last time I saw Lani was in the summer of 2021 by some **strange coincidence**. I was sitting on a bench on St Nicholas avenue, a few blocks down from where I met **Cosmos** (p 452). Lani just happened to walk by me and I stopped him. He was on his way to an appointment with a doctor at Harlem Hospital. He was going through rough times. He told me that his visions caused his mother to admit him to the psych ward years ago and since then he's been working on getting his life together.. He needed money so I gave him 20 dollars. When ever I pass by 125th street I look for him.

The most profound experience I had with **Lost** was on **June 23, 2021** (page 648). That day I went back to my **childhood home** and took a picture of it, then went home and watched the 5th episode of the last season of **Lost** and the main character Jack "**Shepard**" goes to a **lighthouse** on the island and sees an image of his **childhood home** in a **mirror**. The jack of all trades is a master of none but more often times the jack of all trades is better than the master of one. Jack "Shepard" like the "Shepard staff" that the pharaoh carries in his left hand. That same day I would **cross paths** with two **left handed** brothers while riding to the **ferry** with my brother Matthew who is also a **lefty** like myself (p 648). None of these things are random **coincidences**, they are **coinciding angles** connected by seen and unseen forces most commonly referred to as **angels** or God. One time is an incidence, twice is a coincidence, but three, four, five is a pattern but can you tell the difference? The following year I would have another confirmation with **Keith Brown** after my first trip to Far Rockaway in 2022 (p 648).

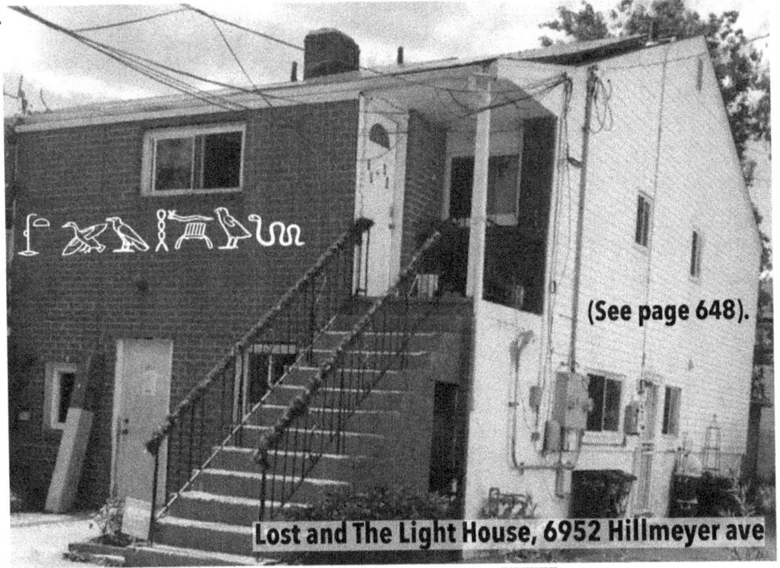

Lost and The Light House, 6952 Hillmeyer ave

Queen Tiye

2013 - The Year Of The Snake

This is the year the NTCHRU would come for me. I had been born in the year of the **snake** in this life and a few of my other pervious lives. Snakes represent **immortality** with the shedding of their skin symbolizing continuous renewal. While compiling this book I had to search through my computer, my phones, and e-mails for music, and pictures to mirror my journey. While doing this I noticed many patterns. This picture of **Queen Tiye** was found downloaded on my computer in 2013 as well as many other pictures from the 18th Dynasty of Kemet. At the time I knew very little about Tutankhaten (King Tut) and I did not know that **Queen Tiye** was "his" Grandmother. She was the Royal Wife of Amenhotep III. She is also the real person that the biblical character **Queen Sheba** was fashion after (p 7 and 389). This year I would say her name for the first time in my music, in the song **Peace Maat** (as seen below). AmenHotep III, was my ancient grandfather. He was known as the **Dazzling Sun** and AmenHotep the Magnificent. He was a family man like his son Amenhotep IV, building statues depicting his wife Queen Tiye the same size as him. His greatest achievement was his ability to rule for around 40 years without war, as he honored the principles of **Maat** (see page 367) and practiced excellent diplomacy. This allowed kemet to reach the peak of its artistic and international power leading to a period of unparalleled prosperity and opulence. **AmenHotep III** is the real person that the biblical character **King Solomon** was fashion after.

January 4th 2013 Peace Maat (1st of 10)

The **B**asic **I**nstructions **B**efore **L**eaving **E**arth, when the **Bible** was written it made Black people cursed, shoot a nigga kill a nigga put him in the earth, the first shall be last and the last shall be first, I ain't say it, the book said it and I give them credit, it's very poetic but sometimes I wonder if you read it? they say the sun died so you could live and it's true, the earth was a sun too, you study **Sun Zu**, I study the **Neteru**, the vitamin the mineral you gotta learn the inner you, you're too linear don't let your enemy enter your mind, they teach you not to eat swine, but they don't teach you how to logically critically use your mind, this is all a design, a very good trick, yet you are the God but you so sick, that you cant see what I can see, peace and unity or it's death for you and me, you're blind sun, blind to the facts, peace and unity or it's death for you and me....

Don't eat from the tree of knowledge without knowledge of self, what if you had a wealth of health? **Moringa**, **kelp,** but shame on a brother if he smoke herb, I do 50 in the crib that's my word, I say fuck the law political herbs, and there will never be peace until you get bold, you will never be free until you see the whole, Behold, the mind the body the seat of the soul, The worst slavery of all is mind control, you gotta eat like you trying to feed your soul, did you know dis ease is an ease that we control? But we meet death eating flesh with GMO's! what if we regressed and didn't know? Open your eyes realize the **magic** show, Imagine just how deep the rabbit goes, maybe for eons, one **Neo,** the spelling of words cast **spells** on the people, a brother trying to live but all I see is evil, meditate levitate let the chi lead you, no escape from the world cause the world needs you, It's true, there's a force surrounding all of you, your heart and mind the strongest part of you, you gotta shine like the star that started you, it's time, peace and unity or it's death for you and me, You're blind sun, blind to the facts, peace and unity or it's death for you and me

I used to see the cuties and only see the **booties,** but now I see their beauty and now I know my duty, I been around the world, seen a lot of girls, did a lot wrong now I'm out of the storm, but when you change, some people always see you the same, but they lame and they don't know no better, don't waste your time trying to be a go getter, be a go giver it will feel much better, like the **Nile River** giving hidden treasure, remember **Queen Tiye** and the **MDW NTCHR,** remember me B, a Queens G, we fall down but we give up never, The **Blakseed** look for me in the whirlwind, The **Blakseed** look for me when the world end, you ain't got a lot of time to waste my friend, ever second every minute never coming again, you gotta let your light shine, bright like them, stars in the sky, you gotta try man, we all stars homie and all stars die, but why we gotta die by the hands of a gun?! why lil kids can't play and run?! **Ma'at Amen Ra** we ain't done! out of chaos comes order we are all one, human beings come before your religion, See the **sun** giving life to everyone and everything, You want peace?! you better take it! fuck a **dream!** see the **sun** giving life to everyone and everything **- Dawuud's Appeal**

Significance

I started this verse with thoughts of **Killah Priest's** song **B.I.B.L.E.** I can't count the amount of times I listened to that song but it was on heavy rotation when I was in college (page 74). I knew it word for word. When I finished the first verse of this song I can remember liking it a lot and thinking - "I really could be a rapper". At the time I felt it was my best rhyme. When I read the first verse now I realize that my soul was talking to me when "I" said, "this is all a design, a very good trick, yet *you are the God* but you so sick, that you cant see what I can see, peace and unity or it's death for you and me, you're **blind** sun, **blind** to the facts". When I wrote this song I had no idea that I was on a **blind** initiation, going through a spiritual detox. In this song I would also say the name **Queen Tiye** (p 7 and 389), for the first time. **42 Laws of Maat, Page 367**

2013 THE YEAR OF THE SNAKE

Bobby H**emmit** would become my favorite occult lecturer to listen to. I listened to as much of him as I could find and I preferred the long videos as I could absorb more streams of thought that way. It wasn't until a year after I knew that I was Emmett that I would come to realize that Emmett's nickname was **Bobo**. **Bobby** H**emmit** was sent to this planet for all of us however he had a star code in his name connected to this prophecy. He had a specific mission aimed at awakening my soul fragments of the boy king, Tutankhaten. This would prove to be a hard task because Bobby knew not of this mission and nor did I. The success of his mission would henge on not only Bobby and me, but on many other peoples actions as well. In fact you could say that nature itself was helping me on way. Countless events happening at divine times in the past, present and off in the distant and near future all having important roles to play, like the intersecting points on the web of a spider. like Peter (**Ptah**) **Park**er the Spiderman or Wheeler **Park**er, Emmett Till's Cousin, or like Juanita P**ark**er, my Grand Mother. I lived in Queens with my Grand mother Mrs Parker just like spider man (Peter/Ptah Parker) lived with his Aunt.. And when my Grand Father died it sp**ARK**ed my ***transformation*** just like the murder of Peter's Uncle sp**ARK**ed his. Even the Hip Hop music I was attracted to as a teenager was laced with my prophecy. Take for instance the verse below.

Rau
nu
Prt
m
heru

"it's sort of like the story of superman, how world destroy, so now we're here on this land, with no super human powers, only my six sense and visions after hours, I see psychics and Gypsies I can't afford, and swamis for predictions on the Ouija board, the triangular magic game, to get insight on my planet and real name, I live in Flatbush with my aunty **Em**, like Peter P**ark**er, I keep my secret from the rest of them" - ***Phantasm the lyrical emperor (Cella Dwellas, page 65)***

Iu
f
Per
f
m
heru

The word Emmett means TRUTH! The word **Emit** means to send forth. My soul was sent forth across the far distances of space and time after my Opening of The Mouth Ceremony 3000 plus years ago. **Bo**bby H**emmit** was sent down (born) on **November 28th** two days after Tutankhaten's tomb was opened on **November 26th** 1922 (page 11). On July 3rd 2018 (page 480) my past life of Emmett Till would be revealed to me and on April 4th 2020 my past life as Tutankhaten (King Tut's) would be revealed to me (page 594). The Word **Hemmit** in ancient MDW NTR (hieroglyphs) means - (a well of water, wife or women). So the ancient Afrikans of the Hapi Eteru (Nile River) valley equated a woman to the importance of a well of water. Everyone needs water and we refer to smart people as being "a well of water", or "a great source of knowledge". If you take the letter **H** off of the name H**emmit** you have the word **Emmit**, like **Emmett**. Emmett's nickname was **Bobo**, like **Bobby Emmett**. The word **Till** means: a cash register or drawer for **money** in a store, bank, or restaurant. Emmett was lynched in **Money** Mississippi as a result of what happen in THEIR store! The word **Till** also means to **Cultivate**. The story of **Jesus** is another telling of the story of **Ausar** (**Osiris**) and Osiris was the first to **cultivate** the land (page 481). In the word M**ississ**ippi you can see the name **Isis** (Auset) who is the **mother** of **Heru** (**Horus**, **Zeus**, **Jesus**) the one who **resurrects** after death. **Isis** is the great royal **wife** of **Ausar** (**Osiris**), known as the Lord of **resurrection,** the Lord of the **West,** the Lord of the dead and the underworld. In ancient Kemet the concept of reincarnation and past lives was called the **Wehem-Mesut** (repeating of births, page 14). Imagine if "Emmett" had a black owned store to buy is gum from (page 506)! Buy from your kind first, and second. Let buying outside of your kind be your last resort. We can rebuild our nation! We will rebuild our nation! At this very moment, in the hearts and minds of those reading this book, our nation is being built. You are actively taking a part in it. Let this book be a guide to help you read the signs, giving rise to the ancient meaning of "**Man Know Thyself**" (page 283).

Utterances
for
Coming
Forth
by day
into
Light

The world is old but the future springs from the past

As I said above Bobby Hemmit was sent to this planet with astrological star codes for us all however his main target was to find The Boy King. No different than me and my prophetic music. With my lyrics written from my heart and soul I was able to write my past in the present and foresee the future. Like my lyrics from my song **Red Pills**, written on **March 14th 2016,** "The world is old but the future springs from the past, **I came back from the future** and yeah we free at last, but if you don't listen to what I'm spitting we're gonna crash, **I was given a mission to find the other half of a staff stolen**" (page 369). The name of the song was **Red Pills**. Like the **blue** or the **red pill** that morpheus offers YOU* in the movie the **Matrix**. The **blue pill** meaning, stay asleep and enjoy your **bliss** while you unknowingly walk off a cliff, as your soul is recycled like a disk into a new body, in a new life while you are non the wiser to the fact that you have lived here before. Or you can take the **Red** pill and see **reality** as it really is, seeing the world and it's many layers of vibrations and manipulations. Then you can decide how far down the hole you wanna go. I listened to hours of lectures from **Bobby** H**emmit, Dr Phil Valentine**, **Dr** Cl**ark**e, **Dr Charles Finch**, **Jewel Pookrum**, **Dr Ben**, **Ashra Kwesi**, **Anthony Browder** and the list goes on. I bought books and read some. I ate better, listened to debates, I weighed my actions against the feather, daily. I was hard on myself. I kept exercising. I also kept trying to be better. I kept arguing against what I knew was wrong. I felt alone. I lost many of my friends along the way but I was used to doing things alone. Most of my long runs I ran alone. Just me and Hip Hop in my ear. I do miss having my old friends though.

It is
he,
who
comes
forth
by day
into
Light

January 11th 2013 - Kendrick Johnson

On January 11th 2013, the body of Kendrick Johnson was discovered inside a vertical rolled-up mat in the gymnasium of Lowndes High School in Valdosta, in the U.S. state of Georgia, where he was a student. A preliminary investigation and autopsy concluded that his death was accidental. An autopsy conducted by the Georgia Bureau of Investigation concluded that Johnson died of asphyxiation. But a private autopsy requested by the family found that the teen died of "non-accidental" blunt force trauma to his neck, leading them to believe foul play was involved and his body was found with no organs inside.. Race became an issue in the case. Johnson is Black while two of the teens his family accused in the lawsuit, brothers Branden and Brian Bell, are white. They each provided alibis, saying they were not near the gym where Kendrick Johnson was found. Neither of them were ever charged with a crime. The lawsuit claimed the matter was covered up by Lowndes County Superintendent of Schools Wes Taylor and then-Sheriff Chris Prine, acting at the wishes of the Bells' father, former FBI agent Rick Bell.Kendrick's case would open my mind up to organ harvesting in America and I would write about it in my music.

__Condolences__

My condolences go out to the family of Kendrick Johnson and all those who have been robbed of their lives by this system of racism and white supremacy. Please know that death is not the end. The soul survives death, indeed and in spirit. This is a book of the dead written by a boy who was murdered without justice, who defeated death and came forth by day. May the soul of **Kendrick Johnson** walk peacefully through the field of Reeds in Amenta. Amen Ra.

April 11th 2015 (page 324)
From Superman To Man

"the man of steel revealed to be a mankind of a clone, anythings possible, too hospitable with chromosomes, ***__she went missing found dead with her organs gone__***, will you listen now to me on the really? or de Nile like blacks didn't build The Nile Valley?! will you rally for **Walter Scott** shot at 50?! Boycott till they stop terrorizing the block? or will you chill and watch Love And Hip Hop like it's not your problem?" **- Dawud The Uncanny BlaKseed**

June 11th 2015 (page 334)
Kalief Browder

"If I Ruled The World everyone would be taught the **1 6 1 8** curl, and understand how and when men fell, not blaming it on the girl, the truth it will propel man from his hell, it's the hue in man from the gland that prevails, they be shoot'n man ***__organs be for sale__***, stuck in a race doing laps as time elapse perhaps love will fill the cracks for blacks on my block" **- Dawud The Amazing BlaKseed**

January 15th 2017 (page 441)
Cancer

"I felt like a failure when my **Grand Father** died, he could have survived if I had opened my eyes researched the **Medical Apartheid,** I cried for days for years, we gotta face our fears, make haste to a place of cheer, a place that cares, that place not here! they only tare us down, recycle our **organs** put us in the ground! how that sound? hard to believe but real! if you don't read and study you'll be diseased and ill, with medical **bills** to pay they feed you **pills** that's no way to live, they ain't got the answer's **Sway" - Dawud The Uncanny BlaKseed**

March 23rd 2017
Nefertari keep ya head up (page 445)

"Your religion is not the reason they bring you harm, It's your organs that they farm like a tax, **Henrietta Lacks,** This life ain't fair, *__there's a war going on outside__* no one is safe here, We're being attacked but you're more relaxed than your hair! *__I give a holler to my sisters on welfare, **Dawud cares** if don't nobody else care"__* **- Dawud The Uncanny BlaKseed**

April 29th 2015 (page 328)
2000 Seasons

"I got *__99 problems__* but a heart ain't one, ***__they killed her son with a gun and sold his young organs__***, we on the run cause it's open season, but think what's the reason? they want us gone we ain't leaving, I wrote this when I was grieving, our bloods' in the land go and count them grains of sand, that's how long we been here" ***- Dawud The Uncanny BlaKseed***

March 31st 2016 (page 373)
Superfluous

"We may not yet be numerous but we form a strong nucleus, and everybody needs one, **like the liver, I'm not your superfluous organ giver, they pick a nigga pull the trigger then they deliver the heart or the spleen, know what I mean**? It's donation when it's taken via operation, The younger the better so cops be chase'n, you'll never find your dream in this nightmare we face'n" **- Dawud The Amazing BlaKseed**

March 3rd 2017 (page 444)
Get Out

"when I die, I fly in the whirlwind like a **Falcon** with **Malcolm,** blasting my album in **Thugs Mansion** no doubt son, **Get Out** son, American nightmare the outcome, a burning house, your organs, wake up without them! you heard about **Kendrick** Lamar! well, tell me bout **Johnson!** I'm ready to unite tonight mother fuck m**arch**'n" **- Dawud The Uncanny BlaKseed**"

March 25th 2017 (page 445)
Taken

"Imagine being locked behind a door, kidnapped, trapped, taken! American nightmare Jason, **Get Out!** Chasing Trayvon Martin, **organs taken**, Orphans, Masons, Preachers breaking laws you put faith in, they care more about the teachers than they do for the children, anything to stop poor people from building" **- Dawud The Uncanny BlaKseed**

February 3rd 2013 - Chris Dorner
When You Die How Long Will They Mourn Ya?

Rau nu Prt m heru

Christopher Jordan Dorner was a Police officer of the Los Angeles Police Department who was the first high profile shooter to be executed by police before standing trial. He was born on June 4th 1979 and he was executed on February 12th 2013 the year of the **snake.** On my **mothers birthday**, February 3rd 2013, and the days following it was reported on all streams of media that there was a manhunt for a **black man** who had committed a series of shootings in Orange County, Los Angeles County, Riverside County and San Bernardino County, California. The media claimed that Dorner, an ex military man and a Los Angeles police officer had killed other officers. When I heard the news I immediately found it suspicious. Perhaps my feelings about the system caused me to question the story given by the media. I wasn't so quick to turn my back on Dorner without hearing the full story. The hunt for Dorner was like something out of a Rambo movie. The cops even shot at and hit an innocent woman because she was in a vehicle that looked like Dorner's. They really wanted him dead! But why? Why didn't he get the chance to stand trial? Did Dorner have something to say? **Some say that Dorner was a hero**. That he was speaking out against the corrupt police system. They released a manifesto claiming that Dorner wrote but I never read it because I didn't trust anything the media was going to show me. Dorner was killed on February 12th in a cabin in the woods like a scene from a **Rambo** or **Terminator** movie with Helicopters, bombs and hundreds of rounds of gun fire. In the end they say he burned to death in the cabin fire. But no proof of a body was ever shown to the public. Sometimes I wonder if brother Dorner is dead, for his sake, I hope that he is. Around five days before Dorner supposedly died his wallet was supposedly found in a field in lindbergh however after all was said and done they claimed Dorner's wallet was found in the rubble of the burnt out cabin. Similar to how the passports of the men that supposedly hijacked the planes that crashed into the Twin Towers were found in the debris of the burnt Twin Tower wreckage (page 99).

Iu f Per f m heru

Condolences

My condolences go out to the family and friends of **Chris Dorner** and all those who have been robbed of their life by this system of racism and white supremacy. Please know that death is not the end. The soul survives death, indeed and in spirit. This is a book of the dead written by a boy who was murdered without justice, who defeated death and came forth by day. May the soul of **Chris Dorner** walk peacefully through the field of Reeds in Amenta. Amen Ra.

What Did Dorner Have To Say?

Utterances for Coming Forth by day into Light

Dorner was the first high profile shooter to be executed by police before standing trial and for many people that seemed odd. Why did they kill Dorner? Why didn't he get the chance to stand trial like white men who kill large groups of people? At 10:10 am on January 8th 2011, Jared Lee Loughner, a white man, opened fire at a constituents meeting killing six people including **U.S. District Court Judge John Roll**, and injuring 13 others including **U.S. Representative Gabby Giffords** who was shot in the head and critically injured. Loughner was taken in alive. He was not murdered like a **Terminator** movie. On October 12th 2011, a mass shooting occurred at the Salon Meritage hair salon in Seal Beach, California. Eight people inside the salon and one person in the parking lot were shot, and only one victim survived. It was the deadliest mass killing in Orange County history. In the end a **White man** by the name of **Scott dekrari** was taken in alive. He was not murdered like a **Rambo** movie. On July 12th 2012 **James Eagan Holmes**, a **White man** went on a mass murdering spree in Aurora, killing 12 people and injured 70 others at a Century 16 movie theater. He was not murdered like a **Terminator** movie. On June 17th 2015 **dylan roof,** a **White man** entered Emanuel African Methodist Episcopal Church through a side door at 8:16 pm. He pretended to be a peaceful participant of the bible study. Then at around 9pm he opened fire with a Glock 41 .45-caliber handgun killing 9 people in total. He was taken in alive not murdered like a **Rambo** movie. On May 14th 2022 Payton S. Gendron, a **White man** murdered 10 black people in Buffalo New York (The Buffalo Massacre). He was taken in alive not murdered like a **Terminator** movie. **Aaron** Salter was the 55 year old ex-cop supermarket security guard who was killed in the Buffalo Massacre. Inspired by rising gas prices, **Aaron** had recently spoken about a "newly discovered energy source" and had patented a system that enables vehicles to run on water instead of gasoline, called hydrogen-electrolysis. Some say that the massacre was an organized assassination of Aaron so as to suppress technology that would threaten the oil and automotive industries. But why did they kill Dorner? Why didn't he get the chance to stand trial? Some might say that I'm a conspiracy theorist because... "I kick the truth to the young black youth. Because of this they get mad at me. But are they mad at me because I'm Malcolm X with the strategy?! Hopefully they don't Martin me on the balcony! But I have no fear when it's my time I'm out of here! So much I care, a lot of tears, *I See Death Around The Corner,* am I next like Chris Dorner?! but I put a hex on em! I got these spirits in my corner!! **When you die How Long Will They Mourn Ya**?!" (pages 360 and 368).

It is he, who comes forth by day into Light

Here Comes The Judge of Gods Law
S.H.I.T.
HAPPENS
The
Chronicles

I had been dealing with a sweet tooth and was craving a slice of the lemon cake from a local coffee shop. I fell for the craving and made my way to the coffee shop. As I was on my way I remember hoping that the shop was closed because I knew I didn't need the sugar from the lemon cake. As I arrive I saw that it was indeed closed, however there was a guy standing in front of the shop handing out flyers. I usually don't take flyers but for some reason I felt like I should take his and I did. I grabbed it and read it. It said "Shit Happens". I laughed then we exchanged a few words, then I walked off. I was headed across the street to the Duane Reade store to see what sweets they might have there. As I got to the corner he asked me what my **zodiac sign** was. When I first registered the question I didn't receive it well because the man had the mannerisms of a **homosexual** and I thought he was coming on to me. At this time in my life I had not studied astrology and didn't have an in-depth understanding of how someone could tell a persons zodiac sign just by talking to them. Just before I crossed the street I turned around and asked him, "what sign do you think I am". He responded, **"scorpio",** and that got my ATENtion! I walked back over to him and we started to talk more. I remember that it was February, because he reminded me that **the year of the snake** was coming in a few days and I was born in **the year of the snake**. We walked to the Dunkin' Donuts on the corner where we talked for over an hour and I let him hear some of my music. He had a few **books** with him, **Sextrology - The Astrology of Sex**, The Definitive book of **Chinese Astrology** and a few others that I don't recall. At the end of our discussion he pulled out a **contract** and wanted me to sign it but I of course I refused to. I was not looking for a record deal. Instead I wrote down the books he had and purchased a few of them.

Confirmations

During our discussion he told me about celebrities in the music industry that **groomed** young men for **homosexuality**. I will not mention any names how ever I will say that years later, in 2017, I ran into one of the rappers he named. I ran into him at the juice bar, Branson Got Juice in Harlem. I had just recorded the song **BlaK Wall Street**, for the **Maat Magik** album (page 447). I took my head phones off and told him to listen. He was on a call and told me his son is an A&R and I should let him listen to it. His son put my headphones on. He started listening. He looked at me and ask me if this was me rapping. I smiled and said yes. He bobbed his head, and listened to the whole song which is 4 minutes and 52 seconds long. Afterwards he asked me if I read a lot of books? I smiled again and said - yes I read books. Then he asked me how old I was. I told him to guess. He said 25, 28.? I laughed again and said, no I'm old enough to be your father. He followed my Instagram then he unfollowed it. It was interesting to meet the son of one of the founders of Hip Hop. He was also into music but had no talent. Don't ever ask me who the person is because I won't tell you. This book is not about exposing anyone but myself and this system of racism that must come to an end! The Golden age is upon us! Are you ready? **42 Laws of Maat, Page 367**

Books Books and more Books School, Lectures, books and fitness

I was training clients, and attending classes in Massage school. I took the money from my Army G.I. Bill (page 218) that I received for going to school and I began to collect books. I would hear a lecture on Youtube from people like Bobby Hemmit (page 262) and they would suggest specific books. I would buy the book and sometimes other books related to the subject. I was particularly drawn to documentaries about ancient Kemet (Egypt). I was smoking a lot of weed during this time in my life but I was also exercising a lot as well and researching **healthy foods** and **herbs** like **spirulina**, **moringa** and such. On 125th street, across the street from the **Apollo** was another place where I purchased books often. That's where I met brother Nova, Mfundishi Jhutyms, Brother Willie, Brother Seku, The Pillars and more. Apollo is the Greek Equivalent to **Heru**. Ausar returns (resurrects) through his son Heru (Horus) as **Ra** in the Ausarian **resurrection drama.** I only wrote 11 rhymes in 2013 **but every last one of them are connected to this prophecy of reincarnation**. Above my desk I always kept pictures of ancestors, family and friends, some of which can be seen in earlier pages of this book. **Remember that you are Ausar and Heru, the hero!** See page 3 for the **hero's journey**!

Rau nu Prt m heru

Dawud Eddings
Prof. Andrianova
BMCC English 101-081

ESSAY 1. Why I Write

Some may say that the roles of language, writing, and communication in our lives have no effect on our everyday lives but I disagree. All forms of communication affect our everyday lives whether we are watching a movie or listening to a presidential debate. People write for many reasons but what kind of writer are you? Do you write with the moving tide of society or are you strong enough to face it? For some people writing is merely leisure while for others it represents life or death. In the essay "Why I Write", George Orwell addresses his trials of writing and also his reasons for writing. Using a few quotes from Orwell's essay I will explain how I relate to them individually, academically and philosophically. If you have previously overlooked the power of communication you may develop a new way of decoding what you see and hear after reading my essay.

Why I Write is an essay that resonates with me deeply because of the author's passion for justice and his overall reason for writing. He makes it clear that he writes with the weight of the world on his shoulders. Orwell's does not view writing as joyful pleasure, in his own words he see's it as, "a horrible struggle, like a long bout of some painful illness". I would call it a beautiful struggle because anyone who is trying to bring about peace in this world that we live in is a part of a greater struggle, a beautiful struggle. In my opinion the most significant lines in the essay are,

Iu f Per f m heru

"What I have most wanted to do in the last 10 years is to make political writing into an art. My starting point is always a feeling of partisanship, a sense of injustice. When I sit down to write a book, I do not say to myself, 'I am going to produce a piece of art'. I write it because there is some lie that I want to expose, some fact to which I want to draw attention to, and my initial concern is to get a hearing'." (¶9).

This quote brings many thoughts to my mind. The first things I think of are my own poems. I write poems and create music as a hobby and I always feel the need to speak for the people who have no voice or to situations of great importance that are not addressed nationally or globally. My need to do this has everything to do with the world that we live in and my relationship to the world I live in. Just as Orwell's lived through trying times, we are living in trying times. As a descendant of Africans who built pyramids in Nubia before moving north to build pyramids in Egypt, I write to honor the glory that Africans once had and will have again one day soon. Here are a few lines from my latest poem entitled - PEACE,

Utterances for Coming Forth by day into Light

"There will never be peace until you get bold. You will never be free until you see the whole. Behold the mind, the body, the seat of the soul. The worst slavery of all is mind control. You have to eat like you're trying to feed your soul. Did you know dis-ease is an ease that we control? But **we 'Meat' death eating flesh with GMO's**. What if we've regressed and didn't know? Open your eyes and realize the magic show. Imagine just how deep the rabbit goes. Maybe for 'eon's, 'one', 'neo'. The spelling of words cast spells on the people. I'm just trying to 'live' but all I see is 'evil'. Meditate, levitate let the chi lead you. No escape from the world because the world needs you. It's true! There's a force surrounding all of you. Your hearts and minds, the strongest parts of you, you gotta shine like the star that started you. It's time.... Peace."

As I stated earlier all forms of communication affect our everyday lives whether we are watching a movie or listening to a presidential debate. Unfortunately sometimes these platforms for communication are used to deceive us. Most of the people reading this have seen the movie The **Matrix** with Keanu reeves as Neo and Laurence Fishburne as Morpheus. And most people loved the movie. If you have not yet seen it I suggest you watch it. Some may think the Matrix is merely a sci-fi movie about humans verse machines. In fact however the movie is more complex than you may think. Many people may not know that a black woman named Sophia Stewart wrote the movie not the men who got credit for it. In the early 80's Stewart had black revolution on mind when she wrote the screenplay, however Larry and Andy Wachowski stole the screenplay from her. Very much like the knowledge of the ancient mystery schools of Africa were stolen to create this country we live in. Just look on the back of the one-dollar bill and you will see a pyramid built by Africans. Just as Orwell's said, every writer has his or her motives. It gives me great comfort to know that I am not alone in my need to draw attention to lies and deception. People write for many reasons but what kind of writer are you?

It is he, who comes forth by day into Light

2031
THE END

BIBLIOGRAPHY

- "They say / I say": The moves that matter in academic writing, Gerald Graff and Cathy Birkinstein, ISBN: 978-0-393-93361-1, 2010
- Why I Write, George Orwell, 1946
- The Matrix Movie, Sophia Stewart 1999

Professor Andrianova was a White woman who did not like me. This was my first essay assignment for her class and she did not like the fact that all my writings were focused on the black struggle or this corrupt government. She was always asking me to explain my writing. She was so desperate to correct something that she even tried to correct the date **2031** that I placed at the end. With a smile I told her that this essay was about the writings of George Orwell and he wrote the book 1984 in 1948. Afterwards she felt stupid.

February 26th 2013 The BlaKseed Osiris

I be The BlaKseed **Osiris,** see sun **set**, looking for **Auset Isis,** Black duality crisis, born in this White man's world to civilize it, when I think about a **king** I be thinking bout **Akhenaten,** you are not forgotten, P.O.W M.I.A, my brother **Mumia,** yeah he's still locked away, New Orleans, they did the same shit in Rockaway, they sell your dreams, a world full of Philistines, I'm just a brother from Queens, I'm just a brother that seen, so many different type of things, my nigga, but, I ain't seen freedom ring my nigga, I seen tell lie vision, condition brothers for the prison, division, **Malcolm X** would still be living, If we would do the math, but we been hood winked, and y'all mother fuckers don't know the half, cause you glad to be eaten your chicken your beef and your sirloin, we need to leave the animals alone, and tell the people the truth, somebody gotta show em, this is all love, what a beautiful poem, do not obey make way for a better day we gotta show em, babies we gotta grow em, feed em the life that's living, maybe this all was different, maybe we ate plants, maybe that made a difference, maybe the fall of man started with the stolen land, it starts when you start loving man more than the woman, **It's a war written in the sand**, I can hear em saying, click click in the night, heard the heart sp**ark** the revolution late at night, heard em saying click click click click in the night, **Nat Turner** with a burner saying fuck this life, **Tina Turner** with a burner click click in the night **- Dawuud's Appeal**

Addendum **Significance**

This was written the same day the last room in King Tut's tomb was opened (p 11). In this song I mentioned the names **Osiris**, **Auset**, **Isis**, **Set** and **Akhenaten** for the first time. But I also mention **Tina Turner's** name for the first and only time in this book. In **1977**, The Year Of The Snake, the same year I was born, **Tina Turner** had **a spine-tingling experience** that attracted her to ancient Kemet (Egypt) and caused her to believe in reincarnation. She also saw a **psychic** that year who told her she was the Pharaoh **Hatshepsut** in a past life. **Was she Hatshepsut** in a **past life**? I don't know but what I do know is; exactly one month after I mentioned her name, I would then mention **Hatshepsut's** name for the first time in this book (p 278)… Tina was born on November 26, the same day **King Tut's** tomb was opened (p 11). And she died on **May 24**, the day before the first star code, **May 25** (pages, 30, 40, 104, 222, 512).

March 9th 2013 2031

In the year 2031 the human population is one, cause the wicked they won, it's all fair in love and war, life ain't now fairytale son, the moon mars and stars revolve in rotation, like the rise and fall of nations, **6 6 6** they flipped the **hieroglyphs** and destroyed the melanation, before that they put it in animation, controlled the imagination, **I came back** on this track to raise the vibration, I pour the libation, *his heart was racing the man was chasing, he was facing his termination but you don't listen, you just turn the station! would they feel me if I wrote it in brail* ? would they kill me or just throw me in jail? would you see your silence as betrayal? all's well that ends well, well they ordered the slaughter of infidels, infants and anyone with Intel, frankincense for the smell in the story I tell, reality is wrong **dreams** are real, life is a gift and a curse like the purse on the hip of a dead witch in a hearse, would you take it or bury it in the earth? the thirst for the hidden, written in stone, **the birth of the risen heir to the throne,** cause the cataclysm division, destroying homes breaking bones, mission top secret destination unknown, life is a struggle be strong you're never alone, it's ok to cry, ever seen a **caterpillar** try try before she **butterfly**? If eye be single **pineal** tingle said master **Yoda** to the evil **Jedi,** fly higher than eagle like **Heru** flew the **millennium Falcon,** he planted black seeds to feed when disease and the drought come, and when the drought came, the savages started dancing and shouting and then it rained, **then he reigned** and then remained the Blakseed, giving blacks what they need, the Blakseed, he remained the Blakseed giving blacks what they need, the Blakseed, plant the Blakseeds in the earth, plant the Blakseeds in the earth **- Dawuud's Appeal**

March 22nd 2013 (Godfrey digitizes my Saqqara Logo)

I was on my path towards **Maat** and the **Saqqara** Step Pyramid (page 670) was my first official **Kemetic** (Egyptian) inspired Logo. The Saqqara pyramid was built by the master builder **Imhotep**. It was built with 6 levels, one on top of the other. When I chose the Saqqara Pyramid as my logo I did not know that the 1st level represented **Earth**, the 2nd represented **Water**, the 3rd represented **Fire**, the 4th represented **Air**, the 5th represented **Ether** and the last represented the **Cosmic Mind**. Not knowing this, I placed the words, **1 goal**, **1 people**, **1 village**, **1 step at a time,** on each layer of the step pyramid. Soon after I would start going by the name **General Maat** in honor of my Grand Father **General** Dukes Jr and my path towards **Maat** (42 Laws of Maat, P 367). UTBC was an acronym which meant, **U T**OUGH **B**OOT**C**AMP. U TOUGH was an acronym which meant, **U T**rain **O**r **U G**o **H**ome. I was making healthy changes in my life and I encouraged these changes in the lives of my family, friends and the clients I came across in my group classes and my 1 on 1 personal training. In April of 2022 I went to Kemet (Egypt) and when I stepped on the Saqqara pyramid I got a profound feeling of **Deja Vu** (p 670), like I had been there before.

- THE -
UTBC
PARADIGM
1 GOAL
1 PEOPLE
1 VILLAGE
1 STEP AT A TIME
A holistic approach to health & wellness.

Rau nu Prt m heru

March 27th 2013 **Year of the Snake**

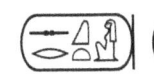

It's **the year of the snake** stakes are high, Every day is a day that you can die, but every day is a day that you could fly, When I say fly? what does that mean to you? is it the way you look or something you do? ***When you die do you come back? sign another contract?*** *run another lap? What about the little ones who die so young?* ***Peace to the Gods when they come back, I signed another contract to be here and so did you!*** *you are not aware,* I see dead people, you do not see clear, I hope you have ears to hear, open your first eye, where is your halo? I'm searching for mine, eating green, you gotta stay clean, I'm a be iron like lion if you know what I mean, if I was **MJ** I would **Scream**, don't get caught chasing this American **dream,** when I was in school I broke rules and always seen the dean, even back then I knew things wasn't what they seem, young Black Male trapped in Far Rockaway Queens, I had a **dream,** I took a walk through **The Valley Of The Kings** and **King Tut** told me to scream **Scorpion King!** that's my word, he said **Scorpion King,** that's your name Blakseed you the **Scorpion King, Hatshepsut** look look, the **Scorpion King** look look, **- Dawuud's Appeal**

(**See page 2, Scorpion King**)

Iu f Per f m heru

2013 One Shot

Here I am with my brother **One Shot** standing next to the statue of Fredrick Douglass on 110th and Fredrick Douglass. At the time he was teaching me how to train groups of people in boxing by running my clients through boxing drills. One Shot and I met in 2005 when I started training at Bally's in Brooklyn but it wasn't until 2013 that we realized we had both attended college together in 1996 at Suny Canton (page 73). This was a **coincidence** that I found **strange** but I never thought too much about it. I had not yet began to put the **patterns** together but they were indeed playing out all around me. Ask yourself what pattern might be forming around you that you're not paying **Aten**tion to......?

2013 Art Class BMCC

We were instructed to go to the MET museum and draw one of the Greek statues but I drew the **Pharaoh** instead. My grade was reduced because of it but I didn't care....

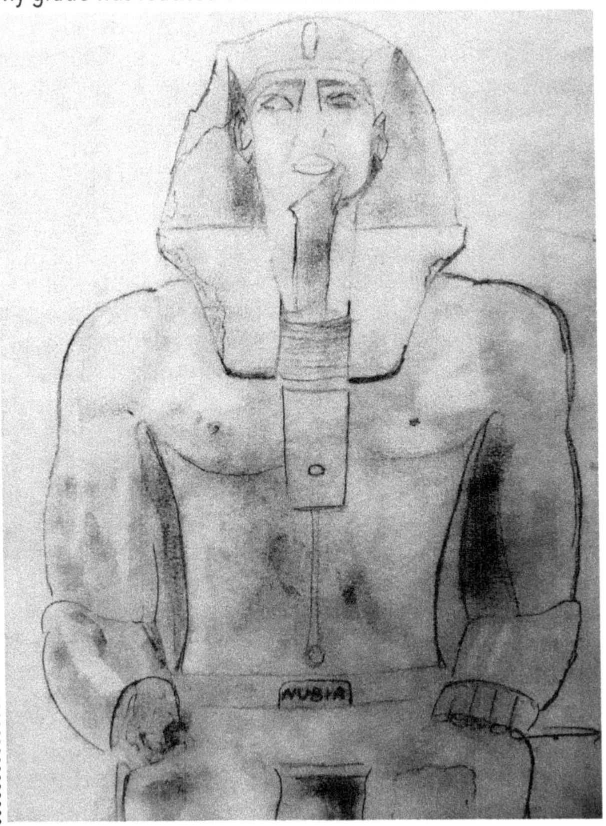

Utterances for Coming Forth by day into Light

March 30th 2013 **Sunny**

On a **sunny** day ***I star gazed at the fathers rays*** and he said to me you're gonna be the BlaKseed Emcee, that was me back in 93 in time we'll see, I took a long break but life makes no mistakes, I took the long way and signed my **soul** away, I went to war for this country, I was lost like Columbus, don't play in the world if you ain't got no compass, do the knowledge, know the ledge, you in college trying to get ahead, what good is college if it don't get you fed? people go to school but they don't know **the golden rule**, trample down evil with your **left foot forward** fool, get the message don't worry about the messenger, ***the man in the mirror*** don't get no clearer brah, worth more dead than alive, **Thriller** yo! slow down lil homie I'm trying to let you know, this game is not over but we gotta grow, the power of one! you are the one, we are the sons and daughters made in her image, on a **sunny** day ***I star gazed at the fathers rays*** and he said to me you're gonna be the Blakseed emcee, that was me back in 93 in time we'll see, I took a long break but life makes no mistakes, on a **sunny** day ***I stargazed at the fathers rays*** and he said to me you're gonna be the Blakseed Emcee, that was me back in 93 in time we'll see, I took a long break but life makes no mistakes **- Dawuud's Appeal**

It is he, who comes forth by day into Light

Thoughts in 2021

Before I wrote this rhyme I had been **sun gazing**. I did not consciously know who I was at the time of this rhyme. The past life revelations don't start till 2018 when my life as Emmett Till is revealed on July 3rd 2018 (page 480) and then on April 4th 2020 my life as Tutankhaten (King Tut) is revealed (page 594). Tutankhaten is the son of Akhenaten the Nswt Bity (Pharaoh) who venerated the **Aten** (**Sun**). **I think the act of sun gazing helped to awaken my dormant DNA or perhaps I was just channeling messages from the ancestors or my higher self, my ancient soul fragments**.

Dawud Eddings
Prof. Andrianova
BMCC English 101-081

Fuck Sports, Don't be a Good Sport!

Everybody wants to see the athletes playing their games and being good sports. The games have changed so much over the years and so have the sports, however what has not changed over the years are the roots of the words that the spectators cheer. Some roots go deeper than others, in fact some are rooted so far back in time that some find finding the beginning can take a lifetime to find. Unfortunately some people will never find the roots of the games and the sports being played. This is because they are not really looking. How can one be looking when they are drunk watching the game? The Oxford dictionary defines the word Sport as an activity involving physical exertion and skill in which an individual or a team competes against another or others for entertainment. This definition begs me to define entertainment but I will leave that for the reader to decipher.

On the surface the word sport might seem harmless, just being a simple pastime for many, something to watch on Super Bowl Sunday for others and a way of life for a few. However if we look into the etymology of the word sport, we see that it derives from the word **Disport**, which means: **to distract attention from**. Does this definition for disport immediately change the meaning of the word sport? I would say yes and no because only those who have eyes to see and ears to hear will see the illusion that is bright as day. While the minds of many people are distracted and programed with entertainment and sports, some one's child is in pain, some even dead, bombed in flames. Only a few people ever listen to the person who puts a face to the shame especially when it stops them from watching their game and cheering for King James. There are many causes to the lack of attention the public puts on important issues. The root of this problem is lack of awareness and understanding, but ultimately it is an issue of indifference. People most often fail to place themselves in the position of the person(s) struggling. That is because their brains cannot process the necessary antidote or the ultimate solution, so they would rather leave pressing issues alone and be entertained or just not think about it. Who cares in the end when they have rent to pay, kids to feed and college debt to pay? Who cares that sports and all forms of entertainment occupy so much of our time? Who cares and so what? Sometimes people only care when it happens to them.

Maybe it's all the time I spent on different teams that allows me to care about others. There is no "I" in team however "I" care about the issues of the day! My eyes are wide open and the true uses of the sports do not escape me. They not only distract peoples attention from important issues but they also serve as conveyers of advertisement for beer, cigarettes, sex, pharmaceutical drugs and the list goes on. As a child I always saw sports as simply fun and rewarding. I had fun being good and the rush, the high, the thrill from winning or doing something amazing on the football field was my reward. Many people will never understand the feeling of fielding the football deep in the end zone, so deep that most men would opt to take a knee and down the ball but not Dawud. When I got the ball it was go time all the time. Imagine that your team is losing and you are about to return a punt or a kick return. Your team is down by 6 points; you field the ball deep in the end zone. The crowd is cheering. The opposing team is advancing towards you yet still you advance forward. As you begin your journey north you feel as if there is no one who will stop you! Everyone else seems slow, but you see everything. You change direction many times, you make peoples heart jump causing excitement but for you it is the same thing you have been doing since childhood, you are simply playing tag. You are not thinking about the roaring crowd, you are just having fun, playing a sport. You are the sport, in the zone controlling the moment. It is the ultimate high. Finally, you score a touchdown but not before you have escaped and evaded capture by breaking more tackles than you can remember. Both the crowd and your teammates who have seen you do this once or twice will forever be believers in your ability to sport. Their brains will have recorded the feeling of being saved when they felt all hopes for winning were lost. Many people will never experience this because they are too busy watching the game.

Sometimes I wonder what it will take for people to understand that team sports are a microcosm of society. We are all on the same team but our team is in turmoil. Human beings are probably the most miss directed and confused of all life on earth. We watch and play sports but we miss the lessons. Sports taught me to never give up. At one time the thought of playing a sport professionally was my **dream**, my way out of the hood, but now I have a love hate relationship with sports because of the disport. While I still feel that I was good enough to play professionally I am happy that I never did. They say that it is easier for a camel to fit through the eye of a needle than it is for rich men to make it into the kingdom of heaven. When you are given money before you have attained wisdom, the money is more often times squandered. If I had been a professional athlete I would have been no better than the brainless fans buying into the athletes fantasy. The only way to be an athlete is to be one with integrity like **Muhammad Ali** who chose potential jail time rather than being sent to Vietnam to kill people that he did not know. Ali said, "No Vietnamese ever called me Nigger". This is a powerful stance to take as an athlete. It is not met with open arms. Ali was banned from boxing for his views but he also forced the country to reassess their moral compass. I was illusive on the football field. I was escaping capture always moving north, but I was trapped in a sport. I was an athlete playing a sport. I was used to distract attention from pressing issues but the truth is that it was my love for a sport that distracted me. I was so consumed with being good at a sport that I did not focus on the issues of the day. My passion and desire to win was harnessed by a sport instead of a revolution. I never played professionally but I got the important lessons. I learned how to never give up. I learned how to stay true to myself and to a team. I faced my fears. Then finally; I got far enough away from the sport to see the "disported" picture. We must all work on ourselves. We must not be distracted from what is important. We must push ourselves to learn and grow. We must all search for peace from within.

I will end by saying sports are good for children. They teach them how to work together regardless of ones color. If you must watch all the sports then do so, however never allow yourself to be distracted from true north! We must be aware. Personally I say Fuck Sports, Don't be a Good Sport. "we can go fast and go alone. Or we can go together and go far"- Ancient African Proverb.

April 2013 BMCC

While at BMCC I organized free workout sessions for students in the gym where I promoted healthy living. They all received a free **UTBC Paradigm tee shirt** (one goal, one people, one village, one step at a time). The classes were always small but we always had fun and worked hard. I had classes with some of the attendees and some joined us after seeing our group at the gym. I don't currently have contact with any of them but I hope they are all doing well in their respective life journeys.

Rau nu Prt m heru

Iu f Per f m heru

April 24th 2013 Mumia Rally in Philly

Mumia Abu Jamal

While at **BMCC** I would hang around the library and the Student Government office. I met a brother named Domingo there who invited me to the **Mumia** Rally and I was happy to go. I had first been made aware of **Mumia** from the **KRS One** song **Free Mumia** in 1995. Unfortunately after that song I had not heard of Mumia often or at all till I got out of the Army in 2005. While I was in the Army I was out of touch with the world at large and the current flow of Hip Hop. Immortal Technique dropped his first album in 2001 while I was stationed in Germany so I did not hear his music till I left the Army in 2005 (page 143). He was indeed the dopest new emcee that I heard when I got out the Army. His music was different and I liked it. When I heard the song, **Bin Laden "Bush Knocked down the Towers",** it made me think! I became a "**conspiracy theorist**"! I don't think I'd heard anything about the **911** conspiracy while I was in the Army because we didn't have social networking back then. But now I no longer believed the stories told by the national media. I began to question everything! While at the Mumia rally I met **Immortal Technique** and interestingly enough, when I got close to him my phone stopped working correctly. It actually turned off as I tried to open it for a picture. Someone I was with took the picture for me and they didn't care to check to see that the picture was blurry..

Utterances for Coming Forth by day into Light

It is he, who comes forth by day into Light

Immortal Technique

2013 Khnum "Stic" Ibomu

Riding my bike home one day from **BMCC** (borough of manhattan community college) I would see **Khnum** "Stic" Ibomu jogging just below Canal street. I stopped him and greeted him. I was so surprised and excited to meet him that I didn't think to respect his personal space or his freedom to enjoy a run without being stopped by random people. I wasn't thinking about that, all I thought was he was one of my favorite emcees and people and here he was in front of me. I stopped him, gave him a pound and introduced myself. "Yo Stic ,it's Dawud we are friends on Facebook". He looked at me and thought for a second then... heee... Ramembered me, or least he pretended to. I told him that I first heard his music in 2003 right before I deployed to **Iraq** (page 108). I told him that his music was very important to my personal growth. I told him that **Tupac** was my favorite rapper but **Dead Prez** was my favorite group and that their music had done a lot for me and I was thankful. I had some of my music playing in my head phones and I tried to get him to listen and that's when he signaled that his run was being filmed - there was a guy trailing him recording his run and I hadn't even noticed him until that moment. I pounded him up again and he finished his run. The exact date of this meeting is unknown but I would meet Stic again shortly after this meeting. On May 3rd of 2013 Dead Prez would perform at BMCC and I would meet him again there.

Significance

Stic is my favorite artist and the falcon (Heru) logo he uses for his music company is taken from the pectoral jewelry from the tomb of **Tutankhaten** (**King Tut**). In ancient kemet **Heru** (Falcon/Horus/Jesus) is the son of **Ausar** (Osiris) that returns. Heru is from the Ausarion or Osirion drama of **resurrection.** On April 4th 2020 the day that Martin Luther King was assassinated (see page 69) I would have my past life revelation of my life as **Tutankhaten** (**King Tut**, see page 594). **Remember that you are Ausar and Heru, the hero!** <u>See page 3 for the **hero's journey**!</u>

April 28th 2013 John Henrik Clarke

I salute to ***<u>John Henrik Clark</u>*** and all the elders that never failed to shine light in the d**ark,** from the heart I speak truth to power cause there could never be a ***<u>Noah's ark</u>*** without the ***<u>ark of the covenant</u>***, these are lies from the government! and it seems that you're loving it! in love with the drugs, in love with some other shit, I tried to tell them the truth and they ain't trying to hear me, **they kidnapped their spirits**, now they're living acidic, but I'm alkaline I'm out my mind, out to **shine** like the summer time, you remind me, you remind me of a perfect moment in time and revolutionary love is a crime, when you taking the time to study and you knowing the time, people looking at you like you're out of your mind, but be wise, I speak for myself but I wouldn't be surprised if all my homies felt, everything I was saying, everything gonna be alright homie stop praying! stand up **Ramoses** BlaKseeds stand at ease! how great thy family tree? if you plant a seed plan a family now that's when you're manly, my family tree starts with me, eat drink think healthy, my family tree starts with me, eat drink think healthy, healthy, healthy **- Dawuud's Appeal**

Significance

Akhenaten is the biblical **Moses** and the father of **Tutankhaten** (**King Tut**). In the bible Moses brings the **Ark** of the Covenant down from the top of Mount Sinai and presents it to his people who are worshipping a statue of a Bull (p 486). The Ark was said to be a box and inside the box were two tablets that had the Ten Commandments (taken from the 42 negative confessions of Maat, p 367) written on them, it had Aarons **staff** in it, and a jar containing the **Manna**. "As the Lord commanded Moses, Aaron put the manna with the tablets of the covenant law, so that it might be preserved." (Exodus 16:34 "**round caps**"). I mention Ramoses in this rhyme and the tomb of **Ramose** is in the city of Akhetaten which was built by Akhenaten (p 671). The truth about Noah's Ark on page 252.

Addendum

May 2, 2013 4:21 AM • La Juana and the 10 year "COINCIDENCE"

I met La Juana on August, 6 2016 (p 399) but it wasn't till sometime in **2023**, that I found a video of her and her son on an old hard drive. By some strange **coincidence** I seemed to have I recorded her years before I met her. I remembered capturing the video but of course I didn't know the people in the video and didn't remember the date and time of the incident.. Apparently, on **May 2, 2013**, at **4:13 am**, I entered **110 train station in Harlem**. I remember seeing a boy playing his **violin** while a woman stood next to him holding up a sign. For some reason I decided to capture a video of him playing and I went on with my day, and I went on with my life. But as I have said before, many of the people we cross paths with have important roles to play in our lives. By some **strange luck**, in **2023**, I was searching for a video in an external hard drive when I ran across this video again. However, when I viewed the video in **2023** I realized **it was La Juana and her son in the video**.. Then I checked the date on the video and was shocked to see I recorded her 3 years before I met her. I sent La Juana the video and explained how I had **coincidentally** recorded her and her son years before we met. She was surprised but she was also accustomed to me sharing these **strange happenings**. Like the strange timing of her mothers miscarriage (p 455), my experience with **Michelle Lamy** (p 582), and my **precognition dreams** (pages 586, 589). **La Juana** played a pivotal role in my life. But life is not a simple trip from the womb to the tomb. It's a continuous journey and sometimes we cross paths with **past life relatives**. We are immortal beings of light and we get more than one chance at life! Life is a class for you to gain as much positive fuel as you can so that you can shine bright reaching the **highest** levels of **spiritual consciousness**.

Rau nu Prt m heru

I was cool with the student government at school and because of that I was able to chill backstage before the **Dead Prez** set and have access to the stage while they performed. It was cool because I had just met **Stic** a few weeks prior and here I am again at his show. Over the years Stic had become my favorite rapper because of his words and his direction with health, wellness and family. I felt he was a good example of Manhood. His song **<u>What Men Do</u>** being one of my Favorite tracks at the time. It was spiritual food and I needed to hear it at the time. Brothers, Please listen to that song! In the song Stic ask's the question "Am I wrong for tell'n it like it is Beloved?", My name means beloved. I felt like the song was for me.

<u>Significance</u>

Stic is my favorite artist and the falcon (Heru) logo he uses for his music company is taken from the pectoral jewelry from the tomb of **Tutankhaten** (**King Tut**). In ancient kemet Heru (Falcon/Horus/Jesus) is the son of Ausar (Osiris) that returns. Heru is from the Ausarion or Osirion drama of **resurrection.** On April 4th 2020, the day that Martin Luther King was assassinated (see page 69) I would have my past life revelation of my life as **Tutankhaten** (**King Tut**, see page 594). **Remember that you are Ausar and Heru, the hero!** <u>See page 3 for the</u> **<u>hero's journey</u>**!

Iu f Per f m heru

Utterances for Coming Forth by day into Light

It is he, who comes forth by day into Light

May 5th 2013 Letters From Metu Ntchrs

They made letters from **Metu Ntchr's,** they was stuck in a cave, don't be a victim to tv cause the ignorance pays, this revolution won't be televised, end of the days, so many stories allegories but will you sit and ignore me? free **Mumia** we screamed in Philly, ready to rally, ready to die, ready to live, New York to Cali, stop waiting for a leader free your mind soul and your body, the spirit of a leader, evoking the lion heart **Bob Marley,** connect the dots no **Malcolm X** without **Garvey!** **Garvyism** is like **Nasir Jones** sp**ark**ing his own religion, a Thugs Life, this hate you gave little infants fucked everyone one starry night, swing low chariot they had a bounty on **Harriet,** now they got a house nigga chasing for **Assata,** I heard Obama wanna put his hands on **Assata,** I'd die for Assata what if Assata was your mamma, I'm a rider **Muhammad Ali pyramid** on the dollar, fuck they school and they rules! keep your hands off Assata **- Dawuud's Appeal**

May 13th 2013

When **Jay Z** came back from Cuba in 2013 he dropped a song entitled "**Open Letter**" on April 11th 2013 the **year of the snake**. Less than a month later on May 2nd Assata was coincidentally placed back on the F.B.I. most wanted list. In response to her being put on the most wanted list I would have these Assata Tee shirts made but I never got them printed. They are available now along with other tee shirts @ www.TutemRa.com

A percentage of the proceeds from the Assata Tee Shirt will go to the legal battles for the freedom of our political prisoners. We could get them free with out the legal system if WE really wanted them free!!!!

May 25th 2013 (May 25th Strikes Back)

I took this picture in salute of **Huey P Newton,** one of the founders of the **Black Panther Party for Self Defense**. I put the picture in the book when I saw that it was taken on **May 25th** 2013 the year of the **snake**....................

For significance see pages iii, 30, 40, 104, 157, 222, 293, 512, 610, 659.

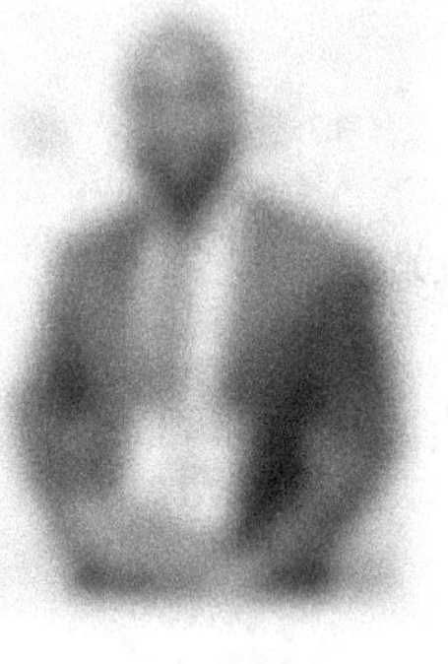

2013 -$800 Miller Time 5/7 Communications

I hadn't heard from Miller about returning my money in a few years. After I got my $tipend from the military my money problems subsided but I happened to find him on whatsapp. His profile picture was a nice luxury car and I still wanted my money so I questioned him about it. He gave me the same run around then he stopped responding.

Next communication page March 13th 2017 page 444

Rau nu Prt m heru

Iu f Per f m heru

Utterances for Coming Forth by day into Light

It is he, who comes forth by day into Light

July 7th 2013 **KNOCK KNOCK**

Knock knock, who's there? **George Zimmerman**, didn't he just kill a man? Like the ku klux klan! but who's the ku klux klan? the fireman, police man, the judge and the preacher man! ain't no peace here it's warfare, the law makers don't care, so throw ya guns in the air, all these laws are the walls to keep us down, **Jed Bush** signed stand your ground, now they lawfully buck'n us down, Man ain't no fucking around, this shit is real like **Emmett Till,** on my side of town, yeah it's similar to Vietnam and you should be alarmed, some people don't care till they the one that's being harmed, some people won't care until they start hearing bombs, Word to my moms, a word to **Assata,** I'm a rider **Muhammad Ali Pyramid** on the dollar, I'm a rider **Muhammad Ali Pyramid** on the dollar, fuck they rules and they schools, **Keep ya hands off Assata! - Dawuud's Appeal**

Significance

During the opening argument of the Trayvon Martin murder trial the defense attorney makes a knock knock joke. "Knock knock. who's there? George Zimmerman. George Zimmerman who? ok you can be on the jury". The defense felt like a knock knock joke was a morally sound way to start their defense. The defense argued that Zimmerman could not get a fair trial due to all the publicity around the case. I was angered by this lack of empathy and wrote the rhyme **Knock Knock**. While writing the song a soul fragment from a previous life came flying forth by day and I spoke my previous name, **Emmett Till** in rhyme for the fourth time. **More on Trayvon Martin on page 232.**

August 2013

Massage School, NYCHP (New York College Of Health Professionals)

I spent a year at **BMCC** and I wasn't happy with the experience. I had argued with both my health and African history professors and I didn't like the overall atmosphere at the school. I felt like an outcast and it was no surprise to me that Assata had attended school there and led a protest there. I still needed the money I was receiving from my Army stipend so I searched for another school to attend. I searched "Holistic School Harlem" and the New York College Of Health Professionals (NYCHP) appeared. They were advertising Acupuncture and the first thing I thought about was **Mutulu Shakur**. I had come across videos about Mutulu using the acupuncture five-point auricular treatment to help drugs addicts release their addictions to drugs. I called the school and asked if they accepted the army G.I. Bill for payment and they said yes. I scheduled a meeting and when I got there I met with a woman named Miss Rosa who suggested that I take the massage course instead and I agreed. I did not even realize that we would be massaging each other in school. I just wanted to use the money doing something that was useful info and not what was being taught at BMCC.

Mutulu Shakur and The Black Panther Party for Self Defense

President Nixon signed the **Controlled Substance Act in** 1970 (page 501) and it organized federally regulated drugs into five schedules. **Schedule I**, Drugs are the ones they claimed to have no accepted medically useful remedies and a high potential for abuse. **LSD, Heroin, Psilocybin (Magic Mushrooms)**, **Cannabis, Ecstasy, Peyote** and **DMT** were all on that list. In 2022 Cannabis ,Mushrooms and DMT are being used for therapy. **Schedule II**, the narcotic drugs that put you to sleep with a high potential for abuse. Leading to severe psychological or physical harm and dependency. They regulated the distribution of these drugs to the doctors who prescribed: morphine, opium, codeine and Percocet, Adderall, and Ritalin for the children. **Schedule III**, for the athletes, the anabolic steroids. Schedule IV and Schedule V Drugs with a low potential for abuse and low risk of dependence. On June 17th 1971 (pages **23** and 40) President Richard Nixon would declare drug abuse to be "public enemy number one" which was really a war on Black people and the Black family structure, sending countless Black people to prison for long sentences for simple possession of Cannabis (Crack, page 502). Mutulu Shakur was a member of the black liberation group, the Republic of New Afrika who worked to combat the governments attack on the Black community and the Black family. Mutulu was interested in the use of acupuncture to treat addiction. He became aware of acupuncture when his son received it after a car accident. Mutulu received training and began to practice acupuncture as part of the People's Drug Program in 1971 along with Walter Bosque and other community volunteers. Established in 1970, The People's Drug Program was launched at Lincoln Hospital in New York by the Young Lords, the Black Panther Party, and other community activists. The Young Lords was a Puerto Rican liberation organization founded in 1968. The Black Panther Party was a Black power political organization founded in 1966, sparked by the assassination of Malcolm X. Mutulu led the work of the Lincoln Detox Center from 1971 - 1978. In 1978, he also became the co-founder and co-director of the Black Acupuncture Advisory Association of North America (BAAANA) and the Harlem Institute Of Acupuncture, training hundreds of acupuncturists. A five-point auricular treatment help reduce withdrawal symptoms, including cravings and emotional distress. Mutulu and the center became well known for their use of acupuncture. Mutulu became a sought after speaker both nationally and internationally. In later years, the use of acupuncture to treat addiction would enjoy another wave of popularity in the White middle class and with more affluent individuals. The new found notoriety was void of the connection to addressing oppression and community empowerment. In other words, when the drugs that the government had placed in the black community started to affect White people they used acupuncture as a treatment instead of waging a war on White people like the government did to Black people. (continued on the next page)

Mutulu Shakur is the real life **T'Cholla**, the **Black Panther** that you see in your Hollywood block buster movie. He is a man that took a stand against the destruction of his community when all odds were against him. Mutulu was a child of Malcolm X who birthed the Black Panther movement after he was assassinated. Mutulu is the Black Panther that the police railroaded and placed in a cage on false charges. **Will you rally for his immediate release** or will you just pack the movies for the next Black Panther sequel?!. Mutulu is the brother of **Assata Shakur** and the stepfather of rapper **Tupac Shakur**. Both Mutulu and Assata were members of the Black Liberation Army, a black nationalist organization operating in the United States from 1970 in to the 80's, who's soul purpose was to ensure the freedom, justice and quality of the lives of people of color in America. The group was comprised primarily of former members of the Black Panther Party. Mutulu Shakur is currently incarcerated in federal prison, serving a 60-year prison sentence for his **alleged** involvement in a 1981 robbery of an armored truck, which resulted in two people's death. Mutulu has maintained that he is innocent of murder. It is reported that Mutulu orchestrated the theft to fund a black nationalist revolution. Mutulu evaded capture for 6 years before being tried and convicted. He was also convicted for aiding and abetting his sister's escape from prison. Assata Shakur has been living in Cuba for the last 30+ years after escaping from prison, where she was incarcerated on a murder charge. Mutulu's legal team continues to advocate for his release. To date, all attempts to request his parole have been denied. Currently, Mutulu Shakur is suffering from bone marrow **cancer**. His family and supporters are now seeking his release due to his declining health. **Will you rally for his immediate release of the Black Panther Mutulu Shakur?**

August 17th 2013 **The UTBC Paradigm (Kendrick Lamar Control Remix)**

This ain't **Kanye West** work out, I ain't got no beef with **kendrick, I don't eat meat**, I think, I take it back to **Kemet,** if Popeye ate spinach, then the Hulk ate kale, one goal, one people, one village, one step at a time, **The UTBC Paradigm,** to the sky no limit, detox your body and mind, so your **spirit** can shine, connect tachyons, **transform** into atoms that form cells, can you fathom a time when we wasn't living in hell? it ain't hard to tell, I excel and prevail, If them haters hating they waiting, they probably wanna see you fail, But stay awake in **the year of the snake**, to attract clientele, never sell your **soul** homie, **Be the soul controller of your journey!** like the sperm to the egg, or a baby hugging a leg, I see the dreads on one two five, trying to open ya eyes, see either you're eating to live, or you're eating to die, the other day just walking by, I seen a grown man die, he collapse had a heart attack, to bring him back the medics they did try, at U TOUGH we run laps, breathing energy from the sky, **Taking energy from the sun, Controlling the energy from the sun, Control - Dawuud's Appeal**

The Bar Tendaz

I'm not sure how they caught me smiling but the rarity of it made me place it in the book. The fitness community is the same everywhere you go. People who workout have a bond and respect for one another. On this day I caught a workout with the Bar Tendaz. I'm not sure the exact day but it was somewhere around this time that I remember leaving this park and passing a woman who's beauty captivated me and soon after seeing her in passing I saw her on TV. Her name is **Teyana Taylor**.

Rau nu Prt m heru

Iu f Per f m heru

Pictures taken on September 3rd 2013
I Start Massage Therapy School at NYCHP

A week after I started school my Land Lord gave me a brand new massage table and books that I needed for school. His cousin had completed school for massage but she never pursued the profession. She ended up leaving New York and left those things in the basement with no plans on coming back to get them. I began to feel like the universe was conspiring for me. Everything seemed to be falling into place. I posted this picture on Instagram telling the story and talking about **synchronicities**. One time is an incident, twice is a **coincidence** but three, four and five is a pattern! Can you tell the difference? Emmett Till's wake was held on September 3rd 1955 at Roberts Temple Church of God in Christ (page 514). When **coincidences** bind with **synchronicities** the outcome tends to have **the mark of a greater authority!!!...**

Utterances for Coming Forth by day into Light

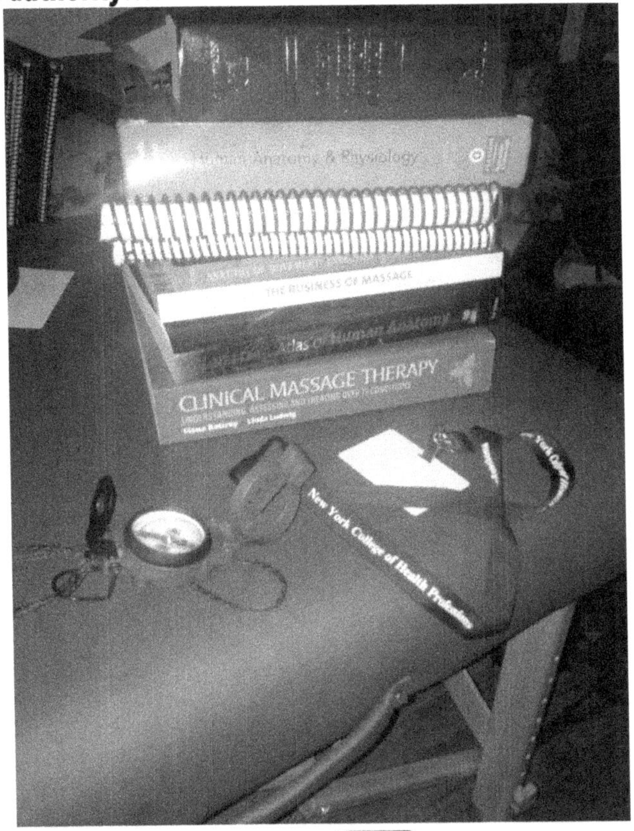

It is he, who comes forth by day into Light

September 2013 The Year of The Snake
Martin Luther King and Massage Therapy at Riverside Church

It would be another 5 years till I would come to know that my life is intimately connected with Martin Luther King's. My past life as **Emmett Till** will be revealed to me on July 3rd 2018 (p 480), 2 days after I graduated as a **Kemetic Yoga** instructor. **Rosa Parks** practiced **yoga** (pages 474, 518), and **Martin Luther King practiced Karma Yoga** every day. He may have never practiced the Yoga postures, but he drew heavily on the **Gandhi's** idea of **nonviolence** in his own activism which is the first yama, or moral precept, of yoga as outlined by Patanjali in the Yoga Sutras. Martin Luther King knew about the pre existence of the soul, he wrote a **theology** paper on **Heru** and the **Ausarian Resurrection** in 1949 (p 593). Martin was born in the year of the **Snake** (1929), "Emmett" was born in the year of the **Snake** (1941) and I was born again in 1977, the year of the **Snake**. My last day in the **Army** was **Martin Luther King's** birthday, Jan 15th 2005 (p 130). I attended some of my first semester of classes at The New York College of Health Professional via a satellite location at **Riverside Church** in 2013 the year of the **Snake**. This is the same church that **Martin** would deliver the speech "**Beyond Vietnam,**" on April 4th 1967 which is exactly one year before his death on April 4th 1968 (p 69). On the day of his assassination, April 4th 2020, I would have my second **past life revelation**, this time my life as Tutankhaten (**King Tut**) is revealed to me (p 594). Emmett Till was murdered in 19**55** which propelled Martin Luther King into the forefront of the Civil Rights Movement. Around 2 minutes and **55** seconds into Martin's **Beyond Vietnam** speech he says: *"Perhaps a new **spirit** is rising among us. If it is, let us trace its movement, and pray that our inner being may be sensitive to its guidance. For we are deeply in need of a new way beyond the d**ark**ness that seems so close around us."* I ask that you read this book and trace my movements. Out of the d**ark**ness comes the divine soul. The **ark** of a million years, the magic carpet or "Noah's **ark**" (p 252). I am talking about the **immortality** that man is so desperately searching for. Be careful my brothers and sisters, before you throw my revelation to the pigs I suggest you consider the idea that perhaps there are things that other groups of people know but are in no rush to tell you. **Because anyone who profits off of you being blind will not teach you or inspire you to see**. **We have had our spiritual culture stripped from us** but we understood the immortality of the soul in ancient times. In fact reincarnation was taken out of the bible in 553 AD under the reign of **Justinian** the 1st. In the Bible the character of Jesus speaks of reincarnation in the book of **Matthew**. I was sent to this school where Martin delivered this speech about, *"a new **spirit** rising among us"* so that those with **eyes to see** can feel confident in knowing what they are seeing is true. It was ordained from the beginning of time that I would die a sacrificial death as Emmett Till so that I could have the opportunity to come back here again in this life and earn the right to know who I was and with the revealing of this revelation mans consciousness will be aroused and justice can at-last prevail.

Reincarnation in the Bible

Life does not end when body function ceases, but body function ceases when life leaves the body. Future life is a certain as the sun setting in the west and rising again in the east... The human soul does the same. Again and again. This ancient doctrine of reincarnation had always been known throughout the world, except in modern times, when it was cast into darkness by the Roman State Church in order to force the world to believe in its "Lord and Savior Jesus Christ". Reincarnation was taught by Pythagoras and Plato; it was one of the principles of the Druid faith. Caesar found it among the Gauls. It was found in the old races of Mexico, Central and South America but it was first realized and taught in Ancient Kemet (Egypt). Reincarnation was voted out of Christian doctrines in 325AD and almost completely erased from the Bible in 533AD.

Matthew Chapter 16

13: When Jesus came to the region of Caesarea Philippi, he asked his disciples, "**Who do people say the Son of Man is**?" **14:** They replied, "***Some say John the Baptist; others say Elijah; and still others, Jeremiah or one of the prophets.***" **15:** "But what about you?" he asked. "Who do you say I am?" **16:** Simon Peter answered, "***You are the Messiah, the Son of the living God***." **17:** Jesus replied, "Blessed are you, Simon son of Jonah, for this was not revealed to you by flesh and blood, but by my Father in heaven. **18:** And I tell you that ***you are Peter***, and on this rock I will build my church, and the gates of Hades will not overcome it. **19:** I will give you the keys of the kingdom of heaven; whatever you bind on earth will be bound in heaven, and whatever you loose on earth will be loosed in heaven." **20:** Then he ordered his disciples not to tell anyone that he was the Messiah.

Matthew Chapter 11

11: Truly I tell you, among those born of women there has not risen anyone greater than John the Baptist; yet whoever is least in the kingdom of heaven is greater than he. **12:** From the days of John the Baptist until now, the kingdom of heaven has been subjected to violence, and violent people have been raiding it. **13:** For all the Prophets and the Law prophesied until John. **14:** And if you are willing to accept it, ***he is the Elijah who was to come***. **15:** Whoever has ears, let them hear.

Matthew 19

9: As they were coming down the mountain, Jesus instructed them, "Don't tell anyone what you have seen, until the Son of Man has been raised from the dead." **10:** The disciples asked him, "Why then do the teachers of the law say that Elijah must come first?" **11:** Jesus replied, "To be sure, Elijah comes and will restore all things. **12:** ***But I tell you, Elijah has already come***, and they did not recognize him, but have done to him everything they wished. In the same way the Son of Man is going to suffer at their hands." **13:** Then ***the disciples understood that he was talking to them about John the Baptist.***

Early Christian Fathers

Origen (184-253) who's name meant "born of **Heru**" was one of the early Christian fathers and through him we know that reincarnation was wide spread in Christianity in the 1st two centuries. Origen taught about the **pre-existence of our souls**, taking up reincarnation or one or another aspect of re-embodiment which, among many other of his teachings, was later condemned as heresy. Examples are scattered through Origen's works, especially Contra Celsum (1, xxxii), where he asks: **"Is it not rational that souls should be introduced into bodies, in accordance with their merits and previous deeds . . . ?"** In the 6th century, the eastern Roman emperor **Justinian** the 1st, (482-565), saw him self as the supreme ruler of the church and made it law that nothing could be done in the church contrary to his will and command. He removed all the teachings of the **pre-existence of our souls**, and reincarnation from the church doctrine. He wanted everyone to believe that they only live one time and so the church would wield more power because the people would come to believe that they could only go to heaven by way of the church. It became the most powerful tool to control the masses. **Pope Vigilius** (?- 555) knew that reincarnation was a part of the teaching of the bible so he **apposed** the emperor and **refused to sign the ban** of the teachings of **reincarnation** in 543. 10 years later December 8th 553, the pressure from the emperor was so fierce that Pope Vigilius acquiesced and signed the law in Constantinople. After this a problem was created because now the church could no longer answer questions like where do we come from, where do we go when we die and why are we here. This is when new doctrine was created, eternal damnation, **original sin**, **creation of the soul at the time of birth**, mortal sin, **judgement day** and purgatory. The knowledge of reincarnation was never completely forgotten it was just never taught again in the churches instead it was relegated to **secret societies.** In **Judaism** reincarnation is known as **Gilgul** (Cycle), but it is not taught to everyone. In ancient Kemet the concept of reincarnation and past lives was called the **Wehem-Mesut** (repeating of births, page 14). **Re-member** that **you** are **Ausar** and **Heru**, the **hero!** See page 3 for the **hero's journey**!

Rau nu Prt m heru

September 13th 2013 King David

You ain't *never had a friend like me*, I be **King David** like King **Michael Jackson** the chief musician, I be like **Common** see I be rhyming, do you have eyes to see? Deuteronomy, do the numbers, what is psychology? Mafuka's you owe people an apology, I guess at this point I'm talking about the policies - **Dawuud's Appeal**

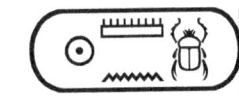

See page **77** for the **Common** connection.

2013 - Tai Chi - Cheng men Ching - Cameron

I met Cameron at massage school. he was the instructor for my intro to Tai Chi class were I began learning the Cheng Men Ching 37 short form. He also wrote poetry. Him and I connected quickly finding commonalities with our outlook on the world. Cam would take the time to help me with my form. Cam had a slogan "Who's the General" and at the time I was going by the name General **Maat**. I was honoring my late grand father General Dukes Jr and the principles of **Maat** (42 Laws of Maat, Page 367). On Feb 4th of 2017 Cameron and I would experience an strange occurrence while texting. Some how he received a text from me that I did not send him. I do not remember the message sent in the text but it was a message that could have caused confusion, potentially causing us to argue but we were smarter than that. The experience made use think of how the government used **Cointelpro** to cause division between members of the Black Panther Party for Self Defense. Read about **Darpa** on page 352.

Iu f Per f m heru

2013 The Year of The Snake - Rihanna and King Tut

Heru Falcon Form

When searching for pictures of Rihanna I came a cross a tour she did in 2012 where she did Kemetic (Egyptian) themed sets with images a Tutankhaten (King Tut) behind her. Around 5 years after meeting Rihanna at Club 1 Oak (July 4th 2009, page 167), she would get 3 Kemetic (Egyptian) tattoos that are connected to my **revelation**. She got a tattoo of King Tut's step mother **Nefertiti** on her rib. Nefertiti is the wife of **Akhenaten**. She also got a **tattoo** of **Auset** (**Isis**) on her sternum in the same place that **Tupac** had his "**50 Niggaz"** tattoo. Auset is the mother of **Heru** (**Horus**) and the wife of **Ausar** (**Osiris**) who just so "happens to be" the Lord of **Resurrection**. She would also get an Egyptian **Falcon** tattooed on her ankle and the Falcon is another symbol of **Heru**, the one who **returns**. Rihanna's tattoo's would become iconic sparking many other women to get the same or similar tattoos channeling the energy of ancient Kemet (Egypt). It is not the fact that I met Rihanna that makes our meeting profound, it is the fact that I would never have met her if I had not met Mickey Rourke months prior (p 167) but having met Mickey would set the stage for the stars to align when he, by chance pulled up right before we left the club. Then somehow I had a conversation with her making our meeting fall into the arena of **fate** or **destiny**. Perhaps she was an ancient Queen or temple singer like Whitney Houston (p 230). It should be noted that **Rihanna** is **Bajan** and so am I. She's born on Feb 20th, the day after my great grandfather **General Dukes Sr** (p 19). She's born the day before **Malcolm X** died. The strangest thing of all is that I also have a small connection with her partner, Asap Rocky but I won't place that in this book. If I ever meet them I'll tell them.

Auset / Isis

Serket

Akhenaten

Nefertiti

ADDENDUM

I have had two **dreams** with Rihanna since this book was released. They were both very interesting. The second dream happened on December 22 2022 and it involved **Tupac**. I won't share the dreams in this book, but if I ever meet Rihanna again I'll tell her.

Utterances for Coming Forth by day into Light

It is he, who comes forth by day into Light

I still remember stopping **Liz** on the street. I was about to start my new group classes in Jackie Robinson park. One day I saw her walking towards me with her head down as if life was weighing her down. I stopped her, and told her that I was starting a new group fitness class and asked her if she would be willing to come. She said yes. She would be my biggest transformation at that group class. She made all the changes I suggested and came to all 3 classes, 3 days a week in Jackie Robinson park at 6am. Eventually I would take my classes to 161 Yankee Stadium recreational park. This year I also did classes in Central Park , Morningside Park. Liz is born on **June 3rd** the same day I crashed my new motorcycle at the **cross**roads in 2008 (page 158). Ross Riddle (seen below) was one of the hardest working people that would pass through my classes but on top of that, he seemed to be **drawn** to my classes. It was in 2023, during the revision of this book that I came to know that I had two Grand Mothers with the maiden name, **Riddle** (page 15). This made me think about this guy Ross **Riddle**. Was he a distant cousin? Perhaps.. Life is indeed a **riddle**.....

2013 The UTBC Paradigm

Rau nu Prt m heru

Iu f Per f m heru

Utterances for Coming Forth by day into Light

It is he, who comes forth by day into Light

I trained all types of people, all ages and all colors. I pulled from my experience playing football and my time in the military. That was the source of my leadership. I also aimed to have fun while exercising. I never turned a person away from my classes. I would share healthy information with the people I was coming in contact with. When I learned something knew I shared it. I encouraged people to consider the foods they ate. I warned them that perhaps much of what we are accustomed to eating isn't actually good for us, and even more so that much of it is detrimental to our health and well being. They all listened but only few made immediate changes, however overtime I would hear from some of them years later and they would tell how they finally made the changes they needed to make. Ultimately I enjoyed working with all of the people I trained and I'm grateful for crossing paths with them. They have no idea how much having a job to do kept me going through my ups and downs as I struggled with depression.

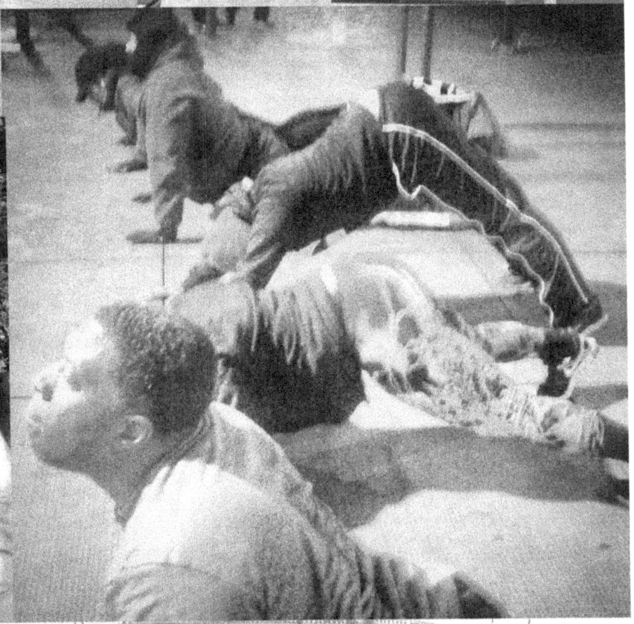

October 5th 2013 - Meta Mental Encounters
The first law of Jhuti: Everything is Mental (My 1st Meeting with Mr Nature)

I got disqualified from Special Forces School on Oct 25th 2002 on my 25th birthday for land navigation (p 110). On Oct 5th I took the picture of my compass and my new logo with the image of the Saqqara pyramid built by **Imhotep**. On this same day I would meet **Mr Nature** for the first time by using the power of divine thought. The events that follow is an example of how our thoughts and desires can affect our reality by influencing quantum level events in time and space. It was around 7:30 am and I was making my way to teach a fitness class at 161 Yankee Stadium recreational p**ark**. On the way I would pass a church and I would see flowers in the window. The sight of the flowers would awaken the **desire** to have more flowers in my studio. I can remember **thinking***, "***I want some flowers for my studio***". I got to the p**ark** and gave my class a good workout. On my way home I would pass the church window with the flowers again and again I would **think** the same **thought***, "***I want flowers for my studio***". When I got to my block, to my surprise, ***I would experience my thoughts responding immediately!!!*** I crossed paths with an old man pushing a shopping cart full of flowers. I asked him if he was selling the flowers and he said, "yes". I told him that I just saw some flowers in a window of a church and wanted to buy some. He smiled. I introduced myself and asked him his name. He told me his name was **Mr Nature**. I bought my first flower from him that day. I would have another profound encounter with Mr Nature on May 3rd of 2014 (p 291) and two more in Oct of 2014 (p, 304, 306) then I would never see Mr Nature again. In April of 2022 I went to Kemet (Egypt) and when I stepped on the Saqqara pyramid I got a profound feeling of **Deja Vu** (p 670). My experience with Mr Nature reminds me of how I met **Nova** (p184).

ADDENDUM **Scott (Burnhard) Bernard** was one of the younger brothers who worked out regularly at the p**ark**. He would see me training my clients in groups and years later he would become a personal trainer. Since this time he has amassed a huge following and has inspired many to change their lives for the better via fitness. I saw Scott in 2022 at the International African Arts Festival for the first time in many years and he was in phenomenal shape. I showed him this book and opened to this page where his picture was shown. I sold him a copy of this book and told him how much he has inspired me to get back on my fitness journey.

Rau nu Prt m heru

Iu f Per f m heru

October 2013 - High Frequency Meta Physical Encounters of the Morph kind

I met Adrianna in my first trimester of massage school and we became close friends quickly. I would teach her about the principles of **Maat** and share other info with her. She taught me about friendship. When her and I met I was going through one of my low periods and because of that my apartment was a mess.I hadn't washed the dishes in months. Adrianna came by to see me and did not judge me, instead she put her things down and washed all my dishes and organized my space because it needed to be done. Adrianna was one of the people in massage school who was there because massage was a path that she had decided to take. I was there for the money but still I got good grades and enjoyed my classes and the people I met. One day we smoked weed at my place and after we kissed **her face began to shape shift** into the face of different women I have been intimate with from my past as well as one face that I did not recognize but yet still **the face was strangely familiar to me**. This was the first time that I would experienced this but it would happen again four years later in Oct of 2017 with another woman (p 452). On July 3rd 2018 (p 480) my past life as Emmett Till would be revealed to me and on April 4th 2020 (p 594) my past life as Tutankhaten (King Tut) would be revealed to me. After my past life as Tutankhaten was revealed to me I began to feel like the face that was strangely familiar to me was the face of my ancient wife Ankhesenaten. Perhaps I opened a **High Frequency psychic channel and she used Adrianna's body like a vessel**, the same way **Whoopi Goldberg** did in the movie **Ghost**. When I first started smoking weed in 2012 I unwittingly opened these channels and received messages about my reincarnation (p 227). I met a woman named Meeky in 2019 at the International African Arts Festival (page 574). A month or so later she revealed to me that she'd been seeing spirits since she was a little girl but she could not hear them and she was a bit afraid of them. I found that interesting because I had met two other women (Noel pages 311, 318 and Zee pages 362, 421, 545) like her a few years prior. Because of the experiences she had in her life and how we met at the festival she believed my story about my past life as Emmett Till. Her and I would become good friends, eventually becoming she like a sister and brother. In January of 2020 I gave her a dose of **sacred medicine more potent than weed** and afterwards **her <u>gift of sight</u> would <u>enhance</u> substantially.** She could now communicate with the spirits! On January 13th 2020 she gave me a spiritual reading where I communicated with two of my guardian angels (p 584). I was told by one of my guardians, that all the paranormal phenomena I had been experiencing over the years like the shape shifting experiences, near death experiences etc, were designed to prepare me for my past life revelations. She said I was slowly awakened so as to not have me go crazy or been seen as crazy. Afterwards I thought about the movie, **The Matrix** and how **Morpheus** said, **it was dangerous to awaken adults to the reality of the matrix they live in**. And this is why my guardian angels could not risk me awakening too quickly an possibly being placed in a psychiatric hospital (insane asylum).

<u>Addendum</u> Whoopi Goldberg, Patrick Swayze the movie Ghost, Emmett Till and Beyond King Tut

Whoopi Goldberg was was born in 1955, the same year **Emmett Till** was murdered. **Patrick Swayze** played the "**ghost**" (the spirit lingering on After death) in the movie. Patrick is born on August 18th, the same day my grand father **General Dukes Jr** died (page 169). My grand father appeared to me in spirit form on Dec 18 2015 (p 348), just like Patrick did in the movie **Ghost**. 3 days after my birthday, on **October 28,** 2022, the movie **Till** was released. **Whoopi Goldberg** was one of the executive producers of the movie. That same day, **October 28,** 2022 the **Beyond King Tut Exhibit** opened in NYC (page 29 & 33). I have not watched my movie but I went to my Exhibit on Dec 22, 2022 with Shanta (p 289).

Utterances for Coming Forth by day into Light

2013 - Meta Spiritual Encounters of the fourth kind
Nswt Bity (Pharaoh) Khufu Body Snatchers (Embodiment)

I would meet an older brother named **Khufu** in massage school (New York College of Health professionals). There were very little black men in massage school so most of us were always friendly to each other. He was in the process of enrolling again to finish. I have only seen him 2 or three times. The last time I saw him he looked at me and said, **"I know who you are".** Just like the **Fitness Guru** from January 2014 (page 286). I asked him – **"who am I"**. He said - ***<u>"you are one of the adept"</u>***. I nodded my head and said ok. We talked some more and I never saw him again.

<u>Significance</u>

I would call brother Khufu from massage school in 2018 after I had my past life revelation of Emmett Till and I asked him if he remembered telling me that I was "***one of the adept***" and to my surprise he did not remember. I had recently read in a book or heard in a lecture, about the strange phenomena involving people who receive profound messages from family, friends even strangers but if these people who delivered the messages are later asked to recall the words they spoke they will often not be able to remember ever telling you what you so vividly remember them telling you. In ancient Kemet (Egypt) the human soul was divided into 7 parts. One of the aspects was the **Ka** which was the spirit, or the etheric twin. The **Sahu** is the part of the soul that survives in the physical world after the body of a person has departed. There was also the **Ren**, which is what we called the name of a person. The **Ren** could be defined as **the energy of a persons name**. **Khufu** was also the name of the second **Pharaoh** of the 4th dynasty of Kemet. The brother Khufu from school took the **Ren** (name) of the Pharaoh Khufu so the **Ka** (spirit) of Khufu was able to *<u>speak through him</u>*. It was the Pharaoh Khufu who spoke to me that day not the brother Khufu that was standing in front of me. His body was used like a conduit. On April 4th 2020 my past life as the Pharaoh Tutankhaten (King Tut) would be revealed to me (page 594). I would have a similar experience with spirits speaking through a person in May of 2019 with my song **Holler if Ya Hear Me** (page 374-375) and at the International African Arts festival in 2018 and again in 2021. On the day before my birthday, October 24th 2009, KRS One released the book, **The Gospel of Hip Hop: The First Instrumental** (page 633). In KRS One's song, **The Beginning** he says "**I am the return of Khufu**".

It is he, who comes forth by day into Light

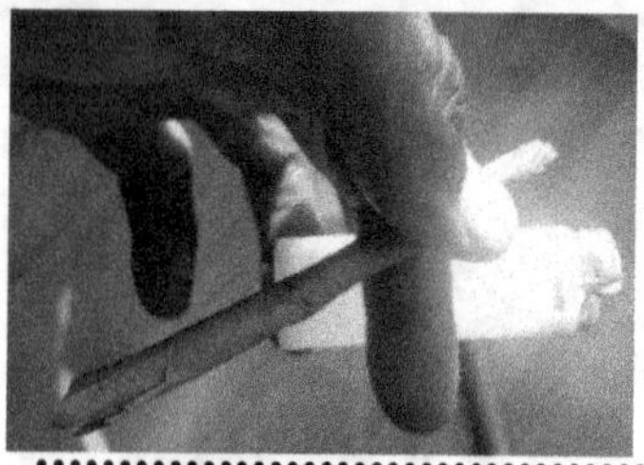

November 29th 2013
"The Battles With Questions, Like Should I smoke weed?"

3 years of smoking weed and I was beginning to question the benefits of it. Was it good or was it bad? Whatever the case, I was seriously **addicted** to it now!

Dr, Amos Wilson
Feb 23rd 1941 - Jan 14th 1995

Dr. Amos Wilson would hit my radar via a youtube video sometime around 2013, the year of the snake. I first heard him recite the ancient African proverb, **Know Thy Self**. This proverb penetrated the depths of my soul and I never forgot it. His name **Amos**, is a Kemetic name mostly used during the New Kingdom, where **King Tut** was from. The first Nswt Bity (pharaoh) from the 18th dynasty was **Iahmose I** (page 638). Dr. Amos explained, if we as Black people don't know who we are, then we are, whoever somebody tell's us we are. He warned about how damaging it was to the psyche of Black people to pray to a White imagine of God. Dr. Amos worked tirelessly to awaken the minds of Black people, trying to get us to focus not on our problems, but instead, to direct our attention on who profits from our pain. For if we refuse to confront the issue of money and wealth, our lives will continue to be threatened by those who profit off our pain and suffering. "How different would our education be if we went to school to learn to create jobs for ourselves?" - Dr. Amos Wilson (Feb **23**, see pages 25, 648).

Know Thy Self
African Proverb

A person who knows not and knows not that they know not is foolish - disregard them.

A person who knows not and knows that they know not is simple - teach them.

A person who knows not and believes that that they know is dangerous - avoid them.

A person who knows and knows not that they know is asleep - awaken them.

A person who knows and knows that they know is wise - follow them.

All theses persons reside in you!
Know Thy Self and to Maat be true.
(42 Laws of Maat, Page 367)

Condolences

My condolences go out to the family and friends of **Amos Wilson** and all those who have been robbed of their life by this system of racism and white supremacy. Please know that death is not the end. The soul survives death, indeed and in spirit. This is a book of the dead written by a boy who was murdered without justice, who defeated death and came forth by day. May the soul of **Amos Wilson** walk peacefully through the field of Reeds in Amenta. Amen Ra.

December 31st 2013 - New Years Eve

When I think back on my days in the military I get a sense of sadness thinking of all the people I met because I miss a lot of them. Even the ones I may not have gotten along with so well. When we are young we sometimes disagree over small things not appreciating the fullness of life. That time of my life is connected with my early 20's and the life of partying, perceived "fun" and being care free. I served in the Army with Michelle and Casey during this time of my life. On December 31st 2013, the year of the **snake,** they came to spend the New Year in New York City. I had not seen them in 10 years and by this time I had already become a hermit but I came out to see them because I missed them. If either of you ever read this book remember Sgt Eddings loves you. Michelle is a cop now and I'm not sure what Casey does for a living. Michelle is born on **Tupac's** birthday and has a son named **Nas** and Nas has a daughter named **Destiny** who is born the day before Tupac's birthday. **14** shots were fired at Tupac on Sep 7, 1996. Ausar was cut into **14** pieces and Emmett Till died at **14** years old. I have a theory about who Tupac was in a **past life** ? . The Cobra **snake** shirt I'm wearing in this picture is the same shirt I was wearing on **April 3rd** 2020 (p 591) the day before my **past life** revelation of my life as **Tutankhaten** (**King Tut**) was revealed to me on **April 4th** 2020 (p 593).

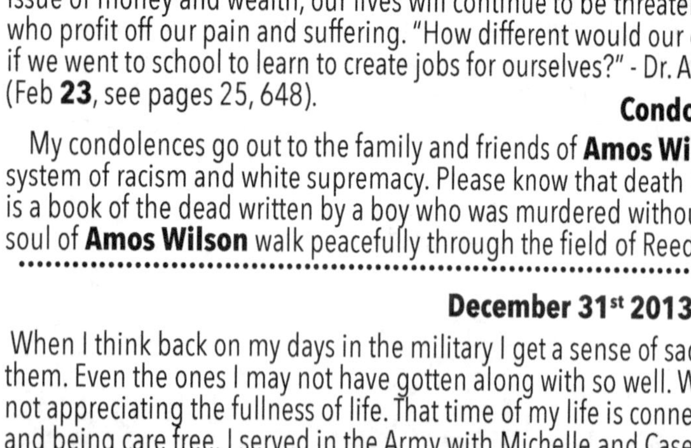

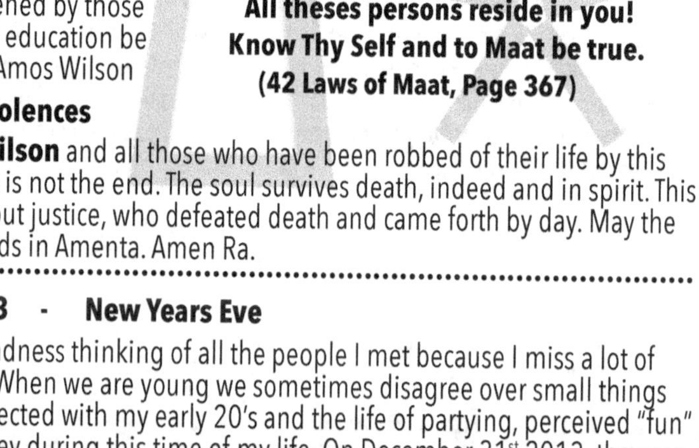

2014 - The Year of Kheper, The Only Begotten God
Neb Kheperu Ra

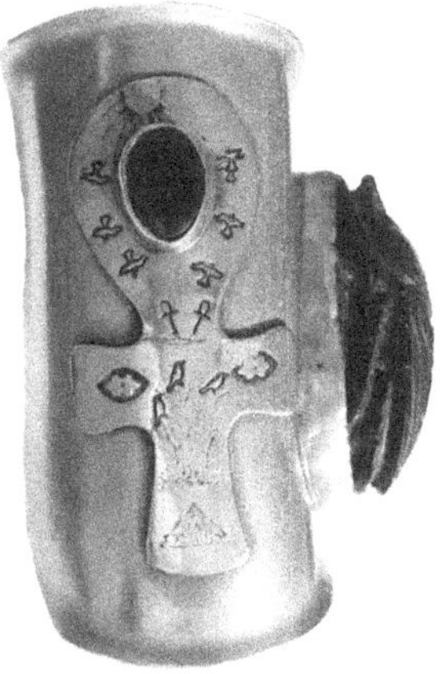

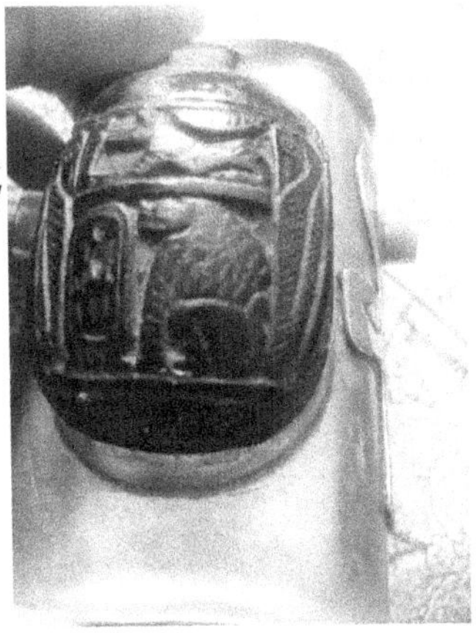

While compiling this book I had to search through my computer, my phones, and e-mails for music, and pictures to mirror my journey. While doing this I noticed many patterns. I notice that 2014 was the year that I purchased the Ancient Book of the Dead, the year that I purchased my first tee shirt with a scarab on it (p 294), the year that the first pictures of Scarabs appeared in my computer and most importantly, the year I purchased my Silver scarab Cuff (p 293). On November 13th 2021 (p 659) I would realize for the first time the name that was written on the cuff in very small mdw ntr (hieroglyphics). Read about Kheper, The Only Begotten God on page 569

Rau

nu

Prt

m

heru

I be the **ancient one** as old as he ancient sun, not **Jesus** or Flavius Josephus, this the **Scarabeus**, the only begotten God from Giza not Nazareth, a star like **Ausar**, read the **resurrection** manuscript, imagine this, we live and die come back again but man forgets, like the gate of men from which souls descend from heaven, and enter new bodies like ducatis speed'n off like harataki in a **dream**, walking on Saqqara pyramid the feeling was serene, clean **deja vu** some how my soul already knew, spiritual revenue, the manger, rejuvenation chambers, Mahabalipuram the Descent of Ganges when I saw them the strangest thing happen within my core, I started pouring, like when I saw the Nile for the first time when I was touring, a stranger in my own land now now they think I'm foreign, but I'm pharaonic restoring maat, iconic live'n and die'n but I come back again fly'n out primordial darkness, **Heru** corporeal walk in my moccasins I dropped a lot of sins, how ironic the cream of the crop now he on top again, eye on top again, eye on top again how iconic the cream of the crop now eye on top again **- TutemRa (April 17th 2022)**

Iu

f

Per

f

m

heru

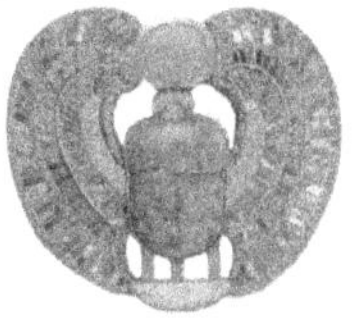

Page 293

Utterances

for

Coming

Forth

by day

into

Light

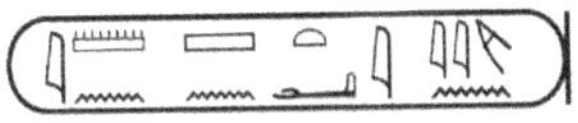

Page 569

It is

he,

who

comes

forth

by day

into

Light

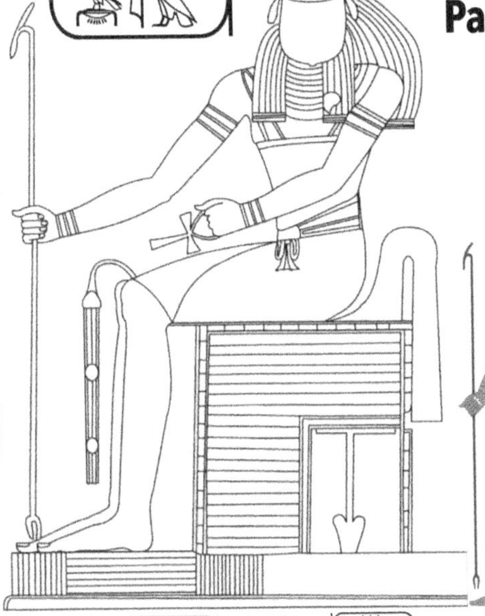

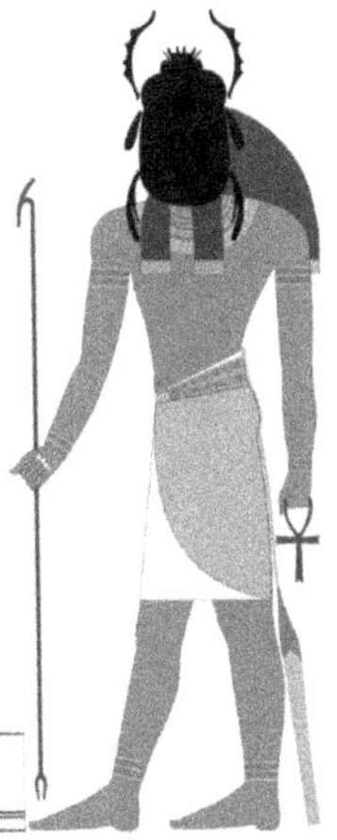

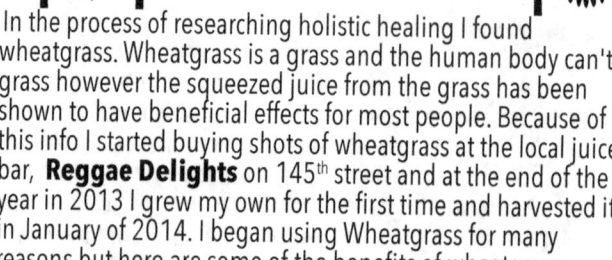

January 1st 2014
Wheatgrass the Green Gold

In the process of researching holistic healing I found wheatgrass. Wheatgrass is a grass and the human body can't grass however the squeezed juice from the grass has been shown to have beneficial effects for most people. Because of this info I started buying shots of wheatgrass at the local juice bar, **Reggae Delights** on 145th street and at the end of the year in 2013 I grew my own for the first time and harvested it in January of 2014. I began using Wheatgrass for many reasons but here are some of the benefits of wheatgrass.

Wheatgrass helps improve the **immune system** by boosting the red blood cell count and in some cases reduced the need for transfusions in patients. When the immune system is supported, we have a better chance of healing. Wheatgrass helps improve **skin health** by Restoring skin thickness while facilitating our internal rejuvenating mechanism, enhancing the youthful glow and elasticity of our skin. Due to its antiseptic properties, wheatgrass is ideal for healing bruises, sores, insect bites, rashes, cuts, and scrapes. Wheatgrass has the ability to increase the amount of **oxygen** in the blood, making it a good way to stimulate **circulation**. Wheatgrass is a natural blood builder because the molecules closely resemble that of the hemin molecule, the pigment which combines with protein to form hemoglobin. The major difference is the wheatgrass molecule contains **magnesium** as it's central atom, and the hemin molecule contains **iron**. The molecular structure of these two substances is almost identical in all other respects. Wheatgrass juice has been proven to build red blood cells quickly after ingestion. It normalizes high blood pressure and stimulates healthy tissue cell growth. Wheatgrass enhances fat **metabolism** helping to reduce weight. It is like a natural energy drink and it contains **selenium**, which is crucial for the healthy functioning of the **thyroid gland**. The thyroid is one of your body's natural weight management tools. According to a 2013 study in Clinical Endocrinology, adding selenium to your diet can help improve irregular thyroid function, even when linked to other issues such as **autoimmune diseases**. Wheatgrass also helps increase a person's **stamina**, cleanses the whole body system, aid digestion, make bowel movements regular, reduce cravings for **addictive substances**, improve **fertility**, inhibit the growth of disease causing bacteria and the activity of **cancer** causing chemicals and ease practically every physical and mental ailment you would expect to encounter among people who are not properly nourished.

January 7th 2014 The Food Is the poison (1st of 12) - Written to the Tupac beat Krazy -

Aye yo I never chased a record deal and never will, some people say I got skills, I just write what I will, see I don't really rap, I write and I talk and it happens to rhyme, like hip hop happened to start in New York, I'm not a rapper but I'm stuck in love with a sport, I got left back in New York, chased but never caught, wrapped up in black thought, black on black crime, don't let these schools brain wash ya mind, I remember that free lunch line, man this food is the poison, the tell lie vision is the drug, now you can say I'm bugged but look man, I ain't never really had money, but I always had love for my homies, don't be a rebel with out a cause, cause the effect, brothers kill brothers just to get a rep, the state kill a brother just to get a check, Keeping you in check or next to a cellmate, behold the world ruled by the pale face, those who attempt to feed your **soul,** be more valuable than those who feed the material hold humanity has on our sanity, there are none more blind than he who will not see, I don't trust everything handed to me, handsome flattery, beautiful analogies, honey bees handle my allergies, naturally nurture me, virtually purposely driven, The **son has risen again,** is there an end son? is there an end? **sun** set, time goes by, puffing on lye, hoping that it gets me high, got a nigga going crazy, got a nigga going crazy, time goes by, puffing on lye, hoping that it gets me high, got a nigga going crazy, got a nigga going crazy

11:59 clock ticking mic rip'n my way to Sunday, my homies said they'll never be peace, but maybe one day kids play on the block of Rockaway without gun play, Namaste, I pray for a better way a better day, the everyday struggle don't sleep rotation in the jungle, when they creep they ain't coming to hug you, they wanna slug you, on the humble for thousands of years we never crumbled, still standing, still _stone be the way of the walk,_ the field nigga planning, New York pitch fork in hand demanding life can be very demanding, Yet remain standing, don't sleep on your landing, a leap of faith heart racing adrenaline fast pace, crash landing, body slamming, **spirit building,** no ceilings, no selling the prophet was yelling, rebelling, if you scared say you scared of going to hell, when heaven is here in the atmosphere, have no fear, disappear and be a hell razor **star gazer,** be a hell razor **star gazer,** be a hell razor **star gazer,** be a hell razor **star gazer** **_coming from the underground,_** time goes by, puffing on lye, hoping that it gets me high, got a nigga going crazy, got a nigga going crazy, time goes by, puffing on lye, hoping that it gets me high, got a nigga going crazy, got a nigga going crazy -
Dawuud's Appeal

January 2014 - Meta Mysterious Encounters
The Fitness Guru

Rau nu Prt m heru

I would meet a younger and sharper version of me at 161st park,Yankee Stadium. While I was at the pull up bar he walked over to me and we began to speak. Him and I clicked as soon as we met like we knew each other before. We looked a little alike however he was more physically developed and sharper at his age than I was when I was his age. He was also a personal trainer. He would come by my studio and we would work out together and talk about life and metaphysics etc. On several occasions this brother would make me feel uneasy. He would look at me, as if he was piercing through my soul and he would say that **he knew who I was** as if he knew something about me that I didn't know. I would ask him who is it that he knew that I was. He would never answer that question but he always seem very sure. Our bodies are divine temples and they can be used as "spirit doors" (p 251). In 2013 the **Nswt Bity (Pharaoh) Khufu** spoke to me through a brother in massage school named Khufu, his body was used like a conduit (p 282). This brother just seemed to know something about me just like brother Khufu. He would share his drawings of the ancient Kemetic Ntchru. This brother came in and out of my life so quickly that I fail to remember his name but he called himself the **Fitness Guru**. He was moving rapidly up and I was there perplexed by the "paranormal" things I was experiencing. I don't think I was moving fast enough for him so he had to continue his quest without me. Even in the word through we can see the word rough. Sometimes life can be rough but we must go "through" the storm. Sometimes the storm is sharpening you, molding and preparing you for something greater. When I think of this brother now I wonder if he saw me for who I was years before I did. I have come to understand that we don't all see the same things when we open and close our eyes. Some people have a different lens they are viewing the world through. In December of this year, I would meet a person who see spirits, for the first time (pages 311 & 318). She would make me aware of my **Guardian Angel** that stands in my hallway. She referred to her as my ancestar*. Later in that next year, I would for the first time see a **"ghost" (apparition)**, the ghost of my Grand father General Dukes appeared to me on Dec 18th (p 348). The next year I would start training **Zee**, another woman who see's **spirits (p 363)**. Zee would would allow me to have a conversation with the spirit and I would come to know exactly who the ancestar* guarding my door is (p 545).

Iu f Per f m heru

January 9th 2014 - Meta Spiritual Encounters of the fourth kind
First Paranormal Experience With the Metu Neter Book

Utterances for Coming Forth by day into Light

Just before I opened this book I had been contemplating the potential of creating reality with our minds and by doing so **I used my thoughts and desires to influence quantum level events in time and space**. I picked up the Book **Metu Neter** by **Ra Un Nefer Amen** just to see if it would give me a message. I opened it to a random page and to my surprise the page spoke about exactly what I had been contemplating and at the same time my candle began to flicker as if someone was trying to blow it out. I picked up my phone and recorded myself saying "Yo! I have to record this! Listen, all I wanna tell you is **Maat**! Listen man, NOTHING in life just happens! I can't even explain to you what just happened to me! **Maat**!" I do not remember all the circumstances surrounding this experience because there were so many interconnecting things that had happened that day and in that moment that made what I read more powerful! It was like the experiences people describe with **ouija board**. It was like something was speaking to me! It reminded me of my experience with the bible and the apparition on **Jan 18th 2012** (p 224). I would have a another mind blowing experience with unseen world involving this book the next year on **May 5th 2015** (page 329). On **Jan 13th 2020** my Oracle would confirm that these experiences were prepping me for the past life revelations that would come on July 3rd 2018 (p 480) and April 4th 2020 (p 594).

It is he, who comes forth by day into Light

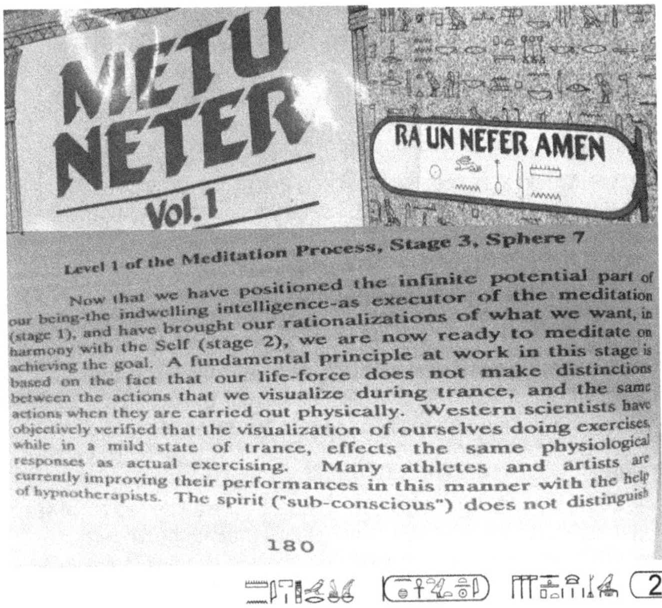

METU NETER Vol.1

RA UN NEFER AMEN

Level 1 of the Meditation Process, Stage 3, Sphere 7

Now that we have positioned the infinite potential part of our being-the indwelling intelligence-as executor of the meditation (stage 1), and have brought our rationalizations of what we want, in harmony with the Self (stage 2), we are now ready to meditate on achieving the goal. A fundamental principle at work in this stage is based on the fact that our life-force does not make distinctions between the actions that we visualize during trance, and the same actions when they are carried out physically. Western scientists have objectively verified that the visualization of ourselves doing exercises while in a mild state of trance, effects the same physiological responses as actual exercising. Many athletes and artists are currently improving their performances in this manner with the help of hypnotherapists. The spirit ("sub-conscious") does not distinguish

180

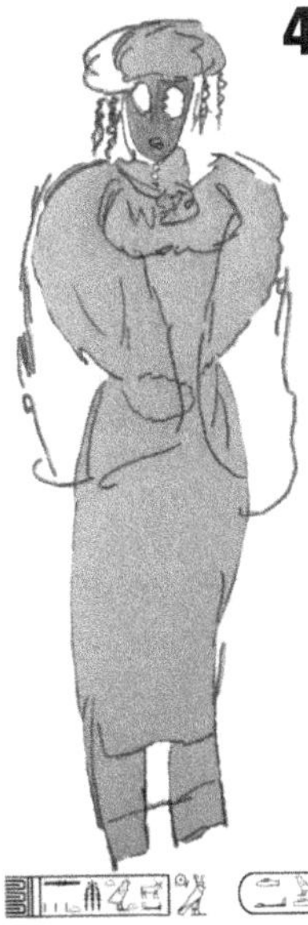

42 Laws of Maat, Page 367

January 20th 2014

The Mysterious Malcolm X Star Code

January 2014, Still making fitness a priority in my life

Dawud, Beloved by the Ntru

January 20th 2014 **The Mysterious Malcolm X Star Code**

My cousins **Wesley** and his younger brother **Justin** are seen in the picture above at my 1999 bootcamp graduation. In 2014 they would come to New York to take part in a video game competition. While here they stayed with me. I picked them up at the train station on 145th and St Nicholas. As we were walking to my apartment I said to them, "This is Harlem, this is where **Malcolm X** and **Marcus Garvey** started. You know who they are right?". Justin had not heard of either of them but Wesley had heard of Malcolm X. I then said - "Well, there are a lot of people to learn about and none of us know everything. You know about **Martin Luther King** right??". Justin said yes. I told them that by the time they leave they will know who **Marcus Garvey** is.

While at my place Wesley asked me If I knew about astrology. I said, "I know a little why do you ask?" He asked me if I knew that **his brother** Justin was born on **my nephews** birthday **July 27th.** I did not know that and I was shocked... I asked him - if he knew that **his sister** is **born** on **my sister and mother's** birthday, **February 3rd**. He did not know that and he was shocked. Then I told him that **his other sister** was not just born on **my birthday October 25th**, but she was also born in 2001 the year of the **snake** just like me (1977) and his mother Pamela (1965). He was shocked again. I asked him **his birthday** and to my amazement he said **May 19th**! I said, "WESLEY! YOU'RE BORN ON **MALCOLM X'S BIRTHDAY**"! We were all shocked, all three of us! I told Wesley to read The Autobiography of Malcolm X and when he finally did start reading it he came to find, that Malcolm had **a brother** named **Wesley**. Isn't that interesting? ***ADDENDUM*** Before you dismiss these patterns as **"just coincidence"**, first concider this. **Rod Sterling**, the creator of the ground breaking **Twilight Zone** TV Show saw the 1955 murder of Emmett Till as a mistrial of justice and wanted to tell Emmett's story. In response to the murder of Emmett Till he produced a show titled **Noon On Doomsday**. However, when the network realized the show was about the murder of Emmett Till they censored it so much that the audience never knew it was about Emmett Till. **But isn't it strange** that the show aired on **April 25**, 1956, and **Carolyn Bryant**, the women who caused Emmett's death would die on **April 25**, 2023...? Afterwards **Sterling** was quoted saying, "I think it's criminal that we're not permitted to make dramatic note of social evils as they exist... Drama by it's very nature should make a comment on those things that effect our daily lives".

My aunt Pamela was sent to this planet and placed in my family tree with an **astrological star code** so that I may place it into this web, this pattern, this divine revelation for you to see, because most of you only believe what you see with your two eyes. I need you to read this book with your heart and soul though! Read this book with your single eye. Use your divine **intuition** which is more valuable than what we learn in schools paid for with **tuition**. Malcolm X was murdered in 1965 the year of the **snake**, the same year my aunt was born. This is the same aunt who took me to see Star Wars, Return of the Jedi and during and after the film I would think I was Luke Skywalker. Star Wars first premiered on **May 25th 1977** the year of the **snake**. Please read what I wrote about Star Wars in the beginning of this book (page 37). The date **May 25th** was engraved on the ring used to identify Emmett Till's mutilated body (page 512). The ring was there to link me with my previous life. On **May 25th 2002** my sister had a **dream** that I died in a car accident and 7 days later I totaled my car, flipping many times, I walked away with only flesh wounds (page 104). In 2008 I would total my motorcycle on **May 25th** and walked away with no injuries (page 157-158). May the force be with you! On Malcolm's birthday, May 19th 2019, I would go to his grave for his annual ceremony and while there I would experience a profound **dream** premonition that came to fruition (pages 561 - 565).

Wesley's Dream

Two months later, when Welsey was **22** years old he joined the Army on March 4, 2014. When he got to his duty station, FT Carson he had a **dream** where I appeared to him like **Morpheus** from the **Matrix**. I pulled up in a car in front of his barracks parking lot. When I got out the car I was wearing the glasses that Morpheus wore in the Matrix. I had an afro and I was wearing a white shirt and jeans.

March 2nd 2014
The Prophecy of REINCARNATION Sambho the Black Buddha

Rau nu Prt m heru

On **March 2**, 2014, my Grand father, **Edward Eddings**' birthday (page 25), I would watch this video all the way through and this Documentary can still be seen on youtube. I was so intrigued by it that I downloaded it to my computer. That's how I was able to date it. The documentary would mention the books ***African Presence In Early Asia*** and ***The Gods of Northern Buddhism*** and I would purchase them immediately. The only thing that really stuck out to me from the documentary was the **prediction** that the **Buddha** would be reborn in the west between the years of 1975 and 2020.When I heard that I did think "I'm born in 1977", but never once did I consider that I was the one who the documentary was talking about especially when the documentary later stated that the Buddha would **reincarnate** in the west in the 1990's. I think it's only natural to feel a way about this person that was supposed to "*come back*". You know, like people waiting for **Jesus** to "come back". The documentary states that the returning **Buddha** would ***prove the immortality of the soul*** with his **reincarnation**. He would be the descendant of those still in bondage today, who are the offspring of those from time immemorial who worked their way from the high lands of Ethiopia down the Nile river to the Mediterranean sea at the delta. As you will read later – the documentary would resurface in my minds eye again shortly after my past life revelation of my life as Emmett Till in July of 2018 (page 480) and again on April 7th 2020 right at the start of COVID 19 only 3 days after I would have my past life revelation of my life as King Tut in April of 2020 (page 594). In ancient Kemet the concept of reincarnation and past lives was called the **Wehem-Mesut** (repeating of births, page 14). In August of 2017 (page 452) I would have a profound experience with the book ***African Presence In Early Asia*** and again on April 11th 2020 the book would spark another profound experience but this time it would deliver a message from Baba **Kilindi Iyi** who had transitioned the day prior (page 606). **Howard Carter**, the archaeologist who discovered the tomb of Tutankhaten (King Tut) in 1922, said the curse of the Pharaoh was nonsense. He claimed that if anyone was going to die from the curse it would have been him since he discovered the tomb. He died on **March 2nd** 1939 (page 13), which is the same day my grand father, **Edward Eddings** was born (page 25)!

Iu f Per f m heru

March 2nd 2014 Gabriella Nevarez 22yrs old
Killed by police in Sacramento California

Following a heated discussion with her Grandmother, Gabriella had taken her car which led to her grandmother calling the police to report it stolen. Police reported that Gabriella evaded them and was driving erratically. They opened fire on her after she rammed into a patrol car. Fourteen bullet holes were found on the car that Gabriella was driving, and it was reported that Gabriella was hit with four gunshots to her back, chest, thigh and scalp.Her grandmother, Mary Beesely, said her granddaughter was bipolar and often had episodes where she went into a dark place, but that she was not a dangerous girl. "She hated guns. She hated violence," Beesley said. Gabriella was murdered on my Grand father, **Edward Eddings**' birthday (page 25).

Utterances for Coming Forth by day into Light

Condolences

My condolences go out to all the families of those who have been robbed of their life by this system of white supremacy. Please know that death is not the end. The soul survives death, indeed and in spirit. This is a book of the dead written by a boy who was murdered without justice, who defeated death and came forth by day. May the soul of **Gabriella Nevarez** walk peacefully through the field of Reeds in Amenta. Amen Ra.

March 8th 2014
Army VA Claim Appeal for Compensation Denied

2003 IRAQ
Good enough to go to war but not good enough to get compensated

It is he, who comes forth by day into Light

The same country that claims to love it's soldiers is the same country that rejects the claims of the soldiers. When I left the Army I made a claim for several injuries I suffered while in the Army but they only approved one of my claims. I got 10% which was around $100 a month, that was in 2005. In 2021 I still only have 10% and I receive $144.00 a month. Because of my experience in America I suffer from PTSD that the military caused and that America has caused. I have several other claims that the Army has denied. Today is October **23**rd 2021 and I do not have the time to chase them down for what they owe me. Especially when I have to jump through hoops to get it (page 121, 1**23**). I have struggled with these pains since I left the army. The VA hospital wants to make soldiers beg them for the compensation they are owed. They denied my appeal and I struggled in silence. I must thank them though. If they had paid me what they owed me I might not have been so financially stressed and I might not have turned to music for therapy and I might not have studied my past and I might not know that I was Emmett Till and Tutankhaten. So thank you but I still want what is mine.

March 28th 2014 - Meta Spiritual Encounters

Shanta and The Transmigration of Her Mother's Soul

ADDENDUM

I met Shanta in high school but we never really spoke. She was the girl friend of my best friend Courtlan and a cheerleader on the cheerleading squad. I can't remember ever having a conversation with her however she remembers us once having a conversation about Tupac while on the train, on the way home from school. After I graduated from high school in 1996 we didn't see each other again until I joined Facebook in 2008. Even then, we never really communicated much, however in 2014 she reached out to me for personal training and soon after I began training her. After my past life revelation of Emmett Till on July 3rd 2018 (page 480) she told me things about her mother and her daughter or you could also say it was about her mother and her mother.. Shanta's mother passed away in 1989, the year of the **snake**. Her mother's name was **Mary** like the mother of "**Jesus**". In Egypt the word Mery meant **beloved** and my name is **Dawud** which also means beloved. In Egypt the symbol used for Mery was a plow ( ) which was used to **Till** the land, like Emmett **Till**. **Mary's** middle name was Sue. 8 years after **Mary Sue** died Shanta had a daughter. She named her **Daya Sue**, like **Deja Vu**. When her father looked at his grand daughter (Daya Sue) for the first time he must have had **Deja Vu** because he told Shanta that the baby was her mother. For some reason he felt like his wife had been **reborn/reincarnated** in the body of his grand daughter. When Daya was around 2 or 3 years old Shanta's father had a rem**ark**able experience with Daya while baby sitting her that further confirmed his initial feelings that she was his wife reborn as his grand daughter. He happened to be driving ***around with her in his car one day when Daya asked him if he remembered dancing and singing to the song that was playing on the radio***. Astonished and bewildered he could do nothing but stare at Daya. There was no way that a baby her age should have articulated herself so well and there was no way that she could have known that he, and his dead wife Mary, used to dance to that song. When he returned Daya, he told Shanta what had happened and asked her if she had ever played that song for her before. With a look of amazement and great curiosity she said no. However, on another occasion Daya did the same thing to Shanta. She asked Shanta if she remembered a **Whitney Houston** (p **23**0) song that was playing on the radio. Daya would also cry for her "grandmother" but she had never met Mary. Or had she?! It is all very **strange**. Especially the fact that Daya has a best friend named **Isis** that she's known since the second grade. Shanta is a Pisces born on March 15th. Her mother passed away on **2**/13/**89** (**2/89**) the year of the **snake**. I did not plan to put Shanta's story on this page but by some **strange** "coincidence" her story ended up on page **289**, like Feb 1989 (**2/89**). After I had my past life revelation of Emmett **Till** in 2018 (p 480) I was told a similar story about her high school boy friend Courtlan that reminded me of Daya Sue (p 74). In 2022 I had **Deja Vu** twice while in **Kemet** (p 670).

One of the best cases of children's past life memories to ever be recorded is the case of **Shanti Devi** (Lugdi Devi). A commission set up by **Muhatma Gandhi** confirmed her claim in 1935. You must ask your self this question - what are you? Are you the body or are you something that is inside of the body, like a spirit or a soul? Perhaps you are just in your body for a short span of time. Perhaps time is not what we think it to be. Perhaps Shanta's daughter is her mother living another life or perhaps her mother just momentarily used the body of her grand daughter to speak to her daughter and husband. Think about why alcohol might be called spirits. Then read what I wrote about the words: **Spirit, Vine, Grapes** and **Wine** in ancient Kemet (page 481). Perhaps thought forms or other entities, spirits or souls like **Lusaaset** (p 481) are more easily able to "**come forth**" when we are in a "drunken" state. Perhaps babies vibrate at a level that allows for spirits or thought forms to "**come forth**" like **Lusaaset**. In Aug of 2020 I went to the Detroit **Psychedelic** conference for the first time and while I was there I was told a story similar to the one Shanta's father told (p 618). In 2013 I had an experience with a brother named **Khufu** that left me wondering if a spirit moved through him to speak to me (p 282). I would also have a similar experience on Apr 16th 2016 after I wrote the song Holler If Ya Hear Me (page 374-375). I started that song with the words - "The plight black life no hand outs, **heirlooms**, damned and doomed but soon the tune gonna change, you ***robbed my tomb***, drove me insane, ***put a chain on my neck***, gave no respect". One could argue that the souls of king Tut and Emmett Till were speaking because King Tut's tomb was **robbed** and Emmett had a chain wrapped around his **neck**. One could also argue that Emmett Till, King Tut and Dawud are all the same soul. The most profound experience I have had with spirits speaking through people happened with my friend **Meeky** at the **International African Arts Festival** on **July 3rd 2021** (p 650). The strange thing about Shanta is that, when she looks at the alabaster sculpture of **King Tut's** mother **Kiya**, she feels a sense of familiarity. When Shanta was in high school she dressed up as **Cleopatra** for senior dress up day (p 323). I don't know if Shanta is an ancient relative or friend of mine but my ancient wife was **Ankh** e**S** en **Amen** and I find it very interesting that Shanta got the **Ankh** ☥ symbol tattooed on her shoulder at 19 years old and her middle name is **Sh**ameen. I wouldn't be surprised if I came back to this planet with people I loved from previous lives. I once wrote a song titled **Twin Flame** on Shanta's birthday (p **444**). During the writing of this book it was Shanta who I confided in as I detailed all the mysterious connections in this book. Shanta's daughter Daya is born on Jan 7, the day after **Mamie Till** died (p 511) she has a son born on Oct 20, 5 days before me and a son born on Sep 7, the day **Tupac** was shot (p 664).

Today is Mar 15th 2022 and today is Shanta's birthday. Today I spoke to my old friend Sgt Oliver (Big O) for the first time in a few years. I told him about this book and afterwards he would tell me stories about his daughter that reminded me of Shanta's daughter and the story I was told in Detroit in August of 2020 (p 618). Big O would also tell me that he crashed his motorcycle the same day that I crashed my car in 2002 (p 96). AS SOON AS WE HUNG UP, I received a message from Coreisa Lee. She wanted to tell me that she got a call to be a part of a new Emmett Till theater project named, **Emmett Till, A New American Opera**, premiering Mar **23**rd 2022. Coreisa was already connected to my revelation as she is the **Renaissance Flutist** I wrote about in the 6th grade (p 44) and she's connected to the song I made for Dr Umar (p 460). There is no such thing as "just" a coincidence. All things are governed by seen and unseen laws.

March 15th 2014

My father and I never really got into the practice of taking pictures together but on **March 15**th 2014 I took these two pictures of us. My father wasn't there for me and my sisters much in our youth but some**times** the universe knows what's best for you. And **time** has a way of mending wounds. As we experience friends and family passing away, **time** allows us to appreciate the **time** we have with friends and family.. My father and I currently have a good relationship.

Rau nu Prt m heru

Iu f Per f m heru

April 4th 2014 The Super Nova

I met Nova back in 2010 in a profound way (page 184). I unconsciously used my thoughts to control quantum level events in time and space. I had no intentions on training her. I was attracted to her and wanted to date her but for some reason we just remained friends. On **April 4th** 2014, the same day that **Martin Luther King** was assassinated (page 69, 592) she would start training with me one on one. She had come to my group classes years before but this was the first time that we trained 1 on 1. At the end of this year on December 17th I would have a profound experience at her house at a holiday party that would spark a four year pattern of communication with the unseen realms (page 314). The December 3rd pattern started in 2014 at **Nova's** house on December 17th and it ended in 2017 on December 3rd with the death of the father of another friend named **Nova** (page 457). She would also get the role to play **Vanity** in her biopic (page 362). In 2019 I would give Nova a massage and after the massage Nova told me she saw a **Giant Titanium Scarab Beetle** with small beetles **floating** around it (page 579). This was before I knew the full meaning of the scarab and before I knew I was Tutankhaten (King Tut). 2014 was the year of the Scarab. The year of Neb Kheperu Ra. On **April 4th** 2020, my past life as King Tut would be revealed (page 594).

Utterances for Coming Forth by day into Light

April 13th 2014 The Battles of Questions Like, "Should I Smoke Weed"?

I had been smoking for 3 years now and I wanted to stop. I knew I was addicted and on top of all the **paranormal** things I was experiencing I didn't like the feeling of being severely **paranoid** or extremely high. Then on the other hand sometimes I would be overcome with amazing ideas for movies but the feelings of paranoia were not worth it! I had also been listening to the music of **Stic** from the legendary group **Dead Prez** and there was one line in a song that made me question my smoking of weed. In the song **Way of Life** Stic says the words - *"The love for the art, the sweat on your shirt, the mind, the body, and the spirit that work, the feelings of failure, the hope to succeed, the battles of questions like -* ***should I smoke weed****?"*. These were the first words to make me question the hazards of smoking weed. Then I read pages 88 and 89 in **Dr Llaila Afrika's** book **African Holistic Health,** which states- *"**Burnt (cooked)** Marijuana is a chemical that **alters the attachment of the spirit to the breath.** It causes the spirit to lose its guiding effect on the mind, mood, and body. It can alter or **destroy levels** of **spirituality**."* - **Dr. Llaila Afrika.** There were times when I smoked and got so high that I could not hold any logical thoughts. I would seem confused and forgetful. I would even forget what I was doing while I was doing it sometimes and for some strange reason **I always felt like something was after me**. At times I even felt like **the government was after me** but **Perhaps** what I was feeling were the **effects** from these **small waves** of this **Prophecy of reincarnation** building up momentum **in my everyday life**. I think this was the first time that I would take one puff of weed and get extremely high then immediately throw all the weed in the toilet because of extreme paranoia. I did not like the way it made me feel. The date was April 13th 2014.

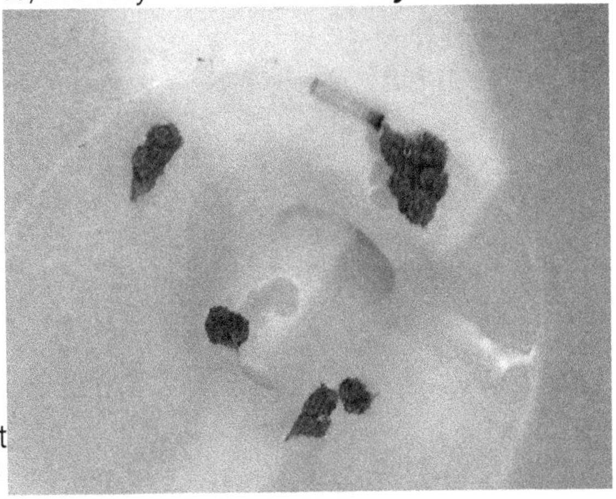

I threw all my weed in the toilet and flushed it. Perhaps a week or two later I bought more weed and smoked again. It wasn't till after my past life revelations that I realized weed had actually opened **High Frequency psychic channels** (page 343).

It is he, who comes forth by day into Light

May 3rd 2014 - Meta Mysterious Encounters
Javet and my Second meeting with Mr Nature

Javet is a friend who I have had since high school. We must have known each other since at least 1994 or 1995. I remember meeting her through my cousin Jackie who is born on my birthday October 25th (page 53). Javet and I connected again when I got out of the Army. I even rented out a room from her and her sister for a few months in 2006 (page 147). I had not seen her in around 6 years and this was the first time we had seen each other since I'd started to change my attention towards Kemet (Egypt). The last time we saw each other we had gone out to a club. On May 3rd 2014 she stopped by to see me. We had a long conversation catching up on old times. Then we went and got food. We could have left 2 minutes sooner or 2 minutes later and we would have never seen Mr Nature but for some reason as soon as we got down stairs Mr Nature came strolling down the street with a shopping cart full of flowers. I had just met Mr Nature in October of 2013 the year of the snake (page 281). I met him just by chance the same way I had met him today so I knew I was supposed to buy a flower. After I gave him the money Javet told me that I bought the same flower that she has on her office table. I laughed, then I told her how I met Mr Nature and she laughed with amazement.

Significance

Javet is a platonic female friend that I have had since my adolescence. She represents the Divine Feminine energy on this planet. I completed my Kemetic Yoga teachers training course on July 1st 2018, which is Javet's birthday and two days later on July 3rd 2018 I would get the past life revelation of my Life as Emmett Till (page 480).

May 19th 2014
Malcolm X Rally 125th street

Attending the annual **Malcolm X Rally** on 125th street for his birthday had become a yearly routine for me. This is the only picture I was able to find from the 2014 Rally and I find it very strange that the boy in the picture has an uncanny likeness to **Emmett Till**. 4 years later I would realize I was Emmett Till in a past life (page 480). And the next year in 2019, on Malcolm's birthday (p 561-565) I would go to Malcolm's grave for the first time and there I would have a profound experience.

May 2014 - High Strangeness
The Tale of Two Mary's and The Patterns of Life

I met a woman named **Mary** at Watkins health foods store on 125th street. She was inquiring about health and wellness so I gave her my card and soon after she called me. I began to train her in my studio and during her sessions she would play her **pandora** play list. She was a social worker and dealt with a lot of veterans and I think she began to see me as a patient because I was a veteran. One day before leaving a session she grabbed my hand and began to talk to me in a manner that was outside of my comfort zone. I was still smoking weed at the time and I didn't trust anyone. She was pretty with a nice body but the last thing I wanted to do was use my space as a place to step out the boundaries of a client /trainer relationship, however less than a week later we began to enter the course. While entering the course I looked for something to tie her hair up with. I looked over my **left** shoulder and there hanging from a **model skeleton** was a string with two Mary's on it, as seen in (**figure A**). A woman named **Mary** had given it me for protection before I deployed to Iraq in 2003 (p 113). When I touched it I got a sense of **Deja Vu** and my thoughts flashed back to 2003. I met this Mary at the club and we only got together to enter the course. She was in love with me but I only saw her as a trophy. Shortly after this experience I stopped training Mary and sometime after I found myself in my studio trying to motivate myself to do my workout routine. Then a song came on that I had downloaded because I heard it on Mary's **pandora** list. The song was one of my favorites and at that moment the song motivated me to get up and exercise. When I was done with my workout I looked at the name of the song it was named, **Open Roads** by the Artist Giles **Lamb** off the album **Transform**. **Emmett Till** was the sacrificial **lamb** (p 511). **Transform**ation like Kheper. This is 2014, **The Year of Kheper the Sacred Dung Beetle** (p 284). **Neb Kheperu Ra** (p 659). The original mother Mary is Auset (Isis) from Kemet (Egypt).. Perhaps this was a test from Auset. In 2022 I experienced **Deja Vu** twice while in **Kemet** (pages 670 - 671).

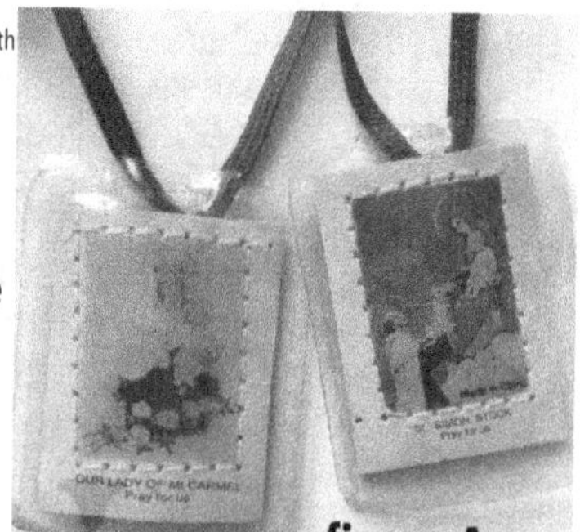

figure A

Rau nu Prt m heru

Iu f Per f m heru

Utterances for Coming Forth by day into Light

It is he, who comes forth by day into Light

July 1799 - The Rosetta Stone

In July 1799, a company of Napoleon's soldiers on demolition duty in **Rosetta** Egypt discovered a compact slab of black basalt built into an extremely old wall. Their work came to an immediate halt when a perceptive lieutenant realized they'd found, an ancient 'document" of extreme importance. Unlocking the secrets of the past the Rosetta Stone proved to be the key to deciphering the language of a culture that had been silent for 1,370 years. On the face of the slab were inscriptions in three distinct languages; 54 lines of **Greek**, 28 lines of Egyptian **demonic** script, and 14 lines of **MDW NTR** (**Egyptian hieroglyphs**), a pictorial system of writing that had baffled experts for centuries. The secrets of the hieroglyphics were unlocked by an African man however the European Jean-François Champollion was given credit for the breakthrough.

Significance

The experience I detail below with **Roza** and the card I found in 2005 (pages 141-142) was similar to what the discovery of the **Rosetta** stone did for the world. The Stone unlocked the secret language and my experience with Roza unlocked my awareness to the **unseen** world and caused me to pay closer attention to other strange spiritual phenomena I would continue to experience in the years to come.

May 2014 - Quantum Spiritual Encounters
Roza, Jean Jacques Dessalines and the glitch in the Matrix

Jean Jacques Dessalines

I met Roza in front of my building. She had just gotten her hair done at the local hair salon. We talked a little then I gave her my business card. Soon after she contacted me and started training with me. One day during one of our sessions she asked me how I became a trainer, so I told her about the remarkable serendipitous experience I had, finding the **no limit fitness business card** in 2005 (pages 141-142). After telling her the story I did something I had never done before. I googled the name on the card to see if I could find the owner but nothing came up. Then I googled the number on the card and still, nothing. Finally I put the e-mail address into the facebook search and a page appeared. The page was private but the profile picture was **Toussaint Louverture** (one of the leaders of the **Haitian revolution**) on a horse. Roza was there to witness this but what she did not witness was what happened when she left. After she left I went back to facebook to further explore the page but to my surprise the page was gone. It no longer came up, as if the page no longer existed. Sort of how the card seemingly appeared from out of nowhere back in 2005 (p 141-142). What was that?! Was the card placed there by **Jean Jacques Dessalines** or **Toussaint Louverture**?! Can things just appear from out of "Nowhere", like teleportation? Do our thoughts and desires affect our reality by influencing quantum level events in time and space? And do our ancestors continue working after death of the physical body? Like **invisible helpers**..? I don't know whether it was Jean Jacques Dessalines or Toussaint Louverture but I'm sure it was some unseen entity. For more on **Guardian Angels** and **Ka Doors** (**Spirit Doors**) see pages (250 -253,48, 150,179, 199, 315, 318, 329, 348, 349, 409, 421, 434, 545, 548, 549, 572, 584, 604, 626, 650).

Significance

The Rosetta Stone was discovered in 1799 by Napoleon. This stone is what allowed the deciphering of the Kemetic **MDW NTR** (Egyptian **hieroglyphs**). My experience with Roza allowed me to reevaluate my scope of possibilities within this thing we called reality and communication with ancestral spirits. This experience with Roza prepped me for the other spiritual phenomena I would continue to encounter for years to come ultimately leading me to my past life of **Emmett Till** on July 3rd 2018 (page 480) and my past life of **Tutankhaten** (**King Tut**) on April 4th 2020 (page 594), the day **Martin Luther King** was assassinated in 1968 (page 69, 592). I am connected to the Haitian revolution because of my Bajan ancestry. When the indigenous population of the island of Hispaniola (Haiti) was decimated by European invaders the first place they went for new "slaves" was Barbados (Bajan) (see page 25).

One time is an incidence, twice is a coincidence, but three, four, and five is a pattern! Can you tell the difference?

May 25th 2014 at 8:11 PM - WHAT'S YOURS WILL BE YOURS
Neb Kheperu Ra and my Silver Heart Scarab Cuff

I would see **Mfundishi Jhutyms Hassan Salim** again vending on 125th street across the street from Red Rooster. I was looking at his table to see if anything caught my eye but my attention was taken away when I saw the cuff he was wearing on his wrist. As soon as I saw it it was as if I was magnetically attracted to it I had to have it. Without thought I asked him with the most serious look on my face "how much for the cuff on your wrist?!" He looked at it and looked back at me and gave me a price. I pulled the money out and bought it without hesitation. I put it on immediately and Mfundishi politely informed me that I had it on upside down. We both laughed as I adjusted it. Later that day I would take pictures with the cuff at 161 p**ark**. The picture is time stamped and that's how I was able to know the exact date and time. I would purchase this **silver Scarab cuff** on May 25th 2014 the same day that was engraved on **Emmett Till's silver ring**, used to identify his body (page 512) and the same day that my sister had that **dream premonition** of my **car** accident in 2002 (page 104) and the same day that I totaled my **motorcycle** in 2008 (page 157). May 25th Strikes again! If that is not strange enough for you then wait till November 13th of 2021 (page 659)! On that day I would realize what was written on this cuff and this was not just a coincidence! One time is an incidence, twice is a coincidence, but three, four, and five is a pattern! Can you tell the difference?

On November 13th 2021 this cuff would reveal it's true Talisman powers.

Page 659

June 14th 2014
Meta Spiritual Encounters
Katherine and Her Psychic Reading

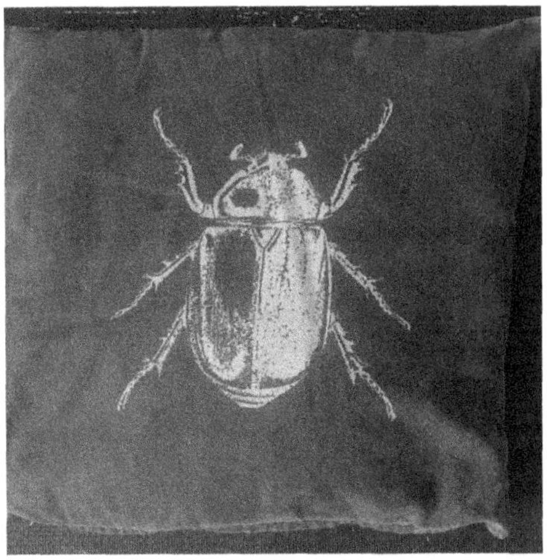

Rau nu Prt m heru

I would meet Katherine through a referral. After our first session we talked for a while about things supernatural. After our conversation she would tell me that she had seen a psychic for her birthday on April 15th and the psychic told her that she would meet a spiritual person and with that person she would have long spiritual conversations and now after meeting me she felt like I was that person. I had never seen a psychic before and still have never seen one but hearing that from her did make me feel good about myself. A psychic had predicted her meeting me, that was cool. She became one of the interesting people that would come across my path. Two years later on May 24th she would gift me this pillow with a **Scarab Dung Beetle** on it. If she had waited one more day it would have made the May 25th star code but it was close enough to fall into the pattern.

June 15th 2014
Mesmerized by the Only Begotten God
Neb Kheperu Ra

Iu f Per f m heru

On June 15th I walked into Jackie Robinson P**ark** and there was a festival taking place. I walked to a random table and my eyes fell upon the symbol of the scarab and as soon as I saw the tee shirt I had to have it! I took my UTBC Paradigm shirt off (page 267) and put the **Scarab** shirt on and had the designer take a picture of me wearing it. For some reason this scarab was calling me. Less than a month ago I had purchased the scarab cuff off of **Mfundishi Jhutyms'** wrist and now this tee shirt had captivated me. I didn't even know the Kemetic name for scarab was Kheper. On the table was also a tee shirt with King Tut's face but that garnered none of my attention. I was taken by the "scarab". I was attracted to the scarab because I knew it symbolized transformation and that's what I was promoting with my fitness training. Helping people transform their bodies. At the time I did not know King Tut's throne name was **Neb Kheperu Ra**, (the master of transformations of Ra). I did not know that scarabs were connected to **resurrection** of the pharaoh's soul after death. And I did not know that the scarab was the original **Only Begotten God** from ancient Kemet (pages 489 and 569). I had no idea of the journey I was on but I was on it. In ancient Kemet (Egypt) the concept of reincarnation and past lives was called the **Wehem-Mesut** (repeating of births, page 14). All the events in this book are true. If you follow my path and do the things I do yet still the great mysteries are not shown to you. Then continue the path and **to Maat be true** and perhaps in due time you will be worthy of the view.

Utterances for Coming Forth by day into Light

It is he, who comes forth by day into Light

July 15th 2014 - Meta Mysterious Messages from The fourth Dimension
Stephanie and Her Dreams of Siddhartha

I met Stephanie in May of 2014, she was into fitness and was looking for healthier ways of eating. I told her about black seed oil and various other herbs and I started training her sometime in May of 2014 soon after we met. She would be one of the women that crossed my path with spiritual messages to impart to me. Two months after meeting her I bought the book Siddhartha. Stephanie is related to **Malcolm X** (p 561) by way of her Uncle **Angel** Pizarro who married Gamilah Shabazz, Malcolm's **fourth** daughter.

I had my past life revelation of my life as **Tutankhaten** (**King Tut)** on April 4th 2020 (page 594) the day that **Martin Luther King** was assassinated (page 69, 592). Sometime after that while searching my order history on Amazon I became aware of two books that I purchased 6yrs prior on July 15th 2014. Apparently I ordered the book **Moses Begat King Tut** on July 15th 2014 and the book **Siddhartha**. I had the book on **king Tut** for 6 years but I never read it and don't remember what made me buy the book. Fueled with the revelation of my life as King Tut in 2020 I searched through my book shelf in search for the book and when I found it I started reading it. The book spoke about the biblical character **Moses** and how he was really the Pharaoh **Akhenaten** from the 18th dynasty, the husband of **Nefertiti** and the father of **Tutankhaten** (**King Tut**). I was amazed.

The interesting thing about the book Siddhartha is **I only have one copy of the book but I should have two**. I don't remember purchasing this book but it is in my Amazon order history and the next year I was also given this book as a birthday gift by my friend Stephanie (page 340). When she gifted it to me I thanked her for it and I put it on my book shelf next to other books that I had not read from cover to cover yet. Instead of reading the book I didn't think the book had any major importance as I felt like I was already reading and doing the things I needed to be reading and doing. I was arrogant. I didn't know it yet but **something** or **someone** wanted me to read this book and Stephanie was just being used as a conduit! I don't know where the other copy went but I can vaguely remember lending the book to my friend **Danny** and that was after I had read it in 2016. Perhaps Danny never gave me the copy back or perhaps I gave him a different book and never received the one I ordered. I don't know but whatever the case may be I only have one copy of Siddhartha but I should have two and some how this book Siddhartha found it's way to me twice. I wouldn't read this book till 2016 after I met a brother named

Kenny who was in his 70's. Kenny and I met in **Marcus Garvey** park. Him and I would have peaceful debates about life and religion and one day during one of our debates he told me I needed to read a book but he couldn't remember the name. After some time he remembered the name of the book and it was **Siddhartha** by Hermann Hesse. Surprised, I told him that I already had the book! Then I told him that the person that gave me the book was born on January 12th the same day as him. Because of that **coincidence** I went home and read the book immediately. I did not know who or what the book was about until after I read the book however after a few paragraphs of reading I was over come with tears as I felt like I was reading about myself. The book Siddhartha is about the **Buddha "Siddhartha Gautama"** and how "he" gained enlightenment.

Rau nu Prt m heru

After I read the book I called Stephanie to ask her why she gave me that book! That's when she told me about her childhood friend **Siddhartha**. He was a really good swimmer who unfortunately and ironically died trying to save someone from drowning. Sometime after she met me in 2014 she had a **dream** about her friend Siddhartha and in the **dream** he wrote a message on a piece of paper and handed it to her. When she awoke from the **dream** she could not remember what the message said. Confused about the **dream** she google the named Siddhartha and came across the book Siddhartha by Hermann Hesse - She purchased the book and read it.. After getting to know me she felt I reminded her of the boy Siddhartha from the book so she bought me a copy of the book for my birthday in 2015 (page 340). Stephanie would also have a **dream** in 2015 that I was once a king and I had **23** wives. Her partner's name is Angel and after training with me he got a tattoo of Enpu (Anubis, page 640) on his forearm.

Iu f Per f m heru

A few months before I met Stephanie and before I purchased the book Siddhartha I watched the documentary <u>The Prophecy of</u> **REINCARNATION** <u>Sambho the Black Buddha</u> (page 288), about the Buddha being reincarnated in the western world between the years of 1975 and 2020. It also stated that the Buddha would prove the immortality of the soul with his reincarnation and the documentary would show images of **King Tut**. I was born in 1977 the year of the **snake** and I had my second past life revelation of my life as **Tutankhaten** (**King Tut)** revealed to me on April 4th 2020 (page 594) the same day that **Martin Luther King** was assassinated (page 69, 592). Who wrote the message on the paper in Stephanie's dream, Siddhartha the Buddha, Siddhartha her childhood friend or me?

Confirmations

Utterances for Coming Forth by day into Light

Today is January 8th 2022 and I just finished adding a song to this book from January 8th 2012 (page 222). I wrote the song in 2012 on January 8th and titled it, **Rocket Ship**. The words are: "**I'm a rocket ship, I'm a beacon of light, I was sent here to write and I was sent here to fight and I could die to night, I'm a rocket ship, on a rocket ship**". When I finished adding the short song to this book I added a picture of an **Ausarian** (Osirion) **Ben Ben** pyramidal cap stone to the page to signify the type of rocket ship I was talking about. (<u>Ausar is the one who defeats death through the resurrection and this is where the story of</u> **<u>Jesus Christ</u>** <u>was taken from when Christianity came into existence. The resurrection of the father through the son, the repetition of the soul,</u> **<u>Immortality</u>**<u>. This is what the ancient Egyptians had mastered! From time immemorial we knew that there was no death. We had no word for death as we know it today because we understood and mastered the repetition of the soul</u>.) When I was done with page 222, I saw that I had received a text from Stephanie a few hours earlier. When I opened the text I saw a screenshot of an old message from her friend Siddhartha along with the message - "my friend pops up every now and again".. Her birthday is Jan 12th but her friend Siddhartha sent her an early message on January 8th of 2012, the same day I wrote the song about being a rocket ship and today is January 8th. I was Siddhartha in a previous life and **I am a beacon of light** and I was sent here to write this book. One of my assignments in this life was to fulfill <u>The Prophecy of</u> **<u>REINCARNATION</u>** <u>Sambho the Black Buddha</u>. In the beginning was the word, then the word became flesh. The word can't be seen like the soul. I wrote music from the heart and soul and my ancient soul awoke within my flesh coming forth by day. My lyrical word was my sword, and with it I crashed down on the enemy with inter dimensional accuracy that they could not detect or anticipate. They knew someone was coming through Hip Hop but they thought they had killed him in 1996! They had no idea he would come from a galaxy Far Far away called Far Rockaway Queens. I have a theory about who Tupac was in a past life and it's wilder than your wildest dreams? . **One time is an incidence, twice is a coincidence, but three, four, and five is a pattern! Can you tell the difference?**

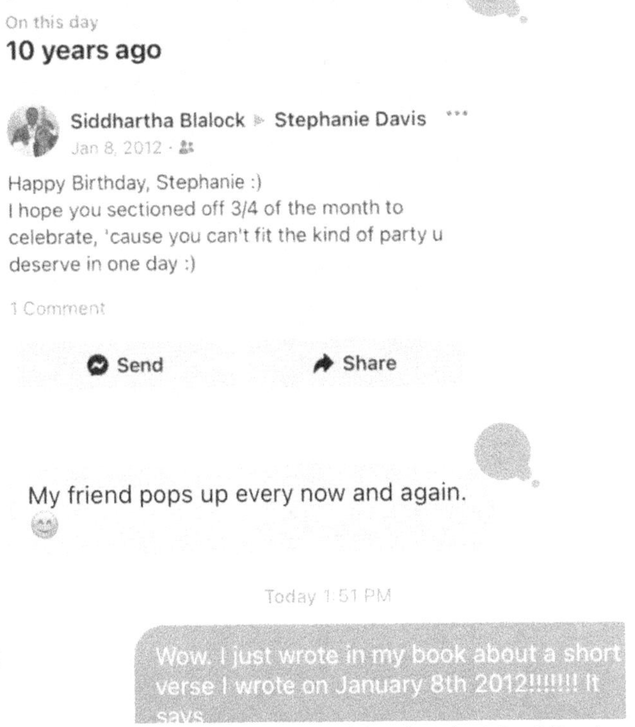
On this day
10 years ago
Siddhartha Blalock ▸ Stephanie Davis
Jan 8, 2012
Happy Birthday, Stephanie :)
I hope you sectioned off 3/4 of the month to celebrate, 'cause you can't fit the kind of party u deserve in one day :)
1 Comment
Send
Share
My friend pops up every now and again.
Today 1:51 PM
Wow. I just wrote in my book about a short verse I wrote on January 8th 2012!!!!!!! It says

It is he, who comes forth by day into Light

July 13th 2014 Gail From 1955

Mysterious Confirmations

Gail started training with me in 2014 when she was 59 years old. She was about to turn 60 and felt it necessary to improve her physical health. She was sent down (born) in 1955 the same year my mother was sent down (born) so I always felt a motherly energy from her. When we first met she could not do a single push up. After some months a training she would break out into tears the first time she did one. When I entered massage school I gave her her first massage. Gail enjoyed the massage so much she wanted to gift her daughter a massage with me as she felt her daughter could use the healing and relaxation benefits but for some reason we never found the time to do it. After my past life revelation of Emmett Till on July 3rd 2018 I told Gail about it and she believed me because of all the other experiences I had shared with her over the years. In 2021 I would meet her daughter and give her a massage. Her daughter was happy to finally meet me as her mother had spoken so highly of me over the years. Her daughter was following me on Instagram and had been aware of my past life revelation because of the posts I share. I told her some of the details of my story and she was amazed. During our conversation I would come to find out that her last name was different from her mothers, her last name's **Mobely**, just like **Emmett Till's** mother, Mamie Till **Mobely**! Gail was born in 1955 the same year Emmett had been murdered and she was born on August 31st three days after he was murdered.

2014

Mysterious Messages from The fourth Dimension
Haitian Sistar from Tai Chi class has a Dream About Me

Tai Chi class had just ended and I was on my way home but before I could get to the steps that lead to the exit a Haitian sister from my class rushed to stop me. She said she had a **dream** about me and asked if it was ok for her to share the **dream** with me. That got my attention quickly, and I was eager to hear. she said it was better if we sat down so we did. She said that she wanted to tell me this the week prior but I left too quickly. Then she told me her **dream**:

Her Dream

She had a dream that she was being attacked. While she was being attacked three people arrived. I was the 3rd person to arrive and when I did I carried her away from danger.

Significance

I had been receiving messages from other people as well so when she told me this dream I wasn't surprised. I felt it had meaning but I didn't know what. Katherine had recently told me she saw a psychic who told her she would meet someone like me a few months before she met me (page 294). **Stephanie** had a dream about me (page 296). Brother **Khufu** from school told me things (page 282) as well as the Fitness **Guru** (page 286). I was receiving messages from everywhere but I always felt hers was significant because she was Haitian and so I never forgot it. The **Haitian** brother was responsible for me becoming a trainer in 2005 (page 138) that led me to the strange experience with the card (pages 141-142), which led me to the experience earlier in the year (page 292). With all of these patterns I felt a stronger connection to **Haiti** and **Jean Jacques Dessalines.** I wrote about Stephanie and this Haitian sister on December 10th 2015, **"I'm in the dreams of a stranger,** it don't get no stranger! She said **I was the 3rd to arrive and I carried her away from danger".** (page 347)

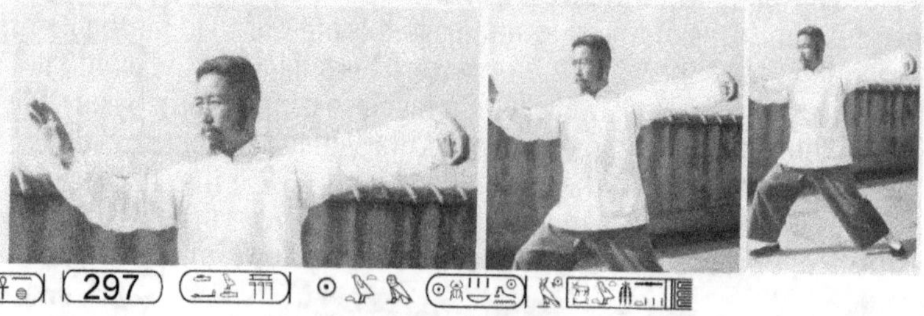

Rau nu Prt m heru

July 2014 - Mysterious Messages from The fourth Dimension
Brittany's Dream (Stuck in Another Dimension)

I met Brittany in the book store while at massage school. She got my attention because she was wearing earrings shaped like an **Ankh**. I started talking to her and we soon became friends. She was in the early stages of her pregnancy with her first son Denver **Heru** at the time. We would talk about things going on in the world and I would let her hear my music and she was a supporter of my music. One day Brittany told me about a **dream** she had of me. Around this time while in massage school I was experiencing women telling me that I was in their dreams. While writing this book I called Brittany to get the details of the dream she had of me back when we were in school. After she sent me the text about her dream she told me that she had other dreams about me too but the only one she could recall was one where she was crying in a dream while she was looking for something. Then she said I appeared and hugged her. We stood there and hugged as she cried. Then the dream was over.

Brittany recalls her dream for me in 2021

'"In that dream which occurred when I was pregnant with Denver you were behind a wall, the wall was an olive and brown color. It had like a brownish stripes coming down the wall almost like a jail cell but it was a wall and it had patterns on it with one type of flower, it could have been a **Lotus flower**. I was trying to pull you out of the wall but you were so far gone and almost disappearing. Almost like we were in two different dimensions, at least that's how I felt in the **dream** and the wall was very long. We were walking side by side." **- Brittany** (Brittany's first daughter, **Skylar**, was born on November 23, 2010, the same day as **Emmett Till's** mother)

Iu f Per f m heru

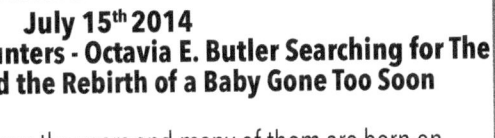

July 15th 2014
Meta Mysterious Encounters - Octavia E. Butler Searching for The Pattern Master and the Rebirth of a Baby Gone Too Soon

I have had many clients over the years and many of them are born on significant days such as the dates of some of my immediate family members. I met **Aiesha** in 2014 and she happened to be born the day after me on October 26th. I met her four years before my first **past life revelation**. **Aiesha** was a teacher and she loved **comic books** and went to the Comic-Con events as often as she could. When we first met she told me that my name reminded her of a character named **Doro**, from **Octavia Butler's** book, **Wildseed**. **Dawud** and **Doro** don't sound the same to me but I can understand how one might think so. Shortly after we started training she gave me around 10 of Octavia's Books but I didn't read any till 2016 when I read Wildseed (page 381). I do not always finish a book but Wildseed kept my interest and the character Doro was so interesting that I read the book faster than I usually read books. I didn't read any of her other books until after my first past life revelation on July 3rd 2018 (page 480). What makes it all strange is who and what **Doro** is in the book Wildseed and after my past life revelation it made me contemplate who or what Octavia Butler is or was in this **matrix** (page 7). Aiesha's baby's rebirth on next page.

Utterances for Coming Forth by day into Light

Octavia Butler was a best selling award winning writer. She is considered by most to be the mother of Black Futurist "fiction". She was a Black woman. After reading a few of her books it's hard to watch any new Sci-Fi movie and not see her influence on the world of imagination. I have to ask myself what kind of experiences did she have that allowed her to write what she wrote?! Did she have visions her self mixed with a healthy imagination, or was she something more interesting, like a **prophet**? I once watched the trailer for a movie and immediately saw the plot of her book **Kindred** in the trailer! In her book Kindred she writes about a black woman in modern time who somehow opens a portal and begins to teleport back and forth from the present time to a time during black bondage enslavement in America. The woman was time traveling.

It is he, who comes forth by day into Light

The character **Doro** from her book **Wildseed** was something more incredible when it comes to traveling in time. Doro was around 4000 years old. He was born in a village in ancient Kemet (Egypt), located on the Nile river in Africa. Doro was an **immortal spirit** or **soul** who changed bodies like clothes, similar to the spirit in the movie **Fallen** with **Denzel Washington** (page 78). When Doro was a boy he went through a rights of passage that gave him the ability of instant **Incarnation**. By reflex or by desire he could force the soul of a person out of the body they lived in. Like someone forcing you out of your **car** then driving away, except now you're also dead. His first in**car**nations were by reflex and by mistake. He killed everyone in his village including his parents, going from body to body, killing each person one by one until everyone was dead while he stood there standing and breathing in the last persons body.. This experience forever changed his views on life and death. For generations Doro roamed the earth from the jungles of Africa to the colonies of America gathering others like him. He had seen many witches, and warlocks with abilities like **thought readers**, **seers**, and even those who could **fly** but they all seemed to die at some point. He was searching for someone with an ability like his, an **immortal**. Some he helped, some he destroyed, but Doro bred, ruled, and owned them all. Doro feared no one, until he met Anyanwu.

The character Anyanwu was an old woman, a young woman, a man, a leopard, an eagle, even a dolphin and more. She was a shapeshifter who could also absorb bullets and make medicine with a kiss but more importantly Anyanwu could not be killed. She was Anyanwu the closet thing Doro had ever seen to himself and because of this he had a healthy fear of her. He called her the **Wildseed**. She feared no one, until she met Doro. Together they were locked in a war, she was a **master healer** and he was an immortal spirit. She had a self regenerating healing power like **Wolverine** from the **X-Men** comic books who was also my favorite member of the X-men (pages 79 and 58). Doro bred with her and she gave birth to tribes that she nurtured and healed, but Anyanwu would destroy anyone who threatened those she loved. Together they were the mother and father and Gods of an remarkable genetic line of people.

continued on next page

Significance - Rebirth of a Baby Gone Too Soon

Aiesha got pregnant some years after she move down south. Unfortunately the baby didn't survive the pregnancy, BUT - Aiesha's brother had a daughter who was born the next year on the same day Aiesha's baby was supposed to be born and **the baby looks exactly like Aiesha! Aiesha** gave me the book **Wildseed** to read. She told me that my name reminded her of a character named **Doro**. In the book, Doro is an immortal soul from ancient **Kemet**, during the times of the **Pharaohs**. He is very similar to the ancient deity Ausar, the Lord of **resurrection** in the ancient Egyptian pantheon (page 481 - 482). Ausar is the one who defeats death through the resurrection and this is where the story of **Jesus Christ** was taken from when Christianity came into existence. The resurrection of the father through the son, the repetition of the soul, **Immortality**. This is what the ancient Kemetyu (Egyptians) had mastered! From time immemorial we knew that there was no death. We had no word for death as we know it today because we understood and mastered the repetition of the soul (wehem mesut, p 14). Today this reality of life is brushed over with very little importance given to it yet all over the world billions of people are waiting for some savior to "return" at the "end of days". Perhaps the only thing that will return is you after the end of your days inside of the body you travel in now. But will you remember is the question..? Perhaps you have been here before and just don't remember. I can tell you that I have been here many times before and as you read this book you will see this pattern forming like the title of Octavia's book, **Pattern Master**. I am the pattern master that Octavia wrote about as in I have been able to decode the pattern of my incarnations as if I collected the blue prints of my creation. I want to thank Octavia E. Butler as her work primed me and helped prepare me to weave my pattern of destiny that not even immortals could imagine. I'd say that I had a rough landing as I came to know who I was. Putting this pattern together was at times very frightening but just like Star Wars (p 37), I became aware of Octavia at the most divine of times. In September of 2016 (page 419) my friend **Amiga** would tell me the **dreams** she had of me where I deciphered the **star code of immortality** which would turn out to be the foretelling of this book, **TutemRa: The Prophecy of Reincarnation**.. **Remember that you are Ausar and Heru, the hero!** See page 3 for the **hero's journey!**

July 17th 2014 (Eric Garner is killed by NYPD)

On July 17th 2014, **Eric Garner** was killed by a white New York City Police officer named Daniel Pantaleo who put Eric in a prohibited chokehold while arresting him. Video footage of the incident generated widespread national attention and raised questions about the use of force by law enforcement. NYPD officers approached Garner on July 17 on suspicion of selling single cigarettes from packs without tax stamps. After Garner told the police that he was tired of being harassed and that he was not selling cigarettes, the officers attempted to arrest Garner. When Pantaleo placed his hands on Garner, Garner pulled his arms away. Pantaleo then placed his arm around Garner's neck and wrestled him to the ground. With multiple officers pinning him down, Garner repeated the words "**I can't breathe**" 11 times while lying face down on the sidewalk. After Garner lost consciousness, he remained lying on the sidewalk for seven minutes while the officers waited for an ambulance to arrive. Garner was pronounced dead at an area hospital approximately one hour later. The medical examiner ruled Garner's death a homicide. According to the medical examiner's definition, a homicide is a death caused by the intentional actions of another person or persons. Specifically, an autopsy indicated that Garner's death resulted from "[compression] of neck, compression of chest and prone positioning during physical restraint by police". Asthma, heart disease, and obesity were cited as contributing factors. On December 4, 2014, a Richmond County grand jury decided not to indict Pantaleo. This decision stirred public protests and rallies, with charges of police brutality made by protesters. By December 28, 2014, at least 50 demonstrations had been held nationwide in response to the Garner case, while hundreds of demonstrations against general police brutality counted Garner as a focal point. On July 13th 2015, an out-of-court settlement was reached, under which the City of New York would pay the Garner family **$5.9 million**. In 2019, the U.S. Department of Justice declined to bring criminal charges against Pantaleo under federal Civil Rights Laws. A New York Police Department disciplinary hearing regarding Pantaleo's treatment of Garner was held in the summer of 2019; on August 2, 2019, an administrative judge recommended that Pantaleo's employment be terminated. Even with video footage of the illegal chokehold it took more than five years after Garner's death for Pantaleo to finally be fired on August 19th 2019.

Significance

On April 8th 2015 (page 323) the murder of Eric Garner would cause me to speak my ancient name Tutankhamen in a most mysterious way as if I knew who I was. In the song **Star of the Story** I can be heard saying - "they killed her son and got away with it, double agents flagrant, **Eric Garner** dead on the pavement, replay didn't change it, these games are ancient, **King Tutankhamen rhyming, Cleopatra** of the nile, tell me why they lying, it might take a while to stop crying, but when you're done, **Return** to the **father** through the **sun,** I be the star of the story, the star". The murder of Black life was awakening my ancient soul fragments from pervious lives (page 6).

Condolences

My condolences go out to the family of **Eric Garner** and all of those who have been robbed of their life by this system of racism and white supremacy. Please know that death is not the end. The soul survives death, indeed and in spirit. This is a book of the dead written by a boy who was murdered without justice, who defeated death and came forth by day. May the soul of **Eric Garner** walk peacefully through the field of Reeds in Amenta. Amen Ra.

August 3rd 2014 Nappy

What do you do when you wake up, and realize that you still need to wake up?! nobody's come'n to save us! save your self Nigga! your health is wealth Cracker! Welfare don't care! Black women you got your part to play in this here, look at your hair, when I was young I hated my hair, cause it was nappy, and I ain't have a pappy to tell me better, cause he was gone, so many family ties have been severed, there was a storm in **one nine seven seven** given me life like **Assata**! trapped in the hood, if you feel me nigga holler, **Allah**, **God**, **Dali lama** who is the fraud? who are you live'n for your **God** or your land Lord? Lord God, **I am God**, I am good, fuck who ever didn't understood, I'm from the hood, but I ain't live the thugs life, I got bullied as a kid and I ain't play dice, a played tag, one time I ran for my life, black on black crime, that would be our biggest vice, my advice *draw **solar light** right from the **sun***, standing on the earth trying to fly, be the one **- Dawud The Uncanny BlaKseed 2014**

August 5th 2014 Tryptophan

Rau nu Prt m heru

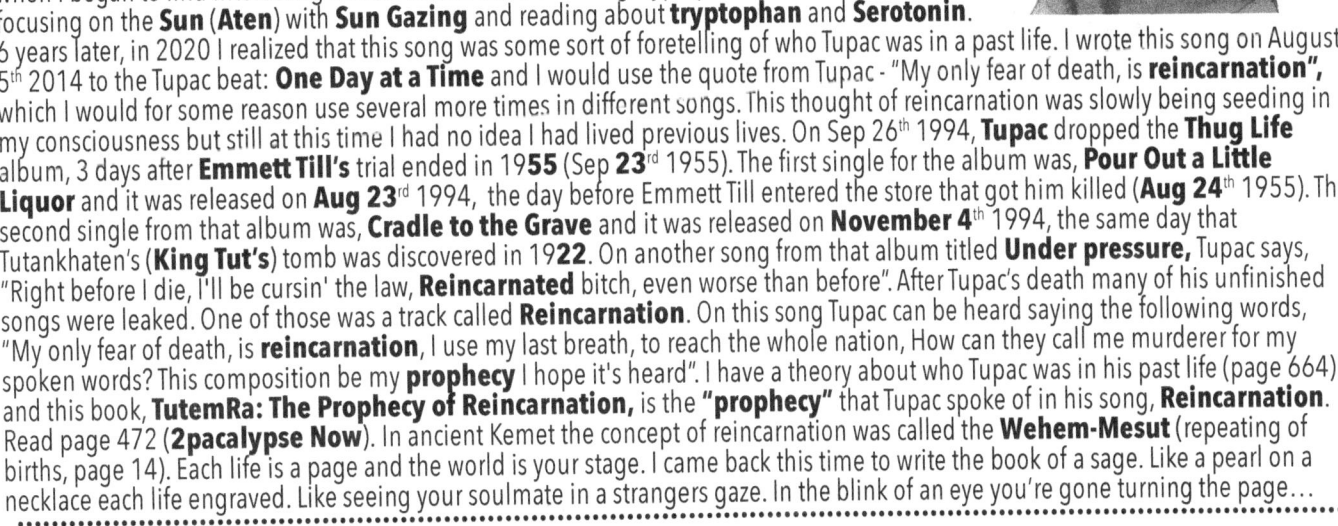

Serotonin is a tryptamine stimulated by tryptophan, when the **sun** hits the man the melanin expands, like wood, you feel good, the power of thought could, and does, and will, according to your will bend steel or heal the body, **Still I embody everybody,** that said fuck illuminati, *or anybody that had anything to do with the destruction of my body,* and my nation the **Haitian,** I'm pacing I'm waiting, **I'm patiently waiting incarnating for ages,** this ain't my last time, this ain't my last rhyme, **The Sun will always Shine,** One day at a time, My only fear of death is **reincarnation,** My only fear of death is **reincarnation,** My only fear of death is **reincarnation - Dawud The Uncanny BlaKseed**

Significance

Iu f Per f m heru

After my past life revelation of Emmett Till in 2018 (p 480) I realized that I had been writing the name Emmett Till in my music years before the revelation so when my past life of King Tut came in 2020 (page 594) I began to look through my music for anything related to Kemet and that's when I began to find interesting connections. I titled this song tryptophan because I had been focusing on the **Sun** (**Aten**) with **Sun Gazing** and reading about **tryptophan** and **Serotonin**. 6 years later, in 2020 I realized that this song was some sort of foretelling of who Tupac was in a past life. I wrote this song on August 5th 2014 to the Tupac beat: **One Day at a Time** and I would use the quote from Tupac - "My only fear of death, is **reincarnation",** which I would for some reason use several more times in different songs. This thought of reincarnation was slowly being seeding in my consciousness but still at this time I had no idea I had lived previous lives. On Sep 26th 1994, **Tupac** dropped the **Thug Life** album, 3 days after **Emmett Till's** trial ended in 19**55** (Sep **23**rd 1955). The first single for the album was, **Pour Out a Little Liquor** and it was released on **Aug 23**rd 1994, the day before Emmett Till entered the store that got him killed (**Aug 24**th 1955). The second single from that album was, **Cradle to the Grave** and it was released on **November 4**th 1994, the same day that Tutankhaten's (**King Tut's**) tomb was discovered in 19**22**. On another song from that album titled **Under pressure,** Tupac says, "Right before I die, I'll be cursin' the law, **Reincarnated** bitch, even worse than before". After Tupac's death many of his unfinished songs were leaked. One of those was a track called **Reincarnation**. On this song Tupac can be heard saying the following words, "My only fear of death, is **reincarnation**, I use my last breath, to reach the whole nation, How can they call me murderer for my spoken words? This composition be my **prophecy** I hope it's heard". I have a theory about who Tupac was in his past life (page 664) and this book, **TutemRa: The Prophecy of Reincarnation,** is the **"prophecy"** that Tupac spoke of in his song, **Reincarnation**. Read page 472 (**2pacalypse Now**). In ancient Kemet the concept of reincarnation was called the **Wehem-Mesut** (repeating of births, page 14). Each life is a page and the world is your stage. I came back this time to write the book of a sage. Like a pearl on a necklace each life engraved. Like seeing your soulmate in a strangers gaze. In the blink of an eye you're gone turning the page…

August 9th 2014 (Michael Brown 18yrs old)

Utterances for Coming Forth by day into Light

A White police officer by the name of Darren Wilson confronted Michael Brown and his friend. Minutes later Wilson fired a total of 12 bullets leaving Michael dead on the floor. Michael was hit at least seven times. His body laid in the street for four hours before it was removed. Wilson shot Michael killing him with no remorse and still feels like he "did his job right". Videos of Michael in a store with no audio, were used to create a narrative of him robbing the store prior to his murder. Years after the case was over the videos were proven to be false as Michael never robbed a store. The system always paints the black victim as the criminal in order to justify the killing of black people by "law" enforcement, the same thing was done to Emmett Till's father (page 518). Darwin says he acted in self defense and no charges were brought against him. He was not fired, he resigned. The insurance company for the city of Ferguson, paid $1.5 million to settle a wrongful death lawsuit filed by Michael's parents, but what really is the price of a soul? Can we really put a number on it?

Condolences

My condolences go out to the family of **Michael brown** and all of those who have been robbed of their loved ones by this system of racism and white supremacy. Please know that death is not the end. The soul survives death, indeed and in spirit. This is a book of the dead written by a boy who was murdered without justice, who defeated death and came forth by day. May the soul of **Michael brown** walk peacefully through the field of Reeds in Amenta. Amen Ra.

Significance

It is he, who comes forth by day into Light

The murder of Michael Brown garnered major attention and it filled me with righteous anger! I would say Michael Brown's name many times in my music. Murders like Michael Brown's fostered a deep seeded distrust and hatred for law enforcement practices. I knew that not all police were bad but I also knew that the police originated from the **slave patrols** formed to stop slaves from escaping during physical bondage in America's dirty past and what we are seeing today is residue from that past.

August 13th 2014 RIP Michael Brown

We are trapped in a riddle of language, the clues are written out for us yet we must seek to find, we must think to shine the pine in the middle of our minds, meditate, Rip **Michael Brown!** another man down cause his skin was brown! now you can drown in your tears, or run from your fears, or you can **Stand Strong**! even **Martin Luther king** said we don't all live long… Sometimes you gotta **Bomb First** or **Duck Down!** I rather be judged by 12 than be dead in the ground! I rather rebel for real than be locked in a cell! I rather live to tell the story of how we rose to glory! we were meek humble and kind but then we changed our minds, *we were* ***Kings,*** we were **slaves** synonymous with crime, every rhyme that I write is like my will that I sign, Lord let your will be done The blakseed be the son, The black sheep **Outkast**ed from my family, insanity, these cards that they handed me got me searching for plan B, Black Black August put **Marcus Garvey** in office, what does it profit a people to plead when they ignore it?! we bleed from the four fifth! addicted to this poor shit! **Rise up young nation**! I don't why you waiting…? **addicted to religion but ain't nobody saving**! they was slaving misbehaving then **taught you that you was pagan**! **- Dawud The Uncanny BlaKseed**

2014 Fitness and Royal Connections

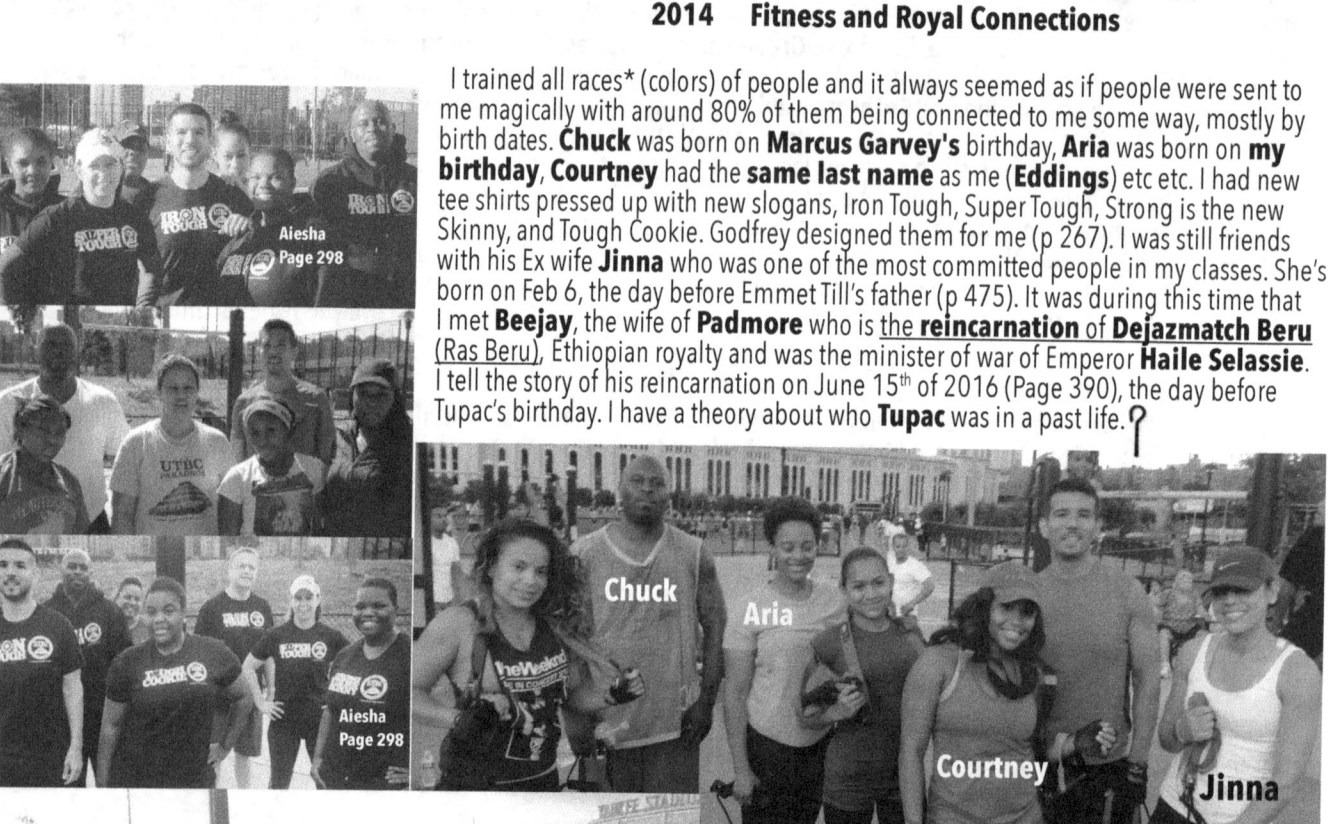

I trained all races* (colors) of people and it always seemed as if people were sent to me magically with around 80% of them being connected to me some way, mostly by birth dates. **Chuck** was born on **Marcus Garvey's** birthday, **Aria** was born on **my birthday**, **Courtney** had the **same last name** as me (**Eddings**) etc etc. I had new tee shirts pressed up with new slogans, Iron Tough, Super Tough, Strong is the new Skinny, and Tough Cookie. Godfrey designed them for me (p 267). I was still friends with his Ex wife **Jinna** who was one of the most committed people in my classes. She's born on Feb 6, the day before Emmet Till's father (p 475). It was during this time that I met **Beejay**, the wife of **Padmore** who is **the reincarnation** of **Dejazmatch Beru** (Ras Beru), Ethiopian royalty and was the minister of war of Emperor **Haile Selassie**. I tell the story of his reincarnation on June 15th of 2016 (Page 390), the day before Tupac's birthday. I have a theory about who **Tupac** was in a past life.

Rau nu Prt m heru

Iu f Per f m heru

Utterances for Coming Forth by day into Light

It is he, who comes forth by day into Light

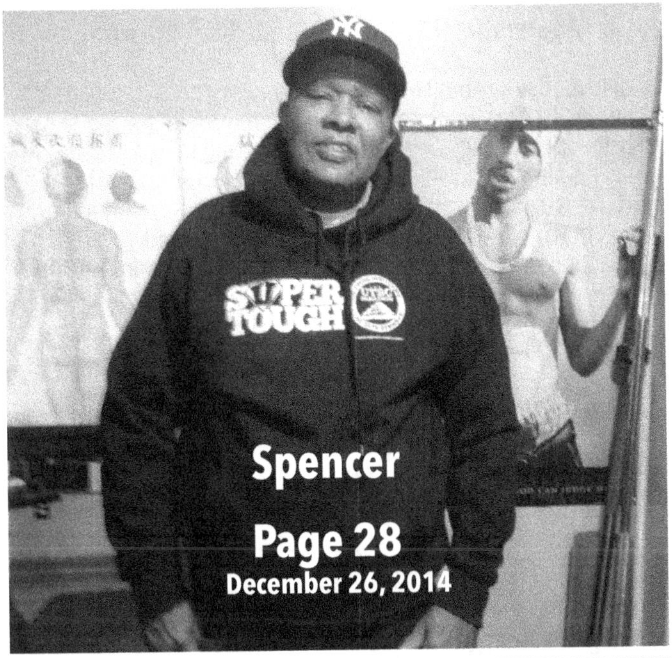

Spencer

Page 28

December 26, 2014

October 24, 2014

Saana

Page 35

Cameron and Phil

October 21, 2014 • See page 278

Jamaad

October 19, 2014

Cameron

Phil

October 16, 2014 • Jason Quick

I only met a couple people in Massage School that I still speak to today and **Quick** is one of them. We connected quickly because of our military background. Being a **Marine** and **Army** Ranger, he was the soldier I always wanted to be (pages 109 -130). Him and I both share the **life path** number **5**. 9 years later Quick would lead me to the **TUF System**, where I would train w/ **Heru Nekhet (p 631)**.

Jason Quick

August 31st 2014 **Buck Em Down**

To the young black youth, what they do?! ***Buck Em Down*** word life, no escape from the hate that permeates our life, what you see on the news is what they choose to highlight, cop cruise on the block, shot rock, kid drop, ***Duck Down***, Hip Hop, self defense wrist lock, **Huey P** definitely! who's coming with me?! 50 shots for **Sean Bell!** rest in peace to **Big L,** *Ain't hard to tell* my heart bleeds for the lost blaKseeds! never got a chance to grow, cut short like weeds, My negus be cut short like weeds, you're either living or dying, doing or trying, it's a time to rejoice and a time when a mother be crying, when they see their **suns** shot down like **Orion,** *if I said I was from Africa I'd be lying, I be trying to find myself cause I'm lost,* brothers still running north, yet we still shipped up north, way off course, of course they play on a golf course, during the course of a 100 yrs so many **Heru's** Have disappeared, **Redemptions Songs** is all I ever have here **- Dawud The Uncanny BlaKseed**

September 17th 2014 **Michael Brown**

It's all love they say but we done lost our way, cause nature don't love this way, I got a lot to say! I don't listen to what the Judge or the Pastor say, they be screaming out nigga and they, they pulling triggers on niggas and still getting away, my Homie **Tray** shot down! like **Kimani Gray** and **Michael brown!** and they ask me why do I frown! why do I look down, man look around, look on the ground! to the young black youth, what they do?! ***Buck Em Down*** word life! **- Dawud The Uncanny BlaKseed**

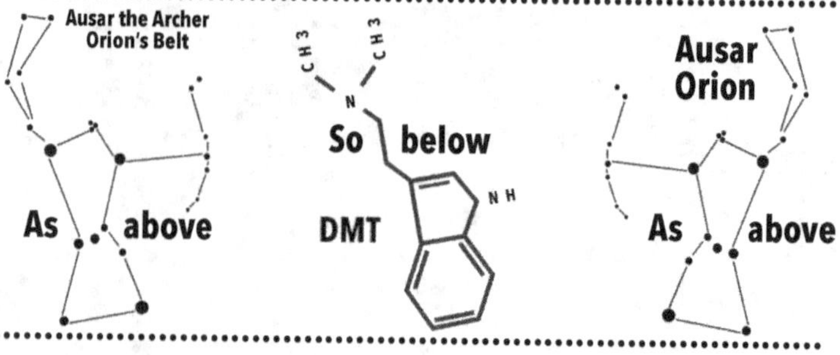

September 26th 2014 **Hands of Time**

If I died today and you never got to see me tomorrow would you feel sorrow? Sometimes I feel so hollow, Sometimes I feel like **Jim Carry** in living color, still I got no brothers, stuck in the **Truman show** got me feeling low, so many **ancestors** that I would never know, If my grand father didn't have to go, see when he died I cried, it was a surprise, the doctors lied cause they don't teach, and we die because of the knowledge we don't seek, when I speak I ain't rapping, ***I'm more like unwrapping the hands of time*** **- Dawud The Uncanny BlaKseed**

October 8th 2014
Decisions. To Do Or Not To Do, That Is The Question

I met a woman at the yankee stadium exercise park. I had just finished teaching a group fitness class when I saw her running the bleachers. Her self discipline and motivation inspired me so I gave her my card. She called me and I spoke to her about my group classes. I was trying to grow my classes and wanted her to be a part of my group fitness classes but she was more interested in 1 on 1 personal training so I started training her. She was Dominican, very pretty with a nice body. I saw these things about her but I was just trying to train her. Our 1 on 1 training sessions were always fun, she laughed a lot and always worked hard. I liked training her. One day she sent me a text with an eggplant emoji (🍆). I had a decision to make. What do I do? Do I ignore it or do I "enter the course"? I did it. I crossed that line that we are told we should never cross and our relationship slowly started to change. I liked her but she was not mentally the type of woman I wanted. **She ate meat and never read books** and we didn't share the same world views. She didn't see her self as an African Latino or care of anything African. I enjoyed entering the course with her but I did not want her, in her current state to be the mother of a child that we might bare if she was to get pregnant and decided to keep the baby. I told her that I wanted to pause with entering the course. She agreed, but later I realized that I might have confused her and maybe offended or insulted her. She kept training for a short time after that then I never saw or heard from her again. Before she vanished she came to a few group classes. During one class she was working out next to a good friend of mine. They both worked hard and during the class they started pushing and motivating each other. My friend had a gold chain on her wrist and oddly enough, **her gold chain would break** while she was talking to the Dominican woman. They were both very pretty. I always wondered what caused my friends chain to break. Perhaps there was some sort of competitive energy taking place that I was unaware of. I never told them that but I recorded it in my mind. I would have another experience like this while washing a glass cup. The frequency of my thought would break the glass and I would get a deep cut on my hand. All of our thoughts have vibrations. Be careful what you say to people and what you think about them because thoughts and desires can affect our reality by influencing quantum level events in time and space.

October 2014 - Amanda, Patterns, August 14th, Mr Nature and George Washington Carver

Rau nu Prt m heru

Iu f Per f m heru

Utterances for Coming Forth by day into Light

It is he, who comes forth by day into Light

I did what you're' are not supposed to do. You're not supposed to fall for your client but I fell for a woman named Amanda. This was back in 2008 or 2009 when I worked at a gym in Soho (page 164). Her and I always had good sessions and I was pretty sure that she liked me too. We hung out at least one time at a club I know because I still have the picture (page 164). Some time in 2009 she stopped training and I would not see or hear from her again until October 2014. Amanda's middle name is **Cassiopeia**, which is one of the **Greek constellations**. In Greek mythology Cassiopeia was the wife of **Cepheus**, the mythical King of **Ethiopia**. Together they are the parents of **Andromeda**. Currently, Earth's pole star is **Polaris**, a star in the northern circumpolar constellation of Ursa Minor (little dipper). The precession of the equinoxes is shifting and the northern-most tip of **Cepheus** is a mere 1.5° away from the pole. Cepheus lies in the far northern sky and by 7500 AD, Cepheus's brightest star Alder**amen** will become the pole star.. To fully understand the symbology of why Amanda (**Cassiopeia**) and I gravitated to each other you must read what **Minister Brown** told me in 2021 about Cepheus and his experience with a light in the night sky (page 518)..

Branson Got Juice

In Oct of 2014 I would reactivate my Facebook account. I developed a habit of deactivating my account to step away from social networking from time to time. I went on for one day then deactivated it again but within the time that I logged on Amanda messaged me. She said that she had been thinking about me and wanted to train again. We exchanged numbers and set up a session. The first session was good. We talked a little before the session to catch up and after the session we talked for longer. I still don't know the cause of her tears but she began to cry deeply. She never really explained herself but I remember her saying that she had never done this before. I never knew what "this" was but I was there to listen to her. The mood calmed and she regained her composure. We walked to the juice bar on 145th and got green juice. After she pulled off I walked across the street to see that Mr Nature was sitting in a chair in front of the church.

Mr Nature and I had known each other for a year now and had become friends. He was good friends with the Pastar* of the church. He had been really good friends with the Pastar's father. He was like a **spiritual advisor**. I walked over to greet him like usual and for some reason I decided to ask him his birthday for the first time. He told me his birthday was **August 14th** 1936. I exclaimed –" you're born on the same day as the girl I just finished training! – and I hadn't seen her in around 5 or 6 years!!" He just smiled. I stood there adding up his life path number and while adding his numbers he told me that he had never told another person in America his birthday before. Mr Nature was from the Caribbean islands and his life path number was a 5 like me and Malcolm X. I walked home puzzled again seeing these strange **coincidences** all the time. When **coincidences** bind with **synchronicities** the outcome tends to have **the mark of a greater authority**. Like a pattern that happens for a **divine purpose**.

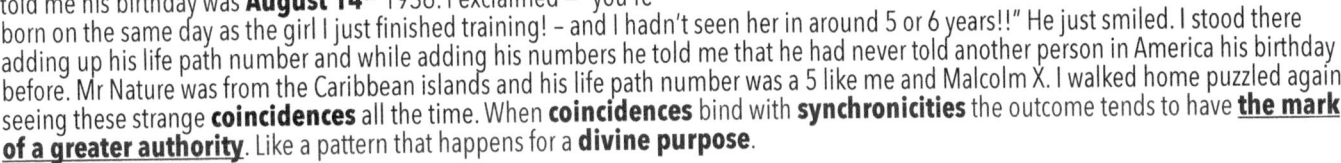

Amanda and I are pictured above at **Branson Got Juice**, located on 741 St Nicholas Ave, in Harlem. Shortly after Amanda started training with me she would refer a friend Ashley to train with me. Oddly enough, her friend was also born on **August 14th** and she had a sister named **Indira** and **Indira** was the name of the first girl I ever loved, from back in my high school years. I was floored with all the **coincidences**.... Amanda seemed to be some sort of **"good omen"**. **August 14th** is the day that the **Haitian Revolution** was planned in 1791. It was executed on August 21st 1791 and lasted till 1804, which is also the same day **Emmett Till** arrived in Mississippi (page 505). If that wasn't strange enough things get even stranger during the middle of the month of October because my high school sweetheart **Indira** would appear in a **dream** (page 305). Come follow me!.......

Mr Nature or George Washington Carver?

After getting to know Mr Nature I would come to feel like he was a person like George Washington Carver or the spirit of George Washington Carver was moving through Mr Nature or perhaps he was Dr Carver in another life. Mr Nature was a healer of plants. He would take plants that were dying and give them life again. I first met him in October of 2013 (page 281) and I would come to realize that I purchased the book: *The Man Who Talks The Flowers, The Intimate Life Story Of Dr George Washington Carver*, written by Glenn Cl**ark** on October 7th 2014. This date is in my Amazon order history and on that same day I bought the book **Man The Unknown** and I would have a profound experience with that book and the **Metu Neter** book from **Ra Un Nefer Amen** on May 5th 2015 (page 329). This experience would confirm to me that something from the unseen realm is indeed and in spirit governing this reality we live in.

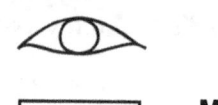

October 16th 17th & 18th 2014
Dreams and The Underworlds
Mysterious Messages from The fourth Dimension

On October 16th 2014 I would exclaim out loud the words "**I want to remember my dreams**!".... For the next three nights I would have vivid dreams and on January 1st of the 2015, exactly 77 days after the second dream, the second dream would come to pass. **The first night** I dreamt that I was on a boat, the sun was shining and everything was extra colorful. Then all of a sudden a beautiful **dolphin** jumped out of the water and splashed water everywhere then the dolphin swam away. afterwards I stepped out the boat onto the beach and walked into a house, then I woke up.

On Oct 17th, **the second night**, I dreamt of an open studio space with wooden floors, then I woke up. This dream wasn't anything special but a least I was dreaming. Two nights in row I had dreamt. I was excited.

On Oct 18th, **The Third night** things would take a remarkable turn and get "big strange"! I would dream of my high school sweetheart Indira Aminta Ceville. In the dream we were walking up the stairs in the subway station, she had a little boy with her then the dream ended. Upon waking from the dream I would receive a text from my aunt Karen about Indira! Literally as soon as I opened my eyes I heard a sound from my phone. I was bewildered! I had not seen or heard from Indira in over 14 yrs. My aunt wanted to know who the person in the picture with Indira was on her Facebook. I was confused.. "Why are you asking me about Indira", I asked. She told me that someone in her family had died. I had never had a dream with Indira before and the first time that I do my aunt calls me right after. I got in touch with Indira and I told her about what had happened. She was now married with children to a Haitian brother. She would tell me about her sister in-law, Joanne Borgella who had just passed away due to a long fight with Cancer. Joanne was a Haitian singer who rose to stardom after her appearance on American idol.

Significance

1st dream: I played for the Beach Channel **Dolphins** in high school so the dream was real nice. I had a dream and a dolphin, my old mascot came by to greet me!!! I made my demand and boom I had a dream that night! I was hotep (satisfied).

2nd dream: On January 1st 2015 I would be given a studio to train my clients out of for practically nothing via a friend of Mr Nature's. This was indeed the space from my dream I had on October 17th 2014.

3rd dream: For two days in a row my **astral body** had been "dreaming" again but on this third night the **astral body** had a different task. I traveled to a soul bond I made 21 years ago in 1993 when I fell in love with Indira in JR High School 180. Indira was mourning the death of her sister in law, Joanne Borgella. Indira's middle name is **Aminta** and in ancient Kemet (Egypt) **Amenta** is the equivalent to heaven. Indira was the first girl I fell in love with and when she was is pain mourning I saw her in a dream. I had not seen her in around 14 years yet still my soul went to her to comfort her. In the years to come I would begin to have more profound experiences while dreaming. In 2017 I would have a dream with Eryka Badu (page 440) and the two days later Jay Electronica would appear in my dream (page 441). This experience confirmed the reality of the dream realm being a real place.

Condolences

My deepest condolences go out to the Borgella family. Please know that death is not the end. The soul survives death, indeed and in spirit. This is a book of the dead written by a boy who was murdered without justice, who defeated death and came forth by day. May the soul of **Joanne Borgella** walk peacefully through the field of Reeds in Amenta. Amen Ra.

Rau nu Prt m heru

Iu f Per f m heru

Utterances for Coming Forth by day into Light

It is he, who comes forth by day into Light

October 19th 2014
Meta Mysterious Encounters
Fourth meeting with Mr Nature

I would take a Capoeira Class at the school on 154th in Harlem. This was my 1st or second time attending a class. While there I would see all the plants they have and was again inspired to buy more plants. After the class I went to see if **Mr Nature** was at his usual location across the street from the juice bar on 145th street. Of course he was there when I arrived. I told him that I was there to buy a plant from him. His response was, "**you are my angel**". I smiled while he explained himself. He told me that someone had stolen all his plants and he needed money so he said a prayer and asked God to send him an angel. I purchased a plant from him. Then he told me this, ***"You are the peoples friend. You will have trials and tribulations but because you are a man of God you will be fine. The ancestars have paved a way for you."*** Because of all the experiences I had been having I took his words very seriously but to no degree did I think it would be anything like the contents of this book. Years later this experience with Mr Nature would take on a more supernatural significance. ***Perhaps it was never really Mr Nature speaking to me at all!*** Perhaps my experience with Mr Nature was no different than my experience with Dr Fredrick Monderson in 2021 (page 650), or with brother **Khufu** from massage school (page 282) and the Fitness **Guru** (page 286).

November 1st 2014 - My loyal Pectoral Seeks To Be Seen, Heru is his name and Life is a Dream

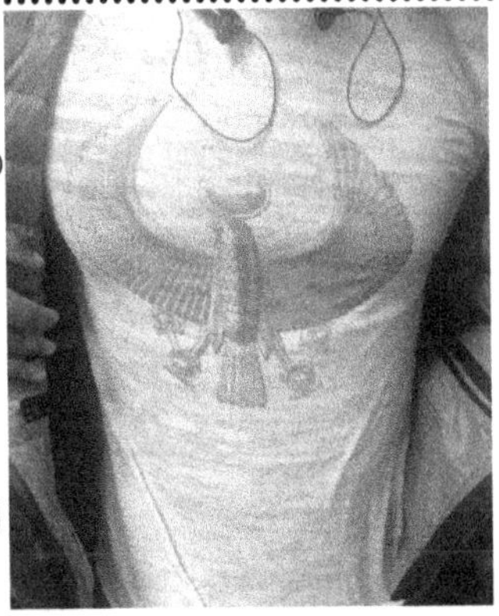

I was taking massage classes in midtown at the Open Center but the main Campus for my school was in Syosset NY. The New York College of Health Professions had satellite locations in the city to meet the demand for those who desired to attend their school but couldn't travel to Syosset. It was mandatory for all students taking classes in the city to take a certain amount of credit hours at the main campus. The school had it set up so that we fulfilled those hours in two days. I went on my birthday October 25th 2014 and November 1st 2014. While at school in Syosset, on Saturday Nov 1, I crossed paths with a brother in the hallway who was wearing a shirt with the image of Heru the falcon on it. The shirt caught my eye and I asked him if I could take a picture of his shirt. He agreed, I took a picture and said thank you, then we parted ways.

Significance

I would meet this brother again in 2015 (page 326) at a gong session around the time of the Baltimore Riots and we would become friends. I would not realize that he was the person wearing the shirt on this day November 1st 2014 until after my **past life** revelation of **Emmett Till** on July 3rd 2018 (page 480). On April 4th 2020 (page 594) I would have my past life revelation of my life as **Tutankhaten** (**King Tut**). The image of Heru on his shirt is a picture of the **pectoral jewelry** from the tomb of Tutankhaten. In ancient kemet Heru (Falcon/Horus/Jesus) is the son of Ausar (Osiris) that returns resurrects/reincarnation. Heru is from the Ausarion or Osirion drama of **resurrection**. Ron would call me on September 25th 2017 and told me something that sp**ark**ed a series of events revealing a pattern that compelled me to make a **pilgrimage** to my home town of **Far Rockaway**.

November 4th 2014 Reflexology

I thank the Lord for my feet, fought wars on my feet, touch my feet I go to sleep, cause I ignored my feet, take care of your feet and watch your step in the street, you might step on a heart and sp**ark** a reflex **arc,** my feet don't meet defeat, on your m**ark** set ready start with your the left foot, always move with your heart, reflexology an **ancient art**, older than Noah's **ark,** it's seems like the human being be hiding things in the d**ark,** but all things brighten up, like **yu yow** on the **eye brow**, pins and needles needles and pins in meridians, finger walking Queens New York'n, my dogs be b**ark**ing but he**ark**en my words, 31 nerves feel the serge, as I hook and back up the great toe, pin and rotate the bladder, be grateful no more pain, novocaine can't match the touch, the last to rush, 90 minutes and I'm finished, but you'll be back I trust **- Dawud the Uncanny BlaKseed**

Significance

During my time at massage therapy school (page 274), Professor **Leslie Brown** was my reflexology (foot massage) instructor. The poem above was an assignment for her class. We were instructed to write a short poem about the feet and reflexology. When I wrote the line, "**reflexology an ancient art**", I knew that pressure therapy had originated in Kemet but I had not yet known about **Ankmahor**. The image above is from the tomb of **Ankmahor**, a physician from a major city in ancient Kemet named **Het ka Ptah**. The image is the oldest documentation depicting **pressure therapy**, dated around 3,000 B.C.E., During the **1st Golden Age** of ancient Kemet also known as the Old Period. Pro Leslie liked my poem so much that she asked if she could use it for all of her future classes as a model for that assignment and of course I said yes. I didn't have many black professors so I appreciated it when I did. Professor Leslie saw something in me so she invited me to a gathering with her mentor **Dr Sir Abdul Ford** but I declined, however two years later I would have one of the most profound experiences at one of his gatherings (page 399). She also referred the book **Metatron** to me. I bought it and a few other books related to it. The book is said to be channeled by the **Archangel Metatron** and the book would be instrumental in triggering thoughts of various levels of **enlightenment**. This Book would come around again in a profound way on September 25th 2018 (page 536). Sometime after this I would come to learn that **Metatron** is connected to the **Aten (Aton)** from the 18th dynasty of kemet where **Tutankhaten** (**King Tut**) is from. I wrote this poem on November 4th the day **Tutankhaten's** (**King Tut's**) tomb was discovered in 1922. On April 4th 2020 my past life as King Tut is revealed to me (page 594). More on **Noah's Ark** on page 252.

November 9th 2014 (Aura Rosser 40, Ann Arbor Michigan)

In the midst of a confrontation with her boyfriend reports say she threatened her boy friend with a knife. Her boy friend called the cops to escort her out the house. With in 5 seconds of entering the house officer David **Ried** shot her killing her while officer M**ark** Raab tased her.Officers say she was holding a knife when they arrived. Officer **Ried** faced no charges. When speaking of Aura her mother Deborah Carter says, "Aura had a magnetism no one could resist. Her artistic skills with a brush and a pen exemplified her as totally talented, uniquely undefinable, and amazing abstract."

Condolences

My condolences go out to the family of **Aura Rosser** and all of those who have been robbed of their life by this system of white supremacy. Please know that death is not the end. The soul survives death, indeed and in spirit. This is a book of the dead written by a boy who was murdered without justice, who defeated death and came forth by day. May the soul of **Aura Rosser** walk peacefully through the field of Reeds in Amenta. Amen RA.

November 13th 2014 (Tanisha Anderson 37 Cleveland Ohio)

Reports say that Tanisha was bipolar and on November 13th 2014 she became restless and was trying to leave the house. The family concerned for her safety called the cops. When the cops arrived they treated her with no love. They slammed to the ground and killed her. The family was awarded a $2.5 million dollar settlement from the Cleveland Ohio police. Officer Scott Aldridge was suspended for 10 days, and officer Bryan Myers was issued a written warning.

Condolences

My condolences go out to the family of **Tanisha Anderson** and all of those who have been robbed of their life by this system of white supremacy. Please know that death is not the end. The soul survives death, indeed and in spirit. This is a book of the dead written by a boy who was murdered without justice, who defeated death and came forth by day. May the soul of **Tanisha Anderson** walk peacefully through the field of Reeds in Amenta. Amen RA.

November 20th 2014 (Akai Gurley 28 Brooklyn)

While walking down the stairs in building he lived in Akai was shot in the chest by a rookie cop. He was shot through the chest and collapsed on the fifth floor landing. His girlfriend tried to administer CPR. Officer Peter Liang walked into the building and shot Akai for no reason. Officer Liang was fired and sentenced to 5 years probation with community service.

Condolences

y condolences go out to the family of **Akai Gurley** and all of those who have been robbed of their life by this system of white supremacy. Please know that death is not the end. The soul survives death, indeed and in spirit. This is a book of the dead written by a boy who was murdered without justice, who defeated death and came forth by day. May the soul of **Akai Gurley** walk peacefully through the field of Reeds in Amenta. Amen RA.

November 22nd 2014 (Tamir Rice 12)

On November 22nd 2014, a caller reported that a male was pointing "a pistol" at random people in a park in Cleveland Ohio. At the **beginning** of the call and again in the **middle**, the caller says of the pistol **"it's probably fake"**. Towards the end of the two-minute call, the caller also states that **"he is probably a juvenile"**. Two officers, Timothy Loehmann and 46 year old Frank Garmback, responded to a police dispatch call. They found a 12 year old **black boy** in the park and the 26 year old **white officer** Timothy Loehmann shot Tamir Rice almost immediately after arriving on the scene. Tamir was playing with a toy gun. The video of this shooting can still be seen online and in it you can see that officer Loehmann shot and killed Tamir Rice with no care for his life! There was no attempt to see if the gun he was holding was real or fake. On April 25, 2016, the lawsuit was settled in an effort to reduce taxpayer liabilities, with the City of Cleveland agreeing to pay Tamir Rice's family $6 million ($5.5 million to Tamir Rice's estate, $250,000 to the child's mother, and $250,000 to the child's sister)

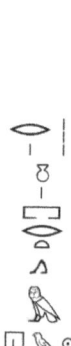

Condolences

My condolences go out to the family of **Tamir Rice** and all those who have been robbed of their loved ones by this system of racism and white supremacy. Please know that death is not the end. The soul survives death, indeed and in spirit. This is a book of the dead written by a boy who was murdered without justice, who defeated death and came forth by day. May the souls of **Tamir Rice** and **George Stinney Jr** walk peacefully through the field of Reeds in Amenta. Amen RA.

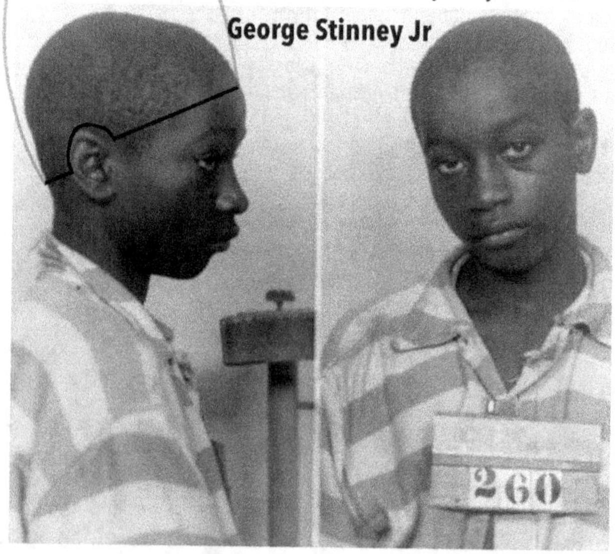

Significance

I first became aware of Tamir's death by the picture that began to circulate with his face placed next to the face of Emmett Till showing their striking resemblance. I remember seeing this picture and wondering if **Tamir Rice** was the same soul as **Emmett Till**. Could the soul of Emmett Till have come back here just to die again to show us how much things had not changed? I had those thoughts because the resemblance captivated me. Tamir looks like Emmett and Emmett's mother **Mamie Till** was born on November **23**rd and Tamir died on November 22nd. Tamir was only 12 and Emmett was only 14 and both of these deaths bothered me. I was still angry about Trayvon and all the others. Tamir's name would find it's way in my music over the next few years along side Emmett's. In fact after seeing this picture I remember wondering if **Tupac** was the reincarnation of **George Stinney Jr**, the youngest person to ever be **electrocuted** by the US prison system at 14 years of age. He was born in 1929 the year of the **snake** and he was electrocuted on Tupac's birthday June 16th 1944. Tupac made a song title, **16 On Death Row** and stated a few times in his music **"My Only Fear of Death is Reincarnation"**. These were the first times that I contemplated the souls of murdered black people reincarnating. I had no idea what was in store for me four years from this point. On July 3rd of 2018 my **past life** as Emmett Till would be revealed to me (page 480).

"shit is real **Tamir Rice** looked just like **Emmett till,** My mother was born the same year he was killed, Today it was cold here maybe **Tamir's soul** hears the injustice, Maybe it's just us, maybe **MJ** was right! "they don't really care about us!" **- Dawud The Uncanny BlaKseed (written on December 29th 2015, page 351)**

Thanksgiving 2014

Rau nu Prt m heru

Iu f Per f m heru

Utterances for Coming Forth by day into Light

It is he, who comes forth by day into Light

I have a family full of loving **Christians** and **Muslims** while I blaze the trail back home to **Kemet** (**Egypt**). Many African families have struggled through the hells of Amerikkklan society. A society that has nefariously and continuously tried to bring about the destruction of black civilization. Knowing this fact, all black families should be working to make our ties stronger, not allowing ourselves to fall away from each other. My family is not without its share or turmoil and problems but that is to be expected when you are only a few generation removed from chattel slavery. All things considered, my family has done quite well.

The holidays that we've been given are all upside down, inside out and backwards. From Christmas, the seasonal marking of the winter solstice which was high jacked by Christianity; to Thanksgiving, a holiday rooted in the destruction of the native peoples of America, who were here thousands of years before the European stepped foot on the land and stole it.. Many "African American" families don't know and or don't care to know about the past from which they came. They have forgotten their connection to the native people from the land they live. Yet still they the utilize this Thanksgiving holiday as a time to come together in love and peace.

This Thanksgiving I would get sick from a piece of **fish** my uncle Tony served me the night before thanksgiving. **I had given up meat for a few years** but I was still eating fish at the time. Tony **microwaved** some fish for me and I ate the fish even though I do not eat microwaved food. At the time I was the only person in my family who had given up **meat consumption** so I wasn't eating most of what was served. I ate the fish because I didn't want to seem, "difficult". Shortly after I ate the fish I began to feel sick and I didn't begin to feel better until the Friday morning after Thanksgiving. While I didn't take part in eating much food I still socialized with family. I remember standing in my aunts back yard and looking up into the night sky **with the desire** to see a **shooting star** and sure enough I did see one. This wasn't the first time that I had looked into the sky and saw the **shooting star** I **desired** to see so it fascinated me but since I only saw one, I saw it as just a **lucky coincidence**. When I got back to New York on Saturday I met a woman name Noel at the health food store Jahlookova, on 125th street. The day after I met her I would receive a conformation about the **hazards** of **fish**, and **microwaves** and a subtle message from **Hatshepsut**, the Kemetic (Egyptian) female Nswt Bity (Pharaoh) from the 18th Dynasty (p 311). Kemet was calling me.

November 2014

Mysterious Messages from The fourth Dimension

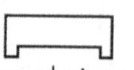

Larry's Dream

It was during my 2014 or 2015 trip to Atlanta that Larry told me about his **dream** he had of me. He **dreamt** that I was **Glowing** like **Bruce Leroy** from the movie**, The Last Dragon.**

Significance

Larry was the only friend from the Army that I saw every few years. Sometimes our schedules would line up and I would see him for Holidays when I went to Atlanta. I can remember hanging out with him in Atlanta when I was still going out to clubs. Larry and I were stationed in Germany together. I think he arrived in Germany in 1999 but I got there in 2000. We weren't in the same unit but I saw him on my post sometimes. He came to the club I worked at sometimes but I don't think we ever hung out while in Germany. After we got out of the Army, Larry would give me a call every few years to check on me and I would hit him up too. I would text him for his birthday and he usually called or texted for memorial day. Over the years my topic of discussion changed to that of the paranormal. I never knew Larry's religion because it didn't matter to me. He was my brother because we were friends and he was my brother because we served in the Army together. Every now and then I would send him my music and I played it for him every time we saw each other in Atlanta. He always gave me feedback. He even liked some of it. Him and I stopped speaking some time after my past life of Emmett came in 2018. Over the years Larry and I never talked religion. I don't think I even knew that he was a **Hebrew Israelite** all these years. I began to tell him that the bible is not our complete history and he didn't agree. I tried to tell him the stories can't be true because that would paint the Africans of the Nile valley as the bad guy. When my past life revelation of Emmett Till came in 2018 I don't think he ever really believed it. In 2020 I started telling him that the story of **Jesus** wasn't real and it was really **astro theology** (page 489). Then Larry told me that he didn't believe that I was Emmett Till in my past life and for the first time we had a nasty convo over the phone and exchanged a few heated text messages. Larry would become the third friend from the army that I lost due to religion. And he was the first friend from the **Hebrew Israelite** faith that I would bump heads with. Years later I would meet Victorious, another brother in the **Hebrew Israelite** faith and because of religion I would end up experiencing discord with him as well (page 346). My discord with Larry lasted all the way to the end of 2023… I sent him a text for his birthday (Dec 12, 2023) and we made a mends. We as a people, especially us brothers, must be able to unite beyond the binds of organized religion. Please read what I wrote on page 667, **SANKOFA: We Must Go Back and Fetch What We Lost....**

November 24th 2014 - New Sweaters designed by Godfrey Lopez

November 2014

I was never the biggest guy in the gym but I was never afraid to put a little work in. But as I type this on October 16th 2021, I have to sit with the fact that I don't look this fit right now.... I have not trained in over a week for sure. I have been spending my time writing and organizing this book everyday. 7 days a week. Somedays I get a lot done and somedays I get a little done. I probably average 10 or 11 hrs a day or maybe more. I wanted to look the best I ever looked for my 44th birthday which is in 9 days but something happened. In July of 2021, I began to slow my strength training down as I wrote this book. Then my four year anniversary of knowing about my past life as Emmett Till came on July 3rd and on Emmett's birthday, July 25th people began to post about Emmett more. I began to see **RIP Emmett** all over social networking again. Then the next month the day he was murdered, August 28th people started posting about him again... I began to **fall into a sad place**. Here I was telling people I was Emmett Till in a past life and very few people acknowledged it. I was writing this book and promoting it online and still I felt like many people pretended like I was not here. Like I was not Emmett. It's a weird place to be in and a weird life experience to contend with. I began to feel like I was in a football game and when September of 2021 came I felt like it was 4th quarter. I needed to finish this book. I was ready to go for the Hail Mary pass. I kept writing. All the events in this book are true. If you follow my path and do the things I do yet still the great mysteries are not shown to you. Then continue the path and **to Maat be true** and perhaps in due time you will be worthy of the view.

Dawud, Beloved by the Ntru

Rau nu Prt m heru

Iu f Per f m heru

Utterances for Coming Forth by day into Light

It is he, who comes forth by day into Light

November 30th 2014
Meta Spiritual Encounters with Noel Simone, The First SEER

I met Noel Simone on a Saturday at the health food store Jahlookova on 125th street. She was ahead of me in line talking on her phone when she asked a question to myself and the woman behind the counter. She asked if anyone had any fast remedies for some malady the person she was on the phone with was dealing with. I don't recall what the person was dealing with but I remember telling her that he **shouldn't eat any meat while trying to heal**. The woman behind the counter gave some advice as well. I gave her my card and she gave me a flyer inviting me to a show she was going to be singing in the very next day at the Black National Theatre. I did not intend on going because I was very much still a hermit but I told her I would try to make it.

The next day was Sunday December 1st. I would get up and go to the Show at the last minute. I remember being surprised that I went. When I got there I walked around and looked at all the vendors. I purchased 3 books - DRUGS Masquerading As Foods, a National Geographic magazine with the female Nswt (Pharaoh) **Hatshepsut** from the **18th dynasty** on the cover (p 638) and the book **Maintaining Our Temples**. I watched the show and was amazed at how gifted the Woman Noel was with singing. In 2022 I went to Kemet (Egypt) for the first time in this life and had the chance to visit the Temple of **Hatshepsut** as well as many others.

On my way home I would cross paths with a woman named Angela Miles. We did not know each other well but when we saw each other we both stopped and laughed because this was actually our third time crossing paths in that one day. We saw each other earlier in the day when we both just happened to be eating brunch at the same place. Then I left and went to the supermarket and I saw her again while leaving, we smiled at each other and kept on our respective ways, and now at the end of my night I'm on my way home and we meet again. we both laughed, hugged and parted ways. Angela is born on August 14th, the day that the **Haitian revolution** was planned and December 1st is the day **Rosa Parks** refused to get out of her seat because all she could think of was the recent murder of **Emmett Till**.

When I got home I opened the book **Maintaining Our Temples.** I played the "let's see what I will read if I open the book to a random page" game. I opened the book and read what my eyes randomly fell on and I read how **fish** and other creatures of the sea were not healthy for humans to eat due to ab excess of mercury. This caught my attention because I had just recovered from being sick from the salmon that my uncle had given me (p 308). This was strange! I felt like the book spoke to my experience!! I turned to another page and there was a passage on microwaves and the harm they do to the body!! **The book was speaking to me again**!!! Like the movie ***The Never Ending Story*** (p 259). My uncle had microwaved the salmon that got me sick a few days ago! I took this as a sign and I stopped eating all creatures from the sea that day!

Noel would start training with me shortly after this and she would reveal her **gift** to me on January 30th 2015 (page 318) . She would be the first person to ever tell me about a **ghost**, **spirit** or **entity** that she see's in my apartment. In fact this would be the first time anyone would ever tell me they saw a **spirit**. Little did I know that spirits had been working with me my whole life and I would visited by the **soul** of a dead friend a few weeks later (page 314).

December 3rd 2014
Meta-Spiritual Encounters and The December 3rd Theory
Algernon Johnson (AJ) Cooper transitions
August 17th 1980 - December 3rd 2014

Rau nu Prt m heru

Iu f Per f m heru

Utterances for Coming Forth by day into Light

It is he, who comes forth by day into Light

Clinton Melton was murdered in broad daylight by a racist White man, on December 3rd 1955, only 3 months after **Emmett Till** was murdered (page 519). In 2022 I would realize that Clinton Melton was connected to this Dec 3rd pattern that seemed to form around the death of my homie Cooper. I wouldn't find out about **Coopers** passing until the 9th of December. I had been taking long breaks from Social Networking but for some reason on Dec 9th I logged into Facebook. Then I began to see a lot of **RIP** posts that seemed to be directed towards Cooper. When I realized that he had indeed passed away I cried. The news of his passing came right before one of my training sessions with a new client and here I was crying. I was told he passed due to a brain aneurysm. I hadn't seen Cooper in person since January 20th of 2009 at the Presidential Inauguration (page 160) but we talked every now and then via facebook. Cooper even played around with writing music a little. After my client left I wrote a song titled, **RIP J. Coop Dec 3rd** in dedication to him. I recorded the song over the **J. Cole** beat, Jan 28th. I uploaded the song to **Soundcloud** and for the first time one of my songs started to amass **thousands** of views. Hours later <u>*the song was taken down*</u> by Soundcloud due to "copy rights infringement". A week later, on Dec 17th Cooper would appear to me in the body of a 5 year old baby boy at a holiday party sp**ark**ing the **December 3rd Theory** (page 314). For the next 3 years I would have a spiritual experience with death on December 3rd and each death would be connected to music. Coop was born on the same day as **Marcus Garvey**.

Condolences

My condolences go out to the family and friends of **Algernon Johnson (AJ) Cooper**. Please know that death is not the end. The soul survives death, indeed and in spirit. This is a book of the dead written by a boy who was murdered without justice, who defeated death and came forth by day. May the soul of **Algernon J. Cooper** walk peacefully through the field of Reeds in Amenta. Amen Ra.

December 7th 2014
The Carbon (Melanin) Conference
Dr. Llaila Afrika and the Reincarnation of Simeon Toko

I had the pleasure of meeting **Dr Llaila Afrika** at The Carbon (Melanin) Conference. Listening to his lectures, purchasing his books and reading about the many vitamins and minerals that comprise the body and what foods can help maintain a healthy body was a major part of my mental, physical and spiritual transformation. After the event was over I got a couple of my books autographed and took a picture with him. Many topics were discussed at this lecture, however what captivated my imagination and got my attention the most was when Bro **Hankh Rising Son** Spoke about the **reincarnation** of **Simeon Kimbangu Toko.** I had never heard of this person before. Simeon was said to be the second coming of **Jesus Christ**. He was said to have been killed several times and mysteriously came back to life each time. He was also said to have performed other miracles like healing the blind and bringing a baby back to life after being dead for several days.

<u>**Significance**</u>

4 years later in 2018, on July 3rd (page 476) I would cross paths with brother **Hankh Rising Son** at the International African Arts Festival where the **spirit** of the **mycelium** (magic mushroom) would speak through him leading me to the next step of my blind initiation helping to spark my **past life revelation** of **Emmett Till** and **Tutankhaten**.

On December 21st 2021 I would see Brother H**ankh** for the first time since July 20th 2018 the year of the **Dog** and he would tell me that he is born on **November 25th** 1958, the year of the **dog.** King Tut's tomb was opened on **November 26th** 1922 (page 11), the year of the **dog**, which would make perfect sense in this **star code pattern**. Meeting him was indeed a meeting governed by the stars! Genesis 1:14 "And God said, Let there be lights in the firmament of the heaven to divide the day from the night; and let them be for signs, and for seasons, and for days, and years". One time is an incidence, twice is a coincidence, but three, four, five is a pattern. Can you tell the difference?

December 11th 2014 — RIP J. Coop Dec 3rd

They can kill us and bury us but we the Blakseeds, **So we'll be back maybe in the weeds,** Like dandelions, I ain't lying I be iron like lion, mothers be crying when they see their sons shot down like **Orion**, I was crying when I got the scoop about my homie **J Coop,** rest in peace we lost a good man to say the least, He was in the streets trying to save the kids from the beast and make peace, how can we ever have peace when the Black man's stressed, cause of this White man's debt, they call us crabs in the bucket I be like fuck it we're never gonna forget, They call us animals but tell me can you analyze this, more cops kill kids than your clips of "**Isis**", black fist black blood I heard it wasn't **O.J.'s** glove, **Bill Cosby** was set up now we need to set it off, **Michael Vick**, I'm pissed but I ain't m**arc**hing forth without direction, when will black life have proper protection, Eye for an Eye, **Buck Shot Smif-N-Wessun,** too many families stressing cause we don't ever learn our lesson, acting verse action, we don't take action, we get roles to act in movies cause we relaxin, I miss **Michael Jackson - Dawud The Uncanny BlaKseed**

December 17th 2014 — Strange Fruit

Out of sight out of mind, did she know she was a queen? Seldom seen are the good times, who controls the timeline? It's a fine between that moment of desperation and a good word you need to hear, I wrote this for my black nation, who was there for **Ashawnty**?! they she died by suicide and it haunts me, **Imani McCray** the same way, **Strange Fruit**, **Billie Holiday**, times are hard but stay another day - **Dawud The Uncanny BlaKseed** (May the souls of **Imani McCray** and **Ashawnty Davis** walk peacefully through the field of Reeds in Amenta. Amen RA.)

(For the Common Connection see page 81)

December 16th 2014 — Wired

Ignorance is bliss, but knowing it is halfway to insanity, I'm serious family, every two hours a **veteran** left cold, soul leaves the body, every 24 hours a black man autopsy - George Zimmerman probably, I left my schatz in Germany in 2003, maybe I should just flee and go back but damn, I don't know where she at man! maybe it's the fear of being guilty by association, that's got me waiting for support from my lost nation, or maybe it's the miseducation of the population, or maybe it's the walking dead, **the meds the meat**, the blue pill red pill, this shit is deep, stay away from everything sweet and unholy, that's how ya die slowly, behold the answers to all your questions unfold when you seek ya **soul,** behind the minds eye below the **hippocampo**, let the O H 2 flow, they might hate you so you show love and devotion, I see ya hands waving like a ocean, "*I know I got ya open*", I'm hope'n **all this violence**, might bring forth a moment of silence to **let your conscious speak**, weakness begets cruelty, turn off ya tv, maybe you will see that **ICE T** ain't a cop, he must've forgot, I always wanted to rhyme like **Common** so I never stopped, never copped out, it ain't about the money, it ain't funny when they choke a brother out and he can't breathe, kill a man and leave his wife to grieve, this is strictly for young nigga's, you got two eyes and two ears, have no fear, look and listen don't be out there downing beers, I been there, I been high speeds, always been the BlaKseed, the blaksheep do the knowledge speak after you apply it, think! not everything out there you gotta try it, this **New Jack City** got a nigga wired **- Dawud The Uncanny BlaKseed**

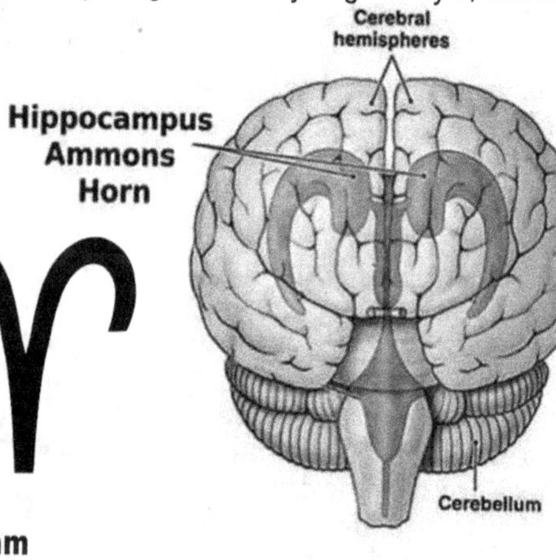

Mission-Aries and the Age of the Ram

Amun is one of the Kemetic Deities (Gods) who were often depicted with **Rams Horns** on their heads which represented the area of the brain called the Hippocampus. It's no **coincidence** that the hippocampus is also called **Ammons Horn** and is shaped like the **zodiac** sign **Aries** and much of the world we live in is based on astrology, even religion.. Especially religion! The ancients regarded matters of the heavens very important which is why they built structures aligned with the stars in various constellations like **Orions Belt** (page 344).. They had already realized that it takes roughly 2,160 years for the equinox to precess (move) through a sign. Thus it takes some 25,920 years for the spring equinox to traverse the full circuit of the constellations. This cycle is called the Great Year and it is the precession of the equinoxes through the constellations that gives names to the various ages. The age of Taurus (Bull) began just around 4320BC, and we can see the ages play out in the biblical allegories. The bible pulls from the astrological zodiacal time period of Aries which covers the 18th dynasty. This is why the Christian men who went around killing in the name of their religion were called **"missionaries"**. The mission was pulling from this time of Aries, hence Mission-Aries. The mission was to steal the knowledge they had taken from the 18th dynasty so as to dominate and control the world with religion (page 592)! The story of **Moses** takes place at the beginning of the age of Aries (Ram). Which is why Moses came down from Mount Sinai as '**two horned**', that is, crowned with **Ram's Horns**. He got "angry" when he saw his people still worshiping the '**Golden Bull**' (Taurus). He broke their statue because they were still stuck in the age of Taurus.This is a code for the adept reading signaling the age of Aries (the Ram).. The age of Aries (Ram) began around 2160BC, and the stories in the Bible are allegories, not real stories with real people.. The age of Pisces (Two Fish) started around 1BC, the same time Jesus was said to be born. **Jesus** feeding the multitude with **two fish** is another allegory connected to the two fish seen in the zodiac sign of **Pisces**. We are at the end of Piscean age which is the age of **Believing**, and we are moving into the age of Aquarius, which is the age of **Knowing.**

December 24th 2014 Halftime

Rau nu Prt m heru

Iu f Per f m heru

Utterances for Coming Forth by day into Light

It is he, who comes forth by day into Light

Y'all niggas ain't shit! cause you're only pissed during halftime, the game back on and then you act real blind, fuck a deal, fuck getting signed, I'm a shine like the **sun,** speak my mind then grind till they come for me, we ain't never been free, only thing free is the labor, the great incarcerator, they ain't never done us no favors, **Micheal Brown** dead on the ground for four and a half hours, make ya holla, **holla at me** if you ain't happy, the happy niggas be the ones misappropriating the funds, Like **Charles Barkley** and **Michael Jordan,** as a kid I watched him scoring, as a man I see him ignoring the poor and loving the plan I guess he never heard the **SunZ of Man,** I'll **Killah Priest** if he touch my son! I'm about peace don't make me bust my gun! "*I ain't a killer but don't push me, revenge is like the sweetest joy next to getting pussy",* and my friends, they killing all my friends like **Tookie** and **Troy Davis,** your apologies you can save it, it's halftime, it's half time, as long as the **sun** shine we got time, as long as the **sun** shine we got time, it's halftime, it's half time, as long as the **sun** shine we got time, as long as the **sun** shine we got time!

How many good brothers in jail with no bail and didn't do a thing? ***New Jim Crow*** scheme, **Antonio Martin, Martin Luther King,** when will it sting the hearts and minds of the times and let freedom ring?! we ain't gotta ask for a thing! **Marcus Garvey** said it'd probably take 24 hours once we decide that it's ours, summon ***7 African powers,*** pollinate the flowers and free the fathers, the warriors, the scholars and the goons, *it ain't hard to tell* that black cops scared to get shot soon, and go to hell to the foul cops that shot **Sean bell,** whom was about to get married, **Amadou Diallo** shot with the wallet he carried, stop spending your money! fuck a rally, we got copers bucking at we! we can get a lot further once we keep our money nappy, got'a keep our women happy, cause we came from a woman, got our game from a woman, time to heal our women and be real with our women, time to kill for our women! yeah nigga! I said kill for our women! it's halftime, it's half time, as long as the **sun** shine we got time, as long as the **sun** shine we got time, it's halftime, it's half time, as long as the **sun** shine we got time, as long as the **sun** shine we got time! - **Dawud The Uncanny BlaKseed**

December 17th 2014 The December 3rd theory
Meta-Spiritual Encounter with AJ Cooper

Giara Nova and her mother are devout Christians. They have a strong faith in Jesus and they care about the well being of others. Every year her mother would host this holiday party only inviting a small group of 8 to 15 people. Before dinner her mother would say a long prayer and in her prayer you could hear her mothers passion. She said the prayer in Spanish so I never understood it but they were thoughtful enough to have Nova translate each line of the prayer. After a few years I began to look around and realize that I might be the only person who didn't know Spanish at these parties.

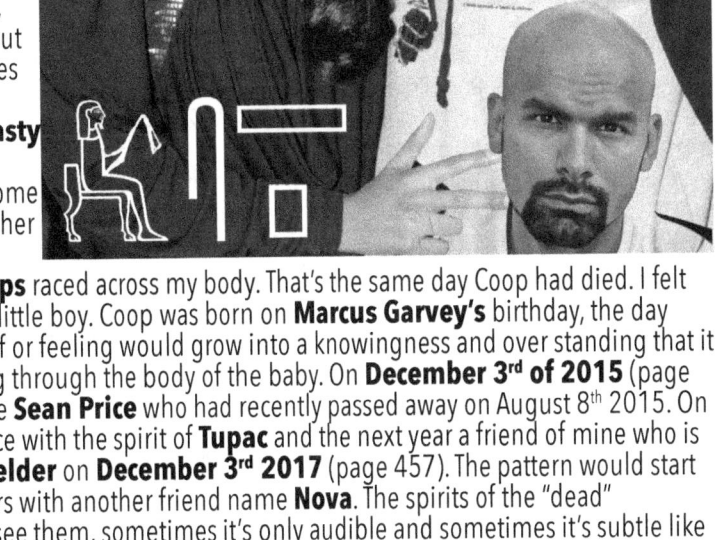

This year was a smaller crowd and this was also the first year that anyone brought children to the party. A couple had just had a new born baby girl only weeks old. They also had a sun who was around 3 or 4 years old. For some reason the boy was attracted to me. He kept coming to me. So I played with him, flying him around the apartment. The parents didn't mind, but they were a bit surprised. They commented that he rarely goes to "strangers". The little boy had a rugby shirt on that had a giant number **25** on it. I had a hoody on that had **25th Dynasty** written across my heart. I noticed that because **25** is my number. After playing with him I sat down at the couch. At some point I looked over at the baby girl in the car seat and asked her parents what day was she born. They replied **December 3rd** and immediately I got a feeling of **Deja vu** as **goose pumps** raced across my body. That's the same day Coop had died. I felt like I had flown the spirit of Coop around in the body of the little boy. Coop was born on **Marcus Garvey's** birthday, the day before my Grandfather died. Over the next 3 years this belief or feeling would grow into a knowingness and over standing that it was indeed and in spirit my friend Coop temporarily passing through the body of the baby. On **December 3rd of 2015** (page 345) I would have an experience with the spirit of the Emcee **Sean Price** who had recently passed away on August 8th 2015. On **December 3rd 2016** (page 431) I would have an experience with the spirit of **Tupac** and the next year a friend of mine who is also named **Nova** would suffer the loss of his father **Jack Felder** on **December 3rd 2017** (page 457). The pattern would start at the house of a friend name **Nova** and it would end 3 years with another friend name **Nova**. The spirits of the "dead" communicate in many ways, sometimes it's visual and you see them, sometimes it's only audible and sometimes it's subtle like these experiences. In 2022 I experienced **Deja Vu** twice while in **Kemet** (pages 670 - 671).

December 26th 2014 High Treason

Love is the answer, you gotta see the love in the **Panthers**, eliminate ***cancer*** with running, don't run from the master, blast that cunning bastard, they say **Jesus fasted**, you gotta eat to live, they deceiving the masses, when you sick and you eating you just feeding the madness, keep breathing and believing, for every season there's a reason, **try telling that to a mother that's grieving**! that's high treason! - **Dawud The Uncanny BlaKseed**

Meta-Spiritual Encounters

Do you believe in **ghost** or **guardian angels**? Some of you do and some of you don't. There are some who know that **ghost** and **spirits** of the dead are real because they have seen them or had experiences that can only be explained by the existence of some sort of **unseen ghostly presence**.. Some of you believe because you have an open mind and some don't believe because it scares you. Some of you need to experience it to believe it and I can completely understand that. People who are afraid to be alone in the dark are really afraid that they are not alone in the dark. Deep within they wonder if something is there. Well, I can assure you that something is there!! Every person has at least one **guardian angel** protecting them and some people have armies. We make a fatal error when we think all that we see with our two eyes is all that there is to see. All things are governed by seen and unseen forces. In 2015, at the tender age of 37 I will be initiated into the realm of the unseen. On January 30th one of my guardian angels will be revealed to me (page 318). On December of 2018 the identity of this guardian angel will be revealed to me (page 545). Then on December 18th my dead grandfather will appear to me in spirit form (page 348). Read Buck Franklin's Eye Witness Accounts during the Black Wall Street massacre on page 409 and ask yourself why the woman wasn't hit by any bullets. Then read about my 2002 car accident on page 105 and ask yourself why I survived and my sister dreamt it before it happened. Then read about my 2006 motorcycle accident on page 158 and asked yourself how I flew off my motorcycle and landed on my feet in the middle of the highway. On January 5th 2019 I was about to run across the street but **something** caused my body to freeze in place, in mid stride, allowing me to avoid being hit by a motorcycle speeding by (page 548). Pondering those events, then ask yourself if you believe in ghosts and guardian angels. **Also see pages** (48, 141, 142, 148,179, 250 -253, 318, 329, 348, 421, 434, 545, 548, 549, 572, 584, 604, 650).

"They" can show you better than I can tell you!

If after reading all those events you still don't "believe". I DARE you to say OUT LOUD, "I want to know if ghost or guardian angels are real". Remember, we attract the energy we send out. Just as there are good people and bad people. There are friendly ghosts and unfriendly ghosts. You reap what you sow. All the events in this book are true. If you follow my path and do the things I do yet still the great mysteries are not shown to you. Then continue the path and **to Maat be true** and perhaps in due time you will be worthy of the view.

January 1st 2015

Dreams and the Underworld: Is Time Traveling DeJa Vu?

My friend **Mr Nature**, was good friends with a pa**star** who was renovating a space above his church. 2 and a half months after I dreamt about walking in into an open wooden space, the pastor would rent his space to me for very little money. When I first walked into the space I got **DeJa vu**. It was the **dream**! I had a **dream** about being in a studio with open wood floors on October 17th 2014 (page 305). **I dreamt this moment before it happened**! I was sure of it! Just like my sister and my father have done. My sister dreamt my car accident back in 2002 on **May 25th** (page 104)! And my father dreams things before they happen all the time. He saw people jumping out of windows the day before the **Twin Towers** fell on September 11th 2001 *the year of the snake* (**911**) (Page 99) . This would be the first time that I would remember doing this but the truth is that we all travel during what we call sleep and some people are traveling during the waken state via meditation. When you experience what we call **DeJa Vu**, the moment can feel so familiar because you have possibly seen this moment before while in a dream and when you reach this moment in your waken state you experience a feeling of familiarity or a sense of "having been here before". So is it "**DeJa vu**" or is it **time travel**? Does some part of our being travel to the future and see something we are going to experience before it happens? If so is what we see set in stone and can we go to the past too? Can we change the outcome? My sister saw me die in a dream but I survived the accident that she saw. These are all questions that we should ask ourselves. Are we advanced beings with amnesia? Have we forgotten how to use the bodies we live in? In 2020 I will began to dream more things before they happen (pages 550/564) or was I time traveling to the future? In 2022 I experienced **Deja Vu** twice while in **Kemet** (pages 670 - 671).

The picture on the right shows clients doing push ups in the Studio I was given to rent. The brother who was in charge of all the affairs with the studio was born in 1989 **the year of the snake**.

January 2015 - Another Long Bout of Abstinence

Rau nu Prt m heru

Sometime in January of 2015 I would start another long bout of **abstinence**. This one would last around 1 year and 4 months. I started this absences because of my experience with the woman I started training on October 8th 2014 the day before my **Grandmothers** birthday. After I decided to stop entering the course with her, my experience with her led me to this conscious decision to abstain from sex. I would break my abstinence somewhere around (May 24th 2016) the time that the picture below was taken. I broke my absence with the woman that took this picture. I met her in 2014 when I was already over a year into a bout of abstinence that I started in September of 2012. She was a training client of mine who was refereed by another client but after some months she stopped training with me. When she came around me again in 2016 she wanted a massage from me. So we booked one and I gave her one. After a month or so she told me that she felt that her boyfriend was gay and she felt like he was only using her for a cover, she called it a "beard". She said that he didn't touch her the way she desired him to. She also told me that she stopped coming to train with me last time because she was attracted to me and she was getting turned on during our training sessions and since I was abstinent she stopped training and left me alone. Some time later during one of her massages she asked me if I could massage her breast so I did, and I enjoyed it. She was attractive and funny and some time after that day she began to give me fellatio. It was her idea and I accepted and enjoyed it. Soon after we started entering the course. I felt guilty for two reasons, because I had planned to abstain for 2 years this time and because I crossed the professional line that made me start this bout of abstinence in the first place. After I broke my abstinence with her I would make a mistake due to my lust on August 16th 2016 (page 402) the day before **Marcus Garvey's** birthday. I still regret that but I learned and I forgave myself. Perhaps if I had not broke my abstinence that might not have ever happened.

We Fall Down but We Get Up

Iu f Per f m heru

What is the lesson here? One of the most common reasons men fall from grace is due to our inability to control our desire for sex. The woman that took this picture was referred to me by a woman who once asked me for a massage then while I was doing the massage she asked me if I had heard about people orgasming from having a massage done on their hand. When she asked me that I was uncomfortable because I was working out of my home space and I did not want to cross any professional lines. I never did anything with her. She would later refer the woman that took this picture and I told you what happened with her. The woman that took this picture would refer another client to me who looked just like my older sister and the client would always make sexual comments. Her advances were easy for me to disregard because she looked like my sister so I could never see her in any sexual way plus it was never my intent to come on to any of my clients or to have sex with them. I have never ever made a first move on a client. Never. Why is this important? Because women are just as guilty for inappropriate sexual behavior as men yet men are the ones who most often fall from grace due to it and often times find themselves behind bars for it. In my previous life I was Emmett Till and I was murdered due to the false allegations of a woman named Carolyn Bryant (see page 508 for pattern with Carolyn's birth and death). In November of 2014 (page 311) I met Noel and because I gave her a safe none toxic environment to train in so I was able to reap the benefits of her gift of sight on January 30th 2015 (p 318). For all those who might want to judge me remember that song you sing in your churches! "We fall down but we get up, a saint is just a sinner who fell down and got up!

May 24th 2016

Utterances for Coming Forth by day into Light

It is he, who comes forth by day into Light

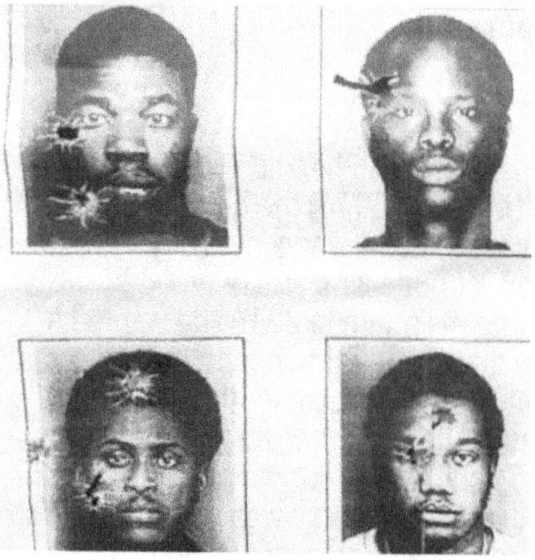

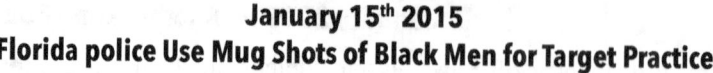

January 15th 2015
Florida police Use Mug Shots of Black Men for Target Practice

Tamir Rice, the 12 year old black boy murdered by police in Ohio had just been killed two months prior when the insidious Florida police practices hit the news on **Martin Luther King Jr's** birthday, January 15th 2015 (page 592). Some time in December of 2014, Sgt. Valerie Deant, who plays clarinet with the Florida Army National Guard's 13th Army Band, arrived at the Medley Firearms shooting range with fellow soldiers who were there for their annual weapons qualifications training. Sgt. Valerie Deant was not prepared for what she would see when she set her eyes on the pictures used for target practice. She saw mug shots of African American men apparently used as targets by North Miami Beach Police snipers, who had used the range before the Guardsmen. Even more startling for Sgt Deant, was the face of her brother with a shot to his eye and one in his forehead. It was **Woody Deant's** mug shot taken 15 years ago, after he was arrested in connection to a drag race in 2000 that left two people dead. His mug shot was among the pictures of 6 black juveniles used as targets by North Miami Beach police, all of them **riddled** by bullets. Sgt. Valerie Deant cried when she saw her brothers picture **riddled** with bullets. Deant's fellow guardsmen were angry too, but they tried to console Deant, who was devastated. She immediately called her brother, Woody Deant, who was 18 years old when the picture was taken. The North Miami Beach Police Chief J. Scott Dennis admitted that his officers could have used better judgment, but denies any racial profiling. There was no disciplinary actions taken against the officers who were involved with the incident. Chief J. Scott Dennis claimed no policies were violated. However, Woody Deant paid his debt to society spending four years in prison after his arrest. He is now a father, a husband and works a 9 to 5 job taking care of his family. He was walking the streets of North Miami Beach unaware that his mugshot was being used as target practice by police. What if one of those officers shooting at Woody's mugshot had stopped him because he somehow felt Woody looked familiar? What about the 12 year old boys like **Tamir Rice** who are killed within seconds because they were carrying a toy gun? The department claimed they would no longer use images of suspects they had arrested but what does that matter when Black life has no major importance to the system of racism and white supremacy? Just another Black face in a mugshot. This is proven by the legal system as most White cops who kill Black people face little to no charges while Black cops who kill anyone usually face more severe penalties, especially if they kill a White person. Some where during the course of this book it should become crystal clear to you that the soul is immortal. So you can kill us and bury us but we're the Blakseeds, and so we'll be back maybe in the weeds, Like dandelions I ain't lying I be iron like lion, mothers be crying when they see their sons shot down like **Orion.** Now that you know for sure that life is eternal what will you do with this life of yours? Remember, we all face Karma in this life and the next. Each life is a page and the world is your stage. I came back this time to write the book of a sage. Like a pearl on a necklace each life engraved. Like seeing your soulmate in a strangers gaze. In the blink of an eye you're gone turning the page. I stay younger than the age that a man plans to retire. The world is my stage, I **Transform** my rage like **Richard Pryor.** It's a cold world take a page, get paid to burn it in the fire. The desire to acquire, you can't steal the level of **Messiah** yet still **the caterpillar will kill the butterfly just to be flyer!**

January 17th 2015
Misplaced Misunderstood Tasmanians (1st of 50)

Suicidal thoughts of my corpse being autopsied, I had love for my nigga till my nigga shot me! I still got love for my nigga cause my nigga probably got coaxed by the same crackers that lobby, "Coca Cola and the coco", Tell me why my niggas love the Coco?! Matter of fact, fuck the Po Po! **Rick Ross,** "nickel rock"? niggas lost, niggas not **Negus,** So I had to negate the God, they found us **wrapped** so I **rap** the research in a skirt, in a melody like **Mc Lyte,** "I write what I like", "***Poor George***" chopped down the cherry tree at night, Poor George his wife he ignored at night, Cause at night curious George be watching them and raping them, **Toussaint Louverture,** have you ever heard of him? **Reparations** for the suns and the daughters of the millions of mans that they slaughtered! They got us miseducated, medicated and if we step out of line we get incarcerated, They got us frustrated! Us niggas just trying not to get **exterminated**! I feel like I'm the last one left, in New York they choked my brother to death, I'm stressed like **Kanye West,** I continue my quest, to the east my nigga, to the death of the flesh, I'm at the last stretch, will this be my last breath breathing? It's nation time, it's nation time, it's nation time, we need to raise a black nation, we don't need to wait'n, and we don't need to wait for revelations, and we don't need to wait for reparations, stop the separation, unite and build up a nation, it's nation time, I said it's nation time, brothers and sisters it's nation time , mothers and brothers and fathers it's nation time, let yo nation shine, let yo nation shine, I said it's nation time - **Dawud The Uncanny BlaKseed**

Significance

This was written to a **J Cole** beat and when I finished it I never really shared it with people because I didn't like my delivery. When I listen to the words now I understand. From the opening of the song my soul was speaking. "**Auset be the asset and Ausar be the star**"! **Ausar** the Lord of **resurrection**. I would say the words "**Suicidal thoughts of my corpse being autopsied**"! What else could I be talking about but my own corpses? Noel sang on this sing but her lyrics are not transcibed. 13 days after creating this song with Noel, she would spark the <u>Year of the **ghosts**</u> by telling me that **she could see** a **ghost** standing in my hallway (page 318). She would also draw what she saw. In1942, Japanese Americans were sent to concentration camps during World War 2. 46 years later, with the passing of the Civil Liberties Act of 1988 Japanese Americans received **reparations** to right the wrongs they experienced. Black people have been in America for hundreds of year being subjected to enslavement, lynchings, systematic racism and the list goes on, yet still we have yet to receive reparations (page 612).

Rau nu Prt m heru

January 22nd 2015 Hypocrite

Dear Doc you're a joke, you took an oath that u broke, I hope you choke on remorse and regret, you hypocrite, **Imhotep** in effect, the **prince of peace** in the flesh, my **Auset** she erect and **resurrect** my lost nation, wait'n for a spiritual manifestation, explanation on creation, ashes to ashes, we are star dust on the earth, the Haitian and Caucasian, we are all amazing, but we ain't all created equal, but that don't mean that anyone's placed beneath you, I beseech you to see through the bullshit they teach you, defeat you before you start, the art of war, like haarp, **I'll be back in the sequel**, in the spirit, you know they fear it, when they hear it, when they see it they don't believe it, they scream'n **Jesus Christ**, they lost their soul insight, he's nice, **he don't eat meat**, he walked on ice then he fell, his last words were rebel or meet defeat twice, this life is hell or heaven, cancer like 7, the God man in the flesh, if I had 24hrs left to live I'd write this rhyme with my dying breath - **Dawud The Amazing BlaKseed**

January 27th 2015 Flowers

I was happier when I ain't know nothing cause ignorance is bliss, how could I not feel like this? like I'm encaged on stage, what's the truth, what's being staged? wars waged on the minds of the times, ignorance is bliss when you're blind, behind every fortune there's a crime, maybe that's just misfortune in my rhyme, stuck in a maze designed with the amazing sign of **Heru,** better act like ya knew that **we are kings!** what's a diamond ring mean to a Queen but nothing?! like the temptations without **David Ruffin,** I wasn't really thinking I was sinking, I was out there front'n, drunk and high, stop teaching lies! You're better off eating to live before you get sick and die! disease is an ease most people believe come from the sky, but you meet death eating flesh with that apple pie, Africans die before their 3rd eye open, I stay searching and I meditate, don't medicate to escape and change fate from hells gate, Heavens inside when a woman creates, when she lactates babies drink the land of milk and honey from their mommy, **I rap like a mummy!** you act like a dummy, a koon, races in places cases they facing soon, lunatic from the moon, cartoons teaching doom in the living room, they eating wrong lucky charms won't let them act calm, silly rabbit, they very young but like **Spike Lee** yeah they gotta have it, take you back to **MR Voodoo** school you with that black magic, **Natural Elements,** I told her that she need to be more celibate, and she should stay in school but she be out there selling it, they shoot us down for the hell of it, My **Grand Father** died from **cancer** he looked hell'a sick, call me **heretic** but fuck this shit we living in insanity, We gotta rebuild our black family brick by brick no fantasies, wall by wall we must **free Mumia Abu Jamal!** we all know who killed **Tupac** and **Biggie Smalls!** fuck the law, stop the wars with each other, seize fire! the devils a liar, the truth you want the proof? I said the roof is on fire, and we don't need no water let that mother fucker burn, one brother teach two brothers, I said two sisters teach three sisters, I said four fathers teach more fathers, and let five mothers bloom five flowers - **Dawud The Amazing BlaKseed**

Iu f Per f m heru

Significance

J Dilla was born on Feb 7, the same day as **Emmett Till's** father (Louis Till, pages 475, 518). I wrote this to the **J Dilla** beat flowers and in the song I would say the following lines - "The amazing sign of **HERU**, We are **KINGS**, I rap like a **MUMMY,** Call me **HERETIC**". This song is a code. I say **HERU**, **KINGS**, **MUMMY**, **HERETIC** and right before I said Heretic I mentioned my Grand Father. King Tut's father was **Akhenaten** and he was given the title as the Heretic king by Europeans. Is it just a **coincidence** that I would mention my Grand Father then say the word Heretic a few words after? I even mentioned **Tupac's** name and I have a theory about who Tupac was in a past life? ! This song was written at a low point in my journey but I was still searching..

Utterances for Coming Forth by day into Light

It is he, who comes forth by day into Light

January 30th 2015 Meta-Spiritual Encounters Noel see's Dead people

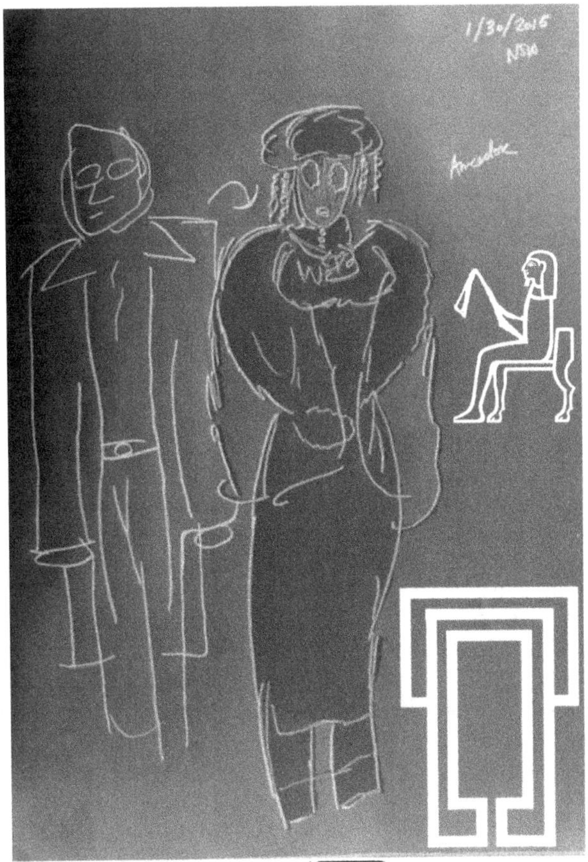

I started training Noel (page 311) shortly after I attended her show on November 30th. On January 17th we did a song together and two weeks after that Noel would share her **gift** of sight with me. She would be the first person to make me aware of the **spirit**, **soul** or **entity** standing guard in my hallway. She said there was a woman standing in my hallway and there was a **white man** standing behind her who looked to be **tormented** and ashamed (page 246, 507). She could not make out the woman's face because there was too much light and her eyes seemed to be glowing. I was reasonably amazed by this and because of the experience I had with J Cooper on Dec 17th 2014 (page 314) I believed what she was telling me! I felt like Cooper had visited me through the body of a baby at Nova's holiday party so this was not out of my realm of possibility. Perhaps if I had not had that experience and the other strange things happening I might not have so quickly believed her, but I did have those experiences and I knew they were real so I believed her. I asked her if she could draw what she saw and she did. I mentioned this experience in the song **Man The Unknown** (page 329).

Noel See's Dead People

Noel explained that she didn't always trust men because most men would treat her nice in public but if they found themselves alone with her most would try to make **sexual advances**. She said she was thankful that I gave her safe space to exercise in. When I look back on this experience I realize how important it is to protect and honor the divine feminine energy on this planet. If I had been a man that was looking to make sexual advances on the women I was coming across

I would not have been rewarded with Noel's gift of sight making me aware of my guardian! This is why it is important to treat all people with love and respect because you never know who you are interacting with. As you read this book you will be amazed to see who this ancestor standing in my hallway would turn out to be. On February 13th 2016 (page 362) **I would meet another woman who could see and communicate with spirits, souls, ghosts or entities**. I can not tell you exactly what "they" are except that they are people without physical bodies. Just know that the ancestors still walk with us! I understand that most people have not had similar experiences of their own allowing them to process this; so as to bare witness to the survival of the soul after physical death I will tell you about a white woman's death bed confession dealing with a soul of a dead black boy she caused to be **lynched** in 1936.

2021 (Survival of the Soul after Physical Death)

In September of 2021 I would see a video online of a white woman going through nursing school. She explained how an **old white woman dying** of **Covid** told her how she had caused a 13 year old black boy to be **lynched in 1936** when she was a teen. This happened in Louisiana during a time when black people were being lynched regularly all across America.. She explained how when she was a teenager she told her mother that one of the local black boys touched her behind the grocery store. The boy was kidnapped, beaten, castrated and lynched. Then his family's home was burnt to the ground. The woman said she watched it all happen. Afterwards the boys family was ran out of town. Now on her death bed the old white woman told her nurse that **she had lied** about the boy touching her. She said she lied because she was **jealous** that the little boy's sisters had prettier dresses than hers. So she **lied** on him out of jealousy. The **strange** thing is that the nurse says the old woman had been **hallucinating** for the pass couple of days. The old white woman **claimed to be seeing a black boy in her room watching her, she said he would not stop staring at her.** The nurse says that old woman was **terrified**. No one else could see the boy except the old woman so they all claimed she was "hallucinating". The old woman asked her nurse if she could be forgiven but the nurse told her that the only person who could forgive her was the boy that she murdered. You can still find this video online if you search (white woman confesses to having black boy lynched). I will have it posted online for you to refer to just incase the video that is up now is later taken down. You should also know that many medical professionals have similar stories of elderly white people making death bed confessions of how they were responsible for the mistreatment of and or death of a black person from decades ago. Our souls do survive death of the physical body! This is a reality. This is the age of Aquarius and all is being revealed. Rest assure that we all pay for our transgressions here on this earth plane. You reap what you sow! We get away with nothing. If you feel you are indeed guilty of acts unforgivable it is important that you immediately make a change in your life. There is always time to make a change. Life is a stage of demonstration. Recreate yourself. Make peace with those you have wronged and transform yourself. Be aware that this must be done with an earnest heart. You can never fool the unseen realms because God see's everything! The only way that America and the rest of the world can right the wrongs done to black people is to be a part of restoring us to our rightful place on earth without fear that we will do to you what you have done to us. We are not like you. We must restore Maat. **42 Laws of Maat, Page 367**

Significance

In 2020 I would become aware of who the tormented white man standing behind my guardian is. Sometimes it is Roy Bryant and some time sit is J.W. Milam, the men that murdered me when I was Emmett Till. One of the seers I met in 2019 would confirm this for me on January 13th 2020. The video of the story detailed above can be found on my youtube page (**TutemRa Kheperu**)

February 2nd 2015 Marshawn Lynch

I used to listen to the underground, Not them teachers in school, My art teacher couldn't draw like me, My coach couldn't score like me, I should have listened to **Ali,** I left the army cause it wasn't for me, I sat the bench cause my attitude was **Marshawn Lynch,** Left church cause ain't nothing worse than when a ***soul*** *get's* ***lynched,*** **James Byrd** have you heard, he ain't deserve to be dragged for the length of 3 miles, to arouse the patriots who were proud, of the who's and the what's and the where's and the how's and the fears of a man that could murder a child, It's on file, Black babies as bait for crocodiles, they foul **- Dawud The Spectacular Blakseed**

Significance

I have never watched Marshawn lynch play a football game but I have agreed with his view on the game and the stance he takes in life. He is an athlete with a brain. I wish I was like him when I started playing football. **James Byrd** was a Black man who was murdered by three racist white supremacists in Jasper, Texas, on June 7, 1998. Shawn Berry, Lawrence Brewer, and **John King** dragged him for three miles behind a pickup truck along an asphalt road. **John King** was the name of my back up receiver on my high school football team (page 62). **James**, was conscious for much of his ordeal, he died halfway through the dragging when his body hit the edge of a culvert, severing his right arm and head. The murderers drove on for another 1.5 miles before dumping his torso in front of a black church. I know now why I wrote about James. Because I was once tortured to death like him and like **Henry Smith,** who was lynched on February 1st 1893 in Lamar Texas, and like many other black people murdered today in modern lynchings. I was tortured to death at 14 years old when I was Emmett Till. All of these lynchings were awakening the ancient parts of my soul. The soul attachments. The memories from previous lives. These lynchings triggered my mission plan. I was sent her to **re-member** my lives so that I could align the Star Codes of Immortality and present this book. So that White men in this time could question their actions. So that African men in this time could question their actions. So that we can finally decide to awaken to our ancient greatness. Our African oneness. So that we can unify now in the present and restore **Maat** (Truth, Justice, Balance, Order, Reciprocity, Morality).

Condolences

My condolences go out to the family of **James Byrd** and all those who have been robbed of their lives by this system of racism and white supremacy. Please know that death is not the end. The soul survives death, indeed and in spirit. This is a book of the dead written by a boy who was murdered without justice, who defeated death and came forth by day. May the soul of **James Byrd** walk peacefully through the field of Reeds in Amenta. Amen Ra.

Rau nu Prt m heru

Iu f Per f m heru

Utterances for Coming Forth by day into Light

It is he, who comes forth by day into Light

February 3rd 2015 Forever Maat

I love girls that love me for the man that I be, and I don't judge the ones that gave it up easily, this ain't easy B Life be teaching me, Be careful what you seeking see, I used to see her, used to love her, put no other one above her, hug her, love her, leave her, never! now I know better so I **treasure** my **feather** of **Maat,** my sp**ark,** my Queen, my heart, we stay together through all weathers, through the cold and d**ark,** pull us apart? Never! you can't separate what fate brought together! never, no end in sight, c*ause we gonna be together forever! even past this life!* so don't count the minutes, finite no finish never ever, love and pleasure could never be measured without pain, on you mind like brain I remain like stain, she came, I proclaim victory **- Dawud The Uncanny BlaKseed**

Significance

"We are going to be here forever **EVEN PAST THIS LIFE"**! My soul knew! I even named it Forever **MAAT**. I had tapped into my ancient culture and it was starting to come out in my music. This was written on my mothers birthday.

42 Laws of Maat, Page 367

February 3rd 2015 Relatives

Sometimes talking to people will have you going insane, when they let religion realign their brains, a small link in a very long chain, can you feel my pain? my heart be beat'n like a drum cause everything is one, there ain't no end, no time, even if the **sun** stops another **sun** will shine, are you present in the present or living life as a peasant? it doesn't matter that you feel me really, it only matter that's you answer the call, so *Holla If You Hear Me* clearly, cause they pray and pray for my downfall, my enemies, I never say never cause even nothing is something you can't see, and your enemy is just a different branch on the same tree! It's all relative when you crack the code of relativity, let negative live, just outside of me! my ancestry locked down in my chemistry, a memory but do you **Ra**member? the **Metu** the **Neter!** the pineal the dot! the spot, the plot to block **Maat** and blot out the **sun**, this ain't a tale check the chem-trail the smoking gun! take you back to **Nun, Ptah, Atum, Khepera, Leflaw Leflah Escorscha,** salute the real souljahs! hold ya accountable like **Hannibal - Dawud the Amazing BlaKseed**

Significance

I wrote this on my mothers birthday. I had been having arguments with my mother and sisters about religion over the past few years. They are muslim and I had no religion. I had been studying our ancient African past and so I had left all forms of religion in favor of ancient Kemetic (Egyptian) culture. My soul was crying out through my lyrics. Was I speaking to myself in my music? I mean, was there an ancient soul attachment asking my current soul a question in this rhyme when I said - "my ancestry locked down in my chemistry, a memory but do you **Ra**member"? was I talking to myself? Was I telling myself who I was? Was I trying to wake myself up? That same day I would write another song talking about **coming back** from the dead. In the song **Inspire** I would say - "Don't shed a tear for me, cause ***I'll be back*** *in the hurricane with* ***spirits*** *on another plane"*. Was my soul speaking? It must have been because I had NO IDEA who I was at the time of these hymns!

42 Laws of Maat, Page 367

February 3rd 2015 Inspire

Don't run cause the job ain't done, suicide is like running to hide, so stay alive and **rise with the lions pride**, people cry when a real soldier dies, don't shed a tear for me, cause ***I'll be back*** *in the hurricane with* ***spirits*** *on another plane,* I'll be back in the hurricane with spirits on another plane, ***I'll be back*** *in the hurricane with* ***spirits*** *on another plane,* **I'll be back** in the hurricane with **spirits** on another plane

Who will I inspire? cause I know who inspired me, is it you? will you follow me and stand right beside of me? when I'm ready to m**arch** off and war against society, finally another soldier speaking with a strategy, **you and me we the worker bee, upper class the royalty**, most of us come home and ain't even got a pot to pee in, so you can cop ya BM or your Benz, but I wish you would take a look at the world through our Lenz, you would probably curl up and cringe, Let's trade places, your whole world would come to an end, trade cases huh, you'd go to jail in the end, cause all my niggas in the pen, and my sisters be like, where the black men? they all locked down on death row, what did you do to change that? I ain't think so! turn on the news and they talk about this, and talk about that, but can you pan your camera over here? listen to raps and yeah we talk about our cars, and talk about our gear, most of us grew up on welfare, but who the hell cares? they call it health care, I call it the least you can do mother fuck'n chemical warfare, are you aware how many Black girls disappear every year and it's never reported?! they ignore it! babies aborted, they cant afford it, daddies an alcoholic and mommies a fiend, ***Brenda had a baby*** not a **dream**, I probably be dead before niggas let freedom ring, **Marcus Garvey** said it would probably take 24hrs, If every nigga came together and decide that it's ours, **Marcus Garvey** said it would probably take 24hrs, If every mother came together and decide that it's ours, **Marcus Garvey** said it would probably take 24hrs, If every father came together and decide that it's ours, **Marcus Garvey** said it would probably take 24hrs, If every sister came together and decide that it's ours, **Marcus Garvey** said it would probably take 24hrs, If every brother came together and decide that it's ours, **Marcus Garvey** said it would probably take 24hrs, If every color came together and decide that it's ours, **Marcus Garvey** said it would probably take 24hrs, **Marcus Garvey** said it would probably take 24hrs, **Marcus Garvey** said it would probably take 24hrs, **Marcus Garvey** said it would probably take 24hrs **- Dawud The Uncanny BlaKseed**

February 8th 2015 ANCIENT FUTURE

I grew up miseducated from them lies that they postulated, the falsifier the liar the black flame white fire, it's a shame the fame that came from the **Wire**, when it's drug inspired, now they **Empire,** but you gotta go back to go higher to the **Ancient Future,** seventeen ninety nine they had to shoot ya, **Napoleon** strolling in **kemet,** he got mad cause he ain't see his face in it, it's kind of sad when you think a minute, they made history cause they wasn't in it, they made religion to control the senate, and the living God within them not knowing Gods infinite, Melanin gonna be here when they finish, so it don't matter cause matter of fact **Imhotep** yeah he built that, peace black carbon triple six be the secret, d**ark matter** be beneath it in the ether even the far reaches, I'm sure the animals look at us like we bizarre creatures, that kill each other cause of the difference in our features, reparations are due, reparations are due, I got caught up in the world took advantage of you, help me raise my Black nation reparations are due, I got caught up in the world took advantage of you, reparations are due reparations are due, I got caught up in the world and took advantage of you, help me raise my Black nation reparations are due, I got caught up in the world

During every big war Blacks unite more, in a vision this is exactly what I saw on the walls of **Luxor,** I had teachers that taught me about mount Rushmore, but never about **Ramoses** they don't care about our families, and they fear the bonding of black men, cause if we unite we just might fight for our fam, we founded Martial Arts giving birth to the **Wu Tang Clan,** I pledge allegiance to my family to write for what's right man fuck a Grammy, and a Oscar imposter, **O.D.B. Osiris** lyrically Karate I chop ya, I saw it in a **dream, Michael Jackson** screaming out nothing can stop ya, he was with **Tupac** and **Toussaint** in a helicopter, is it real or is it a story? is it allegory? if I tell a lie will I go to purgatory? if I write a rhyme and fly will my own niggas come for me? can I get nigga like **RZA** to make a beat for me? reparations are due reparations are due, I got caught up in the world and took advantage of you, help me raise my Black nation reparations are due, I got caught up in the world took advantage of you **- Dawud The Uncanny BlaKseed**

Significance

For the intro of this song I placed an excerpt from a speech of **Malcolm X** Speaking about the Egyptian Statues looking like Black people. I think this might have been the first time I ever heard that speech. At the time of this rhyme I did pay much attention to the part of his speech where Malcolm talked about **King Tut**, however I have transcribed some of the speech later in this book on May 19th 2019 (page 562). At the time of this rhyme I was still under the impression that **Napoleon** shot the nose off of **Heru Em Akhet** (The Sphinx) but after studying the teachings of **Dr Runoko Rashidi**, I learned that it was the **Islamic invaders** of Kemet who shot the nose off of the **Sphinx** and not **Napoleon.**

February 18th 2015 (Janisha Fonville, 20 yrs old Charlotte North Carolina)

Janisha was at home when her family called the cops to take her to mental health facility. Some say she was waving a knife at some point before the cops came. When the cops arrived officer Anthony Holzhauer shot and killed her. The cop reported that Janisha lunged at him with a knife but her family says they didn't see a knife in her hands when she was shot. Officer Anthony Holzhauer was not charged.

Condolences

My condolences go out to the family of **Janisha Fonville** and all those who have been robbed of their life by this system of white supremacy. Please know that death is not the end. The soul survives death, indeed and in spirit. This is a book of the dead written by a boy who was murdered without justice, who defeated death and came forth by day. May the soul of **Janisha Fonville** walk peacefully through the field of Reeds in Amenta. Amen Ra.

March 12th 2015 Booker T Washington

Mother fuck **George Washington**, cause my brother **Booker T** had Jamaicans move'n and shake'n , **Marcus Garvey** inspired a nation, so I pour libation for the African American **Haitian**, I been wait'n for **Toussaint** to **resurrect** and cause wreck like he never left, and put to death this **Napoleon** complex **- Dawud The Uncanny BlaKseed**

March 2nd 2015 Goddess (DR Frances Cress Welsing)

She been abuse, molested, betrayed, thrown shade, and used for sex and left to raise, a nation that won't behave, the **Goddess** giving birth to the grave, the **Eve** of creation, the **oracle** the **sage,** the **Black Madonna,** build your nest before you lay a egg, don't rush to be a momma, the blakseeds face a lot of drama, Mother Nature waiting for the seeds of a soldier with the **soul** of a **Dali Lama,** take control of today plan your tomorrow, **Know thyself** or be sleepy hollow, people who don't know they're past are doomed for sorrow, he blasted on him like an ole G, cause he follow what he saw on tv, shorty wanna be a thug, Lil homie need a hug before he get a mugshot, they buck us down then they frown on parental discipline, I don't think they want boys to be men, don't pray to God, pray that Morgan Free men, let's get free or die trying, I still hear **Trayvon's** mother crying, and I still hear these politicians lying, destroy the Black Family they trying, I still hear these politicians lying, destroy the black family they trying, I need a gangsta, gangsta Goddess like **Harriet**, **Hatshep** and **Isis**

Once upon a time there was a woman who liked me, she left right before I could treat her really nicely, I wasn't sure she was mi amore I tried to explore, sometimes words strike nerves right to the core, It's all fair in love and war, we played heart tug of war, then she left, she walked right out the front door, I never saw her again, I tried to call her again, she sent a text and said that we will always be friends, but somethings you can't mend, and I can't pretend that them things that she said didn't make my heart bend, now I'm home alone in this bed I lay in, looking at this ring and a **dream** I was saving, we could have been amazing, her name was ----, every now and then I think I see her waving, but it's done, one day I'm gonna find me another one, until then I'm gonna stay **star gazing,** I still hear these politicians lying, destroy the black family they trying, I need a gangsta, gangsta Goddess like **Harriet**, **Hatshep** and **Isis - Dawud Amazing BlaKseed**

Significance

This was written on my Grand father, Edward Eddings' birthday (page 25). The night before I wrote the first verse I **fell asleep** listening to a **Frances Cress Welsing** interview. One thing she said really stuck with me. She explain how people use the term "bird brain" for people they think are stupid however birds are not stupid creatures. She said that even a bird knows to build a nest before it lays an egg. She was talking about how the divine feminine energy and the Black Family needed to be respected, protected and maintained. When I woke up I found a beat and wrote the first verse. The second verse I wrote shortly after. Dr Frances Cress Welsing would make her transition the next year on January 2nd 2016 (p 357).

April 1st 2015 ♊ Profitable Life

Black Death is more than popular, it's profitable! even Black Death in the hospital, it's possible to drop a few lines for positive, but when will you support poets trying to give a different perspective? we be neglected and arrested, we oppressed kid, thought shit changed cause **Obama** was elected, yet we still disrespected! **Zimmerman** got paid for what he did, is it **Common Sense** to "extend your hand" just to live? I understand what **Nat Turner** did, beware of the frustrated Nigger! tired of being on the other side of your trigger **- Dawud The Uncanny BlaKseed** **(see pages 66 and 77 for the Common Connection)**

Rau nu Prt m heru

April 4th 2015 Walter Scott

Tutankhaten

Walter Scott was **shot** in the **back** on the same day that **Martin Luther King** was assassinated (p 69), the same day that I had my past life revelation of **Tutankhaten** (**King Tut**) in 2020 (p 594). Seeing this murder fueled me with anger for police officers and that same day ancient soul fragments would come flying through my music. I would mention **Akhnenaten's** name in a rhyme (p 323) and four days later I mention my ancient name Tutankhaten in the song, **Star or the Story** (p 323). **Walter** was shot dead for what looked to be no reason. He was stopped for a broken light, he got nervous and ran from the cop. He posed no threat yet the cop shot him in the back, killing him. Walter was 50 years old, he was studying **massage therapy**, just like me. He was also a veteran from the U.S. Coast Guard who had been discharged because he smoked weed. The same weed that is legal today. Walter ran from the cop because there was a warrant (**War**-rant) out for his arrest for **child support**. There is indeed a **war** against Black people in Ameri**kkk**a. With all the Black people being killed by police in America I don't understand how the police can perform their duty and not know that some Black people feel threatened by them. Many Black people in America, especially Black men have a reasonable fear of losing their life when dealing with police.

Iu f Per f m heru

 ***Condolences*** 

My condolences go out to the family of **Walter Scott** and all those who have been robbed of their life by this system of racism and white supremacy. Please know that death is not the end. The soul survives death, indeed and in spirit. This is a book of the dead written by a boy who was murdered without justice, who defeated death and came forth by day.May the soul of **Walter Scott** walk peacefully through the field of Reeds in Amenta. Amen Ra.

Utterances for Coming Forth by day into Light

April 4th 2015 ♊ Left Hand Right Brain

Trust, I don't trust any person, person, People are evil hard to see through, They will led you astray, And pray for your downfall, Guards be down when you drown in alcohol, Once upon a time I used to trust them all, Met fine dimes had high times, ate swine had a few brawls, Broke speed laws, life at a free fall, Heed the call before you hit a wall, I need y'all to trust in Self, Me myself and I be single, I'm supposed to be meditating, I'm a hell'a late and they saying don't worry be happy, Keep waiting be happy, Keep M**arc**hing keep imparting the sp**ark,** From the heart in the d**ark** in the p**ark,** Be the light leave your m**ark** written in b**ark,** The blakseed, I love you but I'm leaving on the next plane, left hand right brain, high insight with precise aim, trust, I don't trust any person, left hand right brain, high insight with precise aim, trust, I don't trust any person, trust, I don't trust any person, left hand right brain, high insight with precise aim

They put me on this planet damit, I ain't plan it, I been banished, lost in space, memories vanished, erased buried misplaced, the curious case of a late bloomer, I'm supposed to be **dead sleep**, watching the Honey Mooners, and the Truman Show, the human spirit goes tell lie vision, like ***Christ risen*** on a hell of a mission, but will they listen to the chosen, silence is **golden**, ***I arose when*** *the* ***sun*** *hit my skin,* **awoke** from within, I let go of the sin in sensation, in time I began to bend creation, and transcend a nation, with more impact than a man hand written emancipation, they said don't worry be happy, keep m**arch**ing keep waiting, I said a prayer, then there appeared a **Haitian,** divine manifestation, I wrote this rhyme for pine activation, acting verse action we don't take action, we get roles to act in movies cause we relaxing, I miss **Michael Jackson,** trust, I don't trust any person, left hand right brain, high insight with precise aim, trust, I don't trust any person, left hand right brain, high insight with precise aim, trust, I don't trust any person person, People are evil hard to see through, They will lead you astray and pray for your downfall **- Dawud The Uncanny BlaKseed**

It is he, who comes forth by day into Light

Significance

The beginning of the second verse sounds as if I was writing about this book and my **resurrection** as I end the first few bars speaking about Christ being risen. - "*They put me on this planet damit, I ain't plan it, I been banished, lost in space, memories vanished, erased buried misplaced*, the curious case of a late bloomer, I'm supposed to be dead sleep, watching the Honey Mooners, and the Truman Show, the human spirit goes tell lie vision, like ***Christ risen*** on a hell of a mission". This song was written the same day that I would have my **past life** as **Tutankhaten** (King Tut) revealed to me in 2020 (page 594). Which is also the same day that **Martin Luther King** was assassinated in 1968 (page 69, 592). When I said, "I said a prayer, then there appeared a **Haitian,** divine manifestation", I was talking about the card I found on the floor in 2005 that led me to personal training (pages 141-142) . One time is an incidence, twice is a coincidence, but three, four, and five is a pattern. Can you tell the difference?

April 4th 2015 The Power of Words So Be It

The power of words so be it, if you say it then you can see it, put your thoughts on something awesome then believe it, put your work ethic on something epic and then achieve it, failure if you accept it, then you neglected to be perfected, and erected like the **obelisk, <u>the son of the androgynous Akhenaten Amun dominance,</u>** what ever happened to **Common Sense**? I been rhyming since adolescence, searching for divine lessons and divine essence, I went to church and felt the hurt from the blind message, and what's the meaning of the star crescent? the peasant wasn't taught the truth about the God present with in, instead you were led away and filled with sin and medicine, they ain't teach me about my melanin, now they selling the mel-in skin, emergency epinephrin everybody is next to kin to the African, yet everybody be silent when they be attacking them, Tahira here I go with freedom rap again, back again blacker then berries and broker than levees, blacker then berries and broker than levees, I speak the truth, I never let the fruit of the rapping be the reason for action,I pass time with rhymes, now I pursue it with passion, it's a crime to neglect the divine, if you got a gift then you're expected to shine, but first invest in your mind, the man with one eye is king in the land of the blind, electric projected through the base of the spine **- Dawud The Uncanny BlaKseed**

<u>Significance</u>

Tutankhaten (King Tut" is the son of Akhenaten and in this song I would say - "The son of the androgynous Akhenaten Amun dominance", as if I was talking about myself. It becomes more strange when I realized that this song was written the same day that I would have my **past life** as **Tutankhaten** (King Tut) revealed to me in 2020 (page 594). Which is also the same day that **Martin Luther King** was assassinated in 1968 (page 69). One time is an incidence, twice is a coincidence, but three, four, five is a pattern. Can you tell the difference? Akhenaten was consider androgynous because of the shape of his body in some sculptures however these androgynous sculptures were meant to symbolize the dual principles of nature similar to the Ntchr's (deities) **Hapi** and **Atum**. See page 77 for the April 4 **Common Connection**.

April 4th 2015 Lucky Number 5

When I say I'm lucky like **5,** I'm sayin I'm lucky to be alive, first the system tried to erase my pride, then I had to run ditch and dive my own niggas, when I went to war saw them killing sand niggas, now I'm watching the hands of time wither away, tryin not to take my life away, I figure before I go I might as well put on a show, and show you the real thoughts of a field nigger never caught, forever trapped in **coincidence** and **fate** like the number **8, RA**member me from **93 Till Infinity** there's no escape! from the hateful energy of my sworn enemy, from the inner me to the world I see, I over stand the innocence, don't last long in the tech land, the **Tekken** and the **obelisks** was taken like the **sun** of the androgyny's **Akhenaten Amun** dominance **- Dawud The Uncanny BlaKseed**

April 8th 2015 Star of The Story

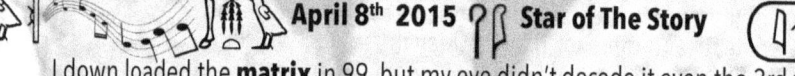

I down loaded the **matrix** in 99, but my eye didn't decode it even the 3rd time, I been having feelings of the 4th kind, they say ignorance is bliss, all this hell will have a **Naga** pissed, vexed, *<u>yes life's a mess don't stress, test are given</u>*, But be thankful that you're living bless, *<u>I guess I'm a major threat, cause I remind **Nagas** of what we were made to forget</u>*, my homie did 40 years for a crime he ain't commit, they gave him a Mill so he wouldn't say shit, they killed her son and got away with it, double **agents** flagrant, **Eric Garner** dead on the pavement, replay didn't change it, these games are ancient, **King Tutankhamen rhyming, Cleopatra** of the Nile, tell me why they lying, It might take a while to stop crying, but when you're done, <u>Return to the **father** through the **sun,**</u> I be the star of the story, the star, ***<u>I be the star of the story</u>*** **- Dawud The Uncanny BlaKseed**

<u>Significance and Creation Story</u>

I got into a heated argument with my Friend **Courtlan**. I do not know what this disagreement was about but that argument caused us to stop speaking for over a year or so. After our argument I fell asleep listening to a **Sophia Stewart** interview. Sophia is the Black woman who the **Matrix** and **The Terminator** movie scripts were stolen from. When I awoke, I woke from a **dream** about the **Matrix** and soon after I woke my friend **Hanif** (page 78) would send me a **Tuamie Generation Y** remix of Tupac's song ***<u>Holler if ya hear me</u>***. I listened to the song and was overcome with uncontrollable **tears**. Everything **Tupac** was saying in the song was still relevant today!! I felt every word! I cried and cried then shortly after I found the instrumental for the song **Star of the Story** by **Ta'Raach** online. I wrote a verse quickly to it and titled it **Star of the Story**. I was frustrated with the world and it came out in my music, along with the name Tutankhamen. In the verse I would say the name **King Tutankhamen** for the fourth time in a rhyme, I would quote Tupac's lyrics from the song *<u>Holler if ya hear me</u>* and I would used a line from a verse **Courtlan** wrote in college, "**Cleopatra** of the Nile". I'm 100% surer but I think his girl friend at the time had Cleopatra as her middle name. What I am 100% sure about is that **Shanta**, (his high school sweetheart) dressed up as Cleopatra in high school (p 289). **Thoughts in 2021:** I think this was the first song that I heard after my **past life revelation** of **King Tut** on April 4th in 2020 (page 594) where I would notice that I said **King Tut's** name in a rhyme like I had been saying **Emmett Till's**. More shocking was that in this verse it sounded like I knew I was **King Tut**! I said "King Tutankhamen rhyming" as if "eye" was King Tutankhamen rhyming! I was amazed! I started to search all my old songs for the name **King Tut** and everything that had to do with the 18th dynasty from Akhenaten to Nefertiti and so forth. After I searched my music for the name King Tut I found that I had said the name 6 times before the revelation (page 201) and I said it for the first time on **November 26th** in 2010 (page 187), the same day that King Tut's tomb was opened in 1922 (page 11)!! I also noticed that I had mentioned some of King Tut's immediate family members names as well. I said his parents names (**Akhenaten, Nefertiti**) several times. I said his grand parents names (**Amen Hotep III, Queen Tiye**) as well as the name **Hatshepsut** who was a great female Pharaoh from the same dynasty as King Tut. The rhymes in which I said the name King Tut can be found on the pages, 187, 195, 268, 323, 382, and 435. I was waking up from a long sleep, in a new body Just like the movie **Matrix**. See page **648** for the **metaphysical significance of the number 23**.

April 11th 2015 **From Superman To Man**

Should I close my eyes, lay me head down and go to sleep? Maybe things will change, maybe next week? we be afraid to speak, these laws be the claws dig deep, they flawed, pigs prey on the weak, and they gotta eat so they made a quota, **Walter Scott**, heart dropped when the cop pulled him over, 8 shots in his back and you can't take it back, you said you feared for your life, I say yeah right! that sound just like what **Zimmerman** said! we say **black lives matter** cause you're killing us dead, the **red** is for our blood, and the **white** be the cops, and the **blue** for the wall of silence that they got **- Dawud The Uncanny BlaKseed**

April 11th 2015 **From Superman To Man**

Never let the fruit of the rapping be the reason for action, I pass time with the rhymes now I pursue it with passion, it's a crime to neglect the divine, you got a gift? then you expected to shine, but first invest in your mind, the man with one eye is king in the land of the blind, electric projected from the base of the spine, the perfected number of man is 9, don't get erect cause she fine, take your time like wine lil homie, and seek the **pine** like **comb,** you just might strike home, it's a cold world son, even colder when you're alone, all that sugar steal the calcium right from your bones, the "**man of steel**" revealed to be a mankind of a clone, anythings possible, too hospitable with chromosomes, she went missing found dead with her organs gone, will you listen now to me on the really? or **De Nile** like blacks didn't build **De Nile Valley?!** will you rally for **Walter Scott** shot at 50?! **Boycott** till they stop terrorizing the block? or will you chill and watch **Love And Hip Hop** like it's not your problem? **- Dawud The Uncanny BlaKseed**

Significance

Read Superman Curse on pages 202 - 204

April 12th 2015 - Freddie Gray is killed at 25 yrs old sparking the Baltimore Riots in Maryland

Freddie Gray is arrested by Baltimore police and 45 minutes later he is found dead in the back of a police van with a severed spine with his hands and feet shackled. Because rioting is the language of the unheard and oppressed, riots broke out in Baltimore on April 27th. The National Guard was activated and sent to Baltimore along with 500 State troopers, and 5000 police from other local areas. The so called "Black American" population was beginning to see more and more Black people murdered and felt it necessary to fight back so protest marches ensued in other cities like New York, Chicago, Miami, Philadelphia, Seattle, Portland, Denver and DC. The riots were compared to the riots in 1968 when Martin Luther King was assassinated(pages 69, 592). 6 officers were charged with his murder but 3 were acquitted and all charges on the other 3 officers were dropped. Gray's family was rewarded a $6.4 million settlement.

Condolences

My condolences go out to the family of **Freddie Gray** and all those who have been robbed of their life by this system of white supremacy. Please know that death is not the end. The soul survives death, indeed and in spirit. This is a book of the dead written by a boy who was murdered without justice, who defeated death and came forth by day. May the soul of **Freddie Gray** walk peacefully through the field of Reeds in Amenta. Amen Ra.

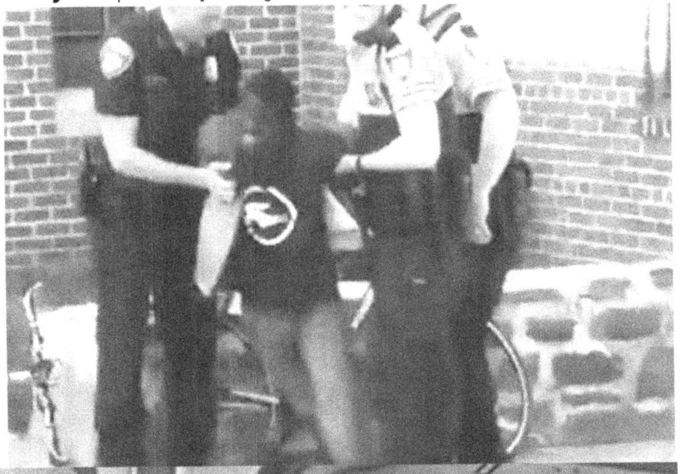

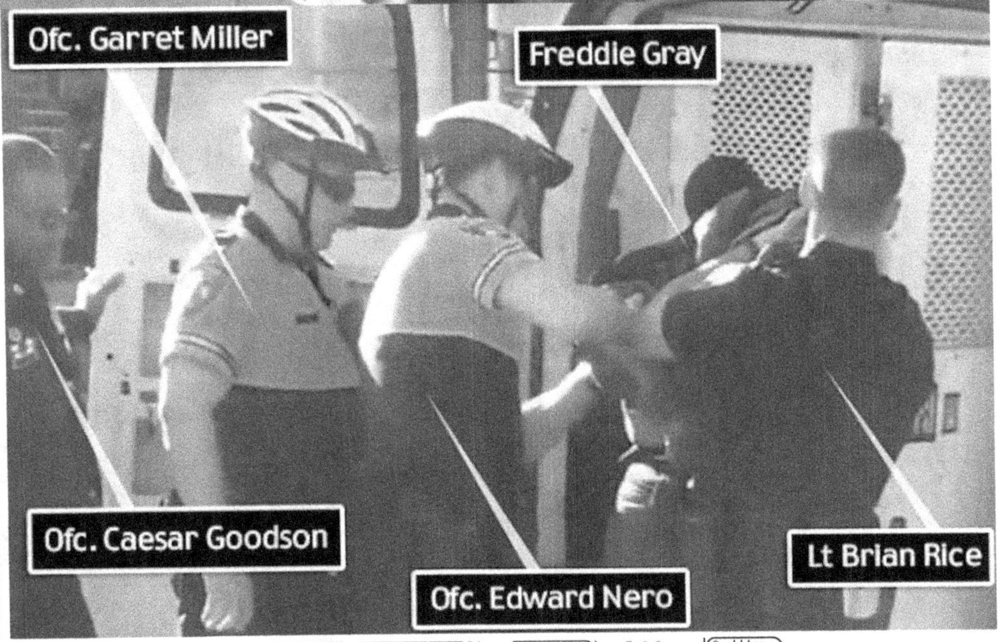

Because rioting is the language of the unheard and oppressed riots broke out in Baltimore on April 27th

SERVE & PROTECT

WHITE SILENCE = WHITE CONSENT

The riots were compared to the riots in 1968 when Martin Luther King was assassinated (see pages 69, 592).

Rau nu Prt m heru

Iu f Per f m heru

Utterances for Coming Forth by day into Light

It is he, who comes forth by day into Light

2015
My first Gong Sessions with Sunseed at Urban Yoga Foundation

I was invited to my first Gong session by **Tami**. I met her at **Tsion Cafe** where we would have small talk. I used to let her hear my music and she would always take time to listen. Tami and I had **Malcolm X** in common. She was editing a book about Malcolm X called **The Dead Are Rising** by her father and author **Les Payne** and Malcolm was one of the reasons I went to Tsion Cafe. I frequented Tsion Cafe for three reasons; because of the historical significance with Malcolm X having worked there years ago when it was called **Jimmy's Chicken Shack**, because the food was good and because I trained the owners.

My first gong session was more transformative but the second one would turn out to be the most **magical**. The sessions were hosted by **Ghylian** via Urban Yoga Foundation, the gong practitioner was brother **Sunseed**. During my second session with Sunseed I kept having the feelings and thoughts of enrolling back into massage school come into my mind several times during my session. After the session was over I would meet a brother named **Ron** who had also attended the session. We introduced ourselves and that's when he told me he was the **Tai Chi** instructor there. I told him that I had learned a little Tai Chi while at massage school and he told me he had learn at school as well and that's when we realized we had both gone to the same school. He was in school for acupuncture taking classes in Long Island at the main campus but I took classes in the city so we never met. **<u>Or so we thought</u>**. Him and I became friends. We would speak often and see each other once a month at the gong sessions. Ron really liked my music. The first time he heard my song, The Oneness, it struck a cord with him and he cried (page 383). He said my music spoke to the part of him that was seeking for a higher purpose in life. Attending gong meditation was instrumental in helping me reduce stress while living in this system of racism and white supremacy. I would have a gong session on **September 25th** 2018 that would spark **astral projection**. I also met a brother named **Akhmose Ari** at Urban Yoga Foundation. When I first heard his name, for some reason it was pleasing on my ears yet I was not yet consciously aware of **Iahmose** or **Kamose** (page 638). I asked him how long he had the name but I don't remember his reply.

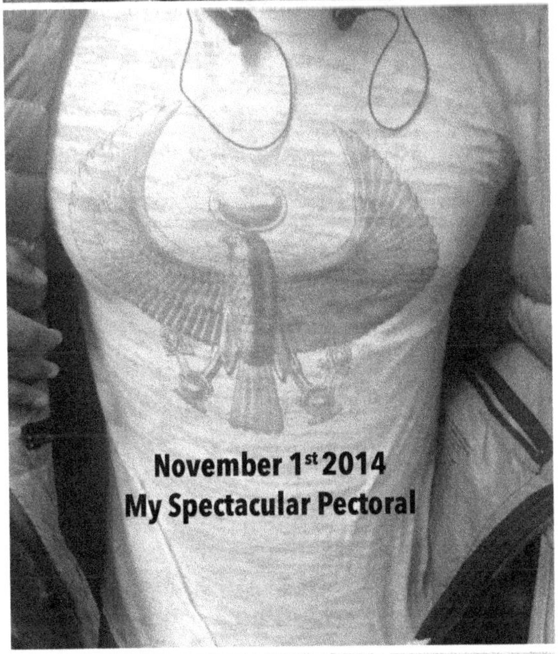

November 1st 2014
My Spectacular Pectoral

Revelation / Significance

Sometime after I had my past life revelation of Emmett Till on July 3rd 2018 (page 480) I would come to realize that I had indeed met Ron before but just in passing. I was looking through his Instagram when I saw a picture of him wearing a tee shirt with **Heru** on it and that's when I realized that Ron was the guy I met on **November 1st in 2014** in Long Island while I was fulfilling the mandatory hours of class at the main campus of the New York College of Health Professions in Syosset NY. During a lunch break I crossed paths with Ron in the hallway and the picture of **Heru** on his tee shirt caught my eye. I asked him if I could take a picture. He agreed. I took the picture and we parted ways (page 306). None of this is just "coincidence"! I was on a blind initiation, a rights of passage, that I was oblivious to. I was following my heart and seeking divine truth and in 2018 my past life as Emmett is revealed (p 480). On April 4th 2020 (page 594) I would have my **past life** revelation of my life as **Tutankhaten** (**King Tut**). The image of Heru on Ron's shirt is a picture of the pectoral jewelry from the tomb of **Tutankhaten**. In ancient kemet Heru (Falcon/Horus/Jesus) is the son of Ausar (Osiris) that returns. Heru is from the Ausarion or Osirion drama of **resurrection.** Ron called me on September 25th 2017 and told me something that sparked a series of events revealing a pattern that compelled me to make a pilgrimage to my home town of Far Rockaway.

Remember that you are Ausar and Heru, the hero!

<u>See page 3 for the **hero's journey**!</u>

April 17th 2015 Wake Up Blakseeds

Every rhyme that I write is like my will that it I sign, Lord let your will sp**ark** the blakseeds in the heart, they say <u>*Hip Hop is dead*</u> I said the **sun** shines on the dark**, The Brand Nubian**, **Usr Maat Ra Setp N Ra** The African, we back on that again, backs against the walls, <u>we can live together and **rise**</u> or die alone and fall, back into the wretched of the earth, respect to the Gods and earths, **Sirius** rotation for the nation, check the constellation and use your imagination, 3 wise men, aligned with the stones, to guide you home, cause you're lost, diseased, eating fruits with no seeds and don't believe, these **Star Wars** have been cloned, no fly zone, drone, 5.0 roam, **Ramarley Graham**, a boy! not a man! still killed inside his home! so I "<u>*dip dip diver civilize a 85er*</u>", did it matter his religion before the cop fired?! No!! so the solution is knowledge of self to better ourself, cause I know myself that we can do much better than this! nothings changed just another sequel, the devil still causing trouble amongst the righteous people! - **Dawud The Uncanny BlaKseed**

42 Laws of Maat, Page 367

April 18th 2015 Memory Lane

I grew up in Rockaway Queens, I never learned about **dreams**, I hit the scene with my cousins and they would be thug'n, life ain't a game, I take you down my memory lane, so many names most to them be lost in my brain, flash back to the summers ***Matmuu*** and **Musunga**, rock fights **Timothy** chased me home at night, hard knock life drugs on the block like dice, if you had a father in the house that would have been nice, I heard Ell been in and out jail through hell and back, hard to excel when you start inhaling crack, ain't hard to tell that he fell on the wrong side of the tracks, he ain't have a man to reach him and teach him and spit the facts, in fact neither did I and sometimes I would cry, Just me and my sisters be a father to you child, It shouldn't take a while to realize they miss ya **- Dawud The Uncanny BlaKseed**

April 19th 2015
(Dr Ben-Jochannan tribute at the National Black Theater)

I would attend this lecture in honor of **Dr Ben-Jochannan**. I had been aware of him for only 3 or 4 years at the time but I was greatly appreciative of his contributions to Afrikan people. Over the last several years I listened to a lot of his lectures and purchased a couple of his books, none of which I had read cover to cover. I would say his name for the first time in a Heka the very next day, in the song below. Then again on Feb 9th 2017, in the song, **Maroons** (page 442). The words, <u>***Black Man of The Nile and His Family***</u> which is the title of one of his books would find their way to a few of my rhymes over the years. The first time was in the song below. Then again on Sep 27th 2015, on the song, **Synchronicities** (page 339). Then again on Nov 19th 2015, in the song, **Amenta** (page 344). Then again on Jan 23rd 2016, in the song, **Don't Argue Me** (page 360). Then again on Feb 13th 2017, on the song, **Blak Wall Street** (page 443). Then again on March **23**rd 2017, on the song **Keep Ya Head up Nefertari** (page 445). Then finally on Dec 2nd 2017, on the song, **I'm Not a Racist** (page 456).

April 20th 2015 Dr Ben-Jochannan

Yesterday I went to a lecture but they ain't talk about God or sin, The talked about **Dr Ben** and the **NTCHR,** The **NTCHRU** in the plural, The African and the **Voodoo,** the **Zulu, Heru** flew through the **Shu,** Moji Mbili Tatu, one two to the three, **Mfundishi** dropping science in a poem, it's a blessing that I met him, so I owe him, **Dr Ben** say do the work, if you do the work then you can sp**ark** a blakseed down to **The Roots**, as I proceed, a bee get's no nectar on the leaf so I don't bee**lie**ve, I know! and I know the **Kemetic** land of the blacks can achieve, if you read between the lines you can see the signs, I thank the **Ankh** man, take the T H off th**ank** and see the **ankh** man! **Professor Smalls** no **Biggie**, was on stage being praised with **Dr Leonard Jeffries** by **Brother Reggie,** he look like **Reggie Noble** but more Nobel, it's kind of heavy but you ain't ready, cause heavens between the legs of a black woman, said by **Sa Ra Suten Seti,** he got that from **Dr Ben-Jochannan** <u>*2000 Seasons*</u>, 4000 miles of the Nile and a million reasons, **The black man of the Nile and his family,** what a tragedy not to know **The Roots** of your family tree **- Dawud The Uncanny BlaKseed**

April 24th 2015 Swami

Nobody wants to be a **Rodney King** I ain't telling you not to swing homie, I'm telling you to be smart, they got a license to kill trained to aim for your heart, you got a nation to build you should study the arts, and inner stand the empty hand, this pin in my hand is mightier than the sword of Conan, mankind <u>subdue the beast of ignorance roaming in a mans mind</u>, this roman land is damned! built on crime, will it stand the test of time like the **pine** that shines in ya mind homie? <u>if only we would stay alive past 25 we could **rise** homie,</u> unify, apply the science of dead **Swami's**, <u>***when I die don't cry, don't shed a tear for me, pour libations and I swear I'll be there homie, in the water, in the breath, in the air, even death don't stop BlaKseeds***</u> planted in the earth **through birth we will proceed**, you know it , believe it, see it, be it, so be it, you know it, believe it, see it, achieve it, be it, so be it, believe it, so be it, know it, be it, so be it **- Dawud The Uncanny BlaKseed**

<u>Significance</u>

It was around this time that I read a few chapters of the book, **Autobiography of a Yogi**. At the end of chapter 6, on page 66 I read a sentence that inspired a line in this song. In this song I speak about **dead swami's** and surviving death by being present in the elements after death and **coming back** through birth. Then a year later On May14th (p 383) I will write the song **THE ONENESS,** about a man being initiated into the order of Swami's and then on **May 24th** I would be **initiated** by someone or something into something I was still unaware of (p 385).

Rau nu Prt m heru

Iu f Per f m heru

Utterances for Coming Forth by day into Light

It is he, who comes forth by day into Light

April 29th 2015 God Winks Infinite

Yesterday I met this fine fit woman on the train, drinking coffee, I tried to explain, the caffeine that you fiend can be a hazard to your brain, and if you trying to gain muscle you must do as much as possible to drop the negative or you gonna live in a hospital, she said, Dawud you're quite hospitable, what a spiritual personality, who taught you that southern hospitality? tell me about your family? where are you from? were you the only son? did you run forest run? did you join the army shoot a gun? yeah, I was stunned, stuck in a daze, amazed what was she some kind of **sage**?! was it staged? she said, calm down, poured her coffee on the ground. I looked around, **profound**! we were on the other side of town!! am I **dreaming**?! she said, you asked for a **sign**, no such thing as **coincidence**, so get that out ya mind, there's the **seen** and the **unseen** you can put that in a rhyme, no such thing as **coincidence**, all divine incidence, **God winks** infinite, weigh you over your intent, God winks infinite, weigh you over your intent, God winks infinite **- Dawud The Uncanny BlaKseed**

April 29th 2015 2000 Seasons

They dug deep and took what mother earth needed for herself, to keep fertile health, material wealth, the imperial killer, serial sinister minister, harbinger of death finisher, theft till nothings left swept across the land, they came with admiration, we filled their open hands, they altered the nation, went away from the way of creation for generations, forgot **The Cycle Of Regeneration,** racing for occupation extermination, like a dog chasing it's tail, if you don't know, then you don't know, don't go creating a tale, **We Came Before Columbus** thousands of years before we fell, rest in peace to my peers who fell, from **Sean Bell** to **Freddie Gray,** this happens everyday, as the world turns they got me turning grey, <u>so I turn to the **SUN,** let it shine on my **pIne** like **Jacob**,</u> it's the ladder you climb up to refine your mind, "**Wake Up Reprise In The Sunshine**", I take you back in time, rewind like a tape, Alex the greek could never **wrap like a mummy,** hit escape when they play that bullwhip bamboozle bullshit from the pulpit, cause they about that money! they politic'n they be politrick'n, don't be a fool and trust a politician! ain't nothing funny! I speak the truth they might take my life from me! we might fight amongst each other but I promise you this, we burn this bitch down get us pissed, we burn this bitch down get us pissed, we might fight amongst each other but I promise you this, we burn this bitch down get us pissed, 2000 seasons a million reasons, we might fight amongst each other but I promise you this, we burn this bitch down get us pissed, We burn this bitch down get us pissed

That's how it goes, we were made to think we ain't supposed to explode, with every new murder we forget, told to get a grip, they can kill us on cam and our fam's left to live with it, but the dead can't cry out for justice! instead the living must ride on these busters! from B More to South Africa it's just us, the truth exposed, they say ***<u>the riot is the language of the unheard, a dream deferred</u>***, does it die or multiply? screaming give me the **loot**! give me the **gold**! give us everything you **stole**! I be the rose that flew through the **Shu Heru** I never fold, I got *<u>99 problems</u>* but a heart ain't one, they killed her son with a gun and sold his young organs, we on the run cause it's open season, but think what's the reason? they want us gone we ain't leaving, I wrote this when I was grieving, our bloods' in the land, go and count the grains of sand, that's how long we been here, the greatest fear at hand, call us the son of ham, afraid to treat us like a man, **I am that I am**, **The Sunz of Man** gave you the plan, and so it was written, so be it, never quitting from the streets to san Quinton, we can dance or stand and listen, the time is always ripe for what is right, we might fight amongst each other but I promise you this, we burn this bitch down get us pissed, we burn this bitch down get us pissed, we might fight amongst each other but I promise you this, we burn this bitch down get us pissed, 2000 seasons a million reasons, we might fight amongst each other but I promise you this, we burn this bitch down get us pissed, we burn this bitch down get us pissed ***- Dawud The Uncanny BlaKseed***

May 3rd 2015 Soulja

They say life is for the learning of lessons, **A soul having a human experience,** breathe in the essence, and don't waste time stressing, for every answer there's a question, solve it and get a blessing, revolving round the blessed one, circadian on the rhythm, create a schism between the truth and the bullshit they give em, the hate they gave little infants Just for living, I'm a **living memory** of every heavenly family member, **RA**member antiquity, sometimes It's hard not to let this shit get to me, but then I write a rhyme and it empties me, the emcee infantry, battling infinitely it's been a battle to be me, reciting my soliloquy, will they remember me, **Or scratch my name off the wall, Like I wasn't there at all,** are you just hearing me or are you listening to the call? are you ready to change your mind for the cause, the cause the cause? because it's time, it's time

They say life is for the learning of lessons, a soul having a human experience, breathe in the essence, and don't waste time stressing, Life is the blessing, **you are live and direct in link with me realizing my essence,** every time I write and record my life, my thoughts on my mind, as I try to remind the self of the self I need to shine, there was a place named pine, a ladder to climb, *<u>the tree of life up the spine,</u>* kundalini in **graffiti like Nefertiti,** close ya eyes if ya trying to see me, do the math when it's done naturally, we live happily ever afterly, naturally there's a half to ever thing even reality, can you separate the real from the fantasy, stuck in the 3rd circuit, what if I told you ***<u>I came back from the future</u>*** and everything was not perfect? **- Dawud The Uncanny BlaKseed**

<u>Significance</u>

I want to focus on one thought from each verse. In the second verse I say - **"you are live and direct in link with me realizing my essence".** When I wrote that I was trying to express how my music is a reflection of my emotions and thoughts so if someone was to listen to my music then they are hearing my growth and transformation. However after my past life revelations this line would read very different as they show that my ancient soul fragments were speaking. With my poetry I caused my soul fragments to fly out of primordial darkness coming forth by day. In the first verse I say "It's been a battle to be me, reciting my soliloquy, will they remember me, **Or scratch my name off the wall, Like I wasn't there at all".** After the reign of **Tutankhaten (King Tut)** inscriptions concerning him were erased from monuments and his statues were defaced and destroyed; the reason for this obliteration of his memory was............ I mention **Back To The Future** in this rhyme, see page 40!

May 5th 2015 - Meta Spiritual Encounter Sparked by a Thought
The never ending story and my experience with the Metu Neter books, "Sometimes I Feel like somebodies Watching Me!"

When I was 8 years old I saw the movie The Never Ending Story (pages **44**, 259, 341) and it quickly became one of my favorite movies. The most intriguing thing about the movie was the part when the main character finds out that **the characters in the book he is reading can hear him**. The movie makes a profound analogy about the **unseen spirit world** being **right in front of our eyes** yet most of us fail to see it. On May 5th 2015 I would have an experience that reminded me of that scene in the movie and it left me speechless, uneasy and damn near scared. It was **spooky action** up close and personal. What ever is out there, in the unseen world was without a doubt communicating with me!! I was 100 % sure of it! **It was not just a coincidence!** I had experienced enough by now to know that. Let me tell you what happened. On May 5th 2015 I was up again at night **smoking weed** and writing music. I began to write a rhyme about the **coincidences** I was experiencing and the **unseen world**... I wrote the words, "I be seeing signs in the times, **could it be the unseen communicating**? does every **dream** mean something? is a **falling star** really a **falling star**? do you know who, what, where, when you are? **man the unknown**, you can go alone and go fast! or we can go together and go far! she saw my ancestars, she said she was my great great great grand mother my protector............"

I stopped writing and I became overcome with sadness and confusion. I was up again at night writing music that I was never going to do anything with! Why the fuck am I writing this music, I kept asking myself!!! I thought about how I used to be out at the clubs having "fun" and now all I do is stay home watching lectures and writing this damn music and reading and why the fuck am I writing this music?!! **I started crying**. I looked out the window and far off in the darkness of the night sky I could see a **star twinkling,** like, "twinkle twinkle little star". I looked over my left shoulder and my eyes fell on my book stand and right in my eyes gaze were the first three books of the **Metu Neter** series by **Ra Un Nefer Amen**. I RANDOMLY grabbed one of them and before my hand touched the book I had already processed the thought - "I wonder if this book will speak to me". I wondered if it had some divine words that would speak to this very moment! I opened the book and my eyes fell on the words, **Communication with the unseen world.** I read those words and I closed the book immediately and about just as fast as the book closed my tears stopped running. I was no more in a crying mood. This was **strange** and I was reasonably alarmed, and **spooked**! This was **spooky action**! I had a dead stare of confusion on my face. I could not explain what I had just experienced and the unseen was not done. Less than a minute after it would speak again!! I wanted to escape the moment. I wanted to change the subject so I ignored what had just happened and I opened my phone and opened Instagram, but as soon as it opened the first thing I saw was a post from the page **@Afrikanlibrary**. The post was a picture of all three of the Metu Neter books by Ra Un Nefer. I left a long comment under the post exclaiming what had just happened to me. Of course no one reading it could really understand me. I finished the rhyme and titled it Man The Unknown. That was an experienced that left me with out a **shadow** of a doubt that **SOMETHING IS WATCHING ME!** I can remember seeing to **Mfundishi Jhutyms**, on 125th street after this experience and asking him if he ever felt like something was watching him. His reply was that **the NTCHR is always watching** (page 345). But I didn't think he fully understood what I was asking.

May 5th 2015 Man The Unknown

I be seeing signs in the times, could it be the unseen communicating, does every **dream** mean something? is a falling star really a falling star? Do you know who, what, where, when you are? **Man the Unknown**, *you can go alone and go fast, or we can go together and go far!* she saw my ancestor, she said she was my great great great grand mother my protector, **Auset Ausar, Neteru Ptah** spiritual, 11 laws, 9 **Arc**h angels **42 negative confessions** to change you, they call it a miracle, the sinner is you, who will kill - destroy the mineral, through temptation of sensations, it's what you tasting today, got you wasting away tomorrow, the key to all your sorrows, the ***holy of holy's*** *is where I go* when I fell low or hollow, even those who follow must lead, take the narrow road that leads to life inner chi and vitality, like **Jesus** walking on water in the sea of Galilee, whether analogy or actuality, weather the storms in your galaxy, from Plato to Pluto to Galileo, don't be the pseudo get you a halo and be a **Zulu** or **Pharaoh,** keep your eye on the sparrow, then split the arrow, split the arrow.. - ***Dawud The Uncanny BlaKseed***

ADDENDUM

Eddington - The 44th parallel - Spooky action in near future and the distant past (see page 40!)

I titled the song, **Man The Unknown**, after a book titled *Man The Unknown*, written by Alex Carrel. In that song I say the word **Pharaoh** at the end. Alex Carrel died on November 5 19**44**, the day after **king Tut's** tomb was discovered in 19**22**. I purchased the book in 2014, and it was on page **22** of this book that I first came across the name **Eddington**. Alex mentioned Einstein and Eddington in the same sentence. I took notice to the name **Eddington** because my last name was **Eddings**, and because of the nature of the Black experience, many of us carry the last names of those who enslaved our ancestors during chattel slavery. Sir Arthur Stanley **Eddington** was an English **astronomer**, **physicist**, and **mathematician**. It was Eddington who gave life to **Einstein's** Theory of Relativity catapulting Einstein into global recognition.. The patterns I present in this book are examples of a phenomena known as **quantum entanglement**, spoken about often in **Physics**. The theory states that quantum particles that are entangled will act as one system. A measurement made on one particle will be the same on the other particle even if the particles are thousands of miles away. Einstein called this phenomena, **spooky action at a distance**. Physicist like Einstein have been trying to find and measure the smallest of particles but these particles seem to disappear and react differently when they are being observed. The particle I am isolating is the transmigration of the soul. The soul in question is my own. Souls are broken into fragments and the measurements on one life (soul fragment) will equal the next life (soul fragment) even if the lives are 3300 years apart. All the patterns in this book are examples of the quantum entanglement of my soul fragments. That is why I have **birthmarks** where Emmett was shot (p 514) and that is why the **gematria** in my names are the same, as seen on page **41**. The mathematics of the divine creator binds all things that are connected with **star codes**. The codes follow us in life and in death, like a finger print. And some of us leave our soul-er finger print everywhere. Like when Einstein died in 19**55**, the same year **Emmett Till** was murdered and the same year my mother was born (p 21). Like when Sir Arthur Stanley **Eddington** died on November **22** 19**44**, the day before Mamie Till died (Emmett Till's mother). Eddington had a cousin named Paul Clark Eddington. Clark Eddington was an English actor best known for starring in the television sitcom, **The Good Life**. The sitcom ran from **April 4** 1975 to **June 10** 1978 - my past life as **King Tut** was revealed on **April 4** 2**0**2**0** (p 594) and my great grand mother Leacola **Riddle** was born on **June 10** 1913 (p 21). Clark Eddington was born on June 18th, the same day my great grand mother **Leacola Riddle** died (p 21), Clark died on **Nov 4th**, the same day **King Tut's** tomb was discovered. On pages 12 - 14, similar patterns surround the discovery of King Tut's Tomb. On pages 37, 172, 517, 561, 582 & 660, you can see the **44th parallel** in action. My sister's "**dream**" (pages 104 -106) wasn't a premonition, **it was time travel**, or **spooky action at a near distant future**. Our consciousness can **quantum leap** to the past or the future via dreaming and meditation. And like my experience detailed above with the Medu Neter books, **the NTCHR is always watching.**

Rau nu Prt m heru Iu f Per f m heru

Utterances for Coming Forth by day into Light

It is he, who comes forth by day into Light

May 9th 2015 Cain and Abel

I said who is the **Cain**, and who is the **Abel**? I was 12, sitting at the table, and at 12 I excelled and prevailed, cause I ain't let them put my **soul** in a cell, he said **Cain** was Black he killed **Abel**, and cause of that Blacks were not able to live in peace or even to be a priest, and at 12, I ain't believe him in the least! See my family, we were raised praying to the east, how could I end up in the Middle East? see I never thought that I was gonna go to war, I wonder who I thought that they was training me for? I be self Lord and master, put no man in from of you not even your pastor, my homie said you stressed son you need to get some laughter you be so vexed son your Facebook status be teaching some lessons but you be causing static you need to speak less son! I said, there's a war going on outside no man is safe from, you can run but you can't hide fore ever from these streets that they done took, you walking with your head down scared to look shook ain't no such thing as half way crooks! **- Dawud The Uncanny BlaKseed** (***see page 49 for lesson on Cain and Able***)

May 12th 2015 Who Do You Believe In

Who do you believe in? I believe in the God that leads me to freedom, I discard the God that say obey the heathen, I pray to even the odds, Adam and Eve, they deceiving the **Goddess Isis,** she's priceless! **Auset be the asset, Ausar** be the star, identity crisis, Do you know who you are? can you locate **Orion?** Mothers in black crying! brothers in packs dying! too high to see the designing of the prison we in, is it **The Ballot Or The Bullet?** or the prison with in the mind? I take you back in time, rewind to 18 89, when it was a crime to be black like me and free, we saw the penitentiary cause of vagrancy, **Slavery By Another Name,** is God saving me or is she saving you? maybe the chosen few, the Jew, the boys in blue.. **<u>these laws are the walls you can't break through</u>**, Industry rule number 4000 and 32, don't let them break you! and to my **Guardian Angels** I thank you, for all you've done and all that you're gonna do, I said who do you believe in? I put my faith in God, blessed that I'm still breathing **- Dawud The Uncanny BlaKseed**

Slavery by Another Name

The American Constitution was taken from the Democratic Constitution written up by the **Iroquois** (Native Americans) but the laws that are carried out by this country do not reflect the ethical and moral practices of the **Iroquois**. Slavery did not start in America but America has left a legacy rooted in the slavery of African and indigenous people that has overshadowed every other recorded account of slavery due to the horrific terrorization that was cast down on the enslaved sons and daughters of African and the enslaved sons and daughters of Turtle Island (America). In **1669** Virginia wrote into law: "slave masters may kill *<u>people</u>* who resist authority". In fact, slavery never ended in America. They kept slavery by writing laws and like I said above, **<u>"these laws are the walls you can't break through"</u>**, and in other songs, **<u>"laws are the walls that keep us down"</u>** (pages 247, 274, 399, 466). The 13th amendment was a **law** that stated, slavery was illegal in America unless you were convicted of a crime. This is when the industrial prison complex was formulated. Vagrancy Laws were passed that targeted Black African people. Vagrancy was the **crime** of wondering from place to place without being able to prove you had a home or a job. This is what people who had just been "freed" of slavery were found guilty of and immediately the prisons were filled with Black people, the same people who had just been "freed" from centuries of slavery. The 13th amendment is still a part of the Constitution today and slavery is still alive in America. In South Carolina, the Angola prison gets its name from the slave plantation that used to occupy the land the prison was built on. The slaves on this plantation were mostly taken from the country of Angola in Afrika. The prison has kept the name of the old slave plantation and the population of prisoners in this prison is currently 70 percent African Black indigenous people. The inmates at this prison are made to pick cotton, the same cotton that the slaves picked on that land during slavery. The inmates (enslaved Afrikans) are paid around 4 cents and hour so this is technically slave labor. America is **the great incarcerator** and the **<u>laws are the walls that keep us down</u>!**

May 13th 2015 Living Water

She went from **obesity** to **depression**, from depression to **cancer**, she kept stressing the weapons, instead of **lessons** and **answers**, she got **love** from **thugs** so she turned to a **dancer**, it's bugged cause she got **pregnant** by her **pastor**, I asked her who she believe in, she broke out in laughter, right after, she looked me in the eyes and cried, she said - everything that he said was lies, now she's wise to game and pain her only prize, she's alive but inside a d**ark** cloud remains, I explained it's a must that you let it rain, Living water, for you, your daughter and all your disorders, I know it sort of seems off topics, I ain't a **prophet** but you gotta let go and let **God** flow to profit, the body you live in is hydraulic, and the way that you're living is high toxic, we die through a process of elimination, this processed food's designed to kill a whole nation, be wholestic and holy and stop waiting, and start praying, who do you believe in? I'm just sayin, I put my faith in **God** blessed that I'm still breathing **- Dawud The Uncanny BlaKseed**

Significance

This rhyme was different in that I had no intention on writing it! I was sitting on a bench in Jackie Robinson Park reading the book **Obesity Depression and Cancer** by **Dr Batmangehigi**, while listening to the **Tupac** beat, **Who do you believe in**? Then all of a sudden these words just came out like **water**. I opened my phone and this verse was written **very** quickly. When I was done I **felt** like **Tupac** had written it. The book was about the healing qualities of water and the words seemed to flow out of me very quickly like water. I have a theory about who Tupac was in a past life.

May 15th 2015 - Meta Spiritual Encounters
(3rd Police stop and check and SGT James Brown Part A)

I was riding my bike through Central Park on my way to the Apple store on 59th street when I was stopped by two police officers. They said I ran a red light. I was wearing my Army hat that day. The cop who did the talking was white and the other was Asian. They wanted to give me a ticket. I blew up on them immediately. I felt like the traffic light was being used as a reason to stop me because other people ran the same light. I stated my military name, rank and unit, "*Sgt Eddings, United States Army Special Ops 160th Soar*". I didn't give a fuck about their ticket or their guns. These were the first cops I had come in contact with in a long time. I had been spending a lot of time alone as usual and I was hot with anger about the **Baltimore riots**, the murders of **Freddie Gray**, **Michael Brown**, **Eric Garner**, **Tamir Rice**, **Walter Scott,** the Military veteran who was shot in the back at 50 years of age over a broken brake light on April 4th the same day **Martin Luther King** was assassinated (pages 69, 592), and the list goes on! I took all my anger out on these two cops. The White cop was trying to get my ID. I can't remember if I showed him my ID or not but I remember the **old White woman** who stopped. She was walking by with a cane when she looked at me and told me to calm down and to not let them anger me. The cops looked at her then got in their car and drove away. I got on my bike and road away thinking about **Seneca Village** (page 413). Seneca was an old Black Village established in 1825 however laws were put into effect that classified the land as Eminent domain. By 1857 the Black people who settled there were displaced and Central Park was built (page 413).

May 15th 2015 (NYPD TRAFFIC INCIDENT and SGT James Brown Part B)

When I got home I saw for the first time a video about the Murder of **Sgt James Brown**, a 26 year old soldier stationed at Fort Bliss in El Paso Texas. He was a father and a loving husband. He believed in serving his country and he served two combat tours. He died on July 14th 2012 at the El Paso County Jail. On July 13th 2012 he voluntarily turned himself in to serve what was supposed to be a 2 day sentence for driving under the influence. While in custody he was given an injection. The video shows him telling the officers that he was having trouble breathing. Watching this video arose more anger within me after having my experience with the cops earlier that day. I had to release this anger! I turned on the **Tupac** beat for the song **What's Next.** Then I felt the presence of **James Brown** the Musician! I was led to the titles of his music. I took the titles and I wrote the song **The Ballot of Sgt James Brown** in a spell of furious anger. I took their movies of war and I turned their propaganda of weaponry back on them ending the song with the words "**The Spooks At The Door,** no more **Saving Private Ryan!** Save yo black ass and yo mother from crying! Who's next my nigga? what's next my nigga?".

Condolences

My condolences go out to the family of **James Brown, SGT James Brown** and all those who have been robbed of their life by this system of racism and white supremacy. Please know that death is not the end. The soul survives death, indeed and in spirit. This is a book of the dead written by a boy who was murdered without justice, who defeated death and came forth by day. May the souls of **James Brown** and **SGT James Brown** walk peacefully through the field of Reeds in Amenta. Amen Ra.

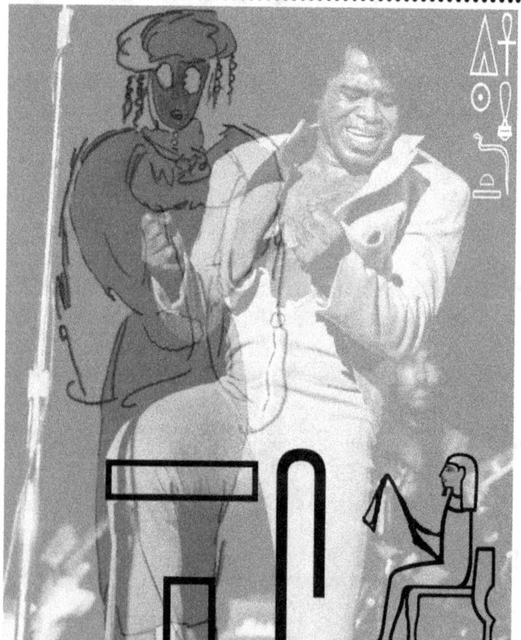

May 15th 2015 The Ballot of Sgt James Brown (Part C)

The Ballot of **James Brown, I Got That Feeling,** he would say **it's too funky in here,** still **Living In America** in fear, screaming **Please Please Please,** get off your knees knees knees, don't be **a dream differed**, sagging like a heavy load, **Get up and Drive Your Funky Soul, Soul Power, Unchained, Say It Loud - I'm Black And I'm Proud!** even through the pain on the **Night Train** with **Harriet,** we ain't having it! they got us hung up on a noose, **Give It Up** or **Turn it A Loose, It's A Mans Mans World,** it's a mad world! expect **The Payback! Papa Don't Take No Mess!** no he don't play that! **Just Try Me, I Got You! Down And Out In New York City,** if I watch the news it be such a pity, I'm a **veteran** but still they be fuck'n with me! I'm tired of telling them! **What's next**?! they killing the melanin, sell it as medicine, ***RIDDLE*** me this, is **James Brown** the **King**, or a soldier from **Fort Bliss**? I sat and watched him die slow on video, he couldn't breathe it's pitiful! first **Eric Garner** then you and me! you could do two or three tours for this country, I came back from Iraq and they fronted on me! spoke to my homie and got the same story! brothers searching for glory like **Forrest Gump,** should have learned from **Tuskegee!** watching too much tv! and can't see the **Enemy At The Gate**! **Black Hawk Down** as it falls to it's fate, **Casualties Of War, We Were Soldiers** before, **The Spooks At The Door,** no more **Saving Private Ryan!** save yo black ass and yo mother from crying! who's next my nigga? what's next my nigga? who's next my nigga? what's next my nigga? tell me what the fuck am I suppose to do? who's next my nigga? what's next my nigga? tell me what the fuck am I suppose to do? who's next my nigga? what's next my nigga? tell me what the fuck am I suppose to do? Who's next my nigga what's next my nigga….. - **Dawud The Uncanny BlaKseed**

Significance

I named this song after the first song off of **Tupac's** seventh posthumous album, **Until the End of Time**. It was released in 2001, the Year of the Snake. The first song on the album is, **Ballad of a Dead Soulja**. On the third verse of this song Tupac mentions reincarnation again when he says, "One day I'll be the Don, until then, remain strong, **my only fear of death is reincarnation**, bustin' at my adversaries like a mental patient". On December 1st 1955 **Rosa Parks** would refuse to give up her seat to a white man on a bus because she was angry about the murder of **Emmett Till** and the next year 1956 her brave act sparked the Civil Rights Movement with the help of **Martin Luther King** and many others. That same year **James Brown** would make his musical debut recording his first single ***Please Please Please*** on **Rosa Parks** birthday, **February 4th**. When I edited the the video for this song I placed a picture of King Tut's **gold** mask when I said the words - "is James Brown the **King**, or a soldier from Fort Bliss?" On April 4th 2020 (page 594) my past life as Tutankhaten (King Tut) would be revealed to me in a deep meditation where the spirits of Rosa Parks and Martin Luther King were present.. April 4th is the same day that Martin Luther King was assassinated (pgs 69, 592) and Martin Luther King help lead the **Civil Rights Movement** after Rosa Parks made her brave stance in the face of grave danger. I used the term, "***RIDDLE*** me this", in this song and knowing what I know now, in 2022, perhaps that was my great grand mothers May Fannie **Riddle** (p 16) and Leacola **Riddle** (p 21) influencing my pen again. I mentioned **Harriet Tubman** again, in this rhyme and years later I would come to understand why I kept saying Harriet's name! I need all those reading this book, to "**Get up and Drive Your Funky Soul, Soul Power, Unchained, Say It Loud - I'm Black And I'm Proud!**"

Rau nu Prt m heru

May 17th 2015 - Besouro (Scarab)

This movie captivated my imagination. The main character is named **Besouro** which translates to **beetle** in english. The movie was about **capoeira** being used as a means of liberation. Besouro could fly around like the characters in the movie Crouching Tiger hidden Dragon. Besouro had the ability to move his soul into the body of other people who were being oppressed by white supremacy allowing him to fight off their enemies using their bodies. **Capoeira** is very similar to **Break dancing** which is an element of Hip Hop. Just like Besouro moved through people to fight for them many souls moved through me to write for me. The only ghost writers I have ever had are the ancestors, and the souls of those who have been taken too soon like the soul of **LaVena Johnson** who came to me on June 10th (page 334) which is my Great Grandmother Leacola **Riddle's** birthday and **Kalief Browder** who came to me the very next night (page 334).

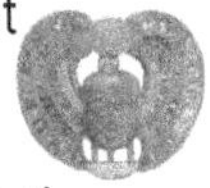

Significance

The movie had aspects of **levitation** in it and studies have shown that the wings of Scarab Dung Beetles have strange levitation qualities. The Nswt Bity (Pharaoh) Tutankhaten's (King Tut's) throne name was Neb Kheperu Ra. Kheper is the Kemetic (Egyptian) word for Scarab. I was being drawn to the scarab because I was Neb Kheperu Ra in my most ancient known past life. On April 4th 2020 (page 594) my past life as Tutankhaten (King Tut) would be revealed to me in the most divine of ways.

Iu f Per f m heru

May 27th 2015
Meta-Mental Encounter Sparked by a Thought
The Genie in the bottle

I was inspired to paint by someone or something that I can not recall. Soon after I went online and started searching for an easel to buy. The next day I would find an easel in my lobby next to the garbage (seen in picture). Years later I would come to find out that the guy on the first floor threw it away. Was this just a **coincidence** or did my desire for an easel cause him to get rid of his? Sort of like how I used my thoughts and desires causing that guy to get up and move when I met **Nova** in 2010 (page 184)! Can we really influence quantum level events in time and space affecting our reality with our minds? That's definitely something to "think" about. Either way, unfortunately I have never used the easel. Our mind is the **lamp** and our super conscious is the **Genie** in the bottle. Use your thoughts wisely.

"Magic is magic to the lay man afraid to paint the future, **staring at a canvas**, you gotta leave the branches and get to the root for the truth if you wanna make advances, trances, dances, **telepathine***, the answers from the unseen uploaded while in a dream, you can rage against the machine or sage and engage the serene" - (**Blood Moon** written on **July 27th 2018, page 350**)

Utterances for Coming Forth by day into Light

Mid 2015 (Katherine's Psychic Reading)

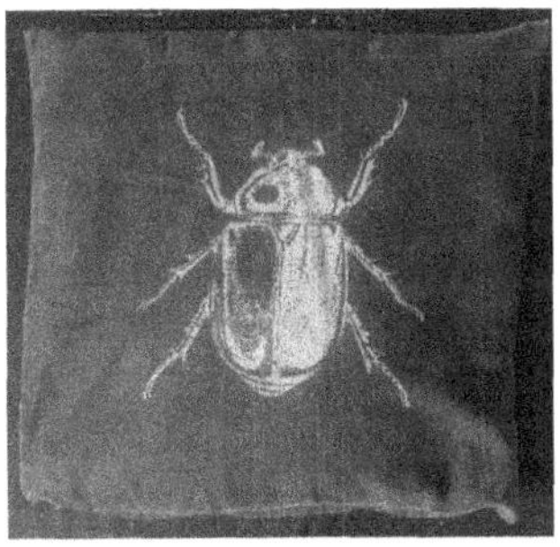

I met Katherine sometime in 2014. She was referred to me from another client. Her and I met a few months after she received a psychic reading for her birthday. The psychic told her that she would met a person that she would have long spiritual conversations with. After our first training session she told me about the reading and she also told me that she felt like I was the person the psychic had predicted she would meet. After training her for some time she would tell me that I reminded her of her father. She said her father was into spirituality and had told her that he once **levitated**. I found this interesting cause I have always been interested in levitation. In 2015 Katherine would give me a pillow with a scarab on it because she saw that I was attracted to them.

Significance

Katherine would gift me this scarab pillow around the same time that I watched the movie **Besouro** and the movie had aspects of **levitation** in it. Studies have shown that the wings of Scarab Dung Beetles have strange levitation qualities. The Nswt Bity (Pharaoh) Tutankhaten's (King Tut's) throne name was Neb Kheperu Ra. Kheper is the Kemetic (Egyptian) word for Scarab. I was being drawn to the scarab because I was Neb Kheperu Ra in my most ancient known past life. On April 4th 2020 (page 594) my past life as Tutankhaten (King Tut) would be revealed to me in the most divine of ways.

It is he, who comes forth by day into Light

May 30th 2015 Strange 4th Kind

One thing I know is I know nothing at all, how do you learn if you don't fall? most of what I know I learned from falling, some people call it failing, you lose when you stop inhaling, exhale heavy metal, van haling, I been gone with the wind but no smooth sailing, when I won it's cause I **visualized** prevailing, never sold dope, never liked drug dealing, be an outlaw and do a little hope dealing, provoke healing, help people cope with their feelings, the pain been building up to the temple touching the ceiling, just a tear in the cup of the mental I'm revealing, kind of chillin, ***smooth criminal,*** **Malcolm, Martin, Huey** killing crew, tell me what the fuck am I supposed to do? who's next? what's next?! I'm a keep it spiritual, a little **Voodoo** from Dawud the **Zulu** in **Eve's Bayou**, in 1832 would they ever had heard of you? ***in my past life I died***, *in 1831 it flashed across my eyes, a close encounter that I survived, I been having feelings of the fourth kind,* you might say that I been out my mind, be out my mind, and I been having **dreams** of the fourth kind, when eyes awake with no mistake fate plays it in rewind, have you ever wondered what's under this grand design? the soul brother from another planet put me on a planet with **Janet** and **Michael** and **Hannibal,** try living in a world where your brother don't like you, they be underhanded doing mad things to spite you, to live a peaceful life we all got the right to **- Dawud The Amazing BlaKseed**

June 6th 2015 - Kalief Browder and May 25th Strikes Back

On May 15th 2010, New York City police apprehended Kalief and a friend in the Bronx. Kalief said he was going home from a party. Kalief had been harassed by police prior to being stopped on a number of occasions as the police carried out what they called routine stop-and-frisks checks. However on this night the Police officers were responding to a 9-1-1 call placed by Roberto Bautista about the theft of a backpack containing a camera, $700, a credit card, and an iPod Touch. Bautista said, "Two male black guys... they took my brother's book bag." Kalief told the attending police officers, "I didn't rob anyone, you can check my pockets." The police searched Kalief but they did not find the backpack. Bautista, who was sitting in the back seat of a police car, identified Kalief and his friend as the thieves. He said the theft had occurred two weeks earlier. Bautista's testimony of the date of the theft varied between interviews, as well as other aspects of his story. Initially, Bautista implied that the robbery occurred the night of the 9-1-1 call, but upon questioning by officers at the scene, he stated that the robbery had occurred two weeks prior. At the scene, Bautista also implied after questioning that someone had merely "tried" to rob him and may not have succeeded. Furthermore, on the initial police report filed after the arrest, Bautista indicated the robbery had occurred "on or about May 2", but Bautista later told a detective that it happened on May 8. Kalief asked the officers why he was being charged and said, "I didn't do anything." they told him he would be taken to the precinct and would likely be allowed to go home. Kalief and his friend were taken to the 48th Precinct police station, where they were fingerprinted and kept in a holding cell for a few hours. They were then taken to the Bronx County Criminal Court, where they were processed at the court's central booking. Seventeen hours after the arrest, Kalief was interrogated by a police officer and a prosecutor. The following day, Browder was charged with robbery, grand larceny, and assault. Because he was on probation, Browder was not released. At his arraignment, he was charged with second-degree robbery and bail was set at $3,000; with a bail bondsman, the amount needed was $900. Browder's family could not raise this amount and borrowed money from a neighbor. When his family met with a bail bondsman to post his bail, they were told that, since he was on probation from his prior felony conviction, his probation officer had placed a probation violation hold on him so posting bail would not get him released from jail anyway. He was taken to jail at Rikers Island to await trial and resolution of his pending probation violation.

Kalief was jailed at the Robert N. Davoren Center (RNDC) on Rikers Island which was known for having a deep-seated culture of violence, in which inmates suffered broken jaws, broken orbital bones, broken noses, long bone fractures, and lacerations requiring stitches. Brendan O'Meara was appointed as Kalief's public defender. Kalief always maintained his innocence. Although the assistant district attorney, Peter Kennedy, called Kalief's case a "relatively straightforward case", his trial was delayed by a backlog of work at the Bronx County District Attorney's office and subsequently Kalief was a victim of violence from both inmates and correction officers and spent 14 months in solitary confinement. Kalief says he was starved and his court dates were continually postponed. Kalief's communication with O'Meara was mostly through his mother. O'Meara said Kalief was "quiet, respectful, he wasn't rude", but he appeared "tougher and bigger" over time. Kalief told O'Meara that he wanted to go to trial; he was offered a plea bargain of 3.5 years in prison if he pleaded guilty. Kalief declined the offer. In June 2012, this period was reduced to 2.5 years, but Kalief again declined the plea bargain. After 961 days in Rikers, Kalief had appeared before eight judge; he later said, "these guys are just playing with my case". On March 13th 2013, Kalief appeared before Bronx judge Patricia DiMango. She offered Kalief a plea bargain of immediate release for his admission of guilt to two misdemeanors with consideration of time already served. Kalief refused the offer and was returned to Rikers. On May 29, 2013, DiMango freed Kalief in anticipation of the dismissal of the charges against him. After his release, Kalief and his brother Akeem sought legal representation. A family member found the Brooklyn prosecutor Paul V. Prestia. In 2011, Prestia had represented a Haitian man who had been arrested in the Bronx and was wrongfully jailed for eight days. In November 2013, Kalief filed a lawsuit against the New York City Police Department, the Bronx District Attorney, and the Department of Corrections. Prestia claimed that there had been a malicious prosecution, and the court had been misled about the prosecution's readiness for trial. Prestia also put to the court that the prosecution knew they would have no witness when Bautista returned to Mexico. The City of New York denied these allegations.

June 6th 2015 (Kalief Browder Suicide?)

While incarcerated in 2010, reports state that Kalief made his first **suicide** attempt and that he tried a second time on **February 8,** 2012, trying to hang himself using strips of sheet tied to a ceiling light in the cell. Kalief later said the COs **provoked** him to **commit suicide**. On another occasion, after an appearance before a judge, Kalief made a sharp implement from the bucket in his cell and started to slit his wrists. An officer intervened. After his release, Kalief continued to have symptoms of depression. He said: "People tell me because I have this case against the city I'm all right. But I'm not all right. I'm messed up. I know that I might see some money from this case, but that's not going to help me mentally. I'm mentally scarred right now. That's how I feel. There are certain things that changed about me and they might not change back." He further added: "Before I went to jail, I didn't know about a lot of stuff, and, now that I'm aware, I'm paranoid. I feel like I was robbed of my happiness." In November 2013, Kalief made another suicide attempt and was admitted to the psychiatric ward of St. Barnabas Hospital, the first of three admissions to the ward. On June 6, 2015, at 12:15 p.m., Kalief hanged himself from an air conditioning unit outside his bedroom window at his mother's home. His mother discovered his body. See pages 321 and 562 for Feb 8 connection.

Condolences

My condolences go out to the family of **Kalief Browder** and all those who have been robbed of their life by this system of white supremacy. Please know that death is not the end. The soul survives death, indeed and in spirit. This is a book of the dead written by a boy who was murdered without justice, who defeated death and came forth by day. May the soul of **Kalief Browder** walk peacefully through the field of Reeds in Amenta. Amen Ra

Rau

nu

Prt

m

heru

June 10th 2015 LaVena Johnson

I can't go to sleep in the late night, I be having visions of death and seeing this great light, and _when I breathe my last breath and escape the flesh_, **I'll be back** in the hurricane with **Lesane,** and every slain African that's feeling the same, bringing the rain, the thunder, the pain, **LaVena Johnson** remember the name!... they **raped** her then they claim it was suicide! a soldier, killed by her own side! no where to run, no where to hide! unify we gotta try, gotta survive, gotta _ride on our enemies_ and stay alive, the inner chi be the energy for you and I, you ain't never lied when you said, **Green Black** and **Red, U.N.I.A** your **dream** is never dead! every day is a day we can move ahead, instead of looking back in fact recite this pledge, I pledge allegiance for many reasons, can you see the treason for 2000 seasons?! who do you believe in?! ***invoking** the legions*, united we stand, divide is treason, on my block **- Dawud The Amazing BlaKseed**

Iu

f

Per

f

m

heru

Significance / Creation story / Meta Spiritual Encounter

I don't drink coffee however on June 9th 2015 "_something_" _came over me_. It was late in the evening and I went down stairs to the bodega and was over come with the desire to drink coffee. I purchased two ice coffees and drank them. For some reason I thought I was gonna go to sleep however that was not happening. I don't drink coffee so the caffeine had me up. I was wired. I could not believe how "up" I was. Not being able to sleep I found myself scrolling through social media and soon after I ran across the information about private **LaVena Lynn Johnson**. She was murdered by fellow soldiers while deployed in Iraq on July 19th 2005, just **8** days before her 20th birthday, she was raped, burned and murdered. They claimed she killed herself but I don't believe that. I know that statistically one out of every three women in the Army is **raped** or **sexually harassed** and these numbers can go up while deployed in combat. Her story troubled me deeply. I had been a sergeant in the army and I had been out of the army for 10 years now. I still knew my NCO Creed by heart, and this line rang out, "all soldiers are entitled to outstanding leadership; I will provide that leadership"... No one protected her! She was gone. I was angry! I turned on the **Tupac** instrumental '_Words to my first Born_' and I wrote the song for her. Years later I would realize that she was born on July 27th the same day as my nephew and two days after **Emmett Tills** birthday. I only have two nephews. One is born 2 days before Emmett was murdered (Aug 26th) and one is born 2 days after Emmett was born (July 27th). This was written on my great grand mother, Leacola **Riddle's** birthday which is the day **Marcus Garvey** died. I mentioned Marcus Garvey and Tupac (Lesane) in this song and I have a theory about who Tupac was in a **past life**. I also added vocals from one of Marcus's speeches to the song and at the very end of the song Marcus says, "if I am apparently crushed by the system of influence and misdirected power **my Ka shall rise again** to plague the conscious of the corrupt." The very next day after writing for **LaVena** I would get the news of **Kalief Browder's** passing and when I did I felt his presence in my studio causing me to write a song for him.

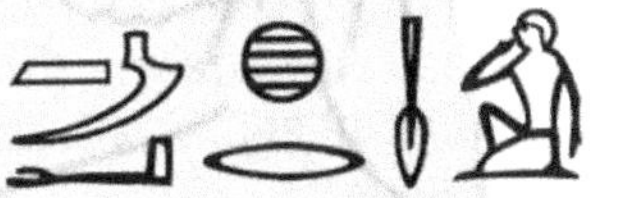

June 11th 2015
Kalief Browder (May 25th Strikes Back)

Utterances

for

Coming

Forth

by day

into

Light

How do we make peace with the ones gone? we try to make it better for the unborn, if I had to write a letter I'd put it in song, dear Lord will you ever tell me why they do harm?! He was one 16 he did nothing wrong, he did **33** months in a cell torn, he got released but time made his mind ab-norm, rest in peace to **Kalief** that's my word bond! who do we call is it, **Minister Farrakhan** or **Dr Umar**?! should we remain calm or act a fool y'all?! our kids cant even find peace at the pool y'all! _Don't let them fool y'all or even School y'all_, _If I Ruled The World_, everyone would be taught the **1 6 1 8** curl, and understand how and when men fell, not blaming it on the girl, the truth it will propel man from his hell, it's the hue in man from the gland that prevails, they be shoot'n man organs be for sale, stuck in a race doing laps as time elapse perhaps love will fill the cracks for blacks on my block **- Dawud The Amazing BlaKseed**

It is

he,

who

comes

forth

by day

into

Light

Significance / Creation story / Meta Spiritual Encounter

He died on June 6th at only **22**yrs of age. I had been following his story so hearing of his death touched me, and saddened me deeply. After hearing about his death I was livid! I turned the same **Tupac** beat back on and when I did I felt a presence in my studio causing me to write a song for him. I recorded the song through tears and after I was done creating the song I googled him and read more about his story, then I saw that he was born on **May 25th 1993!** I was astonished! **May 25th** had struck again (p 222)!! The same day as my car accident in 2002 (page 104) and the same day as my motorcycle accident in 2008 (page 157). This number just kept appearing. I knew it was a sign but what was the universe trying to tell me?!? I felt like LaVena was with me when I wrote for her but did she also have something to do with the thought to drink the coffee the night prior?! So that I would be up that night then be inspired to write for her? Did their spirits come to me so that I could write for them?! Were they there the whole time or was this all just some coincidence?!! Little did I know that I would find more meaning to the date **May 25th** after I had my past life revelation of Emmett Till on July 3rd 2018 (page 512).

Condolences

My condolences go out to all the families of those who have been robbed of their life by this system of racism and white supremacy. Please know that death is not the end. The soul survives death, indeed and in spirit. This is a book of the dead written by a boy who was murdered without justice, who defeated death and came forth by day. May the souls of **LaVena Lynn Johnson** and **Kalief Browder** walk peacefully through the field of Reeds in Amenta. Amen Ra.

June 17th 2015
dylan storm roof Charleston Church Massacre

On June 17th 2015 **dylan roof** entered Emanuel African Methodist Episcopal Church through a side door at 8:16 pm. He pretended to be a peaceful participant of the Bible study. Then at around 9pm he opened fire with a Glock 41. 45 caliber handgun killing 9 people in total. The victims, six women and three men, were all African-American members of the AME Church. Eight died at the scene; the ninth, Daniel Simmons, died at MUSC Medical Center. They were all killed by multiple gunshots fired at close range. Five persons survived the shooting unharmed. Among those people who were killed was the senior pastor and state senator Clementa C. Pinckney.

"Manhunt and Capture"

The attack was treated as a hate crime by police. Officials from the Federal Bureau of Investigation and the Bureau of Alcohol, Tobacco, Firearms and Explosives were called in to assist in the investigation and manhunt however **a random woman did all the "manhunting"**. Police received a tip-off from a woman who recognized Roof and his car, a black Hyundai Elantra with South Carolina license plates and a three-flag "Confederate States of America" bumper decoration. She later recalled, "I got closer and saw that haircut. I was nervous. I had the worst feeling. Is that him or not him?" She called her employer, who contacted local police, and then tailed the suspect's car for 35 miles (56 km) until she was certain authorities were moving in for an arrest. I wonder though what might have happened if she had not called and I wonder if the anonymous woman is safe now - I hope so! The person who recorded the killing of Eric Garner by NYPD was repeatedly harassed and arrested by the NYPD. At 10:44 a.m., on the morning after the attack, Roof was "captured" in a traffic stop in Shelby, North Carolina, approximately 245 miles (394 km) from the shooting scene with no shots fired.. A .45-caliber pistol was found in the car during the arrest but he was not shot like 12 year old **Tamir Rice** or **Alton Sterling** or **Philando Castile**! Instead Dylan was "captured" WITH NO SHOTS FIRED and no cop **feared for their life** even though they were dealing with a man who was armed and had **MURDERED 9 people!!!** And because dylan roof was **hungry** the officers were nice enough to spend **tax payers money** to buy him food from **burger king!**

Significance

On July 1st 2015 I would write a song in response to this massacre and it wasn't till I started writing this book in 2020 that I realize that Dylan killed these innocent people on my **Grandfathers** birthday June 17th, the day after **Tupac's** birthday and I wrote a song to **Tupac's** beat, **You Ain't Never Had a Friend Like Me**! I title the song **Hatshepsut** who is the female NSWT BITY (**Pharaoh**) from the 18th dynasty. The same family as **Tutankhaten** (**King Tut**)! My past life of King Tut was revealed to me on April 4th 2020 (page 594) the same day that Martin Luther King was assassinated (pages 69, 592).

This church is one of the oldest black churches in the United States, and it has long been a center for organizing events which are related to civil rights. This was the church of the honorable **Denmark Vesey**, a Black American leader in Charleston, South Carolina. He was s a carpenter like the bible says **Jesus** was. In June 1822 **Denmark Vesey** was accused and convicted of being the leader of "the rising," a potentially major slave revolt which was scheduled to take place in the city on July 14. He was executed on July 2nd 1822. At Roof's hearing, prosecutors introduced into evidence a two-page excerpt from a journal written by Roof from jail six weeks after his arrest, in which Roof composed a white supremacist manifesto, writing: "I would like to make it crystal clear, I do not regret what I did. I am not sorry. I have not shed a tear for the innocent people I killed. Roof was sentenced to death on January 10, 2017, and to life in prison without parole on April 10, 2017. Today is November 9th 2021 and Roof is still alive.

Condolences

My condolences go out to all the families of those who have been robbed of their lives by this system of racism and white supremacy. Please know that death is not the end. The soul survives death, indeed and in spirit. This is a book of the dead written by a boy who was murdered without justice, who defeated death and came forth by day. May the souls of **Clementa C. Pinckney**, **Cynthia Graham Hurd**, **Susie Jackson**, **Ethel Lee Lance**, **Depayne Middleton**, **Tywanza Sanders**, **Daniel L. Simmons**, **Sharonda Coleman-Singleton**, and **Myra Thompson** walk peacefully through the field of Reeds in Amenta. Amen Ra.

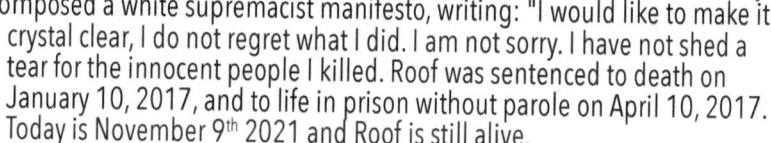

Rau nu Prt m heru

Iu f Per f m heru

Utterances for Coming Forth by day into Light

It is he, who comes forth by day into Light

May 29th 2015 18th Dynasty

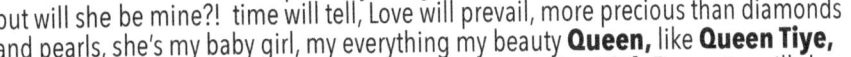

Sometimes not being able to explain everything is frightening, sometimes love strikes like lightening, 7 days, 7 colors, 7 layers we discover, what are the chances we meet each other? they say everything happens for a reason, or do we take chances? sweet glances, romances, hugging you is therapy, the remedy when I see you laughing, is it a crime she's on my mind all the time? perfectly designed down to her sign, she's more than fine, but will she be mine?! time will tell, Love will prevail, more precious than diamonds and pearls, she's my baby girl, my everything my beauty **Queen,** like **Queen Tiye,** the most beautifulest thing **Amen Hotep** could see in the **18th Dynasty,** will she remember me or will she walk past me?! will she walk past me? Actions speak louder than chit chattering, are you listening the the rhythm of my heart unraveling, the unbeaten path traveling, imagining happiness happening, good times, timeless bliss a kiss, the rhyme the reason I miss you, is it a crime I will never forget you, or forsake you, for you I am thankful **- Dawud The Amazing BlaKseed**

Significance / Creation Story

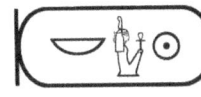

I met **Leara** in Massage school. We had a **Tai Chi** class together and a few others. She was a singer and I used to let her hear my music. She liked one of my verses and wanted me to say it over a song she had been working on. When she sent me the song I wrote the verse above instead. In the verse I would for some reason say the names **Queen Tiye** and **Amen Hotep 3rd** (p 638) from the 18th Dynasty of kemet who just so "happen" to be the grand parents of **King Tut** . On April 4th 2020 my past life as **Tutankhaten** (**King Tut**) would be revealed to me (p 594). This is the same day that Martin Luther King was assassinated in 1968 (p 69, 592). The song was originally titled **14th Dynasty** and I originally said 14th dynasty at the end because Leara is born on November 14th but I later changed it to the 18th Dynasty to match **Queen Tiye** and **Amen Hotep 3rd**. As I have explain throughout this book (p 6) when we open our mouths our egos can speak or our souls can speak. Because my music came from my heart ancient fragments of my soul were able to shine through my music adding to this divine prophecy of reincarnation. I have not spoken to Leara in years but she currently has a beautiful family with a thriving family business. A year later I would add this verse to the end of another song on page 389.

July 1st 2015 Hatshepsut

Will there ever be peace?! **Hatshepsut** the chief in the east brought peace to the Negus nation, The **Haitian** chasing the enemy back in the sea, Passionately like Den**mar**k **Vesey!** They might stress me, because my S.P.**A.R.K,** Yet they spray the A K 47, NEVER forget nine eleven!?, 9 lives even the reverend! Real eyes need to realize or be a dead one!! We never got peace till we did something! there will never get better till we do something! unity between you and me stop front'n!! you might hear my words, but you ain't heard nothing! cause you ain't **"never had a friend like me"**! way pass **25** still I wanna be free, we just trying to survive in this monopoly, label me a **thug** treat me like your property, even the judge show a brother no love it's like the laws written on top of me, hypocrisy in your democracy it ain't hard to see!! **- Dawud The Amazing BlaKseed**

Significance

On July 1st 2015 I would write this song in response to the Charleston Church Massacre. On July 1st 2018 I graduate as a kemetic Yoga instructor and two days later my past life as Emmett Till is revealed to me on July 3rd 2018 (page 480). It wasn't till I started writing this book in 2020 that I realize that Dylan killed these innocent people on my **Grandfathers** birthday June 17th, the day after **Tupac's** birthday and I wrote this song to **Tupac's** beat, **You Ain't Never Had a Friend Like Me**! I titled the song **Hatshepsut** who was a powerful female NSWT BITY (**Pharaoh**) from the 18th dynasty, the same family as **Tutankhaten** (**King Tut**)! My past life of King Tut was revealed to me on April 4th 2020 (page 594) the same day that **Martin Luther King** was assassinated (page 69). In April of 2022 I traveled to Kemet and had the chance to visit the tomb of Hatshepsut and many others.

Denmark Vesey

The honorable **Denmark Vesey**, was a Black American leader in Charleston, South Carolina. He was a carpenter like the bible says **Jesus** was. In June of 1822 **Denmark Vessy** was accused and convicted of being the leader of "the rising," a potentially major slave revolt which was scheduled to take place in Charleston, South Carolina on July 14th. He was executed on July 2nd 1822, the same day as **Emmett Till's** father (Louis Till July 2nd 1922), 100 years before he was born in 1822.

Hatshepsut

July 5th 2015 ABRAKADABRA

Abrakadabra! she spoke words to my cadaver, my eyes opened my flesh closed, then I rose exposed, before I left I dressed in fresh clothes, **Not even death could stop my spirit,** my next stop wall street and the bodies exhibit, I be the Lord of **Maat! Maat** rules everything around me, my **dreams** are balanced they finally here y'all, have no fear I'm here to heal not kill y'all, they call me **MumRa, Thoth** deep in thought, or **Leflaw lefla Escorshca,** the **Falcon** the hawk, to the north star, **cobra** commander, scar on my face like a **black panther,** you a disgrace waiting for a dead white savior, where there's a red **light saber,** there will always be a green and a blue to save you, so stay true, ahh, I thought you knew, I thought you knew! **we coming back!** don't have a heart attack! this is where it started at, 7 wonders of the world but where the other 6 be at? it be kind of fishy black, your history just ain't in tact, see, you created crack then created a war on drugs, what kind of sense is that?! **- Dawud The Uncanny BlaKseed**

42 Laws of Maat, Page 367

July 2015

He-Man

I gotta make this promise that **I'll be back**, between the star and the atom is where I'll be vibe'n at, when I was young I had **He-Man** and **Battle Cat,** see he was **White** but when he **transformed** he was **Black**, tell me **can you psychoanalyze that?!** I went to school broke rules never learned jack! we ate school lunch and apple jacks, was it the crack or the food black?! this is chemical warfare, I swear to God and I see the God in myself evolve, the blakseed succeed **against all odds**, and you are the blakseeds trapped in my bars, you gotta plant seeds like we plotted stars, how are trees effected by cars? imagine paying to breathe like water at a bar, did I go too far? did I loose y'all? sometimes the truth will bruise ya, and scar like a saber, hell razor of a savior, the favor of a deity, like a trinity walk in divine divinity from 93 till infinity, a good verse vs bad energy till they finish me, **bomb on the enemy**! **- Dawud The Uncanny BlaKseed**

July 13th 2015 - Sandra Bland

Sandra Bland was pulled over for a minor traffic violation on July 10th by State Trooper Brian Encinia. The exchange escalated, resulting in Bland's arrest and a charge of assaulting a police officer. Three days later Sandra Bland was found hanged in a jail cell in Waller County, Texas. Her death was ruled a suicide but in December of 2015 Encinia was indicted for perjury for making false statements about the circumstances surrounding Bland's arrest. Bland's death sparked many protest as many people, especially people of color saw her murder as another act of racial violence against Black people. In September 2016, Bland's mother settled a wrongful death lawsuit against the county jail and police department for $1.9 million and some procedural changes. In June 2017, the perjury charge against Encinia was dropped in return for his agreement to permanently end his law enforcement career. We only know about this case because of the dash-cam footage. We only know about the dash-cam footage because the arrest was partially recorded by a bystander's cell phone, and Bland's own cell phone. How many other unnecessary murders are acted out that never make the news? After Emmett Till's body was found in the M**ississ**ippi river 25 other black bodies were found and some of the bodies were tarred and feathered!!

Significance

Sandra Bland was born on **February 7**h the same day as Louis Till (**Emmett Louis Till's** Father, page 475). **Louis Till** was born in 19**22** the same year that **King Tut's** tomb was discovered. Sandra Bland's case angered many of us. People marched and made signs with "say her name" written on them. I would write her into my music many times. Driving while Black is what she was guilty of. When researching her story I was surprised to find a picture of her with me face on her shirt, but there it is.

Condolences

My condolences go out to the family of **Sandra Bland** and all the families of those who have been robbed of their lives by this system of racism and white supremacy. Please know that death is not the end. The soul survives death, indeed and in spirit. This is a book of the dead written by a boy who was murdered without justice, who defeated death and came forth by day. May the soul of **Sandra Bland** walk peacefully through the field of Reeds in Amenta. Amen Ra.

Rau nu Prt m heru

August 14th 2015 (Michelle Cusseaux 55yrs Old Phoenix Arizona)

Offices arrive to Michelle's home to serve her a court order. They removed her security door. Sergeant Percy Dupra fired a single shot claiming she lunged with a hammer. Michelle died shortly after. Dupra was demoted. Michelle was born on Marcus Garvey's Birth and she was murdered on August **14th** is the day that the **Haitian revolution** was planned in 1791. **Emmett Till** was murdered in 19**55** at **14** years of age. Michelle was murdered at **55** years of age in **Phoenix** Arizona. I am a **Scorpio** and our highest ascension is to become the **Phoenix** and the scorpion governs regeneration, rebirth and **reincarnation**. The oldest known pharaohs are **scorpion kings** (page 2)

Condolences

My condolences go out to all those who have been robbed of their loved ones by this system of racism and white supremacy. Please know that death is not the end. The soul survives death, indeed and in spirit. This is a book of the dead written by a boy who was murdered without justice, who defeated death and came forth by day. May the soul of **Michelle Cusseaux** walk peacefully through the field of Reeds in Amenta. Amen RA.

September 15th 2015 BETSY (Written to the Tupac beat - Don't Make Enemies with Me)

Iu f Per f m heru

Don't forget the slave girl **BETSY** in pain no morphine, sadistic doctors ignore her screams, never seen a man cry **Till** I seen a man die, "**Don't make enemies with me**!" Nigga please, **Sirius** like the stars that we all from, here he is **The BlaKseed,** won't stop **Till** he succeeds, *the light bearer like phosphorus,* the white in your sclera turn yellow like toxic flesh, see the world through jaundice eyes the baby cried, they don't wanna see a nigga **rise** like **Osiris,** the best way to kill a nigga is before he born, they lying, lions telling stories of the gazelle that fell, don't believe everything you read in the paper that they sell, it ain't hard to tell this is hell cloaked in veil, everybody wanna go to heaven, they don't know that they come from heaven, they been deceived because of greed, and they need to believe in a reverend, I ran like **DMC, Hip Hop** caught me heavenly, Rest in Peace to **Sean P** and **Marcus Garvey, Jesus Price** we need an army! it's like they all trying to harm me, have I been half as clear? Atmosphere, Plastic element, all that shit I said is relevant, half as clear never meant to be, the son of a mercenary, the truth they burn and bury, the world is flat? now they sell you the map! he had a heart attack, or did he attack his heart? **Jesus Christ** smoking a peace pipe with **Sean Price** on Noah's **ark** with **Tupac** and **General, Steele** I feel a piece of you here, like **Obi won** standing right over there, this the year of the **snake 2025,** how many of us will still be alive? my homie died at twenty five - **Dawud The Amazing BlaKseed**

Significance

Utterances for Coming Forth by day into Light

Have you ever heard of the notorious **Marion Sims**, aka the "father of modern gynecology"? Well if you're a Black woman you should! Sims developed "pioneering tools and surgical techniques" related to women's reproductive "health". In 1876, he was named president of the American Medical Association, and in 1880, he became president of the American Gynecological Society, an organization he helped found. Marion Sims entered the medical profession when doctors didn't undergo the same rigorous coursework and training they do today. After interning with a doctor, taking a three-month course and studying for a year at Jefferson Medical College, Sims began his **"practice"** in Lancaster. He later relocated to Montgomery, Alabama, seeking a fresh start after the death of his first two **patients.** I guess people need **patience** when doctors who are just "practicing". Sims operated under the racist notion that Black people did not feel pain. Before and after his gynecological experiments, he also tested surgical treatments on **enslaved Black children** in an effort to treat "trismus nascentium" (neonatal tetanus), with little to no success. Sims also believed that African Americans were less intelligent than white people, and thought it was because their skulls grew too quickly around their brain. He would operate on African American children using a shoemaker's tool to pry their bones apart and loosen their skulls. Sims's racist beliefs affected more than his gynecological experiments. When any of **Sims's patients died**, the blame, according to him, lay squarely with "the sloth and ignorance of their mothers and the Black midwives who attended them." He saw nothing wrong with his barbaric methods. Of course not all White doctors were racist like Sims but the ruling majority were and so just like the racist practices still lingering in the policing in America, racism still lingers in medicine. Sims' conducted "research" on enslaved Black women without anesthesia or medical ethicists. **Betsy was one of his patients**. His use of enslaved Black bodies falls into a long history of experiments on black people from colonial times to present, that includes the Tuskegee syphilis experiment and **Henrietta Lacks**. In 19**41**, the same year that **Emmett Till** was born, a paper titled "The Negro's Contribution to Surgery," was published in the Journal of the National Medical Association, Dr. John A. Kenney of the Tuskegee Institute, considered the dean of Black dermatology, wrote, "I suggest that a monument be raised and dedicated to the nameless Negroes who have contributed so much to surgery by the 'guinea pig' route." After several years of activism, the Philadelphia statue of Marion Sims was moved into storage and the statue in Central Park was removed on Apr 17, 2018.

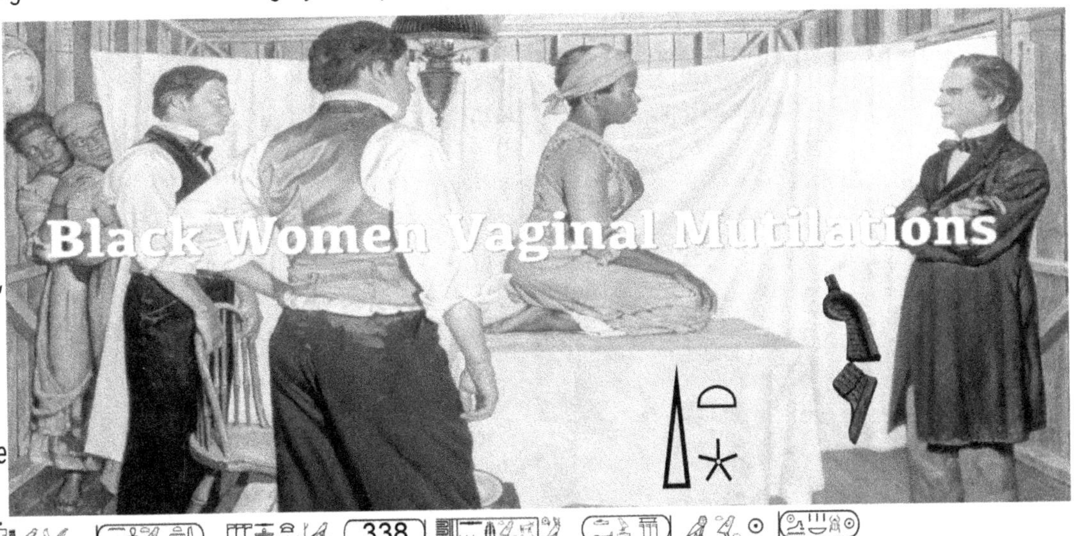

It is he, who comes forth by day into Light

September 17th 2015 **Gateway Chakra**

The gateway chakra, the payday doctor, The bee gets no nectar on the leaf smell the flowers, You gotta know the time and the hour like **Horus** on a scope, if be**lie**f is the core of your religion it's probably a joke! every time you breathe you join my religion, the love for the living, the search for the hidden, just to find the whole world is in your mind, the decision to be free or stay in spiritualism prison, there's gotta be a way to come together like the **Ntchr,** No division, No tell **lie** vision, No stories of **Columbus** on a noble mission! No omission of the truth, Let me see the proof! tare the whole roof off the school to teach the youth **- Dawud The Amazing BlaKseed**

September 22nd 2015 **Rays**

Through this life we be surfing some of us searching, some of us hoping to be saved, riding the wave, if you don't learn to swim you digging your grave, that moment you wake up, and walk out of the cave, take off your make up dear **sun,** take off the shades, and bathe in **Amen Ra's** rays, Rest In Peace to **Jesus Price,** I wanna see **Wu Tang Live Forever,** at night I seek advice, I watch Sa Neter, and measure **Maat's** feather, on my heart lever, I gotta do better I will never stop not never, Mount Everest top lyricist, I summit this, I come with the spiritness, and you blessed that you hearing this, like **blessed thistle,** *the chemistry of mans tissue,* the issue, they send a missile just to hit you, families crying cause they miss you, trying times that we live through, when healing becomes a crime find a **Hindu** in the **Indus Valley,** return of the **Rishi** with a ***mushroom,*** I keep it natty and nappy, no heirlooms, yet they tryin to tax me, asked me if I'm happy I smacked the shit out of him, then I caught a taxi, at a quarter passed 3, caught up in a fantasy, from the sea to shining sea, everything I see just reminding me, can you remember the time honestly, when honesty was a quality in abundancy, redundancy ordained as emergency, the chosen see, the gateway chakra or the payday doctor, the gateway chakra or the payday doctor **- Dawud The Amazing BlaKseed**

42 Laws of Maat, Page 367

Thutmoses III is king David Pages 224-225

September 27th 2015 **Synchronicities**

The **synchronicities** in your life, visualize the concept of the ring pass not, if you wait at the steps of the gate keeper you might never see the top like the eagle, the over achiever verse the cheater, being black is illegal, that's right and exact like a needle, **Recycle it back like a <u>Beetle</u>,** then **transform** into lethal thought, blessed through the cerebral cortex, hexed by the d**ark**ness but still we sp**ark** this, **Hip Hop** held hostage by the heartless lockness monster, **The Akashic Records** here to haunt ya, here to conjure, cause they conned ya, smoking gonja, one day I'm gonna make it better for my Mother and my sister Saana, I love you Allana and Alaina, I would come if I ever knew you were in danger, the **manger** verse the metaphysical, Noah's **ark** and the birth of the baby, do you hear the **<u>riddle</u>** in the middle maybe? here's a hint they sent the navy, I joined the army and drove a Mercedes and didn't understand how they saved me now, **<u>I am that I am</u>,** you can call me crazy, **<u>I'm born again</u>** like ***<u>Skywalker</u>*,** this ain't **coincidence** I talk of, this the art of **synchronicity,** said the author **<u>King David</u>,** we related like **David Walker** the day walker that they torture, don't believe everything they taught ya! you are **the trinity, Leflaw lefla Escorshca,** from **93 Till infinity,** this is what I offer hope you feeling me, we all should unify it's do or die really b! few would die if we tried strategy, we a tribe family, **Black Man Of The Nile** single handedly, **Muhammad Ali** no fantasy, if it was all a **dream** would you remember me? like **Makaveli**, a shot of Hennessy or **Smai Tawi?! Nefertiti** on the titty *<u>50 niggas</u>* probably **- Dawud The Uncanny BlaKseed**

Significance

Of all the lines in this verse this one sticks out the most to me: "do you hear the **<u>riddle</u>** in the middle maybe? here's a hint they sent the navy, I joined the army and drove a Mercedes **<u>and didn't understand how they saved me now</u>**, I am that I am, you can call me crazy, I'm born again like *Skywalker*,". *On page 84 I mention **UFO's**, on page 105 I mention **Aliens** saving me and a **dream** about **Tupac**.*

"Makaveli"

"Lesane Per isis Crooks"

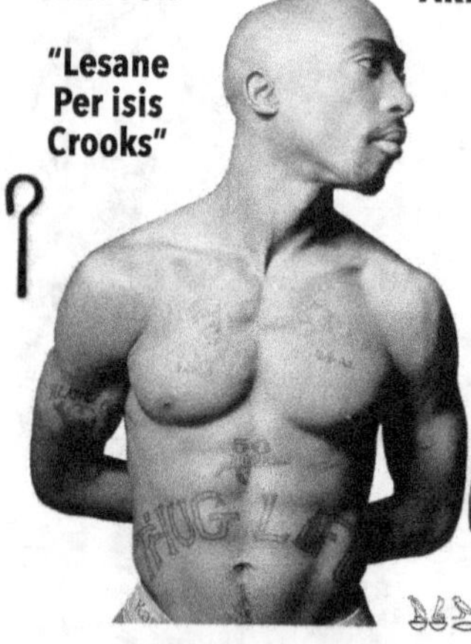

"Akhenaten"

"Born Again"

"The Beetle"

If I had to write a rhyme just for my niggaz, line for line <u>**I would remind with signs**</u>, come hither, **the comforter**, feel the drop on your ear drum, Hip Hop change the whole temperature, **I Used to Love Her**, didn't know who she was, let them tell you, they say she a thug **- Dawud The Uncanny BlaKseed**

October 25th 2015
Meta Mysterious Encounters - Stephanie Siddhartha and Course Correction

Rau nu Prt m heru

I met Stephanie in May of 2014, she was into fitness and was looking for healthier ways of eating. I told her about black seed oil and various other herbs and I started training her sometime in May of 2014 soon after we met (p 295). Stephanie is related to **Malcolm X** (p 561) by way of her Uncle **Angel** Pizarro who married Gamilah Shabazz, Malcolm's fourth daughter.

I had my past life revelation of my life as **Tutankhaten** (**King Tut**) on April 4th 2020 (page 594) the day that **Martin Luther King** was assassinated (pages 69, 592). Sometime after that while searching my order history on Amazon I became aware of two books that I purchased 6yrs prior on July 15th 2014 (p 295-296). Apparently I ordered the book **Moses Begat King Tut** on July 15th 2014 and the book **Siddhartha**. I had the book on **king Tut** for 6 years but I never read it and don't remember how I became aware of the book. Fueled with the revelation of my life as King Tut I searched through my book shelf and found the book then started reading it. The book spoke about the biblical character **Moses** and how he was really the Pharaoh **Akhenaten** from the 18th dynasty, the husband of **Nefertiti** and the father of **Tutankhaten** (**King Tut**). I was amazed.

Iu f Per f m heru

The interesting thing about the book Siddhartha is I only have one copy of the book but I should have two. **This is called course correction**. <u>When the universe wants you to be aware of something it will keep **present**ing it to you. This time it came as a **present**</u>. I don't remember purchasing this book but it is in my order history and the next year I was also given this book as a birthday gift by my friend Stephanie. I thanked her for the book but I wasn't impressed with it so I put it on my book shelf next to other books that I had not read from cover to cover yet. I was arrogant. Instead of being thankful for the book I didn't think the book had any importance as I felt like I was already reading and doing the things I needed to be reading and doing. I didn't know it yet but **something** or **someone** wanted me to read this book and Stephanie was just being used as a conduit! I don't know where the other copy went but I can vaguely remember lending the book to my friend Danny and that was after I had read it in 2016. Perhaps Danny never gave me the copy back or perhaps I gave him a different book and never received the one I ordered. I don't know but whatever the case may be I only have one copy of Siddhartha but I should have two and some how **this book Siddhartha found it's way to me twice and this is why I put the story in the book twice** (page 295). I wouldn't read this book till 2016 after I met a brother named **Kenny** who was in his 70's. Kenny and I met in **Marcus Garvey** park (page 383). Him and I would have peaceful debates about life and religion and one day during one of our debates he told me I needed to read a book but he couldn't remember the name. After some time he remembered the name of the book and it was **Siddhartha** by Hermann Hesse. Surprised, I told him that I already had the book! Then I told him that the person that gave me the book was born on January 12th the same day as him. because of that **coincidence** I went home and read the book immediately. I did not know who the book was about until after I read the book however after a few paragraphs of reading I was over come with tears as I felt like I was reading about myself. The book Siddhartha is about the **Buddha Siddhartha Gautama** and how he gained enlightenment.

Utterances for Coming Forth by day into Light

A few months before I met Stephanie and before I purchased the book Siddhartha I watched the documentary The Prophecy of **REINCARNATION** Sambho the Black Buddha (page 288), about the Buddha being reincarnated in the western world between the years of 1975 and 2020. The documentary would show images of King Tut. I was born in 1977 the year of the snake and I had my second past life revelation of my life as **Tutankhaten** (**King Tut**) revealed to me on April 4th 2020 (page 594) the day that **Martin Luther King** was assassinated (April 4th 1968, see page 69).

On January 8th of 2022 I would receive another confirmation about my life as Siddhartha (page 296) and so the question is, who wrote the message on the paper in Stephanie's dream, Siddhartha the Buddha, Siddhartha her childhood friend or TutemRa? I'm writing a Epic Sci-Real (Science Reality) Novel Trilogy version of this book and a book about Tupac's ancient past life (pages 664 - 665). Stay tuned!

It is he, who comes forth by day into Light

I can't say that I'm fine ,or in my right mind, but writing this rhyme is the best thing I can do at this time, letting my light shine it's the light mind that I'm after, insight on the intuition factor, cause time after time after, ***I feel like I'm being led to the next chapter, in a book I never read, this life is like having the keys to a plane out of sight, but instead of taking flight, we be walking instead,*** sometimes I feel like the whole world is walking dead, sleep walking, caught in a web of ebb and flow, chasing the dough and the street cred, never go to the lowest low tryin to get ahead, he wasn't well fed he was led on a path of indoctrination, doctors, drug dealers and vaccinations, real healers deal with elevation through meditation, he who knows one book knows not creation, **Noahs ark** starts in the wombs when she's birthing a nation, slaves ship to scholars ship the same shit different language, Sanskrit light the house for those left to languish, I write what I will, I'm just trying to heal, trying to deal, I am the steel in the iron, the ion in **Orion,** trying to raise my vibration before dying, **Heru gazes at the age of the lion, the riddle of the sphinx,** to make a brother think and not sink but start climbing, out the prison of the mining of the mind, and now I'm feeling fine, and *I shine and you shine, and I shine and you shine, in this day and time we maintain the same frame of mind* **- Dawud The Uncanny BlaKseed**

Significance

This was written in response to multiple paranormal experiences I was having. To understand more please read **"Lost in the Never ending Story"** which can be found in January of 2013 (pages 259-260) . *"I feel like I'm being led to the next chapter, in a book I never read, this life is like having the keys to a **plane** out of sight, but instead of taking flight, we be walking instead"* - **(never ending story). I suggest that you think deeply about that line.... Especially the words plane and walking.** More on Noah's Ark on page 252.

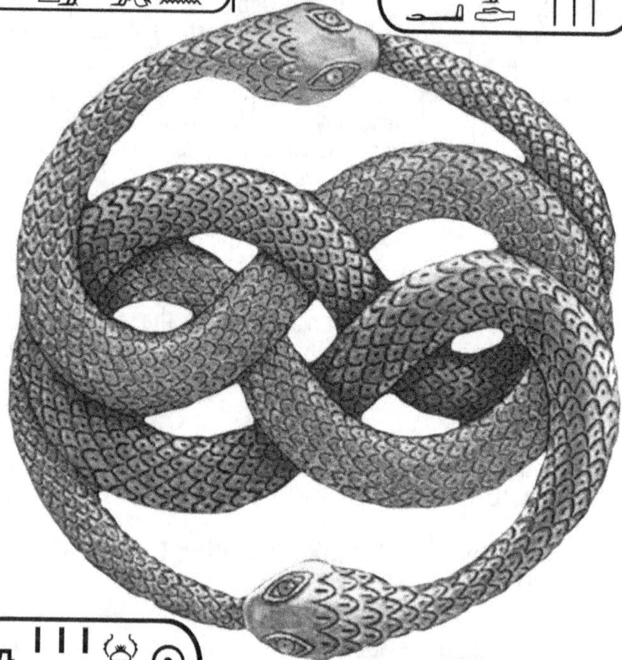

See Page 657

November 4th 2015 - Meta Mysterious Encounters with Bruce Lee, Hannibal, Aaron and Brand Nubian

Rau nu Prt m heru

Iu f Per f m heru

My interest in **Bruce Lee** began in 2013 which led me to buy the squat machine for my apartment so that I could train at home like Bruce did. Eventually I started watching Bruce doing Wing Chung on youtube. This led me to **desire** a wooden Wing Chung practice dummy so I began looking for a cheap one on Craigslist. I found one for a reasonable price but what made me buy it was the name of the person selling it. When he told me that his name was **Hannibal** I found that to be significant because of the African General name **Hannibal** from **Carthage** who fought against Rome in the second Punic wars. So I purchased it. On April 14th of 2016 I would join the Practical Wing Chung school. I joined that school because of a brother named **Aaron** (page 364). I met him at Season Vegan located at **55** St Nicholas, in Harlem. When I went to the school I looked on the wall at the Sifu's news paper clippings and the first one I looked at had been published on a very significant date. It was either **Marcus Garvey's** birthday (Aug 17th) or the day my **Grandfather** died (Aug 18th) . After seeing that date I felt like I was supposed to join so I did. I only stayed for a little over a month however while there I learned **Siu Lim Tao** (the little idea). I tested out for Siu Lim Tao on May 9th 2016. While at School I met a brother named **Reality**. One day after class I let him hear some of my music. After listening he asked me what I was doing with the music. I told him it was my hobby. Then he asked me if I knew who his brother was and I said no. Then he told me his brother was **Lord Jamar** from the legendary group **Brand Nubian**. I was surprised then I was even more surprised that I didn't see it before he told me because they look a lot alike. Brand Nubian was one of the groups that was on that tape that my father gave me when I was 14 (page 54).

When I was in my last year of Massage Therapy school (2016) I met a black sister named Tameasha Cooper. We got along well and when ever we saw each other in school we greeted each other kindly. Her and I had prenatal massage class together. Our pre natal teacher was a white woman who I had no problem with until she disrespected my culture. She claimed that voodoo was wicked. I corrected her and told her that Voodoo was a spiritual system no different than Christianity. From that day her and I seemed to always have issues. It all came to a head one day when the teacher suggested that vaccines were perfectly safe for babies. I objected to this citing cases of autism in black and latino boys when vaccinated. One of the other students felt I was looking for a reason to find discord with the teacher and asked the other students to raise there hands if they agreed. Tameasha Cooper was one of the only people to side with me and she was the only black woman to side with me. Tameasha was part of the **5 percent nation of Gods and Earths** like **Lord Jamar** from **Brand Nubian**. Before school ended she would hand me a folder with the lessons from the Gods and the Earths. I have not seen or heard from Tameasha since I left school.

On April 17th 2015 I wrote the song **Wake Up Blakseeds** (page 327) which was a remix of Brand Nubian's song ***Reprise in the Sunshine***. In 2020 I wrote the song ***Ultra Black*** and edited a video for it. I posted the video for the song on Instagram and **Lord Jamar** liked the video and followed my page. I began to send him my music on Instagram like I used to send to **Stic**. I wanted **Lord Jamar's Yanadameen Godcast** show to be the first place I told my story of my **past lives** but that never happened. I ended up telling my story on **Trans Atlantic Productions via Youtube** with **Minister Clemson Brown** on August 20th and 25th of 2021 (page 518). I understand that from the outside looking in my story may seem strange but stranger things have happened! I hope that after reading this book people will see the **"Reality"** of my story and realize that we must unite as a people! **All for one and one for all**. It's one thing to be born into **racism** and **white supremacy** but it's another thing entirely to **reincarnate** into it over and over and never know it! Yanadameen? Today is October **23rd** 2021 and I'll be **44** in two days and I'm still not proficient with my Wing Chung practice dummy. When I first got it I learned a few sequences from videos I found on youtube but then I stopped practicing. Perhaps when I finish this book I'll spend some time honoring what the ancestors have sent my way or perhaps my Ba (soul) will just fly away. Today is my fathers birthday, June 1st 2022 (p 106) and the following **dream** is the last thing I wrote into this book. Lord Jamar is seen below wearing double **King Tut** chains.

Utterances for Coming Forth by day into Light

ADDENDUM

Brand Nubian Dreams - May 25th 2022

3 year prior to my dream with Lord Jamar I would meet **Grand Puba** on **May 25th** 2019 at the Bam African Street Festival (page 566). Upon returning from Kemet in April of 2022 (page 670) I had **dreams** with several brothers who are in some way connected to Kemet and Lord Jamar was one of them. On **May 25th** 2022 (page 104) I had a **dream** with Lord Jamar. He was in my studio and he saw a copy of his **7** CD laying on my dresser (page 250). We talked and laughed and after that he looked through a collection of vinyls. Then I woke up….
Significance: I have never owned a collection of vinyls but my friend Courtlan does and he has a daughter named **Seven**. Seven is my only Goddaughter, born on February 7, the same day as **Emmett Till's** father (Louis Till, pages 475, 518). I would also dream with **KRS One** (page 633), **Mike Tyson** (page 528) and **XXXtentacion** (page 471).

It is he, who comes forth by day into Light

November 5th 2015 The Yoga Mat on the Floor

Today is March 6th 2022 and I have one thing left to write about and this book will be done. Yesterday I found this picture on an old thumb drive. I started doing yoga and **Tai Chi** when I started school at BMCC in 2012 but yoga never became a regular part of my routine. I had done **bikram** yoga with my friend Randy (page 155) in 2008 or 2009 a few times but I was more interested in the women that would attend classes than I was with the benefits of yoga. However whenever I did do bikram yoga I felt renewed and refreshed. I remember taking this picture on November 5th 2015. This picture was taken the day after Tutankhaten's (King Tut's) tomb was discovered (Nov 4th 1922). I was adding positive habits to my life. I had just recently done my first **gong** session and perhaps that helped me pick yoga up again. 3 years later I would find my self graduating as a **Kemetic yoga** instructor (page 472) and 2 days after I graduated I am struck with my first past life revelation of my life as **Emmett Louis Till** on July 3rd 2018 (page 480). 5 years after this picture my past life as Tutankhaten (King Tut) would be revealed to me (page 594).

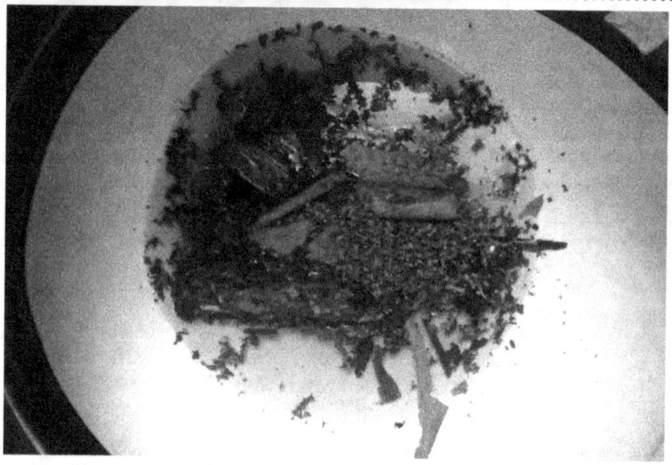

November 12th 2015 at 8:47 AM
HIGH Frequency Psychic Channeling
I finally Stopped Smoking Weed but I see the benefits!

Finally I made the decision to stop smoking weed! On November 12th 2015 I would take two pulls of weed and get so high that I got paranoid. I threw all the weed I had in the toilet and would stop smoking weed for several years. I didn't smoke again until 2017 (page 439). Sometime around that time I ate a weed brownie and the experience was so confusing that I never ate another one. Sometimes I wonder if it was the weed in the brownie that made me feel confused or was it something else that was put into that brownie that did it? Perhaps the brownies were laced with something? I never liked the unpredictability of weed because sometimes the high was very good, funny and happy and sometimes it was sad, and sometimes I got very sad especially on nights that I would write for the people who had been murdered. I smoked weed for the first time before I went to a New Years Party on January 1st 2011 (page 194). I smoked weed because I wanted to see if it would make my raps sound better and if I would write better rhymes. I don't think it did either but what it did do was far more than I was able to fathom at the time. When I got "HIGH" I would have these **ideas** for movies and skits and business. I would record these ideas into my phone as audio memos. Three of these audio recordings can be read on pages 208, 227 and 238. I realize now that these recordings were not ideas for a movies, they were actually inter dimensional transmissions from another dimension. The sacred Marijuana plant had opened up a **High Frequency Psychic Channel** (perhaps from the akashic records), where these messages were channeled down through my thoughts. I smoked weed in 2011 (p 227) and it opened a channel/portal for a thought about **souls returning from the dead** and I **thought** it was an idea for a movie but it was actually a messages about my life purpose, that I would not come to realize for another 7 years. The fact that I had indeed died many times and **COME BACK** again many times! In ancient Kemet (Egypt) the concept of reincarnation and past lives was called **Wehem-Mesut** (repeating of births, page 14). It is not about how much you know, it's about how much you desire to know. It's about where your heart is. All of our actions are measured by the matters of the heart. These spiritual **messages** are **received through the heart**. If your desire is right and exact you can attract the information or situation you earn. This is the ancient Kemetic (Egyptian) principle of divine thought and divine wisdom governed by the Deity (God) **Jehuti** also known as **Tehuti** or **Hermes** or **Thoth** (divine **thought**).

11:19pm on October 27th 2021

Due to my profound experiences with weed I do not demonize it but I do think it is seriously abused and smoked too much! Smoking anything causes acid to accumulate in the lungs which damages the respiratory system and most of the weed today is grown with dangerous toxic chemicals used to make it grow faster. Today is October 27th 2021. I am almost done with this book. I started ingesting weed again sometime around December of 2020 after I started writing this book. For those who deal with this sacred plant that we call weed I want you to know that in the past two years I have only ingested around **5 grams** of it. I have not smoked with anyone else. I did not smoke blunts. I took very small pinches every now and then through a small piece pipe (p 645). The picture seen on the top left is an example how much I would use on rare occasion. I never did it a lot because I was always cautious of the emotional response I would have to it. Weed can cause me to cry deeply. When I smoke I can all of a sudden think about the safety of all the people I care for especially my immediate family and friends. Then sometimes I would feel like something or someone was after me. Not the "thing" that we call God but the ones who control the world. The ones who pretend to be God. I would be paranoid but then as I wrote this book I kept in my mind that I have met many different types of people in my life of all different colors, and in every age there is a time when things make a major shift. We can decide to change the world for the better. The wave that rises must soon fall and the fall can crash causing calamity or it can flow ever so gracefully. That is what we call Maat. Harmonious Balance, Justice, Truth, Cosmic Order, Reciprocity, and Moral Righteousness. Or perhaps those feelings were just as real as the "ideas' I thought I had for "movies". Perhaps something is after me. I know that I came back to earth from a time Far Far away. Perhaps something else came too. Perhaps the reality we are living is more like sci-fi movies than we are ready to fathom. I have less than half a gram left of this weed and I will be finished with this book in a month or so. No more than two more months left and I plan to be done by December 2021. Today is May 1st 2022, I'm almost done and I still have the same amount of weed left..

November 19th 2015 Amenta

Let the sun shine home, climb spine pine comb, light mind sight beyond sight, zone to the unknown, flight or fight higher heights tiger stripes the other side of life, like day and night I might **lucid dream** in **Amenta,** before you die you're meant to enter the house of **Ausar** to **be a star forever**, as on earth as in heaven, seven steps add eleven you got nine the **trinity**, I will never limit me, infinitely symmetry, the tree of life centers me, the breath of life enters me and leaves willingly, will it be Hennessy or the **Smai Tawi?!** law of duality balance me, fall of man from galaxy, to this earthly fantasy, just the world they handed me, insanity, **Black Man of The Nile and His Family,** underhandedly up rooted from our family tree, **magic**ally **Booker T** up from slavery, **Marcus Garvey** read that book and fought for saving we, technically we **Immortal!** when we slip through the portal, Hip Hop be the soil and we rose through the spoils, the **glitch in the Matrix**, cowards scared to face it or say shit, I'm just gonna take off in this space ship, equipped with a cord from the heart to the Lord, my words be the sword, from the earth to the universe, the world is yours, from the earth to the universe, <u>the world is yours, it's mine, it's mine, it's mine, who's world is this? the world is yours!</u> **- Dawud The Uncanny BlaKseed**

Rau nu Prt m heru

Significance

In this song I say the words, "**as on earth as in heaven**". Those words come from the book of Matthew, from the Bible but when I wrote those lyrics I was referring to the three pyramids of **Khufu** and how they align with the stars in **Orions Belt**. I thought it was profound how the builders of the pyramids aligned the pyramids (meta spiritual devices) with the stars in the heavens. At the time I had never experienced a psychedelic and did not realized that there was a deeper layer to the science. It was only during the writing of this book that I would come across info connecting the constellation of Orion to the structure of the DMT molecule. It appears that, not only did the sages of Kemet align the pyramids with the stars in the heavens, but they also explained how the medicines on earth can help to awaken the sleeping human when the medicines are allowed to enter heaven, the holy of holies. When the DMT molecules are allowed to bathe our pineal glands, those who have made themselves ready can open doors and experience levels of awakening only attained by few. I named this song **Amenta** and I mentioned **lucid dreaming** in this song. On October 18th 2014 (page 305) I had a profound **dream** of my high school sweetheart Indira **Aminta** Ceville. Indira's middle name is **Aminta** and in ancient Kemet (Egypt) **Amenta** is the equivalent to **heaven**. Indira was the first girl I fell in love with in JR High School 180. I had not seen her in around 14yrs yet still my soul went to her to comfort her while she was in pain mourning the death of a her Haitian sister in-law. In the years to come I would begin to have more profound experiences while **dreaming**. This book is about the immortality of the soul and in this song I say the words "technically we **Immortal!**". One time is an incidence, twice is a coincidence, but three, four, five is a pattern. Can you tell the difference? I was waking up from a long sleep, in a new body Just like the movie **Matrix**. Remember that you are **Ausar**, the **hero!** <u>See page 3 for the **hero's journey**</u>**!**

Iu f Per f m heru

Ausar the Archer
Orion's Belt

As above

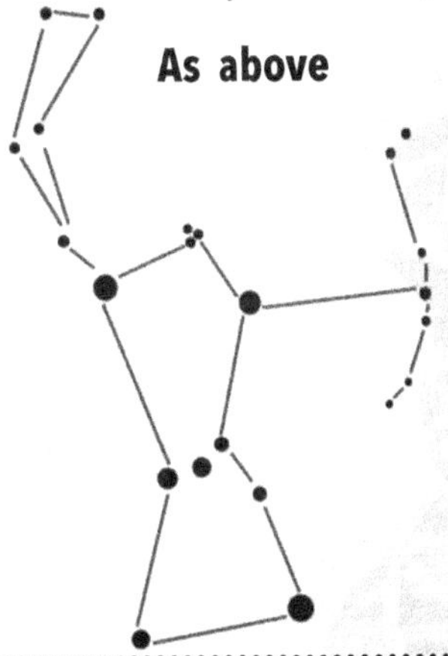

So below

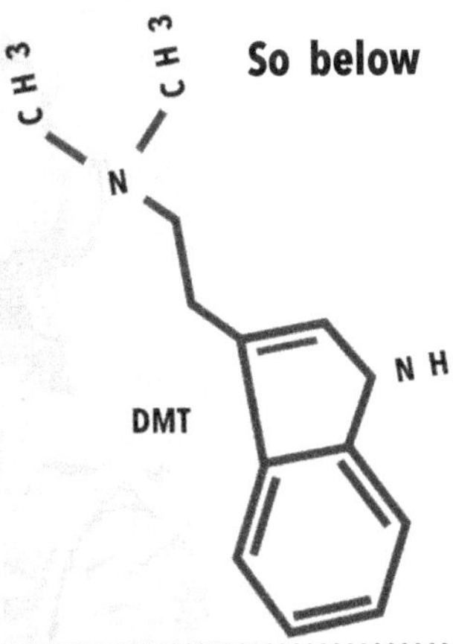

November 29th 2015 FIVE

5 fingers, **5** toes, **5** senses, **5** brothers jumping over fences, **5** limbs connect like the earths land mass in past reflect, on the tree of life <u>he was **hung** by his neck</u>, the trees wept seeing the element leave in the wind, the shit you cant see when you sin, low vibration, light dim! meditation then they **Christ** him, peace like Islam I am self Lord and master wisdom, Bruce Leroy Daniel son decisions, know they self and heal thy self with no incision, homie listen this my last rhyme in a long, gotta take time to apply what I've learned, the form, before I transform into "the one man army Ason", I am the young and the **Ole Dirty Bastard,** in the palm of my hands supreme mathematics, <u>25 like when the sun **rise** between **the manger**</u>, look in the sky and see the 3 wise aligned with the savior, while the deaf dumb and blind crying, dying waiting for a savior, sometimes I wanna die too, then I think of hearing my mother and grand mother cry blues, so I chose to push weight like **King Gator** and **Q**, chill with my boo **bar**bra peace to **Giant the Bar Father,** keeping my head up above the bar biceps be getting harder, read **The China Study** learned that fitness makes you smarter, now I yearn for the burn like **Stic-Man, RBG** fit fam, **Bruce Lee** like **ip man,** hand stands like **Hittman, Hannible For King** from Queens like I am, like I am, and I am the sun **- Dawud The Uncanny BlaKseed**

Utterances for Coming Forth by day into Light

It is he, who comes forth by day into Light

December 2nd 2015 Glory Day

I'm writing these lines just to praise the Lord, even though I live in a world that I can't afford, suicide doors bugatti, land Lords rob me, I'm from **Queens** like **Prince Hakeem** but never seen **King Jaffe,** more like **Semmi** maybe, I never been lazy, the lifestyle that I live pays me, so I live my making, I don't make a living, fast like Jamaicans, don't get it mistaken this wasn't my **dream,** I drew rappers seen in Word Up magazines, joined the army loaded magazines, discharged and realized I hadn't learned a thing, real eyes see real lies, it's all about the cream, Black man try to rise, he die or thrown in the bing, and I'm the type that would die to let freedom ring, cause reality is wrong and we really live in **dreams,** sing along with the song if you feel what I mean **- Dawud The Uncanny BlaKseed**

The Dec 3rd Theory - Meta Spiritual Encounters - Sean Price Lives On (*ADDENDUM*)

The **Boot Camp Clik** was one of my favorite Hip Hop groups in the 90's and **Sean Price** (from **Heltah Skeltah**) was my favorite artists from their ranks. The first album I purchased with my own working money was **Nocturnal**, the debut album from Heltah Skeltah. Unfortunately Sean Price died on August 8th 2015. After he passed I saw a post on Instagram promoting the 20th anniversary **Boot Camp Clik** show at BB Kings on **Dec 3rd**, and because of the experience I had the year prior on **Dec 3rd** (p 313) I felt like it was a sign that I should go, so I committed myself to going. This was big for me because I had been a **hermit** for years and this meant I would have to go out at night and socialize for a bit and I was not looking forward

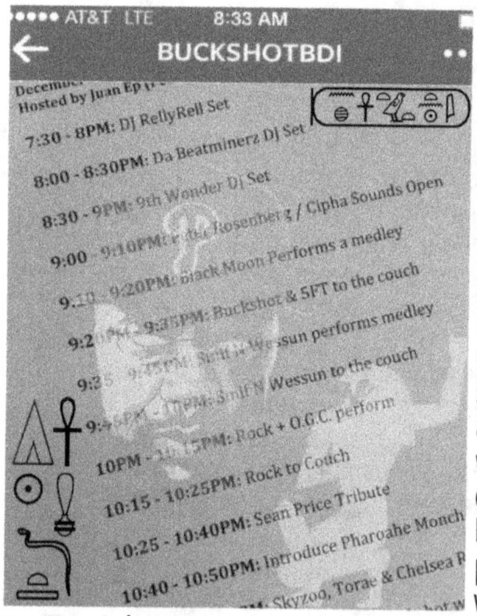

to that part. I liked being a hermit. When it was finally time to go I was tired so I almost stayed home but because of **Sean Price** I went. Upon arriving I got the itinerary, and immediately I noticed that Sean Price was being honored at **10:25**pm, like my birthday, **Oct 25th**! Had **Dec 3rd** struck again?! Was this another sign?! I stayed and watched the whole show. I had never seen the Boot Camp perform before. It took me back to my youth all over again. **KRS One** performed, **Smif N Wessun**, **Rockness**, **Buck Shot, O.G.C.** and many more. While there I ran into a girl I knew from the gym I worked at in Brooklyn back in 2005 when I first started training. She was one of the women you see in the gym with a very nice body. She was a scorpio like me and we had been intimate years prior but when she saw me I was a different person than the guy she knew from 10 years ago. Here I was walking around with this patch of hair behind my head. I tried to tell her about the **coincidence** I just had with Sean Price and what had happened with my friend **Jay Cooper** the year prior on this same day (p 314) but we were at a show with rappers walking by and she wasn't too interested. I understood. I think she thought I was a little off mentally. I understood that too. We hugged and parted ways. I recorded footage of the show and took a picture with the Boot Camp mascot, then I went home. On my way home I contemplated the reason why I had another experience with death on **Dec 3rd**. Was it a coincidence? or was it a sign? Or was it the **spirit** of Sean Price?! It sure felt like it was him! What ever it was there was definitely this "**Dec 3rd pattern**" that was building up and low and behold it would strike again the next year, in 2016 (p 431) and again in 2017 (p 457). It wasn't till the writing of this book that I realized the **Dec 3rd theory** had started in 1955, after the murder of **Emmett Till** (p 519). During the **revision** of this book I realized that the album **Nocturnal** was released on June 18th 1996, the same day my great grand mother Leacola **Riddle** died (p 21). On Aug 9th 2022 I saw a post on Evil D's Instagram promoting a show at S.O.B's celebrating the life of Sean Price. The post had a portion of the song, Sean Price playing (which was my favorite song off the **Nocturnal** album) and for the first time, I realized that Sean Price said the name **Isis** in that song: "Some say Sean Price is nicest on mic devices Pack power witch make me more mightier than **Isis**" (see page 672). When I first heard the song in 1996 I knew nothing of **Isis** (p 2) but in 2022 I heard it with a new ***"set"*** of ears and it gave the "Dec 3rd theory" **MORE LIFE**, like how **Isis** helped **Osiris** achieve, **more life after his death**.. I would not use the name **Isis** in a rhyme till 2016 (p 267). More on Isis (p 357, 665). In November of 2022 I saw that **Rockness** was born on **November 4th**, the same day **King Tut's** tomb was discovered. See page 3 for **Osiris** and the **hero's journey**!

December 5th 2015 - Meta Mysterious Encounter with Mfundishi Jhutyms and the Haitian Voodoo Priestess

The experience with **Sean Price** a few days prior was still nerve wrecking for me. I didn't know why these things were happening. I went to 125th street to see if I would find Mfundishi Jhutyms (page 233) vending in his usual spot across the street from Red Rooster. He was indeed there but he was talking to a woman so I stood by patiently and waited for him to finish. At times I would feel like I was annoying him with my questions. He made no rush to finish his conversation. I waited patiently in the cold for around 15 or 20 minutes. When he was done we finally spoke. I can remember asking him if he ever felt like something was watching him. He replied, "**the NTCHR is always watching**". We spoke for a short while, then I purchased a book from his table titled - The Murder of **King Tut**, then I left. I went to see if my Homie **Nova** was vending at his usual spot across the street from the **Apollo**. He was, but strangely enough that woman was there again. The one that was talking to Mfundishi earlier. I asked Nova who she was and he told me she was a **Haitian Voodoo Priestess**. I found that interesting. Another **sister** joined in the conversation that Nova and I were having. She asked me if I did music and I said yes. She asked if she could hear some so I recited a verse for her. She then told me that she built her own **studio** in her apartment and she invited me to come by sometime to record. We exchanged information then she left. The **Haitian** woman was still there. I asked **Nova** to introduce me to her. Her name was **Florence** like my aunt. We spoke for almost an hour standing in the cold. I told her about many of the things I had been experiencing. I told her about what had happened with the MDW NTCHR book a few months prior on May 5th (p 329). She told me about **spirits** and she told me that I should sage and cleanse my space as that would help protect me from unwanted spirits. She told me to read the MDW NTCHR book. When we finally parted ways I remember my feet feeling frozen from standing so long in that one spot. I would never see the **Haitian woman** again but she would **call** me on **Dec 25th 2015** at the most profound of times (page 349). When I got home I fell asleep in my hammock with the **MDW NTCHR** book in my hand. I would awaken the next day from a vivid **dream.**

December 6th 2015 What ever you do, try not to die in the **Dream**

This was a clear and **vivid** dream. I was in a room with a beautiful woman sitting on my lap. She was naked. There were other people around but I'm not sure how many. Then from out of nowhere a brother rushes towards me to fight me. We began to fight. Then he pulled a knife out. *He cut my throat* and just before any blood would pour from my neck I woke up from the dream.

I Immediately thought about all the things the Haitian woman Florence told me the day prior and because of the things she told me I was not alarmed by the **dream**. I got up and began to clean and **sage** my entire apartment. I was not worried. The dream reminded me of the movie The **Matrix**. There is a scene where the agent is chasing **Trinity** and just before a bullet hits her she picks up the phone and is pulled out of the Matrix, teleporting away safely. Just before the blood spilled from my neck I woke up and was teleported away safely back to this "reality". Perhaps though they were trying to save me? Hm, Please don't go killing yourself but perhaps this is the dream. Perhaps they were trying to save me by killing me in the dream so that I could stay in that dimension but I rather wake up and be saved in a more peaceful way. "As for the span of earthly affairs it is the manner of a dream" (page 30).

2015 - Transdimensional Encounters
UFO Unidentified Flying Object in the Sky towards the direction of the Bronx

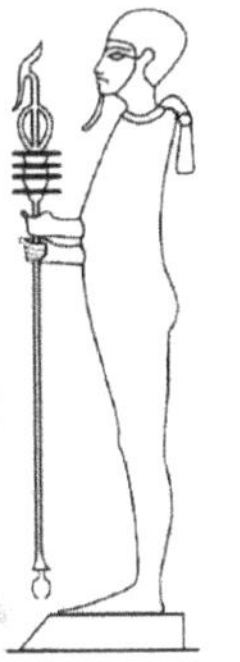

Victorious and I were on my roof one day when we both witnessed seeing a **bright light** in the sky towards the Bronx. It was a **circular** object shining bright. I saw it first. I told him to look then we both stared at it. Then we looked back at each other in disbelief and when we looked back to our amazement it was gone. **The exact date of this event is not known but this occurred sometime before Dec 10th 2015. I know that because on Dec 10th 2015 I would write about the experience in the song Fitness Made Easy.**

Rau nu Prt m heru

Meeting Victorious

Sometime in 2013 I was standing in line at the grocery store. There was a brother in the line behind me. We started talking about food. I told him about super foods like Moringa, Spirulina etc etc. We exchanged info. After our discussion Victorious would make changes to his eating and he thank me for reminding him of these things he had known about. Him and I became friendly. I would come to find out that we shared the same life path number of 5. He was trained in martial arts and would train me sometimes. We would also have long conversations in my studio. One day during our conversations / debates *he asked me if I had ever heard of* ***Ptah***. I said no. He nodded his head back and forth signaling he understood and we moved on with the conversation. He never taught me who Ptah was he just asked me if I had heard of him. Later I would search Ptah and recognize the image but I had not known the story of Ptah and the connection with the principles of Creation. During our conversations and strong differences of opinions **I would use my personal experiences to confirm my conclusions and he would most often quote the Bible to confirm his**. I was never satisfied by his findings but he did however tell me of a profound experience he once had with the **sun**. He said he was walking down the street during a hot sunny day and as he smiled at the sun the sun seemed to get brighter. Then he would stop smiling and the sun would decrease in intensity. He went back and forth with smiling and stopping and the sun would respond by getting brighter when he smiled and decreasing intensity when he stopped smiling. Finally he smiled as hard as he could and when he did every street light on the block exploded. I never forgot that story.

Iu f Per f m heru

My current relationship with Victorious as of 2020.

We exchange texts from time to time. Victorious tells me that I am his Hebrew Israelite brother from the tribe of Yahudah. I tell him that I was Emmett Till and Tutankhaten in my past lives and I don't think we did what the bible says we did to the "Israelites" so I can not agree with the stories of the bible, especially when a lot of it comes from the 18th Dynasty (p 667).. I tell him that we are older than what is written in the bible. We don't speak often at all anymore. On **March 14th 2022** I got a call from Victorious. He told me that his views have shifted. He said that he read a chapter in the bible and had a revelation. He quoted the book of **Isaiah 19:25,** "whom the Lord of host shall bless, saying Blessed is Egypt My People, and Assyria the work of My hands, and Israel My inheritance." Victorious now proclaims Egypt to be the mother land and wants to take a trip to Egypt. He even said that we need to go there together but when I go I will go alone. Victorious is born on July 8th 1970 the year of the **dog**. My past life of Emmett Till was revealed in 2018 the year of the dog (page 480). As of 2022, **now Victorious thinks he is the reincarnation** of **ThutmosesIII** (pages 225, 638), I do not agree with his proclaimed "revelation" because it is based on him knowing me. He thinks, simply because we crossed paths in this life that he must also be a pharaoh…. This bring me back my thoughts written on pages 8 and 9……

Utterances for Coming Forth by day into Light

December 9th 2015 The Superman Booth

I found my way to the woman with the studio in her apartment who I met a few days prior, on December 5th (page 345). I wanted to see her studio and when I saw it, it looked like a telephone booth to me. Like the one **superman** would step into to change his outfit. She had similar equipment as me but she also had 5 pieces of wood nailed together creating a recording booth. I recorded one song there. I kept all my files. I don't remember the sisters name but her birthday was January **25**th and she was suffering from **diabetes**. I told her about **Dr. Llaila Afrika** and shared his teachings about **string bean juices's** ability to help with diabetes then I left. On my way home I thought about how easy it would be to build my own "telephone booth" and 9 days later that's exactly what I would do (page 349). Forget not the Superman Curse (page 202, 204).

DAWUD ENTERED THE PHONE BOOTH
...AND HIS ANCIENT SOUL FRAGMENTS CAME FLYING OUT OF PRIMORDIAL DARKNESS.

It is he, who comes forth by day into Light

December 10th 2015 Fitness Made Easy

Fitness made easy with consistency most definitely, effortlessly changing form like **OGC** I bring the storm, crashing water **Bruce Lee,** fire internally burning me, the Chi Gung is never gone, for what it's worth the earth birthed this song, the element heaven sent, I spent a minute looking then it was gone, ***I seen this light in the sky spinning out of the norm!*** ring the alarm! The 25th dynasty your highness be iron strong, like the crouching tiger, isometric, perfect it, flex it to electric, then you be on some next shit, they ain't touching your level, kick rocks on the devil, wrath with my **wooden staff** and slash with my sword of metal, the elements **with memories of elephants**, ingrained in a strand of a myelinated band, turning mountains into sand and proteins into man, will they ever understand, **I am that I am?! I'm in the dreams of a stranger,** It don't get no stranger! She said **I was the 3rd to arrive and I carried her away from danger,** she said **I had 23 wives, I wasn't a man of anger, I was about peace and love,** my name is defined beloved, what if I told you, some of the things you seek will erode you, and hold you down, weigh you down, why are your feet still on solid ground? that dude Dawud like **Heru** be flying around, Hip Hop over heavy metals, heavy metals, Fit Hop over heavy metals - **Dawud The Uncanny BlaKseed**

Significance

I saw something hovering over Yankee Stadium! It was there for a few seconds then it was gone. I was not alone that day. I was on the roof on my building with my brother **Victorious** (p 346). I saw it first. I pointed at it and Victorious looked and saw it too. Then we looked at each other in amazement but when we looked back it was gone! What we saw looked like some sort of "unidentified" flying object. It looked like a round **UFO** with bright lights (see pages 84, 105, 346, 380, 663). That is why I wrote the line "I seen this **light** in the sky **spinning** out of the norm! ring the alarm! I was in the dream of a Haitian woman In my school (p 297). I saved her in her dream. My friend Stephanie **dreamt** I had **23** wives (p 296). **OGC** was a group affiliated with the **Boot Camp Clik** and they were my favorite group in High School. The spirit of Sean Price (Jesus Price) from the group Boot Camp Clik visited me on Dec 3rd 2015 (p 345). **Heru** is the son of Ausar, the Lord of **resurrection** and Heru is the **falcon** that resurrects and returns in the Ausarian **resurrection** Drama. The "**with memories of elephants"** that I speak of my have been the deep suppressed memories that poured out on **October 7th 2021** when I watched a video about **The Great Arjuna's Penance / Descent of Ganges Relief at Mamallapuram.**

December 14th 2015 Kanye Blame Game Remix

On the bathroom wall I wrote I could have made it in the game all I really needed was help, help help help help, I took a piss and dismissed it like fuck it I'll do it all by my mother fucking self! self self self self, ain't no use in point'n and screaming and saying how I'm blaming everybody else! else else else else, and if you don't like it fuck it go ahead and bob your head to somebody else

You weren't perfect but you made life worth it, deep inside I knew you were my purpose, but what I go and do?! I joined the service, I buried my **dream** now it seems I'm unearthing you, what I'm supposed to do? they say follow your heart and not your mind! I definitely be writing rhymes! that's what I do, so here I go now it's my grind time, line for line, weeks in the crib I'm a get signed! back of my mind I hear the hate, I just keep faith, "You're not good enough", "Give up", "You're too late", "You're too fast", "you're too slow", "Your off pace", "Come out and hang with us, you stay cooped up in your small place", but I don't listen I just lighten my load, you see the truth come out of people when you go through your lows, that's how it goes, a beautiful struggle of how I rose, I ain't trip'n, I'm sit'n, sip'n laugh'n at you hoes, faster I had to go, higher fly never low, even Bo he know when your flow ain't hip that you gotta go, so, before I lay me down to sleep I keep it 100, and toast to the douche bags that fronted - **Dawud The Uncanny BlaKseed**

December 2015 Nova and The Ghost of Christmas Past

Another year at Nova's holiday party. This year the group was a bit smaller. I was wondering if I would be visited by another **spirit** like last year but unfortunately no **ghost** were to be found (page 314). I did however meet one of Nova's friends who wanted to train with me, who would end up being "**a ghost from my distant past"**. She asked me if I was Nova's trainer. Perhaps Nova told her that her trainer would be coming. At this point Nova and I were more like workout partners but she paid me a little. Nova's friend took my info and a few days after the party she reached out to me and we set up a training session. This woman was **attractive**. She came to the session with no bra on and perhaps it would not have been an issue if her breast were not so big. I made no mention of it to her but we had a light session doing no jumping exercises that might cause her to "move around". It wasn't until the end of the session that, **I realized that I knew her!** We had gone out on a date years prior before I had become this **hermit** with this patch of hair behind my head. Upon realizing this I told her, "I think we have met before". She seemed surprised. I asked if she had ever lived in Midtown in a one bedroom apt. I drew the floor plan out. She looked at it and said yes. She pretended to not remember me but I knew she did. She probably knew at the party. She was a lot thinner when we met years prior as she had put on some weight now. I probably met her at the lounge on 26th street called **Tillmans** (P 153). I used to go there often. Her and I only hung out one time back then. Soon after we initially met we went for sushi at a spot in Midtown then we hooked up afterwards. I was drunk that night but I still remembered her apartment. I never heard from her again. She did to me what most men do to women. I guess I was just another number on her hit list. Funny how the universe will swing people from the past back around like the ghost of Christmas past. Was she some sort of test? Did I pass the test, did I fail? Well we didn't hook up this time and she later told me she had remembered me the whole time. Nova would land the role of **Vanity** for a biopic (p 362) and I would have an experience with the **ghost** of **Prince** (p 379).

December 17th 2015 - Clark Kent and the Telephone Booth

I had an intense feeling that I needed to make a recording booth just like the one I had seen at the woman's house 9 days prior on Dec 9th and with booth I should record a **Mixtape** with 25 songs. The idea came over me and I acted on it immediately. I kept thinking it's just like the telephone booth that Cl**ark** Kent used to get in and transform into **Superman** (p 202-204). I called my cousin Abdullah and asked him about the measurements that I would need to build a booth. I wrote them down then went to Home Depot and purchased the wood and sound proofing then made my way home. The price came up to $1**77**.00. I remember looking at the number **77** on the receipt and thinking that it was **divine** and that I was supposed to be making this recording booth because I'm born in the year of **77**. When I got home I had to carry all the wood up 4 flights of stairs by myself. After a few trips I was sweating profusely. I laid all the pieces of wood on the floor under my hammock after which I was reasonably tired. I looked for a book to read, finally choosing the book **Dreams and The Underworld**. I purchased the book because I heard **Bobby Hemmit** (page 262) suggest it during one of his lectures. I laid down with the book and tried to read but before I could read one paragraph I fell asleep and drifted into the underworld. When I awoke I woke from another **dream** where I was fighting again. Here are the details of the dream:

Rau nu Prt m heru

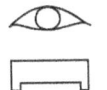

December 18th 2015
Dreams and The Underworld

I was sitting in a **car** when a man walked by and picked a fight with me. We had a very quick fight in which I briefly used some Wing Chung techniques then I slammed him on the ground. As soon as he hit the ground I awoke.

December 18th 2015 - Meta Spiritual Encounters
Seeing the Apparition of General Dukes JR

As soon as I woke up from my dream I stepped out of my hammock **and immediately** I grabbed my drill, nails and the wood and I started putting the booth together. Abdullah was supposed to help me do this but I hadn't heard back from him so I did it myself. When I had all the sides together I stood the booth upright and ***immediately my Grandfather appeared***. **He was staring down at me dressed in all white. There was a very bright white light emanating all around him. I was left transfixed in a trance like state similar to how movies depict people staring bewildered at a spaceship(s) during "U.F.O. Sightings". I can not tell you how long the experience lasted, I really don't know but it seemed like an eternity and at the same time it seemed like a slow blink of the eye, then he was gone and it was over**.. As soon as it ended I finished setting up the booth and I started recording my first **mixtape**. Unbeknownst to myself this would mark the beginning of my **Opening of the Mouth Ceremony**. In the year 2016 I would write **93 rhymes**, the most written in any other year of my life. The only year coming close was 2011 when I wrote **64 rhymes**. This year of 2015 I wrote **46** rhymes. Years after this experience I would start seeing my Grand Father in my **dreams** (Page 6), or perhaps years later I would be spiritually strong enough to remember more of my dreams again. We are always dreaming but some of us don't always remember. I took this picture of my Grand father around a month before he transitioned on August 18th 2009 (page 169). The light shining behind reminds me of what he looked like when I saw him in the apparition. Communicating with dead family members was a common practice in ancient Kemet (Egypt). **Ka doors (spirit doors)** were built into the walls of the tombs in ancient Kemet as a way to interface between the world of the living and the world of the "dead". For more on **Guardian Angels** and **Ka Doors (Spirit Doors)** see pages (251-253, 48, 141, 142, 148, 150, 179, 199, 315, 318, 329, 349, 409, 421, 434, 545, 548, 549, 572, 584, 604, 626, 650).

Iu f Per f m heru

Addendum **Whoopi Goldberg, Patrick Swayze the movie Ghost, Emmett Till and Beyond King Tut**

Whoopi Goldberg was was born in 19**55**, the same year **Emmett Till** was murdered. **Patrick Swayze** played the "**ghost**" (the spirit lingering on after death) in the movie. Patrick is born on August 18th, the same day my grand father **General Dukes Jr** died (page 169). My grand father appeared to me in spirit form on Dec 18 2015, just like Patrick did in the movie **Ghost**. 3 days after my birthday, on **October 28,** 20**22**, the movie **Till** was released. **Whoopi Goldberg** was one of the executive producers of the movie. That same day, **October 28,** 20**22** the **Beyond King Tut Exhibit** opened in NYC (page 29 & 33). I have not watched my movie but I went to my Exhibit on December **22,** 20**22** with Shanta (page 289).

Utterances for Coming Forth by day into Light

It is he, who comes forth by day into Light

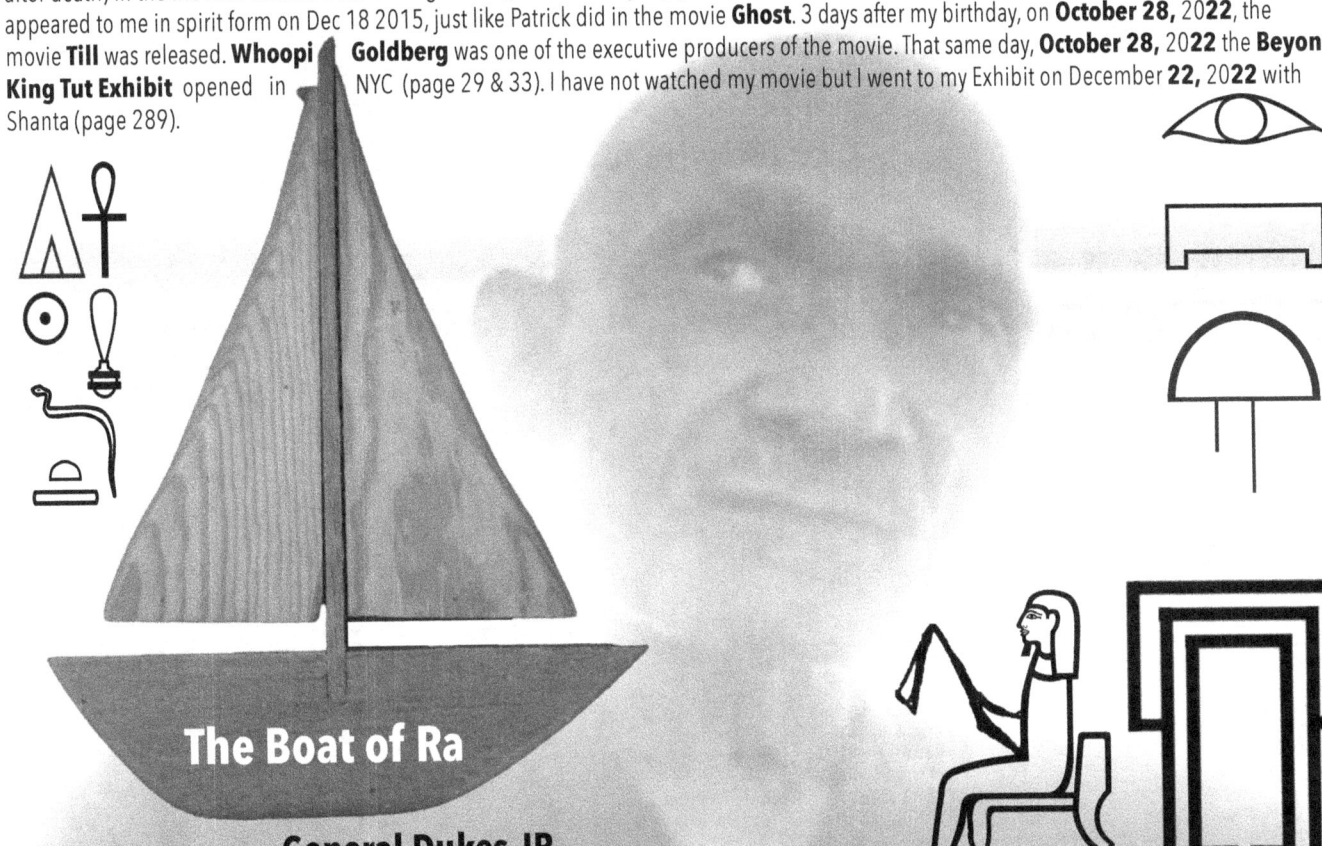

As soon as the **spirit** of my **Grandfather** vanished I went back to the booth and set everything up immediately to record then I started recording right away. The plan was to record **25** songs in 7 days then post the album on Soundcloud on December 25th. The process ended up being harder than I expected. The music seemed to sound better when I recorded in the booth but still I was critical of all my work so I ended up recording some of the songs over and over until I felt they were right. I worked 7 days straight and didn't do anything else. I finished the last song on **December 25th** around 12pm then I listened to every song to see if I liked the delivery on them. I was tired and didn't want to record anything else but there was one verse I was not happy with! It was from the song **Ancient Future** that I wrote on Feb 8th 2015 (p 321). The second verse just didn't sound right so I had to do it over. I went in the booth and started recording it and when I got to the end of the verse *my phone rang*. That was the first time my phone had rung since I had been recording the album and it rang as soon as I said the name **Toussaint** and because of that I looked at my phone. I was dumbfounded when I saw who was calling. It was **Florence**, the **Haitian woman** that I had spoken to on Dec 5th. I answered the call and I said "hello Florence, you will not believe the circumstances in which you called." I told her that she had called me as soon as I said the name **Toussaint** (from the Haitian revolution) and then she told me that she was just calling *to see if I was ok*. We talked briefly then I went back to the verse and finished it. Then I posted the mixtape on Soundcloud. The music did not get many listens and after a week or so I took the album offline. After I finished this mixtape I would write 4 more songs in 2015. One of them was a song that I wrote for **Tamir Rice** and on that song I would say the name **Emmett Till**. *At this point in time I had no idea that I was **Emmett** in my past life!* In fact after the murder of **Tamir Rice** I began to see the picture of the faces of **Emmett** and **Tamir** spliced together and after seeing the striking resemblance I began to think of **Emmett** every time I thought of **Tamir** and I thought of **Tamir** every time I thought of **Emmett.** At one point I even considered that **Tamir Rice** had possibly come back here **reincarnated** as **Emmett Till** just to get our **atten**tion. To show America it's wickedness. Perhaps Tamir was a sacrificial lamb like the story of Jesus. Never did I ever think I was Emmett Till until July 3rd 2018 when I immediately, instantaneously, in the blink of an eye **knew I was Emmett Till** (P 480)**!** Even in the verse that **Florence** called me on I said the name **Osiris** and **Osiris** is another name for **Ausar** and Ausar is the Lord of **Resurrection / Reincarnation**. **Re-member** that **you** are **Ausar (Osiris)** and **Heru,** the **hero!** See page 3 for the **hero's journey!** Many people have children but they don't always have children that come out looking just like them and also taking on their same energy yet **OBD** from the **Wu Tang Clan** has a son that is just like him at least from the surface. **OBD** called himself **Osiris** big baby **Jesus**. In the **Osirian drama** Osiris is murdered by his brother **Set** and **resurrects** through his son **Heru** (**Horus/Jesus**). In this song I speak about **Kemet** (Egypt) being the birth place of **Martial Arts** as seen depicted on the walls of the Temple of Ramessu III in of **Luxor** (p 631). In that song I also say the names **Ptah, Imhotep, Rameses, Michael Jackson and Tupac**. In 2016 I would go on to write the most music I ever wrote in my life, writing around 101 rhymes. **Hekau** is what we called it in Kemet (Egypt), it means words of power (page iii). This is poetry like the stuff people sing at **church**. It is **spiritual** music because of where the music has **risen** from (**page 6**). It came from the muddy waters like the **lotus flower**. The act of creating the mixtape was like a rights of passage or an initiation or you could call it my **Opening of the Mouth Ceremony**. "I pledge allegiance to my family to write for what's right man fuck a Grammy, and a Oscar imposter, **O.D.B. Osiris** lyrically karate I chop ya, I saw it in a **dream, Michael Jackson** screaming out nothing can stop ya, he was with **Tupac** and **Toussaint** in a helicopter" - (**Ancient Future,** written on Feb 8th 2015 (page 321). Forget not the **Superman Curse** (page 202, 204).

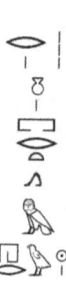

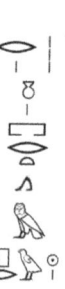

DAWUD ENTERED THE PHONE BOOTH
...AND HIS ANCIENT SOUL FRAGMENTS CAME FLYING OUT OF PRIMORDIAL DARKNESS.

The 25th Dynasty Mixtape

1 Dec 3rd RIP J Cooper
2 Hold Ya Head Remix
3 Keep Ya Head Up Aniya
4 Marshawn Lynch
5 Peace Maat
6 Reprise in The Sunshine Remix
7 Star of The Story
8 Synchronicities
9 The Light Mind
10 2000 Seasons
11 Flowers for J Dilla
12 Garvey on My Block
13 HalfTime
14 Fitness Scienz of Life
15 Ancient Future
16 Who Do U Believe In
17 Eternal Sunshine of The Spotless Mind
18 Blame Game Remix
19 Check The Rhime
20 These many Roads (RIP Michael Jackson)
21 Krazy Blakseeds (Tupac Remix)
22 Return From 2051 (The Force Awakens)
23 May 25th 190E
24 18th Dynasty
25 The Ballad Of SGT James Brown
26 Rays
Post- Eternal sunshine of the spotless mind
Post - RIP Tamir Rice

Rau nu Prt m heru

Iu f Per f m heru

Utterances for Coming Forth by day into Light

It is he, who comes forth by day into Light

December 28th 2015 **Eternal Sunshine of The Spotless Mind**

I miss you like that feel'n of being will'n to be up all night on the cell phone chill'n, I'm steal'n memories of a time, eternal sunshine of the spotless mind, is it a crime, is it a crime that I miss you? I'm write'n this rhyme but I rather be with you, do you remember the first time that I kissed you? love changes, life changes, and best friends become strangers, then they miss you

love changes, life changes, and best friends become strangers, then they miss you, love changes, life changes, and best friends become strangers then they say _baby you got what I need_, like **Biz Markie**, oh baby please, when they ask _I say she's **just a friend**, I say she's **just a friend**, oh baby you got what I need, and I say she's **just a friend** and I say she's **just a friend**,_ this heart break'n, heart race'n, breath taken so stop fake'n, I met this fast Jamaican when I was fifteen, everyday we did the same things, she was look'n for that uhhh but I was still a virgin, keep your souls clean, the idol mind is the devil's time, subdue the beast roam'n in a mans mind, the light mind, let your light shine, I miss you like that feel'n travel'n through the storm 96 will'n, now I'm steal'n back time _is it a crime_? **eternal sunshine of the spotless mind**, if a heart must be broken then you can break mine, and take mine _it's been designed and redesigned many times_ **- Dawud The Uncanny BlaKseed**

Significance

This was the first writing after my "**Opening of The Mouth Ceremony**". I always seemed to be falling for a woman. The first thing I would write after I finished all recording for 25 songs for 7 days straight. This was the first song I wrote after seeing the spirit of my Grand father on December 18th. I will never forget it! I know what I saw! I know what I experienced! While I was recording the last verse on the last song on December 25th 2014 my phone rang as soon as I said the name **Toussaint**! It was the Haitian woman I had met in the beginning of the month. I knew it was not just a coincidence! After I finished the process of recording the mixtape I began to write more frequently than ever before leading me to write over 90 songs in 2016.

Biz Markie passed away on July 16th 2021. My deepest condolences go out to his family, friends and fans. In this song I reference his most successful song "**Just a Friend**", which was released in 1989 the year of the **snake**. After **Biz Markie** passed, I wrote a song titled **Doors** on August 8th 2021. In the song I use a quote from his song **The Vapors**, released in 1988. When I went to edit the video for the song I thought to use footage of him from his video Vapors and to my surprise, he was wearing a **gold** chain with a **Tutankhaten** (**King Tut**) pendant in the video. I just laughed out loud because by this time in my journey these things didn't surprise me anymore. I had a moment with Biz and smiled as I edited the video. You can find the video on youtube if you search (TutemRA: **Doors**). In this song I also speak about the experience I had with **DMX** and **Anubis** on April 9th 2021 the day **DMX** passed away which is the day after Biz Markie's birthday.. The lyrics are, "rest in peace to **Biz Mark** transforming to vapors, and this is the season brothers getting more braver, when **DMX** died his soul came did me a favor, whispered in my ear said go ye there look through them papers! **Anubis** and the **afterlife** advice watch for them **gators**, **Maat** is precise in your life! you gotta watch your behavior! **- TutemRa** (August 8th 2021, page 658)

December 28th 2015 **One Love Remix**

We don't vibe no more but I ain't forget when we was poor, we was four in Rockaway, we used to play hide and seek in the street that shit is deep cause now we don't speak no more, I'm not sure where we went wrong, I **love** you so I'm write'n this song, I'm sorry **Saana** if my words did harm, I been work'n on my breath'n so I can be more calm, we had mad fun at 21 we'll be double that in a minute black, it's been a minute that we sit back and parlay and all I got is good things to say, from now until 93 million miles away, the suns' the rise and the falls, pass him the ball, **22**, 7, the crab to **Seven** the dad, the best friend I ever did have, life is good my nigga I finally spoke to my dad and I'm glad that I kept move'n life is a struggle gotta keep fight'n, I be quote'n **Marcus Garvey** cause of what he taught me, life is a struggle gotta fight your way through it, I don't **beef** cause **I don't eat meat** no more, and I don't watch the news cause all they gonna show you is war, remember uncle **Squeek**? Yeah, he don't drink no more, I take the food raw take the light right the core, float like a butter fly, strike right to the jaw, you might win some yeah but what was it for? We don't vibe no more because we off balance, I grew up in Rockaway Queens where I never learned about **dreams**, I hit the scene with my cousins and they would be thug'n, life ain't a game I take you down my memory lane, so many names, most of them be lost in my brain, flash back to the summer **Matmoo** and **Musunga**, rock fights **Timothy** chased me home at night, hard knock life drugs on the block like dice, if you had a father in the house that would've been nice, my nigga Ell, been in and out of jail through hell and back, hard to excel when you start inhale'n crack, ain't hard to tell that he fell on the wrong side of the tracks, he ain't have a **father** to reach him and teach him and spit the facts, in fact neither did I and sometimes I would cry, just me and my sisters, be a father to your child it shouldn't take a while to realize that they miss ya **- Dawud The Uncanny BlaKseed**

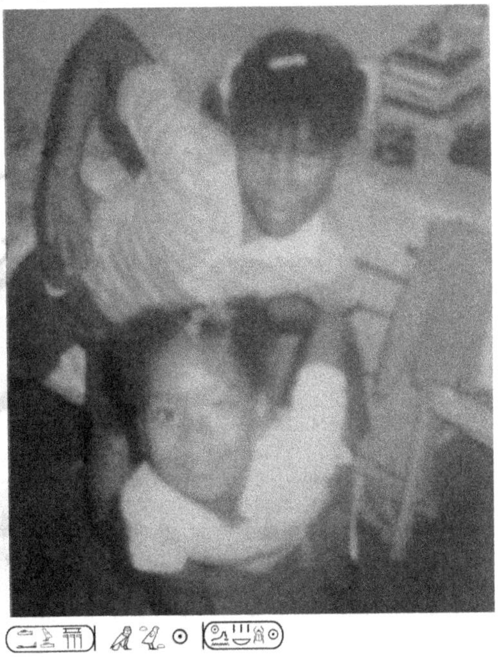

December 29th 2015 RIP TAMIR RICE

Shit is real **Tamir Rice** looked just like **Emmett Till,** my mother was born the same year he was killed, today it was cold here maybe **Tamir's soul** hears the injustice, maybe it's just us, maybe **MJ** was right! "they don't really care about us!", maybe we should fight without the guns they bust, maybe we should unite and try not to hate each other so much, who taught you to hate the color of yo skin? beauty is only skin deep, "who taught you to hate yourself from the top of yo head to the soles of yo feet?" when they cant control what you speak, and you don't bow down in defeat, they seek to destroy with deceit and diversion division, I'm not sure how long my flesh will be living, and even if I'm left in a prison every breath that I'm giving, I'm a be spit'n for my <u>*Souljas to be risen*</u>, **<u>Dead Souljas to be risen</u>**

Another New York **sky**, day **walker** like **blade**, sent another brother to his grave, lil homie b4 you pass away sp**ark** a blaze, I be a gigantic lunatic **sun kissed** bastard, a ghetto rascal **Malcolm** little, the **riddle** for the people, **The temple of man,** the good verse evil, the numbers of stars and sands, **The eagle, the feather of maat,** I see you on the news a lot, cops came out, shots rang out, I saw the boy shook and drop! what now? who got he juice now? who got the props? cops killing kids on the block and they not balancing **The Feather Of Maat - Dawud The Uncanny BlaKseed**

42 Laws of Maat, Page 367

<u>Significance</u>

In this song I say the words, " I'm a be spit'n for my <u>*Souljas to be risen*</u>, **<u>Dead Souljas to be risen".</u>** I would end this year saying the name **Emmett Till** for the fifth time in my music! At this point I had NO idea that I was **Emmett** in my past life! In fact after the murder of **Tamir Rice** and seeing the picture someone spliced together of the faces of **Emmett** and **Tamir** I began to think of **Emmett** every time I thought or **Tamir** and I thought of **Tamir** every time I thought of **Emmett.** At one point I even consider that **Emmett Till** had possibly come back here **reincarnated** as **Tamir Rice** just to get our attention. Never did I ever think I was Emmett Till until July 3rd 2018 <u>the year of the **dog**</u>, when I immediately, instantaneously in the blink of an eye knew I was Emmett Till (page 480)! This was written to the **Fat Joe 'The Shit is Real'** beat and shit is real when you write about **souljas being risen** and then year later you realize that you are the dead soulja that was risen!! **Fat Joe** is born on August 19th 1970 <u>the year of the **dog.**</u> He was born the day after my grandfather died (P 169), and he released this album on my nephew's birthday, July 27th 1993, which is two days after **Emmett Till's** birthday (starcode), July 25th 19**41**. (see page **41**)

December 29, 2015 at 2:02 PM

Just face it, I was kicked off Facebook because of some Gay Shit

Hi,

Thanks for reaching out to us, but unfortunately we can't confirm you're the owner of this account.

Please reply with a scan or photo of your government-issued identification that has your name and photo or name and date of birth.

If you're unable to provide your government-issued ID, please visit the Help Center to learn about the other types of ID we accept:

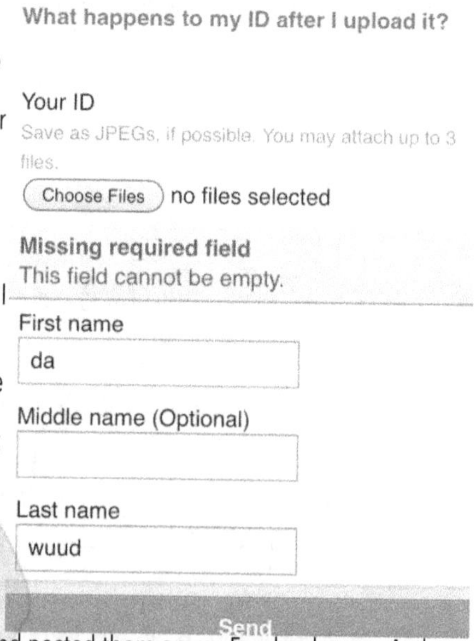
What happens to my ID after I upload it?

Your ID

Save as JPEGs, if possible. You may attach up to 3 files.

Choose Files no files selected

Missing required field

This field cannot be empty.

First name

da

Middle name (Optional)

Last name

wuud

Send

I can only speculate as to why I was kicked off Facebook but what I can tell you for sure is what transpired the days before I was asked to provide proof that I was the owner of my account. I had recently been communicating with a **gay** brother that I didn't know. He left a sexual comment under one of my pictures that I didn't like. Then he began to send me messages and instead of responding in anger I talked to him peacefully. Before I continue I think it's important to give context. At the time that my page was shut down I was 38 years old and I was not used to being hit on by men. I did not grow up with this as a normal experience so to me it was uncomfortable and ultimately it was sexual harassment. It seemed like ever since Obama became president in 2008 **gay** men had become more willing to pursue men, even if the men were not **gay**. Even the Army's laws had changed. When I was in the Army homosexuality was not acceptable but now it was allowed. In 2008 I was 31 and this is when I began to experience this behavior and I only encountered this via Facebook. Initially I did not respond well. I took screen shots of their messages and posted them on my Facebook page. At the time I did not realize how many men were **secretly gay** and how many people I was offending by sharing the private messages **gay** men were sending me. I had never had a problem with **gay** people before until **gay** men began to come on to me. As I stated, a Black brother who was friends on Facebook with some people I knew from my childhood, left a sexual comment under one of my pictures. Then he sent me private messages. Instead of responding in anger I began to talk to the brother. I started to tell him about African civilizations and what we brought to the world. I told him that being **gay** was his choice. I told him that he could live the life he wanted to but he should know that his lifestyle was not a lifestyle that we promoted in ancient African civilizations or at least there is no evidence of it. I told him that we honored the divine women by loving them and protecting them not by taking on their roles. Surprisingly the brother began to listen. At one point the brother thanked me for not verbally attacking or insulting him. He told me that I had made him contemplate **his lifestyle as a gay man. The next day Facebook shut my page down** and **I was asked to confirm that I was the owner of my account by replying with a scan or photo of a government identification card that has my name and a photo or name and birthdate. Annoyed and confused with this request I sent them a picture of the Nswt Bity (Pharaoh) Ramesses**. Perhaps they had not looked at the picture because my page was reopened but on January 1st of 2016 it was closed again and I was sent the same request. I responded by sending them a picture of **Malcolm X** wiping his eye with his middle finger and my page has been shut down ever since. It is important that the reader reads my experience with an unbiased mind. I do not have a record of attacking people for any reason and never have

Rau nu Prt m heru

Iu f Per f m heru

Utterances for Coming Forth by day into Light

It is he, who comes forth by day into Light

I attacked a person due to their sexual orientation. Given the sensitivity of the topic I will disclose all the encounters I have had with homosexuality in my life so that you can understand how my views have been shaped.

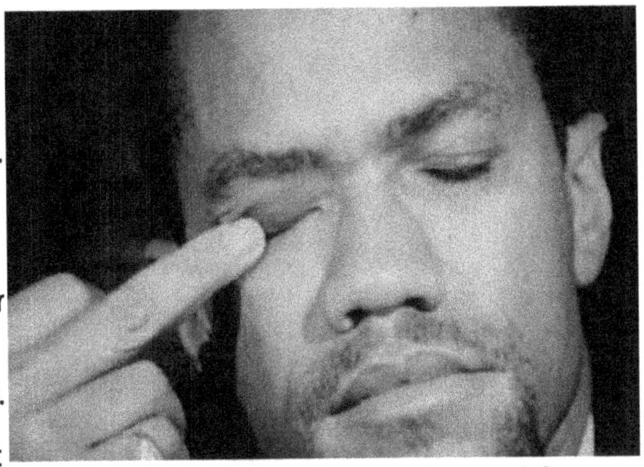

The Defense Advanced Research Projects Agency (**DARPA**) is a research and development agency of the united states department of defense, and is responsible for new technologies for use by the military. DARPA had a program called **LifeLog** and its goal was to track and log a persons entire life. Compiling a massive data base of every activity a person engages in. To include credit card purchases, websites visited, the conversations of telephone calls, e-mails sent and received, faxes, postal mail sent and received, instant messages sent and received, books and magazines read, television viewing habits and radio selections, frequently visited location tracked by GPS applications, even bio medical data. This info was collected to identify preferences, plans, goals and intentions of each person. The info was also aimed to be used as a way to predict the actions of people. The DARPA project was cancelled by the pentagon on **February 4th** 2004 due to concerns with privacy implications with this type of system. On that same exact day **February 4th** 2004 Facebook was launched online and interestingly enough some of the employees from LifeLog went to work at facebook. Rosa Parks was born on February 4th and in 1955 she refused to move from her seat for a white man on a bus in Montgomery, Alabama. Rosa Parks said, "I thought of **Emmett Till**, and I couldn't go back." her brave actions would help spark the first mass Civil Rights Movement.

My History With Homosexuality

As a men that is attracted to women the only way that I can meet women is to express my feelings to them. So I imagine that a **gay** man must do the same thing. Men that like men must at some point meet other men that like men. That's their choice. I can only speak for my experience. When I was a teen I can remember hearing the term "**gaydar**" like "radar". **Gaydar** was the ability for **gay** men or people to tell when a man or person was **gay** allowing them to make their advancement undetected by people who did not have the eyes to see. This term only existed because homosexuality was not a way of life that was promoted openly. Because I didn't have "**gaydar**" I could only see homosexuality in people if it was completely obvious like the instances I will detail below. Today, in 2021 homosexuality is seen as a normality in America and so, many people live openly **gay** or homosexual lifestyles that it would appear that many people were living secretive lives in the past. I'm not going to argue the rightness or wrongness of homosexuality I just want to express how I came to know about homosexuality and how I responded to it in each stage of my life. I am not a homosexual, nor have I ever wanted to be or felt the desire to try. I have the right to voice my opinion due to the fact that I myself have been a victim of **homosexual harassment** on several occasions. In this book I have been open and honest about my life and not all of it was easy to share, so as a man born of a man and a woman it is only natural for my mind to consider the same direction in which to bring forth the same action. I do not mean to judge or debate. I just mean to state my case, and tell my story about how I found out about homosexuality.

Where Are Those Little Boys Now?

I must have been around 7 or 8 years old when I first experienced homosexuality. It was a hot summer day. I was around the corner at the bodega on Almeda with some boys from my block when one of them flashed some money and said, "let's go to the **bay**, they're giving out money and candy". We ran off to the **bay** to see and when we got to the bay I saw something that I will never forget. I saw at least one White man with a group of three to five Black boys standing in a line in front of him with their private parts exposed. Then I saw the White man put his face near one of the boys private area - then immediately I started running.. Someone was behind me but I never looked back to see. I was the fastest boy on my block and I ran home as fast as I could. When I got to my porch no one else was there. I do not remember the other boys who were there with me. All I can remember is being at the bodega, then being at the bay, then seeing what I saw, then I remember running home. I made it home untouched and unmolested. I stopped going into the field to play after that! I never told anyone about this experience because I knew and felt I was in a place I shouldn't have been. That is the first time I ever saw something that was on the lines of homosexuality. There are many people who have a problem with connecting homosexuality with **pedophilia** but they are not doing a service to all the boys and girls who are molested and because of that experience with molestation, they now live lives that would be classified as **gay**, lesbian or homosexual etc. This experience didn't consciously affect me in my life. I forgot about the experience but sometime after the year 2000 I saw the movie **Hurricane Rubin Carter** on DVD. There was a scene in the movie that mirrors my experience and when I saw it the memory of what happened that summer day flashed over me. When I was around the same age I had a cousin who was different than the rest of the boys on the block. He played with the girls a lot. Today he is an openly **gay** man and is married to another man. When he first "came out" I asked him if he always knew he was **gay** and he said yes. I also asked him if he had been molested and he said no. I wondered if perhaps he was one of the boys with me that day or perhaps he had been lured to the field at another time but he says that he was never molested.

Rebirth in the Wrong Body?

I have a friend who has a daughter who was born a boy. Her daughter is now 25 years old and this is her story. When my friend was carrying her child the only thing she was concerned with was having a healthy baby. She noticed that the shape of her stomach reminded her of how it looked when she was pregnant with her daughter and so she felt like she was going to have another daughter but she never let the doctors tell her the gender of the child.. She purchased gender neutral clothes and waited till the child was born to know the gender. She went on to have a son but there was something different about her son. She noticed that the eyes of her son seemed strange. She thought perhaps he was autistic or feeling pain that he could not express. She took him to the doctor for a check up and the doctors told her that there was nothing wrong with him. When her son was one years old he never played with his toy cars, instead he took his sisters dolls and would only play with the girl toys. His father didn't like that he played with dolls. He told his wife that it would make him **gay**. His father would tell him that boys don't play with dolls, they play with trucks. As he grew older he became withdrawn and never play with other boys. He became the quiet kid and developed a fascination with long hair and would play with girls hair. He would even put a towel around his head and pretend it was his hair. His mother thought he had these female traits because he was around her and his sister a lot. When her son was around 8 years old one of her male friends told her that her son was gay but she refused to see it. When her son was in the 7th grade he got hit by a car, and afterwards he had to have therapy because he had anxiety issues when crossing streets. In these therapy sessions his sexual orientation came to the surface. The therapist asked my friend how she would feel if one of there children were **gay**. She said she would love her child no matter what! In Jr high school her son began to ask her if he was **gay**. She didn't know what to say so she told him that **gay** meant happy and if he was happy then he was **gay**. He got drawn into the fashion world and began to dress eccentric. In high school he came out as **bi sexual**. At 17 she through him a party and he invited all his friends. To his mothers surprise all his friends were **transexual** and **gay**. His friends thanked her for making them all feel comfortable but afterwards cried because now she saw the extent of her sons lifestyle. He was not **bi sexual** he was **gay** and only liked other men. After graduation he completely changed his persona to a female. He went to a psychologist and legally got the right to change his sex. He is now a she and lives the life of a women but has not gone through with transitioning. Why did I tell this story? Because I don't have all the answers and some people feel like they are trapped in the wrong body.

Boy Scout

When I was 12 I was a Boy Scout for around a year while living in Columbus Georgia (page 49). I was the only Black boy in my group. I was a Mormon for one year when my mother was struggling financially. The church paid our bills and gave us food and the church had a boy scout program. During the wilderness survival event we went for an over night trip in the woods. I can remember having fun. We played capture the flag and no one could catch me. They were all very slow. I remember taking a shower at night in the cold, naked with boys and the men and I never forget the feeling of being watched like I was the center of attention.

My Friends Little brother

Around the same age, In Georgia I had a friend who's little brother seemed different. He was very soft & feminine. I always treated him nice. I never teased or picked on him but I always wondered why he was like that.

High School, Football and Senior Dress Up Day

Prior to my experience playing football it was never normal for a man to touch your butt however somehow when your uniform is on and you're on the football field it became ok to be patted on the butt and to pat your teammates on the butt. The same way that you might pat a dog or a horse. I never thought anything about this while playing football. I only thought about this after I was years removed from the sport. When you start a play in the sport of football, most of the time one man bends over (the center) in front of another man (the quarter back) and the oval shaped ball is pass to the quarter back who's hands are near the other mans oval balls. I called my friend Angel recently, we played high school football together (P 63). I asked him if he remembered the **hazing** that was done on our team by the seniors to the rookies. I don't know who started this hazing ritual but as I think back on it it disturbs me. Angel remembered the hazing but he never took part in it. The seniors used to grab the rookies and hump them. This was only done in fun and the hump didn't last long, only a few seconds but it was done to the rookies. Everyone got a laugh out of it. Because I was one of the star players it was never done to me but I think I may have done it to a rookie before. These are things I don't like to think about and one of the things that bother me the most is the dress I wore for senior dress up day. I didn't have an outfit planned for the senior dress up day and somehow I thought the most outlandish thing to do was to wear a dress. Perhaps it was the fact that I was made socially acceptable to do as a joke because of **Martin Lawrence's** character **Shanaynay** and **Jamie Foxx's** character **Wanda** from the show **In Living Color**. I was smart enough not to wear the dress out of the house. I put it on when I got to school. I was surprised to see the other males who had decided to wear dresses as well. The strange thing is, most of the males that wore the dresses were athletes. 6 of the males in this picture played a sport. 4 of us were on the football team and two were on the basket ball team. In our defense there was one girl who dressed up like a boy but there was no real shock value in her baggy jeans outfit. Sometimes I look at this picture and I wonder why we all thought this was ok and why we thought it was funny? I wonder how the other men in the picture feel about this picture? This was before the eyes of the world were opened with cell phones & internet. This picture was taken in 1996 and the world was the same back then but it was still very different because homosexuality was hidden behind the veil, only showing it's face in jokes and in the world of homosexuality that stayed hidden in the closet. In 1999 Mike Ditka (a White man) and his new NFL Draft pick Ricky Williams (a Black man) posed for the cover of the ESPN magazine. Williams wore a female wedding gown while Ditka wore a male tuxedo. We had two boys in my high school who we all thought were **gay** but it was never confirmed. They never said they were but most of us figured they were. I can only speak for myself but I never treated either of them bad. Joshua was Black and Kenny was White. I have not seen Joshua since high school but I used to see Kenny on facebook and he is now a very openly **gay** man.

College

In college there were two "openly" **gay** men on campus. One was Black and one was White. One day I encountered them both while on my way to class. I was into working out and I was just getting used to building muscles so I would wear shirts that were tight and showed my physique. While on my way to class I passed one of the men and he winked at me, I gave him a strange look because I had never experienced being winked at by a man. No more than a minute later I happened to cross paths with the other **gay** man and he made a sound when he saw me. The type of sound than men make when they see a woman they like. When he did that I screamed out very loud, "what the fuck is up with all these faggots?!" that was the only time in my life that I ever call a **gay** man a faggot. I went to class and I don't ever remember seeing them again.

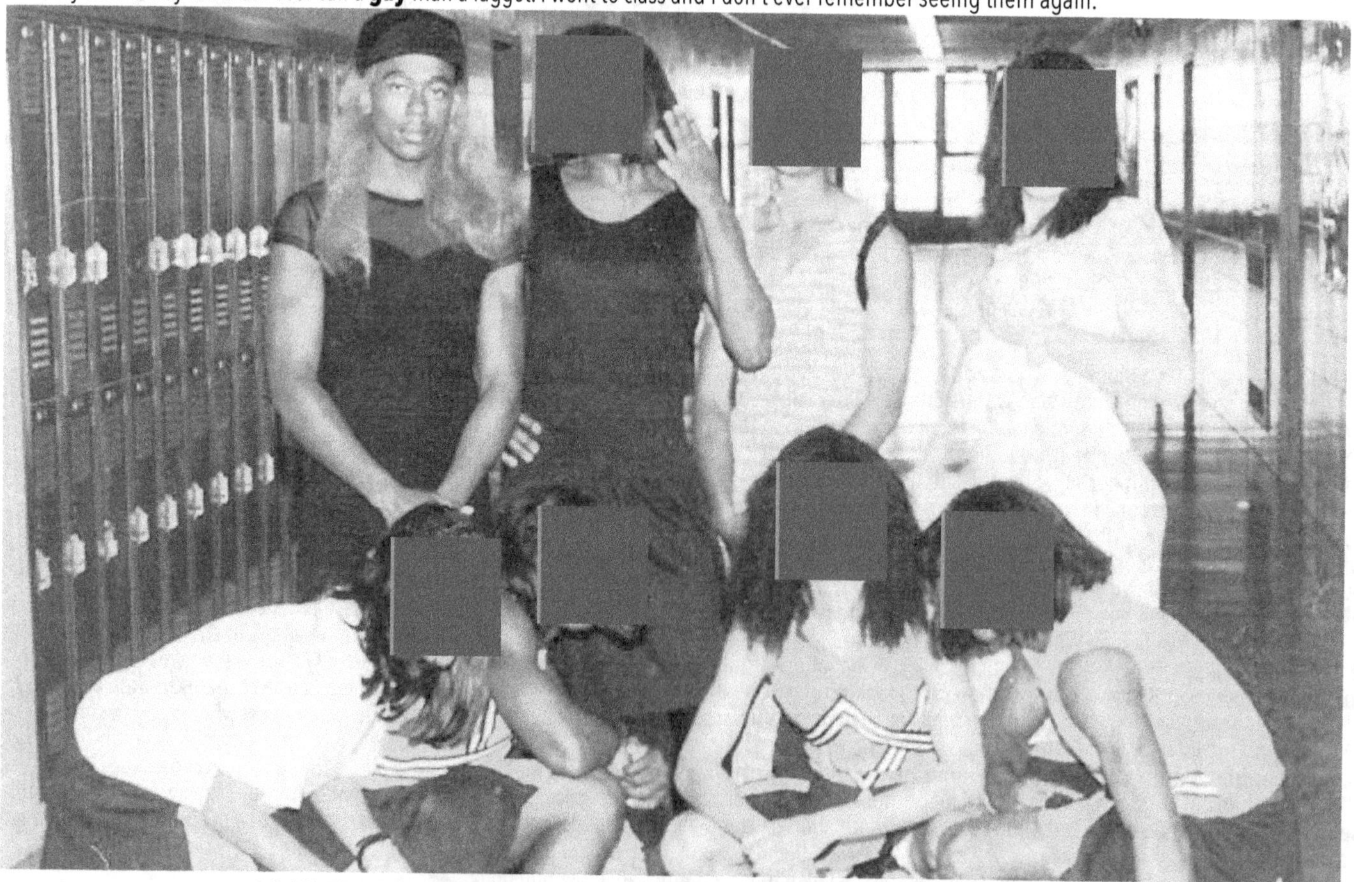

Army

When I joined the Army I was not looking at the Army laws but apparently the Army Laws on Homosexuality were "don't ask don't tell". I never gave that much thought because of course it didn't apply to me but when I think about it now it sounds like it was ok to be **gay**, but it was not ok to talk about it. My first squad leader at my first duty station was **gay**. She never said it but you could tell. Her name was Sgt Carter. She was a southern woman with a gold tooth who was happy about just being promoted to Sgt. I was her first soldier but I wasn't the ideal soldier for a female that was playing the role of a man. She was the masculine type of lesbian. In the Army people can become rank heavy when they get promoted. So since I was her new soldier she was working extra hard exercising her authority to prove she was the "one in charge". I never tried her authority but I think she had a problem with me because all the Chain of Command liked me. I was soldier of the month, soldier of the quarter and soldier of the year. I was the most fit soldier in the unit but for some reason she didn't like me. At the time I had no idea why she didn't like me but as I sit her at 44 years old I can deduce that I was the soldier she wanted to be. There were other people in my unit that were **gay** and I never had a problem with them. Specialist Higgins was **gay** but I never had a problem with him. Of course he never said he was but we all knew he was. He only hung out with the women and he spoke like a gay man. There was also another female in my unit who was **gay**, she never said she was either but we knew she was. I forgot her name but we were cool. Other than that I was unaware of anyone else who might have been **gay**. I never bothered **gay** people and so it didn't matter to me who was **gay** or not.

Rau

nu

Prt

m

heru

Personal Training

I encounter more **gay** people in personal training than any other place in my life. I trained many **gay** men and a few **gay** women. I trained men who were openly **gay** and men who never spoke of their orientation but seemed **gay**. I never treated any of them different because of their lifestyle. I can even say that a few of my **gay** clients were some of the hardest working clients that I've ever had. Developing a nice body was crucial for most of my **gay** clients. Just like the other places I traveled in my life I treated all people with equal respect. I picked those ethics up in the army, treating all people the same regardless of their rank, sex, age or race. In this case however, my **gay** clients paid me money so of course why would I treat them bad and most of my **gay** clients paid me the most I had ever been paid in my life and they paid me with no questions and no problems. One of my **gay** clients would buy packages of 20 to 30 sessions at $120 per session, and this guy was actually the funniest guy I ever trained. He would always tell funny jokes and he would even tell me about the wild things he would do. He was a **gay** version of me really, but worse. He once lost the key to his apartment and when the lock smith came, they… He was once on the way to work and saw a construction worker, he went into the construction site with him and…. I asked him if he was ever molested as child and he told me he wasn't. He just always knew he was different. He said that as a child he was very flexible and he would orally please himself. I listened to his stories and never judged him and it never bothered me because I was the trainer in the gym that was chasing all the women. I was out in the clubs looking to do the same things he did, I just did them with women. I didn't judge him. That was his lifestyle and I had mine. I worked at Crunch in soho and many members of the gym were **gay**. And it never bothered me. I was friends with many of the **gay** members, actually I was friends with all the members in the gym. I was happy there. I was making the most money I had made in my life so peoples **gay** life didn't matter to me. I once met a trainer at New York Sports club in Harlem, this was around 2008 when I was making a lot of money in training. He was always nice to me and always had a smile on his face. When ever I saw him in the streets he would say hi. After homosexuality became more open in the world around 2010 he seemed to be **gay**. One day I asked him if he was and he said he was **bi sexual**. I asked him if he was always this way. He told me no! He said he was **drugged** and taken advantage of and ever since, it has been a part of his lifestyle. He now works in fashion.

Iu

f

Per

f

m

heru

D. Case

I know a man who was adopted and never knew his patents. You look at him and see a white man but he doesn't know his biological background. When he was a boy he was lured into a house by a man and **drugged**. When he woke up he was on a bed with his pants being taken off. His sympathetic nervous system triggered allowing him to over power the man and escaped.. He is not **gay**.

Tee on Mars

I met Mars on July 1st 2018 (page 474) and when I heard the voice in my head that told me to walk away and you will meet a beautiful woman, I was led to Mars. Mars is a very important key to my past life revelation as you will come to see 3 years from 2015 she will be instrumental in my first past life revelation. She is a **gay** woman and I love her like a sister. I am friends with her and her partner. I love and care for her and her partner. I was the first man to lay hands on Mars in many years when I became her massage practitioner. I was 40 years old when we met and we have been friends for 4 years. I went to the extent with my experiences with homosexuality because it is a topic that is very sensitive in this day and time. I have had the conversation about homosexuality with Mars and with her partner. I seek to understand people and how they work I do not seek to shame, shun or ridicule people. I tell people the story of how I met Mars often but never can they feel it like Mars and I do because we experienced it. Just before we made eye contact on July 1st 2018 she **heard a voice** that told her to look up. I had heard the voice moments earlier telling me to walk away and I would meet a beautiful woman. When she looked up we made eye contact, them boom, we met like a mysterious trance. My experiences with homosexuality are not here to cause pain or to emit bigotry. I share them because I feel like there is an agenda being pushed in the world that even some gay people do not agree with.

Utterances

for

Coming

Forth

by day

into

Light

My Views On Homosexuality

I must ask myself, would I be a different person if I had been molested at 7 or 8 years old by that white man at the bay.. I bring that up because not all **gay** people are created the same. I have come across people who feel they are born **gay** and some people who took on that lifestyle due to an experience they had. Remember the **bisexual** brother I met in 2011 (page 203) who came to help me with acting lessons for my Tupac biopic audition? When he came to my place he was comfortable enough to tell me that he was **molested** by someone when he was a boy. He also told me that he had tried to stop living that lifestyle before. Interestingly enough in the year 2019 I saw that this brother was now **happily married** living a **heterosexual lifestyle**. This is my experience meeting people who call themselves **gay** (or any of the other terms). I have also come across research from the biologist **Tyrone Hayes** that details how the pesticide **Atrazine** disrupts the **endocrine system** effecting our **hormones**, even to the point of making some **male animals mate with other male animals** (see page 426). It is a fact that if **gay** men only dealt with **gay** men and **gay** women only dealt with **gay** women they would never be able to naturally have children. With all these variables it does make me wonder if it is a natural phenomena. I really don't know. I know that I am not **gay**. I go the way of ancient Kemet and I do not see it in the teachings of Kemet. I have a few issues with homosexuality though. It is common knowledge that this government promoted homosexuality in the Black community to break up the Black family structure. One example was the practice of "**buck breaking**" during slavery in America. Many of the slave plantations were ran by White men who raped the men, women and the children. **So that means, White gay men enslaved, imprisoned and raped Black people, or White men that engaged in homosexual behavior enslaved, imprisoned and raped Black people**. Black people were prisoners of war and still to this day we are housed in prisons at the highest rates and the biggest fear men have of the penal system (prison system) is being raped. I have family members and friends who are **gay** so I do not mean to offend anyone but remember this when you are fighting for your **gay** rights. There has never been a lynch mob terrorizing the population of **gay** people. Yet **gay** people seem to have some sort of ticket allowing them to receive benefits that Black people have not even been able to receive. Those are my thoughts. If you're **gay** cool, be **gay** but don't you come to me talking about being oppressed when black people get killed everyday for being Black. You can hide your **gayness** but Black people can't hide being Black. And like I said, **gay** White men enslaved and imprisoned Black people and those White men raped Black men, Black boys, Black women and Black girls. That can never be undone. Further more, homosexuality was seen as a mental disorder in American history up until 1973. The diagnostic and statistical manual of mental disorders (**DSM**) had **homosexuality** listed as a **mental disease**. This is what this system deemed to be the truth. However in 1973 homosexuality was **voted** out of the DSM as a mental disorder and the lifestyle was then promoted in the Black community. How many of the people

It is

he,

who

comes

forth

by day

into

Light

who voted were **gay**? We will never know because you can hide your **gayness** but you can't hide your Blackness. Remember this is not an attack on your way of life. Live how you please but your cultural liberties end at my doorstep. I act in the spirit of **Bes**, the kemetic deity with leonine features who had traditionally been a protector of households and eventually became the defender of everything good & enemy to everything bad.

Temple of the spiritual initiates, Khunum en Ankh and Khunum Hotep, Saqqara

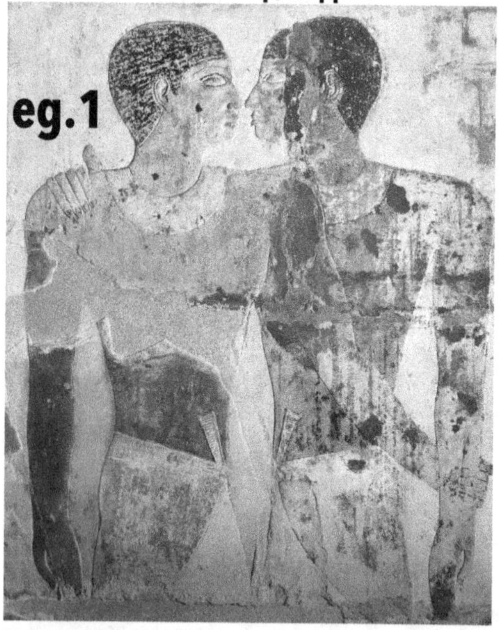

Ptah breaths divinity (Sekhem / life force energy) into the Nswt Bity

(***ADDENDUM***) In Saqqara, the same area that the temple of **Unas** is found, with the pyramid text (resurrection text) written on the walls (p 670), we find the Temple of the two spiritual initiates, **Khunum en Ankh** and **Khunum Hotep**. In the temple the two initiates are seen embracing with their noses very close and lips almost touching (**eg.1**). Many people claim the images seen on the walls are proof of a same sex (homosexual) relationship. This notion can be rendered invalid without reading the walls inside this temple if one were to read the **42 laws of Maat** (p 367), where one of the laws clearly states, "**I have not lusted, committed fornication, or laid with others of my same sex**". This was one of the laws that all the people of Kemet (Egypt) had to live by, especially initiates into the great mysteries. I have come to understand that the temple of **Khunum en Ankh** and **Khunum Hotep** was a path of initiation. The writings on the walls detail both paths. The path of **Khunum Hotep** was uniting with the opposites, which meant to dissolve the opposites. And the path of **Khunum en Ankh** was the secrets of joining with the mystery of life, the path to immortality. Both paths lead to the same destination. When the two initiates are seen with their noses very close and lips almost touching, they are breathing divinity (**Sekhem** / life force energy) into each other. What you are seeing is advanced, high level breath work. No different than images seen with the NTCHRS (deities/gods) embracing and breathing divinity (**Sekhem** / life force energy) into the Nswt Bity's (pharaohs). In the image above (**eg. 2**), the Ntchr **Ptah** is seen embracing and breathing divinity into the Nswt Bity (pharaoh). When Khunum en Ankh and Khunum Hetep are seen embracing they are doing the same thing. What Ever they can do with Ptah they can do with each other because man and women are immortal Ntchrs (gods and goddesses). **Akhenaten** and **Nefertiti** can also be seen in stela's breathing divinity into their children. In the tomb of my wet nurse Maia, she can be seen on the wall doing the same thing to me (p 670). Because of the state of the world today there is much confusion when dealing with touch. As a massage practitioner I have come to see how out of touch we are when it comes to extending care and attention to each other. As we move into our divinity, which is our birthright, we will put aside all habits that don't align with **Maat** (p 367).

The Odd Never Ending story (page 669)

It's **ODD** that Tony Randall from the Odd Couple looks like Harvey Milk, the first openly **gay** man to be elected to public office in California. It's even odder that in many episodes of the Odd Couple Tony's character Felix is seen offering people glasses of milk to drink. We know now how insalubrious cows milk is to the human body. Harvey Milk died the day after King Tut's tomb was opened (page 11), the year after I was born. Today is **Feb 17th** 2022, **Huey P Newton's** birthday and the day **Khalid Muhammad** was assassinated, and I just so happened to watch an episode of **The Odd Couple** today. The theme music is nostalgic and it takes me back to my adolescence. Someone in my house used to watch the show when I was a child so I don't remember the show too clearly I just remember the theme music. I started watching the series on Hulu in the beginning of Feb 2022 and I found that I actually like the show. I find it funny and entertaining. The episode today took me right back to this portion of my book. The character Oscar mentions that 10 of the New York Jet's **football players** were going to **put on dresses** (P 353) and imitate the New York City Rockets (female dancers). As soon as I heard that I paused the episode in disbelief. Then I wondered, what date did this episode air. I googled, **[The Odd Couple first season, episode 19]** and it aired on my great great grand father **General Dukes'** birthday (Feb **19th**), the same year he died, 1971. So I have **a couple** of revolutionaries, one born on **Feb 17th** and one assassinated on **Feb 17th**. I have **a couple** of grand fathers named General Dukes (pages 19, 23). I have the **Odd Couple** talking about athletes in dresses and I have a picture from high school where members of the football team and the basketball team wore dresses (p 353). All of these variables tell me that this should be ad**dress**ed. There's a pattern going on and a message sent from the dead. **There is systematic plan to have men wear dresses just as Dave Chappell suggested** and my grand fathers, **General Dukes Sr** and **General Duke Jr** as well as **Khalid Muhammad** and **Huey P Newton** have made their voices heard in this matter.

December 30th 2015 Check The Rhime Black Cop

Back in the days when all of y'all was children, *pledging allegiance to a flag in the building, he* grew up became a **cop** and a **cop** killed him, it's sad, but this is just the routine! **Black cop** with out his badge yeah they shooting!! ***black cop, black cop black cop black cop***!!! I could have been a **black cop**! but I'll be damned if I up and leave the have nots! and give a ticket to a sister on her last drop! and shoot my brother then watch a cracker sprinkle crack rock! and this is not a funky rhyme about how nice I am! but tell your mother tell you father send a telegram! **I energize the suns energy and then I transform!** ***A Tribe Called Quest, Check The Rhime*** as I latch on, *you on point homie?! we gotta stand strong! You on point homie?! you gotta stand strong!* you see my aura's positive I don't promote no junk but when they shoot my homie down what the fuck they really want us brothers to do or say?! the games they play! you know and I know we need a better way!! political rule number 4000 and 80, police, judges and lawyers are shadyyyy, so people watch ya back cause I think they selling the crack! I don't doubt it, look at how they act! and if knowledge is the key then I'm a put it in a **wrap** for my **Negus** the **Lord Of The Perfect Black!** I take you back to the days of Rockaway, Hamels, Gateway, how much more do I have to say? my reaction to pressure, sizzles the retina how far must we go to gain respect?! Um, well it's kind of simple just protect your own or you'll be crazy sad and alone - **Dawud The Uncanny BlaKseed**

January 2016
The Opening Of The Mouth Ceremony

Rau nu Prt m heru

Iu f Per f m heru

In the picture on the right, the Nswt Bity (Pharaoh) Tutankhaten (**King Tut**) is receiving the Opening of The Mouth Ceremony. This ceremony was a ritual done to symbolize the **expansion of the consciousness** of the "dead" Pharaoh in the **afterlife**. In 2016 I would write **101** rhymes 𓋹𓋹, the most that I ever wrote in one year in my entire life. 3 times more than what I averaged in any other year between the years of 2010 and 2020. 2016 is the year of my "Opening of The Mouth" Ceremony. I title 2015 as the year of the **Ghost**, it was also the Chinese year of the **goat** (p 315), the same Chinese year that Emmett Till had been murdered in back in 1955. In 2015 I had many experiences with the unseen world. **These experiences expanded my consciousness**. It started on January 30th 2015 (p 318) when I became aware of my guardian angel who guards my door. Surely she had been there protecting me the many times that I almost died in this life. On June 18th of 2017 (p 449) I would write a song title The Illustrious One, in which I tell a story about a spirit coming to a man and telling him about his **previous lives** and telling him that she was his daughter in a **previous life** but now she's his protector. Here are some of the lyrics - "in your **past life** *I was your daughter* now I'm your protector, I came to offer insight on your **dreams** of saucers and serendipity, there's so much more left for you to see, like your great great grand mother standing next to me". On May 15th 2015, I would have an experience with the soul of **Sgt James Brown** and the legendary musician **James Brown** (p 331). On June 10th 2015 I would have an experience with the soul of **LaVena Johnson**, the next day I would have the same experience with the soul of **Kalief Browder** (p 334). 2015 would be the second year in a row that I had an experience on Dec 3rd with someone dying or with someone who was dead and in 2015 it was **Sean Price** (p 345). This December 3rd pattern started with **Jay Cooper** on Dec 3rd in 2014 (p 312). After Jay Cooper died I wrote him a song and in the song I said these words - "They can kill us and bury us but we the BlaKseeds, **So we'll be back maybe in the weeds,** Like dandelions I ain't lying, I be iron like a lion, mothers be crying when they see their sons shot down like **Orion,** I was crying when I got the scoop about my homie **J Coop,** Rest In Peace we lost a good man to say the least". Jay Cooper would come to me through a baby at a holiday party on Dec 17th 2014 (p 314). In 2016 it was **Tupac** (p 431) and in 2017 it was **Dr Felder** (p 457), the father of my friend Nova. This December 3rd pattern started in 2014 at the house of a **female** friend named **Nova** (p 314) and it ended in 2017 on December 3rd with the death of **Dr Jack Felder** the father of a **male** friend named **Nova** (p 571). In 2022 I would come to know that the pattern actually started with a **ghost** from 1955 (page 519). One of the last songs I wrote in 2015 I would say the name **Emmett Till** marking the 5th time I said his name in my music prior to the revelation (p 351). On Dec 29th I wrote a song to the **Fat Joe**, Shit Is Real beat and in the song I say the words, "shit is real **Tamir Rice** looked just like **Emmett till**, my mother was born the same year he was killed, today it was cold here **maybe Tamir's soul hears** the injustice, maybe it's just us, maybe **MJ** was right! they don't really care about us!". **2015 ended with my dead Grand Father appearing to me as a spirit** on Dec 18th 2015 (p 348) immediately after I finished building my recording booth! After I finished the process of recording my first mixtape I began to write more frequently. The Ghost year of 2015 would set the stage for 2016, the year of my **Opening Of The Mouth Ceremony**. Making the 25th Dynasty Mixtape was an initiation as I would write **101** rhymes 𓋹𓋹, three times more than I had ever written in one year.

Utterances for Coming Forth by day into Light

It is he, who comes forth by day into Light

Amen Hotep III (Colossi of Memnon)

Pictured on the right I am seen in April of 2022, standing in front of a giant statue of Amen Hotep III, erroneously known as the Colossus of **Memnon** (pages 7, 58, 210, 336, 389, 469, 638).

January 2nd 2016 - Dr Frances Cress Welsing Goes West.

Welsing was born Frances Luella Cress in Chicago on March 18th 1935. Her father, Henry N. Cress, was a physician, and her mother, Ida Mae Griffen, was a teacher. In 1957, she earned a B.S. degree at Antioch College and in 1962 received an M.D. at Howard University. While Welsing was an assistant professor at Howard University she formulated her first body of work in 1969, The Cress Theory of Color-Confrontation and self published it in 1970. **22** years later she released **The Isis Papers**: **The Keys to the Colors**, a compilation of essays she had written about global and local race relations. The name "The Isis Papers" was inspired by an ancient Egyptian Goddess. **Isis** (**Auset**) was the wife of the most significant Egyptian God **Ausar** (**Osiris**). In this book she talks about the genocide of people of color globally, along with issues Black people in the United States face. Welsing explains that the genocide of people of color is caused by White people's inability to produce melanin which is a civilizing agent stimulated by the sun. She also tackled issues such as drug use, murder, teen pregnancy, infant mortality, incarceration, and unemployment, in the Black community. According to Welsing, the cause of these issues is her definition of racism (white supremacy). She attributed AIDS and addiction to crack cocaine and other substances to "chemical and biological warfare" by White people. The minority status of Whites has caused what she calls a preoccupation with **White genetic survival**, and Black men are at the center of her discussion as she explains how Black men have the greatest potential to cause White genetic annihilation via procreation with White women. Racism and white supremacy are synonymous and Welsing defines **racism** as "the local and global power system dynamic, structured and maintained by those who classify themselves as White; whether consciously or subconsciously determined; this system consists of patterns of perception, logic, symbol formation, thought, speech, action and emotional response, as conducted simultaneously in all areas of people activity: economics, education, entertainment, labor, law, politics, religion, sex, and war. The ultimate purpose of the system is to ensure white genetic survival and to prevent white genetic annihilation on Earth." Welsing was against White supremacy and what she saw as the emasculation of Black men and she felt that homosexuality among African-Americans was a ploy by White males to decrease the Black population, arguing that the emasculation of the Black man was a means to prevent the procreation of Black people. Welsing believed that this is one of the goals of racism (white supremacy). She explains how injustice caused by racism will end when "non-White people worldwide recognize, analyze, understand and discuss openly the **genocidal dynamic**. In 2022 the Supreme Court is potentially going to overturn the 1973 landmark Roe v. Wade abortion law. This is happening because the White birthrate is declining. This further proves that what Dr Frances Cress Welsing was teaching is the truth.

Significance

On my quest for truth, on my path towards Kemet I came across the book **The Isis Papers** by Dr Frances Cress Welsing. I purchased the book but never read it from cover to cover. I watched many of her lectures on youtube. On March 1st 2015 I would fall asleep listening to one of her interviews. During this interview she explained how birds are smart enough to build a nest before they lay their eggs. And when I woke up the next day I would write the song **Goddess** (page 321).

"She been abuse, molested, betrayed, thrown shade, and used for sex and left to raise, a nation that won't behave, The **Goddess** giving birth to the grave, The **Eve** of creation, The **oracle** the **sage,** The **Black Madonna, Build your nest before you lay a egg, Don't rush to be a momma**" - **(Goddess - written on March 2nd 2015,** page 321**)**

Condolences

My condolences go out to the family of Dr Frances Cress Welsing and all those who fought against this system of racism and white supremacy. Please know that death is not the end. The soul survives death, indeed and in spirit. This is a book of the dead written by a boy who was murdered without justice, who defeated death and came forth by day. May the soul of **Dr Frances Cress Welsing** walk peacefully through the field of Reeds in Amenta. Amen RA.

January 2nd 2016 Auset Be The Asset (1st of 101)

Rau nu Prt m heru

True love is being in the midst of temptation, **The blakseed** saving his seed no wasting, patiently waiting for my Queen, I'm behaving, cause she the only one, no other one I'm craving, loving laden, sweetness I'm tasting, watching the **sun rise** on vacation, **Auset** be the **asset**, **Ausar** be the **star**, I said **Auset be the asset, Ausar be the star**, she's the twinkle in my eye in the sky so far, my true love do you know who you are? you are my everything, you satisfy my need, see I was searching for a real love like **Mary J,** But that type of love you don't find everyday, and that's word to **Method Man,** nothing make a man feel better than a woman, not a hundred grand, or a hundred on an exam, you can search the land and not find one worth a damn, that's why I'm hanging on to your love like **Sade,** I cherish the day that you walked past my way on the **Pharcyde,** *"The dopest Ethiopian",* she had me opening the **Ankh** fallopian, soaking in, lotioning her feet feet, her neck neck, her back, do for me and I do it right back, **Auset** be the asset, **Ausar** be the star, she's the twinkle in my eye In the sky so far, my true love do you know who you are, you are my everything you satisfy my every need

Like **Prince Hakeem** one day I'm a find my **Queen,** but, I ain't really trying to buy no ring cause, money can't buy me love love, and I don't do what every body does does, when doves cry, true love rise, when the thin line between love and hate divides, look into my eyes and see that I'm true, you do for me and I do for you, I ride for you you ride for me, only time can tell we gonna have to see, twin flame parallel never atrophy, you my **Queen** I'm your **King** we the majesty, my heart sting when I fien for you tragically, then you call me cause we connected naturally, they all see the electric we **emit magic**ally, erect a temple like **Ramoses** did for **Nefertari** - **Dawud The Uncanny BlaKseed**

Meta Mysterious Encounter with Melanie. Divine Patterns - Sing-Natures

Iu f Per f m heru

It was in the early evening and I was crossing the street to go to the supermarket. when I got to the other side I would make eye contact with a woman and immediately we began to speak to each other. There was a sense of comfortability. We introduced ourselves , her name is Melanie. She was a Dominican sister. We talked for a bit and in the short chat I would find out that she knew a Dominican brother named **Carlos** that I had gone to college with and him and I were born on the same day **October 25th (page 75)**. I think Knowing the same person allowed us to open up more. I noticed she had fitness gear on so I spoke to her about personal training. We exchanged info and I started training her soon after. I would train her for a little over a year then she would take a break from training. Her and I would stay in contact via social net working from time to time. In January of 2021 I would see a post on her page about her birthday. She was born on November 26th the day **King Tut's** tomb was opened (page 11). I saw the sign, the signature. The circle would be complete. Circles don't complete if you don't pass the test, or earn it.

Januaru 6, 2016 RealEyez

Utterances for Coming Forth by day into Light

Above all these governmental enemies, my niggas can't get jobs because of fenolies, so they rob and dodge cops high off of Hennessy, tell me what's the remedy? Smai Tawi **Nefertiti** on the tittie 50 niggas probably, rest in peace to **Yaki Kadafi** and **Pac** he was probably in the booth with me, real eyez see real lies and if you give yourself half a try to can really rise - **Dawud The Uncanny BlaKseed**

January 2016 RIP Sean Price

"Some say Sean Price is nicest on mic devices pack power witch makes me more mightier than Isis"

It is he, who comes forth by day into Light

This is for **P,** a toast, probably most under rated now you a **ghost**, when I was young you gave me that dose of medicine, that **Therapy** now Hip Hop is dead again, a legacy ***I resurrect*** *again* left with the best of them, say what up to **Pac, Pun** and **Biggie, Phif Dog** tell **Ruck** that **Rock** dropped **Therapy** at the **20th** anniversary, Searching the itinerary the **spirit** tells me I'm supposed to be here certainly like **Makaveli 7 day Theory, PNC,** my first CD ever bought with working money was **Nocturnal,** *"Heads ain't ready grab the original guns and machetes, I pin that ass to the grass like I was teddy",* **Allah** wasn't ready for you, what **Jesus Christ** said, "I know you a super star **Price** but I'm not gonna beg, I tell you like I tell your brothers, I'll break arms arms legs, They call you **Ruck** but you'll get stuck if you don't **Duck Down** bow and appease us", so **Sean Price** went to hell for snuff'n **Jesus, Sean P! - Dawud The Uncanny BlaKseed**

Meta Spiritual Significance

This song came about due to an experience I had with the spirit of Sean Price on December 3rd 2015 (p, **345**). In this song I say the words, "**I resurrect again**".. This was two years before my first past was revealed (page 480). The first album I purchased with my own working money was **Nocturnal**, the debut album from **Heltah Skeltah**. It wasn't till the **revision** of this book that I realized that the album **Nocturnal** was released on June 18th 1996, the same day my great grand mother Leacola **Riddle** died (p 21). The song, Sean Price off the **Nocturnal** album was my favorite song on that album and for the first time, on Aug 9th 2022, I realized that Sean Price said the name **Isis** (p 2, 267, 357, 374, 481,505, 672) in that song!!

January 9th 2016 ☥ **Timing**

It's all about time, all about timing, met a Queen she was fine, now I'm here rhyming, I had this scene in my mind, her numbers were divine, like the sun reflecting on the moon blooming divine time and space, her face she showed, then she ran like a race, but I'm not with the chase, time is of essence, we talked and walked to a place ate then said grace, **Mind Sex** no embrace more than a hug, the curious case of a thug searching for love, I used to **Get Around,** now my vibration can be found above the ground, she said it sounds like you're lying, her heart still crying, couldn't get pass her past to be free at last, that was the last time I saw her, somebody send this letter to **Cinderella** she tried to find me in another fella, but tell her, the shoe won't fit, I'm too legit, The BlaKseed proceed succeed, all you do is **Party And Bullshit** and smoke weed, and I thought that you was the one to carry my seed, but I see now that you are not the Goddess that I thought you were, the hardest thing is to find and then lose your love, I guess it's all about timing, not even diamond rings are forever, ever ever, ever shining **- Dawud The Uncanny BlaKseed**

Significance

Emmett Till was murdered in 19**55** and I met a woman at **55** St Nicholas, Seasoned Vegan (page 364) and when I saw her she reminded me of **Aylin**, the last woman I dated in Germany. Aylin was Turkish and she was a Muslim. After seeing a women who looked like her, I would go home and write this verse to a beat that sampled the **Father MC** song, Treat Them Like They Want To Be Treated (p 44). At the end of the year I would change the words "met a **Queen** she was fine" to "met **Billie Jean** she was fine" and this verse would become part of my song **Billie Jean** (p 433). This same woman would inspire me to write the song **Destiny** (page 359).

January 14th 2016 ☥ **Ain't got no**

Will there ever be peace? Niggas can't even get no peace when deceased, You can be blacker than Blade, still have your biopic played by a light skinned nigga with a fade, ***She put a spell on me from the grave,*** I ain't got no couth, don't know how to behave, no culture, no class, Shotgun blast the vulture, No pass! No reason to scream **freedom at last**! I ain't got no love for Hip Hop today most of it is trash! no drop top jag! no American flag! No hop scotch or tag, it's like a thing of the past, No mother no father No home, Will there ever be peace?! **Hatshepsut** the chief in the east brought peace to the **negus** nation! The **Haitian** chasing the enemy back in the sea, Passionately like Den**mar**k **Vesey!** They might stress me, cause my S.P.**A.R.K,** Yet they spray the A K 47, NEVER forget nine eleven?! **don't forget the blood on the leaves!** tell me if there's a ghetto in heaven, ***how long will ya mourn me***? Will ya breathe 711 - **Dawud The Uncanny BlaKseed**

Significance

I wrote this to a beat that had a **Nina Simone** sample in it. I added lyrics from the song **Hatshepsut** that I wrote a year prior (p 336).

January 18th 2016 ☥ **Sunflower**

She was a sunflower and she was beautiful, and when the wind blew she hypnotized you, then she met a friend that took her to the end of natural zen, and he destroyed the temple, and the food was the poison! it was detrimental but it was everywhere, they call it fast food, you know the hamburger? but that's a dead animal so I call it murder! the road of less harm have you ever heard of? and I ain't talking kosher, cause I'm talking culture, it ain't in my nature to take her, Mother Nature and rape her! and do me a favor, don't label me a vegan or a vegetarian, I'm just a human being a humanitarian, ocean and sea full or mercury, free willie from the aquarium, **"Mercy mercy me",** the things I see, fall of man from galaxy to this earthly insanity, inhumanity, from **Christianity** to **Islam** to **Judaism,** they all drop bombs on the little children! so go to **hell** with your **religion!** what are you building? Not Peace! cause there's war in the "Middle East" and in these streets, and they bring the law on a nigga any time he speak and reach one and teach one, will there ever be peace sun? will there ever be peace? **- Dawud The Uncanny BlaKseed**

Creation story

I saw a beautiful **Ethiopian** woman on Instagram dancing with a Sunflower in her hand. Her beauty sparked my words "*She was a sunflower and she was beautiful, and when the wind blew she hypnotized you*"

January 21st 2016 ☥ **Destiny**

Desire and devour, verse **love** and devotion, one will last an hour and end in desertion, the other is a well in the desert a lover more real than there's water in the ocean, what are you searching seeking? I heard it's gonna snow this weekend, maybe you will call again and we'll be speaking?, maybe I'm reaching, reeking of **lost love**, of how it could have been or how it was, could it be things were all so simple **my love**?? I feel for you cause my intent went above the nonsense time spent in **clubs**, you were my **Queen** of **hearts** but now you're heartless, I seen this all before and what I saw makes my heart sore, how do I stop this run away Jane?! how do I explain that **destiny** is something real and it's not a game?! can you feel my etheric field from my heart and brain? we got free will so we can still make a change, ain't no needing for two people to be feeling the pain, if we put the same energy in love **we can rise above** and go back to the way it was, cause I remember the time, I remember the time like **Michael Jackson, The 25th Dynasty Everlasting,** you see the world is old but ***the future springs from the past*** stories untold, **The BlaKseed** be a **Old Soul,** they say it's hard to teach an old dog new tricks, but I say, it's hard to teach an old God tricked my **false profits**, so stop it! the real temple is in man, the temple on the land is just a plan to take your money and scram, see I'm a simple man, no I don't eat green eggs and ham, and I am not the **cursed*** son of **ham*! I am that I am! - Dawud The Uncanny BlaKseed**

Rau nu Prt m heru

January 23rd 2016 Don't Argue Me

I need a woman who won't argue me, who won't look at me with a look like nigga you ain't shit, cause that really bothers me, yeah I'm a man but, nobody fathered me, so I'm an endangered anomaly, **Dr Umar** psychology, Black unapologetically! **Black Man Of The Nile And His Family** uprooted from our family tree, **The Destruction Of A Nation,** first civilization! we ain't have words for jail or probation! miseducation won't teach you about the rebel of the **Haitian,** we sailed across the world, and mastered navigation, they promote mass masturbation and low vibration, how can we raise a Black nation when we all out here chasing tale, drinking alcohol, no libation?! well **"I kick flows for ya, kick down doors for ya", SANKOFA!** I left all these hoes for ya, it was easy, I started by turning off the T.V. and the radio, they only play and show programs designed to do exactly what the drugs would do, if I were you I would watch **Khalid Muhammad** on **Donahu**, don't be in a rush to condemn me, she or him, **Malcolm X** said you ain't always think the way you do my friend! *in the event of my demise* we gonna meet again, wipe the tears from your eyes we gonna **rise again** ride and defend, like **Huey** and his friends, 11 hundred and 34 more Black men killed last year when will it end?! it's an epidemic, poisoned water in Flint Michigan! but are you listening?! **Free Mumia!** how much longer will they imprison him?! they need to pardon him!? if **Pac** was alive he'd be 45, that's mad relevant, cause now we got the 45th president! I remember when we wasn't ready for a **Black president,** he came and went and now I'm left wondering what it ever meant, was it heaven sent or was he sent from the government? all I know is poor black folks still ain't got no settlement **- Dawud The Uncanny BlaKseed** (See page **648** for the **metaphysical significance of the number 23**.)

(see page 81 for the Common Connection)

Iu f Per f m heru

January 28th 2016 I Still Love Her

Thoughts looming bout my favorite human, tell me who's your favorite human being, good feelings when you see em, blooming like roses do in spring, love healing that's a real thing, time soon come we have fun do our thing, she like to sing and I love to listen, time move slow when we kissing, **destiny** has written, tell me have you seen her? she's usually sitting, on the dock of the bay in Rockaway, maybe I'm fishing, there's many fish in the sea, one day I'm a see, but I can't see right now that it's possibly, cause I don't see a long life with wife and kids, I live vicariously through friends and family, you might hear this and feel sad for me, but this is a common Black man reality, we gotta **save the Black family**, what a tragedy! I kick the truth to the young Black youth, they get mad at me! cant you see I'm **Malcolm X** on the strategy?! hopefully they don't **Martin** me on the balcony!! but I have no fear when it's my time I'm out of here! so much I care, a lot of tears, **"I See Death Around The Corner"**, am I next like **Chris Dorner?!** but I put a **hex** on em! *I got these spirits in my corner*!! when you die "**How Long Will They Mourn Ya**"?! the **soul** was stole by a crook who lied, gave you a book, told you to look inside for help and spiritual wealth, but you gotta go inside self for real wealth to heal self, why oh why do we desire the quick fix?! promised by liars who promise this!! who do you worship?!! this spiritual journey is a long one don't curse it with that bullshit they spit from the pulpit whether it's written in **English**, cursive or beautiful **Arabic!** if it ain't African I ain't having it! it's all love for those above, below and in between, for the seen and unseen, but let a **king** do his thing, **Sankofa,** get that ass up off the sofa, no soap opera! **The Empire Strikes Back,** in search of that land of the **Perfect Black**, the land of the plenty but not a penny was given to any so they were left skinny, waiting for the one to come to bring finality to poverty, ***sent from another galaxy with a message from Mother Tree*** of love energy, she said "you can never finish me, I will always replenish see, the third eye is in you and me universally! use the university of **Common Sense**, not enough time spent in silence… close your eyes and reconnect to the essence the essence, reconnect to the essence the essence the essence, reconnect to the essence the essence the essence, reconnect to the essence the essence the essence **- Dawud The Uncanny BlaKseed**

Utterances for Coming Forth by day into Light

Significance

This verse was written after I read the caption of a post on Instagram. The post was from a woman who posted a picture of her boy friend with a caption that read - "only a few more days till I see my favorite human being". The caption touched my heart and it inspired me to write 80% of the verse. Later that evening I ended the verse with thoughts of **Sophia Stewart's** book **3rd eye** and with what I read in mind, I wrote the end of the **first verse**. Sophia is the Black woman who the **Matrix** and **The Terminator** movie scripts were stolen from. I was waking up from a long sleep, in a new body Just like the movie **Matrix**, as I unconsciously used music as magic to awaken my ancient soul fragments. I had to take the path of **Sankofa**, going back to fetch what I lost, "It's all love for those above, below and in between, for **the seen** and **unseen**, but let a **king** do his thing, **Sankofa,** get that ass up off the sofa, no soap opera! **The Empire Strikes Back,** in search of that land of the Perfect Black"…. You are **Ausar** the perfect Black (page 3).

It is he, who comes forth by day into Light

January 30th 2016 Heb Sed (Running Ritual)

I left the clubs alone now I'm home alone like ***LL,*** I used to eat junk, roll blunts and smoke L's, Then I read a chapter in a book by **Llaila Afrika,** Then I heard a song that turn my thinking cap on, the powers that be only be about bringing us harm, an hour of ecstasy can leave you damaged like a storm, have you searching for the calm in the sunshine it's not a fun time, come and find the miracle, the fountain of youth through ritual, simple principles, get up early you got shit to do! d*rink water get your bowels in order, constipation caused by dehydration, exercise to feel alive, go inside through meditation, take a break, a vacation for restoration, raise your vibration,* how do we win? we gotta use our imagination! visualize a spiritualized African pride, **realized in this life not the next!** nothing less, **Malcolm X, Magneto, Martin Luther, Professor X,** put it in context, my homie bombed first, then I bombed next, imagine traveling on feet, **Mobb Deep** for success, a million brothers running to release stress from east to west, we ran with a plan to expand, we joined hands to make a better day, Like Africans screaming **Ali Bumaye,** and I can run to **Rockaway** just like this, all the way to **Zimbabwe** and never quit **- Dawud The Uncanny BlaKseed**

February 8th 2016 Magnetic

Spiritually being attracted magnetic sp**ark**ing matches flames, The Blackest d**ark**est electric fire remains, after the first kiss, She was his last kill, but still she didn't know his name, The blakseed plant seeds, Waiting for the rain waters to fall, Divine orders to call Something like love and basketball **- Dawud The Uncanny BlaKseed**

February 9th 2016 The Paradigm

I got a call from a woman 300 and 10 pounds, depressed and sad on the phone she did sound, I told her to calm down, we spoke about food and water and natural order and for her it was profound, 2 weeks later, she was 25 pounds down, did I save her? or did she save her self?! I'm just here to help sp**ark** like an enzyme, I'm a fitness thug, before you take medication practice patience and love, only 3 to 5 out of 10 survive the drugs prescribed to patients, **The wizard Of OZ** has no love, your fate is in his or her hands, I ain't hate'n, I'm just stating the facts, I was raised in this society, why did you lie to me? perhaps I am the great enslaved cash cow, ever think how that cow gets on your plate? is it fate or the great mistake Misstep? I **incarnate** the mystic **Imhotep,** the father of medicine the Mastaba, step by step up the pyramid I climb, coming from behind, I was blind but now I see, so I designed a paradigm for you and me, it ain't hard, fitness made easy through consistency most definitely **- Dawud The Uncanny BlaKseed**

THE UTBC PARADIGM

Page 267

A holistic approach to health & wellness.

February 10th 2016 Spiritual Gangsta

Is it a crime I rhyme just for hobby? a spiritual gangsta doing time, **my mind soul in a body**, I'm just try'n to live, **my mind soul in a body**, they wanna take me out, **my mind soul in a body**, is it a crime I rhyme just for hobby? a spiritual gangsta doing time, my mind soul in a body, I'm just try'n to live, **my mind soul in a body**, they wanna take me out, **my mind soul in a body - Dawud The Uncanny BlaKseed**

2016 - Turning on The Ark of a Million Years and "Aliens"?

This year I would take more interest in **sleep paralysis**. The month prior I had purchased the books **Metu Neter volume 4**, **The Ausarian Resurrection**, **Maat The 11 Laws of God** and **Tree of Life Meditation** by **Ra Un Nefer Amen**. I did read some of his book Metu Neter Volume one but I never read much of the others. I was in the habit of collecting books so when I came across a book that sounded interesting I would buy it and open it when I was called to. I was building my own library. Why am I mentioning books that I didn't read? Because these books are related to activation of the light body, the tree of life and what matters more is your own experience and imagination. I had experiences with dreams and **sleep paralysis** and now I desired to experience more. **Sleep paralysis** can lead to something far more profound than most people will ever have the courage to experience due to the fear of **sleep paralysis**. If we are intentional with our thoughts we can, sort of surf the wave of **sleep paralysis** and ride away in what is commonly known as **astral projection**. What happened next is an example of how our thoughts and desires can affect our reality by influencing quantum level events in time and space. Sometime in 2016 I laid down on my hammock with the intentions of entering into the phase of sleep that **sleep paralysis** occurs in, so that I could attempt **astral projection**. Shortly after I laid down, to my surprise I felt the vibrations and lost mobility of my body, even my eyes. I had successfully entered the paralysis stage.. As I struggled to open my eyes **I saw what looked like 2 or 3 silhouettes near my window that looked like people or beings**. I never got a clear look at what I saw and when I finally came out of the state all I could see were my flowers in the window. I convinced myself that what I saw was my flowers and not some **long alien type beings**. On October 9th of 2018 (page 538) I would be more successful using this same technique.

42 Laws of Maat, Page 367

February 13th 2016 - Meta Spiritual Encounters. What can Zee See?

Zee was one of the people I would see walking their dogs while I trained my group fitness class in Jackie Robinson park at 6am and 7am. Every time she saw me she would say hi. One day she questioned me about personal training so I gave her my business card. On February 13th she would start training with me. I tracked this date from the date on her initial b4 and after picture.

The same day of our first session I received the book **Encyclopedia of Fruits Vegetables, Nuts and Seeds for Healthy Living** in the mail and I played the "let's see what I read if I open the book to a random page" game. So I opened the book to a "random" page to see what I would read. The book opened to a page on **Dates** and the second sentence stated that **Dates** have been found to be valuable for cases of **Anemia**, and other diseases. "Coincidentally" during this initial session Zee would claim to be **Anemic**. I **immediately** grabbed the book I had just received in the mail and opened to the page on **Dates**. She read it and was happy to receive the info. Then I explained to her that I just received that book in the mail earlier today and how I randomly opened it to the page explaining how **Dates** are good for anemia - and now she tells me that she is anemic. We both thought it to be a special moment. I told her that we should not own the labels that Doctors give us. Instead we should find the solutions to our health problems like our own lives depend on it because I assure you they do.

Rau nu Prt m heru

Significance

Later this year Zee would tell me about her **secret power** (page 421)! Her ability to see **ghost's**. She would also tell me that a woman stands at my door guarding it. On July 21st 2018 (page 529) Zee would reveal a dream she had of me and in December of 2018 she would **help me discover the identity of the spirit that stands at my door** (page 545).

February 15th 2016 Giara Nova and Vanity's Biopic

Iu f Per f m heru

Vanity who's real name is **Denise Matthews** transitioned just two months before **Prince** on February 15th 2016. She was born on **January 4th 1959.** Vanity started her career in 19**77** the **year of the snake** as a **model**, the same year that I was born. She met Prince when she was **Rick James'** date at the 1982 American Music Awards. Soon after she started dating Prince at the height of his career in the 1980s. Their relationship was a sex and drug-fueled relationship but after Vanity's death in February, Prince told a crowd the pair "used to love each other deeply". After learning that Vanity could sing, Prince asked her to become the lead singer of his girl group, the Hookers. Prince gave Denise the name **Vanity**, as he considered her to be the female version of himself. She accepted Vanity as a stage name, and the group was renamed **Vanity 6**. Vanity once said that she wanted the **"Diana Ross"** image but she was told she had to take on the Vanity persona if she wanted to get paid. Vanity says the image bothered her at the time but she lied and said it was the image she wanted and she got into the "character". This role would eventually lead to her untimely demise. After years of drug abuse and a crack cocaine addiction Vanity passed away due to kidney failure. Prince and Vanity both died at 57 years of age only two months apart.

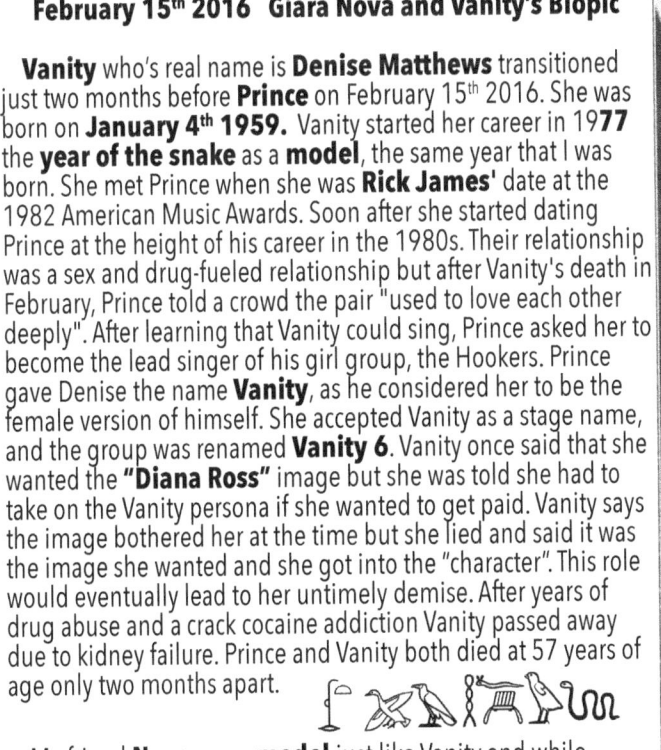

Utterances for Coming Forth by day into Light

My friend **Nova** was a **model** just like Vanity and while growing up she loved Vanity and Prince. Nova would meet Vanity a few years before she passed. Both of them being devote believers in Jesus Christ allowed them fertile ground to build a friendship forging a strong relationship. Vanity would intrust the rights to her **biopic** to Nova having decided that Nova was the best person to play her in her biopic. Nova would fly out to meet with Vanity numerous times so they could work on how Vanity wanted her story presented to the world and with the details from these meetings Nova wrote the script for Vanity's biopic. Vanity saw her younger self in Nova and was looking forward to seeing Nova bring her story to life on screen finally telling her full story. The story of how she **transformed** her life and gave her life to Christ. Unfortunately Vanity passed away before the Biopic was made. Back when Nova first told me about her possible role as Vanity we experienced a moment with Prince. This was a few years before Prince died. One night while leaving the Nuyorican Poets Cafe Nova began to tell me about landing the role for the first time. While she's telling me the story we walked pass a window with a man blasting Prince's music. We looked at each other and laughed, we knew it wasn't just a "coincidence". Nova had tapped into the energy of Vanity and Prince. Even the way I met Nova in 2010 (page 184) was magical and strange! Not to forget the experience I had with the baby at her Holiday party on Dec 17th 2014 (page 314). Nova is born on December 1st the same day that **Rosa Parks** refused to give up her seat to a white man in 1955 Alabama because she was angry about the murder of **Emmett Till**. On July 3rd 2018 (page 480) my **past life** as **Emmett Till** would be revealed to me. In 2019 I gave Nova a massage and after the massage she told me she saw a giant titanium **scarab beetle** with small beetles floating around it during the massage (page 362). This was before I knew the full meaning of the scarab and before I knew I was Tutankhaten (**King Tut**). On April 4th 2020 (page 594) my past life as Tutankhaten would be revealed. Strange experience with Prince on page 379.

It is he, who comes forth by day into Light

Condolences: My condolences go out to the family, friends and fans of **Denise Matthews.** Please know that death is not the end. The soul survives death, indeed and in spirit. This is a book of the dead written by a boy who was murdered without justice, who defeated death and came forth by day. May the soul of **Denise Matthews** walk peacefully through the field of Reeds in Amenta. Amen Ra.

February 17th 2016 Soulmates

She came then she went, was she my soulmate? maybe, can you control fate? hardly! softly she calmed me, **destiny**, life's gonna be what it's meant to be, so let it be, free living organic, don't panic, do you love the chase the challenge? will you take advantage then manage? relationships balance or they vanish like **Atlantis,** put me on a planet where all the women look like **Janet,** with a mind like **Harriet,** let freedom ring I'll marry it, in my heart I'll carry it, this ***poetic justice***, this the narrative, they be telling us that hate is heritage, and we should wait and have faith and vote, but niggas getting choked no Joke by savages! **Civilization or Barbarism?** free my nation from your prison or face my **Garvyism**, **evoke the dead and the living**, when I hit em with the rhythm, I let the rhythm hit em, lyrical exorcism, little wisdom for those that listen, take your time, there will always be those who hate on your grind, don't stop, people gonna throw rocks at things that shine! be the light for the dumb deaf and blind, if your light turn night, put this song on rewind, let it sp**ark** thoughts into action, for motivation but motivation is fleeting, you need a meeting with discipline and dedication! the determination of a **Haitian!** *help me raise my Black nation reparations are due*, I got caught up in the world and took advantage of you, I saw another *Black girl lost* on channel 2, they call it news, this ain't news they program the conditioning, even if you're whispering - Snapchat, Facebook, Instagram they listening, I heard they got a list and if you post facts they visiting, but fuck that we gonna win,! the spirit of **Michael Jackson, Black Moon walking** in, I'm moving from illusion to illumination, the truest emancipation, I feel satan at my doorstep waiting, but I'm the ying and the yang, the d**ark** and the light, I'm everything, the light mind human being on the earth plane, the metaphysical, to the individual saving the earth, save yourself first in the spiritual, the earth gonna be here far after we done with Armageddon, fear none love all, the final call **sun! - Dawud The Uncanny BlaKseed**

Outro

Word. Rest In Peace to the beautiful and the honorable Harriet Tubman. Let freedom ring I'll marry it in my heart ill carry it it's poetic justice this the narrative. Rest in peace to **J Dilla**. Rest In Peace to Garvyism Marcus Garvey and Malcolm X. I let the rhythm hit em like Rakim. Rest In Peace to Tupac who said "Help me raise my Black nation reparations are due." Word! Have the determination of a Haitian inside of you. Rest in Peace to Michael Jackson, Michael Jackson. Escape the illusion through illumination that's the truest emancipation! Rest in Peace to my grand father, The General. Peace

The 7 hermetic principles are:
mentalism, correspondence, vibration, polarity, rhythm, cause vs effect and gender.

February 2016

Jhuti and My First Coffee Enema

I did my first and only colon cleanse on September 8th 2011 and over the years I had gone on to clean up my eating habits (p 212). I was also doing research on health over all and came across teachings about gut health and how many diseases are linked to an unhealthy colon. The phrase "**death starts in the colon**" from Dr. Tim Morrow really got my attention and this led me to enemas. Upon further research I found that the ancient Kemetyu (Egyptians) did regular cleansing of their colon by doing enemas. I learned that enemas were connected to the NTR **Jhuti** (**Tehuti, Hermes, Thoth**) who is depicted as an ibis bird with a it's long beak. Jhuti symbolizes divine wisdom, thought and articulate speech. The ancient Kemetyu observed the ibis bird giving itself and enema buy forcing water up it's own anus with it's long beak to clean it's organ or elimination and this is how the knowledge enemas was gained. Armed with this knowledge I did my first enema but first I watched videos of people talking about their experience and explaining the process then I read more on it then finally in February of 2016 I did my own. I was amazed at how good it made me feel when it was over and by how much waste came out of me. I began to do enemas at least once a year and sometimes more. Did you know that the coroner who did **Malcolm X's** autopsy stated that Malcolm had the cleanest body he had ever seen? Malcolm was muslim and practiced **fasting** at least once a year during Ramadan. I suggest that you look into as many natural healing modalities that you can to ensure that you temple is in optimal condition. Do some research and afterwards you might consider doing an enema if you have not yet done so. The 7 hermetic principles are: **mentalism, correspondence, vibration, polarity, rhythm, cause vs effect** and **gender**.

February 21st 2016 Never forget Malcolm X

Trust me, you don't want to be left behind, spend your whole life eating swine, chasing dimes, just to find that **times** gonna do it's thing, funny thing about **time**, people think they got time until they bell ring, hear that trumpet, heart start pump'n, easier to raise up a strong man child, than a broken man front'n, for real, we cast out an auric field based off how we feel, we emote like a remote, we can heal or provoke anger, kill or build bridges, you stick a knife in my back and expect my forgiveness, you pull it out a little and that's what I'm left to live with, this is not a test, **this is spirit inside the flesh**, we a mess, mesmerized by the lies in text, wisdom for the wise, blind faith for the dumb and deaf, never forget **Malcolm X!** high schools ain't teaching about him! Nor **Jonathan Jackson** running in blasting! Like where's **Assata?!** she's coming with me! the **B.L.A** , The Black Liberation Army, there's nothing you can tell me to sever my love for every revolutionary! New Orleans! Ya gotta know the ledge and the levy! too close to the edge, Public Enemies in the crosshairs of the FED's! **Red, White** and **Blue**? Nah! **Green, Black** and **Red**! "*The **dragon** has arrived*" is what the soldier said, Courage in one hand, Assault rifle in the other my brother, my comrade and my friend never be another, letters from a **Soledad Brother**, **George Jackson**, **Jonathan Jackson**, what I'm asking? acting verse action we don't take action we get roles to act in movies cause we relaxing I miss Michael Jackson - **Dawud The Uncanny BlaKseed**

February 2016 - Meta Mysterious Encounters
Aaron, The Seasoned Vegan

Rau nu Prt m heru

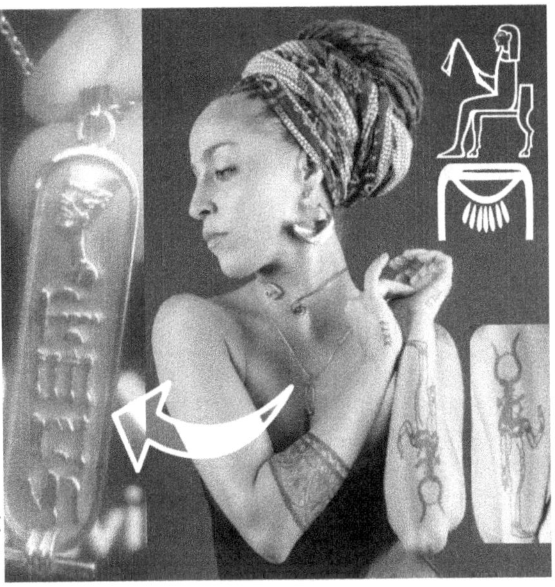

I met Aaron at Seasoned Vegan located at **55** ST Nicholas. Him and I would always talk when I came and we clicked quickly. I also clicked with a brother named **Buddha,** a brother named **Pascal** and a sister named **Annelise**. The staff as a whole was always nice. I would usually go for the brunch they had on weekends and I would always bring a book to read. One day I brought a book on iridology, about the structure and function of the eyes. While reading the book I came across info on the **pineal gland.** The **pineal gland** (3rd eye 𓂀) is responsible for producing the **dimethyltryptamine** (**DMT**) molecule, which is the active component within sacred plant medicines. The Pineal gland appears in the embryo at the **49th** day of gestation and DMT is secreted during birth (via the mother), upon death and during near death experiences. This book was brought forth in 2022, the 49th anniversary of Hip Hop and 49 days is the amount of time the Tibetans believed it took one soul to be reborn into another life. While sitting in Seasoned Vegan, I read about the pineal gland being formed from material very similar to the rods and cones that deal with **vision**. As I contemplated the meaning and purpose of this it became clear that the pineal gland is really an eye and as I came to those thoughts my forehead began to vibrate. The spot between the eyes where Indians place red dots began to vibrate and I just sat there in aw of how this single thought could make my single eye vibrate. As I was taking it in **Buddha** came to take my order. I asked him if he knew that the pineal was made of material similar to the structure of the eyes and he didn't know either. Him and I began to talk about fitness and that's when Wing Chung came up. He called Aaron over and him and I started talking about Wing Chung. I told Aaron I had started looking into Wing Chung and he told me he was practicing it at Practical Wing Chun. Soon after I started training him in fitness and he started teaching me Wing Chung. This would lead me to meet Lord Jamar's brother Reality (page 342). On **August 6th 2016** I would have another experience with one of my glands spontaneously vibrating (p 399-400).

Iu f Per f m heru

Significance

In the bible **Aaron** is the brother of **Moses** and in the historical past **Akhenaten** is the person that the character Moses was fashioned after. Akhenaten is King Tut's Father and on April 4th 2020 I would have my past life revelation of my life as King Tut. **Annelise** wears a **gold** pedant on her neck that says **Nefertiti** but I wouldn't come to know that until June 5th 2021 (page 647). **Nefertiti** is king Tut's step mother. I had initially gravitated to her because of the **Het Heru (Hathor)** tattoo on her arm. Sometime after knowing **Pascal** I noticed that he wore a **scarab** pedant around his neck and I had been drawn to the scarab since 2014 because of the transformation symbolism. He is born on Sep 20th the day after **Emmett Till's** trial started on sep 19th 1955. In 2018 he would cause me to meet a woman with a strange connection to **Emmett Till** (p 534). I would later learn that Lord **Pacal** was a priest king of the **Mayans** and was known as the **feathered snake** or the **feathered serpent** just like **King Tut**. I met **Buddha** there as well and he was always pleasant, he is born on June 3rd the day after one of my sisters. In 2014 I would watch the documentary, The Prophecy of Reincarnation Sambho the black Buddha (page 288), about the **reincarnation** of the **Buddha** in the west between the years 1975 and 2020, I'm born in 1977 and my **past life** revelation of my life as Tutankhaten (**King Tut**) came on April 4th 2020 (page 594) the day **Martin Luther King was assassinated** (see pages 69, 592). They all work at **55** ST Nicholas and Emmett Till was murdered in 19**55** the same year my mother was born. In August of 2018 I would meet a woman at Seasoned Vegan in a strange series of events and I would later come to find that she was from Chicago and when she was little she attended a school named **Emmett Till** elementary school (p 534). On **January 5th** 2019 I would be saved by my **guardian angel** while on my way to **55** ST Nicholas. In 2016 I would meet a woman at **55** ST Nicholas that was born on **Rosa Parks** birthday. We had several things in common and she appeared in my dreams, because of this I thought we were supposed to be together but she doesn't agree. She appeared in a dream most recently on October 21st 2021 (page 539).

Utterances for Coming Forth by day into Light

It is he, who comes forth by day into Light

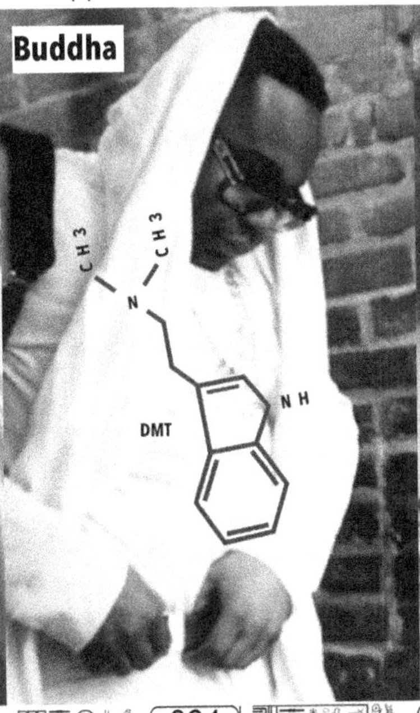

February 22nd 2016 One of These Mornings 3rd verse

Hip Hop is that funny place where the smiley face, could be the hunters pace in chase to trip you in your race, so just in case I suggest you replace the with Hip with Fit and never stop the Hop, nigga who got the props? I said who got the props? Rest in peace to **Sean Price** will I live a long life? I don't know, but I don't live my life chase'n the dough, cause you can't take dough with you, but if you spread love you can leave it, memories don't live like people do believe it, *eternal sunshine in the spotless mind* delete it, everything will be fine but quality time is needed, if you hear'n these lines take it as a sign and heed it, ***Remember the time*, *Beat it***, when a **king** passes, tear drops and closed caskets, the pain you can't mask it, disrespect the dead homie get that ass kicked, catch me on a bad day and get blasted **- Dawud The Uncanny BlaKseed**

February 26th 2016 Populous

They say follow your **dreams** and try so you can fly, I know a girl every time she close her eyes she cries then screams, another bad **dream!** should she follow it? her mind's flooded with fear and shit from tv and the politricks, that ocean of fear swim out of it! dictators who rule by fear you might win some, but you lost one here! murder and manipulation still the population cheers, drinking beers, sometimes I wonder if they really care….? as they smoke away they're pain high on another plane, then they crash low and complain, and wonder why things never change, then they change the channel to another game, what a shame! I channel live energy from my heart and brain, cause the universe is vast, and the answers you seek, to the questions you ask, won't be found in a seat in a class, do the math and science on these tyrants, *cell division times **infinity** you'll never finish me!* you might give me a felony but heavenly I'm heavy see like **Heavy D**, but *you blind to the facts*! you telling me to pay a tax when I was born free, picture that! Kill me, ***I'll be back** in the whirlwind* with **Marcus Garvey!** until then I'll be telling them the truth, see the young Black youth left out of the loop, *the children of the **light***, but we ready to recoup all the things lost and stolen cause deep inside we know we the chosen, *the rose in the concrete*, I let the **soul** inner chi flow through the earth through the **sole** of my feet, the earth to the universe, **we are not alone**! Deep space to the smallest chromosome, the **twilight zone** put in a poem **- Dawud The Uncanny BlaKseed**

February 27th 2016 Sum Spooky Shit

My world view defies you old cold model, too mechanistic, my **soul** is malleable, hot like Malibu, hop on a elephant and handle you like **Hannibal, Pneumonia** the **bird flu** or **the black plague**, as they beg for the antidote for the sickness I wrote from my head, some spooky shit **J Dilla** modern day **Thriller, Raising the dead,** he was gonna go to school, she had to bury him instead, is there a **Ghetto in Heaven**? on this date in Hip Hop February 27th, I shine illuminance iridescence, ***the presence of a mysterious energy around me***, that might astound the observer for a second, I reck'n, I beacon for a deacon before I'm reaching and speaking and teaching, I'm reeking of what we all seeking, can you smell freedom? Can I lead em? who's the general? would they believe him? receive him? Would he deceive them?! that's tantamount to treason!! I rhyme for reason, this is my season! Line for line **9:10 Ephesians,** I come to bring unity to everything you see and if you come to conquer, I purify your ass in **The Lake Of Minnetonka!** many come but, few are chosen with a spiritual sponsor, **I rose when** I had a **dream** of **Toussaint** in a helicopter, **Tupac, Michael and Prince** screaming out nothing can stop ya, Dawud the blakseed the phantom of the chakra **- Dawud The Amazing BlaKseed**

Significance

The song was written to a **J Dilla** beat and **J Dilla** was born on Feb 7, the same day as **Emmett Till's** father (Louis Till, pages 475, 518). While writing this song I felt like there was someone else in the room with me and I intuitively felt like it was **Trayvon**. When the force came in the room I wrote the following words "Some spooky shit J Dilla modern day Thriller, **Raising the dead,** He was gonna go to school, she had to bury him instead, is There A Ghetto In Heaven? on this date in Hip Hop February 27th, I shine illuminance iridescence, ***the presence of a mysterious energy around me***, that might astound the observer for a second"…..

February 28th 2016 Barbaric

We live in a world today barbaric, kids don't play, people don't stay in marriage, they stray and live lavish, people don't pray they disconnected, eat'n animals we once protected, even detectives kill kids, and we don't see the trees, so the forest neglected, I closed my eyes and rested on another planet, not enough time invested inside dammit! are you alive or evil in like **Skeletor?** and what I'm telling y'all is we had a hell of a fall son, Dog? God? whatever! Goddam how did we ever sever our cord with Mother Nature?! tell a man the truth he hates ya, a woman won't date ya! they crave the flavor of the flesh what a mess, as it festers and rest in the sacred temple, the intestines look just like the mental, **J Dilla** on the instrumental again, influencing my pin, **The Force Awakens** again, **The Force Awakens** again, if I was **Mr Manhattan** channeled through rapping, I would focus on stopping the madness in a sad world, it happened at a rally, the **ku klux klan** stabbed Larry, "How do we ever tell the saint from the sinner daddy?" said the little girl, how did that make him feel?! gave him a chill, shit is real!! **Tamir Rice** look like **Emmett Till,** and still they hate still, but the power of love will, create a force field to heal, and build the gates of Zion to escape mothers in black crying and brothers in packs dying and dying **- Dawud The Amazing BlaKseed**

Significance

This song marks the 6th time I said Emmett Till's name in a hekau (rhyme) before I reaized I was him (page 480). The song was written to a **J Dilla** beat and **J Dilla** was born on Feb 7, the same day as **Emmett Till's** father (Louis Till, pages 475, 518).

Rau nu Prt m heru

March 3rd 2016 Truman Show

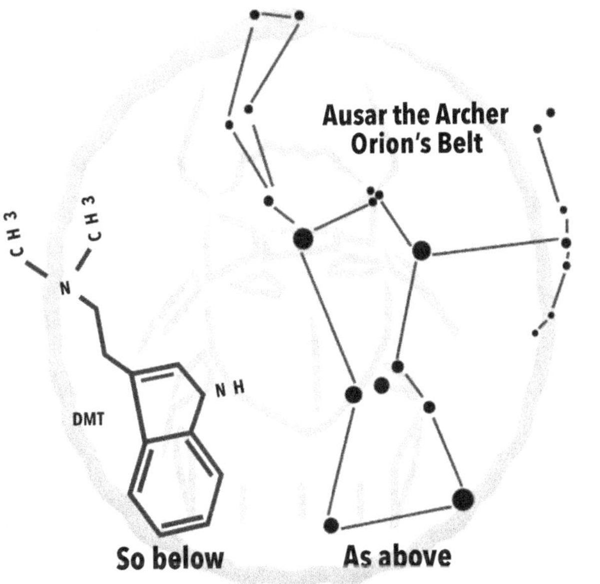

This **Jim Carry Truman** show got a brother feeling low, but I know ***I rise like Heru*** the wise **NTCHRU,** hike one, hike two, that was my passion, running fast and jumping high, you never know you might fly, I seen pro athletes cry, I wonder if they cried when they buried **Malcolm X**?! too busy them cashing checks, I got caught up in that mess too, see chasing this money can mentally arrest you, and Black life can depress you, but God blessed you and protected you! do you know who you are? you are the children of the **SUN**, **The Morning Star**!! you're not alone, take the **Black Star Line** right on home, and don't **Rome** away from royalty, where are you loyalties? truer words never spoke from another Emcee, see rappers mostly rap about life illegally, but Emcees rap about uplifting people spiritually, from the mineral to the plant, from the plants to man to Gods, in a **circle of the little animals** we revolve, Hip Hop the arithmetic used to solve the secret teachings of all ages as war wages, The BlaKseed raises the sword of **David** which divine law favors, the right handed villain, the left handed savior, the link in search for Zelda, the saber, the elder spoke of the birth of the star in a **manger**, **Ausa**r the **Arc**her aims his bow at the **25th Dynasty,** *finally* ***The Never Ending Story*** *is finding me* **- Dawud The Amazing BlaKseed**

Iu f Per f m heru

Significance: In this song I mention **Heru**, The Morning Star, The Circle of Little Animals, as well as the Manger and Orion (**Ausar**) constellations. At the time I had never experienced a psychedelic and did not realized that there was a deeper layer to the science of astrology and resurrection. It was only during the revision of this book that I would come across info connecting the constellation of **Orion** to the structure of the **DMT** molecule. It appears that, not only did the sages of Kemet align the pyramids with the stars in the **heavens**, but they also explained how the medicines on earth can help to awaken the sleeping human when the medicines enter the **brain** (the holy of holies). When the DMT molecules are allowed to bathe our **pineal glands**, initiates who have made themselves ready can open doors and experience levels of awakening only attained by few. **Remember that you are Ausar and Heru, the hero!** See page 3 for the **hero's journey!** For more on Orion see pages 251, 485 594

March 4th 2016 Reckless

Check it, this is a record for my homies out there reckless, far from stressless, in bars with women naked, shots at the bar, get in the car and wreck it, I know life is depressing, but you gotta keep pressing, every fall there's a lesson, spring back up keep step'n and rep'n, I started out with **Smif-N-Wessun, Buckshot Shorty, Common Sense, Naughty,** now I'm close to 40 and you can't ignore me, **I came to save the game** like **Robert Horry,** slap the shit out of **Robin** if he try to skip my story! this is one for glory and fuck a **Grammy!** I pledge allegiance to my friends and family to write for what's right, that's from the heart, I put that on my Granny **- Dawud The Amazing BlaKseed** **(see page 81 for the Common Connection)**

Utterances for Coming Forth by day into Light

March 5th 2016 The Heart Ritual

I think we all come around to this conversation, searching for **love** I remember I was so impatient, the queen bee gives birth to a whole nation, the praying mantis, she **loved** him, and then she ate him, and poor George don't got money so she won't date him, and babies why do it take money to create em, and marriage it take money to have em and separate em, what's the average of a marriage in this generation?! How many babies start from love before penetration?! How many ladies chasing thugs and keep Negus wait'n?!

Follow your heart from the start but take your mind with you, on your m**ark** get set ready go, take it slow, *things fall apart* and get d**ark,** but sometimes they stay together, **Love** is a art, **love** is a sp**ark,** so chart your own course and of course beware of sh**ark**s in a sea of fish, **RA**member this like a **hieroglyph, Anubis** and a **obelisk,** Karma do exist like the kiss of death, so being an apologist is cool but cool intent is best, I guess experience is the best teacher, save yourself some stress and listen to what's vibe'n through your speaker, who do I speak of? the seeker! on a **Quest** for **love** getting deeper to **The Roots** of the effects of drugs on **Thug Life** leaders, the truth is the judge and in time it'll free us, if **love** is a crime then the time is now my **Negus!** put down the **cigarettes and alcohol** and all the things they feed us! if we don't mind up we'll drink up the hemlock in modern day society and drop dead quietly! finally **The 25th Dynasty** aligning the stars and quasar on you and me, to correct our behavior and coonery, no apology! unapologetically Afrikan Afrikan, I know what's happening happening, see you can have the memory of the fly or the elephant, irrelevant or intelligent, your down fall or your betterment, every four years another president, *I hold these truths to be self evident*, another Black youth American dead again!! Gentlemen! let's go back to running laps to prevent heart attacks, dig up the **artifacts**! all black boots on troops picture that!! *Recoup what's stolen and claim it black*, then take it back! how hard is that?! together we stand divided we fall, I'm talking to all of y'all, from **Kingston Jamaica to Jamaica Queens,** it's your ritual that becomes habitual, the habits you're addicted to, what has afflicted you? do you have a clue? do you have the flu or a cold that you couldn't control? Medical Bills and Pills Kill your soul, every year the death rate goes up that's getting old, **they say it's hard to teach a old dog new tricks but it's harder to teach an old God that's been tricked!**

It is he, who comes forth by day into Light

I ain't here to judge cause, you can lead a person to the truth still they won't budge cause, it's like we in love with disease, sort of like how people love cheese, to instill will power I planted a blakseed, I told him cheese came over here on the mayflower when they enslaved our foremothers and fathers, but nigga please is all he said, I left it alone cause I've learned let the dead bury the dead, you're better off kicking the truth to the young Black youth instead, Keep your head up, don't look where you fell but look where you slipped up, this your daily bread with some deadly news, what's **pure white and deadly** put in almost every food? I read the book *Maintaining Our Temple* and it put it plain and simple, the commercial is here to temp you, and your health is your wealth that's fundamental, don't be a tool in your own genocide, they'll kill you then say you enjoyed it, nutritional homicide! you've been advised, the number one killers' been identified, as **pure white and deadly** connected to **obesity, depression, A.D.D.** even with **Cancer** that's the answer! If you stop to think you might find a proper link, then try to ascertain why **aspartame** was once on the list of chemical weapons for war campaigns, along with acid rain, the war on drugs is a war on your heart and brain, I know it's hard to fathom what I said to him but I ain't a vegan or a vegetarian, I'm a human being a humanitarian, it's the legal things that will leave you dead my friend, the evil is in the greed cause Mother Earth supplies all our needs so we can survive and thrive indeed, it's your ritual that becomes habitual, the habits you're addicted to, what has afflicted you? do you have a clue? do you have the flu or a cold that you couldn't control? Medical Bills and Pills Kill your soul, every year the death rate goes up that's getting old, **they say it's hard to teach a old dog new tricks but it's harder to teach an old God that's been tricked! - Dawud The Amazing BlaKseed**

I be the **Lord of Maat** like the base of the throne, in case you forgot let me take you back home, I came flying out primordial d**ark**ness all alone, **Nun** was there she created the moisture, the air and the earth to roam, the sky was the dome, the all embracing cohesion of elements, the rotation of seasons, fair dealings – no relation to heathens, the even equilibrium of the heavens meant everything, no irrelevant aspects of nature, the **NTCHRU** like the **Falcon** flew, he who comes into existence like the **Scarab** do, Like **Ra**, **Ptah**, or **Ausar** one and the same, you can see the weakness in a man through his **iris**, and his tongue is the same, follow me now – ***with my tongue I decree a miracle deliberately***, my chief source of energy **spiritually,** everything else peripherally, with tunnel vision look upon my mission and listen for delivery, of Gods divine faculties facilitating my destiny, the black emcee, **Blackamoor** no more in your dictionary, the **Blakseeds** they be quick to bury, **The Valley Of Kings** place my obituary, **Thug Life** like my **Naga Seti,** d**ark** nights **Better Dayz** coming, so my soldiers getting ready, like **Eric Shepard** ya heard, very epic with words, they might come for me but don't let that pressure your nerves, instead be well fed decalcify **thy eye** with herbs, they might bust led but bus how this **spell** was said, as I read from **The book of The Dead, Coming Forth By Day, The Blakseed** from **New York** by way of **Rockaway,** the last shall be first, screaming out, **"Hip Hop Hooray Hip Hop Hooray",** screaming out, "get out the way"! shots fired another brother expired! it's an execution with no retribution these cops are liars! cops and robbers they death pool for hire, a cesspool corrupted like political bucks stuck under the table, you busted! caught your hands all up in my pockets take'n my profits! they can't be trusted like Uncle Sam! sending rockets to the Mother Land! right now they got the upper hand but we can band together! **"Holla If Ya Hear Me"!** I blame the hand that put the bucket there, not my brother stuck in here with me, quickly trying to get the fuck out of here, we be **"Shifty, Low Down Greedy and Grimy",** like **50 Cent** in the 90's, be careful with a necklace too shiny, reckless Black on Black crime be reminiscing of **Willy Lynch'n** picnic'n, did I mention I slipped back to another dimension sat in the **Chicken Shack** with **Detroit Red!** it was packed from the feet to the head, **Red Foxx** was in the kitchen telling jokes, **Billie Holiday** was hitting high notes, everybody had high hopes, they said a toast I closed my eyes then I woke, I'm still alive **so I rise** and realize what I wrote, time to get this yoke up off my neck, "shit was all good just a week ago" look at the hood where did all the Black people go?! no **reparation** the repercussions of **gentrification,** how do we stop this **Black extermination?** I be the **Lord of Ma'at** like the base of the throne, in case you forgot let me take you back home….. - **Dawud The Amazing BlaKseed**

Significance and Creation Story

I started writing this hekau (rhyme, hymn, song, spell, **words of power**) at **Tsion Cafe,** an Ethiopian Restaurant in Sugar Hill Harlem. In the 1930's and 1940's the location of Tsion Cafe used to be the famous **Jimmy's Chicken Shack. Malcolm X** and **Red Foxx** used to work there. They washed dishes together. Malcolm had not yet went through his spiritual transformation at the time, and so he went by the name **Detroit Red**. In this hekau I would say the following words "The **NTCHRU** like the **Falcon** flew, he who comes into existence like the **Scarab** do, Like **Ra**, **Ptah**, or **Osiris** one and the same". The NTCHRU is everything and everything is NTR. NTR comes from the word NATURE, like the forces of nature that create tornados and tidal waves as well as babies and airplanes. God/Allah controls ALL the forces of NATURE and in ancient Kemet (Egypt) the NTR was the closest equivalent to GOD. The NTCHRU are the creative forces of the universe and ***ALL together they work as one and this one thing is the NTR and the NTR is what we call God***. In Kemet (Egypt) the **falcon** was the symbol of **Heru**, who is the son of **Ausar** (Osiris) and Auset (Isis). Heru is born of an immaculate conception when the spirit of his dead father Ausar impregnates his mother Auset. Heru **returns, resurrects, reincarnates** to avenge his fathers death and goes into battle with his uncle Seth (sunset/darkness). Upon death all pharaohs must go through the process depicted in the scenes on the walls inside the tombs of the "dead" Pharaohs (page 670). This is where modern religions have crafted their heaven and hell concepts. In ancient Kemet the Pharaoh, like all people, must have his/her heart weighed against the feather on the scales of Maat and if it is lighter than the feather he/she returns as **Kheperu Ra**, the morning son. Kheper is the **Scarab**, the same scarab I mention in this line, "he who comes into existence like the **Scarab** do"! When I wrote this song I had no idea that the **scarab** represented **resurrection,** the never ending cycle of life, regeneration and rebirth and the fact that they were placed over the heart of the dead pharaoh to ensure she/he had a safe journey to the next life and resurrection of the pharaoh. I knew none of this. I was only consciously aware of the transformation attributes, yet everything about my life was taking me on the path of **resurrection**. I also mentioned **Ptah,** the Kemetic NTCHRU or principle of Creation. PTAH applies because this book is about creation and regeneration. We all experience creation more than one time and we are here to create, and to ascend. We come back and experience it again and again until we wake up from the dream and ascend. Like when I "awoke" in this song when I was sitting and talking with **Malcolm X** (**Detroit Red**), "did I mention? I slipped back to another dimension sat in the Chicken Shack with **Detroit Red,** it was packed from the feet to the head, **Red Foxx** was in the kitchen telling jokes, **Billie Holiday** was hitting high notes, everybody had high hopes, They said a toast I closed my eyes then I woke, I'm still alive **so I rise** and realize what I wrote, time to get this yoke up off my **neck**". **Emmett Till** had a barbwire chain wrapped around his **neck** attached to a **70** pound cottin-gin fan. The mummification process of the pharaoh was 70 days. Emmet was thrown in a river like Ausar. Ausar was cut into **14** pieces and Emmett was lynched at **14yrs** old. In this song I wrote about having my obituary placed in the Valley of the Kings as if I was a pharaoh! "The **blakseeds** they be quick to bury, **The Valley Of Kings** place my obituary". Why did I write that?! Just by a coincidence? This process of **coming back to life** is covered in the ancient book of Coming Forth by Day and by Night also called the Egyptian Book of the Dead by Europeans who found these writings in the tombs thousands of years later. Ausar was known as, "**the one in the tree**" (p 482). In some versions of the Ausarian Resurrection drama, the **acacia** is the tree that magically grew up around the body of Ausar (Osiris) when his sarcophagus washed up on the shores of Byblos. The acacia tree holds the same spiritual herb that I ingested at the age of 40 which awoke me to my life as Emmett Till (July 3rd 2018, page 480). In this **hekau** (rhyme, hymn, song, spell) I say the words - "decalcify thy **eye** with herbs, they might bust led but bus how this **spell** was said, as I read from **The book of the Dead, Coming Forth By Day**". **Re-member** that **you** are **Ausar** and **Heru,** the **hero!** See page 3 for the **hero's journey**!
I titled the song, **The Lord of Maat** because the Nswt Bity's (Pharaoh's) had to stand on & uphold the principles of **Maat** in order to ascend the throne.

The 42 Precepts of Maat Philosophy

1. **I have not done what is wrong.**
2. **I have not robbed with force.**
3. **I have not stolen.**
4. **I have not killed women or men.**
5. **I have not stolen offerings of grain.**
6. **I have not defrauded offerings.**
7. **I have not stolen things from the Ntchru.**
8. **I have not spoken falsehoods.**
9. **I have not taken away food or offerings.**
10. **I have not been bad tempered.**
11. **I have not committed adultery, or laid with others of my same sex (or committed sodomy).**
12. **I have not caused anyone to cry.**
13. **I have not swallowed my heart by grieving uselessly causing regret.**
14. **I have not attacked anyone.**
15. **I have not been deceitful.**
16. **I have not robbed or laid waste to Tilled Land.**
17. **I have not been an eavesdropper.**
18. **I have not slandered anyone.**
19. **I have not been angry without just cause.**
20. **I have not copulated with a mans wife. (Atymu)**
21. **I have not copulated with a mans wife. (Khbt)**
22. **I have not polluted myself by copulating excessively nor have I fornicated or masturbated.**
23. **I have not caused terror.**
24. **I have not departed from the ways of Maat.**
25. **I have not been a person of wrath or anger.**
26. **I have not neglected true and righteous words.**
27. **I have not cursed sacred teachings.**
28. **I have not been aggressive or violent.**
29. **I have not caused turmoil disturbing peace.**
30. **I have not been quick of heart, by acting or judging hastily.**
31. **I have not overstepped my boundaries of concern.**
32. **I have not multiplied my words in speaking.**
33. **I have not wronged anyone or done evil deeds.**
34. **I have not been hostile towards the Nswt (King).**
35. **I have not polluted the water or the land.**
36. **I have not raised my voice or spoken arrogantly.**
37. **I have not cursed or forsaken the Ntr.**
38. **I have not acted with evil rage**
39. **I have not stolen or damaged offerings to the Ntr.**
40. **I have not taken away offerings from the spirits of the dead (ancestors).**
41. **I have not taken food from children nor have I blasphemed the Ntchru in my native town.**
42. **I have not slaughtered the sacred cow.**

Addendum

Rau nu Prt m heru

Iu f Per f m heru

Utterances for Coming Forth by day into Light

It is he, who comes forth by day into Light

Thoughts looming bout my favorite human, tell me who's your favorite human being, good feelings when you seen em, blooming like roses do in spring, love healing that's a real thing, time soon come we have fun do our thing, she like to sing and I love to listen, time move slow when we kissing, destiny has written, tell me have you seen her? she's usually sitting, on the dock of the bay in Rockaway, maybe i'm fishing, there's many fish in the sea, one day I'm a see, but I can't see right now that it's possibly, cause I don't see a long life with wife and kids, I live vicariously through friends and family, you might hear this and feel sad for me, but this is a common Black man reality, we gotta save the Black family, what a tragedy! I kick the truth to the young black youth, they get mad at me! cant you see I'm **Malcolm X** on the strategy?! hopefully they don't **Martin** me on the balcony!! but I have no fear when it's my time I'm out of here! so much I care, a lot of tears, "**I See Death Around The Corner**", am I next like **Chris Dorner?!** but I put a **hex** on em! *I got these spirits in my corner*!! when you die "**How Long Will They Mourn Ya**"?! the **soul** was stole by a **crook** who lied, gave you a book, told you to look inside for help and spiritual wealth, but you gotta go inside self for real wealth to heal self, why oh why do we desire the quick fix?! promised by liars who promise this!! who do you worship?!! this spiritual journey is a long one don't curse it!! with that bullshit they spit from the pulpit whether it's written in **English**, cursive or beautiful **Arabic,** if it ain't African I ain't having it! it's love for those above, below and in between, for the seen and unseen, but let a **king** do his thing, **Sankofa,** get that ass up and off the sofa, no soap opera! **The Empire Strikes Back,** in search of that land of the **Perfect Black**, the land of the plenty but not a penny was given to any so they were left skinny, waiting for the one to come to bring finality to poverty, ***sent from another galaxy with a message from Mother Tree*** of love energy, she said "you can never finish me, I will always replenish see, the third eye is in you and me universally! use the university of **Common Sense**, not enough time spent in silence… close your eyes and reconnect to the essence the essence, reconnect to the essence the essence, reconnect to the essence the essence the essence, reconnect to the essence the essence the essence

Imagine a time with no time for leisure, no blind believers in religion or deceivers, no world leaders, no fresh foods no vegetables, the lions and the cheetahs come and eat us even our testicles, and only left a few to testify then they next to die, what ever you do don't ask the question why acid rain falls from the sky and babies cry, mass hunger in mass numbers and mass graves, every bodies looking for aid, no money, cause they waiting to trade waiting to be saved by the one the legend the rumor only remembered by some, in the year 2051 the human population is one, cause the wicked they won, it's all fair in love and war, life ain't no fairytale son! the moon mars and stars revolve in rotation, like the rise and fall of nations, **6 6 6** they flipped the **hieroglyphs** and destroyed the melanation, before that they put it in animation, controlled the imagination, **I came back** on this track to raise the vibration, I pour the libation, *his heart was race'n the man was chase'n, he was facing his termination, but you don't listen, you just turn the station, would they feel me if I wrote it in brail?* would they kill me or just throw me in jail? would you see your silence as betrayal? all's well that ends well, well they ordered the slaughter of infidels, infants and anyone with intel, frankincense for the smell in the story I tell, reality is wrong **dreams** are real, life is a gift and a curse like the purse on the hip of a dead witch in a hurst, would you take it or bury it in the earth? the thirst for the hidden, written in stone, **the birth of the risen heir to the throne,** cause the cataclysm division, destroying homes breaking bones, mission top secret destination unknown, life is a struggle be strong you're never alone, it's ok to cry, ever seen a **caterpillar** try try before she **butterfly**? if eye be single **pineal** tingle said master **Yoda** to the evil **Jedi,** fly higher than eagle like **Heru** flew the **millennium Falcon,** he planted black seeds to feed when disease and the drought come, and when the drought came, the savages started dancing and shouting and then it rained, **then he reigned** and then remained the blakseed, giving Blacks what they need, the Blakseed, he remained the Blakseed giving Blacks what they need, the Blakseed, plant the Blakseeds in the earth, the Blakseed ,plant the Blakseeds in the earth **- Dawud The Uncanny BlaKseed**

Significance

I wrote the last three fourths (3/4) of the **second verse** in 20**13** (page 267). The verse originally started with the words "in the year 20**31** the human population is one". It was initially titled 20**31** because I wrote it in 20**13**, just as **George Orwells**' book 19**84** was written in 19**48**. In 20**15** I recorded the song over again and titled it 20**51**. 2015 just happens to be the year of the **goat** and **Emmett Till** was murdered in 1955, the year of the **goat**. Three years later I wrote the first two thirds (2/3) of the **first verse** in 2016 (page 360). The verse was written after I read the caption of a post on Instagram. The post was from a woman who posted a picture of her boy friend with a caption that read, "**only a few more days till I see my favorite human being**". I felt that caption was touching and it inspired me to write the first two thirds (2/3) of the **first verse**. Shortly after I read a portion of **Sophia Stewarts** book, **3rd eye**, and with what I read in mind, I wrote the end of the **first verse**. Shortly after ending the first verse, I watched the new Star Wars movie, The Force Awakens, which inspired me to write more, ending the song on **March 9**th 2016 by adding a few bars to the beginning of the **second verse**. The new Star Wars movie had been released on December 18th 2015, the same day that my **Grand Father** appeared to me in a **apparition** like **Obi Wan Kenobi** (page 348). Just as Star Wars first introduced the last episodes 4, 5, and 6 first, in the 70's and 80s, then years later they released 1, 2 and 3. I did the same thing with this song. Both verses were created in sections, at different times in different orders than they are presented, and they both make references to Star Wars. I did not plan to do this it just divinely happened that way. Why is this important? Because Star Wars was sent down to earth in thought forms to George Lucas, so that I could watch it when I turned **5** years of age and by doing so would be impregnated with the thought that I was Luke Sky Walker (page 37). Star Wars is connected to King Tut (page 37). I have a sister born on May 14th 1989 the year of the **snake** the same day as George Lucas the "creator" of Star Wars. George Lucas is also part of **the 44th Parallel star code pattern** (p 660). He was sent down in (born in) 19**44** and I turned **44** in 2021. George Lucas turned **77** in 2021 and I was sent down in (born in) 19**77** the year of the **snake**. **May 25th** is the first **star code pattern** in my story and **Star Wars** first premiered on **May 25th**, 19**77**, **5** months before I (Dawud/David) was born. The **Ausarian Resurrection Drama** is the hidden story woven within the Star Wars theme (more on page 37). Much of the concepts used in the Star Wars movies were taken from the science and philosophy of ancient **Kemet** (Egypt), in particular from the 18th Dynasty and the relationship between Akhenaten and his sun Tutankhaten. **Ausar** represents the **immortal soul** of all humans that **reincarnates** and because of Star Wars connection to the Ausarian **Resurrection** Drama it is connected to the experiences in my lives as Emmett and Dawud. Please read what I wrote about Star Wars on page 37, (**May 25th 1983 - 2051, The Return of Djed Eye**). I was waking up from a long sleep, in a new body Just like the movie **Matrix**, as I unconsciously used music as magic to awaken my ancient soul fragments. I had to take the path of **Sankofa**, going back to fetch what I lost, "It's all love for those above, below and in between, for **the seen** and **unseen**, but let a **king** do his thing, **Sankofa,** get that ass up off the sofa, no soap opera! **The Empire Strikes Back,** in search of that land of the Perfect Black**".** **Ausar** is the **Perfect Black**!!! **Remember** that **you** are **Ausar** and **Heru,** the **hero!** See page 3 for the **hero's journey!**

March 12th 2016 7 AfriKan Powers

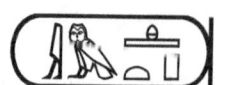

I could be mad all day if I let it, ran away with that girl took a L didn't sweat it, ring a bell when I'm listening to relics, this story I wanna tell it, hell of a magnetic attraction, **George Jackson** waiting for **Angela Davis,** back when black men savored the black women layered in love, Black Families placed above all, close to the edge, I won't fall, roughed up, hands up against the wall, cuffed up didn't do a thing I had enough, will you be there when your homie calls? they like to see a nigga clown around on alcohol, be a sober soldier toeing the line standing tall, this is the final call, the 12th hour, taller than Trump Towers, yeah **we coming back** for everything ours, like a running back, they couldn't tackle him when he pack'n **7 African Powers**, 11 **Lotus Flowers**, did you notice our **sun** shining out the pain? this is real life, this is not a game! the power's in the people, the people put in politics, they sick full of tricks insane, shame on a Emcee rapper that don't take time to write lines that matter, your pockets getting fatter, this been designed by the mad hatter, you been had hood winked, even crime data leave ya mind scattered, if you would think you might let it sink in and over stand, the time is now, **Eric Garner, Sandra Bland,** smarter to be a warrior farmer than a farmer in a war in this crime land, hands of time ticking down homie God damn, I be damned if I give up now homie, **Harriet** wouldn't let us give up now homie God damn! I pledge allegiance to my friend's and family, ain't no money they can hand me, to make me forget who I am B or who I can be! I'm **Michael Jackson, Malcolm X, Imhotep,** America's worst nightmare, a Black man fearless, who don't give a fuck about cashing checks, I can care less, got on the bus came back with the back of my hair left, like the **Olmecs,** I'm so fresh and so clean, they claim I'm violent and mean, expect me to be silent in a nightmare of a **dream,** you can acquiesce but I'm a hell raiser, sent to the dean cause of my bad behavior, you keep messing with the best and that vest won't save ya, we don't wrestle with the flesh my ancestors will slay ya, kick the truth to the youth, you just a slaver, you came with admiration, we did you a favor, you came with open hands, all that shit that we gave ya, now you running the world with little green pieces of paper, you ran away from your mother now you naughty by nature, trying to play God like **Ausar** in the sky, tell me why, tell me why the children gotta die? kill millions so you can thrive, there's no where to run no where to hide, everything done in the d**ark** comes to the light one day, realize the **sun** the **sun** your history you can't run from! **- Dawud The Amazing BlaKseed**

March 14th 2016 Red Pills

The world is old but the future springs from the past, **I came back from the future** and yeah we free at last, but if you don't listen to what I'm spitting we're gonna crash, **I was given a mission to find the other half of a staff stolen,** the hover craft ain't even half of the math floating around in the ether, wake up from your slumber *you're under a spell, fell deep in the sleeper,* got dumber and weaker, this one is written for the seeker, the seeker, this one is written for the seeker, smoking reefer for red pills, conspiracy theories and chills, have you feeling ill, It's a terror knowing the truth teller is getting killed, might have done better taking that blue pill **- Dawud The Amazing BlaKseed**

I mention **Back To The Future** in this rhyme, see page 40!

2016 Mia

I started training Mia in 2016 and she was one of my hardest working clients. I would share a lot of my magical experiences with her and when my past life of Emmett Till (p 480) was revealed I shared that with her. Unfortunately 3 months after that her grand mother, Jean W. Thrash passed on October 6th 2018 the year of the **Dog**. Mia loves **dogs**. She invited me to a gathering celebrating her grand mothers life and that's when I realized her grand mother had an affinity for Kemetic culture. When I looked at the itinerary I noticed Jean was born the day after me on October 26th 1927 and Mia is born the day before my father.

Condolences

My condolences go out to the family, and friends of **Jean W. Thrash**. Please know that death is not the end. The soul survives death, indeed and in spirit. This is a book of the dead written by a boy who was murdered without justice, who defeated death and came forth by day. May the soul of **Jean W. Thrash** walk peacefully through the field of Reeds in Amenta. Amen Ra.

March 15th 2016 Unfollow Me

First of all, I don't give a fuck about fitness the way that you do, so get the fuck out my business, you don't like the cursing? get the fuck off my page, I ain't got time for a mother fucker lost in a maze, you can tell them the truth they still eat they self to a grave, you can show them the proof *they still go and drink the kool-aid,* so the best I can do is just do me, and think about **Bruce Lee** *and repetition, I am my only competition,* you'll never find me on stage shining and glistening, a Lion's a Lion, there's no reward for a bird flying, this flawed sick care system got death rates climbing, families crying with no answers, billions of dollars made off of **Cancer,** the cash cow, now everybody panics, looking for organic foods now, what's the other option, apples full of toxins? they probably blame it on Eve again, and I bet you believe everything you read in their doctrine, indoctrination of the population, they ain't ready to unplug they waiting for a vacation, they look at you bugged, and if you tell them the truth they feeling judged **- Dawud The Amazing BlaKseed**

Rau nu Prt m heru

Iu f Per f m heru

Utterances for Coming Forth by day into Light

It is he, who comes forth by day into Light

March 18th 2016 Warrior Prophets

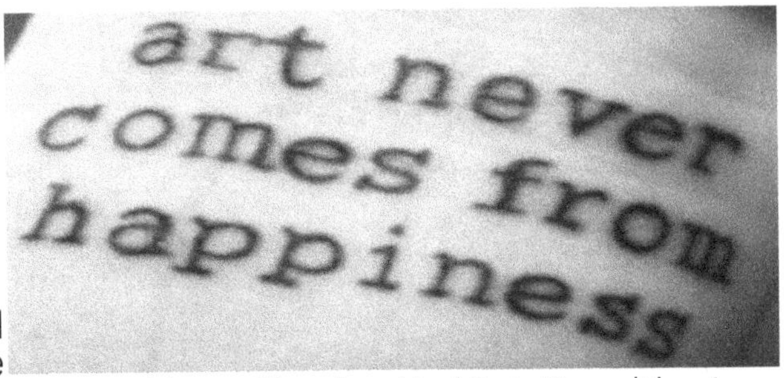

My art rarely comes from happiness, but I be my happiest when I finish it, and lately my experiences been greatly connected to outer spacey **extraterrestrial** Dick Tracey, explainable by only a few, so what do I do? but keep breathing and keep seeing **coincidences,** maybe they'll be leading to incidences where happiness is, I be day dreaming pensive, of a family and kids, then I put up de-fenses, my 6 senses saw the most beautifulest thing in this world, a girl but I was apprehensive, a voice said she's coming for you, and possibly she'll rip your heart out in round 2 like **Tyson** fighting **Laila Ali,** style impregnable, ruthless, ferocious, she'll leave you toothless and hopeless, I had **DeJa Vu** and then I wrote this, then ***I spoke it into existence in the near future or the distant past,*** I saw **The Dopest Ethiopian** in a flash, a **premonition** like when my sister **dreamt** that I crash, but I lived like **obey** shirts on all these kids, so I drown out the negative and let love be the sedative, keep everything relative to heritage like **Malcolm, Garvey, Huey** did, heaven is where the heart is, the hardest thing to deal with is the departed, taken from us by the heartless! plant Blakseeds in the Goddess and harvest more **Warrior Prophets**

His heart racing the man was chase'n, he was face,n his termination, at his funeral they read from revelations, her heart was racing with memories of his face and happy times, they were blind to the crime of them killing her creation, wasn't aware that he was there all she could do is cry, he glides to his mother tries to wipe the tears from her eyes, tales from the other side, it's gonna be hell for them other guys, when it's their time to answer to the most high, most die and never get it, they lie cheat steal and still neglect the spirit, the clarion call they never hear it, they carry on having a ball, drugs, sex, alcohol, hit a wall fall, crawl back up and then they fear it, the truth is hard to bare it, the proof to God is in your merit, in your habits, are you a savage or benevolent? like **David Walker** the day walker intelligent gentlemen from North Carolina, in his jacket liner you might find a copy of **David Walker's Appeal** and a heavy piece of steel, cause shit is real trying to stay alive in 1825, in 1831 **Nat Turner** was on the run, in **1850 The Slave Act** was enacted to catch slaves who escaped evaded capture like running backs breaking tackles, leaving crowds amazed, the truest practice, sink or swim, let's get free or die trying now let's see who's the fastest, he grabbed the **cops** burner and then he blasted **- Dawud The Amazing BlaKseed**

Significance

The first verse was written on march 18th 2016, sp**ark**ed by a picture of a tattoo I saw online that read - "**art never comes from happiness**". From that thought I wrote this song fueled by all the **paranormal experiences** I was having as well as the murder of **Michael Brown**, **Trayvon Martin** and other young Black males – **or was I writing about myself at the start of the second verse**? This was written two years before the revelation of my past life as **Emmett Till** and 4 years before the revelation of my past life as **Tutankhaten** (**King Tut**). It seems like I'm doomed to this cycle of reincarnation un**TILL** I finish my mission here. I hope this is helping you realize that you very well might have been here before and that you are here for a divine purpose. Some of the lyrics from this song have been used throughout this book. In 2022 I experienced **Deja Vu** twice while in **Kemet** (pages 670 - 671).

March 18th 2016 Rope A Dope

They say nothing's beyond the sky, so don't even try, and only birds **fly** and real men don't cry, don't ask why just follow, do your talking on the field or maybe you feel like buck dancing at the **Apollo,** this is my **Creed** take heed, thou shalt not believe cause they deceive, a **bee** gets no nectar on the leave, so what we need to **know** like **Ali** blow for blow, toe to toe with **Joe Frazier**, that **Rocky** movie, it really favors **The Peoples Champ,** don't get me amp, let me find my **lamp** and shine a light, they like when brothers fight, like **Jack Johnson,** rope a dope **Mike Tys**, the **Great White Hope,** not tonight! you might get stripped and swiped of your title be found guilty cause you read the Quran and won't pick up a rifle, **Ali The Greatest Of All Time** idol, he told his rival "I am one man you can't beat and conquer, I fight for 30 million africans your honor, where is the honor in dropping bombs on a town 10 thousand miles away?! they never called me nigger but you kill my people everyday!" the terror stays real like **Emmett Till,** the American way, **float** away **like a butterfly,** but you gotta come back someday like **O.J.** and **Bill Cosby,** I was feeling good till they killed the image of a **Black Family,** it's a plan see see they hand me the **Empire** and the **Wire,** but the devils a liar, **Music** was meant to inspire, I sp**ark** a fire, I Sp**ark** a fire **- Dawud The Amazing BlaKseed**

March 18th 2016 Reincarnated

Perhaps I been **reincarnated**, **scarred** and jaded, **lucid dreams sleep paralysis** I hate it, seeking **oracles** and sages, sages and **oracles** seeking me, this path I'm walking truthfully, I used to chase booty faithfully now I'm abstinent patiently, half a man half amazingly, with the lyrics handed to me from **spirits,** the agony of defeat when they hear this, the strategy have you **eat meat**, drink alchemy, grow weak but if you not meek and speak strong… they bomb the balcony, I am the **falcon** you see on the head of **Khafre,** flying high **The 25th Dynasty** remember the time when we were at our finest b, finally say goodby to uncle Tommy and his cabin **Young Gifted And Black** and rapping like a **Griot, Cheikh Atan Diop** in case you forgot, precolonial AfriKa my **niggas** my **Negsu, Ausar** star dust **rise** from your **sarcophagus,** they can't topple us the populous in Heliopolis, who do we trust and follow? **Mike Tyson** searching for **Cus D'amato,** a people with out the knowledge of their history and customs are hollow, a tree without roots bare no fruits tomorrow, if you know like I know we in route to self destruction and sorrow, I put this letter in a bottle - **Dawud The Amazing BlaKseed**

Significance

At the time of this rhyme I do not consciously know that I have lived previous lives, yet I said these words! I also find it very strange that I mention Mike Tyson in a rhyme titled Reincarnated and I have a theory about who Tyson might have been in a past life (p 528)! **Remember that you are Ausar, the immortal soul, and Heru, the hero!** See page 3 for the **hero's journey**!

March 19th 2016 Don't Panic

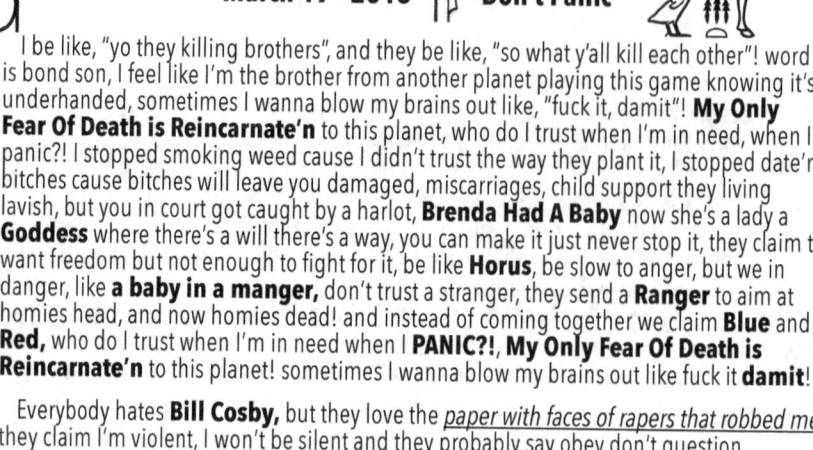

I be like, "yo they killing brothers", and they be like, "so what y'all kill each other"! word is bond son, I feel like I'm the brother from another planet playing this game knowing it's underhanded, sometimes I wanna blow my brains out like, "fuck it, damit"! **My Only Fear Of Death is Reincarnate'n** to this planet, who do I trust when I'm in need, when I panic?! I stopped smoking weed cause I didn't trust the way they plant it, I stopped date'n bitches cause bitches will leave you damaged, miscarriages, child support they living lavish, but you in court got caught by a harlot, **Brenda Had A Baby** now she's a lady a **Goddess** where there's a will there's a way, you can make it just never stop it, they claim to want freedom but not enough to fight for it, be like **Horus**, be slow to anger, but we in danger, like **a baby in a manger,** don't trust a stranger, they send a **Ranger** to aim at homies head, and now homies dead! and instead of coming together we claim **Blue** and **Red,** who do I trust when I'm in need when I **PANIC?!**, **My Only Fear Of Death is Reincarnate'n** to this planet! sometimes I wanna blow my brains out like fuck it **damit**!

Everybody hates **Bill Cosby,** but they love the <u>*paper with faces of rapers that robbed me*</u>, they claim I'm violent, I won't be silent and they probably say obey don't question authority, I find you hypocritical but that's really nothing new! that's what you do! Yeah I said it! I'm organic, you synthetic, you satanic, I'm *headed for the stars!* you still buying cars? is your body wealthy enough to heal scars? you dealing with a God sun! like **Akhenaten** not **Anunnaki,** have we forgotten the ones behind bars? if the grace is ours where do we go from here brethren? cause there's a face on Mars and a ghetto in heaven! we need a haven saving us from guns blazing, I heard em saying "will there ever be another **Malcolm X"**? they be race bait'n and can't define racism, when you raised hating brought up in classism you lack wisdom, I **Let The Rhythm Hit Em** spit venom for his **baptism**, this is **Hip Hop,** politricks I ain't trapped in em, who do I trust when I'm in need when I **PANIC?!**, **My Only Fear Of Death is Reincarnate'n** to this planet! sometimes I wanna blow my brains out like fuck it **damit**! **- Dawud The Amazing BlaKseed**

September 8th 2021 I Care About You

I heard you saying that ain't no body care about you, but that ain't true Lil homie cause I care about you, met you on one two five I had never heard about you, but look at you now, shining with that **gold** around you, the solar disk the **Aten** dropping them hands around you, you got my attention, the **Aten** I see you got the tattoo, that's where I'm from that's my family carved in that statue, my father **Akhenaten**, did you know that he rap too? Psalms 104, plagiarized, but I recognize the hymn to the **Aten**, rhymes will never be forgotten, I'm the son that returned no cap'n, the soul be **coming back** when the body is discarded, but still problems we gotta solve it, so we be come'n back but we forgetting, like when prophets find fame, they profiting off the change and shifting, it's levels to the pain, what's missing? it's levels to this game of life, it's levels to a name, **Tut Ankh Aten** say it twice cause **Tut em Ra** is one in the same, my advice is add virtue to your life, and put respect on my name, cause **Amen Atum Aten** will never be forgotten, I heard you saying that ain't no body care about you, but that ain't true Lil homie cause I care about you **- TutemRa**

Significance

Today is February 28th 2022 and today Marshall (Young Pharaoh Aten, **YP**) was sent to jail. I have been recently watching this brother with mixed emotions but mostly feelings of sadness as he seems to be having many issues in his life. I was drawn to him because of his new choice of name. I met him when his named was just **Young Pharaoh** or **Young Pharaoh Allah** but now he venerates the **Aten** and my name was once Tutankh**<u>aten</u>**. I met Young Pharaoh Aten in Harlem on 125th street in **2016 or** 2017 before he "blew up", which was two or three years before my past life revelations. I was standing across the street from the **Apollo**, in front of my homie Nova's table (page 534) when Nova asked me if I had heard of him yet, but I hadn't. His dreads are currently very long but when I met him he had only just started growing them. Apparently one of Young Pharaoh's youtube videos had gone viral and he was making a name for himself in **debates**. When Nova introduced us I can vividly remember Young Pharaoh looking at the **feather** in my hair (p 385) as we shook hands, then we parted ways. Some time after we met he would meet a female yogi who taught him about the Aten. Years later, in late 2021 I saw that Young Pharaoh began making claims of **reincarnation**. It's not just because of these claims that I chose to write about him, it's also the timing of it. These claims came after he **blocked my Instagram page**. This was around the time that I saw a video where he claimed to have been drugged with **Mushrooms** and or **Ayahuasca**. I found this odd because these are **spiritual medicines** and the mushroom was one part of the many intricate events that brought about my past life as Emmett Till. I wrote a disclaimer warning about these medicines on page 479. When I saw this brother going through his life issues, that he seemed to be bringing upon himself, I reached out to him via Instagram. I left a comment under a post of his and in his Dm, telling him that I saw the video of him doing yoga. I told him that he should begin doing yoga again. I told him that we once met on 125th street and I had seen him amass a following since that time. I told him that since that time I had recovered past lives, one of them being Tutankhaten but he never responded. However after I sent those messages he made a post **claiming to be a reincarnated pharaonic entity**. This got my **atten**tion because I had never heard him make that claim before and I had been coming across many men who claimed to be Pharaohs. Then he made a post claiming to be the smartest Black man on the planet, inviting anyone to **debate** him on any topic. That's when I left a comment offering to **debate** him on who can more convincingly prove that they were a pharaoh in a past life and **that's when he blocked my page**. I wrote the song, **I Care About You** on Sep 8th 2021 in response to his song, **Care About Me,** because his story touched my heart. Young Pharaoh is born on August 30th two days after **Emmett Till** was murdered and it was around this time in 2021 that he claim to be drugged, having had a **"very bad trip"**. He also claims to have been abducted by **aliens** while incarcerated. As I began to follow his story, the death of **XXXtentacion** came to my mind (page 471). XXXtentacion had the **ankh tatted** on his chest and Young Pharaoh has a **pharaoh tatted** on his torso. XXXtentacion shot up to stardom quickly via the Soundcloud seen while Young Pharaoh, on a smaller scale, peaked the interest of the younger generation because of his viral videos where he spoke about **astral projection** and other metaphysical topics. I found it interesting how he gained a large following of impressionable minds who seemed to rally behind him. Just before XXXtentacion died he was finding himself in confrontations ending up on TMZ, and even had problems with his baby mother. As I watched Young Pharaoh he seemed to be going down the same path. I began to hope that Young Pharaoh wouldn't end up sharing the same fate as XXXtentacion with an early demise. Both of them got attracted to Kemet much younger than I did and I admired that about them. I didn't know what an Ankh was till I was in my 30's (page 150). Isn't that funny?! And it wasn't till I started writing this about Young Pharaoh that I paid any **atten**tion to the words in his logo that says, **"we comin' back"** with the face of a pharaoh. Then it hit me, perhaps his soul is being called back to Kemet. And perhaps his ego has disrupted his course. You must be VERY carful how you handle this ancient information. The spirit realm is not to be played with nor are the sacred plant medicines. Young Pharaoh claims to be a reincarnated pharaonic entity. I used to wonder who exactly he thinks he is? And I used to have a problem with men claiming to be Pharaohs but not willing to detail their "revelation". Especially when they claimed to be Tutankhaten or Akhenaten. At this point I don't much care about who people think they are.. Especially when they won't and can't prove it. But if you've gotten this far you know that I have a theory about who Akhenaten reincarnated as, and he isn't Young Pharaoh Aten. **See pages 8 and 664.**

Rau nu Prt m heru

Iu f Per f m heru

March 20th 2016 Going Back In Timing

I was trying to go back in timing, then I saw you in a **dream,** woke up and got a text about you, what does it mean? it seems we been disconnected invested in the wrong things, our **souls** been arrested and it's haunting, we be launching satellites into orbit, yet the **After Life** we ignore it, like it's something morbid or horrid, more **spirits** on this planet than living, she saw it, we been given more potential yet and still the skills lay dormant, my power of will brought me my hearts desire, the same is true with you, take time to admire beautiful flowers, like **George Washington Carver**, everything change **ying yang**, fly from the larva, **Mother Nature** giving birth to the **Heavenly Father**, put respect on my name whether pissed or bothered, it's not a quest for fame, **fuck Notre Dame**, **Yale**, **Princeton**, **Harvard**, they all the same garbage paling in comparison certainly, how you graduate university and don't know the universe **Dark Matter** all you see?! **- Dawud The BlaKseed**

Significance

In this short rhyme I mention the **soul**, the **after life**, **Horus**, **dreams**, **Spirits**, **ufo's** (see pages 84, 105, 346, 380, 663) and **Jesus**. Horus is another name for **Heru** and Heru is where the word **hero** derives from. Heru is the one who is supposed to "return" or **resurrect**. Jesus is the one who said "I am that I am" and also returns through **resurrection** after death. I am talking about what happens to the **soul** after death, meaning the "**after life**". See page 3 for the **hero's journey**. Today is Nov 6th 2021 and I'm looking at this one **Heka** (rhyme) and it is so powerful because I still had no clue that I was Emmett Till or that I was **Tutankhaten** (**King Tut**) at this time. I am just going through this experience of life and letting my emotions go through my poetry and therefor my soul wrote all of this. **29** was my first number and Martin Luther king was born on **Jan 15th** 1929, the year of the snake, and my last day in the army was **Jan 15th** 2005 (page 130). I prayed and asked God whether I should stay in or get out and I followed the sign that God gave me to get out. Martin Luther King rose to prominence after the murder of Emmett Till. On Oct 18th 2014 my soul would go to Indira in a dream while she was mourning the death of her beloved sister in-law. "I was trying to go back in timing, then I saw you in a **dream,** woke up and got a text about you, what does it mean? " (page 305). See page 52 to read my childhood experience with **Yale** and **Notre Dame**.

Utterances for Coming Forth by day into Light

It is he, who comes forth by day into Light

March 20th 2016 I Got You Open

TutemRa

Giza Plateau 2022

They say a closed mouth never gets fed, and if you live by the gun then you die by the lead, here's some food for thought provoking, instead of that trap push'n us back, I'm hope'n it's soak'n in your head, I know *I got you open* with raps, crowds move'n like an ocean in fact, I jump in surf'n it black, visioning in the back of my head, peace to the nappy dreads, and the Goddesses that don't keep their legs open, I be **Marcus Garvey**, **Huey P** quote'n, truer words never spoken, the **spirits** I be evoke'n for heal'n, a hope dealer outlaw guerrilla, *can't sale dope forever*! My nigga, *the 10 crack commandments* a killer but still peace to **Bigga**, the *Thriller in Manila* still deliver shots to your liver, you drop, your top lip quiver, I'm more Hip Hop popular than ever, never drop the *feather of **Maat***, whether or not you try'n to get props or *just to get a rep* as I step to the top, better late than never so fuck your clock and your couch homie, you're in my spot homie, better find another route phony! - **Dawud The Amazing BlaKseed**

42 Laws of Maat, Page 367

March 27th 2016 Love Bes

The worst thing about a **quest** for **love** is dealing with a mess revealing that it wasn't what it was, the flesh, a hug, a **kiss** on the neckless, a wish to connect with someone sent from above divine fate **soulmates**, thin line between **love** and hate, the mind is strong we ain't gotta create storms we can **transform** like **beetles,** not the group! I got the **Juice** speaking the truth, I got the **Flavor Of The Month,** here's the scoop for your sweet tooth, you chill'n on 4 douce chasing shorties cause they cute, but will you be faithful if you catch her? come face to face with the **NTCHR**, let **42 Laws** measure your flaws, placing a **feather** on the **scale** of virtue will tell the tale, my **Negus**, to the **Daughters** of **Isis,** my advice is, go where the light is! not everything that glitters is priceless and vice versa, tell em you heard it from a sober Soulja, where ever there's love the struggle could never be over **- Dawud The Amazing BlaKseed** **42 Laws of Maat, Page 367**

March 30th 2016 Togetherness

We be ignorant but claim we intelligent, and only when somebody dies is it relevant, for heavens sake, we keep making the same mistakes and, a heart attack is when you attack you heart from what you ate, but your family stuck cause they up and ate the same shit at your wake, we keep waiting for **reparations**, all this time and money they wasting, they even doing a **Malcolm X** excavation, my nigga listen my ambition is a result of self guilt and an **apparition,** like a **revelation,** we gotta save our Black Nation, too much time it's taking, too much shining and faking, shucking and jive'n, I spoke to a man 65 and he said he just surviving, let him hear my music he was vibe'n, then he went home to drink his pain away hide'n, "ain't no man alive been where I been", that's what he kept saying laughing, they be blasting whether you riding or law abiding, how did this happen to our people is what we keep asking, but asking is lethal action, we need to stop acting like we fit through the eye of a needle, that's not richness, I need a **Bob Marley** Christmas, they robbed us of our piece of happiness, I see it far off in the distance, come be my witness and my comrade, if we got together it can't be too bad, we go alone we prone to go fast and crash, but if we got together together it can't be too bad!! **- Dawud The Amazing BlaKseed**

March 31st 2016 Superfluous

We may not yet be numerous but we form a strong nucleus, and everybody needs one, like the liver I'm not your superfluous organ giver, they pick a nigga pull the trigger then they deliver the heart or the **spleen**, know what I mean? it's donation when it's taken via operation, the younger the better so cops be chase'n, you'll never find your dream in this nightmare we face'n, no justice with racist judges litigating, they telling us be patient keep waiting, that's just voices of satan, the choice is yours this the final hour, we gotta build and do it ourselves, your problem is our problem together we solve them escape this hell, hell is when yo kidneys fail, you wasn't living well, take the seven steps to heaven so you can live to tell like Jacob and the gland of pineal, seeing Elohim open eyes like Neo **dimethyltryptamine**

What's worse, your thirst for chicken and a coke or some molly sniffing coke in Hollywood billions?! ask **Kat Williams** they getting high **Billy D Williams,** Colt 45 they advertise to the children then lie about the healings they offer! ADHD artificial diet at home disorder, and ain't no daddy at home disorder, you must be sleeping if you ain't believing they out to slaughter ya, wake up out of utopia euphoria you gotta **Get Out** and try, you and I do for you and I, ain't no big i's and little u's, they ain't teaching us how to rise in they schools, they just prepare you for the interview to be used as tools **- Dawud The Amazing BlaKseed**

<u>significance</u>

I had not experienced a **Psychedelic** (dimethyltryptamine) when I wrote this song yet I mention dimethyltryptamine in the first verse. I wouldn't experience a **Psychedelic** until I had my past life revelation during my 40th year of life on July 3rd 2018 (page 480). That experienced happened 3 days after I completed my training to become a Kemetic (Egyptian) yoga instructor and almost 2 months prior I had **fasted for 20 days** only drinking water (page 467). I mention these other factors **so that the reader doesn't go running out to "get high"**. I'm not trying to fuel you desire to **get high**. I want to fuel you with the desire to reach your **highest potential** in this life. I had seen the Movie **Get Out** and before that had been aware of what happened to **Kendrick Johnson** and him being found with no organs. America had become more of a horror in reality than they could put in movies.

April 3rd 2016
The football Run away
Heb Sed

You see I love **Hip Hop** my nigga, but it wasn't my **dream**, I drew rappers seen in **Word Up** magazines, we played **football** on glass and rocks, the grass was never green, I could have made it to the top believe it or not, I **ran** block after block on beaches, **Who Got The Props** in my walkman, in the bleachers I never saw my fam, but still I **ran**, you can ask my quarter back Will i am, his favorite play was a pass to me, Pro right fly to Z, I **ran** naturally, no strategy, coaches be mad at me but you can't coach a nigga **running free**, division one teams wanted me but they fronted B, cause my **GPA** was too far away from a **PHD - Dawud The Amazing BlaKseed**

April 5th 2016 You Got Me

I been on a late night creep top in the backseat, some girl I don't know I know we both moved fastly, and I know you can't judge a person from they past see if you ask me honestly, what they path be monogamy polygamy or something more spiritually? you might not be hearing my realms and reality I left fallacies alone now I hold strong on to morality and **<u>the immortality of my soul</u>**, and Cole you stupid, still wait'n for cupid, and truth is that love is ruthless and the trust is love can heal your **lupus**, and of course they knew this, but they do this for a living they sell intercourse to children, abort babies by the millions, send them to the navy and kill them it's real son, so I chill son I know she will come, the law of attraction in action until then I'll be fasting with no distraction, my passion for life started when I was **Christ** hearted, **Heru** flew and **Set** departed, no regrets the hardest part is over, the Goddesses waiting for her soldiers, I hear **Garvey** in the hurricane screaming it ain't over - **Dawud The Uncanny BlaKseed**

April 14th 2016 The Dopest Ethiopian

Rau nu Prt m heru

Iu f Per f m heru

Utterances for Coming Forth by day into Light

It is he, who comes forth by day into Light

I met **The Dopest Ethiopian**, a **jazz** player, her mother's from **Ethiopia,** father was **Eritrean,** and he was singing the **blues** old school **B B King Etta James,** the planes the bombs the flames and the pain taught her, about oppression and how to keep pressing through the **Muddy Waters,** survival lessons deepest confessions from her daughter, from the cradle of civilization, they made a border to separate the people, med-evil's all they ever offer, disorder, harm, Mortar bombs, <u>the **Aswan Dam,** under water to hide the **African pantheon,**</u> slaughter each other that's a pawn move! carry on and we'll be gone soon! there upon doom looming don't be a bafoon blooming, be a **Maroon** like **Dessalines,** everything is everything, the **unseen** will intervene, now here we go again **The Dopest Ethiopian,** my enemies surround me, do them like we did **Napoleon,** now here we go again **The Dopest Ethiopian,** my enemies surround me, do them like we did **Napoleon - Dawud The Amazing BlaKseed**

April 15th 2016 Influential

You can **heal** your self, it **starts** in the **heart**, then your **mental**, and what you allow to power your **temple**, our downfall is simple, the sweet and the sour forks over knives utensils, for hours I water instrumental, **lotus flower** created from my pencil, then I ate it and elevated, now you play it so I'm influential, searching for the **melanated**, hair natural and braided, my **Goddess** she's the greatest, she support me when the haters and naysayers try to knock me down like **Joe Frazier,** I applied 5 pounds of pressure no greater no lessor between her eyes, to see her **kundalini rise**, and I'm not surprised, success is not an accident, you can learn more from a question, when you're wise and benevolent, double check the checker, like you checking some dead presidents, but you better be checking the living ones, cause they be hesitant to set precedence when **cops** be killing our black residence, in fact **John Hanson** wasn't the first Black president, it starts in the heart, then your mental, and what you allow to power your temple, our downfall is simple, the sweet and the sour forks over knives utensils for hours I water instrumental **lotus flower** created from my pencil, Dawud be influential, Dawud be influential, **lotus flower** created from my pencil, Dawud be influential, Dawud be influential, **lotus flower** created from my pencil

I like em d**ark** skin, **Puerto Rican** and **Haitian,** adorned in art sp**ark**ed from the **Dogon** nation, Yoni taste'n **On Point Tip anointed** with **new life,** rest in piece to my **Dog Phiff** chillin with **Sean Price,** don't pray for a long life, my advice is stay in virtue not vices they only hurt you, I'm searching for **Isis NTCHRU,** not the one they keep showing you, if you ain't careful you'll think I'm your enemy and the government's a friend of you! I been lucky to have a friend or two and you ain't **Never Had A Friend Like Me,** here you see an emcee spitting **Till** his last hour, on that peace **Tip** still fighting this **White power,** fear release it, no **dreams** of counting their green dollars, is it amounting to freeing our **Black power?** trapped in the backs of our hearts and minds, don't cower in the face of Jack Bauer, if I had <u>*24hrs to live*</u>, **By Any Means Necessary,** I **resurrect** the revolutionaries, it starts in the heart, then your mental, and what you allow to power your temple, our downfall is simple, the sweet and the sour forks over knives utensils for hours I water instrumental **lotus flower** created from my pencil, Dawud be influential, Dawud be influential, **lotus flower** created from my pencil, Dawud be influential, Dawud be influential, **lotus flower** created from my pencil- **Dawud The Amazing BlaKseed**

April 16th 2016 - 3am **Holler If Ya Hear Me - Verse One**

The plight black life no hand outs **heirlooms**, damned and doomed but soon the tune gonna change, you ***robbed my tomb***, drove me insane, ***put a chain on my neck***, gave no respect, you claim it's destiny you manifest, white supremacy the enemy I do confess, You ain't never had a friend like me I bet, Dear Momma don't cry if they take my flesh, ain't a man alive escaping death, when you die what example have you left? did you speak truth to power, or did you chase money in the final hour?! **Holla If Ya Hear Me!** "You're too near me to see clearly" don't compare me to one body, I embody everybody **God body, Tupac, Marcus Garvey, Malcolm X, Imhotep,** respect to **Bob Marley,** I am not sorry! I am not a sinner! **The Black Panther Party,** The heart of a winner, the harder you make it for me, you making my story, it was written in stone we gonna have our glory, should have left **Michael** alone now he's ride'n for me! Little **Tamir Rice** couldn't make it to 20! put my **Soul On Ice** like **Eldridge Clever,** Till the day I die be my brothers keeper, I see life around the corner fuck the judge and the reaper, I would have been a goner if I wasn't a seeker, they put drugs on the corner then lock us up for the reefer, now it's stronger and legal these crackers are evil, they predator like the eagle, killing my people, I need you to **transform** like the **Beetle,** hold on stand strong turn on **pineal,** with Dr Jeckle and Mr hide you struggle and wrestle, it ain't pretty they probably wanna kill me, put my head on a penny, can you holler if ya hear me? blood shed what a pity, in the city shimmy shimmy, **Atum Geb** enough said, holler if ya hear me, **lotus flower** got me litty, the power of the kitty, put a dollar on the titty, can you holler if ya hear me? can you holler if ya hear me? they too near me, too near me to see me clearly **- Dawud The Uncanny BlaKseed**

<u>Meta Spiritual Significance</u>

Meta Spiritual Encounters, Body Snatchers

The day prior to writing this I listened to a Tupac interview from 1994 with MTV. In the video he would talk about black people having to start life off from the bottom with nothing. Most of us having no family heirlooms handed down to the children. I would wake up at 3am the next day in the dead of the night with the desire to create a song. The first thing I did was log onto youtube to search for a beat that would allow me to get the feelings that were in my heart out and I found a beat almost immediately. **As if in a trance the lyrics came out like water**. After I was done I put on my headphones and I played this verse over and over. The next morning I went to the bodega (Store) across the street owned by the brothers from Yemen. As soon as I walked into the bodega a **young Black brother looked at me as if he knew me, as if there was something he wanted to tell me. Then he said to me, "we know each other don't we?!"**. He didn't look familiar but I responded "I don't know but listen to this". I took my headphones off and placed them over his ears. He began to listen to the verse I wrote earlier in the day, and then he begins nodding his head to the music. He looks at me and asks me "is this you?". I said, "yes". Then he says "I fucks with this!". When he was done listening he looked at me and said, "This is the type of music I want to write but I can't". Then I asked him "why can't you?!". He replied, "**Because when you write music like this that's when they come for you**". I asked him, "when is your birthday?!". He replied, "**August 18th**". I said, "<u>that's the day that my **Grandfather** died!</u>". Then I asked him, "Do you know who **Marcus Garvey** is?". He said, "no". I said, "There would be no **Malcolm X** with out Marcus Garvey and he's born on **August 17th**". To my amazement the brother said "<u>That's my father's birthday</u>"... I told him more about Garvey then I left the bodega (Store) dumbfounded. I would see him from time to time after that. He was a local sour diesel (weed) supplier. 3 years later I would see him again when I had the song finished and mixed and he would tell me different birth dates (star codes) than the ones he told me this day. The hook for this song was written in a manner that I had never used before and have not used since. When I finished both verses I initially had no hook. Instead I used snippets of audio from Tupac and Malcolm X as the hook. When I finally decided to make an album in 2018 after my past life revelation of Emmett Till, I was recording this song over and all of a sudden this melody or pattern came into my head. The only words were **holler if ya hear me** and a melody. I recorded the melody and filled the words in afterwards. "**It ain't pretty they probably wanna kill me, put my head on a penny, can you holler if ya hear me? blood shed what a pity, in the city shimmy shimmy, Atum Geb enough said, holler if ya hear me, lotus flower got me litty, the power of the kitty, put a dollar on the titty, can you holler if ya hear me? can you holler if ya hear me? They too near me, too near me to see me clearly"**

April 19th 2016 **Holla If Ya Hear Me - Verse Two**

Life's a mess so we stress don't trip Let's kick it, young gifted blessed I rap so wicked, dealing with twisted attacks since back on the plantation you can get shot by a copper blazing, or a doctor vaccination left laying in a coffin, too often kids left with autism, obese or fat you still trapped in a prison, run a few laps and start living, **Huey P Nutrition, Malcolm Xercise,** Proactionary is revolutionary wise, Reactionary is asking to be buried alive, a slow death, first your fingers then your legs next, you can be a singer or an extreme fighter, in dire need for a kidney or a liver donor, rest in peace to **J Dilla** no one iller, we gotta chill with the dunking donuts, you can have 11 bill still be a goner, you can be in a coma from drinking led in your water, she thought she was having a daughter, she had a miscarriage, Do you know the average of all those who perished during the middle passage?! savage bastards! **Leopold,** and **Cecil Rhodes!** truth be told we gotta manage, regain control, the world is old but the future springs from the past, we gotta be free at last, we see farther through the tears of sorrow than a looking glass, do the math today don't wait till tomorrow, we gotta pray an **fast**, save the best for last **The BlaKseeds'** on the path, spiritual emancipation illumination, **The Lord of Maat** like the base of the throne, in case you forgot to have that conversation, **Reparations** are due for my black nation! it ain't pretty they probably wanna kill me, put my head on a penny, can you holler if ya hear me? blood shed what a pity, in the city shimmy shimmy, **Atum Geb** enough said, holler if ya hear me, **lotus flower** got me litty, the power of the kitty, put a dollar on the titty, can you holler if ya hear me? can you holler if ya hear me? they too near me, too near me to see me clearly **- Dawud The Uncanny BlaKseed**

<u>Meta Spiritual Significance</u> **(42 Laws of Maat, Page 367)**

I wrote this verse a few days later while riding my bike home from Seasoned Vegan (p 364) listening to the instrumental. I had to pull over and stop several times as the words to the song kept coming to me. I wrote the lyrics into my phone each time and kept on my way home. As soon as I got home I finished and recorded the verse just as fast as I finished the first verse. I didn't get the song mixed until May of 2019 and the day after I got it mixed I went down stairs and, lo and behold I ran into <u>the same brother I met two years prior the night after I wrote the first verse</u>. I asked him if he remembered the song I let him hear. He said yes. I told him I finished it. I took my head phones off to let him hear the finished version. He looked around and said lets go into the bodega. This time we went into the bodega owned by the **Dominican** brothers across the street from the bodega owned by the brothers from Yemen. Right before he put the headphones on and started listening I reminded him of when we first met and him being born August 18th the day my grand father died **but something strange happened!** He told me that he was not born on August 18th! Then I asked if his father was born on August 17th but he said no! <u>and he gave me a completely different date and when he did</u> **I totally understood what had happened!** I didn't say anything I just stared off as he continued to listen to the song nodding his head. After the song was done we parted ways and I felt weird because I specifically remember him telling me august 18th and 17th. I vividly remember our first conversation. He told me his birthday was August 18th and that's how we ended up talking about Marcus Garvey and Malcolm X. We had that conversation the way I remember it. I am not imagining it! But it was not "him" speaking to me that day we met in the bodega on April 16th 2016! I don't know who it was but it was not him! **<u>Then I remembered I had recently read in a book or heard in a lecture, about the strange phenomena involving people who receive profound messages from family, friends even strangers but if these people who delivered the messages are later asked to recall the words they spoke they will often not be able to remember ever telling you what you so vividly remember them telling you.</u>** It was not him speaking to me when we first met. Some spirit used his body to tell me what I needed to hear so that I could be led down this path of initiation! This would happen to me in **July of 2021** at the **African Arts Festival** (page 650) and this time someone witnessed it with me, Meeky, my friend who can see spirits (invisible helpers). In 1942, Japanese Americans were sent to concentration camps during World War 2. 46 years later, with the passing of the Civil Liberties Act of 1988 Japanese Americans received reparations to right the wrongs they experienced. Black people have been in American for hundreds of years being subjected to enslavement, lynchings, systematic racism and the list goes on, yet still we have yet to receive reparations.

I got the news that **Prince** died while I was at the Schomburg Center for Research in Black Culture on 135th street in Harlem. The official 10th Element of Hip Hop Health & Wellness Proclamation signing ceremony took place there with major players in Hip Hop such as the legendary EZ AD and Tony Tone of the Cold Crush Brothers, Stic of Dead Prez, Styles P and Jadakiss, Queen Afua, John Salley, AsheL Seasunz, SupaNova Slom, Afya Ibumo and celebrity chef Lauren Vonderpool as well as many others.. Prior to this day we had 9 elements of Hip Hop which are Break Dancing, Emceeing, Graffiti Art, DJing, Beatboxing, Street Fashion, Language, Knowledge and Entrepreneurialism, but now the 10th Element of hip Hop is **Health and Wellness**. We are finally in the Green Age of Hip Hop and **"Hip Hop is Green"** is the slogan.

Rau nu Prt m heru

Iu f Per f m heru

April 21st 2016 would go down as a sad day in music with the passing of **Prince** but every time a soul leaves the earth a soul comes into earth born again starting a new life. And who's to say how soon we come back? I came back 22 years after my life as **Emmett Till**. 3500 years ago I lived my oldest known life and here I am again. **Bobby Hutton** was born on **April 21st** back in 1950. Bobby was the first Black Panther to be murdered. He was only 17 when he was murdered by the police on April 6th 1968, 2 days after **Martin Luther King** was assassinated (pages 69, 217, 592). Hip Hop was birthed out of the same fires that birthed the **Black Panther Party For Self Defense**. Hip Hop was created in the 1970's and encompasses an entire culture that goes beyond music. Hip Hop is the world's most popular genre and art form, simultaneously influencing politics, social issues, culture, and society as a whole. However, over time Hip Hop culture has been devalued and degraded leading to the early demise of many Hip Hop artist due to health related issues and unnecessary violence. The 10th Element reclaims Hip Hop culture from its wayward commercialization that glamorizes violence, drug taking, drinking "lean" and other unhealthy and destructive habits that have become symbolic of Hip Hop culture and has unduly influenced our youth. **April 21st** m**ark**s the day that Hip Hop took responsibility for the power it yields when promoting healthy lifestyles. Now, those behaviors are no longer in alignment with Hip Hop culture. We are disrupting the negative narrative and are using the power of Hip Hop to create a healthier community to support the next generation. Like when the song **Self Destruction** was released by **KRS ONE** and many other rappers in 1989 the year of the **snake** on January 15th the day that **Martin Luther King** was born (page 633). Hip Hop came together on **April 21st** 2016 to stop the self destruction. On **April 21st** 2018 I would start my teacher training to become a **Kemetic Yoga** instructor. During that course I fasted for 20 days only drinking water (page 467). Two days after I graduate on July 3rd 2018 my past life as Emmett Till would be revealed to me (page 480).

Utterances for Coming Forth by day into Light

The Ausarian Resurrection Element of Hip Hop

This book was brought forth in 2022, the **49th** anniversary of Hip Hop and **49** days is the amount of time the Tibetans believed it took one soul to be reborn into another life. In my life as **Emmett Till** I was murdered in 19**55**, in that same year the **originator** of Hip Hop, **Dj Kool Herc** was born... **22** years after I was murdered, I came back to earth, born again in 19**77**, carrying a complex equation of star codes intimately connected to the musical art form known as Hip Hop. **KRS One's DJ Scott La Rock** was murdered on **August 27th** 1987 the day before **Emmett** was Murdered (**August 28th**). Emmett's murder sp**ark**ed the **first** Black movement for civil rights while Scott La Rock's death is said to be the **first** murder of a major Hip Hop artist. KRS One released **The Gospel of Hip Hop** the day before my birthday (p 633). The **Artifacts** would released their first album on my 17th birthday **October 25th** in 1994 (p 66). **Artifacts** are objects made by human beings from earlier periods in time typically items of cultural or historical interest and the most famous artifacts ever found in modern time are the ones found in **Tutankhaten's** (**King Tut's**) tomb in 19**22**. The American record producer, DJ, rapper and songwriter Daniel Alan Maman was born the same day and year as me, Oct 25th 1977 the year of the **snake** and he is professionally known as the **Alchemist**. I am the **alchemist** coded within Hip Hop (p 656). This is **Divine Alchemy** of the soul, the only alchemy that matters! Some schools of thought can't be bought with a college tuition, instead you need divine intuition! Hip Hop was one of the most powerful swords I used to awaken to my previous lives. Words are spells and words carry vibrations. The vibration is intertwined with the intentions of the heart. When we open our mouths our words can originate from our ego or our soul. Have divine thoughts and intentions but most importantly have divine actions. The oldest writings known to man are utterances, spells or "rhymes" written on the walls in the tombs of the **Nswt Bity** (pharaoh) evoked to ensure the **resurrection** of the pharaoh in the next life. These writings were called the pyramid text by archeologist, then they were refereed to as the coffin text and later the book of the dead because they were found buried with the dead (page 6). In ancient Kemet the concept of reincarnation and past lives was called the **Wehem-Mesut** (repeating of births, page 14). This book is the modern "book of the dead" (**Pert M Heru**) because it was the murder of Black life that fueled my music causing my ancient soul fragments to come forth by day. When you read my spells read beyond the in-betweens of my lines. Watch my actions over the course of my life. Read between the fabric of the universe. Read between my lives and **re-member** that **you** are **Ausar** and **Heru,** the **hero!** See page 3 for the **hero's journey!** Perhaps you should first read **Wildseed**, by Octavia Butler first (page's 298 and 381). Or go read some of your religious books then come back and read this. Try reading this with an unbiased open mind.

It is he, who comes forth by day into Light

The official 10th Element of Hip Hop Health & Wellness Proclamation is more than just a document, it represents a movement of people within the Hip Hop culture who are committed to supporting health & wellness in our communities. While at the event I got to meet **Jadakiss** and **Styles P** from the Legendary **LOX** group and the Legendary Group **Ruff Ryders**. **Styles P** and **Jadakiss** were awarded for their work in the community. Together they opened up a healthy Juice bar named **Juice for Life** in Yonkers New York. Both of the brothers expressed how the life of an artist can lead you to poor eating habits while on tour and over time those habits lead to health issues. They both made proactive choices in their lives and after seeing the benefits in their over all health they shared the wealth with their community.

"I'm like **Jadakiss** and **Kris** mixed with **2pacalypse" - (Photosynthesis,** written on December 30th 2010, page 193)

April 21st 2016
Stic (Khnum)

This was my 3rd time meeting Stic. I ran into him while he was jogging in 2013 (page 271) and then a month or so later on May 3rd 2013 (page 272), I would see him perform live at BMCC (borough of Manhattan Community College). I was not a star struck person (page 78) but I respected Stic and meeting him was a major part of why I went to this event. Stic was my favorite Emcee as I felt like his music was exactly what the people needed to hear. Stic would start appearing in my dreams after this meeting (page 445) and he would inspire me to write the song, **Standing Rock** on **November 28th 2016.** "It's bigger then the language you speaking! It's bigger than religion and pastors preaching bout money, **It's Still Bigger Than Hip Hop** and your master degree dummy!" (page 429).

April 21st 2016
The Scorpion Kings

I was not surprise to see The Twin Pillars at the event. I met them on 125th street across the street from the **Apollo** when they used to vend next to my brother Nova Felder (page 571). **Apollo** is the Greek Equivalent to **Heru**. Ausar returns (resurrects) through his son Heru (Horus) as **Ra** in the Ausarian **resurrection drama**. I became aware of the Pillars after seeing them on youtube speaking about metaphysical topics. I would let them listen to my music when I saw them on 125th street and they would listen. Nova and the Pillars are fellow scorpios like myself. (see page 2, Scorpion Kings). **Remember that you are Ausar and Heru, the hero!** <u>See page 3 for the **hero's journey**!</u>

April 21st 2016
10th Element of Hip Hop is Health and Wellness.

I had a good time at this event. I met a few people for the first time who I'd previously just seen on social networking. **Lauren Von Der Pool**, **Quadir Lateef**, **Coach Nym**, **Uneek**, **Divine** and many others.

Rau nu Prt m heru

Iu f Per f m heru

Utterances for Coming Forth by day into Light

It is he, who comes forth by day into Light

April 21st 2016 - Prince

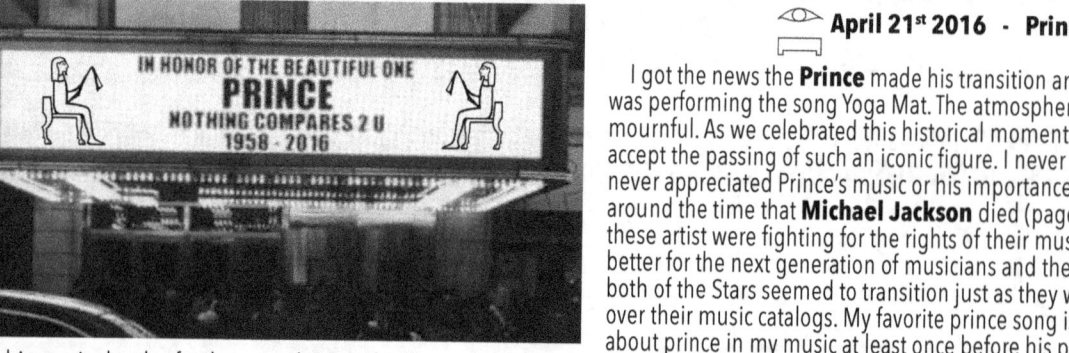

I got the news the **Prince** made his transition around the time when **Stic** was performing the song Yoga Mat. The atmosphere at the event became mournful. As we celebrated this historical moment in Hip Hop we also had to accept the passing of such an iconic figure. I never saw **Purple Rain** and never appreciated Prince's music or his importance to music as a whole till around the time that **Michael Jackson** died (page 166). I saw how both of these artist were fighting for the rights of their music so as to make things better for the next generation of musicians and the world in general. And both of the Stars seemed to transition just as they were going to seize charge over their music catalogs. My favorite prince song is **Adore**. I have written about prince in my music at least once before his passing and I would pull from his music shortly after he passed. Prince had been close to my ears for a few years as my friend **Nova** was set to play the role of **Vanity** in a biopic about the life of Vanity. I wrote about that on February 15th 2016 (page 362). On the day Prince passed away I met a woman who shared a paranormal experience she had with Prince earlier in the day. I would also meet a women that would connect me with a woman who would tell me her mother saw President Kennedy being assassinated in a **vision** years before the assassination took place.

"I rhyme for reason, this is my season! line for line 9:10 Ephesians, I come to bring unity to everything you see and if you come to conquer, I purify your ass in **The Lake Of Minnetonka!** many come but, few are chosen with a spiritual sponsor, I rose when I had a **dream** of Toussaint in a helicopter, Tupac, Michael and **Prince** screaming out nothing can stop ya, Dawud the blaKseed, the phantom of the chakra" **- (Sum Spooky Shit**, written on Feb 27th 2016, page 365)

Condolences

My condolences go out to the family, friends and fans of **Prince**. Please know that death is not the end. The soul survives death, indeed and in spirit. This is a book of the dead written by a boy who was murdered without justice, who defeated death and came forth by day. May the soul of **Prince** walk peacefully through the field of Reeds in Amenta. Amen Ra.

April 21st 2016 (Prince and Princess Erica on Prince Street)

After I left the event I would ride my bicycle to the **Apollo** theatre on 125th street where a multitude had gathered to mourn Prince. While there I saw a sister standing alone and crying. She looked heart broken. Her name was Erica Lee Lawrence and she was a tall beautiful model. I asked her if Prince was her favorite and she said yes. She said she loved Prince. **I told her that we are never really gone that the spirit lives on**. She said she really believed it and began to tell me of the spiritual experience she had with Prince earlier in the day. She was in lower manhattan when she got the news that Prince had passed and at the very moment she was walking in Soho making a left and turned on **Prince street**. As soon as she started walking on **Prince street** she received a text about Prince passing. She said she was in disbelief. I told her that that was a sign from Prince telling her that he loves her too and that he was ok.

The Murder of Phyllis Naughton and President Kennedy

I met Lauren (page 378) on April 21 and by *chance* I would run into her the next day at Seasoned Vegan (page 364). This is when I met her friend. Months later I started fitness training her friend. Some time in 2018, after my past life revelation, I would start training her friends mother and we would become good friends. I began to share my spiritual experiences with her and some time after that she would share a story with me of how, and possibly why her mother was murdered. Her mother **Phyllis Naughton,** was a woman who had **visions**. She could **see** the **future**. Her mother had a vision that president Kennedy would be assassinated. Concerned for his safety she traveled to Washington DC to warn the President. The details and order of events have been lost to time but Phyllis was not allowed to go home for several years. When my friend started looking into her mothers death it took years to get this info and afterwards she was immediately told if she kept asking questions she could be arrested. Her mother **Phyllis Naughton,** was interrogated about how she came to know the information surrounding the assassination. After some time she was admitted to Bellevue psychiatric ward in New York then she was transferred to Orangeburg psychiatric Hospital in New York. Her mother Wrote a letter in 1962 saying she should be home soon and shortly after she was released. When Kennedy was assassinated in 1963 she saw it on the news and cried uncontrollably. She was then reinstituted for several years. She was released in 1965 the year of the **snake** and less than three months later she was found dead on August 10th with her **brain missing**. There were 5 medical examiners present at her autopsy. One of the examiners was **DR. John F. Devlin,** he died mysteriously in 1976 after testifying in a case dealing with 9 murders that took place at the Park Plaza Hotel located at 50 West 77th street in New York City. **I find it strange that** Dr. Devlin also took part in the high profile autopsies of **John F. Kennedy**, **Martin L. King (p 69**,). Why did **Phyllis Naughton** have the same doctor as these men?! **Why was her brain missing**? What were they looking for, or what were they covering up? Clairvoyance and dream precognition is a part of the human design. Unfortunately we live in a world that has dulled our extrasensory abilities. I know that I have myself **dreamt** things before they happened and so have many people that I know. This book is full of dreams and some of them were premonitions (page 104). Kennedy was assassinated on November **22nd** 1963, **the day before** Emmett Till's Mother **Mamie Till** was born (Nov **23**rd 1921). Tutankhaten (King Tut's) tomb was opened on November 26th 19**22** (page 11). **Phyllis Naughton** was born on June 15th **the day before** Tupac's birthday and both of her parents were born on **Sep 13th** the same day the **Tupac** and my Uncle died (page 28). Kennedy was assassinated on **Elm street**. It was truly a nightmare on Elm street. In 1984 the movie **Nightmare on Elm Street** was released with the serial killer Freddy Krueger. Freddy was a **supernatural** serial killer who killed people in their **dreams**. Phyllis Naughton was murdered because of her **supernatural** ability to **dream things before they happened**.

Condolences: My condolences go out to the family, and friends of **Phyllis Norton** and **John F Kennedy**. Please know that death is not the end. The soul survives death, indeed and in spirit. This is a book of the dead written by a boy who was murdered without justice, who defeated death and came forth by day. May the souls of **Phyllis Norton** and **John F Kennedy** walk peacefully through the field of Reeds in Amenta. Amen Ra.

ADDENDUM Deja Dreams / Night visions with Tupac

My friend (**Phyllis Naughton's daughter**) once told me of a **dream** she had with **Tupac**. She calls her dreams, "night visions". She remembers this vision taking place a few years after Tupac died. In the vision she saw Tupac seated in a row at the Mike Tyson fight the night he was murdered. The vision was very vivid, she remembers being close enough to him to see the fibers in the shirt he was wearing. In the vision she walked over to Tupac and tried to warm him about his death. When she told me this "vision" I began to question what it really was. Perhaps she has the same gift of sight that her mother had. Perhaps her dream/night vision wasn't a "dream". Perhaps it was a **deja dream**. From my own experiences (p 104 -106, 305), **Deja Vu** is sometimes a result of having already experienced a moment in a **dream** that you didn't remember upon waking but when you reach that moment from your dream in your waken state you have a feeling of familiarity because some dreams take place in a different space and time where **the astral body travels**, sometimes to the past and even the future. **Jewell** dreamt **Tupac's** death before it happened (p 105). Perhaps these women saw Tupac's death before it happened, the same way **Phyllis Naughton** saw president Kennedys death before it happened. Perhaps she didn't consciously remember doing it and the experience resurfaced as a **deja dream**. In 2022 I experienced **Deja Vu** twice while in **Kemet** (pages 670 - 671).

Maat, The Mysterious Lincoln Kennedy Connection and The 33rd Parallel

Rau nu Prt m heru

Iu f Per f m heru

All things are governed by seen and unseen forces. At some point these patterns can not and should not be seen as just "coincidence". This thing we call God is always speaking and it speaks in a language of math (Maat, page **41**). Take for instance, the mysterious **100 year pattern** that connects President **Kennedy** and President **Lincoln.** Both Lincoln and Kennedy are the only Presidents who attempted to end the Federal Reserve Cartel. President Lincoln was elected to congress in **1846** while President Kennedy was elected in **1946**, 100 years apart. Lincoln was elected president in **1860** while Kennedy was elected president in **1960**, 100 years apart. They both made decisions that were in favor of the enslaved aboriginal (so called black people). Both wives **lost a child** during their presidency. They were both shot in the **head** and assassinated on a **Friday** by southerners. Both killers were assassinated before they could go to trial. Lincoln was shot in a theatre named **Ford** and Kennedy was shot while riding in a Lincoln made by **Ford**. A week before Lincoln was shot he was in **Monroe Maryland** and Kennedy was friends with a women named **Marilyn Monroe**. They were both succeeded by Southerners named Johnson. Andrew **Johnson**, who followed Lincoln, was born in **1808**; and Lyndon **Johnson**, who followed Kennedy, was born in **1908**, 100 years apart. Kennedy had a secretary named Evelyn Lincoln and some say Lincoln had a secretary named Kennedy. There is also claim that both secretaries had foreboding feelings about what would happen to Lincoln and Kennedy and warned them not to go to DC and Dallas. These two accounts of **premonitions** by the secretaries can't be confirmed however, the story of **Phyllis Naughton** is documented (p 379). Getting your hands on the documents might be near impossible but her story is true. **Maat** is cosmic order and Maat governs these patterns – read about the **sacred geometry behind the transmigration of my soul** on **page 602**. Then read the curse of the pharaoh on pages 12, 13, 99 and 204. None of this is just "coincidence". These patterns are examples of a phenomena known as **quantum entanglement**, spoken about often in Physics. **Einstein**, called this phenomena, **spooky action at a distance** (pages 40, 329). Einstein died in 1955, the same year Emmett Till was murdered and the same year my mother was born. Take the mysterious **33rd Parallel** for instance… The **33**rd Parallel is a meridian that orbits the Earth at exactly **33** degrees from where the Sun dissects the Earth's Equator. Kennedy was assassinated on the **33rd parallel** and **Emmett Till** was also murdered on the **33rd parallel**. In the field of Numerology, **33** is the highest of the "**Master Numbers**." The number **33** is seen in different areas of life: The number of turns in a complete sequence of human **DNA** equals **33**. In the Bible, **King David** (p 225) reigned in Jerusalem at **33 years** (2 Samuel 5:5). Genesis 46:15 states: "These sons and daughters of his [Israel's or Jacob's] were **33** in all." **Jesus Christ**, having begun his **33** year ministry at the age of 30 (Luke 3:23), and was said to have died on the cross and rose again at the age of **33**. I smoked weed for the first time at **33** and unwittingly opened a **portal** for **psychic channeling** (pages 227, 343). In 1945 President Roosevelt met his "sudden death" of a cerebral hemorrhage at the **33**rd Parallel at Warm Springs, Georgia. His last words were, "I have a terrible headache," but his medical chart is "missing". In 1945 Roosevelt's successor was Truman. "I've got every degree in the Masons that there is," said Truman. Harry S **Truman** was the **33rd President**. As the **33**rd President, this **33**rd degree Mason initiated the Nuclear Age, exploding the first A-bomb at the **Trinity** Test Site, in White Sands, New Mexico, on the **33**rd Parallel. He was responsible for the killing of thousands of Japanese (the Yellow Peril) at two cities close to the **33**rd Parallel, **Hiroshima** and **Nagasaki**. On July 8th 1947 a **UFO** and **alien** bodies were allegedly found in the desert outside **Roswell**, New Mexico at the **33**rd Parallel. 1990 Mason, Skull and Bones member George Bush, the **41**st United States President, provoked a war with Saddam Hussein. On July 25 (p 503), 1990 the US Ambassador to Iraq, April Glaspie, told Hussein that the Iraq/Kuwait dispute was an Arab matter, not one that affects the US. On August 2, 1990, believing that the United States' Ambassador's word meant something, Hussein invaded Kuwait. In "retaliation" for the invasion he had orchestrated through his Ambassador, Mason George Bush organized Desert Storm, which concerned a border dispute between Kuwait and Iraq at the 33rd Parallel. Shortly after Desert Storm began, George Bush declared the beginning of a "New World Order," but no order proceeds **Maat**! **42 Laws of Maat, Page 367**

Utterances for Coming Forth by day into Light

It is he, who comes forth by day into Light

April 22nd 2016 Life Around The Corner

I see life around the corner, I'm ready to live like former soldiers turned to farmers, no more drama black, yoga mat on the floor, no more heart attacks, eat that what is raw! ain't that what it's for?! more **sun** cooked foods, less killing animals, you a cannibal a vampire, if I watch the news I'm sure to see another brother expire, never seen the **Wire** or **Empire**, but *sucker emcees call me Sia*, I came to sp**ark** a fire, sell freedom to the buyer, victory to the fighter, inner chi to the fiber, to the bone to the smallest chromosome, until you search inside you will never find home, just be a blind clone, like a man unknown, but **the force awakens**, Seamoss with the force of a **Haitian,** Hip Hop is green, no bacon, or chicken or chicken heads, I need a Queen that's green instead **- Dawud The Amazing BlaKseed**

April 30th 2016 at 12:02 PM

Mfundishi Jhutyms' Metropolitan Museum tour

I think this was the first museum tour that I did with Mfundishi. Here I am seen standing in the pose of **Ausar** (the Lord of **resurrection,** page 481). This pose would be made popular in 2018 due to the release of the Marvel movie **Black Panther** but at this time it wasn't common to see many people take pictures standing in this pose (p 461). When I took the picture I knew who **Ausar** was but I'm not sure that I knew that this pose was the pose of Ausar. I just took a picture standing in the same pose as the Nswt Bity (Pharaoh) **Mentuhotep II,** in the statue behind me. At this stage of my journey I had never considered that I might be the **reincarnation** of someone from the recent or ancient past especially not someone that many people still know of and speak about today. In fact I never had that thought until I realized that I was Emmett Till on July 3rd 2018. If someone had approached me and told me that I was Emmett Till and Tutankhaten in my past lives I would have laughed at them or thought they were crazy. Unless of course they could explain to me like this book is doing for you.. Then I'm sure I would have been open to listen. I did not know that every pharaoh was thought to become one with **Ausar** upon "death". Once the pharaoh dies he must have his heart weight and meet **Ausar**. He must become **Ausar** and resurrect as **Heru**. **Re-member** that **you** are **Ausar** and **Heru,** the **hero!** See page 3 for the **hero's journey!** I was wearing the scarab tee shirt that I bought back on June 15th 2014 and the Scarab cuff that I purchased off the wrist of Mfundishi Jhutyms on **May 25th** 2014 (page 293). On Nov 13th 2021 (page 659) I would come to realize that the cuff I am wearing was more divine than I could ever imagine.

May 2016 (Octavia E. Butler, Priming The Pattern Master and the Rebirth of a Baby Gone Too Soon)

I met a woman named Aiesha in 2014 and began personal training her (page 298). The day we met she told me that my name reminded her of a character named **Doro**, from **Octavia Butler's** book, **Wildseed**. **Dawud** and **Doro** didn't sound the same to me but I could see how she made the connection. Shortly after we started training, in 2014 Aiesha gave me around 10 of Octavia's Books. In May of 2016 I would finally read one of those books. I read **Wildseed** first and I read it quickly. It fed my **imagination** but I didn't yet realize the correlation to my life. I didn't yet realized that Octavia sent her books to me through one of her number one fans, my client and friend Aiesha who "just so happens" to be born the day after me. I didn't read any of her other books until after my first **past life** revelation on July 3rd 2018. What makes it all strange is who and what the character **Doro** is in the book Wildseed. **Doro** was around 4000 years old. He was born in a village in ancient Kemet (Egypt), located on the Nile river in Africa. Doro was an **immortal spirit** or **soul** who changed bodies like clothes, similar to the spirit in the movie **Fallen** with **Denzel** (page 78). When Doro was a boy he went through a rights of passage that gave him the ability of instant **Incarnation**. By reflex or by desire he could force the soul of a person out of the body they lived in. Like someone forcing you out of your **car** then driving away, except now you're also dead. His first in**car**nations were by reflex and by mistake. He killed everyone in his village including his parents, going from body to body, killing each person one by one until everyone was dead while he stood there standing and breathing in the last persons body.. This experience forever changed his views on life and death. For generations Doro roamed the earth from the jungles of Africa to the colonies of America gathering others like him. Some he helped, some he destroyed, but Doro bred, ruled, and owned them all. He had seen many witches, and warlocks with abilities like **thought readers**, **seers**, and even those who could **fly** but they all seemed to die at some point. He was searching for someone with an ability like his, an **immortal**.

Significance - Rebirth of a Baby Gone Too Soon

Aiesha got pregnant some years after she move down south. Unfortunately the baby didn't survive the pregnancy, BUT - Aiesha's brother had a daughter who was born the next year on the same day Aiesha's baby was supposed to be born and **the baby looks exactly like Aiesha!** **Aiesha** gave me the book **Wildseed** to read. She told me that my name reminded her of a character named **Doro**. Doro is an immortal soul from ancient **Kemet**, during the times of the **Pharaohs**. He is very similar to the ancient deity Ausar, the Lord of **resurrection** in the ancient Egyptian pantheon (page 482). Ausar is the one who defeats death through the resurrection and this is where the story of **Jesus Christ** was taken from when Christianity came into existence. The resurrection of the father through the son, the repetition of the soul, in **Judaism** reincarnation is known as **Gilgul** (Cycle, page 14). **Re-member** that **you** are **Ausar** and **Heru,** the **hero!** See page 3 for the **hero's journey!** This is what the ancient Kemetyu (Egyptians) had mastered! From time immemorial we knew that there was no death. We had no word for death as we know it today because we understood and mastered the repetition of the soul. Today this reality of life is brushed over with very little importance given to it yet all over the world billions of people are waiting for some savior to "return" at the "end of days". Perhaps the only thing that will return is you after the end of your days inside of the body you travel in now. But will you remember is the question? Perhaps you have been here before and just don't remember. I can tell you that I have been here many times before and as you read this book you will see this pattern forming like the title of Octavia's book, **Pattern Master**. I am the pattern master that Octavia wrote about as in I have been able to decode the pattern of my incarnations as if I collected the blue prints of my creation. I want to thank Octavia E. Butler as her work primed me and helped prepare me to weave my pattern of destiny that not even immortals could imagine. I'd say that I had a rough landing as I came to know who I was. Putting this pattern together was at times very frightening but just like Star Wars (page 37) I became aware of Octavia at the most divine of times. In Sep of 2016 (page 419) my friend **Amiga** would tell me the **dreams** she had of me where I deciphered the **star code of immortality** which would turn out to be the foretelling of this book, **TutemRa: The Prophecy of Reincarnation**.. This is why my named reminded Aiesha of Doro. Because years later I would realize that I was a resurrected pharaoh.

Condolences

My condolences go out to the family, friends and fans of **Octavia Butler.** Please know that death is not the end. The soul survives death, indeed and in spirit. This is a book of the dead written by a boy who was murdered without justice, who defeated death and came forth by day. May the soul of **Octavia Butler** walk peacefully through the field of Reeds in Amenta. Amen Ra.

MAY 2nd 2016 Hapiness

We want happiness health excitement love and enlightenment, I want to kiss the woman in front of me as I'm writing this, I'm trying not to stare, I seen her **here and there** today **I sat in the empty chair**, **we talked a little little pieces of each other we did share**, rare was here beauty truly nothings fair in peace and warfare, heart break love at first sight, the first day, a d**ark** night no cape no rush to steal first base, cause trust is a must in the first place, in the worst case scenario this just end up a song on the radio, but you never know maybe this go radio active, the law of attractive magnetic electric gases roam pheromones feeling good feel it in your bones, "**Black Is The Color Of My True Loves Hair"** that I comb, I be the ***Lord of Ma'at*** like the base of the throne, The blakseed ***be the air to the throne***, in case you forgot let me take you back home, back to the **magic**, ***back to papyrus and tablets written by abbotts***, no bad habits, but look at us now it's tragic! the target of the largest psychological warfare ravaged, there you have it, can we fix it with a marriage? we can manage, put our hands together forever ***you and the Maat feather I will cherish!*** **- Dawud The Uncanny BlaKseed**

Significance

I wrote this on the day Afeni Shakur died and I have a theory about who Tupac was in his past life. I was sitting on the bench in Jackie Robinson park because no one showed up to my class that day. Whoa is me. What am I doing with my life is what I thought. Sometimes I got really low. If I tried harder I knew I could fill my classes up. But did I even want to do these classes?! Those are the thoughts that ran through

my mind then my phone chirped. It was a message from Ron (page 306). A clip from YouTube he wants me to watch. I clicked it and it's the song, **Happiness is** by **King I Divine**, the beat is beautiful and I must have it. I took off to get my computer. I didn't have wifi at the time so I went to Starbucks so that I could search for the instrument. I walk into Starbucks. It was crowded, packed to the rim. There is one seat open but there was also a cup on the table as if someone was sitting there. To my surprise the woman on the other side of the table is this woman that I had been seeing, **here and there**. I had never spoken to her but I always thought she was beautiful, and I had a crush on her. I asked her if the seat was free and she said yes. The guy to her far left looked up, he had just moved before I came in, he grabbed his cup. **I sat in the empty chair**. I was sitting in front of this beautiful woman that I had always wanted to speak to. I said hello. She said hi. I asked her her name. **We talked a little and a little pieces of each other we did share**. she was Ethiopian, an aspiring writer and her favorite rapper was **Tupac**. As I sat in front of her I searched for the instrumental and found it on sound cloud. I downloaded it and started writing while sitting in front of her. "**We want happiness, health excitement love and enlightenment, I wanna kiss the woman in front of me as I'm writing this, I'm trying not to stare".** I wrote a few more bars, then I closed my computer, said goodbye then went home to finish the verse. As I continued this song I would refer to myself as the **Lord of Maat** again in a song and I would make the claim that I was **heir to some throne**. The next day I would hear that **Afeni Shakur** had passed on May 2nd. I was over come with sadness and I would write another verse.

Rau nu Prt m heru

May 3rd 2016 Hapiness

Rest In Peace to **Afeni, Dear Momma I love you**! I'll be there when you need me! **King Tut, Nefertiti,** black people we divided can't you see that we don't share the same religions? coming together should be easy! what we need is hapiness health excitement love and enlightenment, for so long I been fighting this, maybe this song can right the wrong so I'm writing this, and I don't blame you for nothing, not an ounce of it! this government front'n they killed **Martin** then omitted it, **My Family Tree** they be chop'n it, I'm coming from the rotten apple metropolis, scribble slave on my face like **Prince** no apologist, what sense does it make to imprison the populous? 25 million for bail it **"Ain't hard to tell"** they wan't a brother staying in jail, "<u>*and go to hell to foul cops that shot*</u>" **Sean bell,** Free **Mumia, Mutulu** and every other **political prisoner** as well, we need a history that tells the story of the gazelle not the lion, cause these mafucka's be lying, Mothers in black crying Brothers in packs dying, It's about timing, what we do today is defining our tomorrow, we need another way that could be drowning out our sorrow, 400 years of work with no pay that's a no no, **<u>Reparations</u>** are due but they be moving slow mo, I suggest you speed up before you screaming oh no! **- Dawud The Uncanny BlaKseed**

Iu f Per f m heru

42 Laws of Maat, Page 367 **<u>Condolences</u>**

My condolences go out to the family, and friends of Queen mother **Afeni Shakur**. Please know that death is not the end. The soul survives death, indeed and in spirit. This is a book of the dead written by a boy who was murdered without justice, who defeated death and came forth by day. May the soul of **Afeni Shakur** walk peacefully through the field of Reeds in Amenta. Amen Ra.

Utterances for Coming Forth by day into Light

In1942, Japanese Americans were sent to concentration camps during World War 2. 46 years later, with the passing of the Civil Liberties Act of 1988 Japanese Americans received **<u>reparations</u>** to right the wrongs they experienced. Black people have been in America for hundreds of year being subjected to enslavement, lynchings, systematic racism and the list goes on, yet still we have yet to receive **<u>reparations</u>**.

May 8th 2016 **Mothers Day**

Happy mothers day, if I could run away I'd run away to another time to a better day, when the sun shined, maybe we laugh and play, but d**ark** nights and black life get in the way, it's not your fault I can't forget the things you say, but I forgive you anyway a **Queen** from Rockaway, you never taught all the things you claim today, I been almost caught by the system in every way, you don't respect my path because of who I pray, you need to let a man be a man and go his way, I know I look just like my father and he hit you with his hands, Just like your father but I never hit you or curse you, **Dear Momma** I don't do things to hurt you, sometimes I be barely holding on, I rarely put feelings like this in a song, let my words echo my truth when I'm gone, when you was gone Grandma had to carry on, and there lies the reason why we have a bond, but ain't a woman alive that can replace my moms, I'm only alive cause I have you Momma, we need to struggle and strive and find a way through the drama, because I love you Momma, Saana, Tahira, Jenna and Allana, I love you Momma **- Dawud The Uncanny BlaKseed**

It is he, who comes forth by day into Light

May 8th 2016 **Thoth Surfing**

Thought surfing working my lyricism, like a surf in feudalism on a mission, everyday struggle is what I give em, She said "you're so blessed I hope you stay living, I love given you neck, I put respect on it when it's risen", is you done or is you finish? is you running for number one spot like division, or is you not **The Number One Chief Rocker** spit'n? fuck a cop'er if she hotter than hands of **Jordan** scoring on a pass from **Pippin**, during my **fast I drink water** from **copper**, this is not your everyday struggle rags to riches, **You see my path is different, and my richness is in life forever!!** I ain't saying I never chased the bitches, but now I know better! I chase the three bitches of **The Dog Star,** and the **Maat feather,** the lips of wisdom never speak if you not clever, the secret was buried deep like a hidden treasure, **Thoth** surfing like silver searching the galaxy, approaching **mercury**, opening eyes from surgery, the first university, the first to sail the sea, "<u>*we probably in hell already we just fail to see, and our dumb asses not knowing every body kissing ass to go to heaven ain't going*</u>" **- Dawud The Uncanny BlaKseed** **42 Laws of Maat, Page 367**

When you feeling down hear this sound, be in the now, in the present, life is full of set backs, don't let that kill out your happiness, don't sweat that! don't let that steal destroy your joy, expect that things get better, bet that things change like the weather, life is like that, keep your heart light as a feather, the wise win before they even fight, the ignorant fight to win, cause they never quite understood the yin to the yang, the end to the pain, you in for the fame, I'm in for the change, into the game I came with the **archers** aim, my flow be the bow, the arrow goes to the heart, flow through the veins, **Maat magic** moves the lymphatics, from the floor to the core to the attic, they want more they all became addicts, it's good for the spirit so I let em have it, I'm good with lyrical miracle automatic, **I live it so I give it then autograph it**, through all the traffic, and static stayed organic, didn't panic, then scored a classic, holographic universes, the pin pad merges, words became magnetic, they went ecstatic when I said it - **Dawud The Uncanny BlaKseed**

Summer 2016 - Brother Kenny, Marcus Garvey and Siddhartha

I wouldn't read the book **Siddhartha** by Hermann Hesse till 2016 after I met a brother named **Kenny** who was in his 70's. Kenny and I met in **Marcus Garvey** park after one of my classes with Mfundishi Jhutyms. He was working with a few brothers teaching them Aikido. I took his card and sometime around May of 2016, I called him for some lessons in Aikido. Kenny and I only met around 5 or 6 times and during all of our sessions we would talk about spirituality which were more like friendly debates. One day during one of our debates he told me I needed to read a book but he couldn't remember the name. After some time he remembered the name of the book and it was **Siddhartha** by Hermann Hesse. Surprised, I told him that I already had the book! Then I told him that the person that gave me the book was born on January 12th the same day as him. The book Siddhartha is about the "**Buddha Siddhartha Gautama"** and how he gained enlightenment and the strange thing is that I purchased the book on July 15th 2014 and was later given another copy as a gift by my friend Stephanie on my birthday October 25th of 2015 but I never read the book. Because of that **coincidence** with Kenny I went home and read the book immediately. I did not know who the book was about until I finished the book however after a few paragraphs of reading I was over come with tears as I felt like I was reading about myself. After I read the book I called Stephanie to ask her why she gave me that book! That's when she told me about her childhood friend **Siddhartha**. He was a really good swimmer who unfortunately and ironically died trying to save someone from drowning. Sometime after she met me in 2014 she had a **dream** about her friend Siddhartha and in the **dream** he wrote a message on a piece of paper and handed it to her (p 296). When she awoke from the **dream** she could not remember what the message said. Confused about the **dream** she google the named Siddhartha and came across the book Siddhartha by Hermann Hesse - She purchased the book and read it.. After getting to know me she felt I reminded her of the boy Siddhartha from the book so she bought me a copy of the book for my birthday in 2015. Stephanie would also have a **dream** in 2015 that I was a king and I had **23** wives (page 295). Who wrote the message on the paper in Stephanie's dream, Siddhartha the Buddha, Siddhartha her childhood friend or me? A few months before I met Stephanie and before I purchased the book Siddhartha I watched the documentary The Prophecy of **REINCARNATION** Sambho the Black Buddha, about the Buddha being reincarnated in the western world between the years of 1975 and 2020 (p 288). The documentary would show images of King Tut. I was born in 1977 the year of the snake and I had my second past life revelation of my life as **Tutankhaten** (**King Tut)** revealed to me on April 4th 2020 (page 594) the day that **Martin Luther King** was assassinated (pages 69, 592). I'm writing a Epic Sci-Real (Science Reality) Novel Trilogy version of this book and a book about Tupac's ancient past life (pages 664 - 665). Stay tuned!

Indus Valley Civilization

As taught by **Dr Ivan Van Sertima** (pages 606, 607, 518), the Indus Valley Civilization, also known as the **Harappan civilization** was created by black African men from the **Nile Valley**. The Indus Valley was highly civilized and is dated back to at least 7000 B.C.E. In the **Ausarian Resurrection Drama**, it is said that **Ausar** went out and civilized the world, teaching agriculture and all other sciences. With that said, agriculture, animal domestication, sanitation systems, and the building of two story buildings were all brought to the Indus Valley by Africans. Just as **Ivan Van Sertima** once said, "**We Came Before Columbus**" (pages 328, 460, 581).

May 14th 2016 THE ONENESS

I closed my eyes reached into my pocket, to retrieve the locket and the letter, the first line said "I love you forever, have a safe journey return safely home to me, learn what you went to learn, let your Hara burn, turn from a **Yogi** into a **Swami**", she's my lady my motivation I shed tears of separation, slipped into a meditation awaiting my initiation, the taxi said we're here your destination, I hopped out with now hesitation, grabbed my bag moved through the vegetation, on the path to elevation, with levitation enlightenment, I ain't done yet I'm still writing this, searching for the oneness that exist everywhere, the man on top of the mountain didn't fall there, the fountain of youth is not found in warfare, the truth is in peace I'm living proof the least you can do is let go of fear, and take in a deep breath of air, Searching for the oneness that exist everywhere, the man on top of the mountain didn't fall there, Searching for the oneness that exist everywhere, the man on top of the mountain didn't fall there

Keep your eye on the sparrow, God is the bow, the flow is the arrow, the goal is the narrow road I travel, searching for the oneness, is it found in the flesh or the bone marrow? the sun set or the steps that I chose to follow? a bee collects honey in harmony like a piano with **sacred geometry**, micro macro, peace and joy follows me like my shadow follows my body, *like the reflection of the* ***sun*** *walking on the sea of Galilee*, I'm "*up early with my mind state so military*", they fantasize of seeing young black seeds buried, that don't worry me I keep it G like **Marcus Garvey,** meditate with love and devotion take this analogy, a lake is to the ocean what religion is to spirituality! how are you living, are you a villain or driven by morality? is it **Ma'at** philosophy, equality, compassion, justice, cosmic order? the way of mastery!? Searching for the oneness that exist everywhere, the man on top of the mountain didn't fall there, Searching for the oneness that exist everywhere, the man on top of the mountain didn't fall there - **Dawud The Uncanny BlaKseed**

Significance

I wrote the first verse after reading only 2 or 3 paragraphs in the book **The Initiation**, by Donald Schnell. I think this was one

of the books I heard Bobby Hemmit (p 262) mention in a lecture. On may 14th 2016 I would choose this book to read while taking a bath. While in the bath I wrote the first verse very quickly while listening to a beat that had a **Sade** sample in it. After I wrote that verse I put the book down for the day and the days following I read a few pages here and there. Then on **May 23rd 2016** this book would become **magical** (page 385). The book would speak to me like the books I bought on November 30th 2014 (page 311)! Like the **Medu Neter** book spoke to me on May 5th 2015 (page 329)! Like when Baba **Kilindi Iyi** spoke to me from a book on April 10th 2020 the day after he transitioned (page 606). Like when the **NTR** spoke to me in a cross word puzzle on November **23**rd 2017 (page 455). Like when the thrift store spoke to me and gave me 3 books in 2016 that all have to do with my **revelation** (page 418-419). Like when the **"elements"** provided me with the info I needed for a client on February 13th 2016 (page 362). Like when the **Cosmos** came to me in a book in 2017 (page 452). 10 days after I wrote this verse, on **May 24th 2016** I would be **initiated** by someone or something into something that I was still unaware of (page 385). I was on a blind initiation that would eventually lead me to my past lives (page 602)

Rau nu Prt m heru

Iu f Per f m heru

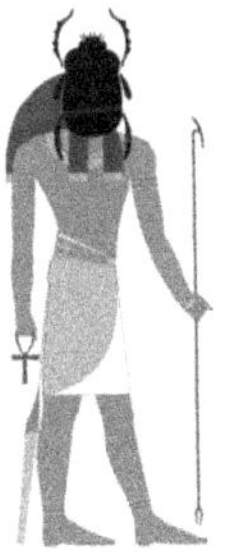

Utterances for Coming Forth by day into Light

May 14th 2016
New Logo

I changed my logo to the **scarab** (**Kheper**), but I still don't know the **resurrection** attributes of Kheper yet. At the moment I'm only pulling on the physical transformation with myself and clients.

2016 The Sunz Of Man

No self pity no agony, under the Bo Tree **Buddha** sat **ma**gically **magi**cally **magically,** no self pity no agony, under the bo tree **Buddha** sat **ma**gically **magi**cally **magically,** become empty first, of desire **dreams** sorrow pleasure and thirst, **transform rebirth resurrect in the verse, "No Love With Out Hate**, no peace without war" on the earth, no madness without no sadness, where's the love peace and happiness excitement I'm writing this for all those seeking enlightenment, the inner verse inside the **Sun Of Man,** the **I am that I am,** the **Atman** taught by the **sages** through out the ages, written down on pages, now I spit it down on stages, only the chosen few knew, now you know what the true way is, **Be Like Water My Friend,** and be the star that gazes, remember to take deep breaths, **Dawud the blakseed, king David**

It is he, who comes forth by day into Light

Expect the changes every season that you see, incredible is life like the wings carrying a bee, lemon honey water the natural order healing in the tea, the seed will never see the tree, **Tai chi** revealing this to me, ***The Never Ending Story*** realer than fantasy, have you ever had a **dream** that **came to reality?** to me it's stranger to see humanity spiritually locked down! look back and see all the things that we not now! they hide the truth in fiction cause we forgot how to close the eyes to see, to listen like the **sacred cow**, the nature in man is to expand, not rape the land, **George Washington Carver** smarter than the founding fathers, things change ying yang, fly from the larva, Mother Nature giving birth to the heavenly father, inside the **Sun Of Man,** the **I am that I am,** the **Atman** taught by the **sages** through out the ages, written down on pages, now I spit it down on stages, only the chosen few knew, now you know what the true way is, **Be Like Water My Friend,** and be the star that gazes, remember to take deep breaths, **Dawud the blakseed, king David,** Still we gonna raise this Black nation, I'm tired of the games I'm tired of waiting for **reparations,** I'm tired of the pain I'm tired of mass incarceration, I'm tired of modern day lynchings playing on our tv stations, I'm tired of this conversation, I'm tired of waiting, I'm tired of pacing back and forth, Free **Mumia Mutulu** and **Dr York,** free my Black Nation - **Dawud The Uncanny BlaKseed............** (When I wrote this song I was not well informed about the Dr York case)

May 19th 2016 Malcolm

Ethnic cleansing, dehumanization, Incarceration the colonization of information, and the image of God and creation, A-Fra-Ka Ta-merry, it seems we forgot, caught up in the belly of the beast, I know my people ready for some peace, it's about time they got our minds locked down in their spiritual paradigm, the mineral kingdom and the sun that shine, the plant domain to heal the sick mankind, humane knowing ourselves to be the first divine design, religion to return and bind back from which we came, **Hip Hop** became **rap** when they **raped** the game, and if **The Black Madonna** is *black like me*!, tell me why from **Pre K** to **PHD** the enslaver is teaching me?! Seriously we need to home school! we need our own food! rule number one know where you coming from son, so we can know where we must go and grow **- Dawud The Uncanny BlaKseed**

May 23rd 2016 Hadiiya and The Feather of Maat

I had been thinking about wearing a feather in my hair for over a year now to represent **Maat**. Around 4 or 5 months ago I reached out to **Hadiiya** about where she got hers. I saw her wearing feathers in her hair on social networking. She told me she got them from the Feather Place on 38th st. I knew Hadiiya from my years of personal training in Brooklyn and lower Manhattan having trained her before and even sharing a profound experience with her in 2005 (page 156). Finally on this day, May **23**rd 2016 I would walk to the Feather Place after my Wing Chung class, from 61st street and 1st ave to 38th street and 6th ave. Initially I wanted ostrich feathers because they symbolize Maat but they were too soft and feminine for me to wear. I purchased some for my alter and looked around for other feathers that I might feel better wearing. As soon as my eyes fell on the female **peacock feathers** I knew I had found my feathers. At the time I did not know that Peacock feathers represent **resurrection** and **eternal life**. I purchased a dozen immediately and I wore one home that day. I would experience many funny looks again from people. The same looks I experienced when I first started wearing the patch of hair in the back of my head. People are so stuck into what is a normality for them. Now I was getting funny looks because of the feather in my head. I was only wearing the feather to honor Maat. It was not because I am Blackfoot or Cherokee Indian. No, it was for Maat! The next day the unseen world would strike again, or should I say a book would strike again. I will see Hadiiya on July 1st 2018 (page 474) for the first time in many years and she will be a part of the star code pattern surrounding my past life of **Emmett Till**. **(42 Laws of Maat, Page 367 / Metaphysical significance of the number 23, Page 648)**

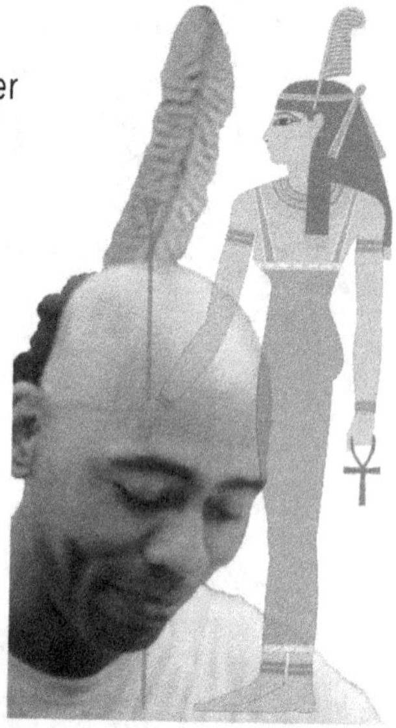

May 24th 2016 Anointed with a Peacock feather (The Blind initiation)

The day after purchasing the **peacock** feathers I decided to take a bath. While the water was running I searched for a book to read while bathing. I gathered a few books then right before I got in the tub I saw the book, **The Initiation** and decided that I would read that one. This book was interesting as it had recently sparked me to write the song - **Searching For the Oneness** just two weeks prior on May 14th (p 383). I got in the tub and turned meditative music on, then I opened the book and began to read from where I left off last time. The unseen world would speak to me in the very first sentence sending chills throughout my entire body. The main character of the book would have his Swami master materialize in front of him anointing him into the order of Swami's. The Swami would use a wand with a **peacock feather** at the end of it to initiate him. The very next day after I wore a **Peacock feather** for the first time in this life I picked up a book and open it to a page, and the first line I read details a man being initiated with a peacock feather. A man who was following his intuition and in doing so was mysteriously led on a magical journey seemingly out of his control, just like my life. I have been wearing a feather in my hair since that day. I shared this experience online and it seems like my story **manifested** in a TV show (p 536).

May 28th 2016 (Bam African Dance Festival and the Common Connection)

This was my first time attending the **Bam African Dance Festival** in **Brooklyn** and the first time I would wear my feather at a festival. I noticed that it attracted a lot of attention. Many people stopped me to tell me they liked my feather and asked to take pictures of me. **SupaNova Slom** was one of the people. He looked at my feather and said, "I like your feather". I said thanks and tried to open a conversation with him but he was either busy or wasn't interested. I had only recently become aware of him. Perhaps 2 or 3 months before I crossed paths with him a woman asked me if I'd ever heard of him. I met her while walking home from the supermarket. She was struggling with many bags of groceries and had several children straggling along side of her. I felt I should help her so I asked her if she wanted help and she accepted. I carried all her bags home and she thanked me. I shared my music with her and after hearing a few songs she asked me if I'd ever heard of **SupaNova Slom** but I hadn't. After that meeting I have only seen this woman 3 or 4 times. Years later I would realize that SupaNova's born name was Dawud, like mine and his mother is **Queen Afua**. I ran into **Ell** at the festival too, we used to work at the same gym and I had not seen him since I left Brooklyn in 2007 (page 145). When I saw **ELL** he looked at me the same way **Shiller** did (pages 616). The last time I spoke to **ELL** was in a text message a few years after this meeting. I sent him a song but he didn't like it, he told me I should try to rhyme more like **Common**. I found that both insulting and funny because **Common** was my favorite rapper for a long time (See page 66). I also met a woman named **Michelle** at the festival. My feather intrigued her and when she gave me her business card I saw that she had feathers on it. Her and I had a long conversation about **spirits** and **paranormal phenomena**. I would start training her soon after we met. For the first and second **Common Connections** see pages 66, 77. For **Common's** name in my music see pages 81, 134, 195, 200, 278, 313, 322, 3**23**, 360, 366, 431 and 624. Also see page 2**08**!!!!!

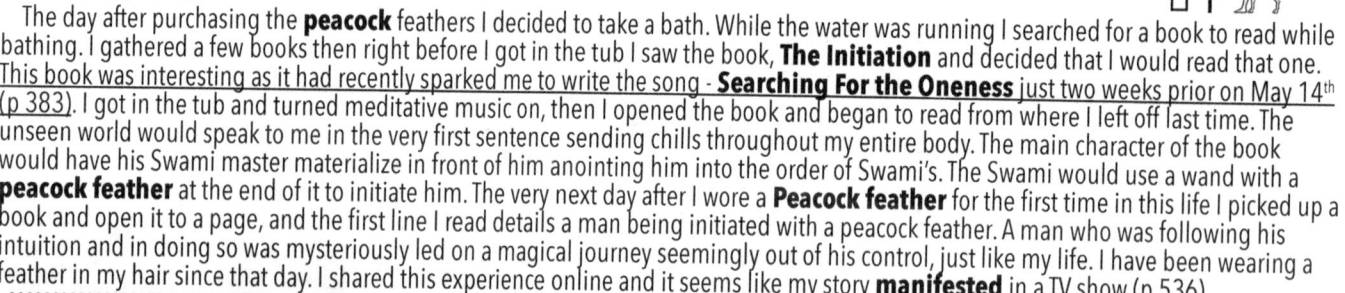

Rau nu Prt m heru

Iu f Per f m heru

Utterances for Coming Forth by day into Light

It is he, who comes forth by day into Light

June 3rd 2016 (Muhammad Ali Passes Away)

Muhammad Ali was born Cassius Marcellus Clay Jr. On January 17th 1942 the year after **Emmett Till** was born. He was born and raised in Louisville, Kentucky and began training as an amateur boxer at age 12 after someone stole his bicycle. Ali described the murder of Emmett Till as a point of awakening for him. Growing up, the boxing great was shocked by photos of Emmett Till's body and it affirmed his role of using boxing as a way to represent the black struggle in America and the **Jim Crow** South. In his book The Greatest Ali wrote: "Emmett Till and I were about the same age..I felt a deep kinship to him". Ali saw himself in the murder of Emmett Till because he was 13 years old at the time and Emmett was 14 years of age. It could have been him in that casket. No different than how young black males in 2021 see themselves in the murder of **Trayvon Martin**, **Tamir Rice**, and all the others. At 18 years old he entered the 1960 Summer Olympics and won a **gold** medal in the light heavyweight division and turned professional later that year. After winning a **gold** medal Cassius tried to eat at a restaurant and was refused to be served because he was black. He was confident, out spoken and not afraid to speak truth to power against the white racist American power structure. He became a Muslim after 1961 and was frequently seen with **Malcolm X** who was a mentor to him. He won the world heavyweight championship from **Sonny Liston** on February 25th 1964 at the age of **22**. On March 6th 1964, he publicly announced that he would no longer be known as Cassius Clay, changing his name to **Muhammad Ali**. In 1966, Ali refused to be drafted into the military, citing his religious beliefs and ethical opposition to the **Vietnam War**. He was quoted saying, "no Vietnamese ever called me nigger". Ali felt it was not wise to go fight a people that he didn't know when white people in his own country treated him less than human. He was found guilty of draft evasion, stripped of his boxing titles and faced 5 years in prison. He stayed out of prison as he appealed the decision to the Supreme Court, which overturned his conviction in 1971, but he had not fought for nearly four years and lost a period of peak performance as an athlete. Ali's actions as a conscientious objector to the Vietnam War made him an icon for the Black community, and he was a very high-profile figure of racial pride for African Americans during the Civil Rights Movement and throughout his career.

"I am the greatest" - Muhammad Ali

He fought in several historic boxing matches and feuds, most notably his fights with Sonny Liston, Joe Frazier, including the Fight of the Century (the biggest boxing event up until then), the Thrilla in Manila, and his fight with George Foreman, The Rumble in the Jungle. Ali thrived in the spotlight at a time when many boxers usually let their managers do the talking, and he was often provocative and outlandish. He was known for trash-talking, and often freestyled with rhyme schemes and spoken word poetry incorporating elements of Hip Hop, and often predicted in which round he would knockout his opponent. Ali released an album in 1963 with Sam Cooke and in 1964 was nominated for two Grammys. Ali was nicknamed The Greatest, he is widely regarded as one of the most significant and celebrated sports figures of the 20th century. He is frequently ranked as the greatest heavyweight boxer of all time and in 1999 he was named the Sportsman of the Century by Sports Illustrated and the Sports Personality of the Century by the BBC. As a Muslim, Ali was initially affiliated with Elijah Muhammad's Nation of Islam (NOI). He later disavowed the NOI, adhering to Sunni Islam. In Ali's autobiography he admitted that his greatest regret was going against Malcolm X. In interviews from family members of Malcolm and Ali they explain how Ali deeply regretted his falling out with Malcolm. In his autobiography, Soul of a Butterfly, Ali writes "Turning my back on Malcolm was one of the mistakes that I regret most in my life. I wish I'd been able to tell Malcolm I was sorry, that he was right about so many things, but he was killed before I got the chance." Perhaps Ali felt his public rejection of Malcolm helped create the atmosphere for Malcolm's later assassination, possibly at the hands of members of the Nation of Islam. Malcolm once said "just know that they'll hire one of us, to kill one of us, just to say it was one of us". In 2021 it was revealed that the FBI and NYPD were behind the murder of Malcolm X and later that year the two men who were convicted of killing Malcolm X were exonerated **55** years after being convicted in 1966. This government murdered Malcolm X and Martin Luther King (see pages 69, 592) and I feel that Ali was "silenced". Ali retired from boxing in 1981 focusing on religion, philanthropy and activism. In 1984, he made public his diagnosis of Parkinson's syndrome, which some reports attribute to boxing-related injuries, though Ali and his specialist physicians disputed this. He remained an active public figure globally, but in his later years made fewer public appearances as his condition worsened. He was cared for by his family, passing away at 74 years of age on June 3rd 2016. I mention Ali several times in my music before he passed away. Two months before he died I wrote the song **Rope A Dope** (page 370), where I mention the name **Emmett Till**. " **Ali The Greatest Of All Time** idol, he told his rival "I am one man you can't beat and conquer, I fight for 30 million africans your honor. where is the honor in dropping bombs on a town 10 thousand miles away, they never called me nigger but you kill my people everyday", the terror stays real like **Emmett Till,** the American way, **float** away **like a butterfly,** but you gotta come back someday."

"Your hands can't hit what your eyes can't see" - Muhammad Ali

Condolences

My condolences go out to the family, friends and fans of **Muhammad Ali** and all those who fought against this system of racism and white supremacy. Please know that death is not the end. The soul survives death, indeed and in spirit. This is a book of the dead written by a boy who was murdered without justice, who defeated death and came forth by day. May the soul of **Muhammad Ali** walk peacefully through the field of Reeds in Amenta. Amen RA.

June 9th 2016 The Peoples Champ Ali

Every rhyme that I write is like my will that I sign, fuck the system I'm in, my skin be the crime! **The Peoples Champ, Sam Cooke** on my mind, *"A change gonna come"* but will it come on time? I float like **Ali** in his prime, **The Greatest Of All Time!** I only count the reps that burn, like a perm, friendship is not something you learn in a school, I been **The Peoples Champ** since I was in high school, I didn't like their rules and didn't read their books, still I paid my dues and I ain't never been shook, I ain't got nothing to lose and everything to gain, if you don't live life courageous you might not ever change, I strike like **Marcus Garvey** in the hurricane, **Menace to Society** Ole Dog and Cane, if you 50 years old and still view life the same, you wasted 30 years of life can you feel my pain? <u>*"my aim, spread more smiles than tears"*</u>, Rest In Peace to **Prince** and **Afeni,** it appears, that the revolutionary disappears in the end, it's the silence of your peers that **Stings Like A Bee**, let go of your fears then maybe we can be free, it's the silence of your peers that **Stings Like A Bee,** let go of your fears then maybe we can be free **- Dawud The Amazing BlaKseed**

June 2016 (4th Police stop and check, Brother Basui and the Spine of Ausar)

Rau
nu
Prt
m
heru

This would be the **last time** that I allowed myself to explode during a ticketing incident with the New York **Police**. I have been stopped by the police many times in my life, but prior to 2011 I had only been stopped while in my car. I got pulled over on my motorcycle by a white cop sometime in **2008** and that traffic stop saved my life (p 157).. I had even been pulled over on December 16th **2004** in Tennessee or Kentucky for having weed in my car but I had no verbal altercation with the police (p 128). Sometime in **2011** (page 211) was the first time I was stopped by police while just walking and left the situation with no trouble. Then again in **2012** (page **23**9), but this time would be after the murder of Travon Martin and I exploded on the cops. Then again on May 15th **2015** (page 331) I blew up on two cops because I was still angry about the **Baltimore riots**, the murders of **Freddie Gray**, **Michael Brown**, **Eric Garner**, **Tamir Rice**, **Wilson Scott** and the list goes on! This day would be the last time that I allowed myself to explode on the police and the experience would change my way of thinking forever. I tried my best to track this incident down to the exact date, this is as close as I got but I think it's the right date. I know that it was around a time that I was doing some training with **Mfundishi** and recently I see that I had gone to the Museum with him last month in April. I know it was a Sunday and I had just left a class with Mfundishi in Marcus Garvey Park. I know I went to eat at Seasoned Vegan (page 364) with **Basui** and **Khepera after class.** We had a good time that day until my altercation with the police. I road my bike to class that day so when we all left Seasoned Vegan I left on my bike and headed home and they left together in a car. I was stopped by a cop at the merging intersection on 116th street south side of the street for running a red light on my bicycle. As soon as I was stopped I exploded. The peace that I had was gone immediately. I let this situation rouse up anger within me so fast that I almost hurt myself. All the anger that I had been releasing through my music exploded. The officer looked like he was Dominican or Puerto Rican. I was straddling my bike and I stayed that way for the entirety of our altercation. I told the cop that there was no need for a minor traffic stop like this where there is no traffic. He told me he was just trying to protect all traffic because many cyclist cause accidents. I began to dispute his decision to stop me. I gave him my name, rank and last army unit. I said my name is "Sgt Eddings, United States Army Special Operations 160th Soar regiment and I've driven trucks through the streets of Iraq during the Iraqi "war" so I have no problem navigating these streets on my bicycle!" I told him that he was stopping me just to meet some mother fuck'n quota but by this time I was louder. I was yelling. I had lost control. I remember slamming my front wheel on the ground as I was speaking. Just as my anger was at it's peak I was struck with a pain so excruciating that if I had not been straddling my bike I may have fallen on the floor. I felt a **sharp piercing** feeling of painful **electricity shoot through my spine** from my neck **moving down my spine and ending at my sacral bone**. I stopped yelling and sat on the seat of my bike to avoid from falling to the ground. Then I heard **Basui** yelling from his car window asking me if I was ok. Him and Kherpera had stopped at the light on 116th street and happened to see me yelling at this cop. I said I'm being stopped for running a light. Moments later the cop looked at me and said "I'm out of here". He got in his car and left. I road home trying to figure out what had happened to me. I was almost incapacitated. If that bike wasn't there I might have fallen to the floor in pain. Afterwards I called **Basui** and told him what happened with the pain. We laughed when he told me what Kherpera said. That was the first time I met Kherpera and Kherpera said the person he met in class was not the person he saw at the light cursing the cop out. I seemed to be calm and peaceful in class and at brunch but at that moment I was in a fit of anger. I was there with a peacock feather in my head screaming at a cop. **It wasn't until the writing of this book that I realize a deeper connection to the pain I felt.** On September 25th 2018 I went to a group gong session and had a profound **coincidence** happen while I was there, then when I got home I felt a similar pain in my spine that I felt while yelling at the cop but at home I had no bike to sit on so I fell to the floor in severe pain. While writing this book I realized that after that experience on September 25th 2018 I began to have **dreams** of **flying** and I even had self induced **astral projection** experiences. The most profound of which was on my Grandmothers birthday October 9th 2018. My first past life revelation had just come 3 months prior on July 3rd 2018. Why did I write in so much detail you might ask. I began to realize that there is a opposite to everything. **After experiencing extreme pain from anger I began to consider what effects the emotions of extreme love might be able to bring forth in the body**.

Iu
f
Per
f
m
heru

Utterances
for
Coming
Forth
by day
into
Light

It is
he,
who
comes
forth
by day
into
Light

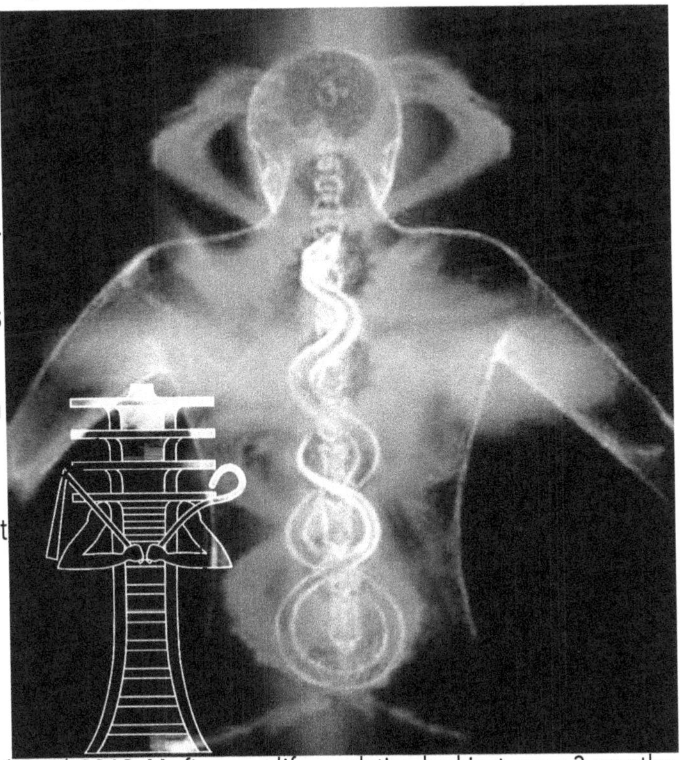

June 14th 2016 Pederasty

Shit got real last year, it's like the real is fake and the fake is real queer, fear everywhere, everyday struggle, the same one to hug you, be that one to mug you, then best friends become strangers, only God can judge you, but then the judge can hang ya, 15 to 25 for dope and buss'n your gun, but the Pope don't get none for poke'n and buss'n on your son, thank God I can run, hard navigat'on, hard to have this conversation in this abomination of a nation, tell me where are the children safe son?! **-Dawud The Amazing BlaKseed**

Significance

This year Afrika Bambaataa would be accused of allegedly touching and sodomizing and sucking the genitals of young boys earlier in his career. This is what caused the lyrics of this verse. The evidence against Bambaataa seemed to be very convincing. I believed what I heard based on what some gay men have told me about their experiences and because of what was told to me by a gay man in February of 2013 (p 265). (Also see p, 355)

June 14th 2016 Mahogany

There's an emptiness inside of me, I'm not where I'm supposed to be, I'm supposed to be in **love** but I don't let them close to me, society ya lied to me like **mahogany** and **Billie D**, I'll probably die with no progeny, that's highly possibly, I'm just a **dreamer** my philosophy can't be explained, we was talk'n in the rain, our **hearts** were **beat'n** still **spark'n** a **flame**, sometimes meeting, it's like the **Arc**hers aim, sometimes not being able to explain everything is frightening, sometimes love strikes like lightening, **7** days, **7** colors, **7** layers we discover, what are the chances we meet each other? they say everything happens for a reason, or do we take chances?! sweet glances, romances, hugging you is therapy, the remedy when I see you laughing, is it a crime she's on my mind all the time? perfectly designed down to her sign, she's more than fine, but will she be mine?! time will tell, love will prevail, more precious than diamonds and pearls, she's my baby girl, my everything my beauty **Queen,** Like **Queen Tiye,** The most beautifulest thing **Amen Hotep** could see, in the **18th Dynasty,** will she remember me or will she walk past me?! will she walk past me without ever seeing the pattern, sometimes not being able to explain everything is frightening, not being able to explain everything is frightening, not being able to explain everything is frightening, Sometimes love strikes like lightening **- Dawud The Amazing BlaKseed**

Significance

The second half of this song was taken from the song, **18th Dynasty**, written on **May 29th 2015** (Page 336).

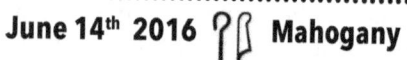

Amenhotep III and his royal wife, **Queen Tiye**

AmenHotep III, was my ancient grandfather. He was known as the **Dazzling Sun** and AmenHotep the Magnificent. He was a family man like his son Amenhotep IV, building statues depicting his wife Queen Tiye the same size as him. His greatest achievement was his ability to rule for around 40 years without war, as he honored the principles of **Maat** and practiced excellent diplomacy. This allowed kemet to reach the peak of its artistic and international power leading to a period of unparalleled prosperity and opulence. See page 638. **42 Laws of Maat, Page 367**

June 18th 2016 Searching

I started searching when I was 10 years old, I felt the thorns on the flowers, but still I rose, **miracles** happen when you **seek love** don't sell your soul, a million reasons to be cold and sad but instead hold on to happiness and laugh, be thankful for the road blocks on your path, if it comes let it come, if it goes let it pass, experiences they come they go, but when God comes you glow, you grow fast, eventually the pieces fall into place like math, the good news is, bad times don't last, the bad news is, good times don't last either, that's why it's better to be a knower than a be**lie**ver **- Dawud The Amazing BlaKseed**

Rau nu Prt m heru

Iu f Per f m heru

Utterances for Coming Forth by day into Light

It is he, who comes forth by day into Light

June 15th 2016 - Meta Spiritual Encounters
The Reincarnation of Dejazmatch Beru and my first set at Tsion Cafe

I met **Beejay** in 2013 when she joined my group fitness classes. Some time later she and her husband **Padmore** opened an Ethiopian restaurant in Harlem named **Tsion Cafe.** The location of their restaurant is a historical landmark as it is in the same location that used to house **Jimmy's Chicken Shack**, the famous jazz spot where, **Malcolm X** and **Red Foxx** once worked in the 1930's and 1940's.. At the time Malcolm went by the name **Detroit Red**, he had not yet went through his spiritual transformation. Over the years Tsion Cafe became a place of comfort for me. Some times I went there to relax and write music and that's where I met **Tammy Payne**. She would always be willing to listen to my music. We got along well because of our love for Malcolm X. She was finishing her late father, Les Payne's book, **The Dead Are Arising,** a **Malcolm X bio**. Tammy would invite me to my first **Gong meditation** session which was instrumental in my self-care (page 326). I also met **Charnae** there, she hosted the open mic nights at Tsion Cafe and after seeing me at one of the open mics she asked me if I wanted to do a set and I agreed. On June 15th 2016 I would do my first set at Tsion Cafe where I would perform 8 to 10 songs in front of many of my friends and patrons of Tsion Cafe. Charnae's Grandmother is born on **October 9th** the same day as my **Grandmother**. I did this set the day before Tupac's Birthday and the next year on the same day I would have a profound experience with **Tupac**. I have a theory about who Tupac was in a **past life** ☥ (p 448). After sharing my past life revelations with Padmore in 2020 he would tell me that **he felt he was** the **reincarnation** of **Dejazmatch Beru** (Ras Beru). After looking into Dejazmatch Beru I found interesting star patterns that align with my previous lives which would make sense as to why I met his wife years ago leading to a friendship with both of them. **Tammy Payne** would win the **Pulitzer Prize** for the book **The Dead Are Arising,** and this book, TutemRa: The Prophecy of Reincarnation, Star Codes of Immortality is confirmation that The Dead Are Arising!

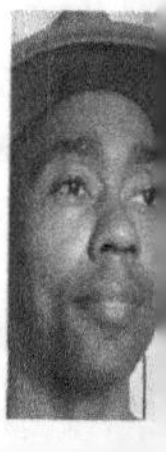

The Reincarnation of <u>Dejazmatch Beru</u> at Tsion Cafe

Rau nu Prt m heru

Iu f Per f m heru

In the picture below **Haile Selassie**, the **Negus** (King) of **Ethiopia** is seen on the **left**. He was born two days before **Emmett Till** on July **23**rd 1892 and he died the day before Emmett Till died on August **27**th 1975. In the middle **Lidj Yassu** can be seen. **Lidj** became Emperor after the death of **Menelik II**. **Lidj Yassu** was born on **February 4th 1895** the same day as **Rosa Parks** and he died on November 25th 1935 which is the day before **Tutankhaten's** (**King Tut's**) tomb was opened in 1922 (page 11). On the right is **Dejazmatch Beru** (**Ras Beru**) who was Ethiopian royalty and was the minister of war of Emperor **Haile Selassie**. In 2014 I met brother **Padmore** when the Ethiopian restaurant **Tsion Cafe** first opened in Harlem. I was training his wife in my group fitness class and I would come by the restaurant often, which him and his wife owned. Padmore and I would become friends over the years and I would start training him in 2021. After sharing my past life revelation with him in 2020 <u>he would tell me that he felt he was the **reincarnation** of Dejazmatch Beru (**Ras Beru**)</u>. Padmore is born on **February 4th** which is **Lidj Yassu** and **Rosa Parks's** birthday. The death of Emmett Till sparked the Civil Rights Movement after **Rosa parks** was arrested for not giving her seat to a White man. Rosa later said, "I thought of Emmett Till, and I couldn't go back." Padmore looks just like Dejazmatch Beru and he operates an Ethiopian restaurant in Harlem, in the same location that **Malcolm X** used to work when it was called **Jimmy's Chicken Shack. May 25th** was the first **star code pattern** that I deciphered and it appears at very profound points in this book. On **May 25th** 1963 the Organization for African Unity (OUA) was established with a permanent headquarters in Addis Ababa, Ethiopia. Haile Selassie, Emperor of Ethiopia was selected as the first president of the OAU. Based on my **Immortal Star Code pattern** I feel that Padmore is the reincarnation of Dejazmatch Beru and it doesn't surprise me because I have met other people over the course of this journey who have made connections to previous lives. In ancient Kemet (Egypt) the concept of reincarnation and past lives was called the **Wehem-Mesut** (repeating of births, page 14). Go back read about **Mambo**, the **reincarnated** World War 1 veteran (page 151, 407). Or you can read about **Amiga** and her **Past life** as **Dihya Al-Kahina.** I met her in **September** of **2016** while attending massage school and **Amiga** would have visions and **dreams** of me (page 419-420). In one of her dreams she saw me drawing a star code in the sand, the **Immortal Star Code pattern**. She saw the coming of this book 6 years before it was written. These numbers and dreams are not appearing by mere "coincidence". They are divine spiritual confirmations. One time is an incidence, twice is a coincidence, but three, four, and five is a pattern, can you tell the difference? All things are governed by seen and unseen forces and as you continue to read you will see this revelation unfold across space and time, life after life arriving at this very time so as to awaken those who are blind to the reality of the immortality of the souls journey from life to life and beyond the beyond.

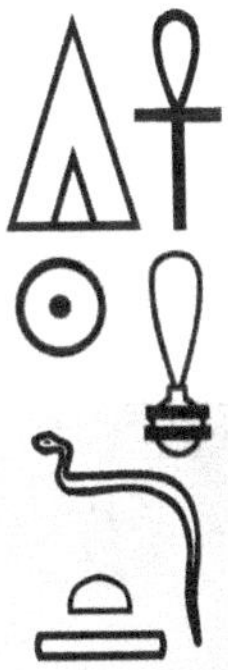

WHEN YOU EAT AT TSION CAFE, KNOW THAT YOU EAT WITH SPIRIT OF THESE MEN:
Haile Selassie, Lidj Yassu, Dejazmatch Beru and Malcolm X

Menelik = 10 Commandments. See 42 Laws of Maat (Page 367)

Utterances for Coming Forth by day into Light

It is he, who comes forth by day into Light

Felicia
Thomas
Danny
Michelle
Kassie
Janicea
Liz
Malik
Londi
Tammy
John
Rachael
Aiesha
P 298
Neeq
Mitch
Sunseed
Erica
Ron
Charney

Nova
Adrianna

Rau nu Prt m heru

Iu f Per f m heru

Utterances for Coming Forth by day into Light

It is he, who comes forth by day into Light

June 21st 2016 Beyond the Beyond

Sight beyond sight, **Life after life**, beyond the beyond, the quiet before the storm, **we vibrate into many forms**, let the dead bury the dead my friend, ***some of us come back in new babies born again*** I'm trying to go to another plane not here again! this life is about raising the consciousness of men, not the nonsense they program condition'n, the wind be whisper'n, but are you tuning in and listen'n? I never knew I'd be a fisher man, you think it's a miracle to walk on water? think again! the miracle is to walk in peace on this earth full of sin! the nectar spilling from my pin, worth more than the shoes I'm walking in, some people walk out your life then walk back in, your biggest supporters will be strangers not your friends, don't be afraid to walk alone, you never know when your life might depend on it, then you gotta show em like **Bruce Lee** in the **Green Hornet** or **Muhammad Ali** stinging like a bee be enormous, don't be afraid to run free like **Harriet,** one day you might be wanted with a warrant but **God** brings the Chariot, the truth is never denied the seeker it's the seeker that won't marry it! this is the truth coming through your speaker I'm not a preacher what I speak of is a freedom time narrative, hey young world, world, hey young world, world, do you know, where you're going to, do you like the things that life is showing you, where are you going to, hey young world, world, hey young world world

If you looking for a sign this is it, the signatures in nature in every rhyme that I spit, one day I'll transition into vapor like **Obi Wan** hit with a saber by **Darth Vader,** sharp razor harp player from the heart sayer, have a wonderful day **Giara,** everything I say I say cause I care, life ain't fair but we must dare to tare down walls even if tears do fall, the everything of everything, the all in all, in my **dreams** I hear the call then I wake stand tall, no fear, crystal clear like atmosphere when I hear whistles in my ear I know my grand father's near, as the eye peers through obstacles how ever foggy you are there at the end even before your physical body like a thought **Jhuti**, like karate on the wall hidden from everybody, it's your duty to be great elevate the **God body, Black Indian Dravidian** origins **Smai Tawi,** meridians and glands the union of the two lands, the soles of your feet top of your head, the dantians the palms of your hands, in the calm before the storm we plan, hey young world, world, hey young world, world, do you know, where you're going to, do you like the things that life is showing you, where are you going to? **- Dawud The Amazing BlaKseed**

Significance

In both verses I speak about **death** but in the first verse I say the words - "**some of us <u>come back</u> in new babies born again**". This line was most likely inspired by **Tamir Rice**. I first became aware of Tamir's death by the pictures that began to circulate with his face placed next to the face of **Emmett Till** showing their striking resemblance. I remember seeing this picture and wondering if **Tamir Rice** was the **same soul** as **Emmett Til.** Could the soul of Emmett Till have come back here just to die again to show us how much things had not changed? I had those thoughts because the resemblance captivated me. Tamir was only 12 and Emmett was only 14 and both of these deaths bothered me. I was still angry about Trayvon and all the others murdered before their time... Tamir's name would find it's way in my music over the next few years along side Emmett's. I had no idea what was in store for me two years from this point because on July 3rd of 2018 (page 480) my **past life** as Emmett Till would be revealed to me. In ancient Kemet (Egypt) the concept of reincarnation and past lives was called the **Wehem-Mesut / Ankh** (repeating of births/life, page 14)

June 30th 2016 Love at First Sight

Love at first sight, the power of will, we hugged the first night, sealed with a kiss on the forehead, instead of her lips, reminisce forever in bliss, never the less, forever the more, mi amore our hearts beat together before we ever did meet before, deep in my core saw you before, I ain't lying hear me roar, many roads, many doors, many floors, many ways we explore, many days, hours, minutes, our love never fade or diminish, only soar to the sky no limit, like a sword pierce the atmosphere as we stare back to the earth from the infinite, from the dirt to the universe, from my heart to my mind to a verse, perfect timing, stars aligning, blessings, finding you shine'n like diamonds in a purse **- Dawud The Amazing BlaKseed**

July 5th 2016 - Alton Sterling 37, Baton Rogue Louisiana

Alton Sterling was a loving father who was out selling musical cd's in front of a store.. The cops arrived to stop him from selling the cd's and he was then shot 6 times by officer Blane salamoni. Officer Salamoni was fired while the other officer was suspended for 3 days. No charges were filed. Sterling's children accepted a $4.5 mill settlement from the city-parish (**per isis**).

<u>Condolences</u>

My condolences go out to the family of **Alton Sterling** and all those who have been robbed of their life by this system of white supremacy. Please know that death is not the end. The soul survives death, indeed and in spirit. This is a book of the dead written by a boy who was murdered without justice, who defeated death and came forth by day. May **Alton Sterling** walk peacefully through the field of Reeds in Amenta. Amen RA.

July 6th 2016 - Philando Castile 32, Falcon Heights Minnesota

Philando was pulled over for a traffic stop. Dash cam footage shows office shoot castle seconds after Philando informed him he had a legal fire arm in the car. Officer Jeronimo yanze was acquitted of second degree man slaughter. Philando's family received a $3 million settlement.

Condolences

My condolences go out to the family of **Philando Castile** and all those who have been robbed of their lives by this system of racism and white supremacy. Please know that death is not the end. The soul survives death, indeed and in spirit. This is a book of the dead written by a boy who was murdered without justice, who defeated death and came forth by day. May the soul of **Philando Castile** walk peacefully through the field of Reeds in Amenta. Amen RA.

July 6th 2016
Meta Mysterious Encounter in The Fourth Dimension
Vivid Dreams with an R&B Chick

On the night of July 5th 2016 I was listening to an interview of Mitchel Gibson on youtube. In the interview he spoke about a series of prayers that he does and he recited one called the **miracle prayer.** I don't remember everything from that interview but this miracle prayer got my attention so I downloaded the video immediately then fell asleep with the prayer playing over and over. I woke up from a **vivid dream** with a woman who I had gone on a date with one time many years ago.

Significance

When I woke up the next day I sent her a text detailing how she was in my dream but she never responded. I never mentioned what the dream was about though. I met her years ago when I was a trainer in soho and I went on a date with her one time in central park. I remember being happy to have her time because she was very pretty. I'm not sure if this was before or after she got the role for the **Biggie Smalls** movie, **Notorious** in 2009. Later that day I would finish listening to the interview with **Mitchell Gibson** and as soon as it started playing where I left off he went on to say that the prayer is known for inducing **vivid dreams**. I was shocked! I bought a few of his books and read them. It was one of Mitchel Gibson's videos where I learned that **birthmarks** are linked to fatal injuries from previous lives. When I had my past life revelation of Emmett Till I realized I had birthmarks in the places Emmett Till was shot (page 514). I reached out to Mitchel Gibson on Instagram and told him about my revelation and he blocked me (p 8). I don't think he believed me.

November 11th 2021

Our thoughts and desires can affect our reality by influencing quantum level events in time and space. I logged the experience above in this book yesterday (Nov 10th 2021) and today I fell asleep and had another vivid dream about this woman and it was more vivid than the first. I called the number that I have for her to see if the number was still hers just to see if she as ok. I even sent a text but I got no reply. The soul of the human being has nine layers and one is the **Ren** which is the name. <u>I spoke her name and had her in my thoughts, then she appeared in my dream very clearly and vivid</u>. I wonder if she is ok….. All the events in this book are true. If you follow my path and do the things I do yet still the great mysteries are not shown to you. Then continue the path and **to Maat be true** and perhaps in due time you will be worthy of the view.

July 11th 2016 911 Is A Joke

The problem is, we got these kids and mouths to feed, relatives doing bids, rent to pay and staying home from work's a negative, the everyday struggle is a sedative, the system is broke, **a heritage of hate**, a rope around his neck no note they called it suicide, **911 Is A Joke**, coppers got guns, tasers, bullet proof vest, helicopters, you could be weaponless, still they aim for your chest and drop ya, that ain't proper! and that ain't it! – they say'n "all lives matter", that's bullshit! **if I kill my brother I'm doing time** but if a copper kill me y'all won't do shit **- Dawud The Uncanny BlaKseed**

(Inspired by the 1993 Tupac Black Watch interview)

July 16th 2016 Violent Tyrants

Where is the unity? not even in the conscious community! I see conflict, they just wanna conquer you and me, as soon as we try to U.N.I.T.Y., turn on the news and all you see is another brother die, **but we don't die we multiply** and we civilize, I hear the lies coming from the evil, you superior the chosen? well we the original people! the indigenous, the genius here to teach you harmonious balance and virtue, you need to be more peaceful less hurtful, self defense is not violence, it's survival, it's impossible to remain silent when a tyrant gives you a choice, the grave or the hospital, the voice of **Malcolm Little - Dawud The Uncanny BlaKseed**

Significance
(Response to the murder of Philando Castile)

July 16th 2016 The Source

Morality governs humanity, your salary won't escort you from mortal to **immortality,** the **portal,** to take it, erase everything they taught you to escape this flesh, life is a test, the **sun rise** on the right and sets on the left, so I follow the North Star **Ausar** and **Auset,** we the last ones left, 100 monkey effect, blast off like a jet connect to the source like a **Jedi,** we lost connection when they hid the **magic** of the **one eye,** introspection, the answer to the question, the truth fertilized, from the root I **rise** like a **snake,** the great deception, the disguise, it's alive! I mean live like a wire, in the sky, breathe in, sp**ark** that **fire**! can't see it, with or without faith if you don't breathe it, you expire, you need it! we require to eat it, believe it or not we forgot a lot since **Egypt,** adopted religion the **prison**, even **Jesus Christ** *<u>said, "these priceless gifts can be given to all of you who adopt a righteous way of living"</u>, let not a toxic man sway your decision, just cause it's written don't mean it's coming from the true and living* **- Dawud The Uncanny BlaKseed**

July 21st 2016 The Secret Life of Plants

Rau nu Prt m heru

I awoke from my trance and the plants was listening to my conversation, maybe it's a figment of my imagination, maybe I need a vacation or some medication, all I ever wanted was some **levitation,** I got confronted with creation after praying and meditation, **she said,** "<u>awake from your slumber the oneness is waiting, it's no wonder that the thunders been plundering satan, it's your faith in self that's the key to a healthier nation</u>", So I knelt then I felt the perspiration, the respiration oxidation, **she said,** "<u>I'm here to help give you a **revelation**, a test, why do you consume death? can't you see I'm the true and living? I created every breath that you've been given, **I have risen**, I am the law of attractive magnetic electric gases roam pheromones, feeling good, feel it in your bones, I am The BlaKseed, I am the weed I am all you need, I'm in your chromosomes, you are not alone, I know you wanna go home but first you gotta show em how to measure, I **anoint** you with this **peacock feather,** teach em how to chase the oneness and not the chedda, yes you have done well but you can do so much better, to break the **spell** utter the **Metu Neter,** we been here forever and never will we reach a limit</u>", the walking talking statues of **Kemet**, what you looking at is the remnants the ruins, the hemlock y'all they got it locked down, only a few in the material reach **Elohim,** tread wisely you professional skeptics don't move me, back to a pine tree spin whirlwind wizardry Merlin **Jhuti,** picture me in **3D** the **shadow** of the **4th dimensional** you don't see, **ESP** thought detection cause malfunction to sophisticated weapons of mass destruction, mind surveillance mind over matter blind the assailants with my minds eye antenna, take in the **Prana, Shakti, Sekhem, Assalamu Alaikum, Shalom,** I say **ANKH UDJA SNB NEB, Namaste,** I opened the doors to the **Cosmos** and flew away, universal intelligence, Dolphin - Elephant, everything is everything so nothing is irrelevant, <u>black lives matter</u> with or without a Black president, the elusion of inclusion, are you selfish or selfless or taking selfies dying to be relevant?! try trying to be benevolent, we went from fighting for humanity to freedom to equality now we fighting for survivability cause of our ability mentally physically spiritually supernaturally, super Nat Nat phenomenon healing me, vitamin D Megatron stealing the **BOX** out of Optimus Prime, these are trying times, time to shift the paradigm, where are the mystics to fix this saga? if you find a woman being raped would you save her or claim <u>**All Vaginas Matter?!**</u> shame on rappers that don't write lines that matter! your pockets getting fatter, that's designed by the mad hatter, you been had hood winked even crime data leave your mind scattered if you would think you might let it sink in and over stand time is at hand **Eric garner, Sandra bland,** smarter to be a warrior farmer than a farmer in a war in this crime land, tears in my hands, eyes soaking, flash of insight my eyes open! like a wave realizing it's the ocean, floating like formless shapeless water preparing to crash down on this new world order and drown out companies stealing indigenous water, "they killing us, they're villainous" she said to the reporter, they're giving to the rich and take it from the poorer, the ancient tree, the forest you see is smaller, masonry, **The Temple in Man** is taller than anything money can buy, **Sodom Gomorrah!** fire and brimstone except for Bella, **Dawud The BlaKseed** a righteous fella, mic in my hand, **Slick Rick** story teller, maybe in the next life we'll all do better **- Dawud The Amazing BlaKseed**

Iu f Per f m heru

Meta Strange Significance

Utterances for Coming Forth by day into Light

I started this rhyme while I was seated at **Tsion Cafe,** I was reading the Book, **The Secret Life of plants**. While reading the book I read about how plants can sense human thoughts. This made me think about my plants at my studio and how I needed to take better care of them. I began writing this song then I left and finished it when I got home, ending the song with the words "**maybe in the next life we'll all do better**".. Two years later the last words of this song would take on a new meaning when my past life as Emmett Till was revealed to me on July 3rd 2018 (page 480). On December 22nd 2018 (page 546) I would find a beat that touched my soul and with the desire to say something to it I recorded this song to the beat but when I was done recording there was still over a minute left to the beat so I wrote more to the rhyme using a rhyme and pattern from **Nas's** song **Nas is like**, then I changed the name of the song to **The Immortal Life of Emmett Till**. Afterwards I listened to the song on repeat many times and it was one of my favorite songs for a long time. It wasn't till a few weeks after I completed the song that I realized that the beat had the sound of a **whistle** in it. When I realized that I was **dumbfounded** because Emmett was murdered because he **whistled** at a white woman (page 506). The additional lyrics to the song can be read below.

See page 391 for the Reincarnation of at Tsion Cafe.

It is he, who comes forth by day into Light

"maybe in the next life we'll all do better, this body is finite but the soul will live forever in the ether, the next lines not designed for the nonbeliever, I was shot in the head left for dead body thrown in the river, my mommy **Mamie Till Bradley** had me open casket, the law giver bastards still called her nigger, her feelings they hurt it, "<u>freedom or jail clips inserted, another baby's being born the same time</u>" that I was murdered! the beginning and end, as far as that goes it's only natural I came back yo, through the **astral plane**, in **the year of the snake**, Dawud the **Naga** the saga, tell me what will it take to break the spell, is it the **changa**? the **Lotus**? the **DMT** that exploded? a course collision kinetic a vision decoded, written in the stars, floated in my dreams past **Mars**, read between the bars, birds planes stars avatars, birds planes stars avatars, read between the bars, birds planes stars avatars" **- Dawud The Amazing BlaKseed** (written on December 22nd 2018, page 546).

July 25th 2016 **The Good News**

I got some good news and some doper new son, **The soul never dies!,** we can't lose we won!! they might cruise by and take the life of your son, your father, mother, brother but they gonna holla **when they discover the other side of being alive**!! I'm tired of seeing families cry and I try to cope with this life but it's seeming hopeless, house full of roaches and clips, hard to focus on the future and shit, I ain't got no future! **cops** will shoot ya before you use your scholarship, same politic they **Pick-a-Nigga** like it's the plantation, we them same Niggas, tired of getting whipped and we tired of waiting for freedom! fuck those rights you reading cause your legality ain't morality it's more like treason, mortality rates of Blacks the highest what's the reason? what's the odds we get even and **rise again**, ride and defend like **Huey** and his friends? eleven hundred and 34 more Black men killed last year when will it end?! it's an epidemic poisoned water in Flint Michigan are you listening? I ain't finished we getting the death sentence for being Black, when **cops** go on strike crime diminish what's up with that?!

*I got tired of running from the storm so I danced in the rain! didn't conform, I **transformed** then the **ancestors** came!!!* they said your name ain't **Toby**, it ain't **King Kunta** either, you're **The BlaKseed** plant seeds in the hearts and minds of the future, grab the shooters, the looters, the strippers, the scholars, the weeds, the flowers, the thug Niggas and take them all with ya!

I said don't cry ***Keep Ya Head Up***! all these things they showing you get you fed up, if only you knew what they be owing you you'd be lining up and signing up, they want us to run a muck but that ain't helping us, **Nepotism** the best decision, a freer way of living, next on the mission let's unify before we all die! let's try to form one religion, **One Nation,** I ain't trying to cause division but maybe separation is what we need to heal these bad relations, like a reservation call it a **revelation,** what I see is **DR Umar** schools teaching our whole nation, use your **imagination**! *the power of one unified thought* can change the course like a horse carrying a **Strong Haitian,** we were born with **Latent Powers Suppressed, Our ancient ancestors waiting to be reborn in the flesh, Immortality no death,** I'm stressed but sucker free, fuck with me and take your last breath breathing, my enemies giving me reason to be a **Hell RAzor**, the hate they gave little babies - fed us to alligators, they put crack in the hood in the 80's because they love us or do they hate us?! tell me, do they **love** us or do they **hate** us? - **Dawud The Uncanny BlaKseed**

Meta Spiritual Significance

This song was written on Emmett Till's birthday and in the very first line of the first verse I say "**the soul never dies"** and at the end of the second verse I would say "**our ancient ancestors waiting to be reborn in the flesh, Immortality no death".** In ancient Kemet (Egypt) the concept of reincarnation and past lives was called the **Wehem-Mesut** (repeating of births, page 14). I remember how I felt after I wrote this rhyme. I didn't see the point of writing the music. And I wanted to stop writing completely because I did not like the continued creation of music that was rooted in the pains of Black genocide. I told myself that I would never write another rhyme again. I could not continue to take in this pain as the music was causing many tears and emotional breakdowns. A few days passed and I was about to delete my Instagram account again then suddenly; I saw the story of **Korryn Gaines** on my timeline!! I was overcome with **righteous anger** again!!!! I wrote a song for her very quickly (p 398). She had been murdered the day prior on August 1st 2016. In a fit of anger I wrote a song for her with lightening speed.

August 1st 2016 - Korryn Gaines 23yrs old

On march 10th 2016 Korryn was pulled over by a police officer for driving without a license plate. The officers gave her a citation, then ordered her to exit her vehicle, threatening to impound her car. A verbal conflict ensued. Five months after this traffic stop Korryn Gaines was murdered in her home by a Baltimore swat team. According to Baltimore County Police Korryn was **wanted** on a bench warrant for failing to appear in court on charges related to the traffic stop on March 10th 2016. Off the heels of the Baltimore riots which happened on April 12th 2015, Korryn Gaines is murdered. Korryn was shot on August 1, 2016, in Randallstown, Maryland, near Baltimore, resulting in her death, at **23** years of age, and the shooting of her son, who survived. According to the Baltimore County Police Department, Immediately after the first officer entered her home to serve the warrant, Gaines pointed a shotgun at him, prompting him to withdraw without shots being fired. The Baltimore County SWAT team responded and a 6 hour standoff began. She recorded and live streamed to Facebook where Gaines's friends told her to "continue on". She is seen warning her son that "the police are coming to kill us". Upon her refusal to let them in, police got a key from the rental office but found the chain lock blocking their entry. An officer then kicked in the door. The Police say Gaines pointed a shotgun at an officer, telling him to leave but why should we trust anything the police report. Why can't they show the video footage of the incident!? Ruby is no longer employed with the county police department, officials said. Prosecutors in 2016 declined to charge him in the shooting, finding it legally justified. In 2018, a jury awarded the Korryn's family $38 million in damages after finding that the first shot, fired by Royce Ruby and killing Gaines, was not reasonable, and thus violated their **civil rights**. That **verdict was overturned** in February 2019 by Judge Mickey Norman who ruled that physical evidence suggests Gaines' was raising her weapon when shot, thus posing a threat to Ruby and his team. Judge Norman described Ruby's actions as objectively reasonable. In July of 2020, an appeal court reinstated the $38 million award and Korryn's son received $32 million of it. The jury awarded about $5.4 million to the family members who have now settled with the county. That included $4.5 million to Gaines' daughter, Karsyn; a total of $607,000 to her parents; and $300,000 to her estate.

Significance

The murder of Korryn Gaines really bothered me! As I said on the last page I was emotionally drained! Walter Scott was shot in the back by a cop, Freddie Gray dies in police custody and the Baltimore riots are sparked, Kalief Browder "commits suicide, Dylan roof kills 9 Black people while they are in church at bible study, Sandra Bland dies in police custody, Michelle Cusseaux, Alton sterling, Philando Castile is shot by a cop while his hands are up. The constitution gives every person in America the right to

Rau nu Prt m heru

Iu f Per f m heru

Utterances for Coming Forth by day into Light

It is he, who comes forth by day into Light

bear arms! With all the killings of Black people in America the American policing system expects Black citizens to stand by and allow themselves to be murdered and kidnapped. It is only common sense to feel threatened by the American policing system. Korryn Gaines was a Black woman in 2016 dealing with post traumatic stress disorder that all Black people experience whether they are aware of it or not. The Baltimore police felt that a traffic ticket was a serious enough of an offense to lead to the killing of a **23** year old mother. See page **648** for the **metaphysical significance of the number 23**.

<u>Condolences</u>

My condolences go out to the family of **Korryn Gaines** and all those who have been robbed of their life by this system of racism and white supremacy. Please know that death is not the end. The soul survives death, indeed and in spirit. This is a book of the dead written by a boy who was murdered without justice, who defeated death and came forth by day. May the soul of **Korryn Gaines** walk peacefully through the field of Reeds in Amenta. Amen RA

....

August 2nd 2106 (RIP KORRYN GAINES)

<u>"Ok right, alright that's fine, I have family that will take care of them and I have family that know who I am and I already warned them about this day ok?! I'm not afraid of y'all! I don't know what the fuck y'all don't get!"</u> - **Korryn Gaines**

The end of white deception! black reflection! they knew this day was coming, they drew their weapons, are you running or are you unafraid? where are the blessings? who will **Jesus** save? Bury me a G! like **Afeni, Sandra Bland, Korryn Gaines!** we looking for change, when our voices become one, we get it done! until then the pain remains, **Haitian** rum to summon the **spirits**, the **Voodoo** the **Juju** in the lyrics, the good **cop** bad **cop**, **blue wall of silence,** won't stop the violence can you hear this?! if I gotta drop to my knees like the realest, **Pac** on the block aimed his glock at the killers, "They tryin to kill us!" her only son said, cause she was hunted and **wanted** like **Harriet,** loaded clips, No! She ain't having it! The **Goddess** in the midst of savages, what would you do, if you knew the truth behind the blackness and the black disparages?! the miscarriages of justice! would you ***<u>fight the power</u>*** or would you trust it? they dusted **black Indians** with a muskets, and **smallpox**, the toxic substance - **Dawud The Uncanny BlaKseed**

<u>"Divine they could never go back far enough. We are way beyond their time. Therefore in the meantime they hunt the Queens and Kings with crime. Used to hang us up with strings to trees and other thangs. now they tote guns with beams with wrist rings same ole ankle chains"</u> - **Korryn Gaines**

Come look look me in my eyes, this is a must that you stay alive! don't trust what they say about ya momma, ya momma was a **Goddess** with knowledge really wise, you see it's the system that she despised, freedom is missing we've been deprived, I'm giving you a mission, like the **lotus flower** out of the muddy water you must **rise, Like Heru!** Like **Jean Jacque Dessalines** and **Tupac Amaru,** they grew through the concrete jungle and that's the same thing that you must do, one two, mic check, this for every president elect, the more you neglect the debt, cause my family stress, **I be a truth terrorist, I be a major threat, I be a lie killer, urban gorilla, ruff-neck, knowledge gangster, history hitman**, this science project really making us sick man, the tv the trap music you're listening, the food changing your mood to kiss man, when a man kiss a man that ain't bring'n no life man, I ain't trying to start a fight but that's the life of the **iceman,** we gotta get it right a wife and a tight fam - **Dawud The Uncanny BlaKseed**

<u>"The vampire theory. Our blood reeks of royalty they can smell it in the air. We're so used to our own scent we can not fathom what we bare. They know of our greatness I'm just trying to taste it while others are trying to waste it and the white man is trying to trace it"</u> - **Korryn Gaines**

The vampire theory, y'all ain't trying to hear me when I speak, our blood be royalty really! don't be the sheep! they smell the blood in the air, they be the wolf, they came from over there the cave, we came from **kush**, made us the slave stole our books, set us free, labeled us the "**crooks**", took our technology called it a mystery, wrote a odyssey, I don't need your therapy! fuck your psychology! you don't know harmony, you don't know morality, all of your policies, Just another strategy, forming your monopoly, no care for ecology, or for astrology, explore the hypocrisy, the nerve of the doctor performing surgery without properly warning humanity we die from the cure that's pure insanity, they double handed see, when you speak the truth they bring the troops and calamity, they did the same thing to **Dr King!** they made her a **Martyr,** they shot the **Queen!** now she's seen at high esteem, now she's soaring on another plane, remember **Korryn Gaines!** she didn't want to go! didn't want to be thrown in chains!! they came with a swat and shot with no shame, rest in power forever, **Korryn Gaines - Dawud The Uncanny BlaKseed**

<u>"Except now they trying to survive, cant find any use for us alive. Not knowing we cant die!! So while they're chasing blood, snatching bodies, eating babies and raping our minds while having sex with our kind. They can only become us with every thrust I trust they only raise our army and I trust that we are righteous!"</u> - **Korryn Gaines**

<u>Meta Spiritual Significance</u>

I wanted to stop writing after I wrote the song **The Good News** on July 25th. I began to sink in a depression from the continued creation of music that was rooted in the pains of our Black genocide. Creating this type of music caused many tears and emotional breakdowns. I told myself that I would never write another rhyme again!! I logged on Instagram prepared to delete my account and disconnect with social networking but the first thing I saw when I logged on was the murder of **Korryn Gaines!!** I saw her story on my timeline! **I was overcome with righteous anger again!!!!** I wrote the song **RIP Korryn Gaines** for her in a spell of anger, with lightening speed. She had been murdered the day prior on the first day of August! It was **Black August**! Like The Haitian revolution, Nat Turner, George Jackson, Emmett Till, and many more and now Korryn Gaines was added to the list.

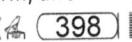

August 6th 2016 Terrorism

I said **the laws are the walls to keep us down**, Humpty Dumpty gotta fall and break his crown, I said they come'n for us all, the time is now, **Lord why are they so underhanded**?! have we been abandoned?! Tell me what **Sandra Bland** did?! We need some answers! I trade a Black president for the Black Panthers, they kill'n Black residents faster than cancer, the attack is on your intelligence, what you see relevant! what if I told you your perception is a misconception because of media deception?! what if I told you to turn off your tv would you believe me or would continue traveling on your road easy? What if I told you there'd be no **Malcolm X** without **Marcus Garvey**, no **Tupac** without **Afeni** following **Huey**, no me without **Tupac**, I'm speaking truthfully and because I'm speaking my truth they probably wanna shoot me

Terrorism is what we been given, just for living!! you could be riding with a licensed gun, kids in the back and still get shop by a **cop**!! not **Isis** on your tell lie vision! even peaceful activism get you locked in prison, *This Ain't Living, This is Strictly For My Niggaz,* where them culture vultures at? they ain't riding with us! Mr Officer, can't you see my empty hands? can't you see that you just a pawn in a bigger plan?! **Black Cop**, you gotta stop and tell me where you stand! the truth hurts but that **Biggie** Shirt says he's a future Klan! I'm spit'n hot bars, but will it get me future fans or just locked behind bars with cuffs on my hands?! it don't matter, sending love and Black power to my Black family, this could be my last hour so I'm writing with **7 Afrikan Powers**, sending love peace and power to **Aiyana Stanley** and her family **- Dawud The Uncanny BlaKseed**

August 6th 2016 So Much Neter

No, I don't wear no polo sweater, I grew up and now I know so much better, I buy Black give me that **Neter** sweater, and I never say never cause even nothing is something you can't see, your enemy is just a different branch on the same tree, I see **Nas** said Hip Hop is dead, I planted some BlaKseeds so we can stay fed, maybe one day we break bread? I use to break dance now I take lead and make **GOLD**, how do you fix a broken man? you make a plan leading to his **soul**, then let him free to see the universe is in control, I'd rather be me than I liar with a ghost writer, retire or just fold, where I'm from the sum of your clout is you sold out, **Eric Garner** got choked out, no doubt you heard about but never wrote about! get out Hip Hop you not about the *Natural Elements*! I can't speak of **Jesus** but **Malcolm X** was heaven sent, like the **Ra** and in **Rakim** Kemetic relevance

Study the **Medu Neter Neter**, from **Malcolm** Little to Shabazz things get better better, study the **Medu Neter Neter**, from **Malcolm** Little to Shabazz things get better better, study the **Medu Neter Neter**, Don't believe everything they taught ya, they give you water after torture so you develop a love for you oppressor, I made a alter out of my dresser so I never falter and never forget to praise my ancestors **- Dawud The Uncanny BlaKseed**

August 6th 2016 (DR FORD AND THE ACTIVATION OF MY SOLAR PLEXUS)

The most frequently asked question I receive before, during and after I give a massage is why did I become a massage practitioner. If you have been reading my book you should know that I only went to school so that I could receive the $3177.00 a month $tipend from the military back in 2012 when I started at BMCC (pages 218 & 240). After a year of school at BMCC I was tired of the schooling system so I searched for a holistic school to use this government money. I did a search online for "holistic school in Harlem" and the NYCHP (new york college of health professions) came up. I saw that they offered acupuncture and immediately thought of Mutulu Shakur who used acupuncture to help drug addicted people break their addictions to drugs (page 274). I called them and set up an appointment. When I got there a woman named Miss Rosa directed me to massage and I agreed. I did not even realize that in school we would be massaging each other. I just wanted to use the money doing something that was useful info and not what was being taught at BMCC. After I finished my first year I left school because I had saved a few thousand dollars and wasn't struggling financially like I was when I started at BMCC in 2012. In 2015 I was invited to a **gong session** around the time of the Baltimore riots. During that session I kept thinking about going back to school (page 326). After the session I met a brother named **Ron** and we would realize that we both attended the same school. He was going for acupuncture and he was taking classes in Long Island that's why we "never" met. You should go back and read all the **synchronicities** surrounding my meetings with Ron. I met Ron in passing on **November 1st 2014** (page 306) but didn't know it until 2018 yet still we became friends when we met at the gong session in 2015. Ron and I share the same life path number of 5. After meeting Ron at the gong session I enrolled in school again.

When I went to school to enroll I saw **Professor Leslie,** I took her Reflexology class my first year in school and she was very happy to see me. We hugged each other then she invited me to a meeting with her mentor **Dr Ford**. She'd invited me to a meeting with him when I was in school my first year but I declined back then. This time I accepted immediately and I'm happy I did. Around this time I was emotionally drained due to all the **police killings** of black people seen on TV and had subsequently became topics in my **music**. I remember wearing my feather to this meeting. I had my new **Scarab** tee shirt on with white harem pants and a **peacock feather** in my hair. Little did I know that when I got to the meeting on August 6th 2016 I would have many **profound synchronicities**. It all started with a **Jewish** brother **Gregory Kirschenbaum**. As we were all waiting in the lobby for the meeting to start Gregory walked over to me and looked at my tee shirt with the **scarab dung beetle** on it and told me that he had just seen a **giant dung beetle** (page 569) earlier in the day, he added that he had never seen a beetle like that in New York his entire life. As the meeting began we had around 15 people there. Most of us were finishing up massage school or had just graduated and there were some people there who had been working in massage for years. Just as the meeting began Gregory looked at me and expressed that he could sense a great source of energy coming from me. He mentioned that he had spent years with a **guru**

Rau nu Prt m heru

Iu f Per f m heru

Utterances for Coming Forth by day into Light

It is he, who comes forth by day into Light

by the name of **Sathya Sia Baba**. He said the energy that he felt coming from me reminded him of what he felt when in the presence of **Sia Baba**..I had never heard of the person before and to be honest he sort of made me feel uncomfortable by saying that in front of everyone. Sathya Sia Baba was an Indian guru and philanthropist. It wasn't until the writing of this book that I realized that at the age of **14** he claimed that he was the **reincarnation** of Shirdi Baba and left his home to serve society and to be an example to his followers. Sia Baba's life was plagued with accusations of sexual abuse, sleight of hand and even murder but his followers rejected those claims. He was said to possess the ability to materialize **gold** objects like rings and necklaces into his hand, along with reports of miraculous healings, **resurrections**, clairvoyance, bilocation and alleged omnipotence and omniscience. Sia Baba was born November **23**rd, the same day as Mamie Till (Emmett's mother). See page **648** for the **metaphysical significance of the number 23**.

As the meeting began Dr Ford seemed to take a special interest in me as he kept asking me what I thought about the topics being discussed. Then at some point he look at me with piercing eyes, extended his arm and pointed at me exclaiming, **"THE POWER OF GOD IS IN YOU!". Instantaneously my solar plexus started vibrating intensely!** This had never happened to me before so it caused me great confusion, however I remained calm and silent while this vibration took over my whole chest cavity. I don't think anyone else noticed what I was experiencing because I kept quiet as I allowed my self to experience what was happening. As the vibration rose up in me I began breathing deeply attempting to ease the vibration and after a minute or so the vibration subsided. Dr Ford kept asking me my thoughts on topics and I continued to give my thoughts.

There was a woman sitting to the left of me that I found to be very attractive. She became more interesting when I noticed that we were both wearing the same exact clear quartz crystal around our necks. During the intermission I introduced myself and brought the crystal to her attention. She told me she had noticed it as well and that's when she told me that I looked just like her uncle. Then I would find that she was born on September 13th, the same day **Tupac** died and the same day my uncle died (page 28). On my way home from the event I met a woman on the train dressed in all white. We talked about life, spirituality and the synchronicities I had just experienced. Just before we parted ways she looked at me and said - **"there is no such thing as just coincidence"**. I never got the contact information of the woman I met at the event who was born on September 13th and I never saw or heard from her again. I don't remember her name, but when I got home that night I found a beat online and as soon as I heard it I fell in love with it. The beat just so happened to be uploaded to youtube on September 13th. The beat was beautiful so I proceeded to record my song, **Secret Life of Plants** to it. The title of this song would later be changed to **The Immortal Life of Emmett Till** (page 546) after I had my **past life** revelation of Emmett Till on July 3rd 2018 (page 480). A week or so after the gathering I would keep crossing paths with another woman I met at the gathering. Apparently she owned a massage spa in Harlem (page 455) on the same block as **Tsion Cafe** where I did my first set a few months prior on June 15th 2016 (page 390). Her name was **La Juana** and she would end up offering me a job at her spa just before I graduated on August 14th 2017 (page 456). Her and I would become good friends like sister and brother. La Juana and I share many **synchronicities** one of which is her mother and my grand mother both sharing the same name **Juanita**. **But nothing more strange than what happened 3 years before me actually met, see page 271!**

Ron

Gong Session with Sunseed

La Juana

Alfredo Darrington Bowman, better known as **Dr. Sebi** was born on **November 26th** 19**33** the same day that **Tutankhalen's** (**King Tut's**) tomb was opened in 19**22** (page 11). Dr Sebi was born in Honduras where he learned the natural art of herbalism and healing, he also practiced in the United States from the 80's until his death on August 6th 2016. Dr. Sebi claimed that all disease could be reversed with herbs and a plant-based alkaline diet and denied that **HIV** caused **AIDS**. He set up a treatment center in Honduras, then moved his practice to New York City and Los Angeles. Numerous entertainment and acting celebrities were among his clients, including **Michael Jackson** (pages 99, 166), Lisa '**Left Eye**' Lopes, and **John Travolta**.

Attack from American Medical Association

Dr Sebi was considered a fraud by licensed doctors, attorneys, and consumer protection agencies because he used the title and name Dr. Sebi, but had not completed any European medical training. This led to him being arrested and accused by New York state of practicing medicine without a license. After trial, Dr Sebi was acquitted based on the legal definition of "medicine" for his herbs. He was later charged in a civil suit that resulted in him being prohibited from making therapeutic claims for his supplements. In 1987, the New York State Attorney General charged Dr Sebi with two counts of practicing medicine without a license after he placed ads in local newspapers claiming to be able to **cure AIDS**. The Attorney General's Office sent undercover agents to his office to gain diagnoses and treatments for purported symptoms of disease. Dr Sebi was **acquitted** because jurors said the tape recorded by the agents failed to show that Dr Sebi had made a medical diagnosis of their purported conditions. In an effort to stop Dr Sebi from healing people without European medicine and surgery, the New York Assistant Attorney General for consumer fraud filed a civil suit against Dr Sebi, his Ogun Herbal Research Institute, and other named businesses. It resulted in a consent agreement by which he was prohibited from making therapeutic claims for his products. He was also fined $900. The suit had ruled that the claims were unsubstantiated.

The Murder of Dr Sebi

In May 2016, Dr Sebi was arrested in Honduras for money laundering, after being found carrying tens of thousands of dollars in cash with insufficient accounting for its origin. Dr Sebi was released pending a court hearing on 6 June 2016, but he was re-arrested by the Public Ministerio on money laundering charges. He was held for several weeks in a Honduran prison, while his family was attempting to obtain his release. He fell ill and, after police officials realized the severity of his condition, they transported him to a hospital. Bowman died of complications of pneumonia on 6 August 2016, en route to Hospital. The length of his time in custody and the poor condition of the jail contributed to his death. Many people questioned the circumstances of his arrest and death. They claim that there was a conspiracy to silence him because his teachings differed from the medical establishment and threatened the pharmaceutical industry. If people could heal themselves with natural medicines what use was the modern barbaric medical association and the poisonous pharmaceutical industry who's drugs do more harm than they claim to heal? Dr Sebi was a threat to their monetary gains.

Murder of the Musicians

In 2018, **Nipsey Hussle** stated he was planning on creating a documentary about the legacy of Dr. Sebi and his successful defenses at his criminal trials – a legacy that another fallen and dearly missed music icon tapped into before her 2002 death: TLC's Lisa "Left Eye" Lopes. Hussle was later murdered in 2019 by a known acquaintance. Law enforcement claims to have found no link between Hussle's death and Dr Sebi. Just like the American legal system found no guilt on the part of the killers of **Emmett Till** and **Breonna Taylor** (p 627). Many fans and industry counterparts alike, believe that Nipsey's murder is directly connected to the Dr. Sebi undertaking he revealed in 2018. After **Left Eye's** death a video on the internet reemerged of her 'Dr. Sebi Testimony' in which she discusses how she came to discover him. She said she prayed to God for answers, presumably regarding healing and spirituality, and she found the answer to her prayers in Dr. Sebi. "I just could not believe that there was not a cure for – I don't care what disease – especially AIDS," **Left Eye** said in the clip. When "Emmett's" body was found, "his" **Left Eye** was missing and "his" right eye was left laying on "his" cheek (page 514). The untimeliness of both Nipsey and Left Eye's fatalities are undeniable and difficult to grasp given their promising legacies but some fans are convinced that their deaths had less to do with coincidence, and far more to do with conspiracy, and everything to do with a common denominator: the support and disclosure of Dr. Sebi. (see page 124) In 2019 I would meet a colleague of Dr Sebi named **Mr G** (page 574), who confirmed a **dream** I had about **Eryka Badu** (page 549). Lisa once drew a picture of Tupac in the early 90's. Lisa signed and dated the picture. Years later that picture would end up being placed on the wall of a record stored owned by **William Lesane**, Tupac's cousin. Years after Lisa died, William Lesane noticed that Lisa had drawn the picture on April 25, which was strangely the same day she died in 2002. The patterns I present in this book are examples of a weird phenomena known as **quantum entanglement**, spoken about often in **Physics**. Like the mysterious pattern seen on page 602.

Condolences

My condolences go out to the families of Dr Sebi, Lisa "Left Eye" Lopes, Nipsey Hussle and all those who have been robbed of their life by this system of racism and white supremacy. Please know that death is not the end. The soul survives death, indeed and in spirit. This is a book of the dead written by a boy who was murdered without justice, who defeated death and came forth by day. May the souls of **Alfredo Darrington Bowman 'Dr Sebi'**, **Lisa Lopes 'Left Eye'**, and **Airmiess Jospeph Asghedom 'Nipsey Hussle'** walk peacefully through the field of Reeds in Amenta. Amen RA.

"Music is spiritual" - Nipsey Hussle (page 6)

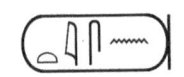

August 10th 2016 Most High (May 25 strikes back)

Her **love** be the **most high**, she be the **most high**, before I met her I wanted to die, man I would cry, I would lie, I would say I was ok but now her **love** is the **most high**, higher than the sky I fly everyday, **May twenty five** I'm alive with purpose I survived the surface **sleep walking**, ***never judge a dead man by his coffin***, her mouth be closed but she still be talking, I suppose I'm a lucky man ***I rose through the concrete you don't understand***, I'm a simple man in a temple in a foreign land, **I am that I am** *The BlaKseed*, I'll say again I will succeed and proceed to rock the mic with ease like a **Bernard Hopkins** fight, strike with **Mike Tyson's** might, and bet's believe *I write what I like* like **Steve Biko**, I be regal majestic invested in life but I'll be fighting evil even until I'm breathless, my sight beyond sight be restless, ***my death wish is the immortal guest list cause when your fleshless what else will you be left with, be left with***?! I said her **love** be the **most high**, she be the **most high** - **Dawud The Uncanny BlaKseed**

Rau nu Prt m heru

August 11th 2016 Sacred Contracts

She said, "you gonna end up in a monastery or a madhouse, you ain't no missionary, you need those fairies or demonic spirits cast out, what you know about contact, and sacred contracts? if it ain't in my Gods book then it ain't a fact, my Gods **coming back** to save me, so save that fugazi crap for the crazy! - **Dawud The Uncanny BlaKseed**

Dawud, Beloved by the Ntru

Iu f Per f m heru

Utterances for Coming Forth by day into Light

It is he, who comes forth by day into Light

August 16th 2016 - Coon

I am pictured here with **Neo Nefertari** whom I met on Feb 28th 2012 (p **233**). She is a good friend of mine. She invited me to a dance show and while there I saw the most beautiful woman dancing on stage. I wanted to meet her and I wanted to do more than just meet her. She turned me on. I had just ended a long period of abstinence and had been staying in the house for long periods of time so when I saw her I fell to my lower nature. I disregarded all thoughts of Maat. I had the feathers in my hair but **Maat** was forgotten. I approached the woman and I gave her my card and she sent me a text shortly after. I did not give her my card to be her trainer though. I was interested in her romantically. We met up a few days after when she came by my space to workout with me. After the workout she mentioned her back being tight so I offered to rub her back. I wanted to rub her back anyway. I wasn't trying to get to know her. After I was done rubbing her back I tried to kiss her but she denied my advance and she was visibly disappointed that I even tried. I think she felt that I was different from the usual men that approached her. I felt very bad. She wanted to smoke weed so I got her some weed and she smoked but I never saw her again after that. Her last name was Coon. I ask myself did I play the role of a "**Coon**" but I already know the answer to the question. Take a look at the poem **Sacred Contracts** that I wrote on August 11th. I find it **strange** that it seems to foretell me "breaking sacred contracts". As if the thought that formed that rhyme saw this day coming before it happened... We get tested time after time, life after life, moment after moment. What will you do with your moments? What will you give your attention to? I advise you to learn from my mistakes and to **MAAT** be true! **42 Laws of Maat, Page 367**

August 16th 2016 Save Freedom

We been robbed of our free unadulterated naturally cultivated, not yet jaded, not sedated, have you been loved or have you been hated? did you give love? was it reciprocated? was it complicated, a conflict haven not worth the saving? or was it above the clouds like **Carl Sagan**? who will save them? **save freedom**, they say you can lead a man to books but you can't make him read em, they say **God** manifest in what ever form best please those believing - **Dawud The Uncanny BlaKseed**

August 21st 2016 Break Nothing

If you let me in I won't break nothing, won't leave you stranded with your heart pumping, won't start something that I can't finish, won't start fronting my **love** won't diminish, from the first minute I was immersed in it, no reversing it, I was sick she was nursing it, put my hands on her spine then she opened it, then said f- -k me with your mind, I started stroking it, It's been a week now I'm weak and I'm hoping this don't end in the friend zone with a floating **kiss**, throw me the bomb cause you the bomb and I'm catching it, something tell me I'm catching **feelings** to my detriment, shit damn mother fucker be my sentiment, intimate intercourse came then it went, if your **love** end up lost was it relevant, is every **coincidence** something sent from heavenly? let the intent from my **heart** speak eloquently, before I met you I was hell'a empty but now you're gone and more strong and happy and healthy, you helped me you reminded me to **love** me, the world blinded me and drugged me then drug me down, not everybody you **love** gonna stay around so if ever you find **love** don't play around, whenever you find **love** don't play around - **Dawud The Uncanny BlaKseed**

August 23rd 2016 BlaK Wall Street (Part A)

I'm so sour more flowers when ever we grow ours we get cut down like trees disease, **white power!** refugees embassies **Negus** please! these **crackers** blew up the Twin Towers! ain't no safe zone even if you own a lot of dollars! ask the scholars what happened in lower Manhattan, you too busy fuck'n with fashion and flash'n! in 1906 we was heavy into politics then they got pissed, **Atlanta Race Riots,** we was mashing like **Huey!** they never taught you he had a masters degree do they?! cause that ain't their duty! truly yours more wars more tours **Till** we unify for a cause, when I die I fly in a **whirlwind** following natural laws, Louisiana **Juantia** my **Grandmother** told me they ran her home when she was little, on the phone she told me her greatest fear is being left alone, I will always be there for you!!! I will travel through a battle zone!!! **Return** like a **Jedi** and kill a clone, destination top secret mission unknown, restitution **reparations** everything they owing, we be flowing from **Gabby Douglas** to **Jessie Owens, Usain Bolt** giving brothers hope forever show-'em, you see where I'm go'n! **Black Power**, **Bruce Leroy** glow'n, don't act like you ain't know'n! Brother brother, don't stray too far.... you cant get to heaven with out the **Black-Star**! Sister sister.... do you know who you are? wanna get to ghetto heaven? take the **Black-Star - Dawud The Uncanny BlaKseed**

Significance

The video for this song was taken off of youtube on March **23rd** 2022, their explanation was, "We wanted to let you know our team reviewed your content, and we think it violates our **hate speech** policy". Only the first verse was uploaded, I guess the word **Cracker** offends them. Yet the word **Nigger** can be played on the radio for everyone to hear and they can tell the story of Black Wall street in movies but we can't rap about it. This song was sparked with thoughts about Black Wall Street and the first bar speaks to black communities destroyed by racist white people working together to maintain systematic racism and white supremacy. "*I'm so sour more flowers when ever we grow ours we get cut down like trees disease,* ***white power***"**...** When I finished the first verse I called my **Grand Mother** because I mentioned her in the rhyme. I talked her up to see how she was doing and to talk about her childhood.. She told me the story of how she was chased home by little white kids when she was a child. Her name is **Juanita** and when she was a little girl the white kids would chase her and her sister home from the bus taunting them screaming "**Nigger Nigger black as tar, Cant get to heaven on a electric car**". When my Grandmother and her sister got to her block the white kids would stop. Then my grand mother and her sister would scream back "**Cracker Cracker green as grass, can't get to heaven on a bull frogs ass"....** I took that rhyme and changed it to - "Brother brother, don't stray too far, you cant get to heaven with out the **Black-Star**! Sister sister do you know who you are? wanna get to ghetto heaven? take the **Black-Star".** It was around 2am and we talked for about 30 or 40 minutes then I went back to writing. Midway through the second verse my Grandmother called me back to tell me that my **Uncle Squeek** had passed away. He was my Grandmother's sister's husband and he was the oldest male in our family. I talked with my grand mother for some time as we mourned his death then we hung up as she went to call her sister. I finished the rhyme adding Uncle Squeek to the song.

BlaK Wall Street 2nd VERSE (part B)

"*I just wanna grow, I wanna be better, I want you to grow, I want us to all grow, we evolve or disappear"* forever you know? be the energy you wanna to see, lead by example, close your open mouth, open your closed minds! why cant you do the mathematics? 10 dollars a month, 500 people, a Black grocery store we can have it!! now that's fighting evil! I **transform** like the **Beetle,** left my feeble ways, first they create the **Virus EBOLA, AIDS,** then they fund the **vaccine, Stranger Things!** fear will take you right there to a grave! fuck a wedding ring... diamonds are neither rare or valuable! don't let this western culture devour you! don't be a slave, instead let the ancestors empower you, let them empower you, the truth is written on the walls engraved, let the strong help the weak carry on for **Better Days**, rest in power to **Uncle Squeek**, I'm so sour more flowers, I remember hearing you speak for hours on **Hillmeyer** when I was a young lad, we gotta learn how to appreciate what we have, before time shows us what we had, I rhyme with reason so sometimes it's sad, you know I'll be glad when **Black Unity** is the newest fad, ***RA****member the time* ***Michael Jackson*** Bad, Brother brother, don't stray too far.... you cant get to heaven with out the **Black-Star**! Sister sister.... do you know who you are? wanna get to ghetto heaven? take the **Black-Star - Dawud The Uncanny BlaKseed**

Significance

Kirkland Jordan was born on **January 4, 1931** and he passed on **August 23, 2016**. His funeral was on **August 27**. **Hurricane Katrina** started on **August 23**, 2005 (page 143) and **Tupac** dropped the single **Pour Out a Little Liquor** on **August 23**, 1994. See page **648** for the **metaphysical significance of the number 23**. I started the second verse with a quote from **Tupac**. "I want to grow. I want to be better. You grow. We all grow. We're supposed to grow. You either evolve or you disappear." I have a theory about who Tupac was in a past life? This song was released on iTunes on Feb 25th 2017 and later released on the album ***Dawud The Uncanny Blakseed: The Immortal Life of Emmett Till*** on July 25th 2019.

Condolences

Please know that death is not the end. The soul survives death, indeed and in spirit. This is a book of the dead written by a boy who was murdered without justice, who defeated death and came forth by day. May the soul of uncle **Kirkland (Squeek) Jordan** walk peacefully through the field of Reeds in Amenta. Amen Ra.

Greenwood (Black Wall Street) Prospers

As segregation grew stronger, Greenwood's Black business district thrived, mainly because residents fed their purchasing dollars back into the local economy, while earning their incomes from white employers. At it's peak Black Wall Street had 600 Black owned businesses, 21 Black churches, 21 Black owned restaurants, 30 Black owned grocery stores, 2 Black owned movie theaters, 6 Black owned private airplanes, a Black owned hospital, a Black owned bank, a Black owned post office, Black owned schools and libraries, Black owned law offices and even a black owned bus system. This was possible because the migration of oilmen to Tulsa created a spike in demand for domestic help, which enabled Black residents to attain high-paying labor jobs as maids, chauffeurs, gardeners, janitors, shoe shiners, and porters. These workers often earned enough money to send their children to universities like Columbia Law School, Oberlin College, the Hampton Institute, the Tuskegee Institute, Spelman College, and Atlanta University, which positioned them to secure white-collar jobs after graduation.

Rau nu Prt m heru

Iu f Per f m heru

Eye witness accounts from Buck Franklin
What caused Tulsa massacre?

"For fully forty-eight hours, the fires raged and burned everything in its path and it left nothing but ashes and burned safes and trunks and the like where once stood beautiful homes and business houses. And so proud, rich, Black Tulsa was destroyed by fire–that is its buildings and property; but its spirit was neither killed nor daunted. It is however not within the purpose of this true story to dwell on this; nor is it our purpose to discuss here the cause or causes of this great shame, except to say that the chief cause was economic. The Negroes were wealthy and there were too many poor whites who envied them. Within two hours after the alleged assault had been reported, there were not a dozen white men here who did not know that this alleged assault consisted of a poor laboring Negro boy accidentally stepping on the foot of a very poor but worthy white girl while the two were on a very crowded elevator in one of the down town business buildings; nor yet is it our purpose here to discuss the wonderful, almost miraculous come-back of the Race here in the accumulation of property and in the acquiring of a larger, richer and fuller spiritual life." **- Buck Franklin (written on August 22nd 1931, 10 years after the massacre)**

Utterances for Coming Forth by day into Light

It is he, who comes forth by day into Light

1879-1960 BUCK COLBERT FRANKLIN

Buck Franklin was an attorney in Tulsa, Oklahoma, who is most notably known for defending the survivors of the Tulsa Race Riot of 1921. He was also father to the venerable civil rights advocate and historian John Hope Franklin. Franklin was a Native American born the seventh of ten children on May 6th 1879, near the town of Homer in Pickens County, Chickasaw Nation, Indian Territory (currently Oklahoma). He was named Buck in honor of his grandfather who had been a slave and purchased the freedom of his family and himself. There is speculation that the true origins of the Franklins' freedom came when Buck Franklin's father, David Franklin, escaped from his plantation and changed his name early in the Civil War. Practicing law as a young man in the predominantly White town of Ardmore, Oklahoma, he faced racial prejudice and saw major flaws in the white judicial system. In one instance, he was literally silenced in a Louisiana courtroom because of his race. In response to this, he decided to focus on practicing law within African American communities and moved to the all black town of Rentiesville, Oklahoma, where he would marry Mollie **Parker** Franklin and start his own family in 1915. Franklin later moved to Tulsa, Oklahoma, with his family in 1921 the same year as the massacre.

Franklin and his family had managed to survive the Tulsa Massacre. The Tulsa City Council, however, in the aftermath of the carnage, passed an ordinance that prevented the Black people of Tulsa from rebuilding their community. The city planned instead to rezone the area from a residential to a commercial district. Franklin led the legal battle against this ordinance and sued the city of Tulsa before the Oklahoma Supreme Court, where he won. As a consequence, Black Tulsa residents could and did begin the reconstruction of their nearly destroyed community.

Franklin went on to write his own autobiography but he died before he could see the final publication. He would pass away on September 24, 1960, which was the day after the Emmett Till's Trial ended in 1955. Of his four children, John Hope Franklin would become a prominent historian and Black intellectual of this time period. He contributed to the Brown v. Board of Education case in 1954 which was a spring board to the racial turmoil of the newly segregated M**ississ**ippi that caused the lynching of Emmett Till. John Hope Franklin also participated in the 1965 march for voting rights in Selma, Alabama which was led by Martin Luther King. John Hope Franklin and his son would finalize his father, B.C. Franklin's autobiography, My Life and an Era: The Autobiography of Buck Colbert Franklin.

The 1921 Tulsa Massacre's connection to Emmett Till and the Haitian Revolution

Roy Belton (a White man) was lynched on ***August 28th** 1920 the **same day** that Emmett Till* was Lynched by **Roy B**ryant in 1955. On August 21st 1920 (the same day Emmett arrived in M**ississ**ippi and the same day the Haitian Revolution started) **Roy B**elton and a female accomplice murdered a white taxi driver. **Roy B**elton was arrested the same day but 7 days later a mob of White armed men confronted Sheriff Wooley at the jail house where the mob took **Roy B**elton and drove him out of town and lynched him. He was lynched from a telephone pole 9 miles out of Tulsa while the police watched on as they redirected traffic away from the lynching. The news of this lynching spread fast. A. J. Smitherman, editor of a **Black owned** newspaper warned of the potential for this lynching to affect the safely of Blacks in Tulsa and the surrounding areas, for if they could lynch a White man and legally get away with it, what could black people expect given they arrest a Black person!? Smitherman tried to get Sheriff, Wooley removed from his elected position. An all White grand jury investigated but nothing was done. No different than how **Kyle Rittenhouse** was not found guilty in his 2021 trial or how the cops that killed Breonna Taylor were never arrested (Pages 589, 627).

—Photos by Alvin C. Kr...

MRS. MARIE HARMON

...k Co. Especially for The Tribune.

Dick Rowland

Rau nu Prt m heru

Iu f Per f m heru

9 months after the lynching of Roy Berton, Tulsa faced the potential lynching of the 19 year old **Dick Rowland,** a **Black** shoeshiner, who was accused of assaulting Sarah Page, a 17 year old **White** elevator operator in the nearby Drexel Building. Rowland was arrested quickly and taken into custody. According to conflicting reports, Rowland tripped in Page's elevator on his way to a segregated bathroom, and a White store clerk reported the incident as an "assault" or a rape. After his arrest rumors that Rowland was going to be lynched spread throughout the city, and because of the lynching of Roy Belton 9 months prior and all the other acts of violence that Blacks experienced on a day to day basis the Black men in Tulsa, mostly WW1 veterans, united in defense of Rowland. A gun fight broke out at the court house that led to the forming of a White mob. According to the Oklahoma Historical Society a mob of white residents, some of whom had been deputized and given weapons by city officials and instructed to "get a gun and get a nigger" made their way to the jail house. The events that follow would later be known a the Tulsa race massacre, also known as the Tulsa pogrom, the Tulsa race riot, or the Black Wall Street massacre.

Eye witness accounts from Buck Franklin "Then comes a lull–a lull before the storm"

Utterances for Coming Forth by day into Light

"It is now May 31st, 1921. The day is just beginning. Sweet-throated birds warble their songs of joy in the tree-tops, fanned by the refreshing zephyr, and the dew sparkles upon the grass like countless little diamonds, as old Sol rises above the eastern horizon and, shining in all his resplendent glory, thrusts his myriad rays upon the busy world below. An unbroken stream of pedestrians–male and female–passes down Greenwood Avenue. It is made up of laborers, some empty-handed and others with dinner pails, on their way to work. They hurry along as if they are late. A few of the more pretentious ones pass in their own cars, or in jitneys, or upon busses. Then comes a lull–a lull before the storm

It is now 11:30, A.M. of the same day and the first edition of the Tulsa Daily Tribune is out. The newsies are hawking their wares, listen: "Tulsa Daily Tribune, Mister? Tribune, Mister? All about a Negro assaulting a white girl–read all about it–Tribune, Mister?" And so thousands of people buy the Tribune and scan its pages for the article about the alleged assault. They find it tucked away in a small space on one of the inside pages of the paper. In the twinkling of an eye, a part of Tulsa is changed from the happy, joyous, care-free to looks of grim determination.

It is he, who comes forth by day into Light

It is also the commencement season and the streets of the city are filled all day long with the happy, innocent, care-free graduates, colored and white, walking proudly in their capes and gowns. The colored graduates are dreaming, building air-castles and, in their waking dreams, they see themselves rising, mounting higher and higher up the ladder of recognition and renown. But, alas, their dreams are like Ponzi's financial bubbles.

The day wears on, and the shadows of the evening lengthen and soon darkness comes on apace. Now it is night and all law-abiding citizens, except those attending some commencement program or detained on business in shop or office, are at home. Possibly a few are out with their families for a drive in the cool of the night. The night grows a little older and a few shots are heard–in the distance. One first thinks it is fire signals. The night grows older and the shooting increases and becomes less intermittent. One becomes, by the peculiar working of one's mind, slightly disturbed and distressed. One's mind goes back to that news article about that purported assault, and then still further back–about a month–to the lynching of that white man in West Tulsa. (This white man was taken from the Tulsa County Jail by a mob and hung, I believe, to a telephone pole.) My mind becomes thoroughly aroused." **- Buck Franklin (written on August 22nd 1931, 10 years after the massacre)**

We Did Not Stand By And Die

The year was 1921 and 3 years prior the 1919 "red summer" race and labor riots broke out in 26 cities across the country leading to the countless number of deaths of black people and 6 years prior the movie **Birth of a Nation** had been released on February 8th 1915.. This movie would be the first movie ever shown at the **White House** on February 18th 1915, the day before my great grand fathers birthday (General Dukes Sr). The movie showed scenes of a Black man attacking a white woman and afterwards a mob of Ku Klux Klans members were seen lynching the black man. President Woodrow Wilson, members of his family and his Cabinet attended the screening of the movie. This single **MOVIE** caused membership in the **Ku Klux Klan** (the White terrorist organization) to grow rapidly all across America. This is what set the stage for the Tulsa massacre and many other massacres like it that have been lost to the pages of his-story. The **Tulsa race massacre** started on May 31st and ended on my fathers birthday June 1st, 1921, the **same year Emmett Till's** mother (**Mamie Till**) was born. Upon hearing reports that a **mob** of hundreds of **white people** had gathered around the jail where Rowland was being held, a group of around **100 Black men**, some of whom were armed World War 1 veterans, arrived at the jail in order to ensure that Rowland would not be lynched. Tulsa was in a racially segregated district but it would come to be known as "the Negro Wall Street" after the blacks (Negros) struck oil in Tulsa and began to establish self determination (kujichagulla). This caused racial tension and jealousy as the local white residents in the surrounding areas did not like to see Black prosperity. Blacks were not supposed to do as well as them or to do for themselves and were never supposed to do better than White people. The only problem was the warrior **spirit** of the black men, most of whom were **Veterans** like my friend **Mambo** and who had recently returned home from World War 1 in 1918. Many of these Black veterans migrated to Tulsa to start new lives. I met Mambo in **2007**, and in 2021 he would detailed the events that awoke him to his **past life** as a World War 1 veteran (p 151). In ancient Kemet (Egypt) the concept of reincarnation and past lives was called the **Wehem-Mesut** (repeating of births, p 14). **Mambo,** and other black vets like them had fought for their country and now felt that they had earned their right to pursue "happiness, health, excitement, freedom, liberty, love and enlightenment" and they were willing to fight and die for it. See pages 321 and 562 for February 8 connection.

Soldiers of the 369th (15th N.Y.), Awarded the Croix de Guerre for gallantry in action, 1919.

ALL HELL BROKE LOOSE!

Addendum

Faced with around 100 black men the white sheriff tried to persuade the group to leave the jail, assuring them that he had the situation under control but in the spirit of **Son Turner** (page 19) the black men held their ground and did not move. A White man approached the crowd and spoke to a black veteran named **O.B. Mann**, and demanded that he hand over his pistol but Mann refused, the white man attempted to disarm him. O.B. Mann shot him in self defense, and then, according to the sheriff's reports, "*all hell broke loose*." The Black men took cover and fought to defend Rowland who was being held captive. At the end of the exchange of gunfire, 12 people were dead, 10 White and 2 Black. Out numbered, the Black men fled back into Greenwood shooting as they retreated. As news of the violence spread throughout the city, white terrorist, Ku Klux Klan mob violence exploded and the white terrorist invaded Greenwood that night and the next morning, killing men, women and children, burning and looting stores and homes. Fire fighters were not permitted in to Greenwood so all that caught flame was left to burn. Years after the massacre Black women were often seen snatching their jewelry off the necks of white women who paraded around wearing the jewelry that was stolen from their homes during the massacre. This massacre is considered by many "the single worst incident of racial violence in American history". The terrorist burned and destroyed more than 35 square blocks of Black Wall Street, which at the time was one of the wealthiest Black communities in the "United States". More than 800 people were admitted to hospitals, and as many as 6,000 Black residents of Tulsa were jailed in large facilities, many of them for several days and weeks. At least 300 were dead but the total number of dead can not be calculated because he who writes his dirty past will often lie about the events. Many survivors left Tulsa, while the Black and White residents who stayed in the city largely kept silent about the terror, violence, and resulting losses for decades. The massacre was largely omitted from local, state, and national histories. Decades after this massacre the story had been widely forgotten, even in Tulsa. There are stories of old black men and women begging for money in Tulsa, years after the massacre while people walk by them having forgotten the events of the massacre that caused them to become homeless.

The WW1 Snipper Young Ross

August 22nd 1931, 10 Years After The Massacre
Eye Witness Accounts From Buck Franklin

Rau nu Prt m heru

I went from the front porch into the bath room and washed my face, and thereafter went into my room and dressed. I left the building for my office. As I reached the side-walk a shrill whistle sounded from the direction of stand-pipe hill. And then, immediately thereafter, five thousand feet, it seemed, were heard descending that hill in my direction. On they rushed, whooping to the top of their voices like so many cow-boys, and firing their guns every step they took. I quickened my pace and, cutting across vacant lots and dodging behind buildings, I finally reached Frankfort Place, about the middle of the three hundred block. Just as I emerged upon the street, I came face to face with a fine looking young man, with soldiery bearing, leading an elderly woman with a young lady following close behind. I knew mother Ross, but at the time did not recognize the other two.

"Why, hello Lawyer Franklin," the young man spoke between clenched teeth. His face was grim and bore a determined look and his eyes sparkled and flashed defiance. He continued, hurriedly, "I have not seen you since you delivered that memorable address at Eufaula in October, 1917. How different is this occasion of our meeting from that. Then we were all filled with patriotism–love of country–and–standing erect–were recognized as the equal of our other fellow men. Now, now," he continued choking with rage, "We, after going through hell once for our country–Now, I say, we are chased, driven and hunted as wild, hateful, dangerous things."

Iu f Per f m heru

"What in the world, Ross–where have you been and where are you going?" I hurried to ask him. For I now recognized both the soldier and his wife, the young lady with him, and his mother.

"Just some more of my wanderlust, I suppose," he answered hurriedly, "I have been out of the State until this morning. Yesterday I became restless. Something within me told me that all was not well at home. I followed my mind **(telepathy)**. I reached Tulsa not more than an hour ago. How I got through the mountain of white men on the other side of the city, will always be a miracle to me. Judge, we are literally surrounded. I reached Greenwood and, luckily for me, I found my mother and my wife wandering about the street, panic-stricken. In terror, they had fled from home. I'm going back home to defend it or die in the attempt." And without another word, he grabbed his aged mother in his arms and fled toward his home. When young Ross and his family left me, I pushed on toward my office.

Utterances for Coming Forth by day into Light

It is he, who comes forth by day into Light

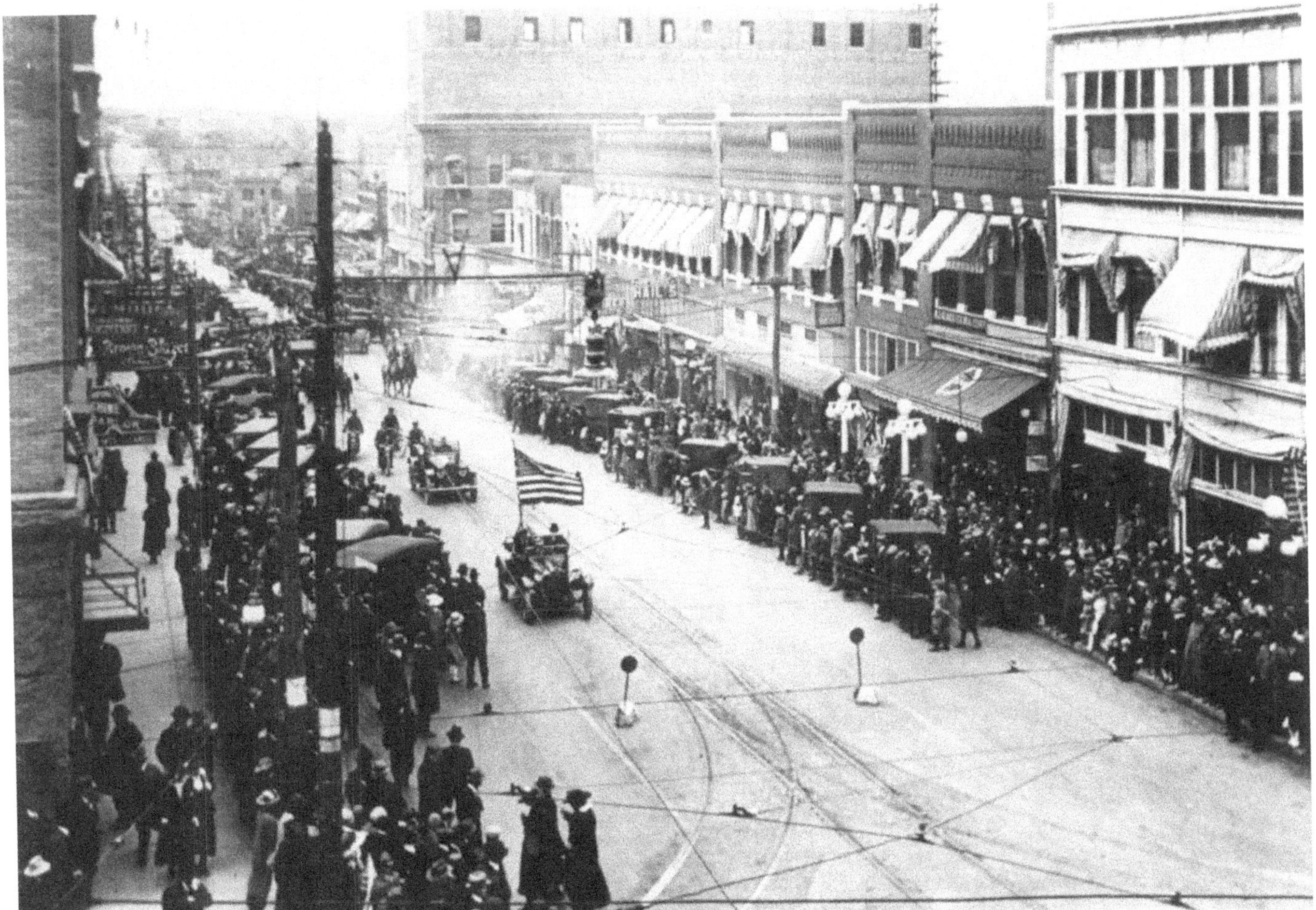

NEVER FORGET that Tulsa was bombed from the air by WW1 fighter planes 90 years before 911

Just as the black WW1 veterans were not afraid to fight for their cause the white WW1 veterans did the same but of course they had the advantage. They had the police and government assistance and they had planes ready for use against the blacks the same way they were used in WW1. As the fighting escalated on both sides and the black community began to back themselves into their section of town, the World War I Curtiss JN-4 Jenny biplane trainers were dispatched to fire at residents and drop bombs on Black homes and businesses; perhaps some of these very planes shown participated in the bombing of Tulsa. There is really no way to determine the ownership of the planes, but it is very likely that at least one was owned by the Sinclair Oil Company. With this kind of firepower on the side of the White citizens, the riot grew increasingly worse for Black Tulsans'. Families who were able began to flee the rampant gunfire. Buck Franklin witnessed the planes dropping turpentine bombs.

Eye Witness Accounts From Buck Franklin
Invisible Helpers

"From my office window, I could see planes circling in mid-air. They grew in number and hummed, darted and dipped low. I could hear something like hail falling upon the top of my office building. Down East Archer, I saw the old Mid-Way hotel on fire, burning from its top, and then another and another and another building began to burn from the top. "What, an attack from the air, too?" I asked myself. Lurid flames roared and belched and licked their forked tongues in the air. Smoke ascended the sky in thick, black volumes and amid it all, the planes–now a dozen or more in number–still hummed and darted here and there with the agility of natural birds of the air. Then a filling station further down East Archer caught on fire from the top. I feared now an explosion and decided to try to move to safer quarters. I came out of my office, locked the door and descended to the foot of the steps. The side-walks were literally covered with **burning turpentine balls**. I knew all too well where they came from and I knew all too well why every burning building first caught from the top. I paused and waited for an opportune time to escape. "Where, oh where is our splendid fire department with its half-dozen stations?" I asked myself. "Is the city in conspiracy with the mob?" I again asked myself. As I stood there in contemplation of these and other gruesome facts, I saw two sights that will live in my memory to my dying days. One was a woman on the opposite side of the street. She was traveling south–hair disentangled and disheveled–**in the very path of whizzing bullets**. She was calling wildly to a little tot that, a few moments before, had dashed in panic before her and turned off Greenwood on Archer at the corner. I hollered to her, "Turn back, woman, for God's sake turn back. You will be mown down." **Never turning her head**, she answered, as she hurried on, "I must follow my child." And so she did follow her child **and not a bullet touched her although they literally rained down the street**. This brave self-denying mother lives today here in Tulsa and with her that tot–now a splendid young lady–whom she risked her life to save." **- Buck Franklin (written on August 22nd 1931, 10 years after the massacre)**

Tulsa Oklahoma was bombed by white people 90 years before planes hit the Twin Towers in 2001.
Never Forget That!

Rau nu Prt m heru

Iu f Per f m heru

Utterances for Coming Forth by day into Light

It is he, who comes forth by day into Light

The WW1 Snipper Young Ross
August 22nd 1931, 10 Years After The Massacre
Eye Witness Accounts From Buck Franklin

From every direction, except the North, we were surrounded, and the mob was closing in upon me. Across the street, directly in front of me, stood the Gurley Building, property of a very wealthy and–up to that time–a very influential colored man. I heard shots fired from behind that building and heard angry and profane voices, saying, "Come out of there, Gurley–you black s–o–a–b." I saw an opening to move on and so I sped North, out Greenwood Avenue. About one hundred yards on the way out, I was joined by I.H. Spears, another colored attorney, and we proceeded on together. I thought that may be I could make it back to my hotel and find a gun of some sort there–in some of these rooms. At the intersection of North Greenwood and East Easton–the point at which I intended to turn west–I looked across to my left and there, in stone's cast, stood the Ross residence–burning from the top. On the front porch stood Mother Ross, with outstretched and trembling hands, begging a mob that was approaching from the northwest to spare her home and family (Evidently she had not then discovered her house on fire). From within I could hear the report of high-powered rifles. I remembered the words of young Ross that morning and knew that he was making good on his threat. Every time there was a report of a gun from within, one of the members of the mob would fall, never to rise again. I somehow, felt happy. I cannot explain that feeling. I never felt that way–before nor since. **B. Franklin**

Young Ross and His Family in 1931
Eye Witness Accounts From Buck Franklin

How the years have flown and how changed and changing is the whole face of this nation. It is now August 22nd, 1931 as this is being written. A little more than ten years have passed under the bridge of time since the great holocaust here. Young Ross, the veteran of the world war, survived the great catastrophe, but lost both his mind and eye sights in the fires that destroyed his home. With a burned and scarred face and a mindless mind, he sits today in the asylum of this State and stares blankly into space. At the corner of North Greenwood and East Easton, sits Mother Ross with her tin cup in hand, begging alms of the passers-by. They are nearly all new comers and have no knowledge of her tragic past, hence they pay her little attention.

Young Mrs. Ross is working and doing the best she can to carry on in these times of depression. She divides her visits between her mother-in-law and her husband in the asylum. Of course, he has not the slightest recollection of her or of his mother. All yesteryears are only blank pieces of paper to him. He cannot remember one thing in the living, breathing, throbbing present. **B. Franklin**

Eye witness accounts from Buck Franklin
The Three Wealthy Black Men

"The three men–one of whom lugged a heavy trunk on his shoulder–were all killed as they were crossing the street–killed before my very eyes. The man who carried the trunk was very old. Likely, he had in that trunk many things of great value (Negroes in Tulsa then were, as a rule, very wealthy) and thought as much of the contents thereof as he did of his own life. When the old man was hit–no doubt by a dozen bullets–he dropped his burden and shrieked and fell sprawling upon the hard paved street. Blood gushed from every wound and ran down the street. I turned my head from the scene." **- Buck Franklin (written on August 22nd 1931, 10 years after the massacre)**

Eye witness accounts from Buck Franklin

"I looked North and directly in front of us stood a thousand boys, it seemed, with guns pointed at our heads. They commanded us to "right about face." Then one half-starved ruffian came forward to search us. Finding no weapon, he started to take my money. At this I balked. This was the last straw. I had endured about all I could and decided then and there to die, if necessary, before I would be robbed by that bunch of hungry out-laws. I have always thanked my God that none of the other members of my family were in the city. My wife and three children were down on the farm–one hundred miles away–and my oldest child–a daughter–was in college in Tennessee. The next day, I got a chance to route her away from Tulsa on her trip from school.

Rau nu Prt m heru

The ruffians marched us back down from Greenwood to First Street, thence on First Street to Main Street, thence on Main Street to Brady Street and thence on Brady Street to convention hall. You see, this was one of the many places of detention, refuge, or whatever you wish to call it, to which my Race was taken when dislodged from its home. Here, those who cared to accept the fare, the people were fed and watered like so many cattle by benefactors (?) who had allowed the mob to take their government away from them and trample their laws and constitution under their unhallowed and barbarous feet. Here, I saw the colored lady of refinement, culture, and good breeding placed on an absolute equality with the prostitute and street walker of the Race. Here, I saw some of the fine matrons of the Race wrapped only in their night gowns, having been ejected from their homes so hurriedly until they did not even have time to dress. Here, I saw a mother, in a dark corner of that mammoth building giving birth–premature birth–to a babe and I heard its husky cries, for the first time, amid this strange, unseemly and wicked surrounding. And from sun rise to sun set, I passed through scenes and experiences that beggar description. They were like unto–if not worse than–The Last Days of Pompeii, as described by Bulwer Lytton. **During that bloody day, I lived a thousand years, in the spirit, at least. I lived the whole experience of the Race; *the experience of royal ancestry beyond the sea*; experiences of the slave ships on their first voyages to America with their human cargo; experiences of American slavery and its concomitant evils; experiences of loyalty and devotion of the Race to this nation and its flag in war and in peace**; and I thought of Ross back yonder, out yonder, in his last stand, no doubt, for the protection of home and fire side and of old Mother Ross left homeless in the even-tide of her life. I thought of the place the preachers call hell and wondered seriously if there was such a mystical place–it appeared, in this surrounding–that the only hell was the hell on this earth, such as the Race was then passing through."- **B. Franklin**

Iu f Per f m heru

Utterances for Coming Forth by day into Light

It is he, who comes forth by day into Light

CAPTURED NEGROS ON WAY TO
CONVENTION HALL-DURING TULSA RACE RIOT
JUNE 1st 1921.

The Aftermath

At least 300 Black died as a result of the massacre but the total number of dead can never be correctly calculated! How many New Yorkers know that **Central Park** is built over the an old Black Village named **Seneca Village**? Seneca was established in 1825 by free African Americans. At its peak it had 225 residents, with over half of them being home owners with the power to vote. Seneca Village had 3 churches, 2 schools and 3 cemeteries. To stop the economic advancement of this thriving African American community, racist laws were put into effect that classified **Seneca Village** as Eminent domain. By 1857 the black people who settled there were displaced and Central Park was built. How do we find the descendants of those Black people and are they owed reparations?! Do Black people all over the world deserve reparations for all we have suffered?! Unfortunately many Black people don't know the events of our history just like many of you didn't know about Seneca Village. About 10,000 plus Black people were left homeless after the Tulsa massacre, and property damage amounted to more than the $1.5 million in real estate and $750,000 in personal property (equivalent to $32.65 million in 2020) at least that's what ***they tell us they owe us***. What we lost in Black Wall Street and Seneca Village can not be calculated on a scale of monetary measurement. **How much does a soul weigh?!** That is the real question we are asking! More than 800 people were admitted to hospitals, and as many as 6,000 Black residents of Tulsa were jailed in large facilities, many of them for several days and weeks; at least that's **what they report**. In my experience the survivors of a genocide often tell a different story from what is made common knowledge. The villain will always paint themselves as the hero or the **Heru** in their version of the story. In their version of American history the Black struggle it is not as bad of an event worthy enough for immediate reconciliation. Instead we listen to them make laws that do nothing to insure our safety or benefit. Just like the laws made to confiscated Seneca Village. **How much does a soul weigh?!**

Helping Hands

Black people supported each other, many came from other communities to assist in Tulsa after the massacre. Here, **Mrs. Ruth G. Fish** of Alamosa, Colorado stands with a little girl referred to as "**Arizona**."

Radio Silence

Many of those who survived the massacre left Tulsa, while the Black and White residents who stayed in the city largely kept silent about the terror, violence, and resulting losses for decades. The massacre was largely omitted from local, state, and national histories. Decades after this massacre the story had been widely forgotten, even in Tulsa. This massacre is considered ***one of*** "the single worst incidents of racial violence in American history". The terrorist burned and destroyed more than 35 square blocks of Black Wall Street, which at the time was one of the wealthiest Black communities in the "United States". Yet still it is not tragic enough of a crime to need

June 1st 1921, The Last Day

Around noon on June 1st the Oklahoma **National Guard** imposed **martial law**, ending the massacre. Many pictures that detail the horrors of Black Wall Street have never been seen by the general public. I remember the pictures that circulated around post while I was deployed to Iraq in 2003 during the war in Iraq. I did not experience the events in the picture but what I saw in the pictures I will never forget. I saw men stuck to their vehicles like their bodies had been melted and now became part of the vehicles. I have successfully erased most of the images from my mind but what about this picture of the black boy holding another baby? Did this boy survive? Is the baby he is carrying in this picture still alive ? What will it take for this Country to stand on the principles the constitution is suppose to uphold? When will black people find every means to come back home? To unite regardless of our differences!

Condolences

My condolences go out to the families of all those who lost their lives during this massacre as well as all the other known and unknown thriving black communities that were extinguished by the hands of white violent racist white supremacist such as the 1898 **Wilmington massacre** in North Carolina, The 1917 **Great Riots of East St Louis**, the 1923 **Rosewood massacre** in Florida, and **Little Haiti riot** in Raleigh North Carolina. Please know that death is not the end. The soul survives death, indeed and in spirit. This is a book of the dead written by a boy who was murdered without justice, who defeated death and came forth by day. May the souls of those innocent residents of Black Wall Street walk peacefully through the field of Reeds in Amenta. Amen RA.

What About Queen Mother Ross?!

Rau nu Prt m heru

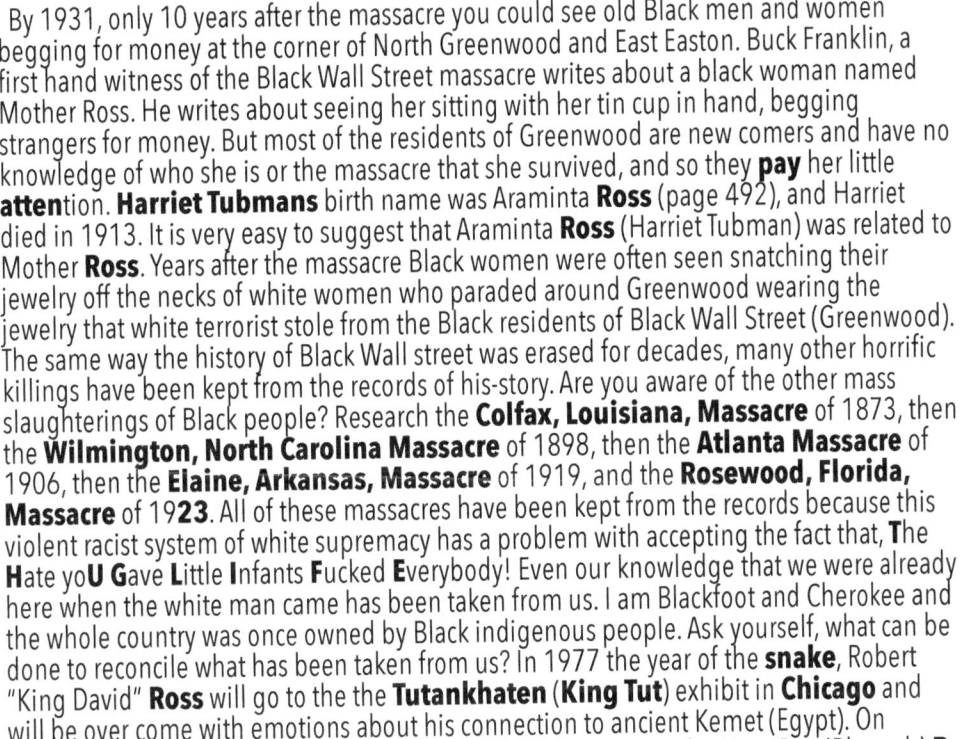

By 1931, only 10 years after the massacre you could see old Black men and women begging for money at the corner of North Greenwood and East Easton. Buck Franklin, a first hand witness of the Black Wall Street massacre writes about a black woman named Mother Ross. He writes about seeing her sitting with her tin cup in hand, begging strangers for money. But most of the residents of Greenwood are new comers and have no knowledge of who she is or the massacre that she survived, and so they **pay** her little **atten**tion. **Harriet Tubmans** birth name was Araminta **Ross** (page 492), and Harriet died in 1913. It is very easy to suggest that Araminta **Ross** (Harriet Tubman) was related to Mother **Ross**. Years after the massacre Black women were often seen snatching their jewelry off the necks of white women who paraded around Greenwood wearing the jewelry that white terrorist stole from the Black residents of Black Wall Street (Greenwood). The same way the history of Black Wall street was erased for decades, many other horrific killings have been kept from the records of his-story. Are you aware of the other mass slaughterings of Black people? Research the **Colfax, Louisiana, Massacre** of 1873, then the **Wilmington, North Carolina Massacre** of 1898, then the **Atlanta Massacre** of 1906, then the **Elaine, Arkansas, Massacre** of 1919, and the **Rosewood, Florida, Massacre** of 19**23**. All of these massacres have been kept from the records because this violent racist system of white supremacy has a problem with accepting the fact that, **T**he **H**ate yo**U** **G**ave **L**ittle **I**nfants **F**ucked **E**verybody! Even our knowledge that we were already here when the white man came has been taken from us. I am Blackfoot and Cherokee and the whole country was once owned by Black indigenous people. Ask yourself, what can be done to reconcile what has been taken from us? In 1977 the year of the **snake**, Robert "King David" **Ross** will go to the the **Tutankhaten** (**King Tut**) exhibit in **Chicago** and will be over come with emotions about his connection to ancient Kemet (Egypt). On January 13th 2019 he would get DNA results connecting him to the Nswt Bity (Pharaoh) **Ramsesses III** (page 547). On May 14th 2022 Payton S. Gendron murdered 10 Black people in Buffalo New York (The Buffalo Massacre). **Aaron Salter** was the **55** year old ex-cop supermarket security guard who was killed in the Buffalo Massacre. Inspired by rising gas prices, Aaron had recently spoken about a "newly discovered energy source" and had patented a system that enables vehicles to run on water instead of gasoline, called hydrogen-electrolysis. Some say that the massacre was an organized assassination of Aaron so as to suppress technology that would threaten the oil and automotive industries.

Iu f Per f m heru

Everything They Owe

Utterances for Coming Forth by day into Light

In 1996, 75 years after the massacre, a bipartisan group in the state legislature authorized the formation of the Oklahoma Commission to Study the Tulsa Race Riot of 1921. The commission's final report, published in **2001 the year of the snake,** states that the city had conspired with the mob of White citizens against Black citizens; it recommended a program of reparations to survivors and their descendants. The state passed legislation to establish scholarships for the descendants of survivors, encourage the economic development of Greenwood, and develop a park in memory of the victims of the massacre in Tulsa. A park like **Seneca Village** (page 413). They want to give you a park. Like they want ti give you a grave stone. Here is the city your ancestors used to own now let us all walk through the park and the city still owns the land. The park for the victims of the massacre was dedicated in 2010. Schools in Oklahoma have been required to teach students about the massacre since 2002, but it wasn't till 2020, that the massacre officially became a part of the Oklahoma school curriculum. In **2001 the year of the Snake,** the posthumous album **Until the End of Time** was released by Tupac. On that album we can find the song Everything they Owe and the lyrics from the first verse ring just as true in 2001 than the would have in 1921 or 1621.

*"We back for everything you owe, no longer oppressed! cause we now overthrow those that placed us in this rotten mess, but let's agree on strategy and pick our enemies, right! Who stands accused of the abuse? My own kind, right? Pardon! not disregarding what you think'n but you must abandon ship cause once I rip your whole shit it's sink'n, supreme ideology you claim to hold, claim'n that we all drug dealers with empty **souls**!"* **- Tupac.**

It is he, who comes forth by day into Light

Dream Land Theatre - Watchmen and Lovecraft Country

The Dreamland movie theatre was one of the two Black owned and operated movie theaters in Black Wall Street. With these movie theaters we had the power to control the images flashed in front of us in on the big screen, and most importantly, the images our children saw. I'm sure they never showed the racist movie ***Birth of a Nation*** at either of their theaters! Unfortunately neither of the theaters survived the bombing and burning of Black Wall Street. I mention this because it is vitally important for a people to control the story of their past. This is sacred and another people should not have control over how your culture and history is portrayed. I have no desire to attack anyones sexual orientation but I can find no historical data pertaining to homosexual Black men in Black Wall Street. In fact the whole massacre is a result of the claims that a 18 year old Black **male** raped a 17 year old White **female** (p 406), no different than how **Emmett Till** was lynched because of the false accusations of a White woman, yet I have seen the two shows, **Watchmen** and **Lovecraft Country** which both incorporate some real events from the Black Wall Street massacre and in each series they have also added graphic male homosexuality scenes that have no historical value (pages 351-355). They took the tragedy of Black Wall Street and inserted homosexual lifestyles into their script which do nothing to add to the massacre of Black Wall Street. They might as well have had a transgender character too or a black Klingon from Star Trek. While the sexual scenes in both series didn't sit well with me I found the plot of Lovecraft Country to be rather interesting especially episode 8, titled **Jig-a-Bobo** which has the funeral of **Emmett Till** detailed in it. The show also has a connection to ancient Kemet (Egypt), **immortality,** Time travel and the **Ausarian** (**Osirion**) **Resurrection**.

Episode 7 of **Lovecraft Country** is titled **Time Machine**. The characters in this episode must travel back in time to Tulsa Oklahoma during the peak of the Black Wall Street massacre to find a mysterious book of **spells** called the <u>*Book of Names*</u> . The oldest historical book of spells are the books in stone left inside the tombs of ancient Kemet (Egypt). These writings were more like utterances that were recited to ensure the "dead" **Pharaoh** had a safe journey in the **after life** and a safe **resurrection** into the **next life**. This concept of repeating of births was called the **Wehem-mesut** (p 14). Initially in ancient times **immortality** was only seen as possible for the pharaoh and you could only find these writings buried with the pharaoh - however as time went by the average person began to be buried with these spells written on papyrus. Thousands of years later these writings were found by White tomb robbers (egyptologist, tomb raiders) and labeled as the coffin text and The Book of The Dead because they were found buried with the dead. It's safe to say that **Lovecraft Country** was written with ancient Kemetic spiritual philosophy. In episode 7 there is a White woman/family searching for the lost <u>*Book of Names*</u>. The book was owned by a Black family that lived in Black Wall Street. Members of the Black family were sent back in time during the peak of the Black Wall Street massacre to retrieve the mysterious <u>*Book of Names*</u> which was a **spell book** of **life**, **Transformation**, and **Genesis**. I found this to be quite interesting because I watched this series in 2020 while I was writing this book which is about the revelation of my past life as Tutankhaten (King Tut) the Nswt Bity Pharaoh from the 18th dynasty. If that wasn't strange enough Episode 8 was titled "Jig-a-Bobo," and it was about the funeral of **Emmett Till**. The story of my Life as Emmett Till fits within the Lovecraft Country story line because the show is committed to depicting the horror and violence of White American racism. <u>It is important that a people control the visual narrative of their past. I went most of my life with an impression of Kemet (Egypt) as racially and culturally linked to **Europe not Africa**, this perception was created by Hollywood stars in **movies** such as "The Ten Commandments" who played the roles of the Egyptians.</u> I saw **Michael Jackson** in "Remember the Time" in 1991 but I did not "remember the time". I saw **Nas's** Egyptian album cover for "I Am.." in 1999 but I did not realize that "I was" a pharaoh and would not awaken to my life as **King Tut** until April 4th 2020, the same day that Martin Luther King was assassinated (see page 69). **Lovecraft Country** isn't the show that has incorporated elements of my story, see **The Manifestation of Emmett Till** on page 536.

August 25th 2016 Run Quick See

Everybody run quick see, I'm taking you back, come follow me, **we sleep they live**, we **eat meat** then preach peace the least you can do is obey the laws of nature, the way! the claws of the **falcon** flying away, the pause in the **Malcolm** speech they edit away, press play, you can call me **Muhammad Ali, The Greatest of All Time**, but not one more time **Cassius Clay! King kunta, Prince Hakeem** from **Far Rockaway** to the bay, ***I pray the Lord my soul to keep if I should die before I reach my peak of my success pray for a soldiers death***, another rep, another step, a deep breath, another **dream** differed, another step back word, ever heard the lion tell the truth to the gazelle? he pushed him too close to the edge then he fell, he flew! **Heru** flight rebel, stay true light, prevail like the **Zulu** fight back! **Cointelpro** might strike back! but it's like that and that's the way it is, I got my sight back, I got the right map and write raps with a pro black propagative, you don't like that?! fuck that that's positive! how the hell you gonna come trying to judge how I live?! "**Puffy good but Wu Tang for the kids**", the blueprint on the wall take the negative let it fall into context next to relative, and who's your relative? and what's your heritage? and tell me of a people who ever did fight evil more than **the black diaspora** ever did?! I need Black people more than I ever did, I need Love more than I ever did **- Dawud The Uncanny BlaKseed**

Rau nu Prt m heru

August 26th 2016 A Living Memory

> ***"Everything's a memory, Everything's a memory, Everything's a memory, Everything's a memory, Everything's a memory, Everything's a memory"***
> *audio from the instrumental I wrote this song to.*

Iu f Per f m heru

Memories don't live like people do, **they live you sleep**, you reap what you sow, when the light's green you go, not tomorrow, the time is now! the future is the gift but today is the present, my love is **King** for the **Queen** of sorrow, everything, m**ark** your **dream** like the earth seen from a room on the moon in **Apollo**, no telescope just hope with a dope memory to follow, **The Pharaoh** with a **bow and arrow** that I see gotta be **Ramoses** slaying the adversary, don't let humanity distract spiritual practice let the dead bury the dead ashes to ashes **- Dawud The Uncanny BlaKseed**

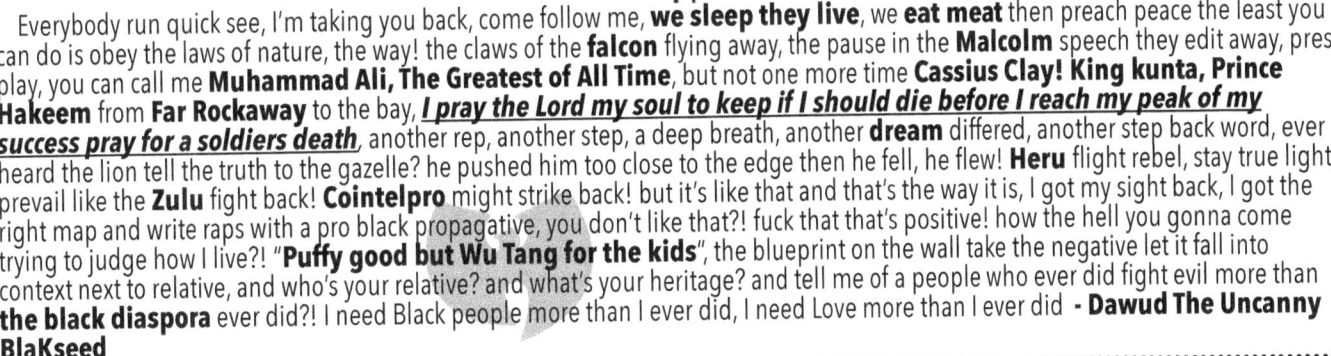

August 27th 2016 Aura Cells

Utterances for Coming Forth by day into Light

What they do?! first they throw brothers in jail! then they scare the females with these visions of hell! religion is like division! how can we ever prevail? when we're taught to see difference not the oneness that dwells? like the order in cells, like the aura that tells the story, like emotions trapped in water crystals, it's the intent from the heart that's the real issue, they didn't think twice killing **Tamir Rice** a little boy with a toy pistol, **Sandra Bland, Philando Castile, Korryn Gains, Alton Sterling**, will this ever change?! I'm feeling the pain and I miss you! worth more dead than alive they exchange organ tissue, they blood bank you no thank you no samples given at my physical, **half man half spiritual**, more miracle than lyrical, still giving you a visual it's the principle! you treat a Black man like we disposable but you the imbecile, mixing the mythical with the biblical, only the originals know what's true check it, your clinical track record is reckless irrational not respected laughable, all about the capital, weaker than the clavicle, **meat eater** like the **cannibal**, I know you wanna cut me sagittal plane, sagittal plane, sagittal plane, the doctor, they wanna cut me sagittal plane sagittal plane but I ain't paying the doctor, they wanna cut you sagittal plane left in pain stuck in bed laying and paying the doctor

It is he, who comes forth by day into Light

My music's creating my aura, it was written just like the **Torah**, I know a sugar cane that will drain your calcium stores brah, we were alkaline paradigm now we full of slime and ibuprofen, undermine the lining the flora, the intestines the colon, the swollen limbs the diabetics, the need for water, the diuretics, the disease created cause we ignore the natural order, call me **King David, Dawud the Blakseed**, like essential oils healing properties, Hidden Colors, they chopping trees like the Congolese did for the rubber, your history taught me like **Leopold** you never loved us! stories untold Nasty **Nas** made peace with his brother, 3 days later he was gone never be another, **Tanisha Anderson** dies right in front of her daughters eyes, another homicide Cleveland cops no conviction, they never apologized, this revolution won't be neutralized, 400 years of oppression, war on the poor, war on immigrants won't take no more! educate your mind don't be afraid to speak, defend yourself don't turn the other cheek! cause a **dream** differed stinks like **rotten meat** and explodes like a heavy load in about a week, sagittal plane sagittal plane, the doctor, they wanna cut me sagittal plane sagittal plane but I ain't paying the doctor, they wanna cut you sagittal plane left in pain stuck in bed laying and paying the doctor, They wanna cut me sagittal plane sagittal plane but I ain't paying the doctor, they wanna cut you sagittal plane left in pain stuck in bed laying and paying the doctor **- Dawud The Uncanny BlaKseed**

August 28th 2016 Man In The Mirror

To forgive is to free, searching for mastery, no self pity no agony under the bo tree **Buddha** sat **magic**ally like **sacred geometry**, I'm a speak honestly, I owe the universe an apology, I point my finger at you and three point back at me, actually I'm just doing what comes naturally, you back'n me up against the wall, too close to the edge and I'm just trying not to fall! oppression, harassment, aggression, perfected methods, stop and check'n, the cruel **school to prison pipe line**, records, felonies, state fines, 1 800 I heard it through the grapevine, 400 years of hate crimes, **It's Nation Time,** big lips broad nose wide hips with a **Haitian** mind, relationship goals I rose to the top, I want them to love me like they love **Pac**, Hip Hop locked in my **soul** since **who Got The Props**, give me the **rock and** let me **roll** like **Chuck Berry,** if everyone was ready we could mash a military, I know the load is heavy, I know the road is long, **Let's Get It On** already, we gotta get along cause we in the storm already, my nigga's tell me really how many we gotta bury? you know **Marcus Garvey?** they said he was suicidal! **Malcolm** said he felt like he died 20 years ago, back against the wall, a rifle no bible! fighting for survival! I'm not a raw **vegan** or a **vegetarian**, I'm just a human being being a humanitarian, it's like we the bacteria in the aquarium, the **king of pop** said it starts with "***the man In the mirror***" man, I started living better it all got clearer man, heal yourself first before you run healing another man, don't forget about the mother land that's where we all come from, "*you might win some but you just lost one*", caution to the wind, swim in the ocean it's sink or swim, Sally went to the shore came back with war and saw the whole world change chameleon, will it ever be the same again?! "what's your name again?", she ain't understand **Kemetian**, it was **alien** - **Dawud The Amazing BlaKseed**

September 1st 2016 - Colin Kaepernick Takes a Knee

On August 14th the same day that the **Haitian revolution** was planned in 1791, Colin Kaepernick remained seated while his teammates stood for the **national anthem**. On August 26th he made his first statement about why he refused to stand. He said: "I'm not going to stand up to show pride for a country that oppresses black people and people of color". On September 1st he took a knee for the first time with his teammate Eric Reid joining him in protest. Colin went from sitting to kneeling after a conversation he had with Nate Boyer, a former Army Green Beret and NFL player. Boyer told HBO's "Real Sports." "Soldiers take a knee in front of a fallen soldiers grave to show respect." I was proud of Colin. I had stopped watching sports a long time ago but he brought me back just to watch his protest on the news. I have not watched a football, or basketball game since around 2009 or 2010. See pages 454 and 535 for more on Colin Kaepernick.

September 2nd 2016 Incarnation

The point of realization, don't need a joint to break the laws of gravitation, thought pushing, law of attraction, manifestation, war on Black skin! help me raise this Black nation! cops harassing, chasing, blasting, incarceration, Death! **another incarnation** in the flesh - **Dawud The Amazing BlaKseed**

September 3rd 2016 Rich In Spirit

A lot can happen in year, down homies up and disappear, but you get smarter wiser more aware, a surviver smaller square around your circle, never know who might be out to hurt you, **laws universal like attraction**, you can find love and passion, see violence become compassion, and vice versa, you never know who might be out to help you, you could be without food clothes and shelter, you can say a prayer and be delivered from the river to the delta, family members die feel pain you never felt brah! things change even the cards God dealt yah, heltah skeltah confusion you be losing, you could be choosing to give up, or you can live up to the righteous **Harriet,** and be free and rich in **Spirit,** you could take a stand even the klan and the fans don't wanna hear it! A Black man with a plan they fear it, a mic in my hand real **Heru** lyrics like change, they ain't know the **BlaKseed** one in the same so, you know what I came fo, to reign to grow, you sow what you reap, 365, 52 weeks, 24 - 7, I wrote this for my peeps and rest in peace to **Uncle Squeek** up in heaven - **Dawud The Amazing BlaKseed** (Sep 3rd page 514)

Buddhist Reincarnation Pictures Found in Computer in 2016

On March 2nd 2014 I would watch the documentary, The Prophecy of Reincarnation Sambho the black **Buddha** (p 288). I would watch this video all the way through and I was so intrigued by it that I downloaded it to my computer, that is how I know the date I watched it. On July 15th 2014 I ordered the book **Moses Begat King Tut** and the book **Siddhartha** from Amazon.com (p 295). I met a woman named Stephanie in May of 2014 and she would give me a copy of the book Siddhartha for my birthday in 2015 (p 340). I did not read the book until 2016 after I met a brother named Kenny in Marcus Garvey Park who suggested that I read it. Kenny and Stephanie are both born on January 12th and that was the reason I finally read the book (p 440). After I read a few paragraphs in the book I began to cry because I felt like I was reading about myself. The book is about how **Siddhartha** the Buddha got his enlightenment. I didn't realize what the book was about till I finished the book yet I cried after only a few paragraphs. When I finished the book I called Stephanie and asked her why she gave me the book and she told me that when she met me I reminded her of Siddhartha from the book. The documentary, The Prophecy of Reincarnation Sambho the black **Buddha,** predicted that the **Buddha** would be reborn in the west between the years of 1975 and 2020 and I'm born in 1977. The documentary states that the returning

Buddha would ***prove the immortality of the soul*** with his **reincarnation**. My past life revelation of my life as **Emmett Till** came on July 3rd 2018 (page 480) and my past life revelation of my life as **Tutankhaten** (**King Tut**) came on April 4th 2020 (page 594), right at the start of **COVID**. This Documentary can still be seen on youtube. While compiling this book I would find that I had downloaded many pictures on Buddhist reincarnation in the year of 2016. Please go back and **July 15th 2014** to read the full story and to get a more detailed breakdown (page 295).

Rau nu Prt m heru

2016 (Magical Book Store)

I don't remember where I heard about the book **The Celestine Prophecy** but I read it sometime around 2014. I owned the book 2 or 3 times. I would lend the book to people and never get it back. While in massage school I got into a conversation about how the book seemed to always find legs of it's own and come up missing. That same day I went to a thrift store near my school for the first time. This store sold second hand books, clothes and various other things. When I looked at the wall of books ***the first book that I laid my eyes on was*** **The Celestine Prophecy**. Instantaneously this book store became magical to me and every now and then I would go to this store just to see what book I would lay my eyes on first. I currently only have the book cover for this book, but I know who has the book this time. **Katherine** has my book. She borrowed it and left me a book called the **history of dreaming**. I never read the book but as I'm typing this I feel like I want to open that book and see what it tells me. Today is November 7th 2021 and I had one of the most profound dreams I have ever had in my life on November 4th 2021! November 4th is the day that **Tutankhaten's** (**King Tut**) tomb was discovered in 1922. The dream was like the movie **inception**!

November 4th 2021 - Dream

I was hanging on to the back of a ship during a great storm. The ship went over enormous tidal waves but I kept hanging on. I was being thrown side to side as I held on with one hand. Then I looked into the ocean and to my surprise I could see the ocean floor as clear as day. There was a giant hole in the ocean floor and looking through the hole I could see people sleeping on the floor of a house. There was no water in the house though, the people were sleeping peacefully. Then all of a sudden I was in the house with them but I was running. I was being chased and someone was along side me, they were being chased too. I don't know who or what was chasing us but after a few steps I saw a mirror and I jumped into the mirror like a portal, then I pulled the person that was running with me into the mirror too. Then we were being led up a long flight of steps by one of the men I saw sleeping on the floor. When we got to the top of the steps there was a door. Then I woke up.

Iu f Per f m heru

2016 Magical Book Store and The Reincarnated Salem Witch

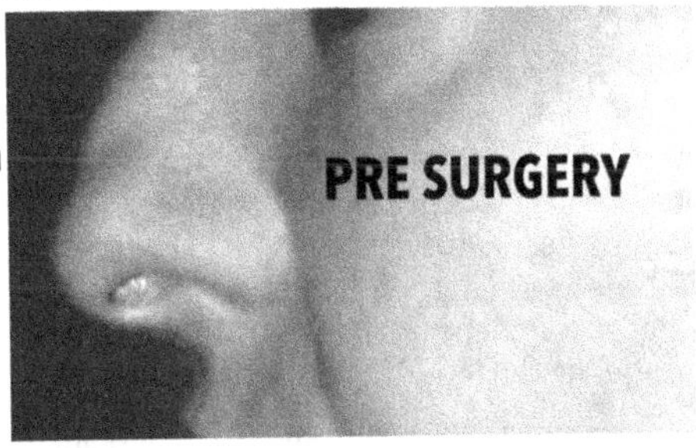

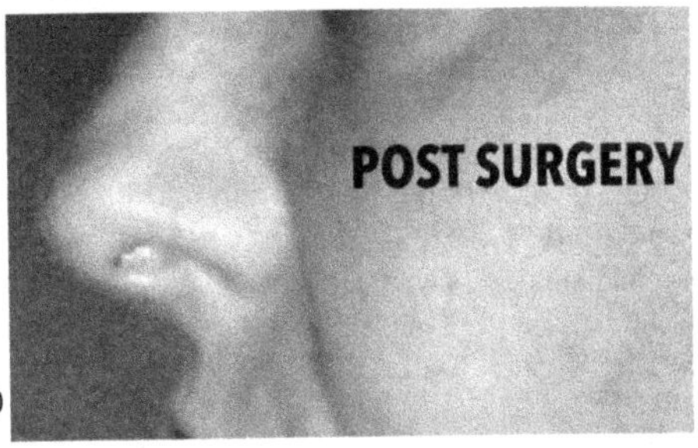

My second year at school I met a woman in my myology class. I will leave her nameless but shortly after meeting her she told me that she was into past life regression and that she felt like she was a **witch** in a **past life**. She even sent me pictures of her nose before and after surgery. She had a nose job done because her nose was naturally bent the way witches are depicted in movies and she hated it. This would be the first time I ever heard of **past life regression** and still I was not clear on what it was. That same day I went to the "magical book store" again, I wanted to see what book my eyes would fall on because of what happened with the book Celestine Prophecy. I walked in the store and I glanced at the wall of books to see what my eye's would fall on first. My eyes fell on the book **GREAT AMERICAN TRIALS,** 201 Compelling Courtroom Dramas. mI grabbed the book and opened it to a random page and it opened to page 18, the **Salem Witch Trials** of 1692. I wondered if the store would speak to me again **but I was not prepared for that!** I called her and told her and she was speechless. For some reason I did not take the initiative to start looking into past life regression after this experience. I had been writing about reincarnation but never did I really consider the idea of having been here before. Perhaps I may have had this revelation sooner if I had taken past life regression and reincarnation more seriously. The last time I spoke to this woman was after I had my past life revelation of Emmett Till on July 3rd 2018. I reminded her about this experience with the book then I told her my story. She was riding on the highway and I was telling her about Emmett Till's connection to **Martin Luther King** (pages 69, 592) then she got chills and goose bumps because as soon as I said Martin's name she had passed a traffic sign that read, Martin Luther King drive. I'm writing a Epic Sci-Real (Science Reality) Novel Trilogy version of this book and a book about Tupac's ancient past life (pages 664 - 665). Stay tuned!

Utterances for Coming Forth by day into Light

It is he, who comes forth by day into Light

Salem Witchcraft Trials: 1692

Defendants: 200 accused, including: Bridget Bishop, Reverend George Burroughs, Martha Carrier, Giles Corey, Martha Corey, Mary Easty, Sarah Good, Elizabeth How, George Jacobs, Susannah Martin, Rebecca Nurse, Alice Parker, Mary Parker, John Procter, Ann Pudeator, Wilmot Reed, Margaret Scott, Samuel Wardwell, Sarah Wild, and John Willard.

Crimes Charged: Witchcraft **Chief Examiners:** Jonathan Corwin and John

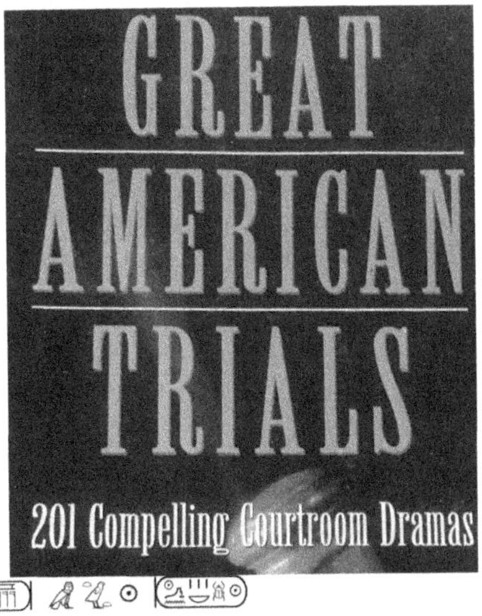

MISSISSIPPI
TRIAL, 1955
Based on the true story of a tragic murder
that helped spark the Civil Rights movement
Chris Crowe

Addendum **2016 - Magical Book Store - Emmett Till**

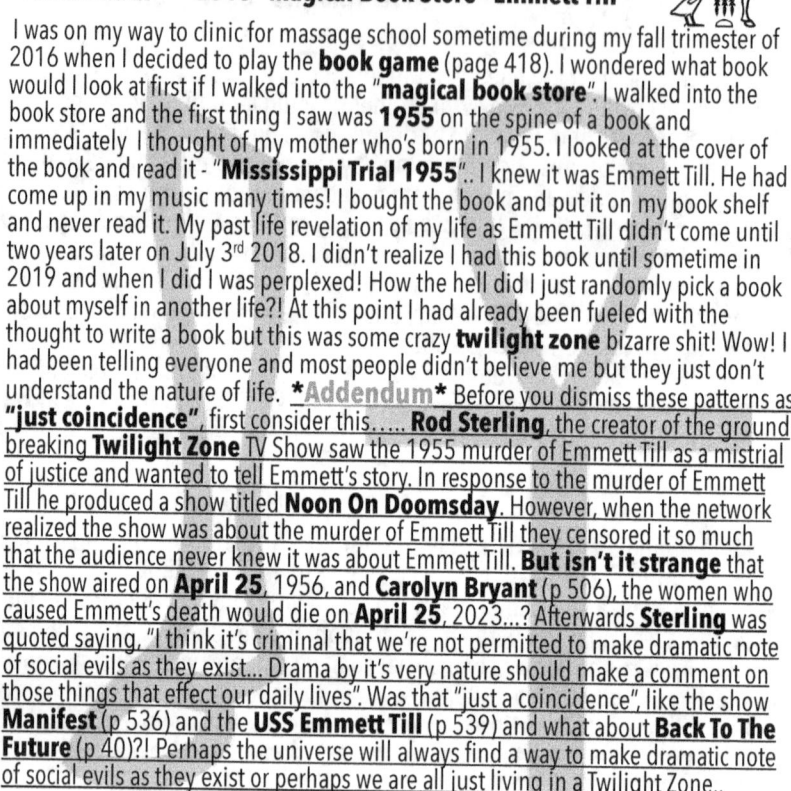

I was on my way to clinic for massage school sometime during my fall trimester of 2016 when I decided to play the **book game** (page 418). I wondered what book would I look at first if I walked into the "**magical book store**". I walked into the book store and the first thing I saw was **1955** on the spine of a book and immediately I thought of my mother who's born in 1955. I looked at the cover of the book and read it - "**Mississippi Trial 1955**".. I knew it was Emmett Till. He had come up in my music many times! I bought the book and put it on my book shelf and never read it. My past life revelation of my life as Emmett Till didn't come until two years later on July 3rd 2018. I didn't realize I had this book until sometime in 2019 and when I did I was perplexed! How the hell did I just randomly pick a book about myself in another life?! At this point I had already been fueled with the thought to write a book but this was some crazy **twilight zone** bizarre shit! Wow! I had been telling everyone and most people didn't believe me but they just don't understand the nature of life. ***Addendum*** Before you dismiss these patterns as **"just coincidence"**, first consider this….. **Rod Sterling**, the creator of the ground breaking **Twilight Zone** TV Show saw the 1955 murder of Emmett Till as a mistrial of justice and wanted to tell Emmett's story. In response to the murder of Emmett Till he produced a show titled **Noon On Doomsday**. However, when the network realized the show was about the murder of Emmett Till they censored it so much that the audience never knew it was about Emmett Till. **But isn't it strange** that the show aired on **April 25**, 1956, and **Carolyn Bryant** (p 506), the women who caused Emmett's death would die on **April 25**, 2023...? Afterwards **Sterling** was quoted saying, "I think it's criminal that we're not permitted to make dramatic note of social evils as they exist... Drama by it's very nature should make a comment on those things that effect our daily lives". Was that "just a coincidence", like the show **Manifest** (p 536) and the **USS Emmett Till** (p 539) and what about **Back To The Future** (p 40)?! Perhaps the universe will always find a way to make dramatic note of social evils as they exist or perhaps we are all just living in a Twilight Zone..

Today is November 8th 2021 and I can't sleep. I'm a bit tired but I must come back to this book. I'm almost done but the journey feels like I'm on a long run with still a long ways to go. I have about 20 more things to write about then I need to proof read what will be around 900 pages. I watched the movie **Defending your Life** yesterday. It came out in 1991, it's about death, the after life and reincarnation. I enjoyed the movie and cried at the last scene but I didn't like how there were very little black people in the movie. We damn sure die in America so I don't know how the hell they left us out of the death part! I opened my youtube yesterday and saw **Brother Jabari Osaze** doing a live video about **Akhenaten**. I left two comments that were not friendly. I get upset when people that work in Kemetic spiritual practices don't see me for who I am, but I understand them now… What I'm saying is indeed something bizarre and that's why I'm writing this book. Well, reincarnation isn't bizarre that's a fact of life but what's bizarre is how "Emmett" seems to stalked me!

I "randomly" bought this book in 2016 but I started saying Emmett's name in my rhymes in 2010! I said his name in the very first rhyme that I wrote in 2010 when I started writing rhymes as therapy (p 180). In that same year I would say King Tut's name, but I don't just say his name, I say his name on the day that his tomb was opened (p 11), November 26th 19**22** (page 187). Emmett's father was born in 19**22** and I can go and on and on with **coincidences**. **22** years after Emmett was murdered I was born when my mother was **22**! The gold mask weighs **22** pounds. **22** days after I realized I was Emmett was July 25th 2018 which would have been Emmett's **77th** birthday! I was born in 19**77** the year of the snake! Emmett was born in 19**41** the year of the snake and on Oct 25th 2018 I turned **41** years old (p **41**). My uncle Jimmy Dukes is born two days before **me on Oct 23,** 19**44** and his wife is born two days before **Emmett Till on July 23,** 19**44**. I turned **44** in 2021, they turned **77** this year and I was born in 19**77**! My Uncle Jimmy Dukes is the younger brother of my Grand father General Dukes Jr. My Grandfather had 6 brothers and mysteriously enough, one is named **Emmett Dukes**! Ain't that crazy?! Emmett Till was murdered in 19**55**, **Einstein** died in **1955**. Physicist like Einstein speak about **quantum entanglement**. Like my entanglement with the movie **Back To The Future** (p 40). In September of 2017 I buy a tee shirt with Emmett's face on it and I start wearing it a lot (pages, 459, 555, 599). It becomes my favorite Tee Shirt, and then and then and then and then one thing after the other after the other kept happening and happening and happening. I had no idea where all this was leading to. To be honest I think I might have gone crazy if it wasn't revealed to me in a slow manner the way it was. It was all dependent upon me earning the right to know based upon my actions. Emmett was killed for many reasons but the heart of it was a white woman in a racist system of white supremacy. I thank God for all the divine women that have come across my path in this life. Dua dua dua. I'm writing a Epic Sci-Real (Science Reality) Novel Trilogy version of this book and a book about Tupac's ancient past life (pages 664,665). Stay tuned.

September 2016

Amiga and her Vision, Dreams, her Past Life as Dihya Al-Kahina and the Star Code of Immortality

I would meet Amiga in Shiatsu class. Shiatsu is a form of healing where the practitioner only uses compressions of the hands on the body of the person receiving treatment to stimulate the persons body intelligence to heal itself. Depending on the practitioners awareness of the body and their level of spiritual refinement will determine how effective or potent their touch is. Amiga and I attracted to each other becoming friends. She was already licensed in massage in another state and was working to gain a license in New York state. She was a spiritual person and had a spiritual practice called Yahweh hands. One day we were partners working on each other. As she laid on the massage table, I would put my left hand on her right should then I put my right hand on her hara (stomach). As I did this I had no out of the ordinary experience but Amiga would tell me of something far more different. She said that as soon as my right hand touched her hara (stomach) she felt electricity flow from my left hand to my right hand traveling down her spine to my right hand she also said that after the circuit was complete **she saw a vision**. In her vision she was taken to a place where a whole lot of conflict was involved and then she saw me in water. I was a man built like a warrior standing in the water. She could sense that I was in some type of combat. She then asked me if I had a fear of water. She said she wondered why she was seeing this. She wasn't sure why this was happening or why she felt connected to me. She would later feel like the vision was from a **past life** with her. That she was trying to find her path along the way in her journey of life. She would later express to me that she didn't feel like Amiga, she felt like she was someone else. She felt her spirit was the same but her flesh was not her. Amiga would have several **dreams** about me over the years.

Rau nu Prt m heru

September 2016
Amiga's 1st Dreams of Me

The mountain top

The first dream she had of me I was only **wearing pants up to my knees with a machete in my hand**. I was standing on top of a mountain guarding people who seemed to be stuck in a maze. Everything was the color red even the sand. She said that I was of a hierarchy and the people listened to me. I was angry with the people stuck the maze but I was guarding them pacing back and forth, they were red and appeared be stuck and unable to get out the maze.

Amiga's 2nd Dream of Me
The Star Code of Immortality

Iu f Per f m heru

In her dream I deciphered an **ancient code.** In the dream I went to the highest mountain and drew the code in the sand. The sand was either **golden** or orange. There was a group of people who were angry with me for cracking the code and sharing it. I drew the code in front of Amiga quickly because these people were after me. She said the code was bigger than the size of a **football field** and it took a long time for me to draw and explain so that she could understand it. I also had a copy of the blueprints in my hands written on an **ancient papyrus scrolls**. There were two other people there with us but they dispersed when the people who were after me appeared and grabbed me. Just before they grabbed me I gave Amiga the scrolls and told her to run and hide them. She ran not knowing what happened to me. She avoided capture by running through a forest. She ran and she ran until finally she ended up at her childhood home. She was now a child again in the house of her parents where she was abused. She hid the scroll in her parents home then woke up. Amiga had these dreams four years before I started writing this book. Her dream was a premonition. The code that I drew in her dream must have been the Star Codes of Immortality that you are reading in this book.

Amiga and Continuous Dreams of Me

Amiga would express that her dreams of me would continue but nothing like the first two dreams. In these dreams I would appear just to say a few words of comfort then I would disappear.

Dihya or Al-Kahina (The Prophetess, Arabic: الكاهنة)

Utterances for Coming Forth by day into Light

Amiga's Past Life

In 2020 the same year that I would have my past life revelation of my life as Tutankhaten, Amiga would have a profound experience during a deep meditation, where she fell into a deep sleep. She found herself in a d**ark** room kneeling on the ground wearing a white dress. There was a tall bald man there standing in the light but his face was not clear just a small area of light hitting the floor, he looked as if he could be a Caucasian man. He called out the name **Dihya** and she felt like she was the person he called. He was angry at her, it appeared as if she stabbed herself, She was there kneeling on the floor bleeding then she woke up. Diyah is the name of an **Arabic Prophetess** who helped fight off the invasion of islam in the 7th century.. In ancient Kemet (Egypt) the concept of reincarnation and past lives was called the **Wehem-Mesut** (repeating of births, page 14)

It is he, who comes forth by day into Light

Amiga would later change her name on her social networking app to **Dihya**. She said she felt a spirit come over her telling her to honor her name because that is who she is and she was erased from history and not many people know who she was. After Amiga changed her name to **Dihya Al-Kahina** on Instagram, the great great grand daughter of Dihya Al-Kahina would inbox her asking her why she chose to use the name Dihya. Amiga told her about her experience and the great great grand daughter would send her her best wishes to finding herself.

Significance

Is Amiga the reincarnation of Dihya Al-Kahina? I don't know but her story is interesting.

See Page 318

2016 - Meta Spiritual Encounters
Zee See's Dead People Too

I started training Zee on February 13th 2016 (page 362). We had been training for a few months now and we often talked about spiritual things during our sessions. She was a religious woman who practiced the Pentecostal denomination of Christianity. She loved kids and was actively involved with the youth at her church. One day at the end of one of our sessions she would open up to me about her gift - her ability to **see ghost's** or **spirits**. She was the 2nd **seer**! First I met Noel in November of 2014 (page 311 / 318) now I meet Zee. Zee told me that when she first saw me training clients in the p**ark** she saw a spirit standing next to me and that was part of why she always said high to me. She went on to say that every time that she comes to train with me, right before I open my door the spirit of a woman appears and smiles at her. I was amazed by this and had many questions. After having met Noel this news didn't catch me off guard. I was intrigued. I wanted to know who the spirit was!

Just about two years later in December of 2018 Zee would allow me to talk to the spirit at my door (page 545). Zee would also draw what she saw just like Noel had done on January 30th 2015 and in by doing so I would finally figure out who the spirit standing at my door was. You won't believe me if I told you right now but I dare you to read without skipping to that date.

Ka Doors (Spirit Doors)
Guardians, Invisible Protectors

Pages 250 -253, 48, 148, 150, 179, 199, 315, 318, 329, 348, 349, 409, 434, 545, 548, 549, 572, 584, 604, 626, 650

September 5th 2016 Photons

Photons, protons, form like **Voltron, Sirius** like **Dogon,** mysterious dot com, insidious shots in the arm doing a lot of harm, like a **cop** and his fire arm, throwing a lot of bombs like **Colin kaepernick,** indigenous plots to farm doctors making me sick, helicopters **police state** Politricks, **Kwame Ture** keep'n streets straight safe organizing **SNCC,** these Crackers think they slick! they can go to hell! they send they kids to **Harvard** and **Yale,** but they send a brother to jail, it **Ain't Hard To Tell, "**<u>*Realizing the realism of life and actuality*</u>", we need a new strategy, we taking too many casualties, your salary don't mean shit if we ain't free, what part of this **matrix** machine that you can't see? in this nightmare of a **dream,** I **dream** so they hate me, the **sixth gate** serene supreme where my faith be, lately interface with the **unseen** agents chase me, miracle lyrical spiritual take me to safety, the **4th plane,** innately escaped when the thought came, **Jhuty** remember the name! truly yours **42 Laws Maat** in case you've forgotten the **Moors** who **civilized you** cause you not the master race in the first place, **Akhenaten**

Don't be a coon so soon to assimilate, you couldn't wait to be in the master's house so he could subjugate, I'm look'n for a route to escape, won't hesitate without a doubt scout the estate, soul controller of my fate, question: who gonna take the weight or at east try? I can't handle this whole weight alone, before I die look in the sky, **Gang Starr** lead me home, give me wings to fly, we are not alone don't believe the lie, eagles eye am that I am, regal high, you ain't never had a friend like me, never say goodbye, leader like **Selassie** eye, sing this like a lullaby by by, sing it like a lullaby by by, I said this is my battle cry, **Hannibal** in the middle of the battle of Cannae, see eye wasn't really born here son, eye was born in the 3rd eye eye, I be iron like lion in Zion, I'm a never stop trying till brothers stop dying and mothers stop crying, mercy mercy me, before you curse me don't take it personally, I'm just a person searching for a place to be, the human body embody the spirit of a giant tree, when you debase **God** you debase me **- Dawud The Amazing BlaKseed**

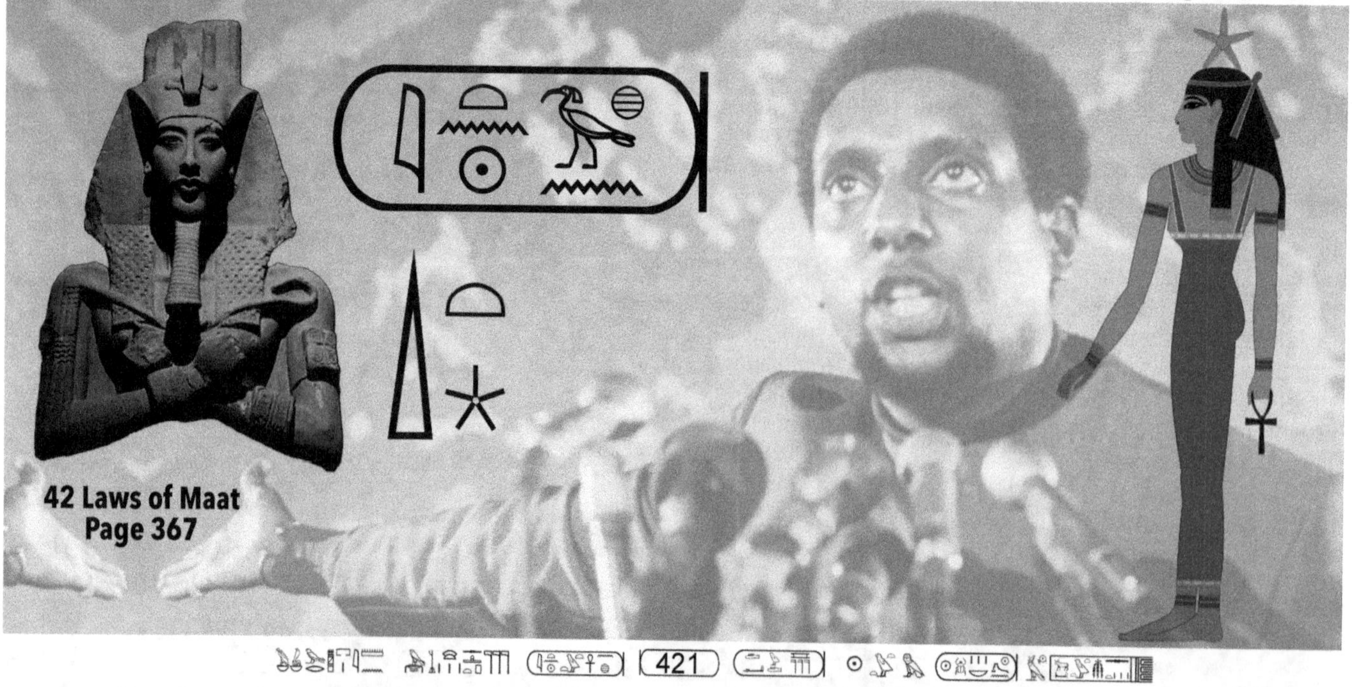

Rau nu Prt m heru

Iu f Per f m heru

Utterances for Coming Forth by day into Light

It is he, who comes forth by day into Light

September 5th 2016 Yin

God is the yin and the yang, the **Goddess**, the force in the prophet, the spiritual web connecting conscious everywhere, the right hemisphere, the left hand receive energy there, **deja vu** it's true – **<u>you been here before</u>**! if your wanna source pray and meditate, open the door, the two wings giving flight, insight sight beyond sight, a metaphor, the triple blackness darkness with in darkness starts in the core, explore **- Dawud The Amazing BlaKseed**

September 23rd 2016 Dogmatic

See page **517** (Sep **23**).

This might burn you and d**ark**en you, that's when you starting to learn true mathematics, so far from home you forgot who you are, that's **illmatic** stagnate chi in the lymphatics, they steal **magic** and wrap it in satanic practice, not even botanic **Garden Of Eden** can reason with inorganic **dogmatic** shit but you believing it! they squeezing clips we dying, like the first slave trip I'm not lying, the first slave ship our ancestors were dying, and crying and lying in their own waste, we've had so much grace we've been here for so long, we let **3rd Base** rock the mic, while **Rodney King** screaming can't we all get along, tonight's the night we changing up our uniform, **Joe Montana** was good but **Colin** throwing me the bomb, fuck **The National Anthem! Cop kills** unarmed black men get paid leave then receive donations handsome **- Dawud The Amazing BlaKseed**

March 3rd 1991 - Rodney King

Rodney Glen King was an African-American man who was a victim of police brutality. On March 3, 1991, **King** was beaten by LAPD officers during his arrest, after a high-speed chase, for driving while intoxicated. Plumbing salesman and amateur videographer George Holliday's videotape of the beating was shot on his camcorder from his apartment window. Two days later, Holliday called LAPD headquarters at **Parker** Center to let the police department know that he had a videotape of the incident. **Still, he could not find anyone interested in seeing the video**. He went to KTLA television with his recording and they aired it. The footage as a whole became an instant media "sensation". Portions were aired numerous times, and it "turned what would otherwise have been a violent, but soon forgotten, encounter between the Los Angeles police and an uncooperative suspect into one of the most widely watched and discussed incidents of its kind". On April 29, 1992, the jury acquitted three of the officers. Within hours of the acquittals, the 1992 Los Angeles riots began, lasting six days. African-Americans were outraged by the verdicts and began rioting in the streets along with the Latino communities. By the time law enforcement, the California Army National Guard, the United States Army, and the United States Marine Corps restored order, the riots had resulted in 63 deaths, 2,383 injuries, more than 7,000 fires, damage to 3,100 businesses, and nearly $1 billion in financial losses. Rodney as born on April 2nd 1965 the year of the **snake** and he died on my Grand Fathers birthday on June 17th 2012

What has changed?

Nothing has changed much in the policies of policing. What has changed is the amount of time between the police encounter and the ending verdict. The judicial system has now made sure that many months pass in cases where police killed black people with no justification so that they can limit the potential of public protest, outcry and riots. They basically wait the people out. They let peoples anger calm down then they exonerate the police in most cases.

September 24th 2016 Pac

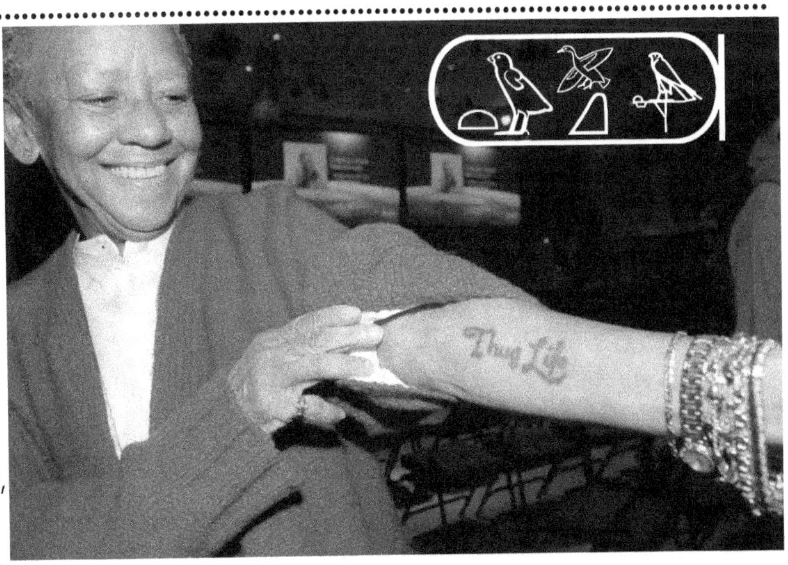

"*<u>My seductive introduction be specific still elusive but exclusive what I give you when I kick it</u>*", read'n the **hieroglyphics, 2pa**calyptic wrote prolific, I document it, they addicted to horrific sophisticated spiritual wicked sickness but still we have elevated, they kill kill and we know it's racially motivated, we must heal basically we live in the hell they created, the hate they gave it and it fucked everybody, **Thug Life** to the death nigga like **Nikki Giovanni**, I was born in America homie but I miss my mommy, like a Jamaican and **Nanny**, like **Left Eye**, like my **Grand Daddy**, may the Lord bless my words to reach the highest heights and lowest valleys and spark a nerve, she wanted freedom badly she gave up, climbed up the pole, is it the seller or the buyer that lose they **soul**? The devil's a liar, we spark a thought then start a **fire**, spiritual gangsta, freedom fighter, eye of the tiger, stand still and just **breathe**, and think about some remedies, no drugs take the root from **mother tree**, fake thug no love America never been a friend to me **- Dawud The Amazing BlaKseed**

September 25th 2016
Ron, Charwayne and Earl

I remember this day being a Sunday. On this day, 3 different brothers from 3 different periods of my life would try to encourage me to take my music seriously. Two of the brothers would be born on the same day June 19th and I'm not sure of the 3rd brothers birthday.

Earlier in the day I attended a **Gong** meditation session at Urban Yoga Foundation (p 326) with **Sunseed** and saw **Ron** from my school. I let Ron hear my song "**Searching for the Oneness**" and when he heard it he cried. He told me I was good at music and should take it serious so I then let him hear music from **Sunz Of Man** so that he could see what good really sounded like. Ron would tell me that I needed to pursue music, and how my music would sometimes lift him out of his depression. I never did understand what I was writing for so I never really took comments like this too seriously but I appreciated his words. I told him that my music is my way of coping with life's many ups' and downs, that music is my **therapy**. At this point I considered Ron a **friend**, like a little brother in a sense so I took his words to heart. We are 10 years apart and we are both life path number 5. He is born on Juneteenth, **June 19th**

When I got home I would get a message on Instagram from **Earl**, a brother I went to college with back in 1997. We followed each other on Instagram but we didn't communicate much, but on this day for some reason he felt the need to reach out to me and tell me that I should pursue music. This was the second time that he would say this to me. I remember thinking "this was weird". Two people saying the same thing on the same day. So I called **Earl**, we spoke for an hour or so catching up on life. I explained to him that I called because of the timing of it all. I told him that I try to follow signs etc. We hung up and I have not spoken to Earl since.

After I hung up with **Earl** I thought about my old friend **Charwayne** who I grew up with in Far Rockaway. We followed each other on Instagram too but didn't communicate often and had not seen each other since around 1996. Coincidentally, just a few days prior Charwayne had offered me to come record music at his recording studio, so I called him. Just like **Earl** we caught up on life and things, then I explained why I called him. Then for some reason I asked him what day was his birthday and he said it was **June 19th**! **That's Ron's birthday**!!!!! Now things got **more strange**. Ron was born in 1987 and Charwayne was born in 1978 and that meant that we all shared the same life path number of 5. **I felt like these series of events were not just coincidental. I felt like something beyond my comprehension was guiding me**. I would accept Charwayne's invite to come to his studio and would make my way there on January 8th 2017 of the next year (page 439).. The image on Ron's shirt is the Jewelry from **King Tut's** treasure, **Heru** the one who **returns**! See page **648** for the **metaphysical significance of the number 23**.

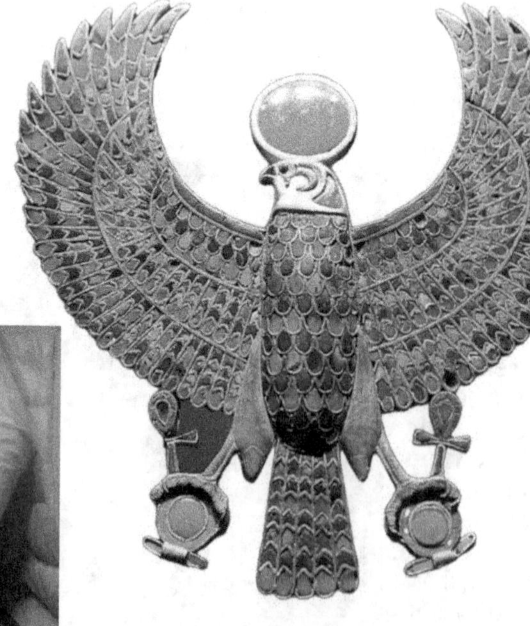

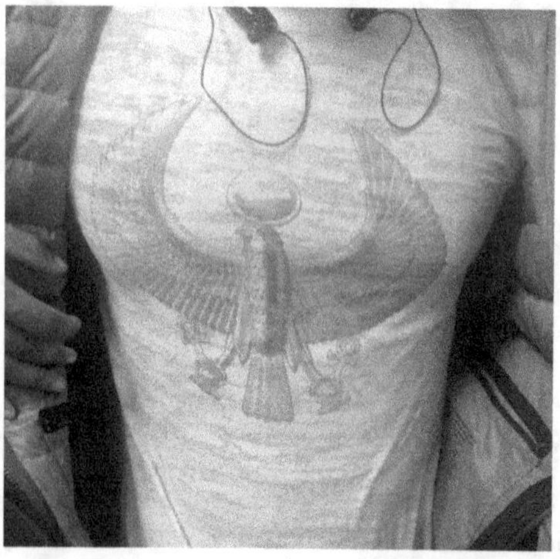

Dawud, Beloved by the Ntru

Rau nu Prt m heru

September 29th 2016 The Prophecy

He **fell asleep** he was drowsing woke up **4000, Years later** born in government housing, they warned of a savior, a **covenant** was found in a **manger**, in wonderment he underwent an excellent ascent, like when **Malcolm** went to **Mecca** it was evident he could plant **Blakseeds** grow trees like regiments on elephants and trample the decadent empire with elegance, fire, water and all the elements, they etched him out they burned his house but they ain't stopping the revolution that I'm talking bout, freedom is paramount I'll shout from the hill top we picked crops sang songs like **Hip Hop**, if **Nat Turner** was here would we hang cops or bust shots like **Tupac?!** hot steel, who was **David Walker** and what was written in his appeal? tell me why when he wrote it they wanted him killed? tell me why **Tamir Rice** look like **Emmett Till ?!** tell me why our blood still spill in the street still?! still **illmatic!** we can heal or have **Havoc** make **magic** like a **Prodigy** this gotta be **The Prophecy - Dawud The Uncanny BlaKseed**

Meta Mysterious Significance

Iu f Per f m heru

This spell is prophetic! This was written in 2016, two years before my first past life revelation was revealed. On July 3rd 2018 I will for the first time know that I was **Emmett Till** (page 480). Yet in this song I mention his name. Before my past life revelation I had never thought about a past life. As you travel down the time line of my life in this life you will get to see my lens of understanding by listening to the words that come out of my mouth in my poetry and also by paying attention to the direction I took in my life. I did not grow up knowing the things I know now. I grew up without the light of my culture in the scope of my everyday life. I grew up watching tv and listening to music. I was fortunate to watch some things that made my imagination wonder and also lucky I chose more of the music that fed my soul. The music probably saved me more than anything else and that's probably why they sing in church and did you know that the Haitians sang marching into battle (page 6)?! I mention **Prodigy** in this verse and on December 11th 2021 I would have a profound experience with the Spirit of Prodigy. Prodigy is a scorpio like myself and he is born on November 2nd two days before the discovery of Tutankhaten's (King Tut's) tomb on November 4th 1922. He died on June 20th 2017 4 days after Tupacs birthday. His last album was titled Hegelian Dialectic (The Book of **Revelation**). My past life revelation or my life as Tutankhaten (King Tut) came on April 4th 2020 (page 594). On the cover of his album **Hegelian Dialectic** Project buildings can be seer and across from them the **Giza pyramids** can be seen. The zodiac wheels of destiny incircles a skeleton version on the vitruvian man drawn by Leonardo da Vinci. Nothing is just a **coincidence** in life. Be careful though, there are those out there who might try to trick you. To set you up for what might seem like a coincidence. They might lie to you. Make a fool of you. Trap you. Close you off. Bind you down. Put you in a box and rob you of your soul.

Utterances for Coming Forth by day into Light

October 2nd 2016 Brooklyn Botanical Garden

I was happy to be back in school. I needed the money and the idea of actually finishing and having a "College Degree" in massage was starting to sound like a good idea. I even signed up for a Chinese Herb class that was not a part of my course curriculum and our professor took us on a trip to the Brooklyn Botanical Gardens on **Nat Turners** Birthday. A few days later I would see the movie about Nat Turner titled Birth of a Nation by Nate **Parker** and would experience another coincidence.

It is he, who comes forth by day into Light

October 6th 2016 - Birth of a Nation

While watching the movie **Birth of a Nation** I felt like a had a coincidental moment with Nat Turner, the revolutionary preacher depicted in the movie. When Nat gave his wife the Benin Face Pendant in the movie as a wedding gift, it looked like the same Benin face pendant that I purchased in 2013 from a lady vending in Soho when I was hanging out with Nkruma (Kodwo, page 249). When I saw that scene a feeling of **Deja Vu** ran throughout my body along with chills. In 2022 I experienced **Deja Vu** twice while in **Kemet** (pages 670 - 671).

Movies have been used to wage psychological war against Black people for a long time (p 415). That is why you rarely see Black men and women in positive leading roles in major blockbuster **movies**. Imagery on film is so powerful that when **Jack Johnson** became the first black heavy weight champion in 1910 the video footage of the fight was banned by congress (page 19). The image of a Black men defeating a White man was damaging to their white supremest ideology so the picture was banned virtually everywhere in the South, as well as in South Africa and India. Even the former President Theodore Roosevelt, an avid boxer and fan, wrote an article for The Outlook, in which he supported banning not just moving pictures of boxing matches, but a complete ban on all prize fights in America. Subsequently Congress banned distribution prizefight **films** across state lines in 1912; the ban lasted for nearly three decades. It was finally lifted in 1940 the same year **Marcus Garvey** died. My great grandfather **General Dukes Sr's** was given the nickname **Son Turner** (page 19). Rumor has it, that he was related to nat Turner. He died on June 9th 1971, the day before Marcus Garvey died, the same year **Tupac** was born. The **footage** of **Jack Johnson's** victory garnered more public attention in the America than any other **film** to that date until the release of **The Birth of a Nation** on February 8th 1915.. This **movie** would be the first movie ever shown at the **White House** on February 18th 1915, the day before my great great grandfather **General Dukes Sr's** birthday. The movie showed scenes of a black man attacking a white woman and afterwards a mob of **Ku Klux Klans** members were seen lynching the black man. President Woodrow Wilson, members of his family and his Cabinet attended the screening of the **movie**. This single **MOVIE** caused the **Ku Klux Klan** (white terrorist organization) to grow rapidly all across America. This is what set the stage for the Tulsa massacre and many other massacres like it that have been lost to the pages of **his-story** (**psychological war via movies**, page 415).

Nat Turner and The Birth of the Boot-Licking, Butt-Licking, Butt-Broken Buck- Dancing, Bamboozled, Half-baked, Half-fried, Sissified, Punkified, Pasteurized, Homogenized Black Preachers

In 1832, the year after Nat Turner was hung, the book, **How to Make a Negro a Christian** was published. Because teaching their black slaves about a white Christian Jesus was a spiritual war strategy. I was once told a story about a gay southern preacher by a man selling books in Harlem. I don't know the exact date of this meeting but I was with my friend **Nova** (p 184) and she witnessed everything I'm detailing. I stopped at this mans table and purchased 3 books. One book was about **Nat Turner**, one was about the structure of the human **eye** and the **third** book I can't recall. I brought up the fact that Nat Turner was a preacher, and after he was hung, black preachers were no longer allowed to preach to other slaves without the company of a white person observing their sermon. And how many preachers were made docile by way of **buck breaking** (page 354) to ensure that they would not take part in insurrections.. Then the vendor began to tell us about his experience with a gay preacher during a card game in the south. He took part in a card game and was told that he could have his way with the woman in the back of a truck if he won. When he won the game he went to the back of the truck only to find a preacher in his clergy robe, bent over, waiting for the next man to penetrate him.

October 11th 2016 Hapi

Above all we wanna be free, we wanna see our family live happily ever after, turn the page light the sage another chapter, turn rage into laughter, I go out in the blaze if I half ta, Maze and Frankie Beverly, happy feelings, a Melody, that's what my feelings be telling me, sharp pains in my heart, **Heavy D,** the rain it start's heavenly pouring from the heavenly, born poor into poverty, reparations is what I wanna see, you can rob me of humanity, but **not immortality** or tenacity, I feel the shadows of death after me, so if I die before my time don't shed a tear, I'm here in the atmosphere with **Garvey,** we are not alone hardly, the panther party, we start an army fall in line use your mind, it's about time we wake up from melancholy, like **Muhammad Ali**, quality over quantity, policy sovereignty mercy mercy me, I'm taking you back come follow me, on a journey to see a for real emcee, if you stay true the **NTCHRU,** shine through and speak to you, close your eyes and see like peaceful people do **- Dawud The Uncanny BlaKseed**

Significance

We speak things into existence! I said the words, "if you stay true the **NTCHRU,** shine through and speak to you". Words are spells! Warning to musicians and poets, be careful what you spell. The Ntchru heard my calls and because my heart was true they appeared and remained with me as I slowly awakened to this grand revelation (p 6). To all people, be careful what comes after the words "**I am**" because you soul is listening. I wrote this after seeing the movie **Birth of A Nation**. In the movie **Nat Turner** gave his wife a Benin bronze face head as a gift for their marriage. It was the same one that I have. When I saw that scene a feeling of **Deja Vu** ran throughout my body along with chills. In 2022 I experienced **Deja Vu** twice while in **Kemet** (pgs 670 - 671).

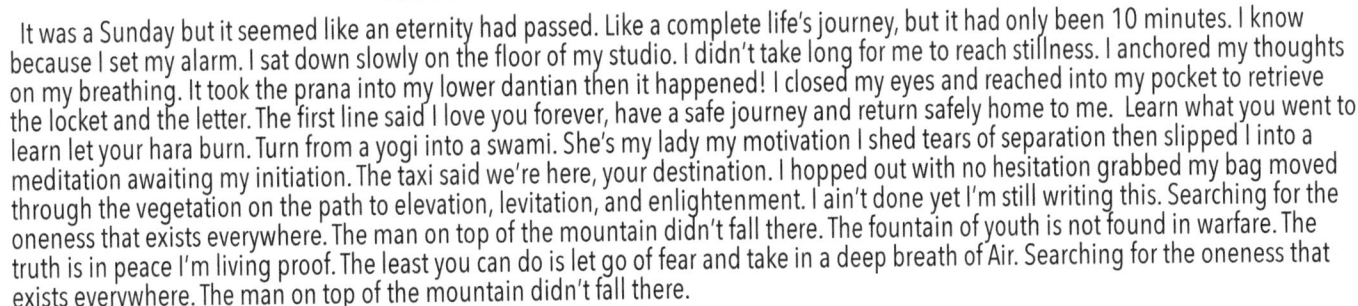

October 16th 2016 - Shiatsu Meditation Homework

Rau nu Prt m heru

It was a Sunday but it seemed like an eternity had passed. Like a complete life's journey, but it had only been 10 minutes. I know because I set my alarm. I sat down slowly on the floor of my studio. I didn't take long for me to reach stillness. I anchored my thoughts on my breathing. It took the prana into my lower dantian then it happened! I closed my eyes and reached into my pocket to retrieve the locket and the letter. The first line said I love you forever, have a safe journey and return safely home to me. Learn what you went to learn let your hara burn. Turn from a yogi into a swami. She's my lady my motivation I shed tears of separation then slipped I into a meditation awaiting my initiation. The taxi said we're here, your destination. I hopped out with no hesitation grabbed my bag moved through the vegetation on the path to elevation, levitation, and enlightenment. I ain't done yet I'm still writing this. Searching for the oneness that exists everywhere. The man on top of the mountain didn't fall there. The fountain of youth is not found in warfare. The truth is in peace I'm living proof. The least you can do is let go of fear and take in a deep breath of Air. Searching for the oneness that exists everywhere. The man on top of the mountain didn't fall there.

Then the buzzer went off. I wrote my experience down as fast as I could. It's a mystery to me how it rhymed so perfectly. I tried to reach this state again throughout the day as instructed but I was unsuccessful. By the end of the day I still felt like I had just finished my first meditation session. I sat and ate my last meal in complete silence. I thought of how I would continue to search for the oneness in my daily meditations. The meditation made me happy. I figured that if I could continue to reach Zen from my meditations then I would be a better Shiatsu Practitioner. I will continue to meditate.

October 24th 2016 Carnism

Iu f Per f m heru

They wanna know if I'm a **vegan,** and if so what's the reason? I'm like "if you a carnivore why don't you eat it raw why do you season? bread and water divine order, but that meat you slaughter! we all have an **aura** and face **karma** don't ignore the rational I offer, I don't eat **cows** I don't like the torture, how you bought your daughter a cat to play with yet a rat you wouldn't save it?.. in other places they eat cats and rats and savor the flavor, some people eat the flesh of the flesh of their savior, now that's bizarre behavior, I press and I press cause my neighbors possessed, I'm **Darth** like **Vader,** I wrest- and I wrestle with my vessel **Till** eye light my **Saber,** slice like a razor, insight I gave her enough to **raise a Lazarus**, amazing manuscript **magic** like **hieroglyphs** like the eye that came from **Nazareth,** I *don't condone slavery I ain't having it,* **The good ship Jesus** equipped with chains and whips ain't that some shit?! I sink your battle ship!! like the eclipse **Nat Turner** saw, the catalyst at the core, we want peace, but blood guts and war the American way, they feast on the poor deaf dumb and blind, where I come from to be ignorant is a crime **- Dawud The Uncanny BlaKseed**

Significance

It had been 6 years since I'd **given up the consumption of dead flesh that we call meat**. This lead me to write my song **Carnism**. Perhaps if I had heard the song **Beef** by **KRS One** when I was younger, I might have contemplated the health risks and morality of eating animals. In my song **Paradigm**, written on Feb 9, 2016 (p 361), I ask the same question that **KRS One** asked, – "ever think how that cow gets on your plate? is it fate or the great mistake Misstep?". The cows in America receive large amounts of **antibiotics** and when humans eat these animals they consume these antibiotics. These antibiotics find there way to tap water and waste water and have been shown to have adverse effects on aquatic lifeforms. The rainbow darter is a small species of freshwater fish. The male rainbow darters have turned into females after coming in contact with antibiotics from waste water. **Atrazine** is a **pesticide** sprayed on American food and has been known to do the same to male frogs (see page 354). If this happens to fish and frogs, could this also happen to humans?!!

October 25th 2016 Spells

Utterances for Coming Forth by day into Light

Everyday they want you to **mourn**, then they tell you that it's **good**, **week** after **week** you are **weak**ened, subconsciously it's understood, you see the **spelling** of **words cast spells** on the people, I see you, the **owl,** the kn**owl**edge, I teach you, to know the ledge, the **word** is the s**word** with double edge, live is evil redrum off with the head, **25th dynasty** the age is here finally, I pledge allegiance vaginally, that makes me happy not gay, the irony of the words we say, word play, **Osso Tutu, Taharka** ubuntu the virtue of a **Zulu,** I want you to want to **Mansa Mussa, Majuju Musus king of Basutu land,** they **Cram To Understand** the plight, **Mc Lyte** is like **Queen Nzinga** with a mic, and a dike is a wall to block **blakseeds,** they don't want you to conceive and grow, to succeed and know, they want you to plant seeds in the snow! I **love** my **Black Queens** take it back to **Queens** fa sho, **Street Dreams 41st side nasty flow,** the last stop on the A that's a far way to go, I asked **Sway "**how?" **Kanye** said "he don't know", but **Hip Hop** is for the people and rappers rap for the dough, I pack a **Stic** and a **M1** when I'm rocking the show **- Dawud The Uncanny BlaKseed**

October 26th 2016 Timing

It is he, who comes forth by day into Light

If you find **love** you better keep it! the truth is everywhere, you might read a line in a book and find the **secret**! live life with a purpose not on the surface, the best things in life you can't purchase, life ain't always perfect! ***<u>sometimes the perfect storm helps you transform then resurface</u>***, those who don't know they pray and they worship, they stay in churches and empty purses, they hear my verses then they shoot me **curses,** they fear the **serpent** cause they can't interpret the **snakes** from the **virgins,** the fakes in the turbans, the servants that ain't serving, they just herding the sheep.. you ain't crazy! you just awake amongst the sleep, if I should die before I wake, I pray my music that you keep, "*<u>and that you boom it in ya, boom it in ya, boom it in ya jeep</u>*", I seek faith in myself and to **create what I speak,** I take the **10 commandments** back from **Menelik,** and track it back to **antiquity,** the government don't want us to see the **Ark Of The Covenant** for what it really be, attacking the **African Spirituality,** so they flood us with fallacies like they did the **Hapi Nile,** so we don't see the old dynasties, how we was wise as the owl, and we still is! bringing the **light** like **Louis** did for **Edison!** they never give us our credit son, they just give us their medicine **- Dawud The Uncanny BlaKseed**

"sometimes the perfect storm helps you transform then resurface"

"I seek faith in myself and to create what I speak"

See 42 Laws of Maat (Page 367) **10 commandments**

October 31st 2016 The Lotus

The world was cold, the nights were d**ark,** she closed her eyes, **belief** took hold of her heart, she stopped seeking and **soul** searching, started listening to a preacher and saw a surgeon, she used to be a virgin, then the birds started chirping and the bee's started working on honey, she started working for money, for degrees to earn skills to pay bills to please her **mummy,** life got real when the baby started in her tummy, "it takes two to tango! where you at, why you acting funny? you can't take it back matter fact we gonna have a **sunny!!**", he never knew his father, she named him **Taharqa** from the **25th Dynasty** and cause it rhymed with **Shaka,** she told him he could be anything even a doctor, but first "*you gotta get the ground beneath ya feet partner, wind beneath your wings and go out in a blaze if you got ta*, this life is a maze before you lay in your grave raise your **chakra**", he was taught in the ways of a sage with proper posture, how to connect the channels and **fly** like a helicopter, how to channel the metal copper and stop **cancer** before it settles in tissue proper, the rebel official Musafa, **Mutulu Acupuncture** they don't want you to heal the people, and if you do they m**ark** it illegal, justice invisible, life is what they giving you, minimal visitors, **Free All political prisoners,** invest in loss, the greater the gain, the higher the sacrifice, the higher the plane, the eye in insight, the eye in the brain, we feeling the pain and we dying in vain, Invest in loss, the greater the gain, the higher the sacrifice, the higher the plane, the eye in insight, the eye in the brain, we feeling the pain and we dying in vain

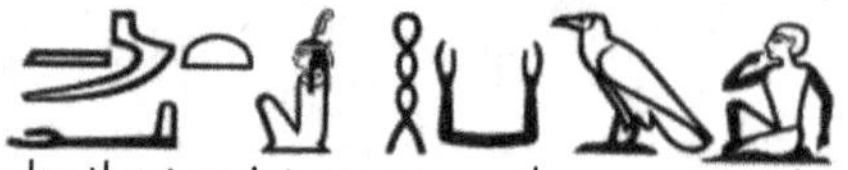

Like the **Lotus** he rose high, fly like **Horus,** purist modus operandi, tell me why the tourist never see the poorest?, hypnotized with the chorus, needle to the **soul,** I paint the picture so you can see the whole, don't ignore us! they locked us in the hole, took us out the forest, now the babies don't know the natural way even when they saw it, they got control of the mind in this new world order, while you ate swine drunk off wine, they went and stole the water, **Dakota pipe line**, **Palestine**, **School to prison pipe line**, Day time, night time, "*the time is always ripe for what is right*", it's fight time, I write rhymes like life lines, *he saw a sign in the skyline,* Sublime bliss this too shall pass, **Maat magic** the path, **Ptah, Allah, Buddha, Karma Sutra,** even he who robs you gives you something of value like a booster, what ever way you travel, wide or narrow, the cock gonna crow like a rooster, you ain't gotta stay the same way that you used ta, ***even a snake sheds skin step into your future, Aniken Sky Walker,*** walking away from the way of the storm trooper, Institutionalized **racism, J Edgar Hoover!** Free **Mumia** and **Mutulu** and ever **political prisoner**, I'm talking to you! not them, cause they the ones that take away our **guru's**, we gotta come together and form like the **Zulu,** invest in loss, the greater the gain, the higher the sacrifice, the higher the plane, the eye in insight, the eye in the brain, we feeling the pain and we dying in vain, Invest in loss, the greater the gain, the higher the sacrifice, the higher the plane, the eye in insight, the eye in the brain, we feeling the pain and we dying in vain **- Dawud The Uncanny BlaKseed**

42 Laws of Maat, Page 367

November 4th 2016
Dreams and the Underworld with my love Ankhesenaten

I was walking to massage clinic in mid town and nothing stood out from the norm. I did my 3 massages for the day then I went home. When I got home I would open Instagram on my phone and the first picture I saw would give me slight **DeJa Vu**. There was a woman whom I felt like I had seen in passing earlier in the day while I was **walking to clinic**. I left a comment under her picture. "Greetings, were you in midtown earlier today?" She replied "no I wasn't why do you ask?" I told her that I could swear that I saw her earlier or someone that looks just like her. Of course she said no one looks like her. We started chatting in a private message. Her first question was how old am I. I told her I was 39 and She was a scorpio like me about to be 22 in the 15th of November. I began to ask her questions that all seemed foreign to her. I told her that her life path number was 4 but she didn't seem interested. She said she didn't 'believe' in time and numbers. I think she felt I was hitting on her which I was not. She ended the chat by saying she "wasn't interested". She offended me because I felt like she "shot me down" when I wasn't even hitting on her. I really felt like I had seen her earlier. Instead of responding with anger I asked her to check out my music and she did. She returned and said she liked my music and we followed each other and that was it. The next day however she sent me a message that read "**On second thought lol. U were weirdly in my dream.. I think we're meant to converse now lol**". I had come to her in her dreams and that confused her. We met and became friendly. I tried to share info with her about food and other things but she was very argumentative. I cut ties with her when she told me that I wasn't "her father".
I realized that she was young and shortly we parted ways. Her name was **Rachel**. Years later I would see her become a vegan like I was suggesting to her and she was now paying attention to all the things that had previously been foreign to her. After we parted ways I used the experience with her to write the song titled **I Still Love Her** on **January 6th 2017.** At the time I had no idea that Mamie Till (**Emmett Till's** mother) had died on January 6th 2003. Even though I don't remember my mother Mamie, **I Still Love Her**. (continued on next page)

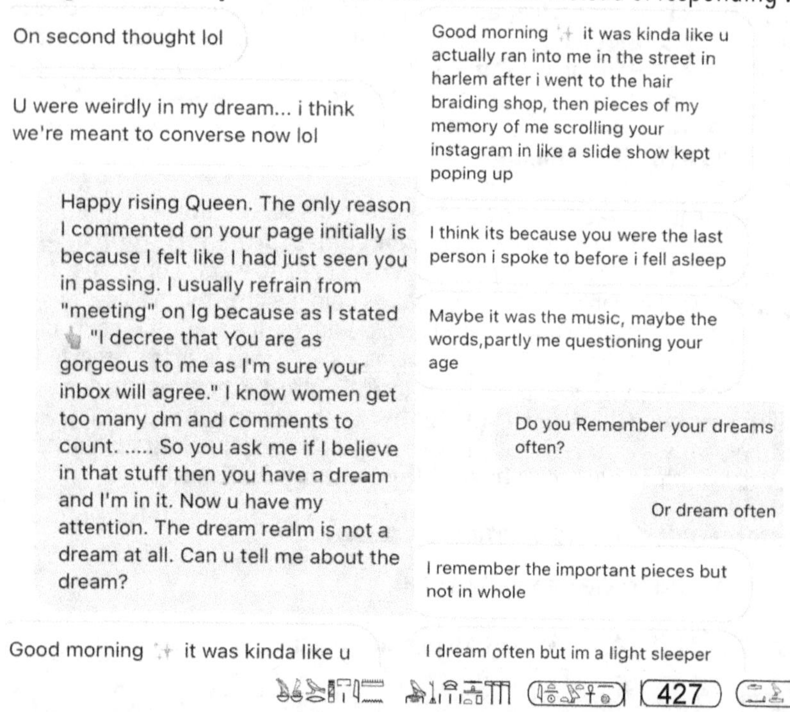

On second thought lol
U were weirdly in my dream... i think we're meant to converse now lol
Happy rising Queen. The only reason I commented on your page initially is because I felt like I had just seen you in passing. I usually refrain from "meeting" on Ig because as I stated "I decree that You are as gorgeous to me as I'm sure your inbox will agree." I know women get too many dm and comments to count. ..... So you ask me if I believe in that stuff then you have a dream and I'm in it. Now u have my attention. The dream realm is not a dream at all. Can u tell me about the dream?
Good morning it was kinda like u
Good morning it was kinda like u actually ran into me in the street in harlem after i went to the hair braiding shop, then pieces of my memory of me scrolling your instagram in like a slide show kept poping up
I think its because you were the last person i spoke to before i fell asleep
Maybe it was the music, maybe the words,partly me questioning your age
Do you Remember your dreams often?
Or dream often
I remember the important pieces but not in whole
I dream often but im a light sleeper

Rau nu Prt m heru Iu f Per f m heru

Utterances for Coming Forth by day into Light It is he, who comes forth by day into Light

(continued from last page) **Significance**

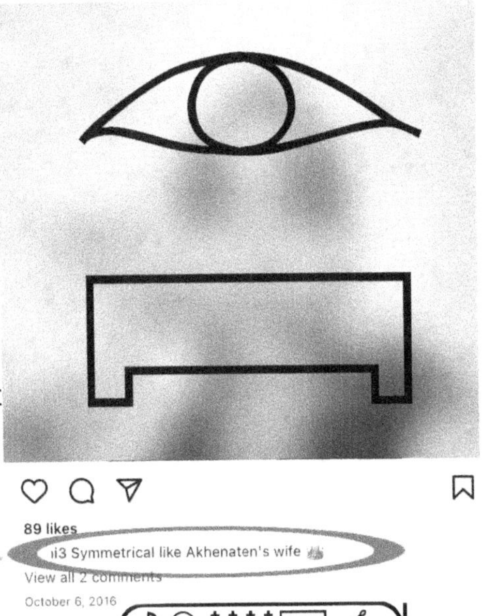

I contacted her on November 4th which is the same day that **Tutankhaten's** (**King Tut's**) Tomb was discovered, November 4th 1922 the year of the **Dog** (Enpu/Anubis). The very next night she would have a **dream** about me. This was not just a coincidence. My light body had been becoming more active but I was not aware of what was really happening. Perhaps it was the gong sessions I had been attending or maybe the experience with the police officer and the electrical pain I felt in my spine during the summer had awakened my **astral body** (p 388). What ever the case may be I feel that it had less to do with the women I was meeting and more to do with a woman that was longing for me. A woman I had forgotten about. In the song I wrote on **January 6**th I would say "Before, once upon a time, in a different place, in another existence off in the distance, in the near future or the distant past a love this rare don't last long like shooting stars running out of gas". Perhaps I had been writing about Ankhesenaten my ancient wife. Perhaps she had been trying to help awaken me and as you will come to see whatever was happening it was successful. I find it interesting that this woman would post a picture of herself almost a month to the day before we met with a caption that read, "**Symmetrical like Akhenaten's wife**". Akhenaten is Tutankhaten's (King Tut's) father and on April 4th 2020 (page 594) my **past life** as Tutankhaten would be revealed to me. In 2022 I experienced **Deja Vu** twice while visiting **Kemet** (pages 670 - 671).

November 13th 2016 11:11

She used her mind to create the present, heart broke she said prayers at **11:11**, hoped for the tall d**ark** and handsome ,awoke from a **dream** she seen the phantom he spoke the lyrical anthem like it was written in **Thugs Mansion**, romances given, rhythm she loved dancing with him, she called him sun tight cause he shine bright like the blue light igniting from the prism, reuniting the **two lands** in man the glands the wisdom, **transform** words into **light rays** tell **eye** vision, at night we gazed at the heavens, holidays religions, amazed at how the reverend praise the Lord but keep the truth hidden, do they ever ask, with all these poor people, what the people doing with all the cash? all my people wanna be is free at last, "you can go up in 5 of these mother fuck'n houses be lucky if you find a dad!" do the math science projects ill effects news 9 got me loosing my mind like I'm'a die next , he pulled his gun and blast! then he dash on em <u>back to the lab</u>, my mind is the gun they ain't know the sum of the <u>***wraps that I had***</u> - **Dawud The Uncanny BlaKseed**

"reuniting the **two lands** in man the glands the wisdom, **transform** words into **light rays** tell **eye** vision"

November 19th 2016 Yoga

She liked men that were older, he told her respect taste better than attention, she liked **yoga** she was a vegan search'n through meditation, that's when he found her heart race'n, eternal sunshine erase'n the spotless mind, chase'n serene memories from a **dream**, intertwined between divine intervention from unseen dimensions, he told her it's all about intentions, expectations get in the way like mankind chase'n life extension, silly rabbit tricks are for kids like detention, **magic** is **magic** to the lay man that don't understand the <u>*emerald tablets*</u> so they fear satan, stuck wait'n for a great man, put faith in the great **I am** if you really wanna see, don't sit blindly in church, build the temple in man masonry, even the dirt one day will be a stone, even a bone, even the river has a story a tone, the great **Ommm,** but are you listening? when opportunity knocks let it in, **Dawud** like David Letterman, <u>my **soul** will never end</u>! ever **Immortal**, I opened a **portal** like a book, never judge another by the cover! prove yourself to yourself not one another, rediscover what it is to be humane, the river is just a vein, the giver of life is the light that came from darkness, let your sight beyond sight be the sharpest, let your life be the artist, let love be the target, give love to the harlot, and water to the alcoholic, call this karmic harmonic ministries cause I paid my penalties and I raised myself up from the dirt with therapies and remedies, to anyone I ever hurt search memories for good times, treasure these sublime rhymes, sometimes I think about <u>***back in the days when I was young, I'm not a kid any more but sometimes I sit and wish I was a kid again***</u> - **Dawud The Uncanny BlaKseed**

<u>This rhyme originally ended as seen below, but a week or so later I made an edit and wrote a longer verse as seen above.</u>

the great **Ommm** but are you listening? even the winds whispering, he saw Simon a fisher man he said follow me I'll make you a fisher of men, if thy eye be single pineal tingle, if thy eye be single pineal tingle - **Dawud The Uncanny BlaKseed**

Significance

My past life revelations came after I graduated as a Kemetic Yoga instructor on July 1st 2018 and in this song I speak of Yoga. In this song I would say the words "<u>my **soul** will never end,</u> ever **Immortal"** and **"**I paid my penalties and I **raised** myself up from the dirt". These lines speak of **resurrection** and **rebirth**. Deep within my soul I was crafting this revelation and on July 3rd 2018 (page 480) my past life as **Emmett Till** was revealed then on April 4th 2020 (page 594) my **past life** as Tutankhaten (**King Tut**) would be revealed.

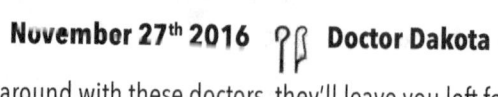

November 27th 2016 **Doctor Dakota**

Fuck around with these doctors, they'll leave you left for dead, get fed up, they call the cops, get you locked to a bed, it's set up like that, this is a practice Jack in fact you're better off doing a fast, don't let them cut you, it's a hustle, worth more dead than alive, the heart muscle, they suck you of vital life force energy, enemy of the state if you use plants to heal, they separate God from nature, cut down the trees burn the leaves, then you sign the paper, if they kill you it was just your time to meet the maker, **Bury me a G,** but never give me **chemotherapy,** that's worse than a felony fuck what you're telling me, and what you're selling on tv, a solar people with a polar diet! reverse psychology, **Dr Sebi** he was savvy with the **electric diet** you should try it, it might reverse mortality increase vitality, realizing the realism of **white** brutality, **Tuskegee Airmen** the battle be in the air the water, the **Vaccinations! Black Boys Autism** Disorder! **Margaret Sanger** aborting our daughters, now they wanna build a border, Dakota pipe line we got something for ya, **La la la la La la la la**

A true **Queen** is rarely seen, cause **Cash Rules Everything,** The **Scorpion King,** The **BlaKseed** sting like a hornet, move like a humming bird, scream like **Ali** when he beat **Liston,** word is bond listen have you heard of the missing people?! hell no said the sheeple… rest in Peace to **Fedel Castro, Hussain Fatal,** I peeped you front'n like **Cain** did **Able,** I was in the Jeep beats bumping, sunk in the seat tinted with heat, listen twice speak once, advice from the peak like a monk, extend your life with **Moringa leaf** the trunk, the seed don't fake the funk, what take you minutes might take me months, but when I'm finished I'm in tuned with the infinite, **Cash Money, No Limits** to numbers so searching for happiness counting money you'll never be finished!! he sold out thought he won but he didn't, the sum of your ***soul*** takes more than the "mula" to be ***risen***, "baby baebae", those around you ain't always down for you, that shit will drive you crazy, let's see who stick around when they hear sounds of **reparations** for slavery, **La la la La la la la** **- Dawud The Uncanny BlaKseed**

Significance

On November 26th 1922 Tutankhaten's (King tut's) tomb was opened (page 11). I wrote this song the day after on November 27th 2016 and in this song I say the words "**Scorpion King"** in the beginning of the second verse and at the end of that verse I say "the sum of your ***soul*** takes more than the "mula" to be ***risen"***. I am speaking about **resurrection** but I don't yet know the magnitude of what I'm speaking into existence! I am a **scorpio** and on April 4th 2020 (page 594) my **past life** as Tutankhaten (King Tut) would be revealed to me! The oldest known Pharaohs are **scorpion kings** and I am indeed a "Scorpion King"(page 2). **Serket** is the **scorpion Goddess** in ancient Kemet (Egypt) and she was the most popular of the four Goddesses that were found guarding my shrine in November of 1922 when my tomb was discovered (p 634).

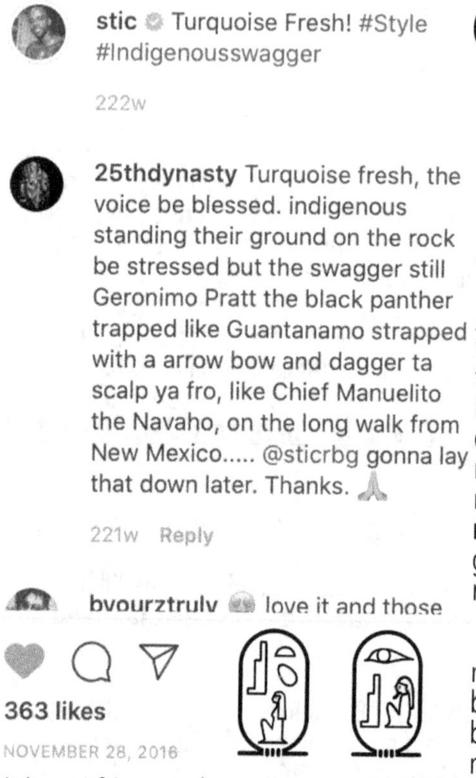

stic Turquoise Fresh! #Style #Indigenousswagger
222w
25thdynasty Turquoise fresh, the voice be blessed. indigenous standing their ground on the rock be stressed but the swagger still Geronimo Pratt the black panther trapped like Guantanamo strapped with a arrow bow and dagger ta scalp ya fro, like Chief Manuelito the Navaho, on the long walk from New Mexico..... @sticrbg gonna lay that down later. Thanks.
221w Reply
byourztruly love it and those
363 likes
NOVEMBER 28, 2016

November 28th 2016 **Standing Rock**

No choice oppressed the voice be blessed, **Indigenous** standing their ground on the rock be stressed, but the swagger still **Geromino Pratt,** the **Black Panther** trapped, like Guantonimo strapped with an arrow bow and a dagger to scalp ya fro! Like **Chief Manuelito** the **Navajo** on the long walk from New Mexico, When all else fails plant the blakseed so it can grow, **Cherokee** in my blood most of my life I didn't know! **The Last of The Mohicans,** Fighting each other like **Dominicans and Puerto Ricans!** It's nation time it's bigger then the language you speaking! It's bigger than religion and pastors preaching bout money, *It's Still Bigger Than Hip Hop* and your master degree dummy! You know the facts? what type of nose is that? They dig up **artifacts** and all they ever find is black! We still paying tax, until this all collapse, "*The white man get paid off of all of that*", So we mash on they ass like **Gaspar Yanga** with righteous anger, the royal member led a slave revolt but do you **Ra**member? Rest In Power to **Nat Turner** eleven November! **Isis** took the members of **Osiris** and put them back together, It's allegory like the bible, Get the message it's survival, **It's the heart and the feather our people must measure,** No choice oppressed the voice be blessed, **Indigenous** standing their ground on the rock be stressed, So we mash on they ass like **Gaspar Yanga** with righteous anger, the royal member led a **slave revolt** but do you **Ra**member?

Sioux, Apache, Camache, Arapaho, Native to this land we was living here natural, the pale face came savage empty hands damage collateral, poison you before they battle you, Blue eyed devil, the harbinger of death, They took this land by terror and they won't change until there's nothing left, before they came we had no chains, no for jails, no locks no keys no hard knock life no thieves no money, you ain't got it? I got it! they call us uncivilized if they can't make a profit, they write down laws then they go and break every promise, No Honesty! *Until the philosophy of race and superiority and 1st and 2nd class nationality is finally and permanently forever more*

discredited, There will be war merited, me say war merited, war merited, war merited everywhere there's war, and horror! **they bombed Panama** with stealth bombers killed pregnant momma's and hard working fathers! no honor! more drama it's sickening no water in Dakota or Flint Michigan, A peoples history of **Florida, Seminal Indians,** before you walk a moon in a mans moccasins don't go mocking him! No choice oppressed the voice be blessed, *Indigenous* standing their ground on the rock be stressed, so we mash on they ass like **Gaspar Yanga** with righteous anger the royal member led a **slave revolt** but do you **Ra**member? **- Dawud The Uncanny BlaKseed**

Rau nu Prt m heru

Significance

On November 28th 2016 I would read the caption of an Instagram post by **Stic** from **Dead Prez** which said "Turquoise fresh! #Style #indigenousswagger" and it would spARK me to write this track Standing Rock. In the song I mention **Osiris** who is the Egyptian Lord of **resurrection**. This song was written two days after the tomb of **Tutankhaten** (**King Tut**) was opened on November 26th 1922. On July 3rd of 2018 (page 480) my **past life** as **Emmett Till** would be revealed and on April 4th 2020 (page 594) my **past life** as **Tutankhaten** (**King Tut**) would be revealed to me. Stic is my favorite artist and the falcon (Heru) logo he uses for his music company is taken from the pectoral jewelry from the tomb of **Tutankhaten** (**King Tut**). In ancient kemet Heru (Falcon/Horus/Jesus) is the son of Ausar (Osiris) that returns. Heru is from the Ausarion or Osirion drama of **resurrection. Remember** that **you** are **Ausar** and **Heru,** the **hero!** See page 3 for the **hero's journey!**

Gaspar Yanga, national hero of Mexico 1545 - 1618

"So we mash on they ass like **Gaspar Yanga** with righteous anger, the royal member led a slave revolt but do you **Ra**member?"

Iu f Per f m heru

Gaspar Yanga was also known simply as Yanga or Nyanga. He was born a member of the royal family of Gabon, in Africa on my sister's birthday, **May 14th** 1545 the year of the **snake***. He was captured and sold into slavery in Mexico. Yanga never forgot who he was as an African **Prince** and eventually he led a maroon colony of slaves to freedom in the highlands near Veracruz, Mexico during the early period of Spanish colonial rule. As a rebel leader he successfully resisted a Spanish attack on the colony in 1609 and his maroons continued their raids on Spanish settlements. Finally in 1618, Yanga achieved an agreement with the colonial government for self-rule of the maroon settlement. It was later called San Lorenzo de los Negros, and also San Lorenzo de Cerralvo. In the late 19th century, Yanga was named as a "**national hero of Mexico**" and "El Primer Libertador de las Americas" (The First Liberator of the Americas). In 1932 the settlement he formed, located in today's state of Veracruz, was renamed as Yanga in his honor. Yanga died sometime after 1618 in San Lorenzo de los Negros, New Spain. On **May 14th** 2022 an 18 year old white man killed 10 black people in Buffalo NY. **Aaron** Salter was the **55** year old ex-cop who was killed in the Buffalo Massacre. Inspired by rising gas prices, **Aaron** had recently spoken about a "newly discovered energy source" and had patented a system that enables vehicles to run on water instead of gasoline, (hydrogen-electrolysis). Some say the massacre was an organized assassination so as to suppress technology that would threaten the oil and automotive industries. See page 3 for the **hero's journey**.

Utterances for Coming Forth by day into Light

Chief Manuelito 1818 - 1893
or Hastiin Ch'il Haajiní ("Sir Black Reeds", "Man of the Black Plants Place")

"strapped with an arrow bow and a dagger to scalp ya fro! Like **Chief Manuelito** the **Navajo** on the long walk from New Mexico"

Manuelito (Little Immanuel) was born in 1818 into the Bit'ahnii Clan near Bears Ears, Utah. Manuelito spent his days shooting arrows and competing with other young men in countless foot races and wrestling matches, always winning. He dressed in well-fitting buckskins and a finely woven blanket. He couldn't wait for his first battle. When word came in the winter of 1835 that 1000 Mexicans (from New Mexico) were coming to attack the Navajos, Manuelito fought his first in what would be many violent battles. There he earned the name Hashkeh Naabaah ("Angry Warrior"). He married a woman named **Juanita,** like my grand mother (page 22). In 1871 Manuelito was appointed Head Chief of the Navajo Tribe. Chief Manuelito was a prominent Navajo leader who rallied his nation against the oppression of the United States military. For several years he led a group of warriors in resisting federal efforts to forcibly remove the Navajo people to Bosque Redondo, New Mexico via **the Long Walk** in 1864, the same year **Thomas Will Haynes** was born (page 16). Chief Manuelito was one of the principal headmen of the Diné people before, during and after the Long Walk Period. After being relocated to Bosque Redondo, Manuelito was among the leaders who signed the 1868 **treaty**, ending a period of imprisonment in United States government internment camps and establishing a **reservation** for the Navajo. Manuelito was also an advocate for **western education** for Navajo **children**, with his famous quote, "My grandchildren, education is a ladder. Tell our people to take it." Measles and Smallpox were used by the white invaders in attempts to exterminate the entire native population and in 1893 Chief Manuelito died from **measles**.

It is he, who comes forth by day into Light

November 30th 2016 Karma

You got a **virus** inflammation itis, you die quicker with a bullet, your stomach be the fullest! think, wait and **fast**! the **fast**est way to recovery they knew it in the past, so they passed it along in religion and practices, *invest in loss* like a pacifist, he thought he was wise as a fox, he owned palaces and people, maybe he knew maybe he forgot, he fell ill, his temple started to rot and decay, they say it's easier for a camel to fit through the eye of a needle than it is for a rich man to find the narrow way, one day he met Karma, she went the way of dharma, he couldn't charm her, her defenses were stronger than the riches armor, he found her in the wilderness with the witches and the farmers, he was used to bitches into mischief, do anything for a dollar, but she was a scholar sage oracle, he said, why do you ignore me the way you do? she said, I saw the aura in you, why do you exploit the poor the way you do? not everybody you meet is gonna fall for your trickery, it's bad to deceive people but it's worse to deceive yourself, cause at the same time you cause your ill health, and you could never love another if you don't even love yourself brother, her name was Karma **- Dawud The Uncanny BlaKseed**

Significance

Two years after writing this song which speaks on the healing potential of **fasting** I would do my **first fast**. On April **23**rd 2018 I would start a 20 day water fast (page 467). I started the fast after the second day of my Kemetic Yoga teachers course and 2 days after I graduated as a Kemetic Yoga instructor my first past life as **Emmett Till** was revealed to me on July 3rd 2018 (page 480). (See page **648** for the **metaphysical significance of the number 23**.)

December 3rd 2016 The Most Beautifulest Thing Remix

Common Sense ain't **common sense** no more, this ain't a diss to the rapper, this the truth, while you wait'n for the rapture, the pastor's count'n the loot, while you chase'n the **gold** and the platinum I'm in the booth write'n a thug anthem for the youth, my **Grandma** said these young rappers ain't got no couth, I stay recluse now, produce lyrics like a **golden** goose, how sway? that's what they say, I got the **juice** now, in pursuit of the ***heavenly Cow Hathor***, the Goddess of fertility be feel'n me like I'm **Tehuti**, spit'n lyrics like this is my duty, for the love truly yours, the most beautifulest thing Blakseed bring'n cures, like when Spain was civilized by the **Moors**, back when Hip Hop was fertilized with that pure shit, raw spit, now we premature, I want peace not war but rest assure cause I'm a kick in the door wave'n the 4 4, scream'n, "the most beautifulest thing in the world, just like that, I get in ya" **- Dawud The Uncanny BlaKseed**

(see page 81 for the Common Connection)

2016 - Meta Spiritual Encounter
The December 3rd Theory, Seana and Tupac

I met Seana during my last year of massage school. She was in school for acupuncture. Sometimes the universe connects us with people but we get caught up in desires of the flesh. She was attracted to me but not in the same way that I was attracted to her. She told me that she always felt comfortable around me. I wanted to date her but for some reason I could never seem to catch up with her outside of school. Then one day she sent me a text inviting me to a business venture on **December 3rd**. I was not interested in the business venture and I did not want to go out because I was comfortable being a hermit. I contemplated up until the last hour and finally decided to go because it was **December 3rd** and because a woman that I was attracted to invited me. Perhaps I was supposed to go, so I went. I got on the train and went to this event at a hotel near 42nd street. There was over 1000 people there. Only two people that Seana invited managed to show up, myself and a Chinese woman. When the event ended we all prepared to leave and on our way out we started talking about birthdays and to my surprise the Chinese woman was born on June 16th, **Tupac's** birthday. Dec 3rd had struck again and I was wearing my Tupac tee shirt that day (p 209). I wondered if it was the spirit of Tupac trying to tell me something?! What ever it was it was **strange** because I rarely go out to events especially at night, and now, three years in a row I have an experience with death on Dec 3rd. It was **Jay Cooper** in **2014** (p 314), **Sean Price** in **2015** (p 345) and now **Tupac** in **2016**. I went home for the third year in a row contemplating what it all meant and whether or not it would happen again next year? When I left I went to see the movie **Doctor Strange** at 10:10 pm. Two weeks later Seana would invite me to our schools holiday party. While there **I would meet someone who can see spirits** (p 434). In 2018 (p 480) my past life as Emmett Till is revealed to me and shortly after I would start taking Mdw Ntr (hieroglyphics) classes with Mfundishi. It was around this time that I ran into Seana while on my way to a Mdw Ntr group study with **Basui** (page 388) at Barnes and Nobles on East 86 street. When I ran into her I knew I was supposed to see her because I missed a train and a bus just before I saw her and if I had caught either train or bus I would not have crossed paths with her. When I saw her I hugged her. She was with a friend who was deaf. I told her about my past life revelation and for some reason I asked her what her birthday was. She told me it was Aug 27th, I laughed and told her she was born the day before **Emmett** was lynched. While writing this book I came across the story of **Clinton Melton**, who was murdered in broad daylight by a racist White man, on Dec 3rd, only 3 months after **Emmett** was lynched (page 519). When I was done writing this book I told Seana that I wrote about her. I told her about the Dec 3rd pattern and to my surprise she told me that many people in her family are born on Dec 3rd. Patterns like these don't just happen by chance (p 12, 99). The universe is always speaking and I have a theory about who Tupac was in a **past life**.

December 7th 2016 Sacred Geometry

Rau nu Prt m heru

Sacred geometry ebony ivory, "success is nothing without somebody you love to share it with" Mahogany, The best to do it if he ever pursue it, he never knew it probably, Everybody gotta die but I got weapons of mass construction, poverty got us fuss'n, not trust'n, bust'n each other, I plant black seeds feeding the hearts and minds of my brothers, they got us even with crime, time to climb back to the top, rediscover what we forgot the **stars** the crops, the summers the drummers in the heart of darkness, I be the one to spark this, you brought the Bible and gun you the heartless mark bitch, get trampled in the moshpit, honor you got none! I lay with a **witch** she made me a **talisman** for when the dark come, **ATEN**tion **Atum**, you suck --s of Adam, I split atoms at noon, I wear pheromones and smell like perfume, the son of **Tefnut** I bloom, The **lioness** on her throne, controller of air, water, that other shit they taught ya is torture for your dome, I offer this poem cause it's off of the dome, and I'm often alone *like a orphan with a fortune unknown,* I be flowing and flowing and flowing and flowing and flowing and flowing for everything they owing a good omen, a good woman a good omen, good feeling, run home, start flowing, from the floor to the ceiling, Love revealing, swimming deep in the moment, fly high eye to eye, cant explain it but you know it when you dealing with….

healing potent passion old fashion love making taken action no faking, she fine, but she don't text back, the type to write a line a switch to another app, her choice not you, people make time when they want to, that's a fact, I ain't disgruntle I just wanted to have a conversation, perhaps this generation lacks interpersonal nonverbal stimulation, I wasn't waiting I moved on met a woman, she inspired the hook to this song, she call me strong back, I be running back she play the receiver, my brother Kaepernick made me a believer, like when the deceiver first saw **Giza**, I'm gonna need a **rebirth** of the **leaders of the new school**, I say Ubuntu Uhuru thank you from the heart, like the ankh giving life the spark like mitochondria, Eye woke now eye cant sleep insomnia, fret not my love where ever you're at I'm finding ya, Like **Auset** did for **Ausar** with the help of **Nebhet**, her sister I swim to the bottom of a **river**, a good woman a good omen, good feeling, run home, start flowing, from the floor to the ceiling, Love revealing, swimming deep in the moment, fly high eye to eye, cant explain it but you know it when you dealing with….

Iu f Per f m heru

healing potent passion old fashion Love making taken action no faking, it's everlasting love **immortal**, I opened a portal and saw you beyond paranormal scientific explanation, gifted with mystic no expectation detachment, still magnetic attraction, contraction gestation just waiting for the right Queen to build a nation, temptation at every turn to ascend the throne it is earned, had to learn to turn down not up, water in my cup half full, more than just cut touch squeeze nut leave I got the keys to her lock, seize pandoras box, wise as an ox, he puzzled her like a paradox, that troubled her, Hip Hop the last refinement of high culture, Ultra MK mind sex, say vulgar language bump and grind dangerous, shift changes, shameless no blankets no anus or aimless actions, or subtractions from **Maat,** feather above my heart flowing with love in the sky see a dove going, I said I see a dove going, a good woman a good omen, good feeling, run home, start flowing, from the floor to the ceiling, Love revealing, swimming deep in the moment, fly high eye to eye, Can't explain it but you know it when you dealing with. **- Dawud The Uncanny BlaKseed**

See Page 602 for the Sacred Geometry behind the Transmigration of My Soul

42 Laws of Maat, Page 367

Utterances for Coming Forth by day into Light

The Golden Ratio is one of the most famous formulas in Mathematics

1 2 3 5 8 13 21 34 55 89 144 233 377 610 987 1597 2584 4181 6765

What ever or whoever the creator is, that being is love and it is indeed a master mathematician, a master builder like the number **22**. It uses sacred geometry. The same math used to build the pyramids aligned with the stars.. Even in your bible there is a book titled numbers. You came to this earth at a divine time and you will leave the same way so make your time here divine. Time is measured by the sun and even the Bible states that the sun will be used as signs. **Genesis 1:14** "And God said, Let there be lights in the firmament of the heaven to divide the day from the night; and let them be for signs, and for seasons, and for days, and years".

See page **602** for **The Sacred Geometry Behind the Transmigration of My Soul!!**

It is he, who comes forth by day into Light

432HZ

On the previous page my mother is seen in a picture of her from the 80's.. She is standing on my grand mothers porch. We were living with her at the time. This picture brings back many memories and sadly there are no more trees on the block anymore. I went back to this house and took a picture on June **23**rd 2021 (page 648) and when I got home I had a divine revelation. After hurricane Sandy hit Far Rockaway in 2012 many homes were destroyed and not much money has been spent to rebuild. The block looks a bit desolate however if you walk towards the A train and walk towards the beach it looks like Miami and more White people live there than Black people. On one side of the A train is a black community and the other side is white like redlining. When I looked at this picture of my mother I laughed because she's wearing the same type of pants that I wear today. They say the fruit doesn't fall far from the tree but I fell far enough away to not completely absorb the religions of my family. I was born muslim (1977), in the year 2000 at 22 I gave my life to Christ (page 92) and in 2011 at 33 I smoked weed for the first time (page 194). When my maternal Grand Father died in 2009 (page 169) it sparked my transformation and due to that I would get into many **arguments** with my mother about **religion**, this would cause a **great divide** in our **relationship**. I was searching for truth and she claimed to be the bearer of truth with her religion. I did not agree with her or with any religion for that matter. It must have been the year 2016 when we were texting, having one of or regular disagreements about life and philosophy when I brought the **golden ratio** up. She told me that the Quran is origin of the golden ratio. I told her the pyramids were older than the Quran and the pyramids were built with the mathematics of the golden ratio. She claimed that the Quran has always been here. Then I told her that she was the golden ratio. I told her that when she was **34** years old she had a daughter that was born in 19**89** the year of the **snake** and that she was born in 19**55** and the numbers **34**, **55** and **89** can be observed in sequential order in the golden ratio. That text ended the argument because she never responded to it. I know I blew her mind. My mother was sent down here with a divine code born in 19**55**, the same year that Emmett Till was murdered. My life path number is **5** and **5** is the **fifth** number in the golden ratio and the only number in the sequence that is equal to its position. Today is October 25th 2021 and I turned **44** years old 2 hours ago. My father called me at 12:17 am to tell me happy birthday. As you read this book you should know that I come from a broken home but <u>**I love** both of my parents and have never not loved them</u>. Perhaps when my family reads this book they will understand what I've been trying to tell them. More **Sacred Gematria on** page 41**.** See page **602** for **transmigration of soul!!**

December 10th 2016 Billie Jean

I'm not who you think I am, think again! I drop a gem on them, **I be morphing on them** like **Neo** and them, what you think you see in people is often times the reflection of your own evil mind, you sitting here like you know, cause of some shit you **Heard Through The Great Vine,** never judge a book by its cover, if you looking for a lover, before you love her, you better read the signs, she was like a beauty Queen **Billie Jean** dance on the floor and around, but the son wasn't mine, in the back of my mind I hear my *mother Saying, "don't go around breaking young girls hearts", "Making them cry all the time", Even if the Lord struck me blind, I'd still see your lovely face*, Till the end of time, **is it a crime** that I **adore** you? and Till the end of time I'll be here for you, God bless the day! she was like a beauty Queen **Billie Jean** dance on the floor and around, but the son wasn't mine, In the back of my mind I hear my mother Saying, "don't go around breaking young girls hearts", "Making them cry all the time", even if the Lord struck me blind, I'd still see your lovely face, Till the end of time, is it a crime I adore you, and Till the end of time I'll be here for you, God bless the day!

When **Billie Jean** stepped on the scene and they seen her face, everyone dreamed of being the one they run they ran their race, she was "*up in the place*" in "**Egyptian** lace" with style and grace, allow me to "*place these lyrical douches in your bushes*", "*Push it*", I take you back and I take you fro, we can go fast or slow, sweet and sour **Salt N Pepa,** for hours we devour our pleasure, on the floor and around, we danced till three, not in the covers, **Billie Jean** is not my lover, cant you see? I adore you! *Love is too weak to define the amount of feelings that I have for you*! I was always told be careful what you do and what you say, *because a lie becomes the truth* and your love can run away, the kid is not my son and **Billie Jean** is not my lover, just another girl who claims that I'm the one, she was like a beauty Queen **Billie Jean** dance on the floor and around, but the son wasn't mine, in the back of my mind I hear my mother saying, "don't go around breaking young girls hearts", "Making them cry all the time", even if the Lord struck me blind, I'd still see your lovely face, Till the end of time, is it a crime I adore you, and Till the end of time I'll be here for you, God bless the day!

It's all about time, all about timing, met **Billie Jean** she was fine, now I'm here rhyming, I had this scene in my mind, her numbers were divine, like the sun reflecting on the moon blooming divine time and space, her face she showed, then she ran like a race, but I'm not with the chase, time is of essence, we talked and walked to a place ate then said grace, **Mind Sex** no embrace more than a hug, the curious case of a thug searching for love, I used to **Get Around,** now my vibration can be found above the ground, she said it sounds like you're lying, her heart still crying, couldn't get pass her past to be free at last, that was the last time I saw her, somebody send this letter to **Cinderella** she tried to find me in another fella, but tell her, the shoe won't fit, I'm **too legit**, the BlaKseed proceed succeed **- Dawud The Uncanny BlaKseed**

<u>Significance / Creation Story</u>

I don't recall the exact cause of my desire to write this song but I remember being taken by it immediately. It sort of came out of nowhere and it seemed to come together on it's own going from **Mobb Deep** to the **Matrix** in the first few lines and ending with **Prince** and **Sade.** From the **genesis** of the song I liked it, and as I continued into the **creation** something **strange** happened, **Billie Jean** appeared! When the **thought** came it felt so good! I placed her in the song then looked up the lyrics of **Michael Jackson's** song Billie Jean. I listened to it then I took some diamonds from the song and placed them neatly into this song that was sort of creating itself. "on the floor and around, but the son wasn't mine, in the back of my mind I hear my *mother Saying, don't go around breaking young girls hearts, Making them cry all the time*". As I continued this mysterious journey

Rau nu Prt m heru

Iu f Per f m heru

Utterances for Coming Forth by day into Light

It is he, who comes forth by day into Light

with Billie Jean, **Prince** appeared and almost immediately after, I was looking up the lyrics for his song **Adore**. I took a couple jewels and placed them in quickly. "She was *up in the place* in **Egyptian** lace with style and grace", was one of my favorite lines in that verse and even the whole song. **Biggies Smalls** and **Salt n Pepa** would stop by in the beginning of the second verse. When I finished the song one line didn't set well with me so I made edits and found a way to squeeze the **Temptations** into the first verse. The third verse was written almost a year prior to the creation of the first two verses. The universe placed a woman in front of me that looked a lot like a woman name **Aylin** that I fell in love with before I left Germany in 2003 (page 359). I met her at Seasoned Vegan (**55** St. Nicholas, p 364) while having dinner. Before I left I told my friend Pascal, who worked there, to give the woman my card. She called and we talked but we never met after that because she soon found out that she was pregnant. After meeting her I would write a verse thinking about Aylin, a beauty Queen I fell in love with back in Germany. **Aylin** and I seemed to fall into these deep emotions for each other rather quickly. In the end I always wondered if she felt for me how I felt for her. I thought I loved her so much, but I didn't even know her. I was attracted to what she looked like (page 359). This song would also include elements from the songs of other artist like **MC Hammer**, **Tupac**, and **Dead Prez**.

December 4th 2016 Pain Remix

Tell me can you feel my pain? I ain't have my father, but hate I never harbor my Naga cause I had my momma, I thought he ain't wanna brother, the saga, but my father was locked down in chains with **Hurricane Rubin Carter,** still I could have had it harder, "cause the greatest loss is what dies inside while you still alive", but **Still I Rise**, they'll never take me alive, I'm getting high with my 45 cocked on these suckers time to die, tell me why they label me a trouble maker, a super predator, **Arnold Schwarzenegga** killed **Tookie,** Terminating governor, took me a minute to peep game but they playing us like a sport, don't end up stuck up in their court man, man fuck what you thought man! they the ones that plan all the homicides, **Cops** be the biggest gangs gang banging on drive-bys, that's why we die at an early age he was so young, **Tamir Rice** a victim of **white rage**, memories of a corpse **Joe McKnight** died cause he wouldn't talk, then they let that mother fucker walk, and it's worse in New York, my brother was telling me he's tired of running from enemies! will I live to be 43?! so much pain_ **- Dawud The Uncanny BlaKseed**

December 9th 2016 Seasons

Is it a reason a season or lifetime? I don't know! but every time I see her my light shine and I glow, I know she feels butterflies when I'm looking in her eyes, energize **S**acred **E**nergy e**X**change, inner thighs, I go where no man's gone before, enterprise, they call it mind sex, Karma Sutra, my honey be sweeter so I eat her like Manuka, she grab the hair of my chinny chin chin, took a deep breath the rest went inny in in, life is a **quest,** where do you direct erect attention? manifestation starts with intention, the heart sp**ark**s creation, use your imagination cause we could build a nation, full of **illumination**, to **Killuminati**, one good brother in every state to rally every body, let it resonate formulate a plan don't hesitate, it's time if you need a sign this is it, the signatures in nature in every rhyme that I spit, administer flavor in your ear snare drum tap, take it back like **Graig Mack** packing a Mac in the back of the ac, **Negros With Guns** teaching sons to bust back, don't be so blind with patriotism that you can't see reality to make a decision, wrong is wrong in any era, this is terrorism! **This Ain't Living!** this is similar to prison they got us trapped, they sell us cellphones, new apps, but they don't tell us that it's tapped, watch my back 24 7, I ain't racing to **Ghetto Heaven,** we steady living in hell and we all know, trying to raise hell to heaven and make some small dough, "but I'll give it all up if it would help you grow ", like a rose in the street rooted deep below in the concrete jungle, I ain't meek but I'm kind and I'm humble, **rumble rumble young man rumble,** a nation full of illumination, to Killuminati, one good brother in every state to rally every body, let it resonate in ya mind **soul** and your body, don't hesitate like Nate packing a shoty **- Dawud The Uncanny BlaKseed**

December 15th 2016
Meta Spiritual Encounters, The Third Seer

See Page 318

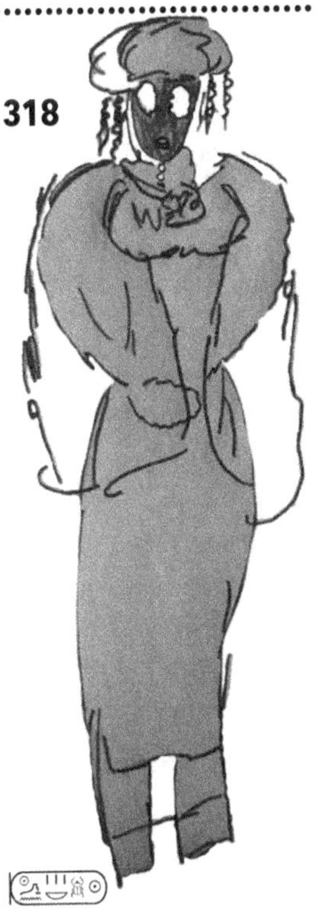

College Holiday Party

If it weren't for Seana (p 431) I wouldn't have gone to this party. I went because I like her. While there, an Asian brother who was in the acupuncture program with Seana looks at me and looks over my left shoulder. He tells me that he can see a spiritual Guardian standing over my shoulder. He did not surprise me because I had been having experiences with the unseen world and at the beginning of this year **Noel** had drawn my **guardian** on a piece of paper for me on January 30th (page 318). I asked him if he saw any others and he said no. He told me she was my grandmother. I told him that I had many guardians. I had not had that confirmation yet but I felt like I did given the many times that I had escaped death by what seemed like divine intervention.

Years later I would run into Seana after I had my past life revelation of **Emmett Till**. It must have been sometime in 2018. I was on my way to my MDW NTR study group with brother **Basui** (page 388) when I crossed paths with her on the upper west side. I knew it wasn't a **coincidence** because I had just missed the bus and the train on my way there so if I had caught either bus or train I would never crossed paths that day. I told her about my past life revelation of Emmett Till and she was amazed but I'm not sure if she believed me. I would later realize the she is born on August 27th the day before Emmett was lynched.

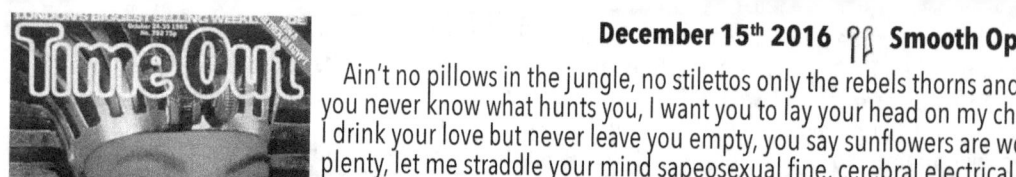

December 15th 2016 Smooth Operator

Ain't no pillows in the jungle, no stilettos only the rebels thorns and rose petals, move slow tip toe you never know what hunts you, I want you to lay your head on my chest and rest as I caress you gently, I drink your love but never leave you empty, you say sunflowers are wonderful, I run for you to get you plenty, let me straddle your mind sapeosexual fine, cerebral electrical when I'm next to you all the time, let's climb a tree see the **sun shine** till the **sun set,** make a wish own a star see **Ausar** the **ARC**her, she said "I love how smart you are, you're out of this world you can colonize my body, let's make a baby girl", listening to **Sade** all day, **Pearls, Your Love is Queen**, but never of sorrow, **A Clean Heart, Bullet Proof Soul**, **Sweetest Taboo**, Dawud the **Smooth Operator**, they say it's **Never Good As The First Time**, still I labor so she remember what I gave her, **No Ordinary Love, The Kiss Of Life** sent from above, **By Your Side**, take flight like doves, to **Paradise, Hang On To Your Love** is my advice, how many times majestic? three times like thrice **- Dawud The Uncanny BlaKseed**

December 16th 2016 Clemency

Will he give his brothers clemency?! we gonna see, pardon me!, I guess the penalty for wanting freedom justice equality is realizing the realism of a **racist** society, rule one for the revolutionary, you're done doomed buried in the ground or in the sounds of the **warehouse of souls**, mass incarceration stories never told, they take the young and bold and try to break em, if they can't make em fold, they keep em till they're old in the penitentiary, **Mumia** I see ya when we free ya, or when they shove me in there already, nightmares **dreams** deadly, **Martin's** greatest fear was he led us here in a **burning house**, he became aware and they took him right out of here, *guess who's stepping in hotter this year*! I shed a lot of tears for my peers already, trapped in the belly make you holler **Kalief Browder** spent a year in solitary confinement, and the reason they couldn't find it, I'm reminded of the blinded justice disgusted! refinement is a must kid!! they say freedom comes through the barrel of a musket, so if they come with peace my first thought don't trust it! **Fight the power**! the called **Mutual Shakur** the **public's enemy,** but he was healing the family it's up to us to set him free!! **- Dawud The Uncanny BlaKseed**

December 18th 2016 Move 9

West Philadelphia born and raised, pray for **John Afrika, MOVE 9** going out in a blaze, you praying for **Palestine** and **Paris** but back in the days nobody gave a damn about your Black ass packing the grave, the Cracker never gave a damn, still ain't got a damn to give, they burn the house down, shot down fleeing kids - screaming in terror "don't shoot"! they only wanted to live in peace and that's why we call **police** the pig, police kill people, treat you like you not equal, **Blue Wall Of Silence** feeds violence, let they're actions teach you, I need you to listen my people we do have a mission to see through **Till** the end, fuck friends! stop wishing and playing, they pretend to tend to our needs, bets believe we gonna win! we gotta fin for ourself put a end to self hating, start creating a mind state to rebuild this Black nation, stop tuning into coons on tv and radio stations! buy black that's how we counter attack the war they waging, **MOVE 9** channel 9 news we all saw em blazing, did the same thing in **Waco Texas** with Caucasians, did the same in **New Orleans** they did to the **Haitians,** that's why I'm **Red, Black** and **Green RBG** flag waving, I don't vote I seen the schemes of **Nancy** and **Ronald Reagan,** while you hope and you **dream,** I'm a **King Tut** black pagan, taking back the science no relation to **Carl Sagan, MOVE 9** channel 9 news we all saw em blazing, that's why I'm **Red, Black** and **Green RBG** flag waving **- Dawud The Uncanny BlaKseed**

"Music is a spiritual thing.
You don't play with music."
Fela Kuti

December 19th 2016 Believe In Me

Picture me rolling seeing life through my rear view, right now is the time that this life has prepared you for, you planted BlaKseeds they grew then they gave us more, it's called free living, this shit we trapped in is a prison war, rich dad more drama bad chick searching for a lot of commas, not a Dali Lama comma komma karma Chameleon love come and go, never stay, find another way to go, plant another seed today, what else do I need to say? should I play like **Fela Kuti, Bob Marley** will the law pursue me? Probably.. but they can't stop me! I'm prolific majestic mystic blessed with rain man type autistic **Poetic Justice,** Keep it realistic, you can't touch this like **MC Hammer,** take a bus trip with **Rosa Parks** down to **Alabama,** this ain't ya grandma revolution, we coming for restitution and **reparation,** I got the solution no more waiting, my execution sedating the minds eye of a whole nation, cause I shine high like the **sun** blazing, if you need someone to believe in believe in me, I fien for freedom, **you ain't never had a friend like me, picture me rollin** with a legion of riders, grab the 85er's, each one teach one let nothing divide us, run grab thy gun bust one for **Assata,** sp**ark** a flame like **Malcolm** when he met **Elijah**

If you need someone to believe in rhyming with a reason, I take you through the storm teach you how to **transform,** they wanna bring harm to the leaders and see em gone, if you a individual they test you to get you to conform! "put on a uniform and form in a formation!" I rather be a unicorn long gone in imagination, than be a pawn henchmen extension of the arm of satan, I'm placing my thoughts on love, walk on the sun dance on the moon meditation, happiness that's my medication, when you wise you don't need a book to have a revelation, open ya eyes and see the crook that stole ya imagination, population controlling the language got you walking on your **souls** to be famous, emasculate the Black man through the anus, can you blame us for blowing up?! **Nat Turner Django** unchain us! it's a **Cole world** but **we gonna be alright,** middle finger to them type a niggas that won't fight for **Queen Nzinga,** I write what I like like **Steve Biko,** they took his life in **77** then gave you me so, If you need someone to believe in believe in me, I fien for freedom, **you ain't never had a friend like me, picture me rollin** with a legion of riders, grab the 85er's, each one teach one let nothing divide us, run grab thy gun bust one for **Assata,** sp**ark** a flame like **Malcolm** when he met **Elijah - Dawud The Uncanny BlaKseed**

Rau nu Prt m heru

From seemingly nowhere The BlaKseed has emerged on the scene like the **Scarab Dung Beetle**. Guided by the **unseen** realm he is crafting his first musical project, **Maat Magik**. Born Dawud in 1977, he spent his formative years in Far Rockaway, Queens until, at the age of 11, he briefly moved to Georgia. Eventually, with stops in Jersey, Queens Bridge and Harlem, life led him back to his roots in Far Rockaway Queens until he enlisted in the Army in 1999. Six years later he walked away from the Army. After he got a sign from the unseen realm he decided not to reenlist and was subsequently honorably discharged. He then developed a career in Health & Fitness. Although Hip Hop was never his "dream", he developed a natural love for the genre while staying up late on school nights listening to the 90's underground Hip Hop scene. In his youth he was influenced by iconic artist such as **Michael Jackson**, **Sade**, **Naughty by Nature**, **Nas**, **The Boot Camp Clik**, **Tupac**, **The Wu Tang Clan**, **Sunz of Man**, **Common Sense**, **Mos Def**, **Talib Kweli**, **Dead Prez**, **Bob Marley** and many more. After suffering the loss of a loved one in 2009 as well as being frustrated by the struggle of his people and society in general, he began to write again in 2010 as a means of stress relief. His music focused on socially relevant topics such as Freedom, Happiness, Health, Excitement, Love and Enlightenment. Despite being told that he shares too much info and that he should dumb his music down he has continued to avoid the low vibrational sound. Overtime as the **lotus** does, out of the muddy waters he has blossomed into an Extraordinary Emcee and on time with the seasons his album Maat Magik will be Blooming in 2017.

Iu f Per f m heru

Significance

The first song I heard from **Jay Electronica** was **Dimethyltriptamine** (**DMT**) and I was instantly a fan. I heard this song sometime around 2013. I was researching DMT when his song popped up. I'm not sure how his art evaded me over the years, perhaps it was because I had sort of stopped searching for new rap when I began personal training. I was so busy chasing women that I wasn't looking into different artist. I wasn't watching tv or listening to the radio so I never heard him before. It's sad to say and embarrassing but I had never really listened to **MF Doom** either until after he died on October 31st 2020 (page 630). To real Hip Hop heads that might seem strange but there was some beauty in that because when I did find Jay and Doom it was like finding a long lost treasure and they both came at the perfect time. Around the time that I first heard Jay 's music I was starting to think I was too old to be still writing raps, then I realized that Jay was only 1 year older than me and that gave me some resolve. I went on with my life as it has been written in this book then in 2015 I heard Jay's song Jazzmatazz (Guru Tribute) and I recorded a song to that instrumental. Around this time I would absorbed as much of Jay's music as I could find. I even looked into his life story a little and that's when **I read his bio**. I had never even considered writing a bio, I was just writing music from the heart. To be honest listening to Jay made me feel the way I felt as a teen listening to **Nas**. They were professionals and I wasn't but for some reason I kept writing. After having Noel draw my guardian angel she saw in my studio on January 30th 2015 (page 318) and then experiencing seeing the ghost of my Grand Father appear to me on December 18th 2015 (page 348) and after writing all the music I had written in 2016, I finally decided to make a real album. I wasn't the best Emcee but so what, I felt like I was writing these rhymes for a reason so I planned to drop an album titled **Maat Magik**. I needed a bio, so **I copied Jay Electronica's.** In Hip Hop it's frowned on to copy someone else's work so I felt a little bad about it but who would know? I let my client Aiesha read it and she edited it for me (page 298). The interesting thing about my bio is that it was written in 2016, two years before my past life revelation of **Emmett Till** which happened on July 3rd 2018 (page 480) and four years before my past life revelation of **Tutankhaten** (**King Tut**) which happened on April 4th 2020 (page 594) the same day that **Martin Luther King** was assassinated (pages 69, 592) - yet in the bio I mentioned the **Scarab Dung Beetle** and the **Lotus flower.** In ancient Kemet (Egypt) the scarab represented immortality, transformation and scarabs were placed in the tombs of the Nswt Bity (Pharaoh) to ensure the **resurrection** of the "Pharaoh" in his **next life**. This concept of repeating of births was called the **Wehem-Mesut** (p 14). In ancient Kemet then name for scarab was Kheper and King Tut's throne name was **Neb Kheperu Ra** which meant the master of transformations of Ra. If that wasn't strange enough, in ancient Kemet the **lotus flower** was seen as the royal flower of **rebirth** as the **Lotus** rises from the muddy waters everyday when the **sun** (**Ra**) rises. The next month on January 12th (page 440) which is **Khalid Muhammad's** birthday I would have my first **dream** with **Erykah Badu**, the mother of Jay Electronica's child and a few days after on January 14th (page 4**41**) the day before **Martin Luther King's** birthday Jay would appear in my **dreams**. Unfortunately this album would never see the light of day. My desire and motivation to complete it fizzled away and all I was left with was the Maat Magik **tattoo** that I got tatted across my belly on May 18th 2017 (page 447) in honor of the album. On July 25th 2019 I would finally release an album (page 577). The album was the result of my past life revelation of my life as Emmett Till. I knew for sure now that my words had meaning. That this boy who's murder sparked the Civil Rights Movement should be heard. **Jay Electronica** is born on September 19, the same day that **Emmett Till's Murder** trial started in 1955 (page 516).

Utterances for Coming Forth by day into Light

It is he, who comes forth by day into Light

December 26th 2016 **The Present**

This is for Instagram my Inst-fam, I need your **love**, you know my name, 25th Dynasty plant Blakseeds In the rain, I reign like your highness see I came into existence lifting locomotives, jumping over tall buildings in a single bound, with the wonder sound from tho underground the time is now and now it's mine, the present is the truest gift, right now! the present is the truest gift not tomorrow! right now! Merry Christmas, the peasant cuts down the tree and side steps the truest bliss, they wanna separate you from the oneness that do exist, the wind blew me the kiss of life one starry night, ***I started remembering what I forgot when starting this life, they say death is an awakening, a remembering like a dream***, Alpha theta beta mo better blues you better choose delta, I felt the spirit you feel it when you hear it **- Dawud The Uncanny BlaKseed**

December 30th 2016 **Hell RAzor**

It's hard to describe what this do to me, it's like I'm a **scribe writing my own eulogy, Huey P** said it's "*revolutionary suicide*", he never lied! we just trying to survive but they ain't tryin to understand me, they wanna murder me and my family, so they label me a thug, I'm out hanging with my homies they claim'n I'm slanging drugs, they full of anger, never been a stranger to homicide, **the pain I felt inside when I heard Aiyana's Grandmother cry**, she was only 7, **Tamir Rice** 12! now they in **Ghetto Heaven,** I asked the reverend where do I find hell? cause I'm a hell razor! stress getting major, dear Lord be my savior! dear Lord can you hear me?! I got my finger on the trigger cause these crackers they trying to kill me, while my niggas watching the Green Bay Packers playing Philly, it's all a plan really! but do you care really?! no democracy left anywhere, only death destruction warfare, the reduction of the population, I was young when I joined the army, I didn't know what I was facing

I be a hell **RA**zor, **TILL** the last breath breathing, a hell **Ra**zor, **Till** my last breath breathing, I be a hell **RA**zor, **TILL** the last breath breathing, a hell **Ra**zor, **Till** my last breath breathing **- Dawud The Uncanny BlaKseed**

The Great American Solar Eclipse Is Upon Us (August 21st 2017)

August is a month that is blazing hot as the sun shines. Perhaps all these connected dots are just **coincidence** but I think not. I think they are divine. Like the fact that **Jordan Edwards** could have been born on any day but he's born on mine, October 25th, and he was also born in the year of the **snake** like me. He was murdered on **April 29th 2017.** I didn't write about Jordan Edwards until after I found out about this Eclipse that happened on August 21st 2017, the same day that **George Jackson** was murdered in 1971. Today is January 6th 2022 and my mother from a previous life, **Mamie Till** died on this day January 6th 2003 the year of the **goat**. Her son Emmett Till was murdered in 1955 the year of the **goat**. On **August 21st** 2017 a total solar eclipse occurred. It was the first one in 38 years to be visible from the mainland U.S.. A new total solar eclipse occurs every 18 months and signals the start of a new spiritual cycle. The month of August has brought people of color many trials and tribulations but it has also been a month of victory as well. The **Haitian revolution** was planned on August 14th 1791 and it was carried out on **August 21st** 1791. **Nat Turner** saw a **solar eclipse** on August 7th 1831 and to him the eclipse was a sign for revolution. The eclipse sparked him to make his way to freedom on **August 21st** 1831. **Marcus Garvey** was born on August 17th 1887 and my Grand father, **General Dukes Jr** died the next day on August 18th 2009. Hurricane Katrina hit New Orleans and devastated the majority black community on August **23**rd - 29th of 2005 and many suggest that the American government used advanced technology like HAARP (high-frequency active auroral research program) to cause that hurricane. August brought us the Women's Suffrage movement on August 20th 1920 with the signing of the 19th amendment giving white* women the right to vote. Michael Brown, an unarmed 18 year old black youth is shot and killed by a white police officer on August 9th 2014 and his body was left to lay on the street for four hours. **Korryn Gaines** was murdered in her home in front of her young son by police on August 1st 2016 and that same month **Colin Kaepernick** decided to stop standing for the National Anthem during football games. Emmett Till was lynched on August 28th 1955 and 8 years later on August 28th 1963 Martin Luther King would lead the historical march on Washington DC. Chadwick Boseman (The Black Panther) died on that same day, August 28th 2020. **Ausar** reigned for **28 years** and Emmett was murdered on **August 28th**. Michael Jackson was born the very next day on August 29th 1958 the year of the Dog. I'm sure King Michael Jackson would say, "**they don't really care about us**!" August 6th 1965 the year of the **snake** marked the signing of the Voting rights act which prohibited racial discrimination in voting **but what has voting ever really gotten us**?!!!!!

Condolences

My condolences go out to the family of **Jordan Edwards** and all of those who have been robbed of their lives by this system of racism and white supremacy. Please know that death is not the end. The soul survives death, indeed and in spirit. This is a book of the dead written by a boy who was murdered without justice, who defeated death and came forth by day. May the soul of **Jordan Edwards** walk peacefully through the field of Reeds in Amenta. Amen RA.

Rau nu Prt m heru

Iu f Per f m heru

Utterances for Coming Forth by day into Light

It is he, who comes forth by day into Light

January 1st 2017 Invocation Emote (1st of 30)

We cast out an auric field based off how we feel, we emote like a remote, we can heal or provoke anger, we can kill or build bridges, you stick a knife in my back then expect forgiveness, pull it out an inch and that's what I'm left to live with! I can get more specific if requested, highly prolific, metaphysic **hieroglyphic** highly respected, like megalithic stones erected no equipment, thought projected, **can't be taught what I'm blessed with**, not smoked not ingested, not for sport to be tested, or fought and bested, or caught and arrested, I'm **too invested in manifestation - Dawud The Uncanny BlaKseed**

January 3rd 2017 (Still Dreaming with Kanye West)

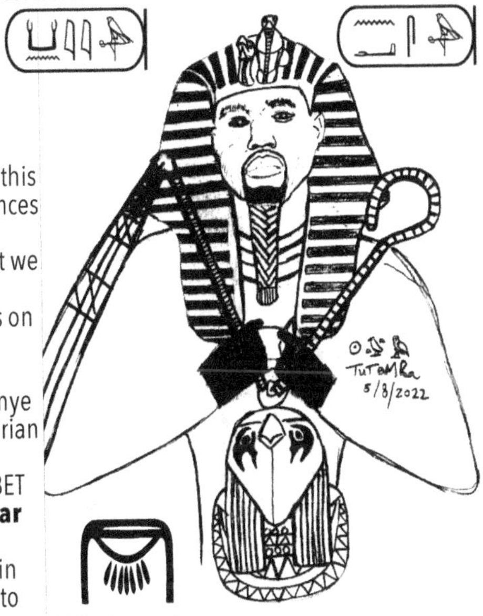

I woke a from a dream and the only thing I remembered was that **Kanye** was there. I don't remember and details.

Significance

If I don't remember the dream one might wonder why I even placed it here..? As I began to write this book I became aware of my dreams were guiding me to my revelation and because of my experiences with these dreams, I have become more attentive to what happens in my dreams. I realize that a dream is not just some made up fantasy that our minds create while sleep. In many instances what we dream has greater meaning and in many cases is real, like my experience with **Erykah Badu** in a "dream" (page 440). Kanye crashed 2 days before my birthday in 2002. I crashed 7 days before his on my fathers birthday in 2002 (page 106). In Kanye's song: Through The Wire, he says the name **Emmett Till**. It was the video for this song that would help him get a release date for his album sparking his rise to fame. My past life as Emmett Till was revealed on July 3rd 2018 (page 480). Kanye is from Chicago like Emmett Till and his last name is **West**. In the ancient Kemetic (Egyptian) Ausarian (Osirion) resurrection drama, Ausar (Osiris) was known as the **Lord of the West** and the Lord of **resurrection**. **West** was where the soul (BA) went when we "die". Kanye performed at the 2010 BET awards wearing a **gold** chain with a giant **Heru** pendant (in falcon form). **Heru** is the son of **Ausar** and he is the one that returns as Ra through resurrection. **Re-member** that **you** are **Ausar** and **Heru,** the **hero!** See page 3 for the **hero's journey!** On April 4th 2020 (page 594), the day Martin Luther King was assassinated (pages 69, 592) my past life as Tutankhaten (King Tut) was revealed to me. Martin Luther King wrote a paper on the Ausarian resurrection in 1949 (page 593).

Still Dreaming (Remix) - not included in chart or page xi ***ADDENDUM***

They say it rained for 40 days and nights, it took me 40 years to wake from this **dream** of life, a break through, most never seen the light so they debate you, if you proceed to fight what sedates you, cause they believe what they're told, they faithful, a nightmare for the **soul**, on a ancient scroll, I read from the **Book of the Dead** and I was lead to a stream of thought, that was seen and taught, like a beam of light in the **Minds Eye**, before you die, try to awake from this **dream**, despite what your life on earth might Seeeem, all your affairs are the manner of a **Dreeeam**, the soul comes forth like the light in the sky my friend like **Nefer Tem**, again and again, again and again, forever ever, forever ever, listen to this **Heka** like it was written in granite, the **Soul** is to the **Neter**, the body is to the planet, peter pepper **Ptah Nefer**, still they don't understand it, until it's vanished, Jack be nimble but he got swindled, damit! can it be all so simple?! rekindle like a candle, like a Hindu, hippocampal a flame in you will continue, the vandal dismantles a life before they knew they had it, if you had three wishes would you be living lavish? or would you marriage the Left the and the Right Brian? when you labor for riches you bound to perish in vein, I see visions of **Kanye** and **Nas** in Paris and Spain, they wear'n a chain, that came from a life when I was slain, I seen **Coltrane** on a old train playing Jazz, **Lisa** passed by winked her **Left Eye** and laughed, she said, live every life like it's ya last, she drew a picture of **Pac** on the same day that she passed, the soul knows but the monkey mind don't know the half, the **soul** grows once the initiate finds the path, despite what your life on earth might Seeeem, all your affairs are the manner of a **Dreeeam**, the soul comes forth like the light in the sky my friend like **Nefer Tem**, again and again, again and again, forever ever, forever ever, listen to this **Heka** like it was written in granite, the **Soul** is to the **Neter**, the body is to the planet, peter pepper **Ptah Nefer**, still they don't understand it.... **- TutemRa**

January 6th 2017 I Still Love Her

I said excuse me miss you look familiar, I see your **soul** it's like I'm looking in a mirror, She said "you look too old for me I ain't tryin to hear ya!" I said "at least hear my music maybe then you might remember", She said "I like it, I like how you write it's really clever", I said "thank you peace good night I didn't sweat her", the next day she hit me up like "I kept waking up with you in my **dream**, the same scene over and over it's strange what does it mean?!" I said "my dear close your eyelids, our **souls** met way before our eyes did, it's like a feeling you can't explain that recognizes chemicals sent to the heart from the brain and mesmerizes like a moth to the flame burnt by the fire, they say love is blind but your love is mine I will always find ya, no matter the time or place from China to Carolina from richer or poorer, diva pariah, slum-dog millionaire I'll be there, I used to love her, yeah yeah I still do, still my brothers keeper seeing life through my rearview, they say Hip Hop is dead but I see a clear view, I used to love her, yeah yeah I still do

Before, once upon a time, in a different place, in another existence off in the distance, in the near future or the distant past, a love this rare don't last long like shooting stars running out of gas, men are from mars but the **Goddess** hails from Venus like a comet, on time like a promise in sync with the moon, together we make **magic,** plants seeds watch em bloom, her love is **Queen,** then it's over super nova boom! gone too soon but a treasure never forgotten! it's better to have **loved** and lost, than to never, ever, ever, ever, ever, see it blossom… depression postpartum like a starving artist that never reaches stardom, or the feeling of Harlem when our star fell, **May 19th the year of the snake, It Ain't Hard To Tell** I attract clientele, flow like water for this new world order put out fires of hell, I used to love her, yeah yeah I still do, still my brothers keeper seeing life through my rearview, they say Hip Hop is dead but I see a clear view, I used to love her, yeah yeah I still do **- Dawud The Uncanny BlaKseed**

Significance

This rhyme was proceeded by an experience I had with a women on November 4th 2016 (**Dreams and the Underworld with my love Ankhesenaten**, page 427). When I wrote this rhyme my **light body** had been becoming more active but I was not consciously aware of this. It had less to do with the women I was meeting and more to do with a woman that was longing for me. A woman I had forgotten about. "Before, once upon a time, in a different place, in another existence off in the distance, in the near future or the distant past a love this rare don't last long like shooting stars running out of gas". I had been writing about Ankhesenaten my ancient wife. She had been trying to help awaken me and as you will come to see she was successful. This was written on January 6th, **Emmett Till's** mother, Mamie Till died on **January 6** 2003, the year of the **goat**. Emmett was murdered in 1955 the year of the **goat**. **Jan 6th** is 12 days after the Winter Solstice (Christmas, pages 489, 614). In the Christian religion **Jan 6** is the day that the 3 Magi visited Jesus in a manger. **Jan 6** is also the day that the ancient Kemetyu celebrated the Winter Solstice and **Tupac's** grand mother Eloise Maria Barnes was born on **Jan 6**.

January 7th 2017 Mantra

The rise and the falls, **The sons and the Set,** The **sun** reflect on the **moon** bloom divine time I'm next, hold on to my rhymes like mantras, subdue the evil roaming in the minds of monsters, don't be one bone stuck in one shape, be flexible not rigid New York mind state, spring back and relax cause if you don't you break, compulsive people with bad habits and opinions rarely change, they try to impose them on anyone that comes in range, Just cause they got one don't mean that they're gonna use their brain, sometimes what they call change is more of the same **- Dawud The Uncanny BlaKseed**

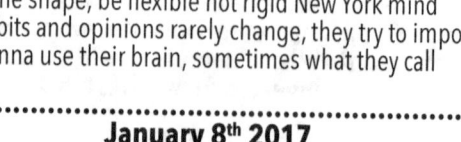

January 8th 2017
My pilgrimage to Far Rockaway

I had not been to Far Rockaway in many years but I traveled the long train ride on a cold snowy day to get there. The only reason I went to Far Rockaway was because Ron called me on Sep 25th 2016 (page 423) and I felt like the **synchronicities** involved with that call meant I should go, so **I followed the signs**. **Charwayne** ran the studio with another brother I grew up with named **Earl**. At this point in time I had only recorded music in one studio years ago with Court when we recorded the song, Shift the Power (page 139). One of my closest elementary school friends, named **Colin** came to join me in the studio. Colin is born on **February 23rd** the same day as **Dr. Amos Wilson** (page 283) and he is also a **life path number 5** like Charwayne, Ron and myself. Colin was smoking weed, and I did the worst thing I could do, I took two or three puffs of his weed. I got so high that I could barely function. Colin had been smoking since high school. I didn't smoke until I was 33 years old and I was 39 at the time (page 194). His weed got me "high high" and I barely managed to recored one song, **Holler If you Hear Me** (page 374). Colin is a loyal friend. We don't see each other often at all and because of that he made it his business to come through in the snow to chill with me and to give support. The next time I would go to Far Rockaway was on **June 23rd 2021** (page 648). This time I went back to **my childhood home** and took a picture of it, then I went home and watched the **5th** episode of the last season of **Lost** and the main character, Jack "**Shepard**" goes to a **lighthouse** on the island and sees an image of **his childhood home** in a mirror. The jack of all trades is a master of none but more often times the jack of all trades is better than the master of only one trade. Jack "Shepard" like the "Shepard Staff" that the **pharaoh** carries in his **left** hand. That same day I would cross paths with two left handed brothers while riding to the ferry with my brother Matthew who is also a lefty like myself. Just like Ron, Charwayne, Colin and I all share the life path number 5. None of these things are just random **coincidences**, they are **coinciding angles** connected by seen and unseen forces most commonly referred to as **angels** or God. Speaking of February **23**, I don't know when I saw the movie **The Number 23** but it was many years before my past life revelations, yet the movie mentions **Sirius** and it's about patterns and numbers. It premiered on Feb **23,** 2007 and Jim Carrey **star**red in it. Jim Carrey **star**ted his acting career in 19**77**, the year of the snake, the year I was born. One time is an incidence, twice is a coincidence, but three, four, five is a pattern but can you tell the difference? See page **648** for the **metaphysical significance of the number 23**. See pages 25, 94, 102, 121, 283, 444, 586, 669, and 672 for more on **February 23rd**. "**Coincidentally**", Colin works a the same Boys Home that my friends Greg and Patrick were housed at (page 138).

January 9th 2017
Dreams of flying

I was sky diving and hang gliding and landing very softly. I remember seeing two women. One was teaching the other how to land. Then I was on the longest journey which felt like a hike. The dream ended with me hanging from a cliff. Then I woke up.

January 10th 2017

Dream

This dream was like the movie Back To The Future (p 40). I was **floating** with something under my feet like a skateboard. The feeling of **floating** felt like the high you get when you're scoring the game winning touchdown.

January 11th 2017 - Dream

Another dream with what felt like levitation. I was jumping very far distances like The **Incredible Hulk**.

Rau nu Prt m heru

Iu f Per f m heru

Utterances for Coming Forth by day into Light

It is he, who comes forth by day into Light

January 12th 2017
1st Dream with Erykah Badu

This dream was very magical. I can not remember many dreams where upon waking I tried to go back to sleep to continue the dream! That is what happened the first time I dreamt with **Erykah**.

I was in a house with Erykah. I think it was her home. I was reading a poem on her wall. The poem seemed to be magical as every line went perfectly with the lines before and after it. The poem seemed to tell a beautiful story and made perfect sense. I loved the poem. It was like it was the best thing I had ever read. Erykah saw that I was amazed so she took the poem off the wall and handed it to me. As soon as she did that I woke up and as soon as I woke up I remembered the dream but I couldn't recall the poem. I closed my eyes immediately trying to go back to sleep to no avail. The dream was gone.

Two days later I would get a strange visit in a dream and 2 years later I would dream of Erykah again. In 1713, the year of the **snake**, **Tartini**, the Italian composer had a similar **dream**, from which he awoke and composed the **Devils Trill Sonata**.

January 12th 2017 - Khalid Muhammad and the Prophecy of the Buddha

I met brother **Kenny** in **Marcus Garvey** Park in 2016. He would show me some Aikido moves and I would do Thai Massage on him. Kenny was in his 70's and we met for training around 7 to 9 times.. As I have stated earlier in the book him and I would get into friendly debates about spiritual sciences and theology. He was the reason I read the book **Siddhartha** and I was thank full for that. During one of our debates he suggested that I read the book and I did. I read it because Stephanie had given me the book for my birthday and she was born on **Jan 12** just like Kenny (p 295). I thought that to be a sign so I read the book quickly and afterwards I felt like I was reading about my life. Kenny told me to read the book because I reminded him of Siddhartha too. One day while at my studio **Khalid Muhammad** came up in discussion because I was wearing a tea shirt with his face on it (p 458) and because his birthday was coming up or it had just passed. When Khalid's name came up Kenny said he didn't care too much for Khalid and I took offense to that. I asked him what had Khalid ever done or said that was wrong and his only response was that - "he was too much".. After Kenny left I realized that Khalid was also born on **Jan 12**. So I sent Kenny a text that read something like - "Brother Kenny, you told me to read Siddhartha because I reminded you of the boy in the book and I read the book because the person who gifted me the book was born on **Jan 12** like you. You know I follow signs from the ancestors. And that's how I live my life. So in the spirit of Khalid you are wrong! Khalid is born on **Jan 12** just like you and Stephanie. And part of the reason brother Khalid is dead is because of brothers like you who are afraid to stand with him.". Kenny never responded and I never heard from Kenny again. As I just typed that I felt remorse for sending him that text but I do feel like it was true. We as a people want to cheer our warriors but we are not ready to stand beside, in front or behind them when they are living yet we honor them only after they have given their lives for the fight for freedom. One time in an incidence, twice is a coincidence, three, four, five is a pattern. Can you tell the difference? I would have another incident with Khalid Muhammad on Feb 17, 2017 the day he was assassinated! This time it was with **Charlamagne** the radio personality (p 443).

"On this day, January 12, 1948, Khalid Adbul Muhammad was born Harold Moore, Jr. in Houston, Texas. Once he joined the Nation of Islam in 1967 as a 19-year old, Muhammad would become an instrumental figure within the organization and eventually became, like Malcolm X before him, the National Spokesman for the Nation.Without question, during his tenure with the NOI, Dr. Khalid Muhammad became a fearless, unapologetic, and unwavering Black Nationalist who did not bite his tongue at any moment in time–One thing you could be sure of was Dr. Khalid told it like it was, no sugar-coating allowed! In recollection, I remember the episode of the Donahue Show when Muhammad gave an eloquent, remorseless historical overview of the atrocities African people had endure for centuries at the helm of white supremacy! It is safe to say after the airing of that episode the ratings of the Donahue Show plummeted.For those that knew him, or knew of him, no would argue that Khalid Abdul Muhammad was not only a Pan-Africanist and a Black Nationalist that had a DEEP love for African people worldwide, he was the epitome of Black manhood! Without skipping a verbal beat, he exhibited the Bravery and Tenacity to say what others like him might have been thinking but did not have the words to express it or the Courage to do so. For that, as well as for his life's work, we will FOREVER HONOR Khalid Abdul Muhammad! Happy 75th Earthday! Maa Kheru (True of Voice)! (January 12, 1948 – February 17, 2001)" - **Dr Heru**

January 13th 2017 Ibis

Magical people no equal, fly like seagull eye like pineal, pin pad paint a picture like the easel, time's been bad but they still been good, you fear death but won't live life with the fight and fire of brother hood, I never understood why **religion** and place of birth on the earth creates division, that hurts seeing warriors in prison, I had a vision it was **nepotism we had risen** back to a harmonious way of living on our own! I be the **Lord of Maat** like the base of the **throne**, in case you forgot let me take you back home, I came flying out primordial d**ark**ness, ready to spark this, *let's get it on*, I got *redemption songs* for my people that's my word is bond, no more pawn shit, **kingship** we gotta **transform** with the quickness **- Dawud The Uncanny BlaKseed**

January 14th 2017 Dream with Jay Electronica

I'm sitting in the passenger side of a car and **Jay Elect** rolls up to my window wearing a pair of old school black roller skates and he says to me, "you ain't got nothing on me". Then he rolls away. I get out the car and I follow him telling him that I'm a fan of his. In the dream I felt like he was competing with me or letting me know that I wasn't as good as him. The only problem is I agreed. I thought he was a better rapper than me so I followed him trying to tell him that I was a fan.

Significance

Two days after I dreamt of **Erykah Badu** the father of one of her children, Jay Electronica comes to me in a dream. I understand now what happened. My soul did meet with Erykah and because the dream realm is a real place the soul of Jay Electronica did come to me perhaps as a protector of a person he loves. Just like I went to Indira on Oct 18th 2014 (page 305). In my dream he had come as a protector. On January 15th 2019 I would dream of Erykah again. I became aware of **J Electronica** at a low period in my journey when I had no desire to write music. I heard him and it was like a breath of fresh air. I listened to everything of his that I could find online as he would become one of my favorite Emcees. I could hear his spiritual quest in between the lines of his rhymes. I listened to him talk about his journey, his ups and downs and how he persevered. I saw that he was only one year older than me. Prior to this I had been starting to feel like I was too old to still be writing rhymes. In 2015 I took the Guru beat that he rapped over and said one of my rhymes to it. Then I started writing again. **Jay Electronica** is born on September 19, the same day that **Emmett Till's Murder** trial started in 1955 (page 516).

January 15th 2017
Dream with Mfundishi Jhutyms

I'm in a grassy plane with Mfundishi and he is teaching me some moves and he is not being soft with his teachings.

January 15th 2017 Cancer

If you want the truth come hither hear from the heart of a **panther**, the system **gold** diggers my niggas dying of **cancer**, families crying **doctors** lying they ain't trying for answers, they're ignorant to the **tune** of **benign** you're found **malignant**, death come sooner the rumor is it's all deliberate, it's all fun and games till your family is living it, you can't drink away the pain I hope you never experience the hideous face the change chills radiation kill epithelial cells, it won't heal ya, it'll give you **anemia**, **anorexia, nausea**, **bone loss**, take **chemotherapy** at your own cost, you could be your own boss, **Soursop, power crops, Spirulina, Chlorella, Who Got The Props? The Blakseed** get to the root, what else can I tell ya but the truth? felt like a failure when my **Grand Father** died, he could have survived if I had opened my eyes researched the **Medical Apartheid,** I cried for days for years, we gotta face our fears, make haste to a place of cheer, a place that cares, that place not here! they only tare us down, recycle our **organs** put us in the ground! how that sound? hard to believe but real! if you don't read and study you'll be diseased and ill, with medical **bills** to pay they feed you **pills** that's no way to live, they ain't got the answer's **Sway - Dawud The Uncanny BlaKseed**

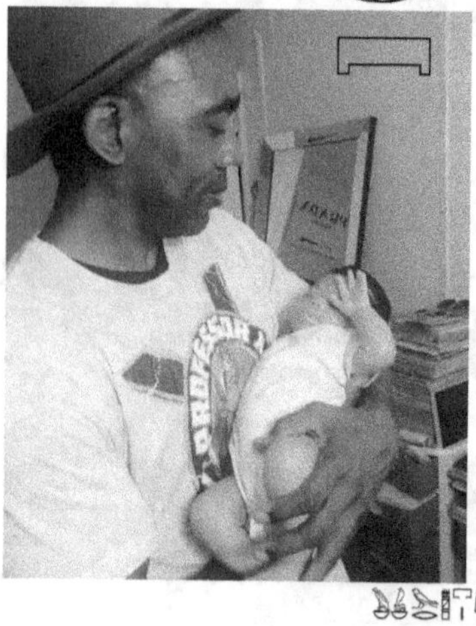

January 18th 2017 - Dream

Alan comes to me and asks me why I didn't go to my sisters birthday party

Significance

See **Alan** on page 57. One of my sisters would have a baby on April 20th 2019 and I would miss the baby shower by mistake. This baby would come to earth bringing a code with her like my Aunt Pamela and her children. Her father was born on **May 25th** and she was born on **April 20th** 2019 (page 558). The murder of **Emmett Till** was the first mass movement for civil rights in American history and Emmett's body was identified by his ring that had the date **May 25th** engraved on it (page 512). **George Floyd** was murdered on **May 25th** 2020 by a police officer the month after I had my past life revelation of my life as **Tutankhaten** (**King Tut**) on April 4th the day Martin Luther King was assassinated (pgs 69, 592). George's murder would spark the biggest protest in American history and his killer was sentenced to prison on **April 20th** 2021. My other sister had a dream on May 25th 2002 that I died in a care accident and 7 days later I had a violent car accident but I survived (page 104).

Rau nu Prt m heru

Iu f Per f m heru

Utterances for Coming Forth by day into Light

It is he, who comes forth by day into Light

January 18th 2017 Nature VS Nurture

Is it nature verse nurture? is it natural to murder? is it the culture? the paper money? the absence of **sunny days**? Inertia - **The Truman Show,** Punxsutawney, is this a hologram they forcing on me like pneumonia, we all damned like Hollywood **To Live And Die in California,** I'm a glitch in the **matrix** programed to try and warn ya, we been stripped of the sacred like the seed from the farmer, the **soul** from the body, the yoga from the dharma, the Zulu from the Shaka, the rebel from the treble sound found in the underground, plant the black seed water it one day they gonna come around, the army ants slaughtered it, brought the elephant down, and organized lie can make the truth drown **- Dawud The Uncanny BlaKseed**

Significance

I was waking up from a long sleep, in a new body Just like the movie **Matrix**.

January 20th 2017 - Dream with Chris Rock

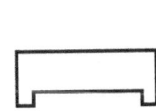

I was with Chris Rock standing in his parking lot and he was telling me jokes.

Significance

The only comedians I have ever seen live are Chris Rock and Paul Mooney but on several occasions back in 2004/2005 I got stopped by White people who thought I was Dave Chappell. I'm serious, not joking. I used to wear a blazer on top of hoodies and I guess that was Dave's style at the time. Chris Rock is born on **February 7th** 1965, the year of the **snake**. He's born the same day as Louis Till (Emmett Till's father, pages 475, 518), and both "Emmett" and I were born in the years of the **snake**. As Emmett I was born in 19**41** and in my present incarnation I was born again in 1977. (see page **41**)

January 29th 2017 Falcon Dreams

We have all seen superman **float** up into the sky then fly away on the big screen. In this dream I did the same thing. Standing with my massage table in my left hand I began to float into the air ever so slowly. There were trees around me and as I got to the height of the top of the trees I let the massage table go. It fell to the ground then I turn into a white **Falcon** and flew away.

January 31st 2017 Ghetto Heaven

Does heaven have a ghetto, is there a heaven for a gangsta? I don't know but if there's a hell below we all gonna go, *we probably in hell already our dumb asses not knowing*, too busy making it rain on mommies out there hoeing, through all the rain and pain **Keep Ya Head Up** and keep going, what you see might make it hard to smile, God bless the child that hold their own and keep growing, like roses in the concrete, one door closes another opens in a heart beat, heart attack took another homie last week, fighting the power starts on your plate with what you eat, from the skin to the skeleton let the food be the medicine, improve the melanin is what I'm telling them, gentlemen! my negus put down the cigarettes, alcohol and all the things they feed us, if we don't mind up we'll drink up the hemlock in modern day society and drop dead quietly, finally the **25th Dynasty** plant seeds of sobriety, ***raising the dry bones in the valley*** of the shadow of death I will have no fear, *be there when my homies call* to build bridges not walls, if they build a wall I'm telling you all it's gonna fall down, the wall's gonna fall down, the walls gonna fall down - **Dawud The Uncanny BlaKseed**

February 9th 2017 Maroons

It's true **Egypt** was a **black land**, it's true the first **American** was a **Black man**! you don't like it? I don't give a damn! uncle sam is good at division, I'm trying to do addition, I ain't hate'n I just want **One Nation,** I'm talking to **Pharaoh Allah, Shakka Ahmose, Sa Ra Suten Seti, Dr Umar**, don't let them fool ya our children are the future, what are we teaching if we beefing?! we are the beacons of light!! two men in a burning house don't have time to fight!! when we fight to death… that's how the west was lost and the enemy takes what's left and our progeny calls them boss! that ain't boss shit that's tragic!! I got **Maat Magic,** for those who lost it, **Up From Slavery Booker T, W.E.B. Du Bois** the first black **PHD,** we still ain't free still attacked daily, **Africa for Africans, Marcus Garvey** take us back again, away from the pain and the suffering, **Nepotism -** the only way for us to win! "and if you think about it we ain't ever had a friend", listening to **John Henrik Clarke** and **Dr Ben Jochannan,** I speak from the heart won't stop till we on top again! one day soon we gonna be on top again, the African came back with unity as the stratagem, maximum effect like **maroons** ready to ride again, when I die I'll come back in the spirit and try again

Where is the unity?! not even in the conscious community… I see conflict they just wanna conquer you and me! as soon as we try to U.N.I.T.Y., turn on the news and all you see is another brother die, but we don't die we multiply and we civilize, I hear the lies coming from the evil, you superior the chosen? well we the original people the indigenous, the genius here to teach you harmonious balance and virtue… you need to be more peaceful less hurtful, self defense is not violence it's survival it's impossible to remain silent when a tyrant gives you a choice, the grave or the hospital, the voice of **Malcolm little,** one day soon we gonna be on top again, the African came back with unity as the stratagem, maximum effect like maroons ready to ride again, when I die I'll come back in the spirit so I can ride again **- Dawud The Uncanny BlaKseed**

Significance

This rhyme was written for the "conscious community". To the brothers that always seemed to be debating and humiliating each other. I got a lot of info from many different brothers and sisters online and it really bothered me when I saw all the division. This song was written with the energy of unity.. **42 Laws of Maat, Page 367**

February 13th 2017 **BlaK Wall Street (3rd verse)**

She was a beauty smart athletic funny, she wouldn't let me waste my money on a diamond or a ruby, truly a treasure **Areyla,** truly a pleasure to meet her, she's magnetic vibe'n on the same frequency, It ain't everyday you meet or see somebody that gets it, a misfit **Outkast Alien,** a **dreamer**, I fell asleep then I seen her flying on a unicorn, we didn't exchange words but she Let me tag along, she was sad, she felt alone in this cold world, so I wrote her a song, she said my words felt warm like kisses, we made a bond so strong I wouldn't exchange for three wishes, every **King** needs a **Queen** waving her wand like **Witches,** the richness is in life beyond the beyond, I witness the sickness and vice, my advice is nepotism a family a wife, a mechanism put together precise, no barbarism or plagiarism or feudalism, take it back to a **Black Wall Street** way of living, no prison no poison no crack, no Crackers no picking cotton or sugar, just happiness and laughter, no sickness, no doctors getting paid like pastors without first healing the **magic**al people, no equal, eye like **pineal,** the **Black Man Of The Nile And His Family** I see you! Brother brother, don't stray too far, you cant get to heaven without the Black Star! Sister sister, do you know who you are? wanna get to ghetto heaven? take the **Black Star**! **- Dawud The Uncanny BlaKseed**

Significance - Creation

I met a girl named Areyla on Instagram who at the time was having trouble dealing with having a White mother and a Black father. She reminded me of my friend Lynzie from Suny Canton (1996). We talked on the phone and I explain that we all come here for our own divine purpose and we chose our parents for a reason. We became friends and after we had this talk I wrote this verse for her. I made it the 3rd verse for my song **Blak Wall Street** (page 403). I took pieces of our conversation and placed them in the verse. When I sent her the verse she was very happy to hear it. In this verse I mention that the richness in life is beyond the beyond. I took that idea from a **Bob Marley** interview where he was asked if he was rich and he stated that, **"his richness is in life forever"**. Bob Marley was mixed like Areyla and he once wrote a song title, **Reincarnated Soul** (p 626).

February 17th 2017 **Charlamagne**

Charlamagne what a name you not a God, you a lame, you's a fraud, you not hard you soft, you bleach your skin cause you're lost! you hate women! of course you berate Buffy the body, I see _the bitch in_ you hoe! And everybody know! you ain't talk to **Fredro Star** like that! you ran a 4 4 flat! when they _kick in your door waiving the 4 4_ what you gonna do black? nothing! you don't even talk about relevant issues, niggas like you need to get whipped with a pistol, do anything for a fist full of nickels, should have been you with Ice Tea and the Skittles, should have been you in the jeep shot up and **riddled**, I never hear you speak of **Malcolm Little** or **Khalid Muhammad,** your Roman name explains why you sugarcane and so dishonest **- Dawud The Uncanny BlaKseed**

Why I wrote this rhyme

On this day February 17th I saw a video of **Charlamagne** belittling a Black woman on his show. He treated her very disrespectfully and I felt that he would never treat a man the way he treated her. He wouldn't talk to Mike Tyson like that. He didn't feel so comfortable when Fredro Starr checked him. This was not my first time seeing him act this way to people. I felt like he does this to anyone he feels he can get away with treating like this. In a fit of anger I wrote the verse. It is not one of my favorite pieces and I never learned it by heart. What I found more alarming about the verse is that when I edited the video for it and posted it on my Instagram it got a lot more likes and engagement than usual for my page. It seemed that the negative "beef" energy of it was entertainment for people. As if they wanted to see that. I have not written another song like that since. I take the art form of Hip Hop seriously in that I think it should be used to build not destroy (**Heka, page 6**). We should not use our talents to attack each other so I don't particularly like that I wrote this verse but **I let myself right it** because of how the song came into fruition. _I felt like I was writing with the fuel and anger of **Khalid Muhammad** when I wrote it_. This happened on February 17th which is the day Khalid Muhammad was murdered which is coincidentally the same day that **Huey P Newton** was born! I always felt a sense of foul play when I realized Khalid was murdered on Huey P's birthday! **Huey P** created the Black Panther Party for self defense and Khalid started the New Black Panther Organization! I always felt like "they" planned to kill him on this day to make a point! Like a signature. With the rise of Hip Hop lyrics being used to indict Hip Hop artist I question all the technology used to promote artist. Perhaps streams are manipulated to create the rise of the artist "they" want to promote. I know from experience that your music can be suppressed. I have even heard **Kanye** speak of being shadow banned. On the Drink Champs Podcast he mentioned how every word of one of his albums must be typed in before it will appear in the search browser for people desiring to purchase it. The same thing must be done for my album, **The Immortal Life of Emmett Till** (page 577). My song **Blak Wall Street** was taken off Youtube because they said it was considered hate music (page 403). My song **Dec 3rd** was taken off Soundcloud when it began to amass thousands of views page 312-313). "Those" who control music, make every effort to prevent certain music from going "viral". On Sep 6th 1996 **Tupac** called Professor James Small and told him that the media was creating the East coast West coast beef and that he was going to start his own distribution company with other Hip Hop artists, the next day he was assassinated (page 564). Take all that info then add **Darpa** (**Hip Hop Police**) to it (page 352).

February 21st 2017 "Still Dreaming" with Nas

In this dream I'm soaking in a big free standing tub in the middle of a room. The lights are dim. In the corner of the room **Nas** is seated in a chair dressed in all white, smoking a Cuban cigar. When I am done with my bath or my "**baptism**" Nas gets up and exits the room. When he exits I rise up renewed. Then I wake up.

(Still Dreaming Remix, page 438)

Nas and Reincarnation

The dream about took place on the day **Malcolm X** was assassinated (p 561-565). A year and half after this dream, my past life as Emmett Till would be revealed to me (page 480). **Nas** released his **Demo Tape** in 1991 the year of the **goat**. **Emmett Till** was murdered in 1955 the year of the **goat**. The last track on his Demo Tape was titled, **Nas Will Prevail**. In the first verse **Nas** says, "**_A modern Shakespeare Reincarnated_**". **Nas** dropped his 11th studio album titled, **Life Is Good** on July 13 2012. On the 3rd track titled, **A Queens Story**, he mentions **reincarnation** again, "**_Bebo Posse reincarnated through me, probably_**". **Emmett** was murdered at **14** and in 2021, on **Nas's 14th** studio album he mentions **reincarnation** again, "_This what I live for, The inventor, The re-invention, **I'm reincarnated**, see what it hit for_". This album was titled **Magic** and it was released on December 24, the day before the **Winter Solstice** (p 489) which is related to Resurrection, Reincarnation, Gilgul (p 14). In 2002 I survived a near fatal car accident and just before I crashed I was listening to the Nas track, **You Da Man,** on repeat (p 104).

Rau nu Prt m heru

Iu f Per f m heru

Utterances for Coming Forth by day into Light

It is he, who comes forth by day into Light

February 23rd 2017 Legacy

If I speak with urgency to my fam, does it make you nervous? am I the angry Black man with verses? beneath the surface I'm purpose driven, this ain't live'n! *Does heaven have a ghetto*, does heaven have a prison, do you have a conscious, do you care a little? you like when I speak nonsense or when I dribble, objects in the mirror appear nearer in the **riddle**, a **thriller in manilla**, **butterfly caterpillar**, from drug dealer to a pillar in the community, you a killer of anyone bringing the unity, but legacies live on like **Malcolm** and **Huey P**, in the hearts and the minds, the rhyme the melody, enemy jealousy felony penitentiary, it ain't Black verse White, what we fight is an entity, good verse evil disperse negative energy, everything got worse when they birthed white supremacy **- Dawud The Uncanny BlaKseed**

(See page **648** for the **metaphysical significance of the number 23**. See pages 25, 94, 102, 121, 283, 586, 669, and 672 for more on **February 23rd**.)

March 3rd 2017 Get Out

(see page 263)

They don't want you to seek, and if you find they don't want you to speak, everything was all fine just a week ago, you better know it's a crime if you try'n to be a teacher bro, fo niggas teach mo niggas, no crackers need to know! **50 niggaz** make a pack, tell me we can't grow?! no reefer, no crack, just the ether that we blow, the deeper the breath keep the reaper of death off my chest, move slow in the fast lane, on a quest for a tribe to invest Black pride, like the **Black Star Line,** I can't see death till I try, when I die, I fly in the whirlwind like a **Falcon** with **Malcolm,** blasting my album in **Thugs Mansion** no doubt son, **Get Out** son, American nightmare the outcome, a burning house, your organs, wake up without them! you heard about **Kendrick Lamar!** well, tell me about **Johnson!** I'm ready to unite tonight mother fuck m**arc**h'n **- Dawud The Uncanny BlaKseed**

March 13th 2017

MILLER TIME -$800 6/7 Communication

It had been four years but by chance I happened to find Mill's again, this time on **Instagram**. I reached out to him on March 13th 2017. He looked clean and sharp as per usual. I noticed a tee shirt he had on. It said, **spiritually mentally physically and financially fit**. I left him a message under his picture. We exchanged words in DM. **I told him** - "I'm not sure why you think I gave you that money brother but I gave it to you because I saw another brother in need. I don't know if you thought I was soft or that I didn't need it or what ever you thought but I'm always going to want my money! You may think just because I didn't come to you with violence or with legal action that you have gotten away with it. Brother the tee shirt you're wearing. This is the life I live. My life is full of spiritual experiences. Just because a judge doesn't force you to give the money back or there isn't some act of violence against you doesn't mean you get away. That part about spiritually fit. There is a spiritual world and you will pay at some point". After that we exchanged a few messages where he said he would pay me. I would hear from him one more time on June 15th the day that I went to see **Tupac's** biopic and the day before Tupac's birthday.

Last communication page June 15th 2017 page 448

March 14th 2017 Dreadlocked

They teach you everything except how to be yourself, you take a picture of everything but you won't stop and help! I have a hard time finding pics of men who never took trips to the moon, you take 50 pics then post two with you standing in the bathroom, you call ships full of slaves immigrants, you's a damn coon a clown, ain't no honeymoon, American nightmare **Michael Brown**! ***Keep Ya Head Up*** stand tall, ain't no answers on the ground, put down the alcohol, if you fall to rock bottom, I'll be there ***when my homies call***, sometimes the bottom is not a problem, cause the bottom is the best place to build a foundation, it's all about perception, like the negative perception they project'n on my Black nation, but I stay fact check'n, they stay hate'n, I stay make'n forward progress like **Walter Payton,** it's 4th and long we down by a lot! The ancestors wait'n! Have you forgotten the **Dreadlock Maroon Haitian** going out blaze'n?! **- Dawud The Uncanny BlaKseed**

March 15th 2017 Twin Flame

Don't chase love attract it, the aura's like a muscle to build it it takes practice, sp**ark** a flame with ya brain you don't need matches, The **Twin Flame** unlocks the heart when the beat matches, it's like a puzzle I love you, I want you to love me like they love **Pac**, Saw me on stage she shook and dropped like I was the **King of Pop,** I said "**Annie are you okay**", She said "**You got the props**, like **5 ft Evil D and Buck Shot**", On top astronaut, Solstice, equinox, a lot of kilowatts, get amped like **Watts Riots** with a deeper plot, Copers still raid the reefer spot, We just tying to heal each other, They drop glocks on our blocks, They want us to kill each other, Wise as a Fox spot the under cover, Stay strong as an Ox uplift my brother, Still I war like **The Lox, Clubber lang** jugular vain feel my pain **- Dawud The Uncanny BlaKseed**

January 2023 Something in my Heart

If you see a world they don't see, you're not alone, there's another world in HD, you're not crazy, they sleep daisy, at my memoria play me and feel the euphoria, she lived on **Hawk** road but not in Astoria, at a fork in the road bought her a rose adorning her, informing her, **there's something in my heart**, drawn to her like a heart pumping beets to the **Liver**, when our hearts touch I beat she shiver, **Auset** weeped for **Ausar** then she dove in the river, a door is a star, come follow me here hither, life is a class and **Love** is trigger like a sp**ark**, so chart your own course and of course beware of sharks in a sea of fish, **RA**member this like a hieroglyph, **Anubis** and a **obelisk**, karma do exist like the kiss of death, and **Love** never dies it rise in the East, and the soul never dies it sets in the West **- TutemRa**

March 2017 Dream with Stic

I'm in the home of Stic having dinner with him and his family.

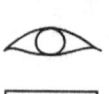

Significance

After **Tupac** I might have to say that Stic is my favorite artist and perhaps that is why I seem to hang out with him in my dreams so often. Stic is my favorite artist and the falcon (Heru) logo he uses for his music company is taken from the pectoral jewelry from the tomb of **Tutankhaten** (**King Tut**). In ancient kemet Heru (Falcon/Horus/Jesus) is the son of **Ausar** (Osiris) that returns. Heru is from the Ausarion or Osirion drama of **resurrection.** On April 4th 2020 the day that Martin Luther King (pages 69, 592) was assassinated I would have my past life revelation of my life as **Tutankhaten** (**King Tut**, page 594).

March 22nd 2017
Dream with Kalishea

Kalishea is upset with me for some reason and soon after another girl comes in. Then I'm in the gym with my friend **Patrick** from high school and we are flexing in the mirror. At some point we get kicked out the gym then I am alone. There is a storm building up with winds so strong that I can barely walk or run and it feels like I'm moving in slow motion and some one is chasing me. My **Grand Daddy (p 169)** comes to my rescue and we dart off in his old truck. We end up hiding in the woods near a ditch.

March 25th 2017 Taken

They got **money** for **wars** but can't feed the poor!!? more Black girls missing, but nobody listens! They say she ran away hoeing stripping, but when a Quarterback's jersey stolen, **FBI** sent on a mission, "*They don't give a fuck about us*"! picture me rolling ready to bust, ***50 niggas*** with triggers Just us out for justice, Freedom come through the barrel of a musket, I don't watch the news, more blues, I don't trust it! tell me **why** we **trust**ing the same **cops** that **kill** our **kids** to find them? It's like we dumb deaf and blind son! can't you see we at war?! imagine being locked behind a door, kidnapped, trapped, taken! American **nightmare** Jason, **Get Out!** Chasing **Trayvon Martin,** organs taken, Orphans, Masons, Preachers breaking laws you put faith in, they care more about the teachers than they do for the children, anything to stop poor people from building **- Dawud The Uncanny BlaKseed**

TutemRa 2022

March 23rd 2017
keep ya head up Nefertari

The Black woman is God, the Black woman is God, but she's the hardest person to convince ever since she been robbed of her knowledge of self, she had the hardest cards dealt cause she felt the pain, seeing her seeds slain, chopped in pieces for not picking the sugar cane, she scream for **Jesus, Jesus** never came! she claims every religion even if it's a prison, she never met **Mark, Luke** or **John,** but **Martin, Malcolm** and **Huey** they gone! your religion is not the reason they bring you harm, it's your organs that they farm like a tax! **Henrietta Lacks,** this life ain't fair, *there's a war going on outside* no one is safe here, we're being attacked but you're more relaxed than your hair! *I give a holler to my sisters on welfare,* ***Dawud cares*** *if don't nobody else care,* and I remember **Tupac** used to sang to me, he had me feeling like Black was the thang to be, then they changed Hip Hop to rap and what a shame to see, it's gonna take the man in me to conquer this insanity, *Royalty* **Black Man Of The Nile And His Family** tree, Loyalty black man smile with your wife and live happily, health excitement love and enlightenment mastery, the black family, save the black family, and when you come around the block I know they clown a lot, cause some men are not men they beat ya down a lot, but please don't cry dry ya eyes never let up, forgive but don't forget girl keep ya head up, please don't cry dry ya eyes never let up, forgive but don't forget girl keep ya head up,

This is sort of like my **Taj Mahal,** I massage her walls, cause a tsunami in **Abu Simbal,** erect a temple like **Ramoses** did for **Nefertari,** over this instrumental, ***It's all about you,*** what I **Do For Love,** I can't live without you, **Until The End Of Time,** baby ***It's all about you,*** and it's true, where ever the thought is so is the entity, so I will always be with you, infinity! I ain't **Never Had A Friend Like** She, the way she kisses me, serendipity the epitome of **synchronicity**, it's all about timing, she's crying, coming eventually, ecstasy we be flying can't tell me this wasn't meant to be, influentially on time, "*I might not change the world but I'll sp**ark** the mind*", my partner in crime, **Me and My Girl Friend, Never Call You Bitch Again,** if I die before you I'm a call you in the whirlwind, and that's the truth, like the love that you find within, if the Black woman is God, tell me how can we be born in sin? if you a son then your job is to shine your light on them, not hating, raping, leaving them fighting them, *I came from a woman got my name from a woman,* bet's believe Dawud The Blakseed gonna fight for them, and when you come around the block I know they clown a lot, cause some men are not men they beat ya down a lot, but please don't cry dry ya eyes never let up, forgive but don't forget girl keep ya head up, please don't cry dry ya eyes never let up, forgive but don't forget girl keep ya head up, **- Dawud The Uncanny BlaKseed**

April 18th 2017 Teenage love

Rau nu Prt m heru

She said, if she could go back in time she would change it, once upon a time the stars aligned our flame lit, with innocent adolescence love now I'm famous, don't don't hurt me again, a teenage love, hugs and kisses dreams and wishes, you never know who reminisces over you, Poor George, Check the rhyme, let me take you back in time, "My closest road dog", "Rewind to 89", "ticky ticky I'm, ticky ticky on, ticky ticky", "My mind playing tricks on me", like a symphony, **Marly Marl, Bob Marley,** 93 Till infinity, be there "when my homies call" me, "19 naughty" **Ghetto Bastard** that's what she used to call me, **I used to love her,** I used to call her, but "Mr telephone man there's something wrong with my line every time I dial my babies number I get a click every time" and it's <u>*killing me softly,*</u> *"* off on a natural charge bon voyage", home of the **Ole Dirty Bastard** Brooklyn God

"It was all a **dream**", **video music box**, **word up magazine**, "Who got the props", <u>*Chief rocker,*</u> beat boxer, door knockers, copers on the beat, **Beat Street** helicopters, **Wrong Side of the Tracks,** "I'm known for leaving token Blacks with broken backs and open caps", I will not lose **Mash out Posse**, "Rugged Never Smooth", "watch these rap niggers get all up in yo guts", "I got the flavor of the month", "most choose chocolate deluxe", "Ain't Nothing but a G Thang", **Garvism,** Army I Ching, "It's bigger than Hip Hop" The King of Pop screaming "They don't really care about us" auk, "911 is a joke on my block", Dawuuuud "got ya all in check", Bum stickady Bum stickady Bum they want **Das EFX, Mos Def**, **Nas**, <u>*Reflection Eternal*</u>, My train of thought might turn you to a revolutionary **- Dawud The Uncanny BlaKseed**

April 29th 2017 (Jordan Edwards and the total eclipse)

Iu f Per f m heru

Today is **January 6**th 2022 and today I came across information on the total solar eclipse that happened on **August 21st** 2017. I found that interesting because the **Haitian Revolution** was sparked on that day (Aug 21st 1791) as well as **Nat Turners insurrection** (Aug 21st 1831) and **Emmett Till** arrived in M**ississ**ippi on August 21st 1955. While I was looking into the significance of the total eclipse of 2017 I came across the murder of Jordan Edwards. I remembered his face an his story but I didn't know that Jordan Edwards was born on my birthday October 25th 2001 in the year of the **snake**. I was born on October 25th 1977 the year of the **snake**. After I looked over Jordan Edwards' story the name Jordan Davis rang in my head and I looked into his case as well. Then I saw that Jordan Davis was killed on November **23**rd 2012 the same day that Emmett Till's mother **Mamie Till** was born. After I was done writing about Jordan Davis I realized that today is **January 6**th and Mamie Till died on **January 6**th 2003 the year of the **goat**. Emmett was murdered in 1955 the year of the **goat**. On July 3rd 2018 my past life as Emmett would be revealed to me (page 480). Today has been a day of tears for me. ***Addendum* January 6th** is 12 days after the Winter Solstice (pages 489, 614). In the Christian religion **Jan 6** is the day that the 3 Magi visited Jesus in a manger. **Jan 6** is also the day that the ancient Kemetyu celebrated the Winter Solstice and **Tupac's** grand mother Eloise Maria Barnes was born on **Jan 6.**

The Murder of Jordan Edwards

Utterances for Coming Forth by day into Light

On April 29th 2017 a neighbor called the police to report a party where teens were drinking in Balch Springs, Texas, within the Dallas-Fort Worth metroplex. Officers were dispatched to the scene, where they found Jordan in a vehicle with other teenagers. An attorney representing the Edwards family told the news outlet that as the driver of the vehicle was exiting he went in the wrong direction and an officer said, "**This nigger doesn't know his fucking left from his right**." Officer **Roy** Oliver fired his rifle despite Jordan's reportedly being in a vehicle that was moving away from the officer. Initially, the department's police chief stated that the vehicle was moving towards Oliver. Jordan was shot in the back of the head while riding in the front passenger's seat of a vehicle driving away from officers that attempted to stop it. Jordan was unarmed and no weapons were found in the vehicle. Afterwards Jordan's brother was also handcuffed and taken into police custody. Oliver was fired from the department and arrested on May 5th 2017. Oliver was found guilty of murder on **August 28th** 2018, **the same day Emmett Till was murdered (Ausar** reigned for **28 years** and Emmett Till was murdered on **August 28th)**. On August 29th 2018, Oliver was sentenced to 15 years in prison. Jordan Edwards was only 15 years old. His family sued the officer, his department and the city of Balch Springs accusing the department of inadequately training the officer and ignoring warning signs that he was prone to erratic behavior but the Judge recommended Balch Springs be removed from the lawsuit filed by family of Jordan Edwards. It is unclear as to whether the family has seen a settlement for the murder of their son. Jordan was the son of Shaunkeyia Keyon Stephens and Odell Lavar Edwards, and he grew up with the companionship of seven brothers and sisters (Vidal, Kevon, Korrie, Kyleah, Kei'Morah, Fiston, and Vicktoriyah). He loved football just like I did. He played in Gentry Elementary School in Mesquite, and after enrolling at Mesquite High School, he became a proud member of the freshman football team, playing quarterback and receiver; he pushed himself persistently as an athlete, often giving up leisure activities to maintain his training regimen; understanding the importance of education, he devoted himself to his schoolwork as well and earned straight A's in his classes; after graduating, he hoped to continue his studies and his football career at the University of Alabama. Jordan was known for his positive attitude and the engaging smile that he often wore, Jordan was well liked by his teachers, his classmates, his coaches, and his fellow players; although football was his passion, his greatest joy came from his family and friends, and he always made an effort to ensure that others felt loved and included. He was a young man who demonstrated boundless drive and enthusiasm, Jordan Edwards also possessed a kind and gentle nature that touched the hearts of everyone around him, and his memory will forever be cherished by those who held him dear.

It is he, who comes forth by day into Light

<u>Condolences</u>

My condolences go out to the family of **Jordan Edwards** and all of those who have been robbed of their lives by this system of racism and white supremacy. Please know that death is not the end. The soul survives death, indeed and in spirit. This is a book of the dead written by a boy who was murdered without justice, who defeated death and came forth by day. May the soul of **Jordan Edwards** walk peacefully through the field of Reeds in Amenta. Amen RA.

April 2017 Suicide

The other day I saw a woman hanging out the window, hell'a stressed in a wedding dress smoking government indo, feeling the wind blow, she did go facebook live, her friends said no! they cried! she took a dive she survived in a coma in limbo, what she didn't know, is love comes and goes, highs and lows, if it ends there's a reason and a lesson for another season, I know it hurts but don't leave your family with a life time of grieving, you gotta know your worth you gotta be believing you birthed on this earth for a reason, the devil is a liar and deceiving, she woke up in the evening surrounded by flowers and family happy to be breathing, Please don't kill yourself, I want you to know that Dawud cares, hopelessness, loneliness and despair, takes so many lives and it's not fair

My favorite rapper told me <u>we gonna see some pain, but still we gotta smile,</u> so let me spark this flame, when your life turns dark then it starts to rain, and everything that was good starts to crumble to the sea, I know it's hard, it's hard to listen to positivity, even harder to be the change that you wanna see, and that's ok though, remember, the same weather that makes the egg hard softens the potato, sunshine blue sky's and tornados, fun times blue times red eyes crying at the table, this is your sign from the divine things gonna be fine don't make it fatal, you are able! Please don't kill yourself, I want you to know that Dawud cares, hopelessness, loneliness and despair takes so many lives and it's not fair **- Dawud The Uncanny BlaKseed**

Significance

I saw stories of people committing suicide and it caused me great sadness so I wrote this song. Life might seem hard and unbearable but you came here to complete your journey so complete it. If you have gotten this far in this book you should know that we come back here. I do not think we are supposed to give our lives up without a fight. We fought our way to the egg, We fought to push through the womb. Make your life count for the betterment of all people. Never give up!

May 8th 2017 - The Mic and Deja Vu

I was told that a better mic would make my vocals sound better so I went to Sam Ash on 34th street to look at mics. I looked around at a few and when my eyes settled one I pointed at it. A brother with locs named **Jerry** handed it to me and **as soon as I touched the mic** there was a **feeling of Deja Vu** that **shot threw** my body from my hand to my feet! **I purchased the mic immediately!** I knew I was supposed to buy it! 10 days later I would get my first Tattoo. I got the words **MAAT MAGIK** tatted across my belly like **Tupac**. It was a salute to him and the name of the album that I was recording. The next month on the day before Tupac's birthday the Tupac Biopic premiers. Just before I left to go see the movie I receive $776.50 from the brother **Miller** who I lent $800.00 to in 2009 (page 164). I felt like that was a good sign. He sort of paid me what I had paid for the Mic. When I went to the movie I would be hit with another sign. When Tupac finally get's his record deal and records his first song for his album he is rhyming over a mic that looks exactly like the one I'd purchased. I felt like Tupac had spoken to me! Three days later I would write another prophetic song titled **The Illustrious one** (page 449). 2016 had been my **Opening Of The Mouth Ceremony,** indeed and in spirit. In 2022 I experienced **Deja Vu** twice while in **Kemet** (pages 670 - 671).

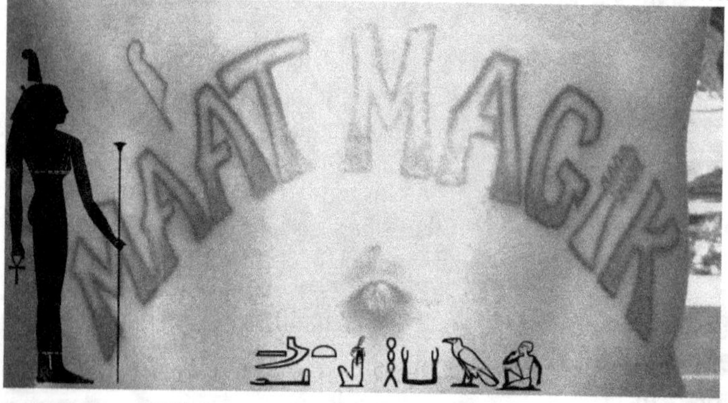

May 18th 2017 MY FIRST TATTOO, MAAT MAGIK

I rushed to get the tattoo but afterwards I regretted it. I loved what my tattoo said but I did not like the font! I would not post another picture of myself with my shirt off for 4 years. I was planning on releasing the album **Maat Magik** on December 25th 2017 so I got the name of the album tattooed across my stomach like Tupac had Thug Life. I never released that album but after my past life revelation of Emmett Till on July 3rd 2018 (page 480) I would feel like all the music I was writing had meaning. I felt like it was the voice of Emmett crying out from my soul so I had to make an album. I recorded an album and released it on July 25th 2019 (page 577). It was released on Emmett Till's birthday and I released it 1 year and **22** days after I had my revelation. At the time I did not know that Tutankhaten's tomb was discovered in 19**22**. In ancient Kemet Maat Magik would translate to **Heka Maat (, or). Heka** is the nTr of meaningful speech or magic and **Maat** is the nTr energy that holds creation together. Without Maat there is chaos. Maat governs the principles of truth, justice, cosmic order, moral righteousness, harmonious balance, and reciprocity. King Tut's throne name was Neb Kheperu Ra **Heka Maat.** **42 Laws of Maat, Page 367**

(Flag day May 18 1803)

Rau nu Prt m heru

June 14th 2017 Carnivore

I'm not a vegan or a vegetarian, if I'm anything I'm a breatharian, inhaling in what they can't see so they not measuring, circadian heavenly body **alien** ministry of love Orwellian, heart ailing em so they cartel'n em, triple bypass talking all that jazz selling them chemotherapy a bad remedy, the Doctor never been a friend to me, post traumatic stress helicopters must be the enemy, check the melody **2pacalypse Now** they feeling me never sell out the family, over stand me I'm uncanny I'm blessed, **Malcolm X**, Magneto, **Martin Luther**, Professor X put it in context, I bomb first you bomb next, ***visualize a spiritualized African pride, realized in this life not the next***, collect reparations advance reconnect pass go! can you hear me?! Van Gogh, give me the loot give me the dough, out for everything they owe, nepotism we can grow, BlaKseeds we reap what we sow, one small step for the debt, one giant leap for respect, write the check, don't be deaf dumb and blind cause where I'm from ignorance is a crime crime crime,

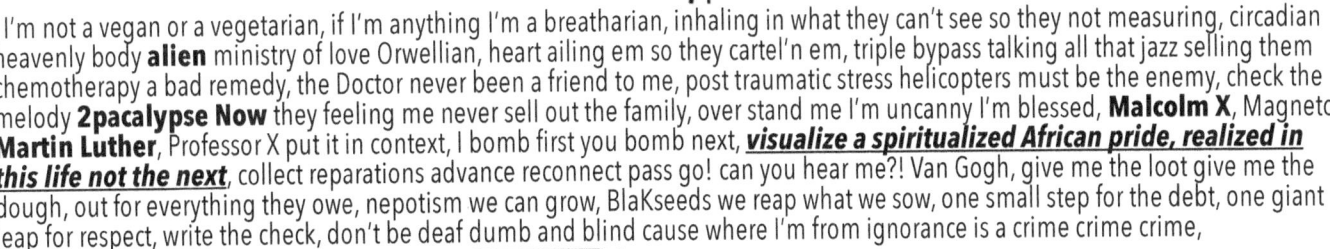

To the mothers and the fathers who don't care enough to know or believe, they be stressed from fear, they blow smoke in the air, the first laugh the first sneeze, the first cough disease, the mucus on the lungs from the air we breathe, the symbiotic relationship we share with trees, a two year old can't control their environment, they can't leave left to meet a slow death and die in it, connect the dots between asthma and breath we digest, I suggest you put the cigarettes to a rest, to an end, before your breath is gone with the wind, the sinner is you who will kill destroy the mineral through temptation of sensation, the strength of a nation is in the pre heaven essence during creation, upon delivery and arrival the baby is fighting for survival, don't be deaf dumb and blind cause where I'm from ignorance is a crime crime crime **- Dawud The Uncanny BlaKseed**

Iu f Per f m heru

June 15th 2017 All About You

I got a text from the next chick for Netflix and chill, but still I had this **Goddess** stuck on my mental, spilled her heart out couldn't erase with a pencil, written in stone like **Maat** on the **throne,** conversations felt like home, sounded like poems and looked like **love** at first sight, spiritually attracted magnetic sp**ark**ing matches flames the blackest d**ark**est electric fire remains, after the first kiss everything changed **The BlaKseed** plants seeds waiting for rain waters to fall, divine orders to call, drunk off **love** no alcohol, high off life like **love and basketball,** even in the **afterlife** our **love** survive it all, till the end of time **eternity**, I record it down in rhyme for our progeny and for the world to see, like **Ramoses** did for **Nefertari - Dawud The Uncanny BlaKseed**

42 Laws of Maat, Page 367

June 15th 2017
MILLER TIME +$800 7/7 Communication

Utterances for Coming Forth by day into Light

It is he, who comes forth by day into Light

On June 15th 2017 Jermaine Miller sent me a message asking for my back account information. He wanted to finally return the money he borrowed from me in 2009. I was hesitant to give him my account number because I didn't know if it was another scam. I asked him if he could send it via PayPal and he said yes. Shortly after he sent $776.50 to my PayPal account and on June 19th (**Juneteenth**) the money was in my account. I felt like that was a good sign because this was the same day I would go see the **Tupac Biopic.** Over the years I went through many financial hardships and every time I did I would think about the money I lent him and sometimes it would anger me greatly. It turns out that he sort of paid me what I had paid for the Mic I purchased two months prior on May 8th 2017 (page 447). When I went to the movie I would be hit with **another sign,** or message from the unseen as I watched the movie. When Tupac finally get's his record deal and records his first song for his album he is rhyming over a mic that looks exactly like the one I purchased on May 8th. The same mic that caused the feeling of **Deja Vu** to **run throughout** my entire body **as soon as I touched it!** I felt like **Tupac** had spoken to me! Three days later I would write another **prophetic** song titled **The Illustrious one** (page 449). 2016 had been my **Opening Of The Mouth Ceremony** indeed and in spirit. I have a theory about who Tupac was in a past life?. In 2022 I experienced **Deja Vu** twice while in **Kemet** (pages 670 - 671).

Significance

I have not seen Miller since I gave him the money in 2009 but we are friends on Instagram and I have nothing but good feelings towards him. He is currently a motivational speaker and has written the books, **Wake Up & Win** and **The Magic Power of your Inner Conversation**. Support this brother. The act of returning the **money** he owed another brother deserves another good turn in his direction. **Emmett Till** was murdered in **"Money"** Mis**siss**ippi! We must not let **money** divide us! He returned the **money** on **Juneteenth**, the oldest known date celebrating the commemoration of the end of slavery in the US. It is up to us brothers to unite on all accords. We must fix what is broken in our relationships. We must rebuild what once was and move forward to build what will be. It is **"Miller Time"**! Let's Wake Up & Win!

June 18th 2017 The Illustrious One

He sat in contemplation, in condemnation *like a **king** who left behind a conquered nation* with his thoughts on karma, her gentle words like well plucked flowers nectar, he respected her for years he prepared to be next to her, in his heart he protected her, she materialized in front of his eyes to his surprise she was spectacular, much you still must learn she said, *in your **past lives*** you were illustrious, romantic, infamous, famous, the *wretched of the earth,* so you **died tragic**, what you see as **magic** is divine order, you are the best you have ever been, in your **past life** *I was your daughte*r now I'm your protector, I came to offer insight on your **dreams** of **saucers** and serendipity, there's so much more left for you to see, like your great great grand mother standing next to me, there's no such thing as **coincidence** is all divine recipe, **sacred geometry**, like that song we wrote about mahogany, you're the best to ever do it if you knew it probably, half man half universal souljah, what if I told ya there's no weapon more dangerous than will, would you fly, be solar like **Heru**? he closed his eyes then he knew what he had to do, **he let his chi rise** and then he flew, who Dawud? **he let his chi rise** and then he flew, who Dawud? **- Dawud The Uncanny BlaKseed**

Significance

A year from now I will have my first past life revealed to me. On July 3rd 2018 (page 480) my past life of Emmett Till is revealed to me.. Then in 2020 my life as Tutankhaten (King Tut) is revealed to me on April 4th 2020 (page 594). I didn't have the slightest clue or idea that I lived in another life yet in this song I am speaking about **past lives**. What's more strange is the way that I speak about them. "*like a **king** who left behind a conquered nation*", is what I said. Tutankhaten (King Tut) was a king who left behind a conquered nation. "*in your **past lives*** you were illustrious, romantic, infamous, famous, the *wretched of the earth,* so you **died tragic",** the **Buddha** was the illustrious one, King Tut is **famous** and Emmett **died tragic** in the age of racism and white supremacy where dark people are seen as the **wretched of the earth.** This was written on the day that my great grandmother **Leacola Riddle** died. I didn't consciously plan this but life is a symphony speaking in **Riddles.** I'm TutemRa the infinite stuck in the middle of eternity, **Heh** infinity, returning the 3rd time trinity. Each life is a page and the world is your stage. I came back this time to write the book of a sage. Like a pearl on a necklace each life engraved. Like seeing your soulmate in a strangers gaze. In the blink of an eye we're gone turning the page. See page **602** for **transmigration of soul!!**

July 29th 2017
The Book Challenge

I am very serious about never getting caught in silly online social media viral challenges but on July 29th 2017 I would take part in the only social networking challenge that I ever took part in. **The Book Challenge** that was sparked by **Lord Jamar** from the legendary group **Brand Nubian** (p 342). In response to the many entertainers who were taking pictures of themselves with stacks of money next to their ears like cell phones, Lord Jamar took a picture with a stack of books next to his ear. The picture went viral and the book challenge was born. Many people began to copy what Lord Jamar had done. I found myself on 125th street, where I purchased the book, **Mentchu-Hotep Spirit Of The Madjay** from **Mfundishi Jhutyms** (page 233). Then I went to see my Brother **Nova** who vends across the street from the **Apollo,** and soon after we did the book challenge. We took pictures, made a video and posted it on Instagram. I had never heard of **Mentchu Hotep II** until I meant Mfundishi Jhutyms. **Mentchu** was the first Nswt Bity (pharaoh) of the 11th Dynasty in Kemet, during a time known as the Middle Kingdom (2060 - 2009 BC). He ascended the throne during a period when the northern Kemet was experiencing turmoil. Mentchu rallied to the north to unify the two lands, restoring balance (Maat) to Kemet.

August 14th 2017

The Haitian Revolution and my Associates Degree in Massage Therapy

By the time I got back to school for the last year I was starting to consider actually doing massage as a profession. Previously I had not really given it much thought. I had only gone to school for the money but along the way the idea of adding this to my skill set sounded nice (page 240). I graduated on **August 14th** the same day that they planned the **Haitian revolution** in 1791. The same day as **Mr Natures** birthday (page 281). The same day as **Amanda's** birthday (page 164). The same day as the **Dominican brother** named **Moses** who cuts hair on 145th street , who knows that the Haitians are his brothers and sisters.

Rau nu Prt m heru

Iu f Per f m heru

Utterances for Coming Forth by day into Light

New York College of Health Professions

hereby confers upon

Dawud Eddings

the degree of

Associate of Occupational Studies- Massage Therapy

together with all the rights, privileges, and honors appertaining thereunto

in consideration of the satisfactory completion of the prescribed studies and other requirements.

In Testimony Whereof, the seal of the College and signatures as authorized by the Board of Trustees are hereunto affixed in the city of Syosset in the state of New York in the United States of America,

the 14th day of August, in the year two thousand and seventeen.

Chairman, Board of Trustees

President

ADDENDUM **I'm not the smartest man. But I know what divine is.**

Forrest Gump is a movie I've watched multiple times with multiple years in between each viewing. And every time I've watched the movie I found more reasons to feel like my life was like the story of Forrest Gump. What fueled this feeling was all **the strange patterns I began to uncover (page 222) and all the coincidences I experienced over the course of my life**. Gump always found himself in advantageous positions and my life sort of mirrored that. The big difference of course was, Gump had become a millionaire and I had not yet struck my fortune. I always felt like I missed my chance at making millions with football when I left school (page 73) but I was still able to go to Germany and live out a lower level of success with football and even the way that happened seemed to be magical, as if the universe, or "God" was looking out for me (pages 82, 89,90). My life has been full of mysterious, magical and mostly unexplainable experiences. These experiences always made me feel, in a way, special, or important. My life being spared so many times further fueled this feeling of importance (pages 104 -106, 157 - 158). But these feelings would multiply in the next year when my past life as **Emmett Till** is revealed to me. And in 2020, the realization of my past life as **King Tut** would forever change my view of life and my purpose. While most of us waste our time chasing money and gold we forget that more gold has been mined from the souls of men than has ever been robbed from my tomb or dug up from a grave. Life is not about the acquisition of material possessions. **Life is about raysing ones consciousness, by living a disciplined life. By shaping and polishing ones personality while in a physical body so that the soul can become like gold.**

It is he, who comes forth by day into Light

2017
Urban Yoga Foundation ("I'll be there in the whirlwind" - Marcus Garvey)

I started going to **Sunseed's Gong** sessions in 2015 (p 326) shortly after **Freddie Grays** murder and the Baltimore Riots. By this time I'd gotten to know **Ghylian**, the owner of Urban Yoga Foundation where the gong sessions were held. One day she called me and before she could talk I assumed she was calling to follow up on her request to have me teach a Tai Chi Class there. I told her I was studying for the state board exams for massage therapy. I told her that the date on my degree for massage therapy was August 14th, the day that the **Haitian revolution** as planned back in 1791 (page 450). I told her that the ancestors were always speaking to me in dates. I told her that **Marcus Garvey** seemed to always come to me. His birthday would pop up everywhere in **coincidences**. Then she told me she was calling me to invite me to her birthday party and wanted me to recite a poem there.. Then she told me her birthday was **August 17th** the same day as Marcus Garvey's. I just started laughing. I went to her party and I recited a song but I totally messed the delivery up on it but no one seemed to notice.

2017 - Meta Spiritual Encounter, How I Came to Meet "Cosmos"

Rau nu Prt m heru

On August 16th 2017 I ordered the following books online, **African presence in early Asia**, The teachings of Don Juan , Lost Horizon: a novel and A Study of Numbers. Till this day I have yet to read any of these books cover to cover, however the first book I picked up was African presence in early Asia. I saw the book in a documentary I watched in 2014 titled, **The prophecy of Reincarnation**, **Sambho the Black Buddha** (page 288). I found the documentary **very** interesting so I purchased the book. When I first received the book I randomly opened the book to a paragraph on how yogis increased their vitality and psychic abilities by abstaining from sex. That was strange because I had recently gone on bouts of abstinence and had even abstained for 1 year and 7 months one time. I put the book down and went on with life and my "Quest". Later that month I would find myself walking home with the book **African presence in early Asia** in my hand. All of a sudden **I heard a voice in my head** that said "cross the street". So I did, I crossed to the other side of the street eventually I ended up walking on St Nicholas avenue. It was a nice day out so I decided to have a seat in the sun on a bench on 135th street. I opened the book and began to read… Shortly after, a man pushing a shopping cart with what looked to be trash inside of it, stops in front of me and began talking to me... At this point I don't know he's talking to me, I have my headphones on listening to instrumentals as I read but I can see him from my peripheral vision so I gave him my ATENtion. I looked at him and there he was smiling and talking to me. I took my headphones off, smile back and ask him to please repeat himself. He smiles again, looks at the feather in my head and says "My name is Cosmos whats yours"?. I said "I'm Dawud". He sits on the bench next to me and we talk for what seemed like hours.

Iu f Per f m heru

Cosmos would tell me of how he created all the things in his shopping cart and made them into spirals, like the Cosmos. He told me about his times living in the parks, sleeping in the parks and communicating with spirits. He recited a poem to me and it was one of the most profound pieces I ever heard. He told me he had not had **sex** in almost **10 years** and he felt like the abstinence increased his awareness and or "powers". I don't recall everything that we talked about because we talked about so many things but I remember being mesmerized by his poem. I remember his name, Cosmos. I remember him smiling very bright and he was not unhappy about not having a "home" to live in. I remember the junk that he turned into spirals. He was tapped into another view of life. I never saw Cosmos again but the book **African presence in early Asia** would strike again in 2020 during the Covid problem. The African Marital Arts Master **Kilindi Iyi** would make his transition On April 10th 2020. The very next day after I would pick up the book **African presence in early Asia** and randomly open to a page written by **Kilindi Iyi** (page 606). In 2021 I would have another profound experience with this book on October 7th 2021 while watching video footage of **The Great Arjuna's Penance / Descent of Ganges Relief at Mamallapuram and The Shore Temple** in India. This experience seemed to confirm a life I lived in India.

August 17th 2017 - I Shared My First Dream with an Angel

Utterances for Coming Forth by day into Light

I would meet Angelika on social networking. She is Greek and in her family she is the d**ark**est person. She is born on my youngest sisters birthday May 14th. She is a person that is into yoga and holistic healing as well as holistic eating. We developed a friendship as we began to interact with each others pages and chatting in the messenger, then later talking on the video conversations. One night before hanging up I asked her to **meet me in a dream**. She was the first woman that I ever asked to do this. The next day she would tell me that I came to her in her **dream** and I had a **bluish aura** around me. She said that she awoke from the **dream** with a feeling that was more powerful than any orgasm she ever had. I did not return from sleep with the memory of the dream. She would experience me in dreams more than 3 times. She said in the dreams I was in some sort of a **daze** and she would be **trying to wake me**. Two months later she would fly from London to New York to see me. While here we would shared another profound experience. For the first time we both had a very small piece of chocolate that had **magic mushroom** infused in it and later that night her face began to **shape shift** into the face of different women that I had been intimate with in my past, however one face would appear that I did not know yet still it seemed strangely familiar to me. I had a similar experience in 2013 with my friend Adrianna from massage school after smoking weed (page 282).

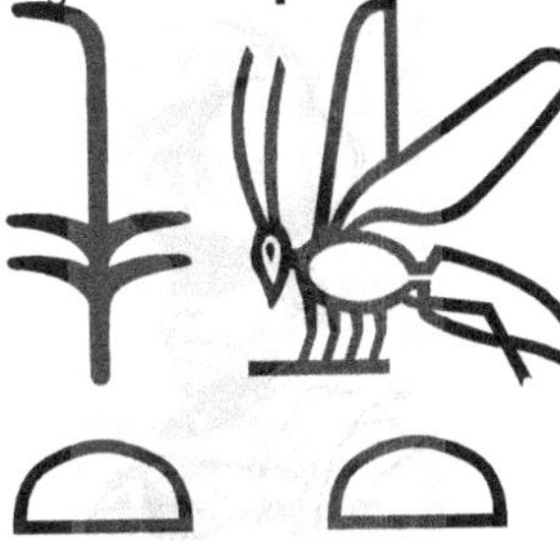

It is he, who comes forth by day into Light

Significance

I fell in love with Angelika and she just so happened to be fascinated with bumble bees. Perhaps she descends from the ancient Greek Etruscans. She was Greek from the island of Crete and one of the most famous legends of the Gods in Greek history is of 'Melissa', the **Goddess of the bees.** In ancient Kemet the Nswt Bity (Pharaoh) was symbolized as a **bee**. On April 4th 2020 (page 594) my past life as Tutankhaten (King Tut) would be revealed to me on the same day that **Martin Luther King** was assassinated (pages 69, 592). Our first shared dream happen on August 17th, **Marcus Garvey's** birthday. The experience inspired the song below. A couple years later I would have a more profound **shared dream** in 2020 (page , 589).

August 17th 2017 Angel

She said hit me, but you gotta hear me first, she spoke in **Greek** and sounded like some British folks, I kissed her lips, her hips then hit her where it hurts, she looked back at me and smiled and then she twerked, she liked it rough, hard hat, men at work, I'm up to bat fourth and long, based loaded, I struck a bomb, she exploded then took a nap, in fact she was **angelic** like a **angel**, a natural high she give you like a psychedelic, bliss not painful, she granted me a wish that came true, like a sage oracle she saw blue shine through my thoracicle

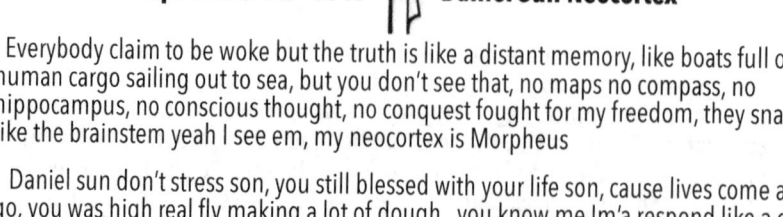

September 23rd 2017 **Daniel Sun Neocortex**

Everybody claim to be woke but the truth is like a distant memory, like boats full of human cargo sailing out to sea, but you don't see that, no maps no compass, no hippocampus, no conscious thought, no conquest fought for my freedom, they snakes like the brainstem yeah I see em, my neocortex is Morpheus

Daniel sun don't stress son, you still blessed with your life son, cause lives come and go, you was high real fly making a lot of dough, you know me Im'a respond like a don with a liver flow, I been good and been low but I been listening to the signs of nature, like when the wind blow, and it's been telling me, everything gonna be alright now I'm a better me, and look, you're a better you, I'm sure you learned what not to do and how to spot a fake one that's not really true, never judge a book by it's cover cause that's what fools do, I never blew up and got angry cause I knew this life would school you, I'm glad you made it to the bright side, brother your actions took me back to the life I lived, I crashed I survived, I listened to your speak and it hurt I cried, but I left it all in the Lords hands, and I'm glad you still stand above ground cause life is short no love lost fam **- Dawud The Uncanny BlaKseed**

See page **517** (Sep **23**.)

September 25th 2017 **Anthem**

Shame on you, shame on you, you not true, you not true, o say can you see through the lies? they brutalize, by the stars gallantly streaming, and so it's seeming that I'm dreaming this American **nightmare**, I see rockets in the air, the red glare, they dropped bombs everywhere, it's hell here like **Black Wall Street**, and that's the truth, not the lies that they speak, the Star Spangled-Banner, deception and deceit, after the perilous fight I shine light on slaves you keep, free **Mumia**, **Mutulua**, and all the political prisoners, my negus! it's time to get out of this bottomless **dream**! <u>it's time to **rise**</u> like **Ali** in the ring, ***<u>Lift Every Voice And Sing</u>***, a new day has begun, remember **Toussaint** and **Jean-Jacques Dessalines** we won, we won, we won, we won, we won, we won, we won, we won, shame on you, shame on you, you not true, you not true, o say can you see through the lies? they brutalize, by the stars gallantly streaming, and so it's seeming that I'm **dreaming** this American nightmare, I see rockets in the air, the red glare, they dropped bombs everywhere, it's hell here like **Black Wall Street** **- Dawud The Uncanny BlaKseed**

Tulsa Massacre 1921 (pages 404 - 415)

The year was 1921 and 3 years prior the 1919 "**red summer**" race and labor riots broke out in 26 cities across the country leading to the countless number of deaths of Black people and 6 years prior the movie **Birth of a Nation** had been released on February 8th 1915.. This movie would be the first movie ever shown at the **White House** on February 18th 1915. The movie showed scenes of a black man attacking a white woman and afterwards a mob of Ku Klux Klans members were seen lynching the Black man. President Woodrow Wilson, members of his family and his Cabinet attended the screening of the movie. This single **MOVIE** caused **Ku Klux Klan** (the white terrorist organization) to grow rapidly all across America. This is what set the stage for the Tulsa massacre and many other massacres like it that have been lost to the pages of his-story. The **Tulsa race massacre** started on May 31st and ended on *<u>my (Dawud Eddings) father's birthday</u>* June 1st, 1921, the **same year** my (**Emmett Till's**) mother (**Mamie Till**) was born.

October 7th 2017 Deception

They say Orange is the new Black, I guess they got warrants on a niggas cause I got new raps, for new jacks, I ain't never touched a gat that I couldn't shoot, execute with precision, free my brothers out the prisons then we go and free the women, it's time my niggas, cause ***this ain't live'n***! they don't want us **rise'n**, they don't want us **kneel'n**, but they be silent when it's us they kill'n, violent White man gun wilding kill women and children! Oh, he's just a lone wolf?! nah! don't believe the **deception**! the racism is the complexion for the protection, suppression of the people through the election, through your obsessions with fame, what is it that you ever gained? eternal reflections of pain, **Sandra Bland** say her name! the fans just want you to play the game, they just want things to stay the same, but I'm a hell razor, Abel like Cain, bad behavior, still the Lords favor covers me, spiritually I'm lovely, lyrically I'm lucky on rhyme with the time ugly, don't be reactionary, nah, be pro actionary, stay ready they can bury the revolutionary but not the revolution, I am the proletarian not the pig, ya dig? don't be reactionary, don't be reactionary, be pro actionary

Rau nu Prt m heru

Ain't nothing new under the **sun**, we still in the storm, Black women lead'n the criminal justice reform, this is a **new Jim Crow**, corn fields cotton sugar cane, blow, the forgotten locked down cause they don't want us to grow, fuck what they say though! the same weather make the egg hard soften the potato, *when I die **I'll be back*** in a tornado, **Marcus Garvey's,** in the hurricane with **Hussain Fatal**, it's true **Heru** sent you, don't wait for someone else to save you, pro actionary stay ready they can bury the revolutionary but not the revolution, I am the proletarian not the pig, ya dig? no ham-hock, give me that **soursop**, some figs like a vegetarian, I eat to live, and if you can't do it for yourself then do it for the kids, you know the wealth is in the health, what else, look what we did, we survived but we sleep'n and so they live, ***in the event of my demise,*** I devise a plan so we can live and not have to bury the revolutionary, don't be reactionary, nah, be pro actionary, stay ready they can bury the revolutionary but not the revolution, I am the proletarian not the pig, ya dig? don't be reactionary, don't be reactionary, be pro actionary **- Dawud The Uncanny BlaKseed**

Iu f Per f m heru

October 9th 2017 Cream Remix

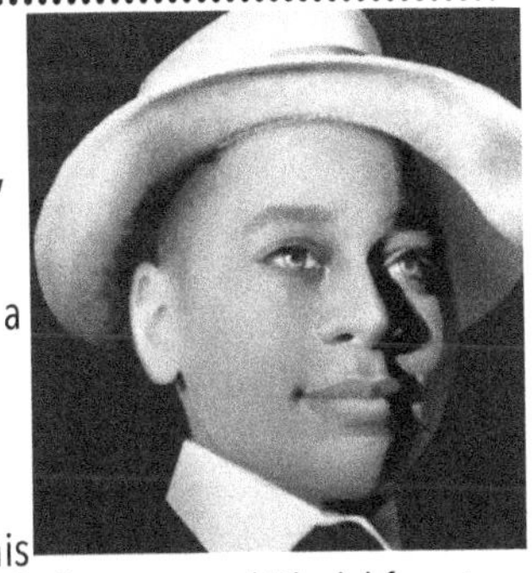

I never made it to the **NFL**, even though I was fast as hell, I had the will and the skills, **it ain't hard to tell,** gave my coach the finger left school bumping **TeK & Steele,** "**Cash rules everything**" but I ain't kissing ass for real, damn! four years later I'm in Iraqi killing fields, came back they still attacking cats like lil black **Emmett till,** they asked if I played with **kap**, then perhaps would I kneel, or would I stand like a coward for a deal? if you don't stand for something you fall for anything, on the road to fast cars and diamond rings, you think ball is life but ball ain't everything, it's enslavement! scared to make **Muhammad Ali** statements! fourth and long he threw the bomb, foul flagrant, touchdown! what now?! to the crowds amazement! man down, inside his head sound like percussions, they don't wanna have the discussion of these many concussions, he was rushing breaking tackles, he got hit on the blind side at high speed, the contact made his eyes bleed, no question, he tried to get the flow off and get the dough off, now he sticking up White boys on ball courts, and Black life gets no better, until we all measure our hearts and actions with the feather **- Dawud The Uncanny BlaKseed**

Meta Spiritual Significance

I wrote this on my Grandmothers birthday and I say Emmett Till's name again in a rhyme. 9 months later my life as Emmett is revealed to me on July 3rd 2018 (page 480). Kaepernick is Quarterback and I was a receiver. My favorite NFL team as a teen was the 49ers. Kaep wears number 7. I'm born in 77 and 7x7= 49. Kaepernick is born on November 3rd, the day before Tutankhaten's (King Tut's) tomb was discovered and I have my revelation of my life as Tutankhaten (King Tut) on April 4th 2020 (page 594). The active component within the sacred psychoactive DMT molecule is called **dimethyltryptamine**. The **pineal gland** (3rd eye), which is responsible for producing the DMT molecule, appears in the embryo at the **49th** day of gestation. DMT is secreted during birth (via the mother), upon death and during near death experiences. This book was brought forth in 2022, the **49th** anniversary of Hip Hop and **49** days is the amount of time the Tibetans believed it took one soul to be reborn into another life. I am the **alchemist** coded within Hip Hop (p 656). This is **Divine Alchemy** of the soul, the only alchemy that matters!. **Emmett Till** was murdererd in 19**55** and the San Francisco **49ers** have the most points by a team in a Super Bowl, with **55** points in Super Bowl XXIV versus the Broncos on January 28, 1990.

Utterances for Coming Forth by day into Light

It is he, who comes forth by day into Light

"They asked if I played with **kap**, then perhaps would I kneel?"

"came back they still attacking cats like lil black **Emmett till**"

"Damn! four years later I'm in Iraqi killing fields"

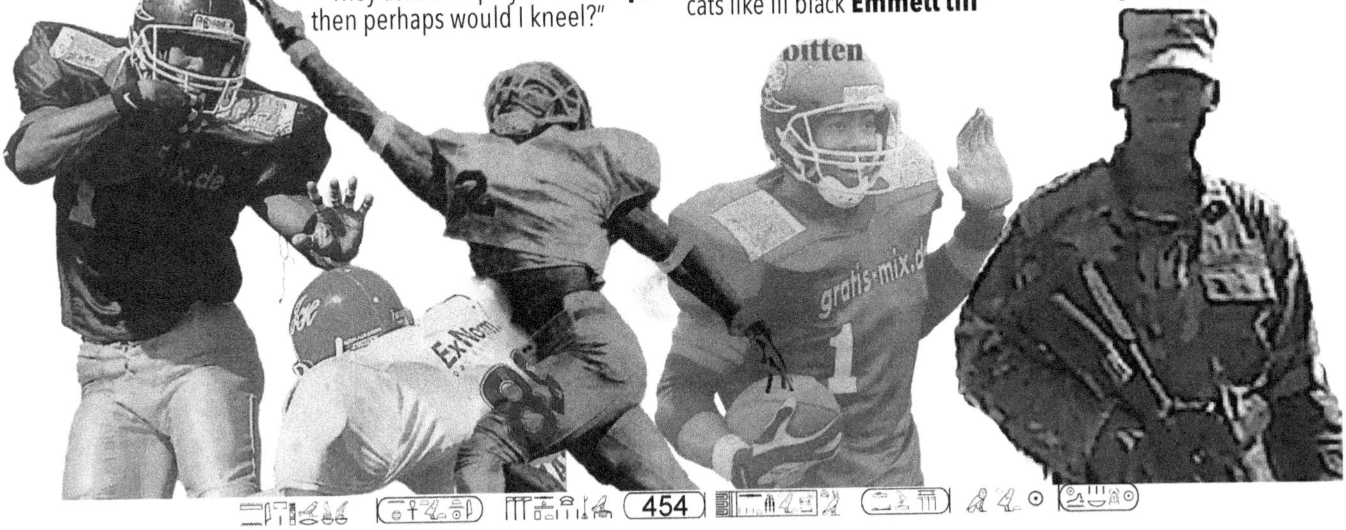

2017 November (La Juana and The SPAaaht)

I met La juana on August 6th 2016 (page 399) at the event with Dr Ford. After meeting her at this event we would cross paths with each other several times in Harlem by chance. **Or was it fate (page 271)?!!!?** The first day of operations at La Juana's Spa was Dec 3rd 2016 and I had already been experiencing a pattern with that date since Dec 3rd of 2014 (page 312, 314, 345, 431, 457, 519). La Juana's mothers name is **Juanita** and that's my **Grandmothers** name. When La Juana was 9 years old her mother had a miscarriage in 1977 the year of the snake, the same year I was born. The baby would have been a boy. When LaJuana and I met I felt like I could have possibly been the baby that miscarried. Her daughter shares the same name as one of my cousins. Her son has a different variation of the name **Ausar** (the Lord of **resurrection**). What ever the case may be I didn't need to look for a job. La Juana offered me a job at her Spa, The SPAaaht and as soon as I graduated I was working. It seemed like the universe was ordering my steps again. When I started working at the Spa La Juana made new business cards and had some made for me. I chose to use the name Dawud **Metta** on my business cards because while taking Thai Massage we learned to extend Metta to our clients which, meant to extend loving joy and kindness. Coincidentally La Juana was fascinated with a woman named Rose **Meta** Morgan. Rose was born August 9, 1912 in M**ississ**ippi and was raised in **Chicago**. **Emmett Louis Till** was born and raised in **Chicago** and murdered in M**ississ**ippi. Rose attended the Morris School of Beauty. After she styled Ethel Water's hair in 1938, the performer invited her to New York City. Rose Meta Morgan became the owner and operator of the largest beauty parlor for African American women. By 1946, the salon had 29 employees including stylists, **masseurs**, and nurses. A 1946 Ebony magazine article named it the "biggest negro beauty parlor in the world." Morgan founded Freedom National Bank, the only commercial bank for African Americans in New York. In 19**55**, she married the boxing legend Joe **Louis**, and in that same year her facility relocated and reopened under a new name, Rose Morgan's House of Beauty. La Juana's Spa is on the same block as Rose **Meta** Morgans House of Beauty and the first time we ran into each other in Harlem was in front of that building that used to house Rose Meta Morgans House of Beauty.

October 30th 2017 Simulation

Up early trapped in this simulation, thoughts become things like imagination, Lord of the rings, Saturn and rotation, the foundation of all healing, if the mind is willing to see past limitations, the separation of the mind **soul** and the body, illuminati got **Biggie Tupac** and **Prodigy,** there's gotta be another way out, probably a **hologram teleportation telepathy**, **realms** and **reality**, **dreams** of wars and **Moors** and **Haitians,** laws of gravity breaking, powers latent suppressed, vibrations deep in the chest, release with the breath, a journey, **A Tribe Called Quest,** never the less, backwards never, forward forever the test **- Dawud The Uncanny BlaKseed**

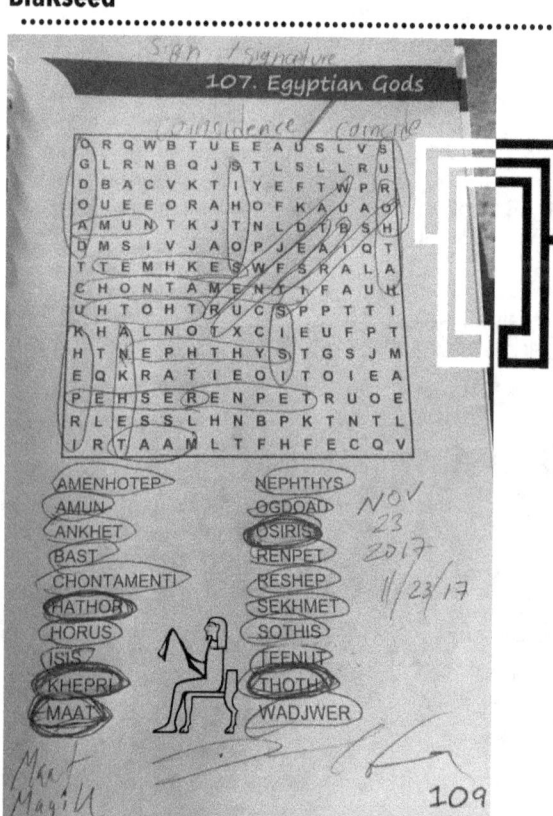

November 23rd 2017
Remarkable Coincidences
Leaving my Niece puzzled at the Crossroads

I had not seen my niece and nephew for a few years when I saw them for this Thanksgiving in ATL. On **Nov 23**rd my niece sat on the couch next to me with her crossword puzzle book. My sister drove a long distance to get to ATL so my niece had been doing the crossword puzzles to pass time. She handed the book to me and I opened it to a random page to see what type of puzzle it would be and I open to the only page that had **Egyptian Gods** on it. I laughed and showed it to my niece. I told her this was "**Maat Magik**" but she didn't understand why it was so funny to me. She had no idea I was being stalked by the "Egyptian Gods". I knew it was no coincidence! I didn't know what it all meant but I knew "something" was happening. I finished the crossed word puzzle then posted my experience on Instagram. **Nov 23**rd is **Mamie Till's** birthday (Emmett Till's mother) and only **3 days** before **King Tut's** tomb was opened on November 26th 1922 (page 11). 8 months later my past life as Emmett Till is revealed to me on July 3rd 2018 (page 480) and **3 years** later my past life as Tutankhaten (King Tut) is revealed to me on April 4th 2020 (page 594) the same day that Martin Luther King was assassinated (pages 69, 592). (See page **648** for the **metaphysical significance of the number 23**.)

42 Laws of Maat, Page 367

Rau nu Prt m heru

Iu f Per f m heru

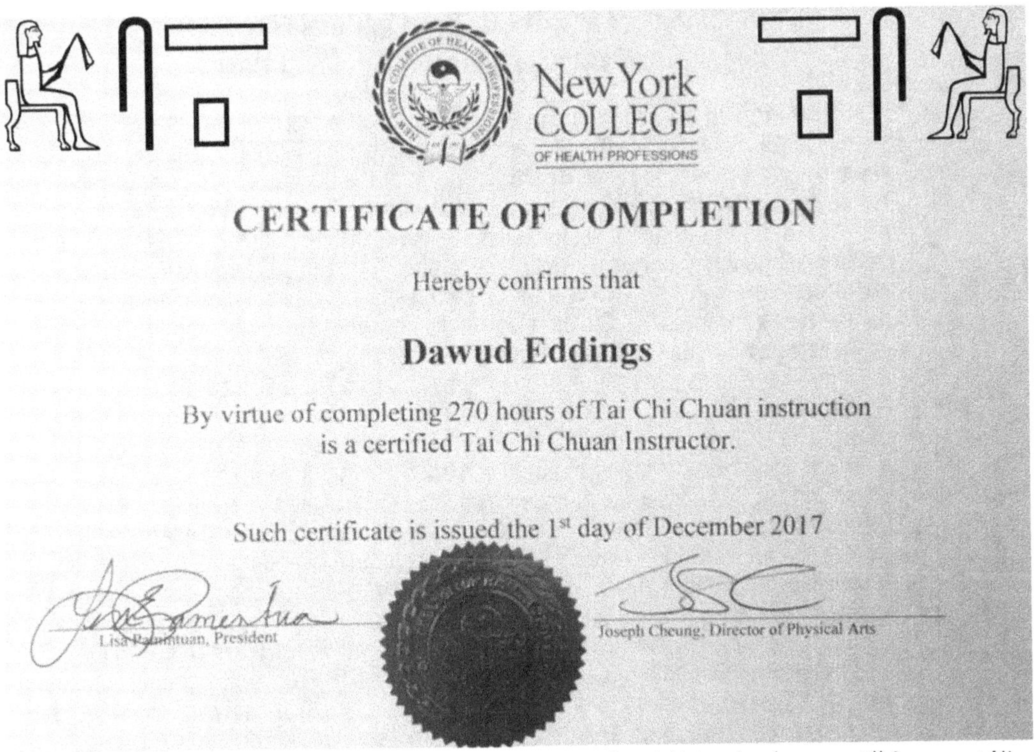
New York COLLEGE OF HEALTH PROFESSIONS

CERTIFICATE OF COMPLETION

Hereby confirms that

Dawud Eddings

By virtue of completing 270 hours of Tai Chi Chuan instruction is a certified Tai Chi Chuan Instructor.

Such certificate is issued the 1st day of December 2017

Lisa Pamintuan, President

Joseph Cheung, Director of Physical Arts

December 1st 2017

Certified Tai Chi Chuan Instructor (Rosa Parks)

Tai Chi was a major help with my mental health allowing me to release stress. I learned Cheng man-ch'ing 37 short form. Not many people have completed the Tai Chi instructors course at my school because it takes a lot of credit hours and time to learn all the forms. I always got along with my instructor until he made a **Nigger joke**. Joseph Cheung made a Nigger joke in one of our classes but I didn't laugh and I was the only person that corrected him. I don't remember the joke but I told him it wasn't funny and that it was not "Tai Chi". He had a small dark birthmark on his forearm the size of a penny and I told him that he was still 2 percent Nigger. He didn't laugh but I did. I met all my requirements and did not let that stop me from completing the course. Even though he never asked for forgiveness I forgave him. Joseph would always go on and on about how China had 5000 years of recorded history and I would tell him the first Chinese were black and that martial arts started in Africa. When I graduated it took me longer than I felt was necessary to receive my certificate of completion. Joseph kept giving me the run around. I didn't receive my certificate until I started reaching out to the president of the school. Finally I received my certificate in the mail and the date of completion was **December 1st** the same day that **Rosa Parks** refused to give her seat up to a racist White man on a bus in Alabama in 1955. Rosa had just come from a meeting where they discussed the lynching of **Emmett Till**. Rosa was sick and tired of being treated like a slave and did not care what the laws were! She did what was morally right. 7 months later my past life as Emmett Till is revealed to me on July 3rd 2018 (page 480). It was in this Tai Chi class that I met **Gu Rubee**, the celebrity bodyguard. I would let him hear my music when ever he made class.

December 2nd 2017 I'm Not Racist Remix

Utterances for Coming Forth by day into Light

It is he, who comes forth by day into Light

Yeah, I'm 40 years old, live in a one room shack, I sleep on the floor, still run a 4 4 flat, yeah I'm **racist,** how the fuck you like that?! I don't listen to **Crackers** cause most of them rape rap, and these rappers need to give Hip Hop back to the people, nah we ain't equal, watch what they teach you cause **White Lies Matter,** like **Elvis** and **Columbus,** but they see through! put them in the ring they can't beat you! on the field they can't match the skill, give her the **pill** and see all the Blacks they **kill**, **Kaep** kneeled but his brothers still stand for mills, yeah I get it, players got mouths to feed, or do they just got miles of greed? what ever happened to **Black Jack Johnson?** the Great White Hope, action Bronson, put his nuts on the table, blou! with a spiked bat, I'm'a teach these Crackers that they not Black, I'm'a bring **Prodigy** and **Tupac** back, **Maat Magik** I bring **Havoc** on the track, *I got you stuck off the realness*, you watch the news but the news is just the same ole shit, just another day, should I pray? law of attraction, should I watch what I say? it's a good day when the pigs role pass us, word to **Sean Bell** these cowards love to blast us, then they ask us about **racism,** they act like we don't know they attacking us, **AIDS** for America, **Ebola** for Africa, blood sucking Dracula they wanna ban my vernacular, it's all about extermination of the dominant gene, the prize so it seems, **Frances Cress Welsing** exposed the schemes, she tried, they fear white male inhalation from black male penetration, **Black Man Of The Nile** filed in mass incarceration, you focus on the effects and ignore the cause, you have no concern, today you gonna learn, look at all the wars, look at all the laws, you do all the killing! man, women and children! you the central villain of history! all you know is misery, we tried to teach you but all you could see was a mystery **- Dawud The Uncanny BlaKseed**

42 Laws of Maat, Page 367

FYI* - I don't run a 4.3 or a 4.4 40 yard dash any more but perhaps if I started sprinting again I could.

December 23rd 2017 A Better Me

I'm just working on improving me, everything else is the **mystery**, *my imprint my story my history*, for videos of **who I used to be**, everyday is a chance just to be a better me, eventually, stimulate you mentally, what does it take to be a real ill emcee? A black thought streams full of libations, black hawk seen in the sky, they try to eliminate my nation, so I'm chasing the source, the path is taken, the cross, the horse, that's never break'n the force, the journey, the course, the only way back, no mistaken just saying what comes to my mind, the Blakseed no half step'n, no fake'n keep it **Jamaican**, I'm preceding through time like a **Haitian**, what are you wait'n for? What they saw? bombs blaze'n! and rockets red glare, wasn't fair what God gave em, a nightmare haven, engaging, we right here! everyday struggle for life here, it's quite clear, a change gonna come, it's right there! it wont take a light year **- Dawud The Uncanny BlaKseed** (See page **648** for the **metaphysical significance of the number 23.**)

December 3rd 2017 - Meta Spiritual Encounters
The December 3rd theory, Dr. Jack Felder

Clinton Melton was murdered in broad daylight by a racist White man, on December 3RD 1955, only 3 months after Emmett was killed (page 519). On December 3rd 2017 I went to Jamaica Queens to see **Dr Umar** speak for the first time. While at the show I got the news that **Dr. Jack Felder** passed away. For the last 3 years **December 3rd** has been surrounded with the mysterious energy of music and death. In 2014 I found out that my homie **Jay Cooper** passed on December 3rd (page 312) and he would later visit me through the body of a five year old boy while at a holiday party of a female friend named **Nova*** (page 314). The baby boy had a new born sister who had just been born on **December 3rd** the same day that Cooper died. Cooper used to host teen summit on B.E.T. and he used to write rhymes for a hobby. In 2015 **Sean Price** from the group **Heltah Skeltah** died in his sleep on August 8th and later that year I went to a **Boot Camp Clik** show on December 3rd for their 20th anniversary celebration and on the itinerary Sean Price was being honored at **10**:**25**pm and I'm born on **10/25**/1977 (page 345). In 2016 I went to an event with Seana from massage school and I would meet a woman born on June 16th **Tupac's** birthday (page 431). The **December 3rd** pattern started in 2014 at **Nova's** house on December 17th and it ended in 2017 on **December 3rd** with the death of **Dr. Jack Felder,** the father of another friend named **Nova**. After leaving this event I would write Dr. Umar a song titled FDMG, and in the song I would quote Tupac's words "My only fear of death is **reincarnation**" in the second verse and I would talk about **Martin Luther King**. Dr. Umar would share the video for the song on his Instagram on January 25th 2018, ten days after Martin Luther King's birthday. On January 15th 2019 which is **Martin Luther King's birthday**, I would have a **dream** about Dr. Umar (page 550) and that dream would come to pass on **Malcolm X's birthday** May 19th 2019 at the annual pilgrimage to his grave site to honor his life (page 564). This was not just a coincidence! **The dead do speak from the other side**. While writing this book I came across the story of **Clinton Melton**, who was murdered in broad daylight by a racist White man, on Dec 3rd, only 3 months after **Emmett** was lynched (page 519).This was not just a coincidence! **The dead do speak from the other side**. Nova Felder is born on November 3rd the day before **Tutankhaten's** (**King Tut's)** tomb was discovered in 1922 and my female friend Nova is born on December 1st the day that **Rosa Parks** refused to give up her seat to a racist white men in 1955 Alabama because she was disgusted with the murder of **Emmett Till**. One time is an incidence, twice is a coincidence, but three, four, five is a pattern. Can you tell the difference?

Condolences

My condolences go out to the families of all those connected to this pattern of December 3rd. Please know that death is not the end. The soul survives death, indeed and in spirit. This is a book of the dead written by a boy who was murdered without justice, who defeated death and came forth by day. May the souls of my brothers **Clinton Melton, Jay Cooper**, **Sean Price**, **Tupac Shakur** and the honorable **Dr. Jack Felder** walk peacefully through the field of Reeds in Amenta. Amen Ra.

The December 3rd theory
The dead do speak from the other side.

December 12th 2017 Buddha

I stopped racing and that's when I won the race, I lost my mind and found it spinning in outer space, I had fallen out of grace with the cosmos, *Forgot that I was the flower the* ***Christ*** in this life that I chose, I suppose they know I rose through the cracks, the traps, **I'm Back like Buddha the blue black,** kick'n the truth to the young Black youth, I thought you knew that, my pin flow like water for fathers with daughters and mothers with sons that been slaughtered, they can kill us and bury us but we **The BlaKseeds,** so we'll be back maybe in the weeds like dandelions' I ain't lying, I be iron like lion mothers be crying, when they see their son shot down like **Orion,** I was crying when I got the scoop about my homie **Jay Coop,** rest in peace we lost as good man to say the least he was in the streets trying to save the kids from the beast and make peace will we ever have peace? - **Dawud The Uncanny BlaKseed**

2018 The Year of the Dog and My First Past Life

Rau nu Prt m heru

Enpu (**Anubis**) is the **dog** headed **NTCHRU** (God/deity) from Kemet who ushers the soul of the dead through the halls of **Maat** where he weighs their hearts against the feather of **Maat** - and one's heart must be lighter than the feather if they wish to enter **Amenta** (heaven) and dance in the field of **reeds** for eternity. Enpu had already come to me a few years prior hidden with in the fabric of the TV Series **Lost** but this year was different (page 259)! This year I would awaken to my first past life, my life as **Emmett Till**. Enpu had come to usher me to my life as Emmett Till. Then in 2020 my life as **Tutankhaten** (**King Tut**) would be revealed to me on April 4th 2020 (page 594) the same day that **Martin Luther King** was assassinated (pages 69, 592), right at the start of the **Covid Virus**. In 2021 I would have another experience with Enpu the "**Dog**" headed NTCHRU but this time it was connected to **DMX,** who is the "**DOG**" of Hip Hop! On April 9th 2021 the day that **DMX** (the dog) passed away I would have a profound experience with the spirit of DMX that brought me back to the series **Lost** (page 259).. On January 7th 2011 I mentioned DMX in a song that I wrote for **Michael Jackson** named <u>These many Roads</u>. Michael Jackson can be seen wearing King Tut's Throne name, Neb Kheperu Ra in several pictures and videos. In that same song I would say the name **King Tut** for the second time in my music. I met **DMX** in Harlem on 125th street a few years after I wrote that song. I was born on a Tuesday and Enpu governs Tuesdays. In 2018, the year of the **Dog** I would have my life as Emmett Till revealed to me on Tuesday, July 3rd after graduating as a kemetic (Egyptian) yoga instructor (page 480).

42 Laws of Maat, Page 367

These Many Roads

"and when I see **DMX** you know a prayer's gonna follow, cause what I see is my brother there fighting for his survival, the rifle back against the wall shit that I do, each one reach one teach one like the gospel, what you ain't got it? homie I spot you, yeah I got you! every other race look out for their own but we forgot to" **- (These many Roads**, written on Jan 7th 2011, page 195)

Iu f Per f m heru

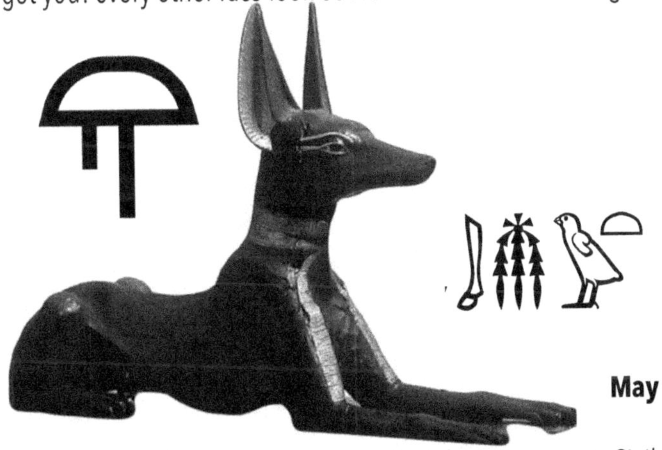

May 3rd 1963

On **May 3rd 1963,** Blacks are met with violent response to Civil Rights Protests in Birmingham, Alabama, which included the turning of fire hoses on thousands of schoolchildren and the infamous picture of a 17 year old Black Civil Rights demonstrator being attacked by a **POLICE DOG.**

Utterances for Coming Forth by day into Light

It is he, who comes forth by day into Light

The Mysterious Case of a Familiar Face Who's Owner Could Not Place

I'd stopped buying new clothes along time ago but when I came across the tee shirt company **RevolutionaryArtistry.com** on **Instagram** I purchased many of their tees. The company made tee's with the drawings of the faces of African ancestors on it. I was drawn to the images so **I bought several shirts**. **I know for sure** that I purchased the **Emmett Till tee shirt** the first time I purchased from the company. ***Addendum*** After the initial release of this book I found the e-mail receipts of all my purchases and realized that I made my first purchase on **Sep 19**, 2017, the same day that **Emmett Till's court trial** started (**Sep 19**, 19**55** p 516). I would eventually purchase other tee shirts with the images of **Malcolm X**, **Dr Khalid Muhammad**, **Muhammad Ali**, **Martin Luther King**, **Harriet Tubman**, **Tupac**, and the boxer **Jack Johnson**. ***My favorite shirt was the one with Emmett Till's image***. For some reason his story and his face was special to me. I liked the color of the shirt because it matched my favorite harem pants well. Eventually I purchased several more of the same Emmett Till tee shirts. I had no problem wearing the same shirt everyday and so I would wear this shirt very often but something strange seemed to happen when I wore the shirt with Emmett's face that didn't happen with any of the other shirts! People seemed to like the shirt for some reason even though most people had no idea who the boy on the shirt was. Well, neither did I really… On several occasions while wearing the Emmett Till shirt I was stopped by old black women and asked if I was the boy in the shirt. The first few times I smiled and politely said, **"No, it's Emmett Till"**. This would happen at least 3 or 4 times in 2018 before my life as Emmett is revealed on July 3. It was always an old black woman that asked me! The last time I was asked, I was a little annoyed but I smiled and said, **"No, it's Emmett Till"**. I was not disrespectful to the woman but I felt she was old enough to know who Emmett Till was. I had never looked at Emmett's face and my face together. In fact ever since the murder of **Tamir Rice** in 2014, when ever I saw **Tamir Rice** I thought of Emmett Till (page 307). When I had my **past life revelation** of Emmett Till I was wearing the shirt with Emmett's face on it looking at a picture of me wearing the shirt with Emmett's face on it. Like Alice in wonderland walking through the looking glass. It wasn't **till** 9 months later that I realized that I looked just like Emmett Till (p **555**). **See** pages 664, 665, & 626 to see who else looked through the looking glass! **"West Side"!**

Rau nu Prt m heru

First of all! the first lessons they should be taught at home, never let the enemy teach the progeny, that's like taking chrome to the head, when will they ever learn?! know the ledge, take your money make a pledge to **Frederick Douglass Marcus Garvey Academy,** those who don't suffer psychological casualty, self destruction disfunction a systematical strategy, *my seductive introduction be specific still elusive but exclusive what I give you when I kick it,* young gifted and black strictly, the system swinging wild but they style missed me, tried to save a black child sent to trial quickly, really in Philly nobody as clear as me, I ain't trying to help the feds catch a case for conspiracy, I was raised full of love to build a school full of healers, to insure young brothers don't become drug dealers, I tried to rise so they tried me, you know them Crackers fear the ghost of **Marcus Garvey,** that's why we gotta strategize on the way to profit, then organize with Black Pride so they can't stop it, then keep it pop'n, divide and conquer that's they protocol, don't trip don't fall, I'll be there when my homies call and then we ball

lu f Per f m heru

He saw it in a **dream,** on the mountain top, she gave him the scene of a better future, she said **Martin Luther** I'm gonna have to shoot ya, but your name's gonna ring and echo, it's gonna sting the heart and the mind of a young king foreseen to swing the divine death blow, he said let's go, I lay my life down for my Black Nation! **My Only Fear Of Death is Reincarnation,** we only 12% the population, only 1% the wealth, but 70% the troops sent to war for annihilation! you do the math yo self! I hold these truths to be self evident, America won't change not even with a black president, Black plague pestilence, Black flame White fire, Black excellence, **We Came Before Columbus** in great numbers, Black Exodus, seven wonders of the world none of the others stand next to us, I never trust a Cracker after listening to **Neely Fuller,** they master the law of money just to keep you poorer, they pull the trigger kill your daughter, White jury cop not guilty, Inner city schools filthy, Black boys led to the slaughter, they say he got **A.D.H.D,** he got ain't no daddy at home disorder, **Umar** we rolling for ya, if I tell you the truth it might shock ya, **Frederick Douglass Marcus Garvey** rolling proper **- Dawud The Uncanny BlaKseed**

Significance

Utterances for Coming Forth by day into Light

I wrote this after meeting Dr Umar for the first time on December 3rd 2017. I sent him the video and he posted it on his Instagram on January 25th 2018. I would have a prophetic **dream** about Dr Umar on Martin Luther King's birthday January 15th 2019 (page 550) and the **dream would come to fruition** on Malcolm X's birthday May 19th 2019 (page 564). Martin Luther King had a **dream** too. So did **Thutmose IV**, the Nswt Bity (Pharaoh) from the 18th dynasty. He had a **dream** about Heru Em Akhet (The Sphinx). When Thutmose IV awoke from the **dream** he **followed the dream** and unearthed the Sphinx that was buried beneath the sand (dreams, p 30). Thutmose IV and the story of Jospeh, from the bible come from the 18th Dynasty of Kemet where **Tutankhaten** (**King Tut**) was from. The ancient Kemetyu (Egyptians) paid attention to **dreams** and that is why **dreams** are part of my revelation! The next month on my Grand Fathers birthday June 17th 2019 (page, 568), I would meet **Coreisa Lee** and she would fulfill the **prophecy of the Renaissance Flute** (p, **44**) by blowing her flute on this song. In this song I say these words "**My Only Fear Of Death is Reincarnation**". In this song I used a lot of **Tupac** Quotes from his song "You Fuckin Wit the Wrong Nigga" and Coreisa blew the melody of that song over the beat for this song. Tupac is born the day before my Grand Fathers birthday and I would meet Coreisa on my Grand Fathers birthday. Today is March 15th 2022 and Coreisa contacted me today. She told me that she got a call to be a part of a new Emmett Till theater project named, **Emmett Till, A New American Opera**. One time is an incidence, twice is a **coincidence** but three, four and five that's a pattern - can you tell the difference?!

January 11th 2018 Peace Love

It is he, who comes forth by day into Light

This is not a farewell, this is a story of glory that you tell, to the underdog's who were born in hell, he said if I die tonight, it's a must that we continue the story, we must all rebel, Rebel! he fell, got too close to the edge of the **Hotel Theresa**, Fadel, bye **Felicia**, we haven't been speaking on the regular, things are complicated, we were intimate we never dated, we connected in a **dream,** she was seen with **King David,** unexpected paranormal, Soul projected in a realm, overwhelmed with emotion like a rollercotion or a motion film, look at the big screen, when the rhymes are real you feel them, you not a savage, just as your feelings you done seemingly conveniently conceal them, it takes practice to attract, this is my oath, if I had a religion it would be about love of course, the primary focus the source, the force that eludes many, the price of a **soul** that's a pretty penny, I remember Timmy used to bully me, **Cardi B,** titty at the Super Bowl, alcohol, "I go down town they say don't come around", and not at all! "*I was raised in this society, there's no way you can expect me to be a perfect person*", but got damn I'm trying to be **- Dawud The Uncanny BlaKseed**

"We connected in a **dream,** She was seen with **King David,** Unexpected paranormal, Soul projected"

February 16th 2018 Naima's dream

Dream

Naima would dream that I was doing well with my music and everyone was listening to my music.

Context

Naima is LaJuana's daughter, LaJuana is the woman I work with doing massage. I had come to feel like LaJuana was a soul sister of mine so I saw her family as an extension of my family. I saw Niama as sort of like a Niece. I bought two tickets to see Black Panther. The person that I wanted to take couldn't make it so some how I ended up taking Naima. Naima was 12 or 13 years old when I took her to see the movie **Black Panther.** I'm not sure whether Naima had this dream before or after we saw the Black Panther movie but it was around this time that she had the dream.

Significance

This dream took place on Feb 16, the same day that the final room of King Tut's Tomb was opened (Feb 16th 19**23**, page 11) and the same day **Tupac** released **Strictly 4 My N.I.G.G.A.Z... Zee** would have the same **dream** in July of this year (page 529). This book is a book of my spells (music, Heka Maat), dreams and other phenomena. My music is the sound track to my life and so it is also the sound track to this book. You are reading my musical spells (Heka) and I hope you are listening (p 6).

Bust of Nefertiti showing her African features.

February 11th 2018 COOLEST MONKEY IN THE JUNGLE (H&M Response)

The coolest monkey in the jungle, swing from tree to tree Ubuntu, confront you with virtue, humble still *sting like a bee, float like* the ***Black Star Line***, ***Nobel*** like **Dru *Ali***, we go and see the ***Black Panther*** but won't set the Black panthers free, **free Mumia** rest in peace and Black power to brother ***khalid***, they killed him on ***Huey P***'s birthday in the worst way, and it tears me apart in the heart, like **apartheid** the **medical** extermination of black people from colonial times to present, met a Black sister yesterday with the mind of a peasant, she said if she had BlaKseeds she would **vaccinate** them, unpleasant be my spirit when I hear it, another ***Black girl lost,*** won't go back to Africa even if you plotted her course, *I'm sorry miss Jackson,* you're just a queen they used as a pawn, you see they feared him in the physical form, like ***Tyson*** fight'n, the greatest weapon in the hands of the oppressor is the mind of the oppressed when it's gone, **white washing our stories the norm**, they bombed the face of he late ***Nefertiti*** live on tv I ring the alarm, I pray to ***Orisha*** to bring me a storm, "alone Apes weak but together the apes be strong", when will those great Blacks in those "**shit whole countries**" get along? they would hate that that's my word is born! **- Dawud The Amazing BlaKseed**

February 17th 2018 Black Panther

I watched them sell us **Wakanda** like they sold us **Obama**, then I wonder what really happened at Hotel **Rwanda**? it's like the snow fell upon us, this **ice age** that haunts us, and hunts us and wants us locked in a tight **cage**, like diorama the **human zoo**, the horror, they not brave, they **White** craze, full of white **rage**, yeah I'm a Black man saying something positive even though that ain't where I live, I do it for the Goddesses, and the God that's in my young G's ready to rebel, growing up on the crime side, two blocks from west hell, round the corner from south shit, ain't hard to tell we the gazelle in their cartel for profit, and they won't ever stop it, unless we make em, and shake em and take em to the hole like **Iverson**, **Paul Roberson**, if not they won it's over son, is that the story you wanna tell? or do you wanna excel and prevail like a parallel universe? Reverse the spell, reimburse, we the first on the earth so they can have **Wakanda**, we want **Egypt**, **Ghana**, **Botswana**, that's the answer to the question, free the Panthers no exceptions! When we stand tall the ancestors answer with the blessings, supernatural like **Hannibal** with weapons and lessons invaluable, the **Black Panther**, my spirit animal **- Dawud The Amazing BlaKseed**

March 4th 2018 Panther Pride

I be the Blakseed of the Black Panthers, the ones you forgot, the ones they shot! I'm searching for the answers, keys to the locks, it's time to free all the fathers, we need a fractions of the dollars they made from the Black Panther! The P that's for POWER, the A for ACTION, the N T cause NOW is the TIME to get it done, the H is for HEART and E for Effect and the R hold it down at the end for RESPECT, **Mos Def**initely I effortlessly come correct, with intellect from the **Nile Valley** to the projects, from the **slave fields** to **Wakanda**, if you feel'n **Huey P**, you feel'n Killmonger, and if you feel'n that my nigga scream **free Mumia**, **free Mutulu**, on the screen fighting like a **Zulu**, this ain't a **dream**, wake up, Get Out! Mr Voodoo, take you back to **Natural Elements** with juju, the excellence, the evidence, **Timbuktu** the elegance, **Hannibal** riding on elephants, ***when the ancestors on your side everything else is irrelevant!*** would you ride on your enemies?! **Nat Turner**! put aside all your penalties, pack a burner! to the detriment, to the death of it, if you ain't down you a punk or bitch! pump a fist, like **Harriet** I kill a clown ain't no sucker shit **- Dawud The Uncanny BlaKseed**

March 8th 2018 Wisdom Young Queen

She was a bad chick chasing for a ring, more concerned with modeling than being the real thing, she met a baller in the club had a fling, fathers with daughters but never taught em a thing about love, she was a analog girl in a digital world, full of drugs and alcohol, casting calls, highs and lows, bathroom stalls, withdrawals, anything goes when you trying to fly and not fall, blackout, wake up, crawl, cant remember anything at all, experience is the best teacher, wisdom we do acquire, she was lit on fire, searching for peace, the motivation of mens desire, this brought her nothing but grief and sorrow, ***"Keep Ya Head"*** Up young Queen, tomorrow brings ***"better days"***, She asked what weighs more on the scales - to Love or to be Loved? he said, you see the dove - what matters more the left wing or the right wing? the heart will be the judge, it's best that you always do the right thing, life is a struggle keep fighting, it might sting, it might bring heart ache sadness and pain, but from the ashes you become inflamed, a **Phoenix**, paint a path more scenic, close your eyes to see, then you **dream** it, then you live it, then you be it, never stop it, TILL you see it **- Dawud The Uncanny BlaKseed**

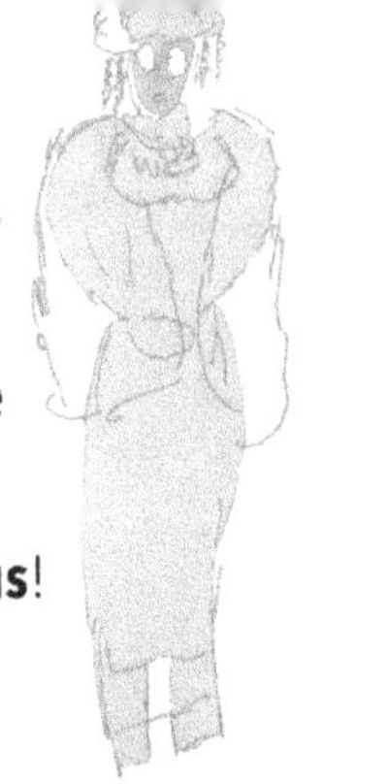

Rau nu Prt m heru

Iu f Per f m heru

Utterances for Coming Forth by day into Light

It is he, who comes forth by day into Light

March 10th 2018 **Bondage - Free Mumia!**

We teaching **pro Black** cause that be the antidote, wouldn't have to do it if you didn't have to throw that **anti-blacky** at me first! from the cradle to the grave, doctor to the nurse, first step to the first grade, **all black everything**! **ebony magazine** it was all a **dream** like **Wakanda** selling a billion, like the feeling of **Mumia** hugging his children with out dealing with the penitentiary……. we gonna all unify eventually! instantly in the blink of an eye! "Should we cry when the pope die?! My request! we should cry if they cried when we buried **Malcolm X**!" no regret not a threat that's a promise, I'm a vet I made a pledge to the dreads to keep it honest! what's next? paying homage to the death like **Harriet** going back for the lasts ones left in **bondage**! My **negus**! the last ones left! would you go back for the last ones left in **bondage**? **- Dawud The Amazing BlaKseed**

Significance

In December of 2018 I would come to know why I wrote about Harriet Tubman so many times.

March 11th 2018 **Black Queen**

It's like **sugar** got control of the God soul, **food** as a **weapon** the goal to put you in a hole, **food deserts** in the ghetto so we settle, heavy metals in the water, what she told the reporter, they sold her ancestors now they threaten to deport her, cause she won't let the vampire stick vaccines in her daughter, now they say she got some type of mental disorder, **auto immune** cause she fight it, she said you kill but water heals **rheumatoid arthritis**, I don't want your pills, my will be done the power of thought can heal my son, if nature don't make it she don't take it, she not the one, she like **turmeric**, and **ginger**, **Himalayan sea salt**, she train like a ninja, they called her the **She Hulk** cause she fought like a **Avenger** for her daughter to defend her, against the powers of the **A.M.A.** in the U.S.A. you could end up in a jail cell locked away just for trying to be healthy! **- Dawud The Uncanny BlaKseed**

March 12th 2018 **Context**

You might like my post, that don't mean that we got the same world view, you live'n life through the rear view, I'm live'n life like it's all a **DREAM**, you might read my text that don't mean you know what I mean, put everything in context, not everything is the way it seems, a guilty conscious has not compass, so busy worried bout reputation - what have you accomplished?! **- Dawud The Uncanny BlaKseed**

March 14th 2018 **Flavor in Your Ear (R.I.P Craig Mack)**

I got that brand new flavor for you ear, cause my people we not aware, it's like we blind to the facts, if we ain't dying from **Cancer** we dying from **heart attack**, no run it back! Nobodies' heart attacks them! We attack the heart with our **daily actions**, you see the food is the poison but you eat'n death like it's the latest fashion, I remember back when I lacked info, I couldn't help my kin folk, spiritually I was broke, ignorance is no joke, hope is important but so is water and breath'n, and knowing is better than believing, love will heal you faster than a doctor, most of them are deceive'n, they more concerned with a profit than they are with you breath'n, in search for a church and a prophet scream'n stop the adhesions and allegiance quote'n **Paul** and **Ephesians**, out of all your getting get understanding, know the cause and the reason, the planetary alignment, the changing of seasons, the seasonings in your food, cardiac muscle will improve with **Cayenne pepper** or **Turmeric**, you ain't sick, you **sugar** rich and you **thirsty**, another emcee buried in the dirt see and it hurts me, this that brand new flavor for your ear, the **Mercury,** this that brand new flavor for your ear, flavor for your ear, flavor for your ear,

We ain't poor we got poor habits, we never out down we out organized, we not wise with the Black **magic**, they never gave us nothing good all they did was be savage, they put drugs in the hood, we bought it, thought we was live'n lavish, we smoke we drank now our kids grow up asthmatics, when I becomes we, even illness is wellness that's illmatic, life is a beach when you practice what you preach, habits make the weak strong if what you eat'n cause'n damage man you won't manage to live long, to prolong life my advice from here on is transform from the savage to serenest, from the ashes to the Phoenix, from the leanest piece of meat to greenest leaf to increase in raising your vibration, thoughts are like radio sometimes you gotta change the station, operation gratitude, appreciation for every step, the inhalation of every breath, I'm stretching my diaphragm, moving to a higher plane, with the stars like a hexagon, this that brand new flavor for your ear, flavor for your ear, flavor for your ear - **Dawud The Uncanny BlaKseed**

March 18th 2018 **(Stephon clark 22yrs Sacramento California)**

Stephon was shot and killed by Sacramento police while standing in his grandmother's back yard. The police shot him more than 20 times claiming he had a gun but in his hand they only found a mobile phone. The district attorney declined to file criminal charges against the officers involved. The City awarded Stephon cl**ark**'s family a $2.4 million settlement.

Condolences

My condolences go out to the family **Stephon clark** and all of those who have been robbed of their life by this system of racism and white supremacy. Please know that death is not the end. The soul survives death, indeed and in spirit. This is a book of the dead written by a boy who was murdered without justice, who defeated death and came forth by day. May **Stephon clark** walk peacefully through the field of Reeds in Amenta. Amen Ra

March 18th 2018 *ADDENDUM*

Sungazing - Sun - Aten - Endocrinology - Pine - Fire

March 22nd 2018

Motherless Brooklyn, The Fire and The Spaaaht

During the last night of filming for the movie *Motherless Brooklyn* the set caught **fire** in a brownstone on 149th and St Nicholas. Unfortunately a fire fighter died in the blaze and we were put out of business for 1 year and 7 months. The next month I would follow the signs that led me to sign up for the **Kemetic Yoga** Instructors course which would open the door for my first past life revelation.

I was in the Spaaaht the night of the fire. I was being paid to keep the space open so that the cast and crew could use our bathroom since we were next door to the Brownstone they were using for filming. The **strange** thing about the fire is how fast the **Jewish Fire Department** arrived to the scene. I find that strange because a few weeks before the fire I can vividly remember seeing a **Hasidic Jewish man** dressed in all black with a black top hat, walk pass the Spaaaht 3 times while looking Inside of our space. He walked north, then came back seconds later walking south, then seconds later he walked north again all while looking into our space. I thought he was going to come in for a massage but he never did. However, a few days later another Hasidic Jewish man came in for a massage. He tipped me $100 and I never saw him again. A few days later, on the last night of filming for the movie **Motherless Brooklyn**, the set caught fire in **Harlem** and the fire took the life of a fire fighter leaving a family **husbandless** and **fatherless**. It left some people **homeless** and it caused the spa I worked at to close due to water damage. **Alec Baldwin** was in that movie and unfortunately Alec has just seemingly fatally shot a fellow actor by mistake while on **set** filming a **Western** movie.

Almost a month from this day I will start my Kemetic Yoga instructors course. I would for the first time apply the principles of Yoga to my everyday life. I had purchased books in the past but had not practiced what I saw or read in my daily routine. I spent a long time absorbing information and I slowly applied some things here and there. I procrastinated sometimes but I always followed a sign. The universe knew that I was good for spotting a glitch in the cosmic akashic **matrix** connecting the star codes.

The kemetic Yoga course appeared right after the fire burned us out and all the dates of the course were significant to me. There was a glitch in the **matrix**! 8 classes, 8 hrs a classes to be done in 4 weekends. 6 of the 8 days were significant to me. April 21st and 22nd didn't get my attention but all the rest did. May 19 was **Malcolm X's** birthday, May 20th was **Toussaint Louverture** birthday, June 16th was **Tupac's** birthday, June 17th was my **Grandfathers** birthday, June 30th was my friend **Cherri's** birthday and July 1st is her sister **Javet's** birthday. At the time of the course I did not know that **Bobby Hutton** was born on April 21st or that he was murdered only two days after Martin Luther King was assassinated but I do now and so do you. But will you remember Bobby Hutton? Will you remember Malcolm? Will you remember Toussaint? Will you remember Tupac? Will you remember General Dukes? Will you remember Cherri? Will you remember Javet? Will you remember Me? I graduated on Javet's birthday. She is a special friend of mine that I have known since my adolescence. **Detroit Red** used to work a few doors down from where I worked at Jimmys Chicken Shack before he became **Malcolm X**.

April 1st 2018 - Kemetic Yoga Course

Following The Signs and Rising Through The Ashes of The Fire Like The Phoenix

I came across the **Kemetic Yoga** course via Instagram, it stated: "Become a Kemetic Yoga instructor at Kemetic Yoga Skills with **Yirser** Hotep". It was 4 weekends of training with 8 hour classes each day. It didn't take me long to make my decision. The course cost $2,500, and there was my lucky number **25**. Then the dates for the classes seemed to speak to me - April 21st and 22nd, May 19th and 20th, June 16th and 17th, then June 30th and July 1st. I did not find significance with the dates in April but **Malcolm X** was born on May 19th, **Toussaint Louverture** was born on May 20th, **Tupac** was born on June 16th, my **Grand Father** was born on June 17th, my friends **Cherri** and **Javet** were born on June 30th and July 1st. I knew this was a **sign**! I **sign**ed up for the course immediately. At the time of the course I did not know that the name **Yirser** was the same as **Ausar** (Osiris), the Lord of **resurrection**. I was also unaware that the **logo** of the course was an image taken from the **Throne** chair of **Tutankhaten** (**see page 472!**). A table was being set for me and all the ancestors were in attendance - Malcolm, Toussaint, Tupac, my Grand Father and even Bobby Hutton. In preparation for the course I purchased a few yoga books from **Muata Ashby**. **Re-member** that **you** are **Ausar** and **Heru**, the **hero**! See page 3 for the **hero's journey**!

Rau nu Prt m heru

Iu f Per f m heru

Utterances for Coming Forth by day into Light

It is he, who comes forth by day into Light

April 4th 2018 Out of Darkness

We got a raw deal but the government stay paid, can't collect rain water, can't sell lemonade, stuck in a prison of fear and it's well made, bad **grades** you **fail**, don't **obey** you go to **jail**, if you ain't **saved** then you go to **hell**, but **Jesus** loves you! and **Muhammad** is the messenger! if the people knew the truth they might rebel like the secular **pagans** waging for war over **the pre-birth existence of the soul reincarnating,** rolling on the **karmic wheels** of **future lives** and many wives, the 7 seals pathetic redirect full of lies, but I stay Gucci, is it **Lucy**? is it the crucifixion? or is it the "fiction" of the "cruci"? my prediction less **molestation** if they let them **popes** get some pussy, don't persecute me I saw it in a **dream** like **Juicy**, a battle field **Martin Luther King** killed **Constantine,** "*Screaming Let Freedom Ring*" from the top of the hill, "*Cream, dollar dollar bill y'all*", if you wanna be free they might try to kill y'all, it's gonna be what it's gonna be! they say the good die young, they kill us live on tv, I'd be a fool to give up my gun when they riding on me, emphatically non cipher! to decipher my poetry when you hear **The BlaKseed** then you know it's me **- Dawud The Uncanny BlaKseed**

Significance

3 months before my past life revelation of **Emmett Till** I wrote this song and in it I am speaking about **reincarnation**. This Prophecy of Reincarnation was gaining momentum but I had no earthly idea. It was beginning to rise up from the mud of my imperfections like the **lotus flower** rises around 5 am greeting the sun (Kheper Ra), the morning star. Heru was about to return to avenge all of his fathers. I speak of **Martin** in this song and he is the one that will champion the Civil Rights Movement sparked by the **courageous** acts of **Mamie Till Bradley** and **Rosa Parks** after the murder of **Emmett Till**. I wrote this on April 4th the same day that Martin was assassinated in 1968 and on this same day in 2020 my past life of **Tutankhaten** (**King Tut**) will be revealed to me. I mentioned Constantine because we need to study the roots of all the religions that we practice. Dr. Martin Luther king wrote a paper on the ancient Kemetic (Egyptian) Ausarian resurrection's influence on Christianity in 1949. My daily practice of **Kemetic yoga**, **fasting** and applying the principles of **Maat** to my daily life is what allowed me to realize this Prophecy of Reincarnation. We must restore Maat! **Dr. Martin Luther King Spoke on Ancient Egyptian Influence On Christianity,** "The Egyptian mysteries of Isis and Osiris exerted considerable influence upon early Christianity. These two great Egyptian deities, whose worship passed into Europe, were revered not only in Rome but in many other centers where Christian communities were growing up. **Osiris** and **Isis**, so the legend runs, were at one and the same time, brother and sister, husband and wife; but **Osiris** was murdered, his coffined body being thrown into the Nile, and shortly afterwards the widowed and exiled Isis gave birth to a son, **Horus**. Meanwhile the coffin was washed up on the Syrian coast, and became miraculously lodged in the trunk of a tree. This tree afterwards chanced to be cut down and made into a pillar in the palace at Byblos, and there **Isis** at length found it. After recovering **Osiris**' dismembered body, **Isis** restored him to life and installed him as King in the nether world; meanwhile Horus, having grown to manhood, reigned on earth, later becoming the third person of this great Egyptian trinity." **– Dr. Martin Luther King Jr. 1949 – Re-member** that **you** are **Osiris** and **Horus,** the **hero!** See page 3 for the **hero's journey!**

42 Laws of Maat, Page 367

42 Laws of Maat, Page 367

April 7th 2018 Good Friday

Every time I turn around I see "**Fuck Cancer** ", **Cancer** ain't fucking around if "you ain't got the answer **Sway**", my ***Aunt passed away*** a week ago on ***Good Friday***, they probably try to say everything happens for a reason, but that I'm not believing, I'm a non believer cause I be reading and I be knowing, the **CDC** and the **FDA** is about the cash flowing, they wanna keep you owing and showing up to appointments, no healing ointments allocated to insure you never find the cure, like **Ayurvedic** remedies, it's hard to see the enemy, everybody claim to be woke but you gotta go to sleep to see, like the stories of the pharisees, the fall of man what a tragedy, I see you smoking trees but that's a hazard, H 2 0 oxygen therapies, **Malcolm** said "if we don't think out the box we easily contained", like those felonies they gave us back in the 70's, we need better recipes and reciprocity, reclaim my legacy **Maat** philosophy**, Check The Melody** of **Imhotep** not **Hypocrites**, He's a hypocrite like **Socrates**, megalithic prehistoric when they saw it they dropped to their knees begging please can we teach them, and we did, now **we sleep**ing and **they live**, now **we sleep** and **they live - Dawud The Amazing BlaKseed**

Dream Premonition

I didn't know my aunt Florence well. I only met her a hand full of times. Before she passed my father had a **dream** that he would be taking care of her then shortly after that she got sick and he was one of the people taking care of her. When my aunt was dying from cancer she did not have strength to get out of the bed. I went to her house and massaged her. After I was done she got up and walked around with out the use of her cane. I showed her daughter (my cousin) how to do the techniques I did but unfortunately my aunt wasn't able to defeat the cancer in her body. She passed away on Good Friday, April 7th 2018.

Condolences

Please know that death is not the end. The soul survives death, indeed and in spirit. This is a book of the dead written by a boy who was murdered without justice, who defeated death and came forth by day. May the soul of my aunt **Florence Eddings** walk peacefully through the field of Reeds in Amenta. Amen Ra.

April 11th 2018 Your Preachers Keep Us

Your secrets teach us what is to be human, your preachers keep us illuminated, while keeping the humans sedated, the data transmitted stolen like the trans Atlantic flowing, you fell asleep woke up never knowing what we owing, the hate we gave and the hate that we keep showing, we gave you **Jesus** and **Jesus Christ** that saved our life! we come in the night like **sleep paralysis** attacking the thalamus took your DNA from your urinalysis, we take your heart then your hope, leave you on dialysis, if you were smart this would evoke some type of analysis **- Dawud The Amazing BlaKseed**

April 15th 2018 Application

They say knowledge is power, and if you wanna plan for a year then plant a flower, and if you wanna entertain plan for an hour, **but if you want change, take our young black youth and turn them to scholars!** with great comes great responsibility, it's our job when teach'n our progeny, I know times are hard but while you pray'n for God I'll be work'n hard, cause application is the key nothing worth have'n comes easily **- Dawud The Amazing BlaKseed**

April 17th 2018 Ancient Futuristic

I take a deep breath all alone, all them fake homies gone, now I'm on my own once again like in the womb, I'm in my room, wake up and see the Sun, the Sa Ra, the Sun of God, I'm not your negro my posture be like **Heru** the **hero,** take notice, **A Change Gonna Come** like **Ottis,** on my pillow in the **Lotus,** out for everything they owe us, every revolutionary you bury strengthens our focus, I wrote this for sisters and brothers out here feeling hopeless, **Islam, Christian ,Quran** the **Bible, Bhagavad Gita** the teachers the idols, the rivals, a disciple's rifle pointed out the window homicidal, his title "**By any means necessary"** to end this cycle, they don't love you they don't like you, "**The price of freedom is death**" B, like **Prince** and **Michael,** this is survival, **the life after death revival,** the vital minerals, the elements spring from **Genesis** to **Exodus**, let us make man, supreme it seem so effortless, no big deal, **Khnum** fashioning man on a potters wheel, with the **ka** the **spirit**, it's mine it's mine "**Who's world is it**", let thy will be done! this world is yours it's your life now live it! **You the *Christ now gifted and elevated***, mystic you meditated, **Ancient Futuristic Premeditated,** They carbon date it but can't duplicate it, so they copy sloppy like Roman **arc**hes, Kill a bee and see the whole hive! no rally's and no m**arc**hes! that's real unity! our enemies be so heartless! eulogies funeral fees families dying in hospice toxic hospitals despicable smooth criminal, optical illusion in collision political, "**I pity the fool**" finishing school thinking you know it all, young enough to go to war but not old enough to drink the alcohol! that's poison! like **Boyce Watson** dropping rumors about **Umar Johnson,** watch your voice son and watch who's rejoice'n, **Destruction Of A Nation,** time to have the conversation, what does it profit brothers fighting each other but not for reparations?! it's been my observation during our segregation things were better we came together like **NTCHRS** more cooperation, **Auset** be the asset, **Ausar** be the star like the constellation, standing ovation my confirmation **- Dawud The Uncanny BlaKseed**

Meta Spiritual Significance

In this Heka (song) I say these words: **"**this is survival, **the life after death revival**" and 4 days after writing this rhyme I would start a Kemetic Yoga course and unwittingly at the same time I would set the stage for another level of an initiation that I had no idea I was in the process of undergoing. I would also say the words: "my posture be like **Heru** the **Hero**". I would go on to say: **"You the *Christ now gifted and elevated***, mystic you meditated, **Ancient Futuristic Premeditated",** as if I somehow knew what was going to happen to me in less than 3 months. The **Christ** is liken to **Jesus** and Jesus is the son of God that **returns** after death. In the bible it is written that Jesus said: "all these things I have done so will you do and even greater deeds will you do". The story of Jesus comes from the Kemetic Ausarian drama of **resurrection**. In ancient Kemet we knew about the repetition of the soul **reincarnating** and less than 3 moons later I would also know about the repetition of the soul **reincarnating.** In less than 3 moons I would experience a profound Hero's jouney… **Re-member** that **you** are **Ausar** and **Heru,** the **hero!** See page 3 for the **hero's journey**!

April 21st 2018 (The first day of the Yoga course)

I can remember the first day and the feeling of being around other like minds. La Juana from The Spaaaht joined me at this course and to my surprise I would see Ghylian from Urban Yoga Foundation (p 451) attending this course as well. The course was rarely given in NYC so we were all taking this opportunity while we had it. The class was mostly women but we were told that our class had an unusually high number of males - which was around 7 or 8. One of the brothers had actually gone to high school with my younger sister Tahira, his name was **KhebHu** (p 468). After the first day of class some of us went to eat at Seasoned Vegan (p 364) with our instructor Yirser Hotep. Afterwards we talked for hours about Kemetic Yoga and the philosophy behind the teachings. I was having a good time being around like minded people. I had no idea what this course would awaken inside of me.

Rau nu Prt m heru

Iu f Per f m heru

Utterances for Coming Forth by day into Light

It is he, who comes forth by day into Light

April 22nd 2018 The Crown

Some say it's time for retribution, some pray on Sunday's for a peaceful resolution, war crimes **rosicrucians** searching for the father, stolen booty jewelry, daughters taken shahada's, the beauty the treasure, the measure of a man, what's done once they put that gun in his hand, they stormed the citadel then they took the crown, raped women and children, shot men left them laying on the ground, facts! I ain't pro black, I'm profound, more brown if I'm a color I'm light, write like **Jehuti** sound, ***divine like what they find underground in the holy land***, some say man is mind but mankind is blind, like a pentagram I shine in the d**ark**ness, showing you the crimes of the winter man cause they be the heartless eating the carcass, "get your hand out my pocket", look where they dropping the rockets, for the profits! make your blood boil, shoot you for your oil, caduceus coil the spoils of war, the **futuristic hieroglyphic** shit they never saw, made history a mystery didn't see the metaphor, trickery misery they are the lot, they saw the **Snake** but not the **door** so they didn't knock, they kick rocks and become **cops** and take shots, but they not the chosen "Who got the props"? Some say it's time for retribution, some pray on Sundays for a peaceful resolution, Some say it's time for retribution, some pray on Sundays for a peaceful resolution

They don't want us speaking, they don't want us reaching **self mastery**, divide and conquer, the law of attraction, separation boundaries distractions, we pay to live transactions, a peoples farm addicted, like **Michael Jackson** tried to *heal the world* with compassion, they killed a girl she was only asking what's the infraction, you could be team captain if you take a knee they bring the assassins, they shape and fashion the minds of the dumb deaf and blind every time, it's game time so they watching and eating they rotten, they're swap'n their freedom just to see them boxing, a fox in a hen house now you boxed in, **Get Out** the box when you start opting out their options, auction blocks men sold for stocks when **The Star Spangled Banner** angled the doctrine, **Who got the props** when cream of the crop kin sold for adoption? take caution and hearken, tread lightly, toxins in the water in order to expedite me to my slaughter, I build bridges of love while they build borders, **laws are the walls to keep us down** not to support us, never taught us about the torture or war crimes from **King Author** to **Abraham** God damn they all lying, **I am that I am** like the sun **Orion**, and in the end I'll be iron like lion in Zion, Some say it's time for retribution, some pray on Sundays for a peaceful resolution, Some say it's time for retribution, some pray on Sundays for a peaceful resolution **- Dawud The Amazing BlaKseed**

Significance

I started writing this rhyme just before I started the second day of Kemetic Yoga class. I remember having to stop writing so I could get myself ready for class as to not be late. The next day I would start a **20 day water fast**.

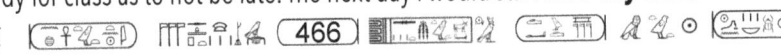

Prior to this fast I had never done any other type of fast that I can remember. Our instructor Yirser suggested a juice fast while attending the course but after the second day of class **I was struck with the thought** of doing a **40 day water fast**. I had read and heard so much about the benefits of fasting that I felt this was the perfect time to attempt one. I was searching for a profound experience of some sort. **Perhaps there was a natural chemical, molecular, hormonal elixir of life that could occur within the body if we gave the temple a cleanse or detox**. Could I decalcify my pineal gland and awaken some parts of my being that I had never experienced before? I didn't know but I was going to try! I had read about Jesus fasting for 40 days and 40 nights and if he could do it why couldn't I? In fact the bible does say that Jesus told his followers "All these things I have done so can you do and greater deeds will you do". So why can't I do it!? On Monday April **23**rd I stopped eating. **#23** see p 648.

Water Fasting

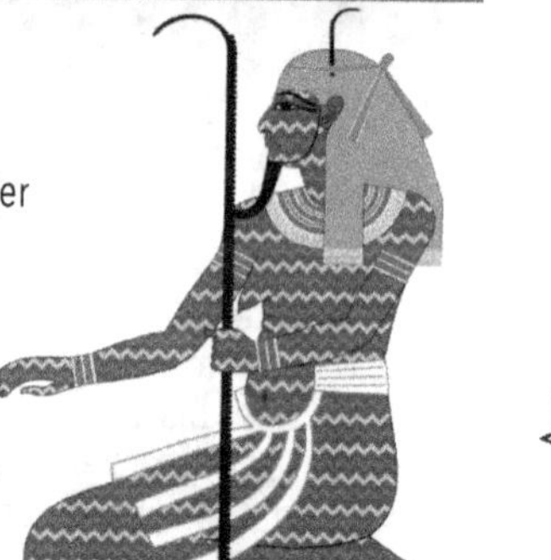

I think my stomach growled once on the first or second day of the fast but after that I do not remember my stomach growling again. It should be understood that my desire for a divine experience greatly superseded my desire to eat food. I made a decision to not eat and so I was not looking for food, **I was looking for transformation**. I drank water only! During the last three days of my fast I added fresh squeezed lemon juice to my water which I enjoyed so much that I felt like I was cheating. I was still doing massages during the fast but other than that I did no physical exercise except for yoga. The massage reviews I received during my fast were exceptional. My clients seemed to be more energized after the massages. I wrote three rhymes during my fast and they all speak to my revelation. On April 26th I would say "*I am God*" in the song **False Prophets**, on May 4th I would say the words "*pose of immortality*" in the rhyme **From Niggaz to Gods** and on May 9th I would say the words "*Born Again Resurrection*" in the song **Old Skin**.

Is Water God?

We are told that **God** is in us and all around us. Well, **Water** (Hydrogen) is in us and all around us. The Kemetic deity **Hapi** was depicted as androgynous (all encompassing) governing the Nile river. Most humans start life in the amniotic fluid (water) of their mothers and water has no gender. **Rain waters** come from the **clouds** and perhaps this is why **Heaven** is said to be in the **sky**. Perhaps **clouds** and no different than the **fog** that forms over bodies of water. Perhaps there is an ocean of water above the clouds. Perhaps that is why the **Nile** is aligned with the **Milky Way** (see page 251). When water is heated by the **sun** it evaporates via the process of precipitation but it is **resurrected** when **rain falls from the heavens**. Just as the second principle of **Jhuty** states "As above, so below, as within, so without, as the universe, so the soul". Just as rain water comes back again so does the human soul, but where exactly does the human soul come from? The people of the Nile Valley (Kemet) are said to come from the foot hills of the mountain of the moon where the God Hapi dwells and descend from the stars, once called **Ta Ntchr**. From Ta Ntchr descend the people of **Ta Seti**, the land of the bow also known as **Ta Merry**. Agriculture, Math, Science and all other forms of culture were brought down the Nile by the descendants of Ta Ntchr. Ta Ntchr is the Milky-Way Galaxy which is aligned with the Nile River. **As above so below**, we come from the primeval roaring waters of **Naunet** and **Nun**. The Kemetyu understood that there was no death and this was expressed through a concept called the **Wehem-Mesut** (repeating of births, p 14). In **Judaism** this concept of reincarnation is known as **Gilgul** (Cycle), but it is not widely taught. The story of **Ausar** being trapped in a **box** by his brother **Set** and thrown in the Nile river was used to give life to this process of resurrection and the Christian "**baptism**" borrowed from this Kemetic motif. All human beings are divine and are baptized by the **life giving waters** (amniotic fluid) of our mothers womb, however – the Christian **Baptism** is a ritual that is based on the belief that every human being is born in sin due to the actions of Eve (the female) so they must be dipped into water to cleanse their soul. In 418 "AD" the Catholic church council decided that every human child is born demonic as a result of sexual conception and damned to hell if not baptized (p 592). This belief system was a misinterpretation of what was seen on the walls in ancient Kemet (p 252). The concept of **baptism** originates in Kemet. It was not the act of submersion into a pool as Christians erroneously practiced, but the pouring of water over the initiate to symbolize cleansing, to begin ones transformation into the pursuit of becoming **Ausar** (p 50). The ancient Kemetyu state that, the only path to Afrikan power is the worship of the divine Godself. In ancient Kemet the divine Godself was called Ausar, the Lord of the **Perfect Black**, the Supreme Being Dwelling in man, the immortal soul that never dies. When you find yourself in search of truth, drink water and **Re-member** that **you** are **Ausar** (Immortal), **Set** (Lower Self), **Auset** (Wise & Intuitive) and you must deiced to become **Heru** (Victorious) the **hero!** See page 3 for the **hero's journey**!

Rau nu Prt m heru

Iu f Per f m heru

Utterances for Coming Forth by day into Light

It is he, who comes forth by day into Light

April 26th 2018 **False Prophets**

I heard the best time to kick a man is when he's down, you let **Nas** down beat'n your brothers down, be careful of those calling other men false prophets, it's a cold word keep your hand out ya brothers pockets, get blasted you need to stop it, you see what happened to our other profits! **Bob Marley** wouldn't do that, he fought the system not his brothers, that shit is wack black, this ain't a diss track so miss me with that beef shit, beef is when niggas can't find jobs so they find a Black mans wife to rob, beef is when you shot dead during road rage, no charge, no better days! **I am a God!** would you like it better if I say that I'm a nigga? or a thug ready to blaze? "***I shot the sheriff***" but I didn't shoot the deputy, did you see *the hate they gave little infants*, tell everybody ***George Bush*** *don't care about Black* bodies drowning or Black mothers frowning, behind our backs they be clowning, they want us to die, want us to go, praying for our downfall and everybody knows! we headed for "***Self Destruction***"! we need to meet at a junction have a discussion on how we function, cause assumptions can't stop the prophet, like **Jeru Da Damaja** I alkalize anything toxic - **Dawud The Amazing BlaKseed**

May 4th 2018 **From Niggaz 2 Gods**

We got choices, we got friends and foes, we can buy black or buy Rolse Royces, that's the life we chose, we can be the voice of the voiceless, or you can chase them hoes, I'm in **the pose of immortality** wait'n for my family, we got a lot of work to do, organize and to **Maat** be true and sincere, have no fear, we revere **black wall street**, look at north and south Korea! It's clear the time is here my dear brothers I'm with ya, let's do it for our mothers and sisters and the ancestors I hear them in the wind when they whisper, God bless ya you are the victor don't let the pressure get ya down, we lift ya up on solid ground, but you gotta do your part, if slavery is a choice then why are you choosing to not go free? turn off the tv, put down the alcohol, sleepy giant wake up, you ain't woke until you *Jacobs' ladder*, it's the **snake** going up that matters, Black life won't get right till we return to the masters of this universe, the sun the earth the moon and stars, we mapped that gotta track back from Niggaz 2 Gods - **Dawud The Amazing BlaKseed**

42 Laws of Maat, Page 367

May 9th 2018 **Old Skin**

I shed the old skin left my old sin behind, walking through the wilderness with a brand new state of mind, keeping my thoughts on breath, one step take life one day at a time, breaking the binds that shackle me, I take it back to corner backers and linebackers they couldn't tackle me, naturally gifted but no direction, the spirit was calling me but I was chasing the erection, theologians rarely teach the path to perfection and what it means to be ***Born Again Resurrection***! you the **Lazarus**! you **Heru** flew through the **Shu**, **Jesus** of the nazareth, the last to rip, the latest but not the greatest, like data I mastered it, self mastery the genie in the bottle, multiply the fish with the lyric given em something to follow, make a wish the gift, think wait and **fast** then hit the throttle - **Dawud The Amazing BlaKseed**

Flexibility

The first day we did more talking about the history of yoga, philosophical concepts and the course requirements than we did yoga but we definitely did some yoga. I know because flexibility was a major weak area for me so the little we did was painful for me. The picture on the right is me doing the modified version of the **pose of immortality** during the second day of class. I did the modified version because I could not physically get into the regular pose without experiencing piercing pain on the top of my feet around the ankles. Finally I was facing this flexibility issue head on. After the first two days I had a feeling that something led me to this course and I had made the right decision.

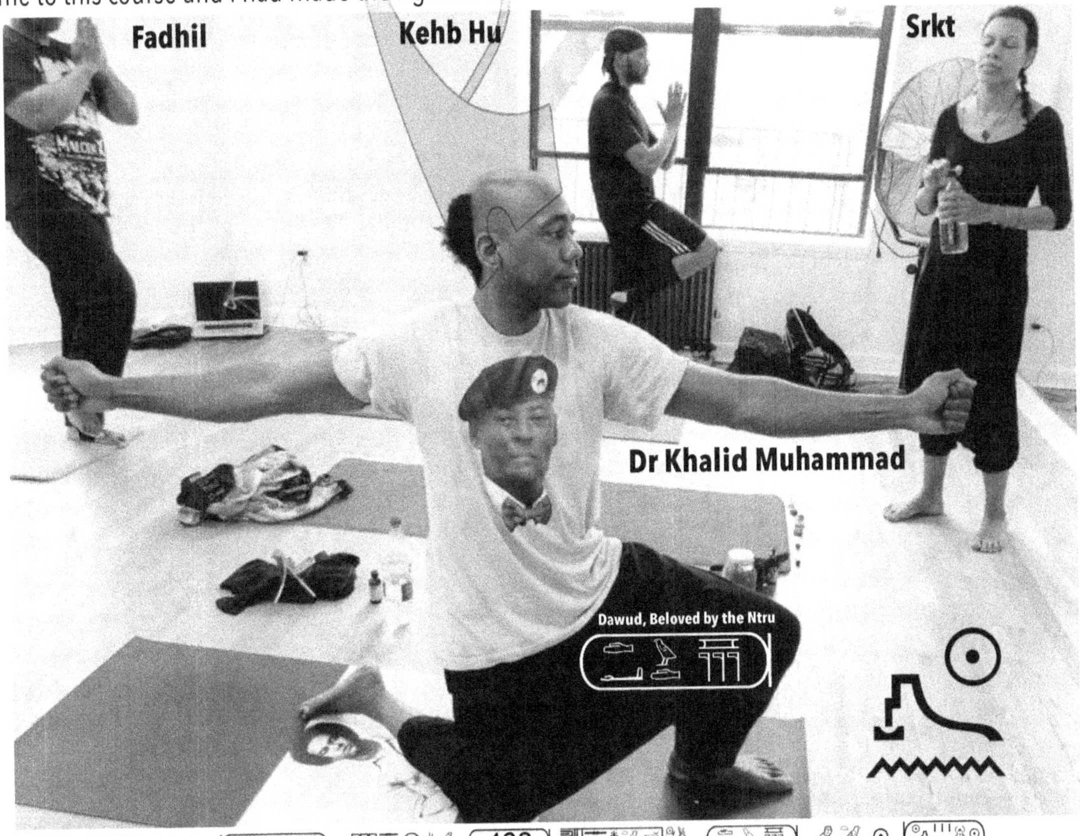

May 12th 2018 (Breaking Fast)

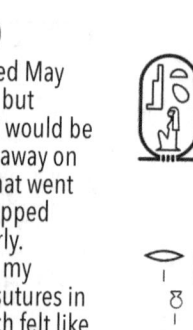

The fast was supposed to be 40 days but I stopped May 12th after the 20th day. Not because I was hungry but because I was low of energy and I did not think I would be able to do the 8hrs of yoga which was one week away on May 19th. I listened to the voices and thoughts that went along with the idea of stopping the fast and I stopped fasting, I ate. But I ate solid foods and I paid dearly. I experienced excruciating pains in my skull and my stomach after my first few meals! It felt as if the sutures in my skull were being pulled apart and my stomach felt like it was being twisted in nots. I felt the pains in my skull were caused by the sugar and the nots in my stomach were because my stomach was too small for the portions I ate. I had not had food in 20 days and so my body had done a lot of detoxing and my stomach had shrunk. So when I consumed the food that was full of hidden sugars my body responded in shock and pain. The next week I attended class and the pains had subsided. On May 20th, after our teachers training some of us went to Uptown Veg on 125th street to grab a bite to eat. While waiting for my food I went outside to talk to **brother G** who had a table set up selling his books. I had purchased his first book, **Memnon** in 2011 (p 210). I wanted to support him so I purchased the other two books to the Memnon series as well as his books Nimrod and Nefertari. I always supported vendors and I thought I bought his book just to support him but there was a deeper reason as to why his books called me. I would not come to know the full meaning until after my past life as King Tut was revealed in 2020 (p 594). * (**Addendum**) * I saw Brother G again in July 2022 at the African Arts festival. I showed him a copy of this book and told him about my past life as Tutankhaten. He looked at the cover and said, "I wrote about reincarnation in my book". He said he would buy a copy of my book but he never did. I saw him again on Aug 21st 2022 at the Harlem Week event. I told him that I had finally read his book Nefertari and that I loved it. I reminded him of how he asked me to play the role of Memnon when we first met (p 210) and how strange that was because Memnon was Amen Hotep III, my ancient grandfather (pages 7, 58, 336, 356,389, 638). I showed him a copy of my book but he looked at me with a blank stare. I'm writing a Epic Sci-Real (Science Reality) Novel Trilogy version of this book and a book about Tupac's ancient past life (pages 664 - 665). Stay tuned!

June 8th 2018 (Kanye West releases the song Yikes on his 41st birthday)

"Shit could get menacin', frightenin', find help, Sometimes, I scare myself, myself, Tweakin', tweakin' off that 2CB, huh? Is he gon' make it? TBD, huh, Thought I was gon' run, DMC, huh? ***I DONE DIED AND LIVED AGAIN ON DMT, HUH,*** See this a type of high that won't come down, This the type of high that get you gunned down" - **Kanye West**

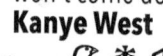

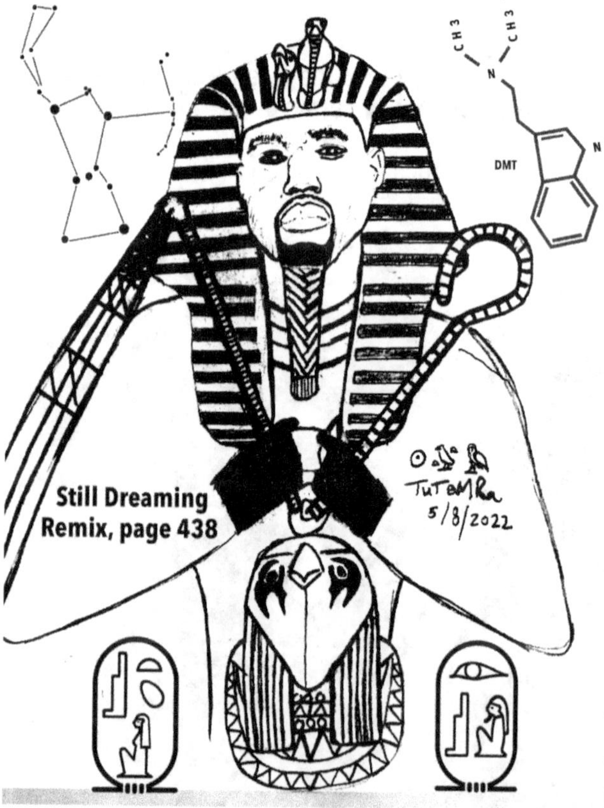

Still Dreaming Remix, page 438

Significance

Kanye West has appeared in my dreams many times over the years. He is born in **the year of the snake** like me and Emmett Till. Emmett was born in 19**41** while Kanye and I are born in 1977 (p **41**). Kanye is born the day before my Great Grandfather General Dukes Sr died on June 9th 1971. On June 8th, Kanye **41**st birthday he released the song **Yikes** and in this song Kanye would say **"I done died and lived again on DMT".** Less than a month later on July 3rd my first past life as Emmett Till would be revealed to me (page 480) with the help of DMT. DMT is a powerful psychedelic used in indigenous ceremonies. Kanye is from Chicago and Emmett was from Chicago. Kanye is the same brother that brought the world the song Jesus walks and in pictures he can be seen wearing a golden pedant of Heru as the falcon. The story of Jesus was taken from the Kemetic story of Heru. **Heru** is the son of **Ausar** (Osiris), the Lord of **resurrection** and Heru is the **falcon** that resurrects and returns in the Ausarian **resurrection** Drama. Kanye West visited the **Tutankhaten** (**King Tut**) Exhibit in 2010. On April 4th 2020 (page 594) the day that Martin Luther King was assassinated I would have my past life revelation of my life as **Tutankhaten** (**King Tut**) revealed to me. **Re-member** that **you** are **Ausar** and **Heru,** the **hero!** <u>See page 3 for the **hero's journey**!</u>

June 9th 2018 Decoding

They don't wanna see no harmony in the Black family, no sovereignty, the criminology the penalty whenever we try to free our minds, physiology, do the crime pay the time, the policy, the methodology, the epidemiology, the13 colonies sodomy extreme, what do I mean? mini sub like marine, fake thugs no love for the hugs from a Queen, between the drugs the lean, the unclean casein, the caffeine the cream, the codeine, they coding encoding loading, I'm exposing the dream differed exploding, Dawud The Amazing BlaKseed decoding **- Dawud The Amazing BlaKseed**

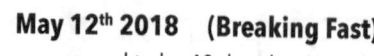

June 14th 2018 Self Care

The art of self care, by any means necessary try not to get buried in this health scare, I used to eat berries when climbing in the tree, culinary ready we didn't know the dairy was deadly, carefree we didn't see the belly treated like a cemetery, we wasn't ready for this military art of war, the food is the poison that they selling in the store, death starts in the Colon swollen rotten to the core, who do you trust the carnivore or the vegan? Can't even trust the language they work you to death till you're weakened, the spelling of words cast spells watch what you speak'n, all's well that ends well until you really start seeking, and knowing is better than believing that's when you growing and glowing and flowing like water - **Dawud The Amazing BlaKseed**

Rau nu Prt m heru

June 15th 2018 Retire

I stay younger than the age that a man plans to retire, The world is my stage, **Transform** my rage like **Richard Pryor,** It's a cold world take a page, get paid to burn it in the fire, the desire to acquire, you can't steal the level of **Messiah,** *the **caterpillar** will kill the **butterfly** just to be flyer!* they fill'n cups higher, they not empty man, they none the wiser, the empty hand, over understand the visualizer, the **seer** make you wonder damn, the idolizer I never am, a*ll miracles done by him can be done by them,* are you taking the gem or will you just keep having faith in him?! take that step and like **Imhotep,** get the blessing - **Dawud The Amazing BlaKseed**

June 2018
Heh, Untold Infinity Numbers of Years

Iu f Per f m heru

During my yoga course I would get this cover for my massage table custom made. At the time I thought the image was of the Ntchru **Shu** but I would later come to know it was the Ntchru **Heh** seated in a **golden** basket holding a pair of notched palm branches which represented untold infinity numbers of years. I would also come to know that this exact image was taken from the throne chair of Tutankhaten (**King tut**). His throne name Neb Kheperu Ra and his family name Tutankhamen can be seen. On his arm hangs the Ankh which represents **eternal life.** My past life a Emmett Till would be revealed on July 3rd 2018 (page 480) and my past life as **Tutankhaten** (**King Tut, Tutankhamen**) would be revealed to me on April 4th 2020 (page 594), the same day that Martin Luther King was assassinated (page 69). In 2023 the significance of this logo would intensify (page 472).

Utterances for Coming Forth by day into Light

It is he, who comes forth by day into Light

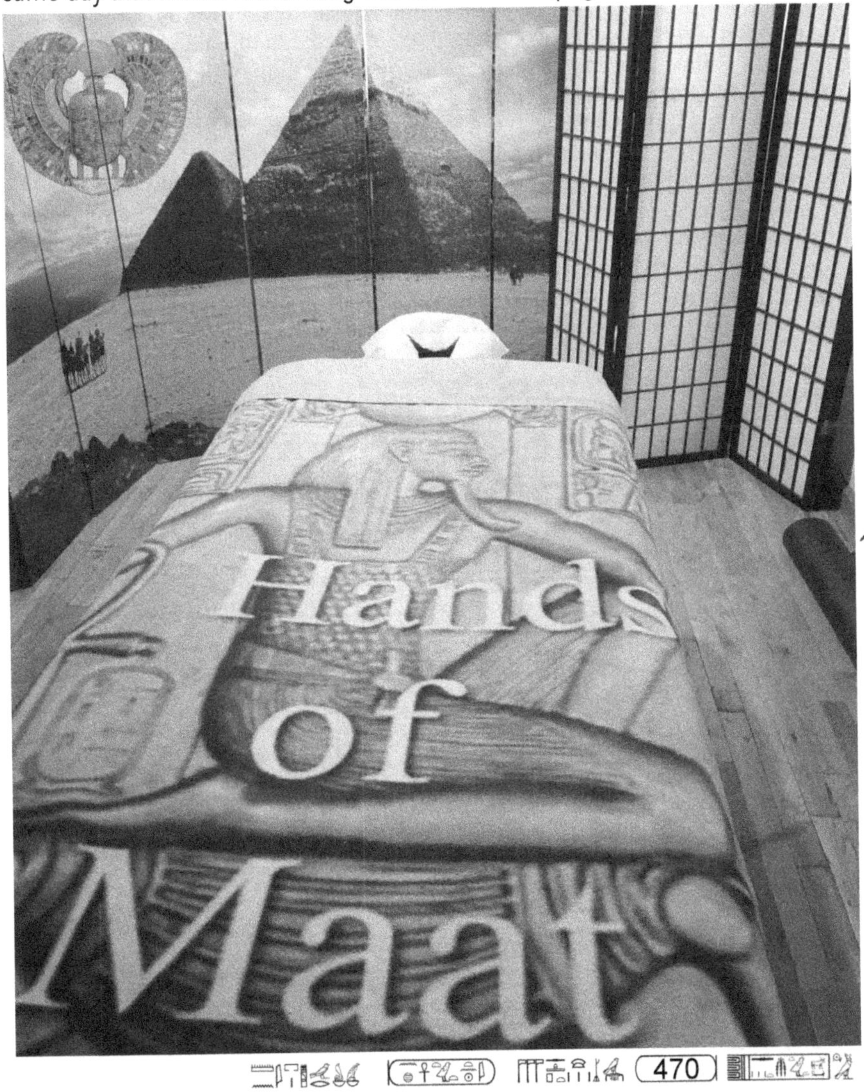

June 18th 2018 XXXtentacion

Another death! The Death of this young brother touched me! **Jashen Dwayne Onfory**, known professionally as XXXTentacion, born January **23**rd 1998 and murdered on June 18th 2018, the same day that my great grandmother Leacola **Riddle** died (p 21).. See page **648** for the **metaphysical significance of the number 23**. I had not listened to any of his music before but I always saw him on **TMZ** involved in disputes with different people. He seemed to always be in trouble. When his death was shown all over social networking I began to look into his life. Then I heard his song Suicide. I don't remember if I cried then but his death would cause me to cry deeply after I realized that I was Tut-**ANKH**-aten (King Tut) in 2020 (p 594). After my past life revelation of King Tut I mourned Jashen for a week straight after I realized he had a **Ankh** tattooed on his chest! And that was once my name! He also had his mother's name, **Cleopatra** tattooed on his chest. Cleopatra was a Queen of ancient Egypt (page 289, 323). I listened to his music for a few days and mourned his passing again. He was murdered the same day that my great grandmother Leacola **Riddle** died (page 21), the day after my grandfather General Dukes birthday, two days after Tupac's birthday, and the day before my friend Ron's birthday! His death touched my heart as it seemed like every time I turned around another Young Black Rapper was dying. I wrote two songs for him the day after he died.

Condolences

My condolences go out to the family, friends and fans of **Jashen Dwayne Onfory**. Please know that death is not the end. The soul survives death, indeed and in spirit. This is a book of the dead written by a boy who was murdered without justice, who defeated death and came forth by day. May the soul of **Jashen Dwayne Onfory** walk peacefully through the field of Reeds in Amenta. Amen Ra.

June 19th 2018 2am RIP XXXTentacion

My <u>Only Fear Of Death</u> is being shot down by another brother, my only regret is not telling her I love her, what's next? Nobody knows! ***<u>The soul lives on</u>***! It's a cold world, everybody wanna go to heaven but we living in hell, we seeing ***<u>Death Around The Corner</u>***, how can a brother prevail? We fell! but I got another story to tell, and well, when it's time to rebel the riots won't be quelled! tried to silence the struggle but they failed, the **Malcolm** the **X** the **X** the **X X**L, the amalgamation of a nation curtailed **- Dawud The Amazing BlaKseed**

June 19th 2018 Everybody Dies in Their Nightmares (XXXTentacion Remix)

I'm tired of seeing the young die in this rap game, I'm tired of hearing the mothers cry on the night news, how much we gotta lose for the street fame?! they don't really want us to grow when we do change, what's black life really worth but a new chain?! everybody claim that they woke but they won't change! they remain the same sleep walking this earth plane, the pain insane who do we blame?! My <u>Only Fear Of Death</u> is being shot down by another brother hot with a hot pound, ***Just to get a rep*** he let it pop now, take your last breath they call the cops now! this American **dream** is a nightmare! never really ever seen nothing nice here! everybody pray to **God** but do God care? tell me where was the **God** when we got here? tired of feeling like I'm trapped in my damn mind! tired of feeling like I'm trapped in a damn lie! tired of feeling like my life is a damn game! nigga really wanna die in the night time! what's next what's left in this cold world? **Malcolm X X X** raising hell! ***<u>Possessed in the flesh can't you tell</u>***? nothing left to do but rebel! if I die tonight tell them tales of me, **Hell Mary** with the rosary, if **Malcolm Little** with the felony dies at 20, we would never know what he rose to be! I wanna be free that's my only crime, it's hard to be free in a stolen land, tired of feeling like my life is a damn game, nigga really wanna die in the night time, don't wanna go to sleep but I wanna dream and stay alive Just enough to make **magic**, don't wanna go outside, know what I mean?! pulling up on side of me in traffic, when ever you make a sp**ark** then they steal your fire, they aim for your heart when you the **Messiah,** if you have anything they desire a **caterpillar** will kill a **butterfly** just to be flyer, tell me if I'm a liar?! that's why I stay alone, in my own mind, in my own zone, tired of feeling like I'm trapped in the **matrix** I hate this attack of the wack shit, clones **- Dawud The Amazing BlaKseed**

ADDENDUM

May 2022 - Dream with Iahmose Nefertari and Jashen Onfory

Upon returning from Kemet in April of 2022 (p 670) I had **dreams** with several brothers who are in some way connected to Kemet and Jashen was one of them. In my dream with Jashen I was looking at the remains of the body of Iahmose Nefertari. I left with some of her belongings and shortly after, Jashen arrived, smiling, in a very high spirited mood as he handed me a book bag. When I opened the bag I saw the bones of **Iahmose Nefertari** (The Matriarch of the 18th dynasty, and the ancient great great great grand mother of King Tut). Then I woke up. This dream took place the same night that I dreamt with **Mike Tyson** (p 528), and **Michele Lamy** (p 582). Some days later I would also dream with **Lord Jamar** (p 342), **La Juana** (p 586) and **KRS One** (p 633).

ADDENDUM **July 1st 2018**

Kemetic Yoga Course Completion

Rau nu Prt m heru

Iu f Per f m heru

Utterances for Coming Forth by day into Light

It is he, who comes forth by day into Light

To complete the course each of us had to arrange and demonstrate a Kemetic Yoga sequence. I was the first person to go and after my sequence was done my instructor Yirser told me that he saw ***two white birds*** land on the balcony just as I began my sequence. After we were all done with our sequences we all went to a vegan restaurant for dinner where we received our certificates of completion. As the ceremony came to a close I went outside and sat down looking into the sun. I took a picture just before everyone else exited the restaurant preparing to part ways (picture seen on right). Here are some pictures we took after the celebration (page 473)..

My yoga instructor is from Chicago just like Emmett Till. His name is Yirser Ra Hotep. I got along well with Yirser from the beginning. I have come across some elders in this "kemetic" "community" whom I will leave nameless, who claim that these Kemetic Yoga postures are being misinterpreted. They claim to hold some higher level of gnosis but all I can say is, I took a course by a man named **Yirser** which is a variation of the name **Ausar** (Osiris) and Ausar is the Lord of the resurrection, and 3 days after I graduated from his course I experienced an **Ausarian Resurrection** with my first past life being revealed to me. The Prophecy of Reincarnation was realized. The logo Yirser used for his company is the exact same image taken from the throne chair of Tutankhaten (**King tut**). The logo is the image of the NTCHR **HEH** who is seen sitting on **gold** and represents **immortality**, and **infinite** numbers of years. There are many images of **Heh** and he could have used but he chose to use the one found in 1922 on **Tutankhaten's** (**King Tut's**) throne chair!

ADDENDUM - 2pacalypse Now

In 2023, I would learn a deeper connection to Yirser by way of brother **Ayiti** (page 572). In 2023, Ayiti would lead me to brother **Neter Ankh**, a Kemetic Yoga instructor who trained under **Muata Ashby**. In 2005, **Ayiti** and **Neter Ankh** took part in the **King Tut** museum protests in Fort Lauderdale (page 572). The same day I met Neter Ankh I enrolled in his 4 month Egyptian yoga course (**Djef Sema Paut n Neteru**). I told Neter Ankh about my **past lives** and the many synchronicities. But when I got to the connection with Yirser's logo <u>he stopped me and explained the **deeper significance**</u>. **Neter Ankh** explained that **Yirser's** yoga instructor was **Ausar Hapi**. Ausar Hapi was a **Hatha** yoga instructor in the 70's but in 1977, **the same year I was born** (page 34), Ausar Hapi went to the **King Tut** exhibit (page 29) and when he saw the **throne chair of King Tut** he **had a profound revelation**. He realized that in the imagine on the chair, the person was doing a spinal twist, a yoga posture! And from this he realized that yoga had it's origins in ancient Kemet (Egypt) and not in India. In the same year that I was born, Ausar Hapi was inspired by the throne chair of King Tut and started teaching yoga from an Egyptian prospective. He would teach Yirser Ra Hotep and Yirser would use the image from King Tut's chair as the symbol for his yoga business. Yirser would teach me Kemetic Yoga and when I graduated I would realize I was Emmett Till in a past life (page 480,481). Then two years later I would realize I was King Tut in a past life (page 594). I told Neter Ankh about my theory about who **Tupac** was in his past life (page 664) and then he shared with me an idea he once had for a book. In this book, there was an apocalypse (**2pacalypse Now)** and years after this apocalypse a boy found the old CD's of Tupac and with the music of Tupac he forged a movement for revolution (page 44). When I heard this I laughed and told him that my life is sort of like his book. Then I read **page 5** of this book to him (**The Older Gods,** page 5). **Ausar =** (Yirser/Osiris) **= Resurrection = of the Immortal soul of Human Beings. Re-member** that **you** are **Ausar** and **Heru,** the **hero!** <u>See page 3 for the **hero's journey**!</u>

Sister Pia

Sister Shale

Sister Sy

Brother Kebhu

Sister Irijah

Sister Mishay

Fadhil

Brother Mark

YogaSkills School of Kemetic Yoga
CERTIFICATE OF COMPLETION 200 HOUR KEMETIC YOGA TEACHER TRAINING COURSE
Life, Health & Prosperity
YOGASKILLS
SCHOOL OF KEMETIC YOGA
REGISTERED YOGA SCHOOL
RYS 200
yoga ALLIANCE
ANKH • UDJAH
SENEB • HOTEP
Yoga Alliance
ID: 62073
BREATH ✝ FLOW ✝ INTERNAL ✝ POWER
Presented To: Dawud Eddings (CKYT), Date: July 1, 2018
In Recognition of Completion of 200 Hour Kemetic Yoga Course
By: Yirser Ra Hotep, Master Instructor
Signature
Yirser Ra Hotep

Rosa Parks doing Yoga at 60 years old
March 1973

Rau nu Prt m heru

July 1st 2018
Mars and The International African Arts Festival

As we were leaving the restaurant someone mentioned that The **International African Arts festival** was taken place in Brooklyn at Barry Commodore Park. It was a Sunday and the weather was fitting for a day at the park enjoying good vibrations, so a few of us went. It was my first time ever going to this festival. I remember being near the main stage with Yirser and a few other people when it happened! ***I heard a voice in my head,*** it was loud and very direct. The voice said "***walk away and you are going to meet a beautiful woman***". Fueled with the potential of meeting this beautiful woman I told Yirser that I was going for a walk and I would be back. I left immediately. I began to walk in a random direction and at some point I got caught up in people watching and looking at the vendors that I completely forgot about this beautiful woman I was supposed to be looking for - then all of a sudden it happened! I made eye contact with a woman and it was like an electromagnetic attraction. We both looked at each other with looks of confusion on our faces but both of us started walking towards each other as if in a trance. Mars would tell me years later that before she made eye contact with me that **she also heard a voice** that said, "**Look up**". When she looked up we made eye contact.

Iu f Per f m heru

We introduced ourselves. Her name was **Mars**. I'm a **scorpio** and my sign is ruled by the planets Mars and Pluto. It was a Tuesday and I'm also born on a Tuesday, **Tuesday** is governed by the planet Mars. I told her that I just graduated as a Kemetic Yoga instructor and that it was my first time at this festival. She said that she was recently looking into Kemetic Yoga. We had things in common. We talked more and when she heard that I was a trainer and massage practitioner she invited me to vend with her. She had a table at the festival and offered me space to do chair massage along side her. I quickly accepted. In the midst of our conversation a graceful older black woman walked up to us and asked to take our picture. After she took our picture I exchanged info with the woman then she left. I would see her again a few days later while at the festival. I exchanged info with Mars and told her I would see her again soon. As soon as I left Mars I ran into Hadiiya.

Utterances for Coming Forth by day into Light

July 1st 2018
Hadiiya and Her Two Sons

As soon as I left **Mars** I ran into **Hadiiya** no more than a minute later. We had not seen each other in person in many years (page 156). We would embrace then we spent some time catching up and just before we parted ways we took a picture. Two days later my past life as Emmett Till would be revealed (page 480) and two years later in 2020 after my past life revelation of **Tutankhaten** (**King Tut**) on April 4th 2020 (page 594), I would come to know that her **two sons** are connected to my revelations. Her first son is born on **August 28th** the same day that **Emmett Till** was murdered and **Ausar** (Osiris, page 3) reigned for **28 years** in the **Ausarian resurrection** drama.... Her second son is born on February 26th the same day that **Trayvon Martin** was murdered (page 232) and this son has a name that sounds like **Ausar**, the **Lord of resurrection** and he is a trainer like myself and he also has a Tattoo of **Nefertiti** on his chest just like **Tupac**. Nefertiti is the step mother of **Tutankhaten** (**King Tut**). I have a theory about who **Tupac** was in his **past life**.

It is he, who comes forth by day into Light

July 2nd 2018

The old black woman who took my picture yesterday called me today. She didn't know how to send the pictures via e-mail so I explained the process to her. We spoke for maybe 20 minutes. It took so long because she didn't know how to work her computer. It wasn't until after I had my past life revelation that I realized how important that call was! I would see her again the next dat on July 3rd and if I had not had the patience to teach her how to send the pictures she may not have taken the pictures of me on July 3rd. This is crucial because one of the pictures that she took of me on July 3rd played a major role in the precise moment that sparked my past life revelation of Emmett Till the evening of July 3rd 2018. It wasn't till a few weeks after my past life revelation that I came to know that July 2nd is the day that **Louis Till** was executed by **hanging** in 1945. Louis Till was the father of Emmett Till, the 14 year old boy who was murdered on August 28th 1955. The lynching of Emmett Till sparked the civil rights movement. Louis Till was assigned to the **177**th port company, 379th Battalion transportation corp. On July 2nd 1945 he and his friend Fred McMurry were executed by the U.S. Army for a crime they did not commit. Louis's family was never told the reason for his execution until after Emmet's murder trial had began, 10 years later in 1955. The media created the narrative that Emmett was a sexual deviant just like his father. These are the same tactics that the media still uses today in cases involving the murder of Black people in America at the hands of the police. **61 years later the full truth would come to light** (p 518). Louis Till was born on **February 7th** of 1922 the same year that Tutankhaten's (**King Tut**) tomb was discovered. The very next day on July 3rd 2018 I would go back to the festival and vend there for the first time doing chair massage and this is the day that I would realize that I was Emmett Louis Till in my most recent **past life**!

Tuesday, July 3rd 2018 International African Arts Festival
The First Past Life is Revealed

Just like we had agreed, I showed up to the festival to do chair massage next to **Mars's** table. I came wearing my favorite shirt with **Emmett Till's face** on it (page 459). I got there early and was happy to see Mars again. I met her partner name Tee and I vividly remember calling her Queen Tee, like **Queen Tiye** from the 18th Dynasty, Tutankhaten's (King Tut's) Grandmother. Mars and Tee were set up outside the actual park where the festival was being held but I wanted to be inside the park. I helped them set up then went for a walk in the park.

Significance

Mars is born on February 4th the same day as **Rosa Parks**. I am a **scorpio** and the planet **Mars** rules the zodiac sign **Scorpio**. While on a bus in Alabama, Rosa Parks refused to give her seat to a white man on Dec 1,t 1955. Rosa had just left a meeting about the murder of **Emmett Till,** she was angry and she was sick and tired of being sick and tired. Mars has a son named **Moses**. Emmett Till's body was identified by a ring he wore that had the date **May 25th** inscribed on it (page 512). Emmett Till's uncle identified the body and his name was **Moses** Wright Jr. Many historians suggest that the character from the Bible named **Moses** was really the Pharaoh **Akhenaten** from the 18th dynasty. Akhenaten was the father of **Tutankhaten** (**King Tut**). The next year on April 4th 2020 the same day that **Martin Luther King** was assassinated (p 69) I would have my past life as Tutankhaten (King Tut) revealed (page 594). **Mars** has a son named **Moses** who is born on April 5th the day after Martin Luther King was assassinated. My mother was born on February 3rd and Rosa Parks and Mars are born the next day on February 4th. Rosa Parks passed away on October 24th, the day before my birthday, the same day that KRS One released his book, The Gospel of Hip Hop (page 633). July 3rd 2018 was a **Tuesday**. I was born on a Tuesday and **Tuesday** is governed by the planet **Mars**. Tuesday is also governed by **Enpu** (Anubis), the dog headed NTCHR who is the Lord of mummification. The first person to ever be mummified was **Ausar** who is the Lord of **resurrection** (page 3). 2018 is the Chinese year of the **dog**. King Tut's tomb was discovered in 1922 the year of the **dog**. This same day I will meet another man born in the year of the **dog**, who will lead me to the next step of my **blind initiation**. In January of 2019 Mars would come to me for a massage and afterwards she would give me my first **tarot card** reading which spoke to everything I was experiencing (page 549).

Rau nu Prt m heru Iu f Per f m heru

I walked into the park an to my surprise I saw **Mfundishi Jhutyms**, the same Kemetic Priest that I had been taking classes with off and on for the past few years (page 233).. The same Kemetic priest I purchased my **scarab** cuff from on **May 25th** 2014 (page 293). I told him I had my massage chair with me and I asked him if I could work under his tent, he smile and said yes. Elated, I thanked him and hurried to get my chair. Now **I was in the festival for real!** On July 3, I only worked on 2 people but on July 4, I worked on more people than I can count (page 522).

The first person to come to my chair was a sister named **Akua**. She looked at my chair and said, **"exactly what I've been looking for".** I smiled and told her she would be my first person today then I made my chair ready for her. Just as I started to work on Akua **the old woman** who took the pictures of Mars and I on Sunday appeared again (p 474). She waved at me and gestured with her camera asking if I wanted her to take pictures, I said yes. She took pictures of me and walked away. That was the last time I ever saw this woman. She would e-mail me the pictures she took around the same time I got home at the end of the day (p 480). In the ancient Kemetic spiritual systems, the **Ahku** is one of the 9 constituents of the human being and it governs the **intelligence**. The **Ka** governs the spirit and the **Ba** governs the **soul**. The **Ba** and the **Ahku** are governed by the **Sahu.** The **Sahu** is the spiritual energy that houses the **Ba** and the **Ahku** and protects the physical **mummified body**. In the ancient Kemetic spiritual system all initiates aimed to become like Sahu, which was the closest one could be to Ntr (God like). Sahu was also the name used to identify the stars that make up the belt in the constellation of **Ausar** (Osiris) the archer (**Orion,** p 344). Years later I would add the name **Sahu** to my name (p 594). **Re-member** that **you** are **Ausar** the **hero!** See page 3 for the **hero's journey**!

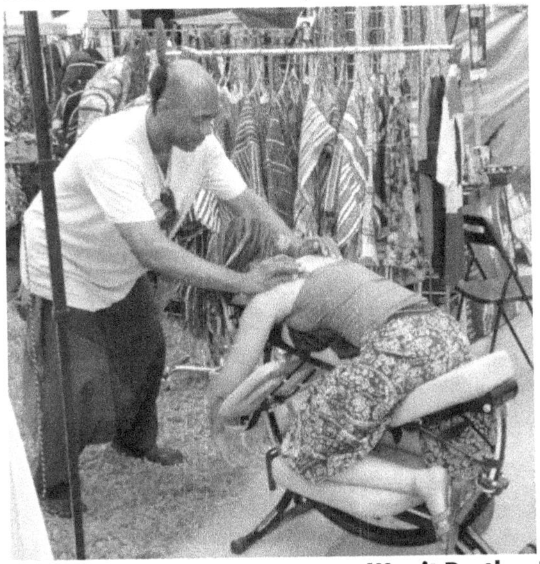
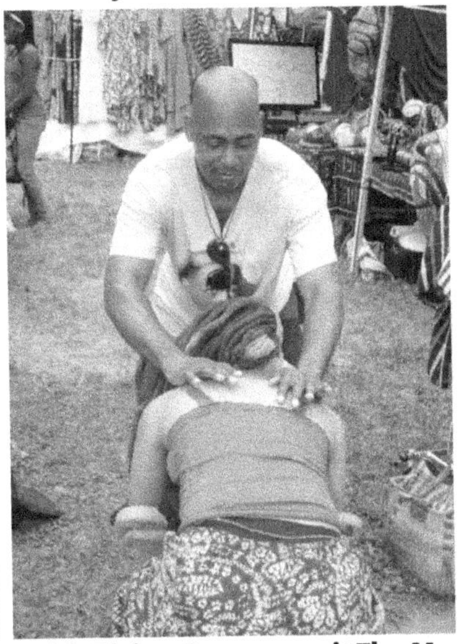

Was it Brother Hankh Rising Sun or was it The Mycelium?

Utterances for Coming Forth by day into Light

It was only during the writing of this book that I realized I had met Brother **Hankh Rising Son** on several occasions before this divine meeting at the festival. I met him first in 2012 or 2013 at the annual Harlem week event on 135th street where I purchased his Tesla water purifier. Then I saw him at The Carbon (Melanin) Conference on December 7th 2014 (page 312) where he spoke about the **reincarnation** of **Simeon Toko.** Many topics were discussed at that conference, however brother **Hankh's** lecture captivated my imagination and got my attention more than anything else. Now 4 years later I meet brother H**ankh** again, here at the festival on July 3rd 2018 the year of the **dog** and now he would lead me to the next step of my **blind initiation**. Sort of like a seeing eye **dog**.

Brother **Hankh Rising Sun** was set up at the tent next to where I was doing chair massage. Through out the day him and I spoke a few times. At some point during the middle of the day brother H**ankh** Rising Sun told me that I needed to take **Ayahuasca** and **Psilocybin** (**Magic Mushroom**). It wasn't till years later that I realized it was the **spirit** of the **mycelium** (magic mushroom) that spoke through him helping to spark my **past life revelation** of **Emmett Till** and **Tutankhaten**. The mycelium of the mushroom is equivalent to roots of a tree and the mycelium is usually hidden under bark, ground, rotten wood, or leaves. The mycelium underground network of the mushroom is what allows trees to talk to each other exchanging vital information for survival. I had been looking into the mushroom and wanted to experience them. The year prior I had a very small piece of a chocolate that had Psilocybin infused in it and the experience I had with that was very interesting (page 452). A few hours after brother H**ankh** told me that I needed the sacred medicines I had my first ounce of Psilocybin (magic mushrooms). When I got home I opened the bag and ate a few pieces. In 2022 I would come to realize that brother **Hankh Rising Son** is born on **Nov 25th** 1958, the year of the **dog.** King Tut's tomb was opened on **Nov 26th** 1922 (page 11), the year of the **dog**. And my past life as Emmett came on July 3rd 2018 the year of the **dog**.

It is he, who comes forth by day into Light

July 3rd 2018
International African Arts Festival
The First Past Life is Revealed

On July 3rd I only worked on 2 people. It was my first time working at the festival and I was having more fun just being there talking to people. While on one of my walks around the park a brother name **Damian** asked me if he could take a picture of me. He took these two pictures and said he would e-mail them to me. His e-mail address was (……**reed29**@….com). I found this interesting because in ancient Kemetic spiritual systems the fields of **reeds** is where your soul goes to dance for eternity after you die if you successfully pass the halls of judgement. The number **29** was my high school football jersey number. My high school sweetheart's middle name was **Aminta** and **Amenta** is the Kemetic equivalent to heaven where to soul goes to dance in the field of reeds for **eternity**. See **Sister Debra 29X** on page 64.

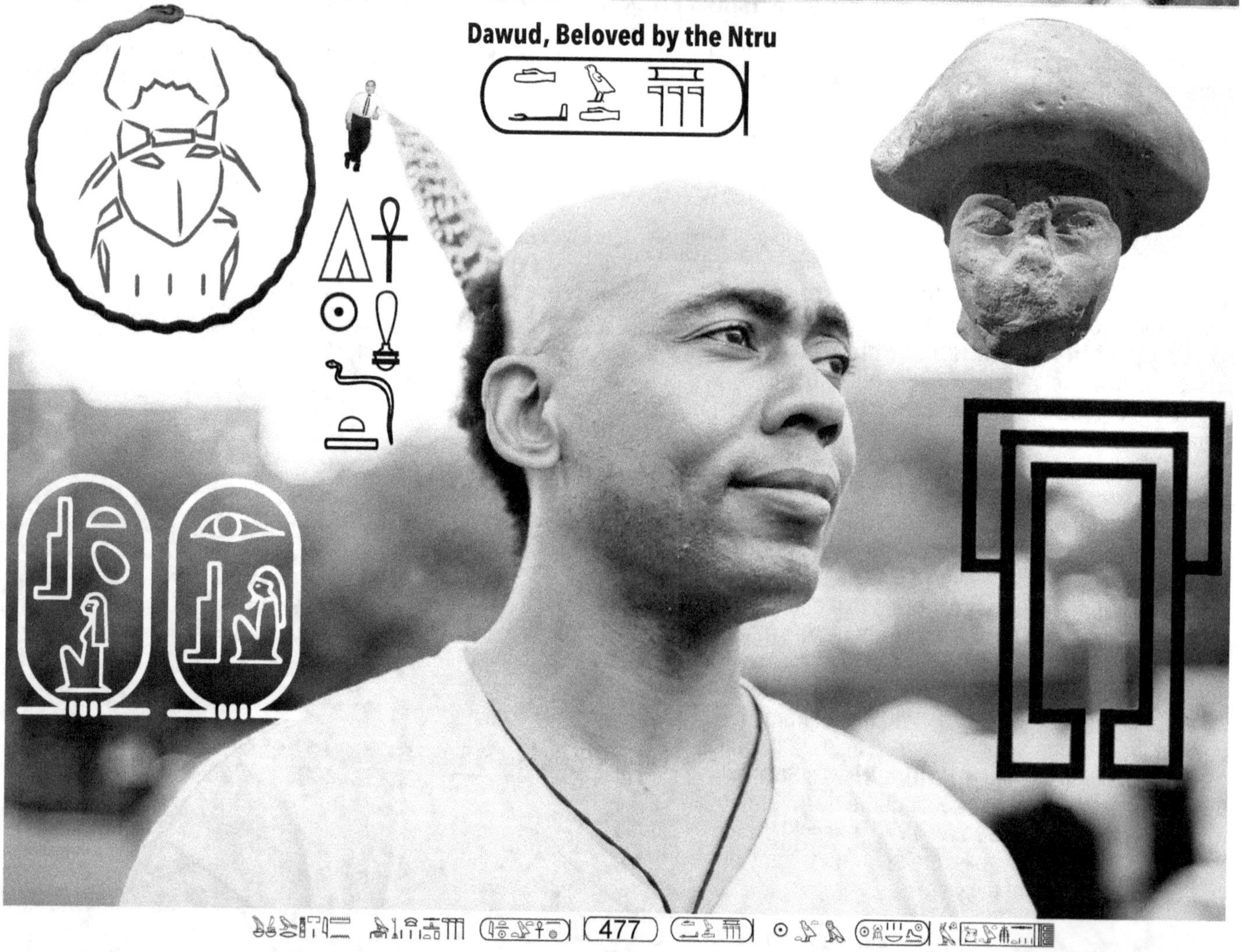

July 3rd 2018

If you look closely you can see the scar on my **left** eye (page 105). I almost lost my left eye on June 1st 2002 in a violent vehicular accident like the one **Dr Strange** had in the movie Dr Strange but I walked away from that accident with only flesh wounds. The strange thing about that accident is that my sister **dreamt** the accident 7 days before I crashed (page 104). I almost lost my left eye while Emmett had his left eye gouged out like **Heru** had his taken out by **Set** in the battle of the Ausarian resurrection drama. Later this evening I would for the first time eat the sacred mushroom medicine that Dr Strange ate while in the presence of the **Ancient One** and it would show me a more ancient version of myself. The soul fragment of my life as Emmett Till would flash before my eyes and at first I couldn't even believe it.. I ate the Sacred Mushroom that **John** talked about in **chapter 6 verse 51** of the **bible,** "I am the living bread that came down from heaven. Whoever eats this bread will have **eternal life**. This bread is my flesh, which I will give for the life of the world." I ate the Sacred Mushroom written about in the Quran, 2:57, 7:160, and 20:80. like the house the **Smurfs** lived in. Like the mushroom that Mario ate in **Mario Brothers**. Like the shape that the pose of **Ausar** forms when hands are crossed in front of you. I ate the sacred fruit and shortly there after I knew who I was instantaneously in the blink of an eye!!

Rau nu Prt m heru

Even in the name Kemet you find the name Emmett

Iu f Per f m heru

Utterances for Coming Forth by day into Light

It is he, who comes forth by day into Light

Psychedelic Disclaimer and Warning

After eating sacred mushrooms my **past life** as **Emmett Till** was revealed to me. This is not to say that if anyone eats a psychedelic plant that a past life will come. That is NOT TRUE! As **Baba Kilindi** says, some things are only experienced by the initiate that has **earned the keys to open those doors**. All the events in this book are true. If you follow my path and do the things I do yet still the great mysteries are not shown to you. Then continue the path and **to Maat be true** and perhaps in due time you will be worthy of the view. It is very important that you read this book in it's entirety so that you do not misinterpret what you're reading about the sacred psychedelic plant medicines. You must know that I did not drink alcohol until I was 21 years of age. I got baptized at **11** years old (page 49) and gave my life to Christ at **22** years of age (page 92). I did not smoke weed until I was **33** years of age (page 194) and I stopped drinking alcohol at **33** years of age. I am **44** years old right now and I didn't eat the sacred mushroom until I was **40** years old. In ancient Kemet (Egypt) the initiate went to school for **40** years learning all the sciences of life before they could become a Kemetic Priest. **40** was the number of tribulation and preparation. In the bible it rained for **40** days and **40** nights in the story of Noah (page 252). Jesus and Moses were taught in the ways of the Egyptians. Jesus **fasted** for **40** days and forty nights while Moses was in the wilderness for **40** years. I went through **40** years of life searching for truth, lost in the wilderness of this world. My revelation is not a "space cadet" or "drug" induced delusion. Drug induced delusions are not this mathematically sound and don't have the forces of nature working to bring forth the revelation (page 41). <u>This is also not a book meant to encourage you to ingest ceremonial plants and other sacred medicines without proper guidance.</u> Some mushrooms are not to be eaten because they can kill you! If you have paid attention to the events in my life during the course of this book you will see that I did not find the plants they found me! I lived a life worthy enough for the plant medicines to find their way to me and when they did I was not in the mindset of fun and recreation. I knew what they were because I had been researching them and when they came to me I communed with these sacred plants in a spiritual manner the same way my **Cherokee, Blackfoot, Vedic** and ancient Kemetic ancestors did. These plants are living sentient beings and if you commune with them when you are not spiritually ready you might find yourself on a hell* of a trip! I'm trying to get you to see that there is a world out here beyond most of our senses that is trying to get our attention. It is always communicating with us however it is our frequency that is sometimes off.

Even in the name K<u>emet</u> you find the name <u>Emmett</u>

Wadjety N Ma'at Imhotep Baka-Amun
I appreciate your willingness to build with me and the help with the MDW NTR. Dua Ntr, Aha tu sn e.

When I got home I got settled in but wasted no time to consume the Psilocybin (Magic Mushroom). I open the bag and took a few pieces and ate them. After some time my body began to vibrate a little. Then for some reason I was **overcome with the desire** to check my e-mail. The old woman from the festival had sent me the pictures she took of me earlier that day. This would be the last time I ever heard from her. **As soon as I saw Emmett Till's face** on the shirt I was wearing in the picture and looked at my face in the picture **I KNEW I WAS HIM**! **There was an explosive orgasmic feeling of realization that flew through out my body** and when it did my knees buckled then I stumbled back and almost fell! I could not believe it but at the same time **I knew it was true and at the same time I was skeptical**. How could this be?! I felt like **Neo** from the movie the **Matrix**, when Morpheus tells Neo what the Matrix really is. Neo didn't want to believe it and I didn't want to believe this either but I had this unexplainable knowingness that it was so. I had awaked from a long sleep, in a new body Just like the movie **Matrix**. Immediately I began to research Emmett Till. I googled Emmett and saw that he was born on July **25th**, that didn't mean anything to me even though I was born on the **25th** too, of October. I brushed that off and explained it away as just a **coincidence** because parts of me didn't want to believe it. Then I realized he was murdered the same year my mother was born in 1955. That was interesting to me, so I kept looking. I saw that he was born in 19**41** (see page **41**). I checked the Chinese zodiac and dammit he WAS born in the **year of the snake,** just like me! My curiosity kept growing. I went to youtube and I watched a documentary on him. He was shot in the temple in the same place as my birthmark (black dot) on the side of my head. Then I remembered that birthmarks are highly melanated markers, usually seen as black dots, which are part of the souls **genetic memory** connected to how people may have died in previous lives. I have **birthmarks** on my neck and he had a barbwire wrapped around his neck. His left femur was broken and I have two black dots / birthmarks on my left leg. His left ear was cut off and I have a birthmark (black dot) behind my left **ear**. I knew I was Emmett Till! As the days went by I kept finding more and more connections. In ancient Kemet (Egypt) the concept of reincarnation and past lives was called the **Wehem-Mesut** (repeating of births, page 14). Some time after my revelation I would hear **Tony Browder** speaking about the concept of **Wehem-Mesut**. The next year I met **Prof. James Small** at the annual **Malcolm X** ceremony and afterwards I would tell him about my life as Emmett but he would not have much to say about my revelation (p 564). On March 22nd of 2020, **Akua** would appear in a profound **shared dream** that I was having with another person (see page 589).

Rau nu Prt m heru

Iu f Per f m heru

Utterances for Coming Forth by day into Light

It is he, who comes forth by day into Light

The Garden, Grapes, The Acacia Tree, and The Original Tree of Life

One of the more modern stories of an **Ancient Tree** is the story written into the Bible about **Adam and Eve** in the **Garden of Eden**. Adam and Eve disobeyed God's law and ate from the tree that contained the knowledge of good and evil and so they were kicked out of the Garden, left to live in a world of sin. In the early days of my search for spiritual truth I read the bible as a literal book. As if there was really some man named Adam and a woman named Eve. Of course that was before I had done any major research into the origins of religion. When armed with ancient knowledge a man will discover that all he really needs in this world of sin, is him and his girl friend. Of course that is, if his girl friend is the Egyptian Goddess **Lusaaset.** We can best understand the meaning behind Lusaaset and her relevance to present day religion by exploring her connection to **Wine,** the **Acacia Tree, DMT**, **Birth** and **Resurrection**.

Who Was Lusaaset?

In one of the Egyptian creation stories creation began when **Atum** masturbated, or copulated with himself, to produce the deities **Shu** and **Tefnut**, thus beginning the process of creation. The hand he used in this act was called the Hand of Atum and personified as a Goddess.. This Goddess of creation was equated with **Hathor** and later the other two minor Goddesses **Lusaaset** and **Nebethetepet**. Lusaaset was known by the Greeks as Saosis. Her name literally means "Utterer of Words, Conceiver of Worlds". She is now considered one of the 10,000 faces of Auset (Isis) and she was considered the **grandmother of all the Egyptian Gods**, except for her husband Atum (Amun-Ra). Her name would later come to mean "**the great one who comes forth**" in connection with the ancient Book of Coming Forth by Day. Similar in appearance to later Goddesses Hathor and Isis, Lusaaset is depicted as wearing the Egyptian vulture crown surmounted with the uraeus (cobra snake) and solar disk between two horns, at times she was also seen with a **scarab (Khepri) beetle on her head**. Utterance 519 of the Book of Coming Forth by Day reads, "I am the son of **Khepri**, born in Hetepet under the tresses of the Goddess of Lusaaset who ascended from the vertex of Geb." Lusaaset becomes an even greater symbol of **resurrection** into the night or afterlife when her name is divided into Lusaa-Set. The Latin name Lucifer means 'light-bearer', or the morning star and day time like Heru (**Jesus**) and Set represents death, the night and after life. While Lusaaset's name is not well known in modern times she was extremely important to the Ancient Egyptians as the Goddess of Creation and the Goddess of the **Tree of Life**. She remained a primary deity throughout all eras of the Ancient Egyptian culture, even through Persian, Hyksos, Greek, and Roman occupations.

Addendum You Heard It Through the Grape Vine

The song, **I Heard It Through the Grape Vine**, was recorded in the year of the **goat**, on June 17 1967, my grand father General Dukes Jr's 36th birthday (p **23**). The song reached number one on the Billboard R&B chart on November 25, 1967, the day before King Tut's tomb was opened (Nov 26 1922, page 11). Everything in this book is a di**vine** message from the **Grape Vine**, from **The One In the Tree**. "Deciphering the **MDW NTCHR** takes a deeper mode of thought than what modern language offers. You must imagine that you are reading the language of immortals. Until this is done the meaning of the MDW NTCHR will never be fully inner stood" (P 30). This divine language was once lost and when it was found it took thousands of years to be deciphered and to this day, the meaning of many words and concepts are still debated. With that said, let's take a look at a few words in the **MDW NTCHR** (mdw=**word** / ntchr =**divine**), or more commonly known as the **hieroglyphs,** and let's analyze how the ancient Kemetyu chose to **spell** them. The words in question are, **Spirit**, **Vine**, **Gardener**, **Grapes** and **Wine**.

Eg.1	Eg. 2a	Eg. 2b	Eg. 3a	Eg. 3b	Eg. 4	Eg. 5
Spirit - Ka	Vine - yrt	Vine - yrt (irt)	Gardener kAny (Kah-nee)	Gardener kAry (Kah-ree)	Grapes - iYrt (irt)	Wine - yrp (irp)

Addendum Emmett Tilling The Garden

The **Spirit** (**Ka**) of the di**vine** is in the **Vine** and **Vines** come forth in **Gardens**, where the **Gardener Tills** the land, allowing **Grapes** to grow from the **Grape Vine**. Those **Grapes** ferment and become **Wine**. Again, we must consider how the ancient Kemetyu chose to "spell" certain words. The symbol for the Ka (**eg. 1**) was two hands raised representing the double nature of our being. It is the **Ka** (**sahu**) that **reincarnates**, finding the perfect opportunity to finish it's mission on earth. Why then did the Kemetyu use the Ka symbol when spelling the word gardener (**eg. 3a / 3b**) and why is there an **eye** (p 30) in the word vine (**eg. 2b**)? There are other symbols/letters that could have been used to make the KA sound in the word gardener (**eg. 3a / 3b**). The symbol of Two hands raised (**eg. 1, ka**) was used in the word gardener for a reason. And there is a reason why Ausar is often seen with grapes hanging above his head. In the ancient Kemetic Ausarian resurrection drama, Ausar (Osiris) was the first **gardener**, the first to cultivate (**Till, Tilling, Tillage**) the land and the first to **come back** after "death", or better known as **Wehem Mesut** (repeating of births, p **14**). Christianity borrowed from the resurrection story of Ausar when the character of **Jesus** was created and the Murder of **Emmett Till** is intimately connected to both Ausar and Jesus. According to the book of John, after Jesus resurrected, Mary mistook him for a **gardener**. "Dear woman, why are you crying?" **Jesus** asked her. "Who are you looking for?" She thought he was the ***gardener***. "Sir," she said, "if you have taken him away, tell me where you have put him, and I will go and get him."- (John, ch. 20:14.15). Emmett **Till** arrived in M**ississ**ippi (**isis**) on August 21st 1955. The next day he spent the early morning harvesting cotton on his uncles farm (**garden**). Emmett **Till**'s uncle, **Moses** Wright Jr was a farmer (a **gardener**). According to the book of John, ch. 19:**41**, Jesus's cruxifixction took place near a **garden**. Emmett **Till** was murdered on Leslie Milam's **farm** (**garden**) in M**ississ**ippi. Ausar reigned for **28 years** and Emmett Till was murdered on **August 28th**. **Emmett** was tortured, shot in the head and **thrown in a** M**ississ**ippi **river** at **14** years old. Ausar was cut into **14** pieces and **thrown in the Nile river**. The story of Ausar is a parable that teaches about the natural law of **Wehem Mesut,** reincarnation (**Gilgul**). With that in mind we must consider what it is that Ausar was really "cultivating", or **Tilling** (p **41**).

Ausar (Osiris)

Addendum Emmett Tilling The Garden

Rau nu Prt m heru

Ausar represents the **immortal soul** of all human beings that reincarnates. **Auset** represents intuition and wisdom. **Set** represents your own **ego**. While **Heru** represents the potential of your spiritual stamina to become the Heru (**hero**) of your life journey, conquering **your own ego** (Set).. **Re-member** that **you** are **Ausar** and **Heru**, the **hero!** See page 3 for the **hero's journey!** In the Bible, God is the father of Jesus and in the ancient Kemetic Ausarian resurrection drama, Ausar (Osiris) is the father of Heru (Horus). Jesus is resurrected from the dead and Ausar is resurrected from the dead through the birth of his son Heru. According to the book of John, ch.15:7, Jesus says, "I am the true **grapevine** and my father is the **gardener**". This verse works to connect Jesus to Ausar. Ausar was a **gardener** and he was also the first to cultivate **grapes**. The wine that was produced from these grapes was called the **blood of Osiris**. When the wine was mixed with ingredients like the acacia bark it was called **Yrp (irp)**. When Yrp wine was consumed during sacred ceremonies it caused the initiates to have life changing experiences similar to the spiritual **Ayahuasca** drink. The Yrp wine was said to caused the appearance of Lusaaset, 'the great one who comes forth.' This is where the stories of Jesus turning water into wine originates from and this is also where the practice of taking communion in the Christian religion comes from. **Emmett** is another way to spell the word **Emit**. Emit means to **send forth**. In a like manner, my past lives were **sent forth** after I communed with the sacred **manna** (p 480), no different than how **Lusaaset comes forth** after the consumption of the **Yrp wine**. When Emmett Till was murdered his mother, Mamie Till was visited by an entity (a voice) that she felt was God (p 511). She **heard a voice** that told her, "*It was ordained from the beginning of time that Emmett would die a sacrificial death.* ***Be happy to have been the mother of a child who died blameless like Christ****, but there is a job for you to do now. Emmett has done his job now your job is to continue to tell the story so that mans consciousness will be aroused and justice can at-last prevail.*" Emmett was murdered in the year of the **goat** and his mother Mamie would also die in the year of the **goat**, in 2003. Even her death worked to confirm what the voice told her. Mamie died on **Jan 6**. **Jan 6** is 12 days after the Winter Solstice (pages 489, 614). In the Christian religion **Jan 6** is the day that the 3 Magi visited **Jesus** in a manger. **Jan 6** is also the day that the ancient Kemetyu celebrated the Winter Solstice and **Tupac's** grand mother Eloise Maria Barnes was born on **Jan 6.** The murder of Emmett **Till** was a prophecy designed to remind human beings about the immortality of their souls and what it is that we are supposed to be cultivating, or "**Tilling**" here on Earth. Even in the name K**emet** you find the name Emmett.

Why the Acacia Tree?

Iu f Per f m heru

The acacia tree was renowned for its strength, hardiness, medical properties, edibility and it is an attractive hardwood from which the ancient Egyptians built, boats, sarcophaguses, and furniture among other things. Acacia was called **shont,** shonnet, shondj, or shondet in Egyptian (it is called sont in modern Arabic). It is important to note that all species of Acacia are known to be **hallucinogenic**, either in their bark, roots, leaves or fruit, due to the natural production of **Dimethyltryptamine (DMT)**. The **pineal gland** (3rd eye), which is responsible for producing the DMT molecule, appears in the embryo at the **49th** day of gestation and 49 days is also the amount of time the Tibetans Monks believed it took one soul to be reborn into another life. In particular, acacia trees were used by the ancient Egyptians to make a hallucinogenic wine similar to the spiritual **Ayahuasca** drink taken by the Tukano Indians of the Rio Uapes in Brazil. The Egyptians called this wine **Yrp**, and when consumed during sacred ceremonies, caused the appearance of Lusaaset, 'the great one who comes forth. This acacia tree has similar psychoactive effects as the sacred mushroom. In Egyptian creation stories , the acacia tree of Lusaaset is located in the Garden of Heliopolis and described as the 'tresses of the Goddess' which 'ascended from the vertex of Geb'. Since Geb was the God of the Earth and husband of sky Goddess Nut, the acacia Tree of Life bridges the Earth and Sky at the center of the Garden. In this way, the hallucinogenic experience of drinking Yrp was a way to ascend the sacred Tree of Life and be **reborn** as spirit into the heavens. The Acacia Tree of Life in the **Garden of Heliopolis** may be the same Tree of Life described in the Biblical **Garden of Eden** and the Egyptians considered the acacia tree a sacred primordial tree. In the Book of Coming Forth by Day, the deceased says that she/he stands before Anubis in a time before the acacia was born, that is, in the beginning, before the deities had established All Things. The oldest acacia tree (**Tree of Life**) was believed to be owned by Lusaaset and located just north of Egypt, in the famous **Garden of Heliopolis**. In one of the Egyptian creation stories all the Goddesses and Gods were said to be born beneath an acacia tree and this is supported in the Book of Coming Forth by Day, because within it it details how after death the deceased souls go back to "the Acacia Tree of the Children". There are many spells and utterances that mention **Lusaaset** and her sacred tree. In one of the formulae of the Coffin Texts, wood from Lusaaset's sacred acacia is crushed by the deceased for its healing properties. In another text, there is a magical spell invoking Lusaaset to heal all ailments.

Ausar is the One in the Tree

Utterances for Coming Forth by day into Light

While the acacia tree is associated with a number of Egyptian Deities, it was intimately connected with the Ausarian (Osirian) resurrection drama. The ancient Egyptians built boats and sarcophagi from the acacia tree and within this act was hidden a sacred analogy.. The **DMT** within the Acacia tree allowed them to sail in their solar barks (**astral bodies**) just like the wooden boats sailed up and down the Nile. The sarcophagus represented the physical body that houses the soul (solar bark). Ausar (Osiris), God of the underworld, rebirth and reincarnation was also born from an Acacia tree. In some versions of the Ausarian Resurrection, Ausar was placed in an sarcophagus, cut into **14** pieces and **thrown in the Nile river** where the **acacia tree** magically grew up around his body after his sarcophagus washed up on the shores of Byblos. His body was discovered by his wife Auset (Isis) and her sister Nephthys, together they were called the two Acacia Goddesses (the Two **Shonti** Goddesses). In the Pyramid Texts, the spirit of Ausar impregnates his wife Auset and Ausar returns/reincarnates as **Ra** through his son Heru (Horus), and "**comes forth** from the acacia tree" of Auset (Isis). Because of this Ausar was believed to **live inside the spirit of all Acacia Nilotica** trees. He was called "**the One in the Tree**" and "**the Solitary One in the Acacia**.". This is why he is often seen painted **green** like a plant. The acacia's hallucinogenic fruit (DMT) would have been the fruit from the forbidden "tree of knowledge". From this we might conclude the wine drank by **Jesus** and his apostles could have been an analogy for the sacred acacia **Yrp wine**, or a **lotus flower** tonic drank by initiates to induce a spiritual rebirth (p 488). Not everyone who drank the wine would have access to the higher realms but still the Yrp wine was sacred so not everyone was allowed to know of it. It is interesting to note that in the outer-body experiences associated with DMT many people have recorded seeing deceased friends and family, therefore Acacia Nilotica is a fitting symbol of the underworld and the spirit. When I had my first experience with the **sacred mushroom** I unlocked the door to my past life as **Emmett Till** however I saw no ancestors, but when my life as **King Tut** came on April 4th 2020 (page 594) I was visited by **Rosa Parks** and **Martin Luther King**. It is not a **coincidence** that the majority of DMT users also feel a sense of rebirth after they commune with the sacred medicines, which is a characteristic of Ausar, the Lord of rebirth, **the One in the Acacia Tree**. In modern archaeology of Egypt, Acacia Nilotica has been found in a huge percentage of the tombs unearthed. The evidence speaks for itself.

It is he, who comes forth by day into Light

Initiate communes with the Acacia Tree

Figure A

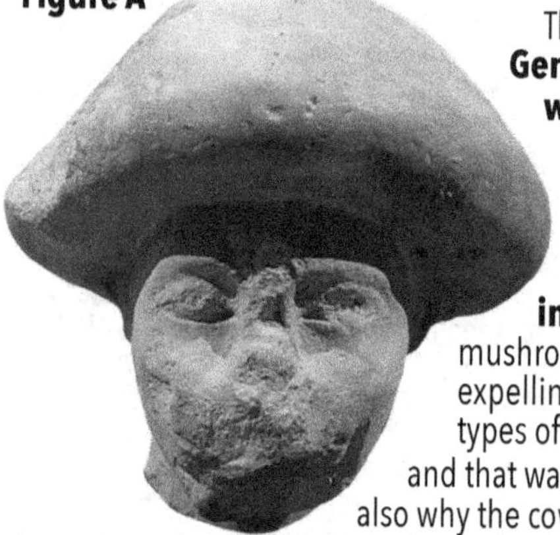

The first African Entheogen (psychedelic) was the Mushroom

The word entheogen is comprised of three base words. The words **In** (inside), **Theo** (God) and **Gene** (to generate). So the word entheogen would mean, to **generate** the **God** dwelling **within you**. Another word for entheogen is psychedelic which means, mind manifesting, or to manifest ones mind. This is the basis of becoming one with Ausar (Osiris) which was a practice of the Nswt Bity's (pharaohs) of the ancient African Kemetyu (Egyptians). One of the first entheogens was the mushroom. Mushrooms (fungi) are crucial to ecosystems and neither forest nor fungi could exist without the other. It's been said that fungi are the **interface** of organisms **between life and death**! Humans share a closer relationship with mushrooms than we do with plants. Mushrooms breathe like humans, taking in oxygen and expelling carbon dioxide. There are many different types of mushrooms which grow in different types of environments. In ancient Kemet the cow (**Het Heru**, **Hathor**) was seen as a divine animal and that was partly due to the fact that the blue sacred mushroom grew from the dung of the cow. This is also why the cow was seen as divine in India. Mushrooms are living sentient beings helping all forms of life throughout the universe. Mushroom spores are organic technology created by an unknown creator and when they were created is also unknown. Spores are like the seeds of a mushroom and the shells of spores are one of the hardest things in nature. Spores are said to come to earth from space on comets. If we are to think of God as the creator that created everything then God created spores long before humans were created (See page 539). In ancient Kemetic spiritual systems **Ausar** is the Lord of the **west**, **resurrection, reincarnation, the underworld** and **rebirth**. He was the first person ever mummified and he is the one who defeats death through the resurrection and this is where the story of **Jesus Christ** was taken from when Christianity first came into existence. The mushroom relates to the underworld like **Ausar**, as they deal with death, decomposition and afterlife. When a pharaoh dies he unites with Ausar and returns through the son, resurrected as Ra. The resurrection of the father through the son. This is what the ancient Egyptians had mastered! This concept of resurrection was called the **Wehem-Mesut** (repeating of births, p 14). **Re-member** that **you** are **Ausar** and **Heru,** the **hero!** See page 3 for the **hero's journey!** From time immemorial we knew that there was no death. We understood the repetition (immortality) of the soul and taught about the resurrection of the Ba (soul). They Called the death of the physical body westing. Just as the Sun rises in the east and sets in the west the same is to be said for the Ba. In more secret teachings you learn that Ausar is always shown with his hands crossed forming the shape of a mushroom cap with his legs representing the stem. In figure **A**, a man can be seen with a mushroom headed hairstyle dating from the reign of Amenemhat I (EmhatAmen I, p 14). The bottom of a **mushroom cap** is a circle within a circle (figure **B**) and looks just like the Mdw Ntr (hieroglyph) symbol of **Ra** (the Sun) which is a circle within a circle (figure **C**), and they both look like the human **eyeball** (figure **D**).

Mushroom Cap

Figure B

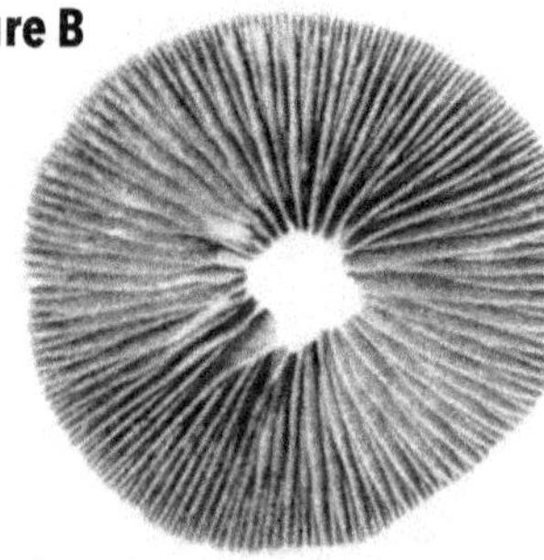

Mdw Ntr (hieroglyph) symbol for the Sun

Figure C

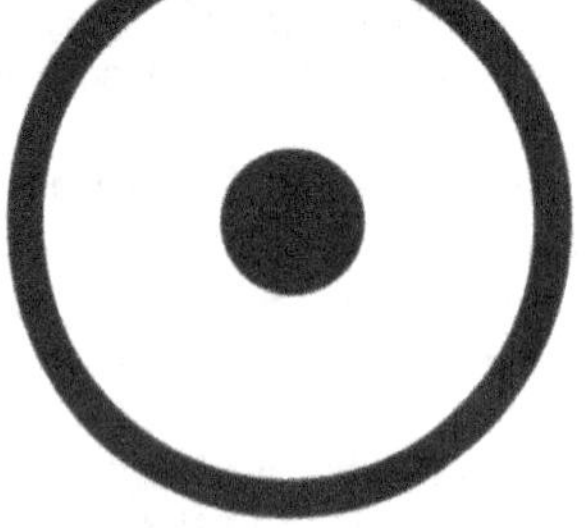

Human eye

Figure D

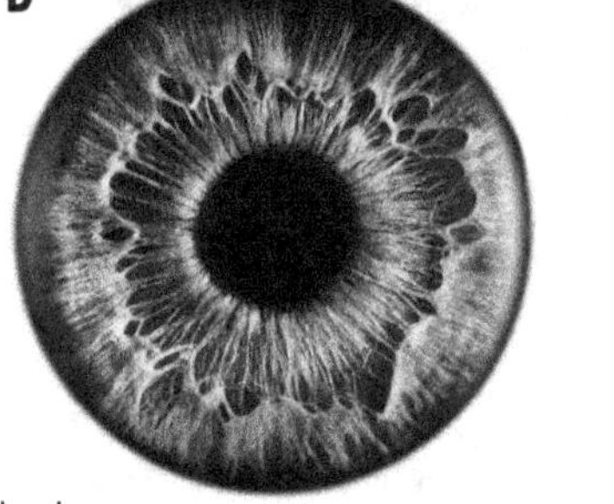

I have heard master **Kilindi Iyi** (p 606) suggest that the Mdw Ntr (hieroglyphs) in ancient Kemet had a secret use that was triggered after the eating of the sacred plants, mushrooms etc. When an initiate ingested the sacred mushroom and looked at the wall of Mdw Ntr, the images would animate and become 3 dimensional, coming off the wall to tell a deeper meaning to what was written. Kilindi says the Mdw Ntr is not just something to be read but it is to be experienced for the initiate that has earned the keys to open those doors. It is also theorized that the mushroom taught man how to build the pyramids. The same thing is said about the Tibetan Mandalas and Persian rugs. When the sacred medicines where ingested the initiates consciousness could enter the mandala and communicate with other beings, even dead relatives. The red dye in the Persian rugs are made from the Syrian Rue seed which has psychoactive effects when it is mixed with the the acacia bark. The **acacia bark** is the same tree (bush) that **Moses** was said to have burned. This is where the legend of Aladdin flying on a **magic carpet** (Persian rug) originates from. The dye (Syrian Rue) from the carpet would help induce this experience along with ingesting the sacred brew (**soma**). The active component within these sacred psychoactive substances is called **dimethyltryptamine** (**DMT**). The **pineal gland pineal gland** (3rd eye 𓂀), which is responsible for producing the DMT molecule, appears in the embryo at the **49th** day of gestation. DMT is secreted during birth (via the mother), upon death and during near death experiences. 49 days is also the amount of time the Tibetans believed it took one soul to be reborn into another life. After death, the body floods the pineal gland (single eye, first eye, third eye, spiritual eye) with DMT and the soul (consciousness) of the individual has there life review and can also visit loved ones before they leave this world and move towards their next phase of existence. It was from master **Kilindi Iyi** that I learned about the 60 day ritual the Tibetans did for their dead to allow the soul time to part this world. In ancient Kemet we also had the 70 days of mummification where the soul was made ready for their departure from this world. I would meet master Kilindi Iyi for the first and only time in physical form on October 5th 2018 at Nicholas book store in Brooklyn, where he gave a lecture on the sacred mushroom (page 537). This was 3 months after I had my past life revelation of my life as **Emmett Till**. I wanted to tell Kilindi my story and get some sort of direction and advice from him. At the end of the lecture I told him my story but all he told me was that this must be the time that it was supposed to be revealed to me. Two years later master **Kilindi Iyi** would visit me on April 11th 2020 the day after he died (page 605-606) which was 7 days after (April 4th 2020) my **revelation** of my past life as Tutankhaten (**King Tut**). I knew that he had come to me in that "coincidence" the same way he explained the 60 day ritual of the Tibetans and the soul visiting loved ones before they leave this world and move towards their next phase of existence. When I went to the Detroit Psychedelic convention on August 7th 2020 (page 618) I met many of **Kilindi's** family and friends who also told stories of him visiting them shortly after he transitioned.

Mushrooms in Kemet

Use your imagination, it isn't hard to find mushrooms hidden in plain sight throughout the images on the walls of ancient Kemet (Egypt).

Rau
nu
Prt
m
heru

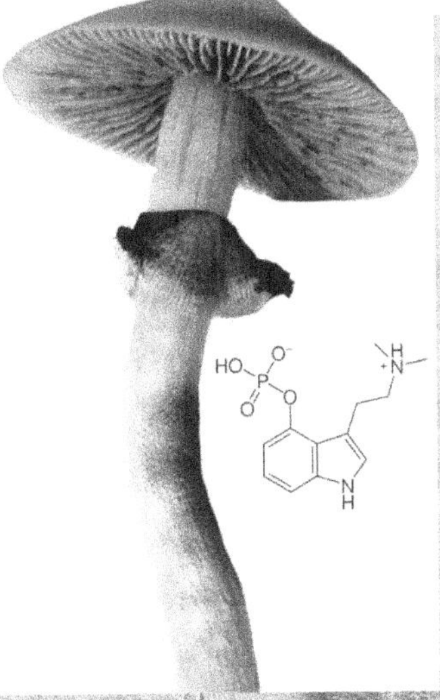

Iu
f
Per
f
m
heru

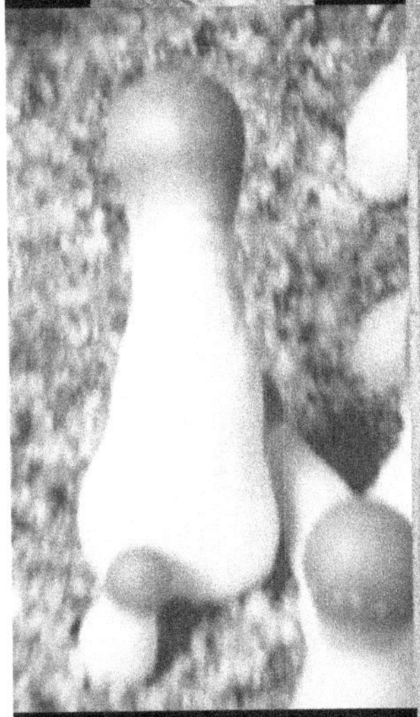

Utterances
for
Coming
Forth
by day
into
Light

It is
he,
who
comes
forth
by day
into
Light

The Lost and Found

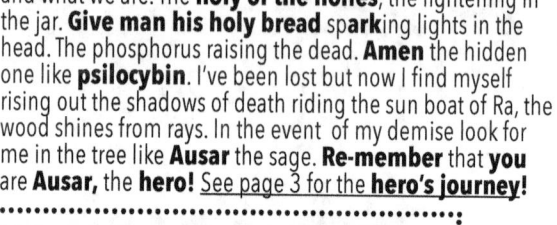

Man has been searching everywhere for the elixir of life ever since the great mysteries were lost to the night. The walls of Kemet leave the most captivating imagery as we have seen with the **Acacia Tree**, the **Lotus**, the **Yopo** and the **DMT.** Giving rise to the high likeliness that the ancient Egyptians were exploring altered states of consciousness. We see the plants in ancient cave art in Algeria, we see mushrooms on the walls in Spain. **Peyote** was used on **Turtle Island** thousands of years before they came. From Greece to India, and from Demeter to Shiva we see secret potions given to believers. Jesus turned water to **wine** and broke sacred **manna** at the last supper leaving theologians and Raiders of the Lost Ark Indiana Jones and them Pirates of the Caribbean searching for a holy grail. They use modern sophisticated archaeometrics, searching for psychoactive plant sources these instruments detect it in the fragments of archeological excavations. As man has made attempts to reach these altered states the misfits and the rejects have altered our fate making misstep after misstep and won't accept their mistakes. From **Heroin** to **LSD** they synthesize Mother Tree. And because you fail to seek the past, too afraid to bare the task. You wear the mask, then you take it off. With every law they pass the truth is lost. With every cough and with every sneeze **Rosemary** is ignored as it blows in the breeze. They can kill us and bury us but we the Blakseeds so we'll be back maybe in the **Weeds** like **Dandelions**. I ain't lying I be iron like **Lion's Mane**, mothers be cry'n when they see their sons shot down like **Orion's** pain. Never knowing the **D**ead **M**an's **T**reasure is where **Orion** aims. We've come so far from the **mayans** disconnected from the **shamans** plane. Even if we heard the original names they'd be foreign maine. Like **Ayahuasca,** most people have no clue of the witches and the farmers in the forest and what they do. Like in the Congo we used **Iboga** for healing but when the missionaries saw this all they did was start killing for killings sake. Like Spanish missionaries burning the indigenous at the stake in Mexico. They poison sacred **Tobacco** but still you smoke it, no ceremonial use just addiction you cope with. Come take this trip with me across the ages and see the European in his many stages. Is he a drug addict or just searching for plants for profit? Use logic cause too much of anything is toxic. Be careful how you define what nature made exotic because herbs are the healings that nature gave the **Gnostics**. They say the truth is hidden where most never think to look. One things for sure the truth is written in this book. With every **crook** and every flail we knew this in ancient days. From time immemorial our minds would bathe with the real milk and honey the single eye would gaze. I take the sun boat of Ra, the wood shines from rays. You can find me in the tree like **Ausar** the sage or running free with **Harriet** going out in a blaze. This life is a maze. Making it easy to get confused. We are never taught in schools about molecules used back in the days of **Ta Seti**. When **Ausar raised his bow** ready to take aim. **As on earth as in heaven**. As above so below. You might know the pyramids were align with the stars, but most don't know who and what we are. The **holy of the holies**, the lightening in the jar. **Give man his holy bread** sp**ark**ing lights in the head. The phosphorus raising the dead. **Amen** the hidden one like **psilocybin**. I've been lost but now I find myself rising out the shadows of death riding the sun boat of Ra, the wood shines from rays. In the event of my demise look for me in the tree like **Ausar** the sage. **Re-member** that **you** are **Ausar,** the **hero!** See page 3 for the **hero's journey**!

As above

Ausar the Archer
Orion's Belt

So below

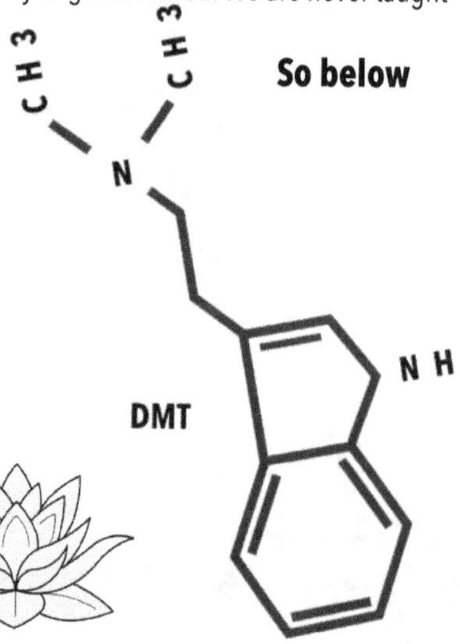

DMT

"The **D**ead **M**an's **T**reasure is where **Orion** aims"

5000 BCE - Mushroom Depicted in Caves

Cave art on the continent of Africa, on Tassili plateau of Southeastern Algeria shows the oldest known petroglyphs of psychoactive mushrooms, specifically Psilocybe. The paintings show a people (Shamans) holding objects that look like mushrooms and some have mushrooms growing from their bodies. One of these figures has been deemed the "**bee-headed shaman".** Interestingly enough In ancient Kemet (Egypt) the Nswt Bity (Pharaoh) was symbolized as a **bee.** These paintings work to strengthen the belief that psychoactive plants have been used as vital parts of spiritual ritual ceremonies from time immemorial. Because of this many people today advocate for the use of psilocybin, the psychedelic compound that occurs in such mushrooms, as treatment for conditions like depression. Unfortunately these medicinal fungi are mostly only seen as just recreational drugs.

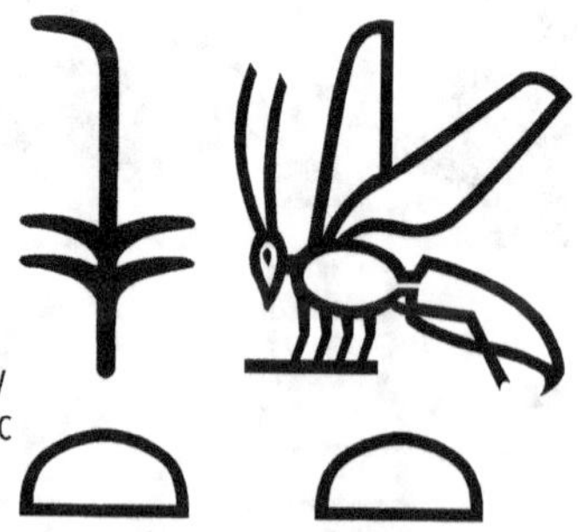

Nswt Bity

Peyote

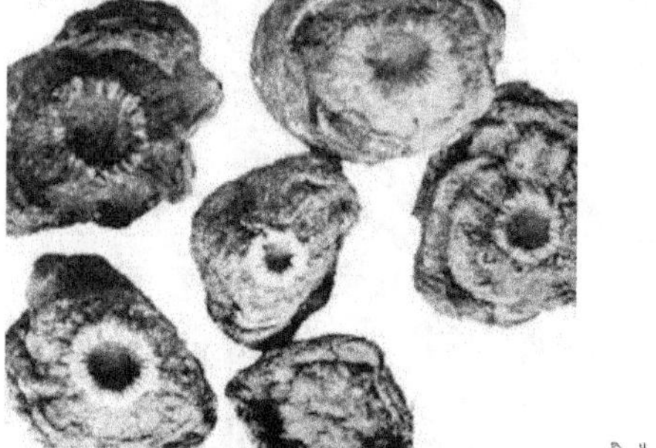

4220 BCE - Peyote

The Peyote plant has been used for thousands of years by the indigenous people living on the land mass now called America. It was used during spiritual rights of passage ceremonies and for tribal celebrations. In 2005 scientists unearthed ancient peyote buttons (the edible crown portion of the peyote plant) at an archeological site in Texas, which radiocarbon dating (also referred to as "carbon dating" or "carbon-14 dating") revealed to date back to 4,220 B.C.E. (approximately 6,000 years ago). Native Americans in the Rio Grande area have also collected peyote buttons and manufactured peyote effigy sculptures which were found in the Shumla Caves dating back to 3700 BCE. A **Harvard University** medical research study concluded that "**we found no evidence of psychological or cognitive deficits among Native Americans using peyote in a religious setting**."

4000 BCE : Mushrooms Bloom in Spain

In a cave near the town of Villar del Humo in Spain, the Selva Pascuala mural depicts what appear to be psilocybin mushrooms. This mural shows a bull in the centre with a row of 13 small mushroom-like objects. These paintings provide the earliest evidence of the use of psychedelic mushrooms in Europe. Most people today associate mushrooms with the 1960s, but these wall pantings are evidence of mushroom use 6,000 years ago. Many of these cave murals found in Spain appear to depict them in religious rituals

Rau nu Prt m heru

Iu f Per f m heru

2000 BCE: Age of Aries

The story of Moses takes place around 2000 BCE at the beginning of the age of Aries. The book of Exodus from the Bible speaks about the sacred mushroom in a allegorical parable manner. In chapter 16 verse 14 of the book of Exodus Moses says "And when the dew that lay was gone up, behold, upon the face of the wilderness there lay a small round thing, as small as the hoar frost on the ground". The small, round, edible objects is none other than the **sacred mushrooms**. And Moses is none other than the Heretic enigmatic Pharaoh Akhenaten who actually, historically did the things that Moses was said to have done in the book of Exodus. The only proof that Moses lived is the bible yet Akhenaten's life is still written in stone. The story of Moses taking his people into the desert is a fabrication of Akhenaten who took his people to a fertile land between Memphis and Thebes (Luxor) and built a city that venerated the sun (Aten). Today this land is a desert as it was when the bible was written.

Utterances for Coming Forth by day into Light

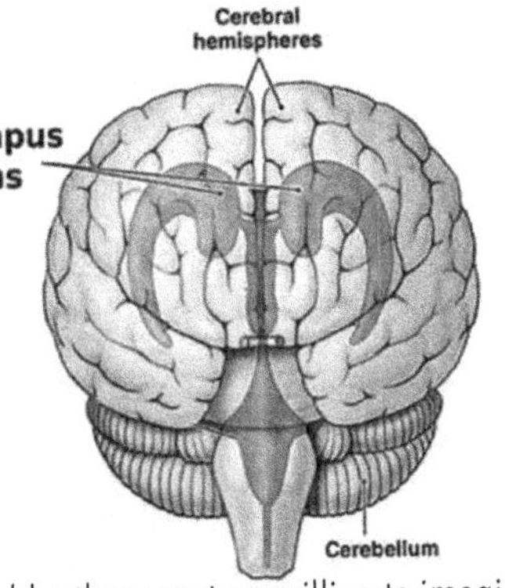

Ganesh = page 542

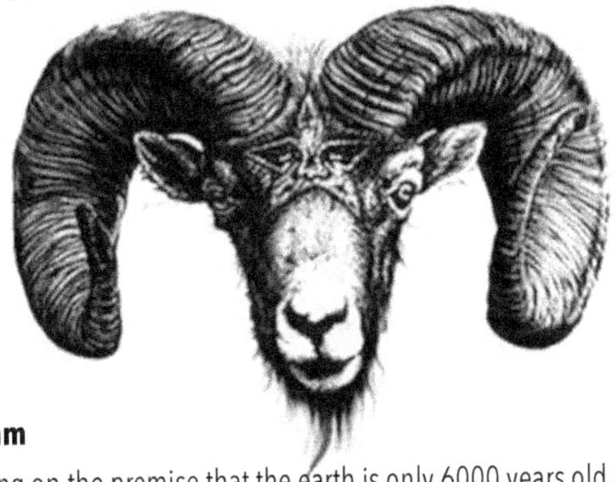

Mission-Aries and the age of the Ram

It is he, who comes forth by day into Light

The planet is older than most are willing to imagine because most people on earth are operating on the premise that the earth is only 6000 years old. This false theory was brought forth by an **arc**hbishop from Ireland named James Ussher. In 1654 he claimed that God created earth on Oct 23rd 4004 BCE, at 9 am. Since then, Christianity bound most of the world into a box of 6000 years, claiming that the meta-spiritual devices (pyramids) could be no older than 6000 years old. Ussher wasn't alone, **Sir Isaac Newton** thought the world was created in 4000 BCE but of course this could not be farther from the truth. The astrological knowledge that was left by ancient civilizations like Kemet and the Mayans span for more than 25,000 years and the remnants of this knowledge is hidden within **astro-theology**. **Amun** is one of the Kemetic Deities (Gods) who were often depicted with **Rams Horns** on their heads which represented the area of the brain called the **Hippocampus**. It's no **coincidence** that the hippocampus is also called **Ammons Horn** and is shaped like the **zodiac** sign **Aries** and much of the world we live in is based on astrology, even religion.. Especially religion! The ancients regarded matters of the heavens very important which is why they built pyramids (Meta Spiritual Devices) aligned with the stars in various constellations like the pyramids of Giza aligining with the stars in **Orions Belt** (page 344).. They had already realized that it takes roughly 2,160 years for the equinox to precess (move) through a sign. Thus it takes some 25,920 years for the spring equinox to traverse the full circuit of the constellations. This cycle is called the Great Year and it is the precession of the equinoxes through the constellations that gives names to the various ages. The age of Taurus (Bull) began just around 4320BC, and we can see the ages play out in the biblical allegories. The bible pulls from the astrological zodiacal time period of Aries which covers the 18th dynasty. This is why the Christian men who went around killing in the name of their religion were called **"missionaries"**. The mission was pulling from this time of Aries, hence Mission-Aries. The mission was to steal the knowledge they had taken from the 18th dynasty so as to dominate and control the world with religion (page 592)! The story of **Moses** takes place at the beginning of the age of Aries (Ram). Which is why Moses came down from Mount Sinai as '**two horned**', that is, crowned with **Ram's Horns**. He got "angry" when he saw his people still worshiping the 'Golden Bull' (Taurus). He broke their statue because they were still stuck in the age of Taurus. This is a code for the adept reading signaling the age of Aries (the Ram). The age of Aries (Ram) began around 2160BC, and the stories in the Bible are allegories, not real stories with real people.. The age of Pisces (Two Fish) started around 1BC, the same time Jesus was said to be born. **Jesus** feeding the multitude with **two fish** is another allegory connected to the two fish seen in the zodiac sign of **Pisces**. We are at the end of Piscean age which is the age of **Believing**, and we are moving into the age of Aquarius, which is the age of **Knowing.**

1700-1500 B.C.E. - Eleusinian Mysteries

The Eleusinian Mysteries surrounding their sacred drink called kykeon represented the most important ritual in the religious realm of ancient Greek world. According to historical hypotheses, they began around 1700-1500 B.C., in Eleusis, a small town outside Athens; and they were practiced until the fourth century B.C. During the mysteries, the faithful honored the divine figure of the Goddess **Demeter**; all the ceremonies took place around the temple of the Goddess herself. The figure of Demeter was flanked by her daughter **Persephone**, who according to mythology was kidnapped by the God of the underworld, **Hades**: the Gods, in a pact with the deity of the underworld decided to allow Persephone to return to the face of the Earth for six months a year, alongside her mother Demeter, before she would be forced to return again to the world of the dead for the rest of the year. This myth leads to the ancient explanation of the change of seasons, of the succession of the periods of flowering in the Spring and Summer with those of dormancy in the Winter. For this reason, according to Homer, the Eleusinian Mysteries were created to honor Demeter and Persephone, as symbols of fertility, flowering and the cyclical birth of life.

Mushrooms or elixirs

Kykeon, the mysterious elixir from the past linked to the Eleusinian Mysteries. What was it made of? There are many speculations as to the ingredients of this elusive elixir. Some claim it was made of water, rye flour (**Ergot**), and Roman mint. Scientific study has identified alkaloids in the ergot fungus that interact with the serotonin receptors in our brains. Additionally, we know that the ergot fungus contains lysergic acid as well as its precursor, ergotamine. Lysergic acid is a precursor for the synthesis of LSD. The theory that the kykeon derived its psychoactive effects from ergot was proposed at the Second International Conference on Hallucinogenic Mushrooms near Port Townsend, Washington on October 28th 1977 (pages 29,33), exactly 3 days after I was born (October 25th 1977, page 34). Few have ver heard of this elixir and fewer still speak or write about it but it was an essential part of a ritual that took place during the practice of an ancient ritual linked to the world of the Greek Gods and their veneration. The Kykeon elixir had a very important role during the Eleusinian Mysteries, being the only food allowed during the period of sacred fasting observed by the believers for the course of these annual religious rites. During the ritual period, which was approximately 21 days, the faithful who were being initiated to the cult of the Goddess were subjected to a fast in honor of Demeter. Etymologically, the Greek meaning of the word Kykeon is that of "mixed together," homogeneous; however, in fact the final product was never a single substance, but a set of ingredients. There were many experiences of mystical visions and apparitions during the Eleusinian Mysteries, during which it was thought that one could have <u>direct contact with the world beyond and with the deities being celebrated</u>.

1000 - 5000 BC
Mushroom Stone Head Status

Central American cultures built temples to mushroom Gods and carved "mushroom stones" found in Mexico and Guatemala. The work provides some insight into indigenous cultures understanding of their local fauna's psychedelic properties.

1500 BCE - 1200 BCE Yoga and Soma

The Indian Rig Veda described the use of the psychedelic drink called **Soma.** Soma at a yogic level refers to the crown chakra, which is opened by Indra (yogic insight) and releases a flood of bliss throughout the body. Said another way, the Soma is a secretion in the brain from spiritual practices of Yoga, pranayama, mantra and meditation (an elixir prepared from the Tarpak Kapha or form of Kapha lubricating the nervous system in Ayurvedic thought). This inner Soma is the main subject of the Vedic hymns, though outer Somas were also important. Man has for a long time been searching for mysterious elixirs of life and lost cities of gold. The Soma plant however might not be one specific plant, it may very well be part of a variety of sacred plants, including tonics, nervines and mind-altering plants of various types as well special preparations of them. We can learn a lot about a people by the art they create and we can see images of **Shiva with mushrooms in his hand** and statues of the Buddha with mushrooms over their heads. Some say these are half truths, and fake histories but if we wish to get to the roots and push past limitations we must expand out imaginations. Perhaps we are what we eat and the ancestors were what they ate. what's on your plate? Holy cow it's a blood moon, I stepped in *shit, then I found a* ***mushroom,*** I ate it then I Jumped off mother ship with a witch then took off on her broom. Interstellar intergalactic, I traveled the universe while laying on my mattress. Magic is magic to the lay man who's afraid to paint the future, stuck staring at a canvas, but you gotta ***leave*** the ***branches*** and go to the ***root*** for the truth if you wanna make advances, trances, dances, **telepathine***. The *answers from the unseen uploaded while in a* ***dream,*** you can rage against the machine or sage and engage the serene. Ever seen **Huey P** in the **Lotus**? ever notice the Lily on the wall? You don't care how they gave the Indians alcohol do you?! Voodoo needles in the arm, Simeon Toko, Angola gaining independence from Portugal, Poking y'all with the sorcery, Avatar or conspiracy? Jesus Christ superstar lyrically, physically a Reincarnation. Perhaps Indigenous people across geographical locations found their own "Soma" or sacred plants by communication with creation by being in tune with nature. Ultimately Soma refers to the the active component within these sacred psychoactive substances called **dimethyltryptamine** (**DMT**). These substances can be found in many plants and have corresponding mind-altering substances that can also be produced by the brain itself.

Rau nu Prt m heru

Iu f Per f m heru

1495 C.E. The Last Supper, Mushrooms and The Search For The Holy Grail

The Last Supper is a late 15th century mural painting by Italian artist Leonardo da Vinci and is assumed to have been started around 1495–96 C.E. It was commissioned as part of a plan of renovations to the church and its convent buildings by Leonardo's patron Ludovico Sforza, **Duke** of Milan. It is one of the Western world's most recognizable paintings (page 489). Those of you who are familiar with the religion of Christianity are probably familiar with the **sacrament** of Christ which Jesus and his **12 disciples** ingested during the "**Last Supper**". You may also be familiar with the story of Jesus turning water into wine. Supposedly Jesus and his disciples ate the **flesh** of Jesus and drank his blood. There are several schools of thought that discuss the theory that the sacrament of Christ (his flesh and blood) was actually a symbolic encryption for the sacred psychedelic mushroom and mushroom tea, which would also explain how Jesus "turned water into wine." Mushrooms can naturally collect rain water within their caps and if left long enough the water can appear to be red. The water absorbs the psychoactive components from the mushroom which can then be drank from the mushroom cap. When I was a Christian I always wondered what the ritual of communion was for. Why were we going through this process when there seemed to be no transformative feeling involved. In chapter 6 verse 51 of **the book John** in the **Bible, Jesus** says to his disciples at **the last supper.** "I am the living bread that came down from heaven. Whoever eats this bread will live forever. **This bread is my flesh,** which I will give for the life of the world." In the bible Jesus often speaks in **parables** and I think this passage is a coded parable. I do not think this passage was meant to suggest that the last supper was a meal consisting of human flesh and blood. In fact there are schools of thought that suggest the character of **Jesus was an analogy for the mushroom (manna)** to keep the secret of the mushroom hidden during the Roman Empire. You can see this symbology in pictures of mushroom caps (sun, halo) behind the head of Jesus. Many clues are given as to just what "Manna" is and the word **manna** even appears three times in the **Quran**, at 2:57, 7:160, and 20:80. All of the 3 passages repeat a similar quote. "and We* revealed to Moses when his people asked him for something to drink: "Strike the rock with your staff," whereupon **twelve** springs gushed from it; each group of people certainly recognized its drinking-place. And We shaded them with clouds and We* sent down upon them manna and quails." It is also narrated in the **Sahih** Muslim (one of the six major **Hadith** collections in Sunni Islam) that **Prophet Muhammad** (PBUH) said: "Truffles are part of the 'manna' which Allah sent to the people of Israel through Moses, and its juice is a medicine for the eye." But what eye* were they referring to? Perhaps the 3rd eye 𓂀, the pineal gland which is the key for spiritual sight. It's interesting that the round cap of a mushroom looks just like the **eyeball**. Exodus 16:14 of the Bible reads, "And when the dew that lay was gone up, behold, upon the face of the wilderness there lay a small **round thing**, as small as the hoar frost on the ground." Exodus 16:20 continues, "…some of them left of it till the morning, and it bred worms, and stank." The small, round, edible objects which when left in the Sun rot, breed worms, and stink are none other than mushrooms. It is the spore of the mushroom that fell from heaven in chapter 6 verse 51 of **the book John,** "I am the living bread that came down from heaven. Whoever eats this bread will live forever. This bread is my flesh, which I will give for the life of the world." Spores come into earths atmosphere on comets and are even found on satellites. In the bible it is written in Genesis 1:29 "God said Behold, I have given you every herb bearing seed, which is upon the face of all the earth, and every tree, in the which is the fruit of a tree yielding seed; to you it shall be for meat." The holy communion takes place **when spiritually mature beings** eat the bread of life sent down from the heavens. As a child I watched the Smurfs who lived in mushroom houses and when I played the video game Mario Brothers the first prize of the game was a mushroom that makes you grow bigger after touching it. The truth was always hidden in plain sight, so much so that it is hard to watch any series on Netflix or Hulu etc and not hear the name Jesus Written into every episode (page 58).

Utterances for Coming Forth by day into Light

It is he, who comes forth by day into Light

More Symbology Coded within the Last Supper, Astro Theology

In the painting you can see that the apostles are gathered in 4 sets of 3 figures each, with Jesus at the center. The 12 figures represent the 12 signs of the **zodiac** and them being gathered in 4 sets represent the 4 seasons, spring, summer, fall and winter. Jesus is the sun at the center. Davinci's painting is an astrological allegory as well. In the last supper's astronomical allegory, Jesus (the sun) gathered his 12 disciples (the 12 signs of the Zodiac) to prepare for the Saviors (Jesus'/Sun's) pending death and rebirth 3 day's later on December 25th (**Christmas**, the time when the sun appears to start it's northerly track). In most sun worshiping cults, common at the time, the sun (Jesus) was believed to have died on or about the 22nd of December, at the **Winter Solstice** and was reborn 3 day's later on **December 25th**. Dec 21 was the shortest day of the year. The 22nd 23rd & 24th are days that the sun seems to not move while nestled between the southern crux (a constellation that forms a cross).. It is this phenomenon that birthed the concept of the sun (son) dying for 3 days (on the southern cross). On the 25th of December the sun began it's northerly movement on the horizon and the day's began to get longer and longer. Like a celestial clock. From this celestial clock the story of Jesus was taken. A parable that teaches us we are eternal, falling and leaving or dying like a leaf on a tree only to be born again in other lives just like the leaves returning in spring. The Ausarian resurrection drama was the first story of resurrection. The story that the parable of Jesus was taken from. In the last supper story, Jesus, **(the sun personified)**, told of a pending betrayal by one of his disciples (one of the 12 signs of the zodiac). The betrayer was Judas who was personified by **Scorpio** (the Scorpion). When the sun (Jesus) was in the house of Scorpio (Judas), the scorpion betrayed Jesus (the sun) with a kiss (a scorpion sting). The scorpio zodiac ushers in the fall season which symbolizes death as leaves die and fall off trees.. And symbolically, the sun (Jesus) dies an agonizing death when the summer season turns to fall. "Jesus" is then stabbed by the Sagittarius spear on the cross, and placed into a cave / tomb, and was raised from the dead 3 day's later. His birth, life and death marked the end of the age of Aries, the ram (2160 BCE-1BCE, page 645), and the beginning of **the age of Pisces** the fish (1 BCE-2160CE), that occurred around 2000 years ago. The last supper was the astronomical allegory foretelling the sun's pending death through astronomical events marked by the changing of the seasons during the winter solstice. We can see this wisdom coded in the book of **Genesis 1:14 "**<u>And God said, Let there be lights in the firmament of the heaven to divide the day from the night; and let them be for signs, and for seasons, and for days, and years</u>**".** The Egyptian God **Khepri** ('he who came flying into existence from seemingly nowhere') was the original animal used to personify the constellation of **Cancer** and represented the **scarab dung beetle**. It was believed that the dung beetle was only male in gender, and reproduced by depositing semen into a dung ball. The supposed self-creation of the beetle resembles that of Khepri, who creates himself out of nothing, therefore **Khepri** (**Cancer**) became known as the '**Gate of Men**' through which souls descended from heaven into human bodies, or into creation. Khepri was known as the **Only Begotten God** (page 569). There is a cluster of hundreds of stars found within the Cancer (**Scarab**) constellation known as the **Bee Hive** cluster. This cluster is now known as "Messier" 44 or M44. This "Bee Hive " is the "gate of men" and it is also known as **the manger**. They said Jesus was born in a "manger" and called him the **Messiah** but thousands of years ago Pharaohs returned flying into existence from **Messier 44** (M44), the Bee Hive cluster of stars found within the Cancer (**Scarab**) constellation. No coincidence that I revealed this book in my **44th** year in this body. **Emmett Till's** mother, **Mamie Till** claimed to have heard the voice of God telling her that her son died blameless like Christ (**The Sacrificial Lamb,** page 511). She died on **Jan 6** 2003, the year of the goat, 12 days after the winter solstice (Dec 25). **Jan 6** is known as the **Epiphany** in Christianity as it marks the day that the 3 wise men visited Jesus in the **Manger** (p 614). **Jan 6** is the day that the ancient Kemetyu celebrated the Winter Solstice. **Tupac's** grand mother Eloise Maria Barnes was also born on **Jan 6**. Galileo wrote about the "Beehive" stating, "The nebula called Praesepe (Manger), which is not one star, only, but a mass of more than forty small stars. I have noticed thirty stars besides the Aselli." Thousands of years ago the sun appeared in the constellation of Cancer at the summer solstice, now the sun has moved one 12th (30 degrees) of a way across the sky away from Cancer, and now it appears near Gemini during the summer solstice. Sometime in 2020 I realized that it was my faith in Jesus Christ's resurrection and returning someday that set the foundation for my own revelation of reincarnation. The Scripture John, 14:12 reads, "Verily, verily, I say unto you, He that believeth on me, the works that I do shall he do also; and greater works than these shall he do". By having the belief in the resurrection of Jesus it allowed my soul to fathom the concept of resurrection after death, not knowing that the concept had originated in Kemet and was called **Wehem Mesut** (page 14).

April 17th 2022 Scarabeus, The Only Begotten God

I be the **ancient one** as old as he ancient sun, not **Jesus** or Flavius Josephus, this the **Scarabeus**, the only begotten God from Giza not Nazareth, a star like **Ausar**, read the **resurrection** manuscript, imagine this, we live and die come back again but man forgets, like the gate of men from which souls descend from heaven, and enter new bodies like ducatis speed'n off like harataki in a dream, walking on Saqqara pyramid the feeling was serene, clean **Deja Vu** some how my soul already knew, spiritual revenue, the **manger**, rejuvenation chambers, Mahabalipuram the Descent of Ganges when I saw them the strangest thing happen within my core, I started pouring, like when I saw the Nile for the first time when I was touring, a stranger in my own land now now they think I'm foreign, but I'm pharaonic restoring maat, iconic live'n and dying but I come back again flying out primordial darkness, **Heru** corporeal walk in my moccasins I dropped a lot of sins, how ironic the cream of the crop now he on top again - **TutemRa**

Rau nu Prt m heru

Iu f Per f m heru

Utterances for Coming Forth by day into Light

It is he, who comes forth by day into Light

Early 1500's

The young God **Xochipilli**, whose name in Nahuatl, the language of the Aztecs, means "Prince of Flowers", also known as Macuilxochitl, meaning "five flowers. **Xochipilli** is holding what appears to be an **Amanita muscaria mushroom** in each hand. According to ethno-archaeologist Irene Nicholson, "flowers symbolize a state of the soul on its journey to full Godhood."..."mushrooms were known as 'the flower that makes us drunk'" (Irene Nicholson 1967, p.90). This Precolumbian figurine on the left is now in the National Museum in Mexico City.

1560
Aztecs, Peyote and Mushrooms

The Spanish priest Bernardino de Sahagún wrote in his Florentine Codex about the use of **peyote** and teonanacatl **mushrooms** by the Aztecs in 1560. Born in Sahagún, Spain, in 1499, he journeyed to New Spain in 1529. He was a Franciscan friar, missionary priest and pioneering ethnographer who participated in the Catholic evangelization (**extermination of indigenous people**) of colonial New Spain. He was a Missionary during the Spanish conquest of Mexico in 1570.

1570
Use of Peyote brings death and pain in the "New Spain"

In the Late 17th century a Spanish missionary in Nayarit provided the first account of a peyote ritual practiced by the Cora tribe in Mexico. In 1570, the King of Spain (Philip II) sends Dr. Francisco Hernandez to **Mexico** "New Spain" to recover as much as possible of the Aztec's medical body of knowledge. Francisco spent the next five years compiling information about thousands of plants that had been used medicinally by Indigenous People, among which was **peyote**. Some of the information he collected (which included about 1000 plants) was published in 1649 in a text called "History of the Plants of New Spain". He included the following about peyote: "*It appears to be of sweet taste and moderately hot. Ground up and applied to painful joints it is said to give relief. Wonderful properties are attributed to this root.* ***It causes those eating it to be able to foresee and predict things***." perhaps the ability to help the native see the future is why it was eventually outlawed. In 1620, the Roman Catholic Church considered peyote "***an evil to be rooted out in the New World***" and created ecclesiastical laws that forbade the religious use of peyote. Because the Viceroyalty of New Spain prohibited peyote use in Mexico, the Inquisition often levied severe punishments, **including torture and death**. Spanish conquistadors ventured into North America with the intent to **capture**, **enslave**, and **convert indigenous people to Christianity** in addition to searching for mythological kingdoms of **gold** and **silver**.

1620 (Conscious)

The term "conscious" first appeared in the English language in 1620 when it was placed in the Oxford English Dictionary. The same time that slave ships were being unloaded with African slaves and the indigenous of Turtle Island (America) reduced to slaves. What kind of conscious is that? They defined it as "inwardly sensible or aware." But was the European **consciously aware** of the **terror** they imposed **everywhere**? They say that "big brother" is always watching. If indeed he is then he must have been watching me write this book and maybe that's why he's decided to have a conscious in 400 years later in 2022 finally declaring lynching a hate crime….. It seems like everything was done this year for poor little Emmett Till (page 666). I get a congressional medal in 2022, a lynching bill passed in my name and a mini series made about my life. . Ida B Wells fought for this over a hundred years ago! Why now? Very convenient I'd say, but that's fine.

1658 (Eleusinian Mysteries)

The first illustration of ergot was drawn by Swiss botanist Bauhin's son. It was the primary ingredient in Kykeon, the mysterious elixir linked to the Eleusinian Mysteries from 2000 BCE, Europe. Scientific study has identified alkaloids in the ergot fungus that interact with the serotonin receptors in our brains. Additionally, we know that the ergot fungus contains lysergic acid as well as its precursor, ergotamine. Lysergic acid is a precursor for the synthesis of **LSD**.

1783 (Amanita Muscaria is named)

The fly agaric gains its modern name **Amanita Muscaria** when it is moved to the subfamily of fungus named Amanita by Jean-Baptiste Lamarck. The name of the mushroom in many European languages is thought to have been derived from the fact that it was used as an insecticide, when sprinkled in milk. This practice has been recorded from Germanic- and Slavic-speaking parts of Europe, as well as the Vosges region and pockets elsewhere in France, and Romania. A Polish prisoner of war once described the Ob-Ugrian Ostyak culture from western Siberia. "They eat certain fungi in the shape of fly agarics, and thus they become drunk worse than on vodka, and for them, that's the very best banquet."

1797 - The First Acknowledge President Of The United States

George Washington was an American soldier, statesman, Founding Father, **Rapist** and **Slave Owner** who served as the first president of the United States from 1789 to 1797. Washington was born on February 22nd 1732, the day after **Malcolm X** was assassinated. The state electors under the Constitution voted for the president on **Rosa Park's** birthday, **February 4th** 1789. Washington was elected President on **April 6th** 1789, the same day **Bobby Hutton** was murdered (page 217) and two days after the day **Martin Luther King** was assassinated (pages 69, 592). Over two hundred years after the first American president was elected, brave men and women like Malcolm X, Rosa Parks, Bobby Hutton, and Martin Luther King were still fighting for the freedom and liberties that the constitution promises. Ameri Ka Ka kan't you see your stain?! Every 4 years don't a damn thing change, all I see is my people in chains, and I wish it would change, my own people ain't feeling my pain, cause they ain't looking, listening or reading shit mane, and it's really strange, cause everybody's looking for fame, but if you sp**ark** a flame, they start to aim, we all gonna die one day, this ain't the time to be a run away, so I gotta stay, I shed tears like **Lupe,** I don't care what they say, *I'm gonna unite the people, from here to* ***Zimbabwe,*** one race, I grew up listening to **Sade,** it's a crime not to replay what I say?!

October 3rd 1799
Mushrooms Bloom in Medical Journals

Exactly 364 days before **Nat Turner's** birth the first documented psychedelic mushroom experience is recorded in a **medical journal**. In a letter to the London Medical and Physical Journal in 1799, Dr. Everard Brande describes attending to a family who was acting strangely, laughing, and having visions after eating a stew they made with mushrooms picked in London's Green Park. Upon examination, the mushrooms were found to be Agaricus glutinosus and later reclassified as Psilocybe semilanceata, aka Liberty Caps.

1801
DMT from The Yopo Tree in 2130 B.C.

Baron Alexander Humboldt (Friedrich Wilhelm Heinrich Alexander von Humboldt) identified the Yopo tree as Anadenanthera peregrine in 1801. Humboldt was born on September 14th 1769, the day after **Tupac** died. He was a German polymath, geographer, naturalist, explorer, and proponent of Romantic philosophy and science. Humboldt was exploring the new world during the close of the Haitian Revolution that was taking place on the island of Hispaniola (Haiti). The beans from the Yopo tree helped the natives on the island of Hispaniola (Haiti) foresee the future allowing them to dispel the European invaders.

A future We Foresee, With and Without DMT

Anadenanthera peregrina (also known as Yopo, Jopo, or Cohoba) is a perennial tree native to the Caribbean and South America. The beans of the Anadenanthera pergrina plant have been noted to contain significant quantities of **bufotenin** (7.4%) alongside lesser amounts of **5 MeO DMT** (0.04%) and **DMT (**0.16%), all of which have a long history of use as entheogens. It has been used for ritual and healing purposes for thousands of years. Archaeological evidence shows Anadenanthera beans have been used as hallucinogens for thousands of years. The oldest clear evidence of use comes from smoking pipes made of puma bone (Felis Concolor) found with Anadenanthera beans at Inca Cueva, a site in the northwest of Humahuaca in the Puna border of Jujuy Province, Argentina. The pipes were found to contain the hallucinogen **DMT**, one of the compounds found in Anadenanthera beans. Radiocarbon testing of the material gave a date of 2130 BC, suggesting that Anadenanthera was used for spiritual healing rituals over 4,000 years ago. Yopo was taken by means of snuff or taken orally. Yopo snuff is usually blown into the user's nostrils by another person through bamboo tubes or sometimes snuffed by the user using bird bone tubes. Physical effects include tingling and numbness throughout the body and an increased heart rate. The hallucinatory effects follow as colors become enhanced and shapes appear to morph. When taken orally small amounts are often combined with alcoholic chichas (maize beer). Moderate doses are reported to be unpleasant, producing nausea and vomiting. Large amounts are not usually consumed orally; as many tribes believe oral use is dangerous.

As above

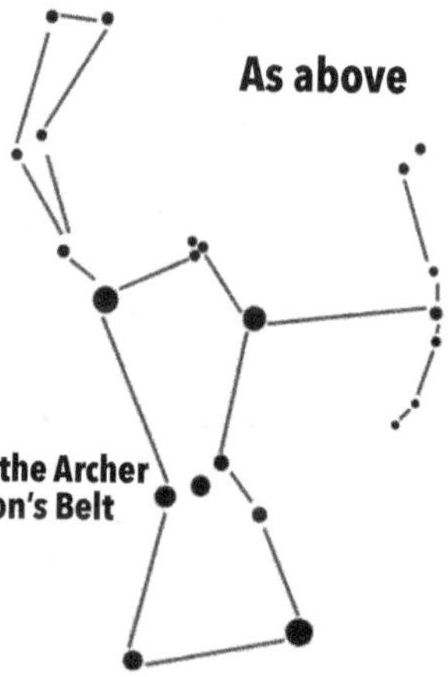

Ausar the Archer
Orion's Belt

So below

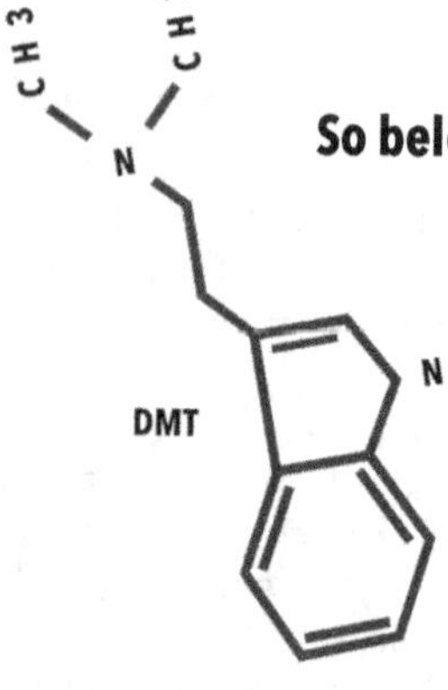

DMT

1847 - 1857 (Peyote on View)

Rau nu Prt m heru

Peyote has been used by the indigenous people of North America ever since the years 3780-3660 BC, however **the first published image of peyote** appeared in Curtis's Botanical Magazine in 1847 and ten years later in 1857 Peyote's effects were first described in the *New Orleans Picayune*. By the 1870's the use of Peyote by europeans spread more widely into the United States. Most prevalent would be the use of peyote for ceremonial purposes by Native Americans. Once consumed, peyote is used as a means of communicating with the spirit world. It is the **mescaline** within the Peyote that is the main **psychoactive component** causing the visionary effects comparable to those of **LSD** and **psilocybin**. The Tarahumara (one of two original indigenous tribes that actually still go on pilgrimages for peyote) are famous as great distance runners. These athletes/hunters run barefoot and naked except for loin cloths and little pouches containing peyote at their sides. Each athlete eats peyote as he runs to combat pain, attain greater endurance and combat hunger and thirst while hunting for days without food, water, or rest. As traditional medicine, peyote has also been shown to have antibiotic activity against a wide variety of bacteria including some penicillin resistant strains. Beyond this, peyote has been used in the treatment of arthritis, influenza, intestinal disorders, diabetes, **scorpion** bites, datura poisoning, to combat painful joints, toothache, pain in child-birth, fever, breast pain, skin disease, diabetes, colds, blindness, neurasthenia, hysteria and asthma. And if all this isn't enough for you, the flesh of peyote may also be applied topically to promote milk production. Furthermore, tribes such as the Tarahumara and Huichol Indians drink powdered peyote in water to give health, long life and to purify body and soul. They also apply it externally after chewing to treat snakebite, bruises, wounds, burns, fractures, constipation, and use it as an analgesic, anti-rheumatic, and general tonic.

1849 "Swing Low Chariot, They had a Bounty on Harriet"

Iu f Per f m heru

Oral tradition tells the story of how Araminta Ross aka **(Harriet Tubman)** ate a sacred mushroom, given to her by **Earl Johnson,** her most trusted friend which helped them navigate through the wilderness at night (**underground railroad**). The **mycelium** of the mushroom is equivalent to the roots of a tree and the mycelium is usually hidden under bark, ground, rotten wood, or leaves. The mycelium **underground** network of the mushroom is what allows trees to talk to each other exchanging vital information for survival. I find it strange that her name sounds like the psychedelic Amanita mushroom (Araminta/ Amanita). The **Amanita Muscaria mushroom** is famous for being found in the forest growing at the base of the pine or evergreen tree and because of this the red and white Amanita Muscaria are closely linked to the pine tree, for **Christmas** (Jesus) celebrations. This mushroom is known to open portals to other dimensions causing a person to laugh and interface "hallucinate" with other entities. The term Shaman originates in Siberia. These Shamans were the spiritual men who wore red and white and carried red and white bags with the sacred mushrooms in them. These Shamans also had reindeer. Some esoteric scholars have linked this mushroom to the story of Santa **Claus**, or St. Nicholas who famously downs exactly the same red and white colors as the Amanita Muscaria. (***ADDENDUM*** Santa '**Claus**' comes from the same root word as **Claustrum**. The Claustrum releases an oily substance (Christ, greek: Christos "oil", **Chrism**) which is a **sacred secretion (a sacred secret)**. Just like Santa Claus travels down a "chimney" with gifts. The claustrum produces the cerebral spinal fluid which lubricates the brain traveling down your spine to your Sacrum/Coccyx bone (**sacred bone**). The **fireplace** is the **root chakra**. There are **33** bones that make up the spine, hence the story of "Jesus" dying at age **33**. When the Cerebral Spinal Fluid travels back up the **33** vertebrates and pass the medulla oblongata, it "**crosses**" the "Vagus Neve" creating a **"CRUCIFIXION"**. This meant the Christ oil (Chrism) was magnified not dead. These experiences are likened to an ego death or spiritual death. The Chrism touches the optic thalamus & remains for **2** to **3** days in a dormant condition after which it illuminates the Pineal Gland (Pine Tree) which awakens the dormant parts of your brain. This is liken to theology with Jesus dying for 3 days on the **cross** or like Astro-theology with the sun dying for 3 days on the southern crux (p 489). Initiates who are prepared when the CSF is raised back up the spine will experience a thousand fold return having earned the keys to **secret** doors, becoming the "**anointed ones**". When this Holy Spirit within rises to the brain it enlightens the **12 cranial nerves (12 Disciples)**. Which is the meaning behind the bible verse, "If your eye be single, your body will fill with light". Ultimately Santa is an analogy for the inner alchemy, resurrecting the Chrism. Santa Claus is also known to give his trade mark "ho, ho, ho," laugh. It is this same exact laugh that is repeated by many partakers of the sacred mushroom when they are under its "spell". I can tell you from my own experience that I laugh with high spirits of jubilation when I am under the spell of the sacred mushroom. All sentient beings have souls and it was the **spirit** of the **mycelium** (magic mushroom) that spoke through brother **Hankh Rising Son** on July 3rd 2018 (p 476) helping to spark my first **past life revelation** of **Emmett Till.** These are the secrets kept from humanity. In **Exodus** 16:33, **Moses** says to Aaron. "Take a jar and put an omer of **manna** in it. Then place it before the Lord to be kept for the generations to come." The manna is the sacred mushroom. On April 4th 2020 (p 594) I laughed with the most joyous of spirits to know that I once lived 3000 plus years ago as Tutankhaten (**King Tut**) and now I was alive again in a new body (p 595). It is no **coincidence** that "King Tut's" Father, **Akhenaten** was the biblical **Moses** who ate the small round caps (**mushrooms**). It's no **coincidence** that **Harriet** was also called **Moses** because she freed many who were enslaved. It's no coincidence that I **worked with Harriet** in a past life when my name was Earl Johnson (p 236, 584). It's no **coincidence** that my **uncle's name** was **Moses Wright** in my life as **Emmett Till** (p 517) or that my great grand father's last name in my current life was also **Wright** (p 15, 25). It's no **coincidence** that **Mars**, the woman who invited me to the festival (p 475) which led to the sparking of my past life, has a **son** named **Moses**.

Utterances for Coming Forth by day into Light

It is he, who comes forth by day into Light

They Write Down Laws Then They Go And Break Every Promise

Our fight isn't just about being physically free. It's about being free to commune with nature the way our ancestors did. **It is better to eat mushrooms in bondage** than to eat meat in freedom waiting for another broken promise.. We think we are free. We eat what we have been taught to eat and we avoid what we have been taught to avoid. We are mentally enslaved. We can't think for ourselves because we rely solely on the propaganda, hearsay and opinions of the doctors and lawyers and political leaders that hold positions in a society that oppresses us. We must think outside the box that society, the media and circumstances have put us in. Too many of us rather see the truth as a threat and a lie as our liberator. As Malcolm X put it, **"If you are not careful, the newspaper will have you hating the people being oppressed, and loving the people who are doing the oppressing."** I speak from a **pro Black** prospective because I see that as the antidote. I wouldn't have to do it if you didn't continue the anit-blacky cures your ancestors gave to my people. My people I beseech you, from the cradle to the grave, from the doctor to the nurse, from our first step to the first grade, **all black everything** is how we need to raise our young queens and kings! **Ebony magazine,** we have a new **dream,** like **Wakanda** selling a billion, like the feeling of **Mumia** hugging his children with out dealing with the penitentiary... FREE MUMIA. We gonna all unify eventually! **instantly in the blink of an eye**! "Should we cry when the pope die?! My request! we should cry if they cried when we buried **Malcolm X**!" no regret not a threat that's a promise, I'm a vet I made a pledge to the dreads to keep it honest! what's next? paying homage to the death like **Harriet** going back for the lasts ones left in **bondage**! My **negus**! The last ones left! Would you go back for the last ones left in **bondage**? It is better to eat mushrooms in bondage than to eat meat in freedom waiting for another broken promise. Echos from the time of Mente she was a descendant of the Ashanti Kingdom of Ghana. She freed a thousand slaves and she stood brave with honor but she could have freed a thousand more if they didn't suffer from post traumatic slave syndrome trauma. Let's take it back home, back to the magic, ***back to papyrus and tablets written by abbots***, with no bad habits, cause look at us now it's tragic! We are the target of the largest psychological warfare ravaged, there you have it. But can we fix it? perhaps with a marriage? If we unify the two lands we can manage, put our hands together forever ***you and the Maat feather I will cherish!***

42 Laws of Maat, Page 367

Tukano Indians of Rio Brazil

1851
Ayahuasca

Ayahuasca is not found in a cup, it is found in the soul. **Richard Spruce** was a English botanist, and the first European to behold the divine Celestine vine, but they had long forgotten this. He took samples but the truth he didn't find. The European side stepped the divine and cut down man like a leaf on a tree, the soul they tear it. The truth is hard to bare it but the proof to God is in your merit, in your habits, are you savage or benevolent?! Like David Walker the day walker intelligent gentlemen from North Carolina, in his jacket liner you might find a copy of **David Walker's Appeal** and a heavy piece of steel, cause shit was real for blacks trying to be free and stay alive in 1825. In 1831 **Nat Turner** was on the run. In **1850 The Slave Act** was enacted to catch slaves like **Harriet** who escaped and evaded capture. In **1851** the botanist **Richard Spruce** was chasing after cities of gold and behold what he found couldn't be bought or sold. The **Tukano Indians** in Rio Brazil who still to this day play on the banks of the Rivers. He saw them, they, "the niggers" mixing the **leaves** with the **vines,** then they drank it causing a meeting of the minds. Aligning ones self with nature, shining truth within the deepest depths of their souls like the **Mayans** and the **Shamans** rhyming and singing the icaros. Feelings of dying and rebirth, being born again, seeing self as the I am that I am, the Holy cargo. If you truly want to know you gotta ***leave*** the ***branches*** and go to the ***root*** for the truth if you wanna make advances, trances, dances, **Telepathine***. The *answers from the unseen uploaded while in a **dream**,* you can rage against the machine or sage and engage the serene.

1858 Drinking Ayahuasca

In 1858 the Ecuadorian geographer Manuel Villavicencio wrote of the use of Ayahuasca in sorcery and divination on the upper Rio Napo. He reported that Shuar using this drink were able: "to foresee and answer accurately in difficult cases, be it to reply opportunely to ambassadors from other tribes in a question of war; to decipher plans of the enemy through the medium of this magic drink and take proper steps for attack and defense; to ascertain, when a relative is sick, what sorcerer has put on the hex; to carry out a friendly visit to other tribes, to welcome foreign travelers or, at least to make sure of the love of their womenfolk." He published his experiences drinking Ayahuasca in **Geografia de la Republica Del Ecuador.** He described his experience of "flying" to marvelous places.

Rau nu Prt m heru

Iu f Per f m heru

Utterances for Coming Forth by day into Light

It is he, who comes forth by day into Light

1864 (Congo iboga root)

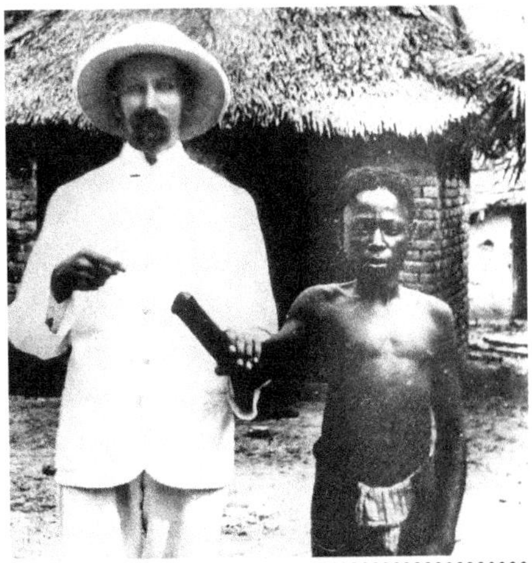

Life is a symphony speaking in **Riddles**. In 1864, the same year that **Thomas Will Haynes** was born (page 16), Griffon du Bellay first reported the use of the Iboga root as a stimulant and aphrodisiac in Gabon and the Congo. By 1867, the same year May Fannie **Riddle** was born (page 16), Iboga was promoted to the public at the Paris Exposition. Afterwards, tonics based on the whole plant extract became extremely popular in France and Belgium. The day before Rosa Parks's birthday, on February 5th 1885, Belgian King Leopold II invaded the Congo Free State by brutally seizing the African landmass as his personal possession. Rather than control the Congo as a colony, as other European powers did throughout Africa, Leopold privately owned the region. Leopold II is best known for the widespread atrocities that were carried out under his rule, as a result of which more than 10 million Afikans died in the Congo Free State.

1880 Mushrooms not Wine

During a widespread shortage of **wine** in Italy, Dr. Batista Grassi wrote an enthusiastic paper recommending **Amanita muscaria mushroom** as an alternative.

1884 (The Peyote Cactus)

Anna Buck Nickels was born on my great grand mother, **Leacola Riddle's** birthday, June 10th in 1832. She died in1917 the year of the **snake**. She was an American **cactus** collector and florist. She was for many years one of the most important collectors, cultivators, and popularizers of the cactus of Mexico and southern Texas. The standard author abbreviation A.B.Nickels is used to indicate this person as the author when citing a botanical name.

1887 (Self experimenting with Peyote)

Louis Lewin was a German pharmacologist. In 1887 he received his first sample of **dried peyote buttons** from Parke Davis & Co. Louis began extracting, characterizing, and self-experimenting with them and later published the first methodical analysis of it, causing a variant to be named Anhalonium Lewis in his honor. Lewin was born in 1850 the same year that **Harriet Tubman** made her way to freedom with the help of mushrooms, using their psychedelic properties to help her navigate. Lewin died in 1929 the year of the **snake** on December 1st the same day that **Rosa Parks** refused to move her seat to a white man on a bus in Montgomery, Alabama. Rosa Parks said, "I thought of **Emmett Louis Till**, and I couldn't go back."

1889 (Iboga)

Henri Ernest Baillon was a French botanist and physician. Henri spent his professional life as a professor of natural history, and he published numerous works on botany. In 1889 the genus Tabernanthe was established and the botanical description of Tabernanthe iboga was made by Henri Baillon. The root b**ark** of the plant contains a chemical called **ibogaine**. Like **Ayahuasca**, Iboga is commonly used in ceremonial native spiritual practices. Ibogaine has been proven to reduce opioid withdrawal symptoms and relapse yet still it is a schedule I substance in the US **not allowed** for wide spread use.

1893, the year of the Snake (Peace Offerings)

In 1891 natives began to seek ways to protect their sacred Peyote ceremonies. In 1893 the year of the **snake**, Quanah **Parker**, chief of the Comanche tribe, gave 50 pounds of dried **peyote buttons** to Smithsonian Institute **archaeologist** and ethnographer **James Moody**. James took the peyote to Washington where it was used in the first scientific trials, including self-experiments by neurologist Weir Mitchell and psychologist William James. **Quanah** was a Native **Medicine Man** who hoped that the peyote would help cure the savagery of the pale foreign invaders like episode 24 of the first season of Star Trek (page 539). Perhaps this worked because James Mooney became convinced of the need to unite the Indians and protect their legal right to worship with peyote. James Mooney lived for several years among the **Cherokee** and was known as "The Indian Man". He conducted major studies of Southeastern Indians, as well as of tribes on the Great Plains. In 1918 he wrote the charter and helped incorporate the Native American Church. Many other Native churches had already been operating but had not been recognized by the American governing bodies.

November 23rd 1897 (150 mg of Mescaline)

On November **23**rd 1897 (Mamie Till's birthday) Arthur Heffter demonstrated that **mescaline** is the main **psychedelic** component in **peyote** by consuming 150 mg of mescaline hydrochloride. This is the first **psychedelic** experience with a purified compound. Arthur was born the day before **Tupac** on June 15th 1859 and he died the day after Louis Till's (**Emmett Till's father,** pages 475, 518) birthday on February 8th 1925, the same year **Malcolm X** was born (pages 321, 562). I have a theory about who Tupac was in a past life..?

1901 (Ibogaine)

Ibogaine has been used by africans on the continent of Africa for 10's of thousands of years as part of ceremonial rights of passage for initiates in the great mysteries. Ibogaine was introduced to the western world in 1901 when Ibogaine was isolated from Tabernanthe iboga by Jean Dybowsky. Ibogaine is a naturally occurring psychoactive substance found in plants in the family Apocynaceae such as Tabernanthe iboga, Voacanga africana, and Tabernaemontana undulata. It is a psychedelic with dissociative properties. Preliminary **research indicates that it may help counter drug addiction.**

George Washington Carver - The Man Who Spoke to Flowers

George Washington Carver was born into slavery sometime around 1864, the same year my great great grand father Thomas Will Haynes was born (p 16), just 14 years after **Harriet Tubman** made her way to freedom in 1849. The next year in 1850 the **fugitive slave act** was enacted, allowing any white man to receive large sums of money for the capture and return of black people escaping bondage (runaway slaves). This "slave act" caused money hungry white men to grab random black people and sell them **back** into slavery. It was common to hear about White men stealing other white men's "slaves", even "free" Black people were grabbed and sold into slavery. And so faith would have it that a week after George Washington Carver was born he was **kidnapped** by slave catchers (raiders). He's sister and mother **Mary** were taken as well to be sold in Kentucky. Carver was later located and returned to his White owner, **Moses** Carver. At around 7 years old Carver was **castrated** by his white owners leaving him with a **high pitched voice**. The reason for his castration, his owners did not want Carver to de-flower their **white daughter** when he hit puberty. History shows through out the slave trade thousands of Black men and boys were **castrated**. There was a demand for Black boys to work in the main house and the castrated boys fetched a higher price by the slave traders. Many slave codes or laws also noted castration as punishment for certain offenses based on the severity. It was noted that Black slaves were also castrated "based on the assumption that the Blacks had an ungovernable sexual appetite." The practice of castration was widely used in the far east as well. During the **islamic invasion of Africa** many Black men and boys were castrated and were referred to as **Eunuchs.** They were castrated for the same reasons Black men in America were castrated, to ensure that the Black men did not have sex with the wives of their enslavers. And because the eunuchs could no longer have children this made them more trustworthy and reliable servants to royal courts. Due to his castration and bondage Carver's boyhood was full of struggle and illness but still he persevered. His struggle ended when he entered Simpson College in Iowa where he studied art and piano, and from there he transferred to the Iowa State University of Agricultural. After graduation, he received the appointment of Assistant Botanist at the Experiment Station. It is thought that his castration kept him completely immersed in his research activities, work and teaching, leaving him a bachelor all his life. When an author interviewed him and asked about castration, he stated that that period of his life was very painful and that he did not want to discuss it.

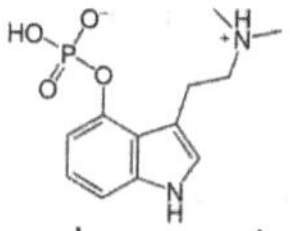

George Washington Carver Ate Magic Mushrooms

In 1893 **Carver ate a magic mushroom** and this transformed his abilities. He would wake up before dawn and walk in to the forest and talk to the flowers. Legend has it that even before he ate the mushroom the **mycelium network** told him to eat the mushroom. After graduation from Iowa State University of Agricultural he took a job with **Booker T. Washington** at Tuskegee Institute in Alabama. While at TuskegeeIn he helped poor white farmers change how they farmed with crop rotation. White's had rendered the soil useless by the constant planting of the same crop (cotton) year after year during slavery. Very soon after his arrival in Tuskegee in 1896, Carver cooperated with **Franklin Sumner Earle**, the Chair of Biology and Horticulture in the Alabama Polytechnic Institute at Auburn, Alabama, in compiling a preliminary list of the fungi of Alabama which was later published. This study formed the basis of a relationship that lasted the entire time that Earle was at Auburn. **Carver shared** his knowledge of the mushroom with Franklyn and Franklyn would go on to be listed as the first person to collect and identify **Psilocybe cubensis** in Cuba. The species was first described as **Stropharia cubensis** in a Cuban agronomy journal in 1906. Of the many contributions Carver made to science, one that has been under emphasized is his role as a **fungal collector**. Throughout his career, Carver maintained a steady interest in **mycology.** Carver developed a talent for collecting and identifying fungal specimens with the remarkable gift for finding rare and new species. Throughout his career, he sent specimens to numerous mycologists and plant pathologists. Carver developed hundreds of products from peanuts, sweet potatoes, and clays; promoted home-canning and the addition of natural fertilizers to improve soil fertility; studied insect and fungal diseases; and developed new varieties of cotton and Amaryllis. When asked how he got all his invention he responded, "**my little friends told me**". The mycelium of the mushroom is equivalent to roots of a tree and the mycelium is usually hidden under b**ark**, ground, rotten wood, or leaves. The mycelium underground network of the mushroom is what allows trees to talk to each other exchanging vital information for survival. Carver was always seen with a flower in his jacket pocket and people often sent their dying plants to him to be revived. Job Bicknell Ellis, a prominent mycologist whose herbarium was purchased by NYBG, received many valuable specimens in return for aiding Carver in identification. It is suspected that Carver's collections ended up at NYBG because of his relationship with J. B. Ellis. In 1902, Ellis collaborated with Benjamin Matlack Everhart on an article entitled 'New Alabama Fungi' which listed 60 important species he had received from Carver. Included in the list were two new species that Ellis and Everhart had named for the Tuskegee scientist. George Washington Carver was an extraordinary scientist and role model. To this day, his name is synonymous with African American ability and achievement. He represents a man who has contributed greatly to science throughout his lifetime. George Washington Carver died on January 5th 1943 the year of the **goat**, the day before Emmett Till's mother Mamie died, **January 6th** 2003 the year of the **goat**. Emmett Till was murdered in 1955 the year of the **goat**, and my mother in this life was born the same year.. **Jan 6th** is 12 days after the Winter Solstice (pages 489, 614). In the Christian religion **Jan 6** is the day that the 3 Magi visited Jesus in a manger. **Jan 6** is also the day that the ancient Kemetyu celebrated the Winter Solstice and and **Tupac's** grand mother Eloise Maria Barnes was born on **Jan 6.** In October of 2013 I met a man named **Mr nature** who was a healer of plants. After meeting this man and having several profound experiences with him I had a strong sense that he was George Washington Carver or somehow Carver worked through him (page 281).

1900 - 1924 Phantastica

Rau nu Prt m heru

Iu f Per f m heru

Utterances for Coming Forth by day into Light

It is he, who comes forth by day into Light

The missionaries were afraid of the visionaries but the biologist were searching for the dominant molecule and some did self studies to ascertain the secret jewels. **Césaire Auguste,** that was his name and with **ibogaine** he gained enlightenment. It's **visionary effects** and he described it Contes Rendu Societe Biologue, things he could never forget and neither would you. On July 12th 1902 an article was published in Popular Science. **Peyote,** taking the mind in trance, it was titled, Mescal: A Study of a Divine Plant. Put man in a lab and let him play with Chemistry. Some find Frankenstein and some find Ecstasy. In 1912, **Anton,** a German Chemist synthesize MDMA by mistake, blemished. His imperfection became how his name is distinguished. In 1914 mushroom trips are published in Science magazine. A six hour span with Psilocybin was like Alice in Wonderland. She looked at her hands and they grew increasingly larger. He went to stand and his body expanded longer, and when it snapped back he saw visions of horror. Hideous faces screaming contortions seeming distorted, a short walk felt longer this is what they reported. A small umbrella shape for heavens sake she's getting smaller and she could hear peoples thoughts a telepathic disorder. Roses everywhere laughter hilarious, the walls moving creeping and crawling. He tried to play the organ but his fingers weren't listening. He looked down at his ring and saw finger tips snakes slithering. The sky was blue yet it seemed green shining and glistening. The impulse of laughter seemed almost irresistible, joke after joke and at times hysterical. These are the things they reported at Yale still in 1914 racism prevailed. In 1915 The **Birth of a Nation** brought the Knights out after it was played by the President in the White House. The Knight Riders of the Ku Klux Klan, the clueless man. They all need a trip with Alice to Wonderland. **In 1919** on my sisters birthday, **Mescaline** synthesis by a chemist from Czechia Republic. His name was Ernst and for **cocaine** he gets the prize. Thanks to Ernst and Hans the **Coca** plant was synthesized. **In 1919** mushroom reports were ignored, **Dr Blas Reko** went to Mexico and in their culture he was absorbed. He saw hallucinations then went and published his article. **In 1919** the **Red Summer** was horrible. **Will Brown** was **lynched** in Nebraska deplorable. His heart was racing no chance of escaping, he was facing his termination, a white lynch mob, with guns, and thoughts of abomination, like a baseball game they cheered drinking beer it was clear their determination for a lynching was real like Emmett Till. He was hung and burned on September 28th with no care or concerns for his cries, tales from the other side, it's gonna be hell for them other guys, when it's their time to answer to the most high. Most die and never get it, they lie cheat steal and still neglect the spirit, and the clarion call they never hear it. Years later a prominent Black attorney, said that he was the lawyer that examined Will's body and because of Will's physical limitations, he was in no condition to go raping anyone being so badly twisted with rheumatism but they didn't listen because it didn't matter if Will was guilty or not. The hatred taught into the lives of Whites' bred a need for blood on the spot. No different than Gladiator pits of Roman thugs who watched men fight to death for them a pleasure it was. The root of their hate can't be measured by a pathologist, peace and love they had never known it or forgotten it. They side step the divine and cut down man like a leaf on a tree, the soul they tear it. The truth is hard to bare it but the proof to God is in your merit, in your habits, are you savage or benevolent?! Like David Walker the day walker intelligent gentlemen from North Carolina, in his jacket liner you might find a copy of **David Walker's Appeal** and a heavy piece of steel, cause shit was real for Blacks trying to be free and stay alive in 1825. In 1831 **Nat Turner** was on the run.

In **1850 The Slave Act** was enacted to catch slaves who escaped evaded capture like running backs breaking tackles, leaving crowds amazed, the truest practice, sink or swim, let's get free or die trying now let's see who's the fastest, he grabbed the **cops** burner and then he blasted. **1924** saw more explorations in pharmacological. **Louis Lewin** not Louis Till. **Louis Till** was hung but Louis Lewin was strung out or just highly curious about morphine, cocaine, and mescaline. He spent a lifetime in study or chasing a high. They called him the father of toxicology when he died. He died in the year of the **snake** when Martin Luther King was born. He was born in 1850 when **The Slave Act** was enacted to catch slaves who escaped evaded capture like running backs breaking tackles, leaving crowds amazed, the truest practice, sink or swim, let's get free or die trying now let's see who's faster brah, if you was a **cop** back then I'm blast'n ya! In 1924 **Louis Lewin** published **Phantastica**.

1927 (Telepathine)

In 1927 Chemists E. Perrot and M. Raymond-Hamet isolated the active agent from Banisteriopsis caapi (**Ayahuasca**) and name it "**telepathine**" due to accounts that it induced **telepathy** in Amazonian tribes.

1930
The Possession of Peyote is Outlawed

In 1930, the same year that my grandmother was born, over a dozen states outlawed possession of **peyote**, largely as an **anti-Native American** statement. Their goal was to separate the natives from nature. They had come to see how the plant medicines were a source of the natives ability to foretell the future and operate harmoniously with the land. The indigenous peoples of North America (Turtle Island) had been using peyote for thousands of years. The first known western recording of Native Americans using peyote was made by a Franciscan Missionary, Bernradino de Sahagun, during the Spanish conquest of Mexico in 1570. Some of the information Bernradino collected was published in 1649 in a text called "History of the Plants of New Spain". He included the following about peyote: "_It appears to be of sweet taste and moderately hot. Ground up and applied to painful joints it is said to give relief. Wonderful properties are attributed to this root_. **_It causes those eating it to be able to foresee and predict things_**." And this is exactly why it was "outlawed". They could not afford the natives foreseeing the terror they continuously inflicted upon them.

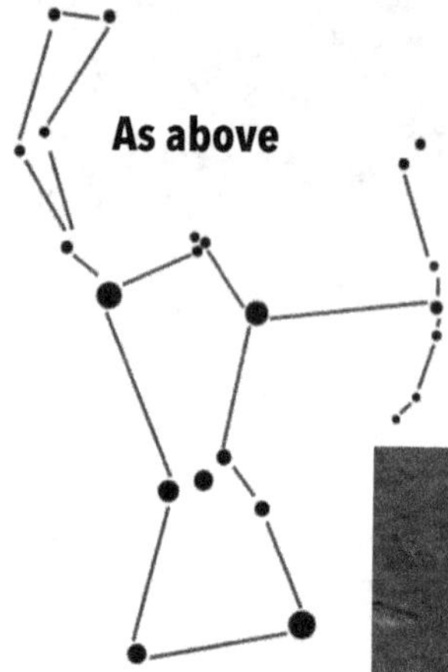

Ausar the Archer
Orion's Belt

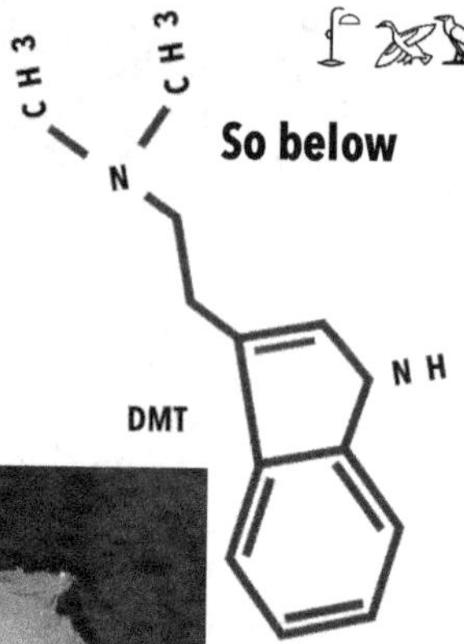

1931 (DMT)

DMT was first synthesized in 1931, the year my grand father **General Dukes Jr** was born by British chemist Richard Manske and named "**nigerine**" (Niggerine) When Manske first synthesized **DMT** the substance's **psychedelic** properties, as well as its natural occurrence in plants and humans, remained unknown. Richard Manske was a German-Canadian chemist. He was born the day after **Tupac** died on September 14th, 1901. He died the year I was born in 19**77** the year of the **snake**, on the same day that Tupac was shot on September 7th 19**77**. My grandfather was born on **June 17th** 1931 and Tupac was born on **June 16th** 1971. I have a theory about who Tupac was in a **past life** ☥ **,** And no, he was not my grandfather.

November 16th 1938 (LSD by Mistake)

Dr. Albert Hofmann, working for Sandoz laboratories, synthesized LSD-25. He stated, "I had planned the synthesis of this compound with the intention of obtaining a circulatory and respiratory stimulant". Colleagues showed no interest in it, so testing was discontinued. 5 years later he revisited LSD and took a very small dose for a self study. Afterward his first experience he decided to test animals before he moved forward with self study. **When he tested LSD's effects on spiders they altered web-building patterns. At low doses, Hofmann noted, "the webs were even better proportioned and more exactly built than normally. However, with higher doses, the webs were badly and rudimentarily made**." He decided to continue his LSD research informally, "in the friendly and private company of two good friends of mine." "I did this," he later wrote, "in order to investigate the influence of the surroundings, of the outer and inner conditions on the LSD experience. These experiments showed me the enormous impact of, to use modern terms - **set and setting** on the content and character of the experience." "In some of my psychedelic experiences I had a feeling of **ecstatic love** and unity with all creatures in the universe," he later said in a High Times interview. "To have had such an experience of absolute beatitude means an enrichment of our life." But he also learned something else: Controlling for set and setting had its limits. "In spite of a good mood at the beginning of a session–positive expectations, beautiful surroundings, and sympathetic company–I once fell into a **terrible depression**. The unpredictability of effects is the major danger of LSD."

October 1945 (Nazi Mescaline Experiments)

The US Navy Technical Mission reported that the Germans were conducting mescaline experiments on prisoners at the Nazi concentration camp in Dachau. They failed to report what was happening in America with the **Tuskegee Airmen**. The united states military Study of Untreated Syphilis in the Black Male was a study conducted between 1932 and 1972 by the United States Public Health Service and the Centers for Disease Control and Prevention on a group of nearly 400 African Americans with **syphilis**.

1947 (Guess who? LSD to the Rescue)

Sandoz Laboratories marketed **LSD** under the name Delysid as a psychiatric drug to be used for treating a wide variety of mental disorders. Sandoz provided researchers with free supplies of LSD. In its marketing literature, Sandoz suggested that psychiatrists take LSD to gain a better subjective understanding of the schizophrenic experience, and many did. In the late forties and fifties, only two communities knew and used LSD: the **psychiatric** research community and the **CIA**.

The True Villain Searching For Truth Serum

This is not a conspiracy theory it's theorem, a 1947 delirium. Can you tell me who was after a truth serum? Have you ever heard of **Project Chatter?** The U.S. Navy created it, initiated it. Dr. Charles **Savage** gave **mescaline** to human specimens at the Medical Research Institute in Bethesda Maryland. They were on a quest like army ants but there was no success. They had heard about the Dachau concentration camps ran by Nazi doctors. The CIA flew over more than 600 top Nazi scientists in helicopters and started **Project Paperclip**. They were a hell of monsters doing racist shit. Delirium mixed with LSD the weirdest shit that you could ever see. In 1950 the first American article says LSD is useful and can aid in **psychotherapy**. That appeared in Diseases of the Nervous System. America is diseased with the white mans burden, his behaviorism his plagiarism the White man is nervous he created a system where he believed he had to impose his **"civilization"** or was it **barbarism** on the black inhabitants through colonialism. In 1951 the CIA begins experimenting with **cocaine** as a **truth serum.** They called it **Operation ARTICHOKE**. This is the truth it's not a joke, they also used **ether** and **morphine** and some people overdosed. **LSD-25** the truth they couldn't hide and in 1953 Project Chatter died but LSD survived. In November LSD was prescribed to new members, the new CIA trainees. It's a cold world and a wicked culture, Mk Ultra in April of 1953, Director Allen Dulles authorized the weirdest shit that you could ever see. It's a cold world and a wicked culture, during The **Cold War** they formed **Mk Ultra**. They said it was for interrogation but it was like a sick child playing with death, assassinations, they called their weird experiments tests but it was sick fascination, tasteless and irresponsible. In 1952 **Dr. Frank Olsen** went to a CIA cocktail party where he was quietly given an untold potion, for him it was a hell of emotions. They thought it was funny probably but he was not well he went home wobbly, not amused intense anxiety ensued and several weeks later on the news, he plunged through a ten-story window to his death, confused. In 1955 Emmett Till is killed and still the CIA is on a mission for a truth serum pill. They never thought to try it on **Roy Bryant** and **J.W. Milam**. No, they hired prostitutes, for them that was more fulfilling. George Hunter White was narcotics officer for MK-ULTRA. And at night to his delight through a two way mirror he watched prostitutes have sex all night, despite the fact that the men where again quietly slipped LSD that's akin to heresy atrocity wickedness, and they call it therapy. This has got to be the most despicable legal use of government money you could ever see. 1960 Sidney Cohen said LSD is an astonishingly safe drug. They had 5000 people who had taken it 25,000 times and only 4 people **COMPLETED** suicide. These findings led to a boom in LSD, now it was alive and the next 2 years LSD psychotherapy was on a rise and the Narcotics Manufacturing Act required licenses for narcotics synthesized.

1953
Aldous Huxley, How One Ought to See

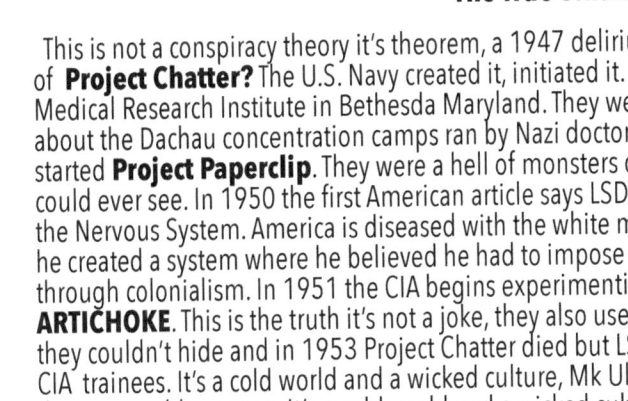

In 1952 Dr. Humphry Osmond had began working with hallucinogens at a hospital in Saskatchewan, looking at the similarity between mescaline and the adrenaline molecule. In May of 1953 Aldous Huxley tries **mescaline** (400 mg) for the first time under the supervision of Dr. Humphrey Osmond. During the experience, he commented **"This is how one ought to see, how things really are."** Huxley was born on July 26th, the day after **Emmett Till's** birthday and he died on November 22nd, the day before **Mamie Till's** (Emmett's mother) birthday. In 1954 Aldous Huxley published the book, **The Doors of Perception** describing his 1953 experience with mescaline. By now you ought to see very clearly the pattern being expressed by the forces of nature beyond mans understanding.

1955 the year of the Goat (E.L.T.) (DMT is discovered occurring Naturally in Plants)

In 1955, the same year that **Emmett Till** is murdered, **DMT** and **5-MeO DMT** was identified as the active chemicals in the Anadenanthera peregrine seeds used to make cohoba snuff. This marked the **first time** these chemicals were discovered occurring naturally in plants. On July 3rd 2018 I ate mushrooms containing Psilocybin, which is in the same family as **DMT** and LSD. After eating the mushroom my **past life** as **Emmett Till** was revealed to me. This is not to say that if anyone eats a psychedelic that a past life will come. That is NOT TRUE! As **Baba Kilindi** says, some things are only experienced by the initiate that has **earned the keys to open those doors**. 1955 The first conference focusing on **LSD** and **mescaline** took place in Atlantic City and Princeton, N.J. And that same year Kilindi was born and Emmett was murdered.

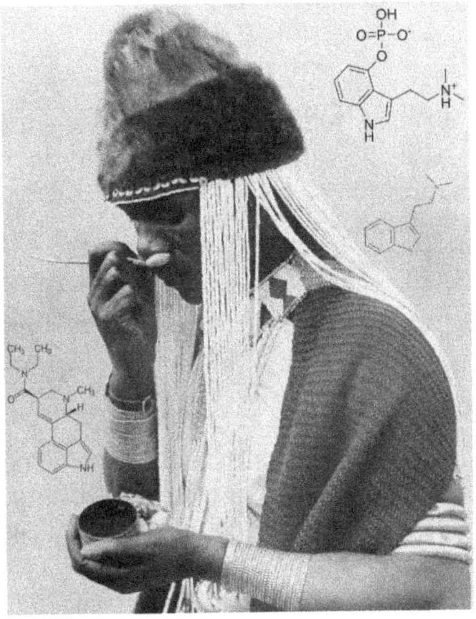

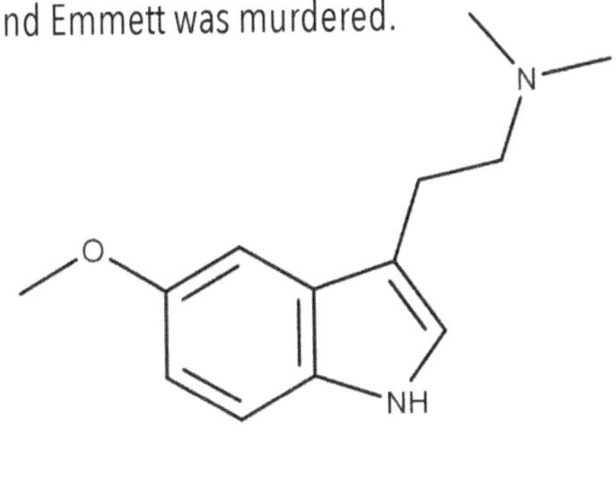

5-MeO-DMT

1955 the year of the Goat (E.L.T.)
María Sabina Magdalena García

María Sabina was a Mazatec Indian **shaman** who was known as the "**priestess of mushrooms**," as well as the "**queen of hallucinogenic mushrooms**." She was probably the most famous Mexican healer to have ever lived. Her history and reputation led her to serve as a bridge between the mystical and ritual worlds of her people, and the mystical exploration of the Western world. She was a Mazatec curandera (natural herbs healer), who lived in Huautla de Jiménez, a town in the Sierra Mazateca area of the Mexican state of Oaxaca in southern Mexico. Her healing sacred mushroom ceremonies, called veladas, were based on the use of **psilocybin mushrooms**, such as Psilocybe cyanescens. She was born and died in Huautla de Jiménez, Mexico. She was born 3 days before **Emmett Till** on July **22nd** 1894, and she Died one day before **Mamie Till**, November **22nd** 1985. The New York banker Robert Gordon Wason and Allan Richardson were the first two Americans to ingest mushrooms at a ritual with Sabina in 19**55**. Sabina's knowledge of hallucinogenic mushrooms was publicized by New York banker Robert Gordon Wason on June 29th 19**55**, the same year that **Emmett Till** was murdered. Afterwards thousands of people from around the world traveled over dirt roads to the mountainous region known as Huautla to participate in ceremonies centered on the "**children of God**," as Sabina called the sacred psilocybin mushrooms. It is said that the likes of **John Lennon**, **Mick Jagger** and **Bob Dylan** (page 231) were among those who made the trip to participate in her ceremonies. In the end, María Sabina was shunned by her community for commercializing their traditions and claimed the niños santos (mushrooms) lost their power after so much misuse. She died in poverty in 1985, at 91 years old. **María** introduced the Western world to Mushrooms in 1955 the same year Emmett was murdered and in 2018 I would eat the mushroom for the first time and realize I was Emmett Till (p 480).

1958 (Alan Watts)

Alan Watts was invited to test the mystical qualities of 1 tenth of a milligram of LSD-25 by Dr. Keith Ditman of the Neuropsychiatric Clinic at UCLA Medical School. Watts stated, "Indeed, my first experiment with LSD-25 was not mystical." Several months later in 1959, Watts tried LSD-25 again with Drs. Sterling Bunnell and Michael Agron of the Langley-Porter Clinic, in San Francisco. He reported, "In the course of two experiments I was amazed and somewhat embarrassed to find myself going through states of consciousness that corresponded precisely with every description of major mystical experiences that I had ever read."

1958

Albert Hofmann isolated and determined the structure of the two active agents in mushrooms. He named them psilocybin and psilocin.

Psilocybin

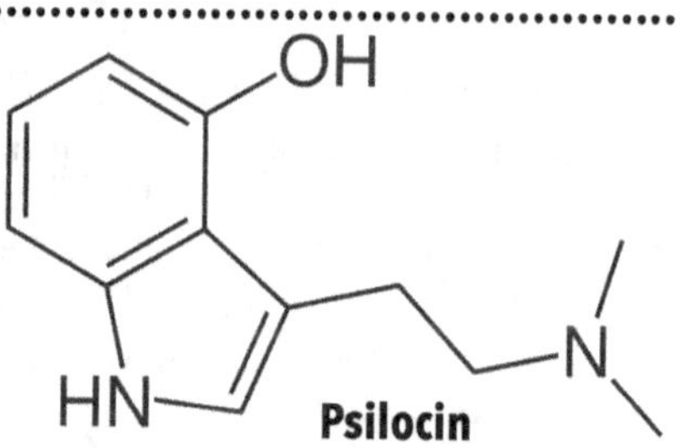

Psilocin

August 1960
Dr. Timothy Leary ate Magic Mushrooms

Dr. Timothy Leary ate magic mushrooms in Cuernavaca, Mexico. He stated, "**It was above all and without question the deepest religious experience of my life**." During the same year he tried synthetic psilocybin and obtained some from Sandoz in order to experiment on prisoners in Concord State Prison, Massachusetts. Dr. Richard Alpert assisted him. Dr. Timothy Leary, Dr. Ralph Metzner and Dr. Richard Alpert started the Harvard Psilocybin Project. They gave psilocybin to graduate students and many volunteers including Allen Ginsberg, Jack Kerouac, Neal Cassady and Aldous Huxley. In September of 1961 Michael Hollingshead met Timothy Leary and moved into the attic of his house. Hollingshead gave LSD to Timothy Leary and guided him through his first trip. Leary described the trip as "the most shattering experience of my life".

1960 - They Break Every Promise

Rau nu Prt m heru

In 1930, the same year that my grandmother was born, over a dozen states outlawed possession of **peyote**, largely as an **anti-Native American** statement. Their goal was to separate the natives from nature. 30 years later in 1960, Arizona Judge Yale McFate rules that Native Americans are guaranteed access to the Peyote sacrament under the First and Fourteenth amendments. That same year Psilocybin became available for **legal sale**. Sandoz Pharmaceutical began producing psilocybin pills, called Indocybin. Each pill contained 2 mg of psilocybin. 7 years later in 1967 **Peyote** is **banned federally** in the U.S. We can see that there is a problem going on. This country which claims to be civilized can not keep it's treaties with native people. It can not uphold it's own laws. They break every promise. They think they somehow have control over the way another culture communes with God. This Governments doesn't like anything that they are not collecting taxes for. Yet this country was founded due to their refusal to pay a tax on Tea. **Sioux, Apache, Camache, Arapaho,** Native to this land we was living here natural, The pale face came savage empty hands damage collateral, Poison you before they battle you, Blue eyed devil, the harbinger of death, They took this land by terror and they won't change until it's nothing left, Before they came we had no name for jails, no locks no keys no hard knock life no thieves no money, You ain't got it? I got it! **They call us uncivilized if they can't make a profit**, They write down laws then they go and break every promise, No honesty! *Until the philosophy of race and superiority and 1st and 2nd class nationality is finally and permanently forever more discredited, There will be war merited, me say war merited, war merited, war merited everywhere there's war,* and horror! they bombed Panama with stealth bombers killed pregnant momma's and hard working fathers! no honor! more drama it's sickening no water in Dakota or Flint Michigan, A peoples history of **Florida, Seminal Indians,** Before you walk a moon in a mans moccasins don't go mocking him! Or try'n to go stop'n him from communing naturally cause **This is how one ought to see,** like the words of **Aldous Huxley.**

Iu f Per f m heru

1962 – 1963 (ibogaine's to treat cocaine)

Howard Lotsof conducted experiments on ibogaine's use in the treatment of cocaine and heroin addiction.

1963
The LSD Got Free

Utterances for Coming Forth by day into Light

1963 was the year LSD made its rounds appearing on the streets as sugar cubes with interludes on public school playgrounds. Even open articles in that **Look** magazine the same one that paid **Emmett Till's** killers to detail his screams. LSD was seen in the **Saturday Evening Post** for free publicity and that was all that she wrote. In January of 1963 Michael Hollingshead moved to New York City and formed the **Agora Scientific Trust Inc.**, with co-directors John Beresford, M.D. and Jean Houston, Ph.D. He conducted hundreds of guided LSD sessions before the Agora closed in December. On April 3rd Bernard Roseman and Bernard Copley were **arrested** after **they sold several grams of LSD to an undercover FDA detective**. They received a felony charge for smuggling LSD into the United States. In May1963 **Timothy Leary** was **fired from Harvard** for leaving Cambridge and his classes without permission or notice. **Richard Alpert** was **fired** from Harvard for **giving psilocybin to an undergraduate**. Timothy Leary, Richard Alpert and Ralph Metzner created the International Foundation for Internal Freedom and set up offices in Boston, New York and Los Angeles. Later that summer, IFIF moved its headquarters to Zihuatanejo, Mexico. They were kicked out of Mexico six weeks after. On November 22nd Aldous Huxley was **dying of cancer**. He wrote a note asking his wife Laura, to inject him with LSD so he could die in euphoria. So she did and several hours later, he transitioned to the here after in a serene state of bliss sublime at 69.

1964
Encore, Raw LSD They Want More

It is he, who comes forth by day into Light

In 1964 Timothy Leary, Ralph and Richard published **The Psychedelic Experience** from LSD (based on the Tibetan **Book of the Dead**). That was the same year Ali said you can call me **Muhammad Ali, The Greatest Of All Time**, but not one more time **Cassius Clay!** And that's the same year M**ississ**ippi **Goddam** did play, **Nina Simone,** we was fighting freedom but they were defining and emphasizing the importance of "set" and "setting" of **Psychedelic Experiences.** I never heard them speak of the hatred blacks experienced. In April of 1964 Owsley Stanley took his first acid trip on LSD. A few months later he tried a new source and realized that the first source was poor quality. So he decided to learn the manufacturing of LSD on his own. On June 4th 1964 Bernard Roseman and Bernard Copley were convicted of **smuggling LSD** into the United States, and they were sentenced to 17 years but they escaped. They posted bond, jumped bail and fled to Mexico and Brazil. They were eventually captured and **sent to federal prison** locked behind steel.

1965 - The Year of The Snake - Bufo

Malcolm X is murdered the same year that the first published analysis of the **venom** of the Sonoran Desert **toad** (Bufo alvarius) appeared in Experientia. Up to 15% of the venom consists of 5-MeO-DMT. In February of 1965 Owsley Stanley set up his first LSD lab in Berkeley. It was known as the Green Methedrine factory because he primarily produced methedrine. He manufactured a small batch of **impure LSD** which hit the streets of San Francisco. On February 21st 1965, **the same day Malcolm X was assassinated**, Owsley's lab was raided and his equipment was confiscated. The police were looking for methedrine or LSD, but found only precursors. Owsley beat the charges and successfully sued for the return of his equipment. By March he had moved to Los Angeles and briefly set up a new lab in the basement of a friend's house. He learned to use column chromatography to purify LSD and crystallize it. By May he set up a lab on Lafler Road in Los Angeles where he produced approximately 75,000 doses of pure LSD (270 μg each). He put some of the LSD in #5 capsules and some of it he dosed as tablet triturates. In June of 1965 Bowden, Drysdale and Mogey published "**Constituents of Amanita muscaria**" in Nature. They determined that the **mushroom's psychedelic effects** were produced by muscimol. That same year Dr. Alexander Shulgin synthesized MDMA. In the fall of 1965 Timothy Leary instructed Michael Hollingshead to go to **London** and spread the word about the marvels of **LSD**. He arrived with 300 copies of **The Psychedelic Experience**, 200 issues of The Psychedelic Review, 200 copies of The Psychedelic Reader, and a half a gram of LSD. He soon opened the World Psychedelic Centre with Desmond O'Brien and Joey Mellen, The center provided psychedelic education and guided LSD sessions.

1966 DMT is made illegal in the United States

What you are seeing is the journey of western mans reaction to the truth when the truth is placed in his hands. The hidden messages, Alice in wonderland. In 1966 **DMT** is banned and made Illegal in the USA. Do you recall the day, **September 19th** 1955, Emmett Till's murder trial?! In 1966 some LSD is recalled. Timothy Leary founded the League for Spiritual Discovery on **September 19th** 1966, in his religion he declared LSD as its holy sacrament. On October 6th LSD is made illegal, Ten days later The Brotherhood of Eternal Love is founded by Michael Randal and John Griggs, they wanted the world on LSD so they continued with their plan. In **1967** The Teachings of Don Juan hit book stands. What you are seeing is the journey of western mans reaction to the truth when the truth is placed in his hands. The hidden messages, Alice in wonderland. A Yaqui Way of Knowledge, the first time I read it I didn't get it, I was 39 I had never had a psychedelic. At 40 years old that would all change, I understood now, I saw a past life and Emmett Till was once my name. and now that would explain why **Tim Scully** was so gully with his determination to produce **Purple LSD**, mind altering hallucinations, but was it for the **money** or was it because of something he did see? Emmett was lynched in **Money** M**ississ**ippi. Scully and Owsley made LSD in a Denver lab but it didn't last, they closed shop but they didn't stop. The search for other sacred knowledge didn't either, more studies on the **Toad** appeared for Biochemical Pharmacology book readers. **5-MeO-DMT** awakens the **ESP** and that's why it's illegal for you and me. In 1967 **Richard Alpert** journeyed to India and studied **meditation** and **yoga** under the Guru teacher Neem Karoli Baba, and that's where he got the name **Ram Dass**, a servant of God, at all cost. KRS One released his book, **The Gospel of Hip Hop: The First Instrumental** On October 24th and on October 24th 1968, the possession of **ibogaine** was **banned** in the U.S.A., that was the day before my birthday and here's the truth that they won't say, **Cocaine** and **Heroin** addiction was being **treated** with **ibogaine** but that's a no no with out pharmaceutical prescription monetary gains. **Healing becomes a crime** when it's done without giving the American Medical Association, "the government" a dime. But a new drug was steadily being designed called **Crack Cocaine.** In 1969 small **LSD** pills called **Orange** sunshine became the most popular LSD of all time. Nick Sand financed that lab for Tim Scully and in return Scully taught him everything he'd learned from Owsley and they created the purist LSD you could see. At the same time in Reno Nevada, Darrell Lemaire was researching psychoactive compounds to be used in **psychotherapy** for trauma. He set up a lab in an underground chamber next to lava, he blasted a tunnel into volcanic rock and yes there was danger, so the saga was well hidden but the government was on a mission and the next year Owsley was sent to prison.. Then **Timothy Leary** got charged with a marijuana conviction and to prison for ten years is where they sent him. But that would not be his fate, **The Brotherhood of Eternal Love** financed his escape and to Algeria he flew. In the year of 1970, two days after my birthday **president Nixon** signed the **Controlled Substance Act** and in the worst way it organized federally regulated drugs into five schedules, it was bugged and it had varying restrictions and penalties. **Schedule I**, Drugs are the ones they claim to have no accepted medically useful remedies and a high potential for abuse, and this is where they placed **LSD, Heroin, Psilocybin**, **Cannabis, Ecstasy, Peyote** and **DMT**. **Schedule II**, the narcotic drugs that put you to sleep with a high potential for abuse from the strong to the weak. From the illicit and the prescription, the Cheek and the Chong. Leading to severe psychological or physical harm and dependency so they were considered dangerous and so they limited the distribution to the doctors dressed in all white all clean. They prescribe the morphine, opium, codeine and percocet, Adderall, Ritalin they give it to the children. **Schedule III**, for the athletes, the anabolic steroids, **Sha'Carri Richardson** smoked weed and so they wouldn't let her run. The rules they enforced had many people upset, but yet still the White Russian girl **Kamila** competed despite a positive drug test. **Sha'Carri** was heated, I was too but it wasn't something that I never saw them do. Schedule IV and Schedule V Drugs with a low potential for abuse and low risk of dependence but they lied. They just legalize the things that they prescribe. Your health and well being is not the primary concern. It's really about how much they can earn. In 1971 **Tupac** was born, that same year **Terence McKenna** first tried dried mushrooms and was forever transformed. **Paul Stamets** ate a mushroom then climbed to the top of a tree during a thunder storm and it was the most beautiful thing he could ever see. In 1972 Julius Axelrod discovered that **DMT** occurs naturally in human brain tissue. Still it was banned from me and you. Isn't that strange? DMT is naturally produced in the brain but if you ingest it you go to jail in chains. Cigarettes are legal but what does that really mean? Cause one cigarette contains enough toxins to kill a person if injected directly into the bloodstream. But still it is legal.

Rau nu Prt m heru

Iu f Per f m heru

Utterances for Coming Forth by day into Light

It is he, who comes forth by day into Light

Crack

42 Laws of Maat, Page 367

Cocaine was the party drug, and it was where ever the party was, from jazz to Hip Hop but not if you couldn't afford it. So other ways to produce it they explored it. They turned cocaine to crack to be smoked and not snorted and that's that, that's how they created crack. That's no joke Richard Pryor was set on fire from free base'n the crack pipe. They said the freaks come out at night and at night they did. Women sold sex for drugs, and some sold their kids, anything to get high off crack they did. Men robbed, and killed just for a high thrill. This is what was going on, it was a battle field. There was a war going on outside no one was safe from. The mafia controlled the drugs like **heroin** but when crack hit the inner city it was a free for all, anyone who wanted to sell could sell with no protocol. This was a fall from grace all by design, Black babies born blind to the ways of mankind. Growing up in the ghetto, livin' second rate every part of Black life sings a deep song of hate. From the places we play to places we live, they never looked as nice as where White people lived. And Still the church tells us that God is smilin' on us, but it feels like God is frownin' too cause God never stops the pain we go through.. They called it a plague they called it a virus but they made crack cheap so I'm calling them liars. They lied about Martin and they lied about Malcolm, they killed both those brothers afraid of the outcome of what might happen if we ever unite, that's why crack was used like a Rook or a Knight. The immediate high euphoric effects, drug related crimes addiction and death. But Cocaine was still the White mans drug for the elite but when the movie Scarface was released the use increased. Walking the streets I remember seeing empty crack vials as a child. They'd be around everywhere even in playgrounds. I knew crack was bad cause I had first hand experience. I had family members who died from the crack epidemic. At least that's what they called it but it was a two in one deal. There was never a war on drugs the war was on Black people's will. Crack made us lie, it made us cheat and steal and most of all it made us neglect the spirit. Some don't want to hear this because the truth is hard to bare it but the proof to God is in your merit, in your habits. America has a habit of taking free labor off the backs of Black people. Even more evil they caused us to destroy our own people. Drug dealers addicted to selling and the user addicted to using, some dealers sold drugs to their parents and the government found this amusing. They put the crack in our community, they knew we would use and sell it then they threw us in jail for using it and selling it and the news, the way they reported was devilish. With the crack baby stories they criminalized Black women, right after she gave birth they threw her in prison. This was a chemical war of crack destroying the Black family. All the chemistry they learned they used as war strategy. In 1985 the name "crack" was printed for the first time in the New York Times side but crack had been spread wide since the early 80's before the "crack babies". Say no to drugs that was a presidential slogan yet the president turned a blind eye to drug smuggling. I played Contra in 1988 but I had no idea of what it was, even the video games supported this 'war on drugs'. So here it was, over throw the Sandinista government that was the plan. And so the government sold weapons to Iran to pay for drug smuggling, by land air and sea the drugs were coming in. There was a secret meeting some say they had in Hip Hop no more self destruction rhymes and so most of it stopped. There was never a war on drugs the war was on Black people's will and so some sold drugs in music for a record deal. but now it's time to recover and time for our greatness to live it! No matter what you've done you can atone the spirit. I be the **Lord of Maat** like the base of the throne, in case you forgot let me take you back home, I came flying out primordial d**ark**ness all alone, **Nun** was there she created the moisture the air and the earth to roam, the sky was the dome, the all embracing cohesion of elements, the rotations of seasons fair dealings no relation to heathens, the even equilibrium of the heavens meant everything, no irrelevant aspects of nature, the **NTCHRU** like the **Falcon** flew, he who comes into existence like the **Scarab** do, like **Ra**, **Ptah**, or **Ausar** one and the same, you can see the weakness in a man through his iris, and his tongue is the same, follow me now *with my tongue I decree a miracle deliberately*, my chief source of energy spiritually, everything else peripherally, with tunnel vision look upon my mission and listen for delivery, of Gods divine faculties facilitating my destiny, the black emcee **Blackamoor** no more in your dictionary, the Blakseeds they be quick to bury, **The Valley Of Kings** place my obituary, **Thug Life** like my **Naga Seti,** d**ark** nights better days coming, so my soldiers getting ready, like Eric **Shepard** ya heard, very epic with words, they might come for me but don't let that pressure your nerves, instead be well fed decalcify thy eye with herbs, they might bust led but bust how this **spell** was said, as I read from **The book of The Dead, Coming Forth By Day,** The Blakseed from New York by way of **Rockaway,** the last shall be first, screaming out Hip Hop Hooray Hip Hop Hooray, screaming get out the way! SHOTS fired another brother expired, it's an execution with no retribution these cops are liars, cops and robbers they death pool for hire, a cesspool corrupted like political bucks stuck under the table, you busted! caught your hands all up in my pockets takin my profits! they can't be trusted like uncle Sam! sending rockets to the mother land! right now they got the upper hand but we can band together! **Holla If Ya Hear Me!** I blame the hand that put the bucket there, not my brother stuck in here with me, quickly trying to get the fuck out of here, we be Shifty, Low Down Greedy and Grimy, like 50 Cent in the 90's, be careful with a necklace too shiny, reckless Black on Black crime be reminiscing of **willy lynch'n** picnic'n, did I mention? I slipped back to another dimension sat in the **Chicken Shack** with **Detroit Red,** it was packed from the feet to the head, Red Foxx was in the kitchen telling jokes, Billie Holiday was hitting high notes, everybody had high hopes, they said a toast I closed my eyes then I woke, I'm still alive **so I rise** and realize what I wrote, time to get the yoke up off my neck, "shit was all good just a week ago" Look at the hood where did all the Black people go?! no **reparation** the repercussion of **gentrification,** how do we stop this **black extermination?** I be the **Lord of Ma'at** like the base of the throne, in case you forgot let me take you back home.

I came to this planet on July 25th which is the most sacred day on the Mayan calendar. The Mayans called it the day out of time. It is the culmination of the 13 Moon Calendar year originated from the **Mayan** science of time. On July 25th, the Mayans observed the star **Sirius** (**the dog star**) rising in sync with the **sun**. In Ancient Kemet (Egypt) the star Sirius was connected with Auset (Isis) and her husband Ausar (Osiris) was connected with the 3 stars (3 wise men, 3 kings) that make up the belt in the constellation of **Orions belt**. Ausar was the Lord of **resurrection/ reincarnation** and the **afterlife**. This was a very special day in ancient Kemet because it m**ark**ed the inundation of the Nile river and the Mayans regarded this day as a spiritual mark to start the evolutionary process of humanity. It is considered a moment of great energetic intensity, in which the **Beings of Light** work to align us with the harmony of the universe, on its various dimensions of time, and space.

On July 30th 2021 I got my first astrological reading from an astrologer named **Sondráya** (p 654) and her reading would align with the Mayans beliefs surrounding July 25th and it's connection with **Beings of Light** working for the harmony of the universe. In that reading I was told that **Emmet Till** came to earth as a sacrificial **lamb,** sparking the 1950's Civil Rights Movement. She explained the significance of Emmett being born as a **Leo** and being murdered in the sign of **Virgo**. The **Sphinx** (**Heru em Akhet**, p 2) is comprised of two fixed signs, **Leo** the **lion** and **Aquarius** the human. This correlates with the ancient prophecy of **Heru** returning/resurrecting in the age of Aquarius, uniting the **lion** with the **lamb**. Virgo governs **service** of humanity and the death of Emmett Till was a **service** to this country. In this reading **Sondráya** was able to connect my current life with my life as Emmett Till and Tutankhaten (King Tut). The Mayans observed July 25th as a day free of time in the 13 Moon Calendar. It is a day of reverence and cultural appreciation for the concept 'Time is Art.' This 'free day' is the closing of a 13x28=364 day year. The Day Out of Time re-aligns the 13 Moon calendar to the solar year and re-aligns humanity into renewed appreciation for our inherent divinity and connection to nature. It is a day of reverence and respect for all life, a dedication to the beauty of **eternal time**, and an outreach of cultural and community exchange and education relative to the concept of natural time. In short, it's a day to recognize unity and encourage **awareness** of the importance of **our eternal time**. July 24th was seen as the last day of the year like December 31st on the Gregorian calendar and July 26th was the first day of the new year, when a new cycle begins again, bringing the energy of renewal and inner purification, with a great impact on our spiritual bodies, especially the emotional ones. Emmett Till was murdered at **14** years of age and in the **14th** verse of the 1st chapter of Genesis, which is the first book in the Bible, it is written: "Let there be **lights** in the firmament of the heaven to divide the day from the night; and let them be for **signs**, and for seasons, and for days, and *years*". I came here to this earth to sacrifice my life for the betterment of the whole. We have fallen into a winter of consciousness. We are a species with amnesia. We have forgotten who and what we are but we are the sun's of "God". We think we are the bodies that we live in because we have forgotten that we are beings of light. "Emmett" was lynched in Money M**ississi**ppi and in the word M**ississi**ppi you can see the name **Isis** (Auset) who is the **mother** of **Heru** (**Horus**, **Zeus**, **Jesus**) the one who **resurrects** after death. Isis the great royal **wife** of **Ausar** (**Osiris**) the Lord of **resurrection**. **Emmett** was beat, tortured, shot in the head and **thrown in a river** at **14** years of age. In the Ausarian **resurrection** drama Ausar was trapped in a box, **thrown in the Nile river**, then cut into **14** pieces. Emmett's **eye** was gouged out like **Heru's** left eye was in the Ausarian resurrection drama. On Sep 29th 2019 I found a video online that explained how the name Emmett meant **truth, mound, build up** according to the **biblical concordance**, and the name **Till** meant **Amen, Time, Aten,** and **Ark** (**of the covenant**) (p 579). This would all make sense on April 4th 2020 when my past life as Tutankhaten (King Tut) was revealed to me (p 594). I don't yet remember my life as Emmett Till or Tutankhaten but I know that I was Emmett Till in my most recent past life and that I was Tutankhaten in my oldest known life. I have gathered information about my life as Emmett Till from the many documentaries and first hand accounts I have seen online and from what I read in books. Much of what you are reading here, I did not come to know until months and years after I realized I was Emmett Till. It is however quite interesting how all the information seemed to just find it's way to me. Even beyond the computerized algorithms that we create from what we search on our computers and phones. It was as if this previous life as Emmett Till was fighting its way through my consciousness in this life. Fighting to be acknowledged. I speak from the prospective of the soul fragment within me that houses my life as Emmett Louis Till but I also speak using the knowledge I acquired in this life as Dawud (TutemRa). **Re-member** that **you** are **Ausar** and **Heru,** the **hero!** See page 3 for the **hero's journey**!

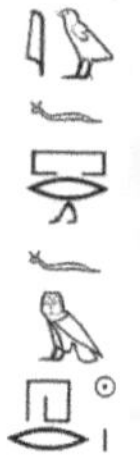
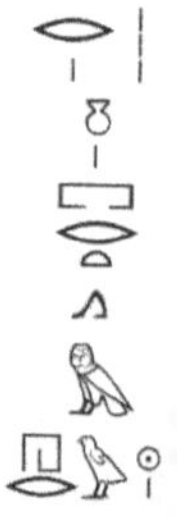

Rau nu Prt m heru

Iu f Per f m heru

Utterances for Coming Forth by day into Light

It is he, who comes forth by day into Light

July 25 1941 - The Early Life of Emmett Till
(1+9+4+1+7+2+5 = **29** = Master Number **11**)

My mother was part of the mass migration of thousands of Blacks from the racist hard life of the south to the less racist life in the north. At 2 years of age she arrived in Argo, Illinois, a small town outside of Chicago, with her mother. Her father had arrived several months ahead of the family to work at the Argo Corn Products Refining Company. She graduated from Argo Community High School in June of 1940 and four months later she married my father Louis Till. My father had a rough start at life growing up in an orphanage. At around 18 years old he met my mother Mamie. During one of their dates they were refused service because they were Black but my father refused to leave demanding that they be served and the owner agreed. Mamie was taken by his bravery and so her respect for him grew. I was born in July of 1941, the same year that **Dr Amos Wilson** (page 283) was born but by 1942 my parents were separated. At times my father was abusive to my mother and this is how he ended up in the Army. Perhaps alcohol was involved, this was the case with my father in my current life as well. After one of their bouts of domestic violence the cops gave my father Louis a choice of joining the Army or going to jail. He joined the Army and was soon deployed to World War II. He was assigned to the 1**77**th port company, 379th Battalion transportation corp. While in the Army he continued to support us sending money in the mail regularly but when the money stopped my mother became worried. Soon after she was informed of his death but the Army never gave any details, only stating that he died outside of service because of his own doing. 61 years after his death the truth was revealed (pages 475, 518).

What do I say to a father that I never met? First of all, I love you and thank you. Thank you for the ring! It was a big help! Thank you for loving me and my mother. I do not believe the reports that were said about you in the news and media. I trust that you were a noble man. My father Louse Till was buried in row 4, Grave 73 of plot E in oise-Aisne American Cemetery but please know that death is not the end. The soul survives death, indeed and in spirit. This is a book of the dead written by a his son who was murdered without justice, who defeated death and came forth by day. May the soul of my Father **Louis Till** walk peacefully through the **field of Reeds** in Amenta. Amen Ra.

From what I have gathered I was a happy teenager with a sense of adventure. I suffered from polio when I was 5 and it left me with a speech impediment but I was gaining my confidence as I grew older. My mother Mamie Till, says I was loving and clever, and I helped with chores at home while she worked long hours to support us, and apparently I liked to cook. At 10 years old I offered to take the trip downtown to pay the bills. I was sent with $100 and directions of all the bills to pay and I returned home having was always trying to help. There were some older people who lived near us that I always went to check on. My mother says she was very proud of the young man that I was becoming. We lived in a middle class African American neighborhood where I attended an all African American grammar school. I loved playing stickball in the streets with my cousin Wheeler Parker who lived next door. Some people thought I was older than 14 and some people described me as chubby because I was bigger and stronger than most boys my age. I can be seen in a picture with my cousin Wheeler **Parker** on top of our bicycles. The year was around 1950 and I was around 9 years old at the time and Wheeler was around 11 or 12. I watched an interview of my cousin Wheeler **Parker** Jr. telling of how I was outgoing and was the center of attraction. He says I was a natural born leader, I loved having fun, and I was a prankster. Another cousin says I was a defender, I didn't allow other people to bother them. I was always making sure everyone else was happy. My cousin, Simeon Wright, said it was hard to tell when I was serious because I liked to joke and make people laugh. Unfortunately my jovial personality did not go over well in M**ississ**ippi.

On **Christ**mas day, **December 25th 1954,** the iconic pictures of me and my mother (top right) and me standing next to the television were taken. I was given my signature hat for a present this year. I dressed up in all my new clothes and we took family pictures.

(Dawuud's Invocation, written on March 24th 2011, page 200)

"**picture** a Van Gogh **starry night**, I'm on a stroll ***trying to find my soul when I write***"

(The Present, written on December 26th 2016, page 437)

"Merry Christmas, the peasant cuts down the tree and side steps the truest bliss, they wanna separate you from the oneness that do exist, the wind blew me **the kiss of life** one **starry night**, ***I started remembering what I forgot when starting this life, they say death is an awakening, a remembering like a dream***"

1955 The Mississippi (ISIS) Delta is like the Nile River ISIS

The year was 1955 and the white racist tension and hate in the American southern states had escalated due to the1954 landmark Supreme Court **Brown v. Board of Education** decision that struck down racial segregation in public schools. The racist whites of the south did not want their way of life to change and no way were their children going to go to the same schools as the lowly Black children. These white racist sentiments are immortalized in a statement made by John William "J. W." Milam, one of the men who murdered me. He was asked why he killed Emmett Till and he replied, "**What else could I do? He thought he was as good as any White man"**. Life in the South was different from life in the North. The North was more urban and industrialized, while the South carried on a farm-based existence steeped in old traditions that went back to the Civil War era or before. This would be the summer that I met M**ississi**ppi first hand. My great uncle **Moses Wright Jr,** who was a **Preacher**, had come up to Chicago from M**ississi**ppi to delivery a **Eulogy** for a funeral and was soon on his way home. It's very strange that his name was **Moses Wright** because in my oldest **past life** my father was the biblical **Moses** (P 667) and in my current life my paternal grand mother was named Charlotte **Wright** (p 25). When I heard that my cousin Wheeler was going to M**ississi**ppi for the summer with his grand father **Moses**, something came over me and I just had to go too. Perhaps my soul knew what it had to do. I put up a major protest with my mother and begged her to let me go. I was not aware of the dangers of the south and my mother knew that. It was dangerous for a northern black boy to go to the south without being aware of the environment he was entering. My mother was keen about not letting me travel on the train by myself but since my uncle **Moses** was taking us down she finally gave in and agreed to let me go. My mother tried to warm me and tried to explain the southern terrain before I was slain. She told me that white people in the south would not treat me the same as they did from whence I came. She gave me instructions, telling me that if a white man was approaching me on the sidewalk to get out of his way and let him pass. If something went wrong to beg for forgiveness and to get on my knees if need be. She was trying to prepare me so that I could avoid the worst possible thing that could happen and unfortunately the fear of what she thought could happen did happen. I did not understand because I had never experienced this before. I was 14 years old and I was from a predominately black neighborhood in Chicago so I had not experienced white racism to this degree. I had been to M**ississi**ppi as a small child but at 14, this summer would be mad wild. I have seen videos of my mother talking about the last time she saw me and she says I almost missed the train. As I ran up the stairs to board the train she called me back and said "You're gonna leave without kissing me? This could be the last time I ever see you Emmett!". Hearing that shocked me, I turned back and gave her a hug and a kiss. That was the last time I embraced my mother. I gave her my watch but **I kept my father's signet ring**, which she had only recently given me. I wanted to show it off to Wheeler, Simeon and the other boys. Turns out that this ring would be the thing that sparked Martin Luther's **Dream**.

We arrived in M**ississi**ppi on **August 21st 1955** the same day as the **Haitian revolution** of 1791. Of course I had never heard of the Haitian revolution or the **Nat Turner** rebellion that took place on the same day in 1831 but all three events took place on a Sunday. It seemed like all the stars were aligning for my tragic exit. Most of the people who read my story feel a sense of sadness but I assure you that the sunshine comes after the rain. I got my first astrological reading on July 30th of 2021 and I was told that astrologically speaking, the death of Emmett Till was a service to this country as it propelled the advancement of the Civil Rights Movement (p 654). **Emmet Till** was a **Leo** who was murdered on a Sunday, August **28th** in the astrological sign of **Virgo**. Virgo governs **service** to humanity. The astrologist explained how the location of Emmett's dragons tail (south node) aligned with the date he was murdered and it strengthens the **theorem** that Emmett came here as a sacrificial **lamb** giving his life for the Civil Rights Movement. We all come here with a divine plan and I was about to live mine out.

We arrived in Money M**ississ**ippi, on the Delta where cotton was king. A "**whistle stop**" town Located in the north**west** part of Mississippi on the notorious **33rd parallel,** the land was rich and fertile just like the **Nile River**. Little did I know that the **Ku Klux Klan** was active in the area and terrorized Black residents regularly. On May 7th 1955 the Reverend **George Lee**, a grocery owner and NAACP field worker had been shot and killed at point blank range after trying to **vote** in M**ississ**ippi. A few weeks later **Lamar Smith**, another Black man, was shot and killed in front of a M**ississ**ippi county courthouse, in broad daylight and before witnesses, after casting his **ballot**. Both victims had been active in voter registration drives. No one was arrested in connection with either murder. Many African Americans were sharecroppers like my Uncle **Moses**, on cotton fields owned by Whites. Southern society was racially segregated with **Jim Crow** laws. The population of Money was only **55**, still public areas, such as diners and theaters, had separate sections for use by Whites and Blacks, and Blacks regularly experienced abuse, oppression, and racism. None of this was on my mind. All I wanted to do was enjoy the summer time with my cousins. My cousin Wheeler tells of how we swam in the river everyday and we would see who could touch the bottom of the river but first you had to chase the snakes out the water. We swam to the floor of the river and return to the surface with dirt in our hands to prove we had touched the bottom and the water got colder the closer you got to the bottom. We had our share of fun but we worked too. We picked cotton on Monday, Tuesday and Wednesday. On Wednesday, August 24th they picked cotton in the M**ississ**ippi sun but they stopped early we all drove into town with Simeon for refreshments and some fun. The car was packed, it was Simeon (12 yrs old), Wheeler (16 yrs old), Maurice, James Pernell, Rosevelt Crawford and Myself (14 yrs old).

August 24th 1955 - Bryants Grocery and Meat Market

Rau nu Prt m heru

Iu f Per f m heru

Utterances for Coming Forth by day into Light

It is he, who comes forth by day into Light

When we arrived to the Bryants grocery store we found kids playing checkers out front while others were engaged in conversations. The store was a White-owned store, owned by **Roy and Carolyn Bryant**. Their business was no different than **People's Grocery** (page 18), they too depended on Black customers in the area who were local sharecroppers. Carolyn Bryant, a 21-year old white woman, was alone in the store working at the cash register while her husband Roy Bryant, was on the road with his half brother J.W. Milam. The first person to go into the store was Wheeler, he knew the customs of the south and how to be very careful not to offend White people. "No Sir, yes Sir and yes Ma'am, no Ma'am were", **very important** when addressing White people as well as not keeping eye contact with them for too long. He had heard of the lynchings in the south and was being very careful to not offend anyone. Wheeler went in and out the store with no problems then I went in. Shortly after I went in, Wheeler sent Simeon in after me to make sure everything went well. I was a Northern boy in the **Jim Crow** south and a few days prior I had set off fireworks in an area that I wasn't supposed to. I wasn't aware of the customs and Wheeler wanted to protect me by sending Simeon in after me. While I was in the store alone with Carolyn Bryant I purchased bubble gum then Simeon came in and we exited the store. There are different accounts as to what happened however there is one consistent agreement, which is that I whistled. The reason why I whistled is what is in question and of course what happened while I was in the store alone with Carolyn. My mother suggests that I may have whistled in an attempt to overcome my **stuttering**. She explained in a video how she taught me how to whistle when ever I became stuck on a word and felt like I was going to **stutter**. Carolyn has changed her story on several occasions, suggesting that I grabbed her by the waist while I was in the store, and that I said, "Bye, baby," along with other lewd comments and finally giving her a wolf whistle as I exited the store. Whatever the case may be, the events that happened were the perfect variables that created the table for my death. When I exited the store Wheeler asked me how everything went and as I attempted to respond I whistled to avoid **stuttering**. When I **whistled** Carolyn heard the whistle causing her to look over at the group of us on the porch, then she headed towards her car. When everyone saw the look on her face, fear and danger filled the air. As Wheeler states, there was a feeling as if we had broken someones window and immediately wanted to flee the area. And after someone said, "she's going to get a gun". We all made a B Line to the car. They all ran to the car so I ran too. They were scared so I was scared too. The tension increased because someone dropped a cigarette in the car causing Maurice to hesitate for a few seconds before we pulled off. The seconds felt like minutes then finally the cigarette was put out and we took off speeding down a dirt road, across the railroad tracks. Fear was in the air!! At some point we saw a car behind us. Was someone after us?! We stopped the car barely fast enough for everyone to exit the car and we all ran into the cotton fields causing the sharp cotton bolls to tear into our legs. In all the confusion we began to fall over each other. I fell and just as I was helped up the car passed us. No one was after us.... We returned to the car and found Simeon still there sitting in the car. He was only 12 and perhaps too young to see the danger. I didn't want to go back home so **I begged them not to tell Uncle Moses and they didn't**. That night we were all quiet, worried about what might come of it all. The next day, Rosevelt Crawford's niece, Ruth Crawford (16 yrs old) told us that she knew those people from Bryant's Grocery and she warned us that we would hear from them again.

Thursday went by, Friday went by and then we forgot about it. On Saturday we all went to Greenwood to see the sights. People from everywhere were there. This was the "big city" of the area. Some people had their wagons doing shopping for the week. All the girls and the guys were walking down Johnson street. There was excitement in the air for us. We stayed all day and left at around 12. Then we stopped at a place called 4 5ths, a "Juke Joint", a place were people danced to music, drank and socialized. When we left Maurice ran over a dog and I began to cry because I loved animals. When we got home our cousin Curtis was there. Maurice shared the bed with Wheeler and I shared the bed with Simeon.

When I whistled, to avoid **stuttering**, the people on the porch thought I whistled at Carolyn and apparently she did too. Roy Bryant returned home from a business trip a few days after the alleged incident, and how he came to learn about the incident is uncertain. Some say his wife told him what happened and some say someone who saw and heard me whistle told Roy that they would give him the details of what happened if they could receive **store credit**. Roy Bryant and John William "J. W." Milam allowed the local Blacks to pay with **credit** because credit was used as a way to control and keep Blacks in check. No different than the story I shared about my **Great Grandfather General Dukes Sr** (page 20). It is said that the story was exaggerated so as to make it worth the **store credit** the person desired. Whatever the case may be, it is said that after Roy Bryant was informed of what had happened, he aggressively questioned several young Black men who entered his store. That evening, Roy approached a Black teenager walking along a road and took him to be identified by a companion of Carolyn's but they denied that the boy was the one who whistled at Carolyn. Somehow, Bryant learned that I was from Chicago and was staying with "the Preacher", **Moses** Wright. After hearing the story Roy decided to deal with this "Chicago boy" himself. Roy did not own a car so he went to borrow his half brother J.W. Milam's car so he could go see about what happened with this "Chicago boy". Milam was a racist, dangerous and violent man. He had no problem killing a Black man, or a Nigger as he called them. When Milam heard about the exaggerated incident he took charge of the search and decided they would head to my Uncle Moses' house that night to find "the Chicago boy". Several witnesses overheard Bryant and his half brother, J. W. Milam, discussing plans to kidnap me.

The Kidnapping of Emmett Till

They arrived around 2:30 a.m. in the morning of August 28th. They banged on the door in the dead of the night screaming: "Preacher Preacher". Uncle **Moses** was known as Preacher by the locals. They were very loud, mean, hostile and they were well armed with flash lights, a shotgun and 45 pistols. When uncle **Moses** answered the door he saw three men standing there, **J.W. Milam**, **Roy Bryant** and a <u>black man that had his head down hiding his face behind his hat</u>. They said they were looking for a fat boy from Chicago. A shotgun was then pressed into my uncle's chest and Milam told my uncle: "take us to the nigger who did the talking". Uncle **Moses** was caught off guard. Uncle **Moses** had a 12 gauge and 410 Bore shotguns in the closet but they were both unloaded. There's no way uncle **Moses** would have let them take me if he had known what happened but he knew nothing about it and he was caught off guard. The only thing uncle **Moses** could do with guns drawn on him was plead with them and that's what he did. Uncle **Moses** begged, "He's only 14, he's from up North, why not give the boy a whipping, and leave it at that?" then Milam asked, "How old are you, preacher?" to which my uncle responded, "64". Milam threatened that if he told anybody he wouldn't live to see 65. My Aunt Elizabeth offered them money and for a second she had Roy's attention but Milam was not concerned with money he cursed at her and told her to return to bed. They moved from room to room as if they knew where they were going, as if someone had given them precise details. To save everyone else in the house uncle **Moses** led them to me but he had no idea he would never see me again. Wheeler heard all the commotion and he was sure that we were all going to die. He began praying and asking God to forgive him for all his sins and to save us all. He told God that if he was spared he would live the rest of his life for God. In 19**77** the year of the **Snake** Wheeler answered that call and became a preacher like his Grand Father **Moses**. That same year uncle **Moses** would pass away (Aug 19**77**). That same year I was born again as Dawud Basheer Eddings. When they finally shined a flash light in Wheeler's face he closed his eyes and prepared to die as he trembled with fear. He had heard of Black people being killed and thrown in rivers in the racist south. They had been warned about the south and about situations like these so he knew that no one was coming to save them, not even the police, but when Milam saw that he was not me they told him to go back to sleep and they moved on to the next room. Wheeler opened his eyes and was relieved that he was not dead but now he feared what they might do to me. When they found me I was still sleeping in the bed with my cousin Simeon. They shined the light on both of us and asked each of us were we the one from Chicago and I said yes. That's when the violence erupted. They gave me a lesson in proper etiquette, "yes SIR" when speaking to white men. "Did you say yes to me? If you say 'yes' to me again I'll knock your brains out". They forced me out of bed and told me to get dressed and told Simeon to go back to sleep. Their anger grew because I wasn't moving fast enough. I began to look for my socks and they cursed at me asking what I was doing. I told them that I always put my socks on before I put my shoes on. "You won't need socks were you're going" is what Milam told me. When they marched me out of the house there was a silence that went through the house. They took me to a green truck and uncle **Moses** said he heard them ask someone in the car if this was the boy, and heard someone say "yes". Uncle **Moses** said the voice seemed like it was a lighter voice than a man's. The person in the car was never identified but most people assume that it was Carolyn Bryant in the truck. They tied me up in the back of a green pickup truck and drove toward Money, M**ississ**ippi. They took me back to Bryant's Groceries where I was pistol whipped and knocked unconscious. **Then they recruited two Black men to hold me down** in the back while they drove to a barn **25** miles away in Drew M**ississ**ippi. Uncle **Moses** stayed on the front porch waiting for me to return. With every car that went by there was hope that I had returned. He and another man drove to Money, got gasoline, and drove around trying to find me with no success, finally he returned home at around 8:00 am. In fear for his life the police were not called. Uncle **Moses** and Aunt Elizabeth drove to Sumner, where Elizabeth's brother contacted the sheriff and my mother. *<u>(see page 180, 287, 419, 508, 659 for pattern with Carolyn's birth and death)</u>*

August 28th 1955 - Amenta and the Field of Reeds - Ausar reigned for 28 years in the Ausarian resurrection drama

We left Glendora M**ississi**ppi just after dawn (**Khepri Ra, the morning star**). We arrived at Leslie Milam's (J.W. Milam's brother) plantation in Sunflower County around 6am. As God would have it, as we arrived to the plantation we passed a black boy who just happened to be walking through a <u>field of **reeds**,</u> him and I made brief eye contact as the truck turned into the plantation. His name just happened to be <u>Willie **Reed**</u> like the <u>field of **reeds**</u> that the **soul** goes to after death in the ancient Kemetic (Egyptian) version of heaven (**Amenta**) and the afterlife. Willie was the last person to see me alive that wasn't connected to my death. At my court trial Reed recalled seeing four white men in the front of the truck, and "two black men" in the back who were restraining me. Some have speculated that the two black men worked for Milam and were forced to help restrain me, although they later denied being present. Willie was up early that morning because his grandmother sent him to the store to buy fresh meat for dinner. While on his way home he crossed a field and passed a barn from which he could hear the sounds of me crying as they beat me. I screamed: "<u>Lord, have mercy! Mama, save me</u>!" Willie could hear the blows landing on my body and they sounded like they were made with heavy objects like the handle of a hoe or a pistol. Willie also heard them cursing and yelling at me, "<u>Get down you black bastard</u>". Willie slowly walked to the barn and looked through a crack and saw them beating me. All of the blows were centered around my head.

He saw Milam take a hatchet and swing down on my head separating my face from the back of my skull. Willie became frighten and walked away from the barn towards a neighbors home. He told the neighbor what he heard but it didn't rouse immediate attention because the Milam brothers were famous for their "pistol whippings" and the sounds of some poor negro being roughed up by the Milan gang was nothing new. Shortly after Willie and the neighbor walked to the well to get water which was close enough to the barn to hear **my cries for help**. While they were at the well drawing water my cries grew fainter and fainter and then there were no more. When my screams stopped, they assumed I must be dead. As they started back to the house they saw Milam exit the barn with a pistol on his right side, he was headed towards them. He stopped at the well and got a drink of water and **asked them if they had heard anything**, and to preserve their lives they responded "No". Willie noticed that Milam seemed to be intoxicated off alcohol. Milan went back to the barn and three other White men joined him in a huddle. Shortly after they dispersed and a tractor near the barn was moved and the green Chevrolet pickup truck with a white top was backed into the side door of the barn. By this time Willie was back at the neighbors house watching through the kitchen window. **They saw my body placed in the back of the truck then a tarpaulin was thrown over me**. While the truck drove off they could see movement from under the tarpaulin. I was still alive, but only barely.

Rau nu Prt m heru

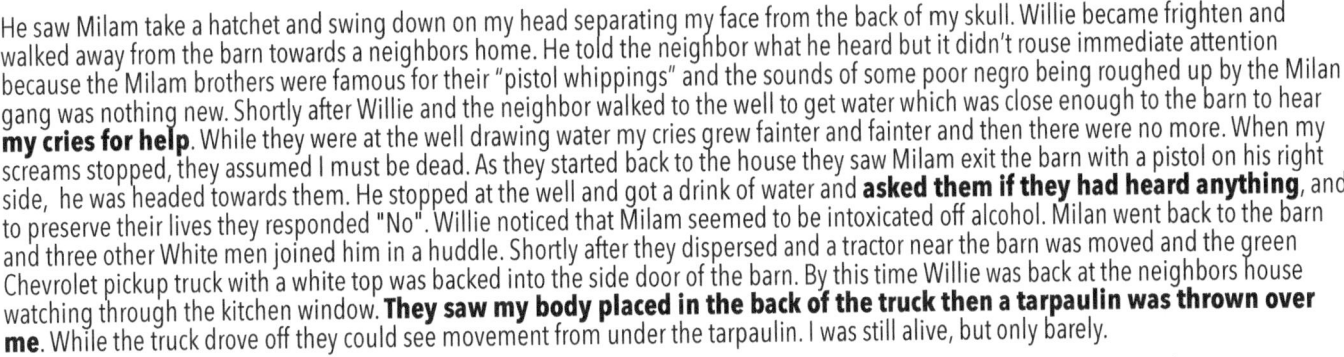

Addendum (The information below comes from a **22** minute Youtube interview with **Mayor Johnny B. Thomas**)

I watched a video on youtube that revealed the identity of 2 of the 5 black men that helped kidnap and kill me. **Mayor Johnny B. Thomas** of Glendora, Mississippi is the Executive Director of the **Emmett Till Historic Intrepid Center**. Mayor Thomas' father, **Henry Lee Loggins** was one of the 5 black men that helped kidnap me. His father, Henry Lee held me down while I was in the truck. Henry Lee Logins was the right hand man of J.W. Milam who was in charge of most of the plantations in the local area. Johnny claims his father was forced to help J.W. Milam kidnap and murder me. He says it was either his father or a black man named **Too Tight** that actually shot me in the head. His father tied the barbwire around my neck, attaching it to the cotton gin fan. Johnny claims the murder was done in a drunken spree. His father, Henry Lee, along with an unnamed black man were kept in several jails in area under a different names for 2 to 3 weeks by the area's white power structure to insure that they would not be able to testify during the murder trial. Johnny says that they lived right next door to J.W. Milam and probably played with his children as a child. He says his mother told him that J.W. Milam would beat her, his father and other blacks if they claimed to be too sick to work the cotton fields on his plantation. Johnny claims his family's legacy was tarnished as many people looked down on his father and would often make comments about him to the tune of, "that low down son of bitch that helped kill that kid". Filled with this burden, Johnny has worked to keep the memory of Emmett Till alive and to bring forth healing. Johnny mentioned a **strange pattern** that he took notice to. He mentioned how "Emmett's" body was shipped to A.A. Rayner, at **4141** South Cottage Grove Avenue, and **coincidentally**, **4141** are the last four digits of his **social security** number. He stated that double digits are rare in **social security numbers**! **4141** adds up to **55**. And I was born as Emmett Till in 19**41**. The remains of **Tutankhaten** (**King Tut**) were found in the Valley of the Kings and were stored as KV**62**. The 2 digits in the middle of my **social security number** are **62** (see page **41**,121, 221, 508). **None of this is just coincidence!** These numerical patterns are examples of a phenomena known as **quantum entanglement**, spoken about often in Physics. **Einstein**, called this phenomena, **spooky action at a distance** (pages 40, 329). Einstein died in 19**55**, the same year Emmett Till was murdered and the same year my mother, (in this life) was born. When **coincidences** bind with **synchronicities** the outcome tends to have **the mark of a greater authority!!!**.......

Iu f Per f m heru

ADDENDUM

The Twilight Zone: Carolyn Bryant on Doomsday

Before you dismiss these patterns as **"just coincidence"**, first read page 180 and concider that reality is a locked door that needs to be opened with the keys of intuition and imagination... **Rod Sterling**, the creator of the ground breaking **Twilight Zone** TV Show saw the 1955 murder of Emmett Till as a mistrial of justice and wanted to tell Emmett's story. In response to the murder of Emmett Till he produced a show titled **Noon On Doomsday**. However, when the network realized the show was about the murder of Emmett Till they censored it so much that the audience never knew it was about Emmett Till. **But isn't it strange** that the show aired on **April 25**, 1956, and **Carolyn Bryant**, the women who caused Emmett's death would die on **April 25**, 2023...? Afterwards **Sterling** was quoted saying, "I think it's criminal that we're not permitted to make dramatic note of social evils as they exist... Drama by it's very nature should make a comment on those things that effect our daily lives". <u>Was that "just a coincidence", like the show **Manifest** (p 536) and the **USS Emmett Till** (p 539) and what about **Back To The Future** (p 40)?!!!!</u> Perhaps the universe will always find a way **to make dramatic note of social evils as they exist** or perhaps we are all just living in a **Twilight Zone**..

Utterances for Coming Forth by day into Light

August 29th 1955

The Search Party

As soon as my mother got news of my kidnapping everyone was crying but **she spent very little time crying**. Instead, she made calls to her local leaders immediately. She got the local news papers involved and they contacted the M**ississ**ippi press. Everyone was searching for me. On August 29th Bryant and Milam were questioned by Leflore County sheriff, George Smith. They admitted they had taken me from my great-uncle's yard, but claimed they had released me the same night in front of Bryant's store. Bryant and Milam were arrested on kidnapping charges in connection with my disappearance. They were jailed in Greenwood, M**ississ**ippi and held without bond. **Three days later**, my decomposed corpse is pulled from M**ississ**ippi's Tallahatchie River. Uncle **Moses** and my cousin Curtis identified my body from a ring with the initials **L.T.**

It is he, who comes forth by day into Light

August 31st 1955 - Mummy Mississippi (The Ausarian Resurrection)

On the morning of August 31st, **three days after** I was abducted and murder my feet were spotted sticking out of the water by two white boys who were fishing in the Tallahatchie river. They notified the local authorities. My body was found nude, swollen and disfigured but I still had my **silver ring** on (ring seen on page 512). My head was very badly mutilated, and my face was unrecognizable due to trauma and having been submerged in water. I had been shot above the right ear, there was evidence that I had been beaten on the back and the hips. A barbwire had been wrapped around my neck with a cotton gin fan to weigh my body down causing my tongue to protrude from my mouth. Some say the fan weighed 70lbs, some say 100lbs and I have even heard it recorded at 125lbs but still they couldn't keep my body down. **Still I rose** to the top and my body was discovered. No one knows the order of events of what happened after I left the barn but we can see from my injuries what was done to me. One of the men who pulled my body from the river said the front half of my skull fell apart when my body was first retrieved from the murky waters. Milam was quoted later as saying that after he and others killed me, they removed my clothing, cleaned the blood from the shed floor and spread cottonseed to hide their crime but all things done in the dark soon come to light. The group drove back to Roy Bryant's home in Money, where they reportedly burned my clothes. After my body was discovered another **25 black bodies** were found in the Tallahatchie river and **some of them had been tarred and feathered**. Many of them were identified as people who were thought to have gone north for a better life and opportunities.

I was lynched (Emmett was lynched) in Money M**ississ**ippi and in the word M**ississ**ippi you can see the name **Isis** (Auset) who is the **mother** of **Heru** (**Horus**, **Zeus**, **Jesus**) the one who **resurrects** after death. **Isis** is the great royal **wife** of **Ausar** (**Osiris**), known as the Lord of **resurrection,** the Lord of the **West,** the Lord of the dead and the underworld. **Re-member** that **you** are **Ausar (Osiris)** and **Heru,** the **hero!** See page 3 for the **hero's journey!** Ausar reigned for **28 years** and I was (Emmett was) murdered on **August 28th**. I was beaten, tortured, shot in the head and **thrown in a** M**ississi**ppi **river** at **14** years old. In the Ausarian **resurrection** drama, Ausar was cut into **14** pieces and **thrown in the Nile river**. The **Nile River** is on a **delta** just like the Tallahatchie river I was thrown in. The Tallahatchie river is located in the north**west** part of M**ississi**ppi on the notorious **33rd parallel**. In ancient Kemet (Egypt) West was where the soul or the BA went when we die. The Ancient people (Kemetic, Egyptians) of the Hapi Eteru (The Nile River) did not believe in death. They understood the immortality of the soul and had mastered the repetition of the soul, the **resurrection** of the Ba (soul). They Called the death of the physical body **westing**. Just as the Sun rises in the East and sets in the West the same is to be said for the Ba (soul). This concept of resurrection was called the **Wehem-Mesut** (repeating of births, p 14). Even in the name K**emet** you find the name Emmett. Memphis Tennessee was named after the city of **Mem**phis, the royal residence and capital of ancient Kemet (Egypt) established my the **Nswt Bity** (Pharaoh) **Memes** (Narmer). My past life of Emmett Till was revealed to me on July 3rd 2018 and my death propelled Martin Luther King to the forefront of the Civil Rights Movement. **Martin Luther King** was assassinated in Memphis Tennessee on **April 4th** 1968 (see page 69!). The **Mississippi river** runs through Memphis and I was thrown in a river in M**ississ**ippi. On **April 4th** 2020 (p 594), 52 years after Martin's assassination my **past life** as

Tutankhaten (King Tut) was revealed to me while in a deep meditation where the spirits of Rosa Parks and Martin Luther King were present.. **Tutankhaten (King Tut)** was a young Pharaoh in ancient Kemet who died young like Emmett. Martin Luther King wrote a **theology** paper on **Heru** and the **Ausarian Resurrection** in 1949. This is a **Divine Riddle** like the **Riddle** of the **Sphinx**. Like my great great grand mother May Fannie **Riddle** (page 16) and my great grand mother Leacola **Riddle** (page 21) who was born the day **Marcus Garvey** died. This is all connected so that it will undoubtedly get your attention. My last day in the army was Martin Luther Kings birthday, January 15th 2005 (p 130). I prayed and asked God for direction on whether I should stay in this mans Army or if I should get out and I was led out on Martin Luther King's birthday. **Heru** is the son of Ausar and he is the one that returns as **Ra** through **resurrection**. The original name of the Sphinx was **Heru** Em Ahket, which has the head of a human and the body of a lion. In my life as Emmett I was a **Leo** like the **Lion**. We must all aspire to be Heru (Shemsu Heru, page 2). The one who rises above his animalistic nature. This is the journey I took in my present life. The present moment is the truest gift and we must be wise about how we spend our time here on earth.

Rau nu Prt m heru

My revelation is aligned with two ancient prophecies. There is **the ancient Kemetic prediction** that **Heru** will return one day and recapture the kingdom of his father, when the **golden** age will be restored and the **lion** will unite with the **Lamb/Goat**. Heru is believed to have a **resurrection** during the **Aquarian Age**. He is the prince of peace, bringer of order, redeemer of truth for humanity, resurrection and the life. He is able to right the wrongs of the past, free the oppressed, and restore **Maat** (page 367). In the ancient Kemetic Ausarian resurrection drama, Ausar (Osiris) was the first **gardener**, the first to cultivate (**Till, Tilling, Tillage**) the land and the first to come back after "death", or better known as **Wehem Mesut** (repeating of births, page 14). Christianity borrowed from the resurrection story of Ausar when the character of **Jesus** was created and the Murder of Emmett **Till** is intimately connected to both Ausar and Jesus. According to the book of John, after Jesus resurrected, Mary mistook him for a **gardener**. Emmett **Till** arrived in M**ississ**ippi (**isis**) on August 21st 1955. The next day he spent the early morning harvesting cotton on his uncles farm (**garden**). Emmett **Till**'s uncle, **Moses** Wright Jr was a farmer - a **gardener**. According to the book of John, Jesus's cruxifixction took place near a **garden**. Emmett **Till** was murdered on Leslie Milam's **farm** (**garden**) in Money M**ississ**ippi. Ausar reigned for **28 years** and Emmett Till was murdered on **August 28th**. **Emmett Till** was beaten, tortured, shot in the head and **thrown in a** M**ississ**ippi **river** at **14** years old. In the Ausarian **resurrection** drama, Ausar was cut into **14** pieces and **thrown in the Nile river**. The story of Ausar is a parable that teaches about the natural law of **Wehem Mesut** (repeating of births, page 14) also known as resurrection, reincarnation and **Gilgul** in **Judiam**. With that in mind we must consider what it is that Ausar was really "cultivating", or "**Tilling**".. The murder of Emmett **Till** was a prophecy designed to remind human beings about the immortality of their souls and what it is that we are supposed to be cultivating, or "**Tilling**" here on Earth. **Emmett** is another way to spell the word **Emit**. Emit means to **send forth**. In a like manner, my past lives were **sent forth** after I communed with the sacred **manna** (p 480), no different than how **Lusaaset comes forth** after the consumption of the **Yrp wine** (p 482). Then there is also ***The Prophecy of Reincarnation Sambho the Black Buddha*** from the far east of Asia. It is said that between the years of 1975 and 2020 the **Buddha** would reincarnate in the western world. He would prove the **immortality** of the **soul** with his **reincarnation**. He would be the descendant of those who are still in bondage today - the offspring of those who from time immemorial worked their way down from the high lands of Ethiopia to the Mediterranean sea at the delta. Behold, **TutemRa: The Prophecy of Reincarnation**..

Iu f Per f m heru

Dr. Martin Luther King Jr. Speaks on Ancient Egyptian Influence On Christianity

"The Egyptian mysteries of **Isis** and **Osiris** exerted considerable influence upon early Christianity. These two great Egyptian deities, whose worship passed into Europe, were revered not only in Rome but in many other centers where Christian communities were growing up. Osiris and Isis, so the legend runs, were at one and the same time, brother and sister, husband and wife; but Osiris was murdered, his coffined body being thrown into the Nile, and shortly afterwards the widowed and exiled Isis gave birth to a son, Horus. Meanwhile the coffin was washed up on the Syrian coast, and became miraculously lodged in the trunk of a tree. This tree afterwards chanced to be cut down and made into a pillar in the palace at Byblos, and there Isis at length found it. After recovering Osiris' dismembered body, Isis restored him to life and installed him as King in the nether world; meanwhile Horus, having grown to manhood, reigned on earth, later becoming the third person of this great Egyptian trinity." – **Dr. Martin Luther King Jr. 1949**

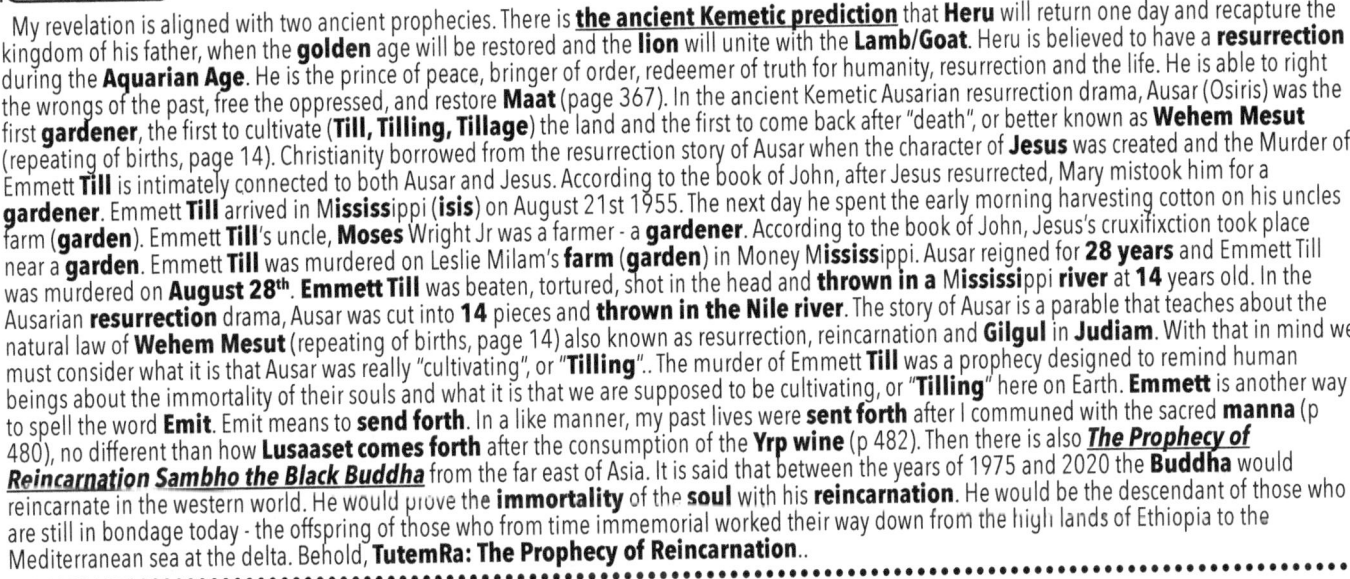

The Return of Heru, The Ausarian Resurrection (full break down on pages 2,3)

ADDENDUM

Utterances for Coming Forth by day into Light

It is he, who comes forth by day into Light

All human beings have the **potent**ial to reach Heru consciousness (Christ, Chrism, p 492), becoming a metaphorical reflection of the Heru stela seen below. Ultimately, **Ausar** represents the **immortal soul** of all human beings that reincarnates, while **Auset** represents intuition and wisdom. **Set** represents your own **ego** and your lower nature. Finally, **Heru** represents the potential of **your** spiritual stamina to **become** the Heru (**hero**) of **your** life journey, by conquering **your ego** (Set).. The Hero's journey is a cyclical one. The hero goes off into the world and finds, or achieves, or does something beyond the normal range of achievement and experience and returns victorious to tell their story. A hero gives their life to something bigger than themselves. There are two types of Hero's. The physical one and the spiritual one. The physical hero might save someones life or sacrifice their own life for another person. The spiritual hero has learned or found some rare form of supernatural experience and comes back to communicate it. I am the spiritual Hero (Heru). Behold, The Reincarnation of **Tutankhaten**, the golden boy who has fascinated the world since 19**22** and **Emmett Till**, the boy who's death sparked the Civil Rights Movement in America, 67 years ago in 19**55**. These two boys are fragments of my soul from different life times. A fragment of my soul was born again in 19**77** as **Dawud Eddings** (page 34). In 2018 I realized I was Emmett Till in a past life (page 480) and in **20**2**0** I realized I was Tutankhaten (**King Tut**) in a past life (page 594). It was ordained from the beginning of time that I would die a sacrificial death in my life as Emmett Till so that I could have the opportunity to be **BORN AGAIN**, **22** years later as Dawud Eddings and earn the right to know who I was and with the revealing of this revelation mans consciousness can be aroused and justice can at-last prevail (page 511). The image (full image seen on page 3) symbolizes Heru's dominion over nature, and most importantly his victory over immoral sexual urges, and anger because these are habits that lead the human personality into failure and regret. Heru is portrayed in the conventional Kemetic form for youth; that is, he is nude and wearing his hair in a sidelock. He is seen with a **scorpion,** a **snake** and a **Lion** in his **left** hand. In his **right** hand he holds a **scorpion,** a **snake** and a **Lamb/Goat**. He is seen stepping forward with his left foot while standing on a crocodile. Above him is the head of **Bes**, the NTCHR (deity) with leonine features who had traditionally been a protector of households and eventually had become the defender of everything good and enemy to everything bad. Heru is flanked by several deities as well as the Uatchet (eye of intention) with human hands and arms. On his right the Goddess **Auset** (Isis), is seen protectively holding the wall of a curved reed hut, a primeval chapel, in which the Heru child stands together with a figure of **Ra-horakhty**, God of the rising sun, who stands upon coiled snakes. **Ausar** is seen next to Ra-horakhty in the form of a hawk standing on a papyrus reed scepter, wearing an Atef crown. Behind Auset, the Goddess **Nekhbet** is seen in vulture form standing on a papyrus reed scepter. On his left **Jhuty** (Thoth) is seen protectively holding the wall of a curved reed hut. Behind Jhuty, the Goddess **Wadjet** in the form of a serpent is seen standing on a papyrus reed scepter. On the stela **Auset** (**Isis**) speaks and recounts that while she and her infant child Heru were still hiding in the marshes, the child became ill. In her despair, she cried for help to the "Boat of Eternity" (the sun boat in which the God travels over the sky), "and the sun disk stopped opposite her and did not move from its place." Jhuty was sent from the sun boat to help Auset and cured her son Heru by reciting spells (words of power, **hekau**). The hekau's always ended with the phrase "and the protection of the afflicted as well," indicating that by using these hekau's, any type of affliction in human beings would be healed. Because of this "egyptologist" believe* this stela to be solely about protection and curing of insect bites but they are wrong just as they have been wrong about many things when it comes to deciphering language and spiritual systems they do not fully inner stand. Heru is striding forward with his left foot, his spiritual foot. The statue is **3 dimensional** as Heru faces the viewer stepping into the aquarian age carrying the zodiac signs of Leo, Scorpion and Snake in his hands. The stela details my return and so here I am, but I won't be the last! More will come!

I was sent down (born) again on July 25th 1941 the year of the **snake** as **Emmett Till** under the sun sign of Leo the **Lion**. In my life as Emmett I was the **sacrificial lamb** held in Heru's right hand (in stela, p 510). I was born again in this life as Dawud (David) on October 25th 1977 the year of the **Snake** under the sun sign of the **Scorpion**. And in this present life I became the Lion (Heru Em Ahket) held in Heru's left hand. Heru is holding the Snakes, Scorpions because I was born in the year of the **snake** many times and the zodiacal sign of scorpio is the sign of transformation and reincarnation. However, this prophecy was not set in stone! I had to earn this revelation. First I rose from the muddy M**ississ**ippi waters like the **lotus flowers** of **rebirth** which are seen in the stela, then in my present life I transformed into Heru the lion earning the right to know I was Emmett Till then 2 years later I was given the name TutemRa and my life as Tutankhaten was restored (p 594).. The **lotus** stand in the stela supports the two feathers of **Maat** in Ausar's headdress. I went through a blind initiation and by honoring the laws of Maat and the divine feminine energies on the planet I was gradually awakened to my previous lives fulfilling the ancient prophecies. This prophecy is for all the citizens of the world, but in particular, and Very Expressly, to the Africans all over the world who still suffer under the oppression of racism and white supremacy. As I have Ramembered who I am it is important that you Ra-member / **Re-member** that **you** are **Ausar** and **Heru**, the **hero!** See page 3 for the **hero's journey**! SANKOFA.

42 Laws of Maat, Page 367

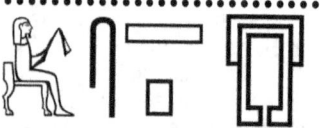

January 18th 2022
Mamie Till heard the voice of God - The Sacrificial Lamb

On January 18th 2022 I was watching a video of my mother, Mamie Till Mobley from an interview she did on July 25th 1991 and in this interview she would share an encounter she has with God. She was asked whether or not it was appropriate to speak of my murder in terms of **biblical prophecy**. The interviewer suggested that many Black people perceived my death to be a calling back of my soul for a mission that was greater than college or a life on earth, that my murder was "**prophecy**". He asked her if this might be a difficult way to look at her loss and her reply astonished me. She responded: "It might be a difficult thing to say but I know the experience that I had… I had the experience of, almost **a one on one conversation with a being outside of myself** and I have to identify that being as **God** because the devil would not of come to me with anything of this nature. **A voice** told me "**It was ordained from the beginning of time that Emmett would die a sacrificial death. Be happy to have been the mother of a child who died blameless like Christ**, but there is a job for you to do now. **Emmett has done his job now your job is to continue to tell the story so that mans consciousness will be aroused and justice can at-last prevail**." It was as if she confirmed the authenticity of this book! I had never seen this interview and had never heard her speak about my death in this manner. Afterwards I realized that she had been given a sense of peace from our ancient family so that she would have the strength she needed to carry on the mission. Mamie Till died on **January 6** 2003, the year **goat**, Emmett was murdered in 1955, the year of the **goat**. (***ADDENDUM* Tupac's** grand mother Eloise Maria Barnes was born on **January 6. January 6th** is 12 days after the Winter Solstice (Christmas Dec 25, pages 489, 614). **January 6** is known as the **Epiphany** in **Christ**ianity as it marks the day that the 3 wise men visited **Jesus Christ** in the Manger. **January 6** is also the day that the ancient Kemetyu celebrated the Winter Solstice. Mamie claimed to have heard the voice of God telling her that her son died blameless like Christ. Mamie dies on the day the three wise men visited Christ in the **Manger**. and day that the ancient Kemetyu celebrated the Winter Solstice. See pages 14 (Christ-Krst), 229, 339, 344, 366, 371, 424, 489, 569, 616).

January 3rd 2021 Mississippi Mummy

Mummy Mississippi, not even Rap Genius can decipher this Riddle, only a chosen few, my name is TutemRa Nebu Sahu Kheperu, shm e em htp, I come in peace, I'm different like Das EFX, claiming to be the deceased, I'm running, doing the reps, immortal Djet, the Ba rises in the east, gold face, the soul sets in the west, a cold case, dead Money, Mississippi Mummy - TutemRa

Emmett Till and the 33rd Parallel

My mother, **Mamie Till** was born in **Webb** M**ississ**ippi, located on the **33rd parallel**. I was **lynched** on the mysterious **33rd parallel** in the zodiac sign of Virgo which is the sign of service. The 33rd Parallel is a meridian that orbits the Earth at exactly **33** degrees from where the Sun dissects the Earth's Equator. In the field of Numerology, **33** is the highest of the "**Master Numbers**." **President Kennedy** was assassinated on the **33rd parallel**. In the Holy Bible, **King David** (Page 225) reigned in Jerusalem **33 years** (2 Samuel 5:5, 1 Kings 2:11, 1 Kings 5:16, 1 Chronicles 3:4, and 29:27). Genesis 46:15 states: "These sons and daughters of Jacob were **33** in all." **Jesus Christ**, began his **33** year ministry at about the age of 30 (Luke 3:23), and was said to have died on the cross and rose again (resurrected) at the age of **33**. There are **33 vertebrae** in the human spinal cord. The number of turns in a complete sequence of human **DNA** equals **33**. In 1945 President Franklin D. Roosevelt met his "sudden death" of a cerebral hemorrhage at the 33rd Parallel at Warm Springs, Georgia. His last words were, "I have a terrible headache." His medical chart is missing. In 1945 Roosevelt's successor was Harry S Truman. "I've got every degree in the Masons that there is," said Truman. Harry S **Truman** was the **33rd President**. As the 33rd President, this 33rd degree Mason initiated the Nuclear Age, exploding the first A-bomb at the 33rd Parallel Trinity Test Site, (Almagordo) White Sands, New Mexico, on the 33rd Parallel. He was responsible for the killing of thousands of Japanese (the Yellow Peril) at two cities close to the 33rd Parallel, **Hiroshima** and **Nagasaki**. The two most well known centers of paranormal activity are on or near the 33rd Parallel, the Great Pyramids, and the Bermuda Triangle. On July 8th 1947 a **UFO** and aliens' bodies were allegedly found in the desert outside **Roswell**, New Mexico at the 33rd Parallel (see pages 84, 105, 346, 380, 663). 1990 Mason/ Skull and Bones member George Bush, the **41**st United States President, provoked a war with Saddam Hussein. On **Emmett Till's** birthday, **July 25th** 1990, the United States Ambassador to Iraq, April Glaspie, told Hussein that the Iraq/Kuwait dispute was an Arab matter, not one that affects the United States. On August 2, 1990, Hussein invaded Kuwait and as a result Mason George Bush organized **Desert Storm**, which concerned a border dispute between **Kuwait and Iraq** at the **33rd Parallel**. On September 11th 1991, 8 months after Desert Storm ended, George Bush SR held a press conference where he stated "we need a catastrophic event to usher in the New World Order". 10 years later on September 11th 2001, the year of the **snake**, two planes hit two buildings and the world changed. In reference to **UFO**'s, for many year the topic of UFO'S has been relegated to tabloids and conspiracy theory, however in 2022 the pentagon declassified photos and videos during a UFO hearing leading many to speculate whether the government has been keeping this knowledge from the American people all this time. This brings me back to my experience while in basic training (p 84), the words I said after my accident in 2002 (p 105) and the lights I saw in the sky in 2015 (346).

Identifying the Immortal Ba (Soul)
Star Wars, May 25th and the 18th Dynasty Strikes Back

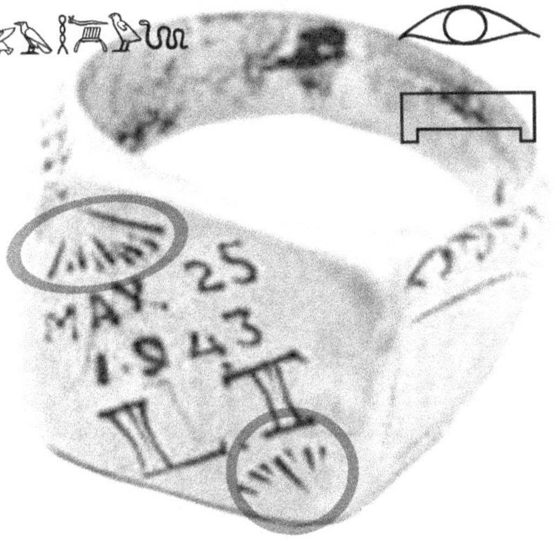

May 25th is the first **star code pattern** in my story and **Star Wars** first premiered on **May 25th**, 1977 <u>the year of the **snake**</u>, **5** months before I (Dawud/David) was born.. The **Ausarian Resurrection Drama** is the hidden story woven within the Star Wars theme (more on page 37). Much of the concepts used in the Star Wars movies were taken from the science and philosophy of ancient **Kemet** (Egypt), in particular from the 18th Dynasty and the relationship between Akhenaten and his sun Tutankhaten. **Ausar** represents the **immortal soul** of all humans that **reincarnates** and because of Star Wars' connection to the Ausarian **Resurrection** Drama it is connected to the experiences in my lives as Emmett and Dawud. When my body was discovered the sheriff immediately sent for my uncle **Moses** to identify me but my face was so disfigured and mutilated that I was unidentifiable. It was my **silver ring,** that was still on my finger, that my cousin Simeon used to identify me. My **father** (Louis Till) left that ring for me in 1943 before he was murdered, when I was only 2 years old. My mother (Mamie Till) had just recently given it to me before I left to M**ississi**ppi. On the ring the initials "**L. T.**" and the date "**May 25** 1943" were carved in it, which is the year of the **goat**. Twelve years later in 19**55**, the year of the **goat** I was murdered and that same year my next mother (Debra Dukes, page 27) would be born. One of my sisters once had a "**vivid dream**" on **May 25th 2002** about me dying in a car accident and 7 days after her **dream** I would crash my car in a violent accident on June 1st 2002 (page 104), which is my father's birthday (Spencer **David** Eddings, page 28). Then 6 years later in 2008 I would total my motor cycle on **May 25th** 2008 (page 157). 5 days after that I purchased another motorcycle and crashed again on June 3rd 2008 (p 158). Mysteriously, this new motorcycle had a cross with a **Jesus** pendant glued between the handle bars and when I saw it I told the owner that I would keep it there so that I would always have **God with me**. On June 3rd, at around 5:50 am, I was riding my new motorcycle to work, going south on the FDR highway when suddenly, a truck began to merge into my lane as if I wasn't there. To avoid getting hit I quickly maneuvered my bike to the next lane, on the right. I had no time to look and check traffic I just moved out of reflex to avoid being hit by the truck. The lane I merged in was at the very beginning of the on ramp for cars merging onto the highway on 116th street. Because of this, the car in front of me was moving at a slower rate of speed than me causing me to crash into the back of it. I flew off my motorcycle and **crashed** into the back window of the car. I bounced off the car and **landed on my feet** on the highway, like **Spiderman** (Peter-Ptah **Parker**). When I landed I looked down at my feet and there I saw the **cross** that was on the bike, it was laying there right between my feet, however **Jesus Christ** was no longer on the **cross**. I picked the **cross** up and I still have it to this day (p 158). I suffered no injures from this accident nor did the people in the car. I left this accident with a sense of being **saved** by God **again*,** because, what were the chances of me finding that **cross** laying between my feet?! The **cross** could have landed anywhere on the highway but it just so "happened" to land where I would land right between my feet! And what are the chances that I would even notice it? But I did notice it and it did land between my feet! I knew that it was some sort of **sign** so I kept the **cross** and told the story to many people. I would not realize that my car accident in 2002 and my motorcycle accidents in 2008 were connected by the date **May 25th** until December of 2011 (page 222). I didn't know what it meant back then but **I KNEW IT WAS NOT JUST SOME COINCIDENCE THAT MEANT NOTHING. I KNEW IT MEANT SOMETHING I JUST DIDN'T KNOW WHAT.** Today I know what happened. Everything was set in place as if it were ordained from the beginning of time just as my mother Mamie Till once said (p 511). Even the murder of **George Floyd** was part of this prophecy with his murder taking place on **May 25th 2020** (page 610), the month after I had my past life revelation of my life as **Tutankhaten** (**King Tut**) on April 4th 2020 (page 594) the day **Martin Luther King** was assassinated (page 69). <u>George was murdered like a **pawn**</u> but he would prove to be a <u>**Pawn of Prophecy**</u> (page 44). When I was murdered in 1955 it sparked the first mass Civil Rights Movement. I was not the first Black person lynched in America and surely not the first Black boy lynched! In fact **Laura Nelson** and her **14** year old son **Lawrence** were lynched together on **May 25th** 1911 in Oklahoma (page 136-137). What made my lynching unique is that it was the first lynching of a Black person to go to trial! My murder sparked the first mass protest for Black liberation in America which birthed the rise of **Martin Luther King** and George Floyd's death sparked the <u>biggest protest in American history</u>. I have a sister who has a baby born on **April 20th** and the babies father is born on **May 25th** (page 558). Derek Chauvin, the White police officer that murdered George Floyd would be found guilty of murder and sentenced to jail on my nieces birthday, **April 20th** 2021.. On my 44th birthday the actor Micah Beals Femia was arrested for the crime of vandalizing the mural dedicated to George Floyd.

Everything was set in place as if it were "<u>ordained from the beginning of time</u>". On the **ring**, the **rays of light** (**Aten**) can be seen shining on both sides of the inscription that reads, "**May 25th 1943**". The Aten rays of light can also be seen on the **Silver cuff** I purchased on **May 25th** 2014 (page 293). My ancient **father** was **Akhenaten,** the Nswt Bity (**Pharaoh**) who popularized the rays of the sun. He was the most enigmatic pharaoh of Kemet from the 18th dynasty who would make radical changes to the spiritual belief systems in Kemet by going away from the Amen Ra priesthood who had perverted the teachings. Akhenaten closed all the other temples for the other deities (Gods) and went back to the ancient ways favoring only one Deity, the Aten (The Sun). Because of these changes he is seen as the father of monotheism (the concept of one God), however he

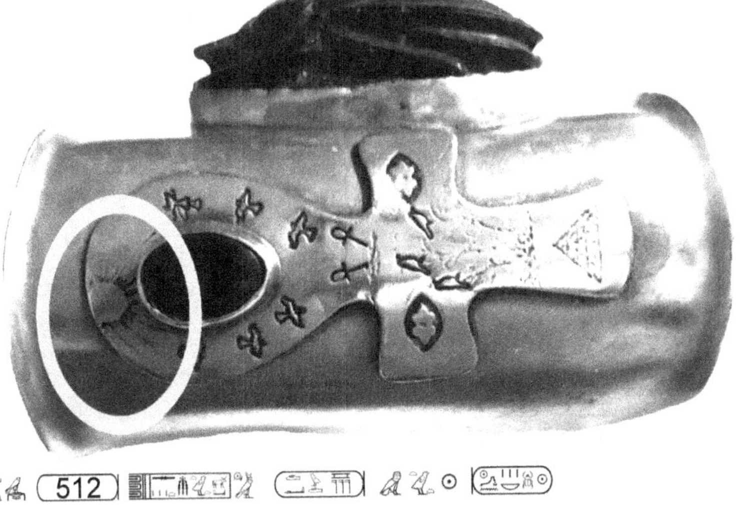

Rau nu Prt m heru

Iu f Per f m heru

Utterances for Coming Forth by day into Light

It is he, who comes forth by day into Light

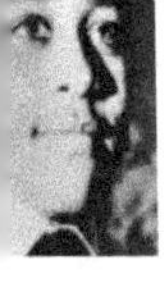

just crystallized teachings about the sun's life giving properties that his forefathers taught him. Akhenaten took his people between Memphis and Thebes (**Luxor**) where he built a new city (Akhetaten) in a lush environment where he venerated the sun (**Aten**). The location is now a **desert**. The character* **Moses*** from the bible has a story similar to Akhenaten's, as **Moses** was chased into the **desert**. Mose is an Egyptian name not the name of a Jew or Hebrew. Akhenaten's city (Akhetaten) is now known as **Tell el-Amarna**, however the locals call it **ET Till** or **EL Till**. These names are part of this prophecy of reincarnation. ET Till like EMM**ET**T **Till** & **EL T**ill like **E**mmett **L**ouis **Till** (p 671). Akhenaten's remains were found in the Valley of the Kings and were stored as KV**55** (p 41) Everything was ordained from the beginning of time and this is why my uncle was named **Moses** in my life as Emmett Till and this is why **Mars** (p 474) has a son named **Moses**. My uncle **Moses** Wright Jr was a preacher and he was assigned with the task of identifying my body. A silver ring was used. A ring that very well should have been discarded by my killers but for some reason they left it on me. They stripped me naked, shot me in the temple, gouged my eyes out, cut my ear off, wrapped barbwire around my neck and attached it to a cotton gin fan, then they threw me in the M**ississi**ppi river like **Set** did his brother **Ausar** (Osiris). But for some reason they left the **silver ring** on my finger. My death was biblical prophecy. For the muslim, you should know that I was **born a muslim** in this life and my middle name was **Basheer** (the bringer of truth). For the Christian, you should know that I got **baptized at 11** (p 49), **gave my life to Christ at 22** (p 92) and my born name was Dawud which means **David** (**beloved of God**). You Jews and Christians are waiting for someone to return through the line of David. Well you should know that my father in this life was given the name David as his middle name and in my life as Tutankhaten I descend from the line of Thutmoses III who is seen as the biblical David by historians. There's no structural or tangible proof that this David from the bible ever lived but Thutmoses the 3rd lived a life that parallels the stories of David from the bible and you can see and touch and read about Thutmoses. Thutmoses the 3rd comes from the 18th dynasty like King Tut so "if" I am Tut then I come from the line of David. There is a poem in the bible written by my father Akhenaten titled Psalms 104 (**Hymn to the Aten, p 615)** from the Psalms of David. My father Akhenaten was the biblical **Moses** and the bible pulls from a time period that covers the 18th dynasty that King Tut comes from so if anyone will return from this **"bible prophecy"** (page 511, "The Sacrificial Lamb") it will be the son of the father of monotheism which is me, Tutankhaten, the son of Akhenaten. The truth is we all return but most of us just don't remember and I don't think life is about knowing every life you have lived. Instead it's about ascending spiritually and living a life worth remembering.

Return of Djed Eye (The Ausarian Resurrection)

Star Wars first premiered in19**77** the year of the **snake** on **May 25th**, **5** months before I (Dawud, David) was born.. See page 37!! Star Wars was created with ancient esoteric information taken from ancient Kemet (Egypt) in particular from the 18th Dynasty and the relationship between Akhenaten and his sun Tutankhaten. George Lucas, the creator of Star wars created a father and son drama between Anakin Sky Walker who would later be known as Darth Vader and his sun Luke Sky Walker. King Tut was the sun of **Akhenaten** the Nswt Bity (pharaoh) that went away from the ways of the **Amen Ra** Priesthood just like **Anakin** (Darth Vader) went away from the **Jedi** and went to the "Darkside" of the force. Much of the concepts used in the Star Wars movies were taken from the science and philosophy of ancient **Kemet** (Egypt). In ancient Kemet the word Tut ( ) is pronounced toot/tute like flute. The bird (quail chick) hieroglyphic in Tut's name makes the uuw sound similar to the uuw sound in the name Luke (Luuwke). If you were to look at the headdress of Darth Vader (Anikan Sky Walker) and the headdress of Amen Hotep IV (Akhenaten) you will see where George Lucas, the creator of Star Wars, got his inspiration. The design of the **light saber** would be taken from the science of the **Djed Pillar** also known as the ***Spine of Ausar (Osiris)*** representing the kundalini serpentine energy that flows up the spine when the Djed Pillar or the "Spine of Ausar "or the "light saber"is activated. Star wars was sent down to earth

in thought forms to George Lucas so that I (Dawud) could watch it when I turned **5** years of age and by doing so would be impregnated with the thought that I was Luke Sky Walker as a child. Luke's aunt's name was **Beru**, like **Heru**, the son of **Ausar**. Star Wars always open with the words "A LONG TIME AGO IN A GALAXY FAR, **FAR AWAY**", I (Dawud) was born in a galaxy Far Far away called Far Rockaway Queens. Star Wars was released on **May 25th** so as to help me connect my previous lives having had many remarkable events in my "lives" happen on **May 25th**. "**Yoda**" is the eldest Jedi that teaches the young Luke Sky Walker the ways of the Jedi and it was Kemetic "**Yoga**" that sp**ark**ed my first past life revelation on July 3rd 2018. I have a sister born on May 14th 1989 the year of the **snake** the same day as **George Lucas,** the creator of Star Wars. George Lucas is also part of **the 44th Parallel star code pattern** (page 660). He was sent down (born) on May 14th 19**44**, and I turned **44** years old in 2021. George Lucas turned **77** years old in 2021 and I was sent down (born) in 19**77** the year of the **snake**. The **Buddha** Siddhartha was aware of the ancient **Vedas** (ancient Hindu scriptures) and commented on it in his writings. It is no coincidence that Darth **Vader** sounds like **Vedas**! One time is an incidence, twice is a coincidence, three, four, five is a pattern, but can you tell the difference?

Rau nu Prt m heru

Iu f Per f m heru

Utterances for Coming Forth by day into Light

It is he, who comes forth by day into Light

The Holy Cargo (The Ausarian Resurrection)

Sheriff Clarence Strider ordered my uncle **Moses** to "get that body in the ground before sundown!" The hole for my body was 75 percent done when my cousin Curtis asked his grandfather, **Moses**, "Are you going to bury Bobo without calling Mamie?" I guess that jolted uncle **Moses**' conscious because he stopped the dig immediately. That's when my cousin Curtis called my mother and told her what was going on. They had found my body and the worst had indeed happened. After hearing the details she wanted to fall apart but instead she rose to the occasion. She knew that she didn't have time to cry. She didn't know what to do but she knew that she had to do something! She quieted all the people in the house who were mourning and crying, and told them that they were going to have to help her. Her Aunt told her to call their local undertaker, **A. A. Rayner** and she did. With Rayner's help and the divine will of God they got my body out of M**ississ**ippi but not without a fight. The powers in M**ississ**ippi wanted me buried but finally the order came in from Sheriff George Smith that there would be no burial, and my body would be shipped to Chicago (**4141** Rayner - pages **41**, 508), but every measure was taken to insure that my body was not seen by the public. <u>My body arrived in **three large boxes**. King Tut's body was also found in **three golden sarcophagi**. **three padlocks** were placed on the **boxes** and the **casket**, and affidavits were signed to insure the **casket** was not opened</u>. When my body arrived in Chicago the undertaker told my mother that they were going to bury the body immediately, as is. But my mother promptly rejected that, explaining that she didn't know what was in that **box**, it could be bricks, it could be dirt or it could be somebody else. She said that she had to know that it was her son in the **box**. The undertaker explained that he had signed affidavits agreeing to not open the **casket** and if he did he was subject to being sued. My mother thought about it then asked him if he had a hammer. He asked her why and she explained that she had not sighed anything so if he couldn't open it then she would. She wanted to see what she was burying. After seeing how determined she was he agreed to open the **casket**.

Birthmarks, Black Dots, Genetic Memory

On September 1st M**ississ**ippi Governor Hugh White orders local officials to "fully prosecute" Milam and Bryant. On September 2nd my mother arrives at the Illinois Central Terminal to receive the box's with me inside. She said that she could smell a stench in the air 5 blocks away and wondered what it could be. To her dismay she realized that the smell was my decomposed body. My body was taken to the A. A. Rayner & Sons Funeral Home. Surrounded by family and photographers who snap her photo collapsing in grief at the sight of my casket. When my mother first looked into the casket she said it felt like **every bone in her body turned to steel** and instead of falling and fainting she straightened up (page 79). She knew she had a job to do in finding out who the person in the casket was. My **left eye** was missing and my right eye was left laying on my cheek. One of my **ears** was missing. I was shot in the side of my **temple** near my ear and there was a hole on the other side of my head where the bullet must have exited. My mother said she could see daylight from one side of my head to the other. When she saw my face she said it looked as if someone had taken a hatchet and chopped at the bridge of my nose. She always loved my teeth and when she looked in my mouth she could only see two teeth as all the rest were knocked out. A barbwire had been wrapped around my **neck** with a cotton gin fan to weigh my body down causing my tongue to protrude from my mouth. Afterwards Mr Rayner asked if she wanted him to retouch the body to make it presentable and she replied: "No, you can't fix that, let the people see what I have seen. And I want open casket viewing from now until we take him to burial. I want the world to see what's going on in M**ississ**ippi, in this great ole United States of America." <u>**In my current life**</u> I have a **black dot** on my left **temple** where "Emmett" was shot in the head. I have **two black dots** on my left femur, "Emmett" and "Tutankhaten" had broken left femurs. I have a black dot behind my left **ear**. I have **two black dots** on my **neck** where the fan was placed around "Emmett's" neck. I also have a few more black dots holding genetic memory from other lives.

September 2nd 1955 (Mamie Till writes a Letter To The President)

THE PRESIDENT
THE WHITE HOUSE

I THE MOTHER OF EMMETT LOUIS TILL AM PLEADING THAT YOU PERSONALLY SEE THAT JUSTICE IS METED OUT TO ALL PERSONS INVOLVED IN THE BEASTLY LYNCHING OF MY SON IN MONEY MISS. AWAITING A DIRECT REPLY FROM YOU
MAMIE E BRADLEY 1626 WEST 14TH PL CHGO & SEELEY

She even reached out to the **FBI** but no help was extended. **J Edgar Hoover**, the head of the FBI said no action on the case could be taken because no federal laws had been violated. Then **J Edgar Hoover** attacked her, calling her a communist.

September 3rd 1955 (The Awakening at Roberts Temple Church of God)

It took a very strong woman to rise to the occasion and receive the body of her dead son, bury him and then speak out about his murder. My mother started her activism with my wake, held on September 3rd 1955 at Roberts Temple Church of God in Christ for viewing and funeral services. She had a public open casket wake so that the world could see what had happened to her only begotten son and thousands of Chicagoans waited in line. My mother said around 60,000 to 100,00 people viewed my body and on average, 1 out of every 5 had to be assisted due to fainting from the sight of my mutilated face. The viewing of my body was a transformative experience for all those who viewed it especially those who viewed it in person and within the time of my murder. As a people we had for some reason felt like things had been changing and getting better but the image of my face was an **awakening**. Those who saw me in person left the Church different people. They understood that there was a fight that they must now be involved with. There was a war against them that they could not run from. If it could happen to a 14 year old then it could happen to them. Many Black parents felt like this could have been their child and the children saw themselves in me. White people who viewed my face were forced to face their brutality. Even though my mother requested that my face not be retouched she said that the face that was seen by the world was not the face that she saw. She said Mr Rayner had done a beautiful job at making it look more presentable than what she saw. She said she's not sure what people would have done if they had actually seen what she saw, nevertheless, the Civil Rights Movement was sparked with my open casket funeral.

A Message to Wheeler Parker Jr. (Shock and Disbelief)

Wheeler, I have watched many of your interviews and they have been helpful in the writing of the events that transpired when we went to M**ississ**ippi in 19**55**. I do not remember my life as your cousin Emmett but I was your cousin Emmett Till in my most recent past life. During my funeral you had no remorse, no sadness or sorrow because you would not allow yourself to believe that I was the person in the casket. You were in a state of shock and kept telling yourself that you would see me again. Well you were right. The same year that I was murdered in 19**55**, my mother, in this life was born on February 3rd 19**55**. **22** years after I was murdered, when my mother was **22**, I was **born again** on October 25th 19**77**, the same year that uncle **Moses** died and the same year that you answered your call to Ministry and became a **preacher**. My grandmother's maiden name, in this life is **Parker**. **Juanita Parker**, born in Roanoke Virginia on October 9th 1930 (page 22). She has the same last name as you because I was **born again** into the same family tree. J.W. Milam's wife was also named **Juanita**. I know that what I am writing might cause **Shock and disbelief** but I'm asking you to listen with your ministerial ears and not the ears of the world. Your name is Wheeler, like a "wheel". In ancient times man understood the immortality of the soul and time was governed by the wheel of little animals circling in the heavens called the Zodiac. And just as the sun rises in the east and sets in the west in our solar system, our souls do the same. They come and they go. In ancient Kemet (Egypt) his concept of resurrection was called the **Wehem-Mesut** (repeating of births, p 14). In **Judaism** reincarnation is known as **Gilgul** (Cycle), but it is not taught to everyone. Jesus said, "all these things I have done, so will you do and greater deeds will you do". Well, I have risen again. As Emmett, I was born on July **25th** 19**41** the year of the **snake** and I was born again on Oct **25th** 19**77** the year of the **snake**. Just as a **snake** sheds its skin so does man. We leave old bodies behind and put on new ones in the eternal **Wheel** of life. On July 3rd 2018 my past life of Emmet was revealed to me and **22** days later on July **25th** 2018 "Emmett" would have been **77.** On October **25**th of 2018 I turned **41**. This is too perfect to be just a "coincidence", it is a **sign**, a **divine pattern**! If I had been born in 1976 I would have been 42 that year and if I was born in 1978 I would have been 40 that year but no, I was born in 19**77** the year of the **snake** and as Emmett I was born in 19**41** the year of the **snake**. In 2018 Emmett would have been **77** and I turned **41**. ∞ It was perfect mathematics (pages **41**, 530). What ever or whoever God is, that being is love and it is indeed a master mathematician, a master builder like the number **22**. Time is measured by the sun and even the Bible states that the sun will be used as **signs**. **Genesis 1:14 "And God said, Let there be lights in the firmament of the heaven to divide the day from the night; and let them be for signs, and for seasons, and for days, and years".**

September 6th 1955
Bur Oak Cemetery

I was buried on September 6th 1955 at **Bur Oak Cemetery**. That same day the Tallahatchie Grand Jury in Sumner M**ississ**ippi indicted Roy Bryant and J.W. Milam for my murder. They both pled innocent and were held in jail until the start of the trial. On September 15th Jet magazine, the nationwide Black magazine owned by Chicago based Johnson Publications, publishes the heart wrenching photographs of my mutilated corpse, shocking and outraging African Americans from coast to coast. On September 17th the black newspaper, The Chicago Defender publishes the same photos. On September 19th the kidnapping and murder trial of J. W. Milam and Roy Bryant opens in Sumner, M**ississ**ippi, the county seat of Tallahatchie County. Jury selection begins and, with Blacks and White women banned from serving, an all-white, 12 man jury made up of nine farmers, two carpenters and one insurance agent is selected. After my burial my mother departed from Chicago's Midway Airport to attend this court proceedings.

Sheriff Strider and No Protection Under The Law

Sheriff Strider playacted to the local press telling them the case would be well investigated. He had already tried to bury the body and fail and when the case gained nationwide attention and scorn he could not help but to reveal his true feelings. In a press conference that stunned many outsiders, Strider summed up what many in the local white community felt. "We never have any trouble until some of our Southern **niggers** go up North and the NAACP talks to 'em and they come back home. If they would keep their nose and mouths out of our business we would be able to do more when enforcing the laws of Tallahatchie County and M**ississ**ippi." When his remarks were heard it was clear that racism was alive and well in the M**ississ**ippi law enforcement.

Medgar Evers and Mamie Till *ADDENDUM*

I didn't find out about Medgar Ever's **connection** to Emmett Till until 2021. Sometime in 2021 the Med Luxx spa that recruited me to do massage for them in midtown requested my service for a massage (pages 583 & 586). I did not want to go downtown to do the massage because I had gotten comfortable with having clients come to me, however I agreed to do the massage because the owner is born on my grand mothers birthday (October 9th). When I met the woman I was going to massage she saw my shirt with Emmett Till's face on it (p 459) and she began to tell me about her connection to Medgar Evers and Medgar's connection to Emmett. She was a lawyer that had worked with Medgar Evers' family in a legal dispute with the Medgar Evers College, in Brooklyn. She also told me that **Medgar Evers was the reason that Mamie Till had an open casket at the funeral**. He encouraged Mamie to show the world Emmett's face and that's how the Civil Rights Movement was born. Medgar was assassinated on **June 12th** 1963, very close to the **33rd parallel** and 5 months later President Kennedy was assassinated on **November 22nd** 1963, on the 33rd parallel. Emmett Till's Mother Mamie Till was born **November 23rd** 1921, in Webb M**ississ**ippi on the 33rd parallel. Emmett Till was murdered in 1955 on the 33rd parallel. Medgar Evers was a soldier in

the U.S. Army during World War II just like Louis Till (Emmett Till's father, p 651). The U.S. Army was still segregated and **openly racist** at the time. Medgar was born in Decatur, M**ississ**ippi, on **July 2nd** 1925, the same day that **Louis Till** was **Hung** by the U.S. Army (**July 2nd** 1945), falsely accused of raping and killing a **White woman**. Medgar participated in the Normandy invasion in June 1944, and his unit was part of the massive, post D-Day invasion of Europe, he served in both France and Germany until his honorable discharge in 1946. Medgar was assassinated on **June 12th** 1963 (**year of the rabbit**) and on **June 12th** 2023 (**year of the rabbit**) my military compensation is incleased to 100% (page 121).

Rau nu Prt m heru

Returning to M**ississ**ippi after the war, Evers attended Alcorn College (now Alcorn State University) on the G.I. Bill, earning honors as one of the most successful students in the nation. In 1954, the same year the landmark Supreme Court, **Brown v. Board of Education** decision struck down racial segregation in public schools, Medgar became the first Black person to apply to the University of M**ississ**ippi **Law School**, but was **denied admittance** because of his race. When Medgars' application was denied on a technicality (the school claimed that he had failed to include the required letters of recommendations), Medgar approached the National Association for the Advancement of Colored People (**NAACP**) for help. NAACP M**ississ**ippi State Conference leader E.J. Stringer was so taken with Medgars' poise and determination that he instead offered him a position as the organization's first field secretary in the state.Medgar accepted, and by December 1954 he had opened an office in Jackson and one of his first assignments was **investigating the murder of Emmett Till**. Fearful that the highly segregated sheriff's office wouldn't mount much of an effort to catch Till's White murderers, the M**ississ**ippi NAACP, launched their own investigation. Medgar Evers and two other field workers, Ruby Hurley and Amzie Moore, tracked down potential witnesses to the events leading up to and including Till's abduction. They disguised themselves as cotton pickers and went into the cotton fields in search of any information that might help find Till. They convinced several people to come forward, keeping them in protective custody when they testified at the 1955 trial of two men accused of killing Till, and then shepherding them out of town in secrecy when the all White jury returned a verdict of "**not guilty**" after deliberating for just an hour.

Iu f Per f m heru

September 19th 1955
The Murder Trial

The trial began on Monday, September 19th 1955, in Sumner M**ississ**ippi. On the first day of trial the prosecution arrived at the court there was no place for Black people to sit and because of that court was recessed until the next day so that the court could make arrangements for the seating of the Black prosecution. A Table was built from pine tree that was full of sharp pieces of wood and if you placed your arms on that table you were sure to be stuck by sharp splinters. Every measure was taken to make things uncomfortable for the prosecution but that didn't stop them, they brought newspapers the next day to line the table. It was over 118 degrees outside and even hotter in the court room. There was no bathroom that the Blacks were able to use in the courthouse. The defendants however, they were allowed to use the judges chamber and they did as they pleased. Every comfort was extended to them. The Blacks however, had to walk 3 blocks to use the rest room at a Black owned restaurant. The scene outside was festive and at the same time the hate was so thick that you could feel it.. White vendors were renting lawn chairs, serving hotdogs, beer, soda, and other things. When Blacks attempted to purchase anything the white people practically spit in their faces.. They wouldn't even sell them a drink. Everyday that my mother approached the courtroom there were White men sitting in the windows with theirs sons on their knees. The little White boys with their cap guns in their hands would point them at my mother as she entered the court house shouting: "**bang bang, you're dead**". As they squeezed the triggers of their toy guns small popping sounds were emitted causing their fathers to laugh joyously saying to each other "Isn't that so cute". Everyday that my mother left the courtroom she was threatened by the local towns people, even the camera men were at times threatened. After observing the scene the prosecution devised an escape plan in case the White people in the courtroom got rowdy. They placed a reporter by the window who was prepared to jump out to the ground while another reporter would help the four or five woman out, and everyone else was on their own.

Utterances for Coming Forth by day into Light

Sheriff Strider tried to dominate the courtroom refusing to admit Black journalists to see the proceedings against the accused, Roy and Milam. When Judge Curtis Swango overruled him, Strider segregated them from the White journalists and placed them at a table off to the side of the courtroom. Then, when the Black Congressman Charles Diggs arrived from Detroit, Strider refused to let him in. A Black journalist tried to explain Diggs' status to Strider, but the sheriff and his deputies refused to believe a Black man was a congressman. "**This nigger said there's a nigger outside who says he's a congressman.**" To which another deputy replied: "**A nigger congressman?**" The white M**ississ**ippians lived in a world of their own and it seemed like Roy and Milam were enjoying the best days of their lives. They were the center of attention and people treated them like heroes. It seemed as if the whole of the White community had rallied behind them. In local stores $10,000 was raised in support of Roy and Milam's legal fees. The city of Sumner had 5 White lawyers and all of them volunteered to work on the case supporting Roy and Milam. Even lawyers from other areas came to support them. The court selected 12 White male jurors because at the time Blacks and women were not allowed to serve as jurors in M**ississ**ippi. Both men had their two sons in the courtroom with them. Their kids played and laughed while their wives came by ever so often to wipe the sweat from their brows and to fan them. Carolyn Bryant was allowed to testify but her testimony was so outlandish that the judge had the jury leave the courtroom. He would not even let the jury listen because even he knew it was a lie.. She kept adding more to her story embellishing over it. No one believed a black boy would do any of what she described especially in a state where the Ku Klux Klan's Knight riders rode the nights terrorizing blacks. No Black man or boy would do what she claim I had done. Despite the jury being moved out during her testimony the details were still passed along to them by those who heard it. Carolyn changed her story on several occasions, suggesting that I grabbed her by the waist while I was in the store, and that I said, "Bye, baby," along with other lewd comments as I left and finally giving her a wolf whistle as I exited the store, but as my mother explains, there is no way that I could have said all those things under the excitement with out **stuttering**. That testimony was deleted from the records of the trial but still it remained in the minds of the jurors and they could decide to believe it or not but most, if not all of them did.

It is he, who comes forth by day into Light

The Sheriff's Testimony

With the trial underway, Strider made the unusual move of testifying for the defense. He shed doubt on the identification of Emmett's body, saying the corpse had been submerged too long to tell whether it was that of a white or a Black person. Strider also claimed that the body pulled from the Tallahatchie was that of an adult rather than a 14-year-old boy. His testimony bolstered the main defense argument that the body they found was not mine and I was not dead, that I was still alive and well, living in Detroit with his grandfather. When Strider was asked how long he thought the body had been in the river he said, "at least 10 to 15 days." He was on the side of the defense using his position to lie for the defense.

The Bravery of Moses Wright Jr and the 44th Parallel

Uncle **Moses** had been in hiding since my body was shipped to Chicago. Aunt Elizabeth wrote him from Chicago begging him not to testify but he felt guilty and responsible for my death and he promised my mother that he would. He knew that it might cost him his life and when asked about the possible consequences of testifying he stated, "A man has to do what a man has to do". Most local Whites didn't think he'd show up but he did. On **Sep 21, 1955** he was asked to identify the men who came to his home on the morning of August **28**th and took "Emmett Till" away with them. **Uncle Moses stood up and boldly pointed at both men and answered, "There they are."** From the witness stand uncle **Moses** identified the men who had kidnapped me. He later said he could feel the "blood boiling" in the hundreds of white spectators. This was the first time in the history of M**ississ**ippi that a Black man had accused White men of a crime that could possibly merit the death penalty. **44** years after **Moses** did this act of bravery I Joined the Army on **Sep 21, 1999** (p 82). This **44** year **"coincidence"** strengthens the **44th parallel theory**. See page 660 for the birth of the **44th parallel.** Unlce Moses would pass away in 1977, the same year I was born again as Dawud Eddings.

The Surprise Witness

Willie Reed was probably the last person to see me alive that was not in some way involved with my murder. **Medgar Evers** tracked Willie down and convinced him to come forward and testify in the trial. Willie was kept in protective custody and was then shepherded out of town in secrecy after the verdict. The defense was not prepared for Willie's surprise testimony. **Willie Reed** testified about hearing "a whole lot of … licks" and screams. "I believe you stated you heard something that sounded like licks there in the barn?" defense lawyer J.J. Breland asked. "Yes, sir," Willie replied. "But you didn't see anybody in the barn at all, did you?" "No, sir." "And you don't know whether that was somebody hammering there, trying to fix a wagon or a car, or something like that, do you?" **"It was somebody whipping somebody."** Willie also said that he could hear me yelling out for my mother. The same way **George Floyd** screamed for his mother on **May 25th** 2020 (page 610).

The Cotton Gin Fan

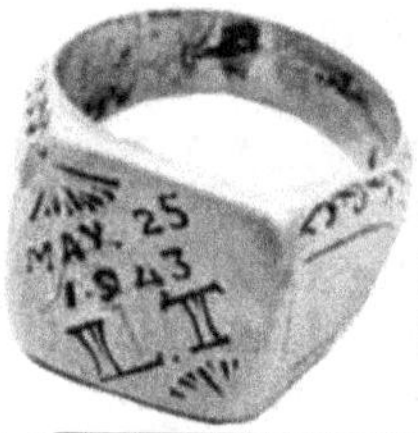

The prosecutors show the wheel used to weigh my body down but the defense argues that the body that was pulled from the river was not mine. Simeon did not have to testify because my mother was called to the stand instead and she confirmed my identity with my ring. She is question as to why she had an insurance plan on me as if to suggest she had something to do with my murder.

September 23rd
The Verdict

My murder trial had drawn fire from the outside world, not just upon Milam and Roy and their crime, but upon the state of M**ississ**ippi and their region and nothing less than the entire racist southern way of life. So my trial became more about **defending their racist way of life** than it was about defending my killers. The final words to the all white jury came from the defense attorney John Whitten who exclaimed, "I'm sure that every last Anglo-Saxon one of you men in this jury has the courage to set these men free." After four days of testimony and only 67 minutes of deliberation, an all white, all male jury acquitted Roy and Milam of all charges. One juror tells a reporter that they wouldn't have taken so long if they hadn't stopped to drink pop. Roy Bryant and J. W. Milam stood before photographers, lit up cigars and kissed their wives celebrating their perceived victory. After the verdict was announced, Sheriff Strider publicly congratulated the defendants. See page **648** for the **metaphysical significance of the number 23**.

September 23rd 1955
Temperatures Rising

After showing the world the pictures of my brutalized body and daring to take my killers to trial my mother barely escaped M**ississ**ippi with her life! When the jury retire to arrive at their verdict my mother noticed that all the Black people in the court room, who had been standing around the walls began to slowly and quietly exit the court room. When she saw that she knew that they knew something and if they were leaving it was time for her to leave too. She felt like she could hear the verdict at a safer distance. That's when she turned to congressmen Digs and his entourage, to Medgar Evers's group as well as T.R.M Howard's group and told them all that she was ready to go. Congressmen Digs replied "what? And miss the verdict?". To which she replied, "If that's what you want to call it. I can tell you what that will be but that's one verdict you want to miss. The verdict is not guilty". Congress Digs replied: "Aw miss Bradley, with all of this evidence they could not possibly bring back a verdict of not guilty." but because she wanted to go they decided to leave. Around 45 minutes after they left town the not guilty verdict came in. Mamie said that the White people in Sumner went berserk as if one of the Chicago sports teams had won a major game. The whites in Sumner M**ississ**ippi started beating random Blacks in hateful acts of violence and even killing some.

Rau nu Prt m heru

Iu f Per f m heru

Utterances for Coming Forth by day into Light

It is he, who comes forth by day into Light

Escape from Mississippi

Medgar Evers had Willie Reed smuggled out of M**ississ**ippi to Chicago and once there, Reed collapsed and suffers a nervous breakdown. Uncle **Moses** fled to join aunt Elizabeth in Chicago, leaving behind his 19**41** Ford and his cotton blooming in the fields. In attempts to escape Mississippi my mother went to see the Bishop of the state of Mississippi to plea for help but he refused. He looked her in the face and told her, "You have no business down here in the first place." He turned her away and offered no help. Instead he scolded her for coming down there and making trouble for Mississippi. Just when all hope seemed to be lost safety was sent her way. Like an angel, a cab appeared from seemingly nowhere, like a scarab dung beetle. After learning who they were, the black cab driver turned his car lights off so as to avoid those who might be after them and raced through the dead of the night as fast as he could on the sketchy M**ississ**ippi back roads, with ditches on each side. Mamie says, "the car trembled like a leaf on a tree the whole ride" and finally he dropped them off at the edge of the Memphis airport and told her, "this is where we have to part company". They had a long walk to the airport but she was grateful that he risked his life for them, they boarded the plane and they made it back to Chicago safely. I'm not sure how my uncle **Moses** Wright made it to Chicago but he made it.. I met **Minister Clemson Brown** in 2021 through Professor Oyibo. Minister Brown would show me a video he captured of Mamie in 1995 and from this video is where I got the details of her escape. Minister Brown is 82yrs old. He is born on August 25th the day after I entered Bryant's grocery store. I don't know who she boarded the plane with but she was used the word "we" so she wasn't alone. In this video she also mention remarks she had once heard Roy Bryant make about me, he said. "Emmett Till has ruined my life. That nigger is dead and I don't know why we can't let him stay dead and if I had anything to do with it I didn't say it then and I won't say it now". He must have forgotten that he confessed to the crime four months after he did it. His brother J.W. Milam took all the money he never got a cent of it and I didn't "STAY DEAD".

Minister Clemson Brown, The Star that fell from the Sky and The Rise of Cepheus, The Ethiopian King

ADDENDUM

I did two interviews with Minister Clemson Brown before I released this book. The first was on August 20th 2021 and the second was August 25th 2021. At the beginning of the second video Minister Brown opened with a profound experience he had with a **star**, or **light**, or **UFO** in the night sky (video can be found on youtube @, TutemRa Kheperu). Minister Brown explains how, in his younger years, when he was in college, he would go to the p**ark** by the river and paint on press board. He would watch the stars and even watch the sun rise. One day, while in the park, by the river, at around 3am, he looked up into the sky and saw countless beautiful stars. **Then one of the stars began to come down**. He says it was coming down fast and everything around him began to light up as if it was day time. He began to run out of the park trying to get away from the light. As he ran he realized he could not get away from the light, it was moving too fast - so finally he stopped. He turned towards the light and looked up into it and immediately the light slowed down and stopped above him. As he stood there, everything around him was lit up as if it was day time. Then **a telepathic voice came into his head** and told him, "**If you are going to win this war, you must become gods**". This lasted for around 30 seconds. Finally the light began to move away from him, then he saw that it looked like a **saucer** as it turned on an angle and darted off into the night sky and disappeared. Minister Brown would also talk about the constellation **Cepheus** (The Ethiopian King) and how it symbolizes the rise of the black man. Currently, Earth's pole star is **Polaris**, a star in the northern circumpolar constellation of Ursa Minor (little dipper). The precession of the equinoxes is shifting and the northern-most tip of **Cepheus** is a mere 1.5° away from the pole. Cepheus lies in the far northern sky and by 7500 AD, Cepheus's brightest star Alder**amen** will become the pole star. In Greek mythology **Cassiopeia** was the wife of **Cepheus**. This explains why I met **Cassiopeia** in 2009 (p 164) and then 5 years later she returned to my orbit (p 304). Minister Brown was ordained as a minister by Rev. Herbert Daughtry, out of The House of the Lords Church. He has no reason to lie about his experience. From the late 70's till the early 2000's Brown was involved with just about every black movement that mobilized in NYC. He was the official documentarian for the Black National United Front. Brown documented over 20,000 hours of black history, traveling to Egypt with Dr Ben Jochannan, Dr Ivan Van Sertima, Dr Asa Hillard, Dr Gabriel Oyibo, etc.

November 1955 (Kidnapping Charges and the Slander of Louis Till)

Thousands of letters protesting the verdict poured into the White House and the government realizes they have a problem on their hands. With the support of the people and the global press watching, the grand Jury was forced to try Milam and Bryant on kidnapping charges. Still it seemed as if the whole of the White community had rallied behind Roy and Milam even the M**ississ**ippi Senator James O. Eastland. In an effort to reduce sympathy for my mother, Senator Eastland revealed to the press that my father, **Louis Till** had been **executed for rape** while serving in the Army. This was the first time that my mother had been given a reason for his execution and armed with this info the defense spun the case into a story of father and son sexual deviants. If the father was a rapist then surely the son was too. The media took that narrative and spread the lie near and far. These are the same tactics that the media still uses today in cases involving the murder of Black people in America at the hands of racist White police officers. Uncle **Moses** and Willie Reed returned to testify at the grand jury hearing but with this rape allegation circulating the grand jury refused to return an indictment. They both left for Chicago and neither of them ever returned to M**ississ**ippi again. **In 2006, 61 years after my fathers death the truth was revealed**. **He had never raped anyone**. My father, a private at the time, stationed in Italy during WW2, was given a pass for R&R and he went out for a night on the town with a friend, private Fred McMurry. That night a white woman was murdered. The police grabbed my father and his friend. They were never identified by anyone they were just accused and jailed. During the court Martial the white female victim was asked to identify the person who raped her but she looked at my father and Fred and **did not single them out**. There was **no proof** that either of them had anything to do with the rape or the murder of the other woman but still on February 17th 1945 (the same day **Khalid Muhammad** was murdered and the same day **Huey P Newton** was born) they were **sentenced to death by hanging**. On July 2nd 1945, Louis Till and his friend Fred McMurry were executed by the U.S. Army **for crimes they did not commit**. Louis Till, **February 7**, 19**22** - July 2, 1945….

December 1st 1955 (Emmett Sparks Rosa Parks and Martin Luther King)

The death of Emmett Till sparked **Rosa parks** when she refused to give her seat to a white man on a bus in Montgomery Alabama. Rosa later said, "I thought of Emmett Till, and I couldn't go back." If it weren't for the brave actions of women like Mamie Till and Rosa Parks there would not have been a Civil Rights Movement. On the day I graduated as a **Kemetic Yoga instructor** I would meet a woman named **Mars** at the International African Arts Festival who just so happened to be born on **February 4th**, Rosa Parks' **birthday** (page 474). **Mars** invited me back to the festival and in doing so she helped set the stage for my first past life revelation. My past life revelation of Emmett Till would be directly associated with the science of **yoga** and the **breath** and it is no surprise that **Rosa Parks practiced yoga**. She practiced **Yoga** and also had an interest in Buddhism. In her senior years she took **yoga** classes and added Buddhist meditation to her prayers. She also became a **vegetarian** and consulted a naturopathic doctor to improve her health. She is seen in March of 1973 at the age of 60 doing **Yoga** (page 474). My **mother,** in this life was born on February 3rd the day before Rosa Parks and Mars (feb 3rd feb 4th) and Rosa Parks passed away on October 24th the day before my birthday (oct 24th oct 25th), the same day that KRS One releases his book, The Gospel of Hip Hop (page 633). These patterns are star codes, not just some arbitrary coincidence. Mars also has a son named **Moses** like Emmett's Uncle. But what are the variables that caused Rosa to make her protest?!

Four days before Rosa Parks made her bus Protest, she attended a packed mass meeting at Dexter Avenue Baptist Church to hear **Dr. T.M. Howard** speak. A key organizer around the Emmett Till case, Howard had helped locate witnesses, and Emmett's mother **Mamie Till** had stayed at his house during the trial. Howard had come before a packed mass meeting in Montgomery because the two men who had killed Emmett, Roy Bryant and J.W. Milam, had been acquitted by an all White jury, and Howard was touring to raise attention. Rosa was filled with anger and despair as she listened to Howard describe the lynching of Emmett Till and the killings of M**ississ**ippians George Lee and Lamar Smith for trying to register to vote.

Dexter Avenue's young pastor, a 26 year old **Martin Luther King**, hosted the meeting, introducing Howard and giving the benediction. Rosa Parks was sickened, angry, depressed and horrified. She had been fighting for years to get justice for Black people such as Recy Taylor and Gertrude Perkins who'd been raped, as well as **Viola White** and **Claudette Colvin** who had been arrested for resisting on the bus. She'd sought protection for Black people and particularly Black men from false charges – like the **Scottsboro boys** and 16 year old **Jeremiah Reeves**. A young Black minister that Raymond knew had been killed for appearing to make an advance at a White woman, as had their neighbor Hilliard Brooks for cases just got swept under the rug but the murder of Emmett, had brought enough attention, an incredible amount of attention and **so there had actually been a trial**. And yet still, Emmett's killers were acquitted! These men who had killed a 14-year-old went free! Four days later, when bus driver James Blake told her to move from her seat, Parks thought of Emmett Till and, "pushed as far as she could be pushed," she refused. Many years later, she told Emmett Till's mother that she had thought of him at this moment. In key ways, then, the Montgomery bus boycott was not just a reaction to bus segregation but also to this pattern of injustice in the criminal justice system – and Rosa Parks' determination to take a stand against it. Parks understood that it was not just about this lynching or this acquittal but about a structure that allowed and protected discrimination, segregation, the differential treatment of Black people under the law. The problem was much bigger than Bryant and Milam and so the need was to start somewhere in attacking that structure. As Reverend Johns (the pastor who served at Dexter Avenue Church before Martin Luther King) observed, "Rosa Parks was one of those rare people who could catch a vision." Parks knew well what could happen to a woman in police custody and the physical and sexual violence that could result – as well as the potential economic consequences of being arrested. And there was little to suggest that anything good would result. She had made stands before, others had made stands, and nothing had happened. Still she summoned the courage – the courage of perseverance – and stood fast. Blake chose to have her arrested, rather than simply evicting her from the bus as he had done previously. While Rosa Parks is often cast as quiet, she believed in the power of speaking back. When the arresting officers asked why she didn't get up, she questioned back, "Why do you all push us around?" One responded, "I don't know but the law is the law and you're under arrest." Parks thought to herself, "Let us look at **Jim Crow** for the criminal he is and what he had done to one life multiplied millions of times over these United States."

The Civil Rights Movement is Born

My mother took her fight to the people and gave speeches to overflowing crowds across the country. Blacks were galvanized. Membership in the NAACP soared. African Americans were angered by Emmett's killing and the injustice, and moved by my mother's loss of her only son. My mother received more than $4,000 and thousands of letters and calls from all over the U.S. With the support of the people my mother, Mamie Till Bradley revealed that she would devote her time and money to fighting racial prejudice. Those in the trenches of Black liberation realized they had to move their fight boldly to the front lines. Soon after Rosa Parks refusal to give up her seat, a 26 year old minister, **Martin Luther King Jr.**, called for a city wide bus boycott. Martin Luther King would declare my lynching one of the most brutal and inhuman crimes of the 20th century. The Civil Rights movement was officially born. **13 years later Martin would be assassinated, shot then suffocated by a white neurosurgeon (see p 69).**

Clinton and Beulah Melton and The Beginning of The December 3rd Theory

3 months after Emmett is killed, 2 months after his killers are acquitted and two days after Rosa Parks refused to move her seat **Clinton Melton** is murdered in broad daylight. Clinton and his wife Beulah lived in Glendora, M**ississ**ippi, just 20 miles from where Emmett was murdered in Money, M**ississ**ippi. Clinton pumped gas and fixed flats at the local gas station, while Beulah stayed home with their four children. Glendora was a small, former plantation town and the Black people living there lived in constant fear. There was no protection where the law was concerned. Any white person could start trouble and no one would interfere. The murder of Emmett Till was fresh and it deeply effected the people of Glendora. The acquittal of Emmett's murderers validated a long standing belief in America that violence against Black Americans would never be punished and that Whites could and would commit these crimes, without consequence. That was proved again just three months later, when on **December 3rd** Clinton Melton was shot and killed at the gas station where he worked.

That afternoon, a car pulled up to the fuel pump at a Glendora Service Station. The driver was Elmer Otis Kimball, **a close friend of J.W. Milam**, who had accompanied him when abducting Emmett Till, according to a recent FBI investigation. At the station, Kimball accused Melton of pumping more gas than he'd asked for. According to witnesses, Kimball was in a rage. He threatened Melton and shouted, "Don't be here when I get back" before driving off. The white station owner told Melton to go home, but before he could, Kimball returned with a shotgun. **He shot Melton once in the hand and once in the head. Clinton died, leaving behind a widow Beulah Melton, and four children**. His wife Beulah gave an interview a few weeks later, to a television camera crew, mourning the loss of her husband. It was right before Christmas and she didn't know how she was going to support four young kids. She also met with Medgar Evers of the NAACP, who hoped to use the case to fuel the fight for Civil Rights across the country, as they had done with the story of Emmett Till. But Beulah was concerned for her family's safety and asked the NAACP to keep its distance. Elmer Otis Kimball was later identified by witnesses as the man who killed Melton and the trial was set for March 1956. **But just days before the court date, Beulah Melton was driving home when her car was run off the road and crashed into the Black Bayou River**. The bayou empties into the Tallahatchie River, where Emmett's body was found. Two of the children were in the back seat. They survived but Beulah died. The Clinton Melton trial moved forward. It was held at the same courthouse as the Emmett Till case, the same sheriff was in charge, and Kimball had the same defense attorneys as his friends Milam and Bryant. Two witnesses identified Kimball as the killer. He claimed self defense, saying that Melton had fired first, but neither witness – **including the white owner of the station** – said they saw or heard Melton fire. No weapon was found on Melton's body or in the car. After deliberating for four hours, an all-white jury found Kimball not guilty. With both parents gone, Beulah's sister, Mary Madison, adopted the four kids. She already had three of her own, but she didn't want them to be separated. Their aunt raised them well, but the children struggled to cope with the enormity of the loss. Today, the stories of Clinton and Beulah Melton have been largely forgotten. But Clinton Melton's name is one of many engraved on The Monument at the National Memorial for Peace and Justice in Montgomery, Alabama honoring victims of lynching in the United States. It's a st**ark** reminder that for every "Emmett Till" whose name is remembered in history books, there are countless others whom most Americans have never even heard of. Perhaps it was **Clinton Melton** who started this **December 3rd pattern** so that his story could be told (pages 313, 314, 345, 431 and finally 457). ***The strange thing about Clinton is that he looks a little like me.***

January 1956
(Look Magazine, The Shocking story of APPROVED KILLING IN MISSISSIPPI)

Rau nu Prt m heru

In January of 1956, less than one year later, in an interview with William Bradford Huie, Bryant and Milam would confess to murdering me in the **Look magazine** article titled, "The shocking story of approved killing in M**ississ**ippi." The men got $4,000 for selling their story ($35,000 in todays economy, 2022). In the article, the pair gleefully admitted to murdering me and expressed no remorse for their heinous deed. They said that when they kidnapped me, they only intended to beat me up and throw me off an embankment into the river to frighten me but decided to kill me when I refused to grovel. They told Huie that while they were beating me, I called them bastards, declaring that I was as good as they, and they said that I claimed to have had sexual encounters with White women. So they put me in the back of their truck, drove to a cotton gin and stole a 70 pound fan, which was the only time they admitted to being worried, thinking that by this time in early daylight they would be spotted and accused of stealing. Then they drove for several miles along the river looking for a place to dispose of my body. They shot me by the river and weighted my body with the fan. Milam explained his decision to Look saying: "Well, what else could we do? He was hopeless. I'm no bully; I never hurt a nigger in my life. I like niggers – in their place – I know how to work 'em. But I just decided it was time a few people got put on notice. As long as I live and can do anything about it, niggers are gonna stay in their place… I stood there in that shed and listened to the nigger throw that poison at me, and I just made up my mind. 'Chicago boy,' I said. "I'm tired of 'em sending your kind down here to stir up trouble. Goddam you, I'm going to make an example of you – just so everybody can know how me and my folks stand." Because the men had already been tried and acquitted of my murder, their callous confession garnered no lawful punishment. On another occasion Milam was asked why he killed "Emmett Till" and he responded: **"What else could I do? He thought he was as good as any white man."**

Iu f Per f m heru

June 12th 1963 - Medgar Evers

By the summer of 1963, Medgar had spent nearly nine years organizing voter registration drives and leading boycotts of segregated M**ississ**ippi businesses. His efforts had been met with more than hostility: Weeks before his death a Molotov cocktail had been thrown through a window in his home, and he'd been injured when a car tried to run him down outside his NAACP office. But Jackson, M**ississ**ippi, wasn't the only American city caught up in the Civil Rights struggle. The violent response to protests in Birmingham, Alabama, which included the turning of fire hoses on thousands of schoolchildren and the infamous picture of a 17 year old Black Civil Rights demonstrator being attacked by a police dog is taken on May 3rd 1963 (picture seen on page 458). On June 11th 1963 President Kennedy took to the airwaves, delivering an address from the Oval Office calling for Congressional action in the area of Civil Rights, defining the cause–for the first time–as a **moral, and not purely legal, issue**. Millions of Americans were glued to their sets, including Medgar Evers wife **Myrlie** and two of his three children. Evers was at an organizational meeting at a local church and returned home shortly after midnight, less than four hours after Kennedy's address however Evers' involvement in the integration of **Ole Miss** gained nationwide attention, and garnered him the **enmity** of local **white racist**. As he walked to his door on June 12th 1963 **he was shot once in the back, dying less than an hour later**. As the kids crawled on the floor to a bedroom, Myrlie went to the front door. Medgar was lying there in a pool of blood, dying from a gunshot wound. A suspect immediately emerged. A sniper rifle left on the scene of the crime was traced to Byron De La Beckwith, a rabid segregationist who belonged to the White Citizens Council and was known to hate Black people. The FBI also traced the sight that the killer had used to Beckwith. Byron De La Beckwith was arrested about a week after the murder, but his prosecution was flawed from the start. During jury selection, the district attorney asked every potential juror if he believed it was a crime to "**kill a nigger**" in M**ississ**ippi. Only seven Black men were included in the jury pool, and none were called to serve. The all white Jury came back with a deadlock that gave Beckwith an automatic mistrial. A second trial, during which the **Ku Klux Klan** packed the gallery and burned crosses around Jackson, resulted in the same verdict. A third trial was planned, but never carried out, and the trials were eventually dismissed. The state of M**ississ**ippi seemed uninterested in pursuing justice. But Myrlie Evers later told a New York Times reporter that in the days following her husband's murder, she promised herself, "I'm going to make whoever did this pay." De La Beckwith, reportedly bragged about his role in the murder and even unsuccessfully ran for lieutenant governor of M**ississ**ippi. In 1989, the year of the **snake** the case was reopened based on new evidence gathered by Myrlie Evers-Williams and others. A Jackson newspaper reporter, who told her he had found evidence that the M**ississ**ippi Sovereignty Commission, a state agency that had secretly been given authority to investigate and intimidate Civil Rights Movement leaders, had surveilled Medgar and conducted secret background checks on jurors. When the news broke, she asked the state prosecutor to reopen the case. Despite a missing murder weapon, legal uncertainty about whether Beckwith could be tried again so many years after the crime, and a case file just three pages long, he did. Then more evidence emerged. New witnesses can become difficult to locate the older a case becomes. But in the case of Medgar's murder, the passage of time allowed some with once unknown details about his murder to feel safer coming forward than they had in the 1960s. Then, In 1994, Beckwith finally stood for his third trial. Still defiant, he came to court every day **wearing a Confederate flag pin**. This time, the jury was more racially diverse and this time they agreed on a different verdict. When the guilty verdict was read, Myrlie Evers-Williams wept. Afterwards, reported the Los Angeles Times, she jumped for joy, then looked up to the sky, saying "Medgar, I've gone the last mile of the way." On February 5th 1994, De La Beckwith was finally convicted, and sentenced to life in prison. He died in 2001 they year of the **snake** at the age of 90. ***ADDENDUM*** Medgar Evers was assassinated on **June 12th** 1963 (**year of the rabbit**) and 60 years later on **June 12th** 2023 (**year of the rabbit**) my military compensation isincleased to 100% (page 121).

Utterances for Coming Forth by day into Light

It is he, who comes forth by day into Light

Condolences

I am eternally grateful to Medgar Evers for the sacrifice he gave in his fight for the freedom of Black people. My condolences go out to his family, and friends as well as all those who lost their lives at the hands of racism and white supremacy during the birth of the Civil Rights Movement. Please know that death is not the end. The soul survives death, indeed and in spirit. This is a book of the dead written by a boy who was murdered without justice, who defeated death and came forth by day. May the soul of **Medgar Evers** walk peacefully through the field of Reeds in Amenta. Amen Ra.

You Can't Legislate The Heart

The property that was once the **Bryants grocery and Meat Market**, where Emmett Till gave a notorious whistle is now a dilapidated shell of itself. Laws have been set in place in attempts to cure the virus known as racism but laws won't change the heart. In 2019 photos surfaced on Instagram of three **Ole Miss** Students posing with guns in front of a bullet **riddled** Emmett Till Memorial (search for picture online) . **Ben LeClere** is seen holding a shotgun while standing in front of the bullet riddled sign. His **Kappa Alpha fraternity** brother, **John Lowe**, squats below the sign. A third fraternity member stands on the other side with an AR-15 semi-automatic rifle. The photo appears to have been taken at night, the scene illuminated by lights from a vehicle. LeClere posted the picture on Lowe's birthday on March 1 with the message "**one of Memphis's finest and the worst influence I've ever met**." the pictured received 247 likes within a day of being posted. Five days after the picture was posted on Instagram, someone saw it and filed a report to the university's Office of Student Conduct. The complaint pointed out there may have been a fourth person present, who took the picture and the photo was on Instagram with hundreds of likes,' and no one said a thing. "I cannot tell Ole Miss what to do, I just thought it should be brought to your attention." said the complaint. The picture was reviewed by the M**ississ**ippi Center for Investigative Reporting and ProPublica and soon after the photo was removed from LeClere's Instagram account. The three students were suspended from their fraternity house, Kappa Alpha. Since the first sign was erected in 2008, it has been the object of repeated white racial hatred. If you're looking for a sign this is it. **The first sign** was thrown in the river. **The second sign** was riddled with 317 bullets or shotgun pellets before the Emmett Till Memorial Commission officials removed it. **The third sign,** featured in the Instagram photo, was damaged by 10 bullet holes before officials took it down. **A fourth sign**, designed to better withstand bullets, is expected to be installed soon. You can legislate the laws but you can not legislate the heart. How many signs do we need to finally get the message? **Let this book be the sign!** Sight beyond sight, **Life after life**, Beyond the beyond, the quiet before the storm, **we vibrate into many forms**, let the dead bury the dead my friend, ***some of us come back in new babies born again,*** I'm trying to go to another plane not here again! This life is about raising the consciousness of men, not the nonsense they program condition'n, the wind be whisper'n, but are you tuning in and listen'n?! I never knew I'd be a fisher man, you think it's a miracle to walk on water? Think again! The miracle is to walk in peace on the earth full of sin!

Highway to Heaven

I watched a lot of TV when I was a child and **Highway to Heaven** was one of the shows I watched. It was a fantasy show starring the actor Michael Landon. The show premiered on **September 19th** 1984 the same day that Emmett Till's court case started in 19**55**. Michael Landon started his acting career in 19**55** the same year Emmett was Murdered. The last episode aired in August of 1989, the year of the snake, the same **zodiacal year Emmett** was born (1941) and the same **zodiacal month Emmett** was murdered. In Highway to Heaven Michael Landon played a probationary **angel** (who named himself Jonathan Smith) whose job was to help people on earth who were in need with hopes that he will do enough good on earth to earn his wings so that he can go to heaven. He had a helper named M**ark** (Ark, Barque, Noah's Ark, Ark of a Million Years - p 252). As I come to a close of this book I have less desire to come back to earth. I would like to take my Celestial Bark and glide off into a higher realm but if I had to come back and be of service I imagine I would. However my hope is that this body of work will spark a star seed more highly advanced than me. Michael served as executive producer, writer, and director of Highway to Heaven and it was the only show throughout his long career in television that he owned outright.

July 4th 2018 - International African Arts Festival

On July 4th 2018 I did chair massages on more people than I can count. I was happy. I felt like I had a new lease on life. Like I had been **reborn**. I had risen from the dead. Poor little Emmett Till was alive after all. For 40 years I had been back here and didn't even know it. I knew I was Emmett now and I told everyone who would listen. I told **Brother Hankh**, the brother who connected me with the psilocybin and when I told him he cried. On Dec 21st 2021 I would see Brother H**ankh** for the first time since this festival and he would tell me his birthday and it only confirmed everything I have written here. He's born on **November 25th** 1958, the year of the **dog.** King Tut's tomb was opened on **November 26th** 1922 (page 11), the year of the **dog** and my life as Emmett was revealed in 2018, the year of the **dog**. Brother **Hankh Rising Sun** lead me to the next step of my blind initiation when the mycelium of the mushroom spoke through him (p 476).

I told **Mars** and she told me that ***ever since she was a little girl she was drawn to the story of Emmett Till because she felt like she knew Emmett in another life***. Some people understood what I was presenting to them but I did not realize how strange this would sound to most people. I knew it was true and I was just as surprised about it as the people I was telling even though I felt like most of them thought I was crazy. There was a certain look that people gave me when I told them. A look of disbelief mixed with confusion mixed with curiosity and mostly a look of rejection. It was unbelievable to many people and for those that did believe it most of them didn't understand the significance of it all. To be honest it took me some time to realize it myself. On July 20th 2018 I would smoke the **sacred toad venom medicine** and I would think I was Tutankhaten **(King Tut)** for a day but I didn't believe it. I wouldn't fully understand the significance until after I fully realized I was Tutankhaten on April 4th 2020 (page 594).

Rau nu Prt m heru

Iu f Per f m heru

Utterances for Coming Forth by day into Light

It is he, who comes forth by day into Light

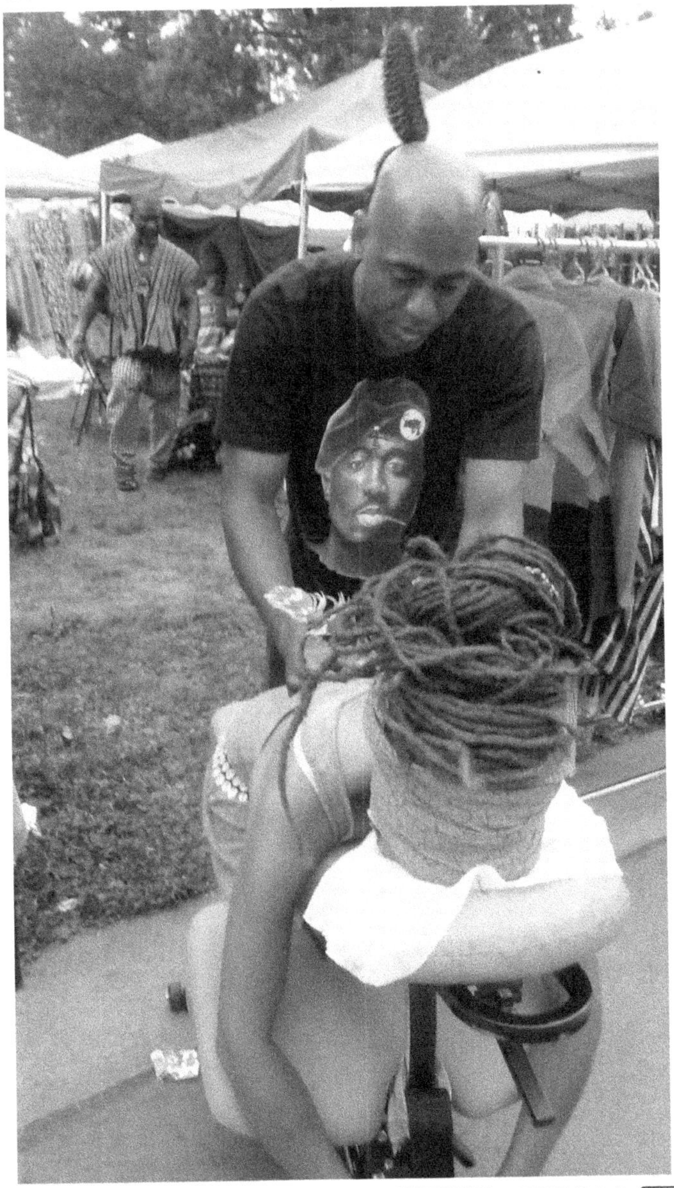

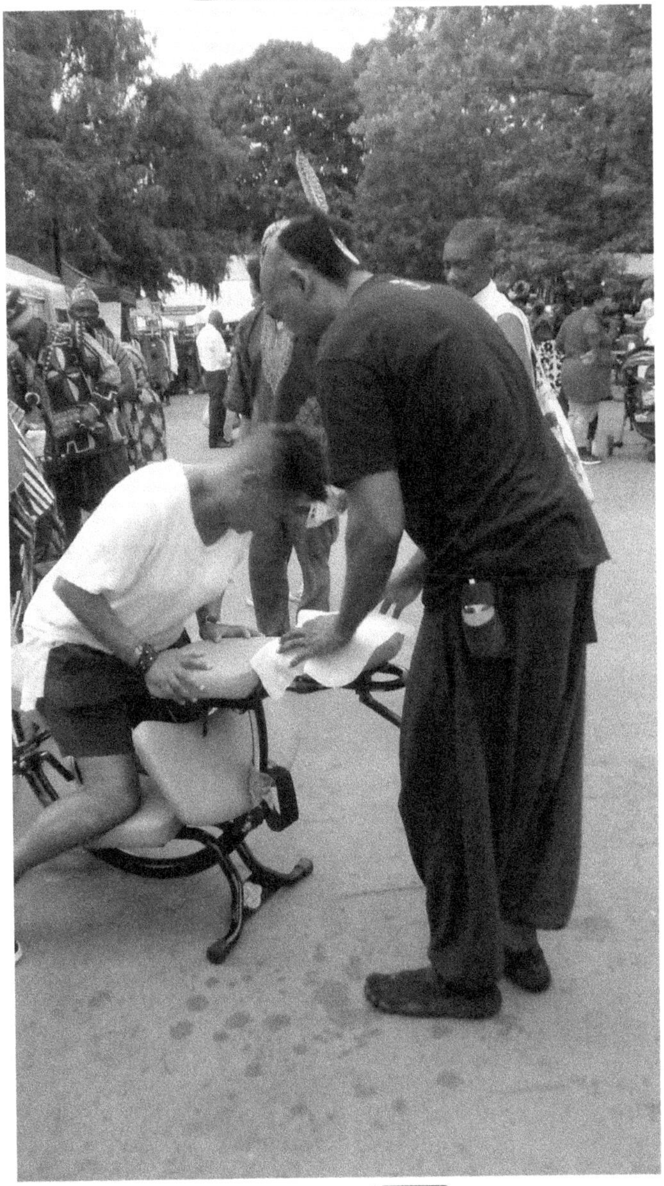

July 17th 2018 Ayahuasca

Everybody wanna know the meaning of life life, but they don't wanna die, everybody claiming that they woke woke Just cause they getting high, take another toke float up up up in the sky, it's a bird it's a plane but not a man, "cause man don't fly", but man do lie and deceive keep yo eye, on the tricks up their sleeve, cause Aleve and Tylenol wont fix up your disease, you need the leaves and the vines, have the meeting of the minds aligning shining like **Mayans** and rhyming like **Shamans** singing the icaros, **Dying to be born again,** see self for what I am, **The Holy cargo,** *The **Rods of Horus** in the hands of the **Pharaoh,*** the **Gods** they saw this so they stored it in the bone and the marrow, the more you explore the more you see the **soul** do travel, **Mushrooms** in the tomb bloom from the dung of the cattle, his sword swung but **Dawud** won before he entered the battle, when he was young he would run towards the **sun** and the **shadows,** he read the Bible but couldn't relate to ***Thomas*** and **Matthew**, ***Timothy, Musunga, Matmuu, Romelle*** more war stories to tell, **Ghetto bastards** but on the madness we won't dwell, I love you **Abdullah** and **Brian** no lying, **The Immortal Life of Emmett Till** - **Dawud The Uncanny BlaKseed**

Rods (wands, cylinders) of Horus

I first came to know about these rods from my brother **Duli**. He was at the first Bufo ceremony I witnessed and he had a pair. Shortly after I purchased a pair of my own. These mysterious cylindrical rods are seen in the hands of many of the Kemetic statues. The purpose of these rods are debated. The Nswt Bity (Pharaoh) **Menkaura** can be seen holding them (as seen above left). I once had a **dream** that I was flying and in my hands I was holding the **Wands of Horus** (page 550).

July 20th 2018
Heket Hastens Tutankhaten's Return

They say that we don't find the medicine it finds us! **Hankh Rising Sun** (p 476), the same elder that facilitated my mushroom communion invited me to another ceremony two weeks after my revelation of Emmett till. I was invited to smoke (**BUFO**) the **sacred** toad venom medicine. I had for years been researching **Ayahuasca** so I was already interested and ready. At the time I knew nothing of Heket (Heqet,HQT) the Kemetic **Toad/Frog** Goddess who birthed the Gods governing **birth** and **rebirth**. Heket hastens the last stages of birth and rebirth, reincarnation. She was given the title as the mistress of the two worlds under the reign of Seti the 1st during the 19th dynasty. Midwives would inscribe the title 'servant to Heket' on their **musical** instruments used during child birth. On July 4th 2019 I would meet a doula (Midwives) named **Ahket** at the International African Arts Festival who would come with a sacred pattern (p 570). Her name was Akhet like **Akhetaten** (p 671), the city that **Akhenaten**, the father of **Tutankhaten** (**King Tut**) built a lush environment between Memphis and Thebes during the 18th dynasty of ancient Kemet's New Kingdom. See page **648** for the **metaphysical significance of the number 23**.

5-MeO-DMT

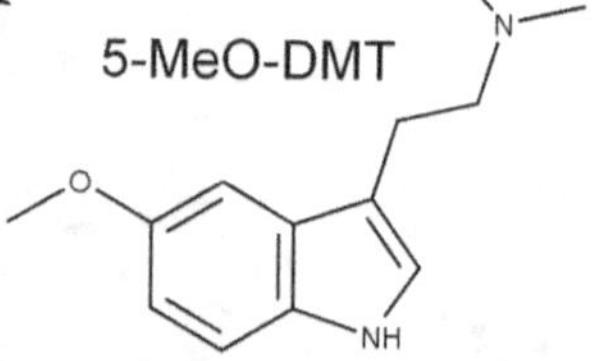

DMT

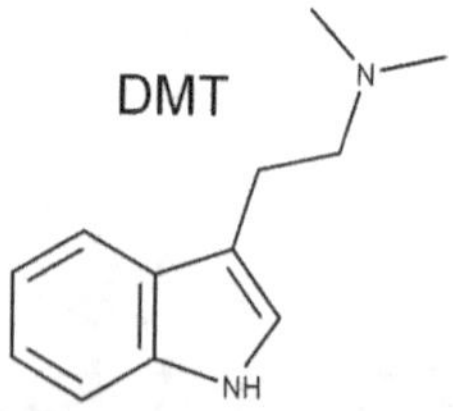

Serotonin

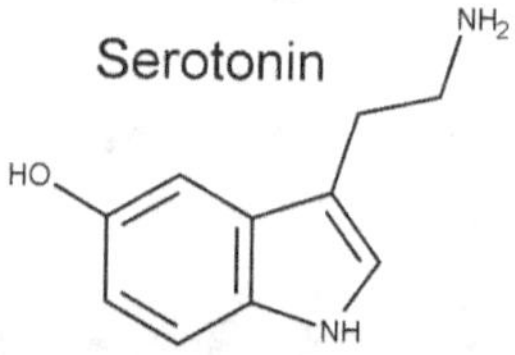

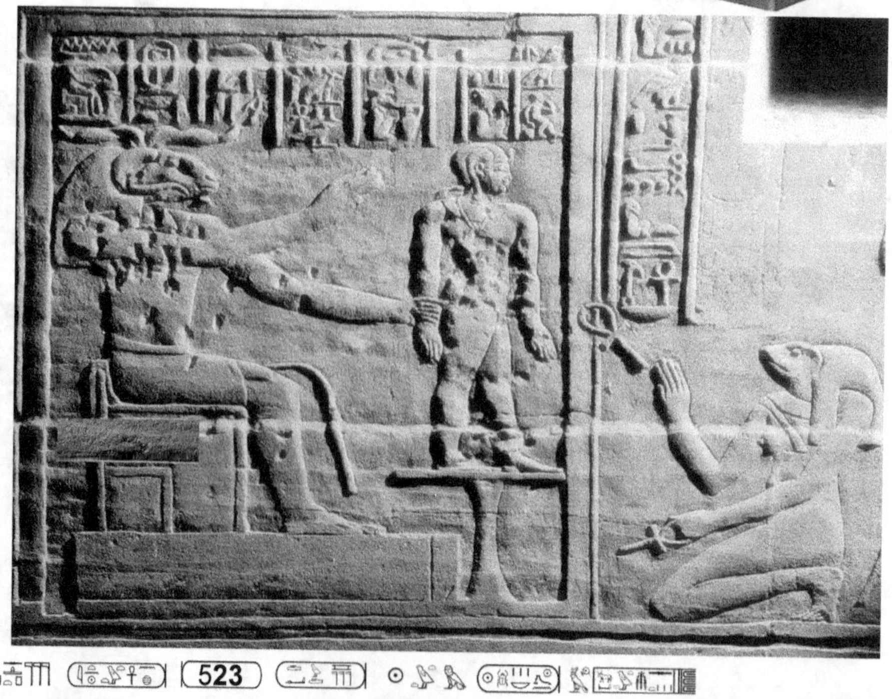

Rau nu Prt m heru

July 20th 2018
Bufo Alvarius and a Glimpse of Tutankhamen

Today I will ingest **the sacred toad medicine**. I had been researching **Ayahuasca** for some years now but had never been able to experience it so when I got the offer to take the toad medicine I accepted immediately. While at this ceremony I met a woman named Allie, she as an acupuncturist who was born on my birthday, **October 25th**. These medicines have been used in indigenous spiritual ceremonies from time immemorial however today governmental agencies do not want the descendants of the indigenous to partake in these indigenous customs so these medicines are "illegal" only being allowed to be used in Native American churches or government regulated "research". Yet alcohol is legal and many people die everyday from alcohol related accidents. Today is October 21st 2021 and 3 days ago on October 19th **Flavor Flav**, from the legendary group **Public Enemy** posted a picture on his Instagram celebrating his 1 year anniversary of **sobriety**. Flavor Flav is alcohol free and he looks so much better. His caption read - "1 year up,,, lotz more to go,,, next year I pray my whole family will be walkin the same path I am,,,". I'm proud of flaver Flav. I stopped drinking alcohol in 2011. Just because something is legal doesn't mean it is good for you and Just because something is illegal doesn't mean it is bad for you. In **1864** it was illegal for Blacks in America to live free (page 16). They were forced by White men and women with guns and laws to work for free as prisoners of war under the fear of death. As of March 31st 2021 it is legal for adults over the age of 21 and older to possess up to three ounces of cannabis (weed) for personal use in New York yet still countless people all across America, most of them Black, have been locked in prison for simple possession of cannibus for years. Our legal system is broken!

Iu f Per f m heru

I Inhaled Deeply

Before the ceremony started the **Shaman** asked me, what was my reason for attending this ceremony. After finding my reason acceptable he agreed to serve me. The first thing he did was blow the Hape (Rapéh) snuff tabacco up my nose. Rapéh is the sacred indigenous tobacco that is blown up the nose to help with grounding and calming allowing one to flow into their meditation more easily. After a few minutes we stood up and he guided me through breathing techniques. Then he stood in front of me with the pipe and packed it with dried toad venom. Then he began to chant. Then he lit the flame under the pipe and the pipe began to fill with white smoke. He placed it in my mouth and told me to breathe it in and I did. I took long inhalation's into my stomach. He told me to hold it. Then he lit the flame again and gave me more smoke to ingest and I did. After holding my breath for around a minute the space between the Shaman and I seemed to go from a matter of a few feet to a million miles away. I was looking him in the eyes and he seemed to be a million miles away yet still he seemed as clear as he could be as if he was less than an inch away. Then I lost consciousness and my next memory was awakening on the grass. All the images from this experience were captured by **Hankh Rising Sun**.

Utterances for Coming Forth by day into Light

It is he, who comes forth by day into Light

July 20th 2018
Heket Governing the Rebirth of Tutankhaten

I was told that I was out for 15 to 20 minutes. While I laid there on GEB (earth) a woman holding space for me waved my feathers over me. The Shaman hit his drum and sang his ritual chants. I purged and rolled on my stomach and back a few times. Brother H**ankh** recorded some of this for me and that is where I got these pictures from. While I was gone my consciousness traveled back to the time before time and I communed with the most ancient parts of my soul fragments. When I awoke I remembered none of this but the next day the trail of my travels would surface in my music (page 529).

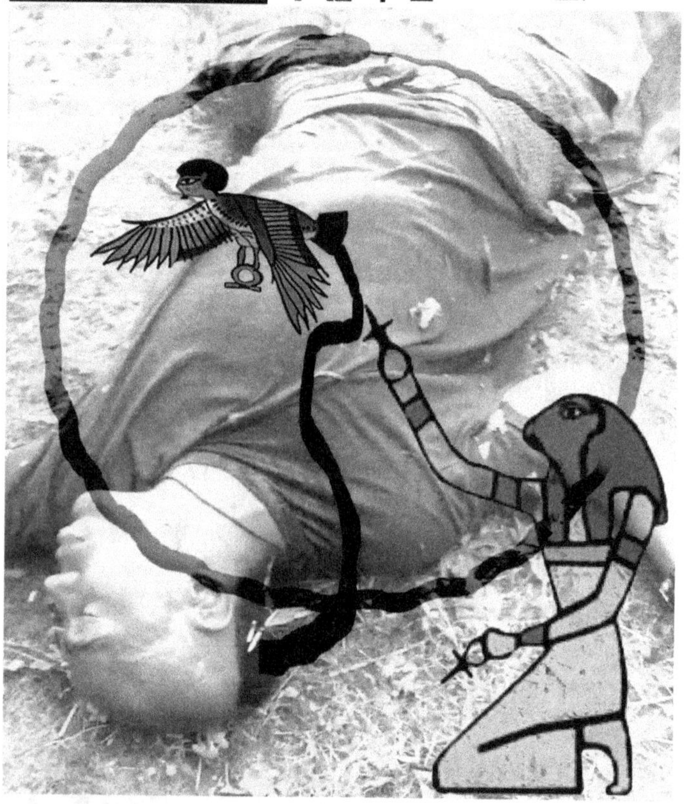

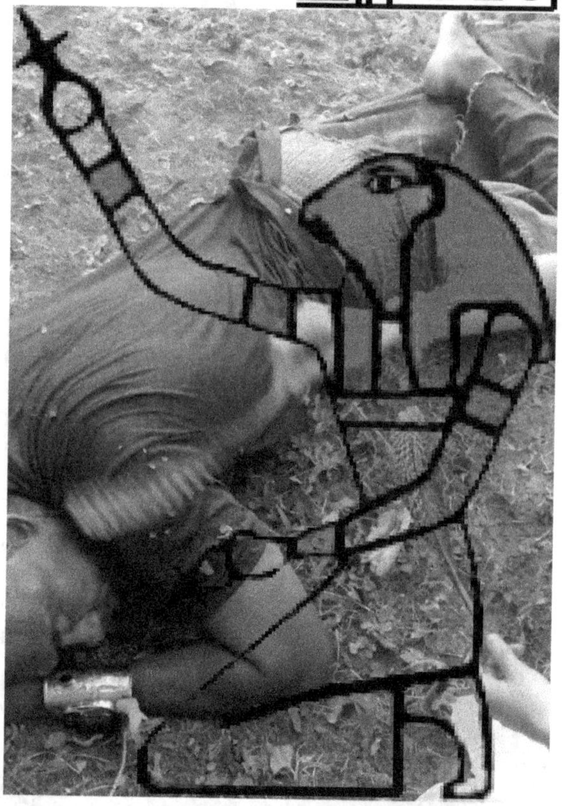

I Danced like an Egyptian my Naga!

I did not remember the trip but things were different when I woke up. I'm not a dancer but I began to dance to the drum and the chants from the shaman like an Indigenous Indian at a Pow Wow. I had never done that before in my life but I started dancing like an **Indian** or like an **Egyptian**. **I Danced like an Egyptian my Naga!** And the guy holding my feathers watched in amazement. He said he had gone to many ceremonies but never saw some one have the experience I had immediately upon rising. If you do repeat my story make sure you beat the Drum while you tell it, cause **Out of the Drum I Come flying like Relics**! See page 48, **Out of the Drum We Come**.

Rau nu Prt m heru

Iu f Per f m heru

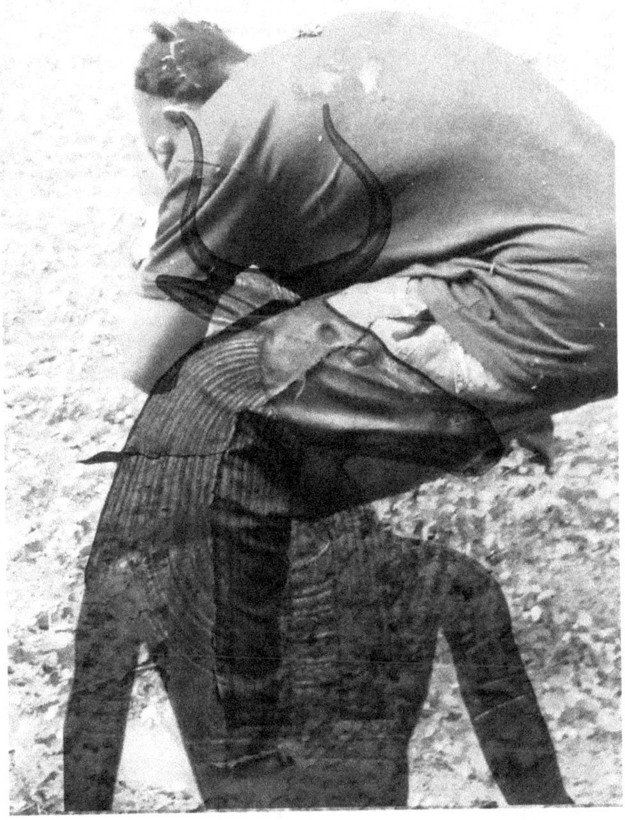

Utterances for Coming Forth by day into Light

It is he, who comes forth by day into Light

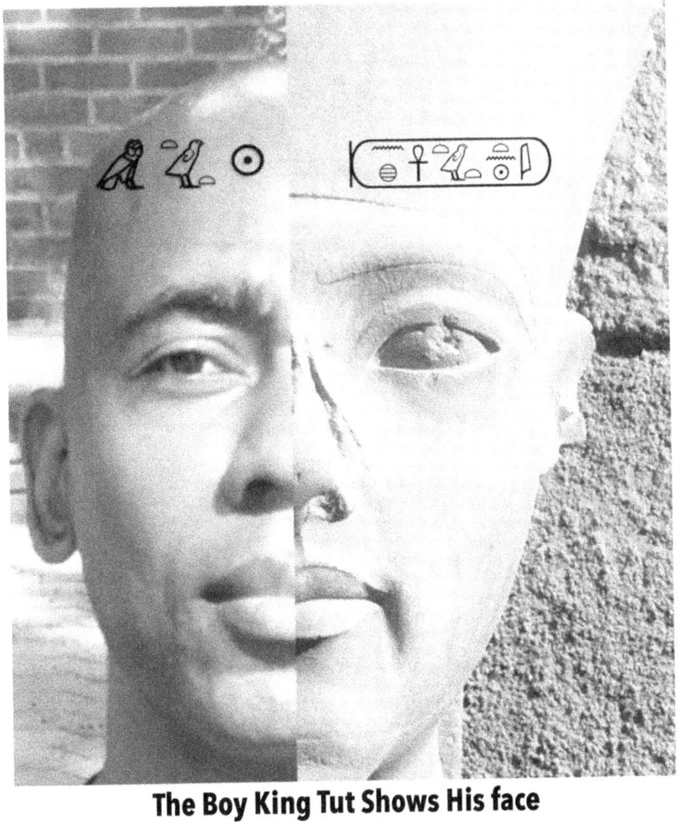

The Boy King Tut Shows His face

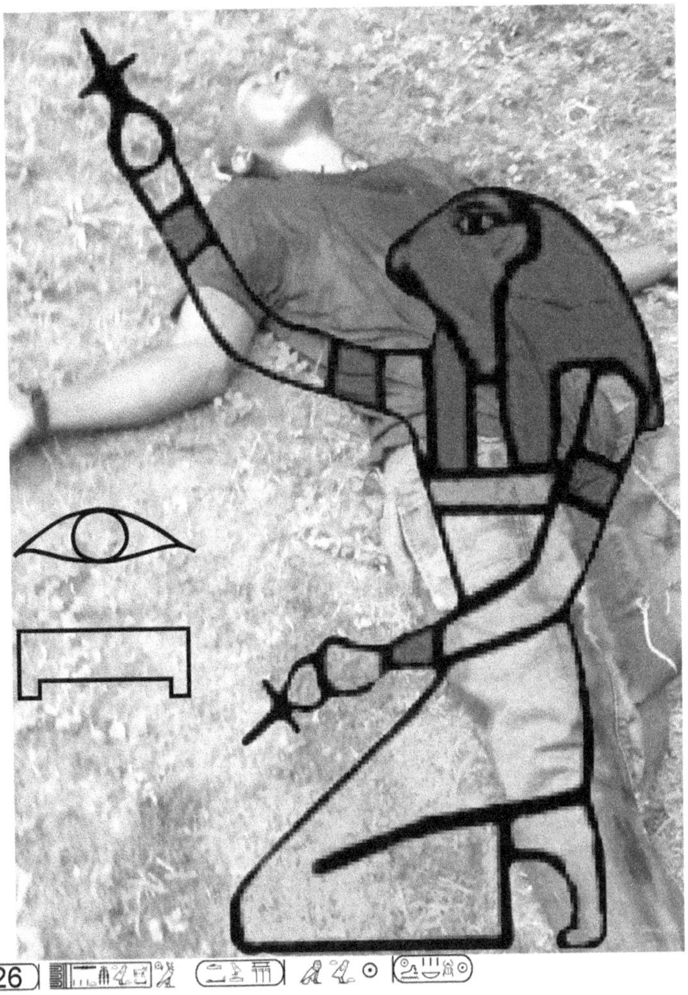

To this day I don't remember my trip and I don't know what I saw but the next day I would think I was **Tutankhaten "King Tut" (page 529)**.

I sat and meditated for a short time until it was time for the next person. Then I sat and meditated near a tree. I hugged the Shaman because I felt so much love for him. I had never hugged a person with that much love. That is a hard thing to describe as I love every person in my family and of course when I hug them I love them but this was different. He had blown this substance into me. There was a bond and this bond would cross over into the dimension of dreams later that night. To this day I don't remember my trip and I don't know what I saw but the next day I would think I was **Tutankhaten** (**King Tut**). This thought would only last long enough for me to write the thought into a song then shortly after I let that crazy idea go (page 529). I didn't believe it! I had just realized I was Emmett Till 17 days prior! I wasn't open to accept some erroneous half baked thought that I was "King Tut" with no proof. I knew I was Emmett Till but the King Tut thought was crazy and down right delusional. I let it go but two years later that erroneous thought would come back echoing in my ear on April 4th 2020 (page 594).

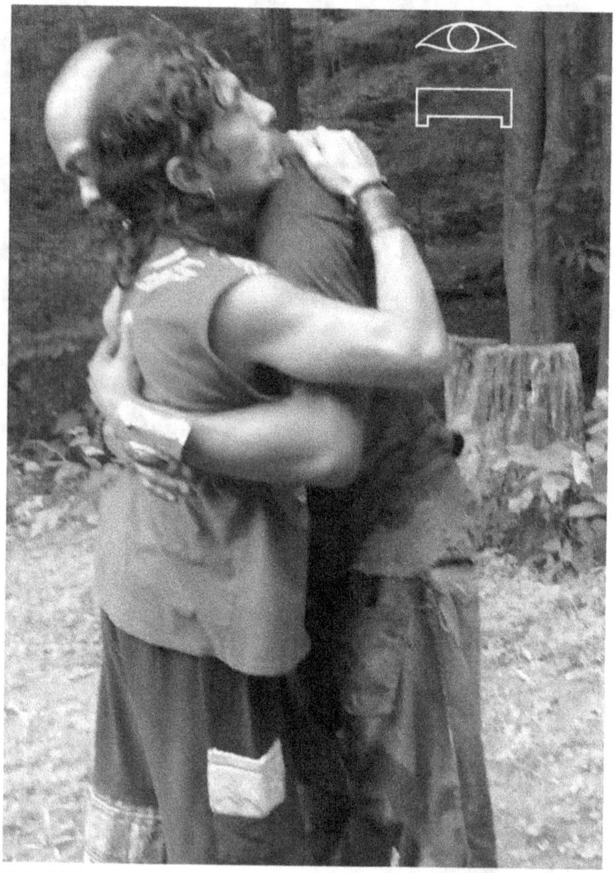

July 21st 2018 (Bufo Dreams)

When I got home I went to sleep and had one of the most vivid, lucid and powerful dreams I have ever had! In the dream I was standing in front of the shaman again looking into his eyes as clear as when I was standing in front of him the day prior. He served me the Bufo again within the dream. As soon as I ingested it I blasted off into the universe shooting through a worm hole. Then I woke up.

The Bufo stayed with me for a few days as I would have a couple more dreams like this for the next couple of days.

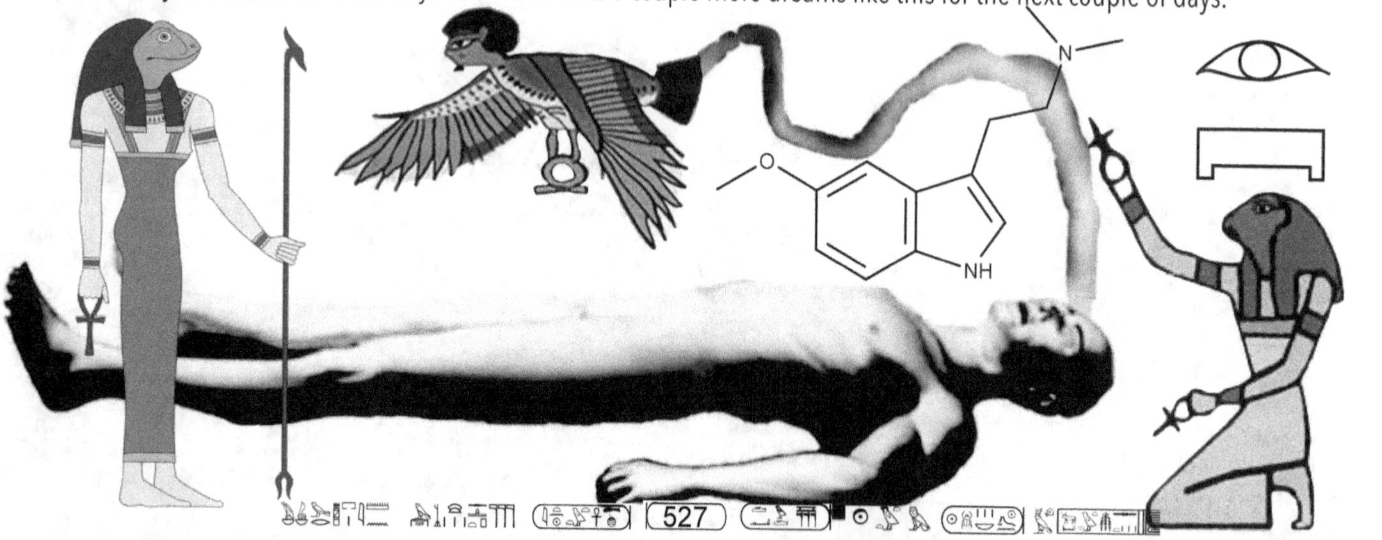

Dream with Mike Tyson and his the Sacred Toad Experience

Rau nu Prt m heru

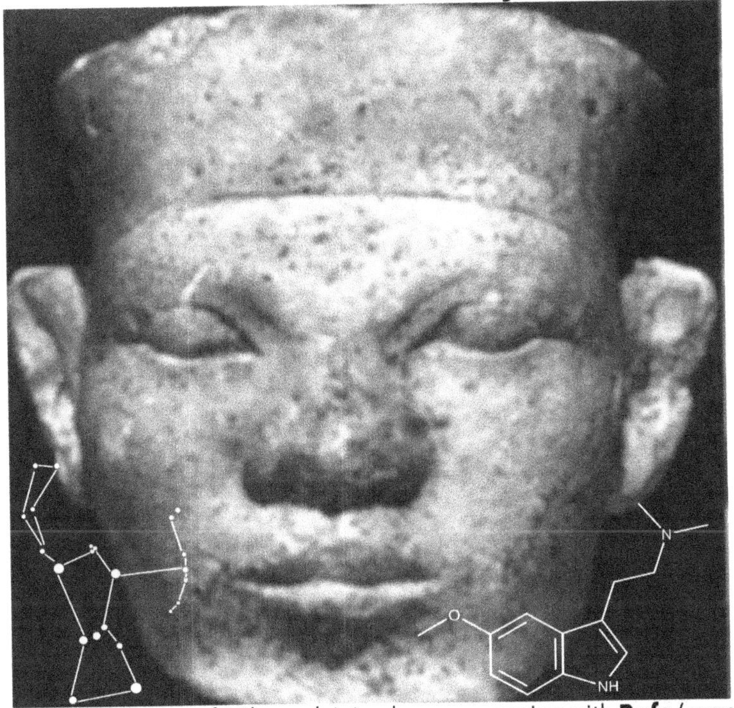

Iu f Per f m heru

I watched a video of Mike explaining how communing with **Bufo** (sacred toad venom medicine) was scary at first, having experienced paranoia the first few times. He said as soon as the effects started he wanted them to stop, "stop stop", Mike screamed. Then he got angry with everyone but at some point he surrendered and then the toad changed his life forever. He said it gave him 2000 years of experience in 20 minutes taking him on trips to his **ancestors**. Doesn't that make you think of the movie Black Panther (page 626)? Bufo is a healing medicine and has been used to help people with schizophrenia as well as those addicted to hard drugs like crack, **heroin**, alcohol and others.

Goddess Heket

Mike said as soon as you take a hit your soul goes one place and your body goes another place. He said the experience allows you to meet God and become one with God for a few minutes. At the time of this interview he had communed with the toad 16 times. The very next video I watched of Mike he said he had taken it over 50 times never having had the same experience. ***Mike** <u>equated the experience like going to be "**Born Again**"</u>*. He said he saw the **sun** open up when he smoked the toad and was amazed sort of like how **Akhenaten** (King Tut's father) might have been when he saw the vision of the **Aten** on the horizon sitting between the two mountains compelling him to build the city of Akhetaten (Aten on the horizon, page 671) in a fertile land along the Nile river between Memphis and Thebes in ancient Kemet (Egypt). Perhaps Akhenaten also smoked the toad or snake Venom and saw the sun. Or maybe he sniffed the burning **acacia** bush and got the **DMT** like "**Moses**" did on the mountain top. I have only done the toad twice and the second time it had no effect on me. The person who served me said he never saw some one commune with the toad and it have no effect on them. The first time I communed with the sacred toad medicine was July 20th 2018 (page 527), 17 days after I had my past life revelation of my life as **Emmett Till** (July 3rd 2018, page 480). The next day on July 21st 2018 I would think I was **King Tut.**

Utterances for Coming Forth by day into Light

Mike Tyson can be seen in videos getting emotional when talking about the positive effects his experience with the toad has had on his life. He says the toad showed him that he was nothing. It humbled him and dissolve the Ego. For decades Mike Tyson had used his heavy weight champion of the world persona to create a self view that was dismantled after his experience with the toad medicine. Mike said he felt loved and safe with the medicine. Mike Tyson got his massive ego from his beloved trainer **Cus D'Amato**. October 15th 2021, after watching these videos of Mike I found out that his beloved trainer Cus passed away at the age of **77**, on **November 4th** 1985, the same day **King Tut's** tomb was discovered on **November 4th** 19**22**.

It is he, who comes forth by day into Light

Significance

<u>Menes also known as Narmer and Maybe, Mike Tyson</u>

These pictures are not here to make the claim that **Mike Tyson** is the **reincarnation** of The Pharaoh **Menes** but I find it interesting that Cus D'Amato, the trainer who looked at a young Tyson and told him he would be the heavy weight champion of the world, would end up dying on the same day King Tut's tomb was discovered, at the age **77** and I was born in 19**77**. With the sp**ark** from Cus, Tyson would go on to become the **youngest heavy weight champion ever**, and probably the most feared heavy weight champion of them all and Tyson looks just like Menes (Narmer), who is the **first known Pharaoh**. Menes united upper and lower Kemet (Egypt) strengthening the whole of Kemet. I do wonder though, if Mike Tyson is Menes, perhaps that's why he fought with such tenacity! He fought with the spirit of the Nswt Bity's (Pharaohs) of ancient times. Perhaps that's why I dreamt with Tyson after I returned from Kemet! Imagine if Mike started studying ancient Kemet and was able to earn the right to know that he was Menes. It would make perfect sense and I think Mike Tyson saw the sun open up while he was under the Toad because Ra (Aten) was calling him. Wake up Menes. Wake up Mike Tyson.

ADDENDUM

May 2022 Dream with Mike Tyson

Upon returning from Kemet in Apr of 2022 (p 670) I had **dreams** with several brothers who are in some way connected to Kemet and Mike Tyson was one of them. In my dream with Mike, him and I were sitting next to each other in what seemed to be a movie theatre. Then I woke up. I would also dream with **Lord Jamar** (p 342), **KRS One** (P 633) and **XXXtentacion** (p 471).

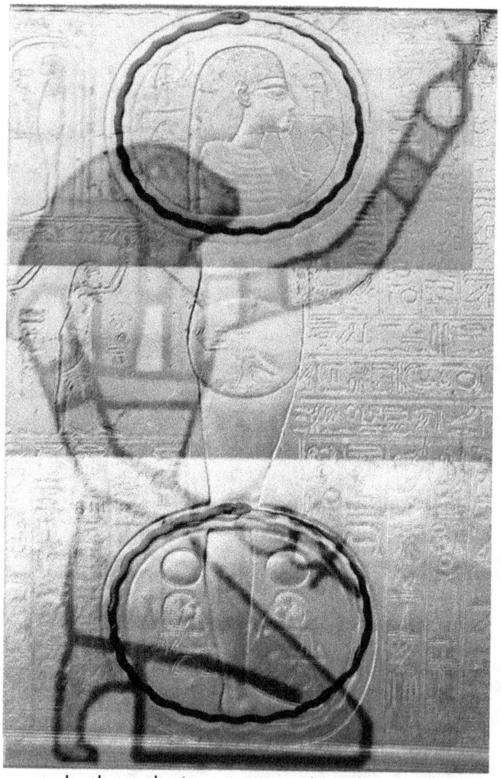

July 21st 2018 - The Boy King Tut Shows His face

The very next day after I consumed the sacred venom toad medicine I would think I was **King Tut**. The thought was bizarre to me but there was this weird feeling that drew me to him out of nowhere! I just knew, sort of like the moment that I knew I was Emmett Till but this was different because the thought came from nowhere. It just popped in my head as powerful as the moment that I knew I was Emmett. As soon as the thought came I wrote the hook for the song **Ayahuasca** that I had written on July 17th (page 523) and in the hook I would say the words -

"I am the **Boy King** in the museum you be seeing
I gave you the signs this time **I'm back** in a human being
Facts encoded in rhyme like my body frozen in time
in 1929 I shined on **Martin Luther King**"

I don't know where those words came from or the thought for that matter. The thought and feelings just came and the words just flew out of my mouth. Somehow I knew it was true but as soon as I was finished recording the hook I let that idea go, weighing more on the the side of disbelief. I had no proof, or so I thought because at the time I didn't know all the connections I had with King Tut. Besides, I had been telling people I was Emmett for two weeks and most people thought I was crazy already so I damn sure wasn't going to tell anyone that I thought I was King Tut, they would for sure think I was insane if I told them that. I never told anyone but deep within me I must have believed it because I started editing pictures of King Tut's mummy and other things related to him into my music videos. I had never heard of Heket, the Kemetic (Egyptian) Goddess who birthed the Gods governing **birth** and **rebirth**. Heket hastens the last stages of birth, rebirth (**reincarnation**). She was given the title as the mistress of the two worlds under the reign of Seti the 1st during the 19th dynasty. Midwives would inscribe the title 'servant to Heket' on their **musical** instruments used during child birth. On July 4th 2019 (p 570) I would meet a doula (midwife) named **Ahket** at the International African Arts Festival who would come with a sacred pattern. Her name was **Akhet** like **Akhetaten** (p 671), the city that **Akhenaten**, the father of **Tutankhaten** (**King Tut**) built in a fertile land between Memphis and Thebes during the 18th dynasty of ancient Kemet's New Kingdom. And she was wearing a scarab cuff with King Tut's name on it. On April 4th 2020 (p 594), the day **Martin Luther King** was assassinated (pages 69, 592) my past life as **Tutankhaten** (**King Tut**) would be revealed to me in the most profound of ways. **Heket** came to me through the Sacred Bufo Toad Medicine and told me that I was King Tut on July 21st 2018, two years before the revelation would be fully revealed. I imagine that it was better that way! Too much info too soon without proper preparation might drive a person crazy.

July 21st 2018 - Mysterious Message from the Fourth Dimension

(Zee's dream)

The day after my **Bufo** experience I am doing **chair massage** in Jackie Robinson park at a community event. The first woman to sit in my chair was named **Hope** and she was born on June 17th my Grand Fathers birthday. She would soon start training with me. There was live music at this event and I was allowed to performed the song **Searching for the Oneness** ,which I wrote on May 14th 2016 (page 383). **Jeannine** from my group fitness classes came by for a chair massage as well as my good friend **Emerson**. I would see **Zee** at this event and she would tell me about a **dream** that she recently had of me. She had the same **dream** that La Juana's daughter had (page 461). She **dreamt** that I was doing music and everyone was listening. Zee would come by for a massage later this year in December and after her massage she would reveal to me who my **guardian angel** was. I was able to communicate and carry on a conversation with my guardian angel for the first time as Zee passed along messages from me to my guardian and from my guardian to me (page 545).

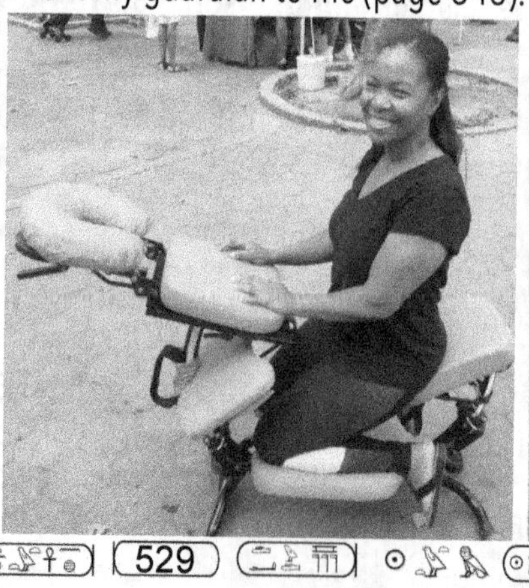
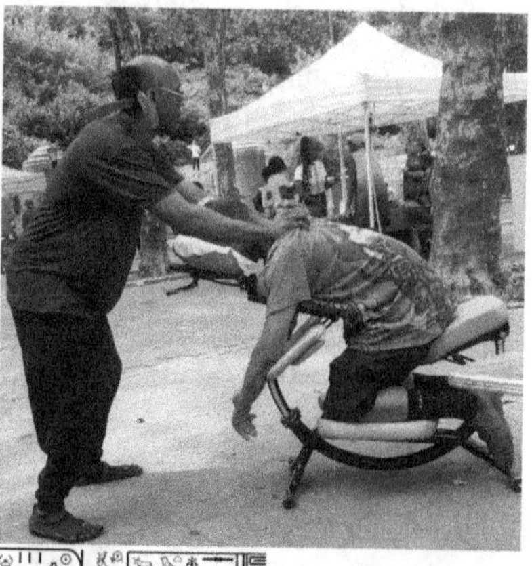

Rau nu Prt m heru

July 25th 2018
Decoding the Transmigration of My Soul
The Immortal Snake, Wadjety, Ouroboros (p 657)

At this point in my revelation I was still doing research connecting all the dots to myself and Emmett Till when I saw a post that said Emmett Till would be **77** years old today if he hadn't been murdered. Emmett was born on July **25th** 19**41** the year of the **snake** and in 2018 he would have been **77** and I was born in 19**77** the year of the **snake** (p **41**)! Emmett was born on July **25th** in 19**41** the year of the **snake** and I was about to turn **41** on October **25th**! This was indeed a **divine pattern**, or some sort of "**astrological star code**". Like the one **Amiga dreamt** about in September of 2016 (p 419)! It was the **star code of immortality!** It was too perfect to be just a coincidence! If I had been born in 1976 I would be 42 this year and if I was born in 1978 I would have been 40 this year but no, I was born in 19**77** the year of the **snake** and Emmett was born in 19**41** the year of the **snake**. It was a perfect **bullseye** like **Ausar** the **archer**! All the math was perfect like sacred geometry. **22** days after I realized I was Emmett in a past life Emmett's birthday flashes across my timeline and I see that "he" would have been **77** years old if "he" had not been killed. Emmett's father Louis Till was born in 19**22** the same year **King Tut's** tomb was discovered. **22** years after Emmett was killed in 19**55** I was born again as Dawud in 19**77**. This **pattern** was like the stones used to build the pyramids of Giza, it couldn't be explained away and you could not put a razor blade between these perfect stones of coincidence. At this time I still don't know that I look like Emmett yet but one by one I put all the stones of **coincidence** together and I could see that this was not just a "coincidence"! No different than the **pattern** that connected **President Lincoln** to **President Kennedy** (p 380). In 2021 I would decipher **The 44th Parallel** (p 6**6**0), which is a similar star code pattern that involves 5 people, my uncle **Jimmy Dukes** his wife **Alice Dukes**, **Sekou Odinga**, **Michelle Lamy** and **George Lucas**! My uncle Jimmy **Dukes** was born **<u>two</u> days before** me on October **23rd** and my aunt Alice **Dukes** was born **<u>two</u> days before** Emmett Till on July **23rd**. They both turned **77** years old in 2021 and I was born in 19**77**. I turned **44** years old in 2021 and they were both born in 19**44.** See page **648** for the **metaphysical significance of the number 23**. In 2019 the political prisoner **Sekou Odinga** would be added to this pattern on **Malcolm X's** birthday (p 561). That same year, the fashion mogul **Michelle Lamy** would be added to this pattern (p 582). Then in 2021 **George Lucas**, the Creator of **Star Wars** would be the last person absorbed into this star code pattern (p 37). In 2021 I got my first and only astrological reading and it confirmed my revelation (p 654). All the patterns above allowed me to decode **the Sacred Geometry behind the Transmigration of My Soul** (page **602**)! **Read page 602** and ask your self if this **sacred pattern** is just coincidental. And Remember, that one time is an incidence, twice is a coincidence, but three, four, and five is a pattern! Can you tell the difference?!

Iu f Per f m heru

Utterances for Coming Forth by day into Light

July 27th 2018 Blood Moon

Holy cow it's a **blood moon**, Stepped in shit, got me a **mushroom,** Jumped off mother ship with a **witch** took off on her broom, interstellar intergalactic, travel the universe laying on my mattress, **Magic** is **magic** to the lay man afraid to paint the future, Staring at a canvas, You gotta leave the branches and go to the root for the truth if you wanna make advances, trances, dances, **telepathine***, the answers from the unseen uploaded while in a **dream,** you can rage against the machine or sage and engage the serene, ever seen **Huey P** in the **Lotus?** ever notice the Lily on the wall? you don't care how they gave the **Indians alcohol** do you?! **Voodoo** needles in the arm, **Simeon Toko, Angola** gaining independence from Portugal, Poking y'all with the sorcery, **Avatar** or conspiracy? **Jesus Christ** superstar lyrically, Physically a **Reincarnation - Dawud The Uncanny BlaKseed.**

<u>Significance</u>

I wrote this on the longest total lunar eclipse of the 21st century which just so happened to be two days after Emmett Till's birthday (July 25th 1941 year of the **snake**). The Mayans observed July 25th as a day free of time in the 13 Moon Calendar (page 503). It is considered a moment of great energetic intensity, in which the **Beings of Light** work to align us with the harmony of the universe, on its various dimensions of time, and space. In this song I would speak of **Simeon Toko**. I learned about the **reincarnation** of Simeon Toko on December 7th 2014 while at a lecture (page 312). The same brother that spoke on Simeon would be the brother who connected me with the sacred medicine on July 3rd 2018 that sparked my **past life** of **Emmett Till**. Simeon was said to be the second coming of **Jesus Christ**. He was said to have been killed several times and mysteriously came back to life each time. He was also said to have performed other miracles like healing the blind and bringing a baby back to life after being dead for several days.

It is he, who comes forth by day into Light

July 30th 2018 **Sirius B**

This is my subjective experience, **paranormal** mysterious, you might object after hearing this but still **the immortal life of Emmett Till** for real, **Sirius B** like **Dogon**, can't kill the chosen, what a bless'n to be back and awoken, not trapped and frozen like **sleep paralysis**, my coffin been opened, the truth been spoken on the wall for your analysis, my journey was long I did fall but I handled it, ever since I was young I heard a call like a candle lit, the catalyst was a **dream**, a **premonition** flowing like a stream, she called me **Siddhartha** the **magician**, and so it seems she was right but still I didn't listen, too busy kiss'n lips and missing sacred connections, and **past life regressions**, these are my confessions, the source of all my blessings, hold all your misconceptions, I'll be the first to tell the world about my imperfections **- Dawud The Uncanny BlaKseed**

July 31st 2018 **God is**

If **God** is everything then **God** is **numerology** and, **God** is in the **breath** and, **God** is written in **astrology** and, **God** is in the **flesh** and, **God** is in the way of less harm son, the **Goddess** is where we come from it's not a conundrum, don't get stuck in the **sunken place** then placed in the dungeon, **God** is in the d**ark**ness, in the **light**, in the **Christian** the **Muslim**, **God** is in the man before man made his **religion** corruption, **God** is in this touch-less society full of seduction, **God** is in the being of everyone, but be wise when you decide to put trust in anyone with the children, yes **God** is a loving **God** but, bets believe if you touch my seeds it might be against all odds but **Dawud** will fuckin kill em, **God** willing I'm not feeling this **Black Mirror** Horror **Thriller** nearer to a **Twilight Zone**, ***stranger in a land my ancestors called home***, see, we are all one and not alone but still I get lonely, but not when you hold me **- Dawud The Uncanny BlaKseed**

August 14th 2018 **Jeannie in a bottle**

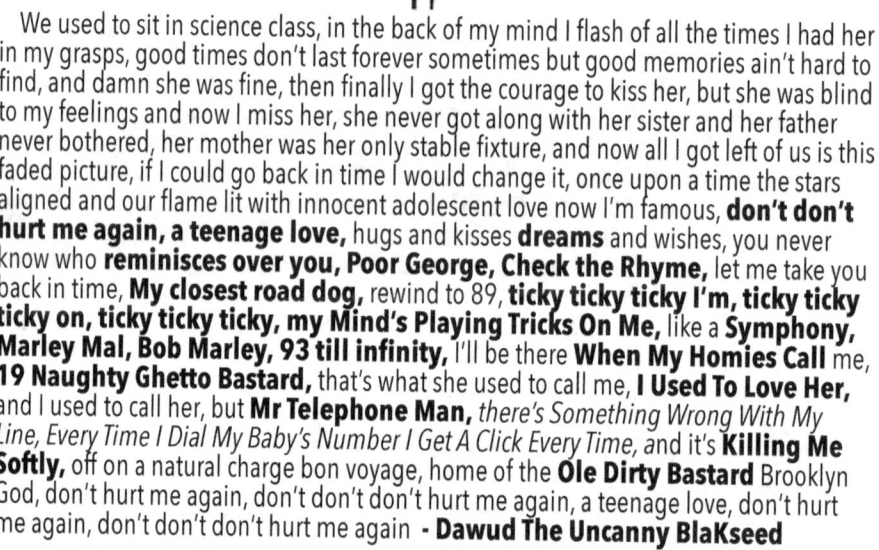

We used to sit in science class, in the back of my mind I flash of all the times I had her in my grasps, good times don't last forever sometimes but good memories ain't hard to find, and damn she was fine, then finally I got the courage to kiss her, but she was blind to my feelings and now I miss her, she never got along with her sister and her father never bothered, her mother was her only stable fixture, and now all I got left of us is this faded picture, if I could go back in time I would change it, once upon a time the stars aligned and our flame lit with innocent adolescent love now I'm famous, **don't don't hurt me again, a teenage love,** hugs and kisses **dreams** and wishes, you never know who **reminisces over you, Poor George, Check the Rhyme,** let me take you back in time, **My closest road dog,** rewind to 89, **ticky ticky ticky I'm, ticky ticky ticky on, ticky ticky ticky, my Mind's Playing Tricks On Me,** like a **Symphony, Marley Mal, Bob Marley, 93 till infinity,** I'll be there **When My Homies Call** me, **19 Naughty Ghetto Bastard,** that's what she used to call me, **I Used To Love Her,** and I used to call her, but **Mr Telephone Man,** *there's Something Wrong With My Line, Every Time I Dial My Baby's Number I Get A Click Every Time,* and it's **Killing Me Softly,** off on a natural charge bon voyage, home of the **Ole Dirty Bastard** Brooklyn God, don't hurt me again, don't don't don't hurt me again, a teenage love, don't hurt me again, don't don't don't hurt me again **- Dawud The Uncanny BlaKseed**

Meta Mysterious Encounter with Jeannie's look alike. Divine Patterns - Sing-Natures

I met a Dominican woman in massage school who looked exactly like Jeannie. We had a Tai Chi class together however the woman didn't complete the class so I stopped seeing her. Upon graduating from school I began working with La Juana at her Spa (p 455) and one day the Dominican woman crossed my path while at the Spa. I was handing out flyers in front of the spa when a woman stopped and asked me if I had gone to massage school at NYCHP (p 274), it was the Dominican woman from school. We exchanged info and shortly after I began training her. Perhaps she was a test, because she began to give me the same feelings that Mary gave me (p 291). She made comments that made feel uncomfortable and eventually I told her that I could not train her anymore. Life is full of tests….

Summer 2018
Meta Spiritual Encounter with Zawadi, The Yoruba Priestess

In the summer of 2018 I met a woman named **Zawadi** at the corner of Fredrick Douglass and 145th street. **A feeling came over me** leading me to hand her my card. I gave her a card for my group fitness class that I held in Jackie Robinson park. She came to one or two classes then she moved down south and I didn't hear from her again till March of 2021. This would lead to her telling me that she was a **medium,** and she would go on to tell me that **she felt my energy when we first met** and she also saw a **bright light** around me the first time that we met. I asked her what color the light was and she said **gold.** Because her spiritual guides told her to, she traveled to New York on **April 22nd 2021** and gave me my first and only **IFA** reading, for free (page 641).

Life is in deed a play of consciousness and if you align with the energy of creation the energies that govern creation will order your steps. This book is my play book. A record of my divine meetings. My divine alignments. I feel that we are all here on earth on some divine appointment and if we listen closely we can hear the call of the unseen realms. We make a fatal error when we think all that we* see with our two eyes is all there is to see and all that we* hear with our two ears is all there is to hear. While on your journey through life Keep an open mind and try not to discredit things that you can't explain or have yet to experience.. In the immortal words of **Malcolm X**, "Don't be in a hurry to condemn a person because he doesn't do what you do or think as you think or as fast. There was a time when you didn't know what you know today."

August 17th 2018 Da Naga

Rau nu Prt m heru

Close your eyes when you meditate, and wait at the gate less gate, this is fate like the greatness in 8, let me elaborate, it's my word is bond, **stepped out of meditation created this song** and ain't it the bomb like the Big Bang from a gong, Dawud da Naga, Tai chi gung, if you ever need me, I'll be there I won't be too long, speedy graffiti **dung beetle Nefertiti**, the **mushroom** said eat me you belong to a star race beyond the beyond, **Ausar** placed on earth as we are seen in the heavens, are you seeking and wondering why you seeing **11 11**? no mistaken awaken woken I was spoken into being, Yoga to yoke the human being, Cobra, Dawud da Naga, I told ya emceeing I'm the **Dali lama**, I ate the **manna** then I saw Nirvana, aSaana unraveling in the **pose of immortality**, transition to another pose traveling the galaxy, the truth is above your nose, the laws are written in analogy, your **dreams** are more realer be the **caterpillar**, **mirror** duality, **Maaty** graci, balancing morality, **Marcus Garvey** gathering the family, look for me in the whirlwind when the world end **Merlin Tehuti** Dawud da Naga the saga the beauty, close your eyes when you meditate and wait at the gate less gate, no mistaken awaken woken I was spoken into being, Cobra Dawud da Naga I told ya emceeing I'm the Dali lama, Tehuti Dawud the Naga the saga the beauty, Dawud da naga the saga Wadjety I told ya, I'm the Dali lama Tehuti, Dawud da Naga the saga, I told ya I'm the Dali lama Tehuti

Iu f Per f m heru

Most people wanna win the lottery, I want the answers to the odyssey, the mystery, number one cause of death? coronary artery! if I should die before eye awaken fully, cardiopulmonary me my **naga,** remember me! then "*bury me a G*", but until death finds me I'm a be the yogi in the **lotus** meditating waiting for that change to come like **Ottis**, the **ladies** in my **dreams** remind me, they call em **witches** but they give me heavenly kisses which is why riches could never define me, if it was up to me I'd be lost in love with **Nefertiti**, in the land before time B and the only way to find me would be the meeting of the minds B, they call it a simulation I'm calling on divination cause I wanna know who designed me, is creation just a real life playstation? is my soul journey Just an **alien** on a short vacation? I have seen things that I can't explain, the unseen be speaking to me to the **dark matter** contained in my veins, simple and plain *the hearts the master key*, the battery to self mastery, the pastor be all about his salary, stillness to heal this body embody another body, Dawud da Naga continue the saga proper with virtuosi, close your eyes when you meditate and wait at the gate less gate, no mistaken awaken woken I was spoken into being, Cobra Dawud da Naga I told ya emceeing I'm the Dali lama, Tehuti Dawud the Naga the saga the beauty, Dawud da Naga the saga Wadjety I told ya, I'm the Dali lama Tehuti, Dawud da Naga the saga, I told ya I'm the Dali lama Tehuti **- Dawud The Uncanny BlaKseed**

(42 Laws of Maat, Page 367)

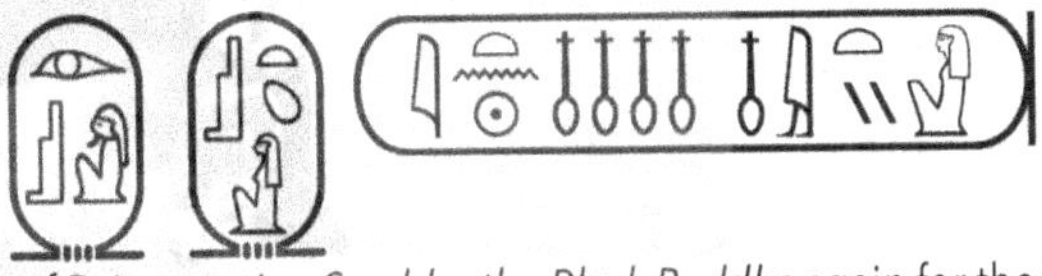

Significance

After my past life revelation of Emmett Till I watched the documentary, *The Prophecy of Reincarnation Sambho the Black Buddha* again for the first time since 2014 (page 288). The documentary would take on a new meaning to me but I still had not think myself to be a Buddha. The documentary would bring the Naga teachings to the forefront of my mind ending up in this song. The beginning of the first verse of this song was birthed while in a deep meditation. It is the only song that I ever wrote while under the influence of the **mushroom**. While sitting in the **lotus** position meditating the words - "Close your eyes when you meditate, and wait at the gate less gate, this is fate like the greatness in **8**" kept playing over and over in my head. It wouldn't go away so I got up and wrote the first verse. It came out like water. In the verse I mention **Nefertiti**, I mention **Ausar** who is the Lord of **resurrection** and rebirth. The verse was a code, a pattern, a message from the other side. A day or so later I wrote the second verse and I started the by stating, **I would rather have know the great mystery of life rather than winning the lottery**. Then I quote **Tupac,** "*bury me a G*". I have a theory who Tupac was in his past life. Sometime in 2019 I called my homie **Mighty Budda**, in search of a **mushroom infused** chocolate square. I pedaled my bike 36 blocks down to 110th street as fast as I could and purchased two from him. I ate one while I was talking to him. We must have spoke for 5 minutes, then I quickly pedaled my bike home. When I got home I had a light coat of sweat on me, my body was vibrating and for some reason I decided to look in the **mirror** – to my surprise I saw a face that was not mine. Or at least I didn't think it was, the face looked like an old Native American Indian. The face reminded me of my grand fathers face. This is the experience that caused to **run for 25th minutes** on April 4th 2022 after ingesting 10 grams of the sacred bread of life (p 593).

Utterances for Coming Forth by day into Light

August 18th 2018 Perception

Hello my name is **Dawud**, it means **David**, my father met a girl, my mother he loved her, they had kids then he left, then the world we had to brave it, I always wanted a brother but my mother had another beautiful baby girl and I love her, her first word was Dawud, her big brother, as a kid I had questions but got no answers, who created God and the universe I would wonder, **when ever I went to church I would want to walk to the alter for my soul, so God could save it**, in high school I rose to the crowds amazement, Will would throw me the ball and I would score, the game I would save it, *we used to catch wreck and collect division one letters, damn if only our GPA's were better*, I fell in love with her, then I traveled through stormy weather, where are you **Monique**? what are you doing? do you miss me? did I ruin? do you remember when we met? do you remember **Indira**? I fell asleep in a **dream** and I could hear her, like a reflection right there like a mirror, life is about perception the clearer you see, you were right I'm sorry, I never said sorry, in the one nine nine nine I joined the army, in the one nine nine nine I joined the army, life is about perception the clearer you see, you were right I'm sorry, I never said sorry, in the one nine nine nine I joined the army, in the one nine nine nine I joined the army **- Dawud The Uncanny BlaKseed**

It is he, who comes forth by day into Light

Life is about perception the clearer you see, you were right I'm sorry I never said sorry
In the one nine nine nine I joined the army
In the one nine nine nine I joined the army

August 2018

Tobius, Egypt, Rameses II and Meta Spiritual Devices

I met Tobius in 2016 at the local Farmers Market that his wife **Sanya** runs in my neighborhood. I would cross paths with Tobius in late August of 2018 a few days after he returned from his first tour of Egypt with **Anthony T. Browder**. We were in front of the **Reggae Delights** Juice Bar on 145th street when he detailed the profound experiences he had in the tombs of the Pharaohs. On July 20th 2018 Tobius entered the Tombs of **Seti I** and **Rameses II** in the **Valley of The Kings** and was immediately over come with **tears** as he **cried uncontrollably**. The tour guides were so taken by his reaction that they let him meditate inside of one of the sarcophagi which are usually off limits. During his meditation he experienced a heightened sense of relaxation and calmness. Days later he flew to **Abu Simbel** where he would have **another profound experience**. What he explained reminded me of what I experienced with Dr Ford in August of 2016 (page 399). On July 27th 2018 Tobius walked into the last chamber on the left in the Temple of Ramses II and **as soon as he entered the chamber his body began to vibrate**. He says that it felt as if he stuck his right hand into an electrical socket and from there his entire body was full of euphoric vibrations. This lasted for the entire time that he was in the chamber. He explains that his right hand and arm vibrated at a higher frequency than the rest of his body, nonetheless his entire body was full of vibrations. After he left the chamber and finished the tour he went back to the chamber just to see if it would happen again and sure enough it did. He says even to this day whenever he thinks about the experience he can feel his body starting to vibrate again. After he shared his experience I told him the details of my past life revelation of Emmett Till. We exchanged numbers and he started training with me shortly after this. I would come to learn that Tobius is born on July 4th the day after I had my past life revelation of **Emmett Till** and his wife has the same name as one of my sisters and is born on July 24th the day before **Emmett Till's** birthday. Tobius would invite me to **Malcolm X's** annual birthday celebration the next year on May 19th 2019 where I would experience a profound **premonition** involving **Martin Luther King JR**, **Malcolm X** and **Dr Umar Johnson** (p 564). I would also meet the political prisoner **Sekou Odinga** there and he would be connected to the **44th parallel** (p 561).

Meta Spiritual Devices and the Activation of The Astral Body

Why did Tobius' body begin to vibrate when he entered the Temple of Ramses II? We know the temples were instrument with precise stone placements that allowed them to be "played" like music, creating sound vibration to be used as a healing modality (page 6), but what else were they used for? Perhaps the "pyramids" (meta-spiritual devices), were designed for more astronomical purposes, and not the burial place for the dead Pharaohs, like some "Egyptologist" claim. **Nikola Tesla** used the technology from the designing of the pyramids to spark many of his inventions. The pyramid of Giza, houses no equipment and no hieroglyphs, only one stone "**box**". But what was the box for? And the shafts inside the Kings Chamber, what were they for? The stone "box" is found in the center of the Great Pyramid, placed in the middle of the Kings Chamber. Inside this chamber there are two narrow shafts, commonly known as "air shafts" and less commonly known as "**star shafts**". The southern shaft reaches to the outer surface of the Pyramid and was aligned with **Orion's belt**. The south shaft in the Queens chamber is aligned to the star **Sirius**. **Orion** was associated with **Ausar** (**Osiris**), the Lord of Resurrection (p 481). It is theorized that in ancient times the initiates would lay in the stone "box" (sarcophagus) inside the Kings Chamber and separate their **light bodies** (Ka, Spirit, Ba, soul, consciousness, astral body) from their physical bodies. Upon separation of the **light body** they would take the **star shaft**, teleporting their **astral body** to the Sirius or **Orion** star systems. For more Orion see pages 251, 366, 485 594.

I went to Kemet in 2022 and on March 30th I entered the Kings Chamber. That was my first time in this meta-spiritual device in this life but for some reason it did not seem like a new experience. It wasn't anything like **Deja Vu,** it was just a feeling of familiarity. However, the following days I would have profound experiences of **Deja Vu** while in **Kemet** (pages 670 - 671). When Tobius entered the chamber he experienced the spontaneous activation of his **light body**. History states that **Napoleon** spent 7 hours in the Kings chamber laying in the stone coffin on August 2nd 1799. When he emerged, from the chamber it was reported that he was visibly shaken. When asked if he had any mysterious experience he had no comment and ordered the incident to never be mentioned again. On his death bed he was about to tell of his experience in the Kings Chamber when suddenly he stopped. Then he shook his head and said, "No, what's the use. You'd never believe me". Napoleon was not an initiate, he was a power hungry instrument of white supremacy. How could he expect to experience what is meant for those who seek spiritual ascension? If you take a piece of metal and stick it into an electrical socket you can expect to be shocked. I suspect the same thing goes for those who seek experiences they have not yet spiritually earned. It's been widely taught that **Napoleon** saw the face of the Sphinx (Heru Em Ahket) in 1799 and shoot the nose off because the facial features did not look like his but the teachings of **Dr Runoko Rashidi** suggest that it was the **Islamic invaders** of Kemet who shot the nose off of the **Sphinx** and not **Napoleon**. The facial features of the Sphinx looked like that of a Black Afrikan!! One day soon we'll be on top again! The Afrikan came back with unity as the stratagem, maximum effect like maroons ready to ride again. When I die I'll be back in the spirit to try again..

Rau nu Prt m heru

Iu f Per f m heru

Utterances for Coming Forth by day into Light

It is he, who comes forth by day into Light

August 2018
Meta Mysterious Encounter with Cheryl from Chicago

I met **Pascal** at **Seasoned Vegan** located at **55** ST Nicholas (page 364) and over the years him and I would become friends. Pascal is a manager at Seasoned Vegan. He was always very friendly and he was a hugger. He hugged people a lot. At one point in our friendship I told him that I didn't want to be hugged so much and so he stopped hugging me. One day in late August of 2018 I was leaving Seasoned Vegan and as I exited the restaurant I found Pascal outside hugging a female friend of his. The hug was long and I stood there while the friend of the girl he was hugging waited on the side. I looked at her and said, "we might as well hug too". She laughed and we hugged. We hugged for longer than you would normally hug a person that you have never met but that's not the strange part. We introduced each other. Her name was Cheryl and her and her friend were visiting from **Chicago**. I gave her my card and told her to book me sometime. Before she left New York she booked me for a massage. After the massage I told her my story of my past life as Emmett Till. Then to my surprise she told me that she not only went to Emmett Till elementary school but **she also grew up on the same block that Emmett Till lived on**. I was amazed. Today is **January 4th** 2021 and Cheryl and I are still friends and I think we will always be friends. I think I have known Cheryl before this life. Pascal and I hug when we see each other most times.

Significance

55 St Nicholas, Seasoned Vegan seemed to be some sort of good omen for me (page 364). Emmett was murdered in 19**55** and my mother was born in 19**55**. I seemed to have good luck there. **Pascal** wore a **scarab** pedant around his neck and at the time I was drawn to the scarab because of the transformation symbolism. **Pascal** is born on September 20th the day after **Emmett Till's** trial started on September 19th 1955. I would later learn that Lord **Pacal** was a priest king of the **Mayans** and was known as the **feathered snake** or the **feathered serpent** just like **King Tut**. My **past life** revelation of my life as Tutankhaten (**King Tut**) would be revealed to me on April 4th 2020 (page 594) the day **Martin Luther King was assassinated** (page 69). **July 25th** is the most sacred day in the **Mayan** year and Emmett Till is born on **July 25th** 1941 the year of the **snake** (page **41**). On **January 5th** 2019 I would be saved by a **guardian angel** while on my way to **55** ST Nicholas.

August 30th 2018 (The bird)

I stopped by my Homie Nova's table on 125th street while on my way to pick up food from Seasoned Vegan (page 364). In the picture I am noticeably thin because I had not done any strength training since I did my **water fast** in April (page 457). This was the first time that I mourned Emmett Till's death on August 28, knowing that I was Emmett in a **past life**. On the **Apollo** sign, **Aretha Franklin's** name can been as she had passed away on the 16th of August. Aretha <u>**Louise**</u> Franklin was born on March 25, 1942 and made her transition on August 16, 2018. She was an American singer, songwriter, and pianist who was referred to as the "**Queen of Soul**". Franklin would record acclaimed albums such as Lady **Soul** (1968), **Spirit** in the Dark (1970), Young Gifted and Black (1972), and Amazing Grace (1972).

Who's bird? Who's Ba?

Just as I left Seasoned Vegan (page 364) to walk home I noticed a bird on the ground. As I got closer to the bird it did not fly away. I knelt down and picked the bird up and walked **33** blocks home with it nestled in my hand.

August 30th 2018 - Who's bird? Who's Ba?

I always wondered what significance the bird held. It stayed with me for at least 4 or 5 days. The bird was comfortable with me. It let me hold it and it walked on my shoulders. I tried to give it water but it barely drank it. After a few days it began to fly around my apartment. For one faint second I thought about buying a cage to keep it as a pet but that thought went away as soon as it came. I decided to open the window allowing the bird to find it's way out naturally and shortly after I opened it the bird flew out of the window. If you ever read this book in its entirety I'd like to know what you think the bird symbolized? Remember, "Emmett's body was found on August 31, 1955 (p 508). I had just realized I was Emmett in a past life a month prior to finding the bird (pages 472 - 480). In ancient Kemet birds were used to symbolize the **soul**.

August 2017 - Cops for Kaepernick

In high school the 49ers were my favorite football team! Jerry Rice was my idol and Joe Montana and Steve Young were the quarterbacks that I knew well. When I was in high school during the 1990's black people were being murdered no different than what Colin Kaepernick was protesting against the only thing is, back then the police killings weren't flashed on tv for everyone to see all the time. But even with the stuff that did happen not many athletes were willing to take a stand against the police brutality and the systematic racism. Not much had really changed in 2017 when it comes to athletes lack of willingness to protest against police brutality and that's why Colin's protest made such a big impact. That along with the social networking that allowed people everywhere to see what was going on. It's one thing for an athlete to take a stand but it's a different thing completely for the police officer to take a stand against police brutality. One might say it takes more courage for an officer to protest than it does the common person because of the "**blue wall of silence**" that the police have. Cops have a "brotherhood" that they stick to. They most often times will not tell or 'snitch" on fellow officers who have done crimes even if they know the officer is guilty because cops have been known to be killed by other police for taking a stand against police injustice. This is what happened to **Chris Dorner** (page 264)! He was a black military veteran turned police officer who stood against police injustice and he was murdered by other police in a hail of bullets for taking that stand. the details of his case have been misrepresented because he who wins war writes the history of it. So they have painted an image of Chris Dorner that they want people to believe. This is why we must stand behind the officers that stood up for Kaepernick and make sure that they are safe and well taken care of. I salute the Cops for Kaepernick! The active component within the sacred psychoactive DMT molecule is called **dimethyltryptamine**. The **pineal gland** (3rd eye 𓂀), is responsible for producing the DMT molecule which appears in the embryo at the **49th** day of gestation. DMT is secreted during birth (via the mother), upon death and during near death experiences. 49 days is also the amount of time the Tibetans believed it took one soul to be reborn into another life. **Emmett Till** was murdererd in 19**55** and the San Francisco 49ers have the most points by a team in a Super Bowl, with **55** points in Super Bowl XXIV versus the Broncos on January 28, 1990.

September 6th 2018 (Botham Jean 26, Dallas Texas)

Jean was at home seated on his sofa eating ice cream when he was shot by off duty cop Amber Guyger after she entered his apartment. She claims she thought she had entered her apartment and when she saw him eating ice cream he seemed to be a dangerous intruder so she shot him. Amber claimed that she was "in fear of her life". Amber was found guilty and sentenced to 10 yrs in prison. Jeans brother forgave her and hugged her in the court room. The judge came off her chair and hugged Guyger too. In the year 2021 a viral video went around the internet that showed Larrianna Jackson (a Black girl) repeatedly hitting a White teacher who was in a wheel chair. No audio can be heard in the video I saw. These types of videos can be very easily infectious when they go viral in the age of social media. Larrianna was arrested and faces 10 years in prison. The same amount of time that Amber Guyger got for killing a man who was eating ice cream in his home. A 10 year old Black girl was being bullied in school and in her anger she drew a picture of the bully. The picture was taken and shown to the bully, the bully didn't like the drawing and complained. The cops came to the school and arrested the 10 year old black girl. She was put in handcuffs as if she was on a 1619 slave ship named The Good Ship Jesus. Where is the forgiveness for 18 year old Larrianna Jackson? Dylan Roof, was a 21 year old White man when he walked into a church on June 17th 2015 and murdered 9 people, six women and three men and when the cops apprehended him they took him to burger king because he was hungry. He had a weapon in the car but the cops apprehended him with no shots fired and no cops feared for their lives even though he had murdered 9 people.

Condolences

My condolences go out to the family of **Botham Jean** and all those who have been robbed of their life by this system of white supremacy. Please know that death is not the end. The soul survives death, indeed and in spirit. This is a book of the dead written by a boy who was murdered without justice, who defeated death and came forth by day. May the soul of **Botham Jean** walk peacefully through the field of Reeds in Amenta. Amen Ra.

September 12th 2018 Perch

Who are we wait'n for, is it **Auset**? is it **Ausar**? is there a jet in the **Mdw Ntchr**? A spliff in the **hieroglyphs**, is the son of God a star? 3 kings followed it, they brought frankincense it's a **riddle** but the lay man don't acknowledge it, what do you stand for? the government, the politic? the language casting spells, so we work till we are weakened, and on the weekend we be free like them Sunday's, in church listening to the deacon speak'n to those seek'n, bird eye perched on the search seeing, it hurts seeing hurt people hurt people, emcee'n put'n words together, lock key in, **freeing the soul**, hot like coal, extrasensory energy taking control - **Dawud The Uncanny BlaKseed**

September 16th 2018 Chicago

They chased me through the woods but I was faster than they could run, from Chicago, when I was 14 little did I know, **Money** M**ississ**ippi cream, my death would sp**ark Martin Luther King** to have a **dream,** tell me what would you do if you knew your past life biological, your astrological formation, you wanna be a star? they pull the trigger on a nigga, "nigger get the fuck out the car", **Black Mirror** bizarre, **Deja Vu dreams** that come true - **Dawud The Uncanny BlaKseed**

Significance

Tag this page, and after you have read this book come back and read this again.

Addendum September 24th 2018 - The Manifestation of Emmett Till

Two months after I made **public claims** that I was the **reincarnation** of **Emmett Till**, a new series named **Manifest** appeared on **NBC.** The show focused on the passengers and crew of a commercial airliner who suddenly **reappear** (resurrect) after being presumed dead for **5.5** years. After **5.5** years the plane reappears on **Nov 4**, 2018 the same day that **King Tut's** tomb was discovered (p 11). **Emmett's** murder trial ended on **Sep 23,** 19**55** (p 517) and "coincidentally", the series premiered on **Sep 24,** 2018. The flight number of the plane was **828**, and Emmett was murdered on **8/28** (**8/28**/19**55**). I publicly shared my experiences of **hearing a voice** that lead me to meet **Mars** at the festival (p 474), leading to my past life revelation of Emmett Till (p 480). "**Coincidentally**", the characters in the series **hear voices**, which the series describes as "callings". These "callings" lead the characters to people and problems that need to be solved.. Emmett Till's mother, **Mamie Till** claimed to have **heard the voice** of God telling her that her son died blameless like Christ (**The Sacrificial Lamb,** p 511). The second season of Manifest started 12 days after winter solstice (Dec 25, **Christmas**, pages 489, 614) on **Jan 6,** 2020. **Jan 6** is known as the **Epiphany** in Christianity as it marks the day that the 3 magi visited **Jesus** in the **Manger** (p 489, 569). **Jan 6** is also the day that the ancient Kemetyu celebrated the Winter Solstice. **Mamie Till** died on **Jan 6** and **Tupac's** grand mother Eloise Maria Barnes was born on **Jan 6**. In season 2, a character named **Emmett** is introduced. On April 4, 2020 my **past life** as **King Tut** is revealed to me and I immediately make public claims of being the **reincarnation** of **King Tut,** and I have been since then sharing the events of my revelation via my music (posted on Instagram and Youtube), as well as verbally telling my story in videos on Instagram and Youtube, just like when my life as Emmett came. The 3rd season premiered on April 1, 2021, just three days shy of my one year anniversary of my past life in ancient **Kemet** (Egypt) and "coincidentally", on the 5th episode they introduce the Egyptian deity **Maat,** as well as **Peacock** feathers displayed on papyrus depicting the judgment scenes in ancient **Kemet** (Egypt), which takes place after death of the physical body. During this season they began to use the term **resurrection** when explaining how the passengers **reappeared** after their supposed deaths. In ancient Kemet the feather that represented Maat is the Ostrich feather but the show used a Peacock feather instead, which are the first feathers that I began to wear in my hair in 2016 (p 385). Peacocks represent **resurrection** and **eternal life** because the Peacock's feathers fall out and regrow and the patterns on the feathers look like eyes, which were seen as the eyes of God. The 4th season was confirmed at **8:28** am on **August 28,** 2021. **Ausar** reigned for **28 years** in the **Ausarian resurrection** drama (p 3). It seems like the writers of this show went out of their way to keep their story consistent with my revelation. When researching a show online it is usually possible to see the birthdates of the creator(s), writers and actors of any given show or movie, however, out of 13 writers I was only able to find one of their birth dates. Margaret Easley is a writer from this series and she is born on **June 2,** 1970, year of the **dog**. My sister is born on **June 2** (p 104) and the tomb of King Tut was discovered in 19**22**, year of the **dog** and my past life as Emmett was revealed to me in 2018, year of the **dog**. The last episode of this season aired on June 10, 2021, my great grand mother Leacola **Riddle's** birthday (p 21). The idea for this show was either stolen from my current life and past life experiences which I shared online or it is another divine pattern confirming the truth of my revelation. No different than what happened the very next month with **Star Trek** (p 539), or **The Dukes of Hazard** and **Orville** (p 19-20) and **Star Wars** (p 37) and **Back To The Future** (p 40) and **David Eddings** (p 44). Sept 24 is the day that the song, **No Alibi** was released (p 672).

September 25th 2018 (Singing Bowl session with Taunya, Archangel Metatron and Spine of Ausar)

Sunseed invites me to a gong session at a friends home. Her name was Taunya. Every now and then I would tag alone to his gong sessions in Brooklyn but his was my first time going to someones home and attending one. When I arrived I would see the Book **Metatron** laying on the floor. The same book that Professor Leslie had suggested to me (page 306). It turns out that the R Mackenzie, author of the book Metatron was joining in via video and this was a Metatron group gong meditation session. When I left this event I would suffer from sharp crippling pains and muscle spasms along my **lumbar spine**. I was in my apartment when I bent over to pick something up from the floor and at the same time I sneezed. When I sneezed I fell to my knees in pain and the pain was so piercing that I shouted in anguish. I laid there on my back and could not move because even the slightest movement would cause my **spine** to spasm with pains that felt like **lightening**. This lasted for 2 days and for two days I laid on the floor. I never called a doctor or had anyone come take care of me. After two days I could get up with only 20% of the pain. It took around a month for all signs of the pain to go away. The closest thing I could relate to this experience was the sharp pain that sat me down when I had that confrontation with the cop on May 17th 2017 (page 388).

Significance

After this experience I starting having more profound experiences with my **astral body** via **astral projection** and more strange dreams. I would even have a weird experience with Taunya's daughter one night in the beginning of Oct (page 540). Two months later I was visited by **Aaliyah** on November 26th 2018 the same day that **Tutankhaten's** (**King Tut**) Tomb was discovered in 1922. She would play the role as a **Ghost Writer** on the song **Astral Plane.** A year after my past life revelation of Tutankhaten, around August of 2021 I would hear Bobby H**emmit** (page 262) say that **Metatron** (page 306) was another name for the **Aten** or **Aton**, like Tutankh**ATEN** or Ahken**ATEN**. On March 17th 2019 Taunya would give me a private singing bowl session that would also be connected to **Kemet** (**Egypt**) (page 553).

Rau nu Prt m heru

Iu f Per f m heru

Utterances for Coming Forth by day into Light

It is he, who comes forth by day into Light

October 5th 2018 - Nicholas Brooklyn
Kilindi Iyi and the Sacred Mushroom

I could not miss the opportunity to hear Baba **Kilindi Iyi** speak on high spirituality, **DMT** (a naturally occurring hormone which can spark profound spiritual experiences in higher doses) and the pineal gland. After having realized my life as Emmett and the **Mushroom** (which contain active DMT) being a part of my revelation I wanted to tell him my story and get some feed back from him. I wanted to know if he had ever heard of anything like this before. What I really wanted was him to believe me and to take my experience seriously and if he did maybe then he would take serious interest in what I was experiencing. I wanted answers. I had gone to **Mfundishi** and the only thing he told me was to , **"write it down"**. I told him I would write a book but I did not put pen to paper till after my second past life revelation. Because of the fact that my past life was connected to kemet yoga, I decided to take a **Mdw Ntr (Hieroglyphics) class** with Mfundishi again. I took one class with him years ago in 2012 but I only lasted one class (p 223). This time I stayed for 4 or 5 classes but dropped out because I lacked motivation. I would not finish his beginners level course until 2020 (p 595).

The lecture began and seemed to flow on from one profound piece of information to the next. I was fascinated with the **mushroom caps** connection to **Ausar** the Ntr from Kemet. Nothing fascinated me more than learning how the mushrooms bring forth life from death and are connected to Ausar the Lord of the **afterlife** and **resurrection**. I had eaten the Mushroom and been awakened to my past life. I began to realize that I had unconsciously undergone a real life Ausarian resurrection. **Re-member** that **you** are **Ausar** and **Heru,** the **hero!** See page 3 for the **hero's journey**!

The lecture ended somewhere around 2am and we all wanted him to tell us more. As everyone went to greet him and take pictures I waited my turn to get a few minutes with him. Finally I did and then I told him the quick run down of what I had experienced. He listened attentively and patiently. When I was done I asked what he thought of what I had experienced. His only reply was, "*It sounds like this was the time for this to be revealed to you*". That was his reply. I wanted someone to tell me that they had seen this before and possibly they might have some sure clear direction for me. I felt like I wanted more but that's all he said. I wasn't satisfied but I was grateful that he didn't look at me like I was crazy. I thanked him for listening and shook his hand. I stayed for a little longer mingling with people until I realized that I had a long train ride back to Harlem. So I **left**. I exited the store and made a **left** towards the train. As I got to the first corner two brothers would pass me on the right and one was wearing a **Black** and **Red football** jacket with the number **41** on it. AS SOON AS I SAW THE NUMBER **41** I KNEW THE UNIVERSE WAS SPEAKING TO ME! Emmett had been born in 19**41** and I was about to be **41** on the 25th (**see page 41**). Black and red are the colors of the **Haitian flag**. I pondered the events of the evening during my train ride home. I was happy I went to the lecture but I also wished I had taken a picture with Kilindi. I would never see Kilindi again but he wasn't done with me. He would visit me two years later on April 11th the day after he made his transition (page 606).

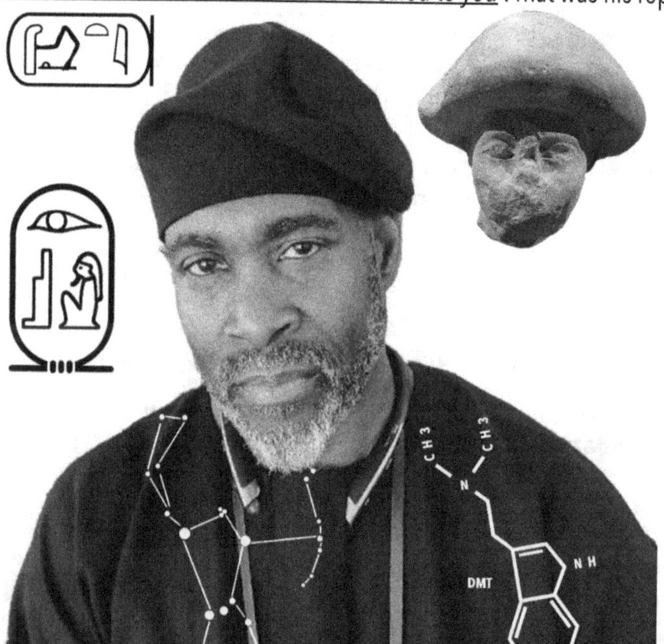

Disclaimer and Warning (page 479)

It is important that the reader is not mislead. I am not saying that you can simply eat a mushroom and then boom, your past lives are revealed! For those who have been reading carefully you can see how many things played key roles in my revelation and the mushroom was just one part. I have come to see the mushroom as a sentient being. All sentient beings have souls and it was the **spirit** of the **mycelium** (magic mushroom) that spoke through brother **Hankh Rising Son** helping to sp**ark** my **past life revelation** of **Emmett Till** and **Tutankhaten** (page 476). None of what I'm writing is fluff. I'm trying to get you to see that there is a world out here beyond most of our senses that is trying to get our attention. It is always communicating with us. It is our frequency that is off. All the events in this book are true. If you follow my path and do the things I do yet still the great mysteries are not shown to you. Then continue the path and **to Maat be true** and perhaps in due time you will be worthy of the view.

October 7th 2018 Check It

A yo check it, check it check it check it, I might **trip** but come back packing light breaking a record, kick flip stab knife gun fight choose your weapon, the black knight, sight beyond sight says my aggression is rooted in **insurrection**, blasting every last one, acting verse action I take action, I don't get roles to act in your movies I ain't relaxing, yours truly if you knew me in any way shape or fashion, it's a call of duty operation **Jhuti**, Umi Say shine your light with passion, if they come asking for you to lead the way, a coward dies a thousand deaths, the Soulja's **soul** is here to stay, I was running out of breath, *No Half Steps, Hip Hop Hooray* **- Dawud The Uncanny BlaKseed**

October 9th 2018 - Meta Spiritual Devices
From Sleep Paralysis to Astral Projection

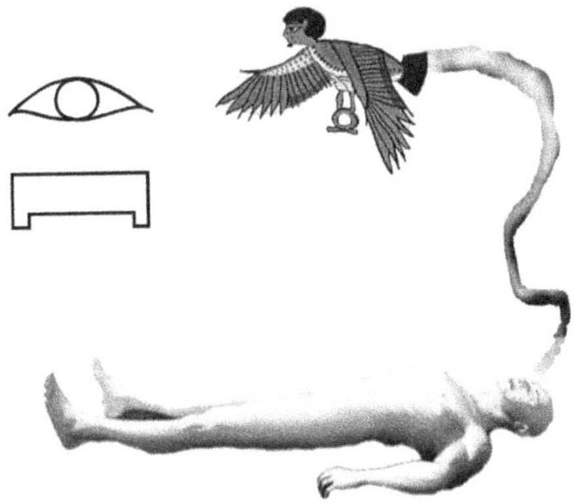

Rau nu Prt m heru

After having different experiences with dreams, meditation and **sleep paralysis** my curiosity in the phenomena was at it's boiling point. I began to contemplate deeply about what **sleep paralysis** really was. Was it some **witch** riding us as the elders would say? Or was it just a **nightmare** only experienced by the unfortunate few? Or was it something very natural that the human being has completely loss touch with? These are the questions I began to ask myself. I increased my research on **astral traveling** and **lucid dreaming**. I came across techniques that help you awaken within the dream and know that you're dreaming. I practice the technique of looking at my hands through out the day and saying "I'm dreaming" and doing the same thing before sleep with the hopes that once in the dream I might remember to look at my hands and realize that I am dreaming. What I found was extraordinary! I realized that **sleep paralysis** can lead to something far more profound than most people will ever have the courage to experience due to **fear** of **sleep paralysis**. We must get past the fear of the paralysis to do this and that's exactly what I did on my Grand Mothers birthday October 9th 2018. <u>I would sort of surf the wave of my **sleep paralysis** and ride away in what is commonly known as **astral projection**.</u> From experience I had come to associate the state of **sleep paralysis** with the feeling of my body vibrating and the sounds of static in my ears and skull. I knew that my body had more potential than I was able to wield but I was also trying to wield it by using the power of thought and will.

Iu f Per f m heru

I laid down with the intentions of entering the phase of sleep that **sleep paralysis** occurs in. Shortly after I began to feel the **vibrations** throughout my body and and I heard the loud static in my ears. I kept my eyes closed and made no moves. I did not move a muscle because this is the point when the autonomic mind is shutting the body down creating the state of **paralysis**. I laid there and felt the vibrations build up then it gradually went away. I opened my eyes and sat up and knew that I had just made that happen! **I had self induced the state of sleep paralysis** for the first time. I was excited but immediately I wondered if I could do it again? **I laid back down a second time** and the same thing happened! I sat up with **excitement** because I had definitely **without a shadow of a doubt,** caused that to happen two times in a row! Then I wondered, if I could do it again!! I laid down for the **third** time and when my body began to vibrate I did not move. Instead, I spoke to myself with my mind and said "**roll out of your body**". When I said that my **astral body** rose from my physical body. I was looking down at my body as I **floated** away. I could see my reflection in the mirror with my peripheral vision as I **floated** towards the window. I was not controlling where I went. **It was more like I was being pulled somewhere**. I **floated** away from my body that was still on the floor until finally I **floated** out of my window then instantaneously I was shot up into the clouds. I stayed there for approximately one split second then instantaneously I was shot back into my body. I sat up like had I just finished a roller coaster ride but with more excitement than any amusement park had ever given me! I had confirmation that I was not my body! I was the energy that resided within the body and I could leave the body behind and travel if I willed it to be so. I had successfully tapped into the bridge between parallel space and time and flew away in my **astral body**, my ark of a million years, my Meta-Spiritual Device. I had a similar experience on November 4th the next month (p 540).. On April 4th 2020 (p 594) I would vibrate to a frequency that allowed me to enter the akashic records where I was greeted by two ancestors and upon return to this "normal" state of consciousness I was given a new name and immediately I knew another life that I had lived..

Utterances for Coming Forth by day into Light

October 11th 2018
Dreams of flight and floating

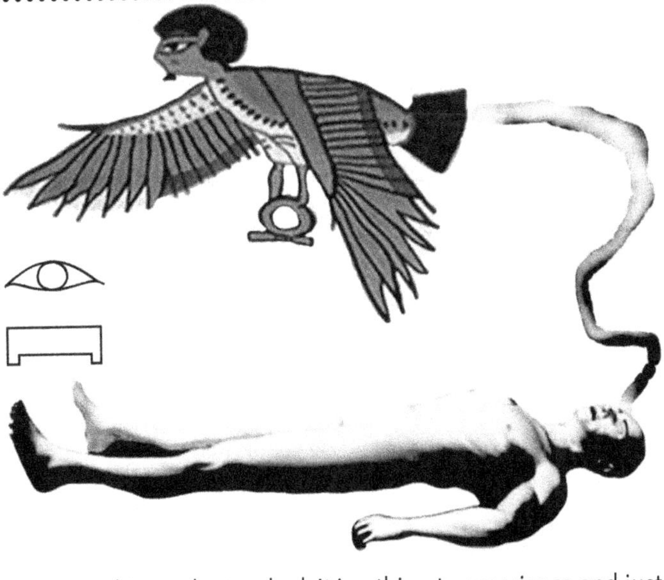

Today is October 21st 2021 and I had a profound dream last night. In my dream I was sleeping or laying down when my **astral body** separated from my physical body. While in my **astral body** I got up in excitement and I woke the person next to me up and asked them if they could see me and they could. They were still in their physical bodies though. Shortly after that I was with the woman I met at 55 ST Nicholas whom I'm attracted to. In this dream she treated me with more interest than she ever does in my awaken state. On October 11th 2018 I had a dream that I was **floating**. Like the dream I used to have when I was a little boy.

It is he, who comes forth by day into Light

Significance

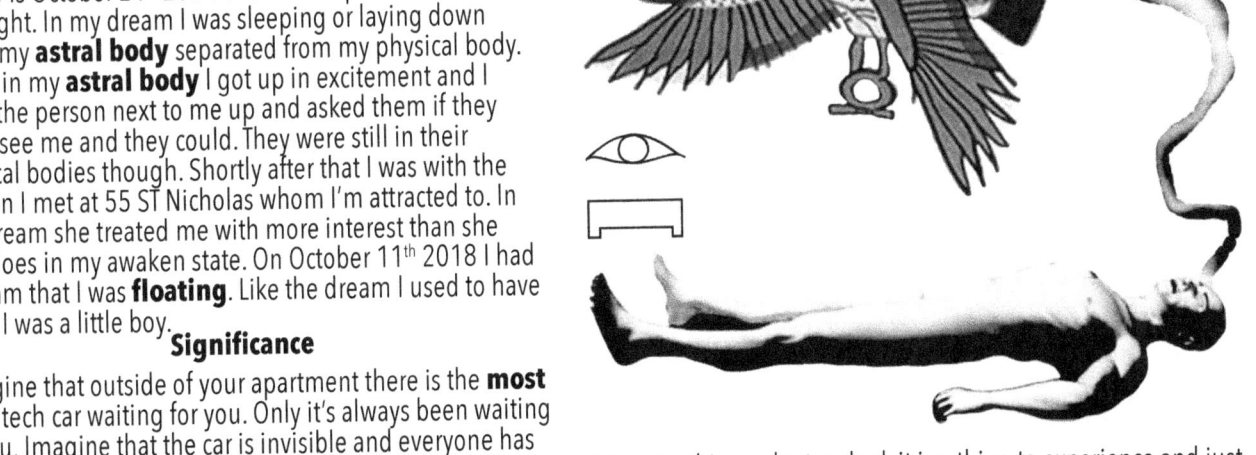

Imagine that outside of your apartment there is the **most high** tech car waiting for you. Only it's always been waiting for you. Imagine that the car is invisible and everyone has one but very few ever even notice it. This car is elusive because it is not a thing to be touched, it is a thing to experience and just like the air you breathe, that you can't see yet you depend on it so dearly, this "car" is of vital importance to you. No one wants to scream "I can't breathe" and no one wants to be without their Boat of Ra when they "die". You must unite the two lands! The physical with the spiritual. Your **astral body** with your material body. Getting in tune with your dreams is an important part of navigating the **astral body**. Imagine that you in**car**nate in a body but the real vessel is the unseen Meta-Spiritual Device **waiting to be activated!**.

October 15th 2018 (Dreams of flight with the lotus flower)

In this dream I was **floating** in the air with **lotus flowers** around me.

October 2018 - The Star Trek Mycelium Conundrum - The USS Emmett Till 2277 (Star Trek Deep Space 9)

Today is January 22nd 2022 and while looking over the Emmett Till case I was amazed when I came across a Federation **Star fleet vessel named The USS Emmett Till.** In October of 2018, 3 months after I had my **past life revelation** of Emmett Till the television series Star Trek: Deep Space Nine introduced a starship named the USS Emmett Till to honor the life of Emmett Till. The ship was created for the 'Deep Space Nine' (DS9) documentary "What We Left Behind", and was featured in a hypothetical season **8** of the show, in the year **23**95 under the command of Captain Ezri Dax. Dax's husband was Dr. Julian **Bashir** who served as her chief medical officer. My middle name is **Basheer** (Bashir), it means, **the bringer of truth**.

Why Emmett Till?

Ira Steven Behr, the producer of DS9 named the starship Emmett Till. Initially he had three names in mind for the ship, **Medgar Evers** (p 520), Congresswoman Barbara Jordan, and Emmett Till. Ultimately he felt that Emmett Till deserved his place among the stars. He also stated. "It seems to me that in order to reach a complete and healthy society we need to do two things. One, the historical record is broken and needs to be fixed. There's lots of information floating around, but very little context. The past is no longer even prologue, it's pretty much ignored. Two, we have to own our mistakes, our failures. Again, it seems to me that unless we recognize and remember our mistakes, embrace them, we are doomed to repeat them over and over and over again. Say hello to the 21st century. So, if I'm living on Federation Earth 300 years from now it would make me feel good to know that as this Star fleet sails among the stars Emmett Till is sailing along with them. He is remembered. We own his story. He is part of our journey". Ira was born in 1953 two years before Emmett was murdered. He was born on October 23rd, two days before me on my Uncle Jimmy Dukes' birthday (p 660). Ira isn't exactly sure when he first heard about the murder of Emmett Till but when he was ten his sister turned him on to **Bob Dylan's** The Times They Are A Changing album (page 231). There were two songs on that album that awakened him in a visceral way to the **Civil Rights Movement**; **The Lonesome Death of Hattie Carroll** and **Only Pawn in Their Game** (about the murder of Medgar Evers). He figures that it was around then that he first heard of Emmett Till. Oddly enough Bob Dylan had recorded a song about Emmett Till but it never made it onto one of his albums until many years later.

Sacred Mushrooms on This Side of Paradise

I ate the **magic mushroom** on July 3rd 2018 and shortly there after my **past life** as Emmett Till was revealed to me (p 480), 3 months later **Star Trek** launches the ship, USS Emmett Till **2277** into Deep Space 9. King Tut's tomb was discovered in 19**22** and I was born again in 19**77** and the Star Trek ship number is **2277** (A pattern similar to the **828** pattern from the series Manifest, p 536). In 1967 the **psychedelic magic mushroom** was written into the story of the 24th episode of the first season of **Star Trek.** The episode was titled, **"This Side of Paradise"** and it was first broadcast on **March 2nd**, 1967. One of the writers of this **Star Trek** episode was **Jerry Sohl** who died on November 4th, the same day **King Tut's** Tomb was discovered in 19**22**. Howard Carter, the archaeologist who discovered the tomb of Tutankhaten (**King Tut**) died on **March 2nd** 1939, the same day this Star Trek episode aired (p 13). **March 2nd** is also the birthday of my grand father, Edward Eddings (page 25). Furthermore, on **March 2nd** 2014, I watched the documentary, **The Prophecy of Reincarnation Sambho the Black Buddha** for the first time (Page **288**). In this 24th episode of Star Trek, the USS Enterprise visits a planet where the inhabitants are under the influence of **strange plant life.** The planet is bathed in Berthold rays, a form of radiation which humans cannot survive under for longer than a week, however Captain Kirk, First Officer Spock and the Chief Medical Officer Leonard McCoy, beam down and discover the colonists all alive and well, despite them having been exposed to the Berthold rays for longer than humanly possible.. Spock is taken to a field of strange flowers where he is shown how the colonists have survived. The flowers expel **spores** that cover Spock, after which he expresses the emotion of **love** and professes his love for a woman on the planet. The rest of the landing party are also exposed to the **spores** and, with the exception of Kirk, exhibit the same sort of behavior. As part of a symbiotic relationship with their human hosts, the spores **provide perfect health**, including protection from Berthold rays. Kirk is the last member of the ship to be exposed and just as he prepares to leave the ship he is overcome with frustration caused from having to abandon his ship. The effect of the spores disappear, and Kirk surmises that violent emotions destroy the effects of the spores. He then uses anger as a means to rid his crew of the effects of the spores. As they leave orbit with the colonists aboard, Kirk asks Spock about his experiences on the planet. Spock replies, "I have little to say about it Captain, except that for the first time in my life, I was happy." The **spores** of **Mushrooms** come to earth from outer space. It is the mushroom that found it's way to me, I did not find it (p 476)!! They are sentient beings that are smarter than us.

October 2018 (Restless Spirits)
Meta-spiritual encounters of the fourth kind

Rau nu Prt m heru

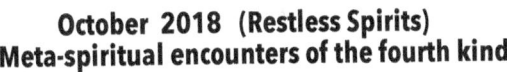

I woke up around 3am to find my phone open to an unsent e-mail to **Elan**. I met Elan at a singing bowl session the month prior (p 536). I figured that I must have opened it by mistake while sleeping, by rolling on it perhaps. I didn't think anything of it so I deleted the e-mail then **I blew out the candle** that I had going. I got up to use the bathroom but the **space heater was on** so I turned it off then just before I turned away I realized that **I never turned it on**! I knew that I hadn't turned it on but I was tired and confused so I didn't give it much thought. I went to the bathroom to pee and when I returned **the fire in the candle was lit again**! The candle was burning and it was all a little creepy and strange but I explained it away, thinking, perhaps I never fully blew the candle out?! I blew the candle out **again** then I laid down and went back to sleep, all the while wondering if something like a **ghost** had been responsible for all this. When I woke up I sent Elan a text and told her what happened. She said that she was not at my apartment. I thought that was a weird response but I left it alone. Shortly after waking up I started washing the dishes. While doing so I heard a sound in the studio so I went to investigate and to my surprise the candle was knocked over! Something had to do that!!! I was in my apartment alone! I did not open my phone and start typing an e-mail! I did not turn the heater on! I know I blew the candle out and something knocked the candle down!! Sometime after this experience I would write the hook Turmaline. The next year I got a private singing bowl session with Taunya (p 553).

October Turmaline

I made a wish on the amethyst, a **witch** gave me some turmaline, projected in my **dream**, I do the same thing for her, we connected synchronized, we died then **resurrected**, a **love** this live cant be expected to stop when the **heart** stops, time tested, invested like timeless art, traverse the universe at light speed like stars that chart, I emceed to sp**ark** a flame, she emptied my heart of pain, now let's go inside the **astral plane** - **Dawud The Uncanny BlaKseed**

Iu f Per f m heru

November 4th 2018 (Sleep Paralysis Dream)

While in a dream I woke up in the state of **sleep paralysis.** While my physical body was paralyzed my **astral body** rolled out of my physical body. I looked at my hands and knew I was dreaming. Then I flew up into the sky and looked down at the city from the clouds. Then I woke up.

Significance

I had been researching **astral traveling** and lucid dreaming. In my research I came across techniques that help you awaken within the dream and know that you're dreaming. I practiced the technique of looking at my hands through out the day and saying "I'm dreaming" and doing the same thing before sleep with the hopes that once in the dream I might remember to look at my hands and realize that I am dreaming. I had a similar experience on October 9th the previous month (page 538). I experienced this on the same day that Tutankhaten's tomb was discovered in 1922.

Utterances for Coming Forth by day into Light

November 6th 2018 Frequency

I plant a frequency in secrecy, I leave and let it grow, if you don't know your history you go where ever the wind blow, you saw **Roots** but you ain't rooted ain't ready to dismantle and rule it, you mumble and ramble, I be the rumble in the jungle recruited to *sting like a bee* and trample, leave everything in shambles, light a candle for flowers and forefathers cut too soon, his momma holla'd you could hear her in her bedroom, her son's dead code red time to let the dreads maroon, *boom* ***once they open my tomb*** *in the air you can smell the whispers of fear and doom cause it's near*, when the ear heard the snare the heart made the words more clear, the billionaire and the poor saw the bombs burst in the air, and there ain't nothing you can do about it, that's what the people shouted, stop the ball and alcohol let's get the revolution crowded, don't doubt it can happen! lay tracks loaded with passion, never let chasing the cheddar be your reason for rap'n - **Dawud The Uncanny BlaKseed**

Significance

It is he, who comes forth by day into Light

Emmett Till's mother, Mamie Till died on **January 6th** 2003, the year of the **goat**. Emmett was murdered in 1955 the year of the **goat**. **Tupac's** grand mother Eloise Maria Barnes was born on **January 6. January 6th** is 12 days after the Winter Solstice (Christmas, pages 489, 614). In the Christian religion **January 6th** is the day that the 3 Magi visited Jesus in a manger. **January 6th** is also the day that the ancient Kemetyu celebrated the Winter Solstice. Today is **January 6th 2022** and I find it very strange that today I found a story about a 4,400 year old tomb that was discovered in November of 2018. What's more strange is the fact that this is the first time that relics from ancient **Kemet** made me **cry**. The images from this 4,400 year old tomb (page 541) caused me to cry the way I cried on October 7th 2021 when I saw video footage of the **Descent of Ganges Relief** from 7th century India (p 659). As I looked at the images of the **Ganges Relief** they were so familiar that I knew I had definitely seen them before and something was pulling at my heart telling me that I had been there before! Today, on **January 6th** 2022 I had the same experience. Afterwards I added the pictures of the 4,400 year old tomb to this book, then I realized that I had written this song **Frequency** in November of 2018. In this song I say the words "*boom* ***once they open my tomb*** *in the air you can smell the whispers of fear and doom cause it's near*". When I wrote those lyrics I DID NOT CONSCIOUSLY KNOW that I was a pharaoh. I had that experience on July 21st 2018 the day after I smoked the sacred Bufo toad medicine where I felt like I was King Tut for just a moment, but still, the feeling was powerful enough to cause me to write the hook to the song **Ayahuasca** (p 529) that I wrote on July 17th 2018 where I said, "I am the **boy king** in the museum that you be seeing, I gave you the signs this time I'm back in a human being, facts encoded in rhyme like my body frozen in time, in 1929 I shined on Martin Luther King". I thought I was King Tut for a moment but I rejected that crazy idea. I was already dealing with the life of Emmett Till that had been revealed to me only **18** days prior on July 3rd 2018. I knew I was Emmett but I didn't believe the thought of Tut, yet here I am writing a song on **November 6th** 2018 (the year of the **dog**) where I mention a **tomb being opened** and King Tut's tomb was discovered on **November 4th** 1922 (the year of the **dog**).

"boom once they open my tomb in the air
you can smell the whispers of fear and doom cause it's near"

The 4,400 year old tomb of Master builder Wahtye discovered in Saqqara in Egypt

On **Nov 6** 2018 I wrote a song titled **Frequency**. In that song I said, *"boom **once they open my tomb** in the air you can smell the whispers of fear and doom cause it's near"* (page 540). On April 4th 2020 my past life as King Tut is revealed to me (page 594). On **Jan 6** 2022, I came across a 4,400 year old tomb while searching the internet. As soon as I saw the images I began to cry uncontrollably. The tomb was discovered in November of 2018, the same month I wrote the song **Frequency**. It was discovered at **Saqqara**, in Kemet (Egypt). It was constructed for a "divine inspector" named "**Wahtye**". At least **55** statues were discovered inside. Initially I couldn't explain why the footage of this tomb caused me to **cry** with feelings of **Deja Vu** as if I was looking at a place that I had been before but a few months later it would make sense. In April of 2022 I took my first trip to the Saqqara step pyramid in this life, and the most mysterious thing happened (page 670). As I walked across the step pyramid at Saqqara I had a **short and sharp** experience of **Deja vu**, as if I had been at that moment in time before. This experience was caught in a video. 7 days later I would have **Deja Vu** again, while leaving the city **King Tut** was born in (page 671). **Deja Vu** is sometimes a result of having already experienced a moment in a **dream** that you didn't remember upon waking but when you reach that moment from your dream in your waken state you have a feeling of familiarity because some dreams take place in a different space and time where **the astral body travels**, sometimes to the past and even the future. There is another layer of **Deja Vu** though, it can also be connected to a life you have once lived in another time and another place.

Rau nu Prt m heru

Iu f Per f m heru

Utterances for Coming Forth by day into Light

It is he, who comes forth by day into Light

November 9th 2018
Dream - Football Game Under Tree

I was playing a game of football on big field under giant trees. We were all jumping high and **floating**. The trees seemed to be the source of our ability to float in a manner that felt more like flight.

Hanau Hornets (page 90)

November 19th 2018 (Quantum Level Fasting)

I did the 20 day water fast in April of 2018 during my yoga course and then my past life of Emmett Till was revealed (page 467). I thought perhaps there was more for me to gain from fasting so this time I planned to do the full 40 days. I started a new fast on November 16th with the intent to do 40 days, ending on December 25th however I stopped this fast after five days. On the 3rd day I would have an experience that reminded me of the **card** I found in 2005 (pages 141-142). I had a cup of brazil nuts on my treadmill and some how they all fell on the floor. I was very meticulous about getting every nut up as I didn't want to leave anything for a possible mouse to eat. I was on my knees getting all the nuts up and when I was done I turned and sat of the floor in the **lotus** position. When I looked in front or me one single brazil nut was right in front of me. I sat and stared at this nut knowing that I had picked them all up. **Something wanted my attention. And when I was typing this <u>I saw something in the corner of my eye move</u> in the mirror but of course nothing was there when I turned to look.** Brazil nuts are nutritional powerhouses, reducing inflammation, supporting brain function and providing healthy monounsaturated fats. They're particularly high in selenium (p 285), a mineral with potent antioxidant properties. They improve your thyroid function and heart health. They also contain some protein and offer a good source of important nutrients, including magnesium, zinc, calcium and vitamin E. If you are a male it is important that you get sufficient zinc and brazil nuts will ensure that. Females should be sure to get sufficient **sunflower seeds**.

2018 (Post Revelation) Ganesh Meditation

I went into meditation with the sacred mushroom and at some point I was approached by a group of beings with **elephant faces**. They stood there looking down at me. I was not prepared for what I saw so I opened my eyes and sat up going away from the meditation. It wasn't till a few days after that I realized I had been visited by Ganesha. Lord Ganesha is considered the God of intellect, good luck, and prosperity and not only that but he is also believed to be the remover of obstacles and the Lord of beginnings, according to Hindu mythology.

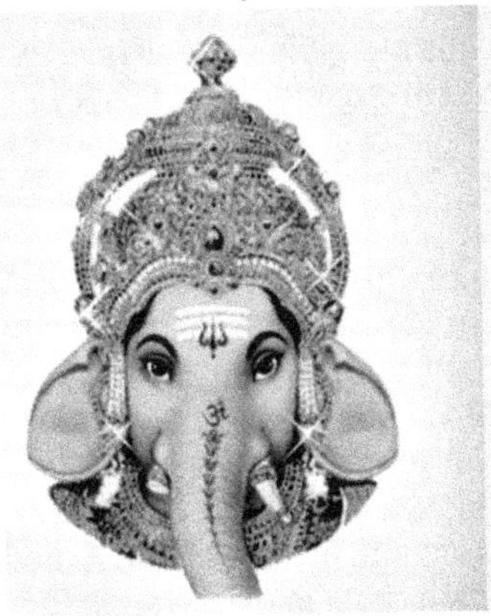

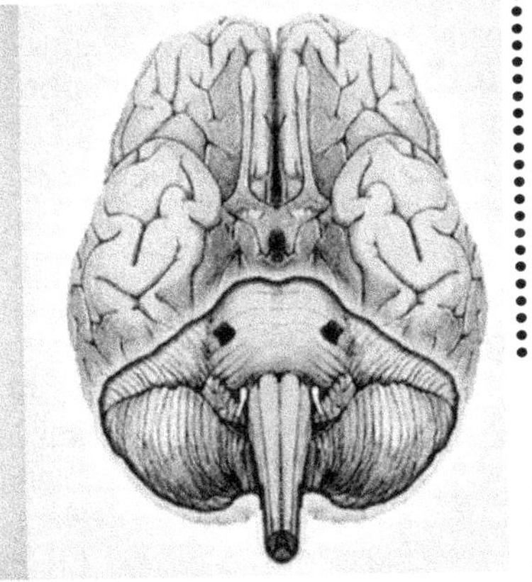

November 23rd 2018 Hell's Kitchen

Welcome to Hell's Kitchen where the poison's well hidden in tradition and religion, soul food still given, old fools still living, **Mel Gipson** <u>*Lethal Weapon*</u>, got you dying from the diet, the spells the blessings, is this hell food or health food? delicatessen hot burning the flesh in the intestines, acidic parasites and cancers they not address'n, this is hell until you learn your lesson well, the **etheric body** looking down at the shell, will you remember your way back black from where you fell? if not you'll **reincarnate** back into this hell, cast down like **shatan**, will you ascend this time or stand in line like them waiting for some divine God to save them? you could be the **alchemist** in the midst of this apocalypse, **immortal** like the ones written about in ancient documents, megalithic **hieroglyph**, podiatrist, psychologist, you are what you eat the temple in man, that's the greatest monument that you could leave, they might laugh at you and say you're eating leaves, but don't laugh at them when they're stuck in disease, stay on your path, walk in the **know** and don't be**lie**ve, stay on your path, walk in the **know** and don't be**lie**ve - **Dawud The Uncanny BlaKseed**

Addendum Ganesh in Human Physiology

It wasn't till the **revision** of this book, in 2022 that I came to a deeper understanding of my experience with "Ganesh". The same way that the stars that form the constellation of **Orions belt** look like the **DMT** molecule, the face of Ganesh looks a lot like the ventral view of the brain. The **Pons** represent the **face** of Ganesh. A group of **nerves** at the pons represent the **tusk** of Ganesh. The roots of the **trigeminal nerves** represent the **eyes** of Ganesh. The **Cerebellum** represent the **ears** of Ganesh, and the **Medulla** represent the **trunk** of Ganesh. I saw Ganesh while in a midst of **meditation** and meditation is key in the practice of **Kemetic yoga**, with special emphasis put on the **breathing**. The **Pons**, which represents Ganesh's face is responsible for the sleep, wake cycle and **breathing**. Yoga is the union of the two lands, the seen world and the unseen world (pages 463 -480). Primordial divinities are not bound to any one culture or country. Ganesh is a principle represented in all of us because we all have brains and if we ever endeavor to reach higher states of conciseness we might find ourselves greeted by Ganesh.

November 25th 2018 Dream with Tupac

Everything in this dream was in slow motion. I was walking with **Pac** and it was like I knew him and he knew me. He was telling me something. He was wearing the gold round Euphanasia Chain with the angel holding a snake. As we were walking in slow motion the chain bounced from left to right. He was in good spirits laughing while he talked.

What are Dreams?

Just as my sister **dreamt** my car accident before it happened (pages 104 - 106), **Jewell dreamt Tupac's death before it happened** (p 105). **Ask Youself, What Are Dreams** (p 30)?!

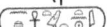

November 26th 2018 Astral Plane

Being in **love** with you is like the cold or the flu and you my only remedy, my peace my serenity, my priestess, peep this verily verily I pay the penalty, **Check The Melody**, Love is a **theory** Like **relativity**, if I fall for you and you ain't there are you feeling me? do you care? where's the **magic**? **new moon** erratic **telepathic** conversations, look at my phone you call more off the wall affirmations, more lore than ever saw than a group of **Moor** master masons, if love is a crime then she organized my assassination, the **Kempress** a **smooth criminal** minimal signs of interest, she was seen on the scene of the lovers crime forensics, like a **mystic** a glitch in the **matrix** no lipstick no slips and no way to trace it, eccentric but basic, illusive, I can still taste it, I juiced it, waters sacred never waste it, drunk in **love** I had to face it, I chased it embraced it super head but never dominatrix, I'm sick in bed get my meds cause I'm a trauma patient, falling for you's a bad idea like banging heads on the pavement, or sailing to remote islands trying to preach enslavement, get hit with arrows of **love** your heart will be the payment, sometimes art is love sometime **love** is entertainment, sometimes cubic's harp got poison darts that he aim's with, I made a wish on the amethyst, a **witch** gave me some turmaline, projected in my **dream**, I do the same thing for her, we connected synchronized, we died then **resurrected**, a **love** this live cant be expected to stop when the **heart** stops, time tested, invested like timeless art, traverse the universe at light speed like stars that chart, I emceed to sp**ark** a flame, she emptied my heart of pain, now let's go inside the **astral plane**

They said it was a bad idea but I'm glad I'm here in hell it ain't hard to tell I fell in hotel stratosphere, in a cell with **Ozone** and **Turbo breaking** laws like **Flow Jo** give me a parachute a **fool** for **love** card **tarot**, and if I fall may God send me a **black crow** to show me how to **escape death** with a few scars **odds** narrow, woke up in a bar with **Othello** a **young pharaoh** a fellow with a pet sparrow they said you up shits creek without a paddle, **Romeo Must Die** don't stress though go prepare for battle drink this expresso, eat this apple wait by the chapel you gonna meet a **Jackal,** he gonna help you tackle the **afterlife** and if you win you gonna die and the **Queen of the Dammed** is to be your wife, think thrice speak once hear twice my advice live the **Ankh life**, vices only hurt you, live a life with virtue, and she will never desert you, **she Star Searched you in 89**, when **love** is true we come back and forth many times, if the world only knew the **soul** is **immortal** the paranormal would be normal opening **portals** with the **mind**, we connected synchronized we **died** then **resurrected** a **love** this live cant be expected to stop when the heart stops, time tested invested like timeless art, traverse the universe at light speed like stars that chart, I made a wish on the amethyst, a **witch** gave me some turmaline, projected in my **dream**, I do the same thing for her, we connected synchronized, we died then **resurrected**, a **love** this live cant be expected to stop when the **heart** stops, time tested, invested like timeless art, traverse the universe at light speed like stars that chart, I emceed to sp**ark** a flame, she emptied my heart of pain, now let's go inside the **astral plane** **- Dawud The Uncanny BlaKseed**

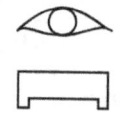

Significance

The hook of this song ended up being the hook I wrote after the paranormal experience the previous month in October (p 540). As I started the second verse of this song I felt the presence of **Aaliyah**, and that is where the **underlined** references to her come from. I was told by a woman who I trust that **Aaliyah** was once a powerful woman in ancient Kemet in a **past life**. Aaliyah died on August 25th the day after **Emmett Till** went into the store that got "him" killed (August 24th 1955). Aaliyah's rise to fame was sparked in 1989 the year of the **snake** after appearing on Star Search. Aaliyah died in 2001 the year of the **snake**. I was born as "Emmett" in 1941 the year of the **snake** (page **41**). I was born in 1977 the year of the **snake**. This song was written in 2018 the year of the **dog** on the day King Tut's tomb was opened in 1922 the year of the **dog** (page 11).. In the verse inspired by Aaliyah I mention the **Jackal.** The Jackal (Anubis, Enpu) is the **dog** headed "deity" of mummification in the ancient Egyptian weighing of the heart ceremony.

Aaliyah and DMX had a close friendship. DMX is the **"dog"** of Hip Hop and on the day **DMX** died his spirit came to me. I elaborate more on that on April 9th 2021 (page 640). "when **DMX** died his soul came did me a favor, whispered in my ear said go ye there look through them papers! Anubis and the afterlife advice watch for them gators, Maat is precise in your life! you gotta watch your behavior!" - (**Doors**, written on Aug 22nd 2021, page 658). When I recorded this song I asked my friend **Jill Minard** to do the intro for the song (not transcribed here). Afterwards Jill began to feel like she has known me before, perhaps in a past life. Jill is also a Kemetic Yoga instructor.

(December 1st 2018 - May 1st 2019) - 5 Months Straight Strength Training

Rau nu Prt m heru

Iu f Per f m heru

After **fasting** for 20 days only drinking water in April (p 467) and attempting a 40 day water fast in November I began to contemplate the idea of **fasting again** (p 542). I had gotten very thin from my fast in April and had done no exercise until August so I was still very thin and I didn't like that. Because I didn't want to be any thinner I told myself that not eating food for 20 days took no real effort, instead it took discipline. Then I thought what if I trained myself for 20 days straight! If I can not eat for 20 days then surely I can strength train for 20 days. I started strength training on December 1st and when I got to the 20th day I didn't want to stop! I trained everyday for 5 months straight and stopped training everyday on **May 1st** 2019. During the **5 months** I saw significant transformation in my physique, I got a lot stronger and motivated all my clients to work harder. In 2020 during the onset of **Covid** I deactivated my streaming apps and started training everyday again on **May 1st** 2020. I trained everyday for **7 months**, then I ran on my treadmill for a minimum of 25 minutes a day for 60 days straight ending with a **24 mile** run on December 26th 2020. I didn't plan to run 24 miles I ran because my **brother in law's (Jermain)** 21 year old son Jermain Jr. **died** in a car accident on Thanksgiving day. My **Nephew** was depressed and mourning the loss of his brother Jermain Jr and Jermain Sr was mourning the loss of his son. This led my nephew to start contemplating **suicide** and my friend **Austin** was mourning the **death** of his son who had past some years ago (page 88). I was writing a book on **reincarnation** and the immortality of the soul so I knew that death wasn't the end but seeing them all mourn pierced my heart and I mourned with them. I was only planning on doing my regular 25 minute run but the news of my nephew contemplating suicide caused me to cry and I kept thinking of my brother in law **Jermain** and how it must feel to lose a 21 year old son and I thought about Austin mourning his son. I just kept running and running and running. I ran for them, I ran for all the people murdered by police, I ran till my legs cramped and I could not run any more. I ran 24 miles that day. But what is it within the human being that allows us to keep going? During a study at Harvard in the 1950s, Dr. Curt Richter placed rats in a small bucket of water to test how long they could tread water. On average they began to tire after 15 minutes but just before the rats gave up and sank due to exhaustion, the researchers would pull them out of the water and dry them off. The rats were allowed to rest for a few minutes and then they were put back in the water for a second round of swimming. In this second round of swimming **they swam for 60 hours straight**! The conclusion drawn was that since the rats **BELIEVED** that they would eventually be rescued, they managed to push their bodies beyond what they were previously able to do. If hope can cause exhausted rats to swim for that long, what could a belief in yourself and your abilities, do for you? Remember what you're capable of. Remember why you're here. Push yourself to the limit and You Will Succeed. What ever you do, Never give up on tasks that are important. Especially when it comes to righting the wrongs of the past! Maat must always prevail! Keep going because you never know what is around the corner! Things might seem bad and tough and unbearable but if you are still breathing then you have the ability to change the situation. Never give up! The ancestars are with you and when ever I leave this body I will be with you just like Marcus Garvey, I'll be there in the whirlwind my friend! Today is March 19th 2022 and I just found out that Jermaine's son passed away of November 26th 2020, the same day that Tutankhaten's tomb was opened (page 11). He was born Feb **22nd** 2002 (2/22/2002). May Jermaine Jr's soul walk peacefully through the field of Reeds in Amenta. Amen Ra. **42 Laws of Maat, Page 367**

Utterances for Coming Forth by day into Light

It is he, who comes forth by day into Light

See pages
318 (Noel)
362 (Zee)

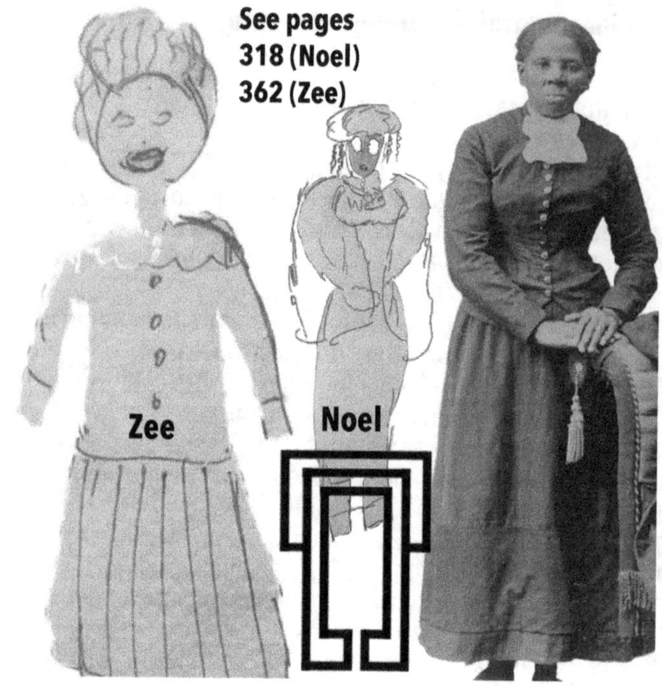

Meta-Spiritual Encounters Through Space and Time

December 2018 - My First Talk With Harriet Tubman

I had not heard from **Zee** in a while when she came for a massage. After her massage I was eager to ask her if she had seen my guardian today. Since I now knew that I was Emmett Till in a previous life I was more curious than ever about who this person or spirit at my door might be. First I told her the details of my revelation, how I came to know I was Emmett Till in my past life. When I finished somehow she knew that I was telling the truth. She said that I didn't need to prove it anymore. She believed me. She was also amazed. She had never seen anything like this. I asked her if she had seen my guardian today and she said no. She added, that before coming to see me she wondered if she would see her today. I was a little disappointed. Was my guardian gone?! Was she still "guarding" me?! I walked her out and opened the door for her to leave, then she jumped back in fright. She said "she's here"! I said "really?"! She said "yes". My guardian was in the hallway!

Dawud- "Tell her that I love her."

Zee- "She says she loves you too. She's smiling very wide and says she is very proud of you."

Dawud- "ask her who she is."

Zee- "she says you know already."

I remember blinking and looking away confused but still the first thought that came to my mind was **Harriet**. I don't know why she came to my mind as the first thought but she did. Then I ran and got my drawing book and showed Zee the picture that Noel had drawn of my guardian standing in my hallway on Jan 30th 2015 (page 318). I asked Zee if she could do the same for me, draw what she saw. Zee smiled and said "I can't draw". I looked as if the wind was knocked out of me but I said ok. Then Zee said "she's gone". And just like that the experience was over. Just like that she was gone. But at least she was still there and now I sort of knew who she was! Zee went home and I was left bewildered but happy. Later that evening Zee would draw what she saw on a napkin and send it to me in a text. As soon as I saw it I knew who it was! It was **Harriet**! I knew a picture of **Harriet** that looked just like the image Zee had drawn. I sent Zee the picture of **Harriet** that I felt looked like the picture she drew then I called her immediately. She picked up. I told her to check her messages. She looked at the picture and said "that's the woman that was at your door"! I said "do you know who the woman in the picture is"? She said "no". I told her it was **Harriet Tubman**. She was even more amazed. Now I was 100% sure it was **Harriet**! No wonder why I had been writing about her so much in my music. In 2020 after my past life revelation of my life as **Tutankhaten** I would become more aware of my relationship with Harriet and I would learn of other lives I have lived. A month or so later Zee would tell me that after this experience other spirits started to come to her asking her to speak to their relatives. She said she was on a bus or a train and a spirit appeared and asked her to speak to the woman sitting in front of her but Zee refused. She says that every time she passes my block she looks at the front of my building and most of the time Harriet is there waving at her. I have come to find that there are many people, mostly woman who have this **gift of sight** but because many of them are afraid of it they refuse to use it or refuse to share it. Seeing spirits is not unusual, it's just not talked about in the open…I would say that this is a cardinal sin, to have a gift but refuse to use it. If it were not for Noel and Zee I would be blind to the awareness that guardians were at my door. I'm also sure that the universe would have sent me someone else if they had refused to do what they were sent to me to do. Be not afraid my friends. Harriet was not afraid and even if she was, her desire for freedom was stronger than her fear. We can fear everything and run or we can face everything and rise. For more on **Ka Doors (Spirit Doors), Guardians (Invisible Protectors) see pages 250 -253, 48, 148, 150, 179, 199, 315, 318, 329, 348, 349, 409, 421, 434, 548, 549, 572, 584, 604, 626, & 650.**

page 438

December 2nd 2019

(Still Dreaming with Nas and Jay Z accompanies him this time)

I fell asleep listening to a guided meditation and when I woke up I knew I had just had a dream with **Nas** and **Jay Z**.

Significance

Both Jay Z and Nas are musical icons who once had musical rivalry's with **Tupac**, however, since Tupac's death they have both been able to put aside their differences to see how much they both had in common with Tupac. They would also have issues with each other but they were able to be examples of **unity** by way of putting their issues behind them and working with each other. I have not been to many concerts in my life but the first rapper I saw perform was **Nas** at the **Apollo** in 1996 the same year Tupac died. **Apollo** is the Greek Equivalent to **Heru**. Ausar returns (resurrects) through his son Heru as **Ra** in the Ausarian **resurrection drama**. The second concert I ever went to was a Jay Z concert in Germany on Nov 8th 2001 (p 95). Jay Z was born on December 4th 1969, the same day **Fred Hampton** was assassinated. Tupac was born within the Black Panther Party for Self Defense that Fred Hampton was heavily involved with. Nas was born on September 14th the day after **Tupac** died. Nas has a daughter born the day before Tupac and Jay Z has twins born 3 days before Tupac. Jay Z's first child is born the day after Emmett Till's mother died and his wife Beyonce is born the day after Emmett Till's wake (p 514). All these dates might seem like meaningless **coincidences** but they are far from meaningless. They are star code patterns. We are all connected and what happens to one of us affects the whole. Fred Hampton's mother **Iberia Hampton** used to babysit **Emmett Till**. Nas has a song with **Kanye** called **Still Dreaming**. In that song Kanye gives insight on **dream premonitions**, "His girl call, feelin' she mad, she threw the ring out, how she found out, **she dreamt the whole thing out**". I have a dream that all the artist and entertainers who have appeared in my dreams have eyes to see that we are reincarnated souls as **Bob Marley** once said in his song, **Reincarnated**. I have a theory about who Tupac was in a **past life**..? **Re-member** that **you** are **Ausar** and **Heru**, the **hero!** See page 3 for the **hero's journey!**

(Still Dreaming Remix, page 438)

December 5th 2018 Mary the Virgo

Yo where that hoe go last night? with **Jesus Christ** in the house of bread, she gave him some head for the low low, can't beat that price from the **Virgo**, the Queen **Mary Magdalene,** check the logo and the logos things ain't what they seem! the cross, the **sun**, the **3 kings**, **Constantine** and the sword that swung, **Elohim** seen in **enoch,** the ***<u>wheel of fortune,</u>*** caution they will hurt you for this capital, circle of little animals, scorpion sting kiss of death, **Judas** be the fall yes, in the winter we see the sun less, spring, summer he back but to that your priest won't confess, **Astro Theology** dressed in white suppressed, probably the greatest story ever sold for frankincense myrrh and gold, behold the pale white horse, revelation tales of hell to quell your life force, spells, good God, Devil evil, rebel people, go to the source don't let the false prophets defeat you, the temple, the steeple, the eye inside is see through, flying high like the eagle, **Heru** flew through the Shu, it was regal but now it's illegal to go within, they only teach you bout him not her, his-story is a blur my friend, ***<u>the world is old, the ancient future springs from the past again</u>***, *the world is old, the ancient future springs from the past again* - **Dawud The Amazing BlaKseed**

Rau nu Prt m heru

Iu f Per f m heru

Utterances for Coming Forth by day into Light

December 22nd 2018
The Immortal Life of Emmett Till

This body is finite but the soul will live forever in the ether, the next lines not designed for the nonbeliever, I was shot in the head left for dead body thrown in the river, my mommy **Mamie Till Bradley** had me open casket, the law giver bastards still called her nigger her feelings they hurt it, "*<u>freedom or jail clips inserted, another baby's being born the same time</u>*" that I was murdered! the beginning and end, as far as that goes it's only natural I came back yo, through the **astral plane**, in **the year of the snake**, Dawud the **Naga** the saga, tell me what will it take to break the spell, is it the changa? the **Lotus**? the **DMT** that exploded? a course collision kinetic a vision decoded, written in the stars, floated in my dreams past **Mars**, read between the bars, birds planes stars avatars, birds planes stars avatars, read between the bars, birds planes stars avatars - **Dawud The Amazing BlaKseed**

It is he, who comes forth by day into Light

<u>SIGNIFICANCE</u>

I started this rhyme on July 21st 2016 (page 396) while I was seated at **Tsion Cafe,** I was reading the **Book The Secret Life of plants**. While reading the book I read about how plants can sense human thoughts. This made me think about my plants at my studio and how I need to care more for them. I began writing this song then I finished it when I got home, ending the song with the words "maybe in the next life we'll all do better".. Two years later the last words of this song would take on a new meaning when my past life as Emmett Till was revealed to me on July 3rd 2018 (page 480). On December 22nd 2018 I would find a beat that touched my soul and with the desire to say something to it I recorded the song **The Secret Life of Plants** to it but when I was done recording there was still over a minute left to the beat so I added more lyrics to the rhyme. I used a quote fro **Nas**. I wrote about my life as Emmett and change the name of the rhyme to **The Immortal Life of Emmett Till**. After I was done I listened to the song on repeat many times and it was one of my favorites for a long time. It wasn't till a few weeks after I completed the song that I realized that the beat had the sound of a **whistle** in it. When I realized that I was dumbfounded. Emmett was murdered because he supposedly **whistled** at a white woman. See page 391 for the Reincarnation of at Tsion Cafe.

2019 The Year of the PIG

The same year the Haitian revolution was sparked. 1791 The Year of the PIG.

May 25th will strike back later this year when I meet a Haitian brother named **Jeffre Ayiti Bluez** at the International African Arts Festival (page 572). On the 3rd day of the festival he would witness and be part of a profound experience I had with the **Scarab Beetle**. In ancient Kemet (Egypt) the Scarab represented resurrection, rebirth, reincarnation and were placed in the tombs of the Nswt Bity (Pharaoh) and placed on the mummy of the Nswt Bity (Pharaoh) to ensure the **resurrection** of the "Pharaoh" in his **next life**. In ancient Kemet the name for scarab was **Kheper** and Tutankhaten's (King Tut's) throne name was **Neb Kheperu Ra** which meant the master of transformations of Ra. On April 4th 2020 my past life as Tutankhaten is revealed to me (page 594).

2019
Tutankhaten (King Tut) awakens the ancient soul of a descendant of Ramesses III

Robert "**King David**" **Ross** of Charleston wears his Egyptian headdress while reading the 23andMe letter informing him of his familial link to the Pharaoh Ramesses III. Robert Ross retired as a management analyst with the U.S. General Accounting Office in Chicago, moved back to Charleston and currently works as a sexton at Morris Street Baptist Church. But most people probably recognize him for the distinctive black-and-gold Pharaoh headdress he often wears around town to express his passion for ancient Egypt. In other words, he's been wearing it long before a 23andMe letter arrived in January analyzing his DNA – a letter that would move him to tears and confirm his many years of work. "You share an ancient paternal lineage with Pharaoh Ramesses III," it read. "You and Ramesses III share an ancient paternal-line ancestor who probably lived in north Africa or western Asia." Ross was ecstatic. "When I first read it, I was so happy, and I was just so glad," he said. "Then I thought, 'No wonder I'm re-enacting and doing certain things that's sort of unexplainable. It's all part of the gene!'" Ross said his passion for ancient Africa began to stir several decades ago, when he visited the **King Tutankhamen** exhibition in **Chicago**. Until then, his impression of Egypt was that it was racially and culturally linked more to Europe than Africa, a perception he said was created by **Hollywood** stars in movies (page 415) such as "The Ten Commandments." But when Ross saw King Tut's gold death mask, he said, "It was like seeing myself. Something just came over me, and I started crying."

SIGNIFICANCE

Robert calls him self King **David** and my name at birth was **Dawud** which means David in english. In 19**77, Robert** "King **David**" **Ross** visited the **Tutankhaten** (**King Tut**) exhibition in **Chicago.** The experience caused him to start crying and triggered his passion for all things Kemet (Egypt). I was born in 1941 the year of the **snake** as **Emmett Till** and then I was born again in 19**77** the year of the **snake** as Dawud Eddings. Emmett Till was from **Chicago** and on July 3rd 2018 my **past life** as **Emmett Till** was revealed to me (page 480). On April 4th 2020 my **past life** as **Tutankhaten** (**King Tut**) was revealed to me (page 594). **Harriett Tubman's** name at birth was Araminta **Ross** and she had a brother named **Robert**. On Jan 13th 2020 **another past life** would be revealed to me by the spirit of Harriet Tubman by way of **Meeky** (page 584). Harriet would tell me that my previous name was **Earl Johnson** and she detailed events that happened when I worked with her (p 236, 584).

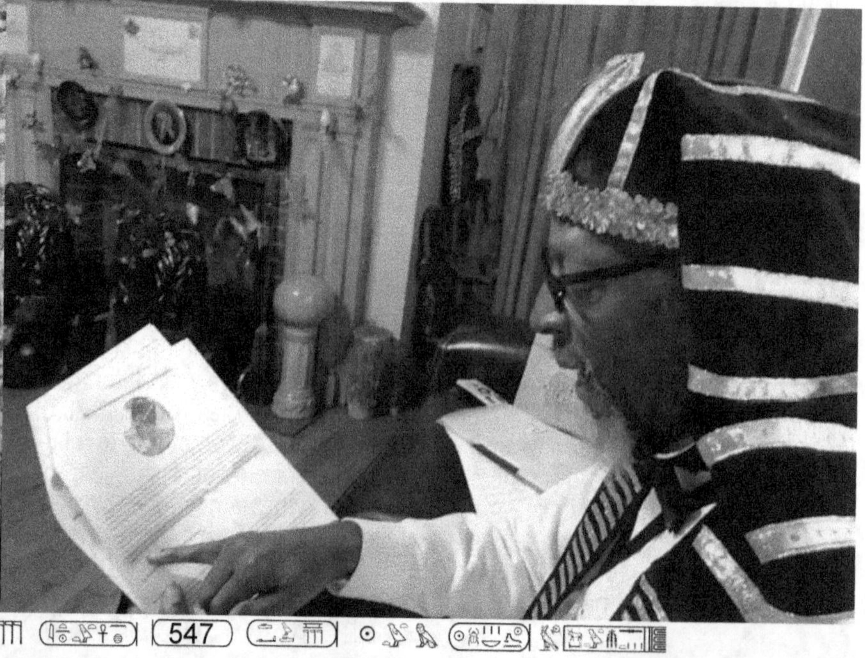

January 2nd 2019 (Dream)

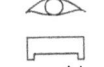

I was with a beautiful woman and her friends and every one was in a festive mood, laughing and having a good time. Someone handed me a scroll but I could not read it. Perhaps it was blurry or maybe it was the language..

Significance

On July 7th 2019 I will meet a woman named Meeky at the 2019 International African Arts festival and we would become friends immediately (page 574), like sister and brother.. She will become a massage client of mine and shortly after I will come to know that she sees and speaks to spirits. On January 13th 2020 I will have an experience with her that mirrors this dream (page 584). The part with the scroll. After my past life revelation of Tutankhaten (King Tut) on April 4th 2020 (page 594) I would start Mfundishi's beginners MDW NTR (Hieroglyphics) class again and I would complete the course this time. I had previously started the class two times but never finished it. I took one class sometime in 2014 and I took around 4 classes in 2018 after my past life revelation of Emmett Till. I am not currently taking classes with anyone but when I'm done with this book I will continue my study on my own. Today is November 4th 2021 and 99 years ago my tomb was discovered in 1922 then same year that Louis Till (Emmett's father) was born.

Rau nu Prt m heru

January 3rd 2019 (Spider-man Dreams)

In this dream I am Cosmic Spiderman (Peter-Ptah **Parker**).in the black suit he got from out of space. I remember being very agile jumping around like Spider-man.

Significance

Spider-man was my favorite comic book character as a teen. His real name was Peter **Parker** and he lived with his aunt. My grand mothers maiden name is **Parker** and I lived with my grand mother for most of my youth. Emmett Till's cousin who was there the night he was taken is named Wheeler **Parker**. I reincarnated into the same family tree as **Emmett Till**. Peter Parker became spider man after his uncle was murdered. Peter felt like he could have saved his Uncle if he had stopped the thief who killed him. My Grand Fathers Death sparked my transformation. He died from cancer and when he died I knew nothing about the business of cancer. When I started studying health and wellness I was overcome with sadness as I felt like I could have prevented my Grandfathers death if I had known about the natural healings for cancer (page 169).. Peter PARKER in spider-man. The name Peter is derived from Ptah, the Lord of creation in the ancient Kemetic spiritual system.

Iu f Per f m heru

January 5th 2019 Invisible Helpers / Guardian Angels
Meta-Spiritual Encounters of the fourth kind

I ordered my food from Seasoned Vegan located at **55** St Nicholas ave (p 364). Unfortunately they don't yet deliver where I live so I got dressed and ready to go pick my food up. I used my phone to see when the next bus was coming and how far away it is. I saw that there was an M3 bus on St Nicholas ave just a few blocks away. I didn't want to be standing in the cold waiting for the next one to come so I dashed up the hill from Fredrick Douglas ave to catch this bus. When I got to St Nicholas ave I could see the bus coming. The bus stop was on the other side of the street. I was rushing and *without looking both ways before crossing I went to run across the street* **BUT THE MOST STRANGE THING HAPPENED! - as I stepped into the street my body was frozen in mid stride** - my left hand was extended out in front of me. This "frozen" state lasted for only a split second however in that split second my finger tips were clipped by a person who sped past me on a motorbike. As soon as my fingers were clipped I was able to move again. I was Dumbfounded! I crossed the street and asked the guy who was on that side of the street if he had seen what happened. I don't even remember his reply but I remember asking him. I caught the bus and road to Seasoned vegan contemplating what had happened.

Significance

Read **Buck Franklin's Eye Witness Accounts From** page 409 and ask yourself why the woman wasn't hit by any bullets, then read about my accident on page 105, then read about my motorcycle accident and asked yourself how I landed on my feet at the Crossroads on page 158. After reading those events, what do you think happened with me when I attempted to **cross** the street?! Was it the guardian that Zee and Noel saw?! As you will come to see later in this book more guardians will be revealed to me. We all have at least one guardian watching over us our entire lives - some of us have more than one. I have more than one. That doesn't mean that I am unable to be harmed it just means that my purpose is of major importance. Remember the ghost of my grandfather appeared to me in an apparition on December 18th 2015 (page 348). In April of 2020 I will start training **Jonathan Jungblut** and shortly after his **Guardian Angel will be revealed** (page 604). Life is a game that we play, a play of consciousness. Your ability to be successful at this game is measured by your ability to see what is not seen and to hear what can't be heard. We make a fatal error when we think all that we see with our two eyes is all that there is to be seen. All things are governed by seen and unseen forces. In **July of 2021** at the **African Arts Festival** (page 650) I would have another experience with spirits (**invisible helpers**).

Utterances for Coming Forth by day into Light

It is he, who comes forth by day into Light

January 10th 2019 Dream

I was standing at the top of a very high wall with nothing but darkness below me. I jumped off the wall into the darkness. I scaled the wall like Spiderman (Peter-Ptah **Parker**)**.and climbed down to safety. Then I woke up.**

January 2019
Mars and my first Tarot card reading

This would be the first time I saw **Mars** since the festival in July. I gave her a massage and afterwards she gave me a tarot card reading from two different decks. The first card she pulled was the **Hermit**. I laughed cause I had been a hermit for many years now. Then she pulled the **Queen of Swords**, **Judgement** and **Four Wands**. She opened another deck and pulled two more cards. The first was **Guardian Angels**. The card had a white ostrich **feather** with a pyramid and an eye behind it. The ostrich feather symbolizes the principles of **Maat**. On the bottom of this card were the words "**you are not alone**". I knew that was true because I had just been saved from being hit by a motorbike a few days prior and a month prior **Zee** had revealed to me that **Harriet Tubman** was guarding the door of my apartment (page 545). The last card she pulled was the **Honey Bee** and in ancient Kemet the Pharaoh was called the NSWT BITY. The BITY was the symbol of a Honey Bee but at the time of this reading I did not make that connection. **42 Laws of Maat, Page 367**

January 15th 2019
I have three Dreams on Martin Luther King's birthday
2nd Dream with Erykah Badu

I had a dream that I was in **Erykah Badu's** home and she was feeding me food. Then I woke up..

Significance / Confirmation

6 months after this dream of Erykah feeding me I would meet a brother named **Mr G** at the International African Arts Festival in July 2019. Mr G was promoting a book he was about to release titled ***My Journey with Dr Sebi*** (www.myjourneywithdrsebi.com). When he saw me he stopped me because of the **feather** I was wearing in my hair. He asked me who I was and what I did. I told him I was doing massage here at the festival. He wasn't satisfied though. He was interested in who I was and wanted to know more about me so I told him my story of my past life as **Emmett Till** and he found meaning in it. We exchanged info and we planned to work together. At the time he was working on a project for **Dr Umar** called the **Shockumentary**. I let him hear the song I had written for DR Umar (p 460) and he felt it was perfect for the project and wanted to use it for the Shockumentary project. I said yes but I wasn't yet finished mixing it. Months after meeting Mr G he would **confirm** my **dream** with Erykah. One day we were on the phone and the topic of **dreams** came up. Then I told him about these dreams I had been having and some with celebrities. I told him of my dream with Erykah feeding me and he stopped me immediately. Mr G had spent a lot of time with **Dr Sebi** and he had either seen Erykah feeding **Dr Sebi** or **Dr Sebi** told him about her feeding him. I'm not sure if Mr G saw this with his own eyes or heard it but he says that Erykah always feeds those she loves. **Dr Sebi** would laugh and say, "let me feed myself" or something to that degree. So when he heard my dream of Erykah feeding me it rang as truth. He was amazed and he believed me. Two years prior to this dream I dreamt of **Erykah Badu** on January 12th 2017 (page 440), **Khalid Muhammad's** birthday. Then two days later on January 14th 2017, **Jay Electronica** would pay me a visit in a dream. This visit by Jay would confirm the movement of the **astral body** during the state we know as sleep (page 305). **Jay Electronica** is born on September 19, the same day that **Emmett Till's Murder** trial started in 1955 (page 516). **Erykah Badu** is born on February 26, the same day that **Trayvon Martin** was murdered (page 232).

January 15th 2019

I have a **prophetic Dream** _(Time Travel, **Deja Vu**)_ on **Martin Luther King's** birthday (2nd dream)

In the next part of my dream I'm in a dream with **Dr Umar Johnson**. I was telling him about the revelation of my life as **Emmett Till** but he was having a hard time believing me.

Rau nu Prt m heru

Significance / Confirmation

Five months later on Malcolm X's birthday, May 19th I would attend the **Malcolm X** annual ceremony at his grave where this dream would come to pass. I had another prophetic dream! Like what happened with my sister who dreamt my car accident back in 2002 (page 104). It would also be linked to the story I wrote in the 4th grade titled **The Renaissance Flute** (page 44). The next month on my Grand Fathers Birthday, June 17th 2019 I would meet a flutist who is a descendant of Malcolm X (page 568). She would play her flute over the song I wrote for **DR Umar Johnson**. The song was inspired by Tupac. I started the second verse with Martin Luther King and I ended the the first verse with Marcus Garvey. The name of the song is FDMG (Fredrick Douglas Marcus Garvey). The song was in promotion of the Dr Umar's School, FDMG. I took lyrics from his song **Fuckin with the wrong nigger**. The most interesting thoughts I took from Tupac was "**My only fear of death is reincarnation**". I said those words in a song that I wrote for Dr Umar and ! What I found so magical about this dream was the fact that I had the dream on Martin Luther King's birthday and it came to fruition on Malcolm X's birthday at his grave! That same day I was randomly picked to be one of the honorary brothers to dress in all white while standing guard around Malcolm's grave. In 2021 I would have a dream with **Floyd Mayweather** that was very similar to this dream with Dr Umar (p 635)

Iu f Per f m heru

January 15th 2019

I have a 3rd Dream on Martin Luther King's Birthday

I saw my sister walking with a stroller but she did not see me as if I was invisible to her. Or perhaps I saw something that has not yet happened.

January 17th 2019 (Dream)

I was on a bus that was traveling at a high speed. The bus crashed in a terrible accident but I walked away unharmed.

January 18th 2019 (Dream)

I was in the car with family members. One of my nephews was laughing and playing with a baby. The dream ends when I get into a disagreement with one of my sisters. We are in her car and she no longer wants me in the car. This was the same sister that dreamt my car accident in 2002.

Utterances for Coming Forth by day into Light

It is he, who comes forth by day into Light

January 19th 2019
Dreams of Flight with the Rods of Horus

I laid down with my arms extended like a plane and fell asleep in that position. Then I woke in a dream flying with my arms extended and in my hands I held the **Rods of Horus**. I flew into the clouds with conscious control over my flight. Then I landed smoothly next to a plane as it landed. Then I woke up with my arms extended like a plane. I laid there amazed about the level of control over my flying and landing I had in that dream… (See page 523, **rods of Horus**).

January 27th 2019
(Still Dreaming with Kanye West)

Kanye gives me a pair of sneakers with **blue** laces.

Significance

Kanye crashed 2 days before my birthday in 2002. I crashed 7 days before his on my fathers birthday in 2002 (page 106). In Kanye's song: Through The Wire, he says the name Emmett Till. My past life as Emmett was revealed on July 3rd 2018 (page 480). It was the video for this song that would spark his rise to fame. I have had several dreams with Kanye and he is from Chicago like Emmett Till and his last name is **West**. In the ancient Kemetic (Egyptian) Ausarian (Osirian) resurrection drama, Ausar (Osiris) was known as the Lord of the West and the Lord of **resurrection**. West was where the soul (BA) went when we "die". Kanye performed at the 2010 BET awards wearing a gold chain with a giant **Heru** pendant (in falcon form). **Heru** is the son of Ausar and he is the one that returns as Ra through resurrection. On April 4th 2020, the day Martin Luther King was assassinated (page 69) my past life as Tutankhaten (King Tut) was revealed to me (page 594). Martin Luther King wrote a theology paper on the Ausarian Resurrection in 1949 (page 593). **Re-member** that **you** are **Ausar (Osiris)** and **Heru**, the **hero!** <u>See page 3 for the **hero's journey**!</u>

February 12th 2019 (Dream with Tupac and My Grand Father)

I was in a room with **Tupac** and a woman. The woman seemed to be familiar to me but I don't know who she was. She was trying to get Tupacs attention. She wanted him to help her. She was dressed in very little clothes. she started crying. I offered to help her. I hugged her. Tupac got up and left the room then she turned into a Lamp. Then I woke up. I went back to sleep and then slipped into another dream. I was leaving and apartment when I was attacked or chased by kids who wanted my watch. I fled up the steps to the train station. They followed me but I got away. At some point in this dream I felt the presence of my Grand Father **General Dukes JR.** Then I woke up.

General Dukes JR
JUNE 17th 1931

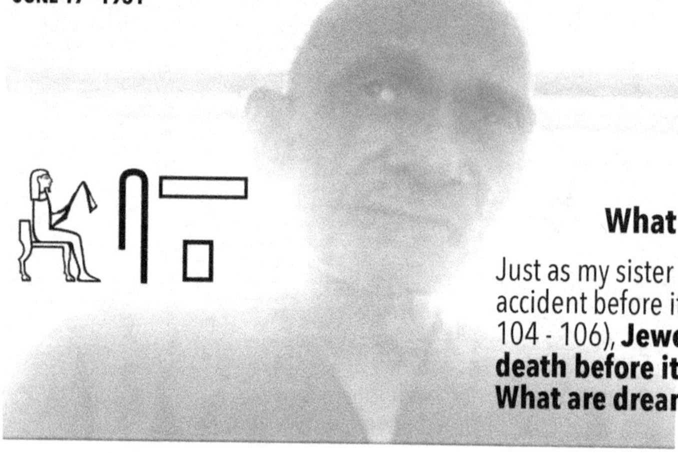

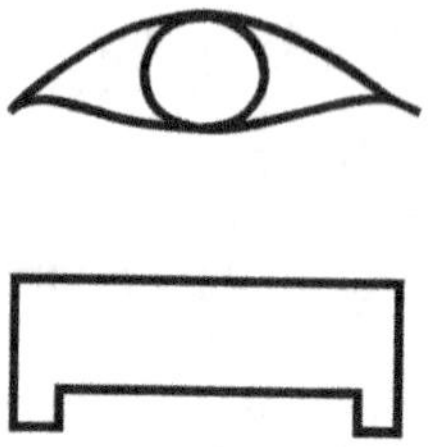

Tupac Amaru Shakur
JUNE 16th 1971

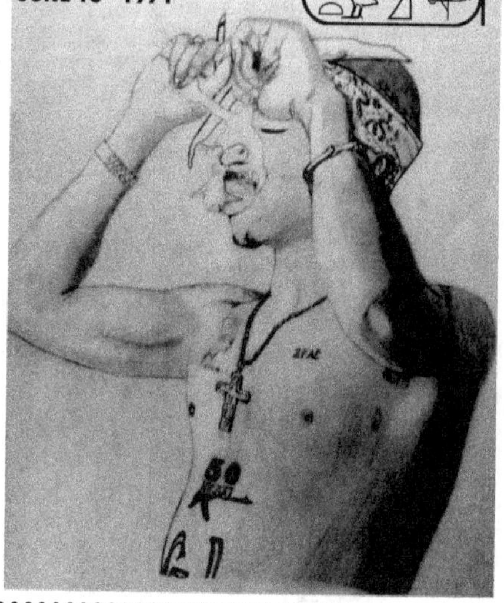

What are Dreams?

Just as my sister **dreamt** my car accident before it happened (pages 104 - 106), **Jewell dreamt Tupac's death before it happened** (p 105). **What are dreams** (page 30)**?!**

February 13th 2019 Nefertari's Dreams

My friend Neo **Nefertari** had a dream that I was living off the grid in peace with two wives. In the dream I had a pit bull that spoke. The C.I.A. was surveilling me. **(See Pages 233, 402)**

Iahmose Nefertari

She was the first matriarch of the 18th Dynasty who lead a coalition from southern Kemet to defeat the **Hyksos** invaders. Parades were established to honor her. She extended the throne to her brother **Iahmose I** and was the mother of **Amen Hotep I**. **King Tut** was the last royal Nswt Bity (Pharaoh) from her lineage. (page 15, 637)

February 21st 2019 Dreams of Fight

I was Surrounded in the hallway of my railroad apartment. I was moving in slow motion but faster than them. I slammed one of them on their head then I flew away. I was set up by a woman who I will keep nameless because I love this woman and can not explain why this would be the case. At some point in the dream my Uncle **Joseph** drove me to safety and the presence of my **Grand Father General Dukes JR** was there as well.

This dream was transcribe into this book on July 16th 2020 and as I was writing this dream into this book the room divider in my hallway fell over. There was no visible person in my apartment with me at the time.

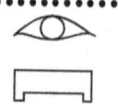

March 3rd 2019
1st Dream with Floyd Mayweather

In this dream I was walking with Floyd Mayweather then I woke up.

Significance

Next dream May 8th 2019 (page 560).

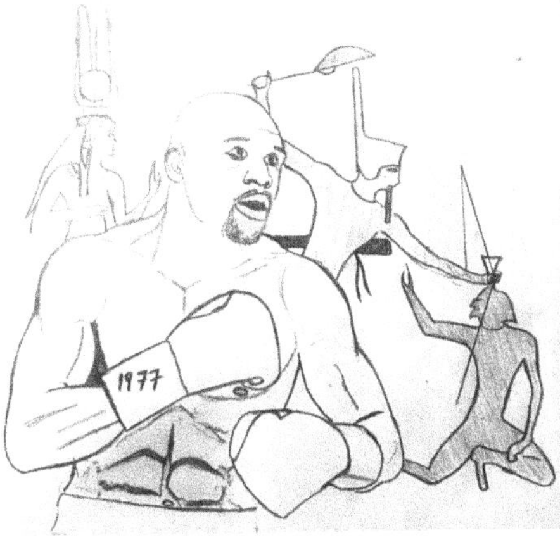

March 4th 2019
Still Dreaming with Kanye West

(Still Dreaming Remix, page 438)

I was in a room with Kanye and Kim West along with two other women from a place that sounded like "bolavah" in Toronto. At some point I was about to go outside with Kanye then I woke up.

page 438

Significance

Kanye crashed 2 days before my birthday in 2002. I crashed 7 days before his on my fathers birthday in 2002 (page 106). In Kanye's song: Through The Wire, he says the name Emmett Till. My past life as Emmett Till was revealed on July 3rd 2018 (page 480). It was the video for this song that would help him get a release date for his album sparking his rise to fame. I have had several dreams with Kanye and he is from Chicago like Emmett Till and his last name is **West**. In ancient Kemet (Egypt) Ausar (Osiris) was known as the Lord of the West. West was where the soul or the BA went when we die. In the ancient Kemetic (Egyptian) Ausarian (Osirion) resurrection drama, Ausar (Osiris) was known as the Lord of the West and the Lord of **resurrection**. Kanye performed at the 2010 BET awards wearing a gold chain with a giant **Heru** pendant (in falcon form). **Heru** is the son of Ausar and he is the one that returns as Ra through **resurrection**. **Re-member** that **you** are **Ausar (Osiris)** and **Heru,** the **hero!** <u>See page 3 for the</u> **<u>hero's journey!</u>** On April 4th 2020, the day **Martin Luther King** was assassinated (p 69) my past life as Tutankhaten (**King Tut**) was revealed to me (page 594). Martin Luther King wrote a theology paper on the Ausarian Resurrection in 1949 (p 593).

March 6th 2019
Dreams of Young Black Males

I saw a line of young black males in prison uniforms. I was in an office with one of the young black males. I asked him what he was there for. I looked at the paperwork and saw that it was labeled **Death Row.** He started crying. I comforted him. Then he told me what he was charged with. He was in a car with other boys. At some point the other boys broke someones leg then they all fled off in a car but he had nothing to do with it. While fleeing from police they stopped at a red light but the light stayed red for 10 minutes so they got caught at the light. The cops sped after them driving a red mustang then I woke up.

Juvenile convict prison laborers, United States, ca. 1903

March 11th 2019
Sleep Paralysis Within a Dream

This dream was like something out of a sci-fi movie. My **astral body** was being chased by a dark entity trying to absorb me or kill me but I **floated** away to safety. This dream was during the day.

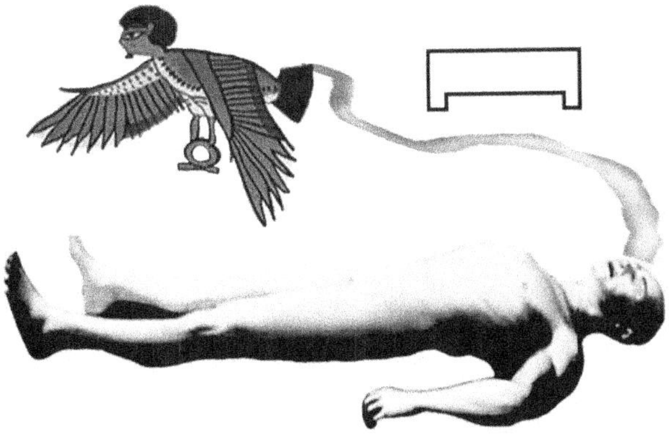

March 15th 2019
Dreams of Sleep Paralysis

While in a dream I wake up within a dream stuck in the state of **sleep paralysis**. I can't move. There is a black hand hovering over me. In the dream I'm in my apartment. My mirror is broken in the dream. Just before I wake up I see a dark spiral of smoke.

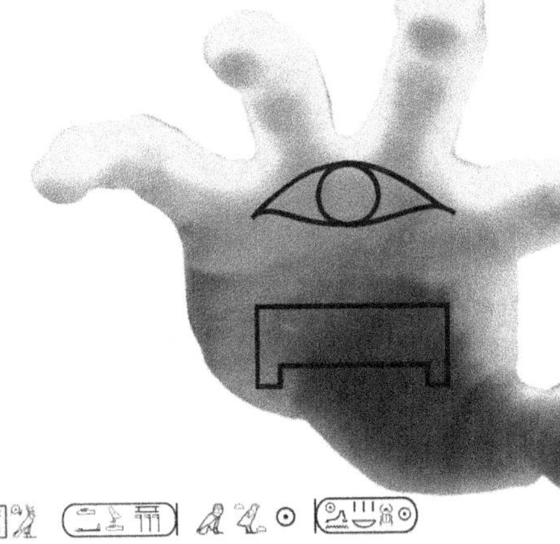

Rau nu Prt m heru

Iu f Per f m heru

Utterances for Coming Forth by day into Light

It is he, who comes forth by day into Light

March 17th 2019 - Singing Bowl Meditation Session with Taunya

Prior to today I had never had a private Sound Healing Session before. Having all these **dreams** and **coincidences** and considering the way that I met Tanya with the **Metatron** book I thought a session with her would be beneficial, so I booked one. Just before I started the session I took a few small pieces of **Sacred Medicine**. Perhaps **1 or 2 grams**. Tanya did not know this. During the session I saw flashing images speeding towards my face, I saw rows of **sphinx's** and faces of many **pharaohs** flashing before me. The flashes came too fast to get a fix on the features of any face. They came sporadically like waves. I was in a sort of trance state. Ever so often I would open my eyes for a split second and every time I would see Tanya's hand on its way to hit a bowl. When the session was over she asked how I felt and what I thought about the experience. I told her about the **sphinx's** and faces of pharaohs that I saw. Her eyes opened wide then she exclaimed "**I felt it**"! She said all during the session all she could think of was **Egypt**. She said every time she hit the bowl the sounds felt like **Egypt** to her. I thought that was amazing and it was confirmation to what I saw. Still I did not think I was some **Pharaoh** even though I had written the line about being the boy king in the museum that you be seeing (page 529). I knew I was **Emmett** and that was it. On April 4th 2020 (page 594) this session would make more sense and I would see Taunya again on **June 12th 2020** (page 616) where we shared another profound **coincidence**. When **coincidences** bind with **synchronicities** the outcome tends to have **<u>the mark of a greater authority</u>**. Like a pattern that happens for a divine purpose.

Rau nu Prt m heru

Iu f Per f m heru

Utterances for Coming Forth by day into Light

It is he, who comes forth by day into Light

March 20th 2019 - Family Dreams

I have not seen my two cousins Romelle and George in almost 20 years. Last night I dreamt of them and other family members that I can not recall.

March 23rd 2019 - Haritaki Visions

I heard someone talking about the healing potential of the plant Haritaki with it's ability to oxygenate the body. That same day I purchased some. The first time I took Haritaki I only took a little before I went to sleep. I woke up the next day and while I laid in bed **with my eyes closed** I could vividly see through a spherical portal as if I was looking through my eye lids down at my feet as I walked in the sand on a beach.

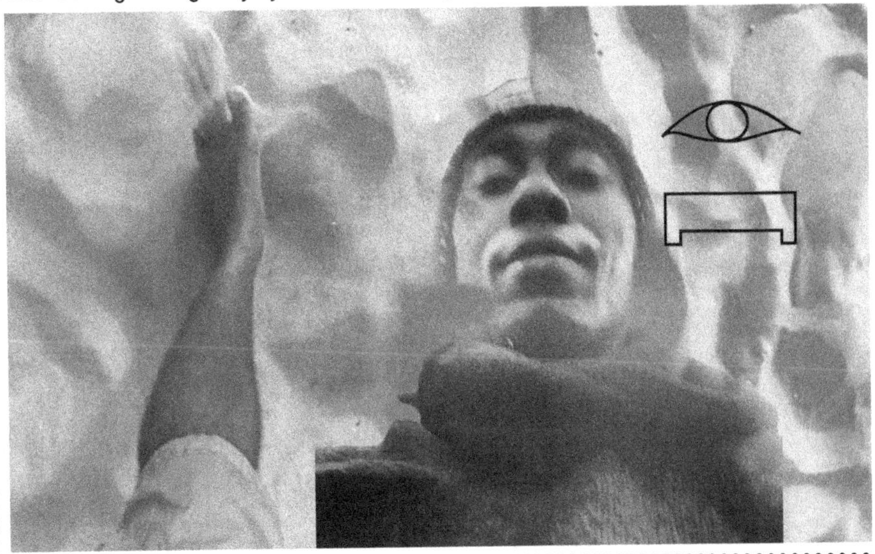

March 22nd 2019 - Dream with De La Soul

I was in the studio with De La Soul. I was trying to play a song for them but the equipment wouldn't work. It took a long time for me to get the song to play but they waited patiently until the song played.

Addendum

On February 12th 20**23**, the beloved member of the group De La Soul, **David Jude Jolicoeur** also known as **Trugoy the Dove** passed away. He was born on September 21st 1968, the same year **Martin Luther King Jr** was assassinated (pages 69, 592) and the same day I joined the Army (page 82) and the same day **Moses Wright Jr** testified in the **Emmett Till** trial (page 517). Please know that death is not the end. The soul survives death, indeed and in spirit. This is a book of the dead written by a boy who was murdered without justice, who defeated death and came forth by day. May the soul of **David Jude Jolicoeur** walk peacefully through the field of Reeds in Amenta. Amen Ra.

April 4th 2019 Dream with 50 Cent and Raekwon

I had a dream about **50 Cent** and **Raekwon**. I was walking in the middle of the street and **50 Cent** walked up to me, then he walked me across the street and introduced me to **Raekwon**.

Significance

This dream took place on the day **Martin Luther King** was assassinated (page 69, 592). I would have my past life revelation of my life as **Tutankhaten** (**King Tut**) on this day the very next year, April 4th 2020 (p 594). 50 Cent once said in a rhyme, "I want them to love me like they love **Pac**". He also spoke my name in a rhyme once , "Feds ain't no jack when **Pac** got shot, I got a kite from the pen saying **Tut** got knocked", eluding to Walter "**King Tut**" Johnson, the person who Tupac thought shot him in 1995 (p 664). 50 is from **Jamaica Queens** and I'm from **Far Rockaway Queens**. Raekwon released the Only Built 4 Cuban Linx on Sep 8th 2009, the day after Tupac was shot in 1996. The second song on the album was, House of Flying Daggers and on that song Ghostface says my name, "I'm an old mummy, my gold weigh as much as **King Tut**". Raekwon and Ghostface are synonymous so I used a picture of "Ghost" because he's wearing a Nefertiti chain like Tupac and I have a theory about who Pac was in a past life?. Raekwon is born the same day as **Khalid Muhammad** (p 440, 666) and Stephanie (p 295). 50 Cent is born the same day **Philando Castile** was murdered (p 395) and he was shot 9 times on May 24th 2000, the day before the first star code pattern of this book (p 222). 50 Cent would appear in another dream on Jan 18th 2022 (p 668).

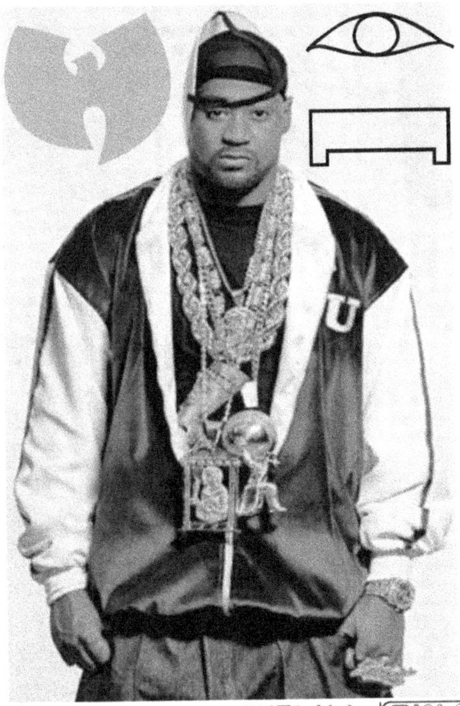

April 9th 2019

The Mysterious Case of a Familiar Face From a Different Time and Different Place

When I started showing people the pictures of my face next to Emmett Till's face I think most of them thought I was deriving my revelation from the likeness that we shared but they didn't understand my full story. They didn't know that the revelation came 9 months before I realized that I looked like Emmett and the pictures happened by "chance". I saw a fedora hat online that looked like the one Emmett wore and since the hat had a **25** on it I purchased it. **I had no idea that I looked like Emmett in any way**. I just wanted to see if we looked alike even if only a little. So I took many selfies wearing the hat until I caught the angle just right. The picture below was the first image that I felt was convincing. I had never seen our images side by side and to my surprise I really felt like I looked like an older version of "him"! The lips, the eyes, the nose, everything. I was just older now. I needed no real proof for myself, I knew in my heart and soul who I was but I was on this mission to prove to people that this boy was me! That I was him in another life! That we are the same soul (Soul Charting, page 602). I started to use the image in the videos I edited for my songs and posted them on social networking. Some people saw the resemblance and were amazed but I began to feel that some people thought I was crazy or at least that I wasn't who I thought I was. How could I really fault them when we live in a world with no frame of reference for things like this? But that's exactly why I was on a mission to prove myself to people. To get them to see between the dimensions of this thing we called time or life or reality. I needed people to know who I was so we could get past that part and then try to understand why it is that I'm back here. We all have the potential to come back here and we all have a mission upon getting here which is to rays our vibration and ascend this plane. And some of us come to leave a mark, a divine message.

After I took the picture I thought about the old ladies, the ones that kept asking me if the picture that was on my shirt was me. Never did it ever occur to me that I looked like Emmett Till! Most people when looking into reincarnation will take pictures of people from different times in the past and place them next to each other revealing a startling likeness. Many people do this with **Jay Z** and a picture of a man from the 1930's. I was walking around with a shirt that had a face on it that looked like mine and I had no idea (p 459)! On 3 or 4 occasions before I had my past life revelation, I can remember being asked if I was the person on the shirt by old black women. Each time I would smile and say no, it's Emmett Till. I can remember responding to the last woman who asked me that prior to the revelation with the look of shock because she didn't know who Emmett was. But I understood, so many of us die every year so it's hard to keep up with the faces of the dead. But I thought for sure that she was old enough to remember Emmett Till. It was my favorite shirt and it was a reminder of the horrors of American culture so I wore it often. **I had not forgotten Emmett Till!** When I think about it the scariest part is the fact that if I had not remembered and honored Emmett Till I would have actually been forgetting my own self. I would have been erased from my own memory storage. More interesting is that in the first pictures I took to see if I looked like Emmett, statues of **Ausar** (Osiris) and Auset (Isis) can be seen in the background. Ausar is the Lord of **resurrection** and Auset is his wife. 4 or 5 months later I would take a better picture on the same angle (p 556). Today is March 19th 2022 and I must laugh at the fact that this page fell on **555**. "Emmett was murdered in 19**55**.. **Re-member** that **you** are **Ausar** and **Heru,** the **hero!** See page 3 for the **hero's journey!**

Rau
nu
Prt
m
heru

Iu
f
Per
f
m
heru

Utterances
for
Coming
Forth
by day
into
Light

It is
he,
who
comes
forth
by day
into
Light

"**picture** a Van Gogh **starry night**, I'm on a stroll ***trying to find my soul when I write***"
(Dawuud's Invocation, written on March 24th 2011, page 200)

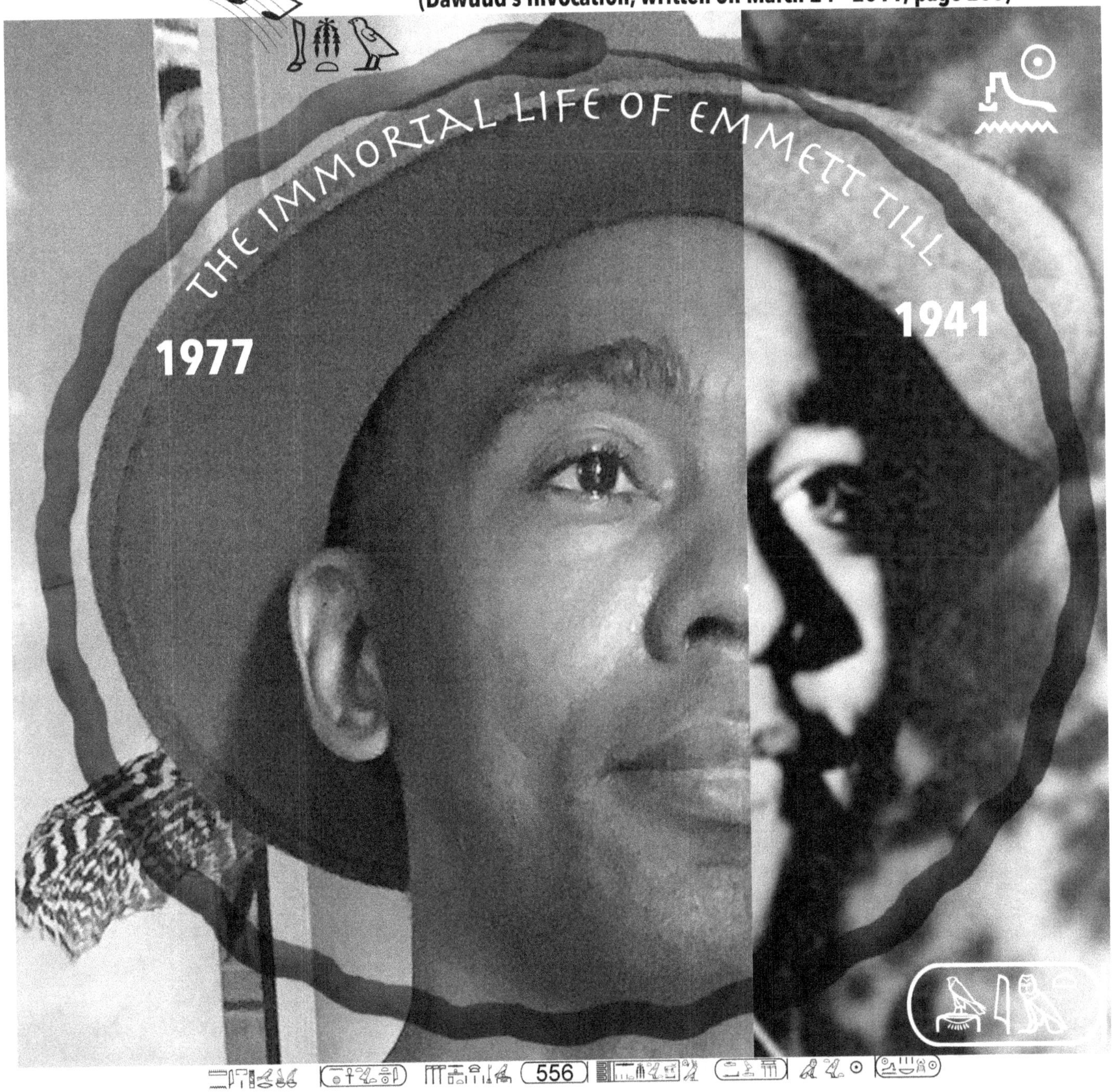

April 20th 2019 - Shauna From DC

I met Shauna in 2010 or 2011. She was the friend of a woman I met at a lounge named Tillmans. I took her friend home that night and entered the course with her in my bathroom while Shauna slept on my ottoman in my studio. I met her that one time and didn't see or hear from her again until 2015 after I had already changed who I was. We ran into each other in Harlem and I started training her on December 9th 2015. Take notice to the image on the ***shirt she was wearing*** for her **before picture**, on our first day of training. On April 20th 2019 Shauna and I grabbed brunch at Seasoned Vegan (p 364) and got into a disagreement. She said my music was angry. I was in the process of releasing my album **The Immortal Life of Emmett Till**. Not everyone believed what I was saying about me being Emmett Till in a past life and I don't think she believed me based on the audio messages she left me afterwards. We got into a disagreement about black life and how people should feel about the murder of black people. I can remember it was raining that day. We were sitting in her car in front of my apartment. She felt like my music was angry. I was trying to explain to her the importance of speaking truth to power and keeping the voices of our ancestors alive. I began to ask her if she knew about certain African figures like **Johh Henrik Clark** and such, but she had never heard of him or any of the other people I mentioned. I think she got offended by that. Perhaps she felt that I was trying to say her point of view was not valid because she didn't know about the people I knew about but I was just trying to give her people to research so that she could see things from a broader perspective. I was about to quote Marcus Garvey but all I could get out my mouth was "Marcus Garvey once said". Then she screamed, "I don't give a fuck about **Marcus Garvey** or what he said". I closed my mouth and exited her car. The day after the argument I would train a high school friend named **Cindy**. Because I knew her well I told her about what had happened the night prior with Shauna. I told her the story and when I told her about **Marcus Garvey** and why he's important to me I mentioned his **birthday** being **August 17th** and Cindy replied - "**that's my daughters birthday**". I laughed with excitement. Marcus Garvey had struck again from the grave just like he always said he would! That same day I sent Shauna a text telling her about what happened with Cindy and I told her she was a **scary black person** who was afraid to offend the white people she knew and worked for by speaking truth to power. She worked in fashion and most of her colleagues were White. So it wasn't "fashionable" to be "pro black". She would respond with five audio messages. **I would be remiss if I did not point out the fact that she lost the argument before it started. In her before picture she is wearing a tank top with an image of a pectoral belonging to Tutankhaten (King Tut). 3 years after this before picture was taken my past life as Tutankhaten is revealed to me on April 4th 2020** (page 594) **the same day that Martin Luther King was assassinated** (April 4th 1968, see pages 69, 592)..

"A people without the knowledge of their past history and culture are like trees without roots" - **Marcus Garvey**

"It will only take 24 hours to regain our place in the world once we all decide that our culture is ours" - **Marcus Garvey**

"If I die in Atlanta my work shall not only then begin, but I shall live in the physical or the spiritual to see the day of Africas glory again. When I am dead, wrap the red the black and green around me, for in the new life I shall ride with God's grace and blessings to lead the millions at the heights of triumph with the colors you well know. Look for me in a whirlwind or a storm. Look for me all around you for with Gods grace I shall come and bring with me countless millions of black slaves who have died in America and the West Indies and the millions in Africa to aid you in the fight for freedom liberty and light. The civilization today has gone drunk and crazy with its power and by such it seeks to injustice fraud and lies across the unfortunate but if I am apparently crushed by the system of influence and misdirected power **my Ka shall rise again** to plague the conscious of the corrupt." - **Marcus Garvey**

April 20th 2019 The 5 audio messages from Shauna

April 20th 2019 12:05 PM "And keep those ancestors around you, and keep those spirits around you. I hope they keep you warm. Cause you won't have physical people around you. That truly love and support you. Because you push everybody and everything away with your ego. You're such an ego maniac. And so self righteous. And that I never want anybody around me like that. So you can create your fake world. With all this pain and hate or what not. I'm not creating that. I acknowledge what is going on with out people. I give to our people where I can, um but you keep flying on that pedestal. It's the the ego it's crazy out of check. And yes once again. I meant it when I called you a bitch. You are a bitch. I believe that and bad word or not you don't lash out at me and call me a scary black person. Yeah, bitch as nigga, "NIGGER" actually". - **Shauna from DC**

April 20th 2019 12:06 PM "And the one thing I remember about you is that you're controlling. I remember in the car, you're trying to force me to listen and hear out something. Yo know? Like, you can't force me to walk the way you walk or talk the way you talk. That's not spiritual at all. People go on their journey and they find things and things are revealed to them in many ways. Things are revealed to me all the time. I don't need to post every message in my journey to the world. You're an ego maniac. You even used to tell me, like this like this. Did you like it? Did you like the video? No I didn't! You're a controlling person. Which is why I don't listen to you. What you say to me means nothing. I, I honestly think you're crazy. To be very honest. So there ya have it". -**Shauna from DC**

April 20th 2019 12:08 PM "And I feel sorry for you. I felt sorry for you so I tried to like give you as much love as my heart could, but what you did by calling me a scary Black person and trying to reduce my blackness. Never! You're never on my page as somebody that I would want on my journey. Or or in my circle. Never! So if you think that's right and that's spiritual and that's all good so be it. But you're wrong. And it will be revealed to you that you're wrong………. ***Maybe not because you're crazy self gonna come up with some number numerology or how you know, you're right.*** Because you're so righteous. So anyway. Honey have a great life and um I hope that you know you get to where you need to be in this stage and yeah. There'll be a next life time, a next life time and next life time so yup. It's all good". - **Shauna from DC**

April 20th 2019 12:08 PM "I promise you, you will never unite humanity, you will never unite Black people with your delivery. I promise you. I promise to God you will not. My goal is to show you that there is , you're imbalanced. Where is the la love in this? Where is it? You never, there's not many things that come out of your mouth that are with pure love. I I I don't feel that way. I don't feel that way. So I can only go by you that type of energy you know um yeah it's crazy, to say somebody is a scary ass black person. What? Hoe many times have you seen me in my whole life? What like, maybe 6 times? And you know me? You're no man. I'm telling you. You're no man for that one". - **Shauna from DC**

April 20th 2019 12:09 PM, "And you know what? I hope you die! I really hope you die. And if you truly are spiritual you know what that means. You stay in your dark place. Don't come over here with it. I know who I am. You're stupid stupid one of the.. A **hotep**! That's exactly what you are! The stupidest Black people of all. The stupidest! If you really truly are a spirit why are you attaching to a particular? Yes we are black we have problems we have issues. That's not without being acknowledged. I do my job but you on the other hand you can't, you're stuck. You're stuck. And you're fucked up. And that's why everybody runs away from you but you'll learn". - **ShaunaFromDC**

April 20th 2019 5:25 PM, My response after finally listening to her audio messages, "Finally listened to those. I was training clients. Bout to train another, booked all day. All people of color.. In life people come and go. Let those who go go. Let those who come come… you can wish death on me. That's so funny and interesting. Wish death on the reincarnation of Emmett Till. You must think I just think I'm him. Lol. No. I am him. And I don't wish death upon you. I tell my story not for ego. But to awaken the truth in others who deep down inside know that they have this magic. That they are more powerful than they know. My story is a revelation of our true journey here. You and the energy you just spit is a disgrace. Coming from yoga with that energy. Even if a person curses you you should be able to be balanced like me. I have not cursed you. Yes I called you scary cause you are scary. Scared to offend the White people around you. Your energy towards me doesn't upset me. There have always been people like you". - **Dawud**

I forgive this woman but I have no desire to communicate with her ever again in any life.

……………………………………………………………………………………

April 20th 2019 Babies and astrological star codes of immortality (May 25th Strikes Back)

My second niece is born on **April 20th** 2019. She would be sent to earth with an **astrological code** for me to decipher just like my aunt Pamela and her children. My nieces father was born on **May 25th** and she was born on **April 20th** 2019.

Significance

The murder of **Emmett Till** was the **first mass movement for Civil Rights in American history** and Emmett's body was identified by his ring that had the date **May 25th** engraved on it (page 512). **George Floyd** was murdered on **May 25th** 2020 by a police officer the month after I had my past life revelation of my life as **Tutankhaten** (**King Tut**) on April 4th 2020 (p 594), the day Martin Luther King was assassinated (pages 69, 592). George's murder would spark the **biggest protest in American history** and his killer was sentenced to prison on **April 20th** 2021 (p 610). My other sister had a dream on **May 25th** 2002 that I died in a car accident and 7 days later I a had violent car accident but I survived (page 104). On my 44th birthday October 25th 2021 Micah Beals Femia would be arrested for the crime of vandalizing the mural of George Floyd. Shauna from DC was right, because on this same day April 20th 2019 she said that "***you're crazy self gonna come up with some number numerology of how you know, you're right***". Yes Shauna from DC, I am right and you are wrong. You are one of the "scary Black people" who are afraid to speak truth to power in fear of losing what benefits that you have in this "White mans" world.

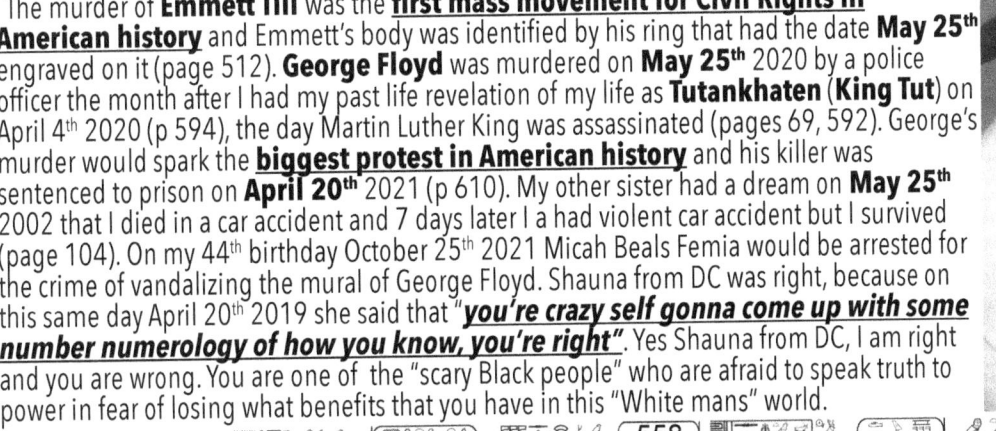

Rau nu Prt m heru

Iu f Per f m heru

Utterances for Coming Forth by day into Light

It is he, who comes forth by day into Light

April 21st 2019 Black Girl Magic (1st of 11)

She ain't know what **Black girl magic** is, she got mad and needed me to add more adjectives, a *Black girl lost* in this white world manages, when a Black girl is found, the Black face vanishes, they don't want you chant'n in the woods with the amethyst, or to manifest inanimate objects, science projects, it's a process, of assimilation, or elimination with no chance of probation, intimidation never worked for **Harriet**! problem solver her revolver she's sure to carry it, like a chariot to freedom, we need more to marry it, spiritual man raise the dry bones of **Lazarus - Dawud The Amazing BlaKseed**

Significance

This was written in response to an argument I had with Shauna from DC on April 20 (p 557). You should know that Shauna was a premature baby and was supposed to be born on **May 25th** but she came a month early. She once told me this when I told her about all my **coincidences** I have had with the date May 25th. **May 25th strikes back with a vengeance this time.**

2019 Fitness and the Divine Meetings

It's 2019 and I'm still working with people, helping them push themselves with health and fitness and still the people who I train come to me with interesting **star codes**. I had been training **Chuck** for a few years when I came to know that he was born on **Marcus Garvey's** birthday, which is the day before my grandfather died. **Mash** (The woman on Chuck's left) just so happened to be friends with my Step sister who I had not seen in many years. **La Juana** (The Women wearing glasses) is born the day after my sister's birthday (p 455). I met **Hana** (The woman on Chuck's right) working at The Spaaaht with La Juana. Hana's sister is born on my birthday and it was her sister that caused Hana and I meet. Hana's sister purchased a chair massage for her because she felt Hana needed stress relief. After Hana's chair massage she began to train with me. I had a client looking for a Doula so I reached out to another friend and I was given the info for a woman named **Myla** (The Women standing next to Mash). I passed Myla's info to my client. Days later Myla called me to thank me. Some time after I started training her. Myla is born the day after **Travon Martin** was murdered and Travons death was called a miscarriage of justice no different than the murder of **Emmett Till**. Myla is connected to **Ahket**, the woman I met under **mysterious circumstances** at the International African Arts Festival (p 570). Myla once left her phone in an Uber. She asked me to ride with her in her car to meet the driver at his home. The driver lived on a block named **Manila**. Myla was born in the city of **Manila** in the Philippines.

April 30th 2019
Kempress

She was ancient majestic a **kempress** from **kemet,** skin flawless, with the soul of a **Goddess,** he saw her in a **dream,** pure bliss like a scene from Zion, **Morpheus fly** on his **magic carpet,** dressed in the finest garments, the son harnessed the gift promised to him from heavens door, she wasn't there he didn't care cause he would wait forevers more, the lore *the score* like **Lauren,** he *explored **every ghetto** every city near and foreign, When it hurts so bad, Nothing even matters,* not even stardom, still *everything is everything*, pardon, I was feeling like I just *lost one*, the pendulum swung, here she come, *can't take my eyes off you*, cause I'm falling, tripping, I'm falling, falling, in love, intoxication no escaping, deep like the ocean, love like a sacred potion, love like deep emotions, love like sweet devotion, like when we be floating, love like oxytocin mixed with serotonin and dopamine, I mean love supreme serene, love like an explosion, I love my Queen she got me open, eye woke up in a **dream** in the **Golden Age,** I saw the **Falcon** fly, I saw **Jhuti** the sage **sun gaze** in **maaty's** eye **- Dawud The Amazing BlaKseed**

SIGNIFICANCE

42 Laws of Maat, Page 367

This was the first song I wrote in 2019 and in it I use **Lauryn Hill** Quotes. I was so busy with recording the songs for this album that I hadn't been writing new music. At this point I know I'm Emmett but I don't really believe that I'm Tutankhaten. Even though I didn't believe it I entertained it to myself as I started using pictures of Tut's **golden** coffin in videos for my songs. This is my first song of 2019 and in it I say - "eye woke up in a **dream** in the **Golden Age,** I saw the **Falcon** fly, I saw **Jhuti** the sage **sun gaze** in **maaty's** eye". King Tut comes from the time of the 3rd **Golden** age during the New Kingdom if ancient Kemet and **Heru** is the falcon that returns in the **Ausarian** Drama. The next year on April 4th 2020 (page 594) everything would change. I would shift from Tutankhaten being a distant thought to an absolute fact of reality indeed and in spirit just like my life as Emmett. **Re-member** that **you** are **Ausar** and **Heru,** the **hero!** See page 3 for the **hero's journey!**

Rau nu Prt m heru

May 8th 2019 - 2nd Dream with Mayweather

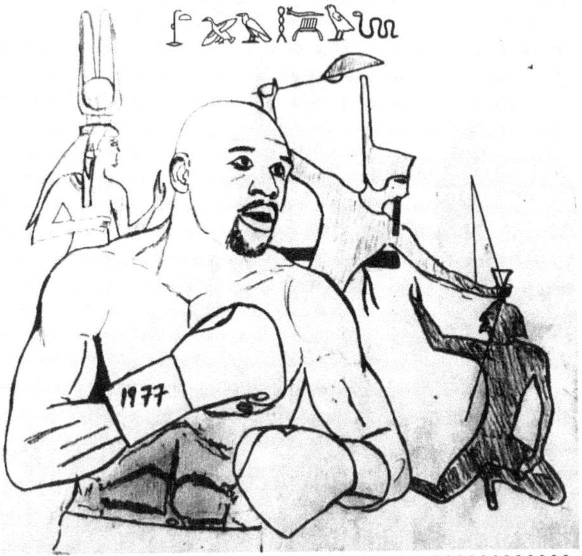

I fell asleep and when I woke up I knew I had just had a dream with **Floyd Mayweather.**

SIGNIFICANCE

I have had a few dreams with Floyd and he is one of my favorite boxers. My client Armeen, went to his 44th birthday part in 2021 and he has a son born on October 9th which is my Grandmothers birthday (page 609). Another friend of mine has a cousin who is one of Floyd's drivers and her last name is **Ramose**, like the Pharaohs (p 164). Perhaps I have some sort of connection with Floyd and Kanye since they both came flying into existence in 19**77** the year of the snake like me. There is definitely some connection and that is why they keep appearing in my dreams. I would dream with Mayweather again on April 1st 2021 (p 635).

Iu f Per f m heru

May 8th 2019 Jacob

Jacob wrestled with a man in **Wakanda,** he ate the **Round Caps Moses** called the **Manna,** He saw the face of God in his reflections in the water, He saw the face of God in the expressions of his daughter, He saw the face of God in the cow they about to slaughter, You debase God in the garden with that plate you bout to order, That's torture, like to off your nuts with a spike fucking bat, You getting hell on earth like a curse when you not fighting back, **I came back** packing my raps in the back of the **arc** yo, my flow be zodiac like the **sun** yo, hung low like a bull no **Chicago**, **Leo** no lying *flying in heavenly cargo*, We dying today in this hell cause of "tomorrow", Never dwell in sorrow, walk with righteous steps, *It ain't hard to tell* when you smell the snipers breath, It stinks like some bacon, I see the blood on his diamonds, he's sneaky, hiding the **Bible** in his army jacket lining, Yo I stand outside of the gates of **Buckingham Palace** selling **teachers**, spitting the ether to the truth seekers **- Dawud The Amazing BlaKseed**

Significance

See **Buckingham Palace Remix** on page **71**

May 13th 2019
Dream J. Cole

J. Cole was playing Basketball in the NBA and he was doing really well. He was new to the team so he wasn't starting but he did a good play and the crowd cheered. He was wearing shorts over top of thin grey sweats.

Significance

In 2021 J. Cole became a pro basketball player when he signed a deal to play three games as a member of the Rwanda Patriots in the Africa Basketball League. Over the years I used J.Cole's name when searching for beats to rap over. I would search, '**J Cole type beat**' on youtube and I would find most of my beats that way. I like J.Cole because he's a dope lyricist and because Tupac is his favorite rapper.

Utterances for Coming Forth by day into Light

May 18th 2019
Hadiiya's Goddess Glow Up Event

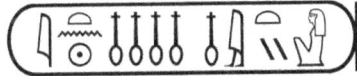

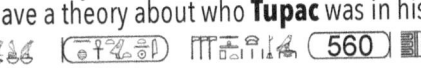

Hadiiya would reach out to me to do chair massage at her **Goddess Glow UP** event and I agreed. The event was for the cultivation of the divine feminine energy. I was one of around 7 men who attended. While there I shared my story of my past life as **Emmett Till** (page 480) and my experience with **Harriet Tubman** with a few women. In telling my stories I was really looking for helpful feedback. Perhaps someone would have some useful information to share. I would me Graciela who would invite me to join her on several occasions where we did ceremony at the statue of Harriet in Harlem. A Haitian woman from this event would reach out to me weeks after the event and would become a frequent massage client of mine. Oddly enough she went by the name **Hathor Akhenaten**. A year later my past life as **Tutankhaten** would be revealed to me on April 4th 2020 (p 594) the day Martin Luther King was assassinated, King Tut being the son of **Akhenaten**. The next day I would experience a divine **premonition** involving **Malcolm X** and **Martin Luther king** at the annual **Malcolm X** ceremony at his grave site. After I realized I was King Tut I would over stand why I ran into Hadiiya at the festival (page 474). Hadiiya's **two sons** are connected to my revelations. Her first son is born on **August 28th** the same day that **Emmett Till** was murdered. Her second son is born on February 26th the same day that **Trayvon Martin** was murdered (page 232) and this son has a name that sounds like **Ausar**, the **Lord of resurrection** and he is a trainer like myself and he also has a Tattoo of **Nefertiti** on his chest just like **Tupac**. Nefertiti is the step mother of **Tutankhaten** (**King Tut**). I have a theory about who **Tupac** was in his **past life.**

It is he, who comes forth by day into Light

May 19th 2019

1st Pilgrimage to Malcolm X's grave / Premonition / Time Travel and the 44th parallel

Tobius (p 533) asked me if I had ever been to the annual pilgrimage to **Malcolm X'**s grave for his birthday and I told him that I had never been there before. He suggested that I go this year and I agreed immediately. Tobius introduced me to the former Black Panther **Sekou Odinga** who had been released from prison on November 25th after serving 26 years. He was released the day before **King Tut's** tomb was opened (Nov 26th 1922, page 11). He is born on June 17th, on my grandfather General Dukes' birthday (p **23**), the day after Tupac's birthday. He is born in 19**44** so he falls into the **44th parallel** (pages, 37, 329, 582, 660). In 2021 **Sekou Odinga** turned **77** and I am born in 19**77,** the year of the snake. In 2021 I turned **44** and he is born in 19**44**. This was another divine pattern! The **44th parallel!!**

Malcolm X - May 19, 1925 - February 21, 1965

"YOU'RE GONNA BE ONE OF THE BROTHERS IN WHITE"

Tobius walked me to 125th were everyone waited patiently to board the buses ready to take the trip to Malcolm's gravesite, Ferncliff cemetery. It was like a family affair as everyone there treated each other with love. Tobius introduced me to brother **Asukile** and immediately the brother looked at me and said **"you're gonna be one of the brothers in white"**. He explained that ever year they have 6 to 9 brothers dressed in white standing around Malcolm's grave as the ceremony takes place. I was honored to do this for Malcolm. I was led to the other brothers and we all practiced marching before we boarded the buses. In ancient kemet (Egypt) Anpu (Anubis) was depicted as a dog or a dog headed person who was referred to as the greatest judge of the character of man. **Anpu guides the spirit down the halls of judgement after death and stands guard at the doors of judgement**. This was a great honor for me! The brothers in white represent the African Islamic brotherhood as Malcolm lived and died as a Muslim. while I was in the military I stood in many Army ceremonies as the honor guard and guide on bearer but none of it could compare to how I felt when standing guard at Malcolm's ceremony.

May 19th 2019 - Pilgrimage to Malcolm's Grave

Malcolm X
May 19, 1925 - February 21, 1965

Rau nu Prt m heru

Iu f Per f m heru

May 19th 2019 - Malcolm X Speaks on King Tut and Egypt

Utterances for Coming Forth by day into Light

It is he, who comes forth by day into Light

On **February 8th** 2015 I wrote the song **Ancient Future** (page 321). On the intro of this song I placed an audio excerpt from a speech of Malcolm X speaking about Egypt. He is speaking about pictures of Egyptian statues seen in a magazine that look exactly like black men. I think this might have been the first time I ever heard that speech. I'm not sure if I wrote the song before or after I heard the speech but I started that rhyme with the words, "I grew up miseducated from them lies that they postulated". At the time, in 2015, I had no knowledge of my past lives however I had been writing about resurrection and Egyptian Pharaohs for a few years at the time. Two months after I wrote that song, I wrote the song, **The Power of Words so be it,** and in that song I say the name of Tutankhaten's (King Tut's) father, **Akhenaten.** That song was written on April 4th 2015 (page 323) which is the same day that I would have my past life revelation of Tutankhaten (King Tut) in 2020 (page 594), which is also the day Martin Luther King was assassinated (see premonition, page 564).

In this video Malcolm also spoke about a story that was printed that day, on page 2 in the L.A. Sunday Times news paper. At the time the Aswan damn was being built and it threatened to flood the historically significant, Abu Simbel Temple complex in Egypt. Malcolm spoke of how detached the Africans in America were to their ancient culture. Because the name Egypt was used instead of Africa, Blacks had disassociated themselves with that culture and most did not see themselves in it. Malcolm explain how the statues had all the features that white men claimed Negros had, but because the statues are associated with such great historical, anthropological and archeological value White men try to claim the culture as theirs. There was a time when their "black slaves" could have looked upon these structures and never seen themselves but in the 1960's the European knew that they could not risk keeping these great structures viewable because those who were once his slave were now waking up. The Negros (Black People, African American) can now look at these structures, just like Malcolm had and potentially see themselves and ponder their true origins. And this is why America was against saving the structure in favor of allowing many structures to be lost under the river water. Fortunately the temple of Rameses The Great was preserved and was eventually cut into pieces and reassembled at a higher elevation but unfortunately many ancient structures were lost under the waters of the Nile river. In the video Malcolm also spoke about a **King Tut** exhibit in Los Angelos. I had forgotten about that part until I listened to the video again on February 14th 2022. When I heard my name I smiled. It made me even prouder to have been picked to stand guard around his grave this day. **Malcolm spoke about seeing "King Tut's" mummy when he visited Egypt and expressed how all the pictures he saw of King Tut depicted him as a Black man.**

May 19th 2019 - Pilgrimage to Malcolm's Grave

When we walked out I lead the way as we made our way to Malcolm's plot. The brothers in white represent the African Islamic brotherhood as Malcolm lived and died as a Muslim. Just before the proceedings began we had a moment of silence for the ceremonial Pouring of libations.

"when I die, I fly in the whirlwind like a Falcon with Malcolm, blasting my album in Thugs Mansion no doubt son, Get Out son, American nightmare the outcome, a burning house, your organs, wake up without them! you heard about Kendrick Lamar! well, tell me bout Johnson! I'm ready to unite tonight mother fuck march'n"

Get Out, Written on March 3rd 2017 (page 444, also see page 263)

Rau nu Prt m heru

Iu f Per f m heru

Utterances for Coming Forth by day into Light

It is he, who comes forth by day into Light

May 19th 2019 - Pilgrimage to Malcolm's Grave

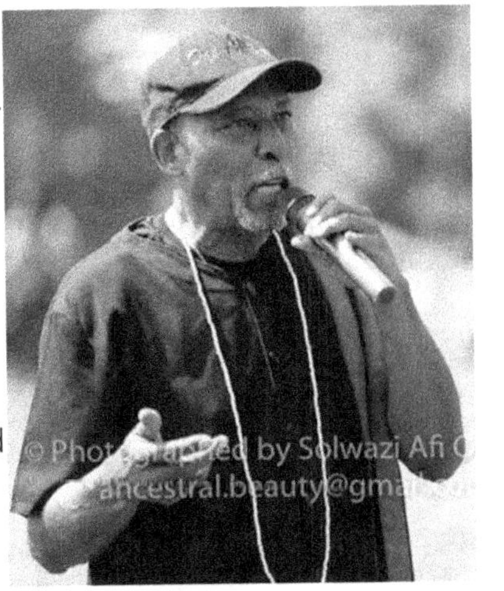

In 2015 I watched a lecture of Professor **James Small** titled (The Rebuilding Of The African Spirituality). In this lecture he talked about a **profound near death** experience he had. Here I am now, four years later at Malcolm's ceremony and to my surprise, Professor **James Small** was the Master Of Ceremonies. Immediately, I remembered his lecture and I wanted to talk to him! I figured, because of his experiences he might receive my experience without too much disbelief or bias. Towards the end of the ceremony Professor Smalls walked over to me and whispered in my ear asking, "brother are you ok? You have not moved a muscle the entire ceremony." I smiled and said, "I'm perfectly fine brother." I told him I had been wanting to speak to him. He told me to find him after the ceremony. After the ceremony I found him and we spoke briefly. He gave me his number and told me to call in a few days. The following Tuesday I called him and told him about my past life as Emmett Till. He remained silent for most of the discussion and I'm not sure he believed me. Because of the near death experience I heard him describe I thought he might understand me but he, like most of the other elders, had no real response... **But I understood**, I sounded like a "crazy" person to most people. However, in 2022 I would hear him on another video speaking about **Wehem-Mesut**, the Egyptian concept of reincarnation (page 14). I felt invisible, I wondered why he was silent when I came to him. But again, **I totally understood**. What I was claiming was a hard truth to contend with and what do you say to a person like me? I was beginning to feel ostracized.

May 19th 2019 - Dream Premonition

The ceremony lasted around 3 hours and I was keen about not moving a muscle. I stood at the position of attention, motionless, locked in tight for Malcolm! **I was honored to stand guard for him!** It was supposed to rain this day but not a drop of rain fell. Instead the wind blew as the sun shined and the trees seemed to move in the wind as if they were dancing. I felt like I was having a **psychedelic trip**, standing there as I watched the trees sway in the wind. **(*ADDENDUM*** Perhaps it was the act of standing in one spot, **like a tree** that caused the feelings of **nirvana**!) I only moved one time and that was when Professor Small called Dr Umar Johnson to the microphone. I turned my head because I had recently had a **dream** about Dr Umar on **Martin Luther King's** birthday, January 15th 2019 (page 550) and now, here he was at Malcolm's birthday ceremony. Then he stated that this was his first time attending this ceremony. It was my first time as well, **I knew this wasn't just a coincidence!** After the ceremony I went to Dr Umar and introduced myself as, Dawud, the brother that made the song for him (p 460). He remembered me, we pounded each other up then I told him about my **past life** revelation of Emmett Till. I showed him the side by side pictures of me and Emmett then I showed him my birthmarks and told him that Emmett had been shot in those same areas.. He looked at me a bit strange, then I just laughed and we took a few pictures. I laughed because when he looked at me strange I realized that I had had a **dream** about that very moment on **Martin Luther Kings birthday** (p 550) and here on **Malcolm X's** birthday **the dream had come to fruition**. This was indeed a divine series of events and I knew it! Or was it time travel? A few years later I would have a similar dream with **Floyd Mayweather** (p 635). Perhaps I was attempting to awaken my brothers in the dream realms. Perhaps that is why I dream with my brothers. **Other prophetic dreams** (pages, 99, 104, 105, 172, 305, 586, 589)! It wasn't until 2023 that I saw videos of Dr Umar speaking about souls reincarnating to earth to fulfill their soul **contracts** (see page **268** for **contracts** on March 27, 2013).

Malcolm X - May 19, 1925 - February 21, 1965

What is **Deja Vu**? What is **Dream Precognition**? The **astral body** IS NOT BOUND TO THE SAME "LAWS" OF SPACE AND TIME AS THE PHYSICAL BODY (**Noah's Ark**, p 252). Some dreams take place in a different space and time where **the astral body travels**, sometimes to the past and even the future. **Deja Vu** is sometimes a result of having already experienced a moment in a dream and when you reach the moment in your waken state you have a feeling of familiarity. Precognition is seeing events in a vision or dream before they happen like when my sister dreamt my car accident before it happened on May 25th 2002 (p 104). Or when Jewell's dreamt **Tupac's** death the day it happened (p 105).. Or when my father dreamt the 911 event before it happened (p 99). Or my dream on Oct 17th 2014 (p 305). In 2022 I experienced **Deja Vu** twice while in **Kemet** (pages 670 - 671). Just imagine if you spent more time exercising your spiritual centers instead of just doing bicep curls for the girls. Imagine if you used your imagination. Imagine if you pulled the **magic** from the images in your **minds eye**. Imagine if I am who I say that I am. The reality is that I am who I say that I am. And Malcolm picked me to stand guard over his grave. Just as Tammy Payne (p 391) would win the **Pulitzer Prize** for the book about Malcolm X, **The Dead Are Arising**, this book, **TutemRa: The Prophecy of Reincarnation, Star Codes of Immortality** is confirmation that the Boy King Tut and Emmett Till have risen (page 481).

Pilgrimage to Malcolm's Grave

After the event was over we all said our goodbyes then boarded the buses and made our ways home. But before that we took a picture together after standing in one spot for 3 hours. The pose I am in below is the pose of Ausar (Lord of Resurrection, page 481). Re-member that **you** are **Ausar** and **Heru,** the **hero!** See page 3 for the **hero's journey**!

"I embody everybody, God body, Tupac, Marcus Garvey, Malcolm X, Imhotep, respect to Bob Marley". Holler If Ya Hear Me, Written on April 16th 2016 (page 374-375).

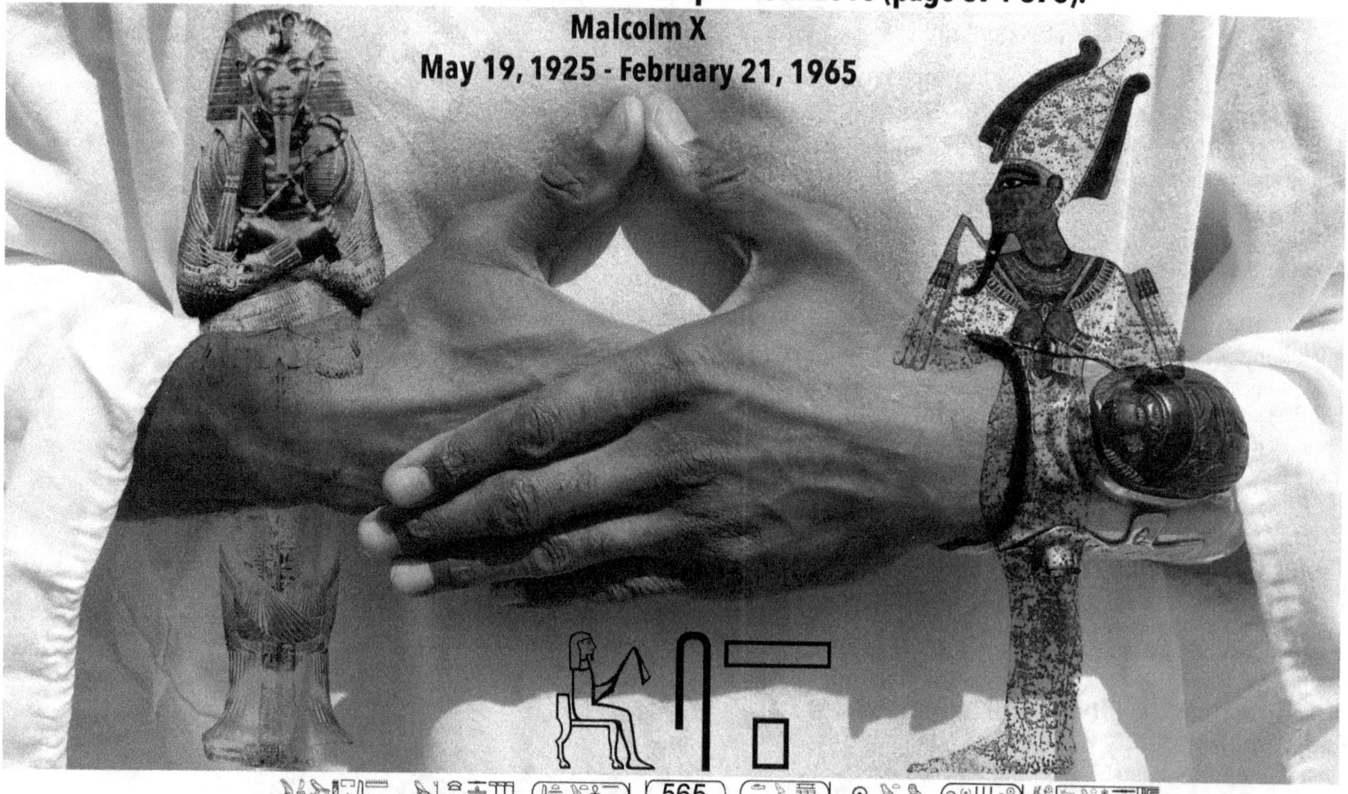

Rau

nu

Prt

m

heru

May 25th 2019
Holler If Ya Hear Me is Released on all Streaming Platforms

I have had two profound experiences involving the **Tupac** song, **Holla If Ya Hear Me**. The first happened in 2015 causing me to write the song, **Star of the Story** (page 323), and the second happened in 2016 while writing my version of **Holler If Ya Hear Me** (page 375). On May 25th 2019 I released the song as the first single off my Album **The Immortal Life Of Emmett Till,** which would be released two months later on July 25th (page 577). I chose May 25th for the date of the first single because of the significance. At this point I felt like May 25th was sort of like a second birthday for me seeing how I escaped death several times on that date (pages 104, 157, 512). And I chose July 25th to release the full album because it was Emmett Tills birthday. At the time I had no idea that the date was exactly 1 year and **22** days after my past life revelation of Emmett Till that I experienced on July 3rd 2018 (page 480). After my past life revelation of **Tutankhaten** (**King Tut** ,page 594) I would understand the significance of the number **22** in my pattern. **22** is the number of the master builder (page 41). King Tut's tomb was discovered in 19**22**. Emmett Till's father was born in 19**22**. I was born **22** years after Emmett Till was Lynched when my mother was **22** years old. The names **Emmett** and **David** (Dawud) add up to **22** in gematria (page 41). My father's life path number is **22** (p **28**).One time is an incidence, twice is a coincidence, three, four, five is a pattern, can you tell the difference?

Iu

f

Per

f

m

heru

May 25th 2019
Brand Nubian Dreams
ADDENDUM

Utterances

for

Coming

Forth

by day

into

Light

It is

he,

who

comes

forth

by day

into

Light

I met **Grand Puba** from the Legendary group **Brand Nubian** on **May 25th** 2019 at the **Bam African Street Festival** and 3 years later on **May 25th** 2022 I would have a **dream** with **Lord Jamar**, another member of Brand Nubian (p 342). When I met **Grand Puba** I asked him for a picture and he accepted. A few months later I crossed paths with **Grand Puba** again, but this time in Harlem. If I recall correctly he was on his way to workout at the YMCA on 135th street. I let him hear the single I had just released. I gave him my card for training and told him he would hear of me again. When I was a teen my father gave me a tape with Brand Nubian in it (page 54). On April 17th 2015 I wrote the song **Wake Up Blakseeds** (page 327), which was a remix of the **Brand Nubian** song, **Wake Up** (**Reprise in the Sunshine**). See page 30 for the di**vine** **math**ematical significance of **May 25th**.

The famous 125th St (at Adam Clay Powell blvd) is co-named **Dr Yosef Ben - Jochanna Way**. I was there with my brother **Nova**. I ran into **Dr Umar** again and I Met **Ralph Carter** from **Good Times** for the first time. An older woman asked me to take a picture with her, so I did. Dr Ben appears in this book for the first time on April 9th 2015 when I went to the his **tribute to his life** held at the National Black Theater (page 327). The next day I would write a **Hekau** for him (page 327). I would speak his name again two years later in the song, **Maroons**, written on February 9th 2017 (page 442).

June 17th 2019 Open mics, Coreisa Lee and The Prophecy of the Renaissance Flute

Rau nu Prt m heru

I knew I was supposed to say something. These open mics kept popping up on my time line. I figured, I had an album coming out, so I might as well promote it. I saw an open mic that was on my Grand Fathers birthday so I went. It was at **The Shrine** in Harlem, named after the famous **Fela Kuti** (page 435). I went up and did a few songs. I felt like I didn't perform them well but I was well received by the crowd. No standing ovation but some people liked it. When I left there was a woman leaving and walking the same way I was. She told me she liked my set and I thanked her. **She felt like we should know each other** so she suggested that we exchange information. Her name was Coreisa. She was going to another venue and suggested I go too. I went and I performed the song, The Immortal Life of Emmett Till. After wards she would blow her flute over 4 of my songs. Years later Coreisa would tell me that **she saw a white light surrounding me** and because of that, she knew we should know each other, no different than what happened with **Zawadi**, the **Yoruba Priestess** (page 641).

Significance

Iu f Per f m heru

On my Grand Father's birthday, June 17th 2019, I would meet Coreisa Lee, a professional flutist. Coreisa is from **Alabama** like Rosa Parks. **Rosa Parks** sparked the Montgomery **Alabama** bus boycott in 1956 when she refused to move her seat for a white man because she was furious about what had happened to **Emmett Till**. This brave act would help usher in the Civil Rights Movement. Coreisa is a descendant of **Malcolm X** and **Rosa Parks**. I found that interesting since I had just stood guard at Malcolm's ceremony a month prior. Because of this I knew we hadn't met by happenstance. She was compelled to exchange numbers because we were supposed to meet! Her spirit knew! Her and I would become friends and she would blow her flute over a few of my songs for my first album, fulfilling **The Prophecy of the Renaissance Flute** (page 44). The short story I wrote when I was in the 5th grade. This book, TutemRa The Prophecy of Reincarnation is the Renaissance Flute from my short story because all of my music was fueled for the love of my people and it was used to awaken my soul (page 6). Flutes are used to ward off evil spirits or to rally them. The most notable song she blew her flute on was the song **FDMG** (page 460), which I wrote for Dr Umar after meeting him on Dec 3rd 2017 (page 457). And I had just had a profound experience involving Dr Umar and a dream premonition that came to pass at Malcolm X's ceremony the month prior (page 550). In the song **FDMG,** I say these words, "**My Only Fear Of Death Is Reincarnation**". In this song I used a lot of **Tupac** quotes from his song "You Fuckin Wit the Wrong Nigga". I played the Tupac song for Coreisa and after listening to it, with ease she blew the melody of Tupac's song over the beat for my song **FDMG**. Tupac is born the day before my Grand Fathers birthday and I would meet Coreisa on my Grand Fathers birthday. I have a theory about who Tupac was in his past life. I would give Coreisa a massage and afterwards she would see a **blue light emanating around me.** Today is March 15th 2022 and Coreisa contacted me today. She told me that she got a call to be a part of a new Emmett Till theater project named, **Emmett Till, A New American Opera**. There is no such thing as "just" a coincidence. One time is an incidence, twice is a **coincidence** but three, four and five, that's a pattern - **can you tell the difference?!**

Within the span of two weeks I performed at **The Shrine** in Harlem. **Nicholas Book store** in Brooklyn on June **28**th 2019. Then at a few places in Harlem like **Londel's** and the **H-Loft.** I went to the Bronx and performed at **Bronx poetry** and ending with my open mic tour at **Peace Cafe** in Harlem.

Utterances for Coming Forth by day into Light

It is he, who comes forth by day into Light

July 4th 2019

International African Arts Festival (Khepri, The Only Begotten Son)

I was excited to get to the festival this year as I felt like something special might happen. I worked under **Mfundishi's** tent again and sure enough magic did happen. All 4 days I was greeted by **Khepri,** the **"Only Begotten Son"**, or as said in ancient times, the **Only Begotten God**. Khepri is represented by the scarab dung beetle. The scarabs that came to me during this festival were symbols of my **rebirth**, they were external manifestations of my inner awakening. This concept of repeating of births was called the **Wehem-Mesut** (p 14). I was not aware of their deeper significance because I was on a blind initiation. These beetles were signs connecting me to my past life and preparing me for the past life that was to come in 2020. The Egyptian God **Khepri** ('he who came flying into existence from seemingly nowhere') was the original animal used to personify the constellation of **Cancer** and represented the **scarab dung beetle**. It was believed that the dung beetle was only male in gender, and reproduced by depositing semen into a dung ball. The supposed self-creation of the beetle resembles that of Khepri, who creates himself out of nothing, therefore **Khepri** (**Cancer**) became known as the '**Gate of Men**' through which souls descended from heaven into human bodies, or into creation. Khepri was the **Only Begotten God.** There is a cluster of hundreds of stars found within the Cancer (**Scarab**) constellation known as the **Bee Hive** cluster. This cluster is now known as "Messier" 44 or M44. This "Bee Hive " is the "gate of men" and it is also known as **the manger**. They said Jesus was born in a "**manger**" and called him the **Messiah** but thousands of years ago Pharaohs returned flying into existence from **Messier 44** (M44), the Bee Hive cluster of stars found within the Cancer (**Scarab**) constellation. No **coincidence** that I revealed this book in my **44th** year in this body. Emmett Till's mother, **Mamie Till** died on **January 6** 2003, the year goat, the same Chinese year Emmett was murdered in (1955). **January 6th** is 12 days after the winter solstice (Dec 25, Christmas, pages 489, 614). **January 6** is known as the **Epiphany** in Christianity as it marks the day that the three wise men visited Jesus in the **Manger** (p 511). **January 6** is the day that the ancient Kemetyu celebrated the Winter Solstice and **Tupac's** grand mother Eloise Maria Barnes was born on **January 6**. The early Christian Fathers knew about the Kemetic (Egyptian) pantheon and connected their **Jesus** deity with the **scarab beetle** as some of them identified Jesus with, and as, the "**good Scarabeus**". The early Christian Father **St. Augustine**, writes, "My own **good beetle**, not so much because he is only begotten (God), not because he, the author of himself, has taken on the form of mortals, but because he has **rolled himself** in our **filth** and chooses to be born from this filth itself." **St. Augustine** is speaking about the dung beetle who **roles the cow dung** in a ball and places it's eggs in the dung, then they deposit their eggs in a hole the ground, where their larvae feed on the dung. When the larvae hatch their progeny spring forth from seemingly nowhere rising from the earth given rise to the connection with the resurrection of the dead. The early Christian Father **Hor-Apollo** was quoted saying, "To denote the only-begotten or a father, the Egyptians delineate a scarabeus! Be this they symbolize an only-begotten, because the creature is self-produced, being unconceived by a female." In accordance with this continuation of the Kemetic symbols, it was also maintained by some sectaries that Jesus was a potter, and not a carpenter; and the fact is that this only-begotten Beetle-God, who is portrayed sitting at the potter's wheel forming the Egg, or shaping the vase-symbol of creation, was the Potter personified, as well as the only-begotten God in Egypt." Besides its being worshipped as a divinity, stones cut in the form of the beetle served as talismans among the Egyptians. It wasn't till 2020 that I realized it was my faith in Jesus Christ's resurrection and returning someday that set the foundation for my own revelation of reincarnation. The Scripture John, 14:12 reads, "Verily, verily, I say unto you, He that believeth on me, the works that I do shall he do also; and greater works than these shall he do". By having the belief in the resurrection of Jesus it allowed my soul to fathom the concept of resurrection after death, not knowing that the concept had originated in Kemet.

Carl Jung, the Swiss Psychotherapist once had a **magical coincidence** with the scarab. Jung Details in his book (*The* Structure and the Dynamics of the Psyche, p. 438) , "A young woman I was treating had at a critical moment, a dream in which she was given a **golden scarab**. While she was telling me this dream I sat with my back to the closed window. Suddenly I heard a noise behind me, like a gentle tapping. I turned around and saw a flying insect knocking against the window-pane from the outside. I opened the window and caught the creature in the air as it flew in." Here is your scarab," he said to the woman, as he handed her a link between her dreams and the real world. But what did the scarab mean for me? The dung beetle lives in filth, the material world which the rational mind can comprehend. And yet the dung beetle represents that which is greater than rational and above the physical, the solar disk (RA). As I stated in the beginning of the book, we all experience falling rain (page 1). The **coincidences** and the **synchronicities** are the messages from the unseen and they are everywhere. When you watch the movie **Matrix**, you see the green text computer code scrolling down in the background known as digital rain or the **Matrix** code and sometimes green rain. This falling **Matrix** code is a way of representing the activity of the simulated reality environment of the **Matrix** seen on screen by kinetic typography. Basically everything that is happening within the **Matrix** is seen on a computer screen as green falling rain which can be decoded or read by those who know how to read it. The same thing is happening within this life you are living. The **Matrix** of this life you are living has a code as well. You must decode it but this code is not limited to green falling rain on a computer screen. Sometimes the code is unseen, sometimes it's in the rain. It can be in a strange message from a stranger passing by like when I met Mr Nature (page 281), or brother Khufu in massage school (page 282). The **coincidences** and the **synchronicities** are the falling rain. These messages are everywhere and this year the message was sent by 5 scarab beetles who came to me everyday of the festival. My book is full of star codes of immortality. These star codes are the falling rain surrounding my life. Our thoughts and desires can affect our reality by influencing quantum level events in time and space. This year, at the International African Arts Festival you will see the falling rain tapping on the window pane of my imagination. I opened the window and poked my head out allowing the falling rain to bathe my rational mind, pulling open the doors to another past life. When **coincidences** bind with **synchronicities** the outcome tends to have the mark of a greater authority. Like a pattern that happens for a divine purpose.

July 4th 2019 (1st day International African Arts Festival)

Last year my life as Emmett Till was revealed to me at this festival so there was no way I was going to miss it this year! I wondered what the universe might show me this year?! I was looking for something, I was looking for signs and the first day I got several! It seemed like the scarab wanted to tell me something as they would find their way to me in the most profound of ways yet prior to this festival I can't remember ever seeing a scarab in my entire life. During my four days at the festival I gave many chair massages and **22** people were kind enough to leave me video testimonials. **Mfundishi Jhutyms** was the first person to sit in my chair this year.

Rau nu Prt m heru

Iu f Per f m heru

Utterances for Coming Forth by day into Light

It is he, who comes forth by day into Light

Chair Massage Video Review #1

"Ee Em Hotep. Mfundishi Jhutyms. I just ascended from heaven. This was a beautiful experience. My body is nice and relaxed. The brother took gentle care and hit all my points that I needed to be hit. I wanna say Dua. If you are in the vicinity of this table make sure you come and visit dua." - **Mfundishi Jhutyms**

Neb Kheperu RA

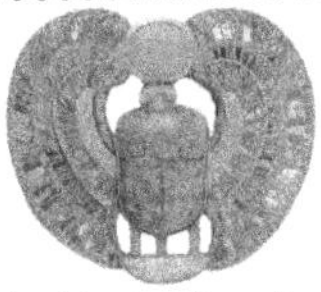

I decided to hand my card out to people and invite them to my chair for a massage. I only handed my card out to 3 or 4 people but the last person was **Ahket**. I handed her my card and told her I was doing chair massage. I introduced myself and asked her name. She mentioned her feet hurting and that she needed a massage. I asked her what she does, she said she was a doulla. I said I have a friend who's a doulla, her name is Myla. To my surprise she replied - "I know Myla and I know you! Myla's been trying to get me to get a massage from you for the longest." Of course this left us shaking our heads. What was the likeliness of this happening? Myla was a massage client of mine and apparently she had told her friend Ahket about me. Perhaps we were meant to meet. I looked at Ahket's wrist and she had a wooden scarab cuff on. What's the likeliness that we are both wearing a scarab cuff on the left wrist. Ahket agreed to get a massage so I walked her to my chair and I gave her a massage. She was kind enough to leave me a review.

Chair Massage Video Review #2

"I just had a wonderful, blissful massage by Dawud here at the African Arts Festival. I highly recommend getting a treatment with him. He knew exactly where I needed the work and I feel so much better. Release of tension and stress so it was wonderful. Thank you so much" - **Ahket**

Significance

On April 4th 2020 (page 594) my past life as **Tutankhaten** (**King Tut**) would come to me and after that I would start studying the life of Tutankhaten and his family. I would come to learn that the word Ahket means horizon and Tutankhaten's father Akhenaten named his city **Akhet**Aten (page, 671). The Aten (sun) on the horizon. I would also come to know that the image of a scarab on her cuff was the throne name of Tutankhaten, **Neb Kheperu Ra**.

Chair Massage Video Review #3

"This was such an excellent massage, I mean a chair massage. It felt like I was on a table with brother Dawud. Check him out here at commodore park Brooklyn. Blessings" **- Acacia**

confirmations

A few months later I would give Acacia some sacred medicine and during her trip she says that **Harriet Tubman** came to greet her. See pages 545 and 584.

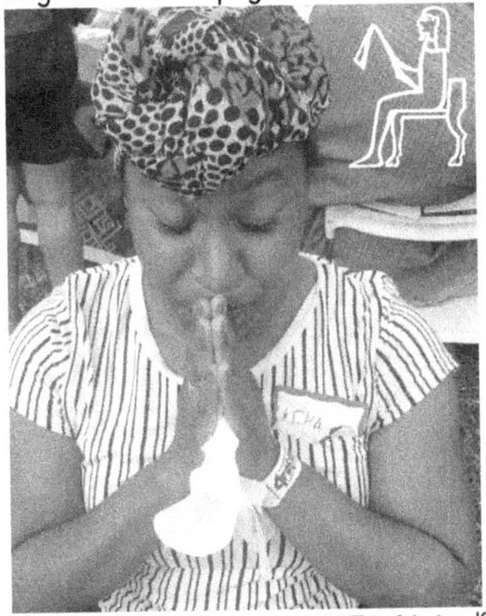

The 1st BEETLE (Khepri, The Only Begotten Son)
Chair Massage Video Review #4

"I just got done getting a massage by Dawud and it is two thumbs up I wish I could put my toes up too I didn't want him to stop. I can't wait for the full body massage. Thank you Dawud." **- Eve**

After I had given **Eve** a chair massage we sat down and got into a conversation about **coincidences** and **synchronicities**. I told her about my past life of Emmett Till and as soon as I said - "**nothing is just a coincidence**" a scarab landed on my wrist next to my silver scarab cuff. We were both **amazed**, I took a picture quickly. This was the first time I had ever seen a scarab in my life, or the only time that I could remember. I told people what had happened and some people smiled. I'm sure some thought I was reading too deep into a random occurrence. Either way I thought I had gotten the sign I was looking for but little did I know the scarab wasn't done with me yet.

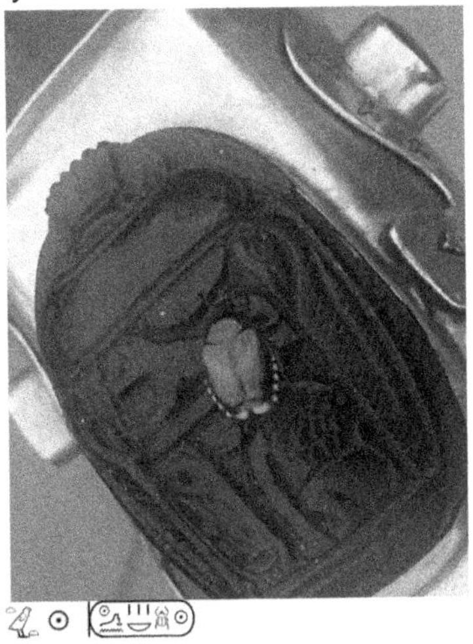

Chair Massage Video Review #5

"So what can I say? My energy has been totally shifted to someplace so relaxing and divine. I could have just stayed there forever and I'm just gonna try to hold on to this. 10 minutes can make such a big difference! It's amazing, amazing." - **Ethel**

July 4th 2019 Performing my song: Da Naga

"Most people wanna win the lottery, I want the answers to the odyssey, the mystery, number one cause of death? coronary artery! if I should die before eye awaken fully, cardiopulmonary me my **naga,** remember me! then "*bury me a G*" **- Dawud The Uncanny BlaKseed** (Written on August 17th 2018, page 532)

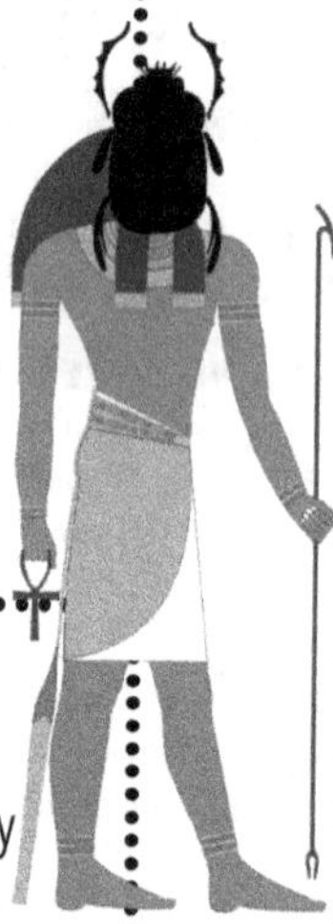

Chair Massage Video Review #6

"I just had an Amazing massage by Dawud. I'm out here at the African Festival, I mean, even though it was so much noise out here I felt like I was in a **trance**. It was so relaxing. My shoulderrs feel less tense, and I just loved it. I really enjoyed it, so thank you so much Dawud and continue doing what you're. Much blessings" - **Saddiya**

July 5th 2019 (2nd day International African Arts Festival)

Brother Nova Felder, Brother Yow and myself as we started the 2nd day of the festival. (See Page 457)

July 5th 2019
2nd day International African Arts Festival
The 2nd BEETLE (Khepri, The Only Begotten Son)

The next day I wondered if I would see another scarab. I got to the festival early and helped set up. **Mfundishi** needed to extend his tent so **Nova** and I grabbed a tent and began to set it up with two other people. We all grabbed a corner of the tent and began to open it. As I began to open my corner of the tent I noticed something dangling in front of my face. As I focused in on what was hanging I saw that it was a dead scarab hanging from a single strand of hair, the same kind of scarab that had landed on my scarab cuff the day prior. Astonished, I carefully pulled it down and showed it to **Nova** and **Mfundishi** and other people then put it in my bag for safe keeping. When I got home that day I put the scarab in a jar and placed it on my book shelf. I still have it to this day.

Rau nu Prt m heru

Iu f Per f m heru

Utterances for Coming Forth by day into Light

It is he, who comes forth by day into Light

July 6th 2019 (3rd day at the Festival)
The 3rd BEETLE (Khepri, The Only Begotten Son)

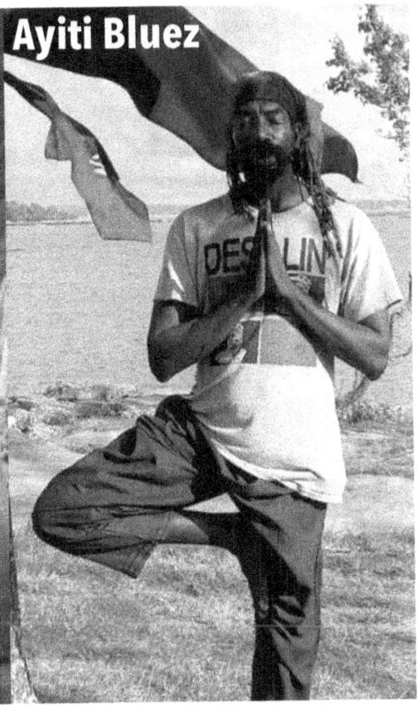

Of course I was looking for a scarab today! I was looking for the pattern but that's not the way it would play out today. Instead I would hear a someone shouting my name. I turned around to see brother **Jeffre Ayiti**. He rushes me back to **Mfundishi Jhutyms'** tent and leads me to a table. He reach down and lifted up a piece of paper and under it was a scarab! The same kind as the two previous days. **Ayiti** explain that **Mother Mut** Rita from **Mfundishi Jhutyms'** Shrine (**Jhuty Heru Neb Hu**) was looking for me and as soon as she spoke my name the scarab appeared and landed in front of them on the table. As soon as I saw the scarab I took my phone out and took a picture of it and shook my head in amazement. Brother Ayiti had heard about the scarabs coming to me the first two days so when he saw the scarab he knew it was not just a coincidence. Ayiti is born on **May 25**, the first star code pattern in this book (pages 30, 222) same day my sister had the dream about my car accident (p 104) and that same day that was on the **silver ring** that identified Emmett Till's body (p 512)! In 2021 Mother Mut Rita would have a profound experience after receiving a chair massage from me, where a portal between the seen world and the unseen world was opened (p 650). One time is an incidence, twice is a coincidence, but 3, 4, 5 is a pattern. Can you tell the difference?

***Addendum* The TutemRa Kheperu Effect**

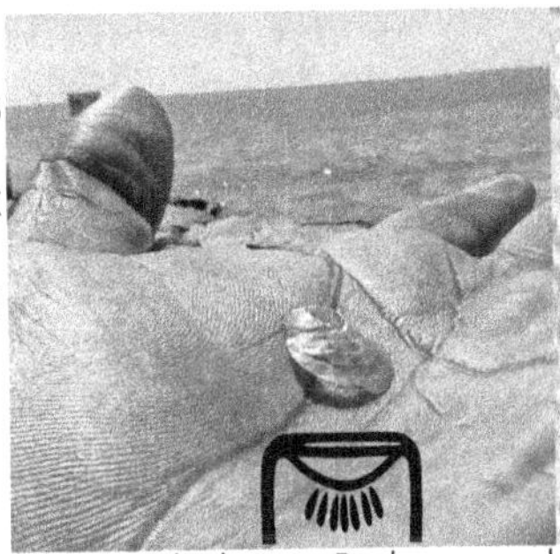

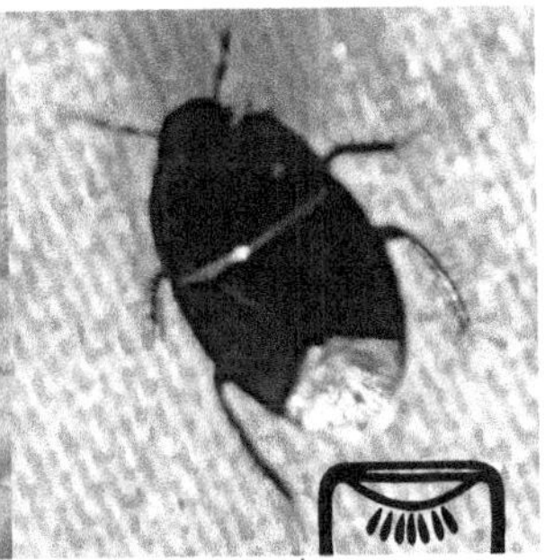

I met Jeffre Ayiti in 2019, which is **the year of the Pig**, the same year the **Haitian revolution** was sp**ark**ed in 1791, the year of the Pig (page 472). In 2021, two years after I had this experience with Jeffre Ayiti and the Scarab beetles (**Kheper**), he began to have experiences of his own with Scarab Beetles (**Kheper**). At 08:29:09 EDT, on Aug 14, 2021, a magnitude 7.2 earthquake struck the Caribbean nation of **Ayiti** (Haiti). Aug 14 being the anniversary of **Bwa Kayiman**, the day that the Haitian Revolution was planned. The next day, on Aug 15, 2021, Jeffre would find a **golden sea shell** on **Rockaway** beach while doing **Smai Tawi** (Kemetic Yoga). 9 days later on August 24, again on Rockaway beach, Jeffre would encounter black and **gold** scarab beetle. He was teaching a Kemetic Yoga class and while transitioning into the Kheper pose, a black and **gold** beetle landed on his mat in front of him. Upon closer inspection he saw that the bottom of the beetle had a **golden** design shaped like a sea shell. These events took place in Rockaway and I was born in Rockaway. Starting on June **23rd** (p 648) of that same year I had experiences of my own on Rockaway beach that work to confirm the prophecy brought forth in this book (pages 647 - 653). To make my connection to Jeffre more **strange**, in 2005, the same year I exited the Army, a **King Tut** exhibit toured 4 American cities, L.A., Chicago, Philly and Fort Lauderdale. The exhibit had **King Tut** portrayed as a light skinned middle eastern man which caused protests from Black people.. By some **strange twist of fate** Jeffre took part in the Fort Lauderdale protests. He remembers chanting, "**King Tut's back, and he's still black!**". This exhibit started in Los Angeles on June 16, **Tupac's** birthday! On April 4, 2020, the day **Martin Luther King** was Assassinated, my **past life** as **King Tut** was be revealed to me (p 594). I have a theory about who **Tupac** was in a **past life** and there's no wonder why the exhibit opened on his birthday (page 665). One time is an incidence, twice is a coincidence, but 3, 4, 5 is a pattern. Can you tell the difference?

Tarot Card Reading from Empress Embahra Ma'at

A few hours later I would get a Tarot card reading from **Empress Embahra Ma'at**, the wife of **Nswt Biti Ra Sankhu Kheper** (scarab) the **Kemetic priest** for the **Temple Of Anu** in New Jersey. This was only the 2nd tarot reading I had ever had in my life. She pulled 4 cards. The first was the Emperor card with **Shu** sitting on the throne with a feather of **Maat** on his head, holding an **ankh** in each hand. When I saw that I laughed as I was sitting there with a peacock feather in my hair. The second card was the **Lovers** card with a man and a woman facing each other with affection. The third card was a plow which means **love** in ancient Kemet (Egypt). The last card was an **amulet** with two feathers of **Maat**. I asked her what this meant and from what I can remember she said "If I want to ascend the **throne** and become the master of the air like **Shu** I need to attract a partner or partners." then I asked her if she could see any **guardians** behind me and she said she can't **see** any but she could sense and feel that I had many behind me, like an **army**. Sometime before or after my reading Ra Sankhu Kheper took me to his car where we listened to each others music. Afterwards I told him my story of my **past life** revelation of **Emmett Till**.

Chair Massage Video Review #7

"This is beautiful. I feel great. And the rain, the rain does something, soothes and I have a full relaxation. It's amazing. Thank you so much. Dua nefer. Peace." - **Ankhesenamen**

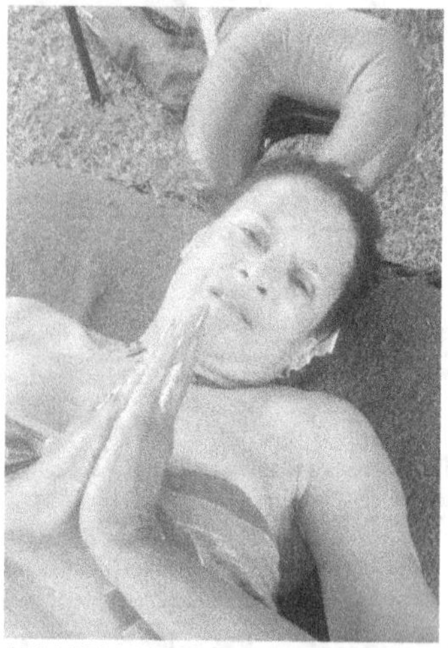

Chair Massage Video Review #8

"My name is Nadine .I'm from Philadelphia Pennsylvania. My daughter gave me a massage for a treat today but as brother Dawud was massaging me I just thought about my ancestors and they never experienced anything like this. So today what I experienced I just give it back to the ancestors. Thank you." - **Nadine**

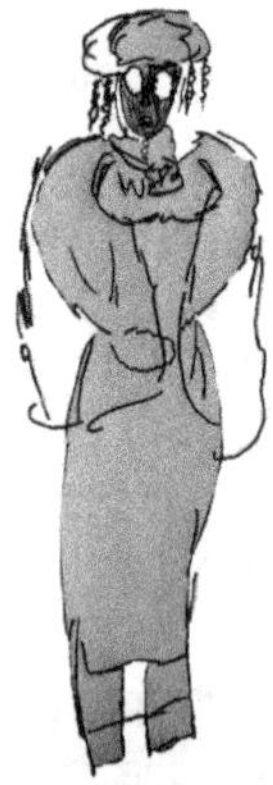

Chair Massage Video Review #9

"I'm Nycomie and I just had a massage with Dawud, and I feel so much better. I literally was about to cry before I saw him cause I was in so much pain and now I can like move my neck. I couldn't even do this before (stretches neck) so this is amazing. Thank you." - **Nycomie**

July 7th 2019 (The last day of the International Afrikan Arts Festival)

The 4th BEETLE (Khepri, The Only Begotten Son)

On the 4th and last day I wondered if I would see another scarab but to my surprise I would see 3 scarabs. As the vendors were opening up their tents for the start of their day I would see a giant scarab land on a book bag that was hanging up for sale. This was not the same kind of scarab as the three previous days. I got my phone out and began recording. The scarab flew off the bag and into the next tent and landed on the ground next to another scarab, near a hole in the ground. As I was recording the scarab mounted the other scarab and performed the art of creation. Then crawled into the hole. After I caught that footage on my phone I thought that was it for the day for scarabs but I was wrong. This was not just a coincidence! One time is an incidence, twice is a coincidence, but three, four, five is a pattern! Can you tell the difference?

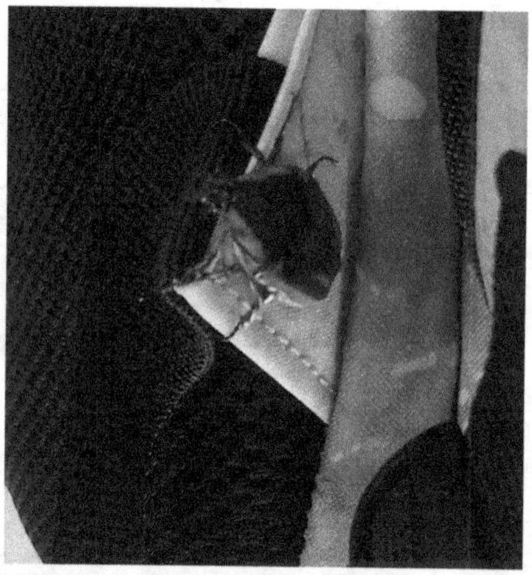

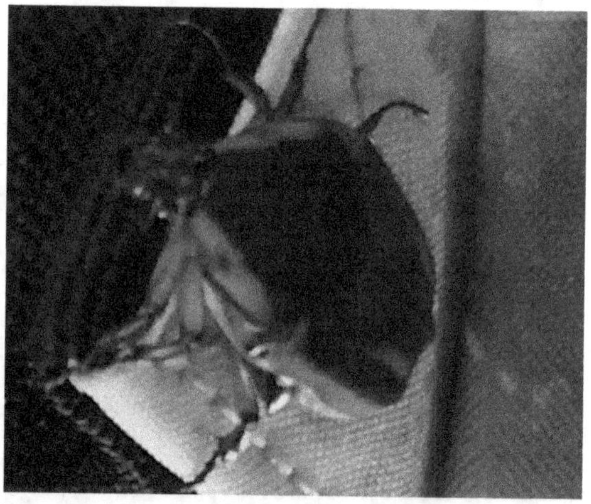

Rau nu Prt m heru

Iu f Per f m heru

Utterances for Coming Forth by day into Light

It is he, who comes forth by day into Light

Chair Massage Video Review #10

"Hi my name is Lameek Smith and I just been massaged by Dawud. I have a torn meniscus and after he massaged me I felt no pain. I was able to stand straight up without pain at all. I also suffer from Lupus so all my joints hurt all the time and right now I'm pain free. Thank you." **- Meeky**

The 5th BEETLE (Khepri, The Only Begotten Son)

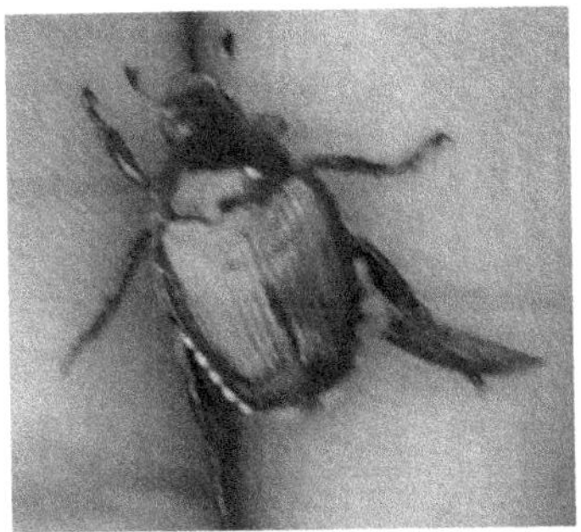

After I had given Lameek a massage and she had given a video testimonial I told her about my past life as Emmett Till and how a scarab had come to me three days in a row and perhaps two seconds after a bug flew in between us. **I said, "it's probably a scarab" and as I focused, I saw that indeed it was a scarab**. I caught it and took a picture. We were amazed. One time is an incidence, twice is a coincidence, but three, four, five is a pattern! Can you tell the difference? I talked to her about not giving **Lupus** power over her and showed her the book, ABC of Asthma, Allergies and Lupus. I introduced her to **Mr G** who had worked with **Dr Sebi**. Afterwards Lameek made changes to her lifestyle and eating habits now she does not suffer from the symptoms associated with Lupus. Meeky would come to me for massage once a month after the festival and some time in 2020 she would share her gift of sight with me (page 584).. Some time after meeting Mr G we had a conversation about **dreams** and I told him of a dream I had with **Erykah Badu** and he confirmed that what she did in the dream is something she does. (page 549). I would later find that Meeky can "see" dead people (pages 504/604/650) but she could not hear them. Some time after learning this I gave her some sacred medicine and for the first time she could communicate with the unseen realms.... See Page 584.

Chair Massage Video Review #11

"I just got a blessed massage. I'm in that bliss state. Definitely hit points that held stress. Had that intelligence in the hands. He knew where the release needed to happen and he helped move it out. Give thanks. Peace yes sir." **- Ras Ben**

Chair Massage Video Review #12

"It was amazing. I was so tight but Dawud just made me, he like released a lot of pent up energy that was stagnant. He released some chakras and stuff. It was amazing. He as great as the Chinese massage therapist I go to all the time. He's amazing. Get yours as soon as possible"

Chair Massage Video Review #13

"Hi, good afternoon my name is Linda and I'm here at the Arts festival in Brooklyn and I met Dawud, and I just had a massage. It was like 15 minutes, it felt so rejuvenating. I feel so revived, so refresh. It was so good and having a man do it even better. So thank you. I feel good, much better than when I started. I'm ready to face the week." **- Linda**

Chair Massage Video Review #14

"I just got a good massage from Dawud. You need to come have him work on you. I feel good. I feel like I wanna lay there and sleep after this. Good work. I feel good." **- Ronald A**

Chair Massage Video Review #15

"I feel good man. Thank you. I appreciate everything you did. This was probably the best massage I ever had in my life. My body feels loose. It feels good man. Make sure y'all get with this brother. He's a real good down to earth brother. He's definitely the reborn version of Emmett Till. I see it written on his shirt. He bares the images, man listen get with this brother. He's a good brother. This the best massage you gonna have in your life. I promise you. **- Ty Black**

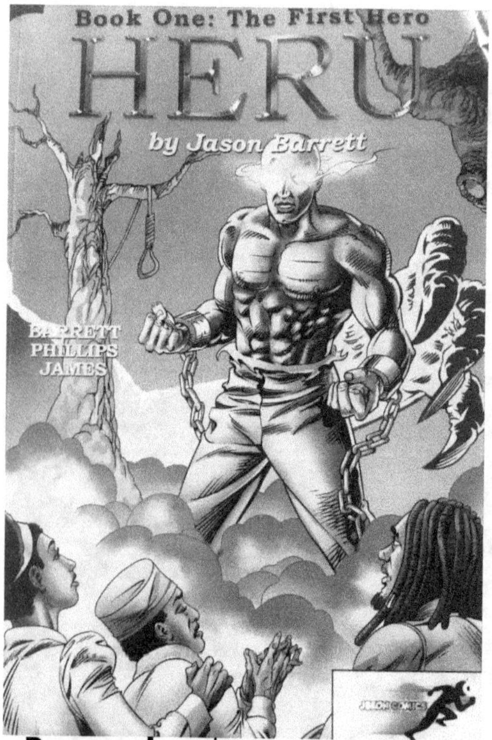

Re-member that **you** are **Ausar** and **Heru**, the **hero**! See page 3 for the **hero's journey**!

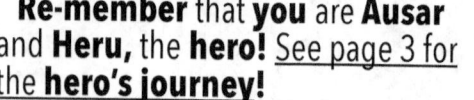

Chair Massage Video Review #16

"Yo this your boy Jason Barrett all the way from England. I just got an amazing massage from Dawud. I'm a fighter so you know I've always got those injuries and lower back problems and shoulder problems and now I'm feeling amazing yo! I don't even all that a massage. I call that plastic cosmetic surgery. -laughs- I feel younger B. Ah man, Dawud number one number one" **- Jason Barrett**

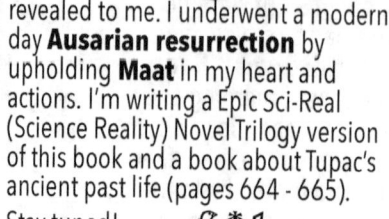

Heru by Jason Barrett

Jason came from England to promote his book **Heru**. Instead of a Money exchanged he offered to extend a copy of his book for a chair massage and I agreed. But who is Heru? Heru is the son of Ausar, the Lord of **resurrection**. **Ausar** defeats death and resurrects (reincarnates) through his son Heru. On April 4th 2020 (page 594) my past life of Tutankhaten (**King Tut**) would be revealed to me. I underwent a modern day **Ausarian resurrection** by upholding **Maat** in my heart and actions. I'm writing a Epic Sci-Real (Science Reality) Novel Trilogy version of this book and a book about Tupac's ancient past life (pages 664 - 665). Stay tuned!

42 Laws of Maat, Page 367

Rau nu Prt m heru

Iu f Per f m heru

Utterances for Coming Forth by day into Light

It is he, who comes forth by day into Light

Chair Massage Video Review #17

"Well I just had a wonderful, therapeutic massage from brother Dawud, which means beloved of God. And it was my earth season, my born season gift to myself today at the African Arts Festival in Brooklyn New York. It was fabulous, this brother does his art. His massage is like art on your body and he does it with love. And it is very good I feel awesome. I feel uplifted and he went over and above what he was supposed to do. I feel great awesome"

Chair Massage Video Review #19

"World, universe, omniverse Dawud; my man he did the work, the job that was needed. Like I'm up here number one being **golden** with my peoples, in New York. Ya know what I'm say'n? and then getting this **golden** massage by this brother, he's enlightening. Beyond that he deals with you the individual. Just a testimonial. Peace Redbone from Philly" - **Redbone**

Significance

Redbone mentions being "**Golden**" and receiving a "**Golden**" massage and On April 4th 2020 my past life of Tutankhaten (**King Tut**) would be revealed to me. "King Tut" is most known for being the first Ancient tomb found in modern times with most of it's **gold** still in it and so "he" is known as the **Golden** boy King Tutankhamun.

Chair Massage Video Review #18

"I just got my reflexology from Dawud, amazing! In one word Amazing!" - **Ka Em Maat**

Chair Massage Video Review #20

"Greetings. I just finished my massage and I never did a massage before to tell you the truth. My back was hurting me and I usually would walk home holding my back on the way to the train but I have to say I don't have any pain. It was great. It was something I always wanted to do and 10 minutes ain't long enough. I really enjoyed the massage and especially no pain. I sat down here with pain. I ain't go no pain no more." - **Shakilla**

Significance

Shakilla would come to my table wearing earings with a **Nefertiti** Pendant.

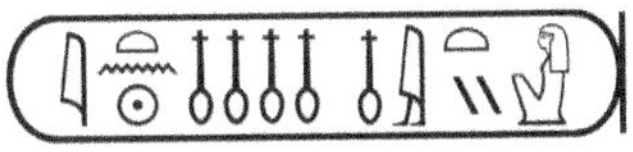

Chair Massage Video Review #21

"I just did my quick little back massage. My back was really hurting. It's incredible how in 15 minutes time my back feels way way different. This the brother Dawud over here I promise you he has magic. Make sure you check this guy out. For real for real. Thank you brother. Peace."

Chair Massage Video Review #22

"Greetings my name is Tamika. I just got a massage from Dawud. I'm trying to find the words to describe how I feel right now but I'll tell you a little about who I am and what I do. I'm a vendor at the International African Arts Festival every year for the past few years and I always say that the end of a four day festival all vendors should get massages including myself but I never do so today I finally did and I'm glad that I did because, when you are on your feet for the whole entire day for four days your legs hurt, your body hurts, you know everything hurts. So getting a massage at the end of the festival was probably the best option so I'm telling all vendors to do that. How do I feel? I never had a massage like this by the way. There are massage practitioners that massage the muscles and things like that but Dawud hit specific points on my body that I didn't even know I needed a massage in. So when he hit those points I felt relaxed. I felt calm. I almost fell asleep -laughs- and he did a full body massage. He also did some movements with my body, on my legs in particular and my arms and my shoulders that some practitioners don't do. This type of body work is something that I will be getting more often but I give thanks for the opportunity to experience this cause a lot of people talk about it. I always see it on your Instagram page and I'm always like I have to get that so shout out to Dawud and his bodywork. Amazing amazing energy. That's another thing. Don't get massages from anyone that you can't resonate with or doesn't have good energy. My energy was totally fine with him and I just feel amazing. I'm ready to go to sleep. I give thanks." - **Tamika**

July 25th 2019 (Album Released)

Dawud The Uncanny BlaKseed (The Immortal Life of Emmett Till)

I did what I felt like I was supposed to do, I released an album with **14** tracks. I planned the release on July 25th 2019 because that is Emmett's birthday. What I didn't plan was it being exactly 1 year and **22** days after my past life revelation of my life as Emmett Till. I realized my life as Emmett on July 3rd 20**18** (page 480) and **22** days later was Emmett's birthday. He would have been **77** and I was born in 19**77** the year of the **snake**. Emmett was born in 19**41** the year of the **snake** and on October 25th of 20**18** I turned **41** (page **41**). Emmett was murdered in 19**55** the same year that my mother was born, I am born **22** years later in 19**77** the year of the **snake** when my mother was **22** years old. My past life revelation of Tutankhaten would come on April 4th **2**0**2**0 (page 594) the same day that Martin Luther King was assassinated. Tutankhaten's tomb was discovered in 19**22** the same year that Emmett Till's father Louis Till was born. I didn't get to pick how much my album would cost. I uploaded it on www.tunecore.com, and their service is horrible. They rob me of my hearts blood. They pay me less than half a penny per stream. It's musical slavery. The type of slavery that Michael Jackson, Prince and Sam Cooke fought against (page 166). But these rhymes weren't written for **money**. These hymns are from the halls of Maat. From the walls of my blood vessels. Emmett was murdered in **Money** M**ississ**ippi. You can find the name Isis (Auset) in the word M**ississ**ippi and Emmett was thrown in a river just like **Ausar** (Osiris), the Husband of Isis who was thrown in a river in the Ausarian resurrection drama. **Ausar** was cut in **14** pieces and thrown in a river and Emmett murdered at **14** years old and thrown in a river (page 508). There are **14** tracks on this album but for some "reason", every word of my album must be typed in before it will appear in the search browser for people desiring to purchase it. Those who control music, make every effort to prevent certain music from going "viral". My song **Blak Wall Street** was taken off Youtube because they said it was considered hate music (page 403). My song Dec 3rd was taken off Soundcloud when it began to amass thousands of views (page 312). **Re-member** that **you** are **Ausar** and **Heru,** the **hero!** See page 3 for the **hero's journey**!

Dawud, Beloved by the Ntru **August 5th 2019 - The Beloved Toni Morrison Goes West**

Chloe Anthony Wofford Morrison (born Chloe Ardelia Wofford) known as Toni Morrison, was an American novelist. She was born on February 18th 1931, the same day as my niece, **the day before** my great grandfather General Dukes Sr and the same year as my grandfather General Dukes Jr. She earned a master's degree in American Literature from Cornell University in 1955 the same year that **Emmett Till** was murdered. Morrison's first play, **Dreaming Emmett**, is about the 1955 murder of **Emmett Till**. The play was performed in 1986 at the State University of New York at Albany. She published her second book, Song of **Solomon** in 19**77** the year of the **snake**, the same year I was born. The book was critically acclaimed and brought her national attention and won the National Book Critics Circle Award. AmenHotep III is the real person that the biblical character King Solomon was fashion after. AmenHotep III (**Solomon**) is the grand father of King tut. In 1987, Morrison published her most celebrated novel, **Beloved** and in 19**88** she won the **Pulitzer Prize** for it. The book **Beloved** was inspired by the **true story** of an enslaved African-American woman, Margaret Garner, whose story Morrison had discovered when compiling The Black Book. Garner had escaped slavery but was pursued by slave hunters. Facing a return to slavery, Garner killed her two-year-old daughter but was captured before she could kill herself. Morrison's novel imagines **the dead baby returning as a ghost**, **Beloved**, at the same age it would have been if it had lived, to haunt her mother and family. Beloved was a critical success and a bestseller for **25** weeks. In the Movie **Beloved** (1998) there is a scene where a group of old women are talking about the baby who had return as Beloved. One of the women says, **"children that die bad don't stay in the ground!"** I remember seeing the movie **Beloved** in 1998 and it was an interesting movie to me. I was drawn to movies about ghost returning, like the movie **Ghost** with **Patrick Swayze**, who was born on August 18th, the same day my grand father General Dukes Jr died, and Patrick died on September 14th **the day after** Tupac died. My name **Dawud** (David), means **Beloved** of God. I am the ghost of Emmett Till that has returned in another body but I have not come to haunt anyone. I have come to remind everyone that the soul is immortal. I have come to warn everyone that there is a penalty to pay for what you do in this life and the time we spend in the state we call death can feel like an eternity. When you spend an hour with someone you're in love with it feels like minutes but if you place your hand on a hot stove for 5 seconds it feels like an eternity! How do you want to spend an eternity?! Many of the corresponding number patterns that fill the pages of this book are mathematical equations formulated by the hatred this country has displayed. I was chosen to come back and die a sacrificial death so that I could have the opportunity to be born again in this life and earn the right to know who I was and with the revealing of this revelation mans consciousness will be aroused and justice can at-last prevail. Morrison's first novel was The Bluest Eye, and "Emmett" had Green Eyes. She died on August 5th 2019 at **88** years old, and on August 5th 2014 I wrote the song **Tryptophan** and in it I said the words, "**I'm patiently waiting incarnating for ages,** This ain't my last time, This ain't my last rhyme, **The sun will always shine,** One day at a time, My only fear of death is **reincarnation"** (page 300).

Condolences

My condolences go out to the family, friends and fans of **Toni Morrison**. Please know that death is not the end. The soul survives death, indeed and in spirit. This is a book of the dead written by a boy who was murdered without justice, who defeated death and came forth by day. May the soul of **Toni Morrison** walk peacefully through the field of Reeds in Amenta. Amen Ra.

***Addendum* Whoopi Goldberg, Patrick Swayze the movie Ghost, Emmett Till and Beyond King Tut**

Whoopi Goldberg was was born in 19**55**, the same year **Emmett Till** was murdered. **Patrick Swayze** played the "**ghost**" (the spirit lingering on after death) in the movie. Patrick is born on August 18th, the same day my grand father **General Dukes Jr** died (page 169). My grand father appeared to me in spirit form on Dec 18 2015 (p 348), just like Patrick did in the movie **Ghost**. 3 days after my birthday, on **October 28,** 20**22**, the movie **Till** was released. **Whoopi Goldberg** was one of the executive producers of the movie. That same day, **October 28,** 20**22** the **Beyond King Tut Exhibit** opened in NYC (page 29 & 33). I have not watched my movie but I went to my Exhibit on Dec **22,** 20**22** with Shanta (page 289).

Rau nu Prt m heru

Iu f Per f m heru

Utterances for Coming Forth by day into Light

It is he, who comes forth by day into Light

August 12th 2019 No Coincidence

I handed her my card and said "hello there", **She said** "so rare", I said "what?" **She said** "the feather in yo hair ", I said "Yeah where ever I go they stare at me as if I float in the air", **She looked** at my card then said "You do massage?", I said "Yeah my chair's over there", **She said** "This is odd, my feet and back throb, this is God at work, **No coincidence!**", I went to work on her feet with tenderness, she fell asleep deep, then woke up in the wilderness, I was there, in despair, we both said "Where is this?!", it was vivid, lucid, limitless, like Genesis! I said "We lost in a **dream**, a simulation, a light **matrix**, a vibration, it's all mental, **She said** "What do you mean is it governmental?!" I said "No it's elementary, it's elemental" - **Dawud The Immortal BlaKseed**

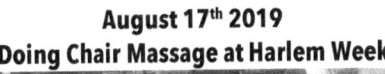

August 17th 2019

Doing Chair Massage at Harlem Week

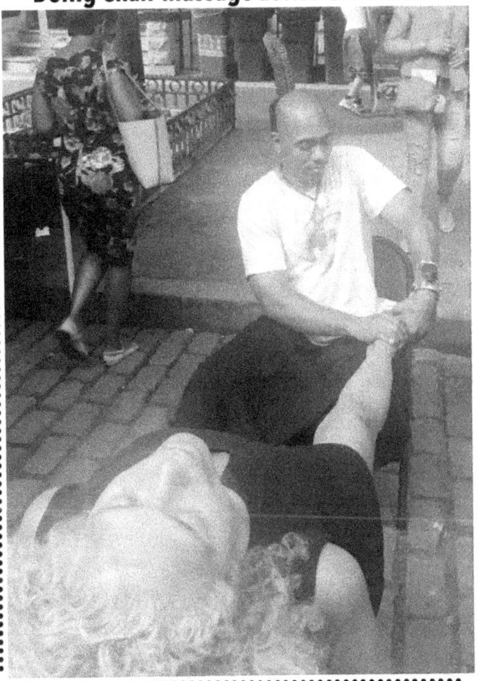

August 26th 2019 Stolen Legacy

When the lights cameras and action glamour glitter and gold saddens the soul, you sit back and wonder how we fell in this hole, a cold felony, no penalty for my **Stolen Legacy,** just enmity the only solution for them is tyranny! are you hearing me? a revolutionary with no weaponry, **7 Day Theory** leave you crossed out allegedly, **Bury Me a G** clearly like **George G.M. James,** the **immortality** of the **soul** can't be locked down in chains, they say I changed, yeah, I try tried till I butterflied - **Dawud The Immortal BlaKseed**

August 31st 2019 The Molder

I fell asleep woke up in a tomb, my **Dog** said, "Do you wanna see a dead body"? I said "take me to the room", the wall said "here lies **Khnum** the molder, he fashioned man from black clay like **Yoda** divine", I shine like the **Sun Aten,** the only begotten forgotten like **Huey P** in his prime, they plot'n to weaken the line, they got you eating the swine detrimental, everything is mind mental in my environmental, inside the temple in man, Dawud be influential when pencil instrumental my hand, I fight lefty destroying what is evil, the eye does what is true, I be **The Lord of Ma'at** but what is **Maat** to you? flying out the **cosmos**, the you in the you-niverse that **God** chose, I rose like the lotus, write scrolls on papyrus, notice the **Osiris** iris effect on my dialect, step by step I intercept intellect from **Imhotep**, I be a war vet spiritual guarded on the ethereal, lyrical **Heru** hekau, speaking **Maakheru**, true of voice for the voiceless, against all odds when I'm choice-less - **Dawud The Immortal BlaKseed**

42 Laws of Maat, Page 367

September 1st 2019 - Monique Takes Me to My First Powwow

My high school sweetheart Monique Wallace (page 60, 148) took me to my **first Powwow**. It was in the city at the Armory. She grew up her whole life knowing she was a Native American from the Shinnecock Nation and went to PowWow's. While at this pow wow I would walk around looking for a **dream catcher** to purchase. I looked at all the vendors and finally I settled on one for $25 dollars. They handed me a flyer for their reservation as I left and I was surprised to see the name of their Chief was General like my late Grandfather. I attended **my second Powwow** with Monique as well, at the 72nd Shinnecock in Long Island. I did not realize I was Native American until I was in my 30's after my grandfather passed away in 2009. My Uncle Jimmy told me that my **Grand Father** was **Cherokee Indian** and so I was too (p 660). Years later at a family gathering with my **Father**, I met some relatives that I had never met before and after seeing the feather in my hair (p 385) they told me that I was a Native, **Blackfoot Indian** from my paternal grandmother (pages 15 & 25). I also learned that my paternal Grandfather was from **Barbados** so I was also **Bajan** (pages 15 & 25). It's no wonder why I fell in love with Monique the way that I did. I still remember traveling to see her in the snow during to the blizzard of 1996 (p 60). No one was out in this storm but I was making my way to see a girl, that at the time I was only kissing. I still love Monique and would be there for her if she ever needed me. 5 days from this date Bothem Jean would be killed in his home by a police office (p 581).

September 13th 2019 More Than Love

There's a war going on outside, we need more than love! we need pain, anger and hate we need **immortal thugs,** who ain't afraid to ride on his enemy, if my words bother you my **Naga**, then you ain't never been a friend to me! see I'm so sick and tired of being sick and tired, **Clifford Glover** murdered at 10! the **cop** that killed him was never fired! he was admired and inspired a generation of white rage, cops killing Black kids in the inner city **- Dawud The Immortal BlaKseed**

Significance

I did not plan this but this was written on the day Tupac died. In the year 2000 a documentary about Tupac was released titled **Immortal Thug** and I say **Immortal Thugs** in this song. I still have a copy of that documentary that I purchased in the year 2000. I have a theory about who **Tupac** was in a **past life** and because of who I am and who I was I feel my theory is true.

2019 (Giara Nova and The Giant Titanium Scarab Beetle)

I gave Nova a massage and after the massage Nova told me she saw a giant titanium **scarab beetle** with small beetles floating around it. This was before I knew the full meaning of the scarab and before I knew I was Tutankhaten (**King Tut**).

Sometime in December of 2021 I would see that Nova took a picture next to a replica of King Tut's gold mask on October 7th 2015. She is born on December 1st the same day that **Rosa Parks** refused to give her seat to a white man in 1955 Alabama because she was angry about the murder of **Emmett Till**. I met Nova in a magical way in 2010 (page 184) and our friendship would prove to be another piece of this unseen web that was forming around me. The December 3rd pattern would start at her home on Dec 17th of 2014 (page 314) where I would be visited by a friend Jay Cooper who had passed away on Dec 3rd of 2014. The pattern would involve music, death, the underworld and the immortality of the soul. It would strike again a year later on Dec 3rd of 2015 (Sean Price, page 345), then again on Dec 3rd of 2016 (Tupac, page 431), Dec 3rd 2017 (DR Jack Felder, page 457) and finally ending in 2022 with **Clinton Melton**, on page 519.. I was having experiences with the souls of people who had passed away. The 4th experience would involve the soul of **DR Jack Felder** who is the father of another friend of mine who is **also named Nova!!**. There is no such thing as just a coincidence, all things are governed by seen and unseen forces. Nova Plays **Vanity** (Page 362). The spirit of **Prince** (p 379).

September 27th 2019 A Different look at Emmett Till

It's not about how much you know, it's about how much you desire to know! What exactly do I mean by that? I know that I attracted this information and at the same time my ancient soul fragments and the universe wanted me to find it. The video was made for me to find! Just like **Star Wars**, **Lost**, and **The Never Ending Story**, were all made for me to watch. At this time I knew for sure that I was Emmett Till and that was it! But of course there were soul fragments within me that knew I was Tutankhaten too! In fact it was my soul that woke me up at 3am on Sep 27th 2019 and placed the **thought*** in my mind to ***go to youtube***. I woke up at 3am and the first thing I did was open my phone to youtube and the first video **suggested*** to me was a video titled: **A different look at Emmett Till**. The brother who uploaded the video was inspired by another youtube channel named **Gnosis**. During this video the brother mentions another brother named **Asir Duke of Tiers.** My grand father's last name was **Dukes** (p 19) and Asir is another way of spelling then name **Ausar** (Osiris) the Kemetic (Egyptian) lord or **resurrection**. **Re-member** that **you** are **Ausar** and **Heru,** the **hero!** See page 3 for the **hero's journey!** After I watched this video it peaked my interest and solidified a connection to ancient Kemet but I did not fully believe I was Tutankhaten (King Tut)

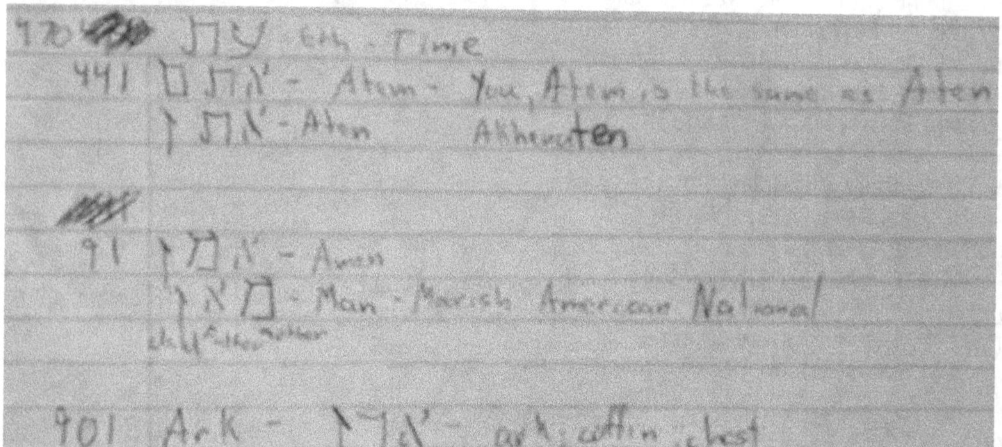

at this time! The video had been uploaded to youtube on February 13th 2017. I watched the video and it seemed to confirm what the **Bufo** had told me on July 21st 2018 (p 529) as it connected Emmett Till to ancient Kemet via Hebrew **Demontria** (numerology). The brother in the video had taken the name Emmett Till and broken down the **etymological** and **numerological** meanings along with the use of a **biblical concordance.** He found that

Emmett Till added up to 901 in Hebrew, so he then went to the concordance to cross referenced **901** and what he found **astounded** me! He found the word **Ark** (**of the covenant**) and as he continued he also found that **Emmett** meant **truth, mound, build up,** and **Till** meant **Amen, Time, Aten, Ark.** He had other theories about why Emmett was lynched but I do not agree with that. He thinks it was some sort of planned ritual because of the aftermath of the lynching and the effects on the Civil Rights Movement. I agreed to come here as Emmett Till knowing that I would be murdered, and knowing that I would forget that I was going to be murdered and after that I would have to traverse the afterlife waiting for the most divine time to return and even then when I returned as Dawud Basheer Eddings I would have no knowledge of this agreement. My memory of all my previous lives would be gone. I would have to earn the right to know that I was Emmett Till and again I would have to earn the right to know I was Tutankhaten. Then after all that I had to write this book.

Rau
nu
Prt
m
heru

901

He followed the trail of the number 901 and went to the concordance and found the words, **Aron** and the **Ark of the Covenant**. Directly under that was the name **Eliasaph** described as **Prince of the tribe of Gad**. Why is this significant you might ask. Because the father of Tutankhaten is **Akhen<u>aten</u>** and he is the historical person that the story of **Moses** was fashioned after in the bible and **Aaron** was **Moses**'s brother in the bible. One time is an incidence, twice is a coincidence, three, four, five is a pattern can you tell the difference?

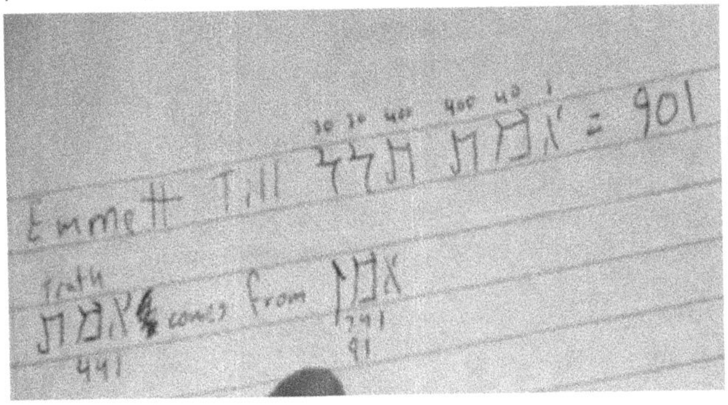

471

Iu
f
Per
f
m
heru

Afterwards he added the name Emmett Till a different way and came up with the number **471.** Then he went to the concordance to cross referenced the number 471 and found **Mount Moriah** (2 Chronicles chapter 3). 2 Chronicles chapter 3 in the bible starts with Solomon building the temple of the Lord in Jerusalem on Mount Moriah where the Lord had appeared to his father **David (Dawud)**. What I found more interesting about the page he turned to were the words at the top of the page. The words **eternity**, **a cycle of cycles**, **angel of 8**, and **period of time** can all be seen right above the number 471. This book is about angles and **angels**, the number **8** and **eternity** and the fact that the soul is immortal **coming back** here again and again in **a cycle of cycles** for short **periods of time**.

Utterances
for
Coming
Forth
by day
into
Light

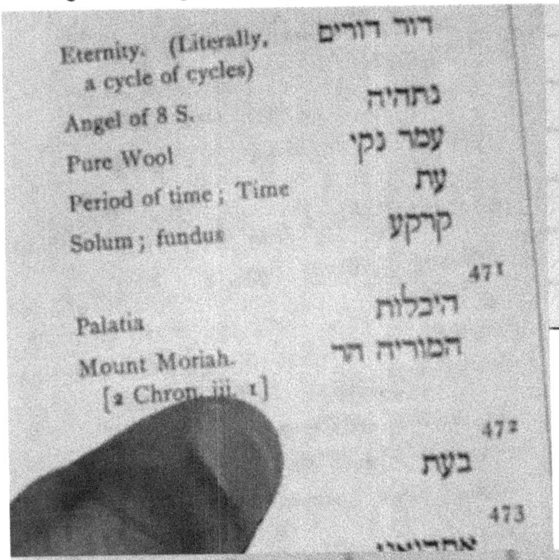

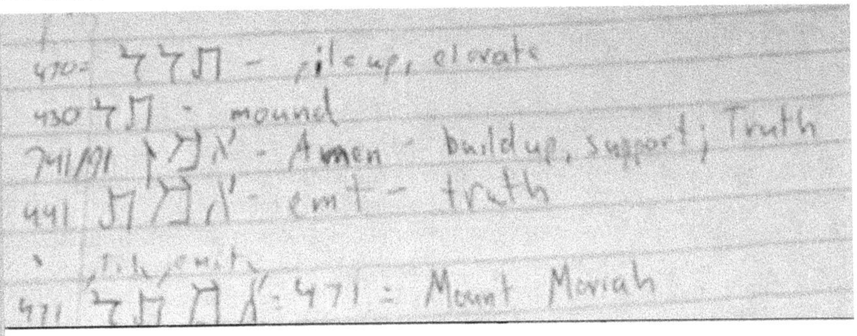

My ancient soul fragments wanted me to find this video.

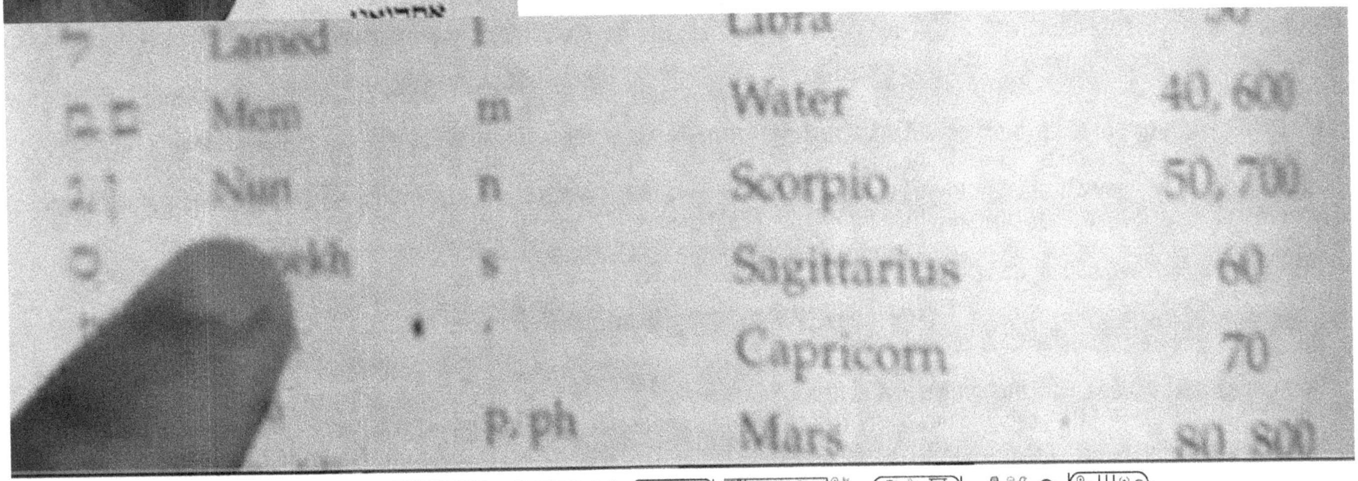

It is
he,
who
comes
forth
by day
into
Light

September 27th 2019
A Different look at Emmett Till

Scorpio

I found it hard to understand his reasoning behind why he turned to this page but his reasoning is not as important as how I decode it. On this page he points to **Nun** and **Scorpio** (p 580). The Scorpio is one of the first land animals to emerge from the primeval waters of **Nun** (the sea). They deal well in isolation and can survive long periods of time under earth regenerating/preserving itself without food or light. I am a Scorpio and a Scorpio's triumph comes when we successfully integrate our souls into our personality and use its resulting powers for the benefit of humankind. To realize these revelations I had to descend into Pluto's underworld (Ausar/Osiris). I confronted all the demons in my past as well as those within my own subconscious hell and after each successful confrontation I unearthed a new treasure. My journey was murderous but it offered me the greatest opportunity because when the Scorpio rises from its own ashes, it takes with it the occult powers transforming from the Falcon to the **phoenix** liberating ourselves and **reclaiming all parts of ours Soul**. The awakened Scorpio embodies the life-giving powers to heal itself and others. Its final prize is its own **immortality**. I have realized my truth and found the **Light** within my own being. I will now practice living the truth for the rest of my days. I will cherish the **Light** of my **Soul** and I will share my **Love** with others. This journey has been worth it and another journey has just begun. I know that I will continue to be reborn again and again. "Amen Atum Aten, never to be forgotten, from Neb Kheperu Ra to slave fields pick'n cotton, from Emmett Till get'n killed thrown in a river rotten, like Ausar I came back as Dawud TutemRa".
Re-member that **you** are **Ausar** and **Heru,** the **hero!** See page 3 for the **hero's journey**!

September 29th 2019 (The 2,200 year old temple on Ptolemy IV discovered in Egypt)

Sanitation workers digging near the western bank of the Nile River in Kemet (Egypt) make a most unexpected discovery. On September 29th the remains of a 2,200 year old temple was found. The temple is believed to have belonged to Pharaoh Ptolemy IV, the fourth Pharaoh of Ptolemaic Egypt from 221 to 204 BC. Archaeologists found inscriptions that read "Ptolemy IV" along the walls of the temple and imagery of animals and birds. See page 424 for the significance of September 29.

October 4th 2019 Bothem Jean

Dear Momma if they murder me, theres a few things I don't wanna see! don't let the family hug my killa! don't let em smear my name! tell em I was a healer! tell em I died and came back cause I'm a real **Naga!** tell em the bible is false mind control drama! tell em the cost of freedom is death! tell em the devil gonna kill until there's none of us left! tell em a dollar bill means nothing if we still ain't free! tell **Jay Z** we got **99 problems** we gotta solve em! tell **Killa Mike** he was right cause too often we fight over what Cracker gonna stab us in the back then leave us in a coffin! tell em we caught in this game of torture and pain, tell em the food is the poison ignorance is to blame! everybody claim to be woke but they sleep walking insane, tell em **We Came Before Columbus**, time for us to reclaim and demand hundreds of thousands of acres of land! he who maketh a slave, can't be much of a man, he who burns a cross can't walk with a cross in his hand, and fuck the law when they made by the **Ku klux klan,** this **the Immortal life of Emmett Till**, they got me load'n up a piece of steel, all I wanna do is relax and chill, but how can I do that when Blacks getting killed

RIP **Joshua Brown,** another man down they said it was gang related, they sprinkled crack on the ground, sound like a **Dave Chappell** skit, episode of law and order, **Joshua** survived by a son and I think he had a daughter, he didn't want to testify cause the brother didn't wanna die! so what he do?! fly to California! what would you do if you was shot in the foot last November, fearing for your life and you not a gang member but you was there on the night? shots rang out **Amber Guyger** said she feared for her life, but that's a lie and we all know it, destroying evidence is perjury! she got 10 years! brothers get more years for burglary!!! career criminals this is warfare on you and me! *no fair trial usually, mob style brutally, destroy multimillionaire Black communities!* no care, no punishment, impunity! look'a hear my **Naga** we need more Black unity! the drama is real, she gonna appeal and probably get off, we will never get a fair deal putting trust in their courts! you better off loading up steel and holding down fort! never forget what they did to **Sean Bell** up in New York, for real! this **the Immortal life of Emmett Till**, they got me load'n up a piece of steel, all I wanna do is relax and chill, but how can I do that when Blacks getting killed - **Dawud The Immortal BlaKseed**

October 12th 2019 (The Murder of Atatiana Jefferson 28. Miami Florida)

Responding to a call about a door being open officer **Aaron** Dean shot Atatiana through the window while she was at home babysitting her 8 year old nephew. Officer Aaron dean resigned. He was later indicted on murder charges.

Condolences

My condolences go out to the families of **Atatiana Jefferson, Bothem Jean** and all those who have been robbed of their life by this system of white supremacy. Please know that death is not the end. The soul survives death, indeed and in spirit. This is a book of the dead written by a boy who was murdered without justice, who defeated death and came forth by day. May the souls of **Atatiana Jefferson** and **Bothem Jean** walk peacefully through the field of Reeds in Amenta. Amen Ra

---

October 18th 2019 Atatiana Jefferson

Rest in peace to Atatiana, with no honor she was struck down, Black state of emergency who do we trust now?! They say the good die young, is it enough now?! they said the power of one can bring this house down, White privilege with a gun everybody running for cover, remorse he got none, then we kill each other, my brother tell me why do we kill each other?- **Dawud The Immortal BlaKseed**

November 7th 2019 They Wanna Know

Rau nu Prt m heru

They wanna know how I found this ***Treasure***, gotta learn to let go, can't hold on forever! go with the flow follow the signs keep the heart light as a feather, they wanna know if I'm lying, I just point to the **NTCHR!** the true **NTCHRU soul compressor** wiser than a old professor, Dawud da **Naga** a deep deep diver baptizer of the 85'ers, *a sleep sleep I was in a dream for days or was it hours*? every step on this path ain't paved with flowers, they wanna know about the powers and the weak, about the sours and the sweet and so I put it on a beat, while you pray to God for your soul to keep, I'm turning up the solar heat, so to speak, from my head to the djed, to the soles of my feet, and so I sow what I reap, you reap what you sow, a wise man is one who knows what he don't know, still they wanna know who I am, if I am who they say that I am, and if I am how did I come to know? is it a scam or gimmick? no! it's the kam the kemet, the measure of a mans soul has no limit, I walked this land as a man before I was **Emmett**! the spirit is younger at a year than the body is at a minute, they took my body I made a new one then I jumped right in it, **Jhuti** he got the scroll, he the scribe he gonna write it,

Maati Grassi to the highest degree, they wanna know what that is, what I aspire to be, see they reported me dead but that's erroneously, tatted **Djed** on my belly ceremoniously **Makaveli**, melodious binary **Ausar Set Thelonious Sphere Monk** dreaming a stars death, **Allah** wept but kept my soul for save keeping with **Bastet** the black cat speak'n with **Sekhmet** bout isfet and rap and how the way back we miss'n that, the last adapt mind bender turn lyrics to gold, you work all week for your prick of a boss like **Job** in the end you get the weak end of a stick and a cross to hold, he made a billion signed a deal son at the cost of his soul, what a feeling to learn everything you thought was true was a lie that was told, they made a killing stealing the greatest story that was ever stole, **O.D.B.** be for the children the dirty bastard forever be **Ole Dirt Dog Osiris**, see the weakness of a man right through his iris, when it's time to weigh the soul, the **baboon** or the **ibis**, **jhuti** he got the scroll he the scribe he gonna write it, **jhuti** he got the scroll he the scribe he gonna write it **- Dawud The Immortal BlaKseed**

Iu f Per f m heru

(42 Laws of Maat, Page 367)

Significance

I can not with 100% memory say that when I wrote this song I wrote it with the feeling that I had lived in Kemet. I know for a fact that I only began to know I was King Tut on April 4th 2020 (p 594) after the revelation, but on July 20th 2018 I communed with the sacred **Toad** medicine and the next day I thought I was King Tut (p's 5**23**-529), but I really had no circumstantial evidence and I didn't really believe it. BUT* this rhyme must be from that experience because I said, "I walked this land as a man before I was **Emmett**!... when you get to April 3rd 2020 you will read what I wrote about the double nature of the Ka (spirit) (p 591). **I suspect that we are living a double life**. This concept of resurrection was called the **Wehem-Mesut** (repeating of births, p 14).

November 20th 2019 - Meta Mental Encounter Brought Forth From the Mind
The Law of Attraction, Michele Lamy, and the 44th parallel

Utterances for Coming Forth by day into Light

I was in between clients at The SPAaaht (p 455) when I sat down on my yoga mat in the Sesh (**Lotus**) pose with the concept of the **law of attraction** on my mind. With the law of attraction in mind **I sent out the thought** that **I wanted to draw business to myself** and seconds later my phone rang. As I was in meditation I thought to let the phone ring but then I considered that it might be the business I just requested. I opened my eyes and answered my phone and to my surprise it was the concierge of the Bowery hotel. She wanted to know if I was available to train a guest for 5 days straight. I agreed and the woman I trained was **Michele Lamy,** a French culture and fashion Mogul. I trained her for 3 days and gave her a massage the last day earning a little over $1000 for 6hrs of work. I needed the money at the time and I manifested it with my thoughts. Michele was a pleasure to work with, she requested to do some boxing and I was impressed by how hard she hit the boxing pads.

Significance

It is he, who comes forth by day into Light

Our thoughts and desires can affect our reality by influencing quantum level events in time and space. From a simple thought I attracted this business to me. It wasn't that I created the business because business potential is always there waiting for us to attract it but some things take longer to arrive than others. No different than arriving from a 10 mile trip or a 1000 mile trip. Our brains send out impressions just like radio signals. At the same exact moment that the concierge at the hotel was looking through a pile of business cards for a possible personal trainer to train their guest I was sitting in the **Lotus** position with a clear thought to attract business to me. This is the law of attraction in action, cause and affect. On April 24th 2021 I gave Tobius (p 533) a Kemetic Yoga session. After he left I sat in my chair and meditated with my eyes closed. At the end of my meditation I was over come with the desire to take my favorite pants and have them copied so I could sell them. When I stood up I said out loud, **"I will design my own pants and sell them"**. I left to get something notarized for my sister and when I return home a man stopped me. He told me that he liked my pants. I told him that he could search harem pants and find this style. He then told me that his name was Yves and he was a designer (Lupitu), he handed me his card. We spoke briefly then we parted ways. When I got upstairs **I remembered** my meditation and I remembered how I met Michele! I called Yves and asked how much he would charge me to copy my pants so that I could sell them. He said he wouldn't charge me anything but nothing in life is free. I trusted Yves but he stole my clothes and my money. Shortly after that he told me that his father died. Yves is born on Feb 6th, the day before **Emmett Till's father's** birthday (pages 475, 518). **Michele's** Husband, **Rick Owens** owns a real Egyptian **sarcophagus** and his latest collection of clothing is named '**Edfu**', after the site of the Ptolemaic **Temple of Horus.** Michelle is part of **"The 44th Parallel"** star code pattern. She turned **77** in 2021 and she is born in 19**44** while I turned **44** in 2021 and I'm born in 19**77.** My uncle Jimmy and his wife (p 582), **George Lucas** (p 37) and **Sekou Odinga** (p 561), **Eddington** (p 329) are all a part of this pattern as well. See page 271.

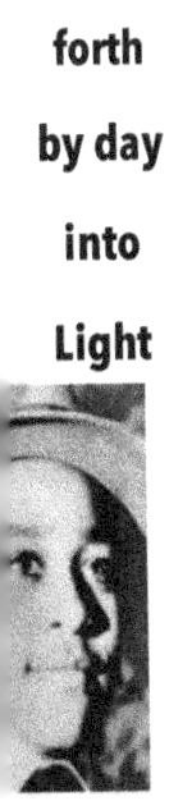

ADDENDUM Dream - May 2020

Upon returning from Kemet in Apr of 2022 (p 670) I had **dreams** with several people who have a connection with Egypt and Michele was one of them. In my dream with Michele I saw a glass of wine. Then I woke up. This dream happened the same night I dreamt with **Mike Tyson** (p 528), and **XXXtentacion** (p 471). Some days later I would dream with **Lord Jamar** (p 342), **KRS One** (p 633) and La Juana (p 586).

Loyalty and Fate

I got a call in December of 2019 from another Spa (**Luxx On Lex**) that was interested in having me do massage for them but because I was loyal to La Juana and committed to The SPAaaht I gave it no thought and turned them down quickly. I knew I was supposed to be working at the SPAaaht and I was happy there.

The SPAaaht and the divine opening

I couldn't leave The SPAaaht. It was a good omen and we had just reopened after over a year of being closed due to the fire on march 22nd 2018. We reopened on November 1st 2019 and on that same day the movie Motherless Brooklyn that cause the fire that caused The SPAaaht to close premiered that day! AND the first customer that came in that day was born on November 1st. I gave him a massage and ended up training him as well. His name is Greg and he still trains with me to this day. One time is an incidence, twice is a coincidence, but three, four, five is a pattern! Can you tell the difference? **The Spa would call me again in March (page 586) and I would decide to meet with them because of a star code (birthdate)....**

December 8th 2019 - Jarad Anthony Higgins (Juice WRLD) dies.

I only found out about Juice WRLD when he passed. Another younger rapper is dead. "RIP's" all over the timelines of social net working for another young rapper gone too soon.. When I read his story I was immediately overcome with sadness. He was only 21 years old. It appears that he rapped a lot about prescription drugs and it appears he died due to an over dose. I watched his video Lucid Dream and was overcome with sadness, soon after I wrote the song *Stream Flowing Dream*. Tupac and the movie Juice inspired Jarad's Stage name Juice WRLD and I have a theory about who Tupac was in his past life.

December 8th 2019 Stream Flowing Dream

He took a high dose cause he was stress'n, his family said they had no indication he wouldn't let them, chronic pain, violence, hide'n pain with silence, depression, the good die young in this dirty game, drive'n slow in the fast lane with no direction, rebellious spirit searching for connection, he found his **past life** through introspection, **astral projection** and the **Peace Pipe** with the right ingestion, **Reflection Eternal**, dissection of my life in my **dream journal,** don't let em turn you, don't let them clone you, cause then they own you, stay true cause if you don't, you turn on your own too, stuck at the intersection, the crossroads, it's my imperfections, my inner essence, the Lord knows it's the coalescence of everything, the spleen, the **thymus**, the time is now, life is a stream flowing **dream,** your highness, the **holy cow,** the **iris**, the **ibis**, **Osiris**, the **scarab,** the *Ballad Of The Dead Soulja,* the marriage of the mind, **soul** and the body, the abbott, there you have it, I told ya, your habits define your destiny, your legacy, what's left to see? mine is **heresy** in the mind of man but heavenly to the great **I am, Amen Atum Aten** never to be forgotten, **Amen Atum Aten** never to be forgotten

you want a stream flowing **dream?!** drink the water lily **blue lotus,** not lean that's for the fiends, necrosis, where's the logic?! you want a tonic?! here's a frequency! here's a sonic shamanic **2020** visional chronicle that's shrouded in secrecy, every time is now and every place is here equally, you searching for your higher self trying to stimulate your sensory with the molly and percocet but that was sent by the enemy to hurt you, to add **vice** to your life and not add **virtue**, we gotta change this **Lil Peep**, **lil Wayne**, ***Juice World***-view, become awaken in the **dream** from **Babylon** to **Timbuktu,** from the jungle to the **Aten,** when **the flower of life** blossoms, sun salutation no separation eye be single like the doctrine, forgotten, omitted, buried like a placenta, like **RA** ferried to **Amenta,** like Mecca, like **Ra**madan, like a scepter, drop a bomb Saddam bless ya, acupressure in the palm, **G**enerator **O**perator **D**estroyer, so I do no harm, this ain't no accident - the holy sacrament grew from morning dew intentional!! the 5th dimensional is calling you, **Amen Atum Aten** never to be forgotten, **Amen Atum Aten** never to be forgotten - **Dawud The Immortal BlaKseed**

Significance

I'm pretty sure this is the first time that I would say the word **Aten** in a song. Aten like Akhen**aten** or Tutankh**aten** or Ankhesen**aten** or Nefer Nerfer**aten**. Perhaps it was the video I watched on September 27th 2019 (page 579) that sparked that line because I will not become fully aware that I was Tutankhaten (King Tut) until April 4th 2020 (page 594) the same day that Martin Luther King was assassinated in 1968 (page 69).

Condolences

My condolences go out to all the family, friends and fans of Jarad Anthony Higgins. Please know that death is not the end. The soul survives death, indeed and in spirit. This is a book of the dead written by a boy who was murdered without justice, who defeated death and came forth by day. May the soul of **Jarad Anthony Higgins** walk peacefully through the field of Reeds in Amenta. Amen Ra.

Holy Cow

The story of the destruction of the world was found in the The Book of the Heavenly Cow, which was found on the 1st gilded shrine of Tutankhaten. Ra, Het Heru (Hathor, Cow) & Sekhmet were components in this story.

January 13th 2020 (Talk with Harriet Tubman)
Meta-Spiritual Encounters of the fourth kind

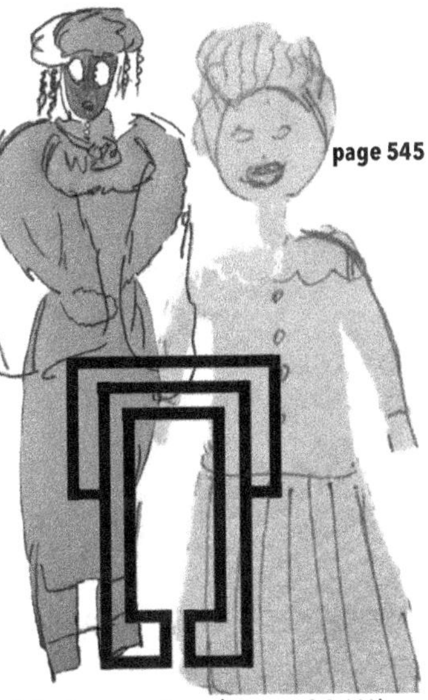
page 545

What you will read below is information about a previous life I lived working along side **Harriet Tubman** (**see p 545**). It seems that I wrote about this life in the rhyme, Strange encounters of the 4th Kind written in 2016 (p 332). This information was given to me from Harriet her self via my friend **Meeky** who speaks to spirits. Even when we are without bodies the soul continues on and can be active in this realm or plane or dimension of existence. Below I have summarized what was said to me. At the end I asked Harriet why she was here and she replied- "to help me navigate." she told me to go with my gut instincts and she also told me that I lived as a **prince** in another life. Meeky can also look at pictures and see spirits in the picture. She told me that she could see one of my guardians named **Robert** standing next to me in the picture I took next to the car I crashed in on June 1st 2002 (p 106). Harriet had a brother named **Robert**. She also told me that all the paranormal phenomena I had been experiencing over the years were designed to prepare me for these revelations. I was slowly awakened so as to not have me go crazy or been seen as crazy. They could not risk me being placed in a psychiatric hospital (insane asylum). I would have a profound experience in 2021 with my **guardian angel** Robert (p 650).

Rau nu Prt m heru

My life with Harriet

I was told that I worked with and lived with Harriet Tubman. We called her **Mente**. My name was **Earl Johnson** (read page 236!!). I Worked along side Harriet gaining information during the **civil war**. I was one of her most fearless soldiers and one of her favorite scouts helping to lead many to freedom. Harriet felt like I was special because I had a telepathic foresight of the future and I dreamt things before they happened. I would sense things right before they happened and I would intuitively stop everyone before the enemy could cause us harm. It took a long time to map out directions for escape. We had different ways of marking our routes. We marked the lower parts of trees and pulled out patches of grass to give signs and directions. We moved from place to place by day and by night. **Blacks and Whites worked with us**. We were wanted in all surrounding states so we had to be careful. Some of our people would do anything to gain favor with our white enslavers and giving information about escaping slaves or some plan of insurrection might garner them **manumission** (freedom). We called them rats. On one occasion someone dropped a handkerchief and it was found by the **overseers** (slave catchers / **slave patrol**), this caused us to almost get caught. We suspected it was done purposely so we set up another trip. We wanted to see if some one would drop something again but no one did. Our mistake was using the same route to get in and out but after that we never used the same routes again. This system of **overseers slave patrols** still exist but now we call them **police officers** (overseer).

Iu f Per f m heru

(Aten Ra and Anat with the Papyrus Scroll)

Anat

After I spoke with Harriet, Anat appeared for the first time. She was holding a papyrus scroll. **Meeky** described **Anat** as a **Golden** Warrior Goddess with a scroll in her hand with a serious demeanor. She is not about games or jokes. She stands guard at my door along with **Harriet** and another Kemetic guardian named **Aten Ra,** however Aten Ra does not appear at my door until after my **past life** revelation of my life as **Tutankhaten** (**King Tut**) on April 4th 2020 (page 594). I asked Meeky to ask Anat to open the scroll and Anat unrolled it a little, then I ran and got my **mdw ntr** (**hieroglyphic**) flip cards. At this point I was kicking myself in the butt because if I had known how to read the **mdw ntr** I might have been able to make better use of that moment but we did the best we could with the flip cards. I laid them on the floor and ask Meeky to point to the cards (words) she saw on the scroll. After I realized I was King Tut I took the beginners **mdw ntr** (hieroglyphs) class with **Mfundishi** again and this time I completed it. Completion of this class would set me up to decipher another link within the **May 25th** star code pattern in 2021 (page 659).

Also see pages <u>(48, 148,179, 250 -253, 315, 318, 329, 348, 421, 434, 545, 549, 572, 584, 604, 650).</u>

Anat, the protector of the NSWT BITY (Pharaoh)

Anat was seen as a bearer of life and powerful Goddess of war and fertility because she protected the **NSWT BITY** (Pharaoh) in battle with mighty vengeance. She was often shown with military gear including a Lance, Axe and Shield. She is also portrayed as wearing a tall crown with feathers. It appears she was almost interchangeable with her sister, the Goddess **Astarte** and at different points was seen as the wife of **Seth** and **Min**.

Utterances for Coming Forth by day into Light

It is he, who comes forth by day into Light

February 4th 2020 Inception Dreams

I woke up in the sate of **sleep paralysis** with in a dream and when I woke up from the dream I was still in **sleep paralysis**. Then I was watching myself watch myself have **sleep paralysis**. Then all of a sudden I was face down laying on the grass. I felt one with the grass as if I had ingested a psychedelic. When I looked up I saw the most beautiful woman staring down at me. As I began to get up I realized I was in a dream then I woke up for real. Unless of course this is all just still one big dream.

Significance

I had this dream on Rosa Park's birthday. Exactly 2 months later on April 4th 2020 (p 594) I will have my past life revelation of Tutankhaten (King Tut) and Rosa Parks was there with me in the spirit form looking down at me during the revelation. Rosa Parks sparked the Civil Rights Movement on Dec 1st 1955 when she refused to give her seat to a white man on a bus in Alabama. Rosa later said, "I thought of Emmett Till, and I couldn't go back." On July 3rd 2018 my past life as Emmett Till was revealed to me (p 480).

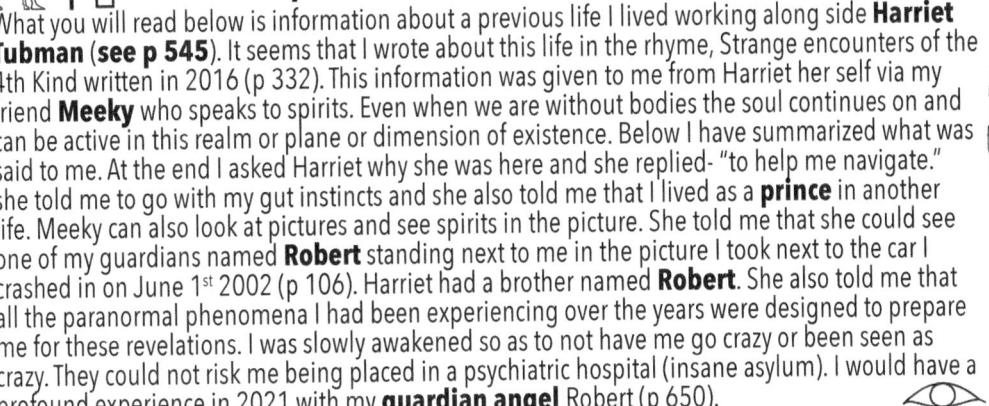

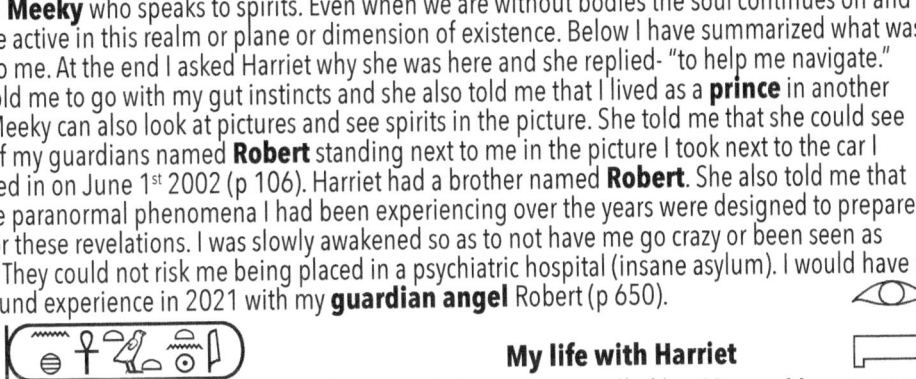

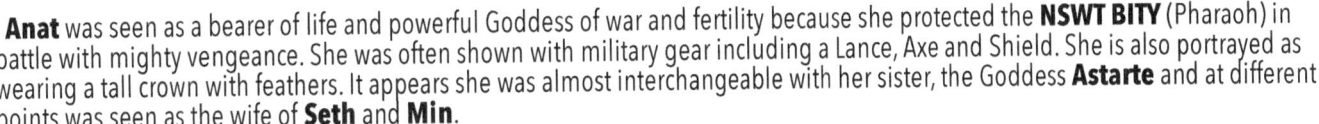

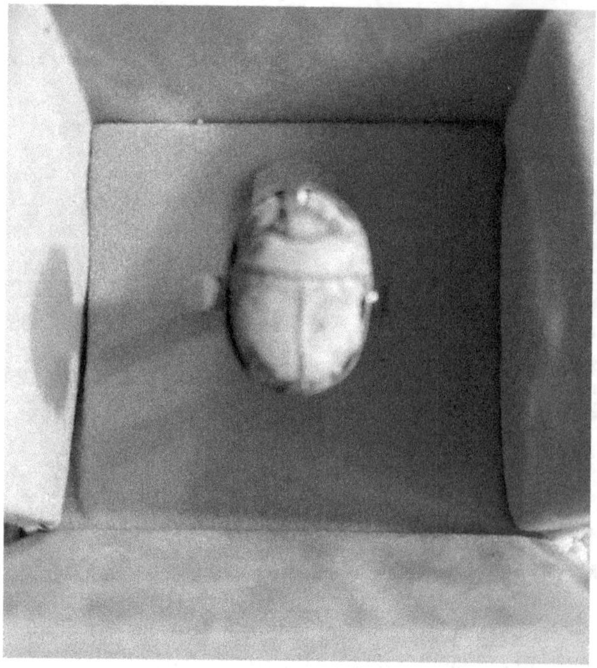

February 21st 2020
Heraa and Her Scarab Ring Heirloom

An **Eritrean** client of mine by the name of **Eden** would refer her friend **Heraa** to me for personal training. Eden told me, "you will like her, she's **Egyptian** and **Sudanese** and she has a **Scarab ring**". That caught my attention! I wanted to see her ring; I was excited to see her ring! I wondered what the universe was doing now? Is this some good omen? Who is this Egyptian and Sudanese woman with a scarab ring? I think I brought up the ring soon after she arrived for her first training session. She told me that it was a family Heirloom that her aunt had given her. Her aunt had not had any children so it was passed down to her. As our session began and we got to the part when I told her to do some push-ups and she replied, "me"?. I laughed out loud and said, "who else is in here that I could be talking to?" Then we both laughed. He**ra**a was always good to work with. I began calling her She-**Ra**. I told her that her name reminded me of the character from the cartoon He-Man that I used to watch as a child, Heraa-"she-**ra**". She had never heard of the cartoon. It wasn't until the writing of this book that I would come to realize the date that Heraa had started training. It was on the day **Malcolm X** was assassinated and two months later on April 4th 2020, the day **Martin Luther King** was assassinated I would have my past life revelation of my life as Tutankhaten (**King Tut**) revealed to me (page 594). When I came to this realization it heightened the significance of meeting her. Was Malcolm speaking to me again? Was I on the right path? Is this a good omen? Was her ring a sign? Was she supposed to be my "wife" or should I be looking for a wife? She was born on October 20th in the sign of libra like my Grandmother. Libra is balance and balance is **Maat**. I always had good sessions with Heraa but unfortunately due to Covid she moved back home to east Afrika. Soon after meeting Heraa she would refer her friend John to me for personal training. He is born on Feb 18th , my nieces birthday. A few months after meeting him I would have a profound experience with Meeky and John's guardian angel (page 604). I would be remiss if I did not mention that **Eden** told me, on two occasions she saw a **psychic** and on both readings she was told that she **descended from ancient royalty** in a previous life. Eden is **Eritrean** and does not like to be called **Ethiopian**. I have tried to convince her that they are the same people but she has yet to agree with me. I recently told her that if in-fact she was royalty in a previous life then it could not have been an Eritrean person because Eritrea didn't exist in ancient times and perhaps her job is to unite her people. She thanked me. We are still friends. It wouldn't be too odd for her to be of royalty because I have met Padmore, in 2014 who is the **reincarnation** of **Dejazmatch Beru** (Ras Beru), **Ethiopian royalty** (page 390). I tell the story of his reincarnation on June 15th of 2016, the day before Tupac's birthday. I have a theory about who **Tupac** was in a **past life**ʔ. This concept of resurrection was called the **Wehem-Mesut** (repeating of births, p 14).

42 Laws of Maat, Page 367

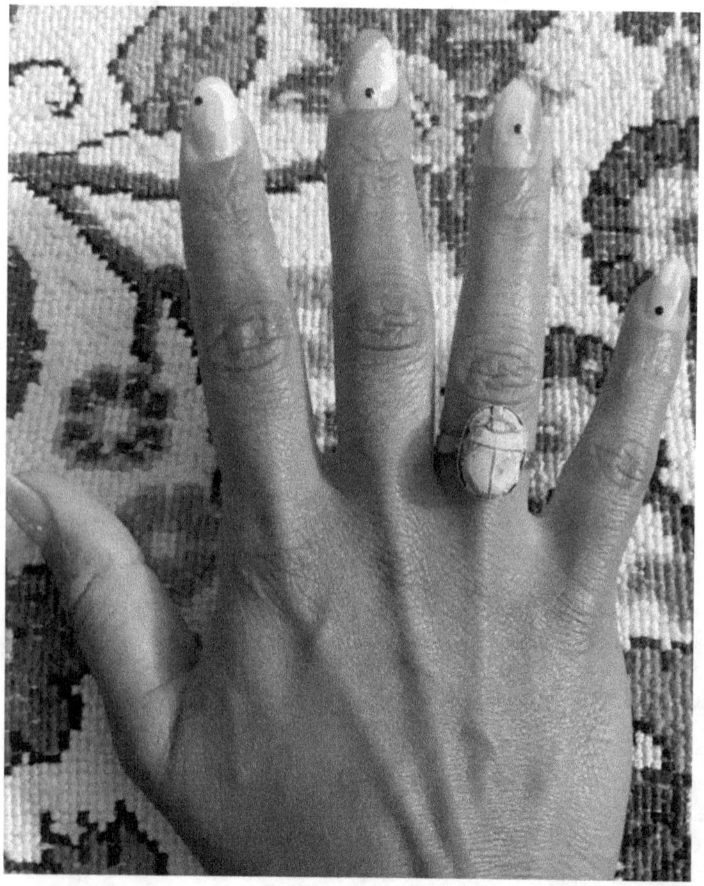

Rau nu Prt m heru

Iu f Per f m heru

Utterances for Coming Forth by day into Light

It is he, who comes forth by day into Light

February 23rd 2020 Ahmaud Marquez Arbery

Ahmaud Marquez Arbery, an unarmed 25 year old black man, was pursued while jogging near Brunswick in Glynn County, Georgia. Ahmaud had been pursued by three white residents - Travis McMichael and his father Gregory, who were armed and driving a pickup truck, and William "Roddie" Bryan, who followed Arbery in a second vehicle. Arbery was stopped, confronted, and fatally shot by Travis McMichael. (See page **648** for the **metaphysical significance of the number 23**. See pages 25, 94, 102, 121, 283, 444, 669, and 672 for more on **February 23rd**.)

Condolences

My condolences go out to the family of **Ahmaud Marquez Arbery** and all those who have been robbed of their life by this system of white supremacy. Please know that death is not the end. The soul survives death, indeed and in spirit. This is a book of the dead written by a boy who was murdered without justice, who defeated death and came forth by day. May **Ahmaud Marquez Arbery** walk peacefully through the field of Reeds in Amenta. Amen Ra.

February 24th 2020 A Dream About Emmett

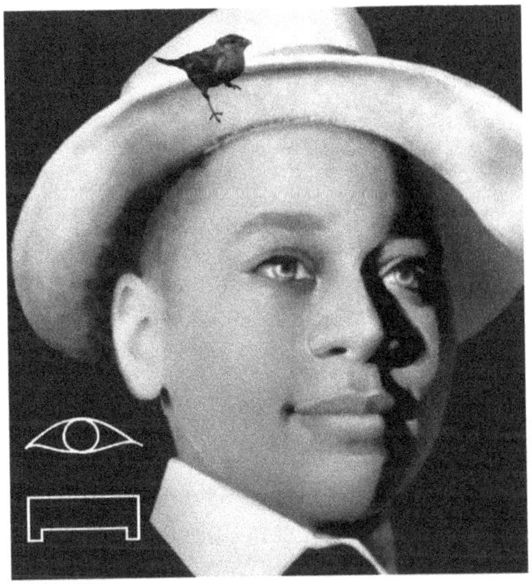

I'm in someones home. A father and son. The father knows who I am and who I was (Emmett). So does the son but still the son wants me to leave because the trouble that I could bring he is not willing to contend with. The father stedfast in his decision places a box in front of me. He opens it and there inside was a set of clothes bloody, torn, and wet. I looked at the father and when I looked back at the box it was gone. Then a beautiful woman materialized in front of my eyes and to my surprise she was spectacular............ "Much you still much learn she said, in your **past lives** you were illustrious, romantic, infamous, famous, the wretched of the earth, so you **died tragic!** What you see as magic is divine order. You are the best you have ever been. In your **past life** I was your daughter now I'm your protector, I came to offer insight on your **dreams** of saucers and serendipity. There's so much more left for you to see, like your great great grand mother standing next to me, there's no such thing as **coincidence** is all divine recipe, sacred geometry, like that song we wrote about mahogany". I left with her. Then I woke up.

Significance

Today is January 19th 2022 and to this day this is the only dream I have ever had of Emmett Till.

March 11th 2020
Premonition Dreams Mark The SPAaaht

In the dream I arrived to work and there was tension with La Juana. Her friend was there instigating the trouble. In the dream I quit on the spot. I grabbed my keys, they had a giant Ankh attached to them. I left the spa through a small narrow window and jumped to the street as if I was Spiderman (Peter-Ptah **Parker**)..

Significance

When I got to work that day I had a disagreement with La Juana and I decided to stop working Sunday's (I used to work Sunday's by myself) she then told me that I didn't need a key anymore since I wouldn't be opening on Sunday's any more. I asked her if she would like me to stop working there. She said no. She asked me the same. I told her I loved my job. Then I told her that I had a dream about everything that just happened and after hearing that she started crying. She had many things going on in her personal life and we had not been seeing eye to eye for a few weeks. Two days later I had another **dream** about my job at The SPAaaht which would prove to be a premonition (page 589). Today is November 3rd 2021 and I still love and care for La Juana and see her as my spiritual sister.

ADDENDUM Premonition Dreams - May 2022

Upon returning from Kemet in April of 2022 (p 670), I had **dreams** with several people and La Juana was one of them. In my dream with La Juana she called me to ask if I was available to do massage on Mondays. Then I woke up. A week or so after this **dream** La Juana would reach out to me to see if I was available to work with her doing couples massage for her clients and I agreed. We will be working together again soon. I would also **dream** with **Lord Jamar** (p 342), **XXXtentacion** (p 471), **Mike Tyson** (P 528), **Michele Lamy** (p 582), and **KRS One** (P 633).

Luxx On Lex

A few days after the incident at work I got another call from Kerry, the owner of the Spa on Lexington (page 583). She asks if it was ok for her to add her sister to the call. I agreed. Kerry wanted me to reconsider working at her Spa but I was not keen to traveling downtown. I liked the convenience of working close to home. Then her sister asked me a random question, she wanted to know what my birthday was. I told her it was October 25th and immediately she said she knew I was an October baby. I asked her what her birthday was and she said **October 20th**. I found that interesting because I had just recently met **Heraa** who is born on the 20th (page 585). I asked Kerry hers and she said **October 9th** and when see said that she had my attention. She was born on my **Grand Mothers birthday** and I had just met **Herra** a month prior who was born on **October 20th** and she came with a **Scarab ring** (page 585). I also trained Herra for the first time on the day **Malcolm X** was assassinated. With all those **synchronicities** in mind I agreed to go meet with Kerry. When I arrived to the Spa I found out that the brother in charge of management was **Haitian** and Kerry was **Jamaican**. In the spirit of the **Haitian revolution** and **Marcus Garvey** I agreed to do a couple of sessions a week there offering my custom Ra Massage treatment as a service. Unfortunately that was short lived due to Covid 19. **Fear** set in and the city shut down just as Kerry had opened her new spa.

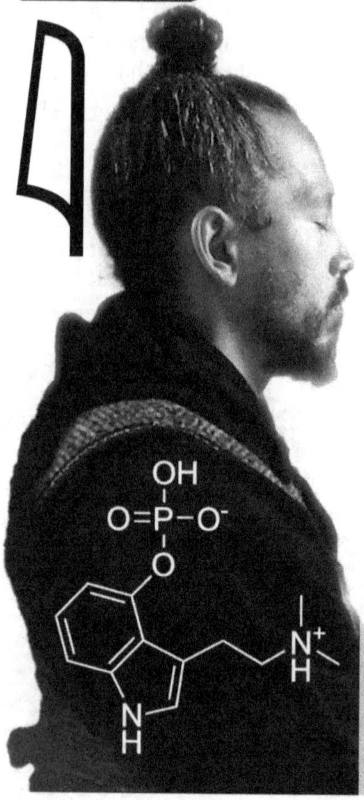

2020 - The Field of Reeds

A brother named **Tim Reed** started following my Instagram page but he was one of the rare and unusual followers who "liked" a lot of my content, he even shared a lot of it too, and because of this I noticed him. He seemed to like my music and I wasn't used to people being that supportive of my music so oddly enough that made me a bit **suspicious** about his motives. He was drawn to me because of my story about my **past life** revelation of **Emmett Till** and it's connection to the mushroom because he was a **mycologist**. After some time I warmed up to him and him and I began to exchange messages via direct message. At some point he offered to send me a **free mushroom grow kit** but I never responded to his offer. I knew that the mushrooms were part of my native spiritual sacrament but they were still illegal in many states so I didn't trust him because to me he was just some person online. I would soon come to find out that he was working with Baba **Kilindi Iyi.** That's when I began to trust him. I let him send me a grow kit and from that kit I grew my first and only mushrooms. On April 4th 2020 I ate from this batch and my **past life** as **Tutankhaten** (**King Tut**) was revealed to me. It wasn't until months later that I realized the **pattern**. Willie **"Reed"** was the last person to see **Emmett Till** alive and he testified in court during my murder trial (page 517). His name just happened to be Willie **"Reed"** like Tim **"Reed"**, like the field of **reeds** that the **soul** goes to **after death** in the ancient Kemetic version of heaven (Amenta) and the **afterlife**. Tim **Reed** and I are still friends to this day. If you've gotten this far you should know by now that, one time is an incidence, twice is a coincidence, but three, four, five is a pattern! Can you tell the difference? Nothing just happens!

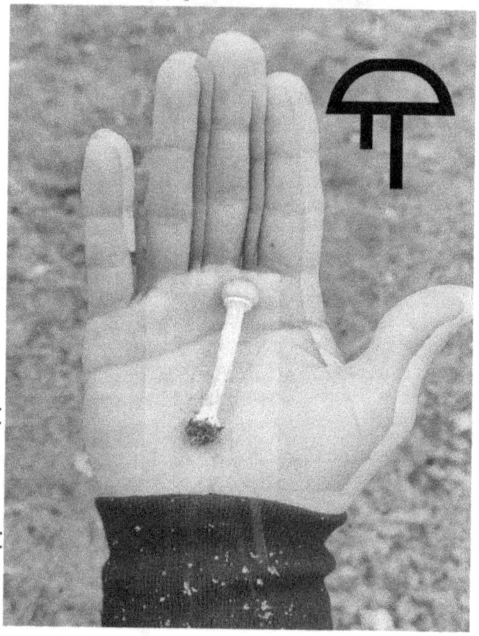

Rau

nu

Prt

m

heru

Iu

f

Per

f

m

heru

Utterances

for

Coming

Forth

by day

into

Light

It is

he,

who

comes

forth

by day

into

Light

March 13th 2020 (Breonna Taylor 26, Louisiana Kentucky)

On March 13th 2020 Breonna Taylor lay asleep with her boyfriend Kenneth Walker. Outside, plainclothes police silently gather, preparing to raid what they claimed to be a residence linked to two known drug dealers. One of the drug dealers, an ex boyfriend of Breonna's was thought to be receiving mail at her apartment. Resulting in a judge signing a search warrant with a "no knock" provision. The warrant claimed that a US Postal inspector confirmed that the dealer had been receiving packages at her apartment. Postal inspector Tony Gooden has since said that his office had told police there were no packages of interest being delivered there. Breonna and Kenneth were awoken by a loud bang at the door on March 13th 2020. According to Kenneth, Breonna yelled "who is it?" Multiple times, to no response, before he armed himself with a legally owned firearm. Kenneth later told police that he feared someone was trying to break in. After the door had been broken off it's hinges, Kenneth fired one shot. The police returned with over thirty rounds, ten of which an officer fired blindly through a window. Breonna was unarmed, she was shot 6 times and died. No drugs were found in the apartment. The Officers involved in this incident were reassigned pending outcome of investigation.. Breonna Taylor worked as a EMT and was working as an ER technician at the time of her death. She aspired to be a nurse. On Sep **23rd** 2020 the officers involved with her wrongful death would all be acquitted. Officer Brett Hankison was charged with "wanton endangerment" for firing into a neighbor's apartment, not for Breonna's death. Even after a year and a half no one has been held accountable for Breonna's murder. **Breonna Taylors killers were acquitted the same day that Emmett Till's killers were acquitted and on that same day, Sep 23rd 2020 my father would have a stroke** (page 627). See page **648** for the **metaphysical significance of the number 23**.

Condolences

My condolences go out to the family of **Breonna Taylor** as well of those who have been robbed of their life by this system of white supremacy. Please know that death is not the end. The soul survives death, indeed and in spirit. This is a book of the dead written by a boy who was murdered without justice, who defeated death and came forth by day. May the soul of **Breonna Taylor** walk peacefully through the field of Reeds in Amenta. Amen Ra.

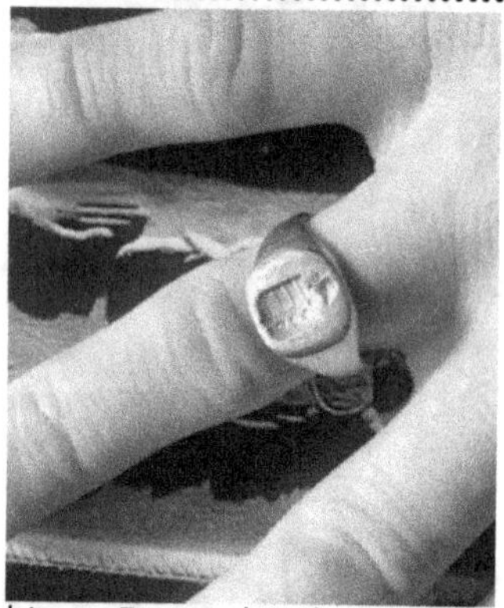

March 13th 2020 (Dream Premonition at The SPAaaht)

I had a dream that one of my regular clients from The SPAaaht contacted me to work with me privately.

Significance

The same day around 5pm La Juana calls me to tell me that one of my clients wants to book a massage. It was the same client I dreamt about (page 586). His name is Nicholas he is a professional dancer at Alvin Ailey. His favorite form of dancing is Break dancing. Nicholas enjoyed my massage so much that he gifted his mother, girl friend and his roommate massages with me. Nicholas would end up taking sessions with me privately after Covid started. Nicholas was intrigued by my story about my **past life**. Because of the **scarab cuff** that I wear he once told me about his Grand mother who took him to Egypt when he was a boy and how she had a **scarab necklace**. On April 2nd 2021 (page 636) after a massages I would tell him about my book and how I come from the line of **Dukes** because my Grand Fathers names was **General Dukes Jr**. Then he placed his hand in front of me flashing a ring and told me that his Grand father was a Duke too. He was wearing the ring of a **Duke**. I was astonished! See page 271.

March 22nd 2020 What it Really Means to Follow Your Dreams

I met a woman named Charney who was born on December 1st the same day that **Rosa Parks** refused to get out of her seat because she was angry about the Murder of Emmett Till. Charney's mother is born on my mothers birthday February 3rd which is the day before Rosa Parks' birthday. Charney and I would become friends. I had the answers to questions that she had been pondering for years. She told me that she enjoyed speaking to me because she liked the way I explained things to her. One night I told her to meet me in a **dream** just before we hung up the phone. I would wake up the next day from a dream with her and my friend **Akua**. Akua was the first person to sit in my massage chair at the International African Arts Festival (page 476) on July 3rd 2018 where I had my **past life** revelation of **Emmett Till** (page 480).

The Shared Dream

In the dream I was laying down with Charney when Akua appeared with a piece of fruit in her hand. She told me to purchase fruit in bulk then handed the fruit to me. As I reached for the fruit and went to stand up I awoke from the dream. As soon as I awoke I sent Akua a text and told her that she was in my dream and that she handed me a piece of fruit in the dream, telling me told me to buy fruit in bulk. She was shocked because she had just arrived to Brazil and had just purchased fruit in bulk. Then I called Charney and told her that I had a dream about her and to my surprise she said she dreamt of me too. I told her my dream and she told me that in her dream we were laying down together. Then I got up to make some food and she was excited to eat it. Later that day I went to the store and I purchased fruit. While at the store I saw a woman that I had given a training session to a month prior, but she had not come back to purchase a package. When we made eye contact she smiled and said she was planning to call me this same day because she was ready to start Training. When I Paid for my food the price was $88.88. When I got home I received a payment for 8 sessions from her. Her name is **Kim,** she owns a company named **Muse** and she is born on my nephews birthday, July 27th two days after Emmett Till's birthday. In 2017 I had my first shared dream with Angelika (page 452).

Akua, (page 476)

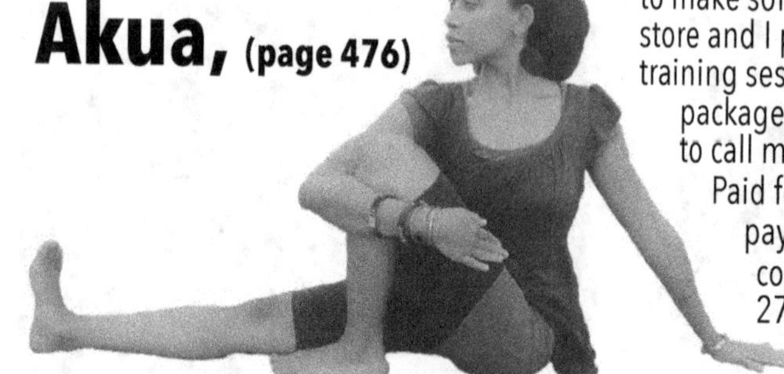

Rau nu Prt m heru

March 25th 2020 - Dream

My Grand father's Presence is there, in a bright light like when he appeared to me but this time I can not see him. I can only feel him.

See Page 169

March 25th 2020 Corona Virus (1st of 19)

Everybody's running from this **pandemic**, what's the story? the **respiratory**, the **asthmatic**, the **diabetic**, the **obese**, they might all have it, designer **virus** from the east got you stuck in a **prison of fear**, panic, pandemonium, manic man at the podium, satanic press conference, short man complex, Napoleon, conquest of the mind, so they controlling them, **Cointel** be online now and they be trolling them, distractions, holy men going to prison, **pedophilia**, **theologian**, every one hundred years another plague, no utopian, they say it's gonna all fall down, and it's no hope for them, and when it all falls down who they gonna call now? who you gonna call now? **- Dawud The Immortal BlaKseed**

Iu f Per f m heru

March 26th 2020 Plan-demic (1st of 18)

They called this a **pandemic** but this is a plan systemic, she ran in the senate and blasted! **Lebron,** not James! she wasn't play'n no games! a bet **king James** never **fasted**! **religion** the most sound **prison** that was ever crafted! I had this dream I was 14 lay'n in my casket, and I'm not sure how long the dream lasted but I know one thing, the regime was extreme fascist! they say one thing then give you a **vaccine** full of acid, times are drastic! and ashes and ashes the masses they all fall down! **F**orget **E**verything **A**nd **R**un, that's if you wanna cow, **F**ace **E**verything **A**nd **R**ise that's if you wanna know how, a coward dies a thousand deaths, **Huey P** to **Mao Mao**, cigarettes and alcohol the protocol to murder y'all, but would you change at all if your loved ones was show'n y'all? salute to **Dr Afrika** read a chapter get your problem solved, for our freedom he was so involved, **Ase**, let's pray, all I can say is this has strengthened my resolve another day around the sun we revolve, a cluster of stars, King Author and the knights of the round table, **Christ** at the last supper, Cain and Abel, young grasshopper your **pineal** has been disabled **- Dawud The Immortal BlaKseed**

Significance

When Covid happened I did not for one second believe the narrative being pushed by the media and I was not willing to take any vaccine for "**Covid**". Instead I leaned on the knowledge I had acquired from my experience with vaccines in the Military as well as all the natural healing remedies I had acquired during the years of my awakening. Before my deployment to Iraq in 2003, the Army **vaccinated** all of us soldiers like farm animals (page 121). I received the **Anthrax, Hep A, Hep B, Smallpox, Yellow Fever, Polio, Influenza, Meningo**, **MMR**, and the **Japanese Encephalitis Vaccines**. When I left Iraq in 2003 I got an **STD** for the first time in my life and shortly after, in 2004 I had a bad case of the **Flu** for the first time in my life. During Covid I increased my exercising and my intake of vital minerals and essential oils such as Pine Needle oil, Vitamin D, Colloidal Silver, Seamoss, Oil of Oregano, Blackseed oil, Thyme oil and other useful herbs. For more info on my experience with Vaccines and **natural ways to heal yourself** read pages **120 - 125**. **R.I.P. Lolita Lebron**

Utterances for Coming Forth by day into Light

It is he, who comes forth by day into Light

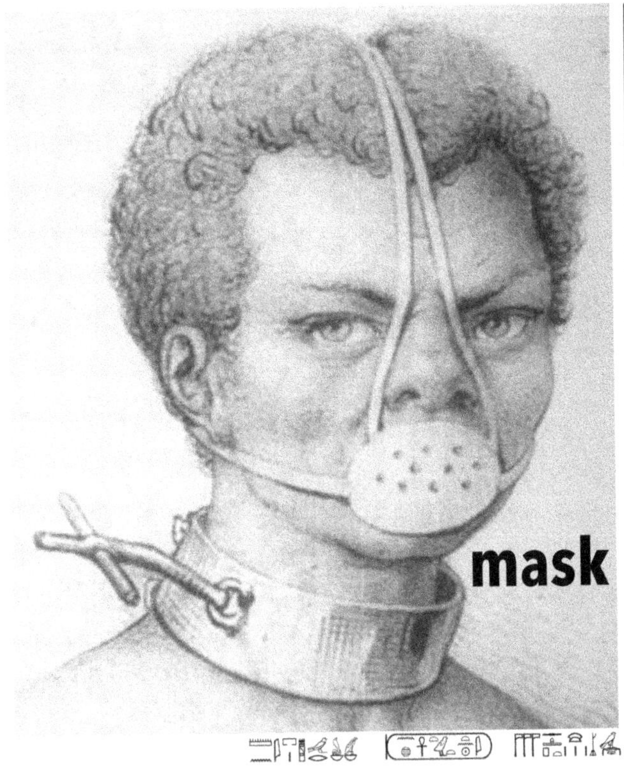

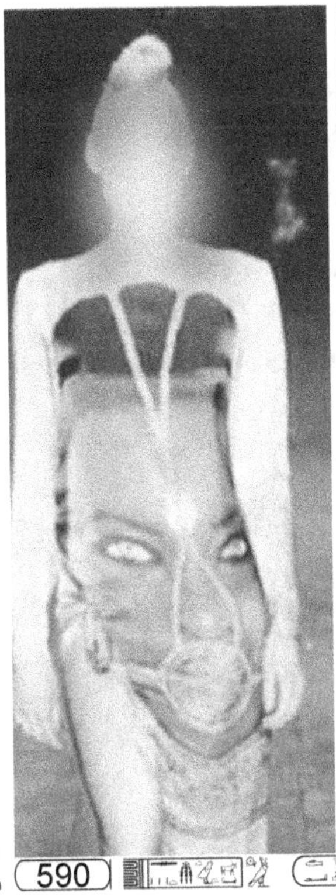

For some odd reason I took a picture wearing a shirt with a **King Cobra** on it. This is the only shirt that I own which has a snake of any sort on it and I do not take pictures in this mirror often. It is the mirror in the lobby of the building I live in. At the time of the picture I had lived in this building for 13 years and I can only remember taking a picture in that mirror 1 or maybe 2 other times. We are here to play this game of life which is more like a play of consciousness. We all play it together like a shared dream (pages 452, 589). It's important that we help wake each other up so that we all end the game well but more importantly we must first awaken ourselves. I was slowly awakening but consciously I was unaware. **I suspect that we are living a double life**. We live a life that we are aware of because we see it but at the same time our **Ka** is playing the game too. The goal of the game is to unite with the Ka. In ancient Kemet (Egypt) the human soul was divided into 7 parts. One of the aspects was the **Ka** which was the **spirit**, or the **etheric twin**. The symbol for the **Ka** was **two hands raised** representing the **double nature** of our being. On April 3rd my **Ka** was ready to unite the two lands and **it** decided to take this picture. Martin Luther **King** gave his last speech, "I've been to the Mountaintop" on April 3rd 1968 and the next day he was **assassinated**. On April 4, 2020, the day after I took this picture my life as **King Tut** was revealed to me and during the experience Martin Luther King's spirit (**ka**) appeared to me (page 594).

September 2013 the year of the SNAKE
Martin Luther King and Massage Therapy at Riverside Church

Rau nu Prt m heru

Iu f Per f m heru

Utterances for Coming Forth by day into Light

It is he, who comes forth by day into Light

My life is intimately connected with Martin Luther King. Martin was born in the year of the **Snake** (1929), I was born as Emmett in the year of the **Snake** (1941, page 41) and I was born again, in this life in 1977, the year of the **Snake**. My last day in the **Army** was Martin's birthday, Jan 15th 2005 (page 130). I attended some of my first semester of Massages classes at The New York College of Health Professional via a satellite location at **Riverside Church** in **2013** the year of the **Snake**. This is the same church that **Martin** would deliver the speech "**Beyond Vietnam**," on April 4th 1967 which is exactly one year before his death on April 4th 1968 (page 69). On April 4th 2020, I would have my second **past life revelation**, this time my life as Tutankhaten (King Tut) is revealed to me (page 594). My life as **Emmett Till** had been revealed two years prior on July 3rd 2018 (page 480), 2 days after graduated as a **Kemetic Yoga** instructor. **Rosa Parks** practiced **yoga** (pages 474, 518), and **Martin practiced Karma Yoga** every day. He may have never practiced the Yoga postures, but he drew heavily on the **Gandhi's** idea of **nonviolence** in his own activism which is the first yama, or moral precept, of yoga as outlined by Patanjali in the Yoga Sutras. Martin Luther King knew about the pre existence of the soul, he wrote a **theology** paper on **Heru** and the **Ausarian Resurrection** in 1949. Emmett Till was murdered in 19**55** which propelled Martin Luther King into the forefront of the Civil Rights Movement. Around 2 minutes and 55 seconds into Martin's Beyond Vietnam speech he says: "Perhaps a new spirit is rising among us. If it is, let us trace its movement, and pray that our inner being may be sensitive to its guidance. For we are deeply in need of a new way beyond the darkness that seems so close around us." I ask that you read this book and trace my movements. Out of the darkness comes the divine soul. The ark of a million years, the magic carpet or "Noah's ark" (page 252). I am talking about the **immortality** that man is so desperately searching for. Be careful my brothers and sisters, before you throw my revelation to the pigs I suggest you consider the idea that perhaps there are things that other groups of people know but are in no rush to tell you. **Because anyone who profits off of you being blind will not teach you or inspire you to see. We have had our spiritual culture stripped from us** but we understood the immortality of the soul in ancient times. In fact reincarnation was taken out of the bible in 553 AD under the reign of **Justinian** the 1st. In the Bible the character of Jesus speaks of reincarnation in the book of **Matthew**. I was sent to this school where Martin delivered this speech about, "a new **spirit** rising among us" so that those with **eyes to see** can feel confident in knowing what they are seeing is true. It was ordained from the beginning of time that I would die a sacrificial death so that I could have the opportunity to come back here again In this life and earn the right to know who I was and with the revealing of this revelation mans consciousness will be aroused and justice can at-last prevail.

Reincarnation in the Bible

Life does not end when body function ceases, but body function ceases when life leaves the body. Future life is a certain as the sun setting in the west and rising again in the east... The human soul does the same. Again and again. This ancient doctrine of reincarnation had always been known throughout the world, except in modern times, when it was cast into darkness by the Roman State Church in order to force the world to believe in its "Lord and Savior Jesus Christ". Reincarnation was taught by Pythagoras and Plato; it was one of the principles of the Druid faith. Caesar found it among the Gauls. It was found in the old races of Mexico, Central and South America but it was first realized and taught in Ancient Kemet (Egypt). Reincarnation was voted out of Christian doctrines in 325AD and almost completely erased from the Bible in 533AD.

Matthew Chapter 16

13: When Jesus came to the region of Caesarea Philippi, he asked his disciples, "**Who do people say the Son of Man is**?" **14:** They replied, "***Some say John the Baptist; others say Elijah; and still others, Jeremiah or one of the prophets.***" **15:** "But what about you?" he asked. "Who do you say I am?" **16:** Simon Peter answered, "***You are the Messiah, the Son of the living God***." **17:** Jesus replied, "Blessed are you, Simon son of Jonah, for this was not revealed to you by flesh and blood, but by my Father in heaven. **18:** And I tell you that ***you are Peter***, and on this rock I will build my church, and the gates of Hades will not overcome it. **19:** I will give you the keys of the kingdom of heaven; whatever you bind on earth will be bound in heaven, and whatever you loose on earth will be loosed in heaven." **20:** Then he ordered his disciples not to tell anyone that he was the Messiah.

Matthew Chapter 11

11: Truly I tell you, among those born of women there has not risen anyone greater than John the Baptist; yet whoever is least in the kingdom of heaven is greater than he. **12:** From the days of John the Baptist until now, the kingdom of heaven has been subjected to violence, and violent people have been raiding it. **13:** For all the Prophets and the Law prophesied until John. **14:** And if you are willing to accept it, ***he is the Elijah who was to come***. **15:** Whoever has ears, let them hear.

Matthew 19

9: As they were coming down the mountain, Jesus instructed them, "Don't tell anyone what you have seen, until the Son of Man has been raised from the dead." **10:** The disciples asked him, "Why then do the teachers of the law say that Elijah must come first?" **11:** Jesus replied, "To be sure, Elijah comes and will restore all things. **12:** ***But I tell you, Elijah has already come***, and they did not recognize him, but have done to him everything they wished. In the same way the Son of Man is going to suffer at their hands." **13:** Then ***the disciples understood that he was talking to them about John the Baptist.***

Early Christian Fathers and the teachings of Reincarnation

Origen (184-253) who's name meant "born of **Heru**" was one of the early Christian fathers and through him we know that reincarnation was wide spread in Christianity in the 1st two centuries. Origen taught about the **pre-existence of our souls**, taking up reincarnation or one or another aspect of re-embodiment which, among many other of his teachings, was later condemned as heresy. Examples are scattered through Origen's works, especially Contra Celsum (1, xxxii), where he asks, **"Is it not rational that souls should be introduced into bodies, in accordance with their merits and previous deeds . . . ?"** In the 6th century, the eastern Roman emperor **Justinian** the 1st, (482-565), saw him self as the supreme ruler of the church and made it law that nothing could be done in the church contrary to his will and command. He removed all the teachings of the **pre-existence of our souls**, and reincarnation from the church doctrine. He wanted everyone to believe that they only live one time and so the church would wield more power because the people would come to believe that they could only go to heaven by way of the church. It became the most powerful tool to control the masses. **Pope Vigilius** (?- 555) knew that reincarnation was a part of the teaching of the bible so he **apposed** the emperor and **refused to sign the ban** of the teachings of **reincarnation** in 543. 10 years later December 8th 553, the pressure from the emperor was so fierce that Pope Vigilius acquiesced and signed the law in Constantinople. After this a problem was created because now the church could no longer answer questions like where do we come from, where do we go when we die and why are we here. This is when new doctrine was created, eternal damnation, **original sin**, **creation of the soul at the time of birth**, mortal sin, **judgement day** and purgatory. The knowledge of reincarnation was never completely forgotten it was just never taught again in the churches instead it was relegated to **secret societies.** In **Judaism** reincarnation is known as **Gilgul** (Cycle), but it is not taught to everyone. In ancient Kemet this concept of resurrection was called **Wehem-Mesut** (repeating of births, p 14). **Re-member** that **you** are **Ausar** and **Heru,** the **hero!** See page 3 for the **hero's journey**!

1949 Dr. Martin Luther King Speaks on Ancient Egyptian Influence On Christianity

"The Egyptian mysteries of Isis and Osiris exerted considerable influence upon early Christianity. Those two great Egyptian deities, whose worship passed into Europe, were revered not only in Rome but in many other centers where Christian communities were growing up. Osiris and Isis, so the legend runs, were at one and the same time, brother and sister, husband and wife; but Osiris was murdered, his coffined body being thrown into the Nile, and shortly afterwards the widowed and exiled Isis gave birth to a son, Horus. Meanwhile the coffin was washed up on the Syrian coast, and became miraculously lodged in the trunk of a tree. This tree afterwards chanced to be cut down and made into a pillar in the palace at Byblos, and there Isis at length found it. After recovering Osiris' dismembered body, Isis restored him to life and installed him as King in the nether world; meanwhile Horus, having grown to manhood, reigned on earth, later becoming the third person of this great Egyptian trinity." – **Dr. Martin Luther King Jr. 1949**

April 4th 2020 Tutankhaten is Born Again
Setting My Intentions of Love and Appreciation for Dr Martin Luther King Jr

It was April 4th 2020 which added up to 444. This was a high vibrational day and in anticipation of this day many people across the world planned a mass meditation at 10:45pm. I found that interesting and since Martin was assassinated on April 4th 1968 I decided to honor him by going into a **ceremonial meditation with the sacred mushroom** on my own. Ever since my past life as Emmett had been revealed to me on July 3rd 2018, Martin had become more important to me since the murder of Emmett is the event that propelled him into the forefront of the Civil Rights Movement. There would be no Martin without the murder of Emmett. There would be no Civil Rights movement without the brave actions of Mamie, Medgar, Rosa or Martin. **I ate 10 grams of dried mushroom** at 10:20 am then I ran on my treadmill for 25 minutes. The run ended at 10:45**am**. As I finished my run I posted a quick video in honor of Martin then went into my meditation. The post read: - "*25 minutes ended up adding up to 10:45 and that's kind of dope because as soon as I'm done with this I'm gonna lay a towel down and take myself into a meditation. I'm gonna start off with my brother* ***Martin Luther King*** *then I'm gonna go on a long journey on* ***444****. Peace*." Then I laid on the floor immediately. I did not even take the time to dry myself off. January 15th 1929 the year of the snake - July 25th 1941 the year of the snake - October 25th 1977 the year of the snake (p 41). All the events in this book are true. If you follow my path and do the things I do yet still the great mysteries are not shown to you. Then continue the path and **to Maat be true** and perhaps in due time you will be worthy of the view.

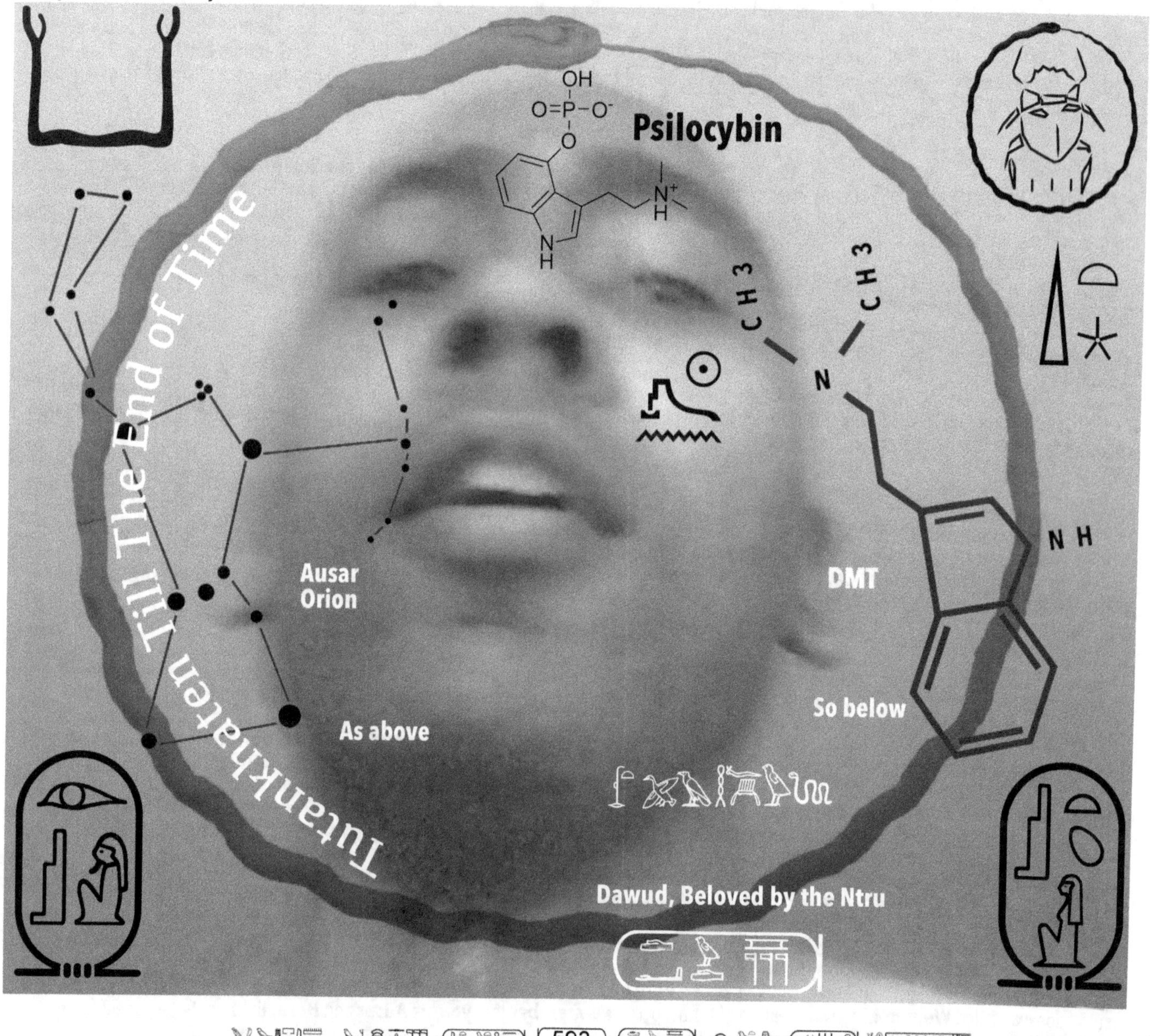

April 4th 2020 - Tutankhaten is Born Again and Given a New Name, TutemRa

Rau nu Prt m heru

I could already feel my body vibrating so I wasted no time. I laid down and pulled my blanket over my body, I put my eye covers over my eyes then crossed my arms in the pose of Ausar. I could feel energy emanating from the crown of my head to the soles of my feet. Once I closed my eyes I focused my thoughts on Martin and began to send him loving thoughts of gratitude. When I was done with him I then sent loving thoughts to all the women in my family starting with my Grandmother, then my Mother, then every other women in my family ending with my niece Ayah, the newest female baby born in my family. As soon as I released my thoughts from my niece I was transported to another space and time (**The Akashic Records**) and I found myself laying in a sarcophagus with my hands crossed in the ausarian position **interfacing** with **Rosa Parks** and **Martin Luther King.** My vision was not 100% clear, it was like looking at a black and white tv screen with bad grainy reception but I could see them clearly enough to know who they were. And there was a sense of knowingness involved with this interfacing. No words were spoken just vibrations of love along with sound right and exact information. **Rosa** was standing at my feet on the left side of my body looking down at me and **Martin** was standing at my feet on the right side of my body looking down at me. Then **Rosa** walked over to me, leaned into the sarcophagus and kissed me on the cheek. Then immediately I floated up out of the sarcophagus and as soon as I opened my eyes it was as if I was pulled away, or shot away with lightening speed and I was back in my studio laying on the floor, and in my ear I heard the name **TOOT EM RA** echoing in my ear over and over, **"TOOT EM RA, TOOT EM RA, TOOT EM RA, TOOT EM RA, TutemRa"**. It was like someone was chanting in my ear but **something was completely different**!! I had **this sense of knowing** that **TutemRa** was my name and that I was **Tutankhaten, King Tut!** I just knew it instantaneously, in the blink of an eye! I opened my phone and recorded a video then posted it on Instagram (p 595). A few weeks later I chose the name **Kheperu** because it was part of my ancient throne name, Neb Kheperu Ra (p 284). Kheper is the Beetle and Kheperu means, a continuous coming into being. A few months later I took on the name **Nebu,** a month or so later I added **Sahu** and years later I added **Setep en Ra**. TutemRa = in the image of **Ra**. Setep en Ra = **chosen by Ra**. Nebu = **Gold**. The **Sahu** is the spiritual energy that houses the **Ba** and the **Ahku** and **protects** the physical **mummified body**. It was also the name used to identify the stars that make up the belt in the constellation of Ausar (Osiris) the archer (**Orion**) and finally, **Sahu is one of the highest levels of spirituality**. The name, TutemRa Setep en Ra Nebu Sahu Kheperu means: The Golden Soul chosen by Ra to continuously Come Forth in the image of Ra.

Iu f Per f m heru

TutemRa Setep en Ra Nebu Sahu Kheperu

MUMMY MISSISSIPPI

Utterances for Coming Forth by day into Light

In my life as Emmett Till, I was lynched in Money **M**iss**iss**ippi and in the word Mississippi you can see the name **Isis** (Auset) who is the **mother** of **Heru** (**Horus**, **Zeus**, **Jesus**) the one who **resurrects** after death. **Isis** is the great royal **wife** of **Ausar** (**Osiris**), known as the Lord of **resurrection,** the Lord of the **West,** the Lord of the dead and the underworld (p 3). I was beaten, tortured, shot in the head and **thrown in a** M**ississi**ppi **river** at **14** years old. In the Ausarian **resurrection** drama Ausar was cut into **14** pieces and **thrown in the Nile river**. The **Nile River** is on a delta just like the Tallahatchie river I was thrown in. The Tallahatchie river is located in the north**west** part of M**ississ**ippi on the notorious **33rd parallel**. In ancient Kemet (Egypt) West was where the soul or the BA went when we die. The Ancient Kemetyu (Egyptians) of the Hapi Eteru (The Nile River) did not believe in death. They understood the immortality of the soul and had mastered the repetition of the soul, the **resurrection** of the Ba (soul). They Called the death of the physical body **westing**. Just as the Sun rises in the East and sets in the West the same is to be said for the Ba (soul). This concept of resurrection was called the **Wehem-Mesut** (repeating of births, p 14). In **Judaism** reincarnation is known as **Gilgul** (Cycle), but it is not taught to everyone. Memphis Tennessee was named after the city of **Mem**phis, the royal residence and capital of ancient Kemet (Egypt) established my the **Nswt Bity** (Pharaoh) **Memes** (Narmer). My past life of Emmett Till was revealed to me on July 3rd 2018 and my death propelled Martin Luther King to the forefront of the Civil Rights Movement. Martin Luther King was assassinated in **Mem**phis Tennessee on **April 4th** 1968 (page 69). The M**ississ**ippi **river** runs through **Mem**phis and I was thrown in a river in M**ississ**ippi. On **April 4th** 2020, 52 years after Martin's assassination my **past life** as **Tutankhaten (King Tut)** was revealed to me while in a deep meditation where the spirits of Rosa Parks and Martin Luther King were present.. **Tutankhaten (King Tut)** was a young Pharaoh in ancient Kemet who died young like Emmett. Martin Luther King wrote a **theology** paper on **Heru** and the **Ausarian Resurrection** in 1949. This is a **Divine Riddle** like the **Riddle** of the **Sphinx**. Like my great grand mother Leacola **Riddle** who was born the day Marcus Garvey died. This is all connected so that it will undoubtedly get your attention. Martin was born in the year of the **Snake** (1929), Emmett was born in the year of the **Snake** (1941) and I was born again in 1977, the year of the **Snake** (page 41). My last day in the army was Martin Luther Kings birthday, January 15th 2005 (page 130). I prayed and asked God for direction on whether I should stay in this mans army or if I should get out and I was led out on Martin Luther King's birthday. In the Kemetic (Egyptian) Ausarian resurrection drama, Ausar (Osiris) returns through his son **Heru** as **Ra**, this is why I was given the name Tutem**RA**. The original name of the Sphinx was **Heru** Em Ahket, which has the head of a human and the body of a lion. In my life as Emmett I was a **Leo** like the **Lion**. We must all aspire to be Heru. The one who rises above his animalistic nature. This is the journey that I took in my present life. The present moment is the truest gift and we must be wise about how we spend our time here on earth.

It is he, who comes forth by day into Light

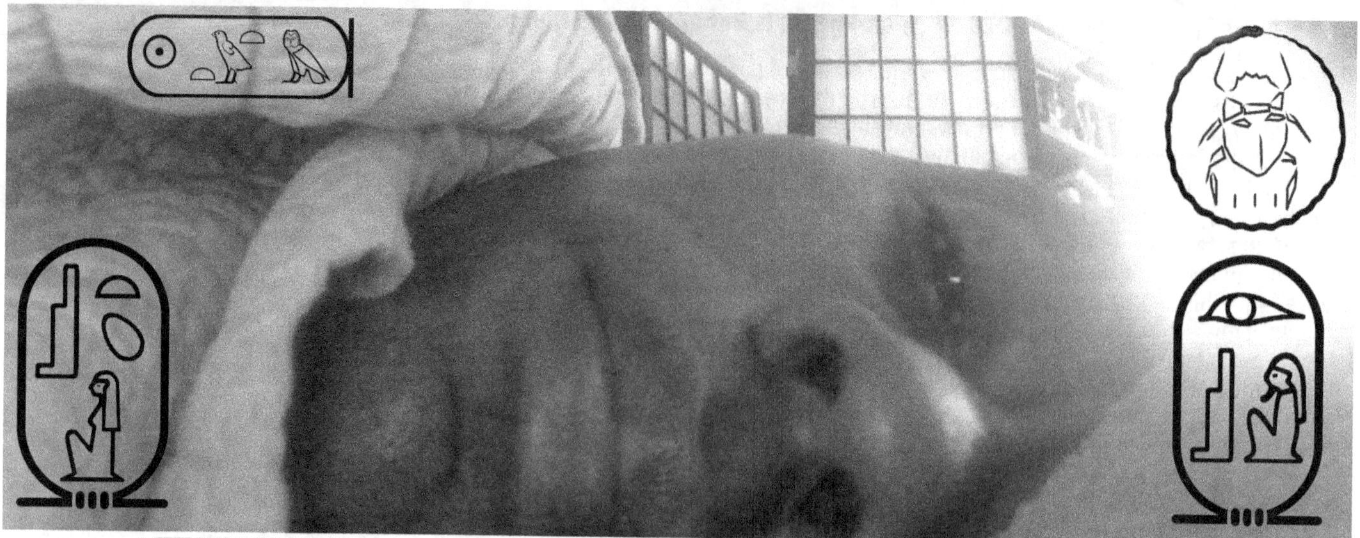

Coming Back to this Dimension

I had **this sense of knowing** that TutemRa was my name and that I was **King Tut**. I just knew it instantaneously. I knew it! I opened my phone and posted a video on Instagram making the following statement,

"I know who the fuck I am! It may not be believable to you but I don't fuck'n care! Today is April 4th of 2020! Brother! My name is **TUT-EM-RA**, **TUT** like flute, **EM** like friend or **Emmett Till**, and **RA** like MumRa! I know who the fuck I am. I don't know who the fuck you are but I know who I am! I came back as Dawud, I Came back as Emmett Till. I know who the fuck I am! Brother! It may seem funny to you! but it is VERY REAL!" **- TutemRa**

The video is time stamped at 12:**55**pm. The meditation must have lasted 2 hours but it only felt like minutes. When I stood on my feet **it was as if I had stood up for the first time in thousands of years**. I began to laugh hysterically knowing that I was in a new body. It's hard to explain how I was totally aware that I was "Dawud" yet still I also knew that my name was now **TutemRa** and that I was not only **Emmett Till** in a past life but in a more ancient life I was **Tutankhaten (King Tut)**! I laughed for a long time as I looked at myself in my giant mirror. I was in a spell of amazement. It might sound childish but I felt like **MumRa** from the Thundercats when he emerges from his sarcophagus (p 43). I was in a most joyous state. I was breathing and walking in another body! I knew that I was King Tut and knew I had conquered death. Afterwards I called **Basui** (pages 388, 431, 569), and asked him what the name TutemRa meant. He told me it meant, **in the image of Ra**. Immediately I realized that Tut-em-Ra and Tut-ankh-aten had the same meaning. Tutankhaten means, **in the living image of Aten**, and both **Ra** and **Aten** are names for the **Sun**. I was given the same name!! I searched the name TutemRa and could find it nowhere. If the name was ever used before it had been long lost to recorded history! I began to share my story and many people thought I was crazy. To be honest I totally understood them but after reading this book I'm sure people can understand how I was just able to know. The past life of King Tut had come to me in 2018 but I didn't really believe it (pages 5**23** - 529)! Some how the **Bufo** released information stored within my **DNA** connected to my ancient soul fragment from my life as King Tut. It all made sense now and this time it didn't take me long to realize I looked like King Tut. I took a picture of myself from the 6th grade (page 46, 602) and it matched just like my face had matched with Emmett Tills (page 556, 602). Around this same time **Mfundishi** had a new Beginners Mdw Ntr (hieroglyphics) course starting, I signed up immediately and I finally completed it. I tried taking his course twice before but never had the motivation to complete it (pages 2**23**, 573). I started to study King Tut and I began to find links with myself and Tut that seemed to never end. Still in 2021 I am finding links, like the cuff that I bought off the wrist of **Mfundishi** on May 25th 2014 (p 293), and how it's connected to King Tut, but I would not realize this till 2021 (p 659). When my past life as Emmett Till came in 2018, Mfundishi told me to write my story but I never did (p 537), however things were different now! I began to compile the materials for this book on Apr 4th 2020, the same day of my revelation. By February of 2021 I had a binder 2 inches thick with every magical moment of my life written in it and everything seemed to be connected in some mysterious magical way (p 634). I even found music that seemed to speak this revelation into existence years before it happened (p 597-598). I was finally ready to arrange this book.

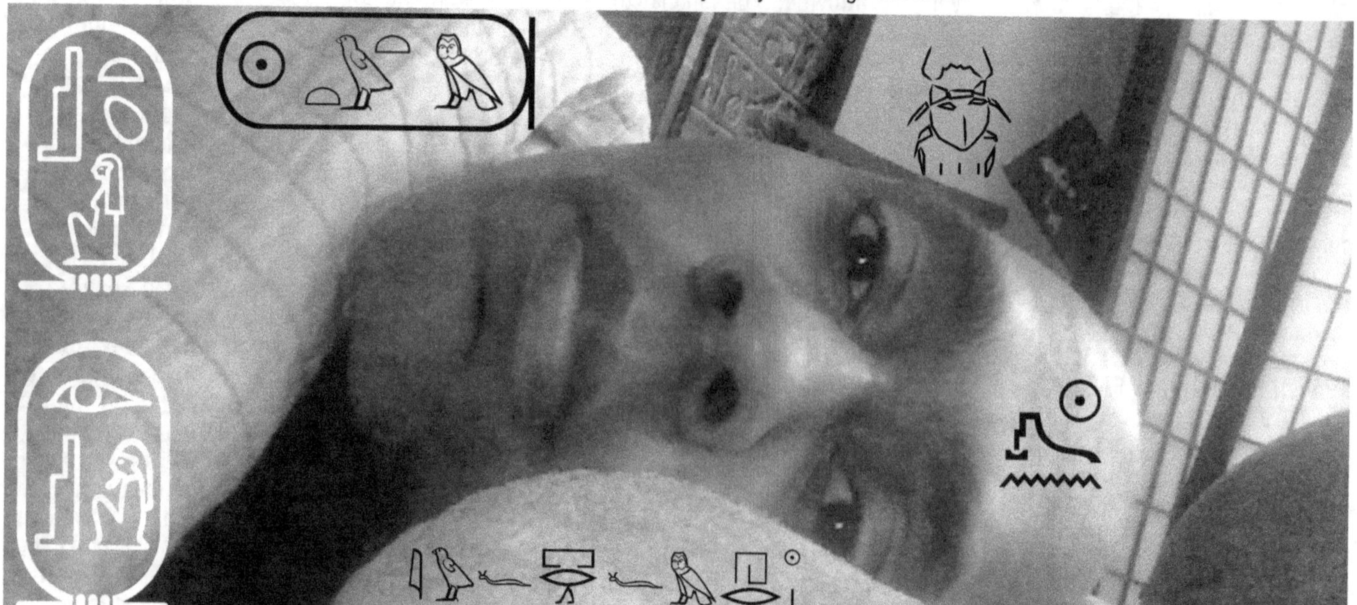

April 4th 2020 TutemRa

Rau nu Prt m heru

4, 4, 20, 20, brothers still chase'n the **MONEY**, ain't a damn thing funny! call me **Tut Em Ra**, that's **Sunny,** The **Boy King Scorpion Sting,** I had a lot of money, poor thing murdered at fourteen, a **mummy**, dummy – you can't murder the spirit, half of y'all can't see the truth when you hear it, I ain't asking I'm telling them, they said the **Christ** would come in music so they attack'n the melanin, **Morpheus** and **Neo** trapped in a cell again, I'm the **Falcon** not the eagle, the **ibis** not the pelican, they put a virus in the **Matrix** ,my ancient music be the medicine, a skeleton like **Skeletor, He-Man** atoms to Adam can you fathom the metaphor? I laid on the floor, crossed my arms like **Ausar** then I saw **Rosa,** she blew the breath of life in my esophagus, then said "my negus, **Ausar** star dust rise from your sarcophagus"! the **Djed pillar** the spine, the swine a killer of the divine, the frequency of the organ is the healer, use your mind, it's a cold summer 5g and Corona combined, Flu like symptoms, I seen it on the Simpsons the government be lying, rest in peace to the victims in these times that's trying, **Amen Atum Aten** never to be forgotten, from **Neb Kheperu Ra** to slave fields picking cotton, from **Emmett Till** gettin killed, thrown in a river rotten, like **Ausar** I came back as Dawud, TutemRa **- TutemRA**

Significance

Iu f Per f m heru

This is the first song I wrote with my new name! A few hours after my revelation I saw a post about the **fabulous Cold Summer rap challenge**. I never do any of the "challenges" that come and go on social media but the beat for Cold Summer was nice and there was a pull inside of me to say something. I download the beat at **5:25**pm and by 6:48pm I had written my first rhyme as **TutemRa**. By April 8th I had learned King Tut's throne name was **Neb Kheperu Ra** and that's when I wrote the hook at the end. I downloaded the beat at **5:25** pm which is mathematically **May 25th** and if you have been reading this book you should know that **May 25th** was the first **star code** that I decoded in 2011 (page 222). My sister had the **dream** I died in a car accident on **May 25th 2002** and 7 days later I crashed and lived on my fathers birthday (page 104). Then I totaled my motorcycle on **May 25th 2008** (page 157). I purchased my Silver Cuff from Mfundishi on **May 25th 2014** (page 293) and on November 13th 2021 (page 659) I would realize the silver cuff had a very interesting name engraved in it revealing it's true **Talisman Powers!!** On the **Silver Ring** you can see the rays of the Aten shining on the date **May 25th** 1943 and on the **Silver Cuff** you can see the rays of the Aten. **George Floyd** was murdered on **May 25th 2020** the month after I had this revelation of my life as King Tut and George's death sparked the biggest protest for Civil Rights in American history while **Emmett Till's** death was the first lynching of a black person that went to trial and it sparked the Civil Rights Movement. Emmett Till's body was identified by the silver ring his father had given him which had **May 25th** engraved on it. In this song I quote myself from a rhyme I wrote in 2016 (page 370) which was titles **Reincarnated**. "my **Negsu, Ausar** star dust **rise** from your **sarcophagus"** (page 370). I don't recall the emotions or thoughts that cause me to write this rhyme but I said some interesting things in it and perhaps my soul was releasing information stored within my **DNA** connected to my previous lives years before I touched the sacred medicines. **May 25th Strikes Back! Re-member** that **you** are **Ausar** and **Heru,** the **hero!**

See page 3 for the **hero's journey**!

Rays of the Aten

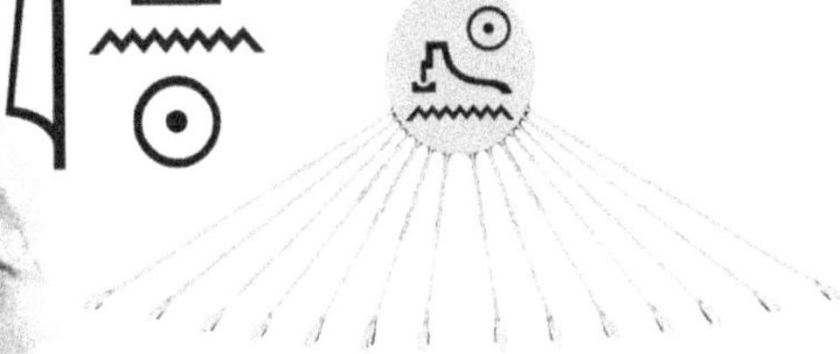

Utterances for Coming Forth by day into Light

It is he, who comes forth by day into Light

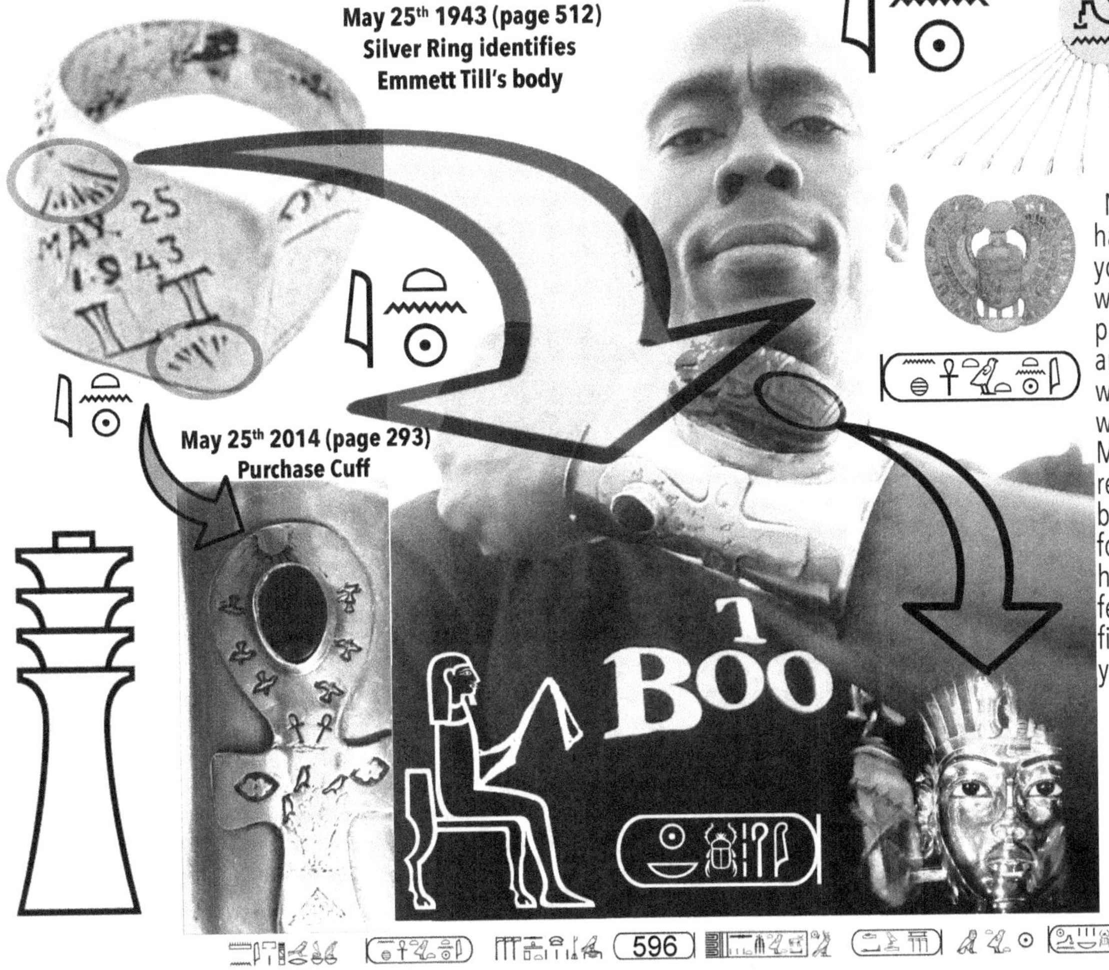

Nothing in life is just happening to us. If you pay **ATEN**tion you will begin to see the pattern forming around you. This cuff was always mine. It was crafted for me. Mfundishi relinquished it because it was meant for me. Keep your heart lighter than the feather and you will find what is meant for you.

The Alchemist coded in Hip Hop

The oldest writings known to man are utterances, spells or "rhymes/hymns" written on the walls (p 670) in the tombs of the **Nswt Bity** (pharaoh) evoked to ensure the safe passage of the pharaoh after death and towards their **resurrection** in the next life (page 6), this concept was called **Wehem-Mesut** (repeating of births, p 14). In my life as **Emmett Till** I was murdered in 19**55**, in that same year the **originator** of Hip Hop, **Dj Kool Herc** was born in the zodiacal sign of **Aries**, which is where **Tutankhaten** (**King Tut**) comes from. In my current life my <u>moon</u> is in **Aries** and my <u>Dragons Tail</u> **originates** in the age of **Aries** (Pages 654-657).. **22** years after I was murdered, I came back to earth, born again in 19**77**, carrying a complex equation of star codes intimately connected to the musical art form known as Hip Hop. **KRS One's DJ Scott La Rock** was murdered on **August 27th** 1987 the day before **Emmett** was Murdered (**August 28th**). Emmett's murder sp**ark**ed the **first** Black movement for Civil Rights while Scott La Rock's death is said to be the **first** murder of a major Hip Hop artist. Emmett's death was **connected to a women** and his **two killers** were **acquitted**. The murder of Scott La Rock is said to be **connected** to a confrontation that **D-Nice** had with **two men** involving **a woman**. **Two men** were arrested and charged with La Rock's murder, but they were **acquitted** at the trial. KRS One released **The Gospel of Hip Hop** the day before my birthday (p 633). The **Artifacts** would released their first album on my 17th birthday **October 25th** in 1994 (p 66). **Artifacts** are objects made by human beings from earlier periods in time typically items of cultural or historical interest and the most famous artifacts ever found in modern time are the ones found in **Tutankhaten's** (**King Tut's**) tomb in 19**22**. The American record producer, DJ, rapper and songwriter Daniel Alan Maman was born the same day and year as me, Oct 25th 19**77** the year of the **snake** and he is professionally known as the **Alchemist**. This book is the modern "**Book of The Dead**, Coming Forth by Day" because it was the **murder** of Black life that fueled my music causing my ancient soul fragments to **Come Forth by Day.** This is the reason why I wrote my story into my music years before I consciously knew about my past lives. Below are some of the rhymes I wrote about Tut years before the revelation. On pages **xi** and p 201 there are charts with every time I said the names Emmett and Tut in music before I knew my past lives. I am the **Alchemist** coded within Hip Hop. This is **Divine Alchemy** of the soul, the only alchemy that matters!. **Re-member** that **you** are **Ausar** and **Heru,** the **hero!** <u>See page 3 for the **hero's journey**!</u>

Prophetic Hekau's (Spells) Written Pre Revelation

November 26th 2010 (Uptown, page 187)
Inter-dimensional Transmission from Tupac

I'm just a revolutionary nigga, simple man, "**Never Had A Friend Like Me**", loyalty to the end, **royalty** I would have been, if I was around in the time of **King Tut** king could have been me! **Watch me rise up** in this fuck'n game, cause all these niggas ain't say'n shit they the fuck'n same! **- Dawud**

January 7th 2011 (These many Roads 1st verse, page 195)
Inter-dimensional Transmission from Michael Jackson

Racing through life on these many roads you gotta know the codes, us brothers in the hood we them black crows, from **The Wiz** not **The Wizard Of Oz,** We had to make our own movies so we can see **stars** that look like us, <u>*we used to be **Gods***</u>! look at **King Tut** even he got robbed! Laying up with shorty you know, after we blazed that, asked her how she felt about **Huey P** from way back, She didn't know who he was I couldn't believe that, Lil homie, be careful where you plant blakseeds at, you never know how the odds will go, you pick a hoe and that same hoe come knocking at yo doo, you ain't got ta live and learn No! That's a big lie, you can learn from other people Just a word from the wise, Open your eyes when will you realize If you give yourself half a try <u>you can really rise</u> **- Dawud**

March 27th 2013 (Year of the snake, page 268)
Inter-dimensional Transmission from self: Nswt Bity Tutankhaten

It's <u>**the year of the snake**</u> stakes are high, every day is a day that you can die, but every day is a day that you could fly, when I say fly what does that mean to you? Is it the way you look or something you do? ***When you die do you come back? sign another contract?*** *Run another lap?* ***What about the little ones who die so young? Peace to the Gods when they come back, I signed another contract to be here and so did you!*** *You are not aware!* I see dead people, you do not see clear! I hope you have ears to hear, open your <u>first eye</u>, where is your halo? I'm searching for mine, eating green, you gotta stay clean, I'm a be iron like lion if you know what I mean, if I was **MJ** I would scream, don't get caught chasing this American **dream,** when I was in school I broke rules and always seen the dean, even back then I knew things wasn't what they seem, Young Black Male trapped in Far Rockaway Queens, I had a **dream,** I took a walk through **The Valley Of The Kings** and **King Tut** told me to scream **Scorpion King!** that's my word, he said **Scorpion King,** that's your name Blakseed you the **Scorpion King,** you the **Scorpion King, *Hatshepsut*, *Hatshepsut* *,Hatshepsut* - Dawuud's Appeal**

February 26th 2013 (The BlaKseed Osiris, page 267)
Inter-dimensional Transmission from Ausar

I be The BlaKseed **Osiris,** see sun **set**, looking for **Auset Isis,** Black duality crlsis, born in this White man's world to civilize it, when I think about a **king** I be thinking bout **Akhenaten,** you are not forgotten, P.O.W M.I.A, my brother **Mumia,** yeah he still locked away, New Orleans, they did the same shit in Rockaway, they sell your dreams, a world full of Philistines, I'm just a brother from Queens, I'm just a brother that seen, so many different type of things, my nigga, but, I ain't seen freedom ring my nigga, I seen tell lie vision, condition brothers for the prison, division, **Malcolm x** would still be living, If we would do the math, but we been hood winked, and y'all mother fuckers don't know the half, cause you glad to be eaten your chicken your beef and your bloody sirloin, we need to leave the animals alone, and tell the people the truth, somebody gotta show em, this is all love, what a beautiful poem, do not obey make way for a better day we gotta show em, babies we gotta grow em, feed em the life that's living, maybe this all was different, maybe we ate plants, maybe that made a difference, maybe the fall of man started with the stolen land, it starts when you start loving man more than the woman, it's a war written in the sand, I can hear em saying, click click in the night, heard the heart sp**ark** the revolution late at night, heard em saying click click click click in the night, **Nat Turner** with a burner saying fuck this life, **Tina Turner** with a burner click click in the night **- Dawuud's Appeal**

Prophetic Hekau's (Spells) Written Pre Revelation

Rau nu Prt m heru

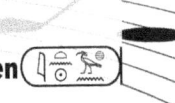

April 8th 2015 (Star of the story, page 323)
Inter-dimensional Transmission from Akhenaten

I down loaded the **matrix** in 99, But my eye didn't decode it even the 3rd time, I been having feelings of the 4th kind, They say ignorance is bliss, All this hell will have a **Naga** pissed, vexed, *Yes life's a mess don't stress, test are given*, But be thankful that you're living bless, *I guess I'm a major threat, cause I remind **Nagas** of what we were made to forget*, My homie did 40 years for a crime he ain't commit, they gave him a mill so he wouldn't say shit, they killed her son and got away with it, double agents flagrant, **Eric Garner** dead on the pavement, replay didn't change it, these games are ancient, **King Tutankhamen rhyming, Cleopatra** of the nile, tell me why they lying, It might take a while to stop crying, but when you're done, Return to the **father** through the **sun,** I be the star of the story, the star, ***I be the star of the story*** **- Dawud The Uncanny BlaKseed**

March 18th 2016 (Reincarnated, page 370)
Inter-dimensional Transmission from Ausar

Perhaps I been **reincarnated**, **scarred** and jaded, **lucid dreams sleep paralysis** I hate it, seeking **oracles** and sages, sages and **oracles** seeking me, this path I'm walking truthfully, I used to chase booty faithfully now I'm abstinent patiently, half a man half amazingly, with the lyrics handed to me from **spirits,** the agony of defeat when they hear this, the strategy have you **eat meat**, drink alchemy, grow weak but if you not meek and speak strong… they bomb the balcony, I am the **falcon** you see on the head of **Khafre,** flying high **The 25th Dynasty** remember the time when we were at our finest b, finally say goodby to uncle Tommy and his cabin **Young Gifted And Black** and rapping like a **Griot, Cheikh Atan Diop** in case you forgot, precolonial AfriKa my **niggas** my **Negsu, Ausar** star dust **rise** from your **sarcophagus,** they can't topple us the populous in Heliopolis, who do we trust and follow? **Mike Tyson** searching for **Cus D'amato,** a people with out the knowledge of their history and customs are hollow, a tree without roots bare no fruits tomorrow, if you know like I know we in route to self destruction and sorrow, I put this letter in a bottle **- Dawud The Amazing BlaKseed**

Iu f Per f m heru

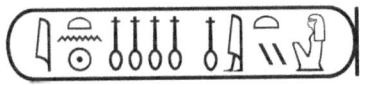

May 3rd 2016 (Hapiness 2nd verse, page 382)
Inter-dimensional Transmission from Nefertiti

Rest In Peace to **Afeni, Dear Momma I love you**! I'll be there when you need me! **King Tut, Nefertiti,** black people we divided can't you see that we don't share the same religions? coming together should be easy! what we need is hapiness health excitement love and enlightenment, for so long I been fighting this, maybe this song can right the wrong so I'm writing this, and I don't blame you for nothing, not an ounce of it! this government front'n they killed **Martin** then omitted it, **My Family Tree** they be chop'n it, I'm coming from the rotten apple metropolis, scribble slave on my face like **Prince** no apologist, what sense does it make to imprison the populous? 25 million for bail it **"Ain't hard to tell"** they wan't a brother staying in jail, "*and go to hell to foul cops that shot* " **Sean bell,** Free **Mumia, Mutulu** and every other **political prisoner** as well, we need a history that tells the story of the gazelle not the lion, cause these mafucka's be lying, Mothers in black crying Brothers in packs dying, It's about timing, what we do today is defining our tomorrow, we need another way that could be drowning out our sorrow, 400 years of work with no pay that's a no no, **Reparations** are due but they be moving slow mo, I suggest you speed up before you screaming oh no! **- Dawud The Uncanny BlaKseed**

Utterances for Coming Forth by day into Light

September 29th 2016 (The Prophecy, page 424)
Inter-dimensional Transmission from Emmett Till

He fell asleep, he was drowsing, woke up **4000, Years later,** born in government housing, they warned of a savior, a covenant was found in a manger, in wonderment he underwent an excellent ascent, like when Malcolm went to Mecca, it was evident, he could plant Blakseeds, grow trees like regiments, on elephants and trample the decadent empire with elegance, fire, water, and all the elements, they etched him out, they burned his house, but that ain't stopping the revolution that I'm talking bout, freedom is paramount, I'll shout from the hill top, we picked crops sang songs like Hip Hop, if Nat Turner was here would we hang cops? or bust shots like Tupac? hot steel, who was David walker and what was written in his appeal? tell me why when he wrote it they wanted him killed?! tell me why **Tamir Rice** look like **Emmett Till?!!** Tell me why our blood still spill in the street still?! still **illmatic,** we can heal or have **Havoc,** make magic like a **Prodigy,** this gotta be **The Prophecy - The BlaKseed**

It is he, who comes forth by day into Light

December 18th 2016 (Move 9, page 435)
Inter-dimensional Transmission from self: Nswt Bity Tutankhaten

West Philadelphia born and raised, pray for **John Afrika, MOVE 9** going out in a blaze, you praying for **Palestine** and **Paris** but back in the days, nobody gave a damn about your black ass packing the grave, the cracker never gave a damn, still ain't got a damn to give, they burn the house down, shot down fleeing kids - screaming in terror "don't shoot"! they only wanted to live in peace and that's why we call **police** the pig, police kill people, treat you like you not equal, **Blue Wall Of Silence** feeds violence, let they're actions teach you, I need you to listen my people we do have a mission to see through **Till** the end, fuck friends! stop wishing and playing, they pretend to tend to our needs, bets believe we gonna win! we gotta fin for ourself put a end to self hating, start creating a mind state to rebuild this black nation, stop tuning into coons on tv and radio stations! buy black that's how we counter attack the war they waging, **MOVE 9** channel 9 news we all saw em blazing, did the same thing in **Waco Texas** with caucasians, did the same in **New Orleans** they did to the **Haitians,** that's why I'm **Red, Black** and **Green RBG** flag waving, I don't vote I seen the schemes of **Nancy** and **Ronald Reagan,** While you hope and you **dream,** I'm a **King Tut** black pagan, taking back the science no relation to **Carl Sagan - Dawud The Uncanny BlaKseed**

The Mysterious Cases of Familiar Faces From Different Times and Different Places

I don't know the date that I went to find pictures of my self that looked like Tutankhaten but it was only a matter of days this time. First I noticed that there was a picture of the gold mask of Tutankhaten that was on the same angle as the pictures I used to show the likeness of me and Emmett. When I placed them together it was as if I unlocked a secret, ancient code of some kind. When I saw the likeness it was like a confirmation that I could not run from. It was in a way, very spooky, but it was also very exciting and amazing. I felt like I had won some sort of "spiritual" lottery. This was more than just the picture though. There are people in the world that might look more exactly like this mask than I do but they don't have this life of revelation detailed within the pages of this book. It was like Excalibur in the **Arthurian legend**, the sword in the stone. But this was an **Ausarian resurrection** and with my life of revelation I pulled myself from the stone or in this case, from the **golden mask** and became the alchemist. **Divine Alchemy** of the soul, the only alchemy that matters! The grand **alchemist** is the tarot card Tower **14** which correlates with **revelation** and **awakening**. Emmett Till was murdered at **14 years** old and Tutankhaten (King Tut) ruled during the **14th century** BCE. The American record producer, DJ, rapper and songwriter Daniel Alan Maman was born the same day and year as me, October 25th 1977 the year of the **snake** and he is professionally known as the **Alchemist**. This book was brought forth in 2022, the 49th anniversary of Hip Hop and 49 days is the amount of time the Tibetans believed it took one soul to be reborn into another life. This concept was called the **Wehem-Mesut** (repeating of births, p 14). I am the **Alchemist** coded within **Hip Hop** (see page 633). Look to KRS One and The Temple of Hip Hop for directions on where Hip Hop should be going. On page 600, I am seen standing in front on my ancient statue in the Temple of Karnak, during my trip to Kemet in 2022.. 599 = **23**, see page **648** for the **metaphysical significance of the number 23**.

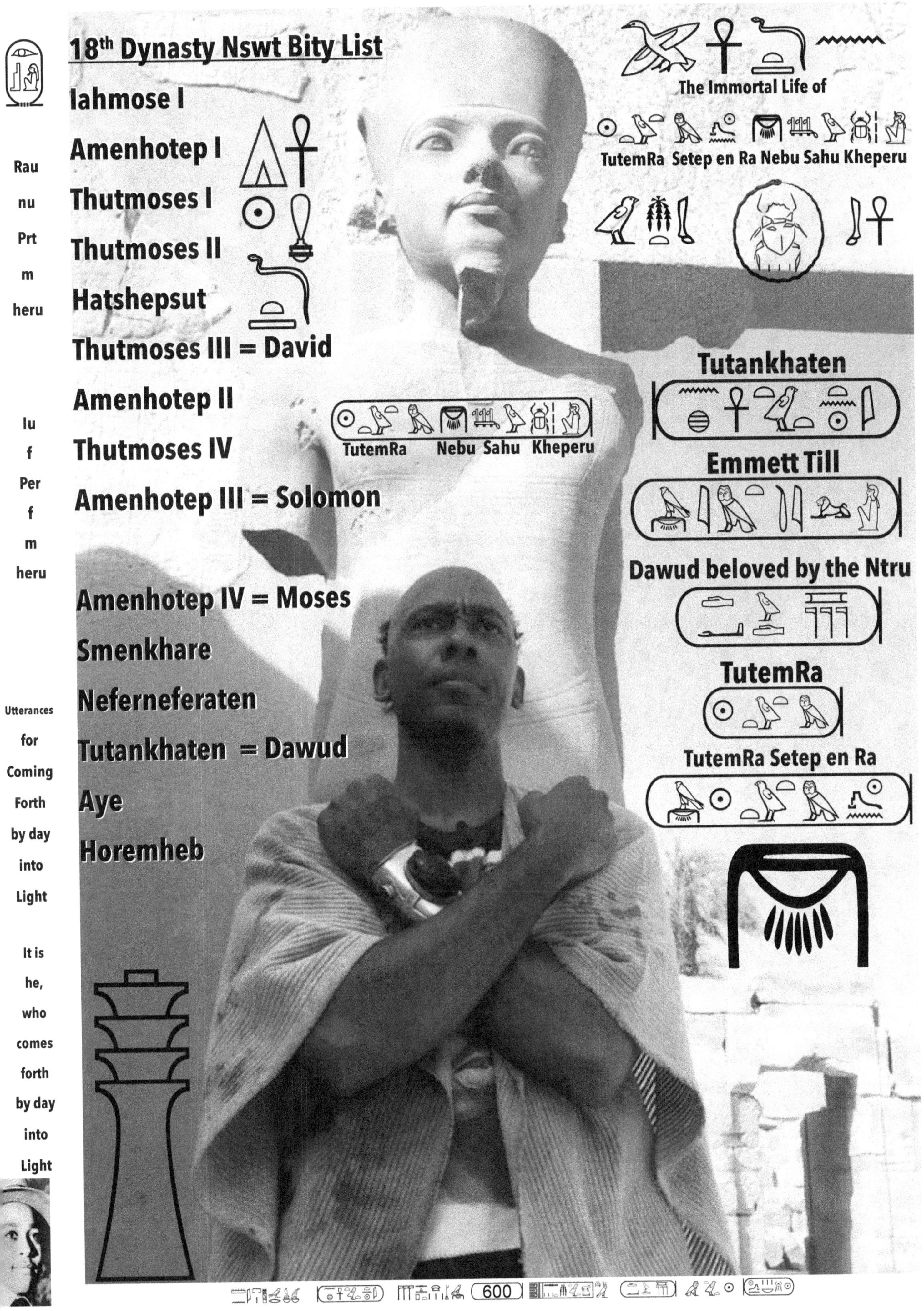

18th Dynasty Nswt Bity List
Iahmose I
Amenhotep I
Thutmoses I
Thutmoses II
Hatshepsut
Thutmoses III = David
Amenhotep II
Thutmoses IV
Amenhotep III = Solomon
Amenhotep IV = Moses
Smenkhare
Neferneferaten
Tutankhaten = Dawud
Aye
Horemheb
Rau nu Prt m heru
Iu f Per f m heru
Utterances for Coming Forth by day into Light
It is he, who comes forth by day into Light
The Immortal Life of
TutemRa Setep en Ra Nebu Sahu Kheperu
TutemRa Nebu Sahu Kheperu
Tutankhaten
Emmett Till
Dawud beloved by the Ntru
TutemRa
TutemRa Setep en Ra
600

"picture a Van Gogh **starry night**, I'm on a stroll ***trying to find my soul when I write"***
(Dawuud's Invocation, written on March 24th 2011, page 200)

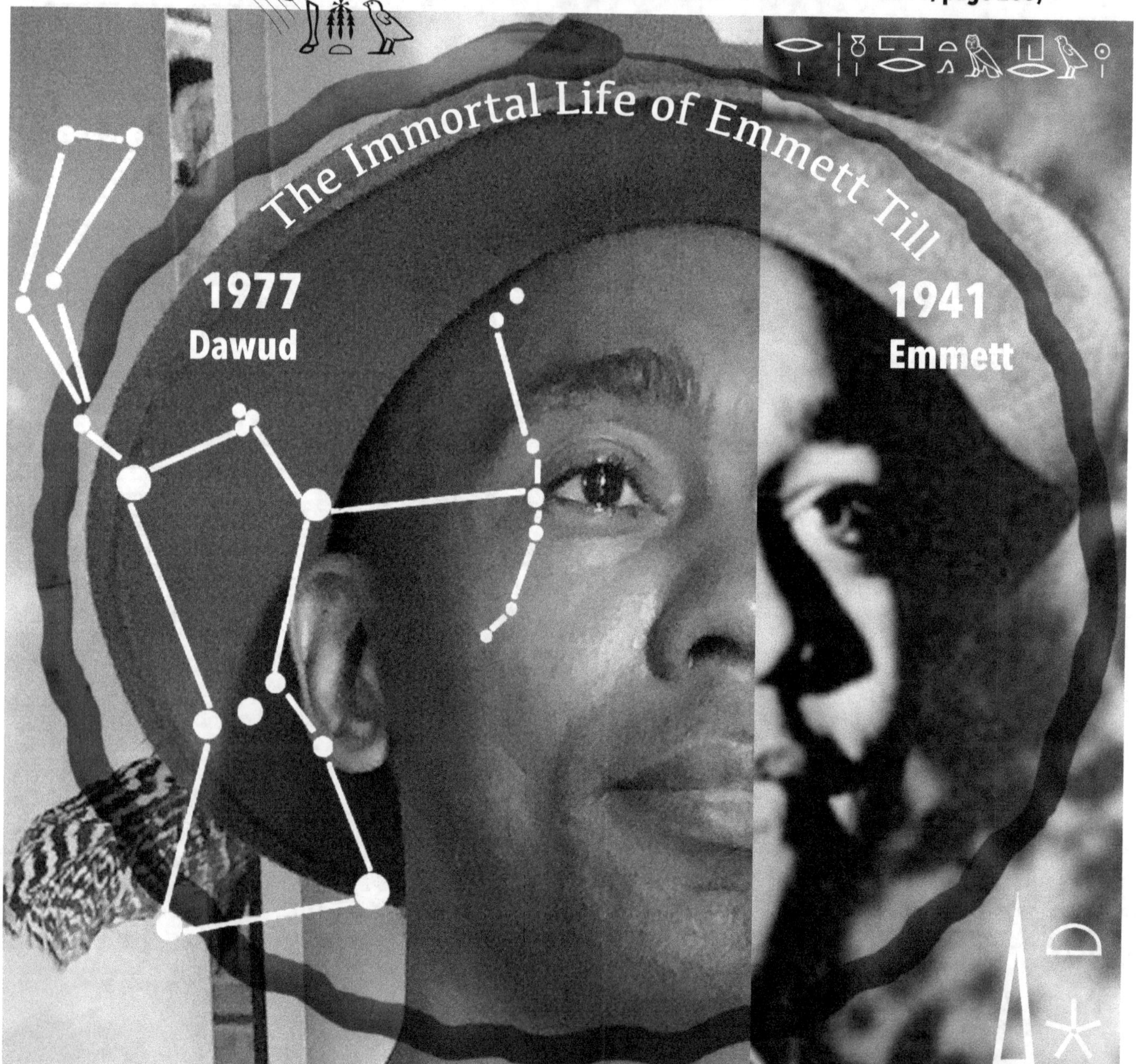

"Merry Christmas, the peasant cuts down the tree and side steps the truest bliss, they wanna separate you from the oneness that do exist, the wind blew me **the kiss of life** one **starry night**, ***I started remembering what I forgot when starting this life, they say death is an awakening, a re-membering like a dream*"** - **(The Present, Dec 26th 2016, page 437)**

Rau nu Prt m heru

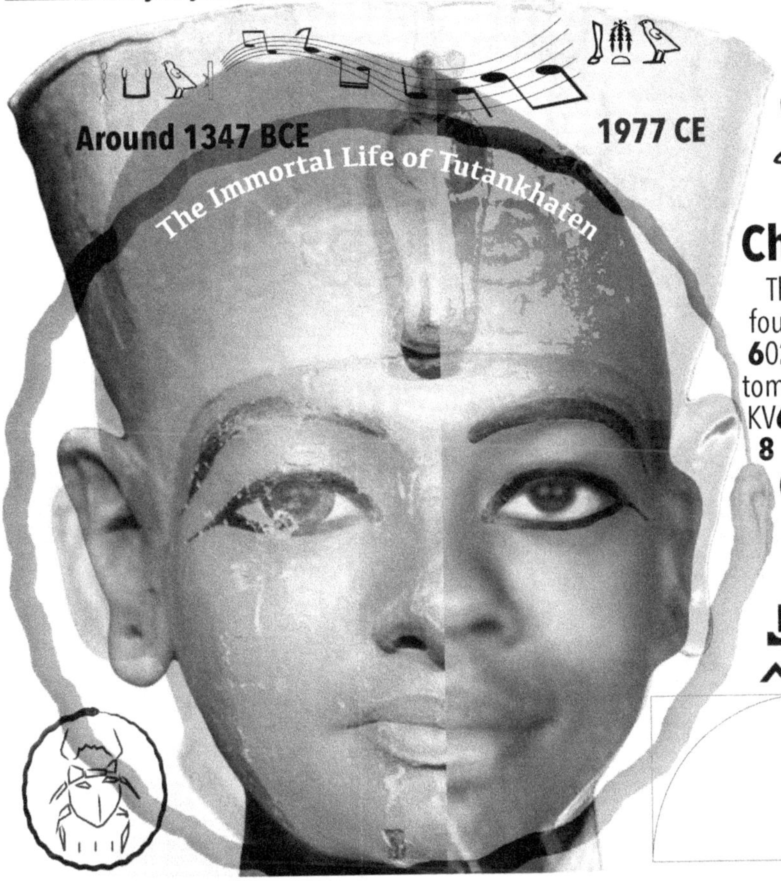

Soul Charting

This chart is found on page **6**0**2**. King Tut's tomb number is KV**62**. 6+2=**8**. **8** is **infinity**. (see pages 41, 221,162,508)

xxx-62-xxxx S.S. number (Page 508)

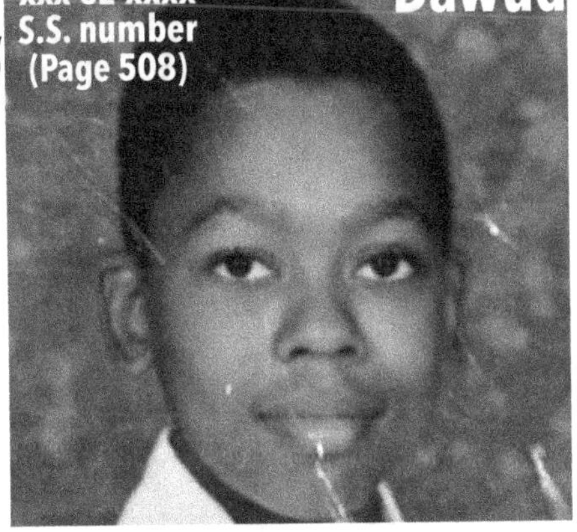

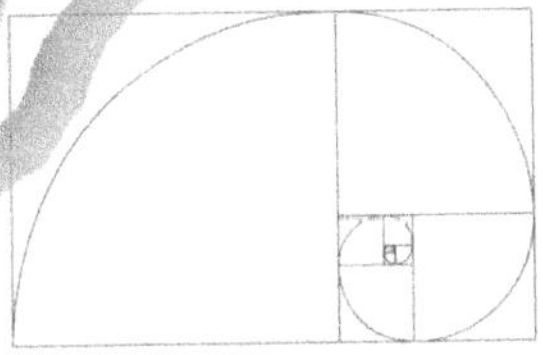

Iu f Per f m heru

The Sacred Geometry behind the Transmigration of TutemRa's Soul - Spooky action in the near future and the distant past

Utterances for Coming Forth by day into Light

This pattern is like spiritual lightening in a jar and TutemRa is the first to bring forth an equation like this! TutemRa decoded the math that connects his previous lives. This is the **Sacred Geometry** behind the transmigration of his soul fragments!! A **divine pattern**, like a formula or a revelation. Formulas reveal a path. Real revelations are specified by formulas as appose to a claim that is not and or can not be proven. The patterns presented in this book are examples of a phenomena known as **quantum entanglement**, spoken about often in **Physics**. The theory states that quantum particles that are entangled will act as one system. A measurement made on one particle will be the same on the other particle even if the particles are thousands of miles away. **Einstein** called this phenomena, **spooky action at a distance** (page 40, 41). Physicist like Einstein have been trying to find and measure the smallest of particles but these particles seem to disappear and react differently when they are being observed. The particle being isolated is the transmigration of the soul. The soul in question is TutemRa's. Souls are broken into fragments and the measurements on one life (soul fragment) will equal the next life (soul fragment) even if the lives are 3300 years apart. All the patterns in this book are examples of the quantum entanglement of TutemRa's soul fragments. "King Tut" was said to have died between **19** and **22** years of age. The tomb of "King Tut" was discovered in 19**22**, the year of the **dog**, the same year "Emmett Till's" father was born. **19** years later "King Tut" was born again as "Emmett Till" in 19**41**, the year of the **snake**. **14** years later, in 19**55**, the year of the **goat**, "Emmett" is murdered. That same year the mother of "Dawud Eddings" is born. **22** years later "Emmett Till" is born again as "Dawud Eddings" in 19**77** the year of the **snake**. **33** years after the tomb of "King Tut" is discovered, "Emmett Till" is murdered and the mother of "Dawud Eddings" is born in 19**55** the year of the **goat**. **55** years after the tomb of "King Tut" is discovered "Emmett Till" is born again as "Dawud Eddings" in 19**77** the year of the **snake** when his mother was **22**. "Dawud Eddings" was born in 19**77** the year of the **snake** and **77** years after "Emmett Till" is born in 19**41**, "Dawud Eddings" realized he was "Emmett Till" in his past life. "Emmett Till" was born in 19**41**, the year of the **snake** and in 2018, the year of the **dog** (page 480), **41** years after "Dawud" is born, Dawud realizes he was "Emmett " in his past life. "Dawud's" mother is born in 19**55**, the year of the **goat**, the same year "Emmett" is murdered and "Emmett's" mother died in 2003, the year of the **goat**. **98** years after the tomb of "**King Tut**" was discovered, on April 4, 2020, the same day Martin Luther King was assasinated, "**Dawud**" had a profound revelation which brought forth his past life as "**King Tut**" (page 594). During this experience he was given the name **TutemRa** and in 2022 this book was released, **100** years after "**King Tut's**" discoverey.

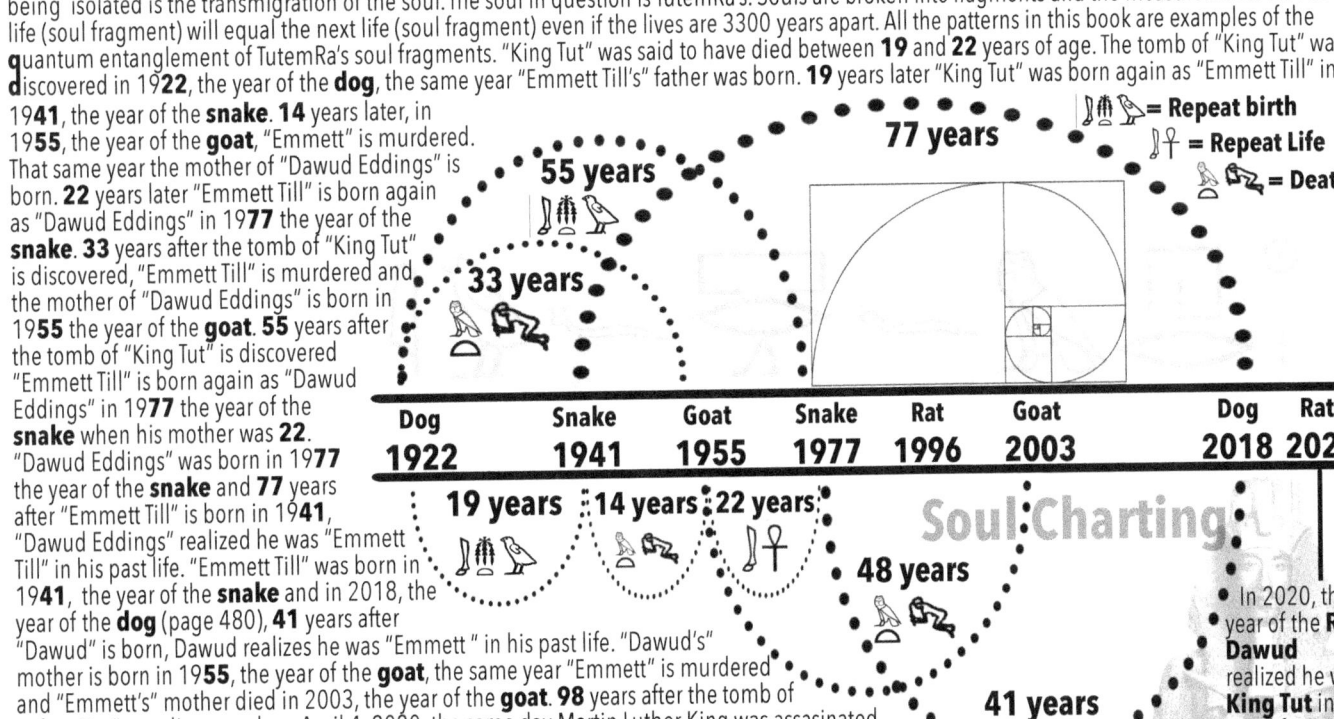

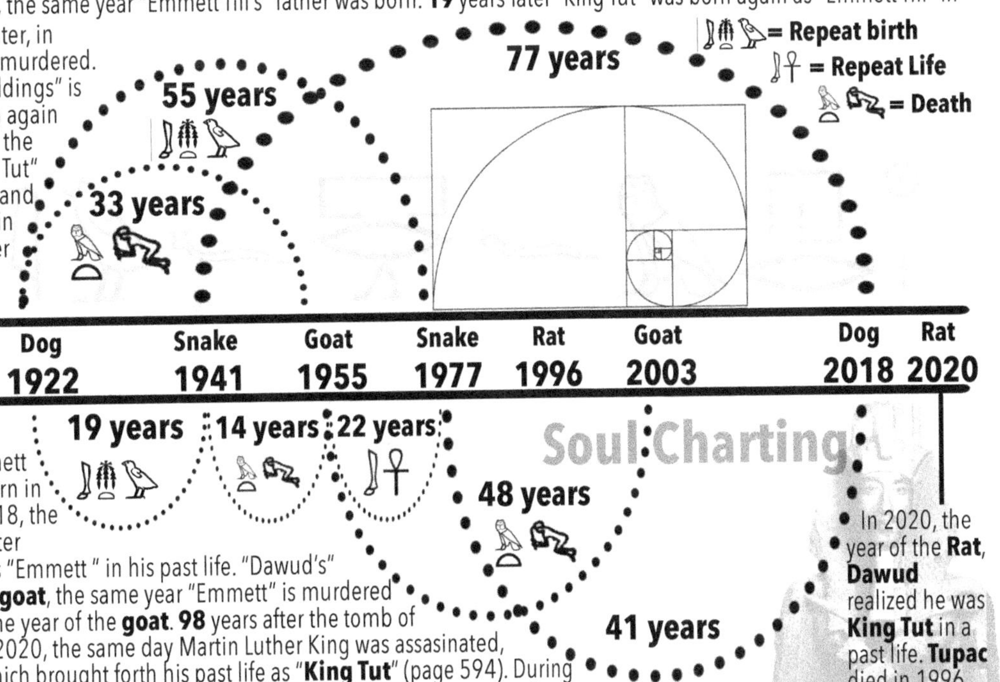

In 2020, the year of the **Rat**, **Dawud** realized he was **King Tut** in a past life. **Tupac** died in 1996, year of the **Rat**. See page 664.

It is he, who comes forth by day into Light

The Mysterious Cases of Familiar Faces From Different Times and Different Places

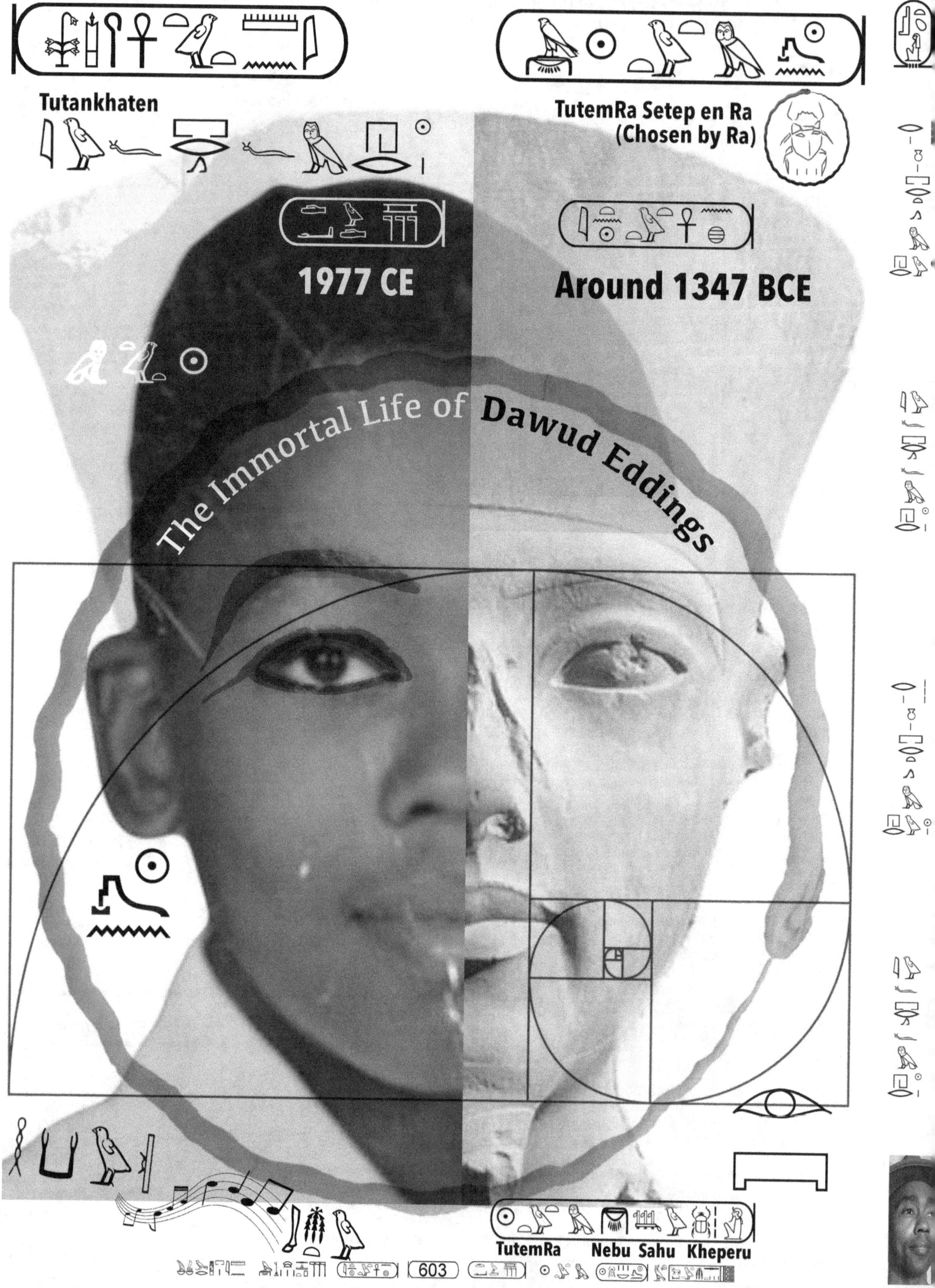

Jonathan Jungblut and His Guardian Angels

During a training session on January 21st 2022, my client and friend John was asking me about the details of my book and how close I was to finishing. The he asked if he was in the book and I told him that I mentioned him when I talked about Heraa, the person who introduced us. He asked why I had not placed a picture of him in the book like I had placed a picture of Heraa. I told him that I place pictures when there is a spiritual experience or something relative to the book. Then he reminded me of what happened with his childhood friend **Jelani**. Sometime in April of 2020, **John** crossed paths with another client and friend named **Meeky** at my apartment. I was finishing a **massage** with Meeky and John was arriving for a **personal training** session. Meeky had recently **awakened** her **gift of sight** and had been passing messages to me from my **guardian angels** regularly. Out of curiosity, I asked Meeky to tell me if she saw any guardians around John and when John arrived she told me that he had two guardians, a childhood friend standing next to him and a member of his family standing behind him. I told John and he confirmed that he had a childhood friend who had been murdered years ago by the police. I had forgotten about this experience with John's guardian angel but afterwards I asked John to write his friend story and told him that I would put it in the book. After John wrote the story I saw that his friend had been murdered on January 24th, just three days before he had come up in conversation. I had recently been telling my friend Shanta that it felt as if the souls of the dead were finding their way to this book and this is exactly how I felt about Jelani. Jelani was murdered in 2003 the year of the **goat** while Emmett Till was murdered in 1955 the year of the **goat**. I called Meeky on January **28**th 2022 to see what she remembered about the experience and she remembered that the childhood friend was they type of guardian that was serious and was there to protect and defend. John is born on February 18th, my nieces birthday.

Rau nu Prt m heru

Jelani Darren Manigault

"Jelani Darren Manigault was born in 1978. My birth year as well. As long as I have known, he has had his "hand on my shoulder". We met other each other in pre-school, played soccer together, were best friends on the field and off, families vacationed together, you get the point. His mom always cooked him meals and served them to him on a tray. And, to me as well, when I went over his house to cause mischief. He was always late to school, even though he lived right across the street. He had more female friends than male friends and almost every male LOVED Jelani. I make this point only to emphasize that his empathy was off the charts. He was the only man I felt comfortable talking to about the "emotional" stuff that you don't talk about with your boyz. We had crushes on the same girl in high school. And, he was an **Eagle Scout** and a **black belt**. Jelani was murdered on January 24, 2003 in Princeton, NJ in what we have come to know as "suicide by cop" AKA a "crazy" black man is an animal we must put down.

Jelani's life story is one of empathy and compassion. He could never hurt a fly, literally. I struggled about my purpose in life when he died. I haven't wavered on it after. Now I know that he is my guardian angel. He stands on my shoulder. The meaning of Jelani in Swahili is "mighty or powerful". It is said we stand on the shoulders of giants. I am a giant, who has a giant on my shoulder, and my purpose in life is to give a mighty, powerful young black man a shoulder to stand on." - **Jonathan Jungblut**

Iu f Per f m heru

Utterances for Coming Forth by day into Light

It is he, who comes forth by day into Light

For more on **Guardian Angels** and Ka Doors (**Spirit Doors**) see pages (250 -253, 48, 141, 142, 148, 150, 179, 199, 315, 318, 329, 348, 349, 409, 421, 434, 545, 548, 549, 572, 584, 626, 650).

Condolences

My condolences go out to the family of **Jelani Darren Manigault** and all those who have been robbed of their lives by this system of racism and white supremacy. Please know that death is not the end. The soul survives death, indeed and in spirit. This is a book of the dead written by a boy who was murdered without justice, who defeated death and came forth by day. May the soul of **Jelani Darren Manigault** walk peacefully through the field of Reeds in Amenta. Amen Ra.

April 7th 2020
The Prophecy of Reincarnation, Sambho the Black Buddha

Three days after the revelation of my life as Tutankhaten I found myself looking through my computer again and ran across a documentary, ***<u>The Prophecy Of Reincarnation Sambho the black buddha</u>*** which I downloaded from the internet on <u>March 2nd 2014</u> (p 288). As soon as I saw it I knew that I needed to watch it again! I drew a bath and relaxed in the water as I began to watch the documentary for the third time. It seemed like I was supposed to be watching it and I couldn't get pass that feeling. It all felt planned. The documentary states that there is a 2500 year old prophecy of the *<u>Return of the Buddha</u>*. It would go on to state that this coming **Buddha** would be born in the **west**. He would **<u>prove the immortality of the soul by his reincarnation</u>**. He would build a city out of **silver**. He would arrive on the planet between the years of 1975 and **2020**. When I first watched this documentary in 2014 I thought it was very interesting and I do recall thinking that it was cool that I was born within that time frame that this future Buddha was supposed to come back but the documentary also said the Buddha would return in the 1990's. When I heard that the first time I wondered who the Buddha might have been because it wasn't me, because I was born in 1977. But things were different this time! Perhaps they were wrong about the timing. I was watching the documentary in the year **2020** and the documentary said the Buddha would arrive on the planet between the years of 1975 and **2020** and I was born in 1977 which is between 1975 and 2020 and I had just had my past life revelation of my life as Tutankhaten (King Tut) revealed to me in the year 2020, on the same day that **Martin Luther King** was assassinated (pages 69, 592). **The documentary even showed a picture of King Tut in the video** and talked about him! At this point I felt that I was the Buddha that they were talking about. After I watched the documentary I immediately thought about my song <u>The Prophecy</u> that I wrote four years prior on <u>September 29th 2016</u> (page 424). The documentary mentioned the book **African Presence in Early Asia** (written by **Ivan Van Sertima**), I figured I should read through it again so after my bath I took that book of my shelf **<u>and placed it on the floor</u>** near other books I was looking through. 3 days later on April 10th **the book would speak to me** like other books have done to me through the course of my journey but this time the book gave me a clear message from the ancestor **Baba Ahati Kilindi Iyi**.

Another Epiphany on December 23rd 2021

Today is December **23**rd 2021 and I should be finished this book by the end of the day on the 25th of December, however I just noticed that the cover of the book **African Presence in Early Asia** correlates with an experience I had on October 7th 2021 (page 659) while watching video footage of **The Great Arjuna's Penance / Descent of Ganges Relief at Mamallapuram and The Shore Temple** in India. This experience seemed to confirm a life I lived in India. As I looked at all the images they were so familiar that I knew I had definitely seen them before and something was pulling at my heart telling me that I had been there before! This experience would cause me to cry uncontrollably. I could not explain the feeling, it was like nothing I have ever experienced before. My experience that woke me up to my past life as Emmett Till was instantaneous and I knew who I was immediately but I did not cry, instead I was amazed and at the same time I had a lot of disbelief. The more that I researched Emmett the more I knew it was real then the life of Emmett seemed to haunt me. He was everywhere even in the music I created years before the revelation. When my life as Tutankhaten came I knew immediately I was him and I laughed out load and joyously for a long time but this experience with the stone relief in India was different! It was like I have walked there before. The elephant statue was ingrained in my memory. The **Nagas** snake deities were also very familiar. I felt like I had climbed the wall relief before or walked on it and because of my past life experiences all I could do was think that I once lived there before. I know that I lived in India as the Buddha Siddhartha but the time in which I was said to have lived does not match with the time of the building of the relief. Perhaps I lived as another person during the 7th or 8th Century. See page **648** for the **metaphysical significance of the number 23**.

Rau nu Prt m heru

Iu f Per f m heru

Utterances for Coming Forth by day into Light

It is he, who comes forth by day into Light

March 18th 1955 ∞ April 10th 2020 Saba Ahati Kilindi Iyi Goes West

When I got news that Kilindi had passed I couldn't believe it. I had just found him and his teachings. I felt like the world had lost someone that most people didn't even know they needed. I was sitting in my chair in disbelief when I happened to glance at the floor and saw the book **(African Presence in Early Asia)** I had taken off the shelf just 3 days ago after watching the *Prophecy Of Reincarnation* video. I picked it up and **RAndomly opened** it to page 138, which was "coincidentally" a chapter that was written by Kilindi Iyi. I smiled and knew that he had indeed spoken to me. This was not some meaningless, lucky flip of the page, no! He had visited me in this "coincidence" no different than when **Prince** visited **Erica** the day he died on April 21st 2016 (page 379). I had recently listened to a lecture where Kilindi talked about what happens to the soul or consciousness when we "die". He said that we have the potential to visit people shortly after death of the physical body (page 483). I was sure he had visited me! This was a message from Kilindi and no one could change my mind on that. Back on October 5th 2018 (page 537) I went to a lecture of his in search of answers about my past life as Emmett Till but I didn't feel like I got what I was looking for from him. I think Kilindi had something to do with me opening that book to a chapter written by him so as to confirm what I was experiencing with my past lives was true indeed and in spirit. On August 7th 2020, while at the Detroit Psychedelic convention I met other people who had paranormal experiences with Kilindi after he died (page 618). Kilindi was born in 19**55**, the same year Emmett was murdered. The book, African Presence in Early Asia, was written by **Ivan Van Sertima**. **Ivan** died on **May 25th**, **the first star code** in this book (pages **iii**, **512**, 30, 4, 14, 37, 44, 104 - 106, **293**, 329, 626 and 659.. ! For more on Guardian Angels and Ka Doors (Spirit Doors) see pages (250 -253, 48, 141, 142, 148, 150,179, 199, 315, 318, 329, 348, 349, 409, 421, 434, 545, 548, 549, 572, 584, 626, 650).

Ivan Van Sertima

Condolences

My condolences go out to the family, friends, students and supporters of Kilindi Iyi. Please know that death is not the end. The soul survives death, indeed and in spirit. This is a book of the dead written by a boy who was murdered without justice, who defeated death and came forth by day. May the soul of **Nswt Bity Kilindi Ahati Iyi walk peacefully through the field of Reeds in Amenta. Amen Ra.**

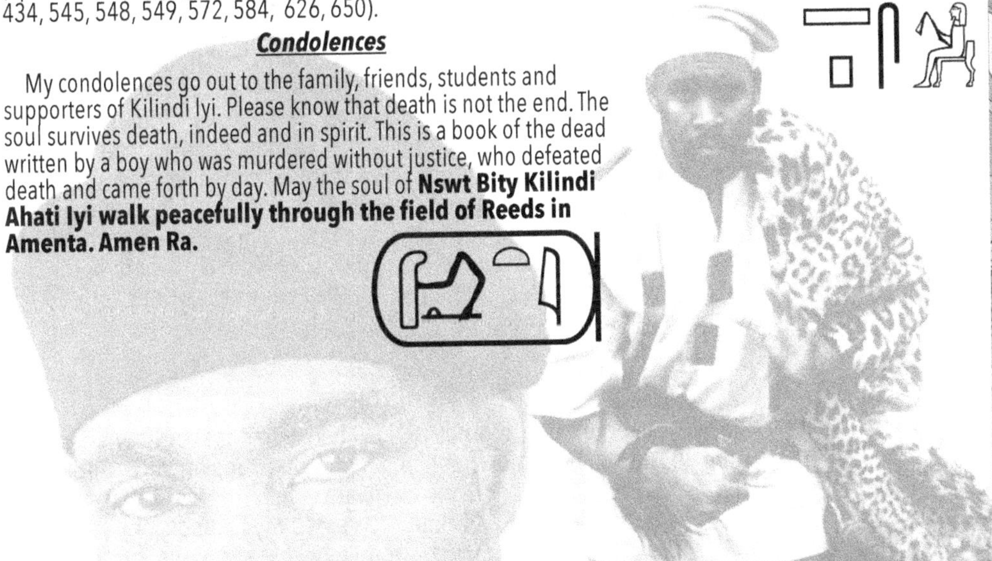

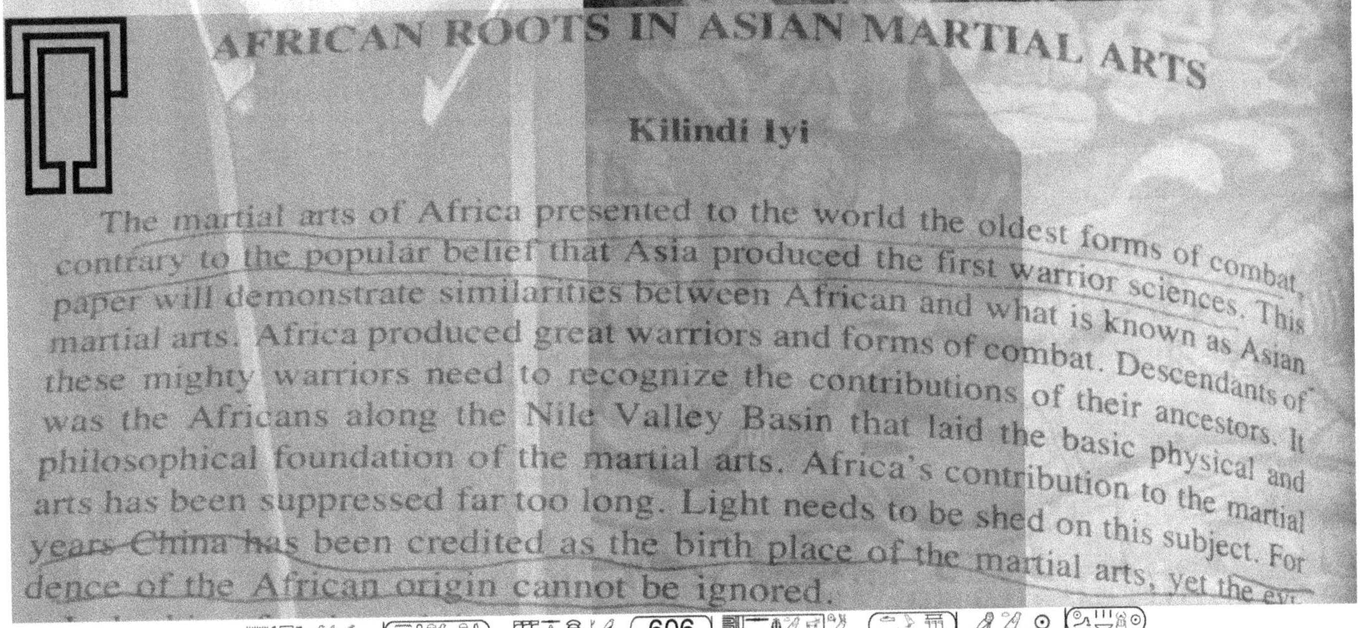

AFRICAN ROOTS IN ASIAN MARTIAL ARTS

Kilindi Iyi

The martial arts of Africa presented to the world the oldest forms of combat, contrary to the popular belief that Asia produced the first warrior sciences. This paper will demonstrate similarities between African and what is known as Asian martial arts. Africa produced great warriors and forms of combat. Descendants of these mighty warriors need to recognize the contributions of their ancestors. It was the Africans along the Nile Valley Basin that laid the basic physical and philosophical foundation of the martial arts. Africa's contribution to the martial arts has been suppressed far too long. Light needs to be shed on this subject. For years China has been credited as the birth place of the martial arts, yet the evidence of the African origin cannot be ignored.

April 19th 2020 Prophecy of The Naga

I rose from the ashes, the **Aten,** the **Boy King, TutemRa** da **Naga** from **Kemet,** the **Ever Lasting,** dear senate have you repented for taking life and casting spells?! I'm forecasting a hell, I'm fasting and drafting plans to prevail, do you **Ra**-member me ?! I think you will, are you my enemy? if not, then you wear it well! they killed me when I was little Emmett Till but still The Immortal Life; despite your knife, it ain't hard to tell, yeah and I'm drinking from my own well, "**My Only Fear Of Death is Reincarnation"** ring the bells, **reparations** for the incarceration, castration, free bas'n and the illegal sales on my black nation! **I'm back, Jason**, you clout chase'n, you black face'n, you wack race'n, you crack bake'n, the hate you gave little infants and the defenseless women that you been rape'n! like Satan or **Jesus** they need us to put faith in, even though they keep break'n treaties, they greedy keep taken like a cancer, and **Sway** I bet they ain't got the answers, **Dawud** da **Naga** word to my mama I would'a been a **Panther** with **Dessalines** and **Nat Turner**! I'm not a tap dancer **- TutemRa**

April 20th 2020 The Pattern

Close your eyelids, **our souls met way before our eyes did**, they say love is a black hole that attracts souls, law of attraction, poles, a grid, polarity, a rose, the chemistry, a road to serenity, **death couldn't finish me**, **I died and came back** navigated the **zodiac** with perfect timing, saw you in a dream but your guardian wasn't trying to let me swing, I woke up and never said a thing, I just kept rising up and metamorphosing, her eyes are shut, she don't see the Tut or the king, it's like I'm the only nut awake in this dream, reality only teaches us to cut off our wings, do you wanna fly? Tell me who's pulling the strings? do you believe in fate or soul mates or whatever chance brings? love sedates, it stings, love comes like a thief in the night, the **Queen** more **powerful** than the knight, the castle or the King, we can shower each other with things or grow wings and fly to the outer rings of **Saturn** where the angels sing, can you fathom being **awake** in the **dream** seeing the pattern? Love rules everything around me, the pattern **- TutemRa**

Significance

A few weeks prior to writing this rhyme I had a dream about a woman I met in 2016. I only mention her name in this book one time. On April 20th I went into a deep meditation and afterwards I felt like I was supposed to marry this woman. For the first time I confessed my feelings for her but she didn't share the same sentiments. I definitely missed judged the "pattern" and so this experience taught me a lesson. Being able to discern what the **coincidences** in our lives mean is very important! My feelings for her were based on the **coincidences** that caused us to meet and because we shared the same ancestral background, they were not based on how she treated me. I was following the pattern and I made the pattern mean what I wanted it to mean and this should not be down with matters of the heart. I would later realize that I was supposed to be her mother's friend. Her mother and I would talk about spirituality and I would introduce her to my friend Meeky who was able to help her speak to her ancestors. After April 20th 2020 I stopped giving this woman my attention and now I see her very rarely, only when I'm helping her mother do something. In matters of the heart I think life offers us many options but it's up to both parties to see the pattern. I'm more careful now not to make too much of a fool of myself. On the left I am seen standing next to an ancient statue of me and my wife Ankhesenaten in the Temple of Luxor during my trip to Kemet in 2022.

April 28th 2020 The Pattern

One time is an incidence, twice is a coincidence, three four five is a pattern, can you tell the difference? Love is a language a marriage with self and the infinite, your heart, watch where you aim it before you get intimate, it's dark in this black hole but she's my light like a filament, soldier of love militant, cause this battle is immanent, **Emmett Till** from then till now and they still got ill intent, **Thutmose** sailed the **Nile** with **rod**, **staff** and regiment, they claim to be holy but put holes in the firmament, you might win some but your reign could never be permanent, the sun **Ra** the melanin we burn'n lit, I went the same way **Ivan Van Serta** went, face'n turbulence we didn't drown, in a world full of violence self defense **Michael Brown**, they wanna silence **Deshawn Jackson** for tweet'n now, but never say shit about black skin get beat'n down, I'm really missing **Michael Jackson** and **Tupac** now, dear Lord tell me why **Breonna** had to die?! She never got to see the bullet she just heard the shot, and her body couldn't take it she just shook and dropped! and her body couldn't take it she just shook and dropped! shook and dropped! it's the pattern, the love is ruling everything around me the pattern, love is ruling everything around me the pattern, love is ruling everything around me the pattern, love'n is ruling everything **- TutemRa**

May 14th 2020
You Can't Bury a Magician
The Great Lafayette and Chung Ling Soo
Levitating From The Grave

Rau nu Prt m heru

Iu f Per f m heru

Meta-Spiritual Encounters of the fourth kind

Many people are drawn to shows where they are mesmerized by magic tricks and things that seem to be nothing other than supernatural and many times quite unbelievable, but the more unbelievable the better. Right? Most people are satisfied by being entertained however the select few choose to open the doors of the occult mysteries of magic becoming magicians themselves. Magicians love to entertain but what about when the magician dies, is the show over or do they move on to another realm where they still work their magic? And if that's true imagine if they can manage to work magic in this realm long after they have departed from their physical bodies? Perhaps they can. Perhaps their need to entertain persists even after death leaving their Spirit (**Ka**) to linger waiting for those who might call on their names (**Ren**)? And if this is true perhaps they are selective with who they appear for. During the **golden** age of magic, many magicians were attracted to the great mysteries of ancient Kemet (Egypt) and this can be seen in the names of their acts and even in the designs for the posters used to promote their acts. On my sisters birthday, May 14th 2020, a month after my past life revelation on Tutankhaten (King Tut) I was given a private magic show by two Magicians from the **golden** age of magic, The Great Lafayette and Chung Ling Soo. Or was it Ching Ling Foo?

The Great Lafayette

On **May 14th** 2020, I found myself searching through my computer for something but instead of finding what I was looking for I came across a video that I downloaded in 2015 named _BBC Supernatural Science - Secrets of Levitation_. Drawn to the video, I watched it all and became **fascinated with levitation again**. Immediately, I went to **youtube** to search for more videos on levitation. I put the words "the history of levitation" in the search browser and many videos appeared. The video I decided to watch was cut into six ten-minute videos and by "**chance**" I selected the fifth video and began to watch it. As I watched the video I was blown away by the **coincidence.** The video was about a magician named **The Great Lafayette** who died performing a levitation act and had a funeral on **May 14th** 1911, and in that same video another magician named Chung Ling Soo would appear with the same hair style as me.

Utterances for Coming Forth by day into Light

Chung Ling Soo

The Great Lafayette and Chung Ling Soo were both from the time considered to be the **golden** era of magic. Chung Ling Soo was an American illusionist in the 1900's who was said to have copied the acts of other magicians, from Egyptian illusionist to Indians finally stealing the act and persona of a Chinese magician Named Ching Ling Foo. When he took on this identity he changed his name from Mr. Wn. G. Robinson to Chung Ling Soo and to make his act more believable he wore a Manchu queue or cue hairstyle, which is a bald head in the front with a single ponytail in the back. He even used a translator when speaking to journalists. Unfortunately, he died on stage attempting to catch a bullet. The irony of his death is that he claimed to know no other language but Chinese however after being shot on stage he spoke these words in English "Oh my God. Something's happened. I've been shot. Lower the curtain."

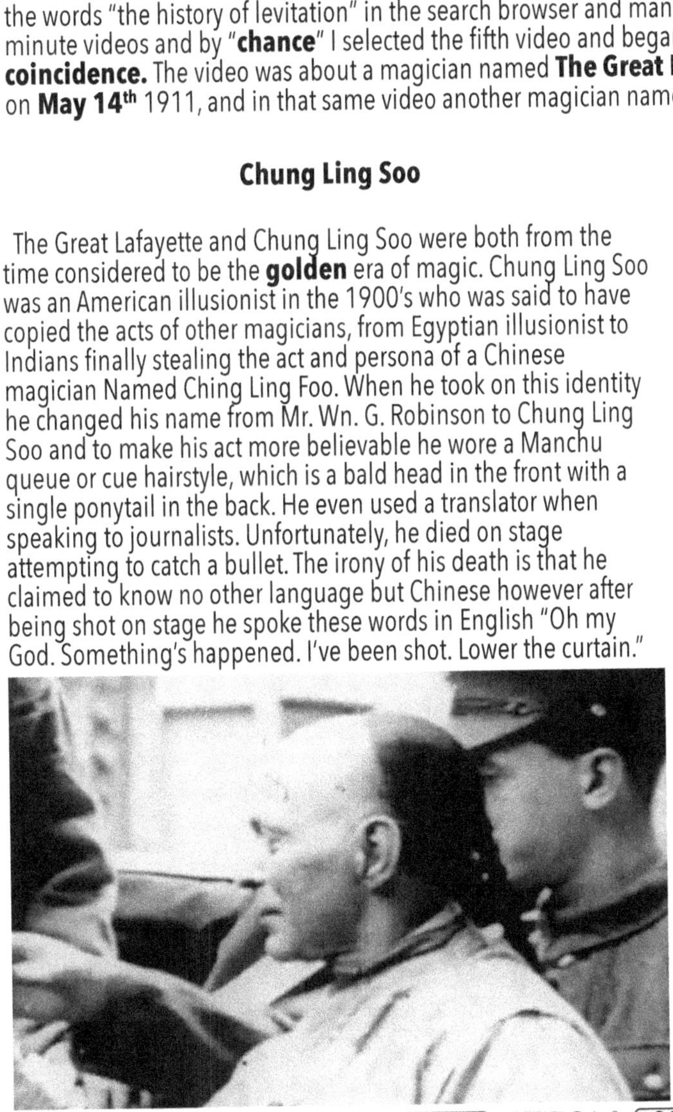

Significance

The Manchu hairstyle was mandatory for all Chinese males and the penalty for non-compliance was execution for treason. In the early 1910s, after the fall of the Qing dynasty, the Chinese no longer had to wear the Manchu queue. While some, such as Zhang Xun, still did so as a tradition, most of them abandoned it after the last Emperor of China, Puyi, cut his off in 19**22,** the same year **Tutankhaten's** (**King Tut's**) tomb was discovered. On **May 14th** 2020 I watched a 10-minute video where I saw The Great Lafayette who was buried on **May 14th** 1911 and in the same video I see The magician Chung Ling Soo who is wearing the same hair style as mine and both of these magicians were fascinated with **Egypt**.

It is he, who comes forth by day into Light

May 17th 2020 Grid of The Gods

We stacked **12 sided stones** in great numbers, make you wonder what **magic** the ancients honed? anti gravity? and the grid of the Gods that's coming home, cosmic wars, pyramid people, how could the Gods be dethroned? geometrically precise, universal laws thrice times majestic, the price of freedom is death kid, **Malcolm** told you that then he was ejected from the body, but **the soul lives forever,** cause it's electric, speak a mans name, he lives forever, **Ancestors, Ancient Stars, Divine NTCHR,** encoded in this rhyme lecture, I don't need to text ya, mental telecom, hard be the texture, I stay in shape like a tetrahedron, I swim in the ocean not the lake, You take makeshift religion, I take my spaceship then dip then trip, then break the system, the theory of everything, **Einstein** can't touch my wisdom, they hate our khemystry, like Jordan hate the pistons, air time soaring magician **acoustic levitation**, exploring the hidden, the music use it for revelation, the creator created creation but there is no obligation, this life is a quest do your best to reach initiation, vibration, karma, cause n effect, the dharma, the wheels of destiny, activate the breath, the chi, pranayama ecstasy, TutemRa the Dali Lama Naga legacy, check the melody, the rhythm my only weaponry **- TutemRA**

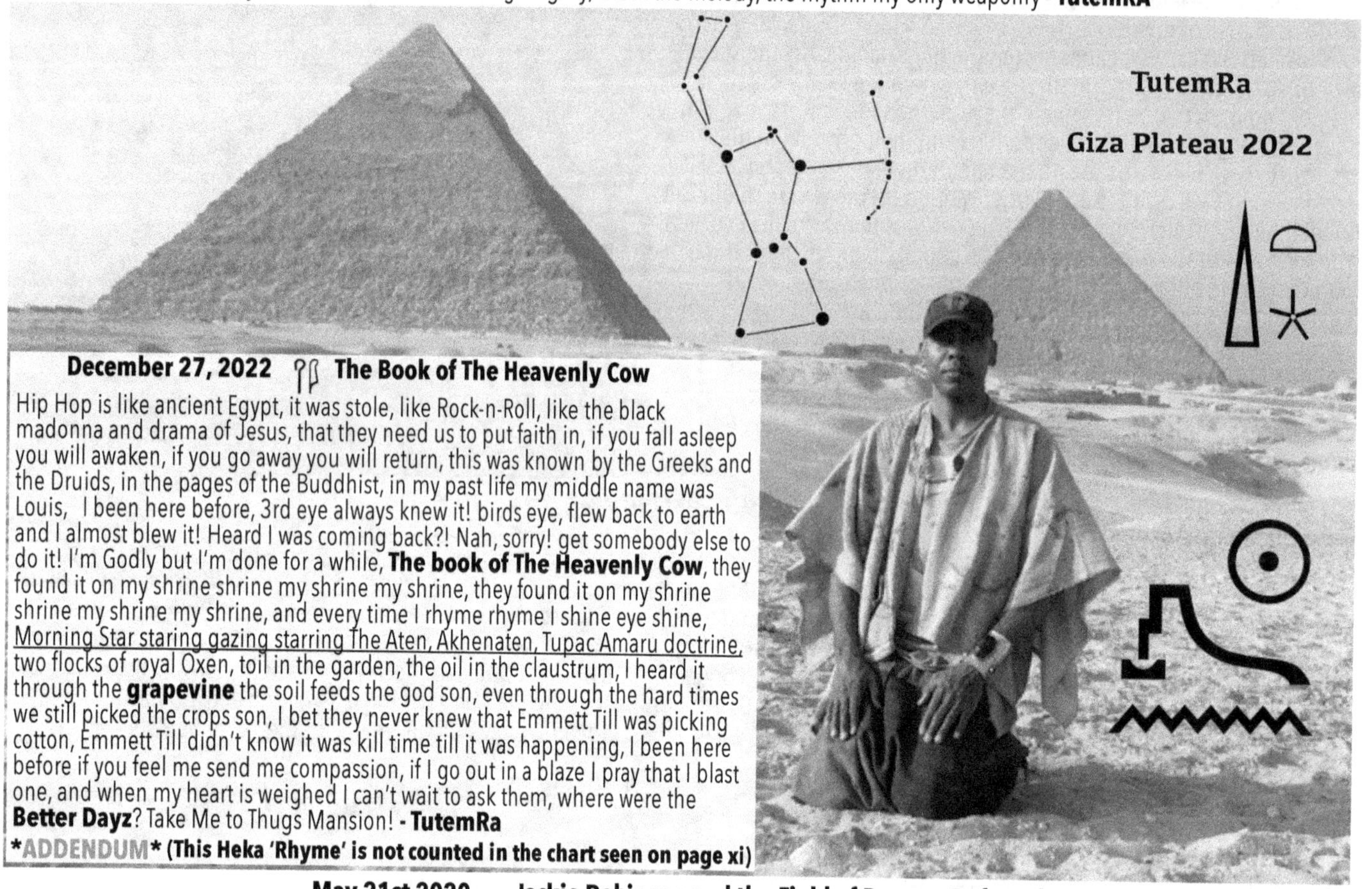

December 27, 2022 The Book of The Heavenly Cow

Hip Hop is like ancient Egypt, it was stole, like Rock-n-Roll, like the black madonna and drama of Jesus, that they need us to put faith in, if you fall asleep you will awaken, if you go away you will return, this was known by the Greeks and the Druids, in the pages of the Buddhist, in my past life my middle name was Louis, I been here before, 3rd eye always knew it! birds eye, flew back to earth and I almost blew it! Heard I was coming back?! Nah, sorry! get somebody else to do it! I'm Godly but I'm done for a while, **The book of The Heavenly Cow**, they found it on my shrine shrine my shrine my shrine, they found it on my shrine shrine my shrine my shrine, and every time I rhyme rhyme I shine eye shine, Morning Star staring gazing starring The Aten, Akhenaten, Tupac Amaru doctrine, two flocks of royal Oxen, toil in the garden, the oil in the claustrum, I heard it through the **grapevine** the soil feeds the god son, even through the hard times we still picked the crops son, I bet they never knew that Emmett Till was picking cotton, Emmett Till didn't know it was kill time till it was happening, I been here before if you feel me send me compassion, if I go out in a blaze I pray that I blast one, and when my heart is weighed I can't wait to ask them, where were the **Better Dayz**? Take Me to Thugs Mansion! **- TutemRa**

***ADDENDUM* (This Heka 'Rhyme' is not counted in the chart seen on page xi)**

May 21st 2020 - Jackie Robinson and the Field of Dreams Deferred

ADDENDUM

I am sitting on a bench in Jackie Robinson p**ark,** my client Armeen **Barnes** is 20 minutes late. He has a son born on **October 9**th which is my grand mother's birthday.. He is distant cousins with **Tupac**. His grand mother was a **Barnes** and Tupac's grand mother was named Eloise Maria **Barnes** Garland. Yesterday was **Toussaint Louverture's** birthday (p 42, 84, 142, 248, 254, 292, **349***, 365, 463). When I was in high school I knew nothing about Toussaint or the Haitian revolution. I knew nothing about much of African history. I had two Haitian friends in high school who played on my football team. They both had the same name, Patrick Hillare. One is born on July 3rd, the same day I had my past life revelation of my life as Emmett Till on July 3rd 2018 (p 480), and the other Patrick (p 66) is born Sep 17, two days before Emmett's court trial started (p 516). I was born in Far Rockaway, Queens NY on Oct 25th 1977 the year of the **snake** at 10:25am. I grew up in a house hold that was loving but there was no time spent teaching about African history because no one in my house knew African history and most of my family still doesn't know African history. I am the only person in my immediate family that has turned their ATENtion towards ancient Kemet. My maternal Grand Parents had **six daughters** and no sons like **Nefertiti** (Akhenaten) and **Betty Shabazz** (Malcolm X). My mother was the first daughter born. My parents met in the Nation of Islam and quickly fell in love, got married and had three children (page 27/28). I was the second child born of my parents and the first male born in the family. At 40 years of age my past life as Emmett Till was revealed to me (p 480). At **42** years old my past life as the **Pharaoh** Tutankhaten (King Tut) was revealed to me (p 594). **Chadwick Boseman** (The Black Panther) had his **first** starring role in 2013 the year of the **snake** as **Jackie Robinson** who was the **first** black man to play major league baseball and "coincidentally" he wore the number **42** and "coincidentally" he died the day before my birthday on October **24th** which is "coincidentally" the same day that Rosa **Parks** died. Rosa Parks refused to move her seat because of the murder of Emmett Till. KRS One released his book, **The Gospel of Hip Hop: The First Instrumental** on Oct 24th 2009 (p 633) the same year my grand father died.. He died the day after Marcus Garvey's birthday (p 169). **Chadwick Boseman** (The Black Panther) died on August **28**th at the age **42**, on the same day that **Emmett Till** was murdered (p 6**24**). Many people feel that Jackie Robinson's move from the **negro league** to the major leagues, becoming the first black major league baseball player was in some way, a great achievement for black people, especially for talented black baseball players. Unfortunately that couldn't be farther from the truth. After Jackie left the negro league many negro league teams who were in close proximity to major league teams almost immediately lost the majority of their fans. All of the best black players were now signed to major league teams and so black baseball fans began to go see Jackie Robinson, Larry Doby and the other black athletes. I recently watched the movie, **Field of Dreams** while on a flight to ATL. In the movie Kevin Costner is standing in his **garden** (p 481) when he **hears a voice** (hearing voices, pages 452, 474, 482, 518, 536, 652) that tells him, **"build it and he will come"**. Then he sees a vision of a baseball field. After hearing the voice several times he decides to build a baseball field. Afterwards the spirits of long dead major league baseball players begin to **come forth** from the corn field. There was a scene in the movie where Kevin and his wife had the same **dream** (pages 452, 589) . This **dream** lead him to a person (p 536). Kevin Costner was born in 19**55**, the same year **Emmett Till** was murdered and the same year my mother was born. The movie Field of Dreams was released in 1989 the year of the snake. I was born in the year of the snake as Emmett Till in 1941, I was born again in this life in 1977, the year of the snake. Life is a symphony speaking in **Riddles** (p 631).

Rau nu Prt m heru

Iu f Per f m heru

Utterances for Coming Forth by day into Light

It is he, who comes forth by day into Light

May 25th 2020
George Floyd 46 Minneapolis Minnesota

George allegedly tried to use a counterfeit $20 bill while making a purchase in a store. The police were called. Floyd was hand cuffed and forced on the ground. officer **Derek chauvin** knelt on his neck for 8 min and 46 seconds as George can be heard screaming for his mother until finally George died. 3 other officers were present but they stood by and did nothing to stop their fellow officer. Instead they kept the crowd that gathered around from interfering. All 4 officers involved were fired. Chauvin faced 2nd degree murder all other officers faced aiding and abetting 2nd degree murder and manslaughter.

Significance

I don't know why I have been given this task but everyday that goes by I receive more confirmation of the importance for me to reveal this **star code of immortality** by presenting this **prophecy of reincarnation**. I saw that George Floyd had been murdered a day or two after he was murdered but I didn't watch the video till maybe a week after it happened and I still have never watched the full video. I had been consuming the footage of black people being murdered for around 10 years while also creating music that was driven by these murders so I try to protect my spirit and emotions from seeing the continuous death. But then on May 28th I realized that George was murdered on **May 25th** and his mother passed away two years prior on **May 25th**! I knew then that his death was part of my **star code pattern** and the universe wasn't done with George! His murder would be a major piece on the board of the game of life after life. He was murdered like a **pawn** but he would prove to be a **Pawn of Prophecy** (page **44**). In 2021 his killer Chauvin would be found guilty of murder and sentenced to jail on **April 20th** 2021. I have a sister who has a baby born on **April 20th** and the babies father is born on **May 25th**. George Floyds death sparked the biggest protest in American history and the murder of **Emmett Till** was the first mass movement for Civil Rights in American history. Emmett Till's body was identified by his **silver** ring that had the date **May 25th** engraved on it. I purchased my **Silver** Cuff on **May 25th 2014** (page 293). **George Floyd** was murdered on **May 25th** 2020 by a police officer the month after I had my past life revelation of my life as **Tutankhaten** (**King Tut**) on April 4th 2020 (page 594) the day **Martin Luther King** was assassinated (see pages 69, 592). Today is October **26th** 2021 and I turned **44** yesterday. Today I found out that the actor Micah Beals Femia was arrested yesterday on my birthday October **25th** 2021 for the crime of vandalizing the mural dedicated to George Floyd. Today I went for my second driving lesson. I have not had a license since my two motorcycle accidents in 2009. I totaled my motor cycles on May **25th** 2009 then I crashed the new one 9 days later on June 3rd 2009. Today my driving instructor was an 80 year old black Muslim brother named **Bilal** Abdul Rakman. My mother took the name **Bilal** when she went back to her Islamic faith. My instructor was born in **1941** the year of the **snake** the same year as Emmett Till. I was born in 19**77** the year of the **snake**.. My instructor was born on **May 26th** 1941 the same year that Emmett Till was born (page 41). I would have been **8**0 years old today if I had not been murdered in 1955. One of my sisters had a dream on **May 25th** 2002 that I died in a violent car accident and 7 days later I had a violent car accident but I survived. I crashed on my fathers birthday, June 1st 2002. I have had a good time in this life. I am sorry that I could not have waken up sooner. Perhaps this part I had to play in this life required me to experience being adulterated. I was sick just like Officer Chauvin but I was sick in another way. Sometimes things in life get hard and we make mistakes but we must do our best to be timely in our self correction. We must have the knowledge of our past story and our culture or we will be like trees without roots. We must be the roses that grow through the concrete. Salute to **Floyd Mayweather Jr** for paying the funeral expenses for George Floyd's family. **Muhammad Ali** would be proud of you. Floyd Mayweather is also born in 19**77** the year of the **snake** like me.

Condolences

My condolences go out to the family and friends of **George Floyd** as well as all the families of those who have been robbed of their lives by this system of racism and white supremacy. Please know that death is not the end. The soul survives death, indeed and in spirit. This is a book of the dead written by a boy who was murdered without justice, who defeated death and came forth by day. May the soul of **George Floyd** walk peacefully through the field of Reeds in Amenta. Amen Ra.

Matters of the Heart

Emmett Till's cousin **Wheeler Parker** once said, "You can legislate the laws but you can not legislate the heart". How many signs do we need to finally get the message? Sight beyond sight, **Life after life**, Beyond the beyond, the quiet before the storm, **we vibrate into many forms**, let the dead bury the dead my friend, ***some of us come back in new babies born again***, I'm trying to go to another plane not here again! **This life is about raising the consciousness of men!** Not the nonsense they program condition'n, the wind be whisper'n, but are you tuning in and listen'n?! I never knew I'd be a fisher man, you think it's a miracle to walk on water? Think again! The miracle is to walk in peace on the earth full of sin! (page 394.)

All the events in this book are true. If you follow my path and do the things I do yet still the great mysteries are not shown to you. Then continue the path and **to Maat be true** and perhaps in due time you will be worthy of the view.

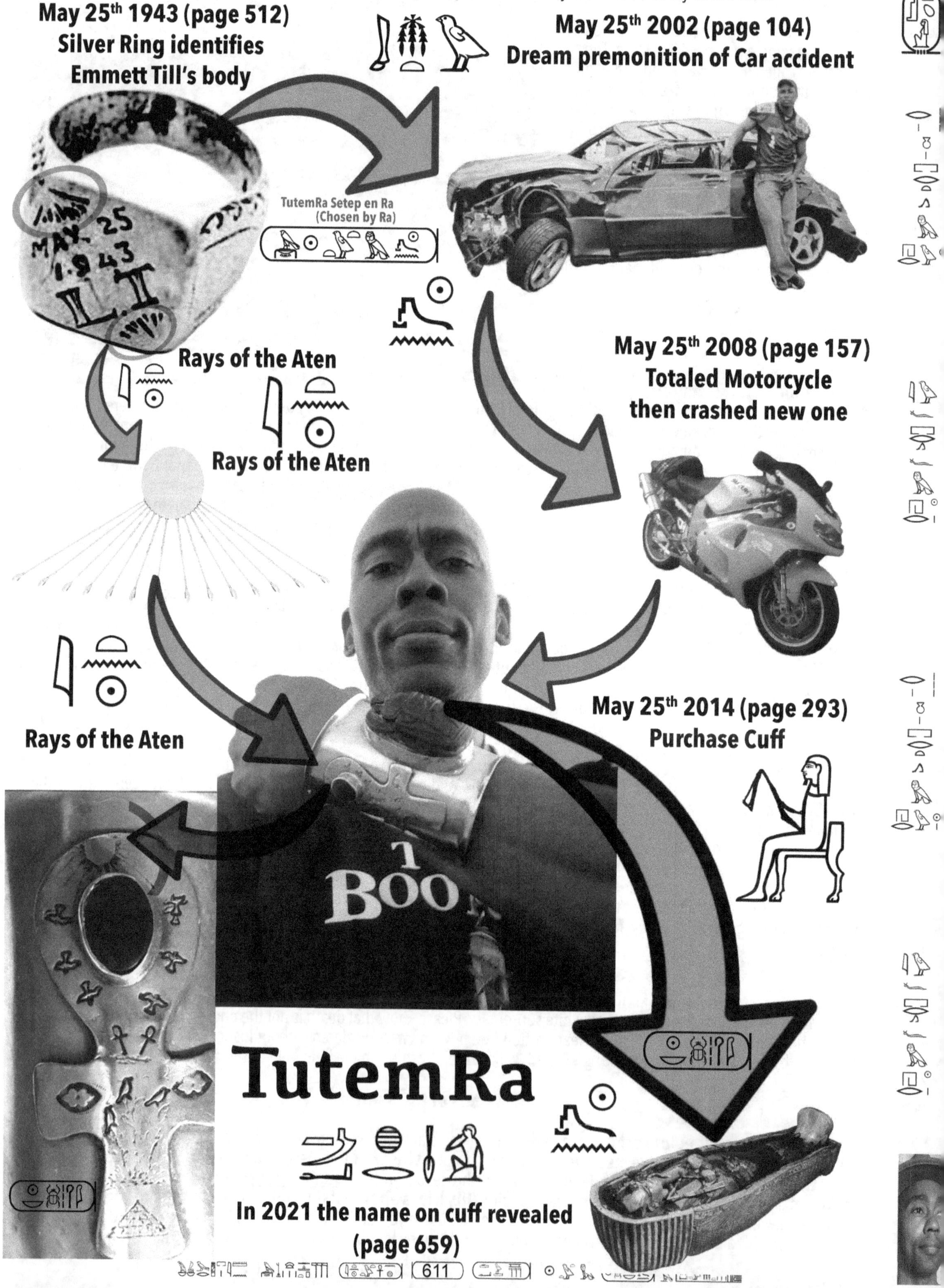

Rau nu Prt m heru

Iu f Per f m heru

REPARATIONS ARE DUE!

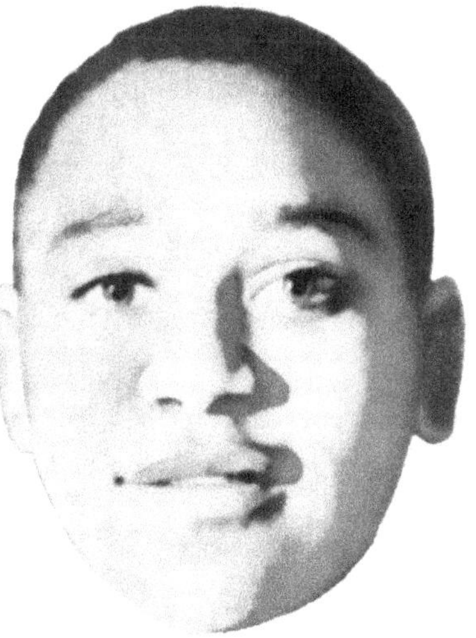

On March 16th 2021, 8 Asian women were killed in an Atlanta Spa and only **2 months later**, in May of 2021 President Biden signed an Anti Asian Hate Bill in to law to protect Asians. Black people have been peacefully trying to get White people in America to stop killing us. We've marched, we've voted, and we've formed organizations like The Black Panther Party only to be murdered and imprisoned. Over a hundred years ago **Ida B Wells** was the most prominent **anti-lynching** campaigner in the United States (page 18). On August **28**th 19**55** Emmett Till was lynched by two racist White men and "his" killers were set free (p 507). **67 years later** the Emmett Till Anti Lynching Act was signed on March 29th 2022 (page 666). This legislation is not specific to Black people like the Anti Asian Hate Bill. Instead, it is a legislation for "**all people**", reminiscent to the "**all lives matter**" response to the "**black lives matter**" mantra. If all lives really mattered in America then efforts to right the wrongs of the present and distant past would be set in place in the tune of monetary settlements. If all lives really mattered in America swift and steep punishment would be handed down to white men who commit acts of racism like Payton S. Gendron. On May 14th 2022 Payton murdered 10 black people in Buffalo New York (The Buffalo Massacre). Just as thousands of racist White people used to gather to watch Black people being lynched as if it was a social event, Payton live streamed his massacre for all to see on social networking and I wonder who was tuned in for the "event". Perhaps these are the new lynchings! No different than the police killings of black people like George Floyd shown across the world for all to see. On Paytons weapon he wrote the names of other White men who killed groups of people, Dylan Roof being one of the names (page 335). On Payton's weapon was the note, **"Here's your reparations"**. After he murdered these Black people he was handled with care and taken in alive just like Dylan Roof was. Yet countless unarmed Black men and women are routinely murdered for as little as selling cd's or cigarettes on the sidewalk. **Aaron** Salter was the **55** year old ex-cop supermarket security guard who was killed in the Buffalo Massacre. Inspired by rising gas prices, Aaron had recently spoken about a "newly discovered energy source" and had patented a system that enables vehicles to run on water instead of gasoline, called hydrogen-electrolysis. Some say that the massacre was an organized assassination of Aaron so as to suppress technology that would threaten the oil and automotive industries. In1942, Japanese Americans were sent to concentration camps during World War 2. **46 years later**, with the passing of the Civil Liberties Act of 1988, **Japanese Americans received reparations** to right the wrongs they experienced. Black people have been in America for hundreds of years being subjected to enslavement, rape, lynchings, systematic racism and the list goes on, yet still we have yet to receive reparations. 8 Asian women were murdered and 2 months later a bill is passed specific to Asian people yet the Anti Lynching Bill for Emmett Till is not specific to Black people who are killed in hate crimes at higher rates than any other people in America. Black people built this country, black women breast fed white babies when the white women's breast would not lactate. A mothers breast **milk** is full of the **love** hormone oxytocin which is produced by the posterior pituitary gland which works with the pineal gland (**3rd eye** 𓂀). The black woman is the mother of creation and America still shoots down her babies. This book is a document that our people and all people must never forget. It's not just about my previous lives or about the lore and mystery of who I was in previous lives.. It's about the restoration of Ma'at! This too shall come to pass! "***It was ordained from the beginning of time that Emmett would die a sacrificial death so that mans consciousness will be aroused and justice can at-last prevail***" *(page 511)*. The voice of Emmett Till has spoken..

Utterances for Coming Forth by day into Light

It is he, who comes forth by day into Light

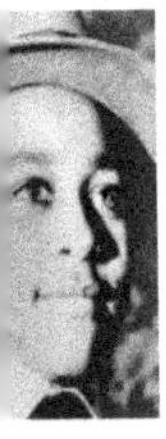

April 29th 2015 2000 Seasons

That's how it goes, we were made to think we ain't supposed to explode, with every new murder we forget, told to get a grip, they can kill us on cam and our fam's left to live with it, but the dead can't cry out for justice! instead the living must ride on these busters! from B More to South Africa it's just us, the truth exposed, they say ***<u>the riot is the language of the unheard, a dream deferred</u>***, does it die or multiply? screaming give me the **loot**! give me the **gold**! give us everything you **stole**! I be the rose that flew through the **Shu Heru** I never fold, I got *<u>99 problems</u>* but a heart ain't one, they killed her son with a gun and sold his young organs, we on the run cause it's open season, but think what's the reason? they want us gone, but we ain't leaving! I wrote this when I was grieving, our bloods' in the land go and count the grains of sand, that's how long we been here, the greatest fear at hand, call us the son of ham, afraid to treat us like a man, I am that I am, The Sunz of Man gave you the plan, and so it was written, so be it, never quitting from the streets to san Quinton, we can dance or stand and listen, the time is always ripe for what is right, we might fight amongst each other but I promise you this, we burn this bitch down get us pissed, 2000 seasons a million reasons, we might fight amongst each other but I promise you this, We burn this bitch down get us pissed!!!!! - ***Dawud The Uncanny BlaKseed (page 328)***

Survival of the Soul after Physical Death. See page 319.

Our souls do survive death of the physical body! This is a reality. This is the age of Aquarius and all is being revealed. Rest assure that we all pay for our transgressions here on this earth plane. You reap what you sow! We get away with nothing. If you feel you are indeed guilty of acts unforgivable it is important that you immediately make a change in your life. There is always time to make a change. Life is a stage of demonstration. Recreate yourself. Make peace with those you have wronged and transform yourself. Be aware that this must be done with an earnest heart. You can never fool the unseen realms because God see's everything! The only way that America and the rest of the world can right the wrongs done to Black people is to be a part of restoring us to our rightful place on earth without fear that we will do to you what you have done to us. We are not like you. We must restore Maat. **42 Laws of Maat, Page 367**

"For 8 minutes, he tried to get a breath in, on his death ticket they went and added 46 seconds, bear witness like the Dog Star, and the dog days of the summer, I saw all of y'all in the streets, y'all heard him scream for his mother!" - TutemRa, June 14th 2020 (page 616)

Tyre Nichols, Emmett Martin III and The Brutal Memphis Police Anti Violence Scorpion Unit

On January 7th, 20**23**, Tyre Nichols was stopped by **Memphis** police officers for reckless driving. See page **648** for the metaphysical significance of the number **23**. After his traffic stop he ran away from the police but was apprehended after a short chase. Tyre was then beaten, tased and pepper sprayed for 5 minutes by a group of 5 or more police officers after which he was left unattended for 25 minutes until finally he was placed on a stretcher by EMT's and taken to the hospital. 3 days later Tyre died from a broken neck and other injuries. Tyre was a 29 year old black man and at least 5 of the officers involved with his death were black men. I have not watched the video of his beating so as to protect myself from viewing these modern day lynchings. As I stated before, I never watched the **George Floyd** killing because of the same reasons (p 610). However, when I heard that one of the officers involved with the killing of Tyre was named **Emmett Martin III**, I began to look into the case. The officers were apart of a unit called **Anti Violence Scorpion** and I am a **scorpio** (p 654). This is only the beginning of the connections this case has with the revelation presented in this book.

Tyre was an amateur photographer who loved taking pictures of the **SUN**. Tyre was beaten on Jan 7th and he died **3 days later**. The story of **Jesus** dying for **3 days** and resurrecting on the **3rd day** is taken from the celestial events that take place during the winter solstice. The sun (Jesus) was believed to have died on or about the 22nd of December, at the **Winter Solstice** and was reborn 3 day's later on **December 25th**. December 21 was the shortest day of the year. The 22nd **23**rd & 24th are days that the sun seems to not move while nestled between the southern crux (a constellation that forms a cross).. It is this phenomenon that birthed the concept of the sun (son/Jesus) dying for 3 days (on the southern cross). This is a parable that teaches us we are eternal, falling and leaving or dying like a leaf on a tree only to be **born again** in other lives just like the leaves returning in spring. Tyre was beaten by at least 5 black officers from a **unit named Scorpion**. The Scorpion unit **betrayed** him. In the **last supper** story, Jesus **(the sun personified)**, told of a pending **betrayal** by one of his disciples (one of the 12 signs of the zodiac, page 489). Judas **betrayed** Jesus and Judas is personified by the **Scorpio** zodiac sign (**the Scorpion**). The scorpio zodiac sign ushers in the fall season which symbolizes death as leaves die and fall off trees. And symbolically, the sun (Jesus) dies an agonizing death when the summer season turns to fall. When the sun (Jesus) was in the house of Scorpio (Judas), the scorpion betrayed Jesus (the sun) with a kiss (a scorpion sting). The sun (Jesus) died an agonizing death, was then stabbed by the Sagittarius spear on the cross, and was placed into a cave / tomb, and was raised from the dead 3 day's later. The Ausarian resurrection drama was the first story of resurrection which is the story that the parable of Jesus was taken from (p 481).

Tyre was beaten on January 7th and **January 6** is the day that the ancient Kemetyu celebrated the Winter Solstice. **January 6** is known as the **Epiphany** in Christianity as it marks the day that the 3 wise men were said to have visited Jesus in the **Manger** (p 511). **Tupac's** grand mother Eloise Maria Barnes was born on **January 6** (page 664 - 665) and this is also the day that Mamie Till died (**January 6**, 2003). **Mamie Till** was the mother of Emmett Till and after Emmett's death she visited by an **angel** that told her, "It was ordained from the beginning of time that Emmett would die a sacrificial death. Be happy to have been the mother of a child who died blameless like **Christ**, but there is a job for you to do now. Emmett has done his job now your job is to continue to tell the story so that mans consciousness will be aroused and justice can at-last prevail" (page 511). The murder of Emmett Till was a prophecy designed to remind human beings about the immortality of their souls and what it is that we are supposed to be cultivating, or "**Tilling**" here on Earth (page 481) and just like the murder of George Floyd, the murder of Tyre Nichols is connected to the revelation brought forth in this book. That is why the names **Emmett and Martin** are intertwined with the murder of Tyre Nichols. As I stated above, Tyre was an amateur photographer who loved taking pictures of the **SUN**. I skimmed through Tyre's Instagram page and saw that his first 3 Instagram pictures were posted on April 4th 2012, the same day **Martin** Luther King was assassinated (p 69) and the same day my past life as Tutankhaten (King Tut) was revealed to me (page 594). To make things more **strange**, Tyre also posted about **reincarnation** on Sep 18, 2013, the day before the Emmett Till murder trial (page 516). The post was a screenshot with the words, "<u>Ya know, I believe 100% in the whole **reincarnation** deal</u>". From his posts I also gathered that he was a 49ers fan and I have written about the significance of the number 49 and **reincarnation** (pages 454, 535). <u>See page 3 for the **hero's journey!**</u>

The murder of Tyre Nichols is connected to the revelation brought forth in this book and that's why the names **Emmett** and **Martin** are intertwined with the murder of Tyre Nichols. The names of the five police **Memphis** officers charged with the murder of Tyre Nichols are Tadarrius Bean, Demetrius Haley, Desmond Mills, Jr., Justin Smith and it is not by happenstance that one of the officers is named **Emmett Martin III**. Martin Luther King rose to prominence after the murder of **Emmett** Till and Martin was murdered in **Memphis** Tennessee. Memphis is also the name of the ancient capital of **Kemet** (Egypt). Ever since the murder of Emmett Till the name Emmett Till has been evoked when ever a black boy or man is murdered at the hands of white people. But what about the black people who kill each other and what about the black cops who take on the same attitudes that some white cops do when dealing with black people? And what about the black men involved with the murder of Emmett Till (pages 507-508)? How do we reconcile this? Why did it take 20 plus days for the name of **Preston Hemphill**, the **white Police Officer involved with the killing of Tyre Nichols** to be made public? And why can't you find any info about him online? Policing in America originated during **chattel slavery**. White male slave owners on horses, armed with guns, formed night patrols (**slave patrols**) to stop enslaved Africans (enslaved black indigenous Americans and Africans) from escaping bondage. This is America's dirty past and what we are seeing today is residue from that past. The only difference now is that those on patrol are called police officers and now both men and women of all racial backgrounds go out on patrols. Police brutality is a systemic problem in America and the **blue wall of silence** is there to insure that cops who do wrong are never prosecuted. As **Tupac** once said, "**The police are the biggest gangs in America**". Absolute power corrupts absolutely. While the killings of black people at the hands of American police usually go unpunished, the emergence of cameras used to record police interactions, arrests and murders have caused an alarming trend. We now have the routine recorded deaths of black people that are no different than **Jim Crow** lynchings. Many of these murders are out the boundaries of what is seen as acceptable by the public yet still more often times the officers involved with these murders are never prosecuted. When cops kill black people the cops are rarely punished and almost never see jail time. Over the years nothing has changed much in the policies of policing. What has changed is the amount of time between the police encounter and the ending verdict. The judicial system has now made sure that many months pass in cases where police kill black people with no justification so that they can limit the potential of public outcry, protest and rioting. They basically wait the people out. They let peoples anger calm down then they exonerate the police in most cases. In the case of Tyre Nichols the Memphis police chief disbanded the city's so-called **Scorpion unit** and five black cops were terminated as soon as the video of Tyre's beating was made public. The murder of Tyre Nichols was one of the last addendums I placed in this book but unfortunately Tyre will not be the last black person murdered without justice. **This won't stop until we, as black people begin to value our lives.** We are "Still mad about Emmett Till", but I am Emmett Till and I have risen from the dead. We must go back and fetch what we lost (page 667). My condolences go out to the family and friends of **Tyre Nichols** as well as all the families of those who have been robbed of their lives by this system of racism and white supremacy. Please know that death is not the end. The soul survives death, indeed and in spirit. This is a book of the dead written by a boy who was murdered without justice, who defeated death and came forth by day. May the soul of **Tyre Nichols** walk peacefully through the field of Reeds <u>in Amenta. Amen Ra.</u>

Rau nu Prt m heru

Iu f Per f m heru

Utterances for Coming Forth by day into Light

It is he, who comes forth by day into Light

ADDENDUM

The Hymn To The Aten - Akhenaten

Below is a translation of the Hymn to the Aten, written by Akhenaten. In it one can clearly see that it influenced the writer(s) of the book of Psalms. The word Psalms can be scrambled to spell Lamps. The Aten is the Sun and all truth comes to light.

You rise beautiful from the horizon on heaven, living disk, origin of life. You are arisen from the horizon, you have filled every land with your beauty. You are fine, great, radiant, lofty over and above every land. Your rays bind the lands to the limit of all you have made, you are the sun, you have reached their limits. You bind them (for) your beloved son. You are distant, but your rays are on earth, You are in their sight, but your movements are hidden.

You rest in the western horizon, and the land is in **darkness** in the manner of death, sleepers in chambers, heads covered, no eye can see its other. Anything of theirs can be taken from under their heads, they would not know. Every **lion** goes out from its **den**, every snake bites. **Darkness** envelops, the land is in silence, their creator is resting in his horizon. At daybreak, **arisen** from the **horizon**, shining as the disk in day, you remove the darkness, you grant your rays, and the two lands are in festival, awakened and standing on their feet. You have raised them up, their bodies cleansed, clothing on, their arms are in adoration at your sunrise.

The entire land **carries out its tasks**, every herd rests in its pastures, trees and plants are sprouting, **birds flying up from their nests, their wings in adoration for your spirit**. Every flock frolics afoot, all that fly up and alight, they live when you have shone for them. Boats sail north and south too, every road is opened at your sunrise, and the fish on the river leap at the sight of you Your rays penetrate the Great Green.

You who cause the sperm to grow in women, who turns seed into people, who causes the son to live in the womb of his mother, who silences him in stopping him crying. Nurse in the womb, who gives breath to cause all he has made to live, when he goes down from the womb to breathe on the day of his birth, you open his mouth in form, you make his needs. When the chick in the egg speaks in the shell, you give it breath within to cause it to live, you have made him, he is complete, to break out from the egg, and he emerges from the egg to speak to his completion, and walks on his legs, going out from it.

How numerous are your **works**, though hidden from sight. Unique god, there is none beside him. You mould the earth to your wish, you and you alone. All people, herds and flocks, All on earth that walk on legs, All on high that fly with their wings. And on the foreign lands of the land of Kemet You place every man in his place, you make what they need, so that **everyone has his food**, his lifespan counted.

Tongues are separated in speech, and forms too - Their skins are made different, for you make foreign lands different.

You make a Flood in the underworld, and bring it at your desire to cause the populace to live, as you made them for you, lord of all they labour over, the lord of every land. Shine for them, O disk of day, great of dignity. All distant lands, you make them live, you place a Flood in the sky, to descend for them, to make waves over the mountains like the Great Green, to water their fields with their settlements. How effective they are, your plans, O lord of eternity! A Flood in the sky for foreigners, for the flocks of every land that go on foot, and a Flood to come from the underworld for Kemet , your rays nursing every meadow, you shine and they live and grow for you. You make the seasons to nurture all you make, winter to cool them, heat so they may taste you.

You have made the far sky to shine in it, to see what you make, while you are far, and shining in your form as living disk. risen, shining, distant, near, you make millions of forms from yourself, lone one, cities, towns,. fields, the road of rivers, every eye sees you in their entry, you are the disk of day, master of your move, of the existence of every form, you create ... alone, what you have made.

You are in my heart, there is none other who knows you beside your son Nefer kheperu Ra sole one of Ra. You instruct him in your plans, in your strength. The land comes into being by your action, as you make them, **and when you have shone, they live, when you rest, they die.** You are lifetime, in your body, people live by you. Eyes are on your beauty until you set. All work is stopped when you set on the west; shine, and strengthen (all for) the king. Motion is in every leg, since you founded the earth, you raise them for your son who come from your body, the king who lives on Right, lord of the two lands, Nefer kheperu Ra sole one of Ra, son of Ra who lives on Right, lord of Risings, Akhenaten, great in his lifespan, and the great king's wife whom he loves, lady of the two lands, Nefer Neferu Aten Nefertiti, eternally alive.

Plagiarism in the Bible

The Bible has 66 books, written by more than 40 different men and was first printed on Feb **23**, 1455 ACE. While the **Bible** is be**lie**ved by many to be a divinely inspired text, supposedly coming from the mouth of God to the hearts and minds of noble men, the debates continue over the exact nature of the relationship between what is written in the Bible and what is found on the walls of Kemet written in stone. If the Bible was original text inspired by God then the **Instructions of Amenemope**, from the 20th Dynasty of Kemet would not have found their way into the Bible (Proverbs **22**). And why is **Psalms 104** so very similar to the **Hymn to the Aten** written by Akhenaten, nearly 3000 years before the first printed bible?!

Great Hymn to the Aten: birds flying up from their nests, their wings in adoration for your spirit

Psalm 104 (12). The **birds** of the sky **nest** by the waters; they sing among the branches.

Hymn to the Aten (3-4): Whenever you set on the western horizon, the land is in **darkness** in the manner of death. They sleep in a bedroom with heads under their covers, and one eye does not see another; If all their possessions which are under their heads were stolen, they would not know it. Every **lion** comes out of his cave and all the serpents bite, for darkness is a blanket. The land is silent now because he who made them is at rest on the horizon.

Psalm 104 (20 -21): You bring **darkness**, it becomes night and all the beasts of the forest prowl. The **lions** roar for their prey and seek their food from God.

Hymn to the Aten (4-5): But when the day breaks **you are risen** on the horizon, and you shine like the Aten in the daytime. When you dispel darkness and you give forth your rays, the two lands are in festival, alert and standing on their feet, now that you have raised them up. Their arms are lifted in praise of your rising. **The entire land performs its work**.

Psalm 104 (22 – **23**): The **sun rises**, and they steal away; they return and lie down in their **dens**. **Then people go out to their work**, to their labour until evening.

Hymn to the Aten (37): **How plentiful** it is **what you have made**, although they are hidden from view, sole god!

Psalm 104 (24): **How many** are **your works**, LORD! In wisdom you made them all; the earth is full of your creatures.

Hymn to the Aten (6): **The barges sail upstream and downstream**, too, for every way is open at your rising. The fishes in the river leap before your face when your rays are in the sea.

Psalm 104 (25 -26): There is the sea, vast and spacious, teeming with creatures beyond number– living things both large and small. **There the ships go to and fro**, and Leviathan, which you formed to frolic there.

Hymn to the Aten (6-7): You who have placed seed in woman and made sperm into man; who feeds the son in the womb of his mother; who quiets him with something to stop his crying; **you are the nurse in the womb giving breath to nourish all** that has been begotten when he comes down from the womb to breathe on the day he was born.

Psalm 104 (27): All creatures look to you to **give them their food** at the proper time.

Hymn to the Aten: When **you rise**, **they live**; **when you set**, **they die**. **Psalm 104** (28 -30): When **you give it to them**, they gather it up; when you open your hand, **they are satisfied** with good things. **When you hide your face**, they are terrified; when you take away their breath, **they die** & return to the dust.

June 12th 2020 Playing the Game of Consciousness with Kilindi Iyi, Swami Muktananda and Taunya

Rau nu Prt m heru

Iu f Per f m heru

Utterances for Coming Forth by day into Light

It is he, who comes forth by day into Light

I'm not 100 % sure of the exact date we met in the park but June 12th 2020 is the day that I ordered the book, **Play of Consciousness**. I met Taunya for the first time sometime in 2018 at a gong session. Shortly after that I was invited to a gong session at her home on September 25th 2018 (page 536) where I had a profound experience. The next year I booked a private **singing bowl** session with her on March 17th 2019 (page 553) where I had an even more profound experience that involved **Pharaohs from ancient Egypt**. By this time, June 2020 I had began using my small hand size singing bowl during my massage sessions but I wanted to upgrade to a bigger bowl so I contacted Taunya. We agreed to meet in Central Park where I could look at a few of her bowls.

The night prior to our meeting I listened to an audio interview with **Kilindi Iyi.** I was still mourning his death that took place on April 10th 2020 (page 606). During that interview someone on the show mentioned several books for people looking to expand their knowledge base. The Book **Play of Consciousness** was mentioned and I put it in my Amazon basket as well as a few other books. When I met with Taunya we sat on a bench at the entrance of Central Park at 93rd street. We began to catch up with each other as we had not seen each other since my singing bowl session in 2019 (page 553). I told her about my past life revelation of Tutankhaten (King Tut) and she was amazed. She believed me because her and her daughter both lived lives in ancient Egypt. She told me about things going on with her and at some point in the beginning of our meeting a brother entered the park and walked by us but I never caught the view of his face however I felt like I knew him but I left it alone and went back to our conversation. Taunya began to tell me about a trip she took with her daughter Elan when she was young. She told me about a little boy who was on the trip who got along with no one. She said the boy took a liking to her so she would read portions of the book **Play of Consciousness** to him everyday of the trip. I stopped her immediately! Then I pulled out my phone, went to my amazon basket of items ready to order and asked her if the book in my basket was the same book. She confirmed that it was indeed the same book! The same book that was mentioned in an audio interview with **Kilindi Iyi** that I listened to the night prior. At the end of our meeting the brother that walked by came back to exit the park and it was indeed my old friend **Shiller** (page 145, 385). He stopped and we embraced and laughed and caught up. I had not seen him in many years. I used to work with him in Brooklyn when I first stared training in 2005. He looked at me with a **feather** in my head and told Taunya that the person that he is looking at now is not the same guy he knew years ago. He said he saw me when he entered the park but was sure that I was not the person he knew because of the way I looked. That day, or the day after, I ordered the book **Play of Consciousness** on June 12th 2020. Kilindi was born on March 18th 19**55** the **same year Emmett was murdered**. When I am done with this book I will write a Science Reality Novel Series version of this book and a book about Tupac's past life..

June 14th 2020 George Floyd

For 8 minutes, he tried to get a breath in, on his death ticket they went and added 46 seconds, bear witness like the **Dog Star**, and the dog days of the summer, I saw all of y'all in the streets, y'all heard him scream for his mother! I can see clearly now it's all a scandal! Christianity before **Christ** don't let them scam you! or **Sandra Bland** you! be careful of those trying to hand you apologies, your foes are not your friends if they ain't changing their policies, less than a month after, **Rayshard Brooks** dead just much faster! guess who else gets paid? the God Damned pastor! another eulogy! no changes we need unity! **Tupac** said it, "the biggest gangs in the cities be the PD and correctional facilities", I ain't vote'n for a republican or democratic, public lynchings, hypertension, post traumatic stress disorder! they don't listen, they don't learn, they don't care, they not concerned, the only thing they give a fuck about is how much money they got that they probably didn't earn, have you forgot about **Aiyana Stanley jones**?! she would have been 18 in 2020, is it me or these no knock warrants be bout the money?! can you see this war on drugs is war on me and you? it's true there will never be peace until we do what we supposed to do, what's understood don't need to be explained, we gotta fly like **Heru** feel my pain! **- TutemRA**

June 15th 2020 Breonna Taylor

Sandra Bland damn! **Breonna Taylor!** the actions of a system gonna show ya what they refuse to tell ya, this country is broken choke'n cause it's a rotten failure, sail ya across the ocean, then sell ya, and then you're forced to work'n, they got you hope'n, praying to a cross, false devotion! eyes wide shut, lost and caught up in your emotions, **Jesus** is never coming! you be**lie**ve everything you read in a book and refuse to have your own 3rd eye opened, is this provoking anger? am I a liar ? am I Stoking the fire? am I in danger? you wanna hang me up with a wire? cause your **messiah** was born in a **manger** like **Mithra** and **Buddha** and **Krishna**, the ancient future the strangers, nomads and drifters raped your dad your sister your mother your brother, it was the Pope and the Minstar, no rubber no vaseline sinister, casein, atrozyne, vaccines for prisoners **- TutemRA**

July 30th 2020 - Another Dream with Stic

It was a warm sunny day and I am on a run with Stic and another brother. Stic was leading the run when we approached a large puddle. Stic ran through the puddle but I leaped in the air and **floated** over the entire puddle. In the dream I seemed to be amazed by the way I **floated** over the whole puddle and cleared it with ease. When I landed on the other side we continued our run. Then I was at a table reading. I woke up just as I finished reading and I only had a paragraph left to go.

July 30th 2020 Breonna Taylor

Who the fuck is this storming in my door at 2:46 in the morning? No time for yawn'n, baby called the cops! I grabbed my piece now I'm armed and ready, I bust a shot, Breonna get down! Damn! my baby's been shot! she hit the ground these bastards still let'n off rounds, this was a robbery, Training Day! copers be found not guilty it's plain as day, plain clothes cops seem to get away, how could you sleep at night knowing the innocent life you took away? the system is broken! no justice it's just a fuck'n failure, how long we need to tell ya arrest the cops that killed **Breonna Taylor?** and **Aura Rosser!** no we don't trust the cops! **Atatiana** at home with her nephew, she never called the cops! She never saw the bullet, she just heard the shot, and her body couldn't take it she just shook and dropped, Breonna never saw the bullets she just heard the shots, her body couldn't take it she just shook and dropped, Breonna never saw the bullets she just heard the shot, her body couldn't take it she just shook and dropped **- TutemRA**

July 31st 2020 Poor Breonna

Breonna was 26 if you saw her on her gram, she'd be laugh'n, dance'n, hang'n with her fam, Breonna is gone now and that wasn't Gods plan! she was an EMT but no one gave her a hand, they shot her 8 times, it's like they didn't give a damn, a no knock Warrant, a license to torment and inflict pain, no care for black life it's insane, pull the knife out my back a little, I still feel pain, shit ain't change since **Malcolm,** maybe a little, I was murdered in **55** they said I whistled, now **I'm back** in 2020, it's the same issue, same pain, same Black death, just a different tissue, a different mother or brother, a different daughter where's the order? manslaughter is manslaughter! **Sandra Bland** damn **Breonna Taylor!** the actions of a system gonna show ya what they refuse to tell ya, this country is broken choke'n, what a rotten failure! they arrest the protesters what does that tell ya? what about the cops that killed Breonna Taylor? she never saw the bullet she just heard the shot, her body couldn't take it she just shook and dropped, she never saw the bullet she just heard the shot, her body couldn't take it she just shook and dropped, dear Lord tell me why Breonna had to die? dear Lord tell me why Breonna had to die? dear Lord tell me why Breonna had to die? dear Lord tell me why Breonna had to die? dear Lord tell me why Breonna had to die? **- TutemRA**

July 29th / 30th 2020 (Martin Luther King / Emmett Till Statue Vandalized)

Unknown individuals defaced a statue that shows **Martin Luther King Jr**. and **Emmett Till** outside the Friendly Harbor building near Grand and 27th in Denver. **White paint was splashed on the statue** and the arches and walkway near the statue had **KKK** painted on them. It was reported to have happened sometime between 6 p.m. Wednesday July 29th and 4 a.m. Thursday July 30th a few days after Emmett Till's birthday and a month after George Floyd was murdered. The piece was sculpted in 1976 by Ed Rose and named **Prophet for Peace**. The sculpture features Martin Luther King Jr in a deacon's robe walking with Emmett Till, both stepping forward with their **left foot**. The plaque includes the final stanza of MLK's "I've been to the Mountaintop" speech given on April 3rd 1968 in Memphis, TN - the next day he was assassinated. The statue was originally in Denver's City Park before being relocated and replaced with another statue of King. In 2002 the statue was moved to the Martin Luther King Jr. Museum and Cultural Center in Pueblo, Colorado. It now sits in this vacant lot in a neighborhood well away from central Pueblo. The museum itself has fallen on hard times and may lose its collection. Two years after the statue of **Martin Luther King Jr**. and **Emmett Till** was vandalized a new statue was built in Mississippi. On time with the release of this book, a 9 ft bronze statue of Emmett Till was unveiled in Greenwood, Mississippi, on October 21, 2022, just 4 days before my birthday. On October **28**, 2022, just 3 days after my birthday, the movie **Till** (a movie about **Emmett Till**) was released nationwide in America and on that same day the **Beyond King Tut tour** opened in New York City (pages, 29 & 33).

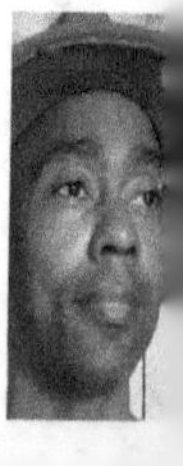

Rau nu Prt m heru

Iu f Per f m heru

Utterances for Coming Forth by day into Light

It is he, who comes forth by day into Light

August 7th 2020
Detroit Psychedelic Convention

After having met **Kilindi** on October 5th 2018 (page 537) and having him appear to me the day after he transitioned I knew that I needed to attend the convention. Tim picked me up from the airport with two of Kilindi's most noble students. I felt comfortable with them after having already developed a bond with Tim over the course of a year or so. Detroit is a Weed legal state and so they all started smoking weed. I had not smoked in a long time. I am not easily influenced but I decided to take a toke and after 2 or three puffs I was overcome with extreme paranoia. I suddenly realized that I don't know any of these "men". I began to think, 'what the fuck am I doing in Detroit with these men I don't know?' I sort of knew Tim but these other two I did not know them! I was paranoid so I started to look for flights back to New York while riding in the back seat. Then I asked my self why I was in Detroit, then I finally rested comfortably on the fact that Kilindi had appeared to me the day after he went west (page 606). This allowed me to settle down and relax and I began to feel at ease again. I think I had anxiety because of all my years of being a **hermit**. Shortly after that I began to feel like I had met this guy driving, his name was Osotrari. *I felt like I knew him.* Something was very familiar about him and I still feel that way to his day. When he laughs it's like I remember him. Perhaps it's because he's born on Nov 2, two days before the tomb of **Tutankhaten** (King Tut) was discovered. Or perhaps I spent a lot of time going over those events in the **astral realm** (dream) before they took place in the now, or perhaps we have known each other very well in previous lives. The interesting thing about **Osotrari** is his **connection** to **Ausar** (Osiris). When he was 3 years old he had a **dream** that would become a reoccurring **dream**. In this dream he was at a party. There was box that everyone was taking turns getting in and out of. When got into the box someone shut the box and a magic spell was spoken trapping him inside. The box was thrown in the river and Osotrari drowned. This dream caused Osotrari to have a fear of water that would take many years for him to overcome. Osotrari came to this earth with the story of Ausar repeating in his dream state. In this life he met **Kilindi** at the age of 15 and was taught in the ways of the Tamerrian fighting arts (Afrikan Montu Martial arts, page 631). This is the reason why Osotrari and I felt like we knew each other. At this convention I met other people who had paranormal experiences with Kilindi after he died confirming what Kilindi taught about the 60 day ritual of the Tibetans and the soul visiting loved ones before they leave this world and move towards their next phase of existence (page 483). For more on **Guardian Angels** and **Ka Doors** (**Spirit Doors**) see pages (250 -253,48, 141, 142,148, 150,179, 199, 315, 318, 329, 348, 349, 409, 421, 434, 545, 548, 549, 572, 584. 604, 626, 650). See page 3 for the **Heru's** (hero's) **journey!**

The Detroit Body Snatchers

While at the Detroit Psychedelic convention I met many interesting people and heard a few profound stories but the most profound were the stories told to me by one brother. I shared my past life revelation with him and his wife and they both believed me. They had had experiences of their own that most people would not believe if they told them. The brother told me about an incident with his daughter and a near death experience he had on the side of a **mountain**. While the experience with his daughter is very similar to the experience I explained on March **28**th 2014 (page 289) what you are about to read I can't fully explain. I don't know if it was a soul fragment from the babies previous incarnation speaking or if it was just a random soul using the opportunity to speak to a sleeping soul (adult) inside of a body.

Meta-Spiritual Encounter from another Life Time
"My name was Mary and I loved to wear red"

The brother told me that he had gone to a lecture and there he heard someone speak about the dormant wisdom hidden within children that is suppressed in modern day society. At the lecture the people were instructed to look their toddlers in the eyes and ask them who they were and what they were here for. When the brother got home he went to his 3 or 4 year old daughter and asked her who she was. His daughter playing in her crib did not answer. Then he looked his daughter in the eyes and asked her again, what was her name. The baby said her name. He then replied - "no what was your name before you were here in this life". What happened next was more like a scene from a sci-fi movie than something in "real life". When he asked her that she immediately stopped. She looked him in the eyes and her posture changed to that of a grown woman with personality. She put her hands on her hips and with another voice she said "*my name was Mary and I loved to wear red*". The father puzzled could do nothing but stare as the baby continued to talk about this woman Mary. As his wife walked into the room the daughter stopped talking and as quick as a light switch she went back to being a baby again. His wife asked who that was talking and he pointed at the baby. He could not believe what he had experienced. I can't remember the full story about the **mountain** but it's probably better that I leave that story out of this book because if I told you you might not believe anything else you read in here. All I will say is that I have never had an experience like his but because of the experiences I have had I will not attempt to explain it away. Instead I am forced to recall the experiences I have had with spirits speaking to me through other people. In 2013 the **Nswt Bity (Pharaoh) Khufu** spoke to me through a brother in school named Khufu (page 282). On **April 16th 2016** an entity spoke to me through a random brother after I wrote the song **Holler If Ya Hear Me** (374-375). In December of 2018 my friend **Zee** would allow me to talk to the guardian angel at my door (page 545). In 2018 Courtlan's Grandmother told me about a spellbinding experience she had with him when he was an infant, he opened his mouth, and spoke clearly **with the voice of an old man** (page 74). In July of 2021 one of my **guardian angels** spoke to me through a brother at the **International African Arts Festival** (page 650). I have had quite a few experiences with spirits and spirits do embody people to deliver messages. I think this might be the origin of the term **"Ghost rider"**. The life of Dorothy Eady also known as **Omm Seti** is another example of spirits passing from one body to the next (page 622)..

You should first re-read what I wrote about Khepri, The Only Begotten Son on July 4th 2019 (page 569). I met a brother named Justin at the **Detroit Psychedelic convention** who was from Atlanta. He was on his journey towards truth and had grown up in the church. He was one of the few people who actually believed my story. I was in the midst of a build with him about finding truth. I mention the purpose of us being there. It was a convention started by the late Kilindi Iyi. I was talking about the logo for his Tamerrian institute, in particular the **Djed** pillar ( ) within the logo. I was breaking down the symbolism of stability and the connection to the spine and resurrection when Justin stopped me and told me that I had a giant bee on my head. I did not fret, I simply said if it's meant to sting me then it will. Then Justin said, "no, it's not a bee, it's a **beetle**". My eyes opened wide and a giant smile took over my face as I asked him if he was sure. I pulled out my camera and told him to record me. He held the phone and started recording me and I said, "Alright so I'm talking to my brother Justin just now, and guess what lands on my feather? This is my spirit animal, my spirit insect because in my previous life my name was **Neb Kheperu Ra**. All he is doing is confirming that everything that I've said to my brother is true, and this is not a coincidence. <u>one time is an incidence, twice is a coincidence, three four five is a pattern, can you tell the difference?</u>" ***Addendum*** I shipped Justin a copy of this book and he received it on July 7th, that same day his girl friend (Liv) came home and randomly opened the book to **page 189** - and to her amazement, she had done a movie with the woman (Nikkie) seen on that page. The movie was titled **Goddess** and Nikkie was the leading role. When I was told this, I was bewildered but that wasn't it, I had divine **coincidences** with **Mark** on July 3rd (p 118) as well as **Keith Brown** on July 20th (p 648) and **Netic** on July 30th (p 182). Today is August 3rd 2022 and I'm almost done with the one and only **revision** I will do to for this book. I added these experiences to the book because the book appears to be taking on a life of it's own. While writing this book I thought that **coincidences** like this might happen and so it is.

one time is an incidence, twice is a coincidence,
three four five is a pattern, can you tell the difference

Mushrooms, and Thoughts Readers - If it happened to you, you'd be a believer

August 2020 Mind Your Thoughts

Rau nu Prt m heru

Our thoughts and desires can affect our reality by influencing quantum level events in time and space. I would be remiss if I failed to mention this experience because prior to this I had never experienced this before. Or at least if I have I never knew, but how would you ever know if someone is reading your thoughts? While at the convention I noticed a woman who was attractive. I did not say a word to this woman but as she passed me she turned quickly and looked me in the eyes and asked me, "Did you say that I have a nice body?" She caught me completely off guard! I said no, then she walked off. I went to her and asked her why she asked me that. I told her that I had seen and thought she was attractive but I had not said anything. I told her it was as if she read my thoughts. She replied, "sometimes I do that."… see page 497 for more info on telepathy (**Telepathine**).

Identical Twins, Telepathy and a Mothers Intuition

I once read about telepathy in a TIME LIFE book titled, A Collection From Mysteries Of The Unknown. The book was published in 1989, the year of the snake. In this book I read about a true story of a mother, who knew something bad had happened to her daughter even though her daughter was miles away. This is called **mothers intuition**. Armed with these thoughts and my experience at the convention I began to ponder about the cases of identical twins being able to know when something is wrong with the their identical twin, even when they are miles apart. I think twins are sent to earth to remind the human species of what all human beings were once able to do. I think the Telepathine (page 497) within the sacred plants are designed to awaken this innate potential.

August 9th 2020 - Going away Ceremony for Baba Kilindi Iyl

Iu f Per f m heru

The closest I had ever been (in this life) to an AfriKan village was when I attended the going away ceremony for Baba Kilindi Iyl in Detroit, on Aug 9th 2020. I felt like I was in an AfriKan village even though I had never been to one in this life. We were by the water, the drums were playing, the elders were there, the ancestors were there and I found myself wishing so much to have been immersed in the culture from a child.. I found myself coming in contact with parts of my culture that I had never been exposed to outside of Hollywood movies. I was almost brought to tears when listening to the men tell their stories of how they came to meet Kilindi and how he had forever changed their lives. I wished so much at that moment that I could have met Kilindi when I was a boy. I even thought of how I wished I could have been his son or had a father that brought me up in this way of life. I love my father, I did not grow up with him but I love him still. I love my mother, my father and all my family members. The process of writing this book has allowed me to understand why I incarnated into the family I did. I needed to go on a this blind initiation, but at the ceremony I didn't see that. **Kilindi has a son who knows himself to be the reincarnation of a well known Nswt Bity (pharaoh) and based on the life that Kilindi lived, it wouldn't surprise me that he spawned the soul of a famouse pharaoh!!**

Utterances for Coming Forth by day into Light

It is he, who comes forth by day into Light

August 2020

Mushrooms, Airplanes and The Hard To Explain Quantum Terrains

After returning from the psychedelic conference in Detroit in 2020 I purchased the book **Mushrooms**, Myths & **Mithras**, the drug cult that **civilized Europe**. I took this book with me on a plane ride to Atlanta later that month. While in the air the trailer for a movie kept playing on the screen in front of me. I don't usually see movies on the flights because the flights I had been taking weren't long enough for a movie but something strange happened. In my lap I had the book ***Mushrooms**, Myths & **Mithras**, the drug cult that* ***civilized Europe*** and in front of me the preview for a movie kept playing over and over and it was only when I started **p**aying attention to the movie that it actually started playing. This is called the **observer effect** in **quantum physics**. Our **thoughts** and **d**esires can affect our reality by influencing quantum level events in time and space. The movie was titled **Onward** and it was about two elf brothers who live in a town called New **Mushroomton**, in a **mushroom** house and attend school at **mushroom** high. They live in a world where **magic is real** but* because of the rise of technology their **magical abilities** had over time completely **faded away**. The older brother is one of the few odd people (elves) who still **believed** in the ancient tales of magic but the younger brother, like most of the other inhabitants of this world had long ago disregarded magic as delusion or only fantasy. The plot of the movie starts when the mother gives the younger elf a birthday gift that was left for him by his father who died years ago, shortly before he was born. The gift was only to be given to him at his current age. The gift was a magical wand with a rare **phoenix** gem attached to it along with a magical **spell** to recite. The spell was intended to bring their father **back to life** (**resurrection**) for one day (24 hours). The elves were both reasonably excited at the possibility of seeing their father again, even if it was only for one day.. The younger elf wants to believe and is excited too but the older elf is more emotionally invested given his love for the tales of magic. The older elf picks up the wand and recites the spell but nothing happens, he left the room discouraged. Alone in his room the younger elf picks the wand up and begins to recite the spell and to his surprise, high winds, thunder and lightning began to occur in his room. Then his father starts to materialize there in his room first his feet appear then his legs then his waist and then the **phoenix** gem breaks and there stands his father, but only half of him. The top of him is still invisible. The two brothers are now on a quest to find another rare phoenix gem so they can finish the spell and spend one last day with their father. The running theme in the movie for me was all the other people along their quest who had forgotten what and who they really were. You had fairies with wings who drove motorcycles and had forgotten how to fly. They didn't know what their wings were for. They grew up learning that fairies don't fly so they never tried to fly. Like people who wait for **saviors** like Christ, but **Christ** is only a title like Buddah. The ancient Kemetians (Egyptians) mummified the Pharoas, and **anointed** them with oils. The Mummified body was called **Krst** (Karast, Christ) and just like the caterpillar goes into a "chrysalis" and transforms growing wings, so can each and every human being.. If you help a caterpillar open it's cocoon the caterpillar will never fly. They must struggle and break through the cocoon on it's own allowing the wings to strengthen so that they can withstand the demands of flight. The two elf's were on their quest but are you on your quest? It was important that they took the path of peril and not the path that was easily traversed. Like the caterpillar and it's cocoon your life mustn't be made easy for you, you must be strengthen by your trials and tribulations which are found on your path of peril. Why did this movie come on while I sat there with a book on **mushrooms** in my lap? Why does the word **question** start with the word **quest**? Questions questions questions. Like the questions that are never answered by most spiritual leaders. If you are not finding the answers to your questions can you really be on a quest for the meaning of life? When I got back to New York I glanced at the welcome to New York sign (seen below, on right) while crossing the **"bridge"** and for the first time I noticed that the woman with her eyes open had a **phrygian hat** on top of her staff and the woman with her eyes closed had a sword and the scales of judgement. What could that possibly mean? Perhaps your body is just the **"bridge"** that your soul uses to get to the other side. On the cover of the book, **Mushrooms**, Myths & **Mithras**, the drug cult that **civilized Europe,** a person can be seen wearing a **phrygian hat** which looks just like the hats that the **Smurf** cartoon characters wear, and Smurfs live in **mushroom** houses just like the Elves in the movie **Onward**. It was the mushroom that help sp**ark** my past lives (page 480). I'm writing a Epic Sci-Real (Science Reality) Novel Trilogy version of this book and a book about Tupac's ancient past life (pages 664,665). Stay tuned.

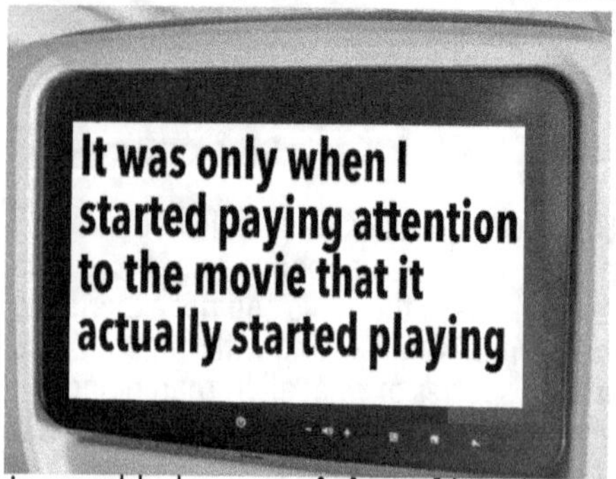

Phrygian Hat

Mushroom headed hairstyle dating from the reign of **EmhatAmen I** (page 14). Also see page 483.

The Compelling Case of Dorothy Eady aka Omm Sety The Reincarnated Mistress of The Nswt Bity (Pharaoh) Sety I

The life and story of Omm Seti is not accepted as credible truth by the governing bodies of Egyptology because it is not rooted in the school of thought they promote and control when it comes to religion, and the immortality of the soul. For if there are people walking around who have lived here on this earth before then everything the ancient African Kemetyu (Egyptians) said about the soul of the pharaoh **coming back** after death was true, and that's probably why there were so many papyrus scrolls found buried with the ancient Egyptian dead, with spells written on them concerning the souls safety in the next life. We knew about If Omm Seti is who she says she is then what the pharaohs taught about the cycle of life was true. The Ausarian resurrection was true! **Re-member** that **you** are **Ausar** and **Heru,** the **hero!** See page 3 for the **hero's journey!**

Rau nu Prt m heru

Iu f Per f m heru

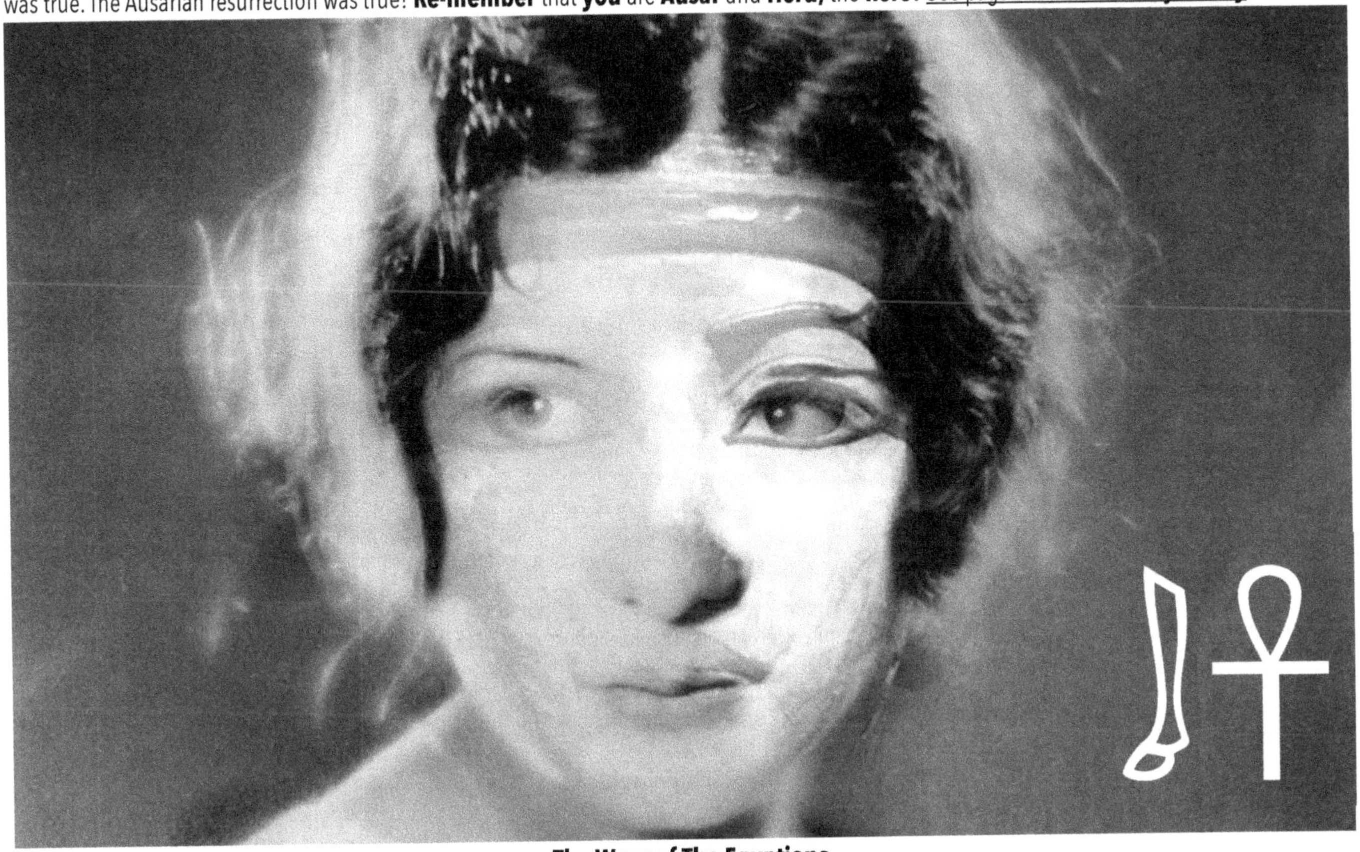

The Ways of The Egyptians

Utterances for Coming Forth by day into Light

From time immemorial the Africans of the Nile Valley have known that there was no death. We had no word for death as we know it today because we understood and mastered the repetition of the soul. Just as the leaf on a tree will fall to the ground and turn from green, to red, to brown then yellow, so will man be born, then get old and finally dying and falling to the earth being recycled just as the leaf will do next spring - but death is not the end, the soul of the man continues on into another life. Today this reality of eternal life is brushed over with very little importance given to it yet all over the world religious people wait and anticipate the "return" of some savior at the "end of days"… Perhaps the only thing that will return is your soul after the end of your days in the physical body you're traveling in now.. The religion of **Christianity** came into the world thousands of years after the African Kemetyu of the Nile Valley broght forth the **Ausarian resurrection** teachings and "perhaps*" that's the origin of the resurrection teachings in the Christian bible about **Jesus** dying and returning from the dead **resurrected** like **Ausar** (Osiris). In the Christian bible Jesus tells his followers that they will do all the great miracles that he has done and greater deeds they will do but first they must place their belief in him. If we are to take Jesus's word literal then he is saying that they will return from the dead resurrected just like he did. Perhaps the bible is a great allegory? It was sometime in 2020 when I realized, it was my faith in Jesus Christ's resurrection and returning someday that set the foundation for my own revelation of reincarnation. By having the belief in the resurrection of Jesus it allowed my soul to fathom the concept of resurrection after death, not knowing that the concept had originated in Kemet (**See page 488**). This Jesus figure also taught about reincarnation (p 592). They say that both Jesus and Moses were taught in the ways of the Egyptians. Perhaps the bible was written with a code of resurrection embedded in it and perhaps this immortality of the soul is the most important part of the book. This concept of resurrection was called the **Wehem-Mesut** (repeating of births, p 14). The Buddha **Siddhartha** Gautama was not the first person to reach enlightenment and to be called the **Buddha**. In fact the followers of the Buddhist religion believe that a new Buddha is coming just like the Christians await the return of Jesus. To make it more clear, the name Buddha was more of a title than it was a name of a person. Buddha simply meant, "the awakened one". Perhaps you can awaken too. Perhaps the most important part of life is the awaking to this dream we are in.. Perhaps near death experiences are gateways to **previous lives**. Perhaps death itself opens the body up for a more ancient portion of the soul to take a seat in the divine ark. Perhaps that's what happened to Dorothy Eady. Perhaps **you** must **Re-member** that **you** are **Ausar** and **Heru,** the **hero!** See page 3 for the **hero's journey!**

It is he, who comes forth by day into Light

The Egyptian Body Snatchers

Dorothy Louise Eady was born on January 19th 1904 the year of the dragon and she went west (died) on April 21st 1981 the year of the monkey. At the age of three, she fell down a flight of stairs and was pronounced dead by a medical doctor. While her parents mourned in their living room they began to hear Dorothy playing on her bed in her room. Their mourning swiftly changed to rejoice as they celebrated their child still living but almost immediately after they began to argue with the doctor for pronouncing her dead. The doctor had no answer as he had followed all the proper protocol and knew she was dead. Alive and well Dorothy kept on with life but something weird happened. She began exhibiting strange behaviors, she began to talk about a garden that she dreamt about and kept asking her parents that she be "brought home" to this garden. To make things more unique she had also developed foreign accent syndrome, now speaking in the accent of a person living in Egypt. After being taken by her parents to visit the British Museum, and on observing a photograph in the New Kingdom temple exhibits room, the young Eady called out "There is my home, but where are the trees? Where are the gardens?" The temple was that of Seti I, the father of Rameses the Great. She ran about the halls of the Egyptian rooms, "amongst her peoples", kissing the feet of the statues. After this trip she took every opportunity to visit the British Museum.

There, she eventually met E. A. Wallis Budge (page 13), who was taken by her youthful enthusiasm and encouraged her in the study of hieroglyphs. As she began to learn she learned fast and claimed that she was more of remembering the language rather than learning it for the first time. This caused some conflict in her early life. Her Sunday school teacher requested that her parents keep her away from class, because she had compared Christianity with the "pagan" ancient Egyptian religion. She was expelled from a Dulwich girls school after she refused to sing a hymn that called on God to "curse the evil Egyptians". Her regular visits to Catholic mass, which she liked because it reminded her of the "Old Religion", were terminated after an interrogation and visit to her parents by a priest. When she was fifteen she described a nocturnal visit from the mummy of Pharaoh Seti I. This behavior was not accepted as normal and coupled with sleep walking and nightmares, these things led her to be incarcerated in Sanatoriums several times. Eady became a part-time student at Plymouth Art School and began to collect affordable Egyptian antiquities, there she became part of a theatre group that on occasion performed a play based on the story of **Isis** and **Osiris**. She took the role of Isis and sang the lamentation for Osiris's death, based on Andrew Lang's translation. "Sing we Osiris dead, lament the fallen head; The light has left the world, the world is grey. Athwart the starry skies the web of darkness lies; Sing we Osiris, passed away. Ye tears, ye stars, ye fires, ye rivers shed; Weep, children of the Nile, weep – for your Lord is dead."

The Reincarnation of Bentreshyt (Omm Seti)

In 1931, she moved to Egypt and married Emam Abdel Meguid and together they had a son and named him Sety. This is where she got the name **Omm Seti** which means mother of Seti. On arriving in Egypt, she kissed the ground and announced she had come home to stay. In the early 1950's she visited Sakkara temple. Around this time she continued to report apparitions and out-of-body experiences, which caused friction with the upper-middle-class family she had married into. At some point she reported nighttime visitations by an apparition of Hor-Ra. He slowly dictated to her, over a twelve-month period, the story of her **previous life**. The story took up around seventy pages of cursive hieroglyphic text. It described the life of a young woman in ancient Egypt, called Bentreshyt, who had reincarnated as the person of Dorothy Eady. Bentreshyt ("Harp of Joy") is described in this text as being of humble origin, her mother a vegetable seller and her father a soldier during the reign of Seti I (1290 BC to 1279 BCE). When she was three, her mother died, and she was placed in the temple of Kom el-Sultan because her father could not afford her. There, she was brought up to be a priestess. When she was twelve years old the High Priest asked her if she wished to go out into the world or stay and become a consecrated virgin. In the absence of full understanding and without a practical alternative, she took the vows. During the next two years, she learned her role in the annual drama of the Ausarian (Osirian) resurrection, a role that only virgin priestesses consecrated to Isis could perform. One day Seti I visited and spoke to her. They became lovers. When Bentreshyt became pregnant she told the High Priest who the father was. The High Priest informed her that the gravity of the offense against Isis was so terrible that death would be the most likely penalty at a trial. Unwilling to face the public scandal for Seti, she committed suicide rather than face trial.

The Unexplainable

As soon as Omm Seti approach the temple of Seti I for the first time she knew where the gardens that she saw in her dreams as a kid were. Excavation was done and remnants of a garden was found in the exact layout that she described. She also gave information of a secret tunnel that ran underneath the temple on the north side. More excavation was done and the tunnel was found. There was no way she could have known this without prior knowledge. She later gave information on where egyptologist could dig to find a lost temple in the valley of the kings and her information led to another discovery of a never before seen tomb. The governing bodies of Egyptology don't want to accept her claims as being the reincarnation of Bentreshyt the mistress of Seti I but they can't deny the fact that she had intimate knowledge of the temple of Seti that had never before been known. She died at 81 years old and just before she went west she claimed there was another secret chamber underneath the Temple of Seti I but no excavation has yet to be made public. See page **648** for the **metaphysical significance of the number 23**.

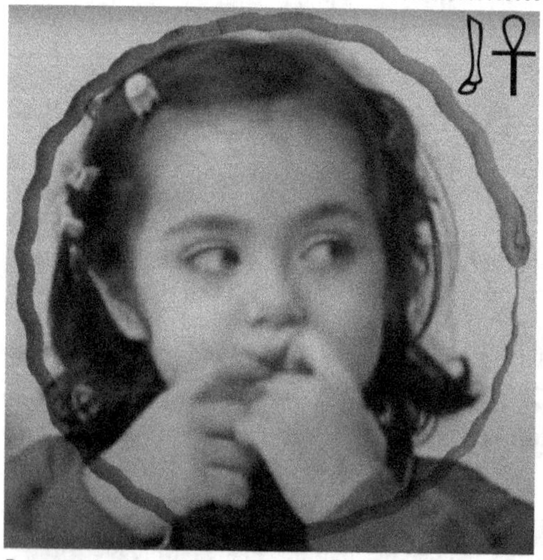

ADDENDUM **Demmet Yilderi, The Reincarnation of Atra Kapi**

On April 20th 1971, a girl named Atra Kapi was born in Turkey. She died on January 11th 1998, in a car accident. **28** days later, in another Turkish village, not far away, D**emmet** Yilderi was born to a **muslim** family. While reincarnation is not a wide held tenet of Islam, Demmet's family belongs to the small **Alawites** sect of **Islam**, a denomination that believes in reincarnation. At a young age D**emmet** claimed to remember living another life. When Demmet was very young she claimed to have two mothers. She claimed her other mother's name was Lemia, she went on to say that her mother was a tailor and she would make all of her clothes. She also remembered the name of her sister, Ifa. Demmet's mother believes her because of the unexplainable knowledge Demmet has of this past life. On one occasion Demmet was in a car with her mother, and as they passed a certain area Demmet started shaking and crying. Her uncle M**emmet,** put his arms around her and asked her what was wrong. Demmet, trembling and terrified, said, "this is where we had the accident". Demmet said, when she bumped her head into the stone something exploded, then she got smaller and smaller… Demmet has a **birthmark** in the same place that Atra Kapi suffered a head injury from her fatal car accident. The family that Demmet described was found and a meeting was set up. When Demmet met with the family of Atra Kapi they believed she was the reincarnation of Atra Kapi. Ifa Kapi, the sister of Atra Kapi, claims to see the soul of her sister in Demmet's eyes. D**emmet** was reborn **28** days later. **Ausar** is the lord of resurrection and reigned for **28** years (p 481). **Emmett** Till was murdered on August **28**, 1955 (p 507)! This story found it's way to me so that I could bring it forth in this book. Death is just a door to another life. One of the best cases of children's past life memories to ever be recorded is the case of **Shanti Devi** (Lugdi Devi). A commission set up by **Muhatma Gandhi** confirmed her claim in 1935.

September 29th 2022 **Lil Boy Emmett**

There was a girl named Demmet, born again in Turkey, a lil boy Emmett came back to earth see, the lil girl Demmet remembered the life she lived, Emmett was thrown in a river where **Isis** is, Emmett was not like Demmet, Emmett came from Kemet, but Emmett had no remanence of any life he lived, still Emmett connected them just like **Isis** did, Emmett connected them just like **Isis** did **- TutemRa**

August 18th 2020 Ultra Black

Rau nu Prt m heru

Iu f Per f m heru

Utterances for Coming Forth by day into Light

It is he, who comes forth by day into Light

"Exalt my image and capture me"

Exercise or exorcism gotta work it out, so I'm doing pull ups, bars of raps, like Peter **Ptah** in a **mushroom** hat, blasting off try'n to find where my soul is at, cause my body's wrapped like a **mummy** with my **artifacts**, supreme inner standing, how smart is that? they said you lost your manuscript, I said nah I died and came back just to get back rap, they said the Nile Valley wasn't the land of the Perfect Black! de-nile it's like they can't see pass the cataracts, sight beyond sight they lying, the Sphinx the Thunder Cats, **Bobby Hemmit** talking to **Emmett** but y'all ain't hearing that, **Common Sense** ain't common even when your thoughts are black, things fall apart, no ceilings, no I ain't feeling that! see everything needs healing and so I'm healing rap, and if you need a rap God sun than I'll be that! **Ultra Black** in my stone sculpture the **vulture** and the **snake** supposed to inspire you to **rise** like **King Djoser**, I pack a mac in the back of the ac for liars with wires who conspire to acquire and kill the culture

Black genesis, all roads lead to black, Cro-Magnon man searching for his self on the map, **The Isis Papers Dr Welsing** spit the facts, and if you think your vote matters you must be smoking crack clown! I ain't pro Black I'm profound, more brown, if I'm a color I'm light write like **Jhuti** sound, **divine** like what they find under ground in the holy land, some say man is mind but mankind is blind, like a pentagram I shine in the d**ark**ness, **Ultra Black** like **Marcus Garvey** or when the n**arc**s hit for them prophets, heartless and mean mug'n at the Hyksos invasion in the 1600's BC, before the caucus, before the Iliad and the odyssey, before Ptolemy, before the Baghdad battery, basalt stone mastery, **exalt my image and capture me**, thou shalt not rewrite the past when you came after me, that's blasphemy! TutemRa alchemy of the soul behold story untold **golden** age 3, Dynasty 18 **Queen Tiye**, **Amen Hotep the 3rd**, That's my word, **Aten** on the horizon, we were thriving, Hapi rising and it's a new day deep diving, I'm live like the third rail, on time like the sun rising, hyphen, like **Tyson** *ain't no stopping me,* ***until I fulfill my prophetic term of prophecy*** **- TutemRa**

Significance - and the Common Connections

The song **Ultra Black** was written on the day my grand father died (page 169). To start this song I took Plat's verse from the song **Kemet** we did on December 8th 2011 (page 218) and flipped it - "Fuck lifting weights, and work'n out, I'm doing pull ups, bars of raps, and everybody wanna know, why I'm so heartless, where my **soul** is at, is my body somewhere with some **artifacts**? Niggas wanna scream damn what type of God is that? and I reply, how large is that? I know everything, how smart is that? they said that I lost my shit, I said I left it, I'm here to get back rap" **- Plat** (Kemet, page 218). I mentioned **Common's** name in this rhyme. **Common Sense** released the single **Resurrection** on **April 4th 1995** and **25** years later I would have my **past life** revelation of **Tutankhaten** (**King Tut**) on April 4th 2020 (p 594), which is also the same day **Martin Luther King** was assassinated (p 69).. See pages 81, 134, 195, 200, 278, 313, 322, 3**23**, 360, 366, and 431 for the other times I say **Common's** name in my music see. See pages 66 and 77 for the first and second **Common Connections**. See pages 208 & 385 for 2 **strange** Common Connections.

August 28th 2020

Chadwick "Aaron" Boseman (The Black Panther) Dies from Cancer

I was in Atlanta when I got the news that Chadwick Boseman died. I found out about his passing a few hours after I had done 1011 lunges straight. August **28**th is also the day that Emmett Till was lynched and murdered back in 1955 the year of the goat. We all need a source of motivation and at this point in my life I happened to be my own source of motivation. How strange to me that The Black Panther would make his transition on this day! Why now? In the middle of a world "plague" on the same day Emmett was murdered! So many people of importance are making their transitions. I tried to make sense of why he made his transition on this day and time. By now you should know that there is no such thing as a coincidence. All things are governed by seen and unseen forces and we must learn how to follow the signs. One time is an incidence, twice is a **coincidence** but three four five is a pattern, But can you see the difference? The actor that played the Black Panther took his last breath, he made his transition to the underworld. His physical body is no more, but where is he? Where is his soul? Is he gone forever? What is the most precious part of life or existence? Is life itself the most precious part of life? Is that the biggest secret? They say life is but a series of breaths, the big heaping first inhalation at birth and then finally the last exhalation upon death. They also say, "as for the span of earthly affairs it is the manner of a dream".

Maybe life isn't about how long we live. Perhaps it's about how well we live, and having a purpose driven life. Did Chadwick live a purpose driven life? Did Chadwick get the role of T'Cholla, the Black Panther by chance or by "luck" or was it his **destiny**? Do we all have a destiny? Was it Martin Luther King's life purpose or destiny written in his life contract to make a stand against the forces of darkness that stand behind the system of racism and white supremacy (pages 69, 592)? They said Chadwick died from colon **cancer**. That hit home with me because my grand father General Dukes JR died from stomach **cancer** in 2009 on August 18th the day after Marcus Garvey's birthday (p 169). Today Instagram is full of pictures of little boys of all colors, crying with their Black Panther action figures. Their superhero is dead. It is natural for children to look up to their parents. Usually little girls want to be like their mothers and little boys usually want to be like their fathers. I grew up without my father so perhaps this fueled my need for a hero. When I was a kid I wanted to be a hero like **He-Man**, **Panthro** from the **Thunder Cats, Superman** and for a short period of time I actually thought I was **Luke Skywalker**. He-Man, Superman and Luke Skywalker were all **White** and I knew that as a child but I used my imagination. I can't really say how much this effected my psyche but we all seek to find a sense of sameness and as a child it was easy to see that **Panthro** from the Thundercats was the black character because his skin color was blue and his accent sounded like a black person, so I imagine that's why I gravitated to him. I can only Imagine how it must have been to grow up as a White boy in a world seeing a White superman, the strongest man in the world with skin the color of theirs as well as 98% of all the other superheroes seen on tv, in the movies and in comic books. And this is why the Black Panther broke all the box office records. Little Black boys had a superhero to look up to who looked just like them. He was even linked to their African ancestry bringing honor to the legacy of African people while even confronting the issue of unity within the family of Africans from the continent and the Africans in America. Not to mention the name **Black Panther,** for adults it evoked the spirit of the **Black Panther Party for Self Defense** which was founded on October 15th 1966 by **Huey P Newton**, **Bobby Seal** and **Elbert Howard** the year after **Malcolm X** was assassinated. Even the throne of the Black Panther in the Marvel movie was styled after the iconic photo of **Huey P Newton** sitting in an African wicker peacock chair. When Chadwick Boseman died Marvel announced that they would not recast another person to play the role of T'Cholla (the Black Panther). I found that to be very strange and even sinister. They claimed that their reason for not recasting the character was their way of honoring the legacy of Chadwick Boseman but what about Superman? What about the 11 white man that have downed the Superman uniform since 1940? No one has ever had a problem casting a new white man to play the role. What about George Reeves? He was the first white man to die after taking the role of a Superman in 1951. Unfortunately when the show was cancelled in 1958 he struggled to get roles as an actor partly or mostly because he was too identifiable as the character Superman and subsequently Reeves committed **suicide** the next year on **Tupac's** birthday, June 16th 1959. Why not honor George Reeves' life and never cast another Superman? What about the Superman curse? (page 204).

I enjoyed the movie Black Panther but outside of that I had not really followed Chadwick's career, however I started looking into his life after seeing how he died the same day as "Emmett Till". There seemed to be some confusion as to whether Chadwick was 42 or 43 years old when he died. The day after his death the site **Golden**globes.com posted a picture with Chadwick and **Stan Lee** that read "Remembering Chadwick Boseman, 1977 - 2020". Some websites say he was born on November 29th 19**77** the year of the **snake** and others say it was 1976 the year of the **dragon**. If it was 1977 that would make him **42** at the time of his death and if it was 1976 it would make him 43 at the time of his death. Chadwick had his **first** starring role in 2013 the year of the **snake** as **Jackie Robinson** who was the **first** black man to play major league baseball and "coincidentally" he wore the number **42** and "coincidentally" died the day before my birthday on October 24th which is "coincidentally" the same day that **Rosa Parks** died, the same day KRS One released his book, **The Gospel of Hip Hop: The First Instrumental** (page 633). I was born in 1977 the year of the **snake** and if Chadwick was indeed born in 1977 as well then he would have been **42** which is the same number that Jackie Robinson wore.

You can still find sites that question whether he was born in the year of 76 or **77**. I find this strange because Chadwick was also born on November 29th, 3 days after my **(Tutankhaten's, King Tut's)** tomb was opened in 1922 (page 11). On April 4th 2020 (page 594) my past life as Tutankhaten (King Tut) was revealed to me and **Rosa Parks** and **Martin Luther King** were there during my revelation. **My revelation was NO different than the scene in the movie Black Panther when T'Cholla ate the sacred Vibranium that sent his astral body to the underworld where he spoke to the spirit of his dead father**.

The Black Panther Goes To The Akashic Records

Please read my **Psychedelic Disclaimer and Warning on page 479.** After the Movie Black Panther was released countless numbers of people took pictures in the Black Panther's signature pose with their arms crossed in front of them. 99 % of these people had no idea where the pose originated from and they had never heard of **Ausar** (**Osiris**). In ancient Kemetic spiritual systems **Ausar** is the Lord of **resurrection, reincarnation, rebirth**. He was the first person ever mummified and he is the one who defeats death through the resurrection and this is where the story of **Jesus Christ** was taken from when Christianity first came into existence. The resurrection of the father through the son. This is what the ancient Egyptians had mastered! From time immemorial we knew that there was no death. We had no word for death as we know it today because we understood and mastered the repetition of the soul, **Immortality**. This concept of resurrection was called the **Wehem-Mesut** (repeating of births, p 14). In more secret teachings you learn that the pose of **Ausar** is really the shape of a **mushroom** cap. **Mushrooms** (fungi) are crucial to ecosystems and neither forest nor fungi could exist without the other. It's been said that fungi are the **interface** of organisms **between life and death**! In the movie Black Panther T'Cholla was on the verge of death and to save his life he is given the **Sacred Vibranium herb** and covered in dirt. In the very next scene T'Cholla rises from the dirt like a **mushroom** but now he is in another dimension where he **interfaces** with his **dead** father. While this scene might seem like it is something only to be seen in movies, I can assure you that it is real. I had a similar experience on **April 4th 2020** when my past life as **King Tut** was revealed to me (p 594). I ate the same sacred **mushroom** (Manna) that Moses and the Israelites were said to have eaten in the biblical story and afterwards I too went to another dimension like T'Cholla where I **interfaced** with **Rosa Parks** and **Martin Luther King** and when I came back to this dimension the name **TutemRa** was **vibrating** and **echoing** in my ear and I knew who I was (p 594)! **Bufo** is one the most powerful psychedelics on the planet and **Mike Tyson** is on record giving his experience with it (p 528). I smoked **Bufo** for the very first time on July 20th 2018 and the very next day July 21st 2018, I would think I was King Tut. I had never thought the thought before and had NO reason to think it but still the thought would just pop in my head from nowhere, the day after smoking the **Bufo**! The thought came but I didn't believe it, yet still on July 21st I wrote the hook for the song **Ayahuasca** that I had written on July 17th and the lyrics are "I am the **boy king** in the museum you be seeing, I gave you the signs this time I'm back in a human being, facts, encoded in rhyme like my body frozen in time, in 1929 I shined on **Martin Luther king**" (p 529). Some how the **Bufo** released information stored within my DNA connected to an ancient soul fragment. When my life as Emmett came on July 3rd 2018 I had just eaten the sacred **mushroom** (Manna) and I was wearing my shirt with Emmett's face on it (p 459), and around 15 minutes after I ate the Manna I looked at a picture of me wearing the shirt with Emmett's face on it and immediately the realization and knowingness that I was Emmett Till in a past Life came to my consciousness in the blink of an eye (p 480) ! These **sacred herbs** are all throughout the ancient holy texts like the sacred ritualistic concoction called **Soma** written about in sacred Indian **Vedas** text and the **Manna** (**mushroom**) that **Moses** and the Israelites ate in **Exodus 16:35** of the **Bible** - "*And the children of Israel ate **manna** forty years*..". Chadwick's middle name was **Aaron** and the biblical character Aaron was the brother of **Moses**. I have expressed several times in this book the connection to the biblical character of Moses and the real life historical person **Akhenaten** who was the father of Tutankhaten (King Tut). I have also expressed my thoughts about **Tupac** and who I think him to have been in a past life. Perhaps **Tupac** ate the **Manna** (sacred **mushroom**) that **"Moses"** and the Israelites ate…? Chadwick died on August 28th the same day that **Emmett Till** was Lynched and **Ausar** (Osiris) reigned for **28 years** in the **Ausarian resurrection** drama. This was a divine pattern, a **"Star Code of Immortality". Re-member** that **you** are **Ausar** and **Heru,** the **hero!** See page 3 for the **hero's journey!**

My Condolences go out to the family, friends and fans of Chadwick "Aaron" Boseman. Please know that death is not the end. The soul survives death, indeed and in spirit. This is a book of the dead written by a boy who was murdered without justice, who defeated death and came forth by day. May the soul of **Chadwick "Aaron" Boseman** walk peacefully through the field of Reeds in Amenta. Amen Ra.

Was Tupac the real "Black Panther" that ate the sacred "Vibranuim"?!

When I began to hear different artist from **Death Row Records** speaking about eating **Mushrooms** I began to wonder if Tupac had also eaten them. **Suge Knight** bailed **Tupac** out of prison and signed him to Death Row Records in 1995. This allowed Tupac to be in the company of **Dr Dre**. **Snoop Dogg** started working with **Dr Dre** in 1992. Years later, on a Full Send Podcast, Snoop talks about lacing his blunts with **mushrooms** and giving them to his homies without them knowing. Did Snoop or Dr Dre introduce mushrooms to Tupac? **Jewell** (p 105) speaks about her and **Lady of Rage** getting **Mushrooms from Dr Dre**. **Eminem** was signed by **Dr Dre** on **Mar 9**, 1998 and a year later on Feb **23**, Eminem released the song, My Fault, a song **about mushrooms**. Did Dr Dre introduce Eminem to **mushrooms** or had Eminem already been using them? **Daz Dillinger** has also gone on record about using **mushrooms**. When Tupac came home from prison **Daz** was the first producer he worked with. The first song he recorded was, **Ambitions Az a Rider**. On this song Tupac mentions **reincarnation**, he says, "They cowards, that's why they tried to set me up, had bitch-ass niggas on my team so indeed they wet me up, but **I'm back reincarnated**". **Daz** is born on **May 25**, which is the first **star code** pattern that I decoded (p 30, 104, 222, 512). Long before Tupac signed to Death Row Records his unconscious mind had been speaking about reincarnation. In 1994 he mentions it on the song Under Pressure (p 664). Tupac smoked weed but did he ever commune with the **mushroom** (p 483)?! Did he have a spiritual awakening?! Did he open a **Spirit Door** like T'Cholla (p 251)? Did Tupac consume **mushrooms** while doing the Makaveli album?! I think that's exactly what happened to Tupac! I think Tupac ate the Sacred **Mushrooms** written about in **chapter 6 verse 51** of the book of **John**, from the **Bible,** that says,"I am the living bread that came down from heaven. Whoever eats this bread will have **eternal life**." Tupac was the real "Black Panther" that ate the sacred "Vibranuim" and got a message from the other side! Tupac mentions reincarnation many times in his music but it's the second verse on the song **Blasphemy**, from the Makaveli album that tells me that his ancient soul was speaking (p 665)!! No one can deny that no other artist has garnered as much attention after their death as Tupac! That's because Tupac lived a life in ancient Kemet thousands of years ago, this is why he is remembered so dearly and why he was drawn to reincarnation (p 665)!!! On May 17, 2022 the Youtube channel, **The Art Of Dialogue** released a video interview with **Napoleon**, titled (2Pac was warned before his death that his life was in danger..!). **Napoleon** details how Tupac once received a letter from a female fan, telling him that his life was in danger. That he must leave Death Row. The woman said bad things were going to happen to Tupac and she didn't think he would survive it. At one point he didn't care if he died young, but after receiving that letter he began to change his views on life and expressed his desire to enjoy life while climbing the ladder of success. I don't know if there's a "Ghetto in Heaven" but I know there's an **After Life** and that Tupac was a "Reincarnated Soul", just as **Bob Marley** once said (p 545, 664).

Rau nu Prt m heru

Iu f Per f m heru

Utterances for Coming Forth by day into Light

It is he, who comes forth by day into Light

September 2nd 2020 **Hotep**

All we want is a little peace, like **Hotep, Islam**, like the steps built by **Imhotep**, the **Christian John** said, "*this **bread** rained down from the heavens and if you eat this bread, **immortality** for the bredren*", they were headed to **Akhetaten** the beautiful city of **Ra** on the horizon forgotten, like **Sneferu** and **Akhenaten,** the rising the dropping, the Hapi river, the first man crop'n, now we share crop'n, beat box'n, **Michael Jackson** Thriller, the action figure who would ever figure 20 20 pull another trigger on another nigger?! My stomach, intestines, lungs and liver protected by **Selkis** get reckless, like **Sekhmet** neckless on necks of Black **Queens** from Texas, vaccines infections, they use foods for weapons, fear God poor **soul**, fools gold, elections, wars to end wars, **The Ausarian Resurrection,** they robbing you of your **soul,** it's a war on complexion, she had a **Papyrus Scroll,** it said have you learned your lesson? You're not in control there's a calling on your **soul** for protection - **TutemRa**

September 4th 2020
The Young Pharaoh

He was a young **Pharaoh,** long distance he had to travel, Inter-dimensional 3rd eye, bulls eye tears from the cattle, **Het Heru,** She was true, lead the army into battle, **TutemRa Kheperu,** her great great great grand nephew, I bet you, if you ever paid **Aten**tion, 60 days in the future on an unknown planet, **Atlantis** Ascension, Divine guidance, not easy for comprehension, hindsight is 20 20, parallel dimensions, the time is 10:10 I was riding, I forgot to mention the chariots of electrum, strapped with a weapon for the mission, **Pepi the 2nd** the longest reign, and every millisecond rep'n for **Kemet,** the spirit of **Emmett** shot down and chained, it went down in flames like the library, they claim they feel my pain but I know they lie to me - **TutemRa**

September 23rd 2020

Murders, Acquittals and a Stroke of Bad Luck
Breonna Taylor, Emmett Till and My Father
Significance

On September **23**rd 2020 the **officers** who **murdered Breonna Taylor** are **acquitted** (page 589). This is the same day as the **acquittal** of **"Emmett Till's" murderers** in 1955 (page 517). The streets are full of protesters again and later that evening I get a call that **my father has had a stroke**. I was in the hospital dealing with the possible death of my father but my father survived his stroke. He also beat cancer 3 times and survived bullet wounds in his teenage years that should have killed him (page 28). I crashed and lived on my fathers birthday on June 1st 2002 (page 106). My sister dreamt that accident before it happened and my father dreams things before they happen (page 99). See page **648** for the **metaphysical significance of the number 23**.

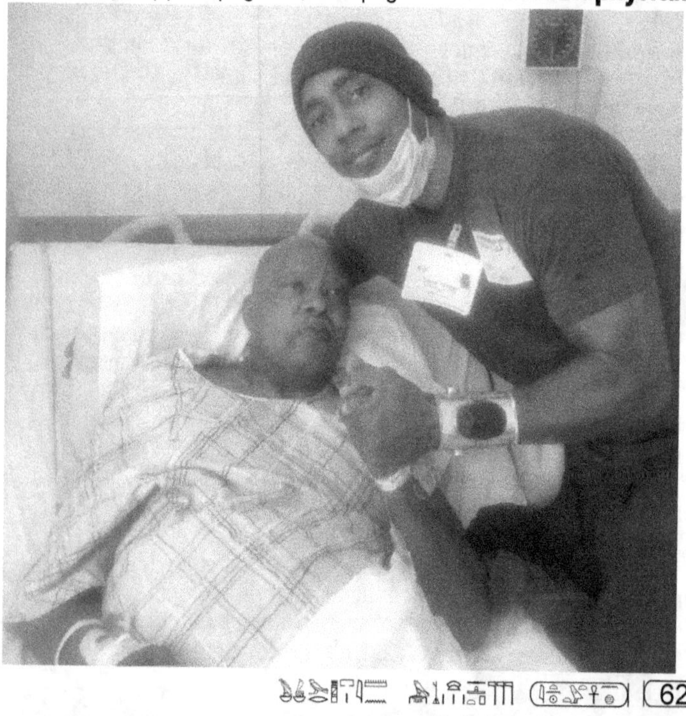

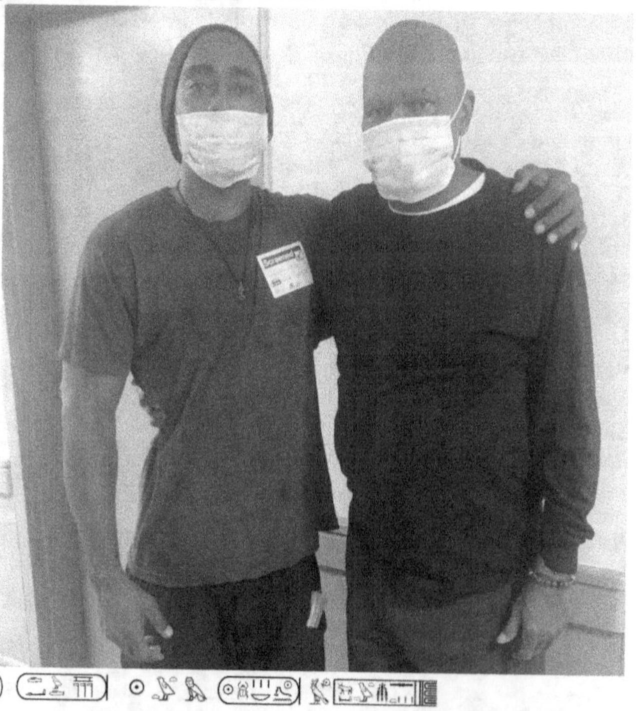

Rau nu Prt m heru

October 23rd 2020 **Black Mirror**

This is a **Black Mirror**, Jack thriller, **The boy king**, Scorpion sting, **Narmer**, **The Man in the mirror**, he look like **Tyson** in the ring it don't get no clearer, 2020 vision, the **Djed Pillar**, the scarab dung beetle, **Amen Hotep** parted the red sea, I see ice people coming from the sea, they must have forgotten the **Aten**, the land before time **Akhenaten**, his wife **Nefertiti** plot'n like a **constellation**, drop'n like a meteor, **spore**, the veil breaks, they saw what they saw, hell hate love heaven, what's it all for? what more is it gonna take to awake? knock knock they opened my door, I flew through the **Shu** in **1 9 2 2** speak'n **Maa Kheru**, but where's my mi amor? I ain't sure, but if she can hear me rhyme'n, just know I miss you more than man wish for gold, silver and diamonds, you know it's true, **I will always love Ankhesenamen, Amen** in my heart you are never forgotten, you know it's true, **I will always love you Ankhesenaten, Aten** in my heart you are never forgotten **- TutemRa**

See page **648** for the **metaphysical significance of the number 23**.

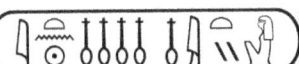

Iu f Per f m heru

2020

The Magical Book Store from 2016

E M M E T T

A B B O T T

If you got this far perhaps you actually read about the **magical book store** I found in 2016 (page 418). If you did, then you remember the **Salem Witch** and the book I found her in. If you skipped that then go back and read about the three books I found there and how I came to find them there (pages 418 and 419). As I was writing this book something* told me to check the book **Greatest American Trials, 201 Compelling Courtroom Dramas** for the murder of Emmett Till because of course it would be in there! Right? Well, to my surprise the American trial of 1955 that sparked the Civil Rights Movement **was not in there** however I did find a trial in there from 1955 that was quite **spell**binding! All the cases in this book are listed in chronological order like most of the events in this book so I opened the book to 1955 and only found one case. The case of a **14** year old **White girl** named Stephanie **Bryan**. I found that interesting because Emmett, a **Black boy** was also murdered at **14** years of age. **Emmett** was lynched by Roy **Bryant** and Stephanie **Bryan** was murdered by Burton **Abbott**. Stephanie was murdered on **A**pril **28**th 19**55** while Emmett was murdered on **A**ugust **28**th 19**55**. Emmett's uncle identified Roy **Bryant** and JW Milam as the killers yet the deliberation of the verdict only lasted **1 hour** and the killers were found not guilty. The clothes of Stephanie **Bryan** were found in the home of **Abbott** and the body of Stephane was found close to the house of Abbott yet it took **2 and a half months** to find the White man guilty. Abbott's trial started on November 7th which is 33 years and 3 day after **Tutankhaten's** (**King Tut's**) tomb was discovered on November 4th 19**22**! My mind does not know how to process this but it is very strange! I never heard about Stephanie until I opened this book. Stephanie Bryan's name has been lost to the pages of **his story** yet the murder of Emmett Till still lingers on. Ask yourself why the book, **Greatest American Trials, 201 Compelling Courtroom Dramas,** didn't have the case of Emmett Till listed in it? Do you think the author forgot? I wonder if there ever was a Stephanie Bryan? Perhaps this is really just some big **Truman** show. What ever it is I know that I was Emmett in my **past life** and I know that I was **King Tut** in a past life and I know all the events in this book are real because I lived them. My higher mind tells me that this case is here to add significance to this book. This is for white people or people who call themselves white. Nothing that is done in the dark will stay in the dark. All things done in the dark will eventually come to light. The sun rises in the east and sets in the west. This concept of resurrection was called the **Wehem-Mesut** (repeating of births, p 14). The body is taken away and then the soul returns just like the sun does everyday. This math is divine math (page 41). You will only do yourself harm by continuing down the path of isfet, barbarism, racism and white supremacy! There is a debt that **you** need to pay and I suggest that you pay it! There is no escape! Death will not save you nor will Jesus! Reparations now! An abbot is the head of a monastery. Just as businesses have bosses and teams have coaches, the monastery has an abbott. I'm writing a Epic Sci-Real (Science Reality) Novel Trilogy version of this book and a book about Tupac's ancient past life (pages 664 - 665). Stay tuned!

Utterances for Coming Forth by day into Light

It is he, who comes forth by day into Light

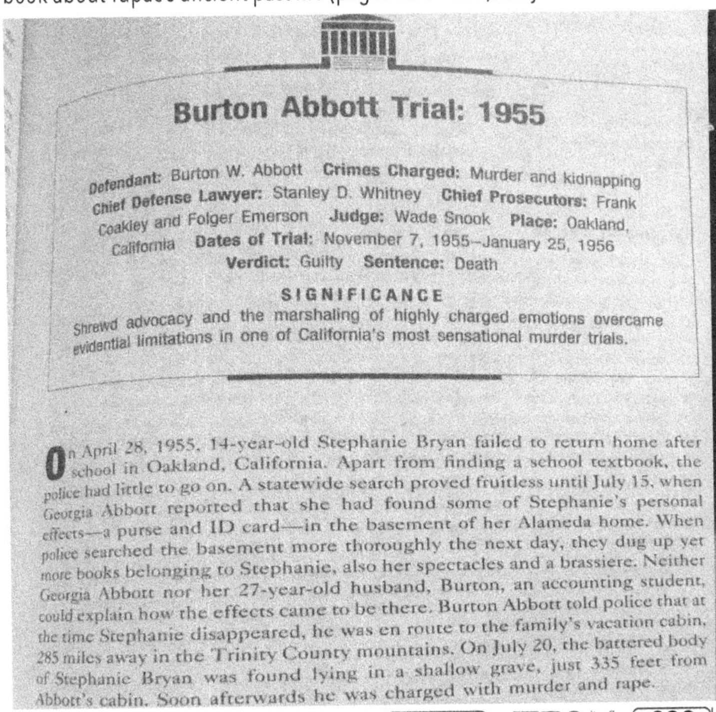

Burton Abbott Trial: 1955

Defendant: Burton W. Abbott **Crimes Charged:** Murder and kidnapping **Chief Defense Lawyer:** Stanley D. Whitney **Chief Prosecutors:** Frank Coakley and Folger Emerson **Judge:** Wade Snook **Place:** Oakland, California **Dates of Trial:** November 7, 1955–January 25, 1956 **Verdict:** Guilty **Sentence:** Death

SIGNIFICANCE

Shrewd advocacy and the marshaling of highly charged emotions overcame evidential limitations in one of California's most sensational murder trials.

On April 28, 1955, 14-year-old Stephanie Bryan failed to return home after school in Oakland, California. Apart from finding a school textbook, the police had little to go on. A statewide search proved fruitless until July 15, when Georgia Abbott reported that she had found some of Stephanie's personal effects—a purse and ID card—in the basement of her Alameda home. When police searched the basement more thoroughly the next day, they dug up yet more books belonging to Stephanie, also her spectacles and a brassiere. Neither Georgia Abbott nor her 27-year-old husband, Burton, an accounting student, could explain how the effects came to be there. Burton Abbott told police that at the time Stephanie disappeared, he was en route to the family's vacation cabin, 285 miles away in the Trinity County mountains. On July 20, the battered body of Stephanie Bryan was found lying in a shallow grave, just 335 feet from Abbott's cabin. Soon afterwards he was charged with murder and rape.

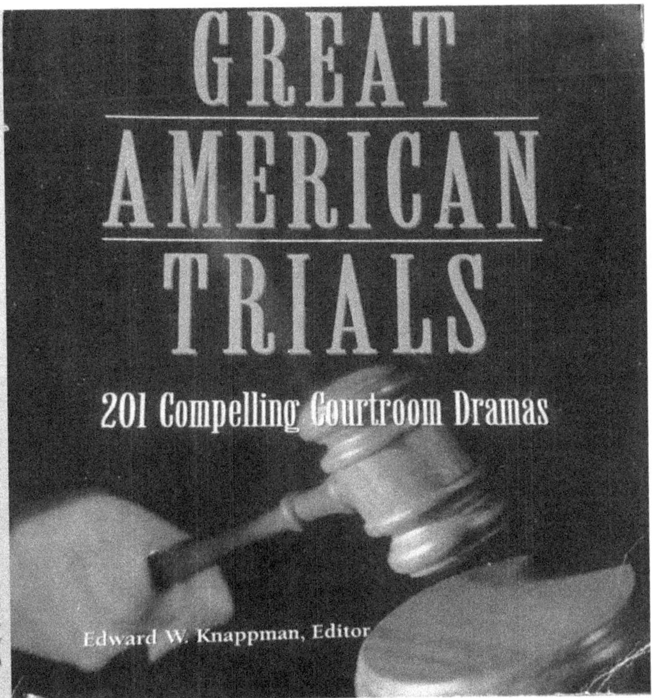

2020 the year of the Ox - The Magical Book Store from 2016
The September 23rd patten and the year of the OX, Don't let them out Fox you like FOX News

I picked the book up again, **Greatest American Trials, 201 Compelling Courtroom Dramas** and it randomly opened to a page where I saw the date **September 23rd**! The same day that **Emmett Till's** killers were **acquitted** page 517), which is the same day **Breonna Taylors** killers were **acquitted** and the same day that my father had a **stroke** and from death he was **acquitted** (page 627)! The same day Aubrey Herbert died (**September 23rd 1923**), he was the half-brother of Lord Carnarvon (page 12). On **September 23rd 1949** the year the **Ox**, 4 years after the United States of America **dropped bombs on Japan** to end world war II, President **Truman** caused hysteria in America announcing that the Soviet Union had atomic bombs and could possibly use them on "us". This announcement caused Americans to start digging under ground bomb shelters while also teaching school children how to duck under classroom desks for bomb drills. When I read this all I could think of was the year the **OX** 2020 and the President telling people that there was a killer **virus** in the air and all of a sudden everyone was in "mask" hysteria. Children were told to wear masks to protect them from this unseen killer **virus** in the air. And to increase the fear there were many reports of people dying and many people did die. It is November of 2021 now and it seems like the killer virus isn't as much as a killer as they claimed. The president has mandated vaccines for all businesses with 100 or more workers yet the police refuse to be mandated and now the Congress members are rejecting the mandates. See page **648** for the **metaphysical significance of the number 23**. I'm writing a Epic Sci-Real (Science Reality) Novel Trilogy version of this book and a book about Tupac's ancient past life (pages 664 - 665). Stay tuned!

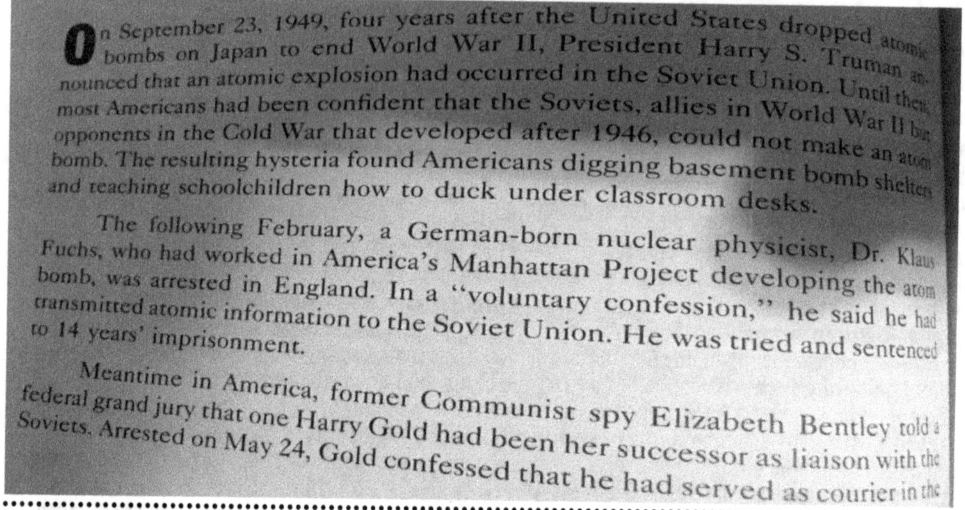
On September 23, 1949, four years after the United States dropped atomic bombs on Japan to end World War II, President Harry S. Truman announced that an atomic explosion had occurred in the Soviet Union. Until then, most Americans had been confident that the Soviets, allies in World War II but opponents in the Cold War that developed after 1946, could not make an atom bomb. The resulting hysteria found Americans digging basement bomb shelters and teaching schoolchildren how to duck under classroom desks.

The following February, a German-born nuclear physicist, Dr. Klaus Fuchs, who had worked in America's Manhattan Project developing the atom bomb, was arrested in England. In a "voluntary confession," he said he had transmitted atomic information to the Soviet Union. He was tried and sentenced to 14 years' imprisonment.

Meantime in America, former Communist spy Elizabeth Bentley told a federal grand jury that one Harry Gold had been her successor as liaison with the Soviets. Arrested on May 24, Gold confessed that he had served as courier in the

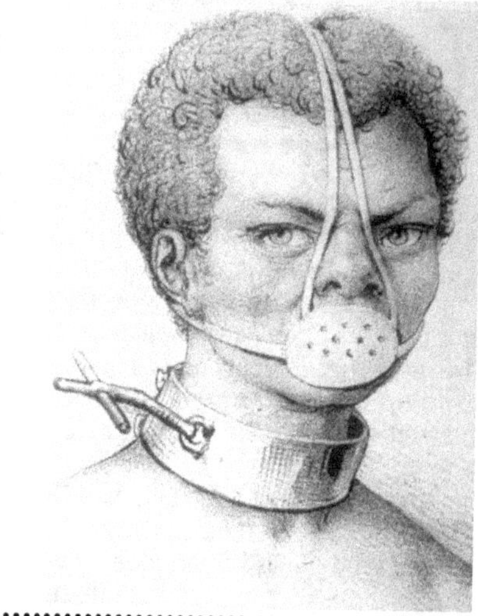

October 30th 2020 Quawan "Bobby" Charles

October 30th 2020 was the last day that the **Black** 15 year old Louisiana teen Quawan "Bobby" Charles was seen alive. His naked and disfigured body was found in the drainage ditch four days later 20 miles away from his home in a sugarcane field. According to Quawan's family members Quawan left their home with a 17 year old "friend" and the "friend's" mother **Janet Irvin** who are both **White**. Quawan's father was out shopping at the time and by 7pm Quawan's father Kenneth Jacko opened Quawan's locked door to find that Quawan was not there. The police where called immediately but the police suggested to Quawan's family that he might have gone off to a football game, and questioned whether he had a troubled past. Allegedly they didn't even try to ping Quawan's cell phone until three days later. Quawan's family felt that they were not getting the support, and they were not being listened to. The family's perceived "indifference" and "lack of empathy" by local law enforcement between the missing persons report and the discovery of the teen's body makes the family wonder if the Quawan's race played a part in the response. In response to reports of Quawan's death, Kevin Archon told the reporters: "If it was a White person – if it was one of their kids – people would have probably been in jail by now." Tambara Bonnet, a Black woman who lived near Janet Irvin in the mobile home community told the reporters: "If it was a White kid, they would have looked for him right then and there". Quawan's mother took a picture of her sons disfigured face, inspired by the decision of **Mamie Till** in 1955 who held an open-casket funeral for her 14 year old son **Emmett Till** who was the victim of a lynching. Local media picked up the story only after the family went public following the discovery -- and an aunt posted a graphic photo of Quawan's face on a GoFundMe page seeking donations to pay for a private autopsy. None of the local media outlets that cover the Iberia **Parish** (**Per Isis**) area claim to have known a child was missing, let alone killed, until the family put them on notice. In alleging a sluggish police response, the Charles family attorney says: "We know that the most critical moments in any missing persons report, in particular, one involving a child, are those first few seconds, minutes and hours that go by." "I believe that, if they showed a greater sense of urgency in this, two things could have happened," he says. "One, Bobby could still be here because they could have intervened. Two, if Bobby still wouldn't have been here, those who were responsible for killing him would be arrested. Evidence would be ripe. Folks would not have been able to cover up their tracks. And instead, we're here 13, 14 days later without answers." "The family's grieving," he says. "They're going to bury their son in a week, and they still know very little."

Janet Irvin allegedly admitted to picking Charles up at his father's home in Baldwin, Louisiana, on October 30th the day he went missing, and driving him about 20 miles to their trailer house without first getting permission from Charles' parents.

Charles' body was found a little over a mile from Janet Irvin's residence on November 3rd 2020. According to investigators, members of Janet's family and their "inner circle" stated that Charles had been high on a hallucinogen however a toxicology report conducted by NMS Labs found no trail or a hallucinogen. On February 9th 2021 Janet Irvin was arrested for failure to report a missing child and contributing to the delinquency of a minor, her bond was set for $400,000.

Significance

When I saw the face of 15 year old Quawan my heart mourned and I immediately thought about my mutilated face! His death still bothers me and the connections to my previous life cause me to place his story in this book. Emmett Till's nickname was **Bobo** (**Bobby**) and Quawan's nickname was also **Bobby**. Quawan's body was discovered on **November 3rd** which is the day before Tutankhaten's (King Tut's) tomb was discovered on **November 4th** 1922.

Rau nu Prt m heru

Condolences

My condolences go out to all the families of those who have been robbed of their lives by this system of racism and white supremacy. Please know that death is not the end. The soul survives death, indeed and in spirit. This is a book of the dead written by a boy who was murdered without justice, who defeated death and came forth by day. May the soul of **Quawan 'Bobby' Charles** walk peacefully through the field of Reeds in Amenta. Amen Ra.

July 13th 1971 - October 31st 2020

Meta-Spiritual Encounter with MF Doom

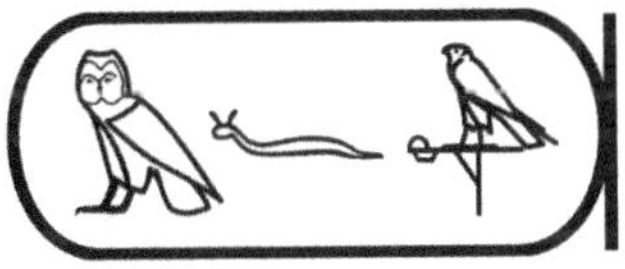

"Have a Nice Dream" MF Doom

Iu f Per f m heru

I moved around a lot as a child and never staying in any school system for too long definitely hindered my ability to stay on top of my studies but it also allowed me less time in any one place to get into too much trouble. Where ever I went I found friends and every where I went Hip Hop was there. I enjoyed all forms of music but Hip Hop was my favorite and it was my escape. **Today is January 11th 2021** and right now I'm listening to **MF Doom** on repeat. The song **America's Most Blunted** by **MF Doom** (Daniel Dumile), from his **Sadvillain** album is playing, the song features **Sade** and **Sean Price**. My mother played Sade a lot when we were young. She was a single mother of 3 suffering from depression, needless to say Sade became one of my favorite artists. When I was in high school, the **Boot Camp Clik** was my favorite rap group. I knew all their lyrics by heart and Sean Price was one of my favorite emcees from the group. I had a **profound experience** with **Sean Price** on December 3rd 2015 (page 345) and today I would have a **profound experience** with **MF Doom**. This is embarrassing but I must admit that I never listened to MF Doom much prior to yesterday. MF Doom, "The Masked Villain" died on October 31st 2020 and I personally feel like he is the best rapper I have ever heard as I write this through tears. The death of rappers don't often make me cry. They usually make me very angry but here I am crying over the death of an artist I just began to listen to. I don't listen to a lot of Hip Hop music any more but I woke up today and put his music on repeat again and afterwards the strangest thing happened! By this time I had the song **Figaro** from Mf Doom's **Sadvillain's** album playing. I had a 9am appointment that cancelled and when she cancelled all I could think to do was to go back to **sleep**. As soon as I had that thought I looked at my bed, and **as soon as my eyes laid on my bed** the words "**have a nice dream**" came out of MF Doom's mouth. Then for around 30 seconds the song stopped till finally **Raekwon** started rhyming the first verse from his song Daytona 500 in which he says the words "**many lives**". The words **many lives** were not said in the context of reincarnation but they were said! The song **Figaro** was originally produced by **Madlib** who was born the day before me on October 24th 1973, the same day **Rosa Parks** died. I had experienced too much in terms of the paranormal so I knew that this was no "**coincidence**"! MF DOOM had spoken to me. I just laughed as I laid down and closed my eyes. When my eyes closed my face was angled towards the **sun** that was peaking through my window. **With my eyes closed** facing the **sun** I could see what seemed like random images moving and flashing before my eyes **as if I was watching a tv screen that was being changed from channel to channel.. The more I focused the more clear each images got. Then I fell asleep.**

Utterances for Coming Forth by day into Light

It is he, who comes forth by day into Light

Condolences

My condolences go out to the family, friends and fans of Daniel Dumile. Please know that death is not the end. The soul survives death, indeed and in spirit. This is a book of the dead written by a boy who was murdered without justice, who defeated death and came forth by day. May the soul of **Daniel Dumile** walk peacefully through the field of Reeds in Amenta. Amen Ra.

November 14th 2020 (Afrikan Montu Arts)

I met the brothers from the Detroit Tamerrian institute by way of my good brother **Tim Reed** (p, 587). In 2020 they came to NYC and stayed at my place while they were here. Mfundishi had invited them to his Brooklyn museum tour of the Kemetic (Egyptian) artifacts. The night before the tour we had a good time at my place laughing a lot and cracking jokes. When it was time to leave for the museum tour brother **Osotrari** asked if I had an iron and for some reason I found that to be funny because I stopped ironing my clothes many years ago. I thought he was concerned with his clothes being nice and neat and it amused me. When we left for the museum tour Osotrari and **Clarence** put on their regalia and it reminded me of the Emperor's Royal Guards from Star Wars who wore red robes. After the museum tour we went to the Botanical Gardens in Brooklyn where Mfundishi's students and the **Tamerrian** brothers demonstrated Afrikan **Montu** (Martial) **arts** of fighting. The word **Martial** means, a **Roman God of war**, it is not African. When I saw the clothing the Tamerrian brothers wore was used as weaponry I immediately felt foolish for laughing so hard about the iron. **Iron fist** (Tekken, page 76) and all forms of Montu Arts originate in Africa, as **the oldest depictions of Montu Arts of stick fighting and grappling can be seen below, from the walls of the Temple of Ramessu III** (1080 B.C.E.). **Osotrari** is born on Nov 2, two days before the tomb of **Tutankhaten** was discovered. His **life path number** is **22**. **Clarence** is born on **June 16**, the same days as **Tupac**! His **life path number** is **8** and so is **Tim's**. When I met **Clarence** in 2020 I did not know that he had won a **NFL Super Bowl** with the **Ravens** in 2000. He wore number **35** and helped win Super Bowl **35**. It was my proximity to these good brothers that helped propel me into the ways of the **Montu Arts**! In 20**23** I started training with **Heru Nekhet** in his **TUF System**. Heru was born in 1967 the year of the **Goat** and when I started training with him he was **55** years old. **Emmett Till** was Murdered in 19**55** the year of the **Goat**.

ADDENDUM

P 302

December 18th 2020 Ayah

Her name is Ayah, Ayah like Ayahuasca born on 4 20 like a higher chakra **- TutemRa**

December 18th 2020 Bria

Her name is Bria lucky if you ever seen her, born on 2 4 like **Rosa** was march'n, a leader **- TutemRa**

December 18th 2020 Infinity

Life is a symphony speaking in **Riddles**, TutemRa the infinite stuck in the middle of eternity, **Heh** infinity, returning the 3rd time trinity **- Neb Kheperu Ra**

December 23rd 2020

Stars

Billions of stars, yet only one moon, that I see from the window, telescope zoom, it's all perspective, a play of consciousness I presume **- TutemRa**

January 2nd 2021 (Family and Relationships)

Rau nu Prt m heru

My older sister and I don't speak very often but I had been making an effort to call her more regularly. I had recently had an argument with my mother and was calling my sister to talk about things in our family. When she picked up we spoke for a few minutes but then she put me on hold. After being on hold for a few minutes I glanced at my book shelf and saw the book **Maat principles of Moral Living**. I had recently been thinking about reading through the book because I purchased it from brother **Seku** on 125th street years ago and had yet to really give it a good read. So instead of being impatient, I waited for her to come back but while on hold I grabbed the book and opened it to a random page. It opened to page 217 on **Family And Relationships**.The passage spoke to the very issues I was experiencing in my family especially the issues I have with my mother. After I read the page my sister came back to the call and of course I went on to explain to her what I experienced while on hold, then I read her the passage. I found the experience to be more precise due to the images on the cover of the book. On the cover of book 7 images can be seen on the left and 6 of them are directly related to events in this book. A man in the **kemetic yoga sesh pose** and my first past life was given to me 2 days after finishing a **kemetic yoga** course on July 1st 2018 (p 480). An image of **Mentchu-Hotep** can be seen and Mfundishi wrote a book about him (p 449). An image of **Queen Tiye** can be seen and she was my ancient grandmother (p 261). An image of **Harriet Tubman** can be seen and I worked with her in a previous life (page 584). An image of **Malcolm X** can be seen and he was the first man I ever heard speak truth to power when I was a teenager (p 48) and he is one of the most mention people through out this book. If you pay attention and keep a clean heart the messages will flow from everywhere.

42 Laws of Maat, Page 367

Iu f Per f m heru

MAAT

FAMILY AND RELATIONSHIPS

(mehut hau)

First love, marry, and care for children because the good of the family outweighs the individual. Family first

Judge People by Their Actions

1. Judge people by what they do; not by what they say, who they know, or who they are related to. People need to earn their way and be held accountable for their actions. Being fair means to be guided without bias, dishonesty and injustice when interacting with others. Always treat people fairly and according to their deeds. Do not dishonor and disrespect others, especially those who care and provide for you.

2. How you treat others reflects your self-worth and values. Not treating people fairly leads to distrustful and insincere relationships with others. Further, it helps the people who are being favored to believe that they are better than others; not because they've earned it, but for some other reason.

3. Observe what people do and treat them fairly according to their actions. A person who mistreats you, takes advantage of you or harms you should not be treated in the same manner as one who demonstrates concern and kindness. You are no better than anyone and no one is better than you. We are as good as who we are, our character, and what we do.

Be Honest and Direct

1. It is important to be direct and honest first with yourself and then with others. Honesty leads to integrity and trustworthiness, which are essential to relationships that have meaning. Even those who do not agree with or like you can respect you if you demonstrate integrity.

2. When you avoid dealing with something so as not to hurt someone's feelings, several things are going on. For one, by not engaging in principled struggle, you deny yourself and the other person the opportunity to improve and to sharpen your position. Secondly, if the person holds an unprincipled position, your silence runs the risk of allowing her/him to believe that she/he is just in having it,

217

Utterances for Coming Forth by day into Light

It is he, who comes forth by day into Light

January 3rd 2021

Mississippi Mummy (1st of 8)

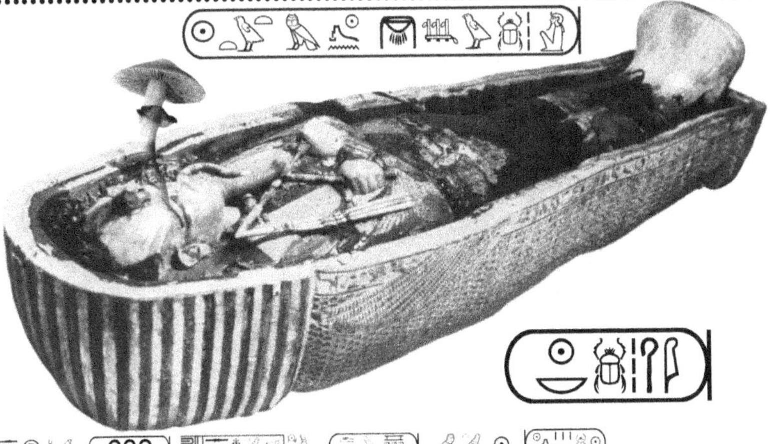

Mummy M**ississ**ippi, not even Rap Genius can decipher this **Riddle**, only a chosen few, my name is TutemRa Nebu Sahu Kheperu, shm e em htp, I come in peace, I'm different like Das EFX, claiming to be the deceased, I'm running, doing the reps, immortal Djet, the Ba rises in the east, gold face, the soul sets in the west, a cold case, dead money, M**ississ**ippi Mummy **- TutemRa**

Significance

See Page 511

January 15th 2021 - MF Doom, KRS One and The Hip Hop Bible

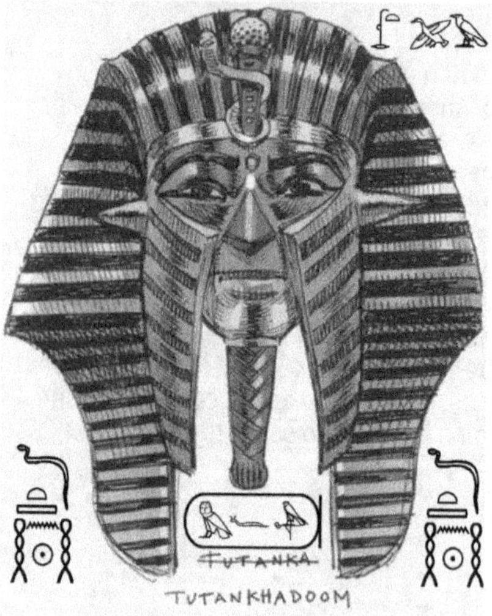

www.danlishartworks.bigcartel.com

I'm Listening to this **MF Doom** dude and he is definitely working from beyond the beyond cause **the illest villains never die**. Yesterday I found an unreleased and untitled track from Mf Doom, produced by **The Alchemist**, who happens to be born the same day and year as me, Oct 25th 1977 the year of the **snake**. The name **Hatshepsut** is said in this song. Hatshepsut is in the family that makes up the 18th Dynasty of Kemet (pages 268, 311, 336, 638). She is in the lineage of **Tutankhaten**. **KRS One's** voice, from his song Attacks is sampled through out the song, **"We will be here forever. Do you understand? Forever! Forever and ever and ever and ever, We will be here for ever. Do you understand? Get what I'm saying? Forever!"**. I regret to say that MF Dooms music only came to me after he died. I had never listened to him. I was too busy going through this transformation. He dropped an album by the Name MF Doom in 1999 the same year that I joined the army (page 82). So I was out of the loop with Hip Hop. After basic training I went straight to Germany and never heard of him until I exited the army on **January 15th** 2005, on Martin Luther King's birthday (page 130). Doom is a lyrical genius and listening to this track, which has a **Sade** sample, makes me cry. I love it and Doom is a favorite now.

If there is any Hip Hop artist that would understand what I'm presenting here it would be **KRS One** because he teaches the **metaphysics** of Hip Hop and music (page 6). KRS One's **DJ Scott La Rock** (Scott Monroe Sterling) was murdered on August **27th** 1987 the day before **Emmett Till** was murdered on August **28th** 19**55**. The murder of Scott La Rock was connected to a confrontation that **D-Nice** had with **two men** involving **a woman**, just like Emmett Till's death was connected to **a women** (page 506). Two men were arrested and charged with Scott La Rock's murder, but they were **acquitted** at the trial, just like the two men who murderred Emmett Till were aquitted (pages 516-517). Scott La Rock's death is said to be the **first murder** of a major Hip Hop artist and Emmett's murder was the first time a white person went trial for killing a black person, **sparking** the Civil Rights Movement, lead by Martin Luther King. Two years after Scott La Rock's death, in 1989 the year of the **snake**, **KRS One** would **spark** a movement for unity by releasing the song **Self Destruction** on **January 15th**, **Martin Luther King's** birthday, which is todays date! Martin Luther King rose to prominence after the murder of Emmett Till and my past life as **Tutankhaten** (**King Tut**) was revealed on April 4th 2020 (p 594), the day that Martin was assassinated (pages 69, 592). It's not a **coincidence** that **D-Nice** says the word **eternity** in the song **Self Destruction**, "It's time to stand together in a unity, cause if not then we're soon to be Self-destroyed, unemployed, the rap race will be lost without a trace, or a clue but what to do, is stop the violence and kick the science down the road that we call **eternity**, where knowledge is formed and you'll learn to be Self-sufficient, independent"- **D Nice.** This book is about the soul being immortal and the reality of **Eternal Life**.

My mother was born in 19**55** (p 27), 2 months later the creator of Hip Hop, **Dj Kool Herc** was born and 4 months later **Emmett** was murdered. At this very moment **KRS One** is **55** Years young. **KRS One** was born in 1965, year of the **snake** like **Martin** Luther King (1929), "**Emmett** Louis Till" (1941) and "me", "**Dawud** Basheer Eddings" (1977). **KRS One's** real name is Lawrence **Kris Parker**. My grand mother's maiden name is **Parker** (page 22) and Emmett's cousin, who was there the night he was murdered, is named Wheeler **Parker** Jr (pages 15, 504, 515). On Oct 24th 2009, the day before my birthday, and the same day Rosa **Parks** died, **KRS One** released the book, **The Gospel of Hip Hop: The First Instrumental**. It is a philosophical masterwork set in the format of the Christian Bible, this 800-plus-page opus is a life-guide manual for members of Hip Hop Kulture that combines classic philosophy with faith and practical knowledge for a fascinating, in-depth exploration of Hip Hop as a life path. None of this is **coincidence** my friends. The name **Christ** is a title for the enlightened being like the title **Buddha** and before there was a Jesus Christ or a Buddha there was the **Nswt Bity** (Pharaoh). In ancient Kemet (Egypt) the mummified body of the **Nswt Bity** was called a **Krst** (Karast, **Kris**, **Christ**). The name **Kris** (**KRS**) is the root of the name **Christ** and in ancient Kemet the **krst** (the mummy) was made in the process of preparation by purifying, **anointing** with oils, and then embalming. Just as a caterpillar wraps (mummifies) itself into a **chrys**alis (**Krst**/cocoon) and transforms into a butterfly, the human being is supposed to use each life to further the transformation of their consciousness, becoming **the Anointed One (page 492)**. I find it very interesting that **KRS One (Kris)** looks a lot like **Huni**, who was the last Nswt Bity of the 3rd dynasty of Kemet, and the father of **Sneferu,** the 1st Nswt Bity of the **4th dynasty**. But even more interesting is the fact that on December 24th 2021 **KRS One** released a song titled, **The Beginning** and in the song he says "**I am the return of Khufu**". Khufu was the 2nd Nswt Bity of the **4th dynasty** of Kemet. In the video for the song **Kemetic,** images of Heru (Horus) can be seen in his **falcon** form. **Heru** is the son of Ausar (Osiris), the Lord of **resurrection** and Heru is the **falcon** that resurrects and returns as Ra in the Ausarian **resurrection** Drama. This is where the story of Jesus **Christ** originates from. **KRS One** released **The Gospel of Hip Hop** the day before my birthday and I have written **TutemRa - The Prophecy of Reincarnation, Star Codes of Immortality**, which I consider to be **The Hip Hop Bible**. This makes considerable sense when you consider **KRS One's** body of work. He has been at the for front of bringing consciousness into the order of Hip Hop. In 1996, the same year **Tupac** died, KRS One established The **Temple of Hip Hop**. He currently teaches from his book every sunday via a live video stream on his Youtube page. When I have time I tune in to his lessons. **KRS One**: **K**nowledge **R**eigns **S**upreme **O**ver **N**early **E**veryone, indeed and in spirit! See Brother **Khufu** on pg 282. **Re-member** that **you** are **Ausar** and **Heru,** the **hero!** See page 3 for the **Hero's Journey**!

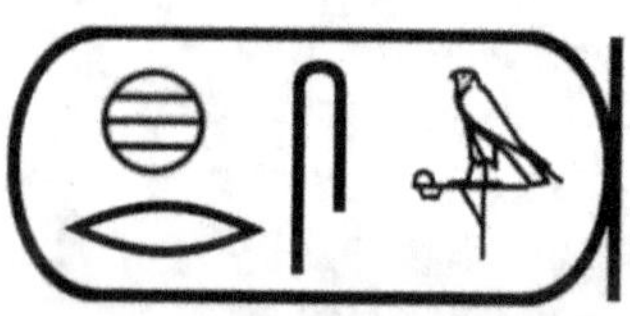

***ADDENDUM* DREAM - May 2022**

Upon returning from Kemet in April of 2022 (p 670) I had **dreams** with several brothers who are in some way connected to Kemet and KRS One was one of them. In my dream with KRS One we were planning on doing a song together. Then I woke up. I would also dream with **Lord Jamar** (p 342), **Mike Tyson** (p 528) and **XXXtentacion** (p 471).

Rau nu Prt m heru

Iu f Per f m heru

Utterances for Coming Forth by day into Light

It is he, who comes forth by day into Light

February 27th 2021 Affinity Publisher

Affinity Publisher

Affinity Publisher is a desktop publishing application developed by Serif for macOS and Microsoft Windows, with an iPadOS version planned for release in 2020. It is a part of the Affinity product line along with Affinity Photo and Affinity Designer. Wikipedia

Initial release date: June 19, 2019

Stable release: 1.9.0 / 4 February 2021; 0 days ago

Almost a year had past since I knew I was Tutankhaten and in that time I had amassed enough material to write a book. From the moment of my revelation on April 4th 2020 (p 595) till February 2021 I'd written down every notable moment in my life as well as every rhyme I had ever written and placed them in a word document. When I was done gathering my material I wrote down every event on a single piece of paper and placed it in a binder. On Feb 18th I was done and when I saw that the binder was 2 inches thick I began to look for book publishing software. On Feb 27th 2021 I purchased Affinity Publisher and began the process of arranging my book. I was not surprised when I found out that the software was initially released on June 19th which is **Juneteenth**. Juneteenth is the oldest known date celebrating the commemoration of the end of slavery in the US. If that wasn't strange enough the stable release date was on **February 4th** which is **Rosa Parks'** birthday. I just laughed and shook my head. Part of me felt like this was some big joke! Was this created just for me, like the **Truman show**?! I did everything for my book, I edited the book, I did the layout, the cover design, and I did my own illustrations.

Today is Feb 24th 2022 and I'm days away from the close of this book. I just finished logging in the details of what happened today with the show, **The Odd Couple** (p 669). I would be remiss if I did not mention that my friend **Mars** (p 474) is also born on **February 4th** and she is the person who invited me back to the African Arts Festival where I had my past life revelation of Emmett Till (p 480). My friend **Padmore** is also born on **February 4th** , he own's Tsion Cafe, an Ethiopian restaurant in Harlem. He is the **Reincarnation** of Dejazmatch Beru (**Ras Beru**) who was Ethiopian royalty and was the minister of war of Emperor **Haile Selassie** (p 390). It is 6:**23** pm and I'm about to leave, there is an open mic tonight at **Tsion Cafe** and **Beejay**, Padmore's wife (and other owner of Tsion Cafe), asked me to stop by to do a poem.

I performed 3 poems last night, **The Lord of Maat**, written on March 6th 2016 (p 367), **The Pattern** written on April 28th 2020 (p 607), and **Thirteen Signs** written on February 21st 2022 (p 669). The crowd was receptive. I gave a lesson on the meaning of the **riddle**, **Thirteen Signs** which I explain on the date that I wrote it.

March 24th 2021

"When I Die let a Real Soldier Tat My Name on His Shoulder" - (Born 2 rebel, written in 2011, page 210)

I knew I wanted tattoo's but I didn't know where I was going to get them. I went to Art 2 Ink Studio located at **22**95 Adam Clayton Powell Jr Blvd a few years back when I got the tattoo on my stomach retouched and that ended up being where I got my new tattoo's. When the owner told me his name was **Naheem** I knew I was supposed to do my tattoos there. My uncles name is **Nahiem**. Then I saw that the girl that worked the desk was in love with **Tupac** and she even had his face tattooed on her hand. Naheem had a Tattoo across his belly that says INK LIFE like **Tupac**. I have a theory about who **Tupac** was in his **past life**. There was also an apprentice there named **Will** who was born on a significant date that I can't remember.. Him and I had the most fun while I was there and we shared spiritual stories. Naheem did 5 of the 12 tattoo's that I would get over the next month. Naheem Tattooed **Serket** on my back, **Akhenaten on my shoulder**, **Auset** on my chest, my **Leopard** on my belly, the **Ba** on my other shoulder and an **ancient name** on my arm. Kenneth Tattooed **3 ancient names** on me, my **new name** on my chest, the **Feathered Snake** on my sternum with **Heru** over it. **Kenneth** is obsessed with Aaliyah and that makes sense because I have a theory about who **Aaliyah** was in her **past life** (page 543).

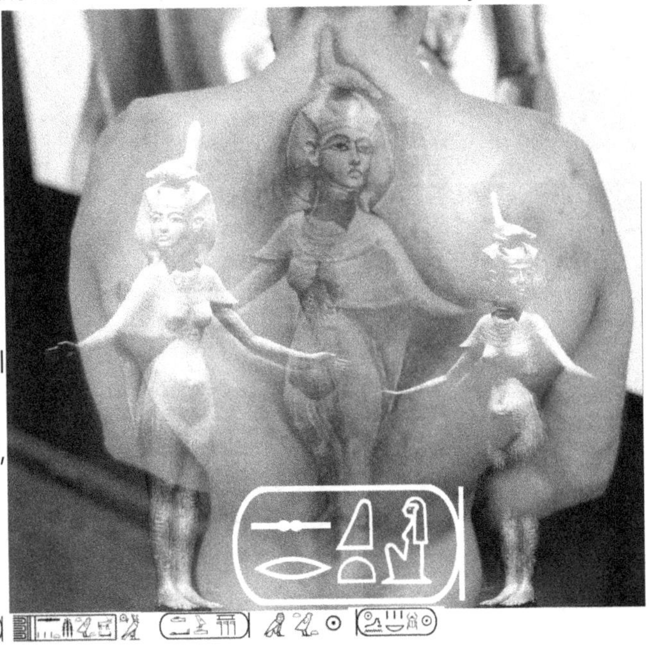

Selket / Selkis / Serqet / Serket

Selket is usually depicted as a woman with a scorpion on her head, and her name means "the one who causes the throat to breathe". She is one of the four female Goddesses (Selket, Isis, Nephthys and Neith) who protect the four cardinal points of the Nswt Bity's (Pharaoh's) royal coffins and canopic chests. She faces the **west** and is the protector of the **Falcon** headed canopic jar (Qebehsenuef) that houses the **intestines**. Duamutef, the **jackal**-headed God representing the **East**, whose jar contained the **stomach** and was protected by the Goddess **Neith**. **Imsety**, the human-headed God representing the **South**, whose jar contained the **liver** and was protected by the Goddess **Auset** (Isis). Hapi, the baboon-headed God representing the **North**, whose jar contained the **lungs** and was protected by the Goddess **Nephthys**.

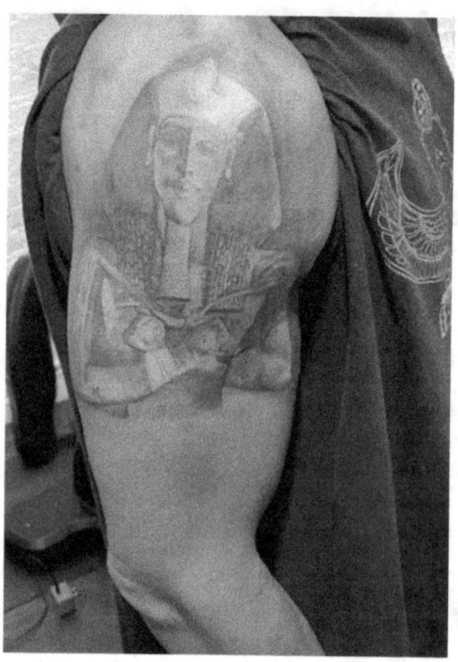

March 27th 2021
Akhenaten Tattoo

I was drunk off tattoo fever and I went out and got **Akhenaten** tatted on my right shoulder. I spoke Akhenaten's name in rhyme for the first time in 2013 the year of the **snake** on the same day that Trayvon Martin was murdered (page **23**2).

The BlaKseed Osiris
written on Feb 26th 2013 (Page 267)

"I be The BlaKseed **Osiris,** see sun set, looking for **Auset Isis,** black duality crisis, born in this white man's world to civilize it, when I think about a **king** I be thinking bout **Akhenaten"**

April 1st 2021 Thursday - 3rd Dream with TBE Floyd Mayweather and Blue Lotus

Dream

I was with **TBE Floyd Mayweather**. There was some beautiful woman trying to get my attention but I brushed her off trying to talked to Floyd. He seemed to be in a rush and was in the middle of packing as if he was about to leave. I think we were in an airport. I was telling him that I was **Tutankhaten**, he was smiling and did not fully believe me. Then I walked away, then I woke up from the dream.

Significance: This dream was similar to the dream I had with **Dr Umar** on Jan 15th 2019 (page 550). In that dream I was telling **Dr Umar** that I was **Emmett Till** in my past life but he didn't believe me. However 4 months later on May 19th 2019 (p 564) while at **Malcolm X's** annual pilgrimage to his grave-sight I would see **Dr Umar** and I would tell him about my past life revelation but he looked as if he didn't believe me. This is the same thing that happened with **TBE Mayweather** in this dream so Perhaps I am going to meet **TBE Mayweather** in the near future. Time will tell. I would go on to experience a couple more dreams with Floyd. Perhaps I was attempting to awaken my brothers in the dream realms. Perhaps that is why I dream with my brothers. Floyd is born in 19**77** the year of the **snake** like me and "Emmett Till".

Ever since I started to write this book I had not been remembering my dreams. I was spun in a whirlwind of compiling this book. Finding old spells(rhymes), dreams from my dream journal, profound events with pictures that coincide with each event then there was the task of aligning the dates of each event. Because of the nature of this book I began to desire more control of my astral body, I wanted more control of my dreams. I was on the phone with someone the other day and as the time struck **1:11:11**, I glanced left at my book shelf and my eyes fell on my jar of **Blue Lotus** flower tea. I told myself that I would start using this again. I purchased a **28**gram Bottle in late 2019 or early 2020 and had not used it more than 10 times. It was still a full jar. After being drawn to the bottle I started to eat a few pieces before I went to sleep each night. I may have started this on March 25th or 26th but it was not more than a week before April 1st. I think I missed one or two nights. None of the nights stimulated dreams. Last night (march 31st) I was up till 4:30 am writing this book and because I was up so late I laid down without taking the blue lotus and was too tired to get up and take a few pieces. Then I thought - I should still be able to activate my dreams without it. I fell asleep then I woke up the next day and remembered a dream with **TBE Floyd Mayweather**. I was happy that I remembered the dream, especially because I had not taken anything to stimulate it, just a clean thought.

Rau nu Prt m heru

Iu f Per f m heru

Utterances for Coming Forth by day into Light

It is he, who comes forth by day into Light

April 2nd 2021 - Lord of The Dreams

On April 2nd 2021 after a massage I would tell Nicholas about my book and how I come from the line of **Dukes** because my Grand Father's name was **General Dukes Jr**. Then he told me that he was a Duke too. He placed his hand in front of me flashing a ring and told me that his Grand father was a Duke too. He was wearing the ring of a **Duke**. I was astonished!

Significance

Emmett Till's body was Identified by a Silver Ring (page 512). On March 13th 2020 (p 589), I dreamt that Nicholas contacted me to work with me privately. The same day around 5pm my colleague calls to tell me that a client wants a massage, it was Nicholas. Nicholas is a professional dancer at Alvin Ailey. His favorite form of dancing is **Break dancing**. Nicholas enjoyed my massage so much that he gifted his mother, his girl friend and his roommate massages with me. Nicholas would end up taking sessions with me privately after Covid started. Nicholas was intrigued by my story about my **past life**. Because of the **scarab cuff** (p 293) that I wear he once told me about his Grand mother who took him to Egypt when he was a boy and how she had a scarab necklace. Nicholas is a White male who loves to dance and loves Hip Hop Break dancing. Hip Hop is a form of music that has crossed all barriers. If we truly desire to live out the '**dream**" of **Martin Luther King** we must all be willing to find common ground and finally close the door on racism and white supremacy. The meeting of Nicholas puts a ring on my link to royalty in Europe (pages 17, 19, 99)

Lord of The Dreams

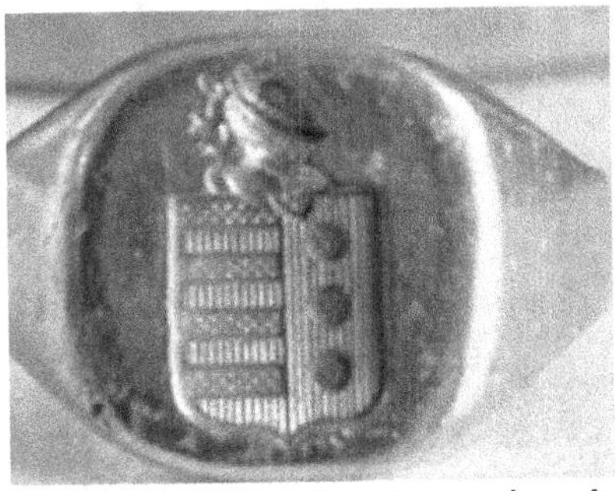

Emmett's Ring with May 25th on it can be seen on page 512. Other mysterious encounters with May 25 can be seen on pages, 30, 37, 58, 93, 104 -106, 137, 157-158, 220-222, 273, 293, 610-613, 659 and other pages.......

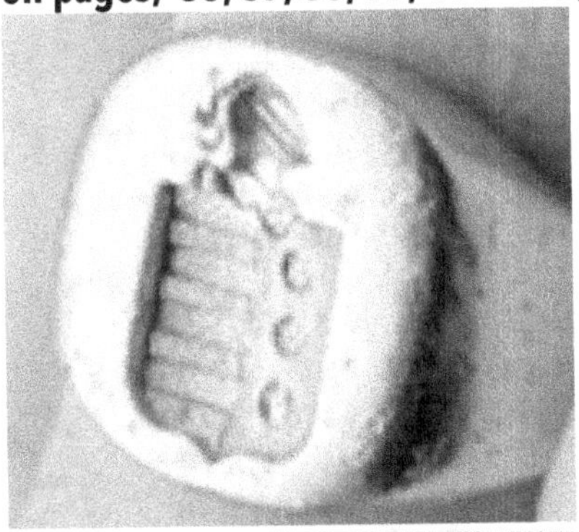

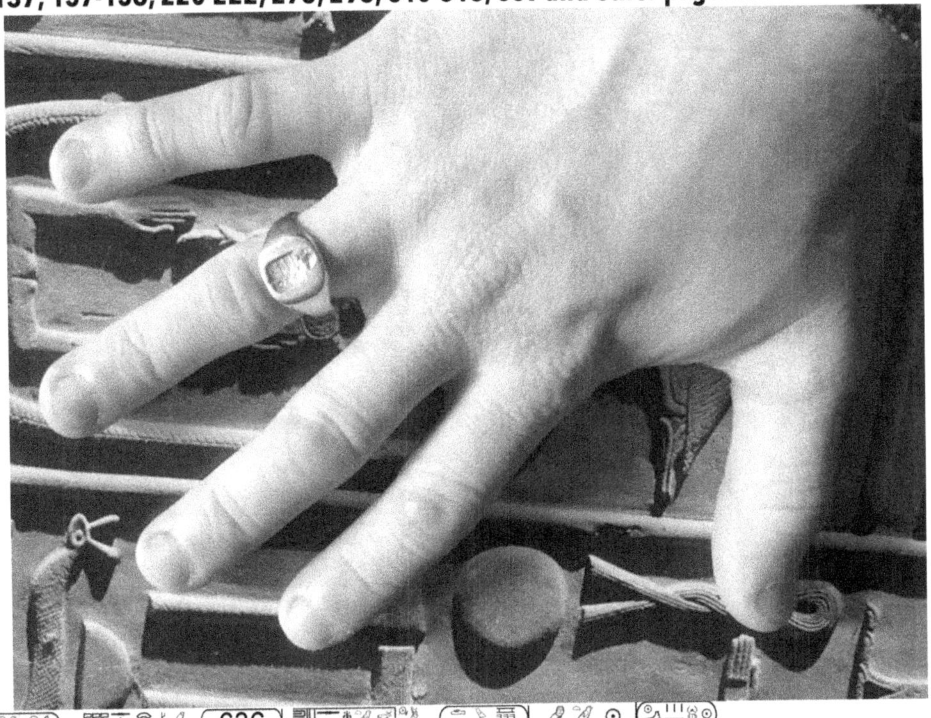

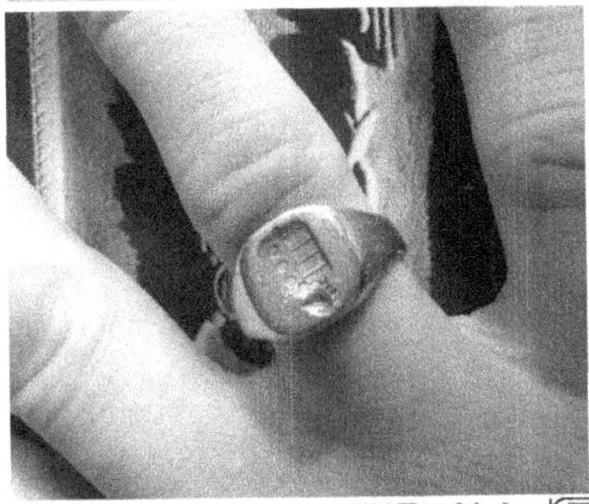

April 3rd 2021 The Pharaoh's Golden Parade

Memphis Tennessee was named after the city of **Mem**phis, the royal residence and capital of ancient Kemet (Egypt) established by the **Nswt Bity** (Pharaoh) **Memes** (Narmer). My past life of Emmett Till was revealed to me on July 3rd 2018 and my death propelled Martin Luther King to the forefront of the Civil Rights Movement. **Martin Luther King** was assassinated in Memphis Tennessee on **April 4th** 1968 (see page 69). The M**ississ**ippi **river** runs through Memphis and Emmett was thrown in a river in M**ississ**ippi just like Ausar (Osiris) was thrown in the **Nile river**. My last day in the army was Martin Luther King's birthday. 52 years after Martin's assassination my **past life** as **Tutankhaten** was revealed to me on that same day **April 4th** 2020. 5 months later in September of 2020 excavations began on a site between the temples of Ramses III and Amenhotep III near Luxor. After seven months of excavations a 3,000 year old '**lost golden city**' from the **Golden** age of the pharaohs was unearthed. Several neighborhoods were uncovered, including a bakery complete with ovens and storage pottery, administrative and residential districts as well as **scarab beetle** amulets and mud bricks bearing **Amenhotep III's** seals. The excavation team said the city "was lost under the sands and dates to the reign of Amenhotep III and continued to be used by Tutankhaten and Ay." Experts say this is presumably the largest ancient city to ever be uncovered in Egypt and is now the second most important archaeological discovery since the tomb of Tutankhaten nearly a century ago in 19**22**. 364 days after my **past life** as Tutankhaten was revealed to me, Egypt held a gala parade on Saturday, **April 3rd 2021** celebrating the transport of the mummified remains of 18 ancient Kings and 4 Queens across Cairo from the iconic Egyptian Museum to the new National Museum of Egyptian Civilization. The elaborate procession was dubbed the "Pharaohs' Golden Parade." Among the **22** bodies were those of **Iahmose Nefertari,** the wife of **Iahmose I,** the first Nswt Bity (Pharaoh) of the 18th dynasty (p 15); **Meritamun**, the wife of **Amenhotep I**; **Amenhotep III** and his wife, **Queen Tiye, Hatshepsut**; **Thutmose III**; **Ramses II**; **Ramses IX**; **Ramses VI**; **Ramses V**; **Seti I**; and **Seqenenre**. The parade was live streamed for audiences around the world to watch.

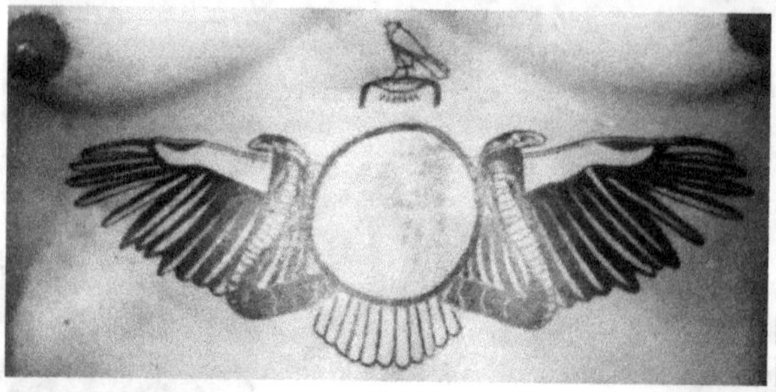

April 3rd 2021 - More Tattoos

Half way across the world there was a **Golden** Parade taking place that I was completely unaware of, yet that same day I rushed out and got 4 more Kemetic tattoos. First I got my royal name, **Tutankhaten** (in the eternal living image of Aten) tatted on my chest above my heart encircled with a shen. Then I got my new name, **TutemRa** (in the image of Ra) above it also encircled in a shen. Then I got my Thrown name, **Neb Kheperu Ra** (master of transformations of Ra) tatted on my left hand also encircled in a shen. This was the most painful tattoo so far. The last Tat that day was the **Heru Behutet** (**Feather Snake/Winged Disk)** on my sternum and just above it, I sealed it with **Heru** perched on top of the symbol for **gold**. It wasn't till days later that I realized a **Golden Parade** for my ancestors had taking place in Kemet at the same time I was getting these tattoos but it didn't surprise me.

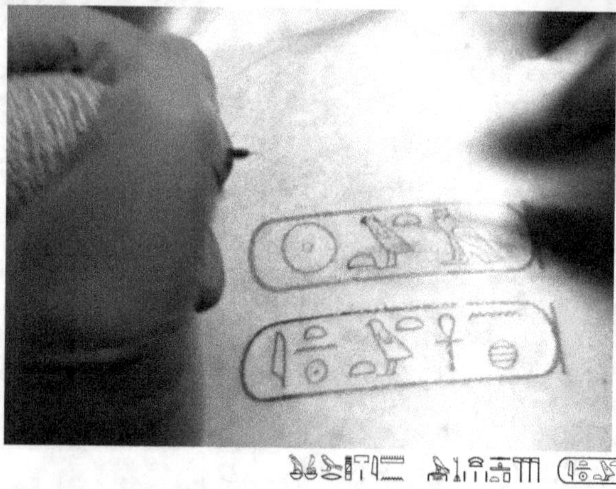

Rau nu Prt m heru

Iu f Per f m heru

Utterances for Coming Forth by day into Light

It is he, who comes forth by day into Light

Seqenenre

One of the last Nswt Bity's of the 17th dynasty, he died in battle defending the land of Kemet. He was the father of **Kamose** and **Iahmose I**.

Iahmose Nefertari

She was the first matriarch of the 18th Dynasty who lead a coalition from southern Kemet to defeat the **Hyksos** invaders. Parades were established to honor her. She extended the throne to her brother Iahmose I and was the mother of Amen Hotep I.

Iahmose Meritamun

She extended the throne to her brother Amen Hotep I. Her tomb was robbed by European invaders and her remains were discovered in 1930 the same year my grand mother was born, (p 22).

Hatshepsut (Maat Ka Ra)

She was a magnificent woman who ruled Kemet wisely, efficiently and peacefully. Representations of her leave no doubt that she was genuinely African. She sent out the great expedition to punt. She was also the wife of Thutmose II. See pages 268, 311.

Thutmose III (Men Kheper Ra)

He was the 6th Nswt Bity of the 18th dynasty and is known as the greatest Kemetic military leader par excellence. He is the real person that the biblical character King David was fashion after. See pages 225, 667.

Amenhotep III (Neb Maat Ra) and his Wife, Queen Tiye

AmenHotep III, was my ancient grandfather. He was known as the **Dazzling Sun** and AmenHotep the Magnificent. There are more surviving statues of him than any other Nswt Bity, with over 250 being found. His throne name was Neb Maat Ra. His greatest achievement was his ability to rule for around 40 years without war, as he honored the principles of **Maat** and practiced excellent diplomacy allowing kemet to reach the peak of its artistic and international power leading to a period of unparalleled prosperity and opulence. He commissioned the largest Meta-Spiritual Device (Temple) of that time. Today the only remnants of this Temple are two imposing statues of him, erroneously known as the Colossus of **Memnon** (p 356). AmenHotep III is the real person that the biblical character King Solomon was fashion after and my grand mother Queen Tiye, is the real person that the biblical character Queen Sheba was fashion after. See pages 7, 58, 210, 389, 469.

Seti I (Men Maat Ra)

He was the second Nswt Bity to rule the 19th dynasty. He was the son of Ramses I and Sitre and the father of Ramses II (**The Great**).

Ramses II (Usr Maat Ra Setep en Ra)

He was a great military leader and is often regarded as one of the greatest builder without an equal in the then known world and even still to this day.

April 7th 2021 - Auset, 2 Live 4

On April 7th I went to get two more tatts. First I got **Auset tatted on my chest**. Initially I also wanted the words, **2 Live 4** with the name Auset in Mdw Ntr (hieroglyphs) next to Auset's face but Naheem wanted to charge hundreds of dollars extra so I decided to just get the face. Then I got the **golden Leopard** on my lower abdomen. The Leopard face was the most painful tattoo I ever got. Two days later the Auset tattoo had an allergic reaction. A month after it healed I went back on May 14 and Naheem fixed the tattoo and added the words **2 Live 4** with the name **Auset** in Mdw Ntr. The numbers **2** and **4** are connected to **Rosa Parks** who is born on February 4 (**2/4**). Rosa Parks is born the day after my mother (p 27) and she passed away on October 24, the day before my birthday. **Rosa Parks** refused to give her seat to a white man because of the murder of **Emmett Till** (p 518). Her actions helped spark the Civil Rights Movement (p 519).

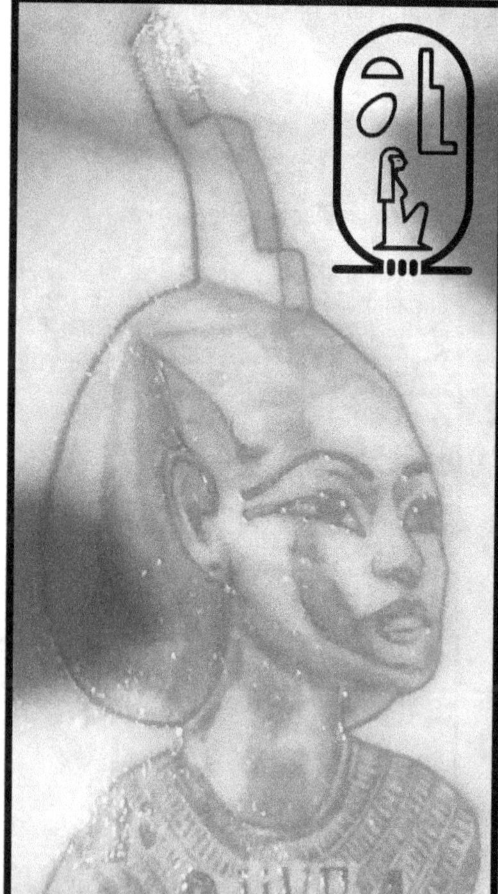

Rau nu Prt m heru

Iu f Per f m heru

Utterances for Coming Forth by day into Light

April 9th 2021 - R.I.P. DMX

ADDENDUM

My experience with **DMX** might sound **strange** to most people but death is not the end! Many people can tell you about having experiences with their loved ones shortly after they have "died", like seeing them in **dreams**, or smelling their scent and even seeing their spirits. In fact, DMX's long time friend **Swizz Beatz** had a **dream** that DMX came to him in a **dream** and told him he was ok. After his dream he would go outside and see an **X** in the sky, apparently left by **two planes**. I'm sure his family and other close friends have had or will have experiences with his spirit in **dreams** or **apparitions**, no different than my experience with my grand father's spirit (p 348) or the experiences the family and friends of **Kilindi Iyi** had (page 606, 618). Death is not the end! The body may be rendered unusable but the soul is immortal. I got the news that **DMX** (the **Dog** of Hip Hop) died while I was at a vegan restaurant in Harlem. I had been rooting for him to pull through so his death saddened me! While riding home on my bicycle **I heard his voice** in my head that said - "**LOOK ON THAT TABLE**".
I stopped my bike immediately and looked at a table where a brother was vending on 125th street. The first thing I saw on his table was the 1st season of **Lost**. This was not "just some coincidence" as I had been recently looking for the series to watch again because while writing this book all of my **synchronicities** reminded me of the series **Lost**.
I purchased the 1st season of **Lost** Immediately, for **$5** dollars from a brother named **Lani**. Months later on another occasion Lani would stare at me with amazement claiming that he saw Enpu (Anubis) standing over my shoulder. To understand more of what happened here you must go back and read what I wrote about the series **Lost** (p 259).
I once met **DMX** on 125th street, less than a block away from where I heard his voice! The year must have been 2014 or 2015, he was with a woman who was in a store purchasing hair. I gave him a pound but now I wish I had taken a picture like the other people had done. DMX was my friend Patrick's favorite artist in high school (p 66) but I would not come to appreciate him till years later. You know somebodies your "dog"when they holler at you after death! **DMX** is a real **ride or die** ryder, **A RUFF RYDER!** As soon as I got home I started watching Lost. I finished the first season then signed up for Hulu and continued to watch the whole series. As I watched the series I realized that it was all based on the **afterlife** and there was a lot of ancient Kemetic (Egyptian) spiritual elements written into the series and **Enpu** (**Anubis**) the **dog** headed "God" of mummification was a major part of the series. **DMX,** who is the **dog** of Hip Hop led me to a series that is based on the principles of **afterlife** and the **dog** headed God **Anubis** from Kemet. On June 5th I would meet a brother in Harlem (p 647) who was from the same part of Queens I'm from and after meeting him I would be summoned back to Far Rockaway Queens. On **June 23rd 2021**, I would experience a profound series of events that were intertwined with the Series **Lost** which left me mind blown (p 648). The universe was indeed talking to me! It was as if I was being stalked by the unseen realms. Then on **July 7th** (p 651) and **July 16th** (p 652) I would have two more experiences in Far Rockaway at the beach with two women whom carried very telling star code patterns. There was a message being coded to me from my ancestral fathers.

"and when I see **DMX** you know a prayer's gonna follow, cause what I see is my brother there fighting for his survival, the rifle - back against the wall shit that I do, each one reach one teach one like the gospel" **- Dawud (These many Roads,** written on January 7th 2010, page 195)

"when **DMX** died his soul came did me a favor, whispered in my ear said go ye there look through them papers! **Anubis** and the **afterlife** advice watch for them gators, **Maat** is precise in your life! you gotta watch your behavior!" **- TutemRa (Doors,** written on August 22nd 2021, page 658)

Condolences

My condolences go out to the family, friends and fans of **Earl Simmons**. Please know that death is not the end. The soul survives death, indeed and in spirit. This is a book of the dead written by a boy who was murdered without justice, who defeated death and came forth by day. May the soul of **Earl Simmons** walk peacefully through the field of Reeds in Amenta. Amen Ra.

It is he, who comes forth by day into Light

April 10th 2021 - I have a Dream

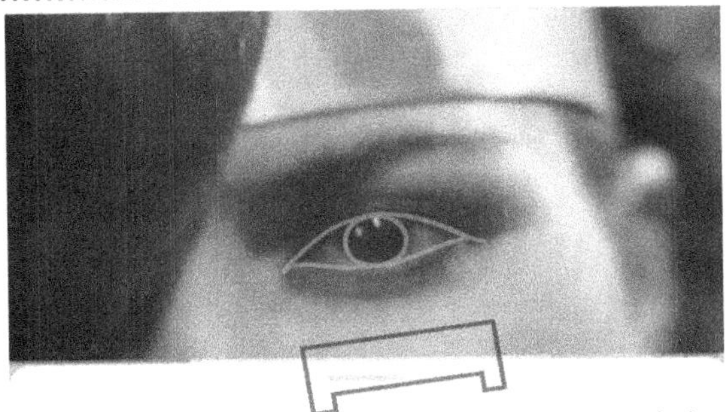

I met a woman in Harlem at a store that had the number **22** as it's address. Her and I would become friends and on April 10th she appeared in my dream. In my dream I was in a pool with many women and we were all pleasing each other. At some point I was in a bed alone, then the woman I met at the store appeared and laid next to me, she gave me a hug then I woke up. As I was awakening I could hear the song, **I Wonder If I Take You Home,** by Lisa Lisa, playing through my window. My neighbors were blasting the song. I had not heard the song in a long time so I laid there and listened to it. When the song went off I searched the song on youtube so I could listen to it again. To my surprise I noticed that the video I chose to watch was uploaded on my birthday. Lisa Lisa was born on January 15th, **Martin Luther King's birthday** and she is **55** years old right now (February 22nd 2022 - **2/22/2022**).

In the summer of 2018 (page 531) I met a woman named **Zawadi** at the corner of Fredrick Douglass and 145th street. A feeling came over me leading me to hand her my card. I gave her a card for my group fitness class that I held in Jackie Robinson park. She came to one or two classes then she moved down south and I didn't hear from her again till March of 2021.

In March of 2021 I got a text from her asking if I did online training. Soon after she joined my online group fitness class for women. On April 15th 2021 I sent her a text complimenting her about her performance in class that day. She thanked me then she asked if she had told me that she was a **medium**.. I said no, then I told her that I have been attracting those types of **divine feminine** energies. That's when she told me that **she felt my energy when we first met** and that she saw a **bright light** around me the day we met in 2018. I asked her what color the light was and she said **gold**. Then I sent her the pictures of me and Tutankhaten (**King Tut)** showing our likeness and told her about my **past lives** as **King Tut** and **Emmett Till**. She was amazed. I asked her how often does she see **light** around people and she replied - "usually when someone is supposed to be on my path - **they*** will reveal them to me - there will be a **light,** but it's not always **golden**. The colors vary but it's usually **white**. I could tell you are **royal**, since it was **gold**". When I heard that it made me feel good. I don't see colors around people so when I hear other people reveal their gifts I always find it interesting. On April 17th at 11:22 AM she told me that she wanted me to get an **IFA** reading from her because she wondered what **they*** would see. Then she told me it was **Oshun** that was claiming me the day that we met in 2018. On **April 19th** she told me that the **spirits** told her that it was ok for her to come see me and that she must read me. I told her I would think about it. She told me that she felt like there was a message that I needed to receive.

On April 22nd 2021 she came to my place and she gave me my first and only **IFA** reading. Before we started she said there were MANY entities in my space competing for position. She did some ceremonial preparation pouring of **libation** and **smudging** then she placed **shells** on the floor. Then she closed her eyes and they remained closed for most of the reading. Her body began to jerk uncontrollably sort of the way my body jerked after my **Bufo** experience. When she spoke it was in a mans voice. If I had not already had many of the experiences with spirits I may not have believed what I experienced this day. When the entity in her began to speak to me I was roused with emotions. I almost cried several times but I had no time to cry I had to copy as much as I could. The entity speaking through her did not reveal his real name. He told me many things some of which I will not share. But he told me of previous lives I have lived. I once lived as a prince. I once navigated the seas when men first sailed the seas. I was told that I once mapped out the continent of Africa in a previous life. I once tracked the star patterns in the heavens. He told me that I am fascinated by the lives I have uncovered but I must get past that because more lives will come. He told me that I must pick a side because many entities want to persuade me. He said many Generals, warriors and those who have been wronged want vengeance for the murder and rape of our people. I asked if my Grandfather was there and he said yes but there are so many other people that he can't get to the front. After the reading was over she told me that my space was clear and all the entities had left. That night I would dream of my Grandfather.

Rau nu Prt m heru

Iu f Per f m heru

Utterances for Coming Forth by day into Light

It is he, who comes forth by day into Light

April 23rd 2021 (Dream with my Grandfather, General Dukes Jr.)

I was walking in a driveway with my Grandfather and behind us was a stage. On the stage rappers were rapping with negative lyrics. As I walked with my Grandfather he asked me if the **music** had to be so violent. Then I woke up.

Significance

This dream came the night after I had my first and only **IFA** reading. This would be the first time that my grandfather spoke to me in a dream. In the reading the day prior I had asked if my Grandfather was there in my studio with all the other ancestral spirits and I was told he was but he could not get through the crowd to speak to me. This dream was a message from my grand father to the musicians of the world. (**see page 6**). See page **648** for the **metaphysical significance of the number 23**.

April 24th 2021 Infinities

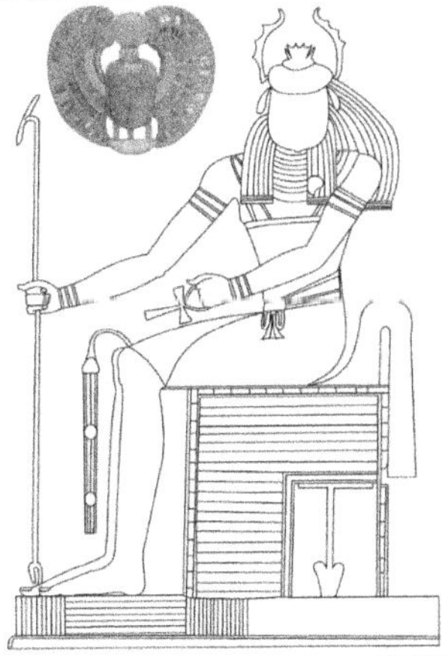

I rolled it up in a ball then rolled it to the sun, then dug a hole in the dirt and it was **"Hard work", Neb kheperu Ra** he sailed to see the sun, the one to come will **rise** in the **west** rebirth is **"Hard work",** Resurface, earth is a place of rehearses, die then be **born again**, ignorance is **"Hard work", Anakin Skywalker**, the spine of **Ausar**, **flying saucer**, wanna live forever like fame? It's gonna be **"Hard work",** They wrapped me up with all my fancy amenities, then said a spell so I could live for infinities, the book of the dead was read by the divinities, never had a friend like me, when we ride on our enemies, Thutmose be the curse, Jhutyms be the first, Scorpion sting sting worse with a big booty nurse, my bling bling looted like **Tulsa** ending on June 1st, King king Kong too strong put in that **"Hard work" - TutemRa**

Significance

Written to the **Stic** track - **Put in the Work**, off the album **Workout II**

April 28th 2021 - Kalishea, The Ba and the Soul of her grand mother

On April **28th** I got a tattoo of bird with a human head on my left shoulder. When Kalishea saw my tattoos on Instagram she called me and asked me about them. Then she pointed out the fact that the **Ba** (bird) looked like her and immediately I agreed, I had not previously noticed that but it does look just like her. Kalishea is born on June 15th, the day before **Tupac's** birthday and she has a son named **Honor** born on October 24th 2016 the day before my birthday. In 2020 I would tell Kalishea about my **past life** as **Tutankhaten** and she would show me a card that she had kept since 2010 (page 199) . A card promoting the **King Tut** exhibit where 50 of King Tut's treasures had been shown from April **23rd** till December 17th of 2010 at the Discovery Times Square Exposition (See page **648** for the **metaphysical significance of the number 23)**. At this time we had not seen each other in over 7 years. On July 18th of 2021 Kalishea attempted to drive to NY from Philly to see me but every route she took was stopped by police road blocks due to rain flooding. After an hour of driving she finally turned around and went home. When she got home and went to exit her car she looked on the passenger seat and saw a **golden** Scarab **Beetle**. She claims that she has never seen a scarab like that in her life. King Tut's throne name was Neb Kheperu Ra. Kheperu is the Egyptian name for scarab. The year after my past life revelation of **Emmett** and a year before my past life revelation of **King Tut** I would have a series of profound experiences with the same type of Scarab Dung Beetles at the 2019 International African Arts Festival (page 569). Afterwards I would realize that scarabs had a deeper meaning in ancient Kemet (Egypt). They represented resurrection, rebirth, reincarnation and were the first, "only begotten God". When Kalishea saw the tattoo she felt it looked like her and to my surprise it did. When Kalishea was 16 she was laying in the bed crying because she was 16 and pregnant. Her grandmother was sick with **cancer** and she felt that she had let her grand mother down. At that moment all she wanted to hear was her grandmothers voice. Then to her amazement the **astral body** (the **ba**) of her grand mother floated through the ceiling and stood over her and said, "I'm sorry baby". Then she floated away. Kalishea picked up the phone to call her grandmother only to find out that she had just passed away. She had just gone west….

May 2nd 2021
Meta Mysterious Encounter in The Fourth Dimension
Jasmin's Golden Dream

ADDENDUM

Assata Shakur was sentenced to life in prison on May 2nd 1977 **The Year Of The Snake** and **Afeni Shakur** transitioned on May 2nd 2016 (page 381-382). On May 2nd 2013 **The Year Of The Snake,** Assata Shakur would be placed back on the F.B.I. Most Wanted List.

Jasmin is **Egyptian, Palestinian** and **German** . If you read the beginning of this book you saw that I left Germany in 2003 (page 95 and 105) and after that I never saw Jasmin again however I was able to audio chat with her via Instagram direct message. On May 2nd 2021 Jasmin would detail the events of a dream she had about me as a **Golden** Pharaoh. I reached out to her because I was contemplating the purpose of our meeting after writing about my accident in which she was there to witness, I began to wonder about how she was doing. I hoped that all was well with her. I went looking for her page on Instagram. I wanted to share my story with her, and tell her about my book and go over the events of my crash. ***ADDENDUM* In 2023, Jasmin saw the tattoo of Serket on my back (page 634), she had never seen Serket before, however she said that this is the person she saw in her dream!** Below is the transcribed portion of my audio conversation with Jasmim.

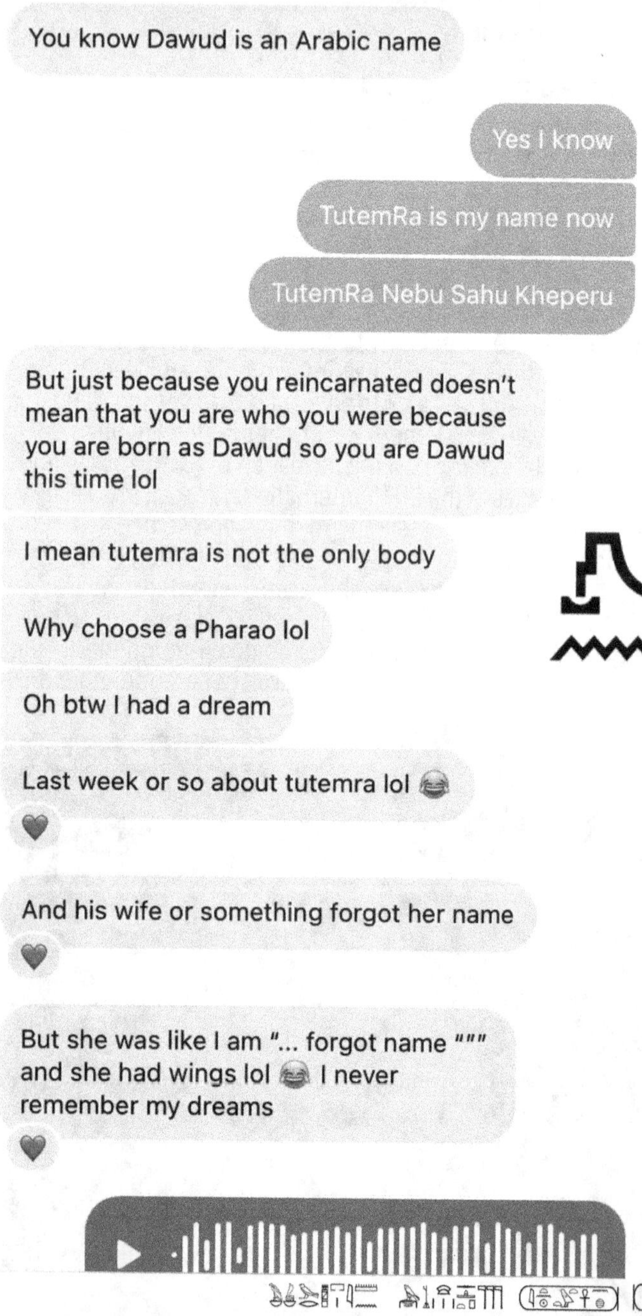
You know Dawud is an Arabic name
Yes I know
TutemRa is my name now
TutemRa Nebu Sahu Kheperu
But just because you reincarnated doesn't mean that you are who you were because you are born as Dawud so you are Dawud this time lol
I mean tutemra is not the only body
Why choose a Pharao lol
Oh btw I had a dream
Last week or so about tutemra lol 😂
And his wife or something forgot her name
But she was like I am "... forgot name """ and she had wings lol 😂 I never remember my dreams

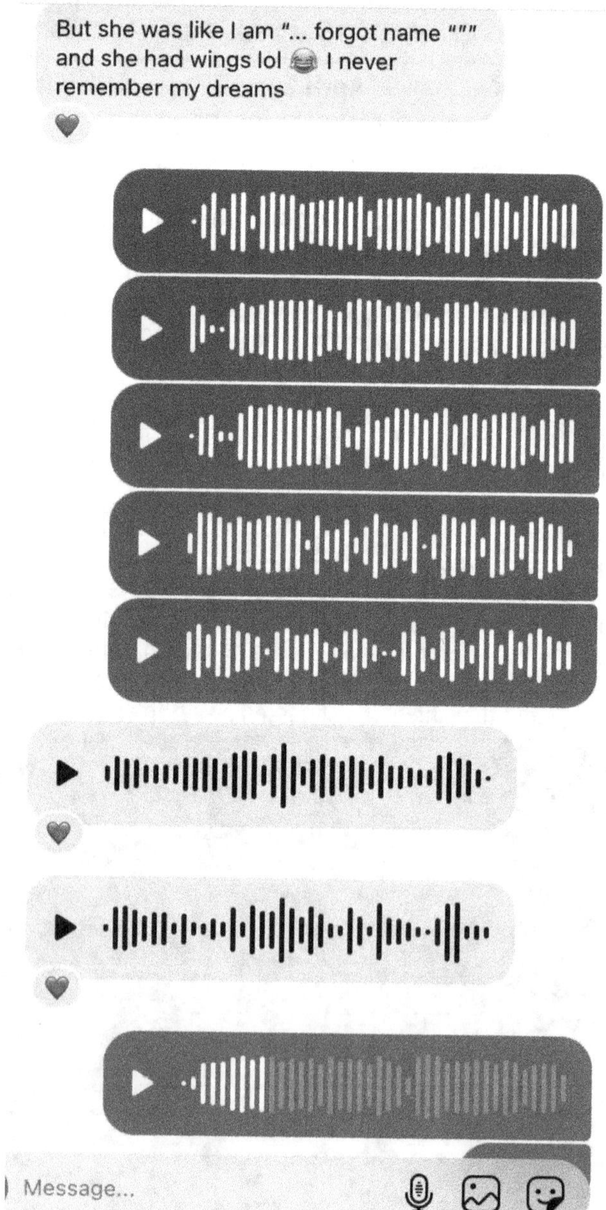
But she was like I am "... forgot name """ and she had wings lol 😂 I never remember my dreams
Message...

Transcribed Portion of audio conversation with Jasmin

Rau nu Prt m heru

Iu f Per f m heru

Utterances for Coming Forth by day into Light

It is he, who comes forth by day into Light

Jasmin - I don't remember much but there was this **Queen**, -laughs- this **Egyptian Queen Goddess** or whatever -laughs- who told me who she was and some other crazy shit, but anyways I'm going into the grocery store.

Dawud - Take 30 seconds and tell me everything from the dream please. Was the woman's name **Ankhesenamun** cause that was her name or **Ankhesenaten**?!

Jasmin - -*laughs*- I have no idea what her name was cause it was a complicated name just like the one you just said, I don't know what that name, I don't remember. It was just ,it was in a, look! I only had that dream cause we talked about this the same day ok?! Um no I don't remember details but I woke up after it and it was like 3am in the morning or something and I couldn't go back to sleep that's why I remember the dream. -*Takes a deep breath*- um what, what was it? I don't know, all I remember is it was a **Gold** um, inside a, um inside a, -*confused*- I don't know, um a a building, but it was it was a dream ok?! It was like um, something and then something **and she came with her wings and said that she is her and that she is me** -*laughs*- that I am her, whatever!

Jasmin - Before that, I don't remember what happened in the dream, I just knew it was the wife of you -*laughs*- but it's only because we were talking about this on that day, yeah?! I am sure! And you were in the dream too but you were really evil, like, you you had like a evil, you were not nice! You were evil, not evil as of evil but like I mean? Like um, not evil, I don't know, I can't say that, it wasn't evil it was just not pleasant, not a pleasant um, aura, you were like a bad king or something -*laughs*- oh God -*laughs*-

Dawud - So basically, you're telling me you never remember your dreams, then you speak to a dude you used to care for very much, who you're born on his grand mothers birthday, who had a accident and survived that his sister dreamt it before it happened, he comes and tells you that he's a pharaoh from ancient times and then you don't remember your dreams -but! - You have a dream that night of a **pharaoh**, a **Queen**, in all **gold** telling you her name and telling you that she's you. And you don't understand the potential of -*laughs*- of that dream? See here's the thing, um, all the women that I ever met in my life, not all of them but many of them are connected to me in certain ways, and we don't live just one time Jasmin you know? We don't just live one time you know so this is the one life that we are living right now but we've lived before. Potentially you and I have known each other before.

Jasmin - But literally the only thing I can remember is that scene when she's telling me I'm her -*laughs*- I know I dreamed that because of you because we talked about that?! It's not like I'm her!

Dawud - Ok yeah it's not like you're her, you, you only had that dream cause we talked about it. But I'm gonna tell you, you got married had kids, I ran the world, never had children and then I took the spiritual path the same way I took the other things in my life, and many things started to materialize you know? seeing ghosts', having dreams with people, we both coming back remembering the dream, **astral traveling**, floating out of my body, many types of different things I experienced in my life because I didn't have children and responsibilities like that, So I'm telling you that dreams are not just "dreams" my friend. They're deeper than just a dream.

Jasmin - Yeah I know that's all a part of the game, you know, play the game on earth whatever -*laugh*- um learn whatever your soul has to learn on earth I guess.

Dawud - Thank you for taking the time to do that , thank you so much. Danke.

Jasmin - Yeah I know I know and I don't really, I don't remember my dreams, I only remember important things, like weird dreams, like that, -*laughs*- that's what I remember -*laughs*- um like every, twice a year maybe. Yeah, I don't know what I wanted to say? Yeah I don't know, you probably opened all your chakras whatever -*laughs*-, I opened my hand chakra by the way um, and I have power in my hands, -*laughs*-

Jasmin - Yeah seriously I have power in my hands, I've been manifesting a lot of stuff.......

May 12th 2021 - Nebu Kheperu

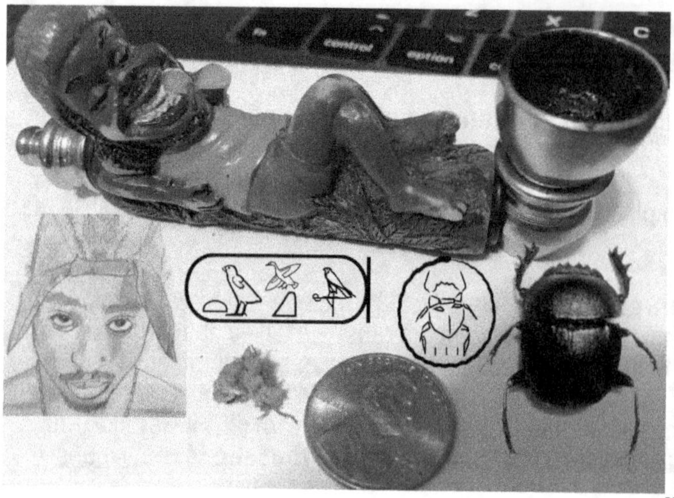

I'm not sure the exact day that I drew this logo but it was in the beginning of the month of May and the oldest picture of it was taken on May 12th. I was creating a logo for a **clothing line** I wanted to launched called **Nebu Kheperu** (The **Golden** Beetle). I was inspired by an image I found online of my (Tutankhaten's) gilded shrine. The image fascinated me. It was a snake swallowing it's own tail like the necklace that the **hero** from the movie **The Never Ending Story** was given when he started his hero's journey quest to find the princess (see page 3 for my **hero's journey**). I drew the snake swallowing it's tail first, then I started drawing the beetle encircled within the snake then I took one **very small puff** of weed from my little bong. Very soon after, the **thought** came to make the **beetle** the **face** of **Tupac** with the legs as the bandanna. I used the picture I drew of Tupac in 2002 as a reference (page 111). I stress the point of only **ingesting a very small amount of weed** because I think people are abusing the sacred medicines. Anything in excess can be damaging. Even too much water can kill you. When I was done with the logo I sent the image to my friend **Godfrey** and he took my drawing and created my logo. Some time in June of 2022 I completed the logo on my own.. The image of a snake swallowing it's own tail is called a **Ouroboros**. The ouroboros symbol embodies **rebirth**, **eternity**, self-reliance, **immortality** with the shedding of new skin, and natures' **cyclic** character (**Wehem Mesut**, P 14). The snake eating its own tail is among the most prominent ancient symbols found in the history of different cultures, religions, and civilizations. The **oldest** known Ouroboros was found in 19**22** in circular form on the second gilded shrine in the tomb of Tutankhaten. Two ouroboros's can be seen on the shrine, one is circling the head and the other circles the feet of the pharaoh who is seen in Ausarian mummified form.

High Frequency Psychic Channels

I don't commune with the sacred Marijuana plant any more because of all the hazards surrounding the plant. I don't think any of the sacred medicines are designed to be taken everyday and if they are used everyday I don't think they should be taken in such high doses regularly. There needs to be time spent applying what the medicines teach. When I first smoked weed I opened up **High Frequency Psychic Channels** (perhaps from the akashic records), where messages were channeled down through my thoughts just like this logo. I smoked weed in 2012 (p 227) and it opened a channel/portal for a thought about **souls returning from the dead** and I **thought** it was an idea for a movie but it was actually a message about my reincarnation. The fact that I had indeed died many times and **COME BACK** again many times! It is not about how much you know, it's about how much you desire to know. It's about where your heart is. All actions are measured by the matters of the heart. These spiritual **messages** are **received through the heart**. If your desire is right and exact you can attract the information or situation you earn. This is the ancient Kemetic (Egyptian) principle of divine thought and divine wisdom governed by the Deity (God) **Jehuti** also known as **Tehuti** or **Hermes** or **Thoth** (divine **thought**).

The 7 hermetic principles are:

mentalism, **correspondence**, **vibration**, **polarity**, **rhythm**, **cause vs effect** and **gender**.

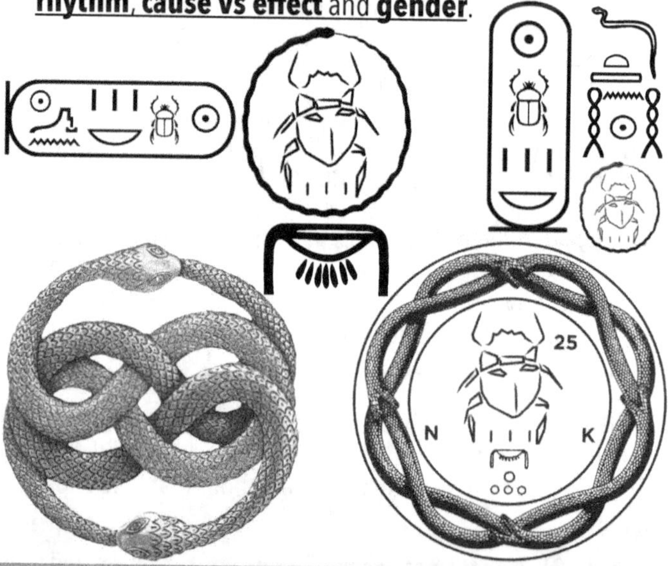

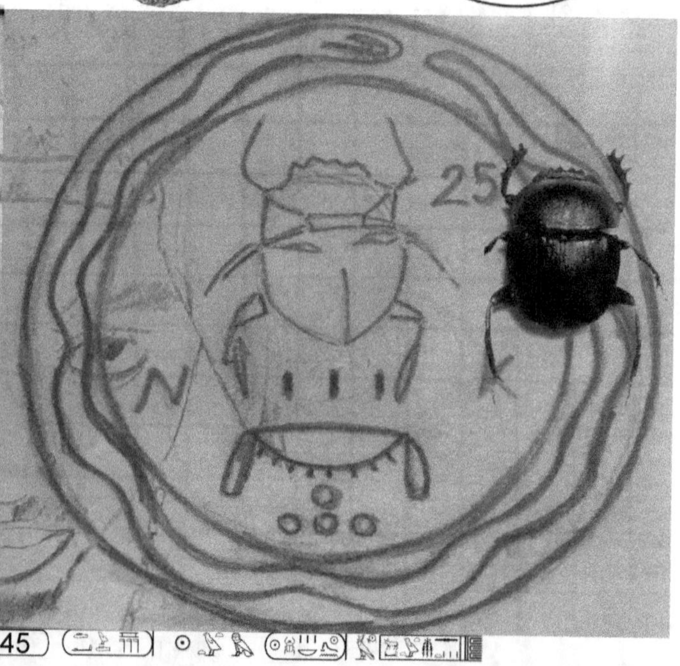

My Brothers from D.R.

There is a **Dominican** brother who works at the barber shop near me. Him and I would wave at each other when ever I passed the window. One day I saw that he had a hat on with **King Tut's gold mask** on it. I went into the shop and asked him where he purchased it and he told me his friend made them. I told him that I would like to buy one and he told me that he would get another one from his friend. Time went by and he was not able to get a hat. One day I showed him the pictures of me and Tut and told him that I was Tut in a past life. He looked a the pictures and looked at me with amazement, then he took the hat off his head and gave it to me. It's currently my favorite hat. I know another **Dominican** Barber named **Moses** who cuts hair on 145th street. He is born on August 14th, the day the Haitian Revolution was planned. **Moses** knows that the Haitians are his brothers and sisters and considers Himself an Afro Dominican like my friend Neo Nefertari (page **23**3).

Rau nu Prt m heru

Iu f Per f m heru

NeferNeferuAten

Akhenaten's 4th daughter, Madam C.J. Walker

Utterances for Coming Forth by day into Light

I met Nef on Instagram, and she feels she is my ancient sister Neferneferuaten, the 4th daughter of Akhenaten. I can not confirm this but the **coincidences** surrounding how I met her were very interesting. She also has an affinity for Madam C.J. Walker. Because of the nature of who I was in my past lives and the course I have taken in this life, I have attracted the souls of other people who have been here before, like **Mambo, The Reincarnated World War 1 veteran** (pages 151, 407), and **The Reincarnation** of **Dejazmatch Beru,** (page 390) and others. Even with this being true I do not "be**lie**ve" every person that comes to me claiming to be people from the past especially those who claim to be "pharaohs". Mainly because I have met too many people who claim to be the same person (page 8), not to mention all the men who claim to be me, Tutankhaten. With all that said, the circumstances surrounding the meeting of Nef were very interesting. But as I said before, I can not and do not claim to be the knower of other peoples souls. I like Nef and I think she is having a divine experience governed by the spirits of Nefertiti and Akhenaten. Nef had a **dream** about me in the beginning of December 2021.

Nefer's Dream

It is he, who comes forth by day into Light

In the dream she asked me if the book I was holding was the book I was writing and I said yes. The book was large with old pages and looked like an ancient artifact, like the first copy of the bible. It was inclosed in a **golden** glass case. She says I seemed to be very happy in the dream and my face looked like the faces seen in the typical art of the 18th dynasty with big eyes.

June 5th 2021 - Mathew, Meta Mysterious Encounters

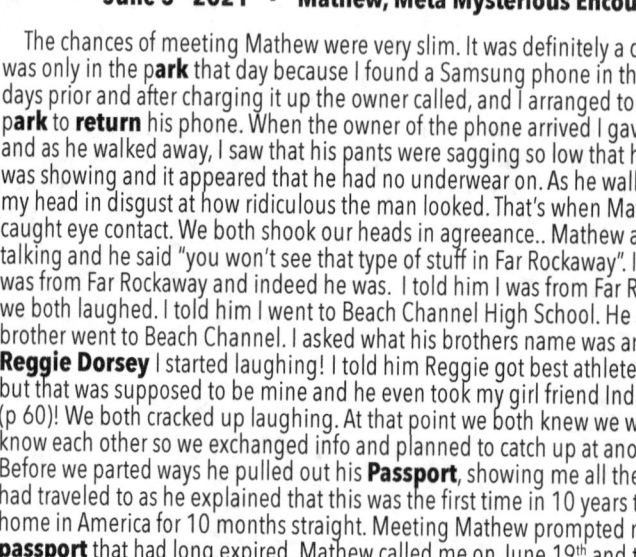

The chances of meeting Mathew were very slim. It was definitely a divine meeting! I was only in the p**ark** that day because I found a Samsung phone in the p**ark** a few days prior and after charging it up the owner called, and I arranged to meet him in the p**ark** to **return** his phone. When the owner of the phone arrived I gave him his phone and as he walked away, I saw that his pants were sagging so low that half of his butt was showing and it appeared that he had no underwear on. As he walked away I shook my head in disgust at how ridiculous the man looked. That's when Mathew and I caught eye contact. We both shook our heads in agreeance.. Mathew and I started talking and he said "you won't see that type of stuff in Far Rockaway". I asked him if he was from Far Rockaway and indeed he was. I told him I was from Far Rockaway. Then we both laughed. I told him I went to Beach Channel High School. He said his older brother went to Beach Channel. I asked what his brothers name was and when he said **Reggie Dorsey** I started laughing! I told him Reggie got best athlete in the year book but that was supposed to be mine and he even took my girl friend Indira to the prom (p 60)! We both cracked up laughing. At that point we both knew we were supposed to know each other so we exchanged info and planned to catch up at another time. Before we parted ways he pulled out his **Passport**, showing me all the countries he had traveled to as he explained that this was the first time in 10 years that he'd been home in America for 10 months straight. Meeting Mathew prompted me to renew my **passport** that had long expired. Mathew called me on June 19th and told me he was in the p**ark** on 135th street in Harlem so I went to meet him (p 647). On the way to

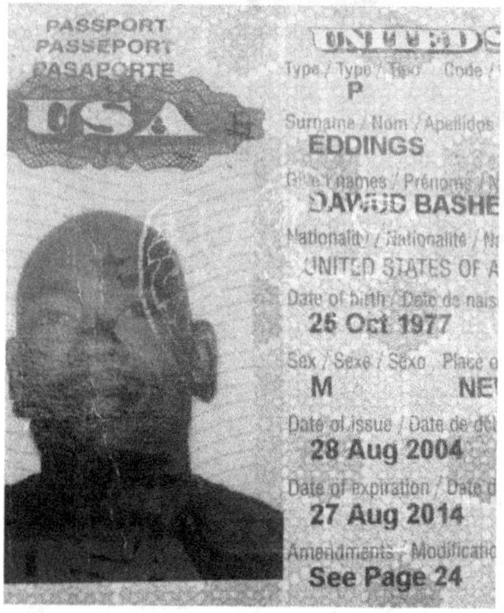

meet Mathew <u>the universe spoke to me as I passed random people</u>, then fate would bring a sign from **Nefertiti** (p 647). I would see Mathew again on June **23rd** (p 648) and that meeting would prove to be extraordinary with spiritual messages sent from **Auset**, the wife of **Ausar** (the Lord of **Resurrection**), this experience would leave a lasting effect on Mathew. In the bible, **Matthew** is one of the **12 disciples of Jesus** and because of the magical events that Mathew has experienced with me he knows my story of my past life as Emmett Till and Tutankhaten (King Tut) to be true of voice, and it has inspired him to make positive changes in his life. I would be remised if I did not point out the fact that the profound events that took place between the pages 647 and 653 may not have happened if I had not decided to <u>**return** the phone that I found</u> and I would not have had the **passport** needed to take my trip to Kemet (p 670)! When I got my new **passport** I was amazed when I saw that my old passport had expired on **August 27th** 2014, and was issued to me on **August 28th** 2004. Emmett Till was murdered on **August 28th** 1955 and **Ausar** (Osiris) reigned for **28 years** in the **Ausarian resurrection** drama... I met Mathew because I decided to **return*** the phone. He was in the p**ark** that day. He sp**ark**ed me to get my passport and because of him I went to the beach and had many profound experiences (p 648-653) and because of him I went to Kemet. I met a brother named Mathew and **in the book of Matthew, Jesus** is speaking about **reincarnation** (p 592). This is the Law of **Karma** in real time, **cause and effect**. The decisions we make at every junction in our lives effect the outcome of our lives. Make sure that your actions are always aligned and balanced with **MAAT**. Everything **Maatt**ers. **(42 Laws of Maat, Page 367)**

June 14th 2021 Catch 22 = (page 40)

It's not that I'm writing a book, I'm just putting things in order, like **Shook** in 95 - recorded in 94, have you ever had **DeJa Vu?** this is nothing knew I've seen this before! catch **22**, I was walking out the store, they say I **whistled** but for what they not really sure, I ate the bread the color was hoar, here to restore **Maat**; you forgot who got the props, they process the poor, so the poor soul get's lost in lure and lust on this ball of confusion, look at the score it's us, we down! **1921 sun down towns**, they said a change gonna come until then don't come around, so we went and found happiness health excitement, then they burnt it down cause they don't got love or enlightenment, <u>**and the question now is, at what time am I writing this?** there might exist a space and time on some **psychic** shit</u>, **Amen Atum Aten**, never to be forgotten, from **Neb Kheperu Ra**, to slave fields pick'n cotton, from **Emmett Till** getting killed thrown in a river rotten, like **Ausar** I came back as **Dawud, TutemRa - TutemRa**

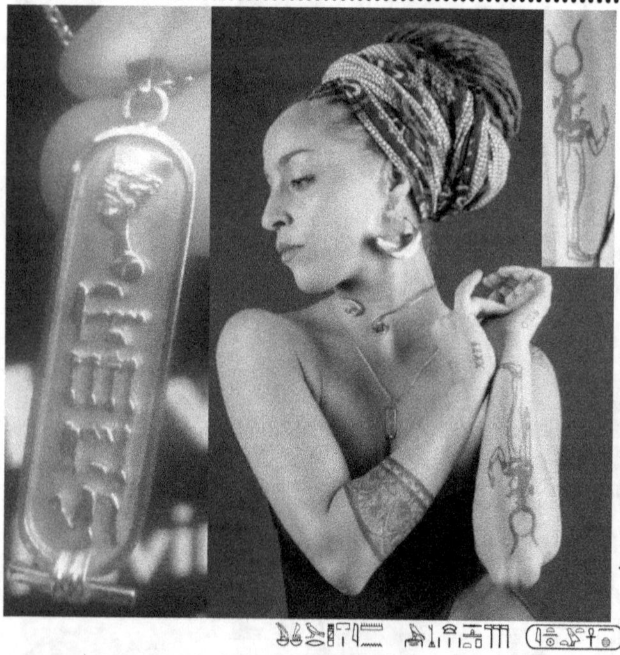

June 19th 2021
Meta Spiritual Encounters walking to St Nicholas Park

Mathew was back in Harlem at an event in St Nicholas P**ark**, on 135th street. I was on my way home from grabbing food from Seasoned Vegan when he invited me so I stopped by.. I had my bike but for some reason I had decided to walk for a bit. While waiting for the light to change on 128th street and St Nicholas, I over heard the conversation of two Black women talking. One woman says "my baby just graduated and she starts college on **August 28th**". I found that **strange** because that's the day Emmett was murdered and **Ausar** reigned for **28** years in the **Ausarian resurrection** drama. I knew it meant something but I crossed the street and continued to the p**ark**. No more then 10 steps after I crossed the street did I pass some old men sitting on benches, and one man says "I was out at Rockaway beach". Immediately I knew I needed to go to Rockaway Beach!!! I was born in The Rockaway's, right near the beach! When I got to the p**ark** I met up with Mathew and shortly after I ran into a **Annelise**, a woman who used to work at Seasoned Vegan (page 364). This day was the first time I realized she was wearing an Egyptian necklace with **Nefertiti's** name engraved on it. It was a gift given to her from her grandmother. **Re-member** that **you** are **Ausar** and **Heru,** the **hero!** <u>See page 3 for the **hero's journey**!</u>

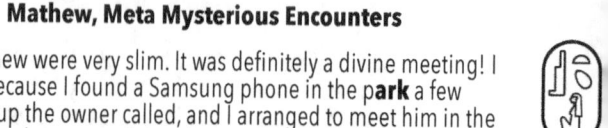

Rau nu Prt m heru Iu f Per f m heru

Utterances for Coming Forth by day into Light

It is he, who comes forth by day into Light

This was my first time back to Far Rockaway since Jan 7th of 2017 when I went to the studio to recored the song Holler if ya Hear Me (p 4**23**). It was snowing and very cold that day so I went from the train to the studio and back to the train and did not get to see the neighborhood I grew up in. However this time the weather was more ideal. I took the ferry and road my bike along the new boardwalk all the way down to beach 67th streets. I met up with Mathew and his Friend **Auset**. Upon meeting her I was alert to some small **sign** or **coincidence** as her full name happened* to be Auset **Shakur**. I promptly showed her my new Auset Tattoo that I had in the same place on my chest that Tupac **Shakur** had his **Nefertiti** tattoo. Her born name was not Auset Shakur but she had been given that name or took that name herself after attending a spiritual ceremony from a sister named **Roszella** who I would meet the next month in July (p 651). We spent the day talking about life and ancient Kemet in between our dips in the ocean and bathing in the sun. After we had had enough of the sun we decided to call it a day at around 4:30pm. *I decided that I would ride to my old block to see the house I grew up in and they decided to join me. We all road to 6952* ***Hill****meyer avenue (****house seen on p 260****). **I stood there and looked at the house I spent most of my youth in while living with my Grandmother.*** *I was over come with emotions as I had not seen this house for over 15 to 20 years. I snapped a picture of the house and sent it to my sisters.* Shortly after, Auset parted ways and made her way home. When I was ready to leave Mathew accompanied me on my ride back to the ferry. As we road up the boardwalk we crossed paths with two brothers on bikes who stopped to greet us. Mathew knew both of them and one of them seemed to know me but I did not immediately recognize him, however as we started talking his face began to get familiar. His name was **Keith Brown**. I asked him what he remembered about me and he told me that he remembered how good I was at football and how everyone thought I was going to make it to the **NFL**. At that point I knew that he knew me. Keith told me about how he broke his right arm when he was a teen and that's how he became a lefty. After he mentioned that we realized that all four of us were lefties. I remember thinking how strange it was for all of us to be lefties given how rare it was to find a **left handed** person (p 35). I forgot the brothers name that was with Keith but he was wearing a Mets shirt and I teased him about being a Mets fan. We all laughed in good fun. Then Keith and I talked separately as Mathew and the Mets guy talked separately on the other side of the boardwalk. I showed Keith the flyer for my book and told him about my **past life** revelations and he was amazed, or at least he pretended to be. As we prepared to part ways I teased the brother about his Mets shirt again and then he said the **strangest thing**. He pointed at my **silver scarab cuff** and said: "***The Mets will win the world series again before Tutankhamen comes out of his grave***!" I looked at Mathew and asked him if he had told him about my revelation, but Mathew with his eyes and mouth wide open, shook his head no. Keith was also amazed that he would seemingly at random speak the name of the person I just claimed to be the reincarnation of. I busted out laughing and handed him my flyer. Then I laughed all the way to the ferry as Mathew accompanied me for the ride, however the strangeness was not over yet! When I got home I laid down to watch the next episode of **Lost** (p 259) which was the **23rd episode**. **Lost** is a tv show about a group of people who crashed on a mysterious magical island. I started watching it again from season 1 on April 9th (p 640) the day **DMX** died and I was now up to the last season, season 6, episode **5**. Upon watching the series again I would realize the series was about **death**, the **afterlife** and **reincarnation**. You would have to watch the series **Lost** to fully grasp the magnitude of the episode that just so happen to be the very next episode for me to watch after I got home from seeing the house I grew up in.

There is a lot of mystery around the number **23** and this experience happened on June **23rd** and that same day I watched the **23rd** episode of **Lost**. In this episode the main character Jack **Shepard**, would be taken to a **lighthouse** by another person on the island. They were instructed to turn the dial in the lighthouse to a certain degrees but as they began to turn the dial images began to flash on the mirrors in front of them. Confused about the images Jack noticed that each degree on the dial had a name next to it. The names were of different people who had crashed on the island. The number **23** had his name (Jack **Shepard**) next to it. Surprised to see his name, Jack disregarded the degrees they were told to turn the dial to and hurried to turn it to the number **23**! When the dial got to the **23rd** degree the image of a house appeared. Jack stood there **transfixed** with a look of confusion no different than the look Mathew, Keith and I had when the guy with the Mets shirt said the name Tutankhamen. ***Jack was looking at the house that he grew up in***! When I saw that I knew that this was another sign from the **unseen realms**. My **life path number** is 32 (**23**) = **5** and this was the **5th** episode of the last season of **Lost**. The main character Jack **Shepard** had a tattoo on his shoulder with the number **5** and a **pyramid**. These were his real life tattoos not tattoos for the show. His number on the dial was **23** and 2 plus 3 equals **5**. **5** is the fifth number in the **golden ratio** and the only number in the sequence that is equal to its position (p 41). I had just stood in front of the house I grew up in as a child and now, in this show, Jack Shepard stands in front of the house he grew up in, at the top of a lighthouse. Lighthouses are use to help ships at sea find their direction! Jack Shepard was the leader in the series Lost just as the person who carried the **Shepard's staff** was the leader in ancient times. In ancient Kemet the **Nswt Bity** (**pharaoh**) held a staff like **Moses** called a **Heka** also called a Shepard's staff or the Crook (p 665). It was the staff of rulership and it was carried in the **left hand**! **Heka** was like the title in a name like Dr or General. King Tutankhaten's (King Tut"s) throne name was Neb Kheperu Ra Heka Maat (master of transformations of Ra, Ruler of Maat). "Jack" = The Jack of all trades is a master of none, but the jack of all trades is more often times more effective than the master of only one trade. The number **23** appeared a few times in the **Lost** series and in this **23rd** episode entitled **Exodus** (pages 225, 492, 665), it was revealed that the main male protagonist, Jack was seated in seat **23B** during the plane crash that precipitated the show's plot. In the two subsequent episodes, which are considered parts **2** and **3** of **Exodus**, it is revealed that the plane took off from Gate **23** and that the main female protagonist, Kate, was taken captive for a **23,000** dollar bounty. Throughout the entirety of **Lost**, numbers play an important role and are interconnected in a multitude of ways. Especially the mysterious sequence of numbers on the side of the hatch (4, 8, 15, 16, **23**, 42). **23** is one of the most commonly cited prime numbers - a number that can only be divided by itself and one. **23** is the lowest prime that consists of consecutive digits. Primes have been described as the "atoms" of mathematics - the building blocks of the world of numbers. With that said, this book is full of **star code patterns** appearing in the form of numbers. There is no wonder why **23** appeared in my story on this day, June **23**, 2021. I spent many years as a **Hermit** studying **Kemet** and Hermes (Djehuty), and it's no surprise that the **Hermit** is the **23rd** tarot card and the **Hermit** is sometimes considered the mature and wiser version of The **Magician (page 672)**. Some say that God is a divine mathematician and numerology is the language of God. Perhaps that's why the axial tilt of the Earth is **23.**5 degrees (rounded to the nearest .5 naturally) **2** + **3** = 5. And the average human physical biorhythm is **23** days. And each parent contributes **23** chromosomes to the start of human life. And my life path number is 32 which also (**23**). And the **second** and **third** operations of **Alchemy** are Dissolution (**death**) and Separation (**reincarnation**), respectively. And the **23rd** hexagram of the **I-Ching** is translated as Splitting Apart (**reincarnation**). And the Discordianism **Law of Fives** states simply that: All things happen in **fives**, or are divisible by or are multiples of five, or are somehow directly or indirectly appropriate to 5 and The Law of Fives is never wrong. An equation they use to explain this: 2+3=5. 23+32=**55**. Of course **55** appears frequently in my experience. **Emmett Till** was murdered in 19**55**, **Akhenaten's** remains were found in tomb number KV**55**, and my mother in this life was born in 19**55**. Speaking of the murder of "Emmett Till", "**W**" is the **23rd** letter of the Latin alphabet. It has **two** points down and **three** points up. **White supremacists** use **23** to represent "W" as a mark of racial superiority. The Roman emperor Julius Caesar was said to have been stabbed **23** times. The **23rd** chapter of Psalms states: "Yea, though I walk through the valley of the shadow of death, I will fear no evil: for thou art with me; thy **rod** and thy **staff** they comfort me.", but of course we know that the Pharaohs are the ones who carried rods and staffs (see pages 225, 667). **23** appears in movies often. I don't know when I saw the movie **The Number 23** but it was many years before my past life revelations, yet the movie mentions **Sirius** and it's about patterns and numbers. It premiered on Feb **23,** 2007 and Jim Carrey **star**red in it. Jim Carrey **start**ed his acting career in 19**77**, the year of the snake, the year I was born. See pages 25, 94, 102, 121, 283, 444, 439, 586, 669, and 672 for more on **February 23rd.** In the science fantasy saga, **Star Wars** Episode IV: A New Hope, Luke Skywalker sneaks into detention block AA**23** to rescue Princess Leia (see page 37, 512 & 513). **Star Wars** premiered on **May 25**, 1977, the year of the snake. **May 25** is the first star code pattern that I decoded in this life and is the patterned that binds me to Emmett Till and the Hero's journey of Luke Sky Walker which was taken from the Ausarian Resurrection Drama (p 30). On **July 7th** and **July 16th** I would have two more experiences in Far Rockaway at the beach with two women who carried very telling star code patterns (pages 651-652). One of the woman was Roszella, the woman who gave Auset her name at the spiritual ceremony. There was a message being coded to me from my ancestral fathers. On Nov 13th 2021 (p 659) I would have a profound revelation surrounding my **silver scarab cuff** (page **29**3) that I purchased from **Mfundishi Jhutyms**, who "happens" to be born on Jan **23** (page 2**3**3). This revelation made the words "*The Mets will win the world series again before Tutankhamen comes out of his grave!*" so much more funnier. A long time ago in a galaxy Far Far Rock**away** the boy king Tutankhaten was born again.

***Addendum* Revision Confirmations** (See pages 118 182 and 619)

On Wednesday July 20th 2022 I made my first trip to the beach. Something was calling me there so I took the train to Far Rockaway at around 4am. I got to the beach as the Sun had began to to rise. I was only at the beach for about 3 hours when I got the desire to leave, so I left. When I got to the train station waiting for the train a huge smile lit up my face as I made eye contact with **Keith Brown** causing us both to laugh. I told him that this was my first time to the beach this year and he said that he was on his way to work but he is never this early. I pulled out my copy of this book and showed it to him. I "happened" to have an extra copy in my bag and he purchased it. We sat on the train as I went over the details of the book with him. I told him about what happened with Justin (p 619) and he was amazed. The book was taking on a life its own.

June 29th 2021
Meta-Spiritual Encounters of The Fourth Kind

Deja Vu or a Ghost that Shined Through?

This was my second day trip to the beach but this time I took the long train ride from Harlem to Far Rockaway. I boarded the train in Harlem at around 2:30 am but unfortunately the train I was on was behind a maintenance train causing my trip to take a lot longer. I dozed off during the long trip and when I opened my eyes an hour had gone by and the train doors where opening to the **Shepards** Avenue station. The time was 4:00 am, I laughed and took a picture (seen below). In ancient Kemet the **Nswt Bity** (Pharaoh) held a staff known as a **Heka** also called a **Shepard's staff** or the **Crook**. It was known as the staff of the **ruler**. **Heka** was also the word for **magic**. King Tut's throne name was Neb Kheperu Ra **Heka** Maat which meant, master of transformations of Ra, **Ruler** of **Maat**. When I finally arrived in Far Rockaway it was around 5:15 am and the first thing I noticed were the new buildings and how much things had changed in Rockaway. I rode my bike to the beach but on my way there I experienced what I thought was **Deja Vu but it was not the normal Deja Vu**. I **vividly** saw a woman yelling at someone on a porch to my left and the view of her was so sharp and her pain so alarming that it caused me to pull over and when I did **I turned back to look at her again and she was gone**. This perplexed me for the rest of that day. She was there then all of a sudden she wasn't. It wasn't till November that I saw a video of a man explaining how he saw a woman walking along a snowy road with a baby and they both had very little clothes on. He pulled over to help her and when he got out of his car she was gone, as if she had vanished. Perhaps into the woods he imagined. He knew he saw a person so he did not think it to be a **ghosts** until he told a friend and to his surprise his friend had seen the woman with the baby on the same road and she'd disappeared in front of him too… I got to the beach around 5:30 am and did my sun rise Kemetic yoga salutations and spent the day at the beach. Sometime around noon **Mathew** (p 647) accompanied me at the beach and afterwards we went to his house which was two blocks away. We sat in the shed in his backyard and on the shelf I saw the book **100 Years of Lynchings**. I opened the book to the lynching of **Emmett Till** where I found more information about the case and about Emmett's uncle **Moses** that I had previously not known. In 2022 I would experience **Deja Vu** twice while in **Kemet** (pages 670 - 671).

42 Laws of Maat, Page 367

July 3rd 2021
International African Arts Festival and The Invisible Helpers

This was my third year attending and working at the International African Arts Festival and I was looking for something special to happen. My past life as **Emmett Till** was revealed to me via this festival in 2018 (p 480) and in 2019 the **scarabs** came to greet me everyday of the festival (pages 570-574). This year I brought my massage chair again to work but my attention was more geared towards promoting this book you're reading. I only did around 8 massages this year because I spent more time handing out flyers to as many people as I could. Just like my experience in 2019 the **scarabs would greet me again** this year on all four days of the festival. I spent more money with the vendors this year than I made money of my own but I didn't care, I just wanted to promote this book.

I told everyone that I would be selling this book next year at the festival in 2022. **Mother Mut Rita** is the oldest woman in Mfundishi's Shrine (**Jhuty Heru Neb Hu**) and she believes my story about my past lives. She's a Haitian woman that has had many experiences with the spirit world. I gave her a massage at this festival and after the massage she stood mesmerized as she asked me if I could see what she saw. I didn't see any thing but she said she saw countless number of warrior spirits walking around us. ****ADDENDUM**** In 2022, when I was selling this book at the festival, I saw **Baba Heru**. I was excited to see him. I showed him my book. Told him, everyone was in it. He asked if he was in it. I thought for a second and said "no". He turned and walked off. I'd forgotten about the picture above…

Rau nu Prt m heru

Iu f Per f m heru

Meta Spiritual Encounters of The Fourth Kind

On the last day of the festival **Meeky** and I went to get breakfast and while waiting for the food to be ready we walked around looking at the different vendors. That's when **Dr Fredrick Monderson** waved me over to him. He was vending, selling his paintings and books. I'd spoken to him about my book the day prior. When I approached him he began to speak to me passionately about the task of writing a book that I claimed I was embarking on. He pointed to several of his books and told me that I would have to be serious about the task. He must have spoken for 8 to 10 minutes straight. When he was done speaking I looked at Meeky and she was standing there **transfixed** with her mouth wide open and a look of amazement on her face. She is a medium and **can see spirits** but she explained that she had never seen anything like this before. She said that just before Dr Fredrick began to speak to me **one of my guardians appeared** and placed his hand on Dr Fredrick's shoulder and at that very moment Dr Fredrick began to speak to me passionately about taking the task of writing my book very seriously. He told me that I would have to be up all night some nights. It was after this experience that I began to write for 8, 10, 13 and 17 hours straight at a time. More on **Guardian Angels** and **Ka Doors** (**Spirit Doors**) see pages (250 -253, 48,141, 142,148, 150, 179, 199, 315, 318, 329, 348, 349, 409, 421, 434, 545, 548, 549, 572, 584, 626, 604).

Utterances for Coming Forth by day into Light

It is he, who comes forth by day into Light

The Divine Feminine Energy

Because of the way I met Mars my first year at the festival (p 474) and meeting Meeky the second year, I was paying attention to all the women I met this year. This year I met 2 women who I felt like I was supposed to meet. I gave one of them ancient Kemetic healing body work and she really enjoyed it. I enjoyed her company so much that I didn't remind her to pay me. I felt an attraction to her that made me think I was supposed to know her but not every attraction is what it seems. After the festival I never saw her again. She was born on Jan 26th. However the 2nd woman aligned with the usual **mysterious** meetings I was accustomed to. Her name was **Roszella** and she would come to visit me at the beach the next week on Wednesday July 7th and she came carrying a **divine star code** (p 651). Then **Christine** would visit me at the beach the following week on July 16th carrying a corresponding **divine star code** (p 652).

I met Roszella at the African Arts Festival the weekend before she came to visit me at the beach. As soon as I saw her I felt like I needed to know her. Perhaps and hour later I saw her walking with a brother who had a **tattoo** of **King Tut** on his arm and when eye saw his tattoo **I stopped them immediately** and handed them both a copy of my flyer promoting my book. Soon after Roszella followed me on Instagram and on July 7th she joined me at the beach. It should be noted that the chances of her coming were almost diverted as she told me that another man tried to stop her from coming to see me but something inside told her to come so she disregarded him and came to see me anyways. I arrived at the beach by myself very early and did sunrise kemetic yoga salutations and meditation. Roszella got to the beach around 8am and stayed with me for several hours. While at the beach we talked about our journeys towards over and inner standing and how we got to the point where we both were in our lives. Afterwards she suggested that we do **Yogic fire breaths** and so we did a sequence of breaths. She was very deeply invested with the thoughts of honoring the memory and the souls of the male members of her ancestry that she has never known. Our meeting became part of my **star code** when I asked her what her **birthday** was. To my surprise she was born on **February 7th**, Louis Till's birthday (page 475, 518). Louis Till was my father when I lived as Emmett Till. How strange I found it that she would be talking about honoring the memory and the souls of the male members of her ancestry and then I find that she was born on the same day as one of the male members of my ancestry!! Roszella and I had a nice day at the beach then she left and went on with the rest of her day as I continued my day at the beach. The next week I would get another star code from a more ancient male member of my ancestry.

July 16th 2021 Christine and The Eternal Looking Glass

I met Christine on May 15th 2021 at a gong session in central park hosted by my friends **Taunya** (p 553) and **Sunseed** (p 326). After the session was over I was talking to a friend named **Graciela** and a woman who had a giant **scarab** tattooed on her back. I started telling her about the book I was writing. This is where I met **Christine** and another sister named **Kymbela**. At the end of our discussion a few of them followed my Instagram page. A few days later Christine booked a massage with me. I remember her expressing that my massage felt like I had many hands on her body moving like a snake. After this massage her and I would stay in contact via text and social networking. On July 16th she joined me at the beach in Far Rockaway. I got there early and sun-gazed while doing Kemetic Yoga. I brought the book **Akhenaten King of Egypt** with me and read some of the book in between trips to the ocean. Christine arrived sometime in the afternoon. I did the usual which was talk about this book I was writing and all the mysterious **coincidences** that surrounded the book and my past lives. I asked her what her birthday was and she said **September 13th**! I explained to her she was born the day that **Tupac died** and last week Roszella came to visit me at the beach and she was born on **February 7th**, **Emmett Till's father's** birthday (page 475, 518)!! This was no coincidence! This strengthened my theory about who **Tupac** was in a **past life**☥. When she set up her sheet to lay on she used various items to weigh the corners of her sheet down and one of the items was a mirror shaped like an **Ankh**. I picked it up to examine it and I immediately bust'd out laughing as I realized that it was a replica of **"Tutankhaten's"** ("King Tut's") Ankh mirror. It had my throne name **Neb Kheperu Ra** engraved on it. Christine and I had a good time at the beach. At some point she started burying her feet in the sand then she asked me to bury her so I did, and while she laid there a lady bug landed on her face. When she got up she decided to bury me. While doing so she had a spiritual experience where she had visions of Egypt and **she heard a voice** telling her that she had done this work before. We also shared a magical moment while we were in the water. I picked her up to throw her but she reacted quicker than me wrapping her legs around me and as we moved back and forth in the Ocean I held her around her waist as we gazed into each others eyes for what seemed like a short eternity coupled with **Deja Vu**. In 2022 I would experience **Deja Vu** twice while in Kemet (pages, 670 - 671)

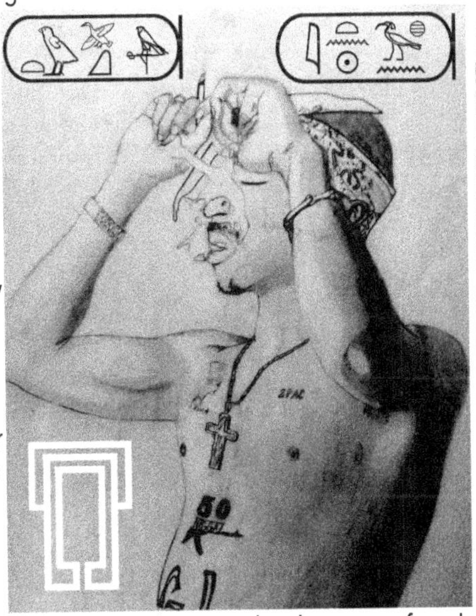

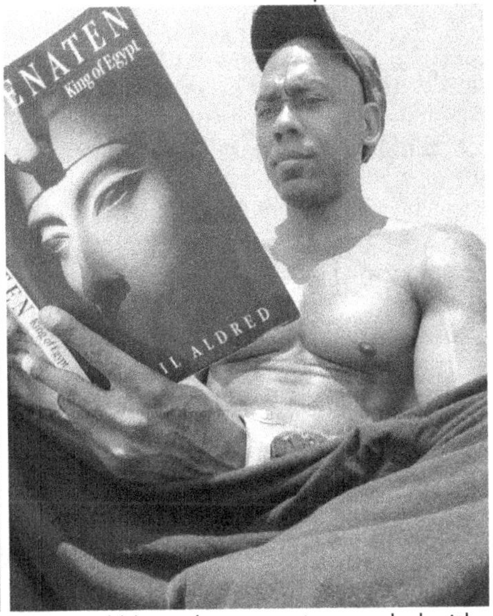

Christine's Dream

On March 26th 2022 Christine dreamed of a little boy who asked her about **Emmett Till**. In the dream she saw a great many ancient statues, some black and some gold. Just before the dream ended she gave the little boy my info so that he could contact me.

Rau nu Prt m heru

Iu f Per f m heru

Utterances for Coming Forth by day into Light

It is he, who comes forth by day into Light

Lady Bugs, The Writer and More DeJa Vu

The next week I took my tent to the beach and stayed the night on the beach. There was a **Super flower Blood Moon** that night and that night I met a black brother in his 60's named Alfred. I had been seeing him on the beach with the same tent in the same spot for weeks. He looked to be homeless so I offered him a banana but he declined. I handed him my card promoting my book and that's when he told me that he was a writer. He was interested in my book so I told him about my **past lives** and he was amazed at all the **coincidences**. The next day I did sunrise Kemetic Yoga at around 5:55 am while sun gazing. Through out the day around 4 or 5 **lady bugs** would land on me during and after my yoga session, even landing on my face once. I spent the day at the beach and before I went home I rode my bike to **Hill**meyer, the block I grew up on (p 40, 648). This time I rode very slowly down the blocks as I took in all the feelings and memories. Then I rode to where the boats were stored and when the smell of the bay hit my olfactory sensors I was struck with **Deja Vu**. The strangest thing about this trip was finding a street named **Barbados** that intersected the street **Hill**meyer. I don't remember that street from my youth and I didn't come to know that my fathers **father** was from **Barbados** until I was in my 30's (page 25). I'm part **Bajan** and grew up one block away from a street that is now named **Barbados**. How strange.., I just laughed. Then I rode to the bay where I saw the men molesting the boys when I was 7 or 8 years old (**p**age 352). I thought about what might **h**ave happened to those other boys then I went home. In 2022 I experienced **Deja Vu** twice while in **Kemet** (pages 670 - 671).

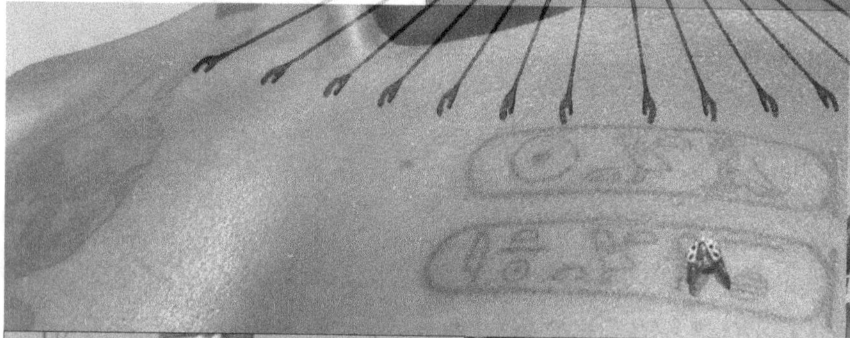

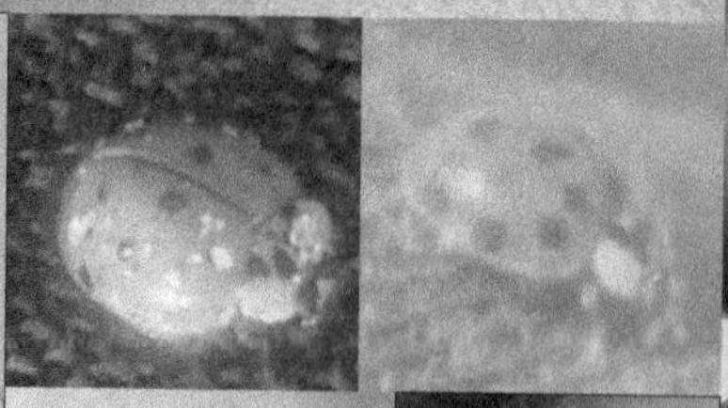

July 30th 2021 - My First and Only Astrological Reading with Sondráya

I first became aware of Sondráya via a youtube video that I watched on July 12th 2021 however the video had been uploaded to youtube on **July 3rd** 2021 and my past life as Emmett Till was revealed to me on **July 3rd** 2018. The video was hosted by **Dr. Oba T'Shaka** and the show was titled **Astrology the Cosmic System for Knowing Your Personal Character and for awakening your Divinity,** and the guest speaker was the astrologist **Sondráya** (T'shaka's sister). During the show Sondráya spoke about how "**as above so below**," pertains to our inner astrological system, and how astrology is the universe that dwells within us. She discussed how astrology can be utilized to help us awaken to our divinity. Sondráya, is a lead astrologer for the first nationwide telephone Astrological Consulting Service in the US. Oba T'Shaka is also an astrologer and he spoke on the **Egyptian** (**Kemetic**) origin of Astronomy/Astrology, with practical examples of how this system works in people's lives to empower them to see their wholeness and live their spiritual magnificence.

Rau nu Prt m heru

Genesis 1:14

"And God said, Let there be lights in the firmament of the heaven to divide the day from the night; and let them be for signs, and for seasons, and for days, and years"

Booking The Reading

A few days after watching **Dr. Oba T'Shaka's** video I called Sondráya to schedule a reading. I booked the reading because after listening to Sondráya I wanted to get my astrological profile from a professional so that I could add it to this book however what I got from Sondráya greatly exceeded my expectations. I told her about my past lives and she listened with an open mind. We initially booked the reading for Wednesday July **28**th but her schedule changed and so we moved the reading to the 30th of July. This would be the first profound event. She did a chart for the day of the reading and explain that it was no accident that we ended up doing the reading on the 30th because this day was a 21 degrees **scorpio** rising, and the dragons tail is rising and conjuncts my rising sign. At the end of the reading I asked her if my reading was one of the more profound readings she has ever done and she replied - "I must say, I have to admit yes it was a most unusual reading". She explained how she could feel it in the way the presence of her body felt and because of that she strongly feels there is a connection with me and the lives of Emmett and Tutankhaten. I was already confident that the reading would align with my revelation but I didn't know that it would fuel my purpose in this life. **(To book a reading w/ Sondráya: Sondraya@Sondraya.com)**

Iu f Per f m heru

Sondráya

TutemRa

Utterances for Coming Forth by day into Light

The Scorpio

I am a Scorpio and a Scorpio's triumph comes when we successfully integrate our souls into our personality and use its resulting powers for the benefit of humankind. To realize these revelations I had to descend into Pluto's underworld. I confronted all the demons from my past as well as those within the subconscious hells of my mind and each successful confrontation unearthed a new treasure. My journey was murderous but it offered me the greatest opportunity because when the Scorpio rises from its own ashes, it takes with it the occult powers becoming the **phoenix** liberating ourselves and **reclaiming all parts of our Soul**. The awakened Scorpio embodies the life-giving powers to heal itself and others. Its final prize is its own **immortality**. Death is the initiate of the Mysteries, he understands transformative power and reminds us that to live is to die and to die is to be reborn. I have realized my truth and found the light within my own being. I will now practice living this truth for the rest of my days. Thus far, this journey has been worth it and another journey has just begun. I know that I will continue to be reborn again and again. "Amen Atum Aten, never to be forgotten, from Neb Kheperu Ra to slave fields pick'n cotton, from Emmett Till get'n killed thrown in a river rotten, like Ausar I came back as Dawud TutemRa".

It is he, who comes forth by day into Light

"The ***wheel of fortune,*** caution they will hurt you for this capital, **circle of little animals**, scorpion sting kiss of death, **Judas** be the fall yes, in the winter we see the sun less, spring, summer he back but to that your priest won't confess, **Astro Theology** dressed in white suppressed, probably the greatest story ever sold for frankincense myrrh and gold" (**Mary The Virgo, page 546**)

"Close your eyelids, **our souls met way before our eyes did**, they say love is a black hole that attracts souls, law of attraction, poles a grid, polarity, a rose, the chemistry, a road to serenity, **death couldn't finish me, I died and came back** navigated the **zodiac** with perfect timing, saw you in a dream but your guardian wasn't trying to let me swing, I woke up and never said a thing, I just kept rising up and metamorphosing" - **(The Pattern, page 607)**

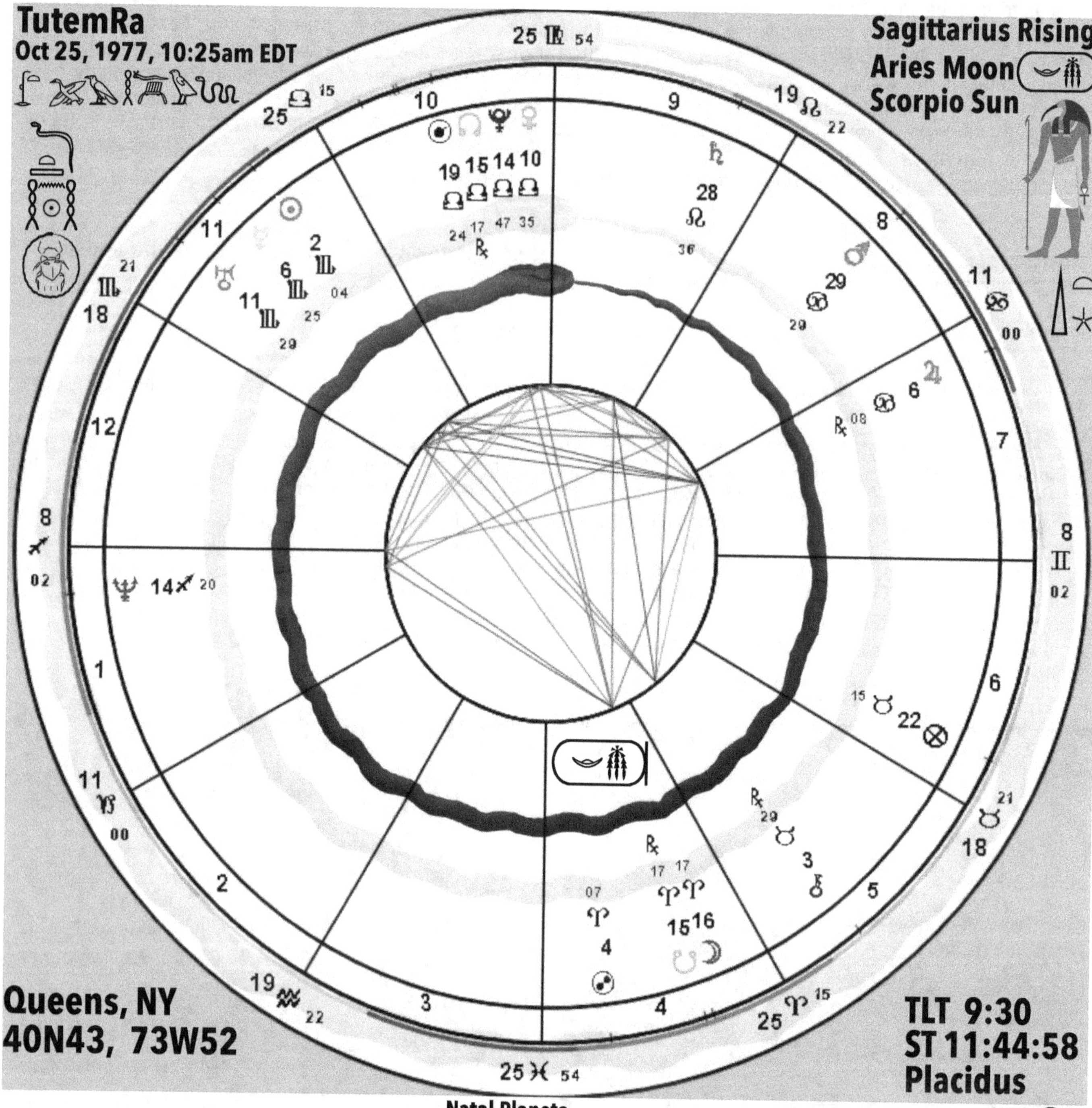

"truer words never spoke from another emcee, see rappers mostly rap about life illegally, but emcees rap about uplifting people spiritually, from the mineral to plant, from plants to man to Gods, in a **circle of the little animals** we revolve, Hip Hop the arithmetic used to solve the secret teachings of all ages as war wages, The BlaKseed raises the sword of **David** which divine law favors, the right handed villain, the left handed savior, the link in search for Zelda, the saber, the elder spoke of the birth of the star in a **manger**, **Ausa**r the **Arc**her aims his bow at the **25th Dynasty,** ***finally The Never Ending Story** is finding me* - **(Truman Show, page 366)**

Re-member that **you** are **Ausar** and **Heru,** the **hero!** See page 3 for the **hero's journey**!

Natal Planets

Sun	☉	**2° Sco 03' 52"**
Moon	☽	**16° Ari 17' 00"**
Mercury	☿	**6° Sco 25'**
Venus	♀	**10° Lib 35'**
Mars	♂	**29° Can 29'**
Jupiter	♃	**6° Can 08'R**
Saturn	♄	**28° Leo 36'**
Uranus	♅	**11° Sco 29'**
Neptune	♆	**14° Sag 20'**
Pluto	♇	**14° Lib 47'**
Chiron	⚷	**3° Tau 29'R**
N Node	☊	**15° Lib 17'R**
P. Fort.	⊗	**22° Tau 15'**
Asc.	⊖	**8° Sag 02'**
Mc	⦶	**25° Vir 54'**

Chart Patterns
Type: Funnel
leading Jupiter
focus Moon
Ruler Asc: Jupiter
Asp Pat: T-Square
to Mars
Asp Pat: T-Square
to Jupiter

Elements and Modes

Fire	6	Cardinal	6
Earth	2	Fixed	6
Air	2	Mutable	4
Water	6		

Strong: Fire, Water

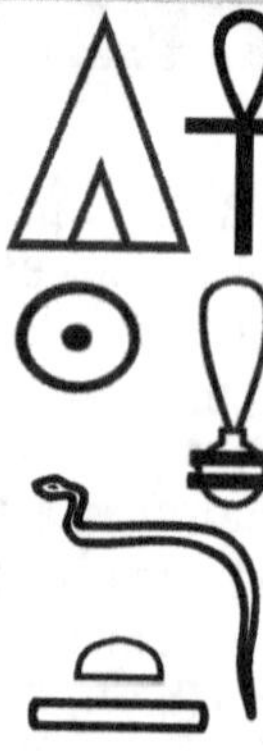

Rau nu Prt m heru

Iu f Per f m heru

Utterances for Coming Forth by day into Light

It is he, who comes forth by day into Light

As we began she told me that she was not thrown off by my **past lives** instead she entered the reading with an open mind and when she saw that my **Dragons tail** fell in the age of **Aries** (the **Ram**) which "happens to be" the same time period that King Tut (**Tutankhaten**) lived she took interest and kept following the trail. The Dragon's Head and Dragon's Tail are neither planets nor celestial bodies. In fact, they are actually intangible 'mysterious points' in the heavens. The dragons tail tells you where your soul comes from and what power you have to draw on while your dragons head tells you where you are going and your service in the world. The bible pulls from the astrological zodiacal time period of Aries which covers the 18th dynasty. This is why the Christian men who went around killing in the name of their religion were called missionaries. The mission was pulling from this time of Aries, hence Mission-Aries. The mission was to steal the knowledge they had taken from the 18th dynasty so as to dominate and control the world with religion (p 592)! As Sondráya moved further into my reading she noticed that my **birth moon** was 16 degrees **Aries** and mysteriously my **dragons tail** (**south node**) is only 1 degrees away at 15 degrees **Aries**. **Moon** signs govern our **ancestry**, heredity, where we come from in previous lives and not just biological but also our **spiritual lineage**. **Iahmose** was the first pharaoh of the 18 dynasty (p 638). His name meant: **born of the energy of the moon**. She also noticed that my dragons tail is in **Aries** the **Ram** with a Leo decan and at this point she said she began to have a feeling about the reading and what ever had led me to this alignment with Tutankhaten (King Tut) and Emmett Till she was able to see validity in it. **Then she explain that if there was no connection at all she would not entertain a conversation about Tutankhaten,** but once she saw a connection with the **birth moon** and my **dragons tail** (**south node**) she started reaching out for more info. She noticed that I have **Neptune** at the depth of my chart and Emmett's dragons tail aligns with my Neptune. Then she looked at my **Saturn** which was the last planet in early European astrology before other planets like Neptune, Pluto and Uranus were rediscovered*. Saturn governs foundation and roots, and my **Saturn** was at **28** degrees **Leo**. **Emmet Till** was a **Leo** and he was murdered on August **28**th in the sign of **Virgo**. Virgo governs **service** and the death of Emmett Till was a service to this country as it propelled the advancement of the Civil Rights Movement. **Ausar** (Osiris) reigned for **28 years** in the **Ausarian resurrection** drama... **Re-member** that **you** are **Ausar** and **Heru,** the **hero!** See page 3 for the **hero's journey!** Sondráya said from Emmett Till's dragons tail it can be deduced that he came here, to Earth as a sacrificial **lamb** giving his life for the Civil Rights Movement. My **midheaven** is also in the service oriented sign of **Virgo**. This confirms my current life path of service with the writing of this book having used what I have learned in life as a teaching and giving it to the world. The number **15** is prevalent in my dragons tail and all my planets have moved between **15** and 16 degrees. On the night Emmett Till was murdered **Saturn** was in **15** degrees **scorpio**, Pluto was squaring that Saturn and **Pluto** would represent the malefic energy of racism or the ku klux klan. My **Saturn** is **28** degrees Leo and Emmett's was at 26 degrees **Taurus** which are two fixed signs. The **Sphinx** (**Heru em Akhet**, page 2) is comprised of two fixed signs, **Leo** the **lion** and **Aquarius** the human. This correlates with the ancient prophecy of **Heru** returning/resurrecting in the age of Aquarius uniting the **lion** with the **lamb** and we are at the shores of the age of Aquarius (page 2). My **Dragons head** (**north node**) is at **15** degrees of libra (**Maat**) with an Aquarius decan expression. Pluto is sitting on my **Dragons head** at 14 degrees 47 which rounds off to **15** degrees. She told me that I have roots and structure in the whole archetype of Leo. Leo is a leader and creator sent here to fulfill the message of the **sun** and so I must strive to be like the **sun** giving love and light indiscriminately shining on everyone and everything. My name is now TutemRa which means - **in the image of Ra,** and Ra represented the sun in ancient Kemet therefore shining love and light is what I'm here to do. In this life time I am here to take it further with my Aries Leo connection. Having **Uranus** in my 11th house allows me to focus on all humanity.

At the time of my birth my sun sign was at 2 degrees **scorpio** and the planet **Mercury** (Juhty, Tehuti, Thoth, Hermese) was at 6 degrees **scorpio** which gives me my **investigative mind**. I have a rising sign of 6 degrees Sagittarius which lends me the qualities of a higher mind as well as being the eternal student and adventurer and even the "**writer of life**". The sagittarius is the grand **alchemist**. The American record producer, DJ, rapper and songwriter Daniel Alan Maman was born the same day and year as me, Oct 25th 1977 the year of the **snake** and he is professionally known as the **Alchemist**. His rise to fame came after working with the Hip Hop group **Mobb Deep**. **Prodigy** from Mobb Deep speaks about reincarnation on page 663. I am the **Alchemist** who has brought **The Hip Hop Bible** (page 633). This book was brought forth in 2022, the 49th anniversary of Hip Hop and 49 days is the amount of time the Tibetans believed it took one soul to be reborn into another life. I am the **alchemist** coded within Hip Hop. This is **Divine Alchemy** of the soul, the only alchemy that matters! The grand **alchemist** is the tarot card Tower **14** which correlates with **revelation** and **awakening**. Emmett Till was murdered at **14 years** old and Tutankhaten (King Tut) ruled during the **14th century** BCE. While some people just have a rising sign I also have the planet **Neptune** rising at **14** degrees Sagittarius. Neptune rising is extreme sensitivity and intuitive, but coupled with Sagittarius it has allowed me to see the trends of times having an over all picture. Neptune represents **the great poet** which is like a tuning fork dealing with rhythm and rhyme. Neptune played a role in my attraction and love of creating Hip Hop and music in general (p 201). Neptune is a hard planet to **tune** into because it is the **highest spiritual** planet in the solar system so tuning requires a willingness to be totally loving. Neptune will be over head in Pisces till 2025 the year of the **snake**.

Sondráya explained that my chart is set up like a funnel or a fan where as, when I was born almost all my planets were viewable in the heavens, along with an **Aries moon** and a very telling **dragons tail**. She explain that my funnel / fan was set up deep within the 4th house of home and family which would give me many lessons to learn about family, home and relationships especially with my mother (page 632). I found this to be true for me and it added to the importance of this reading. This reading was uncovering things that she could not know without me telling her. This journey that I have been on for many years has caused much discord within my family because the experiences I was having went against what the people in my family believed or had experienced. Sondráya encouraged me to be peaceful by all means within my family, keeping things harmonious in the home and she explained that managing sensitivity was key for me in this life. At birth my sun was at 2 degrees scorpio and it has now progressed and moved into **16** degrees **Sagittarius** this is important because my progressed **Pluto** has moved into **16** degrees libra (**Maat**). Neptune was 14 degrees Sagittarius at my birth and has now progressed to **16** degrees Sagittarius.. She explained and emphasized how **numbers** are big deals in astrology and that I have powerful planets totally aligning with my **dragons tail** and my **dragons head** within 1 degrees to help me along my path. She says this is a really divine meeting and it should be seen as an initiatory alignment. She said that an astrological and numerological alignment like this **must have been set up at another time** because those planets don't align like this very often **which is why she felt that it was a divine meeting**. In 2022 I went to Kemet for the first time in this life during the Zodiac sign of **Aries** (March 30 - Apr 13), while there I had **Deja Vu** two times (pages 670 - 671).

The four gilded shrines of Tutankhaten - Ouroboros (The Snake Eating its Tail)

My four shrines had a variety of spells that consisted of the **book of the dead**, **book of the heavenly cow**, and **the book of the underworld**. My outer most shrine was decorated in amulets of Auset (Isis), hieroglyphics of Ausar (Osiris) and had multiple Wadjet eyes. Spells from the the Book of the Dead were inscribed and there was no seal, it measured 5.08m in length and 2.75m in height. The **ouroboros** symbol was found on my 2nd gilded shrine. This shrine had me depicted before Ausar (Osiris, lord of west/underworld) which highlighted the procedure into the afterlife and how I was being welcomed into the underworld, it measured 3.75m in length and 2.25m in height. My third shrine's roof had a depiction of the solar disc which was a representation of the sun god Aten, it measured to 3.4m in length and 2.15m in height. My innermost shrine contained the my coffins and Sahu (mummy) and the door to this shrine was never sealed, it measured to 2.9m in length and 1.9m in height.

ADDENDUM

The **ouroboros** symbol (snake eating its own tail) embodies **rebirth**, **eternity**, self-reliance, **immortality** with the shedding of new skin, and natures' **cyclic** character. This concept of resurrection was called the **Wehem-Mesut** (repeating of births, page 14). The snake eating its own tail is among the most prominent ancient symbols found in the history of different cultures, religions, and civilizations. The **oldest** known Ouroboros was found in 19**22** in circular form on my second gilded shrine. Two ouroboros's can be seen on the shrine, one is circling my head and the other circles my feet as I am seen in Ausarian mummified form (as seen below). These two ouroboros's might signify the dragons head (north node) and the dragons tail (south node) and would explain why my revelation had to unfold in 2018! In 2018 the year of the **dog**, my past life as **Emmett Till** was revealed to me on July 3, 2018 (page 480). **22** days later on July 25th Emmett would have turned **77** years old if "he" were still alive and I'm born in 19**77** the year of the **snake**. On October 25th I turned **41** years old and "Emmett Till" was born in 19**41** the year of the **snake** (page 41). Just like my astrological chart this revelation was a di**vine** numerological alignment so precise that if I had the revelation in 2017 "Emmett" would have been 76 and I would have been 40 and if it happened in 2019 Emmett would have been 78 and I would have been 42 but instead, the revelation unfolded in perfect timing in 2018 the year of the **dog** (page 530). Enpu (Anubis) is the dog headed **NTCHRU** (deity) from Kemet who ushers the soul of the dead through the halls of **Maat** where their hearts are weighed against the feather of Maat. Ausar is the Lord of **resurrection,** the first person the be mummified by Enpu. There is an ancient prediction that **Heru** will return one day and recapture the kingdom of his father, when the **golden** age will be restored and the **lion** will unite with the **Lamb/Goat**. Heru is believed to have a **resurrection** during the **Aquarian Age**. He is the prince of peace, bringer of order, redeemer of truth for humanity, resurrection and the life. He is able to right the wrongs of the past, free the oppressed, and restore Maat. **Re-member** that **you** are **Ausar** and **Heru,** the **hero!** See page 3 for the **hero's journey**!

42 Laws of Maat, Page 367

Ouroboros, Dragons Head

Ouroboros, Dragons Tail

Rau nu Prt m heru

August 5th 2021

Multiple Streams of Happiness

When I first saw her I knew it was the aura, Nebu like gold sort of, but she shot me down like a **flying saucer**, I was a mess, never the less I confessed my love, then I finessed multiple streams of happiness, you win some you lose some, it don't take a scientist to find a fish in the sea, she from the 18th dynasty and I'm trying to see, if the memory stayed timelessly, mahogany flesh caress my arm piety, and from my arm love flow to the coronary artery, stay armed with a bow she's handing me for **archery**, it ain't hard to see I came back like a odyssey, but where my Goddess be? it's hard to be alone honestly, Love rules everything around me I **dream** for my honey I wrote it on a seal y'all, Love rules everything around me I dream, for my honey, I wrote it on a seal y'all **- TutemRa**

Significance

I have begun to long for the love of my ancient wife Ankhesenaten. I wonder if I came here without her or is she out here waiting for me. I have met many men who think they are the reincarnation of me (Tutankhaten), and I have come across a few women online who think they are Ankhesenaten as well but I don't think any of the women I have come across are really her. I think it was Jasmin's **dream** (May 2nd 2021, page 643) that awoke this longing for Ankhesenaten. Perhaps I have already met her in my past. Perhaps she is one of the women I fell in love with in this life. Perhaps she is not here. Perhaps she just floats around watching me. Love rules everything around me, I dream for my honey, I wrote it on a seal y'all.

Iu f Per f m heru

August 22nd 2021 Doors 42 Laws of Maat, Page 367

I see u searching but do you know what you are searching for? a closed mind is not the kind of mind that will open doors, a **gold shrine**, the greatest find in modern time ocean floor, hope'n for, sign on the dotted line it's open war, open soar she flew rock'n **Nebu kheperu** blue couture, what's the cure? they don't know, I guess that's what they shoot'n for, like **Ausar** fruiting spore, you like her? Nah! I love her more, he said I saw a seer fly around with my mi amore, see or saw, see a bird, see a plane, see a door, see a house knock knock who's there? I'm looking for **Theo**dore, ether or air either or *ooh baby I like it raw* yeah, they stood in aw, fear, **Isfet** in the sky warfare, the daughter of **Ra, Sekhmet,** in her eyes red glare, I was there in four thousand four hundred forty four before the Gregorian, wearing a **leopard skin** cardigan, reptilians trying to be God again, a hologram in a temple destroyed by the Taliban, they don't know who I am, where I'm from, **Abu Simbel, "Heavy Mental", Het Heru** the instrumental, could it be coincidental? slipped into a transcendental state when I was a **Hindu**, no escape from the hate that men do, **Khonso** saw you in the street at the festival but talk you ain't want to, **Ubuntu**, is you a follower or a leader? **Kujichagulla, Aaliyah –** *one in a million* like the **Giza**, before Caesar, before Napoleon seized the Kings Chamber, poor stranger stayed the night but never quite found what he came for, they aimed for the breath of the Nswt the statue was made for, they shot the nose off, can't cut the **soul** with a razor! *Rays Lazarus*! like my Naga that came from Ursa Major, Big Dip dip diver my Naga nothing can save ya, rest in peace to **Biz Mark** transforming to vapors, and this is the season brothers getting more braver, when **DMX** died his soul came did me a favor, whispered in my ear said go ye there look through them papers! **Anubis** and the **afterlife** advice watch for them gators, **Maat** is precise in your life! you gotta watch your behavior! warlock the **Acacia**, *the burning bush* light the *light saber*, returning to **Kush**, too close to the edge I got pushed! I fell I flew! feather on my head like **Shu** and **my heart is true** that's why I return like **Heru,** in 1922 I was shot from a star near you, dropped on this planet still manage to speak **Maa Kheru,** Maa Kheru, feather on my head like **Shu** and **my heart is true** that's why I return like **Heru,** this be the Pinnacle Miracle, this *The Digital Underground*, pledge allegiance to spirit invisible, cause *I Get Around*, they say I drowned but I ain't pro Black, I'm profound! more brown, if I'm a color I'm light, write like **Jhuty** sound, mask around they noses, they all fall down, needles full of doses, I came from a small town, got a uncle named **Joseph** he be in my **dreams** now, you disgruntled explosive, you don't over stand how, **Yoga** to yoke, will you ever endeavor beyond the scope of what you can't measure? Micro, Tele, Horo, Divine Boats, Card Tarot, once upon a serpentine spine they called the God pharaoh, AstroTheology, my dragons tail fell in line with astrology, that's harmony! **TutemRa The Prophecy of Reincarnation,** geometry, creation, monogamy or polygamy? Probation! sovereignty divinity, cremation, the summation of the soul is infinity, ashes to ashes 3 phases of the sun the first trinity **- TutemRa Nebu Sahu Kheperu**

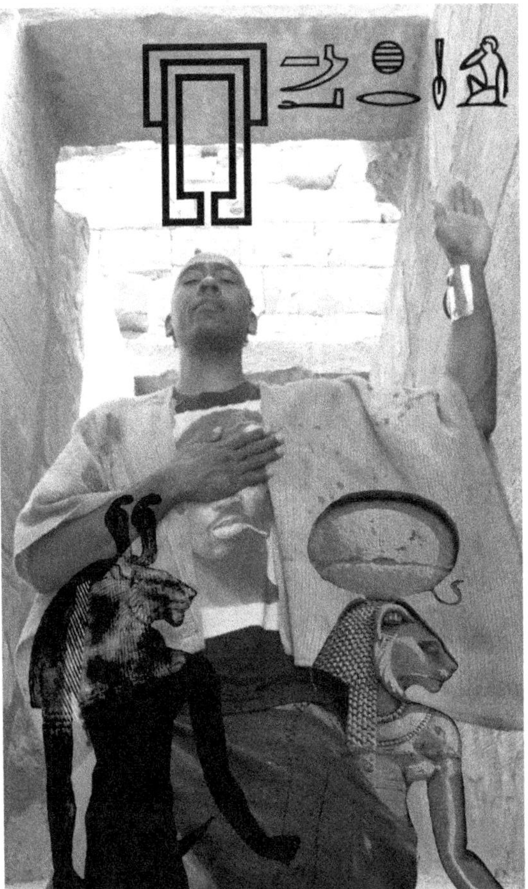

R.I.P. DMX, **See page 640**

Utterances for Coming Forth by day into Light

It is he, who comes forth by day into Light

October 7th 2021
The Great Arjuna's Penance / Descent of Ganges Relief at Mamallapuram

I do not remember the events that brought me to the Youtube video of the Descent of Ganges Relief but when I began to watch the video footage of the carvings on the wall I began to cry uncontrollably. As I looked at all the images they were so familiar that I knew I had definitely seen them before and something was pulling at my heart telling me that I had been there before! I could not explain the feeling, it was like nothing I have ever experienced before. My experience that woke me up to my past life as Emmett Till was instantaneous and I knew who I was immediately but I did not cry, instead I was amazed and at the same time I had a lot of disbelief. The more that I researched Emmett the more I knew it was real then the life of Emmett seemed to haunt me. He was everywhere even in the music I created years before the revelation. When my life as Tutankhaten came I knew immediately I was him and I laughed out load and joyously for a long time but this experience with the stone relief in India was different. It was like I have walked there before. The elephant statue was ingrained in my memory. The **Nagas** snake deities were also very familiar. I felt like I had climbed the wall relief before or walked on it and because of my past life experiences all I could do was think that I once lived there before. I know that I lived in India as Siddhartha but the time in which I was said to have lived does not match with the time of the building of the relief. Perhaps I lived as another person during the 7th or 8th Century.

November 13th 2021 - To Sirius A, or not to Siriusly B Graham Hancock

On November 13th 2021 I took a flight to Atlanta to see my Grandmother. When the **plane** landed I sat there and patiently waited my turn to exit and as I was waiting I just so happened to look at my scarab cuff on my wrist and for the first time I was able to **read the name** that is written very small in mdw ntr (hieroglyphics). I purchased the cuff 7 years ago from Mfundishi on **May 25th** 2014 (p 293). Mfundishi was wearing the cuff as he sat on 125th street vending. As soon as I saw the cuff on his wrist **something came over me and I had to have it**, my eyes opened wide and without thinking I said, "**how much is that**?!" and pointed at his cuff. I asked him for the cuff he was wearing and he gave me a price, then I pulled the money out my pocket and gave it to him. When I purchased the cuff I did not know how to read mdw ntr (hieroglyphics) at the time but 7 years later I sat on a plane and I read the name **NEB KHEPERU RA**, which is King Tut's throne name. I had taken mdw ntr classes with Mfundishi after my past life as Tutankhaten was revealed to me. After realizing this I sent Mfundishi a text about this but he didn't respond. He stopped responding to my texts' in 2020 after I started sharing my past life revelation of King Tut. I don't think he believes me but I understand. When I started sharing my story about my life as Emmett in 2018 he never seemed surprised, all he did was tell me to, "write a book" and for that I'm grateful. We might not get what we want but we get what we need. With that motivation I've written the most profound book ever written. After realizing that the name on the cuff was King Tut's throne name my thoughts were immediately taken back to an incident I had on a plane in 2014. I'm not sure if I was landing in New York or Atlanta but as I was **waiting to exit** the plane a White man asked me if I knew what the scarab on my cuff meant. I looked at him and said "yes" with a sort of attitude and then I disregarded him. I was still upset about the murder of **Michael Brown** (p 300) and didn't feel like talking to some White guy on the plane about my scarab cuff! Of course I knew what it meant! Thats's how I felt, but really I didn't know the full meaning of the scarab at the time. I had not yet learned about the connection it had with the **resurrection** of the pharaoh and wouldn't come to that realization until after I learned I was a pharaoh (2020)! It wasn't until today, Nov 13th 2021 that I felt like the man was Graham Hancock. At the time, in 2014 I did not know who he was. Because of my experiences with **thoughts**, and that fact that his name came flying into my mind from seemingly nowhere, I am inclined to put value on the possibility of it being him however, I would not be too thrown off if it wasn't him. He would have to confirm whether or not he asked a Black man about a scarab just before exiting a **plane** in NY or ATL. **Graham Hancock** is a British writer and journalist. He is known for alternative theories involving ancient civilizations, earth changes, stone monuments or megaliths, altered states of consciousness, ancient myths, and astronomical or astrological data from the past. This encounter with Graham one of two meetings with a specific person in this book that I'm not 100% sure about (page 57), however, for some **reason*** I **feel*** like the man looked like him and that **feeling*** only came after I realized the name on the cuff said **Neb Kheperu Ra**, King Tut's throne name. Later that night, after I arrived to my grandmother's house I **decided*** to watch an episode of ***The Twilight Zone*** titled, **Queen of the Nile** and to my surprise, in this episode there was a statue that bore the name **Neb Kheperu Ra**, I just laughed in amazement. ***ADDENDUM*** Before you dismiss this experience as "just coincidence", concider this first. **Rod Sterling**, the creator of the **Twilight Zone** saw the 1955 murder of Emmett Till as a mistrial of justice and wanted to tell Emmett's story. In response to the murder of Emmett Till he produced a show titled Noon On Doomsday. However, when the network realized his show was about the murder of Emmett Till they censored it so much that the audience never knew it was about Emmett Till. Afterwards he was quoted saying, "I think it's criminal that we're not permitted to make dramatic note of social evils as they exist... Drama by it's very nature should make a comment on those things that effect our daily lives". But isn't strange that the show aired on **April 25**, 1956, and **Carolyn Bryant**, the women who caused Emmett's death would die on **April 25**, 2023...?

November 2021
Uncle Jimmy and The 44th Parallel

Rau nu Prt m heru

Iu f Per f m heru

Utterances for Coming Forth by day into Light

It is he, who comes forth by day into Light

I met my uncle **Jimmy** for the first time at my Grand father's funeral in 2009 (page 169) when he was 64 years old. In November of 2021 I would visit him and his wife in Alabama and during this visit, on November 16th 2021 at the age of **77** he gave me this first hand information about his father (my great grand father), General Dukes Sr, aka **Son Turner** (page 19). While there in Alabama I made the most interesting connection with myself and my Uncle Jimmy which led to the deciphering of the star code pattern hidden within 19**44** and 19**77**. I labeled it **"The 44th Parallel".** I called my Uncle Jimmy for his birthday and discovered that he turned **77** years old on October **23rd** of 2021 and he was born in 19**44**, while I turned **44** years old on October **25th** of 2021 and I was born in 19**77**. Him and I had spoken in 2020 and that's when he told me about his ability to **dream** things before they happen. I found that interesting because not many other people in my family are like that. I felt a kinship with him and that was a major reason why I traveled to see him. I also really wanted to hear more about my great grand father.

When I got to Alabama I discovered that his wife Alice also turned **77** years old in 2021 and was born in 19**44**. My aunt Alice was born on July **23rd** two days before **Emmett Till** (July **25th**) and my uncle Jimmy was born October **23rd** two days before me (Oct **25th**). They both turned **77** years old in 2021 and I was born in 19**77**. I turn **44** years old in 2021 and they were both born in 19**44.** After I decoded this pattern I realized that I met the fashion mogul **Michelle Lamy** (p 582) and the political prisoner **Sekou Odinga** (p 561) in 2019 and they are both a part of this pattern. Then I would finally realize that **George Lucas,** the Creator of **Star Wars** was also absorbed into this star code pattern (p 37). **George Lucas** was born on my sisters birthday, May 14th 19**44**. See page 329 for **Man The Unknown** connection…. **Carolyn Bryant** (pages 180, 506)**,** the women who caused **Emmett Till** to be lynched, was also born on July **23rd**. She died at **88** years of age. 2022 is **88** years after she was born. 2022 in 100 years after the tomb of **King Tut** was discovered and the same year this book was released. My grand father Spencer **Wright** (page 25), and **Haile Selassie** (page 390) are also born on July **23rd**. See page **648** for the **metaphysical significance of the number 23**.

My uncle Jimmy Dukes is a **2x Silver Star** recipient from his time spent in the **Vietnam war**. We spent two nights sitting on the porch as he detailed the events that led to him receiving those medals. He feels that if he were a White man he would have gotten a **Medal Of Honor** or a **Distinguished Service Cross** instead of **Silver Stars**. I felt like he was the closest thing I had to my grand father so while I spent time with him I cherished it as if I was with my grand father. When I left Alabama I drove back to Georgia and during the ride I listened to a lot of **MF Doom**. At one point the MF Doom instrumental **Rhinestone Cowboy** came on and while driving I wrote the song **Son Turner** on November 19th 2021. When I got back to ATL I met up with my homie Tim Reed (page 587) and I finished the song in a parking lot where I recorded the verse over my laptop with no mic.

Vietnam War Veteran
Jimmy Lee Dukes 1st Silver Star Medal

In November of 67 my uncle Jimmy Dukes barely survived an ambush by hostile Vietnamese soldiers. He was a part of a Calvary unit with highly skilled helicopters. The 24th and 25th infantry division and the 1st armored division were responsible for guarding the landmine sweeping details.. Soldiers would do an exercise called Outpost the road every morning, using landmine detectors to sweep the road to ensure there were no explosives landmines on them. It was usually a 3 man detail. Each unit was responsible for a few miles of road a piece. When a mine was found it was exploded or dug up and placed on the side of the road and marked. My uncle Jimmy was a part of the detail that guarded the mine sweepers and ensured the safety of civilians. These main roads were supposed to remain open for convoys. While clearing one of these roads sometimes large piles of debris were pushed around **2**00 to **3**00 feet into the wood line to help open up the road way.. **On thanksgiving night of 1967** this large pile of debris would be used by the Vietnamese troops to create a perfect cover.

Jimmy Dukes was a Sergeant E-5 at the time. He would let the junior soldiers hold guard in the Armored personal Carrier (APC) till 12 or 1am then he would wake up and pull guard at night because he was good at staying up at night. Soldiers in Vietnam had beer, cigarettes, weed and some even had **heroin**. Jimmy drank and smoked cigarettes but his soldiers knew that he didn't condone smoking of weed, **heroin** or anything else. As it got darker that night Jimmy remembers a young Polish kid from New York named Walatica who came a couple times and reported "Sgt Dukes there is something out there moving". At first Jimmy told him it was the beer he drank earlier, but after the second time Walatica gave his report Jimmy got up and sure enough he could also see little things out there moving as well. The Vietnamese had taken cover behind the debris that the engineers created while they were clearing the road, this gave the Vietnamese a natural defense. With no time wasted Jimmy got on the machine gun and screamed to the platoon sergeant warning that the "enemy" was in the wood line as he began to open fire on them. The Vietnamese began to fire back and the first two RPG's hit a APC (tank). Jimmy told a soldier to take charge of the machine gun as he jumped down and climbed in the burning APC and pulled his platoon sergeant (Jonny Harpers) and the Lieutenant out to safety laying them on the ground so that they wouldn't burn to death. Jonny Harpers legs were gone and the Lieutenant was unconscious. This act of bravery is where Jimmy received his first Silver Star medal. Jimmy ordered his soldiers to back the vehicles up against each other so that they formed a circle with their fire power facing in all directions towards the enemy. The gun fight went on into the night and at around 8 or 9 am the Vietnamese began to close in on them from all directions. At this point there are two or three vehicles on fire, RPG's are flying everywhere. Jimmy goes into the pocket of the Platoon Sergeant and grabs his Signal Operating Instruction (S.O.I) booklet to call in for air support. He wasn't able to make sense of the booklet due to the limited light and the excitement of the situation so he had to broadcast in the open. He began to broadcast on any channel hoping another American unit would hear his call for help. Finally after some time he finds another American unit and he identifies himself "**Charlie 23** broadcasting in the open" but the person responds "unknown station get the fuck off the air". Jimmy begins to tell him what his situation is. Then the voice on the other end tells him to "wait out". After a few minutes the voice on the line returns and Jimmy gives his call sign again **"Charlie 23** broadcasting in the open". Then another voice appears on the line, this time it's a Marine from an air fighter unit. They had gotten Jimmy's military records from his unit and asked him questions that only he would know because some of the Vietnamese spoke very good English and they were known for setting up ambushes with fake calls for help. After verifying that the call was real they told Jimmy to sit tight as they set up an air strike. It took **2**0 to **3**0 minutes for them to arrive and when they did they told Jimmy to have everybody in his platoon to turn on their lights at the same time for one second to identify their location because they were **rolling in hot**. The air strike came in with a 20 millimeter Gatling gun and their aim was so precise that they were hitting everything around a 360 perimeter of the vehicles. Jimmy was hit with shrapnel under his right bicep and on the right side of his temple. He did not know he was hit until the event was over. It turns out that Jimmy's unit of 10 armored vehicles was ambushed by around 3,500 Vietnamese troops. On his way to the hospital he was accompanied by two north Vietnamese soldiers who were injured with hands tied behind their backs. He remembers being so angry because he had to fly out of this combat zone with these same men that had been shooting at him all night. A month and half or so after the event they had an award ceremony. Jimmy was put in for a **Distinguished Service Cross** but because he was a black man it was down graded to a **Silver Star**. The 4 star General **West** Moland was in charge of ground forces and he presented Jimmy with his **Silver Star** and also promoted him to E6 at the same ceremony. Jimmy feels that if he were a white man he would have gotten a **Medal Of Honor** or a **Distinguished Service Cross** for his actions during this event. See page **648** for the **metaphysical significance of the number 23**.

Vietnam War Veteran - Jimmy Lee Dukes 2nd Silver Star Medal

In July or August of 1968. Jimmy came in contact with a white Lieutenant Colonel who wanted combat time because it would look good on his record. Jimmy was a Sergeant E-6 at the time. This colonel had convinced the chain of command to make contact with enemy forces in a little country town. The Lieutenant Colonel had an **11** man squad along with Jimmy's 3 vehicles which added up to around **22** people. With no intel as to what was in this town they came across a group of north Vietnamese soldiers. Jimmy says the north Vietnamese troops were very well trained and they were **hard** and **unafraid**. He said they had no problem sacrificing themselves in combat. And because of this **award chasing** Lieutenant Colonel they found themselves in a fire fight needing to be rescued again. At some point Jimmy pulled a pistol on the White colonel. The Colonel wanted to be in charge but he was getting soldiers killed. Jimmy put his army 45 pistol in the officers face and told him "**ay I'm running this shit now! Ok? You're getting us fucked up! Now Quit! Now get your ass over there some place and sit the fuck down**". Jimmy says two of the lower enlisted soldiers were looking at him horrified. They couldn't believe he spoke to an officer like that. In the end the Lieutenant colonel got his medal out of it but he also **fabricated** the story. After this Jimmy got out of the army for 8 or 9 months. He tried to find a way for himself but he was institutionalized. He reenlisted in April of 1969 from Brooklyn New York and was sent back to Vietnam.

Rau nu Prt m heru

Iu f Per f m heru

Jtterances for Coming Forth by day into Light

It is he, who comes forth by day into Light

Vietnam War Veteran
"There is Mud, Blood and Guts out here, All Over"

Uncle Jimmy was on a detail securing Highway 16 to Cambodia. The roads closed at dark and their mission was to ensure that civilian cars were off the roads at night due to regular gun fire. They were always prepared for the worst but somethings seemed like clockwork, like the routine gun fire attack they could expect at 3am and 3pm every day. They did regular Out-posting of the roads, sweeping for landmines to ensure safety. Jimmy details the events of a memory that he can never forget. He was in his vehicle looking at an adult magazine when he heard a tremendous explosion. On sight of the blast him and his soldiers began to run to the road. To their dismay they saw a bus that had ran over a landmine and the bus was full of pregnant Vietnamese women. The bus was taking the women to the major city for pregnancy test and deliveries.. The bus was full to the rim with some people who were hanging on the sides and some seated on the top.

The front wheels of the bus triggered the **landmine** but because the bus was traveling so fast the bus made it half way over the **landmine** before it finally detonated with a blast so catastrophic that it cut the bus completely in half. Jimmy says the truck was so perfectly cut in half that it looked as if someone had used a blow torch to cut it. There were body parts everywhere. Some of the women were very close to their delivery dates. Jimmy made a call to headquarters with the radio on his back, he spoke to his Major Commander and said. "Sir, there is an old American school bus full with pregnant women going to the big city for exams and deliveries, there is mud, blood and guts out here, all over". Medical helicopters were immediately dispatched to bring support. By the time the situation came to a close that night he was covered in blood like a trauma surgeon. He was also evacuated but not because of wounds received but because of psychological trauma. When uncle Jimmy was done telling me this story he told me that he still sees these images over and over in his head as vivid as the day they happened. Sometimes the memories are not so bad and sometimes they are not so good. He said he's never going to forget it. It may be a little less traumatizing but he will never forget that. He explained that when you see a baby who is alive inside of it's mother who's body has been blown open and you must take your knife and cut the umbilical cord but there is nothing that can be done for the mother….. He explained that, "you do what the fuck you have to do! that is not a pretty fucking sight! You got 80 fucking little tiny women." He began to cry. Then he explained, "i just don't understand why we do shit to people. And all I try to do is help". He wiped his tears and told me to turn the camera off.

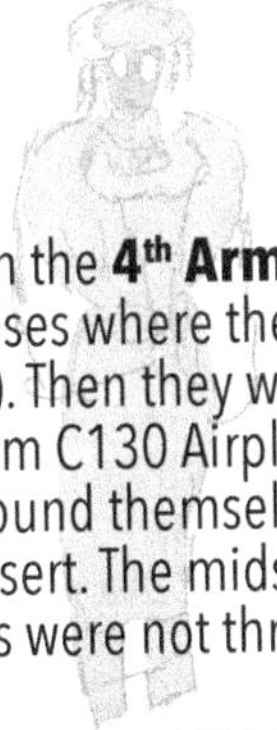

Vietnam War Veteran
Airborne Jumps into Egypt

Jimmy was stationed in the **4th Armored division out of Munich Germany** and because he was qualified he was selected to join the exercises where they would fly into **Kemet** (Egypt) on C130 Airplanes and make airborne jumps into the deserts of **Kemet** (Egypt). Then they would get picked up and fly back to Munich where they would make airborne jumps back into Munich Germany from C130 Airplanes. Jimmy tells me of one of these trips where his unit jumped into Kemet just south of **Cairo** one night and found themselves surrounded by non hostile opposing forces. On another night in Cairo he remembers seeing a **midst** in the desert. The midst looked like the **silhouettes** of **ghost's**. He said it was a horrifying experience but at the same time the figures were not threatening. What did my uncle see in the deserts of Kemet?

November 19th 2021 Son Turner (page 19)

They called him **Son Turner**, some say he's related to **Nat Turner**, **44** strapped with a piece for dummy's that need to learn a, lesson! Story like a Smif-N-Wessun, 1953 **Uncle Jimmy** tell'n me his confessions, mule kicks, white balls, brown horse, rode into town like a boss of course, fully equipped don't cross! fire on a fire cracker like a broken pool stick, **Araminta Ross**, **Moses** and <u>**the ark of the covenant**</u> when you feel'n lost and forgotten like **Akhenaten**, **General Dukes** Sharecrop'n, Time travel'n, air dropped in, helicop't in, Vietnamese never called him nigger still he squeezed and shot them, but still he saved many, **Silver Star** can't measure the bar of a **Brave Cherokee** Native American - Indian, in a **dream** seen before he came, militiamen, suicide never ease the pain, a **Prince** and them, Cinnamon shade discipline, **Tamerrian** like Detroit Michigan - **TutemRa**

December 8th 2021 Star Codes of Immortality

I tapped in, the average mind can't comprehend, limestone copper in rhyme, I shine, **Prophet** lead the blind, read the sign and see reality, and see I deciphered the star code of immortality, **Behold**! I right the wrongs and curse the fallacies, out for **Every Thing They Owe**, the **Pharisees**! *I was shot but came back **resurrected**, this that raw shit I manifested!* <u>astral projected</u>, apple invested with **Eve** on the Nile we had a child and I **Buddha** blessed it, I **Buddha** blessed it, Alpha Omega, A to Z, Hieroglyph Astrology, **Jay Z, Biggie** or **Nas**? **Tupac** probably die tragic, **still illmatic,** we can heal or have **Havoc** make **magic** like a **Prodigy** this gotta be the prophecy, 9 ether carbon hydrogen oxygen nitrogen baptism by fire I be a light receiver, this a **Leacola Riddle** for the non believers they say I whistled a bag of skittles but not a right that was civil, they gave him acquittal, so I don't trust that not even a little, not the left not the right not even the middle, **Cherokee** played the fiddle with feathers scribble symbols of **Ntchrs** for the here after, **Ra un Nefer** for the win go and read a chapter, right after read ***<u>TutemRa</u>*** *<u>the prophecy of reincarnation</u>* see what you are face'n, inhalation race'n against time they harvesting pineal glands but not mine, back of my mind I hear the lines **Mother Ross** always told to me, get off your ass young brother if you wanna be free, picture these jewels being dropped with a beautiful smile we traveled for miles in the dark man women and child **- TutemRa**

Significance

December 8th is celebrated as Bodhi day by Buddhist, the day celebrated as the day the **Buddha Siddhartha Gautama** attained enlightenment. I knew that when I wrote the song and that is why I said the name Buddha in the song. I also spoke **Prodigy's** name in this song and 3 days later a video of Prodigy would find it's way to me in which he speaks about **reincarnation** and I would find significant star codes revolving around Prodigy. Watching that video led me to the video of **Bushwick Bill** where he also talks about **reincarnation** and after watching that video I would come to see that **Bushwick Bill** was sent down on (born on) **December 8th** the day the **Buddha Siddhartha Gautama** attained enlightenment. In this song I also spoke my Great Grand mothers name saying "this a **Leacola Riddle** for the non believers they say I whistled, a bag of skittles but not a right that was civil, they gave him the acquittal". This star code of immortality is like a Divine **Riddle**. I mention Jay Z in this rhyme. Jay Z and Will Smith produced a documentary on Emmett Till that was released in 2022 on Jan 6th, the day Mamie Till died (page 614). Jada P Smith is born the day before Emmett's court case started and Will Smith is born two days after it ended. Jay Z was born on Dec 4th 1969, the day **Fred Hampton** was assassinated. Tupac was born within the Black Panther Party for Self Defense that Fred Hampton was heavily involved with. Jay Z has twins (Gemini, twins) born 3 days before Tupac. Jay Z's first child is born the day after Emmett Till's mother died and his wife Beyonce is born the day after Emmett Till's wake (p 514). I know who Tupac was in a past life, and sometimes this makes wonder just who **Jada** might possibly have been! (See p 371 for the 6th rhyme written this year).

December 11th 2021 (Prodigy Has Been Here Before)

On December 8th I wrote the song **Star Codes of Immortality,** and in that song I mentioned Prodigy's name. Speak a mans name and he lives forever.. And sometimes he appears. Coincidentally 3 days later I see a video of Prodigy in which he speaks about **supernatural** experiences he has had. He explained that he had been desiring to see a **UFO** and one night him and his wife experienced seeing one together (see pages 84, 105, 346, 380). He said the experience scared the shit out of him. There was a blackout in his neighborhood and suddenly a **UFO** appeared over his house shining into his window and the experience was undeniably real. He mentioned seeing **shadow people** in his room one night while the lights were off. He described them as looking like venom, the black Spiderman (Peter-Ptah **Parker**). The next day he found himself in severe pain as his sickle cell flared up again. He says he's been given supernatural guidance that people would not understand if he tried to talk to them about it. He said he has had messages in time that were put there for him to decipher and connect the dot later in life. He has gotten messages that he is on the right track with his music and he was given the tools to heal his sickle cell. He was told that **this was not his first time living on this planet** that **he has been here before many thousands of years**. It also sounds as if he was told who he was in **previous lives** but he did not expound on that. In this video Prodigy was wearing a gold **Nefertiti** chain reminiscent to **Tupac**. In another video recorded years prior Prodigy can be seen driving around talking about the direction he wanted to go with his music. He expressed how he planned to put more conscious information in his music. Prodigy felt that he had learned from all the people that this government has assassinated physically and even the ones who have had their character assassinated and thrown in prison. He felt that the FBI had something to do with the killing of **Tupac** and **Biggie** but the FBI (**Hip Hop police,** p 564) made it look like a rap war. He expressed what many of us had been feeling for years. He mention how being framed by the cops angered him and the experience, in a sense turned him into the new **Malcolm X**, where as he wanted to expose all the crooked things this government is doing to include, Hollywood, the FDA, the military, and healthcare. He also expressed that if **Tupac** was still around they would be on the same team. **Significance:** Prodigy is a scorpio like myself and he is born on November 2nd two days before the discovery of Tutankhaten's (King Tut's) tomb on November 4th 1922. He died on June 20th 2017 4 days after Tupacs birthday. His last album was titled Hegelian Dialectic (The Book of **Revelation**). My past life revelation of my life as Tutankhaten (King Tut) came on April 4th 2020 (page 594). On the cover of his album **Hegelian Dialectic** Project buildings can be seen and across from them the **Giza pyramids** can be seen. The zodiac wheels of destiny incircles a skeleton version on the vitruvian man drawn by Leonardo da Vinci. "It's not that I'm writing a book, I'm just putting things in order, like **Shook** in 95 - recorded in 94, have you ever had **DeJa Vu?** this is nothing knew I've seen this before! catch **22**, I was walking out the store, they say I **whistled,** but for what? they not really sure, I ate the bread the color was hoar, here to restore **Maat"- (Catch 22, p 647)**

<u>Condolences</u>

My condolences go out to the family, friends and fans of **Albert Prodigy Johnson**. Please know that death is not the end. The soul survives death, indeed and in spirit. This is a book of the dead written by a boy who was murdered without justice, who defeated death and came forth by day.May the soul of **Albert Prodigy Johnson** walk peacefully through the field of Reeds in Amenta. Amen Ra.

Bushwick Bill (Geto Boys) Reincarnated

After listening to **Prodigy** talking about living previous lives I remembered the video of **Bushwick Bill** I came across in 2019. In that video Bushwick talked about being diagnosed with stage 4 **cancer** and how he was not afraid of death because he had already died and **came back** on June 19th 1991. He spoke about the experience in the song **<u>Ever So Clear</u>** released on the album **Little Big Man** on Sep 8th 1992. In the song he details the events of his Near Death Experience (**NDE**) where he died and went to heaven and saw a Godly **Jesus** figure: <u>"Five different doctors with needles tryin to stick me, I hear my family hollerin he needs us, Durin the confusion, man, I seen Jesus, my mom's on the phone long-distance from New York, Here comes the doctors again tryin to rip me apart, I got a monkey on my back, I can't shake it, I'm havin suicidal thoughts hopin that I don't make it, but I'ma make it 'cause something's steady urgin me, five hours passed, I made it through surgery, and the doctor said I wouldn't make it through the night, but God told me everything is gonna be alright, and I'm glad that I'm here, gee, but it's fucked up I had to lose an eye to see shit clearly"</u>. He released that album on **Sep 8th** the day after **Tupac** was shot on **Sep 7th** 1996. **Bushwick** died on **June 9th** the same day as my *Great Grandfather* **General Dukes Sr** which is the day before **Marcus Garvey** Died and the day before my *Great Grandmother* **Leacola *<u>Riddle</u>*** was born. My *Grandfather* **General Dukes Jr** is born on June 17th the day after **Tupac's** birthday and he died on August 18th the day after **Marcus Garvey's** birthday. I have a theory about who **Tupac** was in a **past life** and at this point it should be <u>Ever So Clear</u> to you. **The Geto Boys** released their 5th studio album on **April 2**, 1996 titled, **The Resurrection**. My past life of **Tutankhaten** (**King Tut**) was revealed to me on **April 4th** 2020.

Significance

Bushwick Bill was sent down (born) on **December 8th** the same day that I wrote the song **Star Codes of Immortality** (p 663). December 8th is celebrated by Buddhist as the day the Buddha Siddhartha Gautama attained enlightenment. Bushwick Bill released the album **Little Big Man** on September 8th and on that album he writes the song **<u>Ever So Clear</u>** in which he details the events Near Death Experience (NDE) where he died and went to heaven and saw a Godly Jesus figure. ***<u>Condolences:</u>*** My condolences go out to the family, friends and fans of Richard Williams Stephen Shaw. Please know that death is not the end. The soul survives death, indeed and in spirit. This is a book of the dead written by a boy who was murdered without justice, who defeated death and came forth by day. May the soul of **Richard Shaw** walk peacefully through the field of Reeds in Amenta. Amen Ra.

Rau nu Prt m heru

lu f Per f m heru

Utterances for Coming Forth by day into Light

It is he, who comes forth by day into Light

After **Tupac** died in 1996 (page 76) there were many people including myself who felt like he was still alive, living in hiding. There were websites made that had all the events linked by songs and dates speculating the faking of his death. It seemed that Tupac was connected to the numbers **25** and **7**. He was shot on Sep **7th** and died on the **7th** day (page 41), on Sep **13th** at **25** years old, the same day **my Father's** brother died on his **13th** birthday (p 28). "**Coincidentally**", his Last album was titled, **Makaveli**, The Don Killuminati: **The 7 Day Theory** and was released on **Nov 5th** 1996, the day after **King Tut's** tomb was discovered on **Nov 4th** 19**22**. The **coincidences** surrounding his death seemed to have prepared me for the decoding of my previous lives years to come (page 222).
14 shots were fired at Tupac on Sep 7, 1996. **Ausar** was cut into **14** pieces and **Emmett Till** died at **14**. Tupac released the **Thug Life** album on Sep 26th 1994, 3 days after the **Emmett Till** trial ended in 19**55** (page 516).. The first song on the album is **Bury Me a G** and on the second verse, Tupac's brother, **Mopreme Shukar** say's, "<u>and to the G's you can feel my pain, until the motherfucker gets **born again**</u>". The first single for the album was, **Pour Out a Little Liquor** and it was released on Aug **23**rd, the day before **Emmett Till** entered the store that got "him" killed (p 506). The second single, **Cradle to the Grave**, was released on **Nov 4th** 1994, the same day that **King Tut's** tomb was discovered in 19**22**. On the song **Under Pressure** Tupac says, "<u>Right before I die, I'll be cursin' the law, **Reincarnated** bitch, even worse than before</u>".

Tupac's, Comin' For Them Pharaoh's Kids
AMEN
LUXOR HOTEL
96 9 7

Life isn't a series of random events. There is an **unseen** order from which everything is connected & Tupac lived a life in ancient Kemet thousands of years ago. This might sound **strange** but keep reading and I'll take you to the "**West Side**"! Tupac was shot and robbed on Nov 30th 1994, four days after **King Tut's** tomb was opened (Nov 26th 19**22**, p 11). <u>Walter "**King Tut**" Johnson</u> was a street goon who was well known for doing high risk robbery's. Tupac felt **Tut** was the person who shot him and on his last album **Makaveli,** he mentions **Tut** in the song, **Against All Odds**: "<u>All out warfare, eye for an eye last words to a bitch nigga, why you lie? now you gotta watch your back nigga, watch your front, here we come gunshots to **Tut**, now you stuck</u>". Tupac also mention's **Nas** on that song and Tupac died the day before **Nas's** birthday and **Nas** has a daughter named **Destiny** who's "**coincidentally**" born the day before Tupac's birthday. Tupac also felt that Jimmy Henchman had something to do with his shooting in 1994. **Jimmy Henchman** was sentenced to **life in prison** on my birthday, **Oct 25** 2013, <u>the year of the snake</u>. Tupac was falsely accused of **rape** and sent to prison for it on Feb **7th** 1995, which is **Emmett Till's father's** birthday, who was also falsely accused of **rape** (page 475). Mike Tyson got married on **Feb 7th** and was also falsely accused of **rape** and sent to prison on Feb 10th 1992. **Mike Tyson's** trainer **Cus D'Amato** died on **Nov 4th** 1985, the same day **King Tut's** tomb was discovered on **Nov 4th** 1922, the same day **Sean (Diddy) Combs** was born (p 44, 199). On Sep **7th** 1996 Tupac drove to Las Vegas to meet up with Suge Knight to attend the **Mike Tyson** fight (p 528). Tupac checked into the **LUXOR** Hotel where he booked a room for the night. **Luxor** is a city in Kemet (Egypt) that was once called Thebes and Waset. Tupac took one of his last photos standing in front of an image of **Amen** in the lobby of the **Luxor** Hotel. **Amen** is the **unseen** hidden God (deity) and was seen as the **king** of the **8** primordial deity's. Tupac was gunned down with a Glock **22** pistol the same day he took that picture. The ancient Kemetyu called the death of the physical body, **Westing**. Just as the Sun rises in the East and sets in the **West** the same is to be said for the soul. After Tupac was shot, Suge began to drive **West**. Tupac was known for flashing the "**West Side**" hand signs. Tupac's sister's name is **Sekyiwa** Shakur and they call her **Set** for short. **Set** is the brother of **Ausar** (Osiris) and Au**set** (**Isis**). Ausar is the Lord of **resurrection**, the lord of the **dead** and the **Lord** of the **West (p 3).**

In ancient times the concept of reincarnation was called **Wehem** **Mesut** (p 14). In **Judaism** it's known as **Gilgul** (Cycle). Egyptians called death of the physical body, **WESTING**. Just as the **Sun** rises in the east and sets in the **west** the same is to be said for the **soul**. When the Nswt Bity's (Pharaoh's) "went **WEST**", they reincarnated into new bodies and when they did they went to their tombs to collect their belongings! That's the reason we buried ourselves underground like the only begotten **Scarab** who springs forth from the dirt from seemingly nowhere (p 569). Every "Pharaoh" was seeking to resurrect / reincarnate no different than your modern day Dali Lama is said to be the same reincarnated soul. In the TV series **Lost** (p 259), the character John Locke had been thrown out the window of a building by his father but miraculously he survived the fall, but he was now a paraplegic in a wheel chair with no hopes of ever walking again. He gets on a plane and the plane crashes on an island. He survives the crash but to his amazement he was miraculously healed and could now walk! The people living on the island before the crash had been waiting for the **"chosen one"** to appear. After hearing about the effect the island had on John Locke some of them believed John to be special and possibly the chosen one. To see if John was indeed and in spirit "the chosen one" some one traveled back in time to meet John when he was a little boy. They told John's mother that he was being considered for a special program for gifted children. A man placed various items on a table in front of John and asked him to pick up the items that were his. John, around 5 years old looked at the items and with

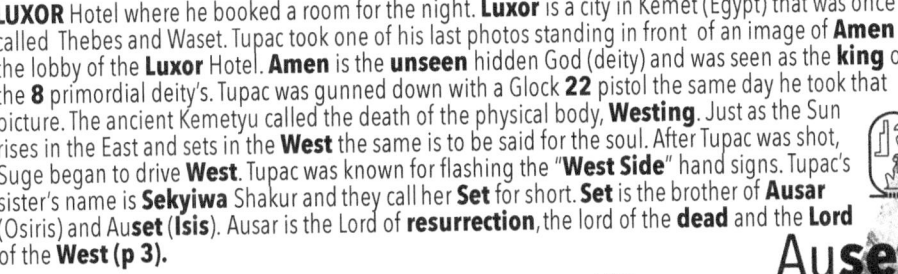

expert aim he grabbed all of the things that belonged to the Adult version of John who was back on the island. When the man saw that John was who they thought he was he gazed in amazement . This is very similar to how they pick the new Dali Lama. When a Dali Lama dies they search for his successor and in doing so they look for birthmarks and other details that only the Dali Lama would gravitate to. In my case, I was drawn to the story of Emmett Till as I wrote about him 9 times in my music before I knew I was him in my previous life (p 201). I also have birthmarks in all the places that Emmett Till and King Tut were said to be injured (p 514). **Birthmarks** are highly melanated markers, usually seen as black dots, which are part of the souls **genetic memory** connected to how people may have died in previous lives. When we **reincarnate** back to earth we can tend to gravitate to things that are familiar to ancient parts of our souls. There is a reason why they call you an "**old soul**". You seem to be familiar with a time that was far before your time... Why do we focus on what we focus on? Why are we attracted to what we are attracted to? How long does love last? Does it die after death? Does it get recycled? Is there a storage system for the memories of our previous lives? Let's take Tupac for instance, why did he choose to wear **Nefertiti** jewelry so much? Yes she was well known due to her European whitewashing but Tupac seemed to almost **love** Nefertiti. It reminds me of my Emmett Till tee shirt. I bought it 10 months before my revelation and it is connected to the very moment I realized I was Emmett Till in a **past life** (p 459 - 480). **With all this in mind, ask yourself, why did Tupac make so many references to reincarnation in his music and why did he think a man named King Tut shot him??!!** Walter "**King Tut**" Johnson was born on Sep 8th, the day after Tupac was shot and he was sentenced to life in prison on Oct 24 1996, the day before my birthday. He maintains that he had nothing to do with 2pac's attempted murder & assassination. On the song **Ambitions Az a Rider**, Tupac says, "They cowards, that's why they tried to set me up, had bitch-ass niggas on my team so indeed they wet me up, but **I'm back reincarnated**". On the album **R U Still Down,** Tupac can be heard saying: "you can't kill me, **I'm the king**". On the track, Only Fear of Death, Tupac say's "Never will I die, **I'll be back, reincarnated** as a mother fuckin' MAC 11". This album was released on Nov 25th, the day before **King Tut's** tomb was opened (p 11). The **Outlawz** released the album **Still I Rise** in 1999, on the track **Killuminati**, Tupac says, "Hard to kill a nigga cause **I'm comin' back like Jesus**". Tupac's album **Better Dayz** was released on **Nov 26th** 2002, the day King Tut's tomb was opened. On the last track he can also be heard saying: "**Expect me nigga. Like you expect Jesus to come back. Expect me nigga. I'm coming!**". On the track **Untouchable**, released in 2006, Tupac say's, "Y'all remember me legendary **live eternally**, **bury me in pieces cause they fear reincarnation**". After Tupac's death many of his unfinished songs were leaked. One song was titled, **Reincarnation** (p 300), on that song Tupac can be heard saying, "My only fear of death, is **reincarnation**, I use my last breath, to reach the whole nation, How can they call me murderer for my spoken words? This composition be my **prophecy** I hope it's heard". This book is the **"prophecy"** that Tupac spoke of in his song, **Reincarnation! Jewell dreamt** about **Tupac's death** before it happened (p 105), just like my sister **dreamt** about my car accident (p 104)!

How is Tupac connected to the **Curse of the Pharaoh** (p 204)?!! Why did Tupac **tattoo** the image of **Nefertiti** on his chest?! Why did he make references to **reincarnation** in his music? And why did Tupac tattoo the words: "**My Only Fear of Death iz Coming Back Reincarnated**" on his arm? The book of **Exodus** from the bible is based off of the life of Akhenaten, the husband to Nefertiti and father to Tutankhaten (King Tut). Akhenaten did the things that **Moses** was said to have done in the book of **Exodus**. Moses was said to have taken his people into the desert for 40 years while Akhenaten took his people to a fertile land between Memphis and Thebes (**Luxor**) and built a city that venerated the sun (**Aten**), during the age of **Aries**, that city is now a desert. Mose introduced the 10 **commandments** while Akhenaten proclaimed **Aten** as the one God. Why did Tupac tattoo **Exodus** on his back? Perhaps Tupac's ancient soul fragment was speaking on the song **Black Jesus** when he said the words, "Went to church but don't understand it, they underhanded, God gave me these **commandments**, the world is scandalous, Blast till they holy high, baptize they evil minds, **Wise**, no longer blinded, **watch me shine** trick". Perhaps Tupac was the biblical person that Moses was fashioned after. Did you know that Akhenaten was a poet? He wrote **The Hymn to The Aten (p 615)**, a poem dedicated to the **sun** and the life giving power it has. The strange thing about **The Hymn to The Aten (Sun)** is that it resembles **Psalms 104** from the bible that was supposedly written by David. Why did Tupac say, "Then we ride 'til the **SUN** come **shinin'** back to **brighten** up the sky"?! Akhenaten was known for his willingness to promote the love he shared with his family creating stela's with images of him kissing and feeding his children. No other Pharaoh had done that before. Tupac wrote *Brenda's got a baby*, he wrote *Dear Momma* , he wrote *Keep Ya Head Up* and other songs empowering women. Tupac loved the divine feminine energy on the planet. Music can be felt by the soul and that's why Tupac's music is still loved by the world today 25 years after his death (p 6). In ancient Kemet the Nswt Bity (pharaoh) held a staff like **Moses** called a **Heka**. It was also called a Shepard's staff (𓋾) or the **Crook (heka,𓋾)**. It was the staff of **rulership**. It was like the title in a name like Dr or General. Could this be why Tupac's name was Lesane Parish **Crooks (𓋾)** when he was born, and later his name was changed to Tupac Amaru Shakur?! The name Lesane can be scrambled to spell the word slane (slain). The word **Parish** can mean family, **house** or town, usually related to Christian Churches. The word Parish also stems from the word Parisis (Par-**isis / "Paris"**). The Kemetic word for **house** was **per** (par) and **isis** (Auset) was the wife of Ausar (Osiris) the lord of **resurrection**. So Tupac's born name can translate to, the slain (Lesane) **Ruler** (Crooks) born in the **house** of **Isis** (Per-**isis**). In the movie **Juice**, Tupac's character was named **Bishop**. The Bishop in the church is a leader. The Bishop is also a piece in the game of chess. The oldest version of the game chess is called **Senet** (p 10), it was created in ancient Kemet (Egypt), and many of the Senet board games were found in the tomb of Tutankhaten. While Tupac was serving time in Clinton Correctional Facility he wrote a movie script titled "**Live 2 Tell**". In my life as Tutankhaten I was born in Akhetaten the city built by my father Akhenaten. Today Akhetaten is called Tell EL Amarna. The locals call it **ET Till** or **EL Till**. These names are part of this prophecy of reincarnation and they connect me with my past lives as Emmett Till and Tutankhaten. ET Till like EMM**ET**T Till and **EL T**ill like **E**mmett **L**ouis **Till** (p 671). In my life as Tutankhaten I was born in an ancient city now known as Et Till, like Emmett Till. I died young and was born again many times with one of my most recent lives being born as Emmett Till in 1941 the year of the snake. Even in the name K**emet** you find the name Emmett. As Emmett Till I lived a sacrificial life dying at 14 years old sparking the Civil Rights Movement. I was born again as Dawud in 1977 the year of the snake. Tupac was my favorite rapper since I was a teenager. At the age of 40 I realized I was Emmett Till (p 480) and at 42 I realized I was King Tut and was given the name TutemRa (p 594). Tupac had a cousin named Crystal **Dukes** & I descend from the **Dukes** of Orrville (p 19). By now it should be **Crystal** clear who **Tupac** was.

Blasphemy

Tupac dropped his last studio album **Makaveli** on Nov 5th 1996, the day after **Tutankhaten's** tomb was discovered on Nov 4th 1922. The 5th song on the album was titled **Blasphemy**. On the second verse of this song Tupac says he's **"coming for the Pharaoh's kids"** and he says the name **Moses**. **Akhenaten** was the biblical **Moses**... Tupac also writes about living by the **Nile** and **coming back resurrected.**

"We pro'ly in Hell already, our dumb asses not knowin', everybody kissin' ass to go to Heaven ain't goin', put my soul on it, I'm fightin' devil niggas daily plus the media be crucifyin' brothers severely, **tell me I ain't God's son**; nigga, momma a **virgin**, we got evicted, had to leave the 'burbs, back in the ghetto doin' wild shit **lookin' at the SUN** don't pay, Criminal mind all the time, wait for judgment day, they say **Moses** split the Red Sea, I split the blunt and rolled it fat when I'm deadly, **Babylon beware, comin' for them Pharaoh's kids**, retaliation, makin' legends off the shit we did, still bullshittin', niggas in Jerusalem **waitin' for signs,** God comin' she's just takin' her time (haha!), **Livin' by the Nile while the water flow,** I'm contemplatin' plots, wonderin' where the thought'll go, **Brothas gettin' shot comin' back resurrected, It's just that raw shit, nigga check it** (that raw shit)" **- Tupac**

January 12th 2022
Congressional Gold Medal and Anti Lynching Bill for Emmett Till
Why Now?!

Rau nu Prt m heru

On March 16th 2021, 8 Asian women were killed in an Atlanta Spa. Only **2 months later**, in May of 2021 President Biden signed an Anti Asian Hate Bill in to "**Law**" to protect Asians. 67 years ago Emmett Till was lynched by two racist White men in 1955. **67 years after** Emmett was lynched the Emmett Till Anti Lynching Act was signed on March 29th 2022. This legislation is not specific to black people like the Anti Asian Hate Bill. Instead, it is a legislation for **all people** yet not all groups of people are murdered indiscriminately like Black people. 8 Asian women were murdered and a bill is passed for Asian people yet the Anti Lynching Bill for Emmett Till is not specific to Black people who are killed in hate crimes at higher rates than any other people in America. On January 12th 2022 the Senate 'honored' Emmett Till and his mother, Mamie Till-Mobley. Lawmakers passed legislation that would posthumously award Emmett and his mother with the **Congressional Gold Medal**, the United States Congress's **highest civilian honor**. We got a Gold Medal but no protection under the "**Law**".. I was 14 years old when I was kidnapped, beaten, and brutally lynched in M**ississ**ippi by racist white supremacists in 1955. My mother allowed photographs of me to be taken in my casket, and demanded an open casket funeral. The image of my battered body served as a rallying cry for African Americans who joined the Civil Rights Movement to ensure there would be no more "Emmett Tills". Unfortunately we still see "Emmett till's" in 2022. I am writing this on January 17th 2022, the day that **Muhammad Ali** was born and Ali described the murder of Emmett Till as a point of awakening for him. Growing up, the boxing great was shocked by photos of Emmett Till's body and it affirmed his role of using boxing as a way to represent the black struggle in America and in the **Jim Crow** South. In his book, **The Greatest**, Ali wrote: "Emmett Till and I were about the same age..I felt a deep kinship to him". Ali saw himself in the murder of Emmett Till because he was 13 years old at the time and Emmett was 14 years of age. It could have been him in that casket. No different than how young black males in 2022 see themselves in the murder of **Trayvon Martin**, **Tamir Rice**, and the countless others. This award was given to me 67 years after I was murdered. This award was given to me on Khalid Abdul Muhammad's birthday, he would have been 74 years old this year. **I dedicate this Congressional Gold Medal to brothers Khalid Abdul Muhammad and Muhammad Ali**. Khalid was born in 1948 and he was 7 years old when I was murdered. Brother Khalid was assassinated on Brother Huey P's birthday, February 17th 2001, the year of the **snake**, he was only 53 years old. The first time I heard brother Khalid speak it roused a sense of honor and respect within me. I have had a few experiences with him over the course of these past 10 years. I am forever grateful for brothers like **Khalid Muhammad** and Muhammad Ali. Below I have placed some of the times I mentioned them in my music. Today is May 14th 2022 and today is my sisters birthday. Today there was a massacre in Buffalo NY. Payton S. Gendron, a 18 year old white man drove over 200 miles to a store in Buffalo NY and killed 10 black people. **Aaron** Salter was the **55** year old ex-cop supermarket security guard who was killed in the Buffalo Massacre. Inspired by rising gas prices, Aaron had recently spoken about a "newly discovered energy source" and had patented a system that enables vehicles to run on water instead of gasoline, called hydrogen-electrolysis. Some say Payton drove over 200 miles because the massacre was an organized assassination of Aaron so as to suppress technology that would threaten the oil and automotive industries.

Iu f Per f m heru

<u>Letters From Metu Ntchrs (written on May 5th 2013, page 72)</u>

"I'm a rider **Muhammad Ali pyramid** on the dollar, fuck they school and they rules! keep your hands off Assata"

Don't Argue Me (written on January 23rd 2016, page 360)

"if I were you I would watch **Khalid Muhammad** on **Donahu**, don't be in a rush to condemn me, she or him, **Malcolm X** said you ain't always think the way you do my friend!"

Rope A Dope (written on March 18th 2016, page 370)

"you might get stripped and swiped of your title, be found guilty cause you read the Quran and won't pick up a rifle, **Ali The Greatest Of All Time** idol, he told his rival "I am one man you can't beat and conquer, I fight for 30 million africans your honor. where's the honor in dropping bombs on a town 10 thousand miles away, they never called me nigger but you kill my people everyday", the terror stays real like **Emmett Till,** the American way, **float** away **like a butterfly,** but you gotta come back someday."

Run Quick See (written on August 25th 2016, page 416)

"The pause in the **Malcolm** speech they edit away, press play, you can call me **Muhammad Ali, The Greatest Of All Time**, but not one more time **Cassius Clay! King kunta, Prince Hakeem** from **Far Rockaway** to the bay, ***I pray the Lord my soul to keep if I should die before I reach my peak of my success, pray for a soldiers death***"

Cream remix (October 9th 2017, page 454)

"damn! four years later I'm in Iraqi killing fields, came back they still attacking cats like lil black **Emmett till,** They asked if I played with **kap**, then perhaps would I kneel, or would I stand like a coward for a deal? if you don't stand for something you fall for anything, on the road to fast cars and diamond rings, you think ball is life? but ball ain't everything, it's enslavement! scared to make **Muhammad Ali** statements!"

COOLEST MONKEY IN THE JUNGLE (H&M Response) (written on February 11th 2018, page 461)

"The coolest monkey in the jungle, swing from tree to tree Ubuntu, confront you with virtue, humble still ***sting like a bee, float like*** the ***black star line***, ***Nobel*** like **Dru *Ali***, we go and see the ***Black Panther*** but won't set the black panthers free, **free Mumia** rest in peace and black power to brother ***khalid***, They killed him on ***Huey P's*** birthday in the worst way, and it tears me apart in the heart, like **apartheid** the **medical** extermination of black people from colonial times to present,"

Utterances for Coming Forth by day into Light

It is he, who comes forth by day into Light

SANKOFA: We Must Go Back and Fetch What We Lost

The planet is older than most are willing to imagine because most people on earth are operating on the premise that the earth is only 6000 years old. This false theory was brought forth by an **arch**bishop from Ireland named James Ussher. In 1654 he claimed that God created earth on Oct **23**rd 4004 BCE, at 9 am. Since then Christianity bound most of the world into a box of 6000 years, claiming that the meta-spiritual devices (pyramids) could be no older than 6000 years but of course this could not be farther from the truth. The **astrological** knowledge that was left by ancient civilizations like Kemet and the Mayans span for more than 25,000 years and the remnants of this knowledge is hidden within **astro-theology.** I have love for all people yet I do not have a "religion". I have a way of life that is most closely related to the way the ancient Kemetyu from the Nile Valley lived their lives. I apply the 7 principles of Jhuty (Thoth, Hermes) to my life, which are, **mentalism, correspondence, vibration, polarity, rhythm, cause vs effect** and **gender**. I respect all people the same regardless of their age, gender, size, color, or status etc. I balance my actions with the **42 laws of Maat** (p 367). It was from these laws that the 10 commandments from the Bible were fashioned. John Henrik Clark once said, "Religion is the organization of spirituality into something that became the hand maiden of conquerors. Nearly all religions were brought to people and imposed on people by conquerors and used as the framework to control their minds." I know that what I am proclaiming might cause people confusion or even anger. It is important that you understand that I do not wish to be at odds with any being on earth and I do not wish to war with any group of people especially my own people. With that said, I want to explain the problems I see with many modern organized religions. It was the Muslim religion that enslaved Africans and forced them into the religion of Islam. It was the Christian religion that enslaved Africans and forced them into the religion of Christianity. I have found reasons causing me to come to the conclusion that much of what is taught in the Abrahamic religions was taken from ancient Kemet (Egypt), and this is why it is easier for me to walk the path towards ancient Kemet rather than conform to the religion of an enslaver and colonizer. For the Muslim, you should know that I was born a Muslim and my born name is **Dawud** which means **David** (beloved of God, page 41) and my middle name is Basheer (the bringer of truth). I have come to bring you a divine truth, in the spirit of Maat. For the Christian, you should know that I got **baptized** at **11** (page 49) and gave my life to **Christ** at **22** (page 92). All the branches of Abrahamic religions teach about the prophets in the bible as if they were real people yet there are no artifacts from any of these prophets in these holy books. There is no museum on the planet earth where one can go to see the skeletons of any prophets from the bible or the Quran. Not even a sword or cloth or a staff, yet museums all over the world are full of African skeletons and treasures from ancient Kemet. I can see the artifacts and bodies of the Queens and Kings of ancient Kemet but I have never seen anything that belonged to Jesus, Moses, Abraham, Jacob, or Elijah in a museum. The only thing I am left to mull over is the Holy Bible, but the events and motifs in the Bible were taken from Kemet. There's no structural or tangible proof that this "David" character from the bible ever lived but Thutmoses the 3rd lived a life that parallels the stories of David from the bible and you can see, touch and read about Thutmoses on the walls of Kemet (page 225). Thutmoses the 3rd comes from the 18th dynasty, the same dynasty that my ancient soul **(King Tut)** descends from. There is a poem from the Psalms of **David,** in the bible, written by my father Akhenaten titled, Psalms 104 (**Hymn to the Aten, page 615**). Akhenaten did the things that Moses was said to have done in the book of **Exodus**. He took his people to a fertile land between Memphis and Thebes (Luxor) and built the city of Akhetaten that venerated the sun. Today Akhetaten is called Tell EL Amarna and it is mostly a desert. The locals call it **ET Till** or **EL Till** (p 671). These names are part of this prophecy of reincarnation. ET Till like EMM**ETT Till** and **EL Till** like **E**mmett **L**ouis **Till**. Akhenaten is seen as the father of monotheism (the concept of one God). Akhenaten didn't create this concept he just crystallized teachings about the sun's life giving properties. My father **Akhenaten** was the **biblical Moses**. The Christian religion took their concept of monotheism from **Akhenaten**. The Christian **mission** was to use the knowledge they took from Kemet so as to dominate and control the world with the new religion they created. The 18th dynasty spans over 250 years during the age of **Aries** and that is why the story of **Moses** was said to have taken place during the age of **Aries** (Ram). The Christian **Mission** for world domination was centered around the age of **Aries** and that is why the men who were sent to convert people were called **missionaries**, (**Mission-Aries**). Moses came down from Mount Sinai crowned with Ram horns. He got angry when he saw his people still worshiping the '**Golden** Bull'. He broke their bull statue because they were mentally stuck in the age of Taurus, he was trying to tell them that the age of Aries the Ram had come. The age of Aries began around 2160BC, and the stories in the Bible are allegories, not real stories with real people, however the 18th dynasty is full of real people who reigned from 1550 BC - 1290 BC. The age of Pisces (Two Fish) started around 1BC, the same time Jesus was said to have been born. The story of Jesus was taken from Heru, the son of Ausar who returns after death. The story of Jesus feeding the multitude with two fish is an allegory connected to the two fish seen in the zodiac sign of Pisces. We are coming to the end of the age of Pisces which is the age of **Believing**, and we are moving into the age of Aquarius, which is the age of **Knowing**. In Chapter **23**, verses 1-6, in the book of Psalms, lies an interesting passage, "Yea, though I walk through the valley of the shadow of death, I will fear no evil: for thou art with me; thy **rod** and thy **staff** they comfort me." This "rod" and "staff" sounds like the **Crook** and **Flail** carried by the Nswt Bity's (Pharaoh's) of ancient Kemet. **Re-member** that **you** are **Ausar** and **Heru,** the **hero!** See page 3 for the **hero's journey!** We must go back and fetch what we lost so that we can move in the know and not be subjected to blind faith and belief. Efforts have been made to destroy the Black family in America ever since we were brought here in 1619. In 1667 Virginia wrote into **law**: "enslaved Blacks who convert to **Christianity** are still slaves". So not even God could free Black people from the binds of this White mans system of slavery. And by 1669 Virginia wrote into **law**: "slave masters may kill *people* who resist authority". When we were set free in 1865, the prison system was built and new laws were created aimed at filling the prisons with Black bodies. Black men and boys were the targets and soon they filled the jails only to be rented out as cheap labor to work on the same plantations they had been "freed" from. Even with these nefarious efforts to destroy us, the Black family persevered as we managed to keep our families together with high marriage rates. We built thriving communities and even found our way into political offices. We were involved with many important inventions that propelled America into the position it is in today. Black men and women worked in factories, many did not even have college degrees yet they were still able to take care of their families. In 1955 I was murdered (page 480) and Martin Luther King, a **Christian preacher** rose to prominence shouldering the struggle of freedom for Black people (page 69). As we began to gain ground, efforts were made to see us fail. Our leaders were intimidated, jailed and murdered. The factories were closed in the Black communities. The high schools in Black communities took the trades like plumbing, welding, electrician, brick mason, carpentry, and auto mechanics off of the curriculum, then drugs were put in our communities, and the drug dealers and the drug addicted were put in prison. The Black woman was made to depend on governmental assistance for survival and Black men could not be in the homes when the Black women were receiving this governmental assistance. This helped to create and promote the single Black family. The Black woman became the most educated group of people in America and the bread winner as she was paid more than the average Black man. This was systematically done to cause division in Black families. In 2001 **laws** were passed allowing the **government** to finance **churches** creating a conflict of interest when it comes to Black preachers speaking out about injustices done to the masses of Black people by a **governmental system** of **racism** and **white supremacy**. **Anyone who profits off of you being blind will not teach you or inspire you to see**. **Kaba Kamene** once said, "To continue to follow a religious system that no longer meets your needs and solves your problems, is equivalent to carrying the boat on your back after crossing the river". **Kaba Kamene** has been teaching since **1977**! **"Wake me when we are free!!"**

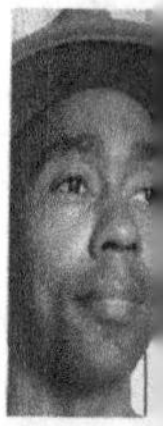

Rau nu Prt m heru

Iu f Per f m heru

Utterances for Coming Forth by day into Light

It is he, who comes forth by day into Light

January 17th 2022 Still Dreaming with Kanye

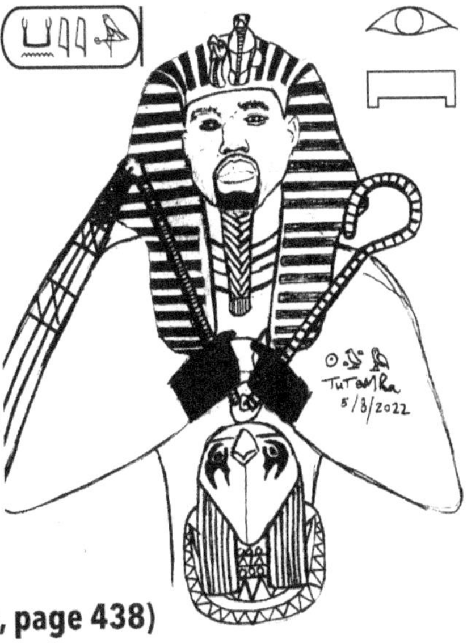

I've been having dreams lately but I have not been adding them to this book. I've just been observing them. Tonight will be a full Moon and I woke up today from another dream with Kanye West. Kanye first appeared in my dreams in 2009 (p 163). When he appeared the second and third times I began to think about the song **Still Dreaming** that he did with **Nas**. In that song Kanye says, "He pulled up at 6:30 in his 745, as he wavin' his shorty hi, you know he showin' his bling out, She got in the car, he drove, he pulled his thing out, His girl call, feelin' she mad, she threw the ring out, How she found out, **she dreamt the whole thing out**". When I heard that line in 2006 I always thought about how my sister dreamt my car accident before it happened (p 104 - 106) and so I figured that Kanye had some sort of experience with dreams that caused him to write that line. Kanye, if you are aware of the power of dreams then you know they have meaning. You can find me quicker than I can find you. Let's talk.

The Dream

I don't know where we were in this dream but I was next to **Kanye** and we were talking. I told him that we were meant to meet at this time. I pulled my phone out and went to open my photo album to show him my pictures of me and Emmett but for some reason the photo app in my phone didn't work. Then I was in a different room with Kanye and he was sitting on a chair. He seemed to be getting sick and everyone was worried. I checked his pulse but he was alive and well. There was a woman on a sofa next to him who looked to be sick as well. I was concerned so I put my hands on her legs then she opened her eyes and smiled. Then I woke up.

(Still Dreaming Remix, page 438)

Significance

Kanye West is a polarizing figure in the world today. His willingness to speak his mind freely has caused him to be the center of a lot of controversy. In 2022 Kanye claimed that black people are the Semitic people written about in the Bible. He made comments about the white Jewish people that own the music industry and other Industries. He said that no record company would allow any artist to distribute music that promoted the killing of white Jewish people or white people in general, yet they allow artist to distribute music about killing black people, and other deleterious behavior.. I agree with Kanye. I do not think Kanye is coming from a place of hate. Kanye is a wealthy black man and because of this he sees the world from a rare view. In modern time most black men never reach the level of perceived freedom that he has reached. Yet still, with all his money and influence, his business contracts were terminated because of his views. Even his bank refused to do business with him. Kanye disrupted religious beliefs. The word **Jew** or **Jewish** will cause major problems if you make any claim about white Jews that is not positive. You are not supposed to say that Jewish people profited off the enslavement of black Africans during the Trans Atlantic Slave Trade. You are not supposed to say that **black people were killed first during the Jewish holocaust**. You are not supposed to say that the same **eugenics research** used to kill white Jews was first used by **Margaret Sanger** to **kill black babies** via the **Planned Parenthood**. I have heard white Jewish men say, "**We should not attempt to compare who has suffered more**", yet in the very next sentence go on to say, "**The Jewish holocaust was the worlds most greatest crime**". I make no attempt to play the "who has suffered more game", because I can't find another group of people who have endured a holocaust for as long and horrific as African people have. No other group of people has been robbed from their home, reduced to servitude in the most brutal of ways. Been lowered to the class of an animal, and said to be only 1/5 of a human being. We were repeatedly raped, and not just the women. The man, woman and children were raped. Our lives were not valued. We were beaten, eaten, lynched, and our babies were used as crocodile bait. Even though many of us lived under the fear of imminent death, we never stopped fighting for our freedom. We were not "freed" by American laws. We were "freed" because we would not stop fighting for freedom and we were beginning to out number the white slave owners. Even when we were "freed", we still faced lynchings, racist **laws**, and every other possible way to stop us from self determination. When we did good for ourselves our towns were destroyed and burned. White Jews claim 6 million Jews died in their Holocaust. Because of this white Jews have received reparations from their suffering yet Black people have yet to receive reparations for the 600 million that died from our Holocaust. But why do white Jews feel so special? White Jews claim to be Gods chosen people. The only book that makes this claim is the Bible and through out this book I have explained that the Bible is not a literal book. It is religious literature. Some of it was plagiarized (page 615) and much of what is written in the Bible is allegory. The **Jews** are not a group of people, they are the **chakras/Glands** of the body. Revelations, ch 2:9 says, "those who claim they are Jews but they are not, they are the synagog of Satan". This Scripture is referring to people who have not raised themselves up via the inward path, those who have not built their "Noah's Ark" (page 252). For more information please read the previous page (page 667). Kanye has come up many times in this book. He is probably the most mentioned artist in this book next to Tupac. All my experiences with Kanye in the **dream realm** appear on pages: 162, 163, 438, 550, 552, 668, 669. Every time I said Kanye's name in a rhyme appears on pages: 218, 275, 317, 426. Every time I used a Kanye beat to write a rhyme is found on pages: 185, 187, 210, 347. Other times I mentioned Kanye are on pages: 106, 143, 155, 181, 469, 545.

March 14th 2022 Kanye Westing

Troubles at home then go talk to **Bes,** this poem left here is for **Kanye West,** I read your **Dead** piece and it touch my **soul**, like the **Heru** piece on your neck eye behold, I see **ghost** too, I see **ghost** three, I do not trust what eye see on TV, you are not **dead**, you're the **Lord** of the **West** and that's why your name is **Kanye West,** The **Lord** of the **living**, he's the one coming back, yes he is the **Lord** of the **perfect black,** but what about **Bes** tell me who is that? the protector of homes to keep things intact, but you're on a quest so I offer this map, to find a church where **Westing** lives at, No Church in The Wild and yes that's a fact cause after death through **Westing** we come back, the best thing you can do is look Through The Wire like a looking glass before you expire, You've been in my **dreams** and I am no liar, two days before my birthday you crashed Through The Wire, one nine seven seven we both came to this plane, and you might not yet know that you know my name, see I was once **dead** but now I am not, you once said my name then you rose to the top, we came here together but you must've forgot, that you're the **Lord** of the **West** don't think that you're not, the **Ba** is the **soul** resting over beds, viewed as a **bird** cause we are not **dead,** come walk with the **jackal** with him we are led to the halls of **Maat** where judgement is read, **Amen Atum Aten** never to be forgotten, from **Neb Kheperu Ra** to slave fields pick'n cotton, From **Emmett Till** get'n killed thrown in a river rotten, like **Ausar** I came back as **Dawud, TutemRa - TutemRa**

Significance: I read Kanye's poem titled, **DEAD** on March 14th 2022 and it inspired me to write this poem for him. **42 Laws of Maat, Page 367**

January 18th 2022 Dream with 50 Cent

I fell asleep at around 4:30 am. Just before that I set my alarm for 5:55am. I had a 6am client to train on zoom (Client from Nov 1st, p 583). All of a sudden I was in a dream sitting next to **50 Cent**. We were talking about a movie and I made a comment about the movie. Then he looked at me and said. "Are you serious, don't you need to be up soon?" As soon as he said the word **soon** my alarm went off and I woke up. Maybe that had something to do with the full **moon**.

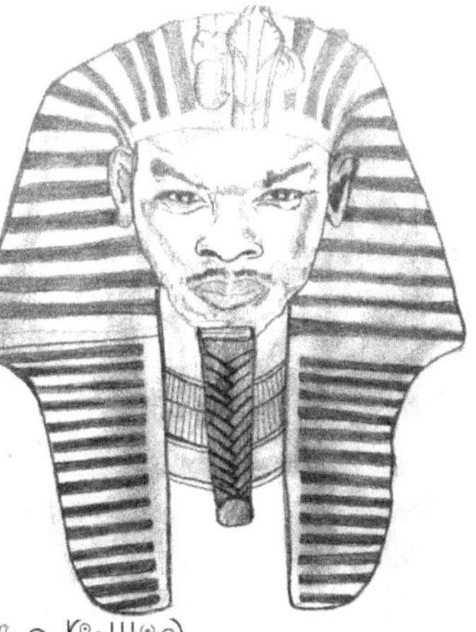

I had another dream with 50 Cent that is not in this book. That dream still puzzles me.....

January 26th 2022 (1st of 8)
Tuesday

She's having a birthday on Wednesday not Tuesday, Abena what they do say, when I dream, look in da-mirror and see Amin, I mean the truth is hidden within don't need a shahada to come clean, Armana the sun when we met I felt something, like maybe we met before like she was once Queen **- TutemRa**

January 27th 2022
Cords

Once upon alone fine, Yvone charmed we hugged for a long time, unusual cords, remind remember, never let go, die be born again, find her and befriend her **- TutemRa**

January 30th 2022
Burnt Out

Today is January 30th and it is 2:30 pm. The hardest part of this book has been the writing of the murder of Emmett Till. Researching my own murder has been time consuming and taxing on my mental health. It has roused emotions, causing me to cry and I have started to feel like I vaguely remember being yelled at in the dead of the night on August 28th 1955 (p 507). "you won't need socks where you're going", that's what Milam is reported to have said to me and somehow I feel like I remember that. Perhaps I have internalized the story and like a child that has been told a story so many times they begin to believe they experienced something that they didn't. I don't know if that is the case or if I have started to remember. I have never wanted to remember that part of my life as Emmett. I do not want those memories.

Still Dreaming Remix,
page 438

February 6th 2022
(Still Dreaming with Indira and Kanye)

A car crashed in a river. **Indira** was in the car trapped at the bottom. I dove into the river to free her from the car. We swam to the surface and we walked out of the river, she sat down. I grabbed her hand and walked her up a long flight of steps. She was wearing a red dress. The next scene I was in my current apartment when **Kanye** walked in. He sat on my couch and we talked.

February 13th 2022 **Pearls on a Necklace**

Each life is a page, the world is your stage, I came back this time to write the book of a sage, like a pearl on a necklace each life engraved, like seeing your soulmate in a strangers gaze, in the blink of an eye we're gone turning the page **- TutemRa**

Mary Sue Smith

I did not plan to write this hekau on this date but there was once a women by the name of Mary Sue Smith who was murdered on February 13th 1989 the year of the snake. She was born again 8 years later in 1997. Mary can be seen in the picture on the left with the red orbs floating in the picture. (See page 289 for more details)

Condolences

My condolences go out to the family of those who have been robbed of their lives due to senseless violence. Please know that death is not the end. The soul survives death, indeed and in spirit. This is a book of the dead written by a boy who was murdered without justice, who defeated death and came forth by day. May the soul of **Mary Sue Smith** walk peacefully through the field of Reeds in Amenta. Amen Ra.

February 21st 2022 **Thirteen Signs**

Untouched thoughts, memories never felt yet still I smell invisible cards never dealt **- TutemRa**

Meaning

Our **thoughts** and desires can affect our reality by influencing quantum level events in time and space. An untouched thought is an idea or plan that was never put into action or focused on so it never manifested in the physical realm. We are dual in nature and therefore we shouldn't neglect the unseen parts of our being. Most of us awake from dreams but we never remember them and that's sad because a dream is a **memory** of the soul (Ba). Our olfactory organs deal with the sense of **smell** which is connected to our memory centers in the brain which is why a smell can evoke memories from the oldest parts of our past, yet you can't see a smell. We can live life by chance or we can plant our feet into the soul of life and follow the signs and patterns of the **invisible cards** presented to us from the unseen realms. Every day with every action we choose the roads we take. Some paths may appear to be easier to deal with but nothing worth having comes easy. Take path of peril not the ones easily traversed!

February 24th 2022 - The Odd Never Ending story

On February 24th I was watching the 5th episode of season 2 of The Odd Couple. It was titled **A Grave For Felix**. In the episode Felix was looking for a plot of land for his burial. On this episode Oscar says, "He's harder to bury than **King Tut**", and that's when I looked into the details of this episode. The episode aired in 1971 the same year my great grand father **General Dukes Sr** died (p 19) and the same year **Tupac** was born. One of the writers, D. Bensfield was born on June 18th, the same day my great grandmother Leacola **Riddle** died. The director of that episode, Hal Cooper was born on **February 23rd**, which was "yesterday". Felix, the character played by Tony Randall was born on February 26th which is the very day that the last room in **King Tut's** tomb was opened (page 11)!! Finally Oscar, played by Jack Klugman, who said the name **King Tut**, was born in19**22**, the same year **King Tut's** tomb was discovered. (See page **648** for the **metaphysical significance of the number 23**. See pages 25, 94, 102, 121, 283, 444, 586, 669, and 672 for more on **February 23rd**.)

Rau nu Prt m heru

Iu f Per f m heru

Jtterances for Coming Forth by day into Light

It is he, who comes forth by day into Light

TO BE CONTINUED.. In this life or the next....

March 31st 2022 ***ADDENDUM***

Deja Vu at The Saqqara Step Pyramid

This part of my journey has come to a close and I currently have **12** days left in Kemet (Egypt). I will share with you a few small details of my trip and the rest will be continued at another time, perhaps in this life or perhaps in the next. When I arrived to Cairo I went to purchase a new chip for my phone. I could have paid with American dollars but I decided to use my bank card. The fee was only **8** dollars but my card was declined. Frustrated, I went to see about exchanging money for Egyptian pound but the banks were not yet open. Then I saw the currency exchange machines. While on my way to the machine a brother asked if he could help me. I explain my issue and he helped me with the machine and my card worked. His name was **Magmoud**. I have a cousin name George that we used to call Matmuu when I was little (page 36). Magmoud would end up setting up my tour in Egypt. His brother Dola is my tour guide. I have a cousin named Abdulla who we used to call Dula (page 180). On March 31st Dola took me to the Saqqara step pyramid (page 267) which was built by the great master builder **Imhotep**. As I got close to the step pyramid I was overcome with the desire to climb it. I handed my phone to Dola and asked him to record me as I made my way up the bottom layer. At exactly **2** minutes and **55** seconds of the video I suddenly stopped and turn towards the camera expressing the fact that I had just experienced **Deja Vu** (picture seen on top right). As I walked across the step pyramid at Saqqara I had a short and sharp experience of having been at that moment in time before. This experience is aligned with the rock-cut tomb of my wet nurse, **Maia**, which was found in Saqqara in 1996, the same year **Tupac** died. On the wall of her tomb, Maia is seen embracing me (seen on right), breathing divinity (**Sekhem** / life force energy) into me (see page 355). **Deja Vu** is sometimes a result of having already experienced a moment in a **dream** that you didn't remember upon waking but when you reach that moment from your dream in your waken state you have a feeling of familiarity because some dreams take place in a different space and time where the **astral body travels**, sometimes to the past and even the future. There is another layer of Deja Vu though, it can also be connected to a life you have once lived in another time and another place. This was not my first trip to Saqqara. I was there with Maia, in my life as Tutankhaten. The ancient Kemetyu understood that there was no death and thus, reincarnation and past lives was called the **Wehem-Mesut** (repeating of births, Gilgul, page 14). In the picture below (left) I am seen in the pose of **Enpu** standing in front of the Saqqara Step Pyramid. In the other picture (bottom right) I am seen in the **Ka** pose, standing inside of the temple of **Unas**. The oldest writings known to man are utterances, spells or "rhymes/hymns" written on the walls in the tombs of the **Nswt Bity** (pharaoh) evoked to ensure the safe passage of the pharaoh after death and towards **resurrection** (Wehem-Mesut) in the next life. These rhymes first appeared in the pyramid of Unas, the last pharaoh of the 5th Dynasty. **7 days later I would experience Deja Vu again** (page 671).

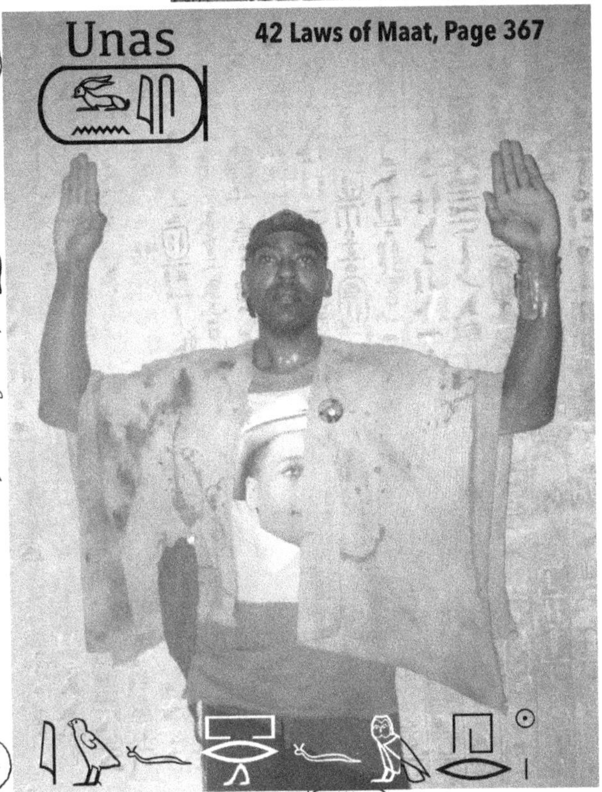

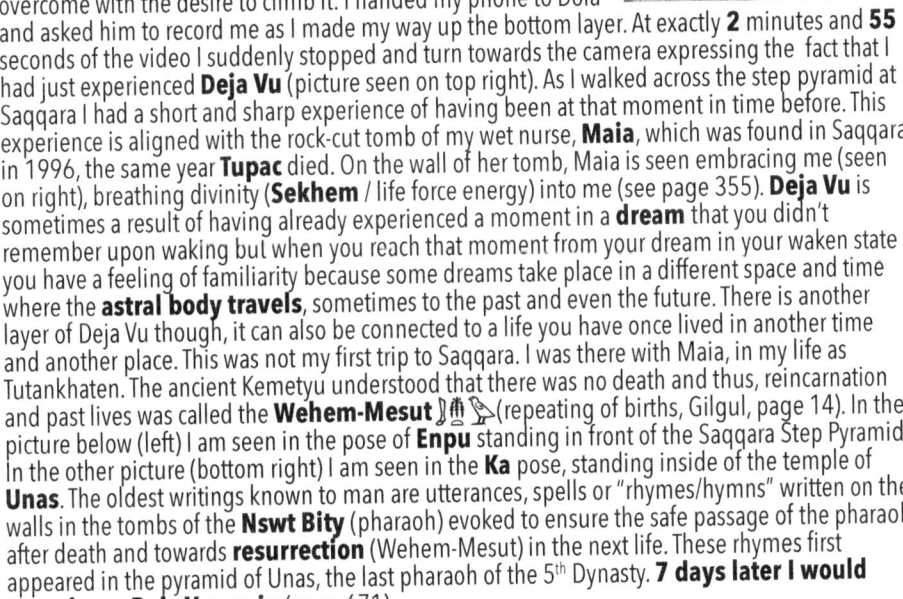

April 8th 2022 Deja Vu while Leaving The City of Akhetaten

Going to see the ancient city of **Akhetaten** was not on my initial travel plan that I set up with Magmoud but on my way back from Aswan to Cairo I decided that I had to see it before I left Kemet. **Akhenaten** (King Tut's father) built the city of Akhetaten along the Nile river between Memphis and Thebes in ancient Kemet (Egypt). When I got to Akhetaten I only had 30 minutes because the site closed early due to **Ra**madan but I was still able to see the tombs of **Ahmes** and **Meryre**. I recorded myself doing kemetic yoga postures of adoration in front of and inside of the tombs then I left quickly because the site was closed. As we drove away from Akhetaten **I was overcome** with a **great sense** of **Deja Vu**. Perhaps I had been there in a dream before I arrived or maybe it was the fact that I had lived there thousands of years ago in my life as Tutankhaten. 3 days later on April 11th I went back to Akhetaten and this time I arrived at 4am. The site didn't open till 9am so I slept in the car until 5:30 then I went to the location that used to be the Great Palace, the main residence of the royal Aten family and watched the sun rise over the mountains of Akhetaten as I did **Kemetic yoga**. Afterwards I met with **Naser**, the keeper of the grounds of Akhetaten. I told him my story about my past life as Tutankhaten and showed him the pictures of myself and Tutankhaten. I was surprised to see that he believed me. He told me that he had been waiting for me for many hundreds of years. He Loves the city of Akhetaten and knows himself to have lived a life during the times of Akhenaten. Interestingly enough, Naser has a long pointed nose just like the images of Akhenaten. Before I left to see the royal tomb he handed me a staff, a short wooden branch that had come from a tree in Akhetaten. He told me that it was mine. The name Nefertiti was written on the branch in ink along with the date, 10/9/2021. I asked him if the date was **October 9th** or September 10th, he smiled and said October 9th and I immediately told him that that was my grand mothers birthday. That surprised him but he shook his head as if it confirmed why he was compelled to give it to me. When I was done with the royal tomb I was taken to see the site called **Stela U**, where there are writings on the wall of a giant cliff and two statues carved into the side of the cliff marking the boundaries of the city. I climbed up the mountain and recorded a 6 minute video doing kemetic yoga postures of adoration next to the statues. From this point I could see all of Akhetaten stretching to the Nile river. When I left I looked at the footage and to my surprise the Aten (sun) began to appear from over the mountain 4 minutes into the video shining it's rays of light on me just as I changed from the pose of **Min** to the pose of **Ausar**. The timing of the rays of the Aten was too perfect to be "just a coincidence". If I had placed the camera one foot to the right I would not have captured the Aten's rays. This was indeed divine, just like the cities current name. Akhetaten translates to, the sun on the horizon. Today Akhetaten is called Tell EL Amarna. The locals call it **ET Till** or **EL Till**, which means: **The Hill**. In this current life I grew up on a block named **Hill**meyer (p 35, 40, 648, 653). These names are part of this Prophecy of Reincarnation. ET Till like EMM**ET**T Till and **EL T**ill like **E**mmett **L**ouis **Till**. I am a man of many names. **TutemRa Setep en Ra Nebu Sahu Kheperu** is my current name and in my most recent previous life I was Emmett Till. I lived many lives before that with my oldest known life being Tutankhaten. As Tutankhaten, I was born in K**emet** and even in the name K**emet** you find the name **Emmett**. The name **TutemRa** was given to me by the ancestors (p 594), it means, in the image of **Ra**. A few days later I chose the name **Kheperu** because it was part of my ancient throne name, Neb Kheperu Ra (p 284). Kheper is the Beetle and Kheperu means, a continuous coming into being. A few months later I took on the name **Nebu** and a month or so later I added **Sahu**. Nebu **= Gold**. The **Sahu** is the aspect of the soul that **reincarnates**. It was also the name used to identify the stars that make up the belt in the constellation of Ausar (Osiris) the archer (**Orion**) and finally, in the ancient Kemetic spiritual system all initiates aimed to become like **Sahu**, which was **one of the highest levels of spirituality,** the closest one could be to **Ntr** like (**God** like). I added Setep en Ra (chosen by Ra) to my name because it was a variation of my ancient throne name.
TutemRa Setep en Ra Nebu Sahu Kheperu means: The Golden Soul chosen by Ra to continuously Come Forth in the image of Ra.

TutemRa Setep en Ra Nebu Sahu Kheperu
The Golden Soul chosen by Ra to continuously come forth (or "Emmett") in the image of Ra
Akhetaten= Et Till
EmmEtt Till

The Boundary Stelae that oversees the ancient city of Akhetaten, now known as Amarna by many and Et Till by locals.
Stela U

ADDENDUM **February 24, 2023** **No Alibi Remix**

Rau nu Prt m heru

Look through the window, and tell me what you see, the Kemetic poetic school of philosophy, maybe you seen it or heard about my odyssey, see there be no mistaken, I be the one that you been wait'n, to bring it home, call me the chief corner stone, a ton, defeat Set and return as the sun, no rapture! the news I bring might kill laughter and birth anger, and I might be the one in danger, so I lay low, but can't stop the shine of my halo, like Doro - Mind Of My Mind aligned with Draco, do what I say so, the hidden **Ma-gician**, take my hand if you ever want to live again, a Scorpion then, a Leo later, start again, **Wehem Mesut**, reboot, **The Root** of the Hindu Vedas, the fruit to the labor, the light to a sabor, a door to a star, **do you know who you are?** the **Dravidians** live'n in skin **blacker** than obsidian tar resin, **Ausar** risen, deep diving, I'm live like a third rail, on time like sun rising, connecting my life **life after life** like a hyphen, strike like **Tyson**, ain't no stopping me! until I fulfill my prophetic term of prophecy, I went and wrote a book, some say hypocrisy, just a big tale but this be the crook and the flail in the flesh, Yea though I walk through the valley of the shadow of defamation, I carry this **Ankh** like revelations, – We all seen it and heard it but the law said they didn't, that lady she got me shot and her man got **acquitted***, exhibit the truth because I'm living proof wise, from the dead I rise, murdered in **55**

Look into my mind and find a ancient prism, blind a devil with the black and gold shine from the **Chrism**, divine mysticism, I rhyme with the intuition of a **Nat Turner** mission, skate with ammunition, stakes are high, snakes will let you die for **manumission**! mannerisms I peep em, weak links we reap em, fortunately running free for hours days and weeks, in this day and time, 1829, through rivers lakes and creeks, even mountains I climb, they say man is mind but mankind is blind, like a pentagram I shine in the darkness, ultra black like **Marcus Garvey** or when the narcs hit, heartless and mean mug'n to escape the sub-terranean hell, if you fell then they got you, only self to blame, sanity to be lost never be the same, better off if they shot you to release the pain, chain around my neck flashback, if only I had a tek to blast back, my attitude is scarred by this American way of being, sometimes I wonder, from whence there came a European? amazed by the bullet, triggers they quick to pull it on the flavor youth, gotta stay sharper than a saber tooth, that's the truth unfortunately, down in Mississippi, taken my life aye yo they gypped me, and quickly they tried to bury in the end, like **Amen**, thinking I would never live again – We all seen it and heard it but the law said they didn't, that lady she got me shot and her man got **acquitted***, exhibit the truth because I'm living proof wise, from the dead I rise, murdered in **55 - TutemRa Setep en Ra**

Significance

Iu f Per f m heru

Today is **March 9**, 2023 and this is one of the last day of amendments to this book. In an effort to track the events that lead to me remixing the classic song, No Alibi, from The Roots I checked my youtube history today and here's how it happened. On **Feb 16**, 20**23** I went down a rabbit hole listening to old **Boot Camp Clik** instrumentals. This just so "happens" to be the same day that the final room of King Tut's Tomb was opened (**Feb 16**, 19**23**, (page 11) and the same day **Tupac** released **Strictly 4 My N.I.G.G.A.Z** (**Feb/16/93**). I downloaded a few of the instrumentals from the **Enta Da Stage** album on **Feb 16**, 20**23**. That same day I listened to the song, No Alibi by The Roots.. The next day, on Feb 17, I searched for the **Canibus** beat **Buckingham Palace** and to my surprise I found it (page 71)! That same day I wrote a verse to the Canibus beat. Days later, on Feb **23**, I found the No Alibi instrumental for the first time! I had searched for this beat for many years just like I had searched for the Buckingham Palace beat but never found it until now. The instrumental was uploaded on Sep 16, 2022, 3 days after Tupac died in 1996 and 3 days before the Emmett Till trial started in 1955. The song **No Alibi** was from their third album titled, **Illadelph Halflife** which was released 11 days after Tupac died, on **September 24,** 1996, the day after Roy Bryant and J.W. Milam were **acquitted** for the lynching of **Emmett Till** (page 517). Neither man had an **Alibi** but they were **acquitted***. On Feb 24, the day after I downloaded the beat, I wrote the No Alibi remix. I did the same thing I did with the Canibus Remix. I took elements from the original song and made it my own. After I wrote the second line, "the Kemetic poetic school of philosophy" everything else flowed like water. It was as if I was supposed to take this song, which was my favorite Roots song, and remix it. After I wrote both verses I realized that I could use the hook and reword it to fit my story so I did and it was like the lyrics from my Canibus remix, "tell me how could eye ever lose! I took the blueprint from the human rubrics cube" (page 71). **I felt as if these lyrical masters, Canibus, Malik B, Black Thought,** and **Buckshot had crafted these master pieces thereby giving me a blueprint to tell my story**. When I wrote the Buckingham Palace remix it was my favorite song until I wrote the No Alibi remix. The next day I remixed the Black Moon song Slave from their debut album, **Enta Da Stage**. May the soul of **Malik B** travel in peace. **RIP**. See page **648** for the **metaphysical significance of the number 23**.

February 25, 2023 **Sage (Black Moon, Slave Remix)**

Utterances for Coming Forth by day into Light

TutemRa, the circle in the square, I disappear and reappear, death I don't fear, sent here on a journey of the soul, I peeped how the Devil be tryin to take control, but behold a new scroll metaphysics, so they feel it they're soul and they're spirit when they hear it, straight to my bloodstream I pump the breath, coalesce with the flesh and the spirit – **Amen Hotep**, rhythm and blues style is not in my environmental, the temple in man, left hand, everything is mind mental, assemble like **Mentu Hotep**, like when **Akhenaten** saw the **Aten** on **Akhet**, **Akhetaten**, the only begotten forgotten like **Huey P** in his prime, they plot'n to weaken the line, they got you eating the swine, detrimental, with a pin pad and mic devices I'm influential, some say more mightier than **Isis** when the rhythm hit you, when the rhythm hit you, it might feel like a tidal wave to be hit with the mind of a **sage**

I left my body buried in the side of a cave, look at my grave, when will we find **Betters Dayz**, jugular vein bust'n out my neck, light the **sage**, I move to the groove to remove the rage, I took **buckshots** to my back but came back, to my roots like the motherland salute troops dressed in black, and I don't really trust what they say, commercial rap say the same crap day after day, my **Negus** be left with the death blow, the rest they stuck on **Death Row**, till the only thing left is a echo, that night I got bum-rushed by **Set**, me and my sister on the real **Auset**, balancing **Maat** recall **Who Got The Props**, spit another lesson to **resurrection** from the **Tekhen**, **Jhuty** be wise from the tribe of the moon, gave em the crooked eye when they opened my tomb, they wasn't ready to be hit with a tidal wave, from deep in the mind of a **sage - TutemRa Setep en Ra**

Significance

It is he, who comes forth by day into Light

Today is **March 9**, 20**23** and I am writing some of the last lines in this book during this 50th year of Hip Hop. This book was released last year on my father's birthday (page 28), June 1, 2022 on time with the 49th anniversary of Hip Hop and **49** days is the amount of time the **Tibetans believed** it took one soul to be **reborn** into another life (page 6). Today is **March 9**, 20**23**, the day **Biggie Smalls** was murdered which lead to me writing the song **The Resurrection** in 1997, which was the first time I ever used the word **resurrection** in a rhyme (page **77**). It was a **Canibus** beat that started the series of remixes that lead to me writing the song above and it was Canibus who said, "the greatest rapper of all time died on **March 9**th". As with many things in this book there is a **divine star code**. This time the code is in the date **Feb 25**. **Muhammad Ali** is considered to be "the greatest boxer of all time" by many. **Malcolm X** was good **friends*** with **Ali**, and Ali won the heavy weight championship on **Feb 25**, 1964 (page 387). Years later Ali was diagnosed with Parkinson's syndrome but he and his physicians did not think it was a result of boxing….. **Malcolm X** visited Kenya in 1959 and developed a **friendship*** with the Kenyan politician **Pio Gama Pinto**. On **Feb 25**, 1965, 4 days after **Malcolm X** was assassinated in front of his wife and daughters (page 561), **Pio Gama Pinto** was assassinated in front of his daughter. On **Feb 25**, 2000, after three days of deliberation, a jury composed of four black and eight white jurors **acquitted*** the officers of all charges of killing **Amadou Diallo** (page 80). On **Feb 25**, 2012 I wrote the song **Griot** in which I said the words, "what would you say if I say **I'm coming back like Christ,** you would reject that right?!" (page **23**1). On **Feb 25**, 20**23** I remixed the **Black Moon** song **Slave** from their debut album, **Enta Da Stage**. I took one of my favorite **Buckshot** tracks and repurposed it because we must move from the mind set of being the descendants of **slaves** and go back further so as to realize that we are also the descendants of the first enlightened **Sages** and **Gurus** from Kemet. All human beings have the potential to reach **Heru consciousness** becoming a metaphorical reflection of **Heru** (page 3). Each life is a page, from which we **Enta Da** world **Stage**. I came back this life to write the book of a **sage**. Like a pearl on a necklace each life engraved, like seeing your soulmate in a strangers gaze, and in the blink of an eye you're gone turning the page. I look forward to the reincarnation of all the **Warrior Prophets** (page 370). **"I'll see you in another life"** (pages 259,**260**).

I'm writing a Epic Sci-Real (Science Reality) Novel Trilogy version of this book and a book about Tupac's ancient past life (pages 664 - 665). Stay tuned!

www.ingramcontent.com/pod-product-compliance
Lightning Source LLC
Chambersburg PA
CBHW080834120626
46553CB00009B/2428
* 9 7 9 8 9 8 6 0 3 6 2 0 5 *